S0-BBS-614

Oxford Dictionary of National Biography

Volume 51

Oxford Dictionary of National Biography

IN ASSOCIATION WITH

The British Academy

From the earliest times to the year 2000

Edited by

H. C. G. Matthew

and

Brian Harrison

Volume 51

Smillie–Sprott

Great Clarendon Street, Oxford OX2 6DP

Oxford University Press is a department of the University of Oxford.
It furthers the University's objective of excellence in research, scholarship,
and education by publishing worldwide in

Oxford New York

Auckland Bangkok Buenos Aires Cape Town
Chennai Dar es Salaam Delhi Hong Kong Istanbul Karachi
Kolkata Kuala Lumpur Madrid Melbourne Mexico City Mumbai Nairobi
São Paulo Shanghai Taipei Tokyo Toronto

Oxford is a registered trade mark of Oxford University Press
in the UK and in certain other countries

Published in the United States
by Oxford University Press Inc., New York

First published 2004

British Library Cataloguing in Publication Data
Data available

Library of Congress Cataloging in Publication Data
Data available: for details see volume 1, p. iv

ISBN 0-19-861401-2 (this volume)
ISBN 0-19-861411-X (set of sixty volumes)

Text captured by Alliance Phototypesetters, Pondicherry
Illustrations reproduced and archived by
Alliance Graphics Ltd, UK
Typeset in OUP Swift by Interactive Sciences Limited, Gloucester
Printed in Great Britain on acid-free paper by
Butler and Tanner Ltd,
Frome, Somerset

LIST OF ABBREVIATIONS

1 *General abbreviations*

AB	bachelor of arts
ABC	Australian Broadcasting Corporation
ABC TV	ABC Television
act.	active
A$	Australian dollar
AD	*anno domini*
AFC	Air Force Cross
AIDS	acquired immune deficiency syndrome
AK	Alaska
AL	Alabama
A level	advanced level [examination]
ALS	associate of the Linnean Society
AM	master of arts
AMICE	associate member of the Institution of Civil Engineers
ANZAC	Australian and New Zealand Army Corps
appx *pl.* appxs	appendix(es)
AR	Arkansas
ARA	associate of the Royal Academy
ARCA	associate of the Royal College of Art
ARCM	associate of the Royal College of Music
ARCO	associate of the Royal College of Organists
ARIBA	associate of the Royal Institute of British Architects
ARP	air-raid precautions
ARRC	associate of the Royal Red Cross
ARSA	associate of the Royal Scottish Academy
art.	article / item
ASC	Army Service Corps
Asch	Austrian Schilling
ASDIC	Antisubmarine Detection Investigation Committee
ATS	Auxiliary Territorial Service
ATV	Associated Television
Aug	August
AZ	Arizona
b.	born
BA	bachelor of arts
BA (Admin.)	bachelor of arts (administration)
BAFTA	British Academy of Film and Television Arts
BAO	bachelor of arts in obstetrics
bap.	baptized
BBC	British Broadcasting Corporation / Company
BC	before Christ
BCE	before the common (*or* Christian) era
BCE	bachelor of civil engineering
BCG	bacillus of Calmette and Guérin [inoculation against tuberculosis]
BCh	bachelor of surgery
BChir	bachelor of surgery
BCL	bachelor of civil law
BCnL	bachelor of canon law
BCom	bachelor of commerce
BD	bachelor of divinity
BEd	bachelor of education
BEng	bachelor of engineering
bk *pl.* bks	book(s)
BL	bachelor of law / letters / literature
BLitt	bachelor of letters
BM	bachelor of medicine
BMus	bachelor of music
BP	before present
BP	British Petroleum
Bros.	Brothers
BS	(1) bachelor of science; (2) bachelor of surgery; (3) British standard
BSc	bachelor of science
BSc (Econ.)	bachelor of science (economics)
BSc (Eng.)	bachelor of science (engineering)
bt	baronet
BTh	bachelor of theology
bur.	buried
C.	command [identifier for published parliamentary papers]
c.	*circa*
c.	*capitulum pl. capitula*: chapter(s)
CA	California
Cantab.	Cantabrigiensis
cap.	*capitulum pl. capitula*: chapter(s)
CB	companion of the Bath
CBE	commander of the Order of the British Empire
CBS	Columbia Broadcasting System
cc	cubic centimetres
C$	Canadian dollar
CD	compact disc
Cd	command [identifier for published parliamentary papers]
CE	Common (*or* Christian) Era
cent.	century
cf.	compare
CH	Companion of Honour
chap.	chapter
ChB	bachelor of surgery
CI	Imperial Order of the Crown of India
CIA	Central Intelligence Agency
CID	Criminal Investigation Department
CIE	companion of the Order of the Indian Empire
Cie	Compagnie
CLit	companion of literature
CM	master of surgery
cm	centimetre(s)

Cmd	command [identifier for published parliamentary papers]
CMG	companion of the Order of St Michael and St George
Cmnd	command [identifier for published parliamentary papers]
CO	Colorado
Co.	company
co.	county
col. *pl.* cols.	column(s)
Corp.	corporation
CSE	certificate of secondary education
CSI	companion of the Order of the Star of India
CT	Connecticut
CVO	commander of the Royal Victorian Order
cwt	hundredweight
$	(American) dollar
d.	(1) penny (pence); (2) died
DBE	dame commander of the Order of the British Empire
DCH	diploma in child health
DCh	doctor of surgery
DCL	doctor of civil law
DCnL	doctor of canon law
DCVO	dame commander of the Royal Victorian Order
DD	doctor of divinity
DE	Delaware
Dec	December
dem.	demolished
DEng	doctor of engineering
des.	destroyed
DFC	Distinguished Flying Cross
DipEd	diploma in education
DipPsych	diploma in psychiatry
diss.	dissertation
DL	deputy lieutenant
DLitt	doctor of letters
DLittCelt	doctor of Celtic letters
DM	(1) Deutschmark; (2) doctor of medicine; (3) doctor of musical arts
DMus	doctor of music
DNA	dioxyribonucleic acid
doc.	document
DOL	doctor of oriental learning
DPH	diploma in public health
DPhil	doctor of philosophy
DPM	diploma in psychological medicine
DSC	Distinguished Service Cross
DSc	doctor of science
DSc (Econ.)	doctor of science (economics)
DSc (Eng.)	doctor of science (engineering)
DSM	Distinguished Service Medal
DSO	companion of the Distinguished Service Order
DSocSc	doctor of social science
DTech	doctor of technology
DTh	doctor of theology
DTM	diploma in tropical medicine
DTMH	diploma in tropical medicine and hygiene
DU	doctor of the university
DUniv	doctor of the university
dwt	pennyweight
EC	European Community
ed. *pl.* eds.	edited / edited by / editor(s)
Edin.	Edinburgh
edn	edition
EEC	European Economic Community
EFTA	European Free Trade Association
EICS	East India Company Service
EMI	Electrical and Musical Industries (Ltd)
Eng.	English
enl.	enlarged
ENSA	Entertainments National Service Association
ep. *pl.* epp.	*epistola(e)*
ESP	extra-sensory perception
esp.	especially
esq.	esquire
est.	estimate / estimated
EU	European Union
ex	sold by (*lit.* out of)
excl.	excludes / excluding
exh.	exhibited
exh. cat.	exhibition catalogue
f. *pl.* ff.	following [pages]
FA	Football Association
FACP	fellow of the American College of Physicians
facs.	facsimile
FANY	First Aid Nursing Yeomanry
FBA	fellow of the British Academy
FBI	Federation of British Industries
FCS	fellow of the Chemical Society
Feb	February
FEng	fellow of the Fellowship of Engineering
FFCM	fellow of the Faculty of Community Medicine
FGS	fellow of the Geological Society
fig.	figure
FIMechE	fellow of the Institution of Mechanical Engineers
FL	Florida
fl.	*floruit*
FLS	fellow of the Linnean Society
FM	frequency modulation
fol. *pl.* fols.	folio(s)
Fr	French francs
Fr.	French
FRAeS	fellow of the Royal Aeronautical Society
FRAI	fellow of the Royal Anthropological Institute
FRAM	fellow of the Royal Academy of Music
FRAS	(1) fellow of the Royal Asiatic Society; (2) fellow of the Royal Astronomical Society
FRCM	fellow of the Royal College of Music
FRCO	fellow of the Royal College of Organists
FRCOG	fellow of the Royal College of Obstetricians and Gynaecologists
FRCP(C)	fellow of the Royal College of Physicians of Canada
FRCP (Edin.)	fellow of the Royal College of Physicians of Edinburgh
FRCP (Lond.)	fellow of the Royal College of Physicians of London
FRCPath	fellow of the Royal College of Pathologists
FRCPsych	fellow of the Royal College of Psychiatrists
FRCS	fellow of the Royal College of Surgeons
FRGS	fellow of the Royal Geographical Society
FRIBA	fellow of the Royal Institute of British Architects
FRICS	fellow of the Royal Institute of Chartered Surveyors
FRS	fellow of the Royal Society
FRSA	fellow of the Royal Society of Arts

FRSCM	fellow of the Royal School of Church Music
FRSE	fellow of the Royal Society of Edinburgh
FRSL	fellow of the Royal Society of Literature
FSA	fellow of the Society of Antiquaries
ft	foot *pl.* feet
FTCL	fellow of Trinity College of Music, London
ft-lb per min.	foot-pounds per minute [unit of horsepower]
FZS	fellow of the Zoological Society
GA	Georgia
GBE	knight or dame grand cross of the Order of the British Empire
GCB	knight grand cross of the Order of the Bath
GCE	general certificate of education
GCH	knight grand cross of the Royal Guelphic Order
GCHQ	government communications headquarters
GCIE	knight grand commander of the Order of the Indian Empire
GCMG	knight or dame grand cross of the Order of St Michael and St George
GCSE	general certificate of secondary education
GCSI	knight grand commander of the Order of the Star of India
GCStJ	bailiff or dame grand cross of the order of St John of Jerusalem
GCVO	knight or dame grand cross of the Royal Victorian Order
GEC	General Electric Company
Ger.	German
GI	government (*or* general) issue
GMT	Greenwich mean time
GP	general practitioner
GPU	[Soviet special police unit]
GSO	general staff officer
Heb.	Hebrew
HEICS	Honourable East India Company Service
HI	Hawaii
HIV	human immunodeficiency virus
HK$	Hong Kong dollar
HM	his / her majesty('s)
HMAS	his / her majesty's Australian ship
HMNZS	his / her majesty's New Zealand ship
HMS	his / her majesty's ship
HMSO	His / Her Majesty's Stationery Office
HMV	His Master's Voice
Hon.	Honourable
hp	horsepower
hr	hour(s)
HRH	his / her royal highness
HTV	Harlech Television
IA	Iowa
ibid.	*ibidem*: in the same place
ICI	Imperial Chemical Industries (Ltd)
ID	Idaho
IL	Illinois
illus.	illustration
illustr.	illustrated
IN	Indiana
in.	inch(es)
Inc.	Incorporated
incl.	includes / including
IOU	I owe you
IQ	intelligence quotient
Ir£	Irish pound
IRA	Irish Republican Army
ISO	companion of the Imperial Service Order
It.	Italian
ITA	Independent Television Authority
ITV	Independent Television
Jan	January
JP	justice of the peace
jun.	junior
KB	knight of the Order of the Bath
KBE	knight commander of the Order of the British Empire
KC	king's counsel
kcal	kilocalorie
KCB	knight commander of the Order of the Bath
KCH	knight commander of the Royal Guelphic Order
KCIE	knight commander of the Order of the Indian Empire
KCMG	knight commander of the Order of St Michael and St George
KCSI	knight commander of the Order of the Star of India
KCVO	knight commander of the Royal Victorian Order
keV	kilo-electron-volt
KG	knight of the Order of the Garter
KGB	[Soviet committee of state security]
KH	knight of the Royal Guelphic Order
KLM	Koninklijke Luchtvaart Maatschappij (Royal Dutch Air Lines)
km	kilometre(s)
KP	knight of the Order of St Patrick
KS	Kansas
KT	knight of the Order of the Thistle
kt	knight
KY	Kentucky
£	pound(s) sterling
£E	Egyptian pound
L	lira *pl.* lire
l. *pl.* ll.	line(s)
LA	Lousiana
LAA	light anti-aircraft
LAH	licentiate of the Apothecaries' Hall, Dublin
Lat.	Latin
lb	pound(s), unit of weight
LDS	licence in dental surgery
lit.	literally
LittB	bachelor of letters
LittD	doctor of letters
LKQCPI	licentiate of the King and Queen's College of Physicians, Ireland
LLA	lady literate in arts
LLB	bachelor of laws
LLD	doctor of laws
LLM	master of laws
LM	licentiate in midwifery
LP	long-playing record
LRAM	licentiate of the Royal Academy of Music
LRCP	licentiate of the Royal College of Physicians
LRCPS (Glasgow)	licentiate of the Royal College of Physicians and Surgeons of Glasgow
LRCS	licentiate of the Royal College of Surgeons
LSA	licentiate of the Society of Apothecaries
LSD	lysergic acid diethylamide
LVO	lieutenant of the Royal Victorian Order
M. *pl.* MM.	Monsieur *pl.* Messieurs
m	metre(s)

m. *pl.* mm.	membrane(s)
MA	(1) Massachusetts; (2) master of arts
MAI	master of engineering
MB	bachelor of medicine
MBA	master of business administration
MBE	member of the Order of the British Empire
MC	Military Cross
MCC	Marylebone Cricket Club
MCh	master of surgery
MChir	master of surgery
MCom	master of commerce
MD	(1) doctor of medicine; (2) Maryland
MDMA	methylenedioxymethamphetamine
ME	Maine
MEd	master of education
MEng	master of engineering
MEP	member of the European parliament
MG	Morris Garages
MGM	Metro-Goldwyn-Mayer
Mgr	Monsignor
MI	(1) Michigan; (2) military intelligence
MI1c	[secret intelligence department]
MI5	[military intelligence department]
MI6	[secret intelligence department]
MI9	[secret escape service]
MICE	member of the Institution of Civil Engineers
MIEE	member of the Institution of Electrical Engineers
min.	minute(s)
Mk	mark
ML	(1) licentiate of medicine; (2) master of laws
MLitt	master of letters
Mlle	Mademoiselle
mm	millimetre(s)
Mme	Madame
MN	Minnesota
MO	Missouri
MOH	medical officer of health
MP	member of parliament
m.p.h.	miles per hour
MPhil	master of philosophy
MRCP	member of the Royal College of Physicians
MRCS	member of the Royal College of Surgeons
MRCVS	member of the Royal College of Veterinary Surgeons
MRIA	member of the Royal Irish Academy
MS	(1) master of science; (2) Mississippi
MS *pl.* MSS	manuscript(s)
MSc	master of science
MSc (Econ.)	master of science (economics)
MT	Montana
MusB	bachelor of music
MusBac	bachelor of music
MusD	doctor of music
MV	motor vessel
MVO	member of the Royal Victorian Order
n. *pl.* nn.	note(s)
NAAFI	Navy, Army, and Air Force Institutes
NASA	National Aeronautics and Space Administration
NATO	North Atlantic Treaty Organization
NBC	National Broadcasting Corporation
NC	North Carolina
NCO	non-commissioned officer

ND	North Dakota
n.d.	no date
NE	Nebraska
nem. con.	*nemine contradicente*: unanimously
new ser.	new series
NH	New Hampshire
NHS	National Health Service
NJ	New Jersey
NKVD	[Soviet people's commissariat for internal affairs]
NM	New Mexico
nm	nanometre(s)
no. *pl.* nos.	number(s)
Nov	November
n.p.	no place [of publication]
NS	new style
NV	Nevada
NY	New York
NZBS	New Zealand Broadcasting Service
OBE	officer of the Order of the British Empire
obit.	obituary
Oct	October
OCTU	officer cadets training unit
OECD	Organization for Economic Co-operation and Development
OEEC	Organization for European Economic Co-operation
OFM	order of Friars Minor [Franciscans]
OFMCap	Ordine Frati Minori Cappucini: member of the Capuchin order
OH	Ohio
OK	Oklahoma
O level	ordinary level [examination]
OM	Order of Merit
OP	order of Preachers [Dominicans]
op. *pl.* opp.	opus *pl.* opera
OPEC	Organization of Petroleum Exporting Countries
OR	Oregon
orig.	original
OS	old style
OSB	Order of St Benedict
OTC	Officers' Training Corps
OWS	Old Watercolour Society
Oxon.	Oxoniensis
p. *pl.* pp.	page(s)
PA	Pennsylvania
p.a.	per annum
para.	paragraph
PAYE	pay as you earn
pbk *pl.* pbks	paperback(s)
per.	[during the] period
PhD	doctor of philosophy
pl.	(1) plate(s); (2) plural
priv. coll.	private collection
pt *pl.* pts	part(s)
pubd	published
PVC	polyvinyl chloride
q. *pl.* qq.	(1) question(s); (2) quire(s)
QC	queen's counsel
R	rand
R.	Rex / Regina
r	recto
r.	reigned / ruled
RA	Royal Academy / Royal Academician

RAC	Royal Automobile Club
RAF	Royal Air Force
RAFVR	Royal Air Force Volunteer Reserve
RAM	[member of the] Royal Academy of Music
RAMC	Royal Army Medical Corps
RCA	Royal College of Art
RCNC	Royal Corps of Naval Constructors
RCOG	Royal College of Obstetricians and Gynaecologists
RDI	royal designer for industry
RE	Royal Engineers
repr. *pl.* reprs.	reprint(s) / reprinted
repro.	reproduced
rev.	revised / revised by / reviser / revision
Revd	Reverend
RHA	Royal Hibernian Academy
RI	(1) Rhode Island; (2) Royal Institute of Painters in Water-Colours
RIBA	Royal Institute of British Architects
RIN	Royal Indian Navy
RM	Reichsmark
RMS	Royal Mail steamer
RN	Royal Navy
RNA	ribonucleic acid
RNAS	Royal Naval Air Service
RNR	Royal Naval Reserve
RNVR	Royal Naval Volunteer Reserve
RO	Record Office
r.p.m.	revolutions per minute
RRS	royal research ship
Rs	rupees
RSA	(1) Royal Scottish Academician; (2) Royal Society of Arts
RSPCA	Royal Society for the Prevention of Cruelty to Animals
Rt Hon.	Right Honourable
Rt Revd	Right Reverend
RUC	Royal Ulster Constabulary
Russ.	Russian
RWS	Royal Watercolour Society
S4C	Sianel Pedwar Cymru
s.	shilling(s)
s.a.	*sub anno*: under the year
SABC	South African Broadcasting Corporation
SAS	Special Air Service
SC	South Carolina
ScD	doctor of science
S$	Singapore dollar
SD	South Dakota
sec.	second(s)
sel.	selected
sen.	senior
Sept	September
ser.	series
SHAPE	supreme headquarters allied powers, Europe
SIDRO	Société Internationale d'Énergie Hydro-Électrique
sig. *pl.* sigs.	signature(s)
sing.	singular
SIS	Secret Intelligence Service
SJ	Society of Jesus
Skr	Swedish krona
Span.	Spanish
SPCK	Society for Promoting Christian Knowledge
SS	(1) Santissimi; (2) Schutzstaffel; (3) steam ship
STB	bachelor of theology
STD	doctor of theology
STM	master of theology
STP	doctor of theology
supp.	supposedly
suppl. *pl.* suppls.	supplement(s)
s.v.	*sub verbo* / *sub voce*: under the word / heading
SY	steam yacht
TA	Territorial Army
TASS	[Soviet news agency]
TB	tuberculosis (*lit.* tubercle bacillus)
TD	(1) *teachtaí dála* (member of the Dáil); (2) territorial decoration
TN	Tennessee
TNT	trinitrotoluene
trans.	translated / translated by / translation / translator
TT	tourist trophy
TUC	Trades Union Congress
TX	Texas
U-boat	*Unterseeboot*: submarine
Ufa	Universum-Film AG
UMIST	University of Manchester Institute of Science and Technology
UN	United Nations
UNESCO	United Nations Educational, Scientific, and Cultural Organization
UNICEF	United Nations International Children's Emergency Fund
unpubd	unpublished
USS	United States ship
UT	Utah
v	verso
v.	versus
VA	Virginia
VAD	Voluntary Aid Detachment
VC	Victoria Cross
VE-day	victory in Europe day
Ven.	Venerable
VJ-day	victory over Japan day
vol. *pl.* vols.	volume(s)
VT	Vermont
WA	Washington [state]
WAAC	Women's Auxiliary Army Corps
WAAF	Women's Auxiliary Air Force
WEA	Workers' Educational Association
WHO	World Health Organization
WI	Wisconsin
WRAF	Women's Royal Air Force
WRNS	Women's Royal Naval Service
WV	West Virginia
WVS	Women's Voluntary Service
WY	Wyoming
¥	yen
YMCA	Young Men's Christian Association
YWCA	Young Women's Christian Association

2 Institution abbreviations

All Souls Oxf.	All Souls College, Oxford
AM Oxf.	Ashmolean Museum, Oxford
Balliol Oxf.	Balliol College, Oxford
BBC WAC	BBC Written Archives Centre, Reading
Beds. & Luton ARS	Bedfordshire and Luton Archives and Record Service, Bedford
Berks. RO	Berkshire Record Office, Reading
BFI	British Film Institute, London
BFI NFTVA	British Film Institute, London, National Film and Television Archive
BGS	British Geological Survey, Keyworth, Nottingham
Birm. CA	Birmingham Central Library, Birmingham City Archives
Birm. CL	Birmingham Central Library
BL	British Library, London
BL NSA	British Library, London, National Sound Archive
BL OIOC	British Library, London, Oriental and India Office Collections
BLPES	London School of Economics and Political Science, British Library of Political and Economic Science
BM	British Museum, London
Bodl. Oxf.	Bodleian Library, Oxford
Bodl. RH	Bodleian Library of Commonwealth and African Studies at Rhodes House, Oxford
Borth. Inst.	Borthwick Institute of Historical Research, University of York
Boston PL	Boston Public Library, Massachusetts
Bristol RO	Bristol Record Office
Bucks. RLSS	Buckinghamshire Records and Local Studies Service, Aylesbury
CAC Cam.	Churchill College, Cambridge, Churchill Archives Centre
Cambs. AS	Cambridgeshire Archive Service
CCC Cam.	Corpus Christi College, Cambridge
CCC Oxf.	Corpus Christi College, Oxford
Ches. & Chester ALSS	Cheshire and Chester Archives and Local Studies Service
Christ Church Oxf.	Christ Church, Oxford
Christies	Christies, London
City Westm. AC	City of Westminster Archives Centre, London
CKS	Centre for Kentish Studies, Maidstone
CLRO	Corporation of London Records Office
Coll. Arms	College of Arms, London
Col. U.	Columbia University, New York
Cornwall RO	Cornwall Record Office, Truro
Courtauld Inst.	Courtauld Institute of Art, London
CUL	Cambridge University Library
Cumbria AS	Cumbria Archive Service
Derbys. RO	Derbyshire Record Office, Matlock
Devon RO	Devon Record Office, Exeter
Dorset RO	Dorset Record Office, Dorchester
Duke U.	Duke University, Durham, North Carolina
Duke U., Perkins L.	Duke University, Durham, North Carolina, William R. Perkins Library
Durham Cath. CL	Durham Cathedral, chapter library
Durham RO	Durham Record Office
DWL	Dr Williams's Library, London
Essex RO	Essex Record Office
E. Sussex RO	East Sussex Record Office, Lewes
Eton	Eton College, Berkshire
FM Cam.	Fitzwilliam Museum, Cambridge
Folger	Folger Shakespeare Library, Washington, DC
Garr. Club	Garrick Club, London
Girton Cam.	Girton College, Cambridge
GL	Guildhall Library, London
Glos. RO	Gloucestershire Record Office, Gloucester
Gon. & Caius Cam.	Gonville and Caius College, Cambridge
Gov. Art Coll.	Government Art Collection
GS Lond.	Geological Society of London
Hants. RO	Hampshire Record Office, Winchester
Harris Man. Oxf.	Harris Manchester College, Oxford
Harvard TC	Harvard Theatre Collection, Harvard University, Cambridge, Massachusetts, Nathan Marsh Pusey Library
Harvard U.	Harvard University, Cambridge, Massachusetts
Harvard U., Houghton L.	Harvard University, Cambridge, Massachusetts, Houghton Library
Herefs. RO	Herefordshire Record Office, Hereford
Herts. ALS	Hertfordshire Archives and Local Studies, Hertford
Hist. Soc. Penn.	Historical Society of Pennsylvania, Philadelphia
HLRO	House of Lords Record Office, London
Hult. Arch.	Hulton Archive, London and New York
Hunt. L.	Huntington Library, San Marino, California
ICL	Imperial College, London
Inst. CE	Institution of Civil Engineers, London
Inst. EE	Institution of Electrical Engineers, London
IWM	Imperial War Museum, London
IWM FVA	Imperial War Museum, London, Film and Video Archive
IWM SA	Imperial War Museum, London, Sound Archive
JRL	John Rylands University Library of Manchester
King's AC Cam.	King's College Archives Centre, Cambridge
King's Cam.	King's College, Cambridge
King's Lond.	King's College, London
King's Lond., Liddell Hart C.	King's College, London, Liddell Hart Centre for Military Archives
Lancs. RO	Lancashire Record Office, Preston
L. Cong.	Library of Congress, Washington, DC
Leics. RO	Leicestershire, Leicester, and Rutland Record Office, Leicester
Lincs. Arch.	Lincolnshire Archives, Lincoln
Linn. Soc.	Linnean Society of London
LMA	London Metropolitan Archives
LPL	Lambeth Palace, London
Lpool RO	Liverpool Record Office and Local Studies Service
LUL	London University Library
Magd. Cam.	Magdalene College, Cambridge
Magd. Oxf.	Magdalen College, Oxford
Man. City Gall.	Manchester City Galleries
Man. CL	Manchester Central Library
Mass. Hist. Soc.	Massachusetts Historical Society, Boston
Merton Oxf.	Merton College, Oxford
MHS Oxf.	Museum of the History of Science, Oxford
Mitchell L., Glas.	Mitchell Library, Glasgow
Mitchell L., NSW	State Library of New South Wales, Sydney, Mitchell Library
Morgan L.	Pierpont Morgan Library, New York
NA Canada	National Archives of Canada, Ottawa
NA Ire.	National Archives of Ireland, Dublin
NAM	National Army Museum, London
NA Scot.	National Archives of Scotland, Edinburgh
News Int. RO	News International Record Office, London
NG Ire.	National Gallery of Ireland, Dublin

NG Scot.	National Gallery of Scotland, Edinburgh
NHM	Natural History Museum, London
NL Aus.	National Library of Australia, Canberra
NL Ire.	National Library of Ireland, Dublin
NL NZ	National Library of New Zealand, Wellington
NL NZ, Turnbull L.	National Library of New Zealand, Wellington, Alexander Turnbull Library
NL Scot.	National Library of Scotland, Edinburgh
NL Wales	National Library of Wales, Aberystwyth
NMG Wales	National Museum and Gallery of Wales, Cardiff
NMM	National Maritime Museum, London
Norfolk RO	Norfolk Record Office, Norwich
Northants. RO	Northamptonshire Record Office, Northampton
Northumbd RO	Northumberland Record Office
Notts. Arch.	Nottinghamshire Archives, Nottingham
NPG	National Portrait Gallery, London
NRA	National Archives, London, Historical Manuscripts Commission, National Register of Archives
Nuffield Oxf.	Nuffield College, Oxford
N. Yorks. CRO	North Yorkshire County Record Office, Northallerton
NYPL	New York Public Library
Oxf. UA	Oxford University Archives
Oxf. U. Mus. NH	Oxford University Museum of Natural History
Oxon. RO	Oxfordshire Record Office, Oxford
Pembroke Cam.	Pembroke College, Cambridge
PRO	National Archives, London, Public Record Office
PRO NIre.	Public Record Office for Northern Ireland, Belfast
Pusey Oxf.	Pusey House, Oxford
RA	Royal Academy of Arts, London
Ransom HRC	Harry Ransom Humanities Research Center, University of Texas, Austin
RAS	Royal Astronomical Society, London
RBG Kew	Royal Botanic Gardens, Kew, London
RCP Lond.	Royal College of Physicians of London
RCS Eng.	Royal College of Surgeons of England, London
RGS	Royal Geographical Society, London
RIBA	Royal Institute of British Architects, London
RIBA BAL	Royal Institute of British Architects, London, British Architectural Library
Royal Arch.	Royal Archives, Windsor Castle, Berkshire [by gracious permission of her majesty the queen]
Royal Irish Acad.	Royal Irish Academy, Dublin
Royal Scot. Acad.	Royal Scottish Academy, Edinburgh
RS	Royal Society, London
RSA	Royal Society of Arts, London
RS Friends, Lond.	Religious Society of Friends, London
St Ant. Oxf.	St Antony's College, Oxford
St John Cam.	St John's College, Cambridge
S. Antiquaries, Lond.	Society of Antiquaries of London
Sci. Mus.	Science Museum, London
Scot. NPG	Scottish National Portrait Gallery, Edinburgh
Scott Polar RI	University of Cambridge, Scott Polar Research Institute
Sheff. Arch.	Sheffield Archives
Shrops. RRC	Shropshire Records and Research Centre, Shrewsbury
SOAS	School of Oriental and African Studies, London
Som. ARS	Somerset Archive and Record Service, Taunton
Staffs. RO	Staffordshire Record Office, Stafford
Suffolk RO	Suffolk Record Office
Surrey HC	Surrey History Centre, Woking
TCD	Trinity College, Dublin
Trinity Cam.	Trinity College, Cambridge
U. Aberdeen	University of Aberdeen
U. Birm.	University of Birmingham
U. Birm. L.	University of Birmingham Library
U. Cal.	University of California
U. Cam.	University of Cambridge
UCL	University College, London
U. Durham	University of Durham
U. Durham L.	University of Durham Library
U. Edin.	University of Edinburgh
U. Edin., New Coll.	University of Edinburgh, New College
U. Edin., New Coll. L.	University of Edinburgh, New College Library
U. Edin. L.	University of Edinburgh Library
U. Glas.	University of Glasgow
U. Glas. L.	University of Glasgow Library
U. Hull	University of Hull
U. Hull, Brynmor Jones L.	University of Hull, Brynmor Jones Library
U. Leeds	University of Leeds
U. Leeds, Brotherton L.	University of Leeds, Brotherton Library
U. Lond.	University of London
U. Lpool	University of Liverpool
U. Lpool L.	University of Liverpool Library
U. Mich.	University of Michigan, Ann Arbor
U. Mich., Clements L.	University of Michigan, Ann Arbor, William L. Clements Library
U. Newcastle	University of Newcastle upon Tyne
U. Newcastle, Robinson L.	University of Newcastle upon Tyne, Robinson Library
U. Nott.	University of Nottingham
U. Nott. L.	University of Nottingham Library
U. Oxf.	University of Oxford
U. Reading	University of Reading
U. Reading L.	University of Reading Library
U. St Andr.	University of St Andrews
U. St Andr. L.	University of St Andrews Library
U. Southampton	University of Southampton
U. Southampton L.	University of Southampton Library
U. Sussex	University of Sussex, Brighton
U. Texas	University of Texas, Austin
U. Wales	University of Wales
U. Warwick Mod. RC	University of Warwick, Coventry, Modern Records Centre
V&A	Victoria and Albert Museum, London
V&A NAL	Victoria and Albert Museum, London, National Art Library
Warks. CRO	Warwickshire County Record Office, Warwick
Wellcome L.	Wellcome Library for the History and Understanding of Medicine, London
Westm. DA	Westminster Diocesan Archives, London
Wilts. & Swindon RO	Wiltshire and Swindon Record Office, Trowbridge
Worcs. RO	Worcestershire Record Office, Worcester
W. Sussex RO	West Sussex Record Office, Chichester
W. Yorks. AS	West Yorkshire Archive Service
Yale U.	Yale University, New Haven, Connecticut
Yale U., Beinecke L.	Yale University, New Haven, Connecticut, Beinecke Rare Book and Manuscript Library
Yale U. CBA	Yale University, New Haven, Connecticut, Yale Center for British Art

3 *Bibliographic abbreviations*

Adams, *Drama*	W. D. Adams, *A dictionary of the drama*, 1: *A–G* (1904); 2: *H–Z* (1956) [vol. 2 microfilm only]
AFM	J O'Donovan, ed. and trans., *Annala rioghachta Eireann / Annals of the kingdom of Ireland by the four masters*, 7 vols. (1848–51); 2nd edn (1856); 3rd edn (1990)
Allibone, *Dict.*	S. A. Allibone, *A critical dictionary of English literature and British and American authors*, 3 vols. (1859–71); suppl. by J. F. Kirk, 2 vols. (1891)
ANB	J. A. Garraty and M. C. Carnes, eds., *American national biography*, 24 vols. (1999)
Anderson, *Scot. nat.*	W. Anderson, *The Scottish nation, or, The surnames, families, literature, honours, and biographical history of the people of Scotland*, 3 vols. (1859–63)
Ann. mon.	H. R. Luard, ed., *Annales monastici*, 5 vols., Rolls Series, 36 (1864–9)
Ann. Ulster	S. Mac Airt and G. Mac Niocaill, eds., *Annals of Ulster (to AD 1131)* (1983)
APC	*Acts of the privy council of England*, new ser., 46 vols. (1890–1964)
APS	*The acts of the parliaments of Scotland*, 12 vols. in 13 (1814–75)
Arber, *Regs. Stationers*	F. Arber, ed., *A transcript of the registers of the Company of Stationers of London, 1554–1640 AD*, 5 vols. (1875–94)
ArchR	*Architectural Review*
ASC	D. Whitelock, D. C. Douglas, and S. I. Tucker, ed. and trans., *The Anglo-Saxon Chronicle: a revised translation* (1961)
AS chart.	P. H. Sawyer, *Anglo-Saxon charters: an annotated list and bibliography*, Royal Historical Society Guides and Handbooks (1968)
AusDB	D. Pike and others, eds., *Australian dictionary of biography*, 16 vols. (1966–2002)
Baker, *Serjeants*	J. H. Baker, *The order of serjeants at law*, SeldS, suppl. ser., 5 (1984)
Bale, *Cat.*	J. Bale, *Scriptorum illustrium Maioris Brytannie, quam nunc Angliam et Scotiam vocant: catalogus*, 2 vols. in 1 (Basel, 1557–9); facs. edn (1971)
Bale, *Index*	J. Bale, *Index Britanniae scriptorum*, ed. R. L. Poole and M. Bateson (1902); facs. edn (1990)
BBCS	*Bulletin of the Board of Celtic Studies*
BDMBR	J. O. Baylen and N. J. Gossman, eds., *Biographical dictionary of modern British radicals*, 3 vols. in 4 (1979–88)
Bede, *Hist. eccl.*	*Bede's Ecclesiastical history of the English people*, ed. and trans. B. Colgrave and R. A. B. Mynors, OMT (1969); repr. (1991)
Bénézit, *Dict.*	E. Bénézit, *Dictionnaire critique et documentaire des peintres, sculpteurs, dessinateurs et graveurs*, 3 vols. (Paris, 1911–23); new edn, 8 vols. (1948–66), repr. (1966); 3rd edn, rev. and enl., 10 vols. (1976); 4th edn, 14 vols. (1999)
BIHR	*Bulletin of the Institute of Historical Research*
Birch, *Seals*	W. de Birch, *Catalogue of seals in the department of manuscripts in the British Museum*, 6 vols. (1887–1900)
Bishop Burnet's History	*Bishop Burnet's History of his own time*, ed. M. J. Routh, 2nd edn, 6 vols. (1833)
Blackwood	*Blackwood's [Edinburgh] Magazine*, 328 vols. (1817–1980)
Blain, Clements & Grundy, *Feminist comp.*	V. Blain, P. Clements, and I. Grundy, eds., *The feminist companion to literature in English* (1990)
BL cat.	*The British Library general catalogue of printed books* [in 360 vols. with suppls., also CD-ROM and online]
BMJ	*British Medical Journal*
Boase & Courtney, *Bibl. Corn.*	G. C. Boase and W. P. Courtney, *Bibliotheca Cornubiensis: a catalogue of the writings … of Cornishmen*, 3 vols. (1874–82)
Boase, *Mod. Eng. biog.*	F. Boase, *Modern English biography: containing many thousand concise memoirs of persons who have died since the year 1850*, 6 vols. (privately printed, Truro, 1892–1921); repr. (1965)
Boswell, *Life*	*Boswell's Life of Johnson: together with Journal of a tour to the Hebrides and Johnson's Diary of a journey into north Wales*, ed. G. B. Hill, enl. edn, rev. L. F. Powell, 6 vols. (1934–50); 2nd edn (1964); repr. (1971)
Brown & Stratton, *Brit. mus.*	J. D. Brown and S. S. Stratton, *British musical biography* (1897)
Bryan, *Painters*	M. Bryan, *A biographical and critical dictionary of painters and engravers*, 2 vols. (1816); new edn, ed. G. Stanley (1849); new edn, ed. R. E. Graves and W. Armstrong, 2 vols. (1886–9); [4th edn], ed. G. C. Williamson, 5 vols. (1903–5) [various reprs.]
Burke, *Gen. GB*	J. Burke, *A genealogical and heraldic history of the commoners of Great Britain and Ireland*, 4 vols. (1833–8); new edn as *A genealogical and heraldic dictionary of the landed gentry of Great Britain and Ireland*, 3 vols. [1843–9] [many later edns]
Burke, *Gen. Ire.*	J. B. Burke, *A genealogical and heraldic history of the landed gentry of Ireland* (1899); 2nd edn (1904); 3rd edn (1912); 4th edn (1958); 5th edn as *Burke's Irish family records* (1976)
Burke, *Peerage*	J. Burke, *A general* [later edns *A genealogical*] *and heraldic dictionary of the peerage and baronetage of the United Kingdom* [later edns *the British empire*] (1829–)
Burney, *Hist. mus.*	C. Burney, *A general history of music, from the earliest ages to the present period*, 4 vols. (1776–89)
Burtchaell & Sadleir, *Alum. Dubl.*	G. D. Burtchaell and T. U. Sadleir, *Alumni Dublinenses: a register of the students, graduates, and provosts of Trinity College* (1924); [2nd edn], with suppl., in 2 pts (1935)
Calamy rev.	A. G. Matthews, *Calamy revised* (1934); repr. (1988)
CCI	*Calendar of confirmations and inventories granted and given up in the several commissariots of Scotland* (1876–)
CClR	*Calendar of the close rolls preserved in the Public Record Office*, 47 vols. (1892–1963)
CDS	J. Bain, ed., *Calendar of documents relating to Scotland*, 4 vols., PRO (1881–8); suppl. vol. 5, ed. G. G. Simpson and J. D. Galbraith [1986]
CEPR letters	W. H. Bliss, C. Johnson, and J. Twemlow, eds., *Calendar of entries in the papal registers relating to Great Britain and Ireland: papal letters* (1893–)
CGPLA	*Calendars of the grants of probate and letters of administration* [in 4 ser.: *England & Wales, Northern Ireland, Ireland*, and *Éire*]
Chambers, *Scots.*	R. Chambers, ed., *A biographical dictionary of eminent Scotsmen*, 4 vols. (1832–5)
Chancery records	chancery records pubd by the PRO
Chancery records (RC)	chancery records pubd by the Record Commissions

CIPM	*Calendar of inquisitions post mortem*, [20 vols.], PRO (1904–); also *Henry VII*, 3 vols. (1898–1955)
Clarendon, *Hist. rebellion*	E. Hyde, earl of Clarendon, *The history of the rebellion and civil wars in England*, 6 vols. (1888); repr. (1958) and (1992)
Cobbett, *Parl. hist.*	W. Cobbett and J. Wright, eds., *Cobbett's Parliamentary history of England*, 36 vols. (1806–1820)
Colvin, *Archs.*	H. Colvin, *A biographical dictionary of British architects, 1600–1840*, 3rd edn (1995)
Cooper, *Ath. Cantab.*	C. H. Cooper and T. Cooper, *Athenae Cantabrigienses*, 3 vols. (1858–1913); repr. (1967)
CPR	*Calendar of the patent rolls preserved in the Public Record Office* (1891–)
Crockford	*Crockford's Clerical Directory*
CS	Camden Society
CSP	*Calendar of state papers* [in 11 ser.: *domestic, Scotland, Scottish series, Ireland, colonial, Commonwealth, foreign, Spain* [at Simancas], *Rome, Milan*, and *Venice*]
CYS	Canterbury and York Society
DAB	*Dictionary of American biography*, 21 vols. (1928–36), repr. in 11 vols. (1964); 10 suppls. (1944–96)
DBB	D. J. Jeremy, ed., *Dictionary of business biography*, 5 vols. (1984–6)
DCB	G. W. Brown and others, *Dictionary of Canadian biography*, [14 vols.] (1966–)
Debrett's Peerage	*Debrett's Peerage* (1803–) [sometimes *Debrett's Illustrated peerage*]
Desmond, *Botanists*	R. Desmond, *Dictionary of British and Irish botanists and horticulturists* (1977); rev. edn (1994)
Dir. Brit. archs.	A. Felstead, J. Franklin, and L. Pinfield, eds., *Directory of British architects, 1834–1900* (1993); 2nd edn, ed. A. Brodie and others, 2 vols. (2001)
DLB	J. M. Bellamy and J. Saville, eds., *Dictionary of labour biography*, [10 vols.] (1972–)
DLitB	Dictionary of Literary Biography
DNB	*Dictionary of national biography*, 63 vols. (1885–1900), suppl., 3 vols. (1901); repr. in 22 vols. (1908–9); 10 further suppls. (1912–96); *Missing persons* (1993)
DNZB	W. H. Oliver and C. Orange, eds., *The dictionary of New Zealand biography*, 5 vols. (1990–2000)
DSAB	W. J. de Kock and others, eds., *Dictionary of South African biography*, 5 vols. (1968–87)
DSB	C. C. Gillispie and F. L. Holmes, eds., *Dictionary of scientific biography*, 16 vols. (1970–80); repr. in 8 vols. (1981); 2 vol. suppl. (1990)
DSBB	A. Slaven and S. Checkland, eds., *Dictionary of Scottish business biography, 1860–1960*, 2 vols. (1986–90)
DSCHT	N. M. de S. Cameron and others, eds., *Dictionary of Scottish church history and theology* (1993)
Dugdale, *Monasticon*	W. Dugdale, *Monasticon Anglicanum*, 3 vols. (1655–72); 2nd edn, 3 vols. (1661–82); new edn, ed. J. Caley, J. Ellis, and B. Bandinel, 6 vols. in 8 pts (1817–30); repr. (1846) and (1970)
DWB	J. E. Lloyd and others, eds., *Dictionary of Welsh biography down to 1940* (1959) [Eng. trans. of *Y bywgraffiadur Cymreig hyd 1940*, 2nd edn (1954)]
EdinR	*Edinburgh Review, or, Critical Journal*
EETS	Early English Text Society
Emden, *Cam.*	A. B. Emden, *A biographical register of the University of Cambridge to 1500* (1963)
Emden, *Oxf.*	A. B. Emden, *A biographical register of the University of Oxford to AD 1500*, 3 vols. (1957–9); also *A biographical register of the University of Oxford, AD 1501 to 1540* (1974)
EngHR	*English Historical Review*
Engraved Brit. ports.	F. M. O'Donoghue and H. M. Hake, *Catalogue of engraved British portraits preserved in the department of prints and drawings in the British Museum*, 6 vols. (1908–25)
ER	The English Reports, 178 vols. (1900–32)
ESTC	*English short title catalogue, 1475–1800* [CD-ROM and online]
Evelyn, *Diary*	*The diary of John Evelyn*, ed. E. S. De Beer, 6 vols. (1955); repr. (2000)
Farington, *Diary*	*The diary of Joseph Farington*, ed. K. Garlick and others, 17 vols. (1978–98)
Fasti Angl. (Hardy)	J. Le Neve, *Fasti ecclesiae Anglicanae*, ed. T. D. Hardy, 3 vols. (1854)
Fasti Angl., 1066–1300	[J. Le Neve], *Fasti ecclesiae Anglicanae, 1066–1300*, ed. D. E. Greenway and J. S. Barrow, [8 vols.] (1968–)
Fasti Angl., 1300–1541	[J. Le Neve], *Fasti ecclesiae Anglicanae, 1300–1541*, 12 vols. (1962–7)
Fasti Angl., 1541–1857	[J. Le Neve], *Fasti ecclesiae Anglicanae, 1541–1857*, ed. J. M. Horn, D. M. Smith, and D. S. Bailey, [9 vols.] (1969–)
Fasti Scot.	H. Scott, *Fasti ecclesiae Scoticanae*, 3 vols. in 6 (1871); new edn, [11 vols.] (1915–)
FO List	*Foreign Office List*
Fortescue, *Brit. army*	J. W. Fortescue, *A history of the British army*, 13 vols. (1899–1930)
Foss, *Judges*	E. Foss, *The judges of England*, 9 vols. (1848–64); repr. (1966)
Foster, *Alum. Oxon.*	J. Foster, ed., *Alumni Oxonienses: the members of the University of Oxford, 1715–1886*, 4 vols. (1887–8); later edn (1891); also *Alumni Oxonienses … 1500–1714*, 4 vols. (1891–2); 8 vol. repr. (1968) and (2000)
Fuller, *Worthies*	T. Fuller, *The history of the worthies of England*, 4 pts (1662); new edn, 2 vols., ed. J. Nichols (1811); new edn, 3 vols., ed. P. A. Nuttall (1840); repr. (1965)
GEC, *Baronetage*	G. E. Cokayne, *Complete baronetage*, 6 vols. (1900–09); repr. (1983) [microprint]
GEC, *Peerage*	G. E. C. [G. E. Cokayne], *The complete peerage of England, Scotland, Ireland, Great Britain, and the United Kingdom*, 8 vols. (1887–98); new edn, ed. V. Gibbs and others, 14 vols. in 15 (1910–98); microprint repr. (1982) and (1987)
Genest, *Eng. stage*	J. Genest, *Some account of the English stage from the Restoration in 1660 to 1830*, 10 vols. (1832); repr. [New York, 1965]
Gillow, *Lit. biog. hist.*	J. Gillow, *A literary and biographical history or bibliographical dictionary of the English Catholics, from the breach with Rome, in 1534, to the present time*, 5 vols. [1885–1902]; repr. (1961); repr. with preface by C. Gillow (1999)
Gir. Camb. opera	*Giraldi Cambrensis opera*, ed. J. S. Brewer, J. F. Dimock, and G. F. Warner, 8 vols., Rolls Series, 21 (1861–91)
GJ	*Geographical Journal*

Gladstone, *Diaries*	*The Gladstone diaries: with cabinet minutes and prime-ministerial correspondence*, ed. M. R. D. Foot and H. C. G. Matthew, 14 vols. (1968–94)
GM	*Gentleman's Magazine*
Graves, *Artists*	A. Graves, ed., *A dictionary of artists who have exhibited works in the principal London exhibitions of oil paintings from 1760 to 1880* (1884); new edn (1895); 3rd edn (1901); facs. edn (1969); repr. [1970], (1973), and (1984)
Graves, *Brit. Inst.*	A. Graves, *The British Institution, 1806–1867: a complete dictionary of contributors and their work from the foundation of the institution* (1875); facs. edn (1908); repr. (1969)
Graves, *RA exhibitors*	A. Graves, *The Royal Academy of Arts: a complete dictionary of contributors and their work from its foundation in 1769 to 1904*, 8 vols. (1905–6); repr. in 4 vols. (1970) and (1972)
Graves, *Soc. Artists*	A. Graves, *The Society of Artists of Great Britain, 1760–1791, the Free Society of Artists, 1761–1783: a complete dictionary* (1907); facs. edn (1969)
Greaves & Zaller, *BDBR*	R. L. Greaves and R. Zaller, eds., *Biographical dictionary of British radicals in the seventeenth century*, 3 vols. (1982–4)
Grove, *Dict. mus.*	G. Grove, ed., *A dictionary of music and musicians*, 5 vols. (1878–90); 2nd edn, ed. J. A. Fuller Maitland (1904–10); 3rd edn, ed. H. C. Colles (1927); 4th edn with suppl. (1940); 5th edn, ed. E. Blom, 9 vols. (1954); suppl. (1961) [see also *New Grove*]
Hall, *Dramatic ports.*	L. A. Hall, *Catalogue of dramatic portraits in the theatre collection of the Harvard College library*, 4 vols. (1930–34)
Hansard	*Hansard's parliamentary debates*, ser. 1–5 (1803–)
Highfill, Burnim & Langhans, *BDA*	P. H. Highfill, K. A. Burnim, and E. A. Langhans, *A biographical dictionary of actors, actresses, musicians, dancers, managers, and other stage personnel in London, 1660–1800*, 16 vols. (1973–93)
Hist. U. Oxf.	T. H. Aston, ed., *The history of the University of Oxford*, 8 vols. (1984–2000) [1: *The early Oxford schools*, ed. J. I. Catto (1984); 2: *Late medieval Oxford*, ed. J. I. Catto and R. Evans (1992); 3: *The collegiate university*, ed. J. McConica (1986); 4: *Seventeenth-century Oxford*, ed. N. Tyacke (1997); 5: *The eighteenth century*, ed. L. S. Sutherland and L. G. Mitchell (1986); 6–7: *Nineteenth-century Oxford*, ed. M. G. Brock and M. C. Curthoys (1997–2000); 8: *The twentieth century*, ed. B. Harrison (2000)]
HJ	*Historical Journal*
HMC	Historical Manuscripts Commission
Holdsworth, *Eng. law*	W. S. Holdsworth, *A history of English law*, ed. A. L. Goodhart and H. L. Hanbury, 17 vols. (1903–72)
HoP, *Commons*	*The history of parliament: the House of Commons* [*1386–1421*, ed. J. S. Roskell, L. Clark, and C. Rawcliffe, 4 vols. (1992); *1509–1558*, ed. S. T. Bindoff, 3 vols. (1982); *1558–1603*, ed. P. W. Hasler, 3 vols. (1981); *1660–1690*, ed. B. D. Henning, 3 vols. (1983); *1690–1715*, ed. D. W. Hayton, E. Cruickshanks, and S. Handley, 5 vols. (2002); *1715–1754*, ed. R. Sedgwick, 2 vols. (1970); *1754–1790*, ed. L. Namier and J. Brooke, 3 vols. (1964), repr. (1985); *1790–1820*, ed. R. G. Thorne, 5 vols. (1986); in draft (used with permission): *1422–1504*, *1604–1629*, *1640–1660*, and *1820–1832*]
IGI	*International Genealogical Index*, Church of Jesus Christ of the Latterday Saints
ILN	*Illustrated London News*
IMC	Irish Manuscripts Commission
Irving, *Scots.*	J. Irving, ed., *The book of Scotsmen eminent for achievements in arms and arts, church and state, law, legislation and literature, commerce, science, travel and philanthropy* (1881)
JCS	*Journal of the Chemical Society*
JHC	*Journals of the House of Commons*
JHL	*Journals of the House of Lords*
John of Worcester, *Chron.*	*The chronicle of John of Worcester*, ed. R. R. Darlington and P. McGurk, trans. J. Bray and P. McGurk, 3 vols., OMT (1995–) [vol. 1 forthcoming]
Keeler, *Long Parliament*	M. F. Keeler, *The Long Parliament, 1640–1641: a biographical study of its members* (1954)
Kelly, *Handbk*	*The upper ten thousand: an alphabetical list of all members of noble families*, 3 vols. (1875–7); continued as *Kelly's handbook of the upper ten thousand for 1878* [1879], 2 vols. (1878–9); continued as *Kelly's handbook to the titled, landed and official classes*, 94 vols. (1880–1973)
LondG	*London Gazette*
LP Henry VIII	J. S. Brewer, J. Gairdner, and R. H. Brodie, eds., *Letters and papers, foreign and domestic, of the reign of Henry VIII*, 23 vols. in 38 (1862–1932); repr. (1965)
Mallalieu, *Watercolour artists*	H. L. Mallalieu, *The dictionary of British watercolour artists up to 1820*, 3 vols. (1976–90); vol. 1, 2nd edn (1986)
Memoirs FRS	*Biographical Memoirs of Fellows of the Royal Society*
MGH	Monumenta Germaniae Historica
MT	*Musical Times*
Munk, *Roll*	W. Munk, *The roll of the Royal College of Physicians of London*, 2 vols. (1861); 2nd edn, 3 vols. (1878)
N&Q	*Notes and Queries*
New Grove	S. Sadie, ed., *The new Grove dictionary of music and musicians*, 20 vols. (1980); 2nd edn, 29 vols. (2001) [also online edn; see also Grove, *Dict. mus.*]
Nichols, *Illustrations*	J. Nichols and J. B. Nichols, *Illustrations of the literary history of the eighteenth century*, 8 vols. (1817–58)
Nichols, *Lit. anecdotes*	J. Nichols, *Literary anecdotes of the eighteenth century*, 9 vols. (1812–16); facs. edn (1966)
Obits. FRS	*Obituary Notices of Fellows of the Royal Society*
O'Byrne, *Naval biog. dict.*	W. R. O'Byrne, *A naval biographical dictionary* (1849); repr. (1990); [2nd edn], 2 vols. (1861)
OHS	Oxford Historical Society
Old Westminsters	*The record of Old Westminsters*, 1–2, ed. G. F. R. Barker and A. H. Stenning (1928); suppl. 1, ed. J. B. Whitmore and G. R. Y. Radcliffe [1938]; 3, ed. J. B. Whitmore, G. R. Y. Radcliffe, and D. C. Simpson (1963); suppl. 2, ed. F. E. Pagan (1978); 4, ed. F. E. Pagan and H. E. Pagan (1992)
OMT	Oxford Medieval Texts
Ordericus Vitalis, *Eccl. hist.*	*The ecclesiastical history of Orderic Vitalis*, ed. and trans. M. Chibnall, 6 vols., OMT (1969–80); repr. (1990)
Paris, *Chron.*	*Matthaei Parisiensis, monachi sancti Albani, chronica majora*, ed. H. R. Luard, Rolls Series, 7 vols. (1872–83)
Parl. papers	*Parliamentary papers* (1801–)
PBA	*Proceedings of the British Academy*

Pepys, *Diary*	*The diary of Samuel Pepys*, ed. R. Latham and W. Matthews, 11 vols. (1970–83); repr. (1995) and (2000)
Pevsner	N. Pevsner and others, Buildings of England series
PICE	*Proceedings of the Institution of Civil Engineers*
Pipe rolls	*The great roll of the pipe for ...*, PRSoc. (1884–)
PRO	Public Record Office
PRS	*Proceedings of the Royal Society of London*
PRSoc.	Pipe Roll Society
PTRS	*Philosophical Transactions of the Royal Society*
QR	*Quarterly Review*
RC	Record Commissions
Redgrave, *Artists*	S. Redgrave, *A dictionary of artists of the English school* (1874); rev. edn (1878); repr. (1970)
Reg. Oxf.	C. W. Boase and A. Clark, eds., *Register of the University of Oxford*, 5 vols., OHS, 1, 10–12, 14 (1885–9)
Reg. PCS	J. H. Burton and others, eds., *The register of the privy council of Scotland*, 1st ser., 14 vols. (1877–98); 2nd ser., 8 vols. (1899–1908); 3rd ser., [16 vols.] (1908–70)
Reg. RAN	H. W. C. Davis and others, eds., *Regesta regum Anglo-Normannorum, 1066–1154*, 4 vols. (1913–69)
RIBA Journal	*Journal of the Royal Institute of British Architects* [later *RIBA Journal*]
RotP	J. Strachey, ed., *Rotuli parliamentorum ut et petitiones, et placita in parliamento*, 6 vols. (1767–77)
RotS	D. Macpherson, J. Caley, and W. Illingworth, eds., *Rotuli Scotiae in Turri Londinensi et in domo capitulari Westmonasteriensi asservati*, 2 vols., RC, 14 (1814–19)
RS	Record(s) Society
Rymer, *Foedera*	T. Rymer and R. Sanderson, eds., *Foedera, conventiones, literae et cuiuscunque generis acta publica inter reges Angliae et alios quosvis imperatores, reges, pontifices, principes, vel communitates*, 20 vols. (1704–35); 2nd edn, 20 vols. (1726–35); 3rd edn, 10 vols. (1739–45), facs. edn (1967); new edn, ed. A. Clarke, J. Caley, and F. Holbrooke, 4 vols., RC, 50 (1816–30)
Sainty, *Judges*	J. Sainty, ed., *The judges of England, 1272–1990*, SeldS, suppl. ser., 10 (1993)
Sainty, *King's counsel*	J. Sainty, ed., *A list of English law officers and king's counsel*, SeldS, suppl. ser., 7 (1987)
SCH	Studies in Church History
Scots peerage	J. B. Paul, ed. *The Scots peerage, founded on Wood's edition of Sir Robert Douglas's Peerage of Scotland, containing an historical and genealogical account of the nobility of that kingdom*, 9 vols. (1904–14)
SeldS	Selden Society
SHR	*Scottish Historical Review*
State trials	T. B. Howell and T. J. Howell, eds., *Cobbett's Complete collection of state trials*, 34 vols. (1809–28)
STC, 1475–1640	A. W. Pollard, G. R. Redgrave, and others, eds., *A short-title catalogue of ... English books ... 1475–1640* (1926); 2nd edn, ed. W. A. Jackson, F. S. Ferguson, and K. F. Pantzer, 3 vols. (1976–91) [see also Wing, *STC*]
STS	Scottish Text Society
SurtS	Surtees Society
Symeon of Durham, *Opera*	*Symeonis monachi opera omnia*, ed. T. Arnold, 2 vols., Rolls Series, 75 (1882–5); repr. (1965)
Tanner, *Bibl. Brit.-Hib.*	T. Tanner, *Bibliotheca Britannico-Hibernica*, ed. D. Wilkins (1748); repr. (1963)
Thieme & Becker, *Allgemeines Lexikon*	U. Thieme, F. Becker, and H. Vollmer, eds., *Allgemeines Lexikon der bildenden Künstler von der Antike bis zur Gegenwart*, 37 vols. (Leipzig, 1907–50); repr. (1961–5), (1983), and (1992)
Thurloe, *State papers*	*A collection of the state papers of John Thurloe*, ed. T. Birch, 7 vols. (1742)
TLS	*Times Literary Supplement*
Tout, *Admin. hist.*	T. F. Tout, *Chapters in the administrative history of mediaeval England: the wardrobe, the chamber, and the small seals*, 6 vols. (1920–33); repr. (1967)
TRHS	*Transactions of the Royal Historical Society*
VCH	H. A. Doubleday and others, eds., *The Victoria history of the counties of England*, [88 vols.] (1900–)
Venn, *Alum. Cant.*	J. Venn and J. A. Venn, *Alumni Cantabrigienses: a biographical list of all known students, graduates, and holders of office at the University of Cambridge, from the earliest times to 1900*, 10 vols. (1922–54); repr. in 2 vols. (1974–8)
Vertue, *Note books*	[G. Vertue], *Note books*, ed. K. Esdaile, earl of Ilchester, and H. M. Hake, 6 vols., Walpole Society, 18, 20, 22, 24, 26, 30 (1930–55)
VF	*Vanity Fair*
Walford, *County families*	E. Walford, *The county families of the United Kingdom, or, Royal manual of the titled and untitled aristocracy of Great Britain and Ireland* (1860)
Walker rev.	A. G. Matthews, *Walker revised: being a revision of John Walker's Sufferings of the clergy during the grand rebellion, 1642–60* (1948); repr. (1988)
Walpole, *Corr.*	*The Yale edition of Horace Walpole's correspondence*, ed. W. S. Lewis, 48 vols. (1937–83)
Ward, *Men of the reign*	T. H. Ward, ed., *Men of the reign: a biographical dictionary of eminent persons of British and colonial birth who have died during the reign of Queen Victoria* (1885); repr. (Graz, 1968)
Waterhouse, *18c painters*	E. Waterhouse, *The dictionary of 18th century painters in oils and crayons* (1981); repr. as *British 18th century painters in oils and crayons* (1991), vol. 2 of *Dictionary of British art*
Watt, *Bibl. Brit.*	R. Watt, *Bibliotheca Britannica, or, A general index to British and foreign literature*, 4 vols. (1824) [many reprs.]
Wellesley index	W. E. Houghton, ed., *The Wellesley index to Victorian periodicals, 1824–1900*, 5 vols. (1966–89); new edn (1999) [CD-ROM]
Wing, *STC*	D. Wing, ed., *Short-title catalogue of ... English books ... 1641–1700*, 3 vols. (1945–51); 2nd edn (1972–88); rev. and enl. edn, ed. J. J. Morrison, C. W. Nelson, and M. Seccombe, 4 vols. (1994–8) [see also *STC, 1475–1640*]
Wisden	*John Wisden's Cricketer's Almanack*
Wood, *Ath. Oxon.*	A. Wood, *Athenae Oxonienses ... to which are added the Fasti*, 2 vols. (1691–2); 2nd edn (1721); new edn, 4 vols., ed. P. Bliss (1813–20); repr. (1967) and (1969)
Wood, *Vic. painters*	C. Wood, *Dictionary of Victorian painters* (1971); 2nd edn (1978); 3rd edn as *Victorian painters*, 2 vols. (1995), vol. 4 of *Dictionary of British art*
WW	*Who's who* (1849–)
WWBMP	M. Stenton and S. Lees, eds., *Who's who of British members of parliament*, 4 vols. (1976–81)
WWW	*Who was who* (1929–)

Smillie [Smellie]**, Robert** (**1857–1940**), trade unionist and politician, was born on 17 March 1857 in Belfast, the second son of John Smillie, a Scottish crofter. Orphaned at a young age, he and his elder brother James were brought up in Belfast by their grandmother, a former countrywoman, who enthralled them with tales of banshees and fairies. Smillie (pronounced 'Smile-y' not 'Smill-ie') spelt his name Smellie until at least his twenties (including on his marriage certificate in 1879).

Smillie's education was affected by the need to add to the household income. Between the ages of nine and eleven he worked part-time as an errand-boy and in other jobs. At eleven he began work in a mill as a half-timer, but after six months worked there full-time. At fifteen he joined his brother in Glasgow, where he worked in a brass foundry and as a riveter in two Clyde shipyards. At seventeen he again followed his brother, this time to the coalmines at Larkhall. Smillie lived at Larkhall during the remainder of his life, declining to move to London when he became president of the Miners' Federation of Great Britain in 1912. His career in the coal industry began with working long hours as a pump man, later as a drawer of coal tubs, and then, after practising in his spare time, as a coal hewer. Before he was twenty-three he was elected a checkweighman. In 1879 he married Anne Hamilton (*d.* 1942), a weaver; they had seven sons and two daughters.

Smillie played a leading part in the revival of mining trade unionism in Larkhall in the mid-1880s. He presided over the mass meeting which in 1885 formed the Larkhall and upper ward of the Lanarkshire Miners' Association, and served as its secretary. When a county federation was formed in 1893, Smillie became its chairman, and in 1894, when the Scottish Miners' Federation was formed, he became its first president. He played a major part in establishing the Scottish Trades Union Congress in 1896, and was elected first chairman of its parliamentary committee (its executive) for three years (1897–9).

Smillie moved from radicalism to socialism in the early 1880s. He had been a warm supporter of Gladstone at the time of the Liberal statesman's election campaign in Midlothian in 1880. However, the bad social conditions in the mining areas, both down the pits and on the surface, as well as his outrage at the eviction of the families of striking miners from tied cottages, helped turn Smillie to socialism. Like many working-class activists of the period he read widely.

A founder member of the Scottish Labour Party in 1888 and of the Independent Labour Party in 1893, Smillie was a close associate of Keir Hardie during their early careers and remained a friend until Hardie's death. He campaigned for Hardie in many of his election contests, including the first in 1888; and Smillie himself stood for parliament on seven occasions between 1894 and 1910. Later, he could have had the nomination for winnable seats in Glasgow but chose to remain with his work for the miners.

Smillie's socialist commitment resulted in the Lib-Lab old guard of the Miners' Federation of Great Britain (MFGB) for many years keeping him out of senior posts in that body. Eventually, in 1909, he became its vice-president and in 1912 its president. In the 1912 national coal strike, which occurred before Smillie became president, David Lloyd George saw him as the key person on the miners' side with whom to reach agreement. In the period before the outbreak of the First World War Smillie helped to establish the 'triple alliance' of miners, railway workers, and transport workers, and when its constitution was approved in December 1915, he became its chairman.

Robert Smillie (1857–1940), by unknown photographer

With the outbreak of war, Smillie found he was in a small minority on both the MFGB and Scottish Miners' Federation in being opposed to it. He vigorously condemned conscription and was the president of the National Council Against Conscription when it was formed in 1915. He also presided over the Leeds Convention of June 1917 which welcomed the Russian revolution of February 1917 and called for the creation across the country of councils of workmen and soldiers' delegates. Smillie combined these activities with committee work aimed at defending the interests of the miners and working people generally. He served on the War Emergency Workers' National Committee, acting as its chairman from September 1915 until the end of the war. In addition he served from February 1915 on the government's committee set up to secure the necessary production of coal during the war, an aim which required some curtailment of the recruitment of miners into the armed forces. When Lloyd George became prime minister in 1916 Smillie declined the post of food controller.

Smillie's career reached its peak in 1919 with the struggle for the miners' post-war demands, including nationalization of the mines. Lloyd George prevented a strike by setting up the Sankey Commission, with Smillie believing the premier had promised nationalization if the majority on the commission recommended it. Smillie gained widespread respect for the skill with which he questioned witnesses before the commission. However, Lloyd George and the government declined to implement the commission's report—and the miners were left to campaign for nationalization after the most propitious time for a strike had passed. With declining health and failing eyesight, Smillie offered his resignation in February 1920. It was declined then and again later in 1920. He remained president during the 'Datum Line Strike' of October–November 1920 over a proposed productivity deal in which bonuses would be automatically paid when specified output levels were reached, but he resigned in March 1921 on grounds of ill health. He nevertheless undertook the presidency of the Scottish Miners' Federation (1922–8) and was elected Labour MP for Morpeth (1923–9), declining office in the first Labour government (1924).

Smillie impressed supporters and opponents alike as 'a man of outstanding ability, force of character and integrity' (Redmayne, *Men, Mines and Memories*, 301). He appears to have spent his later years as an invalid and in poverty, and died on 16 February 1940 from pernicious anaemia at Crichton Royal Hospital, in Dumfries. He was cremated at the western necropolis, Glasgow, after a funeral oration by James Maxton. CHRIS WRIGLEY

Sources R. Smillie, *My life for labour* (1924) · J. R. MacDonald and M. McArthur, *Memoir of James Keir Hardie and tribute to his work* (1915) · R. P. Arnot, *The miners: a history of the Miners' Federation of Great Britain*, 1: … *1889–1910* (1949) · R. P. Arnot, *The miners: a history of the Miners' Federation of Great Britain*, 2: … *from 1910 onwards* (1953) · R. P. Arnot, *A history of Scottish miners from the earliest times* [1955] · R. A. S. Redmayne, *Men, mines and memories* (1942) · R. A. S. Redmayne, *The British coal mining industry during the war* (1923) · H. A. Clegg, A. Fox, and A. F. Thompson, *A history of British trade unions since 1889*, 2 (1985) · A. B. Campbell, *The Lanarkshire miners: a social history of their trade unions, 1775–1974* (1979) · *The letters of Sidney and Beatrice Webb*, ed. N. MacKenzie, 3 (1978) · 'Smillie, Robert', *DLB*, vol. 3 · C. Wrigley, 'Smillie, Robert', *BDMBR*, vol. 3, pt 2 · *DNB* · d. cert.

Archives People's History Museum, Manchester, corresp. and papers | BLPES, corresp. relating to the independent labour party · NL Scot., Larkhall Miners' Association minute books; Scottish Miners' Federation records · People's History Museum, Manchester, Labour Party MSS; War Emergency Workers' National Committee MSS

Likenesses B. Partridge, pen-and-ink caricature, NPG; repro. in *Punch* (29 Sept 1920) · photograph, People's History Museum, Manchester [*see illus.*]

Smirke, Sir Edward (1795–1875), lawyer and archaeologist, was born in Marylebone, the third son of Robert *Smirke (1753–1845), painter and illustrator, and his wife, Elizabeth Russell (*d.* 1825). He was the brother of Sir Robert *Smirke and Sydney *Smirke, architects. He was educated privately and at St John's College, Cambridge, where he graduated BA in 1816 and MA in 1820. In July 1815 he obtained the chancellor's gold medal for an English poem on Wallace, which was printed in that year, and later in *Cambridge Prize Poems* (1820, 1828, and 1859).

Smirke was called to the bar at the Middle Temple on 12 November 1824, went on the western circuit, and attended the Hampshire sessions. At Kensington on 11 September 1838 he married Harriet Amelia (*d.* 1863), youngest daughter of Thomas Neill of Turnham Green. In December 1844 he was appointed solicitor-general to the prince of Wales, and on 5 February 1845 solicitor-general to him as prince of Wales and duke of Cornwall. He succeeded to the post of attorney-general to the prince on 25 June 1852, and was *ex officio* a member of his council. By letters patent under the great seal of England on 2 July 1853 he was constituted vice-warden of the stannaries of Cornwall and Devon, a post he held until 29 September 1870. From 1846 to 1855 he was recorder of Southampton. On his retirement in 1870 he was knighted at Windsor.

Smirke studied charters and the history of mining in the duchy of Cornwall. He was a member of the Royal Archaeological Institute from its foundation, and took an active part at its annual meetings. From 1861 to 1863 and 1865 to 1867 he presided over the Royal Institution of Cornwall. In 1862, when the Cambrian Archaeological Society paid a visit to Truro, he presided over the congress. Smirke was author of several legal works and a prolific presenter of papers to the Society of Antiquaries and the Royal Institution of Cornwall. He died at his home, 18 Thurloe Square, South Kensington, London, on 4 March 1875. W. P. COURTNEY, *rev.* ERIC METCALFE

Sources Boase, *Mod. Eng. biog.* · Boase & Courtney, *Bibl. Corn.*, 2.658, 660 · 'Proceedings at meetings of the Royal Archaeological Institute', *Archaeological Journal*, 32 (1875), 326 · *Journal of the Royal Institution of Cornwall*, 5 (1874–8), 175–6

Archives NL Scot., letters to J. P. Earwaker · RIBA BAL, corresp. with Sydney Smirke, and papers

Wealth at death £25,000: administration, 22 April 1875, *CGPLA Eng. & Wales*

Smirke, Mary (1779–1853). *See under* Smirke, Robert (1753–1845).

Smirke, Richard (1778–1815). *See under* Smirke, Robert (1753–1845).

Smirke, Robert (1753–1845), painter and illustrator, was born in Wigton, Cumberland, on 15 April 1753 and baptized there on 25 May, the son of Richard Smirke (*bap.* 1727, *d.* *c.*1776/7), a peripatetic artist, and his wife, Mary Walker. Little is known about Smirke's early years in Cumberland, but he was brought to London by his father in 1766, where he was apprenticed to the coach-painter John Bromley. Bromley's copy of *A Heraldic Book of Painters Arms* was in Smirke's possession from 1769 to 1770 (BL, Add. MS 30341). He entered the Royal Academy Schools on 30 November 1772 and became a member of the Incorporated Society of Artists in 1775, showing there in 1777 and 1778. On 1 March 1777 Smirke married Elizabeth Russell (*d.* 1825) at St Mary's, Marylebone Road, Marylebone, Middlesex. They had eight children: the antiquarian draughtsman Richard (1778–1815), and Mary (1779–1853), a painter, both of whom are noticed below; the architect Sir Robert *Smirke (1780–1867); Alfred (*bap.* 19 Jan 1794); the lawyer and archaeologist Sir Edward *Smirke (1795–1875); Thomas; the architect Sydney *Smirke (1798–1877); and Sarah (married *c.*1816).

Smirke built his reputation on early commissions for paintings with literary themes and contemporary subjects such as *Recovery of a Young Man Believed Drown after Resuscitation by Dr. Hawes* and *Young Man Lifted from the River Apparently Drown* (both 1787; engraved by R. Pollard, Guildhall Art Gallery, London). For John Boydell's Shakspeare Gallery he painted scenes from plays that were engraved for numerous publications, including *The Picturesque Beauties of Shakespeare* (1783–7) and *A collection of prints from pictures for the purpose of illustrating the dramatic works of Shakespeare by the artists of Great Britain* (1805). Smirke's association with Shakespeare would be enduring; his output was prolific and proved tremendously popular. *Illustrations to Shakespeare by Robert Smirke R.A.*, containing over forty engravings after Smirke, was published in 1821, 1822, and 1825. Smirke mostly painted in oil or in grisaille and he frequently produced works on a small format to facilitate their reproduction as engravings. His style is notable for its flowing, refined drawing, and his use of characterization is typically expressive, revealing playful humour or drama. The Folger Shakespeare Library, Washington, DC, holds fifteen of his paintings, including *The Awakening of King Lear* (*c.*1792, engraved by A. Smith, 1792), in addition to two original wash drawings, *Lady Macbeth Sleepwalking* and *Falstaff Thrown into the Thames* (engraved by C. Taylor and published in *The Picturesque Beauties of Shakespeare*). The Royal Shakespeare Theatre Gallery, Stratford upon Avon, has paintings by Smirke of scenes from *Much Ado about Nothing*, *The Merry Wives of Windsor*, and *Henry IV*. *The Seven Ages of Man* (exh. RA, 1798; engraved by R. Thew, 1801), seven canvases illustrating act II, scene vii of *As You Like It*, are at the Yale Center for British Art, New Haven, Connecticut. At the Shakspeare Gallery sale on 18 May 1805 these works sold for the large sum of 240 guineas, fetching more than major works by Benjamin West and James Northcote and out-priced only by Reynolds.

Smirke exhibited at the Royal Academy from 1786 to 1813. He was elected an associate of the Royal Academy on 10 November 1791 and became a full academician on 11 February 1793; his diploma work was *Don Quixote and Sancho Panza* (1793; RA) Smirke was greatly involved with the corporate life of the academy. However, he held democratic sympathies and anti-monarchist sentiments which came increasingly into view in the 1790s, as is demonstrated by his *The Attempt by Margaret Nicholson to Assassinate King George III* (engraved by R. Pollard and F. Jukes, 1796). The diarist Joseph Farington spoke 'of the effects of S[mirke] contaminating the minds of his daughter and sons with his principles' and referred to Robert and his eldest son Richard as 'Crops (Hair cut short) and democrats' (Farington, *Diary*, 3.1113; 2.404). Certainly by 1795 Smirke's views had reached the attention of George III: 'West spoke to Smirke abt. The King having been informed of his holding democratic principles' (ibid., 1.270), and George III later refused to ratify Smirke's election as keeper of the Royal Academy in 1804. Yet, though democratic in tendency, his views were not unpatriotic, and Farington records Smirke's views on the battle of Waterloo and his condemnation of Napoleon.

Smirke provided a large number of illustrations for literary and historical texts such as Robert Bowyer's edition of David Hume's *History of England* (1792, engraved by Landseer) as well as Joel Barlow's *The Columbiad* (1807). He depicted scenes for publications as diverse as *The Adventures of Gil Blas* (1809, engraved by A. Smith) and James Montgomery's *Poems on the Abolition of the Slave Trade* (1810, engraved by A. Raimbach). *Proofs, from pictures, painted by R. Smirke R.A and engraved by A. Raimbach; the subject taken from the Rasselas of Dr. Johnson* was published in 1805; original drawings for Johnson's *Rasselas*, in brown pigment with white highlights, are at the Yale Center for British Art, New Haven, Connecticut. Smirke also produced illustrations for *Arabian Nights* (1802), exhibited at the British Institution in 1806 and engraved by C. Armstrong, *Adventures of a Hunchback* (1814), and *Don Quixote* (1818). The Tate Collection, London, holds a large number of his original paintings for *Don Quixote*, including *Sancho Panza and the Duchess* (*c.*1797), *The Order of the Knighthood Conferred on DQ by the Innkeeper*, and *Twelve Illustrations to Don Quixote*.

In later years Smirke's relationship with the Royal Academy became strained. Sir Thomas Lawrence suggested to Farington that 'our friend's conduct towards the academy (the elder I mean) is not consistent—it is all contempt or all apprehension' (Thomas Lawrence, letter, 12 Oct 1811, RA). About 1818 Smirke wrote a memorandum on the first fifty years of the academy (RIBA). Authorship was also attributed to Smirke of the satirical *Catalogue Raisonnée of the Pictures now Exhibiting at the British Institution* (1815). He died on 5 January 1845 at 3 Osnaburgh Terrace, Regent's Park, London, and was buried at Kensal Green cemetery, Middlesex.

Richard Smirke (1778–1815), antiquarian draughtsman, was born in January or February 1778. He entered the Royal Academy Schools to study painting on 16 July 1796 'aged 18½' (Hutchison) and gained a gold medal in 1799 for *Samson and Delilah*. Farington's diary indicates that he not only shared his father's political views, but also some of his character traits. The diarist recalled a remark by Frank Horsley 'that Smirke was so constituted that he *could not know the world* and that his late son Richard was so disposed that he *would not know the world*' (Farington, *Diary*, 14.4827). A proposed visit to Paris with his brother Robert in 1800–01 was abandoned as too risky; however, in 1802 they set out on a grand tour that lasted two years and took them to France, Germany, Italy, and Greece, among other countries. Richard Smirke proved to be a skilful antiquarian draughtsman:

> when the wall paintings in St. Stephens Chapel, Westminster, were discovered in 1800, Smirke made a set of beautiful facsimile copies of them in watercolours, on a small scale, which are now in the Society of Antiquaries; he was afterwards employed by the society on similar work. (*DNB*)

Smirke also devoted some time to the study of chemistry, and made some discoveries on the qualities of colour. He did not marry, and died on 5 May 1815 at the Howard Arms inn, Brampton, Cumberland.

Mary Smirke (1779–1853), painter, was born on 22 June 1779. She attended Miss Bates's school, Rickmansworth, and was later taught to draw by her father. She was well-regarded as a painter and Nathaniel Dance and Sir Thomas Lawrence employed her as a copyist. She was a skilled landscape painter, collaborating with Joseph Farington, who although an admirer of her abilities found her 'reserved and unsociable' (Egerton, 1348). She exhibited six paintings at the Royal Academy between 1809 and 1814. A contemporary described her work as 'natural and pleasing … unpretending, but every touch true to nature' (ibid., 1351). She also showed a strong ability with languages, and, with her father's encouragement, translated *Don Quixote*, published in 1818. She also published *Illustrated Translations from the German* (1843, 1853) with her niece Laura Smirke (daughter of Sir Robert Smirke), which included English translations of German poems illustrated with pencil and pen-and-ink drawings and illuminated letters and decorations. A portrait she made of her father was copied by John Jackson (NPG), and engraved by C. Picart. She is not known to have married and died on 14 September 1853. *Valle Crucis Abbey, Denbighshire*, is in the Victoria and Albert Museum, London, and the Royal Institute of British Architects has two topographical drawings. A folio of her landscape pencil drawings and watercolours was sold at Sothebys on 11 April 1991. TINA FISKE

Sources *GM*, 1st ser., 85/1 (1815), 477 • *GM*, 2nd ser., 23 (1845), 317–19 • Farington, *Diary* • J. Turner, ed., *The dictionary of art*, 34 vols. (1996) • *DNB* • Graves, *RA exhibitors* • S. C. Hutchison, 'The Royal Academy Schools, 1768–1830', *Walpole Society*, 38 (1960–62), 123–91 • W. L. Pressly, *A catalogue of paintings in the Folger Shakespeare Library* (1993) • M. Cormack, *A concise catalogue of paintings in the Yale Center for British Art* (New Haven, Conn., 1985) • G. Ashton, *Shakespeare and British art* (1981) • *Concise catalogue of the Tate Gallery collection*, 9th edn (1991) • J. Evans, *A history of the Society of Antiquaries* (1956) • J. Egerton, 'An artist of leisure: Mary Smirke, 1779–1853', *Country Life* (20 Nov 1969), 1348–51 • *IGI*

Archives Hunt. L., letters • RIBA BAL, notes and letters | RA, corresp. with T. Lawrence • Som. ARS

Likenesses R. Smirke, self-portrait, miniature, *c*.1780–1790; Christies, 10 July 1990, lot 156 • G. Dance, drawing, 1793, RA • H. Singleton, group portrait, oils, 1795 (*The Royal Academicians, 1793*), RA • W. Daniell, soft-ground etchings, 1809 (after G. Dance), BM, NPG • J. Jackson, watercolour drawing, *c*.1810 (after M. Smirke), NPG • C. Picart, engraving, 1814 (after J. Jackson), repro. in *The British gallery of contemporary portraits*, 2 vols. (1822) • attrib. E. H. Bailey, plaster bust, *c*.1828, NPG

Smirke, Sir Robert (1780–1867), architect, was born in London on 1 October 1780, the second of the five surviving sons and two daughters of the painter and illustrator Robert *Smirke RA (1753–1845) and his wife, Elizabeth Russell (*d*. 1825).

Education Smirke was educated at a private school at Aspley Guise, near Woburn, Bedfordshire, where he was head boy. Though proficient at Greek, Latin, and French, he preferred drawing and in March 1796 his father secured a recommendation by George Dance the younger to that

Sir Robert Smirke (1780–1867), by William Daniell, pubd 1809 (after George Dance, 1809)

architect's former pupil John Soane, whose office in Lincoln's Inn Fields Smirke entered the following May at the age of fifteen. Soane was rigorous but highly temperamental: Smirke wrote to his father that while 'in one of his *amiable* Tempers' Soane had berated his pupil's drawing as wholly and 'excessively *slovenly*' (Stroud, 65) and ordered him to redraw it on the reverse of the sheet so as not to waste paper. Soane presented Smirke, as he did all his pupils, with a copy of Marc-Antoine Laugier's *Essai sur l'architecture* (1755), which was to influence strongly Smirke's architectural thought and on which he was later to write an unpublished treatise and commentary. Thus began 'his sense of belonging to the French rather than the English classical tradition' (Watkin, *Sale Catalogues*, 223). Although Soane had admitted Smirke to his office without the usual arrangement of a fee-paying apprenticeship, after ten months Smirke was sufficiently discouraged to leave and, while he was not the only pupil so to depart, Soane took his withdrawal as an insult. Instead, Smirke received his training as a private pupil from the ageing Dance and from the London surveyor and measurer Thomas Bush. In July 1796 Smirke had also begun to study at the Royal Academy Schools, where he gained the silver medal and the same year was awarded the honorary palette in silver of the Society of Arts. His design for *A National Gallery for Painting, &c.* won him the Royal Academy gold medal in 1799.

In May 1799 Smirke and his elder brother, the draughtsman Richard *Smirke [*see under* Smirke, Robert (1753–1845)], hoped to accompany Lord Elgin, who was shortly to visit Athens, but with others (including J. M. W. Turner) they were turned down. In 1801, during the Napoleonic wars, the Smirke brothers proposed visiting Paris disguised as Americans, but abandoned the idea as too risky. In September 1802 they set out with the painter William Walker and others on an extended tour lasting over two years to France, the Southern Netherlands, Germany, Austria, Italy, Sicily, and Greece. In Athens, Smirke again encountered Lord Elgin and, although he seems still to have approved of the earl's mission, was deeply affected by the damage caused to the temple by the removal of the Parthenon friezes. As each heavy stone, laboriously dislodged with crowbars, noisily hit the ground, he recorded that 'it seemed like a convulsive groan of the injured spirit of the Temple' (St Clair, 139). This did not deter Smirke from purloining fragments of the neighbouring Erechtheum, having first painted of it a fine watercolour (RIBA drawings collection, London). In 1808, following the great acclaim to which the marbles were exhibited in London in 1807, he conceded that a great opportunity had been missed in not having been Lord Elgin's artist. In his obituary his younger brother the lawyer and archaeologist Sir Edward *Smirke noted the impression that Greek and particularly Athenian architecture made on Smirke: he was everywhere

> forcibly impressed with the simplicity and dignity of the Great Works which 2000 years of decay and destruction had left behind, and the memory of those grand architectural features was ever after present in his mind, counteracting the more popular inclination to superficial decoration. (*The Builder*, 604–6)

The painter and diarist Joseph Farington, who was one of Smirke's supporters at the Royal Academy, certainly thought that no prospective architect in Britain was ever so well prepared as was Smirke on his return to London in January 1805. In that year he became a fellow of both the Royal Society and the Society of Antiquaries and a member of the Architects' Club. An immediate fruit of his travels was the first, and only, part of a projected larger work, *Specimens of Continental Architecture* (1806).

Early career Smirke built up a substantial and growing private architectural practice that was to become, for its time, the largest in London. The rapid success of his early career was largely due to the support and connections of his father and other Royal Academicians, notably Dance and the portraitist Sir Thomas Lawrence, who assisted him in obtaining commissions from noble clients and from leading politicians, especially in the ruling tory party. Lawrence introduced him to Sir Robert Peel, perhaps Smirke's most influential supporter. Smirke's capacity for hard work and skill in controlling the organizational, administrative, and practical elements of his architectural practice soon gained him a reputation for efficient and sound working methods and for professional integrity and reliability. He also possessed in abundance a requisite genial manner which enabled him to accommodate discriminating patrons and to please those who were notoriously difficult to satisfy. Together with his acceptable designs, predominantly though not exclusively in the Greek revival style, these personal qualities ensured his early and continued success throughout most of his long career.

Like most architects of his time, Smirke worked on three main types of building: church, public, and domestic (with public architecture as perhaps the fastest-growing area), and with a requirement to work in a variety of styles over a wide geographical area. Not all commissions comprised completely new buildings: many involved alterations, both external and internal, additions to existing buildings, and other modifications, which included rectifying structural and other defects, even in recent buildings, something for which Smirke's reliability made him much in demand. John Wilson Croker dubbed him (after the celebrated morbid anatomist) 'the Dr Baillie of architects' (Crook, *British Museum*, 84). Several of his buildings have been demolished and some altered, but many remain as he left them.

Smirke launched his career in 1806–7, working on all three types of buildings almost simultaneously, and was elected an associate of the Royal Academy in 1808. His first important country house commission was Lowther Castle, Westmorland (1806–11), in the castellated style employed successfully by James Wyatt and others, for the leading tory William Lowther, first earl of Lonsdale, at a cost of £64,000. In London, Smirke was commissioned by the actor–manager John Philip Kemble to rebuild the Theatre Royal, Covent Garden (1808–9; des. 1856), which necessitated the suspension of work at Lowther and the decline of other commissions. He produced a building that was revolutionary: its giant pure Doric portico to Bow Street, the first on any London building, modelled on the Parthenon (predating, but only just, that on William Stark's Glasgow court house), set against starkly simple blocks with plain walls relieved only by a minimum of openings and decoration, established the Greek revival style in a fashionable and influential venue in the heart of the capital. On such an important building, rather than something 'fanciful' or 'lighter in style', he considered the Doric alone 'appropriate to a Theatre', providing 'Grandeur of effect', with a character 'of dignity & gravity' (Farington, *Diary*, 10.3515). Structural innovations included fireproofing and enabled an audience capacity of 4200. On its rapid completion in eight months at a cost of £150,000 Smirke received £10,000, a figure that became a benchmark, for he was rumoured thereafter to have refused commissions for less. The theatre opened on 18 September 1809 to almost universal applause. Lawrence did not think there was 'a building in so pure a taste in London', and John Flaxman, while disapproving the Doric order on a theatre, considered it 'as fine a building as any in this Country' (ibid., 10.3512–13, 3522).

A dissident voice was that of Soane. In his fourth lecture as professor of architecture at the Royal Academy, on 29 January 1810, he deplored the 'practice of sacrificing everything to one front of a building' at the expense of its other sides and at Covent Garden pointed out 'the glaring impropriety of this defect … contrary to every idea of beauty … of Grecian architecture … a deviation from classical purity' (Soane, 70, 67). The academy was outraged at

Soane's attack on the work of a living artist and following its unanimous condemnation the council, at the instance of Smirke's father, formalized what had been a tacit understanding by passing an academy law prohibiting lecturers from introducing comments on the opinions or work of living British artists. Smirke was not directly involved with Soane in the increasingly acrimonious controversy but, following the submission of *Restoration of the Acropolis of Athens*, his election as Royal Academician on 11 February 1811 clearly indicated the academy's support for him. A public reconciliation was short-lived: within weeks Soane was again ridiculing the younger architect. The whole protracted affair, which originated in debates over the proper use of antique sources, was never properly resolved but undoubtedly enhanced Smirke's reputation. Soane identified the rationalist, geometrical bases of Smirke's neo-classicism and analytic approach to composition, using 'original combinations of primary masses' to produce a 'Graeco-cubic style' (Crook, *Greek Revival*, 125, 113), and, with not a little prescience, foresaw in Smirke's architecture the widespread literal and not always appropriate application of porticoes as metaphors for temples and the repetitious, often indiscriminate, use of a few supposed ideal models.

Major works By 1815 Smirke's commissions for public buildings included: the completion of James Johnson's Royal Mint, Tower Hill (1809–11), where he owed his appointment as architect to the third Earl Bathurst; the county courts, Carlisle, Cumberland (1810–12), begun disastrously by Thomas Telford and others and completed to Smirke's Gothic designs; the market house, Appleby, Westmorland (1811); bridges at Carlisle (1812–15) and Gloucester (1814–17); markets at Whitehaven, Cumberland (1813); and shire halls at Gloucester, where he used the Ionic order for the first time in the recessed portico (1814–16), and Hereford, with its Doric portico (1815–17). He designed the Belgrave Chapel, Halkin Street, London (1812; dem. *c.*1910), and undertook additions and repairs to the cathedrals at Gloucester (1809) and Carlisle (1809–11) and to Strood church, Kent (1812). He enlarged numerous country houses as far apart as Kent and Yorkshire, Sussex and Radnorshire, and Middlesex and Dumfriesshire. In the north wing which he added to Cirencester Park, Gloucestershire (1810–11), for Lord Bathurst he introduced into domestic architecture cast-iron stanchions, beams, and girders, previously used only in industrial buildings; he later used them again at Somerset House, the Union Club, and the British Museum. Like Wilton Castle, Yorkshire (*c.*1807), for Sir John Lowther, Eastnor Castle, Herefordshire (1812–20), which cost over £100,000, was in the castellated style but incorporated such concealed supports. His client here, the second Lord Somers, unlike most of his patrons, was 'a Whig, but a *Country Gentleman Whig*' (Farington, *Diary*, 11.4086), and Smirke spent three weeks in February 1812 in Herefordshire discussing plans, one of thirteen visits between December 1805 and November 1813. He designed Kinmount, Dumfriesshire (1812), for the fifth marquess of Queensberry and, following his only public building in Scotland, the grim Doric Perth county buildings (1815–19), he received five Scottish country house commissions between 1817 and 1828. Whittingehame House, East Lothian (1817–18), for James Balfour, was, like Kinmount, 'blocky' and 'of Graeco-cubic formation'; Strathallan Castle, Perthshire (1817–18), for James Drummond, was castellated; while the largest, Kinfauns Castle, Perthshire (1820–22), for the fifteenth Lord Gray, was a picturesque castle; Cultoquhey House, Perthshire (*c.*1820), for Anthony Maxtone, and Erskine House, Renfrewshire (1828), for the eleventh Lord Blantyre, were 'mixed Tudor' mansions (Crook, '"The New Square Style"', 207, 210). Between November 1814 and June 1816 Smirke made three circuitous coach journeys lasting up to a month to the north of England and Scotland, each covering well over 1000 miles, which made him unwell and exhausted.

In the scramble to succeed Wyatt on his death in 1813 as surveyor of the office of works, Smirke's rivals engaged in a frenzy of intrigue: Wyatt's son and nephews sought a dynastic succession; John Nash petitioned his royal patrons at court; and Soane, 'indefatigable in pursuing any object which He has in view' (Farington, *Diary*, 12.4424), exploited his government connections. Smirke's strategy, in contrast, was to write immediately to judiciously selected factions: to his supporters at the Royal Academy and to patrons in the tory establishment, who in turn mobilized support among influential contacts in royal and government circles. In the reorganization of the board of the office of works in 1815 three posts of attached architects were created, whose occupants were to oversee royal and government buildings on a regional basis, for which they would receive a retaining fee of £500 and a percentage on executed work, while continuing in private practice. The first triumvirate comprised Nash, Soane, and Smirke. Nash told Soane: 'Our appointments are perfectly Constitutional, I the King, you the Lords, and *your* friend Smirke, the Commons' (Crook, *British Museum*, 78). Nash was sixty-three and Soane sixty-two: at the age of thirty-five Smirke had risen to the top of his profession, gaining a major appointment that was to bring him some notable and highly lucrative commissions, including the British Museum and the Post Office. His success was overshadowed by the death on 15 May of his brother Richard, to whom he was close.

The reorganization of the board coincided with the relaxation of building restrictions after Waterloo, and Smirke's practice, increasingly London-based, flourished. He designed temporary rooms (1815–16) for the Elgin marbles at the British Museum (then at Montague House, Bloomsbury), and completed Thomas Hardwick's Millbank penitentiary (1816–19), where, following the failure of the foundations, he pioneered the use of concrete in Great Britain. In 1816 at the Inner Temple, where he became surveyor in 1819, he began alterations which were to occupy him intermittently over the next twenty years. For the third marquess of Lansdowne he remodelled the library at Lansdowne House, London, as a picture gallery (1816–19) while work continued on country houses at

Newton Don, Kelso (*c*.1815), for Sir Alexander Don, Somerset House, Gloucester (*c*.1816; now the judge's lodgings), for John Phillpotts, Luton Hoo Park, Bedfordshire (1816–27), and Cardiff Castle (*c*.1818) for the second marquess of Bute, and Hardwicke Court, Gloucestershire (1817–19), for T. J. Lloyd Baker. He remodelled Armley House, near Leeds, Yorkshire (1818–22), for the millionaire millowner Benjamin Gott, adding an Ionic portico, the only one so to dominate Smirke's country houses and much admired by Karl Friedrich Schinkel in 1826. Other commissions included the legacy duty office, Somerset House (1817–33), the duchy of Lancaster offices off the Strand (1817–23), the astylar and influential United Service Club (1817–19), and the completion of Daniel Alexander's county gaol, Maidstone, Kent (1817–19).

On 19 April 1819 Smirke married at Edgeworth, Gloucestershire, Laura, the fifth daughter of the ten children of the Revd Anthony Freston, rector of Edgeworth, and his wife, formerly Miss Hyde, of Cambridge. They had a daughter, also Laura, baptized on 5 February 1820, at St Marylebone Church, Middlesex. Matthew Brettingham, eldest son of the architect of the same name, was uncle and guardian to the Revd Mr Freston, who as a child changed his name to inherit an estate.

In 1820 Smirke succeeded John Yenn as treasurer at the Royal Academy and became surveyor-general for the south parts of the duchy of Lancaster, in which capacity he oversaw the development in London of the Savoy estate. His contribution to the Church Building (or 'Millon') Act of 1818 comprised several similar churches, some with semicircular porticoes closing long vistas or on awkward axes: St Anne's, Wandsworth (1820–22), St Mary's, Wyndham Place (1821–2), and the almost identical St Philip's, Salford, Lancashire (1822–4), all Ionic; and St James's, Hackney (1821–3; dem. 1958), and St George's, Brandon Hill, Bristol (1821–3), both Doric. Commissions in the 1820s and early 1830s included: the Ionic Royal College of Physicians, Pall Mall East, and the Union Club (now Canada House), Trafalgar Square (1822–7); the county courts in the castle, Lincoln (1823–30); the council house, Bristol (1824–7); and the cubic Normanby Park, Lincolnshire (1825–30), for Sir Robert Sheffield. At the custom house, London (1825–7), Smirke reconstructed the central portion, which had collapsed in 1813 when David Laing's foundations failed. There followed the infirmary (1827–30) and shire hall (1834–7) in Shrewsbury; the approaches to London Bridge (1829–35); King's College, comprising the east wing of Somerset House in the Strand and the completion of Sir William Chambers's design for the river-front (1830–35); the ingeniously combined Doric church and mausoleum at Markham Clinton, Nottinghamshire (1831–3), for Henry Pelham, fourth duke of Newcastle; and Drayton Manor, Staffordshire (1831–5; dem. 1913), in the Elizabethan style, for Sir Robert Peel.

Smirke's General Post Office, St Martin's-le-Grand (1824–9; dem. 1913), was considered one of the most successful of modern buildings. Sydney *Smirke, who later assisted his brother, believed 'that no other age or country can offer such an imposing spectacle of national unity and spirit', providing 'the evidence of national greatness' and 'growing prosperity' (Leeds, 35, 39). J. D. Passavant thought it 'the most successful attempt in this [Grecian] style … in England', a most 'skilfully managed … union … of true antique simplicity with the convenience and arrangements required in the present age' (Passavant, 2.296–7). It seems that columnar screens which dominated earlier Parisian designs (such as that by J.-P. Gisors and F. J. Delannoy for the French Académie de l'Architecture grand prix competition, for which the theme in 1779 was a museum) provided a common source for both Smirke and Schinkel rather than that the latter's near-contemporary Altes Museum in Berlin directly influenced the design of the British Museum (1823–46; completed 1846–52 under Sydney Smirke, who designed the round reading-room, 1854–7). Smirke's articulation of its façade with central giant portico and projecting wings ties the composition essentially to the British Palladian tradition. The Ionic is a synthesis of the orders of several Greek temples and the combination of portico and colonnade round an open court afforded (as Covent Garden did not) 'an area in front sufficiently ample to secure to the façade an advantageous display' (Smirke, 75), enabling Smirke to fulfil his ideal, derived from Laugier, of 'apparent utility' (Crook, *British Museum*, 99–101). £1 million was allowed separately for the General Post Office and the British Museum, Smirke's largest commissions, and his remuneration, normally 5 per cent, was 3 per cent for both. His contractor Henry Harrison found him difficult, but Smirke's ability to keep within estimates was largely due to his using the bill of quantities, by 1830 widely accepted as a sound basis for pricing. He was apparently the first architect to use this system and also, perhaps owing to his training under Thomas Bush, the first to introduce quantity surveying as a distinct aspect of the building process. In 1828, the year Lawrence commissioned Edward Hodges Baily to sculpt a marble bust of him (now in the British Museum, London), the architectural press considered Smirke the country's leader in the field of construction.

In 1832 the office of works was again reformed: the posts of attached architects were abolished and for his services Smirke was knighted by William IV. Thereafter, while still engaged on the British Museum, his reduced commissions included supervising the completion by Benjamin Wyatt of York House (or Gower House; later Stafford House and Lancaster House), St James's (1833–8), for the second duke of Sutherland; the Carlton Club, Pall Mall (1835–6); and, with his brother Sydney, the Oxford and Cambridge Club (1836–8). On the founding of the Institute of British Architects in 1837 Smirke was made an honorary fellow.

Later years Smirke received no new commissions after 1838 but continued to advise his brother Sydney and acted as assessor and adjudicator in the 1839 competitions for the new Royal Exchange, London, and for the Taylor Institution and Randolph Gallery (now the Ashmolean Museum), Oxford. When he retired from practice in 1845 he had completed almost 130 commissions distributed throughout the country. By far the largest number of commissions was for houses, with 48 in the country and 11 in London, followed by 47 public buildings, of which 27 were in the capital and 2, the Wellington Testimonial, Dublin, and the gaol at St John's, Newfoundland, abroad. He worked on almost every available type of building, and only some twenty of his designs remained unexecuted, including those for Grosvenor House, London (1825–7), and the houses of parliament (1834–5).

On Smirke's retirement in 1845 at the age of sixty-five, Sir Robert Peel appointed him to the commission for metropolitan improvements following his work on the London Bridge approaches. In the same year Smirke's former pupils, including William Burn, C. R. Cockerell, William Doull, John Newman, Henry Roberts, Lewis Vulliamy, and Sydney Smirke, commissioned the sculptor Thomas Campbell to make a bust of Smirke, which they presented to him (Royal Institute of British Architects, London). In 1850 ill health forced him to resign as treasurer of the Royal Academy, a post he held longer than anyone else. He was awarded the gold medal of the Royal Institute of British Architects in 1853 and in 1859, 'at the close of a long and prosperous career, in order that he might not hinder other artists from attaining the like dignity', he resigned, 'full of honours', from the Royal Academy (Sandby, 2.268). In that year he left his home in Berners Street, London, and retired to Cheltenham, Gloucestershire, not far from Edgeworth, where his wife, Laura, had family connections. He died at his home, 20 Suffolk Square, Cheltenham, on 18 April 1867, aged eighty-seven, and was buried at Leckhampton church. After over twenty years in retirement he left an estate valued for probate at under £90,000.

Smirke owed his success to consistent patronage and to his reliability, even predictability, rather than to distinction in design. Technically and structurally, he was bold: stylistically, he was less so. As a young man in Greece he wrote to his father that certain temples 'should always be a model' and in viewing them the 'impression made upon my mind … had not in … the least weakened by being frequently repeated' (Crook, '"The New Square Style"', 53). Having settled on a few such models including the Doric Parthenon and Theseum and, above all, the Ionic temple on the Ilissus, he continually repeated their architectural orders, particularly in his public works, and this persistent sober adherence to these models, including as little variation in composition as was absolutely necessary, produced buildings which, while never lacking grandeur, are consequently often dull. His economical repertory and regulated routine, while scorned by critics in the 1840s, contributed greatly to his commercial success, among the greatest of any nineteenth-century architect. To John Eastty Goodchild he was not only complacent but an 'Architectural Manufacturer … a mechanic with no feeling for *art* but working for money' (Watkin, *Cockerell*, xxiii). C. R. Cockerell, Smirke's most talented pupil, found him 'serene, friendly, communicative' (ibid., 145) and 'provokingly rational' (Crook, *British Museum*, 101) but, like his contemporaries, found it difficult to throw off Smirke's spell. Abused as 'an architectural Lazarus' (Crook, '"The New Square Style"', 136–7), A. W. N. Pugin thought his career had gone on 'too long' (ibid.). He lived through a long retirement to see his reputation diminished, but his finest accomplishment remains impressive and undiminished. In its dignified classical grandeur and monumental scale the British Museum stands as one of the greatest architectural achievements of the nineteenth century. RICHARD RIDDELL

Sources Colvin, *Archs.* • J. M. Crook and M. H. Port, eds., *The history of the king's works*, 6 (1973), 403–21, 430–37 • J. M. Crook, 'The career of Sir Robert Smirke, R.A.', DPhil diss., U. Oxf., 1961 • G. C. Tyack, 'Smirke (1) Sir Robert Smirke', *The dictionary of art*, ed. J. Turner (1996) • J. M. Crook, *The Greek revival: neo-classical attitudes in British architecture, 1760–1870*, rev. edn (1995) • J. M. Crook, *The British Museum: a case-study in architectural politics* (1973), 73–104 • [W. Papworth], ed., *The dictionary of architecture*, 11 vols. (1853–92), vol. 7, pp. 91–2 • D. Stroud, *Sir John Soane, architect* (1984), 65–6 • W. Sandby, *The history of the Royal Academy of Arts*, 2 vols. (1862), vol. 1, pp. 391–3; vol. 2, p. 268 • J. Soane, *Lectures on architecture by Sir John Soane*, ed. A. T. Bolton (1929) • W. St Clair, *Lord Elgin and the marbles* (1967) • G. Beard, *Craftsmen and interior decoration in England, 1660–1820* (1981) • S. Smirke, *Suggestions for the architectural improvement of the western parts of London* (1834) • *The Builder*, 25 (1867), 604–6 • M. Passavant, *Tour of a German artist in England*, 2 vols. (1836); repr. with new introduction by C. J. Bailey (1978) • T. H. Shepherd and J. Elmes, *Metropolitan improvements, or, London in the nineteenth century* (1829) • W. H. Leeds, *Illustrations of the public buildings of London* (1838) • D. Watkin, *The life and work of C. R. Cockerell* (1974) • S. C. Hutchison, *The history of the Royal Academy, 1768–1986*, 2nd edn (1986) • Farington, *Diary*, vols. 10–12 • J. Summerson, *Georgian London*, new edn (1988) • A. K. Placzek, ed., *Macmillan encyclopedia of architects*, 4 (1982), 84–7 • J. M. Crook, '"The New Square Style": Robert Smirke's Scottish houses', *Scottish country houses, 1600–1914*, ed. I. Gow and A. J. Rowan (1995), 206–16 • *Dir. Brit. archs.* • A. N. L. Munby, ed., *Sale catalogues of libraries of eminent persons*, 4, ed. D. J. Watkin (1972), 223 • *CGPLA Eng. & Wales* (1867)

Archives RIBA BAL, corresp., incl. family corresp. and papers • RIBA BAL, MS 'Notes on a journal in Greece' • RIBA BAL, architectural notes, sketches, and drawings • Rochester Bridge Trust, corresp. and reports relating to Rochester Bridge Trust • Som. ARS, papers and corresp. | BL, corresp. with Sir Robert Peel, Add. MSS 40349–40608 • Cumberland CRO, Lowther Castle accounts, D/Lons/L., Accs 629 • Herefs. RO, letters to Edward Poole relating to Homend (Herefordshire) • RIBA BAL, letters to John Wilson Croker

Likenesses G. Dance, drawing, 1809, RA • W. Daniell, etching, pubd 1809 (after G. Dance, 1809), NPG [*see illus.*] • E. H. Baily, marble bust, 1828, BM • T. Campbell, marble bust, 1845, RIBA

Wealth at death under £90,000: double probate, Oct 1875, *CGPLA Eng. & Wales* (1867)

Smirke, Sydney (1798–1877), architect, was born in London and baptized on 14 January 1798 in St Pancras Old Church, London, the fifth son of Robert *Smirke RA (1753–1845) and his wife, Elizabeth Russell (*d.* 1825). He was the brother of Sir Robert *Smirke (1780–1867) and of Sir Edward *Smirke (1795–1875). He first became a pupil of his brother Robert, whom he greatly assisted in his later commissions and from whom he gained valuable experience. In 1819 he was awarded the gold medal at the Royal Academy, and in 1820 he visited Sicily and mainland Italy, where, over several years, he sketched and took measurements of classical architecture. In 1828 he was appointed clerk of the king's works at St James's Palace. He married Isabella Dobson, daughter of the architect John *Dobson, on 8 December 1840 in Newcastle upon Tyne. They had four sons and four daughters. He lived at 28 Berkeley Square, London.

Smirke's commissions number about eighty and are very wide-ranging. Some of the earliest include the private mansions Oakley Park, Suffolk, for Sir Edward Kerrison; Thornham Hall, Suffolk, for Lord Henniker; Clumber Park for the duke of Newcastle; Basing Park, Hampshire, for Sir Thomas Lethbridge; and Gunnersbury Park for Baroness Rothschild. His first major commission was the reconstruction of the Pantheon in Oxford Street (1833–4). This was followed by several contracts in Lancashire for rectories at Halsall, Burscough, and Treales and three churches: Holy Trinity, Bickerstaffe; St James's, Westhead; and Christ Church, Treales. Later commissions included the custom houses at Bristol, Shoreham, Newcastle, and Gloucester, and the juvenile reformatory at Parkhurst on the Isle of Wight (1837–46).

After succeeding his brother Robert as surveyor of the Inner Temple in 1841, Smirke completed the restoration of the Temple Church with the assistance of Decimus Burton. Further commissions, which included alterations to Bridewell Hospital, Blackfriars, and the house of occupation, Lambeth, Brookwood cemetery, near Woking, and the galleries of the Horticultural Society in Kensington, led Smirke to develop an interest in the design and construction of imposing club houses in London. Together with his brother Robert, he assisted with the design of the Oxford and Cambridge Club, Pall Mall (1836–7), which was to prove invaluable to him when he came to design the old Conservative Club in St James's Street (1843–5) together with George Basevi. In 1847 Smirke altered and later completely rebuilt the second Carlton Club in Pall Mall (1847–56), taking his inspiration for the design from Sansovino's library of St Mark's in Venice.

After Sir Robert Smirke had successfully restored the choir at York Minster, Sydney took over the prestigious restoration of the minster from his brother in 1840. The cost of the restoration rose to £90,000 and was arguably the costliest ecclesiastical restoration project at the time, which he executed faultlessly. He was also architect to the Bethlem Hospital, to which he made extensive additions, and was later appointed surveyor-general to the duchy of Lancaster. In 1843 he restored the Savoy Chapel and again, after a subsequent fire, in 1860. He was later to rebuild Crown Office Row, Temple (1863–4), and Inner Temple Hall (1868–70).

Perhaps Sydney Smirke's best-known construction is his famous round reading-room in the British Museum. Sir Robert Smirke had collaborated with the trustees of the British Museum as early as 1815, when he was employed by them to build the first wing of the new quadrangular museum, the east wing. They also commissioned him to design and build his elegant gallery to house the large library of George III. The King's Library, described by J. M. Crook as 'one of the noblest rooms in London' (Crook, *British Museum*, 130), was completed in 1827 at a cost of approximately £120,000. The piecemeal construction of the rest of the new quadrangular British Museum, which was executed in an anti-clockwise direction, was continued and virtually completed when Sir Robert retired in 1846. The railings around the perimeter wall had yet to be completed as well as the forecourt and some exhibition galleries in the museum. As on several other occasions, Sydney Smirke took over the project from his elder brother. The Italian political exile Sir Anthony Panizzi was appointed to the post of principal librarian and director of the British Museum in 1856. As keeper of printed books he had insisted that the museum needed a new reading-room and suggested that the area occupied by the inner quadrangle should be utilized, submitting a flat-roofed design to the trustees in 1853. Smirke, in collaboration with Panizzi, drew up a design for a round reading-room based on the Pantheon in Rome; construction began in 1854 and was completed in 1857 at a cost of £100,000. Of considerable architectural importance because of the extensive use made of cast iron, a relatively new building material, in its construction, the round reading-room made Smirke's reputation, and in 1860 he was awarded the RIBA gold medal.

Smirke's last major commission was the addition of a fine range of exhibition galleries for the Royal Academy at Burlington House, Piccadilly, which he began in 1866 and completed in 1870. His published works include *Suggestions for the Architectural Improvement of the Western Part of London* (1834) and 'An account of the Temple Church' in John Weale's *Quarterly Papers on Architecture* (1843–5). He also contributed five papers to the *Proceedings* of the Society of Antiquaries. He was elected an associate of the Royal Academy in 1847 and Royal Academician in 1859. He was appointed professor of architecture at the Royal Academy from 1861 to 1865 and became treasurer in 1871. He was elected a fellow of the Royal Society, the Society of Antiquaries, and the Royal Institute of British Architects. In 1852 Smirke founded the Architects' Benevolent Society, of which he was the president until his death at The Hollies, Frant Road, Frant, near Tunbridge Wells, on 8 December 1877. DENIS V. REIDY

Sources J. M. Crook, 'Sydney Smirke: the architecture of compromise', *Seven Victorian architects*, ed. J. Fawcett (1977), 50–65 · J. M. Crook, *The British Museum* (1972) · J. M. Crook, 'Smirke, Sydney', *Macmillan encyclopedia of architects*, ed. A. K. Placzek, 4 vols. (1982) · *DNB* · P. R. Harris, *The reading room* (1979) · E. M. Paintin, *The King's Library* (1989) · *CGPLA Eng. & Wales* (1878) · m. cert. · d. cert. · *IGI*

Archives LPL, letters · RIBA BAL, corresp., notes, and papers | BL, corresp. with Sir Robert Peel, Add. MSS 40563–40609 · Lambton Park, Chester-le-Street, co. Durham, letters to second earl of Durham relating to Lambton Castle

Likenesses bust medallion, repro. in Crook, 'Sydney Smirke', 50 · print, NPG; repro. in *ILN* (1877) · wood-engraving, BM, NPG; repro. in *ILN* (1859)

Wealth at death under £80,000: probate, 30 Jan 1878, *CGPLA Eng. & Wales*

Smith. *See also* Smyth, Smythe.

Smith [*later* Smith Grant] **family** (*per.* **1824–1975**), distillers and farmers, owned at Glenlivet one of the best-known and most respected malt whisky distilleries in the north-east of Scotland. The earliest records of the family, originally known in English-language documents as Gow (from the Gaelic *gobha*, a smith) identify them as tacksmen of the duke of Gordon, holding lands in Glenrinnes and subsequently Morinsh in Banffshire. In 1776 a member of the family, Andrew (*b.* 1742), farmer, married Margaret Gordon from nearby Glenlivet, and they set up home in the glen. One of their sons, **George Smith** (1792–1871), became a carpenter, and in 1823 obtained a share in the rent of the small farm of Upper Drumin in Glenlivet. The following year, with encouragement and later with some financial assistance from his landlord, the duke of Gordon, Smith converted a barn and began to distil whisky there—the first man in Glenlivet to obtain a licence from the Scottish excise board to do so legally.

Since the 1790s Glenlivet, a remote glen high in the foothills of the Cairngorms, had become a haven for illicit whisky-making, and in 1825 two of George Smith's brothers were prosecuted for possessing an illicit still and assaulting an excise officer. Many local people were hostile to the establishment of a licensed distillery, which would lead to the stationing of excise officials in the glen. Consequently Smith was shunned by many of his neighbours who threatened to burn down his distillery and assault him. He was presented with a pair of pistols by a local landowner, to protect himself on his journeys through the hills carrying whisky to his customers in the south, and he employed members of his family and friends to mount a round-the-clock guard on his farm and small distillery. Illicit distilling and whisky-smuggling were finally stamped out by troops sent to the area during the late 1820s. Smith's Glenlivet distillery prospered thereafter, partly because of the high reputation for quality which had become attached to smuggled whisky from the glen.

During the 1840s George Smith's eldest son, William, took charge of the distillery, and the second son, **John Gordon Smith** (1822–1901), travelled to Edinburgh to work as an apprentice to a lawyer. When William died of consumption in 1846 John Gordon returned home to help his father, with the latter concentrating on the management of his growing farming and cattle-rearing business in the glen. George Smith was a member of the Highland and Agricultural Society of Scotland, and by 1851 he was the tenant of four farms in Glenlivet, comprising a total of 600 acres. He had a famous herd of west highland and shorthorn cattle at Minmore, and in 1856 a Minmore bull won first prize and a gold medal at the Paris Exhibition. George was aware of the importance of railway development in the north-east of Scotland to encourage industry and agriculture, and he became a shareholder in the Morayshire Railway and director of the Strathspey Railway companies. The Glenlivet whisky, which was originally carried south in casks on the backs of ponies, and later sent by coasters from Garmouth on the Moray Firth to Leith and other ports, was delivered to customers by rail after the opening of the Strathspey Railway's station 8 miles from the distillery at Ballindalloch in 1863.

Shortly after John Gordon's return the distillery business became known as G. and J. G. Smith. In 1858 the distillery at Upper Drumin and another briefly operated by the partners at Delnabo near Tomintoul were given up, when G. and J. G. Smith opened a larger, more modern distillery at Minmore. The new plant had a production capacity of more than 1800 proof gallons per week by 1868, and more than double that figure by 1887, as the firm's agents, Andrew Usher & Co. of Edinburgh, increased sales of what was commonly known as Smith's Glenlivet to Scotch whisky blenders and to markets in England and the British colonies. When George died in 1871 the farms and distillery were inherited by John Gordon Smith.

Like his father, John Gordon became an influential figure in the whisky industry, and he was particularly active in litigation to protect the Glenlivet trademark, which he and his father had registered in 1870. He also took his responsibilities in the community seriously, serving as a deputy lieutenant as well as an honorary sheriff-substitute of Banffshire. He helped to organize and was a benefactor of the local volunteer corps, which became the 6th volunteer battalion of the Gordon Highlanders, and he rose to the rank of lieutenant-colonel; on his retirement in 1891 he became honorary colonel. He died at his home, Delnabo, near Tomintoul, on 13 September 1901. He had not married, and the farming, shorthorn cattle, and distilling businesses passed to his nephew, **George Smith Grant** (1845–1911).

By 1901 George was already a prominent local landowner, and, as founder of the famous Auchorachan herd of Aberdeen Angus, a well-known and successful cattle breeder. Smith Grant was a president of the Aberdeen-Angus Cattle Society, a member of the council of the London Smithfield Club, and a chairman of the Clydesdale Horse Club. Although he seems to have left the day-to-day management of the distillery business to the manager, Peter McKenzie, Smith Grant took his responsibilities as a leading distillery owner seriously. He served as president of the North of Scotland Malt Distillers' Association, and in that capacity he gave evidence to the royal commission on whisky and other potable spirits in 1908. Smith Grant was honorary sheriff-substitute of Banffshire and deputy lieutenant of Moray and Banff, and he rose through the ranks of the local battalion of the volunteers from colour sergeant in 1867 to become colonel. Like his uncle before him he was eager to see the construction of a more effective transport infrastructure in the north-east, and was a director of the Great North of Scotland Railway Company. He died in 1911.

George Smith Grant's elder son John Smith Grant inherited the distillery and farming business on his twenty-first birthday, in March 1914. However, the business was left in the hands of the manager, Peter McKenzie, when John left for France with his regiment, the Royal Scots, shortly after the outbreak of the First World War. John subsequently transferred to the Royal Flying Corps, serving in Italy and France and attaining the rank of flight commander before being wounded in September 1917. He was killed in a German bomber raid on the 3rd Canadian stationary hospital at Doullens in France on 30 May 1918.

John's brother, **William Henry** [Bill] **Smith Grant** (1896–1975), served with the Gordon Highlanders in

France, and was twice wounded. He was awarded the Military Cross for 'conspicuous gallantry and devotion to duty' in command of a raiding party at the battle of Arras in 1917. He became the proprietor of the distillery in March 1921. His first years in charge were devoted to steering the business at Glenlivet through a depression in the industry, brought on by economic recession at home and the imposition of prohibition in the USA. However, the distillery's fortunes picked up during the 1930s and Smith Grant toured the USA after prohibition was repealed, seeking agents willing to sell his product as a bottled single malt. The Glenlivet became the best-selling single malt Scotch whisky in the USA before the Second World War, a position it still held at the end of the century. Between 1901 and 1975 the annual production of whisky at the Glenlivet distillery rose from 300,000 to more than 1.2 million proof gallons.

Bill Smith Grant was a member and a commodore of the Royal Findhorn yacht club. By the Second World War he was too old to rejoin the army, but he served as a lieutenant-commander in the Royal Naval Volunteer Reserve. His first wife, Helen Gordon, died in 1946, and he married in 1948 Mrs Margaret (Peggy) Stewart Grant, *née* Anderson. In 1952, as large North American firms began to acquire many old-established distilleries and blending firms, G. and J. G. Smith merged with J. and J. Grant Ltd, proprietors of the Glen Grant distillery in Rothes, to form the Glenlivet and Glen Grant Distilleries Ltd. In 1970 this company merged with the Edinburgh blending firm Hill, Thomson Ltd and the Longmorn Distilleries Ltd to form the Glenlivet Distillers Ltd. Bill Smith Grant remained on the board of the company until his death in 1975. Three years later the Glenlivet Distillers Ltd was finally acquired by a Canadian company, Seagram, which had first approached Bill Smith Grant with a view to purchasing his distillery shortly before the Second World War.

The Smiths and Smith Grants were typical of many distillers in the north-east of Scotland, rising from humble origins as tenant farmers to make considerable fortunes. As leading farmers and industrialists they provided employment for large numbers of men and women, and became respected figures and social leaders in their local community. Partly by the good fortune of beginning in business in Glenlivet, and partly through their talents for promotion and protecting their business, they made the Glenlivet one of the best-known brand names in the Scotch whisky industry. Iain F. Russell

Sources Chivas Brothers Archives, Strathisla Distillery, Keith, Banffshire • E. Francis, *The Glenlivet: spirit of the place* (1997) • J. M. Bulloch, *The Gordons and Smiths at Minmore, Auchorachan and Upper Drumin in Glenlivet* (privately printed, 1910) • genealogy database, Elgin Library, Grant Lodge, Elgin, Scotland, local history department • bap. reg. Scot., Inveravon, Banffshire, NA Scot., RH 21/34/1 [George Smith, John Gordon Smith] • bap. reg. Scot., Kirkmichael, Banffshire [George Smith Grant] • *National Guardian* (16 June 1911) [George Smith Grant] • bap. reg. Scot., Auchorachan, Elgin Library, Elgin, Scotland [William Henry Smith Grant] • bur. reg. Scot., NA Scot., RH 21/35/1 [John Gordon Smith] • *Northern Scot* (22 Feb 1975), 9 [William Henry Smith Grant] • *Northern Scot* (22 March 1975), 9 [William Henry Smith Grant]

Archives priv. coll. • Strathisla Distillery, Keith, Banffshire, Brands Heritage Centre, Glenlivet archives

Likenesses J. H. Lorimer, portrait (George Smith Grant); presented 1909 • portrait (George Smith Grant), Chivas Brothers' Brands Heritage Centre, Keith, Moray • portrait (William Henry Smith Grant), Chivas Brothers' Brands Heritage Centre, Keith, Moray • portrait (George Smith), Chivas Brothers' Brands Heritage Centre, Keith, Moray • portrait (John Gordon Smith), Chivas Brothers' Brands Heritage Centre, Keith, Moray • portraits, priv. coll.

Wealth at death £200,455 19*s*. 9*d*.—John Gordon Smith: confirmation, 1 March 1902, *CCI* • £77,178 6*s*. 8*d*.—George Smith Grant: confirmation, 16 Sept 1911, *CCI* • £145,296.45—William Henry Smith Grant: confirmation, 12 June 1975, *CCI*

Smith, Father. *See* Smith, Bernard (*c*.1628/9–1708).

Smith, Mrs. *See* Woodham, Mrs (*d*. 1803).

Smith of Derby. *See* Smith, Thomas (*bap*. 1720x24?, *d*. 1767).

Smith, Aaron (*d*. **1701**), conspirator and lawyer, was possibly descended from a namesake farmer at Petworth, Sussex, and may have been a protégé of the earls of Northumberland. His friends were roundheads' sons, and in religion he was a dissenter, like Prudentia (or Prudence) Wood (*d*. 1708/9), whom he married at Canterbury on 19 December 1670. They lived in Chancery Lane, London. Three sons and a daughter reached adulthood. By the 1670s Smith was a solicitor practising in chancery and estimated his professional income at £500–£600 a year.

Smith strongly supported the parliamentary opposition to Charles II and belonged to the Green Ribbon Club. In 1677, when the opposition leaders unsuccessfully claimed that the Cavalier Parliament was dissolved, Smith argued this so vehemently in tavern disputes that the House of Lords ordered his detention and, when he temporarily absconded, had a proclamation issued against him on 1 June. According to Roger North he was called 'the furious phanatick', and was 'a furious Party man … a desperate Talker and very bold … a violent monster; and his friends, for his excuse, used to say he was half-mad' (North, *Lives*, 1.189; *Examen*, 75).

Previous interpretations of Smith as coolly cynical in his attitude to Titus Oates and the Popish Plot have confused him with Thomas Smith (*d*. 1681), a leading barrister prominent during the plot trials. Aaron Smith in fact sincerely believed in a Catholic conspiracy, never stirring outdoors but with loaded pistols. When Charles II fell dangerously ill in 1679 Smith and his clerk prepared arms and ammunition. He was one of the ten men who on 13 January 1680 presented to Charles the London 'monster petition' for the meeting of parliament, and that autumn his evidence helped expel Sir Francis Wythens from the Commons for 'abhorring' petitioning.

When the whig Stephen College was indicted for treason in 1681 Smith was his solicitor. The government's determination to convict College made it a dangerous post. When College was tried at Oxford on 17 August 1681 the judges, headed by the lord chief justice, Sir Francis North, enforced the letter of the law that defendants had no right to consult counsel or solicitors. The notes, advice, and inflammatory draft speech which Smith was carrying from counsel to College that morning were seized from him and revealed to the prosecution. One lawyer allegedly claimed that soliciting for defendants accused of treason was in itself treasonable. Cross-examined during the trial Smith burst out 'It is high time for us to look about, for our lives and estates are beset here' (Luttrell, 1.202). He was consequently bound over and on 30 January 1682 was charged with carrying treasonable papers to College. After postponements he was without warning tried in the king's bench in July and convicted of delivering libels and disloyal words. He absconded before sentence.

Believing 'that the King and the cursed Council were resolved to destroy old English liberty and totally extirpate the Gospel' (*CSP dom., July–September 1683*, 42) Smith joined in the radical whigs' plans to rebel. In January 1683 their leaders, the council of six, at Algernon Sidney's suggestion, sent Smith to Scotland with letters to summon leading Scottish plotters to London to co-ordinate their risings, but he endangered the mission by indiscreet talk. He was possibly also involved in the Rye House assassination plot. On 4 July 1683 he was arrested in Axe Yard, Westminster, and was sent to the Tower. He resisted heavy pressure to become the second witness required to convict Sidney of treason, the most solid charge against whom was having organized Smith's mission. Doubtless partly in retaliation the lord chief justice, Jeffreys, on 27 October 1683 sentenced the defiant Smith on his previous conviction to be pilloried twice, fined £500, and imprisoned until he could find sureties for good behaviour. Though the populace spared him, as was intended his pillorying permanently damaged his reputation.

Unable to pay the fine, Smith remained in the king's bench prison for four and a half years. Fellow prisoners included the now disgraced Oates and the whig adventurer Henry Baker. Finally, when he was about to buy a pardon with all he had, William Penn's friend Charlwood Lawton persuaded Penn to solicit James II for one. James, characteristically, at first refused angrily, saying 'Six such men would put his three kingdoms in a flame' (Janney, 302), but then pardoned Smith's fine in March 1688 and received him, saying he persuaded himself that the dissenters would now be loyal to his government. He then appointed Smith one of the commissioners to remodel corporations without examining his real attitudes.

After the revolution the whig Treasury board, on 20 April 1689, appointed Smith solicitor to the Treasury at a salary of £200 a year, to be shared with a deputy. Smith's duties included the routine preparations for state prosecutions and he undoubtedly acted with spiteful hostility towards some persons accused of Jacobitism, including his benefactors Penn and Lawton. He apparently meddled at trials until the attorney-general, Treby, checked him for infringing his authority. Yet, although Smith appointed Oates's solicitor, Thomas Bale, as his deputy, he dutifully steered potential witnesses away from Oates, lest their credibility in court should be damaged. On 14 June 1692, to prevent several recently arrested suspects from being bailed, he made an affidavit indicating that there were the required two witnesses against them for treason, when there was really only one and strong circumstantial evidence. This was done with the connivance of the lord chief justice, Holt, who acted on the affidavit despite knowing its falsity. For this act, however, the House of Lords examined Smith so ferociously on 11 November 1692 that he claimed next day to be sick.

For six years the Treasury apparently ordered money warrants for Smith worth only £17,000 (compared with £52,000 to his predecessor, Burton, over four years) and much of that was never issued. He received no salary after 1691. Besides private legal practice he gained money by taking small bribes from arrested Jacobites for finding their bail acceptable. By mid-1694, with his private credit exhausted, he was pleading desperately for payments for that term's prosecutions: 'I doe my duty with the Hazard of my life daily … I never knew what the want of money was … untill I had the Honr of this Imploymt … distresse of minde … eats up my very spiritts' (Smith to Treasury, 21 June 1694, PRO, T 1/28, fol. 171).

In 1694 Smith may, therefore, have succumbed to temptation, and assisted his former 'fellow-sufferer' Baker in approaching the government with several false witnesses testifying to a Jacobite 'Lancashire Plot', from which they hoped for rich rewards through confiscation of Catholic estates. However, he may, like the ministers, have been honestly deceived, as there was genuine major plotting in Lancashire. Smith's fiercest accuser was John Taaffe, a false witness who changed sides and claimed that as a radical dissenter Smith hoped later to turn the plot against the Church of England. Taaffe's narrative of events, however, varied and Smith did not, as Taaffe sometimes claimed, accompany Baker and the witnesses on their July raid into Lancashire seizing suspects and plundering. The Jacobite propagandist Robert Ferguson, another former whig fellow conspirator, accused Smith in October in *A Letter to Mr Secretary Trenchard* of regularly supporting sham plots to get government money; yet in August, in the first edition of *A Letter to Sir John Holt*, Ferguson had praised him for compassion for the innocent.

Smith's official duty to protect the chief prosecution witness, the swindling bigamist John Lunt, certainly obliged him to bully and to bend the law that autumn. He attended the plot trials at Manchester on 20 October 1694, but on hearing that Taaffe would testify for the defence quickly fell ill and withdrew. Parliament's 1694–5 inquiry into the plot wrongly concluded that it was genuine.

At a treason trial in April 1695 Smith's testifying was objected to because he had been pilloried. What discredited him officially, however, was his almost total failure to keep accounts. On first attending the commission for the public accounts in January 1693 he unwisely pretended to have accounts almost ready, and was repeatedly summoned and rebuked. By 1695 he had alienated the Treasury, and in February 1696 the commission finally made him attend the Commons, which, when he still produced nothing, imprisoned him for two months. He was dismissed by 25 July 1696. Though still making promises to the Commons and commission in 1697 he never passed his accounts. He was not, however, prosecuted for embezzlement, and continued to wind up official business: the Treasury may have suspected that, as his widow claimed, the government owed him money.

Smith died in 1701 between 17 March and 8 October, when his widow, Prudentia, was granted administration of his estate. He was probably buried in Bunhill Fields nonconformist burial-ground, as Prudentia's will, proved on 11 February 1709, directed that she should be. Her will showed modest middle-class prosperity, suggesting that Smith may have recovered the family's finances before his death.

Smith was not 'the "Mephistophiles" of whig intrigue since 1678' or a would-be 'Fouquier-Tinville of the English revolution' (*DNB*), but a fanatical radical whose sheer vehemence thrust him into more exalted political company. Contemporary propaganda and later mistaken identity have unduly blackened his reputation and inflated his significance. PAUL HOPKINS

Sources *State trials*, vols. 8–12 • R. North, *The lives of … Francis North … Dudley North … and … John North*, ed. A. Jessopp, 3 vols. (1890) • R. North, *Examen* (1742) • R. Ferguson, *A letter to Mr Secretary Trenchard* (1694) • R. Ferguson, *A letter to Sir John Holt*, 1st edn (1694) • P. A. Hopkins, 'Aspects of Jacobite conspiracy in England in the reign of William III', PhD diss., U. Cam., 1981 • *CSP dom., 1676–97* • W. A. Shaw, ed., *Calendar of treasury books*, 8–16, PRO (1923–38) • R. Morrice, 'Ent'ring book', DWL, Morrice MS P–Q [vols. 1–2] • J. Redington, ed., *Calendar of Treasury papers*, 1–3, PRO (1868–74) • memorials and letters from Smith, 1692–5, PRO, treasury papers, T 1/18, fols. 91–2; T 1/28, fols. 167–71; T 1/35, fols. 5–7 • N. Luttrell, *A brief historical relation of state affairs from September 1678 to April 1714*, 6 vols. (1857), vols. 1–4 • *The manuscripts of Lord Kenyon*, HMC, 35 (1894) • *The manuscripts of the House of Lords*, new ser., 12 vols. (1900–77), vol. 1 • *The manuscripts of the House of Lords*, 4 vols., HMC, 17 (1887–94), vol. 4 • will, PRO, PROB 11/506, fol. 310 [Prudentia Smith] • admin., PRO, PROB 6/77, fols. 99v, 199v [Aaron Smith] • admin, 30 July 1707, PRO, PROB 6/83, fol. 139 [Aaron Smith, jun.] • admin., 21 April 1715, PRO, PROB 6/91, fol. 67 [Aaron Smith] • admin., 4 Sept 1718, PRO, PROB 6/94, fol. 169 [Moses Smith] • S. M. Janney, *The life of William Penn* (1878) • W. Beamont, ed., *The Jacobite trials at Manchester in 1694*, Chetham Society, 28 (1853) • W. Goss, ed., *The trials at Manchester*, Chetham Society (1861) • minutes of the commissioners for the public accounts, BL, Harley MSS 1491, 1493–1494 • M. Knights, *Politics and opinion in crisis, 1678–81* (1994) • J. Scott, *Algernon Sidney and the Restoration crisis, 1677–1683* (1991) • T. B. Macaulay, *The history of England from the accession of James II*, new edn, ed. C. H. Firth, 6 vols. (1913–15) • S. Baxter, *The development of the treasury, 1660–1702* (1956) • R. L. Greaves, *Secrets of the kingdom: British radicals from the Popish Plot to the revolution of 1688–89* (1992) • M. S. Zook, *Radical whigs and conspiratorial politics in late Stuart England* (1999) • W. Fuller, *The whole life of Mr William Fuller* (1703) • J. C. Sainty, *Treasury officials, 1660–1870* (1972) • *JHC*, 11 (1693–7) • assessments, tax on marriages, 1695, CLRO, 106, p. 14 • *IGI*

Archives PRO, treasury papers

Smith, Aaron (*b.* *c.*1793, *d.* in or after 1852), sailor accused of piracy, was, according to the story he told in court, while in the West Indies made the first mate on board the brig *Zephyr*, which sailed from Kingston, Jamaica, for England at the end of June 1822 when Smith was making for England to marry Sophia Knight, a publican's daughter. The captain ignored advice against taking the shorter, leeward, passage, and the brig was captured by a schooner manned by a Spanish and French crew, who plundered her of whatever seemed valuable. The *Zephyr* was then released, but Smith was detained in the schooner to act as navigator and translator. He was compelled by threats and actual torture to take part in the plundering of the *Victoria*, the *Industry*, and other vessels. On board the *Industry* was a Captain Cook, who was captured by the pirates and transferred to the schooner and who was to figure largely in Smith's later life. Smith escaped from the pirates, but was arrested when recognized in Havana and brought to England in irons on board the *Sybille* to be tried at the Old Bailey on 19 December 1823 on various charges of piracy in the West Indies. He claimed he had been forced into the acts of piracy, and was acquitted.

Subsequently Smith continued at sea and had command of a vessel in the China trade. In 1834 he retired and lived in London, doing some business as an underwriter and a bill discounter. In January 1850 Smith attended a meeting at the London tavern to counter a petition to parliament to do away with 'head money', a bounty paid to those who officially swore that they had killed a Borneo pirate. It was said that the Borneo pirates did not exist, and that innocent fishermen were being killed for the bounty. Smith contradicted this, saying that he himself had been attacked by such pirates. When this opinion by Smith was quoted in a debate in parliament on 23 May, Cobden discounted the statement on the grounds that Smith himself was 'a most atrocious pirate'. Smith employed a Mr E. Garbett to ask Cobden for an interview but this was refused. An angry correspondence followed, reported in *The Times* of 1 and 20 June 1850, in which Captain Cook came forward to support Cobden, saying that he had been captured and ill-treated by Smith, who was undoubtedly a pirate. Smith brought an action for libel against Cook, which virtually turned into a retrial of Smith for the acts of piracy of which he had already been acquitted some twenty-eight years previously. None of the original witnesses could be found and there was no official record of the previous trial; Smith's 1824 publication, *The atrocities of the pirates: being a narrative of the sufferings endured by the author during his captivity among the pirates of the island of Cuba*, was deemed too romanticized for reliability. Smith was again acquitted, but given damages of only £10. He was then living in Camden, where he continued to be recorded in the *London Directory* until 1852, when his name disappears.

J. K. LAUGHTON, *rev.* J. GILLILAND

Sources Allibone, *Dict.* • *The Times* (20 Dec 1823) • *The Times* (1 June 1850) • *The Times* (20 June 1850) • Boase, *Mod. Eng. biog.* • *Morning Chronicle* (20 Dec 1823)

Smith, Abel (1717?–1788), banker and merchant, was baptized on 14 March 1717, the third son of Abel Smith (*d.* 1757) and his wife, Jane, daughter of George Beaumont of Chapelthorpe, Yorkshire. His grandfather Thomas Smith had added to a local mercer's business in Nottingham some banking activities, including remittances for the excise. This banking activity was considerably expanded by the elder Abel Smith and his brothers, but Abel's eldest son, Sir George Smith, baronet, used his inheritance to become a country gentleman. The younger Abel was placed at fifteen as an apprentice in a Hull merchant firm trading to the Baltic. At the conclusion of his apprenticeship he became a partner in this firm, thereafter Wilberforce and Smith. In 1745 he married Mary, daughter of Thomas Bird of Barton on the Heath, Warwickshire, a wealthy silk manufacturer; her sister Elizabeth was to marry his partner Robert Wilberforce, establishing close family ties between the Nottingham and Hull families.

Abel Smith also became a partner in his family's bank in Nottingham, whose management he took over on his father's death in 1757. The firm's expanded volume of government and other remittances made close London connections indispensable. To gain them, in 1758 Smith entered into a partnership with John Payne, a London linen draper, to form the bank of Smith and Payne with offices in London and Nottingham. Smith was already well connected in London through cousins and through his elder brother John, a London merchant and director of both the East India and the South Sea companies. As John Payne was then chairman of the East India Company and his brother Edward a director of the Bank of England, Smith and Payne, almost from its inception, was a prestigious house that could attract the correspondence of country banks and desirable town and country business. (The Paynes' connections were also to prove useful in obtaining for Smith and Payne extraordinary re-discount facilities at the Bank of England.) Smith led in creating additional affiliated banks in Lincoln (1775) and Hull (1784). Despite the difficulties of wars, these precociously integrated firms experienced significant growth during the last decades of the century.

The Nottingham bank attracted the business of neighbouring nobility and gentry as well as that of local hosiery manufacturers and traders. Through his close association with Henry Clinton, second duke of Newcastle, Smith was returned as MP for Aldborough (1774–8), and he later sat for St Ives (1780–84) through the interest of Humphrey Mackworth Praed. He shared in a government victualling contract during the American war, but broke with Lord North on being excluded from the underwriting of government wartime loans. He then supported William Pitt the younger, on whose recommendation he was returned by Edward Eliot as member for St Germans (1784–8).

At his death, on 12 July 1788, in addition to his partnerships in the several Smith banks, in Wilberforce and Smith, and in several other firms, Abel Smith left extensive land holdings, particularly in Nottinghamshire and Lincolnshire, a sugar estate in Jamaica, and £59,953. Five of his six surviving sons (he had no daughters) became MPs. His son Robert *Smith (1752–1838) was created Baron Carrington in 1796. Four of his sons became partners in the Smith banks. These firms survived and prospered until 1902, when they merged with the Union Bank, which in turn was absorbed by the National Provincial Bank.

Jacob M. Price, *rev.*

Sources HoP, *Commons, 1754–90*, vol. 3 • J. A. S. L. Leighton-Boyce, *Smiths, the bankers, 1658–1958* (1958) • L. S. Pressnell, *Country banking in the industrial revolution* (1956)

Wealth at death £59,953 excl. land: *DNB*

Smith, Abel (1788–1859), banker and politician, was born on 7 July 1788, probably in Nottinghamshire, the eldest son of Samuel Smith (1745–1834), banker and politician, and his wife, Elizabeth (*d.* 1835), daughter of Edmund Turnor, of Stoke Rochford and Panton Hall, Lincolnshire. Smith was one of four brothers; he also had nine sisters. In 1801 Smith moved with his family from Nottinghamshire to Hertfordshire when his father purchased the estate of Woodhall Park at Watton, near Hertford. He was educated at Harrow School and Trinity College, Cambridge.

Born into one of England's great banking families, Smith was destined to become perhaps the most respected banker of his generation. In 1810 he became a partner in the London banking house of Smith, Payne and Smith, which conducted business from no. 1 Lombard Street. In addition to this bank, founded in 1758, the Smith family also established banks at Nottingham (1658), Lincoln (1775), Hull (1784), and Derby (1806). In an era when the Bank of England held a monopoly of joint-stock banking, and private banks in both London and the provinces were predominantly single offices with no more than six partners, the interlocking partnerships forged by the Smiths were of especial significance. Smith became a partner in the Lincoln bank in 1829, though his interests and reputation were always closely tied to London.

Despite being a relative newcomer to London private banking, Smith, Payne and Smith weathered the financial storm of 1825–6 (when eighty private banks failed in London and the country) better than most. In the following decades the bank went from strength to strength. The key role played by Smith was highlighted in a memoir in 1859, which noted that:

> during the last half century, the name of Abel Smith has been intimately associated with the banking business of London, and under his able management the house which his grandfather in connection with the late Mr. Payne, founded, attained to a position second to no private bank in the kingdom. No man, probably, in modern times has exercised a greater or a more deserved influence in financial circles than Mr. Smith. He was amongst the shrewdest and most far seeing of those who trade in money. (*Bankers' Magazine*, 205)

Smith's experience of financial affairs was also widely recognized at Westminster, where he was a member of parliament for the boroughs of Midhurst and Wendover and, between 1835 and 1847, the county of Hertfordshire. A nephew of the first Lord Carrington, Smith was in politics a consistent conservative, voting against the Reform Bill in 1832. Though not a natural orator, he carried considerable authority when speaking with his customary brevity on the financial matters of the day. Together with Sir Robert Peel and George Grote, he was a member of the Commons select committee whose inquiry into banking led to the Bank Charter Act of 1844, which sought to stabilize the currency by fixing the volume of bank notes in circulation.

On 28 August 1822, Smith married his first wife, Lady Marianne Melville, daughter of the ninth earl of Leven and Melville. The marriage, which was childless, ended with her death on 22 March 1823. He married his second wife, Frances Anne (*d.* 1885), daughter of General Sir Harry *Calvert, of Claydon Hall, Buckinghamshire, on 12 July 1826. They had four sons and six daughters. Following the death of his father in 1834, Smith inherited the family seat of Woodhall Park and devoted increasing amounts of time to the management of the estate. A JP for Hertfordshire, he maintained a strong interest in improving the social fabric of the locality, particularly through the endowment of livings and provision for the building and renovation of churches in the surrounding rural parishes. However, despite his many duties as a resident landlord, Smith continued to take an active role in the management of the London banking house until his death.

Smith died at Woodhall Park, Watton, Hertfordshire, on 23 February 1859. An obituary in the *Hertford Mercury* (26 February 1859) noted that 'as a landlord he was just and liberal; and as a resident among a population born and employed upon the land, he was not unminded of the obligation imposed upon the rich, of wisely and judiciously helping the poor'. He was buried at Watton, Hertfordshire, on 2 March 1859. Smith died a man of immense wealth, with land and property in no fewer than eight counties, together with his property and banking interests in London and Lincoln. The entailed estate of Woodhall Park descended to his eldest son, Abel Smith (1829–1898), while his shares in the banking establishments passed to his second son, Robert Smith (1833–1894). Remaining property was divided variously between his four sons, with cash legacies granted to his daughters.

IAIN S. BLACK

Sources 'Memoir of the late Abel Smith', *Bankers' Magazine*, 19 (1859), 205–8 • J. A. S. L. Leighton-Boyce, *Smiths, the bankers, 1658–1958* (1958) • *Hertford Mercury* (26 Feb 1859) • private information (2004) • I. S. Black, 'The London agency system in English banking, 1780–1825', *London Journal*, 21/2 (1996), 112–30 • H. T. Easton, *History of a banking house*, 1st edn (1903) • Venn, *Alum. Cant.* • d. cert. • Burke, *Gen. GB*

Archives priv. coll. | NatWest Group, 41 Lothbury, London, archives, Smiths Bank records

Likenesses G. Richmond, oils, 1850, priv. coll. • S. Cousins, engraving (after portrait by F. R. Say), repro. in Easton, *History*, facing p. 24

Wealth at death under £400,000: probate, 9 April 1859, *CGPLA Eng. & Wales*

Smith, Adam (*bap.* **1723**, *d.* **1790**), moral philosopher and political economist, was baptized on 5 June 1723 at Kirkcaldy, a small port on the Forth. His father, also Adam Smith (1679–1723), was private secretary to the third earl of Loudoun, later becoming writer to the signet and a local customs official; his mother, Margaret Douglas (1694–1784), was the daughter of Robert Douglas of Strathenry, the second son of Sir William Douglas of Kirkness, a prominent Fife landowner and Scottish MP until 1706. The marriage, in 1720, was the father's second, his first wife having died in 1717, leaving him with a son, Hugh (1709–1750). The half-brothers do not appear to have had much to do with one another, though Adam inherited Hugh's property when he died intestate.

Childhood and education The death of Smith's father five months before his birth meant that he was brought up by

Adam Smith (*bap.* 1723, *d.* 1790), by James Tassie, 1787

his mother, probably as a sickly child. She had help in the early years from influential relatives and friends who acted as the guardians named in his father's will. They included James Oswald of Dunnikier, a wealthy merchant and landowner in Kirkcaldy, and Smith's cousin, William Smith, the second duke of Argyll's steward at a time when the Argyll family controlled much of the patronage in Scotland.

Smith was put through the grammar school curriculum at the local two-room burgh school, learning Latin and a little Greek, Roman history, rhetoric and grammar, and arithmetic. He later commended the Scottish parish school system, while suggesting that 'geometry and mechanics', rather than 'a little smattering of Latin', were a better supplement to basic skills for the 'common people' (Smith, *WN*, 785). In his own case, however, the introduction to ancient languages was a good foundation for a scholarly career that began in earnest when, at the age of fourteen, he went to Glasgow College. The curriculum consisted of these languages, logic, moral philosophy, mathematics, and natural philosophy, each taught by a specialist professor. Mathematics and natural philosophy were said to be Smith's 'favourite pursuits' (Stewart, 271), but the teacher who was to have most influence on Smith's career was Francis Hutcheson, professor of moral philosophy. Hutcheson was a 'new light' teacher, one of the first to lecture in English rather than Latin, doing so in an inspirational manner that countered rigid

Calvinist doctrines and brought him under local suspicion for so doing.

In 1740 Smith was awarded a Snell exhibition which enabled him to move to Balliol College, Oxford. The Snell foundation was originally intended to support those destined for ordination in the episcopalian Church of Scotland, though the penalties for failing to honour this had fallen into abeyance. Smith spent six years at Oxford, mostly devoted, as far as it is known, to reading widely in ancient philosophy and in English, French, and Italian literature. These were to remain lifelong interests, aided by considerable powers of recall. Smith also acquired something prized by Scots seeking advancement: fluency in accepted English usage of the language. The intellectual conservatism and indolence of Smith's teachers at Balliol contrasted unfavourably with the teaching at Glasgow. Smith's damning verdict on Oxford has become part of the standard indictment of the ancient English universities during the eighteenth century. By family background and education—whig, Presbyterian, and Hanoverian—Smith could not have been in sympathy with the tory, high-church, and Jacobite sympathies of Balliol. Nor could the anti-Scottish prejudices of the place have helped him to feel at home there.

In 1746 Smith returned to Kirkcaldy, where he spent the next two years, having decided to honour the original terms of the Snell exhibition in one respect only, namely by exercising his talents in Scotland. His first opportunity came as a result of an invitation from Henry Home, Lord Kames, to give a course of public lectures in Edinburgh on rhetoric and *belles-lettres*. Such was their initial success that between 1748 and 1751 Smith expanded their content to include the history of philosophy and jurisprudence. It was during this period too that Smith formed or confirmed some of his most important friendships among the Edinburgh literati: with Kames, James Oswald (son of Smith's guardian), Alexander Wedderburn, Adam Ferguson, William Johnstone (later Pulteney), John Millar, William Robertson, and Hugh Blair. More especially, he formed his most important friendship, that with David Hume, his senior by twelve years. The affinities between their respective writings on philosophy, politics, economics, history, and religion show that Hume and Smith formed a closer intellectual alliance with each other than either of them had with the other representatives of what has come to be known as the Scottish Enlightenment.

The lecturer's plan of studies The Edinburgh lectures provided Smith with material that was put to immediate use when he was offered regular employment at Glasgow as professor of logic in 1751, especially since he took on the duties of the professor of moral philosophy as well. He transferred to the latter chair when it became vacant in the following year, but retained the classes on rhetoric as part of his duties. The curriculum inherited from Hutcheson provided the framework for Smith's teaching, especially in the early years of his tenure. It consisted of ethics and a consideration of the rights and duties of man according to the tenets of the law of nature and nations, with politics and some incidental treatment of economic subjects included. There was sufficient latitude here for Smith to develop those special interests and emphases that were to become the basis for what he later published or planned to publish. He was unusual in resisting the temptation to write on topical subjects, except when they served as illustrations for settled philosophical positions. Even his earliest publications—two articles for the first *Edinburgh Review* in 1755—dealt with weighty subjects: Samuel Johnson's *Dictionary*, the *Encyclopédie*, and Jean-Jacques Rousseau's second discourse on inequality. As a consequence of this peculiarity—and in the case of the *Wealth of Nations* the long interval between conception and delivery—the pattern of Smith's teaching and his original plan of studies has assumed special significance.

The main informant on this subject was Smith's pupil John Millar, who reported that Smith taught under four headings: natural theology (on which nothing survives, though a good deal can be inferred); ethics (the subject of Smith's first book, *The Theory of Moral Sentiments*); 'that branch of morality that relates to *justice*' (on which we now have two sets of student notes); and finally, 'those political regulations which are founded, not upon the principle of *justice*, but that of *expediency*, and which are calculated to increase the riches, the power, and the prosperity of a State' (Smith, *EPS*, 274–5), the outcome of which emerged a quarter of a century later as the *Wealth of Nations*.

By ordering the destruction of sixteen volumes of manuscript material just before his death, Smith ensured that attention would be focused on his two longest and most highly polished works, plus the posthumously published *Essays on Philosophical Subjects*, which includes a remarkable essay, 'The principles which lead and direct philosophical enquiries, illustrated by the history of astronomy'. Dugald Stewart attributed this decision to 'an excessive solicitude in the author about his posthumous reputation' (Smith, *EPS*, 327). Yet precisely because that solicitude has been so well rewarded, the missing parts of his original enterprise continue to be of interest, particularly when it is clear that Smith did not regard them as superseded by what was already in print. As late as 1785 he spoke of two projects on which he was actively engaged: 'a sort of Philosophical History of all the different branches of Literature, of Philosophy, Poetry and Eloquence', and 'a sort of theory and History of Law and Government' (Smith, *Corr.*, 287). The first of these represented a return to his beginnings in the *Lectures on Rhetoric and Belles Lettres*. Smith had already published one of these lectures as *Considerations Concerning the First Formation of Languages* in 1761. That *Essays on Philosophical Subjects* was part of the same projected philosophical history was confirmed by the discovery of student notes on the *Lectures on Rhetoric and Belles Lettres* in 1958. Another set of notes on Smith's lectures on jurisprudence was found at the same time, supplementing those published in 1896, both of which are now contained in *Lectures on Jurisprudence*. Although these lecture notes cannot be an entirely faithful record of what was said, they were based on painstaking collation and revision, whether for personal use or for sale. On most significant issues their accuracy can be checked by reference to opinions expressed in the published writings. The various parts of the original plan have acquired separate lives in the histories of rhetorical, ethical, jurisprudential, and economic thinking, but their connections, or perceived lack of them, continue to be central to understanding Smith's aims and achievements.

Rhetoric and astronomy From a literary-historical point of view, the *Lectures on Rhetoric and Belles Lettres* can be seen as Smith's contribution to the promotion of Augustan English in Scotland, together with its associated norms of taste. By responding to this need he also became a founder of the study of English in universities, as well as the kind of critic Romantics in the following century loved to hate. He was a determined advocate of the plain style in prose, taking Jonathan Swift and Joseph Addison as his favoured models, Shaftesburian over-elaboration as its antithesis. But there was a great deal more to the lectures than stylistics and literary criticism. They were innovative in rejecting outmoded branches of knowledge such as ancient logic and the metaphysics of the schools, and that 'very silly set of books' devoted to rules of eloquence and figures of speech (Smith, *LRBL*, 26). Smith was to adopt a similar position towards casuistry when dealing with ethics. The lectures also attest to a more ambitious philosophical goal, described by Millar as follows:

> The best method of explaining and illustrating the various powers of the human mind, the most useful part of metaphysics, arises from an examination of the several ways of communicating our thoughts by speech, and from the attention to the principles of those literary compositions which contribute to persuasion or entertainment. (Smith, *EPS*, 274)

Smith was pursuing the 'experimental' or empirical approach to the 'science of man' that Hume had endorsed in the introduction to his *Treatise of Human Nature* (1739) when speaking of this science as the headquarters from which all other philosophical and literary enquiries could best be explored.

Smith's essay on the formation of languages contributes to a branch of speculative linguistics of the type pursued by Girard, Condillac, and Rousseau. He was chiefly interested in the light shed by the development of language on various mental operations: taxonomy, analogy, abstraction, combination, and the capacity to form systems of grammar. A 'rational grammar' based on such insights, he thought, could provide a foundation for logic; it would also contribute to the 'history of the natural progress of the human mind' (Smith, *Corr.*, 87–8), where this history would take account of variations in types of social existence. When dealing with modes of communication and the methods of presentation appropriate to each of them, Smith distinguished four main types: poetical, oratorical, historical, and didactic. Of these, the last two have the closest bearing on Smith's own writings. Smith's historiographic preferences favoured impartial causal narratives combining the account of actors' motives with external events. Thucydides and Livy were considered the best of the ancients, Machiavelli of the moderns, with Hume now replacing him.

Although historical narrative, as Smith's persistent recourse to it shows, could also serve didactic purposes, didactic discourse proper sought to prove a proposition or set of propositions by expounding all the relevant arguments for and against. It was best exemplified by the 'Newtonian method', which being the 'most Philosophical' approach, was applicable to both natural and moral sciences. It entailed laying down 'certain principles, known or proved in the beginning, from whence we account for the severall Phenomena, connecting all together by the same Chain' (Smith, *LRBL*, 146). That the Newtonian system also emerges as the triumphant conclusion of Smith's essay on the history of astronomy is hardly surprising, though Smith's account remained faithful to the Humean agenda in making the psychological basis for scientific curiosity, and the aesthetic qualities possessed by successful theories, its chief concern. There is a Humean basis too for the role Smith attaches to constructive uses of the imagination in creating systems ('imaginary machines'; Smith, *EPS*, 66) designed to restore tranquillity by overcoming the uncomfortable sensations associated with living in a world of discordant sense perceptions. When successful, such systems provide the simplest as well as most accurate account of the observational evidence. But since they remain a product of our imaginations, there is always the possibility of supersession: hence Smith's disturbingly sceptical hint at the end of the essay on astronomy that Newton might not be the end of the story. If Smith could be sceptical about Newton, perhaps there were other overarching conceptions to which we assent for reasons of mental comfort which have even less foundation. There could be a clue here to the charge that Smith, in performing his duties under natural religion perfunctorily, was adopting a view that was too flattering to human pride.

These early preoccupations with language, history, and the Newtonian method resurface in Smith's two main works, *The Theory of Moral Sentiments* and the *Wealth of Nations*. Indeed, one could say that, in several senses, they lay the groundwork for those works. Most obviously, Newton provided him with something akin to the modern idea of a philosophy of science. It furnished a justification for treating moral and economic behaviour naturalistically, seeking causal regularities that could be verified by an appeal to the external evidence of our senses in the accepted Newtonian manner, as well as by recourse to the introspective knowledge we have of human behaviour as fellow actors. Ready access to the latter kind of evidence accounted for Smith's belief that it was more difficult to impose false causal accounts on others when dealing with moral phenomena than it was in natural philosophy, where the phenomena are more distant from ourselves (Smith, *TMS*, 313–14).

The concern with language and modes of communication also provided more substantive insights into the ways in which individuals and groups interact with one another in society. The auditors and readers of the *Lectures on Rhetoric and Belles Lettres* are replaced by spectators of our moral conduct in *The Theory of Moral Sentiments*. An ability to find the mode of communication that expresses our thoughts and feelings perspicuously for auditors is on a par with the way in which, in our moral dealings, we seek harmony between our own feelings and those of others, modifying our original impulses to bring them into line with those that spectators can share. Similarly, in the *Wealth of Nations*, the oratorical qualities of language provide a basis for one of the central human propensities in that work: the propensity to 'truck, barter, and exchange one thing for another' which underpins the division of labour in society (Smith, *WN*, 25). Language use distinguishes human beings from other animals; it is the medium through which we persuade others to co-operate in serving our wants by meeting their own.

***The Theory of Moral Sentiments* (1759)** Those who attended the lectures on rhetoric at Glasgow would also have heard Smith's lectures on ethics, and they might have judged the latter to be as much an exercise in oratorical as didactic discourse. *The Theory of Moral Sentiments* retains signs of delivery to a youthful audience, though the order of the published parts, it has been suggested by his modern editors, differed from the published version. The final part on the history of systems of moral philosophy was probably delivered first, setting the scene for his own theory by ending with the systems of Hutcheson and Hume. These are the two most important influences on Smith's work, part inspiration, part stimulus to fruitful disagreement. All three philosophers agree that morals are essentially a matter of 'immediate sense and feeling' (Smith, *TMS*, 321) rather than rational calculation. But neither Hume nor Smith accepted Hutcheson's concept of a single 'moral sense' capable of directly apprehending moral verities, nor did they believe that truly praiseworthy moral behaviour could be confined to disinterested benevolence. For Hume the 'natural' virtues displayed in our personal relationships had qualities akin to this, but he devoted more ingenuity to explaining the difficult 'artificial' virtues that underlie many of our dealings with our fellow creatures. From this point of view, Hutcheson had failed to confront the complexities of the main artificial virtue, justice, a virtue of paramount importance in a world where the scarcity of means in relation to human ends placed limits on the capacity for benevolence towards others. Outside the realm of family and friends, then, the claims of *meum* and *tuum* conflict, making rules of commutative justice essential. The virtues that underlie these rules are learned through a process that Hume attributes to an acquired sense of their public utility. Smith follows Hume in distinguishing between beneficence and justice, but consistently rejects Hume's explanations based on utility. These are consigned to the role of an 'afterthought' (ibid., 20), a philosopher's reflection on behaviour, rather than its cause.

Smith also took issue with Hutcheson's refusal to allow prudence in the conduct of one's private affairs to be a virtue, particularly when it is accompanied by a quality that enhances all virtues, that of self-command. The persistent invocation of this quality in *The Theory of Moral Sentiments* imparts that Stoic element to Smith's ethics that has rightly received so much attention in recent years. Even so, Smith assigns an inferior status to prudence, describing it in the final edition (1790) as commanding only a 'cold esteem' (Smith, *TMS*, 216). He does so because self-regard, though a necessary human attribute, is commonplace; it requires no additional social reinforcement for its performance. In recognizing prudence as a virtue, however, Smith had to distinguish his own position from the 'licentious' system of morals expounded by Bernard Mandeville, to whom he devotes a chapter that refutes him while acknowledging his cynical insight into human nature. One of the initial premises of *The Theory of Moral Sentiments* was that Hobbes and Mandeville were wrong in thinking that all moral behaviour could be explained as variations on self-love. Man's sociability, his basic need for the approval of others, and his capacity to form objective moral codes through social interaction, is a central theme in Smith's work.

The book begins with an explanation of how we arrive at notions of propriety and impropriety when judging others. We do so not simply by observing others' behaviour but by imaginatively entering into the situation prompting that behaviour. The sympathy arising from conscientious spectating is never perfect, but our ability to achieve concord if not unison supports that combination of Christian and Stoic ideas of virtue which best epitomizes Smith's position:

> As to love our neighbour as we love ourselves is the great law of Christianity, so it is the great precept of nature to love ourselves only as we love our neighbour, or what comes to the same thing, as our neighbour is capable of loving us. (Smith, *TMS*, 25)

Judgements of the merit and demerit of actions go beyond mere propriety in requiring an additional process of sympathy: with the gratitude of the beneficiary as well as with the motives of the actor. Having arrived at notions of propriety and merit when observing others, we apply the lessons to our own conduct. Without this social mirror we are incapable of forming any idea of our own character, let alone of how it might be improved.

But if we relied solely on the mirror held up by actual spectators we would often merely be vain and rootless conformists. Smith allows that we may well be just this on many occasions. Such behaviour underlies the socially beneficial, though often personally misplaced, desire for social approval that fuels the ambition to rise in the world and leads us to defer to the rich, regardless of their true merit (Smith, *TMS*, 50–61). Nevertheless, it is an important feature of Smith's answer to cynics like Mandeville, and critics of *amour propre* like Rousseau, that we are also capable of distinguishing between mere praise and genuine praiseworthiness. To explain this Smith introduced his concept of an impartial spectator, or 'man within the breast' (ibid., 130), an idea he developed further in each successive edition, possibly as a response to the suspicions of more orthodox Scottish contemporaries that he had not placed enough distance between himself and the 'prudential', selfish, or Epicurean position of Hobbes and Mandeville. Psychologically, the impartial spectator explains the role played by conscience in enabling us to correct the inevitable defects in the social mirror by imagining how our actions would look from a better-informed standpoint. From a more sociological perspective, this striving for an objective position becomes part of an evolutionary process that helps to explain and underpin the stability of moral norms over time.

The Theory of Moral Sentiments has gained interest from being regarded from the Humean or naturalistic standpoint rather than as a providentialist account of overall harmony in human affairs. It becomes an attempt to give a scientific account of the 'efficient' causes of individual behaviour and its various social outcomes. What remains at issue, however, is how we should interpret the arguments Smith adduces when speaking of 'final' causes: are they a rhetorical supplement or an essential element in repairing defects in the 'efficient' mechanisms? Smith clearly does employ deistic arguments from design, showing how the various qualities he finds in human nature, good and bad, produce a harmonious outcome. The passage in which the 'invisible hand' generates a rough equality of happiness from the selfish expenditures of the rich falls into this category (Smith, *TMS*, 184). In other words, *The Theory of Moral Sentiments* deploys teleological arguments that encourage the nineteenth-century view adopted by Leslie Stephen in 1897 when he judged Smith to be a 'sincere theist' (*DNB*). In the language of modern philosophies of science, Smith is resorting to a form of functionalist explanation that cannot be adequately rendered into causal terms (Kleer). Hume, the opponent of arguments from design, may have been drawing attention to such features of the book when he reported that *The Theory of Moral Sentiments* had pleased those 'Retainers to Superstition', the bishops (Smith, *Corr.*, 35). Perhaps Hume's irony can be more accurately expressed by saying that Smith had not aroused the bishops' suspicions, as he was to do in later editions when he removed a reference to divine retribution, possibly in deference to Hume's memory (Raphael, *Adam Smith*; Smith, *TMS*, 383–40).

It is possible to give a Stoic rather than Christian interpretation of Smith's reversion to a use of 'natural', not in the sense of 'normal' or within ordinary human capacities, but as referring to properties conferred by an all-wise Nature or beneficent God. One could also say that the regularities of our social existence are such as to lead us to believe in God; that they are consistent with belief in God; or, more weakly still, that the perceived order is such that we often take aesthetic pleasure from attributing it to God. The last of these resembles Smith's views on astronomy: on the evidence currently available to us, we cannot help but give credence to Newton's account of the physical universe. Whatever gaps this may reveal in Smith's explanations, it cannot be said that they tell us much about his own religious beliefs.

Lectures on Jurisprudence After Smith had published *The Theory of Moral Sentiments*, he shifted his attention as lecturer and would-be author to the third and fourth parts of the curriculum described by Millar. The firm promise made in the final paragraphs of *The Theory of Moral Sentiments* on this subject was retained in all later editions. It announced his intention to establish 'a theory of the general principles which ought to run through and be the foundation of the laws of all nations', where this involved a history and critique of existing systems of positive law on the basis of universally applicable principles of natural justice. The programme contained two elements, only the second of which was brought to fruition. It was to be:

> an account of the general principles of law and government, and of all the different revolutions which they have undergone in the different ages and periods of society, not only in what concerns justice, but in what concerns police, revenue, and arms and whatever else is the object of law. (Smith, *TMS*, 342)

The notes for *Lectures on Jurisprudence*, therefore, explain something about the origins of the *Wealth of Nations*, but are equally interesting as a bridge between this latter text and *The Theory of Moral Sentiments*, as well as providing evidence about the likely shape of the unfinished enterprise.

The moral groundwork for the promised theory of justice was contained in *The Theory of Moral Sentiments*. There Smith had contrasted the strict, though negative, obligations of the rules of justice with the voluntary, though positive, calls on us made by codes of beneficence. He also believed that precise rules could be formulated on the basis of the resentment felt by the impartial spectator when confronted by injuries to legitimate rights. Precision plus consensual resentment was the basis for endowing magistrates, those acting on our behalf, with powers of retributive punishment for civil and criminal offences, thereby avoiding the civil strife that would come from personal revenge. Without rules of justice 'the immense fabric of human society … must in a moment crumble into atoms' (Smith, *TMS*, 86). Beneficence was merely the ornament to this edifice; it made social life enjoyable rather than merely possible. Smith is careful to confine justice, as Hume had done, to those perfect rights which must be protected from injury in all societies. He calls this commutative justice and it embodies a negative virtue because just behaviour consists only in 'abstaining from what is another's, and in doing voluntarily whatever we can with propriety be forced to do' (ibid., 269). Ideas of distributive justice, based on conceptions of relative merit or desert, were insufficiently precise to provide the degree of social consensus required for communal coercion. *Lectures on Jurisprudence* builds on this foundation a new kind of evolutionary history of law and government, owing something to Kames and John Dalrymple, with Montesquieu's *Spirit of the Laws* acting as general inspiration for an approach that relates laws to social circumstance. Smith employs the established natural law categories of rights and duties owing to man as individual, member of family, and citizen to deal with private and public jurisprudence, with a special category being reserved for 'police'—those duties of legislators to achieve what he summarizes as 'cheapness and plenty'. The historical and anthropological evidence complements his theory of rights based on resentment by examining the particular offences recognized by different societies over time.

The feature of the history that most interested twentieth-century commentators was its classification of societies according to four stages, each defined by a specific mode of subsistence: hunter-gathering, pastoral, agricultural (feudal), and commercial. Changes in forms of property, and the resulting inequalities, are linked to changes in forms of government, the most important function of which was to protect property. The four stages feature less prominently in the *Wealth of Nations*, but comparative-historical evidence is widely deployed throughout, especially when dealing with the transition from feudal to commercial society in book III and justice in book V. Smith's historical narrative supplements the sociological relativism of Montesquieu by adding a concern with social change in which economic conditions play a necessary role. It lacks, however, the deterministic and predictive features of later types of materialist history, and retains its original critical purpose in making an understanding of law its chief focus. Civil liberty, defined as security under the rule of law, is treated as the historical outcome of a politico-economic process which makes allowance for the accidents of geography and history. Vigilance in preventing this modern, yet still imperfect achievement from being warped by 'particular orders of men who tyrannize the government' (Smith, *TMS*, 341) is, in turn, a precondition for further economic improvement.

When Smith was honoured by election to the rectorship of Glasgow in 1787, he judged his years there to be 'by far the happiest and most honourable' period of his life (Smith, *Corr.*, 309). Though not as eloquent a lecturer as Hutcheson, Smith's clear and unaffected manner acquired a growing circle of admirers. Since part of his income was derived from student fees (a system he recommended as an antidote to the indolence he found at Oxford), it is fortunate that he attracted students from Ireland and England, some of them from aristocratic families. In such cases they became part of his household, which consisted of his mother and a cousin, Jane Douglas, who acted as housekeeper. Smith was also entrusted by his colleagues with responsible administrative duties, first as quaestor for the library, later as dean of the faculty, and finally as vice-rector. He left a record of institutional loyalty and prudent concern for the university's welfare, even when this meant opposing the election of Hume, his unbelieving friend, to a chair.

Smith had also taken a full part in the life of the town, a thriving port enjoying the access to colonial markets and the carrying trade that came with the Anglo-Scottish Union of 1707. The Union, Smith believed, had done 'infinite Good' to Scotland (Smith, *Corr.*, 68). In addition to commercial benefits it had delivered the middle and lower ranks of Scottish society 'from the power of an aristocracy which had always before oppressed them' (Smith, *WN*, 944), a theme that dominates book III of the *Wealth of Nations*. Smith was a member of various clubs that attracted leading figures from the mercantile community; and the talks he gave on economic subjects to the Literary and Political Economy clubs show that he had begun to develop the sections of his lectures on justice that deal with 'police, revenue and arms' into something more ambitious.

Travelling tutor and independent scholar In 1764, at the age of forty, Smith resigned his chair. He wanted to accept an invitation from Charles Townshend to act as travelling tutor to Townshend's stepson, the third duke of Buccleuch, while on a continental tour. Although Smith criticized this fashionable mode of aristocratic education in the *Wealth of Nations*, the rewards and opportunities attached to the post were considerable: a pension for life of £300 p.a. and his first chance to meet some of the French literary figures whose works he had read and lectured on with warm appreciation. The family ties with the Argylls—Buccleuch was the grandson of the second duke, to whom Smith's cousin and early trustee had acted as secretary—may also have played a part. The tour enabled Smith to collect evidence on the fiscal problems of the world's most powerful absolute monarchy, much of which later appeared in the *Wealth of Nations*, the work he now began to assemble during the intervals left between his duties as tutor and chaperon to an obedient charge.

The tour lasted just under three years, eighteen months of which were spent in the quiet provincial capital of Toulouse, with side-trips to Geneva and the south of France. It was probably in Geneva that Smith met Voltaire, whose philosophical and dramatic writings he had long held in great esteem ('the most universal genius perhaps which France has ever produced'; Smith, *EPS*, 254). The last ten months were spent in Paris, where Smith met a wide range of *philosophes*: D'Alembert, D'Holbach, Helvetius, and Morrellet. Although Smith spoke French badly and was not, otherwise, a prepossessing figure, he was welcomed at the salons of mesdames D'Enville, De Boufflers, Du Deffand, and De L'Espinasse, those circles in which Hume had recently been fêted while serving at the British embassy. The trip coincided with the first signs of interest in translating the *Theory of Moral Sentiments*, a work that proved popular in France, particularly among the women who frequented the salons.

Smith also made his first personal encounter with the *économistes*, then entering into their most influential phase under the leadership of François Quesnay: Dupont de Nemours, Mirabeau, Mercier de la Rivière, and Turgot, a sympathizer, if not a disciple, of Quesnay. Smith had probably read the articles which this group had contributed to the *Encyclopédie* and was to add their journals, *Ephémérides du Citoyen* and *Journal de l'Agriculture*, to his library. Disputes over the national origins of the new science began soon after publication of the *Wealth of Nations*. Many of these turned on what Smith may have borrowed as a result of his contacts with the *économistes*, and his acquaintance with Turgot's *Réflexions de la formation et distribution des richesses* (1766) in particular. The discovery of the notes on Smith's lectures on jurisprudence put an end to charges of plagiarism by revealing how far Smith's own ideas had progressed before his visit to France. Nor can Smith be accused of mean-spiritedness in his treatment of what he called the 'agricultural system'. Not only did he entertain the idea of dedicating the *Wealth of Nations* to Quesnay, but he gave a sympathetic exposition of the *tableau économique*, judging Quesnay's system to be 'the nearest approximation to the truth that has yet been published' (Smith, *WN*, 678).

There are some broad similarities in policy conclusions: the primacy of agriculture (though not, for Smith, a belief in its uniquely productive status), opposition to Colbertism (official encouragement of manufactures), and free domestic and international trade. Beneath this, however, there are significant divergences best summarized by Smith's endorsement of policies that encouraged 'cheapness and plenty' compared with the physiocratic stress on achieving high prices for agricultural goods. There are closer parallels between Turgot's *Réflexions* and some ideas that appear for the first time in the *Wealth of Nations*: chiefly the addition of a circular conception of economic life connected to a theory explaining the rates and shares going to wages, profits, and rents. Smith also borrowed the distinction between productive and unproductive labour, while putting this troublesome terminology to different use when discussing forms of capital accumulation.

Upon his return from France in 1766, Smith spent the next few months in London, partly correcting the proofs of the third edition of *The Theory of Moral Sentiments*, partly continuing to serve his employer, Townshend, who, as chancellor of the exchequer under Chatham, was faced with the problems of public debt and taxation left by the Seven Years' War. As the *Wealth of Nations* was to show, Smith could readily support Townshend's resolve to make the American colonies contribute a larger share of revenue to cover debts incurred in their defence, but there is no evidence that Smith advised the duties on tea that were to become the centre of colonial resentment at Boston in 1773.

Since leaving Glasgow, Smith had experienced the *beau monde* in Paris and been close to those wielding power in London. He was more a man of the world, less the dutiful pedagogue. This observation seems worth making in view of Smith's decision to use his pension and new-found freedom by returning once more to the relative seclusion of Kirkcaldy, where he was to spend the next six years, resisting the entreaties of Hume to visit him in Edinburgh, and enjoying solitary walks and sea-bathing throughout the year. Although this regimen left him 'extremely happy, comfortable and contented' (Smith, *Corr.*, 125), the strenuous exercise may have been an antidote to recurrent illness arising from overwork on the *Wealth of Nations*. Many of the leading ideas for this had been in place for nearly two decades, but Smith was a slow writer, even finding the act of writing painful: hence his use of amanuenses. His main efforts now were to incorporate the historical and contemporary factual material he considered essential to illustrate his principles.

Smith's work was still not completed in 1773 when he set off for London, where he was to spend a further three years before publication. Smith picked up the threads of his earlier social life in London, enjoying the company of other expatriate Scots. He was also admitted to fellowship of the Royal Society and elected to The Club founded by Joshua Reynolds, of which Johnson, Edmund Burke, David Garrick, Edward Gibbon, James Boswell, and Oliver Goldsmith were regular members. The main purpose of the visit, however, was to put the finishing touches to the *Wealth of Nations*. This entailed acquiring up-to-date information on American affairs, some of it derived from House of Commons debates, some from experts such as Benjamin Franklin. The causes and consequences of the dispute between Britain and its colonies were a vital part of Smith's treatment of what he was to call, with pejorative intent, the 'mercantile system'. Although the situation was moving rapidly towards the climax marked by the Declaration of Independence on 4 July 1776, one might not gather that from Smith's calm description of events as the 'present disturbances' (Smith, *WN*, 585). Much to the relief of Scottish friends who knew how much effort Smith had invested in the work, the *Wealth of Nations* was published on 9 March 1776. Its two quarto volumes cost £1 16*s*. Hume, then entering the final months of his life, predicted that such a closely reasoned work would not be an immediate success: 'But it has Depth and Solidity and Acuteness, and is so much illustrated by curious Facts, that it must at last take the public Attention' (Smith, *Corr.*, 186).

***An Inquiry into the Nature and Causes of the Wealth of Nations* (1776)** Hume's prediction proved accurate, though he could not know for just how long Smith's work would hold public attention. Smith awaited the reception with every appearance of Stoic indifference. By the time serious reviews had been received and a second edition had proved necessary, he was merely relieved to find that he was 'much less abused that I had reason to expect' (Smith, *Corr.*, 251). He did not reply directly to any of his critics, though he did make a few minor clarifications in later editions.

The *Wealth of Nations* had no rival in scope or depth when published and is still one of the few works in its field to have achieved classic status, meaning simply that it has sustained yet survived repeated reading, critical and adulatory, long after the circumstances which prompted it have become the object of historical enquiry. As philosopher Smith had taken up the challenge of providing an 'imaginary machine' that would render coherent the everyday appearances of an emerging world. In contrast to the existing systems, agricultural and mercantile, he advanced a 'system of natural liberty' capable of supporting a branch of the 'science of a legislator or statesman' (Smith, *WN*, 428) which had grown in significance in all modern societies where commerce was beginning to dominate their domestic and international economic relations. The object of the science was to amend the related practical art by providing legislators with a set of principles to guide their actions and inactions, partly by advocating improvements in existing policies and institutions, partly by altering the general climate of opinion within which these matters were discussed.

Though often criticized for its rambling structure, historical digressions, and over-abundance of 'curious facts', the work has a single unifying theme which takes on further ramifications as it is unfolded. As the full title makes clear, it is an enquiry into the *nature* of wealth, how its benefits should be measured or judged. This is combined with a causal account of the growth of opulence designed to show why the process had been retarded during the feudal period of European history, why some nations were stationary or in decline, and why those that have made a start have frequently failed to reap the full advantages. The theme is launched by posing a simple though artificially heightened enigma that survives from the earliest drafts. While there is no difficulty in explaining how the rich and powerful come to enjoy the fruits of others' labour, how is it that in civilized societies even the poorest members enjoy more of the necessaries and conveniences of life than an African king? Smith had two superficial pieces of conventional wisdom in his sights: the belief that the luxuries of the few were conditional upon the poverty of the mass; and the impossibility of combining high wages with better and cheaper goods for consumers.

It is a mark of Smith's success in changing the climate of opinion that his answers to this enigma are now easier to grasp than the propositions they were meant to replace. The criterion he supplies for judging opulence is a thoroughly normative one:

> No society can surely be flourishing and happy, of which the far greater part of the members are poor and miserable. It is but equity, besides, that they who feed, cloath and lodge the whole body of the people, should have such a share of the produce of their own labour as to be themselves tolerably well fed, cloathed and lodged. (Smith, *WN*, 96)

Improvements in the absolute, if not relative, standards of consumption available to wage-earners are made possible by the improvements in labour productivity that arise from the division of labour, with capital accumulation supplying the means by which these improvements can be embodied in machinery and new methods of working. The specialization of tasks that is illustrated by means of the 'trifling' example of pin manufacture borrowed from the *Encyclopédie* (ibid., 14) is merely a microcosm of the process of growing occupational differentiation and mutual dependence occurring in society at large. The resulting improvements in 'the skill, dexterity, and judgement with which [labour] … is directed or applied' (ibid., 13) depend on the extent of the market. Markets may expand geographically via exploration and reductions in transport costs, but they do so with more regularity when domestic incomes rise and prices have fallen as a result of prior improvements in productivity. The answer to the enigma, then, could be described by a truism: the division of labour depends on the division of labour—and all that makes this self-sustaining spiral possible.

Smith believed the process had operated in England for the previous 200 years, and while he spoke of a stationary state in which a nation could reach its 'full complement of riches', the only nation in this position, China, had arrived there for reasons connected with inflexibilities in its 'laws and institutions' that were in principle reparable (Smith, *WN*, 111). The limits to growth were political rather than economic. Controversially, in the eyes of some later economic anthropologists at least, Smith assumes that the drive towards improvement in our condition is basic to humanity, regardless of period, race, religion, or country, though circumstances determine how far it can be given free rein: 'Our ancestors were idle for want of a sufficient encouragement to industry', not because they had different motives and values (ibid., 335). Given a tolerable degree of liberty and security of the kind enjoyed in the post-feudal parts of western Europe and North America, conditions existed for slow, spontaneous, but by no means inevitable economic combustion. China's fate was merely an extreme example of how human folly could bring an end to the natural progress of opulence. European history contained other examples that showed how vulnerable prosperity based on commerce was to 'the ordinary revolutions of war and government' (ibid., 427). Wickedness, too, could not be extirpated, though its effects could be minimized by the enforcement of the rule of law and by institutional devices, including the disciplines of the market that harnessed self-interest to public good. We no longer see Smith as an economic determinist or as a sunny optimist.

The novelty of the *Wealth of Nations* in 1776 can be seen in a cumulative series of shifts in the focus of public attention it achieved. The most basic of these was an increase in length of perspective. This allowed Smith to adopt more composure than was characteristic of the popular literature of jeremiad and mercantile panacea. Such writings either predicted ruin and depopulation as a result of the spread of luxury, high wages, and every adverse shift of economic fortune, or immediate benefit from manufacturing, banking, and colonial projects. A growing population remained the mark of prosperity, but Smith argued that this could best be achieved by concentrating investment and attention less on export markets and distant carrying trades, and more on agriculture and the internal trade between town and country, despite the fact that agriculture was less susceptible to improvements in productivity through the division of labour. In place of the zero-sum monetary indicator of national success favoured by mercantile writers, a favourable balance of trade with other nations, Smith proposed an alternative barometer that was independent of foreign trade, yet better adapted to a world of multilateral gain and interdependence: the balance of production over consumption, considered not merely year by year, but over periods of time that could be measured in decades, even centuries. It was this balance—whether nations were maintaining, adding to, or running down their capital stock—that determined their growth prospects.

Progressive states were those in which the labouring poor enjoyed high wages, resulting in a healthier, 'more active, diligent, and expeditious' workforce, a view that ran counter to a popular dictum connecting greater effort with low wages (Smith, *WN*, 99). Smith knew that the quantity of labour embodied in commodities could not explain exchange values in a modern society where the rewards to land (rent) and capital (profits) legitimately take their place alongside wages as components of the 'natural price' of goods, without which, indeed, their supply would not continue. Nevertheless, labour effort provides a guide to 'real price' (ibid., 47); it is the best measure of welfare gains over time. Whereas wages and rents rise with progress, profits should fall, unless prevented from doing so by exclusive privileges or conspiratorial abridgements of competition. Falling profits were a sign of health rather than decay, and since the source of savings depended on that 'uniform, constant, and uninterrupted desire on the part of every man to improve his condition' (ibid., 343), the future sources of accumulation were not in jeopardy. The major threat here came from the prodigality of governments, especially now that they were equipped with techniques of public credit, greatly expanded during a century of intermittent war. Against an eighteenth-century background in which perhaps only England and North America, for very different reasons, appeared to have overcome the problems of feeding their populations on a regular basis, Smith's ability to conceive of the possibility of gradual improvement in the living standards of the mass of society is more remarkable.

Throughout the book Smith's 'system of natural liberty and justice' (Smith, *WN*, 157) plays a pervasive role as explanatory model and regulatory ideal, though the famous image of an 'invisible hand' appears late and only once in the whole work (ibid., 456). A quasi-Newtonian treatment is given to those forces which act like gravity when market price departs from natural price, and it always carries with it a normative implication that policies or practices that prevent these forces from acting are detrimental to the public interest. Monopolies, special privileges, informal combinations by merchants or employers to raise prices and keep down wages, import duties, export bounties, as well as institutions such as apprenticeships and restrictions on labour mobility under the Settlement Acts are all condemned from this perspective. They either entail raising the price above what would otherwise be paid, or subsidizing producers at the expense of taxpayers. By hindering or disturbing the balance that would have been achieved, they injure some natural rights and prevent consumers from enjoying the full benefits that a regime of free competitive rivalry could bestow.

At its most abstract, the system entails an idea that perhaps has Stoic origins, the idea of a beneficial harmony in human affairs arising as the unintended outcome of individuals pursuing, short-sightedly, their own interests. The persistent invocation of natural liberty, equality, and justice that accompany this idea take us back to their origins in natural law thinking. What gives these abstract notions substance, however, is the detailed, persistent, ironic, and even angry manner in which Smith applies them in his analysis of actual events and practices. Nowhere is this clearer than in the extended dissection of 'the policy of Europe' performed in book IV of the *Wealth of Nations*, which he acknowledged to be 'a very violent attack … upon the whole commercial system of Great Britain' (Smith, *Corr.*, 251). He attributed this to the 'pretended doctors' of the mercantile system whose ideas had been taken up by merchants and manufacturers 'with all the passionate confidence of interested falsehood' (Smith, *WN*, 496). Smith's animus derives not from a prejudice against such men as individuals or even as a class. Landowners receive more sympathetic treatment, as a whole, but their insouciance also means that they lack the qualities of application that merchants bring to agriculture when they reinvest in it, as Smith advised they should. The danger posed by the mercantile interest was constitutional; it arose from their capacity to act as an 'overgrown standing army' capable of influencing 'that insidious and crafty animal, vulgarly called a statesman or politician, whose councils are directed by the momentary fluctuations of affairs' (ibid., 471). Hence, too, the corrective purpose of any science directed to the legislator 'whose deliberations ought to be governed by general principles which are always the same' (ibid., 468).

Book V lays down the principles that ought to guide legislators in matters of taxation and when carrying out the essential duties of the sovereign or state. Not only does it reveal how far Smith is from counselling Stoic resignation in the face of benign, impersonal economic forces, the book shows why expenditure on public services is likely to grow in all civilized nations. Abdication from a role that no legislator was wise enough to occupy still left important tasks to be undertaken in the fields of national defence (acknowledged to be of higher importance than opulence), the administration of justice, those public works that were beyond private initiatives, and education. Smith's concern about public prodigality, however, led him to propose various devices for ensuring that performance was matched to reward. But his most interesting suggestions concern education for the people at large. Here the problem is posed as one of minimizing an unintended result of the division of labour which is far from beneficial, the mental and moral 'torpor' that accompanies narrow occupations, where a man's proficiency at his work is purchased at the cost of his 'intellectual, social, and martial virtues' (Smith, *WN*, 782). Besides elementary education, partly at the public expense, it requires other initiatives of a military, ecclesiastical, and artistic kind that reveal the author of *The Theory of Moral Sentiments* beneath the surface. The virtues being undermined by the division of labour are those that make us human and sociable civic beings.

Customs official and adviser The first public recognition of Smith's expertise came in 1778 when he was granted a place as commissioner of customs in Edinburgh. Although Smith spoke of the duties as 'easy and honourable' (Smith, *Corr.*, 252) the record of his attendance at meetings (often over 180 days a year) shows that he did not treat the post as a sinecure. With a salary of £600 p.a. and his pension, Smith regarded his situation as now 'fully as affluent as I could wish it to be' (ibid., 253). He moved into Panmure House on the Canongate with his mother and cousin, along with the cousin's nephew, David Douglas, who became Smith's sole heir. Their style of life was comfortably modest, but it ran to giving weekly dinners, and Smith used his affluence to make several anonymous gifts.

For those who rightly regard Smith as an outspoken advocate of free trade, some irony may attach to his becoming a collector of customs. Apart from noting ruefully how many of his personal possessions were on the proscribed list when he took office, there is no sign that he had any qualms about enforcing laws against smuggling—a 'crime' for which he had given ample economic justification (Smith, *WN*, 898). The irony dissolves when other features of Smith's thinking are taken into account. Given the influence exerted on politicians by special interests that had both created and been created by the mercantile system, he did not expect free trade to be established in Britain. Partial reforms could still be attempted, but only 'by slow gradations, and with a good deal of reserve and circumspection' (ibid., 469). Another favourite maxim was that wise legislators should follow Solon's example: 'when he cannot establish the best system of laws, he will endeavour to establish the best the people can bear' (Smith, *TMS*, 233; Smith, *WN*, 543). It was the duty of philosophers to create systems, but as Smith was to emphasize in the final edition of *The Theory of Moral Sentiments* (233–4), it was dangerous for legislators to attempt wholesale implementation. Smith's post enabled him to make a practical contribution to the public finances by advancing proposals for improving the yield from duties. The only personal by-product of Smith's employment that may have ironic features is that it enabled him to improve the information on which his critique of existing policies was based. The last edition of the *Wealth of Nations* to receive his full attention (the third, in 1785) contained a longer treatment of the deficiencies of the chartered companies and an extra summary chapter.

The new post placed Smith's services at the disposal of various Scottish friends in office and other statesmen who prided themselves on being open to 'enlightened' ideas. Anecdotes about William Pitt the younger deferring to Smith on the grounds that he was Smith's pupil may have been embellished over the years, but there is some evidence that acceptance of free trade could be a conversion experience: Lord Shelburne confessed to having seen 'the difference between light and darkness' as a result of a coach journey to London with Smith (Smith, *EPS*, 347). Political economy was a practical science, and, as the case of Townshend noted earlier shows, the advisory role was not a new one for Smith. In 1778 he wrote a memorandum for Alexander Wedderburn, then Lord North's solicitor-general, on the 'state of the Contest with America' after the defeat at Saratoga, an event that provoked a characteristically phlegmatic response from Smith to the effect that there was 'a great deal of ruin in a nation' (Winch, *Riches and Poverty*, 50). The advice to Wedderburn conforms with opinions expressed in the *Wealth of Nations*, but shows Smith's grasp of *realpolitik*. The utopian plan in the *Wealth of Nations* for an imperial 'states-general' (Smith, *WN*, 933), with representation from the colonies being proportioned to their contribution to imperial revenues, was an exercise in demonstrating the only conditions that could make empire tolerable. Peaceful separation and the restoration of normal trade was the best outcome; it would put an end to what Smith described contemptuously as an imperial project 'fit only for a nation of shopkeepers', a 'golden dream' that no longer accorded with 'the real mediocrity of [Britain's] circumstances' (ibid., 613, 947).

Smith's services to Pitt's administration came initially through another Scottish connection, Henry Dundas. In 1779 Smith fortified the resolve of William Eden and the earl of Carlisle, secretary and president of the Board of Trade respectively, to remove the barriers on Anglo-Irish trade and open up colonial markets to Irish goods. This would be a step in the direction of what he had counselled in the *Wealth of Nations*, namely an Anglo-Irish union along Anglo-Scottish lines. It became the basis for one of his rare and least successful predictions. Just as union had reduced factional strife in Scotland, so he anticipated that it would produce 'one people' in Ireland by delivering the bulk of them from an oppressive division based on religion (Smith, *WN*, 944). Smith also advised on the problems created by loss of the North American colonies in 1783, tactfully overlooking those respects in which official policy differed from his own priorities. Eden's efforts on behalf of freer trade climaxed with the Anglo-French trade treaty of 1786, where again Smith was cited in support. As so often happens, however, Pitt's most fulsome parliamentary tribute came two years after Smith's death.

Smith's late official connections, then, were with tory ministries, though the earlier pattern of his friendships had been predominantly Scottish whig. In the 1780s he enjoyed close relations with Edmund Burke and was sympathetic towards the dilemmas faced by his Rockinghamite faction. Although he spoke dismissively of the politician as a type in the *Wealth of Nations*, there are remarks in letters that show what conduct he most admired in politicians. Nor was he was a political innocent when it came to recognizing the need for 'management and persuasion' (Smith, *WN*, 799)—polite terms for what oppositionists called 'corruption'. It is doubtful if any wider significance can be attached to party labels and personal friendships. Retrospective attempts to link Burke with Smith for this purpose are based more on anecdotal evidence than acquaintance with their actual positions on political and economic issues can support.

More significant insight into Smith's politics in a wider sense can now be gleaned from the notes on the lectures on jurisprudence. These confirm how much of Hume's philosophical politics he shared when rejecting contractual accounts of the grounds for political allegiance. Far less emphasis is given to rights of resistance than one finds in Locke, Hutcheson, and late eighteenth-century radicals such as Richard Price and Thomas Paine. But Smith was more complacent about the durability of the English constitution and the threats posed by public debt than Hume became in old age. The mixture of elements in the constitution was a 'happy' one and the securities against royal influence were now firmly entrenched (Smith, *LJ*, 421–2). While Smith recognized the value of political representation, he remained silent on ways of broadening its base. He disappointed those 'men of republican principles' (Smith, *WN*, 706) among his Scottish friends by appearing to undermine their case for a Scottish militia by supporting the need for standing armies on grounds of their efficiency. Smith, therefore, can rightly be described as a North Briton who regarded Scotland not merely as his home but as the best place from which to observe the affairs of the capital with the minimum of involvement in party politics consistent with belonging to the world in which he lived. Though firmly convinced of the comparative superiority of Scottish clerical and educational institutions, Smith was critical of the oligarchic nature of its burgh politics and the shameful irresponsibility of Scottish landowners in failing to improve their estates. Scottish patriotism in everyday matters was, however, overlaid by the cosmopolitan ambitions of his writings.

Despite his official duties, Smith continued to work on the uncompleted parts of the ambitious plan he had conceived as a teacher. With age and growing signs of illness, these projects took second place to his desire to leave his two main works in the best condition he could manage. Having done this for the *Wealth of Nations* by 1785, he turned his attention to preparing a sixth edition of *The Theory of Moral Sentiments*. These late revisions have been sifted for clues of a last will and testament, as well as for hints of his possible reaction to the revolutionary events beginning in France. *The Theory of Moral Sentiments* acquired a new part (VI) which fortified the earlier treatments given to prudence (distinguishing public from private versions), conscience, and self-command. A chapter was added to emphasize the corruption in our moral sentiments that accompanies the otherwise useful habit of deference to the rich and powerful. Smith made good his claim for the new part to be advancing 'a practical system of Morality, under the title of the Character of Virtue' (Smith, *Corr.*, 320). The theory of the nature of virtue based on propriety, however, has been judged (Raphael, 'Adam Smith, 1790') not to meet the expectations aroused by Smith's fuller treatment of the separate question answered by the theory of moral judgement in the earlier parts of the book.

Late in life Smith's periodic bouts of illness had settled into inflammation of the bladder and piles. On 17 July 1790, a few weeks after the revised version of *The Theory of Moral Sentiments* had appeared, he died in his Edinburgh home, Panmure House, of a 'chronic obstruction in his bowels' (Stewart, 327). His last reported words to friends were: 'I believe we must adjourn this meeting to some other place' (Ross, 406). He was buried on 22 July in the Canongate churchyard with a simple inscription on a tomb designed by Robert Adam, a fellow alumnus from Kirkcaldy.

The man Some elusive, even reclusive, features of Smith's character have already been noted. Unlike Edward Gibbon and Hume, he left no autobiographical reflections and since he was a dilatory correspondent he left fewer epistolary hostages to fortune than most. Even accredited portraits are few and far between, though in appearance he was above average height, well-dressed, eyes heavy-lidded, teeth rather prominent, but with a smile that could be radiant—though this might reflect the one thing everybody noticed, 'absence', or what a French admirer described as 'distraite' (Rae, 212). Anecdotes relate that he was in the habit of speaking aloud to himself, and that he suffered various misadventures due to preoccupation: falling in tanning vats, copying the signature of the person who signed ahead of him instead of writing his own, saluting sentries, mistaking bread and butter for tea when brewing the latter, and finding himself in faraway places as a result of taking long walks while musing. In the absence of firm information about matters that interest posterity, his works have been plundered for insights into the man, with the illustrative portraits of different characters in *The Theory of Moral Sentiments* usually proving whatever the interpreter wishes to prove. Where next to no evidence exists, speculation is unbounded. The fact that Smith did not marry, that he lived with his mother for nearly thirty years and was devastated by her death, instead of being taken as a simple mark of filial love has aroused curiosity about his sexuality. There is evidence that he was attracted to the opposite sex, but all his failure to marry indicates is that he was more attached to the two women in his household than to any he encountered outside it.

The friendships and memberships of various clubs show that absent-mindedness was compatible with sociability, and that it did not prevent conscientious performance of the duties attached to the offices he held. If there is a paradox in Smith's character, it lies in the tension between an emphasis on philosophy as a means of restoring tranquillity (illustrated by his own immersion in private scholarly pursuits) and his assumption of a restless desire for self-improvement in humankind. Philosophers who cultivated knowledge with practical ends in view were accorded an important role by Smith as observers and inventors. Even so, he held that: 'The most sublime speculations of the contemplative philosopher can scarce compensate the neglect of the smallest active duty' (Smith, *TMS*, 237).

That Smith set great store by what he described as 'inflexible probity' (Smith, *Corr.*, 428) is confirmed by various episodes: his insistence on returning fees to students for courses he could not complete; his offer to return his pension to Buccleuch on receiving official preferment; and his negotiations on behalf of friends and students.

Probity of a less attractive kind might account for the accusations of plagiarism he made against contemporaries: Robertson and Ferguson fell under suspicion here, though Blair was given access to the *Lectures on Rhetoric and Belles Lettres* when he was appointed to the chair of rhetoric in Edinburgh. Smith also made one effort, early in his career, to lay claim to priority for his system of natural liberty, but he could be generous to those to whom he felt indebted, as was the case with Hutcheson, Hume, and Quesnay. Kames and Mandeville can be added to this list, though the compliment was a backhanded one in the latter case. Other Scottish contemporaries are conspicuous by their absence; and Smith's decision to treat his main economic rival, James Steuart, to silent rebuttal was parsimonious *and* effective. Smith may have derived more information from mercantile authors than the anger he felt over their influence allowed him to express. What he may have learned from Turgot has been mentioned earlier. Apart from his personal library ('I am a beau in nothing but my books'; Ross, 311), a strong sense of intellectual autonomy could have been Smith's only vanity.

Curiously perhaps, the most serious charges against Smith's character have arisen from his friendship with Hume. The publication of an obituary in which Smith described Hume 'as approaching as nearly to the idea of a perfectly wise and virtous man, as perhaps the nature of human frailty will admit' (Smith, *Corr.*, 221) proved scandalous to some Christian consciences. Smith became the object of abuse, with lasting echoes into the following century. Others have been more perturbed by Smith's failure to accede to Hume's wishes that he should oversee posthumous publication of his *Dialogues on Natural Religion*. The episode has been cited as a case where misplaced solicitude for his friend's reputation was either overlaid by prudential regard for his own, or based on dislike of becoming involved in theological disputes. Intellectual disagreements over the merits of arguments from design seem unlikely to have played any part in Smith's motives on such an occasion.

Reputation Despite Smith's late attentions to his ethical system, his reputation has come to rest chiefly on his economic *opus*, a tribute to its readable qualities as well as to the continued prominence of economic questions in public life. Smith's forecast of the likelihood of implementing free trade proved unduly pessimistic: in Britain the process was completed with the abolition of the corn laws in 1846; and many of Smith's maxims on public finance had become embodied in Gladstone's budgets by the 1860s. Hence, too, the popular association of Smith's political economy with a form of laissez-faire liberalism of a negative variety that exalted individual thrift and self-help. During the centenary of the *Wealth of Nations* in 1876, this Victorianized version was sufficiently diffused for Walter Bagehot to announce that Smith's teachings 'have settled down into the common sense of the nation, and have become irreversible' (Winch, 'A very amusing book'). The *Wealth of Nations* had given rise to a new science capable of separate development—almost unwittingly, given Smith's lack of fervour in seeking disciples and his attachment to other parts of his original enterprise. The succeeding generation of followers, led by Robert Malthus and David Ricardo, accepted the text as their starting point but not as their bible. They were too conscious of those ways in which it failed to address, or provided too loose an analysis of, problems that seemed central to the British economy during and after the Napoleonic wars; chief among these were those connected with monetary issues and the dilemmas posed by population growth and rising food costs. When John Stuart Mill attempted in 1848 to emulate Smith's achievement in his *Principles of Political Economy*, he judged the *Wealth of Nations* to be 'in many parts obsolete, and in all, imperfect' (ibid.). None of this undermined the pieties of the centenary celebrations, dominated as they were by a proper sense of what was due to a pioneering and still popular exposition of the science. Indeed, for some who were opposed to the abstract deductive nature of the Ricardian version of Smith's science, the *Wealth of Nations* became the embodiment of an inductive or historical approach to economics that needed to be revived.

Despite the number of translations of the *Wealth of Nations* that had appeared by then, there was also some concern that the science had acquired fewer adherents abroad, apart from a vigorous brand of economic liberalism in France, largely based on the proselytizing efforts of one of Smith's followers, Jean-Baptiste Say. In Germany, however, where nation building was still a major preoccupation, there had been a revival of interest in *Mercantilismus*, with *Smithianismus* representing a foreign doctrine out of harmony with native *étatiste* and historicist traditions. Two other German intellectual developments also had a bearing on Smith's reputation: the emergence of Marx-inspired forms of socialism and a debate between German commentators centring on 'das Adam Smith Problem', the idea that there was a fundamental conflict between the 'idealism' of *The Theory of Moral Sentiments* based on sympathy and the 'materialism' of the *Wealth of Nations* based on self-interest.

Marx's interest in political economy centred on the labour theory of value as the clue to capitalist exploitation. Smith played a lesser part in this than Ricardo, but 'socialistic yeast' was also detected in the pages of the *Wealth of Nations* (Winch, *Riches and Poverty*, 416). Although Smith's book is innocent of any theory of exploitation that makes it intrinsic to commercial society, anyone looking for a theory of unequal bargaining power, especially between employers and wage-earners, could find a basis for it there. Smith's distinction between productive and unproductive activities could also be readily adapted to suggest that this described the two main classes in society. Twentieth-century interpretations of the relationship between Marx and Smith, however, have focused more on what Marx could have learned from Smith's allegedly materialist version of history and on the similarities between the early Marxian concept of alienation and Smith's remarks on the debilitating effects of the division of labour. If there is now less tendency to portray Smith as the ideological spokesman for a rising class of capitalists, seen within a context dominated by the industrial revolution, that is due to improved understanding of that revolution and of Smith's actual opinions. Smith was more interested in the unfinished agrarian revolution than in its emerging industrial successor. Not only was he antagonistic towards its mercantile advocates, but he failed to give technology the independent role that later interpreters of the industrial revolution felt was due.

The original 'Adam Smith Problem' has suffered a similar fate, though it has been revived in more sophisticated forms in recent decades. Ignorance of the dates during which Smith was pursuing the various parts of his plan of studies accounted for some of the problem. This was compounded by a misunderstanding that led sympathy to be equated with benevolence and treated as a motive that could be contrasted with self-interest. One result of the publication of the Glasgow edition of Smith's works has been a fuller understanding of the connections between the various parts of his enterprise, making schizophrenic interpretations rarer. Nevertheless, there are obvious ways in which the aims and audiences for his two main works differ. The *Wealth of Nations* engages with a smaller range of human motives, without positing that later invention: rational economic man. By contrast, the mechanisms analysed in *The Theory of Moral Sentiments* cover the entire range of human interaction; they include friendship, membership of the family, and those bonds that occupy the public sphere: legal, military, and political, as well as those more anonymous economic relationships where private prudence reigns. Beneath these differences of scope, however, there is a common preoccupation with forms of social collaboration and mutual interdependence. We should not expect the mechanisms and results to be the same in every sphere, but that does not mean there is no overlap, still less that they are in conflict.

During the twentieth century the custody of Smith's reputation was still firmly in the hands of economists, though other academic tribes were beginning to show an interest. Alfred Marshall, the author of the English economic bible at the beginning of the century, had overcome earlier squabbles about Smith's methodological legacy and conferred on him the highest praise a late Victorian could bestow: Smith was the Darwin of modern economics (Winch, 'A very amusing book'). Yet since economics was now firmly committed to proving precisely how the invisible hand achieved general market equilibrium under fairly restrictive assumptions, Smith's rudimentary treatment of this problem left much to be desired. Between the wars, when unemployment and business cycles were prominent concerns, Smith's account of long-term growth, in which savings were always invested, lacked interest for other reasons. After the Second World War, with the return of interest in growth and economic advancement in the developing world, Smith's stock rose again. Economists continue to find the *Wealth of Nations* useful on celebratory occasions, sometimes as a source of inspiration, sometimes for target practice, but they no longer have exclusive rights or even, perhaps, the kinds of interest that enable them to make best use of a work that does not conform with modern tastes. Economic historians have a better claim in this respect. For them the *Wealth of Nations* serves both as a historical source and as a model for dealing with what is still the most important period of transition through which Western societies have passed. It goes without saying that no one interested in any aspect of eighteenth-century intellectual life can avoid encounter with either of Smith's main works.

The revival of interest in Smith's ethics in recent years is largely due to its merits when seen as a contribution to a quasi-social scientific enquiry into some interesting problems connected with the interpersonal formation of moral codes and with their internalization as moral norms. Sociologists and social psychologists have understandably led this revival. Largely as a result of the writings of Friedrich Hayek, others have been attracted to Smith's method of explaining socio-historical outcomes as the unanticipated result of behaviour by individual agents. There is an important insight here into the connections between knowledge, agency, and evolution that survives its cruder uses as an argument against all forms of intervention. The fate of *The Theory of Moral Sentiments* continues to be linked with the *Wealth of Nations* for reasons connected with the remarkable revival of interest in Smith during the last decades of the twentieth century by those who regard him as the patron saint of free market capitalism. This evidence of re-canonization represented a return to 1876 rather than to 1776. The fall of the Soviet empire in 1989 marked another milestone by appearing to confirm the enduring qualities of Smith's vision over the temporary one associated with Marx. Faced with this ideological revival and with persisting doubts about the moral legitimacy of the kind of society being celebrated, *The Theory of Moral Sentiments* has been examined for an alternative source of values. The risk here is of creating another version of 'das Adam Smith Problem': of seeking a reconciliation of ethical dilemmas posed in one realm by recourse to a supposedly higher court of appeal. Smith had a hard-headed, even cynical awareness of the political and moral dilemmas of his own day, and he made many fruitful suggestions designed to minimize if not remove their consequences. When considering later versions of these dilemmas Smith continues to provide a benchmark, but if his work lives on it is as an example of humane speculation at the highest level combined with detailed observation and insight into the human condition. DONALD WINCH

Sources *The Glasgow edition of the works and correspondence of Adam Smith*, 6 vols. (1976–87) [*TMS: The theory of moral sentiments*, vol. 1; *WN: An inquiry into the nature and causes of the wealth of nations*, vol. 2; *EPS: Essays on philosophical subjects*, vol. 3; *LRBL: Lectures on rhetoric and belles lettres*, vol. 4; *LJ: Lectures on jurisprudence*, vol. 5; *Corr.: The correspondence of Adam Smith*, vol. 6, 2nd edn] · D. Stewart, 'Account of the life and writings of Adam Smith', *Transactions of the Royal Society of Edinburgh* (1794) · J. Rae, *Life of Adam Smith*, 1965 edn (1895) · I. S. Ross, *The life of Adam Smith* (1995) · R. H. Campbell and A. S. Skinner, *Adam Smith* (1982) · D. D. Raphael, *Adam Smith* (1985) · A. S. Skinner, *A system of social science: papers relating to Adam Smith*, 2nd edn

(1996) • T. D. Campbell, *Adam Smith's science of morals* (1971) • D. Forbes, 'Sceptical whiggism, commerce, and liberty', *Essays on Adam Smith*, ed. A. S. Skinner and T. Wilson (1976), 179–201 • K. Haakonssen, *The science of a legislator: the natural jurisprudence of David Hume and Adam Smith* (1981) • D. Winch, *Riches and poverty: an intellectual history of political economy, 1750–1834* (1996) • P. Stein, 'Adam Smith's theory of law and society', *Classical influences on Western thought, 1650–1870*, ed. R. R. Bolgar (1979) • R. L. Meek, *Social science and the ignoble savage* (1976) • D. D. Raphael, 'Adam Smith, 1790: the man recalled; the philosopher revived', *Adam Smith reviewed*, ed. P. Jones and A. S. Skinner (1992), 93–118 • D. Winch, 'A very amusing book about old times', *Contributions to the history of economic thought*, ed. A. Murphy and R. Prendergast (2000) • R. A. Kleer, 'Final causes in Adam Smith's *Theory of moral sentiments*', *Journal of the History of Philosophy*, 33 (1995), 275–300 • *DNB*

Archives U. Glas., corresp. and papers | NRA, priv. coll., letters to Lord Shelburne • NRA, priv. coll., letters to Lord John Sinclair • Trinity Cam., corresp. with Henry Beaufay and William Strahan

Likenesses J. Kay, etching, 1787, NPG • J. Tassie, glass paste medallion, 1787, NPG [*see illus.*] • J. Tassie, plaster medallion, 1787, NPG • J. Kay, etching, 1790, NPG • P. Park, bust, 1845, Art Gallery and Museum, Glasgow • T. Collopy, oils, National Museum of Antiquities, Edinburgh • medals, Scot. NPG • oils, Scot. NPG

Wealth at death David Douglas was sole heir to property, incl. valuable book collection; excl. £400 left to another relative

Smith, Sir Albert James (1822–1883), lawyer and politician in Canada, was born in Shediac, Westmorland county, New Brunswick, on 12 March 1822, the third of the seven children of Rebecca Beckwith (1798–1870) and Thomas Edward Smith (1796–1871), a retail and timber merchant. The family were loyalists, originally from New England. Albert Smith attended the local Madras School and the Westmorland county grammar school. He worked briefly in his father's store before embarking upon a legal career, when he was articled in the Dorchester law offices of Edward Barron Chandler, the leader of the New Brunswick government. He was admitted as an attorney in 1845 and was called to the bar in 1847.

An imposing and combative man, Smith seemed destined for a distinguished career in commercial and marine law. A member of the Church of England, he could have carved out a niche within the tory establishment. But in 1852, since he disapproved of the power and privilege of the governing establishment, he stood for election in Westmorland county as an opponent of Chandler's 'compact' government. He won, and was soon in the front ranks of a growing opposition 'party'.

When Reformers won a majority of seats in 1854, Smith became a member of the executive council in Charles Fisher's government; but although he supported his colleagues in advocating electoral reforms and fiscal responsibility, he was at odds with them on other issues. His campaign to remove the seat of government to Saint John and his condemnation of the special privileges accorded King's College led to a bitter feud with Fisher, the registrar of King's College and Fredericton's representative in the assembly. He opposed Samuel Leonard Tilley's Prohibitory Liquor Bill in 1855, but, in 1861, the more conciliatory Tilley, now government leader, appointed Smith attorney-general. However, in 1862, when the executive council proposed to underwrite the construction of an intercolonial railway, the new QC resigned in protest. Thus Smith was not a member of the council when negotiations for maritime union, and later the union of British North America, began in 1864. Nor did Tilley invite him to be a member of New Brunswick's delegation at the Charlottetown and Quebec conferences.

Smith, 'the Douglas of Dorchester', 'the Lion of Westmorland', the incisive lawyer, formulated the opposition platform. He argued that, with a mandate to discuss only maritime union, the delegates had acted unconstitutionally in considering a British North American union. He warned that New Brunswickers would be burdened with heavy taxes to pay the Canadas' debts, incurred in constructing canals and railways. Moreover, representation by population would ensure that 'in a few years we shall be at the feet of Canada—Upper Canada—who will exercise control not only over Lower Canada but also over us' (Wallace, 'Life and times', 45).

The confederation issue cut across party lines, destroying traditional divisions. In the 1865 election, New Brunswickers sent twenty-nine anti-confederates, eleven unionists, and four independents to the legislative assembly. Arthur Hamilton Gordon, the lieutenant-governor, invited Smith, the Reformer, and Robert Duncan Wilmot, a Conservative, to form a government. Their executive council included men who supported union but opposed the Quebec plan, and men who opposed all union schemes.

As premier Smith proved unsuccessful as a leader of men. His debating style was aggressive and confrontational, and, coupled with his hot temper, had earned him a reputation as something of a bully. It is not surprising that Gordon, a British aristocrat who found colonial politicians beneath contempt, had no love for him. Nor is it surprising that Smith failed to hold his disparate coalition together.

Smith's alternative to confederation was neither inward looking nor parochial: he advocated continued reciprocity with the United States, and the construction of both a western extension railway from Saint John to the American border and a rail link between New Brunswick and Nova Scotia. But when financial constraints prevented his government from implementing railway construction schemes and the Americans rejected reciprocity, Smith was left without a programme. Defections and declining support pushed him towards compromise, but the centre would not hold and Gordon forced his resignation. In the 1866 election the anti-confederates were routed.

In the confederation election of 1867, Smith was elected to the House of Commons as an independent. Although a supporter of Sir John A. Macdonald's government by 1872, he opposed the construction of a railway to the Pacific and once again broke with a political party over the issue of railway subsidies. Having returned to the Liberal fold, in 1874 he became minister of marine and fisheries in Alexander Mackenzie's newly elected government. One of the ablest marine lawyers in the country, Smith directed the preparation of Canada's brief, presented before the Halifax fishery commission of 1877, convened under the terms of the treaty of Washington to arbitrate the amount of compensation to be paid by the United States for east coast fishing rights. Canada was awarded $4,500,000, and in 1878 Smith was created a KCMG.

These were satisfying years for Smith. On 11 June 1868 he had married Sarah Marie (1847–1926), the daughter of John Wilson Young, a Halifax merchant. He built a comfortable home in Dorchester, where the couple brought up their son, John Wilson Young Smith.

Although Mackenzie's government was defeated in 1878, Smith easily retained his seat. But he was less visible in opposition, and was defeated in the 1882 election. Out of politics for the first time in thirty years, he seemed to lose direction. His health deteriorated, and, on 30 June 1883, at Dorchester, he died.

As a politician, Smith served his conscience and his province. An independent thinker, he succeeded as a good 'party man' only in support of a leader who was as uncompromising as himself. Smith has not captured the imagination of New Brunswickers as Joseph Howe has captured the imagination of Nova Scotians, yet his opposition to confederation was equally perceptive. When he failed to carry the electorate with him in 1866, he sought to protect the province's interests at the federal level and, returning to his Reform roots, found his place in the federal Liberal Party. GAIL G. CAMPBELL

Sources C. M. Wallace, 'Smith, Sir Albert James', *DCB*, vol. 11 · C. M. Wallace, 'Albert Smith, confederation, and reaction in New Brunswick: 1852–1882', *Canadian Historical Review*, 44 (1963), 285–312 · C. M. Wallace, 'The life and times of Sir Albert James Smith', M.A. diss., University of New Brunswick, 1960 · A. G. Bailey, 'The basis and persistence of opposition to confederation in New Brunswick', *Canadian Historical Review*, 23 (1942), 374–97 · J. K. Chapman, *The career of Arthur Hamilton Gordon, first Lord Stanmore, 1829–1912* (Toronto, 1964) · W. S. MacNutt, *New Brunswick: a history, 1784–1867* (1963) · P. B. Waite, *The life and times of confederation, 1864–1867* (1962) · T. A. Burke, 'Mackenzie and his cabinet, 1873–1878', *Canadian Historical Review*, 41 (1960), 128–48 · Provincial Archives of New Brunswick, Graves MSS

Wealth at death over $100,000: Wallace, 'Smith, Sir Albert James', *DCB*

Smith, Albert Richard (1816–1860), author, public lecturer, and mountaineer, was born on 24 May 1816 at Chertsey, Surrey, the son of Richard Smith (*d.* 1857), surgeon, and his wife, Maria. He was educated at Merchant Taylors' School, London (1826–31), and at Middlesex Hospital (1835–8). In 1838 he qualified as a surgeon and apothecary, attended at the hospital of the Hôtel Dieu in Paris, and joined his father's medical practice at Chertsey. Before returning from France, Smith visited Chamonix, and in 1839 and 1840 he gave descriptive lectures on the Alps to local literary societies in Surrey and the suburbs of London. In 1841 he moved to 14 Percy Street, Tottenham Court Road, London, to begin his own medical practice, but he soon decided to lay down the lancet to try his hand with the pen.

In the 1840s Smith made his living as a journalist and writer. He was a regular contributor to *Bentley's Miscellany* and *Punch* and also wrote many plays, burlesques, extravaganzas, and songs, as well as being the drama critic of the

Albert Richard Smith (1816–1860), by Camille Silvy, *c*.1860

Illustrated London News. With Angus B. Reach, he edited *The Man in the Moon*, a sixpenny monthly, from 1847 to 1849. As publicity for this, Smith made several balloon ascents from Vauxhall Gardens in 1847; during one of these, the balloon burst 7000 feet above London, but the deflated balloon was trapped in its own netting and acted as a crude parachute. He also edited the short-lived *Town and Country Miscellany* in 1850, and *The Month* in 1851.

During the course of his career Smith published nearly thirty books. His novels, more notable for their wit than their plots, enjoyed modest commercial success but little critical acclaim. They included *The Adventures of Mr. Ledbury* (1844), *The Fortunes of the Scattergood Family* (1845), *The Marchioness of Brinvilliers* (1846), *The Struggles and Adventures of Christopher Tadpole* (1847), and *The Pottleton Legacy* (1849), some of which were illustrated by John Leech. He also published two collections of essays—*The Wassail Bowl* (1843), and *Wild Oats and Dead Leaves* (1860)—and wrote many satires on the pretensions and snobbery of social climbers. In the early 1840s he wrote essays on evening parties in the style of the French 'physiologies', and he later expanded this genre with parodies of the 'natural history' of society, which highlighted the uncertain definitions of contemporary social status. *The Natural History of the Gent* (1847) became a best-seller and was followed over the next two years by similar works on 'stuck-up people', the ballet girl, the idler about town, and the flirt.

Smith became best known, however, for his entertaining lectures about his travels in the 1850s. Having journeyed through Europe to Constantinople and Egypt in 1849, he lectured in a comic vein about the overland route to India in 'The overland mail', with illustrations by William Beverley, at Willis's Rooms, King Street, London, in 1850. Smith's entertainment combined elements of the earlier monologue lectures of Charles Mathews with the visual displays of the panoramas and dioramas then popular in Leicester Square. Around this time Smith moved to 12 Percy Street, which he shared with parents, sister, and aunt, who were dependent on him.

On 12 August 1851 Smith climbed Mont Blanc with three Oxford students and sixteen guides. On 15 March 1852 'Mr. Albert Smith's Ascent of Mont Blanc' opened at the Egyptian Hall, Piccadilly, on a stage resembling a Swiss chalet. He interspersed descriptions of his journey to Chamonix with patter songs lampooning British tourists in Europe, and St Bernard dogs roamed the hall during the intermission. The show culminated in his dramatic account of the ascent, again illustrated by Beverley. 'Mont Blanc' was a sensational success and ran for six years. Smith gave several command performances—on 24 August 1854 he put on a performance before the queen and the prince consort at Osborne House—and even acted as guide for the prince of Wales at Chamonix. He earned a fortune from his show, much of it from Mont Blanc merchandise, including colouring-books, fans, games, and miniature replicas of the mountain. He also published *The Story of Mont Blanc* (1853), describing his own and earlier ascents. The lecture programme was changed each year by adding new characters, varying the route to Chamonix, and inserting fresh references to contemporary events. 'Mont Blanc' closed after its 2000th performance on 6 July 1858.

Smith's Mont Blanc entertainment dismayed some critics. John Ruskin referred to his exploits as 'a Cockney ascent of Mont Blanc' (*Works*, 36, 1909, 117–18), and Herman Merivale wrote in 1856 that Zermatt was becoming 'a second Chamonix; but with nothing, as yet, of the Cockneyism, the Albert Smithery, the fun, the frolic, and the vulgarity of that unique place of resort' (*Edinburgh Review*, 104, 1856, 446). Smith's show blurred the boundaries between the insular and vulgar cockney, and the educated and genteel classes. As *Town Talk* reported on 3 October 1859: 'the very "Stuck-up People" whom [Smith] so cruelly abused are now perhaps his warmest friends, the strings of carriages round the Egyptian Hall, and the knowledge that Royalty patronises the entertainment, having for them the greatest attraction'.

Smith's show also inspired many people to visit Chamonix and to climb Mont Blanc. Although the mountain had been climbed first in 1786, ascents were still infrequent events when he climbed the peak. John Murray's *Handbook for Travellers in Switzerland* noted that the ascent 'of Albert Smith, in 1851, has effectually popularized the enterprise' (5th edn, 1852, 336). During Smith's entertainments in the 1850s the ascent of Mont Blanc became common, and mountaineering in the Alps became a popular sport. He was a founder member of the Alpine Club in 1857.

After travelling to Hong Kong in 1858, Smith gave another series of lectures, on China, between 22 December 1858 and 19 May 1860. On 1 August 1859 he married Mary Lucy Keeley (1830–1870), an actress, the daughter of Robert *Keeley, a comic actor. Shortly after their marriage, they moved to North End Lodge, near Fulham Green, Brompton, where Smith died of bronchitis after a short illness, on 23 May 1860. He was buried three days later at Brompton cemetery.

Albert's brother **Arthur William Watson Smith** (1825–1861), theatre manager, was also born at Chertsey. Although he too was educated for a career in medicine, Arthur became an impresario and worked for his brother. He made all of the business arrangements for the Mont Blanc entertainments at the Egyptian Hall from 1852 to 1858, and managed two series of readings by Charles Dickens in 1858 and 1861. Founder of the Fielding fund for relief of the literary and theatrical destitute, he was also active in the Thames Fisheries Protection Society, and in 1861 wrote a brochure for the society called *The Thames Angler*. He died at his home, 24 Wilton Street, Belgrave Place, London, on 1 October 1861, and was also buried in Brompton cemetery. PETER H. HANSEN

Sources J. M. Thorington, *Mont Blanc sideshow: the life and times of Albert Smith* (1934) • R. Fitzsimons, *The baron of Piccadilly: the travels and entertainments of Albert Smith* (1967) • P. H. Hansen, 'Albert Smith, the Alpine Club, and the invention of mountaineering in mid-Victorian Britain', *Journal of British Studies*, 34 (1995), 300–24 • R. D. Altick, *The shows of London* (1978) • R. Hyde, *Panoramania! the art and entertainment of the 'all embracing' view* (1988–9) [exhibition catalogue, Barbican Art Gallery, 3 Nov 1988 – 15 Jan 1989] • A. L. Mumm, *The Alpine Club register*, 1 (1923) • T. S. Blakeney, 'Mountaineering and the British royal family', *Alpine Journal*, 59 (1954), 278–87 • E. H. Yates, *Edmund Yates: his recollections and reflections*, 3rd edn, 1 (1884), 229–30 • Boase, *Mod. Eng. biog.* • *DNB*

Archives BL, letters to Royal Literary Fund, loan 96 • Bodl. Oxf., letters to Bradbury & Evans, Eng. lett. MS d. 398, fols. 70–84 • Harvard TC • NL Scot., letters to Blackwoods • NYPL, Berg collection • U. Lpool L., Sydney Jones Library, letters to John Leech

Likenesses C. Baugniet, lithograph, 1844, BM, NPG • C. Baugniet, lithograph, 1855, BM, NPG; repro. in Thorington, *Mont Blanc sideshow* • C. Baugniet, lithograph, 1858, repro. in Thorington, *Mont Blanc sideshow* • D. J. Pound, stipple and line engraving, 1858 (after photograph by J. Mayall), BM, NPG • C. Silvy, photograph, *c.*1860, NPG [*see illus.*] • wood-engraving, 1873 (after photograph by H. Watkins), repro. in *Illustrated Review* (3 April 1873) • R. J. Lane, lithograph (after F. Talfourd), BM, NPG • P. Naumann & R. Taylor & Co., wood-engraving, NPG; repro. in *ILN* (14 May 1892) • portrait (after photograph by Mayall), BL, Add. MS 35027, fol. 121 • portrait, repro. in *ILN*, 21 (25 Dec 1852), 565 • portrait, repro. in *ILN*, 23 (10 Dec 1853), 493–4 • portraits, Harvard TC • portraits, NYPL, theatre collection • prints, NPG

Wealth at death under £16,000: resworn probate, Sept 1860, *CGPLA Eng. & Wales* • under £9000—Arthur Smith: probate, 28 Oct 1861, *CGPLA Eng. & Wales*

Smith, Alexander (1684–1766), vicar apostolic of the lowland district, was born at Fochabers, Moray, in June 1684, the son of Catherine Wilson; his father may have been Robert Smith, a Roman Catholic surgeon and oculist at Fochabers. He was admitted into the Scots College at Paris in 1698, where he graduated MA in 1703. He returned to

Scotland in deacon's orders in 1709 but was not ordained priest until 1712. He returned to Paris in 1718, and was procurator of the Scots College there until he went back to Scotland in 1730. Owing to ill health he visited Paris again from 1733 to 1735. In 1735 he was consecrated bishop of Misinopolis *in partibus infidelium*, being appointed coadjutor to Bishop James Gordon, vicar apostolic of the lowland district, on whose death in 1746 he succeeded to the vicariate. He published two catechisms for use by the Scottish Catholics, which received the formal approbation of the holy office on 20 March 1750. In exile in England from 1751 to 1752, he died at Edinburgh on 21 August 1766.

THOMPSON COOPER, *rev.* ALEXANDER DU TOIT

Sources J. Darragh, *The Catholic hierarchy of Scotland: a biographical list, 1653–1985* (1986) · C. Eubel and others, eds., *Hierarchia Catholica medii et recentioris aevi*, 8 vols. (Münster and Passau, 1913–78); repr. (Münster, 1960–82) · W. M. Brady, *The episcopal succession in England, Scotland, and Ireland, AD 1400 to 1875*, 3 vols. (1876–7) · J. F. S. Gordon, *Ecclesiastical chronicle for Scotland*, 4 vols. (1867) · 'Vicars apostolic of Scotland', *London and Dublin Orthodox Journal*, 4 (7 Jan–24 June 1837), 82–5

Archives Scottish Catholic Archives, Edinburgh | BL, Carlyle family corresp. · NL Scot., Walter Blaikie collection

Smith, Alexander (*fl.* 1714–1726), compiler of biographies, is known for a number of criminal lives published in the reign of George I. They appeared under the name of Captain Alexander Smith, almost certainly a pseudonym. The first and most successful was *The History of the Lives of the most Noted Highwaymen*, published by John Morphew in 1714. It expanded to three volumes in the third edition during the same year, and reached a fifth edition as *A Compleat History* in 1719–20. The later version included *The Thieves' Grammar*, derived from a work separately published as *The Thieves' New Canting Dictionary* (1719). A German translation of the *Lives* by L. Rost appeared in 1720, and has been edited by A. Schlosser (1987). A new edition of the English text was edited by A. L. Hayward (1926).

Once he had found his formula, Smith stuck to it. His other collections include *The Secret History of the Lives of the most Celebrated Beauties, Ladies of Quality, and Jilts* (1715); an augmented version in two volumes was entitled *The Court of Venus* (1716) and the second volume reappeared as *Court Intrigues, or, An Account of the Secret Memoirs of the British Nobility* (1730). In 1723 he produced *The comical and tragical history of the lives and adventures of the most noted bayliffs in and about London and Westminster*, a compendium of drolleries which was used by Harrison Ainsworth in his novel *Jack Sheppard* (1839). Last came *Memoirs of the life and times of the famous Jonathan Wild, together with the history and lives of modern rogues* in two volumes (1726), an attempt to capitalize on the sensational career of the thief-taker Wild, who had been executed at Tyburn on 24 May 1725. A modern reprint of the book has appeared (1973). As usual, the work is derivative and unreliable, embroidering on the known facts freely. Smith's books are characteristic of the criminal biography written in his age, although less moralistic than some. Nothing is known about the identity of the compiler or compilers of the publications attributed to Smith.

PAT ROGERS

Sources *DNB* · G. Howson, *Thief-taker general: the rise and fall of Jonathan Wild* (1970) · L. B. Faller, *Turned to account: the forms and functions of criminal biography in late seventeenth- and early eighteenth-century England* (1987) · L. B. Faller, *Defoe and crime* (1993) · J. J. Richetti, *Popular fiction before Richardson* (1969)

Smith, Alexander. *See* Adams, John (1768?–1829).

Smith, Alexander (1829–1867), poet and essayist, was the eldest of six children born to John Smith (*fl.* 1800–1890) and Christina *née* Murray (*fl.* 1810–1880), only two of whom outlived them. Alexander was born on 31 December 1829 (a date confirmed by the 1851 census, although previous biographers have favoured 1830) in Kilmarnock, where his father designed printing blocks for calico and muslin. Shortly after the birth of a daughter the family moved to Paisley, where Smith's brief education commenced, and about 1838 they arrived in Glasgow.

Little is known about Smith's formal education except that by the age of eleven he had left John Street School, Glasgow, and was working alongside his father, learning the art of pattern drawing for the burgeoning muslin trade. He summed up his schooling as 'reading, writing, arithmetic never could learn, and English Grammar imperfectly with a slight knowledge of Geography, and a considerable stock of Biblical History. First committed the sin of rhyme when about the age of eleven' (Smith, autobiographical note). Whatever the shortcomings of a parish-school education it must have provided Smith with the basic tool of literacy. A childhood fit left him with a villainous squint in his right eye, but he became a voracious reader in his teens. His wide knowledge of English poetry in particular was commented on by many of the literary and academic figures whom he encountered in later life.

The next twelve years were spent working long hours in ramshackle premises in the centre of an early Victorian manufacturing city during the cotton boom of the 1840s. Smith later wrote evocatively about the highs and lows of growing up in such an environment. More about the working conditions as well as his annual trades fortnight, usually by paddle steamer to a Clyde resort, can be gleaned from the largely autobiographical 'A Boy's Poem' (*City Poems*, 1857).

Smith was clearly self-taught and he seems to have set about the task systematically. Along with a dozen or so young apprentices and others aspiring to middle-class mores he instituted and was the first secretary of the Glasgow Addisonian Literary Society. The minute book of this avowedly evangelical young men's improvement society has survived, showing that it met on a Saturday evening in the upstairs room of a Candleriggs coffee house between 1847 and 1852. It was here that Smith learnt to compose and deliver essays on such diverse topics as 'Earnestness' and 'Whether has the poet or legislator the greater influence on the community?' It was no mean feat for one who was invariably noted for his diffident manner.

Smith's first published poem (in Spenserian stanzas) appeared in James Hedderwick's *Glasgow Citizen* in 1850. By this time Smith had already fallen under the spell of the Revd George Gilfillan, a Church of Scotland minister in Dundee and self-appointed herald of a new breed of young poets. Encouraged by the Addisonians, Smith sent poems to Gilfillan who encouraged him to weld them together into a long poem in semi-dramatic form. Thus was 'A Life Drama' born and subsequently heralded by Gilfillan in *The Critic* in 1851–2 with a series of extracts. By the time it appeared in book form as *Poems* in 1853 it was already something of a sensation. Around this time Smith paid his one and only visit to London to be fêted by literati such as G. H. Lewes.

With £100 in advance royalties from his publisher, Smith had given up the muslin warehouse. 'A Life Drama' catapulted him from total obscurity to being talked of in the same breath as Tennyson and Arnold. He was now one of the most notable names in a loose group headed by Sydney Dobell. The florid diction and sensational subject matter that typified this group (the so-called Spasmodics) in the mid-1850s also influenced Tennyson's *Maud*. Smith had no rich patron; luckily one or two influential figures helped to secure him the post of secretary to Edinburgh College (later University) in 1854. The job allowed him a few spare hours in the day for writing, as well as the long summer vacation, but it was no sinecure, especially when he also took on the duties of registrar and secretary to the university council in 1858. Through the university connection Smith met eminent academics such as John Stuart Blackie, professor of Greek and early Scottish nationalist, and William Aytoun, professor of rhetoric and belles-lettres and noted parodist. But in general he preferred the company of freelance writers and artists such as Horatio McCulloch. These formed the backbone of the Raleigh Club, an informal gathering whose discussions were inevitably accompanied by dedicated smoking.

In 1854 Sydney Dobell (pseudonym Sydney Yendys) was staying in Edinburgh and he and Smith collaborated on *Sonnets on the War* (1855), an unashamedly jingoistic contribution on the Crimean War, based mainly on newspaper reports but also possibly on first-hand accounts by William 'Crimean' Simpson, a Glaswegian lithographic artist who had covered the campaign for the *Illustrated London News*. While this project was being jointly created (each poet doing alternate sonnets with Smith concentrating on the bloodier episodes) both were mercilessly parodied by Aytoun in *Blackwood's Magazine* (May 1854) in a spoof review of a long narrative poem 'Firmilian, or, The Student of Badajoz: a Spasmodic Tragedy' by T. Percy Jones. Further extracts were to follow from Aytoun's wickedly inventive pen: the Spasmodics and Gilfillan were effectively deflated but Smith's original *Poems* continued to reprint.

In 1857 Smith's next collection, *City Poems*, showed that he had taken the criticism to heart and lightened his poetic palette. None the less there was unfavourable criticism. It included some of his best work, including the memorable 'Glasgow', an early example of city poetry. An anonymous letter (now known to be from William Allingham) in *The Athenaeum* had accused Smith of wholesale plagiarism and there was a furious correspondence over several issues contributed by detractors and supporters. The campaign was effectively orchestrated by *The Athenaeum's* literary editor, Henry Chorley, and it set the tone for negative reviews of *City Poems* which Smith had hoped would bring him a useful supplement to his secretary's income.

On 24 April 1857 Smith married Flora Macdonald (1829/30–1873) at Ord House on the Isle of Skye, a part of the world he had been introduced to by Sheriff Alexander Nicolson and also by Horatio McCulloch who had painted a number of studies of the Cuillins, visible from the Macdonald house. Flora, related indirectly to the saviour of Bonnie Prince Charlie, also had relatives in Edinburgh. The couple had to return to Edinburgh soon after the wedding (via a steamer trip to Oban), but it was to Skye that they would return every August for the nine remaining years of the poet's life. These visits, as well as providing the raw material for his best-known work, were to prove essential to sustaining his creativity.

Smith's long narrative poem *Edwin of Deira* (1861) was immediately castigated as a pale shadow of *Idylls of the King*, and although he continued to write poetry Smith realized that he had to turn to prose to make a regular second income and support his growing family. He became a frequent contributor to *Blackwood's Magazine*, *Macmillan's*, and Alexander Strahan's *Good Words*, producing work that was always intensely personal, characterized by a distinctive, even quirky, persona. Montaigne was Smith's inspiration and model for many of these pieces and in particular for *Dreamthorp: a Book of Essays Written in the Country*, published by Strahan in 1863. One of the themes that runs through the individual essays in the collection is an understanding that human finiteness contributes to our awareness of joy and beauty in the everyday. This paradox is powerfully conveyed in 'A Lark's Flight', an episode based on the public hanging of two Irish navvies which took place in the east end of Glasgow where Smith spent his boyhood. A moment before the trap is sprung both the silent crowd and the condemned men are assailed by the spiralling notes of a lark 'out of the grassy space at the foot of the scaffold, in the dead silence audible to all'.

Awareness of mortality was early in Smith's thoughts. In the first stanza of 'Glasgow' (written in 1854) he seems to presage his own untimely death: 'Before *me* runs a road of toil/With my grave cut across'. The latter years of his life were characterized by extreme financial worry. A large house at Wardie, overlooking the Forth (bought for them by Flora's uncle, a Skye-dwelling nabob with an indigo works near Calcutta), must have been a drain and by 1866 Flora had borne four children. Smith began to complain of giddiness and spots before the eyes as his literary labours increased. In the last two years of his life he completed *A Summer in Skye* (1865) which comprised some earlier pieces done for *Blackwood's Magazine* and *Temple Bar*. He also completed a strikingly original prose portrait of Edinburgh; a novel serialized in eleven episodes in *Good Words*; the editing and introduction to the Golden Treasury edition of Burns; the introduction to *Golden Leaves from the American Poets*; as well as poems and essays for which there was now a ready periodical market. He was writing 'in the shadow of the Shade', as Henley wrote of Robert Louis Stevenson, aware that he must leave an inheritance for his dependants.

When Smith complained to some of his closest friends of feeling debilitated few believed him. His natural manner was to be as unobtrusive as possible, and he seemed to emanate rude good health, an impression probably reinforced by his walking the two miles to the registrar's office at the Old College and back if the weather allowed. David Masson described him in 1865: 'Latterly he became stouter about the shoulders and more manly-looking, with a tendency to baldness over the forehead which gave a better impression of mental power. But the most remarkable thing about him was his wonderful quietness of demeanour'. Smith contracted diphtheria in November 1866 and, although he seemed to have recovered by Christmas, he was struck down by typhus that proved too much for his weakened constitution. He died at home on 5 January 1867 at the very beginning of his thirty-seventh year, and was buried six days later in Warriston cemetery, Edinburgh.

Assessing Smith's literary influence is complicated by most of his later output having been written for the periodical market (some of these essays were collected in the posthumous *Last Leaves*). Their studied cadences show little sign of being written within strict editorial limits of time and space. Some of them are wonderfully polished and laced with original insights, perfectly suited to their middle-class readership. Although described as journalism, this style of writing has more in common with the essays of Lamb and Hazlitt.

Although well read in the ballads and poetry of his native land, Smith was nevertheless a product of urban north Britain. It was the introduction in his late twenties to Skye and the west highlands that made him realize the homogenizing effects of urbanization ('Some kindred with my human heart/Lives in thy streets of stone' he wrote in 'Glasgow'). The annual month's retreat on Skye allowed his psychological defences against urban pressures to be lowered. His creative, dionysian side fed on the unpredictable and irrational features of the island: the sudden contrasts of storm and calm, the semi-surrealistic mountain shapes and colours, the superstitions and fantastic tales of its inhabitants. All these went into *A Summer in Skye*, making it a fascinating hotchpotch of travelogue and speculation with no obvious models. In the same way as Scott's poetry had drawn visitors to Perthshire earlier in the century, so Smith's work (allied to the growth in the railway network) benefited the west highland tourist trade.

One can only wonder what Smith the poet would have made of Skye, but he published very little poetry after the débâcle of *Edwin of Deira*. His three volumes of poetry are all startlingly different, suggesting that from his early twenties when 'A Life Drama' appeared Smith was searching for a true poetic voice. It is a tragedy that he was prevented from doing that by the raucous critical reception that greeted each work. Lately his prose output has been brought back into print, but his poetry still remains a closed book. The Edwardians rediscovered some of the shorter pieces, in particular the plangent 'Barbara' which was included in the 1912 edition of the Golden Treasury.

Smith was characteristic of his age and yet in subtle rebellion against it, seeking to extol the affirmative qualities of the literary vagabond and question the accepted cultural mores. He should be seen as one of the most original writers who inhabited the chasm in Scottish letters between the death of Scott and the emergence of Robert Louis Stevenson. SIMON BERRY

Sources P. P. Alexander, 'Memoir', in A. Smith, *Last leaves: sketches and criticisms*, ed. P. P. Alexander (1868), i–cxxiii • T. S. Brisbane, *The early years of A. Smith* (1869) • W. Sinclair, *The poetical works of A. Smith* (1909), v–xxxviii [introduction] • A. Smith, autobiographical notes, 1853, NL Scot. • D. Masson, 'Memoir', *Macmillan's Magazine*, 15 (1866–7) • A. Smith, *A summer in Skye*, ed. L. McL. Watt (1907), ix–xvi [introduction] • S. Berry, 'The Glasgow Addisonians', *Scottish Book Collector*, 3/7 • S. Berry, 'Alexander Smith and *A summer in Skye*', *Scottish Book Collector*, 2/7 • S. Berry, 'Alexander Smith: the forgotten enfant terrible', *Scottish Book Collector*, 1/7 • H. Walker, *The literature of the Victorian era* (1910), ch. 6 • P. Turner, *English literature, 1832–1890: excluding the novel* (1989), vol. 11/1 of *The Oxford history of English literature* (1945–), 171–2 • M. Scott, 'Alexander Smith: poet of Victorian Scotland', *Studies in Scottish Literature*, 14 (1979), 98–111 • m. cert. • d. cert. • census returns, 1851

Archives Ayrshire Archives, papers relating to his work • Dick Institute, Kilmarnock, Glasgow Addisonian Literary Society minute book; letters by Flora Smith and Alexander Smith | BL, letters to Royal Literary Fund, loan 96

Likenesses photograph, *c*.1853, Mitchell L., Glas. • J. Archer, oils, *c*.1856, Scot. NPG • K. Brown, bronze bust, 1910, Glasgow Art Galleries and Museums • W. Brodie, plaster medallion, Scot. NPG • Dalziel, woodcut, BM • J. Moffat, photograph, Scot. NPG • engraving, repro. in *Good Words* (Feb 1867)

Wealth at death negligible: letters from widow to Royal Literary Fund

Smith, Sir Allan MacGregor (1871–1941), employers' leader and politician, was born on 19 May 1871 at 236 Dumbarton Road, Glasgow, the second of eight children of Alexander Smith, master house-painter and a native of Elgin, and his wife, Agnes Welsh Campbell, from Glen Orchy in Inverness-shire. He was educated at Glasgow Academy and at the University of Glasgow, where he took an MA ordinary degree in 1890. He went on to read law, graduating LLB in 1896. His subsequent career, initially as a practising solicitor, and then as the leading figure in the Engineering Employers' Federation (EEF) and as a member of parliament, was to take him to the very centre of industrial politics in Britain.

Smith's apprenticeship began in Glasgow, when he joined the legal practice of Biggart and Lumsden as a managing clerk. Through this firm, which acted for the EEF and some of the chief engineering and shipbuilding companies on Clydeside, Smith was introduced to the world of employers' organizations and to the politics of labour relations. In 1901 his legal and administrative capabilities were recognized when he was made a partner in the firm. In the same year he was named as parliamentary solicitor to the EEF, and he also became assistant secretary to the North-West of Scotland Engineering Employers' Federation and to the Clyde Shipbuilders' Association. In 1908 Smith was made joint assistant secretary to the EEF and two years later, when the federation moved to new headquarters in London, he was appointed sole secretary and treasurer.

Smith first attracted public notice in 1912 when he presented the federation's evidence on trade union agreements to the Industrial Council, a government-sponsored body designed to promote industrial peace. However, with the outbreak of war in 1914, he rose rapidly to national prominence as an employers' leader. In 1916 he was appointed chairman of the EEF's newly formed management committee, effectively becoming the federation's chief executive. During the war Smith served on more than thirty official government committees and acted as an adviser to various ministries and departments, notably the Ministry of Munitions and the ministries of Labour and Reconstruction. At the end of 1918 he was created KBE for his wartime services, and further official recognition soon followed, which confirmed his authority in industry. In February 1919 he was appointed spokesman for the employers' delegation at the National Industrial Conference; in April 1919 he joined the Sankey coal enquiry and a few months later he was chosen as the British employers' delegate on the governing body of the newly formed International Labour Organization, which he served until 1922.

During and immediately after the First World War Smith made several important and lasting contributions to the organization of employers in Britain. Under his efficient direction the EEF increased its membership and influence in the metal industries to become one of the premier employers' organizations in the country and a major force in industrial affairs. Smith was also the leading personality behind the setting up of the National Confederation of Employers' Organizations in April 1919, of which he was chairman between 1919 and 1922 and then an active ex-officio member of its executive council. In addition he played an instrumental role in the establishment in March 1920 of the International Organization of Industrial Employers, based in Brussels, in which he held the post of president during 1921 and 1922. In February 1923 he was elected a companion member of the Institution of Mechanical Engineers in recognition of his services to industry.

Smith's work for the EEF, and on behalf of the employers' movement generally, drew him into active politics. During these years he was a prominent and influential member of several political bodies, notably the British Commonwealth Union (BCU) and the Economic League. In December 1919, with the support of the BCU, he was elected as the Conservative MP for Croydon South; he held the seat until the general election in 1923, when he chose to stand down. Subsequently, he stood unsuccessfully for the Partick division of Glasgow. In the House of Commons, Smith was a member of the parliamentary industrial group, an influential backbench organization sponsored by the BCU, and served as its chairman between 1921 and 1923. In this role Smith spoke on trade and industrial matters and enjoyed the intimacy of some of the important political figures of the day, including David Lloyd George (his chief political patron), Winston Churchill, and Sir Robert Horne. After the war Smith was also able to continue his role as a government adviser, joining the British delegation to the Cannes conference in 1922 as an industrial expert, serving on the Balfour committee on industry and trade between 1924 and 1929, and providing the second Labour government of 1929–31 with advice on trade and employment policy matters. In October 1934 he resigned from the EEF on the grounds of ill health and retired from public life.

In 1919 Smith, at the height of his powers, had been described by one contemporary as a 'star among the professional representatives of capitalism' (Cole, 160–61), and he remained wholly dedicated to this cause. Throughout his career his approach to economic issues was guided by a deep-seated belief in free enterprise and by a ferocious determination to assert the interests of Britain's staple heavy industries. In the arena of industrial relations, where his influence was strongly felt, notably in the engineering dispute of 1922 and in the events surrounding the 1926 general strike and its aftermath, he was opposed to all forms of government intervention and vigorously expounded an approach to labour relations based on the principle of the employer's 'right to manage'. His firm and frequently heard views on these issues, in numerous speeches and in print, earned him a reputation for clear thinking and honesty but also for inflexibility; they also brought him into disagreement with some of the more consensus-minded employers of his day, as well as with Labour leaders and the trade union movement.

A religious and intense man, short in stature but physically strong 'with a face of granite and steel-blue eyes' (Wigham, 291), Smith commanded attention from those around him, if not affection. His closest friends and associates, who were drawn mainly from the engineering industry and from business circles, included Lord Weir, Sir Andrew Duncan, and Patrick Hannon. In December 1901 Smith married Isabella Clow (1869–1933), the daughter of John A. McCallum, one of Scotland's chief coalmasters, and they had a son and two daughters. Smith's social and leisure activities reflected his strong and continuing links with Scotland, which he visited regularly. His interests included music—he was a bagpiper—and sailing, on the west coast of Scotland and as a member of the Royal Thames Yacht Club, as well as deerstalking and fishing. For most of his active career Smith lived with his family in Hampstead, London. He died there on 21 February 1941 at 9 Greenaway Gardens, Hampstead, from coronary failure, and was buried on 26 February at St Andrew's Presbytery Church, Frognal, London.

A pioneering and controversial employers' leader, Sir Allan MacGregor Smith was one of several outstanding business figures from Scottish backgrounds who made a mark upon industrial and political affairs in Britain during and after the First World War. TERENCE RODGERS

Sources *The Times* (24 Feb 1941) • *Glasgow Herald* (24 Feb 1941) • *The Engineer* (28 Feb 1941) • *Engineering* (7 March 1941) • T. Rodgers, 'Smith, Sir Allan MacGregor', *DBB* • T. Rodgers, 'Sir Allan Smith, the industrial group and the politics of unemployment, 1919–

1924', *Business History*, 28 (1986), 100–23 • T. Rodgers, 'Employers' organisation, unemployment and social politics in Britain during the inter-war period', *Social History*, 13/3 (1988), 315–41 • J. Zeitlin, 'The internal politics of employer organization: the Engineering Employers' Federation, 1896–1939', *The power to manage? Employers and industrial relations in comparative historical perspective*, ed. S. Tolliday and J. Zeitlin (1991), 52–80 • E. Wigham, *The power to manage: a history of the Engineering Employers' Federation* (1973) • J. Turner, 'The politics of "organised business" in the First World War', *Businessmen and politics: studies in business activity in British politics, 1900–1945*, ed. J. Turner (1984), 33–49 • K. Middlemas, *Politics in industrial society: the experience of the British system since 1911* (1979) • R. P. T. Davenport-Hines, *Dudley Docker: the life and times of a trade warrior* (1984) • *Beatrice Webb's diaries, 1912–1924*, ed. M. I. Cole (1952) • private information (2004) • b. cert. • m. cert. • d. cert. • *The Times* (27 Feb 1941) [burial]

Archives priv. coll., letters and newspaper cuttings | Bodl. Oxf., corresp. with Sir W. L. Worthington-Evans • CAC Cam., Weir MSS • HLRO, Hannon MSS • Mitchell L., Glas., Strathclyde Regional Archives; North-West Engineering Trades Association records • NA Scot., Steel-Maitland MSS • PRO, PREM 1/30 • U. Warwick Mod. RC, records of the National Confederation of Employers' Organisations; Engineering Employers' Federation records, CBI archive

Likenesses photograph, *c*.1916, priv. coll.

Wealth at death £38,704 0s. 11*d*.: confirmation, 8 July 1941, *CCI*

Smith, Sir Andrew (1797–1872), army medical officer and naturalist, was born on 3 December 1797 in Kirktoun parish, Roxburghshire, to Thomas P. Smith, a shepherd, and Grizzel Tait Winnington. After local schooling he was apprenticed to Mr Graham, a surgeon in Hawick, and studied medicine at the University of Edinburgh before entering the Army Medical Service as a hospital mate on 15 August 1815. After training at Fort Pitt, Chatham, he was stationed in Edinburgh in 1818 and resumed his studies at the university. He graduated MD in 1819 upon completion of a thesis on secondary smallpox.

Smith was sent to the Cape Colony in 1820 as medical assistant to the 72nd regiment. He remained there for sixteen years, and although he continued to serve in the Army Medical Service his reputation was made through his enquiries into the region's zoology, ethnography, and geography. He was appointed founding superintendent of the South African Museum of Natural History in 1825. At the request of the Cape government he investigated the frontier region known as Nama Land, in 1828, and in 1832–3 he led an official mission to Dingane's Zulu kingdom in Natal. In 1834–6 he superintended a fact-finding expedition into the territory north of the Cape Colony, which was financed by Cape merchants and other interested parties. His ethnographic notes and reports on the San, the Khoi-Khoi and other Southern African peoples are richly detailed and highly informative, and his knowledge of the region's zoology was so extensive that Charles Darwin sought out his expertise. His most important publication was *Illustrations of the Zoology of South Africa*, issued in parts from 1838 to 1849, and in four volumes in 1849.

After returning to England in 1836 Smith was stationed again at Fort Pitt, Chatham, where he became staff surgeon and principal medical officer in 1841. Here on 6 March 1844 he married his housekeeper, Ellen Henderson (*c*.1802–1864), and converted to her Roman Catholic faith. In 1845 he was made professional assistant to Sir James McGrigor, the director-general of the army medical department, and at the close of the year he took the position of deputy inspector-general. He was promoted inspector-general on 7 February 1851, when Sir James retired, and on 25 February 1853 he became director-general of the army and ordnance medical departments. During the Crimean campaign he was blamed in the press for the scandalous state of medical care for British troops. Florence Nightingale sought his dismissal, referring to him as 'smoke-dried Andrew Smith'. He defended his conduct before several select parliamentary committees and was exonerated of dereliction of duty. Smith resigned his post as director-general, owing to impaired health, on 22 May 1858, and was on 9 July following created KCB.

Smith was elected a fellow of the Wernerian Society of Edinburgh in 1819, of the Zoological Society of London in 1843, of the Faculty of Physicians and Surgeons of Glasgow in 1855, of the Medico-Chirurgical Society of Aberdeen in 1855, of the Royal College of Surgeons of Edinburgh in 1856, and of the Royal Society, London, in 1857. He also received an honorary MD degree from Trinity College, Dublin, in 1856. He died on 11 August 1872 at his residence, 16 Alexander Square, Brompton, London, and was buried at Kensal Green Roman Catholic cemetery.

DANE KENNEDY

Sources P. R. Kirby, *Sir Andrew Smith, MD, KCB* (1965) • *Andrew Smith's journal of his expedition into the interior of South Africa, 1834–6*, ed. W. F. Lye (1975) • P. R. Kirby, ed., *Andrew Smith and Natal: documents relating to the early history of that province* (1955) • parish register (baptism), 9 Jan 1798, Kirktoun, Roxburghshire • d. cert.

Archives RCS Eng., zoological papers • South African Museum, Cape Town • Transvaal Museum, Pretoria | National Archives of South Africa, Cape Town

Likenesses oils, Royal Army Medical Corps Museum, Farnham • oils, Royal Army Medical College, Millbank, London, mess room

Wealth at death under £3000: probate, 12 Sept 1872, *CGPLA Eng. & Wales*

Smith, (Robert) Angus (1817–1884), applied chemist and environmental scientist, was born in Pollokshaws, near Glasgow, on 15 February 1817, the seventh son and twelfth child of John Smith (1765–1843), a minor manufacturer of Loudoun, Ayrshire, and Janet (1776–1853), daughter of James Thomson, owner of flax mills. Both families were connected to the prominent Napier family of Strathaven. The family was an intensely religious one; the elder Smith espousing a 'deep but narrow' Calvinism. Although two of the elder brothers were ordained, none made his career in the pastorate of the Scottish church. The eldest, John, who supported the family during much of Angus's youth, became an important educator, and headmaster of the Perth Academy, and also an experimenter on optics. James Elishama *Smith became an Irvingite in 1828 and converted most of the rest of his family, only to found his own mystical, pantheistic, universalist sect in the mid-1830s. Micaiah (MA Glasgow, 1827) remained an Irvingite minister.

Education Following his elder brothers, Smith was sent to the Glasgow high school in 1826, and then on to Glasgow University in 1829 to prepare for the ministry in the Church of Scotland. He left Glasgow University after one

(Robert) Angus Smith (1817–1884), by unknown photographer

year, although whether this was for reasons of finance or conscience (he was distressed at the expulsion of Macleod Campbell) is not clear. He spent most of the following decade as tutor to several families, first in the Scottish highlands, and after 1836 in London. It was in this capacity that in 1839 he accompanied the family of the Revd E. Bridgeman to Germany, and stayed on in Giessen to study chemistry at the laboratory of Justus von Liebig; he graduated PhD from there in 1841. He had become interested in the science through attending the lectures of Thomas Graham at the mechanics' institute in Glasgow during the late 1820s, and through the influence of his brother Joseph, who had studied chemistry with Frederick Penny in Aberdeen. From 1841 to 1843 Angus Smith was again in London, tutoring and considering taking holy orders in the Church of England, an option prevented by his lack of the proper university degree.

In 1843 the young chemist Lyon Playfair, who had been a fellow student in Liebig's laboratory, invited Smith to become his assistant in Manchester, where Playfair had recently been appointed professor of chemistry at the Manchester Royal Institution. Smith also assisted Playfair in the massive report on sanitary conditions in industrial Lancashire that Playfair was undertaking as one of the royal commissioners on the health of towns and populous places. Here the role of decomposing matter as a cause of disease, which had been one of Liebig's interests, was central, and it would subsequently become the main theme of Smith's research. Smith also carried out research for the royal commission on the sanitation of the metropolis in 1848, for the royal commissions on mines (1864), and on the cattle plague in 1865, and for the Local Government Board in 1879.

Analytical chemist in Manchester When the ambitious and well-connected Playfair left in 1845 to take up a post at the Royal School of Mines, Smith remained in Manchester as a consulting analytical chemist. During the next two decades he applied for university posts, but without success; as a lecturer he had a tendency to highlight the complexity and uncertainty that others circumvented. His career in private practice was successful, however: in Manchester he was part of a circle of young industrial chemists interested in inorganic industrial chemistry, and in the new commercial possibilities of the distillation of hydrocarbons. These included several fellow Scots—Peter Spence, James 'Paraffin' Young, and Alexander McDougall. With the last, Smith patented in 1854 a disinfectant marketed as McDougall's powder, a combination of carbolic acid with magnesium and calcium sulphite. It was the use of this product in preventing the putrefaction of Carlisle sewage that led Joseph Lister to carbolic acid in his efforts to prevent the sepsis of surgical wounds; his success in these trials led to antiseptic surgery. Another patent of Smith's, for a rust-resistant pitch coating of iron water pipes, was also widely used, though in neither case does Smith appear to have been active in the actual marketing of the products.

By the mid-1850s Smith had become familiar with the heavy chemicals industry through the trials of his friend Peter Spence, who was being sued for the creation of a public nuisance in allowing the passage of ammonia, hydrogen sulphide, and sulphur dioxide gases into the atmosphere in his alum works at Pendleton. Smith's experiences as a defence witness in the case of *R.* v. *Spence* unsettled him deeply and altered the course of his career. He was disturbed both by the abilities of cross-examining counsel to distort the meaning of a scientist's testimony and by the apparent willingness of some chemists to become paid advocates who would state any technical opinion for a fee. 'We stand aside from a man who twists the expression of natural law for his own interest, as from one who, before his eyes, has neither the fear of God, nor the love and admiration of nature', wrote Smith in 1860 (*Journal of the Society of Arts*, 8, 1860, 139). Almost single-handedly he began a campaign for reform in the use of scientific testimony in courts of law, and, by implication, in parliamentary select committees, initially through the National Association for the Promotion of Social Science, subsequently through the British Association for the Advancement of Science (which had a committee on the subject from 1859 to 1867), the Society of Arts, and the Law Amendment Society. The campaign led to no significant reforms, and the concerns still arise periodically.

In an age when testimony to courts on matters of pollution or patents, and to parliamentary committees, was a significant source of income for applied scientists, and particularly for analytical chemists, Smith was unique in refusing to become a 'trading witness'. His uncompromising independence, along with his experience, did, however, make him the obvious candidate for the alkali inspectorate established under the Alkali Act of 1863, a position which Smith held until his death. The act required removal of 95 per cent of gaseous HCl, prior to aerial discharge. When, in 1876, a Rivers Pollution Prevention Act was passed, prohibiting discharge of liquid industrial and urban wastes that had not been treated according to best practicable means, Smith also became one of the inspectors under it. His strategy in both posts was one of facilitating improvement by making available to manufacturers his expertise, rather than of confrontation and prosecution. Though Smith was criticized for his leniency, the strategy was largely successful in the case of the alkali industry, but only because there was increasingly a market for aqueous HCl and for chlorine, and new technologies, in the Gossage tower and the Deacon process, for recovering these materials. It was less successful in addressing the manifold industrial and municipal sources of river pollution.

Wider environmental concerns As well as reporting his regulatory activities, Smith used his official reports as inspector to explore contested empirical, methodological, and theoretical issues that had no direct connection with the immediate business of inspection. In the case of the alkali inspectorate this included research into the normal composition of the urban industrial atmosphere. Little was known about variation of the composition of the air as a result of urban concentration of industrial activity, or about the effects on health of gases not normally present in significant concentrations, such as ammonia. In the case of river pollution, Smith addressed problems of natural sewage purification. Working in the years immediately prior to the discovery of specific waterborne pathogens, he was concerned both with characterizing more precisely the kinds of organic matter that might be present in water and with understanding which stages of organic decomposition were most closely associated with disease. In the cases of both air and water these were problems that occupied him throughout his career, beginning with his earliest scientific paper, on the air and water of towns, published in the *British Association Report* for 1848. Highly sensitive to environmental quality, Smith had argued there that subtle changes in atmospheric composition, related perhaps to processes going on in water and soil, might be significantly undermining health without necessarily causing cases of acute disease.

Much of Smith's work concerned the effects of oxygen demand in both air and water. He worried, for example, that coal smoke might be depriving air of some of its respirable qualities. He worried also about the roles of microscopic life in causing disease and decomposition, and also in completing the process of the decomposition of organic wastes. Smith was one of the few who recognized that Liebig's chemical theory of decomposition-based pathology was not necessarily irreconcilable with Louis Pasteur's biological theory. He became interested not simply in whether microbe species caused diseases, but in the chemical ecology of microbial life, in the environmental factors that either generated pathogenic microbes or harboured and cultivated them between human hosts. Independently, Smith was developing a research programme similar to that which the better known Max von Pettenkofer was developing in Bavaria. Having long experimented with distinguishing water or the washings of particular airs by the growths they produced on standing, Smith had, by the early 1880s, developed means of bacterial water analysis similar to those being perfected by Robert Koch.

Published work As a scientist Smith was idiosyncratic and disorganized. The methods he used were often of his own invention, and rarely found favour with other chemists. His scientific papers often resemble notes rather than polished articles. They are rambling, their conclusions highlighting not what had been learned but how much remained unclear. His books, usually collections of earlier work, were repetitive and sometimes inconsistent. Drawing on a remarkably broad knowledge of classical and Germanic sources on the history and philosophy of chemistry (as well as on sanitary practices), he tended toward metaphysical rather than practical aspects of the questions on which he worked. These factors, coupled with his isolation in Manchester and unwillingness to participate in the political and legal forums of expert testimony in which so much of sanitary science was done, made it possible for his contemporaries largely to ignore substantive aspects of Smith's work. The questions he explored (for example, acid rain) and the approaches he took became mainstream areas of research only in the latter part of the twentieth century and he himself seems not fully to have understood their importance. His most important work is in *Disinfectants and Disinfection* (1869), in which he recognizes the quite different chemical effects of the variety of substances proposed as disinfectants, antiseptics, or deodorizers, and *Air and Rain: the Beginnings of a Chemical Climatology* (1872), which presents the vast body of data Smith had accumulated on the composition of urban atmospheres.

Smith was a fellow of the Chemical Society from 1845, and served on its council in 1870–72 and as a vice-president in 1878–80. He was elected fellow of the Royal Society in 1857 and, toward the end of his life, was a member of the Society of Chemical Industry and the Sanitary Institute of Great Britain (in which he was president of the section on chemistry, meteorology, and geology in 1883). He was much more active in Manchester-based organizations—the Manchester and Salford Sanitary Association, for which he regularly gave popular lectures, and particularly the Manchester Literary and Philosophical Society, an apt home for one whose interests were philosophical, literary, and antiquarian as well as scientific. Almost half of his forty-eight scientific papers appeared in the society's proceedings, and Smith served as secretary in 1852–6, and as a vice-president in 1857–81 except when he was president in 1864–5. Under the auspices of the society he published his first book, a *Memoir of John Dalton* (1856), as well as his *Centenary of Science in Manchester* (1883). As a historian of science he also published *The Life and Works of Thomas Graham* (1884).

Final years In the late 1860s Smith became interested in the antiquities of the Scottish highlands. He acquired a large library of works in Gaelic and wrote *Loch Etive and the Sons of Uisnach*, published posthumously by his niece and long-time housekeeper, Jesse Knox Smith, in 1885. Smith also published privately *To Iceland in a Yacht* (1873), an account of an 1872 trip with James Young. Smith, who was known as thoughtful and gentle, never married; his friends nicknamed him Agnus Smith. Like his friend Sir William Crookes, whose *Chemical News* was one of the few publications to take his scientific work seriously, he became a spiritualist later in his life. Despite declining health through much of the 1880s he kept active almost to the end of his life. He died at Glynwood, Colwyn Bay, on 12 May 1884 of complications of pernicious anaemia and was buried in the churchyard of St Paul's, Kersal, near Manchester. CHRISTOPHER HAMLIN

Sources A. Gibson, 'Robert Angus Smith and sanitary science', MSc diss., University of Manchester Institute of Science and Technology, 1972 • A. Gibson and W. V. Farrar, 'Robert Angus Smith, FRS, and sanitary science', *Notes and Records of the Royal Society*, 28 (1973–4), 241–62 • R. M. MacLeod, 'The Alkali Acts administration, 1863–1884: the emergence of the civil scientist', *Victorian Studies*, 9 (1965–6), 85–112 • C. Hamlin, *A science of impurity: water analysis in nineteenth century Britain* (1990) • E. Ashby and M. Anderson, *The politics of clean air* (1981) • H. Schunck, *Memoirs of the Literary and Philosophical Society of Manchester*, 3rd ser., 10 (1887), 90–102 • *Nature*, 30 (1884), 104–5 • E. Gorham, 'Robert Angus Smith, FRS, and "Chemical climatology"', *Notes and Records of the Royal Society*, 36 (1981–2), 267–72 • J. Eyler, 'The conversion of Angus Smith: the changing role of chemistry and biology in sanitary science, 1850–1880', *Bulletin of the History of Medicine*, 54 (1980), 216–34 • *CGPLA Eng. & Wales* (1884)

Archives RS, letters • UCL, corresp. with E. Chadwick

Likenesses bust, University of Manchester • bust, Manchester Literary and Philosophical Society • photograph, repro. in Gibson and Farrar, 'Robert Angus Smith, FRS' • photograph, Royal Society of Chemistry, London [*see illus.*]

Wealth at death £1953 15*s*. 4*d*.: resworn administration with will, Feb 1885, *CGPLA Eng. & Wales* (1884)

Smith, Anker (1759–1819). *See under* Boydell, John, engravers (*act.* 1760–1804).

Smith, Ann (*fl.* 1682–1686), political activist, was a member of that small minority in seventeenth-century England of women who took an active part in radical politics. Her financial support was the principal factor making possible one rebellion in 1685, and it was an important factor in a second. Nothing is known of her before 1682, nor anything certain of how and why she became involved in politics. In 1682 she was middle-aged with at least one adult son, and married to a well-to-do London sugar baker. She was an active partner in the business, as she showed by arresting the Spanish ambassador's nephew in pursuit of a debt of £3000. She was a fervent Baptist, and it may have been the government's renewed campaign against dissenters, after the failure of the exclusion campaign in 1681, which drew her into politics. She was an associate of the Cromwellian officer, Baptist, and rebel Major Abraham Holmes, and was on good terms with other religious conspirators, such as the preacher Robert Ferguson. In December 1682 she wrote a partially encoded letter to the printer Francis Smith, then in exile in Rotterdam, containing messages for him, the earl of Shaftesbury, and Robert Ferguson.

It was, however, Ann Smith's association with Archibald Campbell, ninth earl of Argyll, which drew her into the politics of treason. In 1681 Argyll had been condemned by the government in Scotland for refusing to support the draconian campaign there against dissenters. Early in 1682 he escaped to England, and through the agency of Major Holmes he was brought to Ann Smith. She hid the earl and his servant, first in a tenement near her house in Battersea, and then more comfortably in a house in Brentford, just outside London. When the hunt for the fugitive earl grew too hot and he fled to the Netherlands, Smith and her husband joined him, and in late 1683 he was staying with them in Utrecht. They accompanied him to Cleves to see another Scottish exile, Sir John Cochrane, and a government report at this time refers to Ann as 'a great fomentor of plots' (Greaves, 413). Some time in 1684 her husband died and the wealthy widow was now able to show the depth of her regard for Argyll by giving him £7000 of the £9000 he needed to raise his highland rebellion. For good measure she also gave the duke of Monmouth the £1000 he suddenly needed for his rebellion, to hire a frigate to escort his two small ships safely to Lyme Regis against James II's now vigilant navy. Smith's son also accompanied Argyll: it is not known whether he survived. When she heard that Argyll had landed safely, in June 1685, she had a sermon preached in her house on Psalm 34: 1–2. Some weeks later, however, she was visited by the preacher Robert Ferguson with the sorry details of the failed expedition. Undaunted, she was still engaged in conspiracy in 1686, but in August of that year received a royal pardon, and nothing more is heard of her.

Ann Smith's relationship with Argyll seems based on the latter's religious principles, and appears to have been profoundly reciprocated by him. As he awaited execution the earl wrote her a farewell letter (twice the length of that to his wife), in which he regrets deeply that her name could not be kept out of his trial, says that her concern for him is 'a Cross greater than I can express', thanks her for all her 'kindness to all saints', and declares that he leaves the world in hope of glory (Wodrow, 2.541).

Ann Smith was one of a dozen or more women known to have been politically active in the 1680s in roles such as couriers, pamphlet distributors, and providers of safe houses. On a lesser scale, political tension in the last ten years of Stuart rule seems to have politicized a minority of women in the same way as the better-known crisis of the 1640s. ROBIN CLIFTON

Sources R. L. Greaves, *Secrets of the kingdom: British radicals from the Popish Plot to the revolution of 1688–89* (1992) • J. Willcock, *A Scots earl in covenanting times: being life and times of Archibald, 9th earl of Argyll (1629–1685)* (1907) • R. Wodrow, *The history of the sufferings of the Church of Scotland from the Restauration to the revolution*, 2 vols. (1721–2) • *CSP dom.*, 1681–8 • R. Clifton, *The last popular rebellion: the western* *rising of 1685* (1984) • Ford, Lord Grey, *The secret history of the Rye-House plot: and of Monmouth's rebellion* (1754) • D. J. Milne, 'The Rye House plot with special reference to its place in the exclusion contest and its consequences till 1685', PhD diss., U. Lond., 1949

Archives PRO, state papers, Charles II • PRO, state papers, James II

Wealth at death probably very little; contributed £7000 to Argyll's expedition and £1000 to Monmouth's in 1685

Smith, Annie Lorrain (1854–1937), mycologist and lichenologist, was born on 25 October 1854 at Halfmorton, Dumfriesshire, a younger daughter of the Revd Walter Smith, minister in the Free Church of Scotland. The family was large and talented; three sons became university professors.

Annie received her early schooling in Edinburgh and studied French in Orléans and German in Tübingen. For a time she worked as a governess, but about 1888 began to study botany, taking classes under D. H. Scott (1854–1934) at the Royal College of Science, London. She was introduced by Scott to the department of botany in the British Museum (Natural History), where she undertook the remounting of the recently purchased de Bary collection of microscopical slides of fungi; this began an association with the museum's cryptogamic herbarium that lasted for the rest of her life. As women were then ineligible for official staff positions, she was always an 'unofficial worker', paid from a special fund.

Although Annie Smith did some early research on seaweeds, fungi were her special interest. Extensive work preparing exhibition stands of microfungi and three years assisting with seed testing, which included examining microfungi associated with germination, expanded her knowledge of the group. Within a short time she became responsible for identifying most of the fungi collections arriving at the museum, especially those from tropical east Africa, Angola, and the West Indies. Her studies on these and on new or rare British fungi were reported in numerous papers published between about 1895 and 1920.

From 1906 Annie Smith also worked extensively in lichenology. Following the death that year of James Crombie, one of the leading British figures in the field, she undertook to complete the unfinished second volume of his *Monograph of the British Lichens*. This appeared under her name in 1911, although it is now thought to have been almost all Crombie's work. However, she then thoroughly revised both volumes one and two for a second edition (1918, 1926). The *Monograph*, which is still an important reference work, quickly brought her wide recognition. Since it lacked workable keys she also published her well-illustrated *Handbook of British Lichens* (1921), the only available set of keys to all known British lichens for almost three decades.

Annie Smith was probably best known for her textbook *Lichens* (1921; repr. 1975), outstanding for its breadth and detail and for more than half a century the standard work in English on the historical development of the field. A reviewer, describing it as 'practically the first modern

Annie Lorrain Smith (1854–1937), by unknown photographer

scientific work devoted solely to Lichens' (*Journal of Botany, British and Foreign*, 1921), rightly predicted it would long remain a classic. Her separate short history of British lichenology appeared in 1922, in the *South Eastern Naturalist*. Also especially appreciated by her contemporaries were the reviews and abstracts of recent work on lichens she regularly contributed to botanical journals for more than thirty years. Her fieldwork in lichenology was limited mainly to the forays of the Essex Field Club and the British Mycological Society, but she took part as lichenologist in the 1909–11 Clare Island survey (co. Mayo, Ireland), one of the most successful large-scale field investigations of the time.

A foundation member of the British Mycological Society, Annie Smith regularly attended annual meetings for thirty-five years and was twice president (1907, 1917). She became one of the first women fellows of the Linnean Society in 1904, and was a council member in 1918–21. In 1922 she was president of the South-East Union of Scientific Societies. At the British Museum, with the staff depletions of the First World War, she became acting assistant in the cryptogamic department with responsibility for fungi and lichens, but still as an 'unofficial worker'.

Vigorous, warm-hearted, and always ready to assist students and younger colleagues, Annie Smith had wide interests and strong views, including a deep commitment to the social and political goals of the women's rights movement. She enjoyed travel and visited both Australia (with the British Association) and the United States. For fifty years she shared her home with an older sister, whose death in 1933 affected her severely. A civil service pension and an OBE, conferred when she retired in 1934, came as recognition of her contributions to cryptogamic botany. She died at her home, 44 Stanwick Mansions, in west London, on 7 September 1937, shortly before her eighty-third birthday, after three years of poor health.

MARY R. S. CREESE

Sources G. Lister, *Proceedings of the Linnean Society of London*, 150th session (1937–8), 337–9 · *Journal of Botany, British and Foreign*, 75 (1937), 328–30 · D. L. Hawksworth and M. R. D. Seaward, *Lichenology in the British Isles, 1568–1975* (1977), 26–7 · *Bulletin of Miscellaneous Information* [RBG Kew] (1937), 442–3 · *The Times* (14 Sept 1937) · review of A. L. Smith's *Lichens*, *Journal of Botany, British and Foreign*, 59 (1921), 331–3 · *The Times* (9 Sept 1937)
Archives NHM, botany library, notebooks and letters
Likenesses photograph, NHM, department of botany [*see illus.*]
Wealth at death £7991 13s. 2d.: probate, 12 Oct 1937, *CGPLA Eng. & Wales*

Smith, Aquilla (1806–1890), numismatist, was born in Nenagh, co. Tipperary, on 28 April 1806, the youngest child of Aquilla Smith (1776–1858) and Catherine, daughter of William Doolan. He was educated privately in Dublin, and entered Trinity College, Dublin, in 1823. He went on to study at the Royal College of Surgeons of Ireland but ill health made him change to medicine, and he was licensed by the King and Queen's College of Physicians in Ireland in 1833. He received the degree of MD *honoris causa* from his university in 1839. Smith was king's professor of *materia medica* and pharmacy in the school of physic from 1864 to 1881, and physician-in-ordinary to Sir Patrick Dun's Hospital. From 1851 to 1890 he represented the Irish College of Physicians on the General Medical Council. On 21 February 1831 he married his first cousin Esther, daughter of George Faucett; they had thirteen children, among them Vincent Arthur *Smith (1848–1920).

Smith was an active member of the Royal Irish Academy from 1835 until his death at his home, 121 Lower Baggot Street, Dublin, on 23 March 1890. In his lifetime he was thought to be the leading authority on Irish coins. He became interested in numismatics early in life, an interest encouraged by his friendship with Richard Sainthill. Nearly 500 of the illustrations in Sainthill's *Olla podrida* (1853) were engraved from drawings by Smith. At his death his large collection of Irish coins and tokens was acquired by the academy for £350. He received a medal from the Numismatic Society in 1884. Smith wrote many articles on antiquarian subjects, in particular on the early coinage of Ireland. He also wrote on the early history of the College of Physicians of Ireland, and he edited manuscripts for the Irish Archaeological Society.

C. L. FALKINER, *rev.* MARIE-LOUISE LEGG

Sources *Numismatic Chronicle*, 3rd ser., 10 (1890), 22–7 · Burtchaell & Sadleir, *Alum. Dubl.* · Burke, *Gen. Ire.* (1958) · *CGPLA Ire.* (1890)
Likenesses S. C. Smith junior, oils, exh. 1891, Royal College of Physicians of Ireland, Dublin · F. W. Burton, engraving, repro. in R. Sainthill, *Olla podrida*, 2 (1853)
Wealth at death £971 18s. 9d. in England: Irish probate sealed in England, 13 June 1890, *CGPLA Eng. & Wales* · £4480 8s.: probate, 22 April 1890, *CGPLA Ire.*

Smith, Archibald (1813–1872), mathematician, born on 10 August 1813 at Greenhead, Glasgow, was the only son of James *Smith (1782–1867) of Glasgow, geologist, and his wife, Mary (1789–1847), daughter of Alexander Wilson, professor of astronomy in Glasgow University. Smith entered Glasgow University in 1828 and distinguished himself in classics, mathematics, and physics. He proceeded to Trinity College, Cambridge, in 1832 whence he graduated BA in 1836 and MA in 1839. In 1836 he was senior wrangler and first Smith's prizeman, and was elected a fellow of Trinity College. He entered Lincoln's Inn on 24 May 1836 and was called to the bar on 25 January 1841. He practised for many years as an equity draughtsman in Stone Buildings, Lincoln's Inn, and became an eminent property lawyer.

While still an undergraduate, Smith had communicated to the Cambridge Philosophical Society a paper on Fresnel's wave-surface, in which he deduced its algebraical equations by the symmetrical method, one of the first instances of its employment in analytical geometry in England. In November 1837, in conjunction with Duncan Farquharson Gregory, he founded the *Cambridge Mathematical Journal*. Between 1842 and 1847, at the request of General Sir Edward Sabine, he deduced from Poisson's general equation practical formulae for the correction of observations made on board ship, which Sabine published in the *Philosophical Transactions of the Royal Society*. In 1851 he deduced convenient tabular forms from the formulae, and in 1859 he edited the *Journal of a Voyage to Australia*, by William Scoresby the younger, giving in the introduction an exact formula for the effect of the iron of a ship on the compass, a problem with which Scoresby had been preoccupied, but had failed to solve. Smith was also the author of *Supplement to the practical rules for ascertaining the deviations of the compass caused by the ship's iron* (1855) and *A graphic method of correcting the deviations of a ship's compass* (1855). In 1862, in conjunction with Sir Frederick John Owen Evans, superintendent of the compass department of the Royal Navy, he published an *Admiralty manual for ascertaining and applying the deviations of the compass caused by the iron in a ship*. This work was translated into French, German, Russian, and Spanish.

In recognition of his services Smith received the honorary degree of LLD from the University of Glasgow in 1864, and in the following year was awarded a gold medal by the Royal Society, of which he had been elected a fellow on 5 June 1856. In 1872 he received a grant of £2000 from the government. In addition he received a gold compass set with thirty-two diamonds from the tsar of Russia, and was elected a corresponding member of the scientific committee of the imperial Russian navy.

In August 1853 Smith had married Susan Emma (*d.* 1913), daughter of Sir James *Parker of Rothley Temple, Leicestershire. They had six sons and two daughters. His fourth son, Arthur Hamilton *Smith (1860–1941), was keeper of Greek and Roman antiquities at the British Museum, while his eldest son, James Parker Smith, was MP for the Partick division of Lanarkshire. Sir Henry Babington *Smith was a younger son. Archibald Smith had once stood as the Liberal candidate for Glasgow, but was unsuccessful. He died at his London home at Riverbank, Putney, on 26 December 1872. E. I. CARLYLE, *rev.* ADRIAN RICE

Sources W. T., *PRS*, 22 (1873–4), i–xxiv · J. Belavenetz, 'Biographical sketch of Archibald Smith, Esq.', in A. Smith, *Deviations of the compass* (1865) · Ward, *Men of the reign*, 822 · Irving, *Scots.*, 483 · *Law Times* (11 Jan 1873) · Burke, *Gen. GB* · Venn, *Alum. Cant.* · *GM*, 4th ser., 3 (1867), 393 · *CGPLA Eng. & Wales* (1873)

Archives Mitchell L., Glas., Strathclyde Regional Archives, family and scientific corresp. · Sci. Mus., notebook on magnetism · Trinity Cam., undergraduate notebooks | CUL, corresp. with Lord Kelvin

Likenesses T. C. Wageman, drawing, 1835?, TCD · Maull & Co., sepia photograph, RS · engraving, repro. in Belavenetz, 'Biographical sketch'

Wealth at death £7682 13*s.* 10½*d.*: Scottish confirmation sealed in England, 28 Feb 1873, NA Scot., SC 58/42/40/227 · £14,850 0*s.* 11*d.*: additional Scottish inventory sealed in England, 18 Feb 1886, NA Scot., SC 58/42/52/938 · trust mortgage: additional inventory, 6 Sept 1887, NA Scot., SC 58/42/53/1137

Smith, Sir Archibald Levin (1836–1901), judge, was born at Salt Hill near Chichester, Sussex, on 26 August 1836, the only son of Francis Smith JP (1806–1872) of Salt Hill, and his wife, Mary Ann Lee, only daughter of Zadik Levin. After receiving private tuition at home and at Chichester, he entered Trinity College, Cambridge, in 1854. He graduated BA in 1858 with a first class in civil law classes, but was best-known as an oarsman, rowing for the university in the boat race three years running (1857, 1858, 1859). A non-swimmer, he had to be rescued in the last of the three races when the Cambridge boat sank. He remained devoted to sport, with a fondness for shooting, fishing, and cricket. He played good class cricket and was president of the MCC in 1899.

Smith had entered the Inner Temple on 27 May 1856, and was called on 17 November 1860, when he joined the home circuit. Encouraged by Lord Chief Justice Cockburn, he rapidly acquired a good junior practice, being largely employed in commercial cases and in election petitions. Though he was 'more forcible than articulate, more prone to rattling expletives than rounded periods' (*Law Journal*), his natural acuteness and energy served him well and his cheerfulness, breezy good humour, and frankness made him a general favourite. In 1879 he accepted the place of junior Treasury counsel offered by Sir John Holker, the attorney-general, which Edward Clarke had declined. The post almost guaranteed the offer of a judgeship in due course and Smith's came unusually quickly, for he joined the ranks of judges of the Queen's Bench Division on 12 April 1883. He was elected a bencher of his inn the same day, and was knighted on 20 April. Firm, courteous, and hard-working, he made a favourable impression.

In 1888 Smith and Mr Justice Day were chosen to form a special tribunal under the chairmanship of Sir James Hannen to inquire into allegations published by *The Times* against Charles Stewart Parnell and other Irish nationalists. The two junior judges maintained an almost complete silence throughout the prolonged proceedings. Smith, believed to be of Conservative views, took no active part in political life.

On 17 June 1892 Smith was promoted, with general approval, to the Court of Appeal. Most of his colleagues there were more learned lawyers, but Smith's modesty, force of character, and great intelligence enabled him to hold his own effectively among them. They found 'a startling nudity in his language' (*The Times*) but if his judgments seldom made a notable contribution to the law, he usually got it right, except in workmen's compensation cases, where he contributed to the court's unfortunate record.

Since Smith was still perhaps the most popular judge on the bench, there was no sign of dissatisfaction when he was appointed in October 1900 to succeed Lord Alverstone as master of the rolls. But the last years of his life were marred by tragedy. His wife, Isabel, daughter of J. C. Fletcher of Dale Park (not far from Salt Hill), whom he had married on 26 September 1867, suffered from a long and distressing illness, and his own health and strength soon began to fail. He was unable to find distraction in sporting pursuits from these anxieties and worries over his own cases and arrears in the court, for whose administration he was responsible. In August 1901, while staying at Wester-Elchies House, near Aberlour, Morayshire, the residence of their son-in-law, Mr Grant, his wife was drowned in the Spey, almost in Smith's presence. Smith never recovered from the shock, and died at Wester-Elchies House on 20 October 1901, a few days after resigning the mastership of the rolls. He was buried at Knockando, Morayshire, and was survived by two sons and three daughters.

HERBERT STEPHEN, *rev.* PATRICK POLDEN

Sources *The Times* (22 Oct 1901) · *Law Times* (26 Oct 1901), 579 · *Law Journal* (26 Oct 1901), 536 · Venn, *Alum. Cant.* · J. Foster, *Men-at-the-bar: a biographical hand-list of the members of the various inns of court*, 2nd edn (1885) · Walford, *County families* (1865–88) · C. Biron, *Without prejudice: impressions of life and law* (1936) · D. Walker-Smith and E. Clarke, *The life of Sir Edward Clarke* (1939) · *GM*, 4th ser., 4 (1867), 672 · Sainty, *Judges* · Sainty, *King's counsel*

Likenesses Spy [L. Ward], caricature chromolithograph, NPG; repro. in *VF* (3 Nov 1888)

Smith, Arnold Dunbar (1866–1933). *See under* Brewer, Cecil Claude (1871–1918).

Smith, Arthur Hamilton (1860–1941), museum curator, was born on 2 October 1860 at 14 Ashley Place, Westminster, the fourth son in a family of six sons and two younger daughters of the mathematician Archibald *Smith (1813–1872) and his wife, Susan Emma (1835/6–1913), daughter of Sir James *Parker and his wife, Mary. His eldest brother was Sir James Parker Smith and a younger was Sir Henry Babington *Smith. His other three brothers achieved distinction in the army, the navy, and the church. He attended Dr Spyers's school at Weybridge and was then a scholar of Winchester College (1874–9). At the end of his time at Winchester he renounced a nomination to the Indian Civil Service, going instead to Trinity College, Cambridge, where he obtained a second class in part one of the classical tripos (1881) and a first class in part two (1883) with special distinction in archaeology, and was captain of the university shooting eight.

After lecturing in Cambridge on early Greek art and

travelling in Asia Minor with W. M. Ramsay, Smith entered the department of Greek and Roman antiquities in the British Museum as assistant, second class, on 30 April 1886 and was promoted assistant, first class, on 11 February 1893. He assisted the keeper, A. S. Murray, in the rearrangement of the sculpture, and produced the *Catalogue of Engraved Gems* (1888); the *Catalogue of Sculpture* (3 vols., 1892–1904); the *Guide* to the department, which ran through several editions; and *White Athenian Vases* (1896) with reproductions by cyclograph, an invention of his own for the photographing of cylindrical surfaces (for which he received a gold medal at the Berlin photographic exhibition in 1896). He also published catalogues of the Lansdowne (1889), Yarborough (1897), and Woburn Abbey (1900) collections. In 1893–4 and again in 1896 he took part in expeditions to Cyprus, the results of which were published in *Excavations in Cyprus* (1900).

On 28 April 1897 Smith married Gertrude Prudence Blomfield (1870–1961), daughter of the Revd Blomfield Jackson, later prebendary of St Paul's Cathedral; there was one daughter of the marriage, Elizabeth. Until 1902 they lived at 121 Bedford Court Mansions and then at 22 Endsleigh Street, also in Bloomsbury, until 1912, when Smith obtained an official residence in the British Museum.

On 11 July 1904 Smith became assistant keeper of his department and on 1 January 1909 keeper. As such he was responsible for the successful measures taken to protect the collections during the First World War. *The Sculptures of the Parthenon*, in two folio volumes (1910), remains a standard work of reference, as does a fully documented article on the Elgin marbles ('Lord Elgin and his collection', *Journal of Hellenic Studies*, 36, 1916, 163–372), published to mark the centenary of their acquisition, which vindicates Lord Elgin from the aspersions of Byron and others. He continued the British Museum tradition of augmenting the exhibition of the sculptures of the Parthenon with casts, models, diagrams, and photographs, and was dismayed by the minimalist exhibition planned in the 1930s for the Duveen Gallery. His acquisitions as keeper could not match the spectacular ensembles of some of his predecessors, but the high quality of many individual objects in a wide range of materials earned the admiration and even the envy of at least one of his successors.

Outside the museum Smith's principal activity was in connection with the Society for the Promotion of Hellenic Studies, of which he was a member of council from 1887 onwards, joint editor of the journal from 1892 to 1898, librarian from 1896 to 1908, and again from 1912 to 1924, vice-president from 1907 to 1924 and again from 1929 until his death, and president from 1924 to 1929. He was also vice-president of the Society for the Promotion of Roman Studies, and was associated with the Byzantine Research Fund.

Smith retired from the museum in October 1925, but in 1928–30 he served as director of the British School at Rome, with which he had been connected since its foundation, and he briefly undertook the directorship again in 1932, when he did excellent service at a time of disciplinary difficulties. He was a good linguist, and established very friendly relations with foreign archaeologists.

Smith's natural quietness of manner was intensified by deafness in one ear and tinnitus, caused by neglected mumps in 1876; but his thoroughness and conscientiousness, added to natural ability, made him a very efficient administrator. He was elected FSA in 1893, FBA in 1924, and an honorary associate of the Royal Institute of British Architects in 1925, and was a corresponding member of the German and Austrian archaeological institutes. He was an honorary member of the Art Workers' Guild and of the Yorkshire Philosophical Society. In 1926 he was appointed CB. In 1932 he settled in Weybridge, Surrey, and he died there, at his home, 2 Balfour Road, on 28 September 1941. He was buried in Weybridge cemetery on 1 October 1941. F. G. Kenyon, *rev.* B. F. Cook

Sources F. G. Kenyon, 'Arthur Hamilton Smith, 1860–1941', *PBA*, 27 (1941), 393–404 • *The Times* (30 Sept 1941) • staff applications, minutes of the standing committee of trustees, 6 July 1912, BM, vol. 56, p. 2, no. 969 • *British Museum: list of the trustees of the standing committee, and sub-committee … also the establishment* (1895) • *British Museum: list of the trustees of the standing committee, and sub-committee … also the establishment* (1905) • cemetery records, Weybridge cemetery, Elmbridge borough council, grave no. 1146 • *WWW, 1897–1915* • *WWW, 1941–50* • 'List of officers', *Journal of Hellenic Studies* • *Proceedings of the Society of Antiquaries of London*, 2nd ser., 14 (1892–3), 277 • *RIBA Journal*, 32 (1924–5), 646 • Principal Registry of the Family Division, London, index of wills, 1913, 1941, 1961; Smith's will • census returns, 1871, PRO, RG 10/716, fol. 42, p. 1; 1881, RG 11/662, fol. 28, p. 1, RG 11/663, fol. 23, p. 40 • *CGPLA Eng. & Wales* (1942)

Archives BM, department of Greek and Roman antiquities, field notebooks from excavations in Cyprus • Trinity Cam., corresp. and personal papers

Wealth at death £7305 12s. 5d.: probate, 13 Jan 1942, *CGPLA Eng. & Wales*

Smith, Arthur Lionel (1850–1924), historian and college head, was born in London on 4 December 1850, the second son of William Henry Smith, a civil engineer, and his wife, Alice Elizabeth, daughter of the painter Jacob *Strutt. Smith's father died young, leaving the family badly off. The widow sent her first son to sea, got Arthur a place at Christ's Hospital (1857–69), and took the other children to Italy; after losing a second husband she moved to Chicago. Arthur, entering the school at six, by default made it his home; he won prizes, honours, and an exhibition to Balliol College, Oxford. He went up there in 1869 just as Benjamin Jowett was beginning his mastership. Smith earned first-class honours in classical moderations (1871) and *literae humaniores* (1873); in 1874 he was placed in the second class in the school of modern history. He won the Lothian prize for history that year. Meanwhile, he became a university and college prizeman, and built up his slight frame so that he could row as Balliol's bow; in 1873 his college went head of the river. He remained a keen boatman, and later took up bicycling, hockey, and skating.

In 1874 Smith became a fellow of Trinity College, Oxford. He taught classics for two years (and rowed in the college boat), and then studied for the bar at Lincoln's Inn until 1879, an important year for him. In it he married

Arthur Lionel Smith (1850–1924), by Francis Dodd, 1915

Mary Florence (*b.* 1855/6, *d.* in or after 1924), eldest daughter of John Forster Baird of Bowmont Hill, Northumberland; left Trinity; and began teaching history at Balliol. He was elected fellow of Balliol in 1882, and remained there until his death. Under Smith's tutorship, the history school grew steadily. Thanks in part to his teaching, Balliol soon needed a second and then a third tutor in the subject. Each week in a normal term, he gave thirty or more hours, famed for humour and personal sympathy, to his pupils. Examination honours, prizes, and fellowships at All Souls College reflected the success of Balliol's methods of recruitment and tuition. Lewis Namier, whom Smith personally admitted to Balliol, described him as 'perhaps the best history teacher of our time', emphasizing his complete commitment to tutorial work and his pupils. Two decades after Smith died, his pupils Maurice Powicke, Keith Feiling, and G. N. Clark held Oxford and Cambridge's leading chairs of modern history.

In Smith's first years, he became a favourite of Benjamin Jowett, who admired his aptitude for training students with poor school records. Many such students lived with the Smith family before matriculating, and became lasting friends. Smith was also skilful at bringing on African and Asian students, who found Balliol (and the Smiths' home) welcoming. Jowett responded by coming to share Smith's taste for sports and games, and consequently developing Balliol's playing fields in Holywell. Near them, the master ordered a spacious home, the King's Mound, to be built for the large Smith family and their many boarders. It was finished in 1893, while Jowett lay dying.

Smith thus had considerable political gifts. On Jowett's death he organized the successful campaign to elect Edward Caird as the new master, though subsequently establishing a firm alliance with J. L. Strachan-Davidson, the dean and internal candidate against Caird. When Caird retired in 1907, Strachan-Davidson almost automatically succeeded, and Smith became dean; Strachan-Davidson's death in 1916 led to Smith's own immediate election as master.

This managerial talent also made Smith a leader in the university at large. From 1884 to 1887, and again in 1895 and 1901–3, he served as an examiner in the final honour school of modern history (he also was external examiner in other universities). He joined Edward Armstrong, Richard Lodge, C. R. L. Fletcher, and others in a strong tutors' association, which came to determine the history school's syllabus and to resist critics like Charles Oman and Charles Firth who sought to give the school a more 'scholarly', professorial tone. In 1907 he built strong ties as a committeeman in Oxford's dealings with the Workers' Educational Association (WEA), and later taught at the WEA's summer school at Balliol. He promoted women's education in the university, and until his death tutored students at Lady Margaret Hall.

Smith long tried to meet his family's claims materially by taking on pupils for cramming, and by personally teaching his daughters. Both habits survived 1906, when he received one of the first two Jowett fellowships, endowed by his friend Lord Newlands to reward exceptional teaching. This nearly doubled his income but did not diminish his commitment to teaching: in the Christmas vacation of 1907, he was giving three extra hours a week to Lawrence Jones, an oarsman and baronet's heir whom he was cramming (unsuccessfully) for the fellowship examination at All Souls College.

During the First World War, as a firm believer in its moral and political rightness, Smith threw himself into the 'war effort', lecturing at workers' meetings and at public schools, making long railway journeys, often in term time. Between 1914 and 1917 he served on the archbishops' committee on church and state, writing with Sir Lewis Dibdin the section of its report on the history of church and state in England. After 1916 he served on another archbishops' committee, on industrial problems, and from 1917 to 1919 chaired the Ministry of Reconstruction's committee on adult education.

Smith thus had scant time for scholarly writing. According to his wife, he mostly wrote late at night, after poring over undergraduate essays and planning the next day's tutorials. His earliest pieces were hack work, as in sections of *Social England*, edited by H. D. Traill from 1893. He also wrote summary notes for students' revision, which he began issuing around 1890; his *Notes on Stubbs's Charters* was published in 1906. The year before, during a row over C. H. Firth's attack on the tutors' association, Smith was invited to be the Ford lecturer in English history. He accepted, he told the Cambridge legal historian, F. W. Maitland, in part to defend the tutors' honour as competent historians. The lectures, published in 1913, were entitled *Church and State in the Middle Ages*, but dealt mostly with quarrels between popes and the Holy Roman Emperor Frederick II, whose life Smith had long been trying to write. The biography survives only as bundles of notes and sketches in the Balliol archives.

The preparation of *Church and State* was delayed by Smith's busy routine of teaching and administration. When Maitland died in 1906, Smith agreed to compile a bibliography of his work, and to give two lectures on it as Oxford's public memorial. Issuing that work in 1908 delayed a promised chapter in volume 6 of the Cambridge Modern History on 'English political philosophy in the seventeenth and eighteenth centuries'. Its publication in 1909 led to an invitation to visit Colombia University, New York, the next winter—his sole sabbatical leave. Smith gave a set of lectures on political discourse, which summed up his years of teaching Hobbes's *Leviathan*, a set text in the history school; he later kept recasting the lectures, but never quite finished the project.

However, Smith had little personal interest in publishing. As one of Oxford's first married dons, free of pressure to be ordained, he was none the less as pastoral a tutor as any cleric. He is said to have defined a good tutorial relationship as one requiring 'muddy boots': tutor and undergraduate hiked across country talking at length. He cared little for outward piety, or until later life for refined theology. Yet his lectures sought common ground between Christian and civic values, and in later years he wrote for Christian socialist publications. Such an approach exemplified a tradition in Balliol, derived from Jowett and T. H. Green and later upheld by Smith's successor in the mastership, A. D. Lindsay.

Few of Smith's known writings, including manuscripts at Balliol, directly show the man himself. His character is best revealed in his family life. Mary Smith showed prowess in managing a man untidy, overworked, generous to a fault; she also excelled as a steward of a family barely living within its means, and as a hostess. In time she became his secretary, and later his official biographer. They had two sons, including the educationist (Arthur) Lionel Forster *Smith, and seven daughters who made notable marriages, for example to Reader Bullard, Henry Clay, and Harold Hartley.

Smith suffered some sporting injuries, but generally enjoyed good health. In 1902 he took a term's leave in Egypt for rheumatism. His war activities combined with his new duties as master ran him down; later, leading the revival of college life exhausted him. Yet he kept teaching, writing, and serving on the university's hebdomadal council, on the board of its endowment fund and as a curator of the Bodleian Library. Smith was a popular master, and his public service restored the national reputation of the post which Jowett had achieved for it. But the circumstances of the war and his subsequent ill health lessened Smith's ability to shape the college internally. He had a major operation in 1921 and died after two months' illness at the master's lodgings on 12 April 1924. He was buried in Holywell cemetery, Oxford. R. L. PATTERSON

Sources [M. B. Smith], *Arthur Lionel Smith, Master of Balliol College, 1916–1924* (1928) • J. Jones, *Balliol College: a history, 1263–1939* (1988) • J. Kenyon, *The history men: the historical profession in England since the Renaissance* (1983) • P. R. H. Slee, *Learning and a liberal education: the study of modern history in the universities of Oxford, Cambridge and Manchester, 1800–1914* (1986) • R. E. Soffer, 'The modern university and national values, 1850–1930', *Historical Research*, 60 (1987), 166–87 • R. Soffer, 'Nation, duty, character and confidence: history at Oxford, 1850–1914', *HJ*, 30 (1987), 77–104 • *CGPLA Eng. & Wales* (1924) • m. cert.

Archives Balliol Oxf., corresp. and papers | HLRO, corresp. with W. G. S. Adams • HLRO, Lloyd George MSS

Likenesses F. Dodd, oils, 1914, Balliol Oxf. • F. Dodd, etching, 1915, NPG [*see illus.*] • F. Watt, oils, *c.*1918, Balliol Oxf. • pastel drawing (after F. Dodd), Balliol Oxf. • photograph, Balliol Oxf.

Wealth at death £4162 19*s.* 6*d.*: probate, 8 July 1924, *CGPLA Eng. & Wales*

Smith, Arthur Norman Exton- (1920–1990), geriatrician, was born on 7 January 1920 in Graham Street, Ilkestone, Derbyshire, the elder of the two sons of Arthur Smith (1881–1975), and his wife, Ethel Mary (1887–1960), daughter of Robert and Augusta Robertson of Nottingham; both the Smith parents were teachers and both sons became medical professors. Born Arthur Norman Exton Smith, he assumed the surname Exton-Smith in 1943, perhaps to distinguish himself from his brother, David Robertson Smith. He was educated at Nottingham high school, Pembroke College, Cambridge, and University College Hospital (UCH), London. He qualified in 1943 and in the following year joined the Royal Army Medical Corps, landing in Normandy the day after D-day.

Demobilized in 1947, Exton-Smith returned to UCH for specialist training. His professor, Max Rosenheim, suggested that he should assist Lord Amulree in a new department of geriatric medicine at St Pancras Hospital, which with the advent of the National Health Service in 1948 had been taken over by UCH from the London county council. The inheritance was bleak: the wards were overcrowded; there were no bed curtains, few chairs, and only primitive bedside lockers. The patients were mostly confined to bed—none had been properly examined; they had simply been labelled 'senile'. It was enough to drive away any ambitious doctor. But Exton-Smith, impressed by Amulree's enthusiasm, stayed. Within a year he published a paper showing what could be achieved even in such a medical backwater. He stressed the interest, the job satisfaction, and the vast field for research—concerns which were to occupy him for the rest of his life. In 1951 he was appointed consultant geriatrician to the Whittington Hospital, and on 29 August of that year he married Jean Barbara Belcher (1924–1990), a nurse; they were to have two children. In 1959 he added to his post at the Whittington that of physician to the Hospital of St John and St Elizabeth. In 1966 he returned to UCH as Lord Amulree's successor, and in 1973 UCH created a chair and he became the first professor of geriatric medicine in London.

In 1955 Exton-Smith published *Medical Problems of Old Age*, a pioneer textbook of geriatric medicine. But he preferred to write in collaboration with colleagues and was an excellent editor. His greatest interests were in nutrition and metabolism, the ageing of the autonomic system, and the regulation of body temperature. In 1964 he chaired the BMA committee which first drew attention to hypothermia and wrote its report. His research also covered many other fields, including organization, nursing, bone disease, pressure sores, and terminal care. Latterly he used computerized testing to study dementia. In every field he made fundamental contributions. Elected a fellow of the Royal College of Physicians in 1964, he became the first geriatrician on the college council and the secretary of its first geriatrics committee, and he persuaded the college to recognize geriatrics as a speciality. He was for sixteen years a member of a government committee on food policy and for fifteen years a consultant adviser on geriatric medicine to the Department of Health. He was also a governor of the Centre for Policy on Ageing.

Exton-Smith became assistant secretary of the British Geriatrics Society in 1952 when it had 100 members, and subsequently became secretary, editorial secretary, and president. When he retired the membership was 1500 and a small medical club had become an influential professional society. He was the first editor of the society's journal (1959–85). He wrote or edited four textbooks of geriatric medicine, four books on nutrition and metabolism, a report on geriatric nursing, the proceedings of several international conferences, and 135 papers. He knew everybody in his field and was an enthusiastic organizer of meetings both nationally and internationally. Through the British Council he arranged courses for physicians from abroad; he set up joint meetings in the USA, Belgium, the Netherlands, Germany, and Italy; and, an immensely hard worker, he even found time to be secretary to a dining club for Cambridge medical graduates.

Exton-Smith received many honours including the appointment as CBE in 1981, the Henderson medal of the American Geriatrics Society, the Moxon medal of the Royal College of Physicians, the Founder's medal of the British Geriatrics Society, the Sandoz prize for research in gerontology, and an honorary DM at Nottingham. He retired in 1985, but returned to the Whittington to conduct research. For the last eight years of his life he suffered from cancer but between operations continued to research, to write, and to lecture. His courage and determination were beyond praise. He died on 29 March 1990 at the Edenhall Marie Curie Home, London, and was cremated at Golders Green. During his life he did more than any other person to bring geriatric medicine from the professional backwater in which it originated to the position of a major speciality of medicine. R. E. Irvine

Sources Munk, *Roll*, 9.160–66 · private information (2004) · m. cert.
Archives British Geriatrics Society, London · Royal Society of Medicine, London
Likenesses photograph (excellent), British Geriatrics Society, 1 St Andrew's Place, London
Wealth at death £293,332: probate, 1 Aug 1990, *CGPLA Eng. & Wales*

Smith, Arthur William Watson (1825–1861). *See under* Smith, Albert Richard (1816–1860).

Smith, Sir (Charles) Aubrey (1863–1948), actor and cricketer, was born on 21 July 1863 at 9 Finsbury Place South, London, the son of Charles John Smith, a doctor, and his wife, Sarah Ann Clode. He was educated at Charterhouse School and St John's College, Cambridge (1881–4), where he studied medicine. Smith earned a great reputation as a cricketer, captaining the university eleven and, on graduating from Cambridge, becoming captain of the Sussex county team in 1886 and subsequently captain of the England eleven on tour in Australia and South Africa.

Aubrey Smith first appeared on the professional stage with A. B. Tapping's company at Hastings in 1892. In 1894 he played Aubrey Tanqueray on tour with Mrs Patrick Campbell's company in Arthur Wing Pinero's *The Second Mrs Tanqueray*; and first appeared on the London stage on 13 March 1895, playing the Revd Amos Winterfield in another Pinero play, *The Notorious Mrs Ebbsmith*. He rapidly became a well-known leading actor, appearing with John Hare, George Alexander, Fred Terry, Mrs Patrick Campbell, Johnston Forbes-Robertson, and other famous actor-managers. On 15 August 1896 he married Isabella Mary Scott (*b*. 1871/2), daughter of Major Alexander Wood.

Between 1898 and 1900 Aubrey Smith was the business manager of the St James's Theatre but returned to acting in 1900. From 1904 onward he began to accept engagements in the United States as well as in London. There was no year, indeed, between 1900 and 1930, when he did not appear in a new production (sometimes of a new play, sometimes of a revival) in either London or New York, his first appearance in the latter city being in 1911. In the pursuit of this international acting career he is said to have crossed the Atlantic over a hundred times—in an age when each journey took five or six days each way.

From 1915 onward Aubrey Smith appeared in numerous silent films and successfully negotiated the tricky transformation to sound films in the 1930s. From then on he became better known as a film actor than a stage actor; he was never a 'film star' but was a very sound and reliable player of supporting 'character' roles, specializing in upper-class English gentlemen, and being seen in dozens of films. These included *Lives of a Bengal Lancer* (1934) and *Clive of India* (1934). Aubrey Smith made his home in the USA during the 1930s and 1940s, where he resided in Beverly Hills, close to Hollywood.

As a stage actor Aubrey Smith was most at ease in light, popular 'entertainment' plays. Unlike his near-contemporary Robert Loraine, who enjoyed and rose to the challenge of playing Strindberg and Shakespeare, he very rarely undertook plays of any very serious import. However, he did once play a Shakespearian role (as Frederick in *As You Like It* in 1896) and he appeared in *Votes for Women!* by Elizabeth Robins at the Court Theatre, under Harley Granville Barker's direction, in April and May 1907. He also played the lead in the first production of Clemence Dane's *A Bill of Divorcement* at the St Martin's Theatre in 1921. St John Ervine, the theatre critic for *The Observer*, noted that he managed in this 'to do what was almost impossible, retain sympathy for a sympathetic character at a moment when that character is behaving in an incomprehensible and unsympathetic fashion' (20 March 1921).

The play was something of a *cause célèbre*. Among the better-known popular plays of the day in which Aubrey Smith also played leading parts were *The Liars* by Henry Arthur Jones (1916), A. A. Milne's *Mr Pim Passes By* (1922), W. Somerset Maugham's *The Constant Wife* (1926, in New York), and J. Galsworthy's *Old English* (1941 and 1943, in San Francisco and on tour in America).

Aubrey Smith was never a great actor, but he was a very popular performer of great charm, technical proficiency, energy, and industry. Early in his career, Max Beerbohm, then a distinguished theatre critic, was struck by his limitations, which sprang from a certain over-solemnity and a trivializing lack of inner seriousness. Reviewing one of his early performances, in *The Finding of Nancy* (1902) by Netta Syrett, Beerbohm wrote that 'Smith, in manner and costume, was more like a cavalry officer than an obscure journalist. He came amiss in the milieu of the play. But he did his best' (Beerbohm, *More Theatres*, 467). Beerbohm was equally critical of his role in Oscar Wilde's *Lady Windermere's Fan* in 1904. As Lord Darlington, Smith had to say 'the extravagant and silly things' for which Lady Windermere reproves him. Unfortunately, Beerbohm considered that he spoke 'with all the portentousness of an eminent physician examining an invalid' (ibid., 103–4). In 1905 Aubrey Smith played Colonel Gray in the first production of J. M. Barrie's *Alice Sit-by-the-Fire*. Beerbohm commented that he 'might surely manage to behave rather more like an amiable and quite ordinary colonel who is glad to be home among his family, and rather less like a distinguished general whose career has just been blasted by failure in a crucial campaign. He might, in fact, play lightlier' (ibid., 155–6).

Even in 1905 Aubrey Smith was an old-fashioned actor: tall, handsome, deft, and assured, he was as immune from the uneasy influence of the new drama of Ibsen, Shaw, Strindberg, Chekhov, Hauptmann, and Schnitzler as he was from the new theatre practices of Antoine, Stanislavsky, Copeau, Craig, and Meyerhold. Sensibly, he recognized his own métier. With the help of his agreeable personality and his abundant native energy he made a busy and successful career, especially in the USA. *Who's Who in the Theatre* lists no fewer than eighteen plays, between 1902 and 1943, in which Aubrey Smith played the part of a titled gentleman. His roles included Lord Darlington, Colonel Gray, Sir Marcus Ordeyne, the Marquis of Tallemont, the Hon. Geoffrey Stoner, Sir Philip Lilley, Sir Christopher Deering, Sir George Knowsley, Sir Theodore Frome, Sir Basil Winterton, and Sir Thomas Ryecroft. Finally, in 1944, he was himself knighted 'for services to the theatre'.

Sir Aubrey Smith died at his home, 629 North Rexford Drive, Beverly Hills, California, on 20 December 1948 at the age of eighty-five. He was survived by his wife and a daughter.

ERIC SALMON

Sources *The Times* (21 Dec 1948) • *The Times* (24 Dec 1948) • I. Herbert, ed., *Who's who in the theatre*, 17th edn, 2 vols. (1981) • M. Beerbohm, *More theatres* (1969) • M. Beerbohm, *Last theatres* (1970) • Venn, *Alum. Cant.* • *CGPLA Eng. & Wales* (1950) • private information (2004) • *WWW* • b. cert. • m. cert.

Wealth at death £1038 19*s.* 2*d.*—effects in England: administration with will, 20 June 1950, *CGPLA Eng. & Wales*

Smith, Audrey Ursula (1915–1981), medical scientist and cryobiologist, was born in India on 21 May 1915, and baptized at Chindwara, India, one of the two children of Alan Kenyon Smith, of the Indian Civil Service, and Gertrude May Smith.

Audrey Smith entered King's College, London, at seventeen years old, and obtained a first class BSc (hons.) degree in general science in 1935. At Bedford College for Women she specialized in physiology, again obtaining a first class BSc (Sp) degree (1936). She returned to King's College holding a research scholarship (1936–7). The following year she spent in the USA, at Vassar College as a demonstrator in physiology, then at the Marine Biological Laboratory, Woods Hole, USA, investigating the action of the neurotransmitter acetylcholine on single muscle fibres.

However, the Second World War interrupted Audrey Smith's research career. She studied medicine at King's College Hospital from 1938 to 1942. Once qualified, she practised as a medical doctor for the rest of the war, at King's College Hospital in 1942, and at associated hospitals in 1943. She worked as a clinical pathologist at King's College Hospital (1943–4), transferring to the Public Health Laboratory, Epsom (1944–5), then the Emergency Public Health Laboratory Service, Nottingham (1945–6). She resumed her research career at the National Institute for Medical Research in London in May 1946, under Professor Alan Parkes, who was working on problems of fertility in animals, and attempting, unsuccessfully, to freeze human and fowl spermatozoa. In 1948 Christopher Polge, a poultry farmer's son with a degree in agricultural science, joined them. Parkes set him to work with Audrey Smith because she 'had already proved to have quite exceptional gifts in practical research' (Parkes, 143).

Together, Polge and Smith made the momentous discovery that a medium containing glycerol allowed the preservation of spermatozoa and red blood cells by freezing, without cell damage upon subsequent thawing. The fertility of the frozen fowl semen was greatly improved by gradual removal of the glycerol by dialysis before insemination. The serendipitous discovery is described in her monograph (*Biological Effects of Freezing and Supercooling*, 1961). Different optimal experimental conditions had to be discovered for bull semen, and for each type of cell and tissue, ranging from bone-marrow stem cells, through skin, cartilage, ovarian eggs, and tissue from endocrine glands. For example, successful long-term, low-temperature banking of corneas to enable their transplantation to blind patients, required many months of experimenting to establish the right conditions for the survival of the corneal endothelium. Peter Medawar remarked 'living cells will do for Audrey things they won't do for other people' (Parkes, 159).

Audrey Smith was awarded a William Julius Mickle fellowship of the University of London (1953–4). She was elected a member of the Physiological Society (1953) and awarded a DSc (1956), and she gained an MD (1962).

Audrey Ursula Smith (**1915–1981**), by unknown photographer, *c*.1950

Audrey Smith became head of the division of low temperature biology in 1967, later renamed the division of cryobiology. When the division moved to the Clinical Research Centre at Harrow in 1970, she did not wish to remain with it because she held strong views against 'experimenting' on patients. In spite of reassurance that she did not need to work with human subjects at the Clinical Research Centre, she transferred to the external scientific staff of the Medical Research Council, at the Royal National Orthopaedic Hospital and the Institute of Orthopaedics at Stanmore (1970–74). She wrote that there she was distracted from fundamental studies in order to work in the growing and most important field of cryosurgery, on problems such as those involved in repairing worn joints with grafts of cartilage and bone (Smith).

Audrey Smith was described by Christopher Polge as one of the main founders of cryobiology, and an outstanding scientist who did not get the recognition she deserved. However, she was extremely modest about her achievements. On accepting the prestigious Kammerlingh Onnes medal in 1973, she remarked 'it is the proudest, happiest day of my entire career, and at the same time I have never felt more humble' (Smith, 91). She felt that she was not in the same class of intellect as the previous winners of the medal. Colleagues had come and gone from the field of low-temperature biology in the previous twenty-five years, while she had become the ageing continuity girl. She thought her main job was to initiate new lines of work, and to help younger scientists get started. They were very appreciative of her advice and help. One wrote 'Despite being superficially untidy, Audrey's chief characteristic was in clarity of thought, which is exemplified in her writings' (Bindman, 139).

Audrey Smith never married, but had many friends and two nieces and two nephews (children of her brother, Colonel Alan Patrick Smith) and a goddaughter, who all received bequests in her will. In her later years her corgi dog Katie was a loved companion who even accompanied her to scientific meetings. Audrey Smith died of cancer in the Edgware General Hospital, London, on 3 June 1981. The vicar of her Anglican church, St Paul's, Mill Hill, led a service on 9 June at her cremation at Hendon Park crematorium, where her ashes were scattered.

LYNN J. BINDMAN

Sources A. U. Smith, 'Twenty-five years of research in low temperature biology', *Koeltechniek*, 67 (1974), 91–100 • C. Polge, *Cryo Letters*, 2 (1981), 225–8 • L. Bindman, A. Brading, and T. Tansey, eds., *Women physiologists: an anniversary celebration of their contributions to British physiology* (1993) • A. Parkes, *Off-beat biologists* (1985) • *CGPLA Eng. & Wales* (1981) • D. Pegg, 'Cryobiology: life in the deep freeze', *Biologist*, 41 (1994), 53–6 • private information (2004) [C. Polge and J. Farrant] • d. cert. • BL OIOC, N/1/406, fol. 159

Archives National Institute of Medical Research, London, MSS and list of publications

Likenesses photograph, *c*.1950, National Institute for Medical Research, London [*see illus.*] • photograph, repro. in *Koeltechniek*, 66 (1973), 315

Wealth at death £134,011—gross: probate, 10 Sept 1981, *CGPLA Eng. & Wales*

Smith, Augustus John (1804–1872), landowner and philanthropist, was born in London on 15 September 1804, the eldest of six children of James Smith (1768–1843), landowner and scion of a Nottingham banking family, and his second wife, Mary Isabella (1784–1823), eldest daughter of Augustus Pechell of Great Berkhamsted. After the death of his half-brother James in 1811, Augustus became heir to his father's considerable property, centred on Ashlyns Hall, Hertfordshire. He entered Harrow School about 1814, and matriculated from Christ Church, Oxford, on 23 April 1822; he graduated BA on 23 February 1826.

Bored with the life of leisure into which he was raised, Smith now threw himself into projects of social improvement in Hertfordshire. He supported the reform of the poor laws instituted nationally in 1834—and had anticipated it in a local reform at Great Berkhamsted—but he felt that its disciplinary impact ought in justice to be accompanied by the ameliorative effects of education. In 1834 he opened a 'school of industry' for boys and girls, and in 1841, after a lengthy lawsuit, he procured the reopening of the long-moribund grammar school at Great Berkhamsted.

Smith's ambitions for these reforms and especially his advocacy of non-sectarian Christian education set him at odds with local tory and Anglican interests, though he was himself a conforming churchgoer. That this antagonism lingered throughout his life was evident in a celebrated episode of 6 March 1866. When the second Earl Brownlow enclosed with strong iron fences about a third of the common land of that parish which was in front of the earl's seat, Ashridge Park, Smith engaged a band of navvies from London, who pulled the fences down. This incident attracted much attention at the time and was the subject of a poem ('A Lay of Modern England') in *Punch*, on 24 March 1866. He vindicated his opposition to the enclosure in *Berkhamstead Common: Statement by Augustus Smith* (1866). In 1870 Smith obtained an injunction against any future enclosure of the common, an early victory for the struggle to preserve open space for public access, in which Smith was associated with the Commons Preservation Society.

In 1834, however, Smith had found an unobstructed field for his projects of social improvement. In that year he obtained, for a £20,000 fine, a lease from the crown (initially for ninety-nine years, contingent on three lives) of the Isles of Scilly. For the rest of his life, he devoted himself earnestly to the development of these poor and neglected islands, where he resided for at least eight months in each year. The church at St Mary's, the principal island, was completed at his expense and according to his own plain design, and when that at St Martin's was nearly destroyed by lightning in 1866, it was rebuilt mainly at his cost. He built a pier at Hugh Town in St Mary's, and constructed for his own habitation the house of Tresco Abbey, with its grounds and fishponds. The magnificent display of sub-tropical plants that he collected at Tresco—unique to the British Isles—began to attract excursionists after railway and steamboat connections were made in 1859.

Throughout the islands Smith consolidated the farm holdings and rebuilt the homesteads, but he would not allow the admittance of a second family in any dwelling; he also imposed compulsory education and industrial training on the young, and a penny rate on his tenants to help to pay for it. But beyond such levies these improvements cost £80,000, and during the first twelve years of his term they absorbed the whole of the revenue. They were set out by him in a tract entitled *Thirteen Years' Stewardship of the Islands of Scilly* (1848), and were controversial among both Scillonians and those in metropolitan intellectual circles, who were bemused by the mix of liberalism and authoritarianism. J. A. Froude and S. G. Osborne were loud in their praise, but J. S. Mill denounced Smith's paternal government as detestable.

In 1852 Smith contested the borough of Truro in Cornwall as a Liberal, but he was defeated by eight votes. In 1857 he was returned without a contest, and he represented the constituency until 1865, when his doubts about parliamentary reform (outlined in his *Constitutional Reflections on the Present Aspects of Parliamentary Government*, 1866) caused his constituents to cool to him; he then retired voluntarily. He was president of the Royal Geological Society of Cornwall at Penzance from 1858 to 1864, and he held the presidency of the Royal Institution of Cornwall at Truro from November 1863 to November 1865. As provincial grandmaster for the freemasons of Cornwall from July 1863, he promoted the establishment of a county fund for aged and infirm freemasons.

Until late in life Smith kept his imposing figure and handsome good looks, and a full head of dark hair, though he ran latterly to fat. Cool and commanding, plain-spoken and unmannered, he never married, yet a few intimates of both sexes penetrated his reserve, notably Lady Sophia Tower (aunt of his adversary Lord Brownlow). In public life his reputation was for over-persistent and often footling controversy (as in a tedious exchange of correspondence and pamphlets with Trinity House over pilotage). His forcefulness in both life and work has inspired at least two works of fiction, explicitly in Ann Schlee's *The Proprietor* (1983) and more loosely in Jim Crace's *Signals of Distress* (1994).

After a severe illness Smith died of pneumonia at the Duke of Cornwall Hotel, Plymouth, on 31 July 1872, and was buried in the churchyard of St Buryan, Cornwall, on 6 August. His will and seven codicils were proved in March 1873, and the lesseeship in the Isles of Scilly was left to his nephew, Thomas Algernon Smith-Dorrien-Smith, who subsequently married Edith, the daughter of Lady Sophia Tower. PETER MANDLER

Sources E. Inglis-Jones, *Augustus Smith of Scilly* (1969) • G. F. Matthews, *The isles of Scilly: a constitutional, economic and social survey* (1960) • [A. Smith], *Thirteen years' stewardship of the islands of Scilly* (1848) • A. Smith, *Apology for parochial education on comprehensive principles* (1836) • R. King, *Tresco: England's island of flowers* (1985) • A. Smith, *A true and faithful history of the family of Smith* (1861) • *DNB*

Archives Tresco Abbey, Isles of Scilly

Likenesses attrib. J. Hoppner or J. Opie, oils, 1807?, Tresco Abbey, Isles of Scilly • oils, 1818?, Tresco Abbey, Isles of Scilly • ivory miniature, 1825, Tresco Abbey, Isles of Scilly • W. Jenkyns, photograph, 1856, repro. in C. Thomas, *Views and likenesses* (1988) • oils, 1863?, Tresco Abbey, Isles of Scilly • oils, 1863?, Freemasons' Lodge, St Mary's, Isles of Scilly • J. Gibson, photograph, 1865–6, repro. in C. Thomas, *Views and likenesses* (1988)

Wealth at death under £60,000: double probate, April 1875, *CGPLA Eng. & Wales* (1873)

Smith, Bartholomew. *See* Scholes, Theophilus Edward Samuel (*c*.1858–*c*.1940).

Smith, Benjamin (1717–1770), merchant and politician in America, was born in the parish of St James Goose Creek, South Carolina, the first of three children of Thomas Smith (1691–1724), a small planter, and his wife, Sabina (1694?–1735), daughter of the second Landgrave Thomas Smith of South Carolina. Little is known of Benjamin Smith's early years in South Carolina. Upon his father's death in 1724, he inherited a 2000 acre plantation in St James Goose Creek along with two slaves, but he was never to devote his principal attention to agriculture. Although he retained possession of this plantation, and later added another plantation on the Ashley river to his portfolio, Benjamin Smith was to make his mark in the mercantile world.

Like many young Carolinians interested in commerce, Smith, in his teens, attached himself to a prominent Charles Town merchant—in this case, to James Crokatt—in order to learn the ways of the counting-house. It is unclear exactly when Smith began working at Crokatt's trading house in Charles Town, but extant records reveal that he was 'at Mr. Crokatt's' by June 1735. In 1738 Crokatt decided to quit Charles Town for London, but, before departing, formed a commercial partnership with Smith and Ebenezer Simmons, another clerk at the trading house. A new house called Simmons, Smith & Co. was created, wherein Crokatt, Simmons, and Smith, equal principals, were to engage 'in the trade and business of Merchandizing' (Rogers, 10), for a period of seven years effective from 1 September 1738.

Over the course of the 1740s and 1750s Smith became not only one of the great merchants of Charles Town but one of the key political powers in the Commons house of assembly, South Carolina's lower house. Smith began his ascent up the mercantile ladder during his years with Simmons, Smith & Co. His varied commercial endeavours, both with this firm, as an independent trader, and as a principal in other mercantile concerns, proved extremely successful, and by the time of his retirement, late in 1762, Smith had become the pre-eminent native-born merchant in South Carolina. Involved in a wide range of business activities—he was very active in the slave trade, as well as the deerskin trade, the importation of general merchandise, and banking and moneylending—Smith, along with men such as Gabriel Manigault, Jacob Motte, and Henry Laurens, constituted the very heart of Charles Town's commercial élite.

Smith's successes in the commercial world were matched by his achievements in the political and social realms. Having been first elected to the lower house of the South Carolina royal assembly for session 1746/7, he quickly assumed a leadership role in this legislative body, and served as speaker for most of the period between 1755 and 1763. When absent from the counting-house or the lower house, Smith likely could be found in a clubhouse of one type or another. A mason, Smith served in a variety of leadership positions in Charles Town's Solomon Lodge, and he was also active in many other fraternal, religious, and philanthropic groups, including the South Carolina Society, the Charles Town Library Society, the St Andrew's Society, and the vestry of St Philip's (Anglican) Church in Charles Town.

Smith married twice. In 1740 he wed Anne Loughton, with whom he had six children, including the arch-federalist William Loughton Smith (1758–1812), before her death on 29 February 1760. On 2 October that year Smith married Mary (*d.* 1777), daughter of Joseph Wragg, one of Charles Town's leading slave traders. They had six more children, the last born in 1769. By then Benjamin Smith was in failing health, and he died on 29 July 1770 in Newport, Rhode Island, while on holiday with his family. He was buried in Trinity churchyard, Newport, soon after his death, but was re-interred in Charles Town in October of that year. At the time of his death Smith was one of the wealthiest inhabitants in the wealthiest colony in British North America. According to extant probate records, he left a huge estate—his personalty alone was valued at well over £50,000 sterling, mostly in the form of bonds and notes—to be distributed among family members and assorted charitable causes. PETER A. COCLANIS

Sources G. C. Rogers, *Evolution of a federalist: William Loughton Smith of Charleston, 1758–1812* (1962) • W. B. Edgar and N. L. Bailey, eds., *Biographical directory of the South Carolina house of representatives*, 2 (1977) • A. S. Salley, 'William Smith and some of his descendants', *South Carolina Historical and Genealogical Magazine*, 4 (1903), 239–57 • J. P. Greene, *The quest for power: the lower houses of assembly in the southern royal colonies, 1689–1776* (1963) • *The papers of Henry Laurens*, ed. P. M. Hamer and others, 15 vols. (1968–) • W. O. Moore, 'The largest exporters of deerskins from Charles Town, 1735–1775', *South Carolina Historical Magazine*, 74 (1973), 144–50 • W. R. Higgins, 'Charles Town merchants and factors dealing in the external negro trade, 1735–1775', *South Carolina Historical Magazine*, 65 (1964), 205–17 • S. O. Stumpf, 'South Carolina's importers of general merchandise, 1735–1765', *South Carolina Historical Magazine*, 84 (1983), 1–10 • *South Carolina Gazette* (16 Aug 1770) • *South Carolina Gazette* (18 Oct 1770) • *South Carolina Gazette* (1 Nov 1770) • *South Carolina and American General Gazette* (17 April 1777)

Archives Mass. Hist. Soc., Smith–Carter papers • University of South Carolina, Columbia, Henry Laurens papers

Likenesses J. Wollaston, portrait, repro. in Rogers junior, *Evolution*; priv. coll.

Wealth at death over £50,000 sterling in personalty [*c.*£380,000–£390,000 Carolina currency]: inventory, South Carolina Archives and History Center, Columbia, inventories of estate, Y, 1769–71

Smith, Benjamin (*d.* 1833), engraver, of unknown parentage, was reputed to have been a pupil of Bartolozzi and also of Benjamin West, but no firm evidence for this has been found. His first recorded print is dated 1787. He worked mainly in stipple-engraving, producing portraits, illustrations, and allegorical and biblical subjects after prominent artists of the day. He frequently worked for the print publisher John Boydell and produced several in the important series of prints illustrating Shakespeare's plays after paintings by British artists which was published by Boydell in 1802. These plates include a scene, 'The Enchanted Island', from *The Tempest* and 'Parliament House' from *Richard II*, both after paintings by George Romney. Smith also engraved illustrations for the frontispiece and introduction of this publication. For Boydell he further produced a large stipple- and line engraving portrait of George III, after Sir William Beechey, which was published in 1804, and two engravings, published in 1799, after the allegorical frescos 'Innocence' and 'Providence' painted by John Francis Rigaud for the common council chamber in the Guildhall, London.

Smith engraved several portraits for the *British Gallery of Contemporary Portraits* (1809–22), issued by Cadell and Davies. He also published some of the portraits that he engraved himself, including those of the dramatist and songwriter Charles Dibdin and his wife, Ann (1801). He is reputed to have had many pupils, including William Holl the elder, Henry Meyer, and Thomas Uwins. He lived and worked in Somers Town, London, first at 21 Judd Place, then at 65 Ossulston Street, where he died in 1833, leaving a widow, Ann, and a son, William Henry Smith.

RUTH COHEN

Sources *DNB* • *Engraved Brit. ports.*, 6.686–7 • W. H. Friedman, *Boydell's Shakespeare Gallery* (1976), 220–45 • Redgrave, *Artists*, 2nd edn, 401 • Thieme & Becker, *Allgemeines Lexikon*, 31.32 • [W. Holden], *Holden's triennial directory for 1805, 1806, 1807, including the year 1808*, 2 vols. (1805–7) • admin., PRO, PROB 6/209, fol. 224v

Likenesses G. Dance, pencil and watercolour drawing, 1796, BM • stipple, V&A • watercolour drawing, BM

Wealth at death under £1000: administration, 1833, PRO, PROB 6/209, fol. 224v

Smith, Benjamin (1783–1860). *See under* Smith, William (1756–1835).

Smith, Benjamin Leigh (1828–1913), Arctic explorer, was born in Whatlington, Sussex, on 12 March 1828, the eldest son of Benjamin *Smith (1783–1860) [*see under* Smith, William (1756–1835)], MP for Norwich, and Anne Longden (1801–1834), a milliner. His sister was the artist and women's activist Barbara Leigh Smith *Bodichon, a co-founder of Girton College, Cambridge. His paternal grandfather was the politician William Smith. The family was wealthy and radical in its views. His parents were unmarried, his father believing that the marriage laws were unjust to women; but because the children were illegitimate many of their relatives refused to associate with them. After the death of his mother from tuberculosis in 1834, Benjamin was brought up by his father first at Pelham Crescent, Hastings, and then at his London home, 5 Blandford Square. Educated first at home by progressive tutors and then at the Unitarian Bruce Castle School, in 1848 Smith was elected a pensioner of Jesus College, Cambridge; he was senior wrangler in 1852. As a nonconformist he was not granted the BA degree until 1857, when he was the first dissenter to be admitted. He was called to the bar at the Inner Temple in 1856.

Smith travelled widely in his youth. He took the Board of Trade licence to command his own ships and, probably inspired by James Lamont, from 1871 to 1882 he sailed in Arctic waters. In 1871 he took the yacht *Sampson* to Spitsbergen and to the Seven Islands, reaching lat. 81°30′ N. In 1872 he could not get beyond the north-west capes of Spitsbergen. His interest was always scientific and not merely that of a hunter or traveller. He had invented an instrument for computing time at sea and, with Captain J. C. Wells, did valuable oceanographic work on the Gulf Stream during his two voyages. On his 1873 voyage he met A. E. Nordenskiöld, the Swedish explorer and scientist, but bad weather forced him home. In 1878 he tried vainly to reach Spitsbergen but it was a close season.

In 1880 Smith built the screw brigantine *Eira* in which he sailed from Peterhead, but because of mist and pack ice failed to make Jan Mayen or east Greenland. Learning that ice on the north coast of Spitsbergen made it impossible to pass Amsterdam Island, he made for Franz Josef Land, recently discovered (in 1873–4) and only partly mapped. He reached and named May Island in August, adding the south-west coast of the new land to the chart. He also made some additions to the chart of the east coast of Spitsbergen. For these discoveries he was awarded the patron's medal of the Royal Geographical Society in 1881. His paper on the voyage of 1880 was read at a meeting of the society and its importance agreed.

In 1881 the *Eira* sailed from Peterhead and sighted Novaya Zemlya and Franz Josef Land, but on 21 August the yacht was nipped between pack ice and land floe off Cape

Benjamin Leigh Smith (1828–1913), by Stephen Pearce, 1886

Flora, and sank within two hours. The crew lived in a makeshift hut, built from materials they had previously deposited on Bell Island, for ten months, before taking to their boats in June 1882 for the homeward passage. They reached Novaya Zemlya where they met the *Hope*, commanded by Sir Allen W. Young, who had been sent to find them following considerable speculation in England as to their whereabouts. The whole crew landed safely at Aberdeen at the end of August 1882, having survived the winter because lack of provisions led them to live on a much healthier diet of fresh meat, and because of Smith's quiet leadership.

Back in England, Smith gave £1000 to the Royal Geographical Society in gratitude for the mounting of the search party. In 1882 he was made an honorary fellow of Jesus College, Cambridge. He made no further Arctic expeditions, and revoked the bequest of £80,000 he had left to the Royal Geographical Society in 1887, in frustration at their neglect of polar exploration. None the less, in 1892 he worked with the society to promote scientific investigation of the Antarctic.

In 1882 Smith married Charlotte Annette (*b.* 1862/3), daughter of Frederick William Seller, wine merchant of Paddington. They had two sons and two daughters, and lived quietly at Scalands, near Robertsbridge, Sussex. He died on 4 January 1913 at 43 Frognal, Hampstead, and was buried in Brightling, Sussex.

A. G. E. Jones, *rev.* Elizabeth Baigent

Sources A. G. E. Jones, 'Benjamin Leigh Smith; arctic yachtsman', *The Musk Ox*, 16 (1975), 24–31 · A. G. Credland, 'Benjamin Leigh Smith: a forgotten pioneer', *Polar Record*, 20 (1980–81), 127–45 · *The Times* (6 Jan 1913) · *CGPLA Eng. & Wales* (1913) · H. R. Mill, *The record of* *the Royal Geographical Society, 1830–1930* (1930) • P. Hirsch, *Barbara Leigh Smith Bodichon: feminist, artist and rebel* (1998)

Archives Scott Polar RI, corresp. and journals • U. Edin. L., journal of Arctic voyage

Likenesses photograph, 1880, repro. in A. G. Credland, 'Benjamin Leigh Smith', 133 • S. Pearce, oils, 1886, NPG [*see illus.*] • J. Eves, oils, *c.*1910, repro. in Credland, 'Benjamin Leigh Smith', 143 • S. Pearce, oils, second version, Jesus College, Cambridge

Wealth at death £110,891 17*s.* 7*d.*: resworn probate, 15 March 1913, *CGPLA Eng. & Wales* • £98,171 14*s.* 10*d.*: resworn further grant, 8 May 1913, *CGPLA Eng. & Wales*

Smith, Bernard [*known as* Father Smith] (*c.***1628/9–1708**), organ builder, may have been born on the continent; arguments have been advanced for him having German or English parentage. The conjectured date of birth stems from a statement that he was 'about seventy-four' in September 1703, when he was involved in a lawsuit with Renatus Harris. Evidence for his German birth in Goslar followed by training at Wettin near Halle under Christian Forner was advanced without substantiation by Rimbault. Clutton and Niland have argued for Smith's English origins. It is known that Smith emigrated in 1657 from Bremen to Hoorn, Holland, where, as Baerent Schmitt, he was appointed organist of the Oostkerk and, as an organ builder, he restored the organ in the Grote Kerk (1660). Between 1662 and 1663 he worked on two instruments at Edam, and in May 1665 he was contracted to build a small organ of six stops for a church in Amsterdam. There are no further references to Baerent Schmitt in Holland after the final payment for this instrument in May 1667. This makes it possible for him to have been the Bernard Smith who was paid to tune the organs of Westminster Abbey, London, that same year. Smith's first wife, Anne (*b. c.*1626), died in 1698, and in the next year he married Elizabeth Houghton.

No record has yet emerged of Smith's being granted British citizenship, which would surely have been the case had he been German by birth. Moreover, in 1671, only three years after becoming established in Britain, he was appointed the king's organ maker.

Contemporary commentators support Smith's north European connections: Anthony Wood, in his memoirs, wrote of his organ for the Sheldonian Theatre (1671) that it 'cost 261 li made by Smith, a Dutchman', and Roger North noted his use of the German pitch names H (for B♮) and Cis and Dis (for C♯ and D♯ respectively). The styles and spellings of his stop lists also concur with those of small and medium-sized organs in north Germany and the Netherlands, and Smith's letters contain idiosyncratic spellings and constructions which point to his German-speaking associations.

In 1676 Smith was appointed organist of St Margaret's Church, Westminster, and became involved in a lawsuit with John Hingston, yet by 1681, in association with Hingston, he was confirmed in his position as organ maker to Charles II, and in 1695 (jointly with John Blow) he became keeper of the king's organs. Smith was sufficiently highly regarded in literary, musical, and scientific circles to be able to enjoy the society of Bentley, Blow, Evelyn, Locke,

Bernard Smith (*c.***1628/9–1708**), by unknown artist

Newton, Purcell, and Wren. The portrait of Smith, by an anonymous artist, that hangs in the University of Oxford faculty of music, portrays him as a characteristic gentleman of the Restoration with a long wig, lace cravat, and red drapery round his shoulders.

Fierce professional rivalry existed between the protestant Smith and the Roman Catholic organ-building family of Renatus Harris (supported at court by Queen Catherine of Braganza). This culminated in the 'battle of the organs', when in 1682 the benchers of the two societies of the Temple commissioned each craftsman to erect instruments in the Temple Church so that it could be determined 'which, in the greatest number of excellencies deserved the preference'. The rival claims were settled in Smith's favour only after an appeal to Lord Chief Justice Jeffreys.

There are some fifty recorded locations in Britain at which Smith is known to have worked, although his name is associated with more than seventy instruments (some of these are unsubstantiated attributions). At least thirty-four were new instruments; the other jobs were repairs or rebuilds. His new instruments include those at the Sheldonian Theatre, Oxford (1670–71); the king's private chapel, Windsor (1673); St Margaret's, Westminster (1675–6); Christ Church, Oxford (1680 or 1685?); St Peter Cornhill, London (1681); the Temple Church, London (1683–7); Durham Cathedral (1684–5); Emmanuel College, Cambridge and St Katharine Cree, London (1686); St Giles Cripplegate, London (1688); St Paul's Cathedral, London (1695–6); St Mary the Great, Cambridge (1698); St Michael's, Barbados, and the Banqueting House chapel, London (1699);

Eton College (1700–01); St David's Cathedral (1704?); Pembroke College, Cambridge (1708); and Trinity College, Cambridge (1708, finished by Schreider).

Smith's strongly architectural casework is the most impressive surviving aspect of his work. Characteristic examples of his cases with the façade pipes disposed within four towers and double-storeyed flats of pipes can be seen in Trinity College, Cambridge, St Paul's Cathedral (divided and altered), Durham Cathedral, Christ Church, Oxford, and St Katharine Cree, London.

An account of Smith's instruments by Sir John Sutton (1847) mentions the 'sweetness and brilliance' of his wooden pipes; Smith used good materials, yet his actions were criticized as 'spongy' and his wind supplies as irregular. His organs, like those of Harris, introduced new timbres to the pre-Commonwealth English organ building tradition, particularly stops such as the cornet, and a greater variety of flutes, and mixtures. The 'sweetness and brilliance' of his wooden pipes may be an indigenous English tradition or one learned through Christianus Smith and reflective of German and Dutch practice. His organ at the Temple Church contained some novel experiments such as the 'Violl & Violin of mettle' and additional split keys and pipes for G♯/A♭ and D♯/E♭, intended to increase the harmonic versatility of the instrument. Smith died in 1708 and was buried at St Margaret's Church, Westminster, London. His successor was his foreman Christopher Schreider, who had married his daughter, but the family craft was also continued by his nephews Gerard and Christian from about 1689 and 1690 respectively.

CHRISTOPHER KENT

Sources A. Freeman and J. Rowntree, *Father Smith, otherwise Bernard Schmidt* (1977) · J. Rowntree, 'Bernard Smith (*c*.1629–1708), organist and organbuilder, his origins', *Journal of the British Institute of Organ Studies*, 2 (1978), 10–23 · J. Boeringer, 'Bernard Smith (*c*.1630–1708): a tentative chronology', *Organ Yearbook*, 6 (1975), 4–16 · E. Hopkins and E. Rimbault, *The organ: its history and construction* (1855) · C. Clutton and A. Niland, *The British organ*, 2nd edn (1982) · W. Sumner, *The organ*, 4th edn (1973) · M. Wilson, *The English chamber organ* (1968) · E. Macrory and M. Muir Mackenzie, *Notes on the Temple organ*, 3rd edn (1911) · *Roger North on music*, ed. J. Wilson (1959) · R. Poole, 'The Oxford music school and the collection of portraits formerly preserved there', *Musical Antiquary*, 4 (1912–13), 143–59 · W. Bannerman, ed., *The registers of St Olave, Hart Street, London, 1563–1700* (1916) · W. Stüven, *Orgeln und Orgelbauer im Halleschen Land vor 1800* (Wiesbaden, 1964) · J. Sutton, *A short account of organs built in England from the reign of King Charles the Second to the present time* (1847) · *The life and times of Anthony Wood*, ed. A. Clark, 5 vols., OHS, 19, 21, 26, 30, 40 (1891–1900)

Archives Bodl. Oxf., receipts for work at York Minster

Likenesses J. Caldwell, line engraving (after oil painting by unknown artist), NPG · oils, U. Oxf., faculty of music [*see illus.*]

Wealth at death rings, jewels, and items of plate: will, Freeman and Rowntree, *Father Smith*, 70

Smith, Boatswain. *See* Smith, George Charles (1782–1863).

Smith, Bobus. *See* Smith, Robert Percy (1770–1845).

Smith, Brian Abel- (1926–1996), economist and social policy analyst, was born on 6 November 1926 at 24 Kensington Court Gardens, London, the younger son of Brigadier-General Lionel Abel Abel-Smith (1870–1946), officer in the Royal Artillery, and his wife, Genevieve Lilac, *née* Walsh,

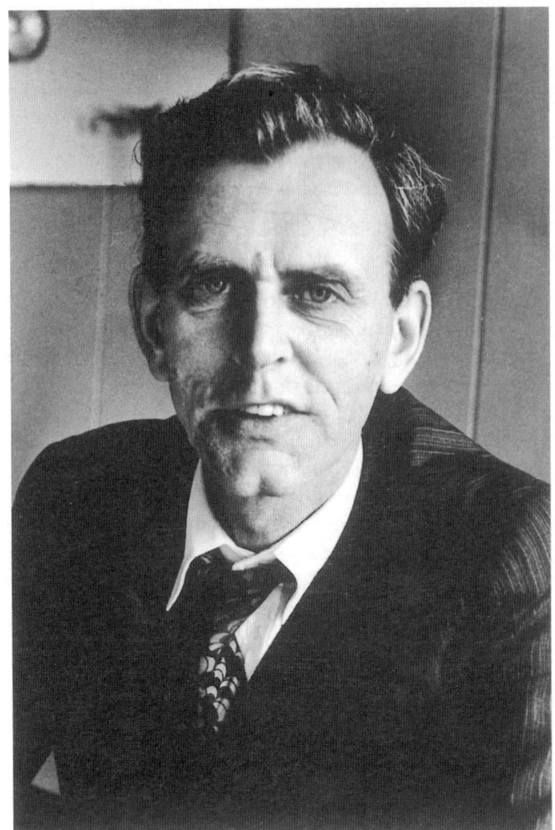

Brian Abel-Smith (1926–1996), by unknown photographer

daughter of Robert Walsh, of Armagh. Through his kinsman Sir Henry Abel-Smith, who was married to Queen Mary's niece Lady May Cambridge, he was distantly related to the royal family. Friends wickedly introduced him as twenty-seventh in line to the crown. Along with his erect bearing and extraordinarily acute command of the skills of diplomacy, that connection seemed to make his embrace of socialism all the more impressive and influential.

Abel-Smith was educated at Haileybury College from 1940 to 1945, before entering the army as a private. He was commissioned in the Oxford and Buckinghamshire light infantry in 1946 and was aide-de-camp to the military governor of the British zone in Austria during 1947–8. He then entered Clare College, Cambridge, where he studied economics from 1948 to 1951 and where he also became secretary of the Cambridge Union. He remained at Cambridge for a further two years to study the cost of the National Health Service (NHS); he was awarded his doctorate in 1955. He served his research apprenticeship from 1953 to 1955 at the National Institute of Economic and Social Research, and at the London School of Economics (LSE) with Professor Richard Titmuss, collecting evidence about the cost of the NHS for the Guillebaud committee. His academic career at the LSE took him from assistant lecturer in 1955 to lecturer in 1957, reader in social administration in 1961, and full professor in 1965. He retired in 1991. In

1968–70 he became senior adviser to the secretary of state for social services, Dick Crossman, was reappointed to a similar post in 1974–8 by Barbara Castle and then David Ennals, and in 1978–9 was the special adviser to the secretary of state for the environment, Peter Shore. During 1960–73 he served on government committees dealing with both health and social security, played a key practical role on the boards of regional and teaching hospital management committees, such as St Thomas's Hospital, and from 1956 until his death was consultant and expert adviser to the World Health Organization (WHO) in its work in many countries.

Some great people are insufficiently appreciated in their lifetime—and among them are those who avoid the limelight quite deliberately. Abel-Smith matched sheer brilliance and assurance with genuine modesty. His contributions to international health and health services, social policy, government administration, and politics read like the considerable careers of four separate people, equally intriguing and displaying enviable versatility.

First, health: it was the NHS that earned Abel-Smith's particular devotion. More than anyone he explained the reasons for its existence—and how it had to be adapted to new circumstances. His early books, *The Cost of the Health Service in England and Wales*, with Richard Titmuss (1956), *A History of the Nursing Profession* (1960), *Paying for Health Services* (1963), and *The Hospitals, 1800–1948* (1964), established a formidable case for a comprehensive public service and remained among the best books on the subject that any student could read. His contribution to better health services was sustained for another thirty years. Twenty-five of his 37 books, and 98 of his 166 published articles and papers were on health. Influential examples from his middle and later years were: *An International Study of Health Expenditure* (1967), *Value for Money in Health Services* (1976), *National Health Service: the First 30 Years* (1978), *The Organisation, Financing and Cost of Health Care in the European Community* (1979), *Planning the Finances of the Health Sector* (1984), and *An Introduction to Health: Policy, Planning and Financing* (1994).

Abel-Smith's work for the Guillebaud committee marked the start of the unrivalled lifelong contribution he made to improvements in health care. Set up by the Conservative government in 1952, this committee, chaired by Claude Guillebaud, an economist who had been Iain MacLeod's tutor at Cambridge, was asked to investigate what at the time was believed to be the uncontrolled rising cost imposed on the exchequer by the NHS and whether this could be avoided while maintaining an adequate service. Abel-Smith showed that, far from rising, the cost of the NHS was in fact falling as a share of gross national product. If the same share of national resources had been devoted to the NHS in 1953 as in its first full year of 1949, expenditure would have been £67 million, or one-sixth higher. The committee confessed themselves unable to make a case for new or higher charges. Instead they recommended increases in expenditure, including capital investment to improve the service. 'In large measure', as one authority testified, 'Guillebaud spiked the Treasury guns' (Timmins, 207).

Abel-Smith's investigation has been described as 'a minor classic of modern social analysis' (Webster, 207). It provided the basis for his subsequent book with Richard Titmuss (also drawn from Abel-Smith's doctorate), *The Cost of the National Health Service in England and Wales* (1951). His work on health became vigorously cross-national and, through the WHO, he visited a stream of poor countries—starting with Mauritius in the 1950s and ending with Indonesia in 1995. This was matched during the same period by his repeated visits around Europe. He influenced overseas developments in health care even more than in his own country. After his death the Mauritius government issued a set of commemorative stamps to mark his contribution to the establishment of the country's health service.

Second, Abel-Smith's contribution to social policy: as an economist he also developed a parallel interest in anti-poverty policies, starting when writing his doctorate on health at Cambridge University. This shaped his contribution to social policy. He began to write extensively, sometimes with Peter Townsend, on poverty, pensions, and social security. They collaborated in writing together as well as independently for eighteen years on these three themes. Their book *The Poor and the Poorest* (1965) has been highlighted as marking 'the rediscovery of poverty' in the UK after people had come to believe that the introduction of post-war welfare measures had resolved pre-war poverty and many other long-standing social problems. The book was based on a new method of constructing a poverty line to track the value of government policies. The method was to specify and assemble the weekly rates of social assistance to which families of different size and composition were entitled as an implicit measure of what the state actually defined as the income required to meet their needs, and then compare these with their actual income (and expenditure). By that standard poverty had increased in the 1950s. The extent of poverty was also shown to be larger than that described by Seebohm Rowntree, in his third book on the subject, *Poverty and the Welfare State* (1951). Rowntree's conclusions were found to be over-optimistic and his data less reliable than in his previous investigations of the subject. Abel-Smith and Townsend's *The Poor and the Poorest* was not just a report drawn from official sources about trends in poverty. It was credited with influencing Labour government thinking in the 1960s and 1970s on social policies generally.

Abel-Smith had that rare ability of combining penetrating mastery of Keynesian (and later monetarist or neo-liberal) theory with detailed understanding of how the welfare state works in administrative practice. He embodied all the strengths of what was taught about the welfare state at the London School of Economics. His early contribution, 'Whose welfare state?', to a book called *Conviction* (1958) had as much of an impact in later years as it did when it was published.

Abel-Smith's wider command of social policy included legal institutions. His capacity for penetrating, indeed adventurous, analysis led to one of the most original contributions to the role of law of the twentieth century. His book with Robert Stevens, *Lawyers and the Courts* (1967), was a sociological study of the English legal system from 1750 to 1965 which showed its social origins and mode of control and helped to make an unanswerable case for root-and-branch modernization. The sequel, *In Search of Justice* (1968), demonstrated the failings of the legal system as a social service and, had the book attracted the attention it deserved, might have led to some of the changes still required in the early twenty-first century.

Abel-Smith's third contribution, to government, was less well known than his contributions to academic social science, but none the less intriguing. Cabinet ministers grew to depend on his total discretion and, unusually for an academic, he earned glowing tributes from career civil servants. His top advisory appointments to successive cabinet ministers—Dick Crossman, Barbara Castle, David Ennals, and Peter Shore—provided glittering opportunities to influence legislation, but also had costs for his academic research career. He was also too much of a socialist to accept a life peerage. Barbara Castle paid high tribute to his experience and skill. He was 'the most outstanding' of the specialists on whom she could draw; and possessed 'an unparalleled mastery of the details of social policy' (Castle, *Fighting All the Way*, 461).

Finally, in the political domain, as government adviser he concealed his regret at not entering a career in politics. He gave the Fabian Society a modern social influence and served it for many years as treasurer and vice-president. For thirty-one years, except when he was a senior adviser to government, and until they were both elected vice-presidents, he and Townsend were elected annually to the executive committee of the Fabian Society. He wrote influential pamphlets on social security and health and, with Peter Townsend in 1955, on the future of pensions: *New Pensions for the Old*. This was picked up by Dick Crossman, who persuaded Hugh Gaitskell and later Harold Wilson to invite Abel-Smith and Townsend, with Richard Titmuss—a trio described by the then Conservative minister of pensions as the Labour Party's 'skiffle group'—to prepare a new detailed plan for national superannuation, published and endorsed at the party's annual conference in 1957. This was the basis of the bill that fell during its parliamentary committee stages when the election was called in 1970 and of the bill eventually passed in 1975. In 1970 Crossman described Abel-Smith as 'my closest personal friend … without [whom] I could have done very little in the past two years' (Crossman, 921). Although Titmuss had the policy judgement and Townsend had some of the necessary sociological knowledge of family living conditions, it was Abel-Smith who had the economic skill and dexterity to make this a visionary as well as a politically appealing plan for the late twentieth century.

Abel-Smith had been picked out by Hugh Dalton, a former chancellor of the exchequer, as someone with a potentially glittering political future, especially in the Treasury. Nevertheless he refused to apply for safe seats, more because of the risk of public humiliation if he was discovered to be homosexual than anything else. In the less censorious climate of the 1990s and 2000s his political gifts would have been regarded as nationally precious. When he was working for Barbara Castle she happened to appoint Jack Straw as political adviser. 'Let me be clear', she said to Straw, 'I have appointed Brian for his brilliance. I have appointed you for your low cunning.' At the end of her cabinet career she wrote that 'Brian's steady, informed and perceptive help is a tower of strength' (*Castle Diaries*, 721).

As a socialist Abel-Smith appreciated the importance not just of creating public institutions but of standing by them through thick and thin in a practical capacity. He played a big part in the foundation of the Child Poverty Action Group. In the early 1960s he and Townsend, with others, had been giving early warnings about the extent of poverty among different groups, and they anticipated some of the findings of *The Poor and the Poorest* in articles and pamphlets in 1962 and 1963. An apparent lack of response from the new Labour government in 1964 and early 1965 led to meetings between social workers and academics who were having everyday experiences interviewing and trying to help people in poverty. The decision to set up a campaigning group and to use the publication of *The Poor and the Poorest* in December 1965 as a rallying message was taken. It was a build-up fomented by the two authors, working with others, including Tony Lynes and Harriet Wilson, during the critical months from February 1965 to the end of that year. Abel-Smith gave a speech to the Society of Friends at Toynbee Hall in March which crystallized intentions. Another practical role for Abel-Smith was as governor of St Thomas's Hospital for many years. He helped to shape the policies and management of this internationally famous teaching hospital. Most importantly he supported the cause of social policy at the London School of Economics, and played a key part administratively for more than three decades. By the end of the century the department of social policy had been ranked as the leading department in the country on the subject.

Affordable but adequate welfare, detailed planning on behalf of the underdog, universal public services—these were Abel-Smith's cardinal values, reflected in one of his last published essays, published in *LSE on Social Science: a Centenary Anthology* (1996). Even more than Titmuss, he saved the National Health Service in its early days from savage spending cuts; it was his resolute defence of the advantages of making health a truly public service that saved the NHS from being weakened irretrievably. He was also the powerful figure, within government administration, behind a list of measures on pensions, disability allowances, and community care, as well as health services, which did much to make Britain a more settled and less divided country in the 1960s and 1970s than it later became.

Abel-Smith's wit could be discomfiting, and could be applied with devastating, but also fundamentally constructive, effects. One evening in the 1960s he unravelled the reputation of Nightingale nurses with a group of them. They were never the same again. He revered Florence Nightingale but showed that some of her ideas had been applied dogmatically or misinterpreted both in her lifetime and later; and had led to a stiff and autocratic regime. To improve standards and obtain public support Florence Nightingale had 'popularised nursing as an occupation for ladies' (Abel-Smith, *A History of the Nursing Profession*, 1960, 241). She created upper-class missionaries who had to prove they were chaste, so that parents of other young ladies would encourage their daughters to become nurses. However, these ladies subsequently sought status and power for women like themselves instead of spreading the advantages of adequate basic one-year training, which Nightingale wanted to establish for women generally. They pulled up the ladder. They became medical mercenaries and imposed a socially distant and inflexible regime for patients in the mass.

Deeply radical people have an ability to analyse individuals like Florence Nightingale, who are almost mythical figures, and turn them into recognizable human beings. Along with Barbara Wootton, Abel-Smith was a relatively neglected creative genius of post-war social policy in Britain. Perhaps this was because he was both a distinguished social scientist and a politician *manqué*, perhaps because he was unreservedly loyal to Titmuss and to the department at the LSE leading the analysis of the maturing welfare state.

Abel-Smith created a wonderful garden in his home in Kent with John Sarbutt, and was a fine cook, as well as skier and raconteur. He died of carcinoma of the pancreas at his home in London, 10 Denbigh Street, Westminster, on 4 April 1996. PETER TOWNSEND

Sources curriculum vitae, 1996, priv. coll. · *The Times* (9 April 1996) · *The Guardian* (9 April 1996) · *The Independent* (9 April 1996) · *Daily Telegraph* (11 April 1996) · *Eurohealth* (London School of Economics, June 1996) · R. H. S. Crossman, *The diaries of a cabinet minister*, 3 (1977) · *The Castle diaries, 1974–1976* (1980) · B. Castle, *Fighting all the way* (1993) · M. McCarthy, *Campaigning for the poor: CPAG and the politics of welfare* (1986) · N. Timmins, *The five giants: a biography of the welfare state* (1995) · C. Webster, *The health services since the war*, 1: *Problems of health care: the NHS before 1957* (1988) · *CGPLA Eng. & Wales* (1996) · *WWW* · personal knowledge (2004) · private information (2004) · b. cert. · d. cert.

Archives BLPES, papers · BLPES, corresp. and papers relating to AEGIS

Likenesses photograph, News International Syndication, London [*see illus.*] · photograph, repro. in *The Guardian* · photograph, repro. in *The Independent*

Wealth at death £712,780: probate, 4 Oct 1996, *CGPLA Eng. & Wales*

Smith, Sir Bryan Evers Sharwood- (1899–1983), colonial governor, was born on 5 January 1899 at College View, Spring Bank, Hull, the son of Edward Sharwood Smith, classics master at Hymers College, and his wife, Lucy Marion Evers. He was educated at Newbury School and Aldenham School, Hertfordshire, from where he won a classical scholarship to Emmanuel College, Cambridge, in 1916. After joining the Royal Flying Corps instead of Cambridge, he served in France and—to his joy as an ardent reader of Kipling's *Kim* and aspirant member of the Indian political service—on the north-west frontier. A hoped-for transfer to the Indian army did not come off. On demobilization, after a brief stint teaching at St Cuthbert's preparatory school in Malvern, he decided not to take up his university place and in 1920 applied for the colonial service.

Assigned to the mandated territory of the British Cameroons in 1921, where the administration was initially very 'northern' in both staff and style, Sharwood-Smith developed 'a long cherished plan' (Sharwood-Smith, 36) to serve in Northern Nigeria, far closer than Southern Nigeria to the India he knew. Inter-regional transfers were unusual except on an exchange basis, but Sharwood-Smith's fluency in Hausa (which he had learned during study leave in Kano in 1924) and an appeal to his lieutenant-governor did the trick. In 1927 he was transferred to Sokoto: over the next thirty years he became every inch a northerner. A promising career—his Hausa nickname, *Mai Wandon Karfe*, 'iron trousers', derived from the common perception that, since he was always too busily pacing about ever to sit down, he must be wearing metal trousers (Imam, 5)—nearly came to grief in 1928, when, having exceeded his authority in handling a murder case, his resident damningly minuted on his file that he must never be allowed to serve in an emirate again. In the event, such a reprimand soon (like its author) evaporated and Sharwood-Smith became successively resident of two of the three premier emirate provinces, Sokoto and Kano, and reached staff grade in 1946; that he never served in Borno was sometimes held against him by those who held senior positions there. He was twice married: to Sylvia Powys-Smith (*b.* 1905/6) on 17 July 1926, from whom he was subsequently divorced (their daughter Sarah was subsequently to marry his aide-de-camp), and on 26 August 1939 to (Winifred) Joan Mitchell (1915–1999), with whom he had a daughter and two sons. During the war Sharwood-Smith reverted to military service and in the rank of captain ran a 'research office' in Kano, a front for a trans-frontier intelligence organization under Captain Rennell (later Lord Rennell of Rodd). Yet another nickname was thus acquired: Sh Sh Hush Hush.

Post-war constitutional changes led to the regrading of the post of chief commissioner northern provinces to lieutenant-governor in 1951. When the office became vacant in 1952 Sharwood-Smith's chances appeared weakened by his total lack of secretariat experience in either Kaduna or Lagos, but in the end the Colonial Office bypassed the more intellectual candidate and came down in favour of him as the safer pair of hands. Two years later the post was upgraded and Sharwood-Smith now became governor of the northern region. His governorship coincided with the rapid advance of the north to self-government. For one who, in the words of his premier, Ahmadu Bello, 'would have made a good governor of the old type … but found difficulty in working with the parliamentary system' (Sharwood-Smith, 210), his relationship with the ministers was frequently strained. For all his vigorous purging of corrupt native authorities, culminating in his bold dismissal of several important emirs in 1953, and his determination to abolish the outdated status of sole native authority, his instinct was to hold the balance between the chiefs and the creeping encroachment on their authority by the politicians. He was particularly anxious about the impact of the appointment of a minister for local government on their traditional administrative role. Together, his views precipitated something of a cabinet crisis in Kaduna, with the emirs dangerously rallying behind the governor. He also had to face a worrying secessionist movement by the non-Muslim provinces, known as the 'middle belt'. A favourite dictum of his was that 'democracy is what democracy does' (private information).

Among Sharwood-Smith's imaginative initiatives were the launching of a 'war against ignorance' campaign, based on adult literacy; a plan for a system of provincial devolution, the 'Twelve Pillars' policy, 'torpedoed' (interview, 19) as soon as he left; the commissioning of a book to arouse interest in the north among professional staff in the UK, including those retiring prematurely from the Sudan, followed by the dispatch of two district officers to Oxford and Cambridge, ostensibly to attend the senior Devonshire course but with a personal brief to stimulate administrative recruitment; and the opening in 1954 of the Institute of Administration at Zaria, whose training programme for local district officers became a model for east and central Africa. His was the inspiration behind the creation of a communications flight to enable ministers and senior officials to fly to distant parts of the north in a three-seater Auster. He derived huge pleasure from taking the controls and flying low over terrain he had once toured on horseback. The queen's visit in 1956 preoccupied him, but for all its visible success the premier somewhat sourly contended that the governor had seized centre-stage and banished his ministers to the background. With two such leaders, each reluctant ever to efface himself, the Kaduna scene was often a tempestuous one. Pro-consular comparativists have to hand a rich experience in contrasting the style and image of Sharwood-Smith with those of his successor Sir Gawain Bell (in a very different constitutional context), as well as their differing relationships with and perceptions by the premier, Alhaji Sir Ahmadu Bello (Sharwood-Smith suspected a certain malice aforethought in the ghosting of the last-named's autobiography).

Sharwood-Smith retired in 1957, to Hythe and then Bexhill. Nigerian and British staff alike recognized that his heart lay in Sokoto and in the pre-war life of the traditional district officer, endowed, in his own words, with 'a warm heart and a cool head' (interview, 46); he had too, in the opinion of the governor-general, 'absorbed much of the Northern attitude' (Robertson, 189). Privately he regretted Sir Frederick Lugard's 1914 amalgamation of the north and south, and cherished the concept of a north on its own but closely supervised by the British, in the manner of Jordan. To some of the political class, perhaps searching for a target of old-fashioned authority, he appeared too set in the imperial mode, but to his field staff, with his long experience as one of them and an unequalled knowledge of emirate administration, he represented the ideal of a true district officer's governor. He was at his happiest away from Kaduna relaxing with a drink and reminiscing with a district officer. A shrewd judge of character, he endeavoured to place his senior administrative staff where they could do most good—and now and again, where they could do least harm. The wealth of Government House anecdote and district lore reflected their affection as well as their admiration, despite his grinding lack of consideration for his personal aides. He was a stickler for punctuality, 'to the second rather than to the minute' (private information). Strong-minded and hugely energetic, with a self-confessed tendency 'to go bull-headed at things' (interview, 5), confident in his own judgement, and just a little suspicious of those who differed, he could be less convincing in conversation than on paper: his deputy found it hard to 'translate his half-expressed musings into definite views' (Maddocks, 90). His gruffness concealed a fundamental shyness, and at the start of every dry season he suffered severely from hay fever. His staff were adept in knowing when to produce a pink gin to ease his instinctive tension over ceremonial occasions. No one who encountered Sharwood-Smith during his thirty-seven years' service in Nigeria would contradict the outsider's view that 'even as a junior officer [he] was not a man of whom it was possible to be unaware' (Heussler, 137).

Sharwood-Smith was quite lost in retirement, apart from twice revisiting Nigeria; and after a disgruntled guest at the annual Northern Nigeria dining club reunion accused him of blocking his promotion a decade earlier, he never attended again. To his immense delight, his memoirs were published in 1969; his wife published hers in 1992. Illness confined him to a wheelchair in his last years. He was made CMG in 1950, KBE in 1953, KCMG in 1955, and KCVO in 1956. He also held the Efficiency Decoration. He died on 10 October 1983 at Battle Hospital, Battle, Sussex. A. H. M. Kirk-Greene

Sources B. Sharwood Smith, *But always as friends* (1969) • interview with Sir B. Sharwood-Smith, 25 May 1968, private archive • J. Sharwood-Smith, *Diary of a colonial wife* (1992) • R. Heussler, *The British in Northern Nigeria* (1968) • A. Bello, *My life* (1962) • K. Maddocks, *Of no fixed abode* (1988) • *The Times* (12 Oct 1983) • *The Times* (17 Oct 1983) • private information (2004) [J. H. Smith, former aide-de-camp] • J. Robertson, *Transition in Africa* (1974) • A. A. Imam, *Auren Zobe: Abuta Nijeriya da Ingila—Tafsirin Mai Wandon Karfe* (Hausa, 1974) • N. C. McClintock, *Kingdoms in the sand and sun* (1992) • J. H. Smith, *Colonial cadet in Nigeria* (1969) • T. Clark, *A right honourable gentleman: Abubakar from the black rock* (1991) • G. W. Bell, *An imperial twilight* (1989) • E. Huxley, *Four guineas* (1954) • *WWW* • b. cert. • m. cert. • d. cert. • *CGPLA Eng. & Wales* (1983)

Archives Bodl. RH, corresp. and papers | SOUND Oxford Colonial Records Project

Likenesses photographs, repro. in Bello, *My life* • portrait, repro. in Sharwood Smith, *But always as friends* • portraits, Northern Nigerian ministry of information, Kaduna, archives

Wealth at death under £40,000: probate, 16 Nov 1983, *CGPLA Eng. & Wales*

Smith, Cecil Blanche Woodham- [*née* Cecil Blanche Fitz-Gerald] **(1896–1977)**, biographer and historian, was born on 29 April 1896 at Tenby in Wales. Though her mother,

Blanche Elizabeth Philipps, was Welsh, she felt Irish, since her father, Colonel James FitzGerald, an Indian army officer who served in the mutiny, belonged to the family of Lord Edward FitzGerald, hero of the Irish rising of 1798. Educated at the Royal School for Officers' Daughters, Bath, until expelled for rebelliously taking French leave to visit the National Gallery, she finished her schooling at a convent in France. At St Hilda's College, Oxford, she took a second class in English in 1917, despite a term's rustication for joining Irish demonstrators in the streets. She then learned typing and copy-writing with an advertising firm.

In 1928 she married a distinguished London solicitor, George Ivon Woodham-Smith, her mainstay as woman and writer. But like so many women of her period, she waited until her children (a son and a daughter) were at boarding-school before beginning her literary career. Meanwhile she wrote pot-boilers under a pen-name. Her gift for fast narrative and human detail, she would say, was learned at the feet of 'Janet Gordon'. To aspiring biographers her advice was: 'Keep the story moving.'

After nine years' research, writing, and rewriting, Cecil Woodham-Smith's first biography, *Florence Nightingale* (1950), won the James Tait Black memorial prize and carried her straight to the top. Wit, empathy, and finely sifted information showed what could be done with a Victorian subject conceived on the grand scale. Lytton Strachey had left Florence Nightingale deftly debunked. (The Stracheys, especially Lytton's brother Oliver, were good friends of the Woodham-Smiths.) Cecil Woodham-Smith built her up again into more than a legend: into a living complex woman. Those who afterwards had occasion to use the Nightingale papers in the British Library found that she had missed nothing.

The Reason Why (1953) was no less dashing than the charge of the light brigade which it described, and became perhaps the most popular of Cecil Woodham-Smith's four masterpieces. It emerged organically from its predecessor, as did all her books; but whereas her *Florence Nightingale* involved much administrative detail, lucidly presented, *The Reason Why* hardly ever touched ground, except to expose low-down intrigues with the most beguiling irony. On television she explained how she wrote the charge itself, working at a gallop through thirty-six hours non-stop without food or other break until the last gun was fired, when she poured a stiff drink and slept for two days.

In *The Great Hunger* (1962), Cecil Woodham-Smith's Irish ancestry caused her to see the potato famine with the savage anger of Jonathan Swift. Her meticulously handled source material produced pictures of the potato disease and coffin-ships at once macabre and memorable. Some of her readers might have preferred to forget them. Historians had wondered whether she had not this time bitten off more than she could chew. But the general verdict was, 'She did not put a foot wrong.' In a review Conor Cruise O'Brien wrote that the book was 'One of the great works not only of Irish nineteenth-century history but of nineteenth-century history in general'. Later a younger school of Irish-born historians argued that Cecil Woodham-Smith was less than fair to the assistant secretary to the Treasury in London, Sir Charles Trevelyan, whom she described as 'virtually dictator of relief in Ireland' (*The Great Hunger*, 105). However, what she told her English readers about the horrors of the Irish famine was what they needed to hear.

The death of her husband in 1968 took some of the elasticity from Cecil Woodham-Smith's writing and great happiness from her life. Nevertheless *Queen Victoria: her Life and Times*, volume 1 (1972), showed remarkable feats of research in the Windsor archives, for which she learned Old German script. A superlatively readable panorama resulted, studded with original case histories of characters like Sir John Conroy, Princess Victoria's bogeyman, and Sir George Anson, Prince Albert's private secretary. Her account of the prince's death was the fullest and most moving ever written. The last sentence of this first volume showed her skill as the composer of biography, for it was both a conclusion and a looking forward. 'What is going to happen now', she quoted, 'to the poor Queen?' Sadly, Cecil Woodham-Smith did not live to answer that query. She died in London on 16 March 1977.

Noel Blakiston, one of Cecil Woodham-Smith's close literary friends, recalled her aristocratic appearance, high-spirited entertaining, and long hours at the Public Record Office, her arrivals and departures made in a chauffeur-driven car. Another friend asked her, near her end, which of Queen Victoria's children she put next to the queen herself. Raising her head, she said with the old flash of her bright blue eyes, 'None!' She was appointed CBE in 1960, received honorary doctorates from the National University of Ireland (1964) and St Andrews (1965), and became an honorary fellow of St Hilda's in 1967.

ELIZABETH LONGFORD, *rev.*

Sources personal knowledge (1986) • private information (1986) • *The Times* (17 March 1977) • *CGPLA Eng. & Wales* (1977)

Archives King's Lond., Liddell Hart C., corresp. with Sir B. H. Liddell Hart • Royal Society of Literature, London, letters to Royal Society of Literature

Wealth at death £96,297: probate, 25 Aug 1977, *CGPLA Eng. & Wales*

Smith, Sir Cecil Harcourt- (1859–1944), archaeologist and museum director, was born at Staines, Middlesex, on 11 September 1859, the second son of William Smith, solicitor, and his wife, Harriet, daughter of Frederic Harcourt, of Ipswich. He was a scholar of Winchester College (1873–8), but did not proceed to a university, and in 1879 he joined the department of Greek and Roman antiquities in the British Museum. He soon became known for his archaeological interests, and in 1887 was a founder editor and contributor (as Cecil Smith) to the *Classical Review*. He later hyphenated his name, and in 1892 married Alice Edith, daughter of H. W. Watson, of Burnopfield, co. Durham. They had two sons, of whom the elder, Simon, was a writer. The younger, Gilbert (1901–1968), became an air vice-marshal of the Royal Air Force.

In 1887 Smith was attached to a diplomatic mission to

Persia, and from 1895 to 1897 he was granted special leave in order to hold the post of director of the British School, Athens. The school had just received a subvention from the Treasury and was able to extend its activities: Harcourt-Smith instituted the *Annual*, and began the school's excavations in the island of Melos, which contributed much to knowledge of Aegean civilizations.

While in Athens, Harcourt-Smith had been promoted assistant keeper of his department in the British Museum, and in 1904 he succeeded A. S. Murray as keeper. He was soon, however, to transfer his activities to another sphere. The collections of applied art at South Kensington, which had accumulated round the nucleus of the objects purchased by the government after the Great Exhibition of 1851, were badly in need of reorganization. In 1908 Harcourt-Smith became chairman of the commission appointed to consider the matter, and his report was so highly approved that he was offered the post of director and secretary of what was henceforward to be known as the Victoria and Albert Museum. He took up his duties in 1909, when the new building had just been completed, and remained director until his retirement in 1924.

In the following year Harcourt-Smith was appointed adviser for the royal art collections and from 1928 until 1936 he was also surveyor of the royal works of art. Among his many public activities, Harcourt-Smith played a leading part in the foundation of the Central Committee for the Care of Churches; he was chairman of the committee of the Incorporated Church Building Society, and vice-chairman of the British Institute of Industrial Art and the British Society of Master Glass Painters. He was also vice-president of the Hellenic Society, president of the Society of Civil Servants, and British representative on the International Office of Museums. He was an honorary member of the British Drama League and an honorary associate of the Royal Institute of British Architects. In addition to his scholarly contributions to the British Museum departmental catalogues, he wrote for the art journals and also published a number of monographs: *The Collection of J. Pierpont Morgan* (1913), *The Art Treasures of the Nation* (1929), and *The Society of Dilettanti: its Regalia and Pictures* (1932), which he wrote as the society's honorary secretary.

It is, however, for his work at the Victoria and Albert Museum that Harcourt-Smith is best remembered. He raised the status of the technical staff and negotiated for them the same rates of pay and conditions as the officials of the British Museum. He established students' rooms in all departments and encouraged the issue of guides and catalogues. He instituted official guide-lecturers, and sponsored special displays such as the Franco-British exhibition of 1921. It was under his directorship that the museum was enriched by the acquisition of the Salting collection, the Talbot Hughes collection of costumes, the Pierpont Morgan stained glass, and the Rodin sculptures (although these were later transferred to the Tate Gallery). His arrangement of the contents of the museum according to their material was hailed as an innovation. It lasted until after the evacuation of 1939, when it was abandoned in favour of a chronological sequence, subdivided into primary and secondary collections, devised by Sir Leigh Ashton and more likely to be understood by the general public.

Harcourt-Smith was a man of striking appearance, tall, slender, and erect. In his youth he was known to some of his friends as 'the light dragoon'; later, with his white hair and moustache, his immaculate clothes, linguistic abilities, and ambassadorial manners, he was an impressive figure on all occasions. He was knighted in 1909, appointed CVO in 1917, and advanced to KCVO in 1934. He also held a number of foreign decorations, and received honorary degrees from the universities of Aberdeen (LLD, 1895) and Oxford (DLitt, 1928). He died at his home, Stoatley, Bramley, Surrey, on 27 March 1944.

JAMES LAVER, *rev.* DENNIS FARR

Sources *The Times* (29 March 1944) • *WWW* • J. B. Wainewright, ed., *Winchester College, 1836–1906: a register* (1907), 301 • private information (1959)

Archives RIBA, papers as vice-chairman of British Institute of Industrial Art | U. Durham L., corresp. with the khedive of Egypt

Likenesses M. Beerbohm, cartoon, 1924, V&A • W. Stoneman, photographs, 1924–34, NPG • Lady Welby, bust, V&A

Wealth at death £3045 8*s*. 11*d*.: administration, 6 July 1944, *CGPLA Eng. & Wales*

Smith, Cecil Lewis Troughton [*pseud.* Cecil Scott Forester] (**1899–1966**), novelist, was born in Egypt at Cairo on 27 August 1899, the third son and fifth child of George Foster Smith, schoolmaster and author of elementary Arabic textbooks, and his wife, Sarah Medhurst Troughton. From an early age he was able to read with ease. With his brothers, he conducted long battles with lead soldiers and naval campaigns with paper ships, drawing up army lists and naval operation orders in Nelsonian style. He frequented the public library, forming the lifetime habit of reading at least one book a day. His omnivorous reading included Gibbon, Suetonius, 'dozens of naval histories', and Harmsworth's *Encyclopaedia*, besides G. A. Henty, R. M. Ballantyne, Harry Collingwood, and Robert Leighton. This, added to rigorous cramming for scholarships at his elementary school in London, revealed the weakness of his eyesight. A Christ's Hospital scholarship having been withdrawn at the last moment because of the size of his father's income, Smith, aged eleven, joined the fourth form at Alleyn's School. After an unhappy start, he did well enough to be offered some public-school scholarships, settling for an internal offer of two years' free tuition. He moved next to the sixth form (science) at Dulwich College. He was a good cricketer and keen games player.

Between the ages of twelve and sixteen, Smith grew 5 inches annually. An army medical examination at seventeen revealed a weak heart, precluding his recruitment in 1917. This was an unhappy time for him. His vivid imagination enabled him to picture his contemporaries' sufferings 'with terrible realism', sharpening his distaste for civilian complacency. Overshadowed by his eldest brother, who had qualified aged twenty, he entered Guy's

Cecil Lewis Troughton Smith [Cecil Scott Forester] **(1899–1966)**, by Howard Coster, 1937

Hospital as a medical student, but he came to the conclusion that he was unfitted for medicine. On 3 August 1926 he married Kathleen Belcher (*b.* 1902/3), the daughter of George Joseph Belcher, a schoolteacher, and they had two sons.

Smith's thought had turned increasingly to writing, and the novelist's instinct triumphed over family opposition. He took the name Forester for professional purposes in 1923, and his first attempts at fiction taught him that 'the better part of the work is done before pen is put to paper'. The artistic standard he set himself (he called it 'beauty') was first met by *Payment Deferred* (1926), a compelling narration of a murderer being accused of a crime he did not commit. In 1931 Charles Laughton acted in a successful stage version, and the story was also later filmed. *Brown on Resolution* (1929) collates the themes of the command of the sea, the service of England, and 'the man alone', which dominate Forester's best work. Yet the story has a curious moral; the heroic death of an illegitimate son, after his mother dies of cancer, advances his father's naval career. Forester's best biography was *Nelson* (1929). *Death to the French* (1932) reveals an acute insight into the British army during the Peninsular War. Rifleman Dodd, separated from his regiment, shows the value of Sir John Moore's training. *The African Queen* (1935) convincingly depicts a dedicated woman's love driving a weak man to heroic efforts on England's behalf. John Huston directed the classic 1951 film adaptation starring Humphrey Bogart and Katharine Hepburn, and, although the ending was altered, this was the best of the various films made of Forester's books.

The General (1936) is Forester's striking study of Lieutenant-General Sir Herbert Curzon, a professional British officer, whose rapid rise to high command in the First World War ends during the German offensive of March 1918. The novel stresses Curzon's devotion to duty and unbending sense of honour, without glozing his narrow outlook and sympathies.

During these years Forester was combining the writing of books with journalism; from 1936 to 1937 he was a correspondent in Spain during the civil war, and he was also in Czechoslovakia when the Germans occupied Prague in March 1939.

In 1937, with the publication of *The Happy Return*, Forester created his best-known character, Horatio Hornblower, a sensitive and gifted individual, the flowering of whose talents within the chain of naval command revealed the author's understanding of Nelson's navy, and of sea power. Forester's command of the historical detail of the period was due to his chance purchase, some time previously, of three volumes of the *Naval Chronicle*, a journal published during the Napoleonic wars. Between 1937 and 1962 appeared twelve Hornblower stories, tracing the rise of the hero from midshipman to admiral. The books were written in a terse, effective style, well suited to the portrayal of the self-doubting but self-disciplined Hornblower, whose complex personality was brilliantly evoked. Hornblower's activities were confined, during the thirty years of the stories (1793 to 1823) to the Atlantic, Baltic, Mediterranean, and Caribbean. In *The Hornblower Companion* (1964), which contains a candid account of the creation and writing of the Hornblower books, Forester explained frankly why this was the case: 'These were the only waters with which Hornblower's biographer was familiar while writing about the closing years of the Napoleonic Wars.' One of the Hornblower novels, *A Ship of the Line*, was awarded the James Tait Black memorial prize for 1938. A television series entitled *Horatio Hornblower*, based on the second of Forester's novels, *Mr Midshipman Hornblower* (1950), was produced by the American Arts and Entertainment television network in 1999. It was aired in the United States to great acclaim, winning an Emmy award for the outstanding mini-series of that year.

During the Second World War, Forester, always conscious of the shared British–American heritage, contributed much to British and American propaganda, producing short stories and articles, illustrating the British war effort, for American publication. When America entered the war he was co-opted as an American propagandist and became a familiar figure in the Pentagon. He accompanied a United States warship on one of its missions. In 1943 he was invited by the British Admiralty to sail in the *Penelope*, an experience which resulted in his writing *The Ship* (1943), of which half a million copies were printed and distributed throughout the fleet. The book was a brilliant portrait of trained individuals working as a team. Forester was also a frequent contributor to the *Saturday Evening Post*, in which *The Commodore* (1945) appeared as a serial.

In 1945 the allied governments foresaw the possibility of protracted Japanese resistance. Forester, now settled permanently in the United States, was given the freedom of the navy department, Washington, with number two priority on air transport. He busied himself with writing 'logistics for the common man', stories about the Pacific war (*The Man in the Yellow Raft*, published posthumously in 1969).

Forester, a shy man, thin-lipped and high-browed, had a quiet sense of humour. He enjoyed bridge and travel. However, arteriosclerosis curtailed his mobility from 1943 onwards. His first marriage had not survived the war; it ended with a divorce in 1944. On 3 May 1947 he married his second wife, Dorothy Ellen (*b*. 1899/1900), the daughter of William James Foster, a retired shipbroker. Forester suffered a severe stroke in 1964, which confined him to a wheelchair, and he died in Fullerton, California, on 2 April 1966. NEIL HUXTER, *rev.*

Sources C. S. Forester, *The Hornblower companion* (1964) • C. S. Forester, *Long before forty* (1967) • *The Times* (4 April–6 June 1966) • private information (1981) • m. certs. • *CGPLA Eng. & Wales* (1968)
Archives Ransom HRC, autobiography, corresp., and literary MSS • U. Cal., Berkeley, Bancroft Library, papers and library | King's Lond., Liddell Hart C., corresp. with Sir B. H. Liddell Hart
Likenesses H. Coster, photograph, 1937, NPG [*see illus.*] • H. Coster, photographs, NPG
Wealth at death £63,405: administration with will, 5 Jan 1968, *CGPLA Eng. & Wales*

Smith, Charles (1713–1777), writer on the corn trade, was born in Stepney, the son of Charles Smith, a corn mill owner of Croydon, Surrey, and his wife, Anne, daughter and coheir of James Marrener, a naval captain with the East India Company. His family had been profitably engaged in the grain trade for two generations. Smith was educated at Ratcliff grammar school, Middlesex, after which he entered the milling trade, moving to Barking in Essex, where the family owned a number of mills. He married twice. The details of his first marriage are not known, but in 1748 he married Judith, eldest daughter of Isaac Lefevre, a wealthy distiller, the son of Huguenot refugees. They had a son, also named Charles, who became MP for Westbury, Wiltshire, in 1802, and a daughter. Smith took charge of the family business in 1761 on his father's retirement, but soon afterwards handed over the day-to-day running of affairs to a younger relative; he became a magistrate and a keen student of the economics of the grain trade and the influence of the corn laws.

The scarcity of corn in 1756–7 and its high prices had led to food riots in several parts of England, making it the subject of much comment in the newspaper and pamphlet press. Many writers declared the season one of artificial scarcity and laid the blame for disorder at the door of farmers, millers, and bakers, aided by middlemen and speculators, who held back supplies from the markets in anticipation of still higher prices. Smith's response was to write *A Short Essay on the Corn Trade and Corn Laws* (1758), which argued that the scarcity had been in the main a real one, occasioned by deficient harvests in the west and north-west parts of England over the preceding three or four years and a general shortfall in the harvest of 1756, and defended as legitimate the actions of the middlemen. This work attracted much attention and praise—David Hume wrote an admiring preface for the Edinburgh edition—and was followed by a second work of 'considerations on the corn laws' (1759), which was privately circulated. In 1766 both these works were reprinted with additional material as *Three Tracts on the Corn-Trade and Corn-Laws*.

Living in the corn-producing and -exporting county of Essex, as well as in close proximity to the important London markets, Smith was well placed to observe agriculture and the corn-dealing and -milling businesses. His work is still cited by modern historians of agriculture and the corn trade. A firm supporter of internal free trade and an export trade encouraged by the payment of bounties, he favoured the discreet use of powers held by magistrates to intervene in the market place, as in the assize of bread, in order to steer a middle course between the interests of producers, bakers, and consumers. Although his writings were not theoretically sophisticated even by the standards of his day, their acute observation and sound reasoning came to the attention of Adam Smith, who, despite considering Smith an exponent of the 'mercantile system', described him as an 'ingenious and well-informed author' (Smith, 1.506).

With the return of scarcity and disorder in 1766 and 1772 the corn trade remained at the centre of public attention and official scrutiny and Charles Smith was called several times to give expert testimony to parliamentary committees investigating the causes of high prices. He spent his final days in partial retirement at Stratford, Essex, where he was a well-respected local figure. He died on 8 February 1777 following a fall from his horse. R. D. SHELDON

Sources G. Chalmers, 'Some account of the life of Charles Smith, esq.', in Charles Smith, *Tracts on the corn trade and corn laws* (1804) • D. R. Raynor, 'Who invented the invisible hand?', *TLS* (14 Aug 1998), 22 • Adam Smith, *The wealth of nations*, ed. R. H. Campbell and A. S. Skinner, 2 vols. (1976) • letter from Charles Smith to Charles Townshend, 23 Sept 1766, BL, Add. MS 32977, fol. 135 • letter from Charles Smith to first earl of Liverpool, 26 Nov 1772, BL, Add. MS 38207, fol. 199 • *Chelmsford Chronicle* (14 Feb 1777) • *DNB* • R. G. Thorne, 'Smith, Charles', HoP, *Commons*
Archives BL, letter to first earl of Liverpool, Add. MS 38207, fol. 199 • BL, letter to Charles Townshend, Add. MS 32977, fol. 135

Smith, Charles (*c*.1715–1762), topographer and county historian, was born in co. Waterford, Ireland, of unknown family origins. He began his employment in Dungarvan, co. Waterford, in 1740 as an apothecary. From 1738 he was involved in an ultimately unsuccessful attempt to publish a natural history atlas of the counties of Ireland, in which he concentrated upon Cork and Waterford. He came to wider attention in 1744 as the co-author of *The Antient and Present State of County Down*, which he wrote with Walter Harris (1686–1761), the editor of Sir James Ware's historical collections of Ireland. As the preface of the book explained, this was not only the first county history of its kind in Ireland but also, hopefully, the first in a complete series. To reach this objective Smith and others founded the Physico-Historical Society in Dublin in May 1744 and he became what is referred to in the minutes as an 'itinerant inquirer' or an active collector of topographical, historical, and antiquarian information for the counties of Munster. Under the society's auspices he published both *The Antient and Present State of County Waterford* (1746) and *The Antient and Present State of the County and City of Cork* (1750). However, following a financial dispute over moneys he argued were owed to him by the society for his work, which was only settled when Smith was given an unmentioned number of copies of his Cork book to sell for himself, he severed his connection with the society in September 1750, two years before its demise. He continued his surveying work, including some cartographic work on the harbours and sea coasts of co. Waterford, and published *The Antient and Present State of County Kerry* in 1756, leaving surveys of another three counties (Clare, Limerick, and Tipperary) unfinished in manuscript form. His mixture of the topographical and historical is sometimes ignored by historians, given some of his eccentric interests in meteorological and natural oddities, but his works also provide both a snapshot of the lifestyles of the protestant gentry of Munster in the middle decades of the eighteenth century and a pointer towards the social and economic improvement of the province.

In July 1756 Smith and some medical friends founded the Medico-Philosophical Society in Dublin to inform others of medical advances and develop areas of intellectual curiosity for physicians. He was the author of the society's *Discourses* (1758), in which he outlined its aims and appealed for more members to support this second attempt to cultivate Irish enlightenment. The society prospered, and Smith enjoyed a happier time than when in the Physico-Historical Society until this was cut short by his sudden death from gout in July 1762 while on a visit to Bristol, where he was buried. EOIN MAGENNIS

Sources minutes of the Physico-Historical Society, 1744–52, Royal Irish Acad. • A. J. Webb, *A compendium of Irish biography* (1878)
Archives Royal Irish Acad., minutes of Medico-Philosophical Society; minutes of the Physico-Historical Society; topography MSS

Smith, Charles (1749–1824), subject and portrait painter, born on 7 November 1749 in Stenness in the Orkneys, was the son of William Smith and Charlotte Whitefoord, sister of the diplomat Caleb Whitefoord. After studying at the Royal Academy Schools, he attempted to establish himself as a portrait painter in London and exhibited three portraits at the Society of Artists in 1776 as a pupil of J. H. Mortimer. However, he was apparently hindered by his extreme and violently expressed political opinions. In 1783 he went to India and travelled extensively in that country. He spent some time in Madras, where Ozias Humphry noted that Smith charged 75 pagodas for a bracelet-sized miniature. He was in Calcutta in June 1785 when John Macpherson, governor-general, gave him letters of introduction to the nawab of Oudh. His self-portrait (exh. RA, 1795, engraved by S. W. Reynolds, 1795), describes him as 'painter to the Great Mogul', and thus suggests that he also travelled to Delhi and met the Mughal emperor. From 1789 to 1797 Smith lived in London and Edinburgh, exhibiting mythological and fancy compositions as well as portraits at the Royal Academy. In October 1798 his musical entertainment entitled *A Day at Rome* was performed at Covent Garden Theatre. He subsequently published this piece in protest at its condemnation and proceeded to write *A Trip to Bengal* in 1802, dedicated to Macpherson in thanks for his hospitality and patronage. Smith died at Leith on 19 December 1824.

F. M. O'DONOGHUE, *rev.* KATE RETFORD

Sources M. Archer, *India and British portraiture, 1770–1825* (1979), 178–85 • W. Foster, 'British artists in India, 1760–1820', *Walpole Society*, 19 (1930–31), 1–88, esp. 72–3 • B. Stewart and M. Cutten, *The dictionary of portrait painters in Britain up to 1920* (1997), 426 • Waterhouse, *18c painters*, 349 • D. Foskett, *A dictionary of British miniature painters*, 2 vols. (1972), 1.519 • Graves, *RA exhibitors* • Graves, *Soc. Artists*, 237 • *Engraved Brit. ports.*, 4.121 • Redgrave, *Artists*, 2nd edn, 401 • Bryan, *Painters* (1903–5) • *IGI* • E. Kilmurray, *Dictionary of British portraiture*, 2 (1979), 196
Likenesses C. Smith, etching, 1776, BM • S. W. Reynolds, mezzotint, 1795 (after self-portrait by C. Smith), BM • C. Smith, self-portrait, exh. RA 1795 • stipple (after self-portrait by C. Smith), repro. in C. Smith, *A trip to Bengal* (1802), frontispiece

Smith, Charles (1786–1856), singer and composer, was born in London in September 1786, the grandson of Edward Smith, page to Princess Amelia, and the son of Felton Smith, a chorister at Christ Church, Oxford. At the age of five, owing to his precocity, he became a pupil of Costellow for singing. Later, in 1796, on the advice of Samuel Arnold, he became a chorister at the Chapel Royal under Edmund Ayrton, and sang the principal solo in the anthem on the marriage of Charlotte Augusta Matilda, the princess royal, to the prince of Würtemberg on 18 May 1797. In 1798 he was articled to John Ashley, and in the following year was engaged to sing at Ranelagh Gardens, the Lenten oratorios, and other concerts. In 1803 he went on tour to Scotland, but, his voice having broken, he gave up singing temporarily, and devoted himself to teaching and playing the organ. He later became deputy organist for Charles Knyvett and John Stafford Smith at the Chapel Royal and for Bartleman at Croydon. On the latter's retirement, Smith was appointed organist there, but shortly afterwards he went to Ireland as a tenor with a theatrical party. On his return, a year later, he became organist of Welbeck Chapel, succeeding Charles Wesley.

In collaboration with Isaac Pocock, Smith next turned his attention to writing for the theatre, and produced in rapid succession the music to several farces, including *Yes or No* (Haymarket, 31 August 1808, published 1809), *Knapschou, or, The Forest Fiend* (Lyceum, 1809), *Hit or Miss* (Lyceum, 26 February 1810), and *Anything New* (1 July 1811). He withdrew from the theatre when Pocock left Drury Lane. From 1813 he sang baritone parts at the oratorio concerts, and in 1815 he married a Miss Booth of Norwich. In 1816 he went to fill a lucrative post in Liverpool. He ultimately retired to Crediton in Devon, where he died on 22 November 1856.

Smith was an excellent organist and a fine singer. Many of his compositions, in particular his songs and ballads, enjoyed widespread success, the most popular being a setting of Campbell's *The Battle of Hohenlinden*, which was reviewed in the *Quarterly Musical Magazine and Review* (2 (1820), 214–20) and described as 'a work of rare and extraordinary merit'. His *Ancient Psalmody, from the Publications of T. Est, Ravenscroft, Morley* … appeared in 1843.

R. H. LEGGE, *rev.* DAVID J. GOLBY

Sources W. H. Husk, 'Smith, Charles', Grove, *Dict. mus.* • *Quarterly Musical Magazine and Review*, 2 (1820), 214–20 • [Clarke], *The Georgian era: memoirs of the most eminent persons*, 4 (1834), 304

Smith, Sir Charles Bean Euan- (1842–1910), army officer and diplomatist, one of several sons of Euan Maclauren Smith of Georgetown, British Guiana, and his wife, Eliza Bean, was born at Georgetown on 21 September 1842. He was educated at a preparatory school near Rugby, and subsequently by an English tutor at Bruges. Appointed ensign in the Madras infantry at the age of seventeen, he was promoted lieutenant in 1861, captain in 1870, major in 1879, lieutenant-colonel in 1881, and colonel in 1885, retiring in 1889. After serving in the expedition to Abyssinia in 1867 he was present at the capture of Magdala. He was secretary in 1870–71 to Sir Frederick Goldsmid during the special mission of the latter to Persia, and, as military attaché, accompanied Sir Bartle Frere in his special anti-slave-trade mission to Zanzibar and Muscat in 1872. He was made CSI in November of that year. Subsequently he was in charge of the consulate-general at Zanzibar from June to September 1875, was first assistant resident at Hyderabad in 1876, and was appointed consul at Muscat in July 1879. During the Anglo-Afghan War of 1879–80 he was on special duty as chief political officer on the staff of Lieutenant-General Sir Donald Stewart, and subsequently took part in Lord Roberts's expedition for the relief of Kandahar, receiving the campaign medal with two clasps and the bronze star for his share in the campaign. During the following years he held political appointments in Mewar, Bansara, Bharatpur, and Karauli.

In December 1887 Euan-Smith was appointed to succeed Sir John Kirk as British consul-general at Zanzibar. He was plunged into thorny discussions concerning territories on the mainland acquired from the sultan by the British East Africa Company: the discussions revolved around German territorial annexations, and the claims of France and other European countries to certain immunities that flowed from their consular jurisdiction in the area. Euan-Smith proved to be a shrewd negotiator. He took swift advantage of the appointment in February 1890 of a new sultan, Ali bin Said, to formalize the British position in Zanzibar by persuading Ali to agree to the island becoming a British protectorate. The explanation given by Euan-Smith to the new sultan of the nature of the proposed new relationship was 'partial and misleading' (Oliver and Mathew, 411). The declaration of the protectorate paved the way for agreements about the settlement of east Africa with Germany and France. Euan-Smith, who had been made CB in 1889, was now advanced to KCB.

The Foreign Office especially valued Euan-Smith's negotiating powers, and Gerald Portal was sent to administer the protectorate, Euan-Smith being moved to the sensitive area of Morocco in March 1891 as British envoy. He was given special instructions, foremost among which was a direction to negotiate a new commercial treaty on a broad and liberal basis. In April 1892 he started from Tangier on a special mission to Fez, taking with him the draft of a commercial treaty, and terms for the ending of slavery. After a long and wearisome negotiation, the mission failed: no treaty or agreement was reached, and Euan-Smith's career was blighted. He was relieved of his post in July 1893. In June of that year the University of Oxford awarded him the honorary degree of DCL and he was made an honorary fellow of St John's College, Oxford. He devoted the rest of his life to commercial business, taking an active part, as chairman or director, in several companies. In July 1898 he was offered by Lord Salisbury and accepted the appointment of minister resident at Bogota, in the republic of Colombia, but resigned it without taking up his post. He married in 1877 Edith, daughter of General Frederick Alexander RA; they had one daughter. He died at his home, 51 South Street, Park Lane, London, on 30 August 1910.

T. H. SANDERSON, *rev.* H. C. G. MATTHEW

Sources *FO List* (1911) • *The Times* (31 Aug 1910) • L. W. Hollingsworth, *Zanzibar under the Foreign Office, 1890–1913* (1953) • R. Oliver and G. Mathew, *History of East Africa*, 1 (1963) • *CGPLA Eng. & Wales* (1910)

Archives BL OIOC, corresp. relating to India, MS Eur. B 311 • Oxon. RO, corresp. and papers | Bodl. RH, corresp. with Lord Lugard and others • SOAS, letters to Sir William Mackinnon

Likenesses wood-engraving, NPG; repro. in *ILN* (12 Jan 1889)

Wealth at death £2132 18*s.* 5*d.*: probate, 7 Sept 1910, *CGPLA Eng. & Wales*

Smith, Sir Charles Edward Kingsford (1897–1935), aviator, was born on 9 February 1897 in Brisbane, Australia, the fifth of the seven children of William Charles Smith (1852–1930), banker, and his wife, Catherine Mary Kingsford (1857–1938). In 1903 the Smith family moved to Vancouver, Canada, where William found clerical work in property and in the railways. There they adopted the composite surname Kingsford Smith: this was an unconventional though practical measure that enabled ease of identification in a new country. The family returned to Australia in 1907, and this time settled in Sydney, where for convenience the revised surname was retained. Between 1903 and 1912 Charles attended elementary school in Vancouver, St Andrew's choir school in Sydney, and Sydney Technical High School. Soon after, at the age of sixteen, he took up an apprenticeship with the Colonial Sugar Refining Company.

The First World War interrupted this career path: in February 1915 Kingsford Smith enlisted with the Australian Imperial Force, in which he served at Gallipoli, in Egypt, and in France, earning promotion to sergeant. In October 1916 he transferred to the Australian flying corps, under whom he trained as a pilot in Britain. In March 1917 Kingsford Smith was commissioned as second lieutenant in the Royal Flying Corps; three months later he joined 23 squadron in France as flying officer. In August 1917, though, his plane was shot down, which left him with a foot wound

Sir Charles Edward Kingsford Smith (1897–1935), by unknown photographer, *c.*1932

that required long-term rehabilitation. Now retired from combat, Kingsford Smith was awarded the Military Cross, but he remained active as a flying instructor for the Royal Flying Corps. Indeed, in April 1918 he was promoted to the rank of lieutenant.

Kingsford Smith saw great potential for civil aviation and so was determined to be a key figure in the development of flying in Australia. However, his initial moves in this direction were modest. Denied a start in the 1919 competition for the £10,000 prize offered by the Australian government for the first flight between England and Australia, he set up a firm offering joy flights to the English public; he then moved to the west coast of North America, where he performed stunt manoeuvres for flying 'circuses' and film studios. Kingsford Smith was, in his own mind, capable of far greater feats than these; indeed, his key aim while in the United States was to raise sponsorship for an inaugural trans-Pacific flight, believing that a spectacular flight was the best way to generate publicity and support for his civil aviation plans.

But in January 1921 Kingsford Smith returned to Australia without financial support and was again obliged to take work as a joyrider. Soon after he found a position as chief pilot with the fledgeling Western Australian Airways, and on 6 June 1923 he married Thelma Eileen Hope McKenna. In 1924 he went into partnership with a fellow pilot, Keith Anderson, to establish an airline under his own control. The pair operated a trucking business, hoping to raise enough capital to purchase two aircraft. By 1926 they had accumulated sufficient funds so they moved to Sydney, where, along with Charles Ulm, they established Interstate Flying Services. This venture stalled; other firms won tenders for airmail services. So Kingsford Smith and Ulm initiated several distance flights to display their capabilities. In June 1927 the duo attracted great public interest as they circumnavigated the Australian continent in ten days and five hours—halving the previous record. Smithy, as he was now known colloquially, then petitioned the New South Wales government to help finance a trans-Pacific flight. It did so by providing a grant of £9000 Australian, with additional sponsorship from Melbourne entrepreneur Sidney Myer.

On 31 May 1928 Kingsford Smith and Ulm, together with two American crew, set off from Oakland, California, for Brisbane in their composite Fokker aeroplane the *Southern Cross*. After stopping to refuel at Hawaii and Suva, they landed in Australia after 83 hours 38 minutes of flying. This feat made Kingsford Smith famous: he was made honorary squadron leader, Royal Australian Air Force, and was presented with the Air Force Cross. The flight also earned the two pilots about £20,000 Australian, though they fell out with Anderson, who petitioned unsuccessfully for a portion of the windfall. The money had practical importance: Kingsford Smith was keen to show that regular airmail and passenger travel were conceivable, so in August 1928 he and Ulm flew east–west across the Australian continent from Point Crook, Victoria, to Perth, then from Sydney to Christchurch in September 1928. Primed by these feats, the pilots then set out on 31 March 1929 to fly to England, where they hoped to purchase planes for an air service in Australia. But they were forced down in the Northern Territory, where they remained until help arrived sixteen days later. Tragically, in one of the aircraft that searched for the pair was Anderson who, along with his co-pilot, perished in the desert after crash landing. Rumours spread that Smithy had faked his disappearance as a publicity stunt, but an official inquiry dismissed such claims. So he and Ulm resumed their flight to Britain, which was completed on 25 June in the record time of twelve days and eighteen hours.

In January 1930 Kingsford Smith launched his own airline, Australian National Airways, and he piloted one of the company's ten planes. But he was never content as a business operator, nor was he particularly able as an entrepreneur. By June 1930 he was again aboard the *Southern Cross*, this time flying from Ireland to Newfoundland in a record thirty-one and a half hours. A reception in his honour followed in New York, and he was presented with the city's gold medal. Further aviational feats followed: in October 1930 he flew a biplane, affectionately named *Southern Cross Junior*, from England to Darwin in less than ten days; in doing so he beat four other competitors and broke the existing record by more than five days. Having divorced his first wife in 1929, he married on 10 December 1930 Mary (*b.* 1911), only daughter of Arthur Powell, merchant and manufacturer of Melbourne. They had a son.

In October 1933 Kingsford Smith flew solo from London to Western Australia in the record time of seven days and five hours, a feat that earned him a commonwealth grant of £3000 Australian. Despite all this he had not prospered; his airline business was in the doldrums during the depression, and a Sydney-based pilot training school in his name folded in 1935 after being in operation for only three years. Yet he was relentless, even obsessional, about etching his name in distance aviation history: in late 1934 he and G. P. Taylor made the first west–east trans-Pacific flight, from Brisbane to San Francisco in a Lockheed Altair. On 6 November 1935 he began another England–Australia journey, again aiming to break the record. But this was his last flight: after passing over Calcutta about midnight on 7 November, heading for Singapore, he and companion J. T. 'Tommy' Pethybridge were lost at sea on 8 November, probably in the Bay of Bengal, off the coast of Burma, where one of the wheels of their plane was washed ashore two years later. His wife (who later remarried and settled in the USA) and son survived him.

Kingsford Smith received numerous honours: in 1932 he was knighted for his pioneering role in distance aviation, and he received an array of awards from flying associations. Smithy was a national figure: his image appeared on an Australian postage stamp in his lifetime, and it later featured on the $20 note. Sydney's airport was named Kingsford Smith, and at Brisbane airport the *Southern Cross* is on public display. DARYL ADAIR

Sources C. Kingsford Smith and C. Ulm, *The great trans-Pacific flight: the story of the 'Southern Cross'* (1928) • C. Kingsford Smith, *The old bus* (1932) • G. Rawson, ed., *My flying life: an authentic biography prepared under the personal supervision of and from the diaries of the late Sir Charles Kingsford Smith* (1939) • E. P. Wixted, *The life and times of Sir Charles Kingsford Smith* (1996) • N. Ellison, *Flying Matilda: early days in Australian aviation* (1957) • B. Sheil, *The Caesar of the skies: the life story of Sir Charles Kingsford Smith* (1937) • P. Davis, *Charles Kingsford Smith: the world's greatest aviator* (1988) • W. McNally, *Smithy: the Kingsford Smith story* (1969) • W. McNally, *The man on the twenty dollar note: Sir Charles Kingsford Smith* (1976) • *AusDB* • *The Herald* [Melbourne] (9 June 1978)

Archives Mitchell L., NSW, logbook of the flight of the *Southern Cross* from San Francisco to Brisbane, June 1928 • NL Aus., memorabilia | SOUND NL Aus., 'Charles Kingsford Smith and Charles Ulm on their trans-Pacific flight, 1928', sound recording from Radio 2VE, Sydney, 1 tape reel

Likenesses S. Miller, drawing, 1930 • photograph, *c.*1932, Hult. Arch. [*see illus.*] • watercolour, 1956, NL Aus. • bronze bust, 1971, Brisbane airport

Wealth at death A$12,875

Smith, Sir Charles Felix (1786–1858), army officer, second son of George Smith (*bap.* 1754), banker, of Burn Hall, Durham, and his wife, Juliet, daughter and heir of Richard Mott of Carlton, Suffolk, was born on 9 July 1786 at Piercefield, Monmouthshire. Elizabeth *Smith (1776–1806) was his sister, and George Smith (1693–1756) his great-grandfather. He joined the Royal Military Academy at Woolwich on 15 June 1801, and was commissioned second lieutenant in the Royal Engineers on 1 October 1802. On 9 October he was promoted first lieutenant and sent to the south-eastern military district, where he was employed on the coastal defences of Kent.

On 16 December 1804 Smith embarked for the West Indies, where he served under Sir Charles Shipley. He was promoted second captain on 18 November 1807. In December of that year he accompanied the expedition under General Bowyer against the Danish West Indian islands, and took part in the capture of St Thomas, St John, and Santa Cruz. In January 1809 he accompanied the expedition under Sir George Beckwith to attack Martinique, and took part in the capture of Pigeon Island on 4 February and in the capture of Fort Bourbon, which led to the capitulation of the island on 23 February. He was wounded, and on his return to England on 31 March 1810 received a wound pension of £100 p.a.

On 25 October 1810 Smith embarked for the Peninsula, and joined the force of Sir Thomas Graham at Cadiz, then blockaded by the French. In the spring of 1811 an attempt to raise the siege was made by sending a force by water to Tarifa near Gibraltar to march on the flank of the enemy. Smith was left behind as senior engineer officer in charge of Cadiz, as well as of La Isla. In spite of the victory at Barossa (5 March 1811) the siege was not raised, and the British retired within the lines of La Isla.

Smith's health suffered at Cadiz, but in October he was sent to Tarifa, where he was commanding royal engineer during the siege by the French. Colonel Skerrett commanded the British and Spanish troops of the garrison. The allied outposts were driven in on 19 December, and in ten days the French batteries opened fire, making a breach after only a few hours. Skerrett proposed to abandon the defence, embark the garrison on board the transports, and sail for Gibraltar. Smith opposed the proposal, and continued preparations for desperate resistance. Details of the situation were sent to the governor of Gibraltar, who promptly removed the transports. On 31 December 1811 the French made an unsuccessful assault. Bad weather damaged the French batteries and trenches, and supply became difficult owing to the state of the roads. On the night of 4 January 1812 it became apparent that the French were preparing to withdraw, and on the morning of the 5th Skerrett assumed the offensive, drove the French from their trenches, and compelled them to retreat. By general consent the chief credit for the successful defence was given to Smith. Napier, in his *History of the War in the Peninsula* (4.59, 60), points out that Skerrett was persuaded by Smith's energy, but with reluctance. 'To the British engineer, therefore, belongs the praise of this splendid action.'

Smith was promoted brevet major for his services at Tarifa from 31 December 1811. He was promoted first captain in the Royal Engineers on 12 April 1812, and returned to Cadiz, where he was commanding royal engineer until the siege was raised in July. In the following year he took part in the action of Osma (18 June 1813), the battle of Vitoria (21 June), and the engagements at Villafranca and Tolosa (24 and 25 June). He accompanied Sir Thomas Graham on 1 July to take part in the siege of San Sebastian. On Wellington's visit on the 12th, he accompanied the duke round the positions as senior officer of Royal Engineers, and his plans of operation met with Wellington's approval. San Sebastian fell on 9 September; Smith was mentioned in Graham's dispatch and promoted brevet lieutenant-colonel on 21 September 1813 'for conduct before the enemy at San Sebastian'.

Smith returned to England in August 1814. He was knighted by the prince regent on 10 November, and received permission to accept and wear the crosses of the royal orders of Carlos III and San Fernando of Spain, given to him for his services in the Peninsula. On 28 April 1815 he was appointed commanding royal engineer of the Sussex military district. On 4 June he was made CB, military division. He received the gold medal with clasp for Vitoria and San Sebastian. His previous pension of £100 was increased to £300 a year on 18 June 1815, as he had partially lost the sight of an eye in the Peninsula.

On 19 June 1815 Smith joined the British army in the Southern Netherlands as commanding royal engineer of the 2nd corps, and took part in the entry into Paris on 7 July. He was one of the officers selected by Wellington to take over the French fortresses to be occupied by the British, and subsequently commanded the engineers at Vincennes. He was the first to import English thoroughbred horses into France for racing, and organized races at Vincennes superior to those under royal patronage in the Champ de Mars. He was an accomplished boxer and a noted duellist, skilled with rapier, sabre, and pistol. During his stay in Paris he was involved in duels that resulted in the deaths of three men.

Smith returned to England on 8 November 1818. He was employed in the south of England as commanding royal engineer until 1 January 1823, when he was appointed commanding royal engineer in the West Indies, with headquarters at Barbados. He was promoted lieutenant-colonel in the Royal Engineers on 29 July 1825, and colonel in the army on 22 July 1830. During his fourteen consecutive years in the West Indies he was acting governor of Trinidad in 1828, 1830, and during the whole of 1831. In 1833 he was acting governor of Demerara and Berbice, and in 1834 of St Lucia. He commanded the forces in the West Indies from June 1836 to February 1837. He was promoted colonel in the Royal Engineers on 10 January 1837.

On 8 May 1837 Smith was appointed commanding royal engineer at Gibraltar, where in 1838 he was acting governor and commanded the forces. He returned to England in the summer of 1840 to go on special service to Syria. He arrived at Beirut on the frigate *Pique* on 1 September. A landing was effected on the 10th, but Smith was too ill to take immediate command. He was invested, by imperial firman dated 30 September 1840, with the command of the sultan's army in Syria, and on 9 October was given by the British government the local rank of major-general in Syria in command of the allied land forces. After a bombardment Beirut surrendered on 11 October. On 3 November, Smith took part in the capture of Acre, where he was severely wounded. He returned the battered fortress to a state of defence and undertook the temporary administration of the pashalic of Acre.

Smith returned to Gibraltar in March 1841, receiving the thanks of parliament and of the government, while the sultan presented him with the Nishan Iftikhar, and diamond medal and sword. He was granted one year's pay for his wound at Acre. Promoted major-general in the army on 23 November 1841, he returned home from Gibraltar on 15 May 1842, and was made KCB (military division) on 27 September 1843. He was employed as a major-general on the staff in Ireland during the 1848 unrest, and was promoted lieutenant-general on 11 November 1851 and colonel-commandant of the corps of Royal Engineers on 6 March 1856.

Smith married, first, in 1821, a daughter of Thomas Bell of Bristol (she died at their residence in Onslow Square, London, on 18 June 1849), and, second, in 1852, Matilda Caroline, eldest daughter of Thomas Croft; she survived her husband. There were no children. Smith died at 8 Bath Buildings, Worthing, Sussex, on 11 August 1858.

R. H. VETCH, *rev.* JAMES FALKNER

Sources *Army List* • W. Porter, *History of the corps of royal engineers*, 2 vols. (1889) • 'Interesting intelligence from the London Gazettes', *GM*, 1st ser., 82/2 (1812), 174 • 'Companions of the order of the Bath', *GM*, 1st ser., 85/2 (1815), 628 • *GM*, 3rd ser., 5 (1858), 310 • R. H. Gronow, *The reminiscences of Captain Gronow*, 4 vols. (1861–6) • T. W. J. Connolly, *History of the royal sappers and miners*, 2nd edn, 2 vols. (1857) • W. F. P. Napier, *History of the war in the Peninsula and in the south of France*, 6 vols. (1886) • *Hart's Army List* • *Colburn's United Service Magazine*, 3 (1849), 300 • Boase, *Mod. Eng. biog.* • *Dod's Peerage* (1858) • *CGPLA Eng. & Wales* (1858)

Archives Bodl. Oxf., letters to Sir William Napier • U. Durham L., letters to Viscount Ponsonby

Wealth at death under £14,000: probate, 22 Oct 1858, *CGPLA Eng. & Wales*

Smith, Sir Charles Hamilton (1776–1859), soldier and natural historian, was born in east Flanders on 26 December 1776, a descendant of a Flemish protestant family. He was at school in Richmond, Surrey, when a revolt occurred in the Low Countries and he was called home to study in the Austrian Academy for Artillery and Engineers at Malines and then at Louvain. He pursued a career as a soldier, serving in the British army as a volunteer before joining the 60th regiment in the West Indies where he was island engineer in Jamaica (1797–1807).

In 1809 Smith was engaged in recruiting at Coventry when he was transferred, as deputy quartermaster-general, to the British force which seized Walcheren (but was subsequently forced to withdraw, after almost half of the 15,000 troops had died of fever). He then served with distinction in Holland and Brabant, before returning to Coventry in January 1811 by which time he had achieved the rank of captain in the 6th regiment. Called to active service again, he returned to the Low Countries. His last posting occurred in 1816 on a mission to the United States and Canada. He retired in 1820 on half pay and ten years later received the brevet rank of lieutenant-colonel. He also became a knight of Hanover in 1834.

From a very early age, Smith had industriously sketched and accumulated data. His interests were wide, so that his sketchbooks included historical, zoological, archaeological, and topographical subjects. His interest in such topics persisted through his time as a soldier; after retirement they became all-absorbing. His manuscript notes (and thousands of watercolour drawings) were made mostly for his own instruction and that of any student who asked to see them. However, during his military career, use was made of his details of roads and towns in the forest of the Ardennes, and a scheme he drew up for the defence of Canada (which was sufficiently regarded as to be printed by the government).

After retirement Smith settled at Plymouth with his wife, Mary Anne (*d.* before 1841), the daughter of Joseph Mauger of Guernsey, whom he had married in 1808. One son, Charles Ferdinand Hamilton Smith, who lived in New South Wales, and three daughters survived their father. The eldest daughter, Emma, looked after her father following the death of her mother.

Smith's numerous publications, with his lectures at the Plymouth Athenaeum, made him well known. He was elected FRS in 1824 and FLS in 1826. His industry enabled him to master several disciplines and his accuracy of observation assisted him in the making of accurate drawings of his subjects. Interested in history, as well as the natural sciences, he often gave information to the theatre managers William Charles Macready (1793–1873) and Charles John Kean (1811–1868) and his brother Edmund (1787–1833) on the correct costumes for their productions. By 1815 he had written two books on the subject of costume worn in Britain and Ireland before the seventeenth century. He also gave Sir Charles Barry some designs for heraldic decorations when the latter was designing the new Palace of Westminster in 1840.

Smith's authorship of historical books on war included the translation of accounts of the Seven Years' War in Germany, a piece on the military exploits of the duke of Marlborough (for Coxe's biography), and a narrative of the retreat of Napoleon from Moscow, which he wrote in French. He also contributed articles on the subject of war to encyclopaedias. Many of these works were illustrated from his own drawings and watercolours. The illustrations in his natural history books were also based on his own original sketches.

Smith was a close friend of the French anatomist Georges Léopold Chrétien Frédéric Dagobert Cuvier (1769–1832), an assistant professor of comparative anatomy in the Jardin des Plantes, also an intimate friend of Richard Owen. He was one of the collaborators who produced *General and Particular Descriptions of the Vertebrated Animals* (1824–35) based on a translation of Cuvier's *Le règne animal* and published under the editorship of Edward Griffith. Some of Smith's drawings were used for the illustrations in a number of volumes which he wrote for Sir William Jardine's Naturalist's Library: two volumes of the *Natural History of Dogs* (1839 and 1840), the *Natural History of Horses* (1841), and *Introduction to the Mammalia* (1842). A *Natural History of the Human Species* (1848) was designed to complement these volumes, and included his engraved portrait for the frontispiece. Besides these major titles, he wrote and illustrated numerous articles for scientific journals.

By the time Smith died on 21 September 1859 at his home, 40 Park Street, Plymouth, Devon, manuscripts, books, and sketchbooks overflowed every room in the house. Following his burial in the family vault at Pennycross, his manuscripts and drawings were sold. Under the terms of his will, his estate of about £4000 and the proceeds of the sale of his effects were to be shared equally between his son and three daughters, Emma Hamilton Smith, Eliza Hamilton Whiteford, and Emily Frances Jane Hamilton King.

Many of Smith's twenty volumes of manuscript notes, chiefly unpublished letters and papers, were deposited in the Plymouth Institution, but were destroyed during a bombing raid in 1941. His collection of nearly 15,000 drawings was put up for sale by Puttick and Simpson on 20 July 1860 as a single lot, and knocked down to 'Smith' for £500. The drawings were classified as general (hunting scenes and trees, 132 drawings), antiquities (3938), ethnology (2184), topography (3253), full-length historical portraits (1048), and natural history drawings. The last amounted to 4893 sheets, with some sheets bearing several drawings. However, it is not known what became of most of the works. CHRISTINE E. JACKSON

Sources notes on life of C. H. Smith, Linn. Soc. [on which the pubd obits. are based] • *Proceedings of the Linnean Society of London* (1859–60), xxx–xxxi • *PRS*, 10 (1859–60), xxiv–xxvi • G. D. R. Bridson, V. C. Phillips, and A. P. Harvey, *Natural history manuscript resources in the British Isles* (1980), 600 • R. McN. Alexander, 'Drawings of vertebrate animals from the collection of Charles Hamilton Smith (1776–1859)', *Archives of Natural History*, 13 (1986), 39–70 • R. N. Worth, *History of Plymouth from the earliest period to the present time* (1890), 471–2 • sale catalogue (1860), lot 1894 [Puttick and Simpson, 20 July 1860] • E. Rundle Charles, *Our seven homes: autobiographical reminiscences of Mrs Rundle Charles, with portraits*, ed. [M. Davidson] (1896)

Archives American Museum of Natural History, New York, drawings and MSS • BM, drawings and watercolours • Harvard U., Houghton L., drawings and MSS • Linn. Soc., notebook • NHM • S. Antiquaries, Lond., antiquarian notes and drawings • V&A, department of prints and drawings, sketches • Westcountry Studies Library, Exeter, sketches of Devon tombs, arms, etc. | priv. coll., Coulton collection, natural history drawings • Royal Museum, Edinburgh, letters to Sir William Jardine

Likenesses W. Brockedon, pencil and chalk drawing, 1830, NPG • J. Scott, engraving, pubd 1841, Plymouth • J. Scott, mezzotint, pubd 1841 (after E. Opie), BM, NPG • E. Opie, oils?; formerly in possession of Mrs Rendle, 1868 • engraving, RS • lithograph, repro. in *Memoir* [pubd Ghent *c.*1860]

Wealth at death under £4000: probate, 6 Oct 1859, *CGPLA Eng. & Wales*

Smith, Charles Harriot (1792–1864), architect, was born in London on 1 February 1792, the son of Joseph Smith, monumental sculptor, of Portland Road, Marylebone. On leaving school at the age of twelve, he entered his father's business and practised drawing and modelling after working hours. He exhibited at the Royal Academy as early as 1809 and in 1813 he became a life member of the Society of Arts. According to Gunnis, he was befriended by Bonomi, the architect, at whose suggestion he entered the Royal Academy Schools, in 1814, aged twenty-two, and in 1817 he obtained the academy gold medal for his *Design for a Royal Academy* (Gunnis, 354). Between 1809 and 1823 he exhibited portrait busts, monumental compositions, and architectural designs at the Royal Academy. He acquired a knowledge of geology, mineralogy, and chemistry, and became an authority on building stones. In 1836 he was appointed one of the four commissioners for the selection of a suitable building stone for the new houses of parliament. Gunnis noted a comment that, while the commissioners' report 'won the admiration of the profession as a great addition to professional knowledge', Smith himself 'secured the lasting goodwill and esteem of his colleagues by his zeal, intelligence and cheerful co-operation' (ibid., 355).

Smith executed the ornamental stonecarving of the Royal Exchange, of the National Gallery, and of Dorchester and Bridgewater houses. In 1850 he carved the capital of Nelson's Column in Trafalgar Square. In 1855 he was elected a member of the Royal Institute of British Architects, to which he contributed numerous sessional papers, of which the most important was entitled 'Lithology, or, Observations on stone used for buildings', which he read in 1842. He also wrote an essay on linear and aerial perspective for Maria Arnold's Library of the Fine Arts. Smith was also interested in science and wrote papers on a variety of subjects. Gunnis noted that he described himself as 'a strange mongrel of art, science, literature and business' (Gunnis, 355). In his obituary one of his workers was said to have remarked 'he never grasped for money, but he did for knowledge which he held fast but nevertheless gave away abundantly' (*The Builder*, 5 Nov 1864, 802).

He died at his home, 24 Hatton Garden, London, on 27 October 1864, leaving his wife, Fanny, and one son, Percy Gordon Smith, who was for many years architect to the Local Government Board.

E. I. CARLYLE, *rev.* M. A. GOODALL

Sources *GM*, 3rd ser., 17 (1864), 805 • [W. Papworth], ed., *The dictionary of architecture*, 11 vols. (1853–92) • Redgrave, *Artists* • Allibone, *Dict.* • Boase, *Mod. Eng. biog.* • *A compendium of Pevsner's Buildings of England*, ed. M. Good (1995) [CD-ROM] • M. H. Port, ed., *The Houses of Parliament* (1976) • R. Gunnis, *Dictionary of British sculptors, 1660–1851* (1953); new edn (1968) • *The Builder*, 22 (1864), 802 • *CGPLA Eng. & Wales* (1864)

Archives RIBA BAL, notebook relating to stone for the Houses of Parliament

Wealth at death under £600: probate, 16 Nov 1864, *CGPLA Eng. & Wales*

Smith, Charles John (1803–1838), engraver, was born in Chelsea, London, where his father, James Smith, practised as a surgeon. He was a pupil of Charles Pye, and became a good engraver on steel of topographical and antiquarian book illustrations, some after his own design. He executed a few of the later plates in Charles Stothard's *The Monumental Effigies of Great Britain* (1817–32), the views of houses and monuments in Edmund Cartwright's 'The parochial topography of the rape of Bramber', in James Dallaway's *A History of the Western Division of the County of Sussex* (2 vols., 1815–30), about half of which were printed as vignettes onto the text page, and several of the plates from illuminated manuscripts for T. F. Dibdin's *A Bibliographical, Antiquarian and Picturesque Tour in the Northern Counties of England and Scotland* (1838). In 1829 Smith published *Autographs of royal, noble, learned and remarkable personages conspicuous in English history, from the reign of Richard II to that of Charles II, with some illustrious foreigners*, with memoirs by John Gough Nichols, and later undertook a serial work, *Historical and literary curiosities consisting of facsimiles of original documents, scenes of remarkable events* (1835–40), which he did not live to complete. He is known to have engraved at least seven of the plates for *Graphic Illustrations of the Life and Times of Samuel Johnson* (1835). He was elected a fellow of the Society of Antiquaries in 1837, and died of paralysis in Albany Street, where he was living in London, on 23 November 1838. He is best remembered for his landscape prints.

F. M. O'DONOGHUE, *rev.* JOANNA DESMOND

Sources B. Hunnisett, *An illustrated dictionary of British steel engravers*, new edn (1989) • Redgrave, *Artists*

Smith, Charles Roach (1806–1890), antiquary, was born at Landguard Manor, near Shanklin, Isle of Wight, on 18 August 1806, the youngest of ten children of John Smith (1758–1812), a tenant farmer, and his wife, Ann (1764–1832), the daughter of Henry Roach of nearby Arreton Manor. His father having died when he was six, Smith was brought up by his mother and sisters. He attended Mr Crouch's school at Swathling, Southampton, and moved with the school to St Cross, Winchester. About 1818 he entered Mr Withers's academy at Lymington. In 1821 he joined the office of Francis Worsley, solicitor, of Newport, Isle of Wight. He showed no aptitude for the law, however, and in 1822 he was apprenticed to John Follett, a chemist in Chichester. In 1827 he joined Wilson, Ashmore, Hodgkinson, and Minshull, wholesale druggists of Snow Hill, London, and in 1834 established a chemist's business at Founders' Court, 48 Lothbury.

In 1840 Smith's premises were compulsorily purchased by the City corporation, and he moved to 5 Liverpool Street. He was joined here by his sister Maria, and the pair lived happily together until she died in 1874; neither was married. In 1856, the business having dwindled, the Smiths retired to Strood, Kent, where he purchased Temple Place, on the Cuxton Road (now the premises of Strood Conservative Club). He also acquired some surrounding horticultural land, which from 1877 was regularly flooded by the River Medway.

A person of manly and handsome appearance, Smith also possessed a fine intellect which was matched by his fierce determination and relentless industry. His kindness, integrity, and gift for repartee gained him many friends, but his outspokenness, strong opinions, a tendency to self-aggrandizement, and the resentment he showed towards persons in authority also made him enemies.

On moving to Lothbury, Smith began to collect the Roman and medieval antiquities which were being recovered in constructing sewers and offices and in dredging the Thames. He eventually amassed more than 5000 items, not for their artistic or monetary worth, but to illustrate 'the institutions, the habits, the customs, and the arts of our forefathers' (*Collectanea Antiqua*, 4, 1855, Appendix, 46). His collection was open to enquirers and, following the publication of his *Catalogue of the Museum of London Antiquities* (1854), Smith's fellow antiquaries urged that it should be preserved for the nation. In 1855 Smith offered it to the British Museum for £3000, but the museum refused to purchase, as it had hitherto collected mainly foreign antiquities, provoking an outcry in the press. Although this sum could have been obtained at auction, Smith accepted the museum's subsequent offer of £2000 to prevent the collection from being dispersed.

Smith made numerous archaeological observations in the City, although from 1841 he was actively obstructed by the City corporation, who were offended by his lambasting them in the press. His work nevertheless amounts to the first sustained campaign of urban site observation in Britain, and it enabled Smith to suggest the development of the Roman City, and to demonstrate the survival of monumental buildings and of Roman work in the City walls, the existence of the Roman riverside wall, and the probability of a Roman bridge over the Thames. His *Illustrations of Roman London* (1859) remained the principal work on the subject until 1909.

Beginning with his 'List of Roman coins recently found near Strood …', an article published in the *Numismatic Chronicle* in 1840, Smith also pioneered the statistical study of Roman coin hoards. He published many new coin types, especially of Carausius and Allectus, and from 1862 to 1863 assisted with Stevenson's *Dictionary of Roman Coins* (1889).

Throughout his antiquarian career Smith made regular excursions in search of field monuments and antiquarian collections. Starting in 1836 in south-east England, these extended to northern France, Hadrian's Wall, and ultimately to Germany and Italy. He published the results in the *Gentleman's Magazine* and his own *Collectanea Antiqua* (7 vols., 1843–80)—the first journal devoted to archaeology in the modern sense of the word. Smith thereby became the first Englishman to study the Roman antiquities of France and Germany and to take an interest in provincial sepulchral monuments depicting scenes of everyday life.

In December 1836 Smith was elected fellow of the Society of Antiquaries of London, and he served on its council from 1840 to 1845 and from 1849 to 1851. He was elected to the London Numismatic Society in 1837, and was an honorary secretary from 1840 to 1844 and from 1847 to 1851. He was made honorary member of the society in 1852, and in 1883 received its first medal for promoting the knowledge of Romano-British coins. He became an honorary member of the Royal Society of Literature in 1853 and of the Archaeological Institute in 1872, and received similar recognitions from many other societies at home and abroad. He published numerous articles in the *Archaeological Journal*, the *Journal of the British Archaeological Association*, and *Archaeologia Cantiana*, and wrote in the *Gentleman's Magazine*, compiling its monthly 'Antiquarian notes' from 1865 to 1868.

In December 1843 Smith joined Thomas Wright in founding the British Archaeological Association, to encourage the recording, preservation, and publication of archaeological discoveries, and to lobby for government assistance. Smith became its first secretary and arranged the first six annual congresses. Although nominally a secretary until 1851, he effectively resigned the post in 1849 after the committee had refused a suggestion that they should raise a testimonial for him. The incident sealed Smith's disillusionment with the association, which he considered had failed through internal squabbling, sycophancy, and the famous schism of 1845. In 1852 he resigned from all subscribing societies, although in 1874 he was elected honorary member of the British Archaeological Association and a year later became a vice-president.

After his resignation Smith set out to prove that he could succeed without societies. Certainly he outstripped them in fund-raising for publications and for his excavations of the Roman forts of Lympne and Pevensey in 1850–52, which he co-directed with M. A. Lower and James Elliott respectively—the first archaeological excavations in Britain to be financed by public subscription. He published the results in *The Antiquities of Richborough, Reculver, and Lymne* (1850) and two slim supplements, which amount to the first systematic investigation of the Roman forts of the Saxon shore. Smith subsequently gave much assistance to J. C. Bruce, author of works on Hadrian's Wall, and, through the abbé Cochet, successfully intervened with Napoleon III to preserve the Roman walls of Dax.

Instead of writing in the *Journal of the British Archaeological Association*, Smith now revived his *Collectanea Antiqua*, wherein he emphasized the importance of facts as a basis for interpretation, and revived the systematic study of provincial Roman and Anglo-Saxon antiquities begun some decades earlier by Revd James Douglas. Smith's excursions had demonstrated the value of studying regional variations in pottery, glasswork, brooches, and other artefacts, and from 1848 to 1861 his international comparative studies, supported by detailed illustrations, achieved international significance alongside those of Worsaae in Denmark. Smith's most important observation—that differences in brooches and other Anglo-Saxon grave goods might reflect the areas settled by the different ethnic groups described in Bede's *Ecclesiastical History*—stands high among the achievements of nineteenth-century archaeology. He engendered a revival of interest in Revd Bryan Faussett's collection of Anglo-Saxon grave goods by editing an illustrated edition of Faussett's notebooks—the *Inventorium sepulchrale* (1856)—which remains a cornerstone of Anglo-Saxon cemetery studies. He also wrote a *Catalogue of Anglo-Saxon and other Antiquities Discovered at Faversham* (1871) for the South Kensington museum.

From 1861 Smith's archaeological work became less original, and he redirected his energies into horticulture and Shakespearian studies, publishing tracts on these subjects. He grew grapes and produced wine at a time when English vineyards were almost unknown. He gave dramatic readings in public, and in 1871 helped found the Strood Elocution Class, to assist the young working men of Strood. His final years were spent writing his *Retrospections, Social and Archaeological* (1883–91), the third volume of which was edited posthumously by J. G. Waller. Arising from his researches and his secretarial work, Smith amassed a huge collection of correspondence, notes, and drawings, which, despite his efforts to secure its future, was dispersed before his death. More than 300 manuscript collections survive in the public domain, but these represent no more than one-third of what formerly existed.

Smith died at Temple Place, Strood, on 2 August 1890, and on 7 August was buried in the same grave as his sister Maria in Frindsbury churchyard, near Strood. Three days before his death, John Evans, president of the Society of Antiquaries of London and of the Numismatic Society, presented Smith with a silver medal from fellow antiquaries to commemorate his 'lifelong services to archaeology'. Despite such acknowledgements, Smith's work was soon forgotten, and not until the mid-1970s did it begin to regain the recognition it deserves.

MICHAEL RHODES

Sources M. Rhodes, 'Some aspects of the contribution to British archaeology of Charles Roach Smith (1806–1890)', PhD diss., U. Lond., 1992 • M. Rhodes, 'Faussett rediscovered: Charles Roach Smith, Joseph Mayer, and the publication of *Inventorium sepulchrale*', *Anglo-Saxon cemeteries: a reappraisal*, ed. E. Southworth (1990), 25–64 • 'Death of Mr Roach Smith, F.S.A.', *Isle of Wight County Press* (9 Aug 1890), 5 • 'Death of Mr Charles Roach-Smith', *Chatham and Rochester Observer* (9 Aug 1890), 5 • G. Payne, *Journal of the British Archaeological Association*, 46 (1890), 318–30 • D. Kidd, 'Charles Roach Smith and his Museum of London Antiquities', *British Museum Yearbook*, 2 (1977), 105–35, pls. 74–98 • H. Smetham, *C.R.S. and his friends* (1929) • Isle of Wight County RO, Newport, Isle of Wight, File FAM /89 (Smith) • C. R. Smith, *Retrospections, social and archaeological*, 1 (1883) • d. cert.

Archives BM, department of medieval and modern Europe • NL Wales, corresp. and antiquarian papers • S. Antiquaries, Lond., antiquarian collection • Sheffield City Museum, antiquarian corresp. | BL, letters to Thomas Wright, Add. MSS 33346–33347 • Bodl. Oxf., corresp. with Sir Thomas Phillips • Ches. & Chester ALSS, letters to Thomas Hughes • Essex RO, Wire MSS • Lpool RO, Mayer MSS • Northampton Library, corresp. with Sir Henry Dryden • Sheffield City Museum, Bateman MSS • Sussex Archaeological Society, Lewes, corresp. with Mark Lower • U. Edin. L., corresp. with James Halliwell-Phillips • U. Newcastle, Robinson L., letters to Sir Walter Trevelyan

Likenesses G. Fontana, marble medallion, 1856, S. Antiquaries, Lond.; identical medallion, Walker Art Gallery, Liverpool • W. T. Taylor, medallion, 1858 • Mayall of Brighton, photograph, 1876, Dorset County Museum, Dorchester; pasted in author's copy of C. Warne, *Ancient Dorset* (1870) • Pincher, medallion, 1890 (struck at behest of John Evans), BM • R. T., wood-engraving, NPG; repro. in *ILN* (30 Aug 1890) • E. Walford, photograph, repro. in E. Walford, *Portraits of men of eminence*, 5 (1866), facing p. 13 • engraving, repro. in C. R. Smith, *Retrospections, social and archaeological*, 3 (1891), frontispiece

Wealth at death £1736 19*s.* 11*d.*: resworn probate, July 1891, *CGPLA Eng. & Wales* (1890)

Smith [*née* Turner], **Charlotte** (**1749–1806**), poet and novelist, was born on 4 May 1749 in King Street, off St James's Square, in London, the eldest of three children of Nicholas Turner (*b.* *c.*1721, *d.* before 1776), a prosperous landowner, and his wife, Anna (*c.*1727–*c.*1752), daughter of William Towers. Charlotte Turner was born into a family whose holdings included the London townhouse in which she was born, two estates (Bignor Park on the Arun, Sussex, and Stoke Place near Guildford, Surrey), and some smaller properties. She was baptized at Stoke church, near Guildford, on 12 June 1749 and spent her childhood moving between London, Stoke Place, and Bignor Park.

Charlotte Smith (1749–1806), by George Romney, 1792

Her sister and future biographer, the children's writer Catherine Ann *Dorset (*d.* in or after 1816), was born in or before 1752. Their mother died giving birth to their brother, Nicholas, when Charlotte was three years old. In the wake of this loss, their father travelled abroad, leaving the children to be raised by Lucy Towers, their maternal aunt.

Youth and marriage When she was six Charlotte attended school in Chichester, where she also took drawing lessons from the landscape painter George Smith. She moved with her aunt and sister to London when she was eight and continued her education at a fashionable girls' school in Kensington. She learned dancing, drawing, music, and acting, and won praise for her performances in French and English plays. Her avid reading habit and early efforts at poetic composition were encouraged by her father, who wrote poetry himself. At six or seven Charlotte began to compose her own poems (none of which survives) and to submit them to the *Lady's Magazine*, which did not print them.

It is unclear when Nicholas Turner returned to England, but his homecoming marked the end of Charlotte's childhood, in the form of financial difficulties that motivated him to sell Stoke Place and some smaller properties, and to remarry. In 1765 Nicholas Turner married Henrietta Meriton of Chelsea, who reportedly possessed both property and £20,000. Her arrival prompted Charlotte's formal entrance into society at the age of twelve, while her education continued at home in London with teachers engaged by her father. Although he refused an offer of marriage on her behalf when she was fourteen, he accepted another when she was fifteen. Benjamin Smith (1743/4–1806) was the second son of Richard Smith, a West India merchant and a director of the East India Company. He was twenty-one years old when he married Charlotte Turner on 23 February 1765.

Richard Smith hoped that Benjamin would join his business, but abandoned this plan as his son's irresponsibility and fiscal recklessness became apparent. Richard Smith was the owner of plantations in Barbados and he and his second wife, Elizabeth, brought with them to England five slaves, who were bequeathed, with their descendants, as property in his will. Charlotte Smith later protested against slavery in such works as *The Old Manor House* and her poem 'Beachy Head', but her new family's annual income of £2000 depended on slave labour. The couple's first home was an apartment over Richard Smith's business warehouse in Cheapside, a location meant to encourage Benjamin's participation in the family business. The family later moved to Southgate and Tottenham.

In the year after her marriage Smith gave birth to her first child, whose name and birth date are unknown. The infant died in 1767, within days of the birth of her second child, Benjamin Berney. Between 1767 and 1785 Smith gave birth to ten more children: William Towers (*b.* *c.*1768), Charlotte Mary (*b.* *c.*1769), Braithwaite (*b.* 1770), Nicholas Hankey (*b.* 1771), Charles Dyer (*b.* 1773), Anna Augusta (*b.* 1774), Lucy Eleanor (*b.* 1776), Sir Lionel *Smith (1778–1842), Harriet (*b.* *c.*1782), and George (*b.* *c.*1785). Only six of these children survived their mother, and two perished as children. Benjamin Berney died in 1777 after a long illness that may have been tuberculosis.

As her family grew, Charlotte assumed a small role in the family business that her husband neglected, by assisting Richard Smith with his business correspondence. Charlotte successfully defended her father-in-law against libel by writing a vindication of him, and she persuaded him to relieve his son of all his ties to the business and establish him as a gentleman farmer in Hampshire. She lived with her husband at Lys Farm for nine years from 1774 to 1783. The ties between Charlotte and Richard Smith were strengthened when he married Charlotte's aunt Lucy Towers in 1767, after Elizabeth's death. Wanting to protect his legacy of approximately £36,000 from his unreliable son and to secure it for his grandchildren, he undermined his own efforts, however, in an intricate will that proved vulnerable to legal challenges. After his death in 1776 the trustees could not agree on its meaning, and a chancery suit was spawned that did not reach even a partial settlement until 1798, and remained open until after Charlotte Smith's death. The estate's anticipated settlement prompted Smith's writing career: she wrote in order to maintain her children's social standing until they received their inheritance.

Poet When Benjamin was sent to the king's bench for debt in December 1783, Charlotte served part of the seven months' sentence with him, leaving their children with her brother, Nicholas. She negotiated the financial arrangements that enabled his release and submitted her first work for publication as a means of raising money. Smith approached the prestigious publishing house of James Dodsley with a collection of sonnets, but received only an offer to print the poems at his expense in exchange for any profits. After approaching Edward and Charles Dilly without success, Smith sent her poems to her Sussex neighbour the poet and biographer William Hayley, whose place in literary history would be secured by his friendship and sometime patronage of artists and writers, including the sculptor John Flaxman, the painter George Romney, and the poets William Cowper and William Blake. When Hayley accepted the dedication, Smith had Dodsley print the poems at her expense. *Elegiac Sonnets, and other Essays by Charlotte Smith of Bignor Park, Sussex* appeared in a slim quarto edition in June 1784 and immediately justified her risk. Within a year a second edition was printed, and by 1800 *Elegiac Sonnets* was in its ninth edition and filled two volumes. In identifying herself as 'Charlotte Smith of Bignor Park' on the collection's title-page, Smith made public her profile as a gentlewoman poet, a role that flattered her conviction that she need only remain in the literary marketplace until her father-in-law's estate restored her family to its rightful position among the landed gentry. Her commercial success as a poet gave Smith the confidence to publish the prose works that followed under her own name, a daring decision for a late eighteenth-century woman writer.

By continuing to add sonnets, other poems, prefaces, and illustrations, Smith enhanced her public profile as a poet. Although her novels, which far outnumbered her poetry collections, garnered the greatest profits and fame, Smith identified herself as a poet, the vocation she deemed best suited to her genteel origins. She prized her verse for the role it gave her as a private woman whose sorrows were submitted only reluctantly to the public. Smith both projected herself publicly and cast herself in her poetry and prose, through the use of thinly veiled autobiographical characters, as a familiar figure from the cultural tradition of sensibility: a woman who suffered a fall into difficult circumstances not of her own making and found solace in her natural surroundings and in sympathizing with other sufferers.

So effectively did Smith adopt the persona of the elegiac poet that Catherine Dorset was moved to correct her sister's self-presentation, by contending that '[c]heerfulness and gaiety were the natural characteristics of her mind' and that '[e]ven in the darkest periods of her life, she possessed the power of abstracting herself from her cares' (Dorset, 53, 54). Dorset provides a striking supplement to Smith's self-portrait as the poet alone in nature:

> In the society of persons she liked, and with whom she was under no restraint, with those who understood, and could enjoy her peculiar vein of humour, nothing could be more spirited, more racy, than her conversation; every sentence had its point, the effect of which was increased by the uncommon rapidity with which she spoke, as if her ideas flowed too fast for utterance. (ibid.)

Dorset recalls that her sister excelled at parody 'and did not spare even her own poetry' (ibid., 54). In the novels, this ability was often turned to satiric ends, her favourite figures of critique being lawyers, whom she held responsible for the irresolution of the chancery case, and thus her family's financial distress and her continued literary labour.

Novelist Soon after Benjamin Smith's release from debtors' prison, the family left England for France, in order to avoid his creditors. Charlotte returned to England shortly after they settled in Dieppe, in Normandy, but this time failed to settle her husband's finances. Back in France during the winter of 1784–5, she began the first of two translations from the French: *Manon Lescaut, or, The Fatal Attachment*, from the Abbé Prévost's *Manon Lescaut*. Later she published selections from François Gayot de Pitaval's court trials, *Les causes célèbres et intéressantes*, as the popular and influential *The Romance of Real Life* (1787). Smith withdrew *Manon Lescaut* from the press in response to criticism of the work's 'bad' morals, and a charge of plagiarism, on the grounds that English translations already existed. Smith acted to protect herself and her publisher Thomas Cadell senior from adverse publicity (the volume appeared anonymously in 1786). For Smith, Cadell was worth sparing, for he proved consistently supportive, and his reputation as a gentleman gratified her sense of her genteel literary standing.

The family returned to England about 1785 and settled at Woolbeding House near Midhurst, Sussex, but in 1787 Smith separated from her husband without obtaining a legal agreement that would protect her earnings from Benjamin's access to them under English primogeniture laws. One of Smith's recurrent concerns in her poetic and prose works is women's status in the English legal system. Smith settled with her children near Chichester and turned to novel-writing as a more lucrative form of publishing, beginning with *Emmeline, the Orphan of the Castle* (1788). The novel, which contained autobiographical portraits of Charlotte and Benjamin Smith as Mr and Mrs Stafford, was a success; the first edition of 1500 copies sold within months, and within a year a third edition appeared. Nine more novels followed in the next ten years: *Ethelinde, or, The Recluse of the Lake* (1789), *Celestina* (1791), *Desmond* (1792), *The Old Manor House* (1793), *The Wanderings of Warwick* (1794), *The Banished Man* (1794), *Montalbert* (1795), *Marchmont* (1796), and *The Young Philosopher* (1798).

Smith's novels develop the form according to Gothic and sentimental traditions (and were satirized by Jane Austen in *Northanger Abbey*). Smith also used her novels to explore social concerns. Critics have noted that Smith often borrows the Gothic setting of the manor house as a metaphor for the nation, and adopts the framework of the courtship novel in order to indict English primogeniture laws which favour empowered men over women, second sons, the impoverished, and the enslaved. From her first novel she examines the relations between social identity and a sense of self, showing how Emmeline's treatment by other characters and ultimately her fate turn on her social position, which begins with her apparent illegitimacy and poverty and ends with the revelation of her identity as the heir to Mowbray Castle.

In her novels and poems Smith frequently adopts the prototypical figure of the wanderer (who may be male or female) as a vehicle for social commentary. For instance in *The Old Manor House* she sends Orlando Somerive to America, where he begins to sympathize with the American Indians, to question English imperialism, and to critique slavery. Smith herself was a wanderer for much of her literary career. After leaving her husband she moved frequently, residing in numerous locations, including the environs of Chichester, Brighton, Storrington, Bath, Exmouth, Weymouth, Oxford, London, Frant, and Elstead, before settling at Tilford, near Farnham, in Surrey. Her wanderings were motivated by various factors, including her fluctuating economic circumstances, her health, which gradually declined from 1793 onwards, and a restlessness that left her, in her sister's words, 'unsettled, moving from place to place in search of that tranquility she was never destined to enjoy' (Dorset, 51).

Politics and later career At Brighton from 1791 to 1793 Smith became involved in radical English circles; the French Revolution and its aftermath provided some of her main themes. She was a republican sympathizer but later modified her opinion as a result of the terror. Her fourth novel, *Desmond* (1792), adopts the epistolary form to tell the story of the title character who travels to revolutionary France and is persuaded by arguments he hears there for revolution abroad and reform in England. The novel appeared from the house of the whig publisher George Robinson in June 1792, the year before war was declared between France and England and before the 'September massacres', news of which helped to turn the tide of English sentiment against the revolution. *Desmond*, the poem *The Emigrants* (1793), and another novel, *The Banished Man* (1794), belong to an era that Florence Hilbish terms Smith's 'French period'. In the two latter works Smith's politics follow in part the shifting tide of much radical sentiment in England, which slowly turned against a France that increasingly seemed to threaten its neighbours. The sympathetic title figures of the poem and the novel's hero are émigrés. Yet in dedicating *The Emigrants* to William Cowper, Smith makes a case against English nationalism and defends the socio-political ideals that initially fuelled the French Revolution. In repeatedly sympathizing with those who have endured social oppression, Smith participated in a tradition of sensibility that bound together the literary and the political by valuing a refined responsiveness to suffering. In recognition of her ability to move readers on social topics, Smith was asked to write *A Narrative of the Loss of the Catharine, Venus, and Piedmont Transports* (1796), an account of a shipwreck of seven ships off Dorset, in order to raise money for the survivors.

Smith's literary fame is displayed in an epistolary tableau provided by the painter George Romney of a gathering at Hayley's Sussex estate, Eartham, in summer 1792, that included Cowper. Romney completed a pastel drawing of Smith in crayons that Smith had copied and then engraved by P. Condé for volume 2 of *Elegiac Sonnets*. During the visit Smith composed *The Old Manor House* (1793), the novel frequently deemed her best. Sir Walter Scott called it her '*chef-d'oeuvre*' (Dorset, 63), and Anna Letitia Barbauld chose it for her edition of *The British Novelists*

(1810). The novel returns to the sentimental themes of her earlier novels and is praised for its development of minor characters. Smith's literary stature may also be measured by her acquaintances and correspondents, who included Charles Burney, Samuel Taylor Coleridge, Erasmus Darwin, Thomas Erskine (later lord chancellor), Mary Hays, Richard Brinsley Sheridan, and Robert Southey. More testimony to her prominence is provided by the number and diversity of periodicals that reviewed her works, including the *Anti-Jacobin*, the *Analytical Review*, the *British Critic*, the *Critical Review*, the *European Magazine*, the *Gentleman's Magazine*, the *Monthly Magazine*, and the *Universal Magazine*.

Smith counted on her literary fame to sustain a buying public's interest, but she also courted the aid of patrons who could attract the genteel readers she cherished as reflecting her status as a gentlewoman poet, and who might act on her behalf in the settlement of her father-in-law's estate. Thrice she ventured subscription, a form of publication that straddled both worlds, for the *Narrative* and both the fifth edition (1789) and volume 2 of *Elegiac Sonnets* (1797). The subscription list for the fifth edition boasts 815 names, including the archbishop of Canterbury, the duchess of Cumberland, Frances Burney, Elizabeth Carter, William Cowper, Mary Delany, Richard Payne Knight, William Pitt, Samuel Rogers, Horace Walpole, and Thomas and Joseph Warton. The embellishment of *Elegiac Sonnets* also testifies to its success: the fifth edition featured five illustrations, two by the prominent Thomas Stothard.

Judith Phillips Stanton estimates that Smith's greatest earning years were from 1787 to 1798 (Stanton, 'Charlotte Smith's "literary business"', 393). When volume 2 of *Elegiac Sonnets* appeared in 1797, the list of subscribers had shrunk to 283 names. A number of reasons have been suggested for the decline in Smith's popularity, including a corresponding erosion of the quality of her work after so many years of literary labour, an eventual waning of readerly interest as she published, on average, one work per year for twenty-two years, and a controversy that attached to her public profile during her 'French period'. Smith drew criticism from both radical and conservative periodicals for her treatments of the French Revolution and its aftermath. Her perseverance in the chancery suit cost her several patrons, including George O'Brien Wyndham, the third earl of Egremont. Moreover, Smith's growing frankness about the details of her autobiographical lyric speaker's melancholy in the prefaces to her later works, combined with her increasing willingness to treat social issues, made her a less universally sympathetic figure.

In her prefaces Smith shared with readers her sorrow at her misfortunes, which included the loss of several children. Braithwaite died of a fever at age sixteen, the same year that William Towers became a writer for the East India Company in Bengal at the age of seventeen. Both he and Nicholas Hankey, who went to Bombay in 1788, pursued successful careers in the civil service and contributed to the family income. In 1792 Charles joined the 14th regiment of foot and in the following year lost a leg at Dunkirk. He recovered to return to the army, but died of yellow fever in Barbados in 1801. Smith's daughter Lucy married a man who proved to be abusive, and after his death she returned home with three children. Smith mourned most publicly for her daughter Anna Augusta, who married an émigré, Alexandre Marc-Constant de Foville, and died aged twenty in 1795. Of her children, Lionel achieved the most public success: he was knighted and became governor of Barbados and then of Jamaica, where he strongly supported the emancipation of slaves that was under way throughout the British empire.

Despite a decline in her popularity, the end of Smith's life found her successfully entering new literary markets. A collection of tales, *The Letters of a Solitary Wanderer*, appeared in five volumes (1801–2) and a comedy, *What Is She?* (1799) was published anonymously, but is generally attributed to Smith. She found her most rewarding new readership in children, by publishing four works for them: *Rural Walks* (1795), *Rambles Farther* (1796), *Minor Morals* (1798), and *Conversations Introducing Poetry* (1804). She also completed two volumes of a history of England, directed to young women (1806; vol. 3 written by another, unknown author). Two works appeared posthumously, *A Natural History of Birds* (1807) and *Beachy Head, Fables, and other Poems* (1807) which included the unfinished but much admired title poem.

Although the immediate cause of Smith's death at fifty-seven is unknown, she suffered from gout, arthritis, neuritis, and pleurisy and her health gradually declined. She died on 28 October 1806 at Tilford, having survived Benjamin by eight months. He died on 22 February 1806 in debtors' prison in Scotland. Their son George died of yellow fever in Barbados in 1806 six weeks before Charlotte (she died before the news could reach her). The final settlement of Richard Smith's estate took place on 22 April 1813, more than thirty-six years after his death and after his estate had been greatly diminished in litigation. Charlotte Smith was buried at Stoke church, Stoke Park, near Guildford.

Although William Wordsworth remembered Smith in the 1830s as 'a lady to whom English verse is under greater obligations than are likely to be either acknowledged or remembered' (*Poetical Works*, 7.351), her influence on her contemporaries and successors is widely documented. Coleridge and others credited her with revitalizing the English sonnet. In her lifetime she was perhaps most frequently praised for her poetic and prose landscapes. Scott said of her novels that she 'preserves in her landscapes the truth and precision of a painter' (Dorset, 64), and Barbauld credits Smith with pioneering sustained natural description in novels. Wordsworth observes that she wrote 'with true feeling for rural nature, at a time when nature was not much regarded by English Poets' (*Poetical Works*, 7.351). As her novels and poetry began to be republished in the late twentieth century, the case for her importance was made again by critics interested in the period's women poets and prose writers, the Gothic novel, the historical novel, the social problem novel, and post-colonial studies. SARAH M. ZIMMERMAN

Sources *The collected letters of Charlotte Smith*, ed. J. Phillips Stanton (2003) • M. Hays, 'Mrs. Charlotte Smith', *Public characters of 1800–1801* (1801), 43–65 • 'Mrs. Charlotte Smith', *Monthly Magazine*, 23 (1807), 244–8 • C. A. Dorset, 'Charlotte Smith', in *The miscellaneous prose works of Sir Walter Scott*, 4 (1849), 20–70 • F. M. A. Hilbish, 'Charlotte Smith, poet and novelist, 1749–1806', PhD diss., University of Pennsylvania, 1941 • J. P. Stanton, 'Charlotte Smith's "literary business": income, patronage, and indigence', *The age of Johnson: a scholarly annual*, ed. P. J. Korshin (1987), 1.375–401 • L. Fletcher, *Charlotte Smith: a critical biography* (1998) • J. P. Stanton, 'introduction', in *The old manor house*, ed. A. H. Ehrenpreis (1989), vii–xxiii • A. L. Barbauld, 'introduction', in *The old manor house*; *The British novelists*, 36 (1810), i–viii • *The poetical works of William Wordsworth*, ed. W. Knight, 7 (1896), 351 • S. T. Coleridge, 'Introduction to the sonnets (1796)', *The complete poetical and dramatic works*, ed. J. D. Campbell (1903), 542–3

Archives Petworth House, West Sussex, legal documents and letters • Princeton University Library, New Jersey, Firestone Library, letters | Hunt. L., letters to Joseph Walker and Sarah Farr Rose • NRA, priv. coll., corresp. with Lord Egremont • Preston Manor Museum, letters to Thomas Cadell and William Davies • Yale U., Beinecke L., letters to Thomas Cadell

Likenesses G. Romney, pastel crayon, 1792, NPG [*see illus.*] • P. Condé, stipple, 1792–7 (after G. Romney, 1792), repro. in C. T. Smith, *Elegiac sonnets*, 8th edn (1797), vol. 2 • Ridley, stipple, pubd 1799, NPG • Ridley and Hall, stipple, pubd 1806 (after J. Opie), BM, NPG • S. Freeman, stipple (after G. Romney), BM, NPG; repro. in *Monthly Mirror* (1808) • stipple, BM

Smith, Charlotte Fell (1851–1937), historian, was born on 2 January 1851 at Pattiswick Hall, Essex, the last surviving child of Joseph Smith (1813–1904), farmer and JP of Woolpits, Great Saling, Essex, and his wife, Mary, eldest daughter of James Christy of Chelmsford. The Smiths were a Quaker family: Charlotte was educated at Friends' schools at Lewes and York. As a young woman she began writing for periodicals, including *Chambers' Magazine* and the *National Review*. Although the *Wellesley index* does not list her as a contributor, she allegedly wrote for the *Cornhill Magazine*, which was edited in the 1870s by Leslie Stephen; this link may explain her role as the most prolific female contributor to the *Dictionary of National Biography*, of which Stephen became editor in 1882. Her first entry appeared in the tenth volume of the *Dictionary of National Biography*, published in 1891; she contributed a further 230 articles, mainly on minor seventeenth- and eighteenth-century male nonconformists, especially Quakers. Written with concision, these entries were well researched (especially in the case of East Anglian figures); Fell Smith often consulted parish registers, wills, and state and other papers in the British Library and the Public Record Office.

Fell Smith's involvement with the *Dictionary of National Biography* inspired several separate publications. While researching the article for John Kendall, she had read the correspondence of the seventeenth-century Quaker Steven Crisp (1628–1692). This manuscript collection, then held by the Colchester monthly meeting, was in a poor condition: Fell Smith seems to have arranged for its cleaning, mending, and binding, and in 1892 she produced a synopsis of the letters, with a lengthy introduction, under the title *Steven Crisp and his Correspondents*. This was followed in 1901 by *Mary Rich, Countess of Warwick (1625–1678): her Family and Friends*. Another figure of local interest (Mary Rich had spent most of her life at Leighs Priory, close to Fell Smith's own childhood home), the countess had already been the subject of one of Fell Smith's *Dictionary of National Biography* entries. Although anecdotal and idealizing—the author waxed lyrical in the preface about the 'gracious, womanly, domestic life' (*Mary Rich, Countess of Warwick (1625–1678): her Family and Friends*, v)—the full-length biography was a more valuable work than that of M. E. Palgrave, whose life of Mary Rich appeared in the same year. In 1906 Fell Smith published a short biography of the Quaker 'martyr' James Parnell (1637–1656), for whom she had also written the *Dictionary of National Biography* entry.

In 1909 Charlotte Fell Smith published another biography, *John Dee (1527–1608)*, written at the suggestion of the physicist and electrical engineer Silvanus Phillips Thompson (1851–1916). Despite its scientific genesis, the biography dwelt on Dee's spiritualist activities rather than his important contributions to geography, science, and mathematics: a reviewer in *The Athenaeum* commented aptly that 'Miss Smith has told the story of his failure: we should have been glad to hear more of his achievement' (Abbott, 590). Although romantic in tone and over-reliant on Meric Casaubon's *A True and Faithful Relation* (1695)—an edition of Dee's diary which put him in an unfavourable light—Fell Smith's biography of Dee set the trend for more sympathetic consideration of his career and remained the standard published account of Dee's life for over fifty years.

By the time of the completion of the 1901 supplement to the *Dictionary of National Biography*, Charlotte Fell Smith was already involved with another publishing project, albeit of lesser stature. In 1892 she had contributed an article entitled 'A group of Essex divines, 1640–1662' to the *Essex Review*, a quarterly antiquarian journal which also included poetry, local news, and reviews of novels. She continued to contribute regularly to the *Review* until 1936, and in 1898 she became its joint editor, with E. A. Fitch, a local antiquary. Fitch's editorship was largely nominal and Fell Smith was almost entirely responsible for the journal, even before his death in 1912 left her as sole editor. She did not retire until 1933, and her obituarist in the *Review* commented that 'It is largely due to the efforts of Miss Fell Smith that … the *Essex Review* survived' after the First World War (*Essex Review*, 133). Her later publications included *Extracts from State Papers Relating to Friends* (1910–11), *An Anthology of Essex* (1911, with I. L. Goude), *Daniel Whittle Harvey* (1915), and *William Bendlowes of Great Bardfield Place* (1915); the last two were reprints from the *Essex Review*. She also contributed pieces on Essex industries to volume 2 of the Victoria county history of Essex and wrote essays on the county's mansions for *Country Life*. Other activities included foreign travel (she undertook a tour of the Mediterranean when over eighty years old), and cataloguing and rearranging the contents of the Colchester and Essex Museum in Colchester Castle.

In old age Charlotte Fell Smith was a shrewd-looking

woman, with large, regular, handsome features and softly waving grey hair. She died unmarried on 7 May 1937 at her home, Five Corners, Felsted; her funeral service was held on 10 May at Felsted church, and was followed by cremation at Ilford. Her active but obscure career as a local historian and as a contributor to one of the great collaborative historical projects of the late nineteenth century reveals the often unacknowledged part played by women in turn-of-the-century historical research.

ROSEMARY MITCHELL

Sources *Essex Review*, 46 (1937), 133–5 • *WWW*, 1929–40 • G. Fenwick, *The contributors' index to the Dictionary of National Biography, 1885–1901* (1989) • G. Fenwick, *Women and the 'Dictionary of National Biography': a bibliography of DNB volumes 1885–1995 and 'Missing Persons'* (1994) • G. F. Abbott, review of *John Dee* by Charlotte Fell Smith, *The Athenaeum* (13 Nov 1909), 590 • P. J. French, *John Dee: the world of an Elizabethan magus*, pbk edn (1984), 16–17 • 'Dictionary of Quaker biography', RS Friends, Lond. [card index] • d. cert.
Likenesses photograph (in old age), repro. in *Essex Review*, 134
Wealth at death £1017 15*s*. 11*d*.: probate, 12 Aug 1937, *CGPLA Eng. & Wales*

Smith, Sir Clement (*d*. 1552), administrator, was the second son of Thomas Smith, gentleman, of Rivenhall, Essex, and Isabel, daughter and heir of William Foster of Little Baddow, Essex. He began his career as the dependant of his prosperous elder brother, John (*d*. 1545), of Cressing Temple, Essex, and Wootton Wawen, Warwickshire, who in 1513 became lord treasurer's remembrancer in the exchequer through the intervention of the incumbent, Edmund Denny. On 4 December 1539 John Smith was advanced to second baron of the exchequer, and subsequently knighted. Clement Smith was granted the office of lord treasurer's remembrancer for life in survivorship with his brother on 2 December 1539. He occupied the office until his death on 26 August 1552. The remembrancer headed one of the principal divisions of the exchequer of audit, responsible for important aspects of accounting and debt collection. Smith had already been active in the exchequer from at least 1531 as a clerk and attorney in the exchequer of pleas.

At some time before 1536, probably during the first half of the decade, Smith married Dorothy Seymour, the youngest daughter of Sir John Seymour (*d*. 1536) of Wolf Hall, Wiltshire. The marriage of his sister-in-law, Jane *Seymour, to Henry VIII on 30 May 1536 thrust Smith towards the centre of court life. The circumstances that produced Smith's marriage are obscure, but his connection to Sir Edward *Seymour, Jane's eldest brother, dated back to 1531, if not earlier, and Smith remembered his long-deceased father-in-law fondly in his will of 1552. The marriage produced three sons and four daughters, including his son and heir Sir John *Smythe (1533/4–1607) of Little Baddow, the diplomat and military writer.

In 1536 Smith began the acquisition of a landed estate in Essex through a combination of private purchases, crown leases, and, in 1544, the purchase of Bourchiers Hall, Coggeshall, Essex, from the court of augmentations. By 1543 he had attained the standing of esquire and was on the Essex commission of the peace. Smith was assessed for the subsidy of 1545 on lands and fees in London valued at £100 per annum (of which two-thirds was his exchequer salary) and another £50 per annum in Essex properties. He continued making purchases in Essex up to 1550, mostly from private individuals but including a favourable exchange of lands with the crown in August 1547. He was knighted by Edward VI on 22 February 1547. Smith sat in the parliaments of 1545 and 1547 for Maldon, Essex; no record of his activity survives. His likely patron for these elections was the Parr family. Smith leased Bradwell Manor from Queen Katherine Parr and was her farmer for the profits of Great Baddow, Essex; his cousin John Smith was a receiver of the queen's lands.

Smith's Roman Catholicism was evident both in his lifetime and in the devout personal language of his last will and testament. In 1550–51, as part of the government's attack on Princess Mary's religion, several prominent court Catholics were singled out for official displeasure, Smith included. He suffered a brief imprisonment in the Fleet in 1550, and was 'chidden' by the king on 24 March 1551. He appears to have been protected earlier by the regime of Edward Seymour, duke of Somerset, and Smith remained a supporter of the disgraced lord protector. In April 1550 he exploited his exchequer office to issue legal proceedings against John Dudley, earl of Warwick, for substantial unpaid taxes. Dudley brought the issue to the privy council and Smith was reprimanded for excess zeal, in what had clearly been a partisan manoeuvre.

Smith wrote his will on 13 July 1551, with a codicil of 10 August 1552. He died at Little Baddow on 26 August 1552. His two younger sons, Bennet and Clement, were assigned life annuities and were to be apprenticed to learned auditors or other officers of the law courts. His heir, John Smith, began immediately in 1553 to sell portions of his inheritance to finance his voluntary exile abroad as a Catholic soldier of fortune. His widow, Dame Dorothy, had already been the recipient of royal munificence, including a lease of the site of the monastery of Coggeshall, Essex, in 1550. She married Thomas Leventhorpe in 1553. On 8 February 1553 she was awarded an annuity of £66 13*s*. 4*d*. to raise her niece Lady Elizabeth Seymour, one of Protector Somerset's four daughters. In his lifetime Smith had been well connected among the mercantile and legal élites of London, and counted two lord mayors—Sir William Bowyer and Sir Thomas White—among his close friends. His executors included the court Catholics John Ryther, cofferer of the household, and Robert Rochester, comptroller of Princess Mary's household.

J. D. ALSOP

Sources HoP, *Commons, 1509–58* • J. C. Sainty, ed., *Officers of the exchequer: a list* (1983), 54–5 • *Literary remains of King Edward the Sixth*, ed. J. G. Nichols, 1, Roxburghe Club, 75 (1857), ccxxvi • *The chronicle and political papers of King Edward VI*, ed. W. K. Jordan (1966), 56 • PRO, PROB 11/19, fols. 235–7; 11/30, fols. 87–89*v*; 11/31, fols. 330*v*–331*v*; 11/33, fol. 58; 11/35, fols. 219*v*–221*v* • PRO, C1/1124/57–60 • PRO, C1/1157/30 • PRO, C1/1264/40 • PRO, C142/98/6 • PRO, E159/315, 318, 322, 323 • PRO, E163/12/14, fol. 36 • PRO, E165/129, fol. 11 • PRO, E314/19/6/4 • PRO, E315/340, fol. 6*v* • PRO, E111/47A • PRO, E368/333 • *LP Henry VIII* • *APC*, 1550–52, 8 • PRO, SP 10/19, fol. 6*v* • J. E. Oxley, *The Reformation in Essex to the death of Mary* (1965), 260 • *DNB* •

P. H. Reaney and M. Fitch, eds., *Feet of fines for Essex*, Essex Archaeological Society, 4: *1423–1447* (1964), 135, 149, 204, 224, 226, 240, 272 · *VCH Essex*, 5.133 · Essex RO, T/A44, fol. 121 · *The diary of Henry Machyn, citizen and merchant-taylor of London, from AD 1550 to AD 1563*, ed. J. G. Nichols, CS, 42 (1848), 24

Wealth at death wealthy: subsidy records

Smith, Colvin (1796–1875), portrait painter, was born on 16 July 1796 in Brechin, Forfarshire, Scotland, one of the three children and the eldest son of John Smith (1764–1837), a merchant, manufacturer, and magistrate, and a descendant of the family of Lindsay (or Smith), heritable armourers to the bishop of Brechin. His mother was Cecilia (1763–1839), daughter of Richard Gillies of Little Keithock, Forfarshire, and sister of Adam *Gillies, Lord Gillies (1760–1842), judge, and John *Gillies (1747–1836), historian and classical scholar. In 1811 and 1812 he enrolled for two sessions at the University of Edinburgh where he attended classes in the humanities. At the age of twenty Smith went to London and enrolled as a student in the Royal Academy Schools in October 1816; he was awarded the academy's silver medal in 1819. He also studied under the sculptor Joseph Nollekens. He travelled abroad to Antwerp where he studied the art of Rubens, and in July 1822 to Paris, where he studied in the Louvre. In 1826 he was in Rome, where he made friends with Sir David Wilkie, whose portrait he painted. The following year he returned to Edinburgh, where he purchased the studio and gallery in York Place, which had once belonged to Sir Henry Raeburn and was later to be used by S. J. Peploe. Raeburn's dramatic portraits were to have a powerful effect on Smith's portrait style, limiting his palette and introducing dramatic lighting into his compositions. Smith first exhibited at the Royal Institution, Edinburgh, in 1826 and again in 1828 and 1829. He was an artist-associate of the Royal Institution but seceded from it in 1829, having become a founding member of the Scottish Academy, of which he was an ardent supporter throughout his long career. From 1830 his work was exhibited at the Scottish Academy (from 1838 the Royal Scottish Academy) every year, except 1867, until 1879.

With such a well-connected family, Smith received many portrait commissions from the wealthiest citizens of Edinburgh. His diploma work was a portrait of John Lord Hope, dean of the faculty of advocates (Scot. NPG), which was exhibited at the Royal Scottish Academy in 1831, along with two more portraits by Smith, *The Rt. Hon. the Earl of Lauderdale in the Robes of the Order of the Thistle* and *The Rt. Hon. the Lord Baron*. The following year Smith exhibited his portrait *Robert, Second Viscount Melville* (Scot. NPG). He also painted and exhibited portraits of Lord Jeffrey, the lord provost Sir James Spittal, the lord justice-general of Scotland in 1850, and in 1853 Robert Handyside, the solicitor-general of Scotland. Among other notable people painted by Smith were Henry Mackenzie, author of *The Man of Feeling*, and Sir James Mackintosh (both Scot. NPG). Smith exhibited his work less often at the Royal Academy in London between 1843 and 1871.

Smith is perhaps best-known for his portraits of Sir Walter Scott, the first of which was painted in 1828 for lord chief commissioner William Adam. Scott had reservations about the likeness: 'My own portrait is like', he wrote of it 'but I think too broad about the jowls, a fault they fall into I suppose, by placing their subject on the high stage and looking up at them, which foreshortens the face' (McEwan, 537). Nevertheless it proved so popular that several of Scott's friends had replicas painted for them, about twenty in all, for some of which Scott gave separate sittings to please his friends. The Ashmolean Museum, Oxford, has in its collections one of these replicas. Painted by Smith in 1829, it was commissioned by Dr Hughes and presented by him to Edward Copleston, bishop of Llandaff. Another version, in the Scottish National Portrait Gallery, came from the artist's family. Yet another was painted for John Hope, lord justice-clerk of Scotland, and another for Lord Jeffrey. The following year Scott sat again to Smith for a portrait that was probably given by Colvin Smith to his uncle, Adam, Lord Gillies. The recipients of these paintings were friends of Scott and it was perhaps on his recommendation that they then chose to have their own portraits painted by Colvin Smith. Caw was scathing of Smith in terms of his lack of originality, clearly seeing too much of Raeburn's style in his portraits. Nevertheless he saw his merits as a portraitist, commending the simplicity of his compositions, his ability to capture the character of his sitter, and his expertise in composition. This is especially evident in his group portraits, such as *Elizabeth Cheape of Rossie and her Two Granddaughters* (exh. Royal Scottish Academy, 1843) and *William Forbes of Castleton and his Son* (exh. Royal Scottish Academy, 1856; both Perth Art Gallery). Smith's draughtsmanship was accomplished and, like Raeburn's, his sitters were not much flattered by extraneous accoutrements and lavish costume detail but portrayed in an honest and straightforward way. Smith achieved this through simplicity of treatment and an impressive ability to grasp and convey the character of his subject. Smith died in his own house, 32 York Place in Edinburgh, on 21 July 1875 and was buried at Brechin. Smith's letters to his nephew R. G. S. Colvin-Smith, included in the latter's *The Life and Works of Colvin Smith R.S.A.*, record his keen enjoyment, to the end of his life, of country pursuits.

L. H. Cust, *rev.* Jennifer Melville

Sources R. C. M. Colvin-Smith, *The life and works of Colvin Smith R.S.A.* (1939) · D. Irwin and F. Irwin, *Scottish painters at home and abroad, 1700–1900* (1975) · P. J. M. McEwan, *Dictionary of Scottish art and architecture* (1994) · J. L. Caw, *Scottish painting past and present, 1620–1908* (1908) · W. D. McKay, *The Scottish school of painting* (1906) · *CGPLA Eng. & Wales* (1875) · C. B. de Laperriere, ed., *The Royal Scottish Academy exhibitors, 1826–1990*, 4 vols. (1991) · S. C. Hutchison, 'The Royal Academy Schools, 1768–1830', *Walpole Society*, 38 (1960–62), 123–91, esp. 169 · F. Russell, *Portraits of Sir Walter Scott* (privately printed, London, 1987) · Graves, *RA exhibitors*

Likenesses C. Smith, self-portrait, oils, repro. in Colvin-Smith, *Life and works*, frontispiece

Wealth at death £29,747 8s. od.: confirmation, 19 Aug 1875, NA Scot., SC 70/1/174, 707–22

Smith, Culling Eardley. *See* Eardley, Sir Culling Eardley, third baronet (1805–1863).

Smith, Cyril James (1909–1974), pianist, was born on 11 August 1909 at 101 Costa Street, Middlesbrough, Yorkshire, the youngest in the family of two sons and one daughter of Charles Ernest Smith, a bricklayer at an iron foundry, and his wife, Eva Mary Harrison. His father played the cornet in a brass band and organized piano lessons from local teachers for his children. Cyril Smith won a scholarship to Middlesbrough high school, and in 1926 was awarded a scholarship by the Royal College of Music, where he studied with Herbert Fryer and won the silver medal of the Worshipful Society of Musicians (1928) and the Dannreuther concerto prize. In 1929, while still a student, he was asked by Adrian Boult to perform the Brahms piano concerto no. 2 in B♭ with the Birmingham City Orchestra, and this led to his first appearance at a Henry Wood Promenade Concert, in 1930, when he again played the Brahms concerto. After leaving the Royal College of Music in 1930, he took a job at the Baird television studio in Long Acre, London, accompanying the entertainment transmitted experimentally by the BBC every night after radio broadcasting had finished. He remained at this job after the BBC took over altogether and moved the studio to Broadcasting House, until 1934, when he was appointed professor of pianoforte at the Royal College of Music.

Cyril Smith became a very successful concert pianist, known especially as an interpreter of Rachmaninov's concertos and *Rhapsody on a Theme of Paganini*. Rachmaninov thought his performances of the notoriously difficult third concerto the best he had heard from an English pianist, and arranged for him to record the work with Malcolm Sargent. Smith was married twice. A first marriage on 11 August 1931 to Andrée Antoinette Marie (*b*. 1903/4), daughter of Elie Paty, a doctor, ended in divorce. On 16 October 1937 he married Phyllis Doreen (*b*. 1911), daughter of George Montague Sellick, an electrical engineer. Phyllis was a pianist who specialized in the twentieth-century English and French repertory; the couple had one son and one daughter. For a few years they continued to pursue independent careers, and during the war he toured for the Entertainments National Service Association, often playing several concerts a week. Smith played at the lunchtime National Gallery concerts while continuing to perform the piano concerto repertory with the leading English orchestras, especially the Liverpool Philharmonic Orchestra under Malcolm Sargent.

Cyril Smith and Phyllis Sellick formed a duet partnership in 1941, when Sir Henry Wood asked them to play Saint-Saëns's *Carnival of the Animals* on the opening night of the 1941 series of Promenade Concerts, the first to be held in the Royal Albert Hall following the bombing of the Queen's Hall. After this, they built up their two-piano repertory, touring together for the British Council and the Entertainments National Service Association and notably making a tour of the Far East for the latter in September 1945. Their repertory increased as British composers began to write works for them: Vaughan Williams wrote *Introduction and Fugue* (1946), 'for Phyllis and Cyril'; Joseph Cooper arranged Vaughan Williams's 1930 piano concerto, and they gave the first performance of this work, entitled *Concerto for Two Pianos and Orchestra*, under Adrian Boult in 1946; and they gave the first performance of Lennox Berkeley's concerto for two pianos, op. 30 (1948), which too was dedicated to them. At the same time, Cyril Smith had a heavy international touring schedule of solo recitals, mainly of pieces by Beethoven, Chopin, Liszt, and Rachmaninov, and performed concertos by Rachmaninov (nos. 2 and 3), Grieg, Tchaikovsky, and Beethoven (nos. 4 and 5). While he worked with many conductors, he had the closest relationship with Malcom Sargent.

In 1956 Cyril Smith and Phyllis Sellick took part in a tour by British musicians of the Soviet Union as part of a cultural mission led by Sir Arthur Bliss, master of the queen's music. In Kharkov, in Ukraine, Smith had a stroke, as a result of which he lost the use of his left arm. This stimulated friends and pupils to take the four-hand piano repertory and rearrange it for three hands: in his autobiography, *Duet for Three Hands* (1958), Smith describes the difficulty of learning to play one-third of the music with his right hand, while his wife had to learn to play one-third with each hand. Their first public performance as a three-handed act was in the summer of 1957, in Birmingham town hall, playing an arrangement of Mozart's concerto in E♭ for two pianos, K365. Sir Arthur Bliss arranged his concerto for two pianos (1924) as a concerto for two pianos (three hands) for them, and they gave the first performance in 1968. Malcolm Arnold was one of several composers who wrote new works: Smith and Sellick gave the first performance of his *Concerto for Phyllis and Cyril* in 1969, and Gordon Jacob wrote a concerto for piano duet (three hands) and orchestra (1969). They recorded a three-hands arrangement of Lennox Berkeley's *Polka, Nocturne, and Capriccio*, op. 5, originally written for two pianos in 1934.

Cyril Smith and Phyllis Sellick were both appointed OBE in 1971. Smith died suddenly on 2 August 1974 at his home, Oak Lodge, 33 Fife Road, East Sheen, London. He was survived by his wife. ANNE PIMLOTT BAKER

Sources C. Smith, *Duet for three hands* (1958) · *New Grove*, 2nd edn · *The Times* (3 Aug 1974) · *WW* · b. cert. · m. certs.
Archives SOUND BL NSA, performance recordings
Likenesses photograph (with Phyllis Sellick), repro. in Smith, *Duet*, frontispiece
Wealth at death £20,155: probate, 25 Nov 1974, *CGPLA Eng. & Wales*

Smith, Cyril Stanley (1903–1992), metallurgist and historian of technology, was born on 4 October 1903 in Birmingham, the third of the four children of Joseph Seymour Smith, a commercial traveller for Camp coffee, and his wife, Frances, *née* Norton (1871–1949). He was brought up in a Methodist household. He was educated by avidly reading the *Children's Encyclopaedia* and also at Bishop Vesey's Grammar School in Sutton Coldfield; an excellent teacher of geometry was influential in forming some of his tastes, and his parents and an uncle provided home laboratory facilities, including a metallurgical microscope. His progress in mathematics was too slow to allow him to study physics, his first choice, and instead he read metallurgy at the University of Birmingham, from which he graduated with a second-class degree in 1924.

Cyril Stanley Smith (1903–1992), by Godfrey Argent, 1970

In 1923 a magazine article describing Bell Laboratories and other research establishments in the USA inspired Smith to emigrate to America, where he went in 1924. He secured admission to the Massachusetts Institute of Technology (MIT) and gained his metallurgical doctorate in only two years. From there, in 1926, he moved to the American Brass Company in Connecticut and spent sixteen contented years undertaking industrial research on alloy development. He obtained some twenty patents and published a number of excellent research papers, of which perhaps the most distinguished was a micrographic study of a phase transformation in the copper–aluminium system.

On 16 March 1931 Smith married Alice Marchant Kimball (1907–2001), then a student of English social history at Yale, from which she obtained her PhD in 1936; she was later a distinguished dean at Radcliffe College. (Her sister's reaction to her marriage was: 'If he didn't go to Oxford or Cambridge, isn't Church of England, and doesn't like sports, you might as well marry an American'; Radcliffe College Archives.) Alice became Smith's devoted partner for sixty-one years. As Smith later said in his only (and fascinating) effort at intellectual autobiography: 'perhaps it was my unsuccessful attempt to turn her towards the history of science that helped spark my own interest in it' (Smith, *Search*, 344–57). He spent weekends in the history library of nearby Yale University, though he never had any formal training in historical techniques, and did not feel the lack of them; in fact, he had disliked history at school. It was during these years that he started (at small cost) his remarkable collection of antiquarian metallurgical texts, which on his death was left to the Burndy Library at the Dibner Institute in Cambridge, Massachusetts. He was naturalized an American in 1939.

In 1942 Smith moved for a short time to an uncongenial desk job in Washington, DC, until Robert Oppenheimer persuaded him to join his team at the Los Alamos laboratory in 1943. There he masterminded metallurgical research, especially on plutonium with its numerous phase transformations. 'We hardly knew ourselves what we had to do, except that at some time, approximately two years in the future, we would have to fabricate some excessively precious, highly radioactive metal of unknown metallurgical characteristics into completely unknown shapes' (Smith, 'Recollections', 3–10). His period at Los Alamos led to several years of high-level committeemanship for the American government and it also led his wife to write a renowned historical book about the atomic scientists' movement, *A Peril and a Hope* (1965).

In 1946 Smith was invited to create an institute for the study of metals at the University of Chicago. Just after he had agreed he was invited, too late, to become professor of metallurgy at Cambridge University. In fifteen years of effort he turned the institute into the leading laboratory of its kind in America with an impressive staff of metallurgists, physicists, and chemists. He himself did not take any students, but published a number of papers, the most important of which was 'Grain shapes and other metallurgical applications of topology' (1952). This provided a key rationalization of the development of metallic microstructures and is still frequently cited.

In 1960 Smith published his historical masterwork, *A History of Metallography*, a study ranging from medieval times to the nineteenth century, relating metallurgical achievements (for example, the Japanese samurai sword) to attempts to understand the scientific underpinnings. His interests were by now firmly historical, and in 1961 he left Chicago and moved to Cambridge, Massachusetts, to become institute professor at MIT, attached to both the metallurgy and humanities departments; there he spent the rest of his long life, devoting himself to a very varied study of the role of materials in history, especially in art. In his own words, 'MIT has been the environment admirably suited to … the final development of my "philosophy" in which structural change—that is, physics and history combined—is seen as the common factor uniting all my previous interests' (Smith, *Search*, 344–57). Many of his best essays on this broad theme were collected in *A Search for Structure* (1981). In the apologia prefacing this book he asserted: 'One cannot hope to understand the nature of interaction between impinging areas without a firm knowledge of at least one of them,' which he amply displayed. Smith was a member of the American Philosophical Society as well as of the National Academy of Sciences. In 1945, working with an expert linguist, he translated Biringuccio's *Pirotechnia*, an early (1540) classic metallurgical text, and over the next forty years he translated a number of other similar texts from Europe and Japan, a country whose art and crafts he venerated. Other key historical compilations which he edited included *The Sorby Centennial Symposium on the History of Metallurgy* (1965), commemorating the great Sheffield microscopist Henry Sorby, and *Sources for the History of the Science of Steel, 1532–1786* (1968).

Smith died at his home, 31 Madison Street, Cambridge, Massachusetts, of colonic cancer, on 25 August 1992. He was survived by his wife, son, and daughter.

ROBERT W. CAHN

Sources C. Smith, *A search for structure: selected essays on science, art and history* (1981) • private information (2004) [Professor Anne Smith Denman, Professor H. Lechtman, Stuart Smith] • *Boston Globe* (29 Aug 1992) • *The Times* (2 Sept 1992) • C. Smith, 'Some recollections of metallurgy at Los Alamos', *Journal of Nuclear Materials*, 100 (1981), 3–10 • C. S. Smith, *A history of metallography* (1960) • C. Smith, 'Metallurgy as a human experience', *Metallurgical Transactions*, 6A (1975), 603–23 • C. Smith, 'On material structure and human history', *Annual Review of Materials Science*, 16 (1986), 1–11 • Alice Kimball Smith, interviewed by Helen Homans Gilbert, 1986–7, Radcliffe College Archives • H. Lechtman, 'Cyril Smith', *Proceedings of the American Philosophical Society*, 138 (1994), 571–3

Archives Massachusetts Institute of Technology, Cambridge, corresp., course notes, drawings, lectures and writings, metal samples, photographs, tapes, etc. | Massachusetts Institute of Technology, Cambridge, Dibner Institute for the History of Science and Technology, collection of antique and classical metallurgical texts | SOUND Massachusetts Institute of Technology, Cambridge, archives, tapes

Likenesses photograph, *c.*1948 • G. Argent, photograph, 1970, NPG [*see illus.*] • photograph, repro. in *The Times* • photograph (in old age), priv. coll.

Wealth at death £32,751—effects in England: administration with will, 31 Aug 1994 • $303,550—book collection willed to the Burndy Library

Smith, David Nichol (1875–1962), literary scholar, was born at Buccleuch Place, Edinburgh, on 16 September 1875, the younger son of Henry G. C. Smith (*d.* 1885), a mathematics teacher and author of several successful mathematical textbooks, and his wife, Camilla Baxter. He was educated at George Watson's College and at Edinburgh University, where he took the new honours course in English, graduating in 1895 with a first class. The regius professor of rhetoric and English literature, David Masson, with the assistance of Smith's elder brother, Gregory Smith, a lecturer in the department (and later English professor at Belfast), designed and taught the new course. When Masson retired in 1895 he was succeeded by George Saintsbury, for whom Smith felt the greatest admiration. Saintsbury gave the young graduate the task of revising the dates in the index to his *History of Nineteenth Century Literature*, an exercise which convinced Smith, as he recalled many years later at a dinner of the Saintsbury Club, that 'the only dates in which Saintsbury could be trusted to be minutely accurate were the dates of vintages' (Sutherland, 449).

A fellowship in English now enabled Smith to pass a year at the Sorbonne, which was mainly spent in studying French literary criticism of the late seventeenth and eighteenth centuries. One of the first-fruits of those studies was an edition of Boileau's *L'art poétique* (1898), a remarkably mature and erudite piece of scholarship for a relatively young scholar. For the next few years he supported himself by editing various texts for use in schools, 'waiting', in his own words, 'for something to turn up' (Sutherland, 455). This Grub Street period ended in 1902 when he was appointed Walter Raleigh's assistant at Glasgow University. In the summer of 1904 Raleigh was appointed to the new chair of English at Oxford, and Smith obtained the professorship of English at Armstrong (now King's) College, Newcastle upon Tyne, shortly after his twenty-ninth birthday. The two men were not to be separated for long, for Raleigh soon invited Smith to join him in editing an old-spelling edition of Shakespeare's plays based on the first folio for the Clarendon Press; and in 1908 took him to Oxford as Goldsmith's reader. Smith already knew a good deal about the textual problems involved in editing Shakespeare from his editions of *Henry VIII* (1899) and *King Lear* (1902), but it turned out to be a more difficult task than either man had expected. Raleigh always thought of the project as a simple job, and on this question the views of the two men could not be reconciled, so that after some years Smith reluctantly decided to abandon the edition. He continued, however, to give Raleigh valuable assistance in organizing the English school, and later helped his successor, George Gordon, in planning the new BLitt course, thereby furthering the development of English as an academic discipline.

In 1915, Smith married Mary Isabella (*d.* 1962), daughter of the Revd George Harford, vicar of Mossley Hill, Liverpool, and honorary canon of Liverpool. They had three daughters, and a son, Christopher, who was killed at Tobruk with the Royal Air Force in 1942.

In 1921 Smith became a fellow of Merton College, Oxford, and from 1929 to 1946 he was Merton professor of English literature. He was elected fellow of the British Academy in 1932 and received honorary degrees from the universities of Durham, Glasgow, Edinburgh, Cambridge, Princeton, Adelaide, and Lyons.

Meanwhile Smith was turning his attention increasingly towards the eighteenth century. His edition of *Eighteenth Century Essays on Shakespeare* (1903) had as its aim 'to give an account of Shakespeare's reputation during the eighteenth century, and to suggest that there are grounds for reconsidering the common opinion that the century did not give him his due' (Sutherland, 452–3). Much of his later work invited further reconsideration of eighteenth-century literature, notably two series of lectures, published as *Shakespeare in the Eighteenth Century* (1928) and *Some Observations on Eighteenth Century Poetry* (1937), the latter being the Alexander lectures at the University of Toronto.

As an editor, and more especially as an annotator, Smith had few equals. His *Characters from the Histories & Memoirs of the Seventeenth Century* (1918) is a fine example of the erudition and editorial precision which he brought to bear on such work. Among his major editions is one of Swift's *Tale of a Tub* (with A. C. Guthkelch, 1920); *The Letters of Jonathan Swift to Charles Ford* (1935); and (with E. L. McAdam) *The Poems of Samuel Johnson* (1941), as well as editions of, among others, Byron, Dryden, Hazlitt, Macaulay, and Wordsworth. An edition of *Gulliver's Travels*, on which he had worked for many years, slowly and meticulously, as was his custom, was left unfinished at his death. Although he ventured outside his favourite period on a number of occasions, maintaining that he was not 'cursedly confined to one century' (Sutherland, 455), he is chiefly remembered for his work in promoting a better understanding of eighteenth-century literature.

In later life Smith travelled a good deal. In 1936–7 he worked at the Huntington Library, San Marino, California, and in 1946–7 he was at Smith College, Northampton, Massachusetts, and at the University of Chicago. On his retirement he lectured at Cairo University and in 1950–51 at the University of Adelaide. He was also Nuffield lecturer in New Zealand. As a lecturer he was judicious, lucid, and endlessly informative rather than brilliant. He was perhaps at his best when supervising the work of graduate students; they used to revisit him in his book-lined study at 20 Merton Street for the rest of his life. He died at the Radcliffe Infirmary, Oxford, on 18 January 1962; his wife died later that year.

James Sutherland, *rev.* Melanie Ord

Sources J. Sutherland, 'David Nichol Smith, 1875–1962', *PBA*, 48 (1962), 449–59 • *BL cat.* • *CGPLA Eng. & Wales* (1962) • NL Scot., Muir MSS

Archives Bodl. Oxf., autograph collection; corresp. relating to Percy letters; essays, lectures, and notes • NL Aus. • NL Scot., corresp. | Bodl. Oxf., corresp. with R. W. Chapman • NL Aus., letters to Hugh Macdonald

Likenesses J. Russell & Sons, photograph, 1940, repro. in Sutherland, 'David Nichol Smith', pl. 22, p. 448 • W. Stoneman, photograph, 1940, NPG • M. Bone, drawing, priv. coll.

Wealth at death £32,448 5s. od.: probate, 4 April 1962, *CGPLA Eng. & Wales*

Smith, Derek Colclough Walker-, Baron Broxbourne (1910–1992), politician, lawyer, and author, was born on 13 April 1910, the second son and third child of Sir Jonah Walker-Smith (1874–1964) and his wife, Maud Coulton Hunter (*d.* 1966). His father was director of housing at the Ministry of Health before winning Barrow in Furness for the Conservatives in 1931. A brilliant student, Walker-Smith won scholarships to Rossall School and to Christ Church, Oxford, where in 1931 he was awarded a first in history. His *The Protectionist Case in the 1840s* (1933), dedicated to Keith Feiling, boasted a preface by Harold Macmillan, and with a good sense of timing concluded by citing Disraeli on protection as 'not dead, but … only sleeping' (p. 91). But academic study did not exhaust his energies; he also published a novel, *Out of Step* (1930), before he left Oxford. He was called to the bar in 1934, and wrote biographies of three eminent lawyers before his thirtieth birthday. He was also editor of the *English Review* for two years. On 26 May 1938 he married Dorothy Ellen Mary Etherton (*b.* 1906/7), with whom he had a son and two daughters.

Somehow Walker-Smith also found time for politics. He attracted notice for his public speaking at the Oxford Union and was active in the university's Conservative Association. Although he supported appeasement—and published *Neville Chamberlain: Man of Peace*, with an enthusiastic preface written as late as November 1939—he threw himself into the military life when war came, even growing a splendid handle-bar moustache. Having begun as a commissioned officer in the Royal Artillery he ended up on General Eisenhower's staff, with the rank of lieutenant-colonel.

Walker-Smith's father lost Barrow at the general election of 1945 but the family was compensated by his own election to a safer Conservative seat: Hertford. However, though he quickly won a reputation as a dangerous critic of the Labour government he made an unusual career move by becoming chairman of the backbench 1922 Committee in 1951. In one respect this was testimony to his high repute among tory MPs because the post seemed better suited to a more experienced parliamentary hand. But it also gave the impression that Walker-Smith was too independent-minded to choose the typical ascent of an ambitious politician, spending years of zealous conformity in the ranks of junior ministers.

In 1955, however, Walker-Smith was given his first government post, as parliamentary under-secretary to the Board of Trade. In November 1956 he succeeded Sir Edward Boyle as economic secretary to the treasury before moving back to trade, as minister of state, in January 1957. This second stint lasted only until September of that year, when he was appointed minister of health. At the time this was not a cabinet post but it was a highly responsible one. Walker-Smith's main achievement was the passage of the Mental Health Act (1959), which introduced new safeguards against improper detention and foreshadowed a more humane treatment of patients.

By July 1960 Walker-Smith seems to have recognized that he would never achieve cabinet rank. Significantly his unexpected decision to leave the government (but not the Commons) came within days of a cabinet discussion on the European Economic Community (EEC). But no clear policy line arose from that meeting, and unless Walker-Smith had a premonition of a major departure in the area it seems more likely that he seized on the impending retirement of the chancellor of the exchequer, Derick Heathcote Amory, as a convenient time to resume his legal career. He had been made a QC in 1955, and though his area of expertise (the building industry and housing) lacked glamour it was a lucrative field. Macmillan accepted his resignation without regret and awarded him a baronetcy, before appointing Enoch Powell in his place. Ironically two years later health was made a cabinet post. Although Walker-Smith had tried hard to accelerate the rate of hospital building Powell's new status meant that the work of his predecessor was soon overshadowed. If he found himself in agreement with Powell on other subjects in later years Walker-Smith disliked many of his policies at health, notably his doubling of prescription charges.

Although Walker-Smith was never recalled to office he was yet to discover the main cause of his political life. He tended to be nit-picking in his approach to constitutional matters; for example in summer 1963 he solemnly presented the ludicrous argument that if Macmillan resigned the queen would dissolve parliament. For one with his legalistic approach to politics the prospect of entry into the EEC had intolerable implications for national sovereignty. Over the next ten years he delivered a series of speeches, at party conferences and in the Commons, that conveyed the same message. After one of his best-known efforts, at the Llandudno conference of 1962, *The Times* compared him to an Old Testament prophet. Certainly his position was open to ridicule; piled high with quotations and sonorous phrases, to his opponents the rhetoric seemed as outdated as his ideas. The prevailing emotion seemed to be nostalgia for a world that was passing; there was no real vision of Britain's future outside the EEC. With anyone but his intimate friends Walker-Smith could also seem stiff and formal in conversation. Yet he could also be witty, and like any good barrister he was particularly sharp in dealing with attempts to deflect his argument.

Perhaps Walker-Smith's greatest parliamentary speech came in the 'great debate' on the principle of EEC membership, in 1971. He backed his views with his votes on every available occasion, and acted as chairman of an informal dissident body, the 1970 Group. Murmurs against him within his constituency party were no deterrent. But once parliament had decided in favour of joining, the legalistic stickler accepted the new *status quo*. Britain had, after all, signed a treaty, and it would have been beneath the dignity of a great nation to backslide. Walker-Smith had pleaded his case as best he could; but the jury had decided against him, and he accepted the verdict. In 1973 he accepted nomination to the European parliament, and served on its legal committee from 1975 to 1979. Without exactly going native he developed a respect for some products of the movement for European co-operation; as a member of the House of Lords he worked unsuccessfully to incorporate the European Convention on Human Rights into British law.

Walker-Smith left the Commons after the general election of 1983, and was made a life peer as Baron Broxbourne. He returned to his writing and in 1987 co-wrote a reference work on building contracts. But his final years were clouded by ill health. He died at Eastbourne on 22 January 1992, succeeded by his son as second baronet; his wife survived him. Perhaps Walker-Smith is best regarded as a man who reached his full potential very early, rather than as a case of talent unfulfilled. By choice he divided his attention between two demanding careers; to have made his mark in both, and to have thrown in some well-received scholarship as a sideline, was no slight achievement. MARK GARNETT

Sources *The Times* (24 Jan 1992) • *The Times* (6 Feb 1992) • *The Independent* (24 Jan 1992) • *WWW* • Burke, *Peerage* (1999) • m. cert.
Likenesses photograph, repro. in *The Times* (24 Jan 1992) • photograph, repro. in *The Independent*

Smith, Donald Alexander, first Baron Strathcona and Mount Royal (1820–1914), businessman and politician in Canada, was born on 6 August 1820 at Forres, Moray, the second of three sons of Alexander Smith, a tradesman of Archieston, and his wife, Barbara, daughter of Donald Stuart of Leanchiol. He also had three sisters. Educated at Anderson Institution, a local grammar school, he joined the office of the town clerk at the age of sixteen. Two years later, in the spring of 1838, he emigrated to Canada to seek employment with the Hudson's Bay Company. Having received a royal charter in 1670, this company conducted a thriving fur trade across the north-western interior of British North America.

Dogged perseverance and blind obedience permitted Smith to toil for thirty years in the most menial and isolated positions in the company. After counting skins at the Lachine warehouse for three years, he was promoted to junior trader at remote Tadoussac on the St Lawrence River and subsequently at even more secluded Mingan. Extremely isolated, often lonely, his frustrations came to a boil in 1846 when he threw many of his possessions, including valued notes and books, into a cabin fire; and again a year later when he deserted his post to seek treatment for sun blindness. When Montreal doctors refused to confirm serious damage to his eyes, an irate Governor George Simpson banished the hapless Smith to Rigolet, a tiny post on the Hamilton inlet of eastern Labrador.

Without complaint Smith toiled there and in North West River for the next seventeen years, engaged primarily in the fur trade but also in a broad range of supplementary activities. He experimented with the export of seal oil, iced salmon, and cranberries. He built a cannery, imported livestock, and grew a variety of vegetables and other crops. In 1853 he married Isabella Sophia (*d.* 1913), daughter of Richard Hardisty, chief trader, then stationed in North West River. The couple had one daughter, Margaret Charlotte. Smith's patience and hard work finally bore fruit in 1853 when the company named him chief trader, and in 1862 when he was promoted to chief factor with control over all of Labrador. In 1869 he became head of the company's Montreal department.

In his new position Smith played a prominent part in the pacification of the Red River uprising of 1869–70. Led by Louis Riel, the local métis—a people descended from aboriginal and European fur traders—protested against the surrender of the Hudson's Bay Company's charter to the newly formed dominion of Canada without consultation. The Canadian government asked Smith to travel to the north-west in mid-winter in search of a settlement. Although placed under house arrest, Smith quietly negotiated with moderate thinkers and inspired a series of meetings which resulted in the federal government's creating the province of Manitoba, with important constitutional guarantees for people of mixed race.

Diplomatic success may have whetted Smith's appetite for politics. He successfully contested the seat for Selkirk, Manitoba, for the federal tories in 1871. He was an indifferent politician, however, making no significant contribution, except for his betrayal of Sir John A. Macdonald in 1872 on the 'Pacific scandal' issue, which led to the prime minister's resignation. Smith won the seat for the Liberals with only a small majority in the 1873 election and even more narrowly in 1878. The supreme court found the latter contest corrupt and declared his seat vacant. Smith lost the subsequent election and left politics. He returned in 1887, running for the tories in Montreal West, allegedly in return for that party's support of the Canadian Pacific Railway. He held the seat until 1896, when he was named Canada's high commissioner in London.

Smith's fame rests largely on his business career. He began to build his fortune while employed in Labrador, investing his own and his colleagues' surplus earnings in outside enterprises, principally the Bank of Montreal. In the early 1870s, already a wealthy man, he used his own funds and those of the trusts he managed to purchase Hudson's Bay Company shares for himself, shrewdly realizing that the company's future lay with the settlement of the north-western prairies. From 1874 to 1879 he served as the firm's land commissioner but his policies were passive, aimed at securing long-term speculative profits. As the Hudson's Bay Company's largest shareholder, Smith moved quickly through the posts of chief commissioner and director to become its governor in 1889. In that post he presided over its gradual and seemingly reluctant transformation from a company solely involved in the fur trade to one dealing in real estate, natural resources, and wholesale and general retail business.

Smith also played an important if shadowy role in the capitalization and construction of the Canadian Pacific Railway. This was intended to tie the interior prairies to the recently confederated Canada and was finally completed in 1885. While his partners looked after the financial details and construction problems, Smith formed the North West Land Company to maximize profits on the railway's land grant. At the same time he took control of the Bank of Montreal and in 1887 he became its president. Through these companies Smith benefited enormously from the immigration boom which resulted in the settlement of the western Canadian prairies at the turn of the century. Although his total wealth was inestimable he was easily the wealthiest Canadian of his time, owning a number of large and ostentatious estates in both Canada and Great Britain.

Smith rounded out his business activities in Canada by founding and managing the Royal Trust Company, and by investing in a Cornish textile mill, a Montreal rolling-stock plant, and a large number of enterprises in Canada and Great Britain. Towards the end of his life he also served as chairman of Burmah Oil, and he was the first chairman of the newly created Anglo-Persian Oil Company. During the First World War, these companies gave the British navy access to safe supplies of fuel oil.

Smith was knighted in 1886 and created Baron Strathcona and Mount Royal of Glencoe and Colonsay in 1897. He became a noted philanthropist and was particularly generous to McGill University in Montreal and Aberdeen University in Scotland; many other institutions of higher learning as well as hospitals also benefited from his generosity. At the outbreak of the Second South African War, Lord Strathcona personally funded an entire mounted regiment, Strathcona's Horse, which distinguished itself in the conflict.

Lord Strathcona died of a stroke at 28 Grosvenor Square, London, on 21 January 1914, only a few months after the death of his wife. He was buried at Highgate cemetery, and survived by his daughter, who inherited the barony. Taciturn and egocentric, obsessed with details and balance sheets, he had been an investor and accumulator rather than an innovative activist and developer; methodically and patiently he had built the foundations of a financial empire which supported Canada's great land boom at the start of the twentieth century.

A. A. den Otter

Sources D. McDonald, *Lord Strathcona: a biography of Donald Alexander Smith* (1996) • P. C. Newman, *Company of adventures* (1991), vol. 3 of *Merchant princes* • B. Willson, *The life of Strathcona and Mount Royal*,

Donald Alexander Smith, first Baron Strathcona and Mount Royal (1820–1914), by Alexander J. Ross, 1885 [centre, driving the last spike at Craigellachie, British Columbia, to mark the completion of the Canadian Pacific Railway]

2 vols. (1915) • J. MacNaughton, *Lord Strathcona* (1928) • W. T. R. Preston, *Strathcona and the making of Canada* (1915) • K. Halliday, 'Donald Smith: an imperialist agent', undergraduate essay, 1989, Memorial University of Newfoundland • J. W. Pedley, *Biography of Lord Strathcona and Mount Royal* (1915) • *CGPLA Eng. & Wales* (1914)

Archives NA Canada, papers relating to Canadian estates • NA Scot. • NRA Scotland, priv. coll., papers relating to Canadian estates | NA Canada, Hudson's Bay Company MSS; MacDonald MSS • NA Scot., Skene MSS • Provincial Archives of Manitoba, Winnipeg, Hudson's Bay Company MSS • U. Birm., corresp. with Joseph Chamberlain • U. Warwick Mod. RC, British Petroleum (Anglo-Persian Oil Co.) archives • Wellcome L., letters to Sir Thomas Barlow | FILM BFI NFTVA, news footage

Likenesses A. J. Ross, group portrait, photograph, 1885, Hult. Arch. [*see illus.*] • Elliott & Fry, photograph, NPG • Spy [L. Ward], caricature, chromolithograph, NPG; repro. in *VF* (19 April 1900)

Wealth at death £418,553 6*s*. 1*d*.: confirmation, 11 May 1914, *CCI* • £3102 3*s*. 5*d*.: eik additional estate, 28 Aug 1916, *CCI*

Smith [*married name* Beesley], **Dorothy Gladys** [Dodie] (**1896–1990**), playwright and writer, was born on 3 May 1896 at Stonycroft, Whitefield, in Lancashire, the only child of Ernest Walter Smith (*c*.1868–1898), a bank manager, and his wife, Ella (Nell) Furber (1874–1914). Her father died when Dodie was two, and her mother took her to live with her grandparents, three uncles, and two aunts at Kingston House, Old Trafford, Manchester. So Dodie enjoyed a charmed childhood at the centre of eight doting adults, who involved her in all their activities, an upbringing to which she later attributed her success as a playwright. The Furbers were dedicated to amusement and passionate about the theatre; they held music and recitation soirées at home, and the uncles acted in productions by the Atheneum, one of Manchester's sixty-four amateur dramatics societies. Here Dodie made her stage début at eight, and fixed on becoming an actress. When her mother remarried in 1910 (her new husband was Alec Gerald Seton-Chisholm), Dodie accompanied them to London, where she attended St Paul's Girls' School. In 1912, at the age of sixteen, she successfully auditioned for the Royal Academy of Dramatic Art, but her first year there was blighted by the death of her mother from cancer at forty.

Despite Dodie's lack of acting talent or beauty (she was only 5 feet tall, with strong features and a heavy bosom; 'my looks had gone,' she always said, 'by the age of seven'), she managed to scrape a precarious existence for several years on the stage. 'I could always talk myself into a part,' she would say, 'and act myself out of it.' Living in a girls' hostel called the Three Arts Club in the Marylebone Road, London, she acted in army concert parties, end-of-pier farces, and touring productions. She took a job at the newly formed Everyman Theatre in Hampstead, London, and was seduced (with her enthusiastic co-operation) by its founder, Norman MacDermott. Eventually, at twenty-six, she decided that a proper job would be preferable to penury and went to work at Heals, the furniture emporium, running its art gallery. Here she embarked with determination upon an affair with the married chairman of the company, Ambrose Heal, who already had an established mistress, Prudence Maufe. Ambrose gave her the Underwood typewriter on which she wrote, in 1929, her

Dorothy Gladys [Dodie] **Smith** (**1896–1990**), by Anthony Buckley, 1953

first play, *Autumn Crocus*. She had been to the Leipzig toy fair to buy goods for Heals, and while there dreamed up a plot about a spinster schoolmistress from Lancashire who falls in love with a married Tyrolean innkeeper. The play was bought by Basil Dean for £100. It made Dodie, who had been earning £4 a week, rich and famous overnight in 1931. 'Shopgirl writes play', proclaimed the billboards.

After an apparently disastrous first night, *Autumn Crocus*, starring Fay Compton and Francis Lederer, ran for a year in the West End, and was later filmed. It was followed by a succession of light comedies: *Service* (1932), *Touch Wood* (1934, the first to be written under her own name instead of the pseudonym C. L. Anthony), *Call it a Day* (1935), *Bonnet over the Windmill* (1937), and *Dear Octopus* (1938), which established Dodie Smith as the most consistently successful woman playwright of her time. She appeared to have a deft touch, knowing just what the 1930s West End audience wanted: well-crafted middlebrow comedies with a skein of sentiment. But with *Dear Octopus*, centred on a family reunion, and starring John Gielgud, Marie Tempest, and Leon Quartermaine, she achieved her biggest triumph. The play, catching the mood of the time exactly, ran for two years; and its moving 'grand toast' speech (originally delivered by Gielgud), a paean to the durability of the family, ensured its place in repertory for the next sixty years.

But at the height of her fame, with her name in lights, Dodie went into exile. At Heals she had met her future husband, Alec Beesley (1903–1987), seven years her junior. Handsome, gentle, and artistic, he gave up his job (as advertising manager of Heals) to become Dodie's business manager and devoted helpmeet for the rest of her life. Beesley, the son of a survivor of the *Titanic* (Lawrence Beesley, author of *The Loss of the 'Titanic'*, and later a consultant on the film *A Night to Remember*), was a pacifist, so the couple decided to leave for the United States as the Second World War loomed. In January 1939 they left their cottage, The Barretts, at Finchingfield in Essex, in the care of the impresario Hugh (Binkie) Beaumont, and sailed for New York on the *Queen Mary* with their pale grey Rolls-Royce and their adored Dalmatian, Pongo. The dog had been a thirty-eighth birthday gift from Alec to Dodie in 1934 when she had jestingly remarked that, since her Regent's Park flat was decorated in fashionable monochrome with white carpets and black curtains, 'All I need now is a Dalmatian.' Pongo was destined for immortality as the hero of *The Hundred and One Dalmatians* after Dodie's friend Joyce Kennedy, the actress, remarked: 'He would make a nice fur coat,' thus unwittingly becoming the prototype for Cruella de Vil.

Dodie and Alec married in Philadelphia in 1940, and spent the next thirteen years in rented houses mostly in Hollywood—Dodie was in constant demand at the film studios, rewriting screenplays—but sometimes in New England. When the war ended, their return home was delayed by her fear of opprobrium for abandoning England in wartime, and by the prospect of quarantining their three Dalmatians. Dodie wrote one new play for Broadway (*Lovers and Friends*, 1942) but the principal features of her years in the United States were her journal writing (one million words, mostly agonizing over having left behind her devoted audience); the birth of fifteen puppies in 1942 to her two Californian Dalmatians, Buzz and Folly, an event later incorporated into *The Hundred and One Dalmatians* (1956); and her close friendship with two fellow British writers in California, John van Druten and Christopher Isherwood. Dodie became one of the few people to whom Isherwood showed his work in progress. More importantly, she had written her first (and finest) novel, *I Capture the Castle* (1949), a captivating story located in a medieval castle she had seen at Wingfield, Suffolk, in 1934, and written in the form of the diary of Cassandra Mortmain, aged seventeen, essentially based on the young Dodie. It was an instant success in the USA and in Britain, and its wit and charm, with its appeal to readers of all ages, has kept it in print ever since: it became a Virago Modern Classic in 1996 and a Folio edition followed in 1997.

Dodie and Alec returned to their Essex cottage in 1953. Having felt viscerally heartsick with nostalgia for England, Dodie could not have chosen a worse time to relaunch herself as a playwright, when the kitchen sink school of drama was shortly to erupt. She had two flops at the Aldwych: *Letter from Paris* (1953; adapted from Henry James's *The Reverberator*) and her own adaptation of her novel *I Capture the Castle* (1954), which closed in four weeks despite universally rapturous reviews for Virginia McKenna as Cassandra. In a spirit of defiance, Dodie Smith wrote a highly praised children's book, *The Hundred and One Dalmatians*, the long-term survival of which was ensured by Disney's subsequent film adaptations: the hugely successful animated feature, *101 Dalmatians* (1961), and the 1996 live film of the same title. In the 1960s two new plays (*Amateur Means Lover*, and *These People: These Books*) failed to come into the West End; a further half-dozen plays were never produced at all. *Dear Octopus* enjoyed a West End revival in 1968, with Jack Hulbert and Cicely Courtneidge as the golden wedding couple, on their own golden wedding anniversary.

But Dodie never stopped writing. Always longing to revive her theatrical success, about which she reminisced indefatigably in her diaries, she consoled herself by writing five increasingly fanciful novels: *The New Moon with the Old* (1963), *The Town in Bloom* (1965), *It Ends with Revelations* (1967), *A Tale of Two Families* (1970), and *The Girl from the Candle-Lit Bath* (1970). She also published two more children's books (*The Starlight Barking*, 1967, and *The Midnight Kittens*, 1978), as well as four autobiographical volumes: *Look Back with Love* (1974; about childhood), *Look Back with Mixed Feelings* (1978; about her twenties), *Look Back with Astonishment* (1979; about her success in the 1930s), and *Look Back with Gratitude* (1985; about America.) Living a hermit-like existence, seeing few friends (among them the actress Gwen Ffrangcon-Davies, and the novelist Julian Barnes, who became her literary executor) Dodie remained alone at her cottage after the death of Alec in September 1987. She died at Finchingfield on 24 November 1990, and was cremated there, leaving an estate valued at £473,833, of which £2000 was willed to the care of Charley, her seventh and last Dalmatian. VALERIE GROVE

Sources V. Grove, *Dear Dodie: the life of Dodie Smith* (1996) · D. Smith, *Look back with love: a Manchester childhood* (1974) · D. Smith, *Look back with mixed feelings* (1978) · D. Smith, *Look back with astonishment* (1979) · D. Smith, *Look back with gratitude* (1985) · D. Smith, fifth volume of memoirs, Boston University, Dodie Smith archive of diaries and letters · private information (2004) [J. Barnes and others]

Archives Boston University, journals, letters, MSS, and photographs | FILM BFI, films of her plays incl. *Autumn crocus* and *Dear octopus* | SOUND BBC, interviews incl. 'Dodie at ninety', 1986

Likenesses A. Buckley, photograph, 1953, NPG [*see illus.*] · D. Bachardy, portrait, priv. coll. · photographs, priv. coll.

Wealth at death £473,833: probate, 3 April 1991, *CGPLA Eng. & Wales* · under £115,000—further grant: 14 May 1991, *CGPLA Eng. & Wales*

Smith, Eaglesfield (*c*.1770–1838), poet and surgeon, was the second of five children of Eaglesfield Smith (*c*.1730–1806) and his wife, Anna Galliard. His father was a Scottish landowner with his principal residence at Langshaw House, in Dumfriesshire. His mother was an English heiress descended from the ancient Bradshaw family of Derbyshire, who brought her husband an estate in Eyam, where the younger Eaglesfield Smith may have been born. On his father's death he inherited both the Eyam estate and Blackwood House (Blacket House), in Middlebie parish, Dumfriesshire.

Nothing is known of Smith's early life, although the poems (many in Scots dialect or on border themes) suggest a primary allegiance to Scotland. He attended two sessions at Edinburgh University, preparing for a career as a surgeon, studying anatomy and surgery in 1792–3 and chemistry in 1793–4. On 1 March 1794 he enlisted in the 3rd dragoon guards, as surgeon's mate, and was posted to serve against the French in Flanders. His military career began badly: on 26 April he took part in Mansel's disastrous charge on the French infantry in the battle near Cateau, described in his poem 'The Death of General Mansel'. Though the French were eventually routed Mansel's company suffered serious casualties and Smith himself was taken captive. As a prisoner of war under Robespierre he languished for months in imminent danger of death, but managed to return to England by 1795. In a prefatory note to his *Poetical Works* (1802), he claimed that many early poems were written to 'amuse the tedious hours of a French prison'.

Smith joined the 29th light dragoons, as surgeon, in March 1795, only to retire from the service in 1796, when his first volume, *William and Ellen*, appeared. He anticipated Walter Scott in adapting the ballad vogue to a historical border legend, the Kirkconnel tragedy of Dumfriesshire fame. Southey reviewed it coolly ('a bad imitation of Bürger's Leonora') but was kinder to Smith's next major poem, *The Scath of France* (1797). A fictitious tale of the French Revolution, the ballad is remarkably sympathetic to the French cause, given Smith's wartime experience. Six more ballad volumes followed, often under the pseudonym 'E. S. J.' (Eaglesfield Smith junior), from *Morcar and Elfina* (1798) to *Rudigar the Dane* (1815). Smith also published a farce, *Sir John Butt* (1798), and numerous lyrics on typical Romantic subjects: beggars, chimney-sweeps, children, despondency, the triumph of liberty, the memory of Burns and of Chatterton.

Some of these lyrics found their way (signed E. S. J.) into the *Gentleman's Magazine*, and Smith's most important, 'The Sorrows of Yamba', appeared in the *Universal Magazine* for 1797. This last, an anti-slavery poem in the voice of a female slave, frequently appears in collections of Romantic era poetry, although neither under Smith's name nor in its original form. Smith, or an intermediary, had apparently sent the poem in manuscript to Hannah More for her Cheap Repository Tracts series, and More published it (after Christianizing the poem and introducing crude dialect terms) as a tract in 1795. Smith's version is a much better poem than More's adulterated one, though it remains virtually unknown.

Smith evidently settled into life as a surgeon in Scotland, where he published several books after 1798, including a treatise, *Bile in Animals*, in 1805. In 1803 H. W. Tytler, a Scottish poet and physician, published an 'Extract' of an avuncular letter to Smith in the *Scots Magazine*, urging the younger poet to abandon the examples of 'Southey, Coleridge, or any other modern *Imaginationist*'. On 14 August 1811 Smith married Judith Elizabeth Irving (*d.* 1828), of Robgill Tower, daughter of Sir Paulus Aemilius *Irving and Lady Elizabeth St Lawrence. They had a daughter, Anna, in 1812, followed by three sons, including Smith's heir, Eaglesfield Bradshaw Smith (1814–1871). Smith published a two-volume collection of his poems in 1822, and died, on 10 December 1838, at Lochvale House, near Dumfries. He was buried in the churchyard of Kirkpatrick Fleming. ALAN RICHARDSON

Sources F. Miller, *Poets of Dumfriesshire* (1910) • memorial inscriptions for Kirkpatrick Fleming, Dumfries and Galloway Family History Centre • matriculation records, U. Edin. L., special collections division, university archives, Da 34 • PRO, war office documents, PRO/WO 12/192, 12/1519, 31/30 • *Army List* (1796) • R. Southey, 'William and Ellen', *Critical Review* (21 Dec 1797) • H. W. Tytler, 'Extract of a letter … Eaglesfield Smith, Esq.', *Scots Magazine*, 65 (Aug 1803) • J. T. [J. Tilley], *The old halls, manors, and families of Derbyshire*, 1 (1892) • J. B. Irving, *The Irvings … an old Scots border clan* (1907) • *Poetical works of Eaglesfield Smith, Esq.* (1802); 2nd edn, 2 vols. (1822) • m. reg. Scot.

Wealth at death £8680 15*s*. 8*d*.—Scotland: inventory, 1839, will • £2103 15*s*. 2*d*.—England: will

Smith, Edgar Charles (1872–1955), naval officer and historian of technology, was born at Green End, Newport Pagnell, Buckinghamshire, on 5 May 1872, the son of George Charles Hooper Smith, a schoolmaster, and his wife, Mary Armstrong. The following year the family moved to Gravesend, Kent, where Smith was educated at his father's school. He entered Finsbury Technical College at the age of sixteen but left in 1889 to work at a relative's walking stick factory at Thrupp, near Stroud. In 1890 he joined the Bristol engineers Strachan and Henshaw, continuing his technical education at evening classes at Merchant Venturers' College. Following a spell at Mumfords, the Colchester engineers, he briefly taught at his father's school before joining the Royal Navy in 1895 as a temporary assistant engineer.

During the next twenty-seven years Smith served on a variety of steamships and on the staff of HMS *Britannia*, the naval college, at Dartmouth, where he took professional examinations in 1903. He saw active service in the Boxer uprising and the First World War, reaching the rank of engineer captain. Finally he served for four and a half years on the staff of the engineering department of Devonport Dockyards, retiring in 1922 at the age of fifty. Between 1917 and 1922 he was an examiner in the history of science to the civil service commissioners.

Smith then embarked on a career of lecturing and writing about technical history and biography. He served as first guide-lecturer at the Science Museum (1924–30), where his lucidity was noteworthy. Since 1907 he had contributed a long series of articles (sometimes anonymous) on technical biography to *Engineering*. In 1919 he was invited to contribute centenary articles about James Watt, and as a result officially represented the naval engineering department during the three-day Watt commemoration in Birmingham, which led to the formation of the Newcomen Society. He was a member of the council of that society from its beginning, served as president (1937–8), and contributed a dozen papers to its *Transactions*.

Smith wrote one book, *Short History of Naval and Marine Engineering* (1937), and a large number of articles for *The Engineer*, *Engineering*, *Edgar Allen News*, and *Nature*, specializing in technical and scientific biography or commemorating anniversaries. For *Engineering* between 1944 and 1946 he wrote an autobiographical serial describing his naval experiences, and preceded it with a serial biographical account of the evolution of the steam navy before the First World War. He married Florence Sarah (*b.* 1871/2), the daughter of John Alfred Funge, a Gravesend river pilot, on 28 January 1902; they had five children. He was a Methodist, artist, musician, and a talented cricketer. Smith was of medium height and build, and was bearded. He was appointed OBE.

Smith died on 13 March 1955 at his home, Dalcouth, Keeper's Corner, Burstow, Surrey, and was buried in the churchyard at Burstow. He was survived by his wife.

A. P. Woolrich

Sources E. C. Smith, autobiographical serial, *Engineering* (29 Jan 1944–27 Dec 1946) • *Engineering* (25 March 1955), 362 [with portrait] • *Transactions* [Newcomen Society], 29 (1953–5), 275–6 • b. cert. • m. cert. • d. cert. • *CGPLA Eng. & Wales* (1955)
Archives NMM • Sci. Mus., papers
Likenesses portrait, repro. in *Engineering*
Wealth at death £2635 16*s.* 7*d.*: probate, 4 July 1955, *CGPLA Eng. & Wales*

Smith, Edmund (1672–1710), poet and playwright, the only son of Edmund Neale, a London merchant, and Margaret, daughter of Sir Nicholas Lechmere, was born either at Hanley Castle, Worcestershire, the seat of the Lechmeres, or at Tenbury, Worcestershire. His father died soon after his birth, and he was brought up by a kinsman named Smith—almost surely Mathew Smith of London, who married Margaret, Sir Nicholas Lechmere's sister. As his guardian treated him as his own child, he adopted his surname. He was educated at Westminster School under the famous Dr Busby and was elected to both Trinity College, Cambridge, and to Christ Church, Oxford, but decided on Oxford, where he matriculated on 25 June 1688, at the fairly tender age of sixteen.

Some evidence of Smith's precocity can be seen in his contributions to collections of Oxford verse on the birth of the prince of Wales in 1688, on the coronation of William III and Mary in 1689, and on William's return from the battle of the Boyne in 1690. These poems were the beginning of his reputation as a poet. In 1690 he entered as a student at the Inner Temple. In 1691 he wrote an excellent Latin ode, published in the second volume of *Musae Anglicanae*, on the death of Dr Edward Pococke, the orientalist. Dr Johnson, who could quote some of its verses from memory, thought it 'by far the best lyric composition in that collection; nor do I know where to find it equalled among the modern writers. It expresses, with great felicity, images not classical in classical diction' (Johnson, *Poets*, 2.12). On 24 December 1694 Smith was publicly admonished for licentious conduct by the authorities of Christ Church and faced expulsion, a fate he escaped for a time.

Smith received the degree of MA on 8 July 1696, and five years later, on 8 November 1701, was elected to give the annual oration in praise of Sir Thomas Bodley, founder of the Bodleian Library (published by William Bowyer in 1711). Smith's outrageous behaviour continued, however, and on 24 April 1700 the dean and chapter declared his place void as he had been 'convicted of riotous behaviour in the house of Mr. Cole, an apothecary' (Johnson, *Poets*, 2.13). Further action was delayed. But when he failed in his candidature for the tutorship of Christ Church, he took revenge for his defeat by satirizing the dean, Dr Aldrich. Dr Johnson wrote that 'Of his lampoon upon him I once heard a single line too gross to be repeated' (ibid., 2.13). Hence, on 20 December 1705, the patience of the authorities exhausted, the long-delayed expulsion took place.

Smith took himself to London and allied himself with the whigs, which brought him to the notice of Addison. He is best known for his tragedy *Phaedra and Hippolitus*, which was the first adaptation of Racine's *Phèdre*, produced on 21 April 1707 at the Queen's Theatre. Three more performances followed that month, one of which was a benefit night, and then the play languished until 1722. From 1722 to 1785, however, there were a further eighteen performances. Smith's dedication of the play to Lord Halifax runs to seven full paragraphs of flattery and hints as to patronage. Addison, some four years after the appearance of the play, wrote in *The Spectator*, no. 18 (21 March 1711):

> Would one think it was possible (at a Time when an Author lived that was able to write the 'Phædra and Hippolitus') for a People to be so stupidly fond of the Italian Opera, as scarce to give a third Days Hearing to that admirable Tragedy?

Dr Johnson disagreed with Addison, writing 'It is a scholar's play, such as may please the reader rather than the spectator; the work of a vigorous and elegant mind, accustomed to please itself with its own conceptions, but with little acquaintance with the course of life' (Johnson, *Poets*, 2.16). The play was published on 17 June 1707, and Smith was the richer by £50, but he had been too lazy personally to present the dedication to Halifax, and thereby lost £300.

Smith was the drinking partner of the poet John Philips, a friend from Oxford days, remembered for his poem *Cyder*. On his death in 1709 Smith wrote an elegy on him, of which Dr Johnson wrote 'justice must place [it] among the best elegies which our language can show, an elegant mixture of fondness and admiration, of dignity and softness'. Dr Johnson further wrote that 'This elegy it was the mode among his friends to purchase for a guinea; and, as his acquaintance was numerous, it was a very profitable poem' (Johnson, *Poets*, 2.16–17). Smith cast about for a subject for another tragedy and decided on one on Lady Jane Grey. His friend George Duckett invited him to his home at Hartham, Wiltshire, as a congenial place in which to write his tragedy. But as a result of too much food and strong ale 'he found himself plethorick' (ibid., 2.17). He prescribed a strong purge for himself, which he took despite the warning of the apothecary, and died in July 1710 and was buried at Hartham. Many years after Smith's death Duckett told John Oldmixon that Smith had been asked to 'forge and insert the alterations' to a corrupted text of Clarendon's *History* (ibid., 2.18). There is no truth to the story. Either because of sloppiness of dress or for some other reason, he was known as Captain Rag. Dr Johnson, in the first sentence of his life of Smith, wrote what may serve as a summing-up and an epitaph: 'Edmund Smith is one of those lucky writers who have, without much labour, attained high reputation, and who are mentioned with reverence rather for the possession than the exertion of uncommon abilities' (ibid., 2.1). ARTHUR SHERBO

Sources S. Johnson, *Lives of the English poets*, ed. G. B. Hill, [new edn], 3 vols. (1905) • *The Spectator* (21 March 1711) • E. L. Avery, ed., *The London stage, 1660–1800*, pt 2: 1700–1729 (1960) • *DNB*

Smith, Edward. *See* Smyth, Edward (*c*.1662–1720).

Smith, Edward (1819–1874), physiologist and social reformer, was born at Heanor, Derbyshire, the son of Joseph Smith, a successful hosier, and his wife, Martha. He was a medical student at Birmingham medical school and graduated MB (1841), BA, and LLB (1848) at Queen's College, Birmingham. His degrees were recognized by London University, where he proceeded MD (1843), and MB and LLB (1848). On 4 May 1843 he married Matilda Frearson Clarke, daughter of William Clarke, draper. In 1848 he made a visit to Texas to report on its potential as a place of settlement for emigrants. He published a report of his findings the next year. After some years of medical practice in Birmingham, Smith moved to London in 1851, when he became FRCS, and from 1852 to 1853 he lectured on botany at Charing Cross Hospital. He was made a member of the Royal College of Physicians in 1854, and was elected a fellow in 1863; he gave the Goulstonian lectures at the college in 1865.

Smith was dismissed from his first two teaching positions at London hospitals after quarrelling with colleagues and administrators. But in 1855 he was appointed assistant physician at the Brompton Hospital for Consumption and Diseases of the Chest, and he remained there for ten years, despite being passed over for promotion. Initially in order to study lung function, he developed an apparatus measuring the volume of air inspired per minute. He next added a device for measuring the output of carbon dioxide. He measured his own output while engaged in different activities, and he was made a fellow of the Royal Society in 1860 after publishing a paper entitled 'Experimental inquiries into the chemical and other phenomena of respiration, and their modification by various physical agencies', in its *Philosophical Transactions* (149, 1859, 681–714). Smith then went on to study the influence of different activities on the metabolism of body nitrogen, and published 'On the elimination of urea and urinary water' in the same journal (*Philosophical Transactions*, 151, 1862, 747–834).

By this time Smith had been concerned for several years about the conditions in British prisons, and the use of a treadwheel for those sentenced to hard labour. He himself worked on the wheel for a short period and found his output of carbon dioxide to be greatly increased. On the other hand, prisoners showed no increase in their nitrogen metabolism during and after working on the wheel compared with their rest days. This was important evidence indicating the error of Liebig's dogma that physical work involved the destruction of protein, and that working men had very high protein requirements. Smith was also concerned that consistent regulations be set out for prison diets, because bread-and-water diets, even for short periods, would, he believed, weaken subjects so that they would be unable to carry out 'honest labour' on their release.

In 1863, when there was great hardship among cotton-mill workers in Lancashire, the government commissioned Smith to investigate whether the hardship could result in 'starvation diseases' and, if aid were to be given, how it could most usefully be provided. Smith worked at great speed, travelling among the mill towns, collecting dietaries, and calculating their contents of carbon and nitrogen. He concluded that men and women had the same needs in relation to body weight, and that the average man required 280 grams of carbon and 13 grams of nitrogen per day (equivalent to approximately 2800 kcal and 80 grams of protein). In his 'Report on the nourishment of distressed operatives' (*Parl. papers*, 1863, 25.320–78) he stated that 24 pence per head per week was the minimum expenditure for an adequate diet; that the poorest diets consisted largely of bread and treacle; and that these could be supplemented most economically with fresh vegetables and skimmed milk.

This pioneering study set a standard for the future, and Smith was commissioned to conduct another investigation, described in his 'Report on the food of the poorer labouring classes in England' (*Parl. papers*, 1864, 28.216–329), for which he obtained 600 sets of diets. Overworked needlewomen in London were in particular distress; and, although agricultural labourers were better fed, Smith thought it wrong that their children were not allowed some of the skim milk (left from making butter) that farmers were feeding to their young animals.

Smith was now appointed as a medical officer to the poor board by Sir John Simon, and drew up plans for dietaries in poor-law institutions. In 1871, with the reorganization of public health administration, he was transferred with Simon to the new Local Government Board. There he published *A Manual for Medical Officers of Health* (1879), which advised that medical officers should make themselves aware of all the influences affecting public health in their district—including ventilation, drainage, water supply, food, and air.

Smith died unexpectedly from double pneumonia, at his home, 140 Harley Street, London, on 16 November 1874, leaving his wife and two daughters, Anne Maria, and Lucy (*d*. 1921), who married Sir George Younger (1851–1929). During his life Smith had shown 'energy and capacity' (Brockington, 243–4), and published several books that were in considerable demand. They included *A Practical Dietary for Family, Schools and the Working Classes* (1864), and *Foods* (1872). However, one obituarist commented that Smith 'met with little success in medical practice, nor did he contrive to conciliate the affection of his colleagues' (*BMJ*, 653). Another biographer, in referring to his surveys of diets around the country, stated that Smith was kept 'on the move from place to place, and free from the irksome quarrels which more sustained associations with his intellectual contemporaries seemed to engender' (Brockington, 243–4). Nevertheless, Royston Lambert judged that Sir John Simon's choice of 'this quarrelsome, diverse and talented man' for the first dietary surveys 'was inspired' (Carpenter, 1518); and C. B. Chapman referred to this as a problem for society of making best use of 'a highly motivated, intellectually gifted man … when talent and genius are accompanied by compulsive and offensive personality traits' (Chapman, 22–23).

KENNETH J. CARPENTER

Sources C. B. Chapman, 'Edward Smith (?1818–1874), physiologist, human ecologist, reformer', *Journal of the History of Medicine and Allied Sciences*, 22 (1967), 1–26 • K. J. Carpenter, 'Edward Smith (1819–1874)', *Journal of Nutrition*, 121 (1991), 1515–21 • C. F. Brockington, 'Public health at the privy council, 1858–71; V, biographical details: Edward Smith', *Medical Officer*, 101 (1959), 243–4 • T. C. Barker, D. J. Oddy, and J. Yudkin, *The dietary surveys of Dr Edward Smith, 1862–3: a new assessment* (1970) • *DNB* • *BMJ* (21 Nov 1874), 653–4 • *The Lancet* (21 Nov 1874), 746–7 • m. cert. • d. cert. • Munk, *Roll* • R. Lambert, *Sir John Simon, 1816–1904, and English social administration* (1963)

Likenesses photograph, *c*.1845, Royal Society of Medicine Library, London; repro. in Chapman, 'Edward Smith', p. 7 • T. H. Maguire, lithograph, 1852, Wellcome L. • photograph, *c*.1870, Wellcome L.; repro. in Carpenter, 'Edward Smith', 1515

Wealth at death under £3000: probate, 19 Dec 1874, *CGPLA Eng. & Wales*

Smith, Edward John (1850–1912), merchant seaman and master of RMS *Titanic*, was born on 27 January 1850 at 51 Well Street, Hanley, Staffordshire, the son of Edward Smith (1805–1885), a potter, and his wife, Catherine, formerly Hancock, *née* Marsh (1809–1893), both Primitive Methodists. Catherine had two children by an earlier marriage; her son Joseph Hancock (1833–1893) was in the merchant navy when Edward was born. In the early 1850s the senior Edward Smith moved along Well Street and took over a shop that may have belonged to his mother, the enhanced prosperity raising the family into the middle class.

Schoolboy to master mariner Smith was educated at the British School, Etruria, established and maintained by Wedgwood Potteries and located within the confines of the Wesleyan chapel. After his death, one of Smith's classmates recalled that 'Teddy was a genial and good schoolfellow, one always ready to give a kind of helping hand in any way to his mates' (*Daily Sketch*, 25 April 1912). Smith left school at twelve and was employed at Etruria Forge, but in 1865 he and a group of friends went to meet his half-brother Joseph Hancock, by this time captain of an American sailing-ship, the *Senator Weber*. On 5 February 1867, with his parents' consent, he was taken on the books of the owners, Andrew Gibson & Co. of Liverpool, and signed on the *Senator Weber* as an ordinary sailor. He spent over three years on the *Weber*, rising from 'boy' to third mate; in October 1870 he signed on the Halifax-registered *Amoy* as an able-bodied seaman. Five months later he transferred to the Liverpool-registered *Madge Wildfire*. During these years he studied hard and in July 1871 passed his competency examination as second mate. After service on several other Gibson ships he obtained his first mate's certificate in 1873, and in March 1875 his master's certificate. In January 1880, while an officer on board the square-rigger *Lizzie Fennel*, he saw the White Star liner *Britannic*. He was so impressed that he declared his willingness to step down a grade if he could serve aboard her and in time rise to command. Several days later he was able to tour the vessel and in March 1880 he joined the White Star Line.

Initially Smith had to relearn his trade, and for the first time he had to deal with passengers. His first posting was in the *Celtic*, then as second officer on the cattle-boat *Coptic*, running to New Zealand and South America. He achieved his ambition when he became second officer on the *Britannic* on the North America run, and in 1885 was first officer on the *Republic*. On 13 January 1887, at the parish church, Winwick, Lancashire, he married (Sarah) Eleanor (1861–1931), the daughter of William Pennington, a farmer. They set up house at 39 Cambridge Road, Seaforth, Liverpool; shortly after the birth of their only child, Helen Melville Smith (1902–1972), they were living at 17 Marine Crescent, Waterloo, Liverpool. Smith continued to progress, gaining his extra master's certificate in 1888, the year that he joined the Royal Naval Volunteer Reserve as a full lieutenant, and secured his first command, in the old *Baltic*.

Smith later asserted, notably in an interview with a *New York Times* reporter in 1907, that he had never experienced any problems at sea. Such remarks to the press ran counter to the White Star Line rule 2, posted on the bridge of their vessels: 'Overconfidence—a most fruitful source of accidents, should be especially guarded against.' Several accidents had in fact occurred under Smith's captaincy. On 27 January 1889, off Sandy Hook on the approach to New York, the *Republic* was grounded for almost five hours. Then after landing her passengers at New York, a furnace flue fractured, killing three men and injuring seven. Smith reported only that damage was slight and that the injured men walked from the ship to the ambulance. In December 1890, in command of the *Coptic*, he ran the ship aground on Main Island as they were leaving Rio de Janeiro bound for Plymouth. His longest service was on the *Majestic* (1895–1904), but in August 1901 fire broke out in a linen closet as she approached New York. A hole was cut in the deck and water poured in—a foolish move as the fire was probably electrical in origin. It was not quenched and continued to flare up, being finally put out with steam five hours later. Captain Smith had not been informed, which suggests that he was not fully aware of events on his ship.

During the Second South African War, Smith was called up as RNR captain of the *Majestic* and twice carried troops to South Africa, receiving the transport medal with South Africa clasp from Edward VII in 1903. In 1904 he was given command of the new *Baltic*, then the largest vessel afloat. White Star Line transferred their operations to the deep-water harbour at Southampton in 1907 and the Smiths bought Winwood, a large house in Winn Road, in the select Westwood Park district of Southampton. In the same year Smith was on the executive council of the mercantile marine, and he also made his first voyage on the

Adriatic. A large, imposing figure, who kept a pet Irish wolfhound, and an inveterate cigar-smoker, Smith was a popular and trusted captain among the prestigious passengers who made regular Atlantic crossings on White Star liners.

In 1907 the White Star Line, by then in US hands as part of J. Pierpont Morgan's International Mercantile Marine, planned to build a trio of grand liners: the *Olympic*, *Titanic*, and *Gigantic*, to be built by Harland and Wolff, Belfast. While the Cunarders *Lusitania* and *Mauretania* were both the largest and fastest liners afloat, the White Star liners would be larger and more luxurious than their British and German competitors. The keels of the *Olympic* and *Titanic* were laid in 1909; as constructed, they were 882 feet long, 92 feet broad, and nearly 106 feet from keel to the top of the captain's house on the bridge. There were eleven steel decks. Fifteen transverse bulkheads with electrically controlled watertight doors rose through the lower of the eleven steel decks, though reaching barely 15 feet above the water-line. Both vessels were designed to carry 3500 passengers and crew. As a result of experience with the *Olympic*, the forward part of the promenade deck on the *Titanic* was glassed in, and a few other modifications introduced, which accounted for her slightly higher tonnage. The *Olympic* was launched in 1910, and after fitting-out went into service in 1911, captained by Smith, now holding the rank of commander.

A serious accident occurred on 20 September 1911 as the *Olympic*, carrying 3000 passengers, passed down Southampton Water. An armed cruiser, HMS *Hawke*, was also passing through the narrow channel and as the *Olympic* gathered speed the surge of water outside and between the two vessels caused the lighter *Hawke* to veer into the *Olympic*, with considerable damage to both. The incident provoked a flurry of letters to *The Times*, arguing for and against the supposed 'suction' which the vast bulk of the *Olympic* created on acceleration. The Admiralty inquiry found that the *Olympic* had been responsible for the accident but absolved Smith of blame, for his ship was under compulsory pilotage.

Master of RMS *Titanic* The *Olympic* was repaired by Harland and Wolff, Belfast, delaying work on the *Titanic*. More delay ensued in February 1912 when the *Olympic* lost a propeller at sea and was once more returned to Belfast. On 2 April, Smith was aboard the *Titanic* for trials. These consisted merely of a half-day's cruise up and down Belfast Lough. The White Star Line was so confident of the quality of its ships that none were rated at Lloyds. The Board of Trade regulations of 1894 had set out the number of lifeboats which vessels over 10,000 tons should carry; no change had been considered necessary although the *Titanic*, at 46,328 tons, was only one among many vessels considerably over this tonnage. She was in fact carrying more than the required number, having fourteen lifeboats on davits, two emergency cutters, plus four Englehardt collapsible boats, but giving capacity for only 1178 persons. It was presumed that in case of emergency the boats would serve to ferry passengers to vessels summoned by radio, now being installed on many liners. There were additionally 3560 cork life-jackets, kept in the cabins.

On 4 April 1912 the *Titanic* arrived at Southampton. The crew were hired by White Star, but there were also other staff, including the musicians, provided by the band leader Wallace Hartley, the restaurant staff under their employer Louis Gatti of the well-known Anglo-Swiss catering family, and the two radio operators employed by the Marconi Company to provide twenty-four-hour cover. The passengers went on board, and Smith's wife and daughter came to see him off. Another accident was narrowly averted when the *Titanic* sailed on 10 April. As she passed the *Olympic* and the smaller *New York* the latter's stern cable parted under the sudden surge of water, allowing her to swing out into midstream. The *Titanic*'s screws were immediately stopped and no harm was done. It should by now have been apparent that in harbours or narrow waterways these large vessels created hydrodynamic effects which were not well understood and that smaller craft were unaware of the hazards involved.

After stops at Cherbourg and Queenstown to take on mail and more passengers, the *Titanic* moved into the north Atlantic carrying 885 crew and 1316 passengers, the majority being emigrants hoping for a better life in the New World. Also aboard were Joseph Bruce Ismay, chairman of White Star Line, and Thomas Andrews, Harland and Wolff's chief designer. Steaming at about 22 knots, the *Titanic* followed the normal route for this time of year, which took account of the ice to be expected around 50°W, south of Labrador. No boat drills were held, Smith being satisfied with the exercise performed before the Board of Trade inspector at departure, where the sailors lowered two lifeboats, then raised them. The voyage was uneventful until they reached the zone south of Cape Race, where in spring and early summer vast quantities of ice are carried out of the Arctic Ocean on the southbound Labrador current, including icebergs which have calved from the Greenland glaciers.

On Sunday 14 April at 9 a.m. *Titanic* time, an ice-warning was received from the eastbound *Caronia*, passing on messages that small and large ice was reported in latitude 42°N, between longitudes 49° and 51°W. Smith acknowledged the message which was posted on the bridge. At 10.30 a.m. he led a protestant church service in the first-class dining-room; the purser held a similar service for the second-class passengers, a Catholic mass being held in second, and later in third class. At this time the crew opened the doors separating passengers in the first and second class from those in the third class, which were normally locked to conform with the US immigration laws intended to prevent the spread of communicable disease.

At 1.41 p.m. a message from the *Baltic* warning of icebergs in the area was passed to Smith, who then happened to meet Ismay and showed it to him. Ismay put it in his pocket, showed it to some of his friends, and returned it only when Smith requested it at about 7.30 that evening. This action was later criticized, for the warning should have been immediately posted in the chartroom. A few minutes later another warning message, from the German liner *Amerika* to the US hydrographic office, was passed via the *Titanic*'s radio operators but was put aside as the operators were busy. Other messages were received: one sent at 7.30 from the Leyland liner *Californian* to the *Antillian* was picked up and delivered to the bridge. It warned of three large bergs, and advised that the *Californian* had stopped engines until daylight, but the *Titanic* was by this time 50 miles west of the position given and again no action was taken. The message from the steamship *Messaba* at 9.40, warning of large icebergs in the immediate area of the *Titanic*, was laid aside while the radio operators were busy with passengers' signals. At 10.55 the freighter *Rappahanock* sent a warning by Morse lamp which the *Titanic* acknowledged. At 10.55 the *Californian* contacted the *Titanic* again, but was told to shut up as the operator was busy sending passengers' traffic.

Smith had gone to the bridge at 9 p.m. and spoken to his second officer, Charles Lightoller, commenting on the calm night and telling Lightoller to wake him if the situation became doubtful. He turned in at 9.30; Lightoller instructed the two men in the crow's nest to keep a sharp lookout, relinquished his watch at 10 p.m., and also turned in.

In the light of the information that had reached him over the course of the day, Smith had had two options—to turn south or to slow down; he did neither. Ismay later denied that Smith had been trying to establish a record for crossing the Atlantic. It seems that Smith's years of experience had convinced him that the lookouts would be able to give ample warning. On clear nights the surf washing round bergs set up a phosphorescence which could be seen from a distance. On this night, however, the sea was calm and there was no moon. When the dark mass of a huge berg was sighted, it was only 500 yards ahead. Orders were immediately given to put the helm over, to go full speed astern, and to operate the switch which automatically closed the watertight doors deep within the ship. Within seconds, and before the *Titanic* had slowed, the collision with the berg forced open the plates along some 300 feet of the hull below the waterline, exposing three holds and two boiler rooms to the inrushing water, which rose faster than the pumps could handle. It soon surged over the bulkheads, and as more compartments flooded, the ship began to go down by the bows. The noise of the collision was clearly heard by the engineers and by some other people on the lower decks; the first-class passengers initially noticed the unaccustomed lack of vibration when the engines stopped.

Smith seems to have been uncertain of the extent of damage until he and Andrews toured the ship. Andrews convinced him that it was doomed. Shortly after midnight Smith gave the order to prepare the lifeboats. The radio operator was warned to stand by, but no radio distress signal was sent until 12.10 a.m. White distress rockets were fired, and these were sighted by the *Californian*, probably some 10 miles distant, but were ignored as the lookouts could see the *Titanic*'s lights and did not take them as indicating difficulties. By this time the *Californian*'s single radio operator had turned in. At 12.20 the order was given to swing out lifeboats; Smith ordered women and children to be put on board, and the first boat was lowered at 12.45. There was confusion, rather than panic; there had been no lifeboat drills, the seamen did not have designated boat stations, and there was no public announcement system, all orders having to be shouted against the increasing noise of steam blowing off. The closest vessel to respond to the radio distress calls, the liner *Carpathia*, was some 58 miles away and it took three and a half hours for her to forge through the ice to the point where the *Titanic* had been struck. Meanwhile stewards roused the passengers and instructed them to don life-jackets, and the women and children were directed to board the lifeboats. Many women were scared of the great drop from davits to sea, others refused to leave their husbands, while some considered the *Titanic* to be unsinkable and preferred to stay on board, especially as they could see the lights of the *Californian*, which they supposed would come to their aid. No signal was given to alert the third-class passengers, many of whom were foreign emigrants, and it was more difficult to rouse them and to get them to the boat deck, a part of the ship normally closed to them. At some stage Gatti's waiters were hustled into a cabin and the door locked; all were lost. In the event, the first boats away were carrying far fewer people than the sixty-five which they were rated for.

While the boats were being loaded, Phillips and Bride, the Marconi operators, continued to send the old CQD ('calling all ships') distress signal and also the new SOS signal which had superseded it in 1908 but was not yet in general use. They gave up only when Smith came into their cabin and told them to make their escape. Both men did leave the radio cabin but ran in different directions. Ismay was one of forty-five in the last lifeboat, claiming that there were no more women in sight. He later confided to a relative that he was encouraged to save himself in order to defend Smith. Another accusation concerned the survivors Sir Cosmo Duff Gordon, fifth baronet, and his wife. It was alleged that she dissuaded the crew from returning to pick up survivors in the water, although there was plenty of room in their boat, but in fact there was a general reluctance among the lifeboat passengers to return to the swimmers lest too many attempt to climb aboard. Lightoller, Bride, and some of the stronger swimmers managed to climb onto one of the collapsible boats which had been swept into the sea upside down.

After a while the *Titanic*'s stern began to emerge from the water, those left on the decks moving back to keep out of the advancing water. After some minutes poised vertically, she plunged into the depths at 2.20 a.m. on 15 April 1912, leaving some people afloat in life-jackets but carrying many more down with her. Smith undoubtedly went down with his ship. His body was not among those subsequently fished from the water, all of whom had life-jackets, which Smith had not been wearing. A witness who claimed to have seen him on deck in the final minutes, George A. Braden, stated:

> I saw Captain Smith when I was in the water. He was standing on the deck all alone. Once he was swept down by a wave, but managed to get to his feet again. Then as the boat sank he was again knocked down by a wave and disappeared from view. (*The Times*, 20 April 1912, 10f)

When the *Carpathia* reached the scene she picked up 703 survivors, of whom 493 were passengers, mostly from the first class, and 210 crew; many more bodies were recovered later by the cable ship *Mackay Bennett*, the majority being found to have died of hypothermia in the icy water. They were brought back to Halifax, Nova Scotia, and buried there. About 1500 persons perished (the exact figure is not known).

Among those saved were the suffragette Elsie Bowerman and Laurence Beesley, a schoolmaster, who was travelling second class and whose detailed account, *The Loss of the RMS Titanic: its Story and its Lessons* (1912), was considered one of the best survivors' reports. Those lost included Thomas Andrews of Harland and Wolff; John Jacob Astor, probably the richest man on board, closely followed by Benjamin Guggenheim; William Thomas Stead, the journalist; Christopher Head, mayor of Chelsea; Charles Williams, a sportsman; Thomas Pears of the soap family; F. D. Millet, painter; and Jacques Futrelle, novelist. Isidore Straus, a director of Macy's department store, and his wife, Ida, made the decision to remain on board together.

The *Carpathia* made for New York where a senate inquiry was held between 19 April and 25 May, before witnesses were released. Ismay said that the first he knew of ice was when he was awakened by the impact. He claimed that he and Smith had agreed that there was no need to speed as it was best to reach New York on Wednesday morning. Captain Roston of the *Carpathia* confirmed that the lifeboats were all new and that everyone had been wearing life-jackets. Lightoller—the most senior surviving officer—said that Smith had joined him on the bridge at 8.55 p.m. and said that if it became hazy they would have to slow down. Smith had left the bridge about 9.20. After the impact Lightoller saw Smith moving about the boat deck. He thought that he last saw Smith walking across the bridge.

The British Board of Trade inquiry, held under John Charles Bigham, Lord Mersey, president of the Wreck Commission, heard evidence from a wider range of experts, including the shipbuilders, and the seamens' union, the last alleging negligence in navigation. The Duff Gordons employed their own lawyer to defend their actions. In his report Lord Mersey remarked that it was irregular for Smith to have handed the first message to Ismay and improper for Ismay to have kept it, but these actions probably had no bearing on later events. Despite the second and third messages never reaching the bridge, Lord Mersey was satisfied that the master and his officers knew that they were in the region of ice; the master should have turned south or reduced speed—why did he do neither? Experience had shown that in clear weather it was acceptable to press on and keep a sharp lookout. There had been no previous disasters, and given the competition on the north Atlantic crossing, and the desire of passengers for a fast run, the practice continued. Captain Smith:

> had not the experience which his own misfortune has afforded to those whom he has left behind, and he was only doing that which other skilled men would have done in the same position … He made a mistake, a very grievous mistake, but one in which, in the face of the practice and of past experience, negligence cannot be said to have had any part; and in the absence of negligence it is, in my opinion, impossible to fix Captain Smith with blame. (*Formal Investigation*, 261)

The best outcome of the inquiry was the decision that in future all ships should carry lifeboats and rafts sufficient to accommodate all on board, and that regular lifeboat drills should be carried out.

Titanic, the afterlife There has always been uncertainty over the sequence of actions on the fatal day, on which ships were in the area and might have heard the radio signals or seen distress rockets, and on how far the inquiries on both sides of the Atlantic were cover-ups. The subject continues to hold people's attention and has given rise to the British Titanic Society, the Titanic Historical Society, and Titanic International. Besides numerous books and, more recently, websites, the play *The Berg* (1929) and J. S. Parker's BBC radio play *The Iceberg* (1975), there have been several films based on the actual or similar events. The best-known among them are *Titanic* (1953), *A Night to Remember* (1958), and *Titanic* (1997). There was also a major exhibition in 1997 at the Mariners' Museum, Newport News, Virginia. In 1985 a US–French expedition under Robert Ballard of Woods Hole Oceanographic Institution and Jean-Louis Michel of the French oceanographic institution IFREMER succeeded in locating the wreck at 3810 metres below the surface and in taking some photographs by means of remote-controlled underwater craft. In the following year Ballard made several descents in the *Alvin*, discovering that the bows of the ship lay at some distance from the remainder, with debris scattered over a wide area. No organic material remained and nothing was removed from the wreck. In 1987, however, a consortium of American investors employed IFREMER to retrieve some 900 artefacts from the site, the first of several such plunderings. In 1996 there was a failed attempt to raise a portion of the hull.

The *Olympic* sailed on, meeting her end in a breaker's yard in 1933. The *Gigantic* was modified, renamed, and launched as the *Britannic* in 1914; it was a brief existence, as she was requisitioned by the Royal Navy and struck a mine in the Aegean Sea in 1916.

Apart from his schoolfriends, Smith was unknown in the Potteries and there was no desire to link his native town to the disaster. A portrait was hung in Etruria school in 1913, and later a small plaque was set up in Hanley town hall. He was eventually commemorated by a statue erected in Beacon Park, Lichfield, against the protestations of some of the town's residents; Lichfield was chosen because it was one of the chief towns of the county and the diocese of his birth. Sculptured by (Edith Agnes)

Kathleen Scott, Lady Scott CVO (the widow of Robert Falcon Scott, whose heroic death at the South Pole occurred just over two weeks before the *Titanic* disaster), the statue was unveiled on 29 July 1914 by Smith's daughter, and curiously bore no mention of the *Titanic*. A stained-glass window was also installed in Liverpool Cathedral. By this time the drums of war were clearly audible and interest in the *Titanic* died down, only to be revived during the 1950s and commemorated by a large mural of Smith and the *Titanic* at the Potteries shopping precinct, Stoke-on-Trent. Immediately after the disaster, Eleanor Smith posted a black-edged notice outside the White Star offices. It read simply: 'May God be with us and comfort us all.' She attended the memorial services after the disaster but seems otherwise to have faded from public view. She was living in Kensington when she was knocked down by a taxi and suffered a fractured skull. She died in hospital on 28 April 1931.

The myth of the *Titanic* From the day of the *Titanic*'s sinking, myths began to accumulate round the event. The White Star Line's publicity leaflet of *c.*1910 for the *Olympic* and *Titanic* had not gone beyond the claim that 'as far as it is possible to do so, these two wonderful vessels are designed to be unsinkable'; a later leaflet of 1911 described the watertight doors as 'practically making the vessel unsinkable'. Before long the qualifying adjectives were dropped and the *Titanic* became simply 'unsinkable'.

The certainty that men had stood back to allow 'women and children first' into the boats was part of the Edwardian code of manly behaviour expected of all British gentlemen. It was apparent that the American and indeed 'foreign' passengers and crew also displayed heroism. Apart from sailors who were a necessary part of the lifeboat crews, those few men who were saved such as Ismay and Sir Cosmo Duff Gordon later had to defend their actions, even though many of the boats pulled away with empty spaces.

It is unlikely that the musicians were playing 'Nearer my God to Thee' as the ship slid beneath the waves. There were two groups of musicians, a quintet led by Hartley and a trio who played outside one of the restaurants. Among their instruments were two pianos, two cellos, and a double bass. Apart from the impossibility of dragging these instruments and their stools up onto a sloping deck where their music could be heard from the lifeboats some distance below and away from the *Titanic*, there were at the time three tunes to which this hymn was sung. The musicians did in fact remain below (and all were lost), the two people who could still hear them being the Marconi operators. According to the survivor, Bride, they were playing 'Autumn', by which he may have meant the ragtime tune 'Songe d'automne', popular then in British dance-halls.

Five accounts circulated about how Captain Smith had died. In the final moment (when most of the remaining people were gathered at the stern, some distance from the bridge) he was said to have exhorted them to 'Be British'—which most were not. This action, and his exhortation, gave rise to numerous patriotic songs and verses. Another account had him swimming towards a lifeboat with a child in his arms which he then placed in the boat. As the passengers tried to pull him in he asked, 'What became of Murdoch?', his first officer, and on being told that Murdoch was dead, he let go and sank into the water. Another improbable account described him as shooting himself. More reliably, Lightoller and Braden, as mentioned above, both saw him on the bridge, where it seems likely that he was pulled down with the ship. ANITA MCCONNELL

Sources *Formal investigation into the loss of the S.S. 'Titanic': evidence, appendices and index* (1912) • *Shipping casualties (loss of the steamship 'Titanic'): report of a formal investigation into the circumstances attending the foundering on 15th April, 1912, of the British steamship 'Titanic', of Liverpool, after striking ice in or near latitude 41° 46'N, 50° 14'W, North Atlantic Ocean, whereby loss of life ensued*, parliamentary command paper, cd 6352 (1912) • *'Titanic' disaster report of the Committee on Commerce US Senate pursuant to S. Res. 283 directing the Committee to investigate the causes leading to the wreck of the White Star liner 'Titanic'*, US senate report, no. 806, 62nd congress, 2nd session (1912) • G. Cooper, *The man who sank the Titanic? The life and times of Captain Edward J. Smith* (1992); 2nd edn (1998) • R. Howells, *The myth of the Titanic* (1999) • D. A. Butler, *'Unsinkable': the full story* (1998) • J. P. Eaton and C. A. Haas, *Falling star: misadventures of White Star Line ships* (1989) • R. Gardiner, *The history of the White Star Line* (2001) • B. J. Ticehurst, *Titanic's memorials, worldwide* (1996) • 'Disaster at last befalls Capt. Smith', *New York Times* (16 April 1912), 7, cols. 4–9 • *The Times* (Sept 1911–1914) [many articles] • R. D. Ballard, *The discovery of the 'Titanic'* (1987) • *West London and Kensington Gazette* (1 May 1931), 5d • b. cert. • m. cert. • *CGPLA Eng. & Wales* (1912)

Likenesses K. Scott, bronze statue, 1914, Beacon Park, Lichfield, Staffordshire • photograph, Keele University Library, Warrilow collection • photograph, Hanley town hall, Stoke-on-Trent

Wealth at death £3186 4*s.* 6*d.*: probate, 15 Nov 1912, *CGPLA Eng. & Wales*

Smith, Edward Tyrrel (1804–1877), impresario and showman, was born on 26 August 1804, the son of Admiral Edward Tyrrel Smith (*d.* 1824). Intended to follow his father's profession, he was appointed a midshipman in Lord Cochrane's ship, but at the last minute was fetched back from Chatham at his mother's insistence. He then joined the Metropolitan Police, as a red-waistcoated Bow Street runner, but subsequently became an auctioneer, restaurateur, licensed victualler, music-hall and theatre manager, land agent, picture dealer, bill discounter, and newspaper proprietor. It was rightly said of him that he was everything by turns, but nothing for long.

As a speculator, Smith turned Crockford's gaming house in St James's Street into a first-class restaurant which he called the Wellington. This venture fell through, however, and eventually it became the Devonshire Club. Smith then acquired an interest in Vauxhall Gardens, during their notorious days of decline. In 1849 he became the proprietor of several taverns, including the Coal Hole, in the Strand, where the tragedian Edmund Kean formed his Wolf Club. When the American Mrs Amelia Bloomer gave the world a new garment, he made the barmaids of his tavern wear it.

Smith's connection with theatres began in 1850, when he took the Marylebone, in Edgware Road, which he held for two years. At the end of 1852 he became lessee of Drury

Lane, at a rental of £3500. This theatre was in poor condition and had been on the market for some time, with the ground lessee even having considered demolishing it, but Smith kept it going for a full decade. He opened with *Uncle Tom's Cabin*, based on Harriet Beecher Stowe's novel, and the pantomime *Harlequin Hudibras*, later mixing opera with Shakespeare, variety, and circus entertainment. Smith introduced morning performances there, and claimed thus to have invented the matinée. In 1855 he became the proprietor of Hernandez and Stone's circus, and E. T. Smith's Leviathan Company, as it was known, toured the provinces, with Eaton Stone as manager.

In 1858 Smith acquired the Royal Panopticon in Leicester Square, which he reopened on 7 February as the Alhambra, with the *Cirque imperial*, starring one of the Berri brothers and James Leach, rivals of Jules Leotard on the trapeze. The company was then sent tenting on a provincial tour. Smith next took over Her Majesty's Theatre in the Haymarket, opening in 1860 with Sims Reave in opera and that Christmas producing *Tom Thumb*, the first pantomime to be staged there. It is said that he lost £21,000 in the first year. Nevertheless, Smith was able to lease Cremorne Gardens from 1861 to 1869, meanwhile becoming lessee of Astley's Theatre (1863–4) and of the Royal Lyceum (1867–9). He introduced the sensational Adah Isaacs Menken at Astley's as Mazeppa on 3 October 1864, for a season of ten weeks. Smith worked her engagement for all it was worth, at one point advertising her as 'the saucy wench in tights' (W. Mankonitz, *Mazeppa*, 1982, 142).

Smith ran the Surrey Theatre for a short season from October 1870, Highbury Barn Gardens, with the associated Alexandra Theatre, from 1871, and not long afterwards the Regent Music-Hall, Westminster. At the sale of any place of entertainment Smith would make the highest bid, flourish a £1000 note to demonstrate his means, and trust to luck to raise the funds afterwards. It was said he hired his £1000 note from a moneylender, for £1 per day. His friends believed that it was spurious. One of them, at a luncheon, produced a genuine £1000 note. Smith took it, rolled it into a ball, dropped it into his soup, and swallowed it.

Smith then turned his attention again to restaurant catering and opened the Cremorne Supper Rooms in Leicester Square, and the Radnor on the corner of Chancery Lane, as well as a dining hall under the vaults of the Royal Exchange which was a conspicuous failure. He owned the *Sunday Times* from 1856 to 1858, and he also started another newspaper, the *Bedfordshire Independent*, but he soon gave up both of these business ventures. He stood for parliament in Bedford in March 1857 but was soundly beaten by a brewer.

Smith was a most wonderful and indefatigable impresario, a kind of English Barnum. He certainly made many friends, who seemed always ready to assist him in his various speculations. Although these were not always successful, his friendships were lasting and his faith and honesty were never doubted. He was a noted character in his day, who liked to see his name in print, and a generous supporter of charities; a great many of his acts were motivated by genuine kindness. He was also a jocular sort of fellow, always ready for a lark.

Smith married late in life and left behind a large family. He died on 26 November 1877 at his home, Oval House, Kennington Park, London, an old man, forgotten and in near poverty; his wife, Isabel, survived him. He was buried in Brompton cemetery on 1 December 1877. Despite the great numbers of people he had helped, there were barely half a dozen at his funeral. JOHN M. TURNER

Sources W. W. Wroth, *Cremorne and the later London gardens* (1907), 12–16 • C. Scott, *The drama of yesterday and today*, 2 vols. (1899) • H. Wilding, *World's Fair* (1 Dec 1923), 18, col. 3 • G. Van Hare, *Fifty years of a showman's life, or, The life and travels of Van Hare*, new edn (1893) • E. Sherson, *London's lost theatres of the nineteenth century: with notes on plays and players seen there* (1925) • M. W. Disher, *Greatest show on earth: as performed for over a century at Astley's (afterwards Sanger's) Royal Amphitheatre of Arts* (1937) • B. Dobbs, *Drury Lane* (1972) • d. cert. • *CGPLA Eng. & Wales* (1877) • Boase, *Mod. Eng. biog.*

Wealth at death under £200: administration, 19 Dec 1877, *CGPLA Eng. & Wales*

Smith, Edwin George Herbert (1912–1971), photographer, was born on 15 May 1912 at 2 St Paul's Road, Canonbury, London, the only child of Edwin Stanley Smith, a clerk, and his wife, Lily Beatrice, *née* Gray. He attended an elementary school in Great College Street, Westminster, which he left at the age of twelve—just after it was discovered that he was severely short-sighted—to attend the Northern Polytechnic, in Holloway, to learn building crafts: bricklaying, carpentry, and decorating. He transferred to the polytechnic's architectural school when he was sixteen, and at eighteen won a scholarship to the Architectural Association. He had to abandon his course two years later, as his mother (whose unhappy marriage had ended in divorce) could no longer support him. Thereafter he worked as an architectural draughtsman for several architects in the offices of Marshall Sisson, notably for R. Myerscough-Walker. From 1935 he turned to the life of a freelance photographer as a potential means of supporting a determined interest in painting. On 7 September 1935 he married Rosemary Monica Louise (*b.* 1914/15), of Mitcham, Surrey, the daughter of Albert Henry Ansell, a confectioner.

Smith's passion for architecture was subsumed in his career as a prolific and gifted photographer. While his reputation rests largely on his acute eye for the essence of the built environment, his repertory was substantially larger than the recording and interpretation of architecture. Stillness and silence are the most widely cited attributes of his photographic work; he has also been described as an English Atget—the French recorder of the architectural details of Paris and its environs. (The only book of another photographer's work that Smith ever purchased was Atget's *Photographe de Paris*, 1930.) His early photographic subjects were London, the mining community of Ashington, in Northumberland, the docks and quays of Newcastle, cats, and the fairground and the circus. By the end of the 1930s he had—from an acquaintance with Paul Nash, the painter, designer, and photographer—learned

Edwin George Herbert Smith (1912–1971), by Howard Coster, 1955

to develop and print his own work. He worked briefly for *Vogue* as a fashion photographer, for which he cared little, and subsequently took pictures for an advertising agency. He conceived the photographer as the self-effacing recorder of reality—a reality recorded in a spirit of admiration and celebration. He wrote, to commission for Focal Press, five photographic handbooks, including *All the Photo Tricks* (1940). His own technical progression had been from a Box Brownie to a Contax II and a Tenax, both 35 mm cameras made by Zeiss. After the war he used a Ruby mahogany and brass stand camera of 1904, with a mahogany tripod for architectural subjects. He worked in black and white but experimented with colour photography. Significant holdings of his original work are in the Victoria and Albert Museum and in the Museum of London.

Smith's best-known photographs are of architecture and landscapes, the results of commissions for publications such as *English Parish Churches* (the first of his visual essays, commissioned by Thames and Hudson in 1950; new edn, 1976), *English Cottages and Farmhouses*, *The English Garden*, *England* (text by Geoffrey Grigson), *England* (text by Angus Wilson), *Scotland* (text by Geoffrey Fraser), and *Ireland* (text by Micheál MacLiammóir). Many had texts by the writer Olive Muriel Cook (*b.* 1912/13), his second wife, whom he married on 7 September 1954, his first marriage having been dissolved in 1943. He and Olive also collaborated on many contributions to the *Saturday Book*; they had first met under the aegis of its editor, Leonard Russell. Smith published over thirty books of his photographs of buildings, gardens, and landscape during his lifetime; a further four were published posthumously. Much of his work was done in continental Europe, notably France, Italy, Greece, and Germany. In her introduction to *Edwin Smith Photographs, 1935–1971* (1984), Olive Cook revealed that her husband spoke of himself 'as an architect by training, a painter by inclination and a photographer by necessity' (p. 5); he was described as a painter on their marriage certificate. Only at the end of his life did he describe himself as a professional photographer; in his heartfelt preference to be regarded as an artist (that is, as a painter, printmaker, or draughtsman) he resembled other photographers such as Atget and Henri Cartier-Bresson. He painted or drew every day, and edited Ralph Mayer's *The Artist's Handbook of Materials and Techniques* (1951, with subsequent editions).

Smith took more than 60,000 photographs. He once said 'I have come to worship with my eyes' (Vaizey, 954); his severe myopia, once corrected, effectively sharpened his vision and enhanced his ability to coax the essence from his inanimate subjects. His images define the ways in which light, from dawn to dusk, illuminates the essential features of land and landscape, garden and building. If they do not recognize his name, millions know his images through the continued publication and exhibition of his photographic work.

Smith died of cancer on 29 December 1971 at his home, the Coach House, Windmill Hill, Saffron Walden, Essex, where he had lived since the early 1960s. His legacy is an imaginative documentation of the countryside, churches, palaces, and vernacular buildings of the British Isles and much of Europe. As his second wife and collaborator—who survived him—described it, he 'lived by looking' (Vaizey, 954). MARINA VAIZEY

Sources personal knowledge (2004) • *Edwin Smith photographs, 1935–1971* (1984) [introduction by Olive Cook] • M. Vaizey, 'Smith, Edwin', *Contemporary photographers*, ed. C. Naylor (1988), 953–4 [with complete bibliography] • b. cert. • m. certs. • d. cert.
Likenesses H. Coster, photograph, 1955, NPG [*see illus.*]
Wealth at death £9341: probate, 20 June 1972, *CGPLA Eng. & Wales*

Smith, Edwin William (1876–1957), missionary and anthropologist, was born on 7 September 1876 in Aliwal North, Cape Colony, where his father, the Revd John Smith (later president of the Primitive Methodist church), was serving as a missionary. He was one of five brothers and two sisters. He completed his education at Elmfield College, York, and returned to southern Africa in 1898 as a mission teacher of the Primitive Methodist church, in Basutoland. In 1899 he married Julia, daughter of James Fitch of Peasenhall, Suffolk; they had one daughter. In 1902 Smith moved to Northern Rhodesia, where he established Kasenga mission. Apart from his evangelistic work Smith made significant linguistic studies and in 1920 published (with Captain A. M. Dale) a classic ethnography, *The Ila-Speaking Peoples of Northern Rhodesia*.

After returning to Europe in 1915 Smith served for a year as a military chaplain in France before joining the British and Foreign Bible Society, first as its secretary in Rome and then in other capacities, rising to be its editorial superintendent (1933–9). During these years, when social and educational policy became important concerns of colonial administration in Africa, he emerged as an articulate spokesman of what might be called 'the progressive missionary outlook'. Smith strongly supported the work of the Phelps-Stokes commissions on African education in 1920–24, and the foundation of the International African Institute in 1926. He took a leading part in the epochal missionary conference at Le Zoute, Belgium, on which he based his study, *The Christian Mission in Africa* (1926).

Smith's most influential book, *The Golden Stool* (1926), which went through five impressions in its first year, addressed the issue of 'culture contact' in Africa. Its theme of 'the disintegration of African social life' pointed to a concept of applied anthropology—'a dynamic science of man in the service of Africa'—which Smith was to advocate over the next two decades. Other writings of his later years spoke more of the missionary in him: the influential symposium he edited, *African Ideas of God* (1950), and a series of missionary biographies, of Robert Moffat (1925), the Mabilles of Basutoland (1939), Lindley of Natal (1949), and Price of Bechuanaland (1957). His *Aggrey of Africa* (1929), a study of a leading African educator in the Gold Coast, is perhaps the best expression of his Christian, liberal, and multiracial ideals.

Smith was elected president of the Royal Anthropological Institute for 1933–5. He was awarded the Rivers memorial medal in 1931 and the silver medal of the Royal African Society in 1939; he gave the Frazer lecture in 1946 and the Henry Myers lecture in 1952. Between 1939 and 1944 he spent several years teaching in North America, at Hartford Seminary and at Fisk University, and he received an honorary DD from Wesley College, Winnipeg.

The variety of Smith's endeavours was informed by a vision of great coherence and simplicity. Tolerance and generosity were the keynotes of his relations with his colleagues and younger associates. He lived in retirement in Deal, Kent. He died in Victoria Hospital, Deal, on 23 December 1957. J. D. Y. PEEL, *rev.*

Sources I. Schapera, *Man*, 59 (1959), 213 • D. Firde, *Africa*, 28 (1958), 93–4 • *Aldersgate Primitive Methodist Magazine*, 96–107 (1915–26) • *Minutes of the Annual Conference of the Methodist Church* (1958), 182–3 • *CGPLA Eng. & Wales* (1958)

Archives SOAS, diaries and papers relating to central and southern Africa

Wealth at death £4831 6*s*. 3*d*.: probate, 27 March 1958, *CGPLA Eng. & Wales*

Smith, Eleanor Elizabeth (1822–1896). *See under* Smith, Henry John Stephen (1826–1883).

Smith, Elinor Bellingham (1906–1988). *See under* Moynihan, (Herbert George) Rodrigo (1910–1990).

Smith, Eliza (*d*. 1732?), writer on cookery, is known only through her book, *The Compleat Housewife, or, Accomplished Gentlewoman's Companion*. This was first published in 1727, four or five years before her death. In it she was identified only as 'E— S—', though in later editions her full name was given. Her work proved popular, running to more than a dozen editions, only passing out of favour towards the end of the century. In 1742 *The Compleat Housewife* became the first cookery book to be published in America, preceding the first book of specifically American cookery by over fifty years.

Virtually nothing more is known for certain about Eliza Smith's life. In the preface to her book, she claimed 'that for the Space of Thirty years and upwards … I have been constantly employed in fashionable and noble Families, in which the Provisions ordered according to the following Directions, have had the general Approbation of such as have been at many noble entertainments'. Shorn of its verbiage, she was a housekeeper. Probably, unlike others of her calling more fortunate than herself, she did not leave to take up a career as a confectioner or to run a school of cookery. There are slight hints in her book of an association with the Netherlands, and Lord Montagu has suggested that she may have worked at Beaulieu (Maclean, 135).

Contemporary female cookery writers can be divided into two groups—those who published or sold their book themselves, and those who used the services of a printer to act for them. Most of the first group were either of near gentle birth or had escaped from the toils of earning their livelihood through housekeeping; Eliza Smith belonged to the second group, composed largely of housekeepers. Her recipes, she claimed in the preface, were essentially English, and 'proper for a frugal, and also for a sumptuous Table', though most would best fit the former category. Nevertheless there were some interesting innovations. She was among the first to use potatoes for savoury dishes, and she even offered one recipe using tea. This was for a caudle or hot drink made with 'strong green tea', white wine, grated nutmeg, and sugar, thickened with eggs like a custard (Smith, *The Compleat Housewife*, 16th edn, 193). Her book ends with a substantial section of medicinal recipes that she called 'family receipts'. Some are identified with members of the gentry, many more with members of the medical profession. Her knowledge of the technicalities of medicine went beyond what might be expected in a book of 'family receipts'.

Little is known of Eliza Smith, as is true of many female writers of cookery books in the eighteenth century, but her book is an outstanding example of the genre, rivalling Hannah Glasse and Elizabeth Raffald in content and contemporary popularity. She died, according to the fifth edition of *The Compleat Housewife* (1733), probably in 1732. NANCY COX

Sources V. Maclean, *A short-title catalogue of household and cookery books published in the English tongue, 1701–1800* (1981) • E. Smith, *The compleat housewife, or, Accomplished gentlewoman's companion*, 5th edn (1732); 16th edn (1758), preface

Smith, Elizabeth (1776–1806), scholar and translator, was born on 27 December 1776 at Burn Hall, near Durham, the second child and eldest daughter in the family of four sons and three daughters of George Smith, banker, and his wife, Julia, daughter and sole heir of Richard Mott of Carlton, Suffolk. Sir Charles Felix *Smith was her brother. Her extensive learning was acquired in spite of many disruptions in her life. In June 1785 the family moved to Piercefield Park, near Chepstow, Monmouthshire; when her father's business collapsed after the declaration of war by France (1 February 1793) the family and its valuable library were broken up. In 1794 her father took a commission in the army, serving for some years in Ireland. For a few months in 1796 she and her mother joined her father in Sligo; here she studied the Irish language. In summer 1799 they moved to Ballitor, co. Kildare, where she had access to a good library. Until they moved to Coniston in 1801 she did not have a settled home, spending much of her time visiting friends in London, Shirley, and Bath.

Aside from a governess who taught her French and a little Italian, from six to eight years of age and again from ten to twelve, Smith was largely self-taught. In 1789 she became governess to her siblings and began an influential friendship with Henrietta Maria Bowdler. In 1794 she began learning Arabic and Persian from her brother's oriental dictionary; in 1796 she studied Hebrew from a Bible belonging to Henrietta Bowdler's mother. Between 1795 and 1799 she learned Spanish, German, Arabic, Persian, Greek, Latin, Hebrew, some Syriac, and Erse, as well as music, mathematics, and astronomy.

Henrietta Bowdler visited Coniston in 1802, introducing Smith to Elizabeth Hamilton, who much admired her. In 1803 Elizabeth Smith completed her translation of Job, and was encouraged to translate F. G. Klopstock's memoirs for publication. She dreaded being called a learned lady: her mother said that 'she was a living library; but locked up, except to a chosen few'. Hannah More, in *Coelebs in Search of a Wife* (1804), praised her acquirements, which were 'beautifully shaded, by the gentle exercise of every domestic virtue'. In 1805 Elizabeth Smith caught a cold, from which she never fully recovered. She died, unmarried, on 7 August 1806 in Coniston.

After Smith's death Bowdler published *Fragments in Prose and Verse* (1808), a selection of Smith's works interspersed with an account of her life; it ran into many editions. The poems, some in imitation of Ossian, are graceful if unremarkable and her reflections conventional but lively. It is in her flowing translations and philological work that she shines. Also published from her papers were: *Memoirs of Frederick and Margaret Klopstock* (1808); her translation of Job (1810), edited by Francis Randolph; and *A Vocabulary, Hebrew, Arabic, and Persian*, edited by John Frederick Usko, vicar of Orsett, Essex, who supplied 'A praxis on the Arabic alphabet' (1814). Usko thought this the first systematic collation of these languages. Selections from her didactic writings appeared in *The Lady's Monitor* (1828).

JUDITH HAWLEY, *rev.*

Sources J. Todd, ed., *A dictionary of British and American women writers, 1660–1800* (1985) • A. K. Elwood, *Memoirs of the literary ladies of England*, 2 vols. (1843) • E. Smith, *Fragments in prose and verse* (1808)
Archives Durham RO
Likenesses W. Ridley, stipple, BM; repro. in *European Magazine* (1809) • T. Woolnoth, stipple, BM; repro. in *Ladies Monthly Museum* (1822)

Smith [*née* Grant], **Elizabeth** (**1797–1885**), diarist, was born on 7 May 1797 at 5 Charlotte Square, Edinburgh, the eldest of five children of Sir John Peter *Grant (1774–1848), laird of Rothiemurchus, advocate, MP, and judge, and his wife, Jane, daughter of Edmund Ironside, rector of Houghton-le-Spring.

Elizabeth Grant's childhood was spent mostly on the family estate of Rothiemurchus, Strathspey, and in London. She was educated by governesses and tutors and entered Edinburgh society in 1814. In 1820 the family returned to Rothiemurchus following the decline of her father's career and fortunes. From about 1826 Elizabeth wrote articles to supplement family finances. Her first article, entitled 'An Old Story', she submitted to *Blackwood's Edinburgh Magazine* under a fictitious name. It was not accepted, but appeared later in *Fraser's Magazine for Town and Country*. Having earned £3 for this first article she wrote other stories for *Fraser's* and for *The Inspector: a Weekly Dramatic Paper*. In 1825 she and her sister Mary earned a total of £40 from their stories for *The Inspector*, some of which received favourable criticism in *The Times*, but which Elizabeth later recalled as 'a bundle of rubbish' (*Memoirs*, ed. Tod, 196). However, it is for her memoirs of these early years, written later in life, for which she is remembered as The Highland Lady.

In 1827 the family moved to Bombay following Sir John Grant's appointment as a puisne judge. In India Elizabeth Grant met Colonel Henry Smith, of Baltiboys, an officer in the 5th Bombay cavalry. They were married in Bombay in 1829. The Smiths returned to Ireland in April 1830 to live on Colonel Smith's estate in co. Wicklow. Elizabeth took an active part in the management and improvement of the impoverished estate and wrote articles for *Chambers's Journal* to supplement estate income. She combined this with raising a family of three children: Jane (*b.* 1830), Anne (*b.* 1832), and John (*b.* 1838). Between 1845 and 1854 she wrote the recollections of her life, concentrating on her years in Scotland and providing a unique portrait of the social life of the highlands. Written initially as a private memoir for her family, the first public edition of *Memoirs of a Highland Lady* was published in 1898, edited and abridged by her niece, Lady Strachey. This first edition was reprinted four times in one year and a second edition followed in 1911, reprinted in 1928. A third edition appeared in 1950, but the first complete and authentic edition did not appear until 1988. *The Irish Journals of Elizabeth Smith, 1840–1850*, published in 1980, was a selection from journals she kept during her married life in Ireland from 1840 to 1885. A more complete edition, *The Highland Lady in Ireland*, was published in 1991, and includes details of the great famine of the late 1840s. In 1996 was published *A Highland Lady in France: Elizabeth Grant of Rothiemurchus, 1843–1845*, which covered the time she spent in France during the early 1840s among British émigré society.

Elizabeth Smith's memoirs and diaries represent an invaluable social and historical document. Her vivid accounts of life in Scotland, England, India, Ireland, and France provide an important insight into a period of dramatic social and economic change. She recorded the figures and lifestyle of the first half of the nineteenth century across the social strata, with observations of both public figures and the working people. Her writings are particularly useful as a rare example of a female account of highland and Irish life. She died on 16 November 1885 at Baltiboys, Blessington, co. Wicklow.

CHRISTINE LODGE

Sources *Memoirs of a highland lady: Elizabeth Grant of Rothiemurchus*, ed. A. Tod, 2 vols. (1988); repr. (1992) • E. Grant, *The highland lady in Ireland*, ed. P. Pelly and A. Tod (1991) • *Memoirs of a highland lady, 1797–1827*, ed. A. Davidson (1950) • E. Grant, *A highland lady in France: Elizabeth Grant of Rochiemurchus, 1843–1845*, ed. P. Pelly and A. Todd (1996) • pedigree of Grants of Rothiemurchus estate, priv. coll. • Burke, *Gen. GB* • *CGPLA Ire.* (1886)
Archives NRA, priv. coll., Grant of Rothiemurchus MSS

Likenesses L. Perez, oils ('The Highland lady'?), priv. coll. • photograph, repro. in Davidson, ed., *Memoirs of a highland lady*
Wealth at death £5807 6s. 5d.: administration with will, 4 March 1886, *CGPLA Ire.*

Smith, Elleine (*d.* 1579). *See under* Essex witches (*act.* 1566–1589).

Smith, Dame Enid Mary Russell Russell- (1903–1989), civil servant and college head, was born at Cato Cottage, The Green, Esher, Surrey, on 3 March 1903, the daughter of Arthur Russell-Smith, corn merchant, and his wife, Constance Mary Dilke. She was educated at St Felix School, Southwold, Suffolk, and at Newnham College, Cambridge (1922–5), where she took a first in both parts of the modern languages (French and German) and medieval languages tripos. She entered the civil service in 1925, as one of the first women to enter through open competition, and joined the Ministry of Health as assistant principal. She served in the Ministry of Health for nearly all her civil-service career. She was private secretary to the permanent secretary, Sir Arthur Robinson, between 1930 and 1934, when she became a principal. She was promoted to assistant secretary in 1939, and after helping to co-ordinate provision for evacuees during the Second World War she was made principal assistant secretary. In 1946 she became an under-secretary, rising finally to the position of deputy secretary in 1957. She was made a DBE in 1953 and retired from the civil service in 1963.

Russell-Smith's work focused consistently on the area of public social services. In the inter-war Ministry of Health, which was battling with the linked problems of poor health, overcrowding, insanitary housing, and poverty, she saw herself and her colleagues 'almost as missionaries deeply involved with the improvement of social conditions and emotionally bound up with the schemes for which they were responsible' (Russell-Smith, 82). Many of these schemes were in their infancy and relied on local government for their implementation. Her early work focused on housing, and in practice she spent much of her time trying to push slow-moving local authorities to act as promptly as the most innovative.

After the Second World War, Russell-Smith helped to introduce the National Health Service and allied social services. From 1950 she took charge of the general practitioners' services, nursing, and local health services division. From 1951 she also had responsibility for the national assistance and blind, deaf, and dumb services division. These were later amalgamated as the home health services division, for which she held responsibility until 1957. In this era she acknowledged that 'the man with a mission is more likely to be a specialist with the general administrator acting rather as a brake than an accelerator' (Russell-Smith, 83). She identified more with the concerns of the generalist, working on early performance review and resource management mechanisms to improve standards and co-ordination in the National Health Service. As deputy secretary she worked on the hospital plan, launched in 1962 to expand hospital care, as well as on the health and welfare plan of 1963.

Russell-Smith's contemporaries in the civil service regarded her with awe. She was physically small and slight but radiated energy and drive and was clearly 'possessed of a brilliant mind' (*The Times*). She was unafraid to offend the cultivated manners of some of her male colleagues with fresh ideas and practical insights. Enoch Powell remembered her from his years as minister for health as a 'memorable presence … she threw herself with a twinkling eye and an enthusiastic spirit into all the work. One came to rely upon her advice and her encouragement' (*St Aidan's Association Newsletter*, 26).

In 1963 Russell-Smith embarked upon a second career, in which she served as principal of St Aidan's College, University of Durham, until 1970. Her main task was to manage the construction of new college buildings and maintain a collegiate atmosphere as student numbers tripled. She also worked as a part-time lecturer in politics at the university until 1986. As a college principal 'she had moral and intellectual certainties which the young of the Sixties were busily discarding. Yet she succeeded triumphantly, presenting herself as a totally unstuffy emancipating force of considerable moral authority' (*St Aidan's Association Newsletter*, 23). As a lecturer she was sceptical of the development of academic theories of public administration and sought to inform the teaching of the new discipline with practical insights. She was a clever and challenging influence, who did not suffer fools gladly, but drew immense loyalty from colleagues and students alike. Her concern for student welfare led her on many occasions to take in as lodgers students who were experiencing difficulties. In recognition of this wide array of contributions to university life she was made honorary DCL at the University of Durham in 1985.

Russell-Smith's *Modern Bureaucracy: the Home Civil Service* was written for the Politics Association in 1974 as an accessible short introduction at a time of considerable debate caused by the publication of the Fulton report in 1968. In it she showed herself to be widely read on the history of British public administration and a keen supporter of the tradition of political neutrality. She had a general faith in the high standards already existing in the British civil service, and the tradition of 'learning by doing' (Russell-Smith, 62) by which intelligent young recruits were inducted into the high ideals of public service, a capacity to communicate, and the 'intuitive knowledge' necessary to deal with a huge array of tasks. Nevertheless, she was strongly meritocratic and welcomed a dilution of the bookish Oxbridge-based culture of the civil service. She identified management as one of the key problems and on this basis cautiously welcomed the Fulton report.

Russell-Smith maintained close links with Newnham College, Cambridge, where she had not only been a star student but also captain of the boat club and the college fire brigade. She was an associate member from 1927 to 1943 and from 1954 to 1967; vice-president of the roll in 1951 and president from 1958 to 1961; and an associate fellow from 1963 to 1973. She was widely considered to be a trusted adviser on college governance and was made an honorary fellow in 1974. Following her retirement from the civil service, she also applied her experience to a number of other voluntary positions. She served as a co-opted member of the Teesside (late Cleveland) education committee from 1968 to 1975, and as chairman of the Sunderland Church Commission in 1971, the Durham County Conservation Trust from 1973 to 1975, and the St Paul's Jarrow Development Trust from 1975 to 1980.

Russell-Smith's wide array of activities included a lifelong interest in judo. She achieved a black belt of the third dan, and when living in London was a senior member of the Kensington Budok-wai Judo Club. In her prime she was regarded as Europe's senior woman judo expert. She made regular contributions to conferences of the physical education association, and later at Durham she taught self-defence classes to her female students. She was a lover of the countryside and a keen walker, embarking on an expedition in the Himalayas when well into her eighties. She remained single, but her friends and legacies were many and varied. One of her contemporaries at Newnham College described her in 1925 as being

> distinctly of a Romantic frame of mind (in the technical and not the vulgar sense). It manifests itself, among other ways, in a great affection for ruins, a passion for Racine and an eye for antiques. As hostess or guest she is always a perfect companion. (*Thersites*, May term 1925, quoted in *Newnham College Roll Letter*, 105)

She died on 12 July 1989 at her home, 3 Pimlico, opposite the cathedral in Durham. JONATHAN BRADBURY

Sources *WW* · *British imperial calendar and civil service list, 1926–1964* · E. Russell-Smith, *Modern bureaucracy: the home civil service* (1974) · *St Aidan's Association Newsletter* [University of Durham] (Dec 1989), 23–8 · *The Times* (18 July 1989) · *Newnham College Roll Letter* (1990), 103–5 · b. cert. · d. cert.

Archives U. Durham L., corresp.

Wealth at death £492,091: probate, 10 April 1990, *CGPLA Eng. & Wales*

Smith, Erasmus (*bap.* **1611**, *d.* **1691**), merchant and educational benefactor, was the son of Sir Roger Smith (1570/71–1655) of Husbands Bosworth, Leicestershire, and his second wife, Anna (1585/6–1652), daughter of Thomas Goodman of London. He was baptized on 8 April 1611 at Husbands Bosworth. In 1631 his father was an alderman of the City of London. Erasmus also gravitated to London where, having served a seven-year apprenticeship to John Saunders, he was made free of the Grocers' Company on 10 February 1635. Subsequently he traded as a Turkey merchant. In 1657 he was elected an alderman, but paid a fine of £420 to be excused. Smith married Mary, daughter of Hugh *Hare, first Baron Coleraine, with whom he had six sons and three daughters; she predeceased him.

During the civil wars Smith acted as a contractor to the parliamentarian armies, particularly to those which, after 1647, were dispatched to Ireland. His family was already involved in this sphere. In 1642 Sir Roger had invested £300 in the original subscription, or adventure, for the reconquest of Ireland. This interest was transferred to Erasmus. Only in the 1650s, after the Cromwellians had regained Ireland, did the investment yield its dividend in the form of Irish lands. Smith's services as a supplier to the armies entitled him to further recompense. He also bought out soldiers and other adventurers in England, impatient of receiving their lands. Like numerous other English recipients of Irish lands, he was uninterested in living on them himself. In 1655 he proposed that some of the profits be used to endow protestant schools. He believed, as did the authorities in Dublin, that the neglect of education had been a cause of the uprising in 1641. Unless remedied, this omission might again lead to rebellion. Accordingly, in 1657 he vested much of his Irish property in trustees. They were to erect five schools. The prime purpose was to teach the sons of Smith's Irish tenants 'fear of God and good literature and to speak the English tongue'. As well as grammar and 'original tongues', utilitarian skills such as reading, writing, and accounts were on the curriculum. The most promising pupils were to be further aided by scholarships to Trinity College in Dublin.

The future of this, one of the most ambitious private philanthropic schemes of the interregnum in Ireland, was thrown into doubt with the restoration of Charles II. The project, thanks to Smith's and his trustees' sympathies, was redolent of the Calvinism in favour during the 1650s, which was less appreciated after 1660. Nevertheless, the evident utility of the scheme, together with Smith's highly placed friends and abundant funds, ensured that he kept much Irish property. Lord Massareene, in particular, helped Smith to special treatment. The presence among the commissioners in Dublin who adjudicated on the fate of disputed estates of a nephew, Sir Edward Smith, also assisted. Erasmus Smith engaged in protracted litigation and himself visited Ireland during the 1660s. In addition, he watched over the concerns of close relations who had acquired Irish property. His contest with the courtier William Legge for possession of Dunleer in co. Louth was one of several which generated numerous lawsuits. His opponents sarcastically styled him 'pious Erasmus with the golden purse' (*Dartmouth MSS*, 1.112; Staffordshire County RO, D 1778/I/i, 125). Smith's readiness to devote a large proportion of his booty to public schemes overcame official opposition. On 3 November 1667 letters patent from the king were obtained for a revised foundation. The number of Irish schools was reduced to three and £100 annually bestowed on Christ's Hospital, then in London and much favoured by the king. In March 1669 the Irish project was formalized with a royal charter, which named thirty-two governors to oversee the enterprise. Many were included *ex officio*; a few survived from the original trust of 1657 and retained leanings towards protestant dissent.

By 1675 the governors had an annual sum of almost £600 at their disposal. Schools were erected in Galway, Drogheda, and Tipperary, still primarily for the children of Smith's protestant tenants and other poor inhabitants, who would be taught free. Money was also directed into the recently established King's Hospital, a school in Dublin. Apprenticeships, twenty scholarships at Trinity College, and a Hebrew lectureship there were to be funded. Smith enjoined the governors to recruit only 'persons zealous in the protestant religion as also of a public spirit devoted to the works of mercy', and some appointed to teach had dissenting backgrounds ('Erasmus Smith's book', GL, Smith MS 13823, fol. 26). The impact of the schools was less than Smith had hoped. The readiest explanation—on which he and his agents in Ireland seized—was the hostility of Catholics in the localities. The payment of the annual subsidy to Christ's Hospital caused problems, some of which arose from the depressed Irish rents but others from resentment on the part of the governors in Dublin to sending money from Ireland to England. A scheme in 1709 to vary the benefaction by erecting a mathematical school in Dublin was frustrated by lobbyists for Christ's Hospital. Instead statutes of 1718 and 1723 ended the obligation to the London institution and diverted surplus income (now considerable) from annual receipts of £1100 into other useful ventures in Ireland. One result, a chair of history at Trinity College, continues to bear Smith's name.

Smith, living luxuriously at St John's Court in St James's parish, Clerkenwell, maintained an interest in local charities, such as Christ's Hospital. He served, too, as a governor in Robert Boyle's corporation for propagating the gospel in North America. He had purchased, from Sir William Scroggs, Weald Hall in Essex, which parish he remembered in his will. He died between 25 August and 9 October 1691. In his will he asked that he be buried at Hamerton in Huntingdonshire. He also revealed his approach to education, as primarily religious but also to instil knowledge of mathematics and 'mechanic arts', in his final instructions for the upbringing of his sons. These same objectives underlay his schools in Ireland.

TOBY BARNARD

Sources copy of will, GL, MS 13829 • K. S. Bottigheimer, *English money and Irish land* (1971) • *The manuscripts of the earl of Dartmouth*, 3 vols., HMC, 20 (1887–96), vol. 1, p. 112 • Staffs. RO, D 1778/I/i, 11B, 113A, 121, 134, 139, 187, 260 • T. C. Barnard, *Cromwellian Ireland: English government and reform in Ireland, 1649–1660* (1975) • M. V. Ronan, *Erasmus Smith endowment: a romance of Irish confiscation* (Dublin, 1937) • *Irish statutes*, 13 vols. (1786), 2.239–347, 3.2–136 • GL, Christ's Hospital, E. Smith MSS, 13822–13831 • M. Quane, 'Drogheda grammar school', *Journal of the County Louth Archaeological Society*, 15 (1963) • priv. coll., Waring MSS • E. H. Pearce, *Annals of Christ's Hospital* (1901)

Archives GL, Christ's Hospital MSS, MSS 13822–13831

Likenesses oils, 1666, Christ's Hospital, Horsham, West Sussex • G. White, mezzotint, BM, NPG

Smith, Sir (James) Eric (1909–1990), marine biologist, was born in Hull on 23 February 1909, the elder son and eldest of three children of Walter Smith, who had a wholesale grocery business, and his wife, Elsie Kate Pickett. He was educated at Hull grammar school, where he was head boy and an all-round athlete. After a short period in his father's firm he entered King's College, London, in 1927, where he gained a first class in zoology.

Smith began his scientific career in 1930, as a student probationer at the Plymouth laboratory of the Marine Biological Association (MBA), where he worked on the invertebrate fauna of the Eddystone shell gravels. He left Plymouth in 1932, and after three years as an assistant lecturer at Manchester University (1932–5) moved to Sheffield (1935–8), and thence to Cambridge as an assistant lecturer (1938–50). He then took the chair in zoology at Queen Mary College, London (1950–65), where he ran a most successful department with a strong marine biological side. Although much of his time was taken up by administrative duties (he was vice-principal of the college from 1963 during a period of expansion), he took an active part in lecturing and continued his research on echinoderms, recognized by his election as a fellow of the Royal Society in 1958.

From Queen Mary College Smith returned to Plymouth as director of the Marine Biological Association laboratory in 1965, a post he held until his retirement in 1974. Soon after he became director at Plymouth the wreck of the oil tanker *Torrey Canyon* in 1967 produced the first large-scale oil pollution incident. The work of the MBA during this episode resulted in a classic account of the incident, which Smith edited. He also acted as one of the three members of the commissions of Australia and of the state of Queensland dealing with possible oil drilling on the Great Barrier Reef. The scientific work for which Smith is chiefly known, the neurobiology of starfish, was begun at Manchester and continued at Cambridge and Queen Mary College. It resulted in a series of monumental papers. The study of the starfish nervous system presented challenging difficulties, and when Smith began only rudimentary information about gross morphology was available. He was undaunted by the difficulties, and was able greatly to advance knowledge of the nervous system by careful histological work. He also made significant contributions to the study of the fine structure of the nervous system in another invertebrate group, the polychaete worms, using the methods he had developed for starfish.

Smith was a kindly and generous man, notable for his obvious and genuine interest in people, and an unusually able and diplomatic negotiator; these qualities made his advice and counsel much sought, and he undertook a good deal of committee work. Both at Queen Mary College and at Plymouth, Smith played an important role in British zoology by his membership of many committees. He was a member of the Science Research Council (1965–7); a council member (1953–6) and vice-president (1954–5) of the Linnean Society; twice a council member of the Zoological Society (1958–61 and 1964–7) and vice-president (1959–61); as well as serving twice (1962–3 and 1972–4) on the council of the Royal Society and as vice-president (1973–4). He was also a trustee of the British Museum (Natural History) in 1963–74 (chairman 1969–74), and chairman of the board of the Millport laboratory. After his retirement his skills on committees were still much in demand, and he acted as a member of the Advisory Board for the Research Councils (1974–7), president of the International Council of Scientific Unions, and chairman of its special committee on problems of the environment (1972). He also chaired the advisory board's important review group on taxonomy in Britain, whose report was published in 1977.

Smith was appointed CBE in 1972 and knighted in 1977; among other honours he received the gold medal of the

Linnean Society in 1971, the Frink medal of the Zoological Society in 1981, and was elected a fellow of King's College, London (1964) and Queen Mary College (1967). He received an honorary DSc from Exeter (1968), and was one of the first fellows of the Plymouth Polytechnic.

Smith was of medium height and build, blue-eyed, and more or less bald early in life. He usually dressed simply, in a sports coat and flannel trousers, and his benevolent demeanour and charming smile made him very approachable. In retirement, as well as spending more time in his garden (he was a keen vegetable gardener), he continued a lifelong interest in the naturalists of the west country, and also worked on periwinkles, collected from the shore below his house at Saltash, and at many sites around the south-west. In 1934 he married Thelma Audrey (*d.* 1989), daughter of John Lillicrap Cornish, auctioneer and house agent. They had a son and a daughter. Smith died in a nursing home in Plymouth, Devon, on 3 September 1990.

QUENTIN BONE, *rev.*

Sources Q. Bone and D. Nichols, *Memoirs FRS*, 38 (1992), 323–43 • *The Times* (10 Sept 1990) • *The Independent* (8 Sept 1990) • *CGPLA Eng. & Wales* (1990)

Archives Marine Biological Association of the United Kingdom, Plymouth, drawings, notes, and journal proofs

Wealth at death £162,719: probate, 18 Dec 1990, *CGPLA Eng. & Wales*

Eric Edward Dorman Dorman-Smith (1895–1969), by unknown photographer

Smith, Eric Edward Dorman Dorman- [*later* Eric Edward Dorman O'Gowan] (**1895–1969**), army officer, was born on 24 July 1895 at Bellamont Forest, Cootehill, co. Cavan, Ireland, the first of the three sons of Edward Dorman-Smith (1870–1947), justice of the peace, and his wife, Amy (1874–1961), daughter of Edith and William Patterson of Liverpool. Dorman-Smith was educated alone at home until he was twelve and then at Lambrook preparatory school, near Maidenhead, and Uppingham School. Distinguished by an unwavering sense of principle, a brilliant mind, and an oblique Anglo-Irish perception of the British establishment, he would at the height of his powers sum himself up, accurately, as a military scientist. His effect on the twentieth century, though, was to be twofold, from the opposite angles of military history and literature.

Sprung with nervous energy, tall, thin, immaculately dressed and as capable of charming as of antagonizing, Dorman-Smith was nicknamed Chink because of his resemblance to his regiment's mascot, a Chinkara antelope. As a real-life hero of the First World War, the embodiment of chivalry, he inspired his friend Ernest Hemingway's lasting preoccupation with the themes of war and honour. And as deputy chief of staff and principal adviser to Claude Auchinleck, commander-in-chief in the Middle East, his operational advice based on Ultra decrypts of enemy Enigma signals was instrumental in halting Rommel's Afrika Korps at the first battle of Alamein in July 1942, now acknowledged as a critical turning point for the allies in the Second World War.

Dorman-Smith passed out of the Royal Military College, Sandhurst, after two terms in February 1914 and joined the Northumberland Fusiliers, with whom he travelled to France at the outbreak of the First World War; he was in battle at Mons within ten days. He was to be badly wounded three times, awarded one of the first MCs at Ypres in 1915, and mentioned three times in dispatches when, with the acting rank of major at the age of twenty-four, he fired Hemingway's imagination at their first meeting in Milan on armistice day 1918. In the twenties his army leaves were spent with Hemingway in Switzerland, Paris, and Pamplona, mingling with John Dos Passos, Gertrude Stein, Ford Maddox Ford, Ezra Pound, James Joyce, and Scott Fitzgerald, and he stood as godfather to Hemingway's first son.

In his parallel army life Dorman-Smith rose rapidly, from adjutant of his regiment (1919) to instructor at Sandhurst (1924), and at the Staff College, Camberley (1927–9), he was awarded 1000 out of 1000 in the tactics entrance paper, a record that was never emulated. In 1931 he became brigade-major to Archibald Wavell at 6th experimental brigade, and from 1934, as brevet lieutenant-colonel, he advanced mechanization development from the War Office. After a spell at the Staff College as an instructor he commanded his regiment in Egypt from 1937, before being appointed director of military training in India (1938–40), Britain's greatest single military commitment.

Fuelled by anger at the losses witnessed in trench warfare, Dorman-Smith determined to right matters through intelligent tactics based on out-thinking the enemy and on speed of mechanization, which set him at odds with the cavalry and traditionalists. At the Staff College, where lasting impressions for future teamwork take shape, his open contempt for orthodoxy and for contemporaries who went 'by the book' gained him a reputation for arrogance, and led some who would later gain high command to detest him. At the War Office he blithely ignored the directive forbidding contact with the military journalist Basil Liddell Hart, whose tactical 'Theory of the Indirect Approach' matched his own conclusions. He took pride in not being a clubbable man, and the social skills of his popular first wife Estelle, *née* Dawson (*b.* 1903), whom he had married in 1927 after her divorce from Sir Thomas Berney, bt, smoothed his path. But in 1940 he chafed at being in a 'schoolmaster's role', as commandant of the Haifa Staff College in Palestine.

Two successive commanders-in-chief, Middle East, however, made use of Dorman-Smith's skill at crucial junctures in the Second World War. Wavell brought him in to plan the initial moves of the small western desert force in October 1940 that resulted in the destruction of the Italian Tenth Army, which had been poised to take Egypt. And from 24 May 1942, when the Eighth Army's defeat at Gazala made the pivotal loss of Cairo and Alexandria appear inevitable, it was his unorthodox counsel that enabled Auchinleck to outmanoeuvre Rommel and plan the Eighth Army's subsequent strategy. But upon Churchill's preferment that August of Bernard Montgomery as general officer commanding, Eighth Army, whose tactical thinking Dorman-Smith scorned as 'taking a sledgehammer to crack a nut', disillusion and the inability to trim led to dismissal and reduction from acting major-general to his substantive rank of colonel; isolation was compounded by rumours of a love affair. Although given command of a brigade in Italy in 1944, he was again dismissed, this time under circumstances traceable to an old Staff College vendetta. *Across the River and into the Trees* (1950), a bleak novel about military disillusion, would be Hemingway's lament.

Dorman-Smith returned to Ireland, changed his name by deed poll to O'Gowan in 1949, and devoted himself to his young family—a son (Christopher) and a daughter (Rionagh), both born to his second wife, Eve Nott, *née* Harben (*b.* 1913), whom he married on 17 May 1949—as well as to correspondence, scholarship, and his classical Palladian home. His first marriage had ended in divorce in 1948. As memoirs of the Second World War emerged he fought the smear of Montgomery's supporters that Auchinleck had been intending to retreat at Alamein if Rommel attacked again. Libel proceedings against Churchill over *The History of the Second World War*, vol. 4, *The Hinge of Fate* (1951), were withdrawn only after Hartley Shawcross, who was advising Churchill, disclosed the prime minister's ill health. Having been implacably against partition since 1921, and having become increasingly bitter at the supremacy of the Montgomery version of wartime events, O'Gowan allowed his estate near the border to be used for IRA training camps in the mid-fifties. Opposing loyalties, however, were compartmentalized, with his knowledge of Ultra and his personal army contacts remaining confidential. As with the intermix of Hemingway escapades and formal regimental life thirty years before, he was adept at keeping two worlds apart. 'I know what I owe to you', Auchinleck wrote privately in the 1960s,

> and realise very clearly, as I have always done, that without your wise and indomitable thinking always at my side and in my head, we could never have saved Egypt … and all the rest … The 'voice' was certainly yours, even if the 'hands' were mine. (Auchinleck to O'Gowan, 5 July 1967, JRL)

O'Gowan died from cancer at Lisdarne Hospital, co. Cavan, on 11 May 1969, and was buried at the church of St John the Evangelist, Dartry, co. Monaghan, Ireland.

Lavinia Greacen

Sources JRL, Dorman-Smith MSS • private information (2004) • King's Lond., Liddell Hart C., contemporary MSS • corresp., J.F.K. Library, Boston, USA, Hemingway MSS • Royal Regiment of Fusiliers Archives, Alnwick, Northumberland • J. Connell, *Auchinleck* (1959) • J. Connell, *Wavell, soldier and scholar* (1964) • C. Barnett, *The desert generals* (1960) • H. Shawcross, *Life sentence* (1995) • F. H. Hinsley and others, *British intelligence in the Second World War*, 2 (1981) • L. Greacen, *Chink* (1989) • McMaster University, Hamilton, Ontario, Canada, John Connell MSS • J. Meyers, *Hemingway* (1985) • C. Baker, ed., *Ernest Hemingway: selected letters, 1917–1961* (1981)

Archives JRL, corresp. and MSS | CAC Cam., corresp. with Correlli Barnet • J.F.K. Library, Boston, Hemingway MSS • King's Lond., Liddell Hart C., various items, incl. corresp. with Sir B. H. Liddell Hart • McMaster University, Hamilton, Ontario, John O'Connell MSS • Royal Regiment of Fusiliers Archives, Alnwick, Northumberland • TCD, corresp. with Hubert Butler | FILM IWM FVA, actuality footage | SOUND IWM SA, oral history interview

Likenesses drawings, repro. in Greacen, *Chink* • family photographs, priv. coll. • photograph, priv. coll. [*see illus.*] • photographs, Royal Fusiliers, Alnwick, Northumberland, archives, *St George's Gazette*

Wealth at death £5031: probate, 30 July 1971, *CGPLA Eng. & Wales*

Smith, Ernest Brammah [*pseud.* Ernest Bramah] (**1868–1942**), writer, was born on 20 March 1868 at 1 Rushton Street, Hulme, Manchester, the son of Charles Clement Smith, a Manchester warehouseman, and his wife, Susannah Brammah. He left school in Manchester to go into training as a farmer at Erith, Kent, but, after two years' training and five years' practice, eventually decided that he had no future in farming. He later explained his reasons in *English Farming, and Why I Turned it Up* (1894), in the preface to which he wrote: 'I can remember the time when people used to talk to me about farming and explain how I ought to go about it. Alas! I now know.' This, like all his other books, was written under the pseudonym Ernest Bramah and gave no clues to his personal life. Throughout his career Smith was extremely reticent about his personal affairs and shunned publicity. He once wrote: 'I am not fond of writing about myself and only to a less degree about my work.' *Who Was Who* gives only his pen-name, a list of his works, and his death date.

His farming having failed, Smith decided to try journalism and, after a brief period as correspondent on a provincial newspaper, he went to London to work as secretary to Jerome K. Jerome. He then joined the staff of Jerome's paper *Today*, a twopenny weekly, which was founded in 1893 and folded in 1897.

The name of Ernest Bramah first came to public notice

with *The Wallet of Kai Lung* (1900), the first of his collection of stories told by a wandering Chinese man in the manner of the *Arabian Nights* tales and in an elaborate Mandarin style ostensibly of Chinese translated into flowery English language. Hilaire Belloc, one of his most persistent champions, wrote: 'These parable-like tales obtain their effect of subtle humour and philosophy by the adaptation of Chinese conventions to the English tongue.' Other Kai Lung books include *Kai Lung's Golden Hours* (1922), *Kai Lung Unrolls his Mat* (1928), *The Moon of much Gladness* (1932), and *Kai Lung beneath the Mulberry Tree* (1940). Smith's creation captured the public imagination to the extent that the Kai-Lung Club was founded in London to celebrate the novels.

In 1914 Smith began an entirely different set of stories with *Max Carrados*, the eponymous hero of which, on the dust jacket of the first edition, is described as 'a detective of a totally new and unexpected type, for he is blind; but the alluring peculiarity of his case is that his blindness is more than counterbalanced by an enormously enhanced perception of the other senses'. Further books in this series include *The Eyes of Max Carrados* (1923) and *Max Carrados Mysteries* (1927).

The Specimen Case (1924) contains stories of both Kai Lung and Max Carrados, the main reason for which Smith, emerging from his usual seclusion, explains in the preface. In consequence of the marked contrast between the styles of the two series, some critics had questioned how such stories could all be the work of one author. Grant Richards enquired in the *Times Literary Supplement*, 'Is there really such a person as Ernest Bramah?' and Rose Macaulay wrote in the *Nation and Athenaeum*, 'The crude stilted Conan Doylish English of the detective stories certainly goes far to bear out the common theory that Ernest Bramah has a literary dual personality'. 'There is one retort still left', wrote Smith, 'whereby to confound the non-existence and the dualists alike—I can produce both a Kai Lung and a Max Carrados between one pair of covers—and here they are.'

As a hobby Smith studied numismatics and published *A guide to the varieties and rarity of English regal copper coins—Charles II, 1671, to Victoria, 1860* (1929). He died at 40 Boulevard, Weston-super-Mare, his home in Somerset, on 23 June 1942. His wife, Maisie, survived him.

H. F. OXBURY, *rev.*

Sources H. Haycraft, *Murder for pleasure: the life and times of the detective story* (1941) • *The Times* (29 June 1942) • S. P. B. Mais, *Some modern authors* (1923) • *Location register of twentieth-century English literary manuscripts and letters*, BL, 1 (1988) • S. J. Kunitz and H. Haycraft, eds., *Twentieth century authors: a biographical dictionary of modern literature* (1942) • d. cert.

Archives Ransom HRC • U. Reading • University of Bristol

Likenesses photograph, repro. in Haycraft, *Murder for pleasure*, facing p. 82

Wealth at death £15,172 13*s*. 9*d*.: probate, 1943

Smith, Sir Ernest Woodhouse (1884–1960), fuel technologist, was born on 13 February 1884 in Cross Lane, Gorton, Manchester, son of the Revd Harry Bodell Smith, Unitarian minister, and his wife, Mary Miranda (*née* Woodhouse). He was educated at Arnold School, Blackpool, and at the University of Manchester. After graduating in chemistry he carried out research at Manchester on the synthesis of hydrogen cyanide by heating carbon rods in the presence of gases containing hydrogen and nitrogen. In 1907 Smith went to Canada, spending a year as chemist to the Gold Dredging Company in Saskatchewan. On his return to England the following year he was appointed to a post at the University of Leeds, under the auspices of the Institution of Gas Engineers, to study the thermal efficiency of gas fires.

In 1910 Smith joined the Birmingham gas department as physicist in charge of a high pressure industrial gas laboratory, but in 1912 he succeeded to the post of chief chemist. On 14 February the same year he married Beatrice (1889/90–1955), daughter of George Arnfield of Dolgellau; they had a son and a daughter. During the First World War, Smith's department served in an advisory capacity to the government in such matters as the extraction of toluene from town gas and the preparation of charcoal for gas masks. He was awarded the silver medal of the Institution of Gas Engineers in 1911 and the degree of DSc of the University of Manchester in 1918.

From 1920 to 1944 Smith was technical director of the Woodall-Duckham companies, manufacturers of equipment for the fuel industry. The companies took out many patents during this period (relating to furnaces, kilns, coal gas manufacture, and coking processes) and Smith also continued to contribute to the technical literature of the industry on such topics as the production of coke and the purification of coal gas. In 1942–3 he was seconded to be director-general of gas supply at the Board of Trade and then at the Ministry of Fuel and Power.

Smith's later career centred on the problems of fuel in post-war reconstruction. From 1949 to 1956 he was technical adviser to district valuation boards of the coal industry (coke ovens division). He was active in the Industrial Coal Consumers' Council from 1947 to 1957 and served a period as chairman. He was treasurer of the Smoke Abatement Society (later the National Society for Clean Air) and its president in 1954–6.

Throughout his career Smith served on many occasions as a governmental adviser and played a prominent part in fuel organizations in Great Britain, particularly the Institute of Fuel (president, 1943–5) and the Society of British Gas Industries (chairman, 1931–2; president, 1954). In 1943 the Institution of Gas Engineers honoured him with its senior award, the Birmingham medal. At various times he served on the councils of the Institution of Chemical Engineers, the Institute of Chemistry, and the Society of Chemical Industry. He was a founder of the Gas Research Board. Smith was also active in international fuel circles, having been honorary secretary of the World Power Fuel Conference, London, in 1928. A. L. Roberts wrote of Smith in the *Dictionary of National Biography* that 'his strong sense of public duty and his avoidance of self-interest. … His long experience, shrewdness and constructive outlook, and his charm and friendliness in particular, inevitably brought him to many high offices in fuel affairs'. Smith was appointed CBE in 1929 and was knighted in 1947. He died at his home, Higham Cottage, Beech Avenue, Effingham, Surrey, on 7 November 1960; his funeral was held at Woking on 10 November. JOHN SHORTER

Sources 'Ernest Woodhouse Smith CBE, DSc, FIC, president elect', *Journal of the Institute of Fuel* (June 1943), 133 • *Journal of the Institute of Fuel* (Dec 1960), 626 • *DNB* • personal knowledge (1971) [*DNB*] • private information (1971) • *CGPLA Eng. & Wales* (1960)
Likenesses W. Stoneman, photograph, 1947, NPG • photograph, repro. in *Journal of the Institute of Fuel* (June 1943)
Wealth at death £147,350 15*s*. 4*d*.: probate, 23 Dec 1960, *CGPLA Eng. & Wales*

Smith, (Thomas) Eustace (1831–1903). *See under* Smith, Martha Mary (1835–1919).

Smith, Florence Margaret [Stevie] (**1902–1971**), poet and novelist, was born on 20 September 1902 at 34 Delapole Avenue, Hull, Yorkshire, the second daughter of Charles Ward Smith (1872–1949) and his wife, Ethel Rahel (1876–1919), daughter of John Spear, a successful maritime engineer, and his wife, Amelia Frances. The couple were described by their daughter as 'ill-assorted', and when his shipping agency collapsed in 1906 Charles Smith left home to join the merchant navy, leaving his family to survive on the remaining Spear inheritance. With her older sister Margaret Annie Spear, Ethel Smith and her two daughters moved to Palmers Green, then a hamlet on the extreme north edge of London, later to become a suburb. Originally taken on a six months' lease, 1 Avondale Road was to be Stevie Smith's lifelong 'house of female habitation', for after her mother's death in 1919, she shared it with the much loved aunt whom she described in her fictions as the 'Lion of Hull' until the latter died in 1966; she then lived there alone until her final illness.

Peggy, as her family knew her (she acquired the nickname Stevie in her twenties), was a delicate child who almost died in infancy, and when five years old developed tubercular peritonitis, for which she was sent to a sanatorium in Broadstairs for three years. Lonely and homesick, the child began to consider suicide, but found the thought that she could choose to kill herself paradoxically strengthening her own wish to live. She was then educated at Palmers Green high school (1910–17), and at the North London Collegiate School (1917–20), where despite her intelligence and love of literature she did not shine academically. She did not go to university, partly for lack of funds and partly because she had no interest in schoolteaching (then almost the only career option for women graduates in humanities). Instead she trained at Mrs Hoster's prestigious secretarial academy, and after a year's work for a consulting engineer, entered the firm of C. Arthur Pearson in 1922, being appointed personal secretary to Sir Neville Pearson, bt (who appears, somewhat idealized, as Sir Phoebus in her first two novels). She had mixed feelings about this job, in which she stayed until 1953. She found her secretarial work boring and unrewarding, but also undemanding enough to leave her plenty of spare time, of which she took full advantage, to read and write seriously. She developed a passion for European literature both ancient and modern, educating herself by omnivorous, solid reading.

Florence Margaret [Stevie] **Smith (1902–1971)**, by Jorge Lewinski, 1966

In 1934 Stevie Smith submitted a collection of poems to the literary agent Curtis Brown, unsuccessfully; but her first major publication, *Novel on Yellow Paper* (1936), made her name almost overnight. Its darker 'sequel', *Over the Frontier* (1938), was almost equally well received, as was her first book of poems, *A Good Time was Had by All* (1937), illustrated like all her poetry collections by her own idiosyncratic line drawings, reminiscent of Edward Lear and James Thurber. *Tender Only to One* (1938) also did well; but *Mother, what is Man?* (1942) was less successful, and the publication of her third novel, *The Holiday*, written in 1943, was delayed until 1949. In the 1940s and early 1950s her writing was unfashionable, and she was often dismissed as a *fausse-naïve* eccentric whose work few editors liked; between 1953 and 1955 *Punch* was almost the only established periodical willing to publish her work, although she was writing much of her finest poetry at this time. Despite many friends in the literary world, including Naomi Mitchison, George Orwell, Storm Jameson, Rosamond Lehmann, and Olivia Manning, she grew increasingly isolated, bored, and unhappy in her office work. The title-poem of *Harold's Leap* (1950), her fourth poetry collection, describes suicide, a subject close to home: in 1953 she became clinically depressed and attempted to slash her wrists in her office. She was then, on medical advice, retired from the company, now called Newnes, and given a modest pension, which she supplemented by reviewing extensively for *The Observer* and various periodicals. She re-emerged from comparative obscurity with the justly successful collection *Not Waving but Drowning* (1957), followed by *The Frog Prince* (1966); thereafter her reputation steadily increased, and in the 1960s she became a distinguished performer at public poetry readings, where she recited or chanted her own poems alongside much younger writers, including the Liverpool 'pop' poets, to delighted audiences. She received the Cholmondely award in 1966, and in 1969 was awarded the queen's gold medal for poetry. Her last collection, *Scorpion and other Poems*, appeared posthumously in 1972.

Throughout her life Stevie Smith retained certain childlike qualities, apparent in her bright, dark eyes, her slim figure, and the 'schoolgirl' style of dress which she adopted in middle age. She needed attention and cosseting from friends as well as the Lion Aunt, and she was emotionally vulnerable, often depressed, yet also capable of much warmth and gaiety. Since her death she has increasingly been recognized as an important writer. The publication of her *Collected Poems* in 1975 was a landmark in establishing her as a uniquely original poet, while both *Me Again*, the 1981 anthology of her uncollected writings, and Hermione Lee's *Stevie Smith: a Selection* (1983) helped to make her widely known. (Hugh Whitemore's 1981 biographical play *Stevie*, which also popularized her name, regrettably helped to perpetuate the legend of Stevie Smith the childlike, eccentric spinster rather than the sophisticated, original writer that she was.) The republication of her three novels as Virago Modern Classics in 1980 introduced them to new readers who acclaimed the autobiographical 'talking voice that runs on' through her novels, especially *Over the Frontier*, which is now recognized as a classic of 1930s writing in its subtle exploration of antisemitism, gender politics, and cruelty.

Stevie Smith said in a 1963 interview that she feared writing novels because they drew her into dangerous psychic depths, whereas in her poems she was free to invent characters and stories. She excelled at 'storytelling poems', sometimes retelling old tales from an unusual angle, as in 'The Frog Prince', sometimes inventing new ones, as in 'Angel Boley'. Often funny and always serious, and for long more popular with readers than with critics, these poems combine a lightly worn literary and psychological sophistication with simplicity, strangeness, and a deceptively casual handling of line and cadence. Her studies of patriarchal egotism, such as 'The River God', or of corruption, such as 'The Last Turn of the Screw', are as psychologically subtle as Robert Browning's monologues, and yet retain the chaste simplicity of true story-telling. As the poet D. J. Enright perceptively observed, her poetry is 'in essence uncluttered' and yet inclusive, dealing with such large subjects as love, estrangement, intimacy, sadism, the lives of animals, and God, who inspired many questioning poems in which her deep feeling for Christianity contends with a tough scepticism about religious myths. Death is also the subject of many haunting poems which hover between irony and melancholy in a stylized world of their own, where a barren Romantic landscape forms a bleak setting for a lonely consciousness that welcomes extinction.

In late 1970 Stevie Smith became ill with a brain tumour. She died at Ashburton Cottage Hospital, Devon, on 7 March 1971. Her funeral was held on 12 March in Holy Trinity Church, Buckfastleigh, Devon; she was cremated in Torquay. JANET MONTEFIORE

Sources J. Barbera and W. MacBrien, *Stevie: a biography of Stevie Smith* (1985) • F. Spalding, *Stevie Smith: a biography* (1988) • *Me again: uncollected writings of Stevie Smith*, ed. J. Barbera and W. MacBrien (1981) • K. Dick, *Ivy and Stevie* (1983) • H. Lee, ed., *Stevie Smith: a selection* (1983) • D. J. Enright, 'Did nobody teach you?', *Man is an onion: reviews and essays* (1972), 137–48 • J. Barbera, W. MacBrien, and H. Bajan, *Stevie Smith: a bibliography* (1987) • L. Severin, *Stevie Smith's resistant antics* (1997) • G. Plain, 'Faith in a watching brief: Stevie Smith and the religion of fascism', *Women's fiction of the Second World War* (1996), 68–84 • J. Montefiore, *Men and women writers of the 1930s* (1996) • b. cert. • d. cert. • *DNB*

Archives King's Cam., letters to John Hayward • Oxon. RO, MSS and corresp. with Madeau Stewart • U. Birm. L., letters • U. Hull, Brynmor Jones L., corresp. with L. Horvat • Washington University, St Louis, Missouri, letters to K. Dick and MSS | SOUND BL NSA, London [recordings listed in J. Barbera and W. MacBrien, *Stevie Smith: a bibliography* (1987)]

Likenesses photograph, 1919, University of Tulsa, McFarlin Library; repro. in Barbera and MacBrien, *Stevie* • three photographs, 1938–*c*.1969, repro. in Barbera and MacBrien, *Stevie* • J. Lewinski, photograph, 1966, NPG [*see illus.*] • portrait, 1971, NPG

Wealth at death £23,834: probate, 26 July 1971, *CGPLA Eng. & Wales*

Smith, Frances. *See* Stephens, Frances (1924–1978).

Smith, Francis (*d.* 1691), bookseller and General Baptist minister, was the son of Francis Smith, a Yorkshire farrier from Bradford. No further information has as yet been discovered about his family background or his birth details. On 3 May 1647 he was apprenticed to Thomas Hazard, a stationer; he was made free of the Stationers' Company on 5 May 1654. By this time Smith was living at or near the Sugar Loaf in Queen's Head Alley, London, whence his first imprint, a Baptist treatise, appeared in 1653. In 1654, with the aid of several General Baptist leaders, he opened business at Flying Horse Court in Fleet Street, engaging primarily in the distribution of Baptist pamphlets. By 1659, however, he had begun to publish politically radical and republican tracts (including Captain William Bray's *A Plea for the Peoples Good Old Cause*) and his premises were being regularly searched. In this year he opened premises near Temple Bar under the sign of the Elephant and Castle; he subsequently became known as Elephant Smith on account of this trademark sign.

The Restoration government regarded Smith as a threat. In 1660 he was imprisoned three times for his involvement, along with Livewell Chapman, in publishing Henry Jessey's *The Lord's Loud Call*, a republican catalogue of providential signs. Simultaneously, however, Smith was preoccupied with pastoral issues. In March he had been a signatory to the General Baptists' seminal *Brief Confession … of Faith*, which he also published. Shortly afterwards he published his own devotional work, *Symptomes of Growth and Decay to Godlinesse*. By this time Smith was married. The background of his wife, Eleanor (*d.* in or after 1696), is unknown. From the time of their marriage, however, she played a key role in her husband's business; she continued his trade during Smith's periods of imprisonment and exile, and emerged as a bookseller in her own right after his death. The couple had at least four children, two of whom, Francis junior and Eleanor junior, also joined their parents' business.

Early in 1661 Smith was accused of involvement in Venner's Fifth Monarchist uprising and consequently endured searches, assaults, and the confiscation of his property. He co-published a Baptist plea for toleration; in August, however, he was convicted of treason and imprisoned with others for collaborating in another collection of providential signs. Held in close confinement until the following spring, Smith petitioned persistently against his illegal treatment; he was also penalized by heavy prison fines and loss of trade. He was arrested on at least two further occasions over the next five years. In 1665 he moved his family for the duration of the plague to Dorking, Surrey, where he was again arrested; he was saved from imprisonment in Windsor Castle by the intercession of Sir Thomas Foster, JP for Middlesex and Surrey and son of Lord Chief Justice Sir Robert Foster.

While he produced relatively little throughout the 1660s, Smith nevertheless emerged during this period as the principal publisher of the works of John Bunyan, who, like Smith, endured persecution and imprisonment for refusing to compromise his convictions. Between 1661 and 1676 Smith published the majority of Bunyan's writings with the significant exception of the author's major work of 1666, *Grace Abounding*. By 1679—when Smith incidentally published the third edition of *Grace Abounding*—his increasing political activity and attendant prosecutions appear to have led Bunyan to entrust his work to more reliable booksellers.

Upon his return to London after the plague Smith's premises were investigated regularly by Roger L'Estrange, surveyor of the presses, and his finances were compromised by further litigation. In 1670 he was questioned about a printed critique of the Conventicle Act. He subsequently preached to a congregation in Goswell Street and was finally arrested for violating the act. He was arrested regularly throughout 1671, eventually relinquishing his trade for six months. However, with the publication of the declaration of indulgence Smith was granted a licence to preach to two General Baptist groups in Cornhill, London, and Croydon, Surrey.

In 1673 Smith relocated—with his trade sign—to premises near the Royal Exchange, Cornhill, operating briefly from this and his old Temple Bar addresses. The following year he fell victim to profiteering by an unscrupulous warden of the Stationers' Company, Samuel Mearne, who confiscated a Baptist treatise from Smith's premises and (in a by no means uncommon piece of corruption) subsequently published it himself in a pirated imprint. The earl of Shaftesbury intervened on Smith's behalf, and the king ultimately ordered compensation; Smith testified against Mearne before the House of Lords in 1677. He continued to be hounded, at great cost to his business, by both Mearne and L'Estrange.

The Popish Plot and exclusion crisis marked a period of intensive political and professional activity for Smith, who associated closely with Shaftesbury and Titus Oates. In 1679 he published Popish Plot narratives, extracts from parliamentary journals, and seditious tracts. Arrested and examined on numerous occasions, he was frequently acquitted by sympathetic whig juries. In October, however, he was imprisoned and fined for selling a stinging exposé of the trial of George Wakeman, the queen's Catholic physician, who had been accused by Oates of plotting to kill the king and whose acquittal of treason after a summing-up by the judge, Lord Chief Justice Scroggs, allegedly loaded in his favour, fuelled allegations that the judge had accepted bribes. Smith was imprisoned again in December for promoting petitions for a parliamentary sitting. Throughout 1680 he distributed numerous opposition tracts and was a key whig campaigner in the shrieval elections. In September he was indicted for publishing a protest against the extravagances of municipal leaders. Despite a sympathetic jury he was detained on Judge Jeffreys's order before being released by proclamation. He testified against Jeffreys before a Commons committee in October; Jeffreys resigned as recorder the following month. Subsequently indicted for publishing Shaftesbury's *Speech Lately Made by a Noble Peer*, which explicitly questioned the integrity of the king, Smith was acquitted by a packed whig jury in January 1681.

Smith's career peaked dangerously in this year. His publications attacked papists and arbitrary power and objected to the dissolution of parliament. *Smith's Protestant Intelligence*, an organ of whig propaganda, appeared on 1 February. A key figure in the whig campaigns, Smith accompanied the party to Oxford in March; he distributed an outspoken anti-government tract, *Vox populi*, gratis to each member of the Oxford parliament. Returning to London upon the parliament's dissolution, he was arrested for treason in mid-April. His *Protestant Intelligence* was terminated, and he was held in Newgate prison until his release—for lack of evidence—in June.

As the tories re-appropriated power, Smith's fortunes declined. L'Estrange headed a viciously successful press campaign which satirized and discredited his 'Anabaptist' *bête noire*. The tory propaganda effort identified Smith with the most fanatical republicanism, or 'Franksmithism' (Crist, 204), and lampooned him in a broadside ballad, *The Leacherous Anabaptist*. Increasingly isolated, Smith nevertheless continued to distribute opposition newsletters and was active in the mayoral elections that September. About this time he co-published Stephen College's libellous ballad, *A Ra-Ree Show*. Upon its author's execution Smith fled the country; he remained in exile, apparently in the Netherlands, for more than two years. His wife and his children, Francis and Eleanor, continued the business in his absence, and were themselves frequently prosecuted.

On returning to England in March 1684 Smith was immediately arrested; he was tried by Jeffreys in June for his hand in *A Ra-Ree Show*. Pilloried and fined £500, Smith was unable to raise either money or security for his release; he remained in prison until January 1688, when he was pardoned by James II. In that year, he moved to Pope's Head Alley, establishing his business once again under the sign of the Elephant and Castle. He published very little, and early in 1689 sought financial aid from a local Baptist church. He petitioned King William for a position in the port of London, and was finally employed as a watchman in October that year. He died two years later, on 22 December 1691, and was buried in Bunhill Fields. Despite his ostensible financial ruin he left to his wife a 6 acre property in Surrey and a collection of books.

Described by his detractors as a 'pestilent' and 'Pernicious' dissenter (*CSP dom., 1680–81*, 358; Smith, *Injurious Proceedings*, 2), Elephant Smith was as much feared as reviled by the state officials who hounded and prosecuted him. As an opposition bookseller and whig activist he stands alone in the tenacity and openness of the uncompromising principles for which he was arrested, imprisoned on innumerable occasions, and financially ruined. Smith's political engagement was rooted in the religious convictions which he held deeply and exercised regularly. Cataloguing the relentless physical and material costs of his prosecutions and imprisonments, his autobiographical writings constantly reproached the authorities who persecuted him, and represented their author—with some measure of truth—as a martyr to his cause.

BETH LYNCH

Sources T. J. Crist, 'Francis Smith and the opposition press in England, 1660–1688', PhD diss., U. Cam., 1977 • F. Smith, *An account of the injurious proceedings of Sir George Jeffreys Knt. … against Francis Smith, bookseller* (1681) • F. Smith, *An impartial account of the tryal of Francis Smith* (1680) • D. F. McKenzie, ed., *Stationers' Company apprentices*, [2]: *1641–1700* (1974) • *CSP dom.*, *1661–92* • F. Smith, *Symptomes of growth and decay to godlinesse* (1660); 2nd edn (1973) • *Ninth report*, 2, HMC, 8 (1884) • Wing, *STC* • J. G. Muddiman, 'Francis Smith, "the elder"', *N&Q*, 163 (1932), 57–62, 206 • C. Nelson and M. Seccombe, eds., *British newspapers and periodicals, 1641–1700: a short-title catalogue of serials printed in England, Scotland, Ireland, and British America* (1987) • T. Crosby, *The history of the English Baptists, from the Reformation to the beginning of the reign of King George I*, 4 vols. (1738–40) • will, PRO, PROB 11/408, sig. 15 • *Bunhill Fields burial ground: proceedings in reference to its preservation* (1867) • *A brief confession or declaration of faith: set forth by many of us whoare, falsely, called Ana-Baptists* (1660); another edn (1854) [repr. in E. B. Underhill, ed., *Confessions of faith and other public documents, illustrative of the history of the Baptist churches of England in the 17th century*, Hanserd Knollys Society, 9 (1854), 107–20] • Greaves & Zaller, *BDBR* • W. H. Hart, *Index expurgatorius Anglicanus, or, A descriptive catalogue of the principal books printed or published in England, which have been suppressed*, 1 vol. in 5 pts (1872–8) • C. Hill, *A turbulent, seditious, and factious people: John Bunyan and his church* (1988) • A. Abrahams, note on Francis Smith, *N&Q*, 13th ser., 1 (1923), 310 • G. Kitchin, *Sir Roger L'Estrange: a contribution to the history of the press in the seventeenth century* (1913) • J. G. Muddiman, *The king's journalist, 1659–1689: studies in the reign of Charles II* (1923) • J. Dunton, *The life and errors of John Dunton … written by himself* (1705) • P. G. Morrison, *Index of printers, publishers and booksellers in Donald Wing's 'Short-title catalogue of books … 1641–1700'* (1955) • *The leacherous Anabaptist, or, The dipper dipt* (1681) • W. T. Whitley, ed., *A Baptist bibliography*, 1 (1916) • H. R. Plomer and others, *A dictionary of the printers and booksellers who were at work in England, Scotland, and Ireland from 1668 to 1725* (1922) • H. R. Plomer and others, *A dictionary of the booksellers and printers who were at work in England, Scotland, and Ireland from 1641 to 1667* (1907) • G. E. B. Eyre, ed., *A transcript of the registers of the Worshipful Company of Stationers from 1640 to 1708*, 3 vols. (1913–14) • E. Arber, ed., *The term catalogues, 1668–1709*, 3 vols. (privately printed, London, 1903–6)

Likenesses group portrait, engraving ('Commonwealthmen')

Wealth at death left books and 6 acre property with house and orchards in West Humble, Mickleham, Surrey to wife and executor, Eleanor: will, PRO, PROB 11/408, sig. 15

Smith, Francis (*bap.* **1672**, *d.* **1738**), architect and builder, was baptized on 4 January 1672 in Tettenhall, Staffordshire, the youngest of the three sons of Francis Smith, a bricklayer of Tettenhall, and his wife, Elizabeth Hitchins. He was trained as a mason, and in 1697 he and his brother William contracted to rebuild the nave and tower of St Mary's Church, Warwick, which had been destroyed in the great fire of 1694, to the design of Sir William Wilson. The work was carried out between 1698 and 1704, and during the course of it Francis settled in the town, with which, as 'Smith of Warwick', he is particularly associated.

Subsequently, continuing on occasion to work in partnership with his brother, Smith developed a business which made him one of the most successful of such craft-based figures in English history. The rebuilding of the town of Warwick after the fire presumably provided him with an initial opportunity, and he was later responsible for a further group of churches and other public buildings; but the predominant element in his practice was the building of country houses for the midlands gentry. Of these he produced a remarkably large number, in almost all the counties of the region, becoming unrivalled as the leading master builder there and establishing a reputation which extended well beyond it. As early as 1707 Hugh, first earl of Cholmondeley, was advised by a surveyor in London that the Smiths did a 'great deal of busness in the Contry and they have done a great deal of work thearabout & in Warwick you may easy hear of them' (Colvin, *Archs.*, 883); and when in the 1730s Sarah, duchess of Marlborough, was building a house as far away as Wimbledon, Surrey, she stipulated that

> Mr. Smith of Warwickshire the Builder may be employed to make Contracts and to Measure the Work and to doe every thing in his Way that is necessary to Compleat the Work as far as the Distance he is at will give him leave to do. (ibid.)

The scope of the operation which enabled Smith to achieve this position was complex and wide-ranging. Its basis appears to have been that, although himself a master of one building trade only, like other leading master builders of the period he was prepared to undertake the erection of a complete house, performing the masonry himself and subcontracting the work of the other trades; and he evidently built up a team of craftsman associates—joiners, carpenters, painters, plasterers—whom he called upon regularly in these circumstances. His favoured method of working was to provide detailed estimates of the costs and to charge a five per cent commission—the usual fee of architects at the time when acting in a supervisory capacity—on the actual expenditure. In addition, he acted as a supplier of set-piece marble masonry works such as chimney-pieces, and, occasionally, funerary monuments, and there is some evidence that he also dealt in timber. As for the actual designs, both he and his brother normally provided these themselves, but he also continued the practice of contracting to build to those of other architects: examples of this are Heythrop House, Oxfordshire (1705–8), designed by Thomas Archer, and a number of buildings by James Gibbs, notably Ditchley House, Oxfordshire (1720–42), and All Saints' Church, Derby (1723–5; later the cathedral)—although in both these cases he appears to have had some influence on the design as well. Whatever role he was playing, however, it is clear that the foundation of Smith's success was a reputation for honesty and reliability. Lord Cholmondeley's correspondent referred to the Smiths as 'very good Workmen', and when Smith died in 1738 Sir Edmund Isham of Lamport, Northamptonshire, lamented the loss of 'our honest Builder Mr. Smith of Warwick' (Colvin, *Archs.*, 883).

What in general cannot be claimed for Smith is a specially high level of distinction as a designer. His houses are always monuments of excellent craftsmanship, but as one eighteenth-century critic who had seen a number of them observed, although 'all of them [are] convenient and handsome … there is a great sameness in the plans, which proves he had but little invention' (Colvin, *Archs.*, 883). His typical product is a three-storey rectangular block, which represents in essence the standard late seventeenth-century 'double pile' brought up to date by the replacement of the hipped roof of the latter by an attic storey and crowning parapet. A repertory of ornament of a vernacular baroque character is applied with varying degrees of restraint, while the interiors, usually arranged with the hall and saloon across the centre and the staircase to one side, are enriched with fine joinery and plasterwork but little in the way of spatial incident. Examples among the many are Meriden Hall, Warwickshire (*c.*1720), and Davenport Hall (1726), Kinlet Hall (1727–9), and probably Mawley Hall (1730), all in Shropshire. Of the relatively few exceptions to the pattern, two which call for mention are Chicheley Hall, Buckinghamshire (1719–21), and Sutton Scarsdale, Derbyshire (begun 1724): the exotic façade of the former probably owes more to the taste of the patron, Sir John Chester, than to Smith's own devising; but Sutton Scarsdale, in part evidently inspired by Gibbs's unexecuted design of 1721 for the university buildings at Cambridge, is his finest work, a wholly convincing essay in the heroic grand manner, in which the giant Corinthian order is handled with total assurance.

Smith suffered periodically from gout—in 1720 he wrote that the drawing of a sketch 'at this time has occasioned me to make many a wry face by reason I could neither sit nor stand to do it' (Gomme, 'Architects and craftsmen', 87)—and in his later years he put on weight: 'It is unlucky that Mr. Smith is grown so unweildy' (Colvin, *Archs.*, 884), commented Dr George Clarke of All Souls College, Oxford, in 1730. He bought a country estate at Knowle, Warwickshire, for £10,000 and he twice served as mayor of Warwick, in 1713–14 and 1728–9.

Smith was married twice: first in 1695 to Mary Morteboys, and second on 13 October 1702 to Anne Lea, a native of Warwick: he had four sons and one daughter but only two of the sons survived their father. Of these the elder, William (1705–1747), to whom he left 'all my stock of Marble and Timber … in my Marble Yard in Warwick' (will), continued in his father's business and built some more country houses in the midlands. Smith was buried at Warwick on 9 April 1738. PETER LEACH

Sources Colvin, *Archs.* • 'Francis Smith of Warwick', *Warwickshire History*, 2 (1972–3) • A. Gomme, 'Architects and craftsmen at Ditchley', *Architectural History*, 32 (1989), 85–104 • A. Gomme, 'Smith and Rossi', *Architectural History*, 35 (1992), 183–91 • will, PRO, PROB 11/690, sig. 162 • *IGI*

Likenesses J. M. Rysbrack, terracotta bust, 1741, Bodl. Oxf. • W. Winstanley, portrait, Bodl. Oxf. • portrait, Court House, Warwick • portrait, Warwick Museum

Smith, Francis (*fl.* 1763–1779), painter, was born in Italy, presumably of English parents, and appears to have spent much of his early career in Naples. He became associated with the notorious Frederick Calvert, seventh Lord Baltimore, whom he accompanied on a visit to the East in 1763. He made drawings of the people, ceremonies, and costumes of the court of Constantinople, and of the inhabitants of Greece and Poland, which also formed part of Calvert's tour. These were engraved and published in London in 1769. It is not known whether Smith accompanied Calvert to London on the final leg of his tour, but he seems to have settled in London by 1768, when he exhibited a view of Vesuvius at the Society of Artists. He exhibited at the Royal Academy in 1770, 1772, and 1773, showing a panoramic view of Constantinople and its environs, and views of Naples and London. He died in London before 1780.

F. M. O'DONOGHUE, *rev.* ROSIE DIAS

Sources E. Edwards, *Anecdotes of painters* (1808); facs. edn (1970) • J. Ingamells, ed., *A dictionary of British and Irish travellers in Italy, 1701–1800* (1997) • M. H. Grant, *A chronological history of the old English landscape painters*, rev. edn, 8 vols. (1957–61) • Redgrave, *Artists* • Graves, *RA exhibitors* • Bryan, *Painters* (1903–5) • M. H. Grant, *A dictionary of British landscape painters, from the 16th century to the early 20th century* (1952)

Smith, Sir Francis Petit (1808–1874), inventor of a screw propeller, was born on 9 February 1808, probably at Copperhurst Farm, near Aldington Knoll, about 6 miles from Hythe, Kent. His father was Charles Smith, postmaster of Hythe, and his mother, Sarah, was the daughter of Francis Petit, also of Hythe. He was educated at a private school at Ashford and began work as a grazing farmer on Romney Marsh, where in 1830 he married Ann, daughter of William Buck of Folkestone, with whom he had two sons. He later moved to Hendon, Middlesex, still as a farmer. While a boy he built many model boats and displayed great ingenuity in developing their propulsion. He continued to devote much time to this subject and by 1835 he had built a model propelled by a screw, driven by a spring, which was so successful that he was convinced that this form of propeller would be superior to the paddle wheel, then universally used by steamships.

The Archimedean screw had long been used as a pump and there had been many proposals going back to at least the seventeenth century for its use in driving a ship. There had been a considerable number of full-scale demonstrations of full-size propellers, notably one by Shorter in 1802, which was manually turned, though the inventor pointed out that a steam engine would be desirable. The novel and difficult achievement by Smith was the integration of a steam engine and a propeller with a driveshaft which would accept the thrust from the propeller while remaining watertight where it passed through the hull.

Smith won technical assistance from an engineer, Thomas Pilgrim, and financial backing from Wright's Bank and took out a patent for screw propulsion (not for a

Sir Francis Petit Smith (1808–1874), by unknown artist

propeller) on 31 May 1836, just six weeks before the different patent of his rival, Ericsson. The two inventors became friends and their sharing of ideas contributed much to the development of a successful propeller. Smith's clockwork model was demonstrated in 1836 at the Adelaide gallery, where it was seen by Sir John Barrow, the influential and progressive second secretary (senior civil servant) of the Admiralty, who advised Smith to approach the steam department. Encouraged by this, Smith built a 6 ton launch, the *Francis Smith*, with a wooden screw of two complete turns, with a length of 2 feet 6 inches and a diameter of 2 feet. There was a single-cylinder engine of 6 nominal horsepower (nhp). Trials began in November 1836 and in February 1837 there was a happy accident in which half the propeller broke off and the speed increased. Fitted with a new, short propeller the *Francis Smith* was taken round the coast to Folkestone in September 1837. It was stormy on the return trip and coastguards' reports on the performance of this small craft heightened Admiralty interest. Ericsson approached the surveyor's department of the Admiralty, where the reactionary Symonds rejected the proposal.

Smith was persuaded by the Admiralty to build a larger ship. She cost £10,500 and Smith believed that the Admiralty promised to buy her if she was successful but this was later denied. The *Archimedes* (237 tons) was completed in 1839 and trials began to find a suitable propeller. The engine, of two cylinders and 80 nhp, was geared up to drive the propeller at 138 r.p.m. In May she ran successful trials against HMS *Vulcan*, but there was an accident to the boiler soon after, followed by a broken crankshaft.

After she was repaired the *Archimedes* ran a series of trials for the Admiralty conducted by Captain Chappell, superintendent of the packet service, and Thomas Lloyd, the chief engineer of the Admiralty steam factory. The *Archimedes* was raced against the fastest paddle mail packets of the day and was beaten only once, by a much bigger and more powerful ship. The *Archimedes* was able to maintain a speed of about 9 knots across the channel. The report to the Admiralty was enthusiastic and pointed out the superiority of the screw in bad weather, the lack of interference with broadside guns, and the possibility of keeping the machinery below water for protection; only the noise and reliability of the gearbox were criticized. The *Archimedes* was later used for a number of demonstrations, as a result of which I. K. Brunel changed the *Great Britain* to screw propulsion.

The Admiralty reacted swiftly and decided to build a sloop with a screw propeller to compare with similar paddle-ships in all aspects of warship capability. There were inevitable delays while the possibility of converting an existing ship was considered and the training tender *Bee* was actually the first ship with a screw ordered by the Admiralty. There was some confusion when the Admiralty hired as consultants both Smith and I. K. Brunel, who for a brief period quarrelled between themselves and with Lloyd. The direct cause of the argument was the proposal to design the ship with fine stern lines to give a good flow into the propeller. Both Brunel and Lloyd claimed the idea as theirs. The evidence is not conclusive but it is an idea which would occur to any good engineer and it is likely that they thought of it independently. These quarrels were soon over and the three great engineers became lasting friends.

Preliminary trials were held at the end of 1843 and after some improvements had been made over the winter the serious work began in February 1844, during which twenty-eight propellers of different geometries from a number of manufacturers were tried. The most successful, a two-bladed design by Smith, is displayed at the Royal Naval Museum, Portsmouth. It is clear that the Admiralty was convinced of the merits of the propeller by this time as a considerable number of screw-ships were ordered, but there was no design method—nor would there be until the Froudes' work of the 1870s—and further trials were needed. The next set took the form of races between *Rattler* and her half-sister, the paddler *Alecto*. They were raced under steam alone, under sail alone, and with both together. Each ship towed the other and, finally, they were fastened, stern to stern, for a tug-of-war. The trials were seen as a clear triumph for the screw, and few more paddle-steamers were built for the navy. Later trials demonstrated that a screw machinery plant led to a considerable weight saving over paddles. Attention, then and now, has focused on the hydrodynamic advantages of screw propulsion but, to a warship designer, the benefits of weight saving and easier arrangement were probably more significant.

The Admiralty's decision not to purchase the *Archimedes* led to the failure of Smith's company and he was only partially compensated by his share of an *ex gratia* payment of

£20,000 by the Admiralty in 1851, to be shared among all propeller designers. His patent expired in 1856 and he retired to Guernsey as a farmer. However, his many friends came to his assistance; he was awarded a civil-list pension of £200 in 1855, and two years later there was a subscription on his behalf as a result of which he received a service of plate and £2678; among the subscribers were Brunel and Lloyd. In 1860 he was offered the post of director of the Patent Office museum (now the Science Museum) and in 1871 he was knighted. He married in 1866 Susannah, daughter of John Wallis of Boxley in Kent.

Smith was a member of the Institution of Naval Architects and of the Royal Society of Arts for Scotland, an associate of the Institution of Civil Engineers, and a corresponding member of the American institute. He died at 15 Thurloe Place, South Kensington, London, on 12 February 1874. David K. Brown

Sources D. K. Brown, *Before the ironclad* (1990) • *DNB* • *CGPLA Eng. & Wales* (1874)

Archives PRO, Admiralty MSS, mainly ADM 12/375 • University of Bristol, Brunel collection

Likenesses W. Boxall, oils, Sci. Mus. • oils, unknown collection; copyprints NMM, NPG [*see illus.*] • wood-engraving (after photograph by Maull & Co.), NPG; repro. in *ILN* (9 Sept 1871)

Wealth at death under £500: probate, 5 March 1874, *CGPLA Eng. & Wales*

Smith, Francis Samuel [Frank] (**1854–1940**), politician and Salvationist, was born in Chelsea, London, the son of Alfred John Smith. He was educated at Oxford House School, Chelsea, and apprenticed as an upholsterer in 1870. Four years later, on 28 September 1874, he married Elizabeth (*d.* 1935), daughter of George Hall, a smith.

Smith first became involved with the social and religious activism which was to dominate his life when he joined the Chelsea Mission, and through that the Salvation Army, in the late 1870s. He soon gave up his successful furnishings business in Sloane Street, London, to enter full-time into the Salvationist cause. As a propagandist and organizer for the army, Smith demonstrated the skills which he was later to use effectively in his political work, and developed a reputation for his calm, yet uncompromising, determination for a cause. He rose quickly in the movement, and was appointed to the rank of commissioner by General William Booth in advance of a mission to the United States during 1884. After returning from this trip, during which he had been influenced by the writings of the American radical Henry George, Smith increasingly moved the focus of his concerns towards the need for social reform.

Smith came into close contact with a number of radical and socialist political leaders through his involvement with the Free Speech Committee associated with the 1887 Trafalgar Square and Hyde Park demonstrations. His social activism and religious commitment seemed for a time to be merged perfectly in his role as head of the Salvation Army's social reform wing, to which he had been appointed by Booth in May 1890, and he increased the army's involvement in food relief, shelters, and employment schemes. Smith, with W. T. Stead, has been credited with being central to the development of the social reform proposals published by Booth in *Darkest England and the Way Out* (1890). Yet Smith came increasingly to be at odds with Booth over the relative importance of social and spiritual work, as well as the extent of autonomy which Smith wanted for the social reform wing of the army. Smith resigned from the Salvation Army over these issues in late 1890.

Smith had written a number of articles on an egalitarian theme for the *War Cry* before his resignation, and he turned to journalism as the means of spreading his now more fully formed political views. In early 1891 Smith joined the Fabian Society and also started the *Workers' Cry*, as an organ for the Labor Army, advocating collectivism and other radical means of alleviating poverty, but this ceased publication in early 1892. Through the press proprietor and MP, William Saunders, Smith gained work as the parliamentary reporter for the *Eastern Morning News*, and was later editor of the *Weekly Dispatch*.

In 1892 Smith sought election as an independent, but under the auspices of the Liberal and Labour associations, for both a London county council (LCC) seat in North Lambeth, which he won, and the parliamentary seat of Hammersmith, which he lost narrowly, standing on a platform largely of taxation reform and the abolition of the existing poor-law system. At this time Smith was developing a close association with James Keir *Hardie, who assisted him in the Hammersmith contest. Smith and Hardie shared a very strong spiritual and idealist basis to their politics, and a continuing interest in mysticism and similar beliefs. Smith, whom Hardie called 'St Francis' (*DLB*, 9.272), has often been seen as having encouraged Hardie's moves towards utopianism and political isolation. Hardie lived in Smith's house in Chelsea after his own election to parliament in 1892, and Smith continued to act as a part-time secretary and election agent for Hardie until the latter's death in 1915.

Hardie encouraged Smith to stand in 1894 as the Independent Labour Party (ILP) candidate in a parliamentary by-election in Sheffield. The seat was won easily by the Liberals, but this was the first of a long line of electoral campaigns for Smith as a Labour candidate in which he stood for propaganda effect, rather than with a real chance of victory. He stood for the House of Commons a further eight times before winning a seat, Nuneaton, in 1929, which he held only until 1931.

In 1901 Smith rejoined the Salvation Army after becoming disillusioned with aspects of political life, and he resigned his LCC seat. Yet by 1905 Smith had returned to political activism, as secretary of a Right to Work Council formed by Hardie and other ILP and Social Democratic Federation members, to pressure the Conservative government on unemployment. Smith also stood again successfully for the LCC in 1907, and attempted, less successfully, to form the 'Labour men' on the council into a distinct body, separate from the Progressive grouping. After the 1910 election, Smith, George Lansbury, and R. C. K. Ensor did form, at least temporarily, their own LCC Labour Party.

During the First World War, Smith concentrated on the

land issue, particularly focusing on the development of the allotment movement. He was appointed parliamentary private secretary to Lansbury, the new commissioner of works, in October 1930, and continued his interest in the plight of the unemployed. Apart from his many journalistic contributions, Smith also wrote a work on the removal of General Bramwell Booth by the Salvation Army's high council in 1929, and published a brief biography of Hardie in 1915.

Although Smith was an important and respected socialist activist of the period, the intensity of his idealism, and the extent to which his religious and mystical beliefs continued to dominate his political approach, made him a somewhat unusual and distant figure within the socialist movement. He undoubtedly found his closest kindred spirit in Keir Hardie. Smith died on 26 December 1940 at his home at 67 Longley Road, Tooting, London.

MARC BRODIE

Sources E. I. Champness, *Frank Smith, M.P.: pioneer and modern mystic* (1943) • *DLB* • P. R. Thompson, *Socialists, liberals and labour: the struggle for London, 1885–1914* (1967) • V. Bailey, '"In darkest England and the way out": the Salvation Army, social reform and the labour movement, 1885–1910', *International Review of Social History*, 29 (1984), 133–71 • *WWW* • K. O. Morgan, *Keir Hardie: radical and socialist* (1975) • *The Times* (26 Dec 1890), 5b • *The Times* (1 Jan 1891), 7a • *The Times* (2 Jan 1891), 5c • *The Times* (6 Jan 1891), 5c • *Labour Leader* (17 Dec 1898) • K. D. Brown, *Labour and unemployment, 1900–1914* (1971) • K. S. Inglis, *Churches and the working classes in Victorian England* (1963) • R. Mace, *Trafalgar Square* (1976) • *Daily Herald* (27 Dec 1940), 5 • m. cert. • d. cert.

Likenesses double portrait, photograph, 1895 (with Keir Hardie), repro. in Champness, *Frank Smith*, frontispiece • photograph, repro. in Champness, *Frank Smith*, cover

Wealth at death £1341 17*s*. 7*d*.: resworn probate, 23 Oct 1942, *CGPLA Eng. & Wales*

Smith, Sir Francis Villeneuve (1819–1909), politician and judge in Tasmania, was born on 13 February 1819 at Lindfield, Sussex, the eldest son of Francis Smith (*c*.1787–1855), a merchant of London, and his wife, Marie Josephine, the daughter of Jean Villeneuve. He adopted his mother's maiden name as a second name only much later, in 1884.

In 1826 the family moved to Tasmania, then known as Van Diemen's Land. Francis later returned to England to complete his education: he entered the Middle Temple in 1838 and graduated BA from University College, London, in 1840. He was admitted to the bar in 1842, and, upon his return to the colony, to the bar of Van Diemen's Land in 1844. His legal ability was soon recognized by influential members of local society, and he played an important role in the constitutional turmoil which erupted in 1845, being retained for legal advice by the 'patriotic six' members of the legislative council who mounted a challenge to the powers of the lieutenant-governor, Sir John Eardley-Wilmot. On 26 August 1851 he married Sarah (*c*.1838–1909), the only child of the Revd George Giles. They had two sons and two daughters.

Having gained favour with Eardley-Wilmot's replacement, Sir William Denison—who in 1848 warmly praised his 'talent and legal knowledge' (Bennett, 451)—Smith became crown solicitor in 1849. In 1851 he was appointed to the legislative council. He succeeded to the position of solicitor-general at the beginning of 1854, and later that year was appointed attorney-general, taking office only 'on condition of being at liberty to oppose the influx of convicts into the colony' (*The Times*), in line with the beliefs of the patriotic six. He was a member of the house of assembly from 1856 to 1860, despite having opposed the introduction of responsible government, and remained attorney-general through three of the four separate ministries during that time, including that formed under his own premiership, between May 1857 and November 1860. Under his premiership there were important developments in the areas of education, land reform, and social welfare.

In 1860 Smith suddenly resigned to take up an appointment to the Tasmanian supreme court. He was knighted in 1862 and became chief justice in 1870. His tenure on the bench has been described as demonstrating 'the extremes of legal ability and personal ineptitude' (Bennett and Green). Drivingly ambitious, Smith had spent no time on personal pleasantries in his legal and political rise. When he was a senior judge, although his judgments were never questioned for their soundness and impartiality, his temper was often let loose from the bench upon lawyers and their clients. He was also involved in controversy over his personal involvement in two cases which came before the court.

In 1883 Smith took leave from the bench to visit his sick mother in England. While there he decided to resign from his post, and did not return to Tasmania. He died of senile asthenia and pneumonia on 17 January 1909 at his home, Heathside, in Tunbridge Wells, and was cremated at Golders Green.

MARC BRODIE

Sources J. M. Bennett, 'The legal career of Sir Francis Smith', *Australian Law Journal*, 49 (1975), 451–63 • *The Times* (20 Jan 1909), 11 • J. M. Bennett and F. C. Green, 'Smith, Sir Francis Villeneuve', *AusDB*, vol. 6 • *IGI* • A. D. Baker, *The life and times of Sir Richard Dry* (Hobart, 1951) • W. A. Townsley, *The struggle for self-government in Tasmania* (Hobart, 1951) • F. C. Green, ed., *A century of responsible government, 1856–1956* (Hobart, 1956) • *CGPLA Eng. & Wales* (1909)

Archives National Archives of Australia, Hobart, MSS | National Archives of Australia, Hobart, Wolfhagen MSS

Likenesses J. W. Beattie, photographs, Allport Library and Museum of Fine Arts, Tasmania • C. Reutlinger, photographs, Allport Library and Museum of Fine Arts, Tasmania

Wealth at death £112,432 11*s*. 4*d*.: resworn probate, 1 March 1910, *CGPLA Eng. & Wales*

Smith, Sir Frank Edward (1876–1970), industrial scientist, was born on 14 October 1876 in Aston Manor, Birmingham, the son of Joseph Smith, an office clerk, and his wife, Fanny Jane Hetherington. Smith was educated at Smethwick Central School, which he left at fourteen to become a laboratory assistant at Smethwick Technical College. He studied part-time at the Birmingham Technical School, where he gained honours in inorganic chemistry and magnetism and electricity. He then won a national scholarship to the Royal College of Science, in the face of keen competition from all the schools in the country. This was the first step in his remarkable career. He studied chemistry, mathematics, and physics with some mechanical drawing, geology, and astrophysics. He was awarded the associateship of the Royal College of Science in physics (first class) in July 1899. He remained at the college as a part-time teacher and demonstrator, and became much involved in the study of electrical measurements.

When in 1900 the National Physical Laboratory (NPL) was opened at the Kew observatory, with Richard Glazebrook as its director, Smith was one of his first assistants. For the next ten years he devoted himself to the establishment of accurate electrical standards and methods of measurement.

The first success was the building of the current balance, which enabled the ampere to be determined with great accuracy. This in turn provided a standard with which to develop a voltmeter better than any then existing. The next problem was to improve the Weston cell as a stable and reproducible electromotive force, which Smith was able to do by a change in the electrolyte. There still remained the problem of the measurement of resistance in absolute units. For this Smith, with financial help from the Company of Drapers and Sir Andrew Noble FRS, developed a method suggested by L. V. Lorenz. The first 'Lorenz machine' was constructed and installed at the NPL.

These developments led Smith to propose an international congress on electrical units and standards, and this was held in London at the invitation of the British government in 1908. The units then decided upon remained substantially those in use at the end of the twentieth century. In 1910 Smith went to Washington to assist the national bureau of standards to implement these decisions. Smith had made his mark.

In 1914 the NPL became involved in war work, and Smith made important technical contributions. Ernest Rutherford, Sir Joseph Thomson, and others persuaded the Admiralty to set up a board of invention and research, into which many scientists from the NPL were drawn. It is known that Smith invented the first magnetic mine which sank a number of German submarines. For this Smith received an award of £2000 from the Admiralty. He became a fellow of the Royal Society in 1918.

In April 1918 the NPL was transferred to the Department of Scientific and Industrial Research. Glazebrook retired, and the following year Smith left to join the Admiralty. In 1920 he was appointed director of the new scientific research and experimental department. The Admiralty research laboratory was constructed at Teddington, under his control. He was responsible directly to the third sea lord, controller of the navy for the general direction and organization of research work for naval purposes. When research reached a stage where its practical results were to be tested, it was handed over to the departments which were to make use of it. Since these departments were dependent on the director of research for most of their scientific manpower, Smith was able to influence the scientific standards throughout. In 1923, three years after Smith's appointment, Sir Frederick Laurence Field, on leaving the post of controller, concluded his report with these words: 'I have no hesitation in stating that the scientific section of the Admiralty, working under the able direction of Mr. Smith, has developed into a most valuable and essential adjunct of the Fleet.'

In 1929 Smith was offered and accepted the post of secretary to the Department of Scientific and Industrial Research. The activities of this department covered many fields. There were boards concerned with building, chemistry, food preservation, transport, forest products, fuel, metallurgy, radio, water pollution, and the geological survey. There were also many other committees for research, and fully operative research laboratories and sub-laboratories in several fields. Smith showed great skill both in organization and consolidation, and in dealing with government departments, politicians, and industrialists. The industrial research associations, which were co-operatives in various fields, were also partly financed by the department. The Road Research Laboratory was taken over from the Ministry of Transport and later became one of Smith's main interests. He remained secretary of the department until 1939.

During these years Smith was active in many other fields. Most scientific organizations set up in the United Kingdom at one time or another had Smith on their governing body, commonly as president. He was on the Royal Society's council from 1922 to 1924, and from 1929 to 1938 was its secretary. He was a member of the Physical Society from 1907, a member of council from 1909, and held many of its offices, including the presidency (1924–6). He was a founder fellow of the Institute of Physics in 1920 and its president from 1943 to 1946. He was prominent in the British Association for the Advancement of Science for most of his life. He was president of the Junior Institution of Engineers (1935–6) and a governor of the Imperial Institute (1930–38). He became chairman of the technical sub-committee of the Television Advisory Council in 1935.

At the age of sixty-two Frank Smith began a new career in industry. He became adviser on scientific and industrial research to Anglo Iranian Oil (later British Petroleum), a post he held for seventeen years. He also had a long association with Birmingham Small Arms Co. Ltd—at first as an unofficial adviser, but in 1944 as chairman of the research committee. In 1947 he became a director, and resigned in 1957 on his eighty-first birthday.

Smith also played an important part during the Second World War on advisory scientific committees to various ministries. He was controller of telecommunications equipment, Ministry of Aircraft Production, director of instrument production of the Ministry of Supply, and controller of bearings production at the same ministry. He was chairman of the technical defence committee of MI5 from 1940 to 1946.

The success of Smith's work was recognized by many honours: OBE (1918), CBE (1922), GBE (1939), CB (1926), KCB (1931), and GCB (1942). He was physically attractive, dignified, friendly, and kindly. On the other hand he was very reserved, or even somewhat aloof, and in later years developed an authoritative and somewhat inflexible manner. The brilliance of his mind was generally acknowledged, and he was an indefatigable worker. His academic honours included ARCSc, DSc (Oxon., 1926; Sheffield, 1936), and LLD (Birmingham, 1930; Aberdeen, 1931). He also received many distinguished medals. His publications were many, but his original contributions were confined to his time at the National Physical Laboratory. After that time his work was organizational and administrative, and his influence in scientific circles enormous. He was a brilliant lecturer, and much in demand.

In 1902 Smith married May (*d.* 1961), daughter of Thomas B. King of Birmingham; they had one daughter. Smith died at Minehead, Somerset, on 1 July 1970.

CHARLES GOODEVE, *rev.*

Sources C. F. Goodeve, *Memoirs FRS*, 18 (1972), 525–48 • private information (1981) • *CGPLA Eng. & Wales* (1970)

Archives ICL, biographical papers | IWM, corresp. with Tizard • Nuffield Oxf., corresp. with Lord Cherwell | FILM BFI NFTVA, current affairs footage • BFI NFTVA, documentary footage

Likenesses W. Stoneman, photograph, 1933, NPG • D. Heath, oils, 1937, National Physical Laboratory, Teddington, Middlesex • photograph, repro. in Goodeve, *Memoirs FRS*, facing p. 525 • photograph, National Physical Laboratory, Teddington, Middlesex

Wealth at death £25,451: probate, 29 Oct 1970, *CGPLA Eng. & Wales*

Smith, Sir Frederick (1857–1929), army veterinary surgeon, was born at West Street, Hull, the elder of twins, on 13 April 1857, the son of John Smith, a coal porter, and his wife, Mary Jane (formerly Wood). John Smith later remarried; he died while Frederick was at school, leaving a widow (Ellen, *née* McCaffery), and three younger children, the other twin having died. At the age of sixteen Smith entered the Royal Veterinary College, London. In April 1876 he obtained his diploma 'with great credit', gaining prizes in physiology and cattle pathology, and the Coleman medal for an essay on specific ophthalmia.

Having passed his army veterinary examination in December 1876 Smith was commissioned to the artillery, and in October 1877 he sailed for India (he became veterinary captain, 1880; major, 1896; lieutenant-colonel, 1899; colonel, 1905; and major-general, 1907). He came home for medical treatment early in 1879, and in the same year married Mary Ann, daughter of Arthur Samuel Briggs, a racehorse trainer of Spigot Lodge, Middleham, Yorkshire. They were to have a son and a daughter. Smith returned to India at the end of 1879, and after investigating the cause of sore backs among the 480 horses of his new regiment, the 12th lancers, he showed that contrary to prevailing opinion the main cause was ill-fitting saddles and not errors of riding. In 1882, with J. H. Steel, he established the *Quarterly Journal of Veterinary Science in India*, which was published for seven years.

In 1886 Smith was appointed professor at the army veterinary school at Aldershot, Hampshire, where he spent five years of strenuous work relieved only by a tour of the continental veterinary schools, one consequence of which was the establishment at Aldershot in 1888 of a vaccine institute which supplied all the calf-lymph required for the army. From Aldershot he wrote forty-nine original papers for the professional journals. He also published *Manual of Veterinary Hygiene* (1887; 3rd edn, 1905), *Manual of Veterinary Physiology* (1892; 5th edn, 1921), and *Manual of Sore Backs* (1891, subsequently embodied in the army's *Manual on the Care and Management of Horses*). The first two works became the recognized textbooks for all English-speaking veterinary students. Among the many papers which Smith published between 1893 and 1898 may be mentioned 'The physiology of the horse's eye', 'The loss of horses in war', and 'The physiology of the horse's foot'. Smith also worked on the control of strangles and pneumonia.

Smith served in the Nile campaign of 1898, and in the following year he went on active service to South Africa. After the war he was for two and a half years principal veterinary officer in South Africa, and he then returned to England as principal veterinary officer, eastern command. In 1907, at the age of fifty, he was appointed director-general of the army veterinary service with the rank of honorary major-general.

An army veterinary corps having already been created, Smith reorganized the system of veterinary stores. He also succeeded in obtaining the inclusion of veterinary cadres in the organization of Viscount Haldane's Territorial Force, and strove to get the veterinary service, then subordinate to the remount department, placed directly under the quartermaster-general. The claim was not conceded until 1911, and Smith had retired in 1910. It can be said, however, that the subsequent development of the service, culminating in its conspicuous efficiency during the First World War, followed naturally on the reforms introduced at Smith's instigation.

Save for the years of the First World War, when Smith was re-employed, first as deputy director of veterinary service, southern command, and then as assistant director-general, the remainder of Smith's life was devoted unremittingly to the completion of his historical works. *A History of the Royal Army Veterinary Corps, 1796–1919* (1927) and *The Veterinary History of the War in South Africa* (1919) are of the highest interest and importance for this branch of the army. Smith saw through the press two volumes of his *Early History of Veterinary Literature* (1919 and 1924), and passed the proofs of the third volume (issued in 1930). The fourth volume (published in 1933) he left in manuscript to F. Bullock, together with all his other papers. He was created CMG in 1900, CB in 1905, and KCMG in 1918. Smith had an interest in biography and made a particular study of the lives of his heroes: Cromwell, Napoleon, and Bismarck, who 'inspired him because each wielded his power with success at a time a despot was needed … He scorned pretence, cant, hypocrisy and plagiarism, and looked upon the word "tact" as synonymous with the word "deception" or "dishonesty"' (*Veterinary Record*, 10 Aug 1929).

Smith died at his home at 5 Warrior Gardens, St Leonards, Sussex, on 27 July 1929; his body was cremated on 31 July at Golders Green in London and his ashes were preserved, together with his heart, at the Royal Veterinary College, London. His fortune of about £12,000 he left, after the life interests of his widow and two children, to the Royal College of Veterinary Surgeons for the establishment of a fund for veterinary research.

F. Bullock, *rev.* Linda Warden

Sources *Veterinary Record* (10 Aug 1924), 689–90 · 'Funeral at Golders Green', *Veterinary Record* (10 Aug 1929), 688 · *Veterinary Record* (3 Aug 1929) · A. G. Todd, 'The Royal Army Veterinary School', *Veterinary Journal*, 34 (1927), 14–29 · J. Moore, 'A review of the army veterinary service', *Veterinary Journal*, 34 (1927), 31–5 · b. cert. · d. cert. · *WWW*

Archives Royal College of Veterinary Surgeons, London · Royal Veterinary College, London, notebooks for proposed biography of Napoleon

Likenesses W. Stoneman, photograph, 1918, NPG · D. Hardy, portrait, Royal College of Veterinary Surgeons, London

Wealth at death £12,292 6*s.* 9*d.*: probate, 4 Dec 1929, *CGPLA Eng. & Wales*

Smith, (William) Frederick Danvers, second Viscount Hambleden (1868–1928), newsagent and hospital reformer, was born at Filey, Yorkshire, on 12 August 1868, the only surviving son and youngest of the six children of William Henry *Smith (1825–1891), newsagent and politician, and his wife, Emily Leach, *née* Danvers (1828–1913). He was educated at Eton College (to whose governing body he was elected in 1902) and New College, Oxford, where he graduated in 1890 with a third class in modern history.

Following his father's death in 1891 Frederick Smith, as he was usually known, succeeded his father as Conservative MP for the Strand division of Westminster. He held the seat from October 1891 until his retirement in January 1910. Although he was never an outstanding parliamentarian, Earl Spencer in 1903 'was struck with the vigorous stand made by "Freddie" Smith in moving the vote of thanks' as a Unionist free trader at the inaugural meeting of the Free Food League (*Red Earl*, 2.317). The famous maiden speech in 1906 of F. E. Smith, afterwards earl of Birkenhead, was preceded by confusion when Speaker Lowther called upon 'Mr Frederick Smith' to speak. 'The Member for the Strand, who had been for many years in the House and was known to us all as "Freddy Smith", assumed naturally that he had been called and commenced to deliver his speech.' Disorder prevailed until '"Freddy", who was by now completely bewildered, could be prevailed upon to sit down' (Lee, 91). In 1913, following the death of his mother (who had been created Viscountess Hambleden in 1891), and as the only male heir (his older brother died in infancy), he took his seat in the Lords as Viscount Hambleden. He was not prominent in the upper chamber.

His father's death also placed Frederick Smith at the head of the family firm of W. H. Smith & Son. Like his father he proved a constructive example in business of the governing partner who cast himself as *primus inter pares*. He trusted those to whom he delegated, and chose them well. The master-stroke of his business life was to recruit in 1893 H. J. St John Hornby, with whom he had rowed in the Oxford eight. Hornby proved a decisive businessman whose work sustained and enhanced the firm's performance. The high point of their collaboration was when Smith supported Hornby in launching a network of bookshops to compensate for the loss of the firm's bookstall contracts with the Great Western and London and North Western railways from 1901 to 1903. On 26 July 1894 Smith married Lady Esther Caroline Georgiana Gore (1870–1955), third daughter of the fifth earl of Arran. They had three sons and two daughters.

Smith was a paternalistic employer, and a man of charitable instincts. He perpetuated his father's benevolent relations with institutions in the vicinity of the firm's headquarters. He joined the council of King's College, London, in 1894, becoming a governor in 1898, treasurer from 1898 to 1928, and fellow in 1907. When W. H. Smith & Son bought the land at Clare Market occupied by King's College Hospital, Smith, now Viscount Hambleden, selected and donated a new site for the hospital at Denmark Hill. He was not only chairman of the hospital, but a stalwart friend of all London voluntary hospitals, and an influential worker for their progress. Hambleden was chairman of the London regional committee of the British Hospitals Association, and founding chairman in 1922 of the Hospital Savings Association. In 1923–4 he sat on the Ambulance Cases Disposal Committee. Having been a member of the council of King Edward's Hospital Fund from 1921, and of its revenue committee from 1923, he was selected in 1927 to chair its inquiry into pay beds in London voluntary hospitals. The Hambleden committee's report (published in July 1928, shortly after his death) heralded a major advance in health care. It recommended that it should be a recognized function of voluntary hospitals to provide additional beds for from 4 to 6 guineas weekly to benefit the professional and middle classes, for which hospital facilities for treatment of serious illness were much scarcer than for the poor. This would require the building of new wings to existing hospitals, and possibly of separate hospitals for patients who would pay fees on graduated scales. As even the most expensive nursing homes lacked the facilities of a well-equipped hospital, his committee proposed that voluntary hospitals should raise revenue by treating richer patients. It advised the introduction of health insurance for people of moderate means.

As a lieutenant-colonel with the Royal 1st Devon yeomanry Hambleden served in Gallipoli and Egypt (1915–16) during the First World War and was mentioned in dispatches. Throughout his life he relished country life in Devon, of which county in the 1890s he had become a deputy lieutenant. In 1906 he commissioned Detmar Blow to design a lavish and extensive neo-Elizabethan manor house at North Bovey, a high tin-mining village on the east edge of Dartmoor. Hambleden paid for the restoration by Sir Charles Nicholson of St John's Church in 1916–18, converted stables into a thatched parish hall, built roads, and improved the cottages. As a result North Bovey has endured as perhaps the best preserved and most picturesque of Dartmoor villages.

Hambleden had reserved manners and a deep sense of duty. He was even-tempered, compassionate, but not to be bluffed. After several operations in London, he died on 16 June 1928, at Greenlands, Henley-on-Thames, and was buried on 19 June at Hambleden, Berkshire.

RICHARD DAVENPORT-HINES

Sources *The Times* (18–20 June 1928) · C. Wilson, *First with the news* (1985) · *The Red Earl: the papers of the fifth Earl Spencer, 1835–1910*, ed. P. Gordon, 2, Northamptonshire RS, 34 (1986) · Viscount Lee of Fareham, *A good innings*, ed. A. Clark (1974) · *The Lancet* (23 June 1928) · *BMJ* (21 July 1928); (18 Aug 1928) · E. Barker, *Age and youth* (1953) · *DNB* · Kelly, *Handbk* (1954), 973 · Viscount Chilston, *W. H. Smith* (1965) · d. cert.

Archives W. H. Smith Ltd, Milton Hill, Abingdon, family corresp. and papers | Harrowby Manuscript Trust, Sandon Hall, Staffordshire, letters to fourth earl of Harrowby and fifth earl of Harrowby

Likenesses J. Russell & Sons, photograph, *c*.1917, NPG · W. Stoneman, photograph, 1920, NPG · photograph, 1920, repro. in Wilson, *First with the news* · photograph, *c*.1927, repro. in *The Times* (18 June 1928) · probably by A. G. Walker, bronze bust, *c*.1930, Lincoln's Inn Fields, London · Spy [L. Ward], lithograph caricature, NPG; repro. in *VF* (8 Dec 1904)

Wealth at death £2,500,000—save & except settled land; £200,908 limited to settled land: probate, 1928, *CGPLA Eng. & Wales*

Smith, Frederick Edwin, first earl of Birkenhead (**1872–1930**), lawyer and politician, was born on 12 July 1872 in Pilgrim Street, Birkenhead, the second of five surviving children of Frederick Smith (1845–1888), estate agent, barrister, and local politician, and his wife, Elizabeth (1842–1928), daughter of Edwin Taylor, rate collector. As a boy F. E. (as he was always known) modelled himself on his father, a swashbuckling political adventurer in his own right, a robust tory, and forceful orator who died at the age of forty-three, just a month after being elected mayor of Birkenhead. He was educated first at a dame-school in Birkenhead, then at Sandringham School in Southport (where he announced, at the age of ten, his intention of becoming lord chancellor), and finally—having failed the entrance exam for Harrow—at Birkenhead School (1887–9). From there he won a scholarship to University College, Liverpool, where he spent four terms (a fact he subsequently suppressed) before winning a scholarship to Wadham College, Oxford, in 1891.

Oxford and early political career To an unusual extent Smith made his name at Oxford. Wadham enjoyed a golden age in the 1890s: F. E.'s contemporaries included the legendary all-round athlete C. B. Fry, the future Liberal politician John Simon, and the Liberal economist Francis Hirst. Between them they dominated both the rugby field and the union. Despite the handicap of his northern background Smith outshone them all, endowing his bare initials with a glamour which lasted all his life. Tall, darkly handsome, unashamedly ambitious, endowed with a scathing wit and an inexhaustible appetite for life and pleasure, he made himself the epitome of the Oxford Union 'swell'. His verbal duels with Hilaire Belloc were the stuff of Oxford legend. He switched from classics to law and became president of the union in his third year but still managed, by a heroic last-minute exertion, to take a first. The following year he won the coveted Vinerian law scholarship and was elected a fellow of Merton, where he

Frederick Edwin Smith, first earl of Birkenhead (1872–1930), by Walter Stoneman, 1919

stayed for three years (1896–9), gaining a depth of legal learning that later surprised critics who thought him merely a flashy politician.

Even while sharpening his wit at the Oxford Union, Smith was already active in national politics in the north-west. Billed initially as his father's son, he spoke on tory platforms all over Lancashire as early as the 1892 general election, beating the Orange drum against Irish home rule. When he finally left Oxford in 1899, having eaten his dinners at Gray's Inn and passed his bar finals with distinction that summer, it was to Liverpool that he returned to set up in practice on the northern circuit. He quickly built a brilliant reputation, and many of his impudent retorts to pompous judges passed into legal folklore. ('Mr Smith, having listened to your case, I am no wiser.' 'Possibly not, m'lud, but much better informed.'; 'What do you suppose I am on the Bench for, Mr Smith?' 'It is not for me, Your Honour, to attempt to fathom the inscrutable workings of Providence.') He began earning fabulous fees; but his sights were firmly set on getting into parliament. He cultivated the local tory boss Archibald Salvidge, and threw himself vigorously into the sectarian disputes which characterized Liverpool politics at this period. When Joseph Chamberlain brought his tariff reform crusade to Liverpool in 1903, Smith seized the opportunity to make a dazzling supporting speech which won him adoption three months later for the working-class constituency of Walton. As a prospective candidate he successfully promoted himself as the champion of the hard-drinking, patriotic working man against the moralizing Liberal coalition of free-traders, pacifists, and temperance campaigners who would curtail his 'harmless relaxations' while selling out Britain's interests to foreigners. In 1906, against the tide of the Liberals' landslide victory, he narrowly held the seat which he continued to hold until the redrawing of boundaries in 1918.

Edwardian politics As one of only 157 demoralized tories facing more than 400 Liberals in the new House of Commons, Smith lost no time in making his mark. His maiden speech on 12 March 1906—one of the most celebrated débuts in parliamentary history—was a masterpiece of impudent satire which made him a star overnight (*Hansard* 4, 153, 12 March 1906, 1014–1023). He was shrewd enough not to try to repeat this first success, but followed it with a sequence of brilliantly argued speeches employing his forensic skills to portray the Liberal government's legislative programme as a series of cynical sops to the various sectional interests which made up its support. His speech on the 1906 Trade Disputes Bill remained the classic exposition of the case against intimidatory picketing and the legal immunity of trade unions right up to the 1980s. His clinical exposure of the anomalies of the education and licensing bills helped destroy the government's will to proceed with them when the House of Lords used its built-in Unionist majority to throw them out. As a sustained assault by a single junior back-bencher on the legitimacy of a government with a huge majority, Smith's achievement between 1906 and 1909 has never been surpassed.

At the same time Smith quickly replicated in London the spectacular success he had already made at the Liverpool bar. He took silk in 1908, and by 1910 was earning more than £10,000 p.a. He represented the soap manufacturer W. H. Lever (Lord Leverhulme) in a lucrative series of cases against the Northcliffe press. He appeared more often than was prudent for Horatio Bottomley. He defended Dr Crippen's mistress, Ethel le Neve (and got her off). He successfully defended the young Arthur Ransome's biography of Oscar Wilde against Lord Alfred Douglas's vindictive libel suit. Strangely, he had no single famous case that made his name, yet in an age of star barristers (Edward Carson, Rufus Isaacs, Edward Marshall Hall) F. E. was the most glamorous of them all.

In 1901 Smith had married Margaret Eleanor Furneaux (1878–1968), daughter of the Revd Henry Furneaux, a classics don at Corpus Christi College, Oxford, and his wife, Eleanor, the daughter of the painter Joseph Severn. They had three children, Eleanor (1902–1945), Frederick Winston Furneaux *Smith, later the second earl of Birkenhead (1907–1975), and Pamela, later Lady Hartwell (1914–1982). They lived first at The Grove, Thornton Hough, on the Wirral; then they moved to 70 Eccleston Square, London. In 1907 he bought a modest country house at Charlton, near Banbury, to which over the years he added stables, tennis courts, and a swimming-pool; and in 1913 a palatial London residence, 32 Grosvenor Gardens, which boasted to the world his extraordinary success. These two houses remained his homes for the rest of his life.

When the House of Lords provoked the great crisis of Edwardian politics by throwing out Lloyd George's 'people's budget' of 1909, Smith had only been in parliament three years. But the tory party, though dominated by the landed interest, had always offered opportunity to clever lawyers who made their way by brains alone, and Smith fitted this archetype perfectly. He quickly forced himself to the forefront of the constitutional battle. Privately he thought the peers wrong to reject the budget. But publicly, as a good barrister, he made a brilliant case for their right to do so, turning the 'peers v. people' argument on its head by mounting an ingenious defence of the upper house as the trustee of the popular will against the otherwise unchecked arrogance of the Commons. Unlike the tory peers whose main concern was to preserve their own privileges, Smith saw that the existing composition of the Lords was indefensible. He took his stand on the need for a reformed second chamber, and denounced the government for proposing merely to curb the powers of the upper house, leaving the Commons sovereign in an effectively unicameral system. From this perspective he was keenly interested in Lloyd George's scheme for a grand coalition: he believed that by giving up the Lords' power to veto Liberal legislation the tories could win concessions on issues of greater national importance such as tariffs and defence. The plan came to nothing—Asquith and Balfour were not prepared to split their parties—but Smith's enthusiasm for it foreshadowed his leading role in Lloyd George's post-war coalition.

When the possibility of compromise broke down, Smith joined Carson, Austen Chamberlain, and other 'diehards' in urging the peers to stand firm against the government's threat to swamp the Lords with new creations. For the rest of his life he maintained that the 1911 Parliament Act was unfinished business which left the constitution permanently unbalanced. Meanwhile his performance in the two general elections of 1910—which destroyed the Liberals' independent majority, leaving the government henceforth dependent on the Irish—forced the new tory leader, Bonar Law, to invite him onto the opposition front bench. At the second general election of 1910 Smith was joined on the tory benches by his brother Harold, who was returned for Warrington. Harold, also a barrister, was never much more than a shadow of his elder brother: he even married F. E.'s sister-in-law Joan Furneaux in 1914 and bought a house near Charlton. He lost Warrington in 1922 and died in 1924, aged forty-eight. F. E. was hard hit by Harold's death.

Amid the exceptional bitterness of party conflict in 1910–14 Smith maintained close friendships across the political divide. From the moment he entered the house he had found a soulmate in his fellow adventurer Winston Churchill (then a Liberal). They attacked each other with relish in public, while enjoying one another's company in private. At the height of the constitutional crisis they founded their own dining club—the Other Club—composed of a dozen of the most congenial members from each party, with a leavening of writers and artists. 'Nothing in the rules or intercourse of the Club', rule 12 declared, 'shall interfere with the rancour or asperity of party politics' (Coote, 20). The Other Club epitomized Smith's approach to the great game of life and politics. Though quintessentially a product of the Edwardian era, the club survived the First World War, F. E.'s death in 1930, and Churchill's thirty-five years later, and still exists today.

Though still disdained by many tories as a jumped-up provincial lawyer, Smith worked hard over the next three years to position himself as Law's heir apparent. He presented himself as a progressive modern Conservative, the heir to the Disraelian tradition of tory democracy. To that end he contributed to various journals a stream of essays collected in 1913 under the title *Unionist Policy* (he had already published in 1909 a volume of his speeches). Building on his opposition to the sectional politics of the Liberal government and his own party's shameless abuse of the upper house to try to block them, he developed a lofty theory of inclusive unionism which should bind all classes in a contract of patriotic unity. He supported the payment of MPs, to allow Labour members to sit in parliament without being dependent on the unions. He supported proportional representation, to end the polarizing distortions of the existing electoral system. He supported Lloyd George's national insurance scheme and advocated a minimum wage. With a number of other younger tories he founded the Unionist Social Reform Committee, which published mildly progressive reports on such matters as the reform of the poor law and working-class housing. 'A contented proletariat', he wrote, 'should be one of the first objects of enlightened Conservative policy' (F. E. Smith, *Unionist Policy*, 1913, 1–20).

The price of social security was military service. Smith's progressive toryism closely reflected Lord Milner's campaign for national efficiency, arising out of the failures of the Second South African War and apprehension of a coming trial of strength with Germany. Smith had no illusions on this subject. He saw international relations as a Darwinian struggle in which Germany was perfectly entitled to challenge Britain's supremacy, and warned that Britain would only retain its possessions if it was prepared to fight for them. He himself joined the Oxfordshire yeomanry—though the training he received at weekend camps with Churchill and other congenial companions was decidedly more convivial than strenuous.

The same belief that force ultimately ruled underlay his opposition to women's suffrage. At one level his attitude was simply the protection of male privilege. Characteristically, however, he rationalized his case on a more philosophic basis, arguing that 'votes are to swords exactly what bank notes are to gold—the one is effective only because the other is believed to be behind it' (*Hansard 5C*, 19, 11 July 1910, 66). On issues such as temperance or national service, men would not accept being outvoted by the weaker sex. Up to 1914 he scornfully opposed the suffragists' demand. To his credit, however, he recognized that the women's contribution to the national war effort destroyed his argument. In 1917 he found himself as attorney-general charged with piloting through parliament the bill that gave women over thirty the vote.

The question of consent likewise underpinned Smith's attitude to the last great crisis of Liberal England—Ulster's resistance to Irish home rule. Again he took up an apparently extreme position, acting as Carson's 'galloper' at the torchlight processions and parades of volunteers which culminated in the signing of the Ulster covenant in September 1912. All his antecedents impelled him to this allegiance: even his birthday was the anniversary of the battle of the Boyne. At a time when Bonar Law was warning the government that 'there are things stronger than parliamentary majorities' (speech at Blenheim, 27 July 1912), Smith was bound to take the same line; and characteristically he did not hold back. But as usual his position was more thoughtful than at first appeared. In supporting Ulster's defiance he was trying to convince the Liberal government to take seriously the message that Ulster could not be coerced. By the same token he recognized that the rest of Ireland could not be coerced either. He did not, like most Unionists, see Ulster as a convenient device to block home rule, but conceded Ireland's right to self-government, so long as the government conceded Ulster's equal right to be excluded. He was one of the first prominent politicians in either party to advocate partition.

In the Commons, Smith brilliantly exposed the anomalies of the 1912 Home Rule Bill and mercilessly denounced the Liberals' cynicism in rediscovering home rule after 1910 only because they were once more dependent on Irish votes for their majority. He regarded its imposition in these circumstances—with the Lords no longer able to refer it to the people as they had done with Gladstone's 1893 Home Rule Bill—as a constitutional outrage. Far from promoting civil war, his purpose was to prevent a bloodbath by convincing the government—beginning with his friends Lloyd George and Churchill—that Ulster's determination to resist was deadly serious. By the summer of 1914 the government was beginning to get the message. Viewed in this light, Smith's championing of Ulster was both realistic and constructive.

Law officer in wartime On the outbreak of war in August 1914 Smith was appointed to the spectacularly inappropriate job of press censor. He was not a success, and lasted only a few weeks. Instead of joining his regiment, however—the Oxfordshire yeomanry, with whom he and Churchill had enjoyed playing soldiers before the war—he secured another incongruous appointment as recording officer to the Indian troops arriving in Europe to fight on the western front. This was a convenient posting which enabled him to observe conditions in the trenches from a position of some personal comfort behind the lines; it exposed him to justified criticism that he was shirking the military duty he was keen to urge on others.

Smith was rescued from this embarrassment by the political crisis of May 1915, which forced Asquith to broaden his government. In the resulting coalition Smith became solicitor-general and, six months later, on Carson's resignation, attorney-general with a seat in the cabinet. This was the turning point in his career: henceforth he was in government for most of the rest of his short life. At the same time, becoming solicitor-general diverted him from the political mainstream into the backwater of the legal offices. From this moment his chance of becoming tory leader or prime minister faded. Thus the war derailed his career as it did so many others. He was compensated with the law officer's traditional knighthood, and became known for the next three years by the unaccustomed title of Sir Frederick Smith.

As attorney-general, Smith was largely occupied with advising the government on matters of international law, conducting cases before the prize court, and prosecuting offenders under the Defence of the Realm Act. But by far the biggest case with which he had to deal was the prosecution for treason of Sir Roger Casement, charged with inciting Irish soldiers to mutiny against the crown. Eighty years on, the conviction and execution of Casement continues to arouse extraordinary odium. In view of his own active identification with Ulster before the war it is questionable whether Smith should have conducted the prosecution himself at all. More important, it is widely believed that Smith conspired to blacken Casement's name by circulating his homosexual diaries, in a vindictive determination to secure a conviction. In fact there is no reputable evidence to associate Smith with the circulation of the diaries. The evidence is rather that he thought their use by the Foreign Office to prejudice opinion against Casement 'a ghoulish proposal' (Reid, 410). He had earlier offered them to the defence to assist a plea of insanity in mitigation of the death sentence. Certainly he wanted to secure Casement's conviction; but he was very apprehensive of the effect on neutral (that is, American) opinion of hanging him. Criticism of Smith's conduct of the Casement trial does not stand impartial scrutiny.

Immersed in his legal functions, Smith played no part in the political crisis of December 1916. Asquith's replacement by Lloyd George, however, brought him much closer to the centre of government. Though not a member of the war cabinet, he was increasingly entrusted with additional functions, including a mission to the United States, in the course of which he travelled some 15,000 miles from coast to coast, addressing forty-eight meetings in five weeks. During his absence he was awarded a baronetcy (24 January 1918). As victory neared, he was closely concerned with the question of how Germany and individual Germans should be punished. Smith favoured a tribunal to try the leading war criminals, starting with the Kaiser; doubtless he saw himself as chief prosecutor. When the Kaiser escaped to the Netherlands, however, it proved impossible to charge lesser scapegoats, and the idea lapsed.

Nevertheless, 'Hang the Kaiser' was a popular cry at the 'khaki' election held in December 1918. Smith's old Walton seat was abolished by boundary changes; but he was comfortably returned for neighbouring West Derby. Never one to undervalue himself, he now demanded a seat in the new cabinet. But Lloyd George had no place to offer him—except the woolsack. This would mean giving up the House of Commons and any hope of becoming prime minister. At least as important to F. E., it would also mean giving up his earning potential at the bar, the only way he could support his extravagant lifestyle. Against this, he had always had the ambition to be lord chancellor. To achieve it at the age of forty-six would make him the youngest holder of the office since Judge Jeffreys. The opportunity was irresistible. The appointment raised a storm of protest. The king asked Lloyd George to think again. The *Morning Post* (11 Jan 1919) complained that it was 'carrying a joke beyond the limits of a pleasantry'. Generally Smith was thought to lack both the legal authority and the moral character for the woolsack. But he was determined to confound his critics—and he succeeded.

Lord chancellor Smith took the title Lord Birkenhead (3 February 1919), and instantly invested his decaying industrial birthplace with the glamour that formerly attached to his initials. Capitalizing on his youth and energy he consciously set out to be a memorable lord chancellor, as he explained to a dinner at Gray's Inn (9 May 1919):

> I think perhaps I have the advantage—it is the only advantage I claim—over the great Bacon that I excel him in levity. I think in relation to Brougham I may perhaps claim that I excel him in gravity. (Campbell, 468)

Or, as he expressed it on another occasion, 'Should I be drunk as a lord or sober as a judge?' (F. W. Hirst, *In the Golden Days*, 1948, 106). In fact he was both. He was determined not to change his hedonistic lifestyle (a row quickly broke out over the refurbishment of his official apartments). He relished the magnificence of the office, but was impatient of the ceremonial flummery, the knee-breeches, and the long hours sitting on the woolsack. He very quickly quashed doubts about his legal ability: this was when his years of academic law at Merton paid their dividend. He firmly defended the independence of the judiciary against political encroachment. His judgments were greatly admired, and he pushed through an important agenda of reforms. At the same time he brought an informality to the office and a whiff of brimstone to the soporific proceedings of the Lords. And on occasion—particularly as he began to get bored with the job and realized that no further advancement was open to him—he began to disgrace himself in public. He had always been a formidable drinker, but before the war ambition ensured that he could hold his liquor. Once he became lord chancellor he had no realizable ambition left. Admiring anecdotes still clustered around his name—his witty sallies were repeated from mouth to mouth; but increasingly they were prefaced with the observation that the lord chancellor had 'dined well'. In drink he could be rude and bullying. So in the end some of the doubts about his suitability were vindicated.

Nevertheless Birkenhead achieved his ambition of being remembered as a great lord chancellor. His judgments in a large number of complex commercial cases, delivered with force and lucidity, have stood the test of time. He showed a bold willingness to overthrow precedent in cases where he considered the law anachronistic—for instance, in allowing money to be left to Roman Catholic communities for the purpose of having masses said for the souls of the dead in *Bourne* v. *Keen* (1919). In his only judgment on a criminal appeal, *Director of Public Prosecutions* v. *Beard* (1920), he set an important precedent himself by disallowing drunkenness as a mitigating factor in rape leading to murder. In several painful divorce cases he displayed remarkable humanity. His most agonizing judgment was in the celebrated case of Archdeacon Wakeford, a canon of Lincoln, convicted of adultery under ecclesiastical law: after minute examination of the evidence Birkenhead reluctantly led the judicial committee of the privy council to reject the archdeacon's appeal.

As head of the judiciary Birkenhead took drastic measures to speed up divorce hearings, even sitting himself to clear the backlog of cases that had built up during the war. In the face of strong legal protectionism he carried the County Courts Act (1919), extending the common-law jurisdiction of the county courts to new areas of litigation, and the Administration of Justice Act (1920) which relaxed a number of outdated conventions. His attempt to streamline the assize system was thwarted by local interests. But his greatest monument as a law reformer was carrying a vast and comprehensive Law of Property Act (1922), bringing the law of property into the twentieth century by finally abolishing such medieval hangovers as copyhold tenure and gavelkind. This was a measure which had been in the legislative pipeline for more than twenty years. Birkenhead never pretended that he had done more than provide the political momentum to complete the work of others. But he did claim that 'We have by the Act established some contact with sanity in dealing with land' (Campbell, 486).

More than most lord chancellors, Birkenhead was a key member of the government, one of the prime minister's most trusted colleagues. In cabinet he spoke rarely, but with an authority which compelled respect. 'He was cautious as well as sagacious', Lloyd George remembered, 'remarkable for his lucidity and brevity … a master of words' (Birkenhead, *Frederick Edwin, Earl of Birkenhead*, 2, 1935, 12). He brought all his advocacy skills to the government's cause in the House of Lords: one of his greatest speeches was a courageous condemnation of imperialist tories who made a hero of General Dyer, the officer responsible for the Amritsar massacre. He also campaigned eloquently for reform of the divorce law. Citing heartbreaking cases of women trapped in long-dead marriages, he argued that once divorce was admitted on any grounds it was nonsense to allow it only for adultery, as if the sexual relationship was the most important part of marriage. Cruelty, desertion, drunkenness, and insanity should equally be allowed as grounds to end a marriage. Despite the opposition of the bishops, a bill introduced by Lord Buckmaster carried the Lords, but was defeated in the Commons.

Birkenhead's greatest contribution as lord chancellor, however, was his part in the signing of the treaty which created the Irish Free State in December 1921. Ireland had moved on since 1914. By the Government of Ireland Act (1920) the government had accepted the logic of partition and established a home-rule parliament for the six counties of north-eastern Ulster, sited at Stormont. In the south, however, Sinn Féin refused to accept partition or home rule: they declared a republic and set out to drive the British from Ireland by terror and assassination. The government responded by sending the notorious Black and Tans to suppress them. For two years Birkenhead defended 'the assertion of force—force in its most extreme and vigorous application' (*Hansard 5L*, 44, 22 Feb 1921, 117). When Lloyd George changed tack and invited de Valera for talks he was sceptical; but ultimately—consistent with his attitude before the war—he accepted the principle of offering the south dominion status, if Sinn Féin would accept it. With his record as a leading opponent of home rule, Birkenhead was the pivotal figure. On the one hand it fell to him, with Austen Chamberlain, to persuade the Unionist Party to swallow a settlement which many saw as giving in to terrorism. By chance the party conference was held in Liverpool that autumn: Birkenhead persuaded his old mentor, Alderman Salvidge, to back the negotiations. On the other hand, he played a crucial role in persuading the Irish to compromise their demand for a thirty-two-county republic. In particular he forged a surprising bond of mutual trust with the IRA leader, Michael Collins. Collins believed he had signed his own death warrant by signing the treaty; he was indeed assassinated eight months later. He also predicted that 'Birkenhead may have said an end to his political life' by signing the treaty (R. Taylor, *Michael Collins*, 1968, 152); and this too was not far from the truth. Bitterly attacked by Carson and other old colleagues in the Lords, Birkenhead made a powerful defence of the treaty, looking forward to Ireland taking its place as a self-governing dominion within the empire; but Unionist die-hards never forgave what they regarded as his treachery.

The Irish treaty was just one factor in the alienation of Conservatives from the Lloyd George coalition. Another was the pervasive smell of corruption in public life—arising particularly from the sale of honours—and the government's increasingly autocratic style, epitomized above all by the lord chancellor. Stories of his boorishness and bullying behaviour multiplied, while his regular steps in the peerage—from Baron Birkenhead in 1919, through viscount (15 June 1921), to the earl of Birkenhead (28 November 1922)—only swelled his self-importance. Since the war his views had become steadily more reactionary: obsessed by the threat of Bolshevism, he supported Lloyd George's attempt to merge his Coalition Liberals with the tories in a single anti-socialist party. When that failed he continued to insist that the coalition must be maintained indefinitely, dealing brutally with anyone who expressed a different view. When tory MPs voted at the Carlton Club in October 1922 to end the coalition, they were revolting as much against the arrogance of their own leaders as against Lloyd George.

Indian summer Out of office, Birkenhead drew fresh notoriety by repeating, with provocative relish, his neo-Darwinian view of international conflict. 'The world', he told the students of Glasgow University (7 November

1923), 'continues to offer glittering prizes to those who have stout hearts and sharp swords' (*America Revisited*, 1924, 200). Five years after the war conventional piety demanded lip-service to the League of Nations: Birkenhead was denounced from pulpits and pacifist platforms up and down the country. Both his lordly lifestyle and his robust philosophy were out of tune with the homely bromides of Baldwin's Conservative Party. (At this time he was also conducting a love affair with Mona Dunn, the daughter of an old Canadian friend of Lord Beaverbrook.) Nevertheless, when the tories were returned to office in October 1924 after the short-lived experiment of the first Labour government, Baldwin was anxious to reunite the party. To the disapproval of the moralists he brought back into his government not only Austen Chamberlain as foreign secretary and Churchill as chancellor of the exchequer, but also Birkenhead as secretary of state for India.

Despite his speech in the Amritsar debate, Birkenhead's view of India was thoroughly reactionary. He did not believe that Indians would soon, or ever, be fit for self-government: he had no regard for Indian politicians and believed the Hindu–Muslim divide to be unbridgeable. His main purpose was to block any further extension of the degree of Indian participation in provincial government granted in 1919 by the Montagu–Chelmsford reforms. To this end he accelerated the appointment of the statutory commission to assess the progress of the reforms—to make sure it was not left to a possible Labour government—and appointed his old Wadham contemporary Sir John Simon as its chairman. But in practice the secretary of state was little more than a figurehead: the day-to-day government of India was the responsibility of the viceroy, from 1926 the much more liberal Lord Irwin. Birkenhead was not stretched by the India Office. His parliamentary private secretary recalled that 'We seemed to play an awful lot of golf' (private information).

Birkenhead did, however, play a full part in the Baldwin cabinet. When he could be persuaded to focus his mind upon a problem the penetration and lucidity of Birkenhead's judgement, his legal authority, and his drafting skill still commanded the admiration of his colleagues. Baldwin used him to arbitrate on interdepartmental disputes, for instance between the Treasury and the Admiralty over the building of cruisers. He also took a prominent role in the government's negotiations with the TUC to try to avert the general strike. Here again, however, he was now a thorough die-hard. His pre-war concern for a 'contented proletariat' had hardened into blunt insistence that the miners must be taught the facts of economic life. He strongly supported the 1927 Trades Disputes Act, which punished the trade unions by requiring members to 'contract in' to the political levy instead of contracting out; and also the home secretary's clumsy raid on the premises of the Soviet trade delegation, alleged to be a nest of spies ('I breathe quite differently now that we have purged our capital of these unclean and treacherous elements'; Campbell, 788).

Though still only in his mid-fifties, Birkenhead now cut a rather pompous figure on the public stage: the cartoonist David Low caricatured him as Lord Burstinghead. Yet his energy was still astonishing. He was in constant demand as a speaker, to audiences ranging from the Royal Society of Medicine to the Motor Cycle Trades Benevolent Fund dinner. He poured out a prolific stream of books of varied quality: serious historical and literary essays—*Points of View* (2 vols., 1922), *Law, Life and Letters* (2 vols., 1927), and *Turning Points in History* (1930); popular law—*Famous Trials of History* (1926) and *More Famous Trials* (1928); and some frank potboilers—*The World in 2030* (1930) and *Fifty Famous Fights in Fact and Fiction* (1932). Though denied the chancellorship, he was still an Oxford legend and spoke frequently at the union; he patronized university athletics and raised funds for the British Olympic team in 1924 and 1928. He delighted in inviting clever young Oxford men—friends of his son Freddie—to Charlton for strenuous days of tennis, golf, and talk. 'Good though the tennis was', Sir John Masterman recalled, 'the talk was better; his was, I am convinced, the most powerful mind with which I have ever been brought into contact' (J. Masterman, *On the Chariot Wheel*, 1975, 166). In this high summer of his life, still a senior cabinet minister, presiding over his little court at Charlton, dispensing generous but demanding patronage to young admirers, F. E. was in his element.

In October 1928 Birkenhead left the government, pleading poverty. He could not support his family on a cabinet minister's salary. In the easy-going climate of the coalition he had supplemented his salary by journalism; but Baldwin's new puritanism had closed that option. When Birkenhead objected, his acquiescence was bought with a discreet subsidy from Conservative Party funds, amounting to £10,000 over two years from 1926: remarkable testimony to the value Baldwin placed on his services. But in 1928 the subsidy was not renewed. His friends found him a number of lucrative directorships (including ICI and Tate and Lyle); but he did not enjoy them very long. After years of abuse his powerful constitution suddenly cracked; his health rapidly declined, and he died of bronchial pneumonia at his London home, 32 Grosvenor Gardens, on 30 September 1930, leaving his family mainly debts. After cremation at Golders Green, his ashes were buried at Charlton on 4 October; there was a memorial service at Westminster Abbey on 6 October.

As F. E. Smith before the First World War and Lord Birkenhead after it, F. E. was one of the most vivid public personalities of the first third of the twentieth century, loved and loathed in equal measure by those who enjoyed the warmth of his friendship or suffered the sting of his tongue. He had an unpleasant streak of arrogance, but he was most highly regarded by those who knew him best. He cultivated the reputation of a cynical adventurer; but behind the cavalier façade he was a more constructive politician than he is often given credit for, as he demonstrated before 1914 in relation to both the House of Lords and Ulster. Diverted into the legal departments by the war, he routed his critics by rising to the challenge of the woolsack: he proved an outstanding lord chancellor, both as judge and as law reformer. Above all, it was his statesmanship and political courage that made possible the Irish treaty of December 1921. That is his most solid achievement. His true immortality, however, is preserved in a hundred well-loved legal anecdotes: more than anyone else F. E. in his prime embodies the golden age of the English bar. JOHN CAMPBELL

Sources J. Campbell, *F. E. Smith, first earl of Birkenhead* (1983) • [F. W. F. Smith, earl of Birkenhead], *F. E.: the life of F. E. Smith, first earl of Birkenhead* (1959) • GEC, *Peerage* • T. Jones, *Whitehall diary*, ed. K. Middlemas, 3 vols. (1969–71) • S. W. Roskill, *Hankey, man of secrets*, 3 vols. (1970–74) • S. Salvidge, *Salvidge of Liverpool: behind the political scene, 1890–1928* (1934) • P. J. Waller, *Democracy and sectarianism: a political and social history of Liverpool, 1868–1939* (1981) • C. Coote, *The Other Club* (1971) • R. F. V. Heuston, *Lives of the lord chancellors, 1885–1940* (1964) • I. Thomas, *Our Lord Birkenhead: an Oxford appreciation* (1930) • A. Chamberlain, *Politics from inside: an epistolary chronicle, 1906–1914* (1936) • Lord Beaverbrook, *The decline and fall of Lloyd George* (1963) • F. Pakenham, *Peace by ordeal* (1935) • M. Cowling, *The impact of labour, 1920–1924: the beginning of modern British politics* (1971) • K. O. Morgan, *Consensus and disunity: the Lloyd George coalition government, 1918–1922* (1979) • B. L. Reid, *The lives of Roger Casement* (1976)

Archives BL OIOC, papers relating to work as secretary of state for India, MS Eur. D 703 | BL, corresp. with Lord Northcliffe, Add. MS 62156 • BL OIOC, corresp. with Lord Goschen, MS Eur. D 595 • BL OIOC, corresp. with Lord Halifax, MS Eur. C 152 • BL OIOC, corresp. with second earl of Lytton, MS Eur. F 160 • CUL, Baldwin MSS • HLRO, letters to David Lloyd George • HLRO, corresp. with Andrew Bonar Law • HLRO, corresp. with Lord Beaverbrook • HLRO, letters to R. D. Blumenfeld • Lpool RO, corresp. with seventeenth earl of Derby • NL Ire., notes on trial of Roger Casement • U. Birm. L., Austen Chamberlain MSS | FILM BFI NFTVA, news footage

Likenesses Nibs, caricature, lithograph, 1911, NPG • E. Knapp, drawing, 1914, Barber Institute of Fine Arts, Birmingham • W. Stoneman, photograph, 1919, NPG [*see illus.*] • H. Mann, oils, *c.*1921, Wadham College, Oxford • C. Sheridan, bronze bust, 1924, Gray's Inn, London • R. S. Sherriffs, ink caricature, 1929, NPG • O. Birley, oil copy, NPG • J. Lavery, oils, Gray's Inn, London • B. Partridge, ink and watercolour caricature, NPG; repro. in *Punch* (7 Nov 1927) • B. Partridge, ink and watercolour caricature, NPG; repro. in *Punch* (21 May 1928) • G. Philpot, oils, Gray's Inn, London • Spy [L. Ward], caricature, lithograph, NPG; repro. in *VF* (16 Jan 1907)

Wealth at death £63,223 1*s.* 6*d.*: probate, 25 Feb 1931, *CGPLA Eng. & Wales*

Smith, Frederick John Jervis- (1848–1911), physicist, was born on 2 April 1848 in Taunton, Somerset, the only child of Frederick Jeremiah Smith, prebendary of Wells, a wealthy philanthropist and educational reformer, and his wife, Anne, daughter of John Glover, gentleman, of Taunton. He was educated privately and, from 1868, at Pembroke College, Oxford, where he read classics but was awarded only a pass degree, graduating BA in 1872. After a time at Wells Theological College he was ordained deacon in 1877 and became his father's curate at St John's Church, Bishop's Hull, near Taunton. He was ordained priest in 1880. He married, in 1874, Annie Eyton, the second daughter of Thomas Taylor, physician, of Taunton, formerly of Adelaide. They had one son.

Smith's main interest was mechanics, his natural talent in which was encouraged by the engineer W. E. Metford. His first patent was taken out in 1875; he constructed dynamometers which won a medal at the 1878 Paris Exhibition, and in 1879 he invented the liquid microphone. Although succeeding his father as vicar of St John's in 1885, he resigned two years later to pursue a scientific career. He had been invited to establish a mechanical laboratory at Trinity College, Oxford, where he became Millard lecturer in experimental mechanics (and later engineering) in October 1885. Equipped at Smith's own expense, the Millard Laboratory opened in January 1886. Smith's course, based on that taught in London by Alexander B. W. Kennedy, was open to the entire university, a fact recognized in 1888 when he was made university lecturer in mechanics.

Smith's own research flourished in its new setting, generating eleven patent applications in the years 1888–99. One speciality was the measurement of high-speed events, such as explosions and gunshots, using his tram chronograph, invented in 1888. This led to his appointment by the home secretary to a commission on explosions of compressed gas cylinders (1895–6). In 1897 he used the chronograph to measure the speed of a vehicle in an Oxford street, and presented the results in court. He also experimented with photography, and did significant early work with X-rays from 1896, and with radio waves from 1897.

On 14 February 1897, on the centenary of the great naval victory of his distant kinsman Admiral John Jervis, earl of St Vincent, Smith changed his name by deed poll to Jervis-Smith. After failing to be appointed to Oxford's new chair of electrical physics in 1900, he worked to achieve similar recognition for engineering. In 1905 a diploma was created, and in 1907 the university finally decided to establish a chair of engineering science. It was not, however, intended for Jervis-Smith, and in April 1908 he retired.

In retirement Jervis-Smith continued his experiments and compiled a book, *Dynamometers* (1915), which was completed posthumously by his friend C. V. Boys. Jervis-Smith's other interests were world travel, anthropology, and music; he was an accomplished organist and pianist. He held the medal of the Royal Humane Society for saving a person from drowning. He was elected FRS in 1894, and in 1898 received an honorary MA from the University of Adelaide. After six months of illness Jervis-Smith died at his home, Battramsley House, near Boldre, Hampshire, on 23 August 1911. He was survived by his wife.

A. V. SIMCOCK, *rev.*

Sources C. V. Boys, *PRS*, 88A (1912–13), iv–vi • *Men and women of the time* (1899) • *The Times* (5 Sept 1911) • *The Times* (21 Sept 1911), 9a • *The Times* (3 Nov 1911), 11b • MHS Oxf., Museum MSS 29, 62 and 89 • *CGPLA Eng. & Wales* (1911)

Archives MHS Oxf., corresp. and papers | Inst. EE, archive, letters to Sir William Henry Preece

Likenesses Maull & Fox, photograph, RS

Wealth at death £37,957 17*s.* 5*d.*: resworn probate, 31 Oct 1911, *CGPLA Eng. & Wales*

Smith, Frederick William (*bap.* 1797, *d.* 1835). *See under* Boydell, John, engravers (*act.* 1760–1804).

Smith, Frederick Winston Furneaux, second earl of Birkenhead (1907–1975), biographer, was born on 7 December 1907 at 70 Eccleston Square, London, the only son and second of three children of Frederick Edwin *Smith (1872–1930), known always as FE, who became in 1922 first earl of Birkenhead, and his wife, Margaret Eleanor (1878–1968), second daughter of the Revd Henry Furneaux, fellow of Corpus Christi College, Oxford. Freddie, as he was called, was a godson of his father's closest friend, Winston Churchill. He was educated at Eton College, where he was elected president of Pop and won the Rosebery history prize, and at Christ Church, Oxford, where he played tennis, squash, and fives for the university. He obtained a second class in modern history in 1931. His father was a powerful and dominant figure. Although devoted to his family and always kind to them, he expected and strongly pressed his only son to follow the legal and political career in which he had been such a brilliant success. Smith's talents did not lie in that direction. Although he inherited FE's dark, almost saturnine good looks and something of his addiction to alcohol, which he later overcame, he had neither his father's gift of oratory nor his boundless energy. He preferred literature to law and biography to politics.

In 1930 Smith succeeded to the earldom and to an alarming load of debt. Although devoted to his father's memory he always resented his extravagance and improvidence. He wrote his father's life in two volumes (1933 and 1935) and produced a revised version, *F.E.* (1959). He followed this in 1938 with an unmemorable life of Thomas Wentworth, first earl of Strafford. He wrote much better about people whom he knew, and the seventeenth century is a minefield for amateur historians.

In 1935 Birkenhead married Sheila, daughter of William Ewert *Berry, first Viscount Camrose, proprietor of the *Daily Telegraph*. A year later his sister Pamela, later a great political hostess, married Camrose's second son, Michael (later Baron Hartwell). Birkenhead's marriage (of which there were a son and a daughter) put his finances and the succession to Charlton, near Banbury, his father's beloved country house, on to a secure basis. The place became after the Second World War a notable social centre for (suitably selected) members of the literary, academic, and political worlds.

After a spell in the Oxford yeomanry, Birkenhead became attached to the British military mission to the Yugoslav partisans in 1944–5, along with Randolph Churchill and Evelyn Waugh. There are many anecdotes about this ill-assorted trio, some recounted by Birkenhead himself in his chapter in *Evelyn Waugh and his World* (1973, ed. D. Pryce-Jones). After the war Birkenhead made biography his main occupation despite a major set-back. His plan, with the apparent co-operation of Mrs Bambridge, the heir and owner of the family papers, was to write a life of Rudyard Kipling, but he unwisely signed a contract with her which gave her sole control over the book as a condition of full access to the papers. After three years' work he submitted a draft only to have it irrevocably vetoed without any intelligible reasons given or any consideration of amendment. Many people read it in typescript. T. S. Eliot found it 'slight', but Sir Roderick Jones, Sir Desmond MacCarthy, Sir John Betjeman, and the author of this entry found her decision incomprehensible. The book was eventually published (as *Rudyard Kipling*) with much acclaim in 1978, after both parties to the dispute had died.

Birkenhead's next book was a most entertaining and vivid memoir (1953) of his highly eccentric novel-writing, Gypsy-loving elder sister, Eleanor (who believed quite wrongly that the family had Gypsy blood). He then embarked on the serious biographies which made his name. The first was of Professor F. A. Lindemann, Viscount Cherwell, Churchill's friend and scientific adviser, *The Prof in Two Worlds* (1961). This was followed by a life of E. F. L. Wood, first earl of Halifax, whom he had served as parliamentary private secretary from 1938 to 1939, published as *Halifax* (1965). Four years later he produced *Walter Monckton* (1969). All three are models of serious 'first' official biographies, carefully researched and admirably written. When he died in Oxford on 10 June 1975 after a long illness, Birkenhead was engaged on a biography of his famous godfather. It was published in 1989 as *Churchill, 1876–1922*. The plan had been for his son (Frederick William) Robin (*b*. 1936), who succeeded as third earl and was himself the author of an excellent life of William Wilberforce, to complete it. But he died suddenly in 1985. His draft, ending in 1940, has been privately published. Robin never married and the earldom became extinct.

ROBERT BLAKE, *rev.*

Sources J. Campbell, *F. E. Smith, first earl of Birkenhead* (1983) • private information (1993) • personal knowledge (1993)

Archives Nuffield Oxf., corresp. with Lord Cherwell • U. Birm. L., corresp. with Lord Avon

Wealth at death £442,305: probate, 2 March 1976, *CGPLA Eng. & Wales*

Smith, Gabriel (1724–1783), printmaker and drawing master, was probably born in London, where he was apprenticed to and then employed by the engraver Gerard Scotin. On the latter's death, Smith advertised that he would continue the drawing school at his late master's lodgings, at the Golden Ball in Broad Court, Bow Street, Covent Garden. However, Scotin's deputy master, Allain Turmeau, also advertised that he would be continuing Scotin's drawing school at the premises of Turmeau Senior, a jeweller, at the Golden Key in Grafton Street, St Ann's, where 'may be seen a great Variety of Drawings by him in the Jewellry Way' (*Public Advertiser*, 21 Dec 1754).

An undated allegorical print inserted in J. H. Anderdon's Society of Artists volumes in the British Museum is lettered 'G. Smith inv' and 'G. L. Smith sculp', and may be attributed to Smith: it shows a figure representing painting holding a portrait, with a rococo print at her feet, and a putto displaying a sheet from a drawing manual. The earliest engravings bearing Smith's full name date from the years shortly after Scotin's death and are in the latter's rococo manner. They include the title-page and a number of designs for John Linnell's *A New Book of Ornaments Useful for Silver-Smith's etc.* (*c*.1755–1760). In the late 1750s Smith is said to have accompanied William Wynne Ryland to Paris, where he learned the method of engraving in imitation of chalk drawings from its greatest practitioner, Gilles

Demarteau, who was producing engravings in this manner after red chalk drawings by François Boucher from 1759. Making use of new types of roulettes and mattoirs on an etching ground and printed in a red or brown ink, this new technique was particularly effective in reproducing not only French *sanguines*, but also the works of Rembrandt and Van Dyck, whose drawings Ryland was successfully copying with this technique back in England by 1762. Although J. C. François was credited with inventing the crayon manner in Paris in 1756, Arthur Pond had used a variation of it to reproduce drawings by Annibale Carracci in 1737 and 1747, and François Vivares produced three drawing books using this technique in 1759–61. However, Smith is generally credited with popularizing crayon manner engraving in England, mainly because he executed a series of plates in this style from designs by Watteau, Boucher, Edmé Bouchardon, and others—including *12 Heads Selected from Monsr. Le Brun's 'Passions of the Soul'*, printed for Robert Sayer—which were all published together on sixty folio copperplates by John and Carrington Bowles and Sayer as *The School of Art, or, Most Compleat Drawing-Book Extant* (1765). There had been no market for the technique when it was first used by Pond, but by the 1760s the English had developed a taste for French drawings. The preface to Smith's drawing book indicates that it appeared not only to fill that market, but also, by placing less emphasis on proportion and perspective and containing more examples of landscapes, rococo cartouches, and flower drawings, to respond to the growing demand for drawing books which catered to the new, often female, type of amateur whose numbers were beginning to increase around this time.

In 1767 Smith produced line engravings after paintings in British collections by Salvator Rosa, Tintoretto, Eustache Le Sueur, and Frans Snyders for the publisher John Boydell. In 1771 he engraved in the stipple technique by then in extensive use by Ryland (whom Smith is said to have assisted) a portrait of the Revd John Glen King, after Pierre Falconet, and he also etched theatrical portraits after his own drawings of David Garrick and Samuel Foote. From 1771 until his death Smith was engaged by Joseph Banks to make copperplate-engravings after the botanical drawings made by Sidney Parkinson on his voyage with Captain Cook from 1768 to 1771. Daniel Mackenzie, the principal engraver, G. Sibelius, and Smith produced 743 copperplates for Banks's *Florilegium*. The entire set was never published, but in 1989 colour prints were taken from the plates which were still in the collection of the Natural History Museum. Smith died in London in 1783. The Victoria and Albert Museum and the British Museum in London and the Public Library in New York hold some of his prints. KIM SLOAN

Sources T. Dodd, 'Memoirs of English engravers, 1550–1800', *c.*1800, BL, Add. MS 33405, fol. 11 • J. Strutt, *A biographical dictionary, containing an historical account of all the engravers, from the earliest period of the art of engraving to the present time*, 2 (1786), 326 • Bénézit, *Dict.* • Thieme & Becker, *Allgemeines Lexikon* • C. le Blanc, *Manuel de l'amateur d'estampes*, 3 (Paris, 1858–88), 532 • T. Clayton, *The English print, 1688–1802* (1997), 175–6 • A. Griffiths, *Prints and printmaking* (1996), 80–81, 97, 119 • *Public Advertiser* (21–4 Dec 1754) • M. Snodin and E. Moncrieff, eds., *Rococo: art and design in Hogarth's England* (1984) [exhibition catalogue, V&A, 16 May – 30 Sept 1984] • J. Martineau, '*Banks's Florilegium*', *Print Quarterly*, 6 (1989), 316 • S. Lambert, *The image multiplied: five centuries of printed reproductions of paintings and drawings* (1987) [exhibition catalogue, V&A]

Smith, Gentleman. *See* Smith, William (1730–1819).

Smith, George (1693–1756), bishop of the nonjuring Church of England, was the son of John *Smith (*bap.* 1659, *d.* 1715), prebendary of Durham, and Mary Cooper, daughter of William Cooper of Scarborough. He was born at Durham on 7 May 1693 and baptized the next day at St Mary-le-Bow Church, Durham. Initially educated at Westminster School, where he boarded with his uncle Hilkiah Bedford, he matriculated at St John's College, Cambridge, in 1709. On 18 April 1711 he migrated to Queen's College, Oxford, where his uncle Joseph Smith (1670–1756) was then a fellow. He also, for a time, studied law at the Inner Temple though with 'no intention of following it as a profession' (Nichols, *Lit. anecdotes*, 1.705).

Smith received a considerable inheritance following his father's death in 1715. In 1717 he bought New Burn Hall, near Durham, which adjoined Old Burn Hall, the estate of his uncle Posthumus Smith. He resided there for the remainder of his life. Having studied Anglo-Saxon and early English history while at Oxford, at the age of twenty-two he undertook the completion of his father's unfinished edition of Bede's historical works. Published in 1722, it was the first critical edition of Bede's work, and served as the standard edition for nearly two centuries, placing his father among the founders of English medieval scholarship (Douglas, 62–4). On 5 April of the same year he married his cousin, Christian Bedford (1701/2–1781), daughter of Hilkiah and Alice Bedford (sister of Smith's mother), at St Anne's, Soho, Westminster. Twelve children died in infancy, though their eldest son, John, lived into adulthood and married Anne Shuttleworth. Among his descendants were Elizabeth Smith (1776–1806), translator, and Sir Charles Felix Smith (1786–1858), army officer.

It is unclear when Smith became sympathetic to the nonjuring cause, though his decision was probably influenced by his father-in-law, Bedford. Smith received orders in the nonjuring Church of England on 22 December 1728 from Henry Gandy. He was then consecrated at Gandy's chapel in London on 26 December 1728 as the titular bishop of Durham by Gandy, Richard Rawlinson, and John Blackbourne, bishops of the nonusager party. He was soon involved in efforts to reunite the two nonjuror parties. In 1729 he began a correspondence with the leader of the usager party, Thomas Brett, whom he had first met seven years earlier, and joined him and his son, Thomas Brett the younger, in consecrating Thomas Mawman as bishop on 17 July 1731. The final instrument of union was drawn up and signed on 17 April 1732. Then in 1741 he joined Mawman and the younger Brett in consecrating Robert Gordon as the last bishop of the regular nonjuror communion.

In addition to his work on Bede's histories, Smith published his strongly worded *An Appendix to Two Discourses*, which answered Roger Laurence's *Indispensable Obligation of Ministring ... the Great Necessities of Publick Worship* (1733). Two later works, *An Epistolary Dissertation Addressed to the Clergy of Middlesex* (1739) and *A Brief Historical Account of the Primitive Invocation or Prayer* (1740), supported Thomas Brett's reply to Daniel Waterland's understanding of eucharistic sacrifice and were intended to bring together all parts of the nonjuror communion (Broxap, 213–14). Smith died at Durham on 4 November 1756 and was buried in the churchyard at St Oswald's, Durham. His wife, Christian, survived him, dying on 23 July 1781, aged seventy-nine. ROBERT D. CORNWALL

Sources Nichols, *Lit. anecdotes* • Foster, *Alum. Oxon.* • Venn, *Alum. Cant.* • H. Broxap, *The later nonjurors* (1924) • A. Chalmers, ed., *The general biographical dictionary*, new edn, 32 vols. (1812–17) • J. H. Overton, *The nonjurors: their lives, principles, and writings* (New York, 1903) • D. C. Douglas, *English scholars, 1660–1730*, 2nd edn (1951) • *IGI*
Archives Bodl. Oxf., letters to Thomas Brett
Wealth at death father's inherited estate valued at £15,000 in 1715: Nichols, *Lit. anecdotes*

Smith, George (1713/14–1776), landscape painter, was the son of William Smith (*d.* 1719), a Chichester tradesman and Baptist minister, and his wife, Elizabeth (*d. c.*1755), daughter of Henry Spencer, a butcher in Horsham, Sussex. George Smith was the second and most gifted of three brothers who all practised painting and were known as 'the Smiths of Chichester'. When a boy he was placed with his uncle, a cooper, but, preferring art, became a pupil of his brother William, whom he accompanied to Gloucester; there and in London he spent some years, painting chiefly portraits, and then returned to Chichester where, under the patronage of the duke of Richmond, he settled as a painter of landscapes and still lifes.

Smith depicted the rural and pastoral scenery of Sussex and other parts of England in a picturesque manner, based on the study of Claude and Poussin, which greatly appealed to the taste of the day, and he was throughout his life a much-admired and influential artist. His reputation extended to the continent, where he was known as the 'British Gessner'. In 1760 Smith gained from the Society of Arts their first premium for a landscape, and repeated his success in 1761 (Cheltenham Art Gallery, Gloucestershire) and 1763. He exhibited with the Incorporated Society of Artists in 1760, but in 1761 joined the Free Society of Artists, of which he was one of the chief supporters until 1774; in that year only he was a contributor to the Royal Academy. On 12 September 1766 Smith married Ruth Southen at the church of St Olave, Chichester.

Many of Smith's works hung at Goodwood and other country houses of Sussex and Hampshire, and were engraved by William Woollett, William Elliott, James Peake, and François Vivares; a series of twenty-seven plates from his pictures, with the title *Picturesque Scenery of England and Wales*, was published between 1757 and 1769. A set of fifty-three etchings and engravings by Smith and his brother John, from their own works and those of other masters, was published in 1770 by John Boydell. A good performer on the violoncello, Smith also wrote poetry: in 1770 he published a volume entitled *Six Pastorals*, of which a second edition, accompanied by a memoir of him, was issued by his three daughters Sarah, Elizabeth, and Ruth, in 1811. He died at St Pancras, Chichester, on 7 September 1776, aged sixty-two, and was buried on 15 September 1776 at Litten cemetery, St Pancras, Chichester.

George Smith (1713/14–1776), by William Pether, pubd 1765 [standing, with his brothers, William Smith (centre) and John Smith]

John Smith (1716/17–1764), painter, was the younger brother of George Smith, and was his pupil. He painted landscapes of a similar character; the two frequently worked on the same canvas. John Smith exhibited with the Incorporated Society of Artists in 1760 and with the Free Society from 1761 to 1764. In 1760, and again in 1761, he was awarded the second premium of the Society of Arts, and in 1762, when his brother George was not a candidate, the first; his premium landscape of 1760 was engraved by William Woollett. He died, apparently unmarried, at Chichester on 29 July 1764, aged forty-seven, and was buried on 7 August 1764 at Litten cemetery, St Pancras, Chichester.

William Smith (1706/7–1764), painter, was the elder brother of George Smith. He was thought to have been born at Guildford, Surrey. Placed by the duke of Richmond with a portrait painter in St Martin's Lane, London, he practised portraiture, first in London and then for eight or nine years at Gloucester. After his return to London he also painted fruit and flowers with success, exhibiting at the Free Society until his health deteriorated, when he retired to Shopwyke, near Chichester. There he died, apparently unmarried, on 27 September 1764, aged fifty-seven, and was buried on 29 September at Litten cemetery, St Pancras, Chichester.

In 1939 the headstones of the brothers' graves were moved to lie close to the east side of New Park Road, Chichester, where they still stand.

F. M. O'Donoghue, *rev.* Brian Stewart

Sources *The Smiths of Chichester* (1986) [Pallant House Gallery, Chichester, exhibition catalogue] · B. Stewart and M. Cutten, *Chichester artists, 1530–1900* (1987) · G. Smith, *Six pastorals*, 2nd edn (1811) · R. Dally, *The Chichester guide* (1831), 96 · J. Turner, ed., *The dictionary of art*, 34 vols. (1996) · W. H. Challen, 'Baldy's garden, the painters Lambert, and other Sussex families', *Sussex Archaeological Collections*, 90 (1952), 102–52 · P. Mitchell, 'George Smith of Chichester', *West Sussex History*, 26 (Sept 1983), 3–8 · tombstones, Litten cemetery, St Pancras, Chichester, Sussex · will, PRO, PROB 11/1024, sig. 439 · will, PRO, PROB 11/903, sig. 406 [William Smith]
Archives W. Sussex RO, research papers on Smith
Likenesses W. Pether, group portrait, mezzotint, pubd 1765 (with William Smith and John Smith), BM [*see illus.*] · J. Hopwood, stipple (after W. Pether), BM; repro. in Smith, *Six pastorals* · G. Smith, self-portrait, oils (with his brother John), NPG
Wealth at death see will, PRO, PROB 11/1024, sig. 439

Smith, George (1792–1871). *See under* Smith family (*per.* 1824–1975).

Smith, George (1797?–1850), naval officer, entered the navy in September 1808 on board the *Princess Caroline* (74 guns), and, remaining in her for upwards of four years, served in the North Sea, Baltic, and channel. In February 1813 he was moved into the *Undaunted* with Captain Thomas Ussher, whom he accompanied to the *Duncan* (74 guns) in August 1814. On 20 September 1815 he was promoted lieutenant. He afterwards served in the Mediterranean and on the coast of South America until his promotion on 8 September 1829 to commander. On 19 June 1830 he was appointed to superintend the instruction of officers and seamen in gunnery on board HMS *Excellent* at Portsmouth. The orders were given by the tory Admiralty board led by Lord Melville and Sir George Cockburn. Smith was advanced to post rank on 13 April 1832 for his services to the improvement of naval gunnery on his relief from the command. His connection with the gunnery school at Portsmouth led him to invent a new method of sighting ships' guns, a lever target, and the paddle-box boats, which were widely adopted on paddle steamers. These large craft were particularly useful for amphibious operations. In June 1849 he was appointed superintendent of packets at Southampton (salary £600 per annum). He was 'distinguished for his hospitality, and was always one of the most welcome guests' (*GM*, 665). He was the author of *An Account of the Siege of Antwerp* (1833) and some minor pamphlets on professional subjects. He died, unmarried, at Southampton on 6 April 1850, and was buried in Southampton cemetery. His brother was Daniel Smith of Waterloo Place, Pall Mall, London, 'the eminent land agent' (*GM*, 665). Although Sir Philip Broke, Sir Howard Douglas, and Sir John Broke Pechell are rightly considered the architects of the first school of naval gunnery, George Smith carried their ideas into effect and established the tradition of professionalism that came to dominate all aspects of the Royal Navy.

J. K. Laughton, *rev.* Andrew Lambert

Sources A. D. Lambert, *The last sailing battlefleet: maintaining naval mastery, 1815–1850* (1991) · J. G. Wells, *Whaley: the story of HMS Excellent, 1830 to 1980* (1980) · O'Byrne, *Naval biog. dict.* · *GM*, 2nd ser., 34 (1850), 664–5
Archives PRO, Admiralty archives

Smith, George (1800–1868), historian, born at Condurrow, near Camborne, Cornwall, on 31 August 1800, was the son of William Smith (*d.* 1852), a carpenter and small farmer at Condurrow, and his wife, Philippa Moneypenny (*d.* 1834). He was educated at the British and Foreign schools at Falmouth and Plymouth, to the latter of which towns his father retired in 1808, when the lease of his small farm expired. In 1812 Smith returned with his parents to Cornwall, and was employed for several years in farm work and carpentering. Having accumulated a small sum of money, he became a builder in 1824, and still further increased his resources. He married at Camborne church, on 31 October 1826, Elizabeth Burrall, youngest daughter of William Bickford (1774–1834) and Susan Burrall. Bickford was a manufacturer, who afterwards invented the Bickford miners' safety fuse, which was patented in September 1831. Smith became a partner in his enterprises, taking out separately or in conjunction with his fellow adventurers several patents for improvements of Bickford's invention. Through his business he amassed a considerable fortune.

Smith's energy largely contributed to the completion of the Cornwall Railway, which ran from Plymouth to Truro and Falmouth, and he was the chairman of the company to January 1864. Throughout his life he was a hardworking student, and his speaking and lecturing earned him local celebrity in Cornwall. In 1823 he became a local preacher among the Wesleyan Methodists, and was deterred from offering for the itinerant ministry only by the need to provide for his parents. He was a distinguished class leader, and a tireless worker for Sunday schools, British Schools, and foreign missions. He was a member of the Royal Asiatic Society, the Society of Antiquaries (23 December 1841), the Royal Society of Literature, and the Irish Archaeological Society. In 1859 he was created LLD of New York.

Smith wrote prolifically in the fields of biblical exegesis and the history of religion (also the tin trade) in the ancient world. He is, however, remembered principally for his *History of Wesleyan Methodism* (3 vols., 1857–61, and much reprinted), an apologetic, even polemical, work which presented on the grand historical scale the views which had inspired his pamphlet attacks on the Wesleyan reformers in 1849. Its permanent value lies in the moderate tone which Smith thought appropriate to a belief that there was indeed a good case for the high Wesleyan doctrine of the pastoral office, and for the evidence it affords of the subconscious assumptions on which that case rested. Viewing the local history of Methodism from the centre (in striking contrast to John Petty's *History of the Primitive Methodist Connexion* (1860) which is primarily a history of local missions), Smith wrote substantially a history of the Methodist conference, and highly esteemed the central institutions of Methodism, which had developed rapidly in his own lifetime. Doctrine, which was not then much disputed among Methodists, figures little in his pages.

Smith died at his house, Trevu, Camborne, a converted parish workhouse, on 30 August 1868, and was buried in the Wesleyan Centenary Chapel cemetery on 4 September. His widow died at Trevu on 4 March 1886, aged eighty-one, and was buried in the same cemetery on 9 March. They had four children, the eldest of whom, William Bickford-Smith, was MP for Truro from 1885 to 1892.

W. P. Courtney, *rev.* W. R. Ward

Sources T. R. Harris, *Dr. George Smith, 1800–1868, Wesleyan Methodist layman* (1968) · [G. Amgove], ed., *"Life's Battle Won": a small tribute to the memory of G. Smith … of Trevu, Camborne* (1869) · J. Odgers, *A sermon on the death of the late George Smith LL.D., late of Camborne* (1871) · *West Briton* (10 Sept 1868)
Archives JRL, Methodist Archives and Research Centre, Bunting MSS
Likenesses N. N. Burnerd, memorial tablet with bust, repro. in T. Shaw, *A history of Cornish Methodism* (1967), 73
Wealth at death under £35,000: resworn probate, Nov 1869, *CGPLA Eng. & Wales* (1868)

Smith, George (1815–1871), missionary and bishop of Victoria, Hong Kong, was born on 19 June 1815 in Wellington, Somerset, the only son and eldest of five children of George Smith (1789/90–1834), a clerk to the collector of excise at Wellington, and his wife, Mary Bridges.

Smith was educated privately at home and matriculated from Magdalen Hall, Oxford, as a commoner, on 17 December 1831. After his father's death he funded his continuing studies by private tuition. He graduated BA in 1837, with third-class honours in the classical schools. He was ordained deacon by the bishop of Peterborough on 20 October 1839 and priest by the bishop of Ripon in July 1840.

Smith worked as a classics tutor at a private school in Doncaster (1839–44) while also serving as curate of Marr, near Doncaster (1839–41), officiating minister at the parish of Hook from November 1840 to May 1842, and chaplain and perpetual curate of Goole, Yorkshire (1840–42). He was Church Missionary Society (CMS) association secretary for their north-eastern district from 1840 to 1844. He obtained his MA in 1843.

Having first become interested in the mission to China in the Doncaster home of Robert Baxter (1802–1889), Smith was one of the first two Church of England missionaries to the newly opened ports of China. Instructed by the CMS to explore and advise on the society's future operations in China, and to settle and begin his own mission pending confirmed instructions, he embarked for China on 4 June 1844, reaching Hong Kong on 25 September 1844.

During the next nineteen months Smith travelled extensively in China, submitting two important reports to the society. But his health forced him to return to England, where he met and wrote to Earl Grey about China, later enjoying some influence with Lord Palmerston. He resumed his former work as a CMS association secretary in early 1847, initially for the second midland district.

George Smith (1815–1871), by Francis Holl (after George Richmond)

Early in 1848 he became an association secretary for special services on a national level. In 1847 his book *A narrative of an exploratory visit to each of the consular cities of China, and to the islands of Hong Kong and Chusan* was published in England.

Smith arranged an agreement between financial donors and church authorities, enabling the establishment of the see of Victoria along with St Paul's Missionary College, in Hong Kong, the bishop to be the college's warden *ex officio*. The new archbishop of Canterbury, Sumner, selected Smith as first bishop, 'on the ground of his proved Missionary zeal' (*Church Missionary Record*, February 1872, 68). Smith was made DD on 1 March 1849 and consecrated bishop of Victoria, Hong Kong, on Whit Tuesday, 29 May 1849.

On 11 July 1849, in a ceremony performed by the archbishop of Canterbury at St George's Church, Beckenham, Kent, Smith married Lydia (1818/19–1904), the only daughter of Andrew Brandram (1791–1850), then rector of Beckenham, a secretary of the British and Foreign Bible Society, and his wife, Elizabeth (*d.* 1855), and elder sister of Samuel Brandram (1824–1892), a reciter. The Smiths' three children—Henry Venn Brandram (*b.* 1851), Andrew Brandram (1853–1855), and Alice Victoria Brandram (*b.* 1854)—were all born in Hong Kong. After considerable personal fund-raising in Britain to support the missionary work of his new post, Smith left England from Portsmouth on 6 November 1849 with his new wife, a team of three assistants, and a printing press. They reached Hong Kong on Good Friday, 29 March 1850, and Smith preached in St John's Church (as it then was) on Easter day, consecrating it as a cathedral soon afterwards. An observer saw the young bishop as a 'tall, thin, pale-looking man' (Bickley, 'The first bishop of Hong Kong', *A Celebration of Faith*, 61). The surviving portraits of Smith (one an oil painting hanging in Bishop's House (formerly St Paul's College), Hong Kong, and one in an album containing photographs of the first Lambeth conference), show fine, somewhat feminine features. He was devout, energetic, enthusiastic, single-minded, self-sacrificing, and scholarly, 'attached by sympathy to the moderate Evangelical party in the Church' (*The Times*, 16 Dec 1871, 5). Morally and financially scrupulous, he learned diplomacy and purposeful rhetoric. He was an affectionate and loyal husband, father, brother, friend, and teacher.

During the next fourteen years Smith took care of Anglican pastoral and missionary work in Hong Kong, as well as St Paul's Missionary College (now St Paul's Boys' School), which replaced an earlier Anglican school established by the colonial chaplain. He had learned Mandarin and conducted both Mandarin and English services. From August 1861 to August 1863 he had the assistance of John Fryer (1839–1928), recommended by C. R. Alford, then principal of the Anglican Highbury College, as schoolmaster. From April 1862 to early 1865, through the CMS, he was also assisted by the Revd Thomas Stringer, their first missionary to the Chinese in Hong Kong. Smith established the first mission to seamen in Hong Kong and was president of the corresponding society of the Bible Society in Hong Kong.

Smith was appointed chairman of the Hong Kong government's education committee in March 1852 and of its successor, the board of education, created on 21 January 1860. Based in England from 16 October 1860 to 4 October 1861, he conducted interviews at his home in Lyme Regis, Dorset, and recommended the appointment of the Scottish theological student Frederick Stewart (1836–1889) to direct a new system of education for Chinese pupils.

Smith visited China frequently for episcopal and missionary work. From Hong Kong and in China he assisted the CMS with business and personnel matters. He travelled extensively—to 'Loochoo' (the Ryukyu Islands) in October 1850, to India and Ceylon between the end of 1852 and March 1853, to India, Ceylon, Singapore, and Batavia between September and December 1855, to Australia between April and September 1859, to Japan between April and June 1860, to the USA and Canada between July and September or October 1860, and to Sweden, Norway, and Russia in the 1860s—on behalf of his own and other Christian organizations (the London Society for Promoting Christianity among the Jews, the CMS, the Society for the Propagation of the Gospel, the Bible Society) and the bishop of London, extending the pastoral care of his diocese to Chinese immigrants in Australia, San Francisco, and the West Indies.

Smith exerted skill and patience to resolve the question of the appropriate translation into Chinese of the word for God and secured agreement among Anglican missionaries for the word 'Shang-te', subsequently used in the Anglican Chinese liturgy. He advocated the use of a Chinese lingua franca rather than local dialects in missionary publications. Smith's own books, several published articles, sermons, speeches, letters, and reports centre on missionary, episcopal, and evangelical subjects, with a special focus on the mission to China and the Chinese, including a baptismal service in Chinese.

Smith had authority and jurisdiction over all Anglican clergy in Hong Kong and China and on vessels no more than 100 miles from the Chinese coast. A lengthy correspondence survives containing demarcation discussions between himself and Bishop W. J. Boone (of the protestant Episcopal church of the USA), at a time when only small areas of China were open to western missionaries.

During her husband's absences Lydia Smith continued his pastoral and missionary work. On a visit to England she recruited Mr Baxter's daughter, Miss Harriet Sophia Baxter, to the Hong Kong mission, and they worked closely together. Lydia Smith is acknowledged as the founder of both the Diocesan Girls' School and the school to which it gave rise, the Diocesan Boys' School, both of which still flourish in Hong Kong. She was largely instrumental in opening the first government day school for Chinese girls in Hong Kong, thus proving without doubt 'the possibility of female education in China' (Lobscheid, 31).

Smith was intensely interested in the Taiping uprising, asserting its Christian tendencies. His previous disappointment at the slowness and paucity of conversions and the absence of Chinese willing to become the ministers of the gospel to their countrymen was offset when he ordained two Chinese deacons in 1863, one in Shanghai and one in Hong Kong.

In February 1864 the Smiths left Hong Kong for the last time. Former St Paul's pupils showed 'such attachment as I little imagined in them' (quoted in Bickley, 'The first bishop of Hong Kong', *A Celebration of Faith*, 63). A large group of Chinese accompanied him and his wife and the local clergy to the ship. He visited Jerusalem on the way back to England.

In January 1865, having been granted a pension of £300 a year by the Hong Kong government (which had never paid him a salary), Smith retired from the see of Victoria because of ill health. In April 1867 he became a vice-president of the CMS. Having seen his surviving son at university, Bishop Smith died after a short illness on 14 December 1871 at his residence, 3 Haddo Villas (now 3 Elliott Vale), Blackheath, Kent, of 'paralysis of the brain' (*The Graphic*), leaving an estate of less than £6000. *The Guardian* described him as 'worn out prematurely by the effect of climate and the hardships incidental to early settlers in the East'. He was buried at Ladywell cemetery, Lewisham, near London, where his wife, Lydia, was buried in 1904. The CMS commended his official life in all its aspects. A memorial stained glass window (now gone) was erected in St John's Cathedral in 1874 or 1875, subscribed for by former pupils of St Paul's Missionary College, many of them influential and esteemed. GILLIAN BICKLEY

Sources G. Bickley, *The golden needle: the biography of Frederick Stewart (1836–1889)* (Hong Kong, 1997) · G. Bickley, 'George Smith (1815–1871), iconoclast bishop who established the see of Victoria and founded St Paul's College' [text of talk given at City Hall, Hong Kong, 10 Nov 2000, copy to be deposited in Hong Kong Baptist University Library] · G. Bickley, 'The first bishop of Victoria: the Right Revd George Smith (1815–1871), lord bishop of Victoria, 1849–1865', *A celebration of faith* (Hong Kong, 1997), 60–63 [copy deposited in Hong Kong Baptist University Library] · G. Bickley, 'The first bishop of Victoria: the Right Revd George Smith (1815–1871), lord bishop of Victoria, 1849–1865: relations with the British navy and naval personnel', *St John's Review* (winter 1997), 11–13 [copy deposited in Hong Kong Baptist University Library] · G. Bickley, 'Mission China: narrative and analysis of events in the establishment of the diocese of Victoria', priv. coll. · G. Bickley, ed., *The development of education in Hong Kong, 1841–1897: as revealed by the early education reports of the Hong Kong government, 1848–1896* (Hong Kong, 2002) · E. J. Eitel, 'Materials for a history of education in Hong Kong', *China Review*, 19 (March–April 1891), 308–24; 335–68 · W. Lobscheid, *A few notices on the extent of Chinese education and the government schools in Hong Kong* (1859) · A. Wylie, *Memorials of protestant missionaries to the Chinese: giving a list of their publications, and obituary notices of the deceased* (Shanghai, 1867); repr. (Taipei, 1967) · *DNB* · Foster, *Alum. Oxon., 1715–1886*, 4.1313 · Allibone, *Dict.* · Boase, *Mod. Eng. biog.* · *ILN* (23 Dec 1871), 618 · *Men of the time* (1868), 741 · *The Graphic*, 125 (10 Feb 1872), p. 126 · *The Times* (16 Dec 1871), 5 · *The Times*, suppl. (13 July 1849), 1 · parish registers, parish of Wellington, Somerset, 17 Oct 1817 [baptism] · *CMS register of missionaries* (privately printed) [copy in U. Birm.]

Archives Diocesan Boys' School, Hong Kong, papers · Hong Kong PRO, papers · LPL, corresp. and papers on St Paul's College, 1869–1881, vols. 169, 178, 185 · priv. coll., archive containing copies of all obtainable writings by and about George Smith (published and unpublished), incl. transcriptions, analyses, tables, and illustrations · PRO, Colonial Office series, incl. scattered signed documents by and/or relating to George Smith, incl. CO 129/31, 112, 119, 128, 166 182 | Bodl. RH, Society for the Propagation of the Gospel archives · Church Missionary Society Library, London, serials, *Church Missionary Record*, *Church Missionary Intelligencer*, contributions by George Smith (sometimes extracted, sometimes edited), journals, and letters to Church Missionary Society · CUL, Society for the Propagation of Christian Knowledge archives · Hong Kong Baptist University, Special Collection, microform of the *Chinese Repository*, east Asia material from the Church Missionary Society Archive · Hong Kong PRO, Diocese of Victoria Archive, incl. register of diocese of Victoria, 1849–1871, diocesan records, HKMS 95, D & S no. 1/23, fols. 22–40 · Hong Kong PRO, microfilms of CO 129, Hong Kong government gazettes, Hong Kong government blue books · LPL, Blomfield papers · LPL, Lambeth conference, 1867 · LPL, Longley papers, George Smith, ALS · LPL, Tait papers, corresp. · PRO, Foreign Office documents, incl. scattered documents relating to George Smith and his work, CO 129 · U. Birm. L., Church Missionary Society archives · University of Hong Kong Library, Hong Kong Collection, microform of the *Friend of China and Hong Kong Gazette*, Colonial Office series 129, Foreign Office materials, *Hong Kong Government Gazette*, Hong Kong government blue books

Likenesses oils, *c*.1849, Hertford College, Oxford · Krumholz?, oils?, 1855, priv. coll. · F. Holl, stipple engraving (after G. Richmond), BM, NPG [*see illus.*] · oils, repro. in G. B. Endacott and D. E. She, *The diocese of Victoria, Hong Kong: a hundred years of church history, 1849–1949* (1949); priv. coll. · photograph, sepia, LPL · sketch, repro. in *The Graphic*, 125

Wealth at death under £6000—no leaseholds: will and grant (1872); York probate sub-registry (1996)

Smith, George (1831–1895), social reformer, was born on 16 February 1831 at Clayhills, Tunstall, Staffordshire, the son of William Smith (1807–1872), a brick maker, and his

George Smith (1831–1895), by unknown engraver, pubd 1879

wife, Hannah Hollins. The Smith household was very poor, with the result that George spent just two years at a village dame-school before, at the age of seven, he went full time into the brickfields. When he was nine he was shuttling from yard to brick-maker's table with 40 pound slabs of clay on his head, labour that sometimes lasted thirteen hours a day. Despite the rigours of his job, he also tended brick kilns at night to pay for books and, when he could fit them in, evening lessons. Such self-discipline and moral seriousness were inspired by the Primitive Methodist faith that animated his home. It was a faith that bred in Smith reverence for steady labour and contempt for any other work rhythm.

In 1857, having risen to become the manager of a large brick and tile firm at Humberstone in Staffordshire, Smith discovered valuable clay deposits under a brickyard in Coalville, Leicestershire. Unfortunately, when he showed mineral samples to those who were about to let him the brickyard, they reneged on the agreement, thereby robbing Smith of his chance to become an owner. From 1857 to 1874 he served as manager for the Whitwick Colliery Company, where his salary rose from £75 to £450 per year. Despite Smith's growing financial security, these years brought other pressures. The early 1860s saw him launch a one-man campaign to bring children employed in the brickyards under the protection of the Factory Acts. In 1863 he won the support of Robert Baker CB, an inspector of factories, and thereafter his campaign found a national audience. Although the death of his wife, Mary, *née* Mayfield, in 1866 left him with three children to bring up alone, Smith pressed on, delivering addresses to the Social Science Association and, in 1871, publishing *The Cry of the Children from the Brickyards of England*. This book inspired both the seventh earl of Shaftesbury and A. J. Mundella to take legislative action. Parliament moved quickly, passing a law in 1871 that provided for the inspection of brickyards and the regulation of juvenile labour therein. Smith's employers in Coalville rewarded their crusading manager by sacking him at the end of 1872. For the next thirteen years Smith again knew poverty.

In 1873 Smith shifted his attention from brickyards to waterways, where one hundred thousand 'bargees' allegedly lived in sin, disease, and ignorance aboard canal boats. His exposé, 'Our canal population', appeared in the *Fortnightly Review* in 1875, and was followed that same year by a book-length treatment of the subject. Among the politically powerful who took up Smith's case for reform was George Sclater-Booth (afterwards Lord Basing), who steered the Canal Boats Bill through parliament. The act that came into force in 1878 aimed to improve the sanitary conditions aboard such craft as well as to provide for the elementary education of boat children. But, because the act of 1877 failed to require adequate inspection of canal boats, Smith continued to denounce what he perceived as the barbarian freedom of 'floating people' until 1884, when amending legislation finally satisfied him. Confident that morality could indeed be legislated, he spent increasingly large amounts of time in London, using the British Museum as his office and a perch in the House of Commons gallery as his command post.

Of all Smith's battles, however, it was his frontal assault on Gypsy culture which gained greatest notoriety. The first of his four books on this issue, *Gipsy Life* (1880), made plain his distaste for a 'race' whom he characterized as the 'dregs and refuse' (4–5) of ancient Indian society. What particularly intrigued the reading public was Smith's eye for the exotic. His popular essay of 1883, *I've been a Gipsying*, titillated its audience with details about a community who fed their children half-hatched blackbirds, abused their donkeys, and committed incest. These 'agents of hell' (p. 8) had to be moulded into respectable citizens, a process that should start, Smith held, with the forcible education of their young and the sanitary inspection of their caravans. Smith's Movable Dwellings Bill, nine versions of which were brought before parliament between 1884 and 1894, never reached the statute book, for it fell prey to obstruction orchestrated by the Liberty and Property Defence League. It was Smith's only political defeat, but a bitter one for him.

George Smith was among late Victorian England's most unlikely philanthropists. The army of moral reformers certainly included others from working-class backgrounds, but most of these individuals had the advantage of trade union networks through which to organize and agitate. Smith stood alone. Yet his activism did not go unrewarded. In 1884, Gladstone, then prime minister, arranged for Smith to receive a grant of £300 from the Royal Bounty Fund. To supplement this stipend W. T. Stead used his *Pall Mall Gazette* to organize a collection for the 'penniless enthusiast' with the flowing white beard (*Pall Mall Gazette*, 21 Nov 1884). These gifts enabled Smith to buy a house, The Cabin, at Crick, near Rugby, where he died of cancer on 21 June 1895. He was buried in Crick churchyard. After his first wife's death, Smith had married Mary Ann Lehman. GEORGE K. BEHLMER

Sources E. Hodder, *George Smith (of Coalville)* (1896) • G. Behlmer, 'The Gypsy problem in Victorian England', *Victorian Studies*, 28 (1984–5), 231–53 • *The Times* (24 June 1895) • D. Mayall, *Gypsy-travellers in nineteenth-century society* (1988) • *DNB*

Likenesses pen-and-ink drawing, repro. in Hodder, *George Smith*, frontispiece • sketch (after photograph by J. Powell), repro. in *ILN* (29 June 1895) • woodcut, NPG; repro. in *The Graphic* (24 May 1879) [*see illus.*]

Wealth at death £345 17*s*. 0*d*.: probate, 16 Aug 1895, *CGPLA Eng. & Wales*

Smith, George (1840–1876), Assyriologist, was born at Chelsea, London, of working-class parents on 26 March 1840. His father was William John Smith, who was resident at Barnsbury, London, in 1876. He was apprenticed in 1854 to Bradbury and Evans of Bouverie Street, London, to learn banknote engraving. Though soon an able engraver himself, he was bored by such routine work. Having been fascinated as a child by historical portions of the Old Testament, he read avidly of the Mesopotamian archaeological explorations of Sir Austen Henry Layard and Sir Henry Rawlinson. Their success in deciphering cuneiform inscriptions particularly inspired him. At every spare moment Smith frequented the sculpture galleries of the British Museum, where recent finds from Nineveh and Babylon were on display, and began to collect books on Assyriology. By 1861 his visits to the museum attracted the notice of Samuel Birch, the recently appointed keeper of oriental, British, and medieval antiquities, who gave him sheets from the forthcoming first volume of Rawlinson's *Selection from the Cuneiform Inscriptions of Western Asia* (4 vols., 1861–75). Having taught himself to read the wedge-shaped script, Smith was, a year or two later, employed by the museum as a 'repairer', whose job was to match inscribed cuneiform fragments and put them together. In 1866 some of his more remarkable achievements were translated, and published by himself in *The Athenaeum*. That same year Smith's success in understanding and organizing these difficult materials led Rawlinson to propose the former engraver as an assistant to Birch and himself in preparing a further volume of cuneiform inscriptions. He was duly promoted.

From January 1867 Smith devoted himself solely to Assyriology. He made a systematic examination of tablets and paper casts of inscriptions found by Layard and Rawlinson, and classified these cuneiform writings by subject matter (history, religion, mythology, and so on). He was particularly interested in historical inscriptions that would supplement portions of biblical narrative. A series of articles by Smith in the *Zeitschrift für Ägyptische Sprache* greatly illuminated aspects of later Assyrian history, in particular the political relations of Assyria and Egypt. In 1870 he was appointed senior assistant to Birch, whose position was now keeper of oriental antiquities.

Much of the third volume of Rawlinson's *Cuneiform Inscriptions* was contributed by Smith, who in the course of preparing it accumulated a great deal of further information. During 1871 Smith published *The Phonetic Values of*

Cuneiform Characters and (with subsidies from friends) his monumental *Annals of Assur-bani-pal*, transcribed and translated from cuneiform cylinders on which he had been at work since 1867. He was also active in the newly founded Society of Biblical Archaeology (of which Birch was president), reading before it a précis of his history of Assurbanipal (6 June) and a paper on the decipherment of Cypriote inscriptions (7 November). His work on the Cypriot language was fundamental to later studies by others. *Notes on the Early History of Assyria and Babylonia* (1872), *Ancient History from the Monuments: Assyria* (1875), and *The Assyrian Eponym Canon* (1875) followed. The fourth volume of Rawlinson's *Cuneiform Inscriptions* (1875) was primarily Smith's work. His *Ancient History from the Monuments: Babylonia* (1877) and *The History of Sennacherib* (1878) were posthumously published. These books were regarded by specialists as invaluable pioneering studies on the chronology and languages of buried civilizations.

The work that made Smith's name familiar to the general public was his discovery in 1872, among cuneiform tablets sent to London from Nineveh by Layard's former assistant Hormuzd Rassam, of the 'Chaldean [Babylonian] account of the deluge'. Smith's translation of that startling find, presented by him before the Society of Biblical Archaeology on 3 December 1872, called attention to obvious parallels between this Babylonian story of a universal flood that few humans survived and the well-known account of Noah and his flood in Genesis. By 1872 geological evidence had largely discredited literal belief in the Noachian deluge. Smith's discovery therefore suggested an alternative way of reading Genesis—as myth rather than history—and would be of profound significance to the entire field of Old Testament exegesis. Later archaeologists, Sir Leonard Woolley in particular, would continue to endorse the reality of a Babylonian flood, but only as a local occurrence.

In consequence of the widespread interest taken in Smith's discovery, largely because of its biblical implications, the proprietors of the *Daily Telegraph* offered 1000 guineas towards sponsorship of further Mesopotamian researches by Smith, provided that he lead the expedition and return ongoing accounts of his work to them. This offer having been accepted by the trustees of the British Museum, Smith took a six-month leave of absence beginning on 20 January 1873. He went to the archaeological site of Nineveh, on the Tigris River at Mosul, which consisted of several mounds, of which Kuyunjik was the most important; in December 1853 the famous bas-reliefs of Assurbanipal's lion hunt had been found there. In the seventh century BC Sennacherib made Nineveh the capital of his Assyrian empire, but the city was later destroyed by the Medes (612 BC). Assurbanipal (mentioned in Ezra 4: 10 and more recently called Assurnasirpal) was Sennacherib's grandson. Smith reached Kuyunjik on 2 March 1873, was prevented by the local pasha from digging there until 7 May, and a week later had the remarkable good luck to find a further fragment of the deluge story among the ruins of Assurbanipal's library.

On his return to England (19 July 1873) with several deluge story fragments and other valuable cuneiform inscriptions, Smith was quickly ordered back to the Middle East, as his hard-won permission to dig at Kuyunjik would not expire until March 1874. Sponsored now by the British Museum only, Smith left London on 25 November and reached Mosul on 1 January 1874. In these further excavations, employing some 600 local men and conducted entirely at Kuyunjik, he recovered several hundred tablets and fragments but had to surrender some of them to the local pasha (whom he had refused to bribe with the necessary baksheesh). None the less Smith returned once more to London with numerous inscriptions, many of which were parts of a great literary epic in twelve books called *Gilgamesh* (after its protagonist), of which the deluge episode formed the eleventh. He reached home, by way of Aleppo and Alexandria, on 9 June 1874.

Early in 1875 Smith published one of his best-known books, *Assyrian Discoveries*, an account of his explorations and discoveries at Nineveh during 1873 and 1874. Dedicated to Birch, his superior, it utilized Smith's newspaper accounts in narrating his travels and researches, with numerous translations from Assyrian tablets included. Smith then spent the rest of his time piecing together and translating highly important fragments in which the traditional Old Testament stories of the creation, the fall of man, and the Tower of Babel all seemed to have Babylonian sources predating the biblical one. His *Chaldean Account of Genesis* (1876) summarized this astounding evidence and further strengthened the interpretation of Genesis as myth.

The value and popular impact of Smith's most recent discoveries induced the trustees of the British Museum to send him on yet another expedition to excavate the remainder of Assurbanipal's library. Smith left for Constantinople in October 1875 but was delayed there for six months by the need to obtain a new firman from the slow-moving Ottoman bureaucracy. He was unable to depart for Mosul and Nineveh until March 1876. While detained at Aleppo by plague, Smith explored the banks of the Euphrates from the Balis northwards, and at Jarabulus discovered the ancient Hittite capital of Carchemish. After visiting several other sites he reached Baghdad, where he bought some 2000 cuneiform tablets from Arabs who had found another ancient Babylonian library near Hillah. From Baghdad he finally arrived at Mosul in July 1876—only to find that further Kuyunjik excavations were no longer possible because of political unrest and the lateness of the season.

Unable to speak much Arabic, headstrong, and impractical by nature, Smith unwisely insisted on crossing the desert by day. He left Mosul for Aleppo at the end of July and, suffering from dysentery, collapsed on 16 August at Ikisji, a small village 60 miles north-west of Aleppo. Through the agency of the British consul, James Henry Skene, Smith was brought to Aleppo and attended there (primarily by Mrs Skene) but he died on 19 August at the age of thirty-six. At some juncture he was married, but no details have been found of his wife, or of any offspring. He was buried in the cemetery of the Levant Company. In his time no one in England had done more to bring the excitement and significance of archaeological discovery before the public. DENNIS R. DEAN

Sources *DNB* • E. A. W. Budge, *The rise and progress of Assyriology* (1925), 106–19 • S. A. Pellis, *The antiquity of Iraq* (1956) • R. Borger, *Handbuch der Krilschrift Literatur*, 1 (1967), 484–8 • R. Borger, *Handbuch der Krilschrift Literatur*, 2 (1975), 262 • D. R. Dean, 'The rise and fall of the deluge', *Journal of Geological Education*, 33 (1985), 84–93 • B. M. Fagan, ed., *The Oxford companion to archaeology* (1996) • G. Smith, *Assyrian discoveries* (1875) • *CGPLA Eng. & Wales* (1876)

Archives BL, notebooks, Add. MSS 30397–30427

Likenesses portrait, repro. in Budge, *Rise and progress*, facing p. 178 • print, BM • wood-engraving (after photograph by N. Briggs), NPG; repro. in *ILN* (10 April 1875)

Wealth at death under £1000: probate, 23 Sept 1876, *CGPLA Eng. & Wales*

Smith, Sir George Adam (1856–1942), Old Testament scholar and geographer, was born on 19 October 1856, the eldest son of Dr George Smith and Janet Colquhoun, daughter of Robert Adam of Sweethillocks, Moray, and great-niece of Alexander Adam. Smith was born in Calcutta where his father was principal of Doveton College for Eurasian Boys and, from 1858 to 1875, editor of the *Calcutta Review*; his many books included *The Student's Geography of India* (1882). The Smith family settled in Edinburgh where in 1875 the elder George Smith became foreign secretary to the Free Church of Scotland; he also helped found the Scottish Geographical Society in 1884 and served on its council. His interest in geography and his faith were shared by his son.

When Smith was two years old his mother brought him and his younger brother home to Scotland. She returned to India, but the boys remained with aunts at Leith where they were joined by other brothers and sisters. Smith was educated at the Royal High School, Edinburgh, and at Edinburgh University, where his studies included political economy, a subject which influenced his later work as a biblical expositor and social reformer. After graduating in 1875 he studied divinity at New College, Edinburgh, in preparation for ministry in the Free Church. There he was particularly influenced by Andrew Bruce Davidson, professor of Hebrew, who introduced him to German biblical criticism. In vacations he studied theology at Tübingen, in 1876, and at Leipzig, in 1878, where he was much influenced by the teaching of Friedrich Delitzsch and Adolf Harnack.

Having completed his studies Smith went to Cairo to work with the American mission. While there he learned Arabic and travelled to Palestine for the first time in the spring of 1880, tramping the country on foot with an Arab muleteer. He returned to Scotland in 1880 to take temporary charge of teaching Hebrew and Old Testament at the Free Church college, Aberdeen, after the suspension of William Robertson Smith on suspicion of heresy. In 1882 he was ordained to the charge of Queen's Cross Free Church, Aberdeen, where he stayed until 1892. In preaching and discussion he tried to reconcile the outlook of an

Sir George Adam Smith (1856–1942), by unknown photographer, 1925

advanced scientific scholar with the spirit of devout reverence, and from his sermons and lectures came a commentary on the book of Isaiah (2 vols., 1888–90), which went through many editions. He maintained his wider scientific interests as secretary of the geographical section of the British Association meeting in Aberdeen in 1885 and as fellow of the Scottish Geographical Society, and he was fully engaged in the debate over the relationship of Darwinism, Lamarkism, and natural theology.

From 1883 Smith regularly visited Switzerland and he became an enthusiastic mountaineer. He was elected to the Alpine Club in 1886, and, while climbing from Zermatt in 1889, he met fellow climber (Alice) Lilian (*d.* 1949), daughter of Sir George *Buchanan (1831–1895), chief medical officer of the Local Government Board in London. They were married on 18 December 1889 and during their long and happy marriage shared many interests and activities. In 1891 they and two companions visited Palestine and travelled from the Negev to Damascus and Baalbek, Smith taking notes on climatology, geology, topography, and biblical sites.

In 1892 Smith was appointed professor of Hebrew and Old Testament exegesis at the Free Church college, Glasgow. In addition to his academic work he helped with the college's settlement in Broomielaw and later took charge of the Toynbee House settlement in the centre of Glasgow. He campaigned energetically against the injustices of sweated labour and was chairman of the Scottish Council for Women's Trades. In 1894 he published his *Historical Geography of the Holy Land*, which was immediately recognized as a major work of scholarship. It reached twenty-five editions during his lifetime, was completely revised in 1931, and was reissued as recently as 1966. In the preface to the first edition Smith declared his hope of enabling students of the Bible:

> to see a background and to feel an atmosphere; to discover from 'the lie of the land' why the history took certain lines and the prophecy and the gospel were expressed in certain styles; to learn what geography has to contribute to questions of Biblical criticism; and, above all, to discern between what physical nature contributed to the religious development of Israel, and what was the product of moral and spiritual forces. (Butlin, 384)

Smith's historical geography of the Holy Land was distinguished by his detailed personal knowledge of the area, his familiarity with historical and archaeological evidence, gained in part from contacts at the Palestine Exploration Fund, founded in 1865, for whose *Palestine Exploration Quarterly* he regularly reviewed books, and because he used modern scientific and critical methods to evangelical ends. The often vivid text was illustrated with maps drawn in collaboration with J. G. Bartholomew.

Smith's *Book of the Twelve Prophets* (2 vols., 1894–6) followed his earlier *Isaiah* in demonstrating that the social and religious concerns of the prophets were relevant to the modern world. During his Glasgow years Smith made four visits to the United States. In 1896 he lectured at Johns Hopkins University, where he came into contact with both theologians and geographers, particularly Daniel Coit Gilman. In 1899 he lectured at Yale and his lectures, published as *Modern Criticism and the Old Testament* (1901), were regarded by some in the Free Church as an 'emphatic challenge to the church for the toleration or tacit approval of … revolutionary opinions … which have awakened deep anxiety and unrest throughout the Church' (Butlin, 383). Proceedings against him for heresy were begun on the grounds that his work undermined the truthfulness, inspiration, and authority of large sections of scripture, but were abandoned after the general assembly of the Free Church declared its confidence in him in 1902.

Smith visited Palestine again in 1901 and 1904. His *Topography, Economics, and Historical Geography of Jerusalem* (2 vols., 1907) contained material on the city which was too abundant to be included in his *Historical Geography*. More detailed and technical than *Historical Geography*, it was less enthusiastically received but became a standard work.

From 1909 to 1935 Smith was principal of the University of Aberdeen, presiding over increases in the numbers of students, academic staff, and research institutes, particularly in science and medicine. He preached regularly in King's College chapel, and cultivated good relations with the city of Aberdeen. He maintained his geographical interests, helping the Geographical Association to establish geography in the school curriculum in the early twentieth century, and in 1915 collaborating with Bartholomew to publish his long-planned *Atlas of the Historical Geography of the Holy Land*.

Smith served on the Haldane commission which led in 1929 to the union of the United Free Church with the Church of Scotland, an event he described with John Buchan in *The Kirk in Scotland 1560–1929* (1930).

As his reputation spread Smith received honorary degrees from universities throughout the United Kingdom and the United States. In 1916 he was moderator of the general assembly of the United Free Church; and he was knighted and elected a fellow of the British Academy. In 1933 he was appointed chaplain to the king in Scotland.

Late in his life Smith adopted his second forename, Adam, as an additional surname, though he continued also to use and be referred to as 'Smith' alone. After his death he was generally referred to by the surnames Adam Smith. In 1935 he and Lady Adam Smith retired to Sweethillocks, Balerno, near Edinburgh, where he died on 3 March 1942, survived by his wife. They had seven children. Of their three sons, the two elder, George and Dunlop, were killed in the First World War; Alick, an agricultural scientist, was created Lord Balerno in 1963. Of their four daughters, Kathleen Buchanan married George Paget *Thomson, and Janet Buchanan Adam *Smith, biographer and critic, married William Edward (Michael) *Roberts. Through his sisters Smith was connected to many of those whom Noel Annan described as the intellectual aristocracy of the period: Janetta Smith became the wife of W. R. Sorley and mother of Charles Sorley, and Ann Smith married Sir Montagu Sherard Dawes Butler and was the mother of R. A. Butler.

George Adam Smith followed W. Robertson Smith in helping to transform Scottish biblical scholarship, bringing to it the critical methods developed in Germany in the late eighteenth and early nineteenth centuries. The particular religious controversies in the Scottish Free Church in which he was involved are now closed, but his work on Old Testament prophets, particularly Isaiah, and on geography, has had lasting value. His account of the relationship between topography and the military tactics of ancient armies in his *Historical Geography* was put to practical use by Edmund Allenby in his Palestine campaign against the Turkish forces in 1917, and throughout the twentieth century his geographical writing excited admiration both for his success in incorporating scientific data into works of considerable literary merit and for the moral purpose he brought to topographical description.

ELIZABETH BAIGENT

Sources L. A. Smith, *George Adam Smith* (1943) • R. Butlin, 'George Adam Smith and the historical geography of the Holy Land', *Journal of Historical Geography*, 14 (1988), 381–404 • D. Middleton, 'George Adam Smith, 1856–1942', *Geographers: biobibliographical studies*, 1, ed. T. W. Freeman, M. Oughton, and P. Pinchemel (1977), 105–6 • S. A. Cook, 'George Adam Smith', *PBA*, 28 (1942), 325–46 • R. A. Riesen, *Criticism and faith in late-Victorian Scotland: A. B. Davidson, William Robertson Smith and George Adam Smith* (1985) • R. A. Riesen, 'Smith, George Adam', *DSCHT* • I. D. Campbell, 'George Adam Smith (1856–1942)', PhD diss., U. Edinburgh, 2001 • T. W. Freeman, *A history of modern British geography* (1980) • *DNB* • *CGPLA Eng. & Wales* (1942) • *WWW*

Archives NL Scot., corresp. and papers | NL Scot., corresp. with Henry Drummond

Likenesses photograph, 1925, British Academy, London [*see illus.*] • W. Orpen, oils, 1927, King's College, Aberdeen • J. M. Aitken, portrait, New College, Edinburgh • J. B. Soutier, oils, Trinity Hall, Aberdeen • photograph, repro. in Middleton, 'George Adam Smith', 105

Wealth at death no value given: confirmation, 24 July 1942, *CGPLA Eng. & Wales*

Smith, George Albert (1864–1959), film-maker, was born on 4 January 1864 at 93 Aldersgate Street, Cripplegate, east London, the child of Charles Smith, ticket writer, and his wife, Margaret Alice Davidson. After the death of his father, his mother moved the family to Brighton. It was there, in 1882, that Smith received public attention for the first time as a result of his activities as a popular hypnotist. This led to a partnership with Douglas Blackburn, a local journalist, within which they developed a 'second-sight act' (Blackburn hid an object in the theatre and then Smith, blindfolded, led him to it) and feats of 'muscle-reading' (Blackburn transmitted to the blindfolded 'medium' on the stage, played by Smith, the identity of objects selected by the audience). Smith claimed that genuine telepathy was practised and representatives of the Society for Psychical Research believed that he had the gift of true 'thought reading'. Blackburn would later admit, however, that the act was a hoax. Smith became part of the society's circle and was appointed private secretary to its honorary secretary, Edmund Gurney. In 1887 Gurney carried out a number of 'hypnotic experiments' in Brighton, with Smith as the 'hypnotizer'. Smith was the co-author of a paper titled 'Experiments in thought-transference' published in the society's journal in 1889.

In 1892, by which time he had left the employment of the Society for Psychical Research, Smith acquired the lease to St Ann's Well Gardens in Hove. This was only a short distance from Brighton and the seafront. He cultivated this site so that it became a popular pleasure garden and the home for his film-making activities. In 1896 Smith saw and appreciated the first Lumiére programme in London, and it is likely that he studied Robert Paul's films during their summer season in Brighton. At the end of that year he acquired his first camera. For Smith, the former hypnotist, film offered a new and very modern form of illusionism. He made only the studio shot of the train carriage in *The Kiss in the Tunnel* (1899), but when he inserted it into Cecil Hepworth's phantom ride *View from an Engine Front: Train Leaving Tunnel*, he created an edited film which demonstrated a new sense of continuity and simultaneity across three shots. His filmic imagination was very adventurous and it continued to develop in the next year. *As Seen through the Telescope*, *Grandma's Reading Glass*, *The House that Jack Built*, and *Let me Dream Again*, all of 1900, were remarkable for their interpolated close-ups, subjective and objective point-of-view shots, the creation of dream-time, and the use of 'reversing' (by which action appeared to happen backwards). Through these experimental films Smith was instrumental in the development of continuity editing. He taught his contemporaries how to create a filmed sequence. James *Williamson (1855–1933) was especially influenced by him.

George Albert Smith (1864–1959), by unknown photographer

Smith's films in the years 1897–1903 were largely comedies and adaptations of popular fairy tales and stories. His work within these genres was influenced by his wife, Laura Eugenia (*b.* 1863/4), daughter of William Bullivant Bayley, a sadler. They had married in Ramsgate on 13 June 1888. Her life in popular theatre before 1897, particularly in pantomime and comic revues, provided Smith with an experienced actress who understood visual comedy and the interests of seaside audiences. Laura Bayley would star in many of Smith's most important films, including *Let me Dream Again* and *Mary Jane's Mishap* (1903). No other actress appears as frequently in British films of this period.

At St Ann's Well, in 1897, Smith adapted the pump house into a space for developing and printing films, and in the grounds, probably in 1901, he built a glasshouse film studio. By the late 1890s he had developed a successful commercial film production and processing business with the assistance of the Brighton engineer Alfred Darling. Smith's largest customer became the Warwick Trading Company. Through this relationship Smith became part of the company and developed a long partnership with its managing director, Charles *Urban (1867–1942). The two-colour additive process known as Kinemacolor would dominate the rest of his career in film. This was developed from 1903 from his new home, Laboratory Lodge, Roman Crescent, Southwick. On 8 July 1908 Kinemacolor was presented in Paris to a gathering of scientists and the Lumière brothers. The first demonstration in England followed at the Royal Society of Arts in London on 9 December 1908. For the system Smith was awarded a silver medal by the Royal Society of Arts. Urban turned Kinemacolor into a new enterprise, the Natural Colour Kinematograph Company. It enjoyed success in the period 1910–13, when it produced over 100 short features from its studios in Hove and Nice, but the system was not taken up by the industry. A patent suit brought against Kinemacolor by William Friese-Greene in 1914 would lead to its collapse and end Smith's life in the film business. The widespread use of true colour film would not begin in the cinema for almost twenty years.

In his later years Smith spent much time peering through his telescope from his Brighton seafront arch. He had long been a fellow of the Royal Astronomical Society. In the late 1940s he was 'discovered' by the film community. He was commemorated by Michael Balcon as 'the father of the British Film Industry' and in 1955 was made a fellow of the British Film Academy. He died, aged ninety-five, in the Brighton General Hospital on 17 May 1959 and was cremated five days later at the Downs crematorium, Brighton. He was survived by his second wife, Edith Kate.

FRANK GRAY

Sources T. Hall, *The strange case of Edmund Gurney* (1980) • H. Sidgwick, E. M. Sidgwick, and G. A. Smith, 'Experiments in thought-transference', *Proceedings of the Society for Psychical Research*, 6 (1889–90), 128–70 • F. Gray, 'Smith the showman: the early years of George Albert Smith', *Film History*, 10/1 (1998), 8–20 • J. Barnes, *The rise of the cinema in Great Britain: Jubilee year, 1897* (1983), vol. 2 of *The beginnings of the cinema in England, 1894–1901* • J. Barnes, *Pioneers of the British film* (1983), vol. 3 of *The beginnings of the cinema in England, 1894–1901* • J. Barnes, *Filming the Boer War* (1990), vol. 4 of *The beginnings of the cinema in England, 1894–1901*; repr. (1992) • J. Barnes, *The beginnings of the cinema in England, 1894–1901*, 5 (1997) • D. M. Thomas, *The first colour motion pictures* (1969) • b. cert. • m. cert. [marriage to Laura Bayley] • d. cert. • *CGPLA Eng. & Wales* (1959) • *Evening Argus* [Brighton] (20 May 1959), 10 • *Brighton Herald* (22 April 1893), 2

Archives BFI • Hove Museum, Barnes collection • Sci. Mus., Charles Urban collection | FILM BFI NFTVA

Likenesses photograph, repro. in Barnes, *Rise of the cinema*, 84 • photograph, BFI [*see illus.*]

Wealth at death £9331 4*s*.: probate, 20 July 1959, *CGPLA Eng. & Wales*

George Barnett Smith (1841–1909), by Mortimer L. Menpes, 1879

Smith, George Barnett [*pseud.* Guy Roslyn] (**1841–1909**), author and journalist, born at Ovenden, Yorkshire, on 17 May 1841, was the son of Titus and Mary Smith. Educated at the British Lancastrian School, Halifax, he went to London as a young man, and worked there as a journalist; from 1865 to 1868 he was on the editorial staff of the *Globe*, and from 1868 to 1876 on the *Echo*. He was subsequently a contributor to *The Times*. A man of literary tastes and poetical ambition, Smith managed to become a contributor to the chief magazines, among them the *Edinburgh Review*, the *Fortnightly Review*, and the *Cornhill Magazine*. Although he lacked scholarly training, he was an appreciative critic. A memoir of Elizabeth Barrett Browning in the ninth edition of the *Encyclopaedia Britannica* (1876) satisfied Robert Browning, with whom Smith became a close friend. It was the poet's custom to send Smith proof sheets of his later volumes in advance, to enable him to write early reviews.

Smith was a thorough chronicler of his age, using *Hansard* and newspaper sources effectively in his lives of Gladstone (2 vols., 1879), John Bright (1881), Queen Victoria (1886), and William I of Germany (1887). His *History of the English Parliament* (2 vols., 1892) showed him out of his depth. He also wrote lives of Shelley (1877) and Victor Hugo (1885), and several works on poets, travel, Victorian heroes, and women. As Guy Roslyn he published verse, and *George Eliot in Derbyshire* (1876). Smith was a competent etcher (see his *English Etchings*, 1884–7), and his etching of Carlyle was bought by the prince of Wales.

Smith was twice married, first to Annie Hodson (*d.* 1868), and second, in 1871, to Julia Hannah, *née* Timmis, who survived him; he had four daughters, two of whom survived him. In 1889 problems with his lungs made him an invalid, and he retired to Bournemouth, being granted a civil-list pension of £80 by the tories in 1891, increased by the Liberals to £150 in 1906. He died at his house, Linda, Alumhurst Road, Bournemouth, on 2 January 1909 and was buried in Bournemouth cemetery. His life of Gladstone, published in various illustrated editions, gained him a historiographical niche.

H. C. G. MATTHEW

Sources *The Times* (4 Jan 1909) • Gladstone, *Diaries* • R. Browning, *Letters to various correspondents*, ed. T. J. Wise, 2 vols. (1895–6) • *DNB* • *CGPLA Eng. & Wales* (1909)

Archives BL, letters to W. E. Gladstone, Add. MSS 44405–44521, *passim*

Likenesses M. L. Menpes, drypoint print, 1879, BM, NPG [*see illus.*] • R. Corder, oils; in possession of his widow, 1912

Wealth at death £150 15*s*. 6*d*.: probate, 18 Jan 1909, *CGPLA Eng. & Wales*

Smith, George Charles [*called* Boatswain Smith] (**1782–1863**), missionary to seafarers, was born on 19 March 1782 in Castle Street, Leicester Square, London, the son of William Smith, a tailor, and his wife, Nancy Wilson. The family were active members of Rowland Hill's Surrey Chapel. His father died when he was twelve, and George spent two years as an assistant to a bookseller in Rotherhithe. In 1796 he persuaded his mother to bind him as apprentice to the master of an American brig, hoping to seek his fortune in the New World. His ship was accosted in the Caribbean by HMS *Scipio*, and he was pressed into service in the

British navy. He subsequently was a midshipman on HMS *Agamemnon*, and served with distinction under Nelson in the battle of Copenhagen in 1801. The following year he was discharged from the navy.

Smith underwent a radical religious conversion in 1803, and felt himself called to the Baptist ministry. In Bath he met Opie Smith, under whose patronage he was enabled to study theology with Isaiah Birt in Devonport between 1804 and 1807. In October of the latter year he was ordained as pastor of Octagon Baptist Chapel, Penzance, and in June 1808 he married Theodosia (*d*. 1866), daughter of John and Rebecca Skipwith. At least nine children were born to them in Penzance, where they lived until 1826. Smith twice enlarged his Penzance chapel, renaming it Jordan Chapel in 1822, and was active in building chapels in the surrounding villages. Since he was himself a former seafarer, his chapel was popular with the mariners of the area; in 1809 a delegation of sailors from the *Dolphin* invited him to preach a sermon on board, having survived a harrowing storm. This was the beginning of his involvement in organized missions to seafarers. Later in that year he launched a naval correspondence mission to minister to Christians on the ships of the wartime navy, publishing episodes from this 'naval awakening' in a series called *The Boatswain's Mate* (1811–12) to publicize what came to be known as the 'Seaman's Cause'. In 1814 Smith served for several months as a voluntary chaplain with Wellington's Peninsular army, and in 1815 played an important part in the relief of famine in the Isles of Scilly. His open-air preaching in the villages of the south-west between 1814 and 1817 led to the foundation of the (Baptist) Home Missionary Society.

From 1817 missions to seafarers became Smith's priority. He began to hold prayer meetings and to preach on board the ships moored on the Thames. He was warmly received, and the massive response to an advertised service on the *Agenoria* gave him the idea for a floating sanctuary for seafarers. The sanctuary was opened the following year on a remodelled sloop, the *Speedy* (which was soon universally known as the *Ark*), by the interdenominational Port of London Society for Promoting Religion among Merchant Seamen, which Smith had been instrumental in founding. Smith enthusiastically endorsed the 'Bethel flag', first used in 1817 as a signal for shipboard worship; through his zealous promotion the emblem came to be a catalyst for organized maritime missions throughout the world. In 1819 he founded the British and Foreign Seamen's Friend Society and Bethel Union. In order to publicize the Bethel movement and work among sailors, in 1820 Smith began publishing the *Sailor's Magazine*, which he was to continue until his death. He published more than eighty other works, but the *Sailor's Magazine* was undoubtedly the most important of his literary ventures.

In 1825 Smith secured the vacant Danish church in Wellclose Square, close to the London docks, where he created the first shore-based seafarers' mission, the London Mariners' Church. He moved his family to London, settling in as the first full-time resident minister to mariners, and determined to transform what he saw as the 'Sodom and Gomorrah of Sailors' into a 'marine Jerusalem'. A stream of initiatives to assist sailors followed, including a Shipwrecked and Distressed Sailors' Family Fund (founded 1824); a destitute sailors' asylum in Dock Street (1828); a sailors' home in adjacent Well Street (1829); a Sailors' Orphan House Establishment (1829); and a Maritime Penitent Young Woman's Refuge (1830) for the rehabilitation of dockland prostitutes. He was a pioneer in the founding of the British and Foreign Temperance Society in 1831, and of the Sailors' and Soldiers' Temperance Union two years later. He also campaigned tirelessly against the inhuman conditions of life and work at sea.

Not content with pen and pulpit, Smith carried his cause into the streets, where his stentorian voice and rousing rhetoric repeatedly caused him to be arrested for breach of the peace. With a burly build and benevolent face, Boatswain Smith became a familiar figure on the metropolitan scene, where he was often accompanied by a troop of orphans dressed in nautical uniforms, singing hymns and patriotic songs. Many of his plans were never realized, becoming casualties of his uncompromising, combative nature, which eventually embroiled him in protracted and often virulent public controversy. Furthermore, although his personal honesty was never in doubt, his refusal to be bound by convention and his chronic inability to keep regular accounts resulted in four terms in debtors' prison between 1836 and 1845. This finally caused him to 'give up the ship' in Wellclose Square, and eventually, in 1848, to return to Penzance. He continued to be dedicated to the cause, making annual preaching missions along the coast. In 1853 he again resigned from Jordan Chapel to devote himself to seafarers, making his home, Jordan House, his headquarters. He was reconciled with his wife, who had separated from him in the 1840s under the stress of his repeated incarcerations, and in 1861 was rapturously received on his tour of seafarers' missions along America's Atlantic seaboard, being fêted in New York as the 'originator and founder' of the worldwide movement. In 1862 a public subscription was launched in London to relieve his grinding poverty, but before he could benefit from it he died on 10 January 1863 at Jordan House, Penzance. Some two thousand mourners attended his funeral in Penzance cemetery on 16 January.

Despite his 'oceanic tempestuous nature' and his somewhat erratic behaviour, Boatswain Smith's position as a pioneer in the realm of maritime missions is unassailable. Never a narrow sectarian, he fulfilled the role of a maritime John the Baptist. To rouse the Christian church to accept its responsibility for the evangelization of seafarers and the improvement of conditions in the maritime industry was the task of a prophet, undaunted by impossible odds.

Smith's eldest son, **Theophilus Ahijah Smith** (1809–1879), was a promoter of charities, initially assisting his father at the London Mariners' Church. He assisted in founding the Havre de Grace British and American Seamen's Friend Society (1831) at Le Havre, the first such body based on the mainland of Europe. He was instrumental in establishing the Church of England Temperance Society in 1839, and served as assistant secretary (1840–47) and then secretary (1865–8) of the Protestant Association. Twice married, from 1847 he played a leading role in the rehabilitation of prostitutes, as secretary of the Female Aid Society (1847–61) and as co-founder of the Midnight Meeting Movement (1860). Permanently disabled by a railway accident in 1868, he died at Cardigan Road, Richmond, Surrey, on 13 January 1879. ROALD KVERNDAL

Sources *Sailor's Magazine* (1820–27) • *New Sailor's Magazine* (1827–63) • G. C. Smith, *The boatswain's mate, or, An interesting dialogue between two British seamen*, 7 pts (1811–12) • G. C. Smith, *A sailor's visit to Surrey Chapel, or, Interesting recollections in early life, on shore and at sea* • Boase & Courtney, *Bibl. Corn.*, 2.664–70, vol. 3 • T. A. Smith, *The great moral reformation of sailors* (1874) • *Sailor's Magazine* [New York] (1862–3), 208 • *Sailor's Magazine* [New York] (1876), 107–11, 129–35, 193–7 • *The Revival* (25 Dec 1862), 303 • *The Revival* (8 Jan 1863), 23 • *The Revival* (22 Jan 1863), 45 • *GM*, 3rd ser., 14 (1863), 260, 390–91 • *GM*, 5th ser., 6 (1871), 619–25 • F. Trestrail, *Reminiscences of college life in Bristol* (1879), 103–8 • R. Kverndal, *Seamen's missions: their origin and early growth* (1986) • private information (2004)

Archives British and International Sailors' Society, Southampton • Penzance Library, Morrab Gardens, Penzance • Seamen's Christian Friend Society, Alderley Edge, Cheshire

Likenesses A. Wivell, mezzotint, pubd 1819, BM • portrait, repro. in Boase & Courtney, *Bibl. Corn*, 2.669 • three portraits, repro. in Kverndal, *Seamen's missions*, 114, 359, 363

Smith, George Charles Moore (1858–1940), literary scholar, was born on 3 September 1858 at Whittlesey in the Isle of Ely, the eldest child of George Moore Smith (*d.* 1870), a solicitor in Whittlesey, and his wife, Elizabeth, only child of the Revd James Clarke Franks, vicar of Huddersfield. His great-uncle was Lieutenant-General Sir Harry Smith (1787–1860) and his maternal grandmother was Elizabeth Firth, godmother to two of the Brontë children.

Moore Smith attended a preparatory school in Dalston, London, from 1868 until 1870, when his father died. The family then moved to Tonbridge, where he and his brothers attended Tonbridge School as day boys. The two headmasters during his time there were both former fellows of St John's College, Cambridge, and it was to this college that Moore Smith proceeded in 1877. He matriculated as an exhibitioner, then held a foundation scholarship from 1880 to 1884, which enabled him to continue his studies after he graduated with a first class in the classical tripos in 1881. He used this opportunity to study English language under W. W. Skeat. There followed a long period of uncertainty in his career before he moved to Sheffield in 1896. He spent some time teaching and studying in Europe, making many friends among German and Danish scholars. His life continued to revolve around Cambridge, however, and he was disappointed that he was never able to obtain a permanent situation there (he was eventually made an honorary fellow of St John's College in 1933). He played a leading part in raising support in Cambridge for the Toynbee Hall settlement in London, and from 1885 onwards he did some work as a Cambridge University extension lecturer, first in Norwich, and later in Northampton and St Albans.

Moore Smith arrived in Sheffield at an important moment in the development of higher education in the city. His first appointment, in 1896, was as professor of English language and literature at Firth College (opened in 1880). But the following year Firth College combined with the technical and medical schools to become University College, Sheffield, and in 1905 this college received its charter as the University of Sheffield. Moore Smith retained his post and played a vital part in building up the social and academic status of the new institution. As honorary librarian from 1896 to 1907 he was responsible for developing its library holdings to more than 10,000 books, many obtained as gifts or legacies through his many contacts. He also founded and edited the magazine *Floreamus*, which solemnly chronicled the affairs of the college and university. His own scholarly publications increased steadily after his appointment, and he came to be regarded as one of the most eminent scholars in the new university. Family connections led him for a while into military history: the relief of Ladysmith (a town named after his great-aunt, Lady Juana Smith) prompted him to edit *The Autobiography of Lieutenant-General Sir Harry Smith* (1901) and the success of this book, which was reprinted several times, led on to *The Life of John Colborne, Field-Marshal Lord Seaton* (1903). But Moore Smith's real interests lay in literary history, particularly in the work of authors who, like himself, had received a classical training at Cambridge. He made a special study of the Latin plays written and performed by Cambridge scholars in the late sixteenth and early seventeenth centuries, and produced scholarly editions of *Pedantius* (1905), *Victoria* (1906), *Club Law* (1907), *Hymenaeus* (1908), *Fucus histriomastix* (1909), and

George Charles Moore Smith (1858–1940), by Elliott & Fry, 1933

Laelia (1910), together with a companion volume, *College Plays Performed in the University of Cambridge* (1923). His other major scholarly works included editions of *Gabriel Harvey's Marginalia* (1913), *The Poems, English and Latin, of Edward Lord Herbert of Cherbury* (1923), and *The Letters of Dorothy Osborne to Sir William Temple* (1928). He received a LittD from Cambridge in 1907 and honorary doctorates from the universities of Louvain and St Andrews, as well as from Sheffield. He retired in 1924 and on his seventieth birthday was presented with *A Bibliography of the Writings of G. C. Moore Smith*, which listed more than 300 published items. It is a striking feature of Moore Smith's career that hardly any of these items were substantial monographs: even the books he had largely written, like *The Life of John Colborne*, were officially only 'compiled' by him. He evidently preferred the role of scholarly editor or glossator to that of critic or author. In this respect, although he was very much formed by Cambridge, Moore Smith's approach to the study of literature was quite antithetical to that of the later 'Cambridge English' tradition. His tastes were uncritically those of Victorian Romanticism and his practice, both as teacher and scholar, was modelled on his early success in classics.

Moore Smith departed from his usual topics to produce *The Story of the People's College, Sheffield, 1842–1878* (1912). He was committed to the 'civic' mission of the university in Sheffield, and so served on several local educational committees, and gave many public lectures. He continued to live in Sheffield after his retirement, but suffered increasingly from arthritis, and died at home on 7 November 1940 from injuries sustained after a fall in his room. After a funeral at St Augustine's Church, he was buried on 9 November in the Sheffield general cemetery, less than a mile from his home at 31 Endcliffe Rise Road which, as a lifelong bachelor, he had shared with his surviving sisters. RICHARD STORER

Sources *A bibliography of the writings of G. C. Moore Smith, Litt.D* (1928) [see esp. D. Hamer's MS annotated copy, University of Sheffield] • J. D. Wilson, 'George Charles Moore Smith, 1858–1940', *PBA*, 30 (1944), 361–77 [see also D. Hamer's MS notes, University of Sheffield, Special Collections, Moore Smith MSS] • A. W. Chapman, *The story of a modern university: a history of the University of Sheffield* (1955) • P. Hobsbaum, 'Universal dullness: a case-history of marginal scholarship', *Universities Quarterly*, 19 (1964–5), 33–40 • *WWW* • *Sheffield Telegraph*

Archives Sheffield Local Studies Library • University of Sheffield, family corresp. and papers incl. papers relating to Thomas Randolph, poet • University of Sheffield

Likenesses photograph, 1912, repro. in *Sheffield Literary and Philosophical Society: portraits of presidents*, III (1889–1917) [Sheffield Local Studies Library] • J. H. Dowd, drawing, 1928, repro. in *Bibliography* • Elliott & Fry, photograph, 1933, British Academy, London [*see illus.*]

Wealth at death £13,305 3*s*. 5*d*.: probate, 14 Jan 1941, *CGPLA Eng. & Wales*

Smith, George Joseph (1872–1915), bigamist and murderer, was born on 11 January 1872 at 92 Roman Road, Bethnal Green, London, the son of George Thomas Smith, insurance agent, and his wife, Louisa Gibson. Little is known about his early life. Caroline Thornhill, his first known spouse, maintained that he was sent to a reformatory in Gravesend when he was nine and that when he left, at the age of sixteen, he returned home to live with his mother and began a career of petty theft. Certainly, on 7 February 1891 he was convicted at Lambeth police court of the theft of a bicycle and sentenced to six months' imprisonment. Smith's activities between 1891 and 1896 are uncertain. An alleged three-year service with the Northamptonshire regiment during this period has never been substantiated.

George Joseph Smith (1872–1915), by unknown photographer

As far as is known, Smith's first and only legal wife was Caroline Beatrice (*b*. 1879), daughter of Edward Thornhill, bootmaker, of Leicester. The two were married there on 17 January 1898, with Smith using the name George Oliver Love. Smith soon led his bride into crime. By providing her with false references he secured positions for her in domestic service in London and on the south coast and then induced her to steal valuables from the households in which she worked. On 9 January 1901, however, he was convicted at Hastings of receiving goods stolen by his wife and sentenced to two years' imprisonment. Thereafter Smith became a professional bigamist. His technique was to ensnare lonely and vulnerable women with promises of matrimony and then to desert them, before or after marriage, as soon as he had gained possession of their money. Between the Thornhill marriage and his last arrest in 1915 he married at least seven women. With only one did he maintain a lasting relationship. The exception was Edith Mabel (*b*. 1878), *née* Pegler, whom Smith married, under his real name, on 30 July 1908 at Bristol. He returned to her between his other marriages, accounting for his long absences by pretending to be an antiques dealer whose business necessitated extended trips around the country and abroad.

Smith murdered three brides. Using the name Henry Williams, he married the first of these, Bessie Constance Annie Mundy (*b*. 1875), at Weymouth on 26 August 1910.

Bessie had inherited a fortune of about £2500 upon the death of her father, George Barclay Mundy, a bank manager at Warminster, but the money was invested in gilt-edged securities and managed for her by a family trust. In May 1912 the couple rented a house at 80 High Street, Herne Bay, in Kent. Smith took legal advice as to how he might secure possession of his wife's legacy and on 8 July he and Bessie executed wills in favour of one another. Two days later Smith brought Bessie to the surgery of Dr F. A. French, a local physician, and told him that she had had a fit. French prescribed bromide of potassium as a sedative. When the doctor last saw Bessie alive, on the afternoon of 12 July 1912, he thought she looked 'in perfect health'. But the next morning he was summoned to Smith's house and found her dead in the bath. An inquest was held before Rutley Mowll, coroner for east Kent, on 15 July. Concluding that 'Mrs Williams' had drowned in the bath after suffering an epileptic fit, the jury returned a verdict of death by misadventure. Smith obtained probate of his wife's will in September and the securities held in trust for her were paid into his hands.

Neither of the subsequent murder victims had substantial financial resources, so Smith persuaded them to take out life insurance. This apart, his procedure was almost identical to that in the Mundy case. The brides were whisked off to places where they were unknown, their uncertain health was established by visits to local doctors, and then they were drowned in their baths. Under his real name he married Alice Burnham (*b.* 1888), daughter of Charles Burnham, a fruit grower of Aston Clinton in Buckinghamshire, on 4 November 1913 at Portsmouth. After she had insured her life for £500 and made a will in Smith's favour, he took her to Blackpool where, on 12 December 1913, he drowned her in the bath at their lodgings at 16 Regent Road. Smith persuaded his last victim, a clergyman's daughter named Margaret Elizabeth Lofty (*b.* 1876), to insure her life for £700. He married her, under the name John Lloyd, on 17 December 1914 at Bath, and murdered her the very next day, at 14 Bismarck Road, Highgate. Inquest juries returned verdicts of accidental death in both cases. Smith realized £506 from the insurance paid under Alice Burnham's will but was not given the opportunity to benefit from that of Margaret Lofty.

Smith's arrest resulted from a report of the Lofty inquest that appeared in the national press. It was seen by Charles Burnham, Alice's father, and by Joseph Crossley, the son-in-law of her Blackpool landlady, and although the names were different both noted the striking similarity between the two cases and communicated their suspicions to the police. On 22 June 1915 Smith was eventually brought to trial at the central criminal court for the murder of Bessie Mundy and, notwithstanding a spirited defence by Edward Marshall Hall, was convicted and sentenced to death. He was hanged at Maidstone Prison on 13 August 1915 and buried there.

Smith stood 5 feet 9 inches in height and moved in what was described as a 'military walk'. He had brown hair and a fair complexion and sometimes sported a ginger moustache. Cruel and unscrupulous, he nevertheless attracted a succession of naïve and impressionable women. One of his bigamously married brides spoke of the hypnotic power of his eyes. Much is explained, however, by his genteel appearance, his pretensions to independent means, and his capacity for unctuous flattery.

PHILIP SUGDEN

Sources E. R. Watson, ed., *Trial of George Joseph Smith* (1922) • A. F. Neil, *Forty years of man-hunting* (1932) • E. Marjoribanks, *The life of Sir Edward Marshall Hall* (1929) • D. G. Browne and E. V. Tullett, *Bernard Spilsbury: his life and cases* (1951) • G. R. Sims, 'The Bluebeard of the bath', *Pearson's Weekly* (21 Aug–23 Oct 1915) • F. J. Lyons, *George Joseph Smith: the brides in the bath case* [1935] • A. La Bern, *The life and death of a ladykiller* (1967) • b. cert. • m. cert. [Sarah Annie Falkner]

Archives PRO, MEPO. 3/225B; CRIM. 1/154–155; HO. 144/1404/273877; HO. 144/1405/273877; DPP. 1/43 | FILM BFI NFTVA, documentary footage

Likenesses double portraits, photographs (with Bessie Mundy), Hult. Arch.; repro. in *Daily Mirror* (24 March 1915) • photograph, Syndication International; repro. in La Bern, *Life and death*, facing p. 109 • photographs, repro. in Watson, ed., *Trial of George Joseph Smith*, facing p. 51 [*see illus.*]

Wealth at death bought and sold various properties: Watson, ed., *Trial*, appx 7, 326 (listing those in Bristol) • however, so poor at trial that solicitors attempted to raise money for defence by selling his story to press (vetoed by home secretary)

Smith, George Murray (1824–1901), publisher, businessman, and founder of the *Dictionary of National Biography*, was born on 19 March 1824 at 135 Fenchurch Street, London, the oldest son and second of the six children of George Smith (1789–1846), stationer and publisher, and his wife, Elizabeth Murray (1797–1878), daughter of Alexander Murray, London glassware manufacturer. His parents were both of Scottish origin. From about 1873 Smith informally adopted Murray as his middle name as a tribute to his mother, and bestowed the name on all his children.

Family background and early life The son of a small landholding farmer in north-west Scotland, George Smith's father first began his working life as an apprentice to the Elgin bookseller and banker Isaac Forsyth. He migrated to London in 1812 and was initially employed by the publisher Charles Rivington, and subsequently became a clerk for John Murray at Albemarle Street. A sober and devout man, Smith senior soon acquired the capital and expertise to establish a stationery business in partnership with another recent arrival from Banff, Alexander Elder (1790–1876), with whom he took up premises at 135 Fenchurch Street in 1816.

Within the year Smith and Elder had begun publishing on a modest scale, their first title the anonymous *Recollections of a Ramble during the Summer of 1816*. For the first few years the firm's publishing policy was of necessity conservative, and few further titles were produced. After several years of cautious expansion, however, Smith and Elder found themselves in 1824 in a position to move to more generous premises at 65 Cornhill. Thereafter publishing activity began steadily to increase.

The turning point came with the acquisition in 1827, from the neighbouring firm of Lupton Relfe of 13 Cornhill, of the rights to publish the popular literary annual

George Murray Smith (1824–1901), by George Frederic Watts

Friendship's Offering. Under the editorship of Thomas Pringle, Charles Knight, and Leitch Ritchie, the annual became over the next two decades the backbone of the Smith and Elder list, securing contributions from an impressive array of author celebrities, including Byron, Coleridge, Mrs Hemans, Macaulay, Ruskin, Southey, and the young Tennyson. Its publication is among some of the son's earliest memories:

> For two or three days before its appearance everybody remained, after the shop had closed. Tables were set out, and we sealed up each copy in a wrapper. When the work was all over we were regaled with wine and cake, and sang songs. (Smith)

At its height the *Friendship's Offering* is reputed to have had a circulation of 10,000, the increased income and reputation generated by its success allowing the firm to branch out into a number of new publishing markets.

Between 1831 and 1835 Smith and Elder also published the annual *Comic Offering*, edited by Louisa Sheridan, including illustrations by Robert Seymour, later to achieve fame as the originator of *The Pickwick Papers*. 'The capital of the firm during these years was limited', Smith later recalled, 'but its courage was high' (Smith). One daring, though largely unsuccessful, experiment was the launch of the Library of Romance, a series of fifteen volumes of cheap fiction which appeared under the editorship of Leitch Ritchie between 1833 and 1835. Purporting, in the words of its editor, to break 'the mischievous prejudice which prevails in the trade against works in less than three volumes', the library was several decades ahead of its time, its financial failure owing more to its uninspiring subject matter than its novel 6*s*. format.

By the 1840s the firm had developed a reputation for finely produced books, largely in consequence of their investment in lavishly illustrated works, usually at the instigation of Elder, who harboured a personal enthusiasm for the fine arts. Early examples include *The Byron Gallery* (1833), Clarkson Stanfield's *Coastal Scenery* (1836), and *The Oriental Portfolio* (1840). With the first volume of *Modern Painters* in 1843, Smith and Elder became publishers for John Ruskin, a connection that was to continue for many years.

Another important niche exploited early on by the company was for colonial reading matter, titles appearing in the 1830s and 1840s indicating a close attention to a clearly focused overseas market. *Facts to Illustrate the Character of Indian Natives*, *China Opened*, *Van Diemen's Land as a Place of Emigration* are all typical and demonstrate something of the geographical extent of Smith and Elder's colonial interests throughout this period. It was also at this time that they began to earn themselves a reputation for scientific publishing, among the most notable titles being a nine-volume edition of Humphry Davy's *Works* (1838). Andrew Smith's *Illustrations of Zoology in South Africa* appeared in several volumes (1838–47), as did a number of works by the young Charles Darwin, including *Zoology of the Voyage of the Beagle* (1840–48). Although the company did not achieve its greatest success until several years later under the second George Smith, the reputation and connections that had been built up by the original partners during these early years were to stand him in good stead, providing the firm base on which the spectacular triumphs of the 1860s and 1870s were built.

In 1820 Smith senior had married Elizabeth Murray, also from Elginshire, and it was above the shop at Fenchurch Street that their eldest son was born in 1824. At the age of six the child had suffered a near fatal attack of 'brain fever' and, advised by the family physician to treat the child with utmost care, the parents appear to have treated him thereafter with inordinate forbearance. George and Elizabeth Smith attempted to provide for their eldest son advantages that had not been theirs. Initially he was sent to a boarding-school at Rottingdean and at ten attended Merchant Taylors' School, London. Thereafter he went to a school at Blackheath, and with his younger brother attended the City of London School in 1837.

Although he later blamed his inauspicious school career on bad teaching, Smith nevertheless appears to have perpetually tried the patience of his masters. A fractious child, he later recounted his disruptive influence on his classmates, early on earning himself a reputation for fighting. Despite this, he seems to have acquired a fair knowledge of Latin and managed to cultivate a talent for chemistry and mathematics. When the inevitable expulsion came—he was prematurely withdrawn at the beginning of the Easter vacation in 1838—it was with his exasperated master's recommendation that the child be sent to sea.

Throughout these years Smith appears to have been closest to his mother, who was more indulgent, and to his mind more intelligent, than his father. Although she harboured hopes for him of university followed by a career at the bar, the son was at the age of fourteen taken into the family firm. From childhood he seems to have had a natural interest in commercial ventures, and by all accounts had little trouble channelling his otherwise wayward energy into his new-found business career.

At about this time the two founders took on a third partner. Patrick Stewart (1808–1852), the son of a prominent Church of Scotland minister, was to join the firm as a junior in 1838, from which time the business became styled Smith, Elder & Co. Stewart, whose guardian was a chief partner in a leading Calcutta merchants, brought with him valuable contacts in the imperial trade, and thereafter the firm found itself engaging in an increased number of overseas speculations.

One of Smith's earliest memories was of the company's dealings with the intrepid entrepreneur Lieutenant Thomas Waghorn (1800–1850), who in 1829 had established the overland route to India. In the 1830s Smith and Elder acted as Waghorn's postal agents, later publishing several of his works, including *Waghorn's Guide Overland to India* (1842). His father's refusal to allow young Smith to ride with Waghorn on the leg between Paris and Marseilles was a disappointment that stayed with him. Later, as proprietor of the *Cornhill Magazine*, Smith was responsible for immortalizing Waghorn in the publication of an account by Thackeray of the adventurer's exploits entitled 'From Cornhill to Cairo'.

To Smith his new master was 'a young man of social tastes and … brilliant gifts' and he admired him greatly (Smith). Stewart became a liveryman of the Clothworkers' Company in March 1837 and in May 1838 took on Smith as apprentice for seven years, without salary as was the custom. At his father's insistence Smith began under Stewart to learn the trade from the bottom up, and soon acquired a range of manual skills, from quill-making to binding. One of the first tasks with which he was entrusted, and from which he later said he learned most about business practice, was to enter up overseas correspondence into copybooks. As he later recalled 'my business hours were from 7.30 in the morning till 8 o'clock in the evening, with half an hour for breakfast, an hour for dinner, and half an hour for tea' (ibid.). Despite such 'needlessly long' hours, Smith continued to find time for recreation. His dinner hours were often spent on horseback at a riding school in Finsbury Square, a pastime that he enjoyed all his life.

It was also at this time that Smith allegedly began to cultivate a taste for 'good' literature. Through Leigh Hunt, for whom he soon published several works, he was introduced to the Museum Club, a select dining club which met weekly near the Strand, and which included the writers Douglas Jerrold, G. H. Lewes, and 'Father Prout'. 'The wit was brilliant, the jokes abundant, the laughter uproarious', Smith later recalled; 'often I came away from a meeting of the club with sides which were literally sore with laughter' (Smith).

Early career In the intervening years the publishing side of the business continued to prosper, and some time in the early 1840s Smith persuaded his father to entrust him with £1500 to speculate on his own publishing ventures. His first two experiments under this arrangement were to publish in 1844 R. H. Horne's *New Spirit of the Age* and Mrs Baron Wilson's *Our Actresses*, both moderately successful.

When his indentures expired in 1846, Smith took up his freedom of the Stationers' Company by patrimony and, following the death of his father and the retirement of Elder in the same year, found himself running the company in partnership with Stewart, who had by this time assumed responsibility for the foreign branch. A major crisis hit the firm only two years later, when Smith discovered that Stewart had for several years been misappropriating a large proportion of the company's profits. After being confronted by his younger partner, the disgraced Stewart was stripped of his partnership and, though he remained with the company for another two or three years, left eventually for India where in 1852 he committed suicide. Deeply affected by the débâcle, Smith devoted a whole chapter of his memoirs to what he called this 'business cyclone', relating that he 'could not, at first, tell whether the firm was solvent or hopelessly insolvent … it was only by limiting my expenditure within the narrowest possible limits, and by working like a slave, that I could pull the business through' (Smith).

For the next few years Smith, then barely into his twenties, supported his mother and sisters by taking on sole responsibility for running the firm. Smith recounts that it was not unusual for him to work until four in the morning and, from time to time, for up to twenty-two hours at a stretch. Dramatic action was called for, and one of the first decisions that the new proprietor took to set the house in order was to terminate his father's liberal publishing arrangements with the infuriatingly prolific G. P. R. James. In the past three years the firm had published no fewer than twenty-seven volumes by James, who wrote so fast, according to Smith, that there was at any given time a backlog of three or four manuscripts in the safe awaiting publication. One of the shrewdest of Smith's decisions in his early working life was to appoint William Smith Williams (1800–1875) as literary adviser in 1847. In Leonard Huxley's words it was Williams 'who was to hold the literary helm' for the next thirty years (Huxley, 54). From the first, Williams played an instrumental role; he had a considerable hand in one of Smith's earliest coups and perhaps the single most important decision of his early career, the purchase of *Jane Eyre* (1847), which arguably made his reputation as a publisher overnight. The stories of the arrival of the fascinating manuscript and of the subsequent visits of Charlotte Brontë to London, where Smith introduced the novelist to her admired Thackeray, are now well known. After the novel's success Smith continued to cultivate his relationship with its author. In 1849 he oversaw the publication of *Shirley*, and over the next few years letters and packages were regularly sent between Cornhill and Haworth. Brontë soon became a close family friend, staying in the Smiths' home on four further occasions; although both Brontë and Smith continued to deny any intimate relationship, there is evidence for some romantic attachment during these years. It is common knowledge that Smith provided Brontë with the inspiration for the character of Dr John in *Villette*, a novel he published in 1852.

It was during this period that Smith began to build up the impressive literary list for which he would later be most famous. The year 1851 had seen the publication of the first volume of Ruskin's *Stones of Venice*, which was followed by a string of critical successes, with Thackeray's *Esmond* (1852) and Leigh Hunt's *Imagination and Fancy* (1852) among the most notable. In 1857, two years after the death of Brontë, Smith published *The Professor*, the manuscript of which the firm had originally declined a decade before; and in the same year Smith published Elizabeth Gaskell's highly successful *Life of Charlotte Brontë*, in which several references to his relationship with the novelist appeared.

On 11 February 1854 Smith married Elizabeth Blakeway (1825–1914), the daughter of a London wine merchant, having met her at a society ball only three months earlier. The couple spent their honeymoon at Tunbridge Wells and later went on to Paris where, ever diligent, Smith continued to work throughout. As he later recalled, 'the charm and exhiliration of our honeymoon did not lull my business faculties into a slumber' (Smith) and, much to the consternation of his young wife, Smith regularly took time to answer the Indian mail and keep up with business developments at home. It was while he was overseas that news broke of the Australian goldrush, prompting Smith to order a consignment of revolvers for export. 'I told my wife' by way of explanation, he later wrote, 'that we may as well extract the expenses of our honeymoon from Australian gold' (ibid.).

Elizabeth Blakeway's beauty was legendary and her 'gifts of mind and character', records Huxley, were no less gracious than her outward presence (Huxley, 82). For the first years of their marriage the couple lived at 112 Gloucester Terrace, London, the home Smith had formerly shared with his mother, and moved in 1859 to 11 Gloucester Square. By all accounts, soon after their marriage Elizabeth Smith took a sympathetic interest in her husband's business activities, providing valuable support and encouragement throughout the rest of his life.

The years of success It was probably through his relationship with the Blakeways that Smith met the man who became his business partner for two decades. Henry Samuel King (1817–1878), who had married Elizabeth Blakeway's sister in 1850, joined the firm as partner for overseas trade three years later in order to allow Smith to concentrate fully on the publishing side of the business. By the time that he arrived in London, King had made himself a reputation for revolutionizing the Brighton book trade through his efficient distribution methods, and under his direction the firm continued to strengthen the colonial connections on which it was coming increasingly to depend. Soon the firm employed 150 clerks to oversee its continually expanding operations as supplies of goods from scientific instruments to newspapers flowed through its agencies at Java, Bombay, and west Africa. According to Sidney Lee 'the widening range of the firm's dealings with distant lands … rendered records of travel peculiarly appropriate to its publishing department' (*DNB*). One consequence of success overseas was increased mutual support between the publishing business and the imperial trade, so far more colonial titles were published. Two of the most successful were the *Overland Mail*, a weekly gazette launched in 1855 to carry British news to the colonies, and the complementary *Homeward Mail*, launched in 1857. Book titles published in these years also indicate attention to several overseas niche markets. Titles such as Cunningham's *Buddhist Monuments in India* (1854), Meadows's *Chinese and their Rebellions* (1856), and McRae's *Manual of Plantership in British Guiana* (1856), for instance, suggest something of the firm's extending geographical reach in its colonial interests throughout the decade.

Such a heavy overseas investment eventually rendered the company vulnerable, and ultimately led to a second financial crisis in 1857. As Smith recalled,

> The Indian Mutiny cost me a fortune. It not merely wrecked one great branch of our business. Our customers were mainly men in the army. We supplied them with pistols, saddles, provisions, books, equipment of every kind. … But in the Mutiny so many of our debtors were killed that a large amount was lost to us. (Smith)

Making a virtue of necessity, the resourceful Smith wasted no time in exploiting his colonial infrastructure even as it was falling apart. Within a year he had already published several titles relating to the mutiny itself. Harriet Martineau's *Suggestions towards the Future Government of India* appeared in 1858, followed later that year by John Chaplain's *Narrative on the Siege of Delhi*, Frederic Cooper's *The Crisis in the Punjab*, and William Edwards's *Personal Adventures during the Indian Rebellion*. In 1859 appeared Mrs Coopland's *Lady's Escape during the Mutinies of 1857*. Recovery after the mutiny appears to have been rapid, however, and while the company never again invested so heavily in the colonial book trade, within a year it had begun to bolster its already considerable reputation for literary publishing.

Perhaps the great *tour de force* of Smith's publishing career was in 1860 to launch the *Cornhill Magazine* and to appoint Thackeray as editor at a salary of £1000 per annum (it was doubled after the astronomical success of the first number). Shortly before its first appearance Thackeray insisted to Smith that 'the Magazine must bear my cachet you see and be a man of the world Magazine' (*Letters and Private Papers*, ed. Ray, 4.150), and in much the same way that the name of Dickens came to be associated with *Household Words*, in most minds the *Cornhill* indeed became 'Thackeray's magazine'. Behind the scenes, though, the editor knew who the real strategist was, and after the immediate success dubbed Smith 'the Carnot of our recent victories' (G. N. Ray, *Thackeray: the Age of Wisdom*, 1958, 300).

Essentially, Smith had arranged a division of labour that would allow him complete financial control over the enterprise while capitalizing on the talents and reputation of a well-connected literary figure. With Thackeray as editor, the publisher knew that he could attract established literary names in ways that a mere businessman could not. This was certainly a factor in negotiations with Tennyson, who as a result was eventually persuaded to crown one of the first issues of the *Cornhill* with 'Tithonus'. Whereas Smith's supplications to the poet had fallen on deaf ears, it took Thackeray's charm and influence to secure the laureate's skills for the enterprise. While Smith reserved an equal power of veto over contributions, it was understood that in future he would concentrate on the business machinery and that Thackeray would be primarily responsible for acquiring talent. Such a partnership had other, more practical advantages of course: it allowed Smith to balance his books in the way that he saw fit and allowed Thackeray to divorce himself from the troublesome and undignified matter of cash transactions. In short, it was the editor's responsibility to court new authors; the publisher's was the more mundane job of paying them. It would be unfair to suggest that this was always the case—Elizabeth Gaskell much preferred dealing directly with Smith than Thackeray, for whom she had little regard—yet such an arrangement was at least true in recruiting that important property of the new magazine, Anthony Trollope. 'I will write to Trollope saying how we want him', the editor announced to his publisher shortly before the launch of the *Cornhill*, 'you on your side please write offering the cash' (*Letters and Private Papers*, ed. Harden, 2.906).

The professed aim of both editor and publisher was to acquire the best serial fiction of the day, combined with the most intelligent occasional writing. Its pages also included some of the most sumptuous illustrations of the period: artists employed in the early years included the likes of Du Maurier, Landseer, Leighton, and Millais. The cost involved in securing talent equal to the project's ambition was an extravagant gamble which remunerated its owner generously, its first issue selling no fewer than 110,000 copies. From then on, few authors could resist the prestige of getting their work into so many hands, and at such handsome prices. The list of contributors to the *Cornhill* was from the beginning formidable by any standard in the nineteenth century, the first number alone containing the first parts of Trollope's *Framley Parsonage*, Thackeray's *Lovel the Widower* and *Roundabout Papers*, and G. H. Lewes's *Studies in Animal Life*. For the second issue Smith secured the additional services of Elizabeth Gaskell and G. H. Sala. By the year's end Tennyson, Ruskin, Laurence Oliphant, George MacDonald, Anne Richie, Fitzjames Stephen, and Charles Lever had all thrown their talent behind the enterprise. The serialization of fiction, on which the *Cornhill* largely depended for its success, gave authors a great deal of power over the reading market, but it gave much more to the publisher. For his initial fee Smith almost always managed to secure the rights to the first book publication, and frequently earned himself first refusal on an author's next production.

Another additional advantage of owning such a prestigious vehicle was that it allowed the publisher to pursue new authors more aggressively than ever. After tempting Thackeray away from Bradbury and Evans, Smith soon made himself a reputation for similar acts of pecuniary generosity. In 1867 he offered George Eliot £10,000 for the rights to *Romola*; Eliot's former publisher, John Blackwood, regretfully admitted that he could not possibly compete with such an offer. After receiving the offer of £5000 for *The Ring and the Book*, an astonished Browning wrote to thank Smith for his 'liberal offer', so liberal in fact that the poet was anxious over whether 'you understand business, and will not harm yourself by your generosity' (Glynn, 184). Such was his financial security by this time that, as Smith himself recognized,

> I could afford to take risks for the gratification of my own literary tastes; and I could afford to pay prices to authors I liked … which an ordinary publisher, who lives solely on his publishing profits, would hardly have ventured. (Smith)

Not only did Smith earn himself a reputation for liberality in financial arrangements, but also for the extravagance of the gifts that he sent to authors with impeccable timing. No end of letters of thanks were sent to the Smith, Elder offices for unsolicited packets of books, bon-bons, paintings, and in one instance an ice-maker. In 1861 the *Saturday Review* commented sardonically that Smith's 'judicious liberality' had given considerable impetus to a genre in which 'things produced with so little trouble are so well paid for' ('Padding', *Saturday Review*, 19 Jan 1861, 63–4). G. A. Sala, who had personal dealings with the magazine, later told of his own firsthand experience of Smith's benevolence:

> Mr. George Smith was a very munificent publisher. In fact, they used to say that he sent Albert Smith as handsome a cheque for an article of such brevity that Albert … warned the too-bounteous bookseller that if he continued disseminating cheques of this kind he would come to poverty. … He was, moreover, a festive publisher, and once a month the contributors and the artists of the *Cornhill* were bidden to a sumptuous banquet, held at a house in Hyde Park Square. (Sala)

Smith's generosity as a social host was another important factor in his growing reputation for extravagance. The scale of the Pall Mall dinners held in honour of his writers became legendary, as were the Sunday 'at homes' at Smith's Hampstead residence, instigated at Thackeray's suggestion.

By the mid-1860s Smith had firmly established himself as one of the leading publishers of the day, his company's annual turnover having increased over the years from £59,500 in 1851 to £627,000 in 1866. The list of names coming to be associated with the firm in these years—Arnold, Trollope, Thackeray, Gaskell, Charles Reade, Wilkie Collins, the Brontës, the Brownings—reads like a who's who of Victorian literature. One of the greatest compliments Smith received in his professional life was when in 1867 he was entrusted with the queen's *Leaves from the Journal of our Life in the Highlands*. Not all was glamour, however; while much is often made of the literary successes of the 1850s and 1860s, there has been little, if any, recognition of the amount of 'bread and butter' publishing in which Smith engaged in the same period. It is not generally known that the publisher of *Jane Eyre* and *The Ring and the Book* was also responsible for bringing to birth such forgotten classics as Scrivenour's *Railways Statistically Considered*

(1851), Fitz-Wyggram's *Notes on Shoeing Horses* (1861), and Forsyth's *The Sporting Rifle and its Projectiles* (1863).

It was with the launch of the *Pall Mall Gazette* in 1865 that the company undertook its largest gamble to date. Some years before, Thackeray had suggested to Smith the idea of establishing a topical newspaper. The notion was revived in the publisher's mind largely at the instigation of Frederick Greenwood, a *Cornhill* contributor who had aspirations of founding a newspaper called the *Evening Review* along similar lines. After taking the idea unsuccessfully to the publisher of *Fraser's Magazine*, Greenwood turned to Smith with his proposal for a non-partisan publication that would, as its publisher later recalled, epitomize 'an honest and courageous daily journalism' (Smith). The aim of the newspaper, according to Sidney Lee, was to provide an afternoon paper that would 'bring into daily journalism as much sound thought, knowledge, and style as were possible … and to counteract corrupting influences' (*DNB*). So adamant was he about the need for scrupulousness that Smith insisted from the first that his books should not be reviewed in its pages. Providing a mixture of news, topical articles, and commentary, the *Gazette* benefited from Smith's ability to enlist the help of a wide circle of acquaintances for its pages. Under the editorship of Frederick Greenwood, whom Smith found to be 'a man full of ideas and energy' (Smith), the early numbers attracted contributions from the likes of Fitzjames Stephen, George Eliot, Matthew Arnold, John Morley, and Charles Reade. Despite this auspicious start, the paper was not an immediate financial success. Soon after its launch a morning edition was tried, but it failed to attract advertising and was dropped after three weeks. Over the next two years, however, sales gradually began to improve, and within five years the *Gazette* found itself on a firm financial footing, prompting Smith again to attempt in 1869 a morning edition in direct competition to *The Times*. After four months the morning experiment had again failed, despite intense efforts on the part of the paper's owner and editor. The profit that the evening edition continued to yield for the firm was nevertheless considerable, leaving Smith at the beginning of the 1870s with more speculative capital than ever.

Despite the continued financial success of the business as a whole, relations between Smith and his partner, King, became throughout the 1860s increasingly acrimonious, doubtless owing something to the latter's remarriage in 1863, less than three years after the death of his first wife, Smith's sister-in-law. The strain on business relations might be said to have begun when in late 1864 King had vetoed the firm's involvement in the *Pall Mall Gazette*, after which the responsibility for the newspaper had passed exclusively into Smith's hands. It is often assumed that it was his Conservative political sympathies that caused Smith's partner to distance himself from the venture. Personal circumstances probably also intervened, and from then on relations became increasingly strained. In 1868 it was decided that the company should be divided, with Smith taking the publishing business to 15 Waterloo Place and King remaining at Cornhill to continue supervising the overseas agency. A contemporary who witnessed the weekly meetings between the feuding partners recalled how

> on alternate Wednesdays Smith would go to Cornhill and King would come to Waterloo Place to settle their partnership affairs. … The brothers-in-law, who detested each other, would meet in the parlour and stiffly bow, take chairs, discuss the business of Smith, Elder, and Co., rise and, again bowing solemnly, would re-enter their respective spheres.

A condition of the separation was that King would agree not to engage in publishing for three years thereafter. Eventually he became a successful publisher in his own right, on his retirement leaving his publishing interests under the control of Kegan Paul & Co.

Later career Like many successful people, Smith appears from an early age to have been sustained by the stresses of hard work. Describing a regular working day in the 1860s, Smith writes:

> On Monday morning I went to my office in Pall Mall, and worked till five o'clock in the evening. I then walked or drove home to Hampstead, dined there; went at nine o'clock to the *Pall Mall Gazette* office—it was then a morning paper—and remained there till it had gone to press—which sometimes was not till six o'clock or even later. I then went to Waterloo Place, where I had a bedroom fitted up; took a cup of soup and went to bed. I slept for two or three hours; rose, took my bath and breakfast; the clerks came in with letters, etc. I dictated the replies and decided all business. I worked in this way till five o'clock; then I went to Hampstead Heath to dine, back again to the *Pall Mall Gazette* office and so *da capo*. (Smith)

Having worked ceaselessly throughout the first twenty-five years of his professional life, Smith found himself at forty-five with a personal fortune and with the social cachet that he had for years pursued. In 1861 he was elected to the Reform Club, his candidature proposed by Sir Arthur Buller and seconded by Thackeray, and in 1865 he joined the Garrick, nominated by Trollope and Wilkie Collins. Always keen to combine sociability with business interests Smith could now for the first time in his life concentrate all of his energies on the publishing that he so much enjoyed. With time on his hands, however, Smith found himself almost immediately in a state of nervous collapse. 'I was like a man who stepped out of his own skin', he writes; 'My condition was morbid to an almost lunatic degree' (Smith). It is likely that the near sudden relaxation of his responsibilities precipitated severe depression, a condition that lasted for the next two years. Various medical remedies were tried and even overseas travel was attempted as an antidote, all to no avail. So severe was his illness that those close to him feared for his life. It was only when, at the suggestion of a lawyer friend, he launched himself into a new business venture that the clouds began to clear. In 1870 Smith took on a partnership with the shipping firm Bilbrough & Co., which thereafter became styled Smith, Bilbrough & Co. Relishing the pressures of decision-making that his new position required, and amused by the new range of personalities with which the shipping business brought him into contact, Smith's recovery was rapid.

Income derived from his publishing successes, not least the *Pall Mall Gazette*, had by this stage provided Smith with the means to invest in a range of business interests and to indulge in virtually any scheme that caught his imagination. His status as shipowner brought with it an opportunity to become an underwriter at Lloyds, a post he soon relinquished owing to its relative low yield. By far the most profitable venture in which Smith was ever engaged involved buying the Apollinaris Company in 1880 to import German mineral water. The shares yielded an average annual profit of £30,000, and Smith sold them between 1897 and 1898 for £600,000. In less than twenty years Apollinaris had yielded him a record profit of £1,500,000.

Like many Victorian businessmen, Smith's sense of social responsibility was heightened by his financial success. In the late 1870s one of Smith's sisters had involved herself in Canon Barnett's philanthropic schemes to provide housing for the poor. Shocked by conditions he had witnessed in the East End, Smith was persuaded to finance the building of a block of low-rent residences in London's George Square Yard in 1883. While the initial outlay was considerable, Smith calculated that by charging a nominal rent the properties would nevertheless yield an annual return of 5 per cent. 'In this way', he reflected, 'the poor would have been helped without any loss of self-respect to themselves; and charity would be shown to have all the recommendations of a sound business investment!' (Smith). Although Smith attributed the eventual failure of the scheme to his unduly generous benevolence, it is more likely that a combination of inefficiency and gradual neglect caused the buildings to be sold off in 1891.

In the meantime the publishing branch went from strength to strength. Never one to rest on past victories, Smith guided the firm into a major new niche market when in 1873 he took on Ernest Hart to advise on developing medical publishing. Apart from an extensive list of monographs, one of their first undertakings was the highly regarded *London Medical Record*, which was followed a year later by the launch of the *Sanitary Record*.

When William Smith Williams retired in 1875 Smith appointed James Payn as literary adviser. Payn's gifts lay at the popular end of the literary market, and under his direction the publishing department continued to extend its sphere of influence in that direction, particularly in fiction. Influential authors who joined the firm under Payn included Henry James, whose *Daisy Miller* and *Washington Square* appeared in the *Cornhill* in 1878 and 1880 respectively. Having published Thomas Hardy's *Far from the Madding Crowd* in the *Cornhill* in 1873, Smith was also responsible for bringing *The Mayor of Casterbridge* to light in 1886. The year 1880 brought Richard Jefferies to the list, when his *Hodge and his Masters* caused a sensation. Thereafter Jefferies published all his books with the firm. In 1887 began George Gissing's association with the company, the year in which *Thyrza* was published. One of Smith's final and most spectacular coups was in 1888 to acquire Mrs Humphry Ward's phenomenally successful *Robert Elsmere*, a book in which he took personal interest, given that Mrs Ward was niece of his long-time close friend Matthew Arnold.

In 1882 Smith arrived at the idea of commissioning the project with which his name and reputation became associated more than any other. The initial ambition—to produce a multiple-volume 'dictionary of universal biography'—was modified when, at the suggestion of Leslie Stephen, Smith was persuaded to restrict his aims to the nevertheless remarkably ambitious 'dictionary of national biography'. Late in 1882 the project was begun, Smith working closely with Stephen as editor. 'In every detail of the work's general management', reports Lee, 'he took keen interest and played an active part in it from first to last' (*DNB*).

It is significant that Smith's parting gesture to the reading world should be a scheme which allowed him to bring together his impulses towards literary excellence and social philanthropy in such a way as to vindicate the ideal of private benevolence. 'I liked the idea of a private individual undertaking a work which was really national', he confessed, 'and which outside England is only possible by virtue of the resources of the state' (Smith). For the final two decades of his life Smith spent the greater part of his energies helping to oversee what he viewed as the most significant of all his publications. Under his management sixty-three volumes of the *Dictionary of National Biography* appeared between 1885 and 1900, with remarkable punctuality at the rate of one every three months. Smith's own account of the task suggests something of the personal vigilance that was required to satisfy such a demanding production schedule:

> Sometimes—say about 4 o'clock in the morning—I would wake and perplex myself with fears that from a literary point of view the work might fail. I was haunted with a dread of inaccuracies. But on the whole the work has been very well done and I am proud of it. I venture to say that no other book involving the same amount of labour and anxiety has ever been published. Nobody who has not been behind the scenes, and witnessed the difficulties we have had to meet, can appreciate the real quality of the work. We have taken infinite pains; we have never grudged toil or expense. … There has been notably, too, a very fine spirit amongst the contributors, a loyalty to the interests of the Dictionary; a zeal to maintain its standard, a generous willingness to take infinite pains in its service. I suppose the sense that they were taking part in a great enterprise acted as some sort of an inspiration. They knew, too, that the Dictionary was not undertaken for commercial ends, nor designed to fill its originator's pocket. They were serving literature when writing for it. (Smith, quoted in Huxley, 186–7)

That he saw the scheme lose something in the region of £70,000 was inconsequential, he believed, to his overall purpose. As Lee pointed out, the *Dictionary of National Biography* more than any other scheme satisfied Smith's 'independence of temper' (*DNB*). Suspending his belief in market values and the profitability of excellence, his rationale for the dictionary was that it should constitute a repayment in kind to the nation that had provided him with a personal fortune and a long and busy life.

Final years Toward the end of his career Smith gradually withdrew from his duties. In 1880 the ownership of the *Pall Mall Gazette* passed to his son-in-law Yates Thompson, and in 1881 his eldest son, George Murray Smith, joined the firm. They were joined by his second son, Alexander Murray Smith, in 1890, and in 1894 by his other son-in-law, Reginald John Smith. Although he kept up an intense personal interest in the *Dictionary of National Biography*, Smith relinquished principal control of the firm thereafter to Reginald and Alexander, the first son having stepped down owing to ill health in 1890. The changing commercial landscape that faced the firm at the turn of the century, Smith himself realized, was almost as radically different as his had been from his father's, publishers now going in hot pursuit of materials in ways that made even this most acquisitive of Victorian businessmen marvel at 'the difference between the old and the new régime' (Smith). The same careful nurturing of fresh literary talent continued to be a governing principle at Waterloo Place, even after his departure, and led to the acquisition of work by emerging talents at the end of the century, including J. M. Barrie, Arthur Conan Doyle, and Robert Louis Stevenson.

After spending his life bringing the literary labour of others to light, Smith in retirement had time to turn to literary work of his own. In the early 1890s he began compiling his 'Recollections of a long and busy life', a fascinating and genial account which—apart from four chapters prepared for the *Cornhill Magazine* with the editorial assistance of the Australian writer William Fitchett—remained largely unpublished. Not a work of great literary skill, the 'Recollections' nevertheless conveys a lively mind, full of tact and intelligence, if a little overbearing in its opinions. It provided the principal source for Lee's lengthy memoir of Smith that prefaced the first supplement to the *Dictionary of National Biography*, and later for Leonard Huxley's *The House of Smith Elder*.

In later life Smith received public recognition for his publishing achievements, and was awarded an MA in 1894 from the University of Oxford for services to English literature. Other honours followed: in May 1900 his role in completing the dictionary was honoured by a small dinner which the prince of Wales attended, and on June 30 a banquet, attended by the great and the good, was held for Smith and his contributors at the Mansion House.

With the exception of the extended bout of depression between 1868 and 1870, and despite the diagnosis some years earlier of a mild heart condition, Smith throughout his life enjoyed relatively good health. In or around 1895, however, he was found to be suffering from what Lee calls a 'troublesome ailment which he bore with great courage and cheerfulness' (most probably a form of cancer). Over the next five years the condition grew worse, necessitating an operation which took place at his home in Park Lane on 11 January 1901. Although the surgery was deemed successful at the time, Smith remained weak, and consequently requested a move to Byfleet, Surrey, in March, in the hope of convalescing in the country. After a continued decline, he died at St George's Hill, Byfleet, of a heart attack brought on by septic absorption on 6 April 1901. He was buried five days later in Byfleet churchyard.

The posthumous tributes were overwhelmingly laudatory. One of the many letters of condolence came to his widow from Lord Rosebery, who wrote of his 'admiration … for Mr. Smith as the founder of the greatest literary monument of the Victorian era [the *Dictionary of National Biography*] and … the publisher of *Jane Eyre*'. Smith was survived by his wife (to whom he bequeathed the dictionary) and children, three girls and two boys. At Reginald Smith's death in 1916 the assets of Smith, Elder & Co. were acquired by John Murray, except that of the dictionary, which passed, at Elizabeth Smith's request, to Oxford University Press.

Of the few images of Smith that have survived, the earliest is a portrait, now at the Brontë Parsonage Museum, showing him in his twenties. Apart from the look of serious determination, there is nothing particularly remarkable about his appearance. A more striking portrait, by George Frederic Watts, shows a middle-aged man with thinning hair and an impressive full beard. A third image, painted by John Collier in 1901, and now owned by the National Portrait Gallery, shows a balding but dignified and handsome man, with neatly groomed white beard and moustache. BILL BELL

Sources G. M. Smith, 'Recollections of a long and busy life', NL Scot., MS 23191 • *DNB* • [L. Huxley], *The house of Smith Elder* (1923) • J. W. Robertson Scott, *The story of the Pall Mall Gazette* (1950) • C. Redway, 'Some reminiscences of publishing fifty years ago', *The Bookman* (1891), 186 • J. Glynn, *Prince of publishers: a biography of George Smith* (1986) • *The letters and private papers of William Makepeace Thackeray*, ed. G. N. Ray, 4 vols. (1945–6) [with 2 vol. suppl., ed. E. F. Harden (1994)] • G. A. Sala, 'Things I have seen and people I have known', *Daily Telegraph* (4 March 1893), 4 • *CGPLA Eng. & Wales* (1901) • d. cert.

Archives John Murray (Publishers), London, corresp. and ledgers • NL Scot., corresp. and business MSS, incl. TS memoir • University of North Carolina, Chapel Hill, North Carolina, corresp. and company file copies, special collections, HM 791–821 | BL, corresp. • Bodl. Oxf., letters from Sir Theodore Martin, MS Eng lett e.307 • Bodl. Oxf., letters from Anthony Trollope, MS Eng lett d.413 • U. Birm., corresp. with Harriet Martineau, HM 791–821, 1206–1210 • U. Durham, Grey of Howick collections, letters to General Charles Grey

Likenesses J. Collier, oils, 1901, NPG • G. F. Watts, oils, unknown collection; copyprint, NPG [*see illus.*] • portrait, Brontë Parsonage Museum, Howarth, Yorkshire

Wealth at death £931,968 13*s*. 4*d*.: resworn probate, March 1902, *CGPLA Eng. & Wales* (1901)

Smith, George Murray (1859–1919), businessman and landowner, was born on 4 February 1859 at 3 Finsbury Circus, London, the son of George Murray *Smith (1824–1901), publisher and founder of the *Dictionary of National Biography*, and his wife, Elizabeth Blakeway (1825–1914). Educated at Harrow School, he was admitted sizar at Jesus College, Cambridge, on 1 October 1878 and graduated BA in 1882. He joined his father's publishing firm of Smith, Elder & Co. in 1881, but though he inherited the business flair for important undertakings, his heart was not in the more meticulous work of business letters and literary detail. Suffering from repeated illness, he was advised to live out of London, and he left the firm in 1890, his place being taken by his brother, Alexander Murray Smith.

On 22 October 1885 Smith married the Hon. Ellen, youngest daughter of Edward *Strutt, first Baron Belper; they had three sons and a daughter. The family settled into country life at West Leake, Nottinghamshire, where Smith became a captain in the South Nottinghamshire yeomanry and stood unsuccessfully as Unionist candidate for the Rushcliffe division of Nottinghamshire in 1895. In 1897 they moved to Gumley Hall, near Market Harborough, Leicestershire. This was prime hunting country and Smith was a keen follower of hounds, besides taking an interest in agriculture and the breeding of pedigree stock. He was active locally, a member of Leicestershire county council, vice-chairman of the Leicester Infirmary, and a member of the Market Harborough board of guardians. In 1901 he became a director of the Midland Railway, where he turned eagerly to railway management, mastering the departmental details so thoroughly in the subcommittees over which he successively presided that in 1911 he was unanimously elected chairman.

Smith steered the Midland through the difficult times of the First World War, when the administration was short-staffed, while undertaking other war duties. He served on a national service tribunal, on the committee of the Endsleigh Palace Hospital for Officers, and on a pensions committee. On 30 August 1918 he was appointed to the royal commission on decimal coinage but died suddenly at his sister's house—50 Park Street, Westminster—on 18 April 1919. His funeral took place at Gumley parish church, near Market Harborough, Leicestershire, on 24 April; a memorial service, attended by representatives of the railway industry, was held simultaneously at St Mark's, North Audley Street, Westminster. His eldest and youngest sons, Lieutenant Arthur Murray Smith, 1st Life Guards, and Lieutenant Geoffrey Murray Smith, Royal Fusiliers, had been killed in the war; his wife and daughter and their second son survived him. ANITA MCCONNELL

Sources *DNB* • *The Times* (21–2 April 1919) • *The Times* (25 April 1919) • L. Huxley, *The house of Smith Elder* (1923) • *WWW* • *The Times* (31 Aug 1918) • *CGPLA Eng. & Wales* (1919) • b. cert. • m. cert. • d. cert.

Wealth at death £315,744 3*s.* 9*d.*: probate, 3 July 1919, *CGPLA Eng. & Wales*

Smith, Sir George Reeves- (1863–1941), hotelier, was born in Scarborough, Yorkshire, on 17 July 1863, one of at least two sons of George Reeves-Smith, who was for a time manager of the Brighton aquarium. Educated at Brighton College, Reeves-Smith was apprenticed to Bordeaux wine merchants, Jean Calvert & Co., before training in the hotel industry. About 1890 he was appointed manager of the Victoria Hotel, Northumberland Avenue, London. By 1893 he was manager of the Berkeley Hotel, Piccadilly, which he subsequently purchased by forming a small syndicate in 1897, taking for himself the office of managing director.

Richard D'Oyly Carte, founder of the Savoy Hotel, sought to rebuild his management team after the departure of César Ritz and Auguste Escoffier. To secure the services of Reeves-Smith, he purchased the Berkeley Hotel in 1900 and appointed him managing director of the Savoy Company. Reeves-Smith held this office, together with that of vice-chairman of the Savoy Company, from 1916 until his death.

Sir George Reeves-Smith (1863–1941), by unknown photographer

Reeves-Smith's style of management was precise, for he was aware of the slightest derogation from high standards of housekeeping or service; yet he was innovative and capable of masterly delegation. Although apparently punctilious and conservative in manner and dress, he had a shrewd business appreciation of practical detail and people's tastes in leisure activities. Some idea of his skill may be gained from *Imperial Palace* (1930), a novel by Arnold Bennett based on the author's knowledge of the Savoy and its chief executive, and dedicated to Reeves-Smith.

Reeves-Smith founded the Hotels and Restaurants Association (1910) and was chairman of its executive (1910–41) and of its council (1931–41). He was connected with several industry-wide associations and committees, as well as being chairman of the London coronation accommodation committee (1937). He was involved in the Preston Hall settlement for tuberculous ex-servicemen in Aylesford, Kent (1919–25), and the British Sanatorium in Montana-Vermala, Switzerland. He was knighted in 1938 for service to the hotel industry, and in the same year he was made a chevalier of the Légion d'honneur. In 1939 he became a knight commander of the Order of the Crown of Italy.

On 16 August 1888 Reeves-Smith married Maud, daughter of Charles Hindle, a Brighton hotelier. They had a son, who was killed in the First World War, and a daughter. They lived in rooms, first in the Berkeley, then at Claridge's (also part of the Savoy group of hotels). Reeves-Smith was an inveterate buyer of books, and it was said that he bought a hotel in Seaford, Sussex, to accommodate his library. He died from pneumonia on 29 May 1941 in his rooms at Claridge's, survived by his wife.

TOM JAINE, *rev.*

Sources S. Jackson, *The Savoy* (1964) • private information (1993) • *The Times* (30 May 1941), 7d • d. cert. • *CGPLA Eng. & Wales* (1941) • Burke, *Peerage*
Likenesses photograph, repro. in Jackson, *The Savoy* [*see illus.*]
Wealth at death £55,409 19*s.* 1*d.*: probate, 28 Aug 1941, *CGPLA Eng. & Wales*

Smith, George Samuel Fereday (1812–1891), industrialist and canal manager, was born on 7 May 1812, at Tipton, Staffordshire, the elder son of the ironmaster Richard Smith (*d.* 1868), and his wife, Elizabeth, daughter of Samuel Fereday, the most prominent ironmaster of the region. Smith was educated at Charterhouse from 1821 to 1830 and Queen's College, Oxford, from 1830 to 1835, where he graduated in maths and physics. He also attended University College, London, and studied mining and geology in Germany.

After working as a railway engineer, Fereday Smith (as he was often called) was appointed deputy superintendent of the Bridgewater Trust at the age of twenty-four. The superintendent, James Loch, had tried to recruit his father, Richard Smith, then mine agent to the earl of Dudley. The son was available; the father was not. Appointed deputy superintendent, G. S. F. Smith served the trust in a senior managerial capacity for over fifty years. In his late thirties he enrolled as a student at the Inner Temple, and was called to the bar in 1852.

Fereday Smith became extremely prosperous, partly through his salary, which increased from £600 a year in 1837 to £1500 by 1864. On 5 March 1845 Smith married Mary Jane, daughter of Richard Hampson of Manchester, who had a private income of about £1000 a year. The couple had two daughters and a son. Smith and his wife benefited from the will of a maternal uncle, and also from that of his father, Richard Smith.

The Bridgewater Canal, administered by the trustees, faced growing competition from the railways, and Fereday Smith's influence was consistently exerted in favour of a strategy of meeting such competition with great vigour. He was a strong supporter of increased capital investment, particularly in terminal facilities at Liverpool, Runcorn, and Manchester, which he pursued against the reluctance of Loch. The results included the Egerton Dock at Liverpool, opened in 1840, to accommodate the trade in imported timber. Runcorn was developed from the late 1850s as a canal port for both coastal and sea-going ships. The salt trade from the River Weaver was facilitated by a new canal parallel to the Mersey, between Runcorn and Weston Point (1859). The Alfred Dock at Runcorn was completed in 1860 to handle the Irish grain trade, and in 1865–7 major improvements were made to the Mersey above Runcorn. Fereday Smith also decided to install the electric telegraph along the banks of the canal. He made a practice of delegating to subordinates and seeking their advice. The one policy issue on which he held firmly traditional views was that of steam traction, which he opposed.

Fereday Smith's firm stance against the railway companies was significant, in that from the mid-1840s a sale of the Bridgewater undertaking to railway interests was periodically contemplated by his trustees. Between 1855 and 1857 the North Staffordshire Railway made a serious attempt to lease the trust's properties, which Smith was instrumental in defeating. The death in 1855 of James Loch, usually suspicious of his subordinate's expansionist approach, considerably increased the influence of Fereday Smith. From that date he became, in effect, general manager, although nominally subject to Loch's less experienced successor, Algernon Egerton. Under Smith's guidance the profits of the canal and its carrying trade rose from £29,857 in 1855 to about £54,000 in 1871, and those of the Bridgewater collieries from £15,075 to about £34,500. Control of the canal passed to the Cheshire lines committee in 1872 following a further growth of railway competition in the 1860s. Smith stayed on until 1887, when the Manchester Ship Canal Company acquired the Bridgewater.

Fereday Smith had wide interests outside the trust. He was a fellow of the Geological Society and the Royal Geographical Society, and a member of the Chetham Society (historical and literary). In politics he was a Conservative, sitting as a member of the police commission in Manchester from 1839 to 1842, and later as a councillor from 1846 to 1849. His public service also included a spell as a borough magistrate, and an active association with both the Manchester Commercial Association, and then the chamber of commerce (after a merger in 1858). In the early 1870s Fereday Smith bought Grovehurst, a country house in Kent, and became high sheriff of the county in 1884. He died from influenza and exhaustion on 26 May 1891 at 7 Sackville Street, Piccadilly, London. Smith was survived by his wife. His son, Richard Clifford Smith, succeeded him as general manager of the Bridgewater Trust in 1887.

GERALD CROMPTON

Sources F. C. Mather, 'Smith, George Samuel Fereday', *DBB* • F. C. Mather, *After the canal duke: a study of the industrial estates administered by the trustees of the third duke of Bridgewater … 1825–1872* (1970) • C. Hadfield and G. Biddle, *The canals of north west England*, 2 vols. (1970) • T. R. Gourvish, *Mark Huish and the London–North Western Railway* (1972) • A. Redford and others, *Manchester merchants and foreign trade*, ed. A Redford, 1: *1794–1858* (1934) • d. cert. • *CGPLA Eng. & Wales* (1891)
Archives Northants. RO, Ellesmere-Brackley MSS • priv. coll., Loch-Egerton MSS
Wealth at death £174,127 1*s.* 11*d.*: resworn probate, Jan 1892, *CGPLA Eng. & Wales* (1891)

Smith, George Vance (1816?–1902), Unitarian minister and biblical scholar, the son of George Smith, a joiner and builder of Willington, near Newcastle upon Tyne, and his wife, Anne Vance, was born in October, probably in 1816 (he himself was not sure of the exact year), at Portarlington, King's and Queen's counties, where his mother was on a visit. Brought up at Willington, he was employed at Leeds, where his preparation for a college course was undertaken by Charles Wicksteed, then minister of Mill Hill Chapel. In 1836 he entered Manchester College, York, as a divinity student; in 1839–40 he was assistant tutor in mathematics. When the college moved to Manchester in 1840, he continued his studies there, graduating BA in 1841 at the University of London, to which the college was affiliated.

Smith's first ministry was at Chapel Lane, Bradford, where he was ordained on 22 September 1841. He then moved to King Edward Street Chapel, Macclesfield, in 1843, remaining there until 1846, when he was appointed vice-principal and professor of theology and Hebrew in Manchester (New) College, once again in Manchester. On the retirement of John Kenrick (1788–1877) from the principalship in 1850 Smith reluctantly accepted appointment as his successor. When the college moved to London in 1853, John James Tayler was made principal and Smith became professor of critical and exegetical theology, evidences of religion, Hebrew, and Syriac. He resigned in 1857, went abroad, and obtained at Tübingen the degrees of MA and PhD. In 1858 he settled in York as assistant and successor to Charles Wellbeloved at St Saviourgate Chapel, York.

In 1870, after Kenrick had declined to serve on the grounds of advanced age, Smith accepted the invitation of A. P. Stanley, dean of Westminster, to join the New Testament revision company. His participation in the celebration of the eucharist in Henry VII's Chapel, Westminster Abbey, on the morning of the first meeting of the company in June 1870 led to much high-church criticism (and to some from Unitarians). This 'act of desecration', giving 'that which is most holy to the dogs', as some Anglican extremists held it (*The Times*, 4 March 1902), led the upper house of the convocation of Canterbury, on the motion of Samuel Wilberforce, bishop of Winchester, to pass a resolution condemning the appointment to either of the revision companies of any person 'who denies the Godhead of our Lord', and affirming that anyone of that view should cease to act; a similar resolution was rejected by the lower house in February 1871. Smith bore all this with an inflexible calmness. His work as a reviser was diligent and conscientious, though he was often in a minority of one. In 1873 the University of Jena made him DD.

On 12 July 1843 Smith married Agnes Jane, second daughter of John Fletcher of Liverpool; they had three sons and a daughter. The eldest son, George Hamilton Vance (1848–1939), became minister at Dukinfield (1875–84), Bournemouth and Poole (1887–90), and Dublin (1890–1910). The second son, Philip Vancesmith (1854–1895), was minister at Hindley (1881–91). Mrs Smith died on 25 July 1893, and the next year he married on 14 September Elizabeth Anne (1846x8–1907), daughter of Edward Todd of Tadcaster. In July 1875 Smith left York for the ministry of Upper Chapel, Sheffield, but in September 1876 he accepted the principalship of the Presbyterian college, Carmarthen, an office he held until 1888, combining with it from 1877 the charge of Parc-y-felfed chapel, Carmarthen. After retiring from the active ministry in 1888, he lived first at Bath and later at Bowdon, Cheshire.

Among Unitarians, Smith's position was one of mild conservatism; hence he was more at home at Carmarthen College than he had been in the period at mid-century when Manchester College was moving towards a reconstructed Unitarianism sceptical of any authority other than that arising within the individual soul. As a translator, he published *The Prophecies Relating to Nineveh and the Assyrians* (1857), with notes on the effects of recent discoveries; and he continued (with John Scott Porter) Wellbeloved's work in *The Holy Scriptures of the Old Covenant* (1857–62) with 1 and 2 Samuel, Ezra, Nehemiah, Esther, Isaiah, Jeremiah, and Lamentations. His abridgement and translation of *The Credibility of the Evangelic History Illustrated* (1844) by F. A. G. Tholuck, professor at the University of Halle (published 1837), buttressed his own contribution to John Relly Beard's collection, *Voices of the Church* (1845), in refutation of the mythical theory of D. F. Strauss. He was an effective critic of orthodox views in *The Priesthood of Christ* (1843), two series of letters to John Pye Smith (1774–1851), the well-known Congregationalist theologian. *English Orthodoxy, as it is and as it might be* (1863) was addressed to a wider audience, as were *Eternal Punishment* (1865; 4th edn, 1875) and *The Bible and Popular Theology* (1865), revised under a slightly altered title in 1892, a commentary on certain Bampton lectures and other widely discussed works of theology which in the two editions strikingly indicates the altered religious context over a generation. Later textual studies are *The Prophets and their Interpreters* (1878) and *Texts and Margins of the Revised New Testament Affecting Theological Doctrine* (1881), relevant to his service in the revision company a decade earlier. Smith died at Cranwells, Cavendish Road, Bowdon, on 28 February 1902, and was buried in the graveyard of Hale Chapel, Hale, Cheshire, on 4 March. ALEXANDER GORDON, *rev.* R. K. WEBB

Sources *Christian Life* (8 March 1902) · V. D. Davis, *A history of Manchester College from its foundation in Manchester to its establishment in Oxford* (1932) · *The Times* (4 March 1902) · G. E. Evans, *Vestiges of protestant dissent* (1897) · m. certs. · d. cert.

Likenesses photograph, repro. in J. E. Manning, *A history of Upper Chapel, Sheffield* (1900), 140 · three photographs, DWL, trustees' album

Wealth at death £13,468 12*s.* 11*d.*: resworn probate, July 1902, *CGPLA Eng. & Wales*

Smith, George William Duff Assheton (1848–1904), quarry owner and landowner, was born on 17 May 1848 in London, the eldest son of Robert George Duff (*b.* 1819), of Wellington Lodge, Isle of Wight, and Mary Astley (*d.* 1874). He had two brothers, Charles Garden Duff (1851–1914) and Henry Assheton Duff (*b.* 1862), and a sister, Louisa Alice. He assumed the surname Assheton Smith (or Assheton-Smith) in 1859, when the Vaynol estate near Bangor in Caernarvonshire, including Dinorwig quarry, was bequeathed to him for his lifetime under the will of Matilda, widow of his great-uncle, Thomas Assheton Smith (1776–1858). He was educated at Eton College and

Christ Church, Oxford. In 1888 he married Laura Alice Stanhope Jones, daughter of Colin Stanhope Jones; they had one child, Enid.

Assheton Smith, who had a moustache and a serious countenance, inherited 36,000 acres of land with an annual rental income of £25,000. In his evidence to the royal commission on land in Wales and Monmouthshire in 1893, the agent Captain N. P. Stewart said that there were about 1600 farm tenants and cottagers on the estate and that about 100 cottages had been built in the previous fifteen years. Many quarrymen lived close to the quarry in Llanberis, but accommodation there was scarce and some of the men lodged in the quarry barracks, returning to homes in Anglesey at weekends. Before the introduction of a workers' train in 1895, many of the men travelled on velocipedes, open vehicles operated by foot or hand along the railway.

Assheton Smith, the squire of Vaynol, took an interest in the improvement of the estate and rarely visited London. He was an animal lover, a keen horseman, and a race-horse owner. He had a menagerie of wild animals in Vaynol Park, but this was given up before his death. His yacht, the *Pandora*, was used for fishing expeditions. He was high sheriff of Anglesey in 1872 and of Caernarvonshire in 1878, and was also a JP and the deputy lieutenant for Caernarvonshire. He supported a branch of the Primrose League in Caernarfon. As one of the wealthiest and largest property owners in Wales, he was an influential figure. The main source of his wealth was Dinorwig quarry, which dated from 1787 and was carved out of the south side of Elidir mountain at Llanberis.

Dinorwig quarry consisted of the early workings, including Allt Ddu, and the main quarry. Tramways ran along open galleries, which were at vertical intervals of about 75 ft, and there were two principal incline systems. Transport was by the Padarn Railway which superseded the Dinorwig tramway in 1843 and was converted to steam in 1848. Its 7 mile track ran from Gilfach-ddu, where in 1870 large workshops were sited, to Y Felinheli ('Port Dinorwic') on the Menai Strait. This harbour, half way between Bangor and Caernarfon, had a large basin and a dry dock where ship repairs were carried out. In 1852 a private branch connected Y Felinheli via the Bangor–Caernarfon Railway to the main-line system, but in 1882 most of the 90,000 tons of slate produced by the 2700 men at Dinorwig was being sent by sea, and in the 1890s the quarry had its own fleet of four steel-hulled screw-steamers.

When Assheton Smith took over the quarry in 1869, his quarrymen told him they would be 'quiet, honest and obedient', but in June 1874 all but eleven of them refused to give up membership of the newly created North Wales Quarrymen's Union (NWQU) and 2200 men were locked out for five weeks. Unwilling to lose profits in a buoyant slate market, Assheton Smith accepted trade unionism so long as it did not interfere with the rights of management. However, a depression in the slate industry led to wage cuts and a smaller workforce. The men resented the stricter discipline imposed by the new chief manager, Colonel James Wyatt, and in 1880 Assheton Smith put pressure on them to contract out of the Employers' Liability Act. After Wyatt's death in 1884, his successor, the Hon. W. W. Vivian, joined with the works manager John Davies in implementing new rules, which the quarrymen saw as an infringement of their liberty. In July and October 1885 groups of men were suspended for leaving early, and a mass meeting held in working hours resulted in a lock-out from 31 October.

When the quarry was reopened on 15 December, the men marched to the quarry and ordered the managers to leave for their own safety. The strikers resisted an appeal from W. J. Parry, the president of the NWQU, to abandon their rebellious attitude, but the exhaustion of their funds and an intervention by John Robinson of Tal-y-sarn quarry in Nantlle led to their surrender in February 1886. The disputed rules remained in force, and 300 men were dismissed. During the dispute Assheton Smith was much criticized by the Welsh radical press, and he incurred further hostility when at Caernarfon assizes in January 1886 he was found guilty of negligence for having accidentally shot and injured N. D. Lambert, a forester, who was acting as a game-beater for a shooting party. The jury rejected the victim's claim for £400 compensation and declared the £30 Assheton Smith had offered to be adequate.

The end of the dispute led to some improvement in labour relations at Dinorwig quarry. In June 1887 Assheton Smith paid the men's fares to London for the jubilee, and on his marriage in June 1888 he remitted six months of his tenants' rent and paid the fares and expenses of a day trip to Liverpool or Manchester for all his employees. Wages were raised by 5 per cent in 1895. Assheton Smith offered an interest-free loan to his friend Lord Penrhyn, in July 1897, to help him in the Penrhyn quarry dispute, but the offer was declined. In December 1901 Vivian retired and was succeeded by E. Neele. In May 1902 the prince of Wales stayed at Vaynol for his installation in Caernarfon as chancellor of the University of Wales, and the quarrymen were given a day's holiday plus payments of 6*s.* to those over twenty and 4*s.* to those under.

Assheton Smith died of heart disease at Vaynol on 22 November 1904 and was buried in the mausoleum in Vaynol Park. He was survived by his wife. The estate passed to his brother Charles Garden Duff, who assumed the surname Assheton Smith. JEAN LINDSAY

Sources J. Lindsay, *A history of the north Wales slate industry* (1974) • R. M. Jones, *The north Wales quarrymen, 1874–1922* (1981) • T. Nicholas, *Annals and antiquities of the counties and county families of Wales*, 2 vols. (1872) • J. I. C. Boyd, *Narrow gauge railways in north Caernarvonshire*, 3 (1986) • A. J. Richards, *A gazeteer of the Welsh slate industry* (1991) • 'Royal commission on land in Wales and Monmouthshire: first report', *Parl. papers* (1894), 36.1, C. 7439; 36.9, C. 7439-I; vol. 37, C. 7439-II • S. Turner, *The Padarn and Penrhyn railways* (1975) • *Slater's directory of north Wales, Cheshire and Shropshire with Liverpool* (1883) • J. Lindsay, *The great strike: a history of the Penrhyn quarry dispute of 1900–1903* (1987) • J. E. Griffith, *Pedigrees of Anglesey and Carnarvonshire families* (privately printed, Horncastle, 1914) • D. C. Carrington, *Delving in Dinorwig* (1994) • M. J. T. Lewis, ed., *The slate quarries of north Wales in 1873* (1987) • census returns, 1861 • *North*

Wales Chronicle (3 Dec 1904) · *North Wales Chronicle* (26 Nov 1904) · d. cert.
Archives Gwynedd Archives, Caernarfon, Dinorwic MS
Likenesses J. Wickens, photograph, repro. in *North Wales Chronicle* (17 Dec 1904) · photograph, Caernarfon RO, CHS/1081/5
Wealth at death £820,413 17*s*. 3*d*.: probate, 7 Dec 1904, *CGPLA Eng. & Wales*

Smith, Georgina Castle [*née* Georgina Meyrick; *pseud.* Brenda] (**1845–1933**), children's writer, was born on 9 May 1845 at 15 Cambridge Terrace, Bayswater, London, the fourth of eight children of a solicitor, William Meyrick (1809/10–1898), and his wife, Eliza, *née* James (*b.* 1817/18). She was a bookish child who suffered from hay fever and asthma. Her father appears in directories as tenant of a series of houses in Bayswater until 1872, when he disappears from them both as householder and as solicitor. It seems likely that he was the William Meyrick who was declared bankrupt on 5 June 1874, and that the appearance of Georgina Meyrick's first children's novel in December 1873, when she was twenty-eight, can be linked to a family financial disaster. Her father, who died abroad, apparently deserted the family.

Georgina Meyrick's first book, *Nothing to Nobody* (1873), published, like all her books, under the name Brenda, was a 'street arab' or 'waif' tale in the tradition of *Jessica's First Prayer* (1867) by Sarah Smith. In *Nothing to Nobody* a Sunday school teacher reforms an orphan called Daddy Long Legs, and its emphasis on practical philanthropy and its mildly evangelical Anglicanism are typical of the author's work. It was successful enough for Georgina to write another street arab tale in time for the following Christmas, a tale which became her most popular work. First advertised in December 1874, *Froggy's Little Brother* was a famous tear-jerker about two orphan boys. Froggy works as a crossing-sweeper to support his little brother Benny, but the climax is Benny's saintly death. It remained in print for most of the next fifty years, becoming a staple 'prize book', and was filmed in 1921. *Froggy* was illustrated by a young solicitor, Castle Smith (1849–1936), whom Georgina Meyrick married shortly afterwards (7 October 1875). They set up house at 49 Avenue Road, St John's Wood, London, and had five children. His forename was Castle, but his wife and family used the surname Castle Smith. Brenda continued publishing fairly steadily: thirteen children's books came out in the next fifteen years, then between 1890 and 1932 another eight books, including two novels for adult readers and a sequel (1914) to *Froggy's Little Brother*. Although she did not entirely abandon the street arab formula, and almost all her books incite the reader to philanthropy, many of her later stories focus on middle- and upper-class children. This is true of two of the most charming, *Five Little Partridges, or, The Pilot's House* (1885), about a middle-class family's annual migration to the seaside, which portrays (family tradition asserts) her own children, and *The Earl's Granddaughter* (1895), about the conversion of an upper-class girl to good works. The last contains a thinly disguised picture of the entire community in Lyme Regis, Dorset, to which town the Castle Smiths retired, and where at her home, the Corner Cottage, she died on 27 December 1933; she was buried in the Lyme Regis cemetery. CHARLOTTE MITCHELL

Sources memoir, priv. coll. · private information (2004) [P. Castle Smith, B. Barnikel] · C. Lennox-Boyd, 'Brenda and her works', *Signal*, 62 (May 1990), 114–30 · *The Times* (3 Jan 1934) · *Boyle's Court Guide* · *Law List* · b. cert. · m. cert. · Law Society, archives · bankruptcy petition book (1874), PRO, MS B6/179 · census returns, 1861, 1871, 1881 · D. Gifford, *The British film catalogue, 1895–1985: a reference guide*, [2nd edn] (1986) · wills of Georgina Castle Smith and Castle Smith · *CGPLA Eng. & Wales* (1934)
Archives priv. coll.
Wealth at death £971 18*s*. 8*d*.: probate, 1 Feb 1934, *CGPLA Eng. & Wales*

Smith, Gerard Edward (1804–1881), botanist and Church of England clergyman, was born at Camberwell, Surrey, the sixth son of Henry Smith. He entered Merchant Taylors' School in January 1814, and St John's College, Oxford, as Andrew's exhibitioner, in 1822; he graduated BA in 1829. Before being ordained he published his principal botanical work, *A Catalogue of Rare or Remarkable Phanogamous Plants Collected in South Kent* (1829). Consisting of just seventy-six pages, this work was arranged on the Linnaean system, dealt critically with several groups, and had five coloured plates drawn by the author.

Smith was vicar of St Peter-the-Less, Chichester, from 1835 to 1836, rector of North Marden, west Sussex, from 1836 to 1843, vicar of Cantley, near Doncaster, Yorkshire, from 1844 to 1846, perpetual curate of Ashton Hayes, Cheshire, from 1849 to 1853, and vicar of Osmaston by Ashbourne, Derbyshire, from 1854 to 1871. He died at Ockbrook, Derby, on 21 December 1881.

Smith was the first to recognize several British plants, describing *Statice occidentalis* under the name *S. binervosa* in 1831, and *Filago apiculata* in 1846. He contributed articles to the *Phytologist* and to the *Journal of Botany, British and Foreign* and formed a herbarium, which passed to University College, Nottingham, on his death. He was also the author of several short theological works, including a discussion of the relationship between religion and science—*Are the Teachings of Modern Science Antagonistic to the Doctrine of an Infallible Bible?* (1863).

G. S. BOULGER, *rev.* ALEXANDER GOLDBLOOM

Sources Desmond, *Botanists*, rev. edn, 636 · C. J. Robinson, ed., *A register of the scholars admitted into Merchant Taylors' School, from AD 1562 to 1874*, 2 (1883), 197 · Foster, *Alum. Oxon.* · *Journal of Botany, British and Foreign*, 20 (1882), 63
Archives Derby Museum and Art Gallery, catalogue of plants · NHM, scrapbook: Missionary Needlework, a volume of natural history drawings, notes, newscuttings, and photographs · RBG Kew
Wealth at death £10,641 19*s*. 11*d*.: probate, 28 Jan 1882, *CGPLA Eng. & Wales*

Smith, Gilbert Oswald [G. O., Jo] (**1872–1943**), footballer and schoolmaster, was born at Chesham House, Warham Road, Croydon, Surrey, on 25 November 1872, the third son of Robert Smith, a merchant, and his wife, Margaret, *née* Bannerman. He was educated from 1886 to 1892 at Charterhouse, one of the homes of association football, where he developed the skills which later took him to four appearances and the captaincy for Oxford against Cambridge. He matriculated on 15 October 1892 at Keble College, Oxford, where he obtained second-class honours in classical moderations (1894) and third-class honours in modern history (1896). As well as representing his university at soccer, he scored a match-winning fourth-innings 132 against Cambridge in the university cricket match of 1896. Sir Pelham Warner later commented: 'As long as there is a history of Oxford and Cambridge cricket the name of G. O. Smith will be emblazoned on its rolls' (*Lord's, 1787–1945*, 1946, 114). Smith also played three matches for Surrey in the 1896 season.

Three months before his innings at Lord's, Smith had, as captain, led England's football attack against Scotland at Glasgow; he subsequently came to be regarded as one of the greatest centre forwards in the history of the game. During his zenith at the end of the nineteenth century, he shared with W. G. Grace the celebrity of being known by his initials only, with G. O. often rendered as Jo. Between 1893 and 1901, a period when only three international matches were played each season between England, Scotland, Wales, and Northern Ireland, he played twenty-one times for England, often as amateur captain alongside and in competition with professional players from the leading professional clubs of his era. In a period of great change during football's development from a recreation to a great international entertainment, he transformed the role of the centre forward from that of an individual striker into a unifier of the whole forward line, and indeed the whole team. Unlike later centre forwards, he rarely headed the ball but instead relied on his remarkable balance and ability to trap and control the ball. He led from the front as captain of school, university, club, and country, scoring over a hundred goals for the Corinthian club, of which he was honorary secretary from 1898 to 1902 jointly with his closest friend, William John Oakley (1873–1934), an Oxford blue and schoolmaster. Both men contributed to the volume on *Football* (1899) published in the celebrated Badminton Library of Sports and Pastimes.

Smith's last appearance for England was against Germany, then an emerging football nation, in the first international game between the two countries in 1901. After graduation Smith had become a schoolmaster, and in 1902 he retired from international football at the age of thirty to become joint headmaster with A. T. B. Dunn, an old Etonian and an earlier international centre forward, at the preparatory school for Eton at Ludgrove, Barnet. From 1918 he was a master at Sunningdale preparatory school.

Smith grew up in a period when social distinctions at all levels in British society were highlighted on the playing fields. The distinction between Gentlemen and Players epitomized the dichotomy between amateurs and professionals, although economic freedom or the absence of other domestic or social demands allowed many amateur sportsmen to display their talents on equal terms with professional contemporaries. Many, like Smith, were schoolmasters, who, along with representatives of the church, the army, and the law, formed the nucleus of the public school–Oxbridge Corinthian football club. Smith died, unmarried, at his home, Yaldhurst, Lymington, Hampshire, on 6 December 1943. EDWARD GRAYSON

Sources E. Grayson, *Corinthians & cricketers* (1957) · B. St G. Drennan, *The Keble College centenary register, 1870–1970* (1970) · F. N. S. Creek, *A history of the Corinthian football club* (1933) · P. M. Young, *A history of British football* (1973) · b. cert.

Likenesses photographs, repro. in Grayson, *Corinthians & cricketers* · photographs, repro. in Creek, *History of the Corinthian football club*

Wealth at death £60,314 3*s*. 9*d*.: probate, 15 Feb 1944, *CGPLA Eng. & Wales*

Smith, Goldwin (1823–1910), journalist and historian, was born on 13 August 1823 at 15 Friar Street, Reading, the eldest of the five children of Richard Prichard Smith (1795–1867), physician and railway company director, and his wife, Elizabeth (*d.* 1833), daughter of Peter Breton, of Huguenot descent. Smith's mother died when he was ten years old, 'the greatest misfortune of my life', in his words (*Reminiscences*, 6), and none of his siblings reached adulthood. His early life was shadowed by the expectation that he too would die young. After being sent away to a preparatory school at eight, he entered Eton College as a colleger in 1836. Somewhat solitary and reserved, though with an early reputation for wit, he pursued the classics and won the Newcastle prize. In 1839 his father married Katherine Dukinfield, daughter of Sir Nathaniel Dukinfield, fifth baronet. Smith was never close to his stepmother, who was perhaps intimidated by his precocious brilliance, but his father, who was prosperous and respected, was reasonably indulgent and his recollections of childhood are sunlit.

The Oxford liberal At fifteen Smith won a studentship to Christ Church, Oxford, but was too young to take it up. He matriculated there in May 1841, before moving to Magdalen College as a scholar the following year. At that elegant academic backwater he employed top coaches such as Richard Congreve, the future positivist leader, to burnish his skills as a classicist. Of his contemporaries, only his friend John Conington was said to rival him in Latin and Greek. Though claiming indifference to academic success, Smith won all the major prizes in classics, graduated with the expected first class in 1845, and, after being turned down for dubious reasons by Oriel and Queen's, was elected Stowell law fellow at University College in 1846. Originally intended for the India civil service, where he had several relatives, he opted for law and was called to the bar at Lincoln's Inn in 1850. However, despite excellent legal connections, not least the close friendship of two future lord chancellors, Roundell Palmer and John Duke Coleridge, he soon decided against pursuing a legal career, for which he felt he lacked the physical stamina.

While at Oxford, Smith joined the young liberal intellectual élite that was beginning to coalesce, particularly after the collapse of Tractarianism. He was a member of its most exclusive discussion society, the Decade, together with Matthew Arnold, A. H. Clough, A. P. Stanley, E. A. Freeman, Benjamin Jowett, Congreve, Conington, and others. The influence of Thomas Arnold was very strong

Goldwin Smith (1823–1910), by Hatch & Son

in this circle, with its élitist social radicalism and inclusionist theological liberalism. Like others, Smith was eager to loosen the clerical grip on Oxford by abolishing the religious tests and college restrictions that made it an Anglican seminary rather than the non-sectarian centre of national intelligence and culture which the country increasingly needed. Fortunately Smith's fellowship did not require him to take holy orders and in 1850 he succeeded his friend A. P. Stanley as tutor of University College, where he was an impressive teacher.

Smith had strong political interests and was among the first of the railway dons (the line reached Oxford in 1844), shuttling between the previously separate worlds of the university, where he was a Rugby-style radical, and London, where he was an Etonian liberal tory, cultivated as a valuable young recruit by the future duke of Newcastle and soon on friendly terms with Edward Cardwell, Sidney Herbert, and William Gladstone. His London base was the Athenaeum, to which he was elected in 1851. In 1850 he became a staff leader writer for the *Morning Chronicle*, recently acquired by a Peelite consortium. When John Douglas Cook, its editor, founded the *Saturday Review* in 1855 he recruited Smith, whom he regarded as the 'ablest pen' among its brilliant staff. The *Saturday* made an important contribution to raising the status of journalism and opening it to young university men as a means of making felt their influence as intellectual and political guides to the nation. Smith became perhaps the most brilliant practitioner of higher journalism—confident, polished, and resonant with historical and literary allusions. Generations of undergraduates would try to emulate the style in their essays. Smith wrote for the *Saturday*, chiefly political leaders, until the divergence of his political and religious views from the journal's led to an amicable severance in 1861. He also wrote extensively for the *Edinburgh Review*, *Macmillan's Magazine*, the *Fortnightly Review*, *Contemporary Review*, and *Nineteenth Century*, as well as for newspapers such as *The Times* and especially the *Daily News*.

Smith was a leading figure in the political agitation for university reform from its inception in 1850. His nine letters to *The Times* as Oxoniensis in May–June 1850 and a petition he co-drafted were instrumental in causing the Russell government to appoint a royal commission in August 1850, of which he and A. P. Stanley were made co-secretaries. Its report recommended various ways of raising the teaching quality and general intellectual standards at Oxford. The Aberdeen government embodied at least some of this in legislation, which Gladstone steered through parliament in 1854, drawing heavily on Smith's assistance. Smith was then appointed joint secretary of the executive commission formed to ensure that the new legislation was enacted at Oxford, a task which occupied him until 1857. Having thus established himself as a capable and conscientious public servant, he was appointed in 1858 by the Derby government to the royal commission on elementary education chaired by the duke of Newcastle. Smith wrote the section of its final report (1862) on charitable endowments, a field in which he had acquired extensive legal expertise. Meanwhile, as a brilliant, handsome bachelor (though young women found him somewhat forbidding), over 6 feet tall, slender, brown-haired, grey-eyed, with a high forehead and fine features, he was a frequent guest at country houses and the fashionable intellectual salons of Lady Waldegrave and Lady Ashburton. He was also a keen huntsman.

Evidently a safe man, Smith was also appointed by Lord Derby in 1858 as regius professor of modern history at Oxford. With this position, unsolicited but much appreciated, he felt his vocation finally fixed in academe, and he had a house built in north Oxford. Though his historical knowledge was extensive, he was not in the mould of the research-orientated scholars who were beginning to make history an autonomous academic discipline. Like his Cambridge counterpart Charles Kingsley, he belonged to the tradition in which history partook of both literature and philosophy. Disturbed by Auguste Comte's ideas, which were then gaining some able adherents at Oxford, Smith had written a long and disparaging review of 'Compte' in *The Times* in 1853 and directed several of his Oxford lectures to proclaiming his own 'philosophy of history' based on 'the moral freedom of man' against the determinist science of history of Comte and Henry Buckle. Yet he expounded a complacently whiggish teleology of moral, intellectual, and material progress. His thinking showed the influence of the liberal Anglican school of history exemplified by Thomas Arnold, whose celebrated lectures as regius professor had enthralled him as an undergraduate. One of Smith's larger themes was that the Reformation was a continuing process of religious freedom, long thwarted by state churches, but now regaining momentum as Christian religions yielded to science its rightful sphere and concentrated upon their true purpose, the progressive improvement of humanity's 'character'. He was above all a historical moralist and a historical journalist who passionately summoned history to immediate concerns, as is best exemplified in *Irish History and Character* (1862), *The Empire* (1863), and *Three English Statesmen* (1867), brilliant extended historical editorials.

Smith viewed history as the subject best suited for preparing young gentlemen for public service—including the vital profession of journalism—by freeing them from the blinkers of sect and party (a young gentleman in his particular care was the prince of Wales, whom he tutored during the prince's sojourn at Oxford: they retained a warm lifelong regard for each other). As a leader of the Oxford reform movement and a member of the intervarsity Ad Eundem club, he campaigned to complete the nationalization of the universities. For him, opening the university to the nation meant opening it to the new élites of commerce and industry, to imbue them with the canonical culture of the nation, and inculcate in them the sense of duty incumbent on wealth and power, however new. Unlike some university reformers, he did not believe that an Oxford education should be made cheaper or more accessible, nor offer vocational 'bread and butter' studies instead of the 'intellectual gymnastic' appropriate for gentlemen. To maintain Oxford's special character he led a successful campaign to keep the Great Western Railway works out of the town in 1865. In pursuing his mission to interest captains of industry in university nationalization he tried to persuade the radical politicians Cobden and Bright, whose friend and admirer he became, to take up the cause. Although unsuccessful, he and his friend Professor Thorold Rogers did at least moderate their suspicion of what Bright once called 'the home of dead languages and undying prejudices' (Harvie, 88).

The discovery of America At this time Smith's life was transformed by the American Civil War. Although initially pro-secession, he came to view it as a crusade against slavery and, greatly inspired by Bright, became morally committed. He made his first public speech on 6 April 1863 in the Free Trade Hall to the Manchester Union and Emancipation Society. He wrote pamphlets and lectured on the moral, religious, and historical bearings of slavery: particularly notable is his *Letter to a Whig Member of the Southern Independence Association* (1864). Many of the university reformers joined him in the pro-Northern camp, placing themselves at variance with polite society. Participation in this cause brought Smith into contact with England's industrial north, where he was gratified by the level of working-class support for the union despite suffering the impact of the cotton famine, and by pro-Northern industrialists such as his new friend Thomas Bayley Potter of Manchester. In 1864 he visited the northern US and Canada; the former impressed him more than the latter. He conveyed his sympathies to the northern states, hoping to moderate their strong anti-English sentiments. He was particularly struck by the egalitarianism and prosperity of the republic, and by the North's determination to win the war at whatever cost. Boston's Brahmans made him feel at home among Anglo-Saxon gentlemen. The visit further radicalized Smith, making him republican in principle and somewhat less nervous about democracy in practice.

Smith regarded nations as almost divinely ordained political units, whose viability depended on cultural and ethnic homogeneity. He saw the United States as an Anglo-Saxon nation whose shortcomings he largely blamed on Irish immigration. He was anxious about the problem of its freed slaves, who he thought might be encouraged to relocate in the Caribbean islands. When in 1865 a black uprising in Jamaica was brutally suppressed by British authorities, Smith was a leading member of the Jamaica Committee formed to prosecute the colonial governor for illegal acts. To raise money for this cause he delivered a series of lectures around the country on Pym, Cromwell, and William Pitt, true heroes of British history, in his view, as opposed to the false hero worship conferred on Governor Eyre by his supporters, among them Carlyle. As *Three English Statesmen* (1867), the lectures became one of his most successful books. Upper-class support for Eyre, as for the South, was an important contributing factor in Smith's growing disenchantment with English society.

At the same time the movement for parliamentary reform was gathering momentum. Smith was by now widely acknowledged as the national leader, along with John Stuart Mill, another Jamaica campaigner, of advanced intellectual radicalism. G. O. Trevelyan's satirical poem 'Ladies in parliament' (1866) described the new breed of Liberal as 'On Bentham nursed, and fed on Goldwin Smith'. Encouraged by the 1865 election to parliament of Mill and several other advanced Liberal intellectuals by constituencies with large popular electorates, Smith, along with many others, became persuaded that enfranchising the trustworthy skilled workers would enable academic radicals such as himself to exercise more effectively their intellectual leadership over the nation. Courted by both the middle-class Reform Union and the trade union-dominated Reform League (although he joined neither), Smith spoke on behalf of both organizations. He also contributed to that most distinctive expression of academic radicalism, *Essays in Reform* (1867), in which he reassuringly expounded the implications for democracy in England of 'The experience of the American commonwealth'. In the 1868 general election, when a number of university intellectuals stood for parliament hoping to further the alliance of 'brains and numbers', he declined a Liberal nomination for the safe new seat of Chelsea but made numerous speeches on behalf of his friends. Their failure to win increased his despondency about the tightening grip of party and plutocracy on British politics.

Smith's growing involvement with public issues in

print and on the platform coincided with a time of private tragedy. In 1865 his father was injured in a railway accident and thereafter suffered recurring fits of insanity during which he could not be left alone and only his son could restrain him. Rather than commit him to an asylum, Smith resigned his professorship in order to live at home with him. But while he was away his father committed suicide by taking prussic acid on 7 October 1867. Smith's own delicate health suffered from the shock. Although he was now without a position, Smith's patrimony of £30,000 was larger than he expected. He decided on an extended visit to the United States and was grateful to be sought out in this dark hour of his life by Andrew White, president of Cornell, who was recruiting a distinguished group of non-resident professors for his newly founded university. In November 1868 Smith arrived in Ithaca as an unpaid honorary professor, an act of faith in the ideal republic that sustained his hopes. Despite the hard climate, isolation, and a vocational, co-educational, and egalitarian ethos utterly unlike Oxford's, Cornell reinvigorated him during his two years there, and he would frequently revisit it with pleasure. Grateful for the prestige his connection conferred, Cornell honoured him, and he later bequeathed to it most of his wealth. But, having come to the United States as a sympathetic mutual interpreter between two Anglo-Saxon nations, he was distressed by the amount of anglophobia he met in the aftermath of the *Alabama* claims settlement. He also found his celebrity onerous.

The Englishness of nearby Canada, where he visited relatives, gave relief both cultural and personal. Smith was a lonely man for whom family connections and a sense of home were important. In 1871 he decided to settle in Toronto, where he moved into, and largely supported, the household of a married cousin. On 30 September 1875 he married Harriet Elizabeth Mann Dixon (1825–1909), the rich, childless widow of William Henry Boulton, a leading Toronto politician. Born in Boston and two years younger than Smith, she was warm and outgoing, an excellent household manager and hostess. The marriage was very successful: but it tied Smith to Toronto, a place he did not altogether like, for the rest of his life since his wife did not wish to move elsewhere. Part of her wealth was The Grange, a handsome Georgian country gentleman's house straight out of Jane Austen's *Emma*, but situated in downtown Toronto in extensive park-like grounds. Here he could live the life of a model English squire, an exemplary patron of culture, a respected benefactor to the community, and the kind master of a household where he was adored by numerous servants, horses, dogs, and cats. From his desk in the fine library which he built onto The Grange, Smith discharged the duties incumbent upon wealth, education, and intelligence by offering guidance to the new and not entirely appreciative nation of Canada.

The awkward Canadian On his arrival, Smith was already well known to informed Canadians as one of the few Englishmen who gave much thought to Canada in the 1860s. The first public issue he had taken up in his own name was the empire in a series of letters to London's *Daily News* in 1862–3 (republished in 1863 as *The Empire*). Here he had advocated the cession of Gibraltar and the Ionian Islands, and the withdrawal of troops from the settlement colonies to encourage them to leave the childhood of dependence and enter the manhood of self-government and self-defence. Only in the case of India did the dubious term 'empire'—which he associated with conquest and tyranny—apply; there alone Britain must provide 'honest and honourable despotism' (G. Smith, *Empire*, 1863, 297). Although stigmatized as a 'doctrinaire' by *The Times*, Smith was saying out loud what many policy makers, notably senior Colonial Office officials, thought and privately said in the mid-Victorian period, when optimism about the inevitable globalization of free trade was at its peak. He was well informed, and close to two colonial secretaries of the period, the Peelites Cardwell and Newcastle. Often characterized as a pattern peace and free-trade man, Smith was not a pacifist, though he abhorred war. From the Crimean War onward, he criticized the endemic russophobia of British policy and opinion for engendering bellicosity. But he was always suspicious of France, as Europe's perennial trouble-maker, and joined the volunteer movement during the French invasion scare of the early 1860s. He viewed Britain's dependencies as potential hostages to her rivals and advocated colonial troop withdrawals in the interests of national security. Canada was a case in point during the American Civil War: he chided Canadians for not supporting an adequate militia, and for depending on Britain for defence when their best defence was independent nationhood.

Canada was a North American democracy committed to equality, he wrote, not an inegalitarian European aristocracy like Britain. On arriving in Canada he became engaged in furthering Canadian nationhood, cultural and political. In 1874 he backed financially and wrote extensively for the newly founded *Canadian Monthly*, a review such as those he wrote for in England. He was a leading member of Canada First, a non-party movement of idealistic, young liberal nationalists, and first president of the National Club, their Toronto headquarters. He wrote for its organ, the weekly *Nation*, looked hopefully to Edward Blake, its rising star, for political leadership, and was seriously disillusioned when Blake defected to the Liberal government. As the country struggled through the next quarter-century of economic depression, he became convinced that Canada's destiny was not independent nationhood but some form of union with the more socially dynamic and economically successful United States. It would be a natural union of Anglo-Saxondom, as mutually advantageous to both partners as the union of Scotland and England. The artificiality of the Canadian nation became a constant theme with him: Canadian politics, he claimed, were dominated by sterile partisanship of two parties with no clear principles separating them. He deplored the patronage and constant propitiation of regional interests, particularly those of Quebec; he regarded French Canada as a major obstacle to Canadian nationhood, which for Smith could only be based soundly on ethnic and cultural homogeneity. As Canada expanded westward with the building of the government-backed transcontinental railway, which he regarded as financial folly, it became for him even more irrational, an affront to the geographical and economic imperatives of north–south trade and communication. For all such nay-saying Smith will always be chiefly remembered in Canadian history as the man who failed to understand, and lacked faith in, the country where he chose to spend most of his adult life.

Smith did not sufficiently appreciate the historic role of loyalism in the making of the Canadian identity and the role played by anti-Americanism (or being-unlike-Americanism) in sustaining that identity, just as he failed to grasp the political dynamics of the two founding nations ideal that, however precariously, bound Canada. Yet he admired the Canadian politician who perhaps better than any other did appreciate these things, Sir John A. Macdonald, and recognized his political genius in working with them. Smith was not the cloistered intellectual that some political critics liked to caricature: he was well informed about Canadian history and politics through wide reading and extensive personal contacts. Moreover, he was not alone in his view of the Canada–US economic relationship: in 1887 he became president of the newly formed Commercial Union League. The widespread national support attracted, particularly among farmers, by the energetic campaign which he led on the league's behalf demonstrated his skills in pressure group politics. The campaign was instrumental in convincing the Liberals to adopt unrestricted reciprocity with the United States as party policy in 1888. Smith threw his support behind the Liberals and, though the 1891 election was lost on that issue, it produced something rare, a campaign manifesto of enduring importance, Smith's *Canada and the Canadian Question* (1891). This brilliant example of historical journalism offers an analysis and international contextualization of the dilemmas of Canadian nationhood that retains its relevance over a century after first publication. It also demonstrates his talent for mobilizing history behind a cause, and remains the best explanation of why he believed in the inevitability of Canadian union with the United States.

The Anglo-Saxon continentalist Smith was maligned as an annexationist, which he was not: such unions, he believed, had to be voluntary. Moreover, he was uncomfortably aware of changes in the United States that clashed with his ideal: the growing ethnic diversity of its population, its increasing commitment to protectionism, and the corruption of 'gilded age' politics counterbalanced a gratifying decline in anglophobia. He even came to see Canadian union with the US as a saving transfusion of Anglo-Saxon values to the latter. Significantly, however, the charges of traitor first flung at him in the early 1870s were a response to his advocacy of independence from Britain. Smith was no enemy of Canadian nationhood: 'No nation can live another nation's life', he wrote in *Empire* (p. 137). One of the things that most dismayed him in Canada was what he called 'colonial flunkeyism' (Wallace, 237)—Canadian subservience to British authority, political, cultural, and social, especially in its aristocratic embodiments. He stated these concerns pungently in *Loyalty, Aristocracy, Jingoism* (1896), declaring that 'in not a few cases … loyalty to the British connection is a fine name for disloyalty to Canada' (p. 17). He remarked that appointing British aristocrats as governor-general gave Ottawa the ambience of a 'petty court' (*Reminiscences*, 458). He deplored the practice of Canadian politicians' accepting knighthoods and contrasted the public-spirited philanthropy of rich Americans with that of Canadians who instead of endowing their own community too often looked forward to retiring with their wealth and honours to England. He was profoundly distressed by the surge of late-Victorian imperialism, and criticized the various schemes for imperial unification that it produced as well as being appalled by Canada's participation in the Second South African War. Opposition to the war among French Canadians markedly raised his opinion of them.

If, for Smith, too many Canadians pursued a false gentrification distorted by the flummery of aristocracy, he tried to exemplify the gentleman as citizen. He was an activist in numerous spheres of civil life: with his interest in public education, and the credentials and prestige conferred by his English experience, he was elected in 1873 president of the Ontario Teachers' Association and in 1874 appointed to the government's council of public instruction, where his secularist views on religious education led inevitably to controversy. He was concerned about the dispersal of university education among competing 'one-horse colleges' around the province and promoted their amalgamation into the University of Toronto, whose autonomy from the government he strenuously advocated. Appointed to its senate in 1873, he was a generous benefactor of that university, though he did not teach there. In 1896 he was nominated for an honorary degree, whereupon rabid loyalists seized the opportunity to protest honouring a 'traitor'. Noting that he was accustomed to the 'manly and generous habits of English gentlemen' able to separate political and social occasions, he withdrew his name to spare the university embarrassment (Wallace, 120). The degree was awarded amid applause seven years later. He was subsequently appointed to a royal commission on the university in 1905, and to its first board of governors in 1906.

Smith was a Gladstonian liberal, suspicious of encroachment on the individual liberty of adult males by national governments, but ready to grant a wider sphere of action to local government—except the enforcement of virtue, a speciality of 'Toronto the Good'. Thus he opposed local sabbatarian and prohibitionist ordinances, but criticized the city's reliance on private charity and the maxims of self-help to cope with the widespread distress structural to a prolonged economic depression. He campaigned long and successfully for the appointment of a city welfare officer, whose salary Smith himself paid for the first two years. He deplored the corruption of civic politics and promoted the American progressives' idea of government by commission or city manager. He claimed that his butler, William Chin, who faithfully served in The Grange for over fifty years, was better informed than he about local politicians and that he voted in accordance with Chin's advice. Smith was generous both with time and money in assisting local social and benevolent organizations. He was a founder, major benefactor, and long-time president of the Associated Charities of Toronto, a co-ordinating agency for the city's various charities. He was a prominent member of the St George's Society until organized loyalist hostility persuaded him to resign in 1893. The Toronto Humane Society, of which he was an officer, and the Toronto lawn tennis club, of which he was a founder and long-time president, were among the other local organizations in which he was active.

In virtually every matter that concerned him, Smith's instinct was to reach for his pen. Journalism was his vocation and he shared Thomas Carlyle's exalted conception of journalists as 'the true kings and clergy' of the age. Significantly, when Smith did once consider entering politics in Canada, it was to gain some insider experience that would make him a more effective journalist. Canada was a newspaper-reading country: with a population in 1880 of some 4 million it had some 465 newspapers, fifty-six of them dailies. He quickly fell foul of Canada's most powerful editor, George Brown of the Toronto *Globe*, whose enormous partisan influence he attacked. Brown reciprocated in full, demonstrating how seriously Smith was taken. Controversy was important to Smith's self-definition and he was unusual among journalists in having both financial and intellectual means. In 1876 he helped to found the Toronto *Telegram* in opposition to *The Globe*, and in 1890 *The Tribune* in Winnipeg, being deeply interested in the Canadian west. His most distinctive contribution to journalism was *The Bystander*, a sixty-six-page monthly with an unprecedentedly wide circulation, which he wrote in its entirety. He published it from January 1880 to June 1881, then as a quarterly from January to October 1883, and again as a monthly from October 1889 to September 1890. He was also the founder and part owner of *The Week: An Independent Journal of Politics, Society and Literature*, which published new voices in Canadian literature. In it he wrote a weekly column as The Bystander from 6 December 1883 to 15 January 1885, and contributed regularly thereafter. In 1896 he bought control of the *Farmers' Sun*, and renamed it the *Weekly Sun*. For this widely read rural newspaper, which became an organ of his continental unionist views, he wrote unsigned editorials and Bystander pieces until the year he died. He also aired his views regularly in American journals, such as the *New York Times*, and especially the weekly *Nation*, with which he had a connection as a reviewer from the 1860s, though it was interrupted between 1884 and 1890; the New York *Sun* became his chief American platform from 1893 onwards. His published bibliography, though incomplete, lists over 1600 items.

The transatlantic old liberal Smith's name remained familiar to English readers through the press. He followed English affairs closely, and returned to England for visits of up to eighteen months in 1873–4, 1876–7, 1881–2, 1888, and 1893–4, fending off the urgings of friends to stay, to enter parliament, or to accept the headship of University College. He threw himself with particular zeal into the Bulgarian atrocities agitation as a convener and mentor of the Eastern crisis conference in December 1876. He saw it as a resurrection of the intellectual coalition that had rallied around the Governor Eyre prosecution, a mobilization of the national conscience in the name of justice and humanity. This context accounts for some of Smith's antisemitic outbursts, which initially owed much to his intense dislike of Disraeli, whom he could never forgive for the fall of his hero Sir Robert Peel. He sniped at him in the *Morning Chronicle*, thwarted his opposition to the Oxford University Reform Bill, and got the better of him over the cession of the Ionian Islands. Disraeli retaliated with scarcely veiled references in parliament to professorial 'prigs and pedants' and the 'wild man of the cloister', and a malicious caricature of Smith in his novel *Lothair* (1870) as a 'social parasite'. Smith viewed Disraeli's eastern policy and the turcophilia of the Jewish community as evidence that the Jews were not part of 'the nation', the coherent moral community idealized by many academic radicals. He viewed Judaism as a tribal religion that exalted exclusiveness rather than universal brotherhood, and saw Jews as contributing significantly to the forces of materialism and plutocracy that were corrupting English politics and life. Russian pogroms and the Second South African War occasioned other outbursts against excessive Jewish influence on British policy and opinion. While his antisemitic utterances were unpleasant, his dozen or so pieces criticizing the Jews, among the thousands of articles he wrote, do not perhaps warrant labelling him, as Tulchinsky has, 'a major disseminator of Jew-hatred' (Tulchinsky, 70). Smith attacked Catholicism, and especially the Jesuits, more frequently and with scarcely less venom as anti-national forces, yet he contributed generously to Catholic charities, just as he contributed to the building of a synagogue in Toronto.

Smith's attitude to Ireland was also closely tied to his Anglo-Saxonism. In *Irish History and Irish Character* (1862) he deplored Britain's long history of misgoverning Ireland and was sympathetic to Irish grievances over religion and landlordism. What he saw as Ireland's cultural and political backwardness he considered largely England's fault. However, home rule was anathema to him mainly on grounds of national security. Unlike the empire, which jeopardized it, Ireland was essential to England's safety: home rule led him, like many academic radicals of his generation, to break with Gladstone—on whom his *Memories of Gladstone* (1904) offers some interesting insights. In 1886 he was an active Liberal Unionist campaigner, but declined once more an invitation to stand for parliament. The worst of Gladstone's scheme was that it maintained the disruptive Irish presence at Westminster. He eventually came to the conclusion that outright Irish independence was preferable, though as he lived in Orange Toronto he was acutely aware of the Ulster difficulty.

Smith's belief in democracy and the people, though real, was always fragile, and became increasingly so as he witnessed the failure of those influences he hoped would keep them on the paths of virtue. The defeat of the 'best men', of principled intellectual private members, by party government, was perhaps the central political tragedy for Smith. Mass party politics led to demagogic socialist policies that eroded individual responsibility and to economic interventionism which increased opportunities for political corruption. It encouraged 'flabby sentiment' in favour of votes for women (which he had initially supported in 1866) and, worst of all, jingoism, the hysterical popular lust for imperial war which led to the Spanish–American and Second South African wars. Soon Joseph Chamberlain had replaced Disraeli as Smith's *bête noire*. None the less, Smith retained some of his faith in the working man. He argued that the irresponsible rich were the real 'dangerous class'. He remained a supporter, both moral and financial, of trade unions, which he regarded as legitimate agencies for the protection of workers' interests, and of attempts by working men to enter parliament (among his labour friends was John Burns). He addressed labour audiences on several occasions, and took pride in speaking frankly to them and not currying their favour. When he was invited to open the Canadian trades and labour congress convention in 1905 his speech received a standing ovation, and on his death the congress passed a formal resolution honouring him as a sincere friend of labour.

On religion Smith's views were as passionate, distinctive, and historicist as on other important matters. An advanced mid-Victorian liberal Anglican of the rationalist stamp, he was still sufficiently orthodox in 1861 to attack the Bampton lectures of Henry Mansel (an Oxford ally of Disraeli) for their allegedly atheistic tendencies, but he soon moved beyond any denominational affiliation. He was opposed to established churches and suspicious of all forms of religious authority, particularly in the realm of thought. He could not accept the chief dogmas of Christianity, such as the Trinity, incarnation, redemption, and atonement, and he regarded the Old Testament as a barbaric relic of primitive belief—another element in his criticism of Judaism. But he held the life and character of Christ to be an ethical force capable of uniting all humanity. This belief, or hope, helped to sustain him amid the encircling gloom of his old age. He wrote extensively on religion in his later years, particularly in the New York *Sun*, and collected some of these writings in *Guesses at the Riddle of Existence* (1897) and *In Quest of Light* (1906). Their titles convey his uncertainties.

Personality and legacy Something of Smith's character is revealed by Arnold Haultain, his private secretary during his last eighteen years. Shy, proud, and intensely serious, Smith was kind in private and greatly loved by those who knew him best, including his old university allies in reform, with whom he remained in touch. He enjoyed whist, tennis, and riding and had a donnish sense of humour. He entered controversy on paper with enthusiasm, but indignation and refutation were his strengths rather than persuasion. His instinctive refusal to seek public office was surely sound, and spared him further disappointment. His position as Canada's leading intellectual of the late nineteenth century seems undeniable but by a certain inverse snobbery, perhaps, his stature is not fully appreciated in Canada, where the problem of Canadian unity which he shrewdly if unsympathetically analysed persists, and the economic union with the United States which he so ardently desired proceeds apace. Smith's intellectual legacy is difficult to assess, in large part because he left behind no 'big book', but a huge volume of circumstantial writing, most of it now barely accessible. He intended to write a history of the 'seventeenth-century English revolution' (as he significantly termed it), but it would probably have been popular rather than scholarly. His *The United States: a Political History* (1893) was intended to interpret American history to the English; his *The United Kingdom* (1899) to interpret British history to Americans. Both sold well on both sides of the Atlantic. He declined Lord Acton's invitation to contribute to the *Cambridge Modern History*, and was elected president of the American Historical Association in 1904. He maintained his facility in the classics, publishing a collection of his translations from Latin poetry in *Bay Leaves* (1890), and from Greek drama in *Specimens of Greek Drama* (1893). His judgement as a literary critic and book reviewer is often astute in the 'man of letters' vein. His warm appreciations of *Cowper* (1880) and *Jane Austen* (1890) do credit to his taste and reveal something of his nature.

On 9 September 1909 Smith's wife died, leaving him bereft. They were childless. In March 1910 Smith fell and broke his thigh. He died at The Grange on 7 June 1910 and was buried in St James's cemetery. The Grange was willed by his wife to the city of Toronto as its art gallery. Smith left his excellent library to the University of Toronto, and the bulk of his fortune, increased to over $830,000 by property investments, to Cornell University, with his private papers. CHRISTOPHER A. KENT

Sources E. Wallace, *Goldwin Smith: Victorian liberal* (1957) • G. Smith, *Reminiscences* (1901) • *A selection from Goldwin Smith's correspondence … written between the years 1846 and 1910*, ed. A. Haultain [1910] • A. Haultain, *Goldwin Smith: his life and opinions* [1913] • P. H. Gaffney, *Goldwin Smith bibliography* (1972) • J. McCarthy, *Portraits of the sixties* (1903), 380–95 • C. Harvie, *The lights of liberalism: university liberals and the challenge of democracy, 1860–86* (1976) • C. Kent, *Brains and numbers: élitism, Comtism and democracy in mid-Victorian England* (1978) • W. R. Ward, *Victorian Oxford* (1965) • B. Semmel, *The Governor Eyre controversy* (1962) • W. Roberts, 'Goldwin's myth, the nonconformist as mugwump', *Canadian Literature*, 83 (1979), 50–71 • F. H. Underhill, *In search of Canadian liberalism* (1960), 85–103 • M. Ross, 'Goldwin Smith', *Our living tradition*, ed. C. Bissell (1957), 28–47 • R. Brown, 'Goldwin Smith and anti-imperialism', *Canadian Historical Review*, 43 (1962), 93–105 • G. Tulchinsky, 'Goldwin Smith: Victorian Canadian antisemite', *Antisemitism in Canada: history and interpretation*, ed. A. Davies (1992), 67–91 • D. Feldman, *Englishmen and Jews: social relations and political culture, 1840–1914* (1994) • R. T. Shannon, *Gladstone and the Bulgarian agitation, 1876* (1963) • D. Forbes, *The liberal Anglican idea of history* (1952) • M. M. Bevington, *The Saturday Review, 1855–1868: representative educated opinion in Victorian England* (1941) • Gladstone, *Diaries* • *DNB*

Archives Cornell University, New York, corresp. and papers • Metropolitan Toronto Reference Library, corresp. and papers • NRA, corresp. and literary papers • Public Archives of Ontario, Toronto, corresp. and papers • University of Toronto, Thomas

Fisher Rare Book Library, corresp. | Berks. RO, corresp. with Sir Robert Mowbray • Bishopsgate Institute, London, letters to George Howell • BL, letters to Richard Cobden • BL, letters to T. H. S. Escott, Add. MS 58792 • BL, corresp. with W. E. Gladstone, Add. MS 44303 • BL, corresp. with Macmillans, Add. MS 55172 • Bodl. Oxf., letters to James Bryce • Bodl. Oxf., letters to William Harcourt • Bodl. Oxf., letters to Frederick Max Muller, MSS Eng. c2806/2, c2808 • Bodl. Oxf., letters to J. E. Thorold Rogers • Co-operative Union, Holyoake House, Manchester, Co-operative Union archives, letters to George Jacob Holyoake • HLRO, letters to Lord Ashbourne • JRL, letters to C. P. Scott • LPL, letters to Lord Selborne • Magd. Oxf., letters to F. Bulley • NL Scot., corresp. with Lord Rosebery • Pembroke College, Oxford, letters to Francis Jeune • U. Durham L., corresp. with third Earl Grey • U. Lpool L., letters to William Rathbone • University of Toronto, Thomas Fisher Rare Book Library, letters to James Mavor • W. Sussex RO, corresp. with R. Cobden

Likenesses M. S. Carpenter, oils, 1841, Art Gallery of Ontario, Toronto • G. Richmond, chalk?, 1847, Eton • C. Lyons, 1848–68 (after G. Richmond?, 1847), Art Gallery of Ontario, Toronto • F. Sandys, charcoal, c.1870, Cornell University, Ithaca, White Library • J. Guggenheim, photograph, 1874, NPG • Lock & Whitfield, woodburytype photograph, 1878, NPG; repro. in T. Cooper, *Men of mark: a gallery of contemporary portraits* (1878) • E. W. Grier, oils, 1894, Bodl. Oxf. • J. Russell, oil replica, 1907, Reading corporation • J. W. L. Forster, oils, Art Gallery of Ontario, Toronto • J. W. L. Forster, oils, Cornell University, Ithaca • Hatch & Son, carte-de-visite, NPG [*see illus.*] • Mayall, photograph, carte-de-visite, NPG • A. Munro, plaster bust, Bodl. Oxf. • G. E. Perine of New York, mixed engraving, NPG; repro. in *The Eclectic* • miniature, Oxf. U. Mus. NH

Wealth at death $832,859: *DNB*

Smith, Sir Grafton Elliot (1871–1937), anatomist and anthropologist, was born on 15 August 1871 in Grafton, New South Wales, second son of Stephen Sheldrick Smith, an English schoolmaster at Grafton, and his wife, Mary Jane, *née* Evans, of Sydney. He was educated at Grafton superior public school, and after the family moved to Sydney in 1883, at Darlington public school, then later at Sydney Boys' High School. After having attended Thomas Anderson Stuart's evening classes in physiology he entered the medical school in the University of Sydney in 1888, attracting the support of John Thomson Wilson. After graduating MB ChM (1892) he held various clinical posts and in 1894 began his career as an anatomist and researcher. Four 1894 papers dealt with the hyatid cyst in congenital hernia, the significance of rare anomalies of nerves, muscles, and blood vessels, and mammalian cerebral commissures, with special reference to the monotremes and marsupials. In 1895 he gained a European reputation and gold medal by his MD thesis on the brain of non-placental mammals and eleven papers on the evolution of the primitive mammalian brain and olfaction.

After coming to England in 1896 on a James King travelling scholarship Elliot Smith (the surname by which he was generally known) continued his research at St John's College, Cambridge (BA, 1898; MA, 1903), under Alexander Macalister, publishing eight papers on cerebral morphology (1896–7), and beginning the descriptive catalogue of the brain collection in the museum of the Royal College of Surgeons which became the source book for a generation of neurologists. On 22 September 1900 he married, in Chelsea, Kate Emily Macredie (*b*. 1873/4) of Sydney. In the same year he became the first professor of anatomy in the new government medical school, Cairo, publishing about fifty anatomical papers over the next nine years on the brains of living and extinct forms. But, to quote Montaigne, his mind was becoming 'a tool adapted to all subjects and [which] meddles with everything'. As consultant to the University of California's Hearst Egyptological expedition (1901) he became critical of the methods of anthropologists, classical scholars, and Egyptologists. With Sir Gaston Maspero, George Andrew Reisner, Dr Frederic Wood Jones, and others he began the archaeological survey of Nubia (1907), involving the examination of 20,000 burials. To palaeopathology and comparative anatomy was added a fascination with ancient customs, religion, and mummification which sowed the seeds of his diffusionist theory that all human culture had originated in ancient Egypt. His Egyptian work also yielded *The Ancient Egyptians* (1911).

Elected fellow of the Royal Society (1907), in 1909 Elliot Smith was appointed professor of anatomy in Manchester University. He now became involved with W. H. R. Rivers and W. J. Perry in further investigating the origins of magic and religion, early human migration, and the diffusion of culture. His deployment of the new inductive methods of human biology soon brought him into conflict with many anthropologists and historians. With the 'discovery' of the now infamous Piltdown skull (1912) came close, sometimes combative, contact with Arthur Woodward and Arthur Keith. (The identification of Charles Dawson as the likely forger was made long after Elliot Smith's death, and a suggestion that Elliot Smith was responsible for the forgery, proposed in Ronald Millar's *The Piltdown Men* (1974), was later universally rejected.) Elliot Smith delivered several Arris and Gale lectures before the Royal College of Surgeons on the evolution of the brain (1909, 1911, 1920) and served on the General Medical Council, representing Manchester University (1913–19), as well as being a leading figure in the Manchester Literary and Philosophical Society. During the First World War he collaborated with Rivers and T. H. Pear (the young professor of psychology at Manchester University) in treating shell-shock, and delivered the 1919 Croonian lectures, 'The significance of the cerebral cortex', at the Royal College of Physicians.

In 1919 E. H. Starling persuaded Elliot Smith to accept the chair of anatomy at University College, London. Henceforth his career centred on the Institute of Anatomy which he established there, with Rockefeller Foundation funding, to reinvigorate the somewhat moribund field of anatomical research (inspired by the American F. P. Mall). Here, he introduced practical courses on histology, embryology, neurology, and X-ray anatomy, and formed liaisons with University College Hospital and the prosectorium of the Zoological Society. Physical, and to a lesser extent, cultural, anthropology were also taught but several factors undermined his aspirations to create a unified human biology programme ranging from sociology to anatomy: the death of Rivers (his closest ally), anthropologists' hostility to his extreme ideas on cultural diffusion, and the apparent failure to establish fruitful links with C. Spearman and J. C. Flügel, University College's psychologists.

The institute became an internationally renowned and influential research centre as Elliot Smith continued to raise Rockefeller funding for anthropological and anatomical research in India, Australia, and, most famously, for his ex-assistant Davidson Black's palaeontological Chinese research which yielded the 'Peking skull' and other human fossils at Choukoutien (Zhoukoudian) (1926). Another ex-assistant, Raymond Dart, discovered the infant hominid Taung skull in South Africa, naming it *Australopithecus* (reported 1925). As these finds revolutionized human evolution research he became, with Keith, a major popularizer of this topic, particularly in *The Evolution of Man: Essays* (1924), *Human History* (1930), *Early Man* (1931), and *The Search for Man's Ancestors* (1931). His diffusionist views were meanwhile propagated in *The Migrations of Early Culture* (1915), *Evolution of the Dragon* (1919), *Elephants and Ethnologists* (1924), and *The Diffusion of Culture* (1933). However, while Rivers had been sympathetic, Elliot Smith's diffusionism was incompatible with developments in mainstream British anthropology and, Perry aside, his views received little academic support and rapidly became marginalized. Mainstream anthropologists and disciplinary historians continue to consider the theory an aberration. Two further aspects of Elliot Smith's work now appear significant. He edited three volumes of Rivers's essays for posthumous publication in which Rivers's biographer Richard Slobodin claims he distorted Rivers's level of support for diffusionism. Less contentiously, in the largely overlooked *The Neural Basis of Thought* (1934), co-authored with G. G. Campion, he presented an account very similar in character to D. O. Hebb's highly influential *Organization of Behaviour: a Neuropsychological Theory* (1949).

Despite contemporary eminence and extensive achievements Elliot Smith's reputation had all but evaporated by the end of the twentieth century. While his biographer in the *Dictionary of National Biography* praised his 'childlike simplicity of approach to scientific truth' an intangible whiff of scandal now seems to pursue his name. This appears to spring not from his championing of Piltdown man—he was not alone in that—but from his handling of Rivers's papers and the style in which he conducted his academic life and responsibilities. That earlier biographer's observation '[H]is work was done in spasms, periods of idleness alternating with bursts of intense activity' surely has the ring of euphemism, while the 1938 tribute volume (edited by W. R. Dawson) is as notable for who failed to contribute as for who did. If never substantiated, he apparently left an impression among British colleagues of tendencies towards sharp practice and rule bending. How far this was true, how much mere prejudice against an Australian interloper of 'charm and imposing presence' (*DNB*, see Blunt, 645–6) into the British medical establishment, is, barring new evidence, impossible to ascertain. None the less, by 1938 more than twenty of his former staff were in anatomy chairs around the world. Given the results of his skills as a financial fixer, his undeniable scientific and institutional contributions to anatomy and medical teaching, and his role as a scientific popularizer, a future, albeit modest, recovery of his reputation remains a possibility.

Elliot Smith revisited Australia in 1914 and 1924, and engineered Rockefeller support for a chair of anthropology at the University of Sydney (1926). In 1932 he was partially incapacitated by a minor stroke, but was appointed Fullerian professor of physiology at the Royal Institution (1933). He retired from the University College anatomy chair in 1936 after being knighted 'for services to the Empire and to science' (1934). Other honours had included the Prix Fauvelle of the Anthropological Society of Paris (1911), a royal medal of the Royal Society (1912), and the Huxley medal of the London Institution (1935). In 1931 he was elected an honorary fellow of St John's College, Cambridge, where he had first become a fellow in 1899. He retired at the end of the session 1935/6, and when his wife suffered burns from the explosion of a gas stove, they moved to Kent, settling in St Michael's Nursing Home, Stone Road, Broadstairs, where Elliot Smith died on 1 January 1937. He was survived by his wife and two of their three sons. GRAHAM RICHARDS

Sources W. R. Dawson, ed., *Sir Grafton Elliot Smith: a biographical record by his colleagues* (1938) · R. Slobodin, *W. H. R. Rivers* (1978) · *The Times* (2 Jan 1937), 12b · *The Times* (4 Jan 1937), 14b · *The Times* (6 Jan 1937), 15c · G. G. Campion and G. E. Smith, *The neural basis of thought* (1934) · J. T. Wilson, *Obits. FRS*, 2 (1936–8), 323–33 · M. J. Blunt, *AusDB*, 11.645–6 · *BMJ* (9 Jan 1937), 99 · m. cert. · d. cert. · *DNB*
Archives Australian Academy of Science, Canberra, letters · BL, corresp. and papers, Add. MSS 56303–56304 · Medical Research Council, London, corresp. · UCL, letters and papers | CUL, letters to Charles Ogden · JRL, corresp. with G. G. Campion · NL Scot., letters to Donald Alexander Mackenzie · Royal Anthropological Institute, London, corresp. with T. C. Johnston
Likenesses W. Stoneman, photograph, 1920, NPG · photograph, repro. in Dawson, ed., *Sir Grafton Elliot Smith* · F. Schmidt, photograph, repro. in *Obits. FRS* · group portrait, oils, repro. in R. Millar, *The Piltdown men: a case of archaeological fraud* (1974)
Wealth at death £4629 13s.: administration with will, 20 May 1937, *CGPLA Eng. & Wales*

Smith, (James) Hamblin (1827–1901), mathematician, was born on 2 December 1827 at Rickinghall, Suffolk, the only surviving child of James Hamblin Smith and his wife, Mary Finch. He was cousin of Barnard Smith, fellow of Peterhouse, Cambridge (BA 1839, MA 1842), rector of Glaston, Rutland, and a writer of popular mathematical textbooks. After grammar school education at Botesdale, Suffolk, Smith entered as a pensioner at Gonville and Caius College, Cambridge, in July 1846. On Lady Day 1847 he was elected to a scholarship. At the quincentenary of the foundation of the college, in 1848, he was selected to write the 'Latin Commemoration Ode'. In 1850 he graduated BA as thirty-second wrangler in the mathematical tripos and in the second class of the classical tripos. He proceeded MA in 1853.

After graduating Smith became a private tutor at Cambridge in mathematics, classics, and theology, a career he pursued until near his death; at some point more than half the candidates for ordinary degrees were said to have been his pupils, and many generations of students knew him as 'Big Smith'. He was lecturer in classics at Peterhouse from 1868 to 1872. His ability to simplify mathematical reasoning is illustrated by an ingenious plan for the conversion into pounds, shillings, and pence of money expressed in decimals (*Notices and Abstracts of … the British Association for the Advancement of Science*, 1902, 2.529). He published many handbooks for his pupils' use in preparing for examination, such as *Elementary Statics* (1868), *A Treatise on Arithmetic* (1872), and *Lectures on Paley's Evidences of Christianity* (1881). He also published *Rudiments of English Grammar* (1876), as well as a Latin and a Greek grammar and works on church history. His elementary mathematical treatises enjoyed a wide circulation.

Smith found time for public work at Cambridge, in which his strong yet conciliatory personality gave him much influence. He was one of the Cambridge improvement commissioners from 1875 until the Local Government Act abolished that body in 1889; in this capacity he agitated for the diversion of sewage from the River Cam. He was a member of the council of the senate from 1876 to 1880, and for many years chairman of the Cambridge board of examinations and a governor of the Perse School. He was one of the earliest members of the London Mathematical Society.

Smith married, on 16 April 1857, Ellen Hales (*d.* June 1912), daughter of Samuel Chilton Gross of Alderton, Suffolk, and sister of Edward John Gross, Cambridge secretary of the Oxford and Cambridge schools examinations board. Three sons and one daughter (wife of John Clay of the Cambridge University Press) survived him. He died at his home, 42 Trumpington Street, Cambridge, on 10 July 1901, and was buried at Mill Road cemetery four days later. His portrait is in the possession of Caius College.

J. D. H. Dickson, *rev.* Alan Yoshioka

Sources Venn, *Alum. Cant.* • *The Times* (11 July 1901) • *The Times* (15 July 1901) • *The Caian* (1902) • private information (1912) • *WWW* • *CGPLA Eng. & Wales* (1901)

Likenesses portrait, Gon. & Caius Cam.

Wealth at death £29,440 12*s*. 10*d*.: resworn probate, Oct 1901, *CGPLA Eng. & Wales*

Smith, Hannah Whitall [*known as* Mrs Pearsall Smith] (**1832–1911**), evangelist and religious writer, was born on 7 February 1832 at Philadelphia, Pennsylvania, USA, the daughter of John M. Whitall (1800–1877) and Mary Whitall, *née* Tatum (1803–1880). Both parents came of established Philadelphia Quaker families of an eighteenth-century quietist tradition. On 25 June 1851 she married Robert Pearsall Smith (1827–1898), who came of another old Philadelphia Quaker family. He was drawn into the prospering Whitall–Tatum glass business and in 1865 became general manager of its plant at South Milville, New Jersey. It was among Methodist workers there that the Pearsall Smiths (from 1858 convinced of the centrality of the doctrine of justification by faith) became exponents of immediate sanctification as described in W. E. Boardman's *The Higher Christian Life* (1859).

In autumn 1872 Robert joined Boardman in a visit to Britain in furtherance of the doctrine of the higher life: Hannah followed the next year. Their eldest son, Franklin, had died in the summer of 1872 and Hannah's commemorative book *The Record of a Happy Life* (1873, subsequently entitled *Frank*) was to herald an impressive literary output. The couple moved in aristocratic and intellectual circles in Britain, and Hannah braved accusations of heresy by denying, at first in private but then in public, the doctrine of eternal punishment. She was supported in this by Georgiana Cowper-Temple (later Lady Mount-Temple) and rapidly established a reputation for her scriptural expositions. As well as holding numerous drawing-room occasions in London and elsewhere, they were leading spirits in the conferences at Broadlands (the Cowper-Temple home near Romsey, Hampshire; 17–23 July 1874), Oxford (29 August – 7 September 1874), and Brighton (29 May – 7 June 1875); Robert Pearsall Smith presided at all three, the attendances being estimated at 100, 1000, and 8000 respectively. The Keswick Convention for the Promotion of Practical Holiness (28 June – 2 July 1875) arose out of these gatherings. The Pearsall Smiths were due to take a large share in it, Robert again presiding, but after accusations that he had at Brighton uttered unsound doctrine and committed a moral indiscretion those responsible asked him 'to abstain at once from all public work' (Barabas, 26–7) and in 1876 they both returned to America.

But 1875, the year of disgrace, was also the year of triumph, for Hannah's *The Christian's Secret of a Happy Life*, published that year, ran to over 100 editions and was translated into many languages. Subsequent books included *The Veil Uplifted, or, The Bible its Own Interpreter* (1886); *Every-day Religion, or, The Common-Sense Teaching of the Bible* (1894); and her spiritual autobiography *The Unselfishness of God* (1903). It was in 1888 that the Pearsall Smiths returned to settle permanently in England.

Hannah's robust common sense was allied to an irrepressible sense of humour, a zest for life, a questioning intellect, and, as she got older, an increasing conviction that the young know best. She felt that the art of being a grandmother was not sufficiently attended to: she did so herself to the delight of her grandchildren. Of her six children Mary (1864–1945) married Frank Costelloe (1855–1899) and Bernard Berenson (1865–1959); Alys (1867–1951) was the first wife of Bertrand Russell; Logan Pearsall *Smith, the writer, was unmarried; the remaining three died in infancy or young manhood. In 1906 she moved to Court Place, Iffley, Oxford, sharing a home with her son. After a short illness she died there on 1 May 1911.

Edward H. Milligan

Sources L. P. Smith, ed., *A religious rebel: the letters of 'HWS'* (1949) [repr. in USA as *Philadelphia Quaker: the letters of Hannah Whitall Smith* (1950)] • R. A. Parker, *A family of Friends: the story of the transatlantic Smiths* (1960) • H. W. Smith, *The unselfishness of God* (1903) • R. Strachey, *A Quaker grandmother* (1914) • C. H. Harford, ed., *The Keswick Convention* (1907) • S. Barabas, *So great salvation: the history and message of the Keswick Convention* (1952) • *The Friend*, new ser., 51 (1911), 311–40 • *Annual Monitor* (1912), 162–6

Likenesses photograph, *c*.1878, RS Friends, Lond.; Whitall album

Smith, Hastings Bertrand Lees- (1878–1941), politician, was born at Murree, North-Western Provinces, India, on 26 January 1878, the second of the three sons of Harry Lees-Smith, a major in the Royal Artillery, and his wife, Jesse Reid. On the death of his father in 1880 he was taken to England to be brought up by his grandfather, and there he was educated first privately and then at Aldenham junior military academy. In 1894 he enrolled at the Royal Military Academy at Woolwich, but a weak constitution meant that he gave up the idea of a military career. He entered Queen's College, Oxford, in 1895 and graduated in 1899 with second-class honours in history. At Oxford he was a Liberal, but he also joined the Fabian Society.

After graduation Smith (as he was styled until the 1920s) secured the position of general secretary at the newly opened Ruskin Hall (later College) in Oxford. Ruskin aimed specifically at working-class education, but student discontent at the lack of a definitely 'socialist' approach grew, and this culminated in the students' strike of 1909. Smith, as a progressive Liberal who took a different view of the relationship between class improvement and education, was a particular target of this agitation. But by this time his day-to-day role in the college had already been reduced by his appointment as a lecturer in public administration at the London School of Economics (LSE) in 1906; he continued to teach at the LSE, with breaks, until his death, and was a reader from 1924. He also visited Bombay in 1909 to advise on the teaching of economics, and he occupied a chair in public administration at the University of Bristol in 1909–10. He wrote a number of works, of which *Second Chambers in Theory and Practice* (1923), which argued for an upper house elected by the Commons on the basis of proportional representation, was perhaps the most substantial.

Smith was elected as Liberal MP for Northampton in January 1910. In parliament he soon emerged as fairly radical, supporting nationalization of certain core industries such as the railways, as well as land reform and a minimum wage for certain classes of workers. But matters changed with the outbreak of war in 1914. Smith became a member of the newly formed Union of Democratic Control (UDC), which aimed to reform policy making in such a way that 'secret diplomacy' became a thing of the past. In September 1915 he joined the army, but chose to serve in the ranks and attained the rank of corporal: this move into the forces did not make him unique among UDC members, but rather showed one of the diverse paths taken by progressive Liberals during the First World War. On 5 November 1915 he married Joyce Eleanor, the second daughter of Sidney Herbert Holman; they had two sons.

Involvement with the UDC, whose leading members included the Labour MP Ramsay MacDonald, along with the increasingly illiberal aspects of the policies of successive governments headed by the Liberals H. H. Asquith and David Lloyd George, increased Smith's discontent with his party. In May 1916, addressing parliament in his corporal's uniform, he opposed the introduction of conscription; in May 1917 he called in the Commons for a compromise peace; and by March 1918 he believed that only Labour had an acceptable peace policy. At the 1918 general election he chose to fight the Don Valley division of Yorkshire as an independent radical. He was defeated, but his break with the Liberals was completed in 1919 when he joined the Labour Party. In January 1920 he joined other former Liberals, such as Arthur Ponsonby and Charles Trevelyan, in publishing an appeal to former Liberals to vote against Asquith in the Paisley by-election.

Lees-Smith won the Keighley (Yorkshire) seat for Labour in 1922. Although he lost the seat narrowly to a Liberal the following year, he regained it in 1924 and held it in 1929. His 1923 defeat disqualified him from office in Ramsay MacDonald's first minority Labour government in 1924, but once he was re-elected to parliament he emerged as one of the more significant second-rank figures in the Parliamentary Labour Party (PLP), being elected to its executive committee each year from 1924. He further cemented his role in the labour movement by serving on the board of the *New Statesman* from 1925; in this role he was prominent in urging the paper to take a more overtly pro-Labour line and in blocking the appointment of G. D. H. Cole as editor in succession to Clifford Sharp in 1929 (Kingsley Martin was appointed instead).

When the second minority Labour government came to office in May 1929, Bertie Lees-Smith did not immediately attain cabinet rank, despite his prominence within the PLP. It appears that his relations with MacDonald had cooled somewhat since their UDC days, not least because of Lees-Smith's continuing advocacy of a capital levy (wealth tax) and subsequently a surtax long after MacDonald had decided that they were electoral liabilities. Lees-Smith was appointed instead as postmaster-general. However, the unexpected resignation of Trevelyan as president of the Board of Education in March 1931 forced the issue, and Lees-Smith was appointed to replace him. But the context was unfortunate: Labour's one definite policy, of raising the school-leaving age, had been effectively destroyed by its own Catholic back-benchers and the House of Lords, and the continuing economic crisis meant that the main pressure on Lees-Smith was to cut expenditure. Although he resisted this as well as he could, even he was forced to accept cuts during the August 1931 crisis. At the fateful cabinet meeting that led to the fall of the government, he appears to have backed the call for a cut in unemployment benefits; but after MacDonald's defection to the National Government he was elected to the PLP executive and served on its economic policy committee. However, at the general election that followed in October 1931 he was heavily defeated at Keighley in the National Government landslide.

Following his electoral defeat, Lees-Smith returned to full-time work at the LSE. However, he remained very active in politics. Towards the end of 1931 he participated in the second round-table conference on India, in London. Later he was a member of the XYZ Club, a secretive grouping of economists, bankers, business people, and politicians which aimed to furnish Labour with a more convincing economic policy for the future. However, he remained essentially orthodox and moderate in his outlook, and was critical of the Labour left. In 1935 he narrowly regained Keighley and was immediately re-elected to the PLP executive. He continued to take an interest in party policy on education, and by 1939 he had come out against the principle of selection at secondary level. But his main focus was increasingly upon defence matters, and in 1937 he was instrumental in changing the PLP's line to abstaining on, rather than voting against, the defence estimates. When war broke out in 1939 he was appointed to liaise with the secretary of state for war on behalf of the Labour opposition.

In the debates within the Labour leadership at the time of the Norway debate (May 1940) Lees-Smith was one of the leading advocates of the decision to divide the house which led to the fall of Neville Chamberlain's government. There was no place for him in the Churchill coalition that followed, but with Labour's leader, Clement Attlee, now in government, Lees-Smith was elected as acting chairman of the PLP and leader of the opposition. The position was an important one in parliamentary terms, and Lees-Smith fulfilled it with quiet competence. However, as winter approached in 1941 he succumbed increasingly to the asthma that had plagued him throughout his life, and he died at his home, 77 Corringham Road, Golders Green, Middlesex, after a bout of influenza on 18 December 1941. He was survived by his wife. His colleagues felt the loss keenly: Hugh Dalton, not known for overgenerosity towards colleagues, noted that Lees-Smith had been 'a first-class colleague, sensible, balanced, kindly, with no sign of bitterness, envy or egoism' (*War Diary*, 336). Lees-Smith was cremated at Golders Green crematorium on 22 December. ANDREW THORPE

Sources *DLB* • P. Yorke, *Education and the working class: Ruskin College, 1899–1909* (1977) • S. Harris, *Out of control: British foreign policy and the Union of Democratic Control, 1914–1918* (1996) • D. Tanner, *Political change and the labour party, 1910–18* (1990) • B. Simon, *The politics of educational reform, 1920–1940* (1974) • A. Thorpe, *The British general election of 1931* (1991) • E. Durbin, *New Jerusalems: the labour party and the economics of democratic socialism* (1985) • H. Dalton, *The fateful years: memoirs, 1931–1945* (1957) • *The Second World War diary of Hugh Dalton, 1940–1945*, ed. B. Pimlott (1986) • *Labour and the wartime coalition: from the diaries of James Chuter Ede, 1941–1945*, ed. K. Jefferys (1987) • *WWBMP*, vol. 3 • *The Labour who's who* (1927) • *CGPLA Eng. & Wales* (1942)

Archives U. Hull, Brynmor Jones L., corresp. and papers | King's Lond., Liddell Hart C., corresp. with Sir B. H. Liddell Hart

Likenesses cartoon, repro. in *Punch* (1936)

Wealth at death £5038 8*s*. 1*d*.: probate, 9 June 1942, *CGPLA Eng. & Wales*

Smith, Helen Zenna. *See* Price, Evadne (1896–1985).

Smith, Henry (*c*.1560–1591), Church of England clergyman, referred to as the Silver-Tongued Preacher or Silver-Tongued Smith, was born into a well-to-do family at Withcote, Leicestershire, the seat of his grandfather John Smith. He was the eldest son of Erasmus Smith of Somerby and Husbands Bosworth and his first wife, Anne Wye (*née* Byard). Admitted a fellow-commoner to Queens' College, Cambridge, on 17 July 1573, he left soon afterwards and on 15 March 1576, aged fifteen, matriculated at Lincoln College, Oxford, where he graduated BA on 16 February 1579. He was probably the Henry Smith who proceeded MA from Hart Hall in 1583. Some time in 1582 Smith had temporarily silenced the utterances of Robert Dickins of Mansfield, who styled himself the prophet Elijah, denouncing him as 'a young divell' and 'a child of perdition' (Walsham, 214). It was upon this occasion that Smith preached the sermon later published as *The Lost Sheep is Found*. In 1583, along with Robert Browne, he took up residence at the home of Richard Greenham, then rector of Dry Drayton, Cambridgeshire, who drew him into the ranks of the godly.

Despite the objections of some who saw him as disregarding his patrimonial inheritance in favour of a life more appropriate to a second son, Smith pursued the Christian ministry, but found that his evangelical scruples barred him from subscribing to the ceremonial of the Church of England. Yet though he disliked some of the usages of the established church, Smith had little time for the separatist notions of his former companion Browne. Eventually he effected a compromise of conscience, and 'unite[d] with them in affections from whom he dissented in judgement' (Fuller, *Life*) and took up the position of lecturer at St Clement Danes without Temple Bar in 1587, having been elected by the congregation. He held this post until 1589 or 1590, just before his death. The parish was in the patronage of William Cecil, Lord Burghley, who was the brother of Smith's stepmother, Margaret, widow of Roger Cave, as well as being the recipient of recommendations from Greenham and others. Greenham wrote to Burghley that Smith was:

> well exercised in the holy Scriptures, religious and devout in mind, moderate and sober in opinions and affections, discreet and temperate in his behavior, industrious in his studies and affairs, and, as he hoped, of a humble spirit and upright heart, joined with the fervent zeal of the glory of God and the health of souls. (Seaver, 135–6)

The lectureship was approved by a vote of the congregation and rector, and maintained from funds provided by the congregation. Burghley proved Smith's protector, as Fuller notes, 'he was often the skreen who saved Mr. Smith from the scorching, interposing his greatness betwixt him and the anger of some episcopal officers'. The most important of these acts of intercession came in 1588 when John Aylmer, bishop of London, from whom Smith held no licence, ordered him to stop preaching, acting on a report that Smith had denounced the Book of Common Prayer and refused subscription to the Thirty-Nine Articles. Smith turned to Burghley for help, declaring that Aylmer had previously caused him to preach at Paul's Cross (perhaps the occasion of his sermon *The Trumpet of the Soule Sounding to Judgement*), and that he had never spoken against the prayer book. Smith further stated that he adhered fully to the articles of religion, and that he never commented on matters of discipline. With both Burghley and the congregation intervening on his behalf Smith was soon restored; he eventually dedicated his sermons to Lord Burghley.

Even before the death of William Harward, the rector of St Clement Danes, the congregation had attempted to secure the benefice for Smith, but one Richard Webster was presented to it in 1589. A large number of the artisans of the parish, many of whom could only make their mark, testified that his preaching 'had done more good among them than any other that had gone before or, which they doubted, could follow after' (Strype, 103). That Smith either refused the living or was not offered it is likely to have been mainly due to ill health. He states that it is 'Because sickness hath restrained me from preaching' that he now finds himself in 1589 taking up the pen (Fuller, 'To the reader', *Sermons of Mr. Henry Smith*). He retired to his family's estate at Husbands Bosworth to edit and revise his sermons, some of which had been copied by their hearers during their delivery and then printed without Smith's consent. Predeceasing his father, he died on 4 July 1591 at Husbands Bosworth, where he is buried. He is not known to have married.

It was his preaching that secured for Smith his reputation. Wood declares that he was 'esteemed the miracle and wonder of his age, for his prodigious memory, and his fluent, eloquent, and practical way of preaching' (Wood, *Ath. Oxon.*, 1.603). Fuller states that 'he was commonly called the silver-tongued preacher, and that was but one metall below St. Chrysostom himself' (Chrysostom means 'golden-mouthed'), and continues: 'His Church was so crouded with Auditours, that persons of good quality brought their own pews with them, I mean their legs, to stand thereupon in the alleys.' Smith's persuasiveness was renowned: preaching upon Genesis he observed that Sarah had nursed Isaac and emphasized that this was a Christian mother's duty. The result was that even 'Ladies and great Gentlewomen were affected therewith' to recall their infants from their wet-nurses (Fuller, *Life*). Smith himself wrote of preaching that 'To preach simply is not to preach unlearnedly, nor confusedly, but plainely and perspicaciously, that the simplest which dooth heare may understand what is taught, as if he did heare his name' (Collinson, 231).

Recent studies of Smith's sermons have focused on his rhetorical strategies and use of techniques rooted in classical rhetoric. These analyses have perceived connections between Smith's homiletical style and his penchant for writing Latin poetry, an exercise in which he had engaged before he became a preacher, but abandoned after entering upon his religious vocation. Fuller writes that in the 'Humane Arts and Sciences … [he] furnished himself plentifully therewith' (Fuller, *Life*). Even after Smith's death, when his fame depended primarily upon his preaching, Thomas Nashe likened him to Ovid, one gifted enough to write ditties for Apollo, and whose death the Muses mourned. Only three of his Latin poems survive: an epigram on vocations, an elegiac poem on a choice of vocations, and his *Vita supplicium*, a Sapphic poem on the unhappiness of poetry that did not find its end in theology. These appeared in translation in Joshua Sylvester's *The Parliament of Vertues Royal* (1614). Many of Smith's sermons were printed separately in his lifetime, or reissued in small collections shortly after his death. *The Sermons of Master Henrie Smith, Gathered into one Volume*, were first published in 1591; three further editions had followed by the end of 1594, and several more afterwards. They were reprinted, with an introduction and a précis of Smith's life, by Thomas Fuller in 1657, and again in 1675. In more recent times James Grant published an edition of Smith's sermons in 1866, apparently reproducing Fuller's edition of 1675, and John Brown a selection of his sermons in 1908. GARY W. JENKINS

Sources T. Fuller, *The sermons of Mr. Henry Smith … learned treatises, all now gathered into one volume; also, the life of the reverend and learned authour* (1675) • Wood, *Ath. Oxon.*, new edn, 1.603–5 • Tanner, *Bibl. Brit.-Hib.*, 678 • T. Nashe, *Pierce penniless, his supplication to the divell* (1592) • W. Haller, *The rise of puritanism: … the New Jerusalem as set forth in pulpit and press from Thomas Cartwright to John Lilburne and John Milton, 1570–1643*, new edn (New York, 1957) • J. Strype, *Historical collections of the life and acts of … John Aylmer*, new edn (1821) • W. Davis, 'Henry Smith: the preacher as poet', *English Literary Renaissance*, 12 (1982), 30–52 • J. L. Lievsay, 'Silver-tongued Smith, paragon of Elizabethan preachers', *Huntington Library Quarterly*, 11 (1947–8), 13–36 • P. S. Seaver, *The puritan lectureships: the politics of religious dissent, 1560–1662* (1970) • J. W. Blench, *Preaching in England in the late fifteenth and sixteenth centuries* (1964), 184–7 • *STC, 1475–1640*, 678 • P. Collinson, *The religion of protestants* (1982) • *DNB* • A. Walsham, *Providence in early modern England* (1999) • J. Nichols, *The history and antiquities of the county of Leicester*, 3/1 (1800); repr. (1971)

Likenesses T. Cross, line engraving, V&A; repro. in *The sermons of Mr. Henry Smith* (1657) • line engraving, BM, NPG; repro. in H. Smith, *Sermons* (1660?)

Smith [Smyth], **Henry** (*b.* **1619/20**, *d.* in or after **1668**), politician and regicide, was the only son of Henry Smith (1589–1622) of Withcote, Leicestershire, and his wife, Frisjoyce (Frideswide) Wright of Snelston. He was descended from Ambrose Smith, silkman to Elizabeth I, and thus related to the puritan preacher Henry Smith and the merchant and benefactor Erasmus Smith. When his father died in 1622 he became a ward of the king. He matriculated from Magdalen Hall, Oxford, on 26 January 1638 at the age of eighteen, graduated at St Mary Hall on 9 June 1640, and then became a student at Lincoln's Inn. About this time he married the daughter of Cornelius Holland, MP for New Windsor in the Long Parliament and future regicide [*see* Regicides]. He occupied one of the places in the six clerks office, where his wife died of the plague in 1644. He and his family were moved to quarantine in the Temple by order of parliament. There is no direct information of his family, but there is evidence of a son, Erastus, and a daughter, Susannah, wife of Joshua Sacheverell and mother of the controversialist Henry Sacheverell.

On 20 November 1645 Smith entered parliament as a recruiter MP for Leicestershire, his fellow county MP being the radical and future regicide Thomas, Lord Grey of Groby. Like Holland, Smith allied himself with a group of Leveller sympathizers in parliament. His most active period as an MP was the period of Pride's Purge and the early days of the Rump Parliament. In December 1648 he was added to the committee of compounding, and in January 1649 to the committee for the army. Most significantly, on 3 January 1649 he became a member of the committee set up to consider an ordinance for creating 'an High

Court of Justice for Tryal of the King'. Later that month, as one of the judges at the trial of Charles I, he attended all the sittings of the court and signed the death warrant [*see also* Regicides]. After the king's execution he made little contribution in parliament. In 1650 he was a major of horse under Grey of Groby and in 1656 became the colonel of a regiment of foot in Oxfordshire. A company of this regiment accompanied him to Hull in 1658 when he took up residence as governor there. He revealed Slingsby's plot to take over the garrison to the council of state and was commended at the subsequent trial as 'a prudent and faithful governor' (Smith, 150). In July 1659 he was appointed to the governorship of Inverness but did not take up his appointment.

At the Restoration in 1660 Smith was excepted from the Bill of Pardon (9 June) but surrendered himself to the serjeant-at-arms on 19 June in the belief that he would thereby escape execution. He was committed to the Tower on 6 August and stood trial at the Old Bailey on 16 October after pleading not guilty to the charge of high treason. At his trial he cut a poor figure. He exasperated his interrogators by claiming he could not remember being present in the painted chamber or signing the king's death warrant. He pleaded ignorance—'What I did was done ignorantly, not knowing the law'—and duress—'There were those about me that were able to call me who were then in authority whom I dared not disobey. If so, I had been in danger also' (Noble, 2.237–8). The lord chief baron contemptuously accepted that 'he was led on even as one silly sheep follows another'. Smith presented a petition begging the court to act as mediator with the king. He was committed to the Tower pending an appeal which was heard in Star Chamber in November 1661 when the sentence of execution was commuted to life imprisonment. He remained in the Tower until 1 April 1664 when he was transported to Gorey Castle in Jersey, where he is presumed to have died. He was still alive in 1668 when Thomas Morgan became governor of the island. Smith's verdict on his career had been that, 'I can speak it seriously that from the first to the last of these unhappy wars, I have been a man of trouble and sorrow' (Noble, 2.238).

K. R. GARDINER and D. L. GARDINER

Sources J. Nichols, *The history and antiquities of the county of Leicester*, 4 vols. (1795–1815) • *JHC*, 3–8 (1642–67) • *CSP dom.*, 1649–61; 1667–8 • M. Noble, *The lives of the English regicides*, 2 vols. (1798) • D. Hasson, *Life of John Milton*, 7 vols. (1877–94); repr. (1965), vols. 3, 5–6 • C. H. Firth and G. Davies, *The regimental history of Cromwell's army*, 2 vols. (1940) • Royal warrant committing Smith to prison in Jersey, PRO, WO 94/001 • C. H. Firth, ed., 'Two letters addressed to Cromwell', *EngHR*, 22 (1907), 308–15 • G. R. Smith, *Without touch of dishonour: the life and death of Sir Henry Slingsby, 1602–58* (1968) • PRO, Ward 7/61/155 • Foster, *Alum. Oxon.*, 1500–1714, 4.1372 • *IGI*

Wealth at death estates confiscated in 1660

Smith, Sir Henry Babington (1863–1923), civil servant and financier, was born on 29 January 1863 at Riverbank, Putney, the London home of his father, Archibald *Smith (1813–1872), barrister and mathematician. His mother was Susan Emma (*d.* 1913), the daughter of Sir James *Parker, who was connected to the Babington and Macaulay families. The Smiths had settled at Craigend, Stirlingshire, as 'kindly tenants' of the dukes of Montrose, and became armourers. Smith's paternal great-grandfather, Archibald Smith, was a West India merchant who purchased the estate of Jordanhill, Renfrewshire, in 1800. His grandfather was James *Smith (1782–1867), the authority on ancient shipbuilding and navigation. Henry Babington Smith was the sixth of seven brothers, all but one of whom distinguished themselves in later life; the exception died in infancy. The eldest, James Parker Smith (1854–1929), a barrister and MP, became a close associate of Joseph Chamberlain in the campaign for tariff reform; the second, Walter Edward Smith (*b.* 1855), was vicar of Andover, Hampshire; the third, Charles Stewart Smith (1859–1934), was consul-general at Barcelona; the fifth, Arthur Hamilton *Smith, was keeper of Greek and Roman antiquities at the British Museum; and the youngest, George Edward Smith (1868–1944), became a brigadier-general in the Royal Engineers.

Smith attended private schools before proceeding in 1875 to Eton College as a king's scholar. There he won the Tomline mathematical prize (1880) and the Newcastle medal (1882). His circle of friends included H. F. W. Tatham, W. R. Inge, A. C. Benson, and Montague Rhodes James. Competent in football and in the boats, he was also captain of school. After travel in Italy and Greece he went up in 1882 to Trinity College, Cambridge, where he gained a first class in both parts of the classical tripos, and won the Browne gold medal for a Latin epigram three times (1884–6). He was elected a fellow of Trinity in 1890. At Cambridge as at Eton, he enjoyed an illustrious company of comrades. He was elected to the Apostles in 1885 (his brothers James Parker and Arthur Hamilton had been Apostles earlier) and belonged to the society in the generation which included Harry Cust, Lowes Dickinson, and Roger Fry. Smith also belonged to TAF (Twice a Fortnightly; its members met for supper twice a fortnight) which included J. K. Stephen, Hugh Benson, Gerald Duckworth, and Walter Headlam. Montague Rhodes James said of Smith, '[n]ever what you call frolicsome, he was in youth and later one who never seemed externally to get any older' (Bushnell, 18).

Smith was an assistant master at Winchester College in 1886, but the next year he joined the civil service as an examiner in the education department, an administrative post appointed not by open competition but on the nomination of the lord president, Lord Cranbrook, who recognized Smith's great distinctions and was 'glad to aid James Parker's grandson' (Sutherland, 36). He became principal private secretary to Goschen, the chancellor of the exchequer, in 1891, but entered the Treasury as a clerk when Lord Salisbury's government fell in 1892. The same year he was appointed secretary to the British delegates at the Brussels silver conference, where he had his first taste of international finance, a field which he would make particularly his own.

In 1894 Victor Alexander *Bruce, the ninth earl of Elgin, newly appointed viceroy of India, selected Smith as his private secretary, and Smith sailed for India. There he married, at Simla, Elgin's eldest daughter, Elisabeth Mary

Bruce (1877–1944), on 22 September 1898. They had four sons and six daughters. He returned from India in 1899 and on the outbreak of the Second South African War the Treasury sent him to conduct an inquiry into the finances of Natal. While he was in South Africa, Salisbury invited him to become the British and Dutch representative on the council of the administration of the Ottoman public debt, of which council he served as president in 1901. He received the Osmanieh order, first class, for his service.

From 1903 until 1909 Smith was secretary to the Post Office, and was the British representative at the postal conference in Rome (1906), at the radiotelegraph conference at Berlin (1906), and at the telegraph commission at Lisbon (1908). He left the civil service in 1909 when, through the influence of Sir Ernest Cassel (whose personal finances Smith came to supervise), the Foreign Office requested him to become *administrateur-directeur-général* of the National Bank of Turkey in 1909. After an initial period of two and a half years the appointment was extended. In 1914 Smith became chairman of the Treasury committee on assistance to traders, and chairman of the Pacific Cable Board.

The government drew on Smith's financial experience during the First World War. In 1915 he was chairman of the royal commission on the civil service and of the board of reference on war profits. The same year he went with Lord Reading on the Anglo-French mission to the United States. In 1916 he served as chairman of the enemy debts committee. In 1917 Smith became chairman of the committee appointed to inquire into the limitation of imports, and presided over the committees on war claims and export trade. In 1918 Smith returned to the United States as assistant high commissioner, and in 1919 he became chairman of the Indian exchange and currency committee. He became a director of the Bank of England in 1920.

Smith was appointed CSI in 1897 and CB in 1905. He was created KCB in 1908 and was made a Companion of Honour in 1917 and GBE in 1920. His proudest honour was to be fellow of Eton. He declined Campbell-Bannerman's offer to become governor of Bombay because it would have meant a peerage. Smith explained to his children: '[n]o man is wise who burdens a large family with such trappings. I did without them and so can you' (Bushnell, 26–7). Botany, archaeology, and photography were among his interests and he was an ardent book collector throughout his life. His collection contained incomparable editions of the *Religio medici*. Smith died of encephalitis lethargia on 29 September 1923 at his home, The Vineyards, Saffron Walden, Essex, and was buried at Eton College. His wife survived him.

WILLIAM C. LUBENOW

Sources G. H. Bushnell, *Sir Henry Babington Smith, G.B.E., C.H., K.C.B., C.S.I., M.A., 1863–1923, civil servant and financier* (1942) • Trinity Cam., H. B. Smith MSS • Mitchell L., Glas., Strathclyde regional archives, Smith of Jordanhill MSS • [J. D. Duff], 'Sir Henry Babington Smith', *Cambridge Review* (19 Oct 1923), 10 • *The Times* (1 Oct 1923), 15 • d. cert. • Burke, *Gen. GB* (1952) • G. Sutherland, *Policy-making in elementary education, 1870–1895* (1973)

Archives Mitchell L., Glas., Strathclyde regional archives, Smith of Jordanhill MSS • Trinity Cam., corresp. and papers | BL OIOC, letters to Lord Elgin, MS Eur. F 102 • BL OIOC, letters to Lord Reading, MSS Eur. E 238, F 118 • Bodl. Oxf., corresp. with Lord Kimberley

Likenesses W. Stoneman, photograph, 1917, NPG

Wealth at death £62,852 17*s*. 9*d*.: probate, 18 Jan 1924, *CGPLA Eng. & Wales*

Smith, Sir Henry George Wakelyn [Harry], **baronet, of Aliwal** (**1787–1860**), army officer and colonial governor, fifth of thirteen children, was born on 28 June 1787 at Whittlesea in the Isle of Ely, where his father, John Smith, was a surgeon. His mother, Eleanor, was daughter of George Moore, minor canon of Peterborough. His favourite sister, Mrs Jane Alice Sargant, was a minor author, and two of his brothers, Thomas Lawrence Smith (1792–1877) and Charles Smith (1795–1854), served with him in the army, including at Waterloo.

Early career After brief service in his home yeomanry, Harry received a commission as ensign in the 95th foot, afterwards the Rifle brigade, on 17 May 1805. Promoted lieutenant on 15 August the same year, he was quartered at Shorncliffe. In June 1806 he embarked for service under Sir Samuel Auchmuty in South America. In January 1807 a landing was effected near the mouth of the River Plate. After some fighting the suburbs of Montevideo were occupied, and the city was captured in February. Smith also took part on 5 July in the disastrous attack on Buenos Aires, after which he returned with his regiment to England in December 1807.

In 1808 Smith embarked with some companies of the 2nd battalion for the Iberian peninsula and landed at Corunna on 26 October. In December he was brigaded with the 43rd and 52nd foot under Brigadier-General Robert Craufurd, and served throughout the retreat to and the battle of Corunna on 16 January 1809. Embarking the same night, he arrived at Portsmouth on the 21st.

In May 1809 Smith sailed with the 1st battalion under Lieutenant-Colonel Beckwith for Lisbon, where they landed on 2 July and joined Brigadier-General Craufurd's brigade. Smith was awkwardly wounded in the ankle at the action of the Coa, near Almeida, on 24 July 1810. In March 1811 he commanded a company in the pursuit of Masséna from the lines of Torres Vedras, and was engaged in the actions of Redinha (12 March), Condeixa (13 March), and Foz d'Aronce (15 March). In the same month he was appointed to the staff as brigade major to the 2nd light brigade of the light division. In this capacity he was engaged in the action of Sabugal on 3 April, in the battle of Fuentes de Oñoro on 5 May, and at the siege and storming of Ciudad Rodrigo on 19 January 1812. After being promoted captain on 28 February 1812, he was also at the siege and storming of Badajos on 6 April. The day after the assault two handsome Spanish ladies, one the wife of a Spanish officer serving elsewhere and the other her sister, a girl of fourteen years of age—Juana Maria de los Dolores de Leon (*d*. 1872)—claimed the protection of Smith and a brother officer. They had fled to the camp from Badajos, where they had suffered violence from the infuriated soldiery, who had torn their earrings from their ears. Only a few days after they had met, the younger sister, Juana, became

Sir Henry George Wakelyn Smith, baronet, of Aliwal (1787–1860), by unknown artist, after 1848

Smith's wife. She accompanied him to the end of the war and on all his subsequent tours of overseas duty, except that to America. She was well known afterwards in Regency society and was the model for *The Spanish Bride* in Georgette Heyer's novel of that name (1940).

Smith took part in the battle of Salamanca on 22 July 1812, the battle of Vitoria on 21 June 1813, the passage of the Bidassoa on 7 October, and the attack on the heights of Vera, and in the battle of Sarre, the attack upon the position of St Jean de Luz, and the attack on the heights of Arcangues in November. He also took part in the battle of Orthez on 27 February 1814, the combat at Tarbes on 20 March, and the battle of Toulouse on 10 April 1814.

On the termination of hostilities with France, Smith was appointed in May assistant adjutant-general to the force sent under Major-General Ross to carry on the Anglo-American War of 1812–14. On 2 June he sailed from Bordeaux on board the fleet of Rear-Admiral Pulteney Malcolm, which carried the expedition. They arrived in Chesapeake Bay early in August, landed at St Benedict in the Patuxent River on the 19 August, and marched on Washington. On 24 August Smith took part in the battle of Bladensburg and in the capture and burning of Washington. He was sent home with dispatches in recognition of his services and was promoted brevet major on 29 September 1814. He left England again at once with reinforcements under Sir Edward Pakenham, and joined the British land and sea forces before New Orleans on 25 December. Pakenham took the command ashore, and Smith resumed his duties as assistant adjutant-general. Pakenham was killed in the unsuccessful attack on New Orleans on 8 January 1815. Sir John Lambert assumed the command, appointed Smith his military secretary, and employed him to negotiate with the enemy. During the night a truce for two days was with difficulty effected by Smith, who passed and repassed frequently between the opposing forces.

Smith sailed with the expedition, on 27 January, to attempt the capture of Mobile, 100 miles to the east of New Orleans. Troops were landed to attack Fort Bowyer. On the completion of the siege approaches to the fort, Smith was sent in with a summons to surrender. On 11 February the commandant, having elicited from Smith that the place would certainly be taken if stormed, capitulated. Hostilities ceased three days later, as news had arrived that preliminaries of peace between Britain and the United States had been settled at Ghent on 24 December 1814.

Smith reached England during Napoleon's 'hundred days' in time to proceed to the Netherlands as assistant quartermaster-general to the 6th division of the army of the duke of Wellington. He fought at Waterloo, where Juana later searched him out on the battlefield, and accompanied the allied army to Paris. He was made CB, military division, and promoted brevet lieutenant-colonel from 18 June 1815. He received the Waterloo medal and the war medal with twelve clasps for the Peninsula. Subsequently he filled the post of town-major at Cambrai, where the duke of Wellington fixed his headquarters during the occupation of France by the allied troops.

At the Cape Smith returned to England in 1818 and served with the 2nd battalion of the rifle brigade in Shorncliffe, Gosport, Glasgow, Belfast, and Nova Scotia. On 23 November 1826 he was appointed deputy quartermaster-general of the forces in Jamaica. On 24 July 1828 he was transferred, in the same capacity, to the Cape of Good Hope, under Governor Sir Galbraith Lowry Cole.

On the outbreak of a Cape frontier war at the end of 1834 Sir Benjamin D'Urban, who had succeeded Cole, appointed Smith to be his second in command in the colony from 1 January 1835. Smith at once rode from Cape Town to Grahamstown. He accomplished the ride of 700 miles, over a rough and almost roadless country, in the extraordinarily short period of six days. The feat is still deservedly remembered. After calming the anxious settler community he left Grahamstown with a force of 1100 men to clear the country between the Fish and Keiskamma rivers of Xhosa warriors. In March he prepared a central camp at Fort Willshire, where 3000 troops were assembled before advancing. Towards the end of April D'Urban and Smith carried operations across the Kei River, into the land of Hintsa, chief of the Gcaleka (Xhosa). Smith put Hintsa under restriction after a parley, but he escaped on 12 May, when riding with Smith on the march with his column. He was pursued and overtaken by Smith, who dragged him from his saddle. Hintsa managed to get away, but was shot the same day on the Ngqabara Stream by Lieutenant George Southey, under circumstances which, though disputed, caused an outcry. The war came to an end in June.

The Kei River was made the new boundary, and the country between the Great Fish and Kei rivers was annexed and secured by a series of forts. On Sir Benjamin D'Urban leaving the front on 10 June he appointed Smith to command the troops and to administer the new province of Queen Adelaide, as he named it. On 17 September a formal treaty with the Xhosa chiefs was concluded by Smith at Fort Willshire, and a commission, over which he presided, was appointed to carry it into effect. As chief commissioner Smith defined the boundaries of the land given to each chiefdom and brought about a semblance of control. But the secretary of state, Lord Glenelg, disapproved of the extension of frontier and reversed it on both financial and humanitarian grounds. In consequence of Glenelg's action, Smith returned to Cape Town and resumed his duties as deputy quartermaster-general on 30 September 1836.

India and Aliwal On 10 January 1837 Smith was promoted brevet colonel and on 6 March 1840 he was appointed adjutant-general of the queen's army in India. In December 1843 he took part as adjutant-general in the Gwalior campaign under the commander-in-chief in India, Sir Hugh (afterwards Lord) Gough, and for his distinguished services at the battle of Maharajpur on 29 December was thanked in dispatches and made a knight commander of the Bath.

Early in December 1845, on the outbreak of the First Anglo-Sikh War, Smith was given the command of a division with the honorary rank of major-general. He took a prominent part in the battle of Mudki on 18 December, and again distinguished himself at the battle of Ferozeshahr on 21 and 22 December. He was mentioned in dispatches for his 'unceasing exertions' on both occasions. On 18 January 1846 Smith, with a brigade, reduced the fort of Dharmkote. He then marched towards Ludhiana and, by means of some very delicate combinations, executed with great skill but severe loss, effected communication with that place. On 28 January he encountered the Sikhs in open battle at Aliwal and, leading the final charge in person, drove the enemy headlong over the difficult ford of the broad Sutlej. He took over sixty pieces of ordnance (all that the enemy had in the field), and wrested from them their camp, baggage, and stores of ammunition and grain. The duke of Wellington, in the House of Lords (3 April 1846), said of Smith's conduct at Aliwal: 'I never read an account of any affair in which an officer has shown himself more capable than this officer did of commanding troops in the field.' Of Smith's dispatch announcing his victory Thackeray wrote in his essay 'On military snobs': 'A noble deed was never told in nobler language.'

Smith rejoined headquarters on 8 February and two days later commanded the 1st division of infantry at the crowning victory of the campaign—the battle of Sobraon. Smith was commended in dispatches, both by the commander-in-chief, Gough, and by the governor-general, Sir Henry Hardinge, who took part in the campaign.

Smith was promoted major-general in the East India Company's army on 1 April 1846. For his services in the First Anglo-Sikh War, and especially for his victory at Aliwal, he was created a baronet, with the special designation 'of Aliwal' added to the title, and given the grand cross of the Bath. He received the thanks of both houses of parliament, of the East India Company, and of the duke of Wellington as commander-in-chief. The freedom of the cities of London and Glasgow was conferred on him, and on 9 November of the same year he was promoted a British major-general. In 1847 Cambridge granted him the honorary degree of LLD at the installation of the prince consort as chancellor.

South Africa again: the years of difficulty On 18 January 1847 Smith was gazetted colonel of the 47th foot, and on 16 April of the same year he was transferred to the rifle brigade as colonel-commandant of the 2nd battalion. He returned to England on sick leave and on 3 September 1847 was appointed governor of the Cape of Good Hope and high commissioner of its dependencies, and promoted local lieutenant-general to command the troops there. On his arrival at the Cape on 1 December 1847 Smith was most enthusiastically received. The 1846–7 Cape Frontier War with the Xhosa, which had been going on for some time, had just ended with the capture of Sandile and other chiefs. Smith hastened to King William's Town, where he arrived on 23 December. He held a meeting of the Xhosa chiefs and released Sandile and the others. He issued a proclamation extending Cape Colony to the Orange and Keiskamma rivers. He also announced himself, as representative of the queen, the supreme chief, or *inkosi inkulu*, of the Xhosa. The chiefs had to make their submission under histrionic circumstances, and Smith ordered the annexed territory to be called British Kaffraria. He then visited Natal in an unsuccessful attempt to prevent an exodus of Boers from that embryo colony.

Pretorius, the Boer leader, objected to a proclamation issued by Smith on 3 February 1848, when in camp on the Tugela, which extended British sovereignty over the country between the Vaal and Orange rivers. Early in July Pretorius raised a commando and established himself at Bloemfontein, from which he expelled the British resident. Smith, who was at Cape Town when the news arrived, acted with vigour by ordering a column to march from Grahamstown to Colesberg. He himself met them near the Orange River on 21 August 1848 and on 29 August arrived with the column at Boomplaats, where he found the Boers, 1000 strong, holding a formidable position. He attacked in the middle of the day and stormed the position. The Boers were completely beaten, and broke and fled. Many of the farmers crossed the Vaal with Pretorius to help establish the independence of the Transvaal (recognized in 1852); the remainder returned to their farms and awaited the course of events. Smith continued his pursuit the following day towards Bloemfontein, where he arrived on 2 September and reinstated the British resident. But costly control measures against Moshoeshoe's

Sotho bedevilled the stability of Smith's Orange River sovereignty and caused its abandonment after his departure. This territory south of the Vaal became in 1854 the republican Orange Free State.

During 1848 and 1849 there was considerable excitement in Cape Town over the proposal by the British government to establish a penal settlement there. After a very strong representation had been made by Smith as governor to Earl Grey on the subject, the secretary of state decided that the ticket-of-leave men who had already sailed in the *Neptune* should nevertheless be landed at the Cape, but that no more should be sent. On the arrival of the *Neptune* on 20 September 1849 shops were closed and business suspended. A committee had been formed to prevent the landing of the convicts and was supported by the community. It was resolved not to furnish the *Neptune*, or indeed anyone connected with government, with supplies. Smith acted with great forbearance but did his best to induce the home government to send the *Neptune* away. In the meantime he would not allow the convicts to be landed. His representations resulted in the arrival of orders in February 1850 to transport the convicts in the *Neptune* to Tasmania. While this convict crisis accelerated the Cape's advance to representative government, it paradoxically frustrated Smith's own attempts to gain colonial acceptance for the new constitution, which only received final approval in 1853, after his departure.

During 1850 there were warnings of a Xhosa rising. Too late, Smith summoned a meeting of chiefs to King William's Town. Sandile refused to attend and was deposed on 30 October by Smith acting on his own authority as high commissioner. Sandile's deposition had no effect other than that of angering the Xhosa. Smith had scarcely returned to Cape Town when he received accounts which made him hasten back to the frontier with all available troops. On 24 December a column of troops moving to arrest the deposed chief was attacked with some success in the Boomah Pass near Keiskammahoek, and on Christmas day a massacre of white males took place in Smith's frontier military villages of Juanasburg, Woburn, and Auckland in the Tyhume valley. At the same time Smith himself was besieged at Fort Cox by the Xhosa. On 31 December he sallied out in disguise with his troops and, making a dash through the besiegers, succeeded in reaching King William's Town. A large body of Khoi of the Kat River joined in the uprising and made it more serious. Smith could do little without reinforcements, but while awaiting them he called all loyal inhabitants, both white and black, to arms. He took the field in person on 18 March and went to the relief of forts Hare, Cox, and White. Reinforcements began to arrive in May, so Smith organized columns to scour the country and attack, with varied success, the strongholds of the Xhosa in the mountains. Nevertheless, on 7 April 1852 Smith was superseded by Lieutenant-General the Hon. George Cathcart, because the home government was dissatisfied with the slow progress made in crushing the rising and with the costs incurred. In a blaze of well-wishes and popularity among the white Cape community, the Smiths departed for Britain.

Final years, death, and reputation On 18 November 1852 Smith was a standard-bearer at the funeral of the duke of Wellington at St Paul's. On 21 January 1853 he was appointed to the command of the western military district, and made lieutenant-governor of Plymouth. He was promoted lieutenant-general on 20 June 1854, and on 29 September of the same year was transferred to the command of the northern military district, which he held until 30 June 1859. He died of angina pectoris and its complications on 12 October 1860, at his residence in Eaton Place West, London. His widow died on 10 October 1872. They had no children. Both Smith and his wife were buried in the cemetery at Whittlesea, the place of his birth. By way of memorial to him the chancel aisle of St Mary's, Whittlesea, was restored in 1862, and a marble monument with his bust was placed there. The aisle is known as Sir Harry's Chapel. The sabre Smith wore from 1835 to 1857 was given on her request to Queen Victoria. The towns Harrismith and Smithfield (Orange Free State), Ladysmith (Natal), Ladismith, Whittlesey, and Aliwal (Cape) commemorate Smith's connection with South Africa.

Smith was not devoid of the self-assertion characteristic of men who fight their own way in the world and owe their successes solely to their energy and ability; but he was popular with his colleagues and subordinates, who were fascinated by his daring energy, histrionics, and originality, and who admired his rough and ready wit.

R. H. VETCH, *rev.* JOHN BENYON

Sources *The autobiography of Lieutenant-General Sir Harry Smith*, ed. G. C. Moore Smith, 2 vols. (1901); repr. (1902) · J. H. Lehmann, *Remember you are an Englishman: a biography of Sir Harry Smith* (1977) · C. W. C. Oman, *A history of the Peninsular War*, 1–5 (1902–14) · *The autobiography of Sir Andries Stockenström*, ed. C. W. Hutton (1887) · H. C. B. Cook, *The Sikh wars: the British army in the Punjab, 1845–1849* (1975) · A. H. Craufurd, *General Craufurd and his light division* (1892) · G. Heyer, *The Spanish bride* (1940) · J. E. Hasted, *The gentle amazon: life of Lady Smith* (1952) · A. E. Du Toit, 'The Cape frontier: a study of native policy with special reference to the years 1847–1866', *Archives year book for South African history*, 1 (1954) · G. E. Cory, *The rise of South Africa*, 1 (1910) · J. S. Galbraith, *Reluctant empire* (1963) · N. Mostert, *Frontiers: the epic of South Africa's creation and the tragedy of the Xhosa people* (1992) · T. J. Stapleton, *Magoma: Xhosa resistance to colonial advance* (1994)

Archives Cape Archives, Cape Town · CUL, MS autobiography · NAM, letters to subordinates [copies] · PRO, corresp., diary, and papers, WO 135 · Rhodes University, Grahamstown, South Africa, Cory Library for Historical Research, corresp. and papers relating to Cape Colony · Royal Green Jackets Museum, Peninsular Barracks, Winchester | BL OIOC, letters to Lord Tweeddale, MS Eur. F 96 · NL Scot., corresp. with Sir George Brown · U. Durham L., corresp. with third Earl Grey

Likenesses miniature, after 1848, NPG [*see illus.*] · G. G. Adams, marble bust, St Mary's Church, Whittlesea, Ely, Sir Harry's Chapel; plaster replica, NPG · J. C. Brewer, portrait, Africana Museum, Johannesburg · E. Dalton, lithographs, BM, NPG · T. Fairbank, print (after H. Moseley, 1847), BL OIOC · F. T. Ions, portrait, Africana Museum, Johannesburg · W. Melville, portrait, Africana Museum, Johannesburg · D. J. Pound, stipple and line (after photograph by J. Eastham), NPG · J. D. Pound, photogravure photograph (after J. Easton, *c.*1854), Mendelssohn Library, Cape Town, South Africa · portrait, South African Library, South Africa, Fairbridge collection · portrait, president's residence, Cape Town, South

Africa · portrait, repro. in Moore-Smith, ed., *Autobiography* · portrait, repro. in Lehmann, *Remember you are an Englishman* · wood-engraving, NPG; repro. in *ILN* (1846)

Wealth at death childless; a lieutenant-general; sometimes financially distressed in younger life

Smith, Henry John Stephen (1826–1883), mathematician, was born on 2 November 1826 in Dublin, the youngest of the four children of John Smith (1792–1828), an Irish barrister, and his wife, Mary (*d.* 1857), one of the fourteen children of John Murphy from near Bantry Bay. After his father died in 1828, his widowed mother moved with the family several times before settling at Ryde on the Isle of Wight in 1831. A precocious child, Smith was educated first by his mother and then, from 1838, by private tutors. He went to Rugby School in 1841, but left after the death of his brother in 1843, when his family moved abroad.

On 29 November 1844 Smith was awarded a scholarship at Balliol College, Oxford, but his early undergraduate career was soon disrupted, when, on successive visits to his family on the continent, he contracted first smallpox and then malaria. None the less, he put his enforced convalescence during 1845–7 to good use. He spoke French and Italian fluently, and had a good command of German. While recuperating in Paris he was able to attend lectures at the Collège de France and the Sorbonne, in particular those of Arago and Milne Edwards. He returned to Oxford at Easter 1847, and the following year won the Ireland scholarship for classics. In 1849, just two years after resuming his studies at Oxford, he gained first-class honours in both classics and mathematics (BA 1850, MA 1855) and was elected a fellow of Balliol. In 1850, after careful consideration, he accepted the mathematical lecturership at the college, and in the following year added the senior mathematical scholarship to the list of his university distinctions.

In 1853, in response to the introduction of the new honour school of natural science, Balliol built the first college teaching laboratory and asked Smith to run it. To equip himself for this task he studied in Oxford with Nevil Story-Maskelyne, who became a close friend, and at the Royal College of Chemistry with August Hofmann. He gave chemistry lectures and practical instruction for two years, until, in December 1855, the laboratory was handed over for the use of Benjamin Brodie.

In 1861 Smith was elected Savilian professor of geometry, in succession to Baden Powell who had died suddenly the previous year, and in the same year he became both FRS and FRAS. However, he could not afford to give up the mathematical lecturership, and it was only in 1873 that his election to a sinecure fellowship at Corpus Christi College enabled him to relinquish his teaching duties at Balliol. (He retained his association with Balliol, however, by virtue of his election to an honorary fellowship.) During the late 1860s, in his capacity as Balliol's lecturer, he collaborated with his colleagues at Merton, Exeter, and University colleges in setting up the first combined college lectures. These served as a model for other subjects and groups of colleges, and formed the prototype for the system of lectures later adopted by the university.

Smith never married, and on the death of their mother in 1857 his sister Eleanor [*see below*] moved to keep house for him in Oxford during the terms, first at 64 St Giles' and, following his appointment as keeper of the University Museum in 1874, at the keeper's house, University Museum, South Parks Road. He was a tall, good-looking man, renowned for his charm, generosity, warmth, and spontaneous wit, who greeted the appointment of a pessimistic friend to high office in India with the words 'How fortunate! It will give him another world to despair of' ('Biographical sketches', xxxiv). It is reported that he broke off one mathematics lecture to observe that 'it is the peculiar beauty of this method, gentlemen, and one which endears it to the really scientific mind, that under no circumstances can it be of the smallest possible utility' (ibid., xxxiii–xxxiv).

Smith, who read widely and retained a strong interest in classics, enjoyed the respect of colleagues who knew little of his achievements within mathematics. His 1855 essay on the plurality of worlds in an Oxford collection was widely admired. John Conington, the professor of Latin, once remarked:

> I do not know what Henry Smith may be at the subjects of which he professes to know something; but I never go to him about a matter of scholarship, in a line where he professes to know nothing without learning more from him than I can get from any one else. ('Biographical sketches', xix)

Charles Pearson described him as 'the only one I have known whose superiority was so incontestable that it extinguished jealousy, and whose popularity was such that he had no personal enemies' (*Charles Henry Pearson*, 108).

Smith sought to promote the natural sciences and research within the university, without compromising its older studies or teaching. His ability to find the acceptable compromise which defuses angry debate, coupled with his unrivalled range of experience, made him an invaluable member of the numerous university committees on which he served. His friends, deploring his lack of ambition, urged him to spend less time on routine chores which could as well be done by others, but his strong sense of public duty forbade this. He saw no conflict of interests, believing that mathematics demanded a concentration impossible to maintain for more than short periods, but he did grow uneasy at the accumulation of unpublished results in his notebooks.

Despite his popularity within the university, the solid Conservative vote of the old members, aware of his Liberal sympathies, ensured Smith's defeat when he stood as a candidate for a university seat in the 1878 by-election. None the less, there were other opportunities for him to use his skills on the national stage. He was first chairman of the Meteorological Council, which he represented at the International Meteorological Congress at Rome in 1879, and sat on the royal commission into scientific instruction (the Devonshire commission) and on the royal commission into the universities. He was president of the mathematical section of the British Association at Bradford in 1873 and of the London Mathematical Society (which he had joined in the first year of its foundation) in

1874–6. His presidential address, 'On the present state and prospects of some branches of pure mathematics' (*Proceedings of the London Mathematical Society*, 8, 1876, 6–29), was influential and often quoted. He received honorary degrees of LLD from the universities of Cambridge and Dublin, and shared the 1868 Steiner prize of the Königliche Preussische Akademie der Wissenschaften (Royal Prussian Academy of Sciences) in Berlin for his solution of a problem on the intersection of quartic curves.

Smith's mathematical work lay mostly within geometry, number theory, and elliptic function theory. One exception is a paper on the integration of discontinuous functions (*Proceedings of the London Mathematical Society*, 6, 1875, 140–53), in which he constructed various fractal sets, including the Cantor set, some eight years before Cantor's own paper. His main contributions were, however, in number theory. The six-part 'Report on the theory of numbers', commissioned by the British Association, and presented at its meetings between 1859 and 1865, provided a systematic account of the subject as it had developed until that time, and was widely acclaimed by continental mathematicians as well as those in Britain. In his paper on systems of linear equations and congruences (*PTRS*, 101, 1861, 293–326) he showed that any matrix with integer entries can be put into what is now often called Smith normal form. This provided an elegant procedure for deciding when a system of simultaneous linear equations with integer coefficients has integer solutions, and to determine them when they exist, thus completing the solution to a problem studied since antiquity.

In 'The orders and genera of quadratic forms containing more than three indeterminates' (*PRS*, 16, 1867, 197–208) Smith applied the same result to find the number of ways in which a given positive integer can be expressed as a sum of some fixed number of squares. Various algebraic and analytic techniques had already provided answers for sums of two, three, four, and six squares and partial answers for five and seven squares. Smith outlined a uniform algebraic method for dealing with all the cases simultaneously and gave the full solutions to the problem for five and seven squares, thus completing the whole project. In 1882 the Paris Académie des Sciences, through some oversight, offered its *grand prix de sciences mathématiques* for this very problem, which Smith had already solved fifteen years earlier. When Smith alerted Charles Hermite to his priority, he was asked to help the *académie* avoid embarrassment by submitting his detailed work for the competition. He complied with this request, but died two months before the announcement that the prize had been awarded jointly to him and to a young Prussian student, Hermann Minkowski. After considerable public discussion of whether Minkowski had plagiarized Smith's earlier publications, a second prize was created so that each winner was awarded a full prize.

Apart from one recurrence of malaria, Smith had generally enjoyed good health, but about 1881 the strain of overwork began to show. He died at home of an abscess of the liver on 9 February 1883 and was buried on 13 February in St Sepulchre's cemetery, Oxford. After his death his mathematical papers were collected and edited by James Glaisher and, prefaced by biographical reminiscences, were published in 1894.

Smith's sister, **Eleanor Elizabeth Smith** (1822–1896), was born on 30 September 1822. Like her brother she travelled widely on the continent, and was a good linguist with an extensive knowledge of European literature. She taught herself Hebrew at the age of seven. In the 1860s, before the foundation of the first women's colleges in Oxford, she persuaded various professors sympathetic to the education of women to give a series of women's lectures and organized the first course in 1866. She was one of the women who gave evidence as expert witnesses to the royal commission on schools of 1864 (published in 1868 as the Taunton report). When the Oxford schools board was set up in 1871 she stood as a non-sectarian candidate and was elected as its first woman member. She remained on the board until 1883 but did not achieve her object of founding a non-denominational board school.

Eleanor Smith helped to found and was one of the original (1879) members of the council of Somerville, the women's college at Oxford, and served for many years as a trustee of Bedford College, London. In 1895 she supported the campaign to open Oxford degrees to women. In addition to her keen interest in women's education, Eleanor Smith gave generous support to schemes for improving the health of the poor. She served on the committees of both the Radcliffe Infirmary and the Sarah Acland Home for Nurses, and was a promoter and director of the Provident Dispensary. She died at her home, 27 Banbury Road, Oxford, on 15 September 1896, and was buried at St Sepulchre's cemetery, Oxford, on 19 September. The jurist A. V. Dicey, a lifelong friend, was her executor.

KEITH HANNABUSS

Sources 'Biographical sketches', *The collected mathematical papers of H. J. S. Smith*, ed. J. W. L. Glaisher (1894) · *The Times* (10 Feb 1883) · *Oxford Magazine* (14 Feb 1883) · *Oxford Magazine* (21 Feb 1883) · *Nature*, 27 (1882–3), 381–4 · *Monthly Notices of the Royal Astronomical Society*, 44 (1883–4), 138–49 · *Fortnightly Review*, 39 (1883), 653–66 · *Comptes Rendus*, 96 (1883), 1095 · *Atti dell'Accademia dei Lincei*, 3/7 (1883), 162–3 · admissions book and minutes of college meetings, Balliol Oxf. · Pearson MSS, Bodl. Oxf., MS Eng. lett. d. 191 · A. G. V. Harcourt, 'The Oxford Museum and its founders', *Cornhill Magazine*, [3rd] ser., 28 (1910), 350–63 · M. E. G. Duff, *Notes from a diary, kept chiefly in southern India, 1881–1886*, 2 vols. (1899) · E. B. Elliott, 'The honour school of mathematics and physics', *The English education exhibition 1900* · H. A. Miers, 'Prof. N. Story Maskelyne', *Nature*, 86 (1910–11), 452–3 · T. Smith, 'The Balliol–Trinity laboratories', *Balliol Studies*, ed. J. M. Prest (1982), 187–224 · K. C. Hannabuss, 'Henry Smith', *Oxford figures*, ed. J. Fauvel, R. Flood, and R. J. Wilson (1999) · W. Stebbing, ed., *Charles Henry Pearson: fellow of Oriel and education minister in Victoria* (1900) · *The Times* (18 Sept 1896) [Eleanor Smith] · *Oxford Chronicle and Berks and Bucks Gazette* (19 Sept 1896) [Eleanor Smith] · *Englishwoman's Review*, 27 (1896), 279–80 [obit. of Eleanor Smith] · *Englishwoman's Review*, 28 (1897), 65–6 [obit. of Eleanor Smith] · M. J. Tuke, *A history of Bedford College for Women, 1849–1937* (1939) · P. Hollis, *Ladies elect: women in English local government, 1865–1914* (1987) [Eleanor Smith]

Archives RS | Bodl. Oxf., Pearson and English MSS · CUL, letters to Sir George Stokes · MHS Oxf., corresp. with Sir B. C. Brodie

Likenesses J. E. Boehm, marble bust, 1883, RS · A. Macdonald, engraving, 1885, repro. in Glaisher, ed., *Collected mathematical papers*, frontispiece · S. Acland, slides (Eleanor Smith), Bodl. Oxf. · J. E. Boehm, stone bust (posthumous), Balliol Oxf.; copy, NPG · S. P. Hall, caricature, Bodl. Oxf. · Story-Maskelyne, photograph, MHS Oxf.; repro. in Morton, *Oxford rebels* · P. Ward-Jackson, photograph, RS · bronze bust, CCC Oxf. · carte-de-visite, repro. in V. Morton, *Oxford rebels: the life and friends of Nevil Story Maskelyne* (1987) · photograph, Sci. Mus., Tucker collection · photograph, Balliol Oxf. · photograph (Eleanor Smith), Bodl. Oxf. · terracotta bust, NPG

Wealth at death £3216 11*s*. 11*d*.: administration, 27 April 1883, *CGPLA Eng. & Wales* · £13,306 3*s*. 4*d*.—Eleanor Smith: probate, 23 Nov 1896, *CGPLA Eng. & Wales*

Smith, Sir Henry Martin (1907–1979), fire officer, was born at 23 Woodland Park Road, Greenwich, London, on 10 February 1907, the son of William Smith, tram conductor, and his wife, Helen, whose previous surname was Killick (*née* Martin). He was educated at Roan School, Greenwich, London. From 1923 to 1939 he held posts of fire protection adviser with two well-known manufacturers of fire appliances and equipment. On 12 June 1937, at the Roman Catholic church of Our Lady Star of the Sea, Greenwich, he married Anita Marie (*b*. 1908/9), daughter of James Patrick Sullivan, mechanical engineer. They had no children.

In 1938 Smith joined the Auxiliary Fire Service as a part-time fireman in London and on the outbreak of war became full-time company officer. His abilities were quickly recognized and in 1940 he was appointed assistant regional fire brigade inspector under the Home Office. In 1941, by then inspector for the southern civil defence region, he was appointed MBE for outstanding administrative ability, bravery, and leadership during the heavy air raids on Portsmouth. On the formation of the National Fire Service in 1941 he became chief regional fire officer of the southern region, a post he held throughout wartime until 1947, and was appointed OBE in 1943.

When control of the fire service reverted to local authorities in 1948 he was offered and accepted the post of his majesty's chief inspector of fire services for England and Wales at the Home Office. The new fire authorities, although inheriting a much more effective fire service than had existed before nationalization, soon realized they had major problems to solve, including recruitment at a time when better-paid full employment was available, and the inheritance of a fleet of pre-war and wartime appliances which needed urgent replacement. Many fire stations were also wartime requisitioned premises, whose facilities were antiquated. Although nationalization had brought advances in the standardization of equipment as well as operational and administrative procedures, along with greater involvement by the service in giving advice on fire protection, it thus became the task of the chief inspector to urge and at times cajole fire authorities and chief fire officers to continue improving standards. Smith's efforts gained him a CBE in 1952.

HM, as Smith was affectionately known by all in or connected with the fire service, had a charming manner that enabled him to relate to every person he met, from senior civil servants to local firefighters. Although his early career had not been within the close-knit circle of professional firefighters, he gained their respect as an individual who could achieve most ends in a pleasant, persuasive manner. Despite having a speech impediment he was adept at public speaking, reputedly using the impediment on occasion to advantage. He was described by Sir Charles Cunningham, a permanent under-secretary of state, Home Office, in the report of the Cunningham inquiry into the work of the fire service (published in 1971) as 'having a unique knowledge of the fire services of many countries; he is, by reason of his post, in close and constant touch with all the fire brigades in England and Wales; and he has the confidence of firemen of all ranks'.

Smith's period as chief inspector saw vast changes in the scope and work of the British fire service. Loss of life in fires in premises representing a range of occupancies prompted the government to transfer to fire authorities responsibilities for the enforcement of statutory fire precautions in factories, shops, and offices. This resulted in the involvement of all firefighters in these duties rather than a few specialist officers. This and other changes required better training facilities, and a new national training college, which Smith helped to plan, was built at Moreton in Marsh, Gloucestershire. It was with justified pride that he could say in his final report to the secretary of state for the Home department in 1971 'the British Fire Service is in excellent shape and I am confident that it will continue to progress and continue to be the finest in the world'. His natural modesty prevented him adding that much of the significant progress made during his time as chief inspector was due to the excellent relationships he had with ministers, Home Office colleagues, fire authorities, chief fire officers, and personnel of fire brigades, as well as representative bodies, the fire equipment industry, and all other fire organizations. He was knighted in 1971 and retired in 1972. He died at the Royal Berkshire Hospital, Reading, on 27 October 1979, and was cremated.

Reginald Haley

Sources *Fire*, 896 (Feb 1980), 472, 494 · *Fire Protection*, 511 (Feb 1980), 13 · *Daily Telegraph* (31 Oct 1979) · *WWW* · H. Klopper, ed., *Who's who in the fire services and fire brigade directory* (1971–2) · C. Cunningham, *Report of the Cunningham inquiry into the work of the fire service* (1971) · *Reports of his/her majesty's chief inspector of fire services England and Wales* (1948–71) · T. H. O'Brien, *Civil defence* (1955) · b. cert. · m. cert. · d. cert.

Likenesses photograph, DMG Business Media Ltd, Redhill, Surrey; repro. in Klopper, ed., *Who's who in the fire services* (1971–2)

Wealth at death £64,468: probate, 8 Jan 1980, *CGPLA Eng. & Wales*

Smith, Henry Newson- (1854–1898), accountant and music-hall entrepreneur, was born on 14 May 1854 at 28 Wyndham Street, Marylebone, Middlesex, the son of Henry George Smith, leather merchant, and his wife, Emily Newson. Smith was educated at the North London Collegiate School, Camden Town, and in 1871 took up employment in a City solicitor's office. In 1876 he married Elizabeth Caroline Louisa, the daughter of Nicholas Powning, a builder, of Truro. The same year he established his own accountancy business at 37 Walbrook in the City of

London (which remained his office throughout his career). His business interests flourished and in 1880 he became a fellow of the Institute of Chartered Accountants. In later life he was known as Henry Newson-Smith.

Newson-Smith's financial acumen became evident in the closing decades of the nineteenth century, when he stimulated a profound transformation of the commercial aspects of the buoyant music-hall business. His initial involvement in popular entertainment came through his role as an auditor of theatre companies, but he soon became more deeply involved in the ownership and management of the London Pavilion during the late 1880s. In partnership with George Adney Payne he purchased the recently built Tivoli in 1891 and his control of the West End variety business was consolidated by the opening on 31 January 1893 of the rebuilt Oxford music-hall. As the guiding force behind this syndicate of halls, Newson-Smith controlled the finances of the most influential and successful theatres of the music-hall boom of the 1890s.

According to *The Era*, Newson-Smith's financial success and his distinctive contribution to the development of popular entertainment in Britain lay 'in the intelligent application of ordinary business principles to a calling which had hitherto been regarded as incapable of such treatment' (*Era*, 14 March 1896, 19). Previous generations of music-hall entrepreneurs had adopted a largely cavalier and providential attitude towards the financial aspects of their activities. Newson-Smith, drawing on his experience outside the entertainment industry, pioneered the adoption of a much more rigorous and prudent approach to music-hall finance. His involvement with the music-hall business was cut short by ill health, however. Newson-Smith resigned his directorships of the London Pavilion, Tivoli, and Oxford music-halls in November 1896, and by the time of his death he had sold off the majority of his interests in these companies.

In addition to his business responsibilities, Newson-Smith was also a deputy lieutenant of London and the honorary auditor of the Music Hall Benevolent Fund. 'Hennie', as he was often known to intimates, was a motor enthusiast, a keen collector of Constable paintings, and an avid follower of cricket. Newson-Smith died from cirrhosis of the liver and acute jaundice on 28 April 1898 at his home, 25 Avenue Road, St John's Wood, London; he was only forty-three. He was buried at the old parish church, Hampstead, on 2 May 1898. He had at least one son, who was at that time a chartered accountant's articled clerk. ANDREW CROWHURST

Sources *The Era* (30 April 1898) · 'Funeral of Mr. Newson-Smith', *The Era* (7 May 1898) · A. Crowhurst, 'The music hall, 1885–1922: the emergence of a national entertainment industry in Britain', PhD diss., U. Cam., 1992 · *The Era* (14 March 1896), 19 · b. cert. · m. cert. · d. cert. · *CGPLA Eng. & Wales* (1898)

Wealth at death £59,842 16s. 5d.: probate, 20 May 1898, *CGPLA Eng. & Wales*

Smith, Henry Spencer (1812–1901), surgeon, born in London on 12 September 1812, was the younger son of George Spencer Smith, estate agent, and his wife, Martha. After education at Enfield he entered St Bartholomew's Hospital, London, in 1832 and was apprenticed to Frederic Carpenter Skey, with whom he lived and whose house surgeon he afterwards became. He was admitted MRCS in 1837, and in 1843 he was chosen as one of the 150 persons on whom the newly established degree of FRCS was conferred without examination.

Smith studied medicine in Paris for six months in 1837, and from 1839 until 1841 he studied science in Berlin. On his return to England he was appointed surgeon to the Royal General Dispensary in Aldersgate Street, London, and he lectured on surgery at Samuel Lane's school of medicine in Grosvenor Place. When St Mary's Hospital was founded in 1851 Smith became senior assistant surgeon. Three years later, when the medical school of St Mary's Hospital was instituted, he was appointed dean, and filled the office until 1860. He also lectured there for seventeen years on systematic surgery. He was a member of the council of the Royal College of Surgeons (1867–75), and of the court of examiners (1872–7); and he was secretary of the Royal Medical and Chirurgical Society of London (1855–88).

Smith translated from the German, for the Sydenham Society, H. Schwann's *Microscopical Researches into the Accordance in the Structure and Growth of Animals and Plants* (1847) and M. J. Schleiden's *Contributions to Phytogenesis* (in the same volume).

Smith was married, first to Elizabeth Mortlock, daughter of John Sturges, with whom he had a son and a daughter; and second to Louisa Theophila, daughter of the Revd Gibson Lucas. Smith died at his London home, 92 Oxford Terrace, Hyde Park, on 29 October 1901.

D'A. POWER, *rev.* MICHAEL BEVAN

Sources *The Lancet* (16 Nov 1901), 1383 · *BMJ* (9 Nov 1901), 1444–5 · private information (1912) · d. cert.

Wealth at death £702 11s. 11d.: administration, 4 Dec 1901, *CGPLA Eng. & Wales*

Smith, Herbert (1862–1938), trade unionist, was born in the workhouse at Great Preston, Kippax, in the West Riding of Yorkshire, on 17 July 1862. His father had been killed in a mining accident a few days earlier and his mother died shortly afterwards. He remained at the workhouse until he was adopted by a childless couple, Samuel Smith (*d.* 1894), also a miner, and his wife, Charlotte (*d.* 1902). Coincidentally, they shared Smith's surname at birth.

After moving with his new family a number of times, Smith began his education at a dame-school at Glass Houghton, near Castleford, going on from there to the British School at Pontefract. At ten years of age he started work in the mine at Glass Houghton. From 1879 he was a member of the Glass Houghton miners' union branch committee. In 1894 he was chosen as checkweighman by the miners, and as a delegate to the Yorkshire Miners' Association. From 1896 to 1904 he was president of the Castleford Trades Council, and in 1902 he was appointed to the joint board of the South and West Yorkshire Coalowners and Workmen. He became president of the Yorkshire Miners' Association in 1906.

Smith also represented his association on the executive

Herbert Smith (1862–1938), by unknown photographer

committee of the Miners' Federation of Great Britain (MFGB), and was president of that body from 1922 to 1929. The federation unified the district associations behind a demand for a minimum wage, an eight-hour day, the nationalization of the mines, and the abolition of mining royalties. In 1914 Smith was central to the formation of the 'triple alliance' of railwaymen, transport workers, and miners, which, however, did not become effective until after the war. He held various Trades Union Congress positions between 1913 and 1931. He visited Russia as a TUC delegate in 1924, and was president of the International Miners' Federation from 1921 to 1929. Smith, with Arthur Cook, the MFGB secretary, was prominent in the national miners' dispute that was central to the general strike of 1926.

Six great colliery explosions in six successive years (1908–13) brought mining conditions vividly to public attention, and Smith achieved considerable fame in connection with rescue work at the Whitehaven disaster (1910) and his cross-examination at the government inquiry which followed. Throughout his life he was involved in rescue work in mines in Britain and elsewhere. Although he was on occasion criticized for being a 'showman' during these incidents, contemporaries also recognized him as an exceedingly brave man. In 1931, although nearly seventy years of age, Smith was again prominent in rescue work after the Bentley explosion, when forty-five men were killed. While attending an international miners' conference at Prague in 1936 he received a telegram stating that a disaster involving fifty-six men had taken place at Wharncliffe Woodmoor; by 6 a.m. next day he had landed by air in Yorkshire, and by 9 a.m. was down the pit.

Smith resigned the MFGB presidency in 1929 in protest over an agreement to lengthen mining hours, to which the Yorkshire miners were totally opposed. He unsuccessfully sought re-election in 1931 and 1932. Nevertheless, a nationwide collection among miners in 1931 paid for a bust of him at the Miners' Hall in Barnsley, and for the building of several homes for aged miners to be named after him.

Smith was also active in public affairs. He served for thirty years (1891–1921) on the Glass Houghton school board; in 1894 he was elected to the local parish council, and in 1895 to the Pontefract rural district council and board of guardians. Attracted to the policies of Keir Hardie, in 1897 Smith became active in the Independent Labour Party. He stood unsuccessfully as a Labour candidate at the general election in January 1910. In 1903 he won a seat on the West Riding county council, focusing in his committee work on public health and education. He also served as a magistrate. In 1916 he moved to Barnsley, and there was elected a councillor, and mayor in 1932, and became a justice of the peace. He also served on a number of local charitable committees.

Of medium height but muscular build, Smith had a sometimes overly blunt manner. His obituary in *The Times* emphasized his 'unyielding, uncompromising' nature and argued that this perhaps lessened his effectiveness as a union leader (17 June 1938). Yet there is no doubt that he attracted great respect and loyalty from miners and their families.

Smith died in his Miners' Association office at 2 Huddersfield Road, Barnsley, on 16 June 1938. He had just returned from voting in a by-election for the local Labour candidate. His funeral took place in Barnsley on 20 June, which was the day of the annual Yorkshire miners' demonstration, and crowds lined the 20 mile route from Barnsley to Castleford cemetery, where he was buried. He was survived by his wife, Sarah Ann Ripley, a maidservant of Castleford, whom he married on 17 March 1885, and with whom he had four sons and five daughters.

MARC BRODIE

Sources J. Lawson, *The man in the cap: the life of Herbert Smith* (1941) · *The Times* (17 June 1938) · *The Times* (21 June 1938) · *DLB*

Likenesses J. Bellman, photograph, 1910, repro. in Lawson, *The man in the cap*, facing p. 164 · Jacobi, bust, 1931, Miners' Hall, Barnsley · *Barnsley Chronicle*, group portrait, photograph (as mayor of Barnsley), repro. in Lawson, *The man in the cap*, facing p. 242 · Barratt's Photo Press Ltd, photographs, repro. in Lawson, *The man in the cap* · photograph, repro. in *The Times* (17 June 1938), 18c · photograph, People's History Museum, Manchester [*see illus.*]

Wealth at death £12,008 17*s*. 6*d*.: probate, 20 July 1938, *CGPLA Eng. & Wales*

Smith, Herbert Luther (*bap.* 1809, *d.* 1870). *See under* Boydell, John, engravers (*act.* 1760–1804).

Smith, Horatio [Horace] (1779–1849), writer and humorist, was born on 31 December 1779 in Frederick's Place, Old Jewry, London, the fifth of eight children of Robert Smith

Horatio Smith (1779–1849), by unknown artist, *c.*1840

(1747–1832), a lawyer originally from Bridgwater, Somerset, where his father Samuel was a custom house officer, and his first wife, Mary Bogle (1748/9–1804), daughter of James French Bogle, a London merchant. On his marriage in 1773 Robert Smith adopted the Presbyterian views of his wife's family, and their children were brought up Presbyterians. In 1782 Robert Smith was appointed assistant to the solicitor to the Board of Ordnance, a post which he retained until 1812; he was elected a fellow of the Society of Antiquaries in 1787 and a fellow of the Royal Society in 1796. Sociable, charitable, and literary, he encouraged his children to write. In 1787 Horatio (always known as Horace) was sent to Chigwell School in Essex to join his elder brothers James *Smith and Leonard; in 1791 he followed James to Alfred House Academy, Camberwell.

Business career and early writings While James took up his father's legal profession, in 1796 Horace became an unsalaried clerk in the counting-house of a merchant, Robert Kingston, in Coleman Street; in 1806, with financial help from his father, he formed the partnership of Smith and Chesmer, merchants and insurance brokers, in Copthall Chambers. He was shrewd in business, and during these wartime years his father's position brought him advance information of political and military developments: he made a lot of money, augmented from 1812 when he severed the partnership and became a member of the stock exchange, from which he resigned in 1820, avoiding the crash of 1825–6 which ruined so many.

The Smith brothers shared a taste for wit, theatre, fashionable entertainments, and light verse. Horace Smith's first literary ventures were novels of contemporary manners, characterized by lively dialogue: *A Family Story* (3 vols., 1800), *The Runaway, or, The Seat of Benevolence* (4 vols., 1800), *Trevanion, or, Matrimonial Errors* (4 vols., 1801), and *Horatio, or, Memoirs of the Davenport Family* (4 vols., 1807). He was introduced into dramatic and literary circles by the dramatist Richard Cumberland, whom he met in 1805, and the brothers became frequent visitors at Thomas Hill's gatherings (styled by Smith his 'Court of Momus') in Sydenham. Like James, he contributed regularly to Hill's *Monthly Mirror*, from 1807 to 1819, to William Combe's short-lived magazine *The Pic-Nic*, and wrote several prefaces to plays in Cumberland's new edition of *Bell's British Theatre*. Two of his own plays were performed, *The Highgate Tunnel, or, The Secret Arch* in 1812 and *First Impressions, or, Trade in the West* in 1813.

Rejected Addresses It was a theatrical occasion of a rather different kind which established Smith's fame. To mark the opening of the rebuilt Drury Lane Theatre after the fire of 1809, a competition was held to find an inaugural ode. 112 addresses were submitted, none of an acceptable standard and 69 featuring phoenixes, so an address was commissioned from Byron. Amid discontent at this insider dealing the Smiths had the idea, aided and abetted by the secretary to the theatre Charles William Ward, of publishing, anonymously, a volume of parodies purporting to make public a selection of the effusions rejected. In six weeks the brothers wrote the twenty-one pieces which made up *Rejected Addresses, or, The New Theatrum poetarum*, 'one of the luckiest hits in literature' according to Smith himself (Smith, 'Memoir', 25) and one of the cleverest volumes of parody to be published in the Romantic period. Ten of the pieces were by Horace Smith, including his original (rejected) submission to the competition, 'An Address without a Phoenix', and parodies of Thomas Moore, Walter Scott, and M. G. Lewis. After rejections of its own the volume was taken up by the dramatic publisher John Miller (earlier involved in *The Highgate Tunnel*) who arranged to give the Smith brothers 'half the profits, *should there be any*' (Smith, 'preface').

The publication of the volume provoked amusing responses from those parodied, such as Scott's conviction that he had indeed written the description of the fire in 'A Tale of Drury Lane', though he had forgotten when. 'On the whole, the only discontented persons were the poets who were left out' ('Biographical notice of James Smith', *Law Magazine*, 23, 1840, 121), although Charles Lamb described the parodists in a letter to Wordsworth of 1819 as 'the sneering brothers, the vile Smiths' (P. Fitzgerald, ed. *The Life, Letters, and Writings of Charles Lamb*, 2.131). *Rejected Addresses* was favourably reviewed, most notably in the *Edinburgh Review* by Francis Jeffrey, who thought this 'little morsel of town-made gayety' (*Edinburgh Review*, 20, 1812, 434) ranked with the celebrated parodies of the *Anti-Jacobin*. *Rejected Addresses*, however, is politically noncommittal, and seizes on stylistic and verbal idiosyncrasy in a manner closer to playful imitation than to corrective mockery. Horace Smith later aptly described it as 'a malicious pleasantry' ('preface'). A revised edition appeared later the same year, and *Rejected Addresses* went into seventeen editions by 1819, though the eighteenth, with an important preface by Horace Smith, did not appear until

1833. Editions by others appeared in 1851, 1871, 1890, 1904, 1929; the most recent was by D. H. Reiman in 1977. Popular throughout the nineteenth century, *Rejected Addresses* was reassessed as a landmark in the history of parody in Walter Jerrold's article 'The centenary of parody' (*Fortnightly Review*, 1912) and Edmund Blunden's *Votive Tablets* (1931), and retains this deserved reputation. To capitalize on its success Miller published as *Horace in London* (1813) a collection of twenty topical pieces originally published in the *Monthly Mirror*, mainly the work of James Smith.

Literary man about town The Smiths were now literary men about town and fêted members of several different social sets. Among their established circle of journalists and editors were Leigh and John Hunt, editors of *The Examiner*, and at Leigh Hunt's house in Hampstead in 1816 Smith met John Keats and Percy Bysshe Shelley. He and Shelley, thirteen years his junior, became close friends: their competition to compose a sonnet inspired by the figure of Rameses II in the British Museum produced Shelley's 'Ozymandias' (*Examiner*, 1 Feb 1818), which has secured some attention for Smith's 'On a Stupendous Leg of Granite' (ibid., 25 Jan 1818). Smith visited Shelley at Marlow in 1817, regularly lent him money, and became his financial agent and mediator during Shelley's years abroad, intervening to sort out an unpaid annuity in 1819 and to resolve the financial crisis caused by a legal suit in 1821. Shelley wrote from Italy in the 'Letter to Maria Gisborne':

> … Wit and sense,
> Virtue and human knowledge; all that might
> Make this dull world a business of delight,
> Are all combined in Horace Smith.

And he asked Leigh Hunt (also financially assisted by Smith): 'is it not odd, that the only truly generous person I ever knew, who had money to be generous with, should be a stockbroker?' (*The Autobiography of Leigh Hunt*, ed. J. E. Morpurgo, 1949, 190).

According to his Victorian biographer Arthur H. Beavan, Smith made a first marriage in 1810 against his father's wishes, set up a little household in Knightsbridge Terrace, Kensington Road, and had two children, Eliza and Horatio Shakespeare. On 14 April 1817 he married Sophia Ford, of a Devon family, and moved to Fulham, where they lived until 1821. They had two daughters, Rosalind (*b.* 1821) and Laura (1828–1864). Rosalind was only a few weeks old when, in summer 1821, Smith set out to join the Shelley circle in Pisa. His wife fell ill in Paris, so they delayed travelling further and set up house in Versailles, where they remained for four years; during this time, in 1823, his young son Horatio Shakespeare died. From Versailles he published in Thomas Campbell's *New Monthly Magazine* (including an account of his French travels, 'Journal of a tourist') and John Scott's *London Magazine*, and remained a regular contributor to both. After Shelley's sudden death, Smith's planned review of *Hellas* for the *Paris Monthly Review* in August 1822 apostrophized the brilliance of his poetry and personal character, becoming a key piece in the reception history of Shelley's work. In 1821, prompted by Hunt's 1820 translation of Tasso's *Amyntas*, he published *Amarynthus the Nympholept: a Pastoral Drama*, which has aroused interest for its intellectual and literary ties with Peacock, Hunt, Shelley, and Keats (ed. D. H. Reiman, 1977).

Novels and later verse On returning from Versailles in 1825 Smith settled briefly in Tunbridge Wells, then, in 1826, in Brighton, where he lived (first in Hanover Crescent, and from 1838 in Cavendish Place) with his wife and daughters. They were prominent in Brighton society and regularly entertained visitors including Charles Kean, H. T. Buckle, Macaulay, Dickens, Harrison Ainsworth, and Thackeray. Smith became a friend of Richard Cobden and an advocate of free trade. During this period he published thirteen full-length novels, two shorter novels (*Love: a Tale of Venice* and *Mesmerism: a Mystery*, published together, 3 vols., 1845), and five long tales (*Tales of the Early Ages*, 3 vols., 1832, one of which, *The Involuntary Prophet*, was published separately in Bentley's Standard Novels in 1835). Several of these novels were historical, the most enduring and most popular being *Brambletye House, or, Cavaliers and Roundheads* (3 vols., 1826), after the manner of Scott, who mentioned it in the introduction to his own civil war novel *Woodstock* (also 1826). *Brambletye House* has sometimes been seen as a continuation of Smith's imitative powers: William Hazlitt thought that as an imitation it 'was about as good as the *Rejected Addresses*' (*Mr Northcote's Conversations*, *Works*, ed. P. P. Howe, 11.254). In turn it was one of the objects of William Maginn's parodic historical novel *Whitehall, or, George IV* (1827). *The Tor Hill* (3 vols., 1826), a tale of the Reformation, and *Reuben Apsley* (3 vols., 1827), set during the revolution of 1688, were followed by *Zillah: a Tale of the Holy City* (4 vols., 1828), which was accused of being an imitation of George Croly's *Salathiel* (1828), *The New Forest* (3 vols., 1829), and *Walter Colyton: a Tale of 1688* (3 vols., 1830), set near his father's birthplace, Bridgwater, and experimenting in west country dialect. Smith also wrote novels of contemporary life and social issues: *Gale Middleton: a Story of the Present Day* (3 vols., 1833), *Jane Lomax, or, A Mother's Crime* (3 vols., 1838), and *Adam Brown, the Merchant* (3 vols., 1843). Especially interesting is *The Moneyed Man, or, The Lesson of a Life* (3 vols., 1841), avowedly 'an Autobiographical Memoir of an imaginary personage' (1.iii) which traces the social history of the years 1790–1840 and expresses views strikingly similar to Smith's own. The final phase of historical fiction comprises *Oliver Cromwell: an Historical Romance* (3 vols., 1840), an account avowedly 'drawn by a friendly hand' (1.xi), *Massaniello: an Historical Romance* (3 vols., 1842), and *Arthur Arundel: a Tale of the English Revolution* (3 vols., 1844).

Just as significant as Smith's work as a novelist was his continuing prominence as a writer of comic and occasional verse and prose. He published three volumes of collected essays and comic tales, as well as the interesting compilation *Festivals, Games, and Amusements, Ancient and Modern* (1831). *Gaieties and gravities: a Series of Essays, Comic Tales, and Fugitive Vagaries* (3 vols., 1825) brings together poems and topical prose pieces, the majority first published in the *London Magazine* and *New Monthly Magazine*. Of special note in *The Midsummer Medley for 1830: a Series of Comic Tales* (2 vols., 1830) is the essay 'Hints to the young novel-writer: with specimens' (of different kinds of fashionable fiction). There are amusing and sometimes pointed definitions in *The Tin Trumpet, or, Heads and Tales, for the Wise and Waggish* (2 vols., 1836). Smith's whimsical metropolitan style was parodied in two pieces in P. G. Patmore's *Rejected Articles* (1826). His *Poetical Works* (2 vols., 1846) were considered at the time 'remarkable for variety in style and manner as also in subject, replete with evidences of a thoughtful mind and gentle spirit, and tinctured by a strong tendency to the humorous' (*New Monthly Magazine*, 77, 1846, 407). Much is occasional verse, fanciful but also questioning (as in 'Address to a Mummy'): recurrent interests include the exotic and ancient and alternative religion, while the longer narrative poems show an interest in scientific projects (as in the three long 'Poetical Epistles' about 'A Very Remarkable Aerial Voyage Made in the Grand Kentucky Balloon'). 'The Sun's Eclipse' is influenced by Byron's 'Darkness', and there are tributes to Southey and Campbell, as well as stanzas supporting the Anti-Corn Law League. The important series of recollections 'A graybeard's gossip about his literary acquaintance' appeared anonymously in thirteen numbers in the *New Monthly Magazine* (vols. 79–82, 1847–8), and describes many of his 'friendly brotherhood' of writers (*New Monthly Magazine*, 82.340). Characteristically, his graybeard's defence of Shelley indicts in passing 'minds all stamped in the same established educational mould, or conforming to it with that plastic conventional hypocrisy which the worldly-wise find so exceedingly convenient' (81.240). He also edited *Memoirs, Letters, and Comic Miscellanies in Prose and Verse, of the Late James Smith* (2 vols., 1840). In a letter of February 1818 Keats mentions that Smith had lent him a manuscript entitled 'Nehemiah Muggs, an Exposure of the Methodists', but it is not known to be extant.

The first signs of failing health came with a severe attack of laryngitis in 1841, and Smith scaled down his literary activities, announcing his retirement from fiction in the preface to *Love and Mesmerism* in 1845. In 1849 the family took a house at 6 Calverley Park, Tunbridge Wells, where Smith died on 12 July, underlying gout having developed into serious heart problems. He was buried in the churchyard of Holy Trinity Church, Tunbridge Wells.

Although he defined 'wags and wits' in *The Tin Trumpet* as 'Lamps that exhaust themselves in giving light to others' (184), Smith managed to combine generosity and hospitality with personal happiness, and was generally liked. In his *Autobiography* Leigh Hunt calls him 'delicious' and describes his figure as 'good and manly, inclining to the robust; and his countenance extremely frank and cordial; sweet without weakness' (*The Autobiography of Leigh Hunt*, ed. J. E. Morpurgo, 1949, 189, 192). P. G. Patmore ranked him 'among the most frank, amiable, and gentlemanly of men' (Patmore, 2.237). He maintained the views of his dissenting upbringing, disliking Episcopalianism in theory and practice, but was socially and intellectually open-minded, and had a particular dislike of religious intolerance and unthinking obeisance to rank and wealth. He held progressive social views, including support for parliamentary reform and working-class education, and opposition to the newspaper tax which impeded the freedom of the popular press. At the same time he was worried when Hunt's *Lord Byron and some of his Contemporaries* (1828) allied him too closely with Shelley's social and political views, and took steps to correct that impression. Smith was actively charitable—in Brighton, he supported the mechanics' institute, the Literary Society, the Mantellian Institution, and Phillips' School of Science—and generous in his literary tastes and judgements. His niece, Maria *Abdy, had been a recipient of Smith's verse as a child, and later achieved a reputation as a poet.

FIONA ROBERTSON

Sources A. H. Beavan, *James and Horace Smith, joint authors of 'Rejected addresses': a family narrative* (1899) • H. Smith, 'Biographical memoir', *Memoirs, letters, and comic miscellanies in prose and verse, of the late James Smith*, ed. H. Smith, 2 vols. (1840), 1–54 • H. Smith, 'preface', *Rejected addresses*, 18th edn (1833) • H. Smith, *Rejected addresses, and other poems … with portraits and a biographical sketch*, ed. E. Sargent (1871) • R. M. Funchion, 'The life and works of Horace Smith', diss., University of Pennsylvania, 1968 • *The letters of Percy Bysshe Shelley*, ed. F. L. Jones, 2 vols. (1964) • W. Jerrold, 'The centenary of parody', *Fortnightly Review*, 98 (1912), 223–34 • E. Blunden, 'The Rejected addresses', *Votive tablets* (1931), 199–204 • P. G. Patmore, *My friends and acquaintances*, 3 vols. (1854) • S. Curran, 'The view from Versailles: Horace Smith on the literary scene of 1822', *Huntington Library Quarterly*, 40 (1976–7), 357–71 • H. Smith, 'A graybeard's gossip about his literary acquaintance', *New Monthly Magazine*, new ser., 79–82 (1847–8), 13 pts • 'The authors of the rejected addresses', *New Monthly Magazine*, new ser., 87 (1849), 23–30

Archives BL • Hunt. L. • Norris Museum, St Ives, Cambridgeshire • PRO • U. Leeds, Brotherton L. | Bodl. Oxf., letters to Henry Colburn and Richard Bentley • NL NZ, Turnbull L., letters to Gideon Algernon Mantell • NL Scot., letters to John Scott and Mrs Blunt

Likenesses G. H. Harlow, double portrait, pencil and watercolour drawing, *c.*1812 (with his brother), John Murray collection, London • J. J. Masquerier, oils, *c.*1825, repro. in A. J. Mathews, *Memoirs of Charles Mathews, comedian*, 2nd edn (1839) • E. F. Finden, double portrait, stipple, pubd 1833 (with his brother James; after G. H. Harlow), BM, NPG; repro. in Smith, *Rejected addresses* • E. F. Finden, stipple and line engraving, pubd 1835 (after J. Masquerier), BM, NPG • E. M. Ward, pencil and wash drawing, 1835, NPG • watercolour drawing, *c.*1840, NPG [*see illus.*]

Smith, Horatio Nelson (1874–1960), entrepreneur, was born on 1 June 1874 at 34 Ackers Street, Chorlton upon Medlock, Lancashire, the third and last child of George Frederick Smith (1832–1906), paper merchant, and his wife, Lucy Harding. Although his elder brother, Thomas Brooks Smith, entered his father's paper business, when H. N. (as Smith was called) was nine, he was sent to Hornsea, in the East Riding of Yorkshire, to live with his uncle, Thomas James *Smith, and his spinster aunt, Amelia Ann. He was educated in Hornsea for four years and then attended the City of London School.

In 1890, at the age of sixteen, Smith started work for £12 a year with a London wholesale draper's and woollen manufacturer's business. On being refused a rise, in January 1896 he joined his uncle's cod-liver oil business in Hull, taking it over entirely after T. J. Smith's death in October that year. He then set a course that made Smith & Nephew a major player in the world health-care market by the end of the 1980s. When Smith began managing his uncle's firm, the principal business was the wholesale supply of cod-liver oil. During his first year of control he quickly changed direction towards medical dressings. By his twenty-fourth birthday, he felt secure enough to marry, at a Baptist chapel in Bromley, Kent, Margaret Syme, the daughter of a builder. Of their three children, Alister, Margaret, and Neil, only Alister, who predeceased his father, held executive positions in the business. However, Margaret became the first female director of Smith & Nephew.

Smith at first shared Hull business premises with his father and brother, and until 1916 worked with their paper firm to the extent of undertaking business for them when visiting the United States. Orders from the Turkish war office on the outbreak of the Turkish–Bulgarian War in 1911, and later from allied governments during the First World War, set Smith & Nephew on an exponential growth path. After the post-war slump Smith began acquiring brand names that would allow continued expansion.

Both Smith and Ernest Buckley, his protégé and long-time accountant, were fluent German speakers, with close friends and associates in Germany, from whom they, and the company, gained greatly. Most important was Johannes Lohmann, from whom Smith acquired the rights to Elastoplast and the plaster of Paris bandage Cellona/Gypsona, respectively in 1930 and 1932. 'Coming to Fahr [Lohmann's home district] is like coming home', he wrote.

Smith was a natural entrepreneur with a flair for making friends and spotting opportunities, though not all of them were profitable. His business exploited medical research and experience, particularly in Germany and in British hospitals, without undertaking any research itself until after the Second World War. He played bridge regularly with medical men such as Arthur Dickson Wright, who provided useful means of test marketing new products. A former chairman of the Filey Road Tennis Club, Scarborough (home of the North of England Tennis Championships), Smith was an enthusiastic player of tennis, table tennis, and bridge. His attachment to table tennis—he was vice-president of the English, and president of the Yorkshire, table tennis associations—led him to employ two officials of the Table Tennis Association.

Smith's love of travelling provided him with many sales opportunities and firmly established Smith & Nephew abroad. He first crossed the Atlantic in 1906 to Boston, obtaining Canadian hospital orders for surgical dressings. Later, during the 1930s, his travels were not always so helpful to company management. Smith took a keen but, owing to his frequent and long absences, spasmodic interest in many details of company business, the board was told in 1937, the year that Smith & Nephew became a public company; it accordingly withdrew his executive authority, placing management in the hands of the chief executive, while Smith continued as chairman. When Smith & Nephew shares were traded on the stock exchange Smith was able to free some of his capital from the business and to channel it into charitable activities. The Smith & Nephew Trust was created the following year.

Smith's parting gift to his company was, in effect, a greater commitment to textiles, just as that industry was contracting in the face of foreign competition. During the First World War he had owned an integrated textile and medical dressing company, which he sold in 1920. His interest initiated the purchase in 1953 of Glen Mills by Smith & Nephew, bringing into the company a management team that was to influence strongly the pattern of development. Smith was introduced to the managing director of Glen Mills, George Whittaker, at a social at the Methodist church at Colne, Lancashire, in 1948. This introduction ultimately culminated in Smith & Nephew's acquisition of Whittaker and his business, and heavy investment by Smith & Nephew in textile production.

Smith was variously described as 'the rudest man you have ever met' (by Stanley Duckworth of Colne), and as having 'the most inquisitive and penetrating mind I had ever come across' (by George Whittaker). He had something of the pirate about him, according to Johannes Lohmann, but that was more than compensated for by his warmth and genuine concern for people, especially, but not only, those who worked for him. He was uninterested in display for its own sake and had simple tastes. His contemporaries appreciated his humour, his insatiable curiosity, and his humanity. He died at his house, Greenacre, Ringmer, near Lewes, Sussex, on 1 September 1960.

JAMES FOREMAN-PECK

Sources J. Foreman-Peck, *Smith & Nephew in the health care industry* (1995) • b. cert. • d. cert.

Likenesses photograph, repro. in Foreman-Peck, *Smith & Nephew*, pl. 2

Wealth at death £240,370 16*s*. 3*d*.: probate, 24 Nov 1960, *CGPLA Eng. & Wales*

Smith, Sir Hubert Llewellyn (1864–1945), civil servant and social investigator, was born in Bristol on 17 April 1864. Of middle-class Quaker extraction, he was the youngest son of Samuel Wyatt Smith, a partner in a wholesale tea business, and his wife, Louisa, daughter of James Scholefield, of Kingsholm, Gloucester. Llewellyn Smith married in 1901 Edith Maud Sophia, eldest daughter of George Mitchell Weekley, of Highgate; they had four sons and two daughters.

Early links with the labour movement Llewellyn Smith (as he was usually known) went up to Corpus Christi College, Oxford, from Bristol grammar school in 1883, becoming immersed in the so-called 'new Oxford Movement' that was committed to investigating and improving the condition of the working classes. A contemporary of Michael Sadler and L. T. Hobhouse, he combined other activities with participating in the Inner Ring, a group presided over by Arthur Acland to discuss social and economic issues, and with hosting parties of working men from Bethnal Green befriended by the University Settlement Movement. Like others of this Oxford circle he became a disciple of John Ruskin, whose ideas on social economics and the promotion of the visual arts and technical skills were important influences.

Sir Hubert Llewellyn Smith (1864–1945), by Walter Stoneman, 1917

In 1884 and 1886 Llewellyn Smith obtained a double first in mathematics. More significantly, in 1886, he won the Cobden prize for an essay on *The Economic Aspects of State Socialism*. This reflected a social radicalism that rejected both free-market and socialist dogma. Instead he advocated a mix of ethical and market imperatives in shaping economic and welfare policy. However, his sympathies clearly lay with the labour movement, and in an address to working men in Bradford in 1887 he admitted that he 'would rather be wrong with Karl Marx than right with David Ricardo' (Kadish, 73).

After leaving Oxford, Llewellyn Smith became a lecturer for the Oxford University Extension Delegacy and the Toynbee Trust, and secretary of the National Association for the Promotion of Technical and Secondary Education. He continued to participate in the Settlement Movement both at Toynbee Hall and later at Beaumont Square, where he founded a sub-colony called the Swarm. Meanwhile, on the survey of the life and labour of the people in London (the Booth survey), at the British Association for the Advancement of Science, and at the Royal Statistical and Economic societies, he collaborated with some of the leading social scientists and investigators of the day, including Charles Booth and Beatrice Potter (later Webb). His contributions to the Booth survey on the relationship between migration, the labour market, and social deprivation powerfully informed contemporary concerns surrounding the threat of 'urban degeneration'.

Meanwhile Llewellyn Smith was increasingly involved in union agitation. In 1888 he helped to mobilize public opinion against the employers in the celebrated Bryant and May's match-girls' strike. In 1889 he provided publicity for Ben Tillett in the dock strike, publishing with Vaughan Nash *The Story of the Dockers' Strike*. The following year he attempted to promote union branches among the rural labourers of Oxfordshire, while in the London omnibus strike of 1891 he co-ordinated strike action for John Burns in east London.

Board of Trade: industrial relations, unemployment, and minimum wages Llewellyn Smith's connections with the trade union movement and with the social scientific community, coupled with his strong involvement with the progressive wing of the Liberal Party, led to his appointment as the first labour commissioner of the Board of Trade in 1893, in charge of a newly established labour department. Although its initial terms of reference were largely that of a statistical bureau, as labour commissioner (1893–7), as deputy comptroller-general and comptroller-general of the commercial, labour, and statistical branch (1897–1906), and finally as permanent secretary of the Board of Trade (1907–19), Llewellyn Smith was to preside over its extension into the fields of industrial conciliation and arbitration, unemployment policy, and minimum wage legislation.

Along with George Askwith, Llewellyn Smith laid the foundations for twentieth-century state intervention in British industrial relations. In collaboration with the positivist Henry Crompton, he drafted the 1896 Conciliation (Trade Disputes) Act which established a voluntary framework for government conciliation and arbitration in strikes and lockouts. Thereafter, by creatively exploiting the Board of Trade's investigative powers under the act to mobilize public opinion, and by developing a pool of expert umpires and conciliators, Llewellyn Smith ensured that, despite the absence of compulsion, the department could mediate in many of the most bitter and damaging disputes of the period.

Meanwhile, under Llewellyn Smith's supervision, a whole series of investigations into the causes and effects of unemployment, and possible remedies, had been undertaken at the Board of Trade. His own *Report on Agencies and Methods for Dealing with the Unemployed* and his evidence before the select committee on distress from want of employment of 1895, by breaking down the volume of recorded unemployment into seasonal and cyclical variations, pioneered modern unemployment analysis. Moreover, despite a continuing belief in the importance of 'character', his work facilitated public recognition of unemployment as a structural problem of industry requiring state intervention.

Llewellyn Smith's second major contribution to developing unemployment policy was to recruit, among other experts, William Beveridge to the Board of Trade and to collaborate with him on memoranda and evidence to the royal commission on the poor laws, proposing a compulsory scheme of unemployment insurance in selected trades. This was to be administered in conjunction with a system of labour bureaux or exchanges and financed by contributions from workers, employers, and the state. Thereafter he played a key role, under the presidentships of Winston Churchill and Sydney Buxton, in steering through parliament the labour exchanges and unemployment insurance legislation of 1909 and 1911, despite considerable opposition from employers, the serious concerns of the trade union and labour movements, constant harassment from the Treasury, and the rival ambitions of David Lloyd George for invalidity insurance.

Llewellyn Smith also contributed significantly to the introduction and development of minimum wage legislation under the Trade Boards Act of 1909. He networked between Winston Churchill, the then president of the Board of Trade, and leading experts in the field of 'sweated' labour and low-income destitution, including Ernest Aves, George Askwith, Sidney and Beatrice Webb, and Charles Dilke. He was also largely responsible for ensuring that the proceedings of the trade boards were for the most part voluntary and autonomous and did not involve the state in imposing an arbitrary statutory minimum on any trade.

At the same time Llewellyn Smith was heavily involved in framing pre-war industrial and trade policies. He negotiated a series of commercial treaties, most notably with Romania in 1905 and with Japan in 1911. In addition he participated in government inquiries into the consular service and the system of commercial attachés, and did much to wrest the control of commercial diplomacy from the Foreign Office. He also helped formulate a wide-ranging programme of industrial legislation relating to issues such as patent and company law, copyright, and the regulation of rail transport and the mercantile marine.

Wartime measures and post-war economic policy Llewellyn Smith was at the forefront in Whitehall's response to the economic and administrative challenges of the First World War. He was primarily responsible for the economic preparations for war. He devised the valuable system of war-risk insurance and in 1915 organized, under Lloyd George, the new Ministry of Munitions. He played a crucial role in wresting munitions supply policy from the War Office and in shaping wartime manpower policy. He did much to relieve the critical shortage of skilled labour by decentralizing munitions production, ending indiscriminate military recruitment, and securing an agreement, however tenuous, with the engineering unions on 'dilution' and on the wartime suspension of industrial militancy and restrictive practices.

After the First World War, Llewellyn Smith remained permanent secretary of the Board of Trade until 1919, devoting his energies to the task of domestic and international reconstruction. Between 1917 and 1919 he played a leading part in the reorganization of the board and the machinery of commercial intelligence. In 1918–19 he headed the British economic section at the Paris peace conference and drafted many of the economic provisions of the treaty. In 1919 he also visited India as president of the viceregal committee on the reorganization of the government secretariat.

In 1919 Llewellyn Smith was elevated to the newly created post of chief economic adviser to the government. He continued to make significant contributions to domestic commercial policy, such as the drafting of the 1926 Merchandise Marks Act and of the Balfour report on industry and trade. However, his work in the 1920s was increasingly devoted to promoting the economic aims of the League of Nations, as British member of the economic committee from 1920 to 1927, economic adviser at the Washington disarmament conference, and substitute delegate to the league assembly in 1923 and 1924. As such, he remained a leading personality in all negotiations affecting international trade and the commercial repercussions of the First World War.

Retirement and assessment After retiring in 1927 Llewellyn Smith remained active in public affairs. He continued to contribute evidence to government inquiries, such as the royal commission on unemployment insurance (1931), and wrote a pioneering history of the Board of Trade (1928). He was also chairman of the National Association of Boys' Clubs (1935–43). In addition he renewed his early interests in east London and social scientific enquiry. For many years he worked on a *History of East London* (1939) and between 1928 and 1935 acted as director of the *New Survey of London Life and Labour*, the sequel to Charles Booth's pioneering inquiry of the 1880s on which Llewellyn Smith had learned his statistical and investigative skills.

Apart from his administrative talents Llewellyn Smith had a strong artistic bent, and sketching was always his favourite leisure occupation. *Through the High Pyrenees* (1898), written jointly with Edward Harold Spender, had been illustrated with his own drawings. From his earliest connections with the craft school movement in east London, he retained a lifelong interest in the crafts and the training of craftsmen. He was a vigorous and pioneering chairman of the British Institute of Industrial Art from 1920 until 1935 and published a short but illuminating study, *The Economic Laws of Art Production* (1924).

Llewellyn Smith was appointed CB in 1903, KCB in 1908, and GCB in 1919. He died at Church Farmhouse, Tytherington, Wiltshire, on 19 September 1945, survived by his wife. In many ways his career recalled that of the great Victorian 'statesmen in disguise'. Lord Salter regarded him 'as beyond question one of the great civil servants of his time … who not only administered policy but exercised a powerful influence in its formation' (*DNB*). Recent research into the history of modern government growth reveals Hubert Llewellyn Smith to have been a major architect of the social and commercial policy of late nineteenth- and early twentieth-century Britain.

Roger Davidson

Sources R. Davidson, *Whitehall and the labour problem in late Victorian and Edwardian Britain* (1985) • R. Davidson, 'Llewellyn Smith, the labour department and government growth, 1886–1909', *Studies in the growth of nineteenth-century government*, ed. G. Sutherland (1972), 227–62 • A. Kadish, *The Oxford economists in the late nineteenth century* (1982) • J. Harris, *Unemployment and policy: a study in English social policy, 1886–1914* (1972) • Lord Beveridge, *Power and influence* (1953) • Lord Askwith, *Industrial problems and disputes* (1920) • R. Davidson, 'Sir Hubert Llewellyn Smith and labour policy, 1886–1916', PhD diss., U. Cam., 1971 • R. Davidson and G. Jenkins, interview, 14 Nov 1968 • T. Ainscough and R. Davidson, interview, 23 Dec 1968 • R. Davidson and H. F. Hill, interview, 22 Nov 1968 • R. Davidson and H. Hutchinson, interview, 3 Dec 1968 • R. Davidson, A. Llewellyn Smith, and H. Llewellyn Smith, interview, 4 July 1968 • R. Davidson and H. Wilson, interview, 8 Jan 1969 • *Economic Journal*, 56 (1946), 143–7 • *The Times* (21 Sept 1945) • *The Times* (25 Sept 1945) • *Journal of the Royal Statistical Society*, 108 (1945), 480–81 • *DNB* • J. Harris, 'Ruskin and social reform', *Ruskin and the dawn of the modern*, ed. D. Birch (1999), 7–33 • *CGPLA Eng. & Wales* (1946)

Archives priv. coll., papers • RIBA, papers relating to work as chairman of British Institute of Industrial Art | BL, corresp. with W. J. Ashley, Add. MSS 42243–42247a • Bodl. Oxf., corresp. with Herbert Asquith • HLRO, corresp. with David Lloyd George • U. Newcastle, Robinson L., corresp. with Walter Runciman • University of Toronto, Thomas Fisher Rare Book Library, letters to James Mavor

Likenesses W. Stoneman, photograph, 1917, NPG [*see illus.*] • photograph, 1919, priv. coll. • photograph, *c*.1921–1922, NPG

Wealth at death £9745 16*s*. 2*d*.: probate, 28 Feb 1946, *CGPLA Eng. & Wales*

Smith, Hugh (*d.* **1790**), physician, probably the son of Hugh Smith, surgeon and apothecary, was born at Hemel Hempstead, Hertfordshire. He studied medicine at Edinburgh University, and obtained the degree of MD on 22 April 1755. He initially practised in Essex, but went to London in 1759, and settled in Mincing Lane. In 1760 he began a course of lectures on the theory and practice of physic, which proved to be extremely popular. These, together with the publication of *Essays on Circulation of the Blood, with Reflections on Blood-Letting* (1761), earned him a wide reputation. In 1762 he was admitted as a licentiate of the Royal College of Physicians. In 1765 he was elected physician to Middlesex Hospital, and in 1770 was chosen as an alderman of the Tower ward, a dignity which he had to resign in 1772, due to the pressures of his other duties.

About this time Smith moved to Blackfriars and devoted himself to a consulting practice at home. He gave two days of each week to the poor, from whom he demanded no fee. He also financially assisted some of his patients. In 1780 he purchased an estate at Streatham in Surrey. Besides the work mentioned above, he wrote *Formulae medicamentorum* (1772). He died at Stratford in Essex on 26 December 1790 and was buried in the church at West Ham. Smith left property and annuities valued at £23,000. His estate in Essex was left to his wife; his house at Stratford to his brother-in-law, Mr Hemet. His sister, Mrs Morley, of Broad Street, also benefited from his will.

Smith must be distinguished from another **Hugh Smith** (1735/6–1789), who graduated MD at Leiden on 11 November 1755, and practised at Hatton Garden, London. He married the wealthy daughter of Archibald Maclean, and she later inherited Trevor Park, East Barnet. He died, aged fifty-three, on 6 June 1789, and was buried in East Barnet church. He was the author of several medical titles, including *The Family Physician* (1760) and *Letters to Married Women* (1774), which was republished in France, Germany, and America. E. I. Carlyle, *rev.* Claire L. Nutt

Sources H. Smith, *Formulae medicamentorum* (1791), preface • *GM*, 1st ser., 60 (1790), 1154, 1213 • Munk, *Roll* • P. J. Wallis and R. V. Wallis, *Eighteenth century medics*, 2nd edn (1988) • *European Magazine and London Review*, 19 (1791), 21–3

Archives Wellcome L., lecture notes, MSS 4636–4637

Wealth at death £23,000 in property and annuities; plus other property: *GM*, 1213

Smith, Hugh (**1735/6–1789**). *See under* Smith, Hugh (*d.* 1790).

Smith, Humphry (*bap.* **1624**, *d.* **1663**), Quaker preacher, was born probably at Stoke Bliss, Herefordshire, where he was baptized on 21 February 1624, the son of Humphry and Elianor Smith, who belonged to a yeoman family with branches in neighbouring parishes in the district between Leominster and Bromyard. To judge from Smith's autobiographical writings, his parents were not sympathetic to either godly protestantism or to study. He spent much time as a youth in contemplation, with, it seems, the ambition of becoming an ordained minister, although he never achieved anything concrete in this direction. He became, like his parents, a farmer, occupying a substantial holding in Little Cowarne, Herefordshire, worth £30 a year from about 1640. He was married, possibly to a woman called Jane, and had children.

On the outbreak of civil war in 1642 Smith's sympathies were evidently wholly with parliament, and at some point after the war began he served in one or other of the parliamentarian armies. The collapse of censorship and church discipline allowed him freedom to preach in his native county, and his oratory was evidently compelling. At this point, in the late 1640s, when almost certainly his only son, Humphry, was baptized in the state church, his theological position was probably nearer to that of the Independents than to any other group. Although the Quaker leader George Fox called him a former priest, there is no evidence that he was ever ordained or even held a living, but was instead simply a local preacher. He preached without maintenance or reward, and increasingly became convinced of the futility of his message and of his own unfitness to minister. He seems to have made a definite decision to stop preaching, announcing to his hearers at Stoke Bliss that he would henceforth be silent. A period of inner crisis followed, resolved by his decision to leave his family and his farm about 1650, which he estimated cost him £150 in lost income. He was in correspondence with other 'seekers', such as the Baptist Edmund Skipp of Todenham, but must also have been in contact with leaders of the emerging Quaker movement.

Smith's first destination after leaving Herefordshire may have been Oxford, where in 1654 he organized a meeting at the house of a sympathizer. But his first clash with authority was in Evesham, Worcestershire, where he arrived on 18 August 1655. He provided an immediate boost to a nascent group of Friends. His intervention provoked the wrath of the conservative mayor and corporation, and he was imprisoned the day following his arrival amid scenes of civic disorder. Smith was interrogated many times, but was adept at somehow gaining access to a printing press, so that Evesham became notorious, attracting visitors on both sides of the conflict. Through the Quakers' own efforts, the case of Smith and his friends attracted the attention of Lord Protector Cromwell, who was more sympathetic to them than was the eminent minister and leader of the local Worcestershire Association of Ministers, Richard Baxter. Smith was still in prison in October 1655, but was eventually released and made his way to Exeter, calling at Painswick, Gloucestershire, to establish a meeting there. The official attitude to Quakers in the south-west was in turmoil in the wake of the case of James Nayler, and Smith was imprisoned in Exeter under the vagrancy laws. Once again, Smith fired off two *ad hominem* publications against the rulers of Exeter and Devon.

Released from Exeter gaol, Smith then wandered east into Dorset and Hampshire, where he spent most time during the few remaining years of his life. From 1657 he held meetings in Lyme Regis, Hawkchurch, Dorchester, Poole, South Perrott, Uphay, Axminster, Sherborne, Tetbury, Andover, Alton, and finally Winchester. In nearly all of these places Smith was abused by townspeople, and often imprisoned or whipped. In Winchester he was imprisoned twice, and spent a whole year in gaol there, from February 1658. During a period of liberty in 1660 he wrote a prophetic work about London, which foretold the great fire and the Dutch attack on the Royal Navy in the Medway. He was one of the earliest 'sufferers', as the Quakers from the first days of the movement called them, and his writings demonstrated a flair for mixing a compelling autobiographical narrative with spiritual insight. His repeated confrontations with the authorities suggest that imprisonment was something he thought contributed to his own spiritual journey. He confided to friends that 'he had a narrow path to pass through; and more than once signified, he saw he should be imprisoned and that it might cost him his life' (Besse, 1.233). Eventually, his health was broken by his experiences of ill treatment. On a return visit to Alton, on 14 October 1662, he was arrested and taken to prison in Winchester. He died there of gaol fever on 4 May 1663 and was buried in Winchester in the same month. Those who observed his last days noted that 'he continued sweetly still and sensible unto the end, and died in perfect peace' (ibid., 1.167). His only son, Humphry, became a Quaker activist in Saffron Walden, Essex.

STEPHEN K. ROBERTS

Sources N. Complin, *The faithfulnesse of the upright made manifest* (1663) • *A collection of the several writings … of Humphrey Smith* (1683) • J. Besse, *A collection of the sufferings of the people called Quakers*, 2 vols. (1753) • N. Penney, ed., *'The first publishers of truth': being early records, now first printed, of the introduction of Quakerism into the counties of England and Wales* (1907) • W. C. Braithwaite, *The beginnings of Quakerism*, ed. H. J. Cadbury, 2nd edn (1955) • S. K. Roberts, 'The Quakers in Evesham, 1655–1660', *Midland History*, 16 (1991) • H. Smith, *Man driven out of the earth* (1658) • A. W. Brown, *Evesham Friends in the olden time* (1885) • *A representation of the government of the borough of Evesham* (1655) • *IGI* • *The vision of Humphrey Smith* (1660)

Smith, Iain Crichton [Iain Mac a'Ghobhainn] (**1928–1998**), poet and writer, was born at 8 Lewis Street, Glasgow, on 1 January 1928, the second of three sons of John Smith (1880–1931), a merchant seaman, and his second wife, Christina, *née* Campbell (1888–1969), a fisher-girl; a stepsister, Christina, about ten years older than Iain, was the daughter of John Smith and his first wife. Both parents were born on the Isle of Lewis in the Outer Hebrides but had left the island to seek work. The family returned to Lewis in 1930 to live in the village of Upper Bayble, about 7 miles from Stornoway. When Iain was three years old his father died from tuberculosis.

Crichton Smith spoke Gaelic until he went to Bayble public school (the local primary school), where he was educated entirely in English. The language opened up a welcome new world for him, though in later years he was to view the imposition of English on infant schoolchildren as 'a blow to the psyche, an insult to the brain' (Crichton Smith, *Towards the Human*, 42). In 1939 he gained a scholarship to the prestigious Nicolson Institute in Stornoway, to which he travelled by bus each day. Writing mainly in English and rejecting as far as he was able what he saw as a stifling and joyless religion, the Free Presbyterianism of his mother, Crichton Smith began to feel isolated from his friends and village interests. 'I moved between two worlds—the world of school and the world of the village', he explained (ibid., 79). His feeling of alienation, of what he sometimes described as schizophrenia, was to inform his writing.

At the Nicolson Institute Crichton Smith read and became excited by the English poets. Shelley and Keats and the other Romantics were his favourites. Among the moderns, Auden in particular appealed to him. At seventeen he went to Aberdeen University, where he read English and graduated MA in 1949. There he began to write poetry seriously, most of it in English. After university he attended Jordanhill teacher training college in Glasgow, before doing his national service in the army education corps. In 1952 he began teaching in Clydebank. In 1955 he moved to Oban to teach English at Oban high school and he also published his first book of poetry, *The Long River*. This was followed by *The White Noon* in 1959. His first book in Gaelic, *Bùrn is aran* ('Bread and water') (1960), a collection of poems and short stories, was published under his Gaelic name, Iain Mac a'Ghobhainn. *Thistles and Roses* appeared in 1961.

Crichton Smith's poetry was influenced by his wide reading and his teaching—his former pupil Donald Meek described him as 'an inspirational teacher of English' (S. MacLean, *Eimhir*, 1999, 7)—and his early poetry tended to use traditional forms: stanzas of three, four, five, and six lines, sonnets, paragraphing, rhymes, assonance. 'For many years', he commented, 'the poem to me was to be an elegant construction … a musical artefact composed of exact language' (Crichton Smith, *Towards the Human*, 77). But his subject matter concentrated on ordinary people, on family relationships, on islands, exile, and language, with many poems exploring and opposing Free Church ideas of law, grace, and duty. He was 'pre-eminently the seeker after the "true" nature of personal identity, in terms of religion, culture and philosophy, in local and global contexts' (MacLean, 9). This struggle for a kind of creative perfection appeared at times to run counter to his island identity, as can be seen in 'Poem of Lewis' from *The Long River*:

Here they have no time for the fine graces
of poetry unless it freely grows

in deep compulsion, like water in the well
woven into the texture of the soil
in a strong pattern.

The major themes of Crichton Smith's writing became established, and included the act of poetic creation itself, isolation, alienation, guilt, old age, religion, and death, his thinking much influenced by his absorbed reading of Kierkegaard. Such themes recur in both his poems and his short and longer novels.

Crichton Smith's identity grew in confidence with the years. 'Studies in Power' from *Thistles and Roses* is made up of two sonnets which juxtapose the fear other men will 'stand like giants by my dwarfish verse' with the resolution that the 'straining forces' within him have at last been 'harmonised'. In 1962 Crichton Smith published the long poem *Deer on the High Hills*, which most critics suggest marked a significant transitional stage in his writing and prepared the way for his later work. Throughout his life it remained his favourite poem. Although it is ostensibly about the deer, it is, more fundamentally, an analysis of the creative process that both appreciates the use of poetic language with its powerful metaphors and simultaneously questions its ability to present reality.

Meanwhile, Crichton Smith began to write prose, publishing a volume of short stories in Gaelic in 1963 before he published his first novel, *Consider the Lilies*, in 1968. This portrays the life of an old woman during the time of the highland clearances. In both his poetry and his prose old women are repeatedly treated with varying degrees of criticism, compassion, or respect. His presentation of them stemmed from his uneasy relationship with his mother. He was haunted by a sense of guilt that her life had been so hard compared with his, but she was also a representative of all that he hated about the Calvinism of his youth. Despite the unease in the relationship, he was the brother who accepted the responsibility of caring for his bitter and disturbed old mother: she lived with him until her death in 1969. In *Consider the Lilies* the protagonist, Mrs Scott, finds that the religion she has almost blindly followed her entire life is insufficient for her needs. It is the atheist Macleod, not the Calvinist minister, who picks her up where she has fallen, takes her into his home, feeds and cares for her. Her church fails her. She is broken outside her religious shelter, and will have to face an uncertain future without her old, hard beliefs. *The Last Summer*, a thinly veiled autobiographical story of a boy growing up in Lewis, followed in 1969. Crichton Smith continued to write and publish in English and Gaelic, often translating his own work, but it was the death of his mother which forced him to reassess both his life and his writing. *Love Poems and Elegies* (1972), the volume inspired by his mother's death, is sharper and tauter than was the earlier poetry, and the volumes which follow have a new energy. The language is more direct, less literary, than before. As he remarks in 'On Looking at the Dead':

This is a coming to reality.
This is the stubborn place. No metaphors swarm
around that fact.

On 16 July 1977 Crichton Smith married Donalda Gillies Logan (*b*. 1939) and became stepfather to Donalda's two teenage sons, Alistair and Peter. At the same time he gave up teaching to become a full-time writer. In 1982 he suffered a severe breakdown, an experience which was later explored in a very directly autobiographical novel *In the Middle of the Wood* (1987). He thought at the time that he would never write poetry again but, after a period in hospital, he returned to writing.

A Life (1986) seems to suggest that Crichton Smith had at last come to terms with his identity. In the final section, which deals with his life in Taynuilt, there is a sense of contentment:

Such joy that I have come home to
after all that measurement.
(p. 14)

In *The Village* (1989) he introduced into his poetry a much lighter atmosphere than previously. He had settled happily with Donalda and his writing reflects acceptance of life as it is lived in Taynuilt, with its black-moustached postman, the children 'building a snowman', the washing hanging out 'like paintings', the lively market with the

cries of the salesmen,
who have to live, don't they,
just like us.

His extended love poem for Donalda, *The Leaf and the Marble* (1998), testifies movingly to the love they shared.

Throughout his adult life Crichton Smith wrote prolifically in both Gaelic and English. He was concerned to provide Gaelic stories for the young where none existed. He wrote plays for Gaelic acting groups and was proud of his development of the Gaelic short story. He also produced masterly translations from Gaelic into English of Duncan Ban MacIntyre (1969) and of Sorley MacLean's *Poems to Eimhir* (1971).

Crichton Smith was a slight, bald, bespectacled figure, who read his work beautifully, and whose infectious giggle regularly demolished any hint of over-seriousness. His audiences increasingly demanded not only readings of his poetry but also musings of his wonderfully anarchic *alter ego*, Murdo. In the 1980s Crichton Smith was a much respected writer in residence at the University of Aberdeen, and received honorary doctorates from Aberdeen, Dundee, and Glasgow universities. He was appointed OBE in 1981 and won the queen's medal for poetry among other honours.

In the late summer of 1998 Iain Crichton Smith was diagnosed with cancer. He died at his home, Tigh-na-Fuaran, Taynuilt, Argyll, on 15 October and was cremated at Cardross crematorium, Helensburgh, on 20 October. The casket with his ashes was buried in Muchairn cemetery, Taynuilt. HILDA D. SPEAR

Sources personal knowledge (2004) • private information (2004) [Donalda Crichton Smith, widow] • I. Crichton Smith, *Towards the human* (1986) • C. Gow, *Mirror and marble* (1992) • I. Crichton Smith, *Critical essays*, ed. C. Nicholson (1992)

Archives NL Scot., corresp. and literary papers • priv. coll., papers

Likenesses A. Moffat, oils, 1980, Scot. NPG • M. Knowles, oils, BBC, Edinburgh

Smith, Ian Scott (1903–1972), rugby player, was born in Melbourne, Australia, on 31 October 1903, the son of John Macpherson Smith, barrister, and his wife, Margaret Alexandrina Cathcart, daughter of James Scott of Girvan, Ayrshire. He attended Cargilfield School, where he first played rugby, and Winchester College, where he proved to be a remarkable all-round sportsman. Winchester did not play rugby. Smith had two seasons in the first soccer eleven, won every race from the 100 yards to the mile, and had a solid season in the cricket team in 1922, when he averaged 20 as an opening bat. He made a joke of the fact that he had dropped four catches before lunch in the big match against Eton at Lord's, but *Wisden* records that a stubborn second innings of 34 helped Winchester narrowly to save the game. He was, according to *Wisden*, 'an ugly player with few strokes, but he watched the ball' (p. 331).

In 1922 Smith proceeded to Brasenose College, Oxford, a college developing a very strong rugby tradition, where he read jurisprudence and took a third in 1925. During his first year he appeared on occasions for the university soccer team. He liked a girl who preferred rugby to soccer. She said she would switch her allegiance from Cambridge, where her father had studied, to Oxford, if Ian won a rugby blue. He sent his father a £1 note, inviting a bet at odds of 50–1 against his getting a blue within twelve months. His father had to pay up.

Smith's assets as a wing three-quarter were a long, high stride, great speed, and sheer determination. On one famous occasion he sprinted 85 yards to score for the Barbarians against Swansea. Initially, his tackling was sketchy and he tended to drop passes. His sheer pace, however, won him a place in an Oxford side without a strong pack; the captain, G. P. S. Macpherson, didn't care how many tries the opposition got so long as Oxford scored more. This worked out against Cambridge in 1923, when Smith got his blue. 'Smith's first try', the historians of Oxford rugby record, 'was a copybook effort' (McWhirter and Noble, 133). Lawton, the fly half, got the ball to the very fast centre Jacob, who broke, then passed to Smith, who ran clean round the defence. Oxford won 21–14.

Injured on a tour of South Africa, Smith missed the 1924 varsity match. But in that year he began his illustrious career for Scotland, during which he was chosen to play on 39 consecutive occasions, actually appeared on 32, and scored 24 tries, a record for all nations which stood until David Campese of Australia broke it in the 1987 world cup. When Scotland beat Wales 35–10 in 1924, Smith ran in three tries. Famously, the entire Scottish three-quarter division had played together at Oxford. Beside Macpherson, a great attacking centre, there were A. C. Wallace, a winger who had previously played for New South Wales against New Zealand and represented Australia after winning nine caps for Scotland, and G. G. Aitken, already capped twice as a New Zealand All Black. These men played together again three times in Scotland's grand slam in the five nations championship of 1925, the country's first such triumph, not repeated until 1984, and one based on cavalier attack. At Inverleith (where Scotland beat France 25–4) Smith scored four tries among Scotland's record tally of seven. In Swansea (where Scotland won against Wales, 24–14) he ran in four out of six. Marking the Flying Scotsman, as Smith was nicknamed, must have preoccupied Ireland, who lost 8–14 in Dublin, and England, who came to inaugurate the Scottish Rugby Union's new stadium at Murrayfield. A crowd of 60,000 spectators, then a record for any rugby match, saw Wallace score his fourth try in consecutive matches. Scotland ran the English team to exhaustion, and won, in a nail-biting finish, by 14–11.

This was one of the bright phases in Scotland's often dark rugby history. The championship was shared in 1926. Smith scored two tries in Scotland's first-ever victory at Twickenham over England. It has been seen as remarkable that backs scored tries at all in this period, when defences had tightened, forwards had settled into the 3–2–3 formation, the blind-side flanker went for the scrum half, the open-side flanker harried the fly half, and number 8 functioned as a defensive sweeper behind his own backs. A contrary view is that it now seems impressive that wingers received the ball so often. In any case, when Scotland were again joint champions in 1927, Smith scored twice against the French and twice against England. He was absent throughout 1928, when Scotland were wooden spoonists, but in 1929 the team gained the championship outright, with Smith scoring against Ireland and twice against England, a feat which he performed yet again in 1931. In 1932 Scotland were wooden spoonists for the third time in five years, but Smith contributed his team's only score in a 16–3 drubbing by England at Twickenham. In 1933 Smith was appointed captain of Scotland. He handled young backs—two from Oxford, two from Cambridge—very sensitively. Since France had been excluded from the championship in 1932 (for sixteen years, as it transpired) because of dalliance with professionalism, the triple crown was all that Scotland could win in the 1933 season. Smith's team achieved this in the match when he gained his final cap, against Ireland in Dublin, hobbling for most of the game.

Smith had acquired a reputation at Oxford as a larger-than-life hell-raiser. His captain on an Oxford tour of France recalled that he tried to get Smith to go to bed before matches, but concluded eventually that he played rather better when he hadn't. He missed his athletics blue as a sprinter when he was dropped for breaking training with alcohol the night before the tournament against Cambridge. He cheerfully admitted that, drink taken, he had driven a car packed with sporting comrades, headlights blazing and horn blowing, down the pavement the length of Princes Street.

Having in 1929 qualified as an accountant in Edinburgh, where he played for the university at rugby from 1925 to 1929, Smith settled down to a professional life, alleviated by weekends in Boulogne gambling at roulette and flights all over Europe as navigator to a friend who was looking for deals in timber. He played for London Scottish while he worked in the City of London from 1930 until 1939, when he joined the Royal Army Ordnance Corps as a second lieutenant. He rose to the rank of lieutenant-colonel attached to the Polish forces in Britain. The Poles were quartered in various parts of Scotland, and Smith was able to arrange his visits to them at times propitious for local fishing and shooting. From 1946 to 1948 he was with the Allied Control Commission in occupied Germany. He wished to return to Scotland, and a friend found a job for him if he qualified as a solicitor; this, in his mid-forties, he smartly achieved. He worked with John Clerk, Brodie & Sons, writers to the signet, in Edinburgh from 1950. He found a home in Kelso, where he rose at 5.30 and fished two or three pools before setting off to reach the office at nine.

Smith gained an apt wife in Dorothy Keld Fenwick. He is said to have proposed to her on the summit of Soutra, having carried up caviare and champagne in anticipation of her acceptance. They kept open house at Walton Hall, Kelso. Serious ill health forced his retirement in 1964. He lost a leg, but continued to fish, shoot, and entertain his friends. In great pain, he never complained. As a friend recalled, 'Seated in his wheelchair, an outsize glass in his hand, he would quiz, mock, and even shock the company, but always with humour and that dazzling smile which was his passport to so many hearts' (Roughead). He died at the Royal Infirmary, Edinburgh, on 18 September 1972. He was buried on a hillside near Melrose, where some of his ancestors had lived. Then and long after rugby commentators still harked back frequently to his prodigious achievements, as others continued to strive to match them. When, in 2000, the five nations, with the admission of Italy, became six, Smith's record of twenty-four tries in the championship still stood, six clear of all rivals.

ANGUS CALDER

Sources [N. Roughead ?], 'Memoir', Scottish Rugby Union library, Murrayfield • T. Godwin, *The international rugby championship, 1883–1983* (1984) • A. Massie, *A portrait of Scottish rugby* (1984) • A. R. McWhirter and A. Noble, *Centenary history of Oxford University Rugby Football Club* (1969) • F. Morris, *The first 100: history of the London Scottish football club* (1977) • J. B. G. Thomas, *Fifty-two famous tries* (1976) • S. Thorburn, *History of the Scottish Rugby Union* (1980) • E. R. Wilson and H. A. Jackson, eds., *Winchester College: a register for the years 1901–1946* (1956) • *Wisden* (1923) • private information (2004) • d. cert.

Wealth at death £458,905.45: confirmation, 1973, NA Scot., SC

Smith, Isaac Gregory (1826–1920). *See under* Smith, Jeremiah (1771–1854).

Smith, James (1604/5–1667), Church of England clergyman and poet, was baptized on 25 July 1605 at Marston Moretaine, Bedfordshire, the third of ten children of Thomas Smith (*d.* 1619), rector of Marston, and his wife, Mary. He matriculated from Christ Church, Oxford, on 7 March 1623 aged eighteen, but soon moved to Lincoln College, where his elder brother, Thomas, was a medical student and a dangerous brawler. Smith was at Christ Church long enough to fall under the influence of the dean, Richard Corbett, who was already a noted poet and whom he followed by composing a lampoon on the unfortunate Mistress Mallett.

Smith left Oxford for London in the mid-1620s; he married Elizabeth (whose surname is unknown) in 1626 and was ordained in time to gain, late in 1627, the chaplaincy to Henry Rich, earl of Holland, during his expedition to relieve the English force then attempting to raise a siege of French protestants at La Rochelle. Holland's relief force never sailed, but Smith may have made the acquaintance in Portsmouth of such long-term associates as Robert Herrick, John Mennes, and John Weeks or Wickes, all of whom were involved in the expedition. Soon after the return of the main English force Smith joined the chorus of poets who celebrated the assassination of its leader, George Villiers, duke of Buckingham, writing a rather laboured poetic defence of the assassin, John Felton, in the latter part of 1627. He was shortly offered a chaplaincy by Thomas Wentworth, earl of Cleveland.

It has been suggested that Smith was the unlicensed curate or lecturer of that name at St Michael-le-Querne in 1628. In 1629 he appears to have been a lecturer at St Botolph, Billingsgate, before being turned out 'for keeping excessive Companye with players', by whom he 'hoped to gett good meanes'. In his defence he insisted that 'there might be as much good many times done by a man in hearinge play as in hearinge a sermon' (PRO, SP 16/240/25). During the early 1630s Smith was a conspicuous figure in the *demi-monde* of London's taverns, playhouses, and bowling alleys: he pulled off cheats and scams, was thrown in prison for debt, and together with a number of players (including, probably, Thomas Pollard of the King's Company) he founded a fraternity, the order or family of the fancy, which specialized in drinking binges, the speaking of nonsense, and the composition of comic poetry. In this milieu Smith composed his mock poems, *The Loves of Hero and Leander* (1651) and his highly regarded *Innovation of Penelope and Ulysses* (first printed in 1658, in *Wit Restor'd*), along with laudatory verses by Philip Massinger, JM (John Mennes), and James Atkins.

Smith's riotous behaviour did not derail his clerical career. On 3 April 1633, as from Lincoln College, he gained the degree of BD of Oxford, and on 27 May 1634 he was installed as rector of Wainfleet All Saints', Lincolnshire, although he probably remained in London for much of the decade. On 17 July 1639 he gained the rectory of King's Nympton, Devon. This was in the gift of Sir Lewis Pollard, with whom Smith may have been involved, along with Thomas Wentworth (son of the earl of Cleveland), in a courtly drinking circle.

During the second bishops' war in 1640 Smith was appointed chaplain to Edward Conway, second Viscount Conway, during the latter's northern command. Smith sent his friends Thomas Pollard and Robert Mering a comic verse epistle from Newcastle upon Tyne on 5 July, poking fun at the ill-preparedness of the army. During the winter, with Sir Kenelm Digby, he lived in Conway's house in Queen Street, Lincoln's Inn Fields, from where he wrote teasing verse epistles to Mennes, who remained in the north. About ten of these were later printed in the miscellanies *Musarum deliciae* (1655) and *Wit Restor'd* (1658). Through these volumes the 'drolling' verse of Smith and

Mennes became fashionable and influenced the burlesques of Samuel Butler and the travesties of Charles Cotton.

Throughout the civil wars, Commonwealth, and protectorate Smith managed to retain his cure at King's Nympton, where he appears to have resided. He continued to keep in contact with Mennes through verse epistles: in one (4 May 1648) he defends himself for adopting the *Directory for the Publique Worship of God*; in another (15 February 1649) he takes Mennes to task for compounding; while in a third (late 1653) he congratulates Mennes 'on a rich prize which he took on the Seas' (*Wit Restor'd*, 46, 43; *Musarum deliciae*, 84).

At the Restoration, Smith petitioned the king, insisting on his loyalty throughout the civil war and interregnum. He was granted the archdeaconry of Barnstaple in 1660, retaining it until 1662, and on 10 July 1660 a canon residency of Exeter Cathedral, where, according to Anthony Wood, he composed a number of anthems, no longer extant. Other appointments followed. He was awarded the degree of DD by Oxford University on 3 July 1661, the rectory of Alphington, Devon, on 18 October 1662 (upon which he resigned from King's Nympton), the precentorship of Exeter Cathedral (perhaps in the same year), and the rectory of Exminster, Devon, on 1 July 1664. He died at Alphington on 20 June 1667 and was buried in the church at King's Nympton. TIMOTHY RAYLOR

Sources T. Raylor, *Cavaliers, clubs, and literary culture: Sir John Mennes, James Smith, and the order of the fancy* (1994) • Wood, *Ath. Oxon.*, new edn, 3.776–7 • Foster, *Alum. Oxon.* • C. W. Foster, 'Institutions to benefices in the diocese of Lincoln', *Associated Architectural Societies' Reports and Papers*, 39 (1928–9), 179–216 • bishops' registers, Devon RO, 23–4 • F. G. Emmison, ed., *Bedfordshire parish registers*, 44 (1953) • PRO, SP 29/7/68 • PRO, SP 16/240/25 • *CSP dom.*, 1663–4 • P. S. Seaver, *The puritan lectureships: the politics of religious dissent, 1560–1662* (1970), 246, 351 • memorial, King's Nympton church, Devon

Smith, James (1644/5–1731), architect, was the son of James Smith (*d.* 1684/5), a master mason who was living in Tarbat, Ross-shire, in 1656 and who became a burgess of Forres, Moray, in 1659. Father and son are recorded as building the town bridge at Inverness (1680–82) on which, among other carved embellishments, their names were to be inscribed. Nothing more is known of the family or of James Smith's early years and education except for his intention to enter the Roman Catholic priesthood. On 3 May 1671 'Jacobus Smith Moraviensis' enrolled at the Scots College, Rome, where he studied rhetoric, philosophy, and theology. He left on 3 October 1675, promising to return 'but became an apostate' (Anderson, 118). Later Smith claimed to have had a 'liberall education at schools and Colledges at home and occasion to know the world by travelling abroad' (Armet, 283), as a receipt for expenses from Sir William Bruce in 1677 proves.

In the next year Smith was working in Edinburgh on the palace of Holyroodhouse, begun in 1671 to the design of Bruce. In 1679 he married Janet, eldest daughter of Robert Mylne, the master mason to the crown of Scotland, who was overseeing the building of Holyroodhouse. By right of his marriage Smith was able to enrol on 17 December 1679 as a burgess of Edinburgh, and is described in the entry as 'archetecter' (Watson, 456). The couple's first child, Elizabeth (*bap.* 12 Aug 1680), was followed by Marian (*bap.* 13 Oct 1681) and James (*bap.* 13 March 1683). Janet Smith, having borne eighteen children, died in 1699. Smith's second wife, Anna, bore fourteen children, one of whom, being born in his father's seventieth year, was named Climacterick Smith. A daughter, Bella, married Smith's cousin Gilbert Smith in 1713. Gilbert had an elder brother, James Smith, and the two James Smiths were associated in building projects. Smith was designated Mr James Smith of Whitehill after the property in Edinburghshire which he purchased in 1686 (and where he built a house). When he was in financial difficulties he sold a portion of the lands of Whitehill in 1706 and the remainder in 1726 to his son-in-law Gilbert Smith.

In 1683 James Smith was appointed, on the recommendation of his client, the first duke of Queensberry, to the post of surveyor and overseer of the royal works in Scotland. In that capacity he designed, within the medieval nave of Holyrood Abbey, the chapel for the chivalric order of the knights of the Thistle which was revived by James II (James VII of Scotland) in 1687. The chapel was completed by 1 May 1688. An engraving in William Adam's *Vitruvius Scoticus* (*c.*1812) shows the throne, beneath a canopy of state at the west end facing 'three image peeces for the high altar', carved by Grinling Gibbons (NA Scot., SP 57/13, 181). The knights' stalls were Corinthian aedicules, surmounted by heraldic achievements, set within the bays of the nave arcade. There had never been such a sumptuous display of classicism in Scotland. It did not survive, for, on 20 December 1688, with news of the landing in England of William of Orange, a mob sacked the chapel and 'broke down all the ornaments' (Forbes Leith, 2.143–4), which were burnt.

For the congregation displaced from the abbey, the king had in August 1688 ordered the erection of a church, with a churchyard, in the adjacent Canongate, for which the town council of Edinburgh was to advance money to James Smith. With a Latin-cross plan, chancel, and apse, the Canongate church was unique in post-Reformation Scotland, being generally accepted as a derivative from Catholic Italy. Yet perhaps the unfluted Doric columns of the interior and the curves of the entrance elevation owe more to contemporary Dutch examples, although the syntax of the Doric entrance porch comes from the publications of the sixteenth-century Italian architect Sebastiano Serlio.

The greater part of Smith's architectural output over thirty years was his half a dozen new country houses, to which can be added several other attributed works and alterations to existing houses. His first new house was Drumlanrig Castle, Dumfriesshire, built in 1679–90 for the duke of Queensberry. Although the courtyard plan with high corner towers was old-fashioned (it was probably a reused scheme by Robert Mylne), it was rendered striking by a show front of pediments and pilasters, perhaps taken from a published view of Jacques du Cerceau's château of Charleval of 100 years before. Also of foreign derivation were the arched basement and horseshoe staircase, which were copied from Pierre le Muet's *Maniere de bien bastir* (1647), published in English in 1670.

More significant for the future course of Scottish and of English architecture was Smith's knowledge of the Venetian architect Andrea Palladio, and his *Quattro libri d'architettura*. Drawings by Smith (in the British Architectural Library drawings collection) show a knowledge of Palladianism that seems to be derived as much from unique personal observation as from textual interpretation. The drawings were later owned by Colen Campbell, who would propagandize for Palladianism in England partly through his own designs but chiefly through the volumes of *Vitruvius Britannicus*, in which Smith was declared 'the most experienc'd Architect' in Scotland (2.3). It should be noted that the parental homes of Smith and Campbell on the Moray Firth were only 12 miles apart and that one of the drawings is an updated scheme for Cawdor Castle, Nairnshire, the seat of Campbell's uncle Sir Hugh Campbell. While the bulk of the drawings are theoretical studies on Palladian themes, such as the Villa Rotonda, Vicenza, a few are for specific Scottish projects by Smith. Plans and elevations have been identified for Whitehill (later Newhailes), Edinburghshire (*c*.1686), and for Raith, Fife (1694), with which Strathleven House, Dunbartonshire (*c*.1690), may be linked stylistically. Each has two storeys over a sunk basement, a three-bay pedimented centre, and harling. Each commands a view of water, possibly as a reminder of the villas lining the Brenta Canal in the Veneto.

Of the greater country houses, three are pre-eminent. The genesis of Melville House, Fife (1697–1702), is complex. There was input from Bruce (a draft which has not survived) as well as Smith's Italianate schemes with loggias or a portico combined with a central plan, all of which gave way to a compact H-plan akin to Belton House, Lincolnshire, completed ten years before. Smith's grandest and largest commissions were Hamilton Palace, Lanarkshire (1691–1701; dem.), and Dalkeith House, Edinburghshire (1701–9). Both were old seats remodelled to suit the semi-regal status of their owners and both have porticoes, perhaps modelled on those of Palladian churches in Venice but hitherto unknown in Scotland.

In his later years Smith worked for a time with Alexander McGill at Yester House, Haddingtonshire (*c*.1700–15), and elsewhere; in 1718 he was appointed to design fortifications in the highlands. Thereafter his last years are a blank. Smith was knowledgeable about hydraulics, about which he was often consulted. It was, however, involvement in a flooded colliery that forced the sale of Whitehill. Smith represented Forres in the Scottish parliament in 1685–6, and after the treaty of Union in 1707 he unsuccessfully sought candidacy in 1715 as an MP. He died in Edinburgh on 6 November 1731, aged eighty-six.

James Macaulay

Sources Colvin, *Archs.* • J. Macaulay, *The classical country-house in Scotland, 1660–1800* (1987) • R. S. Mylne, *The master masons to the crown of Scotland and their works* (1893) • M. Wood and H. Armet, eds., *Extracts from the records of the burgh of Edinburgh, 1680–1689*, [12] (1954) • H. Armet, ed., *Extracts from the records of the burgh of Edinburgh, 1701–1718*, [14] (1967) • W. Forbes-Leith, ed., *Memoirs of Scottish Catholics*, 2 vols. (1909) • C. Fraser-Mackintosh, *Letters of two centuries, chiefly connected with Inverness and the highlands, from 1616 to 1815* (1890) • P. J. Anderson, ed., *Records of the Scots colleges at Douai, Rome, Madrid, Valladolid and Ratisbon*, New Spalding Club, 30 (1906) • C. B. B. Watson, ed., *Roll of Edinburgh burgesses and guild-brethren, 1406–1700*, Scottish RS, 59 (1929) • H. Colvin, 'A Scottish origin for English Palladianism?', *Architectural History*, 17 (1974), 5–12 • A. McKechnie, 'James Smith's smaller country houses', *Aspects of Scottish classicism*, ed. J. Frew and D. Jones (1988), 9–15 • *Caledonian Mercury* (8 Nov 1731)

Archives RIBA | NA Scot., Buccleuch (Dalkeith) MSS • NA Scot., Leven and Melville MSS

Smith, James (1645–1711), vicar apostolic of the northern district, was born at Winchester, the second son of Bartholomew and Frances Smith of Stoke Charity, Hampshire. He received his early education, from 1661, at the English College, Douai, from where he went to St Gregory's, Paris, for higher studies in 1669. He returned to Douai to teach philosophy in 1672. Ordained priest in 1677 he took his DD in 1680 and continued to teach at the college, eventually succeeding Francis Gage as its president on 28 August 1682. During this time he inherited, it is said, his brother's large estate, but surrendered most of it to his younger brother, Bartholomew. As early as 1684 he was being recommended by the chapter for a bishopric, and following his nomination by James II as one of the four vicars apostolic of England in November 1687 he was elected by the Propaganda on 12 January 1688 as bishop of Callipolis *in partibus infidelium* and vicar apostolic of the new northern district of England. His consecration followed on 13 May in the chapel of the queen dowager at Somerset House. He arrived at York on 2 August, where he was received with great ceremonial, including a sung high mass and a public Te Deum. The flight of the king brought in its wake a renewal of persecution. Like his brother bishops Smith went into hiding, but fared better in so far as he was never arrested. What little we know about his movements during this difficult time indicates that he had made Wycliffe Hall, Yorkshire, his base for ministering quietly, if not secretly, to his flock scattered throughout the northern counties which clearly did not experience the full severity of anti-Catholic feeling.

Smith was so highly thought of that on several occasions his name was mentioned for preferment. On the death of Cardinal Howard in 1694 a first attempt was made to promote Smith's succession to his post as cardinal protector of England and again in 1699 James Stuart himself wrote personally to the pope from his court at St Germain requesting a red hat for him. In 1702 his name was also canvassed as a likely successor to Bishop Leyburn of the London district, who had just died. Smith, a very modest and retiring man, resisted all these overtures. He was, as he put it: 'better contented to go his little way than be put in circumstances quite out of his talents and education' (Hemphill, 28). His strenuous visitation of the East Riding in 1710 brought on an illness to which he succumbed ten months later on 13 May 1711 at Wycliffe Hall, the twenty-third anniversary of his consecration as bishop. He was buried probably at Wycliffe without any memorial. Dodd describes him as a 'fine gentleman, a good scholar, and a zealous pastor' (Dodd, 3.468), a tribute which the evidence presently available seems to endorse.

D. MILBURN

Sources G. Anstruther, *The seminary priests*, 3 (1976), 205–7 • B. Hemphill, *The early vicars apostolic of England, 1685–1750* (1954), 27–30 • C. Dodd [H. Tootell], *The church history of England, from the year 1500, to the year 1688*, 3 (1742), 468 • W. M. Brady, *The episcopal succession in England, Scotland, and Ireland, AD 1400 to 1875*, 3 (1877), 243–8 • *Catholic Miscellany*, 7 (1827), 243–9 • *DNB*

Archives Archives of the Northern District • Leeds Roman Catholic diocesan archives, corresp. and papers • Ushaw College, Durham, corresp. and papers • Westm. DA

Likenesses engraving (after portrait formerly in Chapel-House at York), repro. in *The laity's directory* (1819) • oils, Ushaw College, Durham • oils, Douai Abbey, Reading • portrait (after print at Ushaw College, Durham), repro. in Hemphill, *Early vicars apostolic*, facing p. 92 • stipple, NPG

Wealth at death various rents, incl. 2976 livres p.a.: will, Ushaw College, Durham; Anstruther, *Seminary priests*, vol. 3, p. 207

Smith, James (1680–1736), Church of Scotland minister, was born probably in early August 1680 at Denny, Stirlingshire, the son of James Smith and Janet (or Jonett) Wilson. Nothing about his family is known, other than the existence, at his death, of a sister, Margaret, and a nephew, James Smith, who was his heir. Smith entered Edinburgh University in 1698, serving also as a domestic tutor, first to the Dalrymples of Cousland, then the Dundases of Arniston. The nexus with the Dundases, especially Robert, later lord advocate of Scotland, assisted his career until Smith deserted the squadrone cause in 1730. Licensed by Dalkeith presbytery on 26 October 1703, Smith was ordained to Morham by Haddington presbytery on 24 September 1706. At Dunbar, on 19 December 1708, he married Katharine Oswald (1684–1730) daughter of John Oswald and Elspeth Cowan of Denny. Katharine was probably the sister of Margaret Oswald, whose husband, the Revd James Craig of Edinburgh, was the author of two volumes of *Sermons* edited by Smith for publication in 1732.

When the important charge of Cramond became vacant in 1709 political rivals scrambled to arrange a suitable successor. After a manipulative campaign lasting two years and three months, Dundas's allies among the squadrone achieved Smith's settlement on 16 January 1712. Soon after, Smith signalled his support for moderate principles within the kirk by publishing two *Dialogues* (1712, 1713) which refuted evangelical scruples about the abjuration oath. His political and doctrinal credentials now established, he rose to the front rank of church leadership during the ascendancy of the squadrone from 1715 to 1724. A determined opponent of zealotry, he was prominent in the general assembly's firm response to the Auchterarder creed (1717), the Marrow controversy (1720–22), the second Simson case (1726–9), and in his defence of John Glas's deposition in 1730. More important, however, was his central belief that the kirk's authority must outweigh even individual conscience, if peace and order are to be maintained. This conditioned his unyielding attitude towards recalcitrants like the seceders and those who resisted settlements by presentation. In the latter connection his authoritarian stance in the Lochmaben (1724) and West Kirk (1730–32) cases attracted particular opprobrium. Although elected to the moderator's chair in 1723, Smith saw that subsequent advancement was only possible by defection to the Ilay–Argyll interest. Preferment followed swiftly: translation to Edinburgh New North Church on 23 July 1730 (demitted 27 April 1732), the chair of divinity at Edinburgh University on 16 February 1732, moderator again in May 1732, university principal on 18 July 1733, along with readmission to the New North Kirk on 25 July 1733.

Smith was widely respected as probably the most able of his peers, and certainly the best orator. His insistence that the kirk must win respect by respecting its own enactments became a characteristic of moderatism. From 1731 he endured unspecified health problems, which were judged to be responsible for occasional outbursts of undignified ill temper. While returning from taking the hot springs at Bristol he died at Coldstream on 13 August 1736. His wife having died in 1730 without children, Smith's estate of £11,942 7*s.* 1*d.* Scots passed to his nephew, also James Smith.

LAURENCE A. B. WHITLEY

Sources *Fasti Scot.* • *The correspondence of the Rev. Robert Wodrow*, ed. T. M'Crie, 3 vols., Wodrow Society, [3] (1842–3) • R. Wodrow, *Analecta, or, Materials for a history of remarkable providences, mostly relating to Scotch ministers and Christians*, ed. [M. Leishman], 4 vols., Maitland Club, 60 (1842–3) • NA Scot., registers of the presbytery of Edinburgh, 1709–1736, CH2/121/7–13 • NL Scot., Saltoun MSS 16544–16547 • XY [A. Webster], *Observations upon church affairs, addressed to Principal Smith* (1743) • A. Morgan, *Matriculation rolls of the University of Edinburgh* (1934) • NA Scot., will, CC 8/8/98, fols. 259–64 • J. Warrick, *The moderators of the Church of Scotland from 1690 to 1740* (1913)

Wealth at death £11,942 7*s.* 1*d.* Scots: NA Scot., CC 8/8/98, fols. 259–64

Smith, James (1775–1839), writer and humorist, was born in London on 10 February 1775, the second of the eight children of Robert Smith (1747–1832), a solicitor, and his first wife, Mary Bogle (1748/9–1804), and the elder brother of Horatio *Smith (1779–1849). He was educated at Chigwell School, Essex; the nonconformist New College, Hackney; Alfred House Academy, Camberwell; and a commercial academy in Tower Street, London. He was articled to his father in 1792, and succeeded him as solicitor to the Board of Ordnance in 1832. Like Horatio, James greatly preferred theatrical and literary amusement to the details of his legal profession, but he was steady and attentive in his official duties.

Smith's first literary production was a hoax, being a series of letters descriptive of alleged natural phenomena which imposed on the *Gentleman's Magazine*. After this he contributed to the *Pic Nic* and *Cabinet* journals, and wrote prefaces for Bell's *British Theatre*. He was closely connected with his brother in his literary undertakings, writing in particular the larger and better portion of the metrical imitations of Horace, which appeared in Thomas Hill's *Monthly Mirror*, and were subsequently collected and published under the title of *Horace in London* (1813). To the *Rejected Addresses* (1812) he contributed nos. 2, 5, 7, 13, 14, 16, 17, 18, 19, and 20, and the notes to the eighteenth edition (1833). James Smith's contributions to these clever parodies were considered the best, especially his imitations of Crabbe and Cobbett, but he appeared contented with the celebrity they brought him, and never again produced anything considerable. Universally known, and everywhere socially acceptable, 'he wanted', says his brother, 'all motive for further and more serious exertion' ('Biographical memoir', 29). He produced, however, the text for Charles Mathew's comic entertainments, *The Country Cousins*, *The Trip to France*, and *The Trip to America* (1820–22), the two latter earning him £1000. Mathews described him as 'the only man who can write clever nonsense' (ibid., 30). He produced much comic and occasional verse and prose for periodicals, and was a frequent contributor to the *New Monthly Magazine* from 1821. Among his better-known works were his anti-Napoleon parody, *The Mammoth*, and his series of comic reflections, *Grimm's Ghost*. 'A confirmed metropolitan' as Horatio described him (ibid., 42), he wrote extensively about London.

Smith's reputation rested on his character as a wit and diner-out; most of the excellent things attributed to him, however, were, in the opinion of his biographer in the *Law Magazine*, *impromptus faits à loisir* ('H.', 125). Dignified and striking in his personal appearance, he was less genial than his brother, and 'circumscribed in the extent of his information, and, as a natural consequence, more concentrated in himself' (*New Monthly Magazine*, 87.23). Keats, after dining with the Smith brothers and their friends in December 1817, left with a conviction of the superiority of humour to wit (*Letters of John Keats*, 1.193).

Smith was plagued by gout, and after a five-month illness of influenza aggravated by gout he died, unmarried, at his house at 27 Craven Street, Strand, on 24 December 1839, and was buried in the vaults of St Martin-in-the-Fields. His sister's daughter, Maria *Abdy, also achieved literary success as a poet.

RICHARD GARNETT, *rev.* FIONA ROBERTSON

Sources 'Biographical memoir', *Memoirs, letters, and comic miscellanies in prose and verse, of the late James Smith*, ed. H. Smith, 1 (1840), 1–54 • A. H. Beavan, *James and Horace Smith, joint authors of Rejected addresses: a family narrative* (1899) • 'H.', 'Biographical notice of James Smith', *Law Magazine*, 23 (1840), 117–31 • 'The authors of the rejected addresses', *New Monthly Magazine*, new ser., 87 (1849), 23–30 • P. Fitzgerald, ed., *Rejected addresses by Horace and James Smith* (1890) • W. Maginn and D. Maclise, *A gallery of illustrious literary characters, 1830–1838*, ed. W. Bates (1873), pp. 143–6, no. 54 • *The letters of John Keats, 1814–1821*, ed. H. E. Rollins, 2 vols. (1958) • P. G. Patmore, *My friends and acquaintances*, 3 vols. (1855) • A. Hayward, *Biographical and critical essays*, 1 (1858) • G. Kitchin, *A survey of burlesque and parody in English* (1931) • D. A. Kent and D. R. Ewen, eds., *Romantic parodies, 1797–1831* (1992) • d. cert.

Archives BL, letters • Bodl. Oxf., letters • Derbys. RO, letters • FM Cam., letters • Northumbd RO, letters • Trinity Cam., letters • U. Leeds, Brotherton L., letters • Wordsworth Trust, Dove Cottage, Grasmere, letters

Likenesses G. H. Harlow, double portrait, pencil and watercolour, *c.*1812 (with Horace Smith), John Murray, London • E. Finden, stipple, 1833 (after G. H. Harlow), BM; repro. in J. Smith and H. Smith, *Rejected addresses, or, The new theatrum poetarum*, 18th edn (1833) • J. Lonsdale, oils, NPG; repro. in Beavan, *James and Horace Smith* • D. Maclise, drawing, repro. in Bates, ed., *Gallery of illustrious literary characters*, no. 54

Smith, James, of Jordanhill (1782–1867), geologist and biblical historian, was born in Glasgow on 15 August 1782, the eldest of five children of Archibald Smith of Jordanhill (1749–1821), West India merchant, and his wife, Isabella Euing (1755–1855). Smith was educated in Glasgow at the grammar school and the university, where he matriculated in 1795. He became a sleeping partner in the firm of Leitch and Smith, West India merchants, and, following his father's death in 1821, he moved to the family seat, Jordanhill, in Renfrewshire.

On 25 July 1809 Smith married Mary (1789–1847), daughter of Alexander Wilson and granddaughter of Professor Alexander Wilson (1714–1786) of Glasgow University. They had nine children, of whom three survived them: the mathematician Archibald *Smith; Isabella, an accomplished sculptor; and Sabina Douglas Clavering, named after Smith's friends the Arctic voyagers General Sabine and Captain Douglas Clavering.

Smith was typical of the class of Glasgow merchants whose lives encompassed scholarly pursuits. His interests and studies included early voyages of discovery, biblical history, book collecting, sailing, language, geography, geology, archaeology, education, the fine arts, and architecture. Among his friends were Lord John Campbell and Dr John Scouler.

Smith was an accomplished yachtsman and navigator, and his passion for sailing enabled him to combine leisure with his scientific and historical studies. His voyages provided access to, and discovery of, sites of scientific interest and he always carried a dredge in his boat to investigate the sea bed. This interest in sea voyages led him to edit Archibald Campbell's *A Voyage Round the World from 1806 to 1812* (1816), and he communicated D. C. Clavering's *Journal of a Voyage to Spitzbergen and the East Coast of Greenland*, published in 1830. His first paper, 'A whirlwind at Roseneath', was published in the *Edinburgh Philosophical Journal* in 1822.

Smith was a member of the Royal Society, the Geological Society, and the Royal Geographical Society of London. In Glasgow he was president of both the Geological Society and the Archaeological Society. In 1850 he was elected a member of the Société Géologique de France. Smith was renowned for his pioneering geological investigations and conclusions which earned him the epithet 'the father of the post-Tertiary geology of Scotland'. Through assiduous research he was the first to maintain and prove that a colder climate preceded the present one. His first paper on the subject was read to the Geological Society of London in November 1836. In January 1839, the epoch-making 'The late changes of the relative levels of land and sea in the British islands' was read to the Wernerian Natural History Society of Edinburgh. Smith's material evidence provided corroboration for Louis Agassiz's belief in a British ice age. He revised and published twelve of his papers in one volume, *Researches in Newer Pliocene and Post-Tertiary Geology*, in 1862.

Gordon L. Davies, in *The Earth in Decay: a History of British Geomorphology* (1969), assesses Smith's contribution to the

James Smith of Jordanhill (1782–1867), by unknown photographer

study of glacial theory in its historical context and his place alongside his contemporaries, Robert Jamieson and William Buckland. Smith retains his eminent position for his contribution to the study of post-Tertiary geology, cold conditions, and the glacial theory in addition to his support for the pioneering works of fellow scientists, such as Agassiz, Buckland, and Lyell.

From 1839 to 1846 Smith lived abroad for the sake of the health of some of his family. He wintered successively at Madeira (where his daughter Mary died in 1840), Gibraltar, Lisbon, and Malta and took the opportunity to study the geology there. While living in Malta, Smith undertook research for what was to be his greatest literary achievement, *The Voyage and Shipwreck of St Paul*, published in 1848 (4th edn, 1880). He identified the location of the shipwreck with St Paul's Bay, Malta, to which it had been traditionally assigned. It remains a standard work on biblical history, ancient shipbuilding, and navigation. In his introduction Smith acknowledged his sources as his own library, nautical history, and his own practical experience in planning, building, and altering vessels.

Smith was a trustee, manager, and, from 1830 to 1839, president, of Anderson's University in Glasgow, the precursor of what became the University of Strathclyde. One of his most notable achievements as president was the foundation in 1831 of the Andersonian Museum, the interior of which he designed. A major benefactor, he gave coins, medals, and natural-history specimens and was honorary curator from 1848 until his death. In addition to the museum interior, Smith also designed a number of buildings including Craigend (for his cousin James Smith), Govan parish church, and alterations to his own residence at Jordanhill.

Smith of Jordanhill formed a small art collection and supported the fine arts in Glasgow as a member of the Glasgow Institution for Promoting and Encouraging the Fine Arts in the West of Scotland (founded 1821) and as member and president of the Glasgow Dilettanti Society, which was founded in 1825. He was nominated a trustee by the engraver James Haldane in his 1833 *Deed of Constitution* for an academy of the fine arts in Glasgow. In 1859 Smith and his sister, Isabella McCall of Ibroxhill, commissioned a window, *St Paul in Melita*, later removed, for Glasgow Cathedral. A Conservative with liberal views, Smith stood unsuccessfully for parliament in 1837 for Greenock. He was an elder of the Church of Scotland.

Smith enjoyed excellent health until the spring of 1866, when he suffered a slight paralytic stroke. He recovered from this, but another at the end of the year led to his death on 17 January 1867 at Jordanhill. His remains were interred in the family burying-ground, old parish church, Renfrew, on 23 January.

Smith was highly regarded for his personal qualities as well as his scientific and literary achievements. He was described in *One Hundred Glasgow Men* as 'gentle and tolerant, he never made an enemy, and those who knew him will not soon forget his courtly yet genial manners, and his charming conversation and delicate humour, his constant good nature and kindliness, and his unaffected piety' (p. 288). GEORGE FAIRFULL SMITH

Sources Mitchell L., Glas., Glasgow City Archives, Smith of Jordanhill collection · private information (2004) · [J. O. Mitchell, J. Guthrie Smith, and others], 'James Smith FRS', *Memoirs and portraits of one hundred Glasgow men who have died during the last thirty years*, ed. J. MacLehose, 2 (1886), 285–8 · *Glasgow Herald* (24 Jan 1867) · *North British Daily Mail* (24 Jan 1867) · A. Smith, 'Memoir of James Smith', in J. Smith, *The voyage and shipwreck of St Paul*, 4th edn (1880) · H. Crosskey, 'Address in memory of James Smith', *Transactions of the Geological Society of Glasgow*, 2, pt 1/62 (1867), 228–34 · Chambers, *Scots.*, rev. T. Thomson (1875) · Anderson, *Scot. nat.* · T. Annan, J. O. Mitchell, and others, *The old country houses of the old Glasgow gentry* (1870), pl. lix [Jordanhill] · T. Annan, J. O. Mitchell, and others, *The old country houses of the old Glasgow gentry*, 2nd edn (1878), pl. lix ['Jordanhill'] · G. L. Davies, *The earth in decay: a history of British geomorphology, 1578 to 1878* [1969] · *DNB* · P. Macnair and F. Mort, eds., *History of the Geological Society of Glasgow, 1858–1908* (1908) · *BL cat.*, vol. 305 · NA Scot., SC 58/42/34/942–979 · NA Scot., SC 58/42/44/12–14 · NA Scot., SC 58/42/52/935–938

Archives Mitchell L., Glas., Glasgow City Archives · University of Strathclyde, Glasgow | U. Edin. L., letters to Sir Charles Lyell · U. Glas., Archibald Campbell MSS · U. Glas., Euing collection

Likenesses brass plaque, 1899, Renfrew old parish church · T. Annan, photograph (after J. W. Gordon), repro. in T. Annan, *Illustrated catalogue of the exhibition of portraits on loan in the new galleries of art* (1868), cat. no. 311 · J. W. Gordon, oils, priv. coll. · I. Gore Booth, plaster bust, University of Strathclyde, Glasgow · Maclure and Macdonald, engraving (after marble bust by I. G. Booth), repro. in Mitchell, Smith, and others, 'James Smith FRS', 2 · H. Raeburn, oils, Royal Technical College, Glasgow · J. Wilson, oils, Royal Clyde and Northern Yacht Club, Rhu, near Helensburgh · oils (after H. Raeburn), University of Strathclyde, Glasgow · photograph, repro. in Smith, *Voyage and shipwreck*, frontispiece [*see illus.*] • photographs, Mitchell L., Glas., Glasgow City Archives, Smith of Jordanhill collection

Wealth at death £2340 15*s*.: confirmation, 16 Oct 1867, NA Scot. SC 58/42/34/942–979 • £2877 in UK: additional inventory, 12 Aug 1876, NA Scot., SC 58/42/44/12–14 • £14,850 0*s*. 11*d*.: additional inventory, 28 Jan 1886, NA Scot., SC 58/42/52/935–938

Smith, James, of Deanston (1789–1850), textile industrialist and agricultural engineer, was born in Glasgow on 3 January 1789, the son of a Glasgow merchant of a Galloway family, who died two months after his birth. He was brought up by his maternal uncle, Archibald Buchanan of Carston, Stirlingshire, who had served an apprenticeship with Richard Arkwright, and was then managing partner of the Deanston cotton works founded by the Buchanans of Carston in 1785. From the age of seven Smith went to school in Glasgow and attended Glasgow University where he shone at mathematics. He spent his vacations in Ayrshire with his uncle who had by then moved to the Catrine cotton works; it was said that the boy learned industrial processes and engineering in the textile mill and machine shop of the works. Smith also served an apprenticeship with Arkwright, then, at the age of eighteen, became manager of the Deanston cotton mill when it was taken over by the Glasgow textile firm of James Finlay, relatives of his mother and the largest cotton manufacturing enterprise during the first phase of Scotland's 'industrial revolution'. Deanston itself was one of the first of the large-scale factories to be built in Scotland, together with Catrine, Balfron, Stanley, and New Lanark, dispersed but sited for an adequate supply of water before the steam engine became the prime mover.

Over the ensuing thirty-five years, Smith restructured and extended the Deanston mill, adding an engineering shop which built machinery for Deanston itself, Catrine, and other mills in the United Kingdom. He designed and sought patents for textile machinery and developed substantial additional power for the factory by installing four large overshot water-wheels, built in the Deanston works and each capable of a drive of 80 hp, and by constructing a weir on the River Teith, including the device of a 'fish-ladder' to give salmon access to the upper reaches of the river. By 1813 a gasworks had been developed and the factory was lit by gas. The parish minister, writing in 1845, sensed the drama of these changes when he described how local people 'were shy of entering this tower of Babel with its unknown sights and sounds'. Smith and the company built a new village beside the factory for the growing workforce, housing about 1200 by the early 1840s. Planned factory villages were the social element of a new industrial order and the model established by David Dale and Robert Owen at New Lanark was followed by Smith, who also built a school at Deanston, adopting the aspirations of the philanthropic industrialist to better the material situation and elevate the moral condition of the workers.

Smith had acquired a grounding in agriculture as well as textile production with his uncle, who farmed 200 acres at Catrine Bank. In 1811 he made one of the first mechanical reapers which in an improved form won a prize from the Highland and Agricultural Society in 1815. A model of the machine was placed in the society's museum and is now in the collections of the National Museums of Scotland. A further model went to the Imperial Agricultural Society of St Petersburg, which awarded Smith a gold medal. The slow progress of agricultural improvement with much land still cultivated under ridge and furrow prevented the efficient use of machinery such as reaping machines. The statistical accounts and county agricultural reports describe the undrained and waterlogged ground of 'still clays' and 'cold soils'. By the time of the *New Statistical Account* in the 1840s, much of the landscape of Scotland had been transformed by 'Deanstonization', a term coined at the time to describe the thorough drainage system devised by Smith. Having taken a lease of Deanston Farm in 1823, he could state with conviction ten years later: 'The complete drainage of land is undoubtedly the foundation of all good husbandry, and it is, when properly executed, a permanent improvement.' He set out over 100 miles of drain and experimented with different types of drain, drain fillers, and drainage patterns—his 'frequent drain system'—adapting to light or heavy soils, and published the results in his *Thorough Drainage and Deep Ploughing* in 1833. At least 25,000 copies had been printed and distributed throughout Britain by the mid-1840s.

As Smith demonstrated at Deanston, fields that had dried out could be worked with green crops, grain, hay, and fallow, and were ploughed with swing plough and subsoil plough working in tandem, with the consequence that the old system of ploughing up into rigs could be abandoned and the surface of the field laid down uniformly flat and into a form on which machinery could work efficiently. Along with a turn-wrest plough and web-chain harrow, Smith developed a heavy plough, possibly as early as 1823, designed to break up the subsoil without raising it to the surface. A scale model submitted to the Highland and Agricultural Society is now in the collections of the National Museums of Scotland. His system of draining and ploughing received widespread recognition and influenced the government legislation of the 1840s facilitating the raising of money for farm drainage schemes.

Smith, who never married, threw up the lease of Deanston Farm in 1842 and left the mill, having been criticized for his concentration on farming at the expense of cotton and for his benevolent employment regime. He went to London where he began a new career as an agricultural engineer and continued to work on improvements to agricultural equipment and processes until his death on 10 June 1850 while on a visit to his cousin Archibald Buchanan at Kingencleuch, Ayrshire. HUGH CHEAPE

Sources J. C. Loudon, *An encyclopedia of agriculture* (1831) • 'Memoir of James Smith esq. of Deanston', *British Farmer's Magazine*, new ser., 10 (1846–7), 491–6 • 'Subsoil ploughing', *Quarterly Journal of Agriculture*, 10 (1839–40), 123–7 • 'The late James Smith of Deanston', *Quarterly Journal of Agriculture*, 17 (1849–51), 457–74 • G. Mitchell, 'Parish of Kilmadock', *The new statistical account of Scotland*, 10 (1845), 1224–42

Likenesses R. Ansdell, engraving, repro. in 'Memoir of James Smith' • R. Ansdell, portrait, Royal Agricultural Society of England, Stoneleigh Park, Warwickshire • attrib. W. H. Lizart, pencil drawing, Scot. NPG

Smith, James (1805–1872), merchant and mathematician, was born in Liverpool on 26 March 1805, the son of Joshua Smith and Esther Bartley. He entered a merchant's office at an early age, and, after remaining there seventeen years, started in business on his own account. (He retired in 1855.) He studied geometry and mathematics for practical purposes, and made some mechanical experiments with a view to facilitating mining operations. Although his results in this area were not made public, he did publish numerous works relating to his investigations into the geometrical problem known as 'squaring the circle'. This problem—equivalent to finding the exact value of π—was then believed, and has since been proved, to be impossible. In 1859 he published a work entitled *The Problem of Squaring the Circle Solved* which was followed in 1861 by *The quadrature of the circle: correspondence between an eminent mathematician and J. Smith, esq.*. This was ridiculed, anonymously, in *The Athenaeum*, most probably by the mathematician Augustus De Morgan. Smith replied in a letter which was inserted as an advertisement and, from this time, the establishment of his theory became the central interest of his life. He bombarded the Royal Society, the British Association, and most of the mathematicians of the day, including William Rowan Hamilton, George Biddell Airy, and William Whewell, with interminable letters and pamphlets on the subject. De Morgan was selected as his peculiar victim on account of certain reflections he had cast on him in *The Athenaeum*, such as: 'he is not mad. Madmen reason rightly upon wrong premises: Mr. Smith reasons wrongly upon no premises at all' (*The Athenaeum*, 1861, pt 1, 627). Smith was not content to claim that he was able graphically to construct a square equal in area to a given circle, but boldly stated that π was exactly equal to 3.125. In ordinary business matters, however, he was shrewd and capable. He was nominated by the Board of Trade to a seat on the Liverpool local marine board, where he served as chairman for some years, and was a member of the Mersey Docks and Harbour Board. He died at his home, Barkeley House, Seaforth, near Liverpool, of heart disease and exhaustion, on 4 April 1872. He was survived by at least two sons, James Barkeley Smith and Charles Chaloner Smith, both merchants, of Tower Buildings, Liverpool. E. I. CARLYLE, *rev.* ADRIAN RICE

Sources *Men of the time* (1868) • A. De Morgan, *A budget of paradoxes* (1872) • J. Smith, *The quadrature of the circle* (1861), vii–xxv • *The Athenaeum* (1861), 627, 664, 679 • *The Athenaeum* (8 June 1861), 764 • *The Athenaeum* (12 Oct 1861), 477 • Allibone, *Dict.* • *CGPLA Eng. & Wales* (1872) • *IGI*

Archives UCL, letters to William Hepworth Dixon

Wealth at death under £20,000: probate, 25 April 1872, *CGPLA Eng. & Wales*

Smith, James Aikman (1859–1931), rugby administrator, was born on 5 March 1859 at 29 Buccleuch Place, Edinburgh, the son of Andrew Smith, a solicitor before the Supreme Court, and his wife, Christina Aikman. He was educated at the Royal High School, Edinburgh, where he played rugby but was never capped. After leaving school he entered the accountancy firm of Murray and Romanes, and in 1881 was admitted as a member of the Edinburgh Society of Accountants. His business interests included the secretaryship of the Edinburgh and Leith Cemetery Co.

Aikman Smith's entry into rugby administration was less than flattering. At the Royal High School former pupils' football club annual general meeting of 1884, the club was seeking a secretary. The bulky brother of Nat Watt, the club captain, carried the relatively slight Aikman Smith into the meeting and dumped him down with the comment 'Here's your Secretary' (Thorburn, 12). He soon became president of the club. After the sudden death in 1887 of J. A. Gardner, the honorary secretary and treasurer of the Scottish Football Union, his successor A. S. Blair was joined on the union committee by Aikman Smith, who was nominated one of the east representatives. This combination of lawyer and accountant played a special part not only in tidying up the affairs and accounts of the union but also in the councils of the recently formed international board.

Aikman Smith was honorary secretary and treasurer of the union from 1890 to 1910, honorary secretary from 1910 to 1914, and special representative from 1914 to 1925. In 1926, when he was elected president of the Scottish Rugby Union (as the union had been renamed in 1924), the rules that stated that this office-bearer must have been a member of a representative side were waived. Throughout his long association with the government of the game Aikman Smith was a fierce critic of professionalism, and in retrospect he has been viewed as a leading example of the rather rigid officialdom that ran Scottish rugby in the early twentieth century (Massie, 15). He was a prime mover in the Scottish Rugby Union's action against the Welsh Rugby Union following the testimonial paid to the Welsh player A. J. Gould; the international fixtures against Wales were cancelled in 1897 and 1898. His criticisms of the daily expenses payments made to the All Blacks by the New Zealand Union during their tour of Scotland in 1905–6 led to a long period in which no matches were played between the two countries. He upheld the idea that the game should be played by amateurs and schoolboys, and in 1909 spoke out against rule changes proposed by the New Zealand Union to make rugby faster and more attractive to spectators. For the same reason he successfully resisted moves in 1926 to allow Scottish international players to wear numbers, for ready identification by the crowd, declaring 'It is a Rugby match, not a cattle sale' (Thorburn, 28). Numbering was not permitted until 1936, after his death. Yet he was well aware of the growing popularity of the sport of rugby union as a spectator activity, and was far-sighted in ensuring that the Scottish union was the first to own its own ground. He was instrumental in bringing Scottish rugby to Murrayfield in 1925.

On 5 February 1931 Aikman Smith attended the funeral in Edinburgh of Sir Andrew Balfour, president of the Scottish Rugby Union, before travelling to Cardiff with other union officials and Scottish players for the match against Wales. Shortly after leaving Crewe he was taken ill and was removed from the train at Stafford. He died on the same day at the Stafford General Infirmary from a cerebral haemorrhage. He left a wife, Robina Duncan, and at least one son. WALTER ALLAN

Sources A. M. C. Thorburn, *The Scottish Rugby Union* (1985) · A. Massie, *A portrait of Scottish rugby* (1984) · b. cert. · d. cert. · [A. Birrell], ed., *Scottish law list, a legal almanac… for the year 1848* (1849) · *CGPLA Eng. & Wales* (1931)

Likenesses photograph, repro. in Thorburn, *The Scottish Rugby Union*, following p. 30

Smith, Sir James Edward (1759–1828), botanist, was born on 2 December 1759 at 37 Gentleman's Way, Norwich, the eldest of the seven children of James Smith (1727–1795), a wealthy Unitarian wool merchant, and his wife, Frances (1731–1820), only daughter of the Revd John Kinderley.

Education and first botanical activities Being delicate, Smith was at first educated at home. He inherited a love of flowers from his mother, but did not begin the study of botany as a science until he was eighteen, and then, curiously enough, on the very day of Linnaeus's death. He was guided in his early studies by his friends James Crowe of Lakenham, Hugh Rose, John Pitchford, and the Revd Henry Bryant, and, though originally destined for a business career, was sent in 1781 to the University of Edinburgh to study medicine. There he studied botany under Dr John Hope, one of the earliest teachers of the Linnaean system, won a gold medal awarded by him, and established a natural history society. In September 1783 he went to London to study under Dr John Hunter and Dr William Pitcairn, with an introduction from Hope to Sir Joseph Banks, then president of the Royal Society.

On the death of the younger Linnaeus in that year the whole of the library, manuscripts, herbarium, and natural history collections made by him and his father were offered to Banks for 1000 guineas. Banks declined but on his recommendation Smith bought them, with a loan from his father. John Sibthorp, author of *Flora Graeca*, and the empress of Russia also attempted to purchase them, but with no success. In September 1784 Smith took apartments in Paradise Row, Chelsea, where the Linnaean collections arrived in the following month. The total cost, including freight, was £1088. It is stated (*Memoir and Correspondence*, 1.126) that Gustav III of Sweden, who had been absent in France, having heard of the dispatch of the collections, vainly sent a belated vessel to the Sound to intercept the ship which carried them. This apocryphal story is perpetuated on the portrait of Smith published in Thornton's *Temple of Flora* (1799).

'With no premeditated design of relinquishing physic as a profession' (*Memoir and Correspondence*, 1.128), Smith now became entirely devoted to natural history, and mainly to botany. During the following winter Banks and his librarian, Jonas Dryander, went through the collections with him at Chelsea, and Pitchford urged him to prepare 'a flora Britannica, the most correct that can appear in the Linnaean dress' (ibid., 130). Elected a fellow of the Royal Society in 1785, he made his first appearance as an

Sir James Edward Smith (1759–1828), by John Rising, exh. RA 1793

author by translating the preface to Linnaeus's *Museum regis Adolphi Frederici*, under the title *Reflexions on the Study of Nature*. In June 1786 he set out on a continental tour, and after obtaining a medical degree at Leiden (23 June), with a thesis 'De generatione', he travelled through Holland, France, Italy, and Switzerland. He visited Allamand and Van Royen at Leiden, the widow of Rousseau (for whom, as a botanist of the Linnaean school, he had a great admiration), Broussonet at Montpellier, Gerard at Cottignac, the Marchese Durazzo at Genoa, Mascagni the anatomist at Siena, Sir William Hamilton and the duke of Gloucester at Naples, Bonnet, de Saussure, and others at Geneva, La Chenal at Basel, and Herman at Strasbourg. He formed a close friendship with Davall, an English botanist living in Switzerland, and until the latter's death they carried on an affectionate correspondence. During the tour Smith carefully examined the picture galleries, herbaria, and botanical libraries *en route*. His tour is fully described in the three-volume *Sketch* which he first published in 1793.

Foundation of Linnean Society and main publications Before his departure Smith appears to have broached to his friends Samuel Goodenough, afterwards bishop of Carlisle (and the only man to correct Smith's Latin), and Thomas Marsham the idea of superseding a somewhat somnolent natural history society, of which they were members, by one bearing the name of Linnaeus. On his return to England in the autumn of 1787 he left Chelsea with a view to practising as a physician in London, and in 1788 took a house in Great Marlborough Street. There the first meeting of the Linnean Society was held on 8 April

1788. Smith was elected president, and delivered an 'Introductory discourse on the rise and progress of natural history'. Marsham became secretary, Goodenough treasurer, and Dryander librarian. The society started with thirty-six fellows, sixteen associates, and about fifty foreign members, mostly those naturalists whose acquaintance Smith had made during his tour. Banks joined the new society as an honorary member. From this period Smith gave lectures at his own house on botany and zoology, numbering among his pupils the duchess of Portland, Viscountess Cremorne, and Lady Amelia Hume, and about the same time he became lecturer on botany at Guy's Hospital. In 1789 he republished, under the title of *Reliquiae Rudbeckianae*, woodcuts of plants from those woodblocks, prepared by Olof Rudbeck for his *Campi Elysii*, which had escaped the great fire at Uppsala in 1702; during the four following years he issued parts of several illustrated botanical works, which, owing to the lack of patronage, he failed to complete. In 1790, however, he began the publication of what has proved his most enduring work, though as his name did not appear on the first three volumes, it is still often known as Sowerby's *English Botany*, from the name of its illustrator, James Sowerby. It formed thirty-six octavo volumes, with 2592 plates comprising all known British plants with the exception of the fungi; its publication was not completed until 1814.

In 1791 Smith was chosen, by the interest of Goodenough and Lady Cremorne, to arrange the queen's herbarium, and to teach her and her daughters botany and zoology at Frogmore, but some passages in his *Tour*, praising Rousseau and speaking of Marie Antoinette as Messalina, although they were removed from the second edition, gave offence at court. In 1796 Smith married Pleasance, only daughter of Robert Reeve, attorney of Lowestoft [*see* Smith, Pleasance (1773–1877)]. Lady Smith later edited her husband's correspondence. Soon after his marriage he retired to Norwich, only visiting London for two or three months in each year to deliver an annual course of lectures at the Royal Institution, which he continued until 1825. His days were spent in his elegantly arranged museum, containing the old-fashioned cabinets from Uppsala, looking very out of place; there he wrote his books from nine o'clock until three and again from seven to nine at night and replied to his numerous correspondents. He was a deacon at the Octagon Chapel, Norwich, for which he wrote many hymns. He was annually re-elected president of the Linnean Society until his death. After he had completed his important *Flora Britannica*, in three octavo volumes, 1800–04, Smith was chosen by the executors to edit the *Flora Graeca* of his friend, John Sibthorp. He published the *Prodromus* in two octavo volumes in 1806 and 1813, and completed six volumes of the *Flora* itself before his death. In 1807 appeared the first edition of his most successful work, *The Introduction to Physiological and Systematic Botany*, which passed through six editions during the author's lifetime; this work included a preface, expressing his own philosophy of life. In 1808, on the death of the Revd William Wood, who had contributed the botanical articles to Rees's *Cyclopaedia* down to 'Cyperus', the editor applied for assistance to Smith. He wrote 3348 botanical articles, among which were fifty-seven biographies of eminent botanists, including Adanson, Clusius, Peter Collinson, and William Curtis. All were signed 'S.' as he disliked anonymous writing. In 1814, when the prince regent accepted the position of patron of the Linnean Society, Smith was knighted. In 1813, Thomas Martyn was already suggesting that Smith should succeed him as Cambridge professor of botany; some heads of colleges and many influential members of the aristocracy supported him. In 1818 after a lengthy and vicious battle he was finally rejected, ostensibly on the grounds that he was a Unitarian. The incident led Smith to write two somewhat acrimonious pamphlets.

Last works and death What has been described as his 'last and best work', *The English Flora*, occupied Smith during the last seven years of his life, the first two volumes appearing in 1824, the third in 1825, and the fourth in March 1828, a few days before his death. The *Compendium*, in one volume, appeared posthumously in 1829, and the fifth volume, containing the mosses by Sir W. J. Hooker, and the fungi by the Revd M. J. Berkeley, in 1833–6. Smith died in Surrey Street, Norwich, on 17 March 1828, and was buried at St Margaret's Church, Lowestoft, in the vault of the Reeve family, on 24 March.

Smith's easy, fluent style, happy illustration, extensive knowledge, and elegant scholarship, both in his lectures and in his writings, did much to popularize botany. His possession of the Linnaean collections invested him, in his own opinion, with the magician's wand, and he set a value on his judgment in all botanical questions which his own attainments did not wholly warrant. However, their ownership secured him a great influence abroad, and he was elected a member of the Académie des Sciences at Paris, the Imperial Academy 'Naturae Curiosorum', and the academies of Stockholm, Uppsala, Turin, Lisbon, Philadelphia, and New York. His name was commemorated by Dryander and R. A. Salisbury in Aiton's *Hortus Kewensis* by the genus *Smithia*, a small group of sensitive leguminous plants. His library and collections, including those of Linnaeus, were offered by his executors to the Linnean Society for £5000 later reduced to 3000 guineas. Fellows contributed £1500 and the society paid the remainder, thereby incurring a heavy debt not paid off until 1861. G. S. Boulger, *rev.* Margot Walker

Sources W. R. Dawson, ed., *The Smith papers* (1934), vol. 1 of *Catalogue of the manuscripts in the library of the Linnean Society of London* (1934–48) · *Memoir and correspondence of the late Sir James Edward Smith*, ed. Lady Smith, 2 vols. (1832) · M. Walker, *Sir James Edward Smith* (1988) · A. T. Gage and W. T. Stearn, *A bicentenary history of the Linnean Society of London* (1988) · B. Henrey, *British botanical and horticultural literature before 1800*, 3 vols. (1975) · H. D. W. Lees, *The chronicles of a Suffolk parish church* [1949]

Archives Linn. Soc., corresp. and papers · Magd. Oxf., lectures · NA Scot., lecture notes · U. Oxf., department of plant sciences, corresp. and papers · Yale U., Beinecke L., corresp. | BL, letters to A. B. Lambert, Add. MS 28545 · BL, letters to Macvey Napier, Add. MSS 34611–34612 · Linn. Soc., corresp. with James Sowerby · NHM, letters to James Sowerby · NHM, letters to members of the Sowerby family · NRA, corresp. with Sir Joseph Banks · U. Lond., department of plant sciences, corresp. with John Hawkins and

J. Sowerby • U. Oxf., department of plant sciences, corresp. with John Hawkins • U. Oxf., department of plant sciences, corresp. with James Sowerby and James de Carle Sowerby

Likenesses A. L. Lane, crayon and pencil drawing, *c.*1789, Linn. Soc. • J. Rising, oils, exh. RA 1793, Linn. Soc. [*see illus.*] • W. Ridley, stipple, *c.*1799 (after pastel by J. Russell), BM, NPG; repro. in R. J. Thornton, *A new illustration of the sexual system of Linnaeus* (1800) • F. C. Lewis, chalk manner print, pubd 1816 (after W. Lane), BM, NPG • F. Chantrey, marble bust, 1827, Linn. Soc. • P. Audinet, engraving, RS • F. Chantrey, pencil sketches, NPG • W. Say, mezzotint (after H. B. Love; after bust by Chantrey), Linn. Soc. • M. Turner, etching (aged four; after T. Worlidge), BM • engraving, RS

Wealth at death money from sale of collections and books divided into five equal parts to be shared by family; remainder of estate left to wife

Smith, James Elishama [*called* Shepherd Smith] (1801–1857), religious writer and journalist, was born at 17 Drygate, Glasgow, on 22 November 1801 and was the second son of John Smith (1765–1843), probably a weaver, and his wife, Janet (1776–1853), the daughter of James Thomson, a mill owner of Strathaven. Among his brothers was (Robert) Angus *Smith, the chemist. John Smith, who was earnest and contentious in religious matters, sent James to Glasgow University in 1812 expecting him to enter the ministry. He graduated MA from Glasgow University in 1818, but being doubtful about the religion of the establishment preached only occasionally, as a licensed probationer. On becoming a private tutor he taught in the home of a Mr Hagert in Edinburgh from 1826 to 1829. The preaching of Edward Irving in the Scottish capital in June 1828 dramatically confirmed Smith's incipient millenarianism, and he now expected the imminent return of Christ. His enthusiasm was such that his father became a follower of Irving and remained so, long after James had turned aside and begun to associate with some followers of Joanna Southcott. In 1829 this new interest took him to Ashton under Lyne, where for nearly two years he was a follower of John Wroe, who claimed to be Southcott's successor. Being a Christian Israelite involved growing his beard and being circumcised, and Smith's description of this period of his life, in his posthumously published novel *The Coming Man* (1873), is a valuable account of the sect. Disillusioned with the bigotry of Wroe's community, which offended his own eminently tolerant disposition, he returned to Edinburgh in 1831, where he earned his living as an artist and teacher of art, but in August 1832 he moved to London.

At first Smith continued to move in Southcottian circles and for a time preached in the Southwark chapel of John (Zion) Ward, who was another, more radical, claimant to the mantle of the prophetess, but who had recently been imprisoned for blasphemy. However, he soon abandoned his earlier messianism and adapted his universalist message to the socialist millennium envisaged by men like Claude Saint-Simon and Robert Owen. This shift in his thinking is apparent in his 'Lecture on a Christian community' delivered at the Surrey Institution and later at the Blackfriars Rotunda (headquarters of the National Union of the Working Classes). In it he argued that the exclusive Christianity of the rich was Antichrist and that true Christianity must put an end to private property. This radical vision of a new social order was published in 1833 in a selection of Smith's early sermons entitled *The Anti-Christ, or, Christianity Reformed*. The introduction to his translation (1834) of Saint-Simon's *Nouveau Christianisme* (1825), which was made at Joachim de Prati's request, adopts a similar position. In May 1833 he began to lecture on Sunday mornings at Owen's Charlotte Street Institution and from September he was editing Owen's magazine *Crisis*. In the course of 1834 he adopted a more forthright trade unionism, writing, under the pseudonym of Senex, a series of 'Letters on associated labour' in James Morrison's *Pioneer*. By August, however, the disintegration of the Grand National Consolidated Trades Union had quenched his syndicalist enthusiasm and he had fallen out with Owen, who stopped publishing *Crisis*.

Smith's editorial career continued with a series of magazines in which his extremism was now more muted. His earlier universalist doctrine of polarities (holding that good and evil derive from a common source) and his science of analogy (linking the physical with the moral world) surface less prominently in his writing, though his fundamental belief in the millennium as an attainable human system of social love and equality is still apparent. Such ideas, combined with an eclectic approach to the Bible, characterize all his subsequent writings, though in later years these were increasingly interlarded with fiction and 'answers to questions'. *The Shepherd*, which he edited in 1834–5 and 1837–8, earned him his pastoral sobriquet, and his leading articles in the *Penny Satirist* (founded 1837) were aimed at self-improving working men. He flirted briefly with Fourierism, contributing articles to Hugh Doherty's *Phalanx* (1841–2), but his ultimate success was with a predominantly middle-class following when he established, in 1843, his own weekly penny journal, the *Family Herald: A Domestic Magazine of Useful Information and Amusement*, which eventually had some half a million readers. In addition to other millennial themes his work contains a significant feminist thread rooted in his Southcottian experience and reinforced by the Saint-Simonian search for the 'Woman-Messiah'. Smith insisted on the complementarity and equality of the sexes, claiming that the millennium would be the offspring of the male spiritual power of God and the female material world of nature. Smith never married, but had several 'long-distance relationships' (Saville, 144) with wealthy patronesses such as Sophia Chichester and Anna Wheeler and her daughter Lady Bulwer Lytton. In 1854 he attempted to summarize his philosophy in his only substantial book published in his lifetime, *The Divine Drama of History and Civilization*. He died on 29 January 1857 at the house of a Dr Harle, while on a visit to Glasgow.

TIMOTHY C. F. STUNT

Sources W. A. Smith, *Shepherd Smith the universalist: the story of a mind* (1892) • J. Saville, 'J. E. Smith and the Owenite movement, 1833–1834', *Robert Owen, prophet of the poor: essays in honour of the two hundredth anniversary of his birth*, ed. S. Pollard and J. Salt (1971) • J. F. C. Harrison, *Robert Owen and the Owenites in Britain and America: the quest for the new moral world* (1969) • W. H. Oliver, 'From the Southcottians to socialism', *Prophets and millennialists: the uses of biblical prophecy in England from the 1790s to the 1840s* (1978) • D. R. Cook,

'Reverend James Elishama Smith: socialist prophet of the millennium', MA diss., State University of Iowa, 1961 • J. E. M. Latham, *Search for a new Eden, James Pierrepont Greaves (1777–1842): the sacred socialist and his followers* (1999)

Likenesses J. Löwy, photograph, repro. in Smith, *Shepherd Smith*, frontispiece

Smith, James Hicks (1822–1881). *See under* Smith, Jeremiah (1771–1854).

Smith, Janet Buchanan Adam (1905–1999), author and journalist, was born on 9 December 1905 at 40 Westbourne Gardens, Kelvinside, Glasgow, the third of four daughters and sixth of seven children of Sir George Adam *Smith (1856–1942), Old Testament scholar and geographer, and his wife, (Alice) Lilian (*d.* 1949), daughter of Sir George *Buchanan, chief medical officer of the Local Government Board in London. Alick Drummond Buchanan Smith, later Buchanan-Smith, Baron Balerno (1898–1984), animal geneticist, was the youngest of her three brothers; the two elder ones were killed in the First World War.

Adam Smith's parents were keen mountaineers, and in childhood holidays on Arran she acquired a lifelong passion for mountains, developing her skills in the highlands, and then undertaking climbs in the Alps around Zermatt. She was educated, following her mother, at Cheltenham Ladies' College, and won an exhibition to read English at Somerville College, Oxford, from where she graduated with a second-class degree in 1926. She learned to type and in 1928, at the suggestion of Sir John Reith, a family friend, she joined the BBC, becoming in 1929 subeditor and in 1930 assistant editor of *The Listener*. She commissioned reviews, and met numerous young British and American poets, some of whose poems she published in her edited volume *Poems of Tomorrow* (1935). Her family connections brought her many social invitations, repeated because of her lively company. On her journeys back to Aberdeen she would take a train to Aviemore, Kingussie, or Blair Atholl, and traverse the Cairngorms alone.

In 1932 Adam Smith met the poet and critic William Edward (Michael) *Roberts (1902–1948), the son of Edward George Roberts, of Totton, Hampshire, and in 1934 climbed with him in the French Alps. They were married on 22 June in the following year, during which Michael compiled his influential anthology *The Faber Book of Modern Verse* (1936). At first they lived in Newcastle upon Tyne, where Roberts was a sixth-form master at the Royal Grammar School. They had four children, Andrew, Henrietta, Adam, and John. The school was evacuated in 1939 to Penrith, where Adam Smith (who retained her maiden name as a writer) wrote her classic memoir *Mountain Holidays* (1946). In 1941 Roberts went to London to work for the BBC; in 1945 his family joined him when he became principal of the College of St Mark and St John, a teacher training college in Chelsea, London, which they both strove to refurbish, and where T. S. Eliot read comic verse to their children. In December 1948 Roberts died of leukaemia, leaving his *The Estate of Man* unfinished. With typical fortitude Adam Smith bought the lease of 57 Lansdowne Road, Notting Hill, London, as a home for her children and a centre for friends and relations, completed her husband's book (which was published in 1951), edited his collected poems (1958), and with help from friends sent her children to good schools.

In 1949 Adam Smith became assistant to T. C. Worsley, literary editor of the *New Statesman*; she was his successor from 1952 to 1960. In 1953 she delighted her public with her *Faber Book of Children's Verse*, based on consultations with many children, including her own. With her mountaineering friend Nea Morin she translated several mountaineering books, notably Maurice Herzog's *Annapurna* (1952). There were many family holidays in the mountains in the 1950s.

Intellectually Adam Smith was heir to the Scottish Enlightenment and Edinburgh reviewers, and her *Life among the Scots* (1946) was a rich distillation of Scottish culture. (For the same Collins series, Britain in Pictures, she also wrote *Children's Illustrated Books*, 1948). She contributed much to the critical study of Scottish literature. Her brief, vivid biography of Robert Louis Stevenson (1937), her edition of his correspondence with Henry James (1948), and her two editions of Stevenson's poetry (1950 and 1971) did much to revive his critical fortunes. But her masterpiece was her biography of John Buchan (1965), written at the invitation of his family, which her background peculiarly fitted her to write. Sympathetic but not uncritical—she was more radical than Buchan politically—it helped re-establish his status as a serious writer and public figure. She followed it with *John Buchan and his World* (1979).

On 5 August 1965 Adam Smith married John Dudley Carleton (1908–1974), the son of Brigadier-General Frederick Montgomerie Carleton and headmaster of Westminster School, where her three sons had been educated. In the year of their marriage her husband published a history of Westminster School. He was no mountaineer, but happily drove his car to collect descending climbers. He retired in 1970, and she was again widowed in 1974. She remained an active literary journalist, writing into her eighties for the *New York Review of Books*. In the 1960s and 1970s she appeared on radio's *The Critics* and *Critics' Forum*. She was visiting professor at Barnard College, New York (1961, 1964), a trustee of the National Library of Scotland (1950–85), president of the Royal Literary Fund (1976–84), and vice-president of the Alpine Club (1979–80). She was awarded an honorary doctorate by the University of Aberdeen (1962), and appointed OBE (1982). In old age she continued to travel—to India, to the USA, and to the Alps.

Janet Adam Smith shone as 'biographer, mountaineer, critic, literary editor, textual scholar, comic versifier, visiting professor, hostess, anthologist, traveller' (*The Independent*, 13 Sept 1999) and as 'one of the *grandes dames* of literary London' (*The Times*, 13 Sept 1999). With her keen mind and firm standards she could seem severe, but her disciplined diversity included generous feeling, infectious enthusiasm, and a gift for friendship. In June 1999 she was fitted with a pacemaker, but she died peacefully at St Mary's Hospital, Paddington, London, on 11 September, following a stroke. The funeral service was held ten days later at St Columba's Church, Pont Street, London, where she had been an active member of the congregation. She was survived by her daughter and three sons.

JOHN D. HAIGH

Sources J. Adam Smith, *Mountain holidays* (1946); repr. (1996) · *WWW, 1996–2000* · *The Times* (13 Sept 1999) · *The Scotsman* (14 Sept 1999) · *The Independent* (13 Sept 1999) · *Daily Telegraph* (14 Sept 1999) · *The Guardian* (14 Sept 1999) · *The Guardian* (15 Sept 1999) · *The Independent* (20 Sept 1999) · *The Guardian* (17 Sept 1999) · Burke, *Peerage* · b. cert. · m. cert. [John Dudley Carleton] · d. cert. · private information (2004) [Sir Adam Roberts, Andrew Roberts]

Archives NL Scot., corresp. and research papers relating to biography of John Buchan · University of Bristol Library, corresp. and statements relating to trial of *Lady Chatterley's lover* | LUL, corresp. with William Paton Ker · Tate collection, Helen Sutherland papers · University of Tulsa, Oklahoma, Rupert Hart-Davis papers | SOUND BL NSA, Bow dialogues, 8 Feb 1966, C812/6

Likenesses A. Roberts, photograph, repro. in *The Times* · A. Roberts, photograph, repro. in *The Scotsman*

Smith, Janet Seymour- (1930–1998). *See under* Smith, Martin Roger Seymour- (1928–1998).

Smith [Smyth], **Sir Jeremiah** [Jeremy] (*d.* 1675), naval officer, was the third son of Jeremiah Smith of Canterbury (himself the son of John and Letitia Smith of Great Waldingfield, Suffolk) and Catherine Wilkinson, daughter of Daniel Wilkinson. The family presumably moved to Yorkshire, as the younger Jeremiah is first encountered serving on merchantmen out of Hull in 1641–2. He later became a prominent merchant and shipowner there. In 1647 he captained a privateer for Colonel John Moore MP. In 1652 he was in the army in Scotland as adjutant-general to General Monck, who may have been his brother-in-law. He certainly appears to have been a protégé of Monck, following him in and out of naval service in the 1650s and 1660s. By April 1653 he was in the navy and captained the *Advice* in the Dutch war engagements of June and July, still serving under Monck. In 1654, having commanded the *Torrington* and received a medal for his service, he returned to the army. Monck petitioned, successfully, for him to receive a captaincy in his regiment as well as retaining his post as adjutant-general. His wife, Frances, died at Birkin, Yorkshire, on 3 September 1656. During 1656–7 he was at sea as captain of the *Essex*, then the *Dunbar*. Ashore again, he was one of the handful of officers consulted by Monck on news of the suppression of the restored Rump Parliament in October 1659 and signed the officers' declaration opposing the move. Monck employed him to secure Edinburgh Castle and he was involved in purging and reorganizing Monck's cavalry, becoming major of Twistleton's regiment. In early 1660 he was sent by Monck to Hull to ascertain the reaction of the radical governor, Colonel Robert Overton, apparently an old friend, to the readmission of the expelled members of the Long Parliament, and to secure the garrison.

The Restoration saw Smith back again in sea service. In 1662 he bought Prior House, Hemingbrough, Yorkshire, which became his principal residence. In 1664 he took command of the *Mary*. He fought this ship bravely at the battle of Lowestoft on 3 June 1665, placing himself between the duke of York in the *Royal Charles* and a Dutch assailant. Smith lost ninety-nine men and all his officers save the lieutenant and master, the heaviest losses on the English side. The duke promised him 'some great thing' (Pepys, *Diary*, 6.129) and he was knighted on 22 June. Later in 1665 he served under the earl of Sandwich, but had to be landed sick at Lowestoft on 28 August. By 13 September he was back at sea commanding the *Royal Sovereign*. On 19 December he sailed for the Mediterranean, chiefly to defend Tangier. Following the French declaration of war, Beaufort was ordered to intercept him in February, when he was about Malaga and Cadiz. But Beaufort did not sail until April, by which time Smith (recalled in March) was almost home. Smith was still absent when the fleet commands for 1666 were assigned, and the post of admiral of the blue was kept vacant for him. His intended flagship, the *Loyal London*, was not ready for the Four Days' Fight (1–4 June); he remained at Portsmouth and did not go aboard until after 14 June. He joined in the widespread criticism of Monck, now duke of Albemarle, for his conduct of the battle. On the first day of the St James's day fight (25 July) Smith had the worst of his battle. The next day he pursued Tromp until about 7 p.m. when, on the advice of the pilot who feared grounding, he stood out to sea. The red and the white squadrons could not join him to close the trap on the Dutch, who were able to run for home. Admiral Sir Robert Holmes, who had become attached to the Blue squadron, immediately accused Smith of cowardice. Their long-running feud split the service, Holmes being supported by Rupert who called for a court martial, while Monck championed Smith, whose qualities he thought manifest from the high proportion of his casualties. Holmes's accusations were heard before the king and the cabinet council on 21 October. The ruling, on 3 November, cleared Smith of cowardice but censured him for having 'yielded too easily' to the opinion of his own pilot without consulting others, enabling the enemy to escape (*CSP dom., 1666–7*, 236). It was meanwhile reported, on 31 October, that Smith had killed Holmes in a duel; they may indeed have fought, but the appearance of both in Westminster Hall that afternoon disproved the reported fatality. During 1667 Smith served as a 'land-admirall' (Pepys, *Diary*, 8.149) commanding the North Sea squadron and taking a number of prizes. In July he was ordered to Kinsale, returning in October. When parliament investigated the conduct of the war in 1668 Holmes renewed his accusations before the committee for miscarriages on 7 March. On 13 March the MPs viewed a written response from Smith, but declined to hear witnesses or to give any further attention to a matter already judged by the king and the lord high admiral.

In May 1668 Smith was vice-admiral of the Channel Fleet aboard the *Royal Katherine*. That year he bought Osgodby Manor, Yorkshire. The duke of York pressed for his appointment to the Navy Board; the king, reluctant to discount other candidates, eventually agreed and Smith became commissioner for victualling accounts on 17 June 1669. Pepys, while glad that 'a seaman, no merchant' was chosen, considered Smith, 'a silly, prating, talking man', was 'but very moderately qualified' (Pepys, *Diary*, 9.382; *Pepys and the Second Dutch War*, 211) and saw to it that his patent carried a clear job description. Smith was in post until death, and acted as master of Trinity House in 1674. He promoted the interests of Hull, and was a close friend of the town's MP, the poet Andrew Marvell. Smith died at Clapham at 11 p.m. on 3 November 1675 'very peacably and with perfect understanding memory and speech to the last gaspe' (*Poems and Letters of Andrew Marvell*, 2.169). His body was taken to Hemingbrough for burial there on 20 November. He was the father of George (*d.* 1681), Francis, and John, children of his second marriage, to Anne, daughter of John Pockley of Thorpe Willoughby. His will of 31 October 1675 confirmed provisions made in 1673 for his sons, of which Marvell was a trustee. Smith was celebrated as a hero in verse, though Holmes was not alone in questioning his courage. In the 1650s he had praised the energies of his ship's chaplain, possibly hinting at a puritan sympathy which may have been borne out in his forbearance to a pressed Quaker, Thomas Lurting, and which suggests that he was not the 'very loose and wicked man' Lurting alleged him to be (*Narrative of Thomas Lurting*, 17).

C. S. KNIGHTON

Sources T. Burton, *The history and antiquities of the parish of Hemingborough in the county of York*, ed. J. Raine (1888), 322–4 • B. Capp, *Cromwell's navy: the fleet and the English revolution, 1648–1660* (1989), 173 (n. 86), 183 (n. 137), 196 (n. 196), 306 • R. C. Anderson, *List of English naval captains, 1642–1660* (1964), 21 • Pepys, *Diary* • *Samuel Pepys and the Second Dutch War: Pepys's navy white book and Brooke House papers*, ed. R. Latham, Navy RS, 133 (1995), 210–12 [transcribed by W. Matthews and C. Knighton] • *The journal of Edward Mountagu, first earl of Sandwich, admiral and general at sea, 1659–1665*, ed. R. C. Anderson, Navy RS, 64 (1929), 249, 268, 271, 295 • *The journals of Sir Thomas Allin, 1660–1678*, ed. R. C. Anderson, 2 vols., Navy RS, 79–80 (1939–40), vol. 1, pp. 264, 278, 279; vol. 2, pp. xvi, xviii–xix, xxvi, xxix–xxx, 28 • J. R. Powell and E. K. Timings, eds., *The Rupert and Monck letter book, 1666*, Navy RS, 112 (1969) • *The poems and letters of Andrew Marvell*, ed. H. Margoliouth, rev. P. Legouis, 3rd edn, 2 (1971), 9, 68–9, 77, 79, 164, 169, 173, 277, 280, 363n. • *Narrative of Thomas Lurting, formerly a seaman under Admiral Blake* (1821), 17, 18–19 • PRO, SP 29/177, no. 41 • BL, Add. MS 29597, fol. 23r–v • BL, Add. MS 36916, fol. 87 • F. L. Fox, *A distant storm: the Four Days battle of 1666* (1996), 120, 126, 163–6, 369–70 • C. H. Firth, 'Sailors of the civil war, the Commonwealth and the protectorate', *Mariner's Mirror*, 12 (1926), 237–59, esp. 258–9 • R. Ollard, *Man of war: Sir Robert Holmes and the Restoration navy* (1969), 164–5 • M. P. Ashley, *General Monck* (1977), 163 • G. Davies, *The restoration of Charles II, 1658–1660* (1955), 162, 172 • Magd. Cam., Pepys Library, Pepys MS 2877, 163 • C. H. Firth and G. Davies, *The regimental history of Cromwell's army*, 2 vols. (1940) • *The Clarke Papers*, ed. C. H. Firth, 4, CS, new ser., 62 (1901) • D. Syrett and R. L. DiNardo, *The commissioned sea officers of the Royal Navy, 1660–1815*, rev. edn, Occasional Publications of the Navy RS, 1 (1994) • PRO, PROB 11/349, fols. 89v–90v • *CSP dom.*, 1666–7, 236

Likenesses P. Lely, oils, 1662, NMM

Wealth at death £2000 to younger sons; lands in Yorkshire and other counties: will, proved 8 Nov 1675, PRO, PROB 11/349, fols. 89v–90v

Smith, Jeremiah (*bap.* 1653, *d.* 1723), Presbyterian minister, was baptized on 21 December 1653 at All Saints', Maidstone, Kent, the son of Jeremy Smith, a barber-surgeon and later a linen draper, and Sarah Jetter, both residents of the town. He is possibly the man of that name of Kent admitted in 1671 to Corpus Christi College, Cambridge, but nothing definite is known of his early life. Certainly he married a wife, Eleanor, whose surname was probably Skinner and who was to survive him, together with four sons—Skinner, Jeremiah, Thomas, Richard—and a daughter, Eleanor, to whom he was able to leave a total of more than £1000.

After 1700 Smith served as a minister at Andover, Hampshire, the successor to Samuel Say. In 1708 he became co-pastor with Samuel Rosewell of the Silver Street Presbyterian Chapel, London. In 1713, at Salters' Hall, Smith preached *The Right Reformer's Character and Duty* before the Society for the Reformation of Manners in the cities of London and Westminster. Such societies, he thought, were worthy of 'all manner of incouragement and assistance', and their work was 'very pleasing to God, and to all wise and good men'; his text was taken from the epistle of St Jude, 'which might be inscribed "Jude's letter for Reformation of manners"', since it was written 'to stem the tide, or torrent rather, of error and libertinism, which even so early was breaking in upon the churches' (Smith, 1–2). In 1719 Smith was prominent in the Salters' Hall debates over whether ministers should be required to subscribe to a specially formulated statement of orthodoxy on the Trinity. He was one of four ministers, described as 'principal leaders on one side of this dispute' (*A Letter*, 3), to reaffirm the orthodox position in *The Doctrine of the Ever Blessed Trinity Stated and Defended* and his contribution, 'The harmony of the reform'd churches', comprised over half of the main body of text. In this controversy Rosewell was on the opposing side, though it is reported that there was no bad blood between them as a result.

Smith was the author of sections on the epistles to Titus and Philemon in the continuation of Matthew Henry's *Exposition* (1710), and he published funeral sermons on Sir Thomas Abney (1722) and Samuel Rosewell (1723). Towards the end of his life he was assisted in the congregation by a Mr Bures. In 1723, while on a visit to friends, Smith fell ill, but seemed to have recovered enough to return home. However, on 20 August 1723:

> the morning of the day fixed for his intended journey, a violent convulsion seized him at once, and in less than an half an hour, put an end to all his thoughts; without his being able to speak one word to those about him. (Clarke, 9)

Smith's funeral sermon was preached by Matthew Clarke, who wrote that he 'studied to bring down difficult things, high in themselves, to common reach', and that he was 'mild and peaceable in his temper; handsome and ornamental in his carriage and behaviour, and in a word, a pattern of good works' (Clarke, 36–7). Smith's eldest surviving son, Skinner, was minister of the congregation of Gosditch Street, Cirencester, from 1727 to 1730; after serving at Abingdon he died in 1748.

C. W. SUTTON, *rev.* STEPHEN WRIGHT

Sources L. Horton-Smith, *The Rev. Jeremiah Smith, 1653–1723: 'the champion of the Trinity', 1719* [1934]; rev. and enl. version of *N&Q*, 167 (1934), 309–12, 327–30 • *A letter to the Reverend Mr Tong, Mr Robinson, Mr Smith and Mr Reynolds* (1719), 3 • A. Gordon, *Addresses biographical and historical* (1922), 123–53; repr. of A. Gordon, *The story of Salters' Hall* (1902) • W. Wilson, *The history and antiquities of the dissenting* *churches and meeting houses in London, Westminster and Southwark*, 4 vols. (1808–14), vol. 3 • will, PRO, PROB 11/593, fols. 121–3 • M. Clarke, *A funeral sermon occasioned by the much lamented death of the Reverend Mr Jeremiah Smith, who departed this life, August 20, 1723* (1623) • Venn, *Alum. Cant.* • J. Smith, *The right reformer's character and duty* (1713)

Wealth at death over £1000 left to widow and children: will, PRO, PROB 11/593, fols. 121–3

Smith, Jeremiah (1771–1854), headmaster, son of Jeremiah and Ann Smith, was born at Brewood, Staffordshire, on 22 July 1771. His family were prominent tradesmen in the town. He was educated under Dr George Croft at Brewood School. In 1790 he entered Hertford College, Oxford, from where he migrated to Corpus Christi College, where he held an exhibition. He formed friendships with Henry Phillpotts, Edward Copleston, and Richard Mant. He graduated BA in 1794, MA in 1797, BD in 1810, and DD in 1811. He was ordained in 1794 to the curacy of Edgbaston, Birmingham, which he soon exchanged for that of St Mary's, Moseley. He was also assistant, and then, in 1798, second master, in King Edward's School, Birmingham; and on 6 May 1807 was appointed by the president of Corpus Christi College high master of the Manchester grammar school, a position he retained for thirty years. An enduring memorial of his success in reviving the school was the published record of his pupils. They recalled his gentle and courteous manner, and his habit of early rising. A member of the Manchester Pitt Club, Smith was a staunch tory, opposing Catholic emancipation and petitioning against the Reform Bill in 1831. On 27 July 1811 he married Felicia (*d.* 1861), daughter of William Anderton of Moseley Wake Green, and had eight children.

While at Manchester, Smith held successively the curacies of St Mark's, Cheetham Hill, St George's, Carrington, and Sacred Trinity, Salford, and the incumbency of St Peter's, Manchester (1813–25), and the rectory of St Ann's in the same town (1822–37). He also held the small vicarage of Great Wilbraham, near Cambridge, from 1832 to 1847, and was from 1824 one of the four 'king's preachers' for Lancashire, a sinecure office which was abolished in 1845. He was a moderate high-churchman who, after 1833, sympathized with the Oxford Movement. His sole publication was a sermon preached before the North Worcester Volunteers in 1805. Smith died at Brewood on 21 December 1854.

Smith's eldest son, **Jeremiah Finch Smith** (1815–1895), Church of England clergyman, born in Manchester on 1 July 1815, was educated at Manchester grammar school and Brasenose College, Oxford, where he graduated BA in 1837 and MA in 1839. After serving curacies he was rector of Aldridge, Staffordshire, from 1849, rural dean of Walsall from 1862, and prebendary of Lichfield Cathedral from 1884. He published, besides many sermons and tracts, the admirably edited *Admission Register of the Manchester School* (3 vols., 1866–74) and *Notes on the Parish of Aldridge, Staffordshire* (2 parts, 1884–9). In 1847 he married Elizabeth Anne, daughter of Clement Ingleby. He died at Lichfield on 15 September 1895.

The third son, **James Hicks Smith** (1822–1881), antiquary, was born at Manchester on 11 June 1822, educated at Manchester grammar school, and called to the bar by the Inner Temple on 30 January 1852. He lived at Brewood and wrote a number of antiquarian works: *Brewood, a Résumé, Historical and Topographical* (1867); *Reminiscences of Thirty Years, by an Hereditary High Churchman* (1868); *Brewood Church, the Tombs of the Giffards* (1870); *The Parish in History, and in Church and State* (1871); and *Collegiate and other Ancient Manchester* (1877). He died, unmarried, at Brewood on 28 December 1881.

Smith's fourth son, **Isaac Gregory Smith** (1826–1920), Church of England clergyman, born in Manchester on 21 November 1826, was educated at Manchester grammar school and Rugby School, and held a scholarship at Trinity College, Oxford, from 1845 to 1850. He was university Hertford scholar in 1846, Ireland scholar in 1847, and gained second-class honours in classics in 1848; and in 1850 he was elected a fellow of Brasenose College. He was presented to the college living of Tedstone Delamere, Herefordshire, in 1854, and in 1859 he married Augusta, daughter of the Revd G. W. Murray. He was vicar of Great Malvern from 1872 to 1896, rector of the Brasenose living of Great Shefford, Berkshire, from 1896 to 1904, a prebendary of Hereford Cathedral from 1870, and examining chaplain to the bishop of St David's from 1881 to 1897. He wrote a number of works of orthodox divinity including *On Modern Scepticism and its Fallacies* (1864). His other works included *Aristotelianism and Modern Thought* (1887), a history of the Worcester diocese (1882), and historical studies of Christian monasticism (1891). His Oxford Bampton lectures, *The Characteristics of Christian Morality*, were published in 1873. As a diocesan inspector of schools, he published pamphlets on denominational controversies following the Education Acts of 1870 and 1902, and some general *Thoughts on Education* (1880). Edinburgh University conferred on him the honorary degree of LLD in 1886. He retired to Woking, Surrey, where he died on 17 January 1920. C. W. SUTTON, *rev.* M. C. CURTHOYS

Sources J. F. Smith, ed., *The admission register of the Manchester School, with some notes of the more distinguished scholars*, 2, Chetham Society, 73 (1868) • Foster, *Alum. Oxon.* • J. A. Graham and B. A. Phythian, eds., *The Manchester grammar school, 1515–1965* (1965) • Boase, *Mod. Eng. biog.* • Brasenose College register • *Manchester Guardian* (17 Sept 1895) • *Manchester Guardian* (4 Jan 1882) • *Church Review* (6 Jan 1882) • *WWW*, 1916–28 • *Men of the time*

Likenesses Colman, portrait; in family possession, 1897 • G. Hargreaves, miniature, repro. in Smith, *Admission register of the Manchester School*, 93

Wealth at death £6926 3*s.* 3*d.*—Jeremiah Finch Smith: probate, 1896 • £12,896 10*s.* 10*d.*—James Smith: probate, 1882 • £6448 11*s.* 10*d.*—Isaac Smith: probate, 1920

Smith, Jeremiah Finch (1815–1895). *See under* Smith, Jeremiah (1771–1854).

Smith, John. *See* Smythe, Sir John (1533/4–1607); Smyth, John (*d.* 1612); Smyth, John (1567–1641).

Smith, John (1562/3–1616), Church of England clergyman and writer, was a native of Warwickshire. He matriculated from St John's College, Oxford, on 20 December 1577, aged fourteen, graduated BA on 18 November 1581, and proceeded MA on 10 June 1585 and BD on 15 November 1591. On 21 September 1592, following the death of Thomas

Simpson, Smith was instituted rector of Clavering, Essex, on the presentation of Lady Ramsey; on 27 October he supplicated for a licence to preach. On 21 October 1594 he was granted a licence to marry Frances, daughter of William Babbington of Chorley, Essex, yeoman. In 1610 the possessions of the rectory of Clavering were listed as comprising

> a dwelling house with yards, a garden, two barns and other out houses, two closes containing two acres, adjoining to the said house, and 3 acres more in Clavering Mid-field, the third part of the tithes of corn and hay of all the lands in this parish, excepting of the parsonage lands. (Newcourt, 2.156)

Smith seems to have been widely respected for learning and piety. He is reported to have 'succeeded Launcelot Andrews in the lectureship of St Paul's [London], where he was also divinity reader' (Davids, 91). He died in 1616, leaving to his former college many books, including three volumes of St Jerome and five of St Augustine; St John's paid a total of 10*s.* 6*d.* for their carriage from Clavering to London, and thence to Oxford. Probate was granted on 29 November 1616 to his widow. Provision was also made in the will for £80 to be paid to the parish after the death of Frances Smith, who increased the figure to £100.

Smith's *The Essex Dove: Presenting the World with a Few of her Olive Branches*, was published in 1629 with a preface by John Harte, addressed to Lord Keeper Coventry. The book recalls of the author that 'he wrote an infinite, intricate exceeding small abreviated hand, out of all hope to be read'; only with difficulty was his work 'fetched out of the fire, and so brought to this imperfect perfection', so that the reader could taste 'those sweet and excellent strains of learning and piety with which he was most plentifully endowed'. STEPHEN WRIGHT

Sources R. Newcourt, *Repertorium ecclesiasticum parochiale Londinense*, 1 (1708) • Foster, *Alum. Oxon.* • Wood, *Ath. Oxon.*, new edn • W. C. Costin, *The history of St John's College, Oxford, 1598–1860*, OHS, new ser., 12 (1958) • W. Hunt, *The puritan moment: the coming of revolution in an English county* (1983) • J. C. C. Smith, *Some additions to Newcourt's Repertorium, vol. II* (1899) • T. W. Davids, *Annals of evangelical nonconformity in Essex* (1863)

Smith, John (*bap.* **1580**, *d.* **1631**), soldier and colonial governor, was baptized on 9 January 1580 at Willoughby by Alford in Lincolnshire, the son of George Smith (*d.* 1596), whose family was from Lancashire, and Alice Rickard, from a Yorkshire family. A yeoman, George Smith possessed a small farm in the county and leased another property from Lord Willoughby, the lord of the manor, who became one of John Smith's patrons. Smith may have been tutored by Francis Marbury, father of Anne Hutchinson, before attending the King Edward VI Grammar School at Louth. In 1595 he was apprenticed to Thomas Sendall, a wealthy merchant in King's Lynn, but a year later, following the death of his father and the remarriage of his mother, Smith parted with Sendall 'because hee would not presently send him to Sea' (*Complete Works*, 3.154). He served under Captain Joseph Duxbury in the Low Countries for three or four years but was back in England in 1599; he was not yet twenty years of age. He then travelled briefly to France with Peregrine Bertie, younger son of Lord Willoughby, before venturing to Scotland in a

John Smith (*bap.* 1580, *d.* 1631), by Simon de Passe, 1616

vain attempt to secure preferment. Back in Lincolnshire, Smith sought to improve himself by reading selected works and received instruction in horsemanship from Theodore Paleogue, an Italian-born Greek in the employ of the earl of Lincoln, after which he set out once again for the continent, this time in the company of four Frenchmen. Cheated by his companions, Smith made for the Mediterranean where he took passage on a merchant vessel which traded in the eastern Mediterranean. Following an engagement with a Venetian vessel, he acquired a share of the booty and, ever curious to see more of the world, disembarked in Italy.

In late 1600 Smith joined the Austrian forces who were then fighting the Turks in the war of 1593–1606. He was promoted to captain after the siege of Limbach and after killing three Turkish officers in single combat in Transylvania early in 1602 he was granted a coat of arms by Zsigmond Bathory. Wounded in a skirmish with the Tartars, he was taken prisoner and sold into slavery. His purchaser, a Turk, presented him to his young mistress whom Smith called Charatza Trabigzanda. She sent him to her brother so he could learn the language and 'what it was to be a Turk, till time made her Master of her self', but 'he being the last, was slave of slaves to them all' (*Complete Works*,

3.189). Smith murdered the brother and escaped, fleeing across Europe. After numerous detours and a voyage to Morocco, he was back in England by the winter of 1604–5.

Governor of Virginia Seeking new opportunities, Smith now became involved with the men engaged in promoting England's overseas ambitions. He sailed on the first fleet to Virginia, which made landfall in May 1607 when it transpired that he had been nominated to the governing council of the colony. He was not sworn for some weeks, having been held in confinement for most of the voyage for reasons which remain obscure: internal wrangling was to plague the colony from the outset. With a disproportionate number of gentlemen among the first planters, the expedition was ill-prepared to meet the challenge of establishing England's first permanent settlement in North America. As plots and counterplots undermined the settlement, he spent much of the time exploring Chesapeake Bay and establishing trade relations with the Native Americans. In December 1607 he was taken prisoner by some of the local inhabitants and brought before Powhatan, the powerful overlord of the neighbouring tribes. In a ceremony which Smith did not initially describe and which he assuredly did not comprehend, he was adopted into Powhatan's tribe as a werowance (local chieftain) and released. The part played in this drama by Powhatan's young daughter Pocahontas, though unclear, became the stuff of American legend. While Captain Christopher Newport, who held overall authority whenever he was in Virginia, stuck firmly to his instructions, Smith preferred to follow his instincts. He was contemptuous of the time spent searching for precious metals, looking for a passage to 'the south sea', and seeking survivors of the earlier Roanoke venture, but, with the departure or death of some of his rivals, on 10 August 1608 John Smith was elected president of the council.

As *de facto* governor of Virginia, Smith sought to impose order and discipline on the Jamestown settlers, whose apathy and lethargy threatened to destroy the colony from within. This meant motivating men to work, improving defences, providing for the support of new arrivals, preparing the ground for cultivation, and maintaining satisfactory relations with the Native Americans on whose corn the survival of the settlers depended. Stores painstakingly gathered were spoiled by vermin brought over in the company's ships, and during the harsh winter that followed Smith dispersed the settlers to live among the Native Americans. His authority within the colony, however, did not go unchallenged and his relationship with Powhatan was never easy. Smith pursued tactics of intimidation and bullying in dealing with Native Americans, which drew criticism from the Virginia Company for violating its instructions not to give offence to them. Despite the colony's weaknesses Smith refused to countenance 'insolence' from the indigenous population though dispensing threats freely himself, yet he never engaged in wanton violence as did some of his contemporaries and many of his successors. Badly injured in an explosion when his term of office was all but complete, Smith sailed for England on 4 October 1609, unaware that a major role had been reserved for him in the company's latest instructions. His vigorous presidency, none the less, had probably ensured the colony's long-term survival.

Though Smith did not return to Virginia, his sojourn there resulted in three publications. A letter he had sent to a correspondent in England recounting events in Virginia was published in 1608, entitled *A True Relation of such Occurences and Accidents of Noate as hath Happened in Virginia*. It appeared without his knowledge and consent and was badly edited. His first significant work was published four years later in October 1612. *A Map of Virginia. With a Description of the Countrey, the Commodities, People, Government, and Religion* has long been valued by anthropologists, ethnographers, and historians for the details it furnishes on the culture and society of the Algonquian people. Part two of the *Map of Virginia* was published separately as *The Proceedings of the English Colonie in Virginia*, also in 1612.

Promoter of colonization What Smith did back in England is a matter of conjecture, but at some point his interest shifted northwards to New England, then known as Norembega. Entering the employ of a wealthy merchant, Marmaduke Rawdon, he took command of a whaling venture in March 1614. Hoping to establish a new colony, Smith explored and mapped the north-east coast of America. When he returned to England in August, he sought out Sir Ferdinando Gorges, leader of the Plymouth Company, which held rights to that part of America. Smith named the region New England and received the title of admiral of New England. In 1615, accompanied by a small party, he undertook two further voyages, both of which were unsuccessful and on the second of which he fell into the hands of French privateers. In *A Description of New England* (1616) written on board the privateer and based on his 1614 voyage, he emerges as a promoter of colonization. No longer an apologist for the missed opportunities of Virginia and Bermuda, he identified the value of North America to England, not in precious metals but in the products of its seas, rivers, and soils, and he projected New England as a location favourable to the re-creation of English society in America. Yet much to his chagrin and despite his obvious expertise, those who settled at Plymouth declined to hire him, 'saying my books and maps were much better cheape to teach them, than my selfe' (*Complete Works*, 3.17).

Little is known about the last fifteen years of Smith's life except for the fact that he turned increasingly to writing, both because he needed to make a living and because he had things to say. In a series of pamphlets, books, and revisions to earlier works he not only became England's foremost advocate of colonization, but sought to develop a coherent theory of colonization with religion at its core. *New England Trials* was published in 1620 and a revised version appeared two years later. Smith's major work, *The Generall Historie of Virginia, New-England, and the Summer Isles* was published in 1624. Financed by subscription, it was rushed out during the crisis over the Virginia Company which led to the forfeiture of the company's charter. Smith was confident that he knew what colonization required better than anyone else. In his view neither Virginia nor Bermuda with their staple economies and unruly populations offered viable models of colonization but developments in New England were encouraging. The first stage of colonization required soldiers and military discipline to secure the settlement, but they should give way to families and communities as soon as it was feasible. Only the emigration of a cross-section of English society would permit the development of towns and communities recognizably English in character and with a strong moral core. As for the Native Americans, though referred to by Smith as cannibals, they were not so degraded or inhuman as to be incapable of conversion.

Less well known are Smith's seafaring publications, which drew on his maritime experience. He produced a pioneering manual for seamen—*An Accidence, or the Path-Way to Experience, Necessary for All Young Seamen*—in 1626, calling himself Captain John Smith, 'sometime Governor of Virginia, and Admiral of New England'. It was revised and republished one year later as *A Sea Grammar* (1627). His second major work, *The True Travels, Adventures, and Observations of Captaine John Smith*, two-thirds autobiography and one-third a continuation of *The Generall Historie*, appeared in 1630. His final work, *Advertisements for the Unexperienced Planters of New England, or any where*, was published in London in 1631, the year of his death. It represented the sum of his thoughts and experience on the subject of colonization. He died between 21 and 30 June 1631, and was buried in London. He never married.

Much of what is known of Smith's life comes from his writings, which are full of bravado and borrowings from other authors in the tradition of the time. His book *The True Travels* was an early example of the genre of autobiography but it reveals little about his life after 1616 and the precise chronology of his earlier history is uncertain. Nineteenth-century historians in particular regarded the tale of his early wanderings across and beyond Europe with great scepticism. Later researchers have found little to undermine Smith's credibility and much to support it. Though contested by some of his contemporaries, the best-documented years are the two and a half that he spent in Virginia. GWENDA MORGAN

Sources *The complete works of Captain John Smith*, ed. P. L. Barbour, 3 vols. (1986) • P. L. Barbour, *The three worlds of Captain John Smith* (1964) • K. O. Kupperman, ed., *Captain John Smith: a select edition of his writings* (1988) • B. Smith, *Captain John Smith: his life and legend* (1953) [with an appendix by L. P. Striker] • E. H. Emerson, *Captain John Smith* (New York, 1971) • F. J. Fausz, 'The Powhatan uprising of 1622: a historical study of ethnocentrism and cultural conflict', PhD diss., College of William and Mary in Virginia, 1977 • N. P. Canny, '"To Establish a Common Wealthe": Captain John Smith as New World colonist', *Virginia Magazine of History and Biography*, 96 (1988), 213–22 • F. W. Gleach, *Powhatan's world and colonial Virginia: a conflict of cultures* (1997) • H. C. Rountree, *The Powhatan Indians of Virginia* (1989) • A. T. Vaughan, *American genesis: Captain John Smith and the founding of Virginia* (1975) • E. S. Morgan, *American slavery, American freedom: the ordeal of colonial Virginia* (1975) • W. M. Billings, J. E. Selby, and T. W. Tate, *Colonial Virginia: a history* (1986) • C. Bridenbaugh, *Jamestown, 1544–1699* (1980) • B. Sheehan, *Savagism and civility: Indians and Englishmen in colonial Virginia* (1980)

Likenesses S. de Passe, line engraving, 1616, BM, NPG [*see illus.*]

Wealth at death land in Lincolnshire and grant of arms left to Thomas Packer; also bequests to friend, sister-in-law, and cousin; books left to three people; £20 for funeral: Barbour, *Three worlds*, 393–4

Smith, Sir John (1616–1644), royalist army officer, was born at Skilts in the parish of Studley, Warwickshire, the fourth son of Sir Francis Smith (*d.* 1629) of Wootton Wawen, Warwickshire, and Queniborough, Leicestershire, and his wife, Anne, daughter of Thomas Markham of Kirby Bellars, Leicestershire, and Ollerton, Nottinghamshire. In 1643 his eldest brother, Sir Charles Smith (1599?–1665), was rewarded for his loyalty to the king with a peerage as Baron Carrington of Wootton Wawen, and Viscount Carrington of Barrefore in Connaught.

Smith was a Roman Catholic, the younger son of one of the wealthiest recusant families in Warwickshire. His early education was entrusted to a kinsman, and he later completed his studies abroad. He returned home to gain his relatives' permission to follow his military inclinations, but was refused and sent instead to study in the Southern Netherlands. Once there he joined the Spanish army of Flanders and earned a reputation as a brave and accomplished commander in its campaigns against the French and Dutch. When he was invited by Sir John Digby to serve in the bishops' wars he returned to England and served Charles I as a lieutenant in 1640. He took part in a victorious skirmish at Stapleford, and distinguished himself in the battle of Newburn, even though the English were routed. In its aftermath he brought many Scottish captives to York where 'the gallant Lieutenant was received with extraordinary joy and universal acclamations, and general applause for his Heroicall Valour' (Walsingham, 'Life of Sir John Digby', 76). After the conclusion of the treaty of Ripon he retired to his mother's house at Ashby Folville in Leicestershire.

Smith joined the royalists at the outset of the English civil war, and was made a captain-lieutenant under Lord John Stuart (*d.* 1644). On 9 August 1642 he disarmed the people of Kilsby in Northamptonshire, who had declared for parliament, and on 23 September he took part in the fight at Powick Bridge. At Edgehill he served in Lord Grandison's regiment, on the left wing. During the battle Smith retrieved the royal standard after it was taken and its bearer, Sir Edmund Verney, killed. Accounts of the incident vary as to whether he wore a parliamentarian sash, rode into the enemy's ranks, and tricked the secretary holding the standard into parting with it, or retrieved it in armed combat. The deed, for which he was knighted on the field (he was probably the last knight banneret created in England), won him instant renown. He was awarded a medal, with an image of Charles on one side and a banner on the other, which he wore constantly until his death. He also received a troop of his own and was appointed by Lord Grandison major of his regiment. Smith was sent into the south, where he was taken prisoner on 13 December by Sir William Waller on the taking of Winchester Castle, and he was released the following September. He then travelled to Oxford, and was made lieutenant-colonel of Lord Herbert of Raglan's regiment. In 1644 he was dispatched to the western army, as major-general of the horse under Lord John Stuart. On 29 March the royalists under Patrick Ruthven, earl of Forth, and Ralph Hopton, Lord Hopton, engaged the parliamentarians under Waller between Cheriton and Alresford, Hampshire. Both Smith and Stuart were mortally wounded and carried from the field to Reading, and from there to Abingdon, where Smith died the next day, aged twenty-eight; he was buried on 1 April with military honours on the south side of the choir in Christ Church Cathedral, Oxford. According to Clarendon, 'the death of these two eminent officers', Smith and Lord John Stuart, 'made the names of many who perished that day the less inquired into and mentioned' (Clarendon, *Hist. rebellion*). The dismay in the royalist camp at his death was translated into several eulogies of their hero's 'True Matchlesse Valour' (Walsingham, 'Life of Sir John Digby').

E. I. CARLYLE, *rev.* S. L. SADLER

Sources Clarendon, *Hist. rebellion*, 3.336–8 • E. Walsingham, *Britannicae virtutis imago* (1644) • [E. Walsingham], 'Life of Sir John Digby, 1605–1645', ed. G. Bernard, *Camden miscellany, XII*, CS, 3rd ser., 18 (1910) • *The memoirs of Edmund Ludlow*, ed. C. H. Firth, 2 vols. (1894) • G. N. T. Grenville [Baron Nugent], *Some memorials of John Hampden*, 2 vols. (1832), 2.298 • *Bellum civile: Hopton's narrative of his campaign in the West, 1642–1644*, ed. C. E. H. Chadwyck Healey, Somerset RS, 18 (1902), 79, 81 • F. Wortley, *Characters and elegies* (1646), 47–8 • *England's black tribunal* (1765), 229 • D. Lloyd, *Memoires of the lives … of those … personages that suffered … for the protestant religion* (1668), 658 • E. Warburton, *Memoires of Prince Rupert and the cavaliers*, 3 vols. (1849), 2.26 • J. Le Neve, *Monumenta Anglicana*, 5 vols. (1717–19), vol. 1, p. 213 • GEC, *Peerage* • W. A. Shaw, *Knights of England*, 3 vols. (1906), 2.214 • E. Walker, *Historical discourses* (1707), 7 • F. L. Colvile, *The worthies of Warwickshire who lived between 1500 and 1800* [1870], 699–701 • *VCH Warwickshire*, 3.111, 179 • A. Beesley, *The history of Banbury* (1841) • S. R. Gardiner, *History of the great civil war, 1642–1649*, new edn, 4 vols. (1901–5), 1.49–50, 326 • A. Hughes, *Politics, society and civil war in Warwickshire, 1620–1660* (1987) • P. R. Newman, *Royalist officers in England and Wales, 1642–1660: a biographical dictionary* (1981), 348 • P. R. Newman, *The old service: royalist regimental colonels and the civil war, 1642–1646* (1993), 208–9, 229 • Burke, *Extinct peerage*, 497

Smith, John (1618–1652), philosopher, was born in Achurch, near Oundle in Northamptonshire. Little is known about his parents, beyond the fact that they were relatively old, and had been childless until his birth. He was admitted pensioner at Emmanuel College, Cambridge, in 1636, where his tutor was Benjamin Whichcote. His contemporaries at Emmanuel included most of the men who became known as Cambridge Platonists: besides Whichcote, Ralph Cudworth, Nathaniel Culverwell, Peter Sterry, and John Worthington were all Emmanuel graduates who were elected fellows of the college. Smith graduated BA in 1641 and proceeded MA in 1644. In that year, in the wake of the earl of Manchester's purge of Cambridge dons who refused to take the covenant, Smith was appointed fellow of Queens' College along with several other fellows of Emmanuel. After submitting to an examination by the Westminster assembly of divines, he was appointed to replace Mr Appleby on 11 June. At Queens' College, Smith was mathematics lecturer. He died young, shortly after making his will on 3 August 1652, struck down by tuberculosis, for which he sought a cure in vain, consulting, among others, Theodore Turquet de Mayerne. He was buried in Queens' College chapel on 7 August when his funeral sermon was preached by his pupil the future bishop of Ely, Simon Patrick. His friend Samuel Cradock was executor of his will; some land in Achurch was left to his mother.

Since he died before he reached the apogee of his intellectual career, Smith never realized the promise evident in his one published work, his posthumously published *Select Discourses* (1660). This was not prepared for press by Smith, but was edited by John Worthington from papers he left behind at his death. It was Worthington who presented the collection as a set of discourses on ten different topics: ranging from the brief discussions 'Of atheism' and 'Of superstition', to the more philosophical 'Of the existence and nature of God' and 'Of the true way or method of attaining divine knowledge'. The most extensive discourse is that on prophecy. This collection could be described as a summary statement of Cambridge Platonism as a religious philosophy. Smith's emphasis on practical Christianity, his high valuation of reason as an instrument of faith, and his optimistic view of human nature are all features of the tolerant divinity that he inherited from his teacher, Whichcote, and shared with the other Cambridge Platonists. Like them, Smith exhibited the non-dogmatic temper and philosophical openness of mind of his teacher that stands in striking contrast to the austere doctrinaire puritanism that held sway in the 1640s. Like Whichcote, he laid emphasis on interior spirituality rather than the externals of religion. Like his friends Ralph Cudworth and Henry More, Smith drew on both ancient and contemporary philosophy for the intellectual underpinning of his theology. His *Discourses* are suffused with humanist learning: Plato, Plotinus, and Plutarch are favourite sources. Smith was an early admirer of the philosophy of Descartes. This is most evident in his discourse 'Of the immortality of the soul'. He appears to have had a special interest in contemporary French thought: Oratorian texts feature in his book collection. None the less, Smith was no ivory-tower academic: he stressed the importance of communicating in accessible language. In his lifetime he made a practice of visiting his native village of Achurch in order to preach. According to Worthington, Smith's discourse 10, 'Of the Christians conflicts … over Satan', originated as a sermon against witchcraft sponsored by his college and delivered at Huntingdon. Much of the appeal of his *Discourses* is the style in which they are written. The book is a masterpiece of seventeenth-century prose, exemplifying Smith's professed determination to avoid abstruse speculation.

Smith was a man of attractive personality who inspired deep affection and respect in friends and pupils alike. In his preface to his edition of Smith's *Select Discourses* (1660), John Worthington celebrates his friend's learning and his personal qualities. He recalls the 'loveliness of his disposition and temper' and 'the extraordinary amiableness of his outward person'. Simon Patrick declared himself 'transported in my admiration of him' (*Works of Symon Patrick*, 9.421). Patrick celebrates Smith's learning for both its depth and his generosity in imparting it. He was, Patrick states, borrowing Eunapius's description of Longinus, 'a living library'. But, he adds, 'he was not a Library lock'd up, nor a Book clasped, but stood open for any to converse withall that had a mind to learn' (Patrick, *Sermon*, 506). Smith bequeathed his library of 600 books to Queens' College (the inventory is in the college archive). In spite of the brevity of his career, Smith was an important influence on the temper of liberal Anglicanism known as latitudinarianism through his pupil and admirer, Simon Patrick. *Select Discourses* was reprinted in 1673 and again in the eighteenth century. His 'Discourse of prophecy' was translated into Latin by Jean Le Clerc as a preface to his edition of the prophetic books of the Bible in 1731 and printed in English in Bishop Richard Watson's *A Collection of Theological Tracts* in 1791. His later admirers include Samuel Taylor Coleridge and Matthew Arnold.

SARAH HUTTON

Sources J. Smith, *Select discourses*, ed. J. Worthington (1660) · S. Patrick, *A sermon preached at the funeral of Mr John Smith*, in J. Smith, *Select discourses*, ed. J. Worthington (1660) [appx] · J. E. Saveson, 'Some aspects of the thought and style of John Smith, the Cambridge Platonist', PhD diss., U. Cam., 1955 · J. Lagrée, 'John Smith et le Portique', *The Cambridge Platonists in philosophical context: politics, metaphysics and religion*, ed. G. A. J. Rogers, J.-M. Vienne, and Y. C. Zarka (1997), 79–92 · M. Micheletti, *Il Pensiero religioso di John Smith, platonico de Cambridge* (1976), 89–111 · *The works of Symon Patrick, including his autobiography*, ed. A. Taylor, 9 vols. (1858) · J. E. Saveson, 'Descartes' influence on John Smith', *Journal of the History of Ideas*, 20 (1959), 258–63 · J. B. Schneewind, *The invention of autonomy* (1998), 199–202 · J. Twigg, *A history of Queens' College, Cambridge, 1448–1986* (1987) · S. Bendall, C. Brooke, and P. Collinson, *A history of Emmanuel College, Cambridge* (1999) · will, CUL, Baker MSS, Mm.1.37, 215 · Venn, *Alum. Cant.*

Archives Emmanuel College, Cambridge | BL, Add. MSS · CUL, Baker MSS

Likenesses stained glass, 19th cent., Emmanuel College chapel, Cambridge

Wealth at death see will, proved 12 Aug 1652, CUL, Baker MSS Mm.1.37, 215

Smith, John (*fl.* **1631–1670**), writer on trade, the son of George Smith, was apprenticed on 11 March 1631 to Matthew Cradock of the Skinners' Company, merchant, for eight years. Under Charles I efforts were being made to exclude foreign fishermen from British seas, where they were seen to profit greatly from trade based on the herring fishery, while reaching agreement with Scotland over its rights to fish local waters. A Society of the Fishery of Great Britain and Ireland was established in 1632 and the area under Scottish control was divided into two parts: the Hebridean, under the earl of Portland, and the Shetland, under Philip Herbert, earl of Montgomery and fourth earl of Pembroke, who was one of the few to be genuinely interested in the affair. It is not known if Simon Smith, Pembroke's secretary, was related to John.

Smith was sent in 1633 as Pembroke's agent to Shetland to report on its trade and industries, with a view to developing the fishery, with its related boat building and processing industries. He arrived in Shetland in June and gradually made his way north to Uyeasound in Unst, from where after only seventeen weeks he dispatched a cargo of 1655 ling and 834 cod (both these fish could be salted or dried). Smith remained in the Orkneys and Shetlands for more than a year. His account mentioned the islanders' settlements and agriculture and went into detail on the construction of their boats and gear. Cod and ling were taken on lines, and herring was netted offshore. Smith considered that the Shetlanders could take only those few fish that had escaped the large fleet of Dutch herring busses. Smith estimated the Dutch fleet in Shetland waters as about 1500 vessels, a figure now known to have been closer to 500 busses, with some smaller doggers setting lines for cod and ling.

The fishery society itself was a failure due to lack of investment in shipbuilding and allied industries, and it was wound up in 1639. Renewed interest in 1661 led to the constitution of another Royal Fishing Company, which may have caused Smith to publish his report, *The trade and fishing of Great Britain displayed: with a description of the islands of Orkney and Shetland, by Captain John Smith* (1661).

In 1670 Smith included this treatise in a more elaborate work entitled *Englands improvement reviv'd: in a treatise of all manner of husbandry and trade, by land and sea*. Smith claimed that he had 'formerly kept three ploughs in Ireland' ('To the reader') until forced out by the uprising of 1647. He also explained that forestry was a branch of husbandry in which he much delighted and had 'endeavoured to know above 30 years' (ibid.). The work was adorned by a eulogistic preface by John Evelyn and a second edition appeared in 1673. Smith gave detailed instructions for planting trees, showing how costs could be offset by the profits from small interspersed areas of wheat, and by letting fallow land for grazing. He was an earnest advocate of free trade and he urged an increase in trade throughout Britain, drawing attention to the profits that foreigners were making from their monopoly of trade in the City of London. Smith's personal life and the circumstances of his death are unknown.

ANITA MCCONNELL

Sources F. J. Shaw, *The northern and western islands of Scotland: their economy and society in the seventeeth century* (1980) · Skinners' Company apprentices register, GL, MS 30719/2, fol. 103 · *CSP dom.*, *1631–2*

Smith, John (**1630–1679**), physician, was born in Buckinghamshire. He entered Brasenose College, Oxford, on 20 February 1649 and graduated BA in 1651, MA in 1652, and DM on 9 July 1659. He was admitted a candidate of the College of Physicians on 22 December 1659, and a fellow on 2 April 1672.

Smith was the author of *Gērokomia basilikē: King Solomon's portraiture of old age. Wherein is contained a sacred anatomy both of soul and body. And a perfect account of the infirmities of age, incident to them both* (1666). A second edition appeared in 1676, and a third in 1752. The book consists of a commentary on Ecclesiastes 12: 1–6, and argues that parts of the scripture imply that Solomon was acquainted with the circulation of the blood, a claim only understandable in the light of Harvey's recent discoveries.

The author has been doubtfully identified with John Smith, doctor in physic, author of *A Compleat Practice of*

Physick (1656). He died at his house in St Helen's, Bishopsgate, London, in the winter of 1679, and was buried in the parish church. E. I. CARLYLE, *rev.* PATRICK WALLIS

Sources Foster, *Alum. Oxon.* • Munk, *Roll* • Wood, *Ath. Oxon.*

Smith, John (1647/8–1727?), clockmaker and writer, was possibly the son of John Smith who was baptized on 13 April 1648 at Binfield, Berkshire (on the grounds of his connection with that village and his own admission of age in one of his books). The clockmaker Thomas Hatton wrote in 1773 that Smith, 'when a toolmaker was unequalled; his engines are the best in use, both in execution and judgement in the theory' (Hatton, 382). Smith, a member of the Clockmakers' Company of London, lived at the eastern end of Cheapside, close to St Paul's Cathedral in the City of London, though he relates that at one time he lived at New Brentford, in Middlesex.

Stereometrie, or, The Art of Practical Gauging (1673), the first work ascribed to Smith in the *Dictionary of National Biography*, is, from its content and style, probably not his. Smith was, however, a prolific writer. His *Horological Disquisitions Concerning the Nature of Time* (1694) belies its content, which includes several of his earlier works and is a vade-mecum for gentlemen resident outside London who wish to attend to their own clocks and barometers. The failure of such instruments to perform properly was, in Smith's opinion, due either to defective workmanship, for which there was no remedy, or to poor maintenance, which could be avoided by the knowledgeable owner. Smith demonstrated his awareness of current literature and his grasp of mathematics in explaining why the days are not of equal length throughout the year; he described the construction and maintenance of pendulum clocks and the various patterns of mercury barometer, likewise how to transport these without harm. He was in advance of his time in writing to the Royal Society, urging it to keep a standard barometer so that other instruments could be made with similar scales and observations made in a similar manner. In this way, observations would be comparable, and rules for the barometer's rise and fall might be discovered. It is this letter, written from Binfield in 1676, that links Smith with that place (Smith to Royal Society, 5 Sept 1676, Royal Society, early letters, S.1.105). Another series of books dealt with the preparation and application of oil paints and varnishes for domestic woodwork, the manufacture of oilcloths, the painting of sundials, and the application of watercolours.

At the beginning of 1695 Smith, one of those dissatisfied with current religious teaching concerning the nature of the Trinity, published a short treatise entitled *A Designed End to the Socinian Controversy.* Issued without any printer's name, it so incensed the religious authorities that they had it confiscated and burned, and forced Smith to sign a recantation. Francis Gregory, rector of Hambledon, virulently attacked what he considered to be Smith's blasphemous falsehoods, dismissing him as an illiterate mechanic; other churchmen instructed him to return to his hammer and anvil and leave matters of religion to those who understood them. Few copies of this treatise survived, but one was found and reprinted in 1793.

Smith relates that he was seventy-four years of age when his 'shilling pamphlet' on the curative properties of water was published in 1722. This book attracted a good deal of attention, went through at least ten editions in English, and was translated into French and German. After his death his copyright passed to one Mary Smith, who published and sold later editions from the Strand, Westminster. It is probable that John Smith died in 1727; a burial at St Paul's of a John Smith of the parish of St Augustine (which had no burial-ground of its own) is recorded in that year. It is not known whether he married. ANITA MCCONNELL

Sources J. Smith, *Horological disquisitions concerning the nature of time and the reasons why all days, from noon to noon, are not alike twenty four hours long* (1694); facs. edn (1962) • R. Wallace, *Antitrinitarian biography*, 1 (1850), 246, 289–98; 3 (1850), 389–98 • T. Hatton, *An introduction to the mechanical part of clock and watchwork* (1773), 382 • J. Smith, *The curiosities of common water, or, the advantages thereof in preventing and curing many distempers* (1722) • W. E. Middleton, *The history of the barometer* (1964) • G. Clifton, *Directory of British scientific instrument makers, 1550–1851*, ed. G. L'E. Turner (1995), 256 • RS, early letters, S.1.105 • *N&Q*, 9 (1854), 395–6, 575

Smith, John (1652–1743), engraver, was born in Northamptonshire. The date of his birth is established by his memorial plaque in St Peter's Church, Northampton, which states that he died at the age of ninety in 1742 OS (which is elaborated by George Vertue as having been in January 1743). The only evidence for the beginning of his career is given by Vertue from information supplied by Edward Luttrell. Smith was the apprentice, with another future mezzotint engraver, Isaac Beckett, of a calico and tillet (a type of coarse cloth) printer in Morefields:

> Mr John Smith haveing a small knacke at drawing when his time was out, & Mr Becket was set up & got into reputation he applyd him self to him & there learnt the secret [of mezzotint] & workd for him. Afterwards farther instructed by Mr Vander Vaart [the Dutchman Jan van der Vaart]. (Vertue, 1.43)

The chronology of the 300 or so mezzotint plates made by Smith is revealed by his own catalogue of his works, of which a late eighteenth-century copy survives in the British Museum. The dates it gives are confirmed by those written in Smith's own hand in two volumes containing his complete output now in the New York Public Library (formerly in the library of the earls of Derby at Knowsley Hall). This shows that Smith's first mezzotints were made in 1683, when he was over thirty. In the first nine years of his career he worked principally for five publishers: first Richard Palmer, then Edward Cooper, Alexander Browne, Pierce Tempest, and Isaac Beckett and his widow, Grace. Although most of these prints were portraits, there was a significant number of subject plates, as well as two etchings.

The first plates that Smith published himself were in 1687, and from 1692 onwards he worked only for himself or directly for private patrons and never made another plate for a rival print publisher. He was able to do this because of his close association with Godfrey Kneller, a

John Smith (1652–1743), by Sir Godfrey Kneller, 1696

position he inherited from Isaac Beckett after the latter's premature death in 1688. This gave him a constant supply of portraits of all the most important persons in Britain, most of whom became his customers. Smith executed in mezzotint Kneller's portrait, and Kneller in return painted Smith's portrait in 1696 (now in the Tate collection). Smith dedicated to Kneller his translation of Charles Le Brun's *Conference upon Expression* (1698, published in 1701), and in Kneller's will Smith was bequeathed a mourning ring.

Smith was in the first class of mezzotint engravers and raised the standard of the medium to a consistently very high level. He made the mezzotint portrait a serious rival to the traditional engraved portrait, a medium in which the French specialized, and won such international prestige that a collection of Smith's *œuvre* became indispensable to any serious print collection in the first half of the eighteenth century, both in Britain and abroad.

Smith was aided by an acute business acumen. He tried to sell his customers not only portraits of themselves but albums of his entire production (at least five of these survive). By keeping hold of his plates, he was able to refresh them whenever they became worn and thus keep up the quality. He also kept in stock proofs before letter, and bought back his early plates, or, failing that, impressions from them, in order to make up complete collections. As demand increased, so did his prices, about which many complaints were made. He also published plates by other mezzotint engravers, mostly small genre subjects that he bought second-hand and often reworked.

Smith published from rented rooms in the Lion and Crown in Russell Street, Covent Garden, where he died, having (with one exception) given up making new plates after 1724. The wealth he had amassed 'by great industry and parcimonious way of living' (Vertue, 3.113) he invested in government stock and in property in his home county, and his will reveals the fortune that he bequeathed to his son and daughter. It also contains instructions that all his copperplates should be defaced so that his reputation should not be posthumously sullied by worn impressions appearing on the market, a stipulation that was later circumvented. His wife, Sarah, predeceased him in 1717. ANTONY GRIFFITHS

Sources will, PRO, PROB 11/725, fols. 321*v*–323*r* · Vertue, *Note books* · J. C. Smith, *British mezzotinto portraits*, 3 (1880), 1131–1241 · J. E. Wessely, *Kritische Verzeichnisse von Werken hervorragender Kupferstecher, John Smith* (1887), vol. 3 of *Kritische Verzeichnisse von Werken hervorragender Kupferstecher* · A. Griffiths, 'Early mezzotint publishing in England', pt 1, 'John Smith', *Print Quarterly*, 6 (1989), 242–57 · A. Griffiths and R. A. Gerard, *The print in Stuart Britain, 1603–1689* (1998) [exhibition catalogue, BM, 8 May – 20 Sept 1998] · T. Clayton, *The English print, 1688–1802* (1997) · memorial, St Peter's Church, Northampton

Archives BM · NYPL

Likenesses G. Kneller, oils, 1696, Tate collection [*see illus.*] · J. Smith, mezzotinto, 1716 (after G. Kneller), BM, NPG; repro. in Smith, *British mezzotinto portraits*, p. 232

Wealth at death wealthy: will, PRO, PROB 11/725, fols. 321*v*–323*r*

Smith, John (1655/6–1723), politician, was the fourth but only surviving son of John Smith (*d.* 1690), landowner, of South Tidworth, Hampshire, and his wife, Mary, daughter of Sir Edmund Wright, alderman of London. He matriculated from St John's College, Oxford, on 18 May 1672 aged sixteen, and two years later he was admitted to the Middle Temple, London, but he was never called to the bar. On 1 September 1679 he married Anne (1652–1680), daughter of Sir Nicholas Steward, first baronet, of Hartley Mauditt in Hampshire. His second marriage, to Anne (*bap.* 1663, *d.* 1727), daughter of Sir Thomas Strickland, second baronet, of Boynton, Yorkshire, took place on 7 November 1683. They had three sons and four daughters.

Smith's grandfather, Thomas, a successful London merchant, purchased estates in North Tidworth and South Tidworth during the mid-seventeenth century. The family flourished in the county and became well established in political circles. Smith entered parliament in 1679 as MP for Ludgershall in Wiltshire and held the seat until the Convention Parliament of 1689–90. He was described by a contemporary:

> as a gentleman of much honour, a lover of the constitution of his country, a very agreeable companion in conversation, a bold orator in the House of Commons when the interest of his country is at stake, of a good address, middle stature, fair complexion. (*Memoirs of the Secret Services*, 90–91)

He was a staunch whig sympathizer throughout his political career, and a believer in the protestant cause.

In December 1691 Smith entered parliament at a by-election for Bere Alston in Devon. He was an active member, delivering several important speeches on varied matters including finance and the Irish forfeited estates. His support for the ministry was rewarded on 27 April 1694 when he was made a lord of the Treasury. In 1695 he was elected for Andover in Hampshire, and he continued to represent this constituency in the next eight parliaments, until 1713. He was also sworn of the privy council, on 23 May 1695. Regarded by Bishop Gilbert Burnet as 'a man of clear parts and of a good expression', he did not fear voicing his opinions (*Burnet's History*, 228). He was particularly vocal in his antagonism towards the earl of Sunderland during the 1690s. In January 1698, during the debates on Charles Duncombe, Smith narrowly escaped the censure of the house by threatening to pull Speaker Foley by the nose unless he was treated better in the house (*Portland MSS*, 3.596).

As a court supporter and close associate of the Junto administration, Smith was promoted on 31 May 1699 to the post of chancellor of the exchequer. He resigned on 23 March 1701 in the belief that there was insufficient whig support in the House of Commons to sustain his position, but he continued to act as one of the leading whig spokesmen in the chamber.

Smith's name was predominant in discussions for the speakership of the 1705 parliament. The choice of speaker became a striking demonstration of party strife as it became clear that whigs and tories would be fairly evenly matched in the new house. In July 1705 Lord Treasurer Godolphin made it known at a meeting of placemen that Smith, 'a very honest gentleman', was to be put forward as the court candidate. Smith's moderation was stressed as one of his most important characteristics. On the first day of parliament, 25 October, the speakership was debated in a full house. Eventually the house divided on the question for John Smith, and this was passed by 248 to 205 votes, defeating the high-church tory candidate, William Bromley.

Smith was brought to the speaker's chair on a tide of whig support, and court approval continued throughout his tenure. He made no secret of his willingness to assist the court, and because of his continuing close connection with Godolphin, became known as one of the 'Treasurer's Whigs' (Holmes, 110–11). He was one of the commissioners for the union with Scotland and played an active part in the preparation of the treaty passed in January 1707. In October 1707 the first parliament of Great Britain assembled and Smith was elected unanimously as speaker, largely because he had 'contributed so much to the Union of both kingdoms' (*JHC*, 15.393).

While still speaker Smith accepted the post of chancellor of the exchequer in January 1708, though he did not take it up until 22 April, following the close of the parliamentary session. He was replaced by Sir Richard Onslow as speaker in the 1708 parliament, but continued to take an active part in debate. The impeachment of the high-church clergyman Dr Sacheverell dominated the 1709–10 session. Smith helped to lead the attack and was one of the managers of the Commons during the trial. Godolphin resigned later in the session, and in view of their close connection Smith decided to withdraw from office. Smith was rewarded for his services to the government in September 1710 with one of the tellerships of the exchequer, a post which he held until 1712 and then again from 1714 until his death.

Smith returned to parliamentary activity at the start of George I's reign, sitting for East Looe in Cornwall. He remained a whig, joining the supporters of Sir Robert Walpole in opposition to the Stanhope ministry. Smith died on 2 October 1723 and was buried two days later at South Tidworth church. KATHRYN ELLIS

Sources 'Smith, John', HoP, *Commons, 1690–1715* [draft] • G. S. Holmes, *British politics in the age of Anne* (1967) • *DNB* • *Memoirs of the secret services of John Macky*, ed. J. M. Grey, Roxburghe Club (1895) [repr. 1895] • W. A. Speck, 'The choice of a speaker in 1705', *BIHR*, 37 (1964), 20–46 • *JHC*, 15 (1705–8) • *JHC*, 8 (1660–67) • *The manuscripts of his grace the duke of Portland*, 10 vols., HMC, 29 (1891–1931), vols. 1–4 • *Bishop Burnet's History of his own time: with the suppressed passages of the first volume*, ed. M. J. Routh, 6 vols. (1823), vol. 5 • G. D. Squibb, ed., *The visitation of Hampshire and the Isle of Wight, 1686*, Harleian Society, new ser., 10 (1991) • *The historical register*, 8 (1723), 42 • J. L. Chester and J. Foster, eds., *London marriage licences, 1521–1869* (1887) • *IGI* • Foster, *Alum. Oxon.*

Likenesses attrib. T. Athow, engraving, watercolour, NPG • oils (after G. Kneller), Speaker's House, London

Smith, John (1657–1726), judge, was born on 6 January 1657, the third son of Roger Smith (*c*.1613–*c*.1667) of Frolesworth, Leicestershire, and his wife, Anna, daughter of Thomas Cotton of Laughton, Leicestershire. He matriculated at Lincoln College, Oxford, on 12 September 1676, and was admitted to Gray's Inn on 1 June 1678. Although he wanted 'some small time' (Fletcher, 77), he was called to the bar on 2 May 1684 at the request of the Hon. William Mountague, chief baron of the exchequer.

Having been created a serjeant-at-law in November 1700, with Basil Fielding, earl of Denbigh, and Lord Brooke of Beauchamp Court as his patrons, Smith was appointed a justice of the court of common pleas of Ireland on 24 December 1700, and was among the commissioners appointed in 1701 to hear chancery cases in Ireland in the absence of the lord chancellor. On 23 June 1702 he became a baron of the exchequer in England, and between 1702 and 1708 acted from time to time as a commissioner of assize on the Norfolk, northern, Oxford, and western circuits. In the celebrated Aylesbury election case, *Ashby* v. *White*, Smith supported Chief Justice Holt in advising the House of Lords in 1704 to reverse the decision of the majority of the court of queen's bench that determination of the right of election was in the House of Commons alone, though he subsequently dissented from the majority of the judges in advising the queen that a writ of error in the case of a decision of the court of queen's bench against the release of electors committed for contempt of the house was not a matter of right.

On 20 May 1708 Smith was granted leave of absence from the exchequer and an additional salary of £500 upon his appointment, together with John Scrope, as one of the two English barons of the court of exchequer in Scotland, newly established following the Act of Union; Sir Salathiel Lovell was in consequence appointed an additional baron of the English exchequer. Smith's appointment was probably at the choice of the lord treasurer, Sidney Godolphin, Lord Godolphin. In the following year Smith became chief baron of the Scottish exchequer upon the resignation of

James Ogilvie, earl of Seafield. It was said that Godolphin was glad of the opportunity to make an Englishman chief baron, though he may have felt that the court would benefit from the presidency of a professional judge rather than a politician. Smith held the office until his death, while retaining his position in the English court and being re-sworn as an English baron upon the accession of George I. While in Edinburgh, Smith established a chapel, the ministers of which he endowed in a codicil to his will. In the same codicil he endowed a charity to provide houses for widows in Frolesworth, members of the Church of England, who were 'constantly to attend our divine service' (will, PRO, PROB 11/610/153) at the parish church. Initially accommodating four widows in separate houses, the charity eventually came to provide for eighteen. Perhaps unmarried, Smith died on 21 June 1726, and may have been buried in the church of St Mary Aldermanbury, London, on 26 August 1726. N. G. Jones

Sources A. Herbert, 'Frolesworth I: the church', *Transactions of the Leicestershire Archaeological Society*, 12 (1921–2), 180–88 • J. Nichols, *The history and antiquities of the county of Leicester*, 4/1 (1807) • J. Foster, *The register of admissions to Gray's Inn, 1521–1889, together with the register of marriages in Gray's Inn chapel, 1695–1754* (privately printed, London, 1889) • E. Foss, *Biographia juridica: a biographical dictionary of the judges of England … 1066–1870* (1870) • R. J. Fletcher, ed., *The pension book of Gray's Inn*, 2 (1910) • Sainty, *Judges* • Foster, *Alum. Oxon.*, 1500–1714, vol. 4 • will, PRO, PROB 11/610/153 • N. Luttrell, *A brief historical relation of state affairs from September 1678 to April 1714*, 4–5 (1857) • W. H. Bryson, *The equity side of the exchequer* (1975) • *CSP dom.*, 1700–02 • *State trials*, vol. 14 • John, Lord Campbell, *The lives of the chief justices of England*, 2 (1849) • E. Cruickshanks, '*Ashby* v. *White*: the case of the men of Aylesbury, 1701–4', *Party and management in parliament, 1660–1784*, ed. C. Jones (1984), 87–103 • J. S. Cockburn, *A history of English assizes, 1558–1714* (1972) • D. M. Walker, *A legal history of Scotland*, 5 (1998) • P. W. J. Riley, *The English ministers and Scotland, 1707–1727* (1964) • memorial, Frolesworth church, Leicestershire

Archives NA Scot., letters to J. Clerk

Likenesses J. Basire, line engraving (in judicial robes), BM, NPG; repro. in Nichols, *History and antiquities* • engraving, repro. in Nichols, *Illustrations*, 1.221 • oils, Parliament Hall, Edinburgh • portrait (in judicial robes), Faculty of Advocates, Edinburgh; [on loan to Parliament House, Edinburgh]

Smith, John (*bap.* **1659**, *d.* **1715**), Church of England clergyman and historian, was baptized at Lowther, Westmorland, on 10 November 1659, one of the eleven sons of William Smith (*bap.* 1630, *d.* 1676), rector of Lowther, and his wife, Elizabeth (*d.* after 1676), daughter of Giles Wetherell of Stockton, co. Durham. His paternal grandfather was **Matthew Smith** (*d.* 1640), barrister and playwright. Most of what is known about Matthew derives from the account of his life in Theophilus Cibber's *The Lives of the Poets of Great Britain and Ireland* (2nd edn, 1753), which records that he was the son of John Smith of Knaresborough, merchant, and became the husband of Anne, daughter of Henry Roundell esquire. He was, it continues, a barrister-at-law of the Inner Temple and served as a member of the council of the north on the eve of the civil war. He left an annotated manuscript copy of Littleton's *Tenures* and two dramatic pieces, a one-act ballad opera, *The Country Squire*, and a masque, the *Masquerade du ciel*. The latter was, Cibber reports, published in 1640, the year of his death, by his eldest son, John, who dedicated the work to Queen Henrietta Maria. However, much of what is claimed beyond the bare family details is difficult to substantiate from independent evidence, and some looks very dubious. Matthew's name does not appear in the Inner Temple records. The *Masquerade du ciel* was indeed published in 1640, having been entered in the Stationers' register on 24 November. But the name on the title-page is 'J. S.': George Thomason identified the author as 'Chapleine to the Lord Brooks' (Greg, 2.732), while William Sancroft thought the masque was written by John Sadler (1615–1674).

All John Smith's brothers who survived infancy gained distinction, among them Joseph *Smith (1670–1756), who became provost of Queen's College, Oxford, and Postumus Smith (*bap.* 1676, *d.* 1725), an eminent civilian. John Smith was educated at Clayton in the West Riding of Yorkshire, by the ejected minister Christopher Ness, and at the grammar school at Appleby, Westmorland. His father intended to send him to the University of Glasgow, but a providential storm prevented his journey, and he matriculated instead from St John's College, Cambridge, in June 1674. He graduated BA in 1677 and proceeded MA in 1681, and was ordained by Richard Sterne, archbishop of York. He was admitted a minor canon of Durham in July 1682, and was then collated to the curacy of Croxdale and in July 1684 to the curacy of Witton Gilbert, both parishes neighbouring Durham. He spent three years, from 1686 to 1689, as chaplain to Charles Granville, Lord Granville of Lansdown (later second earl of Bath), who was then ambassador in Madrid. In 1692 he married Mary, eldest daughter of William Cooper of Scarborough. They had five sons.

In 1694 Smith became domestic chaplain to Nathaniel Crew, bishop of Durham, who in 1695 collated him to the rectory and hospital of Gateshead, and on 25 September of that year to the seventh prebendal stall of the cathedral. Further promotion followed. Smith became treasurer of the cathedral in 1699, and in 1704 rector of Wearmouth, where he rebuilt the rectory and restored the chancel of the historic church. He had taken the degree of DD in Cambridge in 1696, and published some sermons, but his principal work now was not that of a parish priest nor of an officer of the cathedral but of a historical scholar. Living most of the time in Cambridge he devoted his time to the critical study of the middle ages. With other scholars he assisted Edmund Gibson in his revision of Camden's *Britannia*, and the learned James Anderson, author of *An Historical Essay* (1705) and *Collections Relating to the History of Mary, Queen of Scotland* (1727–8), who shared some of his instincts and acumen.

Smith collected material for a history of Durham, but his chief concern was with a critical edition of Bede's ecclesiastical history of the English people, the foremost historical work of its age. His plans were significantly changed by the availability in England after 1701 of the text known as the Moore manuscript, which George I purchased in 1715 with the rest of the library collected by John

Moore, bishop successively of Ely and Norwich, and presented to Cambridge University Library (CUL, MS Kk.5.16). It is one of only four manuscripts of the history surviving from the eighth century, and Smith decided rightly to put it at the heart of his work. He did not live to finish his edition, which was ably completed, and published in 1722, by his eldest son, George *Smith (1693–1756).

Smith's health failed in 1713, and he died at Cambridge on 30 July 1715. He was buried in the chapel of St John's College. A monument by Edward Stanton, with an inscription composed by Smith's friend and colleague Thomas Baker, was preserved when the chapel was rebuilt by Sir George Gilbert Scott in 1863–9.

Historiae ecclesiasticae gentis Anglorum libri quinque, auctore venerabili Bedae, cura et studio Johannis Smith STP remained the best exemplar of Bede until Charles Plummer's edition of 1896. Plummer observed that Smith had confined his work to insular texts, but was himself unaware of the Leningrad Bede (St Petersburg Public Library, MS Latin Q.v.I.182) which was incorporated in the edition by Bertram Colgrave and Robin Mynors (1969). Smith had, nevertheless, made notably competent use of the material that he had, and his editorial criteria and technique still enjoy respect. G. H. MARTIN

Sources *DNB* [J. S.; Joseph Smith; Geo. Smith; C. Ness; T. Baker] • Venn, *Alum. Cant.* • D. C. Douglas, *English scholars* (1939) • D. McKitterick, *Cambridge University Library, a history: the eighteenth and nineteenth centuries* (1986) • *Cambridgeshire*, Pevsner (1954) • R. Gunnis, *Dictionary of British sculptors, 1660–1851*, new edn (1968) • R. S. Boumphrey, C. R. Hudleston, and J. Hughes, *An armorial for Cumberland and Westmorland*, Cumberland and Westmorland Antiquarian and Archaeological Society, extra ser. (1975) • B. A. Myers, *The rectors of the ancient parish church of Bishop Wearmouth* (1998) • J. F. Haswell and C. S. Jackson, eds., *The registers of Lowther, 1540–1812*, Cumberland and Westmorland Antiquarian and Archaeological Society, parish register section, 21 (1933) • R. Shiels, *The lives of the poets of Great Britain and Ireland*, ed. T. Cibber, 5 vols. (1753), 2.323–4 • W. Greg, *A bibliography of the English printed drama to the Restoration*, 4 vols. (1939–59), vol. 2, p. 732
Archives Queen's College, Oxford, family papers

Smith, John (**1662–1717**), poet and playwright, was the son of John Smith of Barton, Gloucestershire. In 1676 he became a chorister of Magdalen College, Oxford: on 10 July 1679 he matriculated as an undergraduate of the college: he graduated BA in 1683 and proceeded MA in 1686. In 1682 he became a clerk of the college, and in 1689 usher of the college school.

Smith was a contributor to *Odes Paraphrased and Imitated* (1685), and wrote *Scarronides, or, Virgil Travesty: a Mock-Poem on the Second Book of Virgil's 'Aeneis'* (1691), which imitated Charles Cotton's treatment of the first book. In the same year was published a play generally, but not universally, attributed to him: *Win her and take her, or, Old fools will be meddling: a comedy, as it is now acted at the Theatre Royal* (1691). The printing was anonymous, with a dedication written by the actor Cave Underhill to Peregrine Osborne, earl of Danby, and an epilogue by Thomas D'Urfey. Twenty years later Smith published *Poems upon Several Occasions* (1713), dedicated again to Peregrine Osborne, now elevated to the lord marquess of Carmarthen. The collection shows that Smith had written other prologues and epilogues for professional actors, including at least one seemingly for a performance of *Volpone* at Oxford, and that he was an accomplished writer of light verse, including the splendid mock-heroic 'Rhapsody upon a Lobster'.

Smith died at Oxford on 16 July 1717, and was buried in Magdalen College chapel. MATTHEW STEGGLE

Sources Foster, *Alum. Oxon.* • A. Nicoll, *A history of Restoration drama, 1660–1700* (1928) • J. R. Bloxam, *A register of the presidents, fellows … of Saint Mary Magdalen College*, 8 vols. (1853–85)

Smith, John (*b. c.***1700**), Church of England clergyman and historian, matriculated at Trinity Hall, Cambridge, in 1719. He was ordained in Lincoln in 1720, and graduated LLB in 1725. He spent most of his life in Lincolnshire, and may have been the John Smith who became rector of Faldingworth, Lincolnshire, in 1720.

Smith's first work, dedicated to the mayor of Lincoln, was *A discourse on trade, liberty, and taxes. Addressed to all landholders and traders in Great Britain* (1733). He devoted his time to the study of the wool trade, and wrote about it in 1742 in *The Grazier's Advocate, or, Free Thoughts of Wool and the Woollen Trade*. In 1747 he published *Chronicon rusticum-commerciale, or, Memoirs of Wool*, in two volumes, in which he traced the history of the wool trade from the beginning of the seventeenth century. This became a standard work. Smith opposed the restrictions on the export of wool, and argued that the price of English wool was too low. He became involved in a pamphlet war with William Temple of Trowbridge, who attacked Smith's views in *A Refutation of One of the Principal Arguments in 'Memoirs of Wool'* (1750). Smith's reply, *The Case of the English Farmer and his Landlord* (1750) was printed in Lincoln, and dedicated to the nobility, gentry, and clergy of Lincolnshire. Temple replied to this in *An epistle to the Rev Mr John Smith, LLB, or, An expostulatory address to him upon his forgery and chicanery in his 'Memoirs of wool'* (1751). Smith also wrote *A Review of the Manufacturer's Complaint Against the Wool-Grower* (1753).

ANNE PIMLOTT BAKER

Sources J. Bischoff, *A comprehensive history of the woollen and worsted manufactures*, 1 (1842), 51–110 • J. Thirsk, ed., *The agrarian history of England and Wales*, 6, ed. G. E. Mingay (1989), 120 • Venn, *Alum. Cant.* • *DNB*

Smith, John (*bap.* **1711**, *d.* **1795**), university professor, was born at Coltishall, Norfolk, and baptized there on 14 October 1711, the second son of Henry Smith, attorney, and his wife, Elizabeth, formerly Johnson. After three years at Norwich grammar school, followed by six years at Eton College (1726–32), he was admitted as a pensioner at Gonville and Caius College, Cambridge, where he graduated BA in 1735–6 and MA in 1739. Elected to a junior fellowship in 1739, he progressed to a senior fellowship in 1744. He was ordained priest in 1739 and briefly held the curacy at Coltishall. He was collated to the chancellorship of Lincoln in 1783 and held this position until his death.

Smith held numerous college offices, including those of dean (1744–9), bursar (1750–53), and president (1754–64). In that year he was awarded the degree of DD and took up the mastership, which he held thereafter. From 1771 he held the Lowndean professorship of astronomy. As was customary at that time, he neither delivered lectures nor published anything on the subject of astronomy. He did, however, have permission in November 1764 to make alterations to the south parapet of the college in order to employ his transit telescope, and this demonstration of interest may have influenced the university—though his friend William Cole ascribed his appointment to court favour.

Cole, who had been at Eton with Smith, described him somewhat harshly:

> This downright honest man … has no other preferment; but as he is a bachelor, with a private fortune, he lives very hospitably and much esteemed by his acquaintance …. A plain honest man of strong passions when moved … an eternal smoker of tobacco; pretends to a taste in painting, and may possibly understand it, though he looks as if he did not, and has such an inarticulate way of expressing himself that very few people understand what he says. He has a brother's widow and her children who lives with him and keeps his house. (Venn, 3.129)

This was Margaret, widow of Smith's younger brother Joseph.

Smith's argumentative nature led, Cole reports, to an unseemly quarrel in the Senate House with Dr Ewin of St John's, and on another occasion to a dispute over some elections. Smith died on 17 June 1795 in Cambridge and was buried on 21 June in Gonville and Caius College chapel, where a memorial tablet was set up in the ante-chapel. He bequeathed to the university the sum of £200, for the increase of the Wendy fellowship, and a small piece of land in Cheshire, the income from which was to benefit the Lowndean professorship.

ANITA MCCONNELL

Sources J. Venn and others, eds., *Biographical history of Gonville and Caius College*, 2: *1713–1897* (1898), 129–32 • J. Venn and others, eds., *Biographical history of Gonville and Caius College*, 3: *Biographies of the successive masters* (1901), 129–32 • R. A. Austen-Leigh, ed., *The Eton College register, 1698–1752* (1927), 314 • *GM*, 1st ser., 65 (1795), 534

Archives BL, Add. MSS 32961–32989 (Newcastle)

Wealth at death under £5000: Venn and others, eds., *Biographical history*, vol. 3

Smith, John (1716/17–1764). *See under* Smith, George (1713/14–1776).

Smith, John (1747–1807), Church of Scotland minister and Gaelic scholar, was born in July 1747 at Croft-Brackley in the parish of Glenorchy, Argyll, the son of John Smith (also known as John M'Lulich), who was probably a farmer, and Mary Campbell. He was educated at the University of Edinburgh and was licensed to preach the gospel by the presbytery of Kintyre on 28 April 1773. He was ordained on 18 October 1775 upon his appointment to the mission at Tarbert, Loch Fyne. On 3 June 1777 Smith was admitted to the parish of Kilbrandon and Kilchattan, in the presbytery of Lorn, as assistant and successor to the ailing Revd James Stewart. In July 1780 he was presented by the duke of Argyll to the first charge at Campbeltown in Kintyre, Argyll, sometimes referred to as Campbeltown Highland, where he was admitted on 18 April 1781. He was described by the son of his successor at Campbeltown as 'perhaps the most powerful and eloquent preacher at that time in the highlands' (MacLeod, 27).

While awaiting his translation to Campbeltown in 1781, Smith published his first Gaelic work, a translation of Joseph Alleine's *Alarm to the Unconverted*, which he carried out with the encouragement of Lady Glenorchy. It is said that a religious revival broke out among the congregation as he read extracts of his translation in the course of Sunday services. Smith's Gaelic translation of the prophetic books of the Old Testament, published in 1787 under the auspices of the Society in Scotland for the Propagation of Christian Knowledge, has been praised by critics for its impeccable scholarship and its use of idiomatic Gaelic. In the same year he received an honorary DD degree from Edinburgh University and published, with the authority of the synod of Argyll, a Gaelic translation of the psalms and paraphrases, including the creed, the Lord's prayer, and the ten commandments in metre. By 1840 more than thirty editions of Smith's translation of the psalter had been published and it was the favoured version among Gaelic worshippers in his native Argyll. A posthumous volume of Gaelic prayers for family worship, with a collection of hymns, was published in 1808 and was reprinted three times during the nineteenth century.

Smith was involved in the controversy surrounding the poems of Ossian published by James Macpherson, and his *Galic Antiquities* (1780) argues for their authenticity. *Sean Dàna le Oisian, Orrann, Ulann …*, which he published in 1787, claims to be the original Gaelic versions, collected in the highlands and islands, of the English translations which had appeared in *Galic Antiquities*, but modern scholars believe that Smith himself wrote much of the material in *Sean Dàna*.

Smith's other writings fall into two broad categories: religion and political economy. Among his religious publications are *A View of the Last Judgement* (1783), *A Summary View and Explanation of the Writings of the Prophets* (1787), and *Lectures on the Nature and End of the Sacred Office* (1798). His works of political economy include *An Essay of the Advantages of Watering Pasture and Meadow Grounds, in the Highlands* (1792), *General View of the Agriculture of the County of Argyll* (1798), and the article on Campbeltown in Sir John Sinclair's *Statistical Account of Scotland*.

On 3 November 1783 Smith married Helen (*c*.1760–1843), daughter of Coll Macdougall of Ardincaple, with whom he had four daughters and four sons, the youngest of whom served as a minister in Campbeltown from 1826 to 1841. Smith died in Campbeltown on 26 June 1807.

RODERICK MACLEOD

Sources *Fasti Scot.*, new edn, 4.50–51 • D. MacKinnon, *The Gaelic Bible and psalter: being the story of the translation of the scriptures into Scottish Gaelic* (1930), 15, 62 • J. N. MacLeod, *Memorials of the Rev. Norman MacLeod* (1898) • D. S. Thomson, 'Bogus Gaelic literature, *c*.1750–*c*.1820', *Transactions of the Gaelic Society of Glasgow*, 5 (1877), 180–81 • J. MacInnes, *The evangelical movement in the highlands of Scotland* (1951)

Archives U. Edin. L., commonplace book and papers

Smith, John (1749–1831), watercolour painter, was born at Irthington in Cumberland on 26 July 1749. His father was gardener to Susannah Maria Appleby, the sister of Captain John Bernard Gilpin of Scaleby Castle in Cumberland who was an amateur artist. Gilpin gave the young Smith lessons in drawing at his studio in the deanery at Carlisle Cathedral and sent him to St Bees School; subsequently Smith was recommended as a drawing-master to a school near Whitehaven (possibly St Bees). Gilpin's sons, the artists William and Sawrey Gilpin, also instructed Smith and he was one of a group of artists who accompanied William Gilpin on sketching tours from about 1770 to 1776, providing illustrations for the books that Gilpin later published.

While staying in Derbyshire *c*.1775 Smith was introduced to George Greville, second earl of Warwick, an avid collector of art for Warwick Castle. Admiring some views of Matlock drawn by Smith, Warwick agreed to send him to Italy, where he met the artists William Pars, Thomas Jones, and Francis Towne. Although Smith had the highest contemporary reputation it is probable that all four encouraged and influenced one another's work; together they brought a new vividness to some of the finest drawings of the late eighteenth century with pictures such as Smith's *Outside Porta Pia, Rome* (*c*.1777–80, Tate collection) and *Interior of the Coliseum* (British Museum). His Italian pictures, which he continued to produce for many years after his return to England, are considered Smith's best. Between 1792 and 1799 he published *Select Views in Italy, with Topographical and Historical Descriptions in English and French*.

After five years Smith returned to England and made his home in Warwick where, on 6 February 1783, he married Elizabeth Gerrard (*d*. in or after 1831) in St Mary's Church. His sobriquet Warwick derives either from his residence in the town or from the earl. Subsequently he travelled widely and six of his drawings were engraved as illustrations for Middiman's *Select Views in Great Britain* in 1784 and 1785. In 1786 he was paid £247 16*s*. by the fourth duke of Atholl for fifty-six watercolours of Perthshire for Blair Atholl Castle. These were followed by twenty-six drawings of the Isle of Man for the duke, who was governor-in-chief; now in the Manx Museum, they are the most important contemporary pictorial record of Man. Another patron was John Christian Curwen of Workington Hall in Cumberland and Belle Isle on Windermere for whom Smith made 100 drawings between 1789 and 1792, a number of which were published. Between 1784 and 1806 Smith made frequent trips to Wales (Basil Long gives details of his itineraries). William Sotheby's *A tour through parts of Wales, sonnets, odes and other poems, with engravings from drawings taken on the spot* was published with thirteen plates after Smith in 1794 'solely for the emolument of the artist' (Williams, 13). In 1792 he was accompanied by Robert Fulke Greville and Julius Caesar Ibbetson, and fifteen of Smith's drawings from this year were subsequently published in *A Tour to Hafod in Cardiganshire* in 1810 with text by Sir James Edward Smith, the president of the Linnean Society.

For much of his career Smith enjoyed a very high reputation particularly as a colourist. According to Ackermann's *Repository of Art* of 1812 'it may with truth be said, that with this artist the first epoch of painting in water colours originated' (Hardie, 1.116). Twentieth-century opinion is more guarded but, as Martin Hardie pointed out, Smith helped introduce direct colour and his work reflected the departure from classic formalism. Smith was reluctant to join the Society of Painters in Water Colours on its formation in 1804; although elected in 1805 he did not exhibit until 1807, when he entered nineteen drawings and, according to Sir George Beaumont, his view of the Coliseum was the best in the room. However, the watercolour artist Francis Nicholson recorded tartly that Smith's work now seemed very conservative in comparison with that of other artists: 'He could not alter his method of practice and probably thought it beneath him to do so … Stood still and was soon left behind' (Royal Watercolour Society, J69/2). Smith continued his membership of the society after it began to accept oils, serving as president in 1814, 1817, and 1818, as secretary in 1816, and as treasurer in 1819, 1821, and 1822 before he resigned in December 1823 when he was seventy-four. In all he exhibited 154 drawings, of British and continental views, which sold for up to 10 guineas. The 1809 catalogue lists six drawings of 'Bradby Park' (Bretby Park) in Derbyshire, a house Sir Jeffry Wyatville was altering for the fifth earl of Chesterfield.

Smith had been in London for some years; in 1815 he moved from 7 St George's Row, Oxford Turnpike, to 25 Bryanston Street, Portman Square. It is known that he gave lessons to the artist John Glover and presumably he had other pupils. John Warwick Smith died aged eighty-one at Middlesex Place, Marylebone Road, on 22 March 1831 and was buried in the vault at St George's Chapel, Uxbridge Road, by 'the little row of houses which contained his old studio and those of Paul Sandby and Tom Girtin, between whose schools of painting he had in a former age fashioned a connecting link in the historic chain of water-colour art' (Roget, 1.433). Smith's will mentions two sons and a daughter, and bequests included his portrait by Hopner, his painting equipment, and a grand pianoforte by Kirkman. A sale of several hundred pencil sketches and other pictures was held by Christie and Manson on 10 March 1832. An exhibition of 200 pictures by Smith was held at the galleries of the Royal Society of Painters in Water Colours in June 1928. One of Smith's albums was acquired from Warwick Castle by the British Museum in 1936; his work is held also by the Ashmolean Museum, Oxford, the Fitzwilliam Museum, Cambridge, and the Victoria and Albert Museum, which has twelve drawings. SIMON FENWICK

Sources I. A. Williams, 'John "Warwick" Smith', *Old Water-Colour Society's Club*, 24 (1946), 9–18 • B. S. Long, 'John (Warwick) Smith', *Walker's Quarterly* [whole issue], 24 (1927) • M. Hardie, *Water-colour painting in Britain*, ed. D. Snelgrove, J. Mayne, and B. Taylor, 1: *The eighteenth century* (1966), 113–17 • *The English lakes* (1949) [exhibition catalogue, Harris Museum and Art Gallery] • Bankside Gallery, London, Royal Watercolour Society MSS • S. Harrison, ed., *100 years of heritage: the work of the Manx Museum and National Trust* (1986), 90–91 • J. L. Roget, *A history of the 'Old Water-Colour' Society*, 2 vols. (1891) • A. Lyles and R. Hamlyn, *British watercolours from the Oppé collection* (1997), 138–41 [exhibition catalogue, Tate Gallery, London, 10 Sept

– 30 Nov 1997, and elsewhere] • C. P. Barbier, *William Gilpin* (1963), 4–76 • PRO, PROB 11/1791A, sig. 599

Wealth at death bequeathed portrait by Hopner; also painting equipment; grand pianoforte: will, PRO, PROB 11/1791A, sig. 599

Smith, Sir John (1754–1837), army officer, was born at Brighton, Sussex, on 22 February 1754; nothing is known of his parents. He entered the Royal Military Academy, Woolwich, as a cadet on 1 March 1768 and was commissioned second lieutenant in the Royal Artillery on 15 March 1771. In 1773 he was posted to Canada. On the outbreak of the War of Independence, Smith found himself in the garrison of St John's attacked by the Americans. After a two-month siege, during which he was twice slightly wounded, Smith and the other defenders surrendered on 2 November 1775 and were taken prisoner. Smith was exchanged in January 1777, rejoined the British forces at Rhode Island, and subsequently took part in Sir William Howe's Philadelphia campaign, seeing action at Brandywine, Germantown, and the capture of Mud Island. In 1778 he served under Sir Henry Clinton during the withdrawal to New York and saw further combat at the battle of Monmouth.

Smith was promoted first lieutenant on 7 July 1779 and was present at the capture of Charles Town on 12 May 1780. In 1781 he served in Virginia before being forced to surrender at Yorktown on 20 October with the rest of Lord Cornwallis's army. Released on parole, he returned to England and was promoted captain-lieutenant on 28 February 1782. He married, at Chatham on 17 April 1782, Grace Weatherall (1751/2–1832), with whom he had five children. In 1785 he went to Gibraltar and was stationed there for five years; his promotion to captain on 21 May 1790 brought him command of number 6 company, the 1st battalion of the Royal Artillery. On 6 March 1795 he received his majority.

Smith had been appointed second in command of the artillery intended to accompany Lord Moira's expedition to France, but in October 1795 he was ordered instead to the West Indies with Sir Ralph Abercromby. He was present at the capture of St Lucia and St Vincent in 1796, and commanded the artillery at the capture of Trinidad from the Spanish in February 1797. Command of all thirteen companies of the Royal Artillery serving in the West Indies then fell to him, and on 27 August 1797 he was promoted lieutenant-colonel. Sickness compelled his return to England soon after.

In September and October 1799 Smith commanded the artillery park during the duke of York's expedition to the Netherlands. He fought at the battles of 2 and 6 October, received the thanks of the commander-in-chief for his services, and returned to England with the rest of the army at the beginning of November. On 20 July 1804 he was promoted colonel and given command of the artillery at Gibraltar. He remained there ten years, during which time he was promoted major-general (25 July 1810) and twice placed in temporary command of the fortress. On 3 July 1815 he was appointed colonel-commandant of the 7th battalion of the Royal Artillery, was promoted lieutenant-general in 1819, and made a GCH and knighted on 10 August 1831. He transferred to the Royal Horse Artillery as colonel-commandant (1833) and was promoted full general on 10 January 1837. He died on 2 July 1837, aged eighty-three, at Charlton, Kent, and was buried in the churchyard of St Luke's, Charlton, on 10 July.

R. H. Vetch, *rev.* Alastair W. Massie

Sources Smith's service record, PRO, WO 76/360 • J. Philippart, ed., *The royal military calendar*, 3rd edn, 5 vols. (1820) • J. Kane, *List of officers of the royal regiment of artillery from the year 1716 to the year 1899*, rev. W. H. Askwith, 4th edn (1900) • L. M. May, *Charlton: near Woolwich, Kent. Full and complete copies of all the inscriptions in the old parish church and churchyard* (1908) • M. E. S. Laws, ed., *Battery records of the royal artillery, 1716–1859* (1952) • F. Duncan, ed., *History of the royal regiment of artillery*, 2nd edn, 2 vols. (1874) • will, 1836, PRO, PROB 11/1882 (568) • *LondG* (14 Oct 1799), 1044 • *GM*, 1st ser., 102/2 (1832), 531 • W. A. Shaw, *The knights of England*, 2 vols. (1906)

Wealth at death see will, 1836, PRO, PROB 11/1882, fol. 568

Smith, John [*known as* John Smith, youngest] (1784–1849), bookseller and publisher, was born in Glasgow on 28 March 1784, eldest son of John Smith (1753–1833), known as John Smith, younger, and Margaret Bryce. Smith's grandfather, John Smith of Finnieston (1724–1814), the youngest son of the second laird of Craigend, was discharged from the army after being wounded at the battle of Laffeldt, Flanders, in 1747, and founded the bookselling concern of John Smith & Son, Glasgow, in 1751. From Glasgow high school Smith matriculated in 1796 at Glasgow College, where he studied humanities. After apprenticeship in Birmingham with the booksellers Knott and Lloyds, he joined his father as partner in the family business in Hutcheson Street in 1803. It was undoubtedly due to his initiative that from 1808, using particularly his contacts with the university, the bookselling, stationery, and circulating library business was further diversified into the publication of poetry, theology, botany, literary criticism, travel, and medicine, for which he handled personally all the details of the publishing process.

The Smith family were members of the Tron Church, whose new minister, Thomas *Chalmers, began in 1815 regularly to visit them in Stockwell Street, having developed an intense attachment to the 22-year-old youngest son, Thomas. Within a year, Thomas was dead. The fateful and ultimately fatal business relationship between Smith and Chalmers effectively began with the publication, jointly with the Edinburgh bookseller William Whyte, of *Astronomical Discourses* (1817). Within a year nine editions had been printed and 20,000 copies sold, a rate of sale not dissimilar to that of the latest Walter Scott novel. There was also a close friendship: 'Mrs Chalmers and I are both anxious to hear of you and we love you' (Chalmers to Smith, May 1817, in House and Kamm).

A further volume, *Sermons Preached in the Tron Kirk, Glasgow* (1819), failed, in spite of the efforts of the publishers. Chalmers got it into his head that this was due to the terms on which it was offered to the trade. The dispute, fuelled by other grievances and Chalmers's intemperate language, smouldered on for several years, finally going to arbitration on two issues: whether Chalmers had behaved 'handsomely' in his dealings with his publisher, and whether his publisher damaged the sales of *Tron Kirk Sermons* by inadequate trade discounts. Whatever the ultimate judgment, of which all trace is lost (or, like the pages in Chalmers's journal for 1821, destroyed), it is inconceivable from the surviving documentation that it went against Smith on both counts.

The John Smith & Son of the 1820s, of which Smith was now in sole charge, was a wide-ranging business with a circulating library of 20,000 volumes and a 'catalogue of books on sale' of 5000 titles; other services included cataloguing of libraries, bookbinding, and 'foreign orders executed upon the most advantageous terms'. Smith successfully piloted the firm through the recession of 1825, after which he ceased commercial publishing; what publishing he did then was largely for the university. In 1829 the bookshop moved to 54 Virginia Street in Glasgow and the circulating library to 95 Wilson Street. In 1835, when new premises were acquired at 70 St Vincent Street, the circulating library was replaced by the Select Reading Club, from which a membership restricted to 100 could borrow almost any book to order: it was disbanded in 1892.

Smith was appointed secretary of the committee for the relief of the industrious poor in 1826, and was a Glasgow merchant bailie from 1827 to 1834. In 1828 he was a founder member of the exclusive Maitland Club for the production of limited editions of works of historical or literary importance, and served as its secretary from 1832 until his death. Other similar organizations to which he belonged included the Abbotsford Club, English Historical Society, Spalding Club, Percy Society, and Spottiswoode Society.

About 1836 Smith purchased Crutherland House and its estate from an ailing Dr Barr, formerly James Watt's physician, offering 'a sum sufficient to relieve him, and also to provide for the future; but [I] would not allow him to accept the offer for one month after, that in the meantime he might … obtain a larger sum': Smith honoured his commitment in full, even after discovering that the house was in such disrepair that 'I doubt much if I could sell it at what it has cost me to make it residable' (Smith to J. Muirhead, 1846, Glasgow University, 4287/789). In gratitude, Barr presented him with the Partridge portrait of Watt now in the Scottish National Portrait Gallery. Smith was in 1840 made an honorary LLD of Glasgow College, to which he bequeathed over 600 rare books and a unique collection of 104 volumes of tracts relating to Glasgow and the west of Scotland.

Smith died at his home, 120 West Regent Street, Glasgow, at 5 a.m. on 22 January 1849. He never married. After monetary bequests to friends, cousins, and servants, and the establishment of two bursaries at Glasgow College to be administered respectively by the Church of Scotland and the Incorporated Stationers Company of Glasgow, he left £10,000 and the residue of his estate in trust for his delightful niece Mary Brown (1824–1866). Mary, orphaned daughter of Francis Brown (*d.* 1826), planter in Trinidad, and Smith's beloved sister Elizabeth (*d.* 1830), had lived with him from the death of her mother until her marriage in 1842. A man of energy, principle, business acumen, and generosity, who went out of his way to help people (including Chalmers's feckless brother Charles), Smith numbered many literary figures among his close friends.

ANTONY KAMM

Sources J. House and A. Kamm, 'A Glasgow enlightenment: an informal history of John Smith and Son, Glasgow', 1989 [in possession of A. Kamm] • [J. C. Ewing], *A short note on a long history, 1751–1921: John Smith and Son (Glasgow) Ltd* (1921) • W. Hanna, *Memoirs of the life and writings of Thomas Chalmers*, 4 vols. (1849–52) • John Smith & Son, Glasgow, archives • Maitland Club correspondence, 1828–48, U. Glas. L., MS Gen. 294–312 • U. Edin., New Coll. L., Thomas Chalmers collection • U. Glas., Archives and Business Records Centre • John Smith, settlement to trustees, 30 Jan 1849, NA Scot., RD5/825 • bap. reg. Scot. • *Glasgow Herald* (1849)

Likenesses oils, *c.*1810, John Smith & Son, Glasgow • J. G. Gilbert, oils, 1847, repro. in Ewing, *Short note on a long history* • attrib. W. H. Lizars, double portrait, pencil drawing (with James Smith of Deanston), Scot. NPG

Wealth at death £5032 19*s.* 8*d.*: inventory, NA Scot, SC 36/48/5

Smith, John (1792?–1824), missionary, son of a soldier killed in battle in Egypt, was born at Rothwell, near Kettering, Northamptonshire. Apart from Sunday school he had little early education, and he was apprenticed at the age of fourteen to a tradesman in London. Smith was attracted to evangelicalism and underwent a conversion when he was eighteen. He applied to the London Missionary Society to become a missionary and trained under the Revd Samuel Newton in Essex. In October 1816 the London Missionary Society accepted Smith's request to fill a vacant post in Demerara at Le Resouvenir estate. After a spell at the training seminary at Gosport, Smith was ordained at Tonbridge Chapel in London at the end of the year. He had recently married Jane Godden (*d.* 1828), who taught in the Sunday school at the chapel. A few days after his ordination, he and his wife sailed for Demerara.

Smith arrived in Demerara on 23 February 1817. He was warmly received by the slaves at Le Resouvenir but had a difficult first meeting with the governor, Major-General Murray. Murray warned him not to teach the local people to read; otherwise, he would be banished. Smith, however, notwithstanding the undisguised hostility of the white population, laboured among the slaves with considerable success. In August 1823 Smith's health worsened dramatically, and a doctor recommended that he leave the colony. But on 18 August a slave rebellion broke out, and three days later Smith was arrested for refusing to take up arms against the slaves. He was tried by court martial on the charge of having promoted discontent among them. After a trial lasting twenty-seven days, he was found guilty and sentenced to be hanged, though the court recommended mercy. While awaiting the decision of the home government, he was confined in an unhealthy gaol and died there of 'pulmonary consumption' on 6 February 1824, before news that mercy had been granted reached the colony. His wife died in 1828 at Rye, Sussex; they had no children.

News of Smith's imprisonment created a considerable stir in England. The publication of the documents connected with the case by the London Missionary Society intensified the excitement, and more than 200 petitions on his behalf were presented to parliament in eleven days.

On 1 June 1825 his trial was debated in the House of Commons. Lord Brougham brought forward a motion condemning the action of the Demerara government, and asserted that 'in Smith's trial there had been more violation of justice, in form as well as in substance, than in any other inquiry in modern times that could be called a judicial proceeding'. However, the motion was defeated by 193 votes to 146. E. I. CARLYLE, *rev.* GAD HEUMAN

Sources E. V. da Costa, *Crowns of glory, tears of blood: the Demerara slave rebellion of 1823* (1994) • M. Craton, *Testing the chains: resistance to slavery in the British West Indies* (1982) • *GM*, 1st ser., 94/2 (1824), 281 • E. A. Wallbridge, *The Demerara martyr: memoirs of the Rev. John Smith* (1848) • *Missionary Chronicle* (March 1824)
Archives SOAS, London Missionary Society MSS
Likenesses engraving, repro. in D. Chamberlin, *Smith of Demerara* (1923)
Wealth at death very little: da Costa, *Crowns of glory*, 276

Smith, John (1797–1861), singer and composer, was born in Cambridge and educated as a chorister in one of the chapel choirs. In 1815 he entered the choir of Christ Church, Dublin, and on 9 February 1819 was appointed a vicar-choral of St Patrick's Cathedral. On 7 July 1827 the University of Dublin (Trinity College) conferred on him the degree of MusD. He later held the offices of chief composer of the state music, master of the king's band of state musicians in Ireland, and composer to the Chapel Royal, Dublin. He was appointed professor of music at Dublin University in 1845. He is said to have possessed a fine, robust tenor voice, and considerable gifts as a composer of church music. His most important work was considered at the time to be an oratorio, *The Revelation*, and in 1837 he published a volume of cathedral music, consisting of services and anthems, a setting of *Veni creator*, and a Magnificat and Nunc dimittis in B♭, which were well known in English and Irish cathedrals. Of his secular music, the trio *O beata virgine* (*c.*1820) and the quartet *Love Wakes and Weeps* attained considerable popularity. Smith won prizes in the glee clubs of both England and Ireland and also published *A Treatise on the Theory and Practice of Music* (1853). He died in Dublin on 12 November 1861, and was succeeded in his professorship by Robert Stewart.

R. H. NEWMARCH, *rev.* DAVID J. GOLBY

Sources *MT*, 10 (1861–3), 178 • W. H. Husle, 'Smith, John', Grove, *Dict. mus.*

Smith, John (1798–1888), botanist and horticulturist, was born on 5 October 1798 at Aberdour, Fife, the son of Alexander Smith, gardener, and his wife, Mary Pye. A basic schooling at Pittenweem, near Grangemuir, ended prematurely when his father lost an apprentice and saw that as an opening for his son in his place. On completing his apprenticeship, Smith gained experience on a succession of large estates before obtaining a position at the Edinburgh Royal Botanic Garden in 1818 through William McNab, the dynamic principal gardener and friend of Smith's father. McNab encouraged his subordinates to study botany, which led Smith to a particular interest in lower plants. Out of his wage of 9*s.* a week he somehow managed to save enough to buy J. E. Smith's *Compendium florae Britannicae*, as well as a supply of drying-paper. An ardent self-improver, he also obtained tuition in land surveying from a local schoolmaster. In 1820 McNab recommended Smith to his own former employer, W. T. Aiton, for a post in the royal gardens in and around London. After a first brief employment at Kensington, Smith was transferred to Kew, then a mere 9 acres in extent, where he was soon promoted to take charge of the propagation department and hothouses. He married about 1832, but his wife's name is not known.

Smith's burgeoning interest in lower plants now became focused on ferns, at that period the subject of a minor horticultural fashion as various leading gardens competed to master the lately discovered technique of raising them from spore. Kew's fern collection then numbered about eighty species, a total Smith was to raise fivefold over the next twenty years and eventually turn into the richest collection in cultivation anywhere. This uniquely wide acquaintance with living examples led him to propose a new classification of the world's fern genera based on the venation and other vegetative characters (instead of on the shape and position of the reproductive organs, as in all previous schemes). In this he was in advance of everyone else for the next fifty years, though to his misfortune and embarrassment his superior, Sir William Hooker, concurrently espoused a crudely artificial alternative in his massive *Species filicum* (1844–64). Having been elected an associate of the Linnean Society in 1837, a signal honour for a self-educated man, Smith introduced his scheme in a paper read before that body in 1841, which was later published in two botanical journals. He went on to develop it further in a series of authoritative books: *Cultivated Ferns* (1857), *Ferns, British and Foreign* (1866), and *Historia filicum* (1875). He has been justly hailed as one of the great pteridologists of the era.

Though Smith had long been effectively running the gardens at Kew—with a stern and ruthless hand—it was only in 1841, on their transfer to the public service, that his status was officially recognized with his designation as curator, a title he retained until failing eyesight brought about his retirement in 1864. Known familiarly as 'Old Jock' (to distinguish him from his identically named successor), he had long resented being overruled on gardening matters by his directors and following retirement gave vent to his frustration in a history of the Royal Botanic Gardens so candid that it has never been published (but remains in the archives at Kew). With his memory and energy intact to the last he also produced several further books, all in a more popular vein. Smith's wife had died long before his retirement, in 1838, and the only two of their six children to survive childhood also predeceased him. He lived out the rest of his days in lodgings, aided by a part-time secretary. He died suddenly at his home at Park House, Kew, on 12 February 1888 and was buried in the churchyard on Kew Green two days later. His collection of dried specimens of 2000 fern species, purchased by the British Museum in 1866, constitutes his most lasting memorial. D. E. ALLEN

Sources J. Smith, *Gardeners' Chronicle*, new ser., 5 (1876), 363–5 • R. Desmond, 'John Smith, Kew's first curator', *Journal of the Kew*

Guild (1965), 576–87 • R. E. Holttum, 'John Smith of Kew', *British Fern Gazette*, 9 (1967), 330–67 • R. Desmond, *Kew: the history of the Royal Botanic Gardens* (1995) • D. E. Allen, *The Victorian fern craze* (1969), 4–6 • *Proceedings of the Linnean Society of London* (1887–8), 96–8 • *CGPLA Eng. & Wales* (1888)

Archives NHM • RBG Kew, botanical papers, incl. history of Royal Botanic Gardens, Kew • U. St Andr., library, botanical notebooks

Likenesses photograph, RBG Kew; repro. in Desmond, 'John Smith, Kew's first curator'

Wealth at death £384 9*s*. 9*d*.: probate, 14 June 1897, *CGPLA Eng. & Wales*

Smith, John (1825–1910), dental surgeon, was born in Edinburgh on 24 February 1825, the son of John Smith (*d*. 1851), a dentist in Hyndford's Close, Edinburgh. He was educated at the Edinburgh Institution and then studied medicine at the University of Edinburgh, where he graduated MD and LRCS in 1847. After graduating he travelled to Paris, and was there during the 1848 rising. On his father's death in 1851 John took over his dental practice at 12 Dundas Street, Edinburgh; however, he did not entirely forgo his medical interests, since in 1859 he proposed the foundation of what was to become the Royal Edinburgh Hospital for Sick Children. In 1853 he married Elizabeth Marjory, daughter of Dr Peters of Arbroath; they had three sons and two daughters.

In 1856 Smith delivered a comprehensive course of lectures on the teeth at the Edinburgh medical school, the first such lectures to be held in Scotland. He was appointed surgeon dentist to the Royal Public Dispensary in 1857, but resigned two years later to establish an institution devoted to dental treatment, the Edinburgh Dental Dispensary, which opened in 1860. Following his representations the dispensary was recognized as a training centre for the diploma in dental surgery of the Royal College of Surgeons, London, in 1865. The dispensary was incorporated into the Edinburgh Dental Hospital and school in 1879, with Smith, who was regarded as the school's creator, as consulting surgeon dentist. In 1871 he was appointed surgeon dentist in Scotland to Queen Victoria, a post he held until her death in 1901.

An advocate of dental education and the advance of the profession, Smith was a member of the dental reform committee inaugurated in 1876 to promote the regulation and professional education of dentists in Britain. Elected in 1879 to the representative board, which was to be responsible for the foundation of the British Dental Association (BDA), he was subsequently appointed to the first editorial committee of the *Journal* of the BDA, and was BDA president in 1884. As well as numerous articles he published *A Handbook of Dental Anatomy and Surgery* in 1864 (revised 1871).

Smith was elected a fellow of the Royal College of Surgeons of Edinburgh in 1861 and held the office of president in 1883–4. For many years he was a member of the president's committee, and he was an examiner for the triple qualification and the fellowship. He was enrolled as a fellow of the Royal Society of Edinburgh in 1871, and served as president of the Odontochirurgical Society of Scotland in 1881–3. He was awarded an LLD degree by Edinburgh University in 1884.

Smith had an amiable, courteous, and considerate personality, and was gifted in various fields other than dentistry. He wrote numerous songs, many of a medical nature; dramatized *Waverley* by Walter Scott; and wrote three successful pantomimes, which were produced at the Edinburgh Theatre Royal. Smith was a talented painter, and he also enjoyed angling and shooting. He was a Conservative, and a staunch adherent of the Church of Scotland. Smith died in Edinburgh on 15 April 1910; he was survived by his wife. M. A. Clennett, *rev.*

Sources *British Dental Journal*, 31 (1910), 388–93 • *British Journal of Dental Science*, 53 (1910), 430–31 • J. M. Campbell, 'John Smith', *British Dental Journal*, 101 (1956), 33–40 • *WWW* • *CGPLA Eng. & Wales* (1910)

Archives Royal College of Surgeons, Edinburgh, papers

Likenesses J. Paterson, chalk drawing, 1908, Scot. NPG

Wealth at death £1901 16*s*. 10*d*.: confirmation, 26 May 1910, *CCI*

Smith, John [Iain Mac a' Ghobhainn, Iain Phàdraig] (**1848–1880**), poet, was born in Iarsiadar, Uig, on the island of Lewis, the son of Janet (or Joan) MacDonald, a general servant from Bernera. He was recognized as the son of Peter Smith, a sheep farmer; a gift for composing poetry ran in this family. John spent five years at the University of Edinburgh, anticipating a career in medicine, but tuberculosis cut short his university career and brought his life to an early close. About 1874 he returned to Uig, where he died in Crulivig on 27 December 1880.

Most of Smith's surviving poetry seems to have been composed in the last seven years of his life. It has acquired a strong historical relevance because of contemporary events in Uig and the adjoining island of Bernera, from which John's mother came. The Bernera riot took place in 1874, when the island of Lewis was owned by Sir James Matheson and his chamberlain was Donald Munro. In a series of cynical manoeuvres, Munro gradually excluded the people of Uig and Bernera from their grazing and shieling rights on the border between Lewis and Harris, and subsequently also from the vicinity of Iarsiadar, where they had lately built a 7 mile stone dyke to mark off their grazing land from the deer forest. They were given smaller and poorer lands in Bernera at a similar rent and with no compensation. This led to an incursion on Stornoway of some 150 men, led by a piper; when Sir James Matheson was told what Munro had done—apparently without his knowledge or approval—the decision was reversed and Munro was taken to court and dismissed.

Smith's poetry deals powerfully and poignantly with these events, and one poem in particular, 'Spiorad a' Charthannais' ('The spirit of kindliness') can be regarded as the classic condemnation of landlords who inspired or condoned tyranny exercised over small-holders in the highlands. This situation was often associated with the development and protection of sporting estates, and resulted regularly in the clearance of tenants from the land. Practices of this kind had been going on for a hundred years, but the Bernera riot and risings in Skye in the following decade led eventually to the setting up of the

Crofters' Commission, and improved conditions of tenancy for crofters and small-holders. The poetry of Mary Macpherson of Skye is often also cited as an important factor in these developments, but Smith's contribution was earlier and sharper. Of the 'clearers' he says (in translation from his Gaelic original):

> They handed over to the snipe
> the land of happy folk,
> they dealt without humanity
> with people who were kind.
> Because they might not drown them
> they dispersed them overseas;
> a thralldom worse than Babylon's
> was the plight that they were in.

He has the worm reflecting on the banquet it enjoys from the dead landlords and their bailiffs:

> The wriggling worm will praise you then
> for your flesh's enticing taste,
> when it finds you placed before it
> on its table, silent now,
> saying 'This one's juicy flesh
> is good for earthy worms,
> since he made many hundreds thin
> to feed himself for me.'

Smith also composed humorous and satirical verse, a wry commentary on pharisaical Christians, a poem on Bannockburn, and a mock-Ossianic ballad. The survival, and appearance in print, of Smith's surviving work is largely owed to John N. MacLeod, who published a collection of poetry from Lewis in 1916, and gave a detailed introduction, from which the above summary of events is derived. DERICK S. THOMSON

Sources J. N. MacLeod, ed., *Bàrdachd Leòdhais* (1916) • D. S. Thomson, *An introduction to Gaelic poetry*, 2nd edn (1990) • d. cert.
Likenesses photograph, repro. in MacLeod, ed., *Bàrdachd Leòdhais*

Smith, John (1938–1994), politician, was born on 13 September 1938 at Baddarroch, Dalmally, Argyll, the only son and eldest among the three children of Archibald Leitch (Archie) Smith, schoolteacher, and his wife, Sarah Cameron, *née* Scott, commercial artist.

Family, education, and marriage At the time of Smith's birth his father was schoolmaster at Portnahaven, Islay, but two years later he became headmaster of the primary school at Ardrishaig, Argyll, which Smith attended. 'It was always, "Why weren't you top of the class?"', he later recalled. 'In the end, it was easier just to be top of the class' (*The Times*, 13 May 1994). At fourteen he was sent as a boarder to Dunoon grammar school. Four years later he became a student at Glasgow University, where he took an honours degree in history, followed by another in law. Though he had already joined the Dunoon branch of the Argyll constituency Labour Party when he was sixteen, it was in that formative period between 1956 and 1963 that his Labour politics were shaped. He became a scintillating speaker in the university's debating society. In 1962 he and another Glasgow student won the *Observer* mace, awarded annually to the best student debaters in Britain.

After graduation Smith became first a solicitor and then an advocate at the Scottish bar, supplementing his income

John Smith (1938–1994), by Adam Elder

by working as a libel lawyer for the *Daily Record* and the *Sunday Mail*. But his ambition lay much more in the pursuit of a political life. He was always much more than a machine politician. He held strong and fundamental beliefs, being genuinely opposed to social injustice and in favour of greater equality and a greater redistribution of wealth and income. His democratic socialism was very much that of a west of Scotland highlander imbued with a firm commitment to the concept of public service. His faith stemmed in part from his devoutly held Christianity. He was very much a son of the kirk and attended church regularly during the whole of his life. He was never a rebel. A man of the Labour Party's centre-right, and a loyal admirer of Hugh Gaitskell as party leader, he was a natural recruit to the ranks of Scotland's political and legal establishment.

Smith married Elizabeth Margaret (*b.* 1940), the daughter of Frederick William Moncrieff Bennett, an insurance manager in Glasgow, on 5 July 1967, after a five-year courtship. She was herself a graduate of Glasgow University (in French and Russian), and a teacher. They had three daughters, Sarah, Jane, and Catherine, whose privacy Smith protected fiercely as they grew up in their tightly knit family home in the middle-class Edinburgh suburb of Morningside. He never moved the family south to London, but commuted each week to parliament. It was Edinburgh rather than Glasgow that became the centre of his deeply private life. Smith was always a gregarious man with a sense of fun and a wide range of friends, including many from university days. But although he became a national political figure, it was the high-minded ethos of the rural west of Scotland that shaped much of his outlook on life.

Early political career Smith fought his first parliamentary contest while still a student, in 1961, when he was Labour's unsuccessful candidate at the East Fife by-election. He fought the seat again at the general election in 1964, with a similar result. He was finally elected Labour MP for the safe seat of North Lanarkshire at the general election of 1970. He continued to represent the seat (renamed Monklands East in 1983) until his death.

In his first parliament Smith was a loyal opposition back-bencher who devoted much of his time to Scottish affairs. But he carried out one calculated act of rebellion in his first parliament by voting for Britain's entry into the European Economic Community in defiance of his party's three-line whip over the issue. He was not a natural rebel, once describing himself as 'an instinctive party man' (*The Times*, 13 May 1994). But he never regretted what he had done, and unlike many in his party he never wavered on the European question. He was convinced by the merits of the argument that Britain's future lay in EEC membership, and whatever political risks he might incur in expressing that opinion he was determined to stand firm. His single act of defiance failed to cripple his political advance. When a minority Labour government came to office in February 1974, the prime minister, Harold Wilson, showed due recognition of his abilities by offering him the post of solicitor-general for Scotland. Smith displayed further independence of spirit by turning it down. Although eminently well qualified for the job, he was determined to become more than a specialist in Scottish law. Instead he agreed to become unpaid parliamentary private secretary at the Scottish Office under Willie Ross.

It was after Labour's second narrow general election victory in October 1974 that Smith was appointed to his first ministerial position, as a junior minister under Tony Benn at the Department of Energy, with special responsibility for developing a North Sea oil policy. The two men may have seemed an unlikely couple to work harmoniously together at a time when Benn was at the height of his radical powers. But the older man came to appreciate his younger colleague's abilities, despite his different brand of Labour politics. Smith went on to display his formidable parliamentary skills with a close attention to detail in carrying the complex legislation to establish the British National Oil Corporation through marathon sessions in a House of Commons where the government lacked an overall majority.

Smith was rewarded for his patient efforts in the government reshuffle that followed Jim Callaghan's election to succeed Wilson as leader of the Labour Party and prime minister in March 1976. He was promoted to serve under Michael Foot, the new leader of the House of Commons, with the specific task of implementing the controversial proposal to devolve power to elected assemblies for Scotland and Wales. It turned out to be an exhausting and ultimately frustrating assignment, which ended in failure in spring 1979. Although the devolution measure reached the statute book, not enough Scots voted to approve the creation of an assembly in the resulting referendum, while devolution was rejected by the Welsh electorate. Despite the set-back, however, Smith's handling of the issue won him widespread admiration across all wings of the Parliamentary Labour Party. In April 1978 he was made a privy councillor in recognition of his efforts. His Commons performance was also recognized when the prime minister promoted him in November 1979 to become president of the Board of Trade, with a seat in the cabinet. Two months younger than the foreign secretary, David Owen, he was then the youngest cabinet minister. Nevertheless he served only six months in that position before Labour's defeat in the general election of May 1979.

Labour in opposition For a man who had only just begun to relish the work of being a cabinet minister, the next fifteen years in opposition were frustrating and barren. Smith's enforced absence from government was partly compensated for by a return to a career at the Scottish bar during parliamentary recesses. But he looked on with increasing dismay at the Labour Party's descent into political fratricide during the early 1980s. While he supported Denis Healey's failed bid for the party leadership in November 1980 and his successful campaign to remain Michael Foot's deputy against Benn's challenge in the following year, Smith often seemed to play only a nominal role in the centre-right's rearguard efforts to contain and eventually turn back what often seemed like an irresistible left-wing tide. The state of the Labour Party led many of his close colleagues to despair but there was never much likelihood that Smith would defect from its ranks to join the newly formed Social Democratic Party in 1981 despite his clear distaste for the left. Smith used to say it was Labour that he loved and served and identified with. If Labour had fallen into terminal decline he would simply have abandoned politics altogether. He was very much a loyalist by instinct and a pragmatist by inclination: he was a practical politician who wanted to be part of a Labour government in order to get things done.

Nobody could have doubted where Smith stood during those years—on the centre-right wing of the Labour Party. However, while he played his part in its struggles he did not seek to do so in a highly public or aggressive manner. Indeed, his power base was almost entirely confined to the Parliamentary Labour Party at a time when the trade unions and constituency associations were becoming increasingly important in the party's structure of authority. It was among Labour MPs that his forensic, witty rhetorical skills were widely appreciated. He stood only once for election to Labour's ruling national executive committee, and on that occasion (in 1981) he received only a derisory vote from the constituency parties. And, despite his sensitivity towards the views of the trade unions, he did not go out of his way to court their influence. Moreover, he often seemed strangely out of touch and at a distance from the tangled local politics of his Monklands constituency party, with its unseemly sectarian and factional rivalries.

However, during the 1980s Smith became perhaps the only senior Labour figure whom Conservative government ministers really came to fear and respect at the dispatch box. In those barren years of opposition he was moved from one policy portfolio to another—trade, prices, and consumer protection (1979–82), energy (1982–3), employment (1983–4), and trade and industry (1984–7). In those jobs he helped to move party policy more towards the centre without abandoning his core beliefs. But his calm, rational, and logically argued contributions often seemed at odds with much of what Labour at that time seemed to stand for. He was opposed to unilateral nuclear disarmament for Britain and any moves to take the country out of the European Economic Community, but he saw no reason to force such issues into a public prominence that would have seriously divided his party.

In June 1987, after Labour's third successive general election defeat, Smith became shadow chancellor of the exchequer, a position which he held until his election as party leader just over five years later. In that position he sought to reassure the City of London and the business community that Labour could be trusted in government to pursue sound economic policies, while not abandoning his party's commitment to progressive policies such as full employment and higher government spending. He believed in principle in a greater redistribution of income and wealth, and above all in the role of an active state in the strategic management of the economy. He was unrepentant in his conviction that in order to spend what was needed to improve the quality of schools and hospitals, governments needed to raise taxes to fund such improvements. He argued that such priorities as education, regional development, skills training, the National Health Service, and overseas aid to assist the world's poor, all required a firm financial commitment from the Treasury. But he also recognized that there could be no return to the economic policies of the 1970s. He sought to reassure the wider business community that as a Labour chancellor he would not be hostile to the operations of the market economy. During his so-called 'prawn cocktail circuit' among brokers and entrepreneurs he emphasized his belief that private investment and action to improve productivity performance should be at the heart of any successful supply-side strategy to revive the economy.

Smith's efforts to convince the markets that Labour could be trusted were balanced by his sense of the need for a stronger moral commitment in public life. This was often on display not only in his calls for a restoration of the public-service ethic but also in his often scathing criticisms of what he regarded as the decline in standards of those in public life, especially in their relations with the private sector. However, his modest plans to raise taxes, made public in the general election campaign of 1992, were said to have cost Labour many seats. His firm support for Britain's membership of the European exchange-rate mechanism was also criticized, especially when the Conservative government of John Major was forced to abandon its constraints. But there were few reservations about him on display to prevent his landslide election to the Labour Party leadership in July 1992 after Neil Kinnock's resignation. Smith received 90.9 per cent of the votes in the complicated electoral college, with only 9.1 per cent going to his rival, Bryan Gould. He won overwhelmingly among Labour MPs, trade unions, and constituency associations.

Party leader Smith was party leader for only twenty-two months. It was insufficient time for him to make any substantial contribution to Labour's development. But his rather cautious and methodical approach gave rise to some criticisms. Party modernizers feared he was being too complacent in his belief that all it would take to win power at the next general election was 'one more heave'. He seemed determined to lead in an inclusive way, by reaching out to support from his party's left wing. He did not appear to believe that Labour needed radical internal reforms in order to recapture the support of middle-class voters in southern England. However, he was prepared to fight hard for a change in party rules to introduce the principle of one member, one vote for the selection of Labour parliamentary candidates. In his determination to end the use of the trade-union block vote in the process he courted defeat at the party conference of 1993. Privately he warned that this was a resigning issue, but it still required a resort to union arm-twisting to deliver him a narrow victory. On policy issues, he moved slowly. But the increasing unpopularity of John Major's government brought a huge growth in popular support for the Labour Party. By spring 1994 Smith was being talked about widely as the next prime minister. It was starting to look as though public opinion was moving inexorably towards Labour after fifteen years in the wilderness.

The expectation of victory made Smith's sudden death all the more poignant. He had experienced a massive heart attack in October 1988 but he seemed to have made a full recovery through an austere regime of strenuous mountain walking and a draconian calorie-controlled diet. However, on the morning of 12 May 1994 he suffered a second and this time fatal attack, and he was confirmed dead on arrival at St Bartholomew's Hospital, Smithfield. A memorial service was held at Cluny parish church, Edinburgh, on 20 May, and he was buried on Iona the following day. He was survived by his wife, Elizabeth (who in 1995 was made Baroness Smith of Gilmorehill), and their three daughters.

Assessment The night before his death Smith had spoken to a European gala dinner in London where he talked of 'a great hunger among our people for a return to the politics of conviction and idealism'. 'I believe everything is moving our way', he told his audience in that last speech. 'I believe the signs are set fairer for the Labour party than they have been for a very long time' (*The Times*, 12 May 1994).

Smith's Labour Party critics believed that as leader he was too cautious, too conservative, and too complacent, convincing himself that the Labour Party was bound to win the next general election comfortably without any need for a fundamental modernization of its policies and structure. But there were others who argued that his steadying and inclusive style of leadership would have ensured a relatively trouble-free path to the premiership whenever a general election was called. Rightly or wrongly, many came to see Smith as old Labour's last leader, an often eloquent champion of enduring values of equity and social justice that were no longer seen as very relevant to achieving electoral success. His ambiguous political legacy thus became the object of often sharp dispute. His name was often evoked by party modernizers as a warning to Labour of the perils of political timidity, while to others it denoted both moral integrity and intelligence, the triumph of substance over style. Perhaps far more in death than in life, Smith turned out to be inadvertently the touchstone of what centre-left politics were to stand for in what was often seen as a new age.

ROBERT TAYLOR

Sources A. McSmith, *John Smith, a life, 1938–1994* (1994) · G. Brown and J. Naughtie, *John Smith: life and soul of the party* (1994) · *Guiding light: the collected speeches of John Smith*, ed. B. Brivati (2000) · C. Bryant, ed., *John Smith: an appreciation* (1994) · *The Times* (13 May 1994) · *Daily Telegraph* (13 May 1994) · *The Guardian* (13 May 1994) · *The Independent* (13 May 1994) · *The Scotsman* (13 May 1994) · *The Herald* (13 May 1994) · *WWW* · personal knowledge (2004) · private information (2004) · b. cert. · m. cert. · d. cert.
Archives FILM BFI NFTVA, documentary footage
Likenesses photographs, 1976–92, Hult. Arch. · A. Elder, photograph, Scot. NPG [*see illus.*] · Harry Horse [R. Horne], pen-and-ink drawing, Scot. NPG · E. Paolozzi, bronze sculpture, Scot. NPG · photograph, repro. in *The Times* · photograph, repro. in *Daily Telegraph* · photograph, repro. in *The Guardian* · photograph, repro. in *The Independent* · photograph, repro. in *The Scotsman* · photograph, repro. in *The Herald*
Wealth at death £399,633.39: probate, 1995, *CGPLA Eng. & Wales*

Smith, John Abel (1802–1871), financier and politician, was born at Dale Park, Sussex, on 2 June 1802, the elder son of John Smith (1767–1842) MP, of London and Dale Park, and his wife, Mary, the daughter of Lieutenant-Colonel Tucker. He was educated at Eton College and Christ's College, Cambridge (1819–24). His paternal grandfather, Abel Smith of Nottingham (1717–1788), founded Smith, Payne, and Smiths, an important London bank whose partners were to include John Abel Smith's father John, his uncle Robert, first Baron Carrington, his brother Martin Tucker (1803–1880), and his cousin Abel (1788–1859). John Abel Smith is sometimes confused with his cousin Abel Smith, for many years senior partner in the family bank. In actuality, Smith gave up his own partnership there in 1845, after hardly ten years in the firm, principally because the other partners appeared uncomfortable with the wide range of his outside commercial interests.

In 1834 Smith and his cousin Oswald Smith joined Hollingworth Magniac (retired from trade in China) to form the new London merchant house Magniac, Smith & Co. This firm acted as London correspondents for the new Canton (Guangzhou) (later Hong Kong) concern of Jardine, Matheson & Co. (successors to Magniac & Co.) and helped that later great firm survive several major credit crises in the 1830s. When William Jardine returned from China, the London house was reorganized as Magniac, Jardine & Co., but Smith and another cousin, Thomas Charles Smith, remained partners through 1847.

Smith was to develop interests in many other parts of the world, both speculative and philanthropic. He was a friend and patron of Edward Gibbon Wakefield and served as a founder director of Wakefield's New Zealand Land Company (1839) as well as the Church Society for New Zealand (1840). Wakefield, who had accompanied Lord Durham to Canada, was also excited by possibilities for settlement and development in the St Lawrence valley and encouraged several of his affluent friends to buy control of the dormant North American Colonial Association of Ireland, of which Smith became a director. In 1839 this organization purchased the seigneury of Beauharnais, south-west of Montreal (originally 324 square miles), from Edward Ellice the elder, MP, who had inherited it from his father, a land speculator. Unable to make the necessary payments, the association returned the property to Ellice, who in 1842 transferred it for sale to three trustees, including his brother Russell Ellice and Smith.

That same year Smith acquired from the landowner and developer Sir Peter Hesketh-Fleetwood a substantial part of the new town of Fleetwood, Lancashire, which he sought to make into a busy port and trans-shipment centre on a combined rail–sea route to Scotland. In this interest, he also invested in coastal steamships and purchased land on the opposite shore of Morecambe Bay, but the opening of the inland Lancaster and Carlisle Railway in 1846–7 reduced the attractiveness of the Fleetwood route. It is likely that Smith lost money on many of these speculative investments. By the 1860s he appears to have withdrawn from most business except a directorship (held from at least 1847) in the Edinburgh Life Assurance Company. (In the 1840s he had briefly also been a director of the University Life Assurance Society, an organization insuring the lives only of former students at Oxford and Cambridge).

In 1830 Smith began an extensive career in the House of Commons, representing first Midhurst (1830–31) and then Chichester (1831–59, 1863–8). A strong supporter of the Reform Act of 1832, his position was generally that of an orthodox whig libertarian, although his parliamentary activity sometimes also reflected his private interests. In the 1830s and 1840s he frequently asked questions or approached ministers directly on matters relating to China, India, and New Zealand. He introduced his partner William Jardine to the foreign secretary, Lord Palmerston, who later acknowledged the extreme value of the information received from Smith and Jardine in planning the Chinese expedition of 1840–41. In later years his activity in the Commons appears to have been more paternalistic, with a marked interest manifest in both savings banks and temperance.

Smith was a close political ally of Lord John Russell, member for the City from 1847, and acted in the 1850s as his informal political manager in the constituency. He kept Russell informed of opinion in the City and on occasion even acted as an intermediary between Russell and Palmerston. The public issue with which he was most conspicuously associated in these years was the admission of Jews to parliament. Smiths bank had long associations with the Rothschilds and in 1847 Smith was head of the City committee that promoted the election of Baron Lionel Nathan de Rothschild to parliament from London. He introduced Rothschild to the Commons, but was unable to obtain an alteration in the required oath that would permit a Jew so elected to take his seat. Much the same happened at the election of 1852, although Smith had organized a petitioning campaign on Rothschild's behalf and spoke strongly for him in the house. Five times bills on Jewish eligibility introduced by Lord John Russell were passed by the Commons but rejected by the Lords. When in 1858 the law was finally changed and the oath amended, Rothschild was triumphantly escorted into the house by Smith and Russell, his two most conspicuous advocates.

On 26 December 1827 Smith married Anne (*d.* 1858), the daughter of Sir Samuel Clarke-Jervoise bt, and the widow of Ralph William Grey. They had three sons: Jervoise (1828–1884), Dudley Robert (1830–1897), and Hugh Colin (1836–1910). The first two became partners in Smith banks in London and Hull, while the third, a partner in Hay's Wharf, became a director of the Bank of England from 1876 and governor in 1897–9. Smith died at Kippington, near Sevenoaks, Kent, on 7 January 1871. At his death he had houses there and in Chester Square, London. Earlier he had what would seem to have been grander residences in Belgrave Square and Dale Park, Sussex.

Smith's overseas interests often appear to have been more enthusiastic than commercially rational. (In his later years he was warmly interested in the activities of Raja James Brooke of Sarawak.) His entire business career cannot be considered very successful, for he left a personal estate of less than £40,000, hardly a tenth as much as the personalty left by his brother Martin Tucker and his cousin Abel Smith. JACOB M. PRICE

Sources J. A. S. L. Leighton-Boyce, *Smiths, the bankers, 1658–1958* (1958) • M. Greenberg, *British trade and the opening of China, 1800–42* (1951) • *LondG* (1848) • P. Bloomfield, *Edward Gibbon Wakefield: builder of the British Commonwealth* (1961) • *The London journal of Edward Jerningham Wakefield*, ed. J. Stevens (1972) • M. Keswick, ed., *The thistle and the jade: a celebration of 150 years of Jardine, Matheson & Co.* (1982) • J. K. Fairbank, *Trade and diplomacy on the China coast: the opening of the treaty ports, 1842–1854*, 2 vols. (1953) • R. B. Mosse, *The parliamentary guide* (1838) • H. T. Easton, *The history of a banking house (Smith, Payne and Smiths)* (1903) • Boase, *Mod. Eng. biog.* • Burke, *Gen. GB*

Archives W. Sussex RO, corresp. and papers; letter-books relating to Chichester elections and political affairs | BL, letters to Sir A. H. Layard, Add. MSS 39102–39107 • LPL, corresp. with Lady Burdett-Coutts • PRO, corresp. with Lord John Russell, PRO 30/22 • U. Southampton L., corresp. with Lord Palmerston

Likenesses H. Barraud, group portrait (with Lord John Russell introducing Baron L. N. de Rothschild to the House of Commons in 1858) • F. R. Say, portrait, repro. in Easton, *History of a banking house*

Wealth at death under £40,000: probate, 6 March 1871, *CGPLA Eng. & Wales*

Smith, John Alexander (1863–1939), philosopher and classical scholar, was born at Dingwall, Ross-shire, on 21 April 1863, the second son of Andrew Smith, of Dingwall, solicitor and county clerk of Ross, and his wife, Jane Eliza Fraser. He was educated at Inverness Academy, at the collegiate school, Edinburgh, at Edinburgh University (where he was Ferguson classical scholar in 1884), and at Balliol College, Oxford, to which he was admitted as Warner exhibitioner and honorary scholar in Hilary term 1884. He obtained a first class in classical moderations (1885) and in *literae humaniores* (1887). After acting for some years as assistant to S. H. Butcher, professor of Greek in Edinburgh University, he was elected a fellow of Balliol in 1891, and appointed Jowett lecturer in philosophy in 1896. In 1910 he was elected Waynflete professor of moral and metaphysical philosophy at Oxford, and became thereby a fellow of Magdalen College. He was elected to an honorary fellowship at Balliol in 1924.

At Balliol, Smith served under three distinguished masters—Benjamin Jowett, Edward Caird, and J. L. Strachan-Davidson—and was one of a very able company of fellows. These included R. L. Nettleship, Evelyn Abbott, W. R. Hardie, A. A. Macdonell, H. W. C. Davis, and A. L. Smith. Of all that band he was perhaps the most variously accomplished. He taught philosophy, and many Balliol men could bear witness to the width and exactness of his knowledge of the subject and the stimulating quality of his teaching. He was a fine Aristotelian scholar, and in 1908 succeeded Ingram Bywater as president of the Oxford Aristotelian Society. He worked for many years at an edition of the *De anima*, and translated this work for the Oxford translation of *The Works of Aristotle* (vol. 3, 1931); he was joint editor of the volumes published between 1908 and 1912. He lectured regularly on the *Ethics*, and in order to get to the bottom of Aristotle's theory of justice studied deeply in Greek law: the first volume (1920) of the *Historical Jurisprudence* of Sir Paul Vinogradoff owed much to Smith's learning and ingenuity. He made extensive preparations for an edition of the *Poetics*, which appealed to his literary as well as to his philosophical interest.

Smith's Aristotelian scholarship is the more significant part of his contribution to philosophy. He did not satisfactorily develop a distinctive philosophical position of his own. In his general philosophical views he maintained on the whole the idealist tradition established by T. H. Green and Caird, but while much influenced by Hegel he was always a critical disciple. He came very much under the influence of Benedetto Croce and succeeded in generating a short-lived fashion for Croce in Oxford in the years immediately following the First World War. The diversity of interests which made him a fascinating companion militated against the continuous effort needed for working out a consistent system of thought, and his self-critical temper prevented him from writing much for publication. His more notable published works include *Knowing and Acting*, his 1910 inaugural lecture; 'Philosophy and progress as an ideal of action', in *Progress and History* (ed. F. S. Marvin, 1920); *The Nature of Art* (1924); and 'Philosophy as the development of the notion and reality of self-consciousness', his contribution to *Contemporary British Philosophy*, edited by J. H. Muirhead (1925). In 1930 he presided over the seventh International Congress of Philosophy, held at Oxford. He left behind him a very large number of valuable unpublished papers; a selection of those on Greek philosophy was deposited in Balliol Library, and a selection of those on other subjects in Magdalen Library.

The best account of Smith's later position in philosophy is to be found in his contribution to *Contemporary British Philosophy*. After giving an account of his earlier views and interests he describes himself as having received his greatest illumination from Croce and Giovanni Gentile, and states a creed, or rather a set of 'suppositions', of which the chief are that the real is essentially in change, and is an event which occupies the whole of time; that history is throughout spiritual, and yet contains a distinction (of degree rather than of kind) between the mental and the non-mental; that reality manifests itself most fully in self-consciousness; that self-consciousness is not a fact but a process, a process of self-making; and that in making itself it reveals its own meaning.

Smith was not only a philosopher; he was an admirable classical scholar. A conspicuous instance of this is supplied by the testimony of an eminent scholar to the effect that he had often 'discovered unerringly what Pindar meant, where every one else was unconvincing'. He was deeply versed in philology (and, as became a highlander, not least in Celtic philology), and acquired with extraordinary facility at least a reading knowledge of many languages. He had a very acute feeling for the precise meaning, and the development of the meaning, of words. Many years later Harold Macmillan recalled his comment at the outset of his lectures: that undergraduates would hear nothing of practical value to their careers 'save only this, that if you work hard and intelligently you should be able to detect when a man is talking rot, and that in my view is the main if not the sole purpose of education' ('Oxford before the deluge', tape-recorded seminar, Oxford University Archives, 1973).

Smith's ingenuity in conjecture was very great, but a growing love of paradox sometimes led him to views which a calmer judgement would have rejected. He was an admirable talker and raconteur, and skilful at card tricks and other forms of legerdemain; he was never happier than when he was entertaining children. Smith retired from his chair in 1936, and died, unmarried, at Oxford on 19 December 1939.

DAVID ROSS, *rev.* C. A. CREFFIELD

Sources *The Times* (20 Dec 1939) • *Oxford Magazine* (18 Jan 1940) • personal knowledge (1949) • R. Metz, *A hundred years of British philosophy*, ed. J. H. Muirhead, trans. J. W. Harvey (1938), 319–21 [Ger. orig., *Die philophischen Strömungen der Gegenwart in Grossbritannien* (1935)] • S. Muller, 'Smith, John Alexander', *Biographical dictionary of twentieth-century philosophers*, ed. S. Brown and others (1996), 731 • *CGPLA Eng. & Wales* (1940)

Archives Balliol Oxf., MSS • Magd. Oxf., corresp. and MSS | Bodl. Oxf., corresp. with G. Murray; corresp. with J. Myres

Likenesses G. Spencer, pencil sketch, 1936; at Balliol Oxf. in 1949

Wealth at death £9529 13*s*. 5*d*.: resworn probate, 28 March 1940, *CGPLA Eng. & Wales*

Smith, John Benjamin (1794–1879), promoter of free trade, was born in Manchester, the eldest son of Benjamin Smith, a cotton merchant there. A brother, Thomas Smith (*d*. 1864), settled at Colebrooke Park, Kent. Smith married Jemina, daughter of William Durning of Liverpool, who predeceased him. They had two daughters.

Smith inherited his father's business and made enough of a fortune during Manchester's halcyon days of the 1820s and 1830s to be able to retire from business in his early forties. He thereafter devoted his energies full-time to politics, initially in the local institutions of Manchester and Salford. A prominent supporter of Joseph Brotherton's candidacy for the Salford parliamentary seat in 1832, Smith, who was an overseer of the poor, introduced the issue of corn law repeal into an election for the Salford select vestry in 1834. President of the Manchester chamber of commerce from 1839 to 1841, he was prominent in bringing the chamber round to a policy of supporting free trade. He became the first president and was later treasurer of the Anti-Corn Law League, founded in March 1839. He was a leader writer for the *League* newspaper which was founded in 1843. A dedicated student of political economy, he earned the sobriquet of 'Corn Law' Smith.

Smith is credited with being one of those who convinced Richard Cobden to join the league, and did much of Cobden's statistical work leading to repeal in 1846. Smith unsuccessfully contested Blackburn in 1837, and Walsall and Dundee in 1841 as a free-trader. He never achieved the national eminence of his friends and league colleagues, Cobden and John Bright. But in 1847 he was returned for Stirling District, a seat he held until 1852, when he was elected MP for Stockport. He retired from parliament in January 1874.

Politically, Smith was naïve in the sense that he always thought that having logic and figures on one's side would be enough to prevail legislatively. His parliamentary activities reflected his commitment to the typical radical nostrums of 'peace, retrenchment, and reform'. He voted for the repeal of the Navigation Acts in 1847, and took a special interest in commercial, fiscal, and currency questions, supporting reductions in the military establishment and imperial self-defence. He was a signatory in 1861 to the memorial of radical MPs in favour of economy in government expenditure. He was also an energetic promoter of decimal currency to reduce obstacles to international trade, serving as a member of the royal commission on international coinage in 1868. A Unitarian himself, he took the dissenting point of view on ecclesiastical matters, opposing church rates and 'all State grants for religious purposes'. He consistently voted for the ballot, and, late in his career, expanded his interests to include the empire and India. He was on the council of the Social Science Association.

Smith was important during the period when the whig party was evolving into the Liberal Party, and lived to see many of his views prevail. He opposed Lord Palmerston, voting against him on Don Pacifico in 1850, and on the Chinese war in 1857. Unlike many of his political friends, he survived Palmerston's electoral landslide in 1857, but voted for the Liberal compromise of 1859 that again made Palmerston prime minister. In the end a Gladstonian Liberal, Smith died at his long-time home, King's Ride, Ascot, Berkshire, on 15 September 1879.

DAVID F. KREIN

Sources *Parliamentary Pocket Companion* (1850); (1857–8); (1873) • Boase, *Mod. Eng. biog.* • *WWBMP* • N. McCord, *The Anti-Corn Law League, 1838–46*, 2nd edn (1968) • *The Times* (17 Sept 1879) • I. G. C. Hutchinson, *A political history of Scotland: parties, elections and issues* (1966) • *Hansard 3* (1847–74) • *House of Commons division lists, 1836–1910*, House of Commons (1982) • G. R. Searle, *Entrepreneurial politics in mid-Victorian Britain* (1993) • D. Fraser, *Urban politics in Victorian England* (1976) • *CGPLA Eng. & Wales* (1879)

Archives Man. CL, Manchester Archives and Local Studies, political papers and corresp. | BL, letters to John Bright, Add. MS 43388

Wealth at death under £350,000: probate, 6 Oct 1879, *CGPLA Eng. & Wales*

Smith, John Chaloner (1827–1895), civil engineer and writer on art, was born in Dublin on 19 August 1827. His father was a proctor of the ecclesiastical courts, and married a granddaughter of Travers Hartley, MP for Dublin in the Irish parliament. Smith was admitted to Trinity College, Dublin, in 1846, and in 1849 graduated BA. He was articled to George Willoughby Hemans, engineer, and in 1857 was appointed engineer to the Waterford and Limerick Railway. In 1868 he obtained a similar position with the Dublin, Wicklow and Wexford Railway, which he held until 1894. He carried out some important extensions of the line, and was mainly responsible for the loop-line crossing the Liffey, connecting the Great Northern and South-Eastern railways of Ireland. Beyond his reputation as an engineer John Chaloner Smith is chiefly remembered for his *British Mezzotinto Portraits … with Biographical Notes* (4 pts, 1878–84), which consists of a full catalogue of plates executed before 1820, with 125 autotypes from plates in Smith's possession. The latter were also issued separately. The print room at the British Museum contains an interleaved copy with manuscript notes by museum staff. Smith was an enthusiastic collector of engravings, especially first-state impressions, and principally mezzotints; his collector's stamp bears the inscription *MEA SPES EST IN DEO* ('My hope is in God'). However, this does not appear on those of his mezzotints now in the British Museum's collection. A large part of his collection of mezzotints was sold by Sothebys in two parts (1887 and 1888) after the completion of his book. The British Museum bought 106 mezzotints in the Sothebys sale of 21–30 March 1887, and a further fifty-five mezzotints in the Sothebys sale of 25 April – 4 May 1888. The second Baron Cheylesmore also bought from these sales and later bequeathed his collection to the British Museum. The Cheylesmore collection, accessioned in 1902, consists of over 5000 engravings, mainly mezzotints. Some of the best of the examples in the sales at Sothebys (especially those by Irish engravers) were purchased for the Dublin National Gallery through the generosity of Sir Edward Guinness (later Lord Iveagh). Over 200 portrait mezzotints were bought in 1887 and a further 100 in 1888.

For many years Smith took a deep interest in the question of the financial relations between England and Ireland. He published two or three pamphlets on the subject, and in December 1894 he gave evidence to the royal commission appointed to consider the question. He died at Bray, co. Wicklow, on 13 March 1895.

D. J. O'Donoghue, *rev.* Lucy Dixon

Sources A. Griffiths, ed., *Landmarks in print collecting: connoisseurs and donors at the British Museum since 1753* (British Museum Press, 1996) [exhibition catalogue, Museum of Fine Arts, Houston, TX, 1996, and elsewhere] • J. C. Smith, *British mezzotinto portraits*, 4 vols. in 5 (1878–84) • print room register of purchases and acquisitions, 7 June 1886–18 March 1889, BM, department of prints and drawings, vol. 41 • *The collection of mezzotinto engravings formed by John Chaloner Smith* (1887) [sale catalogue, Sothebys, London, 21–30 March 1887] • *The second and concluding portion of the mezzotinto engravings formed by John Chaloner Smith* (1888) [sale catalogue, Sothebys, London, 25 April–4 May 1888] • *The remaining portion of the celebrated collection of engraving by John Chaloner Smith* (1896) [sale catalogue, Christies, 3–6 Feb 1896] • F. Lugt, *Les marques de collections de dessins et d'estampes* (Amsterdam, 1921) • A. Le Harivel, ed., *Illustrated catalogue of prints and sculpture: National Gallery of Ireland, Dublin* (1988) • D. Alexander, 'Dublin print catalogue', *Print Quarterly*, 6 (1989), 431–3 • A. Whitman, *Print collectors' handbook* (1901) • C. Wax, *The mezzotint: history and technique* (1990)

Smith, John Christopher [*formerly* Johann Christoph Schmidt] (**1712–1795**), composer and music copyist, was born in Ansbach, Germany, in 1712, the son of the German music copyist **Johann Christoph Schmidt** (1683–1762/3), later known as John Christopher Smith the elder, and his wife, whose name is unknown but who was apparently wealthy. Both composers are chiefly remembered for their connections with Handel.

Johann Christoph Schmidt was born in Ansbach on 17 March 1683. He attended the University of Halle at the same time as Handel (who entered in 1702), and afterwards became a wool merchant in Ansbach. Handel persuaded him to leave this trade and go to London in 1716. His wife and four children, one of whom was also named Johann Christoph, followed him in 1720; father and son appear to have adopted the Anglicized forms of their names in that year. The elder Smith lived successively in Dean Street (from 1716), Meard's Court (from about 1723 until 1750), and lastly King's Square Court (from 1755). He was Handel's music copyist from 1718, and his treasurer from 1720. The two men worked closely until the mid-1750s, when William Coxe's *Anecdotes of George Frederick Handel, and John Christopher Smith* reported a rift between them: 'they quarrell'd there [Tunbridge Wells] and Smith senior left Handel in an abrupt manner which so enraged him, that he declared he would never see him again' (Coxe, *Anecdotes*, 48). This must have taken place after 6 August 1756, when Handel added a codicil to his will increasing the sum left to Smith senior from £500 to £2000. They were reconciled by Smith the younger three weeks before Handel's death on 14 April 1759, but his will, changed in the aftermath of the quarrel, left the father's legacy—'my large Harpsichord, my little House Organ, my Musick Books' (Highfill, Burnim & Langhans, *BDA*) plus the £2000 of the codicil—to the son. After Handel's death, Smith continued to copy music for his son's performances, as well as acting as treasurer for the Foundling Hospital performance of *Messiah* on 3 May 1759. He died between 16 December 1762, the date of his will, and 10 January 1763, when the will was proved, and he was buried on 12 January 1763.

The younger Smith, on his arrival in London, enrolled at Clare's Academy, Soho Square, and appears to have had some lessons with Handel about 1725. He also studied under Thomas Roseingrave (with whom he lodged in Wigmore Street) and John Christopher Pepusch. He began on his own as a music teacher in 1730, at the age of eighteen, but that year contracted tuberculosis, through which he was nursed by John Arbuthnot, one of the authors of the libretto of Handel's *Acis and Galatea*. Through Arbuthnot, he met many literary figures including Alexander Pope and Jonathan Swift. In 1736 he married Frances, daughter of Edward Pakenham of Pakenham Hall, Westmeath, and Margaret, *née* Bradestan, and sister of Thomas Pakenham, later first Baron Longford, but their children John Christopher and Frances did not survive infancy, and his wife fell victim to tuberculosis in 1742. During the mid-1740s Smith was abroad in charge of an ailing pupil, Peter Walter, who had offered him an annuity of £300 if he would accompany him and his sister to the south of France. About this time he also met Robert Price and Benjamin Stillingfleet, who later provided him with librettos, and who, according to Burney, gave him 'a taste for, and procured him admission into, good company; so that he formed his character on models of a higher class than that of a mere musician' (Small, 23.573).

On his return from the continent in 1751, Smith resumed his connection with Handel when the older composer required assistance to offset his oncoming blindness, though Smith's role went beyond that of an amanuensis. He also became music master to Augusta, dowager princess of Wales, for an annual salary of £200, a sum that George III continued to pay after the princess's death in 1772. With Handel's recommendation, in 1754 he became organist of the Foundling Hospital, a post he held until 1770. In the 1750s he was introduced to David Garrick, and through him was involved in one of many feeble attempts to establish all-sung English opera. After Handel's death in 1759 he composed only oratorios, but the popularity of his oratorio season faded, and in 1769 he was reported as planning to retire to Bath; he purchased a house there, in Upper Church Street, in 1774. Smith had married Martha Coxe, widow of William Coxe and daughter of Paul D'Aranda, after her husband's death in 1760; he thus became stepfather to William *Coxe (1748–1828) and Peter *Coxe (1753?–1844). On the death of his father in 1762 or 1763, Smith had inherited from him an important cache of Handel's manuscripts; they provided Smith and his partner John Stanley with an enormous resource for their oratorio seasons, and these in turn he presented to George III. Following his wife's death in 1785, he moved to the residence of his stepdaughter Emilia Coxe in London, and he died there on 3 October 1795. His will, proved on 13 November 1795, provided for his wife's children from her first marriage; he also left the Denner portrait of Handel, inherited with the manuscripts from his father, to William Coxe.

When Smith the younger arrived in London in 1720, he was accompanied by his two sisters Charlotte and Judith, and by his brother Frederick. In 1733 Charlotte married the flautist and oboist William Teede, who is recorded playing in many London Handel performances during the eighteenth century, and took over John Christopher Smith the elder's copying business on his death in 1762 or 1763. Judith also married a Handel flautist and oboist, one John Rector, about whom little is known. Frederick is thought to have been the Frederick Smith who was the trumpeter and kettledrummer who joined the king's music on 7 May 1740. Like Teede, he was one of the original subscribers to the Royal Society of Musicians, and is recorded playing in eighteenth-century Handel performances.

Smith's music is attractive, but undemanding. His earliest London opera, *Teraminta* (1732), was part of the project to provide a repertory of all-sung operas with English words, associated with the elder Thomas Arne. The one surviving air suggests a light, Italianate style, which can also be found in his next opera, *Ulysses* (1733), an uneven work with many da capo arias. His Metastasian operas remained unperformed—all are either unfinished or survive incomplete—and are difficult to judge, but in his later pieces such as *The Fairies* (1755) and *The Tempest* (1756) there is evidence that he was trying to employ a style suitable to public taste, by shortening arias and including such features as the hornpipe and the fashionable Scotch snap. However, Smith's later oratorios were in a Handelian style that a public largely interested in new music would accept only from Handel himself. Manuscripts of his larger works survive in the Staats- und Universitätsbibliothek, Hamburg.

MICHAEL BURDEN

Sources [W. Coxe], *Anecdotes of George Frederick Handel, and John Christopher Smith: with select pieces of music, composed by J. C. Smith, never before published* (1799) • [W. Coxe], *Literary life and select works of Benjamin Stillingfleet* (1811) • Highfill, Burnim & Langhans, *BDA* • S. McVeigh, *Concert life in London from Mozart to Haydn* (1993) • J. Doane, ed., *A musical directory for the year 1794* (1794) • A. D. McCredie, 'John Christopher Smith as a dramatic composer', *Music and Letters*, 45 (1964), 22–38 • A. Hicks, 'The late additions to Handel's oratorios and the role of the younger Smith', *Music in eighteenth-century England: essays in memory of Charles Cudworth*, ed. C. Hogwood and R. Luckett (1983), 147–69 • A. Mann, 'Handel's successor: notes on John Christopher Smith the younger', *Music in eighteenth-century England: essays in memory of Charles Cudworth*, ed. C. Hogwood and R. Luckett (1983), 135–45 • R. King, 'John Christopher Smith's pasticcio oratorios', *Music and Letters*, 79 (1998), 190–218 • D. Burrows, *Handel* (1994) • B. Small, 'Smith, John Christopher', *New Grove*, 2nd edn, 23.572–4

Likenesses E. Harding, stipple, pubd 1799 (after J. Zoffany), NPG; repro. in Highfill, Burnim & Langhans, *BDA* • J. Zoffany, oils, priv. coll.

Wealth at death provided for children of late wife Martha Coxe; left Denner portrait of Handel to William Coxe: will, 13 May 1786

Smith, John Frederick (1806–1890), novelist, was born on 12 March 1806 and baptized on 28 March 1806 at St Stephen's, Norwich, the son of James Smith, manager of the Norwich Theatre circuit, and his wife, Elizabeth, *née* Taylor (*b.* *c.*1768), the widow of William Coatsworth (*d.* 1794). Elizabeth had had twin boys prior to her marriage to James Smith on 23 November 1801; these were always described as James Smith's sons, and in addition to these two brothers, John Frederick Smith had two sisters, one of whom died in infancy. Although the family was Anglican, Smith was educated at 'Mr Harvin's Presbyterian school', probably because of its liberal ethos and Unitarian leanings; it was favoured by many literati of Norwich. The early years of Smith's Bohemian adult life remain obscure, although it is known that he worked as an actor in England and travelled widely on the continent. Partly educated by a Jesuit, he spent some years in Rome, and rendered services to Pope Gregory XVI, but later he left the Roman Catholic church.

Smith had previously written some plays and two novels—*The Jesuit* (1832) and *The Prelate* (1840)—but his break came when he returned from a continental tour in

1849 to write for the *London Journal*. Smith raised the *Journal's* circulation to 100,000 copies that year, first with his short story 'Marianne, a Tale of the Temple' and then with instalments of his most ambitious novel, *Stanfield Hall*. Subsequently published as a three-decker (1888–9), the novel traces the fortunes of the Stanfield family from the middle ages to the Restoration, and combines historical romance, influenced by Sir Walter Scott, with anachronistic treatment of Victorian inventions. *Minnigrey* (1851–2), illustrated by John Gilbert, is said to have increased sales of the *London Journal* to half a million copies, for which newsagents had to send special wagons to the station.

Other novels include *Amy Lawrence, the Freemason's Daughter* (1851), *Woman and her Master* (1854), *The City Banker* (1856), *Milly Mogue* (1859), *Warp and Weft* (1863), and *Sir Bernard Gaston* (1867). When Smith was enticed away to *Cassell's Illustrated Family Paper* in 1855 he ended his current story by blowing up all the main characters on a Mississippi steamboat. He returned to the *London Journal*, however, ten years later.

Smith's habit was to write in the printing office itself. He would closet himself with a bottle of port and a cigar or pipe, read the end of the previous instalment, and then write the next, drawing his fee when he handed over the text. He raised the tension from episode to episode until the mill girls of the north and midlands had to buy their own copies rather than wait to borrow one. But neither the formulaic quality of his fiction (virtue, for example, is always rewarded) nor the sensationalist action of the weekly instalments was suited to the form of the novel republished in volume format.

Although for a time earning the salary of a parliamentary under-secretary and writing thrilling romances of fashionable life, Smith lived quietly in a Bloomsbury lodging-house, cut off from society through his deafness. Later in life he moved to America, and there England's most popular novelist of the mid-nineteenth century died in obscurity and want, in March (before 4 March) 1890, in New York. He was unmarried.

MICHAEL WHEELER, *rev.*

Sources private information (2004) [Thomas M. Steel] • *IGI* • *The Star* (4 March 1890) • *The Athenaeum* (15 March 1890), 343 • F. Jay, *Peeps into the past*, 2 vols. (1919–21) • *TLS* (25 Dec 1930) • L. James, *Fiction for the working man, 1830–1850* (1963)

Smith, John Gordon (1792–1833), university professor, graduated MD from Edinburgh University in 1810 and in 1812 became an assistant surgeon first in the Peninsular War, then, from 1813 to 1817, with the 12th light dragoons (lancers). He served at Waterloo, where he attended his commanding officer, Lieutenant-Colonel F. C. Ponsonby, who had been left for dead on the battlefield. Smith later published two accounts of his experiences as an army surgeon: *The English Army in France* (1830) and *Santarem, or, Sketches of Society and Manners in the Interior of Portugal* (1832). He was retired on half pay in 1815 and settled in London. His Scottish qualifications, however, prevented him from practising as a physician there and he became librarian to the marquess of Stafford, during which time he wrote *Principles of Forensic Medicine*. Published in 1821, it was one of the first books on the subject in the English language. By 1823 Smith was established as the first, and possibly the only, teacher of forensic medicine in London, at the Webb Street school, St Thomas's Hospital. He later gave further lectures on the subject at the Royal Institution from February 1826 to well into the 1827–8 session, when they alternated with Brande and Faraday's chemistry lectures.

Learning that the planned University of London proposed to offer teaching in medical jurisprudence, Smith gave the new library about 200 volumes on forensic medicine in February 1828. As there were only four or five current books on the subject Smith must have given them unsold copies of his own. He followed up this gift with a letter on the subject of medical jurisprudence and was appointed England's first professor in the subject from October 1828, the gift, no doubt, having been appreciated in the spirit in which it was intended. Smith was a poor lecturer. H. Hale Bellot, in his *History of University College, London, 1826–1926* (1929) noted: 'He was rather inclined to make bluster serve for argument, and the rather rambling account of his own battle to do duty for the methodical exposition of his subject' (p. 160). His inaugural lecture was attended by the *Morning Chronicle*, whose reporter noted: 'Condensation is not a virtue of Dr Smith's' (ibid.). The university did not yet offer medical degrees, but coached for the licentiate of the Society of Apothecaries (LSA). As the society did not examine in the subject no one attended the classes. The most part of Smith's salary was paid from student fees so in 1829 he petitioned the society to make medical jurisprudence a compulsory subject, sending them a copy of his book *Hints for the Examination of Medical Witnesses*. In response, the society recommended only that students diligently avail themselves of this tuition.

In the autumn of 1829 Smith tried to become a candidate for the coronership of Southwark and the City of London and was turned down because he did not have a liberal education (that is, he had not attended Oxford or Cambridge), despite having medical qualifications. Thomas Wakley was also campaigning unsuccessfully to become a medical coroner at this time and brought the subject of medical jurisprudence to public attention in bills posted all over London in the summer of 1830. The high point of the campaign was in August when a large public meeting was held at the Crown and Anchor tavern in the Strand. This took place during the week of a much reported inquest on a young consumptive Irishwoman, Catherine Cashin, who had died at the hands of a fashionable quack, John St John Long. In the wake of this, or perhaps because the Royal College of Surgeons in Dublin had put forensic medicine on its curriculum, the Society of Apothecaries' annual announcement in September 1830 included medical jurisprudence as a three-month second year compulsory course for the LSA from the following January. Smith's anecdotal and rambling style was becoming out of place as a more professional approach was adopted in regard to forensic medicine. For example, cases were now being reported in a style suitable for use as evidence in court, a style which Smith had great difficulty in coming to terms with. Smith became embroiled in emotional arguments with the faculty, the result being that once medical jurisprudence became compulsory, he found himself snubbed by the university. Insult was added to injury when he spotted one of his donated books on the library rubbish heap. Smith's resignation, on 1 November 1830, was received without comment by the council of the university and another Scot, Anthony Todd Thomson, professor of materia medica, was invited to become professor of medical jurisprudence in addition to his other duties, assisted by Andrew Amos, a barrister.

Disappointment made Smith irritable and misanthropic, and he turned to drink, which impaired his health and added to his money problems. He spent his last fifteen months as a debtor in the Fleet prison, London, where he died by 'visitation of God', aged forty-one and apparently unmarried, on 16 September 1833.

JENNY WARD

Sources *The Times* (17 Sept 1833) • *London Medical and Surgical Journal* (1833), 287 • *Nomina eorum, qui gradum medicinae doctoris in academia Jacobi sexti Scotorum regis, quae Edinburgi est, adepti sunt, ab anno 1705 ad annum 1845*, University of Edinburgh (1846) • C. Dalton, *The Waterloo roll call*, 2nd edn (1904), 75–7 • J. Ward, 'The emergence of forensic medicine in London, 1821–31', *Association of Open University Graduates Journal* (1994–5), 5–7
Archives UCL, D. M. S. Watson MSS

Smith, John Gordon (1822–1901). *See under* Smith family (*per.* 1824–1975).

Smith, Sir John Mark Frederick (1790–1874), army officer, son of Major-General Sir John Frederick Sigismund Smith (*d.* 1834), Royal Artillery, and grand-nephew of Field Marshal Baron von Kalkreuth, commander-in-chief of the Prussian army, was born at the Manor House, Paddington, Middlesex, on 11 January 1790. After attending the military school at Great Marlow and the Royal Military Academy at Woolwich, Smith was commissioned second lieutenant in the Royal Engineers on 1 December 1805, and in January 1806 joined his corps at Chatham.

In 1807 Smith went to Sicily, and served in 1809 under Major-General Sir Alexander Bryce, the commanding royal engineer of the force of Sir John Stuart, at the siege and capture of the castle of Ischia and at the capture of Procida in the Bay of Naples. He also took part, in the same year, in the capture of the islands of Zante and Cephalonia under Major-General Frederick Rennell Thackeray, commanding royal engineer of the force of Sir John Oswald. Smith was deputy assistant quartermaster-general and senior officer of the quartermaster-general's department under Sir Hudson Lowe in 1810, in the battle before Santa Maura. He resigned his staff appointment in order to serve as an engineer officer in the trenches during the siege of Santa Maura under Oswald, the only engineer officer in addition to Thackeray and himself—Captain Parker having been wounded. This deficiency of engineer officers threw upon Smith much of the work during the most arduous part of the siege, and he had no respite from duty in the trenches until the place surrendered. He received no special recognition of his services, although the officer who took his place on the staff was given the brevet promotion which Smith himself would have received, had he not resigned the staff appointment for the more dangerous duty. He was warmly mentioned in Sir John Oswald's dispatches, and some years afterwards an effort was unsuccessfully made to secure a brevet majority for his services at Santa Maura.

Smith was promoted second captain on 1 May 1811. He served in Albania and in Sicily, and in 1812 returned to England to take up the appointment of adjutant to the Corps of Royal Sappers and Miners at their headquarters at Woolwich on 1 December. He held this appointment until 26 February 1815. He was promoted first captain on 26 August 1817, and in 1819, on the reduction of the corps of Royal Engineers, was placed on half pay for seven months. Smith had married at Buckland, near Dover, on 31 January 1813, Harriet, daughter of Thomas Thorn of Buckland House, Kent. They had no children.

From 1819 to 1829 Smith was employed on various military duties in England, and was promoted regimental lieutenant-colonel on 16 March 1830, and appointed commanding royal engineer of the London district. In 1831 he was made KH by William IV, a knight bachelor on 13 September of the same year, an extra gentleman usher of the privy chamber in 1833, and on 17 March 1834 one of the ordinary gentlemen ushers. This last post he held until his death.

On 2 December 1840 Smith was appointed inspector-general of railways, and examined and reported on the London and Birmingham and other principal railways before they were opened to the public. In 1841 Smith, with Professor Barlow, made a report to the Treasury on railway communication between London, Edinburgh, and Glasgow. Smith resigned the appointment of inspector-general at the end of 1841, and became director of the royal engineer establishment at Chatham on 1 January 1842.

On 5 July 1845 Smith and professors Airy and Barlow were constituted a commission to inquire whether future parliamentary railway bills should provide for a uniform gauge, and whether existing railways should also adopt this gauge. On 30 March 1846 he was appointed commissioner to report on the various railway projects which proposed to locate a terminus in the London area. On 9 November 1846 he was promoted colonel in the army, and on 1 May 1851 was moved from Chatham to be commanding royal engineer of the southern district, with headquarters at Portsmouth.

In July 1852 Smith was elected Conservative MP for Chatham, but in March 1853 was unseated on petition. He was promoted major-general on 20 January 1854. In 1855 he was transferred from Portsmouth to the command of the Royal Engineers at Aldershot. He was appointed public examiner and inspector of the Military College of the East India Company at Addiscombe in 1856. From 1857 until 1865 he was MP for Chatham and resigned his command at Aldershot, finding his time fully occupied with parliamentary duties. A member of the royal commission on harbours of refuge in 1858, and of the commission on promotion and retirement in the army, he was promoted lieutenant-general on 25 October 1859, colonel-commandant of Royal Engineers on 6 July 1860, and general on 3 August 1863.

Smith was a fellow of the Royal Society, an associate of the Institution of Civil Engineers, and a member of several learned societies. He wrote *The Military Course of Engineering at Arras* (1850), and translated, with notes, a work by Marshal Marmont, published as *Present State of the Turkish Empire* (1839). He died on 20 November 1874 at his residence, 62 Pembridge Villas, Notting Hill Gate, London, and was buried in Kensal Green cemetery.

R. H. Vetch, *rev.* James Falkner

Sources *Army List* • W. Porter, *History of the corps of royal engineers*, 2 vols. (1889) • H. M. Vibart, *Addiscombe: its heroes and men of note* (1894) • *Royal Engineers Journal* (Jan 1874) • *Hart's Army List* • *Dod's Peerage* • *WWBMP*

Likenesses engraving, repro. in *ILN*, 30 (1857), 478 • photograph, repro. in Vibart, *Addiscombe*, 297

Wealth at death under £3000: probate, 11 Dec 1874, *CGPLA Eng. & Wales*

Smith, John Orrin [John Orrinsmith] **(1799–1843)**, wood-engraver, was born at Colchester, Essex, in 1799. About 1818 he moved to London, and for a short time trained as an architect. On coming of age in 1821 he inherited some money, with a portion of which he bought a part-proprietorship in a weekly newspaper, the *Sunday Monitor*, on which Douglas Jerrold worked as a compositor. The rest he invested in property, but by the time he was twenty-four his investments had failed and he found himself penniless. In 1821 he had married Jane Elizabeth, daughter of the fruit and flower painter Joseph *Barney. They had four children.

William Harvey, the engraver and draughtsman, came to Smith's assistance; Smith, who had received some early training in wood-engraving from Colchester-born Samuel Williams (1788–1853), resumed engraving under Harvey's instruction. He achieved some success, particularly in his animal and landscape engravings, although some contemporary printers declared that his cuts were too fine to print. In the late 1820s and 1830s he worked in partnership with John Jackson as Jackson and Smith.

In 1835 came a significant commission from Léon Curmer of Paris to engrave a number of the blocks for his fine edition of Saint-Pierre's *Paul et Virginie* (1835). Wood-engraving had not revived at this time in France as it had under Bewick and his successors in England, and further commissions for French publications followed, and for German work, notably an edition of Herder's *Cid* published in Stuttgart in 1839.

In 1837 Smith prepared engravings for C. J. Latrobe's *Solace of Song*, published by Seeley and Burnside, which marked a new departure in wood-engraving. The high finish, tone, and delicacy of Smith's engravings were a notable contrast with the crisp, somewhat hard work of contemporaries such as Clennell, Nesbit, and Thompson. Where, however, there was gain in refinement, there was doubtless a loss in vigour. Other British publications included two in which Smith was part-proprietor with his one-time apprentice Henry Vizetelly and his friend the artist Joseph Kenny Meadows: *Heads of the People* (1840–41) by Kenny Meadows and Shakespeare's *Works* (1839–43), with nearly 1000 designs by Kenny Meadows. In 1842 Smith embarked on his last major venture, going into partnership with his assistant since 1836, William James Linton; as Smith and Linton they were the principal engravers for the newly established *Illustrated London News*. Engen noted that he signed his engravings 'J. Smith', 'ORRIN SMITH', 'Smith & Linton', 'Smith sculp', and 'OSS' and that some time after 1836 he adopted the name John Orrinsmith. In his memoirs, Vizetelly recalled Smith's enthusiasm for his work and how, with his warm and sociable temperament, he inspired those who worked with him.

John Orrin Smith died at 11 Mabledon Place, Burton Crescent, London from 'apoplexy' brought on by the shock of a shower bath, on 15 October 1843. His wife survived him. Of his four children, Harvey Edward Orrin Smith (later Orrinsmith) also practised wood-engraving from *c.*1849 to 1870, but subsequently joined a firm of bookbinders.

Christopher Marsden

Sources R. K. Engen, *Dictionary of Victorian wood engravers* (1985) • H. Vizetelly, *Glances back through seventy years: autobiographical and other reminiscences*, 2 vols. (1893) • W. J. Linton, *The masters of wood-engraving* (1889) • private information (1897) • Redgrave, *Artists*

Likenesses M. A. Williams, engraving (after E. Belaife), repro. in J.-H. B. de Saint-Pierre, *Paul et Virginie* (Paris, 1838)

Smith, John Prince (*c.*1774–1822), barrister, was the only son of Edward Smith of Walthamstow, Essex. He was admitted on 25 November 1794 a student at Gray's Inn, where he was called to the bar on 6 May 1801. He practised on the home circuit, and as a special pleader and equity draftsman, and was one of Daniel Isaac Eaton's counsel on his trial for blasphemous libel on 6 March 1812. He was appointed in 1817 second fiscal in Demerara and Essequibo, British Guiana, and died at Demerara in 1822, leaving a son, John Prince-*Smith, and a daughter.

Smith edited the *New Law Journal* (3 vols., 1804–6) and published a collection of reports of cases in the king's bench between 1803 and 1806. Among his other works were: *Elements of the Science of Money Founded on the Principles of the Law of Nature* (1813) and *Advice for the Petitioners Against the Corn Bill* (1815).

J. M. Rigg, *rev.* Jonathan Harris

Sources *GM*, 1st ser., 92/2 (1822), 646 • J. Foster, *The register of admissions to Gray's Inn, 1521–1889, together with the register of marriages in Gray's Inn chapel, 1695–1754* (privately printed, London, 1889), 399 • *New Law List* (1802), 32

Smith, John Prince- (1809–1874), political economist and translator in Germany, was born in London on 20 January 1809, the son of John Prince *Smith (*c.*1774–1822), barrister and law reporter. He went with his father on the latter's appointment as second fiscal in Demerara in 1817, before returning to England in 1820 to attend Eton College. Thereafter he was employed by Messrs Daniel, merchants, of 4 Mincing Lane in the City of London. He left in 1828 to work variously as a bank clerk, parliamentary reporter, and journalist in London and Hamburg. On

5 April 1831 he became English and French master in Cowle's *Gymnasium* at Elbing in West Prussia. He resigned in 1840 to take up journalism once more, and gained a reputation for advocating free trade in the *Elbinger Anzeigen*. He was a member of the Cobden Club, and published *System of Political Economy* (1844), an English translation of C. H. Hager. In 1846 he moved to Berlin, where he was elected to the free trade union and, two years later, to the city's common council. He became naturalized, and married Auguste Sommerbrod, the daughter of an eminent banker.

Prince-Smith took an active part at the economic congresses at Gotha (1858), Hanover (1862), and Brunswick (1866). He was president of the Berlin Economic Society from 1862 and of the standing committee of the Lübeck Economic Congress from 1870 until shortly before his death. He served as a deputy for Stettin in the Prussian house of representatives (1862–6) and was returned to the Reichstag for Anhalt-Zerbst in 1870. Doctrinally he was a free-trade absolutist, believing that the unfettered freedom of industry was the sole prescription for general prosperity, and that the role of the state should be confined to the prevention of fraud and violence. As such, according to one critical biographer, he created a desirable counterweight to protectionist opinion in Germany, and he performed a useful function in opposing 'monopolies, unnecessary restrictions and medieval survivals' (Palgrave). He also accomplished useful legislative work in the areas of banks, coinage, and weights and measures.

Prince-Smith died at Berlin on 3 February 1874. His collected works in German (*Gesammelte Schriften*), edited by Braun, Braun-Wiesbaden, and Michaelis, were posthumously published in Berlin (1877–80) with a sketch of his life. Prince-Smith was a proselytizer for free trade rather than an original thinker. This has not conferred longevity on his works, and he was among the omissions from the revision in 1987 of Palgrave's dictionary.

H. J. Spencer

Sources O. Wolff, 'Lebensskizze', in [J. Prince-Smith], *Gesammelte Schriften*, ed. C. Braun, K. Braun-Wiesbaden, and O. Michaelis (1877–80) • J. K. I., 'Prince-Smith, John', in R. H. I. Palgrave, *Dictionary of political economy*, 3 vols. (1894–9) • Boase, *Mod. Eng. biog.* • J. Eatwell, M. Milgate, and P. Newman, eds., *The new Palgrave: a dictionary of economics*, new edn, 4 vols. (1998), appx of omitted articles

Smith, John Pye (1774–1851), Congregational minister, was born on 25 May 1774, the only son of John Smith, bookseller, of Angel Street, Sheffield (*d.* 1810), and his wife, Mary Sheard (*d.* 1829). There were also four daughters. The son had no formal education during childhood apart from Latin lessons from Jehoiada Brewer (1752–1817), but he gathered a surprising amount of information by reading omnivorously among the books in his father's shop. In 1790 he was indentured as apprentice to his father, but did not enter the business at the end of his apprenticeship.

In 1792 Pye Smith was admitted into membership of the Independent Queen Street Chapel, Sheffield, where Brewer was minister until 1796. In January 1796 James

John Pye Smith (1774–1851), by Thomas Phillips, 1839

Montgomery (1771–1854), the editor of *The Iris* newspaper, was found guilty of libel and imprisoned for six months, and young Pye Smith edited the paper from 5 February to 5 August. He now set his heart on becoming a minister and was admitted into the Rotherham Academy, of which Dr Edward Williams (1750–1813) was principal. His academic abilities were a source of wonder to fellow students and of commendation by his teachers. He was appointed resident classical tutor at Homerton Academy in 1800. He taught a surprising variety of subjects, including philosophy, logic, rhetoric, astronomy, physics, Greek, Latin, and Hebrew.

On 20 August 1801, at Tunbridge Wells, Pye Smith married Mary, the daughter of Thomas Hodgson of Hackney. She suffered from severe nervous debility and the marriage was not a happy one. They had six children, of whom two sons and a daughter died before their father. Of the two sons and a daughter that survived, John William married a daughter of Edward Baines MP (1774–1848). Pye Smith's wife died on 23 November 1832, and on 12 January 1843 he married Catherine Elizabeth, the widow of Revd William Clayton (1784–1834). They had no children.

In 1803 the Homerton trustees allowed Pye Smith to open the hall of the college for public worship. This led to the formation of an Independent church on 6 March 1804, and on 11 April Smith was ordained its minister. In March 1811 the church moved to the vacant Old Gravel Pit meeting-house. In May 1806 he was appointed theological tutor, the senior position at Homerton. He continued to discharge his duties as teacher and minister until his health was affected by a stroke on 2 January 1849. He resigned his pastorate in the following December and retired from teaching when Homerton became part of New College in June 1850. On 2 October 1850 he moved to The Elms, Woodbridge Road, Stoke, near Guildford, where he died at seventy-six years of age on 5 February 1851. He was buried at Abney Park cemetery.

Pye Smith was a true polymath. Science was an integral part of his personal culture, as it was of his college courses. Even when many of his dissenting contemporaries feared that the growth of scientific knowledge might undermine Christian faith, he insisted that Christians should welcome established scientific facts as confirming faith. Thus, in *The Relation between the Holy Scriptures and some Parts of Geological Science* (1839) he abandons such traditional positions as the recent creation of the world, the creation of the heavenly bodies after the earth, the derivation of all animals from one centre of creation, and a universal deluge. His eminence in this field was recognized by his election as fellow of the Geological Society in 1836 and his subsequent election as fellow of the Royal Society in 1840. His erudition was wide and deep. His large library reveals his familiarity with books in Latin, French, Italian, Dutch, and German. He was the first among dissenters to make substantial use of the works of German theologians. In him the tradition of Philip Doddridge, with its emphasis on the need to combine piety with scholarship, continued to flourish. At the same time he was one of the founding fathers of the political radicalism that was to characterize Victorian dissent. He promoted total abstinence from alcohol, and was vice-president of the Peace Society. At a time when most prominent dissenters were cautious whigs, shy of involvement in politics, Pye Smith appeared on political platforms at election time. It is true that his increasing deafness hampered his effectiveness both as lecturer and preacher, but it did not inhibit his active participation in public life. He was a towering figure among the dissenters of his generation.

Pye Smith's publications were numerous, consisting of some forty-four titles. Many of them were individual sermons. Others were pamphlets, the products of his controversies, first in 1804 with Thomas Belsham (1750–1829) in defence of the divinity of Jesus Christ, then between 1826 and 1830 with the agnostic Robert Taylor (1784–1844) in defence of Christian faith, and finally in 1834 with Samuel Lee (1783–1852), regius professor of Hebrew at Cambridge, in defence of nonconformity. He provided a significant contribution to biblical exegesis in 1826 when he broached his views about the divine inspiration of the Bible in opposition to Robert Haldane's rigid theory that every part of the Bible was inspired in the same way. Pye Smith restated and refurbished Philip Doddridge's contention that different modes of inspiration are to be discerned in the Bible, some providing a fuller understanding of God's mind than others. His most widely circulated book was *Prudence and Piety* (1820), but the two books which made the most solid contribution to nineteenth-century thought were *The Scripture Testimony to the Messiah* (2 vols., 1818–21) and *The Relation between the Holy Scriptures and some Parts of Geological Science*. He was also a frequent contributor to the *Eclectic Review*. R. TUDUR JONES

Sources J. Medway, *Memoirs of the life and writings of John Pye Smith* … (1853) • J. C. Harrison, 'Reminiscences of Dr John Pye Smith', *The Congregationalist*, 10 (1881), 641–8, 753–8, 816–23 • *Congregational Year Book* (1851), 233 • A. Peel, *The Congregational two hundred, 1530–1948* (1948), 120 • *Evangelical Magazine and Missionary Chronicle*, new ser., 29 (1851), 146–9 • A. Peel, 'Clapton Park Congregational Church as seen in the minutes, 1804–1929', *Transactions of the Congregational Historical Society*, 10 (1927–9), 160–66, 234–42 • G. F. Nuttall, *New College, London, and its library* (1977) • J. H. Taylor, 'Some John Pye Smith letters', *Transactions of the Congregational Historical Society*, 20 (1965–70), 368–9

Archives Bodl. Oxf., continental travel journal • DWL, corresp. and papers • NRA, priv. coll., family and estate corresp. • Wellcome L., autobiography

Likenesses T. Phillips, oils, 1839, DWL [*see illus.*] • bust, DWL

Smith, John Raphael (*bap.* **1751**, *d.* **1812**), printmaker and print publisher, was baptized on 25 May 1751 in St Alkmund's Church, Derby, the younger of the two sons (the elder being Thomas Correggio Smith) of Thomas *Smith of Derby (*bap.* 1720x24?, *d.* 1767), landscape painter and engraver, and his wife, Hannah. Educated at Derby grammar school until the age of about eleven, he was apprenticed from 1762 until 1767 to a linen draper. In 1767 he moved to London to work as foreman in a shop on Ludgate Hill. Some years later he married Ann Darlow (*d.* 1778), with whom he had two surviving children, including the artist John Rubens Smith (1775–1849), active after 1806 in the United States.

Smith's earliest mezzotint, *Pascal Paoli* (1769), after Henry Benbridge (priv. coll.), launched a forty-year career during which he produced at least 400 mezzotints and stipple engravings, most of them (about 279) reproductive. Having established his reputation with *Mr Banks*, after a portrait by Benjamin West (exh. Society of Artists, 1773; British Museum), he became Sir Joshua Reynolds's primary interpreter, and produced such atmospheric mezzotints as *Mrs Carnac* (1778) and *Lieutenant-Colonel Banastre Tarleton* (1782), which Reynolds described as having 'everything but the colouring of my picture' (Carey, 43). An unparalleled master of mezzotint, Smith translated works by many other noted contemporaries, exemplified by George Romney's portrait of *The Children of Earl Gower* (1781); Gainsborough's of *George, Prince of Wales* (1783), which precipitated Smith's appointment in 1784 as 'Mezzotinto Engraver to the Prince of Wales'; *The Weird Sisters* (1785), after Henry Fuseli; *Widow of an Indian Chief* (1789), after Joseph Wright of Derby; and *Slave Trade* (1791), after George Morland. Impressions of these prints may be found in the British Museum. Smith exhibited at the Society of Artists in 1773–9, 1783, and 1790 and at the Free Society of Artists in 1782, and showed chalk or pastel drawings and oil paintings at the Royal Academy in 1779–82, 1784–90, 1792, and 1800–05. He held exhibitions in Norwich in 1784 and in Manchester in 1801, and displayed specimens of his 'new process' in oil-coloured prints at the British School in Berners Street, London, in 1803.

While Smith moved in academic painting circles, he also engaged with the popular trade by producing satires and female genre subjects among his 120 original mezzotints and stipples. Early mezzotints, many published by

Carington Bowles for 1s. 'plain' or 2s. if coloured, include *The Jealous Husband* (1771), a prodigal son set (1775), and a group of prostitute subjects for Bowles's 1776–81 series *Ladies in Fashionable Dresses*. Smith's later prints, and those produced by other printmakers after his designs, centred on images of elegant, if disreputable, women whose observed or imaginary narratives express a dramatist's keen sense of stagecraft and characterization: among them *Promenade at Carlisle House*, a 1781 mezzotint (exh. Free Society of Artists, 1782) based on Smith's chalk drawing now in the Victoria and Albert Museum; *Credulous Lady and Astrologer*, a 1786 stipple by J. P. Simon after Smith's original (exh. Royal Academy, 1785); and *What you Will*, a 1791 stipple after an oil painting by Smith (Ferens Art Gallery, Hull). An exceptional portrait among the non-commissioned subjects is Smith's 1783 mezzotint of his second wife, Emma Johnston (*d.* *c.*1802/3), to whom he was married in 1782 or 1783. The first of the couple's four surviving children was the artist Emma Smith (*b.* 1783, *d.* after 1828), the mother of Julian, Lord Pauncefote, Britain's first ambassador to the United States. In his will, dated 12 January 1812, Smith bequeathed to Hannah Croome, 'now living with me', his personal estate.

From 1781 until he sold his stock in 1802, Smith was a prime mover in London's publishing world, issuing his own prints as well as editions after his work and after other artists by more than thirty printmakers (among them William Blake) whom he hired to produce plates or who worked as apprentices and pupils. From 1776 until 1806 the latter group included William and James Ward, Charles H. Hodges, Thomas Girtin, J. M. W. Turner (taken on to hand-colour prints), S. W. Reynolds, William Hilton, and Peter DeWint. Distributing prints throughout the provinces and in such European centres as St Petersburg, Milan, and Paris (where he travelled with Thomas Rowlandson in 1787), Smith capitalized on the sales appeal of such stipple publications as *Nightmare* (1783) by Thomas Burke after Fuseli, and his 1789 *Laetitia* set after Morland. As with *Laetitia*, Smith frequently invented narratives for painters to execute, recognizing a ready market for their printed reproductions. At his peak he played an important role in generating pictorial ideas and in manufacturing thousands of pictures for domestic and foreign consumption. When the French Revolution caused a drastic decline in exports, Smith partially recouped by opening the Morland Gallery in 1793 at his shop in King Street, Covent Garden, and issuing a catalogue listing thirty-six prints planned for production after Morland's rustic subjects. His firm issued a *Catalogue of Prints* listing 302 other publications dating from 1780 to 1798. Smith moved to Newman Street about 1802, when he exhibited his most renowned pastel, *Charles James Fox* (exh. Royal Academy, 1802; Thirelstane Castle Trust, Berwickshire).

Smith's avocations included 'field sports, pugilism, and the stage; in all of which, if not an adept, he was an excellent judge' ('British school of engraving', 69). A gregarious host, with friends among artists, writers, actors, and politicians in whig circles, he was always ready 'to please those who are fond of a song and a story', wrote Edward Brayley in 1802. Henry Angelo's *Reminiscences* (1828–30) give numerous references to boisterous parties in Smith's house where he served wines imported in exchange for cash income from print sales: he 'was famed for his Burgundy'. However unjudgemental, Angelo's recollections helped to substantiate posthumous criticism of Smith's indifference to retaining wealth and his so-called moral shortcomings. William Carey wrote in 1827 that Smith specialized in themes of 'gay ladies of fashionable notoriety'; moreover, he 'dissipated his time and money with little thought and was incapable of resisting the calls of pleasure'. By dwelling on issues of personality, most commentary for the succeeding 150 years clouded Smith's achievements as an original artist and publisher to assert that the quality of his work and choice of subjects mirrored a dissolute life. On the contrary, plentiful evidence testifies to a man of disciplined habits who rose early to work. Certainly a bon vivant, irreverent towards social conventions, Smith was known for his integrity and generosity. An enormously productive and inventive artist, he shaped his publications with a keen awareness of their market demand and was widely praised for his guidance and advice to young artists. Among those he counselled was Sir Francis Chantrey, who sculpted a plaster bust of Smith (exh. Royal Academy, 1811; Ashmolean Museum) and, in 1825, a marble version (V&A).

After 1808 Smith, who was growing deaf, based himself in Doncaster and travelled largely in Yorkshire on commissions for pastel portraits. Following an asthmatic attack, he died on 2 March 1812 in Doncaster, where he was buried. The most comprehensive museum holdings of his prints may be found in the British Museum, London, and the Yale Center for British Art, New Haven, Connecticut. ELLEN G. D'OENCH

Sources E. G. D'Oench, *Copper into gold: prints by John Raphael Smith, 1751–1812* (1999) · J. Frankau, *John Raphael Smith: his life and works* (1902) · W. Carey, 'Some account of the late William Ward, associate engraver of the Royal Academy, and his master, J. R. Smyth', *Repository of Arts, Literature, Fashions*, 9 (Jan 1827), 41–6 · J. R. Smith, *A catalogue of prints published by J. R. Smith* (*c.*1798) · 'British school of engraving III', *Library of the Fine Arts*, 4 (1832), 68–72 · T. Clayton, *The English print, 1688–1802* (1997) · R. Edwards, 'J. R. Smith and his pupils', *The Connoisseur*, 93 (1934), 96–101 · R. Edwards, 'Pastel portraits by J. R. Smith', *The Connoisseur*, 90 (1932), 299–307 · J. C. Smith, *British mezzotinto portraits*, 3 (1880) · E. S. Smith, 'John Rubens Smith', 1930, NYPL, Division of Art, Prints and Photographs, +ZZ-17098 · Graves, *Soc. Artists* · Graves, *RA exhibitors* · H. Angelo, *Reminiscences*, 2 vols. (1828–30) · *Monthly Magazine*, 33 (1812), 380 · *GM*, 1st ser., 82/1 (1812), 488–9 · general registers (baptism), 1538–1813, Derby Local Studies Library, Derby, microfilm no. 160

Likenesses J. R. Smith, self-portrait, chalk drawing, *c.*1774–1775, BM · J. R. Smith, self-portrait, oils, *c.*1785–1787, Usher Gallery, Lincoln · S. De Wilde, watercolour drawing, *c.*1790, BM · T. Rowlandson, chalk drawing, 1790, Harvard TC · T. Girtin, ink drawing, *c.*1795–1798; sold at Sothebys, London, 7 July 1977 · group portrait, line engraving, pubd 1798 (*Sketch taken at the Print Sales*; after P. Sandby), BM · G. Morland, chalk drawing, *c.*1802, AM Oxf. · J. R. Smith, self-portrait, pastel, *c.*1807–1808, NPG · F. Chantrey, plaster bust, 1811, AM Oxf. · F. Chantrey, marble bust, 1825, V&A · G. Morland, chalk drawing, BM · J. K. Sherwin, etching (*Smithfield*

Sharpers; after caricature by T. Rowlandson, 1787), Yale U., Farmington, Lewis Walpole Library

Smith, John Russell (1810–1894), bookseller and bibliographer, was born on 3 January 1810 and baptized on 10 June at Sevenoaks, the first of two known children of Thomas Smith, millwright, and his wife, Frances, the other child being George Claxon Smith, born on 29 January 1812, also at Sevenoaks. Thomas Smith had married Frances Hunt on 2 October 1808 at St Mary's, Lewisham, Kent. John Russell Smith was apprenticed to John Bryant, a bookseller in Wardour Street, Soho, London. Smith then opened a bookseller's shop at nearby 4 Old Compton Street, most probably in 1833 or 1834. During his Old Compton Street days he was one of the foremost promoters of dialect study, publishing a bibliography on the subject and a book on Westmorland and Cumberland dialects, both in 1839, and William Barnes's *Poems of Rural Life in the Dorset Dialect* in 1844. Smith also published John White Masters's Kentish ballad *Dick and Sal*. Interest in topography led to his *Bibliotheca Cantiana* (1837) and the purchase of William Upcott's topographical collection in 1841. Two copies of *Bibliotheca Cantiana* annotated by Smith are in the British Library.

In 1842 the Archaeological Association was split by a quarrel and some members transferred their publications to Smith, whose business consequently increased. On 3 August 1844 he married, at St Anne's, Westminster, Frances (*d.* in or after 1889), the daughter of a London printer, James Daniel Caigou. The couple had two children, Alfred Russell Smith, born on 30 April 1845, and Edith Charlotte Smith.

In 1852 Smith moved to 36 Soho Square, formerly George Routledge's shop, and from there issued several important catalogues: notably on English broadside ballads (1856), Shakespeare (1864), and America (1865). He also published a bibliography of English works on angling and ichthyology in 1856. Between 1874 and 1880 his son, Alfred Russell Smith, issued catalogues based on his father's extensive stock.

About 1884 Smith retired, and both his copyrights and stock were disposed of. His Library of Old Authors, a series of reprints, was sold to a bookseller, William Reeves, for £1000, and his collection of engravings went to another bookseller, Jonathan Nield. A probable reason for Smith's retirement was his growing blindness; when he made his will on 16 February 1889 he was nearly blind. He died of apoplexy on 19 October 1894 at his home, 40 Leverton Street, Kentish Town, London, leaving both a respectable fortune and a reputation for industry and integrity, as recorded in Frederick Saunders's anonymous *Salad for the Social* (1856), and William Carew Hazlitt's *Four Generations of a Literary Family* (1897). R. J. GOULDEN

Sources *The Athenaeum* (10 Nov 1894), 644 • *The Bookseller* (6 Nov 1894) • parish register, Sevenoaks, CKS [baptism] • P. A. H. Brown, *London publishers and printers, c.1800–1870* (1982) • [F. Saunders], *Salad for the social* (1856), 28 • W. C. Hazlitt, *Four generations of a literary family*, 2 (1897), 367 • b. cert. • b. cert. [A. R. Smith] • b. cert. [E. C. Smith] • m. cert. • d. cert. • *CGPLA Eng. & Wales* (1894)

Archives BL, annotated copies (two) of his 'Bibliotheca Cantiana', as well as a collection of various Kentish ephemera • Boston PL, corresp. | Bodl. Oxf., letters and bills to Sir Thomas Phillipps • U. Edin. L., corresp. with James Halliwell-Phillipps

Likenesses W. J. Alais, stipple, 1883 (after photograph by J. Louis), BM, NPG; repro. in J. R. Smith, *A catalogue of twenty thousand engraved portraits* (1883)

Wealth at death £15,022 1s. 2d.: probate, 10 Nov 1894, *CGPLA Eng. & Wales*

Smith, John Sidney (1804–1871), legal writer, was the son of John Spry Smith of 9 Woburn Square, London. In 1827 he joined his father as a clerk in the six clerks' office in the court of chancery, where he remained until 23 October 1842, when the establishment was abolished. He entered Trinity Hall, Cambridge on 29 July 1842 and graduated BA in 1847 and MA in 1850. Admitted to the Middle Temple in November 1842, he was called to the bar on 7 November 1845. He was subsequently admitted to Lincoln's Inn (11 May 1846) and practised in the court of chancery. He published two works on chancery, one of which went through many editions, and a treatise on equity. He was also the anonymous author of a biography of Mirabeau (1848) and *Men of the Scottish Reformation*.

Smith lived latterly at Wimbledon, where he was chairman of the board of guardians, churchwarden, and engaged in local charitable activities. An active Conservative, he was taken ill chairing a party meeting and died soon afterwards on 14 January 1871 at his home, Sidney Lodge. He left a widow, Ann, and children.

G. C. BOASE, *rev.* PATRICK POLDEN

Sources *Law Times* (11 March 1871), 369 • J. Hutchinson, ed., *A catalogue of notable Middle Templars: with brief biographical notices* (1902) • Venn, *Alum. Cant.* • Holdsworth, *Eng. law*, vol. 15 • Boase, *Mod. Eng. biog.* • W. P. Baildon, ed., *The records of the Honorable Society of Lincoln's Inn: admissions*, 2 vols. (1896) • H. A. C. Sturgess, ed., *Register of admissions to the Honourable Society of the Middle Temple, from the fifteenth century to the year 1944*, 2 (1949) • *Royal Kalendar* [various years] • Allibone, *Dict.* • *CGPLA Eng. & Wales* (1871)

Wealth at death under £35,000: resworn probate, July 1871, *CGPLA Eng. & Wales*

Smith, John Stafford (*bap.* 1750, *d.* 1836), musician and musical antiquary, was baptized in Gloucester Cathedral on 30 March 1750, the son of Martin Smith (*c.*1715–1786), organist of Gloucester Cathedral from 1739 to 1781, and Agrilla Smith, *née* Stafford. Smith was first taught music by his father, who in 1761 sent him to London to sing as a treble in the Chapel Royal under James Nares, and to complete his musical education with William Boyce, a boyhood friend of his father. On 16 December 1784 he was admitted a gentlemen of the Chapel Royal as a tenor, and in the following year he also became a lay vicar of Westminster Abbey. On the death of Samuel Arnold he was appointed organist of the Chapel Royal on 1 November 1802. About 1800 he published *Anthems, Composed for the Choir-Service of the Church of England*, a collection of twenty of his anthems. He succeeded Edmund Ayrton as master of the children on 14 May 1805, resigning in 1817, but he remained organist of the Chapel Royal until his death.

Smith was a skilful exponent of catches and glees, two species of partsong which were peculiar to England, performed in the main by men, and fashionable during the period of Smith's creative life. Smith was five times a winner of prize glees awarded annually by the Noblemen's

John Stafford Smith (*bap.* **1750**, *d.* **1836**), by Thomas Illman (after William Behnes)

and Gentlemen's Catch Club winning a prize each year from 1774 to 1777 and in 1780. He published five collections of catches and glees, the first appearing in 1776. The fifth book (1799) contains his harmonized version of 'To Anacreon in Heaven'. Smith almost certainly composed this song, which was the constitutional hymn of the convivial Anacreontic Society founded in 1766, which met at the Crown and Anchor tavern in the Strand. The song became known in America where new words were supplied in 1814 by Francis Scott Key, who renamed it 'The Star-Spangled Banner'. In 1931 it was adopted as the national anthem of the United States of America.

Smith has special importance as an innovator of what is now called musicology. Like Boyce, Smith gathered an outstanding music library. Among his manuscripts were the Mulliner book of keyboard music and the Old Hall manuscript (BL, Add. MSS 30513 and 57950). Working with Sir John Hawkins on his *General History of the Science and Practice of Music* (1776), he was able to supply Hawkins with many sources from his library. Smith became a member of the Royal Society of Musicians on 6 October 1776. In 1779 he published *A Collection of English Songs, in Score … Composed about the Year 1500. Taken from MSS.*, the first historical anthology of its kind. He followed this in 1812 with a remarkable and more comprehensive anthology in two volumes, *Musica antiqua*, containing compositions with accompanying notes spanning the period from the twelfth to the early eighteenth century.

Smith died at Paradise Row, Chelsea, on 21 September 1836 and was buried in St Luke's churchyard. At his death his library and estate were bequeathed to his daughter Gertrude who eventually became insane, and the entire library was sold at auction on 24 April 1844 for her benefit. It was bundled into lots and inadequately described and advertised so that the larger portion of its contents, estimated at some 2191 volumes, remains unknown.

ROBERT J. BRUCE

Sources *The Harmonicon*, 11 (1833), 186 • J. S. Bumpus, *A history of English cathedral music, 1549–1889*, 2 vols. [1908], 377–81 • J. Hawkins, *A general history of the science and practice of music*, 5 vols. (1776) • F. Blume, ed., *Die Musik in Geschichte und Gegenwart*, 17 vols. (Kassel and Basel, 1949–86), vol. 12, 799–802 • N. Temperley, 'Smith, John Stafford', *New Grove* • Highfill, Burnim & Langhans, *BDA*, 14.153–4 • H. W. Shaw, *The succession of organists of the Chapel Royal and the cathedrals of England and Wales from c.1538* (1991), 15 • D. Baptie, *Sketches of the English glee composers: historical, biographical and critical (from about 1735–1866)* [1896], 35–7 • P. M. Young, *A history of British music* (1967), 379–82 • E. Cole, 'Stafford Smith's Burney', *Music and Letters*, 40 (1959), 35–8 • W. Lichtenwanger, 'The music of the star-spangled banner', *Library of Congress Quarterly Journal*, 34/3 (1977), 136–70 • B. Frith, *John Stafford Smith, 1750–1836, Gloucester composer* (1950)

Archives BL, commonplace books, Add. MSS 34608–34609 • U. Glas. L., letters and ballads

Likenesses T. Illman, stipple (after W. Behnes), BM, NPG [*see illus.*]

Smith, John Taylor (1860–1938), bishop of Sierra Leone and chaplain-general to the forces, was born on 20 April 1860 at Kendal, Westmorland, the second son of James Smith, coal agent, and his wife, Jane. He had two brothers and two sisters. He was educated at Kendal grammar school. When aged twelve Taylor Smith experienced an evangelical conversion, which left upon him a deep and permanent impression. He was actively involved in evangelistic activities from his youth and there are indications that he felt early the call to full-time Christian ministry. Nevertheless he dutifully acceded to his father's desire that he enter a trade through his brother's jewellery business. Taylor Smith finally gave up watchmaking in 1882. The story of his final call to the ministry characterizes Taylor Smith's brand of evangelical religion: providence specially guided him to Carlisle Cathedral, where God spoke through the Old Testament lesson. Taylor Smith trained at the strongly evangelical London College of Divinity at St John's Hall, Highbury (1882–5). He was a poor student academically, but impressed with his ebullient personality and his zeal on college missions. In 1885 he accepted a curacy at St Paul's, Upper Norwood. His vicar, the Revd W. H. Graham, was frequently ill, allowing Taylor Smith ample opportunity to develop. It was at Upper Norwood that his skill as a popular, colourful preacher first blossomed.

In 1889–90 Taylor Smith felt the call to missionary work overseas. He turned down the chance to go to Uganda, but subsequently accepted an invitation to serve with the Church Missionary Society in Sierra Leone. He left England in February 1891, and from 1891 until 1897 was subdean and canon of St George's Cathedral, Freetown; he was also diocesan missioner. The climate took its toll and he suffered severe bouts of fever. Nevertheless he worked hard and was remarkably successful, not least in persuading African Christians to volunteer for missionary work. Unexpectedly Taylor Smith served as chaplain to the

Asante expeditionary force in 1895, and this was undoubtedly the turning point of his career. Prince Henry of Battenberg fell seriously ill and left a message with the chaplain for his wife. When the prince died on 21 January 1896 Taylor Smith travelled to Europe to deliver the message in person. He made a favourable impression not only on Princess Beatrice but also on Queen Victoria: he was subsequently created honorary chaplain to the queen. It was no surprise, therefore, when Archbishop Temple made him the new bishop of Sierra Leone in 1897. The main achievement of Taylor Smith's episcopate lay in the creation of a cathedral chapter. He kept up a hectic round of engagements and suffered further life-threatening attacks of fever.

Thus, when the War Office offered Taylor Smith the post of chaplain-general, friends urged him to accept. At first inclined to refuse, he accepted when he felt 'the Pillar of Cloud' (that is, God) was leading him to a fresh pilgrimage. He was appointed on 1 November 1901. The choice caused great surprise at the time, but may be attributed to two factors: the Church of England was determined to have a bishop as chaplain-general and a group of senior army officers pressed for Taylor Smith's appointment. He was at the War Office for almost twenty-four years. This long period as chaplain-general can be divided into two distinct, though unequal, parts. In peacetime Taylor Smith was successful: he concentrated especially on preaching and mission work in the army, for which he had particular talents, and was unquestionably popular with the regular army.

It is his role as chaplain-general during the First World War which occasions great controversy. Alan Wilkinson marshalled evidence to adjudge Taylor Smith naïve, inefficient, and bigoted. But those contemporaries who testified to this effect, in particular Anglo-Catholics and sophisticated intellectuals, were themselves partial. The truth is that the scale of the challenge which Taylor Smith faced would probably have overwhelmed most men. As it was, he quickly learned to delegate. On 16 July 1915 Bishop Llewellyn Gwynne was appointed deputy chaplain-general with special responsibility for chaplains and troops in France, while Taylor Smith concentrated on administration from London. His success can be measured by the continual supply of sufficient chaplains throughout the war and by his calm resistance to self-interested calls for change and innovation. The First World War aged Taylor Smith greatly. Nevertheless he oversaw a comprehensive reorganization of his department in 1920, which brought about a unified system of administration for all denominations except Roman Catholics, and which brought in Territorial Army chaplains with the regulars.

After his return from Africa in 1901 Taylor Smith involved himself wholeheartedly in the work of numerous evangelical societies. His interest in young people's activities led to involvement in camps for public schoolboys, the Boys' Brigade, and the Children's Special Service Mission. Work for the Alliance of Honour was in line with his desire as chaplain-general to encourage young soldiers to abstain from sex outside marriage. Taylor Smith was also active in the Scripture Gift Mission, the Scripture Union, and the Evangelical Alliance. He spoke regularly at Keswick. Taylor Smith retired in April 1925. From then until his death he led a frenetic lifestyle, being in constant demand as a preacher and missioner. He travelled all over the world, and it was while returning from Australia on board the SS *Orion* that he died on 28 March 1938 and was buried at sea. He had never married.

Taylor Smith was a big, burly man with a powerful preaching voice. His sermons were liberally embellished with stories and anecdotes. He was not widely read and his intellect was limited, but he did have the common touch. His autograph book entries, for example, were homely and comforting, and prized by their recipients for their consolatory messages. Public honours did come in his lifetime (he was made a CVO in 1906, a CB in 1921, and a KCB in 1925) and his achievements were certainly more substantial than has generally been allowed.

I. T. FOSTER

Sources private information (2004) • *The Times* (29 March 1938) • *The Record* (1 April 1938) • *Quarterly Journal of the Royal Army Chaplains' Department*, 2/14 (April 1925), 48–50 • *Quarterly Journal of the Royal Army Chaplains' Department*, 6/46 (July 1938), 94–101 • M. Whitlow, *J. Taylor Smith: everybody's bishop* (1938) • E. L. Langston, *Bishop Taylor Smith* (c.1939) • J. Smyth, *In this sign conquer: the story of the army chaplains* (1968) • A. Wilkinson, *The Church of England and the First World War* (1978) • *WWW* • Crockford • *Army List* (1915) • Cumbria AS, records

Likenesses photograph, repro. in Langston, *Bishop Taylor Smith*, frontispiece • photographs, repro. in Whitlow, *J. Taylor Smith*

Wealth at death £8419 11s. 8d.: resworn probate, 1938, *CGPLA Eng. & Wales*

Smith, John Thomas (1766–1833), printmaker and draughtsman, was born in a hackney carriage bound for his family home at 7 Great Portland Street, London, on 23 June 1766. His mother's maiden name was Tarr; his father was the printseller and sculptor Nathaniel Smith (1740/41–1809), who, for the first part of his career, was an assistant to the celebrated Joseph Nollekens (1737–1823). Following the death of his mother in 1779, Smith entered Nollekens's studio, where he ran errands, prepared clay, and had the fortune to become familiar with many of the leading artists of the day. His experiences in this milieu—as well as Nollekens's character and particular fondness for the young Smith—are all vividly recorded in his anecdotal biography *Nollekens and his Times* (1828), which is one of the most informative accounts of the London art world at the end of the eighteenth century. But since he showed only a modest talent for modelling he went, instead, to study with the successful engraver John Keyse Sherwin, who was so impressed by some pencil copies Smith had made after Ostade and Rembrandt that he took him on at half the usual rate. Between 1781 and 1784 Smith studied engraving with Sherwin, mixed with the society figures who visited his studio, and attended occasional evening lectures at the Royal Academy.

In 1784 Smith's father left Nollekens's studio to establish his own print shop at the sign of Rembrandt's Head, 18 May's Buildings, St Martin's Lane; he soon became a

John Thomas Smith (1766–1833), by William Brockedon, 1832

busy printseller, and his business and connections were integral to Smith's early career. Many of the latter's prints were published and sold by his father, and it was through him that Smith met John Charles Crowle (1738–1811), one of his first regular patrons. Commissioned by Crowle to produce a number of watercolour sketches of some ancient London architecture, Smith refined his talents as a topographical draughtsman and became fascinated with that aspect of antiquarianism which would characterize his whole output. As Crowle employed Smith's delicate and precise views in his extra-illustrated copies of Thomas Pennant's *Some Account of London* (1790), now in the British Museum, Smith also became acquainted with this new fashion in print collecting. Sensing the commercial opportunities arising from extra-illustration, in 1791 Smith brought out his first part-work, a series of ninety-six modest etchings and aquatints entitled *Antiquities of London* (1791–1800), which he innovatively promoted 'to be bound up with Mr. Pennant's *London*' (*GM*, 67, 1797, 157). Such was the success of this marketing tactic that he employed it again for his *Ancient Topography of London* (1810–15), a series of lively, deeply bitten etchings recording scenes of urban poverty and architectural decay; these had a romantic quality as, in reality, the sights were being swept away in the current wave of urban improvements.

Antiquities of London was dedicated to Sir James Winter Lake, a governor of the Hudson's Bay Company, who employed Smith as a drawing-master from 1788 to 1797. It was also in 1788 that Smith married Anne Maria Prickett, and together they settled in Edmonton, where the Lake family lived. There Smith came into contact with a circle of antiquaries and collectors who surrounded Lake; he also employed his free time drawing local cottages and developing his *Remarks on Rural Scenery* (1797), whose preliminary essay proposed a system for picturesque sketching. It is interesting to note that this brief venture into rural, rather than urban, imagery occurred at exactly the moment when Smith first met the young John Constable, who was staying in Edmonton in the summer of 1796. Although Constable had not yet decided to become an artist, his later correspondence (and some rather irritated letters from his mother) reveal the influence that John Thomas Smith had over his decision.

In 1797 Smith left Edmonton and moved to 40 Frith Street, Soho, with his wife and three children. Working with his father, he produced a few independent plates and continued to work on illustrated books of antiquarian subjects, but the next decades remained a period of 'acute financial worry' (Owen, 35). Consequently it is not surprising that, in 1800, he jumped at the chance of engraving the fourteenth-century paintings uncovered by restorations at St Stephen's Chapel. Having completed the sketches in six weeks of solid work, Smith planned to publish a volume including an account written by the antiquary John Sidney Hawkins. A setback arose when the authorities transferred the rights to reproduce these paintings to the Society of Antiquaries. Although Smith eventually went ahead with *The Antiquities of Westminster* (1807), the project was evidently fated, as a fire in Mr Bensley's printing office resulted in the destruction of 400 remaining copies of the work, and Smith lost over £3000 of potential revenue. It seems Smith's finances never entirely recovered from this event; in a begging letter to Lord Hardwick, of 1808, he bemoaned that 'My loss by fire has been so severe … that I fear I am Crippled for life' (Smith to Hardwick, 1 Aug 1808).

Despite obtaining the post of keeper of prints and drawings at the British Museum in 1816, and being an attentive, informed, and engaging figure in that role, Smith found his reputation, in later life, partly shaped by his financial anxieties. It is said that he was motivated to write his biography of Nollekens in revenge for being left out of that wealthy sculptor's will, and at the same time he fell out with his friend Francis Douce, who had been remembered very generously. Similarly, in 1828 he offended Constable by borrowing money and endlessly delaying repayment with assurances of the £200 advance he anticipated from his *A Book for a Rainy Day*. Ironically, Smith's most successful books, *A Book for a Rainy Day* (1845), *The Cries of London* (1839), and *Antiquarian Rambles in the Streets of London* (1846), were all edited and published after his death. And, while they did not ease his immediate financial difficulties, they secured his reputation as a gifted raconteur and chronicler of the more curious gossip and characters of contemporary London life.

Smith died, of an inflammation of the lungs, on 6 March 1833 at his home at 22 University Street, and was buried at St George's Chapel, Marble Arch, on 16 March. The fact that Constable wrote to C. R. Leslie to propose raising a subscription for the support of Smith's widow, 'who [was] left without a shilling' (Constable, *Further Documents*, 106), suggests the ultimate affection and respect many of Smith's contemporaries had for him. LUCY PELTZ

Sources J. T. Smith, *A book for a rainy day, or, Recollections of the events of the years 1766–1833*, ed. W. Whitten (1905) • J. T. Smith, *Nollekens and his times*, 1 (1828); repr. (1929); repr. (1986) • F. Owen, 'John Thomas ('Antiquity') Smith: a Renaissance man for the Georgian age', *Apollo*, 140 (Oct 1994), 34–6 • *GM*, 1st ser., 103/1 (1833), 641–44 • Thieme & Becker, *Allgemeines Lexikon* • J. B. Nicholls, 'Biographical memoir of the author', in J. T. Smith, *The cries of London* (1839), ix–xv • Bénézit, *Dict.* • S. Houfe, *The dictionary of 19th century British book illustrators and caricaturists*, rev. edn (1996) • B. Adams, *London illustrated, 1604–1851* (1983) • *John Constable's correspondence*, ed. R. B. Beckett, 6 vols., Suffolk RS, 4, 6, 8, 10–12 (1962–8) • *John Constable: further documents and correspondence*, ed. L. Parris, C. Shields, and I. Fleming-Williams, Suffolk RS, 18 (1975) • Graves, *Artists*, new edn • Graves, *RA exhibitors* • A. Griffiths, 'Introduction: the department of prints and drawings of the British Museum and the history of print collecting', *Landmarks in print collecting: connoisseurs and donors at the British Museum since 1753*, ed. A. Griffiths (British Museum Press, 1996), 9–18 [exhibition catalogue, Museum of Fine Arts, Houston, TX, 1996, and elsewhere] • J. S. Hawkins, correspondence, *GM*, 1st ser., 73 (1803), 31–2 • archive description, BL, letter from John Thomas Smith to Lord Hardwick, 1 August 1808, Add MS 35647, fol. 288 • *Monthly Magazine*, 13 (1802), 362 • S. T. Prideaux, *A history of aquatint engraving* (1909) • 'Smith's views in London', *GM*, 1st ser., 70 (1800), 970

Archives BL, letters to G. Cumberland, Add. MSS 36507, fol. 262; 3650, fol. 143 • Warks. CRO, MSS

Likenesses G. Cruickshank, etching, after 1816 ('First print room in the Tamley Gallery'), BM • W. Brockedon, pencil and chalk drawing, 2 June 1832, NPG [*see illus.*] • W. Skelton, line print, pubd 1833 (after J. Jackson), BM; repro. in J. T. Smith, *Notes for a rainy day* (1930)

Wealth at death impoverished: *John Constable's correspondence*, ed. Beckett, vol. 3, p. 95

Smith, John Thomas (1805–1882), army officer and engineer, second son of George Smith of Edwalton, Nottinghamshire, and afterwards of Foelallt, Cardiganshire, and his wife, Eliza Margaret, daughter of Welham Davis, elder brother of the Trinity House, was born at Foelallt on 16 April 1805. He was educated at Repton School and at Edinburgh high school, entered Addiscombe College in 1822, and was commissioned second lieutenant, Madras engineers, on 17 June 1824, promoted first lieutenant the following day, and attended the Chatham engineering course. He left Chatham on 4 February 1825 and arrived at Madras on 2 September.

On 28 April 1826 Smith was appointed acting superintending engineer in the public works department for the northern division of the Madras presidency (the appointment was confirmed on 2 May 1828). He began to investigate lighthouse lanterns, devising a reciprocating light. Smith suggested to government the improvement of the lighthouse at Hope's Island, off Coringa, and at the end of 1833 his services were lent to the marine board, for the improvement of the Madras lighthouse. On 11 February 1834 ill health compelled Smith to sail for England on leave. Before his departure the marine board had adopted his plans for remodelling the lighthouses at Madras and Hope's Island. He was promoted captain on 5 March 1835.

Smith remained in England until 28 July 1837, and on 1 June 1837 was elected FRS. He was given an extended furlough to superintend the manufacture of apparatus for the Madras lighthouse. In his spare time he translated J. L. Vicat's treatise on mortars and cements, adding the results of many original experiments; it appeared as *A Practical and Scientific Treatise on Calcareous Mortars and Cements, Artificial and Natural, with Additions* (1837). On his return to Madras on 13 December 1837 he was appointed to command the Madras sappers and miners, but remained at Madras on special duty. On 20 March 1838 he was appointed to the first division of the public works department, comprising the districts of Ganjam, Rajahmundry, and Vizagapatam, and on 24 April he took charge of the office of the chief engineer. He served on a committee on the Red Hills railway and canal, and he surveyed the Ennore and Pulicat lakes, to ascertain the feasibility of keeping open the bar of the Cooum River by artificially closing that of theEnnore River; thereby all the waters collected in the Pulicat Lake would be turned into the Cooum, which he considered would enable the cleansing of the Black Town, besides improving the water communication between Madras and Sullurupeta. Meanwhile he superintended erection of the Madras lighthouse, 'a Greek Doric column' with a light on the reciprocating principle, begun 1838 and completed 1844. On 5 April 1839 he was appointed to the sixth division of the public works department, and on 7 May superintending engineer at Madras.

On 24 September 1839 Smith was relieved of other duties to report on the Madras mint machinery. In February 1840 the mint was re-established with Smith as mint-master. By a thorough reform he soon made the mint highly efficient. He successfully adapted to steam power the old animal-powered machinery, and reduced waste. On 13 January 1846 he visited the Cape of Good Hope on leave, returning to the mint on 28 December 1847. His innovation of adjusting the weights of the blanks by diameters instead of thickness resulted in his design of an ingenious machine, by which blanks could be weighed to half a grain and deposited in a separate cell by a single person with two movements of the hand. After the pieces had been thus sorted they were passed through circular cutters, which removed excess weight, so that almost all the blanks were of the exact weight without further correction. This machine gained an award at the Great Exhibition of 1851.

Smith was promoted major on 2 March 1852, and lieutenant-colonel on 1 August 1854. During the Crimean War he made some ingenious inventions, which he proposed to use for the demolition of Kronstadt; he also invented a refracting rifle sight. On 21 September 1855 he was appointed mint-master at Calcutta. The following year he went to England to arrange about machinery for the mint, but did not return, retiring on a pension, with the honorary rank of colonel, on 23 October 1857. He devoted himself to currency problems, favouring a gold standard for India, and warning of the dangers from the depreciation of silver. He was sent to the international monetary congress at Paris in 1865, and was active in many learned societies.

Smith was for a long time consulting engineer to the Madras Irrigation Company; he was also a director of the Delhi bank and of the Madras Railway Company, of which he was for some years chairman. From 17 May 1866 until its abolition on 1 April 1880 he was a member of the consulting committee, military fund department, at the India Office. Sir Arthur Cotton wrote: 'He was one of the most talented, laborious, clear-headed, and sound-judging men I have ever met' (Vibart, 387–8). He married, on 27 June 1837, Maria Sarah, daughter of R. Tyser MD, and they had five sons and eight daughters. All their sons entered the navy or army.

Smith, a fellow of the Society of Actuaries and of the Statistical Society, and a member of many learned societies, published works on mints, currency, and related subjects. He initiated the *Professional Papers of the Madras Engineers*, and edited volumes 1, 2, and 3 of *Reports, Correspondence, and Original Papers on Various Professional Subjects Connected with the Duties of the Corps of Engineers, Madras Presidency* (1845–55). He contributed to these volumes many papers, mainly on mintage and lighthouse construction. An active supporter of the Church Missionary Society, at Madras he was a member of its corresponding committee, and back in England he rendered valuable help with the society's finances. He died at his residence, 10 Gledhow Gardens, Wetherby Road, South Kensington, London, on 14 May 1882.

Smith's eldest son, **Percy Guillemard Llewellin Smith** (1838–1893), army officer, was born at Madras on 15 June 1838, became lieutenant, Royal Engineers, on 28 February 1855, served in South Africa from August 1857 to January 1862, was promoted captain on 31 December 1861, and was employed on the defences of Portland and Weymouth until 1869, and on the construction of Maryhill barracks, Glasgow, until 1874. On 5 July 1872 he was promoted major, and in 1874 was appointed instructor in construction at the School of Military Engineering, Chatham. He was promoted lieutenant-colonel on 20 December 1879, in which year he became an assistant director of works under the Admiralty at Portsmouth. In October 1882 he succeeded Major-General Charles Pasley as director of works at the Admiralty, and during ten years of office carried out many important works both at home and at Malta, Gibraltar, Bermuda, Halifax, and Newfoundland. Promoted brevet colonel on 20 December 1883, he retired from the army on 31 December 1887 with the honorary rank of major-general, but retained his Admiralty appointment. He was twice married: first to a daughter of Captain Bailey RN; and, second, in 1886, to Miss Ethel Parkyns. He was the author of *Notes on Building Construction*, published anonymously in 3 volumes (1875–9). It was considered the best British book on the subject. A fourth volume, *Theory of Construction*, was published in 1891. He contributed to volumes 16 and 18 (new series) of the *Professional Papers of the Corps of Royal Engineers*. He died at Bournemouth on 25 April 1893.

R. H. Vetch, *rev.* Roger T. Stearn

Sources BL OIOC · *The Times* (17 May 1882) · P. S., *PRS*, 34 (1882–3), xvi–xvii · *PICE*, 71 (1882–3), 422–4 · H. M. Vibart, *Addiscombe: its heroes and men of note* (1894) · *Professional Papers of the Corps of Royal Engineers* · *Professional Papers of the Madras Engineers* · T. A. Heathcote, *The military in British India: the development of British land forces in south Asia, 1600–1947* (1995) · D. R. Headrick, *The tentacles of progress: technology transfer in the age of imperialism, 1850–1940* (1988) · E. W. C. Sandes, *The military engineer in India*, 2 (1935)

Wealth at death £33,013 1s. 11d.: probate, 26 July 1882, *CGPLA Eng. & Wales*

Smith, John William (1809–1845), legal writer, was born on 23 January 1809 in Chapel Street, Belgrave Square, London, the eldest son of John Smith, an official of the Irish parliament, displaced by the Act of Union, who served in several government departments before being appointed in 1830 paymaster of the forces in Ireland. His mother was a sister of George Connor, master in chancery in Ireland. After exhibiting remarkable precocity at Dr Greenhow's school in Isleworth, which he attended from 1817, he passed in 1821 to Westminster School, where he was elected queen's scholar in 1823. Refusing to accept fagging, he left and finished his schooling in Blackheath at an establishment run by Greenhow's son. A place was found for him in Dublin Castle but he soon resigned it to a brother and entered Trinity College, Dublin, in 1826. He obtained a scholarship in 1829, and was awarded the gold medal in classics in the following year.

Smith joined the Inner Temple on 20 June 1827 and, after practising unsuccessfully as a special pleader, was called to the bar on 3 May 1834. He practised without success on the Oxford circuit and at the Hereford and Gloucester sessions. Later, he practised in London.

Smith's ungainly person, harsh voice, and awkward manners obscured mental endowments of a high order. To a talent for the discovery and exposition of legal principles, allied to a retentive memory and an exceptional capacity for sustained hard work, he added erudition not only in the ancient classics, but in the masterpieces of English, Italian, and Spanish literature. He was also well read in theology and a devout Christian; indeed at the lowest ebb in his fortunes, he contemplated abandoning the bar for the priesthood.

In 1834 Smith published *A Compendium of Mercantile Law*, on a subject never before treated as a unit; thirteen editions down to 1931 attested its worth. *An Elementary View of the Proceedings in an Action at Law* (1836) sold even better, mostly as a student text, in fourteen editions down to 1884. However, *A Selection of Leading Cases on Various Branches of the Law* (1837–40) shows Smith's powers at their highest. It was a novel conception to use a comparatively small number of decisions as the basis for an account of the principles of common law and equity, their elaboration and qualification traced through extensive notes. Smith succeeded admirably by judicious selection and lucid explanation. Preparation of the sixteenth (and last) edition in 1929 taught the future Lord Denning 'most of the law I ever knew'.

Smith's writings secured him the post of lecturer at the Law Institution, and in 1840 he was appointed to a revising barristership. His lectures on contract and landlord and tenant were published after his death and went through several editions. His academic reputation brought him briefs in steadily increasing numbers. Overwork accelerated the progress of a consumptive condition and he died, unmarried, in his chambers at 10 King's Bench Walk, Temple, on 17 December 1845. Since his wish to be buried in the Temple was impracticable, he was interred on 24 December at Kensal Green cemetery, with a tablet to his memory in the Temple Church.

J. M. RIGG, *rev.* PATRICK POLDEN

Sources S. Warren, *Miscellanies*, 1 (1855) • J. G. Phillimore, *Law Magazine*, 35 (1846), 177–93 • Holdsworth, *Eng. law* • review of *Memoir of the late John William Smith*, *Law Times* (7 March 1846), 473–5 • A. W. B. Simpson, ed., *Biographical dictionary of the common law* (1984) • A. T. Denning, *The family story* (1981) • *Old Westminsters*, 2.859 • W. P. Baildon, ed., *The records of the Honorable Society of Lincoln's Inn: admissions*, 2 vols. (1896) • Burtchaell & Sadleir, *Alum. Dubl.* • J. Whishaw, *A synopsis of the modern English bar* (1835) • J. Wade, *The black book, or, Corruption unmasked!*, new edn, 2 vols. (1829)

Smith, Joseph (1670–1756), college head and Church of England clergyman, was born at Lowther, Westmorland, on 10 October 1670, the fifth of eleven sons of William Smith, rector of Lowther, and younger brother of John Smith (1659–1715), canon of Durham. Following his father's death his mother moved the family to Guisborough, Yorkshire, where Joseph attended the grammar school. After a period at Durham School he was admitted a scholar at Queen's College, Oxford, on 10 May 1689 and matriculated six days later. In 1693 he was chosen a taberdar; he graduated BA in 1694.

In 1697 Smith accompanied his godfather Sir Joseph Williamson to the Netherlands as his private secretary; there Williamson acted as one of the British plenipotentiaries in the negotiations that ended in the treaty of Ryswick, signed on 20 September 1697. In his absence from Oxford, Smith proceeded MA, by diploma, in 1697 and was elected a fellow of his college on 31 October 1698. Soon after his return in 1700 he took holy orders and was presented to the college living of Iffley, near Oxford. In 1704 he was elected senior proctor and dubbed Handsome Smith to distinguish him from his junior colleague Thomas Smith, of St John's. In the same year he declined to stand for election as provost of his college, and instead supported the successful candidate, his old tutor Dr William Lancaster. The new provost presented him to Russell Court chapel and to the lectureship of Trinity Chapel, Hanover Square, which he held until 1731.

Smith moved to London to minister to his new congregations and became chaplain to Edward Villiers, first earl of Jersey (1654–1711), who championed him at court. Invited to preach before Queen Anne on several occasions, Smith was rewarded with her promise of the first vacant canonry in Windsor chapel, which, however, did not fall vacant during the remainder of her reign. In 1708 he took the degrees of BD and DD, and in November was presented by his college to the rectory of Knights Enham and to the donative of Upton Grey, in Hampshire; in 1716 he exchanged the latter for the rectory of St Dionis, Backchurch, London.

In 1709 Smith married Mary (*d.* 1745), youngest daughter of Henry Lowther, of Ingleton Hall, Yorkshire, and of Lowther, in co. Fermanagh; she was also the niece of Timothy Halton, the former provost of Queen's. They had three children: Joseph, an advocate of Doctors' Commons; Anne, who was twice married; and William, who died young. Smith continued to accumulate preferments under George I: he was appointed chaplain to Caroline, princess of Wales, and in 1723 was made prebend of Durham by his college friend Edmund Gibson, bishop of Lincoln. Following Gibson's transfer to London, Smith acquired the donative of Paddington; the lectureship of the new church of St George's, Hanover Square, in 1724; and the prebend of St Mary Newington in St Paul's in 1728. Smith proved his credentials as a whig with a number of publications in support of Benjamin Hoadly in the Bangorian controversy, and with *Anarchy and Rebellion* (1720), in which his condemnation was clearly aimed at Jacobites. He also took part in the deist controversy, publishing *The Unreasonableness of Deism* in 1720.

In 1730 Smith was elected provost of Queen's College, succeeding John Gibson. He enthusiastically set about trying to reform the academic standards of the college. By 1731 he had drawn up a detailed theological curriculum and in 1744 he composed a comprehensive list of disputation questions on logic, ethics, science, and theology. Reading lists were attached to each list but there is no evidence that they were used in Queen's or adopted elsewhere in the university. Smith involved himself in the gradual construction of the classical front quad that had begun in 1719 and commissioned engravings of the new buildings. Through the influence of Arthur Onslow and Colonel John Selwyn he obtained from Queen Caroline a gift of £1000 towards the building works. In gratitude he commissioned Henry Cheere to sculpt the college's royal patron; placed over the college gateway and covered by an elegant cupola, Caroline's statue remains a landmark in the High Street. Smith also persuaded Lady Elizabeth Hastings to settle several exhibitions on the college, specifically for students from northern England, and procured the foundation of four scholarships by John Michel of Richmond, Surrey.

Mary Smith died on 29 April 1745; Joseph Smith died in college on 12 November 1756, and was interred in a vault in the college chapel.

E. I. CARLYLE, *rev.* S. J. SKEDD

Sources J. R. Magrath, *The Queen's College*, 2 vols. (1921) • Foster, *Alum. Oxon.* • *Hist. U. Oxf.* 5: *18th-cent. Oxf.* • *IGI*

Likenesses B. Baron, line engraving (after oils by J. Maubert) • J. Maubert, oils, Queen's College, Oxford • bust (on monument to J. Smith), Queen's College, Oxford, chapel

Smith, Joseph (1673/4?–1770), book collector and patron of the arts, was probably born in 1673 or 1674 (at his death in Venice in 1770 he was said to be ninety-six). Nothing is known of his antecedents; he used a coat of arms of the family of Smith of Essex and Suffolk but he never established his right to it. He had a younger brother, John, a merchant in London, and a sister, Margaret, who was married to a James Bagwell.

Educated at Westminster School, Smith went to Venice

in 1700 as a junior partner in the merchant banking house of Thomas Williams. He prospered and eventually headed the firm of Williams and Smith. Long ambitious for an official post, he was appointed British consul in Venice in 1744 and, though he retired in 1760, he has ever since been known as Consul Smith. A music lover, he married the beautiful Catherine *Tofts (*d.* 1756), the first English prima donna, who had left London for Venice about 1710 or 1711. A son, John, was born in 1721 but died in 1727. Unfortunately, in later life Catherine became mentally deranged.

Smith was a serious book collector, acquiring some of his early printed books from Italian monasteries and others from prominent Venetian families. In 1724 he published in Padua, in an edition of about fifty copies, a detailed catalogue of 227 incunabula, the *Catalogus librorum rarissimorum*. Richard Rawlinson recorded in his journal for 20 July 1725:

> This day went to see Mr. Smith and his fine library where are above 227 books printed before 1500 many on velum, a large collection of Italian Topography and History, books on the Italian language, and many other curious pieces …
> (Morrison, 32)

A second edition of the *Catalogus* was published by Pasquali in 1737, listing 248 incunabula. Smith's book collecting had a commercial element; he had sold a number of manuscript books to the third earl of Sunderland for £1500 in 1720 and in a contemporary letter about the price he wrote:

> you know the long time I have been collecting them and with what Trouble and Expense, and to this added but a Common Interest for my money (which as a merchant I must consider) they stand mee in a very handsome summ …
> (ibid., 29)

Both editions of the *Catalogus* may have been produced as sale catalogues, although no sale occurred and the books remained in his library until 1762. Smith's collecting eventually resulted in a magnificent library, recorded in the *Bibliotheca Smithiana*, published by Pasquali in 1755. This substantial volume of over 900 pages included reprints of the prefaces of many of his incunabula; indeed Smith was one of the first collectors to catalogue incunabula in detail. His library was rich in sixteenth- and seventeenth-century editions of the classics, of Italian literature, history, art and architecture, as well as contemporary continental and English books.

Early in the 1730s Smith set up, with Giambattista Pasquali as his partner and printer, the publishing firm of G. B. Pasquali. Smith 'financed the firm and controlled and directed every detail of the enterprise' (Vivian, *The Consul Smith Collection*, 13–14). Their firm published a wide range of books and by the mid-century ranked as one of the three great Venetian publishers alongside Albrizzi and Zatta. At this time Smith was living in the leased palazzo Balbi (now the palazzo Mangilli-Valmarana) on the Grand Canal which he finally bought in 1740. From 1726 or 1727 he also leased a villa at Mogliano, near Treviso, which he bought in 1731. Although no trace of it now remains, drawings of it by Visentini are in the Royal Collection.

In the early 1720s Smith began his patronage of contemporary Venetian artists by commissioning paintings for himself and other English clients from Sebastiano and Marco Ricci and from Rosalba Carriera. At some time in the 1720s he began his long and fruitful association with Canaletto. From about 1729 until 1735, Smith controlled his whole output, both buying pictures for himself and commissioning works for other English patrons. Consequently, by the early 1730s Smith owned 'the most important collection of modern art to be found in Venice' as well as 'a growing number of old masters' (Haskell, 304). He also collected drawings and prints. Most of these were contained in volumes in his library and were recorded in the *Bibliotheca Smithiana*.

In the 1740s, Smith commissioned Canaletto to paint the principal buildings by Palladio in Venice. Smith's devotion to Palladianism lasted for the rest of his life. In 1751 he employed Visentini to build a Palladian façade for his palazzo. In 1768, after years of preparation, Smith published a facsimile of the original edition of Palladio's *Quattro libri dell'architettura* of 1570. Goethe was so delighted to buy a copy of it in Padua in 1786 that he made a special visit to Smith's grave in the protestant cemetery on the Lido—'To him I owe my copy of Palladio and I offered up a grateful prayer at his unconsecrated grave' (Morrison, 53).

In the late 1750s Smith's finances suffered from the failure of banks in northern Europe in which he had large commitments and he contemplated selling his collections. After protracted negotiations by Lord Bute and his younger brother on behalf of George III, the king bought the library described in the *Bibliotheca Smithiana* for £10,000 and Smith's collections of pictures for another £10,000. The books, excepting volumes of drawings and prints, were an important part of the Royal Library later transferred to the British Museum by George IV and preserved there as the King's Library (now the centrepiece of the new British Library). Most of the paintings, drawings, and prints remain in the Royal Collection, including Smith's fine collection of Canaletto's paintings and drawings. The sale, as Smith had hoped, has preserved his collections for posterity.

Smith's wife died early in 1756 and in 1757 he married Elizabeth (*c.*1717–1788), sister of John Murray, British resident in Venice since 1754. Although he was about eighty-three years old and Elizabeth forty or so, the marriage was apparently a happy one.

During the later years of Smith's long life he continued to buy books and pictures, maintaining his interest in contemporary, as well as earlier, literature. A letter from a Robert Richie to Smith's brother-in-law John Murray in 1770, the last year of Smith's life, described him as 'going on in his usual way, of purchasing books, medals, pictures and other curiositys' (Morrison, 54).

Although Consul Smith's collections were one of the recognized features of the grand tour, he was disliked by some of his visitors, notably Horace Walpole and Lady Mary Wortley Montagu. Vivian suggests that 'in spite of his [Smith's] learning and sensitive response to art … [he] may have been sufficiently vulgar in manner as to grate on the susceptibilities of elegant and aristocratic connoisseurs like Horace Walpole' (Vivian, *The Consul Smith Collection*, 15). The Adam brothers present a contrasting picture of Smith. Robert Adam was received at Mogliano in 1757 'with open arms' and after 'a very handsome dinner' was shown 'as pretty a collection of pictures as I have ever seen' (Fleming, 236). On the other hand, James Adam, calling on him in 1760, referred to being received 'with much flummery' and wrote that Smith was 'literally eaten up with it [vanity]' (ibid., 270). Smith was for many years a member of an intellectual circle in Venice and Padua, and was friendly with, among others, Dr Richard Mead and Thomas Hollis in England. Haskell has suggested that his relationship with Poleni and others in Padua imply that Smith was 'most at home in scholarly surroundings' (Haskell, 301).

Although Smith commissioned portraits of the artists he patronized, he never commissioned a portrait of himself. In spite of accusations of vanity, no likeness of Smith is known to exist. He died of 'senile fever' (Parker, 16) at palazzo Balbi, Grand Canal, Venice on 6 November 1770 and was buried in the protestant cemetery of St Nicolo al Lido. The bulk of his estate was left to his widow. The collections of books and pictures he had amassed after the sale to George III were auctioned in London in the 1770s. Elizabeth Smith died in Bath in 1788.

STUART L. MORRISON

Sources F. Vivian, *The Consul Smith collection* (1989) • F. Haskell, 'The foreign residents', *Patrons and painters: a study in the relations between Italian art and society in the age of the baroque*, 2nd edn (1980), 299–316 • K. T. Parker, *The drawings of Antonio Canaletto in the collection of his majesty the king at Windsor Castle* (1948) • S. Morrison, 'Records of a bibliophile: the catalogues of consul Joseph Smith and some aspects of his collecting', *Book Collector*, 43 (1994), 27–58 • F. Vivian, *Il Console Smith, mercante e collezionista* (Vicenza, 1971) • L. Hellinga-Querido, 'Notes on the incunabula of Consul Joseph Smith: an exploration', *The Italian book, 1465–1800*, ed. D. V. Reidy (1993), 335–48 • A. Griffiths, 'The prints and drawings in the library of Consul Joseph Smith', *Print Quarterly*, 8 (1991), 127–39 • J. Fleming, *Robert Adam and his circle in Edinburgh and Rome* (1962) • Walpole, *Corr.* • *DNB* • *New Grove*

Archives BL, Add. MS 32834, fol. 133 • BL, Lansdowne MS 841, fols. 98–99

Wealth at death widow sold Palazzo Balbi and collections of books and pictures: Vivian, *Consul Smith collection*, 37

Smith, Joseph (*fl.* 1709–1731), printseller and art bookseller, is of unknown parentage and there is no record of his early life. His son Joland was apprenticed in 1721 and was therefore probably born about 1707. Shortly afterwards, in partnership with Henry Overton, David Mortier, and Daniel Midwinter, Smith bought Leonard Knyff's plates of *Britannia illustrata*. He republished this collection of views of fine houses in 1709 and commissioned further prints of a similar nature. From this date Smith also became London's most visible importer of fine prints from Italy and France, using advertisements in the newspapers to promote his stock. He sold 'all sorts of Prints and Maps, cheap and Ornamental for furnishing Rooms, Stair-Cases and Closets', as well as 'large Books of Prints, proper for publick Libraries, at reasonable Rates' (*Post Boy*, 8–10 Jan 1713). Smith published a large number of portraits and topical and military prints but his chief importance was as the principal 'undertaker' of topographical and architectural projects. Knyff's *Britannia illustrata* was gradually amplified with two more volumes of views of houses, one of cathedrals and churches, and, in its 1724 French language edition, an *Atlas Anglois*.

Smith published histories of St Paul's Cathedral and Westminster Abbey and an English translation of Dugdale's *Monasticon*. But his most important enterprise was *Vitruvius Britannicus*. Responsibility for this volume is usually attributed to its author Colen Campbell, but it has been demonstrated that Campbell became involved at a late stage in a survey of modern British building originally orchestrated by Smith with the encouragement of a group of amateur enthusiasts. The subscription to it was launched in 1714 before the fall of Robert Harley's tory government and its original intention was to promote and celebrate British architecture:

> We travel, for the most part, at an Age more apt to be imposed upon by the Ignorance or Partiality of others, than to judge truly of the Merit of Things by the Strength of Reason. It is owing to this Mistake in Education, that so many of the British Quality have so mean an Opinion of what is performed in our own Country. (*Vitruvius Britannicus*, preface)

Smith retained a third and then a half share in the copyright of this and the succeeding two volumes. By 1724 he was sole proprietor of *Britannia illustrata*. In 1721 Smith apprenticed his son Joland to the bookseller Luke Stokoe and in October 1723 announced that he had 'remov'd from his Shop in Exeter Exchange to a Shop over the Way, within two Doors of the Fountain Tavern in the Strand' (*Daily Journal*, 7 Oct 1723). This shop was called Inigo Jones's Head by 1727. In 1726 he took as his apprentice Dryden, the son of another bookseller, Dryden Leach. Smith was still going strong in 1728 when he published a twelve-plate view of London and Westminster, but he probably retired in 1731 when he sold his share of the copy and plates of *Vitruvius Britannicus*. Harris speculates that he died within a few years and before a reissue of the *Nouveau théâtre de la Grande Bretagne* was advertised in February 1737.

TIMOTHY CLAYTON

Sources E. Harris and N. Savage, *British architectural books and writers, 1556–1785* (1990) • D. Hodson, *County atlases of the British Isles published after 1703: a bibliography*, 2 (1989), 97–147 • T. Clayton, *The English print, 1688–1802* (1997) • I. Maxted, ed., *The London book trades, 1710–1777: index of the masters and apprentices recorded in the inland revenue registers at the Public Record Office* (privately printed, Exeter, 1983) • T. P. Connor, 'The making of *Vitruvius Britannicus*', *Architectural History*, 20 (1977), 14–30 • [L. Knyff and J. Kip], *Nouveau théâtre de la Grande Bretagne* (1708); facs edn with a new introduction, notes, and index as *Britannia illustrata: Knyff and Kip*, ed. J. Harris and G. Jackson-Stops (1984)

Smith, Joseph (1732/3–1790), army officer in the East India Company, was the son of Joseph Smith, an engineer officer in the East India Company's service, and himself joined the company's Madras forces as an ensign in 1749. The company's prolonged but intermittent war with the French in the Carnatic (1750–61) provided many opportunities for a vigorous young officer like Smith to distinguish himself. As early as 1753 he was given the command of an independent detachment aiding the nawab of the Carnatic, but was captured when the nawab's forces deserted him in an action. Soon released from captivity during a truce, Smith was promoted captain in 1754. In 1757 he was in command of the key fortress town of Trichinopoly, controlling north–south and east–west routes in the southern Carnatic. Smith successfully repelled a French siege of the place while he was encumbered with five times as many French prisoners of war as he had European troops. In March 1760 he was ordered to reinforce the troops under Major George Monson besieging Karikal, a French post on the coast, and arrived on 3 April in time to assist in the reduction of the place. In September he was appointed to the rank of major and placed in command of a brigade during the successful British siege of the French headquarters at Pondicherry by Monson and Eyre Coote.

Smith returned to England on leave during 1763, arriving back in India with the rank of colonel in September 1766. He was soon given a field command, to act with the nizam of Hyderabad against their common enemy the ambitious and dynamic upstart soldier-ruler of Mysore, Haidar Ali. The East India Company's council at Madras was anxious for the Carnatic to expand to the west, to secure a stronger frontier and more revenue for their puppet nawab Muhammad Ali, and to cut Haidar Ali down to size. Smith's well-founded suspicion that the nizam was toying with the idea of changing sides was rejected by the Madras council. But Smith cautiously withdrew to the Carnatic frontier in May 1767. With the nizam openly hostile by August, Smith prepared to defend the Changama Pass (120 miles south-west of Madras) to prevent the new Indian allies from debouching from the Deccan plateau onto the rich Carnatic coastal plain.

At the height of the monsoon Smith twice defeated Haidar and the nizam in pitched battles (3 and 26 September 1767); on the latter occasion the allies lost 4000 men and sixty-four guns at a cost of 150 killed and wounded to Smith's forces. Although the nizam withdrew into neutrality in December, Haidar was still in the field but was now more cautious about accepting battle from the redoubtable Smith. Smith, who was commander-in-chief after General Caillaud's return to England in January 1768, could not easily force Haidar to fight, because he suffered under severe logistical difficulties, fighting much further inland than any company army in the south had yet managed, and he often had little or no cavalry to confront Haidar's masses, which consequently could ravage the country around Smith's army at will.

Throughout the first nine months of 1768 the Madras council, unsympathetic to Smith's problems, pressed him to seek a decisive battle, even to attack Haidar's major fortress at Bangalore. They eventually and disastrously sent two civilian councillors to his camp to ginger him up. These men tried to impose their amateur strategic ideas on Smith and goaded him into trying to force Haidar into a confrontation by using a light detachment under Colonel Mark Wood to manoeuvre round his rear, but when Haidar turned his whole army (which greatly outnumbered the total company forces) on Wood, Smith only just rescued him in time (9 October 1768).

An impasse between the main forces set in, with Haidar ensconced behind very powerful fortifications and Smith unable to mount an operation against him without vastly improved logistical services and a large siege train. This was far beyond Madras's resources; indeed, by the spring of 1769 the council no longer had the money to keep its army in the field. Desperately, it proposed that Smith should send long-range raiding parties into Mysore to smoke Haidar out. This policy was adopted, but by Haidar, who, with an élite cavalry force 6000 strong, evaded Smith's army and rode swiftly to the gates of Fort St George, Madras, demanding a peace on his terms, which the alarmed and impecunious councillors were forced to accept in March 1769. The company's directors blamed the over-ambitious council for the failure, not Smith, who was made brigadier-general in 1768 and raised to major-general the following year. Haidar had greatly admired Smith, and asked to meet him when the peace was signed.

Smith remained commander-in-chief at Madras for another six years, with two brief intermissions: his successors became entangled in the increasingly partisan politics of the Madras council and quickly withdrew from the fray, leaving Smith to resume his command. Smith, cool and resolute on the battlefield, was the preferred commander-in-chief of the Madras civilian councillors because, mild of disposition in the council chamber, he allowed himself to be manipulated politically. As part of the developing byzantine relationship the Madras councillors had with the nawab (which were dominated by his large debts to them as private individuals), in 1772–3 Smith (who was evidently on the nawab's payroll) was twice sent in command of military expeditions on behalf of Muhammad Ali to force the wealthy and autonomous raja of Tanjore to disgorge some of his riches to balance the books, an action which was later condemned and reversed by the company directors.

Smith eventually resigned the service in October 1775 and retired to England. He died at his house in the Circus, Bath, on 1 September 1790. During his career Smith had shone in the field, despite being ordered to achieve feats far beyond the means given to him. In later years he had also carried out major reforms in the army and had been much beloved by his men for the care he took of them. One officer said he was 'the common Father of the Army … rec[eive]d with universal Joy' (Major Arthur Owen to Robert Orme, 31 Jan 1773, BL OIOC, Orme MS OV 30, fols. 235–40). John Macpherson, later governor-general of Bengal, declared Smith was 'the most amiable Character that India ever saw from Europe' (Maclean). G. J. Bryant

Sources *DNB* • BL OIOC • BL OIOC, MS Eur. Orme • *GM*, 1st ser., 60 (1790), 861 • J. N. M. Maclean, 'The early political careers of James "Fingal" Macpherson and Sir John Macpherson', PhD diss., U. Edin., 1967

Archives BL OIOC, corresp., MSS Eur. Orme • BL OIOC, India Office records

Smith, Joshua Toulmin [*formerly* Joshua Smith] (**1816–1869**), publicist and lawyer, born on 29 May 1816 at Birmingham, was the eldest son of William Hawkes Smith (1786–1840) of that town, an economic and educational reformer. His great-grandmother was sister to Job Orton, and his great-grandfather was Dr Joshua *Toulmin. From 1854 he used the surname Toulmin Smith. Smith was educated at home and at a private school at Hale, Cheshire, kept by Charles Wallace. An eager student of literature and philosophy, he was at first destined for the Unitarian ministry, but that vocation was abandoned in favour of the law, and at sixteen he was articled to a local solicitor. He moved in 1835 to London, and was entered at Lincoln's Inn with a view to the bar. Meanwhile he showed a precocious literary activity. At seventeen he wrote an 'Introduction to the Latin language' for a class at the Birmingham mechanics' institute, and in 1836 produced *Philosophy among the Ancients*.

In 1837 Smith married Martha (*d*. 1887), daughter of William Jones Kendall of Wakefield, and went to the United States, first settling at Detroit, then at Utica, and afterwards in Boston. At Boston he lectured, chiefly on phrenology and on philosophy. Attracted by Professor Rafn's publication at Copenhagen of the narratives of early Icelandic voyages to America, he published in 1839 *The Discovery of America by the Northmen in the Tenth Century*, a study from the original documents, which he was the first to introduce to English readers; the work gained him the diploma of the Royal Society of Antiquaries of Copenhagen. Several other minor publications, educational and historical, occupied his pen until, in 1842, he returned to England. He settled at Highgate, resumed his legal studies, and was called to the bar in 1849, taking chambers at 68 Chancery Lane. At this period he found recreation in the pursuit of geology. Especially directing his attention to the upper chalk, he printed a series of papers in the *Annals and Magazine of Natural History* (August 1847 to May 1848), issued as a volume in 1848, entitled *The Ventriculidae of the Chalk*. The monograph, which he illustrated himself, was based on laborious microscopic investigations; it attempted to establish the true character, hitherto imperfectly known, of the class of fossils of which it treated. This work drew round him the leading geologists of the day. When the Geologists' Association was formed Toulmin Smith was invited to be president, but, beyond delivering the inaugural address (11 January 1859), he took little active part in its proceedings.

Meanwhile, a cholera epidemic, which began in the autumn of 1847, caused intense attention to matters of health, and Toulmin Smith became leader of effective action in his own neighbourhood of Highgate. His enquiries into the former law and practice on the subject of local responsibilities were the beginning of efforts extending over many years, with considerable success in spite of difficulties, to raise the sanitary condition and municipal life of the suburban parish where he lived. He watched the course of public legislation, and brought to bear on it his researches into constitutional law, joined with his local experience, by means of weighty speeches and a tireless pen. He strongly opposed the Public Health Act of 1848, and that year published *Laws of England Relating to Public Health* (1848). Reform of the corporation of London, the sewerage and administration of the metropolis, highway boards, the maintenance of public footpaths, the functions of the coroner's court, the volunteer movement, parish rights and duties, and the church-rate question are some of the subjects on which his research and action between 1850 and 1860 were incessant. In 1851 there appeared his *Local Self-Government and Centralization*, and in 1854 *The Parish: its Obligations and Powers, its Officers and their Duties*, by the second edition of which (1857) he is perhaps best-known. These works enunciated, in a rather extreme tone, the doctrine of the historical autonomy of English local institutions, such as the vestry, which he traced from the Anglo-Saxon period. The form 'local self-government' was his innovation. His work, *English Gilds*, was published posthumously (1870). *Memorials of Old Birmingham* (2 vols., 1863) recorded his debt to his birthplace.

Toulmin Smith's sympathy was strongly drawn to the Hungarians in their struggle for liberty in 1848–9, and among other aids to their cause he published *Parallels between … England and Hungary* (1849), in which he compared the fundamental institutions of the two countries. Through many years, and to his own detriment, he continued a firm friend to Hungary; he successfully defended Lajos Kossuth in the suit as to paper money which was brought against him by the Austrian government in 1861, issued two important pamphlets on the political position of the country, and was the only person who dared to publish in England the full text of Francis Deák's speeches (*Parliamentary Remembrancer*, vol. 4).

Smith declined an invitation to stand as candidate for parliament for Sheffield in 1852. In 1854 he, with W. J. Evelyn, MP for Surrey, and the Revd M. W. Malet, formed the Anti-Centralisation Union, and wrote the thirteen papers issued during the three years of its existence. He then took a wider means of instructing the public on the attempts and methods of modern legislators, by the establishment of the *Parliamentary Remembrancer* (1857–65), a weekly record of action in parliament, with valuable historical commentaries and illustrations. The great labour entailed by this periodical—which he conducted single-handed, helped only by his family—added to his other undertakings and to his practice at the parliamentary bar, and it finally broke down his health. He was drowned while bathing at Lancing, Sussex, on 28 April 1869, and was buried in Hornsey churchyard. His wife survived him with two sons and three daughters. Among the daughters was Lucy Toulmin *Smith. Toulmin Smith's works have an enduring significance in the historiography of English localism. L. T. Smith, *rev.* H. C. G. Matthew

Sources *The Register, and Magazine of Biography*, 2 (1869), 88 • *Law Times* (29 May 1869) • P. B. M. Blaas, *Continuity and anachronism* (1978)

Archives Birm. CA, corresp. and papers | Co-operative Union, Holyoake House, Manchester, Co-operative Union archive, corresp. with George Holyoake • NHM, corresp. with Sir Richard Owen and William Clift • NL Scot., corresp. with George Combe

Wealth at death under £1000: probate, 19 June 1869, *CGPLA Eng. & Wales*

Smith, Josiah William (1816–1887), legal writer, was born on 3 April 1816, the only child of John Smith (*c*.1800–1870), rector of Baldock, Hertfordshire, and his wife, Elizabeth Frances (*c*.1796–1864). He was admitted to Trinity Hall, Cambridge, on 3 December 1834 and graduated LLB in 1841. He entered Lincoln's Inn on 9 November 1836, was called to the bar on 6 May 1841, and chiefly practised in the court of chancery. In 1844 he married Mary, second daughter of George Henry Hicks MD of Baldock. In later years they lived at Athelstan Hall, Hereford; there were no children.

With H. C. Jones, Smith was the draftsman of the *Consolidated General Orders of the High Court of Chancery* (1860). He is best remembered as the author of the *Manual of Equity* (1845), *Compendium of the Law of Real and Personal Property* (1855), and *Manual of Common Law and Bankruptcy* (1864). These works, clearly and concisely written, went through many editions, and were still standard works at the close of the nineteenth century. In addition he compiled several small manuals of devotion and a *Summary of the Law of Christ* (1859 and 1860).

Having become a queen's counsel on 25 February 1861, Smith was chosen a bencher of Lincoln's Inn on 13 March following, and in September 1865 became county court judge for Herefordshire and Shropshire. Supremely confident in his ability to dispense justice, he shared with many county court judges of that era an impatience with advocates and juries and resented appeals. Undaunted by criticism, he grew increasingly 'impatient of that servile deference to legislation and to the decisions of the (so-called) superior courts which a superstitious profession usually expects' (*Solicitors' Journal*, 1886–7, 438). His defiance at length drew down upon him a rebuke from the court of queen's bench.

Smith, who was a JP for Herefordshire, retired from the bench on a pension in February 1879. He died at 33 Caledonia Place, Clifton, Bristol, Gloucestershire, on 10 April 1887, and was buried at Baldock. He was survived by his wife.

W. R. Williams, *rev.* Patrick Polden

Sources P. Polden, 'Judicial Selkirks', *Communities and courts in Britain, 1150–1900*, ed. C. Brooks and M. Lobban (1997), 245–62 • *Law Times* (1863–79) • *County Courts Chronicle* (1863–79) • *Solicitors' Journal*, 7–24 (1863–79) • *Law Journal* (1863–79) • Venn, *Alum. Cant.* • Holdsworth, *Eng. law*, 15.371 • W. P. Baildon, ed., *The records of the Honorable Society of Lincoln's Inn: admissions*, 2 vols. (1896) • J. E. Cussans, *History of Hertfordshire*, 2/3 (1874) • Boase, *Mod. Eng. biog.* • J. Foster, *Men-at-the-bar: a biographical hand-list of the members of the various inns of court*, 2nd edn (1885) • *Debrett's Illustrated House of Commons and the Judicial Bench* (1868) • *Solicitors' Journal*, 31 (1886–7), 449 • *Law Times*, 82 (1886–7) • *CGPLA Eng. & Wales* (1887)

Wealth at death £10,597 9*s*. 4*d*.: probate, 13 May 1887, *CGPLA Eng. & Wales*

Smith, Julia Cuthbert (1927–1997), television producer, was born at 174 Sutherland Avenue, London, on 26 May 1927, the only child of Edward Cuthbert Smith, a vocalist who became the senior professor of singing at the Royal College of Music, and his wife, Elfriede Frances Gritton Menges. The family home was in Bedford Park, Chiswick. Her uncle, Herbert Menges, was a conductor and director of music at the Old Vic; her aunt, Isolde Menges, was a violinist who also became a professor at the Royal College of Music; and her cousin, Chris Menges, became an Oscar-winning cinematographer. Given that background, a theatrical career beckoned. Evacuated to Wiltshire during the Second World War, Smith later went to the Royal Academy of Dramatic Art. Believing her face to be too solemn to win many leading roles, she turned instead to stage management, initially at the Regent Theatre in Hayes, Middlesex, and then in repertory companies. Work for the Royal Shakespeare Company in the 1950s led to her first contact with the BBC, when she was asked to transfer a stage production to the small screen. After some years in television she went back to Stratford. On 2 April 1962 she married David Maxwell Geary (*b*. 1927/8), radio announcer. The marriage ended in divorce in 1966. Meanwhile, in 1963 Smith returned to the BBC, where over the next thirty years she changed the face of British television and earned herself the nickname 'godmother of soap' (*Guardian*, 20 June 1997).

Initially a production manager on serials such as *Pride and Prejudice*, Smith then took a BBC director's training course. Soon she was directing episodes of *Dr Finlay's Casebook*; two *Dr Who* series, one with William Hartnell and one with Patrick Troughton; and *Compact*, a serial set in a women's magazine, which provided her first taste of twice-weekly soap opera. It was in the late 1960s, when working on *Z Cars*, that she first met the script editor Tony Holland. They went on to forge one of the most influential creative partnerships in television history, fashioning for BBC television drama both its biggest hit (*EastEnders*) and its most resounding miss (*Eldorado*). Their first major collaboration was on the 1970s nursing drama *Angels*, which they changed from a weekly series to a twice-weekly serial. Then came *The District Nurse*, set in the south Wales coalfields. When, therefore, BBC1 decided in 1984 to challenge ITV's *Coronation Street*, it was to Smith and Holland that it turned.

The idea of setting BBC television's first all-year-round soap opera in London's East End came from Jonathan Powell, head of BBC television drama series and serials. 'We were still talking and Jonathan casually mentioned "What about that bend in the River Thames?"', Smith recalled eight years later. '*EastEnders* was born' (*Eldorado* press pack, 13). The infant was shrill from the outset. The first episode, on 19 February 1985, began with the words 'Stinks in 'ere', uttered by the Queen Vic's landlord, Dirty Den, and the discovery of a dead body. But this twice-weekly (plus an omnibus edition on Sunday) serial about the occupants of fictitious Albert Square in the imaginary London borough of Walford quickly proved immensely popular and gained an audience that often exceeded 20 million. Its storylines gripped the nation. Fifteen years later, at the start of the new millennium, it was still the BBC's highest-rating regular show.

EastEnders also proved contentious in a way that *Coronation Street*, just as popular but much warmer, did not. *EastEnders* introduced gritty issues such as abortion, illegitimacy, schoolgirl pregnancy, arson, bribery, rape, and drug-taking. Its dialogue was sometimes crude and violent. 'I believe in showing what does exist and preparing people for the world they live in', was Smith's rationale (*Daily Telegraph*, 20 Jun 1997). 'My prime aim is to entertain, my second is to inform. I do not preach'. Nevertheless, some felt its tone was too dark for 7 p.m. Leslie Halliwell, ITV's main programme buyer and author of the famous film guide, noted that it 'caused much controversy by bringing "adult" language and behaviour into the family hour and Sunday afternoon' (Halliwell and Purser, 239). Others disliked what they sensed was not mere social realism but an unstated liberal agenda. Peter Dawson, general secretary of the Professional Association of Teachers, attacked *EastEnders* as 'an evil influence on the nation because it projects, as normal, highly deviant forms of behaviour such as homosexuality, bad language, crime, infidelity and drunkenness' (*The Times*, 2 Aug 1989). Mary Whitehouse was another fierce critic of the programme in its early years.

With Holland as her script editor, Smith produced *EastEnders* from its inception until 1989. They teamed up again in 1992 to launch a new BBC1 serial, promising 'sun, sand, sangria—and, of course, sex' (*Eldorado* press pack, 4). But there was nothing about *Eldorado* that was paved with gold. Shot entirely on location in Spain, this ill-fated Eurosoap about a multinational community on the Costa del Sol failed to win an audience and was axed after one year.

Charismatic, forceful, and driven, Smith ruled her casts with the proverbial rod of iron, as though they were the unruly children she had never had. 'A producer has to have a strong hand', she remarked. 'You have to be mercurial and make quick decisions' (*Daily Telegraph*, 20 Jun 1997). After the collapse of *Eldorado* she gave lectures about television drama and production. She died of cancer on 19 June 1997, at the Royal Marsden Hospital, Chelsea, London, and was cremated at Mortlake crematorium on 30 June. PAUL DONOVAN

Sources *The Times* (20 June 1997) • *Daily Telegraph* (20 June 1997) • *The Guardian* (20 June 1997) • *The Independent* (21 June 1997) • *EastEnders* press pack, 1985 • *Eldorado* press pack, 1992 • *The Times* (2 Aug 1989) • L. Halliwell and P. Purser, *Halliwell's television companion*, 3rd edn (1986) • M. Whitehouse, *Quite contrary* (1993) • b. cert. • m. cert. • d. cert. • private information (2004)
Archives SOUND BL NSA, current affairs recordings
Likenesses photograph, repro. in *The Times* (20 June 1997) • photograph, repro. in *The Guardian* • photograph, *EastEnders* press pack • photograph, *Eldorado* press pack • photograph, repro. in *Daily Telegraph* • photograph, repro. in *The Independent*

Smith, Lancelot Grey Hugh (1870–1941), stockbroker, was born on 4 August 1870 at 71 Princes Gate, Kensington, London, one of the six sons of Hugh Colin Smith (1836–1910), merchant and banker, and his wife, Constance Maria Josepha Adeane. Both parents came of distinguished and large families; his father was a great-grandson of Abel Smith, who established the bank of Smith, Payne, and Smiths in London, as well as opening branches of the (Nottingham-based) Smiths Bank in Lincoln and Hull. H. C. Smith founded the Hays Wharf Company, an important firm of Thames wharfingers, owned by the family, and he became a director of the Bank of England in 1876 and was its governor in 1897–8. Smith's mother was the daughter of H. J. Adeane and his wife, Maud, daughter of John Thomas Stanley, first Baron Stanley of Alderley.

Lancelot Smith was educated at Eton College and at Trinity College, Cambridge, though he left Cambridge in 1889 without taking a degree. He spent some time in the family businesses, the Hays Wharf Company in London and Smiths Bank in Derby, before visiting the USA in 1897. On that visit he struck up a friendship with Jack Morgan, son of Pierpont Morgan, senior partner of J. P. Morgan & Co. in New York and J. S. Morgan & Co. (later Morgan Grenfell) in London. It was through this friendship that Lancelot's brother Vivian Hugh *Smith (later Lord Bicester) joined J. S. Morgan & Co. in London in 1905.

When he returned from America, Smith, against the wishes of his father, joined the then newly established stockbroking firm of Rowe and Pitman. Tradition has it that the two partners, George D. Rowe and Frederick Pitman, who were both keen oarsmen, needed a non-rowing person to look after the office during the Henley regatta. Lancelot, or Lancey as he became known in the City, fitted the bill in that respect, but of course he offered much more to a new stockbroking firm seeking business. Well known in the City of London and beyond, the ramifications of the Smith clan—consisting not only of his brothers (who came to be strategically placed in Morgan Grenfell and Hambros Bank) but also of his numerous cousins—gave Lancey useful connections in many institutions across the City. Indeed, it has been suggested that all the immense stock-exchange business of the Hugh Smith clan poured through Rowe and Pitman. Stockbroking, it turned out, suited Smith. Summing up his skills, the stockbroker Alfred Wagg noted:

> He certainly had not got the ability of several other members of his family. He had no patience with detail, but he had great flair. He seemed to possess the gift of being able to 'smell out' that a security was attractive before it even occurred to other people. (Kynaston, 312)

In 1910 Smith met the young Jean Rhys [*see* Williams, Ella Gwendoline Rees (1890–1979)], then a chorus girl, and later a novelist. She became his mistress, but the liaison lasted only just over two years before Smith terminated it, and 'paid her off' with a small allowance. He was, according to her biographer, the love of her life, and in her novel, *Voyage in the Dark* (1934), she wrote an affectionate portrait of him as Walter Jeffries. During the First World War Smith served for a time in 1914 as a lieutenant in the Westminster dragoons. He was sent in 1915 as the principal delegate in the British mission to Sweden, and in 1917 he was made a CBE. When he returned he was appointed chairman of the Tobacco Control Board. At the end of the war he returned to Rowe and Pitman.

Smith's flair and his connections in the City continued

to benefit the firm; he was a leading partner and ultimately its senior partner. Rowe and Pitman attracted a large number of well-connected and wealthy private clients: Smith's own clients included members of aristocratic and royal families, both British and European; and in the inter-war years he also built up the firm's corporate finance advisory work. Smith had many friends in the City and, Alfred Wagg remembered, also many enemies, offended by his supercilious manner, his tendency to pomposity, and his air of superiority. He never married, and his personal wealth enabled him to own and enjoy several grand houses in London, in Surrey, and in Norfolk. He was a director of the Australian Agricultural Company, and the National Mortgage and Agency Company of New Zealand.

Lancelot Smith died on 23 March 1941 at his home, Old Hall, Garboldisham, Wayland, in Norfolk. In the week following his death a memorial service was held for him at the Savoy Chapel in London. JUDY SLINN

Sources *WWW*, 1941–50 • D. Kynaston, *The City of London*, 2 (1995) • K. Burk, *Morgan Grenfell, 1838–1988: the biography of a merchant bank* (1989) • Venn, *Alum. Cant.* • J. A. S. L. Leighton-Boyce, *Smiths, the bankers, 1658–1958* (1958) • C. Angier, *Jean Rhys* (1990), 63 • *CGPLA Eng. & Wales* (1941) • b. cert. • d. cert.
Wealth at death £408,999 4*s*. 1*d*.: resworn probate, 30 April 1941, *CGPLA Eng. & Wales*

Smith, Sir Lionel, first baronet (1778–1842), army officer and colonial governor, born on 9 October 1778, was the younger son of Benjamin Smith (1743/4–1806) of Liss in Hampshire, a West India merchant, and his wife, the poet Charlotte *Smith (1749–1806). In March 1795 he was appointed, without purchase, to an ensigncy in the 24th regiment of foot, then in Canada; that October he obtained his lieutenancy. While he was in North America the duke of Kent noted his abilities and assisted his advancement. After being quartered in Canada for some time, his regiment was moved to Halifax, Nova Scotia, and from there Smith crossed to the west coast of Africa to quell an insurrection in Sierra Leone. In May 1801 he obtained his company in the 16th regiment, and in April 1802 was promoted major. He went to the West Indies in 1802 and was present at the taking of Surinam, Essequibo, and Berbice, among others. He became lieutenant-colonel in June 1805, in the 18th regiment, but about 1807 was transferred to the command of the 65th, then at Bombay. In 1809 and 1810 he conducted expeditions against the pirates of the Persian Gulf, and received for his services the thanks of the imam of Muscat. In 1810 he was at the reduction of Mauritius, and he obtained his full colonelcy in June 1813. On 17 November 1817 he commanded the 4th division of the army of the Deccan at the capture of Poona, and he was severely wounded in the cavalry action at Ashta in 1818. On 12 August 1819 he became major-general. Smith's first wife, Ellen Marianne, the daughter of Thomas Galway of Kilkerry, co. Kerry, died in 1814, having had two daughters. On 20 November 1819 he married Isabella Curwen, the youngest daughter of Eldred Curwen Pottinger of Mount Pottinger, co. Down, and the sister of Sir Henry Pottinger; they had a son and four daughters.

After serving for some time on the Bombay staff, Smith left India, and on 9 April 1832 was nominated colonel of the 96th foot. On 3 December of the same year he was created KCB, and in October 1834 was appointed colonel of the 74th regiment. From 27 April 1833 he was stationed at Barbados as governor and commander-in-chief of the Windward and Leeward Islands. The recent enactment of the Emancipation Act had produced much bitter feeling among the Europeans, and Smith incurred much unpopularity in his attempts to reconcile the interests of the 'people of colour', the black people, and the planters and proprietors. His attitude towards the house of assembly was unconciliatory, and he was charged with unconstitutional procedure. In 1836 he succeeded the marquess of Sligo as captain-general and commander-in-chief of Jamaica, and in the same year was appointed KCGH. In Jamaica Smith found even greater difficulties than in Barbados. He viewed with disdain his predecessor's attempts to create a special magistracy and a party based on the people of colour, objecting that the effect of Sligo's encouraging men of colour to run for the assembly would be the elimination of white representatives and the rise of the 'Evils of Anarchy, Confusion, and Bloodshed' (quoted in Heuman, 104). Smith supported an attempt to raise the qualification for sitting in the assembly, but it was overturned by the Colonial Office. The people of colour were thus alienated from Smith's governorship, and, following the replacement of apprenticeship by complete freedom in 1838, the measures he took to restrain abuses by the planters earned him the hatred of the white population as well. It was in this context that the house of assembly refused to legislate on the island's prisons in 1838–9, causing a constitutional crisis in Jamaica, and incidentally providing the trigger for the 'bedchamber' crisis in Britain. In 1839 a modified bill was carried by the local legislature, and as Smith was hopelessly unpopular, Sir Charles Metcalfe was selected to succeed him as governor.

While governor, Smith was appointed a lieutenant-general in January 1837, and in February he succeeded George Cooke as colonel of the 40th regiment. At the coronation of Queen Victoria he was included in the list of baronets, and in 1840 he succeeded Sir William Nicolay as governor of Mauritius. In 1841 he was created GCB. He died at Mauritius on 2 or 3 January 1842, and his wife died three days later. E. I. CARLYLE, *rev.* LYNN MILNE

Sources *GM*, 2nd ser., 18 (1842), 93–4 • G. Paton, F. Glennie, and W. P. Symons, eds., *Historical records of the 24th regiment, from its formation, in 1689* (1892) • G. J. Heuman, *Between black and white: race, politics and the free coloreds in Jamaica, 1792–1865* (1981) • R. H. Schomburgk, *The history of Barbados* (1848) • W. J. Gardner, *A history of Jamaica* (1873) • Burke, *Peerage*
Archives BL OIOC, Elphinstone MSS

Smith, (Arthur) Lionel Forster (1880–1972), educationist, was born on 19 August 1880 at Villa Marx, Baden-Baden, the eldest in the family of two sons and seven daughters of Arthur Lionel *Smith (1850–1924), fellow and tutor (later master) of Balliol College, Oxford, and his wife, Mary Florence, eldest daughter of John Forster Baird, a landowner in Northumberland. From the Dragon School, Oxford, he became a scholar of Rugby School, where he shared a study with William Temple, later archbishop of Canterbury. He won a classical scholarship at Balliol, and took seconds in classical honour moderations (1901) and *literae humaniores* (1903) and a first in history (1904).

Smith was elected a fellow of All Souls in 1904, and in 1908 a fellow of Magdalen, where he had become a lecturer in 1906. He was dean of Magdalen from 1910 to 1913. He was a good teacher, careful and sympathetic, though his pupils, who included the prince of Wales, were not always rewarding for someone from the golden age of a Balliol which had prepared many fine minds for public service; the system at Magdalen encouraged passmen to retain knowledge rather than scholars to develop understanding, and when war came Smith was already dissatisfied.

Soon after the outbreak of war Smith joined the 9th battalion of the Hampshire regiment, serving in India until he was posted to Basrah in 1917. He became involved in the administration of the conquered territory of Mesopotamia, principally in the education department. After an unsatisfying return to Magdalen during 1919, he spent from February 1920 to August 1921 in Baghdad, being appointed director of education in August 1920. He was, however, in England on sick leave for two years, and taught at Harrow School for the first two terms of 1923.

From August 1923 to May 1931, under the British mandate, Smith was in Iraq as adviser and sometimes inspector-general, mediating between largely Shiʿi ministers and their directors-general, principally the Arab nationalist Sati Bey al-Husri. King Faisal admired him and called him a friend. Sati Bey, who respected him and worked well with him, wrote of him in a complimentary manner in his memoir of Iraq. Although it became almost treasonable for Iraqis to speak well of the mandate, Smith's memory was cherished long after he had left the country. And yet it was a losing battle he fought, because there was never any money—law and order mattered far more than education to the British government, and the Iraqis were not ready to accept the widespread and liberalizing education he so desired. Personally, he was loved and respected for his integrity, his sportsmanship, his mind, his friendship, and his devotion to the Iraqis; but professionally when he resigned he had to present to his superiors a masterly paper ('The present state of education in Iraq', 1931, reprinted in *Middle Eastern Studies*, April 1983) which is a damning indictment of the whole system of education—background, policy, examinations, teacher training, and political control—despite what had undoubtedly been achieved.

The directors of the Edinburgh Academy chose Smith as rector in 1931 for his personality and his record, preferring him to another man nearly twenty years younger. Two years later Smith refused the headmastership of Eton College. At the academy his wide learning, ready sympathy, athletic gifts, and fine presence, combined with a genuine shyness and humility, earned him the respect and loyalty of masters and boys alike. He loved teaching and the company of boys, and found the rectorship wholly absorbing. He hated 'humbug' and 'snobs'. He spoke in public unwillingly but well. There was little development in his time, but he held a reduced and scattered school together during the war years. His ideal of education was as something to transform understanding, not to prepare for a function, and boys remembered working under him as a marvellous experience. He brought out the best in other people. He left unwillingly in 1945, which he thought a bad year for changing rectors.

Smith was appointed MVO in 1914 and CBE in 1927. The universities of Edinburgh and St Andrews gave him honorary LLD degrees in 1945 and 1947. He was one of the best amateur athletes of his day; in the Rugby cricket eleven; captain of the Balliol boat club and member of Leander and of a winning visitors cup IV at Henley; captain of the Oxford University hockey eleven; an English international hockey player from 1903 to 1913; a squash player, skater, and walker of legendary endurance and skill in Baghdad and Edinburgh; and he was modest about his achievements. These gifts, and his exceptional good looks, predisposed people to accept him; but his greatness was in his spirit. He had from childhood a simple faith which he lived by naturally. His sternest judgements were tempered by a smile of self-deprecation.

On 9 August 1932, at St Peter's Church, Bywell, Northumberland, he married Mary Fletcher, daughter of Henry Lloyd Wilson, chemical manufacturer, mother of three and widow of his connection George Lloyd Hodgkin, who died in 1918. They had no children, but her affectionate companionship warmed the rest of his long life. He undertook no further duties after the rectorship, but his many large private charities and his love of gardening, walking, birds, and painting continued through his twenty-seven years of retirement in Edinburgh, where he died, at 25 Belgrave Crescent, on 3 June 1972. His wife survived him.

L. E. Ellis, *rev.*

Sources E. C. Hodgkin, *A. L. F. Smith* (1979) [privately printed] • P. Sluglett, *Britain in Iraq, 1914–1932* (1976) • M. Magnusson, *The clacken and the slate: the story of the Edinburgh Academy, 1824–1974* (1974) • *Edinburgh Academy Chronicle* • *The Times* (5 June 1972) • *The Times* (21 July 1972) • private information (1986) • E. C. Hodgkin, 'The man who turned down Eton', *The Times* (4 June 1977) • m. cert. • d. cert. • *CCI* (1972)

Archives St Ant. Oxf., Middle East Centre, archive, corresp. and papers relating to education in Iraq

Likenesses photograph, All Souls Oxf.

Wealth at death £101,544.52: confirmation, 1 Aug 1972, *CCI*

Smith, (Lloyd) Logan Pearsall (1865–1946), writer and literary scholar, was born of Quaker stock at Millville, New Jersey, USA, on 18 October 1865, the fourth child and second son of Robert Pearsall Smith and Hannah Whitall *Smith (1832–1911), daughter of John Mickle Whitall. Robert Pearsall Smith was a partner in his father-in-law's glass-bottle manufacturing company but both he and his wife became increasingly involved in the revivalist movement. They became famous as evangelical preachers and religious writers and travelled widely in England and Europe for the movement. The rich cultural life of the family included not only extensive foreign travel but also a

(Lloyd) **Logan Pearsall Smith** (1865–1946), by Roger Fry

domestic circle which included Walt Whitman. The Pearsall Smiths were a literary family. Mrs Pearsall Smith, who published several books as H. W. S., encouraged her son's emerging talents, and his love of books was developed in the Philadelphia Library, of which his grandfather, John Jay Smith, was librarian and which had been bequeathed to the city by an ancestor, James Logan, who had been secretary to William Penn.

Pearsall Smith was educated at the Quaker Penn charter school (1880), Haverford College (1881–4), Harvard University (1884–5), and the University of Berlin (1885–6). He then worked for a year in a branch of the family business in New York which he disliked, and he resolved to return to literary study. His family had settled in England, and in 1888, on the advice of his brother-in-law, B. F. G. Costelloe, a former member, he went to Balliol College, Oxford, where he obtained a second class in *literae humaniores* in 1891. He was a favourite of Benjamin Jowett's, and was influenced by the writing of Walter Pater.

Pearsall Smith's family home in Sussex was the centre of a dynamic circle which included G. B. Shaw, Sidney and Beatrice Webb, Roger Fry, Bertrand Russell, who subsequently married his sister Alys, and Bernard Berenson, who married his elder sister Mary Costelloe. In 1892 he went to Paris to continue his education and there wrote his first book, *The Youth of Parnassus* (1895), a compilation of short stories in imitation of Maupassant, which, though unsuccessful, led to friendship with Robert Bridges. He returned to England in 1895 after travelling in Europe. For the rest of his life he lived in Sussex and Hampshire and, from 1914, Chelsea, and wrote as critic, essayist, and pioneer of language studies.

In 1897–8, with his sister Mary Costelloe and her future husband Bernard Berenson, Pearsall Smith helped to produce a privately printed periodical, the *Golden Urn*. Among his contributions were four prose sketches and with these began the short pieces which he made into his masterpiece, *Trivia* (1902). He continued working on this collection of reminiscences and musings all his life: a greatly enlarged and revised version of *Trivia* was published in 1918, followed by *More Trivia* (1922) and *Afterthoughts* (1931). In 1933 he rearranged the three in a single volume, *All Trivia*; he was continually revising them until his death. His acumen as a critic can be seen in his biography of Sir Henry Wotton (1907); *The Golden Grove*, a collection of quotations from Jeremy Taylor which reflects his love of anthologizing; and, towards the end of his life, his defence of Milton against critics such as Eliot and Pound in *Milton and his Modern Critics* (1940). Another abiding interest was the study of language. In *The English Language* (1912) he established himself as one of the pioneers of semantic study. He assisted Robert Bridges and others to inaugurate the Society for Pure English in 1913, for which he wrote many pamphlets. *Words and Idioms* (1925) is another important contribution to the study of language. He compiled several influential anthologies, was a regular contributor to the *Times Literary Supplement*, and his autobiographical *Unforgotten Years* was published in 1938. He edited his mother's letters in *A Religious Rebel* (published posthumously in 1949) and wrote other books of reminiscences such as *Reperusals and Recollections* (1936).

Pearsall Smith became a naturalized British citizen in 1913 and although he travelled widely in Europe, north Africa, and the Near East, he returned only once to the United States—in 1921. He never married. For much of his later life he shared a house with his mother and, after her death in 1911, with his sister Alys. Although his conversion at the age of four was recorded in a tract written by his father, he lost his faith when still young but retained a large residue of Quaker virtue. Pearsall Smith inherited 'a mild form of manic depression which shaped his existence with cycles of gloom and elevation' (*DNB*). He suffered an especially severe attack in 1938 while in Iceland with Gathorne-Hardy. He was taken to hospital, quite seriously ill, and obituaries were printed in New York newspapers, to his unending amusement. He died on the night of 2 March 1946 at his home, 11 St Leonard's Terrace, Chelsea, London. SAYONI BASU

Sources *A chime of words: the letters of Logan Pearsall Smith*, ed. E. Tribble (1984) [with foreword by J. Russell] · R. Gathorne-Hardy, 'Memoir', in *A religious rebel: the letters of 'H. W. S.'*, ed. L. Pearsall Smith (1949) · R. Gathorne-Hardy, *Recollections of Logan Pearsall Smith: the story of a friendship* (1949) · *The Times* (4 March 1946) · *A religious rebel: the letters of 'H. W. S.'*, ed. L. Pearsall Smith (1949) · L. Pearsall Smith, *Unforgotten years* (1938) · *A portrait of Logan Pearsall Smith, drawn from his letters and diaries*, ed. J. Russell [1950] · D. MacCarthy, *Memories* (1953) · *DAB* · *DNB* · personal knowledge (1959) [*DNB*] · private information (1959)

Archives Kent State University, Ohio, corresp. and papers · L. Cong., manuscript division, papers · Princeton University, New Jersey | BL, corresp. with Society of Authors, Add. MS 63313 · Bodl. Oxf., corresp. with Robert Bridges · Bodl. Oxf., letters to Jack W. Lambert · Bodl. Oxf., letters to Lewis family · King's AC Cam.,

letters to Roger Fry • McMaster University, Hamilton, Ontario, letters to Bertrand Russell
Likenesses E. Kapp, Chinese ink drawing, 1922, Barber Institute of Fine Arts, Birmingham • R. Fry, oils, Haverford College, Pennsylvania [*see illus.*] • W. Rothenstein, drawing; in possession of John Russell in 1959 • E. Sands, oils • H. Trevalyn, watercolour; in possession of Robert Gathorne-Hardy in 1959
Wealth at death £12,970 8*s*. 8*d*.: probate, 21 Aug 1946, *CGPLA Eng. & Wales*

Smith, Lucy Toulmin (1838–1911), literary scholar and librarian, was born at Boston, Massachusetts, USA, on 21 November 1838, of English parents, Joshua Toulmin *Smith (1816–1869), barrister, and his wife, Martha (*d.* 1887), daughter of William Jones Kendall. Her great-great-grandfather was the eminent Unitarian divine Joshua Toulmin (1740–1815). The family had maintained its Unitarian connections. Lucy was the eldest child of a family of three daughters and two sons. In 1842 the Smiths returned to England and settled at Highgate, Middlesex. Lucy resided there until she moved to Oxford in 1894, except for a brief period in the 1880s when she lived at Hampstead, London, returning to Highgate after her mother's death. She was educated at home to a very high standard; she assisted her father in editing the *Parliamentary Remembrancer* (1857–65), and also completed his volume *English Gilds*.

Other works of Toulmin Smith's pre-Oxford period included Camden Society editions of R. Ricart's *The Maire of Bristowe is Kalendar* (1872), and *Expeditions to Prussia and the Holy Land made by Henry earl of Derby … in … 1390–1 and 1392–3* (1894); an edition of C. M. Ingleby's *Shakespeare's Centurie of Prayse* (1879); and editions of Thomas Norton and Thomas Sackville's *Gorboduc* (1883), the *York Plays* (1885), *A Common-Place Book of the Fifteenth Century* (1886), and *Les contes moralisés de Nicole Bozon* (with Paul Meyer, 1889). She also translated Jusserand's *La vie nomade et les routes d'Angleterre* as *English Wayfaring Life in the Middle Ages* (1889), and wrote a grammar manual (1885). During her Highgate years she was a close friend of her neighbour Mary Kingsley. She helped Kingsley to edit her father's writings for publication, and later read and revised the whole of Kingsley's *West African Studies* in manuscript.

Toulmin Smith also worked as a freelance research assistant, her correspondence with T. F. Fenwick showing the range of her activities. Thus in 1870 she did research for James Gairdner; but her major clients were foreign scholars. Her obituary in the Unitarian journal *The Inquirer* (23 December 1911, 820–21) says, 'Some of these services were paid for, but many others were done out of sheer loyalty to the freemasonry of scholars … or … out of a spontaneous hospitality of mind'. On a different level, she contributed to the girls' magazine *Atalanta*, edited (1887–93) by the novelist L. T. Meade, wife of her brother Alfred.

In 1893 Manchester College's new buildings in Oxford were opened. The library building was a gift from the Unitarian Sir Henry Tate; it housed valuable collections of books, but had no librarian, and a year later the general committee authorized the creation of this post. In September 1894 Toulmin Smith was appointed at a salary of £120 per annum, and Sir Henry Tate increased his annual subscription to the college substantially as a result. The Manchester College annual report for 1894–5 noted that the committee considered it 'a piece of great good fortune to have found a lady of such distinguished attainments as Miss Smith to accept this office'.

In addition to the ordinary running of the library, Toulmin Smith attempted to build up collections of special relevance to the college's heritage. Thus she seems to have expended much effort in a largely successful attempt to complete James Martineau's set of the papers of the Metaphysical Society (1869–80). Likewise she built up almost complete runs of such basic Unitariana as the annual reports of the British and Foreign Unitarian Association, and *The Inquirer*. Toulmin Smith's own scholarly work continued. Its most notable expression was a new edition of *The Itinerary of John Leland*, of which the Welsh volume was published in 1906 and the four covering England in 1907–10.

Toulmin Smith's 'hospitality of mind' has been noted, but she was also characterized by hospitality in the more usual sense, and many scholars were entertained at her home at 1 Park Terrace, Park Town, Oxford. Her obituarist in *The Inquirer* remarks that through her many scholarly friendships she formed a link between Manchester College and the Oxford world at large 'which contributed not a little to the place which it now holds there'.

Lucy Toulmin Smith resigned from the librarianship in November 1911 and died at home on 18 December. She was buried in the Wolvercote cemetery, Oxford, on the 20th. She bequeathed her personal belongings, including her books and papers, to her sister, Frances Toulmin Smith.

D. S. Porter

Sources *The Inquirer* (23 Dec 1911), 820–21 • annual report; minutes of the general committee, Manchester College, Oxford, Harris Man. Oxf. • *DNB* • K. Frank, *A voyager out: the life of Mary Kingsley* (1986) • Willard Brown, *The Metaphysical Society* (1947) • P. Morgan, *Oxford libraries outside the Bodleian: a guide*, 2nd edn (1980) • V. D. Davis, *A history of Manchester College* (1932) • D. Porter, ed., *A catalogue of manuscripts in Harris Manchester College, Oxford* (1998)
Archives Harris Man. Oxf., college library corresp. | Bodl. Oxf., letters to Fenwick family • Bodl. Oxf., Phillipps-Robinson MSS
Likenesses E. Hall, photograph, Harris Man. Oxf.
Wealth at death £4471 11*s*. 11*d*.: probate, 5 March 1912, *CGPLA Eng. & Wales*

Smith [*married names* Wardle, Sheehy]**, Madeleine Hamilton** (1835/6–1928), accused poisoner, was born in 1835 or in the first quarter of 1836, eldest of three daughters and two sons of James Smith (1808–1863), a rich Glasgow architect, and his wife, the daughter of David *Hamilton (1768–1843), architect. Educated for three years at Mrs Gorton's Academy for Young Ladies, a boarding-school at Clapton, near Hackney, until 1853, she was a serious, voracious reader with an independent outlook and a talent for intrigue.

At the end of 1854, or possibly in March 1855, (Pierre) Émile L'Angelier (*b.* 1826?) procured an introduction to her in a Glasgow street. He was a Frenchman who had risen from recent destitution to respectability as a packing clerk in a Glasgow merchant house. This outwardly personable, if volatile, young man was vain of his success with women and hoped to raise his station in life by marriage into the moneyed classes. In 1852 he had made suicidal gestures after being jilted by a prosperous woman. L'Angelier reached an understanding with Madeleine Smith by April 1855. Romantic and self-dramatizing, they maintained a constant, clandestine correspondence (in her case written with perfumed inks) and became secretly engaged. She attempted to break with him in the summer, but L'Angelier responded with sanctimonious reproaches and gently implied that he might send her letters (which she had asked him to burn) to her father. The latter refused consent to their marriage in September 1855. During the winter their surreptitious assignations resumed. Probably on 6 May (possibly 6 June) 1856 they became lovers in the woods at Rowaleyn, her father's country house near Helensburgh. 'If we did wrong last night it must have been in the excitement of our love', she wrote exultantly next day. 'Tell me, pet, were you angry at me for allowing you to do what you did—was it very bad of me. … I suppose we ought to have waited until we were married' (*Trial of Madeleine Smith … for Poisoning*, 96). 'My dearest and beloved wife Mimi', L'Angelier replied with characteristically joyless ingratitude,

> Since I saw you I have been wretchedly sad. … Why, Mimi, did you give way after your promises? … I do not understand, my pet, your not bleeding, for every woman having her virginity must bleed. … Be sure and tell me immediately you are ill next time and if at your regular period. (Wilson, 77)

Later in 1856 Smith's passion cooled, and on 28 January 1857 she privately accepted a proposal of marriage from a prosperous neighbour, William Harper Minnoch. When in February she broke with L'Angelier he refused to return her letters, which he threatened to give her father. Foreseeing her irredeemable ruin she implored L'Angelier not to disgrace her, and contrived a reconciliation. Near the end of that month he was taken ill with a severe stomach upset but recovered after a few days. On 12 March she agreed to marry Minnoch in June; on 6, 18, and 19 March she bought arsenic (telling the chemists variously that it was to kill rats or for use as a face wash); she invited L'Angelier to her house on 21 March (afterwards denying that they actually met), and on 23 March he died. Her letters were soon discovered in L'Angelier's office and lodgings, and his body, when exhumed on 31 March, was found to contain eighty-eight grains of arsenic; she was taken into custody.

On 30 June 1857 Smith's trial opened at the high court of the judiciary in Edinburgh. James, first Baron Moncrieff, who prosecuted her, contended that on three nights she had invited L'Angelier to her father's house at 7 Blythswood Square, Glasgow, and handed drinks of poisoned cocoa or coffee to him from her bedroom window so as to prevent exposure of her transgressions and to extricate herself from a disastrous entanglement. Moncrieff declared the story of her intrigue with L'Angelier 'should carry a chill of horror into every family' (*Trial of Madeleine Smith … for Poisoning*, 132–3). The correspondence read in court, he said, disclosed 'almost incredible evidences of disgrace, of sin, of degradation' (ibid., 128). Certainly the assumptions of the Victorian paterfamilias were brutally affronted by the revelations of her trial, which created a national sensation. Her candid sexual pleasure and deception of her father seemed equally depraved. John Hope, the lord justice clerk, typically condemned the 'ill-regulated, disorderly, distempered, licentious feeling' of her letters and likened her to 'a common prostitute' (Smith, 272–3). Though at times the language of her prosecutors suggests that she was on trial for her virginity, or that she must be punished for her sexual independence, there was indubitably a case for her to answer once arsenic was discovered in L'Angelier's corpse and her efforts to buy it were traced. Smith was superbly defended by John Inglis. He contended that L'Angelier had destroyed himself either deliberately (citing some loose talk of suicide) or accidentally, for L'Angelier was a hypochondriac with a tendency to rash self-medication. Though Smith's situation between her affianced and discarded lovers was desperate, Inglis denied her motive to kill, for there was no advantage in L'Angelier's death as long as her incriminating letters were unretrieved and liable to the exposure which she dreaded. Hope's concluding address indicated that though there could be strong presumptions of guilt, at crucial points the prosecution's case was 'radically defective in evidence' so that 'the guilt could not be brought home to her' (Smith, 254, 271). There was no proof of their meetings (because L'Angelier's appointment book was ruled inadmissible as evidence) and therefore no proof of the administration of poison. On 9 July 1857 the jury returned a majority verdict of not guilty on the charge of feloniously administering poison with intent to murder on 19–20 February, a verdict of not proven on a similar charge of administering poison on 22–3 February, and a majority verdict (13 to 2) of not proven on the third charge of murder on 22–3 March.

Smith was firm, calm, and self-possessed during her ordeal. On 4 July 1861 she married George Wardle (son of Hugh Wardle, druggist), artist and student of medieval art, afterwards foreman-manager of William Morris. They became socialists and had at least one son and daughter (five children by one account). After his death she emigrated to the United States where she married a man called Sheehy, who died in 1926. At the age of ninety she was threatened with deportation as an undesirable alien. She died on 12 April 1928 at 4298 Park Avenue, Bronx, New York, and was buried as Lena Wardle Sheehy in Mount Hope cemetery, New York. She is the subject of Emma Robinson's novel *Madeleine Graham* (1864).

RICHARD DAVENPORT-HINES

Sources *Trial of Madeleine Smith of No 7 Blythswood Square Glasgow for poisoning* (1857) • A. D. Smith, *Trial of Madeleine Smith* (1905) • F. T. Jesse, *Trial of Madeleine Smith* (1927) • P. Hunt, *The Madeleine Smith affair* (1950) • G. Butler, *Madeleine Smith* (1935) • J. G. Wilson, *Not proven* (1960) • W. Roughead, *Mainly murder* (1937) • S. Sitwell, *Splendours and miseries* (1943), 191–216 • L. E. X., *The Maybrick and Madeline Smith cases contrasted* (1889) • N. Morland, *That nice Miss Smith* (1957) • J. B. Atlay, *Famous trials of the century* (1899) • C. J. S. Thompson, *Poison romance and poison mysteries* (1899) • J. Forster, *Studies in black and red* (1896) • M. S. Hartman, 'Murder and respectability: the case of Madeleine Smith', *Victorian Studies*, 16 (1972–3) •

M. Hartman, *Victorian murderesses* (1977), 51–84 • V. Morris, *Double jeopardy: women who kill in Victorian fiction* (1990) • *The Times* (18 April 1928), 13 • *CGPLA Eng. & Wales* (1928)
Archives Mitchell L., Glas. • NA Scot.
Likenesses engraving, 1857, repro. in Morris, *Double jeopardy*, 43 • sketches, Mary Evans Picture Library, London
Wealth at death £468 6*s*. 10*d*.: administration, 25 July 1928, *CGPLA Eng. & Wales*

Smith, Margaret Josephine Dean- [*formerly* Lilian Gracie Copeman] (**1899–1997**), folklorist, was born Lilian Gracie Copeman at 31 Marine Parade, Lowestoft, Suffolk, on 7 November 1899, the daughter of Frederica Henrietta Copeman, mother's help. She was adopted, as Margaret Josephine Dean, on 5 June 1900 by Clara Ellen (Nellie) Dean (*d.* 1944). Following the latter's marriage to Arnold Dunbar *Smith (1866–1933) [*see under* Brewer, Cecil Claude], architect, on 11 August 1911, she was known as Margaret Josephine Dunbar Smith. She formally adopted the name Margaret Josephine Dean-Smith following her stepfather's death on 7 December 1933, though she had frequently used this name before then. One of her most cherished memories was of being present at the belated new year party held by Mary Neal and the Espérance Club in February 1906 at the Passmore Edwards Settlement (later renamed the Mary Ward Settlement), designed by her future stepfather. She had thus been present at what was, in effect, the inauguration of the folk-dance revival, and throughout her life she continued to live in close contact with the personalities and ideas involved in the revival and in the arts and crafts movement generally. She had an exceptionally happy childhood, being educated privately on Parents' National Education Union methods until 1911, when she went to St Albans High School for Girls, which she left in 1917. From 1921 until 1933 she lived in her stepfather's flat above the headquarters of the Art Workers' Guild at 6 Queen Square, London, developing a significant combination of experience and skills. She took a history degree at Birkbeck College, studying under Eileen Power and R. H. Tawney. She also worked at John and Edward Bumpus Ltd, Oxford Street, booksellers, in their private library department. She completed a postgraduate diploma in librarianship at University College, London, in 1933. In 1922 she became a member of the English Folk Dance Society, attending a class taken by Cecil Sharp, another memory to cherish, and became actively involved in English folk-dancing.

By 1935 Dean-Smith had begun what she called her 'career job': 'putting in order non-started or neglected libraries' (Taylor, 390). In 1939 she became chief cataloguer in the gramophone library of the British Broadcasting Corporation, another significant addition to her range of experience. In 1946 she was appointed librarian of the English Folk Dance and Song Society, based at Cecil Sharp House. She had already been responsible for bringing the library back from wartime storage in Leominster, and for overhauling the catalogue. Now, with a devotion which was not fully appreciated at the time, she laboured to transform it into a working tool for scholars. As editor of the society's journal (the *Journal of the English Folk Dance and Song Society*) she also sought to assert the importance of academic standards in this kind of material. The strain of overwork led to her resignation from both posts in 1950, but she had already seen to it that the library and the *Journal* were established on sound foundations. The library, later to become the Vaughan Williams Memorial Library, was essentially her creation.

After her adoptive mother's death in 1944, Dean-Smith was financially independent, and during the 1950s she produced her two major personal contributions to scholarship. In 1954 her innovative *Guide to English Folk Song Collections, 1822–1952* immediately became an indispensable reference book which has never been satisfactorily replaced. In 1957 she published her definitive work, *Playford's English Dancing Master, 1651*, which established her as the leading authority on the subject. Ideally there would have been enlarged and revised editions of both the *Guide* and *Playford*, but this was not to be. Isolated portions appeared, but her energies were never directed towards personal glory. Her greatest pleasure was in the joys of collaborative scholarship. She never failed to respond to enquiries from other scholars. During the 1950s she was particularly influential in giving support to an independent group, led by Alex Helm, seeking to gather together material concerning calendar customs. This was a significant development within folk-life studies, and Dean-Smith's importance in this cannot be overrated, both as facilitator and as guardian of academic standards. From 1967 to 1973 she produced a series of authoritative reviews of folklore publications in the periodical *Music and Letters*. They were small masterpieces of their kind, always sympathetic, lucid, and incisive. Much of her best writing centred on this kind of appreciation of other people's work. In a similar vein she wrote major articles on the work of Lucy Broadwood and Anne Gilchrist from an earlier generation. Later she devoted immense care to producing obituaries for her dearest friends, Alex Helm, Frank Howes, Violet Alford, and Edward (E. J.) Nicol, and these were among her finest work.

Dean-Smith's sight failed her in later years, but she retained her zest for life to the end, never losing her warm concern for other people, and her generous loyalty to old friendships. She died on 9 February 1997 at the Royal Surrey County Hospital, Guildford, and was cremated at Guildford on 18 February following a funeral service at St Anselm's Roman Catholic Church, Hindhead, earlier the same day. She never married. Roy Judge

Sources M. Taylor, 'Margaret Dean-Smith, 1899–1997', *Folk Music Journal*, 7 (1995–9), 388–91 • Vaughan Williams Memorial Library, London, Dean-Smith collection • private information (2004) • b. cert. • d. cert.
Archives Vaughan Williams Memorial Library, London
Likenesses M. Dean-Smith, portrait, *c*.1935, repro. in Taylor, 'Margaret Dean-Smith', cover; priv. coll.
Wealth at death £100,724: probate, 25 June 1997, *CGPLA Eng. & Wales*

Smith, Maria Constance (**1853–1930**), civil servant, was born on 9 July 1853 at Mill Hill School, Middlesex, one of the youngest of the ten children of Philip *Smith (1817–1885), classicist and ecclesiastical historian, and his wife,

Eliza Lydia, *née* Basolen. Sir William *Smith, lexicographer and editor of the *Quarterly Review*, was her uncle. She was educated at home by governesses under the supervision of her father, and she later assisted him with his research.

Smith was appointed as one of the first 'female clerks' in the savings bank department of the Post Office when that department opened its doors to women in October 1875. Her abilities were exceptional, and she was appointed as lady superintendent in May 1876 at the age of twenty-three. She remained in this post for thirty-seven years and reigned supreme over the largest 'clerical battalion' of women in the civil service (E. B., 139), which grew from sixty-four when she was appointed to 1800 when she retired.

The Post Office Savings Bank, established in 1861 to provide a secure haven for the savings of the working classes, was a runaway success, but, as its business grew, the department sought both to increase efficiency and to reduce costs by various means, including the transfer of work to women. Smith was quick to take advantage of opportunities to secure more and better work for her staff. She aimed to win recognition for women's capacities by proving that, when well trained and well supervised, they could equal the work of men in 'adding up figures without making mistakes' (E. B., 140). Moreover, she negotiated the gradual colonization, in the teeth of male clerks' opposition, of the ledger divisions, the site of the department's core activity of recording payments in and out of accounts. This culminated in the 'completer separation' of men's and women's work (PRO, T1/11464/18470/12) and women's takeover of the ledger divisions in 1907–9. Finally, when other departments such as the Board of Education and the National Health Insurance Commission established staffs of women clerks, she placed her lieutenants in key positions and so exported the traditions of her department.

'Essentially a womanly woman' (H. D., 151) and an astute tactician, Smith emphasized the practical and abstained from the political, which brought her in the latter years of her career into conflict with the more ardent suffragists and trade unionists among her staff. She believed in segregation by class, the reservation of the clerical grades to middle-class women, and segregation by gender, the cloistering of women in women-only work situations, and she had little sympathy for the equal opportunities programme of 'a fair field and no favour'.

In her dealings with senior men she commanded recognition of her independence but was content to exercise her considerable powers out of the limelight. For example, in 1911 at the jubilee of the Savings Bank, the success of which she had done so much to foster, she took an inconspicuous place on the platform. She was, though, awarded the Imperial Service Medal in 1902, one of the first women to be so honoured. Smith retired in April 1913 and went to live at Folkestone, where she died at her home, 17 Clifton Crescent, on 16 February 1930.

Smith ruled through the force of her personality. Good-looking, well-dressed, and vivacious, she chose to forward the cause of women not through open advocacy of feminist principles but rather through the demonstration of their capabilities. The Treasury recognized just how much she had done to bring women clerical workers from the periphery to the centre: 'It was long thought that this work was unsuited to a Female Force, and it is greatly owing to the ability and energy of the Superintendent, in mastering the details in training her subordinates that the experiment which has been tried has been so successful' (Raikes, PRO, T1/8251B/15090/86). META ZIMMECK

Sources H. Martindale, *Women servants of the state: a history of women in the civil service, 1870–1938* (1938), 26–7, 176–80 · 'Miss Constance Smith, I.S.O.', *St Martin's le Grand*, 23/91 (July 1913), 322–5 · H. D., 'In memoriam: Constance Smith, I.S.O.', *St Martin's le Grand*, 40/158 (April 1930), 151–2 · E. B. [E. Bennett], 'Miss Constance Smith, I.S.O.', *St Martin's le Grand*, 23/90 (April 1913), 136–41 · *The Times* (21 Feb 1930) · PRO, T1/8251B/15090/86, H. C. Raikes, Post Office to Treasury, 28 Sep 1886 · Post Office to Treasury, 1 Nov 1907, PRO, T1/11464/18470/12 · b. cert. · d. cert.

Archives Post Office Archive, establishment papers, Post Office class POST 30 · PRO, establishment papers, Treasury class T1

Likenesses photograph, repro. in E. B. [E. Bennett], 'Miss Constance Smith, I.S.O.', 23/90 (April 1913), 139

Wealth at death £1365 9*s.* 0*d.*: probate, 21 March 1930, *CGPLA Eng. & Wales*

Smith [*married name* Akehurst], **Marian Wesley** (**1907–1961**), anthropologist, was born on 10 May 1907 in New York, the daughter of Frederic Morris Smith and Lillian Mae Wesley. At the age of three she suffered a severe attack of poliomyelitis that left her with one leg partially paralysed for life. In 1934 she graduated from Columbia University, New York, with a BA in philosophy, and she went on to obtain a PhD in 1938 as one of the last students of the great American anthropologist Franz Boas. A gifted university teacher as well as a scholar, she held various offices, including the presidency, of the American Ethnological Society before the age of forty, and she also held high office in the American Association for the Advancement of Science and in the American Folklore Society.

Smith's major ethnographic monograph was *The Puyallup-Nisqually* (1940). She was one of the last generation of anthropologists to be competent in all fields of the discipline: social–cultural, archaeology, material culture, folklore, and linguistics. Her editorship of the volume *Indians of the Urban Northwest* (1949) exemplified this traditional American generalist approach. She also published *Archaeology of the Columbia-Fraser Region* (1950), which attempted to draw ethnological conclusions from archaeological finds in the American north-west. She undertook fieldwork in north-western India as well. Smith moved to Britain in 1952 when she married H. Farrant Akehurst, a senior executive with British Insulated Callender's Cables. It was a happy marriage: they made their home in London, latterly in a penthouse in Marylebone, and she accompanied him from time to time on his business travels abroad.

In 1956 Smith succeeded the Africanist W. B. Fagg as honorary secretary of the Royal Anthropological Institute in London, to become in effect its unpaid director, and she treated this as a nearly full-time commitment. She was intellectually well suited to the institute, which had always sought to maintain a broad-based definition of the discipline. In 1958, with the help of a gift from Brenda Z. Seligman, she established the institute's first endowment fund, which later enabled it to expand its activities. She organized cross-disciplinary symposia for it on such topics as race relations, the artist in tribal society, and the domestication of cattle. She also taught part-time in the famous anthropology department of the London School of Economics, giving special attention to the relations between psychology and social anthropology and aiming at a balance between the British and the American traditions of anthropology, which at that time diverged considerably. In 1960 a cancer of the lymphatic system struck her. After battling against it in London she died in a hospital in New York on 2 May 1961; her husband survived her.

Marian Smith was an all-round anthropologist who made a contribution not only in her ethnography of Native Americans of the north-west, but also in her work for anthropological associations. Unusually, she spanned the American and the British traditions. According to her colleague W. B. Fagg she 'had a genius for that branch of applied anthropology which deals with the harmonious cooperation of anthropologists in their learned societies', and her obituary in *The Times* (9 May 1961) noted that she combined reforming innovation with a respect for tradition.

Smith earned wide admiration for mastering her physical disability. She was distinguished in the clarity of her mind, and in the unfailing humanity, equanimity, and grace of her temperament. Perhaps her disability, as well as her premature death, explains why she did not publish more major works. It is testimony to the thoroughness of her north-west American field manuscripts—now kept in the Royal Anthropological Institute's archives in London, with microfilm copies available in two Canadian libraries—that forty years after her death they were still being used in litigation about fishing rights and some other issues concerning Canadian Indian groups.

JONATHAN BENTHALL

Sources Lord Raglan, *Man*, 61 (1961), 176–7 • R. Firth, *Man*, 61 (1961), 177–8 • W. B. Fagg, *Man*, 61 (1961), 177 • *The Times* (9 May 1961) • *IGI*

Archives Royal Anthropological Institute, London, anthropological notes, collections, and papers

Likenesses photographs, Royal Anthropological Institute photographic collection • portrait, repro. in *Man*

Wealth at death left library to Royal Anthropological Institute, London

Smith, (Ellen) Marion Delf- (1883–1980), botanist, was born on 31 January 1883 at 6 Capel Road, East Ham, Essex, the daughter of Thomas William Herbert Delf, an insurance secretary, and Catherine Mary *née* Bridges. She was educated at James Allen's Girls' School, Dulwich, and attended Girton College, Cambridge, on several scholarships. At Girton she earned a first class in both parts of the natural sciences tripos, and was joint winner of the Montefiore prize in 1906, her final year. Originally planning to stay at Cambridge to study plant physiology with F. F. Blackman, she instead accepted an offer to teach botany at Westfield College, University of London.

At this time Westfield College offered only elementary and intermediate level courses in science, so students wishing to obtain the BSc degree had to complete their courses elsewhere. Delf's appointment was part of a deliberate attempt by the college to upgrade its offerings in at least one scientific subject, botany. When she arrived she found no money for equipment or assistance in the college's attic laboratory, and a botanical collection consisting of 'eight or ten bottles with bits of plants, mostly in very poor condition' (Sondheimer, 62). She also encountered a strong evangelical religious tradition, exemplified by the college's principal, Constance Maynard. Delf challenged Maynard on the religious question, refusing to attend the principal's divinity lectures, and insisting on teaching her students about the theory of evolution. In spite of these obstacles, Delf was able to raise money to purchase equipment and obtain specimens. In 1910 the University of London approved the Westfield laboratory to prepare students for the final BSc pass examination in botany and granted Delf the status of a recognized teacher of the university. The college was recognized to prepare students for honours degrees in botany in 1915.

During this period Marion Delf also managed to continue her own research, begun so promisingly at Cambridge. Between 1911 and 1916 she studied the transpiration of plants, the process by which plants excrete water, particularly the morphology of *Ulvaceae* or seaweeds, publishing her results in four papers in the *Annals of Botany*. In 1912 she was awarded the London DSc degree for a thesis based on original research, as well as the Gamble prize from Girton for an essay entitled 'The biology of transpiration'.

In 1914 Delf was granted a Yarrow fellowship from Girton to work on transpiration in evergreens. Her fellowship was interrupted, however, by war work. From December 1916 to January 1920 she was a research assistant at the Lister Institute of Medical Research in London. As a member of a team led by Dr Harriet Chick she investigated the vitamin content of foods as pertaining to the rations of the military. In 1920 she went to South Africa as a temporary research fellow attached to the Institute of Medical Research, Johannesburg, where she continued this line of research, investigating the vitamin C content in the diets of local mine workers, 'as a result of which their health was substantially improved' (*Girton College Newsletter*, 32). She was offered a chance to remain permanently in South Africa, but rather reluctantly chose to return to Westfield, when she learned that a new laboratory had just been built for her.

Marion Delf was to remain at Westfield for the rest of her career. She was appointed a university reader in 1921, and became head of the Westfield botany department in 1939. In 1928 she married Percy John Smith, an etcher and book illustrator, from which time she was generally known as Delf-Smith. She moved with him to Haverstock Hill in Hampstead, remaining at Westfield as a non-resident lecturer. Percy Smith died in 1948, the year of his wife's retirement.

Delf-Smith was a life member of the British Association, a fellow of the Linnean Society, a member of the South East London Botany Society, the South East Union of Scientific Societies, and the Association of Women Science Teachers, and served on the advisory algae committee of the Scottish Seaweed Organization. Her interests were, however, by no means narrow. She shared with her husband a love of drawing and gardening, serving as the Westfield garden steward after her retirement. She became devoted to the college, serving on its council and as head of the alumnae association. In 1955 she was elected an honorary fellow, a distinction rarely given. Believing that the job of a teacher was to 'at least awaken the desire amongst students to follow some line of investigation for themselves' (Sondheimer, 62), Delf-Smith taught many students who went on to have scientific careers, including her Westfield colleagues Violet Grubb and Alison Westbrook. She died in the Royal Free Hospital, Camden, on 23 February 1980.

FERNANDA HELEN PERRONE

Sources register, Girton Cam. • b. cert. • J. Sondheimer, *Castle Adamant in Hampstead: a history of Westfield College, 1882–1982* (1983) • E. M. Delf-Smith memoir, Queen Mary College, London • *The Times* (5 March 1980) • Queen Mary College, London, E. M. Delf-Smith MSS • *Girton College Newsletter* (1980) • d. cert.

Archives Queen Mary College, London, Westfield College archives, papers

Likenesses Maull & Fox, photograph, 1912, Westfield College, London • photograph, 1912, Westfield College, London • photograph, *c.*1926, Westfield College, London • P. Smith, etching, *c.*1930, Westfield College, London • photograph (aged ninety), Westfield College, London

Wealth at death £140,786: probate, 30 May 1980, *CGPLA Eng. & Wales*

Smith [*née* Dalrymple], **Martha Mary** [Eustacia] (**1835–1919**), art patron, was born on 14 October 1835 in Madras, India, the eldest daughter of Captain (William Henry) Clarence Dalrymple (*d.* 1838) and his wife, Margaret, daughter of Lieutenant-Colonel Oswald Werge. Little is known of her upbringing: she presumably went to Britain as a small child on the death of her father—a naval captain who in 1835 became master attendant and a member of the marine board in Madras—and may then have grown up on the family estates in Northumberland. Through a distant cousin, Sir John Dalrymple (whose wife, Sophia Pattle, was the sister of Lady Somers and of the photographer Julia Margaret Cameron), Martha Dalrymple gained an entrée to Little Holland House, Kensington, in the 1850s and 1860s the hub of the most vibrant artistic clique of the day. As well as Tennyson and Browning, she would have encountered the young painters Frederic Leighton and Val Prinsep (whose mother was another of the Pattle sisters); G. F. Watts lived in the grounds as painter-in-residence.

In 1855 Martha Dalrymple married **(Thomas) Eustace Smith** (1831–1903), a member of one of Tyneside's most prosperous shipping families. He was born in Newcastle upon Tyne on 3 June 1831, the son of William Smith (*bap.* 1787, *d.* 1860) and Margaret Werge (a cousin of Martha's mother). William, with his elder brother Thomas (*c.*1784–1856), had built up their father's rope making business into a major concern, which came to embrace the ownership of ships and docks as well as shipbuilding. On his father's death in 1860 Eustace Smith became heir to business interests worth £60,000 a year. Eustace and Martha Smith had ten children, born between 1856 and 1868. The latter year also marked Eustace Smith's election as Liberal MP for Tynemouth, a seat he held until his resignation in 1885.

Between about 1865 and 1875 the Smiths assembled one of the most spectacular collections of paintings of the nascent aesthetic movement. Initially, most were hung at Eustace's family home of Gosforth Park, near Newcastle, then after about 1874 in London, at 52 Prince's Gate, opposite Hyde Park in the fashionable suburb of Kensington. There they were installed in interiors designed by George Aitchison, with the participation of Walter Crane and Thomas Armstrong. Their importance is reflected by Whistler's comment in 1876 or 1877, on completing the 'Peacock room' for Frederick Leyland, their neighbour three doors away at no. 49: 'it eclipses Mrs Eustace Smith!' (Wilcox, 49).

Watts's portrait of Ellen Terry, *Choosing* (1865; NPG), was one of the first works to be acquired by Eustace Smith, a purchase datable circumstantially to about 1865. He retained a special affection for Watts, who painted his portrait (*c.*1872; Tate collection). For the remainder of the collection, the surviving records reveal the initiative to have been taken almost entirely by Martha Smith, who adopted the name Eustacia as much as an act of identification with the new classicism in painting as with her husband. Her favoured artist was Leighton, who not only painted her portrait (*c.*1870; priv. coll.) but may also have used her as the model for one of his most provocative nudes, prominently displayed at Prince's Gate, *Venus Disrobing* (1867; priv. coll.). Eustacia teasingly admitted to modelling solely for the feet.

Rosetti's *Pandora* (1869; Faringdon Collection Trust), Albert Moore's *A Garden* (1870; Tate collection), Watts's *The Wife of Pygmalion* (1868; Faringdon Collection Trust), and Burne Jones's *Cupid and Psyche* (1867; Cecil French collection, Fulham Public Library) were all ground-breaking essays for their respective artists and their purchase revealed Eustacia Smith's complete commitment to the avant-garde. She showed more than generosity in supporting two indigent protégés of Leighton, George Heming Mason and the Frenchman Alphonse Legros, whose largest and most ambitious works entered the collection about 1872–3. In the case of Mason's *The Harvest Moon* (1872; Tate collection) the purchase was made posthumously. There is no evidence that any further works were added to the collection after about 1875, although in 1882 Mrs Smith apparently commissioned a statuette from Alfred Gilbert which was never completed.

The adventurousness of Eustacia Smith's collecting also typified her private life. In 1868 she engaged in an affair with Charles Dilke MP, one of her husband's Liberal colleagues at Westminster; the liaison re-ignited briefly in 1874–5 on the death of Dilke's wife. In 1876 Dilke's brother Ashton married the Smiths' eldest daughter, Margaret. The web of connections between the families became fatally tangled when in 1885 Charles Dilke was named as co-respondent in a divorce suit filed by Donald Crawford, the husband of another of the Smiths' daughters, Virginia, a scandal described by Henry James as 'queer and dramatic and disagreeable'. The case against Dilke remained unproven, but the shameful implications led Eustace Smith to sell the Prince's Gate house, complete with the paintings, privately to Alexander Henderson, later first Baron Faringdon. The Smiths spent the next fifteen years in self-imposed exile in Algeciras, Spain, their name virtually unmentionable in English society. They eventually returned to England about 1900 and commissioned from W. R. Lethaby a house, High Coxlease, in Lyndhurst, Hampshire, where they lived a retired existence far from the public gaze. Eustace Smith died there on 5 December 1903 following several years' poor health; his wife survived him and died at High Coxlease on 29 December 1919. TIMOTHY WILCOX

Sources T. Wilcox, 'The aesthete expunged: the career and collection of T. Eustace Smith', *Journal of the History of Collections*, 5 (1993), 43–57 • J. Vickers, *Pre-Raphaelites: painters and patrons in the north east* [1989] [exhibition catalogue, Laing Art Gallery, Newcastle upon Tyne, 14 Oct 1989 – 14 Jan 1990] • D. S. Macleod, *Art and the Victorian middle class: money and the making of cultural identity* (1996) • R. Jenkins, *Sir Charles Dilke: a Victorian tragedy*, rev. edn (1965) • L. Ormond and R. Ormond, *Lord Leighton* (1975) • J. Hawthorne, *Shapes that pass* (1928) • F. G. Stephens, 'The private collections of England', *The Athenaeum* (20 Sept 1873), 372–3 • Burke, *Peerage* • Burke, *Gen. GB* (1953) • d. cert. • *Newcastle Evening Chronicle* (7 Dec 1903) [T. E. Smith] • Madras baptisms, BL OIOC

Archives CAC Cam., Dilke/Crawford/Roskill archive

Likenesses V. Prinsep, black chalk, 1867, priv. coll. • F. Leighton, oils, *c.*1870, priv. coll. • G. F. Watts, oils, *c.*1872 (T. E. Smith), Tate collection • photograph, CAC Cam., archives

Wealth at death £17,693 1*s.* 10*d.*: probate, 31 March 1920, *CGPLA Eng. & Wales* • £123,151 2*s.* 4*d.*—(Thomas) Eustace Smith: probate, 1904, *CGPLA Eng. & Wales*

Smith, Martin Roger Seymour- (1928–1998), poet and writer, was born on 24 April 1928 at Tudor House, Newington Green, Islington, London, the only child of Frank Sidney Seymour Smith (1900–1972), a librarian and bibliographer, and his wife, Marjorie Nellie, *née* Harris (1901–1988), who wrote poetry under the pseudonym of Elena Fearn. As a teenage boy at Highgate School with a passion for poetry, Seymour-Smith made a pilgrimage to visit Robert Graves, who received him kindly. Despite the difference in their ages, Graves became a lifelong friend to Seymour-Smith and a dominant influence on his writing. After military service in Egypt Seymour-Smith went to St Edmund Hall, Oxford; he emerged with a poor degree in history but with a reputation as a poet who had published a pamphlet in the Fantasy Poets series, which was to include some famous names. After graduating Seymour-Smith and his girlfriend, Janet de Glanville, were invited to Mallorca by Graves on a double assignment; he was to act as tutor to Graves's son, and she, a Somerville classics graduate, was to assist Graves with translations for *The Greek Myths*, on which he was then working. The couple were married at the British consulate at Palma de Mallorca on 6 September 1952. Graves was one of the witnesses.

Janet Seymour-Smith (1930–1998), translator and scholar, was a tall blonde woman of striking appearance but retiring personality. She was born on 25 August 1930 at Eastnor, Rolle Road, Littleham, Exmouth, Devon, the daughter of Lionel Richard Gethin de Glanville, a doctor, and his wife, Hilda St Hilary Edith Everard, *née* Mayne. Apart from her work for Graves, she was an active supporter of and collaborator in her husband's later literary activities. After her death, their friend Robert Nye wrote, 'Her mind was his mind in such matters. And what a mind it was—as incandescent as it was delicate and particular' (Nye, *The Independent*). Their first child was born on Mallorca; a second daughter was born in England. The American poet Robert Creeley, who knew Seymour-Smith on Mallorca, depicted him as Artie in his autobiographical novel *The Island*: 'In the night he thought of Artie, tired, worn, smiling man. The shuffling gesture, the sidewise manner, the edged, confidential voice' (Creeley, 59). The impression seems authentic to those who knew Seymour-Smith at that time. In Mallorca Creeley set up the Divers Press, which published Seymour-Smith's *All Devils Fading* in 1954 (though dated 1953), an elegant hand-printed collection of eleven poems. Graves's influence is strong in themes and idiom, though not to the extent of extinguishing Seymour-Smith's personal poetic voice; it was to remain strong in the later poetry, where it is combined with that of Hardy, whom Seymour-Smith regarded as the greatest of twentieth-century poets. Like Graves, Seymour-Smith saw human relations in mythic terms, where the beloved woman is both muse and tormentor. His poetry, from the first collection onwards, is peopled by ghosts, devils, revenants, doppelgängers. The eponymous female figures of his second and third collections, *Tea with Miss Stockport* (1961) and *Reminiscences of Norma* (1970), embody the duality of love and suffering. Like Graves, Seymour-Smith was a poet of formal precision and a delicate, occasionally exquisite, music. But his poetry was often obscure, perhaps because of the pressure of emotions that evaded direct expression. In his last collection, *Wilderness* (1994), there are poems of more direct feeling, such as 'To my wife in hospital' and 'To my daughter'. Seymour-Smith wanted to be seen primarily as a poet; in 1970 he wrote, 'all my critical work stems primarily from poetic experience, and from what I describe as poetic thinking' (Murphy, 982). But his poetry remained a thin stream compared to the vast output of his prose writing.

After Seymour-Smith and his family returned to England in 1954 he worked for a time as a schoolmaster, an unhappy phase of his life reflected in the satirical poem 'What schoolmasters say', which Philip Larkin included in the *Oxford Book of Twentieth Century Verse*. In 1960 he became a professional writer. He brought out a variety of potboiling or educational texts, and a scholarly edition of Shakespeare's sonnets; he was also a prolific reviewer. His most substantial contribution to literary study lies in his long biographies and reference books. He published a life of his mentor Robert Graves, which had the benefit of close personal knowledge; of Kipling, which annoyed many readers by implying that he was a repressed homosexual; and of Hardy, whom Seymour-Smith revered, though he devoted too much space to attacking other Hardy biographers. He was always a combative writer, much given to airing his opinions on all sorts of subjects, but his direct and personal style made him irresistibly readable, even when provoking disagreement.

Seymour-Smith's largest and most ambitious book is *The Guide to Modern World Literature*; the first edition, published in 1973, was big, but the greatly enlarged second edition of 1985 was enormous, running to nearly 1400 pages. It is a rewarding book to dip into, and informative to read in at length, but it has puzzling aspects. Could Seymour-Smith have read all the works he discusses, from thirty-odd literatures? Robert Nye acknowledges that he had not and that some of the entries were written by his wife, Janet (Nye, *The Independent*). The blurb of the 1985 edition says Seymour-Smith had a reading knowledge of some twenty languages; if he had, it may be wondered how and when he acquired this remarkable capacity in a busy life. Certainly there are translations from Hungarian, Polish, and modern Greek poets which appear to be by the author himself, and he can happily be given the benefit of the doubt. But Seymour-Smith was a joker and not everything in the guide is to be taken at face value, such as the reference to the Polish philosopher and novelist 'Herma Newticks', who was allegedly responsible for the propagation of 'hermeneutics' as a critical concept.

Anyone who had read so much literature as Seymour-Smith, and wrote so extensively about it, might be expected to work in a university. But he was a proud, late upholder of the old Grub Street tradition, who never let slip an opportunity to cross swords with academics. Robert Nye described him as 'small and wiry, bright-eyed, bushy-bearded'; on his own admission he was 'angry as a bull when roused' (Nye, 'Martin Seymour-Smith', 13). But he had a gentle side, shown in his love of his cats, whom he named after characters in Hardy's novels. He died at his home, 36 Holliers Hill, in Bexhill-on-Sea, Sussex, of a sudden heart attack on 1 July 1998, and was cremated at Eastbourne on 10 July. Janet Seymour-Smith survived him for only two months. She died on 2 September 1998 at the Kent and Sussex Hospital, Tunbridge Wells, and was cremated at Tunbridge Wells on 11 September.

BERNARD BERGONZI

Sources R. Nye, 'Martin Seymour-Smith: the article the DNB will not print', *PN Review*, 144 (March–April 2002) · *The Times* (4 July 1998) · *The Independent* (3 July 1998) · *Daily Telegraph* (10 July 1998) · *The Times* (July 1998) · R. Creeley, *The island* (1963) · R. Nye, *The Independent* (16 Sept 1998) [Janet Seymour-Smith] · *The Times* (Sept 1998) [Janet Seymour-Smith] · personal information (2004) · R. Murphy, ed., *Contemporary poets of the English language* (1970)

Archives Ransom HRC, corresp. and literary MSS · State University of New York, Buffalo, E. H. Butler Library, corresp. and papers | SOUND BL NSA, performance recordings

Likenesses photograph, 1954, Hult. Arch.

Wealth at death under £200,000—gross; under £40,000—net; Janet Seymour-Smith: probate, 7 Oct 1998, *CGPLA Eng. & Wales*

Smith, Mary (1822–1889), schoolmistress and radical, was born on 7 February 1822 at Cropredy in Oxfordshire, the fourth child of William Smith, a boot and shoe maker, and Ann, *née* Pride, a cook from a prosperous farming family. Ann Smith died in 1824, shortly after the birth of her fifth child, when Mary was two years old. William Smith (who later married his housekeeper) attended the Independent chapel at Great Bourton, for which he and his family were forced to endure much local hostility. Mary Smith attended a Methodist Sunday school and, until the age of seven, was poorly educated at village dame-schools, later moving to a rather more rigorous Methodist day school.

When her father became a district registrar, Mary Smith and one of her brothers took over the family shop. However, when her brother married, Smith's services were no longer required. She found employment as a mother's help in the family of a Baptist minister, J. J. Osborn, and travelled with the young family to Brough, in Westmorland. They remained in Brough for three years, during which time Smith was asked to establish a girls' school—the first in the neighbourhood. She then accompanied the Osborns to Carlisle, but they proved to be difficult employers and Smith found a new appointment in nearby Scotby, looking after the children of a local wealthy Quaker family, the Suttons. This proved to be an important move for Smith. She had access to the Suttons' fine library, which enabled her to continue her own education (she came to be particularly influenced by Carlyle and Emerson), and she pursued her interest in languages, learning French, German, and Italian. (She also published two poems in the Oxonian patois.) The Sutton family also took her to hear popular radical speakers such as James Silk Buckingham and George Dawson. Meanwhile Smith began to achieve limited success as a poet, publishing material in journals such as *Whitridge's Miscellany*, the *People's Journal*, *Cassell's Magazine*, and the *Carlisle Journal*. She often used the pseudonym Mary Osborn.

Smith later returned to assist the Osborn family in running a school, but the relationship remained a troubled one and she finally severed her connection with them in 1852. She then took the decision to open her own school. This proved to be a judicious move. Smith had a natural talent for teaching and was proud of her innovative, child-centred methods, and the school flourished. Smith continued to pursue her love for literature, however, publishing two volumes of poetry, the second of which was particularly well received. Under the name Burns Redivivus she adapted popular Scottish ballads, and in 1868 she published her literary sketches, *Old Castles*. Smith also began to write on social and political issues, often using the pseudonym Z. She reported sermons and lectures for the *Carlisle Examiner* and *Observer*. During general elections she composed anti-tory poems for circulation and, with the editor of the *Carlisle Examiner*, she brought out a small tract to encourage candidates to exhibit more 'Christian feeling' in their campaigning.

Smith's concern to improve the moral and physical well-being of the working classes was well illustrated in the evening classes she established for young working women. The classes proved controversial locally as they were held on a Sunday. Lecturing on such improving topics as childcare, thrift, cleanliness, and cheerfulness, Smith was baffled that she did not attract larger audiences. She also became a vehement champion of other efforts to improve the condition of women's lives. She believed that society as a whole would remain degraded until women were given full civil rights. Inspired and aided by Lydia Becker, Smith established a women's suffrage society in Carlisle, although it does not appear to have thrived. She campaigned in favour of the Married Women's Property Bill and for extending women's employment opportunities. Smith stated that she herself remained single out of a desire for independence and employment. She arranged petitions and delivered lectures to protest against the Contagious Diseases Acts.

Smith believed that her low status as a woman was to blame for her failure to achieve the high literary reputation for which she longed. Her friend George Coward (who edited her autobiography) was probably more accurate when he noted that her literary works tended to be overly didactic and lacking in humour. This would certainly accord with what we know of her character. While she was revered for her innate kindness and humanitarian principles, her school pupils remembered that she was also unsmiling and serious to the point of austerity. She invariably wore a neat, black dress and had formal, correct manners. She was an intensely religious person, although her passion for religious liberty meant that she did not join any particular denomination. She left legacies to a variety of local religious institutions. Smith lived frugally throughout her life. This was partly due to financial hardship—she charged such low fees to her pupils that she never enjoyed financial security—but it was also the product of her ascetic nature. For the last seven years of her life Smith suffered from severe ill health. She died on 9 January 1889 at her house, 2 South Alfred Street, Carlisle, and was buried three days later in Carlisle cemetery.

KATHRYN GLEADLE

Sources *The autobiography of Mary Smith, schoolmistress and nonconformist … with letters from Jane Welsh Carlyle and Thomas Carlyle*, 2 vols. (1892) • *Carlisle Journal* (18 Jan 1889) • H. Rogers, 'Poetesses and politicians: gender, knowledge and power in radical culture, 1830–70', PhD diss., University of York, 1994 • Cumbria AS, Carlisle • *CGPLA Eng. & Wales* (1889)

Wealth at death £1463 19*s*.: probate, 6 March 1889, *CGPLA Eng. & Wales*

Smith, Mary Bentinck (1864–1921), headmistress, was born on 2 November 1864 at Hamburg, the daughter of James Smith (1822–1906), a Congregational minister of great learning, and his wife, Countess (Wilhelmina) Augusta Friederike Bentinck (1834–1922), daughter of Willem, second Count Bentinck in the nobility of the Holy Roman Empire (a great-grandson of Hans Willem, first earl of Portland), and his second wife, Sara Geddes. She had a younger brother, William Frederick Bentinck Smith (*b*. 1872), who became professor of philosophy at Tulane University, New Orleans. Mary was educated privately in England and France, and at the public girls' school at Wiesbaden. In 1890 she won a scholarship to Girton College, Cambridge, gaining a starred first in the medieval and modern languages tripos in 1893, and a second class in English in 1894, later gaining the degrees of MA (1904) and DLitt from Trinity College, Dublin. In the same year she wrote to the University of Edinburgh to ask whether women might be considered for lectureships recently advertised, but the court 'did not contemplate the appointment of women'. She went on to build the first part of her career in the women's colleges.

From 1894 to 1897 Miss Bentinck Smith was lecturer in modern languages at Victoria College, Belfast, and during the next two years in German and philology at Royal Holloway College. She returned to Girton in 1899 as lecturer in medieval and modern languages and became director of studies in 1901. She established an international reputation as a Chaucer scholar. She published an edition of his *Prologue* and *Knight's Tale* (1908), translated *The Language and Metre of Chaucer* from the German of B. Ten Brink (1901), made valuable contributions to the *English Dialect Dictionary* and to the *Cambridge History of English Literature*, and translated O. L. Jiriczek's *Northern Hero Legends* (1902). So far her career was a paradigm of a successful new academic woman.

In 1906 Miss Bentinck Smith was appointed principal of Avery Hill Training College, founded by the London county council in the opulent mansion of a self-made City man, the first and most prestigious of the colleges the new local education authority was empowered to provide under the Education Act of 1902. The principal was to be responsible not only for college 'instruction', but also for the 'board, recreation and social life of the students in residence', with a salary of £500 and residence, calculated at £100. Within two months of taking up the appointment, she was taken ill and 'never returned to her desk' (Shorney, 53). In this short time she had made her mark on the college, insisting on high academic standards while paying close attention to the students' welfare. Forty years later she was still remembered with affection, one of a small number of women who began to transform training colleges from oppressive and restrictive sectarian seminaries into stimulating places of professional education.

In 1907 Mary Bentinck Smith became headmistress of St Leonards School, St Andrews, founded by a Girton pioneer and already flourishing, with high academic standards. Although lacking previous school experience she quickly identified herself with St Leonards. Her staff and pupils appreciated her magnetic personality, her genius for friendship, and her sense of humour. She herself was an original and stimulating teacher. A woman of deep faith, her scripture lessons were especially memorable, and in all her teaching girls remembered that there was 'no spoon feeding'. Pupils were encouraged to read up a subject for themselves, to draw their own conclusions, and form their own judgements.

The whole curriculum was kept under constant review.

Since 1902 the school had been recognized as teaching for the first MB of the University of London. Under Miss Bentinck Smith, one of the pioneers of science teaching for girls, two new laboratories and a lecture theatre were built, and opened in 1908 by Sir Ernest Shackleton. An additional mistress was appointed for science, and it became a separate department under its own head. Vocational education was provided in Spanish and typewriting for those who desired it. Aural culture was added to the music course, already very wide and part of the main curriculum, while art was seriously taught. A special domestic science department was created for girls over seventeen, who continued their general education and were examined for the certificates of the Edinburgh School of Cookery. Above all the academic standards of the school were maintained, and indeed raised to meet the increasing competition for places at the Oxford, Cambridge, and London colleges and the needs of the new Higher Certificate. Help and encouragement were given to girls in relation to higher education and their choice of careers.

Miss Bentinck Smith was one of the first women JPs for the county of Fife. She helped to found the Girls' Club and the Women Citizens' Association in St Andrews. She also served her former college, and in 1916 was elected by the Girton College Roll to the college council. In spite of the long journey from Scotland she seldom failed to attend its meetings, though the war years were a great strain upon her health. Mary Bentinck Smith died at St Leonards School, St Andrews, on 20 December 1921. Her academic record was one of high distinction and Girton, Avery Hill, and St Leonards had all benefited from her clear-sighted policy and optimistic outlook, which helped her to overcome obstacles to progress in women's education. Girton acknowledged her contribution by erecting wrought-iron entrance gates as a memorial. *Ad vitam: Papers of a Headmistress*, a volume of her school sermons and addresses, was published posthumously. It included papers on the educational ideals of H. G. Wells, the education of girls intending to enter the medical profession, and the need to provide support for women wishing to carry out academic research. Her account 'The girls' school in literature and life', reviewing the history of girls' education as depicted in fiction, concluded that there was 'no just reason for excluding [girls] from the practice of any profession worthy of a human being's interest and devotion' (Smith, 108). MARGARET BRYANT

Sources K. T. Butler and H. I. McMorran, eds., *Girton College register, 1869–1946* (1948) • *Girton Review*, Easter term (1924) • D. Shorney, *Teachers in training, 1906–1985: a history of Avery Hill College* (1989) • K. H. McCutcheon, *St Leonards School, 1877–1922* (1989) • C. Dyhouse, *No distinction of sex? Women in British universities, 1870–1939* (1995) • M. B. Smith, *Ad vitam: papers of a headmistress* (1927) [with memoir from *St Leonards School Gazette* (Feb 1922)]

Archives St Leonards School, St Andrews

Likenesses G. Harcourt, portrait, St Leonards School, St Andrews • E. M. Hinchley, drawing, repro. in Smith, *Ad vitam*, frontispiece • photograph, repro. in Shorney, *Teachers in training, 1906–1985*

Wealth at death £7358 13*s*. 7*d*.: confirmation, 31 March 1922, *CCI*

Smith, Matthew (*d.* **1640**). *See under* Smith, John (*bap.* 1659, *d.* 1715).

Smith, Matthew (*b. c.*1665, *d.* before **1723**?), spy and writer, was the eldest son of Matthew Smith (*d.* 1672), mercer of Coventry, and his second wife, Anne (Hanna; 1645–1723), second daughter of William Parkyns of Marston Jabbett, Warwickshire. Though a puritan, Smith's father—who had been sheriff of Coventry in 1637 and mayor in 1648—remained an active alderman and deputy lieutenant after the Restoration purges. The younger Matthew was the eldest son and heir only from 1671, and gentlemanly status obsessed him. He attended Adams' Grammar School, Newport, Shropshire, with the Jacobite Robert Charnock and the writer Tom Brown. On 12 May 1684 he was admitted, following his uncle, the future Jacobite Sir William *Parkyns, to the Inner Temple, where he was comptroller (students' master of the revels). Later he always used the form 'of the Inner Temple', although no longer resident.

On 8 October 1688 Smith was appointed captain of an independent company raised to oppose William of Orange's invasion. He changed sides, garrisoned Windsor Castle when William arrived there, and became a captain in the duke of Norfolk's new regiment in March 1689. He was, however, purged with other officers that summer—for having Jacobite and Roman Catholic relatives, he claimed—after an outlay which, added to his extravagance, left him £1500 in debt. The grievance gave him the entrée among Jacobite plotters. In 1691, bribing key neighbours, he courted a Southwark tavern-keeper, Rachael Graves, *née* Body (*b. c.*1656?, *d.* in or after 1693), at least a decade older, twice widowed, and well off from house property. Smith tricked her on 22 August 1691 into a 'jest' marriage which was legally binding; but after several attempts she had it annulled on 8 December 1693.

In late 1694 Smith offered himself to secretary of state Charles Talbot, duke of Shrewsbury, as a spy on the Jacobites. In December 1694 he reported that Parkyns had arms for a cavalry troop hidden at Marston Jabbett; but the backlash from the failed 'Lancashire plot' trials made it politically impossible then to search it effectively. Unfortunately, Smith's wild boasting and personal silliness led Shrewsbury and his under-secretary James Vernon gravely to underestimate his genuine contacts. This proved disastrous when Sir George Barclay began planning the assassination plot in the winter of 1695–6 with Smith's uncle Parkyns and schoolfellow Charnock. By February 1696 Smith had learned and passed on several of their alternative schemes for 'kidnapping' the king. Shrewsbury, however, doubted these because they were contradictory; he informed William, but without the urgency with which the earl of Portland finally made him listen to Thomas Prendergast. Ill since January, Shrewsbury had left Vernon to manage Smith. Alienated by Smith's demands for money, along with his evasiveness and refusal to be a witness, Vernon proved even more sceptical of the information passed to the government. Although Smith did not know of the first intended attack on the king (15 February 1696) he did give some warning, though still of an implausible ‘kidnapping’, before the second a week later. Shrewsbury had just left to convalesce in the country; the exposure of the plot made this liable to misinterpretation, and showed that many names and claims in Smith’s recent letters had been embarrassingly accurate.

As Smith’s cover remained unbroken, Shrewsbury continued to use him as a spy, though refusing to let him badger for a confession the condemned Parkyns (for whose forfeited estate, finally restored to the family, he later unsuccessfully asked). However, Smith became discontented with his lack of reward, particularly in comparison with Thomas Prendergast, and his threats to appeal directly to William (he boasted he would be made a peer) obliged Shrewsbury to dismiss him.

Smith now approached Charles Mordaunt, earl of Monmouth (from 1697 third earl of Peterborough), Shrewsbury’s secret enemy, who by May 1696 was encouraging his accusations that the duke had stifled the plot. Monmouth had the rival secretary Sir William Trumbull receive Smith’s papers, sealed for protection, and both encouraged him to incorporate them into a narrative of his services, initially for the king’s eye. Sir John Fenwick’s accusations against Shrewsbury of Jacobite involvement, and the latter’s serious illness, made this unexpectedly dangerous. The whig junto were even initially uncertain how William would react. Meanwhile Portland and Sir William Trumbull re-employed Smith as a spy; but, deprived of his personal contacts, he weakened his credit by reporting groundless rumours, ‘Jacobite news’ as William called it (*Downshire MSS*, 1.716).

Smith’s threats to appeal to parliament so alarmed Shrewsbury that the court worked to mollify their agent. William gave Smith access on 9 November, received his ‘book’, and assured him that Shrewsbury had passed on his warnings. Portland promised him, sincerely, an army commission in Flanders and gave him 50 guineas. When the Lords investigated Monmouth’s tamperings with Fenwick, they examined Smith on 11 and 13 January 1697. After Monmouth’s grandiose hints, Smith’s complaints of Shrewsbury’s ingratitude to him were inevitably an anticlimax. The Lords, taking their cue from a dismissive letter Shrewsbury sent them, voted that he deserved no further reward.

Monmouth’s disreputable Commons allies, John Arnold and the Colt brothers, now managed Smith, alongside William Chaloner, as a means of blackmailing Shrewsbury into obtaining profitable office for them, preferably at the Royal Mint. When Portland again offered a commission, Smith demanded instead the post of comptroller there, worth £500–600 a year. His continued threats got him barred from the court. By mid-1697 Smith was circulating manuscript copies of his book, and in December he petitioned the Commons, unsuccessfully, for vindication. In early 1698 Arnold sent him abroad with £100 seeking information to harass the government over Jacobites licensed to return home.

In 1699 Smith finally published his *Memoirs of Secret Service*, dedicated to the House of Commons (to whom he sent a copy on 8 February), in a large edition with many copies distributed free. It set his correspondence with Shrewsbury and Vernon, fairly faithfully reproduced, in a framework of falsified ‘minutes’ of their meetings and distorted commentary. Richard Kingston alleged that Tom Brown was the real author of this and Smith’s later publications, but Smith claimed that very little of Brown’s draft preface was used. The outspoken language provoked public interest, and it was translated, but the Commons treated both the book and a petition to MPs in April with indifference. In November 1699 Smith published *Remarks upon the D— of S—’s Letter to the House of Lords*, which went further in accusing Shrewsbury, and sent the Lords a copy. By including Shrewsbury’s 1697 letter to them, he had committed a breach of privilege; and, although the earl of Peterborough vainly defended Smith, whose lies were exposed by examination, the Lords briefly imprisoned him in the Gatehouse from December 1699 and had the pamphlet publicly burned. In January 1700 Richard Kingston, a former government spy, on his own initiative and against ministers’ wishes, attacked Smith in a scurrilous pamphlet, *A Modest Answer to Captain Smith’s Immodest Memoirs*, to which Smith replied, more effectively, in *A Reply to an Unjust and Scandalous Libel*.

After William’s death Smith composed a violent ‘Case and petition’ for the Commons, virtually accusing Shrewsbury and Vernon, who might now be vulnerable, of treason (and the king of corrupting MPs). Though realizing the error of sending it immediately after William Fuller’s exposure, Smith none the less dispatched his allegations (28 March 1702) to Speaker Robert Harley, who ignored them. With Shrewsbury abroad and Vernon dismissed from office, the issue died.

Smith’s decline was abruptly reversed when in August 1703 he was made judge-advocate of Jamaica by sea and land, evidently the result of the earl of Peterborough’s phantom governorship of the island. The post was presumably executed by deputies. Little more is known of Smith’s life. He was probably dead by 1723, when his mother’s will does not mention him. The Matthew Smith of Coventry (*c.*1667–1731), previously of London, at least thrice married, churchwarden of and buried in St Michael’s Church, was, as his signature shows, a different man. PAUL HOPKINS

Sources M. Smyth [M. Smith], *Memoirs of secret service* (1699) • M. Smyth [M. Smith], *Remarks upon the D— of S—’s letter to the House of Lords* (1699) • M. Smyth [M. Smith], *A reply to an unjust and scandalous libel* (1700) • J. Vernon, letters to Shrewsbury, Northants. RO, Buccleuch papers, vols. 46–8 • M. Smith, petition to MPs, Northants. RO, Buccleuch papers, vol. 77, no. 18 • *Private and original correspondence of Charles Talbot, duke of Shrewsbury*, ed. W. Coxe (1821) • Sir William Trumbull’s diary, 1696–7, BL, Trumbull (Downshire) MSS, Trumbull Papers, Add. MSS 72536–72537; Add. MS 72571 • LPL, Court of Arches records, B5/152; B/12/78; D 1915; Eee fols. 587–92, 615–16, 624–38, 641–5, 657–9 • *JHL*, 16 (1696–1701) • *The manuscripts of the House of Lords*, new ser., 12 vols. (1900–77), vols. 2, 4 • W. H. Rylands, ed., *The visitation of the county of Warwick … 1682 … 1683*, Harleian Society, 62 (1911) • *Bishop Burnet’s History* • J. Freke, letter to J. Locke, 26 Jan 1697, Bodl. Oxf., MS Locke c. 24, fols. 200–02 • *A catalogue of the Harleian manuscripts in the British Museum*, 1 (1808), 1620 • N. Luttrell, *A brief historical relation of state affairs from*

September 1678 to April 1714, 6 vols. (1857) • 'The case and petition of Matthew Smyth Esq.', BL, Harleian MS 6210, fols. 138–47 • C. Dalton, ed., *English army lists and commission registers, 1661–1714*, 6 vols. (1892–1904) • B. Boyce, *Tom Brown of facetious memory* (1939) • PRO, PROB 11/594 [A. Bright: mother], fol. 220 • *Report on the manuscripts of the marquis of Downshire*, 6 vols. in 7, HMC, 75 (1924–95) • *Registers of the church of Holy Trinity, Coventry, Warwickshire*, part 3, *baptisms, 1653–1745*; part 4, *banns 1653–61, marriages 1653–1745, burials 1653–1674*, [n.d.] [Coventry City Libraries, transcripts] • parish register, Bulkington, Warks. CRO, DR 198/1 • R. Kingston, *A modest answer to Captain Smith's immodest 'Memoirs of secret service'* (1700) • R. Kingston, *Impudence, lying and forgery detected and chastis'd* (1700) • will, proved, 27 March 1672, Staffs. RO, probate records • personal index files, Matthew Smith I, Coventry City RO

Archives BL, Trumbull papers, Downshire MSS • LPL, courtship narrative, court of arches records, D 1915

Smith, Sir Matthew Arnold Bracy (1879–1959), painter, was born at 30 Elmfield Terrace, Halifax, Yorkshire, on 22 October 1879, the second of the four sons of Frederic Smith (1849–1914), wire manufacturer, and his wife, Frances (Fanny) Holroyd (*d.* 1912). He was educated at Heath grammar school, Halifax (*c.*1890–1895), and Giggleswick School, Settle, Yorkshire (1895–7). His childhood and youth were dominated by the commanding figure of his father, a strict nonconformist who went to chapel twice every Sunday, ran his business with notable success, and in his spare time passed for a lover of the arts. Frederic Smith's collection of violins was well known to visiting virtuosi; he had published a book of Browningesque verses; and he had commissioned a painting, *Stradivarius in his Studio*, from Seymour Lucas.

Attempts to place his son in the business world were a failure and in the face of his father's intense disapproval Matthew Smith won permission to study applied design at the Municipal School of Technology, Manchester, in 1901. His range of activity was severely restricted—'I was twenty-one', he later said, 'before I saw a good picture' (*Matthew Smith: Fifty-Two Colour Plates*). But an iron determination lay concealed within his frail body and apparently timorous nature and at the late age of twenty-six he was allowed to go to the Slade School of Fine Art in London. He was unhappy there, often being handled roughly by Henry Tonks in front of the entire class, and on his doctor's advice he went to Pont-Aven in Brittany in the late summer of 1908—a decision, he would often say, which marked the true beginning of his life.

Pont-Aven's heyday as an artistic centre had passed, but Smith fell in love with France and with French life, and thereafter never felt really at home anywhere else. Enough of the tradition of Paul Gauguin lingered in Pont-Aven for him to learn the uses of pure colour, as distinct from the tyranny of 'pure drawing' maintained at the Slade. When he moved to Paris he was able to show, in 1911 and 1912, at the Salon des Indépendants in company with Matisse, Kandinsky, Fernand Léger, and Georges Rouault. He was lucky enough, also, to glimpse Matisse and his methods at first hand through attendance at the school, soon to be disbanded, which Matisse had run since 1908; and if his personal contacts with Matisse were slight, the experience was revelatory in the highest degree.

Sir Matthew Arnold Bracy Smith (1879–1959), self-portrait, 1932

Towards 1914 Smith's personal circumstances were radically altered by the death of his mother and father and by his marriage, on 10 January 1912, to (Mary) Gwendolen (Gwen) Salmond (1877–1958), who had studied successfully at the Slade in the 1890s and was a close friend of both Gwen John and Ida Nettleship (Augustus John's first wife). Her two brothers were Sir Geoffrey Salmond and Sir John Salmond.

Smith had yet to show a painting in England, but when the First World War forced him and his wife to interrupt their sojourns in France he took a studio in Fitzroy Street, London, where Walter Sickert and Jacob Epstein were among his neighbours. There he painted the first of the pictures in which the lessons of France were truly digested, and in 1916 Epstein persuaded him to show a painting in the London Group exhibition. In 1917 Smith was commissioned as an officer in the labour corps and that year was wounded by shrapnel during the battle of Passchendaele. Shortly before he was demobilized he met the Irish artist Roderic O'Conor (1860–1940) in Paris. Of all his contemporaries O'Conor provided Smith with the greatest inspiration and support. In 1920 Smith went with his wife and their two sons to Cornwall. At St Columb Major he produced a series of landscapes in which the dark, saturated colour of Gauguin was happily combined with reminiscences of the spatial organization in certain Florentine predella panels. With the two 'Fitzroy Street nudes' of 1916 these constitute his first original contribution to English painting.

Smith had always been delicate, and there was throughout his life an apparent discrepancy between his aghast and tentative approach to the practical aspects of living and the imperious energy which went into his work. Early in the 1920s the normal shortcomings of his health allied with the sense of something unfulfilled in his personal life combined to produce a serious breakdown; and it was not until he found in Vera Cuningham [*see below*] the ideal model for his art that he recovered and, indeed, redoubled his ability to work. He took a studio at 6bis Villa Brune in Montparnasse, Paris, and was soon producing one after another of the long series of female nudes which established him as one of the few English painters ever to master this most exacting of subjects. Of *Femme de cirque* (Scottish National Gallery of Modern Art, Edinburgh) Roger Fry wrote: 'It is a picture planned in the great tradition of pictorial design, and carried through without any failure of the impulse' ('The Mayor and Claridge Galleries', *The Nation and the Athenæum*, 1 May 1926, 126–7).

Vera Irene Walpole Martin Cuningham (1897–1955), herself a powerful artist with a compelling interest in the female nude, was born at Goff's Oak House, Goff's Oak, Hertfordshire, on 6 November 1897, the daughter of William Martin Cuningham (1847–1924), a mechanical engineer, and his wife, Caroline Emily (Lina) Walpole (1860–1949). She studied at the Central School of Arts and Crafts, London, and in 1922 began exhibiting with the London Group, becoming a member in 1927. In 1929 she held her first solo exhibition at the Bloomsbury Gallery. It was through her teacher, Bernard Meninsky, that she was introduced to Smith. After their relationship ended in the mid-1930s, she went on to develop within the English neo-romantic tradition an original interior vision carried out in intense colour, mixing a wide variety of media and techniques. During the Second World War she produced her most assured painting, in between her duties as an air raid warden. It has been suggested that 'in these paintings, gargantuan figures and grotesque nudes seem to caricature the nudes of Matthew Smith, suggesting an alarming tension between her role as artist and as model' (F. Spalding, *20th Century Painters and Sculptors*, 1990, 137). She died of lung cancer at University College Hospital, London, on 3 May 1955 and was cremated on the 10th at Golders Green crematorium.

From 1923 until 1940 Smith enjoyed a period of unbroken creativity. If Paris and the nude were predominant in the twenties, in the thirties his interest shifted to Provence, in geographical terms, and to landscape as his preferred theme. Throughout these years his first responsibility was owed to his work; and although he was a devoted father he was inflexible in his will to cut free from any entanglement which might impair the freedom to work which he had sought for so long and had found only in his middle forties.

In June 1940 Smith had to be evacuated from France by the RAF and he left behind many canvases in Aix-en-Provence. There followed a period of great private unhappiness on more than one count; above all, the loss of his two sons on active service was a blow from which he took a long time to recover. The petty vicissitudes of London life during and after the war found in Smith a most consistent victim; he was troubled, also, by an affliction of the eyes which later caused him to undergo a cataract operation. He found renewed energy painting portraits. Augustus John and the novelist Henry Green sat for him, as did many women, among them the actresses Valerie Hobson and Patricia Neal. The largest and most varied series of works was inspired by Mary Keene, *née* Hunt (1921–1981), who remained close to him until his death. She wrote a novel, *Mrs Donald* (1983), in which the love affair was partly drawn from her relationship with Smith.

Smith's natural toughness empowered him to go on working, and the still lifes and large decorative subjects of the mid-fifties have a grandeur of spirit and an unforced amplitude which put them very high in the canon of his work. In 1955 he developed pancreatic cancer, the illness from which he eventually died; but even when it was clear that life was withdrawing its benefits one by one he went on working as best he could. In his last years there was a general realization that as a master of paint he had had few rivals among twentieth-century English artists. He was appointed CBE in 1949 and knighted in 1954. In 1953 a large retrospective exhibition of his work was held at the Tate Gallery, London, and in 1956 the University of London awarded him the honorary degree of DLitt. Equally precious was the affection and respect in which he was held, not only by such lifelong friends and colleagues as Augustus John and Jacob Epstein but also by younger artists—Francis Bacon above all.

Smith was most often talked of as a colourist, but he did not altogether care for the appellation. 'They all praise the colour', he would say, 'but if the pictures hold together there must be something else, you know. There must be something else' (*Matthew Smith: Fifty-Two Colour Plates*). Tenaciously, though with characteristic discretion, he had studied Ingres, Courbet, Rembrandt, and Tintoretto. His landscape practice was based to a surprising degree on the study of Rubens's landscape sketches. He read enormously in an unstudied way, and although he was the last man to 'keep up with' his friends in a conventional sense, few people have had a securer hold on the affections of others. He spoke, someone once said, 'like a highly intelligent moth' (personal knowledge); but, once his confidence had been won, the high seriousness implicit in two of his given names (Matthew Arnold) was allied in his talk with an idiosyncratic and unforgettable sense of fun.

Matthew Smith died at 23 Acacia Road, St John's Wood, London, on 29 September 1959 and was buried at Gunnersbury, Middlesex. The Royal Academy mounted a memorial exhibition of 255 works in 1960. In 1974 Mary Keene, whom Smith had made his heir, presented over 1000 works to the corporation of London. A section of the Barbican Art Gallery, London, is permanently devoted to the display of part of this collection. The first full biography, Alice Keene's *The Two Mr Smiths* (1995), establishes the facts of Smith's life and work, while the second, Malcolm Yorke's *Matthew Smith: his Life and Reputation* (1997), discusses his unique place within early and mid-twentieth-century British art. JOHN RUSSELL, *rev.* ALICE KEENE

Sources A. Keene, *The two Mr Smiths* (1995) · M. Yorke, *Matthew Smith: his life and reputation* (1997) · *Matthew Smith: fifty-two colour*

plates (1962) • J. Rothenstein, *Matthew Smith (1879–1959)* (1962) • P. Hendy, *Matthew Smith* (1944) • J. Rothenstein, *Modern English painters*, 1: *Sickert to Smith* (1952) • M. Keene, *Mrs Donald* (1983) • *Matthew Smith: paintings from 1909–1952* (1953) [exhibition catalogue, Tate Gallery, London, 3 Sept – 18 Oct 1953] • *A memorial exhibition of works by Sir Matthew Smith, C.B.E., 1879–1959* (1960) [exhibition catalogue, RA, 15 Oct – 7 Dec 1960] • *Matthew Smith* (1983) [exhibition catalogue, Barbican Art Gallery, London, 15 Sept – 30 Oct 1983] • J. Benington, *Roderic O'Conor* (1992) • *CGPLA Eng. & Wales* (1959) • b. cert. • d. cert. • personal knowledge (1971) • private information (2004) • *Debrett's Peerage* • d. cert. [Vera Cuningham]

Archives CLRO, collection • NRA, priv. coll., corresp. and MSS | Tate collection, corresp. with Arthur Tooth & Sons Ltd | FILM BFI NFTVA, documentary footage

Likenesses M. Smith, self-portrait, oils, 1909, Guildhall Art Gallery, London • M. Smith, self-portrait, oils, 1932, NPG [*see illus.*] • A. John, oils, 1944, Tate collection • C. Mann, oils, 1952, NPG • C. Beaton, print, NPG

Wealth at death £173,948 13*s*. 6*d*.: probate, 14 Dec 1959, *CGPLA Eng. & Wales* • £6783 7*s*. 9*d*.—Vera Irene Walpole Martin Cuningham: probate, 10 Aug 1955, *CGPLA Eng. & Wales*

Smith, May (**1879–1968**), industrial psychologist, was born on 29 August 1879 at 44 Russell Street, Hulme, Chorlton, Lancashire, the elder of the two daughters of Thomas Smith, an iron turner, and his wife, Augusta, *née* Mathews. May Smith's father, though austere in his religious views (denouncing pastimes such as dancing as sinful), had equally strong literary and philosophical interests which ensured that discussions on such matters were commonplace within the home. After attending Manchester Science School, where she was also a pupil teacher, Smith won an education scholarship to Owens College, Manchester. Graduating with a BA that had included philosophy (and a little psychology) and a London University (external) diploma in education in 1903, she then taught for the next two years in the practising school associated with the education department.

In 1905 Smith was appointed lecturer in educational psychology at Cherwell Hall, a training college for secondary school teachers in Oxford. Having also arranged to study in Oxford for her Manchester MA in philosophy, she began attending William McDougall's psychology lectures and eventually joined his small group of pupils studying experimental psychology. Although her first taste of research was as McDougall's assistant, Smith soon branched out into independent work on the effects of sleep deprivation on mental functioning. Later, a collaborative study with McDougall concerning alcohol and certain drugs led to an official request during the First World War to examine possible links between drink and prostitution. This lengthy, if inconclusive, inquiry equipped her with valuable interviewing and reporting skills.

Smith's qualities as a researcher were eventually recognized and, at the age of forty, she found herself starting a new career with the newly established Industrial Health Research Board (IHRB), a post she held from 1920 until officially retiring in 1944. She was awarded a DSc by London University in 1930 and appointed OBE in 1945 for her services as a pioneer industrial psychologist. It was entirely characteristic of Smith's pragmatic style of research that to prepare for her first IHRB investigation, on fatigue and working hours in the laundry trade, she experienced the tasks at first hand, incidentally acquiring some basic skills, while spending several weeks as a laundry worker. During the investigation itself, she earned much goodwill and co-operation from managers and workforces alike by shrewdly helping out with the actual laundry work at busy times. Contemporaries, too, found her friendly and unpretentious, praised her good sense and also admired her knack of judging exactly how indiscreet she could be with her gossip.

In the late 1920s opportunities for collaborating with researchers from other fields opened up when Smith and several other IHRB investigators moved into the London School of Hygiene and Tropical Medicine. In addition to a long-standing collaboration with Major Greenwood, professor of epidemiology and vital statistics, a partnership with the professor of medical psychology, Millais Culpin, forged during a study of the condition known as telegraphists' cramp, proved to be especially significant for the development of industrial psychology. Initially, it was assumed that the condition was associated with fatigue until Culpin brought his experience of war neuroses to the work and evidence began to emerge of a psychoneurotic element. Subsequent studies on other groups of workers suggested that a 'nervous' factor contributed similarly to many occupational illnesses. Her book, *An Introduction to Industrial Psychology*, published in 1943, did much to introduce the wider world to the notion that applying psychological ideas could be of benefit in the workplace.

May Smith was anything but idle after leaving the IHRB in 1944. The following year she became a part-time lecturer in applied psychology at Birkbeck College, London, retiring only in 1955. From as early as 1914 she had been a stalwart of the British Psychological Society, serving in various capacities including honorary librarian (1932–59) and deputy president (1948–54). On 21 February 1968 she died, aged eighty-eight, at Otto House, 44 Sydenham Hill, Lewisham, London. She was unmarried.

A. D. Lovie and P. Lovie

Sources M. Smith, 'An autobiography', *Occupational Psychology*, 23 (1940), 74–80 • *Occupational Psychology*, 42 (1968), 255–7 • *Bulletin of the British Psychological Society*, 21 (1968), 205–6 • private information (2004) • b. cert. • d. cert

Likenesses Minder and Faraday?, photograph, repro. in *Occupational Psychology*, 23 (1940), facing p. 74

Wealth at death £8604: probate, 26 April 1968, *CGPLA Eng. & Wales*

Smith, Michael (**1932–2000**), biochemist, was born at 65 St Heliers Road, South Shore, Blackpool, on 26 April 1932, the son of Rowland Smith, a market gardener, and his wife, Mary Agnes (*née* Armstead), who worked in the family boarding-house. Educated at Arnold School, Blackpool, he entered the chemistry honours course at Manchester University in 1950. Having graduated in 1953 he proceeded to research on cyclohexane diols and gained a PhD degree in 1956. Like many others at that time he applied for postdoctoral research fellowships in North American universities; he was at length invited to Canada to work with Gobind Khorana, a young biochemist who had recently discovered a method of synthesizing deoxyribo-oligonucleotides at the University of Vancouver, British Columbia.

Synthesis of nucleic acids Smith realized that nucleic acid chemistry was far more complex than anything he had so far tackled, but he was impressed by Khorana's use of chemical or enzymatic methods as appropriate. His first project was to develop a general procedure for the chemical synthesis of molecules belonging to the biologically important organophosphate groups. This led him to investigate the reactions of carbodiimides with phosphoric acid esters, and to a general procedure for the preparation of nucleoside-3′, 5′ cyclic phosphates whose biological significance had only recently been recognized. In the course of this work he discovered methoxyl-trityl protecting groups for nucleoside-5′ hydroxyl groups, which are still used in automated syntheses of DNA and RNA fragments.

In 1960 Smith married Helen Wood; they had three children, two boys and a girl. In the same year Khorana's group moved to the Institute for Enzyme Research at the University of Wisconsin. Here Smith worked on the synthesis of ribo-oligonucleotides, a challenging problem in nucleic acid chemistry. After a year, wishing to return to the west coast of North America, Smith joined the Fisheries Research Board of Canada in its laboratory at Vancouver. Here he learned about marine biology while sustaining his interest in nucleic acid chemistry with a grant from the US National Institutes of Health. He discovered a new synthetic method for preparing complex phosphates, though the laboratory was not intended for academic research. In 1966 Smith was nominated for the post of medical research associate at the Medical Research Council of Canada. This allowed him to become a faculty member of the department of biochemistry in the University of British Columbia, where he remained during the rest of his career.

The pioneering work which led to site-directed mutagenesis began in the 1970s, when Smith learned how to synthesize oligonucleotides, short single-strand DNA fragments. He also studied how these synthetic fragments could bind to the DNA of a virus, and discovered that even if one of the small molecules in the synthetic DNA fragment was incorrect it could still bind in the correct position in the virus DNA. The idea of getting a reprogrammed synthetic oligonucleotide to bind to a DNA molecule and then having it replicate in a suitable host organism occurred to Smith in 1975–6, during a sabbatical at Frederick Sanger's laboratory of the Medical Research Council in Cambridge. He learned Sanger's 'plus–minus' method of sequencing as a member of a team studying the amino-acid sequence of the *E. coli* phage ΦX174.

Having returned to Vancouver in 1978 Smith used this virus as a model for site-directed mutagenesis using a synthetic oligonucleotide. With his co-workers he succeeded in inducing a mutation in the virus and also in correcting a mutation so that the virus regained its natural properties. Reprogramming the genetic code allowed gene sequences to be altered in designated ways, and it became possible to change any amino acid in a polypeptide sequence that made up the backbone of a protein or enzyme. Thus, by changing the nucleotides in a gene encoding a protein or enzyme of medical or industrial importance, a modified product of predetermined structure could be obtained that was not only more stable than the natural protein or enzyme but also perhaps more active. In 1982 Smith and his colleagues were able for the first time to produce and isolate large quantities of an enzyme in which one amino acid had been exchanged for another. This opened up a new approach to the study of the relationships between structure and function in enzymes, and provided a clearer understanding of how biological systems operate.

Commercial possibilities As a consequence of these discoveries the concept of 'protein design', the construction of proteins with predetermined properties, was introduced. Later applications of this concept have shown, for example, that the stability of an enzyme used in detergents can be improved so that it will withstand the chemicals and high temperatures used in laundry work. Smith's discovery also paved the way for gene therapy, by which hereditary diseases might be cured by correcting mutations in the genetic material. A mutated haemoglobin might provide a new way of replacing blood, while mutated proteins in immune system antibodies might be constructed to neutralize cancer cells. In plants, too, there was the possibility of producing disease-resistant crops that could make more efficient use of atmospheric carbon dioxide during photosynthesis.

Such commercial possibilities led Ben Hall and Earl Davie of the University of Washington to invite Smith to join them in founding a new biotechnology company, Zymos. Funded by the Seattle venture capital group Cable and Howse, this company developed a process for producing human insulin in yeast for the Danish pharmaceutical company Novo. This was successfully accomplished in 1988, and afterwards the Danish company, now Novo-Nordisk, purchased Zymos outright. Renamed Zymo Genetics, the company engaged in research on a wide range of potential protein pharmaceuticals, though Smith's connections with the company ceased with the take-over.

In 1986 Smith was asked by the dean of science at the University of British Columbia to establish a new interdisciplinary institute, the biotechnology laboratory, and he set about recruiting people with expertise in physics, chemistry, botany, zoology, and biology. In 1990 he was also founding director of the Network of Centres of Excellence in Protein Engineering, in which established scientists in the various subdisciplines of biochemistry work together on important problems in protein structure–function analysis. At the same time co-operation with Canadian industry improved technology transfer. In 1991 Smith became acting director of the Biomedical Research Centre, a privately funded research institute operating on the campus of the University of British Columbia. Its source of funding having disappeared, Smith had the unenviable task of managing the centre on a tight budget, negotiating future funding from the provincial government, and helping to ensure the transfer of ownership to the university. As many of the staff had been led to believe that Smith was trying to take over and subvert the activities of the centre, the issue became a 'political football' in an election year. However, he succeeded in negotiating funding, the university took over the ownership, and, after a fraught year, he was able to step down, leaving the centre and its work intact.

Reputation In 1993, the year in which he received the Nobel chemistry prize jointly with Kary Mullins, inventor of another technique in genetic engineering, Smith began to anticipate retirement and was looking forward to the chance to return to the laboratory work which was his first scientific love. Instead he found himself suddenly world-famous as his field of expertise in genetic engineering hit the headlines internationally. Fully aware of public concern about genetic engineering, Smith nevertheless believed that biotechnology was essential for the future welfare of humanity. In 1997 he retired from the university to become director of a new Genome Sequencing Centre at the British Columbian Cancer Agency in Vancouver, a post he held until his death. Convinced of the need to educate the public so that people could better understand the issues, he began to travel the world to promote the ideals of improved general education, especially a better understanding of science. His final illness cut short this aspect of his work.

Smith's many academic honours included election as fellow of the Royal Society of Canada in 1981 and of the Royal Society of London in 1986. Yet Smith never forgot his roots. He visited Blackpool as often as possible and was a lifelong supporter of Blackpool United Football Club. He loved the Pennines and moorland country, and thought that this accounted for his pleasure in the rugged outdoors and natural beauty of British Columbia. Smith, who died in Vancouver on 5 October 2000, separated from his wife, Helen, in 1983; he was survived by his partner, Elizabeth Raines, and by his daughter and two sons.

N. G. Coley

Sources B. G. Malmström, ed., *Nobel lectures: chemistry, 1991–95* (1997), 114–36 • www.nobel.se/nobel/nobel-foundation • P. Wright, 'Michael Smith', *The Guardian* (10 Oct 2000) • K. S. Shenton, 'Professor Michael Smith', *The Independent* (24 Oct 2000) • *WW* (1998); (1999) • *Nature*, 408 (2000), 786 • b. cert. • www.nobel.se/chemistry/laureates/1993/smith-autobio.html, 8 Feb 2002

Smith, Michael Holroyd (1847–1932), engineer, was born on 22 December 1847 at Wade Street, Halifax, Yorkshire, the second of six sons, and the fourth of the eleven children of Matthew Smith (1819–1880), wire manufacturer, and his wife, Mary Sutcliffe, *née* Holroyd, daughter of Richard Holroyd of Halifax. His paternal ancestors were Yorkshire dissenting ministers who had settled in Halifax in the eighteenth century. His father managed a wire mill in Birmingham before returning to Halifax in 1864 to enter into partnership in the wire manufacturing firm of Frederick Smith & Co. founded by his younger brother in 1859. He died during his term of office as mayor of Halifax in 1880. His mother, renowned for her beauty, was a Halifax watchmaker and jeweller's daughter. He was educated at King Edward's School, Birmingham. After serving an apprenticeship with Francis Berry & Sons, machine tool makers of Sowerby Bridge, Yorkshire, he worked with the family firm in Halifax before embarking on a career as a consultant engineer, designing mills, testing engines, and investigating the causes of industrial accidents. He then became a partner in Smith, Baker & Co., of Cornbrook, Manchester, and made some of the earliest telephones, telephone exchanges, and phonographs in Britain. On 22 June 1874 he married, at the English Presbyterian Chapel, Tywyn, Machynlleth, Montgomeryshire, Anne Williams (1848–1934), the daughter of Ebenezer Williams, a Welsh nonconformist minister. He and his wife lived in Wales after their marriage, at Maenan Hall, Llanrwst, Denbighshire. Their eldest daughter was the writer Naomi Gwladys Royde-*Smith.

Smith was considered within the family to have lacked the business acumen of his elder brother, Sir George Henry Fisher-Smith, but he was a brilliant and prolific inventor, who became a pioneer of the electric tramway, earning the sobriquet 'the father of electric traction' (*Halifax Courier*, 6 July 1932). By 1882 he recognized the potential advantages of electric traction over cable traction. In 1883 he built three experimental narrow-gauge electric tramways, one in his father's warehouse, the other two in the grounds of Moorside, Skircoat Green, Halifax, the home of a friend, the carpet manufacturer Louis John Crossley, who had installed a private electrical laboratory in his home. From his experimental work in Halifax Smith arranged a demonstration of a standard-gauge conduit tramway line at his Manchester works and then at the winter gardens, Blackpool. This led to the formation of the Blackpool Electric Tramway Company in 1885 and the commissioning of a 2 mile service along the promenade from Claremont Park to South Shore. This was the first electric tramway for public use in Britain, powered by a conduit in the track which was later superseded by overhead power transmission. Six of the ten directors of the tramway company were from Halifax, including the chairman, Richard Horsfall, and the tramway was constructed by Halifax engineers.

Smith was later responsible for the electrification of the City and South London Railway. He also developed an early interest in aviation, delivering in 1879 a lecture to the Halifax Literary and Philosophical Society illustrated with airborne models, and he contributed to the design of the aeroplane propeller blade. He also designed his own reel for engaging in his favourite sport of angling. He was a prolific lecturer and conducted pioneering evening classes in engineering at the Halifax Mechanics' Institute until 1885, contributing to the development of technical education. He was described by Sir Hiram S. Maxim as 'a very clever and scientific engineer' (Bond, *Transactions of the Halifax Antiquarian Society*, 133). He was affable by nature and regarded by one of his friends as 'the most lovable man I know' (Smith, 88). A photograph of him in middle age reveals a man of slim build with receding fair hair, an aquiline nose, and neatly trimmed moustache. He was deeply religious, attending regularly Sion Congregational Chapel in Halifax, where he became Sunday school superintendent, until his move to Wales. He died at his home, Maenan Hall, Llanrwst, Denbighshire, on 6 July 1932, from gastric influenza and kidney failure.

JOHN A. HARGREAVES

Sources A. W. Bond, 'Michael Holroyd Smith', *Modern Tramway and Light Railway Review*, 32/381–5 (1969–70) · *Halifax Courier* (6 July 1932) · J. R. Moore, 'Halifax corporation tramways', *Transactions of the Halifax Antiquarian Society* (1974) · A. W. Bond, 'Michael Holroyd Smith', *Transactions of the Halifax Antiquarian Society* (1971) · G. H. Smith, 'The Smiths of Halifax', *Transactions of the Halifax Antiquarian Society* (1949), 73–91 · A. Keene, *The two Mr Smiths* (1995), 13–17 · M. Yorke, *Matthew Smith: his life and reputation* (1997), 1–15 · P. Triton, *The godfather of Rolls Royce* (1993), 84–5 · *Evening Courier* [Halifax] (28 Sept 1985) · *Evening Courier* [Halifax] (16 Oct 1990) · *Evening Courier* [Halifax] (24 Dec 1994) · *Evening Courier* [Halifax] (28 Jan 1995) · J. I. Bentley, *Bentley of Southowram and Halifax* (1996), 104–12 · b. cert. · m. cert. · d. cert.

Archives Birm. CL, lecture notes on 'The development of an electric tramway' · priv. coll.

Likenesses M. G. Wilde, photograph, 1884 (with Wallace Bentley) · A. Hughes, photograph (in middle age), repro. in Bond, 'Michael Holroyd Smith', 307 · photograph (as a young man), repro. in *Evening Courier* [Halifax] (28 Sept 1985) · photograph, repro. in *Evening Courier* [Halifax] (28 Sept 1985)

Wealth at death £172 19s. 11d.: administration with will, 20 Sept 1932, *CGPLA Eng. & Wales*

Smith, Michael William (1809–1891), army officer, was the posthumous son of Sir Michael Smith, baronet (1740–1808), master of the rolls in Ireland, and his second wife, Eleanor, daughter of Michael Smith, his cousin german. He was born on 27 April 1809, four months after his father's death. He was commissioned ensign in the 82nd foot on 19 November 1830, lieutenant on 21 February 1834, exchanged into the 15th hussars on 29 August 1835, and was promoted captain on 23 April 1839. In November he obtained a first-class certificate at the senior department of the Royal Military College, Sandhurst. He served several years in India; he became major on 9 February 1847 and lieutenant-colonel on 8 March 1850.

During the Crimean War Smith commanded Osmanli irregular cavalry, and received the Mejidiye (second class). He was made colonel in the army on 28 November 1854. He had exchanged from his regiment to half pay on 25 August 1854, and on 16 June 1857 he became lieutenant-colonel of the 3rd dragoon guards, which served in India during the mutiny. In 1858 he was placed in command of a brigade of the Rajputana field force, and was detached from the main body of that force to assist Sir Hugh Rose (afterwards Baron Strathnairn) in his operations against Tantia Topi. On 17 June he attacked the mutineers between Kotah-ki-sarai and Gwalior, and drove them back after some severe fighting, in which the famous rani of Jhansi was killed. He took part in the capture of Gwalior on 19 June. In August he was sent against Man Singh, raja of Narwar, who had rebelled against Sindhia. His own force proved insufficient, but he was soon joined by Sir Robert Cornelis Napier, who had succeeded Rose in command of the central India force; and he took part in the siege and capture of Paori, and in the subsequent pursuit of Tantia Topi. In November he surprised the camp of Man Singh at Koondrye. He was mentioned in dispatches, made CB on 21 March 1859, and was given a reward for distinguished service on 6 April 1860.

Smith left his regiment and went on half pay on 25 April 1862, after being appointed to the command of the Poona division with the local rank of major-general. He held this command until 1 June 1867. He was promoted major-general on 4 July 1864, lieutenant-general on 19 January 1873, and general on 1 October 1877. On 27 April 1879 he was placed on the retired list. He had been given the colonelcy of the 20th hussars on 22 November 1870, and was transferred to his old regiment, the 15th hussars, on 21 August 1883. In 1830 he married Charlotte, eldest daughter of George Whitmore Carr of Ardross, and he left one son, Major William Whitmore Smith, of the Royal Artillery, and one daughter.

Smith was not only a practical soldier, but thought and wrote with some originality on military, especially cavalry, topics. He published *A Treatise on Drill and Manoeuvres of Cavalry* (1865), *Cavalry Outpost Drill* (1867), *Modern Tactics of the Three Arms*, with illustrations by himself (1869), and *A New System of Perspective* (1881). He died at his home, 11 Medina Villas, Hove, Sussex, on 18 April 1891.

E. M. LLOYD, *rev.* ROGER T. STEARN

Sources *The Times* (22 April 1891) · J. Foster, *The peerage, baronetage, and knightage of the British empire for 1882*, 2 [1882] · G. B. Malleson, *History of the Indian mutiny, 1857–1858: commencing from the close of the second volume of Sir John Kaye's History of the Sepoy War*, 3 vols. (1878–80) · C. Hibbert, *The great mutiny, India, 1857* (1978) · T. A. Heathcote, *The military in British India: the development of British land forces in south Asia, 1600–1947* (1995) · *CGPLA Eng. & Wales* (1891)

Wealth at death £14,884 19s. 1d.: probate, 1 June 1891, *CGPLA Eng. & Wales*

Smith, Miles (*d.* 1624), bishop of Gloucester, was born at Hereford, the son of a fletcher (not, as often described, of a 'flessher' or butcher) and became, about 1568, a student of Corpus Christi College, Oxford, from where he migrated to Brasenose. He graduated BA in 1573 and proceeded MA in 1576. About 1576 he was made a chaplain or petty canon of Christ Church. In 1580 he obtained the prebend of Hinton in Hereford Cathedral, and in 1584 he became vicar of Bosbury and in 1587 rector of Hampton Bishop in Hereford diocese, both livings in the gift of the bishop, while also in 1587 he was made a canon residentiary. Having proceeded BD in 1585, he gained his DD in 1594.

In 1595 Smith was made a prebendary of Exeter Cathedral, where his great friend and former fellow prebendary of Hereford, Gervase Babington, had just become bishop. Subsequently he also held the rectories of Hartlebury and Upton upon Severn in the diocese of Worcester, where Babington had by that time been translated. Meanwhile he retained his Hereford stall, continuing there for the rest of his life, and owning at his death a property near the canon's bakehouse. For two periods (1591–3 and 1608–12) he undertook the duties of claviger: the surviving clavigers' accounts reveal a neat and orderly script from Smith's pen.

Smith gained a widespread reputation both as a classical scholar and as a student of oriental languages. Wood reported that 'Chaldaic, Syriac and Arabic were as familiar to him almost as his own mother tongue' (Wood, *Ath. Oxon.*, 1.417). Extant evidence of Smith's proficiency survives in the marginal notes in his own hand added to the works in Hebrew, Chaldee, and Arabic which he left to Hereford Cathedral Library at his death. From this collection it is also clear that his scholarship extended beyond the text of the Old Testament to the targums and rabbinic commentaries.

With this reputation it is not surprising that Smith was invited to join the teams of translators assembled by King James I to undertake the revision of the English Bible which resulted in the publication of the Authorized Version of 1611, being one of very few outside the universities who were included in this enterprise. He worked on the prophetic books of the Old Testament. Furthermore his biographer relates that 'he began with the first, and was the last man of the translators in the work', for he was on the revision committee, and then shared with the bishop of Winchester, Thomas Bilson, in a final review before being given the task of writing the preface, which 'he did in the name of all the translators … the original whereof I have seen under his own hand' (J. S., 1*v*–2*r*).

No doubt in recognition of his major part in this great enterprise, Smith was appointed bishop of Gloucester and consecrated at Croydon on 20 September 1612. His biographer says that Archbishop Abbot was instrumental in securing this preferment for him. His episcopate was marred by a dispute with William Laud, appointed dean of Gloucester in 1616. It is clear that the cathedral at this date was badly in need of repair and King James gave Laud instructions to set about restoring it. Laud extended his remit to include liturgical reordering, and thus armed was able to persuade the chapter to agree to the communion table's being 'placed altarwise at the upper end of the quier, close unto the east walle' (Gloucester Cathedral chapter act book, 1616–87). Incredibly, Laud neither consulted nor informed his bishop about what he had in mind. It was said by John Langley, master of the cathedral school, that Smith was so angry that he never entered the cathedral again while Laud remained dean, but this has been shown to be incorrect. The subdean, Thomas Prior, became the focus of discontent with the new regime: his sermon at Smith's funeral, which extolled the late bishop's opposition to 'papists, Arminians, and carnal gospellers', indicates the conflict of theology which surfaced in this dispute (M. Smith, *Sermons*, 1632, 303).

Smith has been accused of being a reluctant preacher after he became a bishop; however, some of his published sermons, based on Authorized Version texts, were evidently preached after his consecration. They are certainly erudite (one begins with a discussion of an Arabic gloss on one of the words in the text) but also contain some moving passages, and in places show a lively sense of humour. Perhaps he reveals something of a conscience about preaching in the preface which he wrote for the collected works of his friend Babington (1615; rev. 1622), where he points out that 'he that speaketh profiteth his owne congregation, but he that writeth profiteth all' (*Workes*, 1622, A4*v*). The truth about Smith, as can be seen from his marginal notes in the books he collected to the end of his life, is that he remained at heart a scholar and student of languages.

Smith died at Gloucester on 20 October 1624. He was twice married. With his first wife, Mary Hawkins of Cardiff, he had two sons, Gervase, of the Middle Temple, and Miles. His will mentions two further sons, Robert and Edward, and four daughters, including Margaret Morgan and one whose married name was Sutton. The other two, Elizabeth Williams and Margery Clent, both died in childbirth (1622 and 1623) not long before the bishop's own death. They have charming memorials in the lady chapel of Gloucester Cathedral. Nothing is known of his second wife.

Miles Smith (*bap.* 1618, *d.* 1671), secretary of the archbishop of Canterbury, a kinsman of the bishop, was baptized on 6 October 1618 at St Mary de Lode, Gloucester, the son of Miles Smith, a clergyman. In the Lent term of 1634 he became a chorister and servitor of Magdalen College, Oxford, under George Langdon. He matriculated on 20 March 1635, graduated BA on 3 December 1638, and was created BCL on 4 August 1646. When the civil war began in 1642 Smith took the royalist side and served his king. After the Restoration, and as a compensation for his suffering, he was employed by Gilbert Sheldon, who on becoming archbishop of Canterbury in 1663 made Smith his secretary. John Warner, bishop of Rochester, who died in 1666, bequeathed to Smith all his episcopal robes together with his coach and harness. The name of Smith's wife is unknown but his son, also Miles, entered Trinity College, Oxford, as a gentleman commoner but died at Oxford on 17 October 1682, aged sixteen. Smith's only known publication was *The Psalms of King David, Paraphrased into English Metre* (1668), verses which he composed for singing in church. Smith died on 1 February 1671 and was buried in the chancel of St Mary's, Lambeth. A memorial tablet commemorated his service to Sheldon. JOHN TILLER

Sources PRO, PROB 11/144, sig. 102 • clavigers' accounts, Hereford Cathedral archives, R592, 593, 595–8 • dean and chapter act books, Hereford Cathedral archives, 7031/2 • chapter act books, vol. 1, 1616–87, Gloucester Cathedral archives • Foster, *Alum. Oxon.* • Wood, *Ath. Oxon.*, 1st edn • J. S., biographical preface, in M. Smith, *Sermons of the … bishop of Glocester* (1632) • *The works of the most reverend father in God, William Laud*, ed. J. Bliss and W. Scott, 7 vols. (1847–60) • K. Fincham, *Prelate as pastor: the episcopate of James I* (1990) • D. Pearson, 'The libraries of English bishops, 1600–40', *The Library*, 6th ser., 14 (1992), 221–57 • *The workes of … Gervase Babington*, ed. M. Smith (1615); [rev. edn] (1622) • J. R. Bloxam, *A register of the presidents, fellows … of Saint Mary Magdalen College*, 8 vols. (1853–85), vol. 1, pp. 51–2

Likenesses portrait, Christ Church, Oxford

Smith, Miles (*bap.* 1618, *d.* 1671). *See under* Smith, Miles (*d.* 1624).

Smith, Sir Montague Edward (1806–1891), judge, was born at Bideford, Devon on 25 December 1806, the elder son of Thomas Smith (*bap.* 1756, *d.* 1828), attorney and town clerk of Bideford, and his wife, Margaret Colville, daughter of Commander M. Jenkins RN, of St Mawes, Cornwall. He was baptized Edward Montague, but throughout his adult life used his Christian names the other way round, Montague Edward (his first name was sometimes given as Montagu). He was educated at Bideford grammar school. In 1823 he was articled to his father, and after his father's death he practised on his own as an attorney in New Street, Torrington. In November 1832 he wrote an eight-page letter to Lord Brougham on tithe reform, and, receiving an encouraging reply, a second letter, twelve pages long, making proposals for commissioners and a tithe map and apportionment for each parish, very similar to the scheme finally adopted. Encouraged by W. W. Follett he joined Gray's Inn on 11 November 1830 and was called to the bar on 18 November 1835. He practised from chambers in King's Bench Walk and later 3 Paper Buildings, and joined the western circuit and the Exeter sessions. The western circuit was comparatively weak at that time after the departure of Wilde, Coleridge, and Follett, and Smith quickly developed a large practice. At his first Exeter assizes in March 1836 he had three briefs from north Devon, and he was soon busy in Cornwall, Devon, and Somerset. On 11 May 1839 he was admitted to the Middle Temple.

In 1848 Smith appeared, with Crowder, on behalf of Bishop Phillpotts in his unsuccessful libel action against Thomas Latimer, the editor of the *Western Times*. On 28 June 1853 he was appointed queen's counsel and was elected a bencher of the Middle Temple on 22 November. When Crowder was appointed to the bench in March 1854 Smith became the leader of the western circuit and managed to keep his position throughout that golden age for the western circuit when he and three future attorneys-general, Collier, Karslake, and Coleridge, were competing for the lead. He specialized in commercial law, and was a particular expert in railway law, appearing frequently on behalf of the railway companies. In politics he was a Conservative: he was MP for Truro (after unsuccessful contests in January 1849 and July 1852) from April 1859 until February 1865. He occasionally spoke in the house on legal topics, but took little part in the debates. In 1861 he brought in a bill for the limitation of crown suits, which received the royal assent on 1 August. In 1863, and again in 1864, he called the attention of the house to the inadequate accommodation in the law courts in London. He was treasurer of the Middle Temple in 1863. He was appointed a justice of the court of common pleas by Lord Westbury on 7 February 1865, and was knighted on 18 May. His best-known judgment is the judgment of the court of exchequer chamber in *Readhead* v. *Midland Railway Company* in 1869, holding that railway companies could only be liable to their passengers for negligence, though he was a member of the court in *Fletcher* v. *Rylands* (1868) which introduced strict liability in that case. He suffered from a physical ailment which, though it in no way affected his capacity as a judge, made travelling on circuit a painful duty, and on 3 November 1871 he was appointed a member of the judicial committee of the privy council, with a salary of £5000 a year. On 29 June 1865 he was appointed a commissioner under the Courts of Justice Building Act, and on 12 December 1877 a member of the universities committee of the privy council. He retired on 12 December 1881. In retirement he spent the summers in England and the winters in Cannes. He died, unmarried, at his home, 32 Park Lane, London, on 3 May 1891. Smith was a sound lawyer and a persuasive rather than an eloquent advocate. He excelled in clear analysis of facts and authorities, and made an accurate and painstaking judge. Lord Coleridge called him 'the most sensible, weighty and sagacious of men' (J. D. Coleridge, 'The law in 1847 and the law in 1889', *Contemporary Review*, 57, 1890, 801).

David Pugsley

Sources *The Times* (5 May 1891) · *The Times* (8 May 1891) · T. L. Pridham, *Devonshire celebrities* (1869) · E. H. Coleridge, *Life and correspondence of John Duke, Lord Coleridge*, 2 vols. (1904) · P. A. Howell, *The judicial committee of the privy council, 1833–1876* (1979) · A. Harwood, *Circuit ghosts: a western circuit miscellany* (1980) · UCL, Brougham MSS · parish register (baptism), Bideford, Devon
Archives Ottery St Mary parish church, Devon, Coleridge MSS · UCL, Brougham MSS
Wealth at death £238,867 4s. 5d.: probate, 20 June 1891, *CGPLA Eng. & Wales*

Smith, Muriel (1923–1985), singer, was born on 23 February 1923 in New York. Little is known of her early life. In 1939 she sang at a cocktail party where one of the guests was Elizabeth Westmoreland, of Philadelphia's Curtis Institute of Music. Deeply impressed, Westmoreland arranged for a scholarship and Smith became the first African-American ever to study at Curtis, earning her living expenses by cleaning film in a factory for $15 a week. Then, in December 1943, she made a triumphant Broadway stage début in *Carmen Jones*, Oscar Hammerstein's updated version of Bizet's opera *Carmen* with an African-American cast. At that time, American opera companies were not racially integrated, and training for black singers was practically non-existent. On the first day of rehearsals only one of the 115 cast members had appeared on Broadway before.

In spite of the critical and commercial success of *Carmen Jones*, Smith's chances of a career in opera were extremely remote. During the four years she toured with *Carmen Jones*, she wrote a letter to Laurence Olivier telling him how much she wanted to become an actress. 'I had seen the Old Vic company touring America', she later explained:

> and the dream of being an actress was with me. I certainly did not expect a reply, but a long reply did come, imploring me to carry on with my music. Laurence Olivier said: 'Your music is a readier weapon for your soul's purpose than acting'. (Bourne)

Certainly featured roles in musicals were easier to come by, though she did perform with the American Negro Theatre in 1948.

In 1949 Smith went to London's West End to appear in two Cecil Landeau revues at the Cambridge Theatre: *Sauce Tartare* (1949) and *Sauce Piquante* (1950). These were followed by appearances in two London productions of Rodgers and Hammerstein musicals at the Theatre Royal, Drury Lane: *South Pacific* (1951) and *The King and I* (1953). Theatregoer Ken Sephton, a keen 'first nighter' who had

Muriel Smith (1923–1985), by Tracey, 1957

started attending first nights in the West End in 1944, vividly recalled Smith's appearances, almost fifty years later:

> I was immediately struck by her wonderful voice, presence, beauty and individuality. In *South Pacific* she played Bloody Mary and stopped the show with 'Bali Ha'i'. The audience gave her a fantastic reception. Two years later Muriel stopped the show again, this time as Lady Thiang in *The King and I*. She sang that beautiful song 'Something Wonderful' with such feeling and emotion. The audience adored her. (Bourne)

Though Smith's first love was opera, at home black opera singers were still experiencing discrimination. For instance, Marian Anderson, acclaimed as one of the greatest contraltos of the century, had to wait until 1955, almost at the end of her career, to sing a leading role at the Metropolitan Opera House. After giving a recital at London's Wigmore Hall in 1955, Smith returned to America to star in a New York City Center revival of *Carmen Jones* before fulfilling one of her most cherished ambitions. On 17 December 1956 she made her first appearance on the operatic stage when she opened in London at the Royal Opera House, Covent Garden, as Bizet's *Carmen*. The production was described in *The Times* as a 'brilliant revival', and Smith was praised for the 'sheer seductive beauty' of her voice (*The Times*, 18 Dec 1956). On 27 December 1956 a performance was broadcast live on BBC radio.

When *South Pacific* was filmed in Hollywood in 1958, Juanita Hall, the actress who created the role of Bloody Mary on Broadway, was included in the cast, but her voice was not considered strong enough to cope with the songs. Consequently 'Bali Ha'i' and 'Happy Talk' were 'ghosted' off-screen by Smith. Yet, in spite of the popularity of the film and the soundtrack recording, Smith could not overcome the hurdle that had faced 'ghost' singers since the movies discovered sound: to date, no 'ghost' singer had ever been given any screen credit, or acknowledgement on the soundtrack albums.

For the remainder of her life, though she continued to make occasional film and stage appearances, Smith worked for Moral Re-Armament, a religious organization which campaigned on an international scale for a better understanding between nations. In 1984 she received an arts award from the National Council of Negro Women. She died in Richmond, Virginia, on 13 September 1985. She had been working as a voice teacher at Virginia Union University at the time. In 1996 she was the subject of an hour-long BBC radio tribute, *Something Wonderful*.

STEPHEN BOURNE

Sources S. Bourne, 'Diva kept in the dark', *The Stage* (15 May 1997)
Archives SOUND 'Something wonderful', BBC radio, 1996
Likenesses Tracey, photograph, 1957, Hult. Arch. [*see illus.*]

Smith, Naomi Gwladys Royde- (1875–1964), literary editor and writer, was born on 30 April 1875 at Craven Edge, Halifax, the eldest of six daughters and two sons of Michael Holroyd *Smith (1847–1932), an electrical engineer responsible for the electrification of the City and South London Railway, as well as an inventor of a helicopter and a boomerang, among other things, and Anne (Daisy), *née* Williams (1848–1934), the daughter of the Revd Ebenezer Williams of Penybont, Wales, and 'a zealous student of the Bible' (private information, M. Royde Smith). Matthew Smith, the painter, was a cousin. *In the Wood*, a novel written in 1928, was in part a description of her Yorkshire childhood. When the Holroyd Smith family moved to London (the children all taking the surname Royde-Smith), Naomi and her sisters attended Clapham high school; her education was finished in Switzerland at Geneva, and she then began to earn her living, becoming a well-respected reviewer. She also wrote poetry but did not publish any.

From 1904 onwards Naomi lived in London with her sister Leslie (*b*. 1884) in rooms in Oakley Street, Chelsea (later she also had a cottage at Holmbury St Mary, near Dorking, Surrey) and worked at the *Saturday Westminster Gazette*, both reviewing and writing the 'Problems and prizes page'. By 1912 she had become literary editor, the first time a woman had held this position, publishing early work by, among others, Rupert Brooke, D. H. Lawrence, and Graham Greene. Her large circle of friends included J. C. Squire, William Beveridge, Hugh Walpole, and Middleton Murry.

> Miss Royde-Smith had risen entirely through her own ability and drive. She had a forceful personality, sharp-tongued and sharp-witted; she was extremely well read and, while quite able to tackle men on their own terms, she was also fair-haired, feminine and a successful hostess (Whistler, 173)

wrote the biographer of Walter de la Mare, the poet, who

met Naomi in the spring of 1911 and was to be in love with her for the next five years (writing her nearly 400 letters). On Naomi's part she 'felt a great need to be artist's Muse. She wanted the men she loved to be men of genius. … Her chief usefulness was the confidence she gave him' (ibid., 178, 187); she was, however, ambivalent towards men sexually. A close friend at this period was the novelist Rose Macaulay; in the years after the First World War 'she and Rose, acting jointly as hostesses, received such diverse authors as Arnold Bennett, W. B. Yeats, Edith Sitwell and Aldous Huxley' (Smith, 100) at Naomi's flat, 44 Prince's Gardens, Kensington, where, Mary Agnes Hamilton remarked, 'everybody in the literary world, the not yet arrived as well as the established, was to be met' (Emery, 191) and where Naomi 'dressed à la 1860; swinging ear-rings, skirt in balloons … sat in complete command. Here she had her world round her. It was a queer mixture of the intelligent & the respectable' (*Diary of Virginia Woolf*, 5 June 1921). Rose Macaulay was to satirize Naomi at this period of her life in *Crewe Train* (1926), where she appears as Aunt Evelyn, 'a fashionable, meddling, arch-gossip' (Emery).

It was only after Naomi had given up her job in 1922 that she began to write fiction: *The Tortoiseshell Cat*, which was in some ways her best novel, appeared in 1925, and over the next thirty-five years she went on to publish nearly forty more novels, several biographies (for example of Mrs Siddons and of Maurice de Guérin), and four plays. The novels are admired by some but others are of the opinion that

> in spite of a good style, intelligence and frequent touches of truth to character, her novels have no great imagination. Too often the romantic parts suffer from wish-fulfilment studies in masculine Genius that remind one uneasily of many inferior passages in her letters to de la Mare. (Whistler, 342)

Lovat Dickson wrote that 'none of her novels … is likely to survive' (*The Times*, 30 July 1964) but Betty Askwith responded by saying that *The Delicate Situation* (1931) should be remembered and deserved comparison with Alain-Fournier's *Le grand Meaulnes*. She observed that 'any writer might be proud to have written just one book on that level' (*The Times*, 4 Aug 1964). Other novels that are admired are *For Us in the Dark* (1937) and *The Altar-Piece: an Edwardian Mystery* (1939).

On 15 December 1926, at Lynton parish church, Devon, Naomi married the Italian-American actor Ernest Giannello Milton (1890–1974) and converted to Catholicism; she was fifty-one, fifteen years older than her husband (but pretended to twelve). She gave up her hectic social life, although continuing to review and being for a period art critic of *Queen* magazine, and settled into a surprisingly successful marriage—'a triumph over unlikeliness by the strong-minded, romantic woman she was, and the histrionic, highly-strung, generous-minded actor. He placed her, for life, on a pedestal of admiration, though not by temperament drawn to her sex' (Whistler, 342).

The Miltons lived variously in Hatfield in Hertfordshire, Chelsea in London, Wells in Somerset (during the 1930s), and then (during the 1940s and 1950s) in a house in Winchester once lived in by Nell Gwyn, 34 Colebrook Street in the shadow of the cathedral, and later on nearby at Flat 4, 43 Hyde Street. At this period of her life Naomi Milton was, according to her niece, Jane Tilley, 'hugely amusing, chain-smoked, was large and uncorseted, and wore large patterns'. 'The sheer luxuriance of Naomi's discourse is what stays with me' was the impression of her nephew, Michael Royde Smith. She continued to write in spite of increasing blindness. At the end of her life she and Ernest went to live in London at Abbey Court Hotel, 15 Netherhall Gardens, Hampstead. She died from renal failure at the Hospital of St John and St Elizabeth, Marylebone, on 28 July 1964 and was buried in Hampstead cemetery. Her husband survived her. NICOLA BEAUMAN

Sources T. Whistler, *Imagination of the heart* (1993) · C. B. Smith, *Rose Macaulay* (1972) · J. Emery, *Rose Macaulay* (1991) · private information (2004) [M. Royde Smith; C. Denney; J. Tilley] · *The Times* (30 July 1964) · S. J. Kunitz and H. Haycraft, eds., *Twentieth century authors: a biographical dictionary of modern literature* (1942) · *The diary of Virginia Woolf*, ed. A. O. Bell and A. McNeillie, 2 (1978) · m. cert. · d. cert.

Archives U. Reading L., corresp. | Ransom HRC, letters to W. de la Mare · UCL, letters to Arnold Bennett

Smith, Norman Kemp (1872–1958), philosopher, was born Norman Duncan Smith in Dundee on 5 May 1872. He did not use his middle name (his mother's maiden name) but after his marriage in 1910 to Amy Kemp (*d.* 1936), a schoolteacher, daughter of Francis Kemp, banker, of Manchester, he adopted her maiden name, and thereafter was always known as Norman Kemp Smith. He was the youngest of six children of Andrew Watson Smith, cabinet-maker, and the only one in his family to have a university education. He was educated at Dundee high school and Harris Academy, Dundee, and entered the University of St Andrews in 1888, where he studied classics and philosophy under such teachers as Lewis Campbell, John Burnet, Andrew Seth, William Knight, and Henry Jones. After graduating MA with first-class honours in mental philosophy and winning the Ramsey and later Ferguson scholarships, he spent a year in Jena before becoming assistant to Sir Henry Jones in moral philosophy in Glasgow. After further study in Germany, he returned to Glasgow as assistant to Professor Robert Adamson in logic and rhetoric. Adamson, a Kantian scholar and critical philosopher, was to have a great influence on him. In 1902 Smith published *Studies in the Cartesian Philosophy*, which gained him the DPhil degree from St Andrews. In 1906 he went as professor of psychology to Princeton, and in 1914 was elected McCosh professor of philosophy there. In 1916 he returned, on leave, to Britain, where, until the end of the war, he served in the Ministry of Information. His *Commentary to Kant's 'Critique of Pure Reason'* appeared in 1918, and in the following year he was appointed to the chair of logic and metaphysics in the University of Edinburgh, a post he held until his retirement in 1945.

In 1924 Kemp Smith published his *Prolegomena to an Idealist Theory of Knowledge*. In 1934 his translation of Kant's first *Critique* appeared, and some said that even German scholars found it easier to read Kant in Kemp Smith's translation than in the original German. In 1935 he edited, with a lengthy introduction, Hume's *Dialogues Concerning*

Natural Religion (2nd edn, 1947), followed, in 1941, by his great work, *The Philosophy of David Hume*. This seemed to have completed his major published work, whose power and consistency establish him as one of the greatest Scottish philosophers of the twentieth century. However, he returned to the subject of his doctoral thesis and, at the age of eighty produced a new volume, *New Studies in the Cartesian Philosophy* (1952). Only in one of his published works is he presenting his own thought. In all of the others he is developing it in critical appreciation of earlier philosophers. Yet of his book on Hume it could be said: 'The resulting critical account of Hume's philosophy is no less modern a contribution to thought than any other book of our age' (J. Keay and J. Keay, eds., *Collins's Encyclopaedia of Scotland*, 1994, 774). In 1967 three of his former students (A. J. D. Porteous, R. D. Maclennan, and G. E. Davie) edited and contributed to a memorial volume of his collected papers, *The Credibility of Divine Existence*.

In 1917 Kemp Smith attended in London a lecture by Baron Friedrich von Hügel entitled 'Religion and illusion', which became the starting point for a remarkable friendship and correspondence between the Scottish philosopher, whose religious background was Presbyterian and Calvinist, and the Roman Catholic layman, twenty years his senior. The correspondence continued until von Hügel's death in 1925, and has been edited by Lawrence F. Barmann as *The Letters of Baron Friedrich von Hügel and Professor Norman Kemp Smith* (1981). The spiritual character of his quest for truth is evident in these letters, as is his respect for Calvin and his view of sin. Yet he remained outside the church. In part this was due to his understanding that a professor of philosophy has a responsibility not to seem to commend a particular religious viewpoint.

The *Prolegomena to an Idealist Theory of Knowledge* (1924) attempted, as Kemp Smith put it, 'the formulation of an idealist theory of knowledge on realist lines' (preface, ix). 'Idealist' in the title is used in a particular sense, as opposed to 'naturalist' that is, it holds that 'spiritual values have a determining voice in the ordering of the Universe' and do not simply emerge with evolution (p. 1). Kemp Smith's epistemology was not idealist in the more normal sense. He developed it, as he himself said, 'on realist lines'. He rejected the doctrine of representative perception and the subjectivism of both Descartes and Berkeley. He has been described as 'critico-realist'. Knowledge is not accumulated by adding fact to fact. It develops and changes as we learn to criticize our illusions, our assumptions, in the light of new evidence or experience. In the same way, the history of ideas is not an inevitable progression. As his pupil and friend Professor G. E. Davie has suggested, the depth of his thought came from the Calvinist doctrine of original sin in contrast to the shallow optimism of the idea of progress (Davie, 46–61). He saw that to understand and interpret other philosophers one must see them in their historical context. His own interpretations of Descartes, Kant, and especially Hume showed that his critical method could bring them to contemporary life, and throw fresh light on old difficulties. He had little patience with those who reduced philosophy to 'language games'.

Kemp Smith was a powerful force in the struggle of the Scottish universities in the 1920s to maintain a general, philosophical base to university education against pressure towards early specialization on the English model. Following the Scottish tradition he taught his own general class and each year hundreds of students learned the excitement of philosophical thinking from his rapid-fire lectures and dictated notes. He fired them with his own enthusiasm, and with many it lasted through life. With his honours classes, on the other hand, he preferred the seminar, where he was the listener to their weekly papers, gently disciplining their thought and encouraging them to follow where their ideas led. When A. E. Taylor was ill, and for a term he took the moral philosophy honours class as well as his own, he produced Reinhold Niebuhr's *An Interpretation of Christian Ethics* and had the class study and criticize that.

Although a large presence, Kemp Smith was a shy man with little small talk ('Kemp Smith does not converse, he discourses', said one student after having tea with him). Yet he became close to his honours students, who all revered him, as did his assistants and lecturers. He kept finding new things in literature as well as in philosophy and shared his enthusiasm for a new book with students and friends. 'Sell your bed and buy it!', he would say. He learned to drive a car at the age of sixty-six, and one of his students remembers the engine almost stalling on a steep hill while the distinguished philosopher encouraged it by rocking back and forward behind the steering wheel instead of engaging a lower gear. The sudden death of his wife on 16 December 1936 was a great grief. Although she did not share all his intellectual interests, theirs was a deeply affectionate partnership. Their only daughter, Janet, was very close to her father, and it was a joy to him when, in 1938, she married Dr Martin Ludlam, a member of a Quaker family. From 1940 to 1946 they were in India, but after their return, to Carlisle, he was able to take pleasure also in his grandchildren.

In 1920 Kemp Smith received the honorary degree of LLD from St Andrews, and in 1930 he was made honorary DLitt of Durham. Glasgow conferred its honorary degree of LLD on him in 1951. In 1921 he was elected fellow of the Royal Society of Edinburgh, and in 1924 became a fellow of the British Academy.

In 1957 Kemp Smith experienced a black-out and spent some time in hospital. The problem later recurred, and his last months were spent at 41 Drummond Place, an Edinburgh nursing home, where he died on 3 September 1958. He was cremated at Warriston crematorium, Edinburgh, on 6 September. JAMES A. WHYTE

Sources A. J. D. Porteous, biographical sketch, in N. Kemp Smith, *The credibility of divine existence: collected papers*, ed. A. J. D. Porteous, R. D. Maclennan, and G. E. Davie (1967), 3–37 • G. Davie, *The crisis of the democratic intellect* (1986) • A. C. Ewing, 'Norman Kemp Smith, 1872–1958', *PBA*, 45 (1959), 296–306 • *The letters of Baron Friedrich von Hügel and Professor Norman Kemp Smith*, ed. L. F. Barmann (1981) • *WW* (1958) • A. C. Ewing, *Idealism: a critical survey* (1934) • personal knowledge (2004) • b. cert. • d. cert.

Archives U. Edin. L., Special Collections, corresp., papers and notebooks • U. St Andr., senate minutes | JRL, letters to J. Alexander • U. Glas. L., Archives and Business Records Centre, letters from A. A. Bowman
Likenesses portrait, U. Edin.
Wealth at death £23,557 13*s*. 5*d*.: confirmation, 12 Dec 1958, *CCI*

Smith, O. *See* Smith, Richard John (1786–1855).

Smith, (Margaret) Patricia Hornsby-, Baroness Hornsby-Smith (1914–1985), politician, was born on 17 March 1914 at 315 Upper Richmond Road, East Sheen, near Richmond, Surrey, the only daughter and second child of Frederick Charles Hornsby-Smith (*d*. 1944), saddler and master umbrella maker, and his wife, Ellen Florence, *née* Minter. She was educated at Richmond county school; after leaving school Patricia, or Pat (as she was known), embarked upon a secretarial career.

Hornsby-Smith displayed a precociously active interest in politics. In 1930 at sixteen she joined the Junior Imperial League. In the following year the Conservative Party included her in its team of speakers in the general election campaign. Her youth and gender made her contribution quite unusual: many women helped the party but normally as back-room or front lawn supporters; a girl of only seventeen holding forth on a party platform would have been a remarkable sight. It was not, moreover, a general election in which the Conservatives needed to scrape the barrel for supporters; indeed, although she had joined the party when it was in opposition, it dominated British politics for much of the rest of her life.

For ten years Hornsby-Smith worked as a private secretary in engineering, electrical, and textile firms; she also worked for an employers' federation. The outbreak of the Second World War drew her, like many other women, into voluntary work. She helped to organize a comforts fund for service personnel and to run a Women's Voluntary Services canteen; she was also joint organizer of the National Savings Campaign, and a member of the Barnes war efforts committee. In 1941 she became principal private secretary to Lord Selborne, minister of economic warfare. Her move to Whitehall was part of the government's drive to bring more women into government for the duration of the war, although there was discontent among professional women who felt that their skills were undervalued and underused. The Ministry of Economic Warfare had overall responsibility for the Special Operations Executive (SOE), where women were deployed at all levels—from agents in the field to wireless operators, administrators, and, of course, secretaries. After the war she maintained her links with SOE by joining the Special Forces Club.

Hornsby-Smith was, meanwhile, building up her experience within the Conservative Party. She helped to organize the Surrey Young Conservatives and acted as their chair as well as chair of the Young Conservatives in the south-east area. It was regarded as especially important to attract a new generation into the party. In 1945 she was elected to Barnes borough council, and served as a councillor until 1949, sitting on the predictable committees for a woman such as housing, education, electricity, maternity and child welfare, and nursery, as well as the less predictable ones of finance and general purposes, and library. Between 1947 and 1950 she also sat on the Conservative Party's executive committee. In 1946 she attracted wide attention among Conservatives when she gave a fiery address to the annual conference, where the party was still recovering after the shock (for most people) defeat at the general election the previous year.

For a woman to gain adoption as a prospective parliamentary candidate was difficult, especially in a constituency where there was a chance of winning. Hornsby-Smith was repeatedly rejected, at least on one occasion explicitly because she was a woman. Not surprisingly she believed that selection committees were the 'most potent citadel of prejudice' in all the parties, and that women had to be better than all the men to be selected.

Once adopted for Chislehurst in Kent, Hornsby-Smith's drive revitalized the constituency, and in 1950 she successfully contested the seat in the general election. As a constituency MP she was hard-working and effective at dealing with constituents, and she increased her majority at each general election during the 1950s. Although it had not been easy for her to break into national politics the party was quick to make use of a new, young, attractive, redhead woman MP. In 1951 she made the women MPs' BBC party political broadcast to woo women voters in the general election, focusing on the cost of living and housing. Her broadcast was generally thought to have been an improvement on Florence Horsbrugh's performance the previous year.

Hornsby-Smith was quickly spotted for a government post. In 1951 she was appointed parliamentary secretary at the Ministry of Health where she remained for six years. From 1957 to 1959 she was parliamentary under-secretary at the Home Office, and from 1959 to 1961 joint parliamentary secretary at the Ministry of Pensions and National Insurance. In 1959 she became a privy councillor. She was the youngest woman ever appointed to government and to the privy council—not that the competition for these accolades was very great as there had been so few women ministers—but despite holding a variety of posts for over a decade she never achieved a cabinet post, and was, therefore, never in a policy making position. She was not highly rated by the civil servants at the Ministry of Health, who thought her appointment was a token gesture to increase the number of women in government to two; she was too nervous and inexperienced, and too much of a party politician; but as women ministers often faced hostility from civil servants it is hard to know whether they were making an objective judgement or articulating their prejudice. Conservative prime ministers thought it desirable to have women ministers but, after Florence Horsbrugh's short and sad spell in Churchill's cabinet, not women in cabinet. Her ministerial career ended in 1961 when she was created a dame of the British empire. Her parliamentary career was also interrupted when, as a result of changes in the composition of her Chislehurst constituency and especially the growth of council estates within its boundaries, she lost the seat to Labour in 1966.

Writing in 1968 Hornsby-Smith reflected that the lot of a woman MP was not a happy one. She described not only the difficulty of selection but also the awkward lifestyle, parliamentary conditions, the domestic constraints, meagre salary and costs of nursing a constituency, the way in which women MPs were expected to restrict themselves in debate to certain subjects, and the problems inherent in received notions of domesticity. Such comments have frequently been made; what would have been more interesting would have been her views—as a woman who remained a minister for a decade but never made the leap into cabinet—on the difficulties for women ministers. Perhaps because she was never promoted to the cabinet she was deeply conscious of the prejudice against women in all the parties.

Although Hornsby-Smith faced hostility in the Chislehurst constituency she was readopted after an emotional outburst at a party meeting, and in 1970 she regained the seat. In the early 1970s boundary changes meant that the constituency was carved up, and she stepped aside so that Edward Heath could stand in the newly formed Bexley and Sidcup constituency that now incorporated part of Chislehurst. In February 1974 she unsuccessfully contested Aldridge-Brownhills in the midlands.

This defeat marked the end of Hornsby-Smith's House of Commons career and in May 1974 she was created Baroness Hornsby-Smith. She played an active part in the House of Lords for a number of years, despite ill health. Throughout her political career she maintained her wartime interest in voluntary work. She worked for the Arthritis and Rheumatism Council for Research as chair of the appeals committee from 1966, and from 1974 vice-chair of the council; from 1975 she chaired the Electrical Association of Women, and from 1983 the St Edward's Housing Association. Her appointment to company directorships in the 1960s renewed her earlier interests in industry. She also travelled widely: in 1958 she was a delegate to the United Nations; in 1962 she led a parliamentary delegation to Australasia and another in 1972 to Kenya.

Although she never reached the cabinet Hornsby-Smith was a relatively well-known politician: as a woman MP, minister, and then member of the House of Lords she inevitably stood out among the men, and she was known to a wider public through contributing to the BBC radio programme *Any Questions*. From 1971 she was a fellow of the Royal Society of Arts. She belonged to the Constitutional, Special Forces, and Cowdrey clubs. She died, unmarried, on 3 July 1985. A memorial service held on 29 October 1985 at St Margaret's, Westminster, was attended by her brother's family and numerous politicians, including the prime minister, Margaret Thatcher, who read one of the lessons. HELEN JONES

Sources *The Times* (4 July 1985) • *The Times* (30 Oct 1985) • Bodl. Oxf., conservative party archive • W. D. Rubinstein, ed., *The biographical dictionary of life peers* (New York, 1991) • *WWBMP*, vol. 4 • *WWW*, *1981–90* • P. Hornsby-Smith, 'Women in public life', in *A discussion conducted by the Six Point Group in their own right*, Six Point Group (1968) • D. E. Butler, *The British general election of 1951* (1952), 67, 68, 74 • C. Webster, *The health services since the war*, 1 (1988), 186 • M. Phillips, *The divided house: women at Westminster* (1980), 74, 76, 117 • G. E. Maguire, *Conservative women* (1998) • A. Clark, *Diaries into politics*, ed. I. Trewin (2000) • private information (2004) [Mike Hornsby-Smith, nephew] • *CGPLA Eng. & Wales* (1985)

Archives Bodl. Oxf., conservative party archive, books of election addresses • Bodl. Oxf., conservative party archive, Chislehurst constituency papers | SOUND Bodl. Oxf., conservative party archive, general election sound broadcast, CCO 600/3/4/13

Likenesses photographs, Bodl. Oxf., conservative party archive, election addresses

Wealth at death £63,037: probate, 15 Oct 1985, *CGPLA Eng. & Wales*

Smith, (Frank) Percy (1880–1945), film-maker and naturalist, was born on 12 January 1880 at 15 Elizabeth Terrace, Islington, the son of Francis David Smith, a printer, and his wife, Ada Blaker. In childhood he became fascinated with animal and plant life, its identification and classification, a passion exemplified by a story of him lying face down at a frozen pond, so engrossed in what he saw that he found he had become frozen to the ice and had to be freed by a friend. To please his family, however, at the age of sixteen he became a clerk with the Board of Education. The work was hatefully tedious to him, but it did allow him time to pursue his hobby with ever greater attention. He turned naturally to photographing his subjects, and it was a photograph of a bluebottle's tongue that attracted the attention of film producer Charles Urban. Urban aimed to bring documentary and educational film subjects to the general public, and encouraged Smith to repeat some of the close-up studies he had made on film. On 3 June 1907 Smith married Kate Louise (*b.* 1880/81), daughter of James Ustonson, an optician. Such was his commitment to film-making, however, that he went on honeymoon with a motion picture camera and the instruction to film 'anything that kicks, moves or bites' (Wilson, 62). Smith's wife was his devoted and protective companion, and the only assistant he would allow when working. There were no children.

Smith's initial experiments were followed up by more professional work conducted at home, which Urban started to exhibit in London theatres. Scenes of a fly performing such feats as juggling a cork, in *The Balancing Bluebottle*, astonished and delighted the public, and aroused considerable newspaper interest. Having gained no response from the Board of Education to his proposals for using film as an educational medium, Smith joined Urban as a full-time film-maker in 1910. He set up his self-made apparatus in his Southgate home and began to specialize in the filming of accelerated plant growth, using stop-motion photography, using the hour-wheel of a clock to trigger an electrical circuit to expose a single frame of film, and raising the camera by degrees as the plant subject grew. Such work was always preceded by meticulous research to determine the growth rate, and some films could be a year in preparation before a single frame was exposed.

The first of the plant films, *The Birth of a Flower*, was issued in the Kinemacolor colour film process in 1911. Smith made over fifty nature films for the Urban Science series shown at the Scala Theatre, including several employing microscopy, before the outbreak of the First World War, when he first turned his talents to the production of novel animated war maps. Smith then joined the navy, where he was made a sergeant of kinematography and photographed aeronautical and balloon experiments, as well as the surrender of the German fleet at Scapa Flow. After the war, with Urban now in America, Smith was lucky to find another imaginative producer in H. Bruce Woolfe of British Instructional Films. Smith began work on Woolfe's *Secrets of Nature* in 1922, an enduringly famous series of short documentaries that were popular in cinemas and festivals throughout the 1920s and 1930s, and were for a long time acclaimed as the very best of British film production. Their simple yet meticulous observation engrossed all who saw them, and they became a mainstay of the non-theatrical educational film circuit for many years. He was especially involved in underwater photography and micro-cinematography. Smith wrote *The Secrets of Nature* (1939) and other guides to the subjects of his scientific films with educationist and film-maker Mary Field, a long-time associate. Less publicly, he also wrote magazine detective stories using the pseudonym Maxwell Pyx. Not only in his subject matter but also in his observation, patience, and skill, Percy Smith was a distinguished pioneer of the scientific film.

Percy Smith was an exceedingly private man. Shy and uncommunicative, he was obsessively devoted to working in his Southgate studio, surrounded by camera equipment and the various home-made gadgets that enabled him to capture the secrets of nature on celluloid. His work was initially viewed with some scepticism by the scientific community, which simply doubted the evidence of Smith's films, for they not infrequently overturned long-held assumptions about animal activity. But his methods were impeccable, and from the 1920s onwards his work was widely recognized for its originality and rigour, and he collaborated with such eminent scientists as biologist Dr Julian Huxley and botanist Dr E. J. Salisbury. His attitude may be gauged from the response he gave to Mary Field when she described a creature as a pest: 'If I think anything is a pest, I make a film about it; then it becomes beautiful' (Blakeston, 144). He died on 24 March 1945 at 107 Chase Road, Southgate, after gassing himself. The coroner's certificate recorded that Smith killed himself while the balance of his mind was disturbed.

LUKE MCKERNAN

Sources I. Wilson, 'His name was Smith', *The Cine-Technician* (May–June 1945), 56, 62–3 · V. Peers, 'Percy Smith', *Visual Education* (March 1956), 9 · 'Percy Smith', *Sight and Sound*, 14 (1945–6), 6–7 · F. P. Smith, 'My work and play during 1912 [–15+]', unpublished scrapbook, BFI · O. B. [O. Blakeston], 'Personally about Percy Smith', *Close-up*, 8/2 (June 1931), 143–6 · F. A. Talbot, *Moving pictures: how they are made and worked* (1912) · R. Low, *The history of the British film*, 2: *1906–1914* (1949) · R. Low, *The history of the British film*, 4: *1918–1929* (1971) · 'A kinematographic wizard', *Daily News and Leader* (14 Nov 1912) · Sci. Mus., Charles Urban MSS, File URB 8 · b. cert. · m. cert. · d. cert. · *CGPLA Eng. & Wales* (1945)

Archives BFI | Sci. Mus., Charles Urban MSS

Likenesses photograph, repro. in Talbot, *Moving pictures*, facing p. 192 · photographs, BFI

Wealth at death £3203 2*s*. 6*d*.: probate, 21 Aug 1945, *CGPLA Eng. & Wales*

Smith, Percy Guillemard Llewellin (1838–1893). *See under* Smith, John Thomas (1805–1882).

Smith, Philip (1817–1885), historian, was the son of William Smith of Enfield and younger brother of Sir William *Smith (1813–1893). He was educated at Mill Hill School, and entered Coward College, London, as a student for the Congregational ministry in April 1834. He graduated BA from University College, London, in May 1840 and became a professor of classics and mathematics in Cheshunt College from 1840 to 1850, and pastor of the Congregational church at Crossbrook from 1840 to 1845. Simultaneously, he edited the *Biblical Review* from 1846 to 1851 and frequently contributed to the *Quarterly Review* while his brother William was its editor. He also contributed several articles to the dictionaries of Greek and Roman antiquity, biography, and geography edited by his brother, as well as to the *Penny Cyclopaedia* between 1833 and 1844.

Smith's career in teaching continued and from 1850 to 1852 he was first professor of mathematics and ecclesiastical history in New College, London, and from 1853 to 1860 headmaster of Mill Hill School. After 1860, he devoted himself to historical writing, publishing *A Smaller History of England* (1862), *A History of the Ancient World* (1863–5), and *A Smaller Ancient History of the East* (1871). He then published a series of students' manuals, the most popular of which were *The Student's Ancient History* (1871) and *The Student's Ecclesiastical History* (1878–85). He also edited *The Posthumous Works of John Harris, DD* (1857). He helped in the preparation of Heinrich Schliemann's *Troy and its Remains* (1875), and completed the translation of Heinrich Brugsch's *History of Egypt* (1879), begun by Henry Danby Seymour. Smith died at Putney in London on 12 May 1885.

E. C. MARCHANT, *rev.* NILANJANA BANERJI

Sources *The Times* (13 May 1885) · *The Athenaeum* (23 May 1885), 664 · Allibone, *Dict.*

Archives DWL, letters | UCL, letters to Society for the Diffusion of Useful Knowledge

Smith, (Ida) Phyllis Barclay- (1902–1980), ornithological administrator, was born on 18 May 1902 at 57 Glisson Road, Cambridge, the second of three daughters, with one son, of Edward Barclay-Smith, professor of anatomy at Cambridge University, and his wife, Ida Mary, *née* Rogers. She was educated at Blackheath high school and King's College, London. In 1924 Barclay-Smith became assistant secretary of the Royal Society for the Protection of Birds (RSPB), working in what was then a small society. She addressed the seventh International Ornithological Congress on the subject of oil pollution at sea in 1930.

The International Council for Bird Protection was founded in 1922. Jean Delacour, the European vice-president, later its president, met Barclay-Smith and was impressed by her 'unusual efficiency and enthusiasm'. She left the RSPB to join the council in 1935, at first as British section secretary, then sub-secretary to the secretary, Count Lippens. She was to devote a lifetime to it, apparently in an entirely voluntary capacity. The council consisted of national sections which were devoted to bird conservation and in as many different countries as possible, with a central organizing secretariat. National sections increased from twenty-three in 1930 to sixty-seven in 1974. As Delacour admitted, Barclay-Smith actually organized the activities of the council worldwide, continuing as the pivotal figure of its organization for some forty-five years. Her work was interrupted by the Second World War, during which she took on various government secretarial posts. In 1946 she became the secretary of the international council and later, in 1974, the secretary-general. She ran the secretariat, in two rooms with a few helpers, from the Natural History Museum in London.

Barclay-Smith inspired her colleagues. Professor W. Thorpe noticed a most attractive and direct friendliness combined with boundless dedication, a firm grasp of detail and great mental ability, and forthrightness and toughness when necessary. Dr W. R. P. Bourne eulogized her as wise, knowledgeable, clear-sighted, single-minded, industrious, painstaking, thoughtful, modest, kind, and very good company. She incorporated anyone who seemed useful into an extensive network of helpers, advisers, and contacts, expecting others also to give freely and enthusiastically of their time and expertise. She gradually built up a complex worldwide web of contacts—scientists, academics, politicians, civil servants, and amateur ornithologists—who were called on for help, inveigled onto committees, and assembled in conferences. Her great ability lay in organization. She appeared to inaugurate endless meetings, conferences, and committees, and to publish reports. She founded the advisory committee on oil pollution of the sea, helped set up the International Wildfowl Research Bureau, and organized early awareness of the problem of toxic insecticides. As secretary of the British section she took a broad view, arranging the purchase and setting up of the Cousin Island reserve in the Seychelles.

Barclay-Smith found time to translate several bird books from French and German, and contributed some texts of her own. Although not an active aviculturist, she was persuaded to become editor of the *Avicultural Magazine* in 1938, continuing for thirty-five years, persuading bird keepers to write and helping to establish the connection between aviculture and new approaches to bird behaviour and ecology. She served on the councils of various ornithological organizations and was a corresponding member for some overseas bodies. Her works and personality were recognized with, among others, seven gold and six silver medals from various countries. In 1958 she became MBE for services to conservation, promoted to CBE in 1970, and in 1973 she was appointed a 'Ridder of the Most Excellent Order of the Golden Ark' by Prince Bernhard of the Netherlands. While in the process of handing over her international council responsibilities she suffered a severe stroke on Christmas day 1979, and died at Whittington Hospital, Islington, London, on 2 January 1980. She was cremated.

Colin J. O. Harrison

Sources W. R. P. Bourne, *Royal Society for Protection of Birds Magazine* (1980) • W. H. Thorpe, *The Ibis*, 122 (1980), 374–5 • J. Delacour, *Avicultural Magazine*, 86 (1980), 46–8 • private information (2004) • *WWW* • b. cert. • d. cert.

Archives CUL, corresp. with Sir Samuel Hoare • CUL, corresp. with Sir Peter Markham Scott

Wealth at death £107,077: probate, 9 May 1980, *CGPLA Eng. & Wales*

Smith [*née* Reeve], **Pleasance**, **Lady Smith** (**1773–1877**), letter writer and literary editor, was born on 11 May 1773 at Lowestoft, the fifth child of Robert Reeve (1739–1815), attorney and merchant, and Pleasance Clerke (1739–1820). In 1796 she married James Edward *Smith, founder and president of the Linnean Society. He was fourteen years older than Pleasance and she survived him for nearly forty-nine years, living to the age of 103. There were no children.

The Gypsy portrait painted by Opie in 1797 suggests that Lady Smith was very beautiful. The marriage was a happy one and there are numerous letters from her husband to 'dearest Pleasy', some describing the very original presents he had bought her. She was a great reader of literature and enjoyed contemporary authors such as Scott, Burns, Tennyson, and George Eliot; she read sermons, particularly those of Dean Stanley, and studied the politics of the day, including the progress of the four wars fought during her lifetime. After her marriage she and her husband lived briefly in London, then settled in Norwich in a house built by Thomas Ivory, the architect of the local Octagon Chapel. The house contained Linnaeus's collections and it was said that 'the relics of Mohammed are not enshrined with more devotion' (Walker, 27).

After her husband's death in 1828 Lady Smith moved back to High Street, Lowestoft. Here she edited her husband's memoirs and presented the Linnean Society with nineteen volumes of his letters, destroying those of a personal nature. Her correspondents were legion; many botanist friends of her late husband wrote to her. Both the Hookers wrote and sent plants from Kew; Francis Boott, secretary of the Linnean Society, thanked her for sending Linnaeus's copy of Milton, while Wallich confided in her his fears of returning to the Royal Botanic Garden, Calcutta. Everyone asked her for advice, which she gave freely on matters as diverse as religious questions and new knitting patterns.

One of Lady Smith's most remarkable correspondents was the Revd Charles Lessingham Smith. They first met when she was ninety-eight and he sixty-five and they corresponded weekly until her death; he described their relationship as a 'romantic attachment' which had 'gilded his declining day' (C. L. Smith to Lady Smith, 9 Dec 1872, Linn. Soc.). They discussed every serious subject, but he also never failed to describe the elaborate dresses worn by his patroness, Lady Rosslyn. In her later years Lady Smith became a celebrity on account of her advanced age. On her ninety-ninth birthday she received a card from her great-niece, Alice Pleasance Liddell, the little girl Lewis Carroll immortalized in *Alice in Wonderland*. She died at home in her sleep on 3 February 1877 and was buried on 9 February in the Reeve family tomb, beside her husband, at St Margaret's, Lowestoft, after a grand funeral during which people lined the streets to the church and the shops were closed. A stained-glass window over the altar was installed in her memory. MARGOT WALKER

Sources letters to Lady Smith, Linn. Soc. • C. I. Chapman, *In memoriam, Lady Smith* (1877) • A. Stebbings, *Memoir of Lady Smith* (1877) • H. D. W. Lees, *The chronicles of a Suffolk parish church* [1949] • M. Walker, *Sir James Edward Smith* (1988)

Archives Linn. Soc., corresp. and papers • Suffolk RO, Lowestoft, travel journals

Likenesses oils, 1872 (after photograph), Linnean Society, Suffolk Road, Lowestoft • sepia photograph, *c.*1877, repro. in Stebbings, *Memoir of Lady Smith* • Graf & Soret, lithograph (after J. Opie, 1797), BM

Wealth at death under £20,000: probate, 24 Dec 1877, *CGPLA Eng. & Wales*

Smith, (Joseph) Priestley (1845–1933), ophthalmologist, was born on 29 October 1845 at 2 Frederick Street, Islington Row, Birmingham (which later became 51 Frederick Road, Edgbaston), one of the seven children of Brooke Smith (*d.* 1876), engineer and later town councillor, and his second wife, Sophia (*née* Ryland). Priestley Smith was born into a Unitarian family, which accounts for the choice of his Christian names. On his mother's side he had family connections with the Ryland, the Chamberlain, and the Kenrick families of Birmingham. In later life Joseph Chamberlain, as a patient of Smith, was introduced to the wearing of spectacles as a more effective alternative to his habitual monocle. Smith was initially educated at a school in Lancaster. For four years from 1862 he served an apprenticeship in mechanical engineering with the firm of Walter May & Co., engineers and ironfounders of Berkley Street, Birmingham. During his apprenticeship in the engineering workshops he often became so exhausted that he would sleep for the whole weekend.

At the age of twenty-one Smith abandoned engineering and became a medical student, first at Sydenham College, and from 1867 at Queen's College and at the Queen's Hospital in Bath Row, Birmingham. During his student years he served as dresser to the famous Birmingham surgeon Sampson Gamgee, and as clerk to the physician Thomas Heslop.

In 1870, while still a medical student, Smith volunteered to serve with a medical unit in the Franco-Prussian War. He saw service as a dresser under the German Aid Society and was attached, first to a military hospital at Bingen am Rhein, and later with a larger unit near Cologne. An account of his experiences during the ten months which he spent working in the German Red Cross hospitals was published in the *Birmingham Medical Review* of 1873.

After his return to Birmingham Smith qualified MRCS in December 1871. He soon developed a keen interest in the study of eye disease and his first post was that of house surgeon to the Birmingham and Midland Eye Hospital, then situated in Temple Row. After two years he moved to London, spending several months at Moorfields Eye Hospital as clinical assistant to William Bowman, whose own career in medicine had begun in Birmingham. Smith also worked with Edward Nettleship at St Thomas's Hospital during his short spell in London.

In 1874 Smith returned to Birmingham to take up the post of surgeon to the newly created eye department at the Queen's Hospital, on the recommendations of Sampson Gamgee and Thomas Heslop. He retained this position for some thirty years. He had become interested in glaucoma early in his career, and his researches into its causes, symptoms, pathology, and treatment won him the Jacksonian prize of the Royal College of Surgeons in 1878 and were published in his book *Glaucoma* the following year. Smith can be considered a pioneer in the study of glaucoma and spent the rest of his career investigating it through physical experiments, histological examinations, and clinical study. He also conducted research into the growth of the crystalline lens, visual function by means of perimetry, and the treatment of squint. He was a skilful operator with a fine touch, and possessed the invaluable asset of being ambidextrous. His engineering skills helped him to invent instruments useful to his research, among them being a perimeter and a tonometer. He also invented a set of musical gongs which he patented in Britain and the United States.

In May 1877 Smith married Louisa Mary Russell, daughter of James Russell (*d.* 1885), senior consulting physician to the Birmingham General Hospital, and granddaughter of the surgeon James Russell (1786–1851). He later married Ellen Harcourt Ashford.

In 1881 Smith was one of the founders of the *Ophthalmic Review*, a journal which continued until 1916, when it amalgamated with others to form the *British Journal of Ophthalmology*. From its commencement Smith became a joint editor, remaining so until 1899, when W. G. Sym became editor. Even then Smith remained as a member of the editorial board until 1910, when J. B. Lawford took over as editor. In 1892 Smith had been appointed lecturer in ophthalmology to the faculty of medicine at Queen's College, and in 1897 became professor in that subject at Mason College, which had by then become the venue for Birmingham's medical school.

Foreign visitors to Birmingham who expected to see Smith at the head of a large ophthalmic clinic found instead 'an unassuming enthusiast, working with ten beds in a general hospital with the help of a single house surgeon' (*The Lancet*, 13 May 1933, 1039). 'His style was attractive, a blend of the practical and the artistic. Firm but never dogmatic in his convictions he could be impressive in public debate, but excelled rather in discussing privately matters of interest' (ibid.). Smith was never in robust health or very wealthy (he charged only moderate fees for even difficult operations); in his spare time he enjoyed taking long holidays with his children, horse-riding, and sketching.

Smith's contributions to ophthalmology resulted in many honours, among which were the Middlemore prize of the British Medical Association in 1890, and the first award of the Nettleship gold medal in 1904. He also received the Lucian Howe medal of the American Ophthalmological Society in 1927 and the Gullstrand gold medal of the Swedish Medical Society in 1932. Two of these gold medals may be seen in the City of Birmingham Museum and Art Gallery.

Smith retired from active practice in 1916 owing to a gradually increasing physical disability. He was awarded an honorary LLD by the University of Birmingham nine years later, for his continuing contributions to the science of ophthalmology. This was just one of a number of honorary degrees and fellowships which he received during his career. His devotion to ophthalmology is illustrated by the extent of his experimental work and discoveries, which continued until December 1932, only a very short time before his death on 30 April 1933 from pneumonia at 52 Frederick Road, Edgbaston, the next house to that in which he had been born. He was cremated at the Perry Barr crematorium on 2 May 1933, following a memorial service at the church of the Messiah in Broad Street, not far from his home. On the same day his ashes were interred in the family grave at Quinton church, on the western outskirts of Birmingham. His former secretary, A. E. Remmett Weaver, remembered him as 'a great and cultured gentleman, a fond father, and a genius who never despised labour' (*BMJ*, 898).

ANTHONY G. SABELL

Sources D. J. Derrington, The life and work of Priestley Smith, undergraduate diss., University of Aston, 1966, University of Aston • A. G. Sabell, *Professor J. Priestley Smith, 1845–1933: a short biography* (1975) • *British Journal of Ophthalmology*, 17 (1933), 442–5 • *Transactions of the Ophthalmological Society* • *Archives of Ophthalmology* • *Birmingham Post and Mail* (1 May 1933) • *Birmingham Gazette* (4 May 1933) • *BMJ* (13 May 1933), 850, 898 • *The Lancet* (13 May 1933), 1039–40 • P. Smith, 'Notes from the tent hospitals of the Franco-German War', *Birmingham Medical Review*, 2 (1873), 44–56 • b. cert. • d. cert. • *The Lancet* (10 Oct 1885), 694 [obit. of James Russell] • *Birmingham Medical Review* (Oct 1885), 238 [obit. of James Russell]

Archives priv. coll. • U. Birm., department of anatomy • University of Aston, department of vision sciences

Likenesses H. Speed, oils, Queen Elizabeth Hospital, Edgbaston, Birmingham; repro. in *The Lancet* • photograph, repro. in J. T. J. Morrison, *William Sands Cox and the Birmingham Medical School* (1926) • photograph, repro. in 'The History of the Birmingham School of Medicine, 1825–1925', *The Birmingham Medical Review* (Dec 1925) • photograph, repro. in M. Cheesewright, *'Mirror to a mermaid': photographs of Mason College and the University of Birmingham* (1975)

Smith, Sir Prince, first baronet (1840–1922), worsted machinery manufacturer, was born on 3 September 1840 at Keighley, West Riding of Yorkshire, the only son of Prince Smith (1819–1890), a mechanic, and his wife, Martha, the daughter of John Edmondson, a Keighley contractor. He was educated at Wesley College, Sheffield, until about the age of sixteen and then entered the family business of William Smith & Sons at Waggon Fold, Keighley. William, his grandfather, had commenced business in Keighley in 1795, making precision parts for spinning machines. The firm was expanded in the early 1830s, with the opening of a foundry to provide castings. William had seven sons, of whom two died in their twenties; the others were all apprenticed within the firm and joined their father, and in due course were taken into partnership. Prince Smith's father was the fourth son, and perhaps the most dynamic of William's offspring. At William's death in 1850 the brothers continued the partnership, but it was dissolved in 1865, leaving Prince Smith senior and his brother William in control of the textile machine-making business. They built the large Worth Valley works in Keighley, but dissolved their partnership in 1869.

Prince Smith senior continued the business on his own account, taking his son Prince junior into partnership and acquiring the large Burlington Shed in Keighley from Samuel Cunliffe Lister. Prince Smith junior progressively took charge, and finally assumed control of the firm on the death of his father in 1890. By that stage it had developed into one of the biggest manufacturing firms in the worsted trade. In 1878 it employed around 750 people; by the 1890s the workforce had doubled, making Smiths the largest employer in Keighley and district, a major centre of machinery manufacture. The firm extended its products to the full range of manufacturing for the preparation and spinning of worsted yarn. Smith exerted firm control over the business, believing that success was highly dependent on a trustworthy product and the confidence of his clientele. He relied on the reputation of his machines and on personal contact with his customers. Unlike many of the other textile machine manufacturers of the day, he avoided exhibitions and gave little attention to advertising his products. Much of his business was local to Yorkshire, where the British worsted industry was largely concentrated, but by the 1890s his machines were being exported to all centres of worsted manufacture in the world, as part of what was by then a major trade for the British economy.

Smith married Martha Ann (*d.* 1913), the daughter of John Greenwood, a corn miller, of Skipton in Craven, Yorkshire, in 1864. They had one son and two daughters. Their son, also Prince Smith, born on 13 October 1869, married Maud Mary, the daughter of Henry Wright of Keighley, in 1894, entered his father's business in 1887, and became increasingly responsible for its management in the years before the First World War. During the war he was one of the managers of the national shell factory in Keighley.

Smith himself appears to have been technically very able, but it is not clear that he made any very significant contributions to the development of worsted preparatory and spinning machinery. As a businessman he appears to have shown initiative and judgement, providing direction and purpose in the years of major expansion of the firm. His involvement in other affairs was minimal. Of the Liberal persuasion, he took little interest in local or national politics. Like many in his industry he supported free trade, but was not active in the campaign for it. He was a Wesleyan, and supported local organizations in Keighley—notably Keighley Victoria Hospital. At various times he was a member of the Bradford exchange, a director of the Bradford District Bank, and a JP first for the West Riding and then, on his retirement, for the East Riding. He was created a baronet for his service to industry in 1911. His leisure interests included music and golf. In the 1890s he acquired an estate in Kirkcudbrightshire, Scotland, and about 1907 retired from his home at Hillbrook, Keighley, to an estate at Southburn, near Driffield, East Riding of Yorkshire, where he died on 20 October 1922, following a heavy cold. He was buried in Keighley cemetery on 23 October.

At the time of Smith's death the family firm was at the peak of its business activity. Having engaged in munitions work during the war, it recovered its markets and in 1922 employed 1800 people, making it one of the largest manufacturers of worsted combing and spinning machinery in the world. However, like other textile machinery firms at the period, it later suffered from declining business. Smith's son, the third Prince Smith, who on inheriting the baronetcy changed his name to Sir Prince Prince-Smith by deed poll, took the firm into an amalgamation with Hall and Stells Ltd in 1931, creating Prince Smith and Stells Ltd, of which he served as president until his death in 1940.

D. T. Jenkins

Sources D. T. Jenkins, 'Smith, Sir Prince', *DBB* • *Keighley News* (21 Oct 1922) • *Wool Record and Textile World* (26 Oct 1922) • *Men of the period: England* (1897) • J. Hodgson, *Textile manufacture and other industries in Keighley* (1879) • *Keighley News* (28 Oct 1922) • I. Dewhirst, *A history of Keighley* (1974) • *WWW, 1981–90*

Likenesses A. S. Cope, portrait, 1912

Wealth at death £1,181,705 12*s.* 2*d.*: probate, 19 Dec 1922, *CGPLA Eng. & Wales*

Smith, Reginald Bosworth (1839–1908), schoolmaster and author, born on 28 June 1839 at West Stafford rectory, Dorset, was second son in the family of four sons and six daughters of Reginald Southwell Smith (1809–1896), canon of Salisbury from 1875. His grandfather was Sir John Wyldbore Smith, second baronet (1770–1852). His mother was Emily Geneviève, daughter of Henry Hanson Simpson. From Milton Abbas School, Blandford, Bosworth Smith passed in August 1855 to Marlborough College, where he was head boy. At Michaelmas 1858 he matriculated at Oxford, with an open classical scholarship at Corpus Christi College, and he graduated BA in 1862 with first-class honours both in classical moderations and in the final classical school. In the same year he was president of the union. In 1863 he was elected to a classical fellowship at Trinity College, Oxford, and was appointed tutor. In the same year he published *Birds of Marlborough*, a first testimony to his native love of birds, which he had cherished from boyhood. He proceeded MA in 1865.

On 16 September 1864 Bosworth Smith began work as a classical master at Harrow School, on the nomination of the headmaster, Dr H. Montagu Butler. This position gave him the means to marry, on 9 August 1865, Flora, fourth daughter of the Revd Edward Dawe Wickham, whose fifth daughter, Alice Bertha, was wife of Bosworth Smith's elder brother Henry John (1838–1879); the eldest daughter, Emmeline Wickham, married James Franck Bright, the schoolmaster and don.

In 1870 Bosworth Smith opened a new 'large house' at Harrow, The Knoll, which he built at his own expense. For more than thirty years he mainly devoted his life to his duties at Harrow. His house was always one of the most distinguished in the school. His firm but tolerant government, his enthusiasm and simplicity, his wide interests, and his ready sympathy bound his pupils to him in ties of affection, which lasted long after they had left school. In his form teaching, which never lost its early freshness, he qualified the classical tradition by diverting much of his energy to history, scripture, geography, and English literature, especially Milton. Since he remained a layman, however, he was effectively debarred (like his Harrow housemaster contemporary, Edward Bowen), from the headmastership which his reputation as a teacher would have gained him.

Although brought up in a strict evangelical home, Bosworth Smith tended towards liberal churchmanship. In 1874 he delivered before the Royal Institution in London four lectures on Muhammad and Islam, originally prepared for an essay society at Harrow. They were published in the same year (3rd edn, 1889). He both defended the character and teaching of the Prophet and acknowledged the benefits of Islam to Africa, a positive assessment which drew much criticism from missionary societies. The book was translated into Arabic, and its author was for many years prayed for in the mosques of western Africa.

Carthage and the Carthaginians (1878) collected seven lectures also delivered before the Royal Institution, which gave a graphic description of Carthage as 'queen of the Mediterranean', and defended the character of Hannibal. In 1879 he accepted the invitation of the family of the first Lord Lawrence to write his life. He had met Lord Lawrence, and in two letters in *The Times* in 1878 had defended his Afghan policy. Three years were spent on the accumulated documents and in meetings with Lawrence's former colleagues, though Bosworth Smith never visited India. The book was published in two volumes on 12 February 1883, and had an enthusiastic reception. Subsequently the American government placed a copy in every great public library and on every ship in the US Navy. It was also translated into Urdu, and widely read in India.

Bosworth Smith frequently intervened in current political, religious, and educational controversies, especially through letters to *The Times*. He was a keen Russophobe. In 1885 he urged the permanent occupation of the Sudan by Britain. He was active in the movement opposing the evacuation of Britons from Uganda. He led an important delegation of the British and Foreign Anti-Slavery Society to Lord Rosebery, then foreign secretary.

In the autumn of 1885, in letters to *The Times*, Bosworth Smith publicly defended the Church of England against what he considered Gladstone's and Joseph Chamberlain's menaces of disestablishment; his action drew a reassuring message from Gladstone. Although a broad-churchman, Bosworth Smith's loyalty to the church, especially as it functioned in rural areas, was intense. His letters were published by the Church Defence Institution as a pamphlet entitled *Reasons of a Layman and a Liberal for Opposing Disestablishment* (1885). In the following year his determined opposition to Irish home rule marked a further break from his previous Liberal sympathies.

In 1895 Bosworth Smith purchased an old manor house at Bingham's Melcombe, Dorset, and lived there after his retirement from Harrow in 1901. He was JP for Dorset, a member of the education committee of the county council, and vice-president of the Dorset Field Club. At Harrow he had steadily pursued his lifelong study of birds, making annual expeditions with chosen pupils to neighbouring woods, and occasionally to the Norfolk broads and other places, to observe, but not to rob, birds' nests. In 1905 he published *Bird Life and Bird Lore*.

After many months of illness, Bosworth Smith died at Bingham's Melcombe on 18 October 1908, and was buried beside his parents and brothers in the churchyard of West Stafford, his birthplace. He was survived by his wife, who fully shared all his interests. She copied and recopied every line of his illegible handwriting for publication and transcribed most of his important private letters. They had six sons and four daughters; the second son, Alan Wyldbore Bosworth, lieutenant in the navy, lost his life at sea when in command of HMS *Cobra* (18 September 1901). Bosworth Smith was commemorated by tablets in Harrow School chapel and in the church at Bingham's Melcombe; and in his memory were erected a portion of the reredos in the church at West Stafford and (by friends and pupils) a stone balustrade in the terrace gardens at Harrow.

ERIC GRAHAM, *rev.* M. C. CURTHOYS

Sources E. F. Grogan, *Reginald Bosworth Smith: a memoir* (1909) • *Harrovian* [magazine of Harrow School] (27 July 1901), 76–7 • *Harrovian* [magazine of Harrow School] (14 Nov 1908) • *The Times* (20 Oct 1908) • *Salisbury Gazette* (Nov 1908) • *Marlburian* (Dec 1908) • *Dorset County Chronicle* (22 Oct 1908) • *CGPLA Eng. & Wales* (1909)

Likenesses Elliott & Fry, photograph, 1899, repro. in Grogan, *Reginald Bosworth Smith*, facing p. 193 • H. G. Riviere, portrait; formerly in possession of his widow, 1912 • engraving (after H. G. Riviere)

Wealth at death £29,135 9*s*. 3*d*.: probate, 6 Jan 1909, *CGPLA Eng. & Wales*

Smith, Reginald Donald (1914–1985), radio producer, was born at 84 Wills Street, Aston Manor, Birmingham, on 31 July 1914, the eldest of three sons of William George Smith, toolmaker, and his wife, Annie May Griffiths. Brought up in a working-class district of Birmingham, Reggie Smith, as he was generally known, went to King Edward's Grammar School (1926–32). He entered Birmingham University as an undergraduate in 1932, where he founded the Birmingham Socialist Society and obtained a BA with honours in English literature in 1937. He was one of a group that came under the influence of the poet Louis MacNeice, then a young assistant lecturer in classics. MacNeice shared Smith's political sympathies, he was best man at his wedding to the novelist Olivia *Manning (1908–1980) on 18 August 1939, and they were later to work (and drink) together as members of the features department of the BBC.

Shortly before the Second World War, the British Council appointed Smith a lecturer in Bucharest. In Romania he and his wife witnessed King Carol's abdication and the rise of Fascism. They escaped to British-occupied Greece. When the German armies approached Athens, they were evacuated to Cairo and finally Jerusalem, where Smith became controller of programmes of the Palestine broadcasting station. He later became acting deputy postmaster-general for the Palestine government.

Large, ebullient, and gregarious, Smith was dispassionately portrayed by Olivia Manning as Guy Pringle, the central character in her brilliant sequence of wartime novels collected in *The Balkan Trilogy* and *The Levant Trilogy* and later made into the BBC film *Fortunes of War*, where the Reggie Smith character was played by Kenneth Branagh. Guy Pringle in these volumes is a big-hearted Marxist, just as those who knew and worked with Reggie Smith remember him. The relationship between Guy and his wife Harriet is a central theme of the novels. Guy is maddening: energetic and extrovert, he is promiscuously charming and unimaginatively careless of the wife who waits alone at home while he lavishes infinite time and emotion on anyone else.

Returning to England at the end of 1945, Smith became a radio producer in the newly established BBC features department under Laurence Gilliam. Gilliam, according to features producer Douglas Cleverdon, 'genially tolerated' Smith's membership of the Communist Party and encouraged him to range freely across the bounds of radio. It was a time of great freedom and excitement in radio—a period Asa Briggs has dubbed 'the golden age of wireless'. The Third Programme had just been established and features producers were given virtually free rein: Smith was one of a band of versatile producers who flourished in these conditions.

With his gift for instant companionability, Smith was made for radio in this age. He spent much of his time at The George with other seasoned drinkers Louis MacNeice, Dylan Thomas, Bob Pocock, and Bertie Rodgers. His significant radio work includes *The Easter Rising, 1916* (1966), a programme about the abortive Irish rising of Easter 1916 for the fiftieth anniversary, and one of his later works, *The Pump* (1972), a creative documentary written by James Cameron based on his experiences in hospital for a major heart operation.

According to Smith's friends, as the cold war intensified the BBC hierarchy became uneasy at the idea of a communist in features (though he resigned his Communist Party membership after the Russian invasion of Hungary), and he was transferred to the less contentious drama department in 1954. There he again flourished, as Guy Pringle's production of *Troilus and Cressida* in Bucharest foreshadowed, for Smith had a talent for inspiring enthusiasm in others, gifts which made him a talented director. He was well known for finding parts in the BBC production in hand for all kinds of waifs and strays picked up in the pub at lunchtime.

Friends remember Reggie Smith as a warm, generous bear of a man who would do a good turn for anyone. His extreme friendliness and wit, his warmth and exuberance of character, earned him an enormous circle of friends. He made a habit of disappearing during a dinner party at his St John's Wood home with the cheery message that he was off to the pub, perhaps taking one of the other male guests, or perhaps just going alone (his lifelong Marxist principles required that he always drank in the public bar, not the saloon).

After his retirement from the BBC, Smith was from 1973 to 1979 professor of liberal and contemporary studies at the New University of Ulster and he was made professor emeritus on his retirement. When he moved to Ulster, Olivia Manning stayed in London. From 1979 to 1983 he was visiting professor of literary arts at the University of Surrey. Olivia Manning died on 23 July 1980, and Smith later remarried. He had been close to his second wife, Diana Marjorie (*b.* 1928), for some time. He died on 3 May 1985, aged seventy, at the Royal Free Hospital, Camden, London. JEANETTE THOMAS

Sources O. Manning, *The Balkan trilogy* (1960–65), 3 vols. • O. Manning, *The Levant trilogy* (1977–80), 3 vols. • J. Stallworthy, *Louis MacNeice* (1995) • A. Briggs, *The history of broadcasting in the United Kingdom*, 2 (1965) • private information (2004) • *Fortunes of war*, 1987, BBC [film] • b. cert. • m. cert. • d. cert. • files, BBC WAC

Archives BBC WAC | SOUND BBC WAC

Likenesses photographs

Wealth at death £102,315: probate, 16 July 1985, *CGPLA Eng. & Wales*

Smith, Sir Reginald Hugh Dorman- (1899–1977), politician and colonial governor, was born on 10 March 1899 in Bellamont Forest, co. Cavan, Ireland, the second son of an established farmer, Major Edward Patrick Dorman-Smith (*b.* 1870), and his wife, Amy, *née* Patterson. His elder brother, Eric, was born in 1895. Educated at Harrow School and at the Royal Military College, Sandhurst, Reginald Dorman-Smith served briefly in the Indian army before being invalided out at the age of twenty-one. He married Doreen Agnes Edith Watson (*b.* 1896), the only daughter of Sir John Watson of Earnock, second baronet, on 2 March 1921; they had two daughters.

For twenty years Dorman-Smith devoted his life to agriculture, becoming vice-president of the National Farmers' Union (NFU) at the age of thirty-two, and Conservative MP for Petersfield in 1935. Elected president of the NFU the next year, he was the spokesman for farmers in parliament and a natural choice for minister of agriculture when Neville Chamberlain formed a government in 1939. With the fall of the Chamberlain ministry in May 1940 Dorman-Smith left ministerial office and became a colonel in the home defence executive. During his sixteen months as a minister much of the groundwork was laid for putting British agriculture on a more productive wartime footing, including the ploughing of 1.5 million acres of pasture land and the creation of a reserve of 3000 tractors. His appointment as governor of Burma was a means of rewarding, and deliberately sidetracking, an ambitious younger politician still in the prime of political life.

Sir Reginald (he was knighted in 1937) arrived in Rangoon as governor in 1941, and found a city throbbing with political ferment as nationalist youth pushed the elected Burmese politicians to demand from the British authorities an early transfer of power to a fully indigenous government. (Under the 1935 Government of Burma Act, a form of parliamentary government had come into existence in 1937.) The governor's role was to preside over the European-dominated civil service and military forces in conjunction with a Burmese cabinet formed from a highly factionalized legislature composed of various indigenous and immigrant ethnic groups and British economic interests. The Burmese premier, U Saw, was a wily politician who had created a significant political patronage machine behind him. The two men immediately hit it off. Dorman-Smith, unlike his stiff predecessor, Sir Archibald Cochrane, was open to the arguments of co-operative Burmese nationalist politicians that the best way to defend British interests from both the impending possibility of a Japanese invasion and the leftist rhetoric of young Burmese nationalists was a speeding up of the process of granting Burma a fuller degree of internal self-government within the British empire and Commonwealth.

Before Dorman-Smith and the premier could solidify their political and personal relationship, however, the Japanese invaded early in 1942 and forced the governor and the rest of the British administration to go into exile in India. There Dorman-Smith remained, planning for the economic and political reconstruction of Burma after the devastation of war, until the allies retook Burma in 1945. But U Saw was not with him, having been intercepted on a round-the-world journey and detained by the British in Uganda for the duration of the war, for allegedly treasonous contacts with the Japanese after the start of the war in the Pacific.

Sir Reginald returned to re-establish a civilian government in Rangoon in mid-October 1945. There he found a very different political situation from that which he had left three years earlier. The young nationalists of the 1930s were now experienced soldiers of the Japanese-sponsored Burma Independence Army and its various successors. Led by General Aung San, the eventually martyred hero of Burma's independence struggle, the disorganized but highly popular indigenous forces of Burmese nationalism, which had co-operated with Lord Mountbatten's forces in driving out the Japanese, now claimed their right to establish Burma's independence outside the British empire. Sympathetic to Asian nationalist voices as he was, Dorman-Smith remained loyal to the pre-war politicians with whom he had previously worked. Moreover, his room for manoeuvre was severely constrained by official British government policy toward the post-war reconstruction of Burma. Rather than speeding Burma's independence, the war cabinet had agreed that the country would come under seven years of direct rule by the governor to allow for economic reconstruction. Only after that had been achieved would the country's politics be allowed to return to the semi-parliamentary forms of the 1930s. This was clearly unacceptable to the nationalist forces.

While official Burma policy remained frozen in the mindset of the 1930s, men such as Dorman-Smith were more aware of the strength of nationalist aspirations. Mountbatten appreciated the virtues of young nationalists such as Aung San, and was even more willing to make concessions to internal forces on the left. The governor quickly found himself isolated. He was out of sympathy with the young men who had helped drive him from

Burma in 1942, and equally out of sympathy with the initial unwillingness of the new Labour government in London to consider changing the now totally unworkable policy of direct rule he was expected to implement. Only Mountbatten had sufficient influence in London to effect a change in policy, and by the time he did, Dorman-Smith's credibility in Rangoon and London had been destroyed by his inconsistent attempts to put together a political base from the now discredited pre-war moderate Burmese politicians such as U Saw, who had returned to Burma.

Dorman-Smith sailed for London on 14 June 1946 while convalescing from a severe bout of amoebic dysentery. By the time he arrived in Britain on 13 July his role in Burma had ended. In the interim, government policy had changed: an accommodation was being sought with Aung San and his nationalist forces, and Sir Hubert Rance, who had been military governor of Burma at the end of the war under Mountbatten, was appointed in Dorman-Smith's place. The ignominy of his departure was compounded by the insult of not being received in the formal style of a colonial governor when he arrived in London.

Sir Reginald continued his interest in Burmese affairs after the war, but never regained public influence. He became high sheriff of Hampshire in 1952. However, after attempting to write his own account of his time in Burma, he turned to a popular and prodigious author of books on Burma to provide a sympathetic account of what he had tried to do. But the liberal Maurice Collis in his *Last and First in Burma (1941–1948)* (1956) sympathized more with the Burmese nationalists and the liberal Mountbatten than with the engaging, but ultimately embittered and betrayed tory politician turned colonial governor. To the end Dorman-Smith felt wronged by history and was confident that had he been able to govern without the interference of London, he would have saved Burma for the Commonwealth, which it left at the time of independence on 4 January 1948. He died on 20 March 1977 at the King Edward VII Hospital, Easebourne, Midhurst, Sussex.

R. H. TAYLOR

Sources M. Collis, *Last and first in Burma (1941–1948)* (1956) · *WWW* · d. cert. · *CGPLA Eng. & Wales* (1977)

Archives BL OIOC, papers as governor of Burma, MS Eur. E 215 · IWM, telegrams | BL OIOC, corresp. with Sir D. T. Monteath, MS Eur. D 714 · BL OIOC, corresp. with Sir John Walton, MS Eur. D 545 | FILM BFI NFTVA, current affairs footage · BFI NFTVA, news footage · IWM FVA, news footage | SOUND BL NSA, oral history interview

Wealth at death £41,301: probate, 10 May 1977, *CGPLA Eng. & Wales*

Smith, Reginald John (1857–1916), barrister and publisher, was born at Brighton on 30 May 1857, the second son of John Smith, of Britwell House, Oxfordshire, and his wife, Emily Jane, daughter of George Frederick Cherry, of Denford, Berkshire. A colleger of Eton and scholar of King's College, Cambridge, he took a first class in the classical tripos (1880), and a degree in law; he was then called to the bar from the Inner Temple. In addition to some casual journalism—in 1883 he wrote 'Notes on international copyright' in the *Pall Mall Gazette* and on the ecclesiastical commission in 1887 for *The Guardian*—from 1886 to 1894 he devilled for Sir Charles Russell and, among other cases, acted as his junior in the defence of the accused poisoner Florence Maybrick in 1889. In all his legal work he was distinguished for his painstaking care, lucid arrangement of material, and invincible courtesy.

In 1893 Reginald Smith married Isabel Marion, youngest daughter of George Murray *Smith, whose publishing firm of Smith, Elder & Co. he joined in 1894, at first as a general reader. On leaving the bar he was granted the farewell distinction of silk. In 1899, George Smith and his son Alexander Smith having retired, he assumed sole control of the firm, and in 1901 took Leonard Huxley as his literary adviser. Smith had already in 1898 succeeded John St Loe Strachey as editor of George Smith's *Cornhill Magazine*. In 1904–5 and again in 1916 he was president of the Publishers' Association, in 1905 strongly opposing *The Times* Book Club's threat to the book trade in selling off the new books at second-hand prices. From the first Reginald Smith was in close sympathy with his father-in-law. Without the older man's speculative dash, he shared his ideal of the publisher—in literature a trustee of the public, in business the actual partner and trustee of the author, rendering countless services not in the contract. The possession of independent means enabled him to show more concern for good literature than for profit-making.

Smith's salient characteristic was consideration for the sensitivity of authors. Remembering a letter to Charlotte Brontë by William Smith Williams, reader for Smith, Elder & Co., who rejected *The Professor* but sent a two-page letter of 'appreciative criticism', Reginald Smith frequently sent, in his own or his lieutenant's hand, a letter of kindly criticism with rejected manuscripts. He delighted in telling young authors the private praises given by established writers. The business client often became a personal friend, and he continued George Smith's friendships with the families of Thackeray, Browning, Elizabeth Gaskell, and Mrs Humphry Ward, and published in the *Cornhill* a series of six pieces, 'The book on the table', by Virginia Woolf. Smith introduced both A. C. Benson and the Revd W. H. Fitchett to their English audiences, as well as the Antarctic explorers Robert Falcon Scott and Edward Adrian Wilson (Reginald's cousin was the polar explorer Apsley Cherry-Garrard). Six friends dedicated books to him, 'whom to have known', wrote Sir Edward Cook, 'was, in itself, a liberal education in human kindliness, in thoughtful courtesy, and in love of letters' (Huxley, 217).

As the editor of the *Cornhill*, Reginald Smith resolutely maintained its tradition of national pride, serialized novels, literary essays, and remembrances of past glories, undismayed by the competition of the sixpennies and financial loss. His warmest publishing interest attached to the centenary editions of Thackeray and Browning, the Brontë and Gaskell definitive editions, the Antarctic books of Captain Scott, the disposal of the Brontë relics (among which he secured Branwell Brontë's portraits of his sisters for the National Portrait Gallery), and the thin paper edition of the *Dictionary of National Biography* in 1908. This he initiated in consultation with George Smith's widow, Elizabeth, and carried it through with untiring attention to complex details. All corrections, including those published in the volume of errata (1904), were incorporated in the text under the editorship of Sidney Lee. The original sixty-six volumes were reduced to twenty-one, with a twenty-second volume including the three volumes of the first-supplement edition that had been published in 1901. A second supplement in 1912 spanning Edward VII's reign was thought to be more inclusive than the original dictionary. After Elizabeth Smith's death in 1914 Reginald supervised the dictionary staff under Lee's editorship.

The name of 'Reginald Smith ward' commemorates Smith's long connection with the Poplar Hospital, as a member of the committee from 1910 onwards, and treasurer in 1915–16. During the First World War his unsparing exertions broke down his health and, suffering from temporary insanity, he committed suicide on 26 December 1916 by jumping from a window of his home at 11 Green Street, Park Lane, London. He was survived by his wife; they had no children. Reginald Smith was dark and very tall; in face and figure austerely spare; and he had a certain formality of address. In 1917 Elizabeth Smith's representatives gave the *Dictionary of National Biography* to the University of Oxford, to be continued by the Clarendon Press. The publishing business including the *Cornhill Magazine* was acquired by John Murray despite being seriously overvalued. A. F. Pollard, assistant editor of the *Dictionary of National Biography* from 1893 to 1901, advised H. W. C. Davis, editor from 1919 to 1928, that Reginald Smith should not be in the supplement for the years 1912–21 because 'he really had no claims to distinction, except that he devilled for Sir Charles Russell and married George Smith's daughter' (Pollard to Davis, 29 March 1921). Davis chose to ignore this recommendation.

LEONARD HUXLEY, *rev.* BARBARA QUINN SCHMIDT

Sources L. Huxley, *The house of Smith Elder* (1923) • J. St Loe Strachey, *The adventure of living: a subjective autobiography (1860–1922)* (1922) • A. Conan Doyle, *Memories and adventures* (1924) • [S. Ferrell], 'The *Cornhill Magazine*, 1860–1900', *Wellesley index*, 1.321–415 • J. W. Robertson Scott, *The story of the Pall Mall Gazette* (1950) • A. C. Benson, *Memories and friends* (1924) • B. Quinn Schmidt, 'The Cornhill Magazine', *British literary magazines: the modern age, 1914–1984*, ed. A. Sullivan (1985), 103–10 • B. Quinn Schmidt, 'John Murray', *The British literary book trade, 1700–1820*, ed. J. K. Bracken and J. Silver, DLitB, 154 (1995), 203–15 • B. Quinn Schmidt, 'Smith, Elder and Company', *The British literary book trade, 1700–1820*, ed. J. K. Bracken and J. Silver, DLitB, 154 (1995), 260–69 • J. Don Vann, 'The Cornhill Magazine', *British literary magazines: the Victorian and Edwardian age, 1837–1913*, ed. A. Sullivan (1984), 82–5 • G. Fenwick, *Leslie Stephen's life in letters* (1993) • *The letters of Virginia Woolf*, ed. N. Nicolson, 1–2 (1975–6) • *Thackeray and his daughter: the letters and journals of Anne Thackeray Ritchie*, ed. H. Thackeray and A. Thackeray Ritchie (1924) • J. Glynn, *Prince of publishers: a biography of the great Victorian publisher George Smith* (1986) • R. J. L. Kingsford, *The Publishers Association, 1896–1946, with an epilogue* (1970) • Allibone, *Dict.* • John Murray, London, archives • A. C. Benson, 'Reginald John Smith', *The Cornhill Magazine*, 3rd ser., 42 (Feb 1917), 129–37 • d. cert. • A. F. Pollard, letter to H. W. C. Davis, 29 March 1921, Oxford University Press, Oxford DNB archives, DNB archives, PB/ED/12909/OP1720

Archives John Murray, London • NL Scot. • Scott Polar RI, corresp. | Herefs. RO, corresp. with H. H. Malleson • King's AC Cam., letters to Oscar Browning

Likenesses Lady Scott, bronze statue

Wealth at death £130,635 6*s.* 6*d.*: resworn probate, 1917, *CGPLA Eng. & Wales*

Smith, Richard. *See* Smyth, Richard (1499/1500–1563).

Smith, Richard (1567–1655), vicar apostolic of the English church, the son of John and Alice Smith, was born in November 1567 into a well-off gentry family resident in either Welton or Hanworth, Lincolnshire. He went to Trinity College, Oxford, about 1583, but left three years later without a degree, possibly because of conversion to Catholicism. He moved to Rome via Rheims in 1586, living at the English College and studying philosophy and theology between November 1586 and May 1592, when he was ordained priest. After leaving Rome he continued his theological studies and taught philosophy at Valladolid, where he took his doctorate in theology in July 1598. He then taught philosophy at the English College in Seville until 1602, when he briefly moved to the English College at Douai, assisting his uncle, also Richard Smith, on his deathbed. By January 1603 he had fulfilled his promise to return to England, serving as an assistant to the archpriest, George Blackwell, in Sussex, and living in Battle Abbey as a chaplain to a leading protector of recusants, the dowager Viscountess Montague, whose biography he wrote on her death in 1609.

By then serious divisions, both pastoral and ecclesiological, had surfaced within English Catholicism, especially between the secular and regular clergy. Represented mainly by the Jesuits, the latter regarded the restoration of normal episcopal hierarchy in protestant England as impractical and unnecessary. The archpriest controversy revealed the secular clergy's resentment at the limitations placed upon them by Rome, especially concerning education and university degrees, and the tactics of the Jesuits led by Robert Persons; some seculars, Smith included, even seemed willing to break ranks with the papacy over taking the oath of allegiance to the monarchy. Blackwell, deposed for such an offence in 1607, was succeeded by George Birkhead, who sent Smith to Rome in March 1609 as his agent, to present the secular clergy's position to the pope, though their key demand, the appointment of a bishop with ordinary jurisdiction over clergy and laity, could not be pressed at this time. Smith left virtually empty handed in September 1610, but with his hostility to the Jesuits enhanced. He did obtain papal approval for one much discussed objective: to establish a house of study for English secular clergy wishing to take higher degrees and thus be capable of refuting the controversial writings of James I's protestant supporters at Chelsea College. Smith, already with a reputation as a controversialist, became first head of the new community, but significantly he preferred France to the Spanish Netherlands for its location. Founded in 1611, it was housed in the Parisian College of Arras from 1613 onwards. Its initial lack of funds led him to join the household of the future Cardinal Richelieu in 1611 where, in return for a pension, he acted as his theological mentor, notably on matters of controversy. Their subsequent careers remained closely intertwined thereafter, and although Smith was inevitably caught up in

Richelieu's disgrace, exile, and slow return to favour (1617–24), he benefited crucially from the cardinal's patronage at key moments of his career.

It was French, and specifically Richelieu's, pressure which persuaded a reluctant papacy to appoint Smith, who was not the first choice of the English clergy, as vicar apostolic of the English church, with the title of bishop of Chalcedon *in partibus infidelium*, in November 1624. He inherited an already difficult situation from his short-lived predecessor, William Bishop. His own overt dislike of 'church papists' and evident determination to exercise full episcopal authority in ordinary rather than as a papal delegate (which is what he was) over clergy and laity alike, allied to an evident lack of diplomatic skills, only exacerbated existing divisions after his return to England in April 1625. His efforts soon led to controversy and confusion, with the Benedictines, Jesuits, and finally many lay Catholics openly siding against him. Suspended by Rome in 1628 and threatened with arrest by the English government under the Statute of *Praemunire*, he took refuge in 1629 in the French embassy before returning to France in 1631, when he finally consented to resign his office.

Richelieu's patronage again ensured Smith a household place and lodgings in Paris, as well as the abbey of Charroux in Poitou, which he held *in commendam* from 1637 onwards. Under Mazarin his situation became more precarious, and he lost possession of Charroux in 1648. In the early 1630s his return to France precipitated some heated exchanges, with Gallican divines angrily defending episcopal authority against Jesuit defences of the peculiar (to Gallican eyes) conditions of English Catholicism. Yet Smith's own position within English Catholicism was gradually undermined by continuing divisions, this time among the seculars themselves, not least among the members of the chapter established by his predecessor, Bishop. By the early 1650s the majority of its younger members, the Blackloists and their allies—virtually all originally appointed by Smith—preferred to see the chapter rather than a bishop govern English Catholicism, and the ageing Smith proved unable to use the chapter as a means to sustain his own continuing claim to authority. He had no successor for over thirty years after his death.

Until the end Smith continued to write substantial works of controversy, notably the treatise *Of the Fundamental and not Fundamental Points of the Faith* (1645), in which he argued that the essentials of Catholic doctrine can be established on the basis of scripture alone. He also compiled the most authoritative catalogue of English Catholic martyrs, the Chalcedon catalogue, his last published work (1654). He also remained a central figure in the expatriate Catholic community, helping to found and finance the Paris convent of English Augustinian canonesses, Notre Dame de Syon. They provided him with an apartment adjacent to the convent on the rue des Fossés St Victor during his last years after Richelieu's death in 1642. There he died on 18 March 1655, and was buried in the convent chapel. JOSEPH BERGIN

Sources M. C. Questier, *Newsletters from the archpresbyterate of George Birkhead*, CS, 5th ser., 12 (1998) • *Letters of Thomas Fitzherbert, 1608–1610*, ed. L. Hicks, Catholic RS, 41 (1948) • *Miscellanea, XII*, Catholic RS, 22 (1921) • A. F. Allison, 'Richard Smith, Richelieu and the French marriage', *Recusant History*, 7 (1963–4), 148–211 • A. F. Allison, 'Richard Smith's Gallican backers and Jesuit opponents', *Recusant History*, 18 (1986–7), 329–401; 19 (1988–9), 234–85; 20 (1990–91), 164–205 • A. F. Allison, 'An English Gallican: Henry Holden (to 1648)', *Recusant History*, 22 (1994–5), 319–49 • G. Anstruther, *The seminary priests*, 4 vols. (1969–77) • Gillow, *Lit. biog. hist.*, vol. 5 • G. H. Tavard, *The seventeenth-century tradition* (1968)

Archives BL, letters • Stonyhurst College, Lancashire, letters and papers

Likenesses portrait, English College, Douai; repro. in *Miscellanea, XII* • portrait; at English Augustinian convent, Neuilly, in 1897

Smith [Smyth], **Richard** (*bap.* 1590, *d.* 1675), law officer and book collector, was baptized on 20 September 1590 at Lillingstone Dayrell, Buckinghamshire, one of at least four sons of Richard Smith (*bap.* 1567, *d.* 1638), and his wife, Martha Dayrell (*d.* 1651). He went to school in Abingdon, and spent some time at Oxford without taking a degree.

Smith obtained a post as junior clerk in or about 1608 in the Poultry Compter, one of the combined courts and prisons of the City of London, where his cousin Thomas Bitcliffe was a chief clerk. The Poultry Compter and the City's legal system were the focus of Smith's whole career, and he built up an extensive acquaintance among the personnel of the City's courts and prisons, and also at the inns of court. On 27 February 1622 he married Elizabeth (*bap.* 1600, *d.* 1664), daughter of George Deane of Stepney, and by 1623 they were resident in Old Jewry, close to the Poultry Compter and Guildhall. Smith obtained the reversion of a clerk-sitter's place in one of the compters for his own son John in 1634, and was appointed secondary of the Poultry Compter in 1644. The secondary was the chief officer of the compter, effectively acting as under-sheriff, and head of a staff of law officers and clerks. The office was said to be worth £700 a year, derived from a share of the fees and profits of justice in the compter.

Smith was one of the new professional class of seventeenth-century London—civil servants, lawyers, and doctors—who lived off fees and salaries and who, together with the prosperous merchants of the City, were beginning to create a new urban 'middling sort'. He belonged both to the world of the City, characterized by participation in local affairs and by the everyday mixing of social and occupational groups and activities, and to the new metropolitan culture of taste and educated pleasures and leisures, shared with the urban and country gentry. Smith was an assiduous and discriminating book collector, with many friends and acquaintances in the trade. He was 'constantly known every day to walk his rounds through the [book] shops … where his great skill and experience enabled him to make choice of what was not obvious to every vulgar eye' (Ellis, xii). He collected works of theology, history, philology, classical literature, and medicine; he collated and annotated his acquisitions, and also wrote various works himself, including a compilation, 'The wonders of the world' (BL, Sloane MS 388), and a treatise 'On the art of printing' (BL, Sloane MS 722)

Smith served as secondary at the compter until 1655, when, following his son John's death, he resigned the office and retired. He had moved about 1649 to Little Moorfields, Cripplegate, outside the city wall, where he lived until his death on 26 March 1675. He had five sons and three daughters, of whom only two daughters survived him. A family memorial in the church of St Giles Cripplegate, where he had been buried on 1 April 1675, was destroyed in 1940. Smith's will, in which he described himself as 'gentleman', enumerated bequests totalling over £5000. At his death his collection comprised more than 8000 books, pamphlets, and manuscripts. The sale of his library, in 1682, attracted numerous collectors and raised the sum of £1414 12*s.* 11*d.* Smith's life and connections can be traced in his 'Catalogue of all such persons deceased whom I knew in their lifetime', which lists nearly 2000 deaths of familiar and notable individuals, from 1628 to 1675. It was edited, from a surviving manuscript transcript (BL, Sloane MS 886), by Henry Ellis in 1849, as *The Obituary of Richard Smyth*. The catalogue provides a virtual 'Law-Necrology' (Ellis, xx) for the time, and the names of numerous booksellers and printers. Smith emerges as an attractive character, convivial as well as scholarly, a man of long-standing affections with a strong sense of family attachments and connections and many personal friendships. VANESSA HARDING

Sources *The obituary of Richard Smyth … being a catalogue of all such persons as he knew in their life*, ed. H. Ellis, CS, 44 (1849) • V. Harding, 'Mortality and the mental map of London: Richard Smyth's *Obituary*', *Medicine, mortality and the book trade*, ed. R. Myers and M. Harris (1998), 49–71 • *Bibliotheca Smithiana, sive, Catalogus librorum … Richardus Smith Londinensis* (1682) [sale catalogue, London, 15 May 1682] • repertories of the court of aldermen, CLRO, vol. 39, fol. 296*v*; vol. 57, fol. 234*v*; vol. 62, fol. 178; vol. 64, fol. 422 • will, PRO, PROB 11/347, fols. 289*v*–291 • parish register and records, St Olave Old Jewry, GL, MSS 4399, 4400, 4409/1–2, 4415/1 • parish register and records, St Giles Cripplegate, GL, MSS 6047/1, 6048/1, 6419/5–9 • *An inventory of the historical monuments in London*, Royal Commission on Historical Monuments (England), 4 (1929), 99 • *IGI* [Lillingstone Dayrell and St Dunstan Stepney parish registers] • Wood, *Ath. Oxon.*, new edn, 3.1031–4

Archives BL, book catalogues, obituaries of friends and relations, literary MSS, Sloane MSS 388, 771–772, 786–791, 886, 1024, 1054, 1071 • BL, annotated copy of *Bibliotheca Smithiana*, Mic. A1343

Wealth at death bequeathed over £5000, excl. personal possessions: will, PRO, PROB 11/347, fols. 289*v*–291; estate perhaps inadequate to pay legacies, since library sold at auction in 1682 for £1414 12*s.* 11*d.*, whereas will implies it should not be sold: *Bibliotheca Smithiana*

Smith, Richard (*bap.* **1734**, *d.* **1803**), army officer in the East India Company and politician, was baptized on 15 May 1734 at St Mary's, Marlborough, Wiltshire, the eldest son of John Smith, a cheesemonger, of Jermyn Street, London. His social origins and allegedly poor education were sometimes to be held against him in later life. He arrived in India as a purser's mate on an East Indiaman in 1752, and on 9 December 1752 was commissioned ensign in the East India Company's Madras army, at a time when the council was desperate for 'gentlemen' to officer its rapidly growing army. He was made lieutenant a year later (2 November 1753), captain on 2 June 1756, and major in 1760, following the seniority principle which governed promotion in the company's armed forces. On 25 September 1756 Smith had married Amelia, daughter of Captain Charles Hopkins, a master mariner and later Madras civil servant. They had a son and a daughter. The Carnatic, in south-eastern India, was in a state of discontinuous warfare during these years, largely due to competition between the British and French for the dominance of the province. Smith saw active service throughout, obviously recommending himself to his military superiors, for he was given independent commands of forts and detachments, and in 1758 acted as aide-de-camp to Colonel Stringer Lawrence, the commander-in-chief.

Smith was quick-tempered and haughty, but his disarming candour got him out of a number of scrapes. His experience as a purser's mate and his marriage alliance to a merchant family might also have reflected business talents (certainly they suggest business connections); unusually for a Carnatic officer, he amassed a fortune in the 1750s, perhaps by trade but also through the favourite financial method of many Madras Europeans, who lent money to Muhammad Ali, the nawab of Arcot, at 25 per cent per annum. Clearly also, Smith's political skills and forceful personality had impressed his colleagues and fellow creditors, for he was later appointed their unofficial spokesman in London, charged with securing their financial interests. The nawab, bypassing the enraged directors, entrusted Smith with a letter to the king seeking George III's intercession to get him a better deal with the company.

Smith remained in London until 1764, becoming a prominent member of the company's court of proprietors (shareholders) during the great struggle between Robert Clive and Laurence Sulivan for control of the East India Company (he started in the Clive camp, but ended up a supporter of Sulivan). This, and recognition of his military talents, secured him a royal commission as colonel in the East (11 May 1764) and the appointment to command one of the company's three brigades in the reorganized Bengal army under Clive, the new governor. Smith again fell out with Clive on the voyage out to India, but remained loyal to him during the notorious 1766 'white mutiny' of Bengal officers protesting against the governor's military reforms. None the less, Clive admonished him for his 'great ambition and desire to command those who should command you' (Clive to Smith, 15 Feb 1766, NL Wales, Clive MS 224, fols. 57–60). On Clive's resignation in 1767, his unique appointment combining the roles of governor and active commander-in-chief in Bengal was split between the next senior civil servant, Harry Verelst, a rather weak man, and Smith, now promoted brigadier-general.

Bengal was quiet during Smith's command of the army (1767–70), though there were some alarms that the Afghans intended invading and various schemes for the further military and political penetration of northern India by the company. Smith was enthusiastic both for fighting the Afghans outside company-controlled territory, and for putting the wandering Mughal emperor Shah Alam II back on the throne in Delhi; he probably received a substantial monetary reward from the grateful emperor for espousal of his cause. Clive, back in Britain, warned a director of the company that Smith 'will project distant Conquests and every thing else which Pride and Ambition like his can suggest' (Clive to Thomas Rous, 20 Oct 1767, NL Wales, Clive MS 58, fols. 47–8). Privately, Smith admitted he was bent on 'transmitting his name to Posterity' (Smith to Robert Orme, April 1767, BL OIOC, Orme MS OV 37, fols. 118–19). The Calcutta council's rejection of both these proposals helped provoke a bitter and prolonged dispute between Smith and Verelst over the respective spheres of their authority. Both men eventually resigned and returned to Britain in 1770.

Back in London—allegedly with between £200,000 and £300,000 in his pocket—Smith plunged into East India Company and parliamentary politics, living in Harley Street and buying a country seat, Chiltern Lodge, near Hungerford, Berkshire, and becoming high sheriff of that county in 1779. He made such a flamboyant and arrogant entry into society that he became one of the most notorious of the 'nabobs', the *nouveaux riches* East India Company servants who flung their money around to the great resentment and contempt of 'old wealth'. It was said that he was the model for Sir Matthew Mite in Samuel Foote's lampooning play *The Nabob* (1772); he was also the subject of an attack, complete with the only known likeness of him, in one of the 'Tête à Tête' portraits in the *Town and Country Magazine*, opposite Mrs Elizabeth *Armitstead (no. 20, 1776, 34), and, later, of a hostile spoof entitled *A Vindication of General Richard Smith* (1783) by Joseph Price. Smith became a prominent man of the turf, running racehorses and belonging to the Jockey Club; he also lost a fortune at the gaming table (£180,000, it was said, to Charles James Fox).

Smith's recklessness extended to his parliamentary career. He provoked rage by trying to buy his way into the Shoreham constituency in November 1770, and in 1774 he was disqualified, fined, and gaoled for six months for buying votes to win the election for the seat of Hindon in Wiltshire. He tried other seats before eventually getting into parliament for Wendover in 1780, by purchasing the borough's two seats from Lord Verney (the other went to his son). Speaking ably on Indian issues, Smith made enough noise from the opposition benches to be made chair of the commons select committee on East India affairs in 1781. Burke commented that its seventh report 'owed the greatest part of its merit to the General … and did him infinite honour' (HoP, *Commons, 1754–90*, 450). Smith lost his seat in 1784 as one of 'Fox's Martyrs', and, deprived of parliamentary immunity, he had to sell his estate and flee abroad to escape his creditors. He returned to England in 1786, and to parliament, as MP for Wareham, Dorset, in 1790. He contributed regularly to debates on India, on which he supported government policy, although he was otherwise in opposition. He became a prominent critic of the ministry's war policy against France after 1794, and of its measures to cope with corn price fluctuations at home. He spoke, among other issues, on the abuse of child labour in factories, but supported the slave trade. Smith did not seek re-election in 1796 and, with his finances partly restored to health, died seven years later, on 3 July 1803. G. J. Bryant

Sources V. C. P. Hodson, *List of officers of the Bengal army, 1758–1834*, 4 vols. (1927–47) · L. S. Sutherland, *The East India Company in eighteenth century politics* (1952) · J. M. Holtzman, *The nabobs in England, 1760–1765* (1926) · HoP, *Commons, 1754–90* · Verelst letter books, BL OIOC, microfilm 606 · Bengal secret military and political consultations, 1767–70, BL OIOC, range A, vols. 7–10 · BL OIOC, MS Eur. Orme, OV 37 · BL OIOC, MS Eur. F/128, boxes 1 and 3 · NL Wales, Clive MSS 58, 224, 227 · H. D. Love, *Vestiges of old Madras, 1640–1800*, 4 vols. (1913) · *Memoirs of William Hickey*, ed. A. Spencer, 8th edn, 3 vols. · *DNB*

Archives BL OIOC, letters to John Carnac, MS Eur. F128 · BL OIOC, India Office records · NL Wales, Clive MSS

Likenesses engraving (Tête à Tête portrait series), repro. in *Town and Country Magazine* (1776), 34

Smith, Richard Baird (1818–1861), army officer in the East India Company, born at Lasswade, Midlothian, on 31 December 1818, was the son of Richard Smith (1794–1863), surgeon, Royal Navy, of Lasswade, where he was in successful private practice, and his wife, Margaret Young (1800–1829). He was educated at the Lasswade School and at Duns Academy, entered Addiscombe College, the East India Company's military college, on 6 February 1835, passed out at the head of his term, with first prizes in mathematics and Latin, and was commissioned second lieutenant, Madras engineers, on 9 December 1836. After the usual Chatham engineering course he left on 4 October 1837, having obtained six months' leave to study civil engineering and geology. Nineteenth-century army engineers in India had a great variety of civil as well as military roles, as Baird Smith's career illustrated. He arrived at Madras on 6 July 1838 and was posted to the Madras sappers and miners, joining the headquarters in the Nilgiri hills on 13 July; he was appointed acting adjutant on 20 February 1839. On 12 August, on an increase to the Bengal Engineers' establishment, Baird Smith was transferred to them, and on 23 September was appointed adjutant. A week later he became temporarily an assistant to Captain M. R. Fitzgerald, Bengal Engineers, in the canal and iron bridge department of the public works.

On 6 January 1840 Baird Smith was appointed temporarily a member of the arsenal committee. On 12 August he was appointed assistant to the superintendent of the Doab Canal, Sir Proby Thomas Cautley. He was promoted first lieutenant on 28 August 1841. In October 1844 his meteorological observations were officially praised. When Cautley began the Ganges Canal works in 1843, Baird Smith was left in charge, under him, of the Jumna Canal.

On the outbreak of the First Anglo-Sikh War Baird Smith, with the other canal department officers, joined the army of the Sutlej. He arrived in camp a few days after the battle of Ferozeshahr (22 December 1845). He was attached to the command of Major-General Sir Harry George Wakelyn Smith, and was with him at Badiwal and at the battle of Aliwal (28 January 1846), earning praise and mention in dispatches. He was on the staff at the battle of Sobraon on 10 February. After the campaign he

Richard Baird Smith (1818–1861), by unknown photographer, *c.*1860

returned to his canal duties. Also in 1848 he temporarily supervised the botanical gardens in the North-Western Provinces during Dr Jameson's absence.

In the Second Anglo-Sikh War Baird Smith was with Brigadier-General Colin Campbell at the action of Ramnagar on 22 November 1848. He then joined the force of Sir Joseph Thackwell, which under his direction crossed the Chenab at Wazirabad (1–2 December). Baird Smith took part in the action at Sadulapur on 3 December and marched with Thackwell to Helah, where Lord Gough with the main army arrived a fortnight later. He was at the battles of Chilianwala (13 January 1849) and Gujrat (21 February), and was mentioned in dispatches.

After the war Baird Smith returned to irrigation work on 12 March 1849. On 10 February 1850 he obtained furlough to Europe for three years. In October the court of directors commissioned him to examine (for application to India) the irrigation canals in northern Italy. He was promoted brevet captain on 9 December 1851. In January 1852 he finished his report, which was published (*Italian Irrigation, being a Report on the Agricultural Canals of Piedmont and Lombardy*, 2 vols., 1852). Victor Emmanuel offered him a knighthood of the order of St Maurice and St Lazarus but British regulations forbade acceptance. The court of directors praised Smith's achievement and permitted him to visit the Madras irrigation works before returning to duty. He arrived in Madras on 1 January 1853, and later published a description of the irrigation works there (*The Cauvery, Kistnah, and Godavery*, 1856). He also published *Agricultural Resources of the Punjab* (1849), and contributions to *Papers on various professional subjects connected with the duties of the corps of engineers, Madras presidency*, edited by John Thomas Smith (1839), and *Professional Papers of the Corps of Royal Engineers* (1849).

On 10 March 1853 Baird Smith was appointed deputy superintendent of canals, North-Western Provinces. He was promoted captain on 15 February 1854, and on 16 February brevet major for service in the field. On 17 May he was appointed director of the Ganges Canal and superintendent of canals in the North-Western Provinces, in succession to Cautley, with the temporary rank of lieutenant-colonel while holding the appointment. Baird Smith married, on 10 January 1856, in the cathedral at Calcutta, Florence Elizabeth, second daughter of Thomas De *Quincey, the writer, and they had two daughters, Florence May and Margaret Eleanor.

At the outbreak of the 1857 Indian mutiny Baird Smith was living at Roorkee, the irrigation headquarters. Baird Smith directed defensive measures there; the workshops were converted into a citadel, in which the women and children were accommodated, while the two companies of sappers and miners left at Roorkee were placed in the Thomason College buildings. He probably saved Roorkee from the mutineers. Always hopeful, on 30 May he wrote to a friend in England:

> As to the empire, it will be all the stronger after this storm, and I have never had a moment's fear for it … and though we small fragments of the great machine may fall at our posts, there is that vitality in the English people that will bound stronger against misfortunes and build up the damaged fabric anew.

In the last week of June Baird Smith was ordered to Delhi to be chief engineer, replacing the ineffective and unpopular Major John Laughton, Bengal Engineers. He improvised a body of 600 pioneers to follow him, and, pressed to hasten his arrival so as to take part in the assault, started on 27 June and reached Delhi at 3 a.m. on 3 July to find that the assault had been, as usual, postponed. He already knew the city well, and he at once examined the means of attack. He found the artillery, ammunition, and engineer party inadequate for a regular and successful siege, and urged ineffectually upon the general commanding, Sir Henry Barnard, as had already been done by others, an immediate assault by storming and blowing in certain gates. Baird Smith considered that if the place had been assaulted at any time between 4 and 14 July it would have been captured. On 5 July Barnard died of cholera, and was succeeded by Major-General Reed, who was ill. Reed would not risk an assault, and before he resigned on 17 July two severe actions had been fought and had so weakened the British that the chances of a successful assault had been much diminished, if not altogether destroyed. Baird Smith, however, sedulously attended to the defence of the ridge, strengthening the position by every possible means. His second in command was Captain Alexander Taylor, Bengal Engineers and his brigade major was Lieutenant George Chesney, Bengal Engineers.

Since the beginning of the month a retreat had been discussed, and when Brigadier-General Archdale Wilson assumed command on 17 July it required all Baird Smith's energy and enthusiasm to sweep away Wilson's doubts, and to persuade him not to abandon Delhi but, as he wrote to him, 'to hold on like grim Death until the place is our own' (Vibart, *Addiscombe*, 465). Wilson was ill, 'grown nervous and hesitating' (Roberts, *Forty-one Years*, 117). Baird Smith was brave, energetic, determined, and decisive, but also apparently, 'querulous through ill-health' (Sandes, 333). The relationship deteriorated, and for a time in September Wilson refused to talk to Baird Smith. Baird Smith considered Wilson timid, peevish, childish, and obstructive, and wrote of him on 4 September: 'He combines a wondrous amount of ignorance and obstinacy, is so discouraging … the greatest obstacle extant to the vigorous capture of Delhi' (Vibart, *Richard Baird Smith*, 128). He later wrote: 'I have never served under a man … for whom I had less respect' (ibid., 135). Nevertheless Baird Smith was able to prevail over Wilson and get his way. According to Baird Smith, 'It was only by constantly reminding him that if he interfered with my plans, I would throw the whole responsibility for the consequences on him, that I could get on at all' (ibid., 137). Baird Smith assured him that as soon as a siege-train sufficient to silence the guns on the walls of Delhi could be brought up, success would be certain. On 12 August Baird Smith, ill with diarrhoea and scurvy, was struck by a shell splinter in the ankle-joint. He refused to be put on the sick list, took port, cherry brandy, and opium pills, and did not allow either the wound, which caused intense pain, or his sickness to interfere with his duties as chief engineer. Chesney later wrote that Baird Smith was 'absolutely invaluable as director … Although in very bad health & wretchedly weak, he was always cheery and hopeful of final success and had a potent share in keeping the successive Generals up to the mark' (R14/303, Roberts MSS).

The siege-train arrived on 5 September, and in consultation with Captain Taylor, Baird Smith submitted a plan of attack which Wilson, despite his divergence from Smith's views, had already directed him to prepare. It was supported by Colonel John Nicholson and Neville Chamberlain, the adjutant-general, and the assault was decided upon. Wilson recorded that he yielded to the judgement of his chief engineer. After the war contemporaries and later historians disagreed (the 'Baird Smith–Taylor controversy') on whether the plan was by Baird Smith or his second in command: probably it was a joint effort.

The first siege battery for ten guns was begun on the night of 7 September; others rapidly followed, until fifty-six guns opened fire. After a heavy bombardment practicable breaches were made, and the assault took place on 14 September. A lodgement was made, but at heavy loss, and the progress inside Delhi was so slow and difficult that Wilson, increasingly gloomy and dejected, became convinced the British should withdraw from the city; but Baird Smith told him: 'We *must* hold on' (Roberts, *Forty-one Years*, 131). He deprecated street fighting, and by his advice the open ground inside the Kashmir gate was secured, the college, magazine, and other strong forts gained, and progress gradually made, under cover, until the rear of the enemy's positions was reached, and the enemy compelled to evacuate them on 20 September, when headquarters were established in the palace.

Baird Smith had been ably seconded by Captain Taylor, whose work he unstintingly praised. The picture, however, which has sometimes been presented of Baird Smith disabled, while Taylor did all the work, is incorrect. The error presumably originated in Taylor's energy and zeal, and in Nicholson's deathbed exclamations that if he lived he would let the world know that Taylor took Delhi. Wilson's dispatch stated that in ill health and suffering from a painful wound, Baird Smith devoted himself to the difficult siege operations, and that his thanks were especially due to Baird Smith for having planned and successfully carried out, against extreme difficulties, the attack. Baird Smith's rewards were not commensurate with his services. He was promoted brevet lieutenant-colonel (a rank he already held temporarily) on 19 January 1858, was made a CB (military division) on 22 January, and received the thanks of the government of India.

On 23 September Baird Smith gave up his command at Delhi, then went to Roorkee, arriving on 29 September suffering from scurvy, the effect of exposure, and work, aggravated by his wound. He was laid up for some weeks, and then went to Mussooree to recover. He was appointed to the military charge of the Saharanpur and Muzaffarnagar districts, which he held with the appointment of superintendent-general of irrigation.

On 1 September 1858 Baird Smith was appointed mint-master at Calcutta. On 25 January 1859 he became a member of the senate of Calcutta University, and on 26 April aide-de-camp to the queen and colonel in the army. From 5 August to October 1859 he officiated as secretary to the government of India in the public works department. His mint appointment gave him time for other public services. His crowning service was the survey of the great famine of 1861, the provision of relief, and the safeguards proposed to prevent of relief, and the safeguards proposed to prevent such disaster in future. The labour and fatigue of long journeys, investigations, and reports, followed by the depressing wet season, renewed the illness from which he suffered after the capture of Delhi. Intending to return home, he was carried on board the *Candia* at Calcutta, and died at sea on 13 December 1861. His body was landed at Madras and buried there with military honours. A memorial was placed in Calcutta Cathedral, and another at Lasswade, Midlothian.

Baird Smith's wife and daughters survived him. Of his two brothers, John Young (*d.* 1887) was a deputy surgeon-general in the Bombay army, and Andrew Simpson, a colonel in the Indian army, saw much active service in upper India.

Baird Smith left unpublished the beginning of an account of the siege of Delhi, which was used in E. T. Thackeray's *Two Indian Campaigns in 1857–1858* (1896) and, with extracts from Baird Smith's letters, in H. M. Vibart's *Richard Baird Smith: the Leader of the Delhi Heroes in 1857* (1897). R. H. Vetch, *rev.* Roger T. Stearn

Sources BL OIOC · *LondG* · private information (1897) · H. M. Vibart, *Addiscombe: its heroes and men of note* (1894) · H. M. Vibart,

Richard Baird Smith: the leader of the Delhi heroes in 1857 (1897) • E. W. C. Sandes, *The military engineer in India*, 2 vols. (1933–5) • C. Hibbert, *The great mutiny, India, 1857* (1978); repr. (1980) • Lord Roberts [F. S. Roberts], *Forty-one years in India*, 31st edn (1900) • NAM, Field Marshal Lord Roberts MSS, MS R14/303 • J. W. Kaye, *A history of the Sepoy War in India, 1857–1858*, 9th edn, 3 vols. (1880) • G. B. Malleson, *History of the Indian mutiny, 1857–1858: commencing from the close of the second volume of Sir John Kaye's History of the Sepoy War*, 3 vols. (1878–80) • *The Times* (11 May 1858) • R. B. Smith, *Life of Lord Lawrence*, 2 vols. (1883) • *Fortnightly Magazine* (April 1883) • J. G. Medley, *A year's campaigning in India: from March 1857 to March 1858* (1858) • *CGPLA Eng. & Wales* (1862)

Archives BL OIOC, corresp. and MSS, MS Eur. B 214 • NL Scot., family corresp., MSS 10983–10984 • Royal Engineers, Brompton barracks, Chatham, Kent, papers mainly relating to Indian mutiny

Likenesses photograph, *c*.1860, BL OIOC [*see illus.*]

Wealth at death under £5000: probate, 30 Aug 1862, *CGPLA Eng. & Wales*

Smith, Richard John [*known as* O Smith] (**1786–1855**), actor, the son of an actor named Smith (*d.* 1804), was born in York on 23 January 1786. His mother, whose maiden name was Scrace, played leading parts in Dublin. In 1779, after his father was almost killed in Dublin by an accidental wounding during a stage swordfight, the Smiths moved to Yorkshire. Mrs Smith acted under Tate Wilkinson at Hull, York, and Edinburgh, and also played at Bath.

Richard John Smith is said to have been first seen in Bath, as Ariel in John Hawkesworth's *Edgar and Emmeline*. He played there other juvenile parts. He was then put into a solicitor's office, but neglected his duties, spending his time in the painting room of the theatre. Finally he ran away and became a sailor on the Guinea coast. He had some romantic adventures, and assisted, on the River Gabon, in the escape of some slaves, an incident related in 'A Tough Yarn', which he published in *Bentley's Miscellany*. The governor of Sierra Leone, struck by his ability in painting, offered to befriend him, but the captain of the vessel refused to release him. Following his return to Bath Smith found his parents obdurate, and again ran away, rambling in Wales and Ireland. In Liverpool he was seized by a press gang, but was released on stating that he was an actor and giving a recitation as proof. He was engaged at 12*s*. a week by the elder Macready as painter, prompter, and actor of all work. He nearly died in a snowstorm while travelling on foot from Sheffield to Rochdale. He then went to the theatres at Edinburgh and Glasgow and returned to Bath in 1807, when he played in the pantomimes.

Smith's performance as Robert in the pantomime *Raymond and Agnes* attracted the attention of R. W. Elliston, who engaged him in 1810 for the pantomime at the Surrey. In the title role of *Bombastes furioso*, vacated through illness by another actor, he successfully established his position in burlesque. A performance of Obi, in the melodrama of *Three-Fingered Jack*, won him his sobriquet of 'O' (otherwise Obi) Smith. In 1813 Smith accompanied Elliston to the Olympic, where he played Mandeville in *The False Friend*, a role in which Edmund Kean was to have appeared. After acting at the Lyceum he is said to have been engaged in 1823 at Drury Lane, where he had previously been seen in pantomime. He also seems to have played at Covent Garden. His performance in *The Bottle Imp* at the Lyceum attracted attention, leading him to complain, only half-jokingly, that five years of playing devils, monsters, and murderers had destroyed his peace of mind and exiled him from respectable society. A writer in the *Monthly Magazine* declared him eminent in assassins, sorcerers, the moss-trooping heroes in Sir Walter Scott's poems, and other wild, gloomy, and ominous characters in which a bold, or rather a gigantic, figure and a deep sepulchral voice could be turned to good account. Smith had, however, some ability also in parts requiring tenderness, as his performance in *The Cornish Miners* at the Lyceum showed, when he played a maniac who visits the grave of his dead child. When, in 1828, Yates and Mathews took the Adelphi, Smith joined the company, and his subsequent reputation was chiefly connected with this theatre. In October 1829, in *The Black Vulture*, he played the villain so named. In 1831 at the Adelphi, Edinburgh, he oversaw the production of J. B. Buckstone's *The Wreck Ashore*. In January 1833 he played the title role in *Don Quixote* at the Adelphi, London, a part contrasting strongly with those of which he complained. He had also a part in Holl's *Grace Huntley* and was Newman Noggs in an adaptation of *Nicholas Nickleby*. In 1839 he was Fagin in *Oliver Twist*, in January 1843 Hugh in *Barnaby Rudge*, and in February 1844 the Miser in an adaptation of *A Christmas Carol*. Other roles at the Adelphi included Laroche in E. Stirling's adaptation *Clarisse, or, The Merchant's Daughter* (September 1845), Mongeraud in Holl's

Richard John Smith [O Smith] (**1786–1855**), by Edward Matthew Ward, exh. RA 1834 [in the title role of *Don Quixote* by George Almar]

Leoline, or, Life's Trials (February 1846), Pierre in Peake's *The Devil of Marseilles, or, The Spirit of Avarice* (July 1846), and a cab driver, a pathetic part, in Peake's *Title Deeds* (June 1857). In June 1842 he had, at the Lyceum, given a characteristic performance in John Oxenford's *The Dice of Death*, and on 1 April 1853 he played at the Adelphi in *Mr Webster at Home*. On 20 April 1854, at the same house, he was Musgrave in Tom Taylor and Charles Reade's *Two Loves and a Life*. This appears to have been his last original part.

About 1826 Joseph Smith, a Holborn bookseller, having produced a set of theatrical engravings, applied to 'O Smith, the famous comedian' for an account of the English stage to accompany the plates. An agreement was accordingly drawn up, but the author eventually withdrew from the undertaking. He nevertheless continued to accumulate materials such as theatrical prints, newspaper cuttings, magazine articles, playbills, and catalogues relating to stage history, and also to interleave and annotate theatrical memoirs. By the time of his death his collections filled twenty-five large quarto volumes, which later found their way to the British Library under the title *A Collection of Material towards a History of the Stage*.

Smith died in London, after a long illness, on Thursday 1 February 1855, and was buried on 8 February in Norwood cemetery. JOSEPH KNIGHT, *rev.* KLAUS STIERSTORFER

Sources Genest, *Eng. stage* • J. Tallis, *Tallis's drawing room table book of theatrical portraits, memoirs and anecdotes* (1851) • *Theatrical Times* (26 Sept 1847), 121–2 • *The life and reminiscences of E. L. Blanchard, with notes from the diary of Wm. Blanchard*, ed. C. W. Scott and C. Howard, 2 vols. (1891) • J. C. Dibdin, *The annals of the Edinburgh stage* (1888) • *The Era* (4 Feb 1855) • *The Era* (11 Feb 1855) • *Dramatic and Musical Review* • *Era Almanack and Annual* • Hall, *Dramatic ports.* • G. B. Bryan, ed., *Stage deaths: a biographical guide to international theatrical obituaries, 1850–1990*, 2 vols. (1991)

Archives BL, collection relating to theatre history, Add. MSS 38620–38621 • Bristol Reference Library, theatre playbills, MSS, etc. • University of Chicago Library, corresp. and papers

Likenesses penny plain print, 1827 • twopence coloured print, 1830 • E. M. Ward, oils, exh. RA 1834, Garr. Club [*see illus.*] • portrait, repro. in *Theatrical Times* • prints, BM, NPG • thirty-three prints, Harvard TC • twopence coloured print (as Obi in *Three-fingered Jack*; after portrait by J. Findlay)

Smith, Robert (*d.* 1674/5), composer and singer, was probably one of the first boys appointed to the Chapel Royal following the Restoration in 1660, but there seems to be no record of this or of his subsequent dismissal. James Clifford includes the texts of six anthems by Smith in his 1664 edition of *The Divine Services and Anthems*, describing him as 'one of the Children of his Majesties Chappel'. There his contemporaries included Pelham Humfrey and John Blow. Smith seems to have turned his back on church music after leaving the Chapel Royal and by 1672 was writing music for the theatre. Clearly his talent was noted at court, for on 20 June 1673 he was admitted as a musician-in-ordinary without fee at the behest of 'Mr. [Thomas] Purcell'. Such a move frequently led to a permanent salaried place and on 3 August 1674 Smith was sworn among the lutes and voices in place of Pelham Humfrey, who had died on 14 July. By 22 November 1675, he himself was dead.

In spite of his short career Smith was highly regarded as a composer. His precocious anthems for the chapel have not survived, but many songs from his theatre work of 1672 and 1673 were published by John Playford in *Choice Songs and Ayres* (1673), revised as *Choice Ayres, Songs, & Dialogues* (1676). Three keyboard pieces by Smith were included by Matthew Locke in *Melothesia* (1673), but much of his instrumental music remains in manuscript (often in fragmentary state). At least one suite by Thomas Farmer and Smith was 'made in Oxford' according to a note on the cover; others were probably intended for performance in the theatre or at court. Smith's suite entitled 'New Year's Day' was perhaps written for the annual concert (with ode) given on 1 January in 1674 or 1675. His songs have a 'popular' idiom which no doubt made them attractive to audiences of his day. In D'Urfey's *The Fool Turn'd Critick* (1678) a song is admired as the work of 'one Mr. Smith, and late Composer to the King's Play-house … a very Excellent Fellow … and one the Town Misses very much'.

ANDREW ASHBEE

Sources G. E. P. Arkwright, 'Robert Smith', *Musical Antiquary*, 2 (1910–11), 171–3 • C. L. Day and E. B. Murrie, *English song-books, 1651–1702: a bibliography with a first-line index of songs* (1940) • I. Spink, *English song: Dowland to Purcell* (1974) • C. A. Price, *Music in the Restoration theatre* (1979) • P. Dennison, 'Smith, Robert (ii)', *New Grove* • A. Ashbee, ed., *Records of English court music*, 1 (1986) • A. Ashbee, ed., *Records of English court music*, 5 (1991) • P. Holman, *Four and twenty fiddlers: the violin at the English court, 1540–1690*, new edn (1993) • A. Ashbee and D. Lasocki, eds., *A biographical dictionary of English court musicians, 1485–1714*, 2 vols. (1998)

Smith, Robert (*fl.* 1689–1729), schoolmaster and poet, is of unknown parentage. He was educated at Marischal College, Aberdeen, and may have been the Robert Smith who graduated AM in 1682. Soon after the revolution of 1688 Smith was chosen as schoolmaster of the newly founded school at Kerrow, in Glenshee, in the parish of Kirkmichael, Perthshire, which had been endowed with 100 marks by John Murray, later first duke of Atholl. The heritors failed to provide Smith with a dwelling, and after waiting in vain for some months he showed his resentment by publishing 'A Poem on the Building of the School-house of Glenshee', in which he roundly abused the lairds for their neglect. This provoked a reply from a whig poet, Jasper Craig, who, Smith insinuates, was a disappointed candidate for the post. The dispute continued in several more poetical exchanges between the two and was evidently fuelled by denominational difference, for Smith was an Episcopalian and Craig adhered to the Church of Scotland. Smith published their poems as *Poems of Controversy betwixt Episcopacy and Presbytery* in 1714.

By 1729 Smith had moved from Glenshee to become schoolmaster at Glamis in Forfarshire. In that year he published a catechism for children. He had a son, Robert Smith, who was schoolmaster at Kinnaird, in Perthshire; some of his verses appear in Alexander Nicol's *Rural Muse* (1753). It is not known when or where Smith died.

E. I. CARLYLE, *rev.* S. J. SKEDD

Sources T. G. Stevenson, preface, in R. Smith, *The assembly's shorter catechism in metre*, repr. (1872) • *N&Q*, 4th ser., 4 (1869), 320–21 • A. Nicol, *The rural muse, or, A collection of miscellany poems both comical *and serious* (1753) · *Fasti academiae Mariscallanae Aberdonensis: selections from the records of the Marischal College and University, MDXCIII–MDCCCLX*, 2, ed. P. J. Anderson, New Spalding Club, 18 (1898), 249–50

Smith, Robert (*bap.* **1689**, *d.* **1768**), mathematician and benefactor, was baptized on 16 October 1689 at Lea, near Gainsborough, Lincolnshire, the son of John Smith (*d.* 1710), rector of Gate Burton, Lincolnshire, and his wife, Hannah, *née* Cotes (*d.* 1719). His father, who had been educated at Trinity College, Cambridge, and probably also at Oxford, sometimes tutored students in mathematics. Smith attended Mr Thomas's school in Leicester and was also tutored by his father before himself proceeding to Trinity College, where he was admitted pensioner on 28 May 1708 and scholar on 13 May 1709. Having graduated BA in 1712, he obtained his degrees of MA in 1715, LLD in 1723, and DD in 1739. Elected to a college fellowship in 1714, he was a tutor from 1715 to 1734. In 1716 he succeeded his cousin Roger *Cotes to the Plumian professorship of astronomy and experimental philosophy, a post he relinquished in 1760, in which year he was appointed master of mechanicks to George III, soon after the latter ascended the throne. He acted as vice-chancellor of the university (1742–3) and was master of Trinity from 1742 until his death in 1768. An Anglican, probably of a rather conventional hue, Smith was ordained at Norwich in 1738. He did not publish on theology, though he prepared a response to Zachary Grey's *Examination of the Fourteenth Chapter of Newton's Observations on Daniel*.

Although Smith often visited London, he was very much a creature of Cambridge University. His early career was moulded by his two patrons, Cotes and Richard Bentley (1662–1742). Soon after he entered Cambridge his interest in mathematics and natural philosophy was encouraged by Cotes, who appointed him as his assistant in the Plumian Observatory. When Smith received his fellowship Cotes warmly commended him as one of the few college tutors competent to teach both mathematics and recent developments in the physical sciences. His early reputation outside Cambridge and his first literary productions were due to his executorship of his cousin's will. In that capacity he edited two posthumous works by Cotes—*Harmonia mensurarum et alia opuscula mathematica* (1722) and *Hydrostatical and Pneumatical Lectures* (1738).

In college politics Smith invariably sided with Richard Bentley, the master of Trinity, who carried on a war of attrition against many of the fellows, and after Bentley's death, succeeded him as master. J. H. Monk, Bentley's biographer, claims that Smith was more conciliatory than his predecessor and healed divisions within the college. However, Winstanley shows that Smith's period as master was not without controversy, especially during the campaign to elect the university's high steward in 1763–4. With the impending death of the previous incumbent—the first earl of Hardwicke—the duke of Newcastle mobilized his supporters in favour of Hardwicke's son, Lord Royston. However, Smith threw his weight behind the government's nominee, the widely unpopular earl of Sandwich, whom he invited to dine at Trinity. When many

Robert Smith (*bap.* 1689, *d.* 1768), by John Vanderbank, 1730

of the students absented themselves from the dinner, he called a meeting of senior fellows to instigate disciplinary proceedings. Yet he succeeded in carrying the seniority only by arranging the meeting when some of the supporters of Royston (who had now succeeded to his father's title) were absent. Owing to widespread outrage at his underhand tactics the plan backfired. Winstanley, who described Smith as 'a pinchbeck Bentley', shows that in this incident he was highly unpopular and failed to gain the support of many of the fellows.

Contemporary comments indicate that Smith was a competent teacher of mathematics and natural philosophy but a severe examiner. He was also generous in providing encouragement and patronage to many younger scholars. For example, he supported Richard Cumberland's bid for a college fellowship, encouraged Richard Watson's undergraduate studies, and assisted Israel Lyons's mathematical researches. In elections to the Lucasian chair he supported John Colson (who won) in 1739, and William Ludlam (who lost) in 1760. But Smith's most enduring influence was through his benefactions to Cambridge and particularly to Trinity College. In 1758 he presented to the college library a bust of Cotes by Peter Scheemakers, and paid for improvements to the observatory situated over Trinity great gate. In his will he left £1750 to found the Smith's prizes, which were awarded annually to the two junior students who had made the greatest progress in mathematics and natural philosophy. These prizes were keenly sought after and became the badge of mathematical skill. Through these prizes Smith encouraged scientific studies at Cambridge, and many who later became major figures in British science scored their earliest successes in this stiff contest. Also through his will the Plumian bequest, out of which the professorship was financed, was augmented by £1750. He left South Sea stock worth £2000 to Trinity, which was used to finance a new combination room and a window in the college library depicting George III celebrating Newton. Another beneficiary was Edward Walpole, a close friend from their student days, who also received £2000 in South Sea stock.

The wider scientific community first noticed Smith as his cousin's literary executor and editor. Thus when he corresponded with Isaac Newton in 1718 discussion was restricted to the impending publication of his edition of Cotes's mathematical papers. This correspondence shows that Smith was keen to present his late cousin's work in the best possible light. Likewise, he first came to the notice of the Royal Society of London in November 1718, when one of the secretaries, Brook Taylor, wrote enquiring whether Smith would communicate 'some Curious Discoverys in Geometry' by the late Roger Cotes. In his reply Smith indicated that he was in the process of publishing Cotes's papers. A few weeks later he attended a meeting of the society under Newton's presidency and was proposed as a candidate. Elected on 5 February 1719 he was admitted a fellow on 21 May, together with Nicholas Saunderson, the Lucasian professor at Cambridge. Although he was not active in the society and never submitted a scientific communication, he bequeathed to it the sum of £100.

Newton's successes in optics and mechanics dominated Smith's scientific career, and through his teaching and publications he helped to spread Newton's ideas. Byrom's comment—'I told him [Smith] that he worshipped Sir Isaac'—suggests that his admiration for Newton extended well beyond merely acknowledging his scientific achievements. Yet, unlike several other young mathematicians of the period, Smith was not a direct recipient of Newton's patronage.

Smith's scientific reputation rests on two substantial works, *Compleat System of Opticks* (1738; a shortened version for students was issued in 1778) and *Harmonics, or, The Philosophy of Musical Sounds* (1749; 2nd edn, 1759; postscript, 1762; shortened version, 1778). The former work was dedicated to Edward Walpole and the latter to the duke of Cumberland, whom Smith had instructed in mathematics some twenty years prior to the book's publication. Both books were highly regarded by many later eminent scientists, including Hermann von Helmholtz and Lord Rayleigh, who both praised Smith's optical work. The *Opticks*, which was translated into both French and German, played a key role in the dissemination and systematization of Newton's theory of light. Emphasizing the particulate theory of light and the role of short-range forces, Smith showed how this theory could explain a range of optical phenomena. However, he omitted those aspects of Newton's *Opticks* that did not cohere well with this programme, such as the theory of 'fits'. Although the book opens with a short non-mathematical 'popular treatise', the mathematically informed sections proved more enduring. His extensive discussion of the formation of images by systems of lenses was particularly original. Here Smith exploited the method of image construction employing an unrefracted ray through the centre of the lens and a ray parallel to the optical axis that is then refracted through the focus. Another significant result was what is sometimes known as the Smith–Helmholtz equation, which directly connects the linear and angular magnifications for a system of thin lenses.

Music was both Smith's pastime and his other main scientific interest. He was an accomplished performer on several instruments, particularly the violoncello, and possessed a 'correct ear'. In his *Harmonics* he advocated the mean-tone temperament or method of tuning keyboard instruments. In the same work he contributed to the mathematical theory of music with an extended discussion of equal harmonic intervals. He directed the construction of the organ at the Foundling Hospital, which incorporated his system of alternative notes. Although his system found a champion in A. D. McClure in the 1940s, it has rarely been employed in keyboard instruments because of its complexity and the expense involved in constructing the instruments.

Smith never married but lived with his unmarried sister Elzimar (1683–1758) in the lodge at Trinity College. Although he is often portrayed as a rather reclusive character, Byrom's journal shows that in the 1720s and 1730s Smith could be quite sociable. Yet ill health, particularly gout, took its toll and severely inhibited his academic work and social activities. He died at the lodge on 2 February 1768, and on 8 February he was buried in Trinity College chapel, the funeral oration being delivered by Thomas Zouch. GEOFFREY CANTOR

Sources Venn, *Alum. Cant.* • D. A. Winstanley, *The University of Cambridge in the eighteenth century* (1922) • J. H. Monk, *The life of Richard Bentley, DD*, 2nd edn, 2 vols. (1833) • C. Wordsworth, *Scholae academicae: some account of the studies at the English universities in the eighteenth century* (1877) • *The private journal and literary remains of John Byrom*, ed. R. Parkinson, 2 vols. in 4 pts, Chetham Society, 32, 34, 40, 44 (1854–7) • *Correspondence of Sir Isaac Newton and Professor Cotes*, ed. J. Edleston (1850) • J. Gascoigne, *Cambridge in the age of the Enlightenment* (1989) • H. von Helmholtz, *Physiological optics*, ed. J. P. C. Southall, 3 vols. (1962) • L. S. Lloyd, 'Smith, Robert', *New Grove* • *The correspondence of Isaac Newton*, ed. H. W. Turnbull and others, 7 (1977) • journal book, 1703–13, RS, vol. 11 • parish register (baptism), 16 Oct 1689, Lea, Lincolnshire • *DNB*

Archives BL, corresp. with duke of Newcastle, Add. MSS 32699–32943, *passim*

Likenesses J. Vanderbank, oils, 1730, Trinity Cam. [*see illus.*] • J. Freeman, oils, 1783, Trinity Cam. • P. Scheemakers, marble bust, Trinity Cam.

Wealth at death over £7600 known benefactions

Smith, Robert (1722–1777), carpenter and architect, was born at Lugton, a hamlet 8 miles south-west of Edinburgh, on 14 January 1722, the son of John Smith, a baxter (or baker), and Martha, *née* Lawrie. His parents were poor tenants of the wealthy and powerful duchess of Buccleuch. We know nothing of Robert Smith's boyhood and apprenticeship as a carpenter. He first comes to light in Philadelphia in 1749 working for the governor of Pennsylvania,

James Hamilton, at his showy new suburban establishment, Bush Hill (1749–51). It seems likely that Smith had been recruited in Britain by Hamilton, who referred to him as 'my carpenter'.

Smith soon after got another commission, shared with Gunning Bedford, a house carpenter from Delaware, to design and erect the large Second Presbyterian Church for a 'New Light' congregation on the north side of Philadelphia (1750–52). This impressive brick structure was remarkable for its long-span wooden roof trusses. These were new to Philadelphia and probably account for the large number of commissions Smith won from the religious community in and around the city. One of the first of these was to provide Christ Church with a steeple comprising an octagonal frame faced with shingles. The steeple, which has suffered damage over the years, still survives, and is much admired as one of the architect's major achievements. The skills in structural design that Smith brought to the steeple would again be evident in the late 1760s in his unrealized plan for a multiple-span covered bridge over Philadelphia's Schuylkil River.

Smith's next project for a religious group was at the College of New Jersey, then relocating to Princeton, for which he designed and constructed Nassau Hall (1754–7). Built of local sandstone, three storeys high, and topped by a bell turret, the hall, which served as both a residential and teaching facility, was one of the most ambitious structures completed in mid-eighteenth-century America. Despite suffering two devastating fires, the hall has been twice restored and is still in use. In order to superintend the work Smith moved to Princeton with his wife, Esther Jones (*d.* in or before 1777), whom he had married in December 1749, and their children. During the same period he also built a house for the college's president, which exhibits interior panelling of Philadelphia character.

Back in Philadelphia by 1755, Smith began a long construction programme for the College of Philadelphia. The first phase consisted of dividing up a huge preaching hall—initially built to accommodate the audience of the evangelist George Whitfield—into teaching rooms and lecture theatres. In addition Smith erected a new row of brick structures, the New Building (1761–4), and a large brick house for Provost Ewing (1774–5).

Other public buildings on which Smith worked in the 1750s include the landmark Pennsylvania Hospital, for which construction was organized by the master builder Samuel Rhoades. Smith joined the team early on, and is believed to have drawn up the plans for the first unit, a T-shaped structure, capped with a handsome octagonal cupola, entered from 8th Street. The western stem adjoining contained two storeys of patients' wards, while the cellars were designed for the care of the insane. Smith's involvement in the project may have led to his commission to design the Hospital for the Mad and Insane, later the Eastern State Hospital, at Williamsburg, Virginia (1771).

In 1763 Smith began constructing a house for Benjamin Franklin in a courtyard off Market Street in Philadelphia. During his frequent absences on public business Franklin was represented at the site by his friend Samuel Rhoades, who worked directly with Smith as the architect and builder. The result of their collaboration was a 34 feet square brick house. It was later demolished, but its foundations remain an archaeological curiosity in a tourist park.

The success of the Second Presbyterian Church, praised at the time by Franklin, resulted in Smith's being involved in all Philadelphia's major church-building projects during the 1760s and 1770s. In some instances, like St Peter's (1758–61) on Society Hill, Smith handled both the design and construction, for which we have the documents. For others, like St Paul's (1761), he designed the roof and the bell turret. St Paul's, then the largest house of worship in America, was superseded by Smith's own Zion Lutheran Church (1766–9), with space for a seated congregation of 3000. Other works from this period are a steeple for the Second Presbyterian Church (1762–3), a roof design for the Third Presbyterian, known as Old Pine (1767–8), and the large stone Presbyterian church on the frontier at Carlisle, Pennsylvania, for which he was paid £5.

Later commissions include one of Smith's best-known designs, Carpenter's Hall in Philadelphia (1770–74), which survives as a landmark of the revolutionary era. At the end of his life Smith was deeply involved with the defence of the city from the threat of the British navy. He designed a system of underwater obstructions, which delayed for many weeks the occupation of Philadelphia by the British, severely damaging their war effort. Robert Smith died on 11 February 1777 while working for the continental army on barracks at Billingsport, New Jersey. He was buried in an unmarked grave in a Quaker burial-ground. A notice in the *Pennsylvania Evening Post* (13 February 1777) said '[Smith was] a worthy and ingenious man … Several public buildings in the city and environs are ornaments to his great abilities'. CHARLES E. PETERSON

Sources *An historical catalogue of the St. Andrew's Society of Philadelphia with biographical sketches of deceased members, 1749–1907* (1907) • J. Jackson, *Early Philadelphia architects and engineers* (1923) • C. P. Stacey, 'Smith, Robert', *DAB* • C. Bridenbaugh and J. Bridenbaugh, *Rebels and gentlemen: Philadelphia in the age of Franklin* (1942) • C. E. Peterson, 'Carpenters' Hall', *Transactions of the American Philosophical Society*, 43 (1953), 96–128 • D. R. Smith, *Robert Smith, 1722–1777: Dalkeith to Philadelphia* (1982) • C. E. Peterson, 'Robert Smith, 1722–1777', *Macmillan encyclopedia of architects*, ed. A. K. Placzek, 4 vols. (1982) • S. L. Tatman and R. W. Moss, *Biographical dictionary of Philadelphia architects, 1700–1930* (1985) • C. E. Peterson, 'Robert Smith, Philadelphia builder–architect: from Dalkeith to Princeton', *Scotland and America in the age of enlightenment*, ed. R. B. Sher and J. R. Smitten (1990), 275–99 • C. E. Peterson, 'Smith, Robert', *ANB* • L. Hall, 'Artificer to architect in America', PhD diss., Radcliffe College, Harvard U., 1954 • R. W. Moss, 'Master builders: a history of the colonial Philadelphia building trades', PhD diss., University of Delaware, 1972 • C. E. Peterson, *Robert Smith: architect, builder, patriot, 1722–1777* (2000)

Smith, Robert, **first Baron Carrington** (1752–1838), banker and politician, was born at Nottingham on 22 January 1752, the third but eldest surviving son of Abel *Smith (1717?–1788), banker and merchant, and his wife, Mary, daughter of the silk manufacturer Thomas Bird of Barton,

Warwickshire. He became a partner in his father's banking firm of Smith, Payne & Co. of Nottingham and on the death of his elder brother Abel in 1779 he succeeded him as MP for Nottingham, which he represented in five successive parliaments. He married on 6 July 1780 Anne (*d.* 1827), eldest daughter of Lewyns Boldero Barnard of Cave Castle, Yorkshire; they had one son and eleven daughters. Smith succeeded as head of the banking firm after his father's death in 1788.

From the outset of his parliamentary career, Smith attached himself to the fortunes of the younger Pitt, and a close friendship sprang up between the two. In 1786 Pitt selected Smith to examine the state of his disordered private financial affairs. According to Wraxall, Smith's character was 'without reproach and his fortune ample, but he possessed no parliamentary talents' and 'was considered decidedly Ministerial on all questions' (*Historical and Posthumous Memoirs*, 3.391). He was generous in the use of his wealth; one of his benefactions was to the poet William Cowper for the benefit of the poor at Olney. On 11 July 1796, as a reward for his fidelity and support which he secured to Pitt through his pocket boroughs of Midhurst and Wendover, Smith was created Baron Carrington of Bulcot Lodge in the peerage of Ireland, and on 20 October 1797 Baron Carrington of Upton, Nottinghamshire, in the peerage of the United Kingdom. According to Wraxall, this was the only occasion in which George III's objections to giving British peerages to tradesmen were overcome. In 1802 he was appointed captain of Deal by Pitt, who was warden of the Cinque Ports, and in the following year he became lieutenant-colonel of the 2nd battalion of the Cinque Ports Volunteers.

After Pitt's death Carrington supported Lord Grenville for a time before returning to mainstream toryism. In his later years, when he was unable to attend the House of Lords, he entrusted his proxy to the duke of Wellington. He was created DCL of Oxford in 1810 and LLD of Cambridge in 1819, and was also a vice-president of the Literary Fund, FRS (1800), and FSA (1812). In his eighty-third year he married his second wife, Charlotte (1770–1849), widow of the Revd Walter Trevelyan of Henbury, Gloucestershire, and third daughter of John Hudson of Bessingby, Yorkshire, at Bath on 19 January 1836.

Carrington died at his house, 26 St James's Place, Whitehall, on 18 September 1838 and was buried at High Wycombe on 3 October. He was succeeded by his son, Robert John Smith (1796–1868), who took the name Carrington instead of Smith by royal licence.

A. F. Pollard, *rev.* Stephen M. Lee

Sources I. R. Christie, 'Smith, Robert', HoP, *Commons, 1754–90* • P. A. Symonds and R. G. Thorne, 'Smith, Robert', HoP, *Commons, 1790–1820* • *The historical and the posthumous memoirs of Sir Nathaniel William Wraxall, 1772–1784*, ed. H. B. Wheatley, 5 vols. (1884) • Earl Stanhope [P. H. Stanhope], *Life of the Right Honourable William Pitt*, 4 vols. (1861–2) • Foster, *Alum. Oxon.* • *GM*, 2nd ser., 5 (1836), 305 • *GM*, 2nd ser., 10 (1838), 545–6, 678–9 • *Annual Register* (1838) • GEC, *Peerage* • M. I. Thomis, *Politics and society in Nottingham, 1785–1835* (1969) • *The works of William Cowper*, ed. R. Southey, 8 vols. (1853–4) • *IGI*

Archives Bucks. RLSS, diaries, D/CN/D2 • Norfolk RO, letters • NRA, priv. coll., diaries | BL, corresp. with Lord Grenville, Add. MSS 58983, 69044 • BL, letters to A. Young, Add. MSS 35128–35132, *passim* • CKS, letters to Lord Stanhope and Lady Stanhope

Likenesses M. Gauci, lithograph (after J. Reynolds), BM • M. Gauci, lithograph (in peer's robes), BM • G. Hayter, group portrait, oils (*The trial of Queen Caroline, 1820*), NPG

Wealth at death £120,000: *GM*, 2nd ser., 10, 679

Smith, Robert Archibald (1780–1829), composer, was born on 16 November 1780 in Reading, the only surviving child of Robert Smith, a silk weaver, and his wife, Ann Whitcher. His father, from East Kilbride, Lanarkshire, had been a silk weaver in Paisley, but left Scotland because of the depression in his trade, and settled in Reading in 1774. Smith entered his father's workshop. He sang in a church choir and played the flute in the band of a volunteer regiment. In 1800 the family moved back to Paisley, and Smith and his father became muslin weavers. In 1802 Smith married Mary MacNicol, from the island of Arran; they had five children. He hated his work as a weaver, and in 1803 he gave it up to teach music, especially choral singing, and he also joined the Paisley volunteer band.

In 1807 Smith was appointed precentor of the abbey church, Paisley. The standard of psalm singing at the church had been low, and Smith formed a choir and devoted himself to its training. Its reputation grew, and people came from far and wide to hear the singing; even to be admitted to choir practices required a ticket. In 1817 the Abbey Harmonic Choir gave the first of a series of very successful recitals in the abbey church. But there were some complaints that, in concentrating on the choir, Smith had neglected congregational singing. In 1823 he became precentor and choirmaster of St George's Church, Edinburgh, where Dr Andrew Thomson was minister, and again he improved the singing of psalms. His choir gave concerts both in Edinburgh and elsewhere, including a performance at the York music festival in 1825.

But it was as a composer that Smith was best remembered. A friend of the poet Robert Tannahill, he set many of the latter's poems to music. The most famous was 'Jessie, the Flow'r o' Dumblane'. Smith collected more than 600 songs in the *Scotish Minstrel*, which was published in six volumes between 1821 and 1824 and included, anonymously, many of his own songs. The *Irish Minstrel* appeared in 1825. His collections of church music include *Devotional Music* (1810), *Sacred Harmony for the Use of St George's, Edinburgh* (1820), which he published in collaboration with Dr Andrew Thomson, and *Sacred Music* (1825). Among his most popular works were his setting of the anthem 'How beautiful upon the mountains' and the hymn tune 'Invocation'.

Smith's moving to Scotland was later regarded as the beginning of a new era in the music of the Scottish church. He was seen as the greatest Scottish choir trainer since the Reformation and the most outstanding Scottish religious composer of his day.

After many years of poor health, Smith died in Edinburgh on 3 January 1829, and was buried in St Cuthbert's churchyard there. Anne Pimlott Baker

Sources J. Love, *Scottish church music* (1891) • M. Patrick, *Four centuries of Scottish psalmody* (1949) • P. A. Ramsay, ed., *The poetical works of Robert Tannahill* (*c.*1840) [with memoir of R. A. Smith] • H. G. Farmer,

A history of music in Scotland (1947) • D. Baptie, ed., *Musical Scotland, past and present: being a dictionary of Scottish musicians from about 1400 till the present time* (1894) • D. Johnson, *Music and society in lowland Scotland in the eighteenth century* (1972) • M. B. Foster, *Anthems and anthem composers* (1901), 138 • *New Grove* • *DNB*

Archives U. Glas. L., corresp. with William Motherwell

Likenesses painting, 1822; formerly in possession of his widow

Smith, Robert Cross [*pseud.* Raphael] (**1795–1832**), astrologer and journalist, was born on 19 March 1795 to respectable parents in Abbots Leigh near Bristol. By 1820 he had found work as a clerk in London. In the summer of that year he married Sarah Lucas, with whom he had six children. Known to his readers as Raphael, or Merlinus Anglicus Jun., he was a key figure in the revival of astrology in the nineteenth century. He edited the first weekly astrological journal in 1824 and from 1826 produced a successful almanac, the *Prophetic Messenger*, whose copyright was keenly sought after his death. His style was popular and dramatic: he wrote of astrology as an exclusive and learned practice, but his work linked it to popular tales of the supernatural. Of delicate health, Smith died of consumption at his home in Castle Street East, London, on 26 February 1832. KATHARINE ANDERSON

Sources Raphael [R. C. Smith], *The astrologer of the nineteenth century*, 7th edn (1825), 435–6 • Zadkiel [R. J. Morrison], 'Horoscope of Raphael', *Royal book of fate*, 4th edn (1833), xiv–xvi • E. Howe, *Urania's children* (1967) • P. Curry, *A confusion of prophets: Victorian and Edwardian astrology* (1992)

Archives Wellcome L., papers

Wealth at death £1000: 1833, Zadkiel, 'Horoscope'

Smith, Robert Henry Soden (**1822–1890**), museum curator, was born on 25 February 1822, the son of Robert Smith of Dirleton, East Lothian, Scotland, a captain in the 44th regiment, who served in India, and subsequently settled in Dublin when appointed Athlone pursuivant-at-arms. His son Robert, brought up in Scotland, was sent to Trinity College, Dublin, with a view to ordination, but preferred antiquarian studies. After some time as tutor to John Charles Pratt, earl of Brecknock, later third Marquess Camden, he found a niche at the South Kensington Museum, London, which opened to the public on 24 June 1857.

Smith joined the museum on 19 March 1857 and helped to display the pictures in the collection recently donated by John Sheepshanks. On 25 June he was confirmed in the post of assistant keeper of the art library, reporting to the curator of the museum, J. C. Robinson, whom he assisted in 1862 with the huge, epoch-making loan exhibition, 'Works of art of the medieval, Renaissance, and more recent periods', drawn from British private collections. Unfortunately, tension arose in the museum between the scholarly connoisseur Robinson and the director, Henry Cole, who was intent on advancing design reform, art education, and managerial efficiency. As a result, Robinson was forced out in 1863, and his followers among the staff, including Smith, remained disaffected and out of favour. Doubtless Smith was sustained by what was described as 'eminent courtesy' (*The Athenaeum*, 28 June 1890, 839), 'extreme urbanity' (by his successor, W. H. J. Weale, in *Transactions … of … Second International Library Conference … London … 1897*, 1898, 97), and 'never varying geniality' (by his executor Charles Hercules Read, MS letter to Fortnum, 1 July 1890, Fortnum MSS). Such serenity was constantly needed when, after being transferred in 1863 to South Kensington's Education Museum, he returned in 1866 to head the art library (confirmed in post on 1 April 1868), and found himself obliged frequently to apologize for its cramped quarters. Courageously he highlighted this problem in his annual reports, and in May 1878 work began on a new library. After many building delays, Smith opened the new library on 1 October 1884 in the three handsome rooms which it still occupied at the end of the twentieth century.

As he explained in his thorough reports, Smith's task was to build up the holdings of books on art, architecture, and decorative arts, not forgetting art topography and local antiquities. A series of seventeen classified subject bibliographies, published by the museum from 1875, demonstrates his grasp of this body of literature. From the start, Smith also set himself to collect books that exemplified fine printing, book ornament, bookbinding, and manuscript illumination. Until 1909 the library was also responsible for the museum's graphic holdings, and Smith was active in acquiring prints and drawings by historic and contemporary designers. He pursued with special enthusiasm engraved ornament by the German Little Masters of the sixteenth century, and Japanese book illustration. Photographs were also in his charge.

With Robinson, Smith moved in a circle of antiquarian scholars, such as A. W. Franks (in charge of medieval art at the British Museum), C. H. Read (who worked for Smith before becoming Franks's assistant, and, eventually, successor), and the collector Charles Drury Fortnum. Like his British Museum friends, Smith was interested in the relation of art to ethnology, on which he lectured to the Associated Arts' Institute in 1868. He was elected a fellow of the Society of Antiquaries on 27 February 1862, but was more active in the Archaeological Institute, which he joined about the same time. His many contributions to its meetings are recorded in the *Archaeological Journal*, which considered him 'an accurate interpreter of objects of art of varied interest' (47.418). His eclectic expertise was evident also in the range of his publications, occasional rather than systematically focused. His interests as a collector included finger rings; and the Department of Science and Art's museum at Edinburgh exhibited, with brief catalogues, his collections of Chinese and Japanese bronzes (1889–90), and of English pottery (1889–91), which were sold after his death. In natural history his chosen subject was fresh-water shells. To accommodate his collections in his retirement, he bought a house in Hammersmith, but died while still in office on 20 June 1890, at a nursing home at 12 Hollis Street, Cavendish Square, London, having never married. His superiors discovered that 'there is apparently no relative to whom a letter of regret and condolence could be written' (*Précis*, 20 June 1890).

ANTHONY BURTON

Sources C. D. E. Fortnum, *The Academy* (5 July 1890), 16 • AM Oxf., Fortnum MSS • *First … report of the department of science and art*, 46

vols. (1854–99) [for 1853–1898] • *Précis of the board minutes of the science and art department, 1852–1892*, 8 vols. (1864–93) • *The Athenaeum* (28 June 1890), 839–40 • *Proceedings of the Society of Antiquaries of London*, 2nd ser., 13 (1889–91), 313–14 • *ILN* (12 July 1890), 53 [with portrait] • E. James, *The Victoria and Albert Museum: a bibliography and exhibition chronology, 1852–96* (1998) • *CGPLA Eng. & Wales* (1890)

Likenesses photograph, *c*.1880–1889, V&A; repro. in *ILN* (12 July 1890), 53 • H. R. Hope-Pinker, terracotta medallion, 1884, V&A

Wealth at death £4844 1*s*. 11*d*. in UK: probate, 15 Aug 1890, *CGPLA Eng. & Wales*

Smith, Sir Robert Murdoch (1835–1900), archaeologist and diplomatist, second son of Hugh Smith (*d*. 1856), surgeon and medical practitioner at Kilmarnock, and his wife, Jean, *née* Murdoch, was born at Bank Street, Kilmarnock, on 18 August 1835. He was educated at Kilmarnock Academy and at Glasgow University (where he was a pupil of Lord Kelvin), and in September 1855 he was one of the first to obtain by open competition a commission in the Royal Engineers. In 1856–9 he commanded the party of sappers which accompanied the archaeological expedition under Charles Thomas Newton to Asia Minor, the principal results of which were the discovery of the mausoleum at Halicarnassus and the acquisition—under a firman of the Porte—for the British Museum of the magnificent sculptures from that monument. It was Smith who discovered the real site of the mausoleum. He described the excavations in his *Discoveries at Halicarnassus, Cnidus, and Branchidae* (1862).

In November 1860, with Lieutenant E. A. Porcher, Smith started on another adventurous expedition, at his own expense but under government sanction, to explore the ancient cities of the Cyrenaica in north Africa. For a year the two officers excavated at and about Cyrene, and returned with many valuable Greek sculptures and inscriptions, which they placed at the disposal of the government and which were housed in the British Museum. Smith described the expedition in *History of the Recent Discoveries at Cyrene* (1864), illustrated from drawings by Porcher.

After a period of fortification duties in the War Office Smith was selected in August 1863 for special service on the Persian section of the proposed telegraph line from England to India. Permission to construct the line through Persia had been obtained only after much difficulty and delay, and the officers had to contend not only with great physical difficulties but with Persian hostility and distrust from the shah downwards. All these difficulties, however, were overcome, and the line was successfully completed. Smith acted first as superintendent of the Tehran–Kohrud section. In 1865 he succeeded Major John Bateman Champain as director of the Persian telegraph at Tehran. He filled this post with notable ability and success for twenty years: the working of the line reached a high standard of efficiency, and he was successful in conciliating local feeling. An excellent Persian scholar, he won the esteem and trust of the Persian ministers and princes with whom he dealt, including the shah, Nasir al-Din, who in 1885 presented him with a sword of honour. In 1869 Smith married Eleanor, eldest daughter of Captain John Robinet Baker RN (she died in Persia in 1883). Of their nine children, seven died in Persia—three on three consecutive days at Kashan.

When in Persia Smith developed a real understanding of Persian culture, and devoted much time and attention to collecting Persian art objects for the South Kensington (later Victoria and Albert) Museum. His skill in selecting material and negotiating acquisition was highly regarded. In May 1885 he became director of the Edinburgh Museum of Science and Art, and returned to Britain; he continued director until his death. In 1887 he became director-in-chief of the Indo-European telegraph department on the death of Sir John Champain. In the same year he was sent on a special mission to Persia to resolve the differences with the Persian government over the occupation of Jask by British-Indian troops. This question was settled to the satisfaction of both governments. Other questions were also discussed, and Smith succeeded in obtaining a prolongation to 1905 of the two existing telegraph conventions, which would otherwise have expired in 1888 and 1895 respectively. On leaving Tehran he was presented by the shah with a diamond snuff-box, and on his return to England he was made KCMG (10 January 1888) in recognition of his services in Persia.

Shortly afterwards the office to which Smith had been appointed in 1887 was, on his own recommendation, abolished as unnecessary. He had retired from the army in December 1887 with the rank of major-general. Henceforward his work lay in the Edinburgh Museum. It was greatly enlarged, the administration improved, and many valuable objects, especially in the department of eastern art, were acquired. He was largely responsible for a gradual redefinition of the term 'art' as applied to museum collections. The Edinburgh Museum already had a substantial collection of decorative arts material, but it was perceived and represented largely in terms of industrial art, although there were examples from ancient civilizations and non-European areas. Under Smith's direction collecting in these fields became more deliberate, and this in turn attracted loans and donations. The museum benefited from Scottish enterprise in distant places, and Smith himself brought back collections of Persian art. Smith was a member of the board of trustees for manufactures in Scotland and chairman of the committee of the Scottish National Portrait Gallery.

Among Smith's minor writings were his treatise on Persian art, issued by the Department of Science and Art in 1876, a paper entitled 'The strategy of Russia in central Asia' (*Journal of the United Service Institution*, 17, 1874, 212–22), and a lecture to the Society of Arts, 'The Karun river as a trade route' (*Journal of the Society of Arts*, 37, 1888–9, 561–7), for which he was awarded the society's silver medal. In February 1899 he was awarded the freedom of Kilmarnock. Smith died at his home, 50 Moray Place, Edinburgh, on 3 July 1900, and was buried in the Dean cemetery, Edinburgh. He was survived by two daughters.

George Stronach, *rev*. Roger T. Stearn

Sources W. K. Dickson, *Life of Major-General Sir Robert Murdoch Smith* (1901) • *The Scotsman* (5 July 1900) • G. N. Curzon, *Persia and the*

Persian question (1892) • F. J. Goldsmid, *Telegraph and travel* (1874) • *Scottish Geographical Magazine*, 5 (1889) • *The Scotsman* (26 Oct 1896) • *Royal Engineers Journal* (30 Sept 1900) • private information (1901) • J. B. Kelly, *Britain and the Persian Gulf, 1795–1880* (1968) • D. McLean, *Britain and her buffer state: the collapse of the Persian empire, 1890–1914* (1979) • D. R. Headrick, *The tentacles of progress: technology transfer in the age of imperialism, 1850–1940* (1988) • *WWW* • Boase, *Mod. Eng. biog.* • Kelly, *Handbk* (1893)
Archives NL Scot., corresp. and papers | NL Scot., corresp. with his father, and copies of letters
Wealth at death £13,068 3*s*. 1*d*.: confirmation, 22 Aug 1900, *CCI*

Smith, Robert Payne (1818–1895), orientalist and theologian, was born in Chipping Campden, Gloucestershire, on 7 November 1818, the only son and second of four children of Robert Smith (*d*. 1827), a land agent, and his wife, Esther Argles Payne, of Leggsheath, Surrey. The Smiths and the Paynes were both old but impoverished families of gentry. He attended Chipping Campden grammar school, and was also taught Hebrew by his gifted eldest sister, Esther. In 1837 he obtained an exhibition at Pembroke College, Oxford, where he studied classics, in which he graduated with second-class honours in 1841, and oriental languages. He gained the Boden Sanskrit scholarship in 1840 and the Pusey and Ellerton Hebrew scholarship in 1843; the same year he became a fellow of his college and was ordained deacon, then priest a year later. He was a popular classics tutor but later left Oxford and undertook successively the curacies of Crendon and Long Winchendon, Buckinghamshire, and of Thame. In 1847 he accepted a classical mastership at the Edinburgh Academy. From 1848 he was also the incumbent of Trinity Chapel, Dean Bridge, Edinburgh. In 1850 he married Catherine (*d*. 25 Jan 1894), second daughter of the Revd William Freeman of Langley; they had two sons and four daughters, one of whom, Jessie Payne Smith, married the orientalist David Samuel *Margoliouth and became a noted orientalist herself [*see* Margoliouth, Jessie Payne]. In 1853 he left Edinburgh to become headmaster of the Kensington proprietary grammar school. In London he resumed his oriental studies, learning Arabic and working on the Syriac manuscripts in the British Museum, with the encouragement of William Cureton.

In order to spend more time on Syriac, and because Kensington did not suit his wife's health, Payne Smith accepted in 1857 an assistant sub-librarianship created for him at the Bodleian Library, Oxford, even though this involved a drop in salary from £1000 to £300. He gained the respect of Syriac scholars throughout Europe after he published Cyril of Alexandria's commentary on St Luke's gospel, in Syriac (1858) and English (1859), and a translation, *The Third Part of the 'Ecclesiastical History' of John, bishop of Ephesus* (1860), which Cureton had edited in Syriac. But his main task as sub-librarian was to catalogue the 205 Syriac manuscripts then in the Bodleian; he completed the catalogue in 1864. His work on these publications made him aware of the need for a better Syriac dictionary, and in 1860 he began work on his *magnum opus*, the *Thesaurus Syriacus*, which occupied him for the rest of his life; the first fascicle appeared in 1868. He incorporated into it the unfinished work of several earlier Syriac lexicographers, including S. M. Quatremère, G. H. Bernstein, and Frederick Field, who had handed on their papers to him for this purpose; he also utilized the numerous Syriac texts published in Europe at this period and every other available source. The eventual result was a major monument of lexicography, running to 2258 folio-size pages, and started a new era in Syriac studies.

Payne Smith also began to write on controversial theology, favouring the conservative evangelical side. This led to an unexpected improvement in his fortunes, when his friend Francis Jeune, bishop of Peterborough, who had been master of Pembroke, persuaded him to send a copy of his sermons vindicating *The Authenticity and Messianic Interpretation of the Prophecies of Isaiah* (1862) to Lord Shaftesbury, who was so impressed that he influenced the prime minister to appoint Payne Smith regius professor of divinity at Oxford and rector of Ewelme in 1865. He was made DD in the same year, and in 1869 he delivered the Bampton lectures, published as *Prophecy: a Preparation for Christ* (1870). As regius professor he played a leading part in establishing the new honour school of theology, and was one of the first examiners in 1870. In January 1871 he resigned the chair to accept Gladstone's offer of the deanery of Canterbury. As dean he was noted for his successes both in improving the cathedral services and in the repair and modernization of its fabric, which had been damaged by fire.

Payne Smith had been a delicate child, but cured this at Oxford by taking up rowing and riding, and remained active well into old age. His other outdoor pursuits were walking and gardening. Originally influenced by the Oxford Movement, after 1845 he became a moderate evangelical, and was made one of the Simeon trustees, a group which sought to promote by securing appointments for its members. In 1873 he went to the USA to take part in conferences organized by the Evangelical Alliance in New York. He was respected on all sides for his broad sympathies and genial temper, and was held never to have made an enemy, despite his involvement in some of the most heated ecclesiastical debates of the time, serving as he did on the 1867–8 ritual commission and on the Old Testament revision committee from 1870 to 1885. At Canterbury he endeared himself to nonconformists and even Roman Catholics by making the cathedral more accessible to their use. In politics he began as a strong liberal and ended a conservative, but was always concerned to improve social conditions, especially education. He helped to found both Wycliffe Hall, Oxford, of which he remained chairman of council until his death, and the South-Eastern College, Ramsgate, and was active in setting up the church schools in the Canterbury area that were named the Payne Smith schools in his memory. He was also a founder member of the Palaeographical Society (1873).

Payne Smith died at his deanery on 31 March 1895 and was buried on 3 April in St Martin's churchyard, Canterbury. He had lived to publish nine fascicles of his great Syriac dictionary; the final one was seen through the press

(1901) by his second daughter, Jessie, and her husband. Jessie also brought out an abridged version, entitled *A Compendious Syriac Dictionary* (1903), and a *Supplement to the 'Thesaurus Syriacus'* (1927). Another daughter, Mary, wrote a memoir of her father's life, which she prefixed to his final work, *Sermons on the Pentateuch* (1896). R. S. SIMPSON

Sources R. Payne Smith, *Sermons on the Pentateuch: with a memoir of the author* (1896) • *Robert Payne Smith, D.D., dean of Canterbury*, Canterbury Cathedral (1895) [memorial vol.] • 'The dean of Canterbury', *Church Portrait Journal*, new ser., 5 (1884), 1–4 • *The Times* (1 April 1895), 6d • *The Times* (2 April 1895), 9f • *The Guardian* (3 April 1895) • Foster, *Alum. Oxon.* • Crockford (1895) • Boase, *Mod. Eng. biog.*, 2.1406–7 • W. D. Macray, *Annals of the Bodleian Library, Oxford*, 2nd edn (1890) • 'Margoliouth, David Samuel', *DNB*
Archives Bodl. Oxf., corresp. • Canterbury Cathedral, archives, family papers | BL, letters to W. E. Gladstone, Add. MSS 44408–44416 • DWL, letters to Christopher Walton • LPL, corresp. with A. C. Tait
Likenesses J. Corbett, oils, 1871, the deanery, Canterbury • A. E. Fradelle, photograph, 1884, repro. in 'The dean of Canterbury', 1 • M. R. Corbet, oils, 1886, deanery, Canterbury; repro. in P. Collinson, N. Ramsay, and M. Sparks, eds., *A history of Canterbury Cathedral* (1995), pl. 48 • line engraving (after photograph by Russell & Sons), repro. in *ILN*, 106 (Jan–June 1895), 406
Wealth at death £16,783 11*s*. 5*d*.: resworn probate, Aug 1896, *CGPLA Eng. & Wales* (1895)

Smith, Robert Percy [*known as* Bobus Smith] (1770–1845), judge in India, was the eldest son of Robert Smith (1739/40–1827) of Bishop's Lydiard, Somerset, and Maria (*c*.1750–1801), daughter of Isaac Olier of Bloomsbury, Middlesex, and the brother of Sydney *Smith. He was born on 7 May 1770 and was educated at King Edward's School, Southampton, and from 1782 until 1788 at Eton College. In 1786, with his intimates John Hookham Frere, George Canning, and Henry Fox, third Lord Holland, he launched *The Microcosm*, which ran for forty issues and had the distinction of being bought out by a commercial publisher. In 1789 he entered King's College, Cambridge. He took his BA in 1794 and MA in 1797 and was a fellow of King's from 1792 until 1797. Exceptionally gifted at Latin (which is probably why he acquired the nickname Bobus), in 1791 he was awarded Sir William Browne's medal for the best Latin ode. In 1797 he was called to the bar at Lincoln's Inn.

On 9 December 1797 he married Caroline Maria, daughter of Richard Vernon, MP for Tavistock, and closely related to three of the foremost Whig families in the country: the Russells, the Foxes, and the Lansdownes. The Smiths were poor and in spite of Robert's protestations of independence he was eventually forced to accept help from Caroline's connections. In 1802 Henry Petty-Fitzmaurice, the third marquess of Lansdowne, through his friend Sir Francis Baring, procured for Smith the office of advocate-general of Bengal with a salary of £5,000 per year and an expectation of that much again in private fees. Smith apparently cut a flamboyant figure in India. Sir James Mackintosh reported that 'His fame among the natives is greater than that of any pandit since the days of Manu' (*GM*, 441). He returned from India in 1811 with his fortune enhanced, reportedly to the tune of £150,000, and his reputation for dogmatic and immoderate argument much diminished. He was now able to contribute handsomely to the upkeep of his father (who was not always grateful) and siblings.

In 1812 Smith entered parliament as the member for Grantham. Initially he allied himself with his old schoolfriend George Canning but he disliked party politics and was never obviously a tory or a whig. His maiden speech was a disappointment, especially to those who knew him privately to be articulate and witty, and his most valuable parliamentary service was as a committee man. He was anti-evangelical and in the debates over the renewal of the East India Company's charter he opposed the entry of Christian missions to British India and advocated the education of Indians in their own cultural tradition. In 1814 Canning offered him a seat on the India board but, devastated by the death of one of his daughters, he turned it down. In the general election of 1818 he stood unsuccessfully for Lincoln on a whig interest; subsequently, in 1820, he won the seat. The whigs expected him to vote with them only nine times out of ten. He retired from parliament in 1826.

Smith never attained the fame of his brother Sydney, although many of his friends believed that his originality of thought and wit surpassed those of his brother. He died within a fortnight of Sydney on 10 March 1845 at his house in Savile Row, London. Of his two sons and two daughters, only the elder son, Robert Vernon Smith [*see* Vernon, Robert], survived to adulthood.

E. I. CARLYLE, *rev.* KATHERINE PRIOR

Sources HoP, *Commons* • Venn, *Alum. Cant.* • *GM*, 2nd ser., 23 (1845), 440–41, 667 • P. Virgin, *Sydney Smith* (1994) • BL OIOC, Smith MSS
Archives BL OIOC, corresp., MS Eur. C 247 • BL OIOC, papers, MS Eur. C 231 | BL, letters to Lord and Lady Holland, Add. MS 51801
Wealth at death under £180,000: *GM*, 667

Smith, Robert Vernon. *See* Vernon, Robert, first Baron Lyveden (1800–1873).

Smith, Robert William Innes (1872–1933), physician and medical historian, was born at North Bridge, Edinburgh, on 26 December 1872, the eldest of the three sons of William Smith (1848–1931), chemist and inventor, and his wife, Louisa Selina Campbell-Colquhoun (1847–1923), daughter of John Ferguson of the Lairg, Glenledknock, Perthshire. At birth his father gave him the name of Innes (referring to his own coheiress great-grandmother, a descendant of the twelfth chief of clan Innes). He used Innes as part of his surname from 1895.

Smith was educated in Edinburgh at Daniel Stewart's College and graduated MB CM at Edinburgh University in 1894. He qualified MRCS, LRCP, London, in 1900. He spent a period on postgraduate work at Ancoats Hospital, Manchester, and then at King's College Hospital, London, and gained his MD degree at Edinburgh in 1902. In 1896 he married Blythe Simpson Chalmers (*d.* 1957), with whom he had four children.

Innes Smith spent almost all of his professional life in Sheffield, in general practice. However, he also became surgeon to the major steel firm of Vickers Sons and

Maxim Ltd, and was much called upon there and elsewhere as a result of the expertise he had developed as a medical referee not long after the Workmen's Compensation Act of 1897. At that time, in heavy industry in particular, both management and the workforce were having to adapt to the deep social impact of that act. Because of his special skill Innes Smith was called as an official witness in 1907 at the hearing of the royal commission on the poor laws and relief of distress. He was the moving force behind the initiation of the Sheffield Works Ambulance Movement, having shown that the severe injuries sustained by employees in heavy industry could justify a large firm in running its own ambulance. He was also an Admiralty surgeon for twenty years, a fellow of the Royal Society of Medicine, and a member of the Sheffield Medico-Chirurgical Society; and he was involved in many charitable organizations, becoming honorary secretary (later president) of the West Riding Medical Charitable Society and vice-president of the Royal Medical Foundation of Epsom College, for whom he raised large sums of money.

Throughout his dedicated and busy life Innes Smith took the keenest interest in medical history, and in 1927 he was vice-president of the section of the history of medicine at the 95th annual meeting of the British Medical Association. He wrote monographs on Sir John Eliot MD and on Dr James Mounsey of Rammerscales. He felt that insufficient credit had been awarded to Mounsey as a result of his being confused by some with the eccentric physician Messenger Monsey. Conceived during a period of illness, Innes Smith's *magnum opus* was *English-Speaking Students of Medicine at the University of Leyden* (1932), which was well received internationally at the time of its publication and which remained the standard reference work in its field. In addition to its valuable introduction, the compilation provides the names of about 2000 medical figures, usually with brief, well-researched biographical notes. The groundwork for his Leiden book also provided almost as many names of English-speaking medical practitioners who had attended other European universities. This manuscript listing was at its most developed for Padua, and less so for Rheims and Utrecht; additionally it included such student names as Innes Smith could obtain from Angers, Basel, Bologna, Bourges, Caen, Cahors, Ferrara, Franeker, Groningen, Harderwyck, Helmstadt, Montpellier, Orange, and Pisa. The records for twenty-one other universities had held no English medical names.

Ill health prevented Innes Smith from completing a further work from any of these concurrent researches. He died of cancer at his home, Totley Brook Road, Dore, Sheffield, on 28 April 1933, survived by his wife, and was buried in Crookes cemetery, Sheffield. His scattered manuscript notes, which comprise about 1500 medical names, remained in the archives of the Royal College of Physicians, London until they were collated and published posthumously in 1996, in computer readable form together with several bound printed sets in hard covers under the title *English-speaking students of medicine at continental universities: the work archive of R. W. Innes-Smith*. He was also the biographical subject of a FitzPatrick lecture of the Royal College of Physicians (London).

When his posthumous work is included Innes Smith's biographical listing has provided the best available details of medical students during those centuries when British students often had to go abroad if they sought university medical education, owing to the poor state of medical teaching at home. Innes Smith also collected *carmina* (laudatory verses) composed between 1650 and 1654 by English-speaking students, usually in Latin, in honour of the anatomist and surgeon Antonio Molinetti of Padua. A critical analysis of these *carmina* and a critique of the genre of these fashionable poems have since been published.

Innes Smith amassed one of the largest collections of prints of medical portraits in private hands, and in so doing he effectively illustrated his uncanny gift for remembering and being able to identify a likeness. This helped him to recognize an important portrait of Sir Charles Scarburgh which had been wrongly identified, Scarburgh having been royal physician to Charles II, James II, and Queen Mary. He bought the portrait and presented it to the Royal College of Physicians (London). Most of his iconographic collection of prints and engravings has survived and is in the care of Sheffield University, together with a part of his extensive library on medical history.

During his lifetime Innes Smith's research led to articles in the *Edinburgh Medical Journal* and to shorter submissions or notes to the *British Medical Journal*, *The Lancet*, and the *Proceedings of the Royal Society of Medicine*. After his death Sir Henry Wellcome asked for his cap, gown, microscope, and other items, for the Wellcome Museum. H. T. SWAN

Sources H. T. Swan, 'R. W. Innes-Smith: a man to study', *Proceedings of the Royal College of Physicians of Edinburgh*, 22 (1992), 224–37 [FitzPatrick lecture of the Royal College of Physicians of London] · RCP Lond., Innes-Smith MSS 537–555, 860–892 · Innes Smith personal MSS, Sheffield University Library · H. T. Swan, ed., *English-speaking students of medicine at continental universities: the work archive of R. W. Innes-Smith* (1996) · D. K. Money and H. T. Swan, 'Doctors as poets: laudatory verses addressed to Antonio Molinetti by British medical students at Padua, 1650–4', *Journal of Medical Biography*, 3 (1995), 139–47 · D. K. Money, 'A diff'rent sounding lyre: Oxford commemorative verse in English, 1613–1834', *Bodleian Library Record*, 16 (1997–9), 42–92 · 'Royal commission on the poor laws and relief of distress', *Parl. papers* (1909), 41.321–4, Cd 4835 [statement of evidence as to club practice] · private information (2004) · Burke, *Gen. GB* · b. cert. · d. cert.

Archives RCP Lond., papers · University of Sheffield, personal corresp. and papers · Wellcome L., notes

Likenesses miniature, *c*.1895, priv. coll. · W. Brealey, drawing, 1904, priv. coll. · W. Brealey, drawing, 1906, priv. coll. · W. Brealey, circular plaster relief; lost · Elliott & Fry, photographs, NPG · photographs, University of Sheffield

Wealth at death £18,797 9*s*. 4*d*.: probate, 4 Aug 1933, *CGPLA Eng. & Wales*

Smith, Rodney [*called* Gypsy Smith] (**1860–1947**), evangelist, was born in a tent in Epping Forest, in the parish of Wanstead, on 31 March 1860, the fourth child and second son of Cornelius Smith and his wife, Mary Welch (*d*. 1865). He was baptized in Wanstead church. His Gypsy parents travelled around East Anglia making and selling baskets,

Rodney Smith (1860–1947), by Elliott & Fry [detail]

clothes-pegs, and tinware, and dealing in horses. The death of his mother from smallpox when he was only five greatly affected him and he frequently referred to it in revivalist meetings throughout his life. Soon after this tragedy, both his father and his two uncles were converted and began to hold open-air evangelistic meetings, becoming known as the Three Gypsy Brothers.

At an early age Smith began to hawk the pegs and tinware made by his father and showed himself to be a persuasive salesman. He had his share of boyish mischief, and when he was caught scrumping or in other misdemeanours he was beaten by his father, but also experienced the disconcerting effect of a guilty conscience. However, the strong ties of affection which bound the family together became for the later evangelist an illustration of the heavenly father's love for his children. His only schooling was for a few weeks in Cambridge one winter, so that he could say in later life, 'So I am a Cambridge man' (Smith, 59). He was converted at the age of sixteen during a prayer meeting in the Primitive Methodist chapel in Fitzroy Street, Cambridge, encouraged by the kindliness of an old man which 'did more good than a thousand sermons would have done just then' (ibid., 74). He became known to village housewives as the Singing Gypsy Boy through his eagerness to sing them one hymn after another. His favourite was William Cowper's 'There is a fountain filled with blood'. The name stuck, and he was known—internationally—as Gypsy Smith.

Smith began preaching early in 1877, practising on a field of turnips ('a very large and most attentive congregation') and on people on their way to church (Smith, 76–7). His only books were a Bible, an English dictionary, and Eadie's Bible dictionary, but he made a habit of continually asking questions. An opportunity to go to Spurgeon's College came to nothing, but in June 1877 he left home to serve with William Booth's Christian Mission (soon to become the Salvation Army), first in the East End, then in Yorkshire. His preaching and singing drew large crowds. At Bolton Smith experienced the fierce hostility of the Irish Catholics. His fellow workers there were an educated couple who helped him overcome his very limited schooling. He found a way of coping with the reading of a lesson.

> The plan I adopted was this—I went on reading slowly and carefully until I saw a long word coming into sight. Then I stopped and made some comments, and after the comments I began to read again, but took care to begin on the other side of the long word. (ibid., 96)

Smith became a captain in the newly formed Salvation Army, but felt 'rather uncomfortable and out of place', since 'being born in a field, I could not be crammed into a flowerpot' (*DNB*). It did not help that he had been moved from Whitby as soon as it became known that he was courting one of his converts, Annie E. Pennock (*d.* 1937), the daughter of a merchant navy captain. They were married in December 1879. He had few regrets when in 1882 he was dismissed for accepting a gold watch and other gifts in appreciation of his evangelistic work at Hanley, Staffordshire, which contravened the army's rules. With strong popular support he remained in Hanley for another four years as a freelance evangelist. A committee of local free church representatives engaged the large Imperial Circus Hall, where he preached to crowded congregations.

In 1888 Smith was engaged by Samuel Collier, superintendent of the Manchester and Salford Methodist mission, and the following year paid the first of many visits to America, where he was helped by Dwight L. Moody and Ira D. Sankey, who became his friends. In 1894, during a world tour, he spent some time in Australia. In 1897 he was appointed the first missioner for the National Free Church Council, preaching in most of the large towns, and also in South Africa and America, before resigning in 1912. During the First World War he served with the YMCA in France and elsewhere, and in 1918 was appointed MBE for his services. Later he toured the British Isles under the auspices of the home mission department of the Methodist church. This roving commission put considerable strain on his family life, and he was conducting missions in America when his wife died in England in the spring of 1937. Little more than a year later, on 2 July 1938, he married Mary Alice Shaw of Los Angeles, who was fifty years his junior and had been working as his secretary. Despite predictably adverse comments on the match, she was a valuable companion and support to him in his closing years. He died on the *Queen Mary* on 4 August 1947 on his way to New York.

Gypsy Smith was probably the best-known and most successful international evangelist of his day. His colourful personality and fine tenor voice made him a strong pulpit attraction. Stocky, thick-set, and swarthy, he had a lively imagination, a down-to-earth sense of humour, and the 'wooing note' in preaching. Though unconventional in his methods, he nevertheless avoided sensationalism. His love of nature and first-hand knowledge of Gypsy lore, added to a lifelong study of the Bible, gave his addresses a touch of romantic originality. Perhaps only Sankey himself excelled him in the singing of simple gospel solos.

JOHN A. VICKERS

Sources R. Smith, *Gipsy Smith, his life and work* (1902) · H. Murray, *Sixty years an evangelist: an intimate study of Gipsy Smith* (1937) · D. Lazell, *Gipsy from the forest* (1997) · *CGPLA Eng. & Wales* (1948) · *DNB*
Likenesses Elliott & Fry, photograph, NPG [*see illus.*]
Wealth at death £714 6*s*. 8*d*.: probate, 11 June 1948, *CGPLA Eng. & Wales*

Smith, (Edwin) Rodney, Baron Smith (1914–1998), surgeon, was born at 224 Balham High Road, London, on 10 May 1914, the eldest son of Edwin Smith (1870–1937), a medical practitioner and coroner, and Edith Catherine (*née* Dyer), a professional violinist. He enjoyed his time at Westminster School (1927–31), where he excelled academically (he was king's scholar in 1928), became a good cricketer, and was an exceptionally good violinist. 'He contemplated music as a profession but stayed with surgery because, he was wont to remark, a surgeon could enjoy music, but a musician could hardly undertake surgery as a hobby' (*The Independent*, 28 July 1998). He became a medical student at St Thomas's Hospital where he distinguished himself academically both as the William Tite and Peacock scholar and Grainger prizewinner and athletically at cricket, scoring a double century at the Oval in the Surrey county second eleven. He passed the MB BS London examinations in 1937 but was precluded by the death of his father from securing the honorary house officer posts at his hospital. Smith went into general practice in south London; on 26 March 1938 he married Mary (*b*. 1916/17), daughter of Edward Rodwell, a schoolmaster, and, soon after, secured the FRCS at the earliest possible time. In 1939 he became surgical registrar at the Middlesex Hospital where he came under the influence of Webb Johnson, who was president of the Royal College of Surgeons for six years and was only the third surgeon to be created a peer. In 1941, after joining the Royal Army Medical Corps, Smith obtained the MS (London) and saw active service as a surgical specialist in north Africa, Palestine, Italy, and Yugoslavia. He distinguished himself as a skilled, efficient surgeon but was wounded at the Anzio beachhead.

After the war, Smith was appointed in 1946 consultant surgeon to St George's Hospital, where he soon made a great reputation for pancreatic and biliary surgery. He worked extraordinarily hard and published many articles and books. He was awarded a Hunterian professorship in 1947, the Jacksonian prize of the Royal College of Surgeons in 1951 and another Hunterian professorship in 1952. He was appointed to the Penrose May tutorship of the college in 1957, continuing in this post for six years, until his election to the council of the college where he became the dean of the Institute of Basic Medical Sciences in 1966. He succeeded in modernizing the institute, which was no small task. His multi-volume *Operative Surgery* was published in 1956; he edited this *magnum opus* with Charles Robb of St Mary's Hospital. In 1962 he joined the court of examiners.

Following the failure of his marriage, which was dissolved in 1971, Smith married on 20 May 1971 Susan Fry (*b*. 1931/2), a medical photographer, with whom he had worked. He was elected president of the Royal College of

(Edwin) Rodney Smith, Baron Smith (1914–1998), by George J. D. Bruce, 1979

Surgeons on the sudden death in office of Sir Edward Muir in 1973. From the point of view of the profession, his election could not have occurred at a better time because no sooner had he assumed the office than the profession was plunged into conflict with the Labour government. Through his skilful and non-confrontational approach, peace was restored and Barbara Castle, the secretary of state, was relieved of her office. Smith was knighted in 1975. He was a great success as president of the Royal College of Surgeons and enjoyed every moment of his four years in office.

One of Smith's many ambitions was to follow in the footsteps of his great mentor and hero, Lord Webb Johnson, who was president for six years. Although he did not succeed in this, he was raised to the peerage as Baron Smith in 1978, in recognition not only of his outstanding presidency but also of his vital role in defusing the conflict between the secretary of state for health and the medical profession. Again, his expertise at bridge-playing proved an asset as he partnered prominent members of the Labour cabinet, allowing him easy access to the corridors of power which he used surreptitiously and to excellent effect; he had a close liaison with Lord Goodman. 'His quip that he had been created a peer in order to strengthen the bridge team in the House of Lords may have been modestly meant but the incidental self-congratulation about his bridge prowess was characteristic' (*The Times*, 22 July 1998). Lord Smith continued to show his skill at solving complicated problems when he became president of the

Royal Society of Medicine and he soon established peace among the warring factions. Sadly, his presidency of the British Medical Association was cut short by a stroke which occurred while he was operating; he suddenly found himself completely unable to speak. His second wife, Susan, discovered that the area of his brain concerned with chess and bridge was unimpaired and she methodically tutored him so effectively that he recovered his ability to speak remarkably well. Although the House of Lords is tolerant and courteous, reading from a script at question time is not acceptable and is usually accompanied by shouts of disapproval, and this unfortunately precluded Lord Smith from making many comments in the house, as he found it difficult to speak without a script.

Lord Smith's recovery from this devastating stroke was in no small measure due to his wife, and it came as no surprise that he accepted the presidency of the Stroke Association and fought on their behalf with great enthusiasm. He was able to return to the operating theatre where his expertise in pancreatic and biliary surgery was unrivalled in his day. His achievements were more than recognized by the gold medals and honorary fellowships which were showered upon him. Only Lord Porritt equalled his achievements in receiving honorary fellowships from all the colleges of surgeons in the English-speaking world. He was an excellent golfer, an accomplished chess player, and played bridge for England. Among his hobbies were numismatics and opera and after he retired he took up painting with his usual enthusiasm and skill.

Lord Smith was clearly an ambitious, determined man who took infinite trouble to have things in good order, be it his surgical skills in biliary and pancreatic surgery, his bridge playing, or his diplomacy in the medical hierarchy and among the Labour politicians. His life at the top seemed to preclude many close friends. Lord Smith died on 1 July 1998 at Beaumont House, Beaumont Street, Westminster. He was survived by his second wife, Susan, and three sons and a daughter by his previous marriage.

McColl of Dulwich

Sources *The Times* (22 July 1998) • *Daily Telegraph* (14 Aug 1998) • *The Independent* (28 July 1998) • *WWW* • personal knowledge (2004) • private information (2004) • b. cert. • m. certs. • d. cert. • D. I. Williams, 'Lord Smith of Marlow', *Annals of the Royal College of Surgeons of England* [supplement, college and faculty bulletin], 80 (Nov 1998), 301–2 • H. Ellis, 'Lord Smith of Marlow', *BMJ* (9 Jan 1999), 129

Likenesses photograph, 1975, repro. in *The Times* • G. J. D. Bruce, portrait, 1979, RCS Eng. [*see illus.*]

Smith, Ronald George [Ron] (**1915–1999**), trade unionist, was born in Edmonton, Middlesex, on 15 July 1915, the son of Henry Sidney Smith, postman, and his wife, Bertha Clara, *née* Barnwell. His father, a trade-union official, encouraged him to join the Labour Party at the age of thirteen. After elementary schooling he started work for the General Post Office (GPO) as a fourteen-year-old messenger earning 8*s*. a week. In this he was typical of many postal workers, for employment by the GPO often ran in families. Ron, as he was known, immediately joined the Union of Post Office Workers (UPW). Beginning as a representative of the messengers, he proceeded to hold almost every branch office. He was promoted from messenger to postman in 1934, attended Workers' Education Association classes, and in 1938 was recruited to the staff of a union district journal, the *London Post*. On 11 May 1940 he married Daisy Hope (Nicky) Nicholson (1916–1974), GPO telephonist, daughter of Herbert Leggatt Nicholson, house decorator. They had one daughter, Lesley.

Smith was elected to the UPW executive in 1945 and became a full-time official of the union as postal and telegraph officer in 1951 and treasurer in 1953. He succeeded Charles Geddes as its general secretary in 1957 and was accordingly elected to the general council of the TUC. He was then the general council's youngest member, and proved an important modernizing influence. At the congress of 1962 he proposed an inquiry into trade-union organization which ultimately resulted in overdue reforms. He was a loyal and orthodox Labour supporter, who backed Hugh Gaitskell's stance on nuclear armaments; Gaitskell sent the draft of his memorandum of April 1960 on the nuclear deterrent, 'Labour and defence policy', to Smith for his comments. Ron Smith was occasionally confused with Charles Smith, afterwards Lord Delacourt-Smith, of the Post Office Engineering Union. Most postmen and female telephonists were members of the UPW: most engineers belonged to the Post Office Engineering Union. Ernest Marples, who was postmaster-general in 1957–9, found it was important to 'keep sweet with the two Smiths' (Bevins, 77).

The GPO at this time was a nationalized industry with a monopoly of telecommunications in addition to postal services. It suffered from being a business directed by a government minister and civil servants. For years the capital investment had been spent on the telephone system, and working conditions, especially in older sorting offices such as Mount Pleasant, were unpleasant for the postmen who constituted the UPW membership. At the same time UPW members were reluctant to accept managerial responsibilities or organizational improvements which might impinge on higher pay grades. In July 1961 the Macmillan government imposed a 'pay pause' on public-sector workers which resulted in Smith leading the 171,000 members of the UPW in a month-long work-to-rule in January 1962—the first official industrial action by the union in forty-two years. For many years the director-general of the GPO had told Smith confidentially what pay rises postmen could have and allowed him to handle the public bargaining and negotiations in any way he wished. This was on the understanding that they would eventually settle at the figure privately agreed in the first place. The inflationary pressures of the 1960s strained this arrangement, which would have been resented by his more militant colleagues if they had known of it. There was an outright postal strike in July 1964. Smith was more adept at handling reporters during this dispute than the postmaster-general, Reginald Bevins.

During 1965 Smith came under increasing pressure from dissatisfied UPW members. His negotiations on pay with the new postmaster-general, Tony Benn, were sometimes fraught, but reached a compromise which averted further industrial action. When Benn initiated extensive reforms of the structure of the GPO Smith feared that modernization would leave his members with the unskilled jobs carrying poorer status and financial prospects. Publicly, sometimes in emphatic language, and privately in more effective and conciliatory tones, he criticized the drastic nature of Benn's proposals, which were tempered over the months.

Smith's diligent and constructive outlook resulted in his being drawn into Whitehall work. He served on government committees on student grants (1958–60) and company law (1960–62), the Treasury advisory committee on development areas (1959–60), and the courts of inquiry into the industrial dispute at Ford's of Dagenham (1963) and on the pay and conditions of London Transport bus staff (1963–4). He was one of the original TUC members on the National Economic Development Council formed by the Macmillan government in 1962. He was a member of the civil service National Whitley Council (1957–66), and an executive member of the Postal, Telegraph and Telephone International (1957–66).

In 1966 Smith was recruited as a full-time member of the organizing committee of the newly nationalized steel sector. On the formation of the British Steel Corporation (BSC) in 1967 he was appointed as its director of personnel and social policy, serving under Lord Melchett. The rivalries between white-collar and blue-collar unions in the steel sector caused recurrent troubles to Smith. BSC's decision to give sole national negotiating rights to six big manual workers' unions, and to refuse recognition to the Clerical and Administrative Workers' Union and the Association of Scientific, Technical and Managerial Staffs, provoked a long and intricate inter-union dispute during 1968–9. Smith tried to rationalize the negotiating procedure among the eighteen steel unions, but his proposal for one union to represent all steelworkers was resented by union officials protective of their status and influence. After retiring as director of personnel in 1972 he remained a member of the BSC board, and chaired British Steel Corporation (Industry) Ltd, a management company formed by BSC to establish new industries in areas where steelworkers were being made redundant (1975–77).

Smith was a non-executive director of the state-owned British Overseas Aircraft Corporation (1964–70) and relished his opportunities for international travel. He collected beer mats and wine-bottle labels from all over the world to decorate his house in Surrey. He was appointed CBE in 1973. In his prime he stood 6 foot 2 inches tall with strong features and thick, jet-black eyebrows. 'He is a powerful man physically and temperamentally', Tony Benn described him in 1964: 'one felt one was rubbing shoulders against granite' (Benn, 1.170). Despite his physique and the shuffling gait of a heavyweight boxer, he had mild manners, a gentle character and a reflective outlook. He died on 20 October 1999 at Epsom General Hospital, Epsom, Surrey, and was survived by his daughter.

RICHARD DAVENPORT-HINES

Sources *Daily Telegraph* (23 Oct 1999) • *The Guardian* (25 Oct 1999) • T. Benn, *Out of the wilderness: diaries, 1963–67* (1987) • J. R. Bevins, *The greasy pole* (1965) • *The Castle diaries, 1964–1970* (1984) • *WWW* • b. cert. • m. cert. • d. cert.

Likenesses photograph, 1962, repro. in *Daily Telegraph* • photograph, repro. in *The Guardian* • photographs, Union of Post Office Workers

Wealth at death £247,697—gross; £245,945—net: probate, 2 March 2000, *CGPLA Eng. & Wales*

Smith, Sir Ross Macpherson (1892–1922), aviator, was born at Semaphore, Adelaide, South Australia, on 4 December 1892, the second son of Andrew Bell Smith (1853–1924), a successful pastoralist and station manager, and his wife, Jessie Macpherson, both of whom were Scottish-born. He was educated at Queen's School, Adelaide, and also at Warriston School, Moffat, in Dumfriesshire, Scotland, his father's birthplace, where the whole family stayed for two years (1906–8). In 1910 he toured Britain and the United States of America as a South Australian representative of the Australian mounted cadets. He afterwards joined the 10th Australian regiment, the Adelaide Rifles. In due course Smith and his brothers were all expected to join their father in the management of an estate of some 3000 square miles at Mutooroo. Meanwhile they each sought experience in other fields. The eldest, Keith Macpherson Smith (1890–1955), joined a firm of wool brokers; the youngest, Colin, who died of wounds at Passchendaele in 1917, went into a bank; and Ross entered the Adelaide warehouse of a firm of hardware merchants.

On the outbreak of the First World War in August 1914 Ross Smith enlisted as a trooper in the 3rd Australian light horse and sailed with the first Australian expeditionary force, landing in Egypt in December. His unit was used to support the Gallipoli offensive, and Smith landed on the peninsula on 13 May 1915. He showed conspicuous gallantry there and was commissioned second lieutenant on 5 September. The following month he was invalided to England. He was promoted lieutenant on 1 March 1916 and later that month left England to rejoin his regiment in Egypt. In August he took part in the battle of Romani, during the last attack made by the Turks on the Suez Canal.

In October 1916 Smith was transferred to the Royal Flying Corps and joined 67 (Australian) squadron as an observer in Palestine. In July 1917 he qualified as a pilot at the training schools in Egypt and rejoined his squadron, which in January 1918 was re-equipped with Bristol fighters and designated a fighter squadron. As such it played an important role in General Allenby's offensive against the Turks, and Smith emerged as one of its most successful pilots. He engaged in many combats with German aircraft and took a leading part in the bombing attack on the Turkish headquarters on 19 September 1918 which destroyed the enemy's communications and proved the successful prelude to the offensive that ended Turkey's role in the war. By the end of the conflict he had attained the rank of captain and had been awarded both the Military Cross and bar and the Distinguished Flying Cross and two bars.

While in Palestine Smith flew the giant twin-engined Handley Page O/400 bomber, and after the armistice he was selected to co-pilot the machine in a pioneer flight

Sir Ross Macpherson Smith (1892–1922), by William Beckwith McInnes, 1920

from Cairo to Calcutta. With Brigadier-General (later Air Vice-Marshal) Amyas Eden Borton, a friend and mentor, among the crew of five led by Sir (William) Geoffrey Salmond, Smith left Cairo on 29 November 1918 and arrived in Calcutta on 10 December 1918, an exploit for which he was awarded the Air Force Cross. He subsequently accompanied Borton on a series of reconnaissance missions by sea to survey an aerial route to Australia through Burma, Siam, the Malay states, and the Dutch East Indies. All of this proved invaluable experience the following year, when Smith prepared to join the race to make the first flight from Britain to Australia.

The public interest generated by the transatlantic flight of Captain John William Alcock and Lieutenant Arthur Whitten Brown, in June 1919, encouraged the Australian government to offer a prize of £10,000 for the first flight to Australia from Britain made inside thirty days by an Australian. With his brother Keith as navigator, and sergeants J. M. Bennett and W. H. Shiers as the mechanics, Smith set off on 12 November 1919 in a twin-engined Vickers Vimy, of the type used by Alcock and Brown, powered by Rolls-Royce engines. Bad weather delayed their departure for two weeks, and the aerodrome at Hounslow was covered in snow when they left. Over Boulogne they encountered a thick bank of clouds which forced them to climb to 8000 feet, and Smith later recalled: 'The cold was bitter, 25 degrees of frost, and for three hours our breath froze on our face-masks, and our sandwiches were frozen solid' (Cutlack, 389). Just under four weeks later, on 10 December, they landed at Darwin to claim the prize, having covered 11,340 miles in 135 hours of flying. Their signal achievement was justly honoured: Ross and Keith Smith were each created KBE, and Bennett and Shiers were both commissioned and given a bar to their Air Force crosses. The prize money was equally divided between the four men.

In 1921 the Smith brothers planned to fly around the world, with Lieutenant Bennett as their chief mechanic. With support from the Vickers aviation company they chose a Vickers Viking IV amphibian for the flight, principally because it would lessen their dependence on suitable airfields. On 13 April 1922, as part of the final preparations, Sir Ross Smith made his first trial flight of the amphibian at Brooklands, near Byfleet, accompanied by Lieutenant Bennett, having earlier been shown the controls during a short flight piloted by the Vickers test pilot Captain Cockerell. Smith had not flown for some months, and the amphibian, which had peculiar handling characteristics, was a completely new type to him. At 1200 feet the plane went into a spin, from which it briefly recovered before crashing to the ground in a straight nose dive. Smith and Bennett were both killed. Keith Smith, who had arrived too late to join the flight as planned, witnessed the disaster. To the aviation world the news 'was simply stunning' (*Flight*, 20 April 1922, 223–4). It was concluded that pilot error was to blame: Smith was a careful aviator who prepared meticulously for his flights, and the crash was probably due to a momentary hesitation at a crucial time in unfamiliar surroundings. With more elevation he might have recovered: such tragedies affecting experienced pilots were by no means exceptional.

Smith's *14,000 Miles through the Air*, an account of the pioneering flight to Australia, was published after the accident. There was a memorial service at St Clement Danes on 20 April, and on 15 June Smith was buried in the North Road Anglican cemetery in Melindie, Adelaide. Air Vice-Marshal Borton wrote to his mother: 'His was such a lovable character; so essentially upright and straightforward and as unaffected by distinction and success as he was by dangers and difficulties which he regarded merely as incidents to be met and overcome' (Grenfell Price, 125–6).

H. A. Jones, *rev.* Mark Pottle

Sources A. Grenfell Price, *The skies remember: the story of Ross and Keith Smith* (1969) · *AusDB* · *Flight* (26 Jan 1922), 54, 232 · *Flight* (27 April 1922), 244 · *Flight* (22 June 1922), 358 · *The Aeroplane*, 22/16 (19 April 1922), 275 · F. M. Cutlack, *The Australian flying corps in the western and eastern theatres of war, 1914–1918* (1933) · personal knowledge (1937) · private information (1937)

Likenesses W. B. McInnes, portrait, 1920, Australian War Memorial, Canberra [*see illus.*] · F. B. Hitch, statue, Adelaide · photograph, repro. in Grenfell Price, *Skies remember*, 12

Wealth at death £438 6*s*. 2*d*.—effects in England: Adelaide probate sealed in London, 6 Dec 1922, *CGPLA Eng. & Wales*

Smith, Samuel (1584–1665), Church of England clergyman and author, was born in Dudley, Worcestershire, on 28 February 1584, the son of William Smith, vicar of St Thomas's, Dudley, and his wife, Joane Payton. His baptism on 29 February appears together with his horoscope, written in his father's hand, in the parish register. He matriculated on 1 July 1603, aged nineteen, from St Mary Hall, Oxford, where he was a batteler. It is possible that he was the Samuel Smith who on 6 August 1603 married Margery Burboll at St Thomas, and who baptized a daughter, Mary, there on 25 January 1604, but there is no other evidence of a wife or children, and his subsequent career and publications indicate that, although there is no record that he graduated, he had several years of advanced education.

By 20 July 1614, when he signed the first edition of his popular exposition of Psalm 1, *Davids Blessed Man* (1614), dedicated to Sir Robert Rich and his wife, Frances, Smith was minister of Roxwell, near Chelmsford, Essex. He was also so described in the first and third editions of his *Davids Repentence* (1614 and 1616), dedicated to Sir Richard Weston and Sir Edward Pynchon, but on 30 November 1615 he was presented by Rich's father, Robert Rich, Lord Rich, the future earl of Warwick, to the vicarage of Prittlewell in the same county. He continued to publish sermons and expositions of scripture, including *The Great Assize, or, The Day of Jubilee* (2nd edn, 1617), and *Christs Last Supper* (1620), dedicated to Sir Ferdinando Dudley and his wife, Honor. In 1628 he was still at Prittlewell, but about 1630 he spent a year as curate of Clyro, Radnorshire, before moving in 1631 to a curacy at Cressage in the chapelry of Cound, Shropshire. He was still writing: 1632 saw the appearance of *The Admirable Convert* and *The Ethiopians Conversion*, dedicated respectively to Sir Richard and Dame Anne Greeves of Worcestershire and to Sir Richard Newport of Shropshire.

While at Cressage, Smith made the acquaintance of a young connection of Newport's, Richard Baxter (1615–1691), then at nearby Eaton Constantine. He was one of several 'Reverend peaceable Divines' who assisted and settled the young man; Smith and another godly minister, Francis Garbett, sent him the authors 'that had wrote against the Nonconformists', and thus helped keep him on the straight path of conformity. Baxter considered Smith 'one of my most familiar Friends, in whose Converse I took very much delight' (*Reliquiae Baxterianae*, 1.9, 13), and one of the few truly conscientious ministers in Shropshire at a time when that county was a 'pastoral desert' (Collinson, 94).

In 1647 Smith was approved for one of the presbyteries to be set up in Shropshire, and the following year he signed the declaration of certain Shropshire ministers in favour of the solemn league and covenant. By 18 May 1648 he had become rector of Cound. In the 1650s he also seems to have been curate of Kinver, near Stourbridge. Still close to Baxter, he was with him on 19 October 1652 at Trysull, Staffordshire, praying and preaching at a thanksgiving for the settlement of Thomas Willesby at Wombourn and Trysull. In 1654 Smith became a Shropshire 'ejector' of scandalous ministers and schoolmasters. His last work, *A Paterne of Free Grace*, was published in 1658, but further editions of his other works continued to appear.

Smith left Cressage in 1660, probably having withdrawn rather than been ejected. He went to live in his native Dudley, where he paid the clerical subsidy in 1661. In his will, made on 31 January 1665, he disposed of property in Dudley and Sedgeley. His executor was his cousin John Payton the elder of Dudley, and the witnesses included John Taylor, the town vicar. Smith died in Dudley a few weeks later, and was buried in the chancel of St Thomas's Church there on 17 March. C. D. GILBERT

Sources *Reliquiae Baxterianae, or, Mr Richard Baxter's narrative of the most memorable passages of his life and times*, ed. M. Sylvester, 1 vol. in 3 pts (1696) · *Calamy rev.*, 449 · *Calendar of the correspondence of Richard Baxter*, ed. N. H. Keeble and G. F. Nuttall, 2 vols. (1991) · E. Calamy, *A continuation of the account of the ministers … who were ejected and silenced after the Restoration in 1660*, 2 vols. (1727), vol. 2, pp. 567, 728 · Wood, *Ath. Oxon.*, new edn, 3.656 · Foster, *Alum. Oxon.* · S. Shaw, *The history and antiquities of Staffordshire*, 2 vols. (1798–1801) · P. Collinson, *The religion of protestants* (1982) · *N&Q*, 3rd ser., 4 (1863), 501 · *N&Q*, 3rd ser., 12 (1867), 200, 501 · parish register, Dudley, St Edmund's and St Thomas's, 29 Feb 1584, Worcs. RO [baptism] · parish register, Dudley, St Edmund's and St Thomas's, 17 March 1665, Worcs. RO [burial] · W. A. Shaw, *History of the Eng. church …, 1640–1660* (1900) · will, PRO, PROB 11/317, sig. 567 · *STC, 1475–1640*

Wealth at death see will, PRO, PROB 11/317, sig. 567

Smith, Samuel (1587–1620), writer on logic, was possibly baptized on 2 May 1587 at Swineshead, Lincolnshire, and on 19 October 1604 entered Magdalen Hall, Oxford, as a commoner. He was a demy of Magdalen College in 1606, and became a fellow in 1608; he graduated BA the following January, and MA in May 1612. In that year Smith was among the members of the university to contribute verses on the death of Henry, prince of Wales, and in the following year on the marriage of the elector palatine. His small elementary manual of logic, *Aditus ad logicam, in usum eorum qui primo academiam salutant* (1613), was published in London, several later editions being published in Oxford after his death.

In December 1612 Smith was admitted to study medicine, having shown an aptitude for the subject. He was granted three months leave from March 1614 to pursue his studies, and a further six months from April 1616, by which time he had a licence, in order to practise medicine. His academic licence was granted on 15 April 1620, and he was admitted MB on 25 April; he was appointed junior proctor of the university on 28 April, being then, according to Wood, 'accounted the most accurate disputant and profound philosopher in the university' (Wood, *Ath. Oxon.*, 2.283). He died on 17 June 1620, and was buried in the chapel of Magdalen College.

THOMPSON COOPER, *rev.* ANITA MCCONNELL

Sources W. D. Macray, *A register of the members of St Mary Magdalen College, Oxford*, 8 vols. (1894–1915), vol. 3, p. 136 · Wood, *Ath. Oxon.*, new edn, 2.283 · Foster, *Alum. Oxon.* · F. Madan, *Oxford books: a bibliography of printed works*, 3 vols. (1895–1931); repr. (1964) · *IGI*

Smith, Samuel (1620–1698), Church of England clergyman, was born on 19 December 1620 in London, the son of George Smith, grocer, of London. He was educated at the Merchant Taylors' School between 1631 and 1638. He entered St John's College, Oxford, on 13 July 1638, aged eighteen. He graduated BA in April 1642 and proceeded MA in July 1655; he was also a fellow of his college. In 1656 he returned to London and was appointed rector of St Benet Gracechurch. He was ejected from his benefice for refusing to take the oaths outlined in the 1662 Act of Uniformity. He married Elizabeth Lawrence, the daughter of Matthew Lawrence of Ipswich, on 2 May 1654 and they had a son, Lawrence, in 1674. Some time between then and 1683 Elizabeth died and Smith married Susannah, with whom he had four more children.

In 1675 Smith published *The character of a weaned Christian, or, The evangelical art of promoting self-denial, being an essay, alluding to the severities and advantages of infant-weaning, both pleasant and profitable*. On the title-page Smith described himself as 'Minister of the Gospel in London' (which implies strongly that he was still a nonconformist) and the book was dedicated to Sir Robert Vyner, the lord mayor. The work deployed the weaning of the infant from the maternal breast as an extended metaphor for the weaning of the spiritually new-born from the sensual lusts and temptations of the world. The metaphor was worked through in at times highly literal detail:

> we keck and sputter at earthly delights, when we are griped with Wind in our Bowels … while Divine Providence besmears the World's paps with Soot, and cries out, do not touch them as you love your Life, we shrink back (Smith, *Character*, 21, 29–30)

His links with the City élite and his claim to authority on the topic of exhorting sinners to 'a voluntary Alienation of the heart, from the Love of sin and the World, to place it upon God, in a universal Conformity to his Will' may have stood Smith in good stead the following year (ibid., 29). Following the death of Edmund Cressy the court of aldermen appointed Smith ordinary of Newgate (that is the prison chaplain) on 15 June 1676 at a salary of £65 per annum. To occupy this position Smith would have had to conform to the Church of England.

Smith was perhaps less diligent in his post than he might have been, as an order was entered in July 1677 by the aldermen stating that he should read prayers to the prisoners twice a day. The aldermen do not seem to have been overly keen on paying him his stipend, and Smith was forced to petition them on two separate occasions in order for it to be paid. In May 1685 an administrative arrangement meant that his duty as ordinary of Newgate was spread out among other ministers from around London and Smith was discharged from his post. By the autumn of 1690 he had been returned to favour and his post, albeit on a reduced stipend of £30 per annum, and in October Smith again petitioned the court of aldermen and was successful in obtaining his former stipendiary rate.

In 1680 Smith preached a sermon before the mayor and aldermanic bench (who duly ordered it to be published) entitled *Light out of Darkness*, a standard mix of protestant providentialism and anti-popery which warned its hearers how England must fit itself to God's purposes if it were not to squander His mercies in exposing the Popish Plot. Smith's claim to notice lies rather in the works that he began to produce four years later. In 1684 he, together with the publisher and printer George Croom, began to produce the first accounts of the ordinary of Newgate. These were published under the title *The True Account of the Behaviour and Confession of* … or a close variation on that theme. In their combination of tales of sinners redeemed or unrepentant and crime reporting they built on an existing literature of crime pamphlets (as exemplified, for instance, in the work of Smith's Jacobean predecessor Henry Goodcole), while providing a journalistic innovation in the folio sheets which regularly detailed the lives and crimes of those condemned at the Old Bailey. They appeared on a periodical basis and detailed Smith's ministrations to the condemned as they awaited execution in Newgate. He maintained that the accounts were published at the request of the prisoners to 'give account of their penitency; and to warn others by examples of suffering justice' (Smith, *Behaviour*, 1). However, Smith often recorded the difficulties that he faced in converting and offering solace to recalcitrant sinners. His unique access to the felons and *gravitas* as prison chaplain proved a successful combination. Some twenty-three accounts bear his name, making him the most prolific writer on criminals of the seventeenth century.

Smith elicited some criticism as a man who extracted confessions from the condemned and then sold the results for his own profit, most notably a couple of doggerel epitaphs on 'that most learned and profound casuist' by Tom Brown:

> Thou, reverend Pillar of the tripple Tree,
> I would say Post, for it was prop'd by thee,
> Thou Penny-Chronicler of hasty Fate,
> Death's Annalist, Reformer of the State;
> Cut-throat of Texts, and Chaplain of the Halter,
> In whose sage presence Vice itself did faulter.
> (*Works*, 4.42–3)

Brown cheerfully parodied, with a dubious sense of rhyme, the convention of the ordinary's accounts of how apparently small sins in youth led to the gallows:

> How oft has thou set harden'd Rogues a squeaking
> By urging the great Sin of Sabbath-breaking.
> (ibid., 4.41)

He suggested that Smith would only write a positive account of a felon's last days if he had been paid.

Smith died in London on 24 August 1698, allegedly of a quinsy. After his death, the ordinary's accounts continued to be written well into the eighteenth century, first by his immediate successor John Allen, then by Paul Lorrain and later ordinaries. They have come to be recognized as a fascinating type of popular journalism and an important source for the social and cultural history of crime in late seventeenth- and eighteenth-century London.

CHRISTOPHER CHAPMAN

Sources *Calamy rev.* • Wood, *Ath. Oxon.*, new edn • repertories of the court of aldermen, CLRO, vols. 81–95, esp. 81, 82, 88, 89 and 95 • Foster, *Alum. Oxon.* • PRO, PROB 11/447, fol. 206 • *The works of Mr Thomas Brown*, ed. J. Drake, 3rd edn, 4 vols. (1715), vol. 4, pp. 41–5 • S. Smith, *The character of a weaned Christian, or, The evangelical art of promoting self-denial* (1675) • S. Smith, *The behaviour of Edward Kirk, after his condemnation for murdering his wife* (1684) • S. Smith, *The true account of the behaviour and confession of the criminals condemned* (1686) • P. Linebaugh, 'The ordinary of Newgate and his *Account*', *Crime in England, 1550–1800*, ed. J. S. Cockburn (1977), 246–69

Wealth at death over £50: will, PRO, PROB 11/447, fol. 206

Smith, Samuel (*bap.* **1658**, *d.* **1707**), bookseller and publisher, was baptized on 17 May 1658 in the parish church of St Benedict Biscop, Wombourne, Staffordshire, the youngest child of Edward Smith (*d.* 1679) and his wife, Joan (*d.* 1688); his family were minor landowners. Although nothing is known of his early education, he was later described by his contemporary John Dunton as speaking 'French and Latin with a great deal of fluency and ease'. On 1 February 1675 Smith was apprenticed into the London book trade. His indenture shows him to have been officially bound to the bookseller Samuel Gellibrand but 'turned over' or transferred immediately to Moses Pitt, best known for *The English Atlas*. This construction allowed Smith to join the Stationers' Company, of which Pitt was not a member. Smith became a freeman of the company, and in March 1682 of the City of London. Throughout his career he lived and worked in various premises in St Faith's parish, always under the sign of the Prince's Arms. His publications carry the imprint 'The Prince's Arms in St. Paul's Churchyard'.

As a bookseller Smith appears to have succeeded Robert Scott as the major importer of foreign scholarly works in Latin. The extent of his stock can be judged from his 94-page catalogue of 1695 (*Catalogus librorum domi forisque impressorum*) which contains more than 3000 titles, a large proportion of which are of foreign origin. Part of Smith's incoming business correspondence from the Low Countries and Germany for the decade 1682–92 was preserved by the antiquary Richard Rawlinson. These papers document Smith's transactions with many continental suppliers and provide a valuable insight into the workings of the cross-channel book trade of the late seventeenth century.

In 1692 the book auctioneer Benjamin Walford, who was later to be his brother-in-law, became Smith's business partner. From the beginning of his career Smith had published the *Philosophical Transactions of the Royal Society* and in 1693 he and Walford were officially sworn 'printers to the Royal Society', an appointment they held until their deaths. Despite the use of the term in their title, however, there is no evidence that either Smith or Walford was ever active as a printer. Fellows of the Royal Society such as John Ray, Martin Lister, and Sir Isaac Newton published works with them. In addition to such scholarly works, Smith's list of publications (approximately 250 titles) includes editions of the classics for Eton College, travel literature, dictionaries, and sermons.

On 16 March 1682 Smith married Margaret Crompton at a ceremony conducted by his elder brother Edward, rector of St Michael Bassishaw, London. Seven children were born of this marriage, none of whom entered the book trade. After the death of his first wife in November 1703, Smith married Penelope Symcotts (*bap.* 1664, *d.* 1726) in Henlow, Bedfordshire, on 18 October 1705. There were no children of this marriage and, when Smith died two years later, his property was divided between his second wife and Anne (*b.* 1689) and Benjamin (1696–*c.*1738), the surviving children of his first marriage. Samuel Smith was buried in the crypt of St Faith's Chapel under St Paul's Cathedral on 19 November 1707, according to the provisions of his will. His business activities were continued by Benjamin Walford until his death in early 1710.

Marja Smolenaars and Ann Veenhoff

Sources N. Hodgson and C. Blagden, *The notebook of Thomas Bennet and Henry Clements (1686–1719)* (1956) • J. Dunton, *The life and errors of John Dunton … written by himself* (1705) • parish registers, Clifton and Henlow, Beds., Beds. & Luton ARS • parish registers, Wombourne, Staffs., Staffs. RO • parish register, London, St Faith, GL • Smith's will, PRO, PROB 11/502/139 • journal book, 1693, RS • D. F. McKenzie, ed., *Stationers' Company apprentices*, [2]: *1641–1700* (1974)
Archives Bodl. Oxf., MS Rawl. letters 114
Wealth at death see will, PRO, PROB 11/502/139

Smith, Samuel (1765–1841), dean of Christ Church, Oxford, was born in Westminster, London, on 20 September 1765, the eldest in the family of two daughters and five sons (one of whom died young) of Samuel Smith (1731/2–1808), headmaster of Westminster School from 1764 to 1788, and his first wife, Anna Jackson. He was a pupil at Westminster School from 1772, and (as captain of the school) matriculated from there at Christ Church, Oxford, in 1782; his college tutors were John Randolph and Phineas Pett, later his canonical colleagues. Smith himself was for a few years a tutor at Christ Church, but in 1803 he resigned his studentship to become incumbent of Daventry (a Christ Church living). On 9 August that year he married Anne Brady (1781/2–1826), daughter of William Barnett of Arcadia, Jamaica, where the Smiths sold four slaves in 1825.

Smith returned to Christ Church as a canon in 1807. Appointments as subdean (1809) and treasurer (1813) suggest that he was early marked out for appointment as dean; this came in 1824, when he succeeded the handsome but incapable C. H. Hall, other candidates being Edmund Goodenough, headmaster of Westminster, and Charles Lloyd, another canon of Christ Church. Smith's wife died on 23 February 1826, shortly after the birth of their thirteenth child; this loss made him for some time anxious to resign, and may help to account for the relative lack of distinction of his period of office.

Smith has been dismissed as 'Presence of Mind Smith' from his alleged remark on returning without his companion from a disastrous outing on the river: 'If I had not with great presence of mind hit him on the head with a boathook both would have been drowned', but the story comes from *Reminiscences of Oxford* (1st edn, 1900) by William Tuckwell, who in his second edition (1907) consigned it to oblivion; moreover, there was no charge of murder. As dean, Smith attempted to revert to the practices and manners of Hall's great predecessor, Cyril Jackson, but he lacked the ability to manage those with whom a dean of Christ Church had to deal. He was worsted by George IV in a tussle over appointments to studentships; a riot in 1825 led the duke of Wellington to transfer his two eldest sons to Trinity College, Cambridge, and Smith failed to mobilize chapter and common room to achieve the desired result in the by-election following the resignation of Robert Peel early in 1829, the lead being taken by Charles Lloyd. The Revd Frederick Oakeley, later a convert to Rome, a graduate at Christ Church while Smith was dean, thought him 'remarkable for nothing but his good nature' and 'the most irregular and unpunctual attendant' at college services; however, 'the moral and religious state of Christ Church … was in a state of progressive improvement' under Smith (Quiller-Couch, 319, 329–30). These are tendentious claims: it is clear that men prominent in the political, ecclesiastical, legal, and learned life of later Victorian England were admitted to Christ Church in Smith's day. Gladstone's diary for his Christ Church years suggests that in Smith's period as dean, though there were many distractions, a man of exceptional powers could find like-minded friends at Christ Church and read hard and widely; it was Smith who nominated Gladstone to a studentship. Smith published nothing, and at Christ Church he built nothing. However, in Smith's short reign nine men were admitted to Christ Church who achieved a place in the *DNB*.

Smith exchanged the deanery for the 'golden stall' at Durham with Thomas Gaisford in 1831. At Dry Drayton, near Cambridge, he had succeeded his father as patron and incumbent in 1808, presented his own eldest son, Samuel, in 1829, and himself for the second time in 1831. Like his father Smith was fond of gambling on horses, though with marked lack of success; he shared this propensity with few or no other deans of Christ Church. He had six sons, one of whom died young and four of whom became Anglican clergymen, and seven daughters. Smith died on 19 January 1841 in Dry Drayton, Cambridgeshire, where he was buried. In his last ten years at Durham Smith, though conscientious, was not a prime mover in the origins of the new University. J. F. A. Mason, *rev.*

Sources Cambs. AS, Smith papers · archives, Christ Church Oxf. · inscriptions, Dry Drayton · W. R. Ward, *Victorian Oxford* (1965) · Gladstone, *Diaries* · L. M. Quiller-Couch, ed., *Reminiscences of Oxford by Oxford men, 1559–1850*, OHS, 22 (1892), 319–31 · *GM*, 1st ser., 73 (1803), 788 · *GM*, 1st ser., 96/1 (1826), 285

Archives Cambs. AS · U. Durham L., corresp. and papers | BL, corresp. with Sir Robert Peel, Add. MSS 40361–40398, *passim*

Likenesses H. W. Pickersgill, oils, Christ Church Oxf.

Smith, Samuel (1836–1906), politician and philanthropist, born on 11 January 1836 at Roberton Farm, in the parish of Borgue, Kirkcudbrightshire, was the eldest of the seven children of James Smith, a farmer of Borgue, who also farmed land of his own in South Carleton and other places. His grandfather and an uncle, both named Samuel Smith, served as parish minister of Borgue. The former (*d.* 1816) wrote *A General View of the Agriculture of Galloway* (1806); the latter seceded at the disruption of the Scottish church in 1843. After being educated at the Borgue Academy, and at Kirkcudbright Academy, Smith entered Edinburgh University before he was sixteen, and spent three sessions there. In spite of his literary tastes, he was apprenticed to a cotton broker in Liverpool in 1853. There he spent his leisure in study, frequenting the Liverpool literary societies and speaking at the Philomathic Society, of

Samuel Smith (1836–1906), by William Ewart Lockhart, 1899

which he became president, and forming close friendships with Donald Currie, W. B. Barbour, and W. S. Caine.

In 1857 Smith became manager of the cotton saleroom and began to write with authority on the cotton market in the *Liverpool Daily Post*, under the signature Mercator. In 1860 he visited New Orleans and the cotton-growing districts of North America, of which he published a description. On his return, having made a tour of the leading Lancashire manufacturing centres, he started in business as a cotton broker in Chapel Street, Liverpool, and established the first monthly cotton circular, conducting it until he entered parliament. In the winter of 1862–3 he went to India on behalf of the Manchester chamber of commerce to test the cotton-growing possibilities there, in view of the depletion of the English market owing to the American Civil War. In a communication to the *Times of India* (embodied in a pamphlet published in England), Smith questioned India's fitness to grow cotton. The visit generated a lifelong interest in India and its people. He travelled back slowly by way of the Middle East, Constantinople, and the Danube, and greatly improved his business prospects; towards the close of his career he recommended the growing of cotton in British Africa, Egypt, the Sudan, and Sind. On 1 January 1864 the firm of Smith, Edwards & Co., cotton brokers, was launched, and three months later Smith also became head of the Liverpool branch of James Finlay & Co. of Glasgow and Bombay. Cotton spinning and manufacturing were subsequently added to his activities by the purchase of Millbrook Mills, Stalybridge. On 20 July 1864 he married Melville (*d.* 1893), daughter of the Revd John Christison DD, minister of Biggar, Lanarkshire. They had at least one son.

From an early period Smith was active as a philanthropist. At Liverpool he interested himself in efforts for prevention of cruelty to children, for establishing scholarships to connect primary and secondary schools (1874), and for improving public houses. In 1876 he became president of Liverpool chamber of commerce, and in 1879 he entered the town council, winning Castle ward, as an ardent temperance reformer. A zealous Presbyterian of liberal views, he joined in inviting the American evangelists Moody and Sankey to Liverpool in 1875; presided at a meeting of 4000 held at Hengler's Circus in aid of William Booth's 'Darkest England' scheme in 1890; and received 14,000 American delegates of the Christian Endeavour Society in 1897.

At a by-election at Liverpool in December 1882, Smith was elected as a Liberal by a majority of 309, winning against A. B. Forwood in what was regarded as a Conservative stronghold. In 1885 he was defeated in the Abercromby division of Liverpool, but in March 1886 was returned for Flintshire during his absence in India; he retained the seat until 1905. Gladstone's residence, Hawarden Castle, was in his constituency, and Smith was often there, exchanging views with the statesman. Smith, who seconded the address to the crown at the opening of the session of 1884, frequently spoke in the House of Commons on moral, social, religious, currency, and Indian questions. He was an industrious and well-informed representative of the nonconformist conscience. He pressed untiringly for compulsory evening continuation schools for children leaving school at thirteen, and for the abrogation of payment by results and of overstrain in elementary schools. He was an extreme campaigner against 'Romanism' in the prayer book and the Church of England. He zealously promoted the Criminal Law Amendment Act of 1885, and by his efforts made legal the evidence of young children. The Prevention of Cruelty to Children Act of 1889 embodied reforms that he had advocated in Liverpool. He lamented that his attacks on the opium trade between India and China were not very effective. He violently opposed any form of socialism, debating with Henry George at the National Liberal Club on the subject. He promoted women's suffrage, notably in his unsuccessful bill of 1892, which occasioned an exchange with Gladstone.

Smith gave addresses on bimetallism in many parts of the country, having gradually adopted bimetallic views, and several times raised the question in parliament. On 18 April 1890 he initiated a parliamentary debate in which Arthur Balfour, Sir Edward Clarke, and Sir Richard Webster supported, and Sir William Harcourt and W. H. Smith opposed his resolution (which was lost by 183 votes to 87). Smith contributed 'Three letters on the silver question' to H. Cernuschi's *Nomisma* (1877), and published *The Bimetallic Question* (1887).

Smith revisited India in 1886, and his subsequent articles in the *Contemporary Review* (reprinted as *India Revisited: the Social and Political Problem*, 1886) were answered by Sir Mountstuart Grant Duff, governor of Madras. Thenceforth the grievances of India were a main theme of his in the House of Commons. On 30 April 1889 he carried, by a majority of ten against the government, a motion condemning the liquor policy of the Indian government. The result was a reduction of licences in India. In 1894 Smith's motion for a parliamentary inquiry into the condition of the Indian people was followed by a royal commission, which recommended a reduction by £250,000 of Indian liabilities. He encouraged Indians' claim to a larger share in their government. Other peoples found in Smith a warm champion. In 1892–3 he called attention to the abuses of the Kanaka labour traffic from the New Hebrides to Queensland, and in March 1896 his motion of sympathy with the Armenians following recent massacres was carried unanimously.

Religious questions chiefly occupied Smith's closing years. In parliament he urged disestablishment both in Wales and England, and denounced ritualistic offences with sustained vehemence, publishing pamphlets on the subject, which reached a circulation of 1 million. In the summer of 1901 his health failed, but he retained his seat in parliament until the end of 1905, when he was named a privy councillor on his retirement. He was again in India in 1904–5, and returned there at the end of 1906 in apparently improved health, arriving on 25 December; but after attending some sittings of the Indian National Congress he died suddenly on 28 December at Calcutta. He was buried in the Scottish cemetery there. He bequeathed upwards of £50,000 to various Liverpool institutions. Smith was an effective back-bench politician, representing the old radical tradition of campaigning without seeking office. G. LE G. NORGATE, *rev.* H. C. G. MATTHEW

Sources S. Smith, *My life-work* (1902) • P. J. Waller, *Democracy and sectarianism: a political and social history of Liverpool, 1868–1939* (1981) • *The Times* (31 Dec 1906) • *Liverpool Daily Post and Liverpool Mercury* (31 Dec 1906)

Archives Bodl. Oxf., Gladstone MSS • NL Wales, corresp. with Sir J. H. Lewis

Likenesses W. E. Lockhart, oils, 1899, Walker Art Gallery, Liverpool [*see illus.*] • Annan & Sons, photogravure (after photograph by Elliott & Fry), repro. in Smith, *My life-work* • Spy [L. Ward], caricature, watercolour study, NPG; repro. in *VF* (4 Aug 1904)

Wealth at death £111,107 3*s*. 10*d*.: probate, 1 March 1907, *CGPLA Eng. & Wales*

Smith, Samuel (1872–1949), tea dealer, was born on 22 June 1872 at 62 Lady Pitt Lane, Hunslet, Leeds, the son of William Smith, willeyer and fettler, and his wife, Harriet, *née* Powell. He contributed to the family income from the age of nine by working as a butcher's boy on Friday evenings and Saturdays, and then, at the age of ten, as a half-timer was employed as an errand boy for a local tea merchants. After leaving school he remained in the trade, becoming a traveller 'on the road' for Messrs Stable of Leeds. When the firm was taken over by Ridgways a new marketing strategy was adopted of delivering directly to householders, and Smith rose to be area manager with the firm. Smith married and he and his wife, Ada, had four sons and three daughters.

In 1907 Smith left his home town to establish his own

tea blending, packaging, and distribution company in Third Avenue, Newcastle upon Tyne, in partnership with R. Watson and a fellow former employee of Ridgways in Liverpool by the name of Titterington, modified to provide the name of the business—Ringtons. The firm specialized in door-to-door deliveries of packet tea, and by 1914 it operated eleven horse-drawn vans. Rationing and requisitioning during the First World War dramatically reduced the scale of the operations, but post-war expansion was rapid, the firm moving into a new factory and offices in Algernon Road, Newcastle, in 1926, opening depots throughout the north of England, and finally building another large blending and packing factory in the street where Smith had been born, Lady Pitt Lane, Leeds, in 1935. By 1939 Smith was regarded as the 'tea king of the North', operating over 200 vehicles, all painted in the firm's distinctive livery, and had created a subsidiary company, Northern Coachbuilders, to manufacture these for sale to other firms. He was succeeded in business by his second son, Douglas, and several grandsons.

Smith became renowned in the north-east for his public benefactions, for which he was made an OBE. According to one obituary, his humble origins and early poverty meant that 'he never forgot the needy or the underdog … His gifts to struggling organisations and to needy charities were numerous and their full extent will never be known' (*Newcastle Evening Chronicle*). He also donated many valuable pictures to the Laing Art Gallery in Newcastle, Shipley Gallery (Gateshead), and Sunderland Art Gallery. He was particularly supportive of youth movements, providing a motor yacht for the Admiral Jellicoe sea scouts and a gold cup for the scouts. After one of his sons was killed in 1936 while flying from Newcastle to Liverpool he presented two aeroplanes to Newcastle Aero Club. He was a member of Newcastle rotary club, first president of the Tyneside–Yorkshire Society, and a freemason, being founder member of the Doric Lodge of freemasons and member of Lord Collingwood lodge. He was also JP for the borough.

A prominent north-eastern tea dealer, Samuel Smith died on 12 August 1949 at the home of his son Douglas, 52 Mitchell Avenue, Jesmond, Newcastle; the cause of death was recorded as 'senility'. His wife had predeceased him in 1944, but he was survived by three sons and three daughters. His funeral took place at St George's Church, Jesmond, on 15 August and he was interred at All Saints' cemetery, Newcastle. MICHAEL WINSTANLEY

Sources *Ringtons, established 1907*, Ringtons Ltd (privately printed) [promotional history of firm] · *Newcastle Evening Chronicle* (12 Aug 1949) · *Sunderland Echo* (12 Aug 1949) · *Newcastle Journal* (15 Aug 1949) · b. cert. · d. cert. · D. Forrest, *Tea for the British* (1973) · *CGPLA Eng. & Wales* (1949)

Likenesses photograph, repro. in Ringtons Ltd, *Ringtons, established 1907* · photograph, repro. in *Newcastle Evening Chronicle*

Wealth at death £80,335 5*s*. 5*d*.: probate, 8 Dec 1949, *CGPLA Eng. & Wales*

Smith, Sarah [*pseud.* Hesba Stretton] (**1832–1911**), novelist and short story writer, was born on 27 July 1832 at New Street, Wellington, Shropshire. She was the third daughter of the eight children (three sons died young; four daughters and one son lived to maturity) of Benjamin Smith (1793–1878), printer, bookseller, and the first postmaster of Wellington, and Anne Bakewell Smith (1798–1842), a strict and notably intelligent Methodist. Sarah and her elder sister Elizabeth attended the Old Hall, a girls' day school in Wellington, but gained most of their education from the books in their father's shop. Both qualified as governesses.

Sarah Smith (**1832–1911**), by Hayman Selig Mendelssohn

At twenty-six Sarah Smith began her career as a journalist, using the pseudonym Hesba Stretton (derived from the initials of the siblings' names—Hannah, Elizabeth, Sarah, Benjamin, Anna—and the Shropshire village of All Stretton where her younger sister was bequeathed property). Without her knowledge Elizabeth sent Sarah's first published story to Charles Dickens, editor of *Household Words*. 'The Lucky Leg', a bizarre tale of a widower who proposes to women with wooden legs, appeared in no. 469 (19 March 1859). Stretton contributed by invitation 'The Ghost in the Clock Room' to the first *All the Year Round* Christmas number in 1859 and was successful again in 1864, 1865, and 1866. Although he did not accept all her submissions, Dickens was unfailingly helpful and encouraging. 'The Postmaster's Daughter' (*All the Year Round*, 5 Nov 1859), 'A Provincial Post Office' (*All the Year Round*, 28 Feb 1863), and 'The Travelling Post-Office' (*All the Year Round*, 'Mugby Junction', Dec 1866) reflect many personal and family experiences. Smith published stories, from the authentic and factual to the sensational and romantic, in

Chambers's Journal, the *Welcome Guest*, *Temple Bar*, *Tinsley's Magazine*, and *The Argosy*. Her log books, a journal of continental travels, frequent moves in Manchester and London, and dealings with publishers from 1859 to 1871–2, show her to be tart and censorious, prickly in negotiations about payment, fully aware of her own worth, impatient with servants, and driven by the detection of 'bugs' from one lodging-house to another.

In September 1863 Sarah and Elizabeth Smith left home for Manchester, where Elizabeth worked as a governess (until 1870) and Sarah continued to publish a steady stream of children's books: *Fern's Hollow* (1864), *Enoch Roden's Training* (1865), and *The Children of Cloverley* (1865). The huge success that virtually launched her long career with the Religious Tract Society was *Jessica's First Prayer* (*Sunday at Home*, July 1866), a novel for children and the newly literate, about a London waif neglected by her drunken actress mother. With simplicity and pathos, traits Lord Shaftesbury praised in the story, Jessica exposes the prejudice of the Methodist congregation which initially shuns her and the miserliness of the coffee-stall keeper who eventually adopts her. It sold over two million copies in Stretton's lifetime, spawned the sequel *Jessica's Mother* (1867), was translated into fifteen European and Asiatic languages and published in Braille, depicted on coloured slides for magic lantern segments of Bands of Hope programmes, and placed in all Russian schools by order of Tsar Alexander II, a decree revoked by his successor.

First-hand observation made Smith's pictures of slum poverty accurate and compelling. *Little Meg's Children* (1868) features a ten-year-old dealing with abandonment, destitution, the deaths of her mother and an infant sibling, and teenage prostitution; thanks to Meg's biblical faith and some narrative twists, the story also presents reconciliation and reformation. From the outset Smith underscored the candid, often tragic truthfulness of the child, usually a waif, like the urchin Tony in *Alone in London* (1869), who tries to have the dying child Dolly admitted to an overcrowded hospital, the heroic Tom Haslam in *Pilgrim Street* (1867), who dies rescuing his abusive convict father, trapped in the fire the reprobate himself had set, and the lad Peter in *The Fishers of Derby Haven* (1866), who merits only flogging for his honesty. In addition to illustrating New Testament principles, Smith's stories turn on coincidences, frequently involving money, such as Meg's finding treasure in a dingy attic, the delayed letter that results in the surprise gift of a freehold cottage in *Two Secrets* (1882), and the discovery of hoarded money through an act of charity in *Sam Franklin's Savings Bank* (1888).

In her three-decker adult novels Smith continued the detailed accuracy of locale and dialect and added, as in *The Doctor's Dilemma* (1872), the sentimental elements of conflicts between love and duty, undeclared and protracted romances, women's vulnerability under greedy husbands and guardians, and convenient deaths. Her fiction for the young was more succinct and focused, always hitting hard at social issues: enclosure (*Fern's Hollow*, 1864), young offenders (*In Prison and Out*, 1878), streetwalkers and rescue missions (*The King's Servants*, 1873), alcoholism and parental neglect (*Nellie's Dark Days*, 1870, *Lost Gip*, 1873, *Brought Home*, 1875), the abuse of domestics (*Cassy*, 1874), and the starving of children to make them effective beggars (*The Lord's Purse-Bearers*, 1883). Smith applauded Dr Barnardo's work with street children; with the Revd Benjamin Waugh, editor of the *Sunday Magazine*, she lobbied for the establishment of the Society for the Prevention of Cruelty to Children in 1884, and served on its executive for a decade, before resigning on account of the society's financial mismanagement. Smith collected money (over £900) and wrote books to support the cause of Russian evangelicals (Stundists) and famine victims in the early 1890s.

At the age of sixty in 1892, Sarah Smith settled with her sister Elizabeth in their first permanent residence, Ivycroft on Ham Common, Richmond, Surrey, where they founded a branch of the Popular Book Club to circulate good books among the working classes. Here the inseparable duo spent their last nineteen years. Elizabeth predeceased her sister by eight months. Sarah Smith died at home on 8 October 1911. The *Sunday at Home* obituary praised her 'long, happy, useful and noble life'.

PATRICIA DEMERS

Sources M. N. Cutt, *Ministering angels: a study of nineteenth-century evangelical writing for children* (1979) • J. S. Bratton, 'Hesba Stretton's journalism', *Victorian Periodicals Review*, 12 (1979), 60–70 • L. Salway, 'Pathetic simplicity: Hesba Stretton and her books for children', *The Signal approach to children's books*, ed. N. Chambers (1980) • P. Demers, 'Mrs Sherwood and Hesba Stretton: the letter and the spirit of Evangelical writing', *Romanticism and children's literature in nineteenth-century England* (1991) • H. Friederichs, 'Hesba Stretton at home', *Young Woman*, 2 (1893–4), 327–33 • 'Hesba Stretton', *Sunday at Home* (Dec 1911), 121–7 • D. Webb, 'A personal note', *Sunday at Home* (Dec 1911), 124–5 • A. Lohrli, ed., *Household Words: a weekly journal conducted by Charles Dickens* (1973)

Archives Shrops. RRC, diary and log books | Toronto Public Library, Osborne collection, MS letter to W. Taylor; corresp. relating to Canadian connections

Likenesses H. S. Mendelssohn, photograph, NPG [*see illus.*] • E. Stretton, portrait, repro. in Friederichs, 'Hesba Stretton at home' • portrait (in her sixties), repro. in Cutt, *Ministering angels*, fig. 19 • portraits (at a young age), repro. in Friederichs, 'Hesba Stretton at Home' • portraits (at age of forty, with Elizabeth Stretton), repro. in 'Hesba Stretton', *Sunday at Home*

Wealth at death £9902 7*s*.: probate, 5 Dec 1911, *CGPLA Eng. & Wales*

Smith, (Emily) Sheila Kaye- [*married name* (Emily) Sheila Fry] **(1887–1956)**, novelist, was born on 4 February 1887 at Battle Lodge, 9 Dane Road, St Leonards, Sussex, the elder daughter of Edward Kaye-Smith (1840–1922), general medical practitioner, and his wife, Emily Janet Maclean (1843–1924), daughter of Robert de la Condamine and his wife, Janet. Sheila Kaye-Smith (she never used her first name) grew up in east Sussex, and childhood memories of summers spent with her younger sister, Selina (1889–1924), on local farms were to provide a fertile source of images for her novels set in the region. Photographic portraits of Sheila Kaye-Smith by E. O. Hoppé and Howard Coster reveal a serious yet unassuming woman, her dark hair cut in a short twenties bob. She attended St Leonards Ladies' College and in her teenage years wrote six short novels a

(Emily) **Sheila Kaye-Smith** (1887–1956), by Howard Coster, 1930

year. When she was twenty-one her first full-length novel, *The Tramping Methodist* (1908), was published. It displays themes which were to become characteristic of her work: love of place—specifically the Kent and Sussex borders—and a fascination with the Christian faith. During a career spanning some fifty years, she had thirty-one novels published with many more remaining in manuscript. Among her best-known works are *Tamarisk Town* (1919), *Joanna Godden* (1922), *The End of the House of Alard* (1923) and *The History of Susan Spray, the Female Preacher* (1931). In 1947 *Joanna Godden* was made into a film with Googie Withers in the title role.

As a regional novelist, Sheila Kaye-Smith has much to offer: topographical accuracy, a keen ear for dialect, and a genuine affection for the locale and its people. She knew a great deal about farming life and the harsh conditions of farm workers in the nineteenth century and described their lot with imaginative sympathy. Indeed her evocation of rural life, as in *Sussex Gorse* (1916), is realistic and vivid. However, although her characters are on the whole believable, there is a lack of psychological subtlety throughout. Though popular in their day, regrettably her novels have not found lasting acclaim, although *Joanna Godden* and *Susan Spray* were reprinted by Virago in 1983. Her most successful novel was *The End of the House of Alard*, which was a best-seller in both Britain and America. The theme of Anglo-Catholicism is central to this work as it was in the author's own life, and the declining fortunes of the novel's house of Alard come to symbolize the more general decline of the ruling classes in England following the First World War. Through the character of Gervase Alard, who eventually enters a monastery, Sheila Kaye-Smith expresses her own growing belief in Catholicism as the locus of immutable order and tradition.

On 16 October 1924 Kaye-Smith married the Revd Theodore Penrose Fry (1892–1971), eldest son of Sir John Fry, baronet. They had met at the Anglo-Catholic Christ Church in St Leonards, where he was the curate. It was a church she had secretly visited as a child, attracted by the flickering candles and the smell of incense, visits disapproved of by her Anglican parents. Unable to remain at Christ Church once he was married, Penrose Fry accepted a curacy at St Stephen's, Gloucester Road, London, where a few years later T. S. Eliot became churchwarden. The couple lived first in North and then South Kensington. During this time she wrote a non-fictional study, *Anglo-Catholicism* (1925). In 1929 they returned to Sussex, both deeply dissatisfied with Anglicanism, and were received into the Roman Catholic church. They bought Little Doucegrove, near Northiam in Sussex, a dilapidated oasthouse—which had featured in her early novel *Spell Land* (1910)—together with 50 acres of farmland. This was to be their home for the rest of their lives. There were no children of the marriage.

In addition to her novels, Sheila Kaye-Smith wrote some poetry, an autobiography entitled *Three Ways Home* (1937), and a few works of non-fiction including two books on Jane Austen with G. B. Stern, *Talking of Jane Austen* (1943) and *More about Jane Austen* (1949). Her guide *The Weald of Kent and Sussex* (1953) was part of the Regional Books series and still provides a useful introduction to the region. Sheila Kaye-Smith died suddenly of a heart attack on 14 January 1956 at Little Doucegrove. She is buried beside her husband in the grounds of a small Catholic church which she had built at Little Doucegrove and which was dedicated to St Theresa of Lisieux, about whom she had written in *Quartet in Heaven* (1952). PETER D. SMITH

Sources S. Kaye-Smith, *Three ways home* (1937) · D. Walker, *Sheila Kaye-Smith* (1980) · B. Smith and P. Haas, *Writers in Sussex* (1985) · *The Times* (16 Jan 1956) · R. Thurston Hopkins, *Sheila Kaye-Smith and the Weald country* (1925) · personal knowledge (2004) · private information (2004) · *WWW* · b. cert. · m. cert. · *CGPLA Eng. & Wales* (1956)
Archives Ransom HRC, letters and MSS · W. Sussex RO, papers
Likenesses E. O. Hoppé, photograph, *c.*1925, repro. in Thurston Hopkins, *Sheila Kaye-Smith*, frontispiece · H. Coster, photograph, 1930, NPG [*see illus.*] · H. Coster, photographs, NPG
Wealth at death £13,827 12*s.* 7*d.*: probate, 7 March 1956, *CGPLA Eng. & Wales*

Smith, Shepherd. *See* Smith, James Elishama (1801–1857).

Smith, Sir (William) Sidney (1764–1840), naval officer, was born on 21 June 1764 in Park Lane, London, the second son of John Smith of Midgham, Berkshire, a captain in the guards and gentleman-usher to Queen Charlotte, wife of George III; he was also grandson of Edward Smith, an army officer who was governor of Fort Charles at Kingston, Jamaica, and fought under Wolfe at Quebec. Another relation named Edward had been a captain in the navy who, in command of the *Eltham*, was killed in the attack on La Guayra on 18 February 1743. Sidney Smith's mother was the daughter of Mary Thurlow, a Norfolk heiress, and

Sir (William) Sidney Smith (1764–1840), by John Eckstein, 1801–2

Pinckney Wilkinson, a London merchant, who regarded John Smith as an adventurer but was unable to prevent his daughter eloping with him in 1760. They had two other sons: Charles Douglas and John Spencer. Wilkinson disinherited his daughter and severed all connection with her and her three sons. However, Wilkinson's younger daughter Ann had married Thomas Pitt, first Baron Camelford, and, persuaded by him, Wilkinson relented sufficiently to pay for his grandsons' education at Tonbridge School. John Smith and his wife then quarrelled and she fled to Bath, near where the boys completed their education at a boarding-school, but stayed with their father occasionally in Midgham Cottage in the grounds of Midgham Hall, near Newbury, Berkshire. There Sidney Smith was first observed to be vivacious, quick, daring, and mercurial.

Naval service, 1777–1792 Smith entered the navy in June 1777 on board the storeship *Tortoise*, going out to North America, and in January 1778 moved to the brig *Unicorn*, which with the 44 gun *Experiment* in September 1778 captured the 32 gun American frigate *Raleigh*. On 25 November 1779 he joined the *Sandwich*, flagship of Sir George Bridges Rodney, and in her was at an engagement with a Spanish squadron off Cape St Vincent in January 1780, and at those between the British and French fleets on 17 April and 15 and 19 May 1780. Having passed his examination for lieutenant, in September 1780 Smith was appointed in this rank to the *Alcide* and in her was present off the Chesapeake in September 1781 at Admiral Graves's unsuccessful attempt to relieve the British army at Yorktown, and at the battle of the Saintes in April 1782. In May 1782 he was appointed to command the sloop *Fury* and in May 1783 was promoted to the 32 gun *Alcmene*.

At the return of peace, when the *Alcmene* was paid off, Smith lived for two years in France, for the most part near Caen, and in 1787 travelled through Spain to Gibraltar and Morocco, where, in expectation of future hostilities, he took deliberate note of the sultan's naval forces and bases, then reported on them to the Admiralty.

In 1789 Smith obtained a further six months' leave from the Admiralty to travel to Sweden and Russia, then at war. At the Swedish naval base of Karlskrona he was offered employment in the Swedish navy and, though he had as a condition of his leave agreed to forgo any such opportunity, he returned to London to request that his undertaking be waived, carrying the British ambassador's dispatches and a message from the Swedish king Gustavus III. He and his request were ignored; Smith returned to Sweden and travelled on to the Gulf of Finland, where the summer campaigning season of 1790 had begun, and where, despite his undertaking, he agreed to serve Gustavus as a volunteer. That summer he served both the king on shore and the duke of Sodermanland in the Swedish fleet. The Swedes were short of experienced naval officers and Smith was favoured, but this aroused envy. Early in June Russian naval forces drove back and entrapped the Swedes in the Bay of Viborg and to effect their escape Smith was given command of the Swedish light craft—nearly 100 vessels, predominantly bomb ketches, galleys, and gunboats—with which he cleared the Russians from islands commanding the exit from the bay and enabled the Swedes to break out early in July. An armistice followed and Smith returned to London, where in May 1792, at the request of Gustavus, George III invested him a knight grand cross of the order of the Sword. Thereafter his enemies knew him as 'the Swedish knight', the ill feeling behind which title was perhaps increased by the fact that at least six British naval officers were killed fighting for Russia on 3–4 June 1791.

War in the Mediterranean, 1792–1800 Meanwhile, Smith's younger brother, John Spencer, had been appointed to the British embassy to Sultan Selim III of Turkey, and in 1792 Sidney Smith was authorized to visit his brother; at the same time he inspected the Turkish-ruled coasts in the eastern Mediterranean and Black Sea. Following the French declaration of war against Britain on 1 February 1793, Smith received news of the general recall of British officers at Smyrna. He recruited some forty British seamen, purchased a lateen-rigged vessel, and sailed west; in December he entered the port of Toulon, where a British fleet under Lord Hood, with Spanish and Neapolitan allies, was attempting to support the anti-Jacobin party. When in mid-December a republican bombardment forced the withdrawal of the allied forces, Smith volunteered to burn those ships of the French fleet—thirty-two of the line and fourteen frigates—that could not be removed and were within the inner harbour, close to the naval arsenal. Thirteen of these vessels, including ten ships of the line, were burnt, as too were many of the combustible stores in the naval arsenal. Nevertheless eighteen ships of the line and four frigates survived and had to be abandoned to the republican army. Although Hood gave Smith due credit, others resented his employment and blamed him for the survival of so many French warships. The British had indeed missed an unprecedented opportunity to weaken French naval power. However, Smith was only partly to blame: more advance planning and preparation might have avoided last-minute delegation to one who was regarded as a maverick volunteer.

On returning to London with Hood's dispatches, Smith was appointed to command the new 38 gun frigate *Diamond* in the North Sea. Taking advantage of the opportunity of carrying to Flushing Lord Spencer, who in December 1794 became first lord of the Admiralty, Smith requested command of a flotilla of small craft to operate off the estuaries of northern France. This was given him in March 1795, in which capacity he was employed until April 1796, when, cutting out a French lugger from the mouth of the River Seine, Smith with the boarding party was cut off and taken prisoner. Sent to Paris, Smith expected to be exchanged for an officer of equal rank, as was the practice, but, suspected of complicity in espionage, he was confined in the Temple prison for two years. As his companion he had, ostensibly as his servant, a French royalist émigré, François de Tromelin, a survivor from the Quiberon Bay expedition of 1795 who had entered on board the *Diamond*. The latter contacted his wife, partly through whom Smith was put in touch with the royalist Colonel Louis-Edmond Picard de Phélippeaux. In February 1798, with an order of transfer to another prison, Phélippeaux and Tromelin effected Smith's escape. Via Rouen, Honfleur, and a chartered boat intercepted by the British frigate *Argo*, Smith reached Britain on 7 May.

Meanwhile, Bonaparte's expedition for Egypt was departing from Toulon. News of Nelson's defeat of the French fleet off the mouth of the River Nile on 31 July reached Britain on 2 October. By this time Sidney Smith's brother Spencer had become minister-plenipotentiary at Constantinople, and in October Sidney Smith was appointed to the command of the 80 gun *Tigre* and dispatched to the Mediterranean to act under Lord St Vincent, commander-in-chief there, as senior naval officer in his eastern sector, and also as joint plenipotentiary with his brother. Nelson, by then at Naples, had hitherto had command of vessels in the eastern basin, and St Vincent did not write to Nelson formally to place Smith under his command, while Smith in reaching his station wrote to Nelson assuming the command of a commodore with an authority which encroached upon that of Nelson, unknowingly giving offence. The combination of a diplomatic and a naval role was also confusing. St Vincent placed Smith in his naval capacity formally under Nelson, but reverberations from the reorganization reached back to London.

Smith's combined roles resulted in concentrating command of the allied forces in the eastern Mediterranean. At Constantinople, Smith became party to an alliance between Russia and Turkey, which had declared war on France for her invasion of Egypt; he was made a member of the sultan's inner council, the diwan; and he was given command of Turkish naval and military forces assembling on the island of Rhodes to attack the invading force. On 3 March 1799 he also took command of two British ships of the line at Alexandria blockading French forces on shore. That same evening he learned that Bonaparte had stormed Jaffa on his way into Syria. One of his ships Smith promptly dispatched to Acre (administrative capital of the Ottoman governor of the Levant littoral), which the French army, marching along the coast, reached on 15 March. Smith in the *Tigre* reached the walled city almost simultaneously; the defences had been strengthened but could be manned by only 4000 men, while Bonaparte had 13,000 hardened soldiers. Smith immediately put 800 seamen and marines ashore and mounted ships' guns on the ramparts. Over the next six weeks, strengthened by Smith's reinforcement, the Turkish garrison withstood twelve attacks, the last of which almost penetrated the city.

The siege of Acre was raised on 20 May. Initially resistance was possible principally because the French possessed only field guns; the ships conveying Bonaparte's siege guns eastward were captured by British warships on 18 March. Also, from 7 May Acre's garrison was reinforced by Turkish troops from Rhodes. The defence of Acre nevertheless made Smith's name, and justifiably so, as his courage and determination undoubtedly inspired the defenders. From Britain in September 1799 he received the thanks of both houses of parliament, and in 1801 he received a pension of £1000 a year, backdated to 1799. From the sultan he received a pelisse and the chelingk, or plume of triumph, like that awarded to Nelson.

From Acre Smith sailed for Rhodes, where, as nominal commander of the Turkish forces, he accompanied the Turkish counter-invasion of Egypt that was broken by Bonaparte in July. It is said that the French officer negotiating on board the *Tigre* an exchange of prisoners was shown accounts of French reverses in Europe, which precipitated Bonaparte's departure for France on 23 August. In spite of his departure, at the end of October a second Turkish landing was also routed, while Lord Elgin, the new British ambassador at Constantinople, who arrived in November, recommended use of 'every possible means that can aid in forcing the French out of Egypt' (Shankland, 110). In December Smith thus negotiated a month's truce with the new French commander, Kleber, and on 24 January 1800 the convention of al-ʿArish, by which, under a truce of three months, the French army would be transported back to France at allied expense.

By then French forces in Egypt had been much reduced by deaths, and the arrangement had both economy and humanity to recommend it. However, the British government opposed the prospect of 18,000 hardened troops returning to Europe, and the new commander-in-chief in the Mediterranean, Lord Keith, was instructed not to ratify the agreement; indeed on 18 November 1800 and 27 May 1801 Smith was much criticized in parliament for arranging the convention. The French army in Egypt was instead destroyed in 1801 by the British campaign led by Keith and Abercromby, for which Smith was consulted over the place of invasion and on 7 March commanded the third wave of landing craft. In recognition of his significant role in these operations, at the conclusion of the campaign in September, Smith was selected to carry Keith's dispatches to London.

The height Smith's reputation had achieved after Acre was never attained again. Rather, his career hereafter was constrained by a reputation for impulsive activity that was not completely trustworthy because it was unconventional; an added restraint was the fear and irritation Smith engendered by his tendency not to consult or inform when his energy outran his discretion. The agreement of al-ʿArish did much to discredit him, while his own high opinion of his merits and long accounts of his adventures annoyed other officers.

Parliament and the Mediterranean again, 1801–1809 Nevertheless Smith had acquired a high popular reputation, and at the general election of 1801 he was elected MP for Rochester, an Admiralty borough. There he posed as an independent supporter of the Admiralty, but his maiden speech of 2 December 1802 deplored the peace reductions of Lord St Vincent, then first lord, a disregard for the government interest that had already been demonstrated in 1802 when he was living at Greenwich, where he was rumoured to have had a brief affair with Caroline, princess of Wales. With the resumption of war he considered his appointment to active service a deliberate attempt to prevent him attending the House of Commons and that he was disengaged from ministers. By 1804 he was listed as supporting Pitt, and in 1806 was defeated at Rochester.

Between March 1803 and May 1804, with the rank of commodore, Smith commanded a squadron of small craft blockading the Flemish coast. After striking his flag, he designed and obtained Admiralty approval to build at Dover two prototype catamaran landing craft, a design based on the twin-hulled canoes of the Pacific islands. In the autumn of 1804, with the rank of colonel of marines, he was authorized to attempt a night attack on the French invasion flotilla at Boulogne using Congreve's rockets and Robert Fulton's mines but owing to bad weather and a heavy swell the attack was unsuccessful. It was a failure that prompted Lord Barham, first lord of the Admiralty from May 1805, to observe that 'there seems … such a want of judgement in our friend Sir Sidney, that it is much safer to employ him under command than in command' (Castlereagh, 5.115).

Smith's expenses at Dover had outrun his income, and in 1805 he was temporarily in the king's bench prison for debt. On 9 November 1805, however, he was promoted rear-admiral and in January 1806 he hoisted his flag in the *Pompée* for service in the Mediterranean, where Lord Collingwood employed him on the coast of Naples. The French had once more invaded the kingdom of the Two Sicilies and Smith's first task was to land supplies for the relief of the fortress of Gaeta; he also displaced the French occupying force on Capri with a British one, beginning the British occupation of the island. The king of the Two Sicilies appointed him viceroy of Calabria, when, as 'commander-in-chief on behalf of King Ferdinand', he began supplying and reinforcing the guerrilla war in the mountains, agitating for more financial and military support. The insurgents had one notable success at the battle of Maida. However, General Moore, commanding British land forces in Sicily, thought little of Smith's strategy, believing him the unconscious tool of the Neapolitan royal family, while Collingwood thought his head 'full of strange vapours', believed Barham had sent Smith to him simply 'to be clear of a tormentor' (*Private Correspondence*, 191), and himself found Smith more annoying than the French or Spanish fleet.

In February–March 1807, as third in command, he accompanied the fleet under Sir John Duckworth that penetrated the Dardanelles to Constantinople with the intention of forcing the Turks to end collaboration with the French. The demonstration of naval force had little effect; indeed the fleet had to withdraw under threat of being cut off by batteries in the straits. Smith was consulted by Duckworth but felt his former connection with the sultan, which might have been useful diplomatically, was ignored. He returned to Britain, to be appointed in November 1807 senior officer in the Tagus. At Lisbon he assisted in the evacuation of the Portuguese royal family and the remnants of the Portuguese navy to Rio de Janeiro, where in February 1808 he himself was sent to command the South American station. There, without the co-operation of the British minister, Lord Strangeford, he attempted to raise a Portuguese-backed attack on the Spanish in Buenos Aires and was recalled to London to be reprimanded in August 1809.

Latter years, 1810–1828 Smith was promoted vice-admiral on 31 July 1810 but by then opinion about employing him seems to have been widely unfavourable. 'Beware of *Heroes*—the more you come to know them, the less you will think of them' (*Croker Papers*, 1.350), Sir Roger Curtis advised John Wilson Croker, the new secretary to the Admiralty, with regard to Smith. However, it was Croker who asserted responsibility for Smith's appointment as second in command to Sir Edward Pellew in the Mediterranean in July 1812, claiming that naval members of the board were 'rather averse; for certainly he was not what is called a sailor' (ibid., 1.349). Mainly employed in the blockade of Toulon, Pellew found him 'as gay and thoughtless as ever' (Parkinson, 406), and he was replaced in July 1814.

Smith was not employed at sea again. However, criticism of him continued to grow, as was expressed by the duke of Wellington. In Brussels at the time of Waterloo, Smith arranged the evacuation of some of the wounded from the battlefield, and was subsequently employed in a liaison role by Wellington, who later observed to John Croker at the Admiralty:

> Of all the men whom I ever knew who have any reputation, the man who least deserves it is Sir Sidney Smith. During my embassy at Paris … I saw a good deal of him and had eternal projects from him as long as I would listen to them. At first, out of deference to his name and reputation, I attended to him but soon I found he was a mere vaporiser. I cannot believe a man so silly in all other affairs can be a good naval officer. (*Croker Papers*, 1.348–9)

Smith lived in Paris for much of the remainder of his life. Initially this was to escape his creditors. In 1811 he had been refunded £7375 for past expenses and, on petitioning government from Paris, his pension was doubled. He was accompanied to France by his wife, Caroline, daughter of James Hearn of Shanakill, co. Waterford, and widow of Sir George Berriman Rumbold, British minister to Hamburg; Smith had married her in October 1810 and they had three daughters and a son. He was invested with the KCB in December 1815 and attained the rank of admiral on 19 July 1821. In Paris he formed the order of 'knights liberators' to campaign for the release of Christian slaves from captivity in the piratical states of north Africa. With characteristic enthusiasm, he continued to request naval employment. He was made a GCB on 4 July 1838. His wife died on 16 May 1828, and he died in Paris on 26 May 1840; both were buried in the Père Lachaise cemetery.

Smith's intelligence, imagination, energy, and courage were the principal features of his reputation, but he was also renowned for his eccentricities. He was indeed egotistical and insensitive to others, for which he suffered. For he was also the victim of a naval service that during the Napoleonic wars became increasingly rigorous and bureaucratic in its conventions. The sheer size of the Royal Navy, the scale of its operations, and the co-operation and discipline demanded of its officers acted against Smith. He was an individualist who might have been judged more liberally in an earlier military age; certainly some of his proposals were sound. ROGER MORRISS

Sources *Memoirs of Admiral Sir Sidney Smith* (1839) • J. Barrow, *The life and correspondence of Admiral Sir William Sidney Smith*, 2 vols. (1848) • T. Pocock, *A thirst for glory: the life of Admiral Sir Sidney Smith* (1996) • P. Shankland, *Beware of heroes: Admiral Sir Sidney Smith's war against Napoleon* (1975) • E. F. L. Russell, *Knight of the Sword: the life and letters of Admiral Sir William Sidney Smith* (1964) • *The Croker papers: the correspondence and diaries of … John Wilson Croker*, ed. L. J. Jennings, 3 vols. (1884) • *DNB* • *Memoirs and correspondence of Viscount Castlereagh, second marquess of Londonderry*, ed. C. Vane, marquess of Londonderry, 12 vols. (1848–53), vols. 1–5 • *The private correspondence of Admiral Lord Collingwood*, ed. E. Hughes, Navy RS, 98 (1957) • C. N. Parkinson, *Edward Pellew, Viscount Exmouth, admiral of the red* (1934) • HoP, *Commons*

Archives BL, bills and school accounts, Add. MS 69338A • Hunt. L., corresp. and papers • NMM, corresp. • NMM, family MSS • Portsmouth City RO, letters and papers • Rice University, Houston, Texas, Woodson Research Center, corresp. and papers • U. Mich., Clements L., corresp. | BL, letters to Sir Richard Bickerton, Add. MS 37778 • BL, corresp. with British consul at Mogador • BL, corresp. with Lady Camelford, Add. MS 69292 • BL, letters to Lord Collingwood, Add. MS 40097 • BL, corresp. with Lord Grenville, Add. MSS 58980, 69045 • BL, corresp. with Sir Hudson Lowe, Add. MSS 20107, 20163, 20165, 20189 • BL, letters to Lord Nelson, Add. MSS 34908–34917 • Bucks. RLSS, corresp. with Lord Hobart • CKS, letters to William Pitt • Devon RO, corresp. with first Viscount Sidmouth • NA Scot., letters to Sir Alexander Hope • NL Scot., corresp. with Hugh Elliot • NL Scot., corresp. with Robert Liston • NMM, corresp. with Lord Barham • NMM, letters to Lord Keith • NMM, letters to Sir Evan Nepean • NRA, priv. coll., corresp. with Lord Elgin • PRO NIre., corresp. with Lord Castlereagh

Likenesses J. Opie, oils, 1783, NMM • T. Cheesman, stipple, pubd 1796 (after J. Opie), BM • stipple, pubd 1796, NPG • M. Cosway, etching, 1797 (after P. Hénnequin), BM • J. Eckstein, oils, 1801–2, NPG [*see illus.*] • A. Fogg, engraving, pubd 1802 (after W. Hamilton), NPG • E. Bell, mezzotint, pubd 1803 (after Chandler), NPG • T. Kirk, statue, 1845, NMM • P. D'Angers, stipple and line engraving, pubd 1847 (after medallion by G. and C. Cook), NPG • T. Stothard, pencil drawing, BM • T. Sutton, group portrait, Penicuik House, Midlothian • oils (after P. Hénnequin, 1796), NMM • stipple, NPG

Smith, Sidney (1805–1881), political agent, was born on 30 September 1805 at Leith, Edinburgh, the second son of William Drummond Smith, solicitor. He studied law at the University of Edinburgh and practised as a solicitor there while pursuing his interest in 'social morality and the science of mind', on which he gave public lectures. William Tate, the publisher of his *Principles of Phrenology* (1838) recommended him to Richard Cobden who in 1839 appointed him as a full-time lecturer for the Anti-Corn Law League. He was one of the league's most effective crowd-pullers, and some of his lectures were published in the *Anti-Corn Law Circular* as a model for other speakers. His campaign in the 'enemy' territory of Lincolnshire and Cambridgeshire met with organized disruption and had to be abandoned when the meeting at Cambridge turned into a town versus gown riot. Feeling that he had 'rubbed off a little of the enamel of respectability by becoming a field, or market-place lecturer' (Anti-Corn Law League letter-book, Manchester Central Library, MS F 337, 2A1), Smith returned to Manchester as league secretary and editor of its *Circular*. In January 1841 he moved to London at the invitation of Francis Place to become secretary of the Metropolitan Anti-Corn Law Association, energetically promoting its cause in the press, in lectures at Brixton Unitarian chapel, and in a series of mass meetings at London theatres. He also masterminded the return of a free-trade candidate for the City of London in October 1843. In 1846 he was appointed secretary of the City of London Liberal Registration Association, a post he held for thirty-three years, and from 1847 to 1858 managed the successive electoral campaigns of Baron Lionel de Rothschild which culminated in the bill enabling Jews to take their seats in parliament.

Smith's other published works included two handbooks for prospective emigrants to the colonies and *The Mother Country, or, The Spade, the Wastes and the Eldest Son* (1849), in which he advocated a radical programme of reforms including abolition of the rights of primogeniture and entail. However, his identification with the interests of the City, in which he held a plurality of secretaryships, rendered his Liberalism increasingly illiberal. As adviser to the building and engineering employers he recommended the lock-out which ended the 1852 strike, and he vigorously opposed household suffrage, on the grounds that it militated against 'property and intelligence'.

Smith was twice married. His first wife, Matilda, with whom he had two daughters and a son, died in February 1853. On 8 July 1855 he married Elizabeth Harris, with whom he had three sons and two daughters. He died at his home, the Manor House, Feltham, Middlesex, on 14 March 1881, and was buried in the graveyard of St Dunstan's, Feltham. G. Martin Murphy

Sources memoirs of S. Smith, priv. coll. • microfilm, NA Scot., RH 4/156 • S. Smith's reminiscences of Anti-Corn Law League, Man. CL, J. B. Smith collection, MS 923.2 5333, vol. 1, fols. 120–53, 497–510 • N. McCord, *The Anti-Corn Law League, 1838–46*, 2nd edn (1968), 58–87 • P. A. Pickering and A. Tyrrell, *The people's bread: a history of the Anti-Corn Law League* (2000) • N. C. Edsall, *Richard Cobden: independent radical* (1986), 134

Archives Man. CL, Anti-Corn Law League letter-book, MS F 337.2 A1 • Man. CL, J. B. Smith collection, Anti-Corn Law League letters and MSS, MS 923.2 5333 • NRA Scotland, priv. coll., corresp. and papers | BL, Gladstone corresp. • Man. CL, George Wilson MSS, M 20 • NA Scot., microfilm, RH 4/156

Wealth at death £6008 5*s*. 8*d*.: probate, 25 June 1884, *CGPLA Eng. & Wales*

Smith, Simon Harcourt Nowell- (1909–1996), book collector, was born on 5 January 1909 at Southgate Corner, Southgate Road, Winchester, the second of three sons (there was also a daughter) of Nowell Charles Smith (1871–1961), assistant master of Winchester College and previously a fellow of Magdalen and New College, Oxford, and his wife, Cecil Violet, *née* Vernon-Harcourt (1875–1961), one of the ten children of Augustus George Vernon-Harcourt FRS, patriarch of a minor Oxford dynasty. Simon and his siblings adopted the form Nowell-Smith instead of the single surname of their father. Nowell-Smith was educated at Sherborne School, where his father had become headmaster, and at New College. His Oxford career was undistinguished, but his book collecting developed there. His large account with Basil Blackwell proved, as he said, to be a good investment for both parties, in spite of his father's strong remonstrations to each.

His mother's cousin Sir Bruce Richmond found Nowell-Smith a job at *The Times*, where he worked from 1932 to 1940 on general duties but particularly assisting Richmond on the *Literary Supplement*. He was given the back page of the *Literary Supplement* for bibliographical news and reviews, assisted anonymously by a circle of well-informed bibliophiles who met in an informal dining club, the Biblios (or Biblioboys). The back page became an important feature of the bibliographical world.

On 6 October 1938 Nowell-Smith married Marion Sinclair, *née* Crichton (1914–1977), the orphaned daughter of W. S. Crichton of a prosperous Liverpool shipping family. Early in the war they found Hill House at Ewelme in Oxfordshire, which was their principal home until they moved to Headington Quarry, Oxford, in 1965. From February 1940, however, Nowell-Smith worked at the Admiralty (his eyesight not being good enough for active service), where he edited a *Weekly Intelligence Report* digesting press information. He worked alongside the poet William Plomer, whose posthumously published autobiography (1975) he edited; Ian Fleming, then a journalist, was another colleague. Nowell-Smith served there until February 1946, having decided at the end of 1944 not to return to *The Times*.

Nowell-Smith had long been an enthusiast for the writings of Henry James (his definitive collection is now at McMaster University Library) and compiled a lively biographical anthology about him: *The Legend of the Master* (1947). This enhanced his own literary reputation and in 1950 was influential in his being invited to become librarian of the London Library. He started there in October 1950. It was not an easy time to take over, not least because his predecessor, C. J. Purnell, had been retained to complete a further volume of the printed catalogue. Nowell-Smith had the full support of his committee, which soon felt the presence of a distinctive personality as their librarian: 'he is an odd crotchety little man', the chairman Harold Nicolson wrote in his diary, 'but I like him.' He revived an institution that was still recovering from the war, acquisitions were given a clearer focus, and the printed catalogues were brought up to date. The Nowell-Smiths enjoyed living in London, but he found the job unsatisfying and resigned after only six years, leaving the library in much better shape than he had found it.

Nowell-Smith was short in stature (some friends knew him as 'the Bantam'); he dressed with flair, and there was a sharp and quizzical look behind his round horn-rimmed glasses. He wrote much in bibliographical journals under his own name or as Michael Trevanion. Though he insisted he was an amateur, his combination of detailed technical knowledge and exacting literary taste proved otherwise. In the 1960s he started work on *Martin Chuzzlewit* for the Clarendon edition of Dickens's novels but did not find the effort satisfying: his notes were passed on to another editor. He had a sustained interest in publishing history, anticipating later views of its importance. His main contribution was *International Copyright Law and the Publisher in the Reign of Queen Victoria* (1969) based on his Oxford lectures as Lyell reader in bibliography in 1965–6. It is a concise but authoritative guide to a complex subject. He advised Macmillans on the disposal of the firm's archives, now in Reading University and at the British Library: *Letters to Macmillan* (1967), a well-constructed anthology, is the by-product of his investigations.

From 1956 Hill House at Ewelme again became Nowell-Smith's main home, until he moved to Oxford in 1965, and he wrote of his own library as 'The Ewelme collection'. From the very start he had not been a retentive collector. As with Henry James, he collected Robert Bridges in depth; the latter group is now at the University of South Carolina. He keenly collected what he termed 'the four Georges' (Borrow, Eliot, Meredith, and Gissing). His most sustained interest, however, was in English poetry from Landor to the First World War. He relished rarity but valued readability even more. Latterly he sold many minor items to concentrate on inscribed first editions or association copies of the greatest English poets of his chosen period. A loan exhibition, 'Wordsworth to Robert Graves and beyond', was shown at the Bodleian Library in 1983.

Nowell-Smith's wife died in 1977, and in 1986 he married, second, an art book dealer, Judith (*b.* 1944/5), daughter of the American bibliophile Frederick Baldwin Adams. The marriage did not succeed, and Nowell-Smith and his second wife latterly lived apart. He died of Alzheimer's disease on 28 March 1996 at St Luke's Nursing Home in Oxford where he had spent his final three years. His remaining collection was sold to the London dealers Bertram Rota Ltd, and formed their substantial catalogue number 300 in 2002. ALAN BELL

Sources *The Times* (29 March 1996) · *Daily Telegraph* (4 April 1996) · *The Guardian* (5 April 1996) · *The Independent* (29 May 1996) · *Book Collector*, 45 (1996), 240, 243–4 · S. Nowell-Smith, 'The Ewelme Collection', *Book Collector*, 14 (1965), 185–93 · W. E. Fredeman, 'Two uncollected bibliographers', *Book Collector*, 38 (1989), 464–82 · *Poetry: the Simon Nowell-Smith collection*, Bertram Rota Ltd (2002) · b. cert. · m. certs. [Marion Sinclair; Judith Adams] · d. cert.
Archives priv. coll., MSS, personal documents
Likenesses J. Hedgecoe, photograph, *c.*1990, London Library
Wealth at death £506,247: probate, 25 Feb 1997, *CGPLA Eng. & Wales*

(Thomas) Southwood Smith (1788–1861), by James Charles Armytage, pubd 1844 (after Margaret Gillies)

Smith, (Thomas) Southwood (1788–1861), Unitarian minister and physician, was born at Martock, Somerset, on 21 December 1788, the son of William Smith and Catherine Southwood, strict Baptists who early destined their son for the ministry. He studied with William Blake (1773–1821), who had just succeeded his father (of the same name) as minister of the Presbyterian chapel at Crewkerne, a surprising choice for orthodox parents, as Blake had recently moved from the qualified Arian position on Christ's divinity to Unitarianism.

In 1803 Smith entered the Baptist academy at Bristol, headed by Dr John Ryland (1753–1825), with a Broadmead scholarship awarded him for twice the usual term. Smith eventually rebelled against his inherited Calvinism and left the academy in 1808; his parents cut him off, and he never saw them again. On 25 May 1808 he married Anne Read (*d.* 1812), the daughter of a Bristol manufacturer (*d.* 1811). Two daughters were born, Caroline (1809–1902) [*see* Hill, Caroline Southwood] and Emily (*b.* 1810); in 1812 Anne Smith died of fever.

Early career Smith's career between 1808 and 1812 is obscure. He certainly preached as a supply—*The Benevolence of God Displayed in the Revelation of a Future State of Perfect Happiness* (1808) is described as a farewell sermon in the Mary Street Chapel, Taunton, and Bristol offered important resources for emotional and intellectual support. Blake, to whom Smith remained close, had sent him to John Prior Estlin (1747–1817), minister at the Unitarian chapel at Lewin's Mead for spiritual counsel; Estlin's son, John Bishop Estlin (1785–1855), who in 1808 returned to the city to begin a distinguished career in ophthalmic surgery, would have been one point of contact with the city's lively medical community. But no one had the same impact on Smith as Benjamin Spencer (1755?–1822), who had studied at the Baptist academy, abandoned his pulpit in Alcester, Warwickshire, on turning Unitarian, and then trained as a physician at Edinburgh—a remarkable prefiguring of Smith's career.

In 1812 the Unitarian Fund in London sent Smith to minister to the struggling congregation in Edinburgh, where he too went on to study medicine. He had notable success as a minister, though the historian Alexander Gordon (1841–1931) recalled (in manuscript notes on Edinburgh ministers in the John Rylands Library) that Smith dismissed the *Monthly Repository*'s reports of a crowded chapel as 'highly coloured', since at times his congregation numbered only twenty. On 28 July 1813 the founding meeting of the Scottish Unitarian Association was held in Glasgow, organized by Smith and the then minister at Glasgow, James Yates (1789–1871), who thought Smith 'a sensible & intelligent man, tho' not furnished with the advantages of education' (J. Yates to Richard Astley, 4 Jan 1813, Shropshire Records and Research Centre, 1067/163).

After attaining his MD from Edinburgh University in 1816 Smith settled in Yeovil, Somerset, as physician and minister to the Unitarian congregation. In 1819, when the young John James Tayler (1796–1869) was considering such a double career, he consulted Smith, who called it practicable up to a point, but 'the question is, whether beyond that point, a physician … can arrest the course of his practice' (J. J. Tayler to Richard Tayler, 28 Dec 1819, Dr Williams's Library, MS 24.102). Smith could not. A year earlier he had married Mary (1798–1858), the daughter of John Christie (1775–1858), of Hackney, a London merchant and treasurer of the Unitarian Fund; their only child, Herman (*d.* 1897), was born in 1819. Mary Smith was unhappy in a country town, and early in 1820 they settled in London.

On 25 June 1821 Smith was admitted as a licentiate of the Royal College of Physicians; he became a fellow in 1847.

He practised privately for more than a quarter of a century, while also serving as physician to the Eastern Dispensary and the Jews' Hospital, and, most importantly, to the London Fever Hospital. He continued to preach occasionally and had easy entrée to the radical Unitarian élite. By 1821 he had joined the circle of intimates around Jeremy Bentham (1748–1832).

Philosophical and medical ideas The main outlines of Smith's mental outlook were established well before the move to London. In the amalgam of Unitarian ideas he laid particular stress on the doctrine of universal restoration—the belief that all would attain salvation. A natural reaction for an apostate from Calvinism, it was the defining tenet of the General Baptists, a remnant of which was gradually amalgamating with the Unitarians. The doctrine similarly Smith engaged other orthodox Baptist converts, among them Robert Aspland (1782–1845), who greatly influenced Unitarianism after 1800. At one point in its chequered history, the Edinburgh congregation had been influenced by the smaller universalist sect.

In 1816, on the basis of earlier lectures in Edinburgh, Smith published *Illustrations of the divine government, tending to show that everything is under the direction of infinite wisdom and goodness and will terminate in the production of universal purity and happiness*, which reached a fourth edition by 1826. When a fifth edition was mooted (but not realized) in 1845, he asked Charles Wellbeloved (1769–1858) for help in bringing the biblical illustrations into line with recent scholarship, but otherwise he envisioned no change in a work written 'with the simple and sincere purpose of exhibiting the true meaning and spirit of Christianity' (T. S. Smith to C. Wellbeloved, 25 Nov 1845, Dr Williams's Library, MS 24.81). Although universal restoration is the central theme of the work, Smith also expounded necessarianism, a deterministic and generally materialistic philosophy then adopted by many Unitarians. In this view actions are necessary consequences of motives formed in the mind by prior circumstances; Smith explained how individual morality and responsibility were better accounted for in this scheme than under free will and defended the authorship of evil by a benevolent and all-foreseeing God as a part of the divine plan for the improvement of mankind.

The elaborate dedications of Smith's thesis for the MD degree, *De mente morbis laesa*, also published in 1816, acknowledge his debts to Blake and Spencer, John Evans (1767–1827), minister to the General Baptist congregation in Worship Street, London, and Thomas Belsham (1750–1829). Belsham's *Elements of the Philosophy of the Mind* (1801), a trenchant summary of necessarianism and the associationist psychology advanced by David Hartley (1705–1757) in his *Observations on Man* (1749), was Smith's philosophical guide. Although he later noted Hartley's controversial theory of vibrations as only one (and not the preferred) hypothesis to explain the working of the nervous system, the thesis uses Hartley's schematic exposition of association, and a suggestion of Hartley's (*Observations on Man*, part 1, section 6, prop. 92) that disordering of vibrations might explain mental disturbances appears to underlie Smith's main concern with the genesis of mental illness. Throughout his life Smith retained a deep interest in mental phenomena: an unfulfilled ambition was to write a guide to mental health paralleling his *Philosophy of Health* (1834). Convinced, like all necessarians, that sin and suffering result from disobeying divinely established and discoverable law, he put great emphasis on education for the right formation of motives; sermons, both published and unpublished, demonstrate his early and abiding interest in the criminal law.

Smith's interest in the complex of diseases then lumped together under the term 'fever' was driven by the death of his young first wife in 1812, while his medical radicalism bore the lasting impress of his Edinburgh training. An article in the *Westminster Review* in 1824 on the shortage of cadavers helped to shape the Anatomy Act of 1832, and in that and two further articles Smith asserted the centrality of anatomy to medical training, contrasting continental approaches to retrograde English teaching of the subject. An article entitled 'Medical reform' in 1836 advocated a unified profession as against the English separation into oligarchically run corporations of physicians, surgeons, and apothecaries, and denounced the social presumption underlying much English practice: 'Disease is not aristocratic and plebeian, not to be cured in the gorgeous apartments of the noble and the rich by a refined, elaborate, and recondite skill inapplicable to the chambers of the ignoble and the poor' (*London and Westminster Review*, 4, 1836, 60). He also insisted that doctors, who are or should be inductive scientists, must learn the laws of the human mind.

What London offered was not new convictions but confirmation and expansion of old ones and, above all, opportunity to implement them. Here the Benthamite connection was particularly valuable. While Bentham failed to secure Smith's appointment as professor of mental and moral philosophy in the new University of London—the wealthy evangelical Zachary Macaulay (1768–1838) threatened to withdraw his support from the college if so terrible a heretic were appointed (Augustus De Morgan to the Revd William Heald, 20 Aug 1867, in S. De Morgan, *Memoir of Augustus De Morgan*, 1882, 373)—the Bentham circle offered more important benefits.

In this setting Smith produced the greatly expanded third edition of the *Illustrations* (1822), with its new attention to the evils of the social state, and in particular to the Malthusian principle of population. His first article in the *Westminster* dealt with education: a denunciation of fashionable English schooling but primarily a laudatory account of the day school proposed in Bentham's *Chrestomathia*; Bentham's adoption of the then fashionable monitorial system recalled an institution Benjamin Spencer had established in Bristol for spreading biblical knowledge and which Smith outlined in 1822 in the *Monthly Repository*. He was Bentham's principal adviser on medical and sanitary matters in connection with the *Constitutional Code*, the main preoccupation in the last decade of Bentham's life.

There is, then, a special appropriateness to the lecture

Smith delivered in the Webb Street school of anatomy on 9 June 1832 over Bentham's corpse, prior to its dissection by Smith's friend, the anatomist Richard Grainger (1801–1865). (The resulting 'auto-icon'—Bentham's skeleton dressed in a suit of his clothes and surmounted by a wax head—was kept in Smith's consulting rooms in Finsbury until his retirement, after which it passed in 1850 to University College, London.) He paid tribute to Bentham as the Newton of the moral world, to whose advent he had looked forward in his thesis in 1816: the greatest-happiness principle was the fullest realization of the overarching law for which Smith had been striving all his adult life. As a reviewer of the *Philosophy of Health* put it in the *Monthly Repository*, the 1832 oration 'indicated the progress of his speculations to a matured and systematized form' (n.s., 9, 1835, 155).

Smith's appointment to the London Fever Hospital allowed the amassing of clinical observations and statistics that buttressed his *Treatise on Fever* of 1830 and his influential advocacy for sanitary reform. He held that the exciting cause of fever was a poison or 'virus' arising from putrefaction of organic matter, but what that substance was remained unknown; therefore, following Unitarian understanding of the laws of mind, it was important to concentrate on the secondary, predisposing causes, chief among them being filth and fetid air. As the most prominent medical spokesman for the 'sanitary idea' and for the parallel insistence on the anti-contagionist view of epidemics and quarantine, Smith assumed a dogmatic stance that set him against much professional thinking. However, the doctrine led to positive results and was, moreover, peculiarly susceptible to management by government.

Public Service In 1833 Smith was appointed, with Thomas Tooke (1774–1858) and Edwin Chadwick (1800–1890), to the royal commission on the employment of children, a choice that made Harriet Martineau (1802–1876) rejoice that a necessarian philosopher had entered government (H. Martineau to Lord Brougham, April 1833, University College, London). Reports published under the auspices of the poor-law commission in 1838–9 document the sanitary conditions in Bethnal Green and Whitechapel that led to preventable illnesses among the poor, and when the Liberal Lord Normanby questioned his assertions, Smith took the doubting peer to see for himself. He gave powerful evidence before a select committee on the health of towns in 1840 and served on the royal commission on the employment of children, which reported in 1842–3; he arranged to have the first report, on mines, illustrated with graphic woodcuts, which deeply impressed public opinion. In 1848, as the cholera approached, the General Board of Health was created, and Smith was tardily appointed to remedy the initial lack of a medical member. He was, however, given a salary of £1200 only in 1850, under the Interment Act of that year; he then gave up the last of his private practice.

Throughout two decades after 1833 Smith was closely linked with, and has since been largely obscured by, the powerful figure of Chadwick. Chadwick may have resented Smith's professional standing and thought him a poor man of business, a mere 'man of benevolence', but the positive bonds were stronger: not only was Smith the principal formulator of the 'sanitary idea'—his medical views did not advance significantly after 1830—but he was superb at creating and moulding public and political opinion, as in organizing the Health of Towns Association in 1844, or in his lectures in Edinburgh summarizing two decades of accomplishment: *Epidemics considered with relation to their common nature, and their relation to climate and civilization* (1856). He also undertook extensive voluntary activity for causes he believed in: an appeal for clemency for John Frost (*d.* 1877), the Chartist transported for leading the Newport rising of 1839; The Sanatorium, a pioneering, if unsuccessful, middle-class nursing home opened in Devonshire Place House, Regent's Park, London, in 1842; and the Metropolitan Association for Improving the Dwellings of the Industrious Classes, whose successes Smith chronicled in 1854 in *Results of Sanitary Improvement*.

In 1854 the General Board of Health fell victim to inadequate design, narrow medical doctrine, mounting reaction against centralized government, and resentment of Chadwick's high-handedness. Smith's application for other government positions was refused, and he was denied a pension on the ground that he had had only four years of paid employment. A public subscription was raised in 1856, and two years later he was belatedly given a pension of £300.

Family matters Tensions in Smith's marriage had ended in separation in the late 1820s; Mary and Herman Smith withdrew to the continent, but considerable correspondence about placing their son in a bookselling career suggests some continuation of amicable relations. In the early 1830s Smith went to live with Margaret *Gillies (1803–1887), the painter (who was to draw the illustrations in the 1842 blue book), and her sister, Mary (1800–1870), a writer. The arrangement brought estrangement from old Unitarian friends, apparently fed by Mary Smith's family, though one of Smith's admirers, according to Harriet Martineau, thought him 'the most wrongfully injured of men' (Harriet Martineau to James Martineau, 30 Jan 1834, Harris Manchester College, Oxford). In 1844 Smith and Margaret Gillies set up a house, Hillside, in Highgate, Middlesex; there is ample testimony to the charms of the place and its host.

The daughters of Smith and his first wife had become teachers; Caroline was in London and Emily was in Italy, where she became a friend of Mazzini's. In 1835 Caroline married a widowed merchant and banker, James Hill, whose daughters she was teaching. However, when Hill's once prosperous business failed and he suffered a physical and nervous breakdown, the whole responsibility for the family fell to Smith. He adopted Gertrude Hill (1837–1923), the second of the four daughters of the marriage, who in 1865 married C. L. Lewes, the son of G. H. Lewes (1817–1878), and in 1898 commemorated her grandfather in a nearly useless memoir. Octavia *Hill (1838–1912), the third daughter, was early involved in her grandfather's philanthropic work and became a notable figure in the housing movement.

In September 1854, a time of severe economic stringency for them, Smith and Margaret Gillies moved to The Pines, near Weybridge, Surrey, where they were joined by Mary Smith until her death in 1858. In 1856 Smith visited his daughter Emily in Italy; after returning there in the autumn of 1861 to recuperate from illness, he was stricken with bronchitis. He died in Florence on 10 December 1861 and was buried in the protestant cemetery there.

R. K. Webb

Sources F. N. L. Poynter, 'Thomas Southwood Smith—the man (1788–1861)', *Proceedings of the Royal Society of Medicine*, 55 (1962), 381–92 • R. K. Webb, 'Southwood Smith: the intellectual sources of public service', *Doctors, politics and society: historical essays*, ed. D. Porter and R. Porter (1993), 46–80 • C. Yeldham, *Margaret Gillies RWS: Unitarian painter of mind and emotion, 1803–1887* (1997) • J. R. Guy, *Compassion and the art of the possible: Dr. Southwood Smith as social reformer and public health pioneer*, 2nd edn (1996) [Octavia Hill Memorial Lecture 1993] • will, 1862

Archives BL, speech notes, Add. MS 44919, fols. 131–160 • DWL, letters and MS sermons [in shorthand] • UCL, Wellcome Centre for the History of Medicine | BL, corresp. with Leigh Hunt, Add. MSS 38109–38111, 38523–38524, *passim* • NL Scot., letters to J. H. Burton • Octavia Hill Birthplace Museum Trust, Cambridgeshire, Ouvry MSS • UCL, Bentham MSS • UCL, corresp. with Edwin Chadwick • UCL, letters to Society for the Diffusion of Useful Knowledge

Likenesses J. C. Armytage, stipple engraving, 1844 (after M. Gillies), NPG; repro. in R. H. Horne, ed., *A new spirit of the age*, 2 vols. (1844), facing p. 77 [*see illus.*] • M. Gillies, oils, *c*.1846, repro. in Yelman, *Margaret Gillies*, 172; priv. coll. • J. Hart, marble bust, 1856, NPG • J. T. Hart, bas-relief (in memorial obelisk, designed by M. Gillies), protestant cemetery, Ponta Pinti, Florence • bust, Highgate Literary and Scientific Institute, London

Wealth at death under £4000: probate, 25 March 1862, *CGPLA Eng. & Wales*

Smith, Stanley Alexander de (1922–1974), jurist, was born on 27 March 1922 at 19 Uxbridge Road, London, the elder of two children of Joseph de Smith, a drug merchant, and his wife, Jane Alexander. He was educated at Southend high school and St Catharine's College, Cambridge, where he graduated BA in 1942. In each of his three years at Cambridge he gained a first class in law, and in 1942—when he took part two of the tripos—he was awarded the George Long prize for jurisprudence.

From 1942 to 1946 de Smith was in the armed forces, serving with the Royal Artillery in north-west Europe and proceeding to intelligence work in Germany. In 1945 he was mentioned in dispatches and was awarded the order of Leopold II, *croix de guerre* (1940), with palms. He was demobilized as a captain in 1946 and on 5 May the same year married Catherine Joan Natley, the daughter of Louis and Esther Natley; they had two sons and two daughters. Also in 1946 he began a career of twenty-four years at the London School of Economics, where he was initially an assistant lecturer in law. He became a lecturer in 1948 and a reader in public law in 1954, and in 1959 was awarded his PhD degree at London University, where his research supervisors had been Glanville Williams and latterly Sir

Stanley Alexander de Smith (1922–1974), by unknown photographer

David Hughes-Parry. From 1959 to 1970 he was professor of public law at the University of London.

During his years at the London School of Economics de Smith wrote extensively in constitutional and administrative law. He contributed numerous articles, notes on legislation, and case notes for the *Modern Law Review* in particular. In 1959 there appeared the first edition of his pioneering *Judicial Review of Administrative Action*, based on his PhD thesis. This book was to appear in four subsequent editions, two (in 1968 and 1973) by de Smith himself and two (in 1980 and 1995) after his death, with a further edition underway. His inaugural lecture as professor of public law, delivered on 10 May 1959, which sets out many of his considered views on public law, was published as *The Lawyers and the Constitution*. In 1964 de Smith published *The New Commonwealth and its Constitutions*, which reflected his wide-ranging and exceptionally well-informed approach to developments in the Commonwealth. As early as 1953 he had been a joint editor of *Commonwealth and Dependencies* in the third edition of Halsbury's *Laws of England*, and in 1954 he was secretary of the Buganda Constitutional Committee and Namirembe Conference. In addition he published in 1954 *The Vocabulary of Commonwealth Relations* as an inaugural paper for the Institute of Commonwealth Studies. His advice was often sought in emerging countries in the Commonwealth. From 1961 to 1968 he was active on a part-time basis as constitutional commissioner for Mauritius, and his services to that country before and after independence were recognized by a special memorial which was dedicated in the Pamplemousses Botanical Gardens in 1979.

De Smith's first marriage was dissolved in 1965, and in 1967 he married an academic lawyer, Barbara Lillywhite (*b.* 1936), the daughter of John and Alice Lillywhite of Liverton, Devon; they had two daughters. After having been a visiting fellow at the Research School of Social Sciences in the Australian National University in 1962, de Smith was in 1967–8 a visiting professor at the school of law of New York University and senior fellow at the university's Center for International Studies. His work at the centre led in 1970 to the publication of *Microstates and Micronesia*, a study of America's Pacific islands and other minute territories.

In 1970 de Smith returned to Cambridge as Downing professor of the laws of England—Maitland's chair, as he proudly acknowledged—and was elected fellow of Fitzwilliam College. In 1971 he became a fellow of the British Academy. Also in 1971 his *Constitutional and Administrative Law* appeared; and this popular and informative new textbook continued to flourish in later editions. In 1973 de Smith became editor of the *Cambridge Law Journal*, and he was also the principal joint editor of the new title, *Administrative Law*, in the fourth edition of Halsbury's *Laws of England* (1973).

Stanley de Smith resided latterly in Stapleford, near Cambridge. He died of cancer at Addenbrooke's Hospital, Cambridge, on 12 February 1974, aged fifty-one. He was cremated three days later, and his ashes were scattered in Mauritius. He left a formidable array of books and other publications on constitutional and most of all on administrative law. From the 1960s administrative law was transformed and by 1973 de Smith could claim prophetically in his major work, which became one of the seminal legal works of the twentieth century, that 'administrative law had cast itself adrift from its anchorage, and we are on uncharted waters' (*Judicial Review of Administrative Action*, preface). His scholarship was marked by thoroughness and accuracy, he was determined to seek underlying principles in the law, he was acutely aware of the importance of history, and whatever he wrote was enlivened by his elegant style.

Although one of the most distinguished lawyers of his generation, de Smith remained a modest and generous person. He readily recognized the contributions of others, and he wrote many letters, often witty and incisive, to encourage younger (and older) colleagues. He had many friends and took a wide interest in a variety of topics ranging from political events to association football. In academic matters he was an examiner of impeccable fairness, and greatly enjoyed graduate teaching and the supervision of research students. That he was least happy in lecturing to large undergraduate audiences is largely attributable to his wartime experience, which resulted in impaired hearing for which he was awarded a disability pension, and some difficulty in voice projection.

De Smith had a central role in reshaping public law in the second half of the twentieth century. He anticipated many of the changes in the years from 1974 onwards. He had already addressed the constitutional implications of entry to Europe, and in his writings had anticipated the explosive development of administrative law, the mounting concern for the protection of human rights, and the issues of devolution, electoral reform, and freedom of information. His immense scholarship was underpinned by his prescience and his breadth of vision.

D. G. T. Williams

Sources *WWW* · *The Times* (14 Feb 1974) · H. W. R. Wade, 'Stanley Alexander de Smith, 1922–1974', *PBA*, 60 (1974), 477–84 · personal knowledge (2004) · private information (2004) [Barbara de Smith] · *Cambridge University Reporter* (1940–42) · b. cert.
Likenesses photograph, British Academy [*see illus.*]
Wealth at death £32,078: probate, 13 June 1974, *CGPLA Eng. & Wales*

Smith, Stephen (1623–1678), Quaker preacher and writer, was born on 19 September 1623: his parentage is at present unknown. He was for a time engaged in overseas trade and employed by the Levant Company at Alexandretta (Iskenderun), the port of Aleppo. On returning to England, he married Susanna Purse (1623?–1693) and settled at Pirbright, in the parish of Worplesdon, Surrey, where in 1664 he was paying hearth tax on seven hearths. In 1665 Stephen and Susanna both became Quakers when George Whitehead visited the home of Stephen's Quaker brother John in Worplesdon. Whitehead was later to describe Stephen as 'a simple, plain hearted and sincere man' and 'one truly kind and ready to do good' (Smith, *True Light*).

During his lifetime Smith suffered frequently for his beliefs. He was imprisoned at Southwark with Whitehead and others for a month in 1668 for holding a meeting at Elsted, and in 1670 he was fined £24 for preaching in the street at Guildford when the Quakers were barred from their meeting-house. George Fox stayed with Smith soon after, and speaks in his journal of Smith's losses. Fox obviously knew Smith well, for in 1673 he held a meeting of several hundred people at his home. Smith was arrested a second time in 1670 by soldiers for preaching at Ratcliffe and sent to Newgate for six months. A few years later he was sent to the Marshalsea prison for six months for non-payment of tithes due to Gabriel Offley, rector of Worplesdon, who in 1677 further seized five head of cattle from Smith in lieu of 50 shillings' tithe owing. Some time after this Smith met with Fox in Gloucestershire, where they drew up an account of Quaker sufferings for that county to present to the judges at Gloucester.

During the 1670s Smith produced a number of works including *The Light of Christ* (1678), a defence of Quaker beliefs such as immediate revelation and the sufficiency of the inner light. In *A Faithful Testimony Concerning the Scriptures* (1679) he puts forward the idea that true understanding of the Bible must proceed from the movings of the spirit of Christ. In *Wholesome Advice and Information* Smith drew on his years in the Middle East, drawing a comparison between the Turks and the so-called Christians of England which was overwhelmingly favourable to the former in matters of liberty of conscience, true charity and love for one another, and civility. The Turks 'seem to exceed the Christians in Morality; it being a cause of Laughter unto them to see the Christians Beggarly Airy Behaviours one unto another, in scraping with the Leg, and Doffing the Hat' (Smith, *True Light*, 164–5). Smith's nine tracts, including the three above mentioned, were published together in *The True Light Discovered* (1679), which also includes other works by him.

Stephen Smith died on 22 September 1678 at his house and was buried at Worplesdon four days later. He was survived by three children, John, Robert, and Susan, and by his wife, Susanna. She was among those who contributed their testimonies to him in *The True Light Discovered*, describing him as a man of 'upright heart towards God and man' (Smith, *True Light*). CAROLINE L. LEACHMAN

Sources J. Whiting, *Persecution expos'd: in some memoirs relating to the sufferings of John Whiting and many others of the people called Quakers* (1715) • *The Christian progress of that ancient servant and minister of Jesus Christ, George Whitehead*, ed. [J. Besse?] (1725) • J. Besse, *A collection of the sufferings of the people called Quakers*, 1 (1753) • J. Smith, ed., *A descriptive catalogue of Friends' books*, 2 (1867) • S. Smith, *The true light discovered … in several little treatises* (1679) [unpaginated] • T. W. Marsh, *Some records of the early Friends in Surrey and Sussex* (1886) • *The journal of George Fox*, ed. N. Penney, 2 (1911) • digest registers of births, marriages, and burials, RS Friends, Lond. • 'Dictionary of Quaker biography', RS Friends, Lond. [card index] • will, LMA, DW/PC/7/1679/19 • C. A. F. Meekings, ed., *Surrey hearth tax, 1664*, Surrey RS, 17 (1940) • *DNB*

Wealth at death approx. £1250; plus house: will, LMA, DW/PC/7/1679/19

Smith, Stephen Catterson (1806–1872), portrait painter, was born on 12 March 1806 in Skipton in Craven, Yorkshire, the son of Joseph Smith, a coach painter, and Anne, daughter of Stephen Catterson of Gawflat, Yorkshire. After training at the Royal Academy Schools in London (from 1822), he studied in Paris and gained an early reputation for his skill in black chalk portraits; many of these were made into lithographs and published by R. J. Lane. This proficiency led to royal patronage; he produced a number of drawings for the royal family, including, for example, one of the young Princess Victoria (*c*.1829, Royal Collection). Ten years later he received commissions in Ireland and moved to Londonderry, where he stayed for six years, painting portraits and small genre pictures. In 1845 he moved to Dublin, where he lived for the rest of his life and became portrait painter to seven lord lieutenants; examples of his state portraits hang in Dublin Castle. He married, on 30 September 1846, Anne Wyke (*d*. 1886), a miniature painter and daughter of the artist Robert Titus Wyke; they had ten children, two of whom, Stephen and Robert, also became artists.

For over a quarter of a century Smith was the leading portrait painter in Ireland. Over the years, his sitters came from Ireland's most distinguished families, such as the Leinsters of Carton, co. Kildare, and the O'Conors of Clonalis, co. Roscommon. *Miss Emily Murphy* (*c*.1860, Clonalis House, co. Roscommon) is an example of his capacity to capture an engaging likeness, as well as to paint muslin and crinoline with great liveliness. Civic portraiture was also an important part of his output; the Dublin corporation commissioned a full-length portrait of Queen Victoria (1858, Mansion House, Dublin) from him, while in the 1870s he produced at least two posthumous portraits of Daniel O'Connell, one on request from the royal exchange in Dublin (des. 1908).

Active in the Royal Hibernian Academy, Smith exhibited regularly there from 1841 and twice served as its president (1859–66, 1868–9). His spirited self-portrait (*c*.1841; National Gallery of Ireland, Dublin) and a lively oil portrait of the Young Irelander William Smith O'Brien (1840s; National Gallery of Ireland, Dublin) show that he was capable of occasionally moving away from the smooth set pieces which dominated his career. While hanging pictures for the Dublin International Exhibition of Arts and Manufactures in Earlsfort Terrace he was seized with apoplexy and died at his home, 42 St Stephen's Green, on 30 May 1872. He was buried on 1 June in Mount Jerome cemetery in Dublin; his wife survived him. FINTAN CULLEN

Sources W. G. Strickland, *A dictionary of Irish artists*, 2 vols. (1913) • A. Crookshank and the Knight of Glin [D. Fitzgerald], *The painters of Ireland, c.1660–1920* (1978) • A. Crookshank and the Knight of Glin [D. Fitzgerald], eds., *Irish portraits, 1660–1860* (1969) [exhibition catalogue, Dublin, London, and Belfast, 14 Aug 1969 – 9 March 1970] • m. cert., Ireland

Likenesses S. C. Smith, self-portrait, oils, *c*.1841, NG Ire. • S. C. Smith, self-portrait, Royal Hibernian Academy, Dublin • S. C. Smith, self-portrait, chalk, NG Ire.; repro. in Strickland, *Dictionary* • attrib. J. Stephens, oils, NG Ire.

Wealth at death £1500: administration, 3 July 1872, *CGPLA Ire.*

Smith, Strata. *See* Smith, William (1769–1839).

Smith, Sir Swire (1842–1918), promoter of technical education, was born on 4 March 1842 at Wagon Fold, Keighley, Yorkshire, the elder son of the four children of George Smith (1812–1902), a machine maker, and his wife, Mary Swire, of yeoman stock. He was educated at the local national school and at Wesley College, Sheffield, before serving an apprenticeship with a Keighley worsted manufacturer. By the age of twenty he was in business on his own account.

Smith was deeply stirred by his chance attendance in 1867 at an address on technical education by Samuel Smiles, whose theme, 'that the Germans and French, through their superior general education and by their application of the principles of science and art to manufactures and crafts, were making enormous progress in their industries' (Smith, *Technical Education*) to the future detriment of Britain, was to form the bedrock of his life's work. He promptly undertook the secretaryship of a drawing class at the Keighley Mechanics' Institute, and, shortly afterwards, the secretaryship of an ambitious new Keighley trade school council and of the Mechanics' Institute itself. In 1872, after he and several colleagues had investigated schools and polytechnics in France, Germany, and Switzerland, he published anonymously, for private circulation, *Unofficial Comments on Education at Home and Abroad*. This was followed in 1873 by his signed and more widely circulated *Educational Comparisons*. Realizing that elementary education formed an essential forerunner of any technical advance, he also became prominent in the fight in 1875 for a Keighley school board, and served as chairman for the first three years of its existence.

Smith's local agitation, together with his practical and commercial experience of textiles—almost to the end of his life he operated the substantial Springfield mills at Keighley in two different partnerships and later single-handed—led to his being invited to represent the woollen industry on the royal commission on technical instruction formed in 1880. Its report, presented to parliament four years later, stressed the superiority of European industrial training and in 1889 instigated the Technical Instruction Act, which, in Smith's words, 'did largely for technical education what Forster's Act of 1870 did for elementary education'. His own services were recognized by a knighthood in 1898. Other honours testified severally to the national, regional, and local regard for his work: he received the freedom and livery of the Clothworkers' Company of the City of London, a doctorate of laws from Leeds University, and the freedom of the borough of Keighley.

An indefatigable committee member of the National Association for the Promotion of Technical and Commercial Education, Smith continued to utilize every opportunity for propagating his cause in articles, lectures, and addresses. He was in demand at prize-giving ceremonies of the fledgeling technical schools and colleges; prepared the textile sections of the catalogues for the London International Inventions Exhibition and the Chicago World Fair; and served as vice-chairman of a royal commission on international exhibitions. An outspoken authority also on free trade—together with technical education he thought this 'necessary for promoting the highest welfare and efficiency of the nation and enabling it to resist competition and attack in the industrial sphere'—he was a founder of the West Riding Free Trade Federation and an executive member of the national Free Trade Union.

In 1915, at the age of seventy-three, Smith became Liberal MP for the Keighley division; he made his maiden speech, typically, on 'the real German rivalry' in technical training. At the age of seventy-five he visited the battlefront, coming under fire at Vimy and finding the experience strangely exhilarating.

Fair and lively, Smith always looked younger than his actual age. Although he had an eye for the ladies, he never married. He enjoyed many travels and friendships with such famous contemporaries as John Bright, Lord Morley, and Andrew Carnegie (the last presented Smith's home town with the first Carnegie library in England), yet Keighley remained his permanent residence. 'The townspeople loved him', said his local obituary, 'not only for what he did, but for what he was, genial, buoyant, companionable, with a mirth in his nature that was almost frolicsome' (*Keighley News*, 23 March 1918). He contributed jokes to *Punch*, sang in the choir of his local Congregational church, and up to the year of his death entertained a variety of homely gatherings with humorous recitations.

Smith died of congestion of the lungs in a nursing home at 2 Beaumont Street, London, on 16 March 1918, following an operation on his prostate gland. He was buried four days later in Keighley cemetery. IAN DEWHIRST

Sources K. Snowden, *The master spinner* (1921) • S. Smith, *Technical education: Keighley a pioneer* (1912) • *Keighley News* (23 March 1918) • *Yorkshire Post* (18 March 1918) • [S. Smith], *Unofficial comments on education at home and abroad* (1872) • S. Smith, *Educational comparisons, or, Remarks on industrial schools in England, Germany, and Switzerland* (1873) • *CGPLA Eng. & Wales* (1918)

Likenesses S. J. Solomon, oils, 1913, Cliffe Castle Art Gallery and Museum, Keighley

Wealth at death £74,133: probate, 1918

Smith, Sydney (1771–1845), author and wit, was born on 3 June 1771 at Woodford, Essex, the second of the five children of Robert Smith (1739/40–1827), merchant, and his wife, Maria (*c*.1750–1801), the daughter of Isaac Olier, a Huguenot. He had three brothers and a sister; Smith's elder brother Robert Percy *Smith, known as Bobus, was a major influence.

Early life and education Smith's early life was unhappy. His father was vain, petty, selfish, and tyrannical: after dinner every day he forced his children to sit, often for hours, in motionless silence. For Smith, an energetic boy, the experience was purgatorial. Worse still was watching his mother's attacks of epilepsy. A woman of artistic sensibility and ravishing beauty, Maria Olier was beloved by all her sons. As she grew older the frequency and intensity of her fits steadily increased, and her final hours were gruesome.

Smith's lifelong desire for comfort and financial ease was, at least in part, a reaction against his father's rootlessness and financial imprudence. When Robert Smith was about twenty, he left the family business in Eastcheap in his brother's hands and went off to make his fortune in America. He married in 1768, returning to America shortly afterwards. During the War of Independence his American investments became virtually valueless, but failure did not blunt his entrepreneurial ardour. After his marriage he engaged in commercial ventures as far afield as Europe, India, and the West Indies. Most of his speculations met the same fate as his American investments. The attempts to salvage something from the wreckage necessitated frequent trips abroad, leaving his five children in the care of his dedicated (but increasingly helpless) wife. As though this were not enough, Robert Smith kept moving house. The number of his residences in Sydney's formative years is not known, but was probably more than five.

Smith's early years at Winchester College, where he went as a scholar at the age of eleven, were also painful. The headmaster, Joseph Warton, was brilliant, but also, at sixty, ageing. Winchester, in consequence, was in a state of serious decline. Four years before Smith entered the school there had been 116 fee-paying pupils, but when he left, in 1788, there were only thirty-eight, a third as many. Discipline was poor and there was much bullying. Smith also had other complaints: the curriculum, with its virtually exclusive concentration upon the study of Latin and Greek, was tedious, the way of life monastic, and the food

Sydney Smith (1771–1845), by Henry Perronet Briggs, 1840 [replica; original, 1833]

execrable. He nevertheless did well, carrying off a number of prizes and becoming, in his last year, senior boy, known at Winchester as prefect of hall.

On 6 February 1789 Smith entered Winchester's sister foundation of New College, Oxford, as a probationary fellow, becoming a full fellow after he had fulfilled the residence qualification of two years. Life at New College was easy, but it was also dull. For the four-year period 1789–92 there are only fifteen names in the admissions book. Smith was still faced with the drudgery of writing vast amounts of Latin and Greek verse, and he was not encouraged to think. 'A genuine Oxford tutor', he later wrote, 'would shudder to hear his young men disputing upon moral and political truth, forming and pulling down theories, and indulging in all the boldness of youthful discussion. He would augur nothing from it, but impiety to God, and treason to kings' (*Works*, 1.196).

Curacy, marriage, and formation of the *Edinburgh Review* For a two-year period starting in the summer of 1794 Smith was curate at Netheravon on Salisbury Plain, an isolated hamlet of fewer than fifty families. He was appalled by the desperate poverty of the majority of his parishioners, but could do little to help them because he lacked the financial means. He did, however, start a Sunday school, then considered a bold step, and also set in motion a school of industry for twenty girls. The girls met in the forge of Bendall the blacksmith and were taught to darn, knit, and sew.

Smith was priested soon after his return to New College in the summer of 1796. His whereabouts over the next two years are uncertain but he seems to have been mainly at Oxford, where he learnt thoroughly both French and German. Michael Hicks-Beach, the son of Smith's squire at Netheravon, was intending to set out on a continental tour before going to Oxford, and Smith was to accompany him as private tutor. The invasion of Switzerland by France in February 1798 forced a rethink: Weimar was discarded as a destination in favour of Edinburgh.

Smith set off north with his pupil on 1 June 1798. He did not enjoy his tutorial duties—Beach was a lazy young man of mediocre intellectual ability, whose main interest was socializing with his friends—but he loved Edinburgh and quickly built up a friendship network. A major formative influence was Dugald Stewart, professor of moral philosophy. Stewart was not an original thinker, but he fired Smith's imagination with his eloquent exposition of the enjoyment to be gained from the study of literature and science, and also with his passionate defence of the immortality of the soul. Still more important was the companionship of three ardent young whigs: Henry Brougham, Francis Horner, and Francis Jeffrey.

One evening shortly before the Christmas of 1801, Jeffrey asked Smith and Horner to tea at his house in Buccleuch Place. During the meal Smith suggested, half in jest, that they should start a literary review. The idea was taken up enthusiastically, gaining financial support from Archibald Constable, a leading Edinburgh bookseller. The first issue of the *Edinburgh Review* came out on 10 October 1802. Editorial duties were initially shared among Jeffrey, Horner, and Smith; but after three issues Constable—on Smith's advice—appointed Jeffrey editor on a permanent, salaried basis. It was a wise choice: Jeffrey had persistence and an eye for detail, qualities which Smith lacked.

Smith did much to establish the literary reputation of the *Edinburgh Review*. Of the 101 articles in the first four issues, he was responsible for nineteen; only Brougham, credited with twenty-one, wrote a greater number. Smith ranged wide, writing on matters as diverse as philosophy, travel, drama, and theology. He was the best communicator among the reviewers, and also the one with the most scabrous wit. As he told Jeffrey:

> Too much would not do of my style, but the proportion in which it exists enlivens the Review. I am a very ignorant, frivolous, half-inch person; but, such as I am, I am sure I have done [the] Review good, and contributed to bring it into notice. (Virgin, 3)

By the time the *Edinburgh Review* was floated, Sydney was married. Catharine Amelia Pybus (1768–1852) had long been a friend of Sydney's sister, Maria. Her father, John, had been a member of the council of Madras and was the first English ambassador to Ceylon, while her brother, Charles, MP for Dover, was a lord of the Treasury. The marriage, which took place on 2 July 1800, was a love match. Smith revelled in domestic life, and Catharine adored her husband, giving him strong emotional support during his occasional bouts of depression.

There were five children from the marriage, three sons and two daughters, one of whom died in infancy. Sydney pinned high hopes upon his eldest son, Douglas, a diligent scholar but physically weak. Douglas's death in 1829 at the age of twenty-four was the most serious sorrow that Sydney ever had to face: 'I never suspected', he wrote, 'how children weave themselves about the heart' (*Letters*, 2.496). Sydney's elder daughter, Saba [**Saba Holland** (1802–1866)], was born in February 1802, and became the second wife of Henry *Holland (1788–1873), physician-in-ordinary to Queen Victoria, in 1834. Saba Holland's memoir of her father, who had superintended her education, was published in two volumes in 1855. It records many of Smith's best jokes; his daughter apparently 'possessed no slight share' of his humour (*GM*, new ser., 2, 1866, 844), and also contains valuable reminiscences. Saba died on 2 November 1866, and was buried in Kensal Green cemetery.

Success in London, 1803–1809 Smith left Edinburgh for London on 8 August 1803, settling at 8 Doughty Street, not far from Gray's Inn Road. He lived in the metropolis for the next six years, the final three of them at 18 Orchard Street, just north of Oxford Street.

During the 1790s Smith's elder brother, Bobus, had introduced him to Holland House, the citadel of whig power and influence; now that he was living in London, Smith, along with Samuel Rogers and Henry Luttrell, quickly became known as one of the resident Holland House wits. One of Smith's main specialities was aphoristic analogy. 'Correspondences are like small-clothes before the invention of suspenders; it is impossible to keep them up' and 'Marriage resembles a pair of shears, so joined that they cannot be separated; often moving in opposite directions, but punishing anyone who comes between them' are memorable examples (Holland, 1, chap. 11). On a proposal to surround St Paul's with a wooden pavement, Smith remarked: 'Let the Dean and Canons lay their heads together and the thing will be done' (Pearson, chap. 10).

Some of Smith's *mots* occur in his published books and articles (few other writers have succeeded in making ecclesiastical disputes amusing to a readership almost 200 years later), but many were delivered verbally and recorded by his daughter in her *Memoir*. Several of these *mots* have entered the common currency of British humour, for example, 'I never read a book before reviewing it; it prejudices a man so' (Pearson, chap. 3) and 'I am just going to pray for you at St Paul's, but with no very lively hope of success' (ibid., chap. 13). His humour was reinforced by his incongruous appearance—dark, piercing eyes, a high forehead, and a Roman nose, commanding features that were offset by untidy hair brushed upwards after the contemporary French fashion, a small mouth once unkindly compared to an oyster, careless dress, and clumsy movements.

At Holland House, Smith met royalty, writers, and politicians of all persuasions. He also soon became a close friend of his host, Henry, third Baron Holland, and his formidable wife, Elizabeth. Lord and Lady Holland were, from now on, Sydney's chief patrons. In October 1806 they persuaded Thomas Erskine, lord chancellor in the 'ministry of all the talents', to make Smith rector of the rich living of Foston-le-Clay, 12 miles north-east of York.

During these London years Smith also became a popular preacher. He had the use of three pulpits: Berkeley Chapel in John Street, Mayfair, the Fitzroy Chapel a little further north in the parish of St Pancras, and the Foundling Hospital. Smith's doctrinal views were conventional—he was an uncritical follower of the theology of William Paley—and his sermons were firmly moral in their tone. What made him famous was his fiery delivery. Smith's *Sermons*, in two volumes, were published in 1809.

Starting on 10 November 1804 Smith gave two sets of lectures at the Royal Institution in Albemarle Street. An eyewitness gives a graphic account of the press of people. 'All Albemarle Street and a part of Grafton Street were rendered impassable by the concourse of carriages … Many persons, to obtain seats, came an hour before time' (Holland, 128, n.). Smith's subject was moral philosophy, which he defined in typically cavalier fashion as the study of 'everything which belongs to the human mind'. This allowed him to speak on such favourite topics as the nature of wit and the influence of the passions. He used the lectures to popularize Scottish psychology, putting his case with eloquence, humour, and common sense. A third series of lectures, given in the early months of 1806, attracted significantly smaller audiences. His *Elements of Moral Philosophy* was published posthumously in 1850.

Following the fall of the 'talents' in March 1807, Smith defended the late ministry in ten short, and brilliantly funny, pamphlets, published as *Peter Plymley's Letters*. Although anonymous, authorship was an open secret. The 'talents' had fallen because it had proposed that Irish Catholics should be allowed to serve as officers in both the English army and the English navy. Smith's defence of this ill-fated policy was deft. He appealed to protestant prejudice by ridiculing Catholic ritual: 'How would my admirable brother, the Rev. Abraham Plymley, like to be marched to a Catholic chapel, to be sprinkled with the sanctified contents of a pump, to hear a number of false quantities in the Latin tongue, and to see a number of persons occupied in making right angles upon the breast and forehead?' while, at the same time, he also advanced the thoroughly modern, as well as secular, notion that the state should be indifferent towards the religious affiliation of its citizens. In 1808 *Peter Plymley's Letters* were printed in a collection which quickly ran through sixteen editions.

At Foston-le-Clay, 1809–1829 William Markham, archbishop of York, aged and complaisant, allowed Smith to use his preachership at the Foundling Hospital as an excuse for non-residence in his Yorkshire living of Foston. Markham, however, died in November 1807 at the age of eighty-nine, and was succeeded in the new year by Edward Vernon-Harcourt, who was much more zealous. After a protracted correspondence, Smith set out for Foston in June 1809. For the first five years he hired a house at Heslington, 12 miles from Foston, riding over to his parish on Sundays to take services. But from March 1814 he lived at Foston, in a new parsonage which he had designed himself and upon which he spent about £4000 from his own resources.

Smith was an innovative and unconventional rector,

putting into practice what would later be called the social gospel. He planted a number of small gardens with fruit trees, allowing the villagers to gather the produce, and also set aside part of his glebe as allotments at nominal rents. He excelled as a makeshift doctor, keeping copious notes on all his patients and ordering drugs for them from London. In January 1814 he was made a magistrate, subsequently dispensing his own brand of humane justice in preference to the rigours of statute law. He was especially lenient towards poachers.

Influential articles by Smith on social issues appeared in the *Edinburgh Review*. 'Mad Quakers', in April 1814, was a defence of the therapeutic practice of The Retreat, an asylum for mentally ill Quakers near York: management did away with chains, using instead the earliest form of occupational therapy. Smith's article was partly responsible for the formation of a House of Commons select committee on madhouses in May 1815. The committee came down heavily in support of the regime at The Retreat, and its findings led to revolutionary changes in the treatment of mental illness.

This was the only issue on which Smith managed to play a part in initiating immediate change, yet his ideas on other topics can nevertheless be commended for anticipating the future direction of official thinking. He turned the fire of his righteous anger on the practice of sending young boys up chimneys in order to sweep them, ridiculed the game laws, and advocated important changes in legal procedure, including payment of defendants' costs out of the public purse. He was also an important early feminist. In an article in the *Edinburgh Review* in 1810 he argued that women should participate fully in the economy—'Half the talent in the universe runs to waste, and is totally unprofitable' (*Works*, 1.203); he challenged the assumption of male intellectual superiority and advocated a radical extension of female educational provision. 'A century ago', he concluded mischievously, 'who would have believed that country gentlemen could be brought to read and spell with the ease and accuracy which we now so frequently remark?' (ibid., 1.216). Although he was perceptive and forward-thinking, Smith's social ideas nevertheless lack coherence. He was a pioneer of humane treatment of the mentally ill, but advocated inhumane treatment of those who were in prison: 'We would banish all the looms of Preston jail, and substitute nothing but the tread-wheel, or the capstan, or some species of labour where the labourer could not see the results of his toil' (ibid., 1.440).

During these Foston years Smith's aristocratic connections continued to grow. He paid annual visits to Earl Grey's home at Howick in Northumberland, where he was accepted as part of the family, thus adding a new string to his patronage bow. His relations with Frederick Howard, fifth earl of Carlisle—the master of Castle Howard, 5 miles to the north of Foston—were more ambiguous and also more fraught. In 1823 Carlisle used his influence to persuade the duke of Devonshire to present Sydney to the living of Londesborough, worth the large sum of £800 a year. Before entering the benefice Smith signed a resignation bond, under which he agreed to vacate nine years later in favour of the duke's nephew, W. G. Howard, who would then be of canonical age. This was a thoroughly dubious transaction; in 1828 resignation bonds were made illegal except in cases where both the presentee and the future incumbent were related to the patron of the living either by blood or by marriage. A year after he gained Londesborough there was a rupture with Carlisle, who was incensed by the astringency of Smith's social articles in the *Edinburgh Review*. Smith, much chastened, promised the earl that he would, in future, 'attack less frequently, & joke less severely'.

Rector of Combe Florey and canon of St Paul's, 1829–1840 Early in 1828 Smith, through the patronage of Lord Lyndhurst and John Ward, first earl of Dudley, was made a prebendary of Bristol Cathedral. Desiring further promotion, Smith immediately gave up writing for the *Edinburgh Review*. The next three years were a period of turbulence. In March 1829 Smith exchanged Foston for Combe Florey, 7 miles from Taunton, and the next month he gave up Londesborough. After Grey succeeded Wellington as prime minister in November 1830, Smith entered the political fray, delivering three speeches in favour of the Reform Bill, most famously at a meeting at Taunton on 11 October 1831, where he compared anti-reformers with Dame Partington, an old woman who, some years previously, had tried to hold back a storm at Sidmouth in Devon with a mop and bucket.

Smith hoped for a bishopric, but it never came. Grey, instead, translated him from his prebend at Bristol to a canonry at St Paul's, a move that took place in September 1831. Smith's pride was hurt, but he did have ample financial compensation. His income, in 1832, was almost £2900. Only twenty-five beneficed clergy of a total of 7500 were paid more.

After Grey's resignation in July 1834, the continuing failure of the whigs to offer him a bishopric made Smith exceedingly angry. There was a fierce row with Lord Holland in November 1834: the third baron, with aristocratic nonchalance, let slip that he would have preferred Samuel Butler, the famous reforming headmaster of Shrewsbury, as the new bishop of Bristol to the successful candidate, Joseph Allen. Desertion by Lord Holland was a bitter pill to swallow. More bitter still was Melbourne's support for the ecclesiastical commission, set up by Peel during his brief administration that lasted from November 1834 until April 1835. Smith was enraged by the commission's plans to trim the patronage of cathedral dignitaries, interpreting the move as a personal attack. In three letters to Archdeacon Singleton, published in January 1837, the spring of 1838, and February 1839, Smith put himself forward as the leading opponent of church reform. He made his position clear in the first letter: any measures for change must not exceed 'one thing more than was absolutely necessary'.

The letters won warm approval from the influential section of the whig party, which was strongly opposed to the centralizing tendency of Melbourne's administration, but

Smith's defence of ecclesiastical privilege is a shabby episode. A letter to him from Blomfield, bishop of London, written on 24 January 1837—a week after publication of the first letter—shows that Smith had made informal contact with the ecclesiastical commission, and had given an assurance that he would cease his attacks provided his own rights of patronage, as a canon of St Paul's, were not interfered with.

Smith, although still claiming to be a whig, became more politically conservative in the 1830s. His pamphlet *Ballot*, published in 1839, was a witty defence of open voting. His arguments were eloquent and original. A man, he contended, should be prepared to stand up for his beliefs; it was wrong to 'seek for liberty by clothing ourselves in the mask of falsehood, and trampling on the cross of truth'. *Ballot* was well received. 'Since the days of Pascal', said Smith's brother Bobus 'no such piece of Irony, involving so much wisdom, had ever been penned' (Virgin, 269).

After his appointment as canon of St Paul's, Smith spent Christmas and part of the summer at Combe Florey, but was otherwise in London. He initially rented houses, but in the autumn of 1835 purchased a fourteen-year lease on 33 Charles Street, just south of Berkeley Square, moving in the next February. In 1839 he was again on the move: his new house was 56 Green Street, near Park Lane. Smith's life in London was very sociable. In the early 1840s, when he was approaching seventy, he was dining out eight or nine times a week. He was elected to The Club, the highly prestigious literary club founded in the previous century by Samuel Johnson and David Garrick, and also met most of the leading literary figures, including Charles Dickens. It is from this period that most of Smith's conversational *bons mots* have come down to posterity. He found fame irksome. The poet Tom Moore was amused by Smith's response to the new fashion of lionizing famous authors. 'Here', said Smith, 'is a new man of genius arrived; put on the stew pan; fry away; we'll soon get it all out of him' (*Memoirs, Journal, and Correspondence of Thomas Moore*, ed. J. Russell, 8 vols., 1853–6, 7.52).

Last years and death, 1840–1845 From the autumn of 1840 Smith's letters are full of references to aches and pains, and the dreaded subject of his own death begins to come up for frequent discussion. The former fluency of his pen slows to a trickle, and he shows his old controversial flair only in two minor disputes, both of them conducted in the columns of the *Morning Chronicle*. Three letters, written in May and June 1842, persuaded the directors of the Great Western Railway that they had been wrong to try to protect the safety of passengers by insisting that the carriage doors on both sides of trains should be locked while they were in motion. Perhaps it was just as well that the directors gave in, because Smith was planning a fourth letter in which he intended to depict them looking with satisfaction at a trainload of incinerated passengers: 'a stewed Duke … two Bishops done in their own Gravy … two Scotchmen dead but raw, sulphuric acid perceptible' (*Miscellanies of the Philobiblon Society*, 15, 1872–84, 7.17–18). Smith's two letters of November 1843 attacking the state of Pennsylvania for suspending interest payments on its public debt—Smith had lost £400 on a purchase of Pennsylvanian bonds—were less successful, serving merely to antagonize American opinion.

Smith, always overweight, had a severe heart attack in October 1844 while at Combe Florey. His son-in-law, Sir Henry Holland, hurried down to see him and arranged for him to be moved to his London home at 56 Green Street, where he could be under Holland's constant care. Smith died at Green Street on 22 February 1845. He was buried next to his beloved elder son, Douglas, in Kensal Green cemetery. In one of his best-known *mots*, he had said: '[Lutterell's] idea of heaven is eating *pâté de foie* to the sound of trumpets' (*Sayings*, 198–9).

Personality Like many famous wits, Smith had a depressive streak, of which he was fully aware and which he struggled against. The battle with himself helped to hone his humanity: he was kind, compassionate, full of goodwill, quick to anger, and quick to forgive. Known throughout society as 'Dear Sydney', he was one of the most approachable men of his generation, treating his servants in much the same way as he treated prime ministers. Outgoing and immensely charming, especially to women, Smith was very well liked, had few enemies, and possessed a great gift for friendship. He was at his best with children, speaking to them on their own level and being endlessly amusing.

There were also some contrasts and paradoxes. Although proud, Smith was without the slightest trace of vanity. His language was coarse—he said of a friend called Miss Alcock that 'her Latin name would be *Domina omnis penis*'—and yet he was also capable of revealing, on occasion, an underlying moral earnestness. A man of strong feeling, he was reticent about his deepest emotions. He had a high degree of self-knowledge but there were also some blindnesses—he failed to acknowledge, for instance, that he was ravenously ambitious. It is also true that he failed to outgrow his *nouveau riche* origins; always socially insecure, he was, when occasion offered, money-grubbing. His unique achievement nevertheless stands: an important contributor to the growth of libertarian thought in England, he was also, as G. K. Chesterton later pointed out, the inventor of nonsense, a very English style of humour. PETER VIRGIN

Sources Lady Holland, *A memoir of the Reverend Sydney Smith … with a selection from his letters*, ed. Mrs Austin, 2 vols. (1855) • S. J. Reid, *The life and times of Sydney Smith* (1896) • H. Pearson, *The Smith of Smiths* (1934) • *The letters of Sydney Smith*, ed. N. C. Smith, 2 vols. (1953) • A. Bell, *Sydney Smith: a biography* (1980) • P. Virgin, *Sydney Smith* (1994) • *The works of Sydney Smith*, 3rd edn, 3 vols. (1845) • *The sayings of Sydney Smith*, ed. A. Bell (1993)

Archives BL OIOC • Hunt. L., letters, mainly to his father • New College, Oxford, collected corresp. and papers • NL Scot., letters • NRA, priv. coll., corresp. • priv. coll. • Rice University, Houston, Texas, Woodson Research Center, corresp., engravings, and a sonnet | BL, corresp. with John Allen, Add. MS 52180 • BL, letters to Lord and Lady Holland, Add. MS 51645 • BL, corresp. with Sir Robert Peel, Add. MSS 40368–40554 • Borth. Inst., letters to Earl and Countess Grey • Derbys. RO, letters to Sir R. J. Wilmot-Horton • Glos. RO, letters to Michael Hicks Beach • JRL, letters to Edward Davies Davenport • NRA, priv. coll., letters to Richard York and

Edward York • PRO, corresp. with Lord John Russell, PRO 30/22 • RIBA, letters to C. R. Cockerell • U. Durham L., letters to Charles, second Earl Grey

Likenesses J. Henning, porcelain medallion, 1803, Scot. NPG; copy, Scot. NPG • R. Sharples, group portrait, oils, 1831 (*The trial of Colonel Brereton*), Bristol City Museum and Art Gallery • H. P. Briggs, oils, 1833, NPG • E. Landseer, caricature, pen and wash drawing, c.1835, NPG • E. Morton, lithograph, pubd 1839 (after A. Cookenden), NPG • S. A. D., silhouette, 1839, BM • H. P. Briggs, oils, 1840 (after original, 1833), NPG [*see illus.*] • J. Doyle, caricature, pen-and-pencil drawing, 1840, BM • W. Drummond, lithograph (after marble bust by R. Westmacott), BM; repro. in *Athenaeum portraits* (1836) • E. U. Eddis, oils, New College, Oxford • S. Freeman, stipple (after J. Wright), BM; repro. in *The British gallery of contemporary portraits* (1817) • D. Maclise, lithograph, BM; repro. in *Fraser's Magazine* • Maclise, caricature, Mary Evans Picture Gallery, London

Wealth at death £80,000: will, PRO

Smith, Sir Sydney Alfred (1883–1969), forensic scientist, was born at Roxburgh, in the goldfields of Otago, in New Zealand, on 4 August 1883, the youngest child of James Jackson Smith, contractor to the municipality, making and repairing roads. His father was a Londoner who had emigrated to New Zealand and married another immigrant, Mary Elizabeth Wilkinson, *née* Kynaston, a Yorkshire woman whose first husband had died young, leaving her with six children.

Smith was educated at Roxburgh public school, became assistant to the local pharmacist, then went to Dunedin as an assistant where he qualified as a pharmacist at the age of twenty-three. He at once began to study medicine and as a part-time student in the faculty of science at Victoria College, Wellington, took his first-year chemistry and physics examinations while holding the post of dispensing chemist in Wellington Hospital.

Smith went next to Edinburgh University where he won a Vans Dunlop scholarship in botany and zoology which supported him to the extent of £300 spread over three years. He graduated MB ChB with first-class honours and a research scholarship in 1912. On 20 July 1912 he married Catherine Goodsir Gelenick (1886/7–1962), daughter of a commercial traveller; they had one son, Sydney Goodsir *Smith, and a daughter who became a doctor. After a short period in general practice he rejected this as a career and became an assistant in the Edinburgh department of forensic medicine at the suggestion of Professor Harvey Littlejohn. He obtained his MD in 1914 with a gold medal and the Alison prize. He had already had his first big medico-legal case in the prosecution in 1913 of Patrick Higgins for the murder of his two young sons.

Nevertheless, having already obtained his DPH (1913), Smith returned to New Zealand where he became medical officer of health for Otago at Dunedin. After the outbreak of the First World War his department would not release him, but on transfer to Wellington he combined civil health work with duties in various camps with the rank of major in the New Zealand army corps. In 1917 he was appointed principal medico-legal expert to the Egyptian government with a lectureship in forensic medicine at the School of Medicine in Qasr al-Aini, Cairo. The next period of eleven years was probably the most formative in his life for he made original contributions to forensic medicine in ballistics and firearms, and among other things he was responsible for the successful investigation of the murder of Sir Lee Stack in 1924.

In 1928 Smith succeeded his old chief in the regius chair of forensic medicine in Edinburgh, which he held until 1953, becoming dean of the medical faculty in 1931. In these years his name was associated as an expert witness with many cases, both for the crown and for the defence—the characteristic of a great and unprejudiced man, for these involved conflict with the established and, until then, unchallenged experts in England, not least of them Sir Bernard Spilsbury. Smith's main defence cases in Scotland were in Glasgow, where the two John Glaisters, father and son, were crown witnesses. So great was Smith's reputation that his cases on occasion took him as far afield as Ceylon and New Zealand.

During the Second World War Smith continued in his old expertise and devoted time to investigating the ballistic properties of various types of official ammunition. He also acted as consultant in medico-legal cases to the army, and he made possible the founding of the Polish medical school attached to Edinburgh University. He was a member of the General Medical Council from 1931 to 1956 and after retiring from his chair became consultant in forensic medicine to the World Health Organization. In 1954–7 he was rector of Edinburgh University which conferred an honorary LLD upon him in 1955; and in the following year he was elected an honorary member of the Royal Society of New Zealand. He was also FRSE and FRCP Edin. He was appointed CBE in 1944 and knighted in 1949, and he was appointed also to the order of the Nile, third class, and to the Polonia Restituta, third class.

A burly, cheerful man, Smith possessed great charm and was a natural academic politician. This, with his alert and logical mind, and his wide knowledge and experience, made him an expert witness whose integrity was never challenged. His was the stimulating influence in founding the British Association in Forensic Medicine, of which he was first president. He served on British Medical Association committees on alcohol and road traffic accidents in the 1960s. But he is perhaps best remembered for his writing. His textbook, *Forensic Medicine*, was first published in 1925, went into many editions, was translated into Spanish, and was awarded the Swiney prize in 1929. With John Glaister he wrote *Recent Advances in Forensic Medicine* (1931), and between 1928 and 1956 he edited four editions of *Principles and Practice of Medical Jurisprudence* by A. S. Taylor. Smith's reminiscences, *Mostly Murder*, were published in 1959. He died at his home, Rhycullen, 10 Oswald Road, Edinburgh, on 8 May 1969.

Francis Camps, *rev.* Brenda M. White

Sources *The Lancet* (31 May 1969) • *BMJ* (17 May 1969); (7 June 1969) • *BMJ* (5 March 1966); (12 March 1966); (2 April 1966) • personal knowledge (1981) • private information (1981) • *Medical Directories* • *WW* • *WWW*, 1961–70 • S. A. Smith, *Mostly murder* (1959) • M. A. Crowther and B. White, *On soul and conscience: the medical expert and crime* (1988) • m. cert. • d. cert. • *CGPLA Eng. & Wales* (1969)

Archives Royal College of Physicians of Edinburgh · U. Edin., faculty of medicine
Likenesses W. Hutchison, oils, repro. in Smith, *Mostly murder*; priv. coll. · W. Oliphant, charcoal drawing, Scot. NPG · photograph, repro. in Smith, *Mostly murder*
Wealth at death £166,936 5s.: confirmation, 12 Aug 1969, *CCI*

Smith, Sydney Goodsir (1915–1975), poet and playwright, was born on 26 October 1915 in Wellington, New Zealand, the son of Sir Sydney Alfred *Smith (1883–1969) and his wife, Catherine Goodsir Gelenick (1866/7–1962). In 1928 his father became professor of forensic medicine at the University of Edinburgh; he himself was educated there and at Oriel College, Oxford, where he gained a third class in modern history in 1937. During the Second World War he taught English to Polish troops. By the late 1940s he had emerged as the leading figure of the second wave of the Scottish literary 'Renaissance', and over the ensuing decades he gained a reputation as a convivial and cultured presence in the legendary 'writers' pubs' of Edinburgh, as well as in more conventionally scholarly circles.

Smith's earliest collections of poetry include *Skail Wind* (1941), *The Wanderer and other Poems* (1943), *The Deevil's Waltz* (1946), and *Selected Poems* (1947). Although he was not a native speaker of Scots, Smith succeeded in developing a convincing idiom based on the speech which he heard in the pubs and in the streets, enriched by his absorption of the great medieval Scots makars (makers, poets). The consequent range of registers, from the vernacular to the highly ornamented and stylized, was an invaluable resource for a poet concerned with sudden and contrasting changes of mood and feeling. The sequence *Under the Eildon Tree* (1948) comprises twenty-five poems invoking the great lovers in history, legend, and literature, and setting them beside the poet's own love life; the poems alternate between passion and disillusionment, toughened by Smith's irreverent wit, his abiding awareness that the sublime and the ridiculous are interdependent.

Smith became one of the foremost virtuosi of twentieth-century Scottish poetry, often at his most workmanlike when most playful; he delighted in the plasticity of language, in Joycean verbal pyrotechnics. This is most marked in his semi-novelistic prose work *Carotid cornucopius* (1947), which has been compared to *Finnegans Wake* (1939). The wordplay of *Under the Eildon Tree* is frequently of a macaronic nature; indeed, the sequence amply demonstrates that Smith's love of language was by no means limited to Scots, and testifies to his wider European frame of cultural reference. He translated poems by Tristan Corbière and Aleksandr Blok into Scots, and his celebrated 'The Grace of God and the Meth-Drinker' is the Edinburgh Grassmarket's equivalent of the tatterdemalion grotesqueries of a Villon or a Baudelaire:

There ye gang, ye daft
And doitit dotterel, ye saft
Crazed outland skalrag saul
In your bits and ends o winnockie duds
Your fyled and fozie-fousome clouts
As fou's a fish
(S. G. Smith, *Collected Poems*, 1975)

Smith's reputation grew during the 1950s. He belonged to the group of poets who were associated, as contributors and editors, with the Scottish literary magazine *Lines Review* (published 1952–98). *The Aipple and the Hazel* (1951), *So Late into the Night* (1952), *Cokkils* (1953), *Omens* (1955), *Orpheus and Eurydice* (1955), *Figs and Thistles* (1959), and *The Vision of the Prodigal Son* (1960) bore testimony to a prolific decade as a poet. In addition, he was active as a literary critic and editor. His pamphlet *A Short Introduction to Scottish Literature* appeared in 1951; he edited *Robert Fergusson, 1750–1774: Essays by Various Hands* (1952) and *Gavin Douglas: a Selection from his Poetry* (1959). A lifelong admirer and student of Robert Burns, he co-edited (with James Barke) the bawdy *Robert Burns: the Merry Muses of Caledonia* (1959). In 1966 he followed this up with *A Choice of Burns's Poems and Songs*.

Sydney Goodsir Smith (1915–1975), by Denis Peploe

In 1959 Smith and his poet friends C. M. Grieve (Hugh MacDiarmid) and Norman MacCaig were installed as the 'club bards' of the newly founded 200 Burns Club. In addition to MacDiarmid and MacCaig, Smith's immediate literary circle included Tom Scott and the Gaelic poet Sorley MacLean. He edited, with Kulgin Duval, *Hugh MacDiarmid: a Festschrift* to mark that poet's seventieth birthday in 1962.

Smith's political passions—left-wing, nationalist—were counterpointed by a man-of-the-world scepticism; he allowed them full sway in his verse play, *The Wallace* (1960), which dramatizes the revolt and capture of Scotland's national hero. It was revived by the Scottish Theatre Company at the Edinburgh International Festival of 1985, and is likely to remain Smith's most controversial work. His other plays included *Collickie Meg*, based on characters from *Carotid cornucopius*, and *The Stick-up*, which the Scottish composer Robin Orr turned into an opera; it was performed by the national company, Scottish Opera. In

'The Twa Brigs', composed in 1964 to mark the opening of the Forth Road bridge, the poet makes a plea for greater communication, tolerance, and love between people, but the roguish humour offsets any tendency towards moralizing. Another Scottish composer, William Wordsworth, made a musical setting of this poem for a performance in 1973, while a third, Ronald Stevenson, maintained that he had to restrain himself from setting one Smith poem after another. Smith was no narrow littérateur, but a man who embraced all the arts or was embraced by them.

Later sequences and collections included *Kynd Kittock's Land* (1965), *Fifteen Poems and a Play* (1969), and *Gowdspink in Reekie* (1974), the last volume to appear in Smith's lifetime. With his customary loving mockery, *Kynd Kittock's Land* celebrates the contradictions of his adopted Edinburgh:

This rortie wretched city
Sair come doun frae its auld hiechts.

Smith was a melancholy clown. He was variously nicknamed the Kilted Kiwi, or—more frequently and affectionately—the Great Auk. An accomplished artist in his own right, he was for many years the art critic of *The Scotsman*.

Smith had married Marion Elise Welsh, who predeceased him, and on 28 December 1967 he married a schoolteacher, Hazel Elizabeth Simpson Williamson (*b*. 1927/8), who survived him. He died suddenly, at the Royal Infirmary in Edinburgh, on 15 January 1975; at the time a volume of his *Collected Poems* was in production. It was seen through the press by Tom Scott and published later that year, with an introduction by Hugh MacDiarmid. Smith was buried in Dean cemetery, Edinburgh, on 19 January, and a bronze plaque, bearing his likeness in profile, was affixed to the outer wall of his former residence, 25 Drummond Place, Edinburgh. TOM HUBBARD

Sources 'Sydney Goodsir Smith, 1915–1975', *Scotia Review*, 9 (April 1975) • *The Auk remembered: Sydney Goodsir Smith, 1915–1975, published to commemorate the 80th anniversary of the poet's birth and the 20th of his death* • *Akros*, 10 (May 1969) • J. Calder, 'Sydney Goodsir Smith: a poet for all seasons', *Weekend Scotsman* (17 Aug 1985) • T. Royle, *The mainstream companion to Scottish literature* (1993) • E. Gold, *Sydney Goodsir Smith's 'Under the Eildon tree'* (1975) • H. MacDiarmid and [C. M. Grieve], *Sydney Goodsir Smith* (1963) • *For Sydney Goodsir Smith* (1975) • d. cert. • *CCI* (1975) • m. cert.

Archives NL Scot., corresp. and literary MSS; corresp. and papers | NL Scot., letters to Hector MacIver • U. St Andr. L., letters to Cedric Thorpe Davie | SOUND BL NSA, recordings of readings from his own works by Sydney Goodsir Smith 1966–78 • NL Scot., broadcasts and articles

Likenesses A. Moffat, group portrait, 1980 (*Poet's Pub*), Scot. NPG • G. Michonze, charcoal drawing, Scot. NPG • D. Peploe, oils, Scot. NPG [*see illus.*] • D. Peploe, pencil drawing, repro. in *Auk remembered*, frontispiece • bronze plaque, 25 Drummond Place, Edinburgh • photograph, repro. in G. Wright, *MacDiarmid: an illustrated biography of Christopher Murray Grieve (Hugh MacDiarmid)* • photograph, repro. in *Scotia Review*, 9 (April 1975), frontispiece

Wealth at death £2828.98: confirmation, 6 June 1975, *CCI*

Smith, Theodore (*fl*. *c*.1765–*c*.1810x23), composer and musician, is identified in two widely divergent ways by the musicologists François-Joseph Fétis and Ernst Ludwig Gerber, who provide him with radically differing origins. As Théodore Schmidt and Theodor Schmid he is identified as a violist, violinist, and composer, born in Paris to German parents, who was the leader of the orchestra at the Beaujolais Theatre. As T. Smith, however, he is identified as a keyboard player and composer, 'probably born in Hanover', who 'lived in Berlin in the second half of the eighteenth century' (Fétis, 8.54). Gerber is uncertain whether this is only one person or two, but the list of compositions following each entry confirms only one. Smith's first published works appear to have been printed in Paris *c*.1765, but those in Berlin not before 1780, so it is possible that he was of French birth, not visiting Germany until later in life.

Smith's London début was as the soloist in a harpsichord concerto on 17 March 1766, and on 1 February 1767 he became a member of the Royal Society of Musicians. According to R. J. S. Stevens he studied music under John Stanley, but Roger Fiske suggests that, given the *galant* influences in his compositions, he may have studied with J. C. Bach. Smith was a prolific composer who wrote in a popular style, intended mainly for the various pleasure gardens and drawing-room chamber music.

At some time before 1769 Smith met and married **Maria Harris** (*fl*. 1769–1796), who became an acclaimed actress and singer. Charlotte Papendiek claims that she was taught to sing by Smith, who at this time 'lived by teaching the pianoforte and singing' (*Court and Private Life*, 2.117), while *Grove* states that she had been a pupil of the elder Thomas Linley. Maria Smith made her début at Drury Lane on 20 October 1772 as Sylvia in David Garrick's *Cymon*, and performed with Garrick's company until *c*.1785. Probably owing to her influence, Smith was invited to compose music for Garrick's new production of James Thomson's and David Mallet's masque *Alfred* in 1773, but his appointment was controversial. Garrick's usual composers, Thomas Arne and Charles Dibdin, were infuriated by his decision to use another, relatively unknown composer, and an exchange of impolite letters ensued.

On 20 January 1776 the Smiths christened a son, but later the same year the marriage was over. Maria Smith eloped with 'a Mr Bishop' who 'took her off, and when the first shock had subsided, he prevailed upon Smith to accept a sum of money and be silent, for his wife would never return to him, and he (Bishop) would marry her' (*Court and Private Life*, 2.117). It may be that Smith spent some time in Berlin *c*.1780 following the demise of his marriage, given the number of his compositions published there about that time. Smith also took up positions at a girls' school run by a Mrs Roach near Windsor Castle, and at the Chiswick Lane School where his wife's daughter was a pupil 'for the sake of seeing Mrs Bishop, who sometimes came into the schoolroom' (ibid., 2.117–18). Smith's *Musical Directory* (*c*.1781) was no doubt written for the benefit of some of these students, but *ABC Dario Musico* pilloried its claim to 'teach the harpsichord without the assistance of a master' (*ABC Dario Musico*, 44). He wrote many other works for these students, in particular virtually monopolizing the market for piano duets from about 1779.

Although Mrs Papendiek paints Smith as a somewhat

tragic figure, he seems generally to have been an unscrupulous and unpopular character, denounced by other musicians as a charlatan. The organist and composer William Horsley (1784–1858), who was articled to Smith for five years from about 1800 to about 1805, stated that he was 'passionate and indolent to an extreme degree, and entirely neglected the instruction of his pupil' (Kassler, 2.955).

Maria Smith was active at Drury Lane under her husband's name until *c.*1785 and was still alive in January 1796, although nothing is known of her after this date. Smith took a post as organist at the Ebury Chapel in Chelsea *c.*1795, probably because of financial difficulties, and his compositions continued to be published in London and Dublin until 1823. Otherwise nothing is known of the last years of his life; *Grove* sets the date of his death at *c.*1810 but it may have occurred as late as 1823.

CLAIRE M. NELSON

Sources *Court and private life in the time of Queen Charlotte, being the journals of Mrs Papendiek*, ed. V. D. Broughton, 2 vols. (1887) • J. D. Brown, *Biographical dictionary of musicians: with a bibliography of English writings on music* (1886); repr. (1970) • J. Doane, ed., *A musical directory for the year 1794* [1794]; facs. edn (1993) • R. Fiske, *English theatre music in the eighteenth century*, rev. edn (1986) • E. L. Gerber, *Historisch-biographisches Lexikon der Tonkunster* (1792) • H. D. Johnstone and R. Fiske, eds., *Music in Britain: the eighteenth century* (1990) • J. C. Kassler, *The science of music in Britain, 1714–1830* (1979), vol. 2 • R. R. Kidd, 'The sonata for keyboard with violin accompaniment in England (1750–1790)', PhD diss., Yale U., 1967 • *The letters of David Garrick*, ed. D. M. Little and G. M. Kahrl, 3 vols. (1963) • B. Matthews, ed., *The Royal Society of Musicians of Great Britain: list of members, 1738–1984* (1985) • W. T. Parke, *Musical memoirs*, 2 vols. (1830) • Z. E. Pixley, 'The keyboard concerto in London society, 1760–1790', PhD diss., U. Mich., 1986 • Grove, *Dict. mus.* • R. Fiske and R. E. Cowgill, 'Smith, Theodore', *New Grove*, 2nd edn • F. Blume, ed., *Die Musik in Geschichte und Gegenwart*, 17 vols. (Kassel and Basel, 1949–86) • *ABC dario musico* (privately printed, Bath, 1780) • Highfill, Burnim & Langhans, *BDA* • F.-J. Fétis, *Biographie universelle des musiciens, et bibliographie générale de la musique*, 8 vols. (Brussels, 1835–44) • G. W. Stone, ed., *The London stage, 1660–1800*, pt 4: 1747–1776 (1962) • C. B. Hogan, ed., *The London stage, 1660–1800*, pt 5: 1776–1800 (1968) • *Répertoire international des sources musicales*, ser. A/I, 9 vols. (Munich and Duisburg, 1971–81); addenda and corrigenda, 4 vols. (1986–99) • E. B. Schnapper, ed., *The British union-catalogue of early music printed before the year 1801*, 2 vols. (1957) • L. Baillie and R. Balchin, eds., *The catalogue of printed music in the British Library to 1980*, 62 vols. (1981–7)

Likenesses S. De Wilde, oils (Maria Smith as Sylvia in *Cymon*), Garr. Club; repro. in *Biographical dictionary*, vol. 14, p. 160 • N. Hone, portrait (Maria Smith?), repro. in Highfill, Burnim & Langhans, *BDA*, vol. 14, p. 161; formerly in the possession of Gooden and Fox, 1955

Smith, Theophilus Ahijah (1809–1879). *See under* Smith, George Charles (1782–1863).

Smith, Theyre Townsend (1798–1852), Church of England clergyman, son of Richard Smith (*d.* 1823), a barrister of Middlesex, and his wife (1766/7–1842), was the brother of William Henry *Smith (1808–1872). He was originally a Presbyterian, and from 1821 studied at Glasgow University, but being convinced by reading Hooker that episcopacy was the more scriptural form of church government, he decided to enter the English church. He accordingly matriculated from Queens' College, Cambridge, on 4 January 1823, graduating BA in 1827 and MA in 1830.

After serving a curacy in Huntingdonshire and another in Essex, Smith was appointed assistant preacher at the Temple in 1835. In 1839 and 1840 he filled the post of Hulsean lecturer at Cambridge, and in 1845 he was presented to the living of Newhaven in Sussex by Lord Lyndhurst. In March 1848, when Louis-Philippe took refuge in England after his deposition, Smith received him on his landing at Newhaven. In the same year Thomas Turton, bishop of Ely, who had expressed great admiration of his Hulsean lectures, collated him to the vicarage of Wymondham in Norfolk. In 1850 he was appointed honorary canon of Norwich. He married Rebecca, second daughter of Thomas Williams of Coate in Oxfordshire. Smith died on 4 May 1852 at Wymondham.

Smith published collections of his sermons and lectures, as well as *Remarks on the Influence of Tractarianism* (1851), in which he attacked the Tractarian preoccupation with one Catholic church—an idea he cited as responsible for causing conversions to Rome.

E. I. CARLYLE, *rev.* ELLIE CLEWLOW

Sources Venn, *Alum. Cant.* • *GM*, 2nd ser., 38 (1852), 97, 317 • Boase, *Mod. Eng. biog.* • T. T. Smith, *Remarks on the influence of Tractarianism* (1851) • J. Foster, ed., *Index ecclesiasticus, or, Alphabetical lists of all ecclesiastical dignitaries in England and Wales since the Reformation* (1890) • D. Bank and A. Esposito, eds., *British biographical index*, 4 vols. (1990)

Smith, Thomas. *See* Smythe, Thomas (1522–1591); Smythe, Sir Thomas (*c.*1558–1625).

Smith, Sir Thomas (1513–1577), scholar, diplomat, and political theorist, was born on 23 December 1513 at Saffron Walden, the second son of John Smith (*d.* 1557), a small-scale sheep farmer, and Anne Charnock (*d.* 1547), of Lancashire origins. His health was not good and he applied himself to learning, going to Cambridge at the age of eleven for study on the university fringe before joining Queens' College in 1526.

Education and rise to prominence A precocious intellect, 'the flower of the University of Cambridge' (Cortez, i), Smith graduated in 1530 and proceeded MA in 1532. Coming to the notice of William Butts, the king's physician, he was made a king's scholar and appointed to the office of public orator in 1533. In 1540 he was made regius professor of civil law, a post for which he was unqualified on appointment, but between May 1540 and January 1542 he undertook a European tour visiting Orléans, Paris, and Padua, familiarizing himself with humanist legal scholarship, and he was incorporated LLD and DCL on his return. He had already made his mark among the humanist avant-garde by joining his friend John Cheke in passionately advocating the reform of Greek pronunciation on Erasmian lines. The new system was forbidden by Stephen Gardiner, the more conservative chancellor of the university. Smith was initially inclined to defiance, drawing up in August 1542 his *De recta et emendata Linguae Graecae pronuntatione* (not published until 1568) but he caved in under pressure, perhaps because of his political ambitions. He was rewarded with the post of vice-

Sir Thomas Smith (1513–1577), by unknown artist, *c.*1546–7

chancellor in 1543. Although he had some very distinguished pupils like William Cecil, John Ponet, and John Aylmer, he was increasingly drawn into university and college administration, and this brought him into contact with the court. It was to Smith and his friend Cheke that the university turned in 1546 when it wished to defend itself from the prying eyes of a rapacious king, who was asking awkward questions about its finances.

In February 1547 Smith entered Protector Somerset's household and in March became clerk of the privy council. He was also returned to parliament as a member for Marlborough. Other signs of the regime's favour were the posts of provost of Eton College (December 1547) and dean of Carlisle (January 1548), but it was his appointment as secretary of state in April 1548 that marked his prominence and growing notoriety. He undertook an enormous variety of tasks, pressing successfully for firm action to secure the restoration of English trading privileges at Antwerp in the summer of 1548, supervising the raising of foreign loans, examining Baron Seymour of Sudeley and his associates when they were charged with treason in January and February 1549, and marshalling the arguments for English sovereignty over Scotland in the spring of 1549. He was knighted in April that year. In a strongly evangelical regime, he had a reputation for religious lukewarmness, perhaps because of his continuing sympathy for Gardiner, but he took a hard line against the advocates of transubstantiation at the debates in the House of Lords at which he assisted in December 1548, and he played a key role in the presentation of the government's case against Bishop Edmund Bonner in 1549.

Smith's accumulation of ecclesiastical patronage made him enemies among the reformed, however. Latimer lashed out:

> For what an enormity is this in a Christian realm to serve in the civility having the profits of a provostship and a deanery and a parsonage. But I will tell you what is likely to come of it, it will bring the clergy into slavery. (*Sermons*, 122)

He lost the sympathy of many of his former friends in Cambridge by his involvement in the commission to reform the university, where he emerged as a strong supporter of the unpopular scheme to create a college dedicated to the study of civil law by amalgamating Trinity Hall and Clare College. He was not at ease in the world of politics, for he was simply too clever for his own good, and his abrasive manner, 'high in th'instep' (BL, Harley MS 6989, fol. 141), left him isolated. Among his fiercest critics was the duchess of Somerset, the protector's equally abrasive wife. Late in June 1549 he retreated to Eton supposedly to recover from illness, but the instruction from Somerset to remain there over the summer pending a visit from the king which never materialized suggests that he was being marginalized. It was in fact one of his most creative periods, for he used the enforced leisure to write the *Discourse of the Commonweal*.

Political eclipse Smith returned to court at the end of September 1549, as Somerset's regime began to disintegrate following the badly handled summer rebellions, financial crisis, and a failed foreign policy. He was with Somerset and the king at Hampton Court and later Windsor Castle (to which they soon retreated) as the majority of the privy council moved against the protector. He was responsible for drafting the proclamation of 5 October which inflamed the crisis by accusing the London lords of being traitors and murderers, but then worked with Archbishop Cranmer to pull the protector back from the brink of armed confrontation. As one of the 'principal instruments and councillors that he did use both at this time and always' (*APC*, 1547–50, 343–4), and therefore tarred by Somerset's tendency to ignore the privy council, he was too close to the protector, and too disliked, to survive the coup, and he was deprived of the secretaryship and imprisoned in the Tower on 13 October. He sought comfort in writing psalm paraphrases appropriate to his afflicted condition, but they cannot be counted among the more distinguished examples of mid-Tudor verse. His imprisonment was not long-lasting. The threatened swing to the conservatives was arrested, and he was released on 22 February 1550. The council had contemplated depriving him of the chair of civil law, but less vindictive counsels prevailed.

Smith was suspected of feathering his own nest in Edward's reign. The duchess of Somerset had charged him with being 'a sore and extreme man … an oppressour … a great chopper and chaunger of land' (Nichols, 120–27). But he probably attracted unfavourable comment as a man rising from humble origins, and his economic morality was, as he explained in his own defence, nothing other than conventional. He bought the manor of Yarlington in Somerset from the marquess of Northampton in 1547 on terms so favourable as to suggest a link between the purchase and Smith's membership of the commission to investigate the marquess's divorce; other major purchases were made in 1548 when he acquired a sizeable parcel of lands in Derbyshire and a desirable property in Canon Row in Westminster which he sub-let to Sir William Paget, while he shared a house in Philpot Lane in London with his brother George, a city businessman. In 1550 he acquired in part exchange four manors, including Ankerwyke near Eton, and this became his principal home during the rest of Edward's reign as he busied himself about college affairs. The dowry of 1000 marks from his first wife, Elizabeth Carkeke (1529–1553), the daughter of a London printer, whom he married on 15 April 1548, had financed the purchases of that year. She died on 3 August 1553. He remarried shortly afterwards (23 July 1554); his second wife was another Londoner, Philippa (1522–1578), daughter of Henry Wilford, a London merchant, and widow of Sir John Hampden, an Essex gentleman (*d.* 1553). By this match he acquired the extensive manor of Theydon Mount in Essex with its two houses, Hill Hall and Mounthall, and these became his principal residences in the years ahead.

There were moments in the later years of Edward's and Mary's reigns when it looked as if Smith might be politically rehabilitated. He was employed as a commissioner to inquire into offences against the prayer book in 1551 and he was the key player in the embassy sent to France under the leadership of the marquess of Northampton in May 1551 to conclude a marriage treaty between Edward VI and Princess Elisabeth of France. But he had refused to press the case against Gardiner when called upon to give evidence against him in January 1551, and he never enjoyed the full confidence of the Northumberland regime. Gardiner may have reciprocated Smith's favour under the Marian regime, for although he was deprived of the deanery of Carlisle and the provostship of Eton, Mary agreed to pay a pension to Smith of £100 per annum in May 1554, and 'The memorandum for the understanding of the foreign exchange' (if, as seems likely, authored by Smith) may have been the fruits of his consultation by Gardiner on currency matters in the same year. But Smith had prominent enemies—particularly Bonner—and he was never centre stage.

Ambassador in France It is curious that Smith played only a minor role in the early years of the Elizabethan regime in spite of the prominence of his Cambridge associates in the government. An MP for Liverpool, he served on a committee to prepare legislation for the 1559 parliament, and on a commission to enforce the 1559 settlement, and he attended upon Duke John of Finland when he came to press the suit of his brother Erik XIV of Sweden for Elizabeth's hand. But he does not appear to have played a major role in either the making of the religious settlement (in spite of the recommendation of the author of the 'Device for the alteration of religion' that he should chair a committee of six divines to discuss religious changes) or in the recoinage (an area in which he might claim some expertise). He seems to have quarrelled with Sir William Cecil; over what is not clear, but his enthusiastic support for a domestic match for Elizabeth in his widely circulated 'Dialogue on the queen's marriage' (April 1561) would not have helped his relations with the secretary, who was bitterly opposed to a match with Lord Robert Dudley. Cecil resisted the pressure from the English ambassador in France, Sir Nicholas Throckmorton, for Smith's appointment to replace him in the embassy.

It was only when the immediate danger of a Dudley match had passed that Smith secured the appointment as ambassador to France, and left England on 22 September 1562. Smith's second French embassy (1562–6) was not a success. The Huguenots, assisted by the English who had occupied Le Havre, were suffering military reverses in the first of the French wars of religion. As Smith put it, 'I am set to fly with clipped wings' (PRO, SP 70/44/1000, fol. 770). He was hamstrung by divided counsels at Elizabeth's court, and by tensions with Throckmorton, still present in the prince de Condé's camp and urging full-scale support for the Huguenots, while Smith (sharing with his monarch a non-confessional outlook on foreign policy) interpreted his brief as being to secure the restoration of Calais according to the terms of the treaty of Cateau-Cambrésis of 1559. The English occupation of Le Havre rendered his position at the French court weak, and for lack of contacts he sought information from the papal legate, the cardinal of Ferrara, much to the outrage of the privy council. He was unable to prevent the accord between the French court and the Huguenots which resulted in their co-operating in the campaign for the recovery of Le Havre in the autumn of 1563.

In July 1563 the government had foolishly sent Throckmorton back to France as joint ambassador after a brief interlude in England, and tensions between him and Smith over tactics grew steadily worse. Throckmorton undermined Smith's position at the English court, claiming that he was negotiating secretly with Catherine de Medici, and throwing the English cause away. The two men nearly came to blows when Throckmorton denounced Smith to his face as a 'whoresome traitor' (PRO, SP 70/70/316, fol. 255), for letting slip to the French the existence of revised instructions from Elizabeth offering lower terms. In the event the treaty of Troyes (April 1564) represented a considerable climb-down for the English as the rights of both the English and French to Calais were reserved as in the 1559 treaty. Smith hoped now for his recall, but he was destined to spend another two years in France, following the French court on its progress to pacify the kingdom. There was relatively little important diplomatic business, and he was able to pursue his cultural and intellectual interests, visiting archaeological sites, collecting plants and books, and working up his materials on English linguistics. Most importantly of all, he worked on the *De republica Anglorum*, which Smith completed in April 1565 while recovering from a serious illness at Toulouse.

Smith was recalled from the French embassy in April 1566, but although he had mended his fences with Cecil, who was active on his behalf, he did not find favour with

Elizabeth. He was employed on a brief but fruitless embassy to France in March 1567 to demand the return of Calais: his speech to the French court, 'A collection of certain reasons to prove the queen's majesty's right to have the restitution of Calais', was widely circulated in manuscript. Becoming 'all together a contreyman' (*Finch MSS*, 1.12–13), he busied himself in building projects at Hill Hall, and involved himself in local government. His fortunes turned, however, on the death of his enemy Throckmorton and Cecil's elevation to the peerage as Baron Burghley in February 1571. He returned to the privy council in March 1571, immediately before he re-entered parliament as a knight of the shire for Essex, although Burghley's wish that he take over the secretaryship was not realized for over a year. In the meantime he was involved in the examination of the conspirators around the fourth duke of Norfolk which earned him the queen's approval, in spite of his reluctance to use the torture she insisted upon. He was entrusted with another French embassy in December 1571 to foster the developing Anglo-French accord by pursuing Elizabeth's marriage to the duc d'Anjou. Although the marriage foundered on the question of religion he was able to bring the treaty of Blois to a successful conclusion (19 April 1572): England and France were now pledged to a defensive alliance against Spain. Further signs of favour followed. He became chancellor of the Order of the Garter, and received the secretaryship on 13 July 1572, very soon after his return to England. In spring 1573 he was made keeper of the privy seal.

Secretary of state It was around this time that another of Smith's cherished projects was being brought to fruition. For in November 1571 he had been granted land in the Ards peninsula (in co. Down between the Irish Sea and Strangford Lough) with a view to establishing a colony. The scheme was publicized in a pamphlet—*A letter sent by I. B. gentleman unto his very frende Mayster R. C. esquire, wherein is conteined a large discourse of the peopling and inhabiting the cuntrie called the Ardes, and other adiacent in the north of Ireland and taken in hand by Sir Thomas Smith, one of the queenes majesties privie counsel and Thomas Smith esquire, his sonne*. Consciously following Roman models, Smith proposed colonization of Ireland as a solution to the problem of English overpopulation, and in particular the problem of under-employed younger sons, but (probably under the influence of Rowland White) he also showed a keen interest in the economic potential of Ireland, and argued that the dispossession of the Irish was justified because the English colonists would farm more productively. An expedition to establish the colony was headed by his illegitimate son Thomas *Smith (1547–1573), but its departure was delayed from the spring until the end of August 1572, and it soon ran into difficulties. Smith's scheme for cut-price colonization by private enterprise was supported by the parsimonious queen, but it was at odds with the priorities of the lord deputy, Sir William Fitzwilliam, who rightly foresaw the escalation of conflict with the native Irish, and did little to support the projectors. The scheme unsurprisingly brought rival Gaelic groups together as the Clandeboye O'Neills co-operated with the Tyrone O'Neills to block it, but it also encountered opposition from the 'degenerate' Old English families, like the Savages, whom Smith had hoped to win over. The scheme produced a personal tragedy for Smith, for in November 1573 his son was 'slain in the Ardes … by the revolting of certain Irishmen of his own household, to whom he overmuch trusted' (PRO, SP 63/42, no. 58). Smith continued to draw up plans for the colony, and there was another expedition in August 1574 under the joint command of his brother George and Jerome Brett, but bickering between them contributed to the continuing military set-backs, and in April 1575 Smith surrendered his interests in the Ards to the first earl of Essex.

As secretary Smith never enjoyed the power that Burghley had wielded. Although Burghley had given up some of the more onerous duties of state, he retained a central role in policy formulation, and Smith's role was to act as an intermediary between him, the queen, and ambassadors. It was one of many frustrations in his relations with Elizabeth that she often refused to sign papers until Burghley had approved them, sometimes using this as an excuse for putting off decisions. 'Irresolution and long waiting', he confided to Burghley in a characteristic lament, 'will make opportunity and occasion to flit away' (BL, Lansdowne MS 19/81, fol. 178). The one area of policy on which he did have influence was Ireland, where his personal interests were at stake. Here he pushed hard for Elizabeth to support the expeditionary force under the earl of Essex for the conquest of Antrim.

Death Smith had never enjoyed good health. He was prone to bouts of nervous exhaustion when under stress as in summer 1549 or on the death of his son in November 1573. He had a narrow escape from a very serious fever contracted at Toulouse in 1564, and there were apparent recurrences in 1568 and 1570. He was seriously ill again in March 1572 during the French embassy, complaining of continual vomiting and headaches. He set great store by his own medical remedies produced through the distilling of waters carried on at Mounthall, and he passed them on to fellow sufferers like Burghley. By March 1576 he was suffering from cancer of the throat, and he withdrew from public affairs, but continued his academic interests, recataloguing his library and revising some of his earlier writings. He died on 12 August 1577 at Hill Hall, and was buried sometime before 24 August in the church of St Michael's, Theydon Mount, in a fine tomb designed by himself.

Smith's marriage to Philippa Wilford was childless and they were probably never close. The tensions between them came into the open in the last years of his life as Smith sought to pass on an inheritance to his brother George and his nephews. Lady Philippa had not offered her full support to Smith in his fight against a challenge to the Theydon Mount estate from Henry Ferrers, who claimed that Philippa's first husband, Sir John Hampden, had only given her a life interest in the estate with remainders to his grandson Edward Ferrers and his heirs. Lady Philippa expressed indifference about the outcome, and she had treacherously told Henry Ferrers that she had documents which would support his title. Within a day of her husband's death Philippa was contesting the will. Using the threat of support for the Ferrers claims, she was able to force George Smith to agree more favourable terms. This was not the only dispute to mar the funeral, for Andrew Perne, master of Peterhouse and the preacher of the funeral sermon, became engaged in a furious row with Gabriel Harvey, a protégé of Smith's, over the bequest of some of Smith's books.

Humanist scholar Along with his friend John Cheke, Smith was among England's foremost humanists. In his inaugural lectures as regius professor of civil law at Cambridge in 1542 he argued against the traditional Bartolan method of legal interpretation where the authorities were seen as self-sufficient, in favour of applying the disciplines of history and philology to the texts. Quite to what extent Smith was in a position to implement his programme may be doubted, as his training in the civil law was somewhat sketchy. There is perhaps an element of self-promotion in Smith's espousal of fashionable intellectual causes which can also be seen in his intervention over Greek pronunciation, where Cheke had the edge over him in terms of understanding the philological and phonetic issues involved. But there were serious issues at stake, for Smith argued that custom could not be adopted as the common standard for pronunciation, as it varies from country to country and over time. To recover an 'authentic' Greek pronunciation, it was necessary to pay close attention to its literature. The new system was established on the assumption that single letters were intended to express single sounds, as men would not have invented redundant letters. It formed the basis for the form of Greek pronunciation taught in English schools until the end of the nineteenth century.

Smith's interest in English linguistics was an outgrowth from these studies of Greek pronunciation. He had made notes in the 1540s, but returned to the subject while in France in 1566, publishing his *De recta & emendata Linguae anglicae scriptione, dialogus* in Paris in 1568 alongside the volume on Greek pronunciation he had presented to Gardiner in 1542. In this dialogue a character called Quintus invokes Smith's aid in convincing Obstinatus of the need for phonetic spelling and the reform of the alphabet since the Latin alphabet did not provide for the different sounds of English. The project for linguistic reform in which Smith participated with John Cheke, Roger Ascham, Thomas Wilson, and John Hart (the last a possible identification for Quintus) has been seen as part of the developing sense of English national consciousness.

Social and political analyst *The Discourse of the Commonweal*, written at the peak of the social unrest of Somerset's protectorate in 1549, but not published until 1581, is the most impressive piece of economic analysis produced in the sixteenth century. Formerly ascribed to John Hales, similarities to Smith's analysis of money in his 'Treatise on the wages of a Roman footsoldier' (1562) establish Smith as the author. The *Discourse* adopts his characteristic mode of academic analysis, the dialogue, in this case between a knight, a merchant, a capper, and a husbandman, as representatives of the different social groups, who each promote their sectional interpretation of the causes of inflation. But it is the doctor, a civil lawyer, who provides the answers. Although Smith gives some weight to the conventional explanations of sheep farming, enclosure, the raising of rents, and competition from foreign imports, he sees the main cause of inflation as lying in the debasement of the coinage. Smith recognized that gold and silver coinage had a value represented by the price ascribable to its precious metal content. This view was unwelcome to Somerset who had committed himself to the hypothesis (pushed vigorously by John Hales) that it was enclosure which pushed up prices because it allowed a continuation of the Scottish war which was funded by debasement. By arguing that debasement was to blame, Smith was implying that the Scottish war would have to be abandoned: it is therefore unsurprising that the *Discourse* was written during a period of enforced rustication.

Although recent historians have stressed the long-term impact of the pressure of rising population on limited resources as the underlying cause of inflation, there can be no doubt that Smith was essentially correct about the role of the debasements in explaining the severe short-term inflation of the 1540s. Towards the end of his life he grappled with the question as to why Elizabeth's reform of the coinage had not led to a reduction in prices, and came up with the penetrating suggestion that American silver was to blame. The other striking feature of the arguments of the *Discourse* is the challenge it presented to the traditional view that society had to be organized morally. In contrast to other commentators like Thomas Becon, Hugh Latimer, and John Hales, Smith argued that behaviour could be directed through economic management mobilizing individual goals to the common good. 'Can we devise that all covetousness may be taken from men? No, no more than we can make men be without ire, without gladness, without fear, and without all affections' (*Discourse*, ed. Lamond, 121). Thus he positioned himself against the conventional moralists' attacks upon covetousness. Rather Smith sought to channel people's acquisitive instincts to work to the good of the common weal: arable farming in his opinion should be incentivized by allowing the free export of corn (contrary to received wisdom) and imposing additional duties on wool exports.

Smith's other major work was his *De republica Anglorum*, written between 1562 and 1565 and circulating widely in manuscript, but not published until 1583. Smith explained to his friend Walter Haddon that it was written 'in a style midway between the historical and the philosophical, giving it the shape in which I imagined that Aristotle wrote of the many Greek commonwealths, books which are no longer extant' (*De republica*, ed. Alston, xiii–xiv). Smith offered a brief analysis of English society, and a fuller account of institutions and the legal system. He was able to draw upon his civil law training and experience of the continent to make comparisons to establish the distinctiveness of English institutions. *De republica*

Anglorum's presentation of England as a 'mixed monarchy', however, also owes something to the recent experience of minority and female rule, and the work may have been intended as an intervention in the debate between Haddon and the Portuguese Osorio da Fonseca over the legitimacy of Elizabeth's reformation.

Whatever its immediate polemical purposes, *De republica Anglorum* enjoyed great popularity, going through eleven English editions by 1640; a Latin edition appeared around 1610, and there were further Latin editions printed on the continent in 1625, 1630, and 1641. Robert Beale, in his 'Instructions for a principall secretarie' recognized the utility of the work: 'It is convenient for a secretarie to seek to understande the state of the whole realme, to have Sir Thomas Smithe's booke, althoughe ther be manie defects which by progresse of time and experience he shalbe able to spie and mend' (Read, 1.428). Smith would have been surprised by later suggestions that he had made a case for parliamentary sovereignty against the crown. When he declared that the authority of parliament was absolute, he meant that it enjoyed a monopoly of law-making, and that its acts were binding on the whole population. He saw the monarch as part of parliament; parliament could not therefore be conceived as the two houses working against the monarch. Nevertheless the basically descriptive nature of *De republica* meant that in the parliamentary debates of the next century, it could be mined by both upholders of the royal prerogative and exponents of the liberties of parliament.

Smith's support for learning in his later years was expressed in his patronage of rising stars like Gabriel Harvey, who remembered him with great affection. Smith also founded two scholarships and two fellowships at Queens' College, Cambridge, one in arithmetic and one in geometry. Queens' also received the bulk of his library and 'my greate globe of myne owne makinge' (will, PROB 11/59, fol. 238*v*). He was also involved, along with Andrew Perne and Burghley, in promoting the so-called Corn Act of 1576, which provided some inflation-proofing for the Oxford and Cambridge colleges by requiring that one-third of their existing rents be paid in corn or the cash equivalent at current market prices.

Assessment Smith was never at ease in the courtly milieu. He readily confessed that his bluntness made him few friends; he lacked interest in the courtly arts of dancing and music; and he never shared in the adulation of the queen. His enemies played upon his status anxieties, Throckmorton taunting him as 'having come to court but yesterday a beggarly scholar' (PRO, SP 70/70/316, fol. 255). Nor did he really fit into the pattern of confessional alliances made by Elizabethan politicians, in this respect never sharing the outlook of Burghley and Walsingham in spite of his friendship with them. 'The hardest punishment for all papists by mine advice', he opined, 'should be to confine them into Italy and let them live by sucking the pope's teats' (PRO, SP 70/52/411), but he was not among those who pressed for harsher penal laws. Nor is there any sign of sympathy for the puritan cause. That his funeral sermon was preached by the religiously ambidextrous Andrew Perne, a fellow bibliophile, may be significant. His friends were chosen for their shared cultural interests, not for their religious affiliations or prominence at court.

A library list from 1566 establishes the breadth of Smith's intellectual pursuits. His books were arranged by subject matter with separate sections on theology, civil law, history, philosophy, mathematics, medicine, and grammar and poetry. It is rich in the works of the church fathers and in classical texts, both Latin and Greek, as well as more fashionable works by authors such as Castiglione and Machiavelli. His chemical interests were pursued in his laboratory at Hill Hall, but they led him into one of his more absurd speculations, as he poured money from 1570 to 1572 into the worthless schemes of the chancer William Medley, who claimed he had mastered a new technique for producing copper by boiling iron in sulphuric acid. Smith's interest in architecture was more fruitful. He owned five versions of Vitruvius's *De architectura*, and he may well have been responsible for the innovative design of Hill Hall, rebuilt from 1568 to 1569, but still in progress at his death. Hill Hall was built in the classical idiom, and owed much to French buildings like the château of Bournazel near Toulouse.

Even when closest to the centre of power as part of Somerset's household government from 1547 to 1549, Smith never enjoyed the full confidence of the politicians, and his career provides evidence of the dangers faced by academics in office, and of the importance of personality in politics. His intellectual interests were sometimes faddish and could lead him into ill-conceived schemes like the Irish and copper ventures. But the *De republica Anglorum* became a key text for those who sought to understand the functioning of the commonwealth, and the *Discourse of the Commonweal* contributed to the climate of more rational decision making about the economy in the later sixteenth century. IAN W. ARCHER

Sources M. Dewar, *Sir Thomas Smith: a Tudor intellectual in office* (1964) • J. Strype, *Life of the learned Sir Thomas Smith kt* (1698); repr. (1820) • J. G. Nichols, 'Some additions to the biography of Sir Thomas Smith', *Archaeologia*, 38 (1860), 98–127 • T. Smith, *A discourse of the common weal of this realm of England*, ed. E. Lamond (1893) • T. Smith, *A discourse of the common weal of this realm of England*, ed. M. Dewar (Richmond, VA, 1969) • M. Dewar, 'The authorship of the "Discourse of the common weal"', *Economic History Review*, 2nd ser., 19 (1966), 388–400 • T. Smith, *De republica Anglorum*, ed. L. Alston (1906) • *De republica Anglorum by Sir Thomas Smith*, ed. M. Dewar (1982) • *Sir Thomas Smith: literary and linguistic works*, Stockholm Studies in English, 12, 50, 56 (1963–83), prints • P. Stein, 'Sir Thomas Smith, Renaissance civilian', *The character and influence of the Roman civil law: historical essays* (1988), 186–96 • D. R. Kelley, 'History, English law, and the Renaissance', *Past and Present*, 65 (1974), 24–51 • J. B. Mullinger, *History of the University of Cambridge*, 2 (1884) • E. J. Dobson, *English pronunciation, 1500–1700*, 2 vols. (1957), vol. 1, pp. 46–52 • C. Shrank, 'Rhetorical constructions of a national community: the role of the king's English in mid-Tudor writing', *Communities in early modern England*, ed. A. Shepard and P. Withington (2000), 180–98 • R. Zim, *English metrical psalms: poetry as praise and prayer, 1535–1601* (1987), 74–9, 98–103 • *A letter sent by I. B. gentleman unto his very frende Mayster R. C. esquire, wherein is conteined a large discourse of the peopling and inhabiting the cuntrie called the Ardes* [1572] • H. Morgan, 'The colonial venture of Sir Thomas Smith in Ulster, 1571–1575', *HJ*, 28 (1985), 261–78 • D. B. Quinn, 'Sir Thomas Smith and the beginning of English colonial theory', *Proceedings of the American Philosophical Society*, 89 (1945), 543–60 • D. Armitage, *The ideological origins of the British empire* (2000), 47–51 • A. McLaren, *Political culture in the reign of Elizabeth I: queen and commonwealth, 1558–1585* (1999) • HoP, *Commons*, 1509–58, 3.338–40 • M. R. Pickering, 'Smith, Sir Thomas', HoP, *Commons*, 1558–1603, 3.400–01 • *Essex*, Pevsner (1954) • R. Simpson, 'Sir Thomas Smith and the wall paintings at Hill Hall, Essex: scholarly theory and design in the sixteenth century', *Journal of the British Archaeological Association*, 130 (1977), 1–20 • P. J. Drury, '"A fayre house built by Sir Thomas Smith": the development of Hill Hall, Essex, 1557–1581', *Journal of the British Archaeological Association*, 136 (1983), 98–123 • G. E. Aylmer, 'The economics and finances of the collegiate university, *c*.1530–1640', *Hist. U. Oxf.* 3: *Colleg. univ.*, 535–43 [on the 1576 Corn Act] • V. F. Stern, *Gabriel Harvey: a study of his life, marginalia and library* (1979) • P. Collinson, 'Andrew Perne: Elizabethan turncoat', in P. Collinson, *Elizabethan essays* (1994), 179–217 • *Sermons by Hugh Latimer*, ed. G. E. Corrie, Parker Society, 16 (1844) • C. Read, *Mr Secretary Walsingham and the policy of Queen Elizabeth*, 3 vols. (1925) • M. Cortez, *The art of navigation* (1561) • A. McLaren, 'Reading Sir Thomas Smith's *De republica Anglorum* as protestant apologetic', *HJ*, 42 (1999), 911–39 • N. Wood, 'Avarice and civil unity: the contribution of Sir Thomas Smith', *History of Political Thought*, 18 (1997), 24–42 • *APC*, 1547–50 • *Report on the manuscripts of Allan George Finch*, 5 vols., HMC, 71 (1913–2003), vols. 1–2 • will, PRO, PROB 11/59, fol. 238v

Archives BL, Add. MSS 35831, 48047, 325, 4136, 4109, 4103, 4126, 4135 • BL, corresp. and papers, Cotton MS Caligula B vii • BL, Cotton MSS, Caligula E v, E vi, C iii • BL, corresp. and papers, Harley 660, 253, 6989, 6991, 6992 • BL, Julius F vi • BL, Royal MS 17A xvii • BL, MS of autobiography, Sloane MS Lat 325 • BL, Vespasian F vi • Essex RO, Chelmsford, papers relating to attempted colonization of the Ards in Ulster • NL Scot., corresp. and papers [copies] • PRO, letters, SP 12, SP 63, SP 70 • Queens' College, Cambridge, personal notebooks and portion of library | BL, Lansdowne MSS 8, 15, 16, 102, 171, 19, 21, 29 • Bodl. Oxf., MSS Rawl. C 685, C 268 • CUL, MS Mm,1,48, fols. 394–430

Likenesses oils, *c*.1546–1547, priv. coll. [*see illus.*] • tomb effigy, *c*.1577, St Michael's Church, Theydon Mount, Essex • woodcut, 1578, BL; repro. in G. Harvey, *Lachrymae pro obitu* (1578) • M. Gheeraerts senior, group portrait, etching (*Procession of Garter knights*, 1576), BM • oils, Eton

Smith, Thomas (1547–1573), colonial adventurer, was born on 15 March 1547, probably at Cambridge, the illegitimate son of Sir Thomas *Smith (1513–1577), the influential Tudor intellectual and courtier. Sir Thomas expected much of his only child and heir and dictated the course of his life. The awesome shadow cast by his indefatigable father obscures his early years. Thomas is known only to have accompanied him on his French embassies, and to have served as an officer in Ireland about 1568 before entering into the service of the earl of Leicester. His career began in earnest following his father's plan for a private colonial venture in the north of Ireland in the summer of 1571.

In November 1571 Sir Thomas and his son received a substantial grant of land in the Ards, co. Down, and Upper Clandeboye, co. Antrim. Sir Thomas, then a privy councillor, secured this grant by offering independently to recruit colonists and privately fund the expedition. This was accomplished by the publication and distribution of a broadsheet and book appealing for subscriptions and volunteers. Sir Thomas was undoubtedly the ideological force behind both works, although they were attributed to his son. The intention of father and son was to expropriate the Gaelic clansmen in the area, thus liberating the allegedly tractable Gaelic churl who would remain to till the land. They supposed that the clansmen were the disruptive element in local society, whereas the peaceful, hard-working churl would acquiesce in English law and custom. These publications reached Ireland and provoked resentment from Sir Brian O'Neill of Clandeboye, the Anglophile chieftain whose lands had been granted to the Smiths. The administration at Dublin was less than enthusiastic about the plan and feared that outside intervention would cause a general rebellion in the north. The unexpected dispatch of Sir Thomas to France in December 1571 left the controversial and well-publicized enterprise in the untested hands of his son.

Early in 1572 Smith began gathering volunteers at Liverpool, although his undisciplined handling of them soon caused the mayor to complain of their unruly behaviour. Smith further exacerbated the problems of the already troubled undertaking by tampering with the proposed structure of the colony. He attempted to sell to his friends thirty 'assistantships' allowing them wide powers in the colony. Sir Thomas disagreed with his son's changes and suspended the matter until his return. Smith had no recourse but to borrow money from both his father and London in order to keep the enterprise afloat. Sir Thomas rebuked his son for believing he had 'a bottomless purse or a mine to spend at his pleasure' (Dewar, 162). His return in July saved the enterprise from dissolution and his influence at court at last secured permission for the expedition to embark. The delays over the winter, however, had taken their toll and Thomas Smith set sail for Ireland on 30 August 1572 with but 100 of the 800 men he had gathered.

Smith arrived in Ireland the following day to a cold reception. Fitzwilliam, the lord deputy, offered little assistance. He had not been consulted about the enterprise and did not favour the establishment of a virtually autonomous colony in Ireland. Penniless, Smith was forced to borrow wheat from Fitzwilliam and £100 from Lady Fitzwilliam. Two successive grants in late September, according the Smiths substantial powers, did not improve the situation. Smith sought a meeting with O'Neill, who had been most vocal in his opposition to the prospective colony. O'Neill declined and flatly refused to surrender any land to the brash outsider. Smith reluctantly travelled to Dublin to seek the advice of Fitzwilliam, who convinced Smith to allow the winter to pass before any further provocative movements were made. In October O'Neill, supported by rival Gaelic chieftains who also feared expropriation, ravaged the Ards. Irish hostility then ceased for the winter and O'Neill appeared receptive to negotiation. This, however, was a common tactic employed to frustrate and confuse the enemy. Smith, unlearned in Gaelic warfare, looked confidently toward the spring. Sir Thomas did not share his son's confidence and dispatched 250 soldiers in March. But the reinforcements never reached Ireland and Smith was left unaided.

Smith enjoyed some success in early 1573, attacking O'Neill and negotiating the submission of the MacDonald chief. Fitzwilliam, fearing an Irish confederation, reluctantly granted him command of the Newry garrison to facilitate his offensive. His fears were confirmed when O'Neill burnt Carrickfergus in May. It was clear to all, including Smith, that the colony would not survive without reinforcements. He appealed for assistance but none was forthcoming. Following the mutiny of some of his soldiers, Smith wrote that 'envy hath hindered more than the enemy' (PRO, SP 63/40/75). His authority was further diminished by the dispatch of the earl of Essex to salvage Smith's enterprise and establish colonies in those lands where Smith had failed. Smith, however, could not be saved from the bitter enmity his expedition had caused. On 20 October 1573 an Irishman in his employ killed him with a gunshot at Comber in the Ards. What was to have been an exemplary venture ended in utter failure. The hapless Thomas Smith was at once the victim of his father's innovative but untested colonial ideas and his own ignorance of Irish affairs. His death shocked the Elizabethan court and moved a poet to compose 'The Tumulus of Thomas Smith Killed in Ireland'.

CHRISTOPHER MAGINN

Sources *A letter sent by I. B. gentleman unto his very frende Mayster R. C. esquire, wherein is conteined a large discourse of the peopling and inhabiting the cuntrie called the Ardes* [1572] • *The offer and order given for by Sir Thomas Smyth in his voyage for the inhabiting some partes of the northe of Irelande* (1571) • PRO, SP 63 • *CPR, 1569–72* • *The Irish fiants of the Tudor sovereigns*, 4 vols. (1994), vol. 2 • J. G. Nichols, 'Some additions to the biography of Sir Thomas Smith', *Archaeologia*, 38 (1860), 98–127 • D. B. Quinn, 'Sir Thomas Smith (1513–1577) and the beginnings of English colonial theory', *Proceedings of the American Philosophical Society*, 89 (1945), 543–60 • M. Dewar, *Sir Thomas Smith: a Tudor intellectual in office* (1964) • R. Dunlop, 'Sixteenth century schemes for the plantation of Ulster', *SHR*, 22 (1924–5), 50–60, 115–26, 197–212 • H. Morgan, 'The colonial venture of Sir Thomas Smith in Ulster, 1571–1575', *HJ*, 28 (1985), 261–78 • J. Strype, *The life of the learned Sir Thomas Smith Kt. D.C.L., principal secretary of state to King Edward the sixth and Queen Elizabeth* (1698) • *DNB*

Smith, Sir Thomas (*c*.1556–1609), secretary to Robert Devereux, second earl of Essex, was the son of Thomas Smith, a burgess of Abingdon, Berkshire (who served as mayor in 1583–4), and Joan Jennings. He attended Abingdon School before entering Christ Church, Oxford, perhaps at the suggestion of John Argall, headmaster of Abingdon and student of Christ Church. Smith himself became a student at Christ Church in 1573, graduating BA in 1574 and MA in 1578. Abingdon and Christ Church were both strongly connected with Robert Dudley, earl of Leicester, and Smith sought advancement as part of the earl's extended patronage network. Leicester's hand was clearly evident in his appointment as university orator in April 1582 (a post which he held until 1594) and in his later selection as secretary to Leicester's stepson Robert Devereux, second earl of Essex.

Smith was certainly secretary to Essex by January 1589 (when Alberico Gentili mentioned him in dedicating the second book of his *De jure belli* to Essex) and perhaps as early as 1585–6, when Smith had completed his term as a university proctor (1584–5) and Essex accompanied Leicester to war in the Low Countries. His association with Essex explains his return as an MP for Cricklade in 1589 (presumably as a favour to the earl by Lord Chandos, lord of the borough) and for Tamworth in 1593. Essex's support may also have helped Smith's brother Richard to win a command in the English garrison at Ostend. In 1591, when Essex led an army to Normandy, Thomas made repeated trips to England to assuage the queen's anger against his master. In December, when Hatton's death left the chancellorship of Oxford vacant, Smith rallied university support for Essex to be elected as Hatton's successor, only to be thwarted by a royal command that Lord Buckhurst should have the post. As university orator he played a prominent role when Elizabeth paid an extended visit to Oxford in September 1592, although his contribution to a philosophy disputation proved 'too large' for the queen's taste (Plummer, 252).

As Essex's chief secretary, Smith controlled the earl's privy purse and undertook many delicate tasks for him, including frequent liaison during 1593–5 with the Spanish exile Antonio Perez. Edward Reynoldes played a less free-ranging role as Smith's junior colleague. In early 1595, following a false report of Robert Beale's death, Essex sought to install Smith as a clerk of the privy council. Despite opposition from Beale, who feared that Smith's preferment would come at his expense, Essex secured the appointment by September 1595. Smith's entry into royal service encouraged Essex to hire Henry Wotton, William Temple, and Henry Cuffe to replace him. His clerkship required him to balance his debt to Essex with the practical necessity of forging a close working relationship with Sir Robert Cecil, principal secretary of state. Despite the increasingly bitter hostility between Essex and Cecil, he negotiated the divide with aplomb. Appropriately, Smith took 'Fide et taciturnitate' as his motto. Although he empathized with the 'purgatorie' into which Essex had plunged by late 1599 (SP 12/273/51, fol. 101*r*), he advanced his career and wealth by Cecilian patronage, including the clerkship of parliament in 1597. Cecil's support subsequently won Smith a series of offices and grants under James I, including appointment as Latin secretary in June 1603, a reversion (with Sir Thomas Edmondes) to the secretaryship to the council of the north, the receivership for royal revenues in Dorset and Somerset in March 1604, a pension of £100 p.a., and a mastership of requests in early 1608. Like the other clerks of the council, he was knighted in May 1603. This flood of rewards enabled Smith by 1604 to marry Frances Brydges [*see* Cecil, Frances, countess of Exeter (1580–1663)], the daughter of William, Lord Chandos. Cecil (by now earl of Salisbury) stood godfather to Smith's son Robert in August 1605.

Smith seemed to be on the verge of a brilliant political career, openly taking over part of Salisbury's work as secretary of state in mid-1608. Unfortunately, his hopes of further advancement were blighted by persistent and painful illness. From at least summer 1607 he was plagued by ill health and by unpleasant, expensive, and ineffective medical treatment. He was an invalid during much of 1609. Smith died at his house at Parson's Green, Fulham, on 28 November 1609, leaving a large estate (at the time of his death he was said to be worth £20,000) and a puritan will which included reference to the unreasonably high charges of apothecaries. He was buried at Fulham church, where his widow erected a monument, on 7 December 1609. His colleague Sir Thomas Lake opined that 'the state hath not been of long time served by a more sufficient minister' (*Downshire MSS*, 2.199). Smith's 'young fayre' widow subsequently married Salisbury's older brother Thomas Cecil, the aged first earl of Exeter, whom she survived by forty years. Smith's son Robert died in 1625 and the bulk of his estate passed to his younger child Margaret (*d.* 1633), who married Thomas Carey, second son of another old Essexian, Robert Carey, first earl of Monmouth. The marriage of their only surviving child, Elizabeth Carey (1632/3–1679), to John Mordaunt, ultimately third earl of Peterborough, resulted in Smith's house at Parson's Green being renamed Peterborough House.

PAUL E. J. HAMMER

Sources *Calendar of the manuscripts of the most hon. the marquis of Salisbury*, 24 vols., HMC, 9 (1883–1976) • PRO, SP 12, 14, 16 • G. J. Armytage, ed., *Middlesex pedigrees*, Harleian Society, 65 (1914) • will, PRO, PROB 11/114, fols. 446*r*–448*v* • *Reg. Oxf.*, 2/1–2/4 • P. E. J. Hammer, 'The uses of scholarship: the secretariat of Robert Devereux, 2nd earl of Essex, *c.*1585–1601', *EngHR*, 109 (1994), 26–51 • BL, Lansdowne MSS 79, 85, 89 • GEC, *Peerage* • HoP, *Commons*, 1558–1603, 3.399 • C. Plummer, ed., *Elizabethan Oxford: reprints of rare tracts*, OHS, 8 (1887) • Wood, *Ath. Oxon.*, new edn • PRO, SO 3/2 • *The manuscripts of his grace the duke of Rutland*, 4 vols., HMC, 24 (1888–1905) • W. H. Rylands, ed., *The four visitations of Berkshire*, 2 vols., Harleian Society, 56–7 (1907–8) • W. A. Shaw, *The knights of England*, 2 vols. (1906) • *Report on the manuscripts of the marquis of Downshire*, 6 vols. in 7, HMC, 75 (1924–95), vol. 2 • *The diary of John Manningham of the Middle Temple, 1602–1603*, ed. R. P. Sorlien (Hanover, NH, 1976) • J. Maclean and W. C. Heane, eds., *The visitation of the county of Gloucester taken in the year 1623*, Harleian Society, 21 (1885)

Archives Hatfield House, Hertfordshire, Cecil MSS • PRO, privy council registers, letters, documents, PC 2 • PRO, state papers domestic, letters, documents, SP 12, 14

Wealth at death £20,000, incl. approx. £6000 cash and disposables: *Report on the manuscripts of the marquess of Downshire*, 2.194, 199; will, PRO, PROB 11/114, fols. 446*r*–448*v*

Smith, Thomas (*fl.* 1600–1601), soldier and writer on gunnery, of Berwick upon Tweed, was the author of *The Art of Gunnery*, first published in 1601. The book was dedicated on 2 May 1600 to Smith's commander, the governor of the town and castle and warden of the eastern march, Peregrine Bertie, Lord Willoughby of Eresby, military adventurer by land and sea. In his dedicatory epistle Smith expressed the hope that Lord Willoughby was destined 'long to govern over us' (Smith, *Art of Gunnery*, dedication), but unfortunately his lordship died a few weeks after publication of the book. In his prefatory remarks Smith also insisted that he who knew how

> To performe, execute and obey the lawes and orders of the field, that hath some sight in the Mathematicals, and in Geometricall Instruments, for the conveying of mines under the ground, to plant and mannage great Ordnance to batter or beat down the walls of any Town, or Castle, that can measure Altitudes, Latitudes and Longitudes … may be tearmed in my opinion an expert souldier, though he never buckled with the enemy in the field (Smith, *Art of Gunnery*, preface)

and it seems unlikely that he had ever actually seen military action, notwithstanding the fragility of the peace that existed on the Anglo-Scottish border before 1603. He claimed, however, to have been 'brought up from my childehood under a valiant Captaine in Military profession'. Two or three years prior to publishing *The Art of Gunnery* he had written, so he claimed, another treatise, 'Arithmeticall military conclusions', which he had presented to his captain, Sir John Carey, deputy warden of the eastern marches, and which '(God sparing life) I meane to correct and enlarge, and perhaps put to the Presse'. This work does not appear to have been published.

In 1601 Smith published *Certaine Additions to the Booke of Gunnery, with a Supplie of Fire-Workes* (incendiary devices). In 1628 and in 1643 the two books were reissued in one volume with the overall title *The Complete Souldier*, 'for the benefite of this Kingdome in these troublesome times of Warre' (title-page). The claim that the 1628 edition was 'newly perused and amended' (ibid.) is unsupported by the actual content of the book, and it is unknown whether Smith was still alive at the time of its publication.

SEAN KELSEY

Sources T. Smith, *The art of gunnery* (1600/01) • T. Smith, *Certaine additions to the booke of gunnery, with a supplie of fire-workes* (1601) • T. Smith, *The complete souldier* (1628)

Smith, Thomas (*d.* 1658), shipowner and naval official, was from an obscure but armigerous family. He rose to prominence as secretary to Algernon Percy, tenth earl of Northumberland, lord high admiral from 1638 to 1662. An energetic official, with good contacts at court, Smith maintained close links with Sir John Pennington as well as Northumberland. With his firm puritan leanings, he felt misgivings over the wars against the Scots in 1639 and 1640, welcomed the grand remonstrance in 1641, and pressed for severe measures against papists in the wake of the Irish rising. Smith was also determined to profit from his office. He accepted gratuities while in Northumberland's employ and when accused in 1640 of accepting £40 in bribes replied that he never bargained but that 'what men voluntarily give me my conscience assures me I may take as mere gratuities' (*Naval Tracts of Sir William Monson*, 3.409). According to Pepys, Smith had made £5000 to £7000 in one year as Northumberland's secretary, and in 1640 he was forced to defend himself against the charge of selling an appointment other than his own.

Though the king revoked Northumberland's appointment in June 1642, parliament appointed Smith as secretary to the admiralty while the office was in abeyance (in September) and to the new body of admiralty commissioners established in October. Smith later became secretary to Warwick when the earl was appointed lord admiral in December 1643, and from February 1644 he also served as a collector of prize goods. Smith lost his secretarial position when the admiralty was again placed in commission in April 1645, but was appointed a navy commissioner on 28 August 1647 in succession to Phineas Pett, who had recently died.

The navy commissioners were responsible for the building, repairing, and victualling of the fleet, areas traditionally plagued with graft. Smith was an able administrator, but also used his position for personal financial gain. He took an active role in one of the more controversial practices of the period, whereby parliament hired or freighted, often for lengthy periods and at inflated rates, ships belonging to naval officers and officials. Smith owned shares in at least seven ships hired by the navy in the 1640s at a total cost to the state of £33,258. In almost five years his vessel the *Jocelyn* was unemployed for only fifty-four days; state-owned ships certainly did not remain in commission for this length of time. Despite attacks from contemporaries such as Andrewes Burrell and John Hollond, the practice continued until the end of the decade. At the time of his death Smith was still owed £3140 by the navy for freight in the period 1643–51, although admittedly some of this was purchased debt.

Throughout the 1640s Smith was closely associated with the circle of radical shipowners and merchants including Maurice Thompson, Gregory Clement, and Warwick himself. He was a partner in Thompson's 'Sea adventure to Ireland' in 1642 and his anti-Spanish privateering. Smith was also a prominent figure in the Bahamas colonial project in 1647, and joined Thompson in a bid to take over the customs the same year. He was deeply suspicious of moves to subvert the navy in the king's interests in 1647–8, and played a part in triggering the resignation of its commander, Vice-Admiral William Batten, who later described how he had been 'threatened (by that false man, Mr Smith), to have a charge drawn up against me, unless I would instantly lay down my commission' (*A Declaration of Sir William Batten, Late Vice-Admiral to the Parliament, Concerning his Departure from London*, 1648). This would suggest that Smith enjoyed a degree of authority at a significant level.

Smith died in London in April or May 1658, when his widow, Alice, petitioned the protector for the substantial debts he was owed by the state. ROY MCCAUGHEY

Sources R. McCaughey, 'The English navy, politics and administration, *c.*1640–1649', PhD diss., University of Ulster, 1983 · *CSP dom.* · *The naval tracts of Sir William Monson*, ed. M. Oppenheim, 3, Navy RS, 43 (1914), 409 · M. Oppenheim, *A history of the administration of the Royal Navy* (1896) · W. Batten, *A declaration of Sir William Batten, late vice-admiral to the parliament, concerning his departure from London* (1648) · *JHC* · G. E. Aylmer, *The king's servants: the civil service of Charles I, 1625–1642*, rev. edn (1974) · G. E. Aylmer, *The state's servants: the civil service of the English republic, 1649–1660* (1973) · Pepys, *Diary* · audit office and pipe office (declared accounts), PRO · admiralty committee minute book, 1646–8, PRO, ADM 7 · admiralty committee minute book, 1648, BL, Add. MS 9305 · R. Brenner, *Merchants and revolution: commercial change, political conflict, and London's overseas traders, 1550–1653* (1993)

Smith, Thomas (1614–1702), bishop of Carlisle, was born on 21 December 1614 at Whitewall, Asby, near Appleby, Westmorland, a son of John Smith, a yeoman farmer. He was educated at Appleby grammar school until Michaelmas 1630, when he proceeded to Queen's College, Oxford, where he matriculated on 4 November 1631. 'His early proficiency in his studies gained him a singular repute in the

Thomas Smith (1614–1702), by John Smith, 1701 (after Timothy Stephenson)

University' (Magrath, 2.xvii). After graduating BA on 10 July 1635 and MA on 16 May 1639 he was elected a fellow on 16 December 1639. From this time he built up his substantial library, helpfully inscribing his books with his name, and the date and price. Smith proved himself an able scholar, an excellent teacher, and a loyal friend. He preached before Charles I and before the royalist parliament in Oxford in 1645, but finding Oxford under the Commonwealth uncongenial he withdrew to the north-west about 1652, becoming chaplain to Catherine, *née* Dalston, Lady Fletcher (*bap.* 1606, *d.* 1676), whose son he had taught. She was the widow of Sir Henry Fletcher of Hutton in the Forest, Cumberland, who had been killed in the civil war. Thomas Smith married Lady Fletcher about 1655 and went with her to live in Cockermouth.

At the Restoration Thomas Smith was appointed to the first prebendal stall in Carlisle Cathedral, on 24 June 1660, and was awarded the degree of BD on 2 August 1660. He resigned his Carlisle stall on 16 March 1661 in favour of the fourth stall at Durham Cathedral, where he was installed on 20 July 1661. On 11 December 1661 he was awarded his DD. John Bracken's portrait at Hutton shows Smith at this period with a long pale sensitive face, dark eyes, and shoulder length dark hair. He transferred to the first stall at Durham on 1 July 1668. He divided his time among Durham, Cockermouth, and Oxford, until he was appointed dean of Carlisle on 4 March 1671. There he rebuilt the deanery and became a generous benefactor of all the places with which he was associated. On 16 April 1676 his first wife died at Cockermouth, and on 4 November 1676 Smith signed, as the prospective bridegroom, a marriage bond and affidavit to enable him to marry by licence Anna Wrench (*c*.1631–1698), born Anna Baddeley, widow of Richard Wrench, a fellow prebendary at Durham.

Consecrated bishop of Carlisle on 29 June 1684, Smith used his gifts of friendship, wisdom, gentleness, and generosity to good effect. Although he readily recorded events in his letters, he was careful not to commit his own views to paper. One controversy in which he was involved concerned a society for the reformation of manners in Carlisle. Initially giving it his support, he was made to change his mind by his forceful archdeacon, William Nicolson, who discerned dissenters among its members. Smith outlived most of his contemporaries, many of his ex-pupils, and his second wife, Anna, who died on 6 October 1698. Ill health afflicted his last years, his frailty showing in Stephenson's portrait of 1700. He died at his home, Rose Castle, Dalston, Cumberland, on 12 April 1702. He was buried on 17 April beside his second wife in Carlisle Cathedral. The survival of much of his correspondence in the important Fleming papers, two valued manuscript music partbooks of 1637, the bequest of his library to Carlisle Cathedral, the generosity of his benefactions, and the survival of two excellent portraits, have ensured his grateful remembrance. DAVID W. V. WESTON

Sources J. R. Magrath, ed., *The Flemings in Oxford*, 3 vols., OHS, 44, 62, 79 (1903–24) • *The manuscripts of S. H. Le Fleming*, HMC, 25 (1890) • Wood, *Ath. Oxon.*, 2nd edn • Foster, *Alum. Oxon.* • *DNB* • J. Nicolson and R. Burn, *History and antiquities of Westmorland and Cumberland* (1777) • *Fasti Angl.* (Hardy), vol. 3 • R. S. Ferguson, 'The will of the Right Rev. Dr Smith, bishop of Carlisle, Oct. 8, 1700', *Transactions of the Cumberland and Westmorland Antiquarian and Archaeological Society*, old ser., 4 (1878–9), 6–9 • C. M. L. Bouch, *Prelates and people of the lake counties: a history of the diocese of Carlisle, 1133–1933* (1948) • D. Weston, 'Thomas Smith, 1614–1702', 1998, Carlisle Cathedral Archive, CCA B30 • W. Stubbs, *Registrum sacrum Anglicanum* (1897), 128 • marriage licence bond and allegation, Thomas Smith and Mrs Anna Wrench, 4 Nov 1676, Durham Diocesan Records • J. P. Cutts, Bishop Smith's part-song books, 1972, Carlisle Cathedral Library • parish register, Dalston [baptism], 1/6/1606

Archives Carlisle Cathedral, MSS | Cumbria AS, Kendal, corresp. with Sir Daniel Fleming • Cumbria AS, Kendal, Rydal Hall MSS

Likenesses J. Bracken, oils, 1667, priv. coll. • T. Stephenson, oils, 1700, Rose Castle, Dalston, Cumbria • J. Smith, mezzotint, 1701 (after T. Stephenson), BM, NPG [*see illus.*]

Wealth at death bequests amounting to £2510: will, Ferguson, 'The will'

Smith, Thomas (1624–1661), scholar and theological controversialist, was born in London, the son of Thomas Smith (mother's name unknown), and educated at St Paul's School. He was admitted as a sizar at Christ's College, Cambridge, in 1640, and took the degrees of BA in 1644, MA in 1647, and BD in 1654. He was ordained (presumably covertly) by Bishop Joseph Hall, and instituted as vicar of Caldecote, Cambridgeshire, in 1650. He held the post of praelector in rhetoric at Christ's, and was university librarian from 1659 to his death in 1661.

Smith's particular scholarly interest was in Arabic: he was press corrector for Brian Walton's polyglot Bible, for which he obtained manuscripts from Cambridge. But his principal distinction is as a champion of the Church of England during the interregnum, continuing the work of the Tew circle. Introducing a translation of Jean Daillé's work, entitled *Treatise Concerning the Right Use of the Fathers* (1651), he recalls that the book had been a favourite of Viscount Falkland, to whose unpublished papers he had access. A second translation from Daillé, *An Apologie for the Reformed Churches* (1653), has a long preface by Smith defending the Church of England, and Chillingworth in particular. In 1660 he published *Two Discourses Concerning Episcopacy* by Falkland and Chillingworth, and in the following year reprinted John Colet's *Sermon of Conforming and Reforming* with additional material by Henry Hammond and Lancelot Andrewes. These works demonstrate Smith's adherence to and love for the Anglican church in dark times.

Smith found his own place in church history through his disputes with the nonconformists George Whitehead and John Bunyan in 1659. In May Smith heard Bunyan preaching in a barn in Toft, outside Cambridge, and demanded to know who gave him authority to preach:

> The Church of Christ at *Bedford* … consisting only of women and a few Lay-men is not indeed a Church of Christ; none of them hath power to preach or administer the sacraments, and therefore none of them can give the Tinker power to preach and administer the Sacraments.

Bunyan, thought Smith, subverted not only authority but also learning: 'Away (quoth he) to *Oxford* with your hell bred Logick' (Smith, sig. C3*v* and C*v*). Smith's challenge to Bunyan was published in his pamphlet *The Quaker Disarm'd* (1659), which was chiefly a record of his exchanges with the Quaker George Whitehead. Smith first encountered Whitehead in Westminster 'preaching against *Universities*, *Learning*, and *Tithes*, and the *Clergy*', and argued against him to no effect (ibid., sig. A2*r*).

In August 1659 Smith came across Whitehead again in Cambridge, preaching in the Quakers' meeting-house. Ever pugnacious rather than eirenic, Smith challenged him to a public debate, in which George Fox also participated. There he argued that Whitehead's preaching was heretical, focusing on his understanding of the Trinity, the Quakers' refusal to take oaths, and their lack of formal ordination. The debate provides a fascinating example of contrasting theological rhetoric, since Smith relies on syllogistic reasoning, with which the Quakers have some difficulty, while their more imaginative theological language is mockingly dismissed by Smith as nonsensical or papist.

The verbal debate was continued in a pamphlet skirmish, in which Smith's *The Quaker Disarm'd* and *A Gagg for the Quakers* (1659) were answered by Whitehead's *Truth Defending the Quakers* and his splendidly titled *The Key of Knowledge not Found in the University Library of Cambridge* (1660), along with contributions from others. As Whitehead realized, he and Smith understood quite different things by knowledge, and by authority. Thomas Smith was maintaining Anglican scholarship, episcopal ordination, catholic doctrine, and liturgical prayer, at a time when they were scorned by those who professed the freedom and inspiration of the Spirit. In his will, Smith expressed his 'desire to dye in the ancient Catholic & Apostolic faith professed in the Church of England' and to be buried 'without pomp or sermon but with the Liturgy of the English Church'. By the time that will was signed, on All Saints' day 1660, Smith's beloved church had been restored, along with his king. He died the following year on 27 September 1661 'of the new Desease which spreads all over England but is least in the north' (as John Worthington recorded, Peile, 1.468), and was buried the same day at Kingston. PAUL HAMMOND

Sources P. Hammond, 'Thomas Smith: a beleaguered humanist of the interregnum', *BIHR*, 56 (1983), 180–94 · J. Peile, *Biographical register of Christ's College, 1505–1905, and of the earlier foundation, God's House, 1448–1505*, ed. [J. A. Venn], 1 (1910), 468 · [T. Smith], *The Quaker disarm'd* (1659) · G. J. Toomer, *Eastern wisedome and learning: the study of Arabic in seventeenth-century England* (1996) · will, CUL, department of manuscripts and university archives, vice-chancellor's court, bundle 16

Wealth at death land, books, money, and bonds: will, CUL, department of manuscripts and university archives, vice-chancellor's court wills, bundle 16

Smith, Thomas (1638–1710), scholar, was born on 3 June 1638 in the parish of All Hallows Barking by the Tower, London, one of at least two sons of John Smith, a London merchant; little more is known about Smith's family background. He was admitted a battler at Queen's College, Oxford, in 1657 and matriculated as servitor on 29 October that year. He graduated BA in 1661 and proceeded MA in 1663, when he was appointed master of Magdalen College School. At Magdalen College Smith was to embark on a long and productive scholarly career as an orientalist, an ecclesiastical and an intellectual historian, an antiquary, and a librarian. Throughout his adult life Smith was active as a combative high-church preacher of the Restoration church, regularly publishing sermons and theological discourses.

From his earliest days at Oxford Smith developed a passion for oriental studies, the affairs of the Levant, and the Greek church. In the 1660s he was Hebrew lecturer at Magdalen College. In 1662 he published his first work, *Diatriba de Chaldaicis paraphrastis*, a critical and remarkably erudite thesis about the Aramaic paraphrases of parts of the Old Testament (the Targums). At Oxford Smith enjoyed the encouragement of such leading orientalists as Thomas Barlow, Samuel Clarke, Archbishop Narcissus Marsh, and Edward Pococke. From 1667 onwards Smith corresponded with Henry Dodwell, the later nonjuror theologian, about the Greek church, its leadership, its liturgy, and a possible 'reunion' with the Church of England. Smith's studies of the Greek church undoubtedly influenced the later nonjurors' interest in a unification of the Greek and English churches. Made a probationer fellow of Magdalen in 1666, he was made an actual fellow the following year, but from 1668 to 1671 Smith lived and worked in Constantinople as chaplain to the English ambassador, Sir Daniel Harvey, visiting patriarchs and metropolitans and hunting for Greek manuscripts (three of which he later presented to the Bodleian Library). After his return, Smith, who proceeded BD in 1674, became popularly known as Tograi or Rabbi Smith because of his love for oriental learning and his knowledge of Hebrew. He published his researches, first in Latin in 1672, 1674, and 1676, then in English translation as *Remarks upon the manners, religion, and government of the Turks, together with a survey of the seven churches of Asia* (1678) and *An Account of the Greek Church under Cyrillus Lucaris, Patriarch of Constantinople* (1680). He also published a number of related pieces during these years.

In 1676 Smith briefly travelled in France. A year later he declined a proposal by his friends Bishop John Pearson of Chester, Bishop John Fell of Oxford, and William Lloyd, dean of Bangor, to return to the East to collect manuscripts of the Greek fathers at such places as the monastery at Mount Athos. From 1678 to 1679 he worked as chaplain to Sir Joseph Williamson, secretary of state. He was meant to collate and publish the Alexandrian copy of the Pentateuch in St James's Library, but realization of this project was prevented by the death of its patron, Charles II. It was in these years also that Smith developed a friendship with the royalist historian Sir Philip Warwick (1609–1683), two of whose works he was later to publish anonymously, *A Discourse of Government* (1694) and *Memoires of the Reigne of King Charles I* (1701), together with politically charged prefaces which displeased the government and were taken out of many copies.

As a high-churchman and subsequently as a nonjuror, Smith's career was more than once frustrated through his high-principled political choices, though his attitude in all instances was consistent with the tenets of the established church. In 1682 Smith returned to Oxford to become vice-president of Magdalen College. In 1684 he was presented to the rectory of Standlake, Oxfordshire, but soon resigned. In 1686 he became bursar of his college, and in 1687, although he obtained from Thomas Pierce, dean of Salisbury, the prebend of Heytesbury, Wiltshire, he tried in vain to obtain a recommendation from the king to become president of Magdalen. A difficult dilemma arose when James II's attempt to catholicize the college forced the Magdalen fellows to choose between obedience to a Catholic king and loyalty to the doctrines of the English church. When the college opposed the first royal nominee, Smith submitted to the king's mandate, respecting the Anglican doctrine of passive obedience. He refused, however, to live among Catholic fellows. On 3 August 1688 he was deprived of his fellowship by the Catholic president, Bonaventure Giffard, officially because of his non-residence. He was restored on 25 October, together with the other fellows. Smith kept a diary account of the intricate proceedings at Magdalen College (MS Smith 141), which has become an important source for the history of the college.

After the revolution of 1688 Smith refused to take the

oaths to William and Mary, and on 25 July 1692 his fellowship was finally declared void by John Hough, then president of the college. Smith had already left Oxford for London in August 1689. In London he befriended Sir John Cotton (1662–1702), grandson of the founder of the library, Sir Robert Cotton, and became the unofficial librarian of the Cotton Library. He lived in lodgings in Dean Street, Soho, in the house of his nonjuror friend Hilkiah Bedford. Smith continued to produce scholarly work and maintained his correspondences with scholar-friends from abroad, such as T. J. Van Almeloveen, G. W. Leibniz, Henri Justell, and Jacob Rhenferd. His first work from the Cotton Library, an edition of William Camden's letters together with a biography, was published in 1691 with a dedication to Sir John Cotton. Most important was the publication at Oxford of Smith's *Catalogus librorum manuscriptorum bibliothecae Cottonianae* (1696), the library's first printed catalogue. This was a considerable achievement, executed single-handedly and without a salary. Four large introductory essays, including a 'Life of Sir Robert Cotton' and a history and analysis of the library, are still valuable today. Significantly, the catalogue also described those manuscripts which were severely damaged or destroyed in the 1731 fire at Ashburnham House, which then housed the collection.

In 1702 Sir John Cotton died and the ownership of the Cotton Library was transferred to the state. Humfrey Wanley, later Harley's librarian, aspired to the post and approached Samuel Pepys for his support. Pepys explained to Wanley that he supported his friend Smith, and much regretted that Smith as a nonjuror could not retain his position in the library. On 27 September 1702 Pepys expressed his forebodings to Smith:

> But what shall wee say, if the Oaths shall bee turned to its owne Praejudice by the Governmt. that made them, by praeventing it of the use of the Hand, that has most merited, & is best qualify'd to serve it in the Employement you are praetending to, & that carrys soe little of Politicall in it, for them to feare yor haveing the menagem[t] of it. (MS Smith 53.65)

In the end neither Wanley nor Smith were appointed by the trustees. In fact, the library was locked and no librarian was appointed until 1706.

The grievous disappointment of no longer being able to act as unofficial librarian of his beloved library embittered Smith. He had never been paid for his services as librarian but had lived from his scholarly production and the financial support of friends. Yet he remained active as a scholar and retained the support of old friends such as Bishop Thomas Ken. He also found an important stimulus in the friendship of the nonjuring and Jacobite antiquary Thomas Hearne, then working in the Bodleian Library as the assistant of the librarian John Hudson. Smith initiated what was to become an intense scholarly correspondence with Hearne which would continue to the end of his life. Smith became one of the most important formative influences on Hearne, advising him on his classical and antiquarian studies and giving guidance and support to the young man's determination to pursue what Smith foresaw could become a troubled publishing career at Oxford. Hearne responded strongly to Smith's personal and intimate friendship and always went out of his way to help his mentor whose views on politics, religion, learning, and Oxford academic affairs and personalities he shared to an almost complete degree.

Smith, now advanced in age, began thinking of putting his papers in order. Encouraged by Hearne, he published a number of intellectual biographies. In 1704 he published the biographies of his orientalist friends Robert Huntington and Edward Bernard, mathematician and professor of astronomy at Oxford, whose manuscripts had come to Smith. The *Vitae quorundam eruditissimorum et illustrium virorum* (1707) contained the biographies of James Ussher, John Cosin, Henry Briggs, John Bainbrigge, John Greaves, Sir Patrick Young, Patrick Young junior, and John Dee. The same year his continuing interest in the Greek church was reflected in the publication of an additional volume on Cyril Lucaris, together with a dissertation on Orthodox hymns. Smith enlisted Hearne's bibliographical expertise to help his friends the nonjurors Hilkiah Bedford and George Harbin answer the deist and anti-clerical Anthony Collins's *Priestcraft in Perfection* (1709) with a defence of the twentieth of the Thirty-Nine Articles about the authority of the established church. When Smith took up his earlier plan to publish the letters of St Ignatius together with the unfinished annotations of his friend John Pearson (1613–1686), he met with much opposition at the university press. Smith was aware of the unfinished character of the notes but meant to publish what he deemed a tribute to Pearson and a work in support of episcopacy. The book was finally seen through the press by Hearne and Hudson and published at Oxford in 1709.

Thomas Smith's eyesight had deteriorated gradually until he was practically blind. After a brief illness, Smith died on 11 May 1710 in his lodgings in Dean Street, Soho, London; he had apparently never married. He was buried on 13 May in St Anne's, Soho. Hearne had clearly earned the right to be the recipient of Smith's legacy, consisting of his manuscripts, some printed books, and copies of his own works. He received them with special instructions drawn up for him before Smith's death with the help of Hilkiah Bedford; sixteen of the manuscripts (Edward Bernard's papers and Camden's copies of the *Britannia* and *Annales regnante Elizabetha*) were to go to the Bodleian on Hearne's death. Hearne faithfully followed the instructions and corresponded with Smith's brother Richard, who looked after the dead scholar's other affairs. He began publishing from Smith's materials in most of his publications: Smith's collection of royal correspondence in *Titus Livii Foro-Juliensis vita Henrici quinti* (1716), the discourses of the Elizabethan Society of Antiquaries in *A Collection of Curious Discourses* (1720), and most importantly, *Guilielmi Camdeni annales rerum Anglicarum et Hibernicarum regnante Elizabetha* (1717), the most complete edition of this history, from Camden's copy of the 1615 edition, with Camden's manuscript additions and annotations (MS Smith 2). While the sixteen specified manuscripts went to the Bodleian on Hearne's death in 1735, the rest of Smith's manuscripts went to the library with Hearne's own collections in 1755 as part of Richard Rawlinson's bequest.

THEODOR HARMSEN

Sources Bodl. Oxf., MSS Smith, MSS Rawlinson K (Hearne-Smith), MSS Hearne (diaries) · J. R. Bloxam, ed., *Magdalen College and James II, 1686–1688: a series of documents*, OHS, 6 (1886) · J. R. Bloxam, *A register of the presidents, fellows … of Saint Mary Magdalen College*, 8 vols. (1853–85), vol. 3, pp. 182–204 · *Remarks and collections of Thomas Hearne*, ed. C. E. Doble and others, 11 vols., OHS, 2, 7, 13, 34, 42–3, 48, 50, 65, 67, 72 (1885–1921) · T. Smith, *Catalogue of the manuscripts in the Cottonian Library, 1696 / Catalogus librorum manuscriptorum bibliothecae Cottonianae*, ed. C. G. C. Tite (1696); repr. (1984) · T. Harmsen, 'High-principled antiquarian publishing: the correspondence of Thomas Hearne (1678–1735) and Thomas Smith (1638–1710)', *Lias*, 23 (1996), 69–98 · J. H. Overton, *The nonjurors: their lives, principles, and writings* (1902), 172–8 · P. L. Heyworth, 'Thomas Smith, Humfrey Wanley and the Cottonian Library', *TLS* (3 Aug 1962), 660 · T. H. B. M. Harmsen, *Antiquarianism in the Augustan age: Thomas Hearne, 1678–1735* (2000) · H. Trevor-Roper, 'The Church of England and the Greek church in the time of Charles I', *From Counter-Reformation to Glorious Revolution* (1993), chap. 5 · M. Feingold, 'Oriental studies', *Hist. U. Oxf.* 4: *17th-cent. Oxf.*, 449–503 · T. Harmsen, 'Letters of learning: a selection from the correspondence of Thomas Hearne and Thomas Smith, 1703–1710', *Lias*, 24 (1997), 37–66 · F. Madan and others, *A summary catalogue of Western manuscripts in the Bodleian Library at Oxford*, 7 vols. (1895–1953) · C. G. C. Tite, 'Librarians and aspiring librarians', *The manuscript library of Sir Robert Cotton* (1994) · S. G. Gillam, 'Thomas Hearne's library', *Bodleian Library Record*, 12 (1985–8), 52–64 · P. Simpson, *Proof-reading in the sixteenth, seventeenth and eighteenth centuries* (1935); repr. (1970) · H. Ellis, ed., *Original letters of eminent literary men of the sixteenth, seventeenth, and eighteenth centuries*, CS, 23 (1843) · *A chorus of grammars: the correspondence of George Hickes and his collaborators on the 'Thesaurus linguarum septentrionalium'*, ed. R. L. Harris (1992) · Wood, *Ath. Oxon.*, new edn, 4.597–600 · *The life and times of Anthony Wood*, ed. A. Clark, 3, OHS, 26 (1894) · A. Kippis and others, eds., *Biographia Britannica, or, The lives of the most eminent persons who have flourished in Great Britain and Ireland*, 2nd edn, 5 vols. (1778–93) · R. A. Beddard, 'James II and the Catholic challenge', *Hist. U. Oxf.* 4: *17th-cent. Oxf.*, 907–54 · J. M. Levine, *The battle of the books: history and literature in the Augustan age* (1991) · Foster, *Alum. Oxon.* · E. H. Plumptre, *The life of Thomas Ken*, 2 vols. (1889), chap. 25 · W. D. Macray, *Annals of the Bodleian Library, Oxford*, 2nd edn (1890); facs. edn (1984), 185, 208–9 · [J. Walker], ed., *Letters by eminent persons in the seventeenth and eighteenth centuries*, 2 vols. (1813) · Nichols, *Lit. anecdotes*, 1.14ff.; 5.114; 6.298 · register, St Anne's, Soho, City Westm. AC, vol. 40 [burial]

Archives BL, narrative of visitation of Magdalen College, Oxford, Hg MS 401 · Bodl. Oxf., corresp. and papers · Bodl. Oxf., diary and notebook | BL, letters to Sir Hans Sloane; letters to Humfrey Wanley, Add. MSS · Bodl. Oxf., MSS Rawl. K (Hearne-Smith) · Bodl. Oxf., Ballard MSS; Cherry MSS; Rawl. MSS · Bodl. Oxf., letters to Martin Lister

Smith, Thomas (*d.* 1708), naval officer, was, according to his own statement, born at sea to English parents between England and the Netherlands and brought up in North Yarmouth. Nothing else is known of his origins or early years. He commanded several merchant ships from 1680, and by 1691 had settled at Oreston on the eastern bank of the Cattewater across from Plymouth, Devon. In February 1691 he left the merchant service and volunteered to serve in the navy for ten months on the *Portsmouth* (32 guns) under Captain William Whetstone, who rated him a midshipman while cruising in the squadron under Sir Ralph Delavall off Dunkirk and Calais. He continued under Captain John Bridges, who recommended Smith to the Admiralty for command. He was serving in the *Portsmouth* when she and the *James Galley* took an 18-gun French privateer and engaged some Greenland ships. In the latter action Bridges was wounded and put ashore. With Bridges' departure from the ship Smith was left without a patron and Smith's temporary successor, Lieutenant John Lowen, discharged him with a midshipman's pay ticket.

Shortly afterwards the *St Martin's Prize* (Captain John Evans) called at Plymouth and employed Smith as a pilot on the French coast, where she took two prizes. Smith served as prize master of one vessel, which in 1693 he took into Ribadeo, Spain, where her cargo was sold. Sent home when the ship was taken to Cadiz for sale, Smith claimed that he never received the prize money to which he was entitled. After returning to Oreston he married a sea commander's widow with five children; she lived until about 1705. Obtaining command of a transport, he sailed with munitions and stores to Kinsale. Upon his return he obtained an appointment to serve from February to May 1696 as extra pilot on the advice boat *Mercury* (4 guns, Lieutenant John Lapthorne). On three separate voyages to gain intelligence of French activities at Brest, Smith used his extensive knowledge of the French coast to guide the ship into Le Conquet and Brest Roads. Put ashore with several men near Brest, Smith counted seventy sail of the line preparing to embark 40,000 men to invade England. Promptly reported to the Admiralty, this was the information upon which Lord Berkeley was ordered to blockade Brest and bombard the areas around Camaret Bay and l'Anse de Bertheaume.

Quickly recognizing Smith's service, the Admiralty awarded him £30 in March 1696 and, upon completion of his duty on the *Mercury* in September 1696, gave him command of the advice boat *Germoon Prize* (10 guns). In her he carried the news of the peace of Ryswick to the West Indian islands and returned to supervise her refitting for further service in the West Indies at Deptford. In the same period he was accused of embezzling ships' stores and failing to pay a debt. This may have been paid by an undated entry in the ship's pay book showing that £26 5*s*. 11*d*. was deducted from Smith's account for victualling. Superseded in command on 29 August 1698, Smith did not receive his pay and was not employed again for several years, despite formal applications in 1698 and a memorial of 1699 from the mayor and others at Plymouth attesting that he was a 'Person of a Good Life & Honest Conversation & Well Affected to His Majesty & the Present Government & an Able Mariner Navigator and Commander' (PRO, ADM 1/2439), as well as daily appearances at the Admiralty office from October 1701 to June 1702 complaining of 'being so long adrift and having had no benefit of half pay' (ibid., 12 Nov 1701). Finally, on 30 June 1702, he took command of the sloop *Bonetta* (2 guns). In her he convoyed the corn trade from Lynn and Yarmouth roads to the Nore for fifteen months. In May 1703 he made a formal complaint against his boatswain for drunkenness, and shortly thereafter several officers and men accused him of the same crime along with other irregularities, including lending men to merchant ships for money, keeping his men's money, and making false musters. On this charge a court martial held on the *Expedition* found Smith guilty and dismissed him from his command on 1 September 1703. Later Smith alleged that the men had formally recanted their charges. Unable to persuade the court to reverse its judgment and to allow him to resume his naval service, Smith threatened, 'I must be exposed to seek my family bread in some other nation' (PRO, ADM 1/2441, 10 Jan 1704).

Smith continued to seek employment from the Admiralty and offered himself as a volunteer midshipman on a flagship, but Sir Cloudesley Shovell refused him. He claimed to have served without pay in the *Winchester* (50 guns) under Lord Carmarthen, but no record of this has been found. In 1707 he took passage in the Swedish ship *St Peter*, hoping to obtain employment at Lisbon through Commissioner Lawrence Wright. *En route* the French privateer *Dunkirk* (26 guns, Captain Michel Vanstable) stopped the ship and took Smith off. He remained a prisoner on the *Dunkirk* and after thirty-three days at sea was taken to Dunkirk prison. During his 108-day incarceration the local intendant and the commandant of galleys at Dunkirk repeatedly suggested enticing opportunities to Smith, and he eventually agreed to be 'third captain', probably meaning pilot, on the admiral galley. During the four months when he served in that capacity the galley, with five others, captured the English warship *Nightingale* (24 guns, Captain Seth Jermy) off Harwich on 24 August 1707. In the autumn the Dunkirk galley force went into winter quarters, and by November the comte de Toulouse, grand admiral of France, had signed a privateer's commission for Smith to command the *Nightingale* under the French flag. On 24 December he sailed on his first cruise in company with another privateer, the *Squirrel's Revenge* (26 guns). Off Long Sand on 27 December the *Ludlow Castle* (40 guns, Captain Nicholas Haddock) encountered the privateers and chased them northwards for ten hours, eventually recapturing the *Nightingale* 24 leagues north-east of Orfordness and taking her into Hull. An Admiralty marshal's guard escorted Smith from Hull to the Marshalsea, from which he was moved successively to Newgate and the Old Bailey, where he was tried for treason on 2 June 1708. The court convicted him and he was hanged at Execution Dock on 18 June. Afterwards his body was cut down, and his bowels and heart were removed and publicly burnt. His remains were quartered and left to public view, and were reputedly still to be seen in 1713. Contemporary pamphlets and broadsides recounted Smith's treason with varying degrees of accuracy and sordidness, while the most famous account of the *Nightingale*'s voyage appeared in the memoirs of the Huguenot Jean Marteilhe (1757). Shortly after its first appearance in France, Oliver Goldsmith (1728–1774) published the first English translation in 1758, under his pseudonym James Willington.

J. K. Laughton, *rev.* John B. Hattendorf

Sources J. K. Laughton, 'The captains of the "Nightingale"', *EngHR*, 4 (1889), 65–80 • captains' letters, S, PRO, ADM 1/2438 (1698–1700); ADM 1/2439 (1701); ADM 1/2440 (1702–3); ADM 1/2441 (1703–4) • ships' pay books, PRO, ADM 33/147, *Portsmouth*; ADM 33/219, *Bonetta*; ADM 33/190, 204, *Germoon*; ADM 33/189, *Mercury* • *CSP dom.*, 1698, 178, 323, 331 • T. Smith, *The memorial of Capt. T. Smith … wherein a true state of his case is deliver'd with certificates proving his conduct to this nation* (1708) • *A true copy of the paper delivered by Captain T. Smith alias May, to Mr. R. Clare at Execution Dock … 18 June 1708* (1708) • P. Lorrain, *The ordinary of Newgate: his account of the behaviour, confession, and last speech of Captain Thomas Smith* [1708] • *Captain Smith's letter to the world, whilst under his unhappy state of condemnation* (1708) • *Case of Captain Thomas Smith, late commander of the Nightingal, now a prisoner in Newgate* (1708) • J. Marteilhe, *Mémoires d'un protestant condamné aux galères de France pour cause de religion* (Rotterdam, 1757) • J. Marteilhe, *The memoirs of a protestant condemned to the galleys of France for his religion. Written by himself*, trans. J. Willington (1758)
Archives PRO, ADM 1/2438–2441

Smith, Thomas (*d.* 1716), merchant and politician, was the eldest son of Thomas Smith (*d.* 1707), apothecary of Glasgow. He probably attended Glasgow University in 1693. A merchant involved in the American and West Indian trade, Smith became a bailie of Glasgow in 1707, and he twice held the important office of dean of guild (1709–11 and 1713–15). By 1709 Smith had married Janet Crosse, probably a daughter of John Crosse, a Glasgow merchant and himself a former dean of guild. Smith's historical importance chiefly lies in the commentaries that he made on parliamentary affairs in the period 1710–16. These are preserved in the papers of Robert Wodrow (1679–1734), minister of Eastwood, near Glasgow, in the form of extracts and copies of Smith's personal and official correspondence.

On 27 October 1710 Smith was elected to represent the four-burgh district of Glasgow, Dumbarton, Renfrew, and Rutherglen. At Westminster he became a great admirer of whig politicians such as Robert Walpole, but he nevertheless maintained a degree of independence from party strife. 'There is not a firmer man in the House than the *dean of guild*', reported one Scottish member, 'and I dare say is led by nobody' (NA Scot., Montrose MSS GD220/5/807/12, Mungo Graham to duke of Montrose, 21 Dec 1710). Smith's own contributions to debate show a keen concern for Scottish interests. One of his early successes was to persuade ministers in January 1711 to ameliorate the effects upon Scotland of a proposed export duty on British linen. He involved himself actively in parliamentary business and was assiduous in promoting the interest of his constituents. As a presbyterian Scot he sympathized with English dissenters, but was himself intolerant of the comparable disabilities suffered by Scottish episcopalians, whom he regarded as Jacobites almost to a man. In December 1711 Smith opposed the Occasional Conformity Bill—a high-church attack on the dissenters—and he initially rejected the arguments of some Scottish presbyterians that their own position might be strengthened by having its provisions extended to the established church in Scotland. He disliked the fact that such a move would inevitably lead to a formal toleration for episcopalian worship. He changed his mind at the last minute, however, under pressure from the eminent presbyterian minister William Carstares, and he agreed to move a clause relating to Scotland at the report stage on 20

December. But the speed with which the bill passed through its final stages prevented him from intervening and he ended by giving simple negative to the measure. Also during December Smith was active in a successful campaign to insert a clause in the Land Tax Bill, settling the proportion of tax payable by each Scottish burgh. His continuing opposition to episcopalianism was evident in February 1712 when he voted against the Scottish Toleration Bill.

During the summer prorogation of 1712 Smith returned to Scotland and took a leading role in organizing Glasgow's campaign in support of the new Land Tax Act. Its provisions required implementation by the convention of royal burghs, and it was apparent that the system of assessment based on rental values would be opposed on cynical grounds by Edinburgh because this would reduce the scope for manipulating the poorer burghs by promising to reduce their contributions in return for political support. Indeed, so effective was Edinburgh's opposition that, after several years of wrangling, the scheme was entirely abandoned. Back in London for the parliamentary session of 1713, Smith joined the abortive campaign to prevent the extension of the malt tax to Scotland, speaking out on 22 May against technical errors in the bill. Although disappointed at Scottish failure on this issue, Smith was highly suspicious of the ensuing campaign to dissolve the Union. He was relieved when the initiative petered out, having regarded it throughout as a Jacobite stalking-horse. His other principal concern at this time was to oppose the ministry's commercial treaty with France, and he spoke effectively in defence of Scottish economic interests on 18 June.

Smith was re-elected without opposition at the 1713 election, and in the final months of Queen Anne's reign he gave wholehearted support to the whig cause while welcoming the emergence of Hanoverian toryism. He even acknowledged that anti-Jacobitism was creating common ground among formerly antagonistic Scottish factions. In the famous debate over whether the succession was in danger under the present ministry on 15 April 1714 Smith clashed with the Scottish Jacobite George Lockhart over voluntary arming in western Scotland. He denied that Glasgow was arrogating to itself authority belonging to the queen's troops, maintaining that such actions were prompted by loyalty alone. In the remainder of the session he opposed various Scottish tory measures, including a bill to support episcopalian clergy from crown revenues derived from the former bishops' rents. He was re-elected in 1715 and rewarded for his loyalty to the Hanoverian cause with appointment in August to the minor office of commissioner for stating army debts.

Smith died on 19 January 1716, leaving a wife and son; he was buried in Glasgow. Shortly afterwards his wife petitioned Glasgow council for financial aid on the grounds that, in serving the town, her husband had 'laid aside his private affairs' to such an extent that his business 'dwindled to nothing and he became very much decayed in his estate' (Marwick and Renwick, 597–8). A posthumous grant for Smith's parliamentary expenses was made together with a small endowment for the education of his only son, Thomas. DAVID WILKINSON

Sources HoP, *Commons, 1690–1715* [draft] • HoP, *Commons, 1715–54* • NL Scot., Advocates' MSS, Wodrow MSS • J. D. Marwick and R. Renwick, eds., *Extracts from the records of the burgh of Glasgow, AD 1691–1717*, 4, Scottish Burgh RS, 19 (1908) • NA Scot. • G. Lockhart, *The Lockhart papers: containing memoirs and commentaries upon the affairs of Scotland from 1702 to 1715*, 2 vols. (1817) • *The correspondence of the Rev. Robert Wodrow*, ed. T. M'Crie, 3 vols., Wodrow Society, [3] (1842–3)
Archives NL Scot., Advocates' MSS; Wodrow MSS

Smith, Thomas (1707?–1762), naval officer, the illegitimate son of Sir Thomas Lyttelton (1688–1751), was probably born shortly before the future baronet married in 1708. Nothing is known of his mother, except that she was living in Wapping in 1740 and had relatives in Cornwall. Smith's father saw to his son's education and presumably to his start in the navy and Smith remained an intimate member of the Lyttelton family throughout his entire life.

On 6 February 1728, in the Mediterranean, Smith was appointed by Sir Charles Wager to be junior lieutenant of the *Royal Oak*. In June he was moved to the *Gosport* (44 guns), under Captain Duncombe Drake. The ship lay at Plymouth in late November 1728, when a French corvette entered the sound to find shelter. Upon departing she passed near the *Gosport*, and Smith, who was commanding officer because all other officers were ashore, compelled her captain 'to haul in his pennant in respect to the king of Great Britain's colours'. Having already made an arrangement to salute the citadel the French captain considered this action an insult, and so did French authorities when they presented the captain's letter of complaint to the British government. An Admiralty inquiry verified the French account of the incident, and by the king's order of 27 March 1729 Smith was summarily dismissed from the navy for having 'exceeded his instructions'. Popular dislike of France had been recently heightened by a diplomatic rift, and Smith became a minor hero. On 12 May he was restored to his rank and appointed second lieutenant of the *Enterprise*, something that may have been intended all along.

On 5 May 1730 Smith was promoted captain of the 24-gun *Success*; two years later he was given command of the *Dursley Galley*, a fast frigate of 20 guns, to cruise against Barbary pirates. He continued in her for a decade, mostly serving in the Mediterranean. In 1740 he moved to the *Romney* (50 guns) and went home in her, and he then sailed in March 1741 with the fishing fleet to be governor of Newfoundland. Having returned to the Mediterranean, Smith resigned in April 1742. His stated reasons were to settle his private affairs and to accompany Admiral Nicholas Haddock, who was very ill, on an overland journey home, but Smith had arranged with Haddock for the *Romney* to be given to his cousin and protégé Thomas *Grenville (see Hunt. L., Stowe–Grenville papers, box 192 (16, 17); BL, Egerton MS 2529, fols. 285–8). Though such a vacancy was not strictly allowable the earl of Winchilsea, then first lord, was aware that Smith was a highly regarded officer, and found another excuse as well: 'I soon got over his hasty quitting a ship to make room for a friend', he remarked in a private letter, 'and besides I could not forget his gentlemanly behaviour in Plymouth Sound, when the honour of the English flag was concerned' (Wyndham, 1.144, 167).

Grenville soon captured a rich prize, and in April 1744 he cheerfully consented to Smith's request for a loan of £6000, with interest but no clear stipulation of repayment. After Grenville's death, in the battle of Cape Finisterre (1747), his elder brother George demanded repayment (£4200 in 1749) and thereby apparently alienated Smith from the Grenvilles permanently.

In October 1742 Smith was given the *Princess Mary* (60 guns), and he went to Newfoundland as governor, for a second time, in the following year. The suggestion by the eighteenth-century naval historian John Charnock that he was tried by court martial for converting stores to his own use is implausible and lacks evidence. In early 1744 the *Princess Mary* was in the channel under Sir John Norris and went to Lisbon and Cadiz in June under Sir John Balchen, returning in October. Smith next commanded the 100-gun *Royal Sovereign*, in which he became commander-in-chief at the Nore in September 1745. Jacobite success in Scotland had heightened fears of an invasion of England, and Smith spent much of the time aboard the *Hastings* (40 guns), managing the flotilla that guarded the Essex and Suffolk coasts. On 3 February 1746 he was ordered north to replace John Byng as commander-in-chief on the Scottish coast, and he stayed there until January 1747, when he went on half pay.

'Though I do not personally know Commodore Smith, no one can have a greater regard for him than I have, upon account of the universal good character he bears, both as a seaman and an officer.' The duke of Bedford, first lord, wrote this in November 1746 when explaining to George Grenville why he felt obliged to give the Jamaica command to someone else (*Grenville Papers*, 1.57). None the less Smith was included in the promotions and was made rear-admiral on 15 July 1747. His reputation for naval expertise was supplemented by career wisdom, humanity, even temper, and generosity, which were widely acknowledged by his contemporaries. He was a captain to whom parents confidently entrusted their sons. The list of protégés is long and includes Samuel and Alexander Hood and George Rodney. Smith was more than a mentor; he loaned young officers money and helped them through difficulties. With evident fondness they stayed in touch, and many regarded him as a father.

Promoted to vice-admiral in 1748, Smith continued on half pay until 1755, residing at Rockingham Hall, his house on the Lyttelton estate at Hagley, Worcestershire. He never married. In 1751, however, Lieutenant John (Jack) Midwinter (a protégé from the *Dursley*) and his wife, Dorothy, accepted an invitation to share the house. She remained at Rockingham after her husband died in Jamaica. Aware of the admiral's liking for Dorothy, Jack Midwinter wrote just before departing: 'It never once entered my head that you would cherrish my wife in any other but an honest way' (Wyndham, 2.82–3).

In August 1755 Smith became commander-in-chief in the Downs and regularly served either there or at the Nore on board large ships. In December 1756, however, he was ordered to Portsmouth as president of the court martial that tried Admiral John Byng; this lasted about a month. Horace Walpole, critical of anyone whose effort to save Byng was other than boundless, judged Smith to be 'of no capacity'. Yet the admiral's conduct of the trial, news about which was feverishly reported, generated scant criticism, and there is reason to think that the muddling of the issue of 'negligence' was deliberate—skilfully designed to open a path towards forbearance while avoiding an acquittal that almost no one considered warranted. Publicly and privately (he appealed to the Lytteltons) Smith did all he could to get the court's unanimous recommendation of mercy acted upon.

Promoted to admiral of the blue on 24 February 1757, Smith returned to the Downs. However, poor health forced his retirement in October of the following year. Though he had a London house in Cavendish Square he preferred Rockingham, where Dorothy Midwinter, of 'truly amiable disposition', according to Samuel Hood, looked after him, though her health evidently became almost as bad as his. He died at Rockingham Hall on 28 August 1762 and was probably buried at Hagley. The Grenvilles subsequently made claim on his house furnishings.

Smith's career was that of a 'favourite': he enjoyed an uninterrupted decade of peacetime command, often in the Mediterranean, never went to the West Indies, yet enjoyed regular promotion. His assignments tended to keep him from combat, which he never experienced. Yet he immersed himself in the service and left a significant legacy to later generations of seamen; he appears, for example, to have been the true author of the divisional system that remains a fundamental feature of the internal organization of British ships. His much praised humanity was also shared not only within the officer corps but more broadly, as for instance when he made a strong argument for allowing crews confined aboard ship to have shore leave. In 1755 James Lind sent him his now famous book on scurvy, observing that Smith was 'singularly distinguished for … the greatest humanity towards seamen' (Wyndham, 2.55–6). His chief contribution lay in knowledge of, and veneration for, the navy as an institution.

Daniel A. Baugh

Sources *DNB* · M. Wyndham, *Chronicles of the eighteenth century*, 2 vols. (1924) · memorandum and letters concerning Thomas Grenville's loan, Hunt. L., Stowe–Grenville papers, box 23 (58) · captain's letters, PRO, Adm. 1/2456–8 · *The Grenville papers: being the correspondence of Richard Grenville … and … George Grenville*, ed. W. J. Smith, 1 (1852) · D. Pope, *At twelve Mr. Byng was shot* (1962) · H. W. Richmond, *The navy in the war of 1739–48*, 3 vols. (1920) · *The Vernon papers*, ed. B. McL. Ranft, Navy RS, 99 (1958) · S. F. Gradish, *The manning of the British navy during the Seven Years' War* (1980)

Archives Hagley Hall, Worcestershire, corresp. and letter-books · U. Mich., Clements L., papers and corresp. · Worcs. RO, letter-book | BL, Haddock letters, Egerton STG box 23 (58) · CKS, Stanhope papers, copy of document reviewing the Grenville-to-

Smith loan (1749), U1590 S2/013 • Hunt. L., Stowe–Grenville papers

Likenesses R. Wilson, portrait, 1744, repro. in Wyndham, *Chronicles of the eighteenth century*, vol. 2, p. 42 • J. Faber junior, mezzotint (after R. Wilson), BM, NPG • R. Wilson, oils, NMM

Smith, Thomas [*known as* Smith of Derby] (*bap.* **1720x24?**, *d.* **1767**), landscape painter, lived in Bridgegate, Derby. Nothing is known of his family background, but he may have been one of three Thomas Smiths baptized in Derby between October 1720 and April 1724. He exhibited at the Society of Artists in 1760, 1761, and 1767, and at the Free Society of Artists in 1767, showing landscapes, one with poetic figures from James Thomson's *The Seasons* (1730). He is known principally through engravings of his landscapes made by François Vivares and other notable contemporary engravers, though a few of his paintings are in museum collections in Derby, Bristol, and Manchester, and at Chatsworth, Derbyshire, and Belton House, Lincolnshire. After his death his extensive collection of prints, drawings, and books was auctioned by William Darres in February 1768 in Coventry Street, London, and included numerous works by, or after, European masters. A further sale in London conducted by Langford & Son, Covent Garden, in February 1769 contained seventy-five pictures, mostly landscape views by, or engraved after, himself. He and his wife, Hannah, had two sons, who were both artists: Thomas Correggio Smith (*c.*1750–*c.*1802), miniature painter, and John Raphael *Smith (*bap.* 1751, *d.* 1812), portrait painter and engraver.

Thomas Smith's art contributed to the rise of English landscape painting in the mid-eighteenth century. His views of dramatic scenery and of country houses and parks, published as engravings, reflect an increasing awareness of the English countryside. The views themselves often depict groups of elegant tourists admiring beauty spots in the Derbyshire dales, the Peak District, and elsewhere. His first dated work is his set of *Eight of the most extraordinary natural prospects in the mountainous part of Derbyshire and Staffordshire, commonly called the Peak*, engraved by Vivares and others (including himself) and published in 1743. These views of the valleys, cliffs, and waterfalls at Matlock Bath, Dovedale, Peak Cavern at Castleton, and other Derbyshire beauty spots characterize Smith's fondness for wild and dramatic scenery. Later views include *Gordal at Malham* (one of *Four Romantic Views* engraved in 1751 by James Mason) and *Views of Four Lakes in Cumberland*, engraved by himself in 1761.

Smith's views of country houses and estates include prospects of Chatsworth and Haddon Hall in Derbyshire, engraved by Vivares in 1744; Lyme Park, Cheshire, engraved by Vivares in 1745; and parks at Hagley, Newstead, Exton, and Belton (the latter featuring a grotto, hermit, cascades, and ruins), engraved by Vivares and Mason in 1749. His unusual views of the industrial complex at Coalbrookdale constitute two of the earliest detailed industrial landscapes. Designed by Smith and George Perry, engineer and draughtsman, and engraved by Vivares in 1758, they record in detail the topography, buildings, and activities of Abraham Darby's pioneering ironworks. Many of Smith's engraved views were republished by John Boydell in 1760, and again in 1769, as *A Collection of Forty Views in the Peak, in Derbyshire, &c.* These also include four views of Roman ruins after drawings by James Basire, and six equestrian subjects. A collection of his engravings is in the Museum and Art Gallery, Derby. Smith died in the Hotwells district of Bristol on 5 September 1767.

DAVID FRASER

Sources *A collection of forty views in the Peak, in Derbyshire, &c.* (1769) • T. Clayton, *The English print, 1688–1802* (1997) • J. Harris, *The artist and the country house: a history of country house and garden view painting in Britain, 1540–1870* (1979) • J. Harris, K. Kostival, and S. Orchart, *The artist and the country house: from the fifteenth century to the present day* (1995) [exhibition catalogue, Sotheby's Institute, London, 1995] • *A catalogue of the collection of pictures of Mr Smith, late of Derby, painter, deceased, chiefly painted by himself* (1769) [sale catalogue, Mr Langford & Son, Covent Garden, London, 10 Feb 1769] • *A catalogue of the valuable collection of prints, books of prints and drawings, of the celebrated artist Mr Smith of Derby, lately deceased* [William Darres, Coventry Street, London, sale catalogue, 13–16 Feb 1768] • *Drewry's Derby Mercury* (18 Sept 1767) • name index (baptisms, burials, marriages), Derby Local Studies Library

Smith, Thomas (*bap.* **1752**, *d.* **1815**), lighting engineer, was baptized on 6 December 1752 in Ferryport-on-Craig, Fife, a small village opposite Dundee, the son of Thomas Smith, mariner, and his wife, Mary Kay. In 1764 Smith was apprenticed at Dundee to a metalworker named Cairns, after which he went to Edinburgh, probably in 1770 when building of the 'new town' was in progress, as a journeyman metalworker. By 1781 he was trading as a tinsmith from Bristo Street, where he manufactured oil lamps, brass fittings, fenders, and other household metal articles. His business prospered and by 1790 he had moved to premises in Blair Street, where he employed a larger workforce. He was elected to the Edinburgh Guild of Hammermen in 1789, and became its master and a city magistrate in 1802.

On 19 February 1778 Smith married Elizabeth Couper (1758–1786), daughter of a Liberton farmer. After her death, on 20 October 1787 he married Mary Jack (1762–1791). In the year following her death, on 14 November 1792 Smith married Jean Hogg, *née* Lillie (1751–1820). Jean Lillie had first been married in 1771, to Alan Stevenson (1752–1774), and then in 1777 to James Hogg, an Edinburgh gunsmith, whom she divorced in 1792.

Smith took an interest in improving the illumination of lighthouses in 1786, before the board of commissioners of northern lighthouses was formed in the same year to improve the almost non-existent lighting of Scotland's coast. He had proposed to the chamber of commerce at Edinburgh that a lamp with metallic reflectors be substituted for the coal light at the old private lighthouse on the Isle of May, but they declined their support. On 16 June 1786 Smith wrote 'A comparative view of the supperior advantages of lamps above coal light when applyd to light houses', in which he confirmed that he had 'constructed 2 small reflectors & lamp with a view to demonstrate by experiment what has been only laid down in theory' (NL Scot., MS Acc. 10706, 88). He then petitioned the board of manufactures in Edinburgh on the utility of such lamps and they resolved to allow £20 towards the expense of making a model of a reflector lamp and trying an experiment on Inchkeith, a trial that is believed to have been successful. The Northern Lighthouse Board appointed Smith as their first engineer on 22 January 1787.

After receiving instruction in lighthouse construction and illumination in Norfolk from Ezekiel Walker of King's Lynn, Smith enthusiastically set to work in 1787, without payment, on the provision of new lighthouses for the Northern Lighthouse Board, until 1793 when he was awarded a salary of £60 per annum and his expenses. The board did not regard his lack of building and architectural experience as an impediment, as such skills could be and were brought in under his general direction.

During the next two decades, commencing in 1787 with the conversion of Kinnaird Castle into a lighthouse—followed by the Mull of Kintyre (1788), North Ronaldsay (1789), Eilean Glas (1789), and Pladda (1790) lighthouses—Smith was responsible for providing or improving thirteen lighthouses. Independently of the board he was responsible for harbour lights at Leith and Portpatrick, and on the rivers Clyde and Tay. His last major lighthouses were Start Point, Orkney (1802–6) and Inchkeith (1804), both for the board, and Little Cumbrae (1793), for the Clyde Lighthouses Trust.

From 1797 Smith delegated most lighthouse matters to his apprentice and stepson Robert *Stevenson, who married his daughter Jane, and established the Stevenson dynasty of engineers which practised until 1952. Stevenson formally succeeded him as engineer to the Northern Lighthouse Board on 12 July 1808. This enabled Smith to concentrate on lamp manufacture and the expansion of his shipping and other interests, particularly his general and street lighting business. By 1800 his lamps were lighting much of eastern Scotland and the central belt as far west as Glasgow. In 1804 he was the public lighting contractor for both the Old and New towns of Edinburgh and, by 1807, for lighting the streets of Perth, Stirling, Ayr, Haddington, Aberdeen, and, in 1810, Leith. In 1808 Smith retired from the business, which was then carried on by his son James.

Smith developed and made arrays of parabolic reflector oil lamps. Each lamp had a light source at its focus and a curved reflector formed of small pieces of mirror glass set in plaster that produced a beam of light. His first light, at Kinnaird Head, had an intensity of about 1000 candlepower, which, although feeble compared with its modern counterpart of 690,000 candlepower, nevertheless represented a worthwhile improvement on coal lights. He retained glass-faceted reflectors for new lights until 1801, after which, because of Robert Stevenson's influence, he started to manufacture Argand lamps with silvered copper reflectors. This improvement which produced a significantly brighter light is believed to have been first installed in Scotland at Inchkeith lighthouse in 1804.

Details of Smith's reflectors became more generally known from an article 'Reflector for a light-house' in the supplement to the third edition of *Encyclopaedia Britannica* (1801). In it Smith is described as 'an ingenious and modest man [who] has carried [his inventions] to a high degree of perfection without knowing that something of the same kind had been long used in France'. This tribute was omitted from later editions, including the last carrying the article (1823), after the editor had learned of Ezekiel Walker's prior development of the glass facet reflector lamp concept. Nevertheless, Smith was the first to introduce brighter lights into Scottish lighthouses, and has a good claim to be regarded as Scotland's first lighting engineer. He died on 21 June 1815 at 1 Baxter's Place, Edinburgh, and was buried in the old Calton cemetery.

Roland Paxton

Sources J. Leslie and R. Paxton, *Bright lights: the Stevenson engineers, 1751–1971* (1999) • C. Mair, *A star for seamen: the Stevenson family of engineers* (1978) • D. A. Stevenson, *The world's lighthouses before 1820* (1959) • *Edinburgh Advertiser* (30 June 1815) • *Edinburgh Evening Courant* (1 July 1815) • *Caledonian Mercury* (1 July 1815) • 'Reflector for a light-house', *Encyclopaedia Britannica*, 3rd edn, suppl. (1801) • R. L. Stevenson, *Records of a family of engineers* (1912) • private information (2004)

Archives Edinburgh City Archives, chamber of commerce at Edinburgh MSS • NA Scot., board of manufactures and Carron Co. MSS • NA Scot., northern lighthouse board minute books • NL Scot., business records of Robert Stevenson & Sons, Civil Engineers, MS Acc. 10706

Wealth at death approx. £26,000: private information

Smith, Thomas (1817–1906), missionary and mathematician, was born at Symington manse, Lanarkshire, on 8 July 1817, the eighth of ten children of the minister John Smith (*d.* 1834) and his wife, Jean Stodart (*d.* 1840). Educated at Symington parish school, he went to Edinburgh University at the age of thirteen, where he stayed to study divinity under Thomas Chalmers. He was ordained as a missionary to the general assembly's institution in Calcutta in March 1839. In the same month Smith married Grace, *née* Whyte (*d.* 1886); they had a daughter and four sons.

Smith reached Calcutta in August 1839 but was forced, in December 1841, to withdraw for a year to the Cape of Good Hope in order to recover his health. In 1843, at the Disruption in the Church of Scotland, Smith and the other missionaries at Calcutta joined the Free Church. He continued to work at the Free Church Institution as a teacher. He was also active as joint editor of the *Calcutta Christian Observer* and editor of the *Calcutta Review*. His proposal, first put forward in 1840, for women missionaries to establish zenana missions, was eventually realized towards the end of his time in India. Smith also served as chaplain to the soldiers of the Black Watch during the Indian mutiny of 1857, and accompanied the regiment on its campaigns. In 1858 a bout of cholera ended his missionary career and he returned to Scotland, where he received the same year an honorary MA degree from Edinburgh University.

In 1859 Smith became minister of Cowgatehead Free Church, Edinburgh, a territorial church which had been built and partially endowed by his wife's uncle. This seemed a suitable job for a minister with a missionary vocation, since the district was conspicuously poverty-stricken, and Smith soon encountered the familiar scourges of cholera and smallpox in the area. In 1880, having spent twenty years each in the foreign and home mission fields, Smith became professor of evangelistic theology at New College, Edinburgh. He was the first to deliver the Duff lectures on foreign missions, later published as *Medieval Missions* (1880) and he also published a few biographies, including *Memoirs of James Begg* (2 vols., 1885–8), perhaps his best-known work, and *Alexander Duff* (1883). In 1891 he served as moderator of the general assembly of the Free Church of Scotland, and he retired from his professorial chair in 1893. His ministerial diamond jubilee in 1899 was marked with a public meeting in Newington Free Church, Edinburgh, where one of his sons, William Whyte Smith (1849–1904), was then acting as minister. In 1900 he became LLD, his third honorary award from Edinburgh University, which as well as his MA had conferred a DD degree upon him in 1867. Smith died at his home, 23 Hatton Place, Edinburgh, on 26 May 1906, and was buried nearby in the Grange cemetery.

Smith was the last of the pre-Disruption ministers who had 'gone out' in 1843 and he remained a staunch conservative throughout his life. It was taken as an auspicious sign that he withdrew his opposition to the union with the United Presbyterian church, which took place in 1900, for he had been an effective opponent of the proposal thirty years before. His amiable nature, however, meant that 'in controversy he never lost a friend or made an enemy' (*Scottish Review*, 31 May 1906). A respected mathematician as well as an effective missionary, Smith published *An Elementary Treatise on Plane Geometry* (1857) and *Euclid: his Life and System* (1902); his mathematical work was highly esteemed by Lord Kelvin.

W. F. Gray, *rev.* Lionel Alexander Ritchie

Sources *The Scotsman* (28 May 1906) · *Scottish Review and Christian Leader* (31 May 1906) · *WWW, 1897–1915* · *Fasti Scot.*, new edn, 1.261; 7.707–8; · W. Ewing, ed., *Annals of the Free Church of Scotland, 1843–1900*, 1 (1914), 321–2; 2 (1914), 3 · R. Hunter, *History of the missions of the Free Church of Scotland in India and Africa* (1873) · P. C. Simpson, *The life of Principal Rainy*, 1 (1909), 187–96, 323; 2 (1909), 233, 267 · private information (1912) · parish register (births and baptisms), 8 July 1817, Stonehouse, Lanarkshire · parish register (births and baptisms), 16 July 1817, Stonehouse, Lanarkshire · parish register (marriage), 19 March 1839, St Mary's, Edinburgh · *CCI* (1906)

Archives NL Scot., corresp. and papers

Likenesses J. H. Lorimer, oils, 1903, U. Edin., New College · photograph (in old age), repro. in *Scottish Review and Christian Leader*

Wealth at death £7042 6s. 10d.: confirmation, 28 July 1906, *CCI*

Smith, Sir Thomas, first baronet (1833–1909), surgeon, sixth son of Benjamin Smith (1793–1850), a London goldsmith, and his wife, Susannah, daughter of Apsley Pellatt, a descendant of Thomas Pellett, president of the Royal College of Physicians of London (1735–9), was born in Blackheath, Kent, on 23 March 1833. Two of his brothers became canons of Canterbury, and a third, Stephen, was prime warden in the Goldsmiths' Company in 1885–6. Smith was educated at Tonbridge School, which he entered in Lent term 1844. Following a decline in his father's business fortunes he was apprenticed to Sir James Paget in 1847. Smith was therefore one of the last of the 'hospital apprentices' at St Bartholomew's Hospital. He was admitted MRCS in 1854 and in August became house surgeon at the children's hospital in Great Ormond Street. He resigned this post four months later, owing to ill health.

Taking up residence in Bedford Row, Smith began to coach pupils for examinations and at the same time assisted Paget in his private and hospital practice. For several years after 1857 Smith customarily took a class of students to Paris in the Easter vacation, where, with the help of C. E. Brown-Séquard, he taught them operative surgery. The outcome of this work was *A Manual of Operative Surgery on the Dead Body*, published in 1859. In 1858 Smith was admitted FRCS, and in 1859 he was appointed jointly with George W. Callender as demonstrator of anatomy and operative surgery at St Bartholomew's Hospital. On 27 August 1862 he married Ann Eliza Parbury (*d.* 1879), second daughter of Frederick Parbury; she died shortly after the birth of their ninth child.

Smith was elected assistant surgeon at St Bartholomew's on 24 February 1864 on the resignation of Frederic Carpenter Skey, and for a time he had charge of the aural department. He was appointed surgeon in 1873. In the medical school attached to the hospital Smith lectured on anatomy jointly with Callender from 1871, and in 1880 he instituted the Samaritan Maternity Fund at the hospital in memory of his wife. On resigning his hospital appointments on 10 March 1898 at the retiring age of sixty-five he was appointed a consulting surgeon.

From 1858 to 1861 Smith was also assistant surgeon at the Great Northern Hospital, then recently established in York Road, King's Cross. In September 1861 he was elected assistant surgeon at the Hospital for Sick Children in Great Ormond Street, where he was surgeon from June 1868 to November 1883 and afterwards consulting surgeon. He was also surgeon to the Alexandra Hospital for Hip Disease, in Queen Square.

Smith was surgical secretary of the Royal Medical and Chirurgical Society (1870–2), and he contributed to its *Transactions* his paper 'On the cure of cleft palate by operation in children, with a description of an instrument for facilitating the operation'. The method Smith recommended in his paper governed the technique of the operation for many years. He played an important part in the commission appointed to report on the administration of remedies by hypodermic injection.

At the Royal College of Surgeons Smith was elected a member of the council in 1880. He acted as a vice-president in 1887–8, and again in 1890–91, but he subsequently refused nomination for the office of president. He was chosen a trustee of the Hunterian collection in 1900 and was gazetted surgeon-extraordinary to Queen Victoria in 1895, in succession to Sir William Savory. Smith was created a baronet in 1897. He actively aided the Misses Keyser in founding their home for officers wounded in the Second South African War, and was created KCVO in 1901. Becoming an honorary serjeant-surgeon to Edward VII on his accession in 1901, Smith was in attendance when Sir

Frederick Treves operated on the king on the day appointed for the coronation (24 June 1902).

Smith lived at 7 Montague Street, Russell Square, until 1868; he then moved to 5 Stratford Place, Oxford Street, where he died on 1 October 1909. He was buried in the Finchley cemetery.

D'A. POWER, *rev.* JEFFREY S. REZNICK

Sources *St Bart's Hospital Reports*, 90 (1909) · *The Lancet* (9 Oct 1909) · *BMJ* (9 Oct 1909) · V. G. Plarr, *Plarr's Lives of the fellows of the Royal College of Surgeons of England*, rev. D'A. Power, 2 vols. (1930) · personal knowledge (1912) · Burke, *Peerage* · *CGPLA Eng. & Wales* (1909)

Likenesses J. Collier, oils, 1901, St Bartholomew's Hospital, London, Great Hall · Bassano, photograph, repro. in *BMJ* · J. Brooke, group portrait, photograph (with the council of the Royal College of Surgeons of England), RCS Eng. · H. J. Brooks, group portrait, oils (*Council of the Royal College of Surgeons of England 1884–85*), RCS Eng. · photographs, RCS Eng., council club album · portrait, repro. in *St Bartholomew's Hospital Reports* · portrait, repro. in *The Lancet*

Wealth at death £101,245 1s. 9*d*.: probate, 8 Nov 1909, *CGPLA Eng. & Wales*

Smith, Thomas (1883–1969), physicist, was born on 6 April 1883 at Leamington Spa, the eldest of the four children of William Edward Smith, a schoolmaster, and his wife, Dorothy Ann Jameson. He was educated at Leamington School where his father was headmaster, and at Warwick School. He entered Queens' College, Cambridge, as a scholar in 1902, was sixteenth wrangler in part one of the mathematical tripos in 1905, and obtained second-class honours in the mechanical sciences tripos in 1906. He was a master at Oundle School for one year (1906–7) but, not being happy or successful in this post, he joined the National Physical Laboratory in 1907 where he remained for the rest of his working life. He worked for two years on electricity and on tide prediction, in 1909 he became head of the optics division, and when the light division was formed in 1940 he became superintendent (1940–48). He married, in 1913, Elsie Muriel, daughter of E. M. Elligott, a schoolmaster and a relative of the McElligott of Macgillicuddy. They had three daughters and two sons of whom the elder was also a wrangler in the Cambridge mathematical tripos.

Smith was president of the Optical Society (1925–7), and of the Physical Society (1936–8). He was elected a fellow of the Royal Society in 1932. When the International Commission for Optics was formed in 1946 he was chosen by the general consensus of delegates from many countries to be its first president (1947–9). He gave the Thomas Young oration in 1949. He was made an honorary member of the Optical Society of America in 1957.

Smith was the author (in a few cases, joint author), of about 170 scientific papers. About 150 concerned the design and testing of optical systems and ten were on colorimetry. He was interested in the principles underlying the design of optical systems and limited his contribution to practical design problems to some calculations on doublet lenses. He developed algebraic methods of tracing rays without the use of trigonometrical tables. His methods were equally suitable for skew rays and meridional rays and for both spherical and aspherical surfaces. In the presentation of his work he sought the utmost generality and what he considered the most elegant mathematical form. This made his work readily intelligible to only a few and created a resistance additional to that due to the radical novelty of his approach. His algebraic method is very suitable for machine calculation, as are the iterative methods of calculation which he later developed.

In the later part of his work Smith used the mathematical methods of Sir William Rowan Hamilton to calculate image formation from the eikonal rather than from ray tracing. About 1930 he developed very general formulae for image formation in matrix form. He later found that his main results had been anticipated in substance by the astronomer R. A. Sampson in 1898 and made a full acknowledgement. Although he was not the first in this field, it was Smith's work which led to the later use of matrix methods. Smith came to colorimetry at a time when the logical principles of quantitative colour specification and calculation were being devised. In association with J. Guild he proposed a system of colorimetry which was adopted by the International Commission of Illumination (CIE).

Smith was a tall, well-built man of considerable presence. In general, he was a man of few words and no small talk, though he would laugh heartily at a clever joke. Many people found him forbidding, and on scientific matters he was indeed a severe and formidable critic, but those who approached him on personal matters found him sincerely kind and sympathetic. He died on 28 November 1969 at his home, Buxhall, Prospect Road, Heathfield, Sussex.

R. W. DITCHBURN, *rev.*

Sources autobiographical notes, RS · K. J. Habell, *Memoirs FRS*, 17 (1971), 681–7 [incl. photograph and bibliography] · private information (1981) · personal knowledge (1981)

Archives RS

Likenesses W. Stoneman, photograph, RS; repro. in Habell, *Memoirs FRS*, facing p. 681

Wealth at death £17,061: probate, 18 March 1970, *CGPLA Eng. & Wales*

Smith, Thomas Assheton (1776–1858), quarry owner and sportsman, was born in Queen Anne Street, Cavendish Square, London, on 2 August 1776. He was the second of the nine children of Thomas Assheton Smith (1752–1828), a landowner and MP, and his wife, Elizabeth (*d.* 1814), daughter of Watkin Wynne of Foelas, Denbighshire. The eldest son died in infancy. He was educated at Eton College (1783–94), and while there fought Jack Musters (*d.* 1839), who later became a well-known sportsman. Smith was in residence at Christ Church, Oxford, as a gentleman commoner, from February 1795 until 1798, but did not graduate. In his youth he was an active cricketer: while at Eton in 1793 he was in the school cricket eleven, and at Oxford he played with the Bullingdon Club, appearing in the club's fixture against the Marylebone Club at Lord's on 11 July 1796.

Smith sat as a Conservative MP for Andover from 1821 to 1831, and then for Caernarvonshire from 1832 to 1841. On 29 October 1827 he married Matilda, second daughter of

William Webber of Binfield Lodge, Berkshire; the marriage was childless. On the death of his father in 1828, he inherited estates at Tedworth in Hampshire and Vaynol in Caernarvonshire. As part of the latter, he took over the complex of slate quarries known as Dinorwig quarry, which was situated on Elidir mountain, near Llanberis.

Smith spent most of his time at Tedworth House, but every autumn he stayed at Vaynol House near Bangor, always making a daily visit to Y Felinheli ('Port Dinorwic'), his private port for the quarries, to inspect the books. He had learned accounting not at Eton but from the postmistress at Melton Mowbray. Throughout the year he demanded and received reports on his rent roll, his slate quarries, and his three copper mines—Drwsycoed, Llanberis, and Clogwyn Coch—which employed a total of 230 men in 1832. The Vaynol estate comprised about 37,000 acres and Smith owned half of Snowdon. He built the Victoria Hotel at Llanberis for tourists. He was a friend of the duke of Wellington and renamed one quarry Wellington in the duke's honour.

Smith made considerable improvements to his estates and slate quarries. Initially, he helped to get the duties on slate carried coastwise repealed in 1831, and by introducing mechanization in the slate mills and by improving transport, he took advantage of the expansion in the slate industry. Profits increased from about £8000 in 1828 to an annual profit of about £30,000. In 1832 the quarries employed 706 men and boys; by 1858 the number had increased to 2400. Smith replaced the tramroad of 1824 with the Padarn or Dinorwig Railway, which was opened in 1843 and had two steam locomotives by 1848. Y Felinheli was greatly enlarged so that it could accommodate 120 vessels. A railway connection from Y Felinheli to Bangor was established in 1852.

Development in the quarries was more haphazard than it was to be under his successor, but despite his plain features, strong will, and rough temper in the hunting field, Smith was popular with tenants and quarrymen alike. His generosity to the poor, and his support for the local schools in Tedworth and Vaynol, were well known. According to the *Carnarvon and Denbigh Herald* (6 June 1874), he 'thought more of his white jackets [quarrymen] than even of his greyhounds'.

Smith was an enthusiastic and celebrated huntsman. From 1806 to 1816 he was the master of the Quorn hounds in Leicestershire, and from 1816 to 1824 he was master of the Burton hounds in Lincolnshire. His first pack in Hampshire was introduced at Penton, near Andover, in 1826, and consisted of a selection from the kennels of Sir Richard Sutton and others. In 1834 he purchased a large portion of Sir Thomas Burghley's hounds, and in 1842 he added the duke of Grafton's entire pack. He usually had at this time about one hundred couple of hounds in his kennel. He hunted his own hounds four days in the week, and sometimes had two packs out at the same time. After the death of his father, he moved his stable and kennels to Tedworth, where he extended lavish hospitality to his fox-hunting neighbours. In 1832, in consequence of the Reform riots, he raised a corps of yeomanry cavalry at his own expense.

On 20 March 1840 Smith accepted an invitation to take his hounds to Rolleston, Henry Greene's seat in Leicestershire, where he was received by an assembly of two thousand horsemen and acclaimed as the foremost fox-hunter of the day (*Sporting Magazine*, June 1840, 130–32). In 1845 he built a glass conservatory at Tedworth, 315 feet long and 40 feet wide, in which he rode. He continued hunting up to his eightieth year.

At Vaynol yachting occupied much of Smith's attention. He was a member of the Royal Yacht Squadron until in 1830 he quarrelled with the club committee over their refusal to admit steam yachts. This led him to commission Robert Napier (1791–1876) of Glasgow to build a steam yacht for him, christened the *Menai*, of 400 tons and 120 horsepower. This was the first of eight steam yachts built for Smith between 1830 and 1851. In 1840 the *Fire-king* was constructed for him according to his own model, with long and very fine hollow water-lines. He claimed to have been the originator of this wave-line construction, but much of the credit for the invention must go to John Scott Russell.

Smith died at Vaynol on 9 September 1858, and was buried in the village churchyard at Tedworth. He left all his possessions to his wife, Matilda, who died on 18 May 1859. On her death the Tedworth estate passed to her nephew Francis Stanley, and the Vaynol estate to George William Duff, the eldest son of her husband's niece. On inheriting Vaynol, Duff assumed the additional surname Assheton-Smith. G. C. Boase, *rev.* Jean Lindsay

Sources J. Eardley-Wilmot, *The reminiscences of the late Thomas Assheton Smith, esq., a famous fox hunter*, 6th edn (1902) • Nimrod [C. J. Apperley], *Hunting reminiscences* (1843) • J. Lindsay, *A history of the north Wales slate industry* (1974) • J. N. Fitt, *Coverside sketches* (1878) • J. E. Griffith, *Pedigrees of Anglesey and Carnarvonshire families* (privately printed, Horncastle, 1914) • *ILN* (6 Dec 1856), 571 • [A. Haygarth], *Frederick Lillywhite's cricket scores and biographies*, 1 (1862) • J. I. C. Boyd, *Narrow gauge railways in north Caernarvonshire*, 3 (1986) • W. R. Williams, *The parliamentary history of the principality of Wales* (privately printed, Brecknock, 1895) • D. Bick, *The old copper mines of Snowdonia* (1982) • *GM*, 3rd ser., 5 (1858), 532 • N. Gash, *Robert Surtees and early Victorian society* (1993)

Archives Gwynedd Archives, Caernarfon, estate papers and personal accounts • Som. ARS, corresp. | Gwynedd Archives, Caernarfon, Vaynol MSS • Gwynedd Archives, Caernarfon, Dinorwic quarry MSS • NRA, priv. coll., letters to Drummond family, some relating to hunting

Likenesses Ferneley, group portrait, 1829, repro. in Eardley-Wilmot, *Reminiscences*, p. 173 • W. Beechey, oils, Eton • P. Cooper, portrait, repro. in Eardley-Wilmot, *Reminiscences*, frontispiece • Graves, engraving (after W. Seatie), repro. in *ILN*, 571

Wealth at death under £200,000: probate, 2 Nov 1858, *CGPLA Eng. & Wales*

Smith, Thomas Berry Cusack (1795–1866), lawyer and politician, was born on 15 November 1795, the second son of Sir William Cusack *Smith, second baronet (1766–1836), and his wife, Hester, *née* Berry (*d.* 1832). Like his father and grandfather, Smith became a distinguished lawyer and judge. He received his education at Trinity College, Dublin, from 1809 until he graduated in 1813, at the King's Inns, Dublin, and at Lincoln's Inn. In 1819 he was called to the bar, and in 1830 he became a king's counsel. He married in 1827 Louisa, daughter of James Hugh Smith-Barry of Fota, co. Cork, with whom he had one son.

In September 1842 Smith was appointed solicitor-general for Ireland in Sir Robert Peel's administration, and a couple of months later he succeeded Francis Blackburne as attorney-general. From 1843 to 1846 he sat in the House of Commons as Conservative member for Ripon, having previously contested Youghal unsuccessfully in 1842 against Daniel O'Connell's son. As attorney-general his most important duty was to conduct the state prosecution of O'Connell and his chief followers for conspiracy to repeal the Act of Union. In the course of the trial Smith was stung by the sarcasm of one of the opposing counsel and challenged him to a duel. The matter was brought before the court, where Smith publicly apologized. O'Connell applied his talent for nicknames in calling him Alphabet Smith and the Vinegar Cruet.

This state trial was the great legal event in Ireland during Peel's administration. The proceedings, which became a form of political theatre, extended from autumn 1843 to the end of summer 1844, beginning in the Irish queen's bench and ending in the House of Lords. The crown's indictment was an unwieldy and voluminous document, 80 feet in length; the finding of a true bill took six days, the trial twenty-four days, and a motion for a new trial nine days. At the trial, eleven counsel appeared for the crown and sixteen for the traversers. For the crown, only the attorney-general and the solicitor-general spoke, but for the traversers no less than eight king's counsel addressed the court.

Peel considered Smith's speech in the House of Commons in 1844, defending his action as attorney-general in the O'Connell prosecution, as ranking (with Canning's Lisbon embassy speech and Plunket's on catholic emancipation in 1821) among the three speeches most effective for their immediate purpose which he ever heard (*QR*, 130. 199). In 1846 he was appointed to succeed Blackburne as master of the rolls. Much of the business of that court consisted of issues arising in the relationship of landlord and tenant, and required most careful administration of money, with many issues of practice as well as larger questions.

Smith was a man of harsh manners and rough exterior, but his abilities were of a high order. He was well respected in the office of master of the rolls. An impetuous, irascible, and candid nature at times led him to express himself forcibly in court. He stepped somewhat outside the bounds of judicial office in urging the importance of granting leases to tenant farmers, a class for whom he felt strong sympathy. His death, while he still held office, occurred suddenly on 13 August 1866 at his shooting lodge at Ballied, near Blairgowrie, Perthshire. He was buried at Mount Jerome cemetery, Dublin, on 21 August.

Daire Hogan

Sources F. E. Ball, *The judges in Ireland, 1221–1921*, 2 vols. (1926) • *Irish Times* (14–22 Aug 1866) • M. McDonagh, *The life of Daniel O'Connell* (1903) • W. O'Connor Morris, *Memories and thoughts of a life* (1895) • E. Keane, P. Beryl Phair, and T. U. Sadleir, eds., *King's Inns admission papers, 1607–1867*, IMC (1982) • E. Blackburne, *Life of the Right Hon. Francis Blackburne* (1874) • Boase, *Mod. Eng. biog.* • *CGPLA Ire.* (1866)

Archives BL, corresp. mainly with Sir Robert Peel, Add. MSS 40451–40583, *passim*

Wealth at death under £50,000: administration, 7 Nov 1866, *CGPLA Ire.*

Smith, Sir Thomas Broun (1915–1988), jurist, was born in Glasgow on 3 December 1915, the second of four sons (there was also one daughter, the fourth child) of John Smith DL JP, restaurateur, of Pollokshields, Glasgow, and Symington, Lanarkshire, and his wife, Agnes Macfarlane. He was educated at Glasgow high school and Sedbergh School, went to Christ Church, Oxford, as Boulter exhibitioner, and graduated in 1937 with first-class honours in jurisprudence and the Eldon law scholarship. A year later, having achieved a first class and certificate of honour in the bar final, he was called to the bar by Gray's Inn, which in 1986 made him an honorary bencher.

Smith joined the Territorial Army in 1937 and served throughout the Second World War in the Gordon Highlanders and Royal Artillery, rising to the rank of lieutenant-colonel. He took part in the retreat from Dunkirk, served in the Mediterranean and the Middle East, and moved to intelligence work. He then returned to Scotland, passed advocate of the Scottish bar in 1947, and commenced practice. In 1949 he accepted the chair of Scots law in the University of Aberdeen, where he was very happy, made a great impression on students, and began the movement to change the study of law in the Scottish universities from a part-time complement to office training into a more thorough study. He became a QC (Scotland) in 1956 and in 1958 moved to the chair of civil (Roman) law at Edinburgh, where he transformed the course from classical civil law to its later Romanist developments as the basis of much modern European law. Ten years later, in 1968, he transferred to the chair of Scots law at Edinburgh, which he held until 1972. In 1960 he established the Scottish Universities Law Institute, a co-operative organization of the law faculties of the four Scottish universities, to secure the writing and publication of new, modern textbooks in all the major fields of Scots law. He was its director from 1960 to 1972.

Smith also made many contacts abroad, becoming a visiting professor at, among other universities, Cape Town (1958), Harvard (1962–3), and, as Tagore professor, Calcutta (1977). A member of the Law Reform Committee for Scotland from 1954, he became a commissioner when the Scottish Law Commission was established in 1965 (full-time from 1972 to 1980); on this body his breadth of scholarship made him a stimulating and inspiring colleague. In retirement he took up in 1981 the onerous post of general editor of the new *The Laws of Scotland: Stair Memorial Encyclopaedia* (25 vols., 1986–94).

Smith wrote extensively and entertainingly in journals, and some of his papers are collected in *Studies Critical and Comparative* (1952). His Hamlyn lectures, *British Justice: the Scottish Contribution* (1961), strongly asserted the distinctive nature of Scots law. His biggest book, requested as a chapter on Scotland for a volume, *The United Kingdom*, in a series, The British Commonwealth: the Development of its Laws and Constitutions (ed. G. W. Keeton and D. Lloyd), emerged in 1955 as a full volume. It was also issued as *A Short Commentary on the Law of Scotland* (1962), to provide a better basic textbook for Scottish law students than was then available. In this it was not a success, being too general and discursive.

Physically Smith had a tendency to heaviness, and his cheerful round face and moustache maintained to the end strong traces of his military years. He was a genial and jovial companion, with a lively sense of humour; in discussion he was courteous and stimulating, but tended sometimes to pontificate. He cared deeply about Scotland and Scots law. He was much influenced by T. M. Cooper (Baron Cooper of Culross) whom he revered. In particular he was interested in the influence of civil law on Scots law and the shared tradition of Scots and Roman-Dutch law. He made a great contribution to raising to importance Scots law and Scottish legal scholarship, modernizing them and, more by his contacts than by his writings, making them better known to the world and better appreciated outside Scotland.

Smith's published work gained him a DCL (Oxford, 1956) and LLD (Edinburgh, 1963). He was elected FBA in 1958, FRSE in 1977, and a foreign honorary member of the American Academy of Arts and Sciences (1969). He received honorary LLD degrees from Cape Town (1959), Aberdeen (1969), and Glasgow (1978), and was knighted on his retirement in 1981. The *Juridical Review* for 1982 was devoted to essays in his honour.

In 1940 Smith married Ann Dorothea, criminologist, daughter of Christian Tindall CIE of the Indian Civil Service, of Exmouth, Devon. It was a happy marriage, which produced a son, who died in 1962, and two daughters, one of whom also predeceased Smith in 1976. Smith died of cancer in Edinburgh on 15 October 1988; his remains were cremated. Until near the end he continued to welcome friends and bombard contributors to *The Laws of Scotland* with comments and encouragement.

DAVID M. WALKER, *rev.*

Sources *The Times* (18 Oct 1988) · *Daily Telegraph* (18 Oct 1988) · *The Scotsman* (19 Oct 1988) · *Scots Law Times: News* (4 Nov 1988) · J. Cameron, *Year Book of the Royal Society of Edinburgh* (1988–9), 59–61 · J. O. M. Hunter, 'Thomas Broun Smith, 1915–1988', *PBA*, 82 (1993), 455–74 · *The Independent* (18 Oct 1988)

Likenesses T. A. Cockburn, portrait, U. Edin. · photograph, repro. in *The Times*

Smith, Thomas Daniel [T. Dan] (**1915–1993**), local government leader and criminal, was born on 11 May 1915 at 62 Holly Avenue, Wallsend, Northumberland, the son of Robert Smith, miner, and his wife, Ada, *née* Clifford, charlady. His father suffered unemployment in the inter-war years; both parents held left-wing views, which he inherited. Educated at Western Boys' School, Wallsend, he left to become a printer's apprentice at the age of fourteen. After suffering unemployment himself during the

Thomas Daniel Smith (1915–1993), by unknown photographer

1930s, in 1937 he founded a painting and decorating business, which flourished despite acquiring the local nickname of One-Coat Smith; by 1957 he owned seven companies. On 22 July 1939 he married Ada Simpson (*b.* 1918/19), typist, daughter of George Frederick Simpson, storekeeper; they had one son and two daughters. Smith was a conscientious objector during the Second World War and was active in militant activities (including helping to organize the Tyneside apprentices' strike), opposing the war until after the German invasion of Russia. Meanwhile he enlisted in a succession of left-wing movements, including the Independent Labour Party and the Revolutionary Communist Party, before finally joining the Labour Party.

Elected to Newcastle city council in 1950, Smith became a leading member of its Labour group. He was chairman of the Newcastle Labour Party in 1953–6, and when Labour won the 1958 municipal election became chairman of the council's housing committee. From 1960 to 1965 he was Labour leader on the council, but resigned on appointment as chairman of the Northern Economic Planning Council; he was also chairman of the council's town planning committee. He established a remarkable personal ascendancy as council leader, and acquired a national reputation as a vigorous champion of urban improvement. An obituary described him as

> an abrasive and often ruthless town hall politician who had an intimidating physical presence and a booming voice which didn't brook argument. He could rule a committee room with a rod of iron. He could strike the fear of God into city hall officials. (*Newcastle Journal*, 28 July 1993)

He reorganized council procedures by concentrating power in an 'inner cabinet' of Labour councillors, leaving the Conservative minority without effective influence. In a newspaper article he was quoted as saying that 'The democratic vote is no way to get the sort of changes we need in the North' (*The Observer*, 21 Feb 1965). During his period of control he achieved much for the city, which acquired the nickname of the Brasilia of the north. Slum clearance was accelerated and new housing built at a cost of some £50 million. A new civic centre was created and local higher education and transport facilities were improved. A variety of local organizations, including the Northern Arts Council, profited significantly from his support. He served on the Buchanan inquiry into traffic management and the Redcliffe-Maud royal commission on local government reform.

In 1962, the year in which the *Architectural Review* named him planner of the year, Smith founded the first of a series of public relations companies. Doubts about his integrity had been heard in 1960, when it was revealed that his decorating business had received more than half of the external repainting contracts awarded by Newcastle council. In the next year further disquiet was expressed about his involvement in the award of a lucrative contract to the building firm Crudens. From 1957 onwards he had helped the building contractor Bovis to obtain a number of major public commissions. In 1962 he became associated with John Poulson, an architect of mediocre ability already involved in local government corruption. In the next seven years Poulson paid Smith's public relations companies at least £156,000, ostensibly for organizing exhibitions and conferences for Poulson's clients in the building industry, but in reality for bribing councillors and officials in various parts of the country to steer contracts into the right hands. One of his companies was hired by the Labour Party to support Harold Wilson's 1964 general election campaign in northern constituencies, facilitating acquisition of information about leading councillors in many areas. He was increasingly careless in flouting rules governing local government finance. Initially, he often stayed away from committee meetings that awarded contracts to companies for which he was a paid 'consultant'. As early as June 1962, however, he defended in Newcastle council the award of contracts to Bovis and Poulson without declaring his own financial interest as a paid consultant to both.

It was impossible to keep such widespread malpractices concealed indefinitely. Police inquiries resulted in Smith's being charged in January 1970 with offering employment to a leading Labour alderman in Wandsworth in order to win a contract. He was acquitted in July 1971, but by this time he had either resigned from or lost all his political appointments. In October 1973 he was arrested on a series of further corruption charges arising from the Poulson affair, and pleaded guilty to six charges. Sentenced to six years' imprisonment, he served three years. There is little to suggest that Smith was an innocent enmeshed in the criminal activities of unscrupulous tempters. The evidence suggests that he sought a share in the proceeds, taking advantage of existing corrupt practices in local government. He enjoyed increased wealth, with such trappings as a luxurious hotel suite reserved for him in London and a personalized car number plate.

On release from prison, Smith sought with only modest success to rebuild a career, working for the Howard League for Penal Reform and championing the rights of released prisoners. The local Labour Party, resenting the harm he had done to the party's image, refused to readmit him to membership, and relented only in 1987. His health deteriorated and he died, aged seventy-eight, during an operation following a heart attack, at the Freeman Hospital, Newcastle, on 27 July 1993; he was cremated at West Road crematorium, Newcastle, on 2 August. He was survived by his wife and three children.

NORMAN MCCORD

Sources *Dan Smith: an autobiography* (1970) • R. Fitzwalter and D. Taylor, *Web of corruption: the story of John Poulson and T. Dan Smith* (1981) • press cuttings, 2 vols., Newcastle Central Library, local studies department • A. Potts, 'The man and the legend', *North East Labour History Bulletin*, 28 (1994) • R. Challinor, 'The youthful revolutionary', *North East Labour History Bulletin*, 28 (1994) • D. Byrne, 'The disastrous impact of a liberal authoritarian moderniser', *North East Labour History Bulletin*, 28 (1994) • 'Britain's first town boss', *The Observer* (21 Feb 1965) • *Newcastle Journal* (28 July 1993) • *The Times* (28 July 1993) • *The Independent* (28 July 1993) • b. cert. • m. cert. • *WWW*

Likenesses photograph, repro. in *The Observer* • photograph, repro. in *Newcastle Journal* • photograph, News International Syndication, London [*see illus.*] • photograph, repro. in *The Independent*

Smith, Thomas James (1827–1896), manufacturing chemist, was born in June 1827 in the small village of Whitfield, near Haydon Bridge, Northumberland, and baptized there on 17 June 1827, the eldest of four children of Horatio Nelson Smith and his wife, Jane. T. J., as Smith became known, was apprenticed to a dispensing chemist in Grantham, Lincolnshire, at a time when pharmacy had only just emerged as a distinctive practice from the three separate professions of physician, surgeon, and apothecary. He supplemented his skills by attending University College, London, from 1854 to 1855, passing the minor examination of the Royal Pharmaceutical Society (RPS) in June 1855. In August he passed the major examination, which enabled him to become a member of the RPS. He was formally elected on 6 February 1856 and six months later moved to Hull, Yorkshire, where he bought as a going concern the chemist's shop at 61 Whitefriargate.

At first a general retail pharmacist, Smith developed an interest in the properties of cod-liver oil. This was already in use in British hospitals for combating two of the scourges of the day, rickets and consumption. It normally had a deep brown colour and a strong and unpleasant fishy flavour. Smith aimed to find a method of making the product—for which there was a keen demand—purer and more palatable. His experiments, supported by correspondence with medical specialists, enabled him to market his own oil. He refined his product by blending different oils, then putting the 1½ gallon bottles on a flat roof to be bleached by the sun, a process that also improved the taste.

The various sorts of cod-liver oil were imported to Hull from Norway, where specialists had evolved a process to remove the stearin (fat in its solid form). In 1860 Smith went to Norway to investigate this source of supply in person, being the first Englishman to do so. On this pioneering visit he bought 750 gallons of the best oil at a price 1*s*. 3*d*. cheaper per gallon than in London, at the same time making contracts for further visits.

Back in Hull, Smith decided that the Whitefriargate

shop was too small for the wholesale business to which he had now progressed, and he bought 10 and 11 North Church Street, converting them to a warehouse in 1860. In 1861 he rented premises—a house, shop, and outbuildings—at 10 North Churchside. He was by this time selling a superior product at a lower price than his competitors. In 1880 a London specialist wrote to Smith suggesting that he bottle the oil and sell it under a brand name. Smith's Paragon cod-liver oil thus came into being and the business continued to flourish. Also in 1880 Smith bought the freehold of the North Churchside premises with a £500 loan from his father.

Meanwhile Smith had become an active member of Hull's civic community. He was a town councillor from 1875 to 1882 and again from 1885 to 1892. While on the council he founded the Hull branch of the Charity Organization Society, and served the Hull chamber of commerce for many years as honorary secretary and treasurer, two of them as president (1879–80). He was also a member of the East Yorkshire Conservative Association. A natural development from his interest in medicine was his membership of the sanitary committee, which addressed the problem of pre-empting the epidemics to which Hull, as a growing immigration port and commercial centre, was vulnerable.

By his late sixties, Smith was suffering increasing ill health. He had never married, and lived at Hornsea, on the Yorkshire coast, with his spinster sister, Amelia Ann Smith (1839–1905). In 1896 Amelia invited Smith's nephew, Horatio Nelson *Smith (1874–1960), who had lived with them as a boy and was then working with a firm of London drapers and woollen manufacturers, to join his uncle in the cod-liver oil business. H. N., as he was known, accepted the offer and arrived in Hull in January 1896 for a trial period. Six months later, on 1 July, he became a partner in T. J. Smith & Nephew.

Smith was now a complete invalid, and on 3 October 1896 he died at his Hornsea home, 7 Wilton Terrace; he was buried at St Nicholas's Church, Hornsea. Amelia inherited her brother's half-share of the business, but decided to pass it to H. N. At the time of Smith's death, the firm had a staff of three and a turnover of £3000, of which about £2500 was from cod-liver oil. H. N. Smith was its chief, and it was he who developed the surgical dressings side of the business. Thomas Smith's enterprise was thus relatively modest, and his contribution to society was as much through charity and political administration as the wholesaling of cod-liver oil. It was left to H. N. Smith to have the greater vision that made Smith & Nephew into one of Britain's most successful manufacturing companies in the twentieth century. ADRIAN ROOM

Sources R. Bennett and J. A. Lenvey, *A history of Smith and Nephew, 1856–1981* (1981) · J. Foreman-Peck, *Smith and Nephew in the health care industry* (1995) · G. Tweedale, 'Smith, Horatio Nelson', *DBB* · private information (2004) · d. cert.

Archives Smith and Nephew company headquarters, Temple Place, London · Smith and Nephew Medical Ltd offices, Hull, East Yorkshire

Likenesses photograph, *c*.1875, repro. in Bennett and Lenvey, *A history of Smith and Nephew*

Wealth at death £6097 16*s*. 4*d*.: probate, 17 Nov 1896, *CGPLA Eng. & Wales*

Smith, Thomas Roger (1830–1903), architect, was born on 14 July 1830 at Sheffield, the only son of the Revd Thomas Smith of Sheffield and his wife, Louisa (*née* Thomas) of Chelsea. After being educated privately he entered the office of Philip Hardwick and spent a year and a half travelling before beginning independent practice in 1855. In 1858 he married Catherine, daughter of Joseph Elsey of Highgate. They had one daughter and three sons, one of whom, Ravenscroft Elsey Smith, became his partner and (in 1899) professor of architecture at King's College, London. Until 1891 he was also in partnership with A. S. Gale.

Having been selected to prepare the design for the exhibition buildings in Bombay, Smith travelled there in 1864, though the buildings were abandoned after the contract was signed, because of the cotton famine. Several other important buildings were erected in India from his designs, including the post office and British Hospital at Bombay, and the residency at Gunersh Kind. In Britain his work included the technical schools (and baths) of the Carpenters' Company at Stratford; the Ben Jonson schools at Stepney (1872), as well as other schools for the London school board; Emmanuel Church and vicarage, South Croydon; the sanatorium at Reedham (1883); the North London Hospital for Consumption at Hampstead (1880; enlarged 1892; completed 1903); laboratories at University College, London (opened 1892), forming part of an uncompleted scheme for the Gower Street front of the large quadrangle; many City warehouses; and, besides other domestic work, Armathwaite Hall, Cumberland; Brambletye House, East Grinstead; a house at Taplow for Mr G. Hanbury, and Beechy Lees at Otford, Kent.

Smith devoted much of his time to lecturing on architecture. In 1851 he became a member of the Architectural Association, a body to which he delivered a series of lectures; he was president in 1860–61 and again in 1863–4. At the Royal Institute of British Architects he was elected an associate in 1856 and a fellow in 1863. He took a prominent part in its debates and committees, was for several sessions a member of its council, and in 1899 became chairman of the statutory board of examiners (under the London Building Acts). In 1874 he was made district surveyor under the Metropolitan Board of Works for Southwark and North Lambeth, and he was transferred in 1882 to the more important district of west Wandsworth. At the Carpenters' Company he acted as an examiner in carpentry and was a frequent lecturer and surveyor; in 1901 he became master of the company. He was an examiner in architecture at the Department of Science and Art, in South Kensington, as well as at the City and Guilds of London Institute. He was surveyor to the licensing justices of Wimbledon and Wandsworth; but the most important of his posts was the professorship of architecture at University College, London, which he held from 1880 to his death. His wide practical experience in questions of rights of light brought him frequent work as an expert and arbitrator, and in 1900 he served (as chairman) on a joint committee of the Royal Institute of British Architects and the

Surveyors' Institution, which was appointed to discuss amendment to the law of ancient lights. He was also often an architectural assessor in competitions.

Smith prepared many papers on professional and artistic subjects, and published several works, including *Acoustics in Relation to Architecture and Building* (rev edn, 1895, originally published as a treatise on *Acoustics* in Weale's series 1861), and two handbooks: one, with John Slater, on *Architecture, Classic and Early Christian* (1888; new edn, 1898); the other on *Architecture, Gothic and Renaissance* (1880; repr. 1888). Though afflicted with serious lameness for many years Smith continued his professional work until three months before his death, which occurred on 11 March 1903 at his home, 7 Gordon Street, Gordon Square, London. His wife survived him.

PAUL WATERHOUSE, *rev.* JOHN ELLIOTT

Sources *Building News*, 84 (1903), 369 · *The Builder*, 84 (1903), 289 · *RIBA Journal*, 10 (1902–3), 276–7, 284 · biographical file, RIBA BAL · *Civil Engineer and Architect's Journal*, 27 (1864), 181 · *The Architect and Contract Reporter* (20 March 1903), 186–7 · J. M. Crook, 'Architecture and history', *Architectural History*, 27 (1984), 555–78 · *CGPLA Eng. & Wales* (1903) · *Dir. Brit. archs.*

Wealth at death £6741 6s.: probate, 23 May 1903, *CGPLA Eng. & Wales*

Smith, (Lillias Irma) Valerie Arkell- [*née* Lillias Irma Valerie Barker] (**1895–1960**), sexual impostor and perjurer, was born on 27 August 1895 in St Clements, Jersey, the daughter of Thomas William Barker (1857–1918), gentleman farmer and architect, and his wife, Lillias Adelaide Hill (1868–1923). Her parents moved to Surrey in 1899, where her brother Tom Leslie was born. Valerie was educated at Huxley's School for Young Ladies at Prior's Corner, Surrey, and then at Upavon, Wiltshire, finishing her education at a convent school at Graty near Brussels.

In 1914 Barker took up war work as a VAD attached to St Hilda's Hospital, Haslemere. From 1915 she worked as a horse trainer for the Canadian army at Rodborough Common and then at the Bristol remount depot. She remained working with horses, moving on to a hunting stable near Shrewsbury and then to a stables in Meopham, Kent. While in Kent, Barker met her first husband, Lieutenant Harold Arkell-Smith (*b.* 1882/3) of the Australian 20th battalion. They married on 27 April 1918 but the marriage lasted only six weeks, although they never divorced, and she subsequently returned to her parents' house. On 26 August 1918 she enrolled as a member of the Women's Auxiliary Air Force.

After the war Arkell-Smith worked in a tea-shop in Warminster, where she met her next partner, the Australian soldier Ernest Walter Pearce Crouch (1876–1923), who was married but separated. They lived together in Shepperton, and then from July 1919 in France, where he worked in the Paris office of *The Times*. Their son Tony was born on 27 February 1920 in Paris. Nine months later Pearce Crouch lost his job and they returned to England. On 15 June 1921 their daughter Betty was born. They managed to find work as tenant farmers at Bailiffs Court, an estate in Climping in Sussex. However, their relationship was unsatisfactory and Arkell-Smith spent her time with

(Lillias Irma) Valerie Arkell-Smith (1895–1960), by unknown photographer, 1926

Elfrida Emma Haward (*b.* 1895/6), whom she had met in 1922 in Littlehampton. She left Pearce Crouch in 1923 and began a life as a man under the assumed identity of Victor Barker.

Arkell-Smith checked into the Grand Hotel in Brighton as Sir Victor Barker. The transition was easy for she had already gained a reputation for 'affecting masculine attire, and particularly for wearing men's heavy boots' (*Daily Mail*, 3 March 1929). As Colonel Victor Barker she married Elfrida Haward at St Peter's parish church in Brighton on 14 November 1923. The marriage was conducted by the Revd Laurence Hard, who was apparently unaware of the groom's real identity. 'I told Miss Haward that I was not what she thought I was; I told her that I was a man who had been injured in the war' (*Sunday Dispatch*, 10 March 1929). Elfrida always maintained that she believed her.

As the 'Colonel', Arkell-Smith followed a variety of careers, including that of an actor with the stage name of Ivor Gauntlett, boxing club manager, owner of a secondhand furniture business, dog kennel manager, dairy farm manager, café owner, and orchard worker. Owing to this instability Elfrida left the 'Colonel' in autumn 1928 and returned to her father's house. Arkell-Smith became politically involved with the National Fascisti, a militant breakaway group of Britain's fascist movement, in 1927, running a boxing programme for its members.

In 1929, after Arkell-Smith had changed both her name and rank to Captain Leslie Ivor Victor Gauntlett Bligh Barker, she found work as a desk clerk in the Regent Palace Hotel in London, posing as a retired officer. There she was arrested on a bankruptcy charge and was sent to trial at the Old Bailey in London. Put on remand at Brixton prison, she was found to be a woman. The charges against Arkell-Smith were in consequence increased to include perjury as a result of her marriage to Elfrida Haward.

The trial was sensationalized in the press. The prosecutor, Sir Ernest Wild, revealed that not only had Arkell-Smith married Miss Haward posing as an officer, but she had also been tried as a man two years previously in July 1927 in the Old Bailey for possessing a forged firearm certificate, although found not guilty. With the revelation of the new charges, she was found guilty of perjury and was sentenced to nine months in Holloway prison. Despite her marriage to Elfrida, Arkell-Smith was not charged under the amendments to the 1920 Sexual Offences Act.

When Arkell-Smith left Holloway she reverted to the identity of Victor Barker. After a variety of short-term jobs, calling herself John Hill, by 1937 she was attracting enormous crowds to her show, entitled *On a Strange Honeymoon*, in Blackpool, where she portrayed Colonel Barker.

Under another male identity, that of Jeffrey Norton, Arkell-Smith lived as the husband of Eva Norton. In the early part of the Second World War she worked as a switchboard operator in a hospital outside London, and also joined the Home Guard. After the war the couple moved to Kessingland, Suffolk, where Arkell-Smith called herself Geoffrey and became a shop assistant. She died of Parkinson's disease on 18 February 1960 at 3 Wrights Cottages, London Road, Kessingland, Suffolk, and was buried in the grounds of St Edmund's Church, Kessingland, on 23 February. On her death certificate her name was given as Geoffrey Norton, otherwise Lilias Irma Valerie Arkell-Smith. EMMA MILLIKEN

Sources R. Collis, *Colonel Barker's monstrous regiment: a tale of female husbandry* (2001) • 'Old Bailey acquittals', *The Times* (15 July 1927) • 'Woman's strange life as a man', *Daily Express* (6 March 1929) • 'How the colonel's secret was revealed', *Daily Sketch* (6 March 1929) • 'Colonel Barker prosecuted', *The Times* (28 March 1929) • 'Colonel Barker sent for trial', *Daily Sketch* (28 March 1929) • 'Colonel Barker in the dock at Old Bailey', *Daily Herald* (25 April 1929) • 'Perjury charge', *The Times* (26 April 1929) • 'My amazing masquerade', *Empire News and Chronicle* (19 Feb 1956) • V. Arkell-Smith, 'I posed as a man for thirty years', *Empire News and Chronicle* (19 Feb 1956) • J. Wheelwright, *Amazons and military maids* (1989) • M. Baker, *Our three selves: a life of Radclyffe Hall* (1985) • m. certs. • d. cert. • *CGPLA Eng. & Wales* (1960)

Likenesses photograph, 1926, Mansell Collection, London [*see illus.*] • photograph, BL • photographs, repro. in Collis, *Colonel Barker's monstrous regiment*

Wealth at death £333 6*s.* 3*d.*: probate, 14 Dec 1960, *CGPLA Eng. & Wales*

Smith, Vincent Arthur (1848–1920), historian of India and antiquary, was born in Dublin on 3 June 1848, the fifth of the thirteen children of the Irish antiquary Aquilla *Smith (1806–1890), and his wife, Esther, *née* Faucett, a first cousin to Aquilla. He studied at Trinity College, Dublin, where he earned the degree of BA with distinction, and in 1871, having topped the final examination for the Indian Civil Service, was posted to the North-Western Provinces and Oudh. In the same year he married Mary Elizabeth, daughter of William Clifford Tute of Sligo.

After the usual magisterial and executive postings, including a stint with the land settlement department (which prompted him to write the *Settlement Officer's Manual*, 1881), Smith became district and sessions judge of Gorakhpur in 1895, chief secretary to the government in 1898, and later that year commissioner of Gorakhpur.

Smith had inherited his father's tastes, and his work as a settlement officer soon directed his attention to the antiquities of the Ganges valley; among his earliest published works were articles on the coinage of the Gupta dynasty (1889, 1893) and on Graeco-Roman influence on the civilization of ancient India (1889). An original investigator of considerable skill, he nevertheless saw the need for co-ordinating and collating the results of other scholars, and in 1900 he retired early from the service to pursue this object. He settled first in Cheltenham, but moved in 1910 to Oxford, where he joined St John's College and was appointed a curator of the Indian Institute.

In 1901 he published *Asoka, the Buddhist Emperor of India*, followed in 1904 by the *Early History of India*, covering the period from 600 BC to the Muslim conquest. Embodying the main results of the work during the previous century, it was well received and reappeared in several revised editions during Smith's lifetime. Other major works were a *History of Fine Art in India and Ceylon* (1911) and the *Life of Akbar, the Great Mogul* (1917). Although in private he was genial and outspoken, Smith wrote in what he considered to be a restrained style, consciously eschewing the romantic, picturesque atmosphere evoked by an earlier generation of writers. In spite of its proclaimed objectivity, however, such sobriety was often simply a reflection of his own generation's increasingly mean-spirited vision of Indian society. As Peter Hardy has observed, Smith's portrayal of the great Akbar 'just manages to place him at about the level of the average British viceroy' (Hardy, 263).

In 1919 Smith published his *Oxford History of India*, which was to exert a vast influence over generations of students and which remains in print. In it he stressed the importance of benevolent despotism in the history of India, regretted the recurrent fragmentation of Indian polity, and concluded that a paramount power was essential for the maintenance of India's political integrity, an argument which led Indian scholars to denounce the work as a treatise on imperialism. Ironically, however, another of Smith's concepts, that of 'unity in diversity', was seized upon by nationalist politicians as a slogan encapsulating the secularist promise of independent India, although in coining the phrase Smith himself had in mind only the common cultural inheritance of India's Hindu population and would have vigorously rejected any notion of unity between Hindus and Muslims.

In 1915 Smith became a member of the council of the Asiatic Society of Bengal and in 1919 one of its vice-presidents. The society awarded him its gold medal in 1918. He was disappointed in not being elected to the readership in Indian history at Oxford, but, on the other hand, his CIE (1919), in its recognition of pure scholarship, stood out among the usual official decorations.

Smith died at his home, 6 Fyfield Road, Oxford, on 6 February 1920 and was buried four days later in St Andrew's Church, Oxford. He was survived by his widow and three sons and a daughter.

S. V. FITZ-GERALD, *rev.* KATHERINE PRIOR

Sources *Journal of the Asiatic Society of Bengal*, 2nd ser., 16 (1920) • A. T. Embree, *Imagining India: essays on Indian history* (1989) •

P. Hardy, *The Muslims of British India* (1972) • *History of services of gazetted officers attached to the North-Western Provinces and Oudh* (1900) • [J. H. Todd], ed., *A catalogue of graduates who have proceeded to degrees in the University of Dublin, from the earliest recorded commencements to … December 16, 1868* (1869) • R. Emden, *Imagining India* (1990) • *CGPLA Eng. & Wales* (1920)
Archives Bodl. Oxf., corresp. and papers
Wealth at death £4254 11s. 9d.: probate, 27 March 1920, *CGPLA Eng. & Wales*

Smith, Vivian Hugh, first Baron Bicester (1867–1956), merchant banker, was born on 9 December 1867, at 46 Park Street, Grosvenor Square, Mayfair, London, the eldest of the six sons of Hugh Colin Smith (1836–1910), a merchant, of Mount Clare, Roehampton, Surrey, and his wife, Constance Maria Josepha, *née* Adeane (1845–1918). He was descended from Abel Smith (1717–1788), whose own ancestor founded Smith's Bank at Nottingham in 1658. His father originally worked in the merchant house of Hugh Matheson, and then founded the great port of London wharfingers Hay's Wharf, of which he became chairman; he was a director of the Bank of England from 1876, and governor in 1897–9. Smith's two sisters married Sydney Charles, first Earl Buxton (sometime director of Barclays Bank) and Guy Baring. Two of his brothers entered the navy and retired as admirals; three other brothers reached high eminence in the City with widely dispersed interests.

Smith was educated at Eton College, where his attendance at Ascot races caused a school scandal. Afterwards he was a hearty undergraduate at Trinity Hall, Cambridge, and then entered the family firm of Hay's Wharf. In 1894 he joined the board of Royal Exchange Assurance. He was recruited in 1905 by his cousin Edward Grenfell, afterwards first Baron St Just, as a partner in J. S. Morgan, the London merchant bank intimately connected with the New York finance house of J. P. Morgan; it changed its name to Morgan, Grenfell & Co. in 1910. Smith was described in 1905 by Gaspard Farrer of Barings as 'a charming man … straight as a die, & from a social point of view everything that one wd desire in a partner. His experience in business, however, is extremely limited' (Burk, 61). In the event Smith proved energetic and resourceful at chasing business. He regularly visited Canada and Caucasia to inspect the company's overseas investments, and was booked on the *Titanic*'s maiden voyage in 1912, but fortunately found it inconvenient to travel. Morgan Grenfell and its New York associates were crucial as bankers and buying agents for the British and French governments during the First World War. In 1917 the firm bought the great Anglo-Indian mercantile house of Yule Catto, with Smith later becoming chairman. He was interested in engines and industrial processes, and enjoyed attending mechanical demonstrations. His technological aptitude contributed to Morgan Grenfell becoming in the 1920s the first merchant bank heavily committed to advising and financing industry. He took particular trouble with the metallurgical sector, and as late as the 1950s was involved in planning steel denationalization. He and his eldest son (known as Rufus) were indispensable in sustaining Morgan Grenfell during the Second World War, and he remained chairman until his death at the age of eighty-eight.

As governor of Royal Exchange Assurance from 1914 until 1955 Smith commanded great authority: his involvement in both the strategy and management of the business was more intimate than that of any of his predecessors. He led a keen acquisitions policy, especially in motoring insurance. Although Royal Exchange had traditionally kept its affairs private, he established his addresses to its annual court as occasions for public declarations of attitude and policy. His approach was paternalistic, and his trust in a man was crucial to that man's success as a manager.

The most important of Smith's other interests were his membership of the committee of the Hudson's Bay Company and directorship of Associated Electrical Industries. Although not a partisan spirit, he was chairman of the Conservative Party in the City of London at a time when Edward Grenfell represented the constituency as a Conservative. He was sedulous in fostering sympathies between the City and successive governments. In 1938 he was created Baron Bicester, of Tusmore.

Bicester was the most eminent banker in his family since Robert Smith, first Baron Carrington. He was the embodiment of all that was solid and reputable in the City of London of his epoch. His standards and manners were conventional and conservative; in appearance he was authoritative and deeply English; his judgement was always fair. Cheerful, shrewd, and hard-headed, he was famed as a negotiator who never concealed a material fact or enforced a ruthless settlement. He could be irascible or frightening, yet was never unforgiving, and liked to draw men together to work for common ends. With his great energy and zest he was too busy and self-confident for regrets. He regularly visited Ireland to buy horses and to improve his fund of lively anecdotes. Horses were his great love. When in middle life the effects of a hunting accident prevented him from riding he acquired a fine string of steeplechasers. Silver Fame won the Cheltenham gold cup; Roimond was placed second in the Grand National.

Bicester had married in 1897 Lady Sybil Mary McDonnell (1876–1959), the daughter of the sixth earl of Antrim and first cousin of the banker Guy Dawnay. They had three sons and four daughters. Essentially a countryman, for many years until 1921 he rented Rolls Park, Chigwell, in Essex, from Lieutenant-General Sir Francis Lloyd, and commuted into the City. He then acquired Mitford House in Lennox Gardens, Knightsbridge, and rented Squerryes Court, Westerham, Kent. He was over sixty before finally buying his own estate, Tusmore Park, near Bicester. The square, compact house with an Ionic portico had been built in 1770 to the designs of Robert Mylne. Bicester made various interior and other alterations in 1929; the demolition of the house shortly after his death, and its replacement by a neo-Georgian house designed by the fourth Lord Phillimore, was regrettable. Bicester was lord lieutenant of Oxfordshire (1934–54) and freeman of the city of

Oxford (1955). He died of pneumonia and cancer on 17 February 1956, at Tusmore, and was buried on 21 February nearby at Hardwick church.

RICHARD DAVENPORT-HINES

Sources *The Times* (18 Feb 1956) · *The Times* (23 Feb 1956) · K. Burk, *Morgan Grenfell, 1838–1988: the biography of a merchant bank* (1989) · J. A. S. L. Leighton-Boyce, *Smiths, the bankers, 1658–1958* (1958) · B. E. Supple, *The Royal Exchange Assurance: a history of British insurance, 1720–1970* (1970) · D. Kynaston, *The City of London*, 2 (1995) · A. Fitzroy, *Memoirs* (1927) · Lord Chandos [O. Lyttleton, first Viscount Chandos], *The memoirs of Lord Chandos: an unexpected view from the summit* (1962) · P. M. Johnstone, 'Rolls Park, Chigwell, Essex', *Country Life*, 44 (1918), 172–7 · *CGPLA Eng. & Wales* (1956) · Venn, *Alum. Cant.* · GEC, *Peerage*

Archives priv. coll., MSS | GL, Morgan Grenfell MSS · probably GL, Royal Exchange Assurance MSS · Morgan Grenfell Group, London, Morgan Grenfell MSS

Likenesses photograph, 1900–56, repro. in Leighton-Boyce, *Smiths, the bankers* (1958), facing p. 309 · W. Orpen, oils, 1919, Royal Exchange Assurance, London · W. Stoneman, photograph, 1938, NPG · W. Stoneman, photograph, 1947, NPG · J. Gunn, oils, *c.*1950, Morgan Grenfell Group, London; repro. in Burk, *Morgan Grenfell*, plate 13 · S. Elwes, group portrait, oils, 1955, Morgan Grenfell · A. Munnings, oils, priv. coll.

Wealth at death £212,277 6*s.* 3*d.*: probate, 20 June 1956, *CGPLA Eng. & Wales*

Smith, Walter (*fl.* **1525**), poet, is known only by his work *The Widow Edyth: Twelue Merry Gestys of One called Edyth, the Lyeng Wydow*, printed by John Rastell in 1525 (of which only fragments have survived), and reprinted by Richard Jones in 1573. This verse work relates the adventures of a confidence trickster named Edyth, daughter of one John Hankin, and the errant wife of one Thomas Elly, and who, as Rastell informs the reader, was still alive at the date of publication in 1525. Edyth's geography of fraud ranges from her birthplace, Exeter, to Canterbury and London, and encompasses the households of Sir Thomas Neville, the bishop of Rochester, the earl of Arundel, and Sir Thomas More, as well as various London tradesmen and the author himself. A Walter Smith graduated MA from Oxford University on 29 January 1512, but the identification with the poet is difficult to prove.

CATHY SHRANK

Sources W. C. Hazlitt, *Hand-book to the popular, poetical and dramatic literature of Great Britain* (1867) · W. T. Lowndes, *The bibliographer's manual of English literature*, ed. H. G. Bohn, [new edn], 6 vols. (1864) · J. Ames, T. F. Dibdin, and W. Herbert, eds., *Typographical antiquities, or, The history of printing in England, Scotland and Ireland*, 4 vols. (1810–19), vol. 4 · W. C. Hazlitt, *Collections and notes, 1867–1876* (1876) · J. P. Collier, ed., *A bibliographical and critical account of the rarest books in the English language*, 2 (1865) · Foster, *Alum. Oxon.*

Smith, Walter Campbell- (**1887–1988**), mineralogist and petrologist, was born on 30 November 1887 at 41 York Road, Edgbaston, Birmingham, the second son of George Hamilton Smith (1860–1929), paper merchant, and his wife, Charlotte Eliza (1859–1935), daughter of Henry William Ashford, chairmaker, of Birmingham and his wife, Charlotte. Known always as Campbell Smith, the hyphenated form of the name was formalized by deed poll in 1959.

After attending Solihull School (1895–1906), Campbell Smith entered Corpus Christi College, Cambridge, graduating with first-class honours (1910) and becoming Wiltshire prizeman in mineralogy in 1909. On 1 December 1910 he joined the mineralogy department at the British Museum (Natural History) initially to work on minerals but, with the arrival in 1913 of the geological specimens collected by the *Terra Nova* Antarctic Expedition, he was assigned to describe their physical properties. Thereafter he became first and foremost a petrologist.

In 1910 Campell Smith joined the Territorial Army (Artists' Rifles) and was mobilized on the declaration of war in 1914, serving throughout, mainly in France. In 1917 he was awarded the Military Cross for gallantry on the Blaireville–Ficheux front the previous year. He was demobilized on 11 April 1919 and was made a brevet lieutenant-colonel in 1935. He was later awarded the Territorial decoration.

Between the wars the British Colonial Geological Surveys were investigating the complex geology of Africa and Campbell Smith's help was sought in examining carbonate rocks collected by Frank Dixey from within igneous complexes in Nyasaland. From his microscopical observations Campbell Smith concluded, contrary to contemporary opinion, that these were igneous carbonatites rather than sedimentary limestones. He continued to develop his ideas as more occurrences were investigated and he chose carbonatites as the subject of his presidential address to the Geological Society in 1956. This, together with a similar review by Pecora in the USA, changed world opinion. Since that time many more carbonatites have been discovered and their economic potential has been increasingly exploited. In addition to his Antarctic and African work Campbell Smith wrote about one hundred articles on minerals, meteorites, and other petrological topics. He was also well known for his work on Neolithic jadeite implements and he was awarded the ScD degree in 1939.

On 24 June 1936 Campbell Smith married Susan Finnegan (1903–1995), a zoologist and the first woman to be appointed to the senior staff of the British Museum (Natural History). They had a son (*b.* 1938) who became vicar of Goudhurst, Kent, and an adopted daughter (*b.* 1942). Campbell Smith became deputy keeper of the mineralogy department on 1 April 1931 and keeper on 27 May 1937. He was appointed CBE in 1949 and retired on 30 November 1952.

Campbell Smith was president of the Geological Society (1955–6), secretary (1921–32), and Murchison medallist for 1945. He was president also of the Mineralogical Society (1945–8), general secretary (1927–38), foreign secretary (1959–67), managing trustee (1949–55), and four times a councillor. He contributed greatly to the founding of the International Mineralogical Association.

Slim and erect, Campbell-Smith was regarded highly by his scientific colleagues, his regimental association, and his many friends. The warmth of his personality was such that the word 'gentleman' most accurately describes him. The cordiality and affection of his home meant much to him, as did his personal faith; he was a lifelong member of the Anglican church. Campbell-Smith died of old age at his home, Roof Tops, Back Lane, Goudhurst, on 6 December 1988 and was cremated at Tunbridge Wells on 13 December. His long life and distinguished career were celebrated at a memorial service in the parish church at Goudhurst later that day. A. CLIVE BISHOP

Sources *WWW* · private information (2004) · NHM, archives · D. K. Bailey, 'Carbonate magmas', *Milestones in geology: reviews to celebrate 150 volumes of the Journal of the Geological Society*, ed. M. J. Le Bas (1995), 249–63 · M. J. Le Bas, introduction, *Milestones in geology: reviews to celebrate 150 volumes of the Journal of the Geological Society*, ed. M. J. Le Bas (1995), 3 · W. C. Smith, 'A review of some problems of African carbonatites', *Quarterly Journal of the Geological Society of London*, 112 (1956), 189–219 · P. Bury, *The college of Corpus Christi and of the Blessed Virgin Mary: a history from 1822 to 1952* (1995), 256 · *The Cambridge University list of members up to 31 December 1985* (1986) · membership lists, GS Lond. · membership lists, Mineralogical Society, London · b. cert. · d. cert.

Archives GS Lond., corresp. · NHM, diaries, letter-books, and papers

Wealth at death £16,068: probate, 8 June 1989, *CGPLA Eng. & Wales*

Smith, Walter Chalmers [*pseuds.* Orwell, Hermann Kunst] (**1824–1908**), United Free Church of Scotland minister and poet, was born in Aberdeen on 5 December 1824, son of Walter Smith, builder, and his wife, Barbara Milne. He was educated at the grammar school and at Marischal College, Aberdeen, where he graduated MA in 1841. Abandoning the idea of a career in law, he studied for the ministry of the Free Church of Scotland at New College, Edinburgh under Thomas Chalmers.

After a period as a probationer at Newburgh, Aberdeenshire, Smith was ordained minister of the Free (Scottish) Church in Chadwell Street, Pentonville, London, on 25 December 1850. The congregation did not prosper and Smith returned to Scotland to become minister of a church in Milnathort, in the parish of Orwell, Kinross-shire, in 1854. In 1853 he had married Agnes Monteith, with whom he had three daughters and a son. Smith was translated to Roxburgh Free Church, Edinburgh, in 1858, and in 1862 he succeeded Robert Buchanan as minister of the Free Tron Church, Glasgow. His final move was to the Free High Church, Edinburgh (1876), from which he retired in 1896.

As the representative of a liberalizing tendency which surfaced even in the Free Church, Smith found himself involved in a heresy case when several of his sermons appeared to impugn the authority of Old Testament law. He was 'affectionately admonished' (*DNB*) at the general assembly of 1867 but again ran into trouble over his relaxed view of elders' subscription to the confession of faith. Despite this, and his friendship and support for William Robertson Smith when the latter was attacked for his advanced views, he was judged orthodox enough to be entrusted with the moderatorship of the Free Church's jubilee assembly of 1893, in which role he distinguished himself. Smith was honoured with the degrees of DD from Glasgow University (1869) and LLD from Aberdeen (1876) and Edinburgh (1893) universities. As a poet, Smith used several pseudonyms, Orwell for *The Bishop's Walk* (1861) and Hermann Kunst for *Olrig Grange* (1872), one of his most popular works, as well as his own name. His verse was humorous and unpretentious, and allowed him to deal with religious issues better avoided in the pulpit. A complete edition of his poems appeared in 1902. Smith died at his home, Orwell Cottage, Kinbuck, Perthshire, on 19 September 1908 and was buried in Warriston cemetery, Edinburgh, on 23 September. An obituarist hailed him as 'almost the last of the great Free Church figures, and one of the most original and distinguished of Scottish divines' (*Scottish Review*, 24 Sept 1908).

T. F. HENDERSON, *rev.* LIONEL ALEXANDER RITCHIE

Sources *Glasgow Herald* (21 Sept 1908) · *The Scotsman* (21 Sept 1908) · *Scottish Review* (24 Sept 1908) · A. H. Miles, ed., *The poets and the poetry of the nineteenth century*, 12 (1907), 109–28 · *WWW, 1897–1915* · J. Julian, ed., *A dictionary of hymnology*, rev. edn (1907), 1064 · J. A. Lamb, ed., *The fasti of the United Free Church of Scotland, 1900–1929* (1956) · private information (1912) · *CCI* (1908)

Archives NL Scot., corresp. | NL Scot., letters and poems to J. S. Blackie

Likenesses G. Reid, oils, *c.*1894, Scot. NPG · portrait, repro. in W. C. Smith, *Sermons* (1909), frontispiece · portrait, repro. in *Glasgow Herald* · portrait, repro. in *Scottish Review*

Wealth at death £3090 10s. 3*d.*: confirmation, 20 Oct 1908, *CCI*

Smith, Wentworth (*bap.* **1571**), playwright, was baptized on 9 March 1571 in St James Garlickhythe, London, the son of William Smith. On 29 September 1594 he married Agnes Gymber (*d.* 1602) at St Thomas the Apostle, London; the bride was the daughter of Thomas Gymber of Monkleigh, Devon, where she had been baptized on 6 August 1568. By the time of his marriage Smith was working as a scrivener. On 12 February 1596 he wrote a power of attorney, given by William Kempe MA of Cambridge, to Sir Julius Caesar, master of requests (BL, Lansdowne Collection, Caesar MSS, Add. MS 12504, fol. 291), signing his name Wentwoorth Smith in an Italian hand.

In 1601 Smith began writing plays for Philip Henslowe, usually in collaboration with others. For the Admiral's Men between April 1601 and November 1602 he wrote *The Conquest of the West Indies* (with John Day and William Haughton), *1 Cardinal Wolsey* (with Henry Chettle, Michael Drayton, and Anthony Munday), *1 and 2 The Six Clothiers* (with Richard Hathway and Haughton), *Too Good to be True* (with Chettle and Hathway), *Love Parts Friendship* (with Chettle), and *Merry as May Be* (with Day and Hathway). For Worcester's men between September 1602 and March 1603 he wrote *Albere Galles* and *Marshal Osric* (with Thomas Heywood), *1 Lady Jane* (with Chettle, Dekker, Heywood, and John Webster), *1 and 2 The Black Dog of Newgate* and *The Unfortunate General* (with Day and Hathway), and *The Three Brothers* and *The Italian Tragedy* (alone).

None of these plays is definitely known to be extant, though some have been conjectured to be identical with extant plays on similar themes. Chambers conjectured that *Love Parts Friendship* may be the same as the anonymous *Trial of Chivalry* (printed 1605) and that *Marshal Osric* (written with Heywood) may be identical with *The Royal King and the Loyal Subject*, printed in 1637 with an attribution to Heywood. Chambers says that *1 Lady Jane* is 'doubtless' represented by *Sir Thomas Wyatt*, printed in 1607 with an attribution to Dekker and Webster. Even if any of these identifications are correct there is no way to reliably separate Smith's contributions from those of his collaborators. Wentworth Smith has often been supposed to be the W. Smith who wrote *The Hector of Germanie* (published 1615) but this play was actually written by the herald William Smith. He had also been supposed to be the W. S. who wrote *Locrine* (printed 1595), *Thomas Lord Cromwell* (1602), and *The Puritan* (1607), but these attributions are generally believed to have been aimed at Shakespeare by publishers trying to profit from his fame.

There is no further record of Smith's writing after 1603. He may have continued to write for Henslowe, who stopped recording payments to individual playwrights in that year; in 1605 he witnessed the will of fellow Henslowe playwright William Haughton. On 12 October 1602 Smith's first wife, Agnes, was buried in St Thomas the Apostle, and on 15 May 1607 he married Mary Poteman at St Mary Matfelon, Whitechapel. A daughter, Katherine, was baptized on 14 February 1607 and 'Wentford son of Wentford Smith' (apparently a double error for Wentworth) was baptized on 11 July 1610. The latter child was buried on 27 March 1614 at St Giles Cripplegate as 'Wentworth sonne of Wentworth Smith scrivner'. After this Smith disappears from the record. It is not known when or where he died and no will has been found.

DAVID KATHMAN

Sources E. K. Chambers, *The Elizabethan stage*, 4 vols. (1923), vol. 3, pp. 493–4 · M. Eccles, *Brief lives: Tudor and Stuart authors* (1982), 121 · *Henslowe's diary*, ed. R. A. Foakes and R. T. Rickert (1961) · D. Foster, *Elegy by W. S.: a study in attribution* (1989), 267 · B. Wagner, 'Elizabethan dramatists', *TLS* (28 Sept 1933), 651 · *IGI*

Smith [Smyth], **William** (*d.* 1514), bishop of Lincoln and a founder of Brasenose College, Oxford, was the fourth son of Robert Smyth of Peckhouse in Widnes, Prescot, Lancashire. He received schooling as a boy, but not, as was once thought, as a result of the patronage of Lady Margaret Beaufort, countess of Richmond and Derby, though by 1472 she was his near neighbour and, presumably as a result of this geographical connection, was to have a profound influence on his life. By 1478 he was at Oxford, perhaps residing in Brasenose Hall, or at Lincoln College. In any event, by 1476 he had become bachelor of canon law and, by 1492, of civil law. He was granted a papal dispensation for life to hold two incompatible benefices on 20 April 1476, but there are difficulties in discovering all his preferments, because there are so many clergy of the same name.

Ascent to eminence The accession of Henry VII in 1485 and the consequent rise to prominence of Lady Margaret Beaufort brought Smith and other trusted Lancastrian servants to immediate power. Among other benefices, Smith received, on 24 September 1485, the deanery of Wimborne, Dorset, where Lady Margaret's parents were buried; he was made a canon and prebendary of St Stephen's Chapel, Westminster, on 20 October following and became its dean in 1490; archdeaconries and lucrative churches were given to him and singled him out as a rising cleric. His ecclesiastical advancement in these years culminated in his being provided to the see of Coventry and Lichfield on 1 October 1492. The temporalities were restored on 29 January following, and he was consecrated by Archbishop Morton on 3 February. He was incorporated into the University of Cambridge in 1496, and was made chancellor of the University of Oxford in 1500. These honours were a recognition of the influence he enjoyed with Henry VII and Lady Margaret. He also became keeper of the hanaper of the chancery on 20 September 1485, with a substantial salary, and with a grant in 1486 for the custody of the daughters of Edward IV which he subsequently passed on to Lady Margaret, who was given the task of 'keeping and guiding of the ladies' (*DNB*).

It was a measure of the trust which Henry VII placed in Smith that in 1493 he was appointed a member of Prince Arthur's council in the marches of Wales. The prince largely resided at Tickenhall House, near Bewdley, and his council had the considerable responsibility for keeping order, not only in the principality, but also in the marcher lordships, some of which were in royal hands, but each of which had its own customs and traditions. Prince Arthur's council enjoyed a delegation of royal authority throughout Wales together with the responsibility for the counties of Shropshire, Worcestershire, Herefordshire, and Gloucestershire. This was the training ground of the heir to the throne. The borders of Smith's diocese and of Wales were in many places adjacent, and to preside in the former he could live at Pipe, near Lichfield, or at Bewdley, and still be within riding distance of Shrewsbury and Ludlow, where most of his work for the marches was concentrated.

Ecclesiastical and secular employments This did not, however, mean that Smith was not under considerable stress in balancing the demands on his time and his residence. As bishop, he was on the commission for the peace in Staffordshire, and was sufficiently involved to be mentioned in a case which came before the council sitting in Star Chamber. He took a very great interest in the monasteries of his diocese, and he is found regularly on the move; at the beginning of February 1493 he was in London for his consecration, but by the end of the same month he was at Coleshill in Warwickshire, and thereafter is found taking the Lenten ordinations at Tutbury—all this, despite the need to attend to the judicial functions of the council of Wales during law terms. But his diligence was marked by growing wealth which in turn revealed another side of his character. He was a philanthropist. In November 1495 he refounded the hospital of St John the Baptist, Lichfield, providing for almsmen who were to receive a residence, a garden, and 7*d.* a week. To this he added a school, complete with master and usher, for very poor children.

In that same month, on 5 November 1495, Smith was translated to the diocese of Lincoln, but was not permitted to resign from the council of the marches, nor from his care of Prince Arthur. Lady Margaret Beaufort was reported to have celebrated in style his elevation with a new year's day party in his honour. Smith was heavily involved with the prince: not only did he as chancellor introduce him to the University of Oxford in September

1501, but he also participated in the various ceremonies, both by proxy and in person, of his betrothal to Katherine of Aragon in October of the same year. His new see necessitated the purchase, in his own right, of a property on the border of Wales in order to conduct his affairs there, rather than from the nearest episcopal palace in the diocese of Lincoln, which was at Banbury. He therefore acquired an estate at St John's, Bedwardine, the birthplace of his friend and colleague in royal service, Sir Reginald Bray, and, more importantly, a crucial crossing place of the River Wye.

The pressures of office This purchase indicates how widespread Smith's responsibilities had become. In March 1500, while he was on his way to his belated installation as bishop and to visit his cathedral church in Lincoln, he was summoned to attend to business in Bewdley and his introduction to his diocese had to be postponed. He wrote during this time to Bray of his desire to get to grips with the diocese of Lincoln, where, he said, he had been 'but little' and he lamented his failure to supervise rectories where the incumbent was not resident and to require the provision of a curate and hospitality. He wrote:

> Great places of religion both of the king's foundation and others must be visited, for they be sore decayed in divine service and other things, and all the parsons and vicars for the most part be absent and let down [allow to decay] their mansions and their chancels. (Westminster Abbey Muniments, no. 16038)

Smith did manage eventually, in 1501, to visit his cathedral church, as well as the University of Oxford, and additionally made all the necessary arrangements for entertaining Lady Margaret during the summer at his manor at Buckden, Huntingdonshire. Not surprisingly, he shared with Bray the considerable physical strain he was under; he explained:

> now in myself being old and full of sickness and aches in my bones … [I] cannot do such service to the king's grace as I could if I were able and in good health, and the special cause of this difficulty goes with my absence [from my diocese] and it runneth in my mind both day and night and I cannot take no rest. (ibid.)

The stresses and strains were to culminate in April 1502 with the death of Prince Arthur. Smith had a leading part to play in the funeral rites, which lasted from 23 April for four whole days, as the hearse made its way from Ludlow to Bewdley and on to Worcester. After the death of the prince, the whole responsibility for the exercise of royal power in Wales devolved on the lord president, a post which Smith held from August 1502 probably until his death (he may have resigned in 1512). His proven experience and skill were more important to his royal master than his mental and physical anguish.

Bishop of Lincoln After the death of Prince Arthur, Smith concentrated his energies on the presidency, on the diocese of Lincoln, and on the court. By August 1502 he had ceased to be chancellor of Oxford, and he became increasingly concerned with affairs of state: with the consecration, for instance, of William Warham, as bishop of London; with arranging for the appropriate treatment of those involved in the forgery of a bull of the bishop of St David's; and with presiding over the delegation of authority in his diocese of Lincoln. For this purpose he used servants whom he had learnt to trust. His first vicar-general, his *alter ego* in his diocese, was James Whitstones, who was also a canon lawyer and was president of Lady Margaret's council. Whitstones was succeeded by Charles Booth, who had also been on Prince Arthur's council with Smith, and who became chancellor of the marches of Wales in 1502. The fact that the bishop and his deputy were both involved in the diocese of Lincoln and the marches of Wales meant that they could alternate their residence and responsibility. At any rate, they were good friends and among Smith's bequests was a cup of silver and gilt given him as a present by Booth.

Smith's work at Lincoln was primarily that of an organizer and co-ordinator of others. He resided in, and greatly improved, his episcopal residences: the palace at Liddington was extended by him and bears his coat of arms in its windows. He liked to visit Banbury, and Buckden was a useful staging post when he was required to go to London. Only small fragments remain to suggest his activity and the energy which was required of him. A book of costs for 1508 reports that his leggings were bound for him at London. Thereafter he was at Banbury to see his auditor, his servants, and his barber, but within four days he was off into his diocese on further business. What this business was is largely unknown. Only fragmentary visitation and court proceedings survive for his episcopate, but he certainly visited the monastic house of Osney, and citations survive to suggest he visited other houses as well. Not only did he visit his cathedral church in person in 1501, 1503, 1507, and 1510, but he also, and unusually, visited the collegiate church of St Mary-in-the-Newarke at Leicester in September 1510, together with all its surrounding deaneries.

In Leicester Bishop Smith found the usual state of affairs: some lax lay morality and a neglect of fabric and cemeteries, but nothing as depressing as he had described in his letter to Bray. His cathedral church was altogether different: neither he nor his successors could prevent the residentiary canons squeezing the last drop from the shrinking funds of the cathedral, and its lower clergy persistently refused to improve their learning or, in many cases, their singing, preferring to take target practice at the expense of the windows of the cathedral or to vie with each other at cards or at dice, or to out-drink one another or dally with ladies of the town. Smith was not alone in his despair; his successors shared it.

Smith was one of those bishops described by the protestant Hugh Latimer as 'unpreaching prelates' (*Sermons*, 67), and certainly no sermons of his survive. The martyrologist John Foxe, who was to benefit from Smith's generosity to the University of Oxford, thought him lenient with the Buckinghamshire Lollards, but a number were compelled to wear the faggot as a token of their former errors. A few were burnt, though it must be said that some of those whom Smith pardoned were to be accused again and found guilty by his successor, Bishop John Longland.

The foundation of Brasenose College By 1507, when the fate of the Buckinghamshire Lollards was in question, Smith was turning his mind to other responsibilities; he was planning precisely how he would use his considerable wealth to build institutions which would outlast him and in which he would be remembered. In 1507 he had made provision for a master at Farnworth School in Lancashire, but he was also beginning to work with Richard Sutton, a lawyer with whom he is likely to have been long acquainted, towards the founding of a college in Oxford. At first it was not clear whether he would augment an existing foundation—he gave money to Oriel College and manors to Lincoln College. But by 1 June 1509 work had begun on a new college, on the site of Brasenose Hall and incorporating surrounding properties. Smith intended to benefit the secular clergy, and especially those from the north of England: the twelve fellows of the college were to have been born in the diocese of Coventry and Lichfield, or to have come from Lancashire, if possible from his birthplace of Prescot. All were to be in holy orders, but none were to be religious; Smith's experience of visiting religious communities in both his dioceses convinced him that they were past reformation.

Smith gave to Brasenose the lands of Cold Norton, which were to be valued in 1536 as the college's most lucrative rents. But it would appear that he and Sutton were not totally in accord about the purposes of the foundation. It may be that they were not agreed about the place of the religious in the new college, or it may be simply that Smith died too soon to make a personal mark on their foundation. At any rate Smith's statutes were revised, and he was not commemorated in the style worthy of a benefactor until after Sutton's death. Whatever the disagreements may have been, Brasenose received from Smith a considerable legacy of lands, plate, vestments, manuscripts, and books, though the latter may not have reached the intended recipients, possibly because of the intervention of Cardinal Wolsey.

Friends and relatives On his death, which took place on 2 January 1514 at his manor in Buckden, Smith left behind him a number of relatives whom he had appointed to lucrative benefices in the diocese of Lincoln. It was said that the diocese was peopled with persons named William Smyth, and certainly one such, who was a relative, held the archdeaconry of Northampton and subsequently that of Lincoln; he died after the bishop and made substantial bequests to Brasenose. Another William Smyth was early appointed to the bishop's hospital at Lichfield, and the bishop's use of Brasenose Hall as the basis for his college may not be unconnected with the fact that the last principal of the hall was Matthew Smyth. Later generations have berated nepotism. With Smith it was in part one of the ways in which he survived; he surrounded himself with some relatives, but, more importantly, with a group of friends whom he could trust absolutely, in just the same way as he had himself been trusted by Henry VII and Lady Margaret Beaufort. The latter was said to have been a close personal friend and one of her service books (kept in her inner chamber) was given to Smith, the other to Henry VIII. Smith's endowment of learning may have derived its inspiration from her. His loyalty to her and to Henry VII resulted in Smith's protection from fines incurred in the last years of Henry VII's reign.

Smith signed his letter to Reginald Bray 'your old loving friend', and quite apart from the friends he used as vicars-general in his diocese, most of his contemporaries on the episcopal bench were also his friends, notably Hugh Oldham of Exeter and Richard Fox of Durham and subsequently Winchester. He did not share Fox's enthusiasm for humanist studies, and his college was to promote learning of an older kind. But even if the students of Corpus Christi and Brasenose were literally to fight in Oxford for different approaches to learning, the ideas of their benefactors were at one on an all-important particular: learning must be promoted. Equally, though Smith may have learnt much of his skilful administration from Reginald Bray, so Bray and his successors, notably Thomas Cromwell, learned many of their skills from the well-tried practices of the church. This happened because the most senior churchmen and the most trusted royal servants were from a small group who were mainly friends and sometimes relatives.

How necessary friends were is illustrated by two curious incidents. In 1505 Smith was found guilty by commissioners of sewers at Newark of erecting weirs and mills on the Trent, thereby impeding navigation. He was fined, but the fine was remitted by the king a year later. Such royal protection was tested again when he was accused of having paid gold to a foreigner and was fined heavily. Smith began to pay, but Henry VII's executors repaid the sum. Subsequently he took the precaution of protecting himself against jealous civil servants and a new monarch by procuring in 1509 a general pardon for every conceivable offence which he might have committed in the course of his busy life.

Achievement On his death Smith left most of his lands and wealth to charitable purposes. In addition to his bequests to Brasenose, he made provision for a hospital at Banbury. His extensive collection of vestments and plate was shared between Brasenose and Lincoln Cathedral, where he was to be buried. His wish was to lie beside Bishop William Alnwick, and he left money for a priest to sing for his soul in the chapel of St Sebastian, which was the nearest to his grave. The original inscription on it was removed with the reflooring of the cathedral and a later one now commemorates him. The portrait of him in Brasenose is of a deeply serious man. In a certain sense his was a life which seemed to give the late medieval church a bad name in the eyes of protestant reformers. Apparently not a teacher or preacher, and only at times resident in his diocese, he was a mighty and wealthy prelate who appeared to put Mammon before God. Nevertheless, his sheer hard work, his generosity, and the anguish of his letter to Bray tell a different story: one of little rest or peace and ceaseless devotion to the Tudors, to their government, to the church, and above all to learning, and all of it with the awareness which he expressed to Bray that he was there 'to preach and teach Christ's Gospel' (Westminster Abbey Muniments, no. 16038). MARGARET BOWKER

Sources *DNB* • Emden, *Oxf.*, 3.1721–2 • R. Churton, *Lives of William Smyth, bishop of Lincoln, and Sir Richard Sutton, founders of Brase Nose College Oxford* (1800) • M. Bowker, *The secular clergy in the diocese of Lincoln* (1968) • M. Bowker, 'Historical survey, 1450–1750', *A history of Lincoln Minster*, ed. D. Owen (1994), 164–209 • R. A. Griffiths, *King and country: England and Wales in the fifteenth century* (1991) • M. K. Jones and M. G. Underwood, *The king's mother: Lady Margaret Beaufort, countess of Richmond and Derby* (1992) • [F. Madan], ed., *Brasenose College quatercentenary monographs*, 2/1, OHS, 53 (1909) • C. A. J. Steel, *The council in the marches of Wales* (1904) • H. Anstey, ed., *Epistolae academicae Oxon.*, 2 vols., OHS, 35–6 (1898) • Bishop Smith's register, no. XIII, Lichfield Diocesan Registry • Bishop Smith's registers, nos. 23 and 24; accounts; visitations, Lincs. Arch., Episcopal MSS, bps accts. misc. 6–12, 18; Vj.5 and 6, Viv.6 • Lincs. Arch., dean and chapter MSS, A.3.2., A.3.3 • will, PRO, PROB 11/26, sig. 16 • letter of Bishop Smith to Reginald Bray, Westminster Abbey Muniment Room, London, no. 16038 • I. S. Leadam, ed., *Select cases before the king's council in the star chamber, commonly called the court of star chamber*, SeldS, 16 (1903), • J. Gairdner, ed., *Letters and papers illustrative of the reigns of Richard III and Henry VII*, 2 vols., Rolls Series, 24 (1861–3) • *Sermons by Hugh Latimer*, ed. G. E. Corrie, Parker Society, 16 (1844)

Archives Brasenose College, Oxford, personal collection of MSS of medieval authors • Westminster Abbey Muniment Room, London, letters in his own hand, no. 16038

Likenesses brass effigy, Lincoln Cathedral • portrait, Brasenose College, Oxford

Wealth at death wealthy: will, PRO, PROB 11/26, sig. 16

Smith, William (*c*.1550–1618), herald and playwright, was born in Oldhaugh, Cheshire, one of the nine children of Randall Smith (*d*. 1584) of Oldhaugh and his first wife, Jane (*d*. 1562), daughter of Ralph Bostock of Norcroft, Cheshire. Anthony Wood supposed that Smith attended Oxford or Cambridge, but in fact he was apprenticed as a haberdasher and received his freedom in either 1572 or 1575. In the latter year he described himself as 'citezen and haberdasher of London' (Guildhall Library, London, MS 2463), and Noble says (apparently relying on the early eighteenth-century testimony of John Anstis) that Smith had been a 'merchant and traveller' before becoming a herald (Noble, 217).

While still in his teens Smith evinced an interest in topography, visiting Bristol in July 1568 and taking measurements of the town, which he later included in his 'Particuler description of England'. In 1575 he wrote his earliest known work, 'A breffe discription of the royall citie of London' (Guildhall MS 2463). This vividly written work, revised in 1588, contains a detailed description of the ceremonies surrounding the installation of the lord mayor, illustrating Smith's lifelong interest in pageantry, heraldry, and the London livery companies.

Within a few years Smith had moved to Nuremberg, Germany, where (according to Anstis) he kept an inn with the sign of the goose. Probably about 1580 he married Veronica Altensteig, daughter of Francis Altensteig of Nuremberg; the couple quickly had two children, William (1581–1603) and Jane (*b*. 1583). While in Nuremberg Smith wrote 'Genealogical tables of the kings of England and Scotland, and sovereigns of Europe, to the years 1578–9, with their arms in colours' (Bodl. Oxf., MS Rawl. B. 141), which he followed in 1584 with a similar work listing the arms of all English noblemen since William the Conqueror (BL, Harley MS 6099). In Nuremberg Smith also wrote a Latin description of England, dated 26 April 1580 and dedicated to Christopher Fhurer, a leading figure in the city (BL, Add. MS 10620), and an English treatise, 'How Germany is devyded into 10 Kreises', which the title-page declares was 'Written in Nurmberg, the 20 Decemb. 1582' (BL, Harley MS 994).

After his father's death in 1584 Smith returned to England, at least temporarily. He was in Chester in September 1585 drawing views of the town, but that same year he still described himself as a 'citezen of Noremberg' (Bodl. Oxf., MS Rawl. B. 282). Between 1585 and 1588 he wrote several works on the history and topography of Cheshire, one of which was published posthumously by Daniel King in 1656, along with a similar work by William Webb, as *The Vale Royall of England, or Countie Palatine of Chester*. Smith wrote several other heraldic and topographical works during this time, including the vivid and witty 'Particuler description of England' (1588; published 1879). Meanwhile his family was growing, with the addition of Frances (*b*. 1586), Paul (*b*. 1588), and Hester (*b*. 1590). He was permanently back in England by 1591, when he described himself as 'of London' (Coll. Arms, MS 42/P.b.).

By about 1595 Smith was actively campaigning for a position in the College of Arms. Between 1594 and 1597 he compiled a useful 'Alphabeth or blason of armes' (Washington, DC, Folger Shakespeare Library, Folger MS V.b.217), and about the same time wrote 'A breef description of the famous Cittie of Norenberg in High Germany' (LPL, MS 508), with separate dedicatory epistles to Sir George Carey, to Edward, eleventh Baron Zouche, and to William Cecil, Lord Burghley. In 1597 Smith was finally admitted as Rouge Dragon pursuivant on the recommendation of Carey, after the College of Arms found that he was 'honest, and of a quiet conversation, and well-languaged' (Noble, 218).

Smith was prolific in his first years as a herald, transcribing and supplementing several visitations and compiling many heraldic works of his own. However, he also displayed bitterness and a sharp tongue. In 1605 he presented the earl of Northampton with a pamphlet entitled 'A brieff discourse of the causes of discord amongst the officers of armes' (Washington, DC, Folger Shakespeare Library, Folger MS V.a.157), in which he complained caustically of the ignorance of his fellow heralds and of freelance arms painters. That same year he compiled the arms of all the lord mayors of London in 'The XII worshipfull companies, or misteries of London' (Bodl. Oxf., MS top. gen. e.29), dedicated to the then lord mayor, Sir Thomas Low. At the end of this manuscript is a short poem by Smith, in both Latin and English.

In 1613 Smith wrote a historical play called *The Hector of Germanie, or, The Palsgrave Prime Elector*, in honour of the marriage of Princess Elizabeth and Friedrich, elector palatine. It was published in 1615 with an attribution to W. Smith and a declaration that it had been 'publickly

Acted at the Red-Bull, and at the Curtayne, by a Company of Young-men of this Citie' (sig. A1r). Since the late nineteenth century, this play has usually been attributed to the Elizabethan playwright Wentworth *Smith, but the circumstantial evidence for William Smith's authorship is overwhelming. The dedication to Sir John Swinnerton, lord mayor in 1613, says that the play was 'made for Citizens, who acted it well' and also mentions a previous play by the author, *The Freeman's Honour*, 'acted by the Now-servants of the Kings Majestie, to dignifie the worthy Companie of the Marchantaylors' (sig. A2r). Smith had apparently been familiar with the King's Men for some time, since his 'Brieff discourse' in 1605 mentions two members of that company, Augustine Phillips and Thomas Pope.

Warburton's list of lost play manuscripts includes 'St. George for England by Will. Smithe' (Bentley, 5.1178). The title is suggestive of a manuscript of Smith's called 'Orders for the feast of St. George' (Bodl. Oxf., MS Gough Berks. 12) about the annual ceremonies for the Order of the Garter, which are also depicted in *The Hector of Germanie*. Smith died on 1 October 1618 and was buried in the churchyard of St Alfege, London; no will has been found.

DAVID KATHMAN

Sources H. B. Wheatley and E. W. Ashbee, introduction, in *The particular description of England, 1588, with views of some of the chief towns and armorial bearings of nobles and bishops, by William Smith, Rouge Dragon* (1879), v–xv • M. Noble, *A history of the College of Arms* (1805) • Wood, *Ath. Oxon.*, 2nd edn • G. J. Armitage and J. P. Rylands, *Pedigrees made at the visitation of Cheshire, 1613*, Harleian Society, 59 (1909) • J. Hunter, 'Chorus vatum Anglicanorum', *c.*1842, BL, Add. MSS 24487–24492 • G. E. Bentley, *The Jacobean and Caroline stage*, 7 vols. (1941–68) • L. W. Payne, introduction, in W. Smith, *The Hector of Germanie, or, The Palsgrave prime elector* (1906), 7–60 • W. H. Godfrey, A. Wagner, and H. Stanford London, *The College of Arms, Queen Victoria Street* (1963), 220–21 • *DNB*

Archives BL, papers, Sloane MS 2596; Add. MSS 10620, 27438 • Bodl. Oxf., papers • Folger, peerage arms • GL, brief description of City of London and coats of arms of City officers • LPL, papers • NL Scot., genealogies • Norfolk RO, copy of Robert Glover's visitation of Staffordshire with additions by Smith • S. Antiquaries, Lond., heraldic drawings • Wirral Archives, copies of Glover's visitation of Cheshire

Likenesses W. Smith, self-portrait, BL • W. Smith, self-portrait, Folger, Folger MS V.b.217

Smith, William (*fl.* 1596), poet, dedicated to Edmund Spenser a sequence of sonnets, entitled *Chloris, or, The Complaint of the Passionate Despised Shepheard* (1596). *Chloris*, entered in the Stationers' register to Edmond Bolifant on 5 October 1596, opens with two sonnets addressed to Spenser as 'the most excellent and learned shepheard, Collin Cloute' and a third 'To all Shepheards'; all three are signed W. Smith. Smith concludes in Sonnet 50 with an acknowledgement to Spenser as the patron of his 'maiden verse'. Sonnet 13 of *Chloris* was later reprinted in *Englands Helicon* (1600, 1614) under the title 'Corins Dreame of the Faire Chloris'. Few copies of *Chloris* have survived. One copy preserved in the Bodleian Library was reprinted in Alexander Grosart's *Occasional Issues*, volume 14 (1877); another copy in the Huth Collection, British Library, formerly belonged to Narcissus Luttrell and to Thomas Park. This copy was reprinted in Edward Arber's *An English Garner*, volume 8 (1896).

Smith has also been identified as the author of 'A New Yeares Guifte' and 'A Posie Made upon Certen Flowers', dedicated to Mary Sidney Herbert, countess of Pembroke. In his dedication the author says that his muse

> presumes to offer you,
> although unknowen, yet dutious love, and trewe.

The manuscript (BL, Add. MS 35186) formerly belonged to Richard Heber (sale catalogue 1836, lot 1442) and has been printed along with *Chloris* in *Poems of William Smith*, edited by Lawrence A. Sasek (1970). The author of *Chloris* has also been identified as the 'William Smythe' who wrote 'What time all creatures did by joint consent', an untitled 396-line verse allegory of time in the Osborn Collection, Yale University Library. According to Kent Talbot van den Berg, this manuscript is written in the same hand as that of BL, Add. MS 35186. The author of the Osborn manuscript identifies himself as

> your Ladyshippes
> devoted servante as a stranger
> William Smythe.

This reference to himself as a 'stranger', or foreigner, may indicate that he is not the author of *Chloris* but the William Smith who wrote topographical poems and returned to England in 1591 after twenty years in Nuremberg, Germany.

Numerous poems signed 'W. S.' have been attributed to the author of *Chloris* solely on the basis of initials; these include 'A Notable Description of the World' signed 'W. S., Gent.' in *The Phoenix Nest*, commendatory verses for Nicholas Breton's *The Wil of Wit, Wits will, or, Wil's Wit, Chuse you whether* (1597), and 'My Thoughts are Winged with Hopes' in John Dowland's *The First Booke of Songes or Ayres of Fowre Partes with Tableture* (1597). Plays signed 'W. Smith' have also been attributed to the author of *Chloris*, but these were the work of Wentworth Smith. There is no evidence that 'Sonnets by W. S.', entered in the Stationers' register on 3 January 1600, was related either to the author of *Chloris* or to Shakespeare.

JEAN R. BRINK

Sources *The poems of William Smith*, ed. L. A. Sasek (1970) • 'An Elizabethen allegory of time by William Smith', ed. K. Talbot van den Berg, *English Literary Renaissance*, 6 (1976), 40–59 • L. Celovsku, 'William Smith', *Sixteenth-century British nondramatic writers: second series*, ed. D. A. Richardson, DLitB, 136 (1994), 321–5 • A. B. Grosart, ed., 'Introduction to *Chloris*', *Occasional Issues*, 14 (1877), v–x • A. Rollins, ed., *Phoenix nest* (1931), xix • A. Rollins, ed., *Englands Helicon* (1935), vols. 1–2 • E. Arber, ed., *An English garner* (1896), vol. 8 • *DNB*

Smith, William (*d.* 1673), religious writer, was born in Besthorpe, Nottinghamshire, where he lived for most of his life. Little is known of his parentage and background except that he was 'a man of good esteem in his country, and educated after the manner of the better sort of yeomens' sons' ('Several testimonies'). He served for several years as chief constable of his hundred and became an Independent pastor before joining the Quakers in 1658.

Smith suffered frequent periods of imprisonment, during which time he penned many of his large output of tracts, which number well over fifty. In 1658 he was gaoled for nine weeks for non-payment of tithes. Towards the end of the 1650s he wrote several tracts urging people to change their ways and turn to the light, such as *The Day Sprung from on High* (1659), which is apocalyptic in tone. Another tract deals, among other issues, with the Quaker rejection of social customs such as hat-honour, bowing, and the use of 'thee' and 'thou', Smith stating that Quakers 'cannot respect persons, of what quality so ever they may be reputed; because they that respect persons commit sin' (W. Smith, *The True Light Shining in England*, 1660, 21). At the Restoration, he wrote 'An Alarm beat in the holy mountain', an address to Charles II, which is printed in *The Copies of Several Letters which were Delivered to the King* (1660). In this Smith writes that the king must 'break off the bonds of oppression … undo all heavy burdens which tender consciences cannot bear; give true freedom in the practice of religion' (p. 42).

Smith was arrested, along with many others, in March 1661 for being at a meeting at Worcester, and was kept in prison for some time for refusing the oath of allegiance. He wrote at least five of his books at this time and others were completed while in Nottingham gaol, where he was confined on many occasions between 1661 and 1665. In 1663 he was imprisoned for non-payment of tithes and gives an account of his incarceration in *The Standing Truth* (1663). Of interest are a number of catechisms written in the 1660s which were reprinted later in the decade, including *A New Primmer* (1663) and *A New Catechism* (1664), the latter dealing with central Quaker religious tenets such as the notion of perfection, and the nature of the inner light and its relation to the incarnate Christ. In 1663, during the time of persecution, Smith produced *Liberty of Conscience*, in which he again urged Charles II to keep his promise of liberty of conscience, going on to stress the peaceable nature of Quakerism. In his tract *Universal Love* (1664), Smith writes that God has ordered everyone in his place, and goes on to give advice to various groups, including servants, masters, and parents, on how to conduct themselves.

On 11 March 1666 Smith married his second wife, Elizabeth Newton of Nottingham, who described her husband as 'a man of a meek spirit, loving peace and quietness, yet bold in the truth and power of God' (E. Smith). She noted that he had had six children with his first wife, named Ann (*d.* 1659), and implies that she and William also had children following their marriage.

In the 1670s Smith went on to write a few more tracts, such as *The Baptists Sophistry Discovered* (1672–3), a defence of Quaker tenets, and his collected works were published in 1675 as *Balm from Gilead*, at the front of which are many testimonies from contemporaries, written after his death. Ellis Hookes, recording clerk of the society, wrote the epistle dedicatory, in which he suggests that Smith's work 'shall speak forth his praise to generations', for he was possessed of 'a spirit of true wisdom and understanding'.

Smith died at Besthorpe, Nottinghamshire, on 9 January 1673 following a fever, and was buried there in his own garden. CAROLINE L. LEACHMAN

Sources 'Several testimonies concerning William Smith', W. Smith, *Balm from Gilead: a collection of the living divine testimonies* (1675) • E. Hookes, 'Epistle dedicatory', in W. Smith, *Balm from Gilead: a collection of the living divine testimonies* (1675) • J. Besse, *A collection of the sufferings of the people called Quakers*, 1 (1753) • J. Smith, ed., *A descriptive catalogue of Friends' books*, 2 (1867) • *The journal of George Fox*, ed. N. Penney, 2 (1911) • digest registers of births, marriages, and burials, RS Friends, Lond. • *DNB*

Smith, William (*d.* 1695), actor and theatre manager, was born in Greenwich according to his will. The anonymous *History of the English Stage* (1741) states that he was a barrister at Gray's Inn before he joined the Duke's Company at Lincoln's Inn Fields in 1661, which implies a birth date in the mid- to later 1630s. Nothing else is known of his background, but later commentators stressed the fact that he was a gentleman. His first recorded appearance, in the important role of Antonio in Webster's *Duchess of Malfi* (1614), took place on 30 September 1662.

More than eighty parts can be identified for Smith over the thirty-four years he was active, and since performance records are radically incomplete before the establishment of daily newspapers in London the actual total would have been substantially higher. Most of Smith's roles in his first years were in serious or semi-serious plays: Corrigidor in Sir Samuel Tuke's *Adventures of Five Hours* (1663), Lugo in Stapylton's *Slighted Maid* (1663), Buckingham in Shakespeare and Fletcher's *Henry VIII* (1613), Burgundy in the earl of Orrery's *Henry the Fifth* (1664), Polynices in Davenant's *Rivals* (1664), Banquo in the Davenant adaptation of *Macbeth* (1664), and Zanger in Orrery's *Mustapha* (1665)—a part in which he is highly praised by Pepys on 11 February 1668. The one early role that anticipates his principal line as an actor is Colonel Bruce in George Etherege's first play, *The Comical Revenge* (1664), where he played a handsome, spirited (and in this case honourable) hero.

Plague closed the theatres from June 1665 to the autumn of 1666. The only trace of Smith's activities in this period is unfortunate: on 14 November 1666 Pepys records that the actress Mrs Knipp told him

> how Smith of the Duke's house hath killed a man upon a quarrel in play—which makes everybody sorry, he being a good actor, and they say a good man, however this happens. The ladies of the Court do much bemoan him, she says. (Pepys, 7.369)

In some unknown fashion Smith got off. Downes recalled his merit as Sir William Stanly in John Caryll's *The English Princess*, which Pepys saw on 7 March 1667. Smith played a steady succession of major roles, moving with the Duke's Company to its fancy new Dorset Garden theatre in November 1671.

Smith occasionally took the part of a compromised hero in tragedy—he created Pierre in Otway's *Venice Preserv'd* (1682)—but his great talent was for dashing heroes in comedy, some of them noble and strictly honourable, others sex-mad scamps. In the former category fall such characters as Courtall in Etherege's *She wou'd if she cou'd* (1668), Standford in Shadwell's *Sullen Lovers* (1668), Colonel Bruce in Shadwell's *The Virtuoso* (1676), and Truman in Otway's *Friendship in Fashion* (1678). In the latter category fall Woodly in Shadwell's *Epsom-Wells* (1672), Willmore in

Aphra Behn's *The Rover* (part 1, 1677; part 2, 1681), Rashly in D'Urfey's *Fond Husband* (1677), Courtine in Otway's *The Souldiers Fortune* (1680) and *The Atheist* (1683), and the much-interrupted Ramble in Edward Ravenscroft's *The London Cuckolds* (1681). Sir Fopling Flutter in Etherege's *Man of Mode* (1676) was rather out of his metier, a casting that implies a less effeminate character than some later interpretations of that glamorous if ridiculous fop. Smith took some heroic roles (Muly Hamet in Elkanah Settle's *The Empress of Morocco*, Hector in Dryden's *Troilus and Cressida* in 1679, Chamont in Otway's *The Orphan* in 1680), but this was a secondary line.

Following the death of Sir William Davenant in 1668, operational control of the Duke's Company was assumed by two senior actors, Thomas Betterton and Henry Harris. Between 1677 and 1681, as Harris gradually relinquished his roles and managerial duties, Smith succeeded him as co-manager. The records give no clue as to how he and Betterton divided responsibilities, but for the better part of a decade Smith reigned jointly over a prosperous business. Even before entering the management he was a crucial actor, his place in the company indicated by his ownership of one and a half acting shares (of a total of eighteen) as early as 1674. With Betterton and Charles Davenant (Sir William's heir), Smith represented the Duke's Company in a secret agreement signed on 14 October 1681 with Charles Hart and Edward Kynaston, leading actors of the King's Company. Its purpose was to guarantee their employment if they subverted their moribund company's interests and promoted a union with their far healthier rivals. Smith the manager is much recorded during 1682, signing the union agreement of 4 May, the June lease of the Drury Lane theatre, and a new ground-rent agreement on that theatre. He also spoke Dryden's 'Prologue to his Royal Highness' when the duke of York first attended the theatre after his time in Scotland (21 April 1682).

Within two seasons many of the oldest generation of actors retired, leaving behind successful new works from the King's Company's heyday and their vast collection of pre-1642 plays. From November 1682 until the actors' rebellion of 1694, the possibilities for revivals from this trove led to a very conservative repertory policy, and the United Company staged very few new scripts. Documentation is extremely thin during the 1680s, but Smith played Don Leon in a revival of Fletcher's *Rule a Wife* (1624), Cassius in Shakespeare's *Julius Caesar* (1599), Constantine in Lee's *Constantine the Great* (1683), Lorenzo in Southerne's *Disappointment* (1684), Maximus in Rochester's *Valentinian* (1684), and Armusia in Tate's adaptation of *The Island Princess* (1687). Though some scholars have questioned how active Smith was as co-manager, according to figures complied for a chancery suit he was consistently paid a noticeable fee for those services. Fellow shareholders, always quick to contest their profits, seem unlikely to have granted him a sinecure. Changes in management came from another direction: on 30 August 1687 Charles Davenant sold his interest in the United Company to his brother Alexander, who in November replaced Betterton and Smith with another of the Davenant brothers, the 23-year-old Thomas.

For a year Smith continued as a senior sharing actor, then took a leave for extra-theatrical reasons. Cibber in his *Apology* (1740) and Edward Chetwood in his *General History of the Stage* of 1749 relate stories that show a strong political commitment causing Smith trouble. Cibber makes him an example of the mistreatment of actors by cabals, one of which he claims forced Smith's retirement about 1684 or 1685. Those dates cannot be accurate, but if James II was the king who, according to Cibber, dismissed a courtier for abusing Smith, broader hostilities might have fed a cabal against him. After 1683 Smith did cease to speak new prologues, though not to perform or manage. In his will, dated 19 November 1688, he explained that despite 'a fitt of the stone and strangurie', he was about to enter the army in the service of King James II 'at his own expence' (Highfill, Burnim & Langhans, *BDA*, 14.171, 173). He survived this quixotic choice, but Chetwood, in whose view he was '*zealously* attach'd' to the Jacobite interest, claims that when Smith returned (in 1689 or 1690), the audience refused to accept him back (ibid., 14.170). These late stories are unverifiable, but whether or not a specific confrontation occurred after the revolution of 1688, Smith's presence is recorded only in two hard-to-date manuscript casts, and at an unknown point after 1688 he took the £100 severance payment he was owed by long-standing policy, and retired.

Management of the theatre shifted in 1694 to the lawyer Christopher Rich and the dilettante Sir Thomas Skipwith, whose money had purchased the shares Alexander Davenant temporarily controlled. In December, when most of the senior actors in the United Company joined in the 'petition of the players' to the lord chamberlain against the new patentees, Smith was named as a possible arbitrator. His sympathies, however, were with his old mates, and at the end of April 1695, when 'Betterton's Company' opened at the reconverted Lincoln's Inn Fields Theatre, Smith came out of retirement to become a sharer and principal actor. He took the part of Scandal in Congreve's *Love for Love*, their first offering. Just eight months later, while playing Cyaxares in Banks's *Cyrus the Great*, he fell violently ill; by 26 December he was dead. His will shows him as a generous friend and relative and as a decidedly prosperous actor; thirty-six specific bequests total more than £5300, a very considerable sum at the time.

Although William Smith was an important actor and a powerful figure in the Duke's and United companies, his personal life remains extremely shadowy. He left a son, apparently born about 1684, but nothing is known of his marriage beyond the fact that his wife was alive at the time he made his will in November 1688. A reference there to his 'Mother' Orme may be either to a mother-in-law or to a stepmother. A mysterious £50 bequest to a young man whose name the executors would find in a sealed trunk suggests the recipient was an illegitimate son. Betterton, with whom he had worked in tandem as actor and manager, is described in the will as his 'friend and oldest acquaintance' (Highfill, Burnim & Langhans, *BDA*, 14.172).

Smith had appeared most often as the protagonist's 'friend', but if he played second fiddle to Betterton, he did so with great success, and his sudden death in 1695 was a serious blow to the rebel actors' co-operative.

JUDITH MILHOUS

Sources J. Milhous and R. D. Hume, eds., *A register of English theatrical documents, 1660–1737*, 2 vols. (1991) • W. Van Lennep and others, eds., *The London stage, 1660–1800*, pt 1: *1660–1700* (1965) • J. Milhous, 'United Company finances, 1682–1692', *Theatre Research International*, 7 (1981–2), 37–53 • Highfill, Burnim & Langhans, *BDA*, vol. 14 • L. Hotson, *The Commonwealth and Restoration stage* (1928); repr. (New York, 1962) • C. Cibber, *An apology for the life of Mr. Colley Cibber* (1740) • J. Downes, *Roscius Anglicanus, or, An historical review of the stage* (1708) • T. Betterton, [W. Oldys and others], *The history of the English stage* (1741) • Pepys, *Diary*, 7.369

Wealth at death considerable wealth; £5300 bequests: will, Highfill, Burnim & Langhans, *BDA*, vol. 14, pp. 171–2

Smith [Smyth], **William** (*d.* 1708?), writer, lived at Sileby and, perhaps, Market Harborough, Leicestershire. Little can be said about his family, but it is likely that he was the William Smith of Sileby who appears in Quaker registers as the husband of Constance (*d.* 1696) and father of William (*d.* 1676). In 1655 George Fox visited him at his home where there was a 'great meeting' attended by several Baptists (*Journal of George Fox*, 1.195). Later, in 1662, when Fox again visited Leicestershire, he passed through Sileby and noted that he was with a William Smith in Swannington, where, according to Joseph Besse, they were apprehended and imprisoned for about a month in Leicester gaol for the intention of holding a meeting.

In 1679 Smith wrote *The Wisdom of the Earthly Wise Confounded*, an answer to Thomas Wilson, rector of Arrow, Warwickshire, in which he discussed Quaker ideas on scripture and wrote, 'We are not led by our own conceivings nor imaginations (as the carnal-minded outside professors are) to interpret the holy scriptures but by a measure of the same spirit of truth, from which they were given forth' (W. Smith, *The Wisdom of the Earthly Wise Confounded*, 1679, 7). An interesting manuscript of verses written from Harborough in December 1680 may with some likelihood be attributed to him. These concerned the issue of non-attendance at meetings, which he felt stemmed from 'carelessness and indifferency'. He wrote of those that were lax in going to meetings:

> With other lovers you begin to take
> The bread of God you slight and do forsake
> You satisfy yourselves in things below
> So that to meetings you will hardly go.
> If all should be so flighty in this matter
> How would the people God hath gathered scatter.
> (Portfolio MSS 5, 20, RS Friends, Lond.)

If the probable identification of William Smith is correct, he died in 1708 and was buried on 22 June.

CAROLINE L. LEACHMAN

Sources *The journal of George Fox*, ed. N. Penney, 2 vols. (1911) • J. Besse, *A collection of the sufferings of the people called Quakers*, 1 (1753), 333 • J. Smith, ed., *A descriptive catalogue of Friends' books*, 2 (1867) • digest registers of births, marriages, and burials, RS Friends, Lond.

Archives RS Friends, Lond., verses on non-attendance at meetings, dated Harborough, 1680, Portfolio MS 5/20

Smith, William (1651?–1735), antiquary, was the son of William Smith of Easby, near Richmond, Yorkshire, and his wife, Anne, daughter of Francis Layton (1577–1661) of Rawden, master of the jewel house in the reign of Charles I. He matriculated from University College, Oxford, in May 1668 and graduated BA in 1672; after proceeding MA in March 1675, he was elected to a fellowship in his college. From a passion for antiquarian studies, Smith copied or abstracted all the deeds and charters in University College and drew on manuscript material in the city records and the Bodleian Library and college libraries. He incorporated excerpts from the manuscripts of Anthony Wood, Brian Twyne, Roger Dodsworth, and Matthew Hutton in the Bodleian, and from other private collections and personal sources, and had the exceptional privilege of access to the university archives deposited in the Schools Tower, becoming in the process skilful in deciphering and interpreting ancient documents. These collections were described in a letter of 10 May 1709 addressed to Ralph Thoresby (*Letters of Eminent Men*, 2.164–74). He was incorporated MA at Cambridge in 1678 and held the office of senior fellow for twelve years, refusing the mastership, until presented in 1704 to the rectorship of Melsonby, North Riding of Yorkshire, where University College had recently purchased the advowson. He built a rectory house, and married in 1705 Mary, *née* Greenwood (*d.* 1724), the widow of Gerard Langbaine. There seem to have been no children of this marriage; the child who survived him may have been William Langbaine, born shortly before Gerard Langbaine's death in 1692.

At Melsonby Smith maintained a lively correspondence with his fellow antiquaries, and kept his parish register in Latin. He followed the events at University College when a disputed election to the mastership led to arguments over who the college visitor should be—an appointment which depended on who had founded the college. Anthony Wood claimed that University College had been founded by King Alfred, in which case the visitor would be the representative of the sovereign, a view supported at law. In vain Smith protested against the judgment from the king's bench, which in his view disregarded history and common sense in favour of a fraudulent medieval assertion of Alfred as founder. In 1728 he published *The Annals of University College*, seeking to prove that the founder was William of Durham and that the visitor should therefore be convocation. This aroused the anger of Thomas Hearne, who criticized him for 'making everything spurious that happens to be against himself' (Mallet, 28), but Smith's claim was justified.

Changes in the weight and value of money also interested Smith, but his intention to write a treatise on this subject was forestalled by William Fleetwood's *Chronicon preciosum* (1707). However, he published in 1729 *Literae de re nummaria*, in opposition to the general opinion that Roman denarii were never larger than seven to the ounce. In 1732 he erected some almshouses at Easby. He died at

Melsonby in December 1735, and was buried there on 6 December.

The voluminous collection of manuscripts, together with seven heraldic manuscripts, came into the hands of Thomas Smith of Easby, son of William Smith's brother Thomas, who attempted to sell it through the intermediacy of Thomas Wilson, schoolmaster of Easby. It then passed to another relative, a Miss Croft of York, from whom George Allen FSA of Darlington acquired the larger part (but not the heraldic manuscripts), a further eleven volumes ending up in the bursary of University College. Allen may have been responsible for binding his collection in twenty-eight volumes, and these he presented on 3 May 1798 to the Society of Antiquaries in London, where they are now preserved. ANITA MCCONNELL

Sources E. H. A., 'The Rev. William Smith of Melsonby', *GM*, 2nd ser., 40 (1853), 163–4 • C. E. Mallet, *A history of the University of Oxford*, 3 vols. (1924–7), vol. 3 • *Remarks and collections of Thomas Hearne*, ed. C. E. Doble and others, 11 vols., OHS, 2, 7, 13, 34, 42–3, 48, 50, 65, 67, 72 (1885–1921) • J. M. Levine, *Dr Woodward's shield: history, science, and satire in Augustan England* (1977) • *DNB* • [J. Hunter], ed., *Letters of eminent men, addressed to Ralph Thoresby*, 2 vols. (1832)

Archives Oxf. UA, papers and transcripts relating to archives of University College, Oxford • S. Antiquaries, Lond., collections relating to history of University of Oxford

Likenesses oils, University College, Oxford

Smith, William (1697–1769), lawyer and jurist in America, was born on 8 October 1697 at Newport Pagnell, Buckinghamshire, the first of six children of Thomas Smith (1675–1745), tallow chandler, and his wife, Susanna (1677–1728), daughter of Thomas Odell and his wife, Christiana. He was educated by tutors in the classics and sciences, then emigrated to New York with his father's family in 1715. Shortly afterwards he entered Yale College, graduating AB in 1719 and AM in 1722. Proficient in Hebrew, the classics, and theology, he was hired by Yale as a tutor. He was also religiously devout, professing Presbyterianism and seriously considering the ministry as his life's work. In 1724 he was offered the college's presidency. Instead, he chose to enter law; he was admitted to the bar in New York and went to London to study at Gray's Inn. In 1727 he returned to New York, established a lucrative practice, and quickly achieved prestige as a lawyer. On 11 May 1727 he married Mary Het (1710–1754); they had fifteen children, the eldest of whom was the lawyer and politician William *Smith (1727–1793). He married his second wife, Elizabeth, *née* Scott (1708–1774), widow of the Revd Elisha Williams, on 12 May 1761; they had no children.

Throughout his career Smith was prominent in the whiggish 'Presbyterian faction' of New York politics and jurisprudence. Allying himself with James Alexander and Lewis Morris against the Cosby–DeLancey–Philipse interest, he attempted to curb the powers of the royal governor. In 1733 he and Alexander were retained by Councillor Rip Van Dam to defend him against a claim before the supreme court by Governor William Cosby for Van Dam's salary when the latter acted as governor. Smith immediately attacked the legality of the court, and was sustained by Chief Justice Lewis Morris. However, justices Frederick Philipse and James DeLancey dissented, and no decision was reached. In 1734 Smith and Joseph Murray took their arguments against the court to the colony's assembly, where Smith pleaded his case eloquently.

In 1735 Smith and Alexander were involved in the case of John Peter Zenger, printer of an opposition newspaper, the *New York Weekly Journal*. The two lawyers had supported, and sometimes written, articles for Zenger's paper, which attacked Governor Cosby. When Zenger was charged with seditious libel, Smith and Alexander pleaded Zenger's case before the supreme court. When they argued that DeLancey and Philipse had been illegally appointed to the court, Smith and Alexander were disbarred. Zenger's defence was taken up by Alexander Hamilton, who prevailed upon a jury to acquit his client. Smith and Alexander, meanwhile, appealed to the assembly to have their disbarment overturned and were supported by many influential people. In 1737 the court, taunted with ignorance of the law and ridiculed by the opposition, agreed to set aside the decree against Smith and Alexander if they would forfeit any right to sue for civil damages.

Smith was involved in many other important cases in New York and surrounding provinces. In 1737 he challenged the election of Adolph Philipse to the colonial assembly on the grounds that Jews had been permitted to vote for him when history and theology supported their disenfranchisement. Four years later he was a king's prosecutor in the case against black slaves involved in the 'Negro Plot'. In 1743 he was counsel for Connecticut in litigation against the Mohegan Indians, and he took part in many cases before the mayor's court of New York city. He also held a number of civic posts. In 1736 he accepted the office of recorder and in 1751 he was attorney-general for a year. He was a member of the provincial council from 1753 to 1767; in 1754 he attended the inter-colonial Albany congress and served as a commissioner to settle a boundary dispute between New York and Massachusetts. Although he declined appointment as chief justice of New York in 1760, he accepted an associate justiceship three years later and served in that position until his death.

Smith was an ardent proponent of various educational enterprises. He trained many law students, and in 1732 helped to found the first publicly funded school in New York. He assisted in the founding of the College of New Jersey (later Princeton University) in 1746, and two years later was appointed a trustee for life. In 1751 he was foremost among the founders of King's College (later Columbia University) as a non-sectarian institution, but withdrew his support when the school fell under the sway of Anglicans. Three years later he helped to establish the New York Society Library. He died on 22 November 1769 in New York city. PAUL DAVID NELSON

Sources M. Delafield, 'William Smith: judge of the supreme court of the province of New York', *Magazine of American History*, 6 (1881), 264–82 • W. Smith, *The history of the province of New-York* (1757); repr. M. Kammen, ed., 2 (New York, 1972) • F. B. Dexter, *Biographical sketches of the graduates of Yale College*, 6 vols. (1885–1912) • J. Kross, 'Smith, William', *ANB* • E. A. Jones, *American members of the inns of court* (1924) • E. B. O'Callaghan and B. Fernow, eds. and trans., *Documents relative to the colonial history of the state of New York*, 15 vols.

(1853–87), vols. 6–7 • P. Hamlin, *Legal education in colonial New York* (1939) • S. N. Katz, *Newcastle's New York: Anglo-American politics, 1732–1753* (1968) • M. M. Klein, *The politics of diversity: essays in the history of colonial New York* (1974)

Archives New York Historical Society

Likenesses Wollaston, portrait, 1751, priv. coll. • etching (after Wollaston), repro. in Delafield, 'William Smith', 270

Wealth at death wealthy; 'lucrative' law practice: Smith, *History of the province of New-York*

Smith, William (*b.* 1697/8, *d.* in or after 1727), surveyor, was born in Ireland. Examined by the Royal African Company, he was commissioned on 11 August 1726:

> to take exact plans, drafts, and prospects of all their forts and settlements; as also of the principal rivers, harbours, and other places of trade on the coast of Africa, from Gambia to Whydah … in order to our being the better enabled to represent the state of our affairs at the next session of Parliament. (PRO, T 70/55, p. 34)

He boarded the company's vessel *Bonetta*, commanded by Captain James Livingston, on 20 August and made landfall near Cape Verde on 22 September. The African Company sent letters of instruction to Anthony Turner, its governor of the Gambia, and to Walter Charles, director at Sierra Leone, urging them

> to receive the said Mr Smith in a hansom manner, entertain him at the Publick Table during his stay … and give him all the encouragement and assistance that is in your power towards his performing the service he has undertaken with the utmost exactness. (ibid.)

On his first day, finding himself floundering through deep mud along the shore with huge, venomous ants infesting the mangrove trees and attacked by ferocious wasps, Smith regretted ever having undertaken this survey, but 'having put hand to plough' (Smith, 2) could not look back. Inevitably his actions with measuring wheel and theodolite caused some of the natives to suspect him of witchcraft, but as the survey progressed and he grew accustomed to the terrain he was able to record something of the plants and wildlife, and the various customs of the peoples he encountered. Additional information was drawn from *New Description of the Coast of Guinea* (1705), translated from the original of Willem Bosman. Smith worked for a little way up the principal rivers, taking soundings and marking sandbanks, but otherwise did not venture inland from the coast. *Bonetta* sailed for home on 18 August and anchored at Plymouth on 26 September 1727, whereupon Smith took a coach for London. He received an interim payment of 21 guineas, expenses of £30 9*s.* 9*d.*, and his gratuity of £25 in November, the balance of £65 2*s.* at the end of December.

Thirty Different Drafts of Guinea (1730) was presented to the African Company; the drafts included location charts, followed by prospects and plans of the British forts. Among the subscribers to a published version was Peter Smith, a surveyor of Cork, and the Revd John Smith of Kilmore, who subscribed to six copies; it is possible that these were his brother and father. This was followed by *A New and Correct Map of the Coast of Africa, from Cape Blanco … to the Coast of Angola* (1744), which showed the coastline, its seasonal offshore currents, and the entrances to rivers, together with the forts under Dutch, French, and English control. Smith's narrative of his experiences, *A New Voyage to Guinea*, was also published in 1744. Nothing is known of his later life. ANITA MCCONNELL

Sources PRO, T 70/55, 345, 1439, 92 • W. Smith, *A new voyage to Guinea* (1744)

Smith, William (1706/7–1764). *See under* Smith, George (1713/14–1776).

Smith, William (1711–1787), classical scholar, was born on 30 May 1711 at Worcester, where his father, Richard Smith, was rector of All Saints' Church. He entered Worcester grammar school (Queen Elizabeth's) in 1722, and proceeded in 1728 to New College, Oxford. He was there a contemporary of Robert Lowth (afterwards bishop of London), with whom he enjoyed a lifelong friendship. He graduated BA (1732), MA (1737), and BD and DD (both in 1758). He was married to Elizabeth, *née* Heber, of Essex; they had no children.

Soon after taking his bachelor's degree, Smith had the good fortune to become known to James Stanley, tenth earl of Derby, and resided with him for three years as his reader. In June 1735 he took deacon's orders, and the earl presented him on 11 September to the rectory of Holy Trinity, Chester. His first publication, a translation, *Longinus on the Sublime* (1739), established his reputation in the eighteenth century as a talented classical scholar. Smith also spoke Latin fluently and was highly proficient in Greek and Hebrew. In 1743 he was appointed chaplain to the eleventh earl of Derby, the successor of his former patron. Five years later he became headmaster of Brentwood grammar school; however he disliked the lifestyle and resigned later that year.

In 1753 Smith became one of the ministers of St George's, Liverpool, and in the same year he published his translation of Thucydides. In 1758, mainly through the influence of Lord Derby, he was presented to the deanery of Chester, with which he held other preferments. He resigned St George's, Liverpool, in 1767, and Holy Trinity, Chester, in 1780, but he was rector of Handley from 1766 to 1787, and of West Kirby from 1780 to 1787.

In addition to his *Longinus on the Sublime*, his best-known work, Smith published a *History of the Peloponnesian War, from the Greek of Thucydides, with Notes* (1753) which received an unfavourable review in the *Gentleman's Magazine* (1860). In 1770 there appeared his translation, *Xenophon's History of Greece, by the Translator of Thucydides*, followed twelve years later by his *Nine Sermons on the Beatitudes*. Smith died at Chester on 12 January 1787 and was buried in the south aisle of the cathedral where a memorial was erected by his wife. Smith's friend Thomas Crane issued the posthumous *Poetic Works of William Smith, D.D.* (1788) including a brief memoir of the author, a paraphrase of John Downe's *Third Satyr*, and other trifles in verse, some of which had previously appeared in the *Gentleman's Magazine*.

FRANCIS SANDERS, *rev.* PHILIP CARTER

Sources Foster, *Alum. Oxon.* • *GM*, 1st ser., 61 (1791), 745 • G. Ormerod, *Parentalia: genealogical memoirs … genealogical essays illustrative of Cheshire and Lancashire families* (1851–6) • J. Chambers, *Biographical*

illustrations of Worcestershire (1820) • A. Chalmers, ed., *The general biographical dictionary*, new edn, 32 vols. (1812–17) • Allibone, *Dict.* • PRO, PROB 11/1150, fols. 315v–316v

Archives New College, Oxford, commonplace book

Smith, William (1727–1793), lawyer and politician in America, was born in New York city on 18 June 1727, the first child and namesake of William *Smith (1697–1769), the foremost attorney in New York during the first half of the eighteenth century, and Mary Het (1710–1754), of French Huguenot descent. Like his father Smith attended Yale College, graduating AB, in the class of 1745, whereupon he joined his father's legal practice. On 3 November 1752 he married Janet Livingston, a distant relation of the aristocratic family. Another Livingston, William, also studied law with the elder Smith. The younger Smith and William Livingston published the first collection of New York laws, and with their friend John Morin Scott created a shortlived magazine, the *Independent Reflector* (1752–3), becoming prolific cultural critics of New York provincialism and vibrant exponents of British libertarian politics. In 1757 Smith published *The History of … New York … to … 1732* and began work on a sequel carrying the story down to 1762, which was published posthumously in 1826.

Though the Livingston whigs used the Stamp Act crisis (1765) to discredit their rivals in New York colonial politics, the Delancey faction, Smith did not follow other Livingston politicians into opposition to British authority. Instead he hoped to use his Livingston connections and his seat on the royal council as a base from which to launch a behind-the-scenes campaign to reform the British empire and restore harmony between Britain and the colonies. His campaign was two-pronged. First Smith formulated a bold new theory of empire, his 'Thoughts upon the dispute between Great Britain and her colonies (1767)', which diagnosed the structural flaws of the empire and prescribed a new political language for use in imperial discourse. The colonists believed, Smith declared, that their role in winning the Seven Years' War entitled them, as a matter of natural right, to a generous redefinition of the imperial–colonial relationship; Britain, he noted, had made clear, in an astounding instance of 'palpable blundering', that parliamentary taxation and tighter trade regulation were terms of that new relationship. Both sides in the dispute appealed to the British constitution and accused the other of violating its terms.

> The truth is that the Empire long after the Constitution was formed, acquired a *new adventitious state* … The question therefore is not, what the constitution is, or was, but what, present circumstances considered, it ought to be. The Constitution (be it what it will) ought to bend, and sooner or later will bend.

His plan then proposed the creation of an American parliament. Smith sent copies of his plan to various British officials. He naïvely assumed that, as soon as the king's ministers saw the document, it would become 'the ground work' of a new colonial policy (Calhoon, *Loyalist Perception*, chap. 2).

The second prong of Smith's effort to civilize politics was securing, with guile and subtlety, the ear and trust of successive New York royal governors, especially William

William Smith (1727–1793), by Henry Stubble, *c.*1785

Tryon, who arrived in 1771. The stakes of power were land grants made by the governor on the advice of the council. After thwarting the Delancey family's land grabbing, Smith exulted that he had won Tryon's confidence and made him suspicious of the Delanceys' intentions. During the Tea Act crisis of 1773 Smith used the same methods to guide Tryon through a dangerous political storm. He besieged Tryon with suggestions on how to avoid violence until news of the Boston Tea Party took matters out of Tryon's hands. 'It must mortify Tryon who has spoken so vauntingly and assured [the British] government of the landing' of the tea, Smith noted calmly. But below the surface of his demeanour, Smith was in agony. 'Tryon will think I animated him to render him unpopular. How dangerous it is to give private advice' (Calhoon, *Loyalists in Revolutionary America*, chap. 8).

By 1775 the time had come to merge constitutional reform with political manoeuvre. Smith wrote new proposals for imperial reconciliation—ideas for implementing his 1767 plan for imperial reform. With clinical care he suggested that the colonists devise negotiating tactics: 'feeling the pulse of the ministry', proceeding 'without a word about rights', and exercising exquisite tact and timing. When all of these initiatives came to naught, he responded by writing yet another indictment of past British policy and critique of colonial resistance, blending a defence of colonial liberty with an absolute refusal to sanction armed rebellion. By June and July 1776 those dual commitments immobilized him. 'I persuade myself', he told his hostile neighbours on the Haverstraw committee of safety on 4 July 1776, 'that Great Britain will discern the propriety of negotiating for a pacification' (Calhoon, *Loyalists in Revolutionary America*, chap. 8).

Smith's Livington connections gave him the luxury of equivocating until 1778 before casting his lot with the British. Even in 1778 his embrace of loyalism occurred in slow motion. Smith moved to British-occupied New York city, where the Carlisle peace commission, dispatched by Lord North in 1778 to offer the Americans everything they wanted short of independence, courted Smith assiduously. In a confidential memorandum to the commission, the Church of England cleric John Vardill took the measure of Smith's character and politics: 'He is subtle, cool & persuasive … He may be secured by an application to his ambition.' Another loyalist told the commission that Smith was 'a lawyer of great intrigue and subtlety, an independent republican in church and state [an allusion to his Presbyterian and Livingston attachments], in his heat … avaritious & ambitious … few men so able, if he could be trusted' (Upton, *Loyal Whig*, 121).

Once he embraced loyalism Smith lived up to those acid accolades. In New York city's garrison town politics he became the consummate manipulator. When the British commander in North America, Sir Henry Clinton, declined to make Smith the power behind the throne, Smith began a campaign to undermine him. Exulting in Benedict Arnold's apostasy, Smith wanted Clinton to assign Arnold a major military role. Smith also plunged into the Vermont imbroglio, encouraging Vermont separatists to offer Britain their support in return for commercial concessions.

Following the British surrender at Yorktown in 1781 and the replacement of Clinton with Sir Guy Carleton as commander of British forces in America and administrator of New York city, the analytical and conspiratorial strands of Smith's politics finally came together. Carleton understood subtlety and intrigue, and took Smith on his own terms. Independently, but with increasing trust and mutual support, both men tried to stave off British humiliation in the hope that America might concede some nominal tie to the British crown. When in August 1783 he acknowledged that the United States had actually acquired full independence, Smith put out feelers to the other great whig-loyalist in America, William Samuel Johnson of Connecticut, seeking sanctuary in New Haven. Nothing came of that effort, and on 4 December 1783 Smith sailed to England. It took all of Guy Carleton's skill and political standing to secure for Smith, in 1786, appointment as chief justice of Quebec.

There Smith became caught up in a bitter dispute over the extent to which the Quebec Act of 1774 perpetuated French law in the colony. His ruling in *Gray* v. *Grant* (1786) denied the attempt by Alexander Gray, a Scottish lawyer, to settle his bankrupt father's estate under the more favourable liability provisions of French, rather than, English law. The uproar over the decision exacerbated the deep divisions between Francophone settlers and American loyalist émigrés. Smith died in Quebec on 6 December 1793.

Robert M. Calhoon

Sources L. F. S. Upton, *The loyal whig: William Smith of New York and Quebec* [1969] · R. M. Calhoon, *The loyalists in revolutionary America, 1760–1781* (1973) · R. M. Calhoon, *The loyalist perception and other essays* (1989) · *Historical memoirs from 16 March 1763 to 25 July 1778 of William Smith*, ed. W. H. W. Sabine, 2 vols. (1956–8) · *Historical memoirs from 26 August 1778 to 12 November 1783 of William Smith*, ed. W. H. W. Sabine (1971) · L. F. S. Upton, ed., *The diary and selected papers of Chief Justice William Smith* (1963)

Archives NYPL

Likenesses H. Stubble, miniature, *c*.1785, New York Historical Society [*see illus.*]

Smith, William (1727–1803), Church of England clergyman and educationist, was born at Slains, north of Aberdeen, in 1727, probably on 20 April, the only son of Thomas Smith (*b*. 1692) and his first wife, Elizabeth Duncan. After attending the local parish school Smith was admitted to King's College, Aberdeen, in 1743 and graduated in 1747. His first position, as a teacher in Abernethy, gave rise to his earliest publication, an appeal in the *Scots Magazine* for improved pay and conditions for Scottish teachers. His colleagues asked him to present a petition to parliament, and on 20 December 1750 he left Abernethy for London. He never returned to Scotland. In March 1751 he migrated to New York, and during the next year he published in the colonial press fabular homilies and proposals for the education of Native Americans. It was his extended proposal for the education of white colonists, *A General Idea of the College of Mirania* (1753), that established his name. It was noticed by Benjamin Franklin, who offered Smith the new post of provost at the College of Philadelphia.

As such a position was normally held by a clergyman, Smith visited England in 1753 and took orders in the Anglican church. On his return to Pennsylvania he became active in politics on the side of the proprietary Penn family. He fretted over the activities of the French and Indians on the colony's western borders, and in 1755 and 1756 published two pamphlets attacking the Pennsylvania assembly, then under Quaker control, for failing to protect the colony. He became an ally of William Moore, Pennsylvania justice and politician, but quarrelled with Franklin and, more seriously, with the assembly, which on 6 January 1758 had both Smith and Moore arrested for libel; they were gaoled for three months. While imprisoned, Smith courted Moore's daughter Rebecca (1732–1793). They were married on 3 June 1758 and had eight children.

Later in 1758 Smith visited England to appeal his conviction before the privy council. The visit was a great success. Although he was opposed by Franklin, Smith persuaded the privy council to quash the convictions of Moore and himself, and he was awarded honorary doctorates by Oxford and Aberdeen universities. Four years later he was awarded a third doctorate, by Dublin. Smith's success was doubtless partly due to his connections with the Anglican hierarchy. He had impressed Thomas Herring, archbishop of Canterbury, in 1751 on his first visit to London, and by the end of that decade he had become a trusted colonial servant. In 1762 he was commissioned to report on the state of the church in the colonies. Three years later he published, in Philadelphia, an account of Henry Bouquet's victorious expedition against the Ohio Indians, in which he described new methods of Indian fighting and proposed new schemes for frontier settlement. The pamphlet was an immediate success; it was reprinted in London in 1766 by the geographer royal, came out in three more editions between 1768 and 1770, and appeared in French translations in 1769 and 1778.

As discord grew between Britain and America, Smith attempted to steer a middle course. He denounced British attempts to tax the colonies but thought that independence would be disastrous for America. He developed his view in two pamphlets, *A Sermon on the Present Situation of American Affairs* (1775) and *An Oration in Memory of General Montgomery* (1776), which were widely distributed. They did not endear Smith to the patriots. He was imprisoned briefly in 1776, and in 1779 the charter of the College of Philadelphia was revoked. Unlike many who were loyal to the British crown, Smith did not leave his adopted homeland. Instead he moved to Maryland, took charge of a local school, and transformed it into Washington College. In 1789 the charter of the College of Philadelphia was restored and Smith was reappointed as provost, remaining until the college became the University of Pennsylvania in 1791.

Smith died in Philadelphia on 14 May 1803 and was buried there. Two volumes of his *Works*, consisting of sermons and pamphlets, were published shortly afterwards. On the day of Smith's death Benjamin Rush, his physician and a colleague at the College of Philadelphia, wrote a vivid memoir of him. Smith, he said, 'as a teacher was perspicuous and agreeable, and as a preacher solemn, eloquent, and expressive in a high degree', but in later life he became a drunkard who 'was often seen to reel … in the streets of Philadelphia'. According to Rush, Smith was an 'irritable' and 'avaricious' man

> who lived, after acquiring an estate of £50,000, in penury and filth … On his death bed he never spoke upon any subject connected with Religion nor his future state, nor was there a Bible or prayer book ever seen in his room … He descended to his grave … without being lamented by a human creature. (*Autobiography of Benjamin Rush*, 262–5)

Rush's account may well have been inspired by his intense hatred of alcohol. Reeling or sober, Smith left a legacy of educational and cultural achievement. In 1757 he was instrumental in founding the *American Magazine*, and in 1769 the American Philosophical Society. He fostered many careers, including those of David Rittenhouse, the distinguished astronomer; Francis Hopkinson, the poet who was a signatory to the Declaration of Independence and the designer of the new American flag, and who claimed to be the composer of the first book of music published in America; Thomas Godfrey, another poet, whose play *The Prince of Parthia* became in 1767 the first professionally performed drama in America; and Benjamin West, the painter, who made portraits of Smith and his wife. ROBERT LAWSON-PEEBLES

Sources *The works of William Smith*, 2 vols. (1803) • A. F. Gegenheimer, *William Smith: educator and churchman* (1943) • H. W. Smith, *Life and correspondence of the Rev. William Smith, D.D.*, 2 vols. (1879–80) • *The autobiography of Benjamin Rush*, ed. G. W. Corner (1948), 262–5 • R. Lawson-Peebles, 'The problem of William Smith: an Aberdonian in revolutionary America', *Aberdeen and the Enlightenment*, ed. J. J. Carter and J. H. Pittock (1987), 52–60 • R. Lawson-Peebles, 'William Smith in Aberdeen (1745) and Philadelphia (1778): fratricide and familialism', *Culture and revolution*, ed. P. Dukes and J. Dunkley (1990), 46–59 • T. F. Jones, *A pair of lawn sleeves: a biography of William Smith* (1972) • D. H. Moore, *Six centuries of the Moores of Fawley, Berkshire, England, and their descendants amid the titled and untitled aristocracy of Great Britain and America* (1904) • J. H. Hutson, *Pennsylvania politics, 1746–1770: the movement for royal government and its consequences* (1972) • T. Thayer, *Pennsylvania politics and the growth of democracy, 1740–1776* (1953)

Archives Hist. Soc. Penn. • LPL, Society for the Propagation of the Gospel, MSS • University of Pennsylvania, Philadelphia | LPL, Fulham MSS

Likenesses B. West, oils, 1763, Hist. Soc. Penn. • J. Sartain, etching (after West)

Smith, William [*called* Gentleman Smith] (**1730–1819**), actor, was born on 22 February 1730, the son of William Smith (1700–1782), a wholesale grocer and tea merchant in the City of London. With a view to entering the church, he went in 1737 to Eton College and in 1747 to St John's College, Cambridge. A William Smith received an admonition for 'inebriation and obscene language' (admonitions book, St John's College archives, C5.1, fol. 211) on 17 March 1749. Legend has it that a drunken incident that involved firing an unloaded pistol at a proctor led to his leaving Cambridge.

Striking good looks and social connections probably moved Smith in the direction of the London theatre. He appeared as 'a Gentleman' on 8 January 1753 at Covent Garden Theatre, playing the title role in Nathaniel Lee's *Theodosius, or, The Force of Love* alongside Susannah Cibber and the established Irish actor Spranger Barry. Smith later recalled this performance and wrote to Thomas Coutts on 4 January 1814, 'I can never forget the resplendent Powers of *Barry* & Mrs *Cibber*—I shudder at the thought of so poor a shrub as myself even vegetating under such illustrious excellence'. He continued to Coutts on 24 January 1814, 'I was petrified & coud have died with shame at my attempt—After the Play Mr B— & Mrs C— kindly encouraged me & assured me of their support & promised to give me a part in each play they reviv'd' (Highfill, Burnim & Langhans, *BDA*).

His performances sufficiently pleased the manager, John Rich, that Smith was given four substantial roles during the remainder of the season. Rich engaged him for the 1753–4 season, and he added eleven parts to his repertory, including Orlando in *As You Like It*, Loveless in John Vanbrugh's *The Relapse*, Myrtle in Richard Steele's *The Conscious Lovers*, Florizel in MacNamara Morgan's *The Sheep Shearing*, and Valentine in William Congreve's *Love for Love*. Social connections and his genteel manner engaged interest from the 'town' and earned him the nickname Gentleman Smith.

Among the women attracted to him, Smith pursued one whom he hoped would further his social and financial aspirations. At the end of his first full season in the theatre, on 31 May 1754, he married Elizabeth Courtenay (*d.* 1762), the second daughter of Edward Richard Montagu,

Viscount Hinchinbroke, and sister to John Montagu, fourth earl of Sandwich. She was the widow of Kelland Courtenay of Powderham Castle, Devon, and had three grown children. The *Theatrical Biography* (1772) records the outrage of the family and the proposal by Smith that 'if the family he had so *disgraced*, would allow him for life a sum equal to his theatrical acquisitions, he would cease to dishonour them'. This was rejected, and he continued to act for another thirty-four years.

During the next four seasons Smith added almost forty roles to his repertory. These included, in 1754–5, Careless in Congreve's *The Double Dealer*, Antony in *Julius Caesar*, the title role in *Henry V*, Romeo, and Hastings in Nicholas Rowe's *Jane Shore*. Among his parts in 1755–6 were Plume in George Farquhar's *The Recruiting Officer*, Careless in Colley Cibber's *The Double Gallant*, and Archer in Farquhar's *The Beaux' Stratagem*. In 1756–7 he added the title role in Aphra Behn's *The Rover* and Lothario in Rowe's *The Fair Penitent*, and played Hamlet for his benefit performance. Barry's return to Ireland in 1758 left the stage clear for Smith to command the best roles at Covent Garden for over a decade.

Significant parts added during the 1758–9 season included Palador (Guiderius) in Hawkins's adaptation of *Cymbeline*, Lord Foppington in Cibber's *The Careless Husband*, and Sir Harry Wildair in Farquhar's *The Constant Couple*. Late in this season the Drury Lane prompter, Richard Cross, noted (29 May 1759): 'We borrowed Smith from Cov: Garden to do Osmyn [in Congreve's *The Mourning Bride*]' (Highfill, Burnim & Langhans, *BDA*). The following season he added several roles, among them Pierre in Thomas Otway's *Venice Preserv'd*. The crowning of George III on 22 September 1761 occasioned competing stagings of the coronation; Rich's spectacular version at Covent Garden was deemed to outshine David Garrick's at Drury Lane. To complement *The Coronation*, Rich scheduled a sequence of 'royal' plays, and Smith played *Henry V* (eighteen times) and the Bastard Faulconbridge in *King John* and added the title role in *Richard III*.

Elizabeth Smith died on 11 December 1762. Although her estate devolved to two daughters of her first marriage, Smith received a substantial bequest. In spite of his predilection for horse-racing and fine wine, he was prudent with his theatrical income. He further assured his financial security by hastily marrying, in 1763, another heiress, Martha Newsom, the daughter of a prominent citizen of Leiston in Suffolk.

Smith continued to add new roles during 1762–3, notably Kitely in Ben Jonson's *Every Man in his Humour* and Bajazet in Rowe's *Tamerlane*. The following season added Edgar in *King Lear* and Belfield in Arthur Murphy's *No Man's Enemy but his Own*. During 1964–5 he was Heartfree in Vanbrugh's *The Provoked Wife*, and, although physically and temperamentally unsuited, he played Iago in *Othello*. For the remaining years of the decade, with little competition at Covent Garden, Smith appeared in all the roles he wanted and remained a favourite with audiences. Unlike most actors of his age, he neither toured the provinces during the summer nor did he succumb to the temptation of entering the minefield of theatrical management, although he briefly held a share in the theatre in Bristol in 1769, and was elected chairman of the 'committee' of the Covent Garden Theatrical Fund in 1773.

Smith despised the contemporary taste for costumed processions and initially rejected Garrick's invitation to appear in *The Jubilee*—his celebration of Shakespeare at Stratford upon Avon in September 1769. He finally agreed to take part, although he ensured that preparations did not prevent his attendance at York races. He tried to steer a non-partisan course through the tensions between the managerial factions of George Colman the elder and Thomas Harris at Covent Garden. But longevity and the security of his favour with the audience caused him to try to exert power over benefit choices and to seek an increase in pay. Colman rejected his request for an additional £5 per week, but Smith remained at Covent Garden. Among other roles, by 1772, he had added Mirabel in Congreve's *The Way of the World*, Cassius in *Julius Caesar* (1766–7), Iachimo in *Cymbeline*, Lovemore in Murphy's *The Way to Keep him* (1769–70), Leontes in *The Winter's Tale* (1770–71), and the title role in Jonson's *Volpone, or, The Fox* (1771–2).

Still dissatisfied with his treatment, however, Smith began negotiations with Garrick. Smith's urbane qualities would have consolidated the Drury Lane company, but Garrick would not accede to his salary demands. Tensions rose at Covent Garden when the 74-year-old Charles Macklin was engaged for the 1773–4 season. Smith challenged Macklin to a duel when he was accused of being complicit in the disruption of Macklin's *Macbeth*. Although violence was avoided, rioting gave Colman little option but to dismiss Macklin.

Towards the end of Smith's last season at Covent Garden he left for France in the company of the married actress Elizabeth Hartley. The *New Monthly Magazine* (1837) reported that a 'public journal' published an alleged letter from Smith to his wife which concluded: 'You must pardon me this one slip, and believe me when I declare, that though a momentary gust of passion may hurry me into trifling indiscretions, I never can find real felicity and true happiness but in your arms.' Smith carried the scandal with aplomb and, while appearing with Hartley in Dublin during the summer of 1774, reopened negotiations with Garrick—since returning to Covent Garden alongside Hartley would prove impossible. In consequence Smith opened at Drury Lane as Richard III, on 22 September 1774. With Garrick contemplating retirement, he needed the reliable solidity of Smith's performances, but letters from Garrick show that Smith was still unhappy: 'these frequent Billets of Complaint betray an unsatisfyd Mind' (*Letters*, 3.1044). Tensions continued, especially where Smith's presence was sought in the costumed processions of Garrick's 'entertainments'.

Notwithstanding, Smith stayed at Drury Lane until his retirement in 1788, stubbornly refusing to appear in processions or to perform during race weeks. His most characteristic and remembered role was as Charles Surface in Sheridan's *The School for Scandal* (May 1777); he appeared in all the many revivals of the play until his retirement, and he returned, aged sixty-eight, in 1798 to play the part for Tom King's benefit. The *Monthly Mirror* summed up his achievement and manner:

> His *Charles* ... is a favourable specimen of that sort of acting which commonly falls under the denomination of the *old school*: light, airy, and natural; which excites applause without any anxious endeavour to produce it; which suffers the points to tell of *themselves*, and does not place them as so many *traps* to ensnare the injudicious ... we found him possessed of a full, rich, musical voice, somewhat thick in the melody, but by no means ungrateful to the ear, with an articulation sufficiently distinct, and an extent of tone that surprised us. (*Monthly Mirror*, May 1798)

This echoes the age's judgement:

> in the parts of the unaffected well-bred gentleman, he irreproachably claims the foremost rank ... for uniform elegance, ease, and suitable vivacity ... In tragedy he has too much levity, and want of variation ... yet he possesses great fervour and manly spirit. (W. Hawkins, *Miscellanies*, 1775)

Smith lived for thirty-one years after his retirement, enjoying life as a gentleman in rural Suffolk. Cared for by his wife, and patronized by the banker Thomas Coutts, he continued riding, drinking good wine, and walking until his late eighties. He died at his home, Northgate House, 8 Northgate Street, Bury St Edmunds, on 13 September 1819 and was buried in an unmarked grave in the church at Bury St Edmunds. His will left property and stocks to the value of £18,000. CHRISTOPHER BAUGH

Sources Highfill, Burnim & Langhans, *BDA* • P. H. Highfill, 'Charles Surface in Regency retirement: some letters from Gentleman Smith', *Essays in English literature of the classical period presented to Dougald MacMillan*, ed. D. W. Patterson and A. B. Strauss (1967), 135–66 • G. W. Stone, ed., *The London stage, 1660–1800*, pt 4: 1747–1776 (1962) • C. B. Hogan, ed., *The London stage, 1660–1800*, pt 5: 1776–1800 (1968) • *The letters of David Garrick*, ed. D. M. Little and G. M. Kahrl, 3 vols. (1963) • S. West, *The image of the actor: verbal and visual representation in the age of Garrick and Kemble* (1991) • admission records, St John Cam.

Archives Yale U., Beinecke L., papers

Likenesses J. H. Mortimer, group portrait, 1768 (as the Bastard in *King John*), Garr. Club • J. Roberts, group portrait, oils, 1777 (as Charles Surface in *School for scandal*), Garr. Club • J. Hoppner, oils, *c*.1788, Tate collection • W. Ward, engraving, 1819 (after J. Jackson, *c*.1810), repro. in R. Page, *Essex, Suffolk and Norfolk characters* (1820) • J. Roberts, group portrait, oils (as Hamlet), Garr. Club • prints, BM, NPG

Wealth at death approx. £18,000: Highfill, Burnim & Langhans, *BDA*, vol. 14

Smith, William (1756–1835), politician and dissenter, was born on 22 September 1756 at Clapham, the only son of Samuel Smith (1727–1798) and his wife, Martha Adams (*d.* 1759). His father was a large wholesale grocer in Cannon Street, and his mother came from an old and wealthy City family. The Smiths were Independents, and at the age of eight William was sent to a school at Ware kept by an Independent minister, Mr French. There he met Thomas Belsham, a fellow pupil who would become the leading Unitarian divine of the early nineteenth century. Five years later, in 1769, Smith followed his older friend to the dissenting academy at Daventry, where Joseph Priestley had earlier been a student. Smith remained at Daventry until

William Smith (1756–1835), by Henry Thomson, exh. RA 1814

1772 and it is likely that, like Belsham's, his own later Unitarian beliefs began to take shape there.

Upon leaving Daventry, Smith went into his family's grocery business. He stayed for nine years, becoming a partner in 1777. In 1779 the death of his bachelor uncle James Adams left him independently wealthy. The following year he met Frances Coape (1758–1840), daughter of John and Hannah Coape, both dissenters. She had been orphaned young, and had since lived with her guardian, Mrs Forward, in Clapham. Both intelligent and attractive, she had a taste for religious disputation. They were married on 12 January 1781 at Clapham.

In 1780 Smith temporarily withdrew from business, on the condition that he could succeed his father at the head of the firm when the time came. In the meantime he and his new wife lived a fashionable life at Eagle House, Clapham Common. Partly to acquire pictures for their large and elegant home, they travelled extensively through Britain, and Smith alone to Paris in 1790. At its peak, their collection contained three Rembrandts, Reynolds's *Mrs Siddons as the Tragic Muse*, and assorted works by Cuyp, Hobbema, Ruysdael, Van Dyck, Rubens, Gainsborough, Cotman, and Opie. But it was not only culture that attracted the Smiths. Mines and mills were equally fascinating, and they sought political education as well.

Entry into politics Smith had considered a seat in parliament in 1780, but did not acquire one until 1784. In that year his father played an important part in returning supporters of Pitt to City seats, and the veteran government election manager John Robinson proposed William Smith as the ministerial candidate for Sudbury. The significant dissenting element in Sudbury's electorate may explain part of Smith's appeal but a more certain attraction was the fact that he was in the select group listed by Robinson as willing to spend up to £3000 for a seat.

Smith had already identified himself as a reformer, joining the Society for Constitutional Information in December 1782. Pitt had begun as a reformer, and until 1787 Smith was satisfied with loyal, if largely silent, support of the minister's policies. In that year, however, he first made his mark in politics, on a dissenting issue on which Pitt took the other side. The issue was the renewal, for the first time since the 1730s, of the dissenters' demand for the repeal of the Test and Corporation Acts, which in theory, and to a very large extent in practice, barred them from municipal offices and from all offices under the crown. Smith was a member of the application committee and an active speaker in the debates in parliament. The dissenters were unsuccessful in 1787 and again in 1789. Until then, the campaign had been quiet and discreet, with little or no public agitation, but stung by the taunts of Burke and others that dissenters were not united in their enthusiasm for repeal, the committee was determined to prove them wrong. The resulting public agitation was all too effective, provoking a reaction that harked back to the actions of the dissenters' puritan ancestors during the 1640s and 1650s, and that was to flow all too easily into the subsequent reaction to the French Revolution.

Also in 1787, in June, Smith had been the first outside the organizing committee to declare his support for the abolition of the slave trade. But in religious opinion Smith was moving towards a position sharply different from his evangelical neighbours in Clapham. In April 1791 he declared his allegiance to the new Unitarian Society and its principles. These involved warm support for the recently won liberty of the French. Predictably, in May 1792, when Fox introduced his bill for the relief of non-trinitarians, the sentiments of the Unitarian Society figured prominently in the violent opposition of Burke. Smith responded, reaffirming his adherence to the unitarians, ending with the ringing declaration that 'as long as his name was William, he would stand up for the principles he then maintained, and would support them to the utmost of his ability' (Cobbett, *Parl. Hist.*, 29.1396).

In 1790 Smith had been defeated for Sudbury. In January 1791 he found a seat at Camelford, a pocket borough which probably cost him about £2000. As he later wryly remarked, he had been returned in a manner that would probably 'not be sanctioned by the public approbation' (Davis, 59). But he was back in parliament to take his place with Wilberforce in the slave trade debates in April.

Smith's political allegiance was shifting. His difference with Pitt over the Test Acts, then over toleration of anti-trinitarians, on both of which Fox championed Smith's views, brought increasing estrangement. Still, until April 1792, there was no definitive break. Then Smith became a founding member of the Society of Friends of the People, and on 30 April seconded Grey's espousal of parliamentary reform in the Commons, which Pitt censured. In the following December and January he sealed the breach, stoutly opposing the approaching war with France.

In 1785 Smith had acquired a country estate of several hundred acres, Parndon Hall, near Harlow in Essex. As lord of the manor, he held the right of appointment to the parish church. In 1794 he and his wife left Clapham for 6 Park Street, Westminster, another grand house which had previously proved too expensive for two peers to maintain. Their family continued to grow and the last of their five daughters and five sons was born in 1799.

Radical activities Smith was coming to be seen by many as a radical, indeed a Jacobin. Early in 1794 the Smiths went to Hackney to hear Priestley's farewell sermon. Their eldest daughter remembered: 'My F said, "We shall soon see you here again". Dr Priestley replied, "Or I you in America" and went away' (Davis, 75). As well as his public advocacy of peace, Smith's reputation for Jacobinism was based largely on private initiatives with the same purpose. Through acquaintances in Paris and other business and social connections, he sometimes acted as a go-between. In November 1792 he arranged several interviews between Pitt and Maret, later Napoleon's foreign minister, in a last-minute effort to avoid war. A less happy episode was his involvement, through William Stone, a dissenting chemical manufacturer with French connections, with William Jackson, a French spy. Stone and Jackson were arrested on 3 May 1794. Smith himself was summoned before the privy council, though no charges were brought against him, nor could have been, as his only action had been to write a letter to Stone, scouting any illusion the French might entertain about an English welcome for an invading army. None the less the odour of Jacobinism hung about him for some time.

Smith's radicalism showed itself in his advocacy of a householder franchise for the boroughs, which in the 1790s was the key proposal of the Friends of the People, to which he belonged. No voice was stronger than Smith's in opposition to the restriction of freedom of speech and assembly. Following closely on the riots in Birmingham in 1791, which left dissenting chapels and the house and laboratory of Priestley in smoking ruins, Smith was elected one of the members from Clapham of the protestant dissenting deputies of the three denominations, the official London-based protectors of the interests of dissenters, and a member of their committee. In that capacity he played a leading role in protecting dissenters throughout the country from harassment, which had the broader aim of nipping persecution in the bud. His whig colleagues were warmly supportive and, on this issue, so were successive home secretaries, Henry Dundas and the duke of Portland, with whom Smith worked easily, and by his own testimony, to good effect.

Smith's adherence to the whig opposition, however, grew ever stronger, and he was more active than most, as he did not join the party's secession from parliament for several years after 1797. One important reason was his fervent attachment to the cause of the slaves. Among his services was to summon the disaffected whigs to battle when they were needed. It was one of the few summonses that Fox readily answered. This, among other common sentiments, gained Fox the unswerving loyalty of Smith.

Although Smith was once again returned for Sudbury in 1796, in 1802 he was happy to accept the invitation of whigs and radicals to stand for Norwich, a large constituency with many dissenters and a powerful Unitarian élite. To Smith it was a most desirable seat; and, despite charges of Jacobinism, he led his party to victory.

Electoral defeat and financial failure The next election in 1806 was a bitter disappointment. Smith was defeated on a purely local issue, for he had shown an impolitic indifference to the important matter of the Norwich paving bill. It could scarcely have been a worse time, for the whigs were at last in office. For this reason the prospect for abolition of the slave trade was favourable. Unable to give support in parliament, Smith gave it in a pamphlet entitled *A Letter to William Wilberforce* (1807). In it he summed up the core position of the abolitionists in a manner never bettered and argued that slavery was impious, 'I say impious: for I hold it to be no less, to erect municipal institutions in opposition to the eternal law of nature;—to put property, the creature of man, in competition with man himself, the creature of God' (pp. 29–30).

In January 1805 Smith had been unanimously elected chairman of the dissenting deputies, a recognition of the stature he already enjoyed as the pre-eminent leader of the dissenting interest. On his father's death in 1798, he had duly taken his place as head of the family business. In 1803 the death of his bachelor uncle Benjamin Smith left him richer by at least £60,000. This was his last piece of financial good luck. In 1806 he lost heavily in a fire which destroyed Cooke's distillery at Millbank in which he was a partner. In 1813 the grocery partnership broke up in acrimony. He established another, but that was on the verge of bankruptcy by 1819, saved only by an infusion of cash from his eldest son, Benjamin [*see below*], who had since made a fortune at Cooke's. But Parndon, Park Street, and the art collection all had to go, and in 1823 the firm was wound up, leaving Smith with an income of only a few hundred pounds a year. If he had ever had a talent for business, he did not have the time, and he put his faith in the wrong people.

Parliamentary reform Fortunately, Smith had rich sons and sons-in-law, and his financial reverses put no crimp in his political career. Government scandals in 1805 and 1809 helped to revive a parliamentary reform movement, with a distinctly radical, even anti-monarchical tinge. Smith, like Grey, was alarmed at this extremism, but sometimes, when no other whig would appear at a large London reform meeting, Smith would, counselling restraint to a chorus of boos. He was equally forthright at Norwich, which again returned him in 1807 and 1812. The *Norfolk Chronicle*, no partial friend, remarked on 17 March 1812:

> Whatever differences of opinion may exist among speculative men on points of religion and policy, all honest men agree in offering homage to singleness of heart, to strength of understanding, to simplicity of manners, gentleness of disposition, and uprightness of conduct. (Davis, 147)

But in the great test posed by Lord Sidmouth's bill in 1811, Smith's caution got him into difficulty. Beforehand Sidmouth had been by no means clear about his intention, beyond some adjustment in procedures for the registration of dissenting ministers under the Toleration Acts. When he introduced his bill, however, it was evident that it would give the magistrates discretion on whether to register at all, thereby depriving the applicant who was rebuffed of the acts' protection. Smith, who had seen the effects of spirited agitation in the 1780s, and had benefited from quiet negotiation in the 1790s, favoured the latter course; and that was the course the deputies adopted. But other dissenters, especially those with ties to humbler country evangelicals, and Wesleyan Methodists, those groups likely to be most at risk, reacted vigorously. Petitions flooded in and, with such a display of public opinion, the government of Spencer Perceval quickly disavowed Sidmouth. Those who had organized the petitioning, especially the new Protestant Society and the Methodists, won the day, and Smith and the deputies necessarily suffered by comparison.

The ministers, however, worried that aroused dissenters might join the Roman Catholics in a renewal of agitation against the Test Acts, were anxious to placate them and to work with Smith. In the end the government itself decided to introduce a bill in the next session, fully conceding the dissenters' interpretation of their right to automatic registration. Smith and the deputies also secured the repeal of the Conventicle and the Five Mile Acts. The following year, 1813, he worked closely with the new prime minister, Liverpool, to carry a Unitarian toleration act.

Final years Most of Smith's political activity in the 1810s was in intimate co-operation with Wilberforce and the 'Saints', and he is sometimes mistakenly called a 'Saint'. Smith was as deeply committed as they were to the attempts to reform the criminal law. In January 1823 Smith, with William Allen and T. F. Buxton, met at Zachary Macaulay's to lay the foundation for the London Society for the Abolition of Slavery in our Colonies, thereby helping to launch another great campaign. It was the same year that saw the nadir of his personal fortunes.

Smith's political life, however, ended in a glow of triumph. He crowned his career by presiding over the repeal of the Test Acts in 1828. Once more he deprecated agitation, believing that Catholic emancipation and repeal must come together, and that the former issue was winning its way. He also knew that dissent was seriously divided on the issue, and that any manifestation of anti-Catholicism in its ranks would do their cause great harm. Though success would not have come without agitation, as chairman of the United Committee, Smith managed to keep its tone moderate. The United Committee captured the essence of his character in its tribute to

> their respected Chairman … for the zeal, ability, and urbanity which uniformly marked his conduct in presiding over their deliberations, and in conducting them to that successful issue which his unwearied exertions in Parliament, and in every sphere in which those exertions could promote the great cause of Civil and Religious Liberty, during so many years of a most consistent and honourable public life, have essentially contributed to secure. (Davis, 248)

Smith did not stand again for Norwich in 1830. He retired as chairman of the dissenting deputies in 1832. He died on 31 May 1835 at 5 Blandford Square, London, the house of his son Benjamin.

Benjamin Smith (1783–1860), politician, was born on 28 April 1783 at Eagle House, Clapham Common. Educated at Tonbridge School, he was admitted a pensioner at Trinity College, Cambridge, on 8 October 1802. It is doubtful, however, if he ever resided, and he probably went directly to Cooke's distillery where he made his fortune. Unlike his father, his radical inclinations were clear. He never married, but lived openly with Anne Longden (*d.* 1834), a former milliner's apprentice, whom he adored and who was the mother of his five children, the eldest of whom was Barbara Leigh Smith *Bodichon (1827–1891), and the second Benjamin Leigh *Smith, the Arctic explorer. He built an Owenite school in Vincent Square for poor children, which his children also attended so that they could become monitors to teach younger children in the Lancastrian fashion. Member of parliament for Sudbury from 1835 to 1837 and Norwich from 1838 to 1847, Smith was a staunch Liberal and free-trader. He died at Blandford Square on 16 April 1860. R. W. Davis

Sources R. W. Davis, *Dissent in politics, 1780–1830: the political life of William Smith, MP* (1971) • HoP, *Commons* • *IGI* • *DNB* • Cobbett, *Parl. hist.* • *CGPLA Eng. & Wales* (1860) [Benjamin Smith]

Archives Claydon House, Buckinghamshire, family corresp. • CUL, personal and family corresp. and papers • Duke U., Perkins L., corresp. and papers • DWL, drafts of parliament bills relating to dissenters' marriages • University of Kansas, Lawrence, Kenneth Spencer Research Library, collection of material relating to dissenters | BL, corresp. with Lord Holland, Add. MS 51573 • NA Scot., corresp. as deputy governor of the British Fishery Society • priv. coll., Verney MSS, corresp. with Florence Nightingale • St Thomas's Hospital, London, corresp. with his granddaughter Florence Nightingale • U. Durham L., letters to second Earl Grey

Likenesses V. Green, mezzotint, pubd 1800 (after J. Opie), BM • H. Thomson, oils, exh. RA 1814, St Andrew's Hall, Norwich [*see illus.*] • W. C. Edwards, line engraving (after H. Thompson), BM

Wealth at death under £35,000—Benjamin Smith: administration, with the will annexed, 6 June 1860, *CGPLA Eng. & Wales*

Smith, William [*called* Strata Smith] (**1769–1839**), civil engineer and geologist, was born on 23 March 1769 at The Forge, Churchill, Oxfordshire, the son of John Smith (1735–1777), the village blacksmith, and his wife, Ann

William Smith (1769–1839), by T. A. Dean, pubd 1837 (after Hugues Fourau, 1837)

(1745–1807), also *née* Smith. He was educated at the village school, which he attended until about 1780.

Early work in Somerset In 1787 Smith became assistant to the land surveyor Edward Webb (1751–1828) at Stow on the Wold, learning to measure and value land. Late in 1791 Webb sent Smith to survey estates belonging to Lady Elizabeth Jones (1741–1800) at Stowey in north Somerset. After walking there from Stow, he lodged at Rugbourne Farm, High Littleton, which he later named as the birthplace of his ideas. Much coal was mined around Stowey and Smith soon became involved in underground surveys. These set him thinking about the succession of strata in an area where pioneering investigations had been made, some eighty years earlier, by John Strachey (1671–1743).

Smith's work impressed local landowners. As a result he was asked to survey routes for a planned, double-branched, Somerset coal canal, which was intended to take land-locked coal to the sea and, via other canals, to London. (In March 1794 he was in London, giving evidence in support of their enabling act of parliament.) Technically innovative, in August 1794 the canal proprietors sent Smith and two local coal owners, the surgeon Richard Perkins (1753–1821) and Samborn Palmer (1758–1814), on a fact-finding tour of canal and colliery installations throughout the midlands and north of England. On this Smith continued his embryonic geological investigations.

Canal excavations started in July 1795. These extended west to east along two sub-parallel and deeply incised valleys, about 2 miles apart. The excavations revealed the gently dipping strata one by one, allowing Smith to compare those of one branch of the canal with those of the other. By the end of 1795 Smith had worked out the local (incomplete) order of strata. On 5 January 1796 he recorded his critical observation that some of the strata contained fossils, and those that did could be identified by them. This realization allowed Smith to separate, for the first time, strata which had previously been confused because of a shared lithology. This was a major geological breakthrough. Further, Smith's training as a surveyor led him to realize that he could colour such strata onto maps, since he understood their thickness and dip and thus their geometry. From 1799 he started both to map local strata and to show them on geological cross-sections.

The canal excavations may have provided Smith with valuable geological data, but by 1799 there were more practical and immediate construction problems to be considered. During their fact-finding tour of 1794 Smith, Perkins, and Palmer had seen the half-size caisson erected in Shropshire by its inventor Robert Weldon (1768–1804). The use of such caissons was an idea soon adopted by the Canal Company; each caisson would replace several canal locks and save much-needed water. However, such caissons needed to be constructed to an extremely high standard to remain watertight, and the first and only one, newly built at Combe Hay, failed. After disagreement over this caisson, in June 1799, Smith was dismissed from the Canal Company's employment (for which he was then being paid £450 a year).

Land surveying and drainage Smith now set up, in partnership with Jeremiah Cruse (1758–1819), as a land surveyor in Trim Bridge, Bath. Bath proved a fortunate location for the business, since so many of the landed gentry holidayed there. Between 1802 and 1805, his Bath shop was also the venue at which his fossil collections were publicly displayed.

Immediately after his dismissal by the Canal Company, Smith had dictated a list, the 'Order of the Strata round Bath', to his two local supporters, the Revd Joseph Townsend (1739–1816) and the Revd Benjamin Richardson (1758–1832), and with their encouragement he issued a prospectus in June 1801 for his intended book, *Accurate delineations and descriptions of the natural order of the various strata that are found in different parts of England and Wales*, to be published by John Debrett (*d.* 1822). Smith knew that his stratigraphic ideas had great economic potential since they revealed where coal, iron, clay, and other minerals then so vital to British industrialization should be sought. From 1801 he started travelling all over the country in search both of commissions (by 1801 at 2 guineas a day plus expenses) and of data concerning the ordering of strata further afield.

Smith had first undertaken land drainage work for the Canal Company chairman James Stephens (*c.*1748–1816). By late 1799 he was much in demand as land drainer around Bath, a demand augmented by the wet autumn of that year. In 1800, in Wiltshire, he drained the Tytherton estates of Thomas Crook, in the process discovering another new stratum (the Kellaways Rock) to add to his order. Smith's work here was inspected by the landowner Thomas William Coke (1752–1842) who subsequently invited Smith to Holkham, Norfolk. In summer 1801 Coke introduced Smith to Francis, duke of Bedford (1765–1802), then trying to drain some of his Woburn estates with the assistance of his land steward John Farey (1766–1826). Smith and Farey met in October 1801 and Smith's results greatly impressed Farey with their novelty and economic importance. As a result, in February 1802, Farey brought them to the attention of the landowning president of the Royal Society, Sir Joseph Banks (1743–1820).

Towards a geological map In 1801 (and again in 1804) Smith's prospective publisher, Debrett, was declared bankrupt. So, at the June 1804 Woburn sheep shearing, Banks opened a subscription towards publication of Smith's intended *Geological Map* (inspired by the premium newly offered by the Society of Arts). Unfortunately, this subscription drew little support. Nevertheless, in 1803 Smith established a London office (with, from 1805, his fossil collections on shelves corresponding to the strata), and in the following year he was consulted on the trial for coal at Batheaston. Although unsuccessful it was the first trial at which Smith's newly acquired knowledge of stratification was used. More significantly, on 24 March 1805, Smith was able to inform others, hunting coal in the Oxford Clay near Bruton in Somerset, that they were wasting their time and money, and that they had been misled by simple superficial similarities into digging in a place where no coal could be reached using existing mining technology.

From 1806, after Banks had expressed the wish that Smith's geological map should be finished, Farey began to extol Smith's work in the pages of the *Monthly Magazine* and the *Philosophical Magazine* and in Abraham Rees's *Cyclopaedia*. However, from 1805 to 1807 Smith was based at Norwich, working, at least in part, on management of water meadows. Nevertheless, his time in East Anglia did allow him to become familiar with the fossils of another of his key strata, the Chalk. He added specimens from this stratum to his increasingly large collection of the 'characteristic' fossils of the strata he found to occur in England.

Between 1800 and 1812 Smith's life was highly itinerant and financially precarious. He worked as land and mineral surveyor and drainer throughout England and Wales, as coal hunter in Lancashire, coal prospector in Somerset and Yorkshire, sea-defence builder in south Wales and east England, harbour improver in south Wales, and canal surveyor in Sussex. The difficulty of combining writing with so much travelling meant that Smith was only able to publish one book during this period, *Water Meadows* (1806). However, its publication was unprofitable and he did not commit himself to further unremunerative writing.

Late in 1807 the Geological Society of London was founded. Many of its members remained unconvinced of the value of Smith's work and, from 1808, proposed to publish a rival *Geological Map*. By 1810 they were ostracizing Farey for his outspoken support of Smith. Finally, in 1812, the London map maker John Cary (1754–1835) offered to publish Smith's *Geological Map*. Specially engraved plates were prepared, for which Smith decided topographic details.

Publication and debt The first version of Smith's map was published in August 1815. It was dedicated to Banks, who as landowner had immediately realized the economic significance of Smith's results, in contrast to those at the Geological Society. This map was continually modified until at least 1818. It was, and remains, a truly remarkable achievement for one individual. But the rival, better-supported and now better-informed, 'gentlemanly' map of the Geological Society, when finally published in 1820, resulted in a sharp drop in sales of Smith's. A lack of subscribers to Smith's major proposed works, *Strata Identified* (1816–19) and *Stratigraphical System* (1817), meant that neither was completed, despite the important contribution from his young nephew John *Phillips (of whom he had had charge since his parents died in 1807). By 1819 Smith was in serious financial trouble; in June 1819 he was imprisoned for debt spending almost ten weeks in the king's bench prison in London. This was just a month after his wonderful geological maps of the counties of England had started to appear; the series was never completed.

Smith's financial difficulties were broadly due to a lack of the governmental support that his continental contemporaries enjoyed. However, the immediate cause of Smith's imprisonment had been an unfortunate investment in a quarrying concern near Bath. The disaster was only partially assuaged by the enforced sale of his wonderful fossil collections, at Banks's instigation, to an uninterested British Museum between 1815 and 1818. Smith's library also had to be sold and all his personal papers were rescued only when a friend purchased them for return to Smith.

Later years and eventual recognition Smith now turned his back on London and went north. From 1820, assisted by his nephew Phillips, he once again became the peripatetic geologist. In 1824 and 1825 he and Phillips lectured widely in Yorkshire. In 1828 Smith was offered the position of land steward to Sir John Johnstone (1799–1869) at Hackness, Yorkshire. There Smith produced his last, and probably most underrated, masterpiece, a detailed and wonderfully accurate geological map of the Hackness estate, at 6½ inches to the mile (published in 1832).

In the previous year, 1831, the new generation of fellows of the Geological Society, long aware of the treatment meted out to Smith, awarded him their first Wollaston gold medal in 'recognition of his being a great and original discoverer in English Geology' (*Proceedings of the Geological Society*, 1, 1831, 271). This was presented in 1832 at the Oxford meeting of the new British Association for the Advancement of Science (BAAS), at whose meetings Smith became a regular attender. In 1832 he received a government pension of £100 a year. In 1834 he left Hackness to settle finally at Scarborough, Yorkshire. At the 1835 BAAS Dublin meeting Smith was awarded the honorary degree of LLD from Trinity College. At several of these BAAS meetings Smith presented papers, but they often now only demonstrated Smith's great limitations in the new world of theoretical geology, to which he was now expected to contribute. In 1837–8 Smith was a member of the commission which sought stone for the new houses of parliament. Smith died on 28 August 1839 at the house of George Baker, Gold Street, Northampton, on his way to the Birmingham BAAS meeting, and he was buried on 2 September at St Peter's Church, where a memorial bust was put up in his memory.

Personal life and lasting influence In appearance Smith was strong, muscular, and well-built. He was equally taken to be pugilist, soldier, or walker. A trace of a once broad Oxfordshire accent only left people further confused, whether about his unusual activities or his yeoman origins.

Smith married the mysterious Mary Ann (*c*.1791–1844), probably in 1808. She was described in 1824 as 'as unsuited for being the partner of a meditative philosopher as she could well be' (W. C. Williamson, *Good Words*, 18, 1877, 62). By 1819 she was mentally unstable and she died in 1844 in the lunatic asylum at York. Phillips, Smith's nephew and biographer, wrote in January 1831 to Adam Sedgwick that Smith's achievements had been despite 'long and heavy afflictions. Poverty, disappointment & neglect forced seclusion from the world of science—these have been heightened by a still more severe and invincible torment a mad, bad, wife' (letter, CUL, Add. 7652, IA, 84).

Smith's achievements were enormous. His 1815 map helped inspire the French government to fund an equivalent attempt for France. J.-F. d'Aubuisson de Voisins (1769–1841) wrote in 1819 that

> ce que les minéralogistes les plus distingués ont fait dans une petite partie de l'Allemagne, en un demi-siècle, un seul homme l'a entrepris et effectué pour toute l'Angleterre; et son travail [est] aussi beau par son résultat, qu'il est étonnant par son étendue. (What it has taken the most eminent mineralogists half a century to achieve in a small area of Germany, one man has undertaken and accomplished single-handed for the whole of England; and his work is quite as fine in its results as it is astounding in its scope.) (*Traité de Géognosie*, 1, 1819, 253)

In 1977 the Geological Society of London named its new medal for excellence in contributions to applied and economic aspects of geology after Smith. His lack of contributions to more academic geology has, however, left a fertile field for revisionist historians. But they have failed to ask whether the stratigraphical mistakes Smith certainly made were not also still being made by his contemporaries, to whom he had given such a lead.

H. S. Torrens

Sources L. R. Cox, 'New light on William Smith and his work', *Proceedings of the Yorkshire Geological Society*, new ser., 25 (1942–5), 1–99 · J. M. Eyles, 'William Smith: some aspects of his life', *Toward a history of geology*, ed. C. J. Schneer (1969), 142–58 · J. M. Eyles, 'William Smith: a bibliography', *Journal of the Society of the Bibliography of Natural History*, 5 (1968–71), 87–109 · J. Phillips, *Memoirs of William Smith LL D* (1844) · H. S. Torrens, 'Patronage and problems: Banks and the earth sciences', *Sir Joseph Banks: a global perspective* [London 1993], ed. R. E. R. Banks and others (1994), 49–75 · H. S. Torrens, 'Le "nouvel art de prospection minière" de William Smith et le "projet de houillère de Brewham"', *De la géologie à son histoire: ouvrage édite en hommage à François Ellenberger*, ed. J. Gaudant (1998), 101–18 • G. A. Kellaway, 'The work of William Smith at Bath', *Hot springs of Bath*, ed. G. A. Kellaway (1991), 25–55 • T. Sheppard, *William Smith: his maps and memoirs* (1920) • J. M. Eyles, 'William Smith, Sir Joseph Banks and the French geologists', *From Linnaeus to Darwin* [London 1983], ed. A. Wheeler and J. H. Price (1985), 37–50 • R. C. Boud, 'The early development of British geological maps', *Imago Mundi*, 27 (1975), 73–96 • J. Fuller, 'Strata Smith and his stratigraphic cross sections: 1819', *AAPG Bulletin* (1995) • H. S. Torrens, 'In commemoration of the 150th anniversary of the death of William Smith (1769–1839)', *Travaux de Comité Français d'Histoire de la Géologie*, 3rd ser., 3 (1990), 57–63 • d. cert. • burial register, Northants. RO

Archives Oxf. U. Mus. NH, MSS | Essex RO, Chelmsford, map of Essex • FM Cam., MSS • GS Lond., MSS • NHM, MSS • Oxford University, department of geology and mineralogy, MSS • Scarborough Art Gallery, MSS • Smithsonian Institution, Washington, DC • W. Sussex RO, MSS

Likenesses F. L. Chantrey, pencil drawing, *c*.1830, NPG • J. Jackson, pencil drawing, 1831, BM • T. A. Dean, engraving, pubd 1837 (after H. Fourau, 1837), NPG [*see illus.*] • T. A. Dean, stipple, pubd 1837 (after H. Fourau), BM • H. Fourau, oils, 1837, GS Lond. • M. Noble, bust, 1848, St Peter's, Northampton • M. Noble, bust, 1848, BGS • M. Noble, bust, 1848, Oxf. U. Mus. NH • W. Smith, portrait, repro. in Cox, 'New light on William Smith and his work', pl. 1 • W. Smith, portrait, University of Bristol, Eyles MSS • W. Walker and G. Zobel, engraving (*Men of science living in 1807–8*; after J. F. Skill, J. Gilbert, W. Walker, and E. Walker), NPG

Wealth at death under £300: 1839, administration, 1839, Borth. Inst.

Smith, William (1790–1847), merchant navy officer and Antarctic explorer, was born on 11 October 1790 in Seaton Sluice, Northumberland, the elder child of William Smith, joiner, of Seaton Sluice, and his wife, Mary Sharpe, of Earsdon, Northumberland. Nothing is known about his early years and education but he was probably apprenticed aged fourteen to the east coast coal trade. In 1811 he became owner and master of the *Three Friends* of Blakeney, Norfolk, and in 1812 master of the brig *Williams* of Blyth, newly built for him. In the years 1812–18 he traded to Europe and South America.

Smith sailed from Buenos Aires in mid-January 1819. In rounding Cape Horn he was driven into a high latitude, and on 19 February 1819 he wrote in his journal, 'in latitude 62°40′ S and longitude per Chronometer 60°00′ West, Land or Ice was discovered ahead bearing SEbS distant about two leagues, blowing hard gales with flying showers of snow' (Jones, 448). He named the place New South Britain, a name later changed to New South Shetland. What he had seen was Williams Point on Livingston Island, a black promontory that stood out from the ice cap. On returning to Valparaiso on 11 March 1819, he obtained no credence—'all ridiculed the poor man for his fanciful credulity and his deceptive vision' (Miers, 369). On his second voyage, in the winter (May–June 1819), he saw nothing of New South Shetland. On his third voyage, from Montevideo, Smith saw the same point again on 15 October 1819, as well as Desolation Island. He took soundings, made a landing on North Foreland in King George Island, where he took possession, and examined the northern coast of the islands from east to west.

Smith returned to Valparaiso, where Captain William Shirreff RN ordered Edward Bransfield, a master in the Royal Navy, and three midshipmen to accompany Smith to survey the new land. On his fourth voyage Smith examined the north and south coasts of New South Shetland and, from 30 January 1820, part of the Antarctic continent, the Trinity Peninsula. They had thus sighted the continent a few days later than Bellingshausen's sighting in longitude 2°15′ W. Bransfield's manuscript chart is in the hydrographic department of the Admiralty. From this, in 1941 Lieutenant-Commander R. T. Gould RN was able to plot Smith's course in great detail, round New South Shetland and from Tower Island to the South Orkneys. In 1821 Smith made a fifth voyage to New South Shetland, but found British and American ships there, killing fur seals, which were almost exterminated in the next five years. He returned to London with the *Williams*, arriving with 30,000 sealskins worth £7500. His owners were in difficulties and he was bankrupted. Smith published no account of his voyages, which were recorded only in his manuscript memorial and logbook and in a contemporary account by John Miers.

In 1824 Smith was a Thames pilot, and his licence was later extended to the Downs. The Trinity House records of the time describe him as 5 feet 8 inches tall, with black hair and dark complexion. In 1827–30 he was master of the *William and Ann*, owned by James Weddell, in the Davis Strait's whale fishery; he had little success and did not go again. In these years he often changed his address in the East End of London. In 1838 he was rejected for a place in the Trinity House almshouse, being under age. In 1839 his pilot's licence was withdrawn as 'a pilot reduced by age and infirmity', and he was superannuated. Petitions to the Admiralty for remuneration for his discovery brought nothing. He died in May 1847 at 2 Hungerford Street, St George-in-the-East, London, the exact date not being known. His estate, valued at £100, was left to his wife, Mary, about whom nothing is known. It is not known whether they had any children. A. G. E. Jones, *rev.*

Sources A. G. E. Jones, 'Captain William Smith and the discovery of New South Shetland', *GJ*, 141 (1975), 445–61 • J. Miers, 'An account of the discovery of New South Shetland', *Edinburgh Philosophical Journal*, 3/6 (1820), 367–80 • parish register, Seaton Sluice, Northumbd RO

Wealth at death £100: Jones, 'Captain William Smith'

Smith, William (1808–1876), printseller, was born on 11 July 1808 in Lisle Street, Leicester Square, London, the son of William Smith, also a printseller. The younger William Smith and his brother George went up to Cambridge University but left prematurely in 1835 when their father's death drew them to the family business. In 1836 Smith purchased a collection of prints and drawings from the cloth manufacturer John Sheepshanks which included many important Dutch and Flemish prints. He sold these to the British Museum for £5000, a considerably smaller sum than that offered by individuals in Holland. This was the department of prints and drawings' first substantial purchase. It was also the first of a series of large transactions between the British Museum and private collectors where Smith acted as intermediary. In 1841 Smith helped the museum to acquire many valuable prints from the collection of the Bond Street bookseller Joseph Harding. In 1844–5 he assisted the purchase of engravings by early German and Italian artists from the collection of William Coningham. In 1847 he presented works from the collections of Lord Aylesford and Samuel Woodburn and some very rare etchings by Rembrandt, procured with difficulty from the estate of Baron Verstolk van Soelen in Amsterdam. This was followed in 1848 by works from the collection of William Beckford. He also made donations of his own to the museum. Together these acquisitions transformed the collection of the department of prints and drawings.

By 1848 Smith was rich enough to retire from the printselling business. He then devoted himself to public works and to furthering his knowledge of art. He had been elected a member of the Royal Institution in 1845. In 1852 he became a fellow of the Society of Antiquaries and in 1856 founding member and trustee of the National Portrait Gallery. In 1858 he was elected its deputy chairman. An oil portrait of Smith by Margaret Sarah Carpenter dated 1856 remains in the gallery. In 1861 Smith joined the Royal Horticultural Society, organizing its stand at the International Exhibition of 1862. He championed the National Exhibition of Works of Art held in Leeds in 1868 and was also engaged in the management of the Art Union of London. He was a keen collector of watercolours and acquired many examples by eighteenth-century British artists. In 1871 he invited the Victoria and Albert Museum to select eighty-six of these. Others he presented to the National Gallery of Ireland.

Smith lived at 9 Southwick Street, Cambridge Square, Bayswater, London. He died suddenly in Notting Hill High Street on the way home from a friend's funeral on 6 September 1876 and was buried at Kensal Green cemetery, London, on 13 September. He was remembered by his contemporaries as a generous and conscientious man who had contributed greatly to the British Museum and other institutions. Smith bequeathed his letters, manuscripts, annotated exhibition catalogues, and further watercolours to the Victoria and Albert Museum. Additional correspondence is held at the Bodleian Library in Oxford.

E. I. CARLYLE, *rev.* MARY GUYATT

Sources A. Griffiths, ed., *Landmarks in print collecting: connoisseurs and donors at the British Museum since 1753* (British Museum Press, 1996), 90–100 [exhibition catalogue, Museum of Fine Arts, Houston, TX, 1996, and elsewhere] • *Men of the time* (1875), 910 • *The Athenaeum* (16 Sept 1876), 377 • *N&Q*, 5th ser., 6 (1876), 259 • *The Times* (11 Sept 1876), 1; (16 Sept 1876), 10 • L. Lambourne and J. Hamilton, eds., *British watercolours in the Victoria and Albert Museum* (1980)

Archives V&A NAL, annotated catalogues, letters, manuscript catalogues, and watercolours • V&A NAL, notes and lists of German and Italian prints | Bodl. Oxf., corresp. with William Beckford

Likenesses W. H. Carpenter, etching, *c*.1850, BM • M. S. Carpenter, oils, 1856, NPG • Caldesi, Blanford & Co., carte-de-visite, 1860, NPG • W. Carpenter, etching (after M. S. Carpenter), BM • G. & R. Lavis, carte-de-visite, NPG

Wealth at death under £16,000: resworn probate, Jan 1877, *CGPLA Eng. & Wales* (1876)

Smith, Sir William (1813–1893), classical and biblical scholar, was born in London on 20 May 1813, the eldest son of William Smith, tallow chandler, of Enfield, Middlesex. His parents were Congregationalists, and Philip *Smith (1817–1885) was his younger brother. William initially planned to study theology but then turned to the law and took articles with Mr Parker, a well-known solicitor. After entering University College, London, he showed great enthusiasm for the Greek and Latin classics, obtaining first prizes in both subjects. He registered at Gray's Inn on 8 May 1830, but then abandoned this to teach classics at University College School under Thomas Hewitt Key, and was professor of classics at the Independent college, St John's Wood. In 1834 he married Mary, daughter of James Crump of Birmingham.

Smith next embarked on a wide-ranging writing career, contributing articles to the *Penny Cyclopaedia* and editing popular critical editions of classical texts, among them Plato's 'Apology' (1840) and a selection from Tacitus (1850). His major achievement was to publish concise summaries of contemporary critical scholarship through the medium of dictionaries. A major success came in 1842 with the *Dictionary of Greek and Roman Antiquities* (2 vols.), followed in 1844–9 by the *Dictionary of Greek and Roman Biography, Mythology and Geography* (3 vols.). His *Dictionary of Greek and Roman Geography* (2 vols.) was published in 1857. Besides serving as editor, Smith initially wrote many of the entries, but attracted many leading scholars as contributors. With these publications he won a reputation for the authority of his treatment and for concise and clear presentation. The original editions were followed by smaller, abbreviated ones for school use. In conjunction with his publisher John Murray (1808–1892) he also embarked on a series of textbooks under the general title 'Principia' which, besides drawing on his own experience as a teacher, employed principles learned from Key. Besides a Latin grammar and a Latin–English dictionary he edited the series Student's Manuals of History and Literature, to which he contributed *Student's Greece* (1854).

Success in making contemporary scholarship readily accessible through up-to-date concise summaries of knowledge brought wide acclaim to Smith and encouraged him to turn to the Bible. The publication in 1860–63 of a *Dictionary of the Bible Comprising its Antiquities, Biography, Geography and Natural History* under his editorship marked a significant turning point in popular biblical interpretation. It was for this that Smith's name is best remembered. Originally planned as two volumes, the work was expanded to three once the range of material was recognized. The contributors included most leading British clerical scholars, but its chief appeal was its presentation of the results of recent researches in the biblical lands, especially Egypt and Mesopotamia. Smith stated his purpose in the preface: 'It is a Dictionary of the *Bible* and not of

Theology … It is intended to elucidate the antiquities, biography, geography and natural history of the Old Testament, New Testament, and Apocrypha; but not to explain systems of theology, or discuss points of controversial divinity' (Smith, preface, vii; author's italics). Bible dictionaries had been published earlier, notably by John Kitto (1804–1854), but they lacked the authority and historical definition which Smith sought. His *Student's Scripture History* of the Old Testament was published in 1865, and that of the New Testament in 1866.

An *Atlas of Ancient Geography, Biblical and Classical* was edited by Smith assisted by George Grove in 1875. Smith's significance lay in his demonstration that the same principles of historical criticism which applied to the annals and texts of Greece and Rome were relevant to understanding the Bible. Earlier attempts at this, notably by the liberal Anglicans, had aroused widespread consternation—as with the first volume of H. H. Milman's *History of the Jews* (1829). Smith, like Milman, was an eager follower and admirer of Edward Gibbon. This was expressed in Smith's editorship of a critical edition of Gibbon's *Decline and Fall of the Roman Empire* in 1854–5 (8 vols.) which included, and expanded, the notes of Milman and Guizot.

A Dictionary of Christian Antiquities (2 vols., 1875–80) followed, in which Smith was assisted by Samuel Cheetham, and an *Atlas of the Bible* (1875), prepared with the assistance of George Grove. *A Dictionary of Christian Biography* (4 vols.), produced with the editorial help of the evangelical churchman Henry Wace, followed in 1877–87. A second edition of the *Dictionary of the Bible*, revised with help from J. M. Fuller, was published in 1893. The second and third volumes were unaltered, but the first volume was extensively enlarged to include contributions from younger scholars, strongly reflecting the transformation of biblical scholarship in Great Britain since 1860.

Smith was a classical examiner at London University from 1853 to 1869, and a member of its senate from 1869. He was editor of the Conservative *Quarterly Review*, published by Murray, from 1867 until his death, editing issues from April 1867 to July 1893. Firm and tactful, he maintained its reputation. In 1857 he was elected to the general committee, and on 11 March 1869 he became registrar of the Royal Literary Fund. He was a member of the royal commission on copyright (1875). He received honorary doctorates from Oxford (22 June 1870), Dublin (1890), Glasgow, and Leipzig, and was for many years a member of The Club. He reluctantly accepted a knighthood, and was knighted at Windsor on 2 December 1892. He died at his home, 94 Westbourne Terrace, Bayswater, London, on 7 October 1893.

Smith's achievement in applying to the Bible the canons of historical criticism already established in the classical field marked his Bible dictionary as a significant turning point for biblical interpretation in the English-speaking world. This was quickly reflected in the growing Sunday school movement, where the older catechetical approach was replaced by attention to a core of historical knowledge. Although soon overtaken by the much larger (five-volume) work edited by James Hastings (1852–1922), published in 1898, Smith had helped to bring about a major change in popular perceptions of the Bible. Moreover, some of his works, particularly his *Atlas of Ancient Geography*, continued to be used by classicists into the twenty-first century. RONALD E. CLEMENTS

Sources *DNB* • W. Smith, ed., *A dictionary of the Bible comprising its antiquities, biography, geography and natural history*, 3 vols. (1860–63); 2nd edn (1893) • Boase, *Mod. Eng. biog.* • Foster, *Alum. Oxon.* • *Wellesley index*, vol. 1

Archives BL, letters to W. E. Gladstone, Add. MSS 44413–44785, *passim* • BL, letters to Sir Austen Layard, Add. MSS 38986–39115, *passim* • CUL, letters to Lord Acton • ICL, letters to Thomas Huxley • King's AC Cam., letters to Oscar Browning • NL Wales, letters to Sir George Cornewall Lewis

Likenesses Crellin, carte-de-visite, NPG • C. W. Walton, lithograph, DWL • woodcut (after photograph by Elliott & Fry), NPG; repro. in *Harper's Magazine* (1888)

Wealth at death £22,678 4s. 7d.: resworn probate, Feb 1901, *CGPLA Eng. & Wales* (1893)

Smith, William (1816–1896), actuary and translator, was born in Liverpool of Scottish parents on 30 December 1816. His father died while he was an infant, and he was brought up in Edinburgh by his maternal grandfather, Robert Cumming, who, though a descendant of John Brown (1627?–1685), the martyr of the covenant, was himself a disciple of James Purves. Smith was apprenticed to a bookseller in 1829, and after serving seven years he was for another seven years employed as clerk in a newspaper office. In 1844 he married Martha (*d.* 16 May 1887), daughter of Robert Hardie, the manager of the Edinburgh University printing press. They had nine children, of whom seven survived him.

In 1845 Smith entered the insurance business as head clerk to the British Guarantee Association. In 1847 he became manager of the English and Scottish Law Life Assurance Association, a post that he held for forty-five years; he retired in 1892, and became a director. He became a fellow of the Institute of Actuaries of Great Britain and Ireland in 1846, and of Scotland in 1856. In 1862 he served on the committee for collection of the mortality experiences of British life offices. From 1879 to 1881 he was chairman of the Association of Scottish Managers, and as such drafted the Married Women's Policies of Assurance (Scotland) Act of 1880.

Smith made his mark in literature and philosophy as the translator (1845–9) and biographer (1845) of Johann Gottlieb Fichte (1762–1814), with whose idealism he was in strong sympathy. His translations of Fichte were collected as *The Popular Works of Fichte … with a Memoir* (1849). He had no classical tastes or training, but was widely read in French and German, as well as in English literature. His familiarity with modern European thought was extended by foreign travel. In 1846 he was one of the founders of the Edinburgh Philosophical Institution, and he was for a long time its most active vice-president and chairman of its directors. The selection of its library and the arrangements for its winter lectures owed much to his insight and enterprise. The honorary degree of LLD conferred upon him by Edinburgh University in 1872 was a well-earned tribute to one who, without the aid of an academic career, had done much to foster the true spirit of modern culture.

In politics a strong Liberal, Smith took an active part in the second return of T. B. Macaulay for Edinburgh (1852), in the election of Adam Black as Macaulay's successor (1856), and in the successive elections of W. E. Gladstone for Midlothian. He was a JP for Midlothian. For some time he was an officer-bearer, and subsequently an attendant, at St Mark's Unitarian Chapel. Among his closest friends were Robert Cox and William Ballantyne Hodgson. His genial humour, generous kindness, and steadfast will made him a powerful personality in the circles in which he moved. He died at his residence, Lennox Lea, Currie, Midlothian, on 28 May 1896, and was buried at the Dean cemetery, Edinburgh. One of his sons, William Charles Smith (1849–1915), was an advocate and stood as a Liberal Unionist parliamentary candidate; another, Robert Henry Smith, was professor of civil and mechanical engineering at Mason Science College, Birmingham.

ALEXANDER GORDON, *rev.* C. A. CREFFIELD

Sources *The Scotsman* (29–30 May 1896) • *Christian Life* (6 June 1897), 278 • personal knowledge (1897)
Wealth at death £18,284 4*s.* 2*d.*: confirmation, 22 June 1896, *CCI*

Smith, Sir William Alexander (1854–1914), founder of the Boys' Brigade and businessman, was born on 27 October 1854 at Pennyland House, near Thurso, Caithness, the eldest in the family of three sons and a daughter of David Smith of Pennyland, a director of the Labuan Coal Company in China, and his wife, Harriet, daughter of Alexander Fraser, merchant, of Glasgow. He was educated at the local parish school, the Miller Institution, later Thurso Academy, but little is known of his academic record. In 1868, when he was thirteen, his father died in China; the widowed Harriet Smith sold the Pennyland property and moved with her family into Thurso, accepting the offer of her brother, Alexander Fraser, to take William into his home and warehouse business in Glasgow. He soon settled into the routine of prosperous, middle-class, protestant business life, attending YMCA lectures, revival meetings led by the Americans Dwight L. Moody and Ira D. Sankey, sailing trips, and soirées.

A growing estrangement led to Smith's departure from his uncle's home and business in 1878 to establish the exporting firm of Smith, Smith & Co. with his younger brother Donald. A major factor in his Free Church uncle's disapproval of his nephew's way of life was Smith's enrolment in the 1st Lanarkshire rifle volunteers (he reached the rank of lieutenant-colonel before retiring in 1908), which ran counter to Fraser's pacifist views. In 1881 James G. Findlay, a friend and colleague, entered into partnership with Smith to form the firm Smith, Findlay & Co., dealing in a variety of shawls, plaids, and tartans for export.

Smith was also a Sunday school teacher and, hard pressed, he started the first company of the Boys' Brigade (BB) on 4 October 1883 at the North Woodside mission hall of the wealthy College Free Church in the west end of Glasgow. He used military discipline and drill, acquired in the rifle volunteers, and a simple uniform of haversack, belt, and cap, to instil Christian manliness into unruly boys. The BB, a church-based, interdenominational youth movement, was started twenty-five years before the Boy Scouts first appeared on the scene.

In 1888 Smith, a conscientious and outwardly austere man, gave up his business to become the first full-time secretary of the BB, his salary being donated by prominent Scottish businessmen. The success of the BB, as the world's first voluntary uniformed youth organization, owed much to his tireless stewardship during its first thirty-one years. He toured Canada in 1895 to oversee BB progress at the invitation of his friend and supporter John Gordon, seventh earl of Aberdeen, the governor-general.

On 5 March 1884 Smith married Amelia Pearson (1858/9–1898), daughter of the Revd Andrew Sutherland, a former Presbyterian chaplain to the British army in Gibraltar. They had two sons, both later prominent in the BB. Amelia died in 1898 and eight years later, on 10 April 1906, he married Hannah Ranken (1855/6–1907), daughter of William Campbell, wholesale and retail merchant of Glasgow, a cousin of the British prime minister, Sir Henry Campbell-Bannerman. Smith inspected the United Boys' Brigades of America with her in 1907 but she died in the same year from the effects of an accident, not long after their return. Two years later, in July 1909, Smith absented himself for the shortest possible time during the annual 1st Glasgow company camp at Tighnabruaich to receive his knighthood in London. On 8 May 1914 he attended a meeting of the BB executive in London but was taken ill and admitted to St Bartholomew's Hospital, where he died on 10 May 1914.

JOHN SPRINGHALL, *rev.*

Sources F. P. Gibbon, *William A. Smith of the Boys' Brigade* (1934) • R. S. Peacock, *Pioneer of boyhood* (1954) • B. Fraser and M. Hoare, *Sure and stedfast: a history of the Boys' Brigade, 1883–1983*, ed. J. Springhall (1983) • Boys' Brigade Headquarters, Glasgow, archive • *The Times* (27 Oct 1954) • m. cert. [Amelia Pearson Sutherland] • m. cert. [Hannah Ranken Campbell] • d. cert.
Archives Boys' Brigade Headquarters, Glasgow, archive, diaries, corresp., and MS biography
Wealth at death £5062 8*s.* 4*d.*: confirmation, 15 July 1914, *CCI* (1914)

Smith, Sir William Cusack, second baronet (1766–1836), judge and politician, was born William Smith on 23 January 1766 in Dublin, the eldest son of Sir Michael Smith (1740–1808), an Irish barrister and MP (1783–93), and his wife, Mary Anne (*d.* 1798), daughter of James and Angelina Cusack of Coolmines, co. Dublin, and of Ballyronan, co. Wicklow. Sir Michael was also one of the barons of the exchequer (1793–1801), master of the rolls in Ireland (1801–6), and member of the privy council (1801). In recognition for his and his son's services to the government he was created a baronet of Ireland on 28 August 1799.

Smith was educated at Eton College and at Christ Church, Oxford, where he graduated BA in 1788. While at the university he became friendly with Edmund Burke, who became interested in one of his pamphlets. The two corresponded, and Smith spent a few vacations at Burke's house. In 1792 he dedicated two pamphlets, entitled 'The rights of artisans' and 'The patriot', to Burke.

Smith married Hester Berry (*d.* 4 June 1832), eldest daughter of Thomas and Frances Berry of Eglish Castle, King's county, on 13 August 1787. Of his private life no further details are known. The couple had four children (two sons, two daughters) of whom the elder son, Sir Michael (1793–1859), became third baronet, and the younger son, Thomas Berry Cusack *Smith (1795–1866), became attorney-general of Ireland and subsequently master of the rolls.

Smith was admitted to Lincoln's Inn in 1784 and called to the Irish bar in 1788 and, rapidly acquiring a substantial practice, was made a king's counsel in 1795. In 1794 he entered the Irish parliament for the borough of Donegal as a Liberal, supporting Catholic emancipation. At the same time he was a strong supporter of the government, and became a strenuous advocate of the Act of Union, a fact that the *Freeman's Journal* (29 August 1836) later explained by claiming 'his English predilections … were promoted and fostered by an English education and English associates, against which even the stupendous mind of the illustrious Burke had not been proof'. However, at the first parliamentary debate on the union in 1799 he had voted with the majority against it. His speech in the second union debate in 1799, after his change of mind had taken place, was esteemed one of the ablest on that side, and Lord Lieutenant Cornwallis believed that 'it tended strongly to establish the measure in the feelings of the House; though it could not be expected to alter the decision of the question' (Castlereagh, 2.130). It was later published as a pamphlet. Smith was an active member of the minority of the Irish bar which favoured the union, and wrote a letter of protest against the action of the majority. Several of his letters and pamphlets on the issue were republished in *Tracts on the Union* in 1831.

On 6 December 1800 Smith was appointed solicitor-general in Ireland. While holding that office he was appointed deputy judge of assize, and went on the north-east circuit as the colleague of his own father. In 1801 he became a baron of the exchequer, a position he held until his death. The following year he became a bencher of King's Inns, Dublin. There were rumours in Dublin of favouritism due to his support of the union, though Smith was accounted an 'able, acute and erudite lawyer' (*The Times*, 30 Aug 1836).

After his mother's death Smith added the additional surname and arms of Cusack to his name and arms by royal licence (30 March 1800), and succeeded to his father's baronetcy on the latter's death, on 17 December 1808.

Cusack Smith was 'a politician before he was a judge; and though the former character should have merged in the latter, he united both to his life's end' (*Freeman's Journal*, 29 Aug 1836). The style of his political writings was vigorous, but at the same time very pompous. In his spare time he devoted himself to literature, and as Paul Puck Peeradeal he issued a small volume of verse entitled *The Goblins of Neapolis* (1836). His *Verses* (1830) were privately printed without an author's name; and his *Metaphysic Rambles* (in three 'strolls' or parts, 1835–6) appeared as by Warner Christian Search. Under these pseudonyms and that of A Yeoman he issued many other essays, tracts, and addresses on legal matters, but also on topics such as miracles and metaphysics.

Cusack Smith's personality was characterized by a nervous irritability. He was easily excitable, easily offended, and subject to depression and fits of suspicion. His friendships 'were liable to be sometimes crossed by misunderstandings, which not being founded on any substantial ground, were not the easiest to remove by ordinary means' (Wills, 257). At the same time, he was very sensitive to other people's feelings. As a landlord he was highly esteemed by his tenants and the poor, to whom he was said to have been 'charitable to the extreme' (*Freeman's Journal*, 29 Aug 1836).

Cusack Smith's public conduct was 'public-spirited, judicious, independent, and constitutional' (Wills, 263). He was one of the most popular men in Ireland, according to *The Times* (30 August 1836), because of his impartiality and fairness as a judge, his liberal views, and his support for Catholic emancipation. However, when he attacked the emergence of passive resistance to tithes in the 1830s, his popularity dropped. The reason for this opposition to the tithe war can be found in his strong support for the established church, and his fear that this church was in danger. This view was strongly expressed in his *Metaphysic Rambles*. The *Freeman's Journal* (29 August 1836) commented on this: 'His grand error was in identifying it [the established church] with Christianity.' He made his views on the issue very clear, and also charged grand juries at the assizes in condemnation of the tithe agitation. He felt that he had to make a stand against what he believed to be the intimidation of juries. This strongly aggrieved Daniel O'Connell, and his conduct was brought before parliament. O'Connell used Cusack Smith's habit of holding court at inconvenient hours to support his political objections. On 13 February 1834 it was resolved by the House of Commons, at the instance of O'Connell, to appoint a select committee 'to inquire into the conduct of Baron Smith in respect of his neglect of duty as a judge, and the introduction of political topics in his charges to grand juries'. It was soon felt, however, that such a resolution threatened the independence of the judges. Cusack Smith's friends brought forward the question afresh a week later, when the resolution was revoked by a majority of six, chiefly through the exertions of Sir Frederick Shaw. He received congratulatory addresses on this occasion from nearly every grand jury in Ireland.

In August 1836 Cusack Smith fell ill with a bilious fever and a rheumatic attack while on circuit, and was confined to bed at his country seat in Newtown, King's county. However, a full recovery was expected, and he was still able to entertain visitors. His sudden death there on 26 August 1836 came as a shock to the public, and was blamed by some obituarists on over-exertion in his public duties (*The*

Times, 30 Aug 1836; *Freeman's Journal*, 29 Aug 1836). It caused considerable excitement in Dublin, since it was the first death of a baron of the exchequer bench during the administration of Lord Melbourne, and occurred at a time of widespread tithe agitation, and speculations about his successor were soon rife (*The Times*, 30 Aug 1836). Cusack Smith was buried in the family grave at Geashill, Newtown. The sale of his valuable library took place in Dublin in 1837, and occupied four days.

BRIGITTE ANTON

Sources Burke, *Peerage* • *DNB* • GEC, *Baronetage*, vol. 5 • 'Illness of Baron Smith', *Freeman's Journal* [Dublin] (26 Aug 1836), 3 • 'The late Baron Sir W. Smith', *Freeman's Journal* [Dublin] (29 Aug 1836), 2 • 'Death of Baron Sir William Smith', *Freeman's Journal* [Dublin] (29 Aug 1836), 4 • 'Death of Baron Smith', *The Times* (30 Aug 1836), 5c • 'Sir William Cusack Smith, bart.', J. Wills, *Lives of illustrious and distinguished Irishmen*, 6 (1847) • R. J. Hayes, ed., *Manuscript sources for the history of Irish civilisation*, 1 (1965) • *Memoirs and correspondence of Viscount Castlereagh, second marquess of Londonderry*, ed. C. Vane, marquess of Londonderry, 12 vols. (1848–53) • royal licence, 30 March 1800, Genealogical Office, Dublin, MSS 149, 150 • confirmation of arms of the crest of Cusack, 28/11/1809; copies of grant of supporters to the arms of Sir Wm Cusack Smith, 2/1/1810, 28/2/1810, 4/3/1810, Genealogical Office, Dublin, MSS 105, 149, 150 • pedigree of Smiths and Cusack Smiths, 1740–1910, Genealogical Office, Dublin, MS 114 • grant of baronetage, 1799, Genealogical Office, Dublin, MS 3

Archives BL, corresp. with William Gregory, Add. MSS 40202–40205 • BL, letters to Sir Robert Peel, Add. MSS 40239–40404, *passim* • Sheff. Arch., corresp. with Edmund Burke

Likenesses E. Lyon, wax bust, *c*.1834, V&A

Wealth at death valuable library sold in 1837: *DNB*

Smith, William Henry (1808–1872), writer and philosopher, was born at North End, Hammersmith, in January 1808, the youngest son in the large family of Richard Smith (*d*. 1823), a retired barrister; his mother (1766/1767–1842), to whom he was devoted but about whom little is known, was partly German in descent. He studied with a local clergyman, and then at Radley Academy, a nonconformist institution. In 1821 he enrolled at Glasgow College, where his elder brother Theyre Townsend *Smith (1798–1852) was preparing for the Presbyterian ministry. This taste of a congenial academic life was cut short by the death of his father in 1823, after which he settled in London and was articled to Sharon Turner, an attorney and Anglo-Saxon scholar, though Smith found the law distasteful.

By the late 1820s Smith moved in the circle of Sterling, Maurice, and others connected with the new weekly *Athenaeum*, to which he contributed eight pieces under the pseudonym the Woolgatherer. Smith's subsequent rides on the western circuit were profitless, and, despite being acquainted with many literary men, he drifted into a semi-reclusive life, living at home and writing poetry (the Wordsworthian *Solitude* appeared in 1836, along with *Guidone*) as well as *Ernesto* (1835), which was the final novel in Leitch Ritchie's Library of Romance. Smith's *Athelwold* (1842) failed at Drury Lane in 1843 with Macready and Helen Faucit in the principal roles. Small and unremarkable in appearance, Smith was teased about his slightness

William Henry Smith (1808–1872), by unknown sculptor, *c*.1840s

by his friend G. H. Lewes and later nicknamed himself the Snail.

Through his connection with John Stuart Mill, Smith found his true métier when he began to write for the *Westminster Review* in 1836. His first paper was entitled 'The poets of our age, considered as to their philosophical tendencies', which helped shape the Romantic canon. Samuel Warren introduced Smith to the Edinburgh publishing family of Blackwood, and his first contribution to *Blackwood's Edinburgh Magazine*, or 'Maga', appeared in 1837. His next was 'A prosing upon poetry' in 1840, and subsequently he prosed upon poetry, the law, philosophy, history, travel, and other topics for 'Maga' in over 125 articles and tales published over thirty years, and this work provided him with a frugal living, as well as the time to develop other interests.

In 1839 Smith published *A Discourse on Ethics of the School of Paley*, which attacked Cudworth's ethical doctrine, and then a pamphlet, *Remarks on Law Reform* (1840). After serving his time in the Middle Temple, he was called to the bar in the late 1830s. Throughout the 1840s Smith lived on a modest inheritance, coupled with his periodical earnings. He travelled in Europe producing pieces for 'Maga'. In 1848 or 1849 Smith's legacy was reduced by an unrepaid loan to a relative, and he decided to give up his law practice because he could no longer afford the offices. He retired to Bowness in the Lake District in summers, where he rented rooms, lived cheaply, and read and wrote, and wintered often in Brighton, with members of his family. John Wilson, professor of moral philosophy at Edinburgh, and a principal 'Maga' writer, asked Smith in 1851 if he would occupy his chair while he was on leave. This was probably Smith's greatest opportunity for material advancement and fame, but after a careful self-analysis he turned it down.

Blackwoods published Smith's *Thorndale, or, The Conflict of Opinions* in 1856. It purports to be the jottings of a philosophical invalid, and quietly espouses a 'pious uncertainty' that can be taken as one typical response to mid-Victorian crises of faith. The book earned critical esteem, but did not bring general notice. While writing in lodgings in Borrowdale, however, Smith met Lucy Caroline Cumming (1818–1881), daughter of the blind physician Dr George Cumming of Edinburgh, who supported herself and her family through translation work. In 1861 Smith told G. H. Lewes that they had talked about the 'impossibility' of marrying because of their mutual poverty, 'But', he said, 'it is dangerous, Lewes, to talk even of impossibility' (*George Eliot Letters*, ed. G. Haight, 1954, 3.392). They were married at St John's Church, Notting Hill, on 5 March 1861, and their marriage, though childless, was by all accounts exceptionally happy. Smith very shortly after published his second major volume of philosophical reflections, *Gravenhurst, or, Thoughts on Good and Evil* (1862), and in his remaining years devoted attention to the rising science of psychology, including essays in the *Contemporary Review* posthumously published in 1874 as *Knowing and Feeling: a Contribution to Psychology*.

Smith and his wife spent their years together in the Lake District, with relatives in various places, and in Switzerland. In February of 1869 Smith suffered a first heart attack, and by the winter of 1872 his health had rapidly deteriorated. He died on 28 March 1872 at 1 Norfolk Square in Brighton, and was buried in Brighton cemetery. While Smith had joked with his publisher in 1852 that he intended 'to make the experiment whether I can live upon oatmeal-porridge & prospect of posthumous fame!' (Davis, 201), he is one of the most solid and productive of the denizens of the Victorian literary world to have been completely forgotten. D. E. LATANÉ, JR.

Sources L. C. Smith, 'Memoir', in W. Smith, *Gravenhurst* (1875) • G. S. Merriam, *The story of William and Lucy Smith* (1890) • K. W. Davis, 'Letters of William Henry Smith to the Blackwoods, 1836–1862', PhD diss., Vanderbilt University, 1963 • D. Latané, 'William Henry Smith and the poetics of the 1830s', *Wordsworth Circle*, 20 (1989), 159–65 • M. Oliphant, 'William Smith', *Blackwood*, 112 (1872), 429–38 • J. Tulloch, *Modern theories in philosophy and religion* (1886) • M. J. Milsand, *Littérature anglaise et philosophie* (1893), 173–97 • *CGPLA Eng. & Wales* (1872)

Archives NL Scot., corresp. with Blackwoods

Likenesses marble bust, *c*.1840–1849, repro. in Merriam, *Story*, frontispiece [*see illus.*]

Wealth at death £5000: probate, 13 April 1872, *CGPLA Eng. & Wales*

Smith, William Henry (1825–1891), newsagent and politician, was born on 24 June 1825 at 42 Duke Street, Grosvenor Square, London, the only son of William Henry Smith (1792–1865), and his wife, Mary Ann Cooper. He had six sisters. His father, who was originally a newsagent in a small way of business, had the idea of sending London newspapers to provincial towns and rural districts by the morning mail coaches and by local services of swift horsed carts, rather than by the traditional post office night mails. Later he chartered express trains and on one occasion a boat to deliver the news promptly. Stern and irritable in his personal dealings, Smith senior was meticulous, ambitious, and exacting in business, eventually ruining his health and nerves by the pitch at which he worked.

William Henry Smith (1825–1891), by John D. Miller, pubd 1883 (after George Richmond, 1878)

Newspapers and railways Smith junior was educated chiefly at home, and for a few months in 1839 at Tavistock grammar school. Though brought up a Methodist, at sixteen he wanted to go to Oxford to prepare for holy orders; his father, however, curbed this wish, and set him to work in his news agency in the Strand. As a child he had a precocious understanding of the business, and at the age of twenty-one he became his father's partner.

Although his father wished to confine the business to an agency selling newspapers, Smith rented a bookstall at the London and North-Western Railway's Euston Station in 1848, and in 1851 secured a monopoly of bookstalls on the London and North-Western (LNW) system. Reading, which had been disagreeable on horse-drawn coaches, was a pleasant way to reduce the tedium of rail journeys, and the concourses of the London termini provided incomparable sites for the large-scale sale of reading matter. Smith excluded from his bookstalls all material that was judged corrupting or sensational, which earned him the nickname of the North-Western Missionary. His discrimination brought him praise, and kindled notions of middle-class Victorian respectability, with the result that by the time of his death his name had become synonymous in some circles with a dreary and timid puritanism. In fact he was not specially prudish, but for religious and social reasons believed strongly in the ameliorative results of the British people being better educated, and receiving edification from their reading. The effect of this view was to ratify class mobility by entangling it with the acquisition of superior culture. Smith developed his network of railway bookstalls widely, and by 1862 had secured exclusive bookstall rights on all the important English railway systems. Henry James wrote of a Smith's bookstall at a London terminus:

> It is a focus of warmth and light in the vast smoky cavern; it gives the idea that literature is a thing of splendor, of a dazzling essence, of infinite gas-lit red and gold. A glamour hangs over the glittering booth, and a tantalizing air of clever new things. (James, 36)

Smith made other innovations, often opposed by his father, who receded from the business in the 1850s and formally retired in 1857. He displayed advertisements in his bookstalls, and from 1851 began leasing blank walls on the principal railway stations on which to paper advertisements. He was later given contracts—often on a monopoly basis—for advertising in waiting rooms and booking halls. Smith thus pioneered the lucrative if disfiguring practice of open-air advertisements. The repeal of newspaper stamp duty in 1854 gave a great impetus to the business. Also in 1854 *The Times* granted Smith an effective monopoly of its wholesale distribution outside London for an annual charge of £4000. It was a privilege of enormous commercial value to be 'The Thunderer's' sole country agents. In 1861 Smith started a circulating library to supply people in remote districts with improving (or at least uncorrupting) books. He was animated by ideals that were both businesslike and philanthropic. At a time when many moral reformers were characterized as hypocrites, Smith's sincerity was never challenged. By 1890 Smith's library had a turnover of £52,661. In association with Chapman and Hall, Smith also published cheap, 'yellow-backed' books, entitled The Select Library of Fiction, until this business was sold in 1883 to the publishers Ward and Lock.

In 1850 Smith opened a Dublin branch, and during the 1850s (which was a crucial decade in the development of W. H. Smith & Son) he gave considerable attention to Irish business. Though the business expanded under local management, he took little interest from the 1860s, and seemed cold and detached to his Irish associates. He was, however, unlike his father, a trustful rather than anxious delegator. After he received political office, he passed the daily management of W. H. Smith & Son to others, and it became a unique example of a privately owned business that was nevertheless professionally managed.

Many of Smith's strengths seem like a reaction against his father's excesses and mistakes. He was patient, self-controlled, imperturbable, and rational. Where his father's conversation was passionate and refractory, his own speech was flat and pacific. Though he had entered the business reluctantly, as an act of filial submission, he became one of the best-known Victorian capitalists, whose name in the mid-nineteenth century was a byword for mass distribution.

Philanthropy and marriage After Smith had renounced his desire for holy orders, his religious feelings were expressed in public and philanthropic business. In 1849 he joined the managing committee of King's College Hospital, in 1855 he was elected to the Metropolitan Board of Works, and he was treasurer of the Society for Promoting Christian Knowledge and of the London Diocesan Council for the Welfare of Young Men. He was always a generous subscriber to philanthropic schemes, especially those conducted by the protestant church. He had a strong mistrust of Rome.

In 1858 Smith married Emily (1828–1913), widow of Benjamin Auber Leach, and eldest daughter of Frederick Dawes Danvers, clerk to the council of the duchy of Lancaster. In addition to a stepdaughter whom Smith treated as his own child, they had four daughters and two sons, the younger of whom was (William) Frederick Danvers *Smith. A month after his death in 1891, Emily Smith was created Viscountess Hambleden, with remainder to Smith's male heirs.

Politics and office, 1856–1880 In 1856 Smith contemplated standing as a Liberal at Boston, and in 1857 at Exeter; but he was blackballed as a presumptuous tradesman when seeking election to the Reform Club in 1862, and this rebuff perhaps diverted his political sympathies. In 1865 he stood at Westminster as a Palmerstonian Liberal-Conservative against the whig R. W. Grosvenor, afterwards Lord Ebury, and the radical John Stuart Mill. He was left bottom of the poll; but in 1868 (the franchise having been extended to householders in boroughs) he was returned to parliament for Westminster. His expenses in the second contest amounted to £8900—compared to a total of £2296 for Grosvenor and Mill—and the supposition of bribery led to a petition which caused Smith great nervous strain. His success signified a shift in the political allegiances of the commercial classes, and prefigured the wider rejection of Gladstonian radicalism by middle-class constituencies. He seemed the embodiment of a new school of Conservatism whose leaders were firm and prosperous but not imperious, privileged, or reactionary.

Smith's maiden speech in parliament on 1 April 1869 was on pauperism and vagrancy, and though he was never eloquent or even fluent, he proved a useful, assiduous member, who was widely respected for his plain philanthropic qualities and businesslike powers. He was prominent during the passage of the Elementary Education Bill in 1870, and instrumental in forcing the government to substitute one large school board for London instead of their projected twenty-three school boards: an important step towards recognizing that London government required general rather than local supervision. Smith was elected a member of the first London school board in 1871. It was on account of this expertise that Benjamin Disraeli on forming his administration in 1874 initially contemplated appointing Smith to the Board of Education. In the event Smith became financial secretary to the Treasury (February 1874). On financial policy his advice was dependable, succinct, and shrewd.

On 14 August 1877 Disraeli promoted Smith to the cabinet as first lord of the Admiralty. Commending this appointment to the queen, Disraeli wrote: 'The Admiralty requires a strong man & Mr. Smith is such; combining vigilance & vigour with a perfect temper and conciliatory manners' (Chilston, 95). Disraeli was criticized by his own party for conferring the Admiralty on a London tradesman, and this appointment of 'the Ruler of the Queen's Navee' was teased in the Gilbert and Sullivan comic opera of 1878, *HMS Pinafore*. Smith, who was sworn to the privy council on 13 August 1877, belied all misgivings. The accession of a borough member to Disraeli's cabinet proved an immediate strength. Almost from the outset Smith's opinions on subjects outside his own department were weighed by his colleagues, and he participated in the resolution of large issues. His counsel steadied the cabinet during the Bulgarian atrocity agitation, the crisis with Russia, and the resignations of the earls of Derby and Carnarvon (1878). He was never a jingo. Unlike most great capitalists who enter politics in middle age, Smith was neither aggressive to his opponents, insolent to his colleagues, nor snubbing to his officials. As Lord George Hamilton wrote, 'he knew, felt and assimilated all that was best in the progressive movements of the day. His common sense and perception (amounting to genius) rarely, if ever, failed him in his diagnosis of the agitation of the moment' (Hamilton, *Parliamentary Reminiscences*, 252–3). In his diary Lord Derby wrote of Smith that 'He was a perfectly suitable representative of the middle class to which he belonged: having few ideas, no brilliant ability, but industry, the tradesman's willingness to oblige, and sound judgments within the limits of his capacity' (diary of Lord Derby, 21 Feb 1892, Lpool RO).

Opposition, and further office, 1880–1886 Smith preferred to be at truce with his adversaries rather than at loggerheads. After the Liberal victory in 1880, the official Conservative opposition in the House of Commons headed by Smith, Sir Stafford Northcote, and Sir Richard Cross proved too mild for some of their younger colleagues, known as the Fourth Party, who attacked their own leaders as much as the government. Lord Randolph Churchill in particular mocked Smith for his suburbanism. One of Smith's few opponents to denigrate him was W. E. Gladstone, who called him 'dunder-headed' after his speech against the National Debt Bill (August 1883), and said (privately) after his 'scandalous' speech in the naval debate of December 1884, 'he hoped W. H. Smith would never again become a Minister of the Crown—a position which from being utterly void of statesmanlike qualifications he is unfitted to hold', dubbing him, in a patronizing jibe, Marshall and Snelgrove (the London store) (*Diary of Sir Edward Walter Hamilton*, 469, 746). Smith became secretary of state for war on 24 June 1885 in Salisbury's first administration. He had continued to represent Westminster, but as the result of alterations to the constituency under the Redistribution Act, he was elected in 1885 for the new Strand division, which he continued to represent until his death.

When Salisbury had difficulty in replacing Sir William Hart Dyke, who resigned in December 1885 as chief secretary for Ireland, he turned to Smith, who assumed that invidious office on 23 January 1886. It was a measure of the value attached to Smith's discretion that he retained his seat in the cabinet, although Hart Dyke had not been a member. Though Smith had come to dislike the bulk of Irish politicians, he knew Ireland better than most senior Conservatives: he had made many business or pleasure trips there, once contemplated buying property in Connemara and had in 1882, worked up a plan of land purchase, Gladstone having, most unusually, made civil service expertise available to an opposition politician (Matthew, 200–01). Shortly after Smith's arrival in Ireland his Irish news agency business was transferred to his Dublin manager, Charles Eason, to forestall the possibility of attacks on its premises or employees. This was the most permanent result of his appointment as chief secretary for in February 1886 Smith returned to opposition when Salisbury's government was defeated.

The War Office, and leader of the house, 1886–1892 On the formation of Salisbury's second administration Smith was appointed secretary of state for war in August 1886. In his clashes over War Office estimates with Lord Randolph Churchill at the Treasury, he was clear, adamant, and equable where Churchill was excitable and offensive. In the restructuring of the cabinet, following Churchill's resignation, Smith became first lord of the Treasury and leader of the House of Commons in January 1887. His leadership was an undoubted success: indeed if he had only had more power of political initiative he would have rivalled Sir Robert Peel as a leader of the house. Recalcitrance, provocation, and triumphalism were not his methods. He was content to sit silently for long periods, and his interventions seldom gave a pretext for controversy.

> When he found himself in a difficulty, he made some plaintive appeal to the good sense of the House, or to the better feelings of his opponents, or to the dignity of Parliament; or delivered himself of some homely platitude, which, though it was wont to evoke smiles and even laughter, generally served the purpose of the moment. (diary of Sir Edward Walter Hamilton, 8 Oct 1891, fol. 103)

He was conscientious, disinterested, and prosaic; in the weekly parliamentary sketches of *Punch* by H. W. Lucy, he was given the affectionate sobriquet of Old Morality, by which nickname he became widely known. It was his misfortune to lead the house in a period when the management of the Commons was peculiarly difficult. There were many hotheads, and many contentious occasions. Even after Smith in 1887 introduced a more stringent form of closure motion, the Irish separatists protracted debate, and sittings were often as bad-tempered as they were late. The Parnell commission caused particularly violent and agonized feelings.

Wealth, death, and reputation On 1 May 1891 Smith was appointed lord warden of the Cinque Ports, a post to which he was nominated by Salisbury on the grounds that the expenses of running Walmer Castle were so heavy that his richest colleague deserved the honour (the following year Smith's estate was valued for probate at over £1,773,000). Though Smith had invested some £450,000 in land in Devon and Suffolk since 1877, his country house (Greenlands at Henley-on-Thames which he had bought in 1871) was unpretentious and not the centre of great estates: his hopes of buying Powderham Castle from Lord Devon had been disappointed. In late spring of 1891 Smith's health broke under the strain of the parliamentary session, and on 20 August he was moved to Walmer Castle, where he died of gout and heart failure on 6 October 1891. He was buried at Hambleden on 10 October 1891. Survived by his wife, he was the subject of the elegy by Alfred Austin, 'In Westminster Abbey, October 10th, 1891'.

'The feeling about Smith's death is very marked and wide-felt', indeed 'almost hysterical', E. W. Hamilton noted two days later.

> Smith's leading characteristic was high sense of duty, and his determination to discharge his duties honestly and to the best of his ability. He had much tact, firmness, amiability and above all patience, which qualities made him esteemed by both sides of the House. He knew his own measure, and consequently rarely got out of his depth, which was not profound … He was not as much of a simpleton as some people supposed, for he had a good deal of craftiness and wiliness which he concealed under an honest face; and some of those who came in contact with him were inclined to think that in spite of his kindliness and geniality he was a *faux bon homme*. (diary of Sir Edward Walter Hamilton, 8 Oct 1891, fols. 103–4)

Smith's face was clear and frank-looking with voluminous side-whiskers and resolute eyes. He enjoyed music and the sea. In 1880 he bought the *Pandora*, a steam-yacht of 500 tons built for the duke of Hamilton, which delighted him for the rest of his life. He was public-spirited: it was through his generosity that Sir Michael Hicks Beach in 1886 was able to accept the office of chief secretary of Ireland with its small salary and heavy expenses; during the Baring banking crisis of 1890 Smith offered a personal cheque of £100,000 to the Bank of England's guarantee fund. After his death there was unanimity about his qualities. He had become, wrote one elector, 'the typical exponent of a well-balanced common sense in British political life' (Rodd, 260). His colleague Lord Cranbrook agreed: 'He was a straightforward, honest man & won confidence of all by his character & not genius. He was wise in Council & prudent' (*Diary of Gathorne Hardy*, 210). Queen Victoria recorded after his death, 'Such an excellent, honest, reliable, conciliatory man, and so modest and simple' (*Letters of Queen Victoria*, 2.73).

This veneration by Smith's contemporaries derived from a symbolism perhaps more important than the facts of his domestic happiness, business success, and political ability. He personified the embourgeoisement of a set of political myths which had sustained England since the revolution of 1688. Smith stood for sturdy and straight protestantism rather than the subtle designing of cardinals; distrust of extremism, abstract notions, and intellectual passions; cleanliness from the taint of continental doctrines or Latin sensuality; belief in mending old ways; and respect for every caution conveyed by the catchphrase, 'each case on its own merits'.

RICHARD DAVENPORT-HINES

Sources E. A. A. D. Chilston, *W. H. Smith* (1965) · H. Maxwell, *Life and times of the right honourable W. H. Smith* (1893) · C. Wilson, *First with the news: the history of W. H. Smith, 1792–1972* (1985) · L. M. Cullen, *Eason and Son, a history* (1989) · H. James, *Essays in London* (1893), 36 · *The diary of Sir Edward Walter Hamilton, 1880–1885*, ed. D. Bahlman, 2 (1972), 469, 746 · H. W. Lucy, *Sixty years in the wilderness*, 2 (1912), 297–304 · G. Hamilton, *Parliamentary reminiscences and reflections*, 2: *1886–1906* (1922), 252–3 · J. R. Rodd, *Social and diplomatic memories*, 1 (1922), 260 · *The letters of Queen Victoria*, ed. G. E. Buckle, 3 vols., 3rd ser. (1930–32), vol. 2, p. 73 · *The diary of Gathorne Hardy, later Lord Cranbrook, 1866–1892: political selections*, ed. N. E. Johnson (1981) · H. C. G. Matthew, *Gladstone, 1875–1898* (1995) · diary of Sir Edward Walter Hamilton, 1879–1936, BL, Add. MS 48656, fols. 103–4 [8 Oct 1891] · d. cert. · *The Times* (11 Oct 1891) · Lord Derby, diary, Lpool RO

Archives PRO, papers, WO 110 · W. H. Smith and Son, political corresp. and papers | Beaulieu Archives, letters to Lord Montagu · BL, corresp. with Arthur James Balfour, Add. MS 49696 · BL, corresp. with Lord Cross, Add. MS 51268 · BL, corresp. with W. E. Gladstone, Add. MS 44300 · BL, letters to Lord Halsbury, Add. MS 56371 · BL, corresp. with Sir Strafford Northcote, Add. MS 50021 · Bodl. Oxf., letters to Acland Society · Bodl. Oxf., corresp. with Sir Henry Burdett · Bodl. Oxf., letters to Benjamin Disraeli · CAC Cam., corresp. with Lord Randolph Churchill · CKS, letters to Anetas Akers-Douglas · CKS, letters to Edward Stanhope · CUL, letters to Sir George Stokes · Glos. RO, corresp. with Sir Michael Hicks Beach · Harrowby Manuscript Trust, Sandon Hall, Staffordshire, letters to Lord Harrowby · HLRO, letters to Lord Ashbourne · Hove Central Library, Sussex, letters to Lord Wolseley and Lady Wolseley · NA Scot., corresp. with A. J. Balfour · NL Wales, letters to Lord Rendel · PRO, Hambleden MSS · Suffolk RO, Ipswich, letters to Lord Cranbrook · U. Birm. L., corresp. with Joseph Chamberlain · W. Yorks. AS, Leeds, letters to Lord St Oswald · Wilts. & Swindon RO, corresp. with fourteenth earl of Pembroke

Likenesses G. Richmond, oils, 1878; formerly, priv. coll. · J. D. Miller, engraving, pubd 1883 (after G. Richmond, 1878), NPG [*see illus.*] · H. Furniss, pen-and-ink drawing, *c*.1886, NPG · S. P. Hall, double portrait, pencil sketch, 1887 (with John Bright), NPG · F. Winter, plaster bust, 1891, NPG · Barraud, photograph, NPG; repro. in *Men and women of the day*, 2 (1889) · H. Furniss, caricature, pen-and-ink sketch, NPG · A. B. Joy, marble bust, Palace of Westminster, London · Lock & Whitfield, woodburytype photograph, NPG; repro. in T. Cooper, *Men of mark: a gallery of contemporary portraits* (1881) · Lombardi, carte-de-visite, NPG · Spy [L. Ward], caricature, chromolithograph, NPG; repro. in *VF* (12 Nov 1887) · caricature, chromolithograph, NPG; repro. in *VF* (9 March 1872) · lithograph, BM · lithograph, BM; repro. in *Civil service review* (1876) · woodcuts, NPG, BM

Wealth at death £1,773,388 8*s*. 10*d*.: resworn probate, Sept 1892, *CGPLA Eng. & Wales*

Smith, William Robert [Willie] (1886–1982), billiards and snooker player, was born on 25 January 1886 at 3 Taylor Street, Darlington, co. Durham, the son of William Smith, a journalist who was sports editor of the local newspaper the *North Star*, and his wife, Frances Annie Malkin. Young Willie was introduced to the game on the billiard table at the Old Cock public house in Darlington, which his parents ran. He trained and worked as a linotype operator. At the age of only fifteen he was declared a professional player by the Billiards Association after he accepted half a guinea in expenses for playing an exhibition match at Middlesbrough Conservative Club. His resentment at this high-handed decision was to influence his relationship with officialdom throughout his career; he was constantly at odds with the governing body about contracts or changes to rules and equipment.

Smith played in the world billiards championship only twice, in 1920 and 1923, and won on both occasions. During the intervening years he organized his own provincial tours, arranging matches on his own financial terms. He did enter for the competition again in 1924, but characteristically his entry was submitted two hours late.

Smith did not spare his fellow players from his criticisms. He despised exponents of the 'nursery cannon', a shot where the cue ball 'nursed' the red ball and object-white along the cushion in a series of gentle nudges. He dismissed such players as 'cushion crawlers'. In the 1928–9 season he made fifteen breaks of 1000 or more and recorded a massive 2743 against Tom Newman, his defeated opponent in the 1923 final. This break remains the highest ever recorded without the aid of the nursery cannons which Smith refused to incorporate into his game. During a season of challenge matches in Australia in 1929 against the great Walter Lindrum, cut short on the death of Lindrum's wife, Smith's cue was broken by the Sydney betting fraternity.

The following season Smith reluctantly accepted that he could no longer compete with Lindrum and the other nursery specialists. Players such as Newman and the legendary Joe Davis had developed this aspect of their game but Smith stubbornly refused. His disillusionment with the game grew and he drifted out of the top flight.

Never a snooker fan, Smith was nevertheless a good enough player to reach two world finals, losing to Davis in 1933 and 1935. He was also involved in two snooker milestones: in April 1937 part of his match with Horace Lindrum became the first to be televised and on 22 January 1955 he sat and watched his opponent Davis make history by recording the first official 147 maximum break.

Willie Smith died at his home, 10 Hawks Nest Rise, Leeds, on 2 June 1982. He remained a devoted billiards man to the end; two years before his death he was asked for his views on snooker. He replied: 'The rules should be changed—all of them' (Morrison, 121).

TONY RENNICK

Sources *The Times* (4 June 1982) · *Northern Echo* (3 June 1982) · C. Everton, *The story of billiards and snooker* (1979) · C. Everton, *The Guinness book of snooker* (1982) · I. Morrison, *The Hamlyn encyclopedia of snooker* (1985) · P. Matthews and I. Buchanan, *The all-time greats of British and Irish sport* (1995) · b. cert. · d. cert.
Archives FILM BFI NFTVA, sports footage
Likenesses E. G. Malindine, photograph, 1929, Hult. Arch.; *see illus. in* Lindrum, Walter Albert (1898–1960)

Smith, William Robertson (1846–1894), theologian and Semitic scholar, was born on 8 November 1846 at New Farm, Keig, Aberdeenshire, the second of the eight children of William Pirie Smith (1811–1890), Free Church minister at Keig and Tough, and Jane, daughter of William Robertson, head of the West End Academy, Aberdeen. He had three brothers and four sisters. He never went to school, but was educated at home by his father with a view to entering Aberdeen University, where he won a bursary in 1861. When he graduated MA in 1865 he was awarded the town council's medal for the best student. He had already decided to enter the ministry of the Free Church of Scotland and refused at this stage to consider an academic career.

Illness prevented Smith's entry to New College, the Free Church Theological College in Edinburgh, until 1866, but he spent the intervening time learning German and competing for the Ferguson scholarship in mathematics. During his studies at Edinburgh, Smith also acted as assistant to P. G. Tait, professor of natural philosophy in Edinburgh University, and published scientific papers in the *Proceedings* of the Royal Society of Edinburgh, of which he became a fellow. An interest in social anthropology was kindled by his friendship with John Ferguson McLennan. At New College he was chiefly influenced by the professor of Hebrew, A. B. Davidson, but supplemented his studies there by spending two summers attending lectures in Germany. He was particularly impressed by Albrecht Ritschl, whose lectures on theological ethics he considered by far the best he had ever heard.

In 1870 Smith was elected by the general assembly of the Free Church of Scotland to the chair of Hebrew and Old Testament exegesis at the Aberdeen Free Church College (later Christ's College), and in consequence was ordained to the ministry on 2 November 1870. His inaugural lecture, 'What history teaches us to look for in the Bible', published immediately after delivery, indicated the lines he proposed to take as a professor. The summer of 1872 was spent at Göttingen, where he mastered Arabic under Paul de Lagarde and gained the friendship of Julius Wellhausen. In 1875 he was appointed to the Old Testament section of the committee which produced the Revised Version of the Bible. He had been commissioned to write some articles on biblical subjects for the ninth edition of the *Encyclopaedia Britannica*, and the first two of these appeared in 1875—'Angel' in volume 2 and 'Bible' in volume 3. These articles marked a turning point in his career.

The Bible was regarded by the Free Church of Scotland as 'the supreme rule of faith and life', and so anything that might seem to undermine its authority was bound to arouse opposition. An investigation by the college committee of the Free Church found that Smith's opinions as expressed in the article 'Bible' were hardly compatible with his position as a teacher of candidates for the ministry of the church, but provided insufficient grounds to support a process for heresy. Smith maintained that he accepted that the Bible was the one sufficient and authoritative record of divine revelation, and that his critical views were the fruit of studies carried out under the guidance of his teachers at New College, Edinburgh. He therefore demanded that he be given a formal trial by libel (indictment) for his alleged heresies and errors. In the subsequent protracted proceedings in the various church courts Smith, by sheer dialectical skill, was able to beat back the attack on all points except the authorship and purpose of Deuteronomy. The libel proceedings were eventually terminated, but a vote of no confidence in Smith was passed by the general assembly of 1881 and was followed by his summary removal from his chair.

During the heresy proceedings Smith gave two series of highly successful public lectures in Edinburgh and Glasgow, which were afterwards published as *The Old Testament in the Jewish Church* (1881; 2nd edn, 1892) and *The Prophets of Israel* (1882; 2nd edn, 1895). As a mark of sympathy and esteem a valuable gift of Arabic books and manuscripts was publicly presented to him in Edinburgh in 1881. Soon after his dismissal he became editor-in-chief of the *Encyclopaedia Britannica* and ensured its successful completion in 1888. He continued his interest in Semitic subjects and in 1885 published *Kinship and Marriage in Early Arabia*. From 1883 to 1886 he was lord almoner's professor of Arabic at Cambridge, then chief librarian of Cambridge University, and from 1889 he was Adams professor of Arabic at Cambridge. He was appointed by the Burnett trustees to be their lecturer in Aberdeen for 1888–91. Three series were delivered. The first was published under the title *Religion of the Semites: Fundamental Institutions* (1889; 2nd edn, 1894). The second and third series, edited by John Day, were published in 1995.

Smith died at Cambridge on 31 March 1894 of spinal tuberculosis, and was buried in the churchyard at Keig. A brilliant conversationalist, he had many friends but did not marry. He was short and slightly built, being just under 5 feet 4 inches in height, but until his final illness he was physically robust and enjoyed mountaineering. He had unusually bright eyes and a swarthy, though pallid, complexion. He bequeathed some oriental manuscripts to the Cambridge University Library and the remainder of his books to the library of Christ's College, Cambridge, of which he was a fellow from 1885. HENRY R. SEFTON

Sources J. S. Black and G. W. Chrystal, *The life of William Robertson Smith* (1912) · W. Johnstone, ed., *William Robertson Smith: essays in re-assessment* (1995) · *DNB*

Archives CAC Cam. · Christ's College, Cambridge · CUL, corresp. and papers · U. Aberdeen L., student notebooks with pasted-in newscuttings relating to his trial before Aberdeen Free Church Presbytery | UCL, letters to G. C. Robertson

Likenesses G. Reid, oils, 1877, Christ's College, Cambridge · G. Reid, oils, 1896, Christ's College, Aberdeen · G. Reid, oils, Scot. NPG · photograph, NPG

Wealth at death £9773 6*s.* 9*d.*: confirmation, 30 May 1894, *CCI* · £449 6*s.* 10*d.*: eik additional inventory, 3 Sept 1896, sealed in London 6 June 1896, *CCI*

Smith, William Saumarez (1836–1909), archbishop of Sydney, born at St Helier, Jersey, on 14 January 1836, was the son of Richard Snowden Smith, prebendary of Chichester, and his wife, Anne, daughter of Thomas Robin of Jersey. He entered Marlborough College in 1846, and obtained a scholarship at Trinity College, Cambridge, in 1855. In 1857 he won the Carus Greek Testament (undergraduate's) prize; in 1858 he graduated BA (first class, classical tripos); in 1859 he was placed in the first class (middle bachelors) of the theological examination, won the Scholefield prize, the Carus Greek Testament (bachelor's) prize, and the Crosse scholarship. In 1860 he won the Tyrwhitt Hebrew scholarship and was elected fellow of his college. He proceeded MA in 1862, and he won the Seatonian prize for an English sacred poem in 1864 and 1866.

Ordained deacon in 1859 and priest in 1860, Smith became curate of St Paul's, Cambridge, in 1859. He left the post in 1861, and travelled to India as chaplain to Frederick Gell, bishop of Madras, where he remained until 1865, learning Tamil and associating himself with missionary work. He then returned to Cambridge as curate of Trumpington in 1866, and became vicar there in 1867. He was awarded the Maitland prize for his essay *Obstacles to Missionary Success* (1868). He published *Christian Faith* (1869), and several other theological works. In 1869 he accepted the principalship of St Aidan's, Birkenhead, a theological college then at a low ebb. He raised it to prosperity, wiping out a heavy debt and creating an endowment fund. He also served from 1869 to 1890 as examining chaplain to the bishop of Norwich, and in 1880 was made honorary canon of Chester. Smith married in 1870 Florence, daughter of Lewis Deedes, rector of Braintfield, Hertfordshire; she died in 1890, leaving one son and seven daughters.

In 1889, on the retirement of Bishop Alfred Barry from the see of Sydney, Smith was elected his successor by the Australian bishops, in a muddled election which was eventually decided in his favour. He was consecrated at St Paul's Cathedral on 24 June 1890. He was made DD at Cambridge in that year and at Oxford in 1897. As metropolitan of New South Wales and primate of Australia, Smith, with the approval of the Lambeth conference, assumed in 1897 the title of archbishop. His Australian rule was useful rather than eventful. 'Co-operation' was his watchword (*AusDB*). An evangelical of wide sympathies, a hard worker, and a firm though kind administrator, he died at his residence, Bishop's Court, Randwick, Sydney, on 18 April 1909 and was buried in Waverley cemetery. His *Capernaum and other Poems* appeared in 1911.

A. R. BUCKLAND, *rev.* H. C. G. MATTHEW

Sources *The Record* (23 April 1909) · *The Record* (30 April 1909) · *The Guardian* (21 April 1909) · personal knowledge (1912) · S. Judd and K. Cable, *Sydney Anglicans: a history of the diocese* (1987) · *AusDB* · *CGPLA Eng. & Wales* (1909)

Archives Sydney Diocesan Archives · U. Lpool, papers and press cuttings | LPL, Benson MSS; Davidson MSS

Likenesses memorial tablet, St Andrew's Cathedral, Sydney · portrait, Chapter House, Sydney

Wealth at death £14,183 12*s.*: Australian probate sealed in England, 4 Oct 1909, *CGPLA Eng. & Wales*

Smith, William Tyler (1815–1873), obstetric physician, was born near Bristol on 10 April 1815, the son of William Smith, a baker. He was educated at the Bristol school of medicine, where he became prosector and post-mortem clerk. He graduated MB at the University of London in

1840, and eight years later proceeded MD. He became a licentiate of the Royal College of Physicians London in 1850, and was elected to the fellowship in 1859. He began his career as a teacher in George Dermott's private school in Bedford Square, and became, despite an ungainly manner and bad delivery, an impressive and effective lecturer and speaker. On 16 September 1841 he married Tryphena, daughter of Moses Yearsley, a hotel-keeper; they had seven children, two of whom died in infancy.

For several years Smith was largely dependent on literary work, and his skill as a writer increased his professional reputation and influence. He was on the editorial staff of *The Lancet*, at first only as an occasional contributor, but soon as one of its sub-editors. Among his contributions were papers 'On quacks and quackery', and a series of biographical sketches of the capital's leading physicians and surgeons. With James Yearsley and Forbes Winslow he helped to found the *Medical Directory* in 1845.

Urged by his close friend Marshall Hall, Smith studied the applications of the reflex function to obstetrics, with the result that the practice of obstetrics became, for the first time, guided by physiological principle. The results of his researches were published in *The Lancet* in the form of weekly lectures. The earliest series was collected and issued separately as *Parturition, and the Principles and Practice of Obstetrics* (1849), with a dedication to Hall. Some further lectures similarly contributed to *The Lancet* formed the basis of his *Manual of Obstetrics* (1858). Both books are remarkable considering they were written when Smith had little practical experience. The *Manual of Obstetrics* immediately became, and long remained, the favourite textbook in Britain, despite being defective in certain practical aspects, especially regarding operative procedures.

In addition to the above texts, and to numerous contributions to the *Medico-Chirurgical Transactions*, the *Obstetrical Transactions*, and the *Pathological Transactions*, Smith also wrote *Scrofula: its Nature, Causes, and Treatment* (1844), *The periodoscope, with its application to obstetric calculations in the periodicities of the sex* (1848), *Treatment of Sterility by Removal of Obstructions of the Fallopian Tubes*, and *Pathology and Treatment of Leucorrhoea* (1855).

When St Mary's Hospital was founded in 1851, Smith was appointed obstetric physician and lecturer on obstetrics. He continued his teaching there for the allotted term of twenty years, and on retirement was elected consulting physician accoucheur. He held the office of examiner in obstetrics at the University of London for the usual term of five years. He resided, at first, at 7 Bolton Street, Piccadilly, then moved to 7 Upper Grosvenor Street, and subsequently to No. 21 in the same street.

Smith raised the position of obstetric medicine not only by his teaching, oral and written, but by the foundation of the Obstetrical Society of London (1859). The subsequent success of the society was largely due to his contributions in memoirs and in debate and to his capacity for work. On the death of Edward Rigby in December 1860, Smith was elected president.

Smith was associated with Thomas Wakley in the establishment of the New Equitable Life Assurance Society, and he was one of its first directors. When the society was united to the Briton Life Office, he became deputy chairman of the united companies. He also conceived the idea of turning the ancient Cinque Port town of Seaford, Sussex, into a sanatorium and fashionable watering-place. He purchased a considerable piece of land in and adjoining the town, and leased more from the corporation on the condition that he build sea defences and develop the land. Smith actively promoted the foundation and success of the convalescent hospital at Seaford, and was bailiff of the town in 1861, 1864, 1867, 1868, and 1870. He was magistrate for the town and port from 1861 to the time of his death. He died at Richmond Hospital, Richmond, Surrey, on 2 June 1873, and was buried at Blatchington, near Seaford. W. W. Webb, *rev.* Ornella Moscucci

Sources *The Lancet* (7 June 1873), 825–7 • *Obstetrical Journal of Great Britain*, 1 (1873), 283–8 • J. F. C., *Medical Times and Gazette* (14 June 1873), 644–5 • *BMJ* (7 June 1873), 652–3 • Munk, *Roll* • *CGPLA Eng. & Wales* (1873) • O. Moscucci, *The science of woman: gynaecology and gender in England, 1800–1929* (1990) • m. cert. • d. cert.

Likenesses M. Wynter, carte-de-visite, NPG • engraving, St Mary's Hospital, London • portrait, Obstetrical Society of London

Wealth at death under £10,000: probate, 21 July 1873, *CGPLA Eng. & Wales*

Smith, Willoughby (1828–1891), telegraph engineer, was born at Great Yarmouth, Norfolk, on 16 April 1828, son of Daniel Smith, a warehouseman. Nothing is known of his life before 1848, when he joined the Gutta Percha Company, London; he was to remain in the service of this company and its successor until he retired. Gutta-percha was a vegetable substance similar to rubber, derived from trees growing in south-east Asia. It was a recent arrival on the industrial scene and its qualities and possible uses were as yet imperfectly understood. Smith began by testing gutta-percha as an insulator on iron or copper wire for electrical or telegraph lines, and in 1849 the company had so far succeeded with these experiments that they undertook to supply the 30 miles of copper wire, insulated with gutta-percha, for the first submarine telegraph line to be laid from Dover to Calais, under the English Channel. During 1849–50 Smith was engaged in the manufacture and laying of this line, which was handicapped by imperfect joints between the sections of gutta-percha. By the time that a second line was put down the following year, he had improved the technique, and in 1855 he devised a still better method of joining and insulating the conductor wire, which was in use for many years.

From this time on, Smith was occupied with the manufacture and laying of lines and cables on land and under water, and was especially concerned with the manner in which insulation affected the transmission of signals. Early in 1854 work began on the first cable to be laid in the Mediterranean. Smith had charge of the electrical department during its manufacture and assisted Sir Charles Wheatstone with his experiments on the retardation of signals through this cable, while it was coiled at the manufacturing works of Glass, Elliott & Co., at Greenwich; he then supervised its electrical performance, as it was put down between the Italian port of La Spezia and Corsica, and between Corsica and Sardinia. The following year he similarly oversaw the manufacture and laying of a cable between Sardinia and Bona, in Algeria. On his return he became electrician and manager of the wire department at the Gutta Percha works, and began making 2500 miles of core for a cable from Ireland to Newfoundland. In 1858 he prepared a compound of gutta-percha, Stockholm tar, and resin, which bonded the gutta-percha cladding more effectively than the coal-tar naphtha used hitherto, and came into general use.

In 1864 the works of Glass, Elliott & Co. at Greenwich and the Gutta Percha Company amalgamated to form the Telegraph Construction and Maintenance Company (Telcon), under Sir John Pender's chairmanship. In 1865 Smith was on board the *Great Eastern* steamship for the attempt to lay a cable between Ireland and Newfoundland, which had to be abandoned when the cable parted in bad weather. Early in 1866 he was appointed chief electrician at Telcon, and took part in the second and successful laying of this cable, and the recovery of the cable lost the previous year. Smith was among those to whom the American chamber of commerce presented a gold medal for this feat.

On 5 August 1866 Smith married Catherine Susannah King; they had two daughters and three sons, of whom two followed their father as electrical engineers. Subsequently Smith took charge of the French transatlantic cable expedition, which had also been contracted to Telcon. The cable was laid successfully, but Smith, who had been unwell when he boarded the ship, became embroiled in serious disagreements with his electrical colleagues, Fleeming Jenkin, Latimer Clark, and C. F. Varley, and was unable to work for several months afterwards.

After his return to duty, Smith remained ashore and worked on improving the manufacture of gutta-percha for cable work. Early in the 1870s, while experimenting to find cheaper materials for the resistance coils for testing cable during laying, he tried crystalline selenium, and was at first puzzled to find its electrical resistance so variable. Further experiments showed that this substance responded to light; it was highly resistant in the dark, and far less so in daylight. His letter to Latimer Clark announcing this discovery was read by Clark to the Society of Telegraph Engineers. As Clark explained, Smith had discovered the perfect photometer; in later years the selenium cell was developed into a light meter for photography and other uses. In 1881 Smith was appointed sole manager of the Gutta Percha works, in addition to being chief of the electrical department at Telcon.

Through his development of telegraphy apparatus Willoughby Smith was for many years a customer of the electrical instrument firm of Elliott Brothers of St Martin's Lane, Westminster (unconnected with the Elliott of Glass, Elliott & Co.). His sons William Oliver Smith and Willoughby Statham Smith both held management positions at Elliotts. Smith himself became a partner in the firm in 1873, together with Frederick Elliott's widow Susan, and by the time of his death Smith was the sole proprietor. However, his wish that his sons, who inherited generous legacies, should purchase the firm after his death was not fulfilled, and in 1893 Elliotts combined with another telegraph instrument maker, Theiler & Co.

Smith made many contributions to the technical literature. In 1882–3 he was president of the Institution of Electrical Engineers. Failing health led to his retirement in 1887, but he was able, during 1889, to write *The Rise and Progress of Submarine Telegraphy* (1891), which described his own role in this important field. His home was at 3 North Grove, Highgate, but he died at the Grand Hotel, Eastbourne, Sussex, on 17 July 1891; he was buried at Highgate cemetery on 21 July. ANITA MCCONNELL

Sources W. Smith, *The rise and progress of submarine telegraphy* (1891) · L. Clark, letter, *Journal of the Society of Telegraph Engineers*, 2 (1873), 31–3 · *Electrical Engineer* (24 July 1891), 85 · *Nature*, 44 (1891), 302 · *The Times* (25 July 1891), 7 · H. R. Bristow, 'Elliott, instrument makers of London', *Bulletin of the Scientific Instrument Society*, 36 (1993), 8–11 · J. E. H. Gordon, *Treatise on electricity*, 2nd edn (1883), 2.299 · will, proved, London, 14 Oct 1891 · m. cert. · d. cert. · *DNB*

Wealth at death £63,463 16*s*. 9*d*.: resworn probate, Jan 1893, *CGPLA Eng. & Wales* (1891)

Smith, Worthington George (1835–1917), architectural and botanical illustrator and archaeologist, was born on 23 March 1835 at 19 Aske Street, Shoreditch, London, the only child of George Smith (1804–1877), a civil servant from Gaddesden Row, Hertfordshire, and Sarah Worthington (1809–1891) of Laxton, Nottinghamshire. Following an elementary education at St John's parochial school, Shoreditch, he initially wished to become an architect, and was apprenticed to A. E. Johnson of Buckingham Street, London, and later Horace Jones. With the former he designed ecclesiastical fittings for Roman Catholic churches, but the latter expected him to design drains. On 24 March 1856 Smith married Henrietta White (1831–1917), a bonnet sewer from Dunstable, with whom he had seven children, only three of whom survived early childhood.

In 1861, disenchanted with routine architectural work, Smith became a freelance illustrator. Specializing in wood-engraving and lithography he prepared thousands of illustrations for *The Builder* and similar magazines. Soon, however, he turned increasingly to botanical illustration: his work appeared in the *Gardeners' Chronicle* (he was its chief illustrator until 1910), the *Journal of Horticulture*, and many others. Mycology became a major interest: he lectured and wrote books for the British Museum (Natural History) on fungi, and sometimes risked his family's life by involving them in sampling edible and poisonous varieties. In July 1875 he was credited with discovering the cause of the devastating potato blight fungus and was awarded the Royal Horticultural Society's Knightian gold medal. Six months later the German mycologist, Anton de Bary, proved that Smith had been mistaken and had not found the cause, but the British scientific establishment ignored his evidence and Smith was lauded for the next twenty years, sitting on several government commissions concerned with plant diseases.

Stimulated by reading Sir John Evans's *Ancient Stone*

Implements of Great Britain (1872), Smith combined searching for botanical specimens with seeking prehistoric implements. In 1878 he found a Lower Palaeolithic land surface bearing stone tools in commercial excavations at Stoke Newington Common, and soon traced it over a wide area of north-east London.

Following his heart problems, in 1884 Smith and his family moved to 121 High Street South, Dunstable. Despite the move there was no reduction in Smith's output of botanical drawings, or his work for the Natural History Museum. At that time he also began to observe the local brickearth pits. In 1890 he discovered another Palaeolithic land surface at Caddington, 2 miles from Dunstable, with flint tools lying where they had been discarded between 125,000 and 400,000 years ago. He published his London and Dunstable discoveries in an outstanding book, *Man, the Primeval Savage* (1894). The discoveries at Caddington were followed by others nearby at Whipsnade, Round Green, and Gaddesden Row. Of the five known British Lower Palaeolithic occupation sites listed in a comprehensive survey by Derek A. Roe (1968), four were discovered by Smith. His work encompassed numerous archaeological discoveries of other periods in the Dunstable area and beyond, as well as research in depth into the history of the town and neighbourhood, described in his *Dunstable: its History and Surroundings* (1904).

Ever impecunious, in 1902 Smith was awarded a civil-list pension of £50 per annum 'for services to archaeology' on the recommendation of Lord Avebury and Sir John Evans; on 9 November 1903 he became the first freeman of the borough of Dunstable 'in appreciation of the eminent services rendered to his country in connection with his profession, and his munificent gifts to the Corporation of Dunstable'.

Smith died of pneumonia at his home, The Hawthorns, 121 High Street South, Dunstable, on 27 October 1917, four months after his wife; he was buried on 2 November at Dunstable cemetery. In retrospect his mycological work was overshadowed by that of his contemporaries, but his archaeological research 'represents a pinnacle of Victorian antiquarian endeavour' (White, 913). In the late twentieth century Smith's work has attracted renewed attention, with re-examination and reassessment of his discoveries. JAMES DYER

Sources J. Dyer, 'Worthington George Smith', *Worthington George Smith and other studies, presented to Joyce Godber*, Bedfordshire Historical RS, 57 (1978), 141–79 • T. W. Bagshawe, '"W.G.S.": a man to remember', *Bedfordshire Magazine*, 11 (1967–9), 73–9 • J. Dyer, '"W.G.S." and the potato blight mystery', *Bedfordshire Magazine*, 11 (1967–9), 91–6 • J. Dyer, 'Man, the primeval savage', *Bedfordshire Magazine*, 24 (1993–5), 234–8 • D. A. Roe, 'British Lower and Middle Palaeolithic handaxe groups', *Proceedings of the Prehistoric Society*, 34 (1968), 1–82 • J. Wymer, *Lower Palaeolithic archaeology in Britain* (1968), 293–301 • C. G. Sampson, *Paleoecology and archaeology of an Acheulian site at Caddington, England* (1978) • M. J. White, 'The early Palaeolithic occupation of the Chilterns', *Antiquity*, 71 (1997), 912–31 • press cuttings on W. G. Smith, Luton Museum and Art Gallery • R. Richardson and R. Thorne, *The Builder illustrations index, 1843–1883* (1994) • family tree of W. G. Smith, Luton Museum and Art Gallery • m. cert. • private information (2004)

Archives BM, corresp. and artefacts • NRA, priv. coll. | Beds. & Luton ARS, letters to F. G. Gurney

Likenesses A. E. Smith, photographs, Luton Museum and Art Gallery • portrait, repro. in W. G. Smith, *Dunstable: its history and surroundings* (1904)

Wealth at death civil list, 1902, £50 p.a.

Smith [*née* Veitch], **Zepherina Philadelphia** (1836–1894), nurse and social reformer, was born on 1 April 1836 at Sopley, Hampshire, the elder daughter of the Revd William Douglas Veitch (1802?–1884), vicar of St Saviour's, Paddington, London (1862–73). Both her parents took an interest in the social welfare of the working class and, like many young women of her class and generation, Zepherina was determined to do something useful with her life. Recent reforms had raised the status of nursing as a suitable occupation for ladies and in 1867 Zepherina went to University College, London, to train as a nurse under the All Saints sisters. In the following year she was placed in charge of the surgical wards at King's College Hospital and in 1869 was made superintendent of nurses at St George's Hospital. After a few months she resigned this appointment and took a variety of temporary hospital posts before leaving England in September 1870 to work with the All Saints sisters in Sedan during the Franco-Prussian War. She wrote about her experiences of nursing abroad in letters to her sister, extracts from which were published after her death in the *Nursing Notes* (November 1894). In 1870 she published *A Handbook for Nursing the Sick*, which reached a second edition in 1876. Rosalind Paget, one of the leaders of the Midwives' Institute, described it as the best book for nurses that existed.

On her return to England, Zepherina Veitch became interested in improving the practice of midwifery and the status of midwives, most of whom received little or no training. She qualified as a midwife in January 1873 at the British Lying-In Hospital, Endell Street, and became only the tenth person to obtain the diploma of the London Obstetrical Society (LOS). She continued to work in hospitals, but her mother's ill health meant that she tended to stand in for others rather than taking up a permanent post. Her employment as a professional nurse ended when she married a widower, the surgeon Henry Smith (*b.* 1822/3), son of William Smith, a solicitor, in December 1876.

After her marriage Zepherina Smith put her energies into the cause of midwifery reform. Her aim was to improve the status and efficiency of midwives; she emphasized the importance of training, and argued that a woman should not be able to call herself a midwife unless she was properly trained. She hoped to see well-educated, middle-class women take up the work, not only so that there would be an improved midwifery service for the poor, but also so that midwives could be an 'influence for good' on working-class families. Smith's activities should be seen in the context of the development of a women's movement in the middle decades of the nineteenth century which sought to expand educational and employment opportunities for single, middle-class women. It is hardly surprising, therefore, that when she submitted an article on midwifery to the *Women's Gazette* she immediately came to the attention of the editor, Louisa Hubbard, who took an interest in expanding women's work opportunities and in improving their employment conditions. Zepherina Smith was one of seven midwives, all holders of the LOS diploma, who were called to a meeting by Hubbard in December 1881 to form the Matron's Aid Society, with the aim of improving the training of midwives and securing their registration by act of parliament. The name was chosen because the word 'midwife' was rarely used in 'polite' society, but by the late 1880s the members of the society were confident enough to change the name to the Midwives' Institute (which became the Royal College of Midwives in 1948). Zepherina Smith was the treasurer of the society, which had only a handful of members at the beginning, until it was incorporated in 1889. She then became its first president, serving from 1890 until her death.

Zepherina Smith worked tirelessly to promote the cause of midwife training and registration and used her wide range of personal contacts to good effect. She represented the institute on deputations to the government, and when a committee sat to frame the first Midwives' Bill in 1890 she was asked to attend the sittings to watch proceedings from the point of view of the midwife. This was a new departure, since midwives were rarely asked for their opinions. She also gave evidence to the select committee on midwifery in 1892 and delivered numerous papers to clubs and societies on the subject of midwife registration.

Smith was remembered by friends and colleagues as an eloquent speaker with a bright face and a cheery word for everyone. Her sister recalled that Zepherina found that early years spent in Palestine had taught her how to be adaptable, a skill which was invaluable when nursing in difficult circumstances without the resources of a hospital. On one occasion when she had to attend a very poor patient in her own home she found that there was nothing bigger than a meat tin in which to hold water. 'She at once solved the question of how to wash the baby by making a bath in her lap of a big waterproof apron she wore' (Paget). After several months of ill health Zepherina Smith died on 8 February 1894 at her home, Summerhill, Horsell, near Woking, Surrey. JUNE HANNAM

Sources R. Paget, *Nursing Notes* (1 April 1894) · E. Brierly, *In the beginning* (1933) · B. Cowell and D. Wainwright, *Behind the blue door: the history of the Royal College of Midwives, 1881–1981* (1981) · m. cert. · d. cert. · Foster, *Alum. Oxon.*, *1715–1886* [the Revd William Douglas Veitch]

Archives Royal College of Midwives Archive

Likenesses photograph, repro. in *Nursing Notes* (Aug 1933), 112

Wealth at death £473 18*s*. 2*d*.: administration, 16 May 1894, *CGPLA Eng. & Wales*

Smithells, Arthur (1860–1939), chemist, was born at Bury, Lancashire, on 24 May 1860, the third son of James Smithells, railway manager, and his wife, Martha, daughter of James Livesey. Both his parents were Unitarians and Smithells inherited their belief. In 1868 the family moved to Glasgow.

After playing with a shilling box of chemicals as a boy, Smithells developed an interest in chemistry that never left him. His early education was conducted by private tutors, and between 1875 and 1877 he studied natural philosophy and chemistry at Glasgow University under William Thomson and John Ferguson respectively. He attended the British Association's Glasgow meeting in 1876, beginning a lifelong connection with that body. In 1878 he went to Owens College, Manchester, where he studied chemistry under Henry Roscoe, receiving his BSc (London) in 1881. His chemical training was strengthened during 1882–3 by studying in the laboratories of J. F. Baeyer in Munich and Robert Bunsen in Heidelberg. In the latter year he returned to Owens College as assistant lecturer, and two years later moved to Yorkshire College, Leeds, succeeding T. E. Thorpe as professor of chemistry. Smithells's new appointment gave him the means to marry; in 1886 he married Constance Marie (*d*. 1907), daughter of Frederic Mawe; the couple subsequently had two sons and one daughter. After Constance's death Smithells married, in 1908, Katharine, daughter of Arthur Booth; they had one son.

Arthur Smithells (1860–1939), by Walter Stoneman, 1921

At the Yorkshire College Smithells expanded the chemistry department. As a member of the university court and council, Smithells (who served three periods as pro-vice-chancellor) played a major role in establishing the University of Leeds in 1904. University status broadened the cultural basis of the Yorkshire College while developing its special character as a school of applied science with university standards, and Smithells's pioneering work was widely imitated. His belief in the practical application of science led him to make contacts with the gas industry. One outcome of this activity was the endowment of the Livesey professorship at Leeds in 1910 and of the formation of a joint research committee of the gas industry and the university, with Smithells as chairman, thus securing a fruitful co-operation of unique character.

Smithells's main scientific research was on flame structure and in particular the question of how the characteristic spectra of flames were generated. This topic formed the subject of an extensive correspondence between him and G. G. Stokes during the 1890s. It was also the subject of his only Friday evening discourse, delivered at the Royal Institution in 1897. His work was recognized by his election to a fellowship of the Royal Society in 1901. He served on its council in 1915–17, in 1916–17 as vice-president. In the course of his career Smithells also held a great number of posts in the scientific community. In 1907 he was president of the chemical section of the British Association at its Leicester meeting; he also served four terms on the council of the Chemical Society, three as vice-president. In 1907 he was appointed education adviser on home science and household economics at King's College for Women, London, where the subject later acquired degree status. In 1911 he was elected president of the Society of British Gas Industries. In 1910 he was appointed president of the Indian Guild of Science and Technology and in 1913 was invited as special lecturer to the Punjab University; he accepted willingly, since it provided an opportunity to demonstrate how chemistry might be made to appeal to Indian students so that they could put chemical knowledge into practice.

Smithells was greatly shocked by the outbreak of war in 1914. He became visiting lecturer to northern command in 1915 and later (1916–19) was chief chemical adviser on anti-gas training to the home forces. His experience there led him to appreciate the dangers of gas warfare and in the post-war period he devoted much time to alerting the public to its dangers. His military services were recognized by the honorary rank of lieutenant-colonel and appointment as CMG in 1918. Despite his war work, Smithells did not succumb to the hysterical anti-German feeling so prevalent in the country. For example, as vice-president of the Royal Society he threw his weight against efforts to remove the German-born Arthur Schuster as secretary of the society.

Besides working to foster links between science and industry at university level, Smithells also took a very strong interest in school science. In this area he sought, mainly through his former students, to base school science on objects familiar to children. This interest led him to become president of the Science Masters' Association in 1923. In the same year he resigned his professorship at Leeds to become director of the Salters' Institute of Industrial Chemistry in London. This position included the selection and supervision of promising graduates in chemistry who might receive a further training carefully planned to fit them for responsible work in industry. In this period he interested himself in the Institute of Chemistry, being president between 1927 and 1930; he received the honorary degree of DSc from the universities of Manchester and Leeds in 1923.

Failing health dictated Smithells's retirement in 1937 and his death at his home, 68 Lissenden Mansions, Highgate Road, London on 8 February 1939 ended a career largely spent in continuous efforts to break down the barriers between academic science and industry. He was survived by his second wife. FRANK A. J. L. JAMES

Sources H. S. Raper, *Obits. FRS*, 3 (1939–41), 97–107 • A. J. Flintham, 'The contribution of Arthur Smithells, F.R.S., to science education', *History of Education*, 6 (1977), 195–208 • R. K. DeKosky, 'George Gabriel Stokes, Arthur Smithells and the origin of spectra in flames', *Ambix*, 27 (1980), 103–23 • J. W. Cobb, 'Prof. A. Smithells', *Nature*, 143 (1939), 321–2 • *DNB*

Archives U. Leeds, Brotherton L., corresp. and papers | CUL, corresp. with Sir George Stokes • UCL, corresp. with Sir Oliver Lodge

Likenesses W. Stoneman, photograph, 1921, NPG [*see illus.*] • F. Watt, oils, *c*.1925, U. Leeds • photograph, repro. in Raper, *Obits. FRS*

Wealth at death £10,988 4*s*. 5*d*.: probate, 10 March 1939, *CGPLA Eng. & Wales*

Smithers, Sir David Waldron (1908–1995), radiotherapist, was born on 17 January 1908 at Park Farm, Knockholt, Kent, the younger son in the family of two sons and three daughters of Sir Waldron Smithers (1880–1954), a member of the London stock exchange and Conservative MP for Chislehurst, then Orpington, from 1924 to 1954, and his wife, Marjory Prudence, daughter of the Revd Frederick Page-Roberts, rector of Strathfieldsaye. His paternal grandfather was Sir Alfred Waldron Smithers (1850–1924), Conservative MP for Chislehurst from 1918 to 1922. He was educated at Boxgrove School and Charterhouse School, and went to Clare College, Cambridge, in 1926 to read medicine: he was awarded a BA (ordinary) in 1929, and was placed in the third class in both his principal subjects. He qualified as a doctor at St Thomas's medical school in London in 1933. On 30 June in the same year he married Gwladys Margaret (Marjorie) Angel (1906/07–1992), daughter of Harry Reeve Angel, a paper merchant; they had one son and one daughter.

After working on the radiology of the heart at the National Heart Hospital, in 1936 Smithers moved to the Royal Cancer Hospital in Chelsea (renamed the Royal Marsden Hospital in 1954) to take a diploma in diagnostic radiology, and he joined the radiology department as an assistant in 1937. At this time radiology was being developed as a form of treatment for cancer, as well as a diagnostic tool, and he followed the pioneering work of Ralston Paterson at the Holt Radium Institute in Manchester with interest. While remaining part-time at the Royal Cancer Hospital, Smithers went into private practice for a short time before the war. At the beginning of the Second World War he was appointed acting director of the department, and worked on the treatment of cancer with X-rays, publishing *The X-Ray Treatment of Accessible Cancer* in 1946. In 1943 he presented the first of several memoranda detailing ideas for changes in the organization of the hospital; most of these were adopted, including amalgamating the radium research and X-ray treatment units to form one department of radiotherapy, and creating a separate diagnostic radiology department.

In 1944 Smithers was appointed director of the new radiotherapy department at the Royal Cancer Hospital, and in addition from 1946 was professor of radiotherapy at the Institute of Cancer Research at the University of London. One of his proposals in 1943 had been to create specialist units in the hospital with beds available to all visiting consultants, who could run their own clinics jointly with radiotherapists. This proposal was implemented, and as the new specialist clinics attracted more and more patients, the radiotherapy department grew. He became interested in applying nuclear physics to medicine; with his colleague W. V. Mayneord, director of the physics department at the Institute of Cancer Research, he pressed for the hospital's expansion onto a new site in order to build a national centre for radiation research, where Mayneord could investigate applying radioactive isotopes for therapy and diagnosis. Land was secured in Sutton, Surrey, in 1950, but by the time the building came to be planned it was decided to build a second cancer hospital. As chairman of the building committee Smithers played an important part in planning the new hospital, which opened in 1963, and the clinical research unit soon gained an international reputation.

Smithers was very interested in the ideas of Sir Karl Popper, whose *Logik der Forschung* (1935) was published in English in 1959 as *The Logic of Scientific Discovery*, and he attended his lectures in 1961; he later described Popper as his philosophically guiding star. In 'Cancer: an attack on cytologism', published in *The Lancet* on 10 March 1962, he argued that it was wrong to think there was one disease called cancer and that it would be possible to discover the cause and a cure: he preferred to think of it as a disorder of organization of the human body and to talk of 'cancerous reactions in different tissues' rather than simply cancer. He was afraid that failure to understand the nature of the problem led much cancer research in the wrong direction, in the belief that there could be a cure. Smithers, by contrast, believed that there was no one change in every tumour cell that made it cancerous, and that cancerous reactions had to be dealt with differently, depending on where they occurred.

Smithers's clinical work was more important to him than research. After the new hospital opened he confined his clinical work to the management of lymphomas, including testicular cancer, and Hodgkin's disease. He assembled a team to treat these disorders with a combination of radiotherapy and chemotherapy, and greatly improved the survival rates. He was a skilful diagnostician, and drew up an individual treatment plan for each patient. He impressed on his students the importance of treating patients as people, as well as treating their disorders, and he made a point of talking to his patients about their families, visiting the wards one evening a week in order to meet their relatives.

In the 1950s Smithers did some radio broadcasting, including contributions to the series *Talking about Science* for the BBC Far Eastern and European services, and he hosted the first television programme on cancer, in the series *Matters of Life and Death*. He was invited to many international conferences, and in 1961 he joined a group visiting Russia under the auspices of the British Council to study cancer services in the USSR; in 1974 he was a member of a similar delegation to the People's Republic of China. He was president of the British Institute of Radiology from 1946 to 1947, and president of the Faculty of Radiologists from 1959 to 1961. Among his publications was *A Clinical Prospect of the Cancer Problem* (1960), in the series Neoplastic Diseases at Various Sites which he edited from 1958. He was knighted in 1969.

After his retirement in 1973, Smithers turned to writing. *Dickens's Doctors*, about the fifty medical men who make an appearance in Dickens's novels, was published in 1979, followed by *Castles in Kent* (1980), *Jane Austen in Kent* (1981), *Therefore Imagine: the Works of Clemence Dane* (1988), and *This Idle Trade: on Doctors who were Writers* (1989). His final book was *A History of Knockholt* (1991). He also wrote an autobiography, *Not a Moment to Lose: some Reminiscences* (1989). An enthusiastic rose grower, he planted a new rose garden at his home in Knockholt, and became the first president of the South of England Rose Society. He died on 20 July 1995 at his home, Ringfield, Knockholt, Kent.

ANNE PIMLOTT BAKER

Sources D. W. Smithers, *Not a moment to lose: some reminiscences* (1989) • E. Wiltshaw, *A history of the Royal Marsden Hospital* (1998) • *The Times* (29 July 1995) • *The Independent* (5 Aug 1995) • b. cert. • m. cert. • d. cert. • *WWW* • private information (2004) [Clare College, Cambridge]

Likenesses photograph, repro. in Smithers, *Not a moment to lose*, frontispiece • photograph, repro. in *The Times* • portrait, repro. in Wiltshaw, *History*, 79

Wealth at death £274,133: probate, 16 Nov 1995, *CGPLA Eng. & Wales*

Smithers, Leonard Charles (1861–1907), publisher and antiquarian bookseller, was born on 19 December 1861 at 5 Infirmary Road, Sheffield, Yorkshire, one of several children of John Smithers, a dentist, and his wife, Martha, *née* Watson. He was reared in Sheffield, where he graduated from Wesley College for the Law in 1884. Having been admitted solicitor of the Supreme Court of Judicature, he was employed for several years by the firm of Messrs Meredith Roberts and Mills of Sheffield. While still a law student he had married Alice Edith Oldham on 11 October 1882; they had two children, a daughter, Lena, who died at the age of two in 1891, and a son, Jack, born in August 1891.

Although Smithers gained his livelihood for a time as a solicitor, he was far more interested in books and art than in the legal profession. In his spare time he rummaged through the bookstalls and haunted the antiquarian bookshops of Sheffield and its environs, increasingly adept at ferreting out the odd rarity that he could afford. Books of erotica appear to have been his major interest. As his desire to pursue a career in books grew, Smithers came under the influence of the famous world traveller and diplomat Captain Sir Richard Francis Burton, whose fascination with sexual customs of oriental peoples was well known. Smithers was 'a young solicitor with a taste for erotic literature, frankly fascinated by sexual pathology' (F. Brodie, *The Devil Drives: a Life of Sir Richard Burton*, 1967, 319). He subscribed to Burton's unexpurgated edition of *The Thousand Nights and a Night* when it first appeared in 1885–6; he thereby established a correspondence with the translator of other erotic books such as the *Kama sutra* (1883) and the *Ananga Ranga, or, The Hindu Art of Love* (1873, 1885). By 1888 Smithers, with the aid of a young Sheffield printer and book dealer, Harry Sidney Nichols, had established the Erotika Biblion Society, a fictitious organization modelled on Burton's own Kama Shastra Society. Under this imprint, Smithers and Nichols issued several erotic books, one of which was Smithers's translation of the Latin text of the *Priapeia* (1888). Burton, who showed a great interest in this work, offered to add a poetic translation to Smithers's prose text, a project which was published in October 1890, after Burton's death, in a bowdlerized form demanded by Burton's widow, Lady Burton. The second of their two collaborations, the Smithers–Burton translation of the *Carmina* of Catullus—once again 'cleaned up' by Isabel Burton—appeared in 1894. Despite Lady Burton's insistence on editing her husband's erotic books, Smithers and Nichols were able to gain control of *The Thousand Nights and a Night*, which they brought out in attractive and unexpurgated editions in 1894–5.

Smithers and Nichols, having established a partnership in a rare book dealership and printing business in Sheffield in the late 1880s, moved their business to London in September 1891, the rare bookshop located at 174 Wardour Street, near Oxford Street, and the printing business located nearby at 10 Dean Street, Soho. Here they continued to issue erotic books under the imprint of the Erotika Biblion Society. Uneasy about Nichols's penchant for bringing out books of hard-core pornography, Smithers severed his partnership with Nichols at the close of 1894, establishing himself in business as a rare book dealer and as a legitimate publisher in quarters above his residential flat in Effingham House, 1 Arundel Street, the Strand, in 1895. As his business prospered, towards the close of 1896, Smithers moved his shop to 4 and 5 Royal Arcade, Old Bond Street, and later to premises at 5 Old Bond Street.

On his own, Smithers prospered as a publisher—the renowned bookman Bernard Quaritch toasting him as the 'cleverest' publisher in London at a publishers' dinner in 1897 (O'Sullivan, 117). His love for beautifully bound and illustrated books as well as his excellent taste in book design and typography made him, in the words of one critic, 'the most extraordinary publisher, in some respects, of the nineties, a kind of modern Cellini, who produced some wonderfully finely printed books and was himself just as much a part of the movement as any of its numerous writers' (B. Muddiman, *The Men of the Nineties*, 1920, 41).

After Oscar Wilde went to prison, Smithers almost single-handedly saved the avant-garde writers and artists from extinction, providing them with both employment and encouragement. When in April 1895 John Lane of the Bodley Head succumbed to the ultimatum of his conservative, morally high-toned authors and dismissed Aubrey Beardsley as art editor of the *Yellow Book*, Smithers came to his rescue. He launched a rival journal, *The Savoy*, appointing Arthur Symons literary editor and Beardsley chief artist. The finest aesthetic journal of the nineties, *The Savoy* included stories, essays, and poems by Symons, Ernest Dowson, Bernard Shaw, Max Beerbohm, W. B. Yeats, Edmund Gosse, Ford Madox Hueffer (Ford), Joseph Conrad, and Havelock Ellis, as well as artwork by Beardsley, Beerbohm, Joseph Pennell, Charles Conder, Charles H. Shannon, and James McNeill Whistler.

Smithers declared that he would 'publish anything that the others [London publishers] are afraid of' (O'Sullivan, 113). That audacity enabled him to bring out some of the most important books of the nineties: Symons's *London Nights* (1895) and *Amoris victima* (1897), Dowson's *Verses* (1896) and *Decorations: in Verse and Prose* (1899), as well as Beardsley's finest illustrated books, for example *The Lysistrata of Aristophanes* (1896) and Ben Jonson's *Volpone* (1898), as well as the writings of others whom, like Beardsley, the public had erroneously associated with Wilde and treated as pariahs. As O'Sullivan later wrote, for the 'young poets' Smithers took under his wing, he was 'a benediction. They would have been hard put to it to find another publisher in London' (O'Sullivan, 126). After Wilde was released from prison in 1897, Smithers dared to publish *The Ballad of Reading Gaol*, a work no other publisher would touch. There is little doubt that without Smithers the avant-garde movement of the nineties might have foundered.

During the later nineties Smithers was a familiar personage among the writers and artists of London, Dieppe, and Paris. He was a distinctive figure, described by Wilde as wearing ties

> delicately fastened with a diamond brooch of the impurest water—or perhaps wine, as he never touches water: it goes to his head at once. His face, clean-shaven as befits a priest who serves at the altar whose God is literature, is wasted and pale—not with poetry, but with poets, who, he says, have wrecked his life by insisting on publishing with him. He loves first editions, especially women: little girls are his passion. He is the most learned erotomaniac in Europe. He is also a delightful companion, and a dear fellow, very kind to me. (*The Complete Letters of Oscar Wilde*, ed. M. Holland and R. Hart-Davis, 2000, 924)

But as Smithers poured large sums of money into finely produced books such as Honoré de Balzac's *La fille aux yeux d'or* (1896), illustrated by Conder, and Alexander Pope's *The Rape of the Lock* (1896), decorated by Beardsley, he fell into financial difficulties. Partly as a result of his generosity to impecunious authors such as Wilde and Dowson, Smithers moved steadily downward towards bankruptcy, which occurred on 18 September 1900.

After the bankruptcy, Smithers, in order to survive as a publisher, began pirating books to which he no longer had legal rights. Having vacated his fine premises in Bond Street (as well as his palatial home at 6A Bedford Square), Smithers set up an office at 14 Clifford's Inn, where he continued to do business under various surreptitious names, such as Hampden & Co. and Burton & Co. Moreover, he became associated with an underground printer, Alfred Cooper, with whom he published under the imprint Wright and Jones. After Wilde's death in November 1900, Smithers and Cooper published many pirated editions of Wilde's work. In 1904, under the imprint the Mathurin Press, Smithers published a pirated edition of Wilde's *The Harlot's House* with illustrations by Althea Gyles. Also in 1904, Smithers brought out under the imprint Melmoth & Co. an edition of Wilde's *Salome*.

During his later years, Smithers's problems were augmented by what George Sims called 'muscular Rheumatism' (Sims, 297), the ravages of which drove him to alcohol and narcotics abuse. Smithers died in poverty at 4 Kent House, Peterborough Road, Fulham, on 19 December 1907. He was buried in an unmarked private grave in Fulham cemetery, London, on 27 December; his net worth at the time of his death was a mere £99. His wife and son survived him. JAMES G. NELSON

Sources J. G. Nelson, *Publisher to the decadents: Leonard Smithers in the careers of Beardsley, Wilde, and Dowson* (2000) • M. Pinhorn, 'The career and ancestry of Leonard Smithers', *Blackmansbury*, 1/3 (Aug 1964) • G. Sims, 'Leonard Smithers: a publisher of the 1890s', *Antiquarian Book Monthly Review*, 10 (1983), 248–51, 294–9 • V. O'Sullivan, *Aspects of Wilde* (1936) • *The early life and vicissitudes of Jack Smithers* (1939) • b. cert. • m. cert. • d. cert.

Archives Bodl. Oxf., Walpole Nineties collection • Hunt. L., Edwards Metcalf Burton collection • U. Cal., Los Angeles, William Andrews Clark Memorial Library, Oscar Wilde collection

Likenesses photograph, 1900, repro. in Nelson, 259 • M. Beerbohm, caricature, repro. in Nelson, 281; priv. coll. • photograph, Princeton University Library, New Jersey, Albert Eugene Gallatin collection; repro. in J. G. Nelson, *Publisher to the decadents*, frontispiece

Wealth at death £99: probate, 1 Feb 1908, *CGPLA Eng. & Wales*

Smithies, Catherine (1791–1878). *See under* Smithies, Thomas Bywater (1817–1883).

Smithies, James (1819–1869), co-operative movement activist, was born in Huddersfield, Yorkshire, and baptized on 14 November 1819, the son of Joseph Smithies, a publican, and his wife, Hannah, *née* Howe. His education included instruction in bookkeeping and accountancy. By 1841 he was apprenticed as a wool stapler with Phelps Bros. of Rochdale, and later established his own business. In 1843 Smithies married Penelope Holmes (*b.* 1823), with whom he had at least seven children. During the 1840s he was an active socialist and supporter of Owenite communitarian ideals. A desire to advance more practical measures to relieve distress among local workers led to his involvement in the promotion of co-operative self-help.

Smithies owned copies of William King's journal *The Co-Operator* (1828–30) and would have appreciated the earlier popularity of co-operative ideas. During August 1844 he attended several meetings to establish the Rochdale Equitable Pioneers' Co-operative Society [*see* Rochdale Pioneers], which was to become the inspiration for the modern co-operative movement. He was a director of the new society, and assisted in the opening of a store at 31 Toad Lane, Rochdale, on 21 December 1844.

Smithies' temperament, education, and business experience marked him out for prominence in the development of the Rochdale society. During its formative years he served successively as president, secretary, and superintendent of the store. Initially, the Rochdale Pioneers sold groceries and provisions, but Smithies had ambitions to extend their trade, starting with butchery in 1845 and textiles in 1847. He also led the society's educational activities, initiated in 1845. He directed Sunday instruction in reading and arithmetic and advocated co-operative education for adults and children. In 1850 he helped to establish the Rochdale district co-operative corn mill. He also promoted the Rochdale Co-operative Manufacturing Society of 1854—where he supported profit sharing among the workers—and the Land and Building Company of 1862.

Smithies was an articulate man who often spoke for the Rochdale Pioneers in dealings with external authority, notably in 1855–6 when the society successfully resisted moves to tax its trading surpluses. Among his associates were national champions of social progress, including G. J. Holyoake and Christian socialists such as J. M. Ludlow. Smithies' personal qualities also led to his election to represent Spotland ward on Rochdale town council in November 1862.

From the early 1850s Smithies was involved in the regional and national extension of co-operation. He played a leading role in several abortive attempts to found a wholesale agency supplying northern stores. The successful establishment of a wholesale operation required changes to legislation governing co-operative societies, a cause for which he campaigned during the early 1860s. Ultimately, the North of England Co-operative Wholesale Society (later the Co-operative Wholesale Society) began trading in 1863, with Smithies as its first treasurer. In 1867 he was also involved in the establishment of the Co-operative Insurance Society.

The burden of co-operative, commercial, and municipal duties undermined Smithies' constitution. He resigned as a councillor on health grounds in November 1868 and stepped down as secretary to the Co-operative Wholesale Society the following May. He died from tuberculosis on 27 May 1869, at his home, 14 Clover Street, Rochdale, and was buried in Rochdale cemetery on 31 May. He was survived by his wife—who continued his business dealing in waste wool—and four children. Smithies was regarded as among the most influential co-operative figures of his generation. His optimism, humour, and tolerance brought strength and stability to an emergent movement. MARTIN PURVIS

Sources *Rochdale Observer* (29 May 1869) • private information (2004) [D. Greaves, Rochdale Pioneers Museum, Rochdale] • G. J. Holyoake, *Self-help by the people: the history of the Rochdale Pioneers, 1844–1892*, 10th edn (1900) • B. S. Roper, *The co-op chapel of Rochdale* (1993) • H. F. Bing, 'Smithies, James', *DLB*, vol. 1 • Rochdale Equitable Pioneers Co-operative Society, minute books and purchase book, 1844–8, Rochdale Pioneers Museum • Rochdale Equitable Pioneers Co-operative Society, minute books and purchase book, 1856–63, Rochdale Local Studies Library, C/IND/COOP1 1/1/1 • G. D. H. Cole, *A century of co-operation* (1945) • D. Boydell, *The Rochdale Pioneers* (1944) • A. Pählman, 'Rochdale, 1844: the pioneers',

National Co-operative Archive, Rochdale • P. Redfern, *The new history of the CWS* (1938) • *CGPLA Eng. & Wales* (1869)

Archives Rochdale Local Studies Library, records of Rochdale Equitable Pioneers Co-operative Society • Rochdale Pioneers Museum, records of Rochdale Equitable Pioneers Co-operative Society

Likenesses group portrait, photograph, 1865 (with Rochdale Pioneers), Rochdale Pioneers Museum, Rochdale; *see illus. in* Rochdale Pioneers (*act.* 1844) • photograph, *c.*1868, repro. in Redfern, *New history of the CWS*, following p. 32

Wealth at death under £600: probate, 5 July 1869, *CGPLA Eng. & Wales*

Smithies, Thomas Bywater (1817–1883), campaigner for temperance and for animal welfare, was born on 27 August 1817 in York, the second of ten children of James Smithies and his wife, Catherine, *née* Bywater. Little is known of his parents other than that they were respectable, and were married at St Peter's Church, Leeds, on 23 June 1812 (*IGI*).

Little is known of Smithies's childhood, beyond that as a toddler he would hand out tracts in church; that he was educated at York and Doncaster; and that he was praised for the 'singular beauty of this handwriting' (Rowe, 7). After working as a clerk for the Yorkshire Fire and Life Insurance Company from the age of sixteen, Smithies moved to London in 1849 to join the Gutta Percha Company as a manager. During the intervening years, however, he had worked tirelessly as a Sunday school teacher, a prison visitor, and education reformer. Later he joined the British Temperance League, and became a total abstainer and an ardent supporter of the Band of Hope. By 1850 he had published his first pamphlet on the consequences of intemperance. In January 1851 he issued the *Band of Hope Review*, beginning his lifelong involvement with illustrated temperance publications.

On 1 January 1855 Smithies's major publication, the *British Workman, and Friend of the Sons of Toil*, a monthly 'improving' paper, was launched. The *British Workman* became a highly successful penny paper with a circulation in excess of 200,000 copies per month, recognized for the consistency of its editorial position and the superior quality of its illustrations. The success of the *British Workman* was almost entirely due to the efforts and personality of Smithies who had, through his philanthropic work in the capital, come into close association with, and earned the respect of, a number of influential individuals and organizations. His circle of friends included Charles Dickens, Angela, Baroness Burdett-Coutts, and Lord Shaftesbury, and his continuing religious work brought him into intimate contact with prominent members of the established church, the Society of Friends, and noted political figures such as Samuel Gurney MP. He was also acquainted with eminent artists and engravers such as John Gilbert, Robert Barnes, Harrison Weir, and John Knight, all of whom contributed significantly to the success of the *British Workman*, some coming out of retirement so to do. Smithies edited the *Workman* for the next twenty-eight years, along with several other prominent periodicals including the *Children's Friend* and the *Family Friend*, as well as producing numerous tracts, pamphlets, almanacs, and overseeing the publication of many illustrated books for children.

On moving to London Smithies intended that his parents should join him, but his father died before he was able to make the move. However his mother, **Catherine Smithies** (1791–1878), herself a campaigner for animal welfare, did live with him in his house at Earlham Grove, Wood Green, until her death in 1878. Smithies was devoted to his mother and shared her passion for the well-being of animals, directing his energies and resources in support of the Band of Mercy movement in the foundation of which she had been heavily involved, and the Royal Society for the Prevention of Cruelty to Animals (RSPCA) to whom the rights to the *Band of Mercy* journal (and other properties) eventually transferred (*Animal World*, 1 Sept 1883, 137).

Smithies never married, but devoted his life to his numerous publications and, through them, to furthering his many causes. Despite his many business commitments, he still managed to find the time and energy to undertake lecture tours; to serve on the first London school board (1870), representing Hackney; and to take an active interest in the Drinking Fountains Association, as well as numerous other issues. Not only did he show concern for affairs within the United Kingdom, but also in the condition of black people in America, and that of the people of Ireland.

By all accounts Smithies grew up to be a generous and compassionate man, a lifelong Wesleyan Methodist, a total abstainer, and a vigorous campaigner on behalf of the working classes. Pictorial representations depict him as an elderly gentleman with an earnest countenance, sporting a goatee beard and wearing a skull-cap, seated at his desk. He was a totally committed member of the Lord's Day Observance Society, and was known to chastise others for using public transport on a Sunday in order to 'listen to a sermon' (Keefe, 29). He supported the Early Closing Movement.

On 20 July 1883 at Earlham Grove Thomas Smithies, whose health had for a number of years been gradually deteriorating with a serious heart disease, slipped uncomplainingly into unconsciousness, and died. At his bedside were his five sisters. News of his death was widely announced in the press and at his funeral in Abney Park cemetery on 26 July more than 1000 people gathered to pay their respects. The mourners included officers of the RSPCA and his old friend the earl of Shaftesbury. Smithies left the bulk of his estate to his youngest invalid sister, Elisa, his 'Sunbeam in life' (will); it comprised mainly ownership of periodical titles and properties, but very little money. He had never intended to profit from his business, even though he had opportunities to do so. Such resources as were made available to him through his good fortune, and the blessing of God, he shared with others. An obituarist denominated him 'a gentle guide, a wise counsellor, a true friend' to his fellow man (*British Workman*, 346, October 1883, 182). FRANK MURRAY

Sources G. S. Rowe, *T. B. Smithies: a memoir* (1884) • *Animal World* (Sept 1883) • *British Workman* (Jan 1855) • *British Workman* (Oct 1883) •

British Workman (May 1878) • P. R. Mountjoy, 'Thomas Bywater Smithies: editor of the *British Workman*', *Victorian Periodicals Review*, 18 (1985) • H. J. Keefe, *A century in print: the story of Hazell's, 1839–1939* (1939) • B. Harrison, *Drink and the Victorians*, 2nd edn (1994) • E. Hodder, *The life and work of the seventh earl of Shaftesbury*, 3 (1886) • will • d. cert. • *IGI*

Likenesses wood-engraving, *c.*1883, repro. in *British Workman* (Oct 1883), title-page • wood-engraving, *c.*1883, repro. in *Animal World*, 137 • J. W. Walton, group portrait, oils (with the London school board in 1870), LMA, RN 2001/001 • photogravure, repro. in Keefe, *A century in print*

Smithson [*née* Gill], **Alison Margaret** (1928–1993), architect and writer, was born on 22 June 1928 at 3 Clarkehouse Road, Broomhall, Sheffield, the only child of Ernest Gill (1887–1980), graphic artist and art teacher, and his wife, Alison Jessie, *née* Malcolm (1901–1989), who trained as a weaver. Her father, who was principal of the South Shields School of Art from 1929 to 1950, was English and her mother Scottish. Although fiercely loyal to the north-east, Smithson felt distanced from suburban middle-class provincial life, which she wrote about disdainfully in her autobiographical novel *A Portrait of the Female Mind as a Young Girl* (1966). A gifted student, she attended South Shields High School for Girls and Sunderland Church High School. During the Second World War she lived with relatives in north Yorkshire and in Edinburgh, where she went to George Watson Ladies' College and encountered American magazines—sent by a cousin in New England—whose advertisements impressed her profoundly with their quality and range of expressive imagery. Taught by her father to draw and to make measured drawings, she entered Durham University's school of architecture in Newcastle upon Tyne (later part of the University of Newcastle upon Tyne) in 1944. After graduating with distinction in 1949, she joined the schools division of the London county council (LCC) architects' department. On 18 August that year she married Peter Denham Smithson (1923–2003), the son of William Blenkison Smithson, commercial traveller; he was a former fellow student and LCC colleague, who became her lifelong collaborator. They had three children, Simon (*b.* 1954), Samantha (*b.* 1957), and Soraya (*b.* 1964).

While at the LCC Alison and Peter Smithson entered architectural competitions. Their success in the public competition for Hunstanton secondary modern school, Norfolk (1949–54), brought international recognition, and enabled them to set up in practice on their own. Highly photogenic, the steel-framed school was extensively glazed, disciplined with a formal, axial plan, and carefully detailed in the Miesian manner, while its exposed materials and service elements heralded the new brutalism in architecture. Hunstanton particularly impressed young British architects seeking new directions in materials, techniques, and structures. A prime representative of architectural experimentation endorsed by the post-war welfare state, it nevertheless found less appreciation by those whose priorities were social rather than architectural—a conflict which the Smithsons later tried to resolve. On its completion they were jointly named 'Men [*sic*] of the Year' in architecture. Alison Smithson claimed,

Alison Margaret Smithson (1928–1993), by Godfrey Argent, 1969 [with her husband, Peter Smithson]

'We are the best architects in the country' (*Architects' Journal*, 119, 21 Jan 1954, 72). Nevertheless the frustrating pattern of her career was now in train: a widely acclaimed building, followed by no further prestigious work, but unexecuted competitions (Coventry Cathedral, 1950–51; Sydney Opera House, 1956; Sheffield University, 1957–8), small-scale domestic and commercial work (Sugden House, Watford, 1955–6), and, most dispiriting, abandoned projects (British embassy, Brasilia, 1964–8). This irregular professional rhythm was countered by a steady stream of intellectually passionate, influential essays on architecture and urbanism, and a series of books written with Peter Smithson: *Urban Structuring* (1967), *Ordinariness and Light* (1970), *Without Rhetoric* (1973), and *The Shift* (1982).

In the early 1950s Alison and Peter Smithson collaborated with other young artists, including the sculptor Eduardo Paolozzi and the photographer Nigel Henderson, in staging exhibitions ('The Parallel of Art and Life', 1953, and 'This Is Tomorrow', 1956) in which they showed ideas which they had discussed within the Independent Group (IG; 1952–63). This was an informal organization associated with the Institute of Contemporary Arts, which made claims for the significance of popular culture, including advertising, mass communications, and the everyday, in order 'to face up to a mass-production society' (*Architectural Design*, 27, April 1957, 113). By her own reckoning, Alison Smithson named the architecture that emerged 'the new brutalism', which employed 'ordinary' industrially produced materials, techniques, and services, and led to a radical reassessment of the relationship of art and life—of architecture and society. These ethical and aesthetic ideas related to the Smithsons' architecture were widely circulated in the *Architectural Review* (1955) by fellow IG member and historian Reyner Banham.

The central architectural problem for Smithson and her generation was the provision of public housing. This preoccupied her for over twenty years, from the unexecuted Golden Lane scheme (1952) to the Robin Hood estate, Poplar, London (completed 1972). The latter was a robust but controversial utopian solution, which took specific characteristics of local community life 'as found' and focused the design on a response to users' activities. 'Streets-in-the-air' recast the traditional East End street into modern conditions of high-rise living. Nevertheless, Alison Smithson also questioned the efficacy of high-rise living for families with children. In a series of essays and designs for exhibitions she envisaged low-density housing with integral, easy-to-clean furnishings and fittings, including an interior garden-play space in the highly styled House of the Future which she created, with Peter Smithson, for the Ideal Home Exhibition in 1956. The car as a fact of twentieth-century life was woven throughout the Smithson projects, where it was both means and motive for a vision of the planned reconstructed post-war city. Reconfigured in multiple 'clusters' of differing population densities and housing types, their 'Cluster City' was to be connected by a network of motorways, which in one plan called for the demolition of much of Soho and Covent Garden.

With the concept of the city based on human 'association' and an aesthetic of change, Alison and Peter Smithson and other European architects challenged the old guard of the Congrès Internationaux d'Architecture Moderne (CIAM) and their functionalist urban model. Seeking to renew modernism, but ultimately provoking CIAM's demise (in 1960), the dissidents formed Team 10 in 1956, with Alison Smithson a proactive figure until the group's disbandment, in 1981. She contributed to its ambitious but unfulfilled plans for systematic but more diverse urban development, and edited *Team 10 Primer* (1968).

Alison Smithson was the first woman architect to design a large-scale commercial building in central London. The Economist Building (1959–64) in St James's (with Peter Smithson) is in fact three buildings of different heights, shapes, and functions (offices, bank, residential), set asymmetrically on a raised courtyard. Undisguisedly modern but in keeping with its historic neighbourhood, the textured materials, modulated forms, and low-key interiors (later altered) produced quiet spaces for urban life and work in a restrained group of buildings. After her trip to Japan in 1960 respect for materials as part of reverence for the natural world and an architecture of unobtrusive calm became important themes. Smithson's understanding of history and urban palimpsest, which informed her architecture, was most strongly stated in *The Euston Arch* (1968), which supported the conservation movement's landmark case.

The Smithsons combined domestic and professional life on the model of a small farm, self-sufficient and productive, with the family working together from home. Alison Smithson took her own experience as a mother and used it in her work, drawing on everyday activities to develop ideas about architecture and 'changing the art of inhabitation' (the title of one of her books, published in 1994). Decoration, notably absent from modernist architecture, made a reappearance in her work based on a domesticity that delighted in a sense of occasion and place. Family events, and children's toys and books, provided ideas which provoked exhibitions and publications and reappeared in an architectural scale. The decorative graphic elements in ephemera, such as layering, were rethought and reworked in the Garden Building at St Hilda's College, Oxford (1970).

Strikingly handsome, with almost olive skin, black hair, and large dark eyes, Alison Smithson had an upright carriage that gave the impression of being much taller than her 5 feet 3 inches. Her palpable intellect, careful phrasing (which excluded flippant remarks), and forthright manner often gave the impression of a forbidding, imperious nature. However, to her family and close friends she was a warm, supportive person, ever resourceful and dependable. She lived long enough to see a renewed interest in her work by a younger generation of architects, but from the 1970s until her death built work was scarce and dominated by three commissions for Bath University. She died at the Royal Marsden Hospital, Chelsea, London, of breast cancer, on 14 August 1993. Her body was cremated in London twelve days later. She was survived by her husband and their three children. LYNNE WALKER

Sources A. Smithson, *A portrait of the female mind as a young girl* (1966) • A. Smithson, 'Alison Smithson', *The evacuees*, ed. B. Johnson (1968), 245–51 • P. Cook, 'Regarding the Smithsons', *ArchR*, 172 (1982), 36–43 • D. Robbins, ed., *The Independent Group: post war Britain and the aesthetics of plenty* (1990) • E. Mumford, *The CIAM discourse on urbanism, 1928–1960* (2000) • A. Saint, *Towards a social architecture: the role of school-building in post-war England* (1987) • *The Times* (20 Aug 1993) • *Financial Times* (23 Aug 1993) • *The Guardian* (20 Aug 1993) • *Architects' Journal* (1 Sept 1993) • *Progressive Architecture* (Oct 1993) • *Building Design* (3 Sept 1993) • private information (2004) [Peter Smithson, Soraya Smithson, Bryan and Sandra Richards, Rhoda Brawne] • b. cert. • m. cert. • d. cert.

Archives Canadian Centre for Architecture, Montreal • priv. coll., archive | FILM BFI NFTVA | SOUND BL NSA, 'Signs of occupancy', ICA0027741 • BL NSA, recorded talk

Likenesses G. Argent, photograph, 1969, NPG [*see illus.*] • photographs, priv. coll.

Wealth at death under £125,000: probate, 23 Dec 1993, *CGPLA Eng. & Wales*

Smithson, Annie Mary Patricia (1873–1948), author and nurse, was born on 26 September 1873 at 22 Claremont Road, Sandymount, Dublin, the only child of Samuel Raynor Smithson, barrister, and his wife, Margaret Louisa Carpenter (*d.* 1917). Baptized Margaret Anne Jane, on her conversion to Catholicism in 1907 Smithson took instead the names Anne Mary Patricia. Her mother and father were first cousins and her father died when she was young. About 1881 her mother married her second husband, Peter Longshaw, who owned a chemical factory in Warrington in Lancashire. Smithson disliked her stepfather and referred to him always as Mr Longshaw. There were five children of the second marriage.

Smithson spent the first few years of her life living with her mother and her grandparents in Sandymount, Dublin. On her mother's remarriage the family moved first of all to Warrington, and when her stepfather's business failed they returned to live in Dublin. At this time the family were poor and rented flats at various locations around the city. They also rented a house in Bray in co. Wicklow. After her stepfather's death the family moved to Dalkey, co. Dublin. Smithson believed herself to be poorly educated. She had sporadically attended various day schools in Dublin, Warrington, and Bray, and for a brief period was also a boarder at a girls' boarding-school in West Derby. She was removed from school in Bray at the age of fifteen to take care of the children in the family.

Smithson had wanted to become a journalist. Her maternal aunt Susan Carpenter (*d.* 1929) had been one of the few women journalists working on London newspapers in the first decades of the twentieth century. However, Smithson instead trained as a nurse. She spent fifteen months in the Chelsea Hospital for Women in London and went to Edinburgh in October 1898 to train as a Queen Victoria jubilee nurse. She spent two years at the Royal Infirmary in Edinburgh and returned to Dublin in December 1900 for six months' training as a district nurse. Her first appointment was in Portadown but she moved to the village of Millton in co. Down in September 1901 to take up duty there. Here she worked with Dr James Manton in the local dispensary. She fell in love with Manton, a married man. Deciding they had no future together, she left Millton in January 1906. Smithson remained deeply attached to Manton but, while he continued to write to her, they did not meet again. On her conversion to Catholicism Smithson burnt all of Manton's letters.

Smithson returned to the Royal Infirmary in Edinburgh to continue her training and also worked as a night nurse in a women's hospital in Glasgow. It was while Smithson was in Glasgow that she began to attend Catholic church services. Although brought up in the Church of Ireland, she had attended services of the Plymouth Brethren in Dublin in the late 1880s. On her return to Dublin in January 1907 she continued to receive instruction in the Catholic faith from a Sister of Charity, and in March of that year she was received into the church. While Smithson gives no reason for her conversion, she appears to have been quite unhappy for a time—particularly after the ending of her relationship with Manton.

Smithson's work as a district nurse took her to many different parts of Ireland. For a brief spell in 1913 she suffered from tuberculosis and spent some time in Peamount Hospital. She was sympathetic to the cause of Irish nationalism: she canvassed for Sinn Féin in the 1918 general election and became a member of Cumann na mBan, the women's auxiliary to the Irish Volunteers, to which group she gave lectures on first aid. She supported the republican side during the civil war and acted as a nurse to the republicans in the besieged Moran's Hotel in Dublin at the outbreak of the civil war. She was arrested and imprisoned in Mullingar for about a week while travelling to the west of Ireland to help the republicans there. Her republican sympathies led to a request that she resign from the queen's nurses committee, which she did, and she took up private nursing as a consequence. Smithson's stepsister and her family moved to Dublin in 1932 and she shared a house with them in Rathmines in Dublin until her death.

Smithson was elected a member of the General Nursing Council in 1924. In July 1929 she became the secretary of the Irish Nurses' Union (later the Irish Nurses' Organization). Smithson became a member of the Central Midwives' Board in 1934, and was also active on the National Council of Trained Nurses. She wrote regularly for the *Irish Nurses' Magazine* and edited the *Irish Nurses Union Gazette*. In circumstances that remain mysterious, Smithson was forced to resign from her post as secretary of the Irish Nurses' Union in 1942.

It is as a novelist that Smithson is best remembered. Her first book, *Her Irish Heritage*, was published in Dublin in 1917 and dedicated 'To the memory of the men who died, Easter 1916'. In all Smithson was to publish twenty novels and two collections of short stories. Most of her novels, which are strongly nationalist, were best-sellers. Contrasts are made between Irish and English characters, with the English usually coming out worse. There are often conflicts between Catholic and protestant characters, and conversion to Catholicism is a regular feature. The plots are highly romantic and include many incidents taken from Smithson's own experiences. *Carmen Cavanagh* (1921), for instance, is the story of a district nurse in Donegal. *Sheila of the O'Beirnes* (1929) is narrated by a young girl who runs away from her mother and from her school after her mother's second marriage. In *The Walk of a Queen* (1922), a title echoing a phrase from Yeats' play *Cathleen ni Houlihan*, set in the years 1917–21, the hero, who has unwittingly betrayed the cause of Ireland, substitutes himself for his twin brother and suffers the death penalty. In a number of the works children are orphaned and mothers often appear as selfish, worldly women. Her autobiography, *Myself and Others*, appeared in 1944. Smithson died of heart failure at 12 Richmond Hill, Dublin, on 21 February 1948 and was buried in Rathfarnham cemetery.

MARIA LUDDY

Sources A. M. P. Smithson, *Myself and others* (1944) · b. cert. · d. cert.

Archives Military Archives, Collins Barracks, Rathmines, Dublin, 'Captured documents' series · priv. coll., comments regarding her role on the Central Midwives' Board · priv. coll., minute books of the Central Midwives' Board

Likenesses photograph, repro. in *Fiftieth anniversary souvenir book*, Irish Nurses Organisation (1969)

Smithson [*married name* Berlioz], **Harriet Constance (1800–1854)**, actress, was born on 18 March 1800 at Ennis, co. Clare, Ireland, the second of the three children of William Joseph Smithson (*d. c.*1824), an actor and theatre manager, and his wife, an actress, both originally from Gloucestershire. When she was two she was entrusted to the care of James Barrett, dean of Killaloe, and she lived under his guardianship in Chapel Lane, Ennis, until his

Harriet Constance Smithson (1800–1854), by George Clint, *c.*1822 [as Miss Dorillon in *Wives as they Were and Maids as they Are* by Elizabeth Inchbald]

death in 1808. She was then sent to a boarding-school in Waterford. Her parents, who had been acting in Plymouth, returned to Ireland in 1814, and Harriet made her début as Albina Mandeville in Frederick Reynolds's *The Will* on 27 May 1814, at the Theatre Royal, Dublin.

Harriet Smithson was given a more permanent engagement in 1816 with Montague Talbot's company in Belfast, where she played mostly in comedy. She toured with Talbot and in Dublin added a more serious part, Mrs Haller in Kotzebue's *The Stranger*. She was offered a season at the Theatre Royal, Birmingham, then under the management of the flamboyant and talented Robert Elliston. Beginning on 30 June 1817, she appeared in more than forty roles, and played with three of the greatest comic actors of the period, Charles Mathews, John Liston, and Elliston. On 20 January 1818 she made the transition to London and the Theatre Royal, Drury Lane, choosing Letitia Hardy in *The Belle's Stratagem* for her début. Notices tended to refer to her fine figure and graceful movements rather than the distinction of her acting, but as she became more used to the vast auditorium, which held 3000 spectators, she began to attract more appreciative comments. She was unable to secure a permanent place in the company until 1820, under Elliston's management.

Harriet Smithson became established as a hard-working and useful actress, but one who just failed to be seen as first-rate. She rose very slowly in the hierarchy of her profession, a salary of £5 a week in 1824 giving her the right to use the 'first' green room. Her benefit performances were well attended, and she gained the patronage of a number of well-connected persons. After the death of her father she became an important wage-earner for the family, since her mother secured few stage engagements and there was an invalid younger sister to look after. Her brother Joseph organized an English-language season based in Calais and Boulogne, where Harriet appeared in 1824. Except when she was acting, Harriet's life revolved around her family; exceptionally, there was no hint of scandal attached to her. 'Beautiful beyond the common run of beauty; yet as virtuous as beautiful … *she* has never *coquetted* a manager into favour, nor marted her feelings for the sake of her interest,' declared *Oxberry's Dramatic Biography* (2.206), and the article ended with ecstatic praise of her eyes.

In 1827 an English company was organized to perform at the Théâtre de l'Odéon, Paris. The season began, unsensationally, with Sheridan's *The Rivals*, featuring Liston as Bob Acres, Harriet as Lydia Languish, and Mrs Smithson as Mrs Malaprop. On Tuesday 11 September *Hamlet* was announced, with Charles Kemble as Hamlet and Harriet as Ophelia. Harriet was reluctant to play the role, and offered it to other actresses with a week's salary as an inducement, on the grounds that she had not acted Ophelia for twelve years. However, the performance, and her own acting, enjoyed an enormous success. The French were eager for Shakespeare, especially for Shakespeare in the English style of acting. The French Romantics attended in force: Hugo, de Vigny, Delacroix, Dumas, and Gautier were reportedly present. Kemble's acting, especially in the scenes with the Ghost, drew rounds of applause from the audience; but it was Ophelia's mad scenes which most caught their imagination. Harriet's silent acting, her broken snatches of song, her heart-rending sobs, affected everyone, including those who did not understand the English text: 'There was utter silence among the spectators—and then at the first cry of madness, a great burst of cheering, the most enthusiastic that I have ever heard,' recorded Charles Jarrin (author's translation; Tiersot, 53). Harriet Smithson, perhaps released by the French context from her slight diffidence, and certainly aided by a smaller theatre and an eager audience, found herself famous. She followed up with equally well-received performances of Juliet and Desdemona, and in the title role of Nicholas Rowe's *Jane Shore*. She became the subject of comment in newspapers and journals, and her portrait was painted and engraved and displayed in the print-shop windows. *Souvenirs du théâtre anglais* was published, with a series of lithographs by Achille Devéria and Louis Boulanger, in which she was strongly featured. As 'La Belle Irlandaise', she was the theatrical sensation of the year. Finally, she was granted a prestigious benefit, in March 1828, which included appearances by Mlle Mars and Henriette Sontag: the three stars were named by the *Quotidienne* (5 March 1828) 'les trois grandes puissances dramatiques de Paris'. Notable English actors such as W. C. Macready and

Edmund Kean travelled to Paris to appear with her, and she extended her repertory of Shakespearian roles.

Meanwhile the young composer Hector *Berlioz (1803–1869), who had attended *Hamlet* and *Romeo and Juliet*, had fallen helplessly in love with Harriet. He haunted the theatre where she performed; his apartment at 96 rue de Richelieu faced hers on the corner of the rue neuve St Marc; he composed the song *Élégie en prose*, based on one of Moore's Irish melodies; he sent her a declaration of love. She remained unmoved. Berlioz's artistic response to his torment was the *Symphonie fantastique*, completed on 16 April 1830.

Harriet Smithson's ambitious plans for a continental tour did not materialize, and she accepted an engagement at Covent Garden. In 1830 she appeared again in Paris at the Opéra Comique, playing a role in English within a French play, but the directors absconded, revolution broke out, and she found herself stranded and financially embarrassed. A benefit on her behalf at the Opéra on 5 December 1830 enabled her to leave for England, where she resumed her career, but with diminishing success. In November 1832 she returned to Paris, this time as producer as well as leading actress, and opened a season at the Théâtre-Italien. Her supporting company was weak and the response muted. She was persuaded, perhaps as a distraction, to attend a concert on 9 December. The programme consisted of Berlioz's *Symphonie fantastique*, followed by *Lélio, ou, Le retour à la vie*. Berlioz had, in the interim, spent time in Italy after winning the prix de Rome and survived the anguish of a love affair with Camille Moke. The coincidence of the concert brought him back into Harriet Smithson's orbit. The two met, and soon declared their love for each other.

The next months were fraught with difficulties. Marriage was opposed by both families. Dr Berlioz was especially adamant, and Berlioz had to take lengthy and complex legal steps to avoid being disinherited. Harriet Smithson's debts were mounting, and she slipped on the running-board of a cab and broke her leg, which prevented her from acting. These pressures, aggravated by her indecision and Berlioz's volatile temperament, ensured a stormy period before the two were married, on 3 October 1833 at the British embassy, with Liszt as a witness: Harriet, Berlioz wrote to his sister Adèle, was 'Ophelia herself': he had been right to listen to the voice of his heart (*Correspondance générale*, 2.347).

The couple lived first in Paris, and then for a time in the village of Montmartre. On 14 August 1834 their son, Louis, was born. Only the first few years brought happiness. Harriet Smithson still yearned for a career, but, as she never learned to speak French fluently, both her professional and her social life were limited. She appeared in a mimed role at the Théâtre Nautique, and Berlioz tried to persuade George Sand to create a part for her in a new play, but otherwise she was restricted to occasional benefit performances. Meanwhile Berlioz struggled to pursue his career, a process which Harriet found difficult to accept. Possessiveness turned to suspicion and jealousy as Berlioz became involved with the singer Marie Recio. Harriet's health deteriorated, and she began to drink heavily. After the autumn of 1844 the two separated, and Berlioz maintained two households, with Harriet living in Montmartre. Louis, at first placed *en pension* in Paris, was sent to school in Rouen in 1846, and Berlioz went alone to London for a Drury Lane engagement in 1847. In 1848 Harriet suffered the first of a series of severe strokes. Berlioz continued to visit her, and to be financially responsible for her: she required constant nursing care. She died on 3 March 1854, and was buried the following day in Montmartre. Tributes to the impact she had made as an actress came from, among others, Gautier, Dumas, and Jules Janin, who wrote that 'a whole society stirred to the magic of this woman'; he recalled that she was the inspiration for Delacroix's picture of Ophelia, and, by his quotation 'Throw flowers!', linked her death with the funeral procession of Berlioz's *Romeo and Juliet* symphony (Berlioz, *Mémoires*, 570–1). PETER RABY

Sources *Oxberry's Dramatic Biography*, 2/28 (1825) • H. Berlioz, *Mémoires de Hector Berlioz*, trans. D. Cairns (1977) • *Correspondance générale: Hector Berlioz*, ed. P. Citron, 7 vols. (Paris, 1972–95) • P. Raby, *Fair Ophelia: a life of Harriet Smithson Berlioz* (1982) • D. Cairns, *Berlioz, 1803–32: the making of an artist* (1989) • Genest, *Eng. stage* • M. Moreau, *Souvenirs du théâtre anglais à Paris* (1827) • N. P. Chaulin, *Biographie dramatique des principaux artistes anglais venus à Paris* (1828) • W. A. Donaldson, *Fifty years of green-room gossip* (1881) • J. Tiersot, *Berlioz et la société de son temps* (1904) • C. B. Wicks, ed., *The Parisian stage, part 2: 1816–1830* (1953) • C. B. Wicks and J. W. Schweitzer, *The Parisian stage, part 3: 1831–1850* (1960)

Likenesses G. Clint, portrait, *c.*1822, Yale U. CBA [*see illus.*] • Francis, lithograph, 1827, Theatre Museum, London • A. de Valmont, lithograph, 1827, Theatre Museum, London • Langlumé, lithograph, *c.*1828, Theatre Museum, London • G. Maile, mezzotint, 1828 (after Dubufe), BM, department of prints and drawings • R. Cooper, stipple (as Miss Dorrillon in *Wives as they were and maids as they are*), BM, NPG; repro. in D. Terry, *British theatrical gallery* (1822) • A. Devéria, lithograph, BM, department of prints and drawings • Devéria & Boulanger, lithographs (as Ophelia, Juliet, Desdemona, and Jane Shore), Bibliothèque Nationale, Paris • J. Hopwood, stipple (after R. Drummond), BM, NPG; repro. in *Ladies' Monthly Museum* (1819) • J. Rogers, engraving (after painting by R. E. Drummond), repro. in *Oxberry's Dramatic Biography* • lithograph, BM • oils, Garr. Club

Smithson, Hugh. *See* Percy, Hugh, first duke of Northumberland (*bap.* 1712, *d.* 1786).

Smithson [*formerly* Macie], **James Lewis** (**1764–1829**), mineralogist and benefactor, was born Jacques Louis Macie in Paris in early 1764, the illegitimate son of a long-term liaison between Hugh *Percy (formerly Smithson), second earl and later first duke of Northumberland (*bap.* 1712, *d.* 1786), and Elizabeth Macie, *née* Keate (1728–1800), the widow of John Macie (1720–1761) of Weston House, Bath.

Early life Macie's mother moved from Bath as soon as her pregnancy became obvious, and the boy was brought up in Paris as a protestant, an important precaution since Percy was baptized a Roman Catholic and only converted to Anglicanism after his father's death. Macie returned to London to be naturalized by act of parliament in June 1773, and subsequently lived in Marylebone, Middlesex, under the guardianship of Joseph Gape of the Inner Temple. Macie probably attended Charterhouse School, London, as did his brother Henry Louis Dickinson (1771–1820),

James Lewis Smithson (1764–1829), by Henri-Joseph Johns, 1816

another child perhaps of the liaison between Percy and Elizabeth Macie, but no records for such day scholars survive. The duke of Northumberland had three children within wedlock and two illegitimate daughters, born to a different mother from Elizabeth Macie, Philadelphia Percy (*c*.1770–1791) and Dorothy Percy (*d*. 1794). These two were an acknowledged part of the duke's family and were buried with him in Westminster Abbey, but male children by any wife other than the one who brought him the name Percy could not bear that name. Horace Walpole observed in 1775 that 'his patent does not enable him to beget Percys—a Master or Miss Smithson would sound like natural children' (Walpole, *Corr.*, 24.99).

The young mineralogist Macie matriculated at Pembroke College, Oxford, on 7 May 1782, aged seventeen. His friends at Oxford included the mineralogist William Thomson and Davies Giddy. It was Macie who introduced Giddy, who, as Davies Gilbert, became president of the Royal Society, to the then president, Joseph Banks, in June 1789. Gilbert later noted how 'Macie had the reputation of excelling all other resident members of the University in the knowledge of Chemistry' (Gilbert). Macie was created MA on 26 May 1786. While an undergraduate he travelled all over England and Scotland hunting minerals. His most famous tour was to the west of Scotland in 1784, during which he visited Staffa to see the wondrous basaltic columns; inspiration for Macie's trip had come from Thomson who undertook the same tour in 1782. The tour was made in the company of Barthélemy Faujas de St Fond, the French geologist, and William Thornton from the Virgin Islands, a student at the University of Edinburgh. Macie's letter of introduction (from Thomson) to the Edinburgh chemist Joseph Black noted that Macie's 'proficiency [as mineralogist] is … already much beyond what I have been able to attain to' (28 Aug 1784, Black MSS, Edinburgh University Library). In another letter to Black, written following Macie's return to England late in 1784, Thomson wrote, 'Macie I much esteem & as a gent. of fortune, who dedicates his whole time to Mineralogy, in a rational manner, I think him a valuable character in this country. He is very young [twenty]' (ibid., 15 Sept 1784). Another, unrelated, letter dating from 1784 (from Charles Blagden to Joseph Banks) reveals that it was known that Macie was a natural son of the duke of Northumberland.

In that year Macie, then living at Orchard Street in London, was elected a member of the London Society for the Promotion of Natural History. In 1785 he sent minerals to Black and was first in touch with another important mineral collector, Charles Greville. In 1786 Macie was elected a member of the Chapter House Philosophical Society of London. He was next elected a fellow of the Royal Society of London in April 1787, sponsored, among others, by Henry Cavendish and Richard Kirwan. To this society he presented eight papers between 1791 and 1817, including a paper on zeolites collected on his 1784 tour. In 1788 he was also busy procuring fossils from quarries near Oxford for James Hutton.

European travels Many of Macie's Royal Society papers were written on his European travels. In 1790 his friend Thomson suddenly resigned his position at Oxford University and travelled throughout Europe before settling at Naples. In 1791 Macie started an equally itinerant life, believing that 'the man of science is of no country, the world is his country and all mankind his countrymen' (Rhees, 4). Macie's first base was Paris. His euphoric letter written to Greville on new year's day 1792 noted that he was

> here on the brink of the crater of a great volcano [the French Revolution] from which lavas are daily issuing, but whose effects are widely different from those of the other [Vesuvius then in active eruption]. That is laying waste one of the finest countries in the world [Italy], [&] is threatening with ruin the noblest efforts of human art. While this on the contrary [in France] is consolidating the throne of justice and reason, pours its destruction only on erroneous or corrupt institutions, overthrows not fine statues & amphitheatres but monks and convents … If [this] nation succeeds and I do not see what will conquer and restore to ignorance fifteen million of people resolved upon success or death, this country will compel great changes in every part of the globe. (BL, Add. MS 41199, fols. 82–83)

Similar sentiments were revealed in another Parisian letter of May 1792 to Davies Giddy. Macie spent the winter of 1792–3 in Rome and corresponded with Giovanni Fabbroni. In 1794 he was with Fabbroni at Florence, and from 1796 to 1797 was at Dresden, and collecting minerals for Lady Elizabeth Holland, whom he had met at Florence.

Macie's mother is supposed to have stayed in France after giving birth to him, but she had returned to London by 1780 and was living in Lower Brook Street when she made her will in 1789; she died at Brighton in May 1800. Macie had returned to London by 1798 and on 27 April 1799 was elected a proprietor of the Royal Institution, having been proposed by Joseph Banks. Macie proved his mother's will on 16 May 1800 and, at her special request, announced his change of name to Smithson, his father's, in the *London Gazette* of 16 February 1801.

Smithson, as he now became, had resumed his continental travels by 1805 when he was at Frankfurt; another Royal Society paper (dated 2 March 1806) was sent from Kassel in Hesse. In August 1807 British troops landed in Denmark while Smithson was at Tonningen (now Tönning) in Danish Schleswig-Holstein trying to book his passage home, probably after visiting Copenhagen. In September 1807 the Danes, in formal alliance with Napoleon, declared war on Britain and Smithson was seized as a prisoner of war. In April 1808, through the agency of John Thornton, British agent in Hamburg, Smithson now made his way to that city, only to be imprisoned again. His appeal of 18 September 1808 to Banks to secure his release reached London in November. Banks's letter to Jean Baptiste Delambre was read to the French Institut on 20 March 1809 and Delambre wrote on 16 April asking the French minister of war to release Smithson. This was granted on 18 April and Napoleon's final approval of Smithson's release, after a year and a half, was reported on 19 June 1809. Smithson could now return to London and was present at the Royal Society Club on 23 August 1810 when he was introduced by Humphrey Davy. Smithson's next Royal Society paper, on the composition of zeolite, was dated St James's Palace, 22 January 1811. Some of the specimens used he had collected on Staffa in 1784.

With the end of the Napoleonic wars Smithson again ventured to the continent. In 1816 his miniature portrait was painted at Aix-la-Chapelle. His last paper to the Royal Society was on the colouring matters of vegetables and was read on 18 December 1817. Thereafter there was some break with the society, and he published eighteen further papers outside the organization. By 1819 he was in Rome, and in 1820 was back in Paris.

In 1824 Smithson published a paper on Granville Penn's theory concerning the formation of the newly discovered Kirkdale cave in Yorkshire. In this Smithson noted that 'it is in his knowledge that man has found his greatness and his happiness'. By 1825 Smithson had returned to London and was again at the Royal Society Club, now introduced by Sir George Staunton.

The Smithsonian Institution In 1826 Smithson was living in Bentinck Street, Marylebone, where he made his (now famous) will on 23 October 1826. This left nearly all his property to his nephew Henry James Hungerford, 'son of my late brother Lt. Col. Henry Louis Dickinson' or to any children he might have. If there were no children the whole of his property, subject to an annuity was to go to 'the United States of America, to found in Washington under the name of the Smithsonian Institution, an establishment for the increase and diffusion of knowledge among men' (*The Times*, 10 Dec 1829). Smithson died on 27 June 1829 at Genoa, unmarried and childless. He was buried at the protestant cemetery in San Benigno, Genoa. In 1904 his remains were removed to the Smithsonian Institution in Washington.

The great majority of Smithson's fortune, $508,318 when converted to US dollars in 1838, must have come from his mother's family. It is unclear if he ever had any contact with his father, who died in 1786, although his half-sister Dorothy did leave him £3000 in 1794. His mother, on the other hand, was clearly devoted to her two sons. She was a considerable landowner, selling Great Durnford Manor, Wiltshire, to James Harris in 1791. Her will of 1789 left her entire estate to Macie. Elizabeth Macie also had two younger siblings, Lumley Keate Hungerford (1735–1766) of Studley House, Wiltshire, and Bath, and Henrietta Maria Keate (1731–1803), who in 1769 married George Walker (*d.* 1783) and took the name Hungerford from 1789. Much of their money seems also to have passed to Smithson.

Smithson's place in history is almost unique, since he is one of very few people whose fame is entirely posthumous, through the extraordinary consequences of his will, and the mineral Smithsonite named after him in 1832. With the loss of his archives in a disastrous fire in the Smithsonian Institution in 1865, the context of his outburst that 'the best blood of England flows in my veins … but this avails me not. My name shall live in the memory of man when the titles of the Northumberlands and Percys are extinct and forgotten' (Rhees, 2) remains unknown. It may refer only to his publications, although some wish for posthumous fame may have been a contributory factor in his decision to leave money for a foreign institution. But Smithson knew nothing of the crises which arose before his benefaction was put to use in Washington in 1846, twenty years after his will.

The question arises as to why his money was left to a foreign, American, institution. The romantic, and unexplained nature of the bequest has generated much speculative history, culminating in the fanciful 1934 novel by Louise Wallace Hackney, *Wing of Fame*. Smithson's obvious, if unrecorded, problem with the Royal Society from 1818 explains why he did not leave his fortune to that organization. Louis Agassiz recorded that

> Smithson had already made his will and left his fortune to the Royal Society of London, when certain scientific papers were offered to that body for publication … They were refused; upon which he changed his will and made his bequest to the United States. (L. Agassiz, 'Letter on the Smithsonian Institution', *Science*, 28 March 1919, 301)

Notably Agassiz did not say whether the refused papers were written by Smithson.

Macie's reactions to the French Revolution in letters of 1792 give the best demonstration of his feelings for democratic, republican societies and how he, like others including Percy Bysshe Shelley, saw their great potential. Smithson demonstrated an extraordinary optimism in bequeathing his considerable fortune to the United States, a country quite unknown to him. Smithson had had high hopes for the French Revolution, since a Nation with a constitution, a climate and an extent like this which opens its arms to the natives of every latitude, to the sectaries of every religion & receives them as its children, cannot fail soon to accumulate to its bosom nearly all the arts, commerce and wealth of the world, and other nations can possibly maintain any competition with it only by emulating and, if possible, exceeding it, in its improvements … If the millions of money and the thousands of individuals which are at present sacrificed to war, should be applied to the promotion of sciences and arts, what may we not expect, even in our time. (BL, Add. MS 41199 fols. 82–83)

However, the appalling outcome for Smithson's beloved science in the French Revolution, to which he was witness, and his time as a prisoner of war in Germany are likely reasons why he did not feel the institutions of other European countries were worthy of his money. It is probable that he believed that only a new country could support his extraordinary vision. It is tragic that a fire at the Smithsonian Institution in 1865 should have destroyed his archives and a mineral collection described in 1841 as 'choice and beautiful and the richest and rarest in that country' (Wilson, 193), but his posthumous fame was assured. H. S. TORRENS

Sources D. Gilbert, 'Notices … James Smithson', *American Journal of Science*, 20 (1831), 306–7 • *GM*, 1st ser., 100/1 (1830), 275–6 • W. J. Rhees, ed., *The scientific writings of James Smithson* (1879) • L. Carmichael and J. C. Long, *James Smithson and the Smithsonian story* (1965) • W. J. Rhees, *James Smithson and his bequest* (1880) • A. G. Day, 'James Smithson in Durance', *Pacific Historical Review*, 12 (1943), 391–4 • G. De Beer, *The sciences were never at war* (1960) • D. E. Smith, *Delambre and Smithson* (1934) • W. L. Bird jun., 'A suggestion concerning James Smithson's concept of "increase and diffusion"', *Technology and Culture*, 24 (1985), 246–55 • J. S. White, 'Calamines and James Smithson', *Matrix*, 2/2 (1991), 17–19 • J. Conaway, *The Smithsonian: 150 years of adventure, discovery and wonder* (1995) • A. Geikie, *Annals of the Royal Society Club* (1917) • W. E. Wilson, 'The history of mineral collecting', *Mineralogical Record*, 25/6 (1994), 1–264

Archives American Philosophical Society, Philadelphia, Fabbroni MSS • BL, Greville MSS, letters • FM Cam., Hutton MSS • Sutro Library, San Francisco, Banks MSS • U. Edin., Joseph Black MSS

Likenesses H.-J. Johns, miniature, oils, 1816, Smithsonian Institution, Washington, DC [*see illus.*] • Oxford student copper medallion, Smithsonian Institution, Washington, DC

Wealth at death $508,318—bequest to the Smithsonian: J. Conaway, *The Smithsonian: 150 years of adventure, discovery and wonder* (1995), 18

Smits [Smitz], **Caspar** [*alias* Theodorus Hartcamp; *called* Magdalen Smith] (*c.***1635**–*c.***1707**), painter, was probably of Dutch origin. In England he was called Magdalen Smith, since he was known for his pictures of the penitent Magdalen. His father, Houbraken believed, was an officer in the Dutch army. According to Walpole, Smits came to England shortly after the Restoration. If so, he returned to the Netherlands: he was in Dordrecht from 1675 to 1677. In 1675 he was living under an alias, as Theodorus Hartcamp. Confusion has resulted; there was an Antwerp still-life painter called Theodoor Smits, and since Caspar painted some still lifes it has been assumed that the two were identical; but, on stylistic grounds, this is unlikely. According to Houbraken he had an estranged wife who pursued him, which might explain why he used an alias. He may, too, have had a criminal past; in Dordrecht he was accused of swindling his landlord. Houbraken related that buyers of his art also felt swindled, since his pigments faded fast: he replied that the money they paid him vanished more quickly. He held atheistic views, which he expressed forcefully ('I shit on the Scriptures'; Bredius, 118) shortly before leaving Dordrecht. He possibly headed straight for England, since Vertue reported that he went to Dublin from England, and he was a member of the Dublin artists' guild between 1681 and 1688. According to Vertue, he was still in Dublin at the time of his death about 1707. Among his pupils were the portrait painter William Gandy and James Maubert. A fine still life in the Goldsmiths' Hall in London is signed 'cas … smit.': it is the only work securely ascribed to the artist. Walpole claimed of a Magdalen in the Painters' Hall in London that it was by Smits and signed TS in monogram; but the painting is signed FS or SF and is probably by another hand. PAUL TAYLOR

Sources A. Bredius, 'Onbekende schilders, o.a. Casparus Smits, zich ook genoemd hebbende Theodorus Hartkamp', *Oud Holland*, 33 (1915), 112–20 • Vertue, *Note books* • A. Houbraken, *De groote schouburgh der Nederlantsche konstschilders en schilderessen*, 3 (Amsterdam, 1721) • private information (2004) [F. Meijer] • A. van der Willigen, *Netherlandish still-life painters, 1500–1725*, ed. F. Meijer [forthcoming] • Thieme & Becker, *Allgemeines Lexikon* • H. Walpole, *Anecdotes of painting in England: with some account of the principal artists*, ed. R. N. Wornum, new edn, 2 (1849) • *DNB*

Smollett, Sir James, of Stainflett and Bonhill (*c.***1648**–**1731**), politician, was only son to John Smollett of Stainflett (*d.* 1680), burgess and bailie of Dumbarton, and Jean, second daughter of Bontine of Ardoch. He was educated at Dumbarton grammar school and Glasgow University, graduating in 1664. In 1665 he was apprenticed to Walter Ewing, writer to the signet in Edinburgh, but later returned to Dumbarton to practise as a writer. In 1683 he became provost of the burgh. His parliamentary career began in 1685 when he became burgh commissioner for Dumbarton. Unfortunately, on the intervention of James VII, Smollett lost the office of provost in 1686 and he soon found himself suspected of attending illegal conventicles.

Religion and ambition came together as Smollett supported William of Orange and the revolution of 1689. Again provost of Dumbarton, he attended the convention of estates of 1689 and subsequently sat as parliamentary commissioner for Dumbarton from 1689 to 1707. During this period he sat on a variety of parliamentary commissions and committees. However, his most important commission was as a commissioner for union with England, first in August 1702, and more successfully in February 1706. He not only helped frame the articles of union, but in 1707 was elected member for Dunbartonshire to the first parliament of the united kingdom of Great Britain. He was knighted in 1698. His manuscript 'Memorials of certain passages of the Lord's signal mercies' (*c.*1708) provide his comments on the affairs of the time. Politically, Smollett balanced his undoubted commitment to presbyterianism with a natural loyalty to the crown, although he did support the Scottish parliament in its independent stance over the Darien colony.

Smollett married Jane (*d.* 1698), daughter of Sir Auley Macaulay of Ardincaple, with whom he had four sons and two daughters; their fourth son was father to the novelist Tobias *Smollett. On 9 June 1709 he remarried; his new wife was Elizabeth Hamilton; the marriage produced no children. Smollett was a wealthy man, and he inherited Stainflett and Pillanflatt from his father but purchased Bonhill in Dunbartonshire in 1684. His testament shows him a creditor of more than £17,000 Scots at his death and his estate was left to his grandson James (*d.* 1775), son of his deceased second son James (*d.* 1714), rather than to his third son George (*d.* 1744), advocate, who had proved 'incapable to prosecute and manage the trusts formerly committed to him' (Edinburgh register of testaments, NA Scot., CC 8/8/94). Smollett died at Bonhill in October 1731.

A. J. MANN

Sources J. Irving, *The history of Dumbartonshire*, 2nd edn (privately printed, Dumbarton, 1860), 227–30, 339–42 • NA Scot., Register House MSS, Smollett MSS, RH 15/31 • NRA Scotland, priv. coll., Smollett MSS: Telfer-Smollett of Bonhill MSS, 1386 • J. Smollett, 'Memorials of certain passages of the Lord's signal mercies', NRA Scotland, Telfer-Smollett of Bonhill MSS, 1386, bundle 65 [memoirs] • J. M. Thomson and others, eds., *Registrum magni sigilli regum Scotorum / The register of the great seal of Scotland*, 11 vols. (1882–1914); facs. repr. (1984), vol. 14, p. 63; vol. 15, pp. 36, 66, 210 • F. Roberts, ed., *Roll of Dumbarton burgesses* (1957) • F. J. Grant, ed., *The Faculty of Advocates in Scotland, 1532–1943*, Scottish RS, 145 (1944), 195 • M. D. Young, ed., *The parliaments of Scotland: burgh and shire commissioners*, 2 (1993), 650 • *APS*, *1593–1625* • J. D. Marwick, ed., *Records of the convention of the royal burghs of Scotland*, 4–5 (1880–85) • register of testaments, Edinburgh, NA Scot., CC 8/8/94 • C. Innes, ed., *Munimenta alme Universitatis Glasguensis / Records of the University of Glasgow from its foundation till 1727*, 3, Maitland Club, 72 (1854) • *IGI*

Archives NA Scot., family MSS, corresp., and legal MSS, RH 15/31 • NRA Scotland, priv. coll., memoirs in manuscript with Telfer-Smollett of Bonhill MSS

Wealth at death owed £17,580 (Scots): testament proved 13 March 1732, NA Scot., register of testaments, Edinburgh, CC 8/8/94-129-130

Smollett, Tobias George (1721–1771), writer, was born in March 1721, probably on the 16th, the third child of Archibald Smollett (*d.* 1723/4) and Barbara Cunningham (1694?–1770), at Dalquhurn, near the village of Renton, Dunbartonshire, and baptized on 19 March in the parish church of Cardross.

Lineage, early life, and education The Smollett family had been prominent in the area for several centuries. According to Smollett, his ancestors 'were originally Malet or Molet and came from Normandy with the Conqueror' (*Letters*, 43). One John Smollett was a bailie of Dumbarton in the early sixteenth century and a merchant and shipowner. Proud of the family motto, *Viresco* ('I flourish'), Smollett recounted in *The Present State of All Nations* (1768–9) that one of the largest ships of the Armada, the *Florida*, was blown up off Mull in 1588 by an ancestor, John Smollett of Kirkton.

Pre-eminent among the novelist's forebears was his grandfather Sir James *Smollett (*c.*1648–1731). His fourth

Tobias George Smollett (1721–1771), by unknown artist, *c.*1770

son, Archibald (father of the novelist), was sent to Leiden to complete his education, but contracted a fever there. He married, probably in 1716 (Irving, 1.187), Barbara, daughter of Robert Cunningham of Gilbertfield, Lanarkshire. It was recorded that 'as she was of an amiable character, and respectable family, his father had no reason to be displeased with the alliance, except that it had been entered into without consulting him, and that she had little or no portion' (Anderson, *Life*, 7). Granted an annuity and the lease of Dalquhurn farm, purchased by his father in 1692, Archibald had an annual income of £300.

Tobias was the youngest in a family of three. The eldest, James, an army captain, was drowned when his ship foundered off America. 'Distinguished for his address, and those talents of wit and humour, which afterwards characterised Tobias' (*Statistical Account*, 221), he was sorely missed by his brother, who wrote, sympathizing with John Home's fraternal loss, 'I once sustained the same calamity, in the death of a brother whom I loved and honoured' (*Letters*, 38). Tobias's sister, Jane (*d.* 1788), married Alexander Telfer of Scotstoun and inherited the family estates. Archibald Smollett died when Tobias was two, but the family remained at Dalquhurn until after the death of Sir James in 1731, with the children supported financially by their cousin James Smollett.

Tobias was educated at Dumbarton grammar school, where the master was the noted scholar John Love (1695–1750), author of two treatises on grammar. Love engaged in controversy with Thomas Ruddiman as to the respective merits as Latin poets of Arthur Johnston and George Buchanan. Ruddiman eulogized Love in his obituary in the *Caledonian Mercury*: 'For his uncommon knowledge in classical learning, his indefatigable diligence, and strictness of discipline, without severity, he was justly accounted one of the most sufficient masters in this country' (*Miscellaneous Works*, 1.12n.). Smollett's enduring respect for his schoolmaster is evident from his intercession with Wilkes on behalf of Robert Love, 'son of the man from whose instruction I imbibed the first principles of my education' (*Letters*, 102).

Smollett's wish to enter the army was denied since the family had obtained a commission for his elder brother. At fourteen he was destined for Glasgow University and medical training. Although there is no evidence of his matriculating, it is probable he attended classes in anatomy and medicine, and he may also have had instruction in classics, mathematics, moral philosophy, and natural philosophy (Knapp, 17). In November 1735 he was working in a dispensary in Glasgow, and on 30 May 1736 he was apprenticed for five years to surgeons John Gordon and William Stirling (medical faculty records, Glasgow University). Gordon seems to have been on familiar terms with the Smollett family: on 15 September 1738 he wrote to James Smollett of Bonhill, 'Tobias has a cough, but feels that a week or more in the country will do him good' (Irving, 2.190n. 1). The years of the apprenticeship proved formative: confrontation with disease and poverty fostered an interest in the mind–body relationship and fired the indignation of the satirist. According to John Moore, Smollett's first editor, it was among Glasgow merchants and professionals that Smollett first found targets for his virulent wit and 'gave offence to the more serious part of the citizens' (*Works*, 1.cxi–cxii). There was a tradition in Glasgow that Smollett was 'a restless apprentice and a mischievous stripling' (Campbell, 6.219), and John Ramsay of Ochtertyre was informed that 'Smollett's conversation, though lively, was one continued series of epigrammatical sarcasms against one or other of the company, for which no talents could compensate' (Knapp, 21). The obverse side of his personality was also evident: as a student he formed a friendship with John Ritchie, whose premature death he lamented in a poignant prose elegy (*Letters*, 1–2).

London and the West Indies, naval service and marriage, 1739–1743 Smollett's financial circumstances changed with the death in 1738 of his cousin James Smollett of Bonhill, who was succeeded as head of the family by another cousin James (later to appear in *Humphry Clinker*, 1771, as Commissary Smollett). Tobias was not a beneficiary of his cousin's will. Impending conflict with Spain may have suggested the opportunity of gaining medical experience in the nation's service. In summer 1739, without completing his apprenticeship, Smollett went to London with a letter of introduction to Andrew Mitchell (1708–1771), cousin of James Smollett, under-secretary for Scotland, fellow of the Royal Society, and friend of James Thomson. With aspirations as dramatist, Smollett also took with him *The Regicide*, a tragedy inspired by Buchanan's account of the murder of the Scottish poet-king James I at Perth in 1437 (his struggle to have it produced is represented in the experiences of Melopoyn in *Roderick Random*, 1748, chaps. 62–3).

War with Spain was declared in October 1739, and on 10 March 1740 Smollett obtained from the Navy Board his warrant as surgeon's second mate. On 3 April he boarded the *Chichester*, a large man-of-war of 80 guns and 600 men, which set sail on 26 October 1740 in the squadron of Sir Chaloner Ogle, and arrived at Port Royal, Jamaica, on 10 January 1741. Smollett served during the disastrous attempt to seize the Spanish stronghold of Cartagena, on the coast of modern Colombia. Sustained bombardment led to capture of the harbour fortifications of Boca-Chica, but the attempt to take the fort of San Lazar, dominating the town, was a costly failure. In his 'Account of the expedition against Carthagene' published in *The Compendium of Voyages* (1756) and in his *Complete History of England* (1757–8), Smollett attributed the disaster to disagreements between the naval commander, Admiral Vernon, and General Wentworth, commander of the land forces. Smollett's experience of the Cartagena expedition provided much of the material of chapters 24–38 of *Roderick Random*. Roderick's graphic eye-witness account of the physical realities of warfare anticipates the unsparing realism of chroniclers of later wars, such as Sassoon, Heller, Vonnegut, and Herr, and the representation of conditions on board ship is equally shocking. The *saeva indignatio* of the satirist was to have beneficial effect. Anna Barbauld noted in 1810:

> Smollett has given a strong and disgusting picture of the manner of living on board a man of war. It must give pleasure to the reader of the present day to consider how much the attention to health, cleanliness, and accommodation, in respect to our navy, has increased since that account was written. (Kelly, 291)

Leigh Hunt wrote to Shelley on 20 September 1819, '[Smollett] is understood to have done immense good to the poor wounded sailors in naval fights, by those pictures of pitiless surgery and amputation in *Roderick Random*' (ibid., 334). The effects on Smollett himself were profound and lasting. In *The Present State of All Nations* (8 vols., 1768–9, 8.382) he gave a detailed account of the diseases contracted by the fighting men, including yellow fever, to which more than half the force fell victim.

Smollett sailed on the *Chichester* from Port Royal on 18 June 1741, and reached England on 21 September 1741. He remained on the ship's muster until September 1741 and on its payroll, at £2 per month, until February 1742. It is possible that he saw further service in the Caribbean later in 1742, at La Guaira under Knowles (whom he would later libel in the *Critical Review*). Certainly he revisited Jamaica and there met Anne Lassells (1721–1791), whose family had owned plantations there since the seventeenth century. Anne lived with her mother, by then twice widowed, in Kingston. In letter 34 of *Travels through France and Italy* (1766) Smollett described her as 'a delicate creature, who had scarce ever walked a mile in her life'. No records survive, but the marriage probably took place in Jamaica in 1743. Smollett wrote of his confidence that 'all honest men would acquit my principles, howsoever my prudentials might be condemned' (*Letters*, 2). The need to establish himself as surgeon so that he could support his wife led him to return early in 1744 to London, where he took residence in Downing Street. Enforced separation from his young wife until her arrival from Jamaica in 1747 may have exacerbated Smollett's innate irascibility.

Medicine and literary apprenticeship, 1744–1748 Frequenting the British Coffee House in Cockspur Street, off the Strand, Smollett joined the burgeoning group of Scottish medical men and writers that included William Hunter, John Armstrong, John Clephane, and William Smellie. Alexander Carlyle was there with Smollett when word arrived of the victory at Culloden. So riotous was the mob that they walked home with drawn swords, Smollett counselling silence 'lest the mob should discover my country and become insolent. For John Bull … is as haughty and violent tonight, as a few months ago he was abject and cowardly, on the Black Wednesday when the Highlanders were at Derby' (Carlyle, 98–9). Smollett, recorded Carlyle, 'was not a Jacobite, but he had the feelings of a Scotch gentleman on the reported cruelties that were said to be exercised after the Battle of Culloden' (ibid., 99). These feelings inform his ode 'The Tears of Scotland'. Advised to suppress it, Smollett responded by adding a seventh stanza exuding spirited independence and concern for his native land. Set to music by Oswald, it was, he wrote to Carlyle, 'a performance very well received at London, as I hope it will be in your country which gave rise to it' (*Letters*, 5). Carlyle confirmed that it 'had such a run of approbation' (Carlyle, 99), and another setting was composed by Allan Masterton.

It is typical of Smollett's amplitude that his next publications were the verse satires *Advice* (1746) and *Reproof* (1747), which, he reported, 'made some noise here' (*Letters*, 5). Juvenalian indignation at social corruption merges with the personally splenetic or libellous, and there is a debt to the later satires of Alexander Pope. Smollett employs the device of dialogue between poet and a friend who feigns adherence to the practices which the poet would attack. The satires convey the amalgam of strong feelings prompted by his observation of London society—dismay, outrage, and a keen moral commitment—well encapsulated in a line in *Advice*, 'Two things, I dread, my conscience and the law'. In a series of satirical vignettes Smollett targets individuals from a broad social spectrum: politicians William Pulteney and John Carteret; Sir John Cope and Hawley from the military; profiteers, such as Sampson Gideon (adviser to Walpole) and Sir Joshua Vanneck; the notorious quack Dr Thomas Thompson; writers Colley Cibber and Charles Macklin; and—an especially virulent libel—John Rich. Conversely, there are tributes to opponents of Walpole, such as Sir Richard Temple and Viscount Cobham, and praise for Pope, Chesterfield, Handel, and the Scottish lawyer Daniel MacKercher, whose career would be more fully documented in *Peregrine Pickle* (1751).

Through the 1740s Smollett persevered with his attempts to bring to the stage his tragedy, *The Regicide*, which he had offered to George, Lord Lyttelton, on his arrival in London, only to have the patron of Thomson and Mallet eventually decline. Approaches—all fruitless—were made to Charles Fleetwood, James Lacy, who twice promised to produce it at Drury Lane, and, with the support of Chesterfield, John Rich, who rejected it in 1746 as unfit for the stage, a judgment Smollett attributed to 'the pitiful intrigues of that little rascal, Garrick' (*Letters*, 4). The thwarting of his aspirations as dramatist was deeply wounding, and soured Smollett against theatre managers. His masque, 'Alceste', possibly inspired by George Buchanan's Latin translation of Euripides, had an equally fraught history. On 14 February 1749 he was confident it would 'be acted at Covent Garden next season, and appear with such magnificence of scenery as was never exhibited in Britain before' (ibid., 10). Music was by Handel and scenery, 'for which Rich was at great expense' (Hawkins, 5.324), by Servandoni (creator of the fireworks which, accompanied by Handel's 'Music for the Royal Fireworks', were staged in London in April 1749 in celebration of the peace of Aix-la-Chapelle). By 1 October Smollett was a prey to doubts, labelling Rich 'such a compound of Indolence, Worthlessness and Folly, that I cannot depend upon any thing he undertakes' (*Letters*, 12). Although Smollett received part-payment of £100 from Rich and, according to John Home, full payment of £300 (Home, 1.137), the project failed owing to disputes between author and manager. Handel's response was reported to be 'That Scotchman is ein tam fool; I vould have mate his vurk immortal' (Smeaton, 56). A comedy, 'The absent man', which Smollett submitted to Garrick in May 1750, was never produced, and the manuscript is lost.

About January 1746 Smollett moved to Chapel Street, Mayfair, in the hope of extending his medical practice. His wife, Anne, joined him early in 1747, and their daughter, Elizabeth, was born in spring 1748. At some point in that year the family moved to Beaufort Street, near the Strand.

Three major novels, 1748–1753 There appeared in January 1748 the novel that established Smollett's reputation, *The Adventures of Roderick Random*. To Carlyle, Smollett wrote that it was 'intended as a satire on mankind, and by the reception it has met with in private from the best judges here I have reason to believe it will succeed very well' (*Letters*, 6–7). Apologizing for possible stylistic inaccuracies, he acknowledged that, despite interruptions of several weeks, the book had been written 'in the compass of eight months' (ibid., 8). The speed of composition is matched by the pace of the action-packed narrative. Talfourd observed of the eponymous hero, 'He is the sport of fortune rolled about through the "Many ways of wretchedness" … we seem to roll on with him, and get delectably giddy in his company' (Kelly, 348). In his preface Smollett indicates his intention of fulfilling the criteria of instruction, verisimilitude, and amusement: 'Of all kinds of satire, there is none so entertaining, and universally improving, as that which is introduced, as it were, occasionally, in the course of an interesting story, which brings every incident home to life'. He celebrates the achievement of Cervantes in 'converting romance … [to] point out the follies of life', and, while acknowledging *Gil Blas* as an influence, takes care to innovate rather than replicate Le Sage's text. In particular, he claims that the experiences of Gil Blas prompt mirth rather than compassion, so preventing 'that generous indignation, which ought to animate the reader, against the sordid and vicious disposition of the world'. Thus, writes Smollett, 'I have attempted to represent modest merit struggling with every difficulty to which a friendless orphan is exposed, from his own want of experience, as well as from the selfishness, envy, malice, and base indifference of mankind'.

Whereas the picaro is drawn from the lower social orders and is forced to turn wandering rogue in order to survive in a corrupt world, Roderick has been afforded 'the advantages of birth and education, which in the series of his misfortunes will … engage the ingenuous more warmly in his behalf', and he never endures the hardships whereby the picaro must beg, borrow, or steal as alternatives to starving. The features of the picaresque which Smollett chooses to adopt are the displacement and social mobility of the hero and the episodic nature of the narrative. The social and geographical range of incident is noteworthy: Roderick is press-ganged; shipwrecked; abducted by smugglers to France; enlisted in a French regiment, in which he fights against the British and allied armies; and committed to the Marshalsea. He serves as surgeon on his uncle's ship when they traffic in slaves; finds in Buenos Aires his long-lost father; returns to marry his beloved Narcissa; and, with his father, reacquires the family estate. Traversing the ranks of society, he encounters corruption in a range of disguises and sees integrity traduced: the reputed witch, Mrs Sagely, becomes his moral guardian; the licentious aristocrats Strutwell and Straddle prove that rank is no guarantee of morality.

From the outset commentators were intent on reading *Roderick Random* as autobiography, mainly on the basis of the Melopoyn episodes where Garrick appears as Marmozet—by which he was 'inexpressibly galled' (*Letters*, 8). Smollett wrote to Carlyle, 'I am not a little mortified to find the characters strangely misapplied to particular men whom I never had the least intention to ridicule … on the supposition that I myself am the hero of the book' (ibid., 7). The tyrannical grandfather was identified—unjustifiably—with Sir James Smollett, and Love's indignation at the assumption that he was the model for the barbarous pedant prompted Smollett to insist that:

> no person living is aimed at in all the first part of the book; that is while the scene lies in Scotland, and that (the account of the expedition to Carthagene excepted) the whole is not so much a representation of my life as that of many other needy Scotch Surgeons whom I have known either personally or by report. (ibid., 8)

Fifteen years later he reiterated the point: 'The low situations in which I have exhibited Roderick I never experienced in my own person' (ibid., 112).

Smollett's mastery of English and his residence in London from an early age led to his being habitually designated an English novelist. Yet from the beginning of *Roderick Random* there is evidence of his origins in a distinct, identifiably Scottish, literary tradition. Although the novel opens in stock eighteenth-century autobiographical mode, by the second paragraph there are signs of Scottish literature's fondness for the mingling of contraries, the fluctuation between the real and the surreal whereby the bizarre penetrates the patina of normality. During pregnancy, Roderick's mother:

> dreamed she was delivered of a tennis-ball, which the devil (who, to her great surprise, acted the part of midwife) struck so forcibly with a racket, that it disappeared in an instant; and she was for some time inconsolable for the loss of her offspring; when all of a sudden, she beheld it return with equal violence, and enter the earth beneath her feet, whence immediately sprung up a goodly tree covered with blossoms, the scent of which operated so strongly on her nerves, that she awoke.

Consulted for an interpretation of the dream, a highland seer 'assured my parents that their first-born would be a great traveller; that he would undergo many dangers and difficulties, and at last return to his native land, where he would flourish in happiness and reputation'. Such would not have come from the pen of Daniel Defoe, Samuel Richardson, or Henry Fielding; realistic observation and fanciful exaggeration cohabit closely in the native Scottish literary tradition.

One of the foremost features of that tradition is its relishing of the bizarre. An acute sense of physicality, and above all physical incongruity that approximates to the absurd or grotesque, often represented by means of animal analogies, informs Smollett's caricatures—for instance, Crab, the surgeon (chap. 7); Lavement, the apothecary (chap. 18)—part of his substantial legacy to Charles Dickens. Critics have located such characteristics in the tradition of Jonsonian 'humours'; their true origin is in a tradition characterized by 'a grotesque exaggeration, a reckless irreverence, an eldritch imaginative propensity' (Wittig, 71).

Roderick Random (first published anonymously) was an instant success, and some believed it the work of Fielding. Smollett now had the confidence to proceed with publication of *The Regicide*. He progressed his translation of *Gil Blas*, 'a bookseller's job, done in a hurry' (*Letters*, 10), and of 3000 copies printed in September 1748 fewer than 400 remained unsold after four months. In June 1748 he contracted with two booksellers for a translation of *Don Quixote* and he had completed enough by late 1749 to justify payment, though he continued to revise it up to publication in 1755.

In late June 1750 the Smolletts moved to a wing of Monmouth House in Old Chelsea, their home until 1763. During summer 1750 Smollett visited Paris with Moore and met a painter on whom he modelled the character of Pallet in *The Adventures of Peregrine Pickle*, published on 25 February 1751. Presumably he had written part of the novel prior to the French visit, since even Smollett could scarcely have written 330,000 words in four months. On an even larger scale than *Roderick Random*, *Peregrine Pickle* demonstrates his capacity for creative synthesis of diverse influences: there are Shakespearian echoes in characterization and language; the 'Entertainment in the Manner of the Ancients' owes something to Trimalchio's feast in the *Satyricon* of Petronius; and Crabtree is kin to the Man of the Hill in *Tom Jones*. In his first novel Smollett had created memorable nautical characters, such as Lieutenant Bowling. With Commodore Trunnion, who dominates the early chapters of *Peregrine Pickle*, he achieves a new dimension of characterization. Transcending by far the limits of caricature, Trunnion epitomizes Smollett's imaginative fertility.

Possibly to thwart autobiographical interpretation Smollett made Peregrine an Englishman, a graduate of Winchester and Oxford. Chapters 11–38 recount his childhood and adolescence, and emphasize his odd disposition and fondness for vicious pranks. The account of his subsequent career foregrounds the contests between arrogance and virtue, and between appearance and reality, in both the hero and the strata of society in which he moves. The thirty-three chapters in which Smollett represents Peregrine's experiences abroad (including an encounter at Boulogne with homesick, exiled Jacobites) have been described as 'one great, sustained prose satire on the Grand Tour, every detail of which can be fully substantiated from contemporary books on Continental travel' (Kahrl, 40). The rapid flux of experience is matched by the flux of Peregrine's responses and the impetuosity of his passions. Yet he develops an ability to moralize retrospectively on his misconduct, and, in episodes such as his attempted seduction of Emilia, Smollett, in depicting the conflict in his passions, offers psychological insight. A compulsive need for vengeance leads Peregrine to frame a fierce libel on a minister who has tricked him. Imprisoned, Peregrine realizes that he must find happiness within himself rather than in the corrupt and deluding social masquerade. As ever with Smollett, passion and impulse eventually experience the beneficent influence of reason.

Peregrine Pickle achieved instant notoriety for Smollett's inclusion in it of the 'Memoirs of a Lady of Quality', widely recognized as Frances, Lady Vane (1713–1788). Rumours about the 'Memoirs' created interest in advance of publication. Allegations that Smollett was paid for incorporating the material are unfounded; rather, it seems likely that Lady Vane presented it to him for revision where necessary (Putney). While Elizabeth Montagu recommended the novel on the grounds that 'Lady Vane's story is well told' (Kelly, 80), for Samuel Richardson it represented 'that part of a bad book which contains the very bad story of a wicked woman' (ibid., 48), and Horace Walpole found in it 'a degree of profligacy not to be accounted for; she does not want the money, none of her stallions will raise her credit; and the number, all she had to brag of, concealed!' (ibid., 76).

In *Peregrine Pickle* Smollett also took the opportunity to settle old scores with ruthless personal satires. Akenside, whose demeaning of Scotland he could not forgive, is caricatured as the pedantic doctor; Fielding (Mr Spondy) has his personal and professional integrity impugned; and Garrick, Quin, Chesterfield, and Lyttelton, variously held responsible for Smollett's theatrical failures, are mercilessly burlesqued. Conversely, the account of Daniel MacKercher's role in the Annesley case offers an edifying model of humanitarian conduct. In the revised edition of March 1758 Smollett removed the ridiculing of Garrick's acting and the virulent assault on the reputation of Lyttelton. There were revisions, too, to the 'memoirs', probably instigated by Lady Vane (Buck, 45–7). In January 1752 appeared an anonymous pamphlet entitled *A faithful narrative of the base and inhuman arts that were lately practised upon the brain of Habbakuk Hilding … by Drawcansir Alexander, fencing master and philomath*. Since it mounted a ferocious attack on Lyttelton and Fielding, it was attributed to Smollett in the *Gentleman's Magazine* (January 1752), but there is no conclusive proof of his authorship.

Smollett continued to practise medicine and write on medical matters. In June 1750, with supportive references from other practitioners and having paid the fee of £28 Scots, he was awarded the degree of MD by Marischal College, Aberdeen. In one of several reviews for Ralph Griffiths's *Monthly Review* (5, 1751, 465–6) he extolled William Smellie's pioneering *Treatise on the Theory and Practice of Midwifery* (1751). After a stay in Bath, Smollett published *An Essay on the External Use of Water* (1752), questioning the beneficial effects of the mineral waters. In such work, as in his burlesquing of quack doctors in the novels, Smollett's professional training engaged with the satirist's desire for social reform. It was claimed in an anonymous memoir that his failure to expand his medical practice was 'chiefly because he could not render himself agreeable to women'—surprisingly, since 'he was as handsome and graceful a man as any of the age he lived in' (Kelly, 227). However, his increasing eminence as writer and ever-increasing work as editor, translator, and reviewer may well have determined his priorities, and, though he is portrayed by Verelst in 1756 in physician's garb, he became less active as a medical practitioner after the publication of *The Adventures of Ferdinand Count Fathom*, about 15 February 1753.

The dedication to *Ferdinand Count Fathom*, generally thought to be to the author himself, is startling in the candour of its self-analysis. It also contains the following definition: 'A Novel is a large diffused picture, comprehending the characters of life, disposed in different groups, and exhibited in various attitudes, for the purposes of an uniform plan, and general occurrence, to which every individual is subservient'; integral to this is the presence of 'a principal personage'. After identifying the impulses of fear as 'the most violent and interesting of the passions', Smollett alludes to the role of his principal character as a warning to the unwary and then stresses the importance of contrast in giving 'a Relief to the moral of the whole'. In this most wide-ranging of his novels, both socially and geographically, Smollett offers as 'principal personage' an itinerant and totally amoral chameleon in a world dominated by chance. Walter Scott could not countenance such transgression on the parts of author and character, protesting, 'the picture of moral depravity presented in the character of Count Fathom is a disgusting pollution of the imagination' (Kelly, 354). Scott misses the point: the most telling indictment of the corrupt masquerade that is polite society is that such a being is at its heart: 'Fathom, as usual, formed the nucleus or kernel of the beau monde … [he] was the soul that animated the whole society' (*Ferdinand*, 165).

The most celebrated episode is that describing Fathom's terrifying ordeal in the night journey through the forest and the encounter with thieves who murder their victims. Anna Barbauld acclaimed it as 'the best conceived and the most strongly worked up scene of mere natural horror' (Kelly, 256), and Hazlitt enthused, 'there is more power of writing occasionally shewn [in *Ferdinand Count Fathom*] than in any of his works' (ibid., 337). Contrasted with Fathom is the sentimentalist Renaldo, who, visiting what he believes is the grave of his beloved Monimia, finds his soul 'wound up to the highest pitch of enthusiastic sorrow' (*Ferdinand*, 317)—an early exemplification of the concept central to the age of sensibility, that of 'pleasing anguish'. When representing the experiences of his antithetical central characters, Smollett uses style as a distancing mechanism, with their extremes of behaviour subject to comic reduction.

Editor, translator, critic, 1753–1763 The years 1753–63 were marked by herculean efforts across a range of activities, all to the increasing detriment of Smollett's health. Renowned for his hospitality, he is reckoned to have incurred annual expenditure of £600–£800 in the upkeep of his wing of Monmouth House (*Travels*, xii). A letter to Moore on 19 August 1762 offers stark self-analysis: 'My difficulties have arisen from my own indiscretion; from a warm temper easily provoked to rashness; from a want of courage to refuse what I could not grant without doing injustice to my own family; from indolence, bashfulness and want of economy. I am sensible of all my weaknesses' (*Letters*, 107). In 1752–3 both the generosity and the impetuosity featured in his dealings with one Peter Gordon, whom he had aided professionally and financially. When Smollett challenged the debtor for repayment, Gordon brought an action at the king's bench against his alleged assailant. Although Smollett was acquitted, the trial was costly and he was obliged to seek commissions from booksellers. With Robert Dodsley, Charles Rivington, and William Strahan, on 5 May 1753 he contracted to complete, by 1 August 1754, an anthology of travels in seven volumes, for which he would receive £150; it was published anonymously in 1756 as *A Compendium of Authentic and Entertaining Voyages*, with Smollett later conceding that his contribution was limited (*Letters*, 113). He spent five months in Scotland from June 1753, visiting his mother and sister, and spending time in Glasgow, Edinburgh, and Musselburgh, where Carlyle was a willing host. In February 1754 he published anonymously *Selected Essays on Commerce, Agriculture, Mines, Fisheries, and other Useful Subjects*, translations from the *Journal Œconomique*. By the summer of 1756 he was the driving force behind the *Critical Review*, which he edited until 1763 and which he regarded as 'a small branch of an extensive plan which I last year projected for a sort of Academy of the Belles Lettres' (ibid., 46), an aim that was never realized. However, he wrote much of the *Critical Review*, his forthright reviews prompting disputes and retaliations from such as John Shebbeare and James Grainger. Income from his wife's holdings in the West Indies was offset by the financially crippling venture of the *Critical Review*.

In 1754 appeared the first part of David Hume's *History*. In fourteen months from 1755 to 1757 Smollett wrote his four-volume *Complete History of England*, having instructed his servant 'to deny me to all those with whom I had no express business' (*Letters*, 46). Smollett presented the first three volumes to Garrick and dedicated the work to Pitt. Revised in 1758, the *Complete History* was offered for sale in 100 sixpenny weekly pamphlets, and by 28 September 1758 he noted with satisfaction that weekly sales exceeded 10,000 copies (ibid., 73), realizing £500 for the author. Hume wrote to Andrew Millar, bookseller, of 'this extraordinary run upon Dr. Smollett' (Hume, *Letters*, 1.273), and he jocularly reproved William Robertson for replacing him 'near the historical summit of Parnassus, immediately under Dr. Smollett' (ibid., 1.302). The success of Smollett's *History* may be explained by reference to his statement of intent in his prefatory 'Plan': his approach is factual, not theoretical or philosophical; he will eschew conjecture and national, religious, and political partiality; he will consult only the most legitimate of sources; and his style will make his material accessible. Inevitably there were dissonant voices, and Smollett was accused of being Jacobite and papist, most notably by Thomas Comber. Whig policy towards Scotland, and what he perceived as the corruption of Walpole's administration, had weakened his enthusiasm for the party to which his family was traditionally loyal. Surprised to hear of Glaswegian approval, he predicted 'the last volume … will be severely censured by the west country whigs of Scotland', but he reiterated 'I have, as far as in me lay, adhered to Truth without espousing any faction' (*Letters*, 65). In 1758 he took charge of the production of a *Universal History* and contributed the sections on France, Italy, and Germany.

Smollett was now one of the most distinguished literary men in London. Meeting him with Robertson in 1758, Carlyle observed that Smollett was 'now become a great man … we dined together and Smollett was very brilliant', and Robertson, 'who had imagined that a man's manner must bear a likeness to his books … exprest great surprise at the polished and agreeable manners and the great urbanity of his conversation' (Carlyle, 172). Reconciled with Garrick (*Letters*, 51–3), he had the satisfaction of seeing his farce, *The Reprisal, or, The Tars of Old England*, staged in 1757 at Drury Lane, where, though patriotic, it had only moderate success. However, it found favour in an Edinburgh production on 20 August 1759, and later in North America.

In May 1758 in the *Critical Review* (5.438–9) Smollett launched a devastating attack on Admiral Sir Charles Knowles, who, in a pamphlet, had attempted vindication of his conduct in the abortive and costly expedition against Rochefort in 1757. Knowles sued both Smollett and the printer, Archibald Hamilton, for libel, and the action, with concomitant costs, dragged on until 24

November 1760, when Smollett was fined £100 for defamation and committed for three months to the king's bench prison by Lord Chief Justice Mansfield. There he was able to continue his supervision of the *British Magazine*, for which he had secured both a royal licence in January 1760 and the services of Oliver Goldsmith as contributor. It ran until 1767, and the friendship with Goldsmith may have led him to contemplate in 1761 a history of Ireland, but it was never written. May 1760 saw the first of a projected forty sixpenny weekly issues of Smollett's *Continuation of the Complete History of England*. In July 1760 there was a visit to Edinburgh to receive the honour of burgess and guild-brother. Between 1761 and 1765 Smollett edited, with Thomas Francklin, *The Works of Voltaire*, a translation in thirty-five volumes.

At the end of March 1762 *The Adventures of Sir Launcelot Greaves* was published in book form, having been issued in weekly instalments in the *British Magazine* (January 1760–December 1761) and praised by Goldsmith. Too readily dismissed as a pale imitation of *Don Quixote*, it is important in several respects. The density of the opening description anticipates similar openings in Dickens (Wierstra, chap. 4), and the serialized publication meant that Smollett established a precedent in so structuring material as to guarantee enduring reader interest. The supposed madness of the hero is integral to Smollett's satire: Launcelot employs his reason against the enemies of virtue, with his moderation and piety discomfiting the exemplars of corruption that he encounters, so enabling Smollett to satirize lawyers, politicians, and the conduct of elections, and convey his opposition to the war with Germany and his distaste for both political parties. As habitually with Smollett, the action is resolved with the triumph of reason.

Though ailing, Smollett undertook editing of *The Briton*, which appeared weekly in thirty-eight issues (29 May 1762 to 12 Feb 1763) in support of the widely unpopular Bute ministry. Inevitably, Smollett became embroiled in political controversy and was caricatured, and his commitment to *The Briton* severed his friendship with Wilkes. Subsequently, Smollett referred to 'the absurd stoicism of Lord Bute, who set himself up as a pillory to be pelted by all the blackguards of England, upon the supposition that they would grow tired and leave off' (*Letters*, 137). Aware of his declining health, Smollett wrote on 19 August 1762: 'the laborious part of authorship I have long resigned. My constitution will no longer allow me to toil as formerly' (ibid., 108). Approaches to John Home, secretary to Bute, to secure the consulship of Madrid or Marseilles were ineffectual. The death of his only child, Elizabeth, aged fifteen, on 3 April 1763, probably from consumption, overwhelmed both Smollett and his wife 'with unutterable sorrow' (ibid., 114).

Travels and last years, 1763–1771 Accompanied by his wife, his servant Alexander Telloush, and two friends, Smollett sailed in June 1763 to Boulogne, and journeyed south via Paris, Dijon, and Lyons. During two weeks at Montpellier he met Sterne, also there in search of health, who immortalized Smollett as 'the learned Smelfungus' in *A Sentimental Journey*. From Montpellier, Smollett proceeded to Nice, where he resided from November 1763 to April 1765, making two excursions (one of ten weeks) into Italy. With a more benign climate and, from May 1764, a regime of daily sea-bathing his health improved somewhat, though he suffered from asthma, intermittent bouts of fever, and mild tuberculosis. His characteristic resilience reasserted itself: in February 1764 he set himself to learn Italian in six months, before sailing in a felucca from Nice to Genoa in September. From Genoa he travelled to Pisa, Florence, and Rome, and returned to Nice by mid-November. His health had benefited to the extent that, accompanied by Telloush, he could journey by mule over snow-covered mountains to Turin in February 1765. Late in April he returned through France to England. Once more in London, in Brewers Street, he wrote to Moore:

> I have brought back no more than the skeleton of what I was; but with proper care that skeleton may hang for some years together. I propose to pass the winter at Bath, and if I find that climate intolerable, I shall once more go into exile, and never more think of returning. (*Letters*, 124)

With a resurgence of energy Smollett prepared for publication the fruits of his insatiable curiosity during the two years in France and Italy. His observations, 'thrown into a series of letters' (*Letters*, 125), were printing by November and published, on 8 May 1766, as *Travels through France and Italy*, with extracts in newspapers thereafter. Unsurprisingly, his generalizations about the French drew hostile reactions from that country, but in Britain reviews were favourable, an exception being Philip Thicknesse, who proposed renaming the work 'Quarrels through France and Italy for the cure of a pulmonic disorder, by T.S., M.D.' (Knapp, 273). Accounts of altercations with unhelpful natives are more than offset by the range of Smollett's observations—on climate, arts, religion, agriculture, hygiene, and trade—and by the practical concern underpinning many of his proposals: he recognized the potential as a health resort of the village of Cannes and pointed out the need for a highway along the Riviera (the building of the Corniche road was instigated by Napoleon).

The fifth and final volume of Smollett's *Continuation of the Complete History* was published in October 1765, about the time of his move to Bath. Improvement in health was short-lived—on 13 November he wrote to Moore: 'My disorder is no other than weak lungs and a constitution prone to catarrhs, with an extraordinary irritability of the nervous system' (*Letters*, 126). He went to Hot Wells, Bristol, in February 1766, and was reported in the press to be close to death. However, he recovered sufficiently to pay in summer 1766 the visit to Scotland for which he had longed. In Edinburgh he was reunited with mother and sister, and fêted by such luminaries as Hume, Adam Smith, William Robertson, and Hugh Blair. From Glasgow, where Moore played host, he returned to his birthplace: he stayed with Commissary Smollett in Cameron House, Bonhill, a visit which produced the 'Ode to Leven Water', later incorporated in *Humphry Clinker* (1771). Having returned from Scotland, Smollett resided in Gay Street, Bath, and experienced fluctuating health. To William

Hunter he wrote, on 24 February 1767, with characteristic irony, that his 'circulation would have stopped of itself if it was not every now and then stimulated by the stings of my Grub Street friends, who attack me in the public papers' (ibid., 133).

In summer 1767 Hume attempted but failed to secure from Shelburne the consulship of Nice or Leghorn for Smollett (Hume, *Letters*, 2.151–2). Still active, Smollett oversaw completion of *The Present State of All Nations*, and it appeared in weekly numbers from June 1768. If indeed he was author of *The History and Adventures of an Atom*, published about 1 April 1769, then he must have been working on it in 1768. There is no reference to it in his letters or those of his correspondents, but it was attributed to him in the *London Chronicle* (8–11 April 1769). With echoes of the humour of Rabelais, it is a rumbustious, at times scatological, satire on British political life, transposed to Japan. It may be that Smollett, sensing that his remaining days were few, revived his vituperative energies to target enemies, including Pitt, Cumberland, Mansfield, and Wilkes. If his, it was a pungent valediction. He took his leave of Hume in an affectionate letter of 31 August 1768 before going into 'a perpetual exile' (*Letters*, 136).

With his wife, Smollett left for Pisa, probably in late autumn 1768 (Knapp, 279). On 5 June 1769 he was witness to the wedding of George Renner and Anne Curry in Florence. An unfounded report of his death appeared in the *London Chronicle* on 1 August 1769. He was visited in Pisa early in 1770 by Sir Horace Mann. In the spring of that year the Smolletts moved to a villa, Il Giardino, a few miles south of Leghorn, on the slopes of Monte Nero and overlooking the sea, 'a most romantic and salutary situation' (*Letters*, 138). A walking tour with Armstrong in the south of France was planned but not undertaken; instead, Armstrong spent two weeks with the Smolletts in July 1770, and may have taken the manuscript of *Humphry Clinker* back to London for printing (*Expedition*, 446). Smollett learned of the death of his mother on 7 November 1770. Two letters of 9 January 1771 are significant. To his nephew, Alexander Telfer, he wrote of the violent earthquake in Leghorn, wryly observing that whereas many fled he preferred 'to run some small risque of being smothered quietly in my own warm bed' (*Letters*, 139); the self-portrait in the letter to John Hunter reveals a characteristic union of self-irony, skill in verbal depiction, and sense of the grotesque: 'I am already so dry and emaciated that I may pass for an Egyptian mummy without any other preparation than some pitch and painted linen, unless you think I may deserve the denomination of a curiosity in my own character' (ibid., 140). Smollett spent much of the summer of 1771 at Bagna di Lucca, though still with the energy to revise the *Universal History*.

It is almost certain that Smollett received in Italy copies of *The Expedition of Humphry Clinker*, published in London on 17 June 1771, the copyright payment being £210. With material drawn from his experience of London, Bath, and his Scottish visit of 1766, it was begun in Britain and completed in Italy, an immense achievement, as his widow acknowledged: 'It galls me to the soul, when I think how much that poor dear man suffered when he wrote that novel' (Knapp, 296).

Some of the factual detail of the novel derives from material used in *The Present State of All Nations* (Martz, 104–80), but the fictional treatment is more favourable to Scotland. Smollett may have been influenced by the vogue of travel books such as Martin Martin's *Description of the Western Islands of Scotland* (1703) and Daniel Defoe's *Tour thro' the Whole Island of Great Britain* (1724–7). With the graphic account of Lismahago's ordeals among the Miami Indians he offers a sceptical perspective on the concept of the noble savage, while burlesquing the increasingly popular Gothic romance. A further influence was Christopher Anstey's *New Bath Guide* (1766), verse epistles by a family of visitors. Smollett's novel presents the letters of a diverse group—Matt Bramble, irascible Welsh squire; his spinster sister, Tabitha; his nephew, Jery Melford, an Oxford undergraduate; his niece, Lydia, fresh from boarding-school; and Win Jenkins, maid. Their journey, set *c.*1768, takes them via Bath to London and north by Harrogate, York, and Scarborough to Scotland, thence back to Wales. The accounts of the journey determine the novel's structure, and each of the writers is on a personal quest, with the reader travelling alongside on a journey of understanding. From the picaresque derive the mobility and the episodic structure, but, in a fine irony, the potential picaro, the eponymous Humphry, is the only member of the group denied expression of his perspective via letters, underlining the sense in which the socially deprived are acted upon, rather than being agents. The travels enable Smollett, principally through Matt, to mount scathing attacks on luxury and affectation, and the contrast between the lifestyles of Baynard and Dennison is in the Horatian 'Beatus ille' tradition (*Expedition*, xxvii).

The choice of epistolary mode is a master-stroke. The correspondents comment on each other but also, unwittingly, characterize themselves through their language and subject matter, so that the letters function as ironic monologues: the hypochondriac Matt fulminates against amateur diagnosis, while his spinster sister enjoins her housekeeper to commend chastity to the maids. Developing a technique initiated with Morgan in *Roderick Random* and exemplified with Mrs Gobble in *Sir Launcelot Greaves*, Smollett establishes for each of his characters a distinct idiolect. The riotously comic linguistic and orthographic solecisms of Win and Tabitha are ironically self-revealing and have a psychosexual dimension that prefigures James Joyce's Molly Bloom. Since the writers experience the same events but respond differently, the novel is remarkably modern in its interrogation of truth and its celebration of subjectivity and relativity. Hazlitt's assessment of *Humphry Clinker* as 'the most pleasant gossiping novel that ever was written' (Kelly, 337) warrants expansion: the outstanding feature of *Humphry Clinker* is the fusion of information and individualized perspective, with the concern of modernists such as Virginia Woolf with the relationship of subject and object here anticipated.

Horace Walpole alleged, unjustly, that *Humphry Clinker*

was 'a party novel written by that profligate hireling Smollett to vindicate the Scots and cry down juries' (Walpole, 4.328). One of the book's functions is to introduce Scotland, its people and customs, to southern readers, partners in the Union for a mere six decades. As one reviewer noted, 'that part which deals with the Scotch nation is at once calculated to entertain the most gay, and to give the most serious a very useful fund of information' (Kelly, 208). Courtesy of both Matt and Jery, Smollett takes care to qualify enthusiasm for matters Scottish with advice or criticism.

Humphry Clinker took Smollett's reputation to new heights, albeit posthumously. Enthusiastically received, it appeared within a year in a German translation and even inspired a sequel, *Brambleton Hall: a Novel*. For Dickens, who deemed *Roderick Random* and *Peregrine Pickle* 'both extraordinarily good in their way, which is a way without tenderness', *Humphry Clinker* was 'certainly Smollett's best' (Kelly, 367). Such a favourable view of the mellowing of Smollett's vision was, and is, widely shared.

Smollett died from an intestinal disorder at Il Giardino on 17 September 1771. The diary of Dr Gentili, the doctor attending him, notes, 'he has vigour, fiery temperament, will not drink … he died asthmatic and consumptive without trying to help himself' (Knapp, 298). His final words to his wife were, allegedly, 'All is well, my dear' (Smeaton, 118). He was buried two days later in the English cemetery, via degli Elisi, Leghorn, where, after a plea from his widow, a monument was erected, for which Armstrong supplied the Latin inscription (translated, Knapp, 333–4). Anne Smollett was buried there in 1791. In 1774 James Smollett erected a memorial column beside the River Leven, close to Dalquhurn, with Latin inscriptions by Dr George Stuart, John Ramsay of Ochtertyre, and Dr Samuel Johnson (translated, ibid., 334–5), and an inscription in English added by Lord Kames (ibid., 335).

'Who has displayed a more fruitful genius, and exercised more intense industry, with a loftier sense of his independence, than Smollett?': this perceptive summation came from the pen of Isaac D'Israeli in 1812 (Kelly, 330). Smollett's independence expressed itself in personal, professional, and literary contexts. Appropriately, what is generally agreed to be his finest poem is 'Ode to Independence', published posthumously by Foulis in 1773. Burns enthused, 'Are not these glorious verses? … How wretched is the man that hangs on and by the favors of the Great!' (*Letters*, 2.45). Smollett cherished his independence—of party, patronage, and literary, intellectual, or religious affiliation. Of his *History* he wrote, 'I have kept myself independent of all connexions which might have affected the candour of my intention. I have flattered no individual; I have cultivated no party' (*Letters*, 69). While the prodigious output derives in part from economic necessity, it is also an expression of Smollett's insatiable curiosity and formal and stylistic inventiveness. The tireless assertion of creative energy is also a reaction against the legacy of the Presbyterian fatalism which led him to observe:

> we are all the playthings of fortune, and … it depends upon something as insignificant and precarious as the tossing up of a halfpenny whether a man rises to affluence and honours, or continues to his dying day struggling with the difficulties and disgraces of life. (ibid., 98)

But Smollett was also motivated by the zeal of the reformer. His irritability of the nervous system was perhaps a symptom of a humanitarian idealism. He wrote, 'I have such a natural horror of cruelty that I cannot without uncommon warmth relate any instance of inhumanity' (*Letters*, 69). As with Swift, high idealism when confronted by actuality is moved to protest, but Smollett's writing is informed by a keen practical sense in keeping with the spirit of Scottish Enlightenment thought. Habitually in his fiction Smollett depicts extremes, only to employ reason to effect resolution. Smollett both laughs and shocks because he cares.

Smollett expanded the horizons of the novel in terms of both subject matter and technique. His broad canvases, teeming with originals, were a rich legacy to novelists as diverse as Scott, John Galt, Dickens, and William Makepeace Thackeray. The representation of the subjectivity of individual vision in *Humphry Clinker* marks him as kin to Sterne and a progenitor of modernist experimentation. His achievements as innovator have yet to be fully recognized. KENNETH SIMPSON

Sources *The letters of Tobias Smollett*, ed. L. M. Knapp (1970) · L. M. Knapp, *Tobias Smollett, doctor of men and manners* (1949) · P.-G. Boucé, *The novels of Tobias Smollett* (1976) · R. Anderson, *The life of Tobias Smollett, M.D., with critical observations on his works*, 4th edn (1803) · *The works of Tobias Smollett*, ed. J. Moore, 8 vols. (1797) · R. Chambers, *Smollett: his life and a selection from his writings* (1867) · J. Irving, *The book of Dumbartonshire*, 2 vols. (1879) · L. Kelly, ed., *Tobias Smollett: the critical heritage* (1987) · G. M. Kahrl, *Tobias Smollett, traveler–novelist* (1945) · H. S. Buck, *A study in Smollett, chiefly 'Peregrine Pickle'* (1925) · L. L. Martz, *The later career of Tobias Smollett* (1942) · *The miscellaneous works of Tobias Smollett*, ed. R. Anderson, 6 vols. (1820) · T. Smollett, *The expedition of Humphry Clinker*, ed. T. R. Preston (1990) · A. Carlyle, *Anecdotes and characters of the times*, ed. J. Kinsley (1973) · T. Smollett, *Travels through France and Italy*, ed. T. Seccombe (1919) · T. Smollett, *The present state of all nations*, 8 vols. (1768–9) · F. D. Wierstra, *Smollett and Dickens* (1928) · O. Smeaton, *Tobias Smollett* (1897) · L. Melville, *The life and letters of Tobias Smollett (1721–1771)* (1926) · *DNB* · K. Wittig, *The Scottish tradition in literature* (1958) · C. Anstey, *New Bath guide* (1766) · R. Putney, 'Smollett and Lady Vane's memoirs', *Philological Quarterly*, 25 (1946), 120–26 · R. M. Wiles, *Serial publication in England before 1750* (1957) · J. G. Basker, *Tobias Smollett: critic and journalist* (1988) · A. Bold, ed., *Smollett: author of the first distinction* (1982) · K. Simpson, 'The importance of Tobias Smollett', *The history of Scottish literature*, ed. C. Craig, 2: *1660–1800*, ed. A. Hook (1987), 101–21 · T. Smollett, *Ferdinand Count Fathom*, ed. D. Grant (1971) · *The letters of David Hume*, ed. J. Y. T. Greig, 2 vols. (1932) · *The letters of Robert Burns*, ed. J. De Lancey Ferguson, 2 vols. (1931); rev. edn, ed. G. Ross Roy (1985) · *The works of John Home, esq.*, ed. H. Mackenzie, 3 vols. (1822) · J. Hawkins, *A general history of the science and practice of music*, 5 vols. (1776) · C. Welsh, *A bookseller of the last century* (1885) · M. D. Young, ed., *The parliaments of Scotland: burgh and shire commissioners*, 2 vols. (1992–3) · *The statistical account of Scotland* (1796), vol. 17 · bap. reg. Scot. · medical faculty records, U. Glas., Archives and Business Records Centre · T. Campbell, *Specimens of the British poets*, 15 vols. (1819) · H. Walpole, *Memoirs of the reign of King George the Third*, ed. G. F. R. Barker, 4 vols. (1894)

Archives BL, annotated edition of *Travels through France and Italy*, C 45 d20–21 · NYPL, Berg collection, holograph note on reign of Edward III · priv. coll., papers | BL, letters to John Wilkes, Add.

MS 30877 • NL Scot., letters to Alexander Carlyle • PRO, petition for royal licence, state papers domestic, George II, 145 • RCS Eng., Hunter-Baillie collection, letters to William Hunter

Likenesses W. Verelst, oils, *c.*1756, priv. coll. • N. Dance, portrait, *c.*1764, priv. coll. • oils, *c.*1770, NPG [*see illus.*] • J. Collyer the younger, line engraving, pubd 1790 (after unknown artist), NPG • J. Collyer the younger, line engravings, pubd 1790 (after unknown artist), NPG • F. Alianer, line engraving (after J. Reynolds), BM; repro. in T. Smollett, *Complete history of England* • W. Cochrane, portrait, U. Glas. • Ridley, two stipples (after J. Reynolds), NPG

Smuts, Jan Christiaan (1870–1950), prime minister of South Africa, army officer, and writer on evolution, was born on 24 May 1870 at Bovenplaats, near Riebeeck West in the Malmesbury district of the Cape Colony, the second child of Jacobus Abraham (Kosie) Smuts (1845–1914) and Catharina Petronella Gerhardina (Cato) de Vries (1845–1901). Both their families were of predominantly Dutch origin, and had settled at the Cape in the late seventeenth century.

White South Africa's most outstanding twentieth-century figure, and its most renowned internationally, Jan Christiaan Smuts was a man of remarkable intellectual gifts. The major actor in the unification of South Africa, he helped refashion the modern Commonwealth, established the framework for the League of Nations, and inspired the preamble to the charter of the United Nations Organization. A peacemaker who played a notable role in Paris in 1919 and Ireland in 1921, Smuts nevertheless spent much of his life at war and achieved a reputation within South Africa for high-handed ruthlessness. A philosopher and scientist, he seemed psychologically unable to address South Africa's all-important 'colour question', and in this respect never rose above the racist discourse of the time. If Africa was his emotional mother country, Europe was his intellectual fatherland and throughout his life he retained an almost visceral fear that the fragile European civilization established in South Africa would be overwhelmed by black 'barbarism'. He thus remains a curiously elusive if not evasive figure, as his frequent sobriquet, Slim ('crafty') Jannie, suggests.

Early years and career Smuts grew up in the Malmesbury district of the south-western Cape, where his forebears had farmed since the late eighteenth century, first on the farm Bovenplaats, later on Klipfontein, to which his father moved when he was six. The second of six siblings (four brothers and two sisters), Smuts seems to have had a happy childhood. The love of the mountains and veld acquired then never left him, and in later life he remarked that 'the highest religion is the Religion of the Mountain', and referred to Table Mountain as his 'cathedral'.

Smuts's father was a successful farmer and local notable who represented Malmesbury farmers in the colonial parliament as a member of the Afrikaner Bond, the first Afrikaner political organization in the Cape Colony. His mother was a well-educated and intellectual woman of strong character, the sister of a Dutch Reformed cleric known for his enlightened theological views. Like his younger siblings, Smuts was taught at home by his mother but at the age of twelve replaced his oldest brother, who died in 1882, at boarding-school in Riebeeck West. There he rapidly revealed his intellectual promise and capacity for hard work. Within four years he had taken the school higher examination, and was enrolled to take his matriculation examinations, first at the *Gymnasium*, and then at Victoria College, in Stellenbosch. A brilliant and conscientious student, Smuts was a solitary young man, preferring poetry and plants to people—with one exception, his fellow student Sybella Margaretha Krige (1870–1954), better known as Isie, the daughter of a leading local wine farmer, with whom he fell in love in 1887 and whom he was to marry ten years later, in April 1897. An exceptionally powerful and intelligent woman in her own right, Isie was to provide him with the love, loyalty, and stable home life which made many of his achievements possible—as Smuts himself frequently acknowledged.

Jan Christiaan Smuts (1870–1950), by Elliott & Fry, 1917

Despite a preoccupation with sin and salvation (from which he later claimed to be liberated by his study of Walt Whitman) Smuts soon gave up an early intention of taking orders, and graduated from the University of the Cape of Good Hope in 1891 with a double first in literature and science. His intellectual span was already ambitious and his interests included botany, English and German poetry, and Greek, as well as politics and philosophy. In receipt of the Ebden scholarship to Cambridge, he entered Christ's College in October 1891 to read law. Once again he shone academically. He headed the lists for all the intercollegiate examinations in law in 1892–3, and in 1894 was the first candidate to achieve distinction in both parts of the law tripos. F. W. Maitland believed him to be the most outstanding student he had ever taught. Equally solitary at Cambridge, he none the less established an enduring friendship with his tutor, H. J. Wolstenholme, whose interests in philosophy and politics matched his own.

In October 1894, after a brief visit to Germany to study German philosophy and literature, Smuts entered the Middle Temple and successfully passed the honours examination of the inns of court by the middle of 1895. By this time, too, he had written a book on Whitman entitled 'A study in the evolution of personality', which he was never to publish. In it he began to formulate his philosophy of 'the whole' which he dubbed 'holism'.

The young nationalist In 1895 Smuts returned to a southern Africa in political and economic ferment. Unsuccessful in his attempts to establish himself as an advocate at the Cape bar, he was soon immersed in politics. Like his father, he supported the Afrikaner Bond, then allied to Cecil Rhodes, prime minister of the Cape. The young Smuts had first attracted Rhodes's attention as a Stellenbosch student. In October 1895 he made a somewhat unfortunate political début by defending Rhodes against allegations of opportunism and corruption made by Olive Schreiner and her husband, and by declaring his general agreement with Rhodes's policies. Introducing a lifelong preoccupation, Smuts took the occasion to stress the crucial importance of the 'consolidation of the two Teutonic peoples that have sought a home in this country' given the precarious position of about half a million white inhabitants 'at the southern corner of a vast continent peopled by over 100,000,000 barbarians', 'that vast deadweight of immemorial barbarism and animal savagery' (Hancock and Van der Poel, 1.82–3).

Two months later Rhodes's involvement in Dr L. S. Jameson's invasion of Transvaal transformed the political landscape in South Africa, destroyed the Rhodes–Bond alliance in the Cape, and shattered Smuts's belief in Rhodes and, temporarily, in the possibility of fusing the white 'races' in South Africa. For Smuts the raid constituted a declaration of war and in his many articles in the political journals of the day he called for Afrikaner unity against an aggressive British imperialism. In January 1897 a disillusioned Smuts made his way to the South African Republic. There he soon attracted the attention of the president, Paul Kruger. Not only was the young advocate prepared to defend, against the weight of legal opinion in South Africa, Kruger's recent action in dismissing his chief justice; with his Cambridge background and keen intellect Smuts was also clearly the man to deal with Sir Alfred Milner, the newly arrived British high commissioner in South Africa. In June 1898 Smuts was appointed state attorney, responsible for law and order in the republic and legal adviser to its executive council.

The 28-year-old Smuts soon made his presence felt in the affairs of state and played a critical role in the events that led to the outbreak of the Second South African War. Aware of the need to claim the moral high ground, he swiftly addressed the more justifiable grievances of the mine owners and brought the notoriously corrupt police force under control. While defending the sovereignty of the republic, he also urged franchise reform on a reluctant Kruger, and by August 1899 had almost persuaded Joseph Chamberlain, the colonial secretary, to accept the republic's concessions on the Uitlander vote in exchange for an end to imperial intervention in the Transvaal. Despite these concessions, however, Milner remained intransigent and, in an attempt to pre-empt British action, on 9 October 1899 the republic issued the ultimatum—probably drafted by Smuts—which led to war.

War and the unification of South Africa As war became increasingly inevitable Smuts composed a fierce polemic against the British entitled *A Century of Wrong* issued by the state secretary, F. W. Reitz; he followed this up with a powerful memorandum on military and political strategy. In it he advocated the all-out mobilization of Afrikaners in southern Africa, the establishment of a war economy and the subversion of the British empire. Militarily, he urged a swift incursion into Natal and the Cape, to eliminate the British before they could build up their forces, and where, he believed, the Boers would be joined by international opponents of British imperialism. These hopes were dashed in the early months of the war as international assistance failed to materialize, and as the caution of an older generation of Boer leaders squandered their initial military advantages. Despite early Boer victories, the arrival in the new year of lords Roberts and Kitchener and large numbers of British soldiers enabled a rapid imperial advance northward. By March 1900 the Orange Free State had been invaded and Bloemfontein taken; on 5 June General Roberts entered Pretoria.

With the outbreak of war, Smuts had remained reluctantly at his post in Pretoria, conducting government business and advising on military strategy. When at the end of May 1900 Kruger and his senior entourage escaped to Delagoa Bay, Smuts was left in charge. With the fall of Pretoria, he escaped with Transvaal's remaining gold reserve and joined General De la Rey's commando in western Transvaal. Contrary to British expectations, a new phase of the struggle now began as the Boers turned to guerrilla warfare. In October 1900, when the leaders of the Orange Free State and Transvaal met to review this strategy, Smuts was present in his capacities as state attorney and as political commissar with De la Rey in western Transvaal.

Although not alone in his advocacy, Smuts clearly influenced the decision to invade the Cape Colony along the lines he had originally adumbrated and where he hoped for an uprising of colonial Afrikaners, 'the beginning not only of real independence of the republics, but of the deliverance of the whole of South Africa and the Union of our people into a great nation from Table Bay to the Equator' (Hancock, 1.126). This expansive vision of a united settler southern Africa, inherited from Rhodes, remained with Smuts long after the end of the war and the unification of the southern African colonies south of the Limpopo.

By December 1900 Smuts had emerged as a general in

his own right. Leading a commando in western Transvaal, he stormed the British camp at Modderfontein, capturing 200 prisoners and equipping his men with captured arms and ammunition. His main goal, however, remained to carry the war into the Cape, and after much delay, on 1 August 1901 he set off for the Cape Colony with a small body of hand-picked men. Over the next nine months his commando criss-crossed some 1000 miles, enduring innumerable privations, engaging in audacious exploits, inflicting considerable losses on the British, and intensifying the expropriation of rural black communities. Although the commando failed to rouse colonial rebellion, it attracted hundreds of Cape Afrikaner dissidents and provided a rallying point for defeated Orange Free State forces. With some 2000 men he made his way to the north-western Cape where the proximity of the South-West African border enabled him to maintain contact with the Boer leaders in Europe and with pro-Boer opinion in Britain.

For a man who had a reputation as a child for being frail and who was so deeply steeped in book learning, Smuts showed a remarkable aptitude for war. Cool and courageous, he was a fine tactician and, despite his personal aloofness, an inspiring leader of men. He emerged from the war physically robust, with added authority among Afrikaners and a fearsome reputation among the British as their indomitable foe. Yet even before the end of the war, Smuts was beginning to think once more about reconciliation between Briton and Boer in a new South African 'commonwealth', although it was to be a Commonwealth from which black people were to be firmly excluded.

By mid-1902 the greater resources of the British army had worn the Afrikaners down and their leaders were forced to sue for peace, even if it meant relinquishing all immediate hope of independence. In May 1902, shortly after his capture of Concordia in Nama Land, Smuts was summoned to join the Boer discussions at Vereeniging, and together with General J. B. M. Hertzog, who was to become his most serious political rival, he framed the final draft of the peace settlement. This was only done after impassioned debate. Against those, especially from the Orange Free State, who wished to continue the war for republican independence, the Transvaal generals, Louis Botha, and Smuts argued that to do so would jeopardize the very survival of the Afrikaner people. Behind that recognition lay a harsh reality: rural destruction and the suffering and mortality of women and children in the concentration camps had dire demographic implications; however determined the generals, their support was dwindling, while at least as ominously in the countryside Africans and 'coloureds' were taking the opportunity to wage their own struggles against landowners and overlords. And this had a longer-term significance for white supremacy which Smuts feared: the day would come, he wrote, 'when the evils and horrors of this war will appear as nothing in comparison with its after effects produced on the Native mind' (Hancock and Van der Poel, 1.485).

For Smuts, reconciliation between the 'white races' was thus crucial. Significantly, the first item he noted after a briefing by Kitchener on the proceedings at Vereeniging read 'Natives to be disarmed and no franchise until after self-government' (Hancock, 1.155). This somewhat ambiguous phrase was to be the subject of considerable rewording in the final peace settlement. While Milner drafted the original clause to imply that Africans would be granted the franchise after the restoration of self-government to the former republics, Smuts rewrote it to ensure that the decision about African suffrage would be left to self-governing white colonists themselves. The exclusion of the majority African population from citizenship in South Africa's Act of Union in 1910 was the inevitable result.

That Smuts was prepared to accept the end of republican independence at Vereeniging resulted also from his reading of British politics, and Kitchener's private prediction of a Liberal victory in Britain within two years and the grant of self-government to the Boers shortly thereafter. From his Cambridge days, Smuts had been drawn to the 'England of John Bright', and the activities of the pro-Boer lobby during the war encouraged him to hope for a new dispensation from a Liberal electoral victory. Initially, however, with Milner and his young acolytes in control, the political outlook in Transvaal seemed bleak.

Smuts's first tasks after the war were to rebuild his family and repair his fortune. Two babies, both girls, were born (1903 and 1904), to be followed by four more children over the next ten years—two boys and two girls. Back in Pretoria he soon re-established himself as an advocate and invested his earnings in land, acquiring some dozen or so farms during the next decade and half. Over the years these provided the financial independence he needed for his political activities and his scholarly pursuits. He was soon deeply engaged in both endeavours, beginning work on a manuscript completed in 1912 entitled 'An inquiry into the whole', and joining Botha in opposing Milner's education and language policies and the imposition of a war debt on the Transvaal. It was, however, the storm which accompanied Milner's decision to import Chinese indentured labour to resolve the labour shortage in the mines which provided the Boer generals with their political opportunity. Refusing to join Milner's legislative council, between mid-1903 and the beginning of 1905 Smuts and Botha created the political movement known as Vereeniging Het Volk ('union of the people') or more simply Het Volk. By 1905 Het Volk had become the vehicle for bringing together a wide spectrum of Afrikaner opinion behind the demand for responsible government for both of the conquered republics.

Their break came when the Liberal Party took office in Britain at the end of that year. Smuts hastened to London to urge the immediate grant of responsible government to Transvaal and the Orange River Colony; he was equally concerned to ensure that population size rather than the adult male population would form the basis of the franchise. Only this, he argued, would guard against the corruption of politics by the power of finance capital. More importantly it would end the electoral preponderance of the Rand. For Smuts, his interview with Henry Campbell-Bannerman on 7 February 1906 marked a turning point, both in Transvaal–British relations and personally, for he always regarded this meeting as 'the creative encounter of his political life' (Hancock, 1.215). That it was this visit to England which led to Smuts's deep friendship with the Quaker sisters Alice Clark and Margaret Clark (later Gillett), John Bright's granddaughters, undoubtedly intensified the experience, and quickened his intellectual and emotional bonds with English radicalism. These friendships endured to the end of his life; his correspondence with the Clark–Gillett family provides a unique testimony for the historian.

Whether or not his meeting with Campbell-Bannerman was in itself as decisive as Smuts believed, Transvaal soon achieved self-government, followed by the Orange River Colony in 1907. Het Volk won the ensuing Transvaal elections by a considerable majority, and Botha became prime minister, with Smuts as colonial secretary and minister of education, chief parliamentary spokesman and draughtsman, and Botha's closest confidant. According to Hancock, their political partnership was 'reinforced … by bonds of mutual trust, loyalty and love such as have seldom, if ever, united two political leaders' (Hancock, 1.191). Het Volk's electoral success was in large measure the result of Smuts's and Botha's recognition that in the Transvaal political power depended on dividing British South Africans and securing a degree of their electoral support. Given the demographic balance in the Transvaal, compromise was a political necessity. Thus two of six ministerial places went to their electoral allies, the English-speaking National Party, while, as minister of education, Smuts left Dutch to parental choice in primary schools but, despite Afrikaner accusations of disloyalty, accepted the primacy of the English language thereafter.

Despite his anti-capitalist rhetoric at that time, Smuts was even prepared to woo the mine owners in his pursuit of power and was soon discussing with the magnates, on a friendly basis, the day-to-day problems of the industry. Well aware of the centrality of gold-mining to the economic fortunes of the colony, the cabinet delayed repatriating Chinese labour, and called on imperial troops to help crush a strike of white workers in 1907.

The achievement of responsible government in Transvaal was only a preliminary to Smuts's wider purpose—the creation of a 'United South Africa', in which English- and Afrikaans-speaking South Africa would be brought together and from which imperial influence would be eliminated. It was a goal he shared with the veteran liberal politician John X. Merriman, who became prime minister of the Cape Colony in 1908. Unlike Smuts, however, Merriman's vision left room for the inclusion of at least propertied and educated Africans in the body politic, along the lines of the non-racial, class-based franchise established in the mid-nineteenth-century Cape. Time and again in the remarkable correspondence between the two men in the years running up to union Merriman returned to the iniquity and inequity of a policy that would 'ignore three-quarters of the population because they are coloured' (Hancock and Van der Poel, 2.239). Merriman was no champion of what he saw as 'democratic shibboleths'—for black or white—and he shared the racism of his time. Nevertheless he believed a qualified franchise was a crucial safety valve: 'there is no surer bulwark for all the legitimate rights of any class or colour than representation in Parliament. The only alternative is physical force and the volcano', he wrote to Smuts in March 1906, as African rebellion erupted in Natal. Smuts was equally aware of the centrality of 'native policy' in South Africa; he was, however, totally against any extension of political rights to Africans. 'When I consider the political future of the natives in S. A.', he confessed at this time, 'I must say I look into shadows and darkness'; his response was 'to shift the intolerable burden of solving that sphinx problem to the ampler shoulders and stronger brains of the future' (ibid., 242–4).

In the event, economic and political pressures for closer union pushed Merriman's concerns to one side. The victories of Afrikaner political parties in the Transvaal, Orange River Colony, and Cape Colony in 1906–8 provided a major impetus for the movement. Whatever his earlier suspicions of 'sinister' imperial and capitalist interests, Smuts now found common ground over unification with imperial administrators in South Africa and the more far-sighted capitalists who had long advocated the creation of a unified state in the interests of economic development. At the national convention which met in Durban in 1908 to discuss a South Africa-wide constitution, Smuts's views prevailed, the result of the assistance he received from members of Milner's old 'kindergarten' in South Africa, and his own formidable attention to detail both in his preparations for the meeting and as the major participant in its discussions. According to Hancock, 'More than any other national constitution within the Commonwealth, that of the Union of South Africa bears the imprint of one man's mind' (Hancock, 1.268).

Where Cape and Transvaal interests conflicted, Smuts and Merriman had usually negotiated an agreed position beforehand. Largely as a result of their determination, the new constitution provided for a unitary state with a strong central government, and the contentious issue of African political rights was not allowed to jeopardize the prospect of union. In the heated debate, in which the Cape Colony's non-racial, property-based franchise was repeatedly attacked, Smuts argued for its retention—but only in the Cape. Moreover, only 'persons of European descent' were to be eligible for election to parliament. Despite the protests of black South Africans and the near universal expression of regret at the constitutional colour bar, the draft South Africa Act passed unamended when it came before the British parliament in 1909.

The first cabinet of the Union of South Africa When in 1910 Botha was selected as the new prime minister of South Africa, he headed the new South African National Party (later South African Party); Smuts was once again the centre of his cabinet and in the four years up to the outbreak of the First World War established much of South Africa's legal and administrative framework. As minister of defence he was directly responsible for the 1912 Defence Act which instituted the South African army and made appointments to it. As minister of mines he introduced the 1911 Mines and Works Act which entrenched the colour bar in industry; this, he disingenuously informed members, was a 'purely technical' measure. Finally, as minister of the interior he was largely responsible for handling the continuing crisis over the position of South Africa's Indian minority.

The 'Indian question' had already confronted Smuts in his capacity as colonial secretary in Transvaal, when attempts to impose new Indian Immigration and Registration Acts in 1906–8 had roused the Indian community, under the leadership of Mohandas Karamchand Gandhi, to defy the state. This had resulted in an uneasy compromise agreement which broke down in 1912–13 when the introduction of yet another Immigration Bill in parliament coincided with a controversy over Natal's £3 poll tax on ex-indentured labourers (which Gandhi believed Smuts had agreed to repeal) and a judgment in the courts threatened the legal validity of Indian marriages. These issues provided Gandhi with a mass following for the first time, and when in mid-October 1913 he issued a strike call among Indian coalminers in Natal the response was dramatic, and within two weeks several thousand Natal miners were on strike. Initially conciliatory, Smuts was forced to act when Gandhi and his followers led some 4000 strikers and their dependants illegally across the Transvaal border, and the strike spread to Natal's sugar plantations. He ordered several thousand arrests, including that of Gandhi and his immediate followers, and the strike was called off. Fiercely criticized for his handling of the strike, Smuts appointed a commission of inquiry, which led to the partial removal of Indian disabilities. Gandhi left South Africa shortly thereafter, his reputation greatly enhanced.

Although Smuts and Gandhi were later to forge an admiring if distant friendship, Smuts never wavered in his belief that there could be no equality for Indians in South Africa: 'You cannot', he told the imperial war cabinet in 1921, 'deal with the Indians apart from the whole position in South Africa; you cannot give political rights to the Indians which you deny to the rest of the coloured citizens in South Africa' (Millin, 1.247). The status of South African Indians was to haunt Smuts throughout his life.

Indian strikers were not the only ones to confront the cabinet in 1913. Earlier that year an ill-prepared Smuts had been forced to back down in the face of striking white miners on the Rand, and give way to workers' demands. According to Smuts, 'it was one of the hardest things he ever had to do' (Yudelman, 100). He ensured it never happened again. Thus in the following January, when the white miners struck once more, he swiftly mobilized the newly established Union defence force, declared martial law, and summarily deported the strike leaders. Although he was indemnified by parliament, the episode underlined for white workers Smuts's association with the mine owners. Indeed it was widely suspected, with some justification, that Smuts had deliberately engineered the confrontation and its timing, in revenge for his defeat in 1913 (ibid., 108–9).

For Botha and Smuts, however, it was the division among Afrikaners that was most threatening politically and disheartening personally. From the outset the inclusion of the leading Orange Free State politician General J. B. M. Hertzog, in Botha's cabinet had caused intense strain. Unlike Smuts and Botha, who were concerned to conciliate English-speakers, Hertzog, with his base in the homogeneously Afrikaner Free State, enunciated a 'two stream policy' in which he believed Dutch interests would be more fully protected, but which in its more strident moments sounded like a rejection of English rights. At the end of 1912 Hertzog was ousted from the cabinet, and by the beginning of 1914 had formed the Afrikaner National Party.

The First World War, the Versailles peace treaty, and the League of Nations The outbreak of the First World War seemed to those many Afrikaners who remained unreconciled to the imperial connection, and who had gained little from union, an ideal opportunity to regain their lost independence. When, instead, Botha and Smuts led the Union into war on the British side, and planned to invade South-West Africa, part of the army mutinied and was joined by commandos from the Orange Free State and the poverty-stricken western Transvaal. For Smuts, the suppression of his Second South African War comrades was both painful and a matter of honour. In general, he dealt with the rebel leaders leniently except for one Jopie Fourie, a commandant in the Union defence force, who rebelled without resigning his commission. Despite pleas for clemency, Smuts refused to intervene when Fourie was court-martialled and executed; Afrikaner nationalists elevated Fourie almost at once to martyrdom while Smuts was excoriated as a 'murderer' (Hancock, 1.392).

Nor was Smuts's reputation at home assisted by his exploits abroad. No sooner was the civil war over than Botha took command of the invasion of South-West Africa from the north, to be followed shortly thereafter by Smuts from the south. In a rapid campaign they defeated the heavily outnumbered Germans. Although Smuts eulogized the conquest of South-West Africa as 'the first achievement of a united South African nation, in which both [white] races have combined all their best and most virile characteristics' he returned to an intensely divided South Africa (Hancock, 1.400). While Hertzog had remained on the sidelines during the uprising, and advocated neutrality during the war, all over the country fierce nationalist passions had been kindled and large numbers of Afrikaners flocked to the National Party. In the violently contested general elections of October 1915, during which Smuts narrowly missed being shot, the Nationalists made considerable gains, and the South African Party lost its majority, only remaining in office with the support of the pro-war Unionists.

At the beginning of 1916, at the British request, Smuts accepted command of the troops in east Africa with the rank of lieutenant-general in the British army. For over a year the British troops there had been unable to make much headway against von Lettow Vorbeck, despite superior numbers and equipment. Smuts inherited an inexperienced and heterogeneous army, difficult and disease-ridden terrain, and an unpropitious climate. Nevertheless, and despite his critics, within a month of his arrival the military position had been largely reversed. The fighting was strenuous and the cost in men, especially African carriers, who bore the brunt of the campaign, was extremely high, but a combination of speed and surprise tactics, together with von Lettow's strategy—which was not to hold territory but to tie up large numbers of imperial troops—put Smuts in control of an immense territory. By the end of the year, when Botha asked him to represent the Union in London, the Germans had been pushed south of the Rufiji River. Although von Lettow remained undefeated until the end of the war in Europe, Smuts left claiming he had largely dealt with the military threat in east Africa (Ingham, 84–6).

When in March 1917 Smuts arrived in Britain he found himself showered with honours, and the king made him a privy councillor and Companion of Honour. In the dark days of this war, as during the Second World War, he inspired audiences with his own confidence in the ultimate triumph of right. As Sarah Gertrude Millin remarked, his words had a particular value to the British because Smuts spoke as a 'Boer':

> This gave him a spiritual value which transcended all his own virtues—it made him the symbol of England's righteousness. As they said in England: 'He has done more than any man to recall this country to its great tradition.' (Millin, 2.13)

In the midst of his public duties, Smuts also re-established his ties with his Quaker, Liberal, and radical feminist friends. With them, and especially with the Gilletts in Oxford and Alice Clark in London, he found companionship, peace, and spiritual renewal. They also undoubtedly strengthened his liberal internationalism.

In London, Smuts was soon engrossed in the meetings of the Imperial War Conference and the imperial war cabinet, the first devoted to a miscellany of longer-term imperial issues, the second to the day-to-day conduct of the war and the discussion of peace terms. So profound was the impact Smuts made on his colleagues, and especially on Lloyd George, that when he refused the proffered Palestine command they prevailed upon him to remain in London at the conclusion of the conference as a member of the British war cabinet. Refusing the suggestion that he take a seat in the House of Commons, he retained his position as minister without portfolio in Botha's cabinet and was careful not to intervene in purely domestic politics in the UK. Nevertheless, towards the end of 1917 he successfully resolved a potential strike in the south Wales coalfields, and in 1918 dissuaded the British cabinet from imposing conscription in Ireland before the introduction of home rule.

Smuts's main work, however, was more directly connected with the war effort. He played an important role in advising on military strategy as well as in the establishment of an independent Air Ministry, and thus of the RAF; and he headed the war priorities committee which matched industrial production to the demands of war. He was dispatched to the western front in April 1917, and—to his later regret—supported the Passchendaele offensive in Flanders. In November and December 1917 he reviewed the situation in Italy for the war cabinet; his suggestions for reinforcing the troops after Caporetto were accepted, and he explored the possibilities of a separate peace with Austria. In February 1918 he was in Egypt and Palestine and helped plan Allenby's final advance. After armistice he was responsible for the demobilization plans of all the British departments and for compiling the British brief for the peace conference. In April 1919 he was sent to Vienna, Prague, and Budapest as 'plenipotentiary of the great Powers' in abortive negotiations with Bela Kun over the Hungary–Romanian border, and in the hope—which proved vain—that he would meet with the Russian Bolshevik leaders.

Through 1918 Smuts's experience of the Second South African War and the influence of his radical and pacifist friends deeply informed his opposition to the idea of total war, or indeed total surrender, and his keen advocacy of a new international order, embodied in his pamphlet *The League of Nations, a Practical Suggestion*. He also developed the idea of mandates initially adumbrated by those on the political left, although he never intended mandates in Africa where he hoped for the outright annexation of the German colonies. Somewhat ironically in view of his collaboration with the mining industry in South Africa and his failure to recognize African rights at home, he also drafted Lloyd George's speech on British war aims in January 1918, in which he denounced the capitalist exploitation of colonial territories and proclaimed the relevance of self-determination to the German colonies, and which became embodied in Woodrow Wilson's 'fourteen points'.

At the Paris peace conference, where with Botha he represented South Africa, Smuts continued to argue in vain for a magnanimous peace; he despaired that the Versailles treaty was 'conceived on a wrong basis, that … will prove utterly unstable and only serve to promote the anarchy which is rapidly overtaking Europe' (Hancock and Van der Poel, 4.84). He even threatened to resign as a delegate and lead a campaign against the treaty as 'an abomination'. His private letters reveal his anguish. Nevertheless, when Lloyd George asked pointedly whether he was prepared to return the German colonies in south-west or east Africa, Smuts equivocated—and signed the treaty. Yet there were also hard-headed calculations about the territorial aggrandizement of South Africa behind Smuts's decision to stay in Europe. In addition to holding on to South-West Africa he hoped to fulfil a long-held South African ambition by exchanging territory in east Africa for Delagoa Bay and its hinterland. Control over South-West Africa as a 'C Mandate' was the Union's only acquisition, however.

Prime minister, 1919–1924 In the first week of August 1919 Smuts was back on his farm at Doornkloof, outside Pretoria, where the family had moved in 1909; by the end of the month Botha had died, and Smuts had replaced him as leader of the South African Party, and also as prime minister and minister of native affairs. Away from the maelstrom of Europe, Smuts soon found South Africa as turbulent after the war as it had been before. The urban areas were racked by strikes; in the rural areas Africans resisted land loss and poor farm conditions; and everywhere anti-Indian feeling was rife, undermining the Smuts–Gandhi agreement of 1914. The appointment of an Asiatic inquiry commission at the end of 1919 was one of Smuts's first acts as prime minister, although by 1923 he was forced by the feeling in his own party to introduce fresh anti-Indian legislation. In parliament he found his actions constrained by the growth of support for Hertzog's National Party and his consequent dependence on the pro-imperial Unionist Party, widely seen as representing the interests of mining capital. Within weeks of his return he was on the campaign trail, explaining his support for the British during the war and trying to combat the Afrikaner clamour for secession from the empire by explaining the nature of dominion status.

Although in South Africa, Smuts was constantly vilified as an 'imperialist', he had already helped redefine the nature of dominion sovereignty within the British Commonwealth—a term he and Merriman had first used in the early years of the century—on the basis of freedom and equality. He saw the Commonwealth as an evolving community of autonomous nation states with their own varied cultures, held together by common values, consultation, and loyalty to the crown (Hancock, 1.429–32). Resisting notions of imperial federation, which he realized spelt disaster back home, he ensured the right of each dominion to independent representation at the Paris peace conference and in 1919 secured from Lloyd George the admission that 'the independent nationhood of the Dominions' meant that in some future war the dominions could, if they so wished, remain neutral. Smuts set this out once more in a memorandum to the Imperial Conference which he attended in 1921. Although blocked at that time, his proposals formed the basis for the Balfour declaration of 1926 and the Statute of Westminster in 1931. Ironically it was his political rival, the vociferously anti-imperialist Hertzog, who received the credit.

Smuts's ideas on the changed nature of the Commonwealth also inspired his intervention in Ireland. Before leaving Europe in 1919 he had already spoken publicly in favour of Irish independence. On his return to London in June 1921 he was called on by both sides to intervene. He drafted the king's speech of reconciliation to the Irish people at the opening of the new Ulster parliament, and was invited by de Valera to Dublin, where he urged Irish nationalists to accept a non-republican constitution for southern Ireland and dominion status. In the event, despite the truce and the signing of the Anglo-Irish agreement which followed in December 1921, Smuts's intervention in Ireland was no more successful in resolving conflict than his enunciation of dominion status was in South Africa. Differences there over the Union's relationship with the empire permeated political discourse, connected as they were with deep class and ethnic divisions within the white population. This issue dominated the 1920 elections in which the National Party for the first time overtook the South African Party (SAP) in the number both of voters and of parliamentary representatives. To remain in power, Smuts was forced to rely on the Unionists to an even greater extent than had been evident in the war.

So close was the alliance that by 1921 the Unionists and the SAP had merged, despite a final attempt at reconciling Afrikaners in September 1920. Once more reunion ran aground on Nationalist demands for the right to advocate the secession of South Africa from the British empire, and Smuts's realization that they would hold the upper hand in a unified party. Although the new party won the ensuing election with a large majority, the merger meant that the SAP was seen as representing big capital. This was strengthened as a result of Smuts's handling of a general strike in 1922, an event which threatened the state in South Africa, transformed the nature of white politics, revealed the stark nature of class conflict within the white population, and showed the critical importance of recently proletarianized Afrikaners in the white working class.

During the war, a premium on the gold price had protected marginal mines from the effects of inflation. With the worldwide recession in the early 1920s the price of gold dropped precipitately in real terms and many low-grade mines were in jeopardy. In response, mine magnates determined to reduce working costs by substituting cheaper African labour in place of white by abrogating a wartime agreement which guaranteed an agreed ratio of white to black miners. On 2 January 1922 the coalminers came out on strike against wage reductions and by the 10th they had been joined by 20,000 white goldminers on the Witwatersrand. Despite Smuts's initial reluctance to intervene, the centrality of the goldmining industry to state revenue meant the government could not stand aside in the ensuing confrontation. Some attempts at conciliation were made by the government, but Smuts failed to pressurize employers to compromise, and there were many who believed he had deliberately decided to crush organized labour (Yudelman, 179–80). The strike rapidly became an insurrection, with attacks on the police and black workers. On 10 March, having mobilized the active citizen force, Smuts declared martial law and took command of 7000 troops, supported by planes and tanks. Within three days the armed rising was at an end and the strike was broken. In all, 153 people had been killed: 81 were civilians, the rest members of the police and armed forces.

The 1922 strike was not the only deadly confrontation during Smuts's first premiership. In February 1920 African discontent on the Rand had culminated in a strike by some 70,000 black miners, who were driven back to work at gunpoint, leaving several dead and many more wounded; in October of the same year the African trade union the Industrial and Commercial Workers' Union found its first martyrs when police fired on strikers in Port Elizabeth, killing twenty-three (including three white bystanders) and wounding 126 others. In May 1921 members of an African millenarian sect known as the Israelites, who had peacefully encamped to await their redeemer on location land at Bulhoek near Queenstown in the eastern Cape, were eventually forcibly removed at an even heavier cost of life. Armed with sticks and stones they advanced on the troops, and 119 men, women, and children were shot at close range. Smuts told parliament 'that the law of the land will be carried out in the last resort as fearlessly against black as against white' (Simons and Simons, 254). Nor was the bloodshed restricted to South Africa. In 1922 a confrontation erupted in South-West Africa when the Bondelzwarts people, already in conflict with the government, resisted the arrest of a popular leader. It ended with the dispatch of a punitive expedition armed with machine-guns and field artillery and air strikes against the community. The Bondelzwarts suffered 115 dead, uncounted wounded, and over 100 in gaol.

These events were in sharp contrast to Smuts's lectures on the white man's 'civilizing mission'. For all his liberal rhetoric, however, Smuts gave little thought to the position of Africans in southern Africa, mostly repeating contemporary platitudes about trusteeship and separate or parallel development. Between 1919 and 1924 he was responsible for two major pieces of legislation on 'native affairs': the 1920 Native Affairs Act and the 1923 Urban Areas Act. The first made provision for a three-member expert native affairs commission with power to make recommendations on matters affecting the African population, and also extended the local council system first introduced by Rhodes in the eastern Cape and authorized the administration to convene conferences of 'prominent natives'. The second extended compulsory urban residential segregation and obliged municipalities to provide houses and advisory boards for the rapidly urbanizing African population. In both cases, paternalism was coupled with the extension of state control over African life.

Difficult as he found political conditions in South Africa, in Europe Smuts was the admired peacemaker. In 1923, during the Imperial Conference in London, he once more turned his attention to the aftermath of the war. On 23 October he powerfully denounced French policy in the Ruhr, and nudged a Franco-German compromise forward. Prophetically on the same day, the Indian delegate to the conference, Sir Tej Bahadur Sapru, mindful of the Union's recent anti-Indian legislation, warned that:

> if the Indian problem in South Africa is allowed to fester much longer it will pass beyond the bounds of a domestic issue and will become a question of foreign policy of such gravity that upon it the unity of the Empire may founder irretrievably.

In rejecting Indian proposals, Smuts repeated that 'equal rights for Indians in South Africa would lead to equal rights for Natives, and that would mean the end of South Africa' (Hancock, 2.139, 149).

Smuts's strong stand on the Indian question was not enough to rescue his government, which was now profoundly unpopular. Even white Southern Rhodesians, canvassed in a referendum in October 1922 on that territory's future, rejected their incorporation as a province of South Africa for which Smuts had hoped. In the Union both the Labour and Nationalist parties determined to get rid of a man whom they accused of being a 'butcher and hangman'. Shortly after the 1922 uprising they signed an electoral pact. In 1924, after losing a number of crucial by-elections, Smuts decided to go to the country early. The opposition parties won by about 10,000 votes.

From opposition to coalition In opposition for the first time after seventeen years in power, Smuts was at last able to find time for his more scholarly pursuits. As always his intellectual scope was breathtaking. In 1925, as president of the South African Association for the Advancement of Science, he inspired his audience with a sense of the possibilities of scientific research in southern Africa across the disciplines. A great synthesizer, he was also a respected botanist in his own right, and greatly encouraged the development of science in South Africa. His address to the association was but the prelude to his more ambitious work, completed in eight months in September 1925 and entitled *Holism and Evolution*. It 'contained by implication the entire history up to that time of his intellectual and spiritual Odyssey' (Hancock, 2.178). In it, Smuts attempted to modify what he saw as an over-materialist interpretation of evolution by introducing a sense of the transcendent, and brought together the ideas which had concerned him ever since his long essay on Walt Whitman in the 1890s and his unpublished 1912 manuscript. 'Evolution', he wrote, 'traces the grand line of escape from the prison of matter to the full freedom of the Spirit' (*Holism and Evolution*, 1st edn, 1926, 139). For Smuts, the evolutionary drive towards an ever-increasing unity in an ascending order of perfection provided the ultimate meaning or 'immanent Telos' of the universe. 'Wholes', he maintained, 'are not mere artificial constructions of thought, they point to something real in the universe; and Holism as the creative principle behind them is a real *vera causa*' (Hancock, 2.188). The end of evolution was the perfect human personality. Yet, as writers on scientific racism are beginning to show, Smuts's understanding of holism and evolution also underpinned his racialized political philosophy.

Despite the respect accorded to his ideas by prominent scientists of the time, the book soon came under fire. Although Smuts had attempted to keep abreast of the most recent scientific thinking, and greatly influenced the new science of ecology in South Africa, his work was soon bypassed by the turn of scientific and philosophical thought away from the metaphysical and by the important developments in the 1920s in the areas of genetics and physics. From very different perspectives, some theologians were shocked by what they saw as Smuts's belief in the creation but not the creator, while his political opponents purported to see in 'holism' an analogue of his political beliefs. The book was none the less a considerable achievement for a full-time politician, while his term 'holism' passed into common currency in diverse fields, albeit generally leached of much of the meaning Smuts gave it. Although he never completed the second book on holism and moral values which he intended to write, this formed the subject of Smuts's address to the British Association for the Advancement of Science in 1931, when he became president in its centenary year. He described this event as the greatest honour of his life (Friedman, 88).

If Smuts found in his intellectual endeavours some relief from the tedium of opposition, in 1925–6 he none the less believed that he would soon be back in office. Yet the 1929 elections saw the National Party gain an overall majority of eight seats, despite the majority of votes won by the South African Party. Colour issues dominated what was known as the 'black peril' election. Nationalists accused Smuts of endangering 'white civilization' by advocating black–white equality while his expansionist ambitions for a 'great African dominion' led to his portrayal as 'the apostle of a black Kaffir state' (Hancock, 2.218). Quite how far this was from the truth can be gathered from the Rhodes memorial lectures which Smuts delivered in Oxford in November 1929. In language steeped in the racist and paternalist stereotypes of the time Smuts sketched his vision of the future for Africa. Already in 1924 he had envisaged the creation of 'a great European state or system of States in the highlands of eastern Africa "from the Union to Abyssinia"' (Hancock, 2.223). Intervening in the current debate about the paramountcy of African interests in eastern Africa, Smuts contended that the civilization of the 'backward' if happy-go-lucky native in this region could be effected only by white settlers and their gospel of labour. While distancing himself from notions of African inferiority, he denounced humanitarians who treated the black man as 'a man and a brother': while seeking to advance equality, they destroyed 'the basis of his African system which was his highest good'. The resultant breakdown of African society was fraught with 'possibilities of universal Bolshevism and chaos which no friend of the natives, or the orderly civilization of this continent, could contemplate with equanimity'. The only answer, he believed, was South Africa's policy of 'differential development' or segregation (*Africa and some World Problems*, 73–100).

In fact, the differences between Smuts and Hertzog on what was known as 'native policy' were remarkably small. Both agreed on white supremacy, territorial segregation, a migrant labour system, and the exclusion of the majority of Africans from a direct exercise of the franchise, with some necessary provision for the representation of 'educated natives'. Their greatest difference was on the industrial colour bar which protected white workers from black competition. Although Smuts had himself facilitated the entrenchment of the colour bar in the mining industry in 1911, by the 1920s the merger of the SAP with the party of mining and industrial capital made him more equivocal. While, however, the National Party was unanimously behind Hertzog's version of segregation, Smuts's SAP with its divergent constituencies was far more fractured.

Fusion and the formation of the United Party Despite the ferocity of the 1929 elections, by this time other differences between Smuts and Hertzog had also diminished. By the late 1920s Hertzog believed that the equality of English and Afrikaans cultures in a white South African nation and South Africa's sovereign status in the British Commonwealth had been largely achieved, and there was much talk again of Afrikaner reunion. Smuts remained resistant: the personal antagonism between the two men was legendary and, as Smuts confided to a colleague, he was not prepared to play 'second fiddle' (Hancock, 2.241). Nevertheless, within four years of the 1929 elections he had led his party into a coalition with the Nationalists and, in a remarkable act of self-abnegation, had taken office as deputy prime minister and minister of justice under Hertzog. This turnaround was largely occasioned by the impact of the great depression on South Africa, and the consequent British decision to devalue sterling and abandon the gold standard.

The Nationalist determination to assert South Africa's economic independence by refusing to follow suit was disastrous for an economy already suffering from the worst drought in living memory. When at the end of 1932 a prominent member of the National Party publicly called for the abandonment of the gold standard, there was dramatic flight of capital, and the banks declared that they could no longer defend the gold standard. On the 28 December 1932 the government gave way. The call was now for a government of national unity, and by the end of February 1933 a coalition had been formed, with Hertzog as prime minister and Smuts as his deputy. After the 1934 elections which swept the coalition parties into power they merged to form the South African National United Party (later the United Party). This ensured Hertzog's continuation in power. It also provided him with the two-thirds majority in a joint sitting of both houses of parliament which he needed to abolish the Cape's vexed, if by now vestigial, non-racial franchise, a goal he had pursued persistently but unsuccessfully in a series of 'native bills' since 1926.

In the event Hertzog's somewhat modified Representation of Natives Bill came before parliament in 1936. This drastically diminished the remaining African political rights but only eleven MPs voted against the legislation. Smuts, recently returned from a ringing defence of freedom at St Andrews University, where he was installed as rector, was not among them, despite his earlier opposition to Hertzog's native bills. This was not the only occasion on which Smuts opted to bow to Hertzog's will rather than risk splitting the United Party. In 1937 he supported the Aliens Bill which barred the entry to South Africa of Jewish refugees from Nazi Europe, although he had hitherto both championed the Zionist ideal of a Jewish homeland in Palestine and eloquently denounced an earlier bill with similar objectives. On a series of discriminatory bills on mixed marriages, racial segregation in public places, and Indian land purchase, Smuts also remained silent. Nor did he support his lieutenant, Jan Hofmeyr, when he was forced out of the cabinet and then out of the party caucus for his stand on racial issues. To the dismay of his more liberal followers, Smuts seemed prepared to sacrifice all principle in order to maintain the fiction of unity and remain in power (Friedman, 125–53).

It was widely believed that Smuts refrained from opposing Hertzog because, in the deteriorating international situation, he wanted to ensure that he would be able to take South Africa in on the British side in a European war. This is possible but debatable (see Friedman, 120–21). Although at a distance and with little real power to influence events, Smuts followed global developments and the collapse in the authority of the League of Nations with considerable anxiety in the 1930s; until Hitler's invasion of Czechoslovakia, however, he was more concerned with the threat to world peace from Italy than that from Germany, and continued to hope that peace could be preserved through the league (Hancock, 2.275, 285; Ingham, 192ff.). International considerations apart, for Smuts white supremacy and hence white unity always took precedence over African or Indian rights.

The Second World War The outbreak of the Second World War transformed the political position in South Africa and with it Smuts's fortunes. Britain's declaration of war shattered the United Party, reopening the debate over the dominions' right to neutrality in the event of a war in which Britain was a belligerent. As late as September 1938 Smuts himself enunciated this principle, although he had also repeatedly said that he could not imagine South Africa would isolate herself from Britain and the Commonwealth if they were threatened.

When Hitler invaded Poland, Smuts insisted that in its own interests the Union had to join Britain in declaring war. He was supported in cabinet by a majority of one, and in parliament by a majority of thirteen. Hertzog, who advocated neutrality, was forced to resign, and Smuts was called upon by the governor-general to form a new cabinet. His supporters retained the name the United Party, and he formed a coalition government with the small Dominion and Labour parties. Afrikaner nationalists were again bitterly opposed to participation in the war. Extra-parliamentary pro-Nazi groups sprang up and anti-semitism, the persecution of government supporters, and even sabotage were common. Although the more extreme pro-Nazi dissidents were interned during the war, Smuts, remembering 1914, handled the opposition with circumspection.

Although the outbreak of war found South Africa's defence forces and armaments industry in a parlous state, Smuts rapidly built up her land, sea, and air forces, and by mid-1940 had dispatched battalions to Kenya and thence to the Ethiopian and north African fronts. Smuts himself, who became a British field marshal in 1941, paid frequent visits to Europe and north Africa, and used his influence in allied counsels to support the north African and Middle East campaigns, and to push for the advance into Italy in the second half of 1942 and early 1943. Churchill, long an admirer, now a comrade in arms, consulted Smuts before many critical decisions, and he intervened decisively at a number of crucial phases of the war.

In May 1943, bolstered by allied victories in north Africa, Smuts called an election which he won handsomely. He was now at the height of his power at home and abroad. Yet the electoral results failed to reflect the true potential of the Nationalists, who had won 36 per cent of the vote. Their fierce internal disagreements disguised the fact that the right-wing faction of the old National Party, led by Dr D. F. Malan, had consolidated its hold.

Towards the end of the war Smuts continued to play a significant international role. He was present in San Francisco to participate in the establishment of the United Nations, having first mooted a new international body in a speech to members of the British parliament in November 1943. Despite his alarm at the growing power of Russia from 1944, he advised Churchill to accept Russia's right of veto in the Security Council; and he suggested and provided the draft for its eloquent human rights preamble. He was, however, increasingly despondent about the United Nations, and about the state of the world, especially after the peace conference in Paris in August 1946, which he also attended.

Political defeat and death As during the First World War, Smuts was in his element in wartime and in international circles, but, as noted, his 'prophetic' vision deserted him in domestic politics. This was no less true during and after the war than it had been before it. With the exception of the overburdened Hofmeyr, his cabinet was inept and lacked dynamism, while an ageing and weary Smuts himself approached the manifold problems of peace with little sense of purpose.

Yet the years just prior to and during the Second World War witnessed challenging socio-economic changes in South Africa. Industrialization had proceeded apace, and the urbanization of poor black and poor white people had made segregation a chimera. As Smuts himself announced in 1942, segregation had 'fallen on evil days' (Hancock, 2.475). He did little, however, to find an alternative. During the war years his government followed a contradictory policy of coercion and concession. On the one hand it extended a limited amount of welfare to the poverty-stricken and increasingly militant urban black communities, on the other it introduced draconian emergency anti-trade union legislation which the subsequent Nationalist government was to entrench. As in 1922, Smuts's reaction to striking workers was harsh. In 1946, when between 50,000 and 100,000 African miners came out on strike, they were driven back to work at gunpoint and at least twelve workers were killed and 1200 injured. Not only was this a fatal defeat for African trade unionism, but also, within the state, those in favour of reform lost out to those in favour of the repression of African aspirations, and the possibilities of collaboration even with moderate Africans disappeared.

These contradictions were illustrated also in the 1946 Indian Land Tenure and Representation Act in which Smuts, responding to an outcry in Natal against Indian 'encroachment' on urban property, offered Indians limited representation in exchange for restrictions on their right to purchase and occupy land in Natal. Not only did this fail to satisfy either Indian or white opinion in Natal, it also brought Smuts and South Africa into open conflict with newly independent India, now a fellow member of the Commonwealth. In a supreme irony, at the first meeting of the general assembly of the United Nations in 1946, Mrs Pandit, head of the Indian delegation, quoted Smuts's own words in the preamble to the charter in her indictment of both the treatment of Indians in South Africa and South Africa's plans to incorporate South-West Africa. South Africa was instructed to bring her policies in line with the provisions of the charter and the United Nations mandate. It was a bitter experience for Smuts, so long the darling of the international community. 'Colour', he reflected bitterly in November 1946, 'queers my poor pitch everywhere' (Hancock, 2.473).

All this was grist to the mill of the National Party, which had rapidly recovered its resilience after the war and now made 'race relations' its battleground. Smuts, with no alternative to offer, was constantly forced onto the defensive. His policies served neither to satisfy the demands of the increasingly militant black urban organizations and their liberal parliamentary representatives, nor to allay the fears of the white electorate. Increasingly in the run up to the 1948 elections white political discourse was dominated by the Nationalist slogans of the *swart gevaar* ('black peril') and the *oorstrooming* ('swamping') of the cities. These racial metaphors were successfully articulated as apartheid, an ideology which combined the interests of different Afrikaner classes, fearful of the rise of black nationalism and trade unionism and of the hesitant reformism of the United Party. In May 1948 the Nationalists and their allies won the elections on a narrow margin of seats and a minority of votes. Smuts was defeated in his own constituency of Standerton. This was not only a personal tragedy, it also marked a major turning point for South Africa.

The election results came as a shock to Smuts, who had been confident of victory. Not only had he underestimated the capacity of the Nationalists; he had also failed to take the most elementary political precautions by refusing to alter, while he had a parliamentary majority, the rules of delimitation which in their existing form greatly favoured rural constituencies. For him the constitution of 1910 was a matter of good faith. On the basis of one vote, one value Smuts would have won an easy majority (Friedman, 210–12; Hancock, 2.505–6).

Smuts's inauguration as chancellor of Cambridge University shortly after the election restored his morale, but the sudden and unexpected death of his eldest son, Japie, in October 1948 brought him to the depths of despair. His optimism in *Holism and Evolution* that the universe was orderly and even friendly dissipated as he contemplated 'the power of chaos … at the heart of things' (Hancock, 2.509). Nevertheless he continued as leader of the opposition, struggling to keep a dispirited and divided party together and still hoping that the tenuous Nationalist government would fall; it remained in power until 1994.

In the last two years of his life, now frail and visibly aged, Smuts continued to comment perceptively, and on occasion presciently, on world affairs. Europe and the Commonwealth remained his dominant concerns. He greeted the creation of the state of Israel and recognized it two days before the 1948 election. He regretted the departure of the Irish republic from the Commonwealth, but was unhappy when the Republic of India remained within it, fearing the example this would set South Africa's Nationalists. His outstanding contributions as a world statesman were acknowledged in innumerable honours and medals. At home his reputation was more mixed. A standing ovation from over 2000 students at the Afrikaans University of Stellenbosch and an attentive, if dwindling, audience at the unveiling of the Voortrekker monument at the end of 1949 could not hide his alienation from the dominant mood or the decline of his party. Nevertheless, despite ill health he continued his parliamentary and public commitments. On 29 May 1950, a week after the public celebration of his eightieth birthday in Johannesburg and Pretoria, he suffered a coronary thrombosis. He died of a subsequent attack at Doornkloof, Irene, near Pretoria, on 11 September 1950, and was buried at Pretoria on 16 September. An era in the history of South Africa was over.

More than any other twentieth-century politician, Smuts shaped the destiny and character of the Union of South Africa in the first half of the twentieth century, establishing its constitutional basis, legislative and administrative framework, and international profile. Despite a profound attachment to the physical landscape of South Africa, however, he frequently found his own country and its politics too cramped for his talents. He was always less popular as a politician in the Union, where he was seen as aloof, authoritarian, and somehow less than trustworthy than he was internationally, where he was acclaimed as a scholar, statesman, and soldier.

In South Africa in his lifetime Smuts was reviled by Afrikaner nationalists as the 'handyman of empire', and by South Africa's white workers as a 'lackey of capitalism'; in the apartheid era he was largely forgotten. Outside South Africa, since his death, his overt belief in white supremacy and refusal to accept South Africa's majority black population as fellow citizens greatly tarnished his image. To a post-imperial generation the speeches and writings which struck his contemporaries as profound frequently appear overblown or even banal, while his philosophy of holism seems less than persuasive. Apart from Sir Keith Hancock's magisterial biography published in the 1960s, Smuts has been relatively neglected since death. In the late 1990s, however, as white South Africans once more faced the wider world, and with growing interest among scholars in colonial nationalism, white identity, and the history of race and science, this extraordinarily complex and multifaceted individual was attracting renewed attention. SHULA MARKS

Sources W. K. Hancock, *Smuts*, 2 vols. (1962–8) • *Selections from the Smuts papers*, ed. W. K. Hancock and J. van der Poel, 7 vols. (1966–73), vols. 1–7 • S. G. Millin, *General Smuts*, 2 vols. (1936) • B. Friedman, *Smuts: a reappraisal* (1975) • J. C. Smuts, *Jan Christian Smuts* (1952) • H. C. Armstrong, *Grey steel (J. C. Smuts): a study in arrogance* (1939) • K. Ingham, *Jan Christian Smuts: the conscience of a South African* (1986) • S. C. Crafford, *Jan Smuts: a biography* (1943) • P. Beukes, *The holistic Smuts: a study in personality* (1989) • P. Beukes, *The religious Smuts* (1994) • B. K. Long, *In Smuts's camp* (1945) • P. Meiring, *Smuts the patriot* (1975) • J. C. Smuts, *Africa and some world problems* (1930) • J. V. d. P[oel] and S. I. M. du P[lessis], 'Smuts, Jan Christiaan', *DSAB* • D. Yudelman, *The emergence of modern South Africa: state, capital and the incorporation of organized labor on the South African gold fields, 1902–1939* (1983) • H. J. Simons and R. E. Simons, *Class and colour in South Africa, 1850–1950* (1969)

Archives CUL, microfilm • National Archives of South Africa, MSS • Transvaal Museum, orders, decorations, city freedoms and other honours • U. Lond., Institute of Commonwealth Studies, corresp. | BL, corresp. with Lord Cecil, Add. MS 51076 • BL, corresp. with Lord Herbert Gladstone, Add. MS 46008 • Bodl. Oxf., corresp. with Lionel Curtis • Bodl. Oxf., corresp. with H. A. L. Fisher • Bodl. Oxf., corresp. with Gilbert Murray • Bodl. Oxf., Round Table corresp. • Bodl. RH, corresp. with Sir Graham Bower • CAC Cam., corresp. with J. H. Roskill • CUL, corresp. with Mrs M. C. Gillett, etc. [copies] • CUL, corresp. with Lord Hardinge • Duke U., letters to J. H. V. Crowe • HLRO, letters to David Lloyd George • HLRO, corresp. with Andrew Bonar Law • HLRO, letters to Herbert Samuel • IWM, letters to G. N. Barnes • JRL, corresp. with Sir Claude Auchinleck • NA Scot., corresp. with Lord Lothian • NAM, corresp. with Sir James Stewart • National Library of South Africa, Cape Town, J. X. Merriman MSS • Rhodes University, Grahamstown, South Africa, Cory Library for Historical Research, corresp. with Francis Carey Slater • U. Birm. L., corresp. with Francis Brett Young • University of Cape Town, corresp. with Patrick Duncan | FILM BFI NFTVA, current affairs footage • BFI NFTVA, documentary footage • BFI NFTVA, news footage • IWM FVA, documentary footage • IWM FVA, news footage • IWM FVA, record footage | SOUND IWM SA, oral history talk • IWM SA, recorded talk

Likenesses F. Dodd, charcoal and watercolour drawing, 1917, IWM • Elliott & Fry, photograph, 1917, NPG [*see illus.*] • W. Orpen, oils, *c*.1917–1919, University of Cape Town • W. Stoneman, three photographs, 1917–47, NPG • W. Orpen, group portrait, oils, *c*.1918–1919 (*A peace conference at the Quai d'Orsay*), IWM • J. S. Sargent, oils, *c*.1920, NPG • J. S. Sargent, group portrait, oils, 1922 (*General officers of World War I*), NPG • W. Nicholson, oils, 1923, FM Cam. • J. B. Leighton, oils, 1924, Palace of Westminster, London • A. Jones, oils, *c*.1933, Royal Commonwealth Society, London • Saks, charcoal, 1937, Pretoria city council • H. Coster, photograph, 1941, NPG • F. D. Oerder, oils, 1941, Pretoria city council • S. Elwes, oils, *c*.1943, National Art Gallery, Cape Town • Y. Karsh, photograph, 1943, NPG • J. Bodley, oils, 1949, Bodl. RH • M. Kottler, bronze bust, 1949, NPG • J. S. Sargent, oil study, 1954, NPG • J. Epstein, bronze statue, 1956, Parliament Square, London • D. de Jager, plaster cast, 1962, University of Cape Town • J. M. Coplans, bronze bust, Africana Museum, Johannesburg • S. Harpley, bust, Cape Town • S. Harpley, statues, Public Gardens, Cape Town • S. Harpley, statues, Durban • M. Kottler, bust, Johannesburg • W. Leneke, oils, Pretoria • N. Lewis, oils, Johannesburg • W. Nicholson, oils, Johannesburg Art Gallery • F. D. Oerder, oils, Pretoria Club, Pretoria • A. Pan, oils, Christ's College, Cambridge • A. Pan, oils, South Africa House, London; version, Christ's College, Cambridge • J. Penn, bust, Johannesburg • W. Rothenstein, chalk drawing, NPG • E. Roworth, oils, Cape Town • Roworth, portrait, University of Cape Town • F. O. Salisbury, oils, U. St Andr. • J. Tweed, bronze bust, Africana Museum, Johannesburg • F. Wiles, oils, Houses of Parliament, Cape Town • D. van Zyl, portrait, Bovenplaats, Riebeeck West • caricatures, University of Cape Town, C. J. Sibbert collection

Smyllie, Robert Maire (1893–1954), newspaper editor, was born on 20 March 1893 at 6 Hill Street, Shettleton, Glasgow, the first son and eldest of five children (four boys, one girl) of Robert Smyllie and Elisabeth Follis. His father, though possibly Scottish-born, was then a resident of Sligo, where he worked as a printer; later he became editor/proprietor of the *Sligo Times*. His mother was from co. Cork, and they had married in Sligo on 20 July 1892. The family was adventurous: two of his brothers served in Burma with the British forces; one of them, Walker, was later imprisoned in Britain for IRA activities.

Smyllie was Presbyterian: he went to the local protestant grammar school from 1906 to 1911, when he entered Trinity College, Dublin. He never completed his university career, leaving Trinity in the summer of 1913. In the following year, working as tutor to the children of an American family in Germany, he was caught up in the outbreak of the First World War and was interned in the Ruhleben camp near Berlin for the duration of the hostilities. His time in captivity was spent profitably in reading and in acquiring a deep knowledge of the German language and customs, which later informed his abiding dislike of fascism. Released in 1918, he talked his way into being hired by the *Irish Times* to report the Paris Peace Conference, securing a personal interview with Lloyd George. Two years later he became involved with the editor, James Healy, as secretary of a group which tried unsuccessfully to negotiate in the Anglo-Irish conflict. In 1925 he married Kathlyn Reid, the oldest of three daughters of a landowner from Summerhill, co. Meath: they had no children.

Smyllie's position with the *Irish Times* was secured by his journalistic exploits. These included a noteworthy scoop as a result of which his paper was able to publish the details of a proposed new free state government involving Fianna Fáil and the Labour Party immediately after the 1927 election: Smyllie, seeing labour leaders leaving a hotel where they had been having private discussions, pieced his story together from the contents of the wastepaper basket in their meeting room. In 1927 he inaugurated a new feature—the 'Irishman's diary', which he wrote under a pseudonym, and which is still a feature of the paper. He travelled widely for the paper, particularly in the early 1930s, and by 1934, when Healy died, was seen as his natural successor. As editor, he contributed a widely read weekly column under the pseudonym Nichevo.

Whereas Healy had been a unionist of the old school who had learnt with some difficulty to come to terms with the new Irish constitutional and political arrangements, Smyllie edited the *Irish Times* as an enthusiastic insider in the free state. His most productive period as editor was probably from 1934 to 1945, when he fashioned the *Irish Times* into a paper which promoted cultural liberalism as well as political independence. As editor, he continued to travel widely, and his reportage on pre-war Czechoslovakia earned him one of that country's highest awards, the order of the White Lion of Czechoslovakia, conferred on him in 1939, and the last such honour conferred by that government before the Nazi invasion. During the war itself he fought the sometimes inane government censorship policies with energy and flair. Throughout his period as editor he was also the Dublin correspondent of the London *Times*, which supplemented his meagre editorial salary; during the war, this dual role made him an important confidant of British diplomats in Dublin.

The post-war years were less exciting. His health began to fail, and he moved from Dublin to Delgany in co. Wicklow, his editorial role still colourful but less effective than before. He died of heart failure in the Adelaide Hospital, Dublin, on 11 September 1954, and was buried in Mount Jerome cemetery on 14 September. His widow died in March 1974. JOHN HORGAN

Sources personal knowledge (2004) · T. Gray, *Mr Smyllie, Sir!* (1991) · *Irish Times* (13 Sept 1954) · *Irish Press* (14 Sept 1954) · b. cert. · d. cert.

Likenesses W. Conor, oils, *c.*1945, *Irish Times*, 13–15 D'Olier Street, Dublin

Wealth at death £3581: probate, 28 Jan 1955, *CGPLA Éire*

Smyly [*née* Franks], **Ellen** (1815–1901), philanthropist, was probably born in Dublin, the third daughter of Matthew Franks of Merrion Square, Dublin, and Jerpoint Hill, Thomastown, co. Kilkenny. Little is known of her early life. In 1834 she married Josiah Smyly (1804–1864), a surgeon at the Meath Hospital in Dublin and later vice-president of the Royal College of Surgeons in Ireland. The couple had twelve children, four sons, including Philip Crampton *Smyly, and eight daughters, of whom two died in infancy.

Smyly is best known for her philanthropic work with children. When she was seventeen she engaged in home and hospital visitation of the poor in Dublin, inspired by religious idealism. Her granddaughter later claimed that Smyly 'seemed to hear a voice insistently saying to her "Take these children and nurse them for Me"' (Smyly, 4). She opened her first Bible school in a disused forge in Harmony Row, near Grand Canal Street, about 1850. Smyly was active at a time when the evangelical missionary movement had been revitalized in Ireland, particularly in Dublin, and she became a close friend of Alexander Dallas, founder of the Irish Church Missions. The Irish Church Missions, which aimed to 'communicate the gospel to the Roman Catholics and Converts of Ireland', was a highly organized society which claimed fifty-one local committees in Ireland by 1854. Proselytizing activities made the mission controversial and aroused the ire of Catholics, both clerical and lay. Nevertheless, it was in conjunction with Dallas that Smyly began her day schools in Dublin, which operated in Townsend Street, Grand Canal Street, The Coombe, Lurgan Street, and Luke Street. Each school had its own committee but the same members sat on several of the committees. Smyly and her daughters Ellen, Annie, and Harriet taught in the schools, and, in order to raise money for them, Smyly addressed meetings all over England and Ireland. She also wrote numerous letters and appeals which appeared in newspapers. Thomas Barnardo (1845–1905) became a close friend and was very much influenced by Smyly's work, going on to establish a chain of homes for destitute children in England from 1870.

Once the day schools had been established Smyly opened residential homes in the same areas of Dublin. Working closely with the Irish Church Missions she targeted the very poorest Catholics. She opened an orphanage called the Bird's Nest in 1859 in Kingstown. Here the children were supported from public subscriptions but the teachers were paid by the Irish Church Missions. Smyly also founded the magazine *Erin's Hope*, which was published monthly. She experienced considerable opposition to her enterprises from the Catholic community, and very public battles for 'the souls of children' raged between Catholic and protestant from the pulpits, through the press, and on the street. Ellen Smyly died on 16 May 1901 at her home, 8 Merrion Square, Dublin. She left seven homes and four day schools which were carried on by members of her family. MARIA LUDDY

Sources V. Smyly, *The early history of Mrs Smyly's homes and schools* (*c.*1976) · J. B. Lyons, *Brief lives of Irish doctors* (1978) · M. Luddy, *Women and philanthropy in nineteenth-century Ireland* (1995) · A. Dallas, *The story of the Irish Church Missions continued to 1869* (1875)

Likenesses portrait (in old age), repro. in Smyly, *The early history of Mrs Smyly's homes*

Wealth at death £5292 3*s.* 3*d.*: probate, 18 Oct 1901, *CGPLA Ire.*

Smyly, Sir Philip Crampton (1838–1904), surgeon and laryngologist, was born at 8 Ely Place, Dublin, on 17 June 1838, the eldest son in the family of four sons and eight daughters of Josiah Smyly (1804–1864), a Dublin surgeon, and his wife, Ellen *Smyly (1815–1901), third daughter of Matthew Franks, of Jerpoint Hill, Thomastown, co. Kilkenny. His mother devoted herself to philanthropic work in Dublin, founding and maintaining many schools for poor children. His grandfather, John Smyly KC, a member of the Irish bar, came from a family settled in the north of Ireland from the sixteenth century. A younger brother, Sir William Josiah Smyly, was a distinguished obstetrician and gynaecologist in Dublin. A sister, Louisa Katharine, married Robert Stewart, a missionary to Hwa-Sang, China, where they were both murdered in 1892.

Philip Smyly was educated at home and apprenticed at fifteen to his great-uncle Sir Philip Crampton, and after the latter's death in 1858, to Professor William Henry Porter. During his apprenticeship he attended lectures at Trinity College, Dublin, the Royal College of Surgeons in Ireland, and the Meath Hospital. In 1854 he entered Trinity College, and in 1859 he graduated BA, winning a junior moderatorship and silver medal in experimental and natural science. The following year he proceeded MB, and obtained the licence of the College of Physicians in Ireland. After some months' study in Berlin and Vienna he returned home, and in 1861 was appointed successor to Porter as surgeon to the Meath Hospital, his father being one of his colleagues. This post he retained until his death. In 1863 he graduated MD and was admitted FRCS Ireland.

Smyly married on 1 February 1864 Selina Maria, sixth daughter of John Span Plunket, third Baron Plunket, sister of William Conyngham Plunket, fourth baron (1828–1897), archbishop of Dublin, and of David, first Baron

Rathmore; they had three sons and five daughters. Their eldest son, Sir Philip Crampton (knighted in 1905), became chief justice of Sierra Leone, and his second son, Gilbert Josiah, was professor of Latin in Trinity College, Dublin.

Smyly was a member of the staff of the chief secretary for Ireland from 1869 to 1892. He was president of the Royal College of Surgeons in Ireland in 1878–9, and from 1893 to 1900 he represented that college on the General Medical Council. He was knighted in 1892 and was appointed surgeon-in-ordinary to Queen Victoria in Ireland in 1895, and on her death in 1901, honorary surgeon in Ireland to Edward VII. He received the household medal in 1897 and the Coronation Medal in 1902. He was president of the Laryngological Association of Great Britain in 1889, of the Irish Medical Association in 1900, and of the Irish Medical Schools and Graduates' Association in 1902. He was consulting surgeon to the Hospital for Diseases of the Throat and Ear, the Children's Hospital, Harcourt Street, and the Rotunda Hospital, all in Dublin.

Smyly, though he always practised general surgery, was specially interested in the new field of laryngology. He introduced the laryngoscope to Ireland in 1860 as well as inventing a number of specialized surgical instruments. He also took special interest in abdominal and urethral surgery. He published little except for occasional lectures, and notes read before surgical societies.

A generous and courteous man, he had a large practice which, though lucrative, included those unable to pay. He enjoyed music, and played the violin well. At the time of his death he was president of the Hibernian Catch Club. He obtained high rank in freemasonry. He died suddenly from cerebral haemorrhage on 8 April 1904, at his home at 4 Merrion Square, Dublin, and was buried in Mount Jerome cemetery, Dublin. He was survived by his wife.

R. J. ROWLETTE, *rev.* HUGH SERIES

Sources *BMJ* (16 April 1904), 925–6 • 'Sir Philip Crampton Smyly: honorary surgeon to the king', *The Lancet* (23 April 1904), 1167–8 • *CGPLA Ire.* (1904) • *WWW*

Likenesses T. Jones, portrait, 1876; formerly in possession of his wife, 1912 • photograph, repro. in 'Sir Philip Crampton Smyly', *The Lancet* • photograph, repro. in 'Sir Philip Crampton Smyly', *BMJ*

Wealth at death £7621 16*s.* 11*d.*: probate, 2 June 1904, *CGPLA Ire.* • £879 16*s.* 11*d.*—effects in England: Irish probate sealed in London, 10 June 1904, *CGPLA Eng. & Wales*

Smyth. *See also* Smith, Smythe.

Smyth family (*per. c.*1500–1680), gentry, of Long Ashton, originated at Aylburton in the Forest of Dean, but rose to wealth and the possession of a large landed estate through trade from the port of Bristol during the first half of the sixteenth century. **Matthew Smyth** (*d.* 1526) and his brother Thomas Smyth (*d.* 1542) came to Bristol from Aylburton *c.*1500 and worked as 'hoopers', or the makers of bands for casks. They also engaged in trade, exporting small quantities of cloth and importing wine and fish. Both prospered, and by the time of his death Thomas had purchased land at Shirehampton near Bristol, as well as

Sir Hugh Smyth, first baronet (1632–1680), by Samuel Cooper

property within the town. It was the elder brother, Matthew, who began to lay the foundations of the family's fortune. He married Alice John, daughter and heir of a Bristol merchant, Lewis John, and soon prospered as a merchant himself. In a lay subsidy of 1524 he was listed among the wealthy merchants in the town and assessed at £16. A measure of his success is the fact that his daughter, Elizabeth, married Thomas Phelips, a member of a rapidly rising family of Dorset lawyers. Their youngest son, Edward *Phelips, was to be a highly successful lawyer, speaker of the House of Commons in 1604, master of the rolls in 1611, and the builder of Montacute House, Somerset.

After Matthew Smyth's death in 1526 his widow, Alice, continued to trade profitably on her own account, purchasing wool and yarn, exporting cloth to France and Spain, and importing wine, oil, iron, woad, and alum. Their only son, John *Smyth (*d.* 1556), achieved outstanding success as a merchant and thus completed the rise of the family to the position of landed gentry. His ledger or account book survives for the years 1538–50 and gives details of his many fruitful trading ventures. He traded in woollen cloth, purchased in Gloucestershire, Wiltshire, and Somerset, lead from the Mendip hills, hides, leather, timber, and wheat. Numerous cargoes were exported to France and Spain in his own ship *The Trinity*, which returned with wine, iron, woad, alum, and oil. The impression of Smyth which emerges from his ledger is of an able, hard-working, public-spirited man. He served as sheriff of Bristol during 1532–3 and as mayor in 1547–8 and 1554–5. As mayor he was involved in the acquisition of former chantry lands and property by the corporation, purchases from which Bristol was to derive a substantial income in the future. He invested in extensive lands in north Somerset and south Gloucestershire, among them many former possessions of local monasteries and chantries. By far the most important of these investments was in 1545 when he bought an estate at Long Ashton, near Bristol, from Sir Thomas Arundell for £920. This included the large manor house at Ashton Court with its deer park and much of the surrounding land. By the time of his death in 1556 Smyth was a wealthy man, with a large estate, and his probate inventory lists goods and money to the value of £2263. He evidently regarded himself primarily as a Bristol merchant, and continued until his death to live in his merchant's house in Small Street rather than the manor house at Ashton Court.

Smyth married his wife, Joan, in 1529, but she remains a shadowy figure and her origins and maiden name are uncertain (she may have been a member of the Dowding family). They had two sons, **Hugh Smyth** (1530–1580) and **Matthew Smyth** (1533–1583). John evidently had high aspirations for his sons, and they were expected to adopt a lifestyle quite unlike his. Both were sent to New College, Oxford, in 1545, when Hugh was fifteen and Matthew only twelve. In 1550 they went on to complete their education at the inns of court in London. The temperament and behaviour of John's sons, especially the elder, however, were very different from that of their sober, hard-working merchant father. There are several references to quarrels, fights, and serious trouble in London in which both were involved, and during 1553–4 John had to use the good offices of his fellow Bristolian Dr George Owen, successively Edward VI's and Mary's physician, to extricate the two youths from some major trouble, at a cost of £40.

In 1553 Hugh returned to Bristol while Matthew entered upon a career in law; he remained as a barrister at the Middle Temple, becoming a prominent member of the society and serving as treasurer from 1570 to 1573. In 1553 Hugh married Maud, younger daughter and joint heir of a Somerset landowner, John Byccombe of Crowcombe. Hugh and his wife resided at Ashton Court. He became a justice of the peace and was increasingly involved in local government in Somerset. As a justice he proved to be most unsatisfactory. His violent disposition did not for long enable him to live at peace with his neighbours, and there were numerous complaints to the privy council about his conduct, abuse of his position, and the disorder created by the retainers he kept at Ashton Court who terrorized the neighbourhood. Complaints and warnings continued for several years, and matters culminated in 1578 when Smyth's retainers raided the rabbit warren of his neighbour Sir George Norton of Abbots Leigh. They were interrupted in their night raid by two of Norton's men, and in the ensuing struggle one of Smyth's men was mortally wounded. The affair was sufficiently serious for it to come to the attention of the queen and privy council, and all the parties were summoned to London for trial. While in London, Smyth's health deteriorated rapidly and he died on 2 March 1580. He was buried in the church of St Sepulchre in London, but in 1581 his body was disinterred for a sumptuous second funeral at Long Ashton church which cost £243.

Hugh had no male heir and all his property passed to his brother, Matthew, who was still in practice as a barrister. Matthew had married Jane, daughter of Thomas Tewther of Ludlow, and they had one son, **Sir Hugh Smyth** (1575–1627). The family moved to Ashton Court and Matthew threw himself with enthusiasm into the work of running the estate. He did not long enjoy his new status, however, and died in 1583. His widow managed the estate with energy and efficiency on her son's behalf until her death in 1594.

Under Sir Hugh, who came of age in 1596, the family completed the journey into the ranks of the major Somerset landowning gentry. In 1603 he was one of those gentlemen who were knighted by James VI and I on his progress from Scotland to London, and in 1605 he was chosen to accompany the earl of Hertford on an embassy to the archduke of Austria. He continued the policy of buying land and purchased the Great House, which had been built on the site of the former Carmelite friary in central Bristol, where the family lived for part of each year. Smyth's wealth and position were also recognized in 1604 by his marriage to Elizabeth, eldest daughter of Sir Thomas Gorges of Longford Castle, near Salisbury, which brought the Smyths into an alliance with a family of great wealth and numerous influential connections. The marriage was not a happy one, however, for Smyth was a difficult, melancholy man, preoccupied with his own health and reluctant to receive visitors. His only interests appear to have been horse breeding and the latest London fashions, and his correspondence is full of both subjects. He took little part in local affairs. He and his wife had five daughters and one son, **Thomas Smyth** (1609–1642). In 1622 at the age of thirteen Thomas was sent to St John's College, Oxford. The correspondence between him and his mother, as well as the reports from his private tutor, Thomas Atkinson, provide much information about contemporary life and education. He remained at Oxford until 1626. In 1627, three days before his father's death, he married Florence, daughter of Lord Poulett of Hinton St George. Shortly afterwards, through his father-in-law's influence and in spite of his youth, Smyth became MP for Bridgwater. During the next few years he was also active in local affairs as a justice of the peace and member of several county committees. His exchanges with his bailiff and carefully kept account books make it clear that he took a close interest in the management of his estate; in the 1630s he built a large new wing on to Ashton Court. His household consisted of thirty-seven persons, including a jester.

Smyth had a wide circle of friends, and his correspondence reveals his affable temperament and popularity. The continuing involvement of the family with Bristol was recognized in 1641 when he was granted the freedom of the city. His letters and household and estate records give a detailed account of contemporary events and political affairs, as well as of the running of the estate and the building work at Ashton Court. In 1636 the estate was said to provide an annual income of £2000.

Like his father-in-law, Lord Poulett, and his mother's second husband, Sir Ferdinando Gorges, Smyth was a supporter of the royalist cause. When the civil war began, he and Gorges raised a troop of horse. They took part in a skirmish at Shepton Mallet and in September 1642 were besieged in Sherborne Castle. Compelled to surrender by a superior parliamentary force, they marched to Minehead and crossed to Cardiff. Here Smyth contracted smallpox and died in October 1642. His body was brought back to Ashton Court by Gorges. Smyth and his wife, Florence, had three daughters and two sons, **Sir Hugh Smyth**, first baronet (1632–1680), and Thomas, who was born soon after his father's death. Hugh was ten years old when his father died, and as prominent royalists the Smyths remained under suspicion throughout the next few years. Hugh was obliged to remain quietly at Ashton Court or at the nearby Poulett mansion at Court de Wick. His mother married an Irish soldier of fortune, Colonel Thomas Pigott, in 1647 and lived until 1676. In 1654, soon after he came of age, Hugh's royalist connections were further strengthened by his marriage to Ann, daughter of John Ashburnham of Ashburnham, Sussex, who had been one of the late king's inner circle.

The Restoration in 1660 enabled Hugh to resume his father's tradition of public service. He rapidly became a JP, deputy lieutenant of Somerset, colonel of the militia, and member of parliament for Somerset. In 1661 he was created a baronet, the first member of the family to achieve this honour. His voluminous correspondence, which was carefully preserved in the muniment room at Ashton Court, reveals his involvement in all aspects of local affairs, both in Somerset and in Bristol. He became sheriff of Somerset in 1665 and during the next few years was zealous in imposing the new regime, prosecuting dissenters, and collecting taxes. At the same time he was also supervising the affairs of the large landed estate centred upon Ashton Court. He and Ann had three sons and three daughters. Smyth died on 28 July 1680 at the age of forty-eight. His death was sudden and apparently unexpected, and the family correspondence provides no explanation. He was buried in the family vault at Long Ashton. His eldest son, Sir John Smyth (1659–1726), succeeded to the estates and the baronetcy, and the family continued to live at Ashton Court until 1946. Soon afterwards the estates were dispersed and the contents of the house were sold at auction; in 1959 the house and parkland were acquired by Bristol corporation. J. H. Bettey

Sources J. H. Bettey, *The rise of a gentry family, the Smyths of Ashton Court, c. 1500–1642* (1978) • *The ledger of John Smythe, 1538–1550*, ed. J. Vanes, Bristol RS, 28 (1974) • J. H. Bettey, ed., *Correspondence of the Smyth family of Ashton Court, 1548–1642*, Bristol RS, 35 (1982) • L. U. Way, 'The Smyths of Ashton Court', *Transactions of the Bristol and Gloucestershire Archaeological Society*, 31 (1908), 230–44 • Bristol RO, Ashton Court MSS, AC/F1; AC/F1/1, 4; AC/F2; AC/F7/1–7; AC/F8/1, 12; AC/C4; AC/C18/1–10; AC/C34; AC/C42/1–3; AC/C44/1–4; AC/C48/1–29; AC/C52/1–2; AC/C60/1–22; AC/S1/1a; 36074/2, 3, 46, 68, 72, 73, 74, 76, 78, 79, 140, 156, 158

Likenesses S. Cooper, miniature (Sir Hugh Smyth), priv. coll. [*see illus.*] • S. Cooper, portrait (Sir Hugh Smyth), Courtauld Inst. • portrait (Sir Hugh Smyth and his wife, Elizabeth Gorges), Bristol City Museum and Art Gallery • portrait (Thomas Smyth as a child), Leeds Castle, Maidstone, Kent • portrait (Thomas Smyth as an adult), Weston-super-Mare Art Gallery

Smyth, Agnes (1754/5–1783). *See under* Smyth, Edward (*fl.* 1764–1790).

Smyth, Charles Piazzi (1819–1900), astronomer, was born at Naples, Italy, on 3 January 1819, the second of the nine children of William Henry *Smyth (1788–1865), a naval officer and highly regarded amateur astronomer, and his wife, Annarella Warington (1788–1873), the daughter of the British consul to the kingdom of the Two Sicilies. Sir Warington Wilkinson *Smyth and Sir Henry Augustus *Smyth were his brothers. His godfather, from whom he received his middle name, was the famous Sicilian astronomer Giuseppe Piazzi. The young Charles was inspired by this connection, and when he grew up chose to be known as Piazzi to his family and to couple that name with his surname. He was educated at Bedford grammar school until the age of sixteen, when, in spite of his youth, he was appointed assistant to his father's friend Thomas Maclear, HM astronomer at the Royal Observatory, Cape of Good Hope. Maclear, who needed a hard-working, robust observer, was ideally served by his enthusiastic young assistant, who had learned the skills of a practical astronomer at his father's side. Smyth spent ten years in southern Africa working in positional astronomy and in arduous geodetic surveys of the province. Encouraged by John Herschel, he experimented in early photography and in 1843 succeeded in producing the oldest known calotypes of people and scenes in southern Africa.

Astronomer royal for Scotland In 1846 Piazzi Smyth was appointed—not without parental intervention—to the post of astronomer royal for Scotland and regius professor of astronomy at the University of Edinburgh in succession to Thomas Henderson. He thus gained an impressive title but little else. The Royal Observatory building on the city's Calton Hill was in a sad state of neglect, and, worse, there was a huge accumulation of stellar observations left unreduced by his predecessor. Piazzi Smyth felt duty-bound to complete and publish Henderson's observations, a task that occupied him and his sole assistant for five years, before embarking on an observational programme of his own. This was an ambitious, but ultimately futile, search for stellar motions over several decades. In the early years he introduced a much-needed time service for Edinburgh by erecting a time ball on the nearby Nelson monument and later, in 1861, a time gun fired daily from Edinburgh Castle.

On Christmas eve 1855 Piazzi Smyth married Jessie Duncan (1815–1896), a cultivated Scottish lady who became her husband's devoted assistant in his many scientific endeavours. The first and most important of these was their expedition to Tenerife in 1856. The brilliance of the night sky above the mountains of southern Africa had convinced Piazzi Smyth that the future of astronomy lay in seeking out Isaac Newton's 'serene air above the grosser clouds'. He obtained a grant of £500 from the Admiralty and sailed with his wife in a yacht provided by Robert Stephenson to Tenerife to make the first ever systematic examination of a potential astronomical site. After ascending the peak he made thorough measurements of sky transparency, star-image quality, and intensity of solar radiation at altitudes up to 3200 metres. His results, bearing out his expectations, were published in an official report to the Admiralty (1859) and in a popular account, *Teneriffe, an Astronomer's Experiment* (1858), illustrated by a selection of Piazzi Smyth's own stereo-photographs and believed to be the first book ever illustrated in this way. On the strength of this work he was elected a fellow of the Royal Society in 1857.

'Pyramidology' Piazzi Smyth's next major undertaking was of a very different kind: a survey of the great pyramid of Giza in 1865. His declared motive was connected with an official proposal of 1864 to introduce the French metric system into Britain. The move, supported by most scientists, was opposed by John Herschel, who campaigned in favour of the British inch as a basic unit of length. Piazzi Smyth, who was at one with Herschel, allowed himself to be seduced by a claim then in circulation that the British standard was associated with the sacred cubit of the Bible, a measure allegedly incorporated in the pyramid. That edifice was asserted to be a monument enshrining basic scientific information built under divine guidance by the ancient Israelites—an idea that appealed to Piazzi Smyth, an evangelical Christian. Piazzi Smyth's survey, a prodigious piece of work, was published by the Royal Society of Edinburgh. His misguided interpretation of the data, however, cast a major shadow on his scientific reputation and eventually led to his unprecedented resignation from the Royal Society. His lack of proper mathematical training and his inability to distinguish real facts from chance coincidences showed only too clearly in his popular book *Our Inheritance in the Great Pyramid* (1864), which, however, was written with panache and drew him a huge cult following. The book went into five editions in his lifetime and was reprinted many years later, in 1979.

Spectroscopy Piazzi Smyth now turned his mind to spectroscopy and the 'new astronomy', a term used to denote the area of astronomy later known as astrophysics. After years of pleading he was promised a substantial equatorial telescope for astrophysical research and was given a large official residence which would serve as an extension to the cramped premises on Calton Hill. In this new house on Royal Terrace, where he moved in 1871, Piazzi Smyth set up at his own expense first-rate equipment for solar, auroral, and laboratory spectroscopy. True to his own philosophy, he carried his instruments to favourable sites abroad, including Lisbon and Madeira, his wife, as always, being his assistant. One of his aims, successfully carried out, was to discriminate in the sun's spectrum between absorption lines of purely solar origin and those produced in the earth's atmosphere. Among other researches were studies of the spectra of the aurora (observed from Edinburgh), the zodiacal light (observed from Palermo), and the so-called rainband, due to atmospheric water vapour. In the laboratory he concentrated on the spectra of diatomic molecules and, in collaboration with Alexander Stewart Herschel, deciphered the harmonic structure of the green carbon monoxide band. Unfortunately his continued dabbling in pyramidology and his rift with the London scientific establishment meant that much of this excellent research went unrecognized.

While Piazzi Smyth's private researches flourished, official life at the Royal Observatory deteriorated. The longed-for telescope, delivered by Grubb of Dublin at the end of 1872, turned out to have serious flaws and was never put to use. In his professorial role relations with the university authorities became strained. Funds for the observatory dried up. He had become very deaf and increasingly eccentric. He retired in 1888 at the age of sixty-nine and moved to Ripon in Yorkshire, to Clova, a house large enough to accommodate his scientific apparatus. There he had a new lease of life. He installed a large grating spectrograph for photographic solar spectroscopy and produced a splendid set of ultraviolet solar spectra which was unfortunately never published. He also indulged his lifelong interest in meteorology by securing a series of photographs of cloud formations using a camera of his own design. From these he assembled a magnificent atlas of cloud forms which he presented to his erstwhile antagonist, the Royal Society of London. The large collection of his photographs, his remarkable watercolours, and his journals, records of a long scientific and artistic life, were bequeathed to the Royal Society of Edinburgh. Piazzi Smyth died at his home on 21 February 1900 and was buried beside his wife under a pyramid-shaped tomb in Sharow graveyard, near Ripon. They had no children. HERMANN A. BRÜCK

Sources H. A. Brück and M. T. Brück, *The peripatetic astronomer: the life of Charles Piazzi Smyth* (1988) • B. Warner, *Charles Piazzi Smyth, astronomer-artist: his Cape years, 1835–45* (1983) • H. A. Brück, *The story of astronomy in Edinburgh from its beginnings until 1975* (1983) • *The Scotsman* (26 Dec 1855) • d. cert. • d. cert. [Jessica Smyth] • tomb in Sharow churchyard

Archives NL Scot., notebooks and papers • Royal Observatory, Edinburgh, Piazzi Smyth Archives, corresp. and papers • Royal Society of Edinburgh, Piazzi Smyth bequest [deposited at the Royal Observatory, Edinburgh, with the Piazzi Smyth Archives] | CUL, corresp. with George Airy • CUL, letters to Sir George Stokes • Durban City Library, South Africa • NL Scot., corresp. with Lord Rutherfurd • RAS, letters to Royal Astronomical Society • RAS, letters to Richard Sheepshanks • RGS, letters to Sir David Gill • RS, corresp. with Sir John Herschel • U. Edin. L., letters to David Ramsey Hay • U. Edin. L., letters to John Lee • U. St Andr. L., corresp. with James David and George Forbes

Likenesses C. Piazzi Smyth, self-portrait, sketch, 1847, MHS Oxf. • J. Faed, oils, Royal Society of Edinburgh • photograph, Royal Observatory, Edinburgh • photograph, Royal Observatory, Edinburgh

Wealth at death £24,756 6*s.* 10*d.*: resworn probate, April 1901, *CGPLA Eng. & Wales* (1900)

Smyth, Edward (*c.*1662–1720), Church of Ireland bishop of Down and Connor, born at Lisburn in co. Antrim, was the son of James Smyth of Mountown, co. Down, and his wife, Francisca, daughter of Edward Dowdall of Mountown. After attending Mr Haslam's school, he entered Trinity College, Dublin, in 1676, became a scholar in 1678, and graduated BA in 1681. In 1684 he proceeded MA and was elected a fellow. He afterwards obtained the degrees of LLB in 1687, BD in 1694, and DD in 1696.

In 1689, when Dublin was in the possession of James II, Smyth fled to England, where he was recommended to the Smyrna Company, and made chaplain to their factory at

Smyrna. He returned to England in 1693 with a considerable private fortune, and was appointed chaplain to William III, whom he attended for four years during the war in the Low Countries. There he also attracted the notice of the second duke of Ormond, whose patronage assisted his subsequent preferment. On 3 March 1696 he was made dean of St Patrick's, Dublin. In 1697 he became vice-chancellor of Dublin University, and on 2 April 1699 he was consecrated bishop of Down and Connor. Smyth attended to the problem of dissent and kept Ormond informed of the temper of the local Presbyterians. He was in demand as an official preacher on state occasions in Dublin and at least three of these sermons, in 1698, 1702, and 1703, were printed. In vain he sought translation to Meath. He was elected a fellow of the Royal Society in 1695 and contributed various papers to the *Philosophical Transactions*, chiefly on oriental subjects.

Smyth was related both to Thomas Smyth, bishop of Limerick, and to William Smyth, bishop successively of Raphoe and Kilmore, whose daughter, Elizabeth Smyth, became his first wife. They had two children: Elizabeth, who married James Stopford, first earl of Courtown, and Edward. His second wife, whom he married in Antrim on 20 April 1710, was Mary Skeffington, youngest daughter of Clotworthy Skeffington, third Viscount Massareene, and Rachel Hungerford; they had two sons and a daughter. Smyth died at Bath on 16 October 1720.

E. I. CARLYLE, *rev.* TOBY BARNARD

Sources Burtchaell & Sadleir, *Alum. Dubl.*, 757 • W. King, correspondence, TCD, MS 1995–2008/930/942 • *Calendar of the manuscripts of the marquess of Ormonde*, new ser., 8 vols., HMC, 36 (1902–20), vol. 8, pp. 77–8, 85–6, 136, 173, 274 • BL, Ellis corresp., Add. MS 28927, fols. 134, 175 • *The whole works of Sir James Ware concerning Ireland*, ed. and trans. W. Harris, 2 vols. in 3 (1739–45, [1746]) • Burke, *Gen. GB* • *IGI*

Archives NL Ire., letters to William Smyth

Smyth, Edward (*c.*1745–1812), sculptor, was born in co. Meath, reputedly the son of a stonecutter who went to Dublin about 1750. The younger Smyth was apprenticed to Simon Vierpyl, the English carver taken to Dublin by Lord Charlemont to work on the casino at Marino. In 1772, while employed by Vierpyl, he exhibited a competition-winning model for a statue of the patriot Charles Lucas; the finished piece was installed in the Dublin Royal Exchange in 1779. Smyth next found employment with the stonecutter Henry Darley, carving plaques for chimney pieces and memorials, including the finely wrought memorial to Lieutenant William Dobbs (1780) in Lisburn Cathedral. Darley was a principal contractor at the Dublin custom house (built in 1781–91), where an extensive scheme of ornamental sculpture was proposed by its architect, James Gandon. On Darley's recommendation Smyth made models for the internal decoration of the cupola; these impressed Gandon enough to award Smyth a number of independent commissions for the building, including four sets of the arms of Ireland for which his design was judged superior to a proposal by Agostino Carlini. Smyth's *tour de force*, to carve fourteen keystone heads emblematic of the rivers of Ireland, was aided by the English sculptor Benjamin Schrowder, who settled in Dublin. Smyth also carved two of the figures over the south portico ('Plenty' and 'Industry', damaged by fire in 1921), the statue of 'Commerce' surmounting the dome, and the alto-relievo in the tympanum (after a design by Carlini).

Smyth's subsequent work for Gandon included two keystone heads on Carlisle Bridge (built in 1791–5; the heads were re-erected in the 1880s on a building on Sir John Rogerson's quay); the three statues on the pediment of the House of Lords extension to the Parliament House (built in 1784–9); and internal and external carvings at the Four Courts (built between 1786 and 1802) and the King's Inns (begun in 1800). The work on the Four Courts included five statues above the entrance front and trophies of legal emblems above the gates. Almost all Smyth's figurative stucco-work in the building, including eight medallions of lawgivers and eight allegorical figures on the inner dome, was destroyed in the fire of 1922, just as his plasterwork in the custom house was destroyed a year earlier. Most of his work at the King's Inns is on the west front, where there are three large figurative panels at attic level as well as a pair of caryatidic door-cases. Further statues in stucco adorn the interior of the benchers' dining room. For the executant architect of the King's Inns, Henry Aaron Baker, Smyth had previously carved keystone heads and panels at Bishop's Gate, Derry (1789).

After Gandon's retirement, Smyth was taken up in Dublin by the architect Francis Johnston who commissioned the statue of St Andrew for St Andrew's Church (1803) and the three south pediment statues on the Bank of Ireland (1808). The bank, which had acquired the former Parliament House for conversion, obliged Smyth to work from designs by John Flaxman. At the time of his death in 1812, Smyth was completing work on two other Johnston buildings, the Chapel Royal at Dublin Castle (begun in 1807) and St George's Church, where he had been employed from 1809. At the Chapel Royal he worked on both the exterior (where there are ninety carved heads, as well as several figures) and on the interior stucco-work, being assisted by his eldest son, John.

Individual pieces by Smyth in Dublin include a statue of Earl Temple (1788) in St Patrick's Cathedral, the figure of Hibernia (1798) at the Royal Dublin Society, and busts of William Clement and Thomas Parnell (1789) in Trinity College. A wooden crucifix, commissioned by the inhabitants of Navan, co. Meath, in 1782, is still in the Roman Catholic church there. The Ulster Museum has a pair of marble busts of Francis Johnston and his wife by Smyth. He made at least two sets of wax models of the custom house's riverine heads: twelve heads exhibited in 1802 were subsequently presented to the Royal Hibernian Academy by Gandon, but were destroyed in the 1916 rising; another set survives in the Dublin Civic Museum.

In June 1811 Smyth was appointed master of the Dublin Society school of modelling and sculpture, a post which he held for only a short time. He died suddenly at his house at 36 Montgomery Street on 2 August 1812 and was buried at St Thomas's graveyard, Marlborough Street,

Dublin, two days later. Shy and retiring but sociable among friends, Smyth was the most talented Irish sculptor of his day. However, he had little interest in business matters and left his family 'scantily provided for' (Strickland, 2.390). The name of his wife is not known; they had several children.

John Smyth (*c.*1773–1840), sculptor, who was born in Dublin, studied under his father, Edward Smyth, and enrolled in the Dublin Society's figure-drawing school in 1791. In 1809 he exhibited a bust of King George III, a joint work with his father (now in the National Gallery of Ireland). He executed a number of statues for public buildings in Dublin, including those over the porticoes of the General Post Office (1817) and the Royal College of Surgeons in Ireland (1827), where he also carved the royal arms in the tympanum. He completed his father's work on the Chapel Royal (1814) and succeeded him in the mastership of the Dublin Society's modelling school (1812). His most important piece of stucco-work in Dublin was the *Ascension*, a large figurative composition in the apse of St Mary's, the pro-cathedral (*c.*1823). In St Patrick's Cathedral is a portrait statue of the Rt Hon. George Ogle (*d.* 1814), while three of John Smyth's busts are in the College of Surgeons (George IV; William Dease, 1813; and John Shekleton, 1826). In 1824 he was one of the original associates of the Royal Hibernian Academy. His sons, by his wife, Mary, were William (*b.* 1804) and George (*b.* 1818); they were also sculptors. John Smyth died in March 1840.

D. J. O'DONOGHUE, *rev.* FREDERICK O'DWYER

Sources W. G. Strickland, *A dictionary of Irish artists*, 2 (1913), 383–92 • J. Gandon jun. and T. J. Mulvany, *The life of James Gandon, esq.* (1846) [repr. (1969) ed., M. Craig] • V. B. M. Barrow, 'Edward Smyth', *Dublin Historical Record*, 33 (1979–80), 56–66 • P. Lenehan, 'Edward Smyth, Dublin's sculptor', *GPA Irish Arts Review Yearbook*, 6 (1989–90), 67–76 • H. Potterton, *Irish church monuments, 1570–1880* (1975) • H. G. Leask, 'Dublin custom house: the riverine sculptures', *Journal of the Royal Society of Antiquaries of Ireland*, 75 (1945), 187–94 • H. G. Leask, 'Some less well known works of Edward Smyth, sculptor', *Journal of the Royal Society of Antiquaries of Ireland*, 80 (1950), 73–6 • J. Turpin, *A school of art in Dublin since the eighteenth century: a history of the National College of Art & Design* (1995) • C. P. Curran, 'Mr. Edward Smyth, sculptor, Dublin', *ArchR*, 101 (1947), 67–9 • C. P. Curran, *Dublin decorative plasterwork of the seventeenth and eighteenth centuries* (1967) • A. Crookshank and D. Webb, *Paintings and sculptures in Trinity College, Dublin* (1990) • T. Pope, 'The sculptors, Edward and John Smyth and their works', *Dublin Builder*, 8 (15 Dec 1866), 89 • A. Crookshank and the Knight of Glin [D. Fitzgerald], eds., *Irish portraits, 1660–1860* (1969) [exhibition catalogue, Dublin, London, and Belfast, 14 Aug 1969 – 9 March 1970] • G. Willemson, *The Dublin Society drawing schools students & award winners, 1746–1878* (2000) • burial record, St. Thomas's Church, Dublin

Likenesses J. Comerford, drawing, after 1800 • N. Woodhouse, commemorative medal, *c.*1844 (after J. Comerford), National Museum of Ireland • H. Meyer, stipple (after J. Comerford), NPG; repro. in Strickland, *Dictionary*

Wealth at death family 'scantily provided for': Strickland, *A dictionary*, 390

Smyth, Edward (*fl.* 1764–1790), Methodist preacher, was son of the Revd John Smyth (1697–1781) of co. Limerick, chancellor of Conor, and Anne Drysdale (*c.*1706–1777). His uncle was the archbishop of Dublin, F. A. Smyth. Educated at the University of Glasgow between 1764 and 1770, Smyth was ordained in 1770, which was also the year of his marriage to fifteen-year-old Agnes Higginson, who had been born in Lisburn, the daughter of William Higginson [**Agnes Smyth** [*née* Higginson] (1754/5–1783)]. The couple had five children, three of whom died in childhood. In 1773, disappointed in his hopes of inheriting wealth from his uncle, Edward Smyth took up a curacy in Ballyculter, co. Down. Two years later, following Agnes's introduction to Methodism, he too adopted a much more evangelical approach to religion, attracting large crowds and stimulating revivalist fervour when he preached in local barns. Agnes Smyth, who proved an important influence on her husband's spiritual life, was noted at this time for her 'excessive zeal', disapproving of all frivolous behaviour, adopting plain dress, and, when the opportunity came her way, preaching and leading prayers and hymn singing. Edward Smyth's newly discovered zeal was not, however, appreciated by his patron, Lord Bangor. When the curate publicly admonished Bangor for adultery, he responded by accusing Smyth of erroneous teaching. Smyth was brought to trial in the consistory court of Down, and although the case against him was eventually dismissed, Bishop Trail deprived him of his living in December 1776, and his licence was revoked in 1777.

John Wesley, impressed by Smyth's vigorous and effective preaching, appointed him as a 'general missionary', and when he moved to Bath in 1779 because of his wife's ill health invited him to preach at the chapel there on Sunday evenings. Smyth returned to Ireland for a brief spell and then, in 1782, served as one of Wesley's curates in London. Smyth appears to have been greatly affected by the piety and religious ardour of his wife, Agnes, and her death at Bath on 22 May 1783 must have been a considerable blow. He later married a Miss Dawson, though further details are unknown.

In 1783 Smyth settled in Dublin, where a year later his brother William, a wealthy layman, began the building of the Bethesda Chapel on Dorset Street. At this stage Smyth withdrew from the Methodist itinerancy—his relationship with the connection always somewhat uneasy. In 1778 he had advocated the immediate separation of Methodists from the Church of Ireland, while in Bath his presence caused tensions with the conference appointee, Alexander McNab, resulting in division within the society and McNab's temporary withdrawal. When he was appointed co-chaplain (with John Walker) of Bethesda in 1786 a substantial number of wealthy Dublin Methodists left the local society to join the new congregation. Wesley was aware of the power of Smyth's preaching, referring to him as 'a son of thunder' (*Letters*, 7.209), and he himself preached at Bethesda on several occasions. He was also aware of Smyth's propensity for conflict, however, writing to his brother Charles, 'I doubt Edward "needs a bridle"; but who can put the bit into his mouth?' (ibid., 7.324).

Smyth was the author of several religious pamphlets, including a vigorous defence of his actions at Ballyculter, *An Account of the Trial of Edward Smyth* (1777), and while at Bethesda he also compiled a hymnbook and a prayer book revision. By 1790, however, Wesley was noting a decline in

Smyth's popularity, and he subsequently moved to Manchester, where he became curate of St Clement's and St Luke's, after which no further information is known of his life. Edward Smyth's zealous evangelicalism, interpreted by some as spiritual arrogance, had the power both to alienate and attract. The daughter of his first public opponent, the Hon. Sophia Ward of Bangor, was an early convert, and despite Lord Bangor's wholehearted opposition subsequently bequeathed virtually her whole estate to religious and charitable organizations. The Bethesda Chapel, to which he introduced a Wesleyan element, was to become an important focus of evangelical activity in Dublin. Smyth's religious career reflects some of the tensions both within early Methodism and between the connection and the Church of Ireland, and demonstrates the potential of early evangelical activity for both progress and disruption. MYRTLE HILL

Sources R. Roddie, 'List of (Wesleyan) Methodist preachers and stations', Wesleyan Historical Society, Aldersgate House, Belfast • C. H. Crookshank, *History of Methodism in Ireland*, 3 vols. (1885–8) • *Clergy of Down and Dromore* (1996) • *The journal of the Rev. John Wesley*, ed. N. Curnock and others, 8 vols. (1909–16) • *The letters of the Rev. John Wesley*, ed. J. Telford, 8 vols. (1931) • C. H. Crookshank, *Memorable women of Irish Methodism in the last century* (1882) • J. B. Leslie, ed., *Clergy of Connor: from Patrician times to the present day* (1993)

Smyth, Dame Ethel Mary (1858–1944), composer, writer, and suffragist, was born on 22 April 1858 at 5 Lower Seymour Street, London, the fourth of the eight children of Major-General John Hall Smyth (1815–1894) and his wife, Emma, also known as Nina (1824?–1891), the daughter of Charles and Emma Struth, later Reece. She grew up loving sport and a hearty outdoor life, at her first home in Sidcup, Kent, and from 1867 in Frimley, Surrey. A keen hunter and tennis player from her youth, she took up cycling before it was quite respectable and remained an ardent golfer into old age. Music did not play a large part in her upbringing, although she sang and played like any young girl of good family and was also conscious of a growing interest in music. She first became aware of her musical vocation in 1870, under the influence of a governess who had studied at the Leipzig conservatory. She was educated at home, with her five sisters, but was sent to school in Putney between 1872 and 1875. In spite of musical activities at school, she did not really begin to develop her talent until she returned to Frimley and received tuition from Alexander Ewing. This new friend and mentor encouraged her musical aspirations, while his wife, Juliana, foretold an author's career for their enthusiastic pupil. The fruitful contact was brought to an abrupt end by General Smyth's distrust of Ewing, but Smyth had already made up her mind to study composition in Leipzig.

Early musical and romantic life With her goal set, Smyth chafed at the social obligations of a marriageable young woman. She had tacit support from her mother, but quarrelled violently with her disapproving father and eventually resorted to militant tactics, locking herself in her room and refusing to attend social engagements. General Smyth finally agreed to her demand and she set off for

Dame Ethel Mary Smyth (1858–1944), by John Singer Sargent, 1901

Leipzig in July 1877. This was indeed a victory for a young woman of her class.

At the Leipzig conservatory Smyth found both staff and students dull and uninspiring, and after less than a year she abandoned this institution to study privately with the composer Heinrich von Herzogenberg (1843–1900), from whom she gained a solid background in harmony and counterpoint. Herzogenberg's wife, Lisl, became Smyth's first great love and the two women grew very close; between 1878 and 1885 Smyth became a *de facto* member of the childless Herzogenberg household. Throughout her life Smyth engaged in passionate relationships with women; she wrote openly about these relationships in her published memoirs, stating that: 'from the first my most ardent sentiments were bestowed on members of my own sex' (*Impressions that Remained*, 1.79). The Herzogenbergs were respected members of German musical society, and close friends with Brahms. Through them Smyth was introduced into elevated musical circles, and, with her warm and outgoing nature, she made many friends in Leipzig. She thought the Germans the most musical of races and her acquaintance with eminent German performers and conductors was beneficial throughout her compositional career.

Smyth spent summers at home in England, and also began to travel in Europe. She spent the winter of 1882–3 in Florence, where she met Lisl Herzogenberg's sister Julia and her husband, Henry Brewster (1850–1908), an American writer and philosopher who had grown up in France. She returned to Italy the following winter and found herself reciprocating Brewster's growing affection for her, although she tried to act honourably by breaking off all contact with him. Despite this renunciation, Lisl's loyalties were torn, and in 1885 she severed all contact with Smyth. This rupture of a relationship that had dominated Smyth's life for seven years caused her great anguish, and they were still unreconciled when Lisl died in 1892. It was not until after Julia's death in 1895 that Smyth and Brewster were able to pursue their relationship more openly, although they had met again in 1890. They neither married nor had children, and retained separate homes—she in England, he in Italy—but Brewster was a stable presence in Smyth's often stormy life until his death in 1908, his importance to her unaltered by her concurrent relationships with women. 'Harry was never jealous of my women friends, in fact he held, as I do, that every new affection that comes into your life enriches older ties' (*What Happened Next*, 253). She possessed, apart from her 'passions', a great gift for friendship, testified to by her voluminous correspondence.

An emerging composer Smyth began to make a name for herself as a composer during her Leipzig years, writing lieder, piano music, and works for a variety of chamber ensembles in a style strongly influenced by the Brahmsian tradition; many of these were performed privately, but her violin sonata (op. 7, 1887) and a string quintet (op. 1, 1883) were played publicly at the Leipzig Gewandhaus. She felt musically isolated when in the late 1880s she returned to England, where no one knew of her German success. She launched herself on the English musical scene in 1890 with performances at the Crystal Palace of her *Serenade* (1889) and her *Overture to Antony and Cleopatra* (1889), and excited much interest with the première of her mass (1891) by the Royal Choral Society in 1893. She had been brought up as an Anglican, and had written this work in a period of heightened faith following a religious crisis. Later, however, she claimed that the composition of the mass worked it out of her system, for after its completion in 1891, 'orthodox belief fell away from me, never to return' (*Impressions that Remained*, 2.238). Its music represented Smyth's personal response to central European composers in this genre, including Beethoven, Dvořák, and Brahms.

Patronage and performance Throughout her career Smyth was aided not only by her acquaintances in the music profession but also by a network of influential women. During the late 1880s she had become friendly with her neighbour in Farnborough, the former empress of the French Eugénie, who supported her compositional endeavours in a variety of ways, including funding publication and providing introductions to royalty and aristocracy. Smyth was also helped by Mary Ponsonby, one of Queen Victoria's women of the bedchamber, with whom she conducted a warm and intimate, if at times stormy, friendship for nearly thirty years. Royal influence secured the mass's performance, for the prince of Wales was patron of the Royal Choral Society. The great exposure achieved by the mass's première did not, however, lead to the further performances Smyth had hoped for. The work was to lie forgotten for thirty-one years, until Adrian Boult revived it in Birmingham and London in 1924. It then gained some currency, being performed in London and at the provincial festivals, and its long neglect was deplored. Smyth ascribed the mass's fate to its composer's sex, but the combination of an unconventional genre for the time with the individuality and strength of her compositional voice surely played a role in its rejection by musical committees in the 1890s.

Smyth's mass also revealed a dramatic gift, and she was encouraged by the renowned German conductor Hermann Levi, always a strong advocate of her music, to develop this by composing an opera. Already attracted to the genre, she collaborated with Brewster on a libretto based on a play by Alfred de Musset, *Fantasio* (1892–4). After unsuccessful negotiations with a number of German opera houses, her first opera was accepted for performance at the court theatre in Weimar and eventually made its début on 24 May 1898. The audience received the new work warmly and Smyth took numerous curtain calls. *Fantasio* was revived in 1901 at Karlsruhe under the baton of Felix Mottl, but even in this 'almost perfect performance' she recognized the shortcomings of the work, realizing that her music had 'too much passion and violence' for a comic subject, and she did not pursue further productions (*What Happened Next*, 86).

Der Wald By this time Smyth was already engrossed in her second operatic project. Again in collaboration with Brewster, she developed a brief tragic love story framed by opening and closing scenes where wood spirits sing of nature's eternal round. She composed to this a one-act German opera, *Der Wald* (1899–1901), in which both story and music drew on German Romanticism, although critics saw in it elements of verismo as well as a debt to Wagner. She had one of her most difficult experiences of opera production with *Der Wald*'s première in Berlin, which she describes vividly in her essay 'A winter of storm' (published in *Streaks of Life*). She blamed her problems on a combination of Anglophobia generated by the Second South African War and sex discrimination, but internal problems in the theatre contributed significantly. *Der Wald* was nearly cancelled, and was still under-rehearsed when it finally received its première on 9 April 1902. Despite hissing at the première and harsh reviews from the Berlin critics, Covent Garden took up the new work for performance that same summer. Smyth travelled to America early in 1903 for productions at New York's Metropolitan Theatre and also in Boston, and these were followed by a Covent Garden revival. *Der Wald* made her name as an opera composer, but this achievement was won by great struggle. She wrote to Brewster: 'I feel I must fight for *Der Wald* … because I want women to turn their minds to big and difficult jobs; not just to go on hugging the shore, afraid to put out to sea' (*What Happened Next*, 210).

The Wreckers Although she was based in England from the late 1880s until her death, Smyth travelled regularly to the continent, to arrange performances of her music, to take cures, and to visit friends and lovers. Despite the strong German influence in her musical training, she was connected to French culture through both her mother—who had grown up in France—and Brewster. In the first decade of the twentieth century she made friends with a group of eminent women in Paris, including the arts patron the princesse de Polignac and the poet Anna de Noailles. Her interest in France found immediate expression in four French chamber music songs (1907). Her third opera, *The Wreckers* (1902–4), was also composed with French tastes in mind, as she hoped for a première with French singers under André Messager when he was guest conductor at Covent Garden. Although the subject was English, Brewster wrote the libretto in French, and the score shows the growing strength of Smyth's compositional voice, as she synthesized a variety of influences to create what is perhaps her greatest work. Set on the Cornish coast in the eighteenth century, it is a tragic tale of lovers who try to stop the local practice of 'wrecking'—luring ships onto the rocks by setting false beacons—but are discovered and sentenced to death. Smyth's score displays her skill in orchestration in its powerful evocation of the sea, and her dramatic conception is at its best in the lively chorus scenes. Although her solid compositional technique was gained in Germany, *The Wreckers* also reveals a gift for colour related to contemporary French music. Her growing interest in English themes is manifested in the opera's setting and her introduction of folk melody.

The Wreckers was performed in Leipzig and in Prague in late 1906, but the productions suffered respectively from excessive cuts and under-rehearsal. Despite the candid descriptions in her memoirs of the difficulties surrounding her opera productions, Smyth always represented her German operatic experiences as successful. Her achievement in gaining performance of three operas at German theatres was outstanding, and foreign success remained vital for an English opera composer to be accepted at home. Yet Covent Garden did not accept *The Wreckers*, for its management was unwilling to undertake the financial risk it represented. Smyth exposed this lack of enterprise in the press, and in 1908 she arranged a concert performance of the first two acts, conducted by Artur Nikisch. A rich American friend, Mary Dodge, then offered her financial backing for an independent production at His Majesty's Theatre. The young Thomas Beecham was engaged to conduct, and the English première took place on 22 June 1909. *The Wreckers* was finally staged at Covent Garden in 1910, as part of the Beecham season.

Music and suffragism Smyth's music received more concert performance than ever before in the years preceding the First World War. Her reputation rose, and new works were premièred, including her chorus *Hey nonny no* (1910), the orchestral songs *Three Moods of the Sea* (1913), and her string quartet in E minor (1902–12). She was awarded an honorary doctorate of music by the University of Durham in 1910, and always used the title thereafter. In 1911 she broke off her career in order to devote two years to the fight for women's suffrage in the Women's Social and Political Union, under Emmeline Pankhurst, with whom she established a close relationship. During her two years of active service she provided the movement with its battle hymn, *The March of the Women*, arranged concerts of her own works to raise funds, and even went to gaol for smashing a window. She was exhilarated to be part of a community of women working for such a worthwhile end. She had always fought sex discrimination when she encountered it, but her suffragette experience redefined her public profile; to her reputation as a composer was added the image of Smyth as activist. In the decades that followed she published feminist polemic, such as *Female Pipings in Eden*, and was well known for her outspoken beliefs and her indomitable spirit in the face of obstacles. Her writings expressed her increasing conviction that her career had been stunted by sex discrimination, a belief that verged on an obsession in her old age and which she never tired of expounding.

Later compositions In order to concentrate on composition again, Smyth travelled as far as Egypt in search of peace from the suffrage battle and her constant worry over Mrs Pankhurst's safety as she undertook repeated hunger strikes. Here she composed *The Boatswain's Mate* (1913–14), a comic opera based on W. W. Jacobs's short story of the same name. She had arranged its première, and a revival of *The Wreckers*, in Germany for 1915, but both were cancelled at the outbreak of war, so her new opera was first performed in London on 28 January 1916. Perhaps her most popular work, it was revived after the war and taken into repertory by the Old Vic during the 1920s. She always maintained that audiences appreciated her work, whatever critics might say, and with its comic scenes and attractive use of folk melody *The Boatswain's Mate* found much favour; her development of the story's feminist element was clearly written with the audience she had discovered among the suffragettes in mind. Commercial recordings were made of her conducting both *The Boatswain's Mate* and *The Wreckers*.

During the war Smyth worked as a radiographer in Paris, where she also sought treatment for the first symptoms of the deafness and distorted hearing that were to worsen throughout her old age. At the same time she began to write her memoirs, and *Impressions that Remained* was published in 1919. It met with great success, and she found writing a useful 'second string' in the years ahead when composition was hindered by her ear troubles and she experienced financial setbacks. She was well aware that one of her greatest advantages had been 'a small independent income which rendered possible a continuous struggle for musical existence such as no woman obliged to earn her livelihood in music could have carried on' (*Female Pipings in Eden*, 37). Fortunately, when she needed to supplement it, she found that editors were keen to publish her articles. In her lively and engaging prose style, Smyth expressed her decided opinions as openly as she did in person. She published a further eight volumes of memoir, travel writing, and polemic between 1921 and 1940. She loved hiking and mountain climbing, and her travels, which included a camel journey in the Egyptian desert and adventures in the wilds of Greece, make fascinating reading in such volumes as *Beecham and Pharaoh* (1935) and *A Three-Legged Tour in Greece* (1927). These writings occasioned an unexpected reward, for they brought her music to a new public, whose interest, fired by her tale of struggle and neglect, inspired an increase in performances of her music during the 1920s and 1930s. Her more frequent appearance as conductor of her work also attracted audiences.

Final years Despite her increasing deafness, Smyth composed two small theatre works during the 1920s: a neoclassical 'dance-dream' entitled *Fête galante* (1921–2), based on a story by her friend Maurice Baring, which showed her awareness of contemporary trends in composition and which she later arranged as a ballet, and a 'post-war comedy' entitled *Entente cordiale* (1923–4). These were premièred in 1923 and 1925 respectively, and Smyth arranged orchestral suites from each. In 1926 she composed a double concerto for violin and horn, and her last large-scale work was a cantata for soprano and bass solo, chorus, and orchestra, based on a philosophical text by Brewster, *The Prison* (1929–30). This was a work close to Smyth's heart, and its lukewarm reception upset her greatly. Increasing age and infirmity were accompanied by a growing bitterness that her achievements as a composer had not been recognized, a grievance that is not supported by the record of performances of her works during the last decades of her life. Besides performances of her mass, revivals of her chamber music, and the inclusion of choral works and pieces arranged from the operas in concert programmes, her seventy-fifth birthday was recognized with a festival of her music, some of which was also broadcast. Her claim that most performances resulted from her own efforts does contain some truth, however, and is borne out by the decline in interest in her music after her death. She seems to have remained in the public eye more because of her status as a national character than for her music itself, for in the context of changing styles her compositions were appreciated as historical in value.

Smyth herself was energetic, opinionated, and warm-hearted. She spoke her mind and often acted as impulsively as she spoke. Her dressing was idiosyncratic—she was renowned for her tweed suits and battered masculine hats—and she smoked until 1899. She was also known for her love of large dogs: the first was Marco, and he was followed by a series of old English sheepdogs, all named Pan; Smyth celebrated her beloved dogs in *Inordinate (?) Affection* (1936). She always made an impression, and was described by an Austrian critic, Richard Specht, as:

> This thin, resolute woman, touched by no sense of the 'shocking', who laughs at all the follies of the world, … one is aware that she has lived alone for many years with her big dog … in a lonely cottage and thus has become a piece of English nature herself. ('Die Komponistin Ethel Smyth', *Der Merker*, 2, 1911, 1218)

Although her conversation could be relentless, Virginia Woolf found in her a combination of sincerity and abruptness, both generous and shrewd.

Smyth's forthright manner, idiosyncratic appearance, and reputed eccentricity combined to create an image that inspired literary characters, such as the composer Edith Staines in E. F. Benson's novel *Dodo* and Miss La Trobe of Virginia Woolf's *Between the Acts*—testimony to the late friendship between the two women. The caricatures of Smyth's suffragette activities and forthright manner have proved more memorable than her music, which merits re-evaluation. Recent research, both by scholars of the English musical renaissance and by feminist scholars, has begun to reclaim her position as a composer of worth who stood out from her generation.

Smyth was awarded further honorary degrees by the universities of Oxford (1926) and St Andrews (1928). Her contribution was recognized more publicly in 1922, when she was created DBE in the new year's honours list, but she felt that the only truly valid recognition—frequent performance of her music and revival of her operas—eluded her during her life.

Smyth died from pneumonia at her home, Coign, Hook Heath Road, Woking, on 8 May 1944.

ELIZABETH KERTESZ

Sources E. Smyth, *Impressions that remained*, 2 vols. (1919) · E. Smyth, *As time went on …* (1936) · E. Smyth, *What happened next* (1940) · E. Smyth, *Streaks of life* (1921) · E. Smyth, *Female pipings in Eden* (1933) · E. Smyth, *Beecham and pharaoh* (1935) · C. St John, *Ethel Smyth: a biography* (1959) · L. Collis, *Impetuous heart: the story of Ethel Smyth* (1984) · J. A. Bernstein, '"Shout, shout, up with your song!" Dame Ethel Smyth and the changing role of the British woman composer', *Women making music: the Western art tradition, 1150–1950*, ed. J. Bowers and J. Tick (1987), 304–24 · E. Wood, 'Women, music, and Ethel Smyth: a pathway in the politics of music', *Massachusetts Review*, 24/1 (1983), 125–39 · J. Bennett, 'List of works', *The memoirs of Ethel Smyth*, ed. R. Crichton (1987), 373–81 · D. Hyde, 'Ethel Smyth, 1858–1944: a reappraisal', *New-found voices: women in nineteenth-century music* (1984), 138–65 · b. cert.

Archives BBC WAC · BL, music collections, full score of *The wreckers* and related papers, Add. MSS 68893–68901 · BL, music collections, MSS of compositions and notebook, Add. MSS 45934–45950, 46857–46863, 49196 · Queen's University, Belfast · U. Mich., MSS · University of North Carolina, Greensboro, corresp. | BL, music collections, letters to Percy Pitt, Add. MS 3306 · BL, music collections, letters to John Plesch, Add. MS 61881 · BL, music collections, letters to Sir Henry Wood, Add. MS 56422 · BL, corresp. with the Society of Authors, Add. MSS 56812–56813 · Bodl. Oxf., letters to various members of the Lewis family · Glos. RO, corresp. with H. W. Sumsion relating to festival · Herts. ALS, letters to Lady Desborough · King's AC Cam., letters to E. J. Dent · McMaster University, Hamilton, Ontario, Eric Walter White fonds collection · NL Wales, letters to Madame Lucie Barbier · U. Durham L., corresp. | SOUND BL NSA, documentary footage · BL NSA, performance footage · British Music Information Centre, London

Likenesses H. S. Mendelssohn, cabinet photograph, 1884, NPG · photograph, 1891, NPG · A. Mancini, chalk drawing, 1900, Royal College of Music, London · J. S. Sargent, charcoal drawing, 1901, NPG [*see illus.*] · H. Lambert, photogravure, 1923, NPG; repro. in H. Lambert, *Modern British composers* (1923) · H. Coster, five photographs, 1930–39, NPG · N. Lytton, oils, 1936, Royal College of Music, London · G. Bayes, bust, 1939, Sadler's Wells Theatre, London · H. Coster, two photographs, NPG · photographs, NPG

Wealth at death £17,254 13*s*. 11*d*.: probate, 1 Nov 1944, *CGPLA Eng. & Wales*

Smyth, Sir Henry Augustus (1825–1906), army officer, was born at St James's Street, London, on 25 November 1825, the third son in the family of three sons and six daughters of Admiral William Henry *Smyth (1788–1865) and his wife, Annarella (1788–1873), only daughter of Thomas Warington, British consul at Naples. His elder brothers were Sir Warington Wilkinson *Smyth and Charles Piazzi *Smyth. Of his sisters, Henrietta Grace married Professor Baden Powell, and Jane Georgiana Rosetta married Sir William Henry Flower.

Educated at Bedford grammar school from 1834 to 1840, Smyth entered the Royal Military Academy, Woolwich, on 1 February 1841. He was commissioned second lieutenant in the Royal Artillery on 20 December 1843, was promoted lieutenant on 5 April 1845, and served in Bermuda from 1847 to 1851. Promoted second captain on 11 August 1851, he was at Halifax, Nova Scotia, until 1854, and at Corfu from February 1855. On becoming first captain on 1 April, he was sent in May to the Crimea to command a field battery. He served at the siege and fall of Sevastopol, and his battery did arduous work with the siege train in the trenches. He took part in the third bombardment, was present at the fall of Sevastopol, and remained in the Crimea until July 1856.

After spending more than five years at home stations, principally Shorncliffe, war threatened with the United States over the *Trent* affair, and Smyth took his field battery to New Brunswick in December 1861, landing his horses fit for service after an exceptionally rough voyage. In Canada Smyth obtained a brevet majority on 12 February 1863. While on ordinary leave from Canada he visited the scenes of the American Civil War, witnessing the capture of Richmond and the subsequent pursuit of the Confederate army. After being promoted to a regimental lieutenant-colonelcy on 31 August 1865 he returned home. He later attended, while on leave from India, some of the Franco-Prussian War operations. His observations on these and the American war were officially commended, and partly published in the *Proceedings of the Royal Artillery Institution*.

From 1867 to 1874 Smyth served in India, becoming a brevet colonel on 31 August 1870. In 1872 he presided over a committee at Calcutta which condemned the bronze rifled guns proposed for field service, and conducted valuable research on Indian gunpowders. His services were praised by the governor-general in council in May 1874.

He married at Lillington, near Leamington Spa in Warwickshire, on 14 April 1874, Helen Constance, daughter of John Whitehead Greaves of Berecote, near Leamington Spa. On 16 January 1875 Smyth succeeded to a regimental colonelcy and was sent to the autumn German manoeuvres. He commanded the artillery at Sheerness in 1876, and from 1877 to 1880 the artillery in the southern district. He served on various professional inquiries, including the revision of siege operations in view of the adoption of more powerful rifled guns and howitzers. In 1876 and 1887 he was awarded the gold medal of the Royal Artillery Institution for his essays 'Field artillery tactics' and 'Training of field artillery'.

From 1881 to 1883 Smyth served on the ordnance committee at Woolwich. Steel rifled guns were then introduced on the committee's recommendation. Promoted major-general on 1 November 1882, Smyth was commandant of the Woolwich garrison and military district from 1882 to 1886. He became lieutenant-general on 1 November 1886, and in 1887 went to command the troops in South Africa.

Soon after his arrival Smyth rapidly crushed a rising in Zululand, which had been formally annexed in May 1887. For some eight months in 1889–90 he acted as governor of Cape Colony (between the governorships of Sir Hercules Robinson and Sir Henry Brougham Loch). Smyth was created CMG in January 1889, and KCMG in 1890, when he was appointed governor of Malta. He was promoted general on 19 May 1891.

Smyth left Malta at the end of 1893 on retirement, and settled at a house inherited from his father, St John's Lodge, Stone, Aylesbury, Buckinghamshire. He became a colonel-commandant of the Royal Artillery on 17 October 1894. He was JP for Buckinghamshire, and fellow of the Society of Antiquaries and the Royal Geographical Society. He died on 18 September 1906 at St John's Lodge, and was buried in Stone churchyard. His wife survived him, without children. R. H. VETCH, *rev.* JAMES LUNT

Sources Royal Artillery Institution, Woolwich, Royal Artillery records • PRO, Royal Artillery records • *The Times* (20 Sept 1906)
Archives BL, corresp. with Lord Ripon, Add. MS 43564
Likenesses L. Dickinson, portrait; formerly in possession of Lady Smyth, 1912 • silhouette, NPG
Wealth at death £16,967 3*s*. 3*d*.: probate, 6 Dec 1906, *CGPLA Eng. & Wales*

Smyth, Hugh (1530–1580). *See under* Smyth family (*per.* *c.*1500–1680).

Smyth, Sir Hugh (1575–1627). *See under* Smyth family (*per.* *c.*1500–1680).

Smyth, Sir Hugh, first baronet (1632–1680). *See under* Smyth family (*per. c.*1500–1680).

Smyth, James Carmichael (1742–1821), physician, was born on 23 February 1742 in Fife, the only child of Thomas Carmichael (*d.* 1746), of Balmedie, and Margaret Smyth, of Athenry. He took his maternal grandfather's name and arms in addition to his own. He studied for six years at Edinburgh University, graduating MD in 1764 with a thesis on paralysis, which included a short history of medical electricity. He then visited France, Italy, and the Netherlands, attending lectures there.

In 1768 Smyth settled in London, set up in practice, and was appointed physician to the Middlesex Hospital in 1775. In the same year he married Mary, only child and heir of Thomas Holyland, of Bromley, Kent; they had eight sons and two daughters. Their eldest son was General Sir James Carmichael-*Smyth, and their elder daughter, Maria, married in 1800 Dr Alexander Monro. Smyth was elected a fellow of the Royal College of Physicians in 1788, and of the Royal Society in 1799.

Smyth's main published works were on gaol fever

(typhus), contagion, nitrous acid, and the resultant controversy (1796, 1799, 1805); but he also wrote on swinging as a remedy for consumption in 1787 (better than sea voyages, he thought), edited the works of his friend William Stark (1788), and wrote a treatise on hydrocephalus.

Smyth experimented with nitrous-acid gas for the prevention of contagion in cases of fever. At the request of the government he continued the experiments at the prison and hospital at Winchester, Hampshire, where there was an epidemic of typhus. He conducted a similar experiment to destroy contagion in 1795, on the HMS *Union*, a hospital ship which between September 1795 and January 1796 had taken on board 479 typhus sufferers from the Russian fleet. He heated crude nitre, presumably with carbon, and the oxides of nitrogen given off would, in fact, have been fatal to the lice which spread typhus, a disease not yet distinguished from typhoid. In addition, Smyth thought washing and cleanliness very important.

For his experimental work, parliament voted Smyth in 1802 a reward of £5000. His claim to the discovery was disputed by Dr John Johnstone of Birmingham, for his father, Dr James Johnstone, and by M. Chaptal, for Guyton de Morveau. After a keen controversy, Smyth's claims were upheld. Shortly afterwards he was elected physician-extraordinary to George III. He then went to the south of France for his health, and on his return settled at Sunbury, Middlesex. He died at Sunbury on 18 June 1821.

GEORGE STRONACH, *rev.* JEAN LOUDON

Sources W. Anderson, *The Scottish nation*, 3 (1877), 485–6 • Munk, *Roll* • *GM*, 1st ser., 91/2 (1821), 88–9 • C. Singer, 'An eighteenth-century naval ship to accommodate women nurses', *Medical History*, 4 (1960), 283–7 • P. J. Bishop, 'Smyth on swinging', *Tubercle*, 40/1 (1959), 59–62 • *Nomina eorum, qui gradum medicinae doctoris in academia Jacobi sexti Scotorum regis, quae Edinburgi est, adepti sunt, ab anno 1705 ad annum 1845*, University of Edinburgh (1846) • Burke, *Peerage*

Smyth, Sir James Carmichael-, first baronet (1779–1838), army officer and colonial governor, eldest son of Dr James Carmichael *Smyth (1742–1821), and his wife, Mary, daughter of Thomas Holyland of Bromley, was born in London on 22 February 1779. He was educated at Charterhouse School and entered the Royal Military Academy, Woolwich, on 1 March 1793. He was commissioned second lieutenant, Royal Artillery, on 20 November 1794, and transferred to the Royal Engineers on 13 March 1795.

In May 1795 Carmichael-Smyth was sent to Portsmouth, and in April 1796 to the Cape of Good Hope; he arrived in June, and served under generals Craig and Doyle in the operations that year against the Dutch. Following his promotion to lieutenant on 3 March 1797 he took part, under generals Dundas and Vandeleur, in the operations from 1798 to 1800; and on 1 July 1802 after a visit to England in 1800–1, he was promoted second captain. On the restoration of Cape Colony to the Dutch in 1803 he returned to England, and in October 1805 he joined Sir David Baird's expedition to the Cape of Good Hope as commanding royal engineer. This force arrived on 4 January 1806, and at Carmichael-Smyth's suggestion a landing was made on the beach near Blaauwberg on 7 January. He was detached on the sloop *Espoir* to Saldanha Bay, and was, to Baird's regret, absent from the battle of Blaauwberg on 8 January. On the surrender of Cape Town, Baird appointed Carmichael-Smyth acting colonial secretary, his military duties being unchanged. He was promoted first captain on 1 July 1806, and was employed in strengthening and repairing the defences of Table Bay and Simon's Bay. He relinquished the appointment of colonial secretary on the arrival in May 1807 of the earl of Caledon as governor with a complete staff, and returned to England in September 1808. In the following winter he was with Sir John Moore at Corunna, returning with the remnant of the army to England in February. He then served in Scotland; in April he constructed Leith Fort, and on 20 October 1813 was promoted lieutenant-colonel.

In December 1813 Carmichael-Smyth joined the expedition to the Netherlands under his relative General Sir Thomas Graham (afterwards Lord Lynedoch), as commanding royal engineer. During that month he landed with Graham at Zeyrick Zee, and headquarters were established at Tolen. He was in the action of Merxem on 13 January 1814, and the bombardment of Antwerp early in February. Having carefully reconnoitred the fortress of Bergen-op-Zoom, Carmichael-Smyth advised its assault, which took place on 8 March 1814, when he accompanied the central column. Although the assault was successful, owing to blunders the British retreated at daybreak. Hostilities having ended and the French having withdrawn, Carmichael-Smyth on 5 May took over the fortress of Antwerp and all the defences of the Scheldt; afterwards he was engaged in the reconstruction and strengthening of the important fortresses evacuated by the French. He accompanied the duke of Wellington and the prince of Orange on several tours of inspection of the works, which occupied about 10,000 labourers under a large staff of engineer officers. Early in 1815 he accompanied the prince of Orange to London, but on 6 March, Napoleon having escaped from Elba, Carmichael-Smyth again joined the headquarters of the British army at Brussels as commanding royal engineer. During April and May, under Wellington's immediate orders, he placed the defences of the Netherlands in as efficient a state as possible against the expected French invasion, which occurred on 15 June. At Quatre Bras and Waterloo, Carmichael-Smyth served on Wellington's staff, and on 7 July he entered Paris with him. Carmichael-Smyth was promoted colonel in the army and aide-de-camp to the prince regent on 29 June 1815. He was also made a CB and received the orders of knighthood of Maria Theresa and fourth class of St Vladimir. He remained in command of the Royal Engineers at Cambrai until December 1815, and was then placed on half pay. On 28 May 1816 he married Harriet (*d.* 23 Sept 1870), the only surviving child of General Robert *Morse RE, and they had one son.

On 25 August 1821, on Wellington's recommendation, Carmichael-Smyth was made a baronet. In 1823, with Lord Lynedoch, he inspected the Low Countries, fortresses, and in October he was sent to the British West Indies to report on the military defences and engineering establishments and military requirements there. He arrived with his colleagues at Barbados on 27 November, and visited Berbice and Georgetown in Demerara, Tobago, Trinidad, Grenada, St Vincent, St Lucia, Dominica, Antigua, and St Kitts. Their report was dated 20 January 1824.

In the spring of 1825 Wellington, then master-general of the ordnance, selected Carmichael-Smyth to go to Canada on a similar mission. He embarked on 16 April, returned on 7 October, and wrote an able report on the defence of the Canadian frontier, dated 31 March 1826. Meanwhile, on 27 May 1825, he had been promoted major-general, and on 29 July he had become a regimental colonel. In July 1828 he was sent to Ireland on special service to report on the Irish survey; he returned in September. With this report his career as a military engineer closed. He published various books and pamphlets on military, colonial, and related subjects.

On 8 May 1829 Carmichael-Smyth was appointed governor and commander-in-chief of the Bahamas, and before his departure George IV made him a KCH in recognition of his having been placed in command of the Hanoverian engineers in the last campaign in the Netherlands. After four years' successful administration of the Bahamas, during which he abolished flogging of female slaves, Carmichael-Smyth was transferred to the more important governorship of British Guiana in June 1833. He arrived at Georgetown, Demerara, shortly before the emancipation of slaves, when much depended on the governor. Unmoved by the reckless hostility of a section of the planters, Carmichael-Smyth by a firm, impartial, and vigorous government won the confidence of the slaves. He so closely supervised every department of government that, as he himself observed, he could sleep satisfied that no person could be punished without his knowledge and sanction. Carmichael-Smyth died suddenly at Camp House, Georgetown, Demerara, of 'brain fever', after four days' illness, on 4 March 1838; he was widely esteemed and his death much regretted.

Carmichael-Smyth's son, James Robert Carmichael (1817–1883), on 25 February 1841, by royal licence, dropped the name Smyth and readopted the family surname of Carmichael alone. That year he married Louisa Charlotte, daughter of Sir Thomas Butler, baronet. James Carmichael was chairman of the first submarine telegraph company, and died on 7 June 1883, at his residence, 12 Sussex Place, London; his son, James Morse Carmichael (1844–1902), was third and last baronet.

R. H. Vetch, *rev.* Roger T. Stearn

Sources dispatches, *LondG* • royal engineers' records, Royal Engineers' Institution, Chatham • royal artillery records, Royal Artillery Institution, Woolwich • War Office records, PRO • *GM*, 2nd ser., 10 (1838) • W. Anderson, *The Scottish nation*, 3 vols. (1880) • Burke, *Peerage* (1894) • *Annual Register* (1838) • W. Porter, *History of the corps of royal engineers*, 2 vols. (1889) • T. W. J. Connolly, *The history of the corps of royal sappers and miners*, 2 vols. (1855) • J. Sperling, *Letters of an officer … from the British army in Holland, Belgium and France* (1872) • J. Carmichael-Smyth, *Précis of the wars in Canada, from 1755 to the treaty of Ghent in 1814*, ed. J. Carmichael (1862) • R. Muir, *Britain and the defeat of Napoleon, 1807–1815* (1996)

Archives Duke U., Perkins L., personal and family corresp. and papers • PRO, corresp. and papers, PRO 30/35 • Royal Engineers Museum, Gillingham, comments on campaigns of 1814–15 | NL Scot., letters to Lord Lynedoch

Likenesses T. Hodgetts, mezzotint, pubd 1841 (after E. H. Latilla), NPG • F. Chantrey, bust, Georgetown Cathedral Church, Demerara

Smyth, John (*c.*1500–1556), merchant and local politician, was born around the turn of the sixteenth century to Matthew *Smyth [*see under* Smyth family (*per.* *c.*1500–1680)], a middling Bristol merchant and hooper, and his wife, Alice, the daughter of a local merchant. The common nature of his name makes it difficult to trace his early years with certainty. However, he was almost certainly apprenticed to a Bristol or Bridgwater merchant engaged in the Spanish trade. From 1525 the name John Smyth begins to appear regularly in the Bristol customs accounts in contexts associated with the continental trade. It seems likely that, when he married, it was to Joan White, *née* Hoper (*d.* 1560), the widow of a wealthy Bridgwater merchant; she gave birth to their first son, Hugh, in 1530, and their second, Matthew, in 1533.

After 1530 Smyth became increasingly prominent in Bristol politics. His first major office was that of sheriff, which he held in 1532–3. During this year he had to deal with a town inflamed and divided by the rival preaching of Hugh Latimer and William Hubbardine. As he testified against Latimer in an inquiry held that summer it would seem that he was opposed to religious change at that time. However, his later involvement in the sale of monastic lands indicates that he was prepared to be flexible on this issue.

Smyth's ledger for the years 1538–50 provides detailed evidence of his commercial operations and is one of the best sources in this period for the business activities of an English merchant. The ledger reveals that he had extensive trade contacts with western France, the Biscay region of Spain, and south-west Spain and Portugal. He was involved in the export of cloth, lead, leather, and arable produce and the import of wine, iron, oil, and woad. Most of this trade was conducted in a fairly open and legal manner. However, it is clear that Smyth, along with other prominent members of Bristol's commercial community, was also involved in large-scale and well-organized illicit trade, principally the covert export of leather and arable produce to avoid the heavy licence charges to which these commodities were subject. The normal pattern of this, highly profitable, section of his trade was for a small part of a consignment to be legally declared in Bristol and for the rest to be transported from storage depots up the Bristol Channel to join outbound ships at the point where the Avon meets the Bristol Channel. The danger of capture was avoided by the local customs searchers being bribed before a ship's sailing.

Smyth was also involved in the shipping industry. From at least 1536–46 he was the owner of a ship called the *Trinity of Bristol*. The returns on this vessel were generally good, and he was able to achieve a high price for his freight by allowing Bristol-based merchants to defer freight payments. By doing this he was effectively able to act as a financier to the city's smaller merchants without contravening the usury laws. For obvious reasons, Smyth particularly favoured the use of his own ship when he was conducting illicit exports.

From 1539 Smyth began to invest some of his profits in land and property, much of which become available in the wake of Henry VIII's religious reforms. In 1544 he acquired a grant of arms from the crown, and in 1545 he bought the estate of Ashton Court. This major property overlooked Bristol and was to be the home of his gentlemen descendants until the early twentieth century.

Smyth served two terms as mayor of Bristol, first in 1547–8 and then again in 1554–5. From the inventory of his goods it is apparent that he remained active in commerce until his death, at Small Street, Bristol, on 1 September 1556. He was buried in St Werburgh's Church.

Evan T. Jones

Sources *The ledger of John Smythe, 1538–1550*, ed. J. Vanes, Bristol RS, 28 (1974) • E. T. Jones, 'The Bristol shipping industry in the sixteenth century', PhD diss., U. Edin., 1998 • J. H. Bettey, *The rise of a gentry family, the Smyths of Ashton Court, c. 1500–1642* (1978) • J. Collinson, *The history and antiquities of the county of Somerset*, 3 vols. (1791) • W. Barrett, *The history and antiquities of the city of Bristol* (1789) • E. T. Jones, 'Illicit business: accounting for smuggling in mid-sixteenth-century Bristol', *Economic History Review*, 54 (2001), 17–38 • L. U. Way, 'Family album', Bristol RO, AC/F1/4 • will, PRO, PROB 11/38, sig. 14

Archives Bristol RO, ledger • Bristol RO, letters, official documents, etc.

Wealth at death various properties in Bristol and the surrounding countryside; £2263 14*s*. 0*d*. in goods and money: Bristol RO, AC/F7/3

Smyth [Smith], **John** (*d*. 1612), Baptist minister, was probably the fourth son of John Smyth of Sturton-le-Steeple, Nottinghamshire. In March 1586 he was admitted a sizar to Christ's College, Cambridge; he proceeded MA in midsummer 1593. The presbyterian and future separatist Francis Johnson, before his expulsion in the autumn of 1589, acted as Smyth's tutor. Admitted to a fellowship in 1594, Smyth was ordained by William Wickham, bishop of Lincoln, between 1584 and 1595. In 1597, however, Smyth was in trouble for opposing several Anglican church practices, including use of the surplice, and in 1598 he vacated his fellowship.

On 27 September 1600, following a bitterly disputed election, Smyth became town lecturer of Lincoln. On 2 September 1602 the mayor, Edward Dennys, used the city's seal to confirm him as lecturer for life, an illegal tactic which failed, and by 13 December 1602 Smyth was unseated for 'enormous doctrine and undue teaching of matters of religion' and preaching against 'men of this city'. He was also troubled by Bishop William Chaderton, whose charge that Smyth had preached without authority was upheld on 1 April 1603. Deprived of his post at Lincoln, Smyth's attempts to secure redress at the common law brought compensations but not reinstatement.

Chaderton seems to have restored Smyth's preaching licence, a letter of 3 March 1606 referring to the bishop's 'former favour in sparing to suspend him' (Lincoln diocesan records, Cor B2, no. 19), but his position remained precarious, and though he is reported as preaching at Gainsborough in 1604, he also appears to have become curate at Clifton, Nottinghamshire, just outside the Lincoln diocese. By now he was probably married, though the name of his wife is unknown, two daughters of his being baptized at Gainsborough in 1604 and 1606 respectively. On 5 October 1604, as clerk of Clifton, he was charged at East Retford quarter sessions with illegal assembly, in a dispute over a benefice. In March 1605 he published *A Patterne of True Prayer*, for 'the clearing of myself from unjust accusations, and the satisfying of a few friends' (*Works*, 1.68) and in an emotional passage, Smyth both lamented his personal experience and identified with the zealous ministers in the church: 'persecution is a great discouragement to a minister, and it driveth many a godly man to his dumps, and interrupteth his ministry'; he prayed that the 'godly ministers may be preserved and kept from the persecution of tyrants and wicked men' (ibid., 1.163). While explicitly repudiating separatism, the author was worried that a spirit of formality might pervade set prayers.

However, it was charged that at a meeting at Coventry (possibly later in 1605), Smyth had to be dissuaded from separatist positions; he denied this and it cannot be verified, although the issue was certainly discussed. There is some reason to think that Smyth was in touch with William Bradshaw and his colleagues in the underground literary campaign against Archbishop Bancroft's new canons. His outspoken preaching probably encountered growing official determination to use the rules against those who broke them in the radical puritan cause. Perhaps it was this growing tension which underlay his eventual separation, but for some time he continued a member of the Church of England.

On 18 March 1606 Smyth admitted having preached at Gainsborough while suspended by the bishop. Letters in his favour were received from substantial citizens, and no action was taken. But the following January, Smyth admitted having practised as an unlicensed physician and was fined and suspended. He did not attend an earlier hearing in November, perhaps because of a serious illness, which reportedly struck when he was still considering separation. About February 1607, after nine months of hesitation, Smyth made his breach from the Church of England. Soon after, he attacked his former associate Richard Bernard as an apostate, signing himself 'Pastor of the Church at Ganesburgh'. Others had already followed Smyth's lead, notably Richard Clifton. But England was dangerous for people of their new persuasion.

There are hints that John Smyth arrived in Amsterdam ahead of his followers. Perhaps subsisting on earnings as a physician, he made contact with what had become known as the Ancient Church, the separatist congregation led by Francis Johnson and Henry Ainsworth, though without actually joining it. There is evidence that Smyth's church was also distinct from a third group around Clifton, which came to be led by John Robinson and which soon left for Leiden. The crossing to the Netherlands, however, was probably a joint enterprise. Disagreements between Smyth and the Ancient Church now emerged. Already latent in his *Principles and Inferences* of late 1607, these were more starkly outlined in *The Differences of the Churches* in autumn 1608. Here, Smyth opposed the reading of set texts in the service and attacked the traditional division of labour between the pastoral officers of the church; he laid great stress on the powers of the congregation in all matters, including the admission and expulsion of members. But by the time Ainsworth had printed a response, his critic had adopted yet more radical views.

In or about January 1609, Smyth dissolved and reconstituted his church. In an act so deeply shocking as to be denied by Baptist historians for two and a half centuries, he rebaptized first himself and then his followers, and set out his new views in *The Character of the Beast*, published in 1610. Adopting liturgical practices of the utmost austerity, the congregation soon embraced the doctrine of general redemption, and began to voice ideas reflecting the influence of Dutch Anabaptism. It is clear that in or before summer 1609, they made contact with the Waterlander Mennonite congregation in Amsterdam. Smyth came to feel that this was a true church, that he should have sought his baptism from one of its ordained officers, and that his own self-baptism had therefore been disorderly. He urged his followers to apply to the Waterlanders for membership. This provoked a split, in which Smyth and thirty-one supporters were formally excommunicated by a minority led by Thomas *Helwys. The Amsterdam Waterlanders and their leaders, De Ries and Gerritz, were keen to receive the English, and regarded Smyth's self-baptism as a less serious breach of order than did Smyth himself. A conference was held on 23 May 1610, and a revised version of De Ries's confession of faith may have been discussed there as a basis for unity. Smyth was probably the author, not the translator, of a Latin defence of De Ries's work which has survived.

But the Amsterdam Waterlanders belonged to a wider Mennonite fellowship, which remained suspicious of the strange outlook and customs of the English. Negotiations continued, but Smyth and his friends remained outside the fold. Having disowned the validity of their own constitution, they were forced to operate informally, the victims of their own rigour, meeting in a room at the bakehouse of Jan Munter. Smyth seems to have suffered a terrible crisis of confidence, and came to place much less weight upon outward ordinances. In his *Last Booke*, he retracted all the 'biting and bitter words, phrases and speeches' hurled against earlier opponents (*Works*, 2.754). This was consistent with his most recent views: disavowing the factious emigration, Smyth embraced the eirenic spirit of the Waterlanders. But he did not live to see the admission of his followers to their congregation in January 1615. In summer 1612 he fell ill, probably of tuberculosis, and died at the end of August. John Smyth was buried in the Niewe Kerke in Amsterdam on 1 September 1612.

STEPHEN WRIGHT

Sources *The works of John Smyth*, ed. W. T. Whitley, 2 vols. (1915) • Mennonite Archives, Amsterdam, nos. 1347–1350, 1354, 1357–1364 • W. Burgess, *John Smyth, the Se-Baptist, Thomas Helwys and the first Baptist church in England* (1911) • C. Burrage, *The early English dissenters in the light of recent research (1550–1641)*, 2 vols. (1912) • B. R. White, *The English separatist tradition* (1971) • B. H. Evans, *History of the English Baptists*, 2 vols. (1862) • R. Marchant, *The puritans and the church courts in the diocese of York, 1560–1642* (1960) • J. R. Coggins, *John Smyth and his congregation* (1991) [incl. trans. of Smyth's *Defence of De Ries*] • W. Burgess, *John Robinson* (1920), 409–17 • H. C. Porter, *Reformation and reaction in Tudor Cambridge* (1958) • J. W. F. Hill, *Tudor and Stuart Lincoln* (1956) • J. Peile, *Biographical register of Christ's College, 1505–1905, and of the earlier foundation, God's House, 1448–1505*, ed. [J. A. Venn], 1 (1910) • Venn, *Alum. Cant.*, 1/4.101 • C. W. Foster, ed., *Gainsborough parish registers*, 1 (1920) • *The manuscripts of Lincoln, Bury St Edmund's, and Great Grimsby corporations*, HMC, 37 (1895), 76, 78–9 • Lincs. Arch., Lincoln diocesan records, Cj 14, fols. 30v–41v • Lincs. Arch., Lincoln diocesan records, Cj 16, fols. 32, 97 • bishop's correspondence, Lincs. Arch., Lincoln diocesan archives, Cor B/2 nos. 4, 19, 20 • Notts. Arch., C/QSM 1/66/1 • Nottingham archdeaconry records, U. Nott., court book A15

Archives Mennonite Archive (Wynbrands Memorial B), Amsterdam, MSS | Lincs. Arch., Lincoln diocesan archives • Notts. Arch., quarter sessions records • U. Nott., Nottingham archdeaconry records

Smyth, John (1567–1641), antiquary and parliamentary diarist, was the son of Thomas Smyth (*d.* in or before 1594) of Hoby, Leicestershire, and his wife, Joan Alan. Educated first at the free school in Derby, in 1584 he left in order to attend on Thomas Berkeley, son and heir of Henry, Lord Berkeley, at Callowden, Warwickshire. Five years later he accompanied the young Berkeley to Magdalen College, Oxford. Supported by an annuity from Berkeley's mother, Katherine, Lady Berkeley, Smyth subsequently studied at Clement's Inn, and on 17 August 1594 was admitted to the Middle Temple. However, although evidently an active law student, he continued to serve the Berkeleys, aiding Lady Berkeley in 1595 in her negotiations for her son's marriage to Elizabeth Carey and serving as household steward in the year following her death in 1596. On 4 October 1597 he married Grace Thomas, widow of John Drewe, and that year became steward of the hundred and liberty of Berkeley. Called to the bar on 22 November 1605, he afterwards spent up to half of each year in London, pursuing legal cases. Grace Smyth having died on 9 November 1609, he married on 9 January 1610 Mary Browning, daughter of a Gloucestershire client of the Berkeleys, with whom he had five sons and four daughters.

A steady advance in Smyth's social status owed much to his patrons. When Henry, Lord Berkeley, died in 1613, leaving as heir his grandson George, Smyth remained a vital man of business to the young Lord Berkeley, who rarely resided on his Gloucestershire estates, and to his mother Elizabeth. Granted two manor houses with gardens and parks in Nibley, he lived there for the rest of his life. Nevertheless, Smyth was also able to establish for himself an independent place in county life, undertaking work unrelated to that for the Berkeleys. He was appointed escheator of Gloucestershire in 1601, acted as auditor for the earl of Northumberland between 1605 and 1609, and sat for Midhurst in the 1621 parliament. His diary of the proceedings and his membership of committees on domestic and colonial affairs testify to his active involvement.

With free access to the Berkeley Castle muniments, Smyth indulged to the full his passion for genealogical and antiquarian research. As he put it, 'A continued delight of forty yeares haled mee alonge' (Smyth, *Description*, 34). Of his twenty-six volumes of works, three were published in his lifetime: two as *Lives of the Berkeleys*, chronicling the descent of the barony since 1066, and *A Description of the Hundred of Berkeley*. These, especially the latter, which he completed in 1639, are full of fascinating details about landholding patterns, customs, traditions, popular culture, and folk wisdom in his beloved adopted homeland. Smyth also compiled 'Men and armour', a muster roll of men of military age who were fit for service in Gloucestershire in 1608, together with their occupations. This document affords real insights into the economic life of the county. In many ways, Smyth was one of the earliest social historians; R. H. Tawney calls him 'the learned, lovable, pedantic John Smyth' (Tawney and Tawney, 27).

Although he described Berkeley hundred almost as a rural Arcadia—he barely mentioned the large cloth industry in the area—Smyth was also an astute businessman, who purchased large amounts of land, supplied livestock to the London market, and both organized and financed expeditions to Virginia. He was also a keen estate 'improver', although he disapproved of landowners who enclosed common lands to create parks. As the Berkeley estate manager, his life's work was to rescue the estate from the burden of past follies and the profligacy of both of his masters. In 1632 he bravely spoke up against the formidable dowager Lady Berkeley when she sold Wortley Manor behind his back, although he was unable to prevent this or £11,000 worth of disposals. He also spent much time asserting Lord Berkeley's rights over the 300 acre New Grounds in Slimbridge and Frampton-on-Severn, which were created when the Severn changed its course about 1610. He fought successful suits first against the inhabitants, then, in 1638–9, against Sir Sackville Crowe and other 'projectors' who hoped to profit from asserting the crown's dubious claims to the lands.

Smyth acquired great wealth from his position, so much so that on one occasion the Berkeley family fool tied a string around the church at Berkeley 'to prevent [it] from going to Nibley' (Fosbroke, vi). He himself ruefully quoted the local saying 'Dip not thy finger in the mortar, nor seek thy penny in the water' against his own extravagances in building works (Smyth, *Description*, 28), though in fact he left legacies worth over £1000 on top of his estates in and around Nibley. By the end of his life, Smyth was a friend to most of the leading gentry of Gloucestershire, who consulted with him over the parliamentary elections of 1640. He died at Nibley on 23 February 1641, survived by his second wife, and was buried at Nibley church.

John Smyth (1611–1692), local politician, eldest son of John Smyth and Mary Browning, was admitted to the Middle Temple in 1628 and called to the bar on 27 November 1635. He joined his father in several lawsuits on behalf of the Berkeleys. He married Anne, daughter of Sir Edward Bloomfield, lord mayor of London, with whom he had four sons and a daughter. Smyth took over the administration of the Berkeley estates on his father's death and retained the position until at least 1683, interrupted only by the civil war. In the early stages of the war, he tried to avoid commitment to either side and to hold the Berkeley interests together, but after Gloucester garrison troops seized Berkeley Castle in February 1643, he fled to Oxford and joined the royalists. Indeed, he may have been the 'Smith the Marshal' accused by Edmund Ludlow of mistreating prisoners at Oxford, although other prisoners testified that he intervened to help them. He later compounded for his estates. In late 1645 he helped to block the county committee's proposed demolition of the castle.

As a highly active JP in the 1660s, Smyth took a pivotal role in resisting government attempts to reassert the local authority of the council in the marches of Wales and to impose land carriage duties on parishes in the Vale of Berkeley for the state shipbuilding project in the Forest of Dean. He also encouraged local resistance to the extortions of the hearth tax collectors. He remained active at least until the early 1680s, and died in 1692.

ANDREW WARMINGTON

Sources J. Smyth, *A description of the hundred of Berkeley* (1885), vol. 3 of *The Berkeley manuscripts*, ed. J. Maclean (1883–5) • Gloucester Public Library, Smyth of Nibley MSS I–XVI • D. P. Rollison, 'The bourgeois soul of John Smyth of Nibley', *Social History*, 12 (1987), 309–30 • J. Smyth, *Lives of the Berkeleys* (1883), vol. 2 of *The Berkeley manuscripts*, ed. J. Maclean (1883–5) • J. Broadway, 'John Smyth of Nibley: a Jacobean man-of-business and his service to the Berkeley family', *Midland History*, 24 (1999), 79–97 • A. R. Warmington, *Civil war, interregnum and Restoration in Gloucestershire, 1640–1672* (1997) • T. D. Fosbroke, *Berkeley manuscripts: abstracts and extracts of Smyth's Lives of the Berkeleys* (1821) • H. A. C. Sturgess, ed., *Register of admissions to the Honourable Society of the Middle Temple, from the fifteenth century to the year 1944*, 1 (1949), 66, 120 • A. J. Tawney and R. H. Tawney, 'An occupational census of the 17th century', *Economic History Review*, 5 (1934–5), 25–64 • Glos. RO, D2510 • BL, Add. MSS 33588–33589 • PRO, PROB 11/187, sig. 135, fols. 239*r*–241*r* • W. Notestein, F. H. Relf, and H. Simpson, eds., *Commons debates, 1621*, 5 (1935) • G. A. Harrison, 'Royalist organisation in Gloucestershire and Bristol, 1641–1646', MA diss., University of Manchester, 1961 • *DNB* • monument, Nibley church • GEC, *Peerage*

Archives Gloucester Public Library, Smyth of Nibley MSS I–XVI • NYPL, MSS | Berkeley Castle, Gloucestershire, muniments, accounts • BL, letters and papers, Add. MSS 33588–33589 • BL, diaries of 1621 parliament, Add. MS 34121 • Folger, papers, Z.e.1 • Glos. RO, corresp. and papers • Glos. RO, letters and papers, D 885, D 2510 • W. Sussex RO, Bosham Manor collection • Yale U., papers, a 22, fb 151

Wealth at death considerable; also lands bequeathed to heir: will, PRO, PROB 11/187, sig. 135, fols. 239*r*–241*r*

Smyth, John (1611–1692). *See under* Smyth, John (1567–1641).

Smyth, John (1748–1811), politician, was born on 12 February 1748, the only son of John Smyth (*d.* 1771) of Heath, near Wakefield, Yorkshire, and Bridget, daughter of Benjamin Foxley of London. He was educated at Westminster School and at Trinity College, Cambridge, matriculating in 1766. He married, on 4 June 1778, Lady Georgiana Fitzroy (1757–1799), daughter of Augustus Henry *Fitzroy, third duke of Grafton, and his first wife, the Hon. Anne Liddell; they had four sons and two daughters.

Smyth was closely involved in the petitioning movement in favour of parliamentary reform of 1779–80 that had been initiated by the Revd Christopher Wyvill. In

1783, having turned down a previous invitation in 1780, he stood as a candidate for the borough of Pontefract, Yorkshire, backed by a party of resident householders who were attempting to widen the borough's burgage franchise. He was defeated but seated on petition by the election committee of the House of Commons, which implicitly declared itself in favour of the wider franchise. He went on to represent Pontefract for twenty-four years before losing his seat in the general election of 1807.

Smyth was a supporter of William Pitt the younger but like Pitt he gradually moved away from his initial enthusiasm for parliamentary reform, while retaining his commitment to the abolition of the slave trade. He spoke in the House of Commons only rarely and then usually in an official capacity but he regularly acted as a government teller in divisions and was chairman of a number of parliamentary committees. Considered by George Canning 'a very pleasant, gentlemanly man' (*Letter-Journal*, 69), Smyth was successively a lord of the Admiralty (1791–4) and of the Treasury (1794–1802), describing the latter post as 'quite a sinecure' given Pitt's propensity to undertake, as first lord, all the work himself (Glenberrie, 1.128). He became master of the Royal Mint (1802–4) and was sworn of the privy council (on 22 September 1802) during the administration of Henry Addington. In Pitt's second ministry (1804–6) he initially lost his official position but was later appointed a member of the Board of Trade in May 1805. In 1809 Smyth was appointed a lieutenant-colonel in the Wakefield regiment of the West Riding militia. Smyth died in Bruton Street, London, on 12 February 1811.

STEPHEN M. LEE

Sources R. G. Thorne, 'Smyth, John', HoP, *Commons*, *1790–1820* · E. A. Smith, 'Smyth, John', HoP, *Commons*, *1754–90* · *GM*, 1st ser., 81/1 (1811), 197 · *The diaries of Sylvester Douglas (Lord Glenbervie)*, ed. F. Bickley, 1 (1928), 128 · *The letter-journal of George Canning, 1793–1795*, ed. P. Jupp, CS, 4th ser., 41 (1991), 69 · Burke, *Peerage* (1980) · *IGI* · Venn, *Alum. Cant.*

Smyth, John (*c*.1773–1840). *See under* Smyth, Edward (*c*.1745–1812).

Smyth, Sir John George, first baronet (1893–1983), army officer and politician, was born at Teignmouth, Devon, on 24 October 1893, the eldest of the three sons of William John Smyth (*b*. 1869) of the Indian Civil Service. His mother, Lilian May Clifford (1869/70–1956), was the daughter of a naval captain. At the Dragon School, Oxford, which he attended from 1901 to 1908, 'I had', he recorded in the second version of his autobiography, *Milestones, a Memoir* (1979), 'shown signs of becoming an outstanding athlete, with quite a good brain' (Smyth, *Milestones*, 20) until for two years he was bedridden with a serious illness. 'These two years were, from a character-forming point of view, the most important in my life', he considered. 'I read voraciously and … was not afraid of death … Physical fitness became a *sine qua non* all the days of my life' (ibid., 22).

At Repton, from 1908 to 1911, determined to get into Sandhurst, 'I was', Smyth acknowledged in his original autobiography, *The Only Enemy* (1959), 'that most unpopular of all species … a swot' (Smyth, *The Only Enemy*, 37), but he passed, eighteenth out of 250, into Sandhurst in 1911 and left the Royal Military College a year later, ninth among those passing out and a prize winner. He was commissioned into the Indian army and joined the 15th Sikhs, 'thin as a rail, perhaps rather too serious, but enormously keen' (ibid., 45–6).

When war broke out in 1914, widespread doubt existed about the ability of Indian troops to stand up to modern weapons and trench warfare, but Smyth's regiment rapidly confounded the sceptics. On 18 May 1915, at 'that little cockpit of the Western Front near Richebourg L'Avoue, which the troops afterwards called "the Glory Hole" … littered with the unburied dead of many battalions, stinking to high heaven' (Smyth, *Milestones*, 48), the crucial event occurred of Smyth's life. He was ordered to carry a supply of desperately needed bombs to a small party holding out in a captured section of the enemy front line. Two attempts to cross the intervening 250 yards of fire-swept no man's land had already failed disastrously and Smyth was 'in an absolutely blue funk' (ibid., 49) when instructed to make a third, but 'when I asked for ten volunteers to go with me … the whole company stepped forward'. All ten of those chosen, 'crawling forward, taking what cover we could from the British corpses …' were killed or wounded but Smyth survived, though 'I had bullets through my tunic and cap and my walking-stick had been hit … four times' (Smyth, *The Only Enemy*, 78). He succeeded in his mission none the less and that July he was awarded the Victoria Cross, making him nationally known. His men asserted that 'Smyth Sahib bears a charmed life' (ibid., 82) but he probably owed his survival to his being sent later in 1915 to serve in Egypt (having added the Russian order of St George to his honours) and, in 1916, back to India.

Smyth's 'peacetime' service from 1918 was a misnomer, for it included the Third Anglo-Afghan War (1919–20), in which he won the Military Cross, putting down an insurrection in Mesopotamia, and operations on the permanently restive north-west frontier of India. In all three campaigns he was mentioned in dispatches. From 1931 to 1934 he was an instructor at the Staff College, Camberley, and from 1934 to 1939, following accelerated promotion, he held various staff and command appointments in India.

The start of the Second World War found Smyth on leave in England, where he was appointed general staff officer, grade 1, of the 2nd London division, and then, in February 1940, commander of the 127th infantry brigade. This was also an eventful period in his private life. His marriage, on 22 July 1920, to Margaret Dundas, 'a very beautiful woman with a saint-like character' who 'gave me four wonderful children' (one of his three sons was to be killed in action in Burma in 1944) ended in 1940 in a divorce that 'was certainly not her fault' (Smyth, *Milestones*, 75). On 12 April 1940 he married Frances Mary Blair Read Chambers, the start of a 'really happy' partnership (ibid., 290), which endured until his death.

Two weeks later, on 23 April 1940, Smyth left for France in command of 127th infantry brigade. By 1 June he was back in England, via the Dunkirk evacuations, and, after anti-invasion duties in East Anglia, he returned, during

1941, to India, being promoted acting major-general, at first in command of the 19th division. When, in December, the Japanese invaded Burma, he assumed command of the 27th division, during its withdrawal from Moulmein to Rangoon. On 23 February 1942 he approved the blowing-up of a vital bridge over the wide and fast-flowing Sittang River, which left two-thirds of his men on the far side, at the mercy of the advancing Japanese. Smyth always insisted that 'no educated soldier could have made any other' decision (Smyth, *Milestones*, 189), but he was blamed for what Churchill called 'a major disaster' (Churchill, 4.136). That November he was compulsorily retired from the army, on a colonel's pension, with, added later, the honorary rank of brigadier.

Smyth became in 1943 military correspondent to the *Sunday Times* and other newspapers, and subsequently its tennis correspondent. He proved a prolific and versatile writer. Following his first book, *Defence is our Business* (1945), he produced more than thirty titles, mainly on military subjects, but also on tennis and cats (a lifelong love of his), as well as biographies, children's stories, a play, and *The Story of the Victoria Cross* (1962). He also became chairman of the Victoria Cross and George Cross Association.

In 1945 Smyth began a third career, as a politician, standing as Conservative candidate for Central Wandsworth against the formidable Ernest Bevin. He was beaten by 5174 votes, but in 1950 he stood again, at Norwood, and was elected by a majority of 2075; he remained an MP until 1966. From November 1951 he served as parliamentary secretary of the Ministry of Pensions, and he became joint parliamentary secretary when it was merged with the Ministry of National Insurance in 1953. He had little taste, however, for the ministerial battlefields of Whitehall and Westminster and in December 1955 returned to the back benches at his own request. On 23 January 1956 he was created a baronet and in 1962 he was sworn of the privy council.

Late in life Smyth professed himself 'a happy man' and 'an incurable optimist' (Smyth, *Milestones*, 291). He died on 26 April 1983, at his home, 807 Nelson House, Dolphin Square, London, and was succeeded in his baronetcy by his grandson. He bequeathed his medals to the Imperial War Museum, but the VC was a replica. The original had been stolen and, to its owner's disgust, the War Office had charged him £1 11*s*. 6*d*. to replace it.

Norman Longmate

Sources J. Smyth, *Milestones: a memoir* (1979) • J. G. Smyth, *The only enemy: an autobiography* (1959) • *The Times* (27 April 1983), 12 • *The Times* (21 Sept 1983), 14 • *WWW* • Burke, *Peerage* (1959–70) • *Deeds that thrill the empire* (1917) • W. S. Churchill, *The Second World War*, 4 (1951) • *The Times House of Commons: 1945* (1945) • *The Times House of Commons: 1950* [1950] • D. Butler and J. Freeman, *British political facts, 1900–1960* (1963) • *CGPLA Eng. & Wales* (1983)

Archives IWM, MSS • NRA, diaries and papers | Henley Management College, PowerGen Library, corresp. with L. F. Urwick • King's Lond., Liddell Hart C., corresp. with Sir B. H. Liddell Hart • U. Birm. L., corresp. with Lord Avon | FILM BFI NFTVA, documentary footage | SOUND IWM SA, 'World at war', Thames, 1972, 2812

Likenesses photograph, priv. coll. • photographs, repro. in Smyth, *Milestones*, frontispiece

Wealth at death £29,564: probate, 5 Sept 1983, *CGPLA Eng. & Wales*

Smyth [*formerly* Smyth-Pigott], **John Hugh** (1852–1927), Agapemonite leader, was born at Brockley Court, near Weston-super-Mare, Somerset, on 1 August 1852, the third son of Henry Thomas Coward Smyth Pigott (1823–1858), formerly a captain in the Royal Scots Greys, and his wife, Elizabeth Drummond, *née* Nairne (*d*. 1898). He attended Rossall School, Fleetwood, Lancashire, and matriculated from Pembroke College, Cambridge, where he remained for no more than a year (1871–2). After a restless period, first in the merchant navy, later in Queensland, Australia (as a gold prospector), and in North America, he experienced an evangelical conversion through the preaching of Jerry McAuley of the Water Street Mission in New York. In 1879 he began to study for the Anglican ministry at the London College of Divinity, Highbury. Ordained a deacon in 1882 (and a priest in 1883), he served as a curate at St Jude's, Mildmay Park, but in 1884, seeking a platform better suited to zealous evangelism, he became a staff captain in the Salvation Army, taking part in a mission to Cambridge University (his account of which appeared in *War Cry*, 13 December 1884). He resigned from the Salvation Army in September–October 1885. His engagement and marriage (14 August 1886) to the daughter of Henry Bion Reynolds, Catharine (1852–1936), whose brother Alfred was vicar of Kingsley, Cheshire, may have encouraged his reconciliation with the Church of England. Earlier in 1886 he had returned to Cambridge, where his espousal of an extreme form of Christian perfectionism had been divisive in student evangelical circles. In November he was appointed as a curate at the Church of Ireland mission in Townsend Street, Dublin, but very soon his vicar, W. H. Fiske, 'turned him out' because of his extreme views. In 1887 or soon after, Smyth-Pigott renewed his association with Douglas Hamilton, whom he had known at Cambridge but who had recently joined H. J. Prince's sect, the Agapemone at Spaxton, Somerset. Hamilton appears to have persuaded him that he too was called to work with, and possibly even succeed, Prince as the sect's leader.

Almost certainly Smyth-Pigott visited Spaxton and met Henry Prince but he soon moved back to his former haunts in London. By May 1889 he was living in Stoke Newington and was recognized by Prince as the sect's pastor in Clapton. In 1896 an Agapemonite chapel, known as the Ark of the New Covenant, was opened in Rookwood Road. Here, to the delight of his flock, Smyth-Pigott announced on 7 September 1902 that he was the Messiah. A more public proclamation the following Sunday evoked a scornful reaction from an indignant crowd. Shortly afterwards he moved to Spaxton, where he explained that he was the fulfilment of a process in which Prince had been the herald (or John the Baptist). Smyth-Pigott, the Messiah, had conveniently been born in 1852, just after Prince had rallied his followers with the proclamation 'Behold he Cometh'.

Established as the new head, or 'heavenly bridegroom', of the community, Smyth-Pigott appears to have adopted

Prince's dictatorial and arbitrary role, but the lethargy which had characterized the Agapemone in Prince's later years was transformed by the more active lifestyle of several younger recruits who, impressed by Smyth-Pigott's earlier ministry, brought to the community some fresh energy. Though enjoined to secrecy about the community's activities, members were encouraged to have some contact with their neighbours in Spaxton and to engage in charitable work. The need for secrecy was occasioned, at least in part, by the fact that Smyth-Pigott required his followers, including his wife, to abstain from sexual relations, but, like his predecessor, insisted that some of the female members were to be an order of 'soul-brides', from whose number he would be able to choose 'the bride of the Lamb'. In the summer of 1904 Ruth Ann(e) Preece was designated as Smyth-Pigott's 'chief spiritual bride' and it soon became apparent that the relationship was other than platonic. During the next six years she gave birth to three children, of whom Smyth-Pigott was the acknowledged father.

In January 1909, after a trial in the consistory court in Wells Cathedral on charges of improper behaviour, Smyth-Pigott, who had ignored the summons, was degraded from holy orders in his absence. The extent of Smyth-Pigott's promiscuity in subsequent years may have been exaggerated, but it was said that he abandoned Ruth Preece in favour of other soul-brides. In an attempt to regularize the status of his children, deeds were executed in 1914 whereby Smyth-Pigott and Ruth Preece both changed their surname to Smyth, while his legal wife became known as Mrs Pigott. Although these developments led to some indignant resignations from the community, Smyth did not confine his preaching to Spaxton, and his charm enabled him to retain a significant following in other Agapemonite centres in London and elsewhere, notably in Christiania, Norway, which he visited at least eight times between 1902 and 1926. By 1925, however, his health was failing, and on medical advice he remained abroad for some time. On his return a projected campaign in London had to be shelved, but he initiated some improvements to the buildings of the Abode at Spaxton. Smyth died there on 20 March 1927 and was buried in the grounds of the Agapemone.

TIMOTHY C. F. STUNT

Sources Venn, *Alum. Cant.* • Crockford (1883) • Crockford (1884) • Crockford (1887) • J. J. Schwieso, 'Deluded inmates, frantic ravers and communists: a sociological study of the Agapemone, a sect of Victorian apocalyptic millenarians', PhD diss., U. Reading, 1994 • R. Matthews, *English messiahs: studies of six English religious pretenders, 1656–1927* (1936) • J. C. Pollock, *A Cambridge movement* (1953) • D. McCormick, *Temple of love* (1962) • *Portraits of the Smyth-Pigott family: a catalogue of the oil paintings and busts in Woodspring Museum, Weston-super-Mare*, Woodspring Museum [n.d., 1980?] • b. cert. • m. cert. • *Bridgewater Mercury* (23 March 1927), 12

Archives North Somerset Museum Service, Weston-super-Mare, family archive • Som. ARS, Smyth-Pigott box, Wells diocesan file

Likenesses photograph, repro. in Matthews, *English messiahs*

Wealth at death £3279 14s. 5d.: probate, 24 May 1927, *CGPLA Eng. & Wales*

Smyth, Sir John Rowland (1806?–1873), army officer, was the fifth son of Grice Smyth of Ballynatray, co. Waterford, and his wife, Mary, daughter and coheir of H. Mitchell of Mitchellsfort, co. Cork. Educated at Trinity College, Dublin, he was commissioned cornet in the 16th lancers on 5 July 1821. He was promoted lieutenant on 26 May 1825, and was present at the capture of Bharatpur (18 January 1826). On 22 April he was made captain on the half pay list, from which he exchanged to the 32nd foot on 29 November 1827. He served for ten years in that regiment before exchanging on 10 May 1839 into the 6th dragoon guards (Carabiniers). In 1830, in Dublin, Smyth fought one of the last duels in the United Kingdom. He killed his opponent, a civilian, O'Grady, and he and his second were imprisoned for a year for manslaughter. They were granted a year's leave of absence to serve their sentence.

On 17 August 1841 Smyth obtained a half pay majority, and on 6 May 1842 he returned to the 16th lancers. He served with it in the Gwalior campaign of 1843, commanding the advanced wing of cavalry at Maharajpur, and in the Sutlej campaign of 1846, during which he commanded the regiment. It greatly distinguished itself at Aliwal by routing the Sikh cavalry and breaking a square of infantry, Smyth being severely wounded while leading it. He was mentioned in dispatches, and was made brevet lieutenant-colonel and CB.

Smyth was lieutenant-colonel of the 16th lancers from 10 December 1847 until 2 November 1855, when he exchanged to half pay. He had been given a reward for distinguished service on 1 June 1854, and had been made colonel in the army on 20 June. He became major-general on 22 December 1860 and commanded the central division of the Madras army. He was made KCB on 13 March 1867 and promoted lieutenant-general on 1 April 1870. He was given the colonelcy of the 6th dragoon guards on 21 January 1868.

Smyth married Fanny Alice, second daughter of Charles *Abbott, first Baron Tenterden, on 11 May 1839, and they had one daughter, Penelope Mary Gertrude, who married her cousin, the third Lord Tenterden. Smyth died at Norris's Hotel, Russell Road, Kensington, on 14 May 1873. His wife survived him.

E. M. LLOYD, *rev.* JAMES LUNT

Sources *The Times* (17 May 1873) • H. Graham, *History of the sixteenth, the queen's, light dragoons (lancers), 1759–1912* (privately printed, Devizes, 1912) • *Hart's Army List* • J. D. Lunt, *16th/5th The queen's royal lancers* (1973) • Marquess of Anglesey [G. C. H. V. Paget], *A history of the British cavalry, 1816 to 1919*, 1 (1973) • J. D. Lunt, *The scarlet lancers* (1993) • Burke, *Gen. GB* (1894)

Likenesses print, repro. in Graham, *History of the sixteenth*, 119; copy, priv. coll.

Wealth at death under £5000: probate, 25 June 1873, *CGPLA Eng. & Wales*

Smyth, John Talfourd (*c*.1819–1851), engraver, was born in Edinburgh. After studying painting for a time at the Trustees' Academy under Sir William Allan, he taught himself the art of line engraving and specialized in portraits, landscapes, and figure subjects. His earliest published works were *A Child's Head*, after Sir J. Watson Gordon, and *The Stirrup Cup*, after Allan. In 1838 he moved to Glasgow, but during 1845 returned to Edinburgh, where he worked industriously for the print publishers. Two of his rare book illustrations, *Drummond Castle* and *Killiecrankie*, after J. C.

Brown, appear in J. Browne's *A History of the Highlands and of the Highland Clans* (4 vols., 1837–8). Smyth engraved ten portraits of contemporary painters for the *Art Union* in 1847; Ary Scheffer's *The Comforter* in 1846; Wilkie's *John Knox Dispensing the Sacrament* in 1848; and W. Mulready's *The Last In* and Allan's *Banditti Dividing Spoil* for the *Art Journal* of 1850. He was engaged upon a plate from J. Faed's *First Step* when he died prematurely at Edinburgh, on 18 May 1851. His contemporaries had a high opinion of his potential.

F. M. O'Donoghue, *rev.* Joanna Desmond

Sources B. Hunnisett, *An illustrated dictionary of British steel engravers*, new edn (1989) • R. K. Engen, *Dictionary of Victorian wood engravers* (1985) • *Art Journal*, 13 (1851), 183, 201 • Redgrave, *Artists* • print catalogue [V&A] • P. J. M. McEwan, *Dictionary of Scottish art and architecture* (1994)

Smyth [*formerly* Curzon-Howe], **Sir Leicester** (1829–1891), army officer, born on 25 October 1829, was the seventh son of Richard William Penn Curzon, afterwards Curzon-Howe, first Earl Howe, and his first wife, Lady Harriet Brudenell, daughter of Robert Brudenell, sixth earl of Cardigan. After education at Eton College, he was commissioned second lieutenant in the rifle brigade on 29 November 1845. He joined the reserve battalion at Quebec in 1846, became lieutenant on 12 November 1847, returned to England, and went with the 1st battalion to the Cape in January 1852. He served in the 1852 Basuto War, and distinguished himself in the action at Berea on 20 December. He commanded one of two companies which climbed almost inaccessible heights under fire, and drove a large force of Sotho before them. He was highly praised in dispatches.

On 23 February 1854 Curzon-Howe was appointed aide-de-camp to Lord Raglan, accompanied him to Turkey and the Crimea, and was present at Alma and Inkerman, and throughout the siege of Sevastopol. He was assistant military secretary from 7 October 1854 to 11 November 1855, first under Lord Raglan and afterwards under General Simpson. He became captain in his corps on 22 December 1854, and was made brevet major on 17 July 1855 and brevet lieutenant-colonel from 8 September, having taken home the dispatches announcing the fall of Sevastopol. He continued to serve in the Crimea as aide-de-camp to General Codrington until 30 June 1856. He received the Légion d'honneur (fifth class) and the Mejidiye (fifth class).

Curzon-Howe was assistant military secretary in the Ionian Islands from 23 November 1856 to 23 August 1861. He then rejoined the 1st battalion of the rifle brigade, in which he had become major on 30 April, and served with it at Malta and Gibraltar until 4 August 1865, when he went on half pay. He had become colonel in the army on 9 February 1861. On 12 February 1866 he married Alicia Maria (*d.* 1898), eldest daughter and heir of Robert Smyth JP, of Drumcree, co. Westmeath, and in the following November he took the surname of Smyth. They had no children. He was made CB on 13 May 1867. He was military secretary at headquarters in Ireland from 1 July 1865 to 30 June 1870, and deputy quartermaster-general there from 17 July 1872 to 26 February 1874.

On 7 February 1874 Smyth became major-general (later antedated to 6 March 1868), and on 13 February 1878 lieutenant-general. He commanded the western district from 2 April 1877 to 31 March 1880, and at the Cape from 10 November 1880 to 9 November 1885. In 1882–3 he administered the government and acted as high commissioner for South Africa. He was made KCMG on 1 February 1884, and KCB on 16 January 1886. He was promoted general on 18 July 1885, and commanded the southern district from 1 May 1889 to 25 September 1890, when he was appointed governor of Gibraltar. After a few months there he returned to England on sick leave, and died at his home, 24 South Eaton Place, London, on 27 January 1891. He was buried at Gopsall, Leicestershire.

E. M. Lloyd, *rev.* James Lunt

Sources W. H. Cope, 'General Hon. Sir Leicester Smyth', *The Rifle Brigade chronicle for 1890*, ed. W. Verner (1891), 171–4 • *Hart's Army List* • *The Times* (29 Jan 1891) • W. Cope, *The history of the rifle brigade* (1877) • *CGPLA Ire.* (1891)

Likenesses R. T., wood-engraving, NPG; repro. in *ILN* (7 Feb 1891)

Wealth at death £45,932 12*s.* 5*d.* in England: probate, 17 March 1891, *CGPLA Ire.*

Smyth, Matthew (*d.* 1526). *See under* Smyth family (*per.* c.1500–1680).

Smyth, Matthew (1533–1583). *See under* Smyth family (*per.* c.1500–1680).

Smyth, Patrick James (*c.*1823–1885), politician and journalist, was born at Mount Brown, Kilmainham, Dublin, the son of James Smyth, a native of Cavan and a prosperous tanner, and Anne, daughter of Maurice Bruton of Portane, co. Meath. He received his education at Clongowes Wood College, co. Kildare, where he became friends with Thomas Francis Meagher. In 1844 both joined the Repeal Association while they were studying for the bar. In the dispute between the O'Connellites and the Young Irelanders, Smyth, like Meagher, sided with the latter, and in 1847 was elected on the council of the Irish Confederation. Smyth was actively involved in the 1848 rising in Tipperary, when the *Hue and Cry* described him as '5 feet 9 inches in height; fair hair; dark eyes; fair, delicate face, and of weak appearance, long back; weak in his walk; small whiskers; dresses indifferent' (O'Sullivan, 261). Disguised as a peasant, he managed to escape to America, where he worked as a correspondent for several newspapers. After Meagher's escape from Tasmania in 1852, they persuaded the Irish directory in New York to rescue other Young Ireland prisoners. Consequently, with the code name Nicaragua, Smyth planned and carried out the escape of John Mitchel, and set out for Australia again on 24 December 1853 to effect the release of William Smith O'Brien, who, however, was pardoned when Smyth arrived in Melbourne.

On 8 February 1855 in Hobart Town, Tasmania, Smyth married Jane Anne Regan (*d.* 1887?), daughter of John Regan (*d.* 1869), an Irish settler originally from Cork (O'Sullivan, 264). They moved first to America and in 1856 to Ireland, where Smyth resumed his legal studies. He was called to the bar in 1858, but never practised. For four years (1860–64) he was proprietor of *The Irishman*, a nationalist newspaper, in which he also advocated the cause of the northern states in the American Civil War. Although opposed to the Fenians, he offered to defend the staff of the *Irish People* when they were arrested in 1865. In the same year he moved to Normandy, France, before returning to Ireland in 1867.

Smyth published several pamphlets, among them *Notes on Direct Communication between Ireland and France* (1861), a sketch of Meagher (1867), and *A Plea for Peasant Proprietary* (1871). *The Priest in Politics* was published posthumously in 1885. On 29 August 1871 Smyth was made a chevalier of the Légion d'honneur in recognition of his services to France; he had organized the Irish ambulance aid to that country during the Franco-Prussian War, and had been involved in attempts at reviving the Irish brigade to fight for the French.

As a candidate for Isaac Butt's Home Rule Party, Smyth was elected an MP for County Westmeath in 1871; he sat for the constituency uninterruptedly until 1880, when he became MP for Tipperary. He was considered a possible candidate for the leadership of the Home Rule Party, but by 1873 it was clear that he wanted a complete repeal of the union. Furthermore, he became an implacable and bitter enemy of the Land League, which he described as a 'League of Hell'. The arguments with Charles Stewart Parnell and the Irish party cost him his popularity in Ireland, and he resigned his seat in 1882; he subsequently lived in poverty. On 16 December 1884 he was appointed secretary of the Irish loan reproductive fund, and his acceptance of the post was strongly criticized by Irish nationalists. It appears that he took it to provide for his family. He survived his appointment only a few weeks, and died at 15 Belgrave Square, Rathmines, Dublin, on 12 January 1885, leaving his widow and family in straitened circumstances. A fund was raised for their support. Patrick James Smyth is buried in Glasnevin cemetery, Dublin.

D. J. O'Donoghue, *rev.* Brigitte Anton

Sources T. F. O'Sullivan, *The Young Irelanders*, 2nd edn (1945) · J. Mitchel, *Jail journal, or, Five years in British prisons* [1860–76] · T. J. Kiernan, *The Irish exiles in Australia* (1954) · B. M. Touhill, *William Smith O'Brien and his Irish revolutionary companions in penal exile* (1981) · J. H. Cullen, *Young Ireland in exile* (1928) · D. J. Hickey and J. E. Doherty, *A dictionary of Irish history* (1980) · H. Boylan, *A dictionary of Irish biography*, 2nd edn (1988) · R. J. Hayes, ed., *Manuscript sources for the history of Irish civilisation*, 4 (1965) · R. J. Hayes, ed., *Manuscript sources for the history of Irish civilisation: first supplement, 1965–1975*, 1 (1979) · J. Devoy, *Recollections of an Irish rebel* (1929); repr. (1969) · R. Pigott, *Reminiscences of an Irish national journalist* (1882) · C. G. Duffy, *Four years of Irish history, 1845–1849: a sequel to 'Young Ireland'* (1883) · *Freeman's Journal* [Dublin] (13 Jan 1888) · *Dublin Evening Mail* (14 Jan 1885) · private information (1897) [J. O'Leary]

Archives NL Ire., letters and financial papers · NL Ire., MSS | NL Ire., Hickey collection, typescript copies of papers of the Young Irelanders, incl. some of and about Patrick James Smyth, MSS 3225–3226 · NL Ire., account of the Waterford election, 1870, MS 8197 · PRO NIre., John Martin papers, letters to John Martin, D.2137

Likenesses E. Hayes, watercolour, 1854, repro. in Mitchel, *Jail journal*, 369

Wealth at death left family in straitened circumstances; committee, incl. Father Mechan, raised funds for their support

Smyth, Reginald [*pseud.* Reg Smythe] (**1917–1998**), cartoonist, was born on 10 July 1917 at 52 Union Road, Throston, Hartlepool, co. Durham, the son of Richard Oliver Smyth (*d.* in or before 1949), shipyard worker, and his wife, Florence (Florrie), *née* Pearce. Educated at Galley's Field School, West Hartlepool, he left school at fourteen and worked as a butcher's errand boy. After spending some time in unemployment he joined the Northumberland Fusiliers, with whom he served for ten years and rose to the rank of sergeant. He was a machine-gunner and saw active service in north Africa during the Second World War. There he developed an interest in drawing by designing posters for amateur dramatic productions.

After leaving the forces Smyth settled in London, working as a clerk with the General Post Office (GPO). On 13 August 1949 he married Vera (1916/17–1997), the daughter of George Toyne, woodworker, and formerly the wife of Herbert Whittaker. There were no children of the marriage. While working for the GPO, Smyth again produced posters for amateur plays, but by the early 1950s he had moved to creating cartoons and began to work through an agent. It was at this time that he took up the pen name Reg Smythe. By 1954 he was working for the *Daily Mirror*, designing cartoons for the 'Laughter at Work' series, under the mentorship of Leslie Harding (Styx). This led to full-time employment at the *Mirror* and, in 1957, to the birth of his great creation, Andy Capp.

According to Smyth, Andy Capp was born 'on the A1 road at 60 mph' (*The Independent*). While on a visit to West Hartlepool, Smyth had received a request from the *Mirror* to create a cartoon to boost northern readership, and Capp was created as he returned southwards to work. The rise to fame of his creation was staggering. First appearing in the *Mirror*'s northern edition in 1957 the cartoon swiftly went national in 1958. In the same year the first Andy Capp compilation was also published. By 1960 an Andy Capp strip cartoon was appearing seven days a week—six days in the *Mirror* and one in its sister paper, the *Sunday Pictorial*. Andy's rise to international fame was even more sensational. He appeared in at least 34 countries and 700 newspapers, with text in 13 or more languages. He was Tuffa Viktor in Sweden, Willi Wakker in Germany, André Chapeau in France, and Kasket Karl in Denmark, where small, cigarette-smoking models were snapped up in the early 1960s. Smyth's creation brought him numerous awards, including 'Best British cartoon strip' annually from 1961 to 1965. This honour was awarded by the Cartoonists' Club of Great Britain, of which Smyth was a founding member. He won three major awards in Italy—in 1969, 1973, and 1978—and the prestigious US 'Best strip' cartoon award in 1974.

Hugh Cudlipp of the *Mirror*, the man who persuaded Smyth to create Andy Capp, described the cartoon character succinctly as 'a work-shy, beer-swilling, rent-dodging, wife-beating, pigeon-fancying, soccer-playing, uncouth cadger, setting an appalling example to the youth of Britain' (*The Guardian*). It is perhaps Capp's very political incorrectness that made him wickedly appealing. Smyth said on more than one occasion that Andy and his equally infamous wife, Flo, were based on his own parents. In his personal love of a pint of beer and a cigarette—until 1983, when he gave up smoking—Smyth had something in common with his 'offspring'. Andy Capp's ventures off the printed page proved less successful. There was a West End musical and a television series that commenced in 1988, scripted by Keith Waterhouse, but neither had any lasting effect. Some pundits felt that the opportunity for a successful cartoon television series had been missed.

Smyth was a very private man. At the height of his success he returned to his native Hartlepool, living and working quietly in a secluded bungalow in the middle of a large estate—'reserved to the point of being a recluse' (*The Scotsman*). Following the death of his wife in 1997 he married, on 21 May 1998, a widow, Jean Marie Glynn (*b.* 1928/9), daughter of Thomas Barry, labourer. Smyth died at his home, 96 Caledonian Road, Hartlepool, on 13 June 1998, of lung cancer. He was survived by his wife. Typically for a professional described as a 'one off' (*The Scotsman*) he left a year's worth of cartoons to his employers.

KEITH GREGSON

Sources *The Times* (15 June 1998) · *The Guardian* (15 June 1998) · *Daily Telegraph* (15 June 1998) · *The Independent* (15 June 1998) · *The Scotsman* (15 June 1998) · *WWW* · b. cert. · m. certs. [Vera Whittaker; Jean Marie Glynn] · d. cert.

Archives Hartlepool Reference Library

Likenesses photograph, 1963, Mirror Syndication International, London · photograph, repro. in *The Times* · photograph, repro. in *The Guardian* · photograph, repro. in *Daily Telegraph* · photograph, repro. in *The Independent* · photograph, repro. in *The Scotsman*

Wealth at death £490,654—gross; £459,049—net: probate, 1998, *CGPLA Eng. & Wales*

Smyth [Smith], **Richard** (1499/1500–1563), theologian, was born in Worcester diocese, and went to Merton College, Oxford, where he graduated BA on 5 April 1527. Elected to a junior fellowship (25 February 1527), he was confirmed a full fellow on 1 August 1528. On admission as MA (18 July 1530), he held the office of junior dean in the college (1 August 1531) and *scriba* to the university (admitted 8 February 1532) until given leave to read for the degree of BTh (27 February 1533). Two months later (19 April) Smyth was granted letters dimissory to be ordained in Lincoln diocese. He was installed rector of the Merton living at Cuxham, Oxfordshire, in 1536.

In 1536, in order to take up the newly established royal lectureship in theology at Oxford, Smyth incepted DTh and was the first incumbent of the office. A promising scholar, he added his signature to a declaration on holy orders by convocation later that year. He was university delegate to convocation and a signatory of the Bishops' Book in 1537. Smyth was noted for his forceful sermons and was often called upon to preach, most notably at recantations when such a 'solemnity should not pass without some effectual sermon for the holding up of the mother-church of Rome' (*Acts and Monuments*, 5.455). He first revealed a talent for inopportune public displays of religious conservatism when 'he preached purgatory and condemned the doctrine of Sola Fide' in a university sermon at Oxford in 1536 (*LP Henry VIII*, 10, no. 396). His appointments as principal of St Alban Hall and, in September 1537, master of Whittington College, London, and rector of St Michael Paternoster Royal, however, confirmed his theological credentials and growing national recognition. Two official investigations display Smyth's fierce loyalties to his new patrons, Edmund Bonner, bishop of London, and Henry VIII: bidding prayers 'for our most holye father, the Bishop of London, a founder of the faith of Christ' (8 July 1537) correlate with the equally injudicious claim in September 1538 that as royal vice-commissary he 'represented the king's proper person' and, presumably, that he should be accorded suitable honours (*LP Henry VIII*, 12/2, nos. 534, 308). Smyth's lack of finesse was matched only by his unreformed conservatism, although later evangelical accounts suggest that he occasionally mitigated his views to suit his audience. This is reflected by the contrasting views that he was 'Sophista magis cum Theologus' ('a great sophist and divine'; Humphrey, 43) as well as 'the best school man of his time, a subtle disputant, and admirably well read in the fathers and councils' (Wood, 1.143).

The same conservative tenor also pervades Smyth's first publications, which uphold orthodox eucharistic doctrine and the opinion that tradition was equal to scripture, namely his *Assertion and Defence of the Sacrament of the Aulter* (1546), *Defence of the Sacrifice of the Masse* (also 1546), and *Brief Treatyse Settynge Forth Divers Truthes Left by the Apostles Tradition* (1547). On the accession of Edward VI a few months later these books were burnt by order of council during two public recantations, at Paul's Cross and in Oxford. To mark the retractions of this notorious conservative, two separate accounts of Smyth's recantations were published in London almost immediately: *A Godly and Faythfull Retraction Revokyng Certeyn Errors* and *A Playne Declaration Made at Oxford*. They gained Smyth the scorn of both evangelicals and conservatives, causing Bishop Gardiner to write to Cromwell, 'I was glad of my former judgment that I never had familiarity with him', and to accuse Smyth of hypocrisy and hiding 'by the number' (*Acts and Monuments*, 5.39f.). The recantations also undermined Smyth's position as *praelector*. By spring 1548 he had to vacate his lectureship, and witnessed the appointment of Peter Martyr Vermigli, target of most of his later polemical publications, as his successor. He spent the winter months of 1548–9 attending Martyr's lectures on 1 Corinthians diligently and in later polemical writings often took his line of attack from his assiduous notes.

Following a vain attempt to draw his evangelical successor into an impromptu disputation on the eucharist during the course of an ordinary lecture, Smyth disappeared from Oxford amid wild rumours about the exact reason for his sudden departure. When the king's visitors to the university had finally settled details of the debate, Smyth had already left the country and made his way to Louvain University where he incorporated MA on 4 April 1549. From the safety of his exile he launched two polemical salvos against Martyr, *De coelibatu liber unus, de votis monasticis liber alter* (1550) and *Diatriba de hominis justificatione adversum Petrum Martyrem Vermelium nunc apostatum* (also 1550). The year 1551 saw the publication at Paris of two further polemical tracts against Martyr and Cranmer. These writings, one a revised edition of his first treatises on monastic vows and celibacy, the other an attack on Cranmer's 1550 exposition of the eucharist, were banned by order of archbishop and council. None the less 'a barrel of Dr Smyth's most false and detestable books from Paris' was smuggled into England by Bonner's servants (*Salisbury MSS*, 1.83).

After moving to Scotland in spring 1551 Smyth incorporated at St Andrews (DTh, 7 July). In February 1552 he petitioned Archbishop Cranmer, offering a book in favour of clerical marriage in return for a royal pardon. The exiled theologian claimed that his Scottish patrons required him to compose an attack on the archbishop's eucharistic doctrine 'and all other doctrines now approved in England'. It appears that the exertions of life in St Andrews seem to have shaken even Smyth's commitment to Catholicism, as he concluded his pleas by writing: 'I beseech your grace help me home, as soon as you may conveniently, for God's sake, and ye shall never, I trust by God, repent the fact' (Vermigli, 647). Both the fact that Smyth never issued a book on clerical marriage, as well as his central role at Cranmer's heresy trial at Oxford, emphasize his contempt for the prelate and the cynicism of this missive.

By winter 1552 Smyth was again lobbying for a pardon 'for treasons, heresies and all offences', which he received by spring 1553, though he did not, in fact, return to England until after Edward's death. Following Mary's accession Smyth returned to Oxford, took up his preferments again, and was also created eighth prebendary of Christ Church (23 July 1554), as well as rector of St Dunstan-in-the-East (7 January 1555), Aston Clinton, Buckinghamshire (27 January 1555), and St Lawrence's Frodsham, Cheshire (1 October 1557). A chaplain-extraordinary to Philip and Mary, he expounded on 1 Corinthians 13: 3 ('if I give my body to be burned and have not love, I gain nothing') at the burning of Latimer and Ridley in 1555, and had himself elected vice-chancellor in order to preside over Cranmer's trial at Oxford in person (April–October 1555). The publication in 1554/5 of his *Bouclier of the Catholike Fayth of Christes Church* in two parts only confirms Smyth's description as 'the greatest pillar for the catholic cause in his time' (Wood, 1.143).

Shortly after the succession of Elizabeth I, Smyth attempted to flee to Scotland. He was apprehended in the borders, put under house arrest at Lambeth, compelled to subscribe to the royal supremacy in matters spiritual, and subsequently released on bail by the trusty archbishop-elect, who reported Smyth's latest conversion forthwith. Giving Matthew Parker the slip, however, Smyth reached Louvain, was readmitted 'magister noster' (15 February 1561) and resumed publishing almost immediately. In 1562 his output of polemical works amounted to six volumes, which reveal both the author's fundamental theological concerns as well as his chief opponents. Among his Louvain writings, a refutation of the Calvinist doctrines of infant baptism and justification featured alongside a rejection of Philip Melanchthon's eucharistic theology. Smyth rounded off his comprehensive attack on continental evangelicalism by a work on the sacrifice of the mass. One of the most published Louvain authors of his day, Smyth was installed *premier lecteur* in scripture at the newly established Catholic University of Douai barely fifteen months after his arrival in Brabant (5 October 1562), commended by the founders of the university as a man of 'great dynamism and high reputation, whose profound knowledge of sacred theology is evident' (Bibliothèque municipale de Douai, MS 1304, fol. 76). At the instigation of the regent of the Low Countries, Margaret of Parma, he was made provost of the collegiate church of St Peter and vice-chancellor of the University of Douai (22 December 1562). His strong convictions caused Smyth to take up writing once more, and two notable polemical tracts, one a refutation of Melanchthon's 1543 *Common Places*, the other an attack on the Calvinist doctrine of free will, left the newly erected Douai printing press only months before his death at Douai on 9 June 1563. Richard Smyth was buried in the lady chapel, St Peter's, Douai, where his epitaph recorded his age at death as sixty-three.

Contemporary evangelical sources routinely depicted Smyth as an inconsistent careerist with a strong propensity to contradict his writings by his deeds. A great advocate of clerical celibacy with little sympathy for married ministers, Smyth often found himself accused of sexual laxity. This, rather than his opposition to royal supremacy, was given as the reason for his second dismissal from Oxford in 1559. Bishop Jewel modelled a report to Martyr on a classical oration:

> Smith has gone into Wales, where, they say, he has taken a wife, with the view of refuting all your arguments. He now gains his livelihood by a hired tavern, despised by our friends and his own; by those who know him, and those who do not, by old and young, by himself, by everyone. (Robinson, 1.81)

His Louvain friends and patrons, on the other hand, had a very different opinion of Smyth. In a letter to her brother, Philip II of Spain, Margaret of Parma commended Smyth as 'a person of remarkable doctrine, good faith and highly commended by those at Louvain'. While her claim that 'His Holiness has called him to assist with the council' proves impossible to verify, it speaks strongly of the great esteem in which he was held during his exile (Gachard, 2.419). A noted lecturer at Louvain, Richard Smyth attracted the first colony of English *Louvainists* to follow him to Douai. While the foundation of an English college at Douai lay firmly in the hands of the second generation of divinity lecturers, among them William Allen, Smyth undoubtedly laid that college's foundations by bringing the first English exiles to the new university.

J. ANDREAS LÖWE

Sources CCC Cam., Parker Collection, MS 119, fol. 109 • 'Collegii Mertonensis registrum vetus', Merton Oxf., I, fols. 269*r*, 271*v*, 272*v*, 284*r*, 285*r* • 'Registrum actae congregationis', Oxf. UA, fol. 17f • 'Registrum curiae cancellarii', Oxf. UA, fol. 356*v* • 'Registrum H', Oxf. UA, fol. 261 • battels book, Christ Church Oxf., MS X (1) c.1 •

Reg. Oxf., 1.146 • Registrum Ghinucci, Worcs. RO, II, 70 • G. Hennessy, *Novum repertorium ecclesiasticum parochiale Londinense, or, London diocesan clergy succession from the earliest time to the year 1898* (1898), 334 • P. M. Vermigli, *Duos libellos de caelibatu sacerdotum* (1559), 643 • J. Humphrey, *J. Juelli episcopi Sarisb. vita et mors* (1573), 43 • *The acts and monuments of John Foxe*, new edn, ed. G. Townsend, 8 vols. (1843–9), vol. 5, pp. 39–40 • J. Strype, *Memorials of Archbishop Cranmer*, 2 (1647), 200, 213 • A. Wood, *The history and antiquities of the colleges and halls in the University of Oxford*, ed. J. Gutch, appx (1790), 88–91; appx 93 • D. V. Andreas, *Fasti Academici Lovaniensis* (1650), 85 • *Matricule de l'Université de Louvain*, 4, ed. A. Schillings (1961), 600, 612 • J. M. Anderson, ed., *Early records of the University of St Andrews*, Scottish History Society, 3rd ser., 8 (1926), 254, 296 • M. Parker, *De antiquitate Britannicae ecclesiae et privilegiis ecclesiae Cantuarensis* (1572), [422] • L. P. Gachard, *Correspondance de Marguerite de Autriche* (1881), 2.419, 447 • H. R. J. Douthilloeul, *Galerie douaisienne* (1844), 4 • T. H. J. Leuridan, 'Richard Smith', *Revue des Sciences Ecclésiastiques*, 11 (1904), 1–29 • J. F. Foppens, *Bibliotheca Belgica* (1739), 2.1069 • J. Pits, *Relationum historicarum de rebus Anglicis*, ed. [W. Bishop] (Paris, 1619), 761 • J. A. Löwe, 'Richard Smyth and the foundation of the University of Douai', *Nederlands Archief voor Kerkgeschiedenis/Dutch Archive of Church History*, 79/2 (1999), 142–69 • E. van Nuffel, 'Leuven en Douai: De "splitsing" van 1562', *Wetenschappelijke Tijdingen*, 24 (1964–5), 473–80 • *Calendar of the manuscripts of the most hon. the marquis of Salisbury*, 1, HMC, 9 (1883), 83 • H. Robinson, ed. and trans., *Original letters relative to the English Reformation*, 1 vol. in 2, Parker Society, [26] (1846–7)

Archives CCC Cam., MS 119, fol. 109 • Christ Church Oxf., battels book, MS X (1) c.1 • Merton Oxf., 'Collegii Mertonensis registrum vetus', I, fols. 269*r*, 271*v*, 272*v*, 284*r*, 285*r* • Oxf. UA, 'Registrum curiae cancellarii' • Oxf. UA, 'Registrum H' • Oxf. UA, 'Registrum actae congregationis'

Likenesses woodcut, 1641 (*The burning of Latimer and Ridley*), repro. in *Acts and monuments of John Foxe*

Smyth, Richard (1826–1878), minister of the Presbyterian Church in Ireland and politician, the son of Hugh Smyth, a farmer, of Carncullogh, near Dervock, co. Antrim, and his wife, Sarah Anne Wray, was born at Carncullogh on 4 October 1826. As a child he suffered from rheumatic fever. He was educated locally and at the University of Glasgow, where he graduated MA in 1850, and received an honorary DD in 1871. He studied theology at the English Presbyterian Theological College in London, at the Presbyterian college, Belfast, and at the University of Bonn. R. Buick Knox described him as 'a brilliant, if not the most brilliant, product of the London College' (Knox, 4). He was ordained in Westport, co. Mayo, on 20 June 1855. Two years later he was installed as the collegiate minister of the historic First Derry Congregation, and in 1865 he was appointed professor of oriental languages and biblical literature in Magee College, Londonderry, moving in 1870 to the chair of theology. He was a supporter of W. E. Gladstone's policy of disestablishment in Ireland, and, as moderator of the general assembly in 1869 and 1870, played a crucial part in settling the financial affairs of the church following the withdrawal of the *regium donum*.

A lifelong Liberal in politics, an eloquent advocate of tenant right and of educational, temperance, and penal reform, Smyth was elected MP for County Londonderry on 16 February 1874. The demands of public life, in addition to his academic responsibilities and constant preaching engagements, were too much for his weak constitution

Richard Smyth (1826–1878), by unknown engraver, pubd 1874

and he died, unmarried, at Bushvale, Antrim Road, Belfast, on 4 December 1878 after a brief illness. He was buried in his native Dervock on 6 December. The Smyth memorial lecture was established in Magee College in his honour.

G. C. Boase, *rev.* Finlay Holmes

Sources J. M. Barkley, ed., *Fasti of the general assembly of the Presbyterian Church in Ireland*, 1: *1840–1870* (1986), 70 • Church House, Belfast, Archives of the Presbyterian Historical Society • 'Richard Smyth', *Belfast News-Letter* (5 Dec 1878) • 'Richard Smyth', *Belfast News-Letter* (7 Dec 1878) • *The Witness* (6 Dec 1878) • *The Witness* (13 Dec 1878) • T. H. Witherow and A. C. Murphy, *In memory of Rev. Richard Smyth, D.D., M.P., professor of theology in Magee College, Londonderry* (1878) • J. Smyth, 'Memoir of Rev. Professor Richard Smyth', *Presbyterian Churchman*, 6–7 (1888–9) • J. J. McClure, 'Our own worthies: Professor Richard Smyth', *Presbyterian Churchman*, 7–8 (1890–91) • R. F. G. Holmes, *Magee, 1865–1965: the evolution of the Magee Colleges* (1965) • R. B. Knox, *Westminster College, Cambridge: its background and history* (1983), 4

Archives BL, letters to W. E. Gladstone, Add. MSS 44416–44457

Likenesses engraving, pubd 1874, NPG [*see illus.*] • Hooke of Manchester, oils, Union Theological College, Belfast • photograph, repro. in J. E. Davey, *1840–1940: the story of a hundred years* (1940), 55 • photograph, Magee College, Londonderry; repro. in Holmes, *Magee* • photograph (after photograph by A. Ayton), NPG; repro. in *ILN* (18 July 1874)

Wealth at death under £3000: probate, 17 Jan 1879, *CGPLA Ire.*

Smyth, Sir Robert, fifth baronet (1744–1802), patron of the arts and radical, was born on 10 January 1744 at Berechurch Hall, Essex, the son of the Revd Robert Smyth, vicar of Woolavington, Sussex, and his wife, Dorothy Lloyd. He was educated at Westminster School and was admitted as a pensioner at Trinity College, Cambridge, on 27 January 1762, from where he graduated BA in 1766. He had earlier enrolled at Lincoln's Inn (1761). On 8 December 1765 he succeeded his cousin, Sir Trafford Smyth, as fifth baronet. In 1774 he was elected MP for Cardigan Boroughs, where he remained until December of the following year when he was unseated by petition. Five years later he re-entered parliament as MP for Colchester, close to his estate at Berechurch, for which he sat as an opponent of the North ministry, an enthusiastic member of the association movement, and a supporter of Fox during the Regency crisis.

On 17 September 1776 Smyth had married Charlotte Sophia Delaval Blake (*d.* 1823); the couple had three children, George Henry, Louisa, and Charlotte. Born in Hamburg, Lady Smyth was naturalized by an act of parliament on 12 March 1781, thereby also confirming her marriage jointure. In 1777 the couple undertook an artistic tour of Italy. They arrived in Milan in early November, visited Naples in March 1778, and reached Rome in early April, where they became acquainted with the painters Henry Fuseli and Piranesi, who dedicated a plate to Smyth in his *Vasi, candelabri, cippi* (1778). The ten Italian paintings that descended to Smyth's great-grandson, Thomas George Graham White (sold at Christies on 23 March 1878, lots 1–40), including works by Carracci, Correggio, and Salvator Rosa, seem to have been acquired during this trip. Back in England, Smyth became Fuseli's principal patron, for whom Fuseli produced seven of his finest paintings during the 1780s (dispersed 1878, lots 16–22), most notably *Satan Starting from the Ear of Eve at the Touch of Ithuriel's Spear*, *Lady Macbeth*, and the *Death of Dido*.

Smyth was an ardent supporter of the French Revolution and, 'lik[ing] neither the government nor the climate of England' (Thomas Paine, quoted in Williamson, 247), he settled in Paris in 1791. This may also be when he established his bank in the rue Cerutti now rue Lafitte (not, as asserted by Alger, at the peace of Amiens). During his decade in Paris, Smyth became a 'very intimate friend' of Thomas Paine (Paine, 425). At the famous British dinner at White's Hotel on 18 November 1792, Smyth and Lord Edward Fitzgerald proposed to toast 'The speedy abolition of all hereditary titles and feudal distinctions'—misrepresented in the London press as an actual renunciation of their titles—and signed the subsequent 'address' to the convention. That autumn he helped Lord Wycombe spirit the author Madame de Flahault out of Paris.

In October 1793 Smyth assisted in the drawing up of a petition against the measures enacted against British residents of Paris. Despite his revolutionary sympathies, he was arrested on 18 November 1793; although released on this occasion, he eventually spent almost a year in confinement. During his own incarceration (from December 1793 to November 1794), Thomas Paine was sustained by the correspondence which Lady Smyth initiated with him (from 'the Castle in the Air' [Paine] to 'My Little Corner of the World' [Charlotte Smyth], (Yorke, 2.366)). This 'extremely beautiful correspondence' became 'half the world' to him, continuing, according to Yorke, 'without intermission' until 1802 (ibid., 2.346). Paine's biographers have never reached a definitive conclusion about the exact nature of this intimacy.

In summer 1796 Paine stayed with the Smyths at Versailles when he helped Sir Robert secure a passport to enable him to travel to Hamburg to access funds from England. After Paine's return to America he recommended to Thomas Jefferson that he hire Smyth to help the Americans with their trade affairs. But such assistance was not all one-sided. Smyth consistently gave Paine moral and financial support, and was one of Paine's most frequent visitors when he was living with the Bonnevilles (1797–1802). He was also a silent collaborator in Paine's *Decline and Fall of the English System of Finance* (1796), and forced the builders of the iron bridge over the River Wear at Sunderland (completed 1796) to acknowledge that they had relied on Paine's designs and his materials in its construction. Sir Robert Smyth died suddenly at Paris on 12 April 1802 'of gout in his stomach', and was buried at Berechurch Hall, Essex. His wife died at Versailles in 1823. The baronetcy was inherited by Smyth's son, George Henry, and became extinct at his death in 1852. D. H. Weinglass

Sources J. G. Alger, *Paris in 1789–94: farewell letters of victims of the guillotine* (1902) · *Catalogue of the valuable collection of pictures of Thomas George Graham White* (1878), lots 1–40 [sale catalogue, Christie, Manson, and Woods, 23 March 1878] · G. P. Judd, *Members of parliament, 1734–1832* (1955); repr. (1972) · M. M. Drummond, 'Smyth, Robert', HoP, *Commons, 1754–90*, 3.456–7 · H. R. Yorke, *Letters from France in 1802*, 2 vols. (1804), 346, 347–60 · J. Ingamells, ed., *A dictionary of British and Irish travellers in Italy, 1701–1800* (1997) · *Old Westminsters*, 2.863–4 · T. Paine, *Collected writings*, ed. E. Foner (1995), 425 · *The collected English letters of Henry Fuseli*, ed. D. H. Weinglass (1982) · W. A. Shaw, ed., *Letters of denization and acts of naturalization for aliens in England and Ireland, 1701–1800*, 2, Huguenot Society of London, 27 (1923), 186 (21 Geo. III, No. 27) · J. Fruchtman, *Apostle of freedom* (1994) · D. F. Hawke, *Paine* (1974) · Y. Bizardel, *The first expatriates: Americans in Paris during the French Revolution* (1975) · A. Williamson, *Thomas Paine: his life work and times* (1973), 106 · 'Sir Robert Smyth, formerly M.P. for Chichester [sic], and lately a Banker at Paris', *Annual Register* (1802), 503 · *GM*, 1st ser., 72 (1802), 472 · *The Times* (22 April 1802), 3 · *A catalogue of the entire and very valuable library of the late Sir Robert Smyth* (1809) [sale catalogue, Sothebys, 10–15 April 1809]

Archives Essex RO, Chelmsford, corresp.

Smyth, Robert Brough (1830–1889), civil servant and mining engineer, was born on 18 February 1830 at Carville, near Wallsend, Northumberland, the son of Edward Smyth, mining engineer, and his wife, Ann, *née* Brough. Educated initially at Whickham, co. Durham, Smyth studied mining and geology under his father, brother, and the mining engineer John Buddle, as well as by reading extensively on the subject. He worked as clerk at the Consett iron works of the Derwent Iron Company for five years from about 1843.

Smyth arrived in Victoria, Australia, on 14 November 1852. Unsuccessful at goldmining, he worked as a carter constructing the Mount Alexander Road at Sawpit Gully (Elphinstone) until, on 7 November 1853, he was appointed draftsman in the surveyor general's department. Talented and ambitious, he soon rose to acting senior draftsman, taking over administration of the official meteorological observations in April 1855. In 1857 he fought unsuccessfully to prevent the establishment of a government-supported meteorological and magnetic observatory by the German scientist Georg Neumayer.

Smyth married Emma Charlotte (1820/21–1890), daughter of Charles Hay of Newcastle upon Tyne, at St Paul's Church of England Church in Melbourne on 15 August 1856. They had a son and daughter. In January 1858, Smyth was appointed secretary to the board of science and converted it into a *de facto* mining department by taking over supervision of the mining surveyors, by establishing a systematic mining survey, and by publishing progress reports and mining statistics. He was also appointed honorary secretary to the board of protection of Aborigines on 19 June 1860, later becoming chairman. In December 1860 a mining department was established with Smyth as secretary for mines. He built up a large department during

Robert Brough Smyth (1830–1889), by George Gordon McCrae, 1880s

a period of political instability, at the same time undermining the position of the director of the geological survey of Victoria, Alfred Selwyn, by criticism of the manner in which the survey was carried out. Smyth's views prevailed and the geological survey was abolished in December 1868. The government published Smyth's compilation on Victorian mining, *The Goldfields and Mineral Districts of Victoria*, in 1869. In 1871, the geological survey was re-established under Smyth's supervision.

Smyth's tyrannical administration of his department led in 1876 to a public inquiry which ran for three months and the evidence, extensively reported in the press, led to his disgrace. Many charges against him were substantiated. Though only censured, he resigned on 4 May 1876, devoting his time to finalizing the compilation of *The Aborigines of Victoria*, published in 1878.

In 1878, Smyth was engaged by the Indian government to report on auriferous deposits in Madras presidency, and in May 1880 he became mining engineer with the Daval Moyar Gold Mining Company. His glowing reports induced a disastrous boom in Indian goldmining in which many London investors lost money. When he returned to Melbourne in 1882, Smyth was appointed director of the Sandhurst School of Mines in February 1883, allegedly through political influence, but his harsh attitude to staff led to dissatisfaction and resignations. He resigned in March 1887.

Smyth died at his residence, Medenia, High Street, Prahran, Victoria, Australia, on 8 or 9 October 1889 and was buried on 10 October in St Kilda cemetery. Self-opinionated and officious, Smyth did immense harm to the development of geological science in Victoria, but did much to encourage publication of mining and geological reports. THOMAS A. DARRAGH

Sources M. E. Hoare, '"The half mad bureaucrat" Robert Brough Smyth (1830–1889)', *Records of the Australian Academy of Sciences*, 2/4 (1974), 25–40 • [H. M. Humphreys], *Men of the time in Australia: Victorian series* (1878) • *The Leader* (30 May 1863), 11 • 'The Brough Smith inquiry', *The Argus* [Melbourne] (21 April 1876) • T. A. Darragh, 'The geological survey of Victoria under Alfred Selwyn, 1852–1868', *Historical Records of Australian Science*, 7 (1987–9), 1–25 • Victoria Public Record Series, 28/P2, unit 277, series 41, no. 301 • *The Argus* [Melbourne] (16 Aug 1856), 4 • *The Argus* [Melbourne] (16 June 1890), 1 • *AusDB* • T. A. Darragh, 'Robert Brough Smyth: his early years as revealed by his correspondence with Adam Sedgwick', *Historical Records of Australian Science*, 13 (2000–01), 19–42

Archives State Library of Victoria, Melbourne, La Trobe manuscript collection, papers, MS 8787 | CUL, Adam Sedgwick papers

Likenesses G. G. McCrae, drawing, 1880–89, NL Aus. [*see illus.*] • S. Calvert, wood-engraving (after photograph), repro. in *The Leader* (30 May 1863), 1

Wealth at death £7669 18*s*. 11*d*.: Victorian probate documents, Victoria Public Record Series, 28/P2, unit 277, series 41, no. 301

Smyth, Roger [Rhosier] (**1540/41–1625?**), Roman Catholic priest and translator, was born in St Asaph. He was probably the Roger Smithe who graduated BA at Oxford in 1563. He was at Douai College for some years before 1579. In 1579, after the move to Rome and aged thirty-eight, he sided with Morys Clynnog in the acrimonious dispute at the English College which led to the split between the English and Welsh. The *Liber ruber* records his dismissal in 1579, not being willing to be ordained to return to England as a missionary priest: 'dixit se non paratum' ('he said he was not ready'). He moved to Rouen and later to Paris.

Y drych Cristianogawl, printed on a secret press in Wales in 1586–7, is provided with a preface by 'RS' dated in Rouen; doubtless the initials were meant to suggest Roger Smyth, but his authorship is probably as fictitious as the Rouen imprint. In 1595 Smyth came briefly to England, and in unknown circumstances was incarcerated in Newgate prison. Somehow he escaped, to judge by a letter written to him in Paris by Gruffydd Robert in May 1596, which rejoices in his having been able to 'pick the locks of Newgate'. He is referred to by two of Cecil's spies, first in 1598 in connection with his involvement in an attempt to establish a seminary in Paris, and secondly in 1601. These reports comment on his character and ideas. He is said, in Robert Persons's view, to be 'not fit to be employed in matters of state' 'because he could not keep Persons's counsels in certain causes which he imparted to him' (Williams, 114); and he is reported to be anti-Jesuit, anti-English, and in favour of a republic with freedom of conscience in England and Wales. In 1595 he was by his own account still a layman, but by 1601 he is referred to as a priest. It is not known when he was ordained, nor when he acquired his title of doctor. His death 'last year in Paris' is reported by Lewis Owen in *The Running Register* (1626).

Smyth's first published translation, part of Canisius's greater catechism, printed in Paris, as were all his publications, appeared in 1609. A full translation of the catechism, making use both of the original 1555 version and the 1566 revised version, was published in 1611, dedicated to Cardinal Du Perron. This translation of the catechism may have been produced much earlier: it could be that referred to by Owen Lewis in a letter to Cardinal Sirletto in 1578. In 1612 he published a Welsh translation of Saint Robert Southwell's *Epistle of a Religious Priest unto his Father*, and in 1615, as Rhosier Smyth, *Theater du mond sef iw. gorsedd y byd*, a translation from the French of Pierre Boaistuau's encyclopaedic work on the human condition. This, unlike his other translations, was no part of the Counter-

Reformation agenda and displays far greater literary ambition.

In orthography, in his humanist readiness to coin new words, and in style Smyth was a follower of his one-time associate Gruffydd Robert, though not his equal. His ideas, like those relating to policy for restoration of the faith in Britain, had been formed by 1579. His 1612 translation of Southwell's *Epistle*, however, done at the request of Morgan Clynnog, an associate at the English College in 1579 who had chosen to return as a missionary priest to Wales, shows an accommodation with the post-1580 mainstream of the Counter-Reformation. DANIEL HUWS

Sources *DWB* • R. Smyth, *Theater du mond: gorsedd y byd*, ed. T. Parry (1930) • W. L. Williams, 'Welsh Catholics on the continent', *Transactions of the Honourable Society of Cymmrodorion* (1901–2), 46–144 • *Miscellanea, II*, Catholic RS, 2 (1906) • W. Kelly, ed., *Liber ruber venerabilis collegii Anglorum de urbe*, 1, Catholic RS, 37 (1940) • R. G. Gruffydd, ed., *A guide to Welsh literature*, 3: *c.*1530–1700 (1997) • A. F. Allison and D. M. Rogers, eds., *The contemporary printed literature of the English Counter-Reformation between 1558 and 1640*, 2 (1994) • L. Owen, *The running register* (1626) • J. Ryan, 'The sources of the Welsh translation of the catechism of St Peter Canisius', *Journal of the Welsh Bibliographical Society*, 11 (1973–6), 225–32

Smyth, Thomas (1609–1642). *See under* Smyth family (*per. c.*1500–1680).

Smyth, Sir Warington Wilkinson (1817–1890), mining engineer and geologist, was born at San Giovanni in the kingdom of Naples on 28 August 1817, the eldest son of William Henry *Smyth (1788–1865), then a captain in the Royal Navy, and his wife, Annarella Warington (1788–1873). Charles Piazzi *Smyth, the astronomer, and Sir Henry Augustus *Smyth, army officer, were his younger brothers. He was educated at Westminster and Bedford schools, and at Trinity College, Cambridge, where he gained a rowing blue and graduated in 1839 (MA in 1844). His father was known to have a wide knowledge of geography, and Smyth himself became interested in mineralogy and geology while at Cambridge. After graduation, he obtained a travelling scholarship from the Worts foundation, which he used to make extended visits to Germany, Austria, Sicily (including Mount Etna), Turkey, and Asia Minor, studying geology, mining, and mining education.

In 1844 Smyth was appointed as mining geologist to the geological survey, perhaps owing his appointment to the friendship between his parents and the director of the survey, Henry De la Beche. Working for the survey until 1857, his achievements included the colouring of the geological map of north-west Derbyshire (no. 82) and reports on collieries in Wales and the north of England. In 1851 he joined the newly founded school of mines, first as lecturer in mining and mineralogy, and later as professor, and he continued to teach there until his death. He was particularly noted for his skills as a teacher and for his encouragement of the education of miners. He taught not only mining students but also teachers of mineralogy, and he also contributed to the 'penny lectures' held in the evenings for working men. He also lectured at the Museum of Practical Geology. In 1852 he was appointed as mineral surveyor to the duchy of Cornwall, and was made chief inspector of crown minerals in 1857. He was elected a fellow of the Geological Society in 1845 and a fellow of the Royal Society in 1858. He served as a member of the council of the Geological Society from 1856 to 1866, and he was the foreign secretary from 1873 to 1890 and president from 1866 to 1868. He married Anna Maria Antonia, the third daughter of Anthony Story-Maskelyne, on 9 April 1864, and there were two sons from this marriage.

In 1879, a royal commission on accidents in mines was formed, as a result of growing concern about the number of accidents in coal mines, and especially doubts about the safety of the existing types of miners' lamps, and Smyth was appointed as chairman. The commission made extensive investigations of working practices in mines, and reported to parliament in 1887. As a result the Coal Mines Regulation Act of 1887 was passed, and in recognition of his work with the royal commission, Smyth was knighted in the same year.

Smyth kept a holiday home at Marazion, Cornwall, and spent many summers there. He acquired a detailed knowledge of the minerals and geology of the county, as well as of its mines, described in an obituary as being 'perhaps more profound than that of any of his contemporaries'. He joined the Royal Geological Society of Cornwall in 1857, and from 1871 to 1879, and again from 1883 until his death, served as president. During this time he continued to foster educational causes by helping to establish classes for Cornish miners in the basement of the society's museum in Penzance, together with the assistance of the Miners' Association of Cornwall and Devonshire. In 1887 he headed an appeal to raise funds for a museum at Redruth, Cornwall, in memory of Robert Hunt, which was formally opened in 1891.

Perhaps as a result of Smyth's educational efforts, he had little time to devote to writing. He did however publish a book on some of his travels, *A Year with the Turks*, in 1854. He was also responsible for preparing a catalogue for the Museum of Practical Geology, at Jermyn Street, London, in 1864, and wrote *A Treatise on Coal and Coal Mining*, first published in 1867. Among his published papers were a number in the *Quarterly Journal of the Geological Society*, including his two presidential addresses, in which he gave accounts of the geological surveys of Great Britain, Canada, and the United States of America. He also had papers published in the *Transactions of the Royal Geological Society of Cornwall*. His final address as president of that society in 1889 included a historical account of the various theories about the origin of mineral lodes. He died suddenly at his home at 5 Inverness Terrace, Hyde Park, London, on 19 June 1890, and on the 25th was buried, according to his wishes, at St Erth, Cornwall. He was survived by his wife. DENISE CROOK

Sources 'Report of the council', *Transactions of the Royal Geological Society of Cornwall*, 11 (1895), 253–6 • Boase & Courtney, *Bibl. Corn.* • [W. W. Smyth], 'President's address', *Annual Report* [Royal Geological Society of Cornwall], 61 (1874–5), v–xiv, esp. viii [pubd with *Transactions*, 9 (1878)] • H. E. Wilson, *Down to earth: one hundred and fifty years of the British geological survey* (1985) • H. B. Woodward, *The history of the Geological Society of London* (1907) • A. Pearson, *Robert*

Hunt, FRS (1807–1887) (1979) • F. A. Abel, *Accidents in mines* (1888) • *CGPLA Eng. & Wales* (1890) • m. cert. • d. cert.

Archives GS Lond., map • NL Scot., travel logs | ICL, college archives, letters to Sir Andrew Ramsey • NL Wales, letters to Johnes family

Likenesses oils, 1875, priv. coll. • R. T., wood-engraving (after photograph by A. Lewis), NPG; repro. in *ILN* (28 June 1890)

Wealth at death £9504 3s. 6d.: resworn probate, March 1891, *CGPLA Eng. & Wales* (1890)

Smyth, William (1582–1658), college head, was born in the parish of St Mary Magdalene in Taunton, Somerset, on 4 October 1582, possibly the son of the William Smyth and Marie Smyth who were married there on 24 January 1580. He matriculated from Exeter College, Oxford, on 23 March 1599 when he was said to be only fifteen, a stratagem sometimes used to avoid the oath to the royal supremacy required of those over sixteen, although he must have conformed before graduating BA on 15 July 1602 and proceeding MA on 8 July 1606.

At Exeter College, if not before, Smyth formed an important connection with the Petres, a family of Catholic sympathies; Thomas Petre was a near contemporary. By 1604 Smyth was tutoring in Essex the two elder sons of Thomas's brother William, later second Lord Petre, and in 1611 he took them to Oxford. They matriculated in 1613 from Exeter College, but the rector being the bitterly anti-Catholic John Prideaux, they soon transferred to become the first fellow-commoners of Wadham College, founded by their great-aunt Dorothy Petre and her late husband, Nicholas Wadham. Meanwhile Smyth was admitted at Wadham on 8 June 1613 as the first fellow appointed by the foundress, who then nominated him sub-warden each year. On 24 March 1617 she appointed him warden.

Smyth proceeded BD and DD on 26 June 1619. In his theses he avoided controverted Calvinist doctrines but affirmed the authority of princes and of scripture over that of the pope.

Petre patronage brought Smyth two Essex rectories: Ingatestone, held from 1619 to 1630, and Fryerning, held from 1620 to 1630. As warden he stood up to King James against unstatutory intrusion of a Scot into the fellowship, and was an effective head. In 1624, assisted by Lord Keeper Williams, he procured an act of parliament to confirm the college's incorporation. The crypto-papist Lord Treasurer Weston entrusted his younger son, Thomas, to Smyth's care. In 1626 the warden was joint purchaser of the wardship of Francis Petre of Tintinhull, Somerset, the foundress's great-nephew.

Another connection critical to Smyth's career was that with William Laud, who became college visitor from 1626 as bishop of Bath and Wells, and who by his intervention with the king helped Smyth overcome the machinations from 1627 of one of the fellows, James Harington, who was backed by powerful men at court. Smyth's friend, President William Juxon of St John's College, wrote to Laud on 26 December 1627 that the warden wished to belong to a person of quality and to tender the bishop his service.

In 1629 Smyth was appointed a delegate for Laud's scheme of reform of the university's statutes. Between 1630 and 1632 he was vice-chancellor under Laud's chancellorship, in which office he held a court leet claimed by the city of Oxford to have encroached on its liberties, provoking years of litigation. An incident in the summer of 1631, in which three young men preached against 'Pelagianism', contrary to royal instructions, but which stemmed from a general scheme to thwart new statutes, ranged Smyth, Juxon, and ultimately Laud against the culprits' supporters—Laud's powerful enemies in the university and at court—including Henry Wilkinson of Magdalen Hall, Bishop John Williams, and, indirectly, John Prideaux. The affair was settled by Charles I at Woodstock in August to Smyth's satisfaction, and he continued in Laud's confidence, becoming in 1633 a delegate for the university press.

Meanwhile Smyth had in 1627 been presented to the rectory of Alvechurch, Worcestershire, by Benjamin Thornborough, the bishop of Worcester's son. The same year Juxon became dean of Worcester. On 31 May 1629, through patronage from the Sheldon family, kin of the Petres and also notable for Catholicism, Smyth was presented to the rich rectory of Tredington, then in Worcestershire. On 7 September 1635 he resigned the wardenship of Wadham, which required celibacy, and it was probably then that he married his first wife, Anne (*d.* 1638), the widow of Thomas Moore and daughter of Rowland Berkeley, who had bought the manor of Spetchley, Worcestershire, from the Sheldons. Smyth was a Worcestershire JP in 1636, and on 23 May 1638 the king presented him to a canonry of Worcester Cathedral.

Anne Smyth died in 1638, and Smyth married again, at Oxford in 1642; his second wife was Katherine Clerke, a widow. Both marriages were childless. In 1643, Prideaux having become bishop of Worcester, Smyth resigned from Alvechurch. He was ejected from Tredington in 1646 and lived in Oriel College, 'one of the then sanctuaries of Loyalty in the late times', where he maintained contacts inside and outside the university and was adept 'in reconciling differences among his indiscreet friends, and in encouraging hope' (Lloyd, 541).

Smyth is not known to have published anything other than verses in university collections on royal occasions. In his will, drawn up on 29 August 1657, he left the bulk of his diminished estate to his niece Sarah Paulet or Poulet, wife of George Paulet, and her children William and Barbara. Among other beneficiaries were his stepdaughter Frances Skinner and step-granddaughter Jane Strode, 'daughter of Doctor Strode' (will). He died on 6 May 1658 and was buried in Spetchley church alongside his first wife.

A. J. HEGARTY

Sources Wadham College muniments, 1/5; 2/1; 4/29–31; 4/49–51; 6/2–4; 6/7; 7/2–13 • PRO, SP 16/44, 93r–v; 16/61, 60v–61r; 16/65, 126r–129v; 16/81, 95r–v; 16/82, 11r–v; 16/86, 63r–64v, 66r, 137r–v; 16/87, 58r–v, 68r–69v; 16/91, 61r–v, 84r–85v; 101r–102v; 16/94, 32r–33v, 169r; 16/98, 182r–v; 16/100, 14r–15v; 16/101, 42r–44v, 114r–115v; 16/102, 154r • *Reg. Oxf.*, 1.215, 273; 2.233; 3.237, 380 • *The works of the most reverend father in God, William Laud*, 5, ed. J. Bliss (1853) • N. Briggs, 'William, 2nd Lord Petre (1575–1637)', *Essex Recusant*, 10

(1968), 51–64 • R. B. Gardiner, ed., *The letters of Dorothy Wadham, 1609–1618* (1904) • R. B. Gardiner, ed., *The registers of Wadham College, Oxford*, 1 (1889), esp. 34 • D. Lloyd, *Memoires of the lives … of those … personages that suffered … for the protestant religion* (1668), 541 • T. Nash, *Collections for the history of Worcestershire*, 1 (1781), 33, 64–9; 2 (1782), 358–9, 362, 430, 432 • *Walker rev.*, 386 • M. J. Hawkins, ed., *Sales of wards in Somerset, 1603–1641*, Somerset RS, 67 (1965), 191–3 • W. P. W. Phillimore and others, eds., *Somerset parish registers: marriages*, 9 (1907), 10 [St Mary Magdalene, Taunton, 1558–1812] • Foster, *Alum. Oxon.*, 1500–1714 [William Smith] • will, PRO, PROB 11/279, fols. 283r–284v

Likenesses G. Jackson, oils, 1635, Wadham College, Oxford

Smyth, William (1765–1849), historian, was born in Liverpool, the son of Thomas Smyth, an Irish banker. After receiving his initial education locally, Smyth attended Eton College and received private tuition before entering Peterhouse, Cambridge, in 1783, where he crowned his mathematical studies by graduating eighth wrangler in 1787. With the failure of his father's bank in 1793 he was forced to make ends meet by tutoring R. B. Sheridan's eldest son, Thomas. This brought him into contact with the powerful Holland House whigs. In 1807 their patronage won him the regius chair of modern history at Cambridge, which he held in conjunction with a college fellowship at Peterhouse. His elevation was regarded as a notorious piece of political jobbery, and it was mercilessly lampooned by the cartoonist Gillray; Harriet Martineau later called the appointment 'an act of kindness to the individual but scarcely so to the public' (Butler, 218).

Smyth was a firm believer in the value of history as an education for life and for public service. The study of history, he taught, provided 'instruction and a warning in the erring or guilty conduct of those who have gone before us'; such instruction would 'exhibit to a people the rallying point of their constitution, the fortresses and strong holds of their political happiness'. His *Lectures on Modern History* (1840) was thus a predictably whiggish panegyric on the growth and defence of English liberty from early times, through the revolution of 1688, and up to the reign of George III. As such, they were a refutation of David Hume's much read, 'tory' interpretation of English history.

Smyth's whiggish inclinations were most strikingly demonstrated in his lectures on the French Revolution, a subject which he was the first Englishman to treat as a historian. As a young man he had been in considerable sympathy with the revolution, but later he came to view it as a failed imitation of the revolution of 1688. In this he was heavily influenced by his friendship with John Lewis Mallet, the son of the émigré writer Mallet du Pan. Smyth's objections to the French Revolution were as much moral as political. 'The great rule of morality', he pronounced, 'is, that we are not to do evil, that good may come.' Smyth saw in the bloodshed of the reign of terror and in the apologetic rhetoric of contemporaries and later French historians such as Thiers and Mignet an 'escape from responsibility, by notions of fatalism, and of necessity; by talking of revolutionary tides that must roll on'. If there were certain intellectual tensions between his rejection of 'necessity' in the French case, and his simultaneous confident teleological assumptions about British history, Smyth was not aware of them.

The trauma of the French Revolution decisively moulded Smyth's own historical and political outlook. Historically, he was interested in 'how revolutions are to be avoided while reforms are accomplished'. Politically, he remained an unshakeable gradualist: 'step by step is the proper and only mode for getting things done quietly and securely'. The vision of unchecked popular sovereignty unfolded by the French Revolution appalled him. 'Is there any tyrant unfeeling as a single assembly, so unjust, so immoral?', he asked. Instead, Smyth resorted to an increasingly eulogistic celebration of the 'harmonious', 'permanent', and 'marvellous' British constitution.

Thus, although he could fairly have been described as a radical in his youth and early middle age, Smyth became increasingly conservative. Before 1832 he was an enthusiastic supporter of electoral reform and Roman Catholic emancipation; he later drew the line, however, at universal suffrage and the redistribution of wealth. Bentham, Godwin, and Robert Owen were given short shrift in his lectures. Chartism, republicanism, and socialism were all anathema to Smyth. The idea of female suffrage, 'unsexing the females', filled him with horror. Smyth's move away from radicalism was paralleled by an increased interest in religion. Already in his lectures he had insisted on the 'truth' of Christianity; he even referred to Islam as 'false religion'. Subsequently he was to offer in his *Evidences of Christianity* (1845) a rational defence of Christian belief.

Smyth was not a professional historian in the modern sense. His discursive, rambling, and often repetitive historiographical approach, 'a history of histories' as his lectures were known even in his own time, was a far cry from the new source-based school developing in Germany around Leopold von Ranke. None the less, Smyth was popular among students. William Whewell, writing in 1837, described his lectures as 'eloquent and thoughtful disquisitions which … enjoyed great popularity'; one student diarist (Joseph Romilly) thought them 'admirable', even 'beautiful'. Others, however, spoke of 'poor old Smyth' as a man 'too old to be corrected'.

Apart from history and politics, Smyth's main interest was poetry. His collected verses, published as *English Lyrics* (1797), went through five editions, and even found some favour with Byron. Thanks to his renowned conversational skills, Smyth was much in demand in society, where his eighteenth-century manners and appearance, which have been compared to those of a *marquis* of the *ancien régime*, stood out increasingly. Smyth was also a frequent visitor to London, where he could number such whig luminaries as Mackintosh, Francis Horner, and Brougham among his acquaintances. He remained unmarried and lived the life of a bachelor don at Peterhouse, often talking politics into the small hours of the morning. A collection of his books, which he intended for the use of his successors, became the nucleus of the Seeley Memorial Library. Although he served his time as dean and bursar, Smyth's relations with Peterhouse were not always harmonious. He resigned his college fellowship in 1825 but remained in residence until 1847. He died in Norwich on 24 June 1849, and was buried in the cathedral. BRENDAN SIMMS

Sources *DNB* • *The Athenaeum* (30 June 1849) • K. T. B. Butler, 'A "petty" professor of modern history: William Smyth (1765–1849)', *Cambridge Historical Journal*, 9 (1947–9), 217–38 • W. Smyth, 'Autobiography and memoir', in W. Smyth, *English lyrics*, 5th edn (1850) • Venn, *Alum. Cant.*

Archives CUL | Balliol Oxf., letters to J. L. Mallet • BL, corresp. with G. Thomson, Add. MSS 35263–35265 • BL, Mallet MSS, Add. MS 39809 • Girton Cam., K. T. B. Butler MSS • NL Scot., letters to Sir Walter Scott • Northumbd RO, Newcastle upon Tyne, letters to William Ord • Picton Library, Liverpool, Roscoe MSS • Trinity Cam., letters to William Whewell • U. Lpool L., letters to Elizabeth Rathbone

Likenesses I. W. Slater, lithograph, 1831 (after J. Slater), BM, NPG • E. H. Baily, marble bust, 1851, FM Cam. • Ainemülle, stained-glass window, Norwich Cathedral • oils, Peterhouse, Cambridge • two stained-glass windows, Peterhouse, Cambridge

Smyth, William Henry (**1788–1865**), naval officer and surveyor, born in Westminster, London, on 21 January 1788, was the only son of Joseph Brewer Palmer Smyth and his wife, Georgina Caroline, granddaughter of the Revd Mr Pilkington. William's father claimed descent from Captain John Smith (1580?–1631), and owned large estates in New Jersey, which, as a loyalist who fought against the rebels, he lost on the Declaration of Independence of the North American colonies. At an early age William went to sea in the merchant service, and in 1804 was in the East India Company's ship *Cornwallis*, which took part in the expedition against the Seychelles. In March 1805 the *Cornwallis* was bought into the navy and established as a 50 gun ship under the command of Captain Charles James Johnston. Smyth remained on board, seeing much active service in Indian, Chinese, and Australian waters. In February 1808 he followed Johnston to the *Powerful*, which, after her return to England, was part of the force in the attempted assault on Walcheren, and was paid off in October 1809. Smyth afterwards served in the *Milford* (74 guns) on the coast of France and Spain, and was lent from her to command the Spanish gunboat *Mors aut Gloria* for several months at the defence of Cadiz (September 1810 to April 1811). In July 1811 he joined the *Rodney* off Toulon, and throughout 1812 served on the coast of Spain. On 25 March 1813 he was promoted to the rank of lieutenant, and appointed for duty with the Sicilian flotilla, in which he combined service against the French in Naples with hydrographic surveying and antiquarian research. For this service he was awarded the order of St Ferdinand and Merit.

At Messina on 7 October 1815 Smyth married Annarella (1788–1873), only daughter of Thomas Warington of Naples; they had a large family. One of their sons was Sir Warington Wilkinson *Smyth; another, Charles Piazzi *Smyth, was astronomer royal for Scotland; a third was General Sir Henry Augustus *Smyth. On 18 September 1815 Smyth was promoted commander, and without any appointment to a ship he continued on the coast of Sicily, surveying that coast, the adjacent coasts of Italy, and the

William Henry Smyth (**1788–1865**), by Maull & Polyblank, 1855

opposite shores of Africa. In 1817 his work was put on a more formal footing by his appointment to the converted transport *Aid*. In her he carried out further surveys in Italian, Adriatic, Greek, and north African waters, combining his work with archaeological research. The *Aid* was refitted and renamed *Adventure* in 1821 and finally paid off in 1824, in February of which year Smyth was promoted captain. His work resulted in a large number of published charts, many of which remained in use until the middle of the twentieth century. He also published several books on the topography and antiquities of the areas he surveyed. After paying off the *Adventure* he did not return to sea as his tastes led him to a literary and scientific life.

In 1821 Smyth became a fellow of the Society of Antiquaries and of the Royal Astronomical Society (RAS). On 15 June 1826 he was elected FRS and in 1830 was one of the founders of the Royal Geographical Society (RGS). He built and equipped an astronomical observatory at Bedford, where for many years he carried out systematic observations of stars. In 1845–6 he was president of the RAS and in 1849–50 president of the RGS; he was vice-president and foreign secretary of the Royal Society, vice-president and director of the Society of Antiquaries, and honorary or corresponding member of at least three-quarters of the literary and scientific societies of Europe. He contributed numerous papers to the Royal Society's *Philosophical Transactions*, the *Proceedings* of the RAS and RGS, and from 1829 to 1849 to the *United Service Journal*. He was the author of many volumes, including *The Cycle of Celestial Objects for the Use of Naval, Military, and Private Astronomers* (2 vols., 1844), for which he was awarded the gold medal of the Royal Astronomical Society; *The Mediterranean: a Memoir Physical, Historical, and Nautical* (1854); and *The Sailor's Word-Book*, revised and edited by Sir Edward Belcher (1867). The complete story of his literary activity is contained in *Synopsis of the Published and Privately Printed Works of Admiral W. H. Smyth* (1864).

In 1846 Smyth was retired and in due course was advanced, on the retired list, to rear-admiral on 28 May 1853, vice-admiral on 13 February 1858, and admiral on 14 November 1863. After living for many years near Bedford, he moved about 1850 to St John's Lodge, Stone, near Aylesbury, Buckinghamshire, where he died on 9 September 1865. His wife survived him.

J. K. Laughton, *rev.* R. O. Morris

Sources *The Times* (12 Sept 1865) • L. S. Dawson, *Memoirs of hydrography*, 2 vols. (1885) • G. S. Ritchie, *The Admiralty chart: British naval hydrography in the nineteenth century*, new edn (1995) • W. H. Smyth, *The Mediterranean* (1854) • R. I. Murchison, *Proceedings* [Royal Geographical Society], 10 (1865–6), 193–5 • O'Byrne, *Naval biog. dict.*

Archives American Philosophical Society, Philadelphia, corresp. and papers • NZ NL, Alexander Turnbull Library, naval MSS • RAS, corresp. and papers | American Philosophical Society, Philadelphia, corresp. incl. letters to wife • BL, letters to Charles Babbage, Add. MSS 37190–37201, *passim* • Bodl. Oxf., corresp. with Sir Thomas Phillipps; letters to Mary Somerville • NMM, letters to Sir John Philipport • RAS, letters to Royal Astronomical Society; letters to Richard Sheepshanks • RGS, letters to Royal Geographical Society • RS, corresp. with Sir John Herschel • U. Edin. L., letters to James Halliwell-Phillipps • Yale U., Beinecke L., letters to T. J. Pettigrew

Likenesses W. Brockedon, pencil and chalk drawing, 1838, NPG • Maull & Polyblank, photograph, 1855, NPG [*see illus.*] • R. J. Lane, lithograph (after E. U. Eddis), BM, NPG • wood-engraving (after E. U. Eddis, *c.*1861), NPG; repro. in *ILN* (1865)

Wealth at death under £800: probate, 8 Dec 1865, *CGPLA Eng. & Wales*

Smythe. *See also* Smith, Smyth.

Smythe, David, Lord Methven (1746–1806), judge, was born on 17 January 1746, the son of David Smythe of Methven and Mary, daughter of James Graham of Braco. Having studied for the law, he was admitted advocate on 4 August 1769. He married, first, on 8 April 1772, Elizabeth, only daughter of Sir Robert Murray, bt, of Hillhead; she died on 30 June 1785, leaving three sons and four daughters. From his second marriage, to Euphemia, daughter of Mungo Murray of Lintrose, who was reckoned one of the beauties of her time and was the subject of one of Burns's songs, there were two sons and two daughters. Smythe was succeeded in the estate by Robert Smythe (*d.* 1847), the only surviving son of his first marriage, but as Robert died childless, the succession fell to the elder son of the second marriage, William Smythe (1805–1895) of Methven Castle.

Smythe was raised to the bench on 15 November 1793, taking the title Lord Methven. He was credited with the highest integrity as a judge and an excellent understanding. He was appointed a commissioner of justiciary on the death of Lord Abercromby, on 11 March 1796, but resigned that office in 1804. He died at Edinburgh on 30 January 1806.

A. H. Millar, *rev.* Anita McConnell

Sources G. Brunton and D. Haig, *An historical account of the senators of the college of justice, from its institution in MDXXXII* (1832), 541 • *Scots Magazine and Edinburgh Literary Miscellany*, 68 (1806), 159 • Irving, *Scots.* • F. J. Grant, ed., *The Faculty of Advocates in Scotland, 1532–1943*, Scottish RS, 145 (1944)

Archives NL Scot., corresp. and papers

Likenesses J. Tassie, paste medallion, 1794, Scot. NPG

Smythe [*née* Beaufort], **Emily Anne, Viscountess Strangford** (*bap.* **1826**, *d.* **1887**), military nurse, was baptized on 1 April 1826 at St Marylebone, Middlesex, the youngest daughter of Admiral Sir Francis *Beaufort (1774–1857), hydrographer, and his first wife, Alicia Magdalena (1782–1834), daughter of Lestock Wilson, captain in the East India Company's army. Her brother was Francis Lestock *Beaufort [*see under* Beaufort, Sir Francis]. In 1858, the year after their father died, she and her sister travelled in Egypt, Asia Minor, and Syria, and she received the order of the Holy Sepulchre from the patriarch of Jerusalem to mark her ancestors' involvement in the crusades. In 1861 she published *Egyptian Sepulchres and Syrian Shrines* (2 vols.), to which she contributed both pleasing text and fine illustrations. The book was a popular success, going to several editions, and was reviewed by Percy Ellen Algernon Frederick William Sydney *Smythe, eighth Viscount Strangford (1825–1869), diplomatist and orientalist. The couple subsequently married on 6 February 1862 at All Saints' Church, Norfolk Square, Paddington, London. Her husband had acceded to the peerage in 1857, but continued to live mostly in the Near East, accompanied after their marriage by his wife. Her second book, *The Eastern Shores of the Adriatic* (1864), was a substantial work, part travel book and part discussion of the eastern question, in which she described the journeys that she and her husband made in Albania, Montenegro, Dalmatia, and Corfu.

Her husband's death in 1869 left Lady Strangford childless and alone, and it marked a turning point in her life. In his memory she edited *A Selection from the Writings of Viscount Strangford* (1869) and his *Original Letters and Papers* (1878), but her energies were mainly devoted to nursing. She spent several years as unpaid volunteer in a London hospital, probably University College Hospital. Her experience led her to publish *Hospital Training for Ladies: an Appeal to the Hospital Boards in England* (1874), in which she advocated a change in the organization of nursing training. The system then was suited only to women who intended to make nursing a full-time occupation, and it demanded residence in the hospital and very long hours of work. Strangford advocated a system whereby ladies could undergo part-time training, which would lead them to greater knowledge of and expertise in health care but not necessarily to a career in nursing. Such a change she believed would help ladies like herself who found themselves with no family to care for and no obvious means of learning how to nurse. Her proposals did not appeal, however, to those who were trying to change nursing from the part-time occupation of the amateur lady to the full-time career of the professional woman.

Lady Strangford was a dame chevalière of the order of St John of Jerusalem. She and Florence Lees set up the order's subcommittee on the training of home nurses for the poor about 1874. This was a milestone in the development of district nursing, though Lees's contribution was probably more important than Strangford's. Strangford also founded the National Association for Providing Trained Nurses for the Sick Poor. The order of St John also led Strangford to her interest in war relief and medical aid. In 1876, at the time of atrocities committed by the Turks against Bulgarian Christians, she became involved in the order's Eastern War Sick and Wounded Fund, but she lost her place when the committee was reorganized; instead she set up her own Bulgarian Peasants Relief Fund, which raised an amount variously said to be £5000 or £30,000. She set off for Bulgaria, with which her husband had sympathized, holding that the Bulgarians rather than the Greeks were the natural leaders of south-eastern Europe, to oversee the work of the fund. It eventually subsidized the work of six village hospitals in Bulgaria, one flour mill, and five sawmills, and distributed some tens of thousands of garments. Lady Strangford was helped by four doctors and eight nurses, whom she brought with her. She readily admitted the difficulties she encountered and the often chaotic conditions that resulted. In addition she paid for several Bulgarians to be educated in England. In 1877 she was engaged by the Turkophile British Hospital and Ambulance Fund for the sick and wounded in war, which aimed to tend Turkish soldiers in the Russo-Turkish War of 1877–8. In order to give the wounded the speediest aid possible she opened and maintained her hospitals at the front, with her staff of nurses, and worked in Adrianople, Sofia, and Scutari. Having survived virtual imprisonment by the Russians in Sofia, and various financial crises, she did excellent work; evidently she had learned much from her earlier experiences in Bulgaria. Her work was acclaimed in the British press.

In 1880 Lady Strangford published *The Soldier's Wife as his Nurse*, in which she proposed that army wives be trained by regimental surgeons, in the same way that amateurs were being taught basic nursing by the order of St John's new ambulance association. Summers considers this idea to have been inspired by Sir Edward Sinclair's existing training schemes for army midwives, but Strangford herself declared that Mary Stanley first suggested the idea. The scheme was introduced in 1880, but soon met opposition. Soldiers' wives had long acted as nurses in military hospitals but primarily to army wives and children, not men. This proposed extension of their role threatened the male orderlies, who had traditionally nursed the men, and the class of lady nurses, who were trying to establish themselves within military nursing on the basis of their propriety and professionalism, neither of which qualities they acknowledged among soldiers' wives. Florence Nightingale herself was quick to denounce the scheme, perhaps in part because it was introduced by a friend of Mary Stanley, to whom she was antipathetic, and by a woman whose achievements some elements of the British press judged superior to her own. After 1883, when Sinclair died, nothing more was heard of the scheme, though the general principle of using female civilian nurses within army hospitals rapidly became established.

Lady Strangford's next commission was for the order of St John, which sent her to Cairo with Dr Herbert Sieveking and five English nurses. By the time they arrived the war was over, but none the less in 1882 they established at Cairo the Victoria Hospital for the sick and wounded soldiers of both the khedive and the British expeditionary force, and they were warmly welcomed by both sides in the conflict. On their return to England, Lady Strangford and Sieveking wrote *The Victoria Hospital, Cairo* (report of the Egyptian Relief Fund, 1883), and the Royal Red Cross, instituted in 1883, was conferred on Lady Strangford by the queen.

Lady Strangford continued to be active in a wide range of projects. She established the Women's Emigration Society in Dorset Street, Portman Square, London (with Mrs E. L. Blanchard); founded a medical school in Beirut; and endowed a geography prize in memory of her husband at Harrow, his old school. She prepared for publication the novel *Angela Pisani* (1875), to which she prefixed a memoir, from manuscripts left by her brother-in-law, George Smythe, the seventh Lord Strangford. She wrote a preface for James Finn's *Stirring Times: Records from Jerusalem Consular Churches* (1878). She died of cerebral apoplexy on 24 March 1887 on board the SS *Lusitania*, which was in the Mediterranean *en route* for Port Said; there she was to have set up a hospital, which was being established by subscription, for British seamen. She was buried in London on 18 April at Kensal Green cemetery, where her husband was also buried.

Lady Strangford was an energetic and talented woman, generous with both her time and her money. She was a pioneer in several branches of nursing, but chiefly in relief and war nursing. Her reputation eclipsed even that of Florence Nightingale in the eyes of some contemporaries, but her name soon fell into relative obscurity in Britain, though not in Bulgaria, where both she and her husband were long and affectionately remembered. This obscurity may have been because she lacked Nightingale's gift for self-publicity, or because she readily admitted her failures. This made her the more likeable character but not the more memorable one. ELIZABETH BAIGENT

Sources GEC, *Peerage* • A. Summers, *Angels and citizens: British women as military nurses, 1854–1914* (1988) • *The Times* (28 March 1887), 10d • P. M. Matteev, *Veliki blagodeteli na bulgarskiia narod* (Sofia, 1934) • 'Smythe, Percy Ellen Frederick William', *DNB* • J. Robinson, *Wayward women: a guide to women travellers*, new edn (1991) • Gladstone, *Diaries* • *IGI* • *CGPLA Eng. & Wales* (1887)

Archives Duke U., travel diaries • Hunt. L., corresp. and travel diaries | BL, letters to Sir A. H. Layard, Add. MSS 39015–39033, *passim* • NL Wales, letters to Johnes family • UCL, corresp. with Sir Edwin Chadwick

Likenesses engraving, 1877, Bodl. Oxf.; repro. in Summers, *Angels and citizens*, 147 • albumen print, Duke U. • photograph, repro. in P. M. Matteev, *Veliki blagodeteli na bulgarskiia narod iz zhivota i deinostta na …*, 73

Wealth at death £27,885 12s. 4d.: probate, 4 June 1887, *CGPLA Eng. & Wales*

Smythe, Francis Sydney (1900–1949), mountaineer and author, was born at Ivythorne, Maidstone, Kent, on 6 July 1900, the son of Algernon Sydney Smythe, who owned a timber wharf and considerable property in and around

Francis Sydney Smythe (1900–1949), by unknown photographer

Maidstone, and his second wife, Florence, daughter of Francis Reeves, of Wateringbury Hall, Wateringbury, Kent. His father died when Smythe was two years old. After leaving Berkhamsted School, Smythe entered Faraday House Electrical Engineering College in 1919. In 1922 he was sent to Austria, and spent every weekend and holiday climbing and walking. In 1926 he joined the Royal Air Force and went to Egypt, but was invalided out the following year and cautioned for the rest of his life to walk upstairs slowly. For a year he worked with Kodak Ltd; and thereafter he supported himself by books, articles, and lectures on mountaineering, on which subject he contributed frequently to *The Times*. In 1931 he married Kathleen Mary, only daughter of Alexander Barks Johnson, marine consulting engineer. There were three sons of this marriage, which was dissolved. Later he married Nona Isobel, daughter of David Richard Wilson Miller, owner of a sheep station in Canterbury, New Zealand, and formerly wife of Robert Macdonald Guthrie. This second marriage was very happy, and his second wife had a great influence in widening his mental horizons.

In the Alps, Smythe's finest climbs were the new routes which he and Professor Thomas Graham Brown forced up the Brenva face of Mont Blanc in 1927 and 1928. He took part in six expeditions in the Himalayas, and in 1931 led the expedition which conquered Kamet, the first peak over 25,000 feet to be climbed. He took part in the Everest expeditions of 1933, 1936, and 1938, and in 1933 equalled the height record (*c*.28,000 feet) established by Edward Felix Norton in 1924. In 1946 and 1947 he visited the Rockies and in the latter year carried out some extremely successful explorations in the Lloyd George range of British Columbia. He was taken ill on the eve of a Himalayan expedition and flown back to England, where he died at Moorcroft House, Harlington Road, Hillingdon, Middlesex, on 27 June 1949.

Smythe learned to climb by climbing, for he never once employed a guide. He was not in the first flight as a rock climber, but he was one of the greatest mountaineers of the day, and his knowledge of the mountains was not confined to the summer, for he was a competent, although not a stylish, skier, and had a fine record of alpine ski tours to his credit. Dr Raymond Greene, who joined him in his attack on Kamet, had the highest opinion of his qualities as a leader, and wrote of him:

> At great altitudes a new force seemed to enter into him. His body, still apparently frail as it had been in boyhood, was capable of astonishing feats of sudden strength and prolonged endurance and his mind, too, took on a different colour. At sea-level the mistaken sense of inferiority so unfairly implanted by his early experiences rendered him sometimes irritable, tactless, and easily offended. The self-confidence which flowed into his mind and body, the emanation as it were of the mountains whose strength he so greatly loved, changed him almost beyond recognition. It seemed impossible above 20,000 feet to disturb his composure or his essential quietism.

The same writer also paid great tribute to his leadership on the approach to the north col of Everest as 'the finest piece of ice-climbing I have ever seen'.

Smythe always rose to a great emergency. Surprised by a terrible storm high upon the Pétéret Ridge of Mont Blanc, he led the first successful descent of the Rochers Grüber from the col de Pétéret, and, to quote his companion, Dr G. Graham Macphee, 'was never once at fault descending and crossing the complicated and difficult Fresnay glacier'.

Smythe achieved his widest reputation, one which long survived his lifetime, in the literary field, as perhaps the most popular mountain writer in English that there has ever been. Even fifty years after his death many of his twenty-five mountain books were still widely read. The most distinctive quality of his writing, the mystical, quasi-religious tone which he gave to mountain experiences, has if anything gained in esteem with the passage of time: Smythe was indeed an early exponent of the interest in meditation. Whether or not by his intention, his greatest appeal turned out to be to the non-mountaineering public: the exceptionally high quality, for their time, of his photographic illustrations was an important factor here. Mountaineers too have admired his best work, such as *Climbs and Ski Runs* (1929), *Kamet Conquered* (1932), and *Camp Six* (1937).

Yet an important result of the commercial success of Smythe's writings, and of his economic dependence on them, was the disfavour that this brought in the eyes of the mountaineering establishment of his time. That he was not chosen as leader for any of the three Everest expeditions of the 1930s, in which he played so outstanding a part, must be put down primarily to this disfavour, which outweighed even the proven success of his leadership on Kamet. In addition, expert opinion differed widely on his technical ability as a mountaineer, and even on his personal qualities: some equated his self-sufficiency and love of solitude with arrogance. Those who knew him best found him, especially in the high mountains, unassuming, reliable, and good-natured. For posterity, his mountaineering attainments can be left to speak for themselves: in Himalayan climbing, and especially in the British experience of Everest in the generation between the death of George Mallory in 1924 and the successful attempt of 1953, Smythe remains the dominant and symbolic figure. By his writings he brought a love of mountain adventure into the drawing-rooms of many thousands of the unadventurous. Few others have combined these achievements. ARNOLD LUNN, *rev.* A. M. SNODGRASS

Sources *Alpine Journal*, 57 (1949), 230–35 · *British Ski Year Book* (1950) · private information (1959) · personal knowledge (1959) · H. Calvert, *Smythe's mountains: the climbs of F. S. Smythe* (1985) · W. Unsworth, *Everest* (1981) · *CGPLA Eng. & Wales* (1949)
Archives Alpine Club, London, corresp. relating to Matterhorn accident · RGS, Everest Archives | FILM BFI NFTVA, documentary footage
Likenesses photograph, RGS [*see illus.*] · photographs, Alpine Club, London
Wealth at death £9226 2*s.* 3*d.*: probate, 22 Nov 1949, *CGPLA Eng. & Wales*

Smythe, George Augustus Frederick Percy Sydney, seventh Viscount Strangford (1818–1857), author and politician, was born on 13 April 1818 in Stockholm, the eldest child of Percy Clinton Sydney *Smythe, sixth Viscount Strangford (1780–1855), British diplomatist, and Eleanor (Ellen) Browne (*née* Burke; 1788–1826), daughter of Sir Thomas Burke, first baronet (Ireland). He had two brothers, two sisters, and a half-brother and half-sister from his mother's first marriage.

Smythe's first eight years on his father's diplomatic postings in Stockholm, Constantinople, and St Petersburg were crucial. They gave him ease with languages, a European orientation, and ambition, but they also conditioned him to the eventual enemies of his original promise, instability and defiance of authority. He was 'cradled in commotions' through direct exposure to revolutionary violence in Constantinople (1821) and St Petersburg (1825), and to his parents' volatility. There was unconcealed friction between his father and the Foreign Office; his deep attachment to his Roman Catholic mother was vitiated by his father's incitement to abuse her beliefs; and relentless paternal tutoring was marked by high expectations and severe reproofs which alternately stimulated and discouraged him and left him perpetually 'thirsty for applause'. In 1826 his mother died at St Petersburg of tuberculosis, a disease which also incapacitated Smythe intermittently from boyhood. The family returned to England, where he entered Tonbridge School, Kent (1826–8), and later Eton

George Augustus Frederick Percy Sydney Smythe, seventh Viscount Strangford (1818–1857), by Richard Buckner

College (1830–35). He made lasting friendships with Lord John Manners, Alexander Baillie Cochrane, and John Walter—later known as the 'Young England' group—and was a clever but disruptive pupil. He gave the 1835 Eton Address to the king and was elected to the debating society, but he also took part in school riots and was twice threatened with expulsion.

Smythe's father and his godfather, the third duke of Northumberland, groomed him early for politics. He heard the debates on the Reform Bill in 1832 and from 1833 spent holidays at influential house parties. In 1833, aged fifteen, he published romantic poems in *The Literary Souvenir*. In 1834 his brother Lionel died of tuberculosis, leaving him depressed and apprehensive. He left Eton at Christmas 1835 to read with the volatile and imperious theologian Julius Hare at Herstmonceaux rectory, followed by attendance at St John's College, Cambridge (1836–40), where he began with characteristic brilliance but did poorly in examinations. He spent the summers of 1837 and 1838 in the Lake District, where he and Manners in 1838—inspired by the medieval revival, the Oxford Movement, and the fiery Tractarian Frederick Faber—vowed to revitalize England by restoring lost values, the social bonds and mutual responsibilities which traditionally—though no longer—united aristocracy and people.

At Cambridge, Smythe voiced these ideas as president of the Pitt Club (1838) and as 'a young Chatham' himself in union debates. His ability outweighed evidence of his temper and extravagance—a challenge to a duel, suspension for rioting, debts of £1200—and contributed (with his father's financial backing) to election in February 1841 as

Conservative MP for Canterbury, which he held continuously until 1852. His maiden speech in May was a nervous failure, but by 1842 he could deliver, in an entertaining, allusive style, a polished, well-prepared speech, sometimes 'very radical indeed, & unprincipled as his little agreeable self' (*Disraeli Letters*, 4.13). 'GSS' was small and graceful, rather in the Keats style, with striking blue eyes, a sensual mouth, and reddish hair in fashionable sideburns. His father thought him 'handsome as Adonis', Sir William Gregory careless-looking and dingy (*Autobiography*, ed. A. Gregory, 1894, 88); Disraeli's description is probably most accurate: 'not exactly handsome, but with a countenance full of expression'.

Strangford next planned a wealthy marriage for his son, but Smythe resisted. He had an affair (1840–43) with the countess of Tankerville, thirty-five years his senior; he philandered (1843) with Eugénie Mayer, stepdaughter of Wellington's aide John Gurwood; he embarked on, but shirked (1844), courtships of two heiresses to banks, Coutts's and Drummond's; he contracted liaisons and venereal disease. His one genuine romance (1843–4), with the seventeen-year-old daughter of the Russian ambassador to France, Count Stackelberg, was broken off by her parents.

Smythe nevertheless became known as 'the cleverest' of the Young Englanders and in 1842 agreed to a practical alliance with Disraeli, under whom in 1843–4 they opposed Peel's Conservatism. Smythe, however, was independent-minded enough to support congenial Peelite measures, such as (to the outrage of his archiepiscopal constituency) grants to the Roman Catholic seminary at Maynooth. In 1844 he also acquired literary fame, with articles in the *Quarterly Review* and *New Monthly Magazine*, and a book, *Historic Fancies*, notable for sketches of French Revolutionary leaders which showed he was 'not afraid to do justice to criminals'. He was popularly identified with the highly idealized hero of Disraeli's political best-seller, *Coningsby*, and, though gratified, began in response his own *Angela Pisani*, a semi-autobiographical novel questioning conventional concepts of heroism and love. In October he gave a scintillating speech to the Manchester Athenaeum, stressing (as he had done at Eton and Cambridge) the importance of literature and the need for a 'marriage between industry and intellect'. 'A man who can speak like that', one of his father's friends prophesied, 'may aspire to the highest position in the land.' Peel agreed and in January 1846 lured him from Disraeli by appointing him under-secretary for foreign affairs. 'Think', Smythe wrote apologetically to Disraeli, 'as gently as you can of my fall *upstairs*.' Disraeli's riposte was the duplicitous character Fakredeen in *Tancred* (1847).

Junior office was, however, a souring experience. Smythe was no administrator and for two years before Peel's government fell (June 1846) he had been contemplating journalism as a more effective means of influencing public opinion. A widely publicized liaison with Lady Dorothy Walpole (later Nevill) forced him to Europe in September and barred him from many society circles. In February 1848 he joined the newly Peelite *Morning Chronicle*, sending dispatches from Paris during the 1848 revolution and writing vigorous, intelligent articles praised by authorities as diverse as Metternich, Brougham, and Sir G. C. Lewis. Although nominally Peelite and personally opposed to protectionism, he used his editorials to promote Disraeli's leadership; in increasing ill health, he gave up regular journalism after Peel's death (1850) to assist Disraeli.

In 1844, with J. A. Roebuck, and in 1849, with Richard Monckton Milnes, Smythe had almost succeeded in provoking duels; in 1852 he did fight 'the last duel in England' with his Canterbury colleague Frederick Romilly. His father refused any further election funds and in hopes of a diplomatic appointment he colluded with Disraeli to sell out his constituents and ensure the return of protectionist candidates. The manoeuvre was so blatant that the election was declared void; a subsequent royal commission (1853) found evidence of bribery in all Smythe's previous elections. In November 1852 he sent Disraeli, precariously in office, an editorial, written in 1848, for use in parliament on Wellington's death; but he forgot to mention that it was largely quotation from the French statesman Thiers, leaving Disraeli open to charges of plagiarism. By December Disraeli was out of office, Smythe's sister Louisa (Ellen), marchioness of Sligo, had died of tuberculosis, and Smythe was too depressed and ill to accept Aberdeen's offer of a post in January 1853. He was also unwilling or unable to write regularly for Disraeli's paper *The Press*, though he contributed occasional pieces and at least one major article—a defence of Disraeli in January 1854 against McKnight's hostile biography. His sister Philippa, wife of Henry Baillie, died in June, and in August, Smythe withdrew from Canterbury. In 1855 he succeeded as seventh Viscount Strangford, to find that his father had sequestered most of his money to his illegitimate children.

With health rapidly failing, Strangford travelled in 1856 on the Nile, where he began an affair with Margaret Cunynghame Kincaid Lennox (later Bateman-Hanbury; 1829–1897), daughter of John Kincaid Lennox of Lennox Castle, Stirling. In August 1857 his health broke down completely in France and only Margaret Lennox's care brought back the 'bed-ridden Lovelace' to England. He took refuge at Bradgate Park, Leicestershire, with a former mistress, now countess of Stamford and Warrington, and there, after procrastinating as long as possible, he married Margaret Lennox on 9 November. He died there of tuberculosis on 23 November and was buried at Kensal Green cemetery, London.

Smythe's friend Lord Lyttelton thought him a 'splendid failure', Princess Metternich a more sinister *loup-garou* (werewolf). As champion of Young England, as friend, colleague, or lover, he never reconciled his romantic idealism with the pragmatic opportunism inculcated by his father. He excelled as a speaker but the emotional effort exhausted him. He recognized but avoided responsibility. Contemporaries remembered his charm and wit, were fascinated by his refusal ('failure') to conform, or disapproved his visible shifts of course; later appraisals depict a glamorous but flawed nostalgic, ultimately ineffectual. He was dominated by his father and Disraeli and was disturbingly chameleon-like in his changes of loyalty. Disraeli, however, saw that his true potential had been literary rather than parliamentary and that his health as much as his character had prompted his inconsistencies and defections. His ideas were forward looking: ecumenicalism, free trade, class harmony, the power of the press, alliance with Europe, the importance of the United States. Unfortunately, he gave them most cogent expression in ephemeral journalism and an unfinished novel.

MARY S. MILLAR

Sources Queen's University, Kingston, Ontario, Canada, Disraeli Letters Project • Durham RO, Londonderry MSS • CKS, Stanhope papers • E. B. de Fonblanque, *Lives of the lords Strangford* (1877) • *Benjamin Disraeli letters*, ed. J. A. W. Gunn and others (1982–), vols. 3–6 • E. Strangford, 'Memoir', in G. S. Smythe, *Angela Pisani* (1875), v–xxxi • GEC, *Peerage* • C. Whibley, *Lord John Manners and his friends*, 2 vols. (1925) • R. Faber, *Young England* (1987) • *Disraeli's reminiscences*, ed. H. M. Swartz and M. Swartz (1975) • G. Sydney-Smythe, *Angela Pisani* (1875) • Mrs F. Russell, *Fragments of auld lang syne* (1925) • 'Literary legislators V', *Fraser's Magazine*, 35 (1847), 529–38
Archives Belvoir Castle, Rutland MSS • Bodl. Oxf., Disraeli MSS
Likenesses R. Buckner, oils, Hughenden Manor, Buckinghamshire [*see illus.*] • portrait, repro. in P. Cradock, *Recollections of the Cambridge Union, 1815–1935* (1953), 27 • sketch, Hughenden Manor, Buckinghamshire
Wealth at death under £7000: probate, 1858

Smythe, James Moore (1702–1734), playwright and man of fashion, was born James Moore at the family home at Fetcham, Surrey, the son of Arthur *Moore (*d.* 1730) and his second wife, Theophila (*c.*1676–1739), daughter of William Smythe and Lady Elizabeth, daughter of George Berkeley, first earl of Berkeley. He was educated at Oxford, where he matriculated from Worcester College on 10 October 1717 and graduated BA from All Souls College in 1722. In his youth Moore gained a reputation for 'great Wit and Vivacity', high living, and extravagant dressing, for which he earned the foppish epithet 'Jemmy' (*Characters of the Times*, 13). Such behaviour alienated him from his father, though through his close relations with his maternal grandfather he secured the post of receiver and paymaster to the band of gentleman-pensioners (June 1718). On his grandfather's death two years later he inherited a substantial amount of property on condition that he change his name to Moore Smythe (an alteration not recognized by act of parliament until 1728).

Moore Smythe's inheritance notwithstanding, his profligate lifestyle soon required him to seek ways of earning money to satisfy a growing list of creditors. His play *The Rival Modes* (1727), written for this purpose, was first performed at Drury Lane, London, on 27 January of that year. The production was not well received by the critics. In a letter to Thomas Tickell, the poet Edward Young described the play as 'a bad one', though, as a result of Moore Smythe's former indiscretions and his ruthless packing of the theatre to raise money, it received a 'worse Reception than as a first Performance it deserved' (21 Feb 1727, Tickell, 125). *The Rival Modes* played six times, securing its author £300 from the benefit and a generous £105 from the poet Thomas Lintot after its publication later that year.

The play is now best known for the quarrel it sparked with Alexander Pope. In act two Moore Smythe quoted eight lines of Pope's verse for which the poet had earlier given, but then withdrawn, his permission. Moore Smythe's inclusion of the lines in a format that suggested them to be his own earned him a series of rebukes from Pope, most notably in *The Dunciad*:

> A brain of feathers and a heart of lead
> ... Never was dash'd out, at one lucky hit,
> A fool, so just a copy of a wit,
> So like, that critics said, and courtiers swore,
> A Wit it was, and called the phantom More.
> (A. Pope, *Dunciad*, II, lines 44–5)

Pope's hostility may have been further motivated by the exaggerated praise Moore Smythe received from other critics. A 'very bright promising young Gentleman' he was, wrote one apologist of the young playwright, 'possess'd of a more genteel and witty Turn of Writing by far, than Master *Alexander*' (*Characters of the Times*, 13); 'Another Dryden shall arise in thee' was the fanciful claim of Edward Cooke in *Battle of the Poets* (1729). Moore Smythe himself hit back at Pope in his *One Letter to Mr Pope* (1730, co-written with another of *The Dunciad's* victims, Leonard Welsted):

> With long-brewed Malice warm thy languid Page
> And urge delirious Nonsense into Rage.

This defence reinvigorated the assault by Pope, who maintained Moore Smythe's reputation for plagiarism in several verses in the *Grub-Street Journal* (May and June 1730):

> A Gold watch found on a Cinder Whore,
> Or a good verse on J—my M—e,
> Proves but what either shou'd conceal,
> Not that they're rich, but that they steal.

In the same journal Moore Smythe was described at this time as a 'tall modest young Man, with yellowish Teeth, a sallow Complexion and a flattish Eye; shaped somewhat like an *Italian* in the Shoulders, Hip and back Parts' (*Grub-Street Journal*, 25 June 1730). His death, unmarried and in poverty at Whitton, near Isleworth, Middlesex, on 18 October 1734 was followed with a final attack from Pope in his *Epistle to Dr Arbuthnot*.

PHILIP CARTER

Sources *DNB* • *Characters of the times* (1728) • R. E. Tickell, *Thomas Tickell and the eighteenth-century poets* (1931) • *GM*, 1st ser., 4 (1734), 572
Archives NL Scot., MS of *The rival modes*

Smythe [Smith], **Sir John** (1533/4–1607), soldier, diplomat, and writer, was the eldest son and heir of Sir Clement *Smith (*d.* 1552), administrator, of Little Baddow and Rivenhall, Essex, and his wife, Dorothy (*d.* in or after 1553), daughter of Sir John Seymour of Wolf Hall, Wiltshire, and his wife, Margery. Very little is known about his childhood and youth. Smythe's father remained a practising Catholic to the end of his life, to the displeasure of his court connections, including his brother-in-law, Edward Seymour, duke of Somerset.

Education and early years, 1553/4–1576 Anthony Wood reports that Smythe studied at Oxford University. Smythe seems to have left the university without completing his degree but in his later writings comes across as reasonably well read, citing authors such as Diodorus, Thucydides, Herodotus, Pliny, and Plutarch in the proem to his treatise *Certain Discourses* (1590). Sir Clement Smith died on 26 August 1552 and a year later his widow married Thomas Laventhorpe. Smythe was a competent linguist, being fluent in Spanish, and a keen traveller. 'Being martially inclined', as Wood put it (Wood, *Ath. Oxon.*, 1.649), he left England in the early 1550s and gained military experience as a volunteer in France and the Low Countries, as well as in Hungary, where he fought against the Turkish army in 1566, and came to the attention of Maximilian II. At first he seems to have desired military experience, being wealthy enough when he came into his inheritance by 1555 to live the life of an independent member of the gentry. He appears to have been a Catholic initially but his role among a growing number of English and Welsh gentleman volunteers who desired to fight against the forces of Counter-Reformation Europe, suggests that he embraced protestantism, albeit cautiously. Smythe was certainly anti-clerical. He met Philip II and fought, with protestant volunteers, against the Turks in the Mediterranean. Smythe returned to England by 1572, when he was granted the manor of Little Baddow and the advowson of the church there. He was by this time well versed in a variety of military techniques and practices. It was this experience that shaped his firm opinions on the merits of the longbow over other types of weapons and armed him with the confidence in his own views that became the trademark of his written works.

The Spanish embassy, 1576–1577 Smythe knew Spanish customs well and was very familiar with Spanish military tactics. His status at court may have been assisted by his cousin, Edward *Seymour, first earl of Hertford (1539?–1621), courtier. These factors are likely to have earned him his office as Elizabeth I's special ambassador to Spain at a critical time. He was appointed on 18 November 1576.

Smythe was knighted in 1576, probably as a result of his appointment as ambassador. He had an audience with Henri III on 15 December, while on his way to Spain. His salary was £2 10*s*. per day. Smythe's official role was to convey the queen's offer to Philip to act as an arbitrator between Spain and the Dutch rebels. At the same time he was to secure better treatment for English merchants operating in Spanish territory and the release of English prisoners who did not fare well at the hands of the Spanish Inquisition. In reality, a great deal depended on this embassy: the presence of strong Spanish forces in the Low Countries was alarming, as was the possibility of an alliance between Spain and France. The Dutch revolt in 1576 presented Elizabeth with a unique opportunity. If the offer of mediation was accepted, Spain would be bound by at least a temporary obligation not to act against England. Smythe, as was expected of an ambassador, acted as Elizabeth's eyes and ears at the Spanish court, greatly assisted by his fluency in Spanish and knowledge of Spanish society. In a letter to William Cecil, Lord Burghley, he explained that 'I … allso did make her Majestie privy to the whole state of Spayne' (Ellis, 94). Smythe had his first audience on 24 January 1577.

Smythe's carried out his duties well in tense and difficult circumstances but fought his corner, as when he was involved in a heated exchange of frank insults with the inquisitor Gaspar de Quiroga, archbishop of Toledo, in the latter's residence. Smythe sought in vain to overcome Quiroga's hostility to English subjects. Whereas Philip was persuaded to maintain peace with Elizabeth, Quiroga branded her a heretic and refused to grant Smythe an audience despite a barrage of requests. Smythe grew exasperated. In a moment of bravado he forced his way into Quiroga's house, demanding that his requests be heard, the archbishop and he calling one another 'sirrah', and concluded the meeting by throwing himself into a 'violent altercation which nearly ended in blows', before being dragged off by friends (*CSP Spain*, 1509–25, 540). This is the first serious indication of Smythe's tendency to allow his impulses to override his better judgement. Against Quiroga intimidation was futile, as Gabriel de Zayas, secretary of state reminded Smythe drily in a letter dated 26 June 1577:

> the tribunal of the Holy Inquisition is simply and purely ecclesiastical … the King … does not interfere in any way with it or its proceedings … You will thus see easily what it will be proper to ask of his Catholic Majesty and what he is able to concede. (ibid., 2.541)

Shortly after the incident, on 29 March 1577, Smythe requested a last audience with the king before departing for England. The main reason for his embassy had been settled unexpectedly when Don John of Austria, governor of the Low Countries, came to an agreement with the states general without the need for a mediator. Fortunately, Smythe was able to leave, having received adequate assurances from Philip that Elizabeth's subjects in Spain 'shall not be molested or interfered with' (*CSP Spain*, 1509–25, 537). Also, at least four of the prisoners on whose behalf Smythe had intervened were released and compensated. He could return home with a justified sense of having behaved 'dutifully and dilligently' and was recalled on 28 July 1577 (Ellis, 94).

Return to England, 1577–1588 Smythe returned to the life of a country gentleman of modest means, who was frequently fined for neglecting to maintain his property adequately. Nothing more exciting than a spurious plot to accuse him of fathering a child out of wedlock seems to have marked his life until 1585. The outbreak of war with Spain and the distinct possibility of an invasion of England led to debate at court on the advantages of more direct military intervention versus diplomatic efforts to restore peace. Smythe was summoned once more, this time as the queen's ambassador to Alessandro Farnese, duke of Parma. This, however, proved an unlucky distinction: not only was his embassy cancelled but he also became a target for the enmity of the pro-war party.

Smythe made his comeback to a political arena prickling with tension between the followers of Burghley, who opposed the enormous risk and cost of military intervention, and the 'militants', who lobbied for an English offensive in the Low Countries led by Robert Dudley, earl of Leicester. Smythe was an outspoken critic of anyone who, in his view, squandered good English soldiers in unnecessary foreign wars and may have sided publicly with Burghley, with whom he had hitherto been on good terms. This must have exacerbated the mutual antipathy between Smythe and Leicester. Leicester saw to Smythe's dismissal from his last important assignment in 1587–8, when Smythe was commissioned to train at least 2000 troops over several days in Essex. According to Smythe's own accounts, the training was most successful; however, Leicester's sneering report represented him as a hypochondriac, whose eccentricities won him at best general condescension. Smythe was also accused of erratic behaviour. Leicester spoke of Smythe mustering his men with 'such straunge cryes', believing that 'he was not well' (PRO, SP 12/213/55, fol. 93*v*). Matters were not helped by Smythe's attacks on impressment as disruptive of the social order. He felt the wars consumed young men's lives, were wasteful and drawn out.

The military treatises, 1590–1595 Finding himself on the political periphery, Smythe made sure that his voice, at least, was still heard. His *Certain Discourses* (probably completed in 1586) was published in May 1590. Far from being a dry treatise on the longbow, the book is an amalgam of profound technical detail and vehement criticism of 'some of those new disciplinated men of war' (Smythe, *Certain Discourses*, xxx).

England was one of the last European countries to replace bows with firearms; even so, many deplored the decline of archery. Smythe—who remains an authority on the subject—considered the longbow superior to the newfangled weapons such as the harquebus and the caliver. His faith in the longbow sprang from a blend of well-established facts and his personal interpretation of military history. Thanks to his thorough understanding of the mechanics of archery he appreciated fully the longbow as a reliable, effective, fast (a good archer could fire ten to twelve arrows a minute), low-maintenance weapon. But the longbow was also the weapon that had been immortalized in legend, did excellent service during the Hundred Years' War and impressed the French; for many of its devotees it had become an emblem of Englishness and masculinity. In his proem Smythe voiced with much ardour his concern that England might go down the inglorious route of past empires such as Egypt, whose decline he attributed to 'covetousness, and effeminacies' and the neglect of 'all orders and exercise military' (Smythe, *Certain Discourses*, 8). He warned against listening to the 'public and private persuasions and inducements' of young men 'to reduce all our ancient proceedings in matters military', especially 'their vain and frivolous objections against our archery' (ibid., 4). Archery, he argued, had been the key to many great English victories. In this vein of fierce didacticism Smythe went on to accuse several of Elizabeth's advisers of military ignorance and to question their integrity. Oblivious to his tactlessness, he extended his criticisms to the late earl of Leicester. He was also generally critical of English soldiers who had risen to prominence in the Netherlands. This group amounted to virtually the whole Elizabethan military élite, including enemies of Leicester, such as Sir John Norris, a client of Burghley. Roger Williams attacked Smythe in print in 1590, partly because of his criticisms of Norris, who was also a client of Burghley. This increased Smythe's difficulties.

On 14 May 1590, just two weeks after its publication, *Certain Discourses* was suppressed by Burghley, who had been apprised of its offensive nature. Smythe sent several letters of appeal to Burghley; in one of them (20 May) his bitterness at the ignominious state to which he had been reduced finally bursts out: 'since Leicester's death I … have bene made inferior in all affaires of the Shier to divers that … were but boyes, and went to schole, when I had spent some time in the service of some princes'. He pointed out that he was forced to sell a good deal of his patrimony in order to pay his debtors. 'I have great cause to doubt and feare', he continued, 'that the condemninge [of the book] doth procede, rather uppon some great mislikinge had of me, beeing the autour of the booke, then of the booke yt self' (Ellis, 58–60). Evidently Smythe was aware of the effect his views might have on certain people, but had misjudged, perhaps, his standing at court. His protests notwithstanding he might even have anticipated such a reception. His intended trip to continental spas on—genuine—health grounds may have doubled as a contingency plan in case the reactions of those offended by his book made his absence expedient.

Certain Discourses certainly contributed to the debate on the merits of the bow over the gun, attracting a written response from firearm enthusiast Humphrey Barwick, and comment by Williams, and is reported to have sold at least 1200 copies despite (or because of) its suppression. It was not that Smythe was completely opposed to firearms. Instead, he felt that the soldiers using them were inadequately trained and their commanders too inexperienced to gain sufficient benefit from them. *Certain Discourses* was followed, four years later, by a second treatise entitled *Certain Instructions, Observations, and Orders Military* (1594). The book seems to have sold sufficiently well, as it was reprinted in 1595 even though Burghley refused to patronize it. Here Smythe focused for the most part on military methods; even so he did not wish, or manage, to hold back occasional outbursts of animosity directed at those he considered his enemies.

Imprisonment and final years, 1596–1607 Smythe's financial difficulties mounted and he sold Little Baddow in spring 1596. His bouts of irascibility were to cost him dearly: on 12 June he paid a visit to Sir Thomas Lucas in Colchester, Essex. According to his own account to Burghley, Smythe had foolishly deviated from his frugal diet and spent the night 'drinckinge of wyne, and wyne upon wyne' to alleviate 'a wonderfull payne' in his stomach (Ellis, 90–91). Ironically, the man who had once deplored the effects of the 'detestable vice' of immoderate drinking on worthy men, ended up 'dead drunk, or, as the Flemings say, *doot dronken*' (Smythe, *Certain Discourses*, 28). In this state he rode out to the field and before about 100 of the archers and pikemen Lucas had been training he started inciting the men to disobey any orders to waste their lives in foreign wars—especially those supported by Burghley, whom he accused of nothing less than treason. What is more, he urged the men to follow instead his own kinsman, Lord Thomas Seymour, Hertford's younger son, as a worthier leader. His earlier conversations with the chief baron of the exchequer, Sir Roger Manwood, convinced him that the legality of impressment for foreign wars was questionable. This touched a raw nerve, especially because of the need for more soldiers to fight in the Netherlands, France, and, especially, Ireland. His own retainers probably encouraged Smythe but, as the situation got out of hand, initial backers began to distance themselves from him.

Burghley did not take kindly to this behaviour: he commanded Lucas to arrest Smythe and deliver him to the court, even if this required army reinforcements. Smythe's writings provide plenty of evidence that he was genuinely concerned for the welfare of the common soldier, and in his letters to Burghley from the Tower of London he is adamant that drunkenness alone was the reason for his 'franticke, disordered speeches' (Ellis, 91). None the less, Burghley remained unconvinced. 'It is to be supposed', he wrote, 'that the said attempte proceeded not of his meere rashenes … or sodaine overthrowe of his owne, but from some farther grounde and foundacion of practize and conspiracie'. He ordered that 'all and everie' of Smythe's houses be searched for evidence (*APC*, *1595–6*, 501). The court found Smythe guilty of 'verie seditious wordes' and sentenced him to imprisonment in the Tower (ibid., 459).

The letters Smythe addressed to Burghley during the seventeen months of his incarceration capture the essence of his personality: they range from fearful pleas of pardon and piteous confessions of impecuniousness, to long-winded reminders of his patriotism and past successes, to brazen arguments that, according to his lawyers, he 'might lawfullie advise the people not to goe in service out of the realme at this tyme' (*APC*, *1595–6*, 459). Whether because he was advised to show moderation or because Smythe's failing health and precarious finances broke his spirit, subsequent letters to Burghley are much meeker in tone and most of his requests are backed up by references to his advanced years. On the grounds of Smythe's 'olde yeares and unhealthfulnes', Burghley allowed him to be attended by one of his own servants and to be visited (though only during a three-month period) by his wife, by Lady Susan Bourchier, by Richard Bristow, and by his attorney, Matthew Rudd. He was also given leave to take daily walks in the garden of the Tower and to be seen regularly by a physician, Dr Nowell. Most importantly, Burghley granted Smythe's initial plea, that, by way of punishment, he be confined to a 1 mile radius from his new residence in Little Baddow and have copies of a public apology to Burghley posted in Colchester. The queen ordered Smythe's release on 3 February 1598.

After 1598 Smythe's name hardly occurs in records. The only notable exception is a letter dated 4 March 1600 to Smythe from Sir Robert Cecil, enquiring whether he could provide him with notes and correspondence from his Spanish embassy regarding the Inquisition. Smythe was eager but unable to oblige. Nevertheless Cecil seems to have been amicably disposed to his father's detractor. A few weeks later Smythe's confinement was relaxed to a 5 mile radius and his kinsman Reginald Smythe obtained for him permission to travel to London for twelve days in order to see to his affairs, which were still in poor order. Sir John Smythe probably spent the last few years of his life at Little Baddow. He died there at the end of August 1607, aged seventy-three, and was buried in the church of Little Baddow on 1 September. Nothing is known about his wife. Smythe's preoccupation with the issue of how to use the trained bands and of the military obligations of the English and Welsh people did not die with him, instead, becoming increasingly relevant after 1625.

ARTEMIS GAUSE-STAMBOULOPOULOU

Sources J. Smythe, *Certain discourses … concerning the formes and effects of divers sorts of weapons and other verie important matters militarie* (1590); repr. with an introduction by J. R. Hale (1964) • J. Smythe, *Certain instructions, observations, and orders military* (1594); repr. (1595) • *CSP Spain* • *CSP dom.*, *1598–1601* • H. Ellis, ed., *Original letters of eminent literary men of the sixteenth, seventeenth, and eighteenth centuries*, CS, 23 (1843), 48–65, 88–97 • *APC*, *1595–7* • J. A. Froude, *History of England*, new edn, 12 vols. (1893), vol. 10 • Wood, *Ath. Oxon.*, new edn, 1.649–51 • will, PRO, PROB 11/35, sig. 28 • H. J. Webb, *Elizabethan military science: the books and the practice* (1965) • R. Hardy, *Longbow: a social and military history* (1976); 3rd edn (1992) • R. E. Kaiser, 'The medieval English longbow', *Journal of the Society of Archer-Antiquaries*, 23 (1980) • P. Valentine Harris, 'The decline of the longbow', *Journal of the Society of Archer-Antiquaries*, 19 (1976) • J. Strype, *Annals of the Reformation and establishment of religion … during Queen Elizabeth's happy reign*, new edn, 4 vols. (1824), vol. 4, pp. 64–5 • M. C. Fissel, *English warfare, 1511–1642* (2001) • C. G. Cruickshank, *Elizabeth's army* (1946); 2nd edn (1966) • *The works of Sir Roger Williams*, ed. J. X. Evans (1972) • D. Lloyd, *State worthies, or, The statesman and favourites of England from the Reformation to the revolution*, 2 vols. (1766), vol. 1, pp. 558–9 • W. C. Metcalfe, *A book of knights* (1885), 130 • *Literary remains of King Edward the Sixth*, ed. J. G. Nichols, 2 vols., Roxburghe Club, 75 (1857), vol. 1, p. cccxi • P. Morant, *The history and antiquities of the county of Essex*, 2 (1768) • *DNB*

Archives BL, answer to Humphrey Barwick against his opinion on weapons, Harley MS 135 | BL, Cotton MSS, Titus C.vii • BL, Cotton MSS, Vespasian C.vii • PRO, SP 70

Smythe, Maria Anne. *See* Fitzherbert, Maria Anne (1756–1837).

Smythe, Patricia Rosemary [Pat] (**1928–1996**), showjumper, was born on 22 November 1928 at 24 Shotfield Avenue, East Sheen, London, the only daughter and youngest of three children of Captain Eric Hamilton Smythe (1886–1945), civil engineer and businessman, and his wife, Frances Monica (1904–1952), daughter of the Revd Frank Curtoys. Both parents were from families of well-established lineage, and Eric Smythe, an executive

Patricia Rosemary Smythe (1928–1996), by Haywood Magee, 1952 [with her horse Tosca]

director of an electrical engineering firm, had been decorated in the First World War. The Smythes' first child, Dickie, had died in infancy, and Pat grew up with her parents and elder brother, Ronald. In the early 1930s the family moved a short distance to a larger house, Beaufort, on the edge of Barnes Common, where under her mother's tuition Pat learned riding skills on her pony Pixie. She attended several schools: Oakhill, Wimbledon; Downe House, Seaford; Ferne House, Dorset, and later Fonthill Abbey, Wiltshire; Pate's Grammar School, Cheltenham; St Michael's, Cirencester; and Talbot Heath, Bournemouth. Though she later claimed that the family was 'far from wealthy' (Smythe, *Jump for Joy*, 21), they enjoyed a comfortable middle-class life until her father's deteriorating health and eventual death early in 1945 brought on more straitened circumstances.

Through the enthusiasm and knowledge of her mother, a trainer of polo ponies, Pat Smythe developed the understanding and love of horses that determined her career. An outstanding junior showjumper, who tied for first place in her group at the Royal Richmond show of 1939, she became fully immersed in the world of horses and showjumping during the Second World War, when she moved to the west country to live with farming friends and relatives. Her parents subsequently settled at Crickley Lodge near Cheltenham, an area with which Pat maintained connections for the rest of her life. The war years were a formative period that served so to develop her riding skills at local horse shows and gymkhanas that by 1947 her performance at the first international horse show at the White City won her selection to the British team, a status she maintained throughout the remainder of a career that continued until 1963. Riding initially her own horses, Finality, Tosca, and Prince Hal, which she trained with her mother, and then other owners' horses—Flanagan, Mr Pollard, and Scorchin' being the most celebrated—Pat Smythe, assisted by her groom Pauline Sykes, won a succession of showjumping's prestige individual and team events throughout the world. Among her many honours were leading showjumper of the year (1949), the European championship on four occasions between 1957 and 1961, the celebrated gold button of Algiers (1955), and the British Jumping Derby championship at Hickstead (1962). She was the first woman showjumper to represent Great Britain at the Olympic games in 1956, the year in which she was appointed OBE, and was a member of the British team again at the Rome Olympics in 1960. This, together with her autobiography *Jump for Joy* (1954) and her writing for the *Daily Express*, ensured that she was a household name, both in Britain and in much of the rest of the world, during the 1950s.

The peak of Smythe's career coincided with the emergence of television. Her youth, charm, physical courage, and conventional good looks gave her an appeal that was decisive in transforming a previously élite and largely male sport, with strong military associations, into a popular media spectacle. Her success made it possible for other women riders to progress in the sport, so that what had been an exception when she herself was first making her way was to become commonplace by the late 1960s. She possessed few material advantages or privileges. In spite of help from wealthy family and friends, after her father's death she and her mother earned their living by teaching riding and taking in guests at their home in Miserden, a house with stables on which her mother took a lease in 1949. The early death of her mother in a road accident in 1952 left Pat to manage and finance her showjumping career single-handedly. Her progress became an object lesson in surmounting obstacles through hard work, self-discipline, and determination, a central theme in her final autobiography, *Leaping Life's Fences* (1992). She thus became not only an icon of a more egalitarian Britain, but a precursor of the liberated female of the 1960s. Completely devoid of airs and graces—'she had absolutely no side', according to BBC executive Peter Dimmock (*The Guardian*, 29 Feb 1996)—she seemed to embody the triumph of the 'ordinary woman'. Her popularity was especially marked among countless young girls, for whom she wrote popular adventure stories (the *Three Jays* series) about children and horses.

In 1963 Pat Smythe gave up her sport to marry, on 10 September, a friend she had known since her late 'teens, the divorced Swiss lawyer and businessman (Alphons) Samuel (Sam) Koechlin (1924/5–1985), son of Hartmann Koechlin, chemist. They set up home in Switzerland and had two children, Monica and Lucy. For some twenty years Pat accompanied her husband, a representative of the chemical firm Ciba-Geigy, on business trips around the world, during which she promoted the causes of wildlife and environmental protection. Connections with showjumping were maintained. She served as *chef d'équipe* of British teams, and from 1983 to 1986 as president of the British Showjumping Association. Before the age of forty, however, she had suffered severe hip problems, partly as a consequence of riding accidents; she developed the osteoarthritis that had afflicted her father and, subsequently, osteoporosis and heart problems. Following the death of her husband from cancer in 1985 she returned to live at her English home, Sudgrove House in the Cotswolds, maintaining her activities in the fields of conservation, travel, and the arts until her death at Standish Hospital, Standish, Gloucestershire, from heart failure on 27 February 1996. JEFFREY HILL

Sources P. Smythe, *Jump for joy* (1954) • P. Smythe, *Leaping life's fences* (1992) • P. Smythe, *Jumping round the world* (1962) • *The Times* (28 Feb 1996) • *Daily Telegraph* (29 Feb 1996) • *The Independent* (29 Feb 1996) • *The Guardian* (29 Feb 1996) • *WWW* • J. Uglow, *The Macmillan dictionary of women's biography* (1982) • J. Rodda and P. Dimmock, 'Vaulting ambition', *The Guardian* (29 Feb 1996) • m. cert. • d. cert.
Likenesses photograph, 1950, repro. in Smythe, *Leaping life's fences* • H. Magee, photograph, 1952, Hult. Arch. [*see illus.*] • K. Money, oils, *c.*1960 • photograph, 1962, repro. in *Daily Telegraph* • photo, repro. in *The Times* • photograph, repro. in P. Smythe, *Jumping round the world* • photograph, repro. in *The Independent*
Wealth at death £134,709: administration with will, 14 Nov 1996, *CGPLA Eng. & Wales*

Smythe, Percy Clinton Sydney, sixth Viscount Strangford (1780–1855), diplomatist, born in London on 31 August 1780, was the eldest son of Lionel Smythe, fifth Viscount Strangford (1753–1801), who entered the army and served in America, but in 1785 took holy orders, and in 1788 was presented to the living of Killrew, co. Meath. His mother, Maria Eliza, was the eldest daughter of Frederick Philipse of Philipsbourg, New York.

The family descended from Sir John Smith or Smythe of Ostenhanger, Kent, the elder brother of Sir Thomas Smith or Smythe (*d.* 1625). Sir John's son Sir Thomas Smythe was made a knight of the Bath in 1616, 'being a person of distinguished merit and opulent fortune'; and on 17 July 1628 he was created an Irish peer by the title of Viscount Strangford of Strangford, co. Down. He died on 30 June 1635, having married Lady Barbara, seventh daughter of Robert Sidney, first earl of Leicester.

Percy, the sixth viscount, graduated in 1800 at Trinity College, Dublin, where he won the gold medal. In 1802 he entered the diplomatic service as secretary of the legation at Lisbon. In the following year he published *Poems from the Portuguese of Camoëns, with Remarks and Notes*. Byron, in *British Bards and Scotch Reviewers*, accused the translator of teaching 'the Lusian bard to copy [Thomas] Moore', and described him as:

> Hibernian Strangford, with thine eyes of blue,
> And boasted locks of red or auburn hue.

Strangford soon became *persona grata* at the Portuguese court. In 1806 he was named minister-plenipotentiary *ad interim*. He persuaded the prince regent of Portugal, on the advance of the French in November 1807, to leave Portugal for Brazil. Strangford arrived in Britain on 19 December, and drew up, at Canning's request, a connected account of the proceeding drawn from his own dispatches and published in the *London Gazette* on 22 December. In 1828 Napier, in the first volume of his *History of the War in the Peninsula*, maintained that the credit of the diplomatic negotiations really belonged to Sir William Sidney Smith, and made various charges against Strangford. The latter issued *Observations* in reply, which Sir Walter Scott and even the whig circles at Holland House thought satisfactory (*Journal*, 31 May 1828). Napier responded, and Strangford issued *Further Observations. The Times* (7 August 1828) accused him of utter want of truth. Strangford failed to obtain legal redress for some strong reflections made on him in the same connection by *The Sun* newspaper. Brougham appeared for the defendants at the trial (Napier, 6.222–3).

Strangford received the Order of the Bath, and was sworn of the privy council in March 1808. On 16 April he was appointed envoy-extraordinary to the Portuguese court in Brazil. He was made GCB on 2 January 1815, on his return from the mission. On 18 July 1817 he became ambassador to Sweden. The previous day, 17 July, he married Eleanor (Ellen; 1788–1826), youngest daughter of Sir Thomas Burke, bt, of Marble Hill, Galway, and widow of Nicholas Browne, of Mount Hazel, Galway. They had three sons and two daughters. Before leaving Stockholm, two years later, he induced the Swedish government to agree to the British proposals for an arrangement with Denmark, and discussed with them a new tariff highly advantageous to Britain.

On 7 August 1820 Strangford was appointed ambassador at Constantinople. Here he joined the Austrian minister in urging on the Porte the necessity of pursuing a more conciliatory line towards Russia, and of making concessions to its Christian subjects, then in open revolt both in Greece and the Danubian provinces. In the autumn of 1822 he went to Verona, and laid before the European congress the assurances he had obtained from the sultan. When, in December, Strangford returned to Constantinople, he was placed in sole charge of Russian affairs in Turkey. He obtained from the Porte the evacuation of the Danubian principalities, the conclusion of a treaty allowing Sardinian ships to enter the Bosphorus, and the removal of the recently made restrictions on Russian trade in the Black Sea. In return the tsar promised the resumption of diplomatic relations with Turkey. On 13 September 1824 Wellington wrote to Strangford congratulating him 'upon a result obtained by your rare abilities, firmness, and perseverance'. Greville, on the other hand, charged him with having exceeded his instructions while at Constantinople; but these, Strangford complained afterwards, had been scanty and he in fact did much to avoid war between Russia and Turkey (Temperley, 289). In October he left Turkey, and on 26 January 1825 he was given a United Kingdom peerage as Baron Penshurst of Penshurst, enabling him to sit in the House of Lords—apparently the conclusion of a notable career. But on his return he quarrelled with Canning, who suspected, rightly, that he had shown confidential papers to Metternich and Esterházy. Even so, he was sent as ambassador to St Petersburg in October 1825, although Canning refused to discuss his instructions with him. In trying on his own initiative to organize a collective *démarche* of the five powers at Constantinople he falsified an important dispatch to Canning and was caught out. Further, he showed a vital confidential document to the Austrian ambassador in St

Petersburg. In the face of a humiliating rebuff from Canning, he applied for leave of absence. Sir Charles Webster comments: 'It is seldom that so brilliant a man has merited so stern a condemnation' (Temperley, 293). Lady Strangford died at St Petersburg on 26 May 1826.

Strangford's diplomatic career closed in August 1828 with a special mission to Brazil, where he showed cunning and resource (Webster, 48). For the remainder of his life he was an active tory peer, often taking part in debates on questions of foreign policy. On 29 January 1828 he seconded the address. On 11 August 1831 he complained that the arrangements for the coronation of William IV had not been submitted to the privy council, but only to a selection from it, 'similar to that which our transatlantic brethren call a caucus' (*Hansard* 3, 5, 1831, 1170). He signed, as Penshurst, Lord Mansfield's protest against the Reform Bill, and corresponded with Wellington on that bill and on foreign affairs. On 28 February 1828 he sent Wellington a memorandum recommending a British guarantee of the Asiatic dominions of Turkey as the most likely measure to bring the latter to an accommodation.

Strangford retained a taste for literature throughout his life. His close friends included J. W. Croker and Thomas Moore, and he was a frequent guest at Samuel Rogers's table. In his later years he was a constant visitor to the British Museum and state paper office, and frequently contributed to the *Gentleman's Magazine* and to *Notes and Queries*. He was elected FRS and FSA in February 1825, and was a director of the Society of Arts and one of its vice-presidents from 1852 to 1854. In 1834 he published in Portuguese, French, and English the *Letter of a Portuguese Nobleman on the Execution of Anne Boleyn*, and in 1847 edited for the Camden Society (*Camden Miscellany*, 2) 'Household expenses of the Princess Elizabeth during her residence at Hatfield, October 1551–September 1552'. He also collected materials for a life of Endymion Porter. He was created DCL at Oxford University on 10 June 1834, at the installation of Wellington as Chancellor. He was also a grandee of Portugal and a GCH.

Two of his sons, George *Smythe and Percy *Smythe, succeeded in turn to his titles after his death at his house, 68 Harley Street, London, on 29 May 1855. He was buried at Ashford, Kent. Strangford was a gifted if unreliable diplomatist whose ambition and vanity, combined with his support for a 'Holy Alliance' and European intervention in Turkey, brought about the circumstances of his fall.

G. Le G. Norgate, *rev.* H. C. G. Matthew

Sources GEC, *Peerage* • *GM*, 2nd ser., 44 (1855), 90, 114 • H. Temperley, *The foreign policy of Canning, 1822–1827* (1925) • C. K. Webster, *The foreign policy of Castlereagh*, 2 vols. (1925–31) • W. F. P. Napier, *History of the war in the Peninsula and in the south of France*, rev. edn, 6 vols. (1851) • *The journal of Sir Walter Scott*, ed. W. E. K. Anderson (1972)

Archives BL, corresp. and papers | BL, corresp. with Lord Aberdeen, Add. MS 43081 • BL, letters to Sir Robert Gordon, Add. MS 43213 • BL, letters to Lord and Lady Holland, Add. MSS 51623, 51633 • BL, letters to Sir George Rose, Add. MS 42794 • BL, letters to Thomas Streatfield, Add. MSS 34103, 34105 • BL, corresp. with duke of Wellington, Add. MSS 37291–37293 • Bodl. Oxf., letters to Benjamin Disraeli • Bodl. Oxf., corresp. with Sir Thomas Phillipps • CKS, letters to Lord Stanhope • Devon RO, letters to Henry Addington • Durham RO, corresp. with Lord Londonderry • U. Southampton L., corresp. with George Canning [copies] • U. Southampton L., corresp. with Lord Londonderry • U. Southampton L., corresp. with duke of Wellington • UCL, letters to Lord Brougham

Likenesses Count D'Orsay, pencil drawing, 1841, Gov. Art Coll. • miniature, S. Antiquaries, Lond. • print, BM • stipple, BM

Smythe, Percy Ellen Algernon Frederick William Sydney, eighth Viscount Strangford (1825–1869), diplomatist and philologist, born at St Petersburg on 26 November 1825, was the third and youngest son of Percy Clinton Sydney *Smythe, sixth viscount (1780–1855), and Eleanor (Ellen; 1788–1826), daughter of Sir Thomas Burke, first baronet, and widow of Nicholas Browne, of Mount Hazel, co. Galway. His elder brother was George Augustus Frederick Percy Sydney *Smythe, seventh viscount. During part of his youth he was almost blind. From the first he devoted himself to the study of languages. At Harrow School (1841–3) he taught himself Persian, and at Oxford he learned Arabic. He matriculated from Merton College on 17 June 1843, and then held a postmastership (1843–5). In May 1845 he was nominated by the vice-chancellor one of the two student attachés at Constantinople. He became paid attaché there in 1849, and was oriental secretary from July 1857 to October 1858. He worked hard at his official duties, and his health suffered severely from the strain of work entailed by the Crimean War. Meanwhile he acquired an extremely thorough knowledge of Turkish, modern Greek, Sanskrit, and oriental philology. He spoke Persian and Greek well, and was versed in their dialects. He was also acquainted with Celtic, Romani, classical literature, geography, and ethnology.

On his accession to the peerage on his brother's death in 1857 Strangford took a house in London, but mainly continued for four years in Constantinople, where he lived the austere life of a dervish, a member of a Muslim fraternity vowed to poverty. On 6 February 1862 he married Emily Anne Beaufort (*bap.* 1826, *d.* 1887), youngest daughter of Admiral Sir Francis *Beaufort, at All Saints' Church, Norfolk Square, Paddington, London. As Emily Anne *Smythe she became well known as a promoter of trained nursing and as a founder of hospitals in Turkey and Egypt. In 1863 Strangford travelled in Austria and Albania, widening his knowledge and strengthening his interest in the Eastern question. He opposed the philhellenes and thought that the future of south-eastern Europe belonged to the Bulgarians rather than the Greeks. He was a frequent contributor to the *Pall Mall Gazette* and the *Saturday Review*.

In 1869 Strangford's wife edited two volumes of his *Selected Writings*. They contain the three chapters which he contributed to a book by his wife, *Eastern Shores of the Adriatic*, many contributions to the *Pall Mall Gazette* dealing with the Eastern question, and other miscellaneous pieces. In 1878 Viscountess Strangford published his *Original Letters and Papers upon Philological and Kindred Subjects*, which reveals his extensive knowledge of Afghan, Hindustani, Arabic, Turkish, Persian, and some Slav languages. Strangford was president of the Royal Asiatic Society in 1861–4 and 1867–9. He died suddenly at his home, 58 Great

Cumberland Place, London, on 9 January 1869, and was buried, beside his elder brother, at Kensal Green cemetery. His friend Sir Mountstuart Grant Duff remarked that his death left a vacancy in European journalism which was never filled. He left no children and his titles became extinct. G. Le G. Norgate, *rev.* Elizabeth Baigent

Sources *The Times* (12 Jan 1869) • E. B. de Fonblanque, *Lives of the lords Strangford* (1877) • GEC, *Peerage* • H. Rumbold, *Recollections of a diplomatist* (1903) • Foster, *Alum. Oxon.* • M. E. G. Duff, *Notes from a diary, 1851–1891*, 10 vols. (1897) • d. cert.

Archives Bodl. Oxf., letters to Friedrich Max Muller • JRL, letters to E. A. Freeman

Wealth at death under £3000: probate, 15 May 1869, *CGPLA Eng. & Wales*

Smythe, Sir Sidney Stafford (1705–1778), judge, was born in London, the son of Henry Smythe (1676/7–1706) of Old Bounds in the parish of Bidborough, Kent, and his wife, Elizabeth (*d.* 1754), daughter of Dr John Lloyd, canon of Windsor. His mother subsequently became the wife of William Hunt. He was admitted to St John's College, Cambridge, as a fellow-commoner on 1 July 1721, and graduated BA in 1725. Having entered the Inner Temple on 5 June 1724, he was called to the bar in February 1729, and joined the home circuit. In 1733 Smythe married Sarah (*d.* 1790), daughter of Sir Charles Farnaby, baronet, of Kippington in Kent. Both he and his wife took a great interest in the evangelical movement. There were no children.

In 1740 Smythe was appointed steward of the court of the king's palace at Westminster, in the place of Sir Thomas Abney, and in Trinity term 1747 he was made king's counsel and was called to the bench of the Inner Temple. At the general election of 1747 he was returned to the House of Commons for the borough of East Grinstead, where he sat for only three sessions, until 1750, and made no discernible mark. In January 1749 he served as one of the counsel for the crown in the prosecution of smugglers who were tried for murder before a special commission at Chichester. When news circulated in 1750 that Smythe's was one of two names being considered for judicial appointment, Solicitor-General William Murray (later Lord Mansfield) wrote to a friend:

> I own I wish My Lord Chancellor may recommend Smith [Smythe]; He is a sensible man with Parts & Learning sufficient to make an excellent Judge. Besides, which in my opinion are no small Ingredients, He has Prudence & Temper, is a very honest Man & a Gentleman. (BL, Add. MS 32720, fol. 359)

Smythe was appointed a baron of exchequer after the death of Charles Clarke, and took his seat after receiving the order of the coif on 23 June 1750, being knighted in November. With Heneage Legge he tried Mary Blandy for murder at the Oxford assizes in March 1752. While a puisne baron he was twice appointed a commissioner of the great seal, first (with Sir John Willes and Sir John Eardley-Wilmot) from 19 November 1756 to 20 June 1757, and second (as chief commissioner, with the Hon. Henry Bathurst and Sir Richard Aston) from 21 January 1770 to 23 January 1771. He succeeded Sir Thomas Parker as lord chief baron on 28 October 1772. As Parker continued to enjoy vigorous health after his resignation, while Smythe was often prevented by illness from attending court, Mansfield is said to have observed, 'that lord chief baron Smythe, the successor, should resign to his predecessor' (Holliday, 464). The remark was a mere witticism, as Mansfield and Smythe shared a lifelong friendship and mutual respect. Smythe became Mansfield's favourite assize partner; they rode the circuit together for fifteen summers, the last in 1776. After presiding in the exchequer for five years, Smythe was compelled in November 1777 to resign, owing to infirmities. He was granted a pension of £2400 and on 3 December was sworn of the privy council. He died at Old Bounds, Bidborough, Kent, on 2 November 1778, and was buried at Sutton-at-Hone, Kent. His wife survived him, dying on 18 March 1790.

Smythe was unjustly accused in the *Junius Letters* and in parliament of browbeating a jury at the Guildford summer assizes in 1770 in the trial of John Taylor, a sergeant of the Scots guards, for murder. Instead of improperly refusing to accept the jury's guilty verdict, Smythe learned that the verdict was not unanimous, and necessarily sent the jury back for further deliberation. Smythe's entirely proper conduct was brought out in debate in the House of Commons by George Onslow, who also testified to Smythe's exemplary character and abilities as a judge. He was nevertheless described in a funeral sermon as 'the ugliest man of his day' (De Coetlogon, 25).

G. F. R. Barker, *rev.* James Oldham

Sources *State trials* • J. Holliday, *The life of William, late earl of Mansfield* (1797) • J. Oldham, *The Mansfield manuscripts and the growth of English law in the eighteenth century*, 2 vols. (1992) • Holdsworth, *Eng. law* • *Annual Register* (1778), 227 • Foss, *Judges* • *GM*, 1st ser., 10 (1740) • *GM*, 1st ser., 17 (1747) • *GM*, 1st ser., 20 (1750) • W. Hustler, ed., *Graduati Cantabrigienses* (1823) • E. Hasted, *The history and topographical survey of the county of Kent*, 2nd edn, 12 vols. (1797–1801) • F. Townsend, *Catalogue of knights from 1660 to 1760* (1833) • H. Walpole, *Memoirs of the reign of King George the Third*, ed. G. F. R. Barker, 4 vols. (1894) • Venn, *Alum. Cant.* • J. B. Lawson, 'Smythe, Sydney Stafford', HoP, *Commons, 1715–54* • C. D. De Coetlogon, *Funeral sermon preached by the Rev. C. D. De Coetlogon* (1778) • William Murray, letter, 1750, BL, Add. MS 32720, fol. 359

Wealth at death £2400 p.a.: Foss, *Judges*

Smythe [Smith], **Thomas** (1522–1591), merchant and financier, was the second son of John Smith, clothier and minor landowner of Corsham, Wiltshire, and his wife, Joan, daughter of Robert Brouncker of Melksham. Supported by a small inheritance from his father, who died in 1538, Smythe gained his freedom of the Haberdashers' Company and subsequently of the Skinners, the company of Sir Andrew *Judde, a wealthy City merchant and Kent landowner, whose daughter, Alice (*d.* 1593), he married about 1555. Secure in business and society—he was a merchant adventurer, Muscovy merchant, and MP at the time of his marriage—Smythe abandoned a conventional career in commerce when he took up the collectorship of the subsidy on imports at the port of London in 1558. Through his association with the customs, which earned him the title of 'customer', Smythe entered the realms of government finance, court patronage, and politics. The move was highly profitable, particularly after the negotiation of his first lease of the duties on imported goods at London in

1570. Over eighteen years it is estimated that the farm yielded around £50,000 net profit.

Throughout this period Smythe enjoyed the confidence of the lord treasurer, William Cecil, Baron Burghley, and Robert Dudley, earl of Leicester, from whom Smythe subleased the farm of the duties on the import of sweet wines after 1573. The relationships were indeed so close that suspicions arose that Burghley, who helped Smythe to clear a substantial profit on an alum deal in 1578, and Leicester, who referred in his will to his 'great love' of the 'customer', shared in the profits of the farm. Sir Walter Ralegh was not alone in believing that they were, in his words, 'pensioners to Customer Smythe'. Some of the profits of the farm were put into land in Kent, where he added substantially to properties acquired through marriage, and in Wiltshire, where he built a fine house at Corsham. Smythe also invested in industrial and overseas enterprises. He was particularly active in the affairs of the societies of the Mines Royal and of the Mineral and Battery Works, either as manager or as lessee of their rights. By comparison his interest in overseas enterprise was slight. Shares were bought in the venture of Sir Humphrey Gilbert in 1578 and in the 'troublesome voyage' of Edward Fenton in 1582, but the Thomas *Smythe (*c*.1558–1625) who was associated with the Roanoke voyages and with the Levant Company was almost certainly his son and namesake. Mr Customer Smythe did however acquire a dubious reputation for dealing in prize goods.

Smythe died a wealthy man on 7 June 1591 and was buried at Ashford church. He was survived by Alice and their six sons and six daughters. The eldest son, John, was ancestor of the lords Strangford; Thomas, the second son, was eminent in commerce and colonization. According to the monument erected by John in Ashford parish church his father had cherished 'the professors of true religion' and promoted literature. The mathematician Thomas Hood was one who acknowledged a debt to Smythe. Mention is also made of his lease of the customs and the way 'he presided over them with singular liberality towards those of higher rank'. Of several portraits the finest is in the possession of Queens' College, Cambridge.

Brian Dietz, *rev*.

Sources HoP, *Commons, 1509–58* • HoP, *Commons, 1558–1603* • J. F. Wadmore, 'Thomas Smythe of Westenhanger, commonly called Customer Smythe', *Archaeologia Cantiana*, 17 (1887), 193–208 • will, PRO, PROB 11/78, sig. 78

Likenesses portrait, Queens' College, Cambridge

Wealth at death wealthy: HoP, *Commons, 1558–1603*, 406

Smythe [Smith], **Sir Thomas** (*c*.**1558–1625**), merchant, was born about 1558, the second surviving son of Thomas *Smythe (1522–1591), a merchant, financier, and 'customer' of the port of London, and his wife, Alice (*d*. 1593), the daughter of Sir Andrew *Judde, a skinner and mayor of London. He was educated at Merchant Taylors' School and was initiated early into business by his father, who had improved Elizabethan customs collection, despite constant but unproven allegations of corruption, and left his son enormous wealth. By 1580 he was a freeman of the Skinners' Company and the Haberdashers' Company, of

Sir Thomas Smythe (*c*.**1558–1625**), by Simon de Passe, 1616

which he served as master (1599–1600). He was MP for Aylesbury in the parliament of 1597, a seat earlier occupied by his father and elder brother, and was appointed a trade commissioner to negotiate with the Dutch in 1596 and 1598. In the 1590s he became purveyor for the troops in Ireland. Unlike his father, Smythe did not involve himself extensively in government financial concessions but engaged in more purely commercial activities. By 1600 he was a member of the Company of Merchant Adventurers, a governor of the Muscovy and Levant companies, and first governor of the East India Company (31 December 1600). After succeeding to his father's position of customer of London, he became auditor (1597–8), alderman (1599–1601), captain of the trained bands, and sheriff (6 November 1600).

Political fortunes Smythe's career was abruptly halted in February 1601, when he was seriously compromised, though not actually implicated, in the abortive coup of the earl of Essex, to whom, as a moderate puritan, Smythe was probably personally well disposed. On 8 February Essex had visited Smythe's house in Gracechurch Street, hoping he would use his position as captain of the trained bands to raise the city in support of his rebellion. Smythe was seen talking to him in the street outside before Essex entered his house. Initially he was thanked by the queen for his exertions, but later suspicion caused him to be deprived of his shrievalty and to be placed in the custody of the archbishop of Canterbury (14 February) before being put in the Tower (2 March). In his defence he denied prior knowledge of the plot and said that, far from visiting Essex House on the night before the rising (as was alleged), he had had no communication with the earl for nine years before the fateful day. When challenged about the meeting with Essex at his house, he told his inquisitors that he had merely conveyed a message from the lord mayor and had left home by the back gate to visit him when Essex insisted on entering the premises. Smythe was very lucky to escape with a short prison sentence and a heavy fine.

With the accession of James I in 1603 Smythe rapidly rose again to favour. He was appointed a trade commissioner to negotiate with the empire (1603), was knighted (13 May 1603, in the Tower, where he was still immured on 23 December), and was made joint receiver of the duchy of Cornwall (April 1604) and receiver for Dorset and Somerset (May). In June 1604, probably by reason of the leading role he played in the Muscovy Company's trade to northern Europe, he was appointed special ambassador to the tsar of Russia, and he landed at Archangel on 22 July. Over the winter he obtained a grant of new privileges for the company, and he sailed for England on 28 May 1605. His experiences in Russia were published (1605) and later reissued in a compilation by John Milton.

Administering the trading companies In 1603 Smythe, who had been the main promoter of the company's successful first voyage, was re-elected governor of the East India Company, and, with a single break (1605–7), and despite his protestations of long service, age, and ill health, made as early as 1614, he continued in office until 1621, often at the king's request. For two decades Smythe's house in Philpot Lane was the centre of the company's activities: its general assemblies were held in the great hall, which was hung with an Inuit canoe, and one room was specially fitted as a strongroom. The building was often thronged with sailors seeking recruitment or pay arrears and, when fleets were at sea, with their wives, often to Smythe's great discomfort. At one time he sheltered a Native American girl, who came over with Pocahontas and contracted tuberculosis. On at least five occasions between 1609 and 1619 he was voted sums of money by the company for his efforts, varying from £500 to £800, and in 1609 the king presented him with a chain and medal at the launch of a new company ship. But the company made little headway. Some blamed Smythe for having too many other commitments, but more likely reasons were private trading, interlopers, and troubles with the Dutch. In 1619 Smythe was again appointed a commissioner for the settlement of the company's differences with the Dutch and feasted their representatives at his house. Even after his retirement from the company he was asked (1624) to oversee an enterprise for trade with Persia, but he excused himself because of his age. In the hope of diminishing the length and hazards of East India Company expeditions, Smythe, who was also governor of the North-West Passage Company (1612), promoted voyages for the discovery of a north-west passage, especially those of Hudson (1610) and Baffin (1615), who gave his name to Smith Sound, between Greenland and Ellesmere Island.

Smythe had interested himself in Virginia as early as 1589, and in 1609 he obtained a second charter for the Virginia Company, of which he was treasurer until 1619. Although he showed resource, resilience, and flexibility in helping to secure the survival of the colony at Jamestown, and undertook genuine reforms such as the establishment of a Virginian assembly (1619), there was always conflict within the company between the big city merchants, led by Smythe, and the more numerous small adventurers. Some of the latter, who shared the traditional rivalry of the outports towards London, found leadership in Sir Edwyn Sandys and the earl of Southampton and were supported by some of Smythe's business rivals in the city. Despite his capacity for unhurried judgement, the excessive dependence by the company on the tobacco crop—seen by some as a vice—repeated calls by the colonists for more supplies, discouragement as a result of disasters and persistent ill luck, the development of private plantations, and accusations that the leading promoters were interested only in personal, short-term profit, caused the Sandys faction to demand a special audit of the company's accounts, suggesting that Smythe had enriched himself at the expense of the company. Smythe, by now in poor health, resigned the treasurership (1619), and his effective role in the company was at an end. The audit, which dragged on until 1624, formally exonerated his administration of the Virginia Company and condemned Sandys, his successor as treasurer. However, it found Smythe's bookkeeping unsatisfactory, probably the result of clerical errors. In 1624 his indebtedness to the company was agreed at £800, yet he was put on a new commission to settle the company's affairs.

The other main area of Smythe's involvement was Bermuda, then known as the Somers Islands. They were granted to the Virginia Company in 1612, but three years later, when Smythe was governor of the company and Bermuda was first colonized under the name Virginiola, they became the preserve of a distinct body, the Somers Islands Company, of which Smythe served as governor (1615–21). His name was given to the island on which the settlers first landed, to the first fort built to guard the harbour entrance, and, later on, to one of the parishes. Although his hope of recovering whales off Bermuda to replace those lost in northern Europe through French encroachment on the English whaling monopoly was not realized, profits were soon made from an immense piece of ambergris found on the coast, and by 1616 Bermuda had twice as many colonists as Virginia. Smythe secured an exemption for Bermuda ships from the regular depredations of naval impressment and sent East India Company guns and anchors to help the colonists. Although he was ousted from the governorship by the Sandys faction in 1621, he launched a powerful counter-attack, aided by the earl of Warwick, and he was re-elected as governor from 1623 to

1625. He was also governor of the French Company (1611) and a director of the Spanish Company (1604), and his memorial tomb mentions his leading role in a voyage to Senegal.

National politics Smythe sat in three of James I's parliaments: for Dunwich (1604), Sandwich (1614), and Saltash (1621). On his own admission he was no orator, but he served conscientiously on committees, especially those to do with shipping and foreign trade. As a commissioner for the navy (1618) he helped to expose the corrupt naval treasurer Sir Robert Mansell, and he was in charge of the war waged against the Barbary pirates. He also served on the treasury commission (1619). In general he stood for peace and the interests of big business. The crown relied heavily on Smythe's talents: a grandiose London merchant-prince, he was the main link between government and merchants. For thirty years he was overseer of virtually all the trade that passed through the port of London. Without men like him, prepared to switch financial resources to new fields of enterprise and between different continents, the English overseas empire would have been stillborn. Although he sought royal favour for his activities, he neither proffered loans to the crown nor sought influence and rewards from royal favourites. His integrity and relative frugality were allied to tremendous energy, patience and resolution, skill at organization, a broad vision, and generosity to the promising and needy. He gained the respect of his fellow merchants and was popular with both colonial administrators and the common seamen, who wrote him personal letters and gathered curiosities for his collection. 'Under Sir Thomas's management seamen would go, and with his endorsement, London merchants would subscribe' (Wilkinson, 185). Purchas speaks of him as 'our honourable Smith … at whose forge and anvill have beene hammer'd so many irons for Neptune' (S. Purchas, ed., *Hakluytus Posthumus, or, Purchas his Pilgrimes*, 1626 edn, 487).

Retirement years In 1625 Smythe retired to his house, Sutton (Brooke) Place, Sutton-at-Hone, Kent. (His house at Deptford, Skinners' Place, had been burnt to the ground in 1619.) There he died, on 4 September, probably of the plague, which was raging locally at the time. He was buried in the local church, which he is thought to have rebuilt after a fire in 1615. His memorial is a canopied tomb, with his alabaster effigy in furred aldermanic gown lying on a banded sarcophagus and surrounded by globes and a graceful pattern of sextants, compasses, galleys in full sail, barrels, and corded bales. He married three times. Judith, the daughter of Richard Culverwell, and Joan, the daughter of William Hobbs, both died childless; by 1601 he was already married to Sarah (*d.* 1655), the daughter of William Blount, with whom he had one daughter and three sons—two of whom seem to have predeceased him. After his death she married Robert Sidney, first earl of Leicester. The eldest son, John, survived him and was knighted, though a strain was put on their relationship by his marriage to the sister of the earl of Warwick, for long Smythe's commercial rival.

Smythe amassed a large fortune, a considerable part of which he devoted to charitable purposes. In 1619 he had given Tonbridge School (founded by his maternal grandfather, Sir Andrew Judde) an endowment, to be administered by the Skinners' Company, for increasing the salaries of the headmaster and usher and for a scholarship to enable a poor boy from the school to go to university. He also made gifts for the benefit of the poor of Tonbridge, Bidborough, and Speldhurst. His will made ample provision for these charities through the grant of various properties to the Skinners' Company and provided for six further exhibitions tenable at the universities for poor scholars of Tonbridge School. He left £500 to the Muscovy Company and £100 to build churches in Bermuda and Virginia. Because he encouraged his captains to keep detailed accounts of their voyages—for his friend Hakluyt to record—he was honoured with many dedications, including Thomas Hood's *Lectures on Navigation*, Jourdan's *Discovery of the Bermudas*, Sir Dudley Digges's *The Defence of Trade*, and John Woodall's *The Sirgion's Mate* (1617), which contained his likeness, engraved by Simon de Passe. Smythe's name was evidently pronounced Smith, and was often so spelt, but the man himself always used Smythe.

BASIL MORGAN

Sources H. C. Wilkinson, *The adventurers of Bermuda: a history of the island from its discovery until the dissolution of the Somers Island Company in 1684*, 2nd edn (1958) • J. F. Wadmore, 'Sir Thomas Smythe', *Archaeologia Cantiana*, 20 (1893), 82–103 • *CSP col.*, vols. 1–4 • W. Foster, *John Company* (1926) • S. Rivington, *The history of Tonbridge School*, 4th edn (1925) • S. Spurling, *Sir Thomas Smythe, Knt* (1955) • HoP, *Commons, 1558–1603* • T. K. Rabb, *Enterprise and empire: merchant and gentry investment in the expansion of England, 1575–1630* (1967) • W. F. Craven, *Dissolution of the Virginia Company: the failure of a colonial experiment* (1932) • A. L. Rowse, *The Elizabethans and America* (1959) • J. J. Stocker, 'Pedigree of Smythe of Ostenhanger', *Archaeologia Cantiana*, 20 (1893), 76–81 • GEC, *Peerage*, 7.554

Likenesses S. de Passe, line engraving, 1616, BM, NPG [*see illus.*]

Wealth at death very wealthy: Wadmore, 'Sir Thomas Smythe', 100–103; will, proved 12 Oct 1625, PRO

Smythe, William James (1816–1887), army officer, second son of Samuel Smythe, vicar of Carnmoney, co. Antrim, and his wife, Margaret, daughter of John Owens of Tildary, co. Antrim, was born at Coole Glebe, Carnmoney, on 25 January 1816. He was educated at Antrim until he entered the Royal Military Academy at Woolwich on 11 November 1830. He was commissioned second lieutenant in the Royal Artillery on 20 December 1833. In April 1835 he sailed for the Cape of Good Hope, where he served in the Cape Frontier War. He was promoted first lieutenant on 10 January 1837, and returned to England in October.

From July 1839 Smythe was secretary of the Royal Artillery Institution at Woolwich, until he embarked for St Helena in December 1841 to take charge of the observatory, and to carry out magnetical and meteorological observations under Captain Edward Sabine. The results were published by Sabine in two large volumes, *Observations* (1850 and 1860). Smythe was promoted second captain on 5 May 1845, and returned to England in February 1847.

From 1848 to 1849 Smythe served at Halifax, Nova Scotia, and was promoted to first captain, dated 28 June 1849.

In January 1850 he was appointed to supervise young artillery officers on first joining at Woolwich; this led to the establishment of the department of artillery studies, of which he was the organizer, and the first director until July 1852. He was promoted lieutenant-colonel on 1 April 1855.

Having a good knowledge of French and German, Smythe was selected in October 1854 to superintend the execution of arms contracts in Belgium and Germany. He was withdrawn temporarily from this duty by Lord Panmure, in January 1856, so that he could act as a member of the royal commission sent to France, Russia, Austria, and Italy to report on military education and to consider suitable ways to reform the training of British engineer and artillery officers. The other commissioners were Lieutenant-Colonel William Yolland and the Revd W. C. Lake (afterwards dean of Durham). Smythe advocated entirely separate education for the artillery and engineers, a plan which Yolland opposed. In the end the report was drawn up by Lake and the secretary, Smythe signing 'for the history and descriptions of foreign military schools only'. The report, in two blue books, was presented to parliament in 1857. Smythe then returned to the superintendence of the foreign arms contracts until July 1857. He married, on 15 December 1857, at Carnmoney, Sarah Maria, second daughter of the Revd Robert Wintringham Bland JP. They had no children. He was promoted brevet colonel on 1 April 1858, and the same year was again appointed director of artillery studies at Woolwich. In 1859 he was made a member of the ordnance select committee.

In 1859 Smythe was appointed commissioner to investigate the cession of Fiji to England, which an English consul, W. T. Pritchard, had obtained from King Thakombau, as well as the strategic and commercial value of the islands. Smythe, accompanied by his wife, left England on 16 January 1860, taking with him magnetical and meteorological instruments, and reached Levuka on 5 July. He visited the larger islands, and decided that the representations made to the government on the islands' value were exaggerated, and that Thakombau was not king of Fiji. During his stay Smythe made valuable magnetical and meteorological observations.

On 1 May 1861 Smythe reported against the cession, and arrived home in November of the same year. His report was presented to parliament in 1862 and approved. His wife published *Ten Months in the Fiji Islands* (1864), to which Smythe contributed the introduction and an appendix containing his report, together with his magnetical and meteorological observations.

On 5 August 1864 Smythe was promoted colonel in the Royal Artillery. In 1864 he was elected fellow of the Royal Society, and was for some years a member of its meteorological committee. In 1865 he went to India on military duty, and on 6 March 1868 was promoted major-general. In December 1869 he returned home, and lived at Tobarcooran, Carnmoney, co. Antrim. He was promoted lieutenant-general on 1 October 1877, and made a colonel-commandant of the Royal Artillery on 2 August 1880. He retired with the honorary rank of general on 1 July 1881. In his latter years he advocated Irish home rule, and attempted to promote Irish development. He took an interest in agriculture, and devoted himself to the study, and encouragement of the study, of the Irish language. Smythe died at Tobarcooran on 12 July 1887, survived by his wife. He had erected in the churchyard of Carnmoney an Irish cross of mountain limestone, based on the finest surviving examples and regarded as the most beautiful specimen of Irish ecclesiastical art in the country. He was buried at the foot of this cross. Smythe's will provided money to promote the use of the Irish language.

R. H. Vetch, *rev.* James Lunt

Sources J. H. Lefroy, *Minutes of the Proceedings of the Royal Artillery Institution*, 15 (1887) • W. J. Smythe, 'Determination of the magnetic declination, dip, and force, at the Fiji islands, in 1860 and 1861', *PRS*, 11 (1860–62), 481–6 • *Annual Register* (1887) • *Army List* • private information (1897)

Wealth at death £3376 9*s*. 4*d*.—effects in England: probate, 19 Sept 1887, *CGPLA Ire.*

Smythies, Charles Allan (1844–1894), bishop of Zanzibar and of east Africa, born in London on 6 August 1844, was the second of three sons of Charles Norfolk Smythies (*d.* 1847/8), vicar of St Mary the Walls, Colchester, and Isabella, daughter of Admiral Sir Eaton Travers. When he was three years old his father died of consumption, and in 1858 his mother married George Alston, rector of Studland, Dorset. After attending school at Felsted, from January 1854 to December 1857, and at Milton Abbas, 1858–63, Smythies entered Trinity College, Cambridge, in 1863, and graduated BA in 1867. In 1868 he went to Cuddesdon Theological College, Oxford, at that time under the presidency of Dr Edward King, subsequently bishop of Lincoln. In 1869 he was ordained to the curacy of Great Marlow, and in 1872 he took up work at Roath, a suburb of Cardiff, under F. W. Puller, on whose resignation in 1880 Smythies was appointed to succeed as vicar.

In 1882, on the death of Bishop Edward Steere, bishop of central Africa, Smythies declined the offer of the bishopric of the Universities' Mission to Central Africa (UMCA); but after a year's fruitless search the committee of the mission renewed the offer to him, and he accepted. He received his DD degree from Cambridge University, and was consecrated bishop at St Paul's Cathedral in London on 30 November 1883. In January 1884 he left for Zanzibar, the headquarters of the mission.

From the first Smythies devoted himself to the selection and training of African clergymen. Warm and generous by nature, he took enormous pains to discover their vocation and to give them such education as might qualify them to become the evangelists of their own people. He was equally anxious to keep them free from that veneer of English civilization which was then so often thought to mar the work of African clergy in foreign missions. He was neither a scholar nor a linguist, but he was a man of great energy and, at 6 feet 2 inches, imposing physique, and he visited all the nearer stations of the missions every year and the remote stations every two years. This involved five journeys on foot, performed for the most part without white companions, to Lake Nyasa, some 450 miles distant from the coast.

In 1888, under the pretext of suppressing the slave trade, the coast of east Africa was blockaded by the combined warships of Britain and Germany. This provoked much disturbance on the mainland. The situation became so grave that the bishop was strongly urged by the British consul at Zanzibar to withdraw his missionaries. This he declined to do; he set out himself for the troubled district to strengthen the hands of his clergy and their converts. This nearly cost him his life; on landing at Pangani he was attacked, and was saved only by the goodwill and courage of the insurgent leader, Abushiri.

In March 1890 Smythies was ordered to England on medical grounds. By then he was convinced that it was impossible for one man to supervise his vast diocese. In June 1890 he was made honorary DD of the universities of Oxford and Durham. After a rapid recovery he spoke in October at the church congress, and discussed with Germany's chancellor in Berlin the mission's position in what had become since 1885 largely German territory. Discussions on the future of the diocese took him from Zanzibar a second time, in May 1892, but he was again too ill to assist in raising the endowment to support a division. However, with help from the Society for the Propagation of the Gospel and the Society for the Promotion of Christian Knowledge, supporters raised £11,000 in six months, and Wilfrid B. Hornby was consecrated as first bishop of Nyasa, a title afterwards changed to Likoma. On the division of the diocese, Smythies's title was altered to bishop of Zanzibar and missionary-bishop of east Africa.

After his return to Zanzibar, Smythies's health broke down completely; but in spite of physical weakness he set out in October 1893 on a long inland tour, accompanied by an African deacon and a few African Christians. Smithies relied on the hospitality of the Africans, living in their huts and sharing their food, in a manner attuned to ascetic ideals prominent within the UMCA and increasingly fashionable in the wider evangelical community. The result from a spiritual point of view may have been most gratifying, but it was physically disastrous to the bishop: he suffered a further attack of malarial fever. Although he found his way back to Zanzibar and struggled on with his work for a while, he failed to recover; after a brief sojourn in the mission hospital that he had founded in 1891, he was sent to England in the hope of saving his life. On 5 May 1894 he was carried on board the French steamer *Peiho*, but he died at sea, on 7 May and was buried in the ocean at sunset, halfway between Zanzibar and Aden.

E. F. Russell, *rev.* Andrew Porter

Sources G. Ward, *The life of Charles Alan Smythies*, ed. E. F. Russell, 2nd edn (1899) • A. E. M. Anderson-Morshead, *The history of the Universities' Mission to Central Africa, 1859–1909*, 5th edn (1909) • D. R. J. Neave, 'Aspects of the Universities' Mission to Central Africa, 1858–1900', MPhil. diss., University of York, 1974 • J. T. Moriyama, 'The evolution of an African ministry—the work of the Universities' Mission to Central Africa in Tanzania, 1864–1909', PhD diss., U. Lond., 1984 • *The Times* (11 May 1894), 10 • register of births, marriages, and deaths, St Catharine's House, London • W. W. Rouse Ball and J. A. Venn, eds., *Admissions to Trinity College, Cambridge*, 5 (1913) • Venn, *Alum. Cant.* • C. A. Smythies, *A journey to Lake Nyassa and visit to the Magwanqwara and the source of the Rovuma in the year 1886* (1887)

Archives Bodl. RH, Universities' Mission to Central Africa archives

Likenesses C. Reynolds, oils, 1899, Trinity Cam. • photograph, NPG • portrait, repro. in Ward, *The life of Charles Alan Smythies*, ed. Russell, frontispiece • portrait, repro. in *ILN* (19 May 1894), 611

Wealth at death £2987 14*s.* 2*d.*: probate, 31 Aug 1894, *CGPLA Eng. & Wales*

Smythies, Harriette Maria Gordon (1813?–1883), poet and novelist, was born in Margate, Kent, the daughter of Edward Lesmoin Gordon and his wife, Jane, *née* Halliday. No further information on Smythies's parents or early life has been traced. On 1 March 1842 she married the Revd William Yorick Smythies, a Church of England clergyman who was unable to maintain a steady income and who engaged the family in financially crippling litigation. The couple had five children before Harriette Maria Smythies left her husband about 1860 and moved with her children to London.

Harriette Maria Smythies struggled to support her family, and published two long poems and at least twenty-two novels under a number of variations on her married name. Some of her work was serialized in the *London Journal* and *Cassell's Family Magazine*. Between 1857 and 1860 she wrote advice columns for the *Ladies' Treasury*. While her work has often been dismissed for its melodrama and didacticism, it is notable for its keen satire and sensitive renderings of the economic and sexual dangers besetting young and working women.

Harriette Maria Smythies published her first work, a long poem entitled *The Bride of Sienna*, in 1835. In 1838 she published her first novel, *Fitzherbert, or, Lovers and Fortune Hunters*, and she continued to publish about one novel a year during the next three decades. Her most popular works were *Cousin Geoffrey* (1840) and *The Jilt* (1844).

By the mid 1870s all but one of Harriette Maria Smythies's children had died. Her last novel was published in 1880, and she herself died on 15 August 1883 at her home, 24 Brunswick Square, London.

Clare Cotugno

Sources Blain, Clements & Grundy, *Feminist comp.* • N. Cross, *The common writer: life in nineteenth-century Grub Street* (1985), 188–92 • P. Thomson, *The Victorian heroine: a changing ideal, 1837–1873* (1956), 54–6 • Allibone, *Dict.* • Boase, *Mod. Eng. biog.*

Archives Royal Literary Fund, London, letters to Royal Literary Fund

Smythies, Susan (*b.* 1720), writer, the daughter of Palmer Smythies (*b.* 1691) and Susan Puglet, was born in Colchester, Essex, on 13 January 1720. She was the author of three novels and a children's book. *The stage-coach: containing the character of Mr. Manly, and the history of his fellow-travellers*—a revelatory title—was published in 1753, with the second edition in two volumes in 1755 and in 1789, and a third, also in 1789, in three volumes. The plot, such as it is, is a familiar one. In a stage-coach travelling from Scarborough to London the reader is given the 'histories'—that is short biographies—of the passengers. *The History of Lucy Wellers,*

Written by a Lady (2 vols., 1754; new edn, 1755), was translated into German. Lucy is a servant girl who is rewarded for opting for delicacy rather than passion. Of unknown parentage, after various vicissitudes she ends happily married and with an estate. *The Brothers. In Two Volumes. By the Author of The Stage-Coach, and Lucy Wellers* (1758; 2nd edn, 1759) was a conscious attempt to be a female Samuel Richardson, although with less perfect characters from a lower stratum of society. In the 'Advertisement' prefatory to *The Brothers* Smythies justifies the authorship of novels by women and describes her novel thus:

> Tho' designed to amuse, it sometimes, like comedy, raises its voice, inspires sentiment, mends the heart, humanizes the passions, teaches what dry schools cannot, cheats the man of pleasure into a glow of generosity and tenderness, and gives what wise men have wished to give, the native charms of virtue to the sight, in the modern familiar dress of men and women, with more success than maxims and rules; which, like the stiffened ruff and uncouth drapery of our ancestors, turn dignity into ridicule, and beauty into awkwardness.

The author 'hoped to produce something like Clarissa or a Grandison; but nothing came of it but The Brothers.'

A twentieth-century reader wrote of *The Brothers*:

> The plot, it must be admitted, hardly rises above the commonplace. A young lady of excellent character and attractive person is subjected to the assiduities of a gentleman for whom she has no great relish. He induces her to accept his company upon a journey she is under the necessity of making. Though he discovers her to be the child of his half-brother, he seeks to improve this opportunity through misdirecting the postillion and through subtle and specious reasoning to persuade her to become his mistress. A succession of troubles, of the kind unprotected females in eighteenth-century fiction generally endure, in due time leads the young lady to the arms of an eligible and worthy lover, with a paternal blessing and a comfortable fortune to seal the match. (Black, 'A lady novelist', 181)

All the ingredients of the typical sentimental comedy of the period are here. There are copies of Smythies's children's book, *The history of a pin, as related by itself .... By the author of 'The brothers', a tale for children*, dated 1798 and 1799, that are possibly, but not necessarily, posthumous publications.

Of what is of more than ordinary interest lies in the twenty-six pages of the list of subscribers to *The Brothers*. When booksellers had expressed no interest in publishing *The Brothers*, Richardson 'advised her to try her Friends by Private Subscription' and she had 'succeeded beyond her hopes' (Eaves and Kempel, 464). The subscription list contained the names of, among many others, Richardson, Smollett, Garrick, Dodsley, and a William Franklin of Pennsylvania. Richardson subscribed not only for himself but also for his wife and four daughters (ibid., 531). Of the some 675 names in the list, 35 are from Colchester, and between a quarter and a third represent Essex and Suffolk. The names of 23 military subscribers, 16 MDs, 63 clergymen, with subscribers from Cambridge and Oxford, suggest that Smythies had cast her net wide and that her friends had come through for her. In 1758 the *Ipswich Journal* carried the following letter, dated 'Colchester, October 26th, 1758':

> Miss Smythies' Compliments to all that have done her the honour of subscribing to The Brothers and begs the earliest Remittance of their Names and Titles to the Booksellers mention'd in her Proposals, and hopes that they will immediately transmit them to her; that a regular List may be obtained, and the Publication of the Volume no longer retarded. (Black, *TLS*, 596)

ARTHUR SHERBO

Sources F. G. Black, 'A lady novelist of Colchester', *Essex Review*, 44 (1935), 180–85 • F. G. Black, 'Miss Smythies', *TLS* (26 Sept 1935), 596 • G. Watson, I. R. Willison, and J. D. Pickles, eds., *The new Cambridge bibliography of English literature*, 5 vols. (1969–77) • T. C. D. Eaves and B. D. Kimpel, *Samuel Richardson: a biography* (1971) • *IGI*

Smythies, William (*bap.* **1635?**, *d.* **1715**), Church of England clergyman, was the son of William Smythies, vicar of Walter Belchamp, Essex (*d.* 1652); he was probably the William Smithies baptized in that parish on 3 March 1635 as the son of William and Ann. He was admitted sizar of Emmanuel College, Cambridge, on 1 July 1651, graduated BA in 1660, and was rector of Tacolneston, Norfolk, from 1660 to 1671. He moved to London probably in 1671, when he preached at the Norfolk Feast there. He served as curate of St Giles Cripplegate from 1673 to 1704, where, until 1691, his vicar was Edward Fowler. The two men developed a close rapport, and together they endured retribution during the tory purge of the 1680s because of their sympathies with dissent and whiggery. At some point Smythies married Hepzibah, the daughter of James Palmer of Grundisburgh, Suffolk.

Cripplegate was an extramural parish of some 30,000 people, with acute pastoral problems. Thousands were unchurched and thousands worshipped in illegal dissenting conventicles. Smythies made his mark here as a popular preacher: Sunday audiences of 4000 were reported. His *Unworthy non-Communicant* (1683) encouraged frequent communion and went through several editions. He became zealous for charitable make-work schemes for the poor: he was chaplain to the pesthouse, and in 1688 was reported to be in danger of arrest for debt, so much out of pocket was he in support of the poor. He was appointed morning lecturer at St Michael Cornhill through the patronage of the whig plutocrat Sir Robert Clayton. There he guided one of the religious societies of young men which, like those of the clergyman Anthony Horneck, were a tap root of the post-1688 societies for the reformation of manners. Theirs was an evangelical 'awakening' within Anglicanism that would eventually nurture the Wesleyans. In drawing people into the church, however, Smythies was lax about the rubrics. More dangerously he, with Fowler, turned a blind eye to whig sedition; they allowed into the vestry Charles Bateman, later executed for treason in 1685.

Smythies soon acquired enemies, who described the parish as 'curate-ridden'. The occasional conformity of the parishioners became notorious. At Thomas Rosewall's trial in 1684, when a witness said, 'I do hear Dr Fowler, and Mr Smythies too, sometimes', Judge Jeffreys snapped back, 'That is, when there is no conventicle I suppose'. Vicar and curate were named in January 1683 as among those under threat 'by their being not so violent against the Dissenters as others were' (Luttrell, 1.246). A tory caucus began a vendetta against them. Fowler was humiliated by being suspended for giving the sacrament to excommunicated persons. Meanwhile, from August to October 1684 Smythies's faults were paraded in Sir Roger L'Estrange's ultra-tory newspaper *The Observator*. The charge that Smythies was a political 'trimmer' encouraged the vogue for that term of tory abuse. He was also accused of profiteering by establishing a school for poor children and setting them to work as cooks and spinners, by selling pews, and by benefiting from doles paid to pregnant women because his wife took midwifery fees. His critics further charged him with giving charity to the poor 'without respect to their opinions'. He was held to be 'schismatically inclined', believing that the nonconformists were wrongly oppressed, and was called an 'Oliverian' and a seditious whig (W. Smythies, *A Reply to 'The Observator'*, 1684, 3).

Smythies defended himself in *A Letter to 'The Observator'*, *A Reply to 'The Observator'*, and *The Spirit of Meekness*, all published in 1684. He confessed that he omitted the sign of the cross in baptism and the use of godparents, but claimed that thousands of the poor would otherwise turn to dissent or go unbaptized. He denied that his monthly religious club was a conventicle or that he trimmed to dissenters, but he pleaded for 'meekness' rather than 'a vengeful spirit'. Into this debate Fowler interjected that his own troubles stemmed partly from his refusal to sack Smythies, whose plain-speaking sermons grated on the comfortable of the parish: to remove Smythies would earn 'the curses of hundreds of needy families … never was a parish so obliged to a curate' (Fowler, sig. A4*r*).

It is as a victim of the tory purges that historical sources illuminate Smythies, who (it was said) wore a threadbare cassock; of his later years little is known. In 1690 he published an account of an execution of a criminal whom he and Fowler had accompanied to the scaffold. In 1692 he preached for moral reformation, a righteous magistracy, and frequent communion, and against the insidious dangers of Jacobitism. He was buried at Witnesham, Suffolk, on 29 June 1715. William Smythies, low-church rector of St Michael, Colchester, was perhaps a son.

MARK GOLDIE

Sources M. Goldie and J. Spurr, 'Politics and the Restoration parish: Edward Fowler and the struggle for St Giles Cripplegate', *EngHR*, 109 (1994), 572–96 • Venn, *Alum. Cant.* • J. Woodward, *An account of the societies rise and progress* (1698) • E. Fowler, *The great wickedness of slandering* (1685) • N. Luttrell, *A brief historical relation of state affairs from September 1678 to April 1714*, 6 vols. (1857) • *IGI*

Smythson, John (*d.* 1634). *See under* Smythson, Robert (1534/5–1614).

Smythson, Robert (1534/5–1614), master mason and architect, was aged seventy-nine when he died in 1614, according to his memorial tablet in the parish church at Wollaton, Nottinghamshire, but neither the date nor the place of his birth is known. In the 1660s, at the time of the heralds' visitation of Derbyshire, his great-grandson John Smythson stated that he had 'Armes belonging to his family of Westmorland'. No arms or descent was subsequently registered, but it is possible that Robert was connected with the Smythsons who were tenant farmers in Crosthwaite and Crosby Ravensworth in Westmorland, and who were certainly not armigerous. The fact that his memorial carries the arms of the Masons' Company of London suggests that it was in and around London that he served his apprenticeship, acquired experience, and learned to draw.

Smythson's first recorded appearance is at Longleat House, Wiltshire, where he went to work for Sir John Thynne as a master mason in March 1568. He brought with him his own group of masons and a letter of introduction from Humphrey Lovell, the queen's master mason, according to which he had previously been working for Sir Francis Knollys, probably at Caversham House, near Reading. Smythson stayed at Longleat on and off until 1580. Together with a French master mason, Alan Maynard, he was largely responsible for remodelling the exterior of the house, and for much internal detail; in both cases the design, as well as the execution, was probably due to them. In 1576 there is evidence that he was involved with alterations made at Wardour Castle, Wiltshire, for Sir Matthew Arundell. It may have been this connection that took him to Nottinghamshire in 1580, to work for Arundell's brother-in-law Sir Francis Willoughby at Wollaton Hall. His position at Wollaton was that of surveyor of the work, rather than a practising mason. The surviving building accounts and his own drawings make clear that he was responsible for the execution and design of this remarkable house between 1580 and 1588. Smythson stayed on in the service of the Willoughby family, and was employed by them on administrative and financial business, as well as in his capacity as a surveyor. He is described on his monument at Wollaton as 'architector and survayor unto the most worthy house of Wollaton, and diverse others of great account'; this is the first known occasion on which he was called an architect, a term and function then still only in embryo in England.

Some 150 drawings by Robert Smythson and his son John survive in the drawings collection of the Royal Institute of British Architects. They include an interesting group of survey drawings made by Robert on a visit to London in 1611, but also many original designs (some of them drawings of considerable beauty), which supply evidence about several of the 'diverse other' houses mentioned on his monument. They include Worksop Manor, Nottinghamshire (remodelled *c.*1585), Hardwick Hall, Derbyshire (1590–97), Burton Agnes, Yorkshire (*c.*1601–1610), and designs, only partially carried out, for remodelling Welbeck Abbey, Nottinghamshire. The stylistic evidence of drawings and documented buildings, supported by patronage links and geographical proximity, enables a number of other houses to be attributed to him, including: Barlborough Hall, Derbyshire; Doddington Hall, Lincolnshire; Worksop Manor Lodge, Nottinghamshire; Fountains Hall, Yorkshire; and Wootton Lodge, Staffordshire. There is no evidence that at any of these houses Smythson was involved on the same day-to-day basis as at Longleat and Wollaton; his contribution must often have been limited to the provision of a set of plans and elevations, which were liable to alteration at the whim of the patron and executive craftsmen.

Even allowing for these limitations, Smythson's is the strongest architectural personality to have survived from the Elizabethan and Jacobean age. This is partly because more is known about him, and because his drawings and those of his younger contemporary John Thorpe (a high proportion of which are survey drawings) are the only large collections from this period that still exist, but it is also because of the distinctive and remarkable character of the houses with which he can be connected. Both his drawings and the buildings show that he had, for the Elizabethan period, a capable grasp of the language of classical ornament; he knew and used the works of Serlio, possibly of Palladio, and of the Flemish mannerist Vredeman de Vries, whose designs were extensively adapted at Wollaton. But his drawings and buildings also show an interest in the native Gothic tradition. His achievement was to draw on these two strains, and on the contemporary Elizabethan taste for the kind of ingenious conceits known at the time as 'devices', to produce a creative synthesis. In the resulting buildings classical detail and a considerable degree of classical order can be found joined with dramatic combinations of towers, bay windows, and great expanses of glass, derived from the Gothic tradition, and with the complex and ingenious plans which were the architectural expression of the device. At Longleat, where he worked with Maynard, bay windows and lavish glazing were serenely combined with rich classical detail. Wollaton is the most extraordinary of his houses, but it suffers from an over-abundance of motifs. Hardwick, in its combination of high drama, spatial ingenuity, and classical restraint, must be considered his masterpiece.

Nothing is known about Smythson's marriage, but his son **John Smythson** (*d.* 1634) was working as a mason at Wollaton in 1588. He subsequently pursued a similar career to his father, but in the service of the Cavendish rather than the Willoughby family. In particular he was closely involved with the rebuilding of Bolsover Castle, Derbyshire, between about 1612 and his death; the riding-school range there, however, may be the work of his son Huntingdon Smythson, who died in 1648. Robert Smythson died in Wollaton on 15 October 1614.

MARK GIROUARD

Sources M. Girouard, *Robert Smythson and the Elizabethan country house*, [new edn] (1983) • M. Girouard, 'The Smythson collection of the Royal Institute of British Architects', *Architectural History*, 5 (1962), 23–184 • A. Woodhouse, 'In search of Smythson', *Country Life* (19 Dec 1991), 56–8 • A. Woodhouse, 'Smythson revisited', *Country Life* (26 Dec 1991), 36–9 • J. Summerson, *Architecture in Britain, 1530–1830*, 8th edn (1991) • memorial tablet, Wollaton parish church

Snagge, John Derrick Mordaunt (1904–1996), radio broadcaster, was born at 72 Burton Court, Chelsea, London, on 8 May 1904, the second of three sons of Sir (Thomas) Mordaunt Snagge (1868–1955), barrister, and later county court judge, and his wife, Gwendaline Rose Emily, younger daughter of Sir John Charles Ready *Colomb, of Dromquinna, co. Kerry, Ireland, one of the founders of the Imperial Federation League. His paternal grandfather was Judge Sir Thomas William Snagge. After an undistinguished education at Winchester College and Pembroke College, Oxford (where he rowed for his college, but did not gain a blue), he started work in 1924 as assistant director of the BBC's relay station in Stoke-on-Trent. He made the tea, announced, was an Uncle in *Children's Hour*, organized programmes, wrote scripts, and sang duets on the air with the engineer-in-charge. In 1928 he became an announcer at the Savoy Hill headquarters of the BBC. With a robust manner and a clear, authoritative voice—a voice that gradually mellowed into polished mahogany—he was a natural choice as an announcer in an era when it was taken sufficiently seriously for those who practised it to wear dinner jackets for the evening bulletins. He also showed a growing aptitude for outside broadcasts, then in their infancy.

John Derrick Mordaunt Snagge (1904–1996), by Roger George Clark, 1977

Professionally competent and knowledgeable about rowing, Snagge was regarded as the obvious candidate to take over the Oxford–Cambridge boat race when Gerald Cock, the BBC's first director of outside broadcasts, decided in 1931 that it needed fresh blood. Cock said in a private letter that recent commentaries had been 'rotten'—they had neglected to tell listeners who was leading, or what the winning margin was—and that 'violent efforts' were needed to improve matters (Cock to Charles M. Pitman, 10 Nov 1930, BBC WAC, R30/138). Snagge was put on board the motor yacht *Magician*, following the progress of the crews from Putney to Mortlake, and provided a live running commentary. He was deemed to have been a success and continued to be hired every year (except 1940–45, when the boat race was not held) until he bowed out in 1980. The race was televised from 1938, though it was still Snagge's commentary that was used. Some felt he spoke too quickly and chanted the strokes ('in-out, in-out, in-out') too much. In the intensely exciting 1949 race, when Cambridge won by a few feet, he genuinely did not know and could not see who was ahead because his BBC launch, badly piloted, slid broadside-on into the wash of another launch. His on-air comment, 'I don't know who's ahead—it's either Oxford or Cambridge' (*75 Years of the BBC*, CD2, track 4) was subsequently acclaimed as a classic of its genre. There were other dramas, too: in 1948 the press and BBC launches collided and several people fell into the Thames, and in a snowstorm in 1952 the BBC boat ran out of petrol and narrowly avoided being rammed by pursuing vessels.

During the Second World War Snagge was the BBC's presentation director, running an area that embraced continuity and newsreading and which he aptly described as the shop window of the BBC. He also read many (though by no means all) memorable bulletins. It was Snagge who told the nation about the invasion of north Africa, the fall of Rome, Arnhem, the D-day landings in 1944 (in which year he was appointed OBE), and VE-day. He read many of Winston Churchill's great speeches and announced the deaths of both George VI and Queen Mary.

The year 1953 provided the pinnacle of Snagge's career, when he was the main commentator at the coronation of Elizabeth II. High up in a soundproof box in the triforium, he described the rite and pageantry unfolding under his eyes—the shining gold of the Westminster Abbey plate, the dazzle of the crowns—for four hours. Complementing the words and music of the service that listeners could hear for themselves, his commentary was relayed all over the world. 'John Snagge's description, with those of Howard Marshall and Audrey Russell, had many Americans damp-eyed before their radio sets', reported one newspaper the following day (*Daily Mail*, 3 June 1953). Though the event was a watershed in turning Britain from a nation of listeners into a nation of viewers, it was still via radio that most people worldwide were able to follow it. Snagge's contribution was vital to their enjoyment and understanding. 'Mr Snagge's interjections had the economy, the precision, and at times, it may be added, almost the dignity, of liturgical stage direction', said *The Times*. 'None will regret the one intrusion of human interest which he permitted, a brief reference to the expression of the Duke of Cornwall [that is, Prince Charles, aged four] as he watched the ceremony' (*The Times*, 3 June 1953). Snagge himself summarized the event as 'once in a lifetime' and added: 'After that, one is quite content if one never broadcasts again' (*Desert Island Discs*, broadcast 31 Aug 1959).

Snagge did, of course, broadcast again, despite administrative tasks as head of presentation for the Home Service until 1957, and head of presentation for all BBC radio thereafter. After his retirement in 1965 he was busy freelancing for another fifteen years, taking modest jobs such as reading the *Epilogue* on Radio 4 for £10. He even did a voice-over for a Sex Pistols track, 'Pistols propaganda', the B-side of 'Stepping stone', which reached number twenty-one in the British chart. Very occasionally he appeared on television, including once with Noel Edmonds, though radio was his first love. He was nearly seventy when he began a series called *John Snagge's London* on BBC Radio London, making more than 100 editions over a period of seven years. He also did much for the Lord's Taverners, the charity he helped found in 1950 and of which he was three times chairman.

Snagge, who enjoyed fishing and rowing, was twice married: first, on 19 September 1936, to Eileen Mary Josceylyne (*c*.1905–1980), daughter of H. P. Josceylyne, a dentist, and second, on 6 January 1983, to Joan Mary Wilson (*c*.1921–1992), a retired contracts assistant whom he had known at the BBC, and daughter of William Wilson. There were no children of either marriage. Snagge died of throat cancer on 25 March 1996, at Thames Valley Nuffield Hospital, Wexham Street, Wexham, Buckinghamshire, not far from his home in Dorney, near Windsor. He was survived by a brother. PAUL DONOVAN

Sources BBC WAC • transcript of John Snagge's *Desert island discs* programme (broadcast 31 Aug 1959) • *Daily Telegraph* (27 March 1996) • *The Times* (3 June 1953) • *The Times* (27 March 1996) • *The Guardian* (27 March 1996) • *The Independent* (28 March 1996) • *Daily Mail* (3 June 1953) • *WW* (1963) • [P. Donaldson and M. Jones], *75 years of the BBC* (1997) [CD-ROM] • P. Donovan, *The radio companion* (1991) • *Ariel* [BBC staff magazine] (May 1965) • *Ariel* [BBC staff magazine] (23 April 1980) • *Ariel* [BBC staff magazine] (2 April 1996) • b. cert. • m. certs. • d. cert. • *WWW* • Burke, *Peerage*

Archives BBC WAC | SOUND BBC WAC • BL NSA, documentary recordings • BL NSA, performance recordings

Likenesses photographs, 1949–80, Hult. Arch. • R. G. Clark, photograph, 1977, NPG [*see illus.*] • photograph, repro. in *The Times* (27 March 1996) • photograph, repro. in *Daily Telegraph* • photograph, repro. in *The Guardian* • photograph, repro. in *The Independent* (27 March 1996)

Wealth at death £570,093: probate, 31 May 1996, *CGPLA Eng. & Wales*

Snagge, Thomas (1536–1593), lawyer, was the first son of Thomas Snagge. He was born in Letchworth, Hertfordshire, where his father was lord of the manor. In 1552 the younger Thomas Snagge entered Gray's Inn as a student, and was called to the bar there in 1554. In 1563 he was appointed 'reader', and in 1574 became 'double reader'. He was MP for Bedfordshire in 1571, and seems to have become an effective debater in the House of Commons. His brother Robert was a bencher of the Middle Temple and MP for Lostwithiel, Cornwall, in 1571. Robert inherited the bulk of their father's estate, but Thomas Snagge possessed substantial property in Bedfordshire through marriage and received additional land from his father. He practised law in London and his election for Bedfordshire in 1571 and 1586 and for Bedford in 1589 reflected his status as a substantial landowner in the county, who held the estate of Kempston Daubeney as well as the barony and castle of Bedford. The bishops' report of 1564 confirmed him as a protestant, making him a reliable member of the legal profession and county élite in the eyes of the government. Snagge was an active MP and was appointed to a number of committees, including those for the subsidy, church attendance, treasons, and corrupt presentations in 1571, and dealing with Mary, queen of Scots, in 1586.

On 13 September 1577 Elizabeth I, in a private letter to Sir Henry Sidney, lord deputy of Ireland, nominated Snagge to the office of attorney-general for Ireland, with an addition of £100 above the usual salary, 'being sufficiently persuaded of his learning and judgment in the law wherein he had been in long practice as a counsellor' (Morrin, 2.11). 'The Dutye that he oweth to her Majestie and his Countrye', wrote Sir Francis Walsingham, principal secretary, to Sidney,

> doth make him leave all other Respects and willinglie to dedicat himself to that Service, for the which I thinke him a Man so well chosen both for Judgement and bould Spirit … as hardlie all the Howses of Court could yeld his like. (Collins, 1.228)

Snagge proved himself efficient and able in his new office, retaining the queen's confidence, and he held the office until 1580. Three months after his arrival in Dublin, Sidney wrote of him to Walsingham:

> I fynde him a Man well learned, sufficient, stoute, and well-spoken, an Instrument of good Service for her Majestie, and soche a one as is carefull to redresse by Wisdome and good Discreation soch Errors as he fyndeth in her Majesties Courts here. (ibid., 231)

Snagge appears to have been involved in the military establishment while in Ireland.

Snagge returned to England in 1580, when he was appointed serjeant-at-law. He was treasurer of Gray's Inn for that year, and resumed his large practice at the bar. He was chosen as speaker of the House of Commons on 12 November 1588. Parliament was prorogued on 4 February 1589, but Snagge continued to hold the office until the dissolution on 28 March 1590. In 1590 he was promoted to queen's serjeant.

Snagge died on 16 March 1593 in his chamber at Serjeants' Inn, aged fifty-seven. He was buried at Marston Moretaine, Bedfordshire, in St Mary's Church, where there is a fine alabaster tomb with recumbent effigies of him and his wife. He acquired the large estates of the Reynes family in Bedfordshire by marriage with a coheir of Thomas Dikons. His eldest son, Sir Thomas Snagge of Marston Moretaine, was MP for Bedfordshire from November 1588, received one of the first knighthoods conferred by James I on his accession in 1603, and was sheriff of Bedfordshire in 1607. ANDREW LYALL

Sources J. G. Crawford, *Anglicizing the government of Ireland: the Irish privy council and the expansion of Tudor rule, 1556–1578* (Dublin, 1993), 101, 212, 223, 289 • PRO, SP 63/13/110; 63/14/10 • BL, Cotton MS Titus B XII • J. Hogan and N. McNeill O'Farrell, eds., *The Walsingham letter-book, or, Register of Ireland, May 1578 to December 1579*, IMC (1959) • C. G. Cruickshank, *Elizabeth's army*, 2nd edn (1966), 154 • will, PRO, PROB 11/81, sig. 38 • HoP, *Commons, 1558–1603*, 3.410 • J. Morrin, ed., *Calendar of the patent and close rolls of chancery in Ireland for the reigns of Henry VIII, Edward VI, Mary, and Elizabeth*, 2 vols. (1861–2), 2.11–12 • H. Sydney and others, *Letters and memorials of state*, ed. A. Collins, 1 (1746), 228 • *DNB* • tombstone, St Mary's Church, Marston Moretaine, Bedfordshire

Likenesses alabaster tomb effigy (with wife), St Mary's Church, Marston Moretaine, Bedfordshire

Snape, Andrew (1675–1742), college head, born at Hampton Court, Middlesex, was the son of Andrew Snape (*fl.* 1660–1683), serjeant farrier to Charles II. His father published in 1683 a fine folio on *The Anatomy of an Horse*, with many copperplate engravings, a portrait of the author, drawn and engraved by R. White, and a dedication to the king, in which he speaks of 'being a Son of that Family that hath had the honour to serve the Crown of this Kingdom in the Quality of Farriers for these two Hundred Years'.

Snape was admitted to Eton College in 1683, and was elected to a scholarship at King's College, Cambridge, in 1689. He graduated BA in 1693, proceeded MA in 1697, and was created DD *comitiis regiis* in 1705. As a student he contributed verses to the university collections on the death of Queen Mary, the peace of Ryswick, and the accession of Queen Anne. He became lecturer of St Martin Ludgate, London, and was chaplain to Charles Seymour, sixth duke of Somerset, chancellor of the university, by whom he was presented in 1706 to the rectory of the united parishes of St Mary-at-Hill and St Andrew Hubbard. In 1707 he was deputed by his university to represent the faculty of theology at the jubilee of the foundation of the University of Frankfurt-on-the-Oder. During his stay on the continent he preached a sermon before the Electress Sophia. He was a high-churchman and became one of the chaplains in ordinary to Queen Anne, and held the same office under George I. He preached two spitals, in 1707 and 1718, on the subject of the claims of lunatics on the humanity of the public. In 1711 he was appointed headmaster of Eton, which flourished under his management growing to nearly 400 pupils by the time he left in 1719. By then he was married to Rebecca Sharp (*née* Hervey) (*bap.* 1679), who was the widow of Sir Joshua Sharp, sheriff of London, and daughter of John Hervey, merchant, of London.

Snape was one of the principal disputants in the famous Bangorian controversy, and in numerous pamphlets he attacked with great vehemence the latitudinarian principles upheld by Bishop Hoadly. His first 'Letter to the bishop of Bangor' passed through no fewer than seventeen editions in the year of its publication (1717). His second 'Letter …' alleged that Hoadly had altered the sermon before publication to strengthen his case. The part he took in the controversy gave such offence at court that his name, like that of Dr Thomas Sherlock (afterwards bishop of London), was removed from the list of king's chaplains.

On the death of Dr John Adams, Snape was chosen provost of King's College, Cambridge, in February 1719. He was fêted by high-churchmen and was instrumental in uniting the tory interest at Cambridge at the parliamentary election of 1720. Thomas Hearne wrote that King's had lost the support of the court by electing so unpopular a provost. He was vice-chancellor of the university in 1723–4 and presided over the foundation of a new building at King's in 1724. Conyers Middleton dedicated his *Bibliothecae Cantabrigiensis ordinandae modus quaedam* to him in 1723. Snape edited the sermons of Dean Robert Moss which were published in eight volumes in 1732, with a preface, 'by a learned Hand', contributed by Zachary Grey. Early in 1737 he became rector of Knebworth, Hertfordshire; he resigned that living in August of the same year, when he was presented by the chapter of Windsor to the wealthy rectory of West Ilsley, Berkshire. The latter benefice he held until his death, on 30 December 1742, in his lodgings in Windsor Castle. He was buried in the south aisle of St George's Chapel. His sermons were edited by John Chapman and William Berriman and printed in a collected form, under the title *Forty-Five Sermons on Several Subjects*, in 3 volumes in 1745.

THOMPSON COOPER, *rev.* WILLIAM GIBSON

Sources A. C. Benson, *Fasti Etonenses, a biographical history of Eton* (1899) • J. H. Monk, *The life of Richard Bentley, DD*, 2nd edn, 2 vols. (1833) • *The works of Benjamin Hoadly*, ed. J. Hoadly, 3 vols. (1773) • Yale U., Beinecke L., Osborne collection • *The remarks of Thomas Hearne*, ed. J. Buchanan-Brown (1966) • J. P. Malcolm, *Londinium redivivum, or, An antient history and modern description of London*, 4 vols. (1802–7), vol. 4, p. 416 • Venn, *Alum. Cant.* • *IGI* • C. Hollis, *Eton: a history* (1960)

Likenesses J. Fayer, mezzotint, BM

Snape, Edmund (*c.*1565–1608), Church of England clergyman and evangelical preacher, is of obscure origins and little is known about his early life. His age was given as about forty in the consistory court of Exeter in 1605, and his father's name is recorded as Thomas. He had proceeded BA from St Edmund Hall, Oxford, in 1581–2, and MA from Merton in 1584. This degree was incorporated at Cambridge in 1586. He was ordained at Lincoln on 25 October 1583.

Evidence for Snape's career in the 1580s is largely derived from proceedings in the high commission and Star Chamber between 1589 and 1591. It was probably in the later 1580s that he became curate of St Peter's, Northampton, which he seems to have done his best to convert into a fully reformed congregation, the base for a precocious presbyterian organization in Northamptonshire, linked with London and with the wider ambitions of the arch-Elizabethan puritan John Field. In a statement set down for the satisfaction of certain separatists Snape declared that 'the substance' of his ministry derived from the approval of learned and godly neighbouring ministers and the people's election, episcopal ordination being 'a thing merely civil'. The bishop was simply a magistrate, and he would disregard episcopal suspension from his ministry so long as he enjoyed the backing of a majority of his congregation and the consent of fellow ministers. He further undertook to use 'all holie and lawfull meanes' to make a reality of the calling of lay ruling elders (BL, Harley MS 6849, fol. 222*v*). Witnesses in Star Chamber reported what Snape had on one occasion told his parishioners, sitting in 'the great seat' of St Peter's:

> Howe say yow if wee devyse a way wherby to shake of all the antichristyan yoke and governement of Bisshoppes and will joyntly together erecte the disciplyne by pastors, doctors, elders and deacons, and that in such sorte as they that be against that shall never be able to prevayle to the contrary, but peradventure that will nott be this yeare and half.

He went on to explain that this would be done 'little by little' both in congregations and by local classes and greater assemblies or synods meeting in Cambridge and London (PRO, STAC 5/A 27/33).

John Johnson, a fellow Northampton minister, described in detail how the presbyterian discipline had been practised 'privately' in local classes meeting at Daventry, Kettering, and Northampton, which sent representatives to a county assembly of six where Snape was the 'chief man' and registrar, regularly handling correspondence with London and the universities and co-ordinating a campaign of parliamentary petitioning. Snape seems to have commanded a solid core of support, and significant financial backing, in Northampton. But when he refused to baptize a child with a non-biblical name (there is no evidence that Snape favoured bizarre names of 'godly signification', a practice that seems to have spread to Northamptonshire from Dudley Fenner's parish in Kent), the outraged parents took the baby off to the preacher at All Saints' who would later give evidence against him, John Johnson.

Snape's activities became known in connection with the search for Martin Marprelate and his press. Hearing of 'a serch to have bene intended for bookes not authorized', he disposed of stocks of presbyterian literature (BL, Lansdowne MS 64, fol. 53). Soon he was in the hands of the high commission in London and in prison, warning his fellow conspirators 'that you might be forewarned and forearmed', and identifying Johnson as a Judas 'because … persons and thinges of his time beeing mentioned, hee onely is not named' (Bancroft, 92–3). Before proceedings moved to an inconclusive crown prosecution in Star Chamber, Snape was sentenced by the high commission to be stripped of his orders and declared incapable of exercising any future ministry, although this was later commuted to a ten-year suspension.

After more than two years of imprisonment, which had left many of them broken in health, Snape and the other ministers seem to have been released on bond in the early summer of 1592. Snape denied having ever subscribed the presbyterian Book of Discipline but undertook to have nothing more to do with conferences, which he acknowledged to have been in themselves offensive. Whether this promise was kept is perhaps doubtful, since when he arrived in Jersey in 1595 as chaplain to Mont Orgueil, Snape carried a testimonial from the 'Eglises de la province de Northampton'. His counterpart at Castle Cornet, Guernsey, was Thomas Cartwright, and together the two English chaplains successfully reconciled the long-divided presbyterian churches of the Channel Islands and rewrote their discipline. A long-lived error, which began with the seventeenth-century polemical church historian Peter Heylyn, stated that Snape was a presbyterian minister in the Channel Islands in 1576. As far as is known he had never been there before 1595.

Snape was still in Jersey in December 1599, but in August 1600 he turned up in Exeter. According to Bishop William Cotton it was well known that he had been banished from the Channel Islands for entertaining false doctrine on marriage. He came backed by letters to the city fathers from the countess of Warwick and the widow of

Sir Amyas Paulet. No doubt the Exeter worthy Mrs Anne Prowse, who had dedicated a book to Lady Warwick, was involved in this benevolent conspiracy. On the very day that his ten-year suspension lapsed the Exeter magistrates appointed Snape their preacher, and the bishop, moved against his better judgement by more letters from the court, granted him a licence. For an annual stipend of £50 Snape was to preach in the cathedral (the only church large enough to hold his auditory) twice every sabbath, with a proviso that his salary would be withheld if he were silenced. Snape's divisive preaching presently led to a general suspension, to which he responded by continuing to preach at Crediton and Budleigh and to catechize in private houses within Exeter itself.

Years of legal manoeuvres ensued, which, according to Snape, by 1603 had brought his case to the favourable attention of the privy council and James I. The outcome was that Snape was free to preach anywhere outside the diocese of Exeter, and looked forward to returning to Northamptonshire. But his next employment was as preacher at St Saviour's, Southwark, an appointment that he probably owed to another powerful friend, the Northamptonshire gentleman Sir Christopher Yelverton. Within two years he was again suspended. Snape's last years were spent in the thick of the organized puritan militancy which followed the Hampton Court conference of 1604, a link man between the west-country leaders John Travers and Melanchthon Jewel (who had shared his imprisonment in 1590–92) and Northampton. In 1606 he helped to sway opinion in the House of Commons against a bishops' 'bill for conformity'.

Snape married twice. The surname of his first wife was Beridge, that of his second, a widow, Gawden; no other details have survived. His will, made in March 1608, reveals him as the father of eight children and stepfather of four, a well-connected person of substance with friends in several city companies. His legacies amounted to some hundreds of pounds, but were offset by debts of £410, his creditors including the London preacher and John Field's moral successor, Stephen Egerton. He died in London in the summer of 1608, perhaps in July.

Patrick Collinson

Sources Venn, *Alum. Cant.*, 1/3.117 • court of star chamber, proceedings, Elizabeth I, PRO, STAC 5/A 27/33, 49/34, 56/1 • P. Collinson, *The Elizabethan puritan movement* (1967); pbk edn (1990) • A. F. S. Pearson, *Thomas Cartwright and Elizabethan puritanism, 1535–1603* (1925); repr. (Gloucester, MA, 1966) • [R. Bancroft], *Daungerous positions and proceedings* (1593) • BL, Harley MS 6849, fol. 222*v* • CCC Oxf., MS 294, pp. 205–7, 269–73 • City of Exeter Act Book V, City of Exeter Muniments • BL, Add. MS 38492, fol. 36*v* • BL, Sloane MS 271 • vestry minutes, St Saviour's Southwark, LMA, vol. 2, 1581–1628 • State papers domestic, James I, PRO, SP 14/10A/81 • will of Edmund Snape, PRO, PROB 11/112, sig. 72 • W. J. Sheils, *The puritans in the diocese of Peterborough, 1558–1610*, Northamptonshire RS, 30 (1979) • Foster, *Alum. Oxon.*

Snatt, William (1644/5–1721), nonjuring Church of England clergyman, was born at Lewes, Sussex, the son of Edward Snatt, master of Southover Free School, near Lewes, and his wife, Alice, *née* Page. During the 'Great Rebellion' Edward Snatt, who had taught the diarist John Evelyn, supplanted Francis Atkinson, a loyalist clergyman, in the vicarage of West Firle, near Lewes. After attending his father's school William Snatt matriculated at the age of fifteen from Magdalen College, Oxford, on 14 December 1660, graduating BA in 1664 before returning to Sussex to take holy orders. He was ordained deacon on 20 May 1665 and priest by Henry King, bishop of Chichester in 1669, and became rector of Denton near Lewes in 1672, prebendary of Sutton in Chichester Cathedral, and rector of St Thomas-at-Cliffe in Lewes in 1674, vicar of Seaford and Bishopstone in 1679 (where his successor, Robert Nowell, also became a nonjuror), and vicar of Cuckfield in 1681. On 22 May 1687, while at Cuckfield, he married Mary Jupp.

Snatt looked severely upon those who refused to attend the worship of the Church of England, and attracted the particular hostility of the Quakers of Lewes. While he prosecuted them unrelentingly for non-payment of tithe they, in return, placed a black mark against his name in their registers and in 1676 accused him of keeping 'a Crucifix and other Popish Relicques' in his house (Figg, 91). Like his diocesan bishop, John Lake, and other neighbouring clergy, Snatt found himself unable to take the new oaths of allegiance to William and Mary after the revolution in 1688. As a confidant of William Sancroft, the deprived archbishop of Canterbury, he took part in a farewell service of holy communion in Lambeth Palace Chapel on Whit Sunday, 31 May 1691. Losing all his preferments Snatt became one of the first clergy to officiate to a separated nonjuring congregation. Moving to London, a natural centre for many of the nonjuring clergy, he associated with Hilkiah Bedford and Jeremy Collier, both of whom later became nonjuring bishops. Snatt lived in obscurity until 3 April 1696 when, with Collier and Shadrach Cook, another nonjuring clergyman, he appeared on the scaffold to minister to Sir William Parkyns and Sir John Friend, condemned to death for their alleged complicity in the assassination plot against William III. For publicly pronouncing absolution, in the form prescribed in the order for the visitation of the sick but with an additional ceremonial imposition of hands, and for subsequently publishing an account of the proceedings in which the true Church of England was identified with the nonjuring communion, Collier, with Snatt and Cook, was presented by the grand jury of Middlesex on 7 April 1696, indicted by the court of king's bench, and repudiated as 'irregular and scandalous' in a formally published *Declaration of the Sense of the Archbishops and Bishops now in and about London*.

Collier having absconded, Snatt, together with Cook, was committed to Newgate. Despite the best efforts of a powerful team of defence lawyers, including Sir Bartholomew Shower, Sir Francis Winnington, and Constantine Phipps, the two nonjuring clergymen were tried and convicted of high crimes and misdemeanours on 2 July 1696, but were released on bail in August 1696. It is said that this was a result of intervention by the archbishop of Canterbury, Thomas Tenison. Snatt afterwards lived quietly, apparently in Worcester, but continued to take an interest in the affairs of the nonjuring communion. In 1718, at the time of the nonjurors' schism over the eucharistic liturgy, he joined those opposed to any alteration in the order set forth in the Book of Common Prayer, criticizing the introduction of the four so-called usages (the mixture of water with the wine, the invocation of the Holy Spirit, the oblation, and prayers for the dead) in the ironically entitled tract, *Mr Collier's desertion discuss'd, or, The offices of worship in the liturgy of the Church of England, defended: against the bold attacks of that gentleman, late of her communion, now of his own* (2nd edn, 1719–20). He died on 30 November 1721, noted in the tory press as 'eminent for his Goodness, Piety and Learning, and his steady Assertion of the Rights of the Church &c.' (*Post Boy*, 2–5 Dec 1721). RICHARD SHARP

Sources J. H. Overton, *The nonjurors: their lives, principles, and writings* (1902) • J. H. Cooper, 'The vicars and parish of Cuckfield', *Sussex Archaeological Collections*, 46 (1903), 94–113, esp. 108–13 • N. Luttrell, *A brief historical relation of state affairs from September 1678 to April 1714*, 4 (1857), 40, 45, 75, 80 • Foster, *Alum. Oxon.*, 1500–1714, 4.1386 • *DNB* • W. Figg, 'Extracts from documents illustrative of the sufferings of the Quakers in Lewes', *Sussex Archaeological Collections*, 16 (1864), 65–94, esp. 82–94 • T. Lathbury, *A history of the nonjurors* (1845), 168 ff. • *VCH Sussex*, 2.38, 414 • *Walker rev.*, 353 • H. Broxap, *The later nonjurors* (1924), 315

Snedden, Sir Richard (1900–1970), shipping industry administrator, was born on 18 April 1900 in Edinburgh, the elder son of George Snedden, lawyer, and his wife, Ada Inkpin (*née* Wright). He was educated at George Watson's Boys' College. After army service in 1918, he proceeded to the University of Edinburgh, where he graduated MA in 1921 and LLB in 1922.

In 1923 Snedden joined the National Confederation of Employers' Organizations, later to become the British Employers' Confederation, and ultimately the Confederation of British Industry. This body was responsible for nominating representatives on the governing body of the International Labour Office (ILO) at Geneva and its many tripartite conferences. The ILO was designed to reduce world friction by adopting international conventions to standardize conditions of work. Snedden was an ideal apprentice and later a master craftsman in this semi-political world of industrial relations.

Snedden was called to the English bar by the Middle Temple in 1925. He was a member of the British delegations to all ILO conferences from 1923 to 1969, vice-chairman of the employers' group (1953–60), member of the governing body (1952–60), and leader of the shipowners' group at all maritime meetings in 1942–69. He was vice-president (1955–6) and president (1957–8) of the International Organization of Employers—the international association of employers' organizations.

At Geneva, Snedden attracted the attention of Cuthbert Laws, general manager of the Shipping Federation, the British shipowners' central body for negotiating wages and conditions of seafarers and for the supply of crews. It was a founder-member of the International Shipping Federation grouping similar bodies in other countries. Snedden became assistant secretary of the Shipping Federation in 1929, secretary in 1933, and chief executive in 1936, a post he held until 1962.

Snedden inherited and perfected the system of industrial relations in the shipping industry based on the National Maritime Board. The board had its origins in the First World War as a body where shipowners and the seamen's union met to agree wages and conditions on an industry-wide basis. Replacing conflict with co-operation, it produced long-lasting industrial peace. There was no official seamen's strike between 1911 and 1966 and only a handful of unofficial stoppages. Snedden helped to make the board a success because, while loyal to the Shipping Federation, he could see both sides of any question and was the master of the unexpected compromise. Under his management the Shipping Federation became the largest employers' organization in the country, and in the area of industrial relations the shipping industry was described by so qualified a judge as Ernest Bevin as a model to the rest of the world.

During the Second World War Snedden's international experience enabled him to co-ordinate in a masterly way the crew arrangements of the allied merchant fleets in exile. His success was recognized by his appointment as CBE in 1942, and by a number of foreign decorations. He was also made an honorary captain of the Royal Naval Reserve (RNR). Under Snedden the Shipping Federation also co-ordinated the manning of the 'little ships' of the Dunkirk evacuation in 1940 and of many vessels of the D-day invasion fleet in 1944. For general manning purposes a pool of merchant seamen was established, with men being paid and kept ready for service even when ashore. This led post-war to the merchant navy established service scheme (1947), which did much to end casual labour in the shipping industry.

During Snedden's period of management, the Shipping Federation increased and expanded the provision of training for merchant seamen, and by 1950 the federation was responsible for running fourteen training schools. Snedden was vice-chairman of the Merchant Navy Training Board, 1936–62, and chairman of the national sea training schools, 1944–60.

Both during the war and afterwards Snedden was closely involved with industrial relations policy in the wider national field. He was a member of the minister of labour's advisory committee from 1940 to 1962 and chairman of the industrial relations committee of the British Employers' Federation from 1942 to 1962. Snedden also served as a director of several companies, including Monotype and Consolidated Gold Fields.

Although small and short-sighted, Snedden dominated any gathering, serious or convivial. He was knighted in 1951, appointed CVO in 1967, and was a member of the queen's body guard for Scotland. In 1953 he received an honorary LLD from Edinburgh University. He retired from the Shipping Federation in 1962, but remained general manager of the International Shipping Federation until 1969.

To be chief executive officer of an employers' organization demands special qualities, among them the ability to sink individuality and to carry out faithfully a policy not of one's own making. Snedden's loyalty and integrity explain the confidence union officials had in him and the great influence he exerted in the shipping industry both at home and abroad.

Although generally a quiet speaker, Snedden could be forceful if required and his vigorous style at the 1946 Seattle maritime conference of the ILO led the American press to call him 'the blockbuster'. In 1955 Snedden criticized the post-war proliferation of international bodies, claiming that far too often international co-operation was only a label or a slogan, not a policy. He strongly opposed the admission of employer-delegates from the communist bloc to membership of the technical committees of the ILO.

On 2 September 1926 Snedden married Janet Catherine, only daughter of a wine merchant, Duncan MacDougall, of Kilchoman, Islay. Originally fellow students, their partnership lasted until her death a few weeks before his. There was one son, who was mentally disturbed and brought about the untimely death of his father on 9 March 1970, in an irrational desire to save him from loneliness. Snedden died at Pembury Hospital, Pembury, Kent, from a fractured skull and lacerated brain due to blows from an axe. His son was subsequently found not guilty of murder on the grounds of insanity.

Alan G. Jamieson

Sources L. H. Powell, *The Shipping Federation, 1890–1950* (1950) • A. Marsh and V. Ryan, *The seamen: a history of the National Union of Seamen, 1887–1987* (1989) • R. Snedden, 'Labour relations in shipping', *Journal of the Institute of Transport* (July 1964) • private information (1981) • m. cert. • d. cert. • *CGPLA Eng. & Wales* (1970)
Likenesses P. Bliss, oils, priv. coll.
Wealth at death £83,036: administration with will, 7 Sept 1970, *CGPLA Eng. & Wales*

Snell, Charles (*bap.* **1667**, *d.* **1733**), writing-master, was born in London and was baptized on 27 February 1667 at St Giles Cripplegate, the son of Berry Snell (*d.* in or before 1675), vintner, and his wife, Winifred. In 1675 he was admitted to Christ's Hospital from St Giles Cripplegate; he left the school in 1681 to be apprenticed to the writing-master William Brooks, in the City of London. Here he made his own career as a writing-master; he also published books on bookkeeping and was occasionally employed as an auditor. With his wife, Susannah, he had a son, Charles, who was baptized on 20 October 1698 at Christ Church, Greyfriars, and who predeceased his father.

Snell became a bright star in a contemporary galaxy of writing-masters. In 1694 he published his first copybook, *The Pen-Man's Treasury Open'd*. This contained his first critical attack, following the current practice of vituperation between writing-masters, on the over-elaborate style of 'his brother Quills'. He claimed to have avoided 'the Starch'd affected Flourishes, and illiterate copies that senseless Pretenders have imposed on the world … Such Empericks, by their barbarous Copies, both Written and Printed, have led youth into a Labyrinth of Errors' (Heal, 104).

In 1700 Snell succeeded John Seddon as master of the Sir John Johnson's Free Writing School, where he remained until his death thirty-three years later. The year 1712 saw his second copybook, *The Art of Writing in its Theory and Practice*, with a similarly critical preface. In 1715 he published his own writing rules, rigid and meticulous in form, entitled *The Standard Rules of the Round and Round-Text Hands*. This book became the focus of a notable quarrel with another distinguished writing-master, John Clark, which, with criticisms and counter-criticisms, lasted for several years, incidentally increasing Snell's copybook sales. In 1711 he produced handwriting plates included in *Penmanship in its Utmost Beauty and Extent* (1731), by George Bickham.

Snell has been criticized for causing a decline in handwriting by promoting his dull copperplate style, but his practice and teaching of a simpler and standardized mode of handwriting most effectively met the needs of clerks in the growing number of commercial houses. That is his principal claim to fame. He died at his London home in Sermon Lane in 1733, survived by his wife.

Patrick Nairne, *rev.*

Sources Christ's Hospital children's register, 1669–87, GL • W. Massey, *The origin and progress of letters, an essay in two parts* (1763) • A. Heal, *The English writing-masters and their copy-books, 1570–1800* (1931) • J. I. Whalley, *English handwriting, 1540–1853* (1969) • D. Jackson, *The story of writing* (1981) • *IGI*

Snell, Hannah [*alias* James Gray] (**1723–1792**), sexual impostor, was born on 23 April 1723 in Friar Street, St Helen's, Worcester, the eighth of nine children of Samuel Snell, a hosier, and his wife, Mary Williams. Robert Walker's biography of Snell's life, first published in 1750, provides a clue to what might have shaped Hannah's military ambitions. Three of her brothers were either soldiers or sailors, while five of her sisters married into military families. As a young girl, Hannah often played soldiers with her friends and was known to her neighbours in St Helen's as 'young Amazon Snell'. But following the death of Hannah's parents, and without other relatives to support her, in 1740 she left Worcester to live with her sister Susanah and brother-in-law James Gray in Wapping. There she met and later married at Fleet church on 6 January 1744 a Dutch sailor named James Summs. Soon after the ceremony Summs revealed another side of his character; he stole Hannah's possessions and began keeping company with 'women of the basest character'. Meanwhile, Hannah discovered she was pregnant and was deserted by her husband two months before their daughter, Susanna, was born in September 1746. However, the baby lived only five months, and after her death in January 1747 Hannah decided to undergo her transformation as a man.

Although Hannah's only known reason for her transformation was to find her husband, given their unhappy relationship it seems improbable that this was her only motive. More likely it was practical. Without a child to support, she may have decided to take her brother-in-law's name, James Gray, and escape the poverty of her situation in Wapping. She enlisted under this name with Colonel Fraser's regiment of marines, part of Admiral Edward Boscawen's forces waging war against the French. Her disguise went unnoticed by John Rozier, the captain

Hannah Snell (**1723–1792**), by John Faber junior, 1750 (after Richard Phelps)

of the *Swallow*, lying at anchor in Portsmouth harbour on 23 October 1747. His log notes the arrival of 'a lieutenant of marine and five private centinels' among them, James Gray (Stark, 188).

The ship set sail the following day for the East Indies, and by the time it had reached Lisbon, Hannah had 'became a Favourite amongst them all' for her willingness and skill in performing domestic chores. After three weeks in the dock, the *Swallow* continued on to Cape Town along with another ship, the *Vigilant*, through unusually rough seas. During one violent storm Hannah 'rendered herself so conspicuous both by her skill and intrepidity that she was allowed to be a very useful hand on board' (Walker, 36). The peak of Hannah's military career came during the British raid to seize the French-held fort of Devakottai in 1748. Walker described how Hannah was wounded: 'during the Engagement [she] received six Shot in her Right Leg and five in the Left and what affected her more than all the Rest, one so dangerous in her Groin'. Records confirm that on 2 August 1749 a James Gray was admitted to Cuddalore Hospital and remained there for more than two months. However, historians have argued that Hannah may have been suffering from a disease such as scurvy rather than recuperating from wounds to her groin, which would help to explain how she could have kept her identity a secret while hospitalized. But this period marked the end of James Gray's military career. Upon her release from hospital Hannah joined the *Tartar* bound for Madras, and then transferred back to the *Eltham*, sailing for England on 19 October 1749.

On the journey home Hannah's master, Lieutenant Richard Wagget, died, and she was admitted first into the service of the ship's second-lieutenant, Mr Kite, and then Mr Wallis, third lieutenant. Robert Walker suggests that there was now a greater need for Hannah to disguise her identity from her shipmates, who had begun to tease her about a lack of facial hair. When taunted with the epithet Miss Molly Gray, Hannah would 'return the compliment not just with a smile and an oath but with a challenge of the best Sailor of them all yet it secretly created her many an uneasy Hour,' (Walker, 71–2). To affirm further her manliness Hannah accompanied the crew when they went ashore in Lisbon and played 'the Part of a boon Companion so naturally, and so far distant from what bore the least Appearance of Effeminacy, that she answere'd the End proposed. The Name of *Miss Molly* was here perfectly buried in Oblivion' (ibid., 73). During their shore leave, Hannah and Edward Jeffries met a Portuguese woman, over whom the two sailors tossed a coin to see who would spend the night with her. Fortunately, Hannah lost the toss and thus avoided an awkward situation. The *Eltham* arrived back in Portsmouth on 25 May 1750 and Hannah again used her romantic involvement with a woman, a Miss Catherine, to avoid having to join her shipmates on a drinking spree. The next week Hannah, along with ten other marines, headed north for London and arrived three days later. Back at home, she arrived at her sister's house at Wapping and, at least in private, resumed her life as Hannah Snell.

The public unveiling was more dramatic. After collecting her pay and selling off the two suits Hannah received along with her wages, she retired to a pub frequented by her mess mates. There she told them her secret.

> The Money now being paid, and our Heroine having been determined to raise all the ready Cash she could before she opened a new Scene which she well knew would amuse them … she proposed to reveal before they parted, prudently considering that she should never perhaps have so favourable an Opportunity again of disclosing her Sex to such a Number of Witnesses. (Walker, 155–6)

At first, Hannah's friends refused to believe her, and it was only when her sister and brother-in-law supported her that the story was accepted.

Since she was now forced to give up her career as a sailor, Hannah quickly realized that it would be prudent to exploit her adventures while they were still in the public's mind. Her first act was to petition the duke of Cumberland, the captain-general of the army, for compensation for the injuries (or illness) she suffered while serving in the marines. Dressed in her male clothes, she handed her petition to the duke when his carriage had stopped in St James's Park. After reading the petition the duke immediately ordered Colonel Napier, his adjutant-general, to authenticate her claim. Although a promised pension of £18 5*s*. per annum never materialized, she was made an out-pensioner at the Royal Chelsea Hospital in London and granted 5*d*. a day for life.

Hannah had by then met the publisher Robert Walker, whose publication of her story, *The Female Soldier* (1750), rapidly sold out and was reprinted. In addition to the book, there were also two portraits of Hannah on sale and a ballad celebrating her artful disguise and military skills.

She also took to the stage, and between 29 June and 6 September made sixty appearances at Goodman's Fields Theatre in London. Alongside jugglers and acrobats, Hannah paraded the stage with a flintlock and 'performed the manual exercise of a soldier' before marching her own troop of Amazons across the boards (Dowie, 123–7).

Demand for Hannah's performances, however, did not last beyond 1751, and there is no record of whether she achieved her ambition of opening a pub in Wapping as Walker suggests. And although Hannah is quoted in her biography as being 'resolutely bent to be lord and master of herself, and never more to entertain the least thoughts of having a husband', she was married in 1759 to Samuel Eyles, a carpenter with whom she had two sons. She was widowed by 1772 and married a Richard Habgood on 16 November of that year at Welford, Berkshire. At some point thereafter she moved back to London to live with her son George, his wife, Jane Sympson, and their two daughters. On 6 August 1791 the governors of Bethlem Hospital admitted Hannah as patient, where she died on 8 February 1792. She was buried at the Royal Chelsea Hospital, one of only two women to have ever been granted this honour. JULIE WHEELWRIGHT

Sources J. Wheelwright, *Amazons and military maids* (1989) • R. Walker, *The female soldier* (1750) • M. M. Dowie, ed., *Women adventurers* (1893) • M. Stephens, *Hannah Snell: the secret life of a female marine, 1723–1792* (1997) • S. J. Stark, *Female tars: women aboard ship in the age of sail* (1996) • D. Dugaw, 'Introduction', in R. Walker, *The female soldier*, ed. D. Dugaw (1989) • Bethlem Royal Hospital, Beckenham, Kent, Archives and Museum • register of burials, Royal Chelsea Hospital, PRO, RG4/4330, 1691–1856

Likenesses J. Faber junior, mezzotint, 1750 (after R. Phelps), BM, NPG [*see illus.*] • J. Johnson, mezzotint (after J. Wardell), BM, NPG

Snell, Henry, Baron Snell (1865–1944), politician and secularist, was born on 1 April 1865 at Sutton-on-Trent, Nottinghamshire, the son of Mary Snell, formerly Clark. His father's name was not registered; he was brought up by his mother and stepfather. His education at the village school was sporadic and rudimentary, and from the age of eight he was a cattle minder and bird scarer. By his tenth birthday he was working a twelve-hour day as a farm labourer. When aged twelve he was engaged at Newark hiring fair as an indoor farm servant. Subsequently he moved to Nottingham and worked in several public houses, an experience that helped to make him a thorough abstainer from alcohol and tobacco.

Snell's family background was radical, and as a boy he had been influenced by village nonconformity. In Nottingham he began to read widely, attended evening classes at University College, Nottingham, and free-thought lectures, became an admirer of Charles Bradlaugh, and joined the secularist movement. For a period he attended a Unitarian church, but he was excluded in 1889 as a radical influence. His shift to secularism was complemented by a political commitment to socialism. He joined the Social Democratic Federation and took an active part in John Burns's west Nottingham campaign in the general election of November 1885.

After periods of unemployment Snell obtained a clerical post at the Midland Institution for the Blind through his Unitarian contacts, and in 1890 he moved to London as assistant to the secretary of the Woolwich Charity Organization Society. This move was the result of Snell's friendship with Charles Herbert Grinling, a Nottingham curate, who had moved to Woolwich in 1889 and who became secretary of the Woolwich Charity Organization Society. In Woolwich Snell became acquainted with a group of progressive clergy who helped to give the local labour movement a strongly ethical character. This was very congenial to him, and his socialist activities found expression through the Independent Labour Party (ILP), which formed part of a broader and increasingly successful Woolwich labour organization.

Snell became thoroughly involved in the Ethical Society under Stanton Coit. Politically this was a relatively ecumenical movement that could bring together ethical socialists and progressive Liberals. In 1895 he became secretary to the first director of the London School of Economics and Political Science, W. A. S. Hewins; subsequently he lectured for the Fabian Society. Appointed in 1899 as an organizer and lecturer for the British Union of Ethical Societies, he suffered a nervous collapse. During his lengthy convalescence he spent the spring and summer terms of 1902 at the University of Heidelberg. His commitment to the ethical movement deepened. 'My deepest and most abiding interests were in religion and ethics and to these great subjects, the best thought and work of my life have been given' (Snell, 155). As well as becoming chairman of the British Union of Ethical Societies, he was from 1907 to 1931 secretary of the Secular Education League.

Snell's commitment to socialist politics and his abilities as a propagandist eventually led to his adoption as Labour candidate for Huddersfield. This Liberal seat had returned a significant Labour vote in the 1906 election and in a subsequent by-election. Despite the centrality of the constitutional crisis and the consequential problem of presenting a distinctive Labour position, Snell maintained credible Labour support in both 1910 elections. Although he was active in pre-war peace campaigns, Snell had reservations about the ILP's wartime position. He felt that debate over responsibility for the conflict was irrelevant and considered that Germany was more culpable than the ILP official line suggested. Therefore he would have preferred the party to focus on post-war problems. In 1918 he fought Huddersfield once again; his position on the war perhaps helps to explain his relatively strong performance (he came second to the coalition candidate).

Snell's most significant political roots were in London. He became a London county councillor for East Woolwich in 1919 and was successful again in 1922. His failure to stand three years later was the result of his election to parliament in November 1922 as member for East Woolwich; he retained the seat until he accepted a peerage in 1931. He established a reputation as an industrious and principled back-bencher and, as a founder member of the Labour Commonwealth group, with a particular expertise in colonial affairs. One parliamentary observer felt that his most significant Commons intervention came in the debate on the prayer book measure in June 1928. 'There were sentences in it which with slight alterations might have been spoken by the Midland Puritans from where he comes' (Johnston, 47). Snell insisted that in his view the Reformation was 'the most blessed thing that happened in modern history' (*Hansard* 5C, 218, col. 1087, 13 June 1928).

With the formation of the Labour government in 1929, Snell became chairman of the consultative committee elected by the Parliamentary Labour Party to maintain effective links between back-benchers and the government. The task was difficult, and Snell became highly critical of the ILP left. Although Snell staunchly supported the government, he did not hesitate to take an independent line when he felt this was necessary. In October 1929 he went to Palestine as a member of a four-man commission of inquiry under Sir Walter Shaw, charged with investigating recent disturbances. He signed the report, but attached a twelve-page note of reservations insisting in particular that Palestine's prosperity necessitated agricultural modernization and that this required 'Jewish enterprise' (*Report of the Commission on the Palestine Disturbances of August 1929*, command 3530, March 1930, 178).

Snell entered the government as parliamentary undersecretary at the India Office in March 1931. Following the death of Earl Russell, there was a lack of Labour ministerial talent in the Lords, and the appointment entailed Snell's taking a peerage, as Baron Snell, of Plumstead, Kent. His period in office, the prelude to the second roundtable conference, was little more than five months. When the Labour government resigned, MacDonald asked Snell to join the National Government. He refused partly because he felt he might have to justify a more reactionary policy which he could not influence, but more basically he was loyal to the labour movement. 'I should hate it to be said that one of my first actions on becoming a Peer was to desert the Movement whose servant I had been for only so long as it appeared to serve my purpose' (Snell to MacDonald, 26 Aug 1931, PRO, 30/69, MacDonald papers, file 1315).

Within the House of Lords Snell became an effective member within the small Labour group. His interest in Indian affairs led to his membership of the Linlithgow joint committee on Indian constitutional reform in 1933–4. With the election of a Labour majority to the London county council in 1934, he became chairman for the first four years of Labour rule. He became deputy leader of the House of Lords in 1940. He was appointed CBE in 1930, sworn of the privy council in 1937, and made a CH in 1943. London University conferred upon him an honorary degree in 1936. He died at Highgate Hospital, Middlesex, on 21 April 1944. He never married, and the peerage became extinct.

Snell's character emerges clearly from his readable autobiography *Men, Movements and Myself*. Ethically serious and puritanical, he seemed, despite his criticisms of formal religion, to be the personification of the protestant ethic. His *Who's Who* entry listed his recreations as 'none'.

DAVID HOWELL

Sources Lord Snell, *Men, movement and myself* (1936) • *DNB* • J. Johnston, *A hundred commoners* (1931) • P. R. Thompson, *Socialists, liberals and labour: the struggle for London, 1885–1914* (1967) • *Hansard 5C* (1928), 218.1081–7 [Speech on Prayer Book Measure] • 'Report of the commission on the Palestine disturbances of August, 1929', *Parl. papers* (1929–30), 16.675, Cmd 3530 • P. Kelemen, 'Labour ideals and colonial pioneers: Wedgwood, Morrison and Zionism', *Labour History Review* (spring 1996), 30–48 • *CGPLA Eng. & Wales* (1944)

Archives People's History Museum, Manchester, papers | People's History Museum, Manchester, minutes of parliamentary labour party • PRO, MacDonald papers, letters, 30/69

Likenesses W. Stoneman, photograph, 1931, NPG • F. Dodd, oils, *c*.1935, County Hall, London • M. M. C. Urquhart, oils, *c*.1939, Royal Institute of International Affairs, Chatham House, London • W. Stoneman, photograph, 1943, NPG • F. Dodd, charcoal drawing, Athenaeum, London

Wealth at death £21,487 2*s*. 9*d*.: probate, 30 May 1944, *CGPLA Eng. & Wales*

Snell, John (1628/9–1679), educational benefactor, was born at Pinwherry, Colmonell, Ayrshire, the only son of Andrew Snell (*c*.1591–1663), blacksmith, of Colmonell, and Margaret, his wife, daughter of John Carnahan. Snell had at least one sister. He attended the University of Glasgow between 1642 and 1644 under James Dalrymple, without graduating. While there he signed the solemn league and covenant, but he served on the royalist side in the civil war. After the battle of Worcester he found employment in the Cheshire house of Lady Margaret Hoghton (*d*. 1657). Through her he met the royalist lawyer Sir Orlando Bridgeman, who engaged him as an assistant about 1653. In 1660 Bridgeman was appointed lord chief justice of common pleas, and Snell became a court official. When in 1667 Bridgeman was made lord keeper of the great seal, Snell was nominated as seal-bearer, and continued in that office under Bridgeman's successor, the earl of Shaftesbury, until the latter's fall in 1673. Thereafter Snell was secretary to James, duke of Monmouth (who procured him a Cambridge MA degree, which he took by proxy, in 1674), and acted for him in connection with his Scottish estates; he also undertook similar work for wealthy clients such as Robert, Viscount Cholmondeley (*d*. 1681).

In 1662 Snell married Joanna Coventry (*d*. 1697), daughter of Vincent Coventry, rector of Begbroke, in Oxfordshire. They had one daughter, Dorothy (1663–1738), who married William Guise (1648–1716).

Snell was already a man of means by 1661, when he gave some valuable books to the University of Glasgow, which made him an MA in 1662. He subsequently gave more books and also money. In 1674 he paid £8300 for the manor of Ufton in Warwickshire, where he was a charitable absentee landlord. The source of his wealth is obscure.

Snell died on 6 August 1679 at the house of his brother-in-law Benjamin Cooper (*c*.1623–1701), registrar of the University of Oxford, in Holywell Street, Oxford. He was buried in linen under the chancel of St Cross Church, Holywell, Oxford, two days later. There was a black marble gravestone, now lost or concealed. An imposing monument unveiled near the site of his father's smithy in 1919 (a memorial in Colmonell kirk was dedicated on the same day) was rediscovered thickly overgrown in 1995. The cross flory device on these memorials was taken from Snell's seal; he probably took it from George Snell, archdeacon of Chester (*d.* 1656), perhaps a distant relative.

Snell made his will in 1677, adding finishing touches in a failing hand on his deathbed. His Ufton estate, estimated to be worth £450 p.a., he left in trust for the 'mayntenance and education in some Colledge or Hall' at Oxford of at least five Scots who had spent at least one year at the 'Colledge of Glascow'. They were eventually to be ordained and return to Scotland, the underlying purpose being to bolster episcopacy there. Annuities and other burdens on the estate delayed the introduction of any scheme, and in 1690 presbyterianism became by law the established order of things for the church in Scotland. Snell's daughter, in principle his sole heir-at-law, attempted to claim that because his wishes had been frustrated thereby the estate should revert to her. The ensuing litigation denied her this, and in 1693 a cy pres arrangement was settled on Balliol for the support of Scots from Glasgow without the imposition of any career obligations. Balliol was chosen because it was perceived as a 'Scottish foundation', and already had some exhibitions for Scots intending ordination which had been established by the will of John Warner, bishop of Rochester (*d.* 1666). Snell had been involved in the administration of Warner's will because Bridgeman was the principal executor, and he used it as a model for his own. The first four Snell exhibitioners were admitted to Balliol in 1699. Many of their successors are in the *Oxford Dictionary of National Biography*, including James Stirling, Adam Smith, Matthew Baillie, John Gibson Lockhart, Archibald Campbell Tait, and Edward Caird. After three centuries, despite much litigation and adjustment during the first two, the scheme continues in vigorous existence. JOHN JONES

Sources L. Stones, 'The life and career of John Snell (c.1629–1679)', *Miscellany II*, ed. D. Sellar, Stair Society (1984), 148–220 • W. I. Addison, *The Snell exhibitions: from the University of Glasgow to Balliol College, Oxford* (1901), suppl. (1902) • A. Milroy, *John Snell, his schools, schoolmasters and scholars* (1923) • John Snell, Sept 1679, PRO, PROB 10/1103 • J. H. Jones, *John Snell's exhibitions, 1699–1999: Snelliana from the collections of Balliol College* (1999) • J. Jones, *Balliol College: a history*, 2nd edn (1997)

Archives Balliol Oxf., executors' papers

Wealth at death approx. £10,000; London house; cash; debts: Balliol Oxf.

Snell, Sir John Francis Cleverton (1869–1938), electrical engineer and administrator, was born at Saltash, Cornwall, on 15 December 1869, the son of Commander John Skinner Snell RN (*d.* 1873), and his wife, Mary Henriette, only daughter of Frederick William Pouget Cleverton, of Saltash. He was educated at Plymouth grammar school and at King's College, London, of which he was a fellow from 1929. After four years' pupillage with the electrical firm of Woodhouse and Rawson, he became associated first, in 1889, with Colonel R. E. B. Crompton, who employed him on electricity supply work at Kensington and Notting Hill in London, and also at Stockholm; and then, three years later, with Major-General C. E. Webber, for whom he carried out many country-house and other installations. He married on 28 May 1892 Annie Glendenning Quick (*b.* 1865/6, *d.* in or after 1938), second daughter of Henry Bayly Quick, an outfitter, of Biscovey, Cornwall; they had one son.

In 1893 Snell entered municipal service as an assistant electrical engineer to the St Pancras vestry, and three years later went to Sunderland as borough electrical engineer, becoming also borough tramways engineer in 1899. In 1906 he began to practise in Westminster as a consulting engineer, and in 1910 he joined the firm of Preece and Cardew. During this partnership, which lasted until 1918, he was in request as an expert witness, the most notable case in which he was engaged being the arbitration in 1912 concerning the terms on which the state should take over the National Telephone Company. In that arbitration he was chief technical witness for the Post Office, and was under examination for thirteen days.

During the First World War Snell was a member of a number of government committees, including the water-power resources committee of the Board of Trade and the Ministry of Agriculture's committee on electroculture, of both of which he was chairman. In 1919 he became electrical adviser to the Board of Trade and was appointed chairman of the Electricity Commission established by the Electricity (Supply) Act passed at the end of that year. In that position, which he held until the beginning of 1938, he took a leading part in shaping the electrical policy of Britain, and in bringing about the co-ordinated system of generating electricity and transmitting it by the 'grid' which was provided for by the Electricity (Supply) Act of 1926.

Snell was knighted in 1914 and appointed GBE in 1925. He was president in 1902–3 of the (Incorporated) Municipal Electrical Association; in 1914 of the Institution of Electrical Engineers, which awarded him its Faraday medal in 1938; and in 1926 of the engineering section of the British Association at its Oxford meeting. From 1926 to 1931 he was a vice-president of the Institution of Civil Engineers, but for reasons of health was obliged to decline nomination as president in 1930 and again in 1931. Besides many technical papers, he was the author of *The Distribution of Electrical Energy* (1906) and *Power House Design* (1911 and 1921). He was fond of music, particularly the organ, took a keen interest in geology (he was a fellow of the Geological Society), and was a great lover of birds and animals. He died at the London Clinic, 20 Devonshire Place, Marylebone, in London, after an operation, on 6 July 1938.

H. M. ROSS, *rev.*

Sources *The Times* (7 July 1938) • *The Engineer* (15 July 1938) • *Engineering* (15 July 1938) • *Nature*, 142 (1938), 384–5 • *Journal of the Institution of Electrical Engineers*, 83 (1938) • *Journal of the Institution of Civil Engineers*, 10 (1938–9), 131–2 • d. cert. • m. cert. • *The Times* (5 April 1873), 5e

Likenesses W. Stoneman, photograph, 1930, NPG • portrait, repro. in *Engineering*

Wealth at death £11,925 18*s.* 3*d.*: probate, 11 Aug 1938, *CGPLA Eng. & Wales*

Snelling, Matthew (*bap.* 1621, *d.* 1678), miniature painter and courtier, was baptized on 14 October 1621, the second of three surviving sons of Thomas Snelling (*d.* 1623), an alderman and, briefly, mayor of King's Lynn, and his wife, Margaret, *née* Clarke; they had married at the chapel of St Nicholas, King's Lynn, on 16 December 1613. Thomas Snelling died during his mayoral year, and was buried in King's Lynn on 24 April 1623; his widow subsequently married, on 21 July 1625, as his second wife, Ambrose Blagge (*d.* 1662) of Little Horringer Hall, near Barrow, in Suffolk. Blagge was the grandfather of the virtuous Margaret (1652–1678), wife of Sidney, first earl of Godolphin, and the subject of John Evelyn's posthumous memoir *The Life of Mrs Godolphin* (finished by 1686, first published 1847). Matthew was therefore brought up from the age of four by Ambrose Blagge in Little Horringer Hall.

By 1641, having received a substantial bequest on the death of his elder brother, Snelling had taken lodgings in London, in the parish of St Martin-in-the-Fields, and held an appointment at court as esquire of the body to the king. On 3 December 1663 he married Elizabeth, daughter of Peter Maplisden (*d.* 1672), described as a gentleman of St Margaret's, Westminster (Edmond, 114), at the church of St Dunstan-in-the-West, Fleet Street. They had a son, Peter (*b.* 1664), and a daughter, Isabella (*b.* 1666); a third child, Elizabeth, died soon after her birth in 1667. From 1664 Snelling's London lodgings were in Long Acre.

At the Restoration Snelling was reappointed esquire of the body, and retained the position until 1673. On 24 November 1674 he was granted the reversion of the office of the collector of customs for the port of Ipswich. Throughout this period he seems to have maintained a secondary residence in the country, in the household of his stepfather in Little Horringer, within a circle of amateurs of the arts that had, during his lifetime, included the painters Sir Nathaniel Bacon (1585–1627), Nathaniel Thach (*b.* 1617), and Mary Beale, *née* Cradock (1633–1699). He was apparently not above taking a fee from neighbours for coaching in the gentle art of miniature painting, both in London and the country.

Snelling's background and interests would have given him entry as patron to the art of the miniaturist, and accordingly a portrait of him by Samuel Cooper (dated 1644) is described by George Vertue from sight of it at the second day (3 April 1723) of the sale of the goods of the deceased goldsmith Michael Rosse, father-in-law of the miniaturist Susannah-Penelope Rosse. Contact with Cooper would have stimulated and given direction to Snelling's interest in miniature painting. His earliest certain work is a competent *Charles I* after Van Dyck, signed and dated 1647 (priv. coll.), possibly painted as an exercise for himself or as a model for a pupil. His mature work of the 1660s and 1670s, of which *Susanna, Lady Dormer* of 1662 and *Sir John Dormer* of 1674 (both in the V&A) are excellent examples, has technical resemblances to that of Thomas Flatman, whom Snelling would have known through their mutual friend Charles Beale and through their membership of the wider community of learned amateurs of the arts resident in the Long Acre and Covent Garden area of London. Vertue, however, was uncertain as to whether Snelling should be taken seriously as an artist, noting the gossip that he painted only ladies, and then only to flirt with them. Vertue also recalled the scandal that Snelling had somehow contrived the duke of Norfolk's marriage to Jane Bickerton, daughter of the keeper of the king's wine cellar and mother already of two of his sons, against whom the duke's legitimate sons, in March 1777, raised a petition denying the existence of a lawful marriage. But the surviving work, though scarce, is certainly substantial in terms of skill and style, and there is no doubt that had Snelling, like Cooper, been left a poor orphan he could have earned a decent living in the trade.

Snelling died in 1678, perhaps suddenly, since he left no will, and perhaps out of London, since the record of his burial has not yet been found. The portrait of him by Cooper is not now extant. JOHN MURDOCH

Sources Vertue, *Note books*, vols. 1–6 • E. Walsh, R. Jeffree, and R. Sword, *The excellent Mrs Mary Beale* (1975) [exhibition catalogue, Geffrye Museum, London, and Towner Art Gallery, Eastbourne, 13 Oct 1975 – 21 Feb 1976] • M. Edmond, 'Bury St Edmunds: a seventeenth century art centre', *Walpole Society*, 53 (1987), 106–18
Likenesses S. Cooper, miniature, 1644

Snelling, Thomas (1712–1773), numismatist, is of obscure origins although memorial medals give his date of birth as 1712. He may have been the son of John and Phillis Sneling who was baptized at St James's, Clerkenwell, London, on 19 May 1712 but there is no evidence to corroborate this identity. He was in business as a bookseller and coin dealer in Fleet Street 'next the Horn Tavern' by 1763. When he made his will in 1772 Snelling was resident in the parish of St Dunstan-in-the-West, Fleet Street, with his wife, Elizabeth, a daughter, Mary Lord, who was married to the printseller and engraver John *Thane (1747?–1818), and his sons Young Lord and Thomas. The unusual names of the daughter and elder son allow them to be identified as children baptized at Whitechapel in 1739 and 1741 respectively; and the younger son may have been the Thomas Snelling baptized at St Sepulchre, Holborn, in 1749. Thomas and Elizabeth Snelling had four other children, Elizabeth Hawkins, baptized in 1737 at Whitechapel, and Thomas (*bap.* 1743), William (*bap.* 1745), and Elizabeth (*bap.* 1747), all baptized at St Sepulchre.

The earliest evidence of Snelling's interest in numismatics seems to be an undated letter to the antiquary Joseph Ames (1689–1759) for his *Typographical Antiquities* (1749), on the French manner of distinguishing mints by letters of the alphabet. His name occurs as a purchaser at London coin sales from about 1766, but his publications give evidence of many years' experience. The Revd Joseph Kilner bought extensively from him when forming the cabinet of coins which he left to Merton College, Oxford. When William Hunter (1718–1783) started a coin collection in 1770 he relied on Snelling, and trusted him in 1773 to bid at the sale of James West's collection without any limit on price; his accounts show him spending more than £1370 with Snelling.

Snelling's reputation rests on his publications, starting with *Seventy-Two Plates of Gold and Silver Coin* (1757), which, as H. W. Henfrey showed, were probably printed from copperplates engraved in 1652 for the committee of the mint.

A View of the Silver Coin and Coinage of England (1762) considered silver coins since 1066 with regard to type, legend, denomination, rarity, weight, fineness, and value per pound; a footnote on page 13 is the authority for the Newbury hoard of 1756. *A View of the Gold Coin and Coinage of England* (1763) dealt with the gold coins in the same systematic way as the silver.

Snelling's *A View of the Copper Coin and Coinage of England* (1766) was a remarkably well-documented survey; he was the first to give serious consideration to seventeenth-century tokens, and the text here was much more than mere explanation of the plates. *A View of the Coins at this Time Current throughout Europe* (1766) was intended for the use of travellers and all those who had any correspondence with foreign countries. *The Doctrine of Gold and Silver Computations* (1766), illustrated with examples and tables, shows an impressive grasp of assaying. *Miscellaneous Views of the Coins Struck by English Princes in France* (1769) included sterling imitations (of which Snelling showed an early understanding), imitation nobles, British colonial, Manx, and pattern coins. *A View of the Origin, Nature and Use of Jettons or Counters* (1769) has useful illustrations. In 1771 he sought permission from the British Museum for Charles Hall to take drawings of certain medals.

Snelling, 'known among the Antiquarians for his skill in coins and medals', died on 2 May 1773, aged sixty-one (*GM*, 255). He left to his wife all the copyright, copies, and copperplates of his eleven principal works (of *Thirty Three Plates of English Medals* twenty plates only), as well as 'A curious ancient seal of some religious foundation of King Athelstan'. The interest, dividend, and proceeds of his capital stock of £1500 in 3 per cent new South Sea annuities went also to her, to be divided equally after her death among the three children. His stock in trade was to be sold by his executors, who were Benjamin Bartlet ('my good friend') and Charles Combe, who proved the will before Andrew Coltee Ducarel. The coins, rings, cameos, and antiquities of the 'late ingenious Thomas Snelling' were auctioned by Langford, 31 January to 3 February 1774, making something over £488.

Snelling's son Thomas, a printseller at the same Fleet Street address, published posthumously some of his father's works, principally *A View of the Silver Coin and Coinage of Scotland* (1774), to which were added gold, billon, and copper coins for which no explanatory text could be prepared. Adam de Cardonnel (*d.* 1820), though unflattering about Snelling's plates and descriptions, used his material extensively. Snelling's useful little supplement to James Simon's *Essay on Irish Coins*, including one plate supplied by Matthew Duane, was published in 1767 according to the 1810 edition of Simon, but M. Dolley has shown cause to re-date it to 1776. Snelling's works were highly valuable to collectors, and are still useful to students. Their value lies particularly in the plentiful use of copperplate illustrations, the quality of which varied with the competence of his engravers: Francis Perry, whose plates if rather coarse were accurate; and after his death, Charles Hall, James Kirk, B. Warren, and J. Lodge. The coins illustrated by Snelling have proved trustworthy, the James IV half-unicorn eventually turning up in the 1951 Bute sale. Snelling drew largely on his own stock, though by 1769 he was citing many private collections, had visited Paris to inspect the French royal collection, and had graduated from coin dealer to numismatist. R. H. THOMPSON

Sources PRO, PROB 111/988, sig. 221 · L. Brown, *A catalogue of British historical medals, 1760–1960*, 1 (1980), 41; 3 (1995), 302 · G. Macdonald, *Catalogue of the Greek coins in the Hunterian collection, University of Glasgow*, 3 vols. (1899–1905) · H. W. Henfrey, 'Notes on Snelling's *Seventy-two plates of coins*, published 1757', *Numismatic Chronicle*, new ser., 14 (1874), 159–60 · I. Stewart, 'Two centuries of Scottish numismatics', *The Scottish antiquarian tradition*, ed. A. S. Bell (1981), 227–65 · M. Dolley, 'A Snelling non-bicentenary', *Numismatic Circular*, 75 (1967), 201 · A. Durand, *Médailles et jetons des numismates* (1865) · J. M. Gray, *James and William Tassie* (1894) · BL, T. Snelling to J. Ames, Add. MS 5151 fol. 323 [39] · BL, Add. MS 39255, fol. 81 · Merton Oxf., letters to Joseph Kilner, 1766–7, Arch. coll. fol. MS 2 · *GM*, 1st ser., 43 (1773), 255 · *DNB* · R. Hovenden, ed., *A true register of all the christenings, mariages, and burialles in the parishe of St James, Clarkenwell, from … 1551 (to 1754)*, 2 (1885), Harleian Society, register section, 10 (1885), 65 [christenings, 1701–54]

Archives BL, letters, Add. MSS 5151, fol. 323 (39); 39255, fol. 81 · Merton Oxf., letters to Joseph Kilner, arch. coll. fol. MS 2

Likenesses J. Thane, etching, 1770, BL, BM, NPG · J. Kirk, medal, 1773, AM Oxf., BM · L. Pingo, bronze medal, 1773, AM Oxf., BM; repro. in Brown, *A catalogue of British historical medals*, 3.302 · G. Rawle, medal, 1773, AM Oxf., BM; repro. in Brown, *A catalogue of the British historical medals*, 1.41, no. 178 · C. Hall, line engraving, 1776? (after J. Pingo), BL

Wealth at death £1500 in 3 per cent new South Sea annuities; stock sold for over £488; four lots of silver medals: will, PRO, PROB 11/988, sig. 221; price sale catalogue, BM

Snelus, George James (1837–1906), metallurgist, born on 25 June 1837 at Camden Town, London, was the son of James and Susannah Snelus. His father, a master builder, died when George was about seven. Snelus trained to become a teacher at St John's College, Battersea, but subsequently, while teaching in a school at Macclesfield, he attended lectures on science at Owens College, Manchester, where he came under the influence of Sir Henry Roscoe. In 1864, on winning a Royal Albert scholarship, Snelus began studying at the Royal School of Mines, gaining the associateship in metallurgy and mining together with the De la Beche medal for mining. On the recommendation of Dr John Percy he was appointed, in 1867, chemist to the Dowlais ironworks, a post he held for four years. Also in 1867, Snelus married Lavinia Whitfield (*d.* 1892), daughter of David Woodward, a silk manufacturer of Macclesfield. The couple had three sons and three daughters.

In 1871 Snelus was commissioned by the Iron and Steel Institute to visit the United States to investigate the chemistry of the Danks rotary puddling process, and subsequently drew up a report on the subject (*Journal of the Iron and Steel Institute*, 1, 1872, iii–xxxvi).

It was during this investigation that Snelus realized the possibility of completely eliminating phosphorus from molten pig iron by oxidation in a basic lined enclosure. In 1872 he took out a British patent for such a process, afterwards proving by actual trial the soundness of the underlying idea. In a Bessemer converter, lined with overburned lime, he succeeded in almost entirely eliminating phosphorus from 3 to 4 ton charges of molten phosphoric pig iron; in these trials he made the first specimens of 'basic' steel by the pneumatic process. But he failed to overcome certain practical difficulties inherent in the process and it was not until Thomas and Gilchrist developed their 'basic' process in 1879 that it became commercially practicable. For the conspicuous part which he had played in regard to this invention he was awarded a gold medal at the Paris Exhibition of 1878, and the Iron and Steel Institute awarded him, jointly with Thomas, the Bessemer medal. Snelus was elected a fellow of the Royal Society in 1887. Another conspicuous contribution to metallurgical chemistry was his proof of the true practical value of the molybdate method for the determination of phosphorus in steel, a process which afterwards became universal in steelworks' laboratories.

In 1872 Snelus was appointed works manager (and subsequently general manager) of the West Cumberland Iron and Steel Company, Workington, where he remained until 1900. He also became director of several mining concerns in Cumberland. In 1902 he took out a patent for the manufacture of iron and steel in a basic lined rotary furnace, experiments upon which were being carried out at the time of his death by the Distington Iron Company, but were afterwards discontinued.

Snelus was an original member of the Iron and Steel Institute in 1869, and from 1889 onwards until his death he was a vice-president. His most important contributions to the journal of the institute were those on 'The removal of phosphorus and sulphur in steel manufacture' (1879) and on 'The chemical composition of steel rails' (1882).

He was a member of the volunteer force from 1859 until 1891, when he retired with the rank of honorary major and with the officers' long service medal. He was one of the best rifle shots in the country, being for twelve successive years, from 1866, a member of the English Twenty, and during that period gained a greater aggregate than any other member of the team. He won the first all-comers' small-bore prize at Wimbledon in 1868. He was also a keen horticulturist.

Snelus died at his residence, Ennerdale Hall, Frizington, Cumberland, on 18 June 1906, and was buried at the parish church, Arlecdon, Cumberland.

W. A. BONE, *rev.* IAN ST JOHN

Sources *Journal of the Iron and Steel Institute*, 69 (1906), 273 • J. E. S., *PRS*, 78A (1907), lx–lxi • *WWW*

Wealth at death £17,942 6*s.* 1*d.*: administration with will, 27 July 1906, *CGPLA Eng. & Wales*

Snetzler, John [*formerly* Johann Schnetzler] (**1710–1785**), organ builder, was born on 6 April 1710 at Schaffhausen, Switzerland, the son of Hans Heinrich Schnetzler, miller. He was apparently apprenticed to an organ builder in Passau, Germany, and worked on the cathedral organ there. He settled in England and had established himself in London by 1747. The organ he built for St Margaret's, King's Lynn, in 1753–4 earned him a high reputation: among other features, it introduced several stops new to England. Among the Snetzler organs which survive in a comparatively unaltered state are those of Hillington church, Norfolk (1756), Peterhouse, Cambridge (1765), St Andrew by the Wardrobe, London (1769), and chamber organs in Westminster Abbey, the Smithsonian Institution, Washington, DC, and at Williamsburg, Virginia. Both Charles Burney and John Sutton held Snetzler's work in high regard, commenting on the purity of tone and brilliancy of the chorus stops of his organs. Letters of naturalization were granted to Snetzler on 12 April 1770; he died in Schaffhausen on 28 September 1785.

L. M. MIDDLETON, *rev.* K. D. REYNOLDS

Sources M. Gillingham, 'Snetzler, John', *New Grove* • C. Burney, *The present state of music in Germany, the Netherlands and United Provinces*, 2 vols. (1773) • J. Sutton, *A short account of organs built in England from the reign of King Charles the Second to the present time* (1847)

Snoden, Robert (*d.* **1621**), bishop of Carlisle, was the third son of Ralph Snoden of Mansfield Woodhouse, Nottinghamshire. He entered Christ's College, Cambridge, in 1580 as a sizar, later to be elected as a fellow, graduating BA in 1583 and proceeding MA in 1586, BD in 1593, and finally DD in 1598. He was ordained deacon and priest by the bishop of Lincoln in February 1589 and acquired livings in his native midlands, as rector of Harby, Leicestershire, in 1596 and rector of Hickling, Nottinghamshire, in 1598, on the presentation of Robert Farburn. In 1599 Archbishop Hutton of York collated Snoden to a canonry at Southwell, where he later became the reader of the divinity lecture. About this time Snoden married Abigail, daughter of Robert Orme of Elston, Nottinghamshire, with whom he had three sons and two daughters. One son, Rutland, was baptized at Southwell in November 1600, and in 1615 followed his father to Christ's College. In 1603 Snoden became a member of the York high commission at York, and also served as a JP for Southwell liberty and commissary for Archbishop Matthew in Nottingham archdeaconry. In 1610 he became a chaplain to Prince Henry, joining a circle of staunchly evangelical protestants. That his own views matched these is evident from a sermon he preached before James I at Newstead Abbey in August 1612, in which he identified Rome as the 'throne of iniquity' and the pope as Antichrist. The king was so taken with the sermon that he procured a presentation copy.

The death of Prince Henry in November 1612 did not seriously damage Snoden's search for higher preferment: one backer was Sir John Holles, owner of Newstead, who failed to land him the deanery of Lincoln in 1613, a second was Bishop Richard Neile, who may have had Snoden enrolled as James's chaplain, but it was a third, the young Lord Villiers, who won him the bishopric of Carlisle in October 1616. The fact that Snoden had risen to the episcopate without first serving as an archdeacon or dean explains why he was branded as an unworthy choice by the court gossip, John Chamberlain. On his consecration in November 1616 Snoden resigned his livings and canonry. Although few details survive of his activities as bishop of Carlisle, Snoden certainly resided in his diocese, and personally led his primary visitation in 1617. He preached before James I in Carlisle Cathedral on 5 August

1617, and later that month, at the king's request, submitted a report on the state of his diocese, in which he complained of factious gentry and the 'multitudes of base hirelings' as well as commending some 'grave and learned pastors' among his clergy (Ferguson, 131). He also used his contacts with Villiers to overcome disputes in local government, and became embroiled in disputes over managing the estates of the bishopric. Snoden died in London on 15 May 1621 while attending parliament. He was survived by his wife. KENNETH FINCHAM

Sources BL, Royal MS 17 B. xxv • Venn, *Alum. Cant.* • J. Peile, *Biographical register of Christ's College, 1505–1905, and of the earlier foundation, God's House, 1448–1505*, ed. [J. A. Venn], 1 (1910), 159, 305 • K. Fincham, *Prelate as pastor: the episcopate of James I* (1990) • *The letters of John Chamberlain*, ed. N. E. McClure, 2 (1939), 29, 48 • R. S. Ferguson, *Carlisle* (1889) • C. M. L. Bouch, 'The Lowthers of Rose Causey', *Transactions of the Cumberland and Westmorland Antiquarian and Archaeological Society*, new ser., 39 (1938–9), 109–35, esp. 122–34 • P. E. McCullough, *Sermons at court: politics and religion in Elizabethan and Jacobean preaching* (1998) [incl. CD-ROM] • A. R. Maddison, ed., *Lincolnshire pedigrees*, 3, Harleian Society, 52 (1904) • *The manuscripts of his grace the duke of Portland*, 10 vols., HMC, 29 (1891–1931), vol. 9, pp. 23–4 • *Letters of John Holles, 1587–1637*, ed. P. R. Seddon, 1, Thoroton Society Record Series, 31 (1975), 44 • PRO, C 181/2, fol. 14*r* • *The Fortescue papers*, ed. S. R. Gardiner, CS, new ser., 1 (1871), 124–5 • *Fasti Angl.* (Hardy), 3.242

Archives BL, Royal MS 17 B. xxv

Wealth at death £626—in goods: *The Library*, 6th ser., 14 (1992), 254

Snodgrass, Gabriel (*fl.* 1759–1796), naval architect, is a little known figure although his work and views had an important effect on the maintenance and repair of British warships during the late eighteenth and early nineteenth centuries. The earliest mention of him is as an apprentice in a royal dockyard to a Mr Snell, 'builders' measurer'. He then became a working shipwright in the same yard before he joined the East India Company on the recommendation of Benjamin Slade. After some years in Bengal as superintendent of shipping in that port, he returned to England as chief surveyor to the East India Company in 1757.

For the next forty years Snodgrass was in charge of the building or repair of 989 ships for the company, as a result of which he developed strong views on the economic use of timber and extending the life of warships. During this period, which fell between the American War of Independence and the French Revolutionary War, there was considerable concern over the supply of English oak, but Snodgrass believed that there was sufficient given good management of forests and of the conversion of trees to ships' timbers. The ships had to be durable and to this end they were to be built slowly, allowing time for the wood to season. He was one of the first to use iron for beam knees and other brackets and stiffeners. He argued strongly against spending on major repairs though his figures seem exaggerated. He realized that lack of rigidity was the main factor in the decay of wooden ships and proposed stiffening older ships with diagonal braces in the transverse plane and doubling with 3 inch oak planking to increase their shear strength. In 1805 twenty-two line-of-battle ships and eleven frigates were stiffened in this way. This timely reinforcement enabled the main British fleets off the Scheldt, Brest, and Cadiz to meet the Franco-Spanish alliance with approximately equal numbers of ships.

Snodgrass was opposed to excessive tumble home, the inward curvature of the sides above the waterline, as suitable curved timbers were hard to find and those used were often weakened by cutting across the grain. He thought British warships were too small and advocated an increase in length of about 20 feet. It is interesting that for all his criticism of British ships, he saw them as better, in particular stronger, than the French which he referred to as 'ridiculous'. In addition he was one of several designers pointing out the need for covered building slips, but these were not provided until the 1820s.

Of the 989 ships whose building or repair Snodgrass supervised, only one foundered during his time in office. At that time the life of an East Indiaman was about twelve years during which it would make six round voyages to India—the time for a round trip was reduced by two months when they were sheathed with copper. His views were given to a parliamentary committee in 1771 and amplified to another committee in 1791 and, perhaps, finalized in a letter of 1796 to Henry Dundas, president of the Board of Control, which may have marked his retirement. His wife, Mary (*b.* 1732), died at Blackheath in 1788 at the age of fifty-six and was buried at Charlton. They had one son and two daughters.

Snodgrass suggested many other minor but worthwhile improvements. He was rarely the only important shipwright advocating such changes but his position outside the Admiralty made it easier for him to make his ideas known. Nothing is known of his later life or death.

DAVID K. BROWN

Sources J. Sewell, ed., *A collection of papers on naval architecture* (1791) • J. Fincham, *A history of naval architecture* (1857) • R. Morriss, *The royal dockyards during the revolutionary and Napoleonic wars* (1983) • B. Lavery, *Ships of the line*, 2 vols. (1983), vol. 1 • G. Snodgrass, 'On the mode of improving the navy', *Naval Chronicle*, 5 (1801), 129–53 • J. Sutton, *Lords of the east: the East India Company and its ships* (1981)

Snook, William (1861–1916), athlete, was born at Belle Vue, St Julian, Shrewsbury, on 3 February 1861, the son of George Snook, a road surveyor, and his wife, Mary, formerly Corfield. He was educated at Admaston College, Shropshire, and began competing in sprint handicap races at the age of sixteen, but soon found he was better suited to longer distances. It is said that he once ran a mile on a stretch of road in under five minutes wearing 'ordinary shoes'. He took to running in one-mile handicaps and within two years was off scratch in most races. His form attracted Moseley Harriers, a Birmingham club with a reputation for signing talented distance runners, and he joined them at the age of eighteen.

One of Snook's team-mates at Moseley was Walter George, the most outstanding runner of the day, and together the two men helped the club to win the prestigious English cross-country team championship four successive times from 1881 to 1884. In track races, however, they were rivals, and although George won most of their encounters, Snook recorded a number of significant wins. In the 1883 Amateur Athletics Association (AAA) championship he beat George in the 1 and the 4 mile races, and two days later won the 10 miles, a race George did not contest. Snook was again the winner in the one-mile and half-mile races at Widnes three weeks later.

George regained the ascendancy in 1884 and beat Snook in all major races. He then turned professional and left the field open for his rival to establish himself as top amateur. Snook, who moved to Birchfield Harriers, took full advantage, winning the English cross-country race in March 1885, and four titles at the AAA championships in July that year. His fame, however, was short-lived. When he finished second in the cross-country championships at Croydon on 6 March 1886, the AAA officials decided that he had 'thrown' the race for financial gain and suspended him for life from all amateur athletics. Bookmakers played a prominent part in athletics at that time and Snook had been heavily backed to win. The suspension was seen as a move to clean up the sport by making an example of one of its biggest names, and public opinion sided with the AAA.

After his suspension Snook ran as a professional for three years and was the licensee of at least two public houses in Birmingham before moving to France, where he coached runners and cyclists. His wife, Elizabeth Jane Coleman, whom he had married in August 1884, and from whom he was separated, died in 1900, their only child having died in infancy. Snook eventually returned to England in 1916, destitute and in poor health, and was admitted to the Birmingham workhouse infirmary at Erdington. He died there on 9 December 1916 and was buried in a common grave in Witton cemetery, the funeral fees being paid by Birchfield Harriers. WILFRED MORGAN

Sources *Sports Argus* (16 Dec 1916) • P. Lovesey, *The official centenary history of the Amateur Athletics Association* (1979) • *Birmingham Daily Post* (15 Dec 1916) • b. cert. • d. cert. • *Sporting Mirror*

Archives U. Birm., Centre for Sports Science and History, books and magazines

Likenesses photograph, priv. coll. • photograph, repro. in Lovesey, *Official centenary history of the Amateur Athletics Association*

Snow. For this title name *see* individual entries under Snow; *see also* Johnson, Pamela Helen Hansford [Pamela Helen Hansford Snow, Lady Snow] (1912–1981).

Snow, Charles Percy, Baron Snow (1905–1980), writer and scientific administrator, was born at 40 Richmond Road, Leicester, on 15 October 1905, the second of four sons of William Edward Snow (1869–1954) and his wife, Ada Sophia Robinson (1871–1944). William Snow was a clerk in a shoe factory and a church organist.

Education and early career From Miss Martin's grandiloquently christened Beaumanor School of three small rooms he entered, at eleven, Alderman Newton's School for boys, at £5 a term. He excelled at every subject but woodwork and gymnastics, acquiring a reputation for an astonishing memory and, despite needing thick glasses, prowess at football and cricket. He would remain devoted to cricket and found joy in its statistics.

Charles Percy Snow, Baron Snow (1905–1980), by Mark Gerson, 1966

Although he became an external student in science at London University on scholarship in 1923, the Leicester, Leicestershire, and Rutland University College (later Leicester University) had no chemistry or physics department until 1925. Snow bridged the gap as a laboratory assistant at Newton's, reading, meanwhile, the great European novelists from Balzac to Proust. He followed his first-class degree with an MSc degree in 1928 and secured the nationally competitive Keddey-Fletcher-Warr studentship at £200 p.a., using it at Cambridge for research at the Cavendish Laboratory. Snow became a fellow of Christ's College in September 1930, having completed a PhD dissertation, 'The infra-red spectra of simple diatomic molecules'. The 'Cavendish boys', as he called them, were a brilliant generation with whom Snow would work in peace and in war, putting them into his novels in recognizable guises. 'The place', he recalled, 'was stiff with Nobel Prize winners' (Halperin, 18, 21).

From 1934 to 1945 he was a college tutor, although the title became nominal as he moved into other activities, novelizing his experience in *The Search* (1934). He had already written a never-to-be published novel about 'young men and women at a provincial university' (Weintraub, 1). It would be the germ for *Strangers and Brothers* (1940), which begins in a setting much like Leicester as he knew it. Seeing himself not as a breakthrough scientist of the order of some of his Cambridge peers, with his work on infra-red spectroscopy going nowhere (he had already switched to crystallography), he experimented further in fiction. *Death under Sail* (1932) was a detective thriller set near Cambridge on the Norfolk broads, and *New Lives for*

Old (1933)—published anonymously—was science fiction in the manner of H. G. Wells. It combined two of his interests, biological chemistry and politics, and imagined the social and political repercussions of the discovery of a rejuvenating hormone. *The Search* proved more prophetic of his future, as it dealt with the morality of science and the pursuit of a scientific career (as opposed to the search for scientific truth).

In the mid-thirties—Snow recalled 1 January 1935—he began *Strangers and Brothers*, the title becoming the eponymous *George Passant* when he borrowed the original for his cycle of eleven novels drawing upon his own experience through the later 1960s. As a scientist, he later conceded, 'I should never have been much better than a goodish orthodox English professional—probably looking a bit better than I was because I'm bright' (Halperin, 53). Writing seemed a better path. While at Cambridge he began publishing general scientific articles in *Nature* in 1934 and in *The Spectator* in 1936, and became editor of *Discovery* ('the popular journal of knowledge') in 1937, taking it in April 1938 to Cambridge University Press, where he drew distinguished contributors.

Administrative and political career One of Snow's *Discovery* editorials in 1939 predicted an atomic bomb, a subject he regretted raising when the Second World War broke out, an event which interrupted his novel cycle just as it was emerging into print. *Discovery* itself became a wartime casualty in March 1940, when Snow was already involved in a group organized by the Royal Society to deploy British scientific talent, operating under the Ministry of Labour. By 1942 Snow was its director of technical personnel. Working under Lord Hankey, chairman of the cabinet's scientific advisory committee, Snow expedited the mobilizing of scientists for work on radar, the atomic bomb, and other high-priority military technology.

As the urgency abated, Snow became a civil service commissioner in charge of recruiting scientists to post-war government work. He also returned to writing. A director of English Electric by the late 1940s, he remained part-time until he entered the government in 1964. For his public services he had already become CBE in 1943, and a knight in 1957. In 1964 he became a life peer as Baron Snow of the city of Leicester when he joined Harold Wilson's first government as parliamentary secretary of the newly created (but soon to vanish) Ministry of Technology. When the ministry ceased to exist on the demise of the Wilson regime, Snow became an outspoken back-bencher in the Lords. There he continued what he was already doing in fiction and in public life to interpret science to the laity, and to create a recognition of the crucial role of technology to humanity's future.

'The two cultures' Snow had remained in the public eye through his fiction, book criticism for the *Sunday Times*, and thoughtful pieces for a variety of intellectual weeklies on both sides of the Atlantic. His most influential essay appeared in the *New Statesman* (6 October 1956). In 'The two cultures' he charged that ignorance of modern science by professed humanists was as harmful to society as ignorance of the arts ('the traditional culture') by narrowly focused scientists. The ensuing controversy led to his Rede lectures at Cambridge, *The Two Cultures and the Scientific Revolution* (1959), in which Snow contended that the imaginative insights once the monopoly of philosophers, theologians, and artists were no longer sufficient to accommodate a world in irreversible scientific and technological change.

Continuing to espouse the reorientation of perspectives in education and in decision making, Snow delivered the Godkin lectures at Harvard in 1960, published in 1961 with a postscript as *Science and Government*. Here he warned against the undue influence which scientists with political agendas acquire when political leaders are ignorant of science, pointing to examples from his experience in the Second World War.

Again his message was that the political misunderstandings of the technologically illiterate were as dangerous as the misuse of science, a contention he laid out cogently before the American Association for the Advancement of Science (27 December 1960), published widely thereafter as 'The moral un-neutrality of science'. The doctrine of the ethical independence of science, he argued, could not be sustained, and constituted moral blindness. Whatever the aesthetic elegance of its claimed purity, science in its applications impacted upon society. The 'moral nature of the scientific activity' required moral responsibility.

Inevitably, attacks followed from scientists unwilling to grant any impurity to basic research, and from humanists who saw Snow's inclusive view of culture as debasing values. The most notorious tirade came in the Richmond lecture of F. R. Leavis in 1962, which saw relationships between Snow's pragmatism and the allegedly pedestrian prose of his novels—charges which injured Snow's reputation and clouded Leavis's already controversial reputation as provocateur. Snow's public life went on. His Trollopian novel cycle was still incomplete and his honours had not yet been capped by his peerage.

Personal life Although his affairs with women became grist for his novels, two women whom Snow would subsume into the later fiction did not even enter his life until the sequence was plotted out. Anne Seagrim had been his post-war secretary, and close companion, but their intimacy had been interrupted in 1949 by Pamela Helen Hansford *Johnson (1912–1981), a novelist, then married, whom he had first met in 1941. Known to family and friends by his middle name, he became Charles to Pamela, and kept to it thereafter. After divorcing her first husband, Gordon Stewart, she married Snow on 14 July 1950. (The marriage seemed personally and professionally a success, but in 1957 Snow began seeing Anne Seagrim again. His wife apparently never knew.)

The only child of the Snows, Philip Charles Hansford, was born on 26 August 1952 in Cambridge. They had lived at 20 Hyde Park Place in London with Pamela's two children from her earlier marriage; with the addition to the family imminent they moved to Nethergate, a Jacobean house in the Suffolk village of Clare. (Snow retained a flat for business weekdays in London.) The arrangement failed as neither could drive a car and Pamela felt isolated from the literary scene. In January 1957 they returned to London, leasing the ground floor at 199 Cromwell Road, which they retained until 1968 when, with mounting book earnings and literary status as well as his peerage demanding a more appropriate address, they purchased the lease of 85 Eaton Terrace in Belgravia. The novel cycle was near its close; Snow was overwhelmed by lecturing requests and offers of honorary doctorates; he had become rector of St Andrews University in 1961; he was about to begin a decade of influential weekly reviews for the *Financial Times*. Snow was offered the *Sunday Times* post after writing to Leonard Russell, (who thought he looked like 'everyone's idea of a wizard scientist'): 'For an art to consist of a popular entertainment side and an esoteric prestige side is in the long run death … Books are meant to be read' (H. Hobson, P. Knightley, and L. Russell, *Pearl of Days: an Intimate Memoir of the 'Sunday Times', 1822–1972*, 1972, 222–5). Snow's owlish, spectacled face, heavy jowls, bald dome, and ponderous frame, often accoutered in a shapeless suit, and his inevitable cigarette in hand, were recognizable worldwide.

Snow's novel series The eleventh and final novel of *Strangers and Brothers* appeared in 1970. As early as 1945 he had envisioned a sequence of eleven interrelated fictions with a single narrative voice—a lawyer-bureaucrat and *alter ego*, Lewis Eliot. In various forms, some later discarded, he completed nearly a third of the cycle while the war went on, writing confidently to his brother Philip that March: 'Each of the novels, except perhaps Vol XI, will be intelligible if read separately, but the series is planned as one integral work of art and I should like it so considered and judged' (Snow, 102). Although he planned then to depict a variety of characters from 1920 into 1950, 'from the dispossessed to Cabinet Ministers' (ibid.), and to finish the cycle in five years, events in his life and the need to dismantle portions of the work and reconfigure it kept him writing into the later 1960s, with the narrative running into 1965 and even beyond. In *Last Things* (1970) there is even, as appendix, an 'Announcements—1964–1968', ostensibly in most cases from *The Times*—marriage and birth and death notices for plot strands unaccommodated in the final pages.

In the letter to his brother, Snow had added,

> For each major character, the narrator is occupied with the questions: How much of his fate is due to the accident of his class and time? … All the societal backgrounds are authentic. I have lived in most of them myself; and one or two I have not lived in I know at very close second-hand. (Snow, 102)

Only the first novel had then been published. *The Light and the Dark*, set in the immediate pre-war and early war years, appeared in 1947, and focused upon a manic-depressive but brilliant scholar of Manichaean texts (thus the title) who becomes a bomber pilot in the hope he will be killed. *Time of Hope* (1949) reached back into Eliot's Snow-like early years, and *The Masters* (1951), possibly the most admired work in the series, may be the best academic novel in English. Using the microcosmic world of a Cambridge college in the throes of electing a new master, Snow fashioned memorable portraits of the ambitious and those conspiring on behalf of others, and laid bare the ramifications of power. Externally, the year is 1937 and the political context is that of appeasement and imminent war, the outside world mirroring what Snow called the 'ironic sadness' of the conclusion.

The New Men (1954), fifth to be published, covers the years 1939 to 1946, from the planning for an atomic bomb to the aftermath of Hiroshima and Nagasaki. Moral and career crises intertwine. The major figure is Eliot's politically radical younger brother Martin, whose relationship to a scientist about to defect creates a crisis larger, as it is personal, than the bomb, which is beyond individual control. Implicit in the narrative is the relationship of the American Oppenheimer brothers, Robert and Frank. *Homecomings* (the final letter is omitted in American editions), published two years later, continued the narrator's own story as begun in *Time of Hope*. While the first was in the tradition of man-from-the-provinces novels, and focused upon the conflicts between possessive love and lust for power, perhaps related drives, *Homecomings* concerns ambition and failure, the latter coming early when the unhappy heroine, Eliot's wife, is a suicide. The novel then returns to Eliot's bureaucratic ambitions in wartime, his falling in love again, this time with a married woman, and, after their marriage, the dangerous illness of their child (Snow's novels are full of medical matters), which brings Eliot to consider the relative values of ambition and love.

As traditional in craftsmanship as the others, *The Conscience of the Rich*, finished much earlier, appeared finally in 1958. Based upon a wealthy and talented Anglo-Jewish family to which Snow was close in the 1930s, the novel concerns what Eliot called in *Time of Hope* 'the sick conscience of the rich'—or liberal guilt (Halperin, 65). 'It was the sort of thing', Snow recalled in an interview, 'which fairly prosperous people in the thirties in particular felt rather acutely—that they oughtn't to be rich, and that if they were rich then they ought to be doing something other than what they were doing'. Rich in its domestic atmosphere, it also closely mirrors the external world—it is the period of the Spanish Civil War and the rise of Nazism. Already involved are the sophisticated Marches. Eliot is mesmerized by them, 'fascinated by the sheer machinery of their lives. They were the first rich family I had known. In those first months it was their wealth that took my attention more, not their Jewishness'.

The Affair (1960) returns to the internal politics of Eliot's college as the fellows, many of them mediocrities if not drones, consider what to do about a brilliant—and politically radical—young colleague who, in his rush to forge a career, apparently fakes some of his scientific results. In the twenties and thirties Snow knew such cases, especially the notorious Rupp affair in German physics, but his title, to hint at prejudice beyond science, comes from the Dreyfus affair. Since literal justice requires killing off a more-than-promising career, the quality of justice is central; however, the intrusion of politics into judgements remains a Snow theme.

The title of Snow's ninth novel, *The Corridors of Power* (1964) was to enter the language. Again public and private concerns interact, this time on the ministerial level during the mid-1950s, including the period of Suez, but the public issue, Snow confides in a prefatory note, turns on an 'unresolvable complication'. Eliot, largely here an observer, listens to the ambitious Roger Quaife, whose philosophy is 'The first thing is to get power. The next—is to do something with it'.

Tenth in the cycle was *The Sleep of Reason* (1968), based upon the notorious moors murders that appalled Britain in 1965–6. The novel was as close to a collaboration as spousal authors can achieve without actually writing the same book, as Pamela covered the trial for the *Sunday Telegraph*, publishing afterwards a non-fiction account, *On Iniquity* (1967). Taking his title from a Goya caption to a series of phantasmagoric etchings, 'The sleep of reason produces monsters', Snow fictionalized the repellent material, adding some echoes of the Loeb and Leopold case that mesmerized Chicago in the 1920s—two young homosexuals had sought the near-sexual thrill of killing someone. A powerful near-Dostoevskian novel that returns to the cycle some of its earliest protagonists, it finds Eliot drawn into the case by his unreliable friend George Passant. The book broods upon the doctrine of 'diminished responsibility' and its application to crimes as relatively minor as the case in question but applicable even to Auschwitz. 'Morality', Eliot reflects, 'existed only in action'. Its theme harks back to *The Light and the Dark*.

After nearly 2 million words, the cycle ended with *Last Things* (1970), which brought closure to its characters if not to the questions which Snow had raised, and included an event as autobiographical as any he had written. Eliot 'dies'—but only, his doctor tells him, for 'between three-and-a-half and three-and-three-quarters minutes'. As Eliot was undergoing surgery for a detached retina, his heart had stopped and his chest had to be opened to massage the muscle back into activity. 'Now you know', the surgeon adds. 'I bring you no news from the other world', Eliot responds grimly from beneath his bandages. And the experience—actually its aftermath—reshapes his values about public and private behaviour.

Last years The experience of cardiac arrest was Snow's own, as was the eye surgery, even to the date, as in the novel, of 28 November 1965. He could not forget thereafter, as he confided in an interview, that the nearly four minutes in the beyond were beyond memory as 'Nothing, absolutely nothing' (Halperin, 224). He remained 'a pious unbeliever' (ibid., 10).

Compulsively, Snow kept writing, both fiction and non-fiction. Three further novels appeared—*The Malcontents* (1972), *In their Wisdom* (1974), and *A Coat of Varnish* (1978). His non-fiction included a short life of Trollope (1974), and two biographical collections: *The Realists: Portraits of Eight Novelists* (1975), and posthumously, *The Physicists: a Generation that Changed the World* (1981), both in the vein of his earlier *Variety of Men* (1967), which included memories of friends and acquaintances such as Rutherford, G. H. Hardy, and Einstein. Poor health plagued him but he continued to travel and lecture. Returning from his last American visit in 1978, both he and Pamela had to be deplaned in wheelchairs. Still he remained active as writer and critic until hospitalized on 1 July 1980, dying that afternoon of a perforated ulcer. A private cremation took place three days later at Putney Vale, London. No portraits were painted of Snow, who claimed to be too busy for sittings.

As novelist, Snow will be remembered largely for his *Strangers and Brothers* cycle, its rather flat style mirroring its narrator, who observes, from the inside, English society and politics from the First World War to Suez. His civil servant role during the Second World War was sensitive, secret, and seemingly successful. As a philosopher of science and social organization he publicized in memorable language, and in ways only a highly visible personality could do, some key issues of modern technological civilization, bestriding, and interpreting to each other, the 'two cultures'. STANLEY WEINTRAUB

Sources *DNB* • P. Snow, *Stranger and brother: a portrait of C. P. Snow* (1982) • J. Halperin, *C. P. Snow: an oral biography* (1983) • J. Thale, *C. P. Snow* (1965) • P. Hansford Johnson, *Important to me: personalia* (1974) • S. Weintraub, ed., *C. P. Snow: a spectrum* (1963) • D. Schusterman, *C. P. Snow* (1975) • private information (2004) [P. Snow] • m. cert.

Archives Eton, letters • Ransom HRC, corresp. and literary papers | BBC WAC, television contributors, file 1 • Bodl. Oxf., letters to Jack W. Lambert • CUL, corresp. with W. A. Gerhardie; corresp. with A. V. Hill; letters to Gordon Sutherland • RS, Blackett MSS • U. Birm. L., corresp. with Francis Brett Young; letters to Jessica Brett Young • University of Bristol Library, DM 1107 | FILM BFI NFTVA | SOUND BL NSA • Hunt. L., tapes of Halperin oral history

Likenesses M. Gerson, photograph, 1966, NPG [*see illus.*]

Wealth at death £312,677: probate, 4 Sept 1980, *CGPLA Eng. & Wales*

Snow, Sir Frederick Sidney [Freddie] (**1899–1976**), civil engineer, was born at 2 Caffyn Street, Lambeth, London, on 14 February 1899, the third son of the three sons and two daughters of William Snow, a printer's labourer, and his wife, Sarah Byron, *née* Holmes. He was educated at Brownhill School in Catford, London, leaving at the age of fourteen for manual work as a stone dresser at a pepper mill. In 1914 he joined the Royal Horse Artillery, serving in France in both the artillery and the Royal Engineers before demobilization in 1919. He was twice seriously wounded. On returning to civilian life Snow began his lifelong career in engineering with five years' training in Ipswich. In 1924 he was employed by the large building and civil engineering contracting firm of Holland and Hannen and Cubitts Ltd in London. There the chief engineer recognized his potential. He was sent to classes in the relatively new field of reinforced concrete design at the Regent Street Polytechnic in London, and as his confidence increased he was soon given increased responsibility. On 20 September 1924 he married (Rosetta) Elizabeth Brown (*b.* 1900/01), daughter of Edmund Alfred Brown, a customs officer, of Colchester, Essex. They had two sons, and a daughter who died in infancy.

During his nineteen years in contracting Snow became

an acknowledged expert, first on the timbering of deep excavations, then on foundations in general, particularly those in the London area. In 1936 he wrote 'Foundations of London structures', published in *Structural Engineer*, establishing an ability to express cogent views which could command respect. Before the Second World War there were still many social barriers in place within the construction industries. On the one hand were workmen, craftsmen, and managers; on the other were clients, consulting engineers, and academics. It was generally supposed that the former would confine themselves to strictly practical applications and commercial implications of actual projects while the latter would contribute analysis and conceptual thinking to engineering's professional bodies. In September 1942 Snow wrote a remarkable paper entitled 'Human needs and the engineer' (*Structural Engineer*, 20, 139–73) which was based on his experience in contracting on a number of important works. His paper covered, with great penetration and wide vision, the historical background and current realities of the motivations of labour and of management in the implementation of large construction projects. It was a paper which could be read with both pleasure and profit decades later and illustrated the qualities which made him a great and well-loved figure, uniquely spanning both the practical and commercial world and the professional engineering establishment.

In 1943 Snow founded his own firm of consulting engineers. His services were much in demand in his profession and he acted as a design consultant on a large number of reinforced concrete projects, becoming an authority on heavy foundation and underpinning problems. In 1944 he was engaged on the design of the de Havilland airfield at Hatfield, Hertfordshire. He subsequently gave a paper to the Institution of Civil Engineers (*Airport Paper* no. 12, 1950) detailing the project and giving a wealth of theoretical and practical information. His firm grew and prospered, becoming Frederick S. Snow & Partners in 1951, and branches were established in Norwich and Newcastle upon Tyne. He attracted such partners as G. F. Brian Scruby, who succeeded him as senior partner, and Sir Norman Payne, subsequently chairman of the British Airports Authority, and his firm's growing reputation brought it many notable commissions. It was responsible for the design and supervision of construction of many important airports throughout the world, especially in the Middle East: at Jerusalem, Amman, and Kuwait. But of greatest note, in the mid-1950s, was Gatwick airport where a fine result was achieved, both technically and visually. Working with F. R. S. Yorke and his firm (Yorke, Rosenberg, and Mardall) the 'finger' solution to the loading bays problem enabled subsequent extensions of the airport to be carried out with the least possible interference to existing air traffic. In 1959 Snow presented (co-authored) articles on Gatwick airport development to both *Structural Engineer* and the *Proceedings of the Institution of Civil Engineers*. For both his Institution of Civil Engineers papers on airports he was awarded a Telford premium. The development of Newcastle airport and the London Press Centre were among his firm's projects in the 1960s. In 1965 he published *Formwork for Modern Structures*.

Snow himself was by this time an important figure in the world of technology. He had been awarded the London prize of the Institution of Structural Engineers in 1936 and 1942 and was its president in 1948. He was president of the British section of the Société des Ingénieurs Civils de France in 1955 and of the Reinforced Concrete Association in 1956. In 1966, with the establishment of the Concrete Society, it was natural that Freddie Snow, as he was universally known, should be invited to be its first president. He was a member of the Association of Consulting Engineers and a fellow of the Institution of Mechanical Engineers, the Institute of Arbitrators, and the American Society of Civil Engineers. He was also a member of the permanent committee of the International Association for Bridge and Structural Engineering as well as serving on all major building and civil engineering committees of the British Standards Institution. He was a governor of Hammersmith College of Art and Building and a life vice-president of the Guild of Surveyors. In 1972 he was master of the Worshipful Company of Glaziers and Painters of Glass. He was also highly honoured, for he was appointed OBE in 1954 and CBE in 1958, and in 1965 he was knighted. He won the Istiqlal medal of Jordan in 1968 and was made a chevalier of the Légion d'honneur in 1969. In 1974 he was made an honorary LLD at Leeds University. Snow died on 5 June 1976 at his home, 11 Linkswood, Compton Place Road, Eastbourne, Sussex.

F. A. Sharman, *rev.* Robert Sharp

Sources personal knowledge (1986) • private information (1986) • *WWW* • *The Times* (8 June 1976), 16g • *Sir Frederick Snow & Partners, consulting engineers, 1943–1968* (1968) • b. cert. • m. cert. • d. cert. • *CGPLA Eng. & Wales* (1976)

Wealth at death £39,732: probate, 31 Dec 1976, *CGPLA Eng. & Wales*

Snow, Herbert. *See* Kynaston, Herbert (1835–1910).

Snow, John (1813–1858), anaesthetist and epidemiologist, was born on 15 March 1813 at North Street, York, the eldest of the nine children of William Snow (1783–1846) and his wife, Frances Askham (1789–1860). At the time of Snow's birth his father was a labourer, but he later became a farmer and in 1841 moved to a farm in Rawcliffe, outside York. Snow's early education included the learning of Latin, and at fourteen he was apprenticed to William Hardcastle, a surgeon apothecary in Newcastle upon Tyne. In 1831 Hardcastle was appointed to attend the poor during the cholera epidemic of 1831–2, and Snow treated the miners at Killingworth colliery. It was his first encounter with the disease that was to occupy much of his professional life. Snow attended sessions at the Newcastle school of medicine in 1832–3, and on completing his apprenticeship he became assistant, first to Mr Watson, general practitioner in Burnopfield, and then to Joseph Warburton, general practitioner in Pateley Bridge. Snow had become a vegetarian during his apprenticeship after reading several scientific works on the subject. In 1836 he joined the York Temperance Society, and in 1845 he became secretary of the Medical Temperance Society,

John Snow (1813–1858), by unknown photographer, *c.*1856

which was established by a group of London doctors including Richard Hicks. However, when his health began to deteriorate both he and his friends attributed his illnesses to his diet and he returned to eating animal products and drinking wine in the mid-1840s.

In October 1836 Snow enrolled at the Great Windmill Street school of medicine in London, and he shared lodgings at 11 Bateman's Buildings, Soho Square, with a fellow medical student, Joshua Parsons. Six months' surgical practice at Westminster Hospital completed Snow's training and he became a member of the Royal College of Surgeons in May 1838 and a licentiate of the Society of Apothecaries in the following October. He had applied for the post of apothecary to the Westminster Hospital in July 1838 but failed to obtain it, as the by-laws of the hospital stated it could be held only by a member of the Society of Apothecaries; Snow had been prevented from sitting the examination in July rather than in October, because the society refused to recognize the twelve months' hospital practice he had undertaken in Newcastle. In September 1838 Snow moved to 54 Frith Street, Soho, and set up in practice, while also working in the out-patient department of Charing Cross Hospital and as a medical officer at several sick clubs. In 1845 he became a lecturer in forensic medicine at the Aldersgate school of medicine, though his appointment was short-lived as the school closed in 1848. He kept busy with sick-club and dispensary work, but his private practice did not become well-established until the late 1840s and the arrival of anaesthesia. Snow continued his progress up the hierarchy of medical qualifications by gaining his MB (1843) and MD (1844) from the University of London, and he became a member of the Royal College of Physicians in 1850.

Snow believed he owed his successful practice in London and his medical achievements to his early connection with the Westminster Medical Society, which merged with the Medical Society of London in 1851. He had joined the society in 1837 while still a student and he became its orator in 1853 and its president in 1855. He was also a member of the Medico-Chirurgical Society and held committee posts at both societies from 1844 onwards. He was one of the first members of the Epidemiological Society, founded in 1850, and he served on its council with other notable individuals such as Thomas Addison, Richard Bright, Benjamin Brodie, and Charles Hastings. He was a vigorous debater at society meetings; as early as 1838 he challenged the views of Edward Lonsdale, anatomy demonstrator at the Middlesex Hospital, on the anatomy of the recti muscles. He contributed regularly to medical journals and of particular relevance to his later work on anaesthesia are 'On the effects of carbonic acid', (1839) and 'On asphyxia and the resuscitation of newborn children', (1841), both published in the *London Medical Gazette*. He devised several new instruments, including a pump that could be used for artificial respiration, in 1841, and a trocar and cannula for removing fluid from the chest while avoiding the entry of air, so preventing the collapse of the lung, in 1844.

Among Snow's closest medical friends were Sir Benjamin Ward Richardson, who wrote the first memoir (J. Snow, *On Chloroform*, 'Memoir'); Edwin Lankester, who supported him during the investigation into the cholera outbreak in Broad Street in 1854; and John French, medical officer to Poland Street workhouse from 1830 to 1872. He was also particularly attached to Charles Empson, his mother's brother. Empson, a fine-art dealer, lived in Newcastle during Snow's apprenticeship years and then moved to Bath, where Snow visited him in 1836 while travelling from York to London on foot. Empson also accompanied Snow to Paris in 1856. There Snow (unsuccessfully) entered a copy of his treatise on cholera in a competition at the Medical Institute and was introduced to Emperor Napoleon III.

Snow witnessed the use of ether only nine days after James Robinson had first used it in Britain, for a tooth extraction on 19 December 1846. By mid-January 1847 Snow had used his knowledge of chemistry to research the scientific principles of the inhalation process and the effects of the inhalation of ether on the body's physiological responses. He recognized that an efficient inhaler, which allowed the control of vapour strength, was fundamental to the safe administration of any anaesthetic agent and he went on to develop several instruments. Once he had established the principles of ether administration he lost no time in gaining practical experience. By early February 1847 he had administered ether at St George's Hospital, London, for eight surgical operations.

This marked the start of a successful career as an anaesthetist and he quickly developed a specialist practice working in many London hospitals and with some of the most eminent surgeons of the period, including Robert Liston, William Fergusson, and Caesar Hawkins.

In August 1847 Snow produced his definitive ether inhaler and in October he published *On the Inhalation of the Vapour of Ether in Surgical Operations* (1847). This short work was greeted favourably by reviewers and encouraged him to write a series of eighteen papers in the *London Medical Gazette* between 1848 and 1851 which described experiments with a wide range of anaesthetic agents. One of his most important legacies to anaesthetics was his description of the five identifiable stages of the anaesthetic process. His intention was to provide doctors with the ability to interpret the patient's physiological signs and to adjust the administration of vapour accordingly.

In November 1847 James Young Simpson publicized the use of chloroform, and within a week Snow had carried out experiments on animals, prepared a table on the quantity of chloroform that air would hold at different temperatures, and had himself inhaled the substance. He adopted the use of chloroform without hesitation, though he always held that ether was the safer agent, and he spent much time researching a whole range of possible anaesthetic agents with a view to finding one which combined the efficacy of chloroform with the safety of ether. His experimental research into anaesthesia established administration techniques, technical apparatus, and the overall margins of risk within the procedure. These remained as the first foundations of the specialism. Snow's reputation for safety and skill led to the successful administration of chloroform to Queen Victoria during the births of Prince Leopold (1853) and Princess Beatrice (1857). Given the debate which surrounded the safety of chloroform, and its justification in childbirth, Snow's attendance presented no small professional risk.

Snow's contribution to the establishment of the specialty of epidemiology is also well-recognized, and he is remembered primarily in this context for the discovery that cholera was a waterborne infection. *On the Mode of Communication of Cholera*, which described his theory, received little acclaim from the medical world when it was published in 1849. The second edition (1855) contained statistical evidence which he had compiled from the 1854 outbreak of cholera in Broad Street, London, and from his investigations into the supply of water to south London by the water companies of Southwark and Vauxhall, and of Lambeth. The Broad Street cholera outbreak began on 31 August and claimed over 500 lives in ten days. At its start Snow began to consider the local water supplies, and he suspected contamination of the water pump in Broad Street. He took a list of deaths from cholera from the General Register Office and mapped the location of these deaths around the locality. His analysis showed that the majority of deaths had taken place in the vicinity of the Broad Street pump and he presented this evidence to the local board of guardians. The handle of the Broad Street pump was removed, but although this incident has been recorded as the dramatic halt of the outbreak this was not the case, as the intensity of the epidemic was already receding. What is important about the event is that Snow's evidence succeeded in forcing local government action. A cholera inquiry committee was eventually set up by the parish to investigate the outbreak further, and with the help of Edwin Lankester and Henry Whitehead, the local curate, the original source of contamination of the water pump at the commencement of the outbreak was identified.

Snow's interest in water supplies to south London stemmed from the 1849 epidemic, when he noted that cholera fatality rates were particularly high in the areas supplied by the Lambeth and the Southwark and Vauxhall water companies. In 1852 the Lambeth company moved its waterworks to Thames Ditton, thus obtaining a supply of water quite free from the sewage of London. Snow undertook an investigation to calculate the number of deaths from cholera per 10,000 houses during the first seven weeks of the 1854 epidemic. He recognized the scope presented by such an epidemiological experiment, as it would include 300,000 individuals of both sexes, of varying ages and occupations, and from all social classes. His initial conclusions found that 38 houses out of the 44 where deaths from cholera had occurred were supplied with water by the Southwark and Vauxhall water company and he communicated these facts to William Farr. Farr ordered his registrars of all south districts of London to make a return of the water supply for all houses where there had been a death from cholera. The conclusion of this investigation was that the mortality rate for the houses supplied by the Southwark and Vauxhall company was between eight and nine times greater than houses supplied by the Lambeth company. This investigation was an excellent demonstration of collaborative working between practitioners in medicine and those in the newly emerging social sciences. Snow was unable to obtain the proof he required through traditional medical science, so he turned to the new public health data sources to provide evidence for his argument.

Snow contended that his two investigations completely substantiated his theory, but this was not the view of the medical world at large. Reviewers conceded the importance and quality of his work, but could not accept that, in most cases, infected water was a primary source of the disease. It was only in the twentieth century that the accuracy of Snow's theory, and the quality of his epidemiological investigations, became widely appreciated. His writings on other public health issues, such as the adulteration of food, demonstrate his belief that epidemiology had a vital role to play in raising the quality of human life.

Snow's health had been poor since the 1840s and on 10 June 1858, while completing *On Chloroform and other Anaesthetics* (1858), he suffered a stroke. His condition deteriorated and he died (unmarried) on 16 June that year, at his home at 18 Sackville Street, Piccadilly, London, where he had lived since 1852. His brother, William, was present at his death. Post-mortem examination showed evidence of old pulmonary tuberculosis and advanced renal disease. Snow was buried in Brompton cemetery, London, on 21 June 1858. STEPHANIE J. SNOW

Sources J. Snow, *On chloroform and other anaesthetics: their action and administration*, ed. B. W. Richardson (1858) [with a 'Memoir' by the ed.] • S. J. Snow, 'John Snow MD, 1813–1858: the emergence of the medical profession', PhD diss., University of Keele, 1995 • R. Ellis, ed., *The casebooks of Dr John Snow* (1994) • University of British Columbia, Vancouver, Woodward Biomedical Library, The Clover/ Snow Collection, Section VIII, John Snow, items 1–11 • Medical Temperance Society Circular, 1845, University of Central Lancashire, Joseph Livesey Collection

Archives RCP Lond. • St George's Hospital, London • University of British Columbia Library, Woodward Biomedical Library • Wellcome L.

Likenesses T. J. Barker, oils, 1847, priv. coll. • photograph, *c*.1856, NPG [*see illus.*] • photograph, *c*.1857–1858, repro. in Ellis, ed., *The casebooks of Dr John Snow* • S. Poynter, plaster bust (after photograph), probably Wellcome L.

Wealth at death under £1500: resworn probate, Dec 1859, *CGPLA Eng. & Wales* (1858)

Snow, Sir Thomas D'Oyly (1858–1940), army officer, was born at Newton Valence, Hampshire, on 5 May 1858, the eldest son of the Revd George D'Oyly Snow (*c*.1818–1885) of Langton Lodge, Blandford, and his wife, Maria Jane, the daughter of Robert Barlow. After attending Eton College (1871–4) he went in 1878 to St John's College, Cambridge. In 1879 he obtained a direct commission in the 13th foot (Somerset light infantry), then in South Africa, and saw active service in the Anglo-Zulu War.

Snow served with the mounted infantry regiment of the camel corps in the Nile campaign of 1884–5, and was severely wounded at Gubat (19 January 1885). He was promoted captain in 1887, and attended the Staff College (1892–3). In 1895 he was appointed a brigade major at Aldershot, and, after promotion in 1897 to major in the Royal Inniskilling Fusiliers, accompanied Major-General W. F. Gatacre as his brigade major in the Nile campaign of 1898 (Atbara). He received a brevet lieutenant-colonelcy, and in April 1899 was transferred to the 2nd battalion Northamptonshire regiment as second in command, and so was in India throughout the Second South African War period. He returned home on promotion to substantive lieutenant-colonel in March 1903 but never commanded his battalion, for in June he was promoted colonel and appointed assistant quartermaster-general of the 4th corps (subsequently renamed the eastern command). There he remained until 1914, as assistant adjutant-general (1905) and later brigadier-general, general staff (1906), until October 1909, when he was given command of the 11th infantry brigade. He held it only a few months, being promoted major-general in March 1910.

Early in 1911 Snow became general officer commanding, 4th division. In this appointment his gifts for training and command of troops were clearly manifest. He concentrated on making junior officers criticize each other's work, on movement by night, on march discipline, and on concealment from the air, and produced a set of standing orders for war which were used by other divisions in the 1914–18 war. The 4th division, detained in England for a few days to guard the east coast, had its first battle at Le Cateau, where Snow, agreeing with General Sir H. L. Smith-Dorrien that they must fight, covered the left flank of the 2nd corps, and then successfully brought away his division.

During the battle of the Marne Snow's tired horse (he was a big man of 6 feet 4 inches) fell and rolled on him, and cracked his pelvis; before he had completely recovered, at Kitchener's request he took command in November 1914 of the newly formed 27th division of regular troops from overseas garrisons. When the Germans launched the first gas attack in April 1915 Snow was the only divisional general with headquarters east of Ypres, and to him fell in a great measure the conduct of the defence. The same year he was promoted to the command of the 7th corps. Allegedly he was more scared of general headquarters and Haig than of the enemy. In 1916 Haig ordered Snow to attack Gommecourt with two divisions (46 and 56) as a diversion to the main Somme assault, to capture the salient, meet the counter-attack, and inflict heavy casualties. With inadequate artillery and arguably too few infantry, on 1 July the attackers met uncut wire and enfilading machine-gun fire, and suffered heavy casualties. The attack failed and, possibly as a scapegoat for Snow, Major-General the Hon. Stuart-Wortley (general officer commanding, 46 division) was sent home. In the battles of Arras in 1917 Snow's corps was engaged as right wing of the Third Army. At the battle of Cambrai (November–December 1917) it was the right pivot of the operations, and unfortunately Snow's warnings of the German counter-attack were either overlooked or disregarded. The effects of his fall at the Marne were lasting, his lameness had increased, and as the winter of 1917–18 approached he requested to be relieved, and was appointed general officer commanding-in-chief, western command at home, and promoted lieutenant-general. He resigned in September 1919. Forced to use a bath chair, he left Blandford and settled in Kensington, where he devoted much time to charitable work and became chairman of the Crippled Boys' Home for Training. He married on 12 January 1897 Charlotte Geraldine, second daughter of Major-General John Talbot Coke of Trusley, Derbyshire, and they had two sons and two daughters. Snow was appointed CB in 1907, KCB in 1915, and KCMG in 1917. From 1919 to 1929 he was colonel of the Somerset light infantry. He died at his home, 3 Kensington Gate, London, on 30 August 1940.

J. E. EDMONDS, *rev.* ROGER T. STEARN

Sources *The Times* (31 Aug 1940) • personal knowledge (1949) • J. E. Edmonds, ed., *Military operations, France and Belgium, 1917*, 3, History of the Great War (1948) • T. Wilson, *The myriad faces of war: Britain and the Great War, 1914–1918* (1986) • T. Travers, *The killing ground* (1990) • *The Eton register*, 4 (privately printed, Eton, 1907) • *WWW, 1929–40* • Burke, *Peerage* (1931) • Venn, *Alum. Cant.* • Foster, *Alum. Oxon.*

Archives IWM • Lpool RO, account of Cambrai action of 1917 and corresp.

Wealth at death £15,531 9*s*. 0*d*.: resworn probate, 26 Oct 1940, *CGPLA Eng. & Wales*

Snow, William Parker (1817–1895), mariner and explorer, son of a naval officer, was born at Poole, Dorset, on 27

November 1817. His father died in 1826, leaving the family ill provided for; his mother took the family to Jersey and Normandy, leaving William behind at the Royal Hospital school, Greenwich. Four years later he was sent as apprentice in a small brig bound to Calcutta. The hardships of life at sea sickened him, and at the age of sixteen he decided to emigrate to Canada; the project, however, fell through, and he was obliged to ship on board a barque bound to Australia. At Sydney he got employment in a shop, but, tiring of that and getting into bad company, fled into the bush, where he led a wild life. He returned to Sydney in extreme want, got a berth on board a cargo ship, and returned to England in 1836. His mother was dead, his family and friends dispersed. He fell again into bad company, lost all his money, and entered on board a ship of war. The restraint was irksome, and he deserted; he was arrested, sent on board, and punished.

After a year's service on the coast of Africa Snow obtained his discharge—in reward, it is said, for jumping overboard to save a man from a shark. On his return to England he began to write for the papers, and met with some success. But he was robbed of all his money, and for a time suffered from blindness. When he recovered he married a young woman as poor as himself. They raised enough to emigrate to Melbourne, where they became managers of a hotel. After initial success, Snow's health broke down, and after many wanderings they returned to England where Snow became an amanuensis to several people, including Macaulay, for whom he transcribed the first two volumes of the *History*.

After a year in America, Snow returned to England in 1850 to volunteer for one of the expeditions in search of Sir John Franklin, prompted by a dream, which he believed had shown him the true route. The idea came to dominate his whole life. He served in 1850 as purser, doctor, and chief officer of the *Prince Albert*, a small vessel fitted out at the expense of Lady Franklin, under Commander C. C. Forsyth RN. On his return Snow published *Voyage of the Prince Albert in Search of Sir John Franklin* (1851) and was awarded the polar medal. He was convinced that success had been hindered by Forsyth's refusal to go on, and during the following years he vainly importuned the Admiralty to send him out again in command of any vessel, however small, and tried to organize unofficial searches.

In 1854 Snow went to Patagonia in command of the South American Missionary Society's vessel *Allen Gardiner*, and for two years carried missionaries and their stores between Tierra del Fuego, the Falkland Islands, and stations on the mainland. This service ended in a disagreement between him and the superintending missionary at the Falkland Islands, who deposed Snow from his command for disobedience, and left him and his wife to find their own way to England. On his arrival Snow published *A Two Years' Cruise off Tierra del Fuego* (2 vols., 1857), which had some success, but he spent the proceeds on an unsuccessful action against the missionary society. Left penniless, he went to America, where he declined a commission in the Confederate navy, and for some years lived near New York, working for booksellers, writing his own works and editing the work of others.

On his return to England Snow still brooded over the fate of Franklin, and spent the last quarter of his life compiling volumes of indexes of Arctic voyages, of notes, and of biographical records of Arctic voyagers, while living in want. He died at his home, 1 Victoria Road, Bexleyheath, Kent, on 12 March 1895, leaving a mass of manuscripts, which were purchased by the Royal Geographical Society.

Snow's unsettled life, his series of enthusiasms (including emigration, telegraphy, early closing of shops, and total abstinence), his disagreement (which spilled into print and the courts as well as into unpleasant accusation) with almost all in authority, and above all his obsession with the Franklin search, suggest mental disorder; and suffering from this he could not achieve success, despite his intelligence, talent as a writer, and skill as a mariner.

J. K. Laughton, *rev.* Elizabeth Baigent

Sources *Review of Reviews*, 7 (1893), 371–86 • A. G. E. Jones, 'Captain William Parker Snow', *Polar portraits* (1992), 366–371 [repr. from *The Falkland Islands Journal* (1979)] • d. cert.

Archives RGS, corresp., journals, and papers | BL, letters to John Barrow, Add. MSS 35308–35309 • U. Newcastle, Robinson L., letters to Sir Walter Trevelyan

Likenesses portrait (after photograph), repro. in *Review of Reviews*

Wealth at death £80 17*s*. 0*d*.: administration, 22 Oct 1895, *CGPLA Eng. & Wales*

Snowball, Elizabeth Alexandra [Betty] (**1908–1988**), cricketer, was born at 83 Bank Parade, Burnley, Lancashire, on 9 July 1908, the only child of Thomas Snowball, medical practitioner, and his wife, Elsie Alexandra Scott. Her parents were Scottish and Betty, as she became known, was sent to St Leonards School, St Andrews, which had pioneered cricket as a sport in girls' schools. From there she went to Bedford Physical Training College to train as a physical education teacher, and taught for many years at St Swithun's School, Winchester.

Betty Snowball's father was a keen cricketer and at school she became a proficient wicket-keeper. One of her coaches was Learie Constantine, and it was under the influence of the great West Indian player that she became a fanatical devotee of the game. She was a member of the first England women's side to tour abroad, to Australia in 1934–5. Her reliable work behind the stumps earned her praise from the home press, which dubbed her the female Bert Oldfield, after the legendary Australian keeper. She stood the comparison well, and claimed twenty-one victims in ten test matches, including four stumpings in an innings against Australia at Sydney in 1935. She was also effective with the bat, her favourite stroke being a wristy square cut. Batting against New Zealand at Lancaster Park, Christchurch, in February 1935, she set a record that was to endure for fifty-four years. Opening the England innings with Myrtle Maclagan (a partnership seen as the women's equivalent to Hobbs and Sutcliffe), she scored 189 runs in 222 minutes. It was New Zealand's first test match, but she and her captain, Molly Hide (who scored

Elizabeth Alexandra [Betty] **Snowball (1908–1988)**, by David Savill, 1939 [left, with T. Dutton]

110), showed no mercy in putting on 235 runs for the second wicket, another record. In total she scored 613 runs in test matches (average 40.86).

Only just over 5 feet tall, and with a bright, smiling personality, Snowball was fastidious about her clothes and cricket equipment. Her wicket-keeping pads and gloves were made especially for her. On the field she believed that players had an obligation to assist umpires; at no stage, she believed, should emotion, still less disagreement, be shown at the decisions of overburdened officials. In her view any mistake lay with the fielding side for appealing wrongly. She also represented Scotland at squash and lacrosse.

Snowball was present at the New Road county ground in Worcester in July 1986 when India's opener Sandya Aggarwall edged one run past her 1935 score. Ten years later the New Zealander Kirsty Flavell became the first woman to score 200. But Betty Snowball's innings remains the highest score by an England woman player. She retired to live at Colwall in Herefordshire, which has been called the birthplace of women's cricket, and died there, unmarried, at her home, Evendine House, Evendine Lane, on 13 December 1988. Her body was cremated.

Carol Salmon

Sources archives of the Women's Cricket Association • R. H. Flint and N. Rheinberg, *Fair play: the story of women's cricket* (1976) • J. L. Hawes, *Women's test cricket: the golden triangle, 1934–84* (1987) • *Wisden* (1990) • b. cert. • d. cert. • private information (2004)

Likenesses D. Savill, double portrait, photograph, 1939 (with T. Dutton), Hult. Arch. [*see illus.*] • photographs, repro. in Flint and Rheinberg, *Fair play* • photographs, repro. in Hawes, *Women's test cricket*

Wealth at death £145,332: probate, 5 April 1989, *CGPLA Eng. & Wales*

Snowden [*née* Annakin]**, Ethel (1881–1951)**, socialist, suffragist, and peace campaigner, was born on 8 September 1881 at Gladstone Street, Pannal, near Harrogate, the daughter of Richard Annakin, a nonconformist building contractor, and his wife, Hannah Hymas. She had at least one sister and a brother. Ethel Annakin trained to be a teacher at Edge Hill College, Liverpool, where she was inspired by Revd Dr C. F. Aked of Pembroke Chapel to enter the slums of Liverpool and to give temperance lectures. In 1903 she moved to Leeds to take up a post as a schoolteacher and became a member of the Independent Labour Party (ILP) and the Leeds Women's Suffrage Society. She gave her first socialist lecture to the Keighley Labour Institute in September and this marked the beginning of nearly two decades of propaganda work as a speaker and a writer for socialism, women's suffrage, and peace.

In 1904 Ethel Annakin took a teaching job in Nelson, near Cowling, the home of the ILP chairman Philip *Snowden (1864–1937), whom she had met at the Leeds Arts Club. Because of his mother's disapproval Ethel and Philip were married secretly on 13 March 1905 at Otley register office in the presence of only a few friends and relatives, including Ethel's sister Florence and her close friend from Leeds, Isabella Ford, a prominent socialist and suffragist.

After her marriage Ethel Snowden resigned from teaching to concentrate on helping her husband's political career. She also continued to carry out propaganda for socialism and feminism, although the suffrage campaign increasingly became her main concern. It was her influence, and that of Isabella Ford, which helped to persuade Philip Snowden to give wholehearted support to the suffrage cause, a matter of some importance once he was elected as a Labour MP in 1906. As a member of the executive committee of the National Union of Women's Suffrage Societies Ethel Snowden lectured all over the country and also attended conferences in Europe organized by the International Women's Suffrage Alliance. In 1907 she was asked to give a series of lectures in America and returned there on nine separate occasions.

In this period Ethel Snowden wrote a number of books and pamphlets, including *Women and the State* (1907), *The Woman Socialist* (1907), and *The Feminist Movement* (1913), which attempted to bring together her socialist and feminist views. She argued that the state should assume major responsibility for the costs of childcare, including state salaries for mothers and advocated co-operative housekeeping and easier divorce. Influenced by the ideas of eugenicists she called for state control of marriage, believing that the mentally ill and those aged under twenty-six should not be able to marry. In contrast to these radical views on marriage, however, her moral outlook was far

Ethel Snowden (1881–1951), by Lena Connell

more traditional; for example, she was involved in the campaign to abolish barmaids on the grounds that it was immoral for young girls to serve drinks to men.

At the time of her marriage Ethel Snowden was described by the ILP journal, the *Labour Leader* (17 March 1905), as a:

> second Annie Besant … to her good gifts of dark eyes, golden brown hair and rich colour, Nature has added a sweet singing voice and musical ability of no mean order … she has won the affectionate regard of all those who have come into intimate acquaintance with her by her warm enthusiasm for the cause.

Increasingly, however, her volatile personality, quick temper, and uncompromising stand on many issues caused her to be widely disliked in the labour movement. Ethel Snowden was described by Emmanuel Shinwell as 'the would-be Sarah Bernhardt of the party'. She was, he said, 'small, buxom, and fearsome when crossed, with an unerring knack of squeezing the last drop of drama out of the most trivial incident' (McIntyre, 155). As early as 1903 she led a long campaign against the use of alcohol in the Leeds ILP social club which was greeted with hostility by the male members. In 1909 she accused the ILP of giving only lukewarm support to women's suffrage and resigned when she found that two members of the national administrative council were adult suffragists.

Ethel Snowden rejoined the ILP early in 1915 because the party supported demands for a negotiated peace. The Snowdens were on an extensive lecturing tour of the United States when war was declared, but they both joined the Union for Democratic Control when they returned home in 1915 and Ethel became a member of the executive of the Women's International League. She undertook speaking engagements all over the country in favour of an early and just peace settlement. Inspired by the first Russian revolution, a women's peace crusade was initiated in Glasgow in 1917. The ILP set up an advisory committee, which included Ethel Snowden, to assist local groups to take part in the new movement and Ethel became secretary and treasurer of the crusade.

In the post-war period Ethel Snowden's interest in peace continued. She attended the International Congress of Women in Zürich in 1919, which formed the basis of *A Political Pilgrim in Europe* (1921), and in Vienna in 1921. She was also a delegate to the Labour International at Bern in February 1919 and to the League of Nations conference in the same city in March. She was still active in the ILP, attending conferences until 1920 where she spoke on peace and temperance issues. In a pamphlet, *The Real Women's Party* (1919), she urged newly enfranchised women to join the ILP for general political work and in 1919 she was the ILP women's representative on the Labour Party executive.

Increasingly, however, Ethel Snowden and her husband found themselves out of tune with ILP politics. Ethel Snowden visited Russia as a member of the TUC–Labour Party committee of enquiry and published a critical report entitled *Through Bolshevik Russia* (1920) which was received very badly within the ILP. Philip Snowden left the national administrative council in 1921 because he could not forgive the party for the mounting criticism of his wife, which included accusations of social climbing. His resignation coincided, however, with the Snowdens' sharp rightward turn in politics and Beatrice Webb accused Ethel, whom she disliked intensely, of no longer being a socialist. Indeed, during the 1920s the Snowdens were sympathetic to the idea of a union of radical forces with Liberals such as Lloyd George. Philip Snowden became Viscount Snowden in 1931.

After 1920 Ethel Snowden was no longer active in socialist and feminist causes. She was made a member of the board of governors of the BBC in 1926, but proved to be a continuing thorn in the flesh of John Reith, the director-general. 'What a poisonous creature she is', Reith wrote in his diary. According to Reith's biographer, Mrs Snowden was accorded the distinction of a personalized niche in his biblical demonology, in which she was 'the Scarlet Woman' (McIntyre, 155). Although the relationship improved Reith was 'profoundly relieved' when she was not reappointed in 1932.

Lady Snowden played an important part in the revival of the Covent Garden Opera and was chair of the women's council of the Council of Action for Peace and Reconstruction. After her husband's death on 15 May 1937 Ethel continued to write and speak, largely for the temperance cause, and during the Second World War her main concern was declining moral standards, in particular among service women. In 1947 Ethel Snowden suffered a stroke and was confined to a nursing home, and she died of a second stroke on 22 February 1951 at 28 Lingfield Road, Wimbledon, Surrey. She was cremated and her ashes scattered in the same place as her husband's on Ickornshaw Moor, near Cowling. A plaque in her memory was later attached to the cairn on the moor, just below that honouring Philip. JUNE HANNAM

Sources K. Laybourn, *Philip Snowden: a biography* (1988) • C. Cross, *Philip Snowden* (1966) • J. Hannam, *Isabella Ford* (1989) • O. Banks, *The biographical dictionary of British feminists*, 1 (1985) • J. Liddington, *The long road to Greenham: feminism and anti-militarism in Britain since 1820* (1989) • A. Wiltsher, *Most dangerous women: feminist peace campaigners of the First World War* (1985) • J. Vellacott, *From liberal to labour with women's suffrage: the story of Catherine Marshall* (1993) • M. A. Hamilton, *Remembering my good friends* (1944) • *Labour Leader* (1903–18) • *Common Cause* (1909–18) • I. McIntyre, *The expense of glory: a life of John Reith* (1993) • b. cert. • d. cert.

Archives BLPES, corresp. with the independent labour party • HLRO, corresp. with Lord Beaverbrook • HLRO, letters to David Lloyd George

Likenesses portrait, in or before 1920, repro. in Mrs. P. Snowden [E. Snowden], *The real women's party* [1920], frontispiece • L. Connell, photograph, NPG [*see illus.*] • portrait, repro. in *Common Cause* (22 Feb 1912)

Wealth at death £23,279 6*s*. 1*d*.: probate, 4 May 1951, *CGPLA Eng. & Wales*

Snowden, Philip, Viscount Snowden (1864–1937), politician, was born on 18 July 1864 in a four-room cottage at Middleton, Ickornshaw, a row of cottages near Cowling in the Yorkshire Pennines. He was the only son and third child of John Snowden (1830/31–1889), weaver, of nearby Cowling, and his wife, Martha (*b*. 1834), daughter of Peter Nelson, weaver, also of Cowling; Martha too was a weaver. Until 1879 the family lived in Ickornshaw and nearby Cowling, the former a hamlet of some 160 people in 1871. Ickornshaw was dominated by its textile mill, but it also possessed schools, a chapel, and a public house. Most inhabitants came from a small number of inter-marrying local families. Wesleyan Methodism predominated, providing education (through its Sunday school), support for thrift (through its benefit society), and an analysis of social wrongs (by identifying the malign influence of the demon drink). The Snowdens were deeply embedded in these institutions and values. John Snowden was superintendent of the Sunday school and a committed teetotaller. The family lived carefully, saving £200–300 by the late 1870s. This helped to pay for Philip's education. He attended a local school (described variously as a church school or a private school) before moving to the newly opened board school. Unlike most others he did not work half-time in the mill. Instead he took advanced lessons, including French and Latin, from the schoolmaster, becoming first a monitor and then a trainee pupil teacher in 1877. His knowledge of the classic texts in his father's small library was extended by further reading, which included the novels of Scott, Dickens, Thackeray, and Eliot. His own and much larger library, built up over many years, contains many other classics—notably works by Carlyle and Ruskin.

In 1879 the mill which employed Snowden's parents went bankrupt. The family moved to Nelson, a much larger but still textile-dominated town across the Pennines in Lancashire. Philip found employment as an insurance clerk in Burnley, a short railway journey away. Despite the fact that John Snowden was a committed and informed Gladstonian radical, and Nelson a radical centre, Philip did not turn to politics. After considering training to be a solicitor, he applied to enter the civil service and passed the examination with honours in 1886. He entered the excise department of the Inland Revenue on a salary of £50 per year, and worked in Liverpool, Aberdeen, Carlisle and the Plymouth area, where he was stationed in Redruth. In August 1891 he fell ill. He was reported to have chronic inflammation of the spinal chord and consequent paralysis from the waist down. Tuberculosis is thought to have been a possible cause. He returned to his mother's home in Ickornshaw. Two years later he was walking with the support of two sticks, but he never walked unaided again. He was deemed too weak for office work, despite his protestations to the contrary, and was discharged from the civil service.

Philip Snowden, Viscount Snowden (1864–1937), by Bassano, 1923

Local politician and socialist agitator While recuperating, and apparently studying for the bar, Snowden—as a comparatively educated and well-travelled man—was asked to address various local groups. He made an impression and was elected unopposed to the new Cowling parish council in 1894, becoming its first secretary. In 1893 a new socialist organization, the Independent Labour Party (ILP), had been formed in Bradford. Snowden was asked to give a talk on socialism to the Cowling Liberal club. He did so, arguing that the ILP's form of socialism was rooted in a British radical tradition and in the moral teachings of Christ. Snowden's autobiography suggests that he was converted to socialism at this point. However, there was no dramatic and immediate break with his Liberal friends or his existing Liberal values. His increasingly frequent speeches were strewn with biblical references, nonconformist values, and support for Liberal causes. Lectures on politics alternated with lectures on temperance. He did not join the executive committee of the Keighley ILP until 1899, and was not then its 'leader'.

Snowden established a reputation as a fierce critic of the establishment. He eloquently contrasted the evil conditions resulting from capitalism with the moral and economic utopia of socialism. He ranged a battery of intellectual and statistical arguments against his enemies, impressing his largely ill-educated and less confident audience. He even condemned as 'bloodsuckers and parasites' a host of local Liberal figures, mainly textile employers, who were normally treated with reverential respect as they dominated the local economy and the Liberal Party. His speeches were also enlivened by a sardonic wit and attracted admiration from local newspapers for both their style and their content. None the less they contained few new and constructive ideas, as some journalists recognized. Although Snowden later addressed audiences outside Yorkshire, his analysis and rhetoric were rooted in the conditions and values of the Pennine villages, with their complex mix of deep class divisions and a moderate political culture.

Snowden secured a seat on Cowling school board from 1895 and on Keighley school board from 1899. His aims were substantially less radical than those of socialists in nearby Bradford. He was chosen as parliamentary candidate of the ILP at Keighley in 1895, but withdrew for financial reasons before the poll. Between 1895 and 1899 he established himself as a roving propagandist and journalist, speaking regularly at venues on both sides of the Pennines. The most successful of his political sermons was 'The Christ that is to be'—the title taken from Tennyson's 'In Memoriam'—the sentiments of which form a combination of religious revivalism and socialist utopianism. Published as a pamphlet, it went into many editions. Other speakers were told by hard-nosed local election agents that they should 'put some "Come to Jesus" into it, like Philip Snowden'. Adding a new weapon to his armoury, Snowden became editor of the *Keighley Labour Journal* in 1898. He turned it into a scandal sheet, exposing local waste, pettiness, and corruption. Trade union concerns were of limited interest to Snowden; on the contrary, he assumed that unions were interested in wages and little else and saw this as small-minded and conservative.

Snowden increasingly sought a larger audience. He was the parliamentary candidate of the newly formed Labour Representation Committee at Blackburn and Wakefield (1900, 1902) and was considered for other seats, including Clitheroe. He stood for the national administrative council of the ILP in 1897, was elected in 1898, and was chairman from 1903 to 1906 (he returned to this position during the war). Following a good performance as Labour Party candidate at Wakefield in 1902, he spoke on platforms in London, the midlands, and the larger Yorkshire towns, being fêted as 'the awakener of Wakefield'. In 1902 he moved to Leeds; he made a living thereafter by touring as a political lecturer and from syndicated columns and occasional pieces in a vast array of newspapers and journals. He was elected Labour MP for Blackburn in 1906. He was now a national socialist figure, standing alongside Keir Hardie and Ramsay MacDonald.

Into parliament From 1906 Snowden helped the nascent Labour Party to challenge the Liberals by focusing on financial policy. The parliamentary party came to rely heavily on his expertise. His speaking style was not best suited to parliament, despite calculated efforts to adapt, but pamphlets and articles based on his speeches made a considerable impact. He continued to attack the immorality of capitalism, but also used an array of statistics to expose the limitations of Liberal policy. Significant pamphlets included the 'socialist budget' of 1909 (a rival to that of the Liberal Party) and papers supporting a minimum wage in 1912–13. In both instances he developed a case for going further than the Liberals. At the same time, Snowden retained his roots in a radical Liberal-nonconformist culture. A keen and active temperance reformer throughout his life, he demanded state control of the drink trade in his much quoted pamphlet *Socialism and the Drink Trade* (1907). Having branded the House of Lords a 'standing disgrace to the intelligence of the British people' in 1900 (*Northern Daily Telegraph*, 9 Sept 1900) he supported Liberal policy during the constitutional crisis of 1909–11. He also supported proportional representation, disestablishment, Irish home rule, and extending the franchise to women. He was Labour's most active and prominent supporter of the non-militant movement, and was strongly associated with the women's suffrage campaign. Like many radical Liberals, he argued against increased expenditure on armaments and for democratic control of the Foreign Office.

In many respects Snowden's position was not dissimilar to that of Ramsay MacDonald, effectively leader of the Labour Party after 1910. He served on the national executive committee of the Labour Party alongside MacDonald, and like his leader generally opposed calls to fight the Liberals in every possible by-election. He also served on the national administrative council of the ILP, now affiliated to the Labour Party. Here he was part of a ruling clique. Like Keir Hardie, MacDonald, and James Bruce Glasier, he resigned from the council in 1909, following years of criticism from more radical elements. Like MacDonald, he opposed industrial unrest and class conflict as a means of resolving problems, notably in *Socialism and Syndicalism* (1913), and he had even fewer contacts with trade union leaders. None the less, he often sought to distance himself from Labour's leader. He called for an aggressively anti-

Liberal approach during discussions of national insurance in 1911, minimum wages in 1912–13, and proportional representation in 1914. Although there were genuine political differences between the two men, these attacks were often dismissed as an attempt to curry favour with the rank and file. As Bruce Glasier noted on the first of these occasions, 'The affair is the more reprehensible when one remembers that Snowden himself is under suspicion of having become a mere tuft on the tail of the Liberal party' (B. Glasier, diary, 16 June 1911). During conflicts over election strategy in 1914, Snowden was said to be 'as full of bitterness against Mac as a man can well be' (J. S. Middleton to his parents, 15 Feb 1914, Ruskin College, Oxford, Middleton MSS, MID 12/10). He harboured leadership ambitions of his own, at least until 1931.

Some of Snowden's difficulties within the Labour Party were personal rather than political. On 13 March 1905 he married Ethel (1881–1951) [*see* Snowden, Ethel], a schoolteacher, the daughter of Richard Annakin, a building contractor from Harrogate. She too was politically active, campaigning for socialism, temperance reform, and women's suffrage. By 1906 the Snowdens had moved to London, and they lived in Golders Green until after the First World War. While not extravagant, the couple now needed two homes. Ethel also enjoyed socializing with wealthy friends, which added to their financial needs. The couple extended their journalistic activities. Philip became even more prolific, writing a syndicated column for provincial newspapers and regular items for journals as varied as *Christian Commonwealth*, the *Englishwoman*, and the *Blind Advocate*. He was an expert journalist. Despite his puritanical background, he saw the difficulties of making Labour newspapers successful, when activists 'regard it as inconsistent with their principles to give prominence to sensational news' (H. Richards, *The Bloody Circus: the Daily Herald and the Left*, 1997, 4). Yet it was felt that he contributed too little of this knowledge to the party. As Bruce Glasier put it, with the disdain of the devoted activist, 'Snowden does nothing but write for money. He has become an extinct volcano. His wife goes to rich parties' (B. Glasier, diary, 21 July 1907). Other committed Labour activists disliked the way in which he made 'all these criticisms and attacks', on MacDonald in particular, 'but does not come to Party meetings and thrash them out with his colleagues first' (J. S. Middleton to his parents, 15 July 1911, Ruskin College, Oxford, Middleton MSS, MID 10/33). Like MacDonald, Snowden was attacked for 'betraying' his (and the party's) roots.

In July 1914, disillusioned with politics, Snowden went on a worldwide lecture tour. He focused on the issue of temperance and spent much of the time in Australia. He did not return to Britain until February 1915. Although not a pacifist, he immediately advanced the standard radical critique of the war's origins: that militarism and the arms race had promoted war, and that it had been declared following the secret machinations of unaccountable, largely aristocratic, members of the Foreign Office. Warmongers were now lining their pockets, while the country paid a huge price in money and men. He refused to help with recruiting (although he sat on the government's liquor control board) and took a strong stand against conscription, working through the No Conscription Fellowship. As the fellowship's chief spokesman in parliament he continued to harass the government. His principled stance was unpopular with the public, but it helped his political career. He returned to the national council of the ILP in 1915 and was its chairman from 1917 to 1920. He wrote a weekly column for its main journal, the *Labour Leader*, from 1916 and championed its continuing role in the Labour Party. As ever, he was neither trusted nor liked. To some he put the interests of the ILP above those of the anti-war movement. Leonard Woolf concluded that 'Snowden and the I. L. P.ers are so bitter and truculent that they can see nothing except a tiny segment of the horizon' (Leonard Woolf to Margaret Llewelyn Davies, 25 Aug 1917, in *Letters of Leonard Woolf*, ed. F. Spotts, 1989, 387). Although Snowden lost his parliamentary seat in 1918, he had regained his radical reputation.

Economic views Snowden is best known for his two periods as chancellor of the exchequer. Often dismissed as a Gladstonian Liberal because of his actions in office, Snowden in his pre-war economic pamphlets such as *The Chamberlain Bubble* (1903) and *Free Trade and Monopoly* (1904) did not simply accept Liberal economic theories. Liberals argued that competition lowered prices (a good thing); Snowden argued, by contrast, that excess competition initially brought lower wages, inefficiency, and waste, and that competition was speculative, needed unemployment to keep wages low, and meant duplication of production. Concentration of production, economies of scale, and investment were what Britain needed. In time, the desire for profit would concentrate ownership and power in the hands of a few, who exacted profits they neither earned nor needed. However, as he argued in *Socialism and Syndicalism* (1913), the concentration of production in larger units and fewer firms would also make it increasingly possible (and necessary) for public control to be introduced. Only through public ownership and control—little more than the recuperation of the public's own wealth—could the interests of the community be protected and the country developed. Although Snowden rejected the Marxist idea that class conflict was the motor of history, he argued that change was inevitable, evolutionary, and a natural consequence of these shifts in the economic structure.

Snowden's expression and vocabulary drew more on his nonconformist origins than on his socialist reading. The need to compete for survival, he argued, made mankind selfish and greedy. Industrial slavery crowded out all things of beauty and all good human (and Christian) feelings. Those with money had power, and used this power to retain their ascendancy. Merit was no guide to position, as the existence of the House of Lords testified. The immoral consequences of capitalism were as evident in the behaviour of the poor (who resorted to drink for solace) as in the rich, although the former were forced into this by their circumstances. Changing the economic structure would be morally beneficial not to a single class, but to the whole nation. Snowden merged radical Liberal views with a socialist, or at least Fabian, critique of the capitalist economy. He constructed a reputation as an economic expert. He had no formal training, but valued the supportive comments on his economic analysis made by economic experts.

These ideas formed the basis of books such as *Labour and National Finance* (1920) and *Labour and the New World* (1921). If social ownership would follow naturally from the evolution of the economy towards a position of monopoly, there was little that socialists could or should do to hasten the change. If the basis of prosperity was efficient, rationalized, production as part of a modernized economy, government policy could support these developments only by encouraging amalgamations and extending public services. Thus when economic conditions prevented Labour from forcing the pace of modernization in 1930–31, Snowden had little else to offer.

Other legislation—such as taxing unearned increment—was meant only to modify the unfairness of the current system, not to fund fiscal intervention, and was also deemed inappropriate at a time of economic crisis. Snowden had followed others in advocating a heavy tax on wartime profits in the immediate post-war period. Writing in *Labour and National Finance*, he argued that it was morally and economically right that 'the ill-gotten gains of wartime should be disgorged by their possessors' (p. 67). This was less of a contradiction with his later actions than one might think. He argued in the same text that 'sound finance is the basis of national and commercial prosperity' (p. 7) while 'taxation must be justly levied and the proceeds wisely expended', and must not 'discriminate unjustly between individuals and classes' (pp. 38–9). He made little attempt to find another way forward by consulting expert Labour colleagues. He resented the advice of Labour's internal advisory committees. During 1923 the land policy committee tried to define a workable policy of taxation which would create revenue and use land for the public good. Snowden ignored it, and instead drew up a propagandist private member's bill which called for land nationalization.

Snowden certainly knew the views of radical economists. His library contains a vast collection of economic texts, ranging from the radical (Hobson, Cole, Keynes) to the very conventional. By contrast, there is little on Marxist economics. Indeed, he claimed to have read only summaries of Marx's analysis. In the 1920s he was advised by a strong team of Labour economists, who supplied views on taxation, international finance, and the gold standard which differed in several respects from the 'Treasury view'. He remained committed to the idea that state control of the financial and banking system was essential, and supported a major public role in education and welfare. Although a Labour representative on the National Birthday Trust Fund (a charitable group, committed to reducing maternal mortality), he still insisted that such work was 'the primary responsibility of the state' (Williams, 67).

Into the governing class In 1922 Snowden was elected MP for Colne Valley, another Yorkshire Pennine seat not unlike his home area. He had little to do with the constituency. The Snowdens kept first a house and then a flat in London. From 1923 their main home was Eden Lodge, Tilford, Surrey—a substantial house—purchased, Ethel recorded, with the proceeds of her lecture tours. Philip was also earning more, writing for major newspapers in the USA and in Britain. A neighbour in Surrey, David Lloyd George, became a close friend. The Snowdens mixed freely within the world of politics and finance. In 1923 Ethel received some diamonds as a gift from Lady Rothschild.

Following Labour's election victory in 1923 the party formed a minority government which lasted just eleven months. Snowden was the automatic and inevitable choice as chancellor of the exchequer, taking office in January 1924. His policy was cautious but constructive. He argued that progress could be sustained only if industries affected by excessive competition were modernized. A commission on trade and industry was set up to discuss industrial rationalization. Snowden himself stressed the modernization of electricity generation. Land taxation, a little-studied fixation of Snowden's, was planned but not implemented. He reduced expenditure on armaments, cut import duties on various staple foods, and expanded subsidies for building council houses, but shelved the idea of a capital levy. Moderates inside and outside the party welcomed his first budget—a remarkable achievement, given his limited economic training. He established a relationship of mutual respect with the leading civil servants. Many argued that he simply adopted their views. 'We must imagine', Winston Churchill argued in *Great Contemporaries*, 'with what joy Mr Snowden was welcomed at the Treasury by the permanent officials … The Treasury mind and the Snowden mind embraced each other with the fervour of two long-separated lizards' (Skidelsky, 69).

Government policy reopened old divisions. Snowden's economic caution was attacked by the left. His hostility to MacDonald also resurfaced. He felt that MacDonald was too generous to both France and Russia, and that he had mishandled the Campbell case and the Zinoviev letter in 1924, provoking opposition to claims that the government was sympathetic to Bolshevism and hence leading to Labour's electoral defeat in October 1924. Privately he noted the 'great opportunities … wantonly and recklessly thrown away by the most incompetent leadership which ever brought a government to ruin' (Cross, 213). Ethel Snowden made the same claims publicly on a lecture tour of Canada. Not surprisingly this was widely reported in Britain.

After 1924 Snowden became increasingly dissatisfied with radical critics of his policy. He resigned from the ILP in 1927, complaining that it was 'drifting more and more away from … evolutionary socialism into revolutionary socialism' (Boyce, 198). He became closer, politically and socially, to Lloyd George, whose plans for land taxation he thought particularly important. Ethel Snowden even wrote to Lloyd George expressing her 'sympathy for the idea of a Union of all the Radical forces for common ends' (Ethel Snowden to David Lloyd George, 19 Feb 1924, HLRO,

Lloyd George MSS, LG MS, G18/8/12). Snowden associated himself with attacks on MacDonald's leadership in 1925 and 1927. In attacking MacDonald's 'aloofness' and distance from the party, he claimed to be 'expressing the feelings of all my colleagues who have talked with me on this subject' (Snowden to MacDonald, 14 Oct 1927, MacDonald MSS, PRO, 30/69/1173, fol. 573). Such views were common; but Snowden was not the party's preferred alternative. Moderates who knew Snowden felt that he was no more approachable than MacDonald. He attacked colleagues in 1927 when details of Labour's surtax discussions appeared in the press, and felt increasingly threatened by the rise of Labour economists like Hugh Dalton. Those who wanted a more radical approach would hardly turn to Snowden. George Lansbury found him 'stiff and difficult' over the surtax proposals, recognizing also that Snowden saw this as a means of repaying the war debt, and not as a means of redistributing wealth (Lansbury to D. Graham Pole, 15 Dec 1927, Borth. Inst., University of York, Pole MSS, UL5/1). He had opposed the radical economic ideas of the ILP and argued against the Keynesian ideas that formed the basis of the Liberals' 1929 manifesto, *We can Conquer Unemployment*.

The second Labour government and its aftermath The first year of the Labour government elected in May 1929 was not dominated by fiscal conservatism. Snowden's budget increased taxation of the wealthy. It removed about three-quarters of a million people from taxation. He was under pressure to attack unemployment. Charles Trevelyan at education wanted to raise the school-leaving age; Snowden was felt to be less of an obstacle than MacDonald. Herbert Morrison at transport wanted (and obtained) money for road building. The Unemployment Insurance Act (1930) liberalized benefits, increasing costs to the Treasury by £20 million. Further subsidies for council housing were introduced. Some industries (notably coal) received support (albeit less than they wanted, and more than Snowden proposed). The government pretended to be fiscally conservative in order to sustain the confidence of international financial opinion. However, in other areas, Snowden dug in his heels. Labour's advisory committee on international questions wanted to reduce reparations payments. Snowden opposed this, arguing that Britain was being 'bled white', becoming 'the milch-cow of Europe'. He attacked the 'outrageous' Young plan, antagonizing the Foreign Office and the foreign secretary, Arthur Henderson, but received support from the press (Boyce, 196, 205). In 1930 several Labour ministers supported the introduction of import duties and tariffs, either to protect specific industries (corn, steel, and so on) or to raise revenue. Snowden was 'staggered' by MacDonald's suggestion of a registration duty for imported wheat, barley, and oats in February 1930, stating that 'You do not change a food tax by calling it a registration fee' (Roth, 49). He threatened resignation in October 1930 when the idea of a revenue tariff seemed to be gaining majority support in the cabinet. He opposed tariffs again in April 1931 (ibid., 60), describing them as a device for 'relieving the well-to-do at the expense of the poor'. He also felt that powerful trade unions were trying to protect their members at the expense of others; he was noticeably absent from Labour's regular discussions with the TUC on economic policy and other matters. He was not alone in this thought, but he was increasingly isolated from his own more pliant economic team and became more irresolute. He was now a stubborn obstacle to any policy innovation. Laski among others on the left felt that he was 'an incubus to the party … his days of usefulness are over' (H. Laski to F. Laski, 14 May 1931, University of Hull, Laski MSS, 33/21). MacDonald hoped Snowden would go quietly to the Lords and allow tariffs to be introduced. He proposed a peerage in March 1931, following Snowden's prostate operation (which kept him out of politics for seven weeks). Despite his poor health and declared intention of moving on, Snowden declined the offer. He feared that his job would go to Jimmy Thomas (a supporter of tariffs, whom Snowden also thought unreliable, incapable, and vulgar). Other proposals, notably from Oswald Mosley, were dismissed.

By early 1931 Snowden was firmly convinced that drastic steps had to be taken in order to control the mounting budget deficit. The unemployment benefit fund was exhausted. Its borrowing level had been repeatedly increased to meet its commitments. The Holman Gregory Commission set up by Snowden demanded changes. On 11 February 1931 Snowden warned the House of Commons that 'drastic and disagreeable measures' would have to be taken, while schemes for heavy expenditure would have to wait (Riddell, 149). Following pressure from the Conservatives and Liberals he appointed an all-party committee of seven experts, led by Sir George May, to investigate public expenditure. Recognizing the need for all-party support if radical cuts in expenditure were to be made, he also wanted to pressurize his own party into supporting such actions. His budget in April none the less avoided drastic action, although the Unemployment Insurance Anomalies Act of July 1931 removed the benefit entitlement of married women and many seasonal workers. The 1931 budget did, however, contain proposals on land valuation taxation—still one of Snowden's central concerns. He may have hoped that in time this would generate the income he needed, but with no such income possible before 1933, the proposal offered no short-term solutions. Labour's alleged indifference to the idea none the less fuelled his resentment. He later claimed that cabinet colleagues 'were saying freely in the Lobbies that I was not supported by the Cabinet' (Snowden, 2.915).

Later in July 1931, the May committee reported, projecting a budget deficit of £120 million. It advised expenditure cuts of £96 million, mainly from the social services budget. Once published, the report sparked an immediate run on the pound. The government borrowed, but was told that if the underlying problems continued, reserves would be exhausted and Britain would have to leave the gold standard. International financial confidence would be decimated. By September Snowden was estimating an immediate deficit of £47 million, rising to £170 million (not £120 million as predicted by the May committee) in

1932–3. The cabinet agreed a variety of increases in taxation to cover part of the proposed deficit, and cuts amounting to £76.5 million. This was £20 million short of the amount required by Snowden and the May committee, since the cabinet did not institute its proposed 10 per cent cut in unemployment benefit. Endless discussions reached no solution. The TUC and many Labour ministers remained obdurate. Snowden was told that international opinion, and the leaders of the opposition, demanded cuts in unemployment benefit as evidence of the government's commitment. The cabinet naturally sought alternatives. Snowden again declined to accept the alternative of a revenue tariff. When Christopher Addison, the former Liberal cabinet minister, now in charge of Labour's agriculture policy, suggested leaving the gold standard, Snowden 'was more insulting to him than anyone had ever been in his life before' (Thorpe, 80). He was at least even-handed. The TUC was treated with similar disdain by Snowden in August 1931. Unable to create any agreement within his party on how to tackle the crisis, MacDonald formed a national government to implement the cuts and restore the country's financial position in September 1931.

Snowden had been less than honest with his colleagues. He knew the May committee would report in favour of cuts. Treasury experts told him that it exaggerated the budget deficit by at least £50 million. He kept this from cabinet colleagues. This approach was not unusual. Dalton complained that Snowden 'never gave them any real details of taxation proposals' (*Political Diary*, 3 Sept 1931). Others found him equally inflexible. Frederick Pethick-Lawrence's alternative suggestions for balancing the budget in 1931 were ignored. Philip Noel-Baker's consultations with the economist Pigou and others in 1931 went unheeded. Snowden wanted the cabinet to adopt his proposals—including cuts in unemployment benefit—without amendment. The stated views of international financiers and the opposition (who calculatedly promised support only if the cuts were made) were used to support Snowden's preferred policy. Philip Noel-Baker (among others) felt that the Treasury, Snowden, and the opposition had 'engineered' an 'appalling panic'. The way in which the May report was exploited, he added, 'was a most unpatriotic piece of propaganda' (14 Sept and 14 Oct 1931, CAC Cam., Noel-Baker MSS, 3/62). Snowden had allowed matters to drift, until in the end there was little alternative but to make the cuts. MacDonald had been overwhelmed by the scale of the problems and, in the absence of a clear majority for any alternative within the parliamentary party or the TUC, backed Snowden. Snowden's part in the crisis earned him little support in the Labour Party, and little sympathy from historians.

Snowden did not stand for parliament in the October 1931 election. He went to the House of Lords in November 1931 as Viscount Snowden. The National Government had swept to power with a huge majority. Snowden became lord privy seal. Just fifty-two Labour MPs were returned. Snowden contributed a bitter election broadcast, which attacked his old colleagues and described Labour's new policy as 'Bolshevism run mad'. He also attacked Labour's 'capitulation' to the TUC during the crisis, and his colleagues' 'dishonest' accounts of cabinet discussions during this period. Free from office, he treated old enemies within the party to a characteristically abrasive assault. Following the Ottawa Economic Conference in August 1932, the government introduced a variety of protective tariffs. Snowden wrote to Herbert Samuel, the Liberal leader in the coalition and another free-trader, 'I cannot be dragged any further along this road without a loss of all honour and self-respect' (Wasserstein, 355). He resigned on 28 September 1932.

In opposition Between 1931 and 1937 Snowden launched a stinging attack on the Labour Party, the National Government, and MacDonald. His resignation letter in 1932 contained a bitter assault on MacDonald's alleged compliance with the abandonment of free trade. Reviving his former career as a propagandist and journalist, he continued the attack through the *Sunday Chronicle*, the *Sunday Express*, and radio broadcasts. Discussing MacDonald's repudiation of land taxation following pressure from the tories, he stressed the 'nauseating hypocrisy' of MacDonald's comments, continuing 'there is no humiliation to which he will not submit if they only will allow him still to be called Prime Minister' (Cross, 333). In 1934 he claimed that MacDonald's unemployment policy suggested that 'the unemployed may be dealt with by teaching men … to make mats out of bits of old rope for a few pence' (Laybourn and James, 87). The personal venom continued: 'every time he speaks he exposes his ignorance or incapacity'. Members of the governing class (such as Lord Sankey and Tom Jones) found this bitter invective distasteful, but such sentiments were not shared by the public. The newspaperman Collin Brooks wrote that Snowden 'has become quite the most effective demagogue of our time', delivering vitriolic attacks 'without fairness or logic' which were none the less highly popular and effective (*Fleet Street*, 29 Oct 1935).

The attack was developed in Snowden's two-volume autobiography, published in 1934. Snowden's comments, alongside those of Harold Laski, did much to shape early accounts of the 1931 crisis and Labour's own party myths. Snowden claimed that MacDonald had consciously misled his cabinet in 1931; that he formed the National Government with unnecessary haste because he found the tories politically and socially more congenial. He initiated the much repeated story that following the formation of the National Government, MacDonald 'gleefully' rubbed his hands together, commenting 'to-morrow every duchess in London will want to kiss me' (Snowden, 2.957). Snowden also defended the role of the Bank of England, arguing that those who claimed to understand its actions demonstrated more 'confusion than wisdom' (preface to K. Rosenburg and R. T. Hopkins, *The Romance of the Bank of England*, 1933). He was particularly supportive of the Bank of England's governor Montague Norman, displaying his characteristic loyalty to close friends and an equally characteristic willingness to defend unpopular views with vigour.

Snowden was also loyal to his wife's political values, including her support for women's suffrage and better maternity provision. He continued supporting such causes throughout the 1920s and 1930s, when others shifted emphasis and focused on the 'newer' feminist concerns with birth control provision or family allowances. MacDonald's failure to renew Ethel's place on the BBC's board of governors in 1932 fuelled Snowden's anger. Snowden also continued to campaign for temperance reform, a process which culminated in 1936 with the publication of an important pamphlet, *End this Colossal Waste*. He also continued to campaign for peace (like many others underestimating the threat from Nazi Germany), although he had little to do with the Union of Democratic Control or with newer radical peace movements, preferring to work with non-political groups or Liberal friends.

In 1935 Snowden advised voters to support the Liberal Party, where it put forward a candidate. He supported Lloyd George's version of Roosevelt's 'new deal' in speeches, broadcasts, and pamphlets. Lloyd George's 'new deal' was an updated version of the Keynesian proposals advanced by the Liberals, and derided by Snowden, in 1929. Snowden explained his enthusiasm for this programme as a return to his long-standing economic principles. Policies of this kind, he claimed, had been 'temporarily inadvisable' during the 'quite different' conditions of 1931, when 'national necessity' made substantial expenditure impossible (Laybourn and James, 89).

Death, character, and appearance Snowden's prostate operation in 1931 had not been a success, compounding existing medical problems. He became progressively less mobile, eventually needing permanent nursing care. He died of a heart attack on 15 May 1937 at his home, Eden Lodge, Tilford in Surrey, and was cremated at Woking. On 22 May his ashes were scattered on Cowling Moor near Ickornshaw. There was a memorial service at St Margaret's, Westminster, on 26 May. Few Labour politicians attended either event. Snowden's vast collection of books and pamphlets was given to Keighley Public Library, where it remains. Other papers were destroyed. A cairn was raised on Ickornshaw Moor in 1938, funded by public subscription. Ethel Snowden died on 22 February 1951.

Until his illness in 1891, Snowden had been active and fit, walking and cycling a great deal. After the illness he walked with a limp and with the aid of two sticks. Thin and frail, with a gaunt, almost skeletal, face, thin lips, and 'icy' eyes, he always dressed in a dark suit and bowler hat. He looked like a civil servant, not a propagandist, and spoke like a mixture of the two. He used gestures a good deal and was seen as a 'master of words', but was less successful at the clipped style required for election campaigns or outdoor meetings. In private Snowden could be sarcastic and abrasive even with sympathetic colleagues. He disliked interruption, criticism, and questions, worked on his own, and made many enemies as a result. Jimmy Thomas famously commented following Snowden's prostate operation in 1931 that he was 'ill in the head, as well as ill in the balls'. Such language was not unusual. Snowden was often described as a 'bitter' cripple, these characterizations reflecting contemporary assumptions about disability and the harsh internal world of the Labour Party. Dalton describes him in xenophobic mood in 1929: 'Waving his crutches round and round his head and yelling insults at foreigners amidst rapturous applause from all the worst elements in England' (*Political Diary*, 10–19 Aug 1929). In photographs, Snowden's sticks are often partially or wholly hidden. However, there was little formal public discussion of his disability. He did not become a role model for the disabled. Only close friends saw Snowden's lighter and more charming side. A man with simple tastes (apart from Turkish cigarettes), he enjoyed music and detective novels, told stories in his native Yorkshire dialect, and wrote charmingly attentive letters to people who were not political rivals.

Historical significance Snowden was one of the most important figures in the early history of the Labour Party. As chancellor of the exchequer he faced a hostile political environment and in 1930–31 an economic crisis which many democracies, let alone parties, failed to withstand. Few contemporaries or historians have judged his policies or his personality sympathetically. Paradoxically, given his regular conflicts with MacDonald, the similarities between the two men have been emphasized. Both are often described as little more than radical Liberals. Both have been accused of betraying the party and their roots, seduced by the lifestyle and the values of the political and social élite. Ethel Snowden's apparent enthusiasm for this lifestyle—and for Lloyd George—was used against her husband, illustrating how attitudes to gender could permeate and influence Labour's internal political life. Snowden's career is significant not just because of the positions he held, but because it illustrates the problems of leading a party with radical and democratic traditions into a very different political world.

Many have drawn broader conclusions about the Labour Party based on accounts of its main leaders and their views. The 'ethical socialism' that Snowden represented has been described as essentially vacuous. Labour's policies have been judged similarly. Others have suggested that the failure of Labour's leaders to develop a reforming strategy reflected the failure of socialism in general, and Labour in particular, to accommodate a developing intellectual reformism. Like other socialist pioneers, he claimed that his original emphasis on moral change had been submerged and that the party had lost 'much of its idealistic quality and spiritual fervour' (Snowden, 2.1039). His autobiography reinforces this claim to consistency, arguing that he never advocated material improvements for the people as an end in itself. He had supported state measures to raise living standards before 1930 and after 1932. The period of crisis was an exceptional time, in which 'ordinary' programmes had to be suspended. Snowden's evident ambition, his role in 1931, and the limitations of his autobiography as a source have acted against proper consideration of these claims. However, he was more consistent than many of his colleagues wished to recognize, while neither his views nor his temperament were very unusual within Labour circles.

Re-evaluations of Snowden's career are thus concerned with more than the significance of an individual politician. Snowden was at the heart of Labour's only partially successful transformation from a party of propaganda to a party of government. How far errors of policy reflected more than Snowden's personal weaknesses is thus a question that is central to evaluations of Labour as a credible party of reform between 1900 and 1931.

DUNCAN TANNER

Sources Keighley public library, Philip Snowden collection • P. Snowden, *An autobiography*, 2 vols. (1934) • K. Laybourn and D. James, eds., *Philip Snowden: the first labour chancellor of the exchequer* (1987) • C. Cross, *Philip Snowden* (1966) • U. Lpool L., special collections and archives, J. Bruce Glasier MSS • BLPES, Francis Johnson MSS, Independent Labour Party Archive • PRO, J. R. MacDonald MSS • *The political diary of Hugh Dalton, 1918–1940, 1945–1960*, ed. B. Pimlott (1986) • *The diary of Beatrice Webb*, ed. N. MacKenzie and J. MacKenzie, 4 vols. (1982–5), vols. 3–4 • F. Trentmann, 'Wealth versus welfare: the British left between free trade and national political economy before the First World War', *Historical Research*, 70 (1997), 70–98 • D. Tanner, 'The development of British socialism', *An age of transition: British politics, 1880–1914*, ed. E. H. H. Green (1997), 48–66 • D. James, *Class and politics in a northern industrial town: Keighley, 1880–1914* (1995) • K. Laybourn, *Philip Snowden: a biography, 1864–1937* (1988) • R. W. D. Boyce, *British capitalism at the crossroads, 1919–32* (1987) • N. Riddell, *Labour in crisis* (1999) • P. Williamson, *National crisis and national government: British politics, the economy and empire, 1926–1932* (1992) • R. Skidelsky, *Politicians and the slump* (1967) • N. Thompson, *Political economy and the labour party* (1996) • T. Roth, *British protectionism and the international economy* (1992) • B. Wasserstein, *Herbert Samuel* (1992) • D. Marquand, *Ramsay MacDonald* (1977) • A. Thorpe, *The British general election of 1931* (1991) • *Fleet Street, press barons and politics: the journals of Collin Brooks, 1932–1940*, ed. N. J. Crowson, CS, 5th ser., 11 (1998) • A. S. Williams, *Women and childbirth in the twentieth century* (1997) • R. A. Jones, *Arthur Ponsonby* (1989) • A. J. A. Morris, *C. P. Trevelyan, 1870–1958* (1977) • J. Campbell, *The goat in the wilderness* (1977)

Archives Keighley Public Library, Yorkshire | BLPES, corresp. with F. Johnson • BLPES, corresp. with the independent labour party • HLRO, corresp. with Lord Beaverbrook • HLRO, letters to David Lloyd George • HLRO, corresp. with Herbert Samuel • Labour History Archive and Study Centre, Manchester • PRO, J. Ramsay MacDonald MSS • U. Hull, Brynmor Jones L., corresp. with Union of Democratic Control • U. Lpool L., corresp. with John Bruce Glasier and Katharine Bruce Glasier • Wellcome L., corresp. with National Birthday Trust Fund | FILM BFI NFTVA, documentary footage • BFI NFTVA, news footage • IWM FVA, documentary footage | SOUND IWM SA, oral history interview

Likenesses M. Beerbohm, caricature drawing, 1920, AM Oxf. • O. Edis, photograph, 1920–29, NPG • W. C. Dongworth, miniature, *c*.1920–1930, NPG • Bassano, bromide print, 1923, NPG [*see illus.*] • W. Stoneman, photograph, 1924, NPG • print, 1926 (after D. Low), NPG • D. Low, chalk caricature, *c*.1927–1928, NPG; related pencil sketches, NPG • T. Cottrell, cigarette card, NPG • C. Gill, chalk drawings, Man. City Gall. • B. Partridge, pen-and-ink caricature, NPG; repro. in *Punch* (25 Dec 1929) • S. de Strobl, bronze bust, U. Leeds • cast (after bust by S. de Strobl), Gov. Art Coll. • cast (after bust by S. de Strobl), U. Leeds • photographs, labour party archives

Wealth at death £3366 13*s*. 11*d*.: probate, 11 June 1937, *CGPLA Eng. & Wales*; Cross, *Philip Snowden*, 341

Snowdon, Jasper Whitfield (1844–1885), bell-ringer and author, was born at Ilkley, Yorkshire, on 18 June 1844, the second son of the Revd John Snowdon MA, vicar of Ilkley, and his wife, Margaret, *née* Whitfield. Educated at Rossall, near Fleetwood, Lancashire, he entered an engineering works as a student at the age of sixteen and worked there for fifteen years, during which time he took charge of one of the drawing offices. After two years managing an engineering works at Wakefield, he went into practice with his brother William as consulting mechanical engineers in Leeds from 1877 until 1884. He then managed another company near Leeds until his death in 1885.

Snowdon was a fine sportsman, and was well known for his prowess in athletics and cricket. Although he learned to ring in 1861, he did not ring during the period 1862 to 1870, when he founded the Ilkley Amateur Society, as a result of which he learned change-ringing properly, making rapid progress. He was a good heavy-bell ringer. His first peal (in the sense of a length of 5000 or more changes) was rung in 1872, and his 129th and last in 1884. The methods (systems of producing changes) rung were those current in the area at the time. In the early 1870s a series of increasingly successful friendly meetings of ringers on a quarterly basis led to the foundation of the Yorkshire Association of Change Ringers on 30 October 1875. In recognition of the leading part played by Snowdon, he was elected first president and remained in this position until his death.

Snowdon is best-known for his publications, both historical and technical, which were researched and written in a comparatively short space of time and are still important texts to the present day. He published articles in *Church Bells* from 1872 onwards. A major contribution was a six-part article on Annable's manuscript, lent to him by the Revd H. T. Ellacombe, the first part of which appeared in the issue of *Church Bells* of 9 December 1876. The following year a transcript of the records of the Union Society of London, founded in 1713, was made by Snowdon and Robert Tuke and published as a booklet.

Snowdon's first technical book was part 1 of *A Treatise on Treble Bob*, which included the history of the method and also composition and proof. This was published early in 1878. Part 2, a collection of peals in the method, followed in June 1879. However, his name is best-known for his elementary textbook *Ropesight*, designed to teach the principles of change-ringing using the Plain Bob method alone. The first edition appeared in November 1879 and sold out within a few months. A second edition was published in October 1880. The book has been in print more or less continuously ever since. Clearly there was a need for a continuation of *Ropesight*, giving more advanced methods, and so *Standard Methods* appeared in 1881. This was in two parts, a descriptive letter-press and a book of diagrams, and also remains in print over a century later.

In 1884 Snowdon published a book on Double Norwich Court Bob, which included his researches into the history of the method. When he died in 1885 a manuscript on Grandsire was still incomplete. This was edited by his brother William and appeared in 1888.

Snowdon died from typhoid at Leeds Fever Hospital on 16 November 1885 at the early age of forty-one, and was buried two days later at Ilkley. Many muffled touches in his memory were rung across the country. A memorial window, paid for by the change-ringers of England, was erected in Ilkley to his memory and dedicated on 11 June 1887. JOHN C. EISEL

Sources *Bell News and Ringers' Record*, 5 (1885), 264, 272 · *Bell News and Ringers' Record*, 27 (1907), 505 · *Bell News and Ringers' Record*, 1–34 (1881–1915) · *Church Bells* (1870–84) · *Ringing World* (1911–98) · b. cert.

Likenesses engraving, repro. in *Bell News and Ringers' Record* (1885), 265 · engraving, repro. in J. W. Snowdon, *Grandsire*, ed. W. Snowdon (1888)

Wealth at death £1159 19*s*. 1½*d*.: administration, 1 March 1886, *CGPLA Eng. & Wales*

Soames, (Arthur) Christopher John, Baron Soames (1920–1987), politician, was born on 12 October 1920 in Penn, Buckinghamshire, the only son and youngest of three children of Captain Arthur Granville Soames OBE of the Coldstream Guards and Ashwell Manor, Penn, and his wife, Hope Mary Woodbyne, the daughter of Charles Woodbyne Parish. He was educated at Eton College and the Royal Military College at Sandhurst, and commissioned in 1939 as a second lieutenant in the Coldstream Guards. He served in the Middle East, Italy, and France during the Second World War, winning the Croix de Guerre (1942) while on attachment to the Free French brigade in the western desert, where his right leg was shattered by a mine explosion. In 1946 he was appointed assistant military attaché at the British embassy in Paris. In the following year he married Mary, youngest daughter of Winston Churchill, former prime minister.

In 1950 Soames entered parliament as the Conservative member for Bedford. During Churchill's second premiership (1952–5) Soames acted as his parliamentary private secretary. He did much to keep the government going, masking the seriousness of his father-in-law's illness, when Churchill suffered a stroke in 1953. He went through the ranks of junior ministerial office before becoming secretary of state for war in 1958 (when he was sworn of the privy council) and serving in the cabinet in 1960–64 as minister of agriculture.

Having lost his seat in the 1966 election, Soames was an inspired choice by the government led by Harold Wilson as British ambassador to France (1968–72). Soames took up his post at a difficult time, with President Charles de Gaulle continuing to obstruct British accession to the EC. His term in Paris began inauspiciously with the leaking by the Foreign Office of the contents of a private conversation between him and de Gaulle ('l' affaire Soames'). A year later de Gaulle was gone and Soames was able to establish a much warmer relationship with his successor, Georges Pompidou. This was the crucial period leading to the successful completion of negotiations for Britain's entry into the EC and Soames, himself a convinced European, played a major part in persuading the French government no longer to impede the negotiations. His excellent colloquial French, splendid hospitality, and ebullient personality endeared him to the Parisians.

Immediately following British entry into the EC Soames was the first British vice-president of the European Commission and commissioner for external affairs, from 1973 to January 1977. He was a most effective commissioner. He played a major role in international trade negotiations and in establishing British influence in Brussels.

After a brief return to private life Soames was invited to join Margaret Thatcher's government in 1979 as lord president of the council and leader of the House of Lords. Later that year he was given his most difficult task, being appointed governor of Southern Rhodesia to oversee the ceasefire and elections leading to the independence of Zimbabwe. When he set off from London the ceasefire had still not been agreed, much less brought into effect, and the prospects for the success of his mission were generally discounted by the press. Following the successful conclusion of the Lancaster House negotiations a ceasefire was implemented under the supervision of the largely British Commonwealth monitoring force. Soames had the greatest difficulty with the Rhodesian military commanders on the one hand and sections of the Patriotic Front on the other throughout the period leading up to the elections, which were held in February 1980. He had to exercise responsibility with no more real power than he could win by bargaining with the contending parties. He set out to establish a personal relationship with the black political leaders, assuring Robert Mugabe that, if he won the elections, Soames would take the lead in helping the new government establish itself in a still uncertain, tense, and dangerous situation. When Mugabe did win he invited Soames to continue to serve as governor. In the ensuing period major steps were taken towards bringing together and forming into a single military command elements of the Rhodesian forces and those of the Patriotic Front, which itself was split into two warring factions. Soames left Rhodesia having helped to bring an end to the war and to launch Zimbabwe as an independent nation, amid near-universal plaudits.

On his return to Britain he had to deal with matters far less congenial to him, including a civil service strike. He found himself out of sympathy with the new economic strategy being pursued by Thatcher and with her style of government. In 1981 he was dropped from the government. He remained thereafter very active in business, holding a number of important directorships until his death, including those of N. M. Rothschilds and the National Westminster Bank, and the chairmanship of ICL (UK).

Soames was a figure very much larger than life. His conversation could usually be heard in the next room. His convivial but forthright personality inspired strong loyalties among his friends and some resistance on the part of more sensitive souls. His hospitality and enjoyment of life were legendary. As ambassador in Paris, commissioner in Brussels, and governor of Rhodesia he put up performances which could scarcely have been matched by anyone else. His success in all these capacities owed much to his wife, Mary. They had three sons, one of whom, Nicholas, also became a Conservative MP and minister, and two daughters.

The academic distinctions Soames received included honorary doctorates from Oxford (1981) and St Andrews

(1974). He was awarded the Robert Schuman prize in 1976. He was appointed CBE (1955) and GCMG and GCVO (1972), created a life peer as Baron Soames in 1978, and appointed CH in 1980. He also was awarded, on his departure from Paris, the cross of grand officer of the Légion d'honneur. He died from cancer on 16 September 1987, at his home in Odiham, Hampshire. ROBIN RENWICK, *rev.*

Sources personal knowledge (1996) • private information (1996)
Archives CAC Cam., personal and official corresp. and papers | CAC Cam., corresp. with Lord Gladwyn and typescripts of speeches
Wealth at death £2,218,825: probate, 25 Sept 1987, *CGPLA Eng. & Wales*

Soames, Henry (1785–1860), ecclesiastical historian, was the son of Nathaniel Soames, shoemaker, of Ludgate Street, London. He was educated at St Paul's School, and at Wadham College, Oxford, where he matriculated on 21 February 1803, and graduated BA in 1807, and MA in 1809. He became deacon in 1808 and was ordained by the bishop of London in 1809. He held the post of assistant to the high-master of St Paul's School from 1809 to 1814. In 1812 he was made rector of Shelley, Essex, and in 1821 rector of the neighbouring parish of Little Laver. From 1831 to 1839 he was vicar of Brent with Furneaux Pelham, Hertfordshire. In 1839 he became rector of Stapleford Tawney with Theydon Mount, Essex, where he lived, apparently with his sister, until his death. He was Bampton lecturer in 1830, and was appointed chancellor of St Paul's Cathedral by Bishop Blomfield in 1842. He died on 21 October 1860 at Stapleford Tawney.

One of Soames's more notable works is his revised edition (with additions, 1841), of James Murdock's translation of J. L. von Mosheim's *Institutes of Ecclesiastical History* (1832). This was re-edited in 1845, 1850, and finally by W. Stubbs in 1863. In the latter's preface tribute is paid to the value 'of the notes and additions made to the work by my late venerable friend, Mr Soames'. Soames otherwise concentrated his labour and learning on English ecclesiastical history in Anglo-Saxon times and in the sixteenth century. His *History of the Reformation of the Church of England* (1826–8) and *Elizabethan Religious History* (1839) were well received. His other works include *An Inquiry into the Doctrines of the Anglo-Saxon Church* (1830; Bampton lectures), *The Anglo-Saxon Church: its History, Revenues, and General Character* (1835; revised, augmented, and corrected, 1856), and *The Latin Church during Anglo-Saxon Times* (1848), the last of which received mixed reviews. He also published two sermons and *The Romish Decalogue* (1852).

RONALD BAYNE, *rev.* MYFANWY LLOYD

Sources Crockford (1860) • Foster, *Alum. Oxon.* • J. E. Cussans, *History of Hertfordshire*, 1 (1870) • *GM*, 3rd ser., 9 (1860), 370
Wealth at death under £4000: probate, 17 Nov 1860, *CGPLA Eng. & Wales*

Soane, George (1789–1860), writer, was born in London on 28 November 1789 and baptized on 18 December at St Marylebone, St Marylebone Road. He was the younger son of Sir John *Soane (1753–1837), architect, and Elizabeth Smith (1760–1815), niece of George Wyatt, city surveyor of paving. He was educated at home with his elder brother John and later at Pembroke College, Cambridge, where he graduated BA in 1811. On 4 July of the same year he married Agnes Boaden at Old Church, St Pancras, London, in defiance of both his parents, who felt she was a wholly unsuitable choice.

From 1810 George had become interested in literature and drama, and produced his first novels, *The Eve of St Marco* and *Knight Damon and a Robber Chief*, in 1812. His marriage and choice of career were only two of several incidents that tested the patience of Sir John. Hard-working, self-improving, and difficult, he was continually vexed by the behaviour of his charming and lazy younger son. It is claimed that George was responsible for the pregnancy of his wife's sister, and he was perpetually involved in financial difficulties, being several times imprisoned for debt and once for fraud in 1814. What began as disappointment at his son's disinterest in architecture turned to implacable anger when George wrote two anonymous and defamatory articles damning John Soane's architectural style: 'The present low state of the arts in England, and more particularly of architecture' (*The Champion*, 10 and 24 Sept 1815). When George's ailing mother, Elizabeth, heard of the articles, she is said to have exclaimed: 'It is George's doing and I shall never be able to hold up my head again' (Bolton, xiv–xv). John Soane blamed the articles for her sharp decline, calling them 'death blows', and Elizabeth died shortly after they appeared, on 23 November 1815. The result was George's immediate disinheritance. Soane left the bulk of his wealth to the children of his eldest son, John, and the home in Lincoln's Inn Fields that George notoriously likened to a mausoleum was left in trust to the nation by act of parliament. George opposed the bill at committee stage to little effect: it is now Sir John Soane's Museum.

In addition to feuding with his father, George found time to pursue his prolific, though never financially successful, career as a writer. *The Eve of St Marco* was followed by novels, plays, and translations from French, German, and Italian. Such publications include *The Peasant of Lucerne* (1815), *The Bohemian: a Tragedy* (1817), *The Falls of Clyde: a Melodrama* (1817), *Self-Sacrifice: a Melodrama* (1819), *The Dwarf of Naples: a Tragi-Comedy* (1819), *The Hebrew: a Drama* (1820), *Pride Shall have a Fall: a Comedy* (1824), and *Aladdin: a Fairy Opera* (1826). His later work followed a similar pattern, comprising *The Frolics of Puck* (1834), *The Last Ball and other Tales* (1843), *The Night Dancers: an Opera* (1846), *January Eve: a Tale* (1847), *New Curiosities of Literature* (1847), and *The Island of Calypso: an Operatic Masque* (1850). Soane's versatility as a writer can be evidenced by comparing the translations in *Specimens of German Romance* (1826), which use the inflated language of sensibility, with his dry, detailed *Life of the Duke of Wellington* (1839–40). It is ironic that in spite of his efforts, the piece of writing for which he is best remembered is the vitriolic piece in *The Champion*. He died on 12 July 1860 at his home, 38 Charlotte Street, Portland Place, London, where his daughter Clara Agnes was also resident. EMMA PLASKITT

Sources 'Soane, Sir John', *DNB* • *IGI* • A. T. Bolton, ed., *The portrait of John Soane* (1927) • 'Sir John Soane Museum, Lincoln's Inn Fields,

London', www.bbc.co.uk/dna/h2g2/A708608 · *GM*, 2nd ser., 7 (1837), 321–5 · *GM*, 3rd ser., 9 (1860), 218 · Venn, *Alum. Cant.* · S. Palmer, *The Soanes at home: domestic life at Lincoln's Inn Fields* (1997) · *CGPLA Eng. & Wales* (1860) · d. cert.

Archives Sir John Soane's Museum, London, letters to Sir John Soane and others

Likenesses Van Assen, oils, *c.*1800 (with brother and mother), repro. in Palmer, *The Soanes at home*, facing p. 1 · T. Banks, bust, *c.*1804, Sir John Soane's Museum, London · W. Owen, double portrait, 1804 (with brother, John), Sir John Soane's Museum, London; repro. in Bolton, ed., *The portrait of John Soane*, 170 · portrait (aged thirteen; after drawing by G. Dance), repro. in Bolton, ed., *The portrait of John Soane*, 169

Wealth at death under £600: resworn probate, May 1861, *CGPLA Eng. & Wales* (1860)

Soane, Sir John (1753–1837), architect, was born on 10 September 1753, probably at Goring-on-Thames, near Reading, where his father was employed as a bricklayer. He was the seventh and last child of John Soan (1714–1768) and Martha Marcy (1713–1800). In 1784 he changed his surname to Soane, as part of a deliberate programme of self-improvement, as he was extremely conscious of his humble social origins.

Family background and early training Owing to his reluctance to disclose any details about his family background and early years, little is known of Soane's upbringing, although he was almost certainly educated at the school of William Baker in Reading, while his older brother William joined their father's trade. The diarist Joseph Farington, secretary of the Royal Academy, never a friend of Soane, recounted at a dinner party in 1803 the story that as early as 1767 Soane had 'assisted His brother who was a Journeyman Bricklayer as Hod-boy' (Farington, *Diary*, 6.2028).

At the age of fifteen in 1768 Soane entered the office of the architect George Dance the younger, apparently as the result of an introduction by a member of his family to James Peacock, Dance's assistant. Soane lived in Dance's household for his first few months in London, which possibly gave rise to Farington's subsequent claim that he had been employed as a servant by Dance before entering his office. Although such claims caused Soane embarrassment, there is no doubt that a position in the office of Dance, the most inventive architect of his day in the country, was a tremendous advantage for him. Dance had received at St Paul's School what Soane was conscious of lacking—a fine classical education—and, though only twelve years Soane's senior, had already spent six years from 1758 studying architecture in Italy before succeeding his father as clerk of works to the City of London in 1768.

Soane's connection with Dance was also of vital importance because Dance and his elder brother Nathaniel became founder members of the Royal Academy in December 1768. Soane believed that his own subsequent career depended on his connection with the Royal Academy not only because it sent him on the grand tour, then regarded as a virtually essential part of an architect's training, but also because it was on this tour that he met the patrons to whom he was indebted for many of his most important commissions.

Sir John Soane (1753–1837), by Sir Thomas Lawrence, 1828

In October 1771 Soane was admitted to the Royal Academy Schools, where he heard the lectures delivered by the first professor of architecture at the academy, Thomas Sandby. Here also he became acquainted with William Chambers, the distinguished architect who, with Joshua Reynolds, was the prime mover behind the foundation of the academy. From Sandby, Soane imbibed the doctrine of the expression of appropriate character in architecture, and from Chambers, even more importantly, a belief in the superiority of French architecture, especially public and civic buildings, and of French architectural theory. Chambers viewed the foundation of the Royal Academy as a means of raising English architecture and architectural education to the level of the French; he saw study in Italy as essential for the ablest students, who would receive travelling scholarships awarded as a result of competitions. Soane was among the first and by the far most distinguished beneficiary of the programme devised by Chambers. Since training at the academy was not full-time, Soane joined the office of the architect Henry Holland in 1772, claiming that he needed more practical knowledge than he had been able to acquire in Dance's office. He remained with Holland until 1778, becoming a valued member of his office, to judge from Holland's generous payments to him. He seems also to have lived with the Holland family in Mayfair, first in Half Moon Street and later in Hertford Street. Having formed an important alliance with the landscape designer Lancelot 'Capability' Brown in 1771, Holland was working on numerous country houses while Soane was in his office, including Claremont House, Surrey, for Clive of India, Benham Place,

Berkshire, Cadland, Hampshire, and Brooks's Club, London.

In December 1772 Soane obtained a silver medal at the Royal Academy in the competition for a measured drawing of the façade of the Banqueting House. In 1774 he competed unsuccessfully for the gold medal, but he won this two years later with a magnificent design for a triumphal bridge. His remark that, 'my being employed on the drawings of the bridge preserved me for ever from a watery grave' (Soane, 13–14), was a reference to the fact that, working over the weekend on this important project, he declined an invitation from two friends to celebrate a birthday at a boating party at Greenwich on 9 June 1776. One of the two young men, James King, was accidentally drowned on this occasion, which led Soane (who could not swim) 'to associate divine providence with the work ethic' (Ruffinière Du Prey, 77). The following year, at the annual Royal Academy exhibition, Soane exhibited an ambitious design for an *Elevation of a Mausoleum, to the Memory of James King, Esq.* With its stone dome, colonnades, and rusticated base, this owed much to designs published by the French academician Marie-Joseph Peyre, in his *Oeuvres d'architecture* (1765), a copy of which had been placed in the library of the Royal Academy by William Chambers, a friend of Peyre.

It was also from Peyre that Soane derived much of the grandeur and detail of the design for a triumphal bridge which won him the gold medal. Thanks to an endowment from George III, the academy was in a position to offer a three-year travelling scholarship to Italy, one of which, fortunately, became available in 1777. According to Soane, Chambers brought the young architect's design to the attention of George III, whose support helped him gain the king's travelling studentship. Another indication of Soane's ambition was his proposal in the spring of 1777 to publish a book of his own designs, often in styles derived from Peyre and Chambers, mainly for garden buildings but including his design for the mausoleum for James King. By the time the book appeared in 1778, under the title *Designs in Architecture*, Soane had already set off for Rome.

Grand tour Soane left London to embark on his massive programme of instruction and self-improvement in Italy on 18 March 1778 at five o'clock in the morning. As a measure of the importance he attached to his Italian travels, he celebrated 18 March virtually every year for the rest of his life: indeed, he seems never to have been as happy at any point in his subsequent career as he was when in Italy. After arriving in Rome on 2 May, Soane used as his *poste restante* address the famous meeting-place for British visitors in the piazza di Spagna, the Caffè degli Inglesi, which had been decorated with murals in the Egyptian manner by Piranesi. He had for guidance a letter of advice written in 1774 by William Chambers to his pupil Edward Stevens. Chambers had recommended students visiting Italy to

> Work in the same quarry with M. Angelo, Vignola, Peruzzi, and Palladio … Observe well the works of the celebrated Bernini … Converse much with artists of all countrys, particularly foreigners, that you may get rid of national prejudices. Seek for those who have most reputation young or old, amongst which forget not Piranesi, who you may see in my name. (Bolton, 11–12)

Soane followed all these instructions: first, to learn from the work of architects today categorized as Renaissance and baroque, and not to restrict himself to the study of antiquity, as James 'Athenian' Stuart and his partner Nicholas Revett had done; second, to follow the precepts of the eighteenth-century Enlightenment, with its ideals of international brotherhood and sociability, of intellectual and moral improvement in a secular context; and third, to revere Piranesi, whose vision of ancient Rome, as evoked in his dramatic etchings, was an important catalyst in the creation of the monumental style often known today as neo-classicism. Piranesi gave Soane four plates from his *Vedute di Roma* (*c.*1748–78) when he met him in Rome; the plates survive today in the Soane Museum.

With Thomas Hardwick, Soane now began a laborious course of measuring historic buildings in Rome, from both ancient and more recent times. He also designed a mausoleum for William Pitt, first earl of Chatham, news of whose death on 11 May had recently reached Rome. By the autumn of 1778 Soane had become the protégé of one of the most prestigious of grand tour collectors, Frederick Hervey, bishop of Derry and later earl of Bristol. As a measure of his high opinion of Soane, the bishop gave him copies of Vitruvius's *De architectura* and of Palladio's *I quattro libri* in 1778. With Hervey, Soane travelled to Naples in December 1778, visiting Pompeii and Paestum, where he found the early Greek Doric temples 'exceedingly rude' (Soane, 'Italian sketches 1779', notebook, Soane Museum, fol. 61). It was in the appropriate setting of Paestum on 28 January 1779 that he first met the Hon. Philip Yorke, later third earl of Hardwicke, a valuable future patron. In April 1779 Soane set out for Sicily with five friends, mainly landowners, including Rowland Burdon and Henry Greswold Lewis; like Yorke, they became his employers as well as his friends. The uncompleted fifth-century Doric temple at Segesta, in its stunning mountainous setting, made a tremendous impact on Soane. However, following the advice of Chambers, he was equally alive to the merits of Renaissance and Mannerist architects, and made a large collection of drawings of buildings in Verona by Michele Sanmicheli, which he hoped to publish. In Rome, too, he made careful drawings and plans of the Villa Albani, completed in 1762 as a home for Cardinal Alessandro Albani's collection of antiquities. The objects were displayed architecturally throughout the house, loggias, and gardens, often embedded into the walls or set in front of mirrors, in ways which were to be a profound influence on Soane. In 1780 he gained honorary membership of the Parma Academy with a version of his triumphal bridge design, remodelled in the Greek Doric style in tribute to his visits to the temples at Paestum and Agrigentum.

The only misfortune of his signally successful grand tour was his premature departure from Rome in April 1780 to return to England, where the bishop of Derry, now Lord Bristol, had promised him the commission for a vast new house at Ickworth, Suffolk. His decision to curtail his travelling studentship by eleven months, at the virtual command of Lord Bristol, turned out to be a mistake. Although Soane travelled to Ickworth in July 1780 and then on to Downhill, Ireland, and made designs for houses for Lord Bristol in both places, the commissions came to nothing.

The establishment of the Soane style Soane's career began modestly in 1781 with a commission from Philip Yorke for lodges and a dairy, built in 1783, at his house, Hamels, Hertfordshire. With columns composed of tree trunks below a thatched roof, the rustic dairy, an appropriate setting for Rousseau's 'natural savage', was inspired by the primitive hut held up as a model by Marc-Antoine Laugier in his influential *Essai sur l'architecture* (1753). As well as studying Laugier to the point of fanaticism, Soane frequently read the works of Jean-Jacques Rousseau, and owned the works of both authors in multiple copies. Identifying emotionally with Rousseau as the solitary and sensitive victim of something approaching organized persecution, he gave to Philip Yorke's wife a copy of Goethe's *The Sorrows of Young Werther*. Like the writings of Rousseau, Goethe's novel was a key moment in the development of confessional literature.

In addition to giving him minor commissions, the friends Soane made on his grand tour introduced him to further clients who employed him in the 1780s, particularly in Norfolk and Suffolk, where he built Letton Hall, Saxlingham rectory, Shotesham Park, and Tendring Hall between 1783 and 1788. These are chaste essays in the local white brick with a geometrical tautness of line but show little or nothing of the idiosyncratic and poetic style for which Soane later became famous. That originated about 1787, in unexecuted designs for vaulted top-lit spaces: a saloon at Chillington Hall, Staffordshire, for Thomas Gifford, and a picture gallery at Fonthill 'Splendens', Wiltshire, for William Beckford. These flowered in the Yellow Drawing-room which he provided in 1791–4 at Wimpole Hall, Cambridgeshire, for Philip Yorke, third earl of Hardwicke. In 1778 Yorke had admired the Corsini Chapel, constructed in the 1730s from designs by Alessandro Galilei, in San Giovanni Laterano in Rome. Yorke commissioned Soane to make a drawing of its domed cruciform interior which may have provided some hints for Soane's T-shaped, top-lit drawing-room at Wimpole, first conceived in a drawing of 1791. The high-level lighting at Wimpole creates a subterranean effect which seems related to the fact that ancient Roman interiors were discovered through excavation and were thus seen as underground and funereal, a misapprehension which appealed to the introspective and melancholy side of Soane's character. The architect Marie-Joseph Peyre and his son François had also suggested that ancient Roman domestic architecture was densely planned and essentially one-storeyed, thus necessitating frequent use of top-lighting.

Echoing the design of the guildhall council chamber of 1778 by Soane's master, Dance, the ribbed pendentives of the dome at Wimpole are decorated with a scalloped line like the outer edge of an umbrella, suggesting a light structure such as a tent or parachute. This effect is heightened by the fact that the dome does not rest on piers but seems to float above the viewer's head. Here is the origin of many of Soane's later top-lit interiors at the Bank of England and of top-lit tribunes such as that at Tyringham, Buckinghamshire (1793–*c*.1800). He worked at Wimpole on and off for sixteen years, making additions to the house and grounds which were the fruit of the Enlightenment enthusiasms which he and Yorke had formed in Italy. His work at Wimpole thus included a library, a bath house, and extensive buildings and barns on the home farm, some possibly inspired by drawings of Swiss farmhouses which Hardwicke sent to Soane in 1800.

At the same time as designing the Yellow Drawing-room at Wimpole, Soane rebuilt the medieval hall at Gonville and Caius College, Cambridge, where he introduced a screen pierced with seven oculi or circular openings, allowing light to filter through from the great semicircular window which he formed in the wall behind. This arrangement was inspired by the similar arch introduced by Donato Bramante in the 1490s at the end of the medieval nave of Santa Maria della Grazie, which Soane had probably seen on his visits to Milan in 1779 and 1780. This inclusion of a virtual copy of a Renaissance feature was unusual in Soane's work but was the natural consequence of his early determination to find ways of achieving poetry through concealed light.

Architect to the Bank of England In 1788, in the face of fierce competition, Soane won the coveted position of architect to the Bank of England, with the support of William Pitt. He began to remodel and extend the existing buildings in that year, gradually replacing the existing buildings by Sir Robert Taylor and others. This process continued until as late as 1833, by which time he had doubled its size to 3½ acres. He cannot have guessed in 1788 how lucrative and extensive his work there would be, for the expansion of the bank was partly promoted by the fact that Pitt used it to raise funds to finance the Napoleonic wars. As well as handling the war debt, the bank also had to deal with the introduction of income tax in 1799 and of paper banknotes of low denominations in the same year.

From his Stock Office of 1791–2, worked out in association with George Dance, to the Four Per Cent Office of 1820–24 with its lantern ringed by caryatids, Soane contrived to introduce into rooms designed for mundane activities the poetical effects which were essential to his vision of architecture. Interiors such as the Stock Office were also novel from a constructional point of view: here Soane replaced an office built by Sir Robert Taylor in 1767, featuring a top-lit vaulted ceiling supported by sixteen wooden columns. He whittled down the supports to four slender stone piers, while his dome and vaults were formed of hollow earthenware pots, employed for their light weight as well as their fireproof qualities. The room was also tied together with square iron rods, while the lantern lights were made of copper with quarry tiles above.

The Lothbury Arch of 1800 at the entrance to the Bullion Court took the form of a triumphal arch, probably the first permanent triumphal arch erected in London. Soane wanted it to be the principal public entrance to the bank, where its Roman grandeur would also be appropriate to the daily transport through it of tremendous wealth (the bank was the holder of the only major gold reserve in the banking system). However, the arch was not used for that purpose, since the public entrance remained on the south side of the bank. At the north-west corner Soane provided the impressive Tivoli Corner, an inventive and plastic variant of his favourite antique building, the circular temple at Tivoli; this was probably the first use in modern times of the rich Corinthian order of this temple.

Regarded as a major national monument, the bank was illuminated on great public events such as the peace of Amiens in 1802, the visit to London of the allied sovereigns in 1814, and the battle of Waterloo in 1815. Following his visit to the Bank the tsar gave Soane a ring, while the architect in turn presented him with drawings of the bank. The bank thus partially compensated Soane for the fact that he was able to erect few of the public buildings which he designed for Whitehall and Westminster.

Soane's own houses: Pitzhanger Manor and 12–14 Lincoln's Inn Fields On 21 August 1784 Soane married Elizabeth Smith (1760–1815), niece of the prosperous George Wyatt, city surveyor of paving, for whom she kept house. The couple had four children, all boys, born between 1786 and 1790. Of the two who survived infancy, John, the eldest, was born in 1786, and George in 1789. George Wyatt died in February 1790, leaving much valuable London property to his niece and her husband. As a result, in 1792 Soane bought and rebuilt 12 Lincoln's Inn Fields as a home for his family, with an architectural office at the back. This was the start of a process which, like his work at the Bank of England, was to last for almost the rest of his life, for he acquired the two adjacent houses, nos. 13 and 14, in 1808 and 1823 respectively, and lived in different parts of the three houses at different times as his collection of antiquities, paintings, and books expanded.

In 1801 Soane bought Pitzhanger Manor, Ealing, an eighteenth-century villa extended in 1768 by his master, George Dance. Soane had worked on this project when he was in Dance's office, so that his choice of it for his own country residence was a tribute to Dance. While retaining Dance's additions, he demolished and rebuilt the original villa in 1801–3, partly to serve as a place of architectural education for his sons, who he was determined would follow him in his career as an architect. Soane believed that 'architecture speaks a language of its own … and above all, a building, like an historical picture, must tell its own tale' (Soane Museum Archives 1/259, fol. [7]). It is clear from surviving notes that Soane regarded Pitzhanger as a self-portrait, or at any rate a portrait of the owner of fragments of antique sculpture who wished to preserve them from ruin by incorporating them into an Italian villa. It is also possible that the entrance façade, echoing the form of a triumphal arch, was intended to proclaim the building as the home of the architect of the Bank of England, for it echoes the Lothbury Arch at the bank. In the grounds Soane built an extraordinary series of imitation Roman ruins, recalling those at the Villa Albani; these have disappeared, but the house survives and is open to the public. The decoration of the breakfast room was partly inspired by the wall-paintings in an ancient Roman house excavated in 1777 in the grounds of the Villa Negroni in Rome. Soane had visited this, although the paintings had already been bought by the bishop of Derry, who intended to incorporate them in his house at Downhill.

It had become clear by 1810 that his son John was unsatisfactory as an architect, and that George was not interested in the subject at all, so that Soane sold Pitzhanger in that year. He now concentrated his collection at 12 Lincoln's Inn Fields and in the poetic top-lit dome or 'museum' he had built in 1808–9 at the rear of no. 13. In the interiors of no. 12 in 1792 he had already radically broken with the tradition of interior decoration which had prevailed during the eighteenth century, including his own early works, in which areas of colour were separated by white mouldings. He now introduced graining for the woodwork and painted the walls of the dining-room Pompeian red, a shade derived from a scrap of painted plaster which he had brought back with him from Pompeii.

Following his appointment in 1806 as professor of architecture at the Royal Academy, Soane saw 12 Lincoln's Inn Fields more and more as a demonstration of the history of architecture, assembled and displayed for the benefit of students, rather than for his sons. After building the dome in 1808–9 to house his collections, in 1812–13 he demolished and rebuilt no. 13, creating a library and dining-room opening into each other and separated by a series of hanging arches in the ceiling. The walls were painted Pompeian red, while ingenious use of mirrors created picturesque and deliberately ambiguous spatial effects.

Adjacent is the breakfast room, 'In the centre of which', in Soane's words, 'rises a spherical ceiling … forming a rich canopy' as the climax of 'a succession of those fanciful effects which constitute the poetry of architecture' (J. Soane, *Description of the House and Museum on the North Side of Lincoln's Inn Fields*, 1835–6). Soane had studied carefully Quatremère de Quincy's book of 1803 on the origins of Egyptian architecture and its relation to Greek architecture, which posited the cave, the tent, and the hut as the prototypes of all architecture. The hovering dome in the breakfast room resembles a tent, as does that in his privy council chamber in Downing Street of 1824. The coloured light in the breakfast room fell on a range of objects with resonances in Soane's life and career, thus making the room an intensely personal statement: these objects included souvenirs connected with Napoleon, whom Soane regarded as a romantic hero as well as an important patron of public buildings; elsewhere in the room, he hung engraved plates by Camillo Buti of the Roman wall-paintings at the Villa Negroni. The 'fanciful effects' mentioned by Soane also include the use of over 100 pieces of mirror, the views into the dome and monument court, and coloured light falling from concealed skylights. The creation of atmospheric effects with the help of coloured light reflects the work of Soane's friend Joseph Mallord

William Turner. The complexities and ambiguities of the spaces flowing into each other throughout the house, enlivened by contrasts of light and shade, also recall the techniques of landscape gardening as expressed in Alexander Pope's advice to Lord Burlington:

> Let not each beauty ev'rywhere be spy'd,
> When half the skill is decently to hide.
> He gains all points who pleasingly confounds
> Surprizes, varies and conceals the Bounds.
> (A. Pope, *Poems of Alexander Pope*, ed. F. W. Bateson 3, 1951, 338)

The views expressed by Pope had been formulated into the aesthetic theory of the picturesque in architecture and garden design by Richard Payne Knight and Sir Uvedale Price, who recommended an architecture based on intricacy and surprise. The analogy between architecture and nature was appreciated by Soane's contemporaries, as is clear from the fact that John Britton, in his book on Soane's house—significantly titled *The Union of Architecture, Sculpture and Painting* (1827)—quoted from Pope's lines of advice to Burlington. Furthermore, Soane chose to show his house and museum only on sunny days, almost as though it were a kind of architectural garden.

In 1824 Soane added a picture room at the back of 14 Lincoln's Inn Fields, in which he housed some of the most prized objects in his collection, two sets of narrative paintings by Hogarth: *The Rake's Progress*, which he had bought at a sale of William Beckford's possessions in 1802, and *The Election*, which he bought in 1823. The paintings in this room are hung on screens which gradually fold back until it is revealed that there is no wall behind them. Space flows into the next room which cannot be entered from the picture room because its floor is on a lower level. At basement level are the bizarre monk's parlour and yard, conceived as a shadowy Gothic setting for the fictional 'Padre Giovanni', whose tomb can be seen in the yard near some ruined fragments of his monastery. Padre Giovanni is Soane himself, indulging his sense of gloom and isolation.

Given to moods of brooding melancholy, Soane was a prickly and difficult character, quick to take offence, and full of self-pity. He regarded setbacks in his career as the result of malicious plots against him, a process in which he identified with Rousseau. His disastrous relations with his sons caused him endless suffering. George, who had been imprisoned for obtaining money under fraudulent pretences in 1814, published two anonymous attacks on his father in September 1815. These, so Soane persuaded himself, led to the sudden death of his wife a few weeks later. He framed and glazed the articles, to which he appended the title, 'Death blows', and cut his son out of his will. With the death of his elder son, John, in 1823, Soane now determined to leave his house, museum, and library to John's son, also called John Soane. In the end, however, he decided to draft an act of parliament to transfer the whole to a body of trustees who would preserve it permanently 'for the benefit of the public'. This bill was passed in parliament in 1833, though opposed at committee stage by his son George. The act enabled his grandson John Soane to inhabit the building on reaching the age of twenty-five. He was negotiating with the trustees to do so when he died in Madeira in January 1848, aged twenty-four. Soane's house and museum thus survived intact, and form a unique ensemble which is no less interesting architecturally than for its ingeniously displayed contents: architectural drawings from the Renaissance to the nineteenth century; books; paintings, including works by Canaletto, Hogarth, and Turner; architectural models; prints; and miscellaneous antiquities. His own architectural drawings, notebooks, and accounts are also meticulously preserved at the museum; there is a further important collection of drawings by him and his assistants at the Victoria and Albert Museum.

Professor of architecture at the Royal Academy Having been elected an associate academician in 1795 and a Royal Academician in 1802, Soane was in a position to manoeuvre for the professorship of architecture. Sandby's successor as professor, George Dance, had failed to deliver the required course of six lectures. Soane regarded his appointment as professor in succession to Dance in 1806 as the climax of his professional career. Beginning in 1809, he lectured in February and March, and eventually prepared two courses of six lectures each. He undertook an immense amount of reading for what became a monumental illustrated survey of the history of architecture from primitive times to the present day. The lectures were first published in 1929 and in a more authentic and complete version in 1996. Characteristically, Soane concentrated almost as much on what he saw as the faults as well as the merits in the great masters of the past. In his survey of contemporary architecture, which his students probably found the most entertaining part of his course, he lamented the lack in England of the grand public buildings which had been raised in Paris from the seventeenth century onwards. He was also deeply hostile to the meanness of modern domestic architecture in London and to the shoddy construction of most Gothic revival buildings. In 1810 his criticisms of the lack of relation between the front and side façades of Robert Smirke's newly built Royal Opera House, Covent Garden, were the subject of enormous controversy. This led to the suspension of his lectures on the grounds that the rules of the Royal Academy prevented criticism of the work of living artists. His behaviour at the academy between 1810 and his resumption of lecturing in 1813 was so erratic as to lead some members to believe he was going mad.

Obsessed with the need to express appropriate character in architectural forms and appropriate meaning in architectural ornament, Soane wrestled with the problem of ensuring the survival of the classical language of architecture in the modern world. In common with the Enlightenment authors and theorists whose work he spent so much time studying, he believed that problems could be solved by a return to origins and first principles. He thus studied much eighteenth-century writing on the origins of language, architecture, ornament, religious and sexual symbolism, primitive customs, laws, and religion. But, in Soane's lifetime, his lectures were perhaps best known for their illustrations, all of which survive in the Soane

Museum. Over 1000 of these watercolours were prepared between 1806 and 1820, many of them as much as 3 or 4 feet long, each of which took his pupils at least a week's full-time work. Constituting a comparative history of world architecture unique in its day, they were the product of a public-spirited gesture for which Soane received no payment, but which was part of his endorsement of the Enlightenment cult of civic virtue.

Friends and patrons Soane's career was developed through a network of patronage which was established on his grand tour. It was through his early backing by the bishop of Derry that he became a friend in Rome of Thomas Pitt, later Lord Camelford, an amateur architect who was a nephew of the earl of Chatham and a cousin of William Pitt the younger. The support of the younger Pitt was decisive in securing for Soane the most important office of his career, that of architect to the Bank of England. It was also Pitt who ensured that Soane was successful in his application for the post of clerk of the works at Whitehall, Westminster, and St James's, in 1791. Pitt employed him to make extensive alterations, including a new library, at Holwood House, Kent, in the 1780s and 1790s. Soane made frequent visits there, sometimes travelling with Pitt, who would invite him to dine or breakfast with him at the house.

Through his adoption by William Pitt, Soane also became a friend or acquaintance of other members of the ruling élite such as George Canning, Lord Liverpool, and George Rose, secretary to the Treasury and confidant of Pitt and of George III. He worked on the country houses of Pitt, Canning, Liverpool, and Rose, providing in each case a handsome library. Meanwhile, the high degree of professional competence which he showed in his work at the Bank of England led several of its directors to employ him in a private capacity, including the Thorntons of Albury Park, Surrey, and of Moggerhanger House, Bedfordshire, Henry Peters of Betchworth Castle, Surrey, and, most importantly, William Praed of Tyringham Hall, Buckinghamshire. Of his numerous artistic friends, including John Flaxman, Philippe-Jacques de Loutherbourg, Augustus Callcott, Sir Francis Chantrey, Henry Howard, and George Dance, the closest was probably J. M. W. Turner, who shared his preoccupation with coloured light: Turner was the only friend he chose to see during the Christmas following Mrs Soane's death. On the death of his close friend the landscape painter Sir Francis Bourgeois, Soane designed an impressive mausoleum for him at Dulwich, which he attached to a new picture gallery housing Bourgeois's celebrated collection (1811–14). Faithfully rebuilt after bomb damage in 1944, the mausoleum and gallery are among Soane's few major surviving buildings. The gallery has some claim to be the earliest public art gallery, and its method of top-lighting has been especially influential.

Late works One of Soane's most inventive creations was his national debt redemption office and Pitt cenotaph in Old Jewry of 1818–19 (dem. 1900). In this statement of lofty idealism, Soane expressed his own and his country's gratitude to William Pitt as a great national figure whom he described in 1820 as 'the Saviour of Europe' in a letter to George Canning asking him to accept drawings of the Pitt cenotaph (Soane to Canning, Soane Museum, IV.P.2.1, no. 1). A bronze statue of Pitt by William Westmacott on a Roman marble throne sat at the foot of a tribune surmounted by a ring of free-standing Corinthian columns supporting a glazed lantern. A group of merchants and bankers opened subscriptions for the statue as early as May 1802 in what was probably the first raising of public funds for a memorial to an English statesman.

By contrast, one of the principal disappointments of Soane's career was the shelving of his schemes for a new House of Lords, commissioned in 1794 but abandoned because of the Napoleonic wars and the machinations of James Wyatt. What came as a partial compensation was the grandiose *scala regia* or royal entrance and adjacent royal gallery which he built for George IV at the House of Lords in 1822–7 (dem. 1851). Having visited Paris in 1814 and 1819, he introduced into this work something of the flashy empire style of Charles Percier and Pierre-François-Léonard Fontaine, who had remodelled interiors at the Louvre and the Tuileries for Napoleon. Soane's work at the House of Lords was related to his unexecuted visionary scheme for a processional route or ceremonial way to take George IV from Windsor Castle to his throne in the House of Lords. Identifying with the triumphalist mood following the defeat of Napoleon in 1815, Soane envisaged a route of patriotic and imperial grandeur through Whitehall and Westminster, lined with grandiose public buildings including triumphal arches at the entrances to Downing Street. The only portion executed was his Board of Trade and privy council offices in Whitehall of 1824–6, with an engaged Corinthian order. This partly survives but was heightened and remodelled by Sir Charles Barry in 1845–6.

Near by Soane created new law courts in 1822–5 (dem. 1883), oddly contrived between the buttresses of the medieval Westminster Hall. With their floating, top-lit vaulted ceilings, and especially their panelling in a kind of reduced linen-fold pattern, these seem an attempt to create a language of historical resonance, appropriate to their august setting and solemn function. Like Hawksmoor's All Souls College, Oxford, they spoke a haunting personal language at the margin of classic and Gothic. The same flavour recurred in his privy council chamber (1824–6) in Downing Street, with its hovering diaphanous vault or canopy. There were modest echoes of this quality in the dining-rooms he built at 10 and 11 Downing Street in 1825. The former was commissioned by the chancellor of the exchequer, Frederick Robinson, who invited Soane to the opening dinner in 1826.

Soane's most complex late interior was his Freemasons' Hall of 1828 in Great Queen Street (dem. 1864), which combined his interest in hanging vaults, symbolical ornament, and coloured light. Like the Soane Museum itself, it was partly conceived as a poetical expression of his belief in the union of the arts. An active freemason from 1813,

Soane seems to have found no great appeal in the Anglican church of the day. He supported freemasonry in its role as the religion of the Enlightenment; on the continent masonic lodges were a metaphor for the re-establishment of a natural social order based in ideals of fraternal charity. Soane was himself a generous donor to masonic and other charities.

The interiors of Soane's last country house, Pellwall House, Staffordshire (1822–8), for his friend Purney Sillitoe, showed no diminution of his skills or personal style, while its triangular lodge was another attempt to unite Gothic and classical effects. By contrast, his last work, the state paper office, Duke Street (1830–34; dem. 1862), was a palazzo-like composition influenced by Giacomo Barozzi da Vignola. Soane had long been opposed to the chill papery thinness of Greek revival architects such as Robert Smirke and William Wilkins, whose buildings sometimes resembled plain boxes with awkwardly attached porticoes, an opposition which led him here to anticipate the Italianate revival in which Sir Charles Barry was to respond to the call of the Victorians for a greater surface richness.

Critical reception Opposition to Soane's individual manner began as early as 1796 on the completion of his Lothbury façade at the Bank of England. An anonymous critic now published a poem claiming that Sir Christopher Wren would have been pained to see 'pilasters scor'd like loin of pork … the Order in confusion move, Scroles fixed below and Pedestals above … [and] defiance hurled at Greece and Rome' (Bolton, 62). Soane was furious when James Wyatt read this out at a dinner party given for fellow architects. It was followed by a further pamphlet in which the same author pointed out 'that change is not always improvement, that singularity is not beauty, that an unprincipled passion for novelty is not genius' (ibid., 65). Soane was persuaded that he had a case against the publisher for libel, but his application was dismissed by the court of king's bench in 1799.

The bitterest criticism which Soane had to receive came from his own son George, who published anonymously in 1815 a devastating but not wholly unfair account of the relation between Soane's personality and his architecture. George complained of 13 Lincoln's Inn Fields that,

> The exterior, from its exceeding heaviness and monumental gloom, seems as if it were intended to convey a satire upon himself; it looks like a record of the departed, and can only mean that considering himself as deficient in that better part of humanity—the mind and its affections—he has reared this mausoleum for the enshrinement of his body.
> (*The Champion*, September 1815)

Further condemnation came in 1824 in a facetious article in *Knight's Quarterly Magazine* entitled 'The sixth or Boeotian order of architecture'. Once again Soane instituted an unsuccessful libel action. However, important critical acclaim came from W. H. Leeds, writing in *The Public Buildings of London* (2 vols., 1825–8), by John Britton and Augustus Pugin, and from Britton's sensitive monograph of 1827 on the Soane Museum. On retirement from the office of works in 1831, Soane was honoured with a knighthood. Moreover, the high degree in which he was held for his professional probity led to his being offered the presidency of the Institute of British Architects on its foundation in 1834; he was unable to accept this invitation because the rules of the Royal Academy prohibited members from belonging to similar societies. However, his position as the father of his profession was further recognized in 1835 when he was presented with a gold medal by 350 subscribers at a ceremony in the Freemasons' Hall.

This was a natural climax to a professional career which had included a succession of official appointments, including clerk of the works at Whitehall, Westminster, and St James's, in 1791; deputy surveyor of his majesty's woods and forests in 1795; clerk of the works to Chelsea Hospital in 1807; and one of the three 'attached architects' to the board of works, with responsibility for public buildings in Whitehall, Westminster, Richmond Park, Kew Gardens, and Hampton Court Palace, in 1814. A determined self-publicist, Soane printed privately many polemical writings as well as numerous volumes of his own executed and unexecuted designs. The most important of these, which he distributed, unsolicited, to numerous public figures, were *Designs for Public and Private Buildings* (1828) and *Description of the House and Museum on the North Side of Lincoln's Inn Fields* (1830, 1832, and 1835).

Soane died at 13 Lincoln's Inn Fields on 20 January 1837 and was buried on 26 January at the St Pancras old cemetery, in the tomb which he had designed for his wife in 1815, architecturally the most ambitious tomb of any British architect. Despite his numerous pupils and assistants, his style found few imitators. A typically puzzled reaction to his work came from John Weale, who wrote in 1844 that

> there was but one man, the late Sir John Soane, who dared to be positively original. All others were mad in some particular foreign fashion; but he alone was mad in his own way … [but] there was a method in the old knight's madness.
> (*Weale's Quarterly Papers on Architecture*, 2, 1844–5, 5–6)

Rehabilitation began in the twentieth century with praise from two classical architects: Sir Albert Richardson in *Monumental Classic Architecture in Britain and Ireland during the 18th and 19th Centuries* (1914), and Arthur Bolton, curator of Sir John Soane's Museum from 1917 to 1945, in numerous publications on Soane. Bolton's successor as curator, Sir John Summerson, interpreted Soane as a proto-modernist, responding particularly to the reductionist austerity of buildings such as his Dulwich College Picture Gallery and Chelsea Hospital stables. This interpretation was shared by Professor Henry-Russell Hitchcock and Sir Nikolaus Pevsner, although it meant ignoring Soane's conviction, as stated in his second lecture at the Royal Academy, that 'Art cannot go beyond the Corinthian order' (Watkin, *Sir John Soane*, 509). This conviction was rooted in Soane's acceptance of French eighteenth-century notions of convenance in which a hierarchy led from the simplicity of economical brick buildings such as Dulwich Gallery to the marbled Corinthian richness of royal palaces which represented the climax of architectural achievement.

It has become fashionable for architects on both sides of the Atlantic, modernists, post-modernists, and traditionalists alike, to proclaim their indebtedness to Soane. These include Philip Johnson, Richard Meier, Robert Venturi, James Stirling, and John Simpson, although probably only the last of these has truly echoed Soane's handling of space and light, notably at Ashfold House, Sussex, and Gonville and Caius College, Cambridge. However, the inventiveness which enabled Soane to be modern yet classical is likely to ensure that he will continue to fascinate and influence architects. DAVID WATKIN

Sources A. T. Bolton, ed., *The portrait of Sir John Soane* (1927) • J. Britton, *The union of architecture, sculpture, and painting … with descriptive accounts of the house and galleries of John Soane* (1827) • T. L. Donaldson, *A review of the professional life of Sir John Soane, architect, R.A.* (1837) • H. Dorey, 'Sir John Soane's acquisition of the sarcophagus of Seti I', *Georgian Group Journal*, [1] (1991), 26–35 • P. De la Ruffinière Du Prey, *John Soane: the making of an architect* (1982) • E. Harris, 'Sir John Soane's library: "O, books! Ye monuments of mind"', *Apollo*, 131 (1990), 242–7 • A. Jackson, 'The facade of Sir John Soane's museum: a study in contextualism', *Journal of the Society of Architectural Historians*, 51 (1992), 417–29 • B. Lukacher, 'John Soane and his draughtsman Joseph Michael Gandy', *Daidalos*, 25 (Sept 1987), 51–64 • M. Richardson, 'Learning in Soane's office', *The education of the architect*, ed. N. Bingham, Society of Architectural Historians Symposium (1993), 15–21 • E. Schumann-Bacia, *John Soane and the Bank of England* (1991) • J. Soane, *Memoirs of the professional life of an architect between the years 1768 and 1835 written by himself* (1835) • *Soane and after: the architecture of Dulwich Picture Gallery* (1987) • *Soane and death*, ed. G. Waterfield (1996) • D. Stroud, *Sir John Soane, architect* (1984) • J. Summerson, 'Sir John Soane and the furniture of death', *The unromantic castle* (1990), 121–42 • J. Summerson, 'Soane: the man and the style', *John Soane* (1983), 9–23 • P. Thornton and H. Dorey, *A miscellany of objects from Sir John Soane's Museum* (1992) • D. Watkin, 'Freemasonry and Sir John Soane', *Journal of the Society of Architectural Historians*, 54 (1995), 402–17 • D. Watkin, *Sir John Soane: Enlightenment thought and the Royal Academy lectures* (1996) • G. Wightwick, 'The life of an architect—my sojourn at Bath—the late Sir John Soane', *Bentley's Miscellany*, 34 (1853), 402–9 • T. Willmert, 'Heating methods and their impact on Soane's work: Lincoln's Inn Fields and Dulwich Picture Gallery', *Journal of the Society of Architectural Historians*, 52 (1993), 26–58 • Colvin, *Archs.* • G. Darley, *John Soane: an accidental romantic* (1999) • P. Dean, *Sir John Soane and the country estate* (1999) • M. Richardson and M. Stevens, eds., *John Soane architect: master of space and light* (1999)

Archives Canadian Centre for Architecture, drawings for cottages; notebooks of student attending his classes at the Royal Academy • Norfolk RO, bills for work at Ryston, Norfolk • Sir John Soane's Museum, London, corresp. | BL, letters to Lord Camelford, Add. MS 69328 • PRO NIre., letters to the earl of Abercorn

Likenesses N. Dance, pencil drawing, 1774, Sir John Soane's Museum • C. W. Hunneman, oils, 1779, Sir John Soane's Museum • G. Dance, pencil drawing, 1795, Sir John Soane's Museum • W. Owen, oils, 1804, Sir John Soane's Museum • T. Cooley, four pencil drawings, 1810, NPG • J. Jackson, oils, 1828, Sir John Soane's Museum • J. Jackson, oils, 1828, NPG • T. Lawrence, oils, 1828, Sir John Soane's Museum [*see illus.*] • F. Chantrey, marble bust, 1830, Sir John Soane's Museum • W. Brockedon, pencil and chalk drawing, 1835, NPG • F. Chantrey, pencil drawing, NPG • D. Maclise, drawing, V&A • T. Phillips, oils, Bank of England, London

Sobell, Sir Michael (1892–1993), industrialist and benefactor, was born on 1 November 1892 at Boryslau, Galicia, the only son of Lewis Sobel and his wife, Esther. His family owned factories in the Austro-Hungarian empire and oil interests at Limburg in Germany, but his parents moved to England about 1899 to escape antisemitism. The family settled in Dalston, east London, where Lewis Sobel set up as a confectioner. From 1903 Michael Sobel attended the Central Foundation School at Cowper Street in Finsbury (a school attended by other bright Jewish boys). At the age of sixteen, with money provided by his father, he set up as an importer of fancy leather accessories. He and his father subsequently worked as leather goods manufacturers.

On 28 August 1917, at Stoke Newington synagogue, Sobel married Anna (1896–1987), daughter of Samuel Rakusen, shipper. The Rakusens were a Leeds family renowned in the Jewish community for supplying the unleavened bread called *matzo* eaten at passover. Sobel was an adoring and protective husband, who spent only a few nights apart from his wife in seventy years, and never recovered from her death. He was a strict but often splendid parent to their two daughters, Hilda (who married Stanley Rubin) and Netta (who married Arnold, Lord Weinstock).

After the First World War Sobel took small upstairs offices in Oxford Street and began importing novel American electrical products. His energetic and astute salesmanship built up a flourishing business in six-valve radios and small refrigerators. As one gimmick he fitted a radio set to Gordon Selfridge's motor car which was driven along Oxford Street with music blaring out. However, his importance in business history as well as his personal fortune rested less on his salesmanship than on his participation in the transition of Britain into a consumer society. The proliferation of suburban housing and ribbon developments around London, together with the erection of new blocks of flats, increased the demand during the 1930s for electrical household appliances. Finding that he could not satisfy this demand with imports, Sobel raised the finance to open two factories, one for refrigerators and the other for wireless sets and radiograms, at Stonebridge in north-west London. When the Stonebridge factories (by then producing electrical equipment for the armed forces) were bombed during the Second World War, production was transferred to Amersham in Buckinghamshire (near Sobel's new home). In peacetime Sobel was encouraged by Viscount Hall to rent a factory at Hirwaun, near Aberdâr, Glamorgan. This site was used for the manufacture of radio receivers, and was buttressed with a generous quota for the supply of electronic valves for this purpose.

Sobel's interests prospered during the Second World War, and were consolidated in Sobell Industries Ltd, which was registered on 16 January 1946. The company was called Sobell on the advice of its advertising agency. Sobel adapted his own surname to Sobell accordingly. However, the aftermath of wartime disruption and the austerity policies enforced by the Attlee government prevented Sobell Industries from achieving any great immediate success. Sobell remained a trader *par excellence*, who depended heavily on his chief engineer Kurt Vesely.

In 1946 there were only 15,000 television licence holders in Britain (chiefly in London). However, in 1949 the British Broadcasting Corporation bought sites at Shepherd's

Bush and Lime Grove at which to make their own television programmes, and opened the first provincial television transmitter. The televising of the coronation of Elizabeth II in 1953 was a great spur, and by 1956 there were 5 million British television licence holders. These developments encouraged Sobell to extend his activities to include television receivers. He realized that if his radios were placed in large cabinets, and marketed as radiogramophones, they could be sold in furniture shops. As these shops could not supply servicing, he set up a national mobile service (named Home Maintenance) with 105 vans and guaranteed attendance within 48 hours of being summoned. The radio retail trade believed that direct sales to furniture shops deprived them of business and that Home Maintenance deprived them of repair work. They therefore imposed a boycott on Sobell products which continued until 1960.

Sobell Industries in March 1951 contracted with Great Universal Stores (GUS), the retail chain controlled by Isaac Wolfson, to supply annually from 50,000 to 150,000 television receivers over the next five and a half years. Wolfson insisted on a clause whereby GUS could cancel its contract if the government tightened hire-purchase regulations, and the contract was duly ended when such restrictions were imposed in 1952. Sobell declined a revised contract proposed by Wolfson. GUS instead offered the order to Electric and Musical Indusries (EMI) to supply under their Columbia brand, and EMI subcontracted this order to Sobell, but without the cancellation clause. When GUS later cancelled the contract, with EMI following suit, Sobell was entitled to claim damages. However, in 1953 he proposed a settlement as an alternative to litigation. This deal was finalized, with EMI purchasing his company for £300,000 but Sobell re-purchasing the factory and plant for £75,000.

Sobell and his son-in-law Stanley Rubin contracted to run the old business on EMI's behalf for six months until March 1954, when Sobell recruited his younger son-in-law, Arnold Weinstock, into the business. Subsequently the return of the Sobell trade mark was negotiated in return for paying EMI a future royalty of 4 per cent. Sobell resumed manufacture in 1954 under the name Banner Radio and Television Ltd, and by March 1955 all Sobell Industries' trade-mark rights had been recovered for a total of £78,750. The name of the company was later changed to Radio and Allied Industries.

Radio and Allied (R&A) in 1956 bought McMichael Radio Ltd, a small public company, for £345,000. Kenneth Bond, a partner in the auditors Coopers, was recruited as finance director in 1957. For over twenty-five years, Bond was crucial to the development of R&A and later of the General Electric Company (GEC). David Lewis, Sobell's solicitor since the 1930s, also joined the company and played an important role. As a consequence of Weinstock's better management, R&A's profits exceeded £1 million by 1957. Indeed its profits within five years were equal to one-third of the entire pre-tax profits of GEC, the giant British manufacturing company which had been founded by Hugo Hirst.

Sobell wanted the public flotation of R&A as soon as it had achieved the minimum three-year financial record required by the stock exchange. S. G. Warburg & Co., the company's merchant banker, received applications for 5.5 million shares (offered at 9*s.* each). Only 1.35 million shares were available when the company went public in June 1958, for Sobell and his family retained two-thirds of the shares. They were much enriched.

On 28 February 1961 it was announced that R&A had been acquired by GEC. The value of R&A was put at £8.6 million, or 33*s.* 6*d.* per share. GEC exchanged one of its shares for each share in R&A, paying an additional 2*s.* in cash. This deal gave the Sobell and Weinstock families 2.25 million shares in GEC, representing 14 per cent of that company's share capital. Sobell served on the board of GEC from 1961 until 1966; Weinstock was a director of GEC from 1961, and managing director from 1963 until 1996. Sobell remained chairman of the subsidiary GEC (Radio and Television) Ltd until his death.

Sobell's father had been an Austro-Hungarian cavalry officer and his son-in-law Rubin was joint master of the south Oxfordshire hunt. At the suggestion of John Lewis MP, Sobell in 1957 asked the trainer Sir Gordon Richards to buy him a thoroughbred, explaining that if he and his wife found racing fun, they would invest. A four-year-old colt, London Cry, was bought in the names of Sobell and Weinstock for 3500 guineas. Its first season proved a blaze of glory. In 1960, after the death of Dorothy Paget, Richards convinced Sobell and Weinstock to buy her bloodstock and the Ballymacoll stud Farm with nearly 300 acres in co. Meath, Ireland, for £250,000. This proved another success for the two men. They bred for the classics from top-class mares and sold surplus stock chiefly at the Newmarket sales. Sun Princess won the Oaks, Sun Prince won the St James's Palace stakes, and Dark Court won the Magnet cup. But Ballymacoll's supreme horse was Troy, which won the 200th Derby on 6 June 1979 by the widest margin since 1925. Its prize money in 1979 alone was £450,494. When the stallion was syndicated in that year, thirty-two shares were sold at £180,000 each; unhappily, Troy died in 1983. Sobell bought West Ilsley stables in Berkshire from John Astor in 1971. Twelve years later he sold these stables to the queen. He enjoyed being known as an owner, but seldom visited his stables.

Sobell was, in Lord Zuckerman's phrase, 'the gentle, almost secret, but enormous benefactor to a heap of noble causes' (Zuckerman, 86). Following his enrichment by GEC's acquisition of Radio and Allied, Sobell in 1962 formed the Anne and Michael Sobell Trust to benefit charities concerned with health, medicine, housing, children, and youth. The Michael Sobell Benevolent Trust was established in 1967 to advance education and learning among aged, disabled, or poor persons. When the earlier trust expired, its assets were transferred to the Sobell Foundation in 1977. Sobell himself decided on all the benefactions and endowments made by his charities until the late 1980s, when the burden of responsibility was undertaken by his solicitor David Lewis. For over twenty years he dispensed a fortune with imagination as well as generosity.

In 1968 he gave £1.1 million to the London borough of Islington to build the lavish Sobell Sports Centre. Later the foundation funded a similar centre in south Wales. In 1969 (as a personal tribute to his co-religionist Zuckerman) he donated £250,000 to provide pavilions at London Zoo to house apes and monkeys. He supported the rabbinical seminary at Jews' College, the old people's home Nightingale House, Haifa Technion (a technical research university in Israel), the Mount Sinai day centre at Golders Green and the Mount Sinai primary school at Kenton in Middlesex.

Other Jewish charities received his largesse, but it was perhaps in the field of cancer that he used his money best. Having befriended the duchess of Roxburghe, then chair of the National Society for Cancer Relief (afterwards renamed the Cancer Relief Macmillan Fund), in 1966 he paid for premises at 30 Dorset Square, which he had refurbished as offices (named Michael Sobell House) for the charity. The Anne and Michael Sobell Trust also gave £5000 a year to the charity, and from 1966 paid £200,000 each towards the Michael Sobell cancer hospices at Mount Vernon Hospital, Northwood, and Churchill Hospital, Oxford. Sobell served as president of the National Society for Cancer Relief from 1967 until 1984. He donated £500,000 in 1970 to buy premises for the British Empire Cancer Research Campaign and for the Royal College of Pathologists in Carlton House Terrace. To the Sobell Foundation he bequeathed virtually all his estate, which was valued at £47,556,223. Jeffrey Archer, who had approached Sobell in the late 1960s in connection with fund-raising projects for the National Society for Cancer Relief, later described Sobell as 'one of those men who never forgot his roots, and proved it by giving so much of his wealth to causes that would help the next generation' (private information).

In the political field Sobell promised a donation of £600,000 to the European Movement, but was only called upon for half of this sum, which was paid in April 1971. After Sobell's knighthood was gazetted in the new year's honours list of 1972, Hugh Macpherson alleged in *The Spectator* of 4 March 1972 that Sobell had been offered the honour in return for his donation to the European Movement, a charge repeated in the House of Commons on 16 March by a Labour MP. Edward Heath publicly deplored these 'nasty innuendoes' against 'a very distinguished man who has made this country his home, who has contributed greatly to its prosperity, and who has made a quite outstanding contribution to charities' (*House of Commons Debates*, vol. 833, col. 756). Sobell died of bronchopneumonia on 1 September 1993 at his home, Bakeham House, Bakeham Lane, Englefield Green, Surrey, aged 100. He was survived by his two daughters.

RICHARD DAVENPORT-HINES

Sources private information (2004) [Lord Weinstock] · private information (2004) [Mrs Hilda Rubin] · private information (2004) [Sir Kenneth Bond] · private information (2004) [Lord Archer of Weston-super-Mare] · M. Seth-Smith, *Knight of the turf: the life and times of Sir Gordon Richards* (1980) · Lord Zuckerman, *Monkeys, missiles and men* (1988) · M. Crick, *Jeffrey Archer* (1995) · *The Times* (2 Sept 1993) · *The Independent* (2 Sept 1993) · *The Independent* (11 Sept 1993) · *The Guardian* (3 Sept 1993) · K. Geddes and G. Bussey, *The setmakers: a history of the radio and television industry* (1991) · A. Brummer and R. Cowe, *Weinstock* (1998) · S. Aris, *Arnold Weinstock and the making of GEC* (1998) · m. cert. · d. cert. · H. Macpherson, 'Faith, hope and charity', *The Spectator* (4 March 1972), 350–51

Archives FILM presumed news film of Sobell with his champion horse, Troy

Likenesses J. Gunn, oils, 20th cent., priv. coll.; bequeathed 1993 to Jewish Care · photograph, 1980–89, repro. in *The Independent* (2 Sept 1993) · photograph, 1980–89, repro. in *The Times*

Wealth at death £47,556,223: probate, 15 Sept 1993, *CGPLA Eng. & Wales*

Sobhuza II [Ngwenyama, the Lion] (**1899–1982**), king of Swaziland, was born in Zombodze, Swaziland, on 22 July 1899, one of a large family born to his predecessor, King Ngwane V (Bhuna) and Lomawa Ndwandwe, the monarch's chief wife. His father died a few months after his birth and his grandmother then ruled as regent. He was educated at Zombodze primary school and at the Lovedale Institute in South Africa before assuming the Swazi throne as paramount chief at the age of twenty-two in 1921. Like his predecessor Sobhuza took many wives, and the precise number of his offspring, estimated at some 500, is unknown.

Throughout his long reign, Sobhuza presided over the transformation of his country from British protectorate to independent statehood within the Commonwealth. His survival as a traditional monarch was exceptional in a period when, elsewhere in Africa, tribal authority was denigrated and often pushed aside as an antique obstacle to the path of modernization and national self-determination. Sobhuza, however, possessed political skills in abundance, and he cunningly blended appeal to tribal custom with a capacity to manage economic and social change for his kingdom without weakening his autocratic power base.

Sobhuza's role during the years of British rule was essentially ceremonial; for his people—a largely agricultural community—the king was a source of ritual, ensuring rain and a fertile crop. Yet as early as 1922 Sobhuza demonstrated his political leadership of the Swazi nation by petitioning the British government to nullify a proclamation increasing the land available to the white-settler community.

In the early 1960s the king became a major actor in the events that led to independence for his country in 1968. He strongly opposed the orthodox post-colonial constitution proposed by the British government, in which he was assigned the role of constitutional monarch presiding over a Westminster-style parliament. As he emphasized, 'Western democracy is not suitable for my people … my rule through the tribal council is best for them.' Sobhuza founded his own party—the Imbokodvo ('grinding stone')—and in the pre-independence elections of 1967 won all twenty-four seats in the legislative council and 80 per cent of the popular vote. The nationalist opposition had split into competing factions in the years before the election, and it never effectively challenged Sobhuza's rule thereafter. In the 1972 election the Ngwane national liberation congress won three seats, and this modest revival in nationalist fortunes so disturbed Sobhuza that he promptly abrogated the constitution and for the next six years ruled by decree through the national council, a traditional body of tribal advisers. Sobhuza was appointed KBE.

In 1978 a new constitution was promulgated which provided for an elaborate reversion to a tribal mode of rule involving an electoral college of eighty members chosen by forty local councils (*tinkhundla*), dominated by tribal elements. The parliament (which opened in 1979) was in effect a gathering of the 'king's men' issuing instructions to the cabinet and civil service—'the administrative agents of traditional authority'. Thus, by the time of his diamond jubilee in September 1981, Sobhuza had successfully restored and indeed strengthened the monarch's role as the chief arbiter of decision-making in his kingdom.

The Swazi economy prospered under Sobhuza's leadership. Swaziland is rich in natural resources, and much of the land and mineral wealth originally owned by non-Swazi interests was brought under indigenous control during Sobhuza's reign. His foreign policy displayed a mixture of caution and commitment to the details of the Organization of African Unity. Neighbouring South Africa was the dominant state in the region, and—at Pretoria's insistence—Sobhuza kept a tight grip on the activities of the exiled African National Congress (ANC). A secret accord was signed with South Africa in 1982 which in effect deprived the ANC of sanctuary within Swaziland. Yet, at the same time, Sobhuza maintained cordial relations with his Marxist neighbour, President Samora Machel of Mozambique.

Old and infirm, Sobhuza died on 21 August 1982 in Mbabane, Swaziland. The choice of his successor according to Swazi custom threatened to be prolonged and difficult. He left a stable polity and an economy that, by African standards, was a model of successful, if unbalanced, growth. His achievement was considerable; his intuitive understanding of his people's preference for traditional ways enabled Swaziland to avoid the upheavals characteristic of much of post-war Africa. He was shrewd enough to realize that Western-style government could not easily be grafted onto a chiefly structure profoundly resistant to rapid and uneven modernization. He kept in check the political and economic expectations of his people, but in so doing he may well have placed a burden on his young and untried successor, the fourteen-year-old Makhosetive, his son with Ntombi Latfwala, who was queen regent of Swaziland from 1983 until the prince was crowned King Mswati II in April 1986. J. E. SPENCE, *rev.*

Sources *The Times* (24 Aug 1982) · *The Times* (28 Aug 1982) · *Africa South of the Sahara* (1982–3) [directory] · *Africa South of the Sahara* (1984–5) [directory] · C. Moritz, ed., *Current Biography Yearbook* (1982) · H. Kuper, *Sobhuza II, Ngwenyama and King of Swaziland* (1978)

Archives FILM BFI NFTVA, current affairs footage

Likenesses R. Birkett, group portrait, photograph, 1953, Hult. Arch.

Society of Antiquaries (*act.* 1586–1607) constituted a group of scholars whose coming together was the culmination of a process that had begun with John Leland's *New year's gift to King Henry the VIII* (1546) and his *Itinerary* (1550), and was developed thereafter in works like William Lambarde's *Perambulation of Kent* (1570). These works sprang from anxiety about the loss of objects that in post-Reformation England were in danger of destruction as idolatrous, notably funerary monuments and Catholic books, but which nevertheless deserved preservation for their association with the nation's history. In 1561 a petition led to a royal proclamation against the defacement of tombs, and the attempts to moderate religious fervour inherent in the Elizabethan religious settlement also helped to curtail the losses. But it was the Society of Antiquaries who arguably did most to develop a historical perspective able to accommodate such potentially dangerous survivals from the past.

William Camden and the foundation of the society The dissolution of the monasteries created a landscape full of monuments, signs pointing into a vacuum where a historical and cultural identity had previously been sited. William *Camden describes in the preface to his great chorographical work *Britannia* (1586), the grief and curiosity he felt when as a boy he walked among these ruins. Determined to reconcile Britain to the past represented by these slighted antiquities, he spent years walking across the counties of England, Wales, and Scotland, recording inscriptions, turning over stone heaps to find more, inquiring of gentry what had been taken from monasteries and of farmers what they had turned up when ploughing fields. The *Britannia* was the product of these walks. More continental than British in criticizing a Trojan foundation (even though Camden shrank from rejecting it altogether), the *Britannia* combined Flavio Biondo's archaeology, Guillaume Budé's numismatics, and Conrad Gesner's encyclopaedic bibliography. It defined its subject only with reference to what could be attested in the extant record: objects, inscriptions, interviews, and documents. A nuanced philology helped to reconstruct what could be known about the past, in 'Celtic', Roman, Saxon, Norman, and late medieval times, county by county. As discussions of evidence are nearly as frequent as narrative, the *Britannia* proved a work of massive length, and Camden himself admitted turning his back on refinements of literary style. The result was an abstruse and difficult work whose scholarly Latin is regularly interspersed with Anglo-Saxon, and which embraces languages as distant as Persian. Nevertheless it was surprisingly popular, inspiring poets and playwrights like Edmund Spenser and Michael Drayton.

Camden's *Britannia* exerted a great, even directive, influence on Elizabethan scholars. Its preoccupation with the accumulation of evidence created a long-lived tradition of historiographers who were 'not quite historians' because they insisted on system rather than chronology, and because they collected all facts, rather than those that fitted into a narrative. The *Britannia* was not in fact entirely Camden's work, for he had drawn upon the researches of many scholars. But, as a common enterprise, it helped propagate common skills and habits among the members of the Society of Antiquaries. In particular they were expert in epigraphy and palaeography, and familiar with a wide variety of languages from several periods. The *Britannia* similarly provides a model for their work, which can be best understood as interconnected parts of a vast historiographic programme, rather than as individual, narrative, or even patriotic histories with conventional subjects. Its example did much to promote a collaborative scholarly enterprise—what Lambarde described as 'joining our pennes and conferring our labours' (dedicatory letter, Lambarde, v).

Although the date at which that enterprise first took a settled form is not entirely clear, and the year 1572 was often proposed in the eighteenth and nineteenth centuries, the preface that Sir Henry Spelman wrote in the late 1620s for his treatise *The original of the four terms of the year* implies strongly that it was in 1586 that

> Gentlemen in London, studious of Antiquities, fram'd themselves into a College or Society of Antiquaries, appointing to meet every Friday weekly ... [T]wo Questions were propounded at every Meeting to be handled at the next that followed ... That which seem'd most material, was by one of the Company (chosen for the purpose) to be enter'd in a Book; that so it might remain unto Posterity. (Van Norden, 134–5)

It is possible that the *Britannia* merely gave focus to an informal group that was already meeting, but no satisfactory evidence has been found for the activities of such a group.

Activities and membership Manuscript copies of summonses, discourses, and papers exist from thirty-eight meetings between 27 November 1590 and 21 June 1607; except in the plague years 1594–8 these were held every Friday during the law terms, most often at Derby House, the seat of the College of Arms. Some are reprinted in Thomas Hearne's *A Collection of Curious Discourses* (1720, enlarged edition 1771). Topics for discussion were arranged in advance. Though it was agreed that they should be limited to British sources, they covered a great range of subjects, including legal history, land tenure, numismatics, inscriptions, heraldry, medals, and devices, along with the records, collections, lineages, rights and properties of monarchs and nobles, and of religious foundations, colleges, hospitals, corporations, cities, and towns. Funerary customs, the use of sterling money and the introduction of trial by combat into England were all discussed, as were all kinds of surveys, whether of counties or parishes. While disagreements were not unknown, it seems that the Elizabethan society was as much concerned to collect and preserve antiquities as to deliver definitive judgements upon them.

The exact membership of the Elizabethan society is unknown. Spelman's list identifies at least thirty-seven members but may contain errors and almost certainly suffers from omissions. Hearne's *A Collection of Curious Discourses* identifies others, as does a list in Arthur Agarde's hand (BL, Harley MS 5177, fols. 48ff.). These and other sources indicate that there must have been yet others as well. While the exact membership was probably not a concern to the Elizabethan society, it is undoubtedly greater than the names attested in these sources. As well as Camden the list must include at least the following: Arthur *Agard; Robert *Beale; Henry Bourchier or Bouchier; Robert *Bowyer; Richard Broughton; Richard *Carew; either Richard or John Clyffe; William, second Baron Compton; Walter *Cope; Robert *Cotton; John *Davies (and another man of that surname, unidentified); William *Dethick; Dr Thomas *D'Oyly; John *Dodderidge; Sampson *Erdeswick; William *Fleetwood; William *Hakewill; Abraham Hartwell; Michael *Heneage; Joseph Holland; William *Jones; Charles Lailand; Thomas *Lake; William *Lambarde; Francis *Leigh; James *Ley; Arnold Oldisworth; William *Patten; Robert Plott; John *Savile; Henry *Spelman; John *Stow; James *Strangman; Thomas *Talbot; Francis *Tate; Francis *Thynne; William Thynne or Thinne; Robert Weston; James *Whitelocke; Thomas Wiseman; and also perhaps Lancelot *Andrewes, Edmund *Bolton, Hugh *Broughton, Edward *Coke, and Hayward *Townshend.

Two representative members Of the men listed, many were lawyers, many were or became knights, and many were landed gentlemen, often lords of manors. Almost all were university educated, with slightly more from Oxford than from Cambridge. A notable minority were accused, or even confirmed, recusants. Few were clergy, though some had close connections with the established church. One such man was **Abraham Hartwell** (1553/4–1606), who attended Trinity College, Cambridge, where he matriculated in 1568, graduated in 1572, and became a fellow in 1574. He then entered the service of John Whitgift, accompanying him to Worcester in 1577. By 1583 he was a notary public, by 1584 Whitgift's secretary. No doubt it was thanks to the archbishop that Hartwell became MP for East Looe in 1586 and Hindon in 1593. He had become a member of the Society of Antiquaries by 1600, when he described himself as 'in time the last that was admitted into this society' (Hearne, 1771, 2.375). In that year he contributed to the discussion of epitaphs, referring to one at Lambeth and another at Cambridge, and he is also recorded as presenting a paper on heraldic mottoes.

Hartwell's most important contribution to scholarship was as a translator. Between 1596 and 1604 he published three translations from Italian and one from French, the former all dedicated to Whitgift. The first of these, *The history of the warres betweene the Turkes and the Persians* (1596), is described as completed in 'houres ... stollen from your Grace's graver businesses whereon I should have attended' (sig. A4). It was followed in 1597 by *A report of the kingdome of Congo*, an English version, amplified by woodcut plates and a map, of an Italian translation of the Portuguese original by Duarte Lopes. In his address to the reader Hartwell explains that he had been pressed by Richard Hakluyt to translate it, and presents as his primary motive a desire to advance missionary activity. Then in 1599 he published a translation from the French of a case of fraudulent demonic possession, with a dedication to Richard Bancroft, bishop of London, and finally, on 1 January 1604, in 'this my Quinquagenarian yere of Jubile', he produced a translation, *The Ottoman of Lazaro Soranzo*, describing how he had been prompted to 'thrust it forth' by a question put to him by Whitgift concerning the promotion of the grand vizier at the sultan's court. Hartwell made his will on 7 December 1606 (PRO, PROB 11/109, fols. 47v–49). He named as his executor 'my derely beloved wiefe Elizabeth'. She was the daughter of Robert Garnet of Broxbourne, Hertfordshire, where she inherited lands. They had a son John, who was still a minor when his father died, and to whom Abraham bequeathed purchased estates in Thanet, Kent, and Cheshunt, near Broxbourne. His cousin Robert Wright, parson of Woodford, Essex, received many of his 'books of divinity, humanitie, polymathie or of any other profession whatsoever'. Hartwell had died by 17 December 1606, when he was buried at Lambeth.

Few members of the Society of Antiquaries were heralds. Relations with the College of Arms cannot have been inherently unfriendly, since the Society met at Derby House, but the factious state of the college may have limited the membership of heralds, for fear they would bring their quarrels with them. Many members had heraldic interests, however. A good example is **Joseph Holland** (*d.* 1605), who also illustrates some of the virtues and shortcomings found among the less celebrated members of the society. Born at Weare in Devon, Holland was admitted to the Inner Temple in November 1571, and continued to live in London, where on 16 May 1575 he married Angella Bassano, presumably a member of the celebrated family of musicians. Their son Philip was born on 14 March 1576. Angella had died by 24 October 1584 when Holland married Sara Hewett, also of London, with whom he had two sons and a daughter, and whom he made his sole legatee and executor on his deathbed in November 1605. He was granted a coat of arms on 28 September 1588, appropriately, in the light of his own heraldic collections, which included one for his native county, recorded in the College of Arms in the eighteenth century. He was typical of members of the Society of Antiquaries in that he lived in London (he still had chambers in the Inner Temple in 1601), where a residence was probably essential, since attendance at meetings seems to have been required. As these were held during the law terms, members with country residences might not have been completely excluded, but they would not have been easily able to participate. Holland had become a member of the society by 3 June 1598, when he spoke concerning the antiquity of English cities, declaring that 'I have divers antiquities in coin stamped at several times in England', the oldest 'a British piece of gold' from Colchester (Hearne, 1771, 1.38). He collected documents too, among them a charter of King Edgar and a deed of the Edward, the Black Prince, and manuscript volumes, notably the mid-thirteenth-century almoner's cartulary from Reading Abbey (now BL, Cotton MS Vespasian E.v) which John Dodderidge gave him on 16 May 1605. Holland also noted monumental inscriptions and other physical remains of the past, for instance Maiden Castle, Dorset, and the prehistoric barrows surrounding it. The twenty papers that he is recorded as giving to the society show him to have been a careful observer and assiduous collector, but fallible in his judgements. Thus he confidently derived sterling money from its having been first struck by Edward I at Stirling in Scotland; better-informed colleagues contradicted him.

The historiography of the society The writings of Elizabethan antiquaries circle around a few historiographical poles, notably the use of legal and heraldic sources and the collection of evidence in the form of manuscripts, coins, and marbles. Some authors followed in Camden's footsteps by publishing chorographies, a form defined by a contemporary as 'the description of some particular place, as Region, Ile, citie, or such like portion of the earth severed by it selfe fro the rest' (Mendyk, 23). The results varied widely, embracing John Stow's scholarly and affectionate *Survey of London* and Richard Carew's more exuberant *Survey of Cornwall*, as well as many less personal productions, like the history of Norfolk, in Latin, that Sir Henry Spelman left unfinished at his death. Equally closely linked to antiquarian concerns was a large body of legal writing: many antiquaries searched the evidence of the past to find arguments for legal positions, reaching back as far as the ancient Hebrews for arguments on natural law. Besides religious sources, Spelman cites linguistic and textual evidence from Hebrew, Greek, and Arabic sources. Francis Thynne discusses the legal functions of ambassadors with reference to etymological and philological evidence. William Lambarde comments on the high courts of justice by relating them to Hebrew precedents in the Bible, as well as to what was then known about Anglo-Saxon and Norman courts. Robert Cotton used antiquarian evidence to defend the rights of parliament and to assert the primacy of the king of England over the king of Spain. A few antiquaries, including John Stow and William Thynne, also took an interest in literary editing: Stow and Thynne collaborated on an edition of Chaucer, and Stow published a selection of Skelton's poetry. There was an abiding interest in language.

The work of the Elizabethan Society of Antiquaries has been described as Baconian, or inductive, both in its reasoning style and in its focus on collecting data. Many antiquaries were indeed collectors, involved in determining the provenance of objects from medieval texts to Roman pavements. Both acquisition and cataloguing required serious financial commitment. Robert Cotton is the prime example. His manuscript collection included the Lindisfarne gospels, two contemporary copies of the Magna Carta, the only surviving copy of the poem *Beowulf*, many medieval cartularies and chronicles, and numerous Anglo-Saxon texts. Before the disastrous fire in Ashburnham House in 1731, in which a number of manuscripts were utterly destroyed and still more were damaged, Cotton's collections had been even greater. An eighteenth-century list, complemented by John Speed's

History of Great Britain, indicates that Cotton's coins included Greek, Roman, and ancient British specimens, along with 160 Anglo-Saxon coins (the first scholarly collection of these ever assembled in Britain) as well as Norman and later ones. Cotton's marbles included significant finds from Hadrian's Wall, together with Romano-British inscriptions. Some of the Cotton manuscripts came from the royal library. Stories of antiquaries' acquisitiveness were not uncommon. Unsurprisingly, perhaps, Cotton and his contemporaries were not above failing to return books and manuscripts that had been lent to them.

The demise of the Elizabethan society About 1602 Cotton, Ley, and Dodderidge petitioned Queen Elizabeth for the incorporation of a library and academy to support English historical scholarship, a 'Collegium Antiquariorum'. A draft for a royal charter was composed (BL, Cotton MS Faustina E.v, fol. 12) but the project failed. Some five years later the society itself was brought to an end. The causes of its demise in 1607 are obscure. There is manuscript evidence for society meetings until about 1607—also the year of the sixth and final edition of the *Britannia*. But no documentation survives from the period following 1608, strongly suggesting that the society discontinued its meetings at that time. Spelman's account attributes its cessation to the deaths of members, which is certainly relevant in some cases. On the other hand, his reference to 'some Rules of Government and Limitation' as proposed for a re-formed society in 1614, 'That for avoiding Offence, we should neither meddle with Matters of State, nor of Religion' (Van Norden, 135), also points to possible reasons for the society's earlier discontinuance. At the end of the sixteenth century its discussions had become increasingly concerned with political issues, and in the years immediately after the accession of James I they had been specifically directed towards religious topics as well. It may be, therefore, that government pressure had brought meetings to an end. If so, Spelman clearly hoped that the hiatus would only prove temporary. His optimism would not have been unreasonable. Society members still alive in 1614, like Robert Cotton, had not ceased to be active in the collection and preservation of antiquities. Camden was still publishing. It cannot be supposed that informal discussions had not occurred between friends and colleagues in the years since 1607. Perhaps, then, prudent members planned to refrain from investigating subjects that seemed provocative to James I, whom they believed disliked their proceedings. If so, their hopes of renewed activity were disappointed. Before they could meet again they learnt that 'his Majesty took a little Mislike of our Society' (ibid.) and the attempt to relaunch it was abandoned. Nothing survived except its name when the Society of Antiquaries of London was founded in 1717.

CHRISTINA DECOURSEY

Sources L. Van Norden, 'Sir Henry Spelman on the chronology of the Elizabethan College of Antiquaries', *Huntington Library Quarterly*, 13 (1949–50), 131–60 • G. Camdeno [W. Camden], *Britannia, sive, Florentissimorum regnorum, Angliae, Scotiae, Hiberniae* (1586) • BL, Cotton MS Julius F.x, F.x.i • BL, Cotton MS Faustina E.v, fol. 12 • BL, Harley MS 2077, fol. 138 • BL, Harley MS 5177, fols. 48ff. • wills, PRO, PROB 11/109, fols. 47v–49 • T. Hearne, *A collection of curious discourses* (1720) • T. Hearne, *A collection of curious discourses* (1771) • *Remarks and collections of Thomas Hearne*, ed. C. E. Doble and others, 11 vols., OHS, 2, 7, 13, 34, 42–3, 48, 50, 65, 67, 72 (1885–1921), vols. 1–9 • HoP, *Commons, 1558–1603*, 2.265–6 • J. Stow, *Survey of London* (1598) • J. Evans, *A history of the Society of Antiquaries* (1956) • A. Momigliano, 'Ancient history and the antiquarian', *Journal of the Warburg and Courtauld Institutes*, 13/3–4 (July–Dec 1950), 285–315 • M. McKisack, *Medieval history in the Tudor age* (1971) • L. Okie, *Augustan historical writing: histories of England in the English Enlightenment* (Lanham, MD, 1991) • R. J. Schoek, 'Early Anglo-Saxon studies and legal scholarship in the Renaissance', *Studies in the Renaissance*, 5 (1958), 102–10 • F. J. Levy, *Tudor historical thought* (San Marino, California, 1967) • G. Parry, *Trophies of time: English antiquarians of the seventeenth century* (1996) • R. Brooke, *A discoverie of certain errors published in print in the much-commended 'Britannia'* (1723) • J. Leland, *New year's gift to King Henry VIII* (1546) • J. Leland, *Itinerary* (1550) • W. Lambarde, *Perambulation of Kent* (1570) • R. A. Caldwell, 'Joseph Holand, collector and antiquary', *Modern Philology*, 40 (1942–3), 395–401 • commissary court of London, register of wills, 1603–7, GL, MS 9171/20, fols. 123–124r • S. A. E. Mendyk, *Speculum Britanniae: regional study, antiquarianism and science in Britain to 1700* (1989) • K. Sharpe, *Sir Robert Cotton, 1586–1631* (1979)

Soddy, Frederick (1877–1956), chemist and social commentator, was born on 2 September 1877 at Bolton Road, Eastbourne, the fourth son of Benjamin Soddy (*d.* 1911), a semi-retired London corn buyer, and his second wife, Hannah Green (*d.* 1879), who died when Frederick was eighteen months old. He was to blame this early loss for both a speech impediment and a certain shyness which became disguised as irritability. (Benjamin Soddy had three children from an earlier marriage; his daughter, Lydia, cared for his younger sons after the death of their mother.) The family was strongly nonconformist: they attended Eastbourne Methodist Church regularly, and one of Soddy's brothers became a Methodist minister. This religious background probably contributed to Soddy's inflexible attitude once he believed he was fighting a just cause, although he later said that he lost his faith as a small child. Soddy was educated at local schools and then Eastbourne College where his long-term friendship with Harold Cort Carpenter was established, and where the science master, H. E. Green, inspired Soddy to attempt a career in chemistry. He then attended University College, Aberystwyth, for two years before going to Merton College, Oxford, as postmaster. Although disliking Oxford, he was awarded a first-class honours degree in chemistry in 1898. Despite this success and the publication of a joint paper with R. E. Hughes in 1894 and a paper to the Oxford Junior Science Club, Soddy found no immediate employment. He spent a further year on private research at Oxford before hearing that a chair of chemistry was to be vacant at Toronto.

A rising star Soddy travelled to Toronto to apply in person for this post and, when he realized that he would not be appointed, decided to visit the chemistry department at McGill University in Montreal before returning to England. There, in the spring of 1900, he accepted the post of demonstrator. At McGill he met Ernest Rutherford, who had recently been appointed junior professor in physics,

Frederick Soddy (**1877–1956**), by Walter Stoneman, 1920

and, despite marked differences in character and disposition, they collaborated on research which led to the formulation of the theory of radioactive disintegration, published in eight joint papers in the *Journal of the Chemical Society* and the *Philosophical Magazine* in 1902–3. This discovery revolutionized the understanding of radioactivity and is at the root of all subsequent work. Despite rumours that the personalities of the collaborators made their association difficult, Soddy and Rutherford remained friends, continuing a regular correspondence until Rutherford's death. In 1903 Soddy returned to London where he worked with Sir William Ramsay (1852–1916) on the spectrographic proof of the production of helium from radium, which continued the work he had begun with Rutherford. Their results were published in *Proceedings of the Royal Society* in 1903. This work was to be completed by Soddy during his time at Glasgow with the help of his research assistants, and was presented in a series of nine articles in the *Philosophical Magazine* between 1905 and 1924.

After a year with Ramsay, Soddy became dissatisfied with aspects of the work carried out in the University College laboratories and left, to embark on a lecture tour of Australia. His love of travel was by now established and throughout his life he seized opportunities to visit new countries. The lecture tour was a success and, on his return, he took up the new post of lecturer in physical chemistry and radioactivity at the University of Glasgow which he had previously accepted. He held this post from 1904 until 1914, a period which was most productive and successful, professionally and personally. During his time at Glasgow, Soddy worked, with the assistance of Alexander Fleck, on the systematic investigation of the chemistry of the radio-elements, which led to the formulation of the theory of isotopes and the first use of the term in this context. These findings were published as articles in *Chemical News* and *Nature* in 1913. Soddy was elected FRS in 1910, and awarded the Nobel prize for chemistry for this work in 1921. He also wrote (or co-wrote) a further twenty or so scientific articles during this period. In addition he wrote a number of pieces to explain recent findings in the field of radioactivity to a popular audience and these works brought him notice abroad, especially in Russia.

While in Glasgow, Soddy's interests outside the bounds of science began to grow. He became closely acquainted with George Beilby and through his family with discussion and action on a number of political issues, especially economic questions and the suffragette movement. Through these discussions Soddy was to develop theories he had held since his McGill days about the uses and abuses of science. Some results were illustrated in his *Matter and Energy* (1912), where he attempted to show how scientific discoveries could lead to a Garden of Eden on earth. These ideas were popularized by H. G. Wells in *The World Set Free* (1913), which was dedicated to Soddy. Of more immediate importance, however, Soddy's relationship with Winifred Beilby (*d.* 1936) resulted in their marriage in 1908. They were remarkably happy, sharing many interests as well as politics. They both enjoyed mountain walking, even in the rain; she joined in his scientific work and was a popular hostess.

From Glasgow, Soddy moved to the chair of chemistry at the University of Aberdeen in 1914. Although he did not fight, the war had a tremendous impact on Soddy. The number of young men involved in the fighting led to a drastic reduction in the number of students at the university, and a shift in the gender balance, with more women than men. Wartime restrictions and shortages limited the range of experimentation possible. The organization of scientific support of the war effort led to his questioning of administrative structures and bureaucracies, and as a result his political beliefs moved to the left. He was associated with the Independent Labour Party in Aberdeen and was adopted as the Labour rectorial candidate for Aberdeen University in 1920, the year he announced his complete conversion to socialism, although of a rather unconventional kind.

Into Oxford and into difficulty In 1919 Soddy was appointed Dr Lee's professor of chemistry at Oxford. Although this might have been the crowning point of his career, in contrast to his time in Scotland, he actually achieved very little either professionally or personally. His character was unsuited to the internal workings of the institution. He disliked any kind of intrigue and believed in arguing openly for his case. This would not necessarily, in itself, have diminished his popularity, but the lack of any considerable professional advances by him or those attached to his laboratories lessened the respect he received. He published no more significant scientific work and his later writings were in the field of political economy and monetary theory, following, initially at least, the ideas of Major C. H. Douglas (1879–1952) and the social credit movement. He wrote a number of pamphlets and books on this theme, the first and best known of which was *Cartesian Economics* in 1922. His political beliefs had developed through his wartime experiences and were now consumed by one overriding concern, 'why so far the progress of science has proved as much a curse as a blessing to humanity' (*Cartesian Economics*, 1). His answer was that 'the money system' was at the root of the problem and he turned his attention to the reform of that system, postponing scientific research in the interest of that political end. It is also possible that he had come to the end of the project he had begun with Rutherford, and that developing new directions in the field was difficult for a chemist. For the time being, the field of radioactivity had passed to the physicists, which explains in part the hatred which Soddy developed for physicists during the latter years of his life. In this period his political activities filled a vacuum. In addition, other, younger scientists, particularly at Cambridge, were beginning to show that science and political concerns could be combined. Soddy joined them in their concerns, writing an introduction to the important 1935 collection of essays *The Frustration of Science*.

During his time at Oxford the already irascible Soddy's temper worsened and he became more isolated from the main body of the university. However in private life he was happier and, supported by his wife, he regularly entertained a circle of friends and students. His time at Oxford was brought to an end by the death of his wife from a thrombosis in 1936, which led to a period of reclusiveness, and to his retirement to a rather depressing house in Enstone, near Oxford. There were no children, for which Soddy blamed his experiments with radioactive substances which, he believed, had rendered him sterile.

Social concerns and later life In the 1930s Soddy became involved with the Le Play Society, attracted by its broadly sociological aims and the opportunities it provided for travel with some kind of educational purpose. He attended meetings regularly and, after the death of his wife, joined several excursions. The friends he made through the society provided support and company after his wife's death. Through his connections with the Le Play Society (and his concerns with monetary reform) Soddy became associated with the New Britain Group, an organization committed to peace-keeping and prosperity through a complicated programme of monetary reform, European federalism, and individual development. After his retirement he became more closely involved with them and much of his time was spent lecturing and writing for them. The outbreak of the Second World War confirmed his anxieties about society, and the bombing of Hiroshima and Nagasaki revived his long-term fears about the misuse of scientific discoveries.

Soddy died at the Royal Sussex County Hospital in Brighton, where he had been living, on 22 September 1956. His remains were cremated. He left a considerable bequest, largely the residue of his Nobel prize money, to found the Frederick Soddy Trust, which is dedicated to providing opportunities for groups of young people to travel and experience other societies, continuing the interests which had led him to the Le Play Society. The trust has been instrumental in assisting some hundreds of groups and through this his concerns with society are remembered. As a teacher, his conventional approach precluded close ties with many of his students. However, those who could penetrate the forbidding manner of an essentially shy man found a warm, caring individual who could become a permanent support and friend.

Memories of Soddy have been mixed. There was considerable regret among scientific colleagues that he abandoned his scientific career at such an early age, and among political acquaintances there was some feeling that he might have achieved more if he had not joined a relatively obscure group. However, since the early 1970s his work and thought have gradually been re-evaluated. A special 'Soddy session' was held at the conference of the British Society of the History of Science at Edinburgh in 1979, and since then Soddy's writings have been placed firmly within a different tradition from that of the natural scientists. To the post-1960s generation of ecologists and green activists his political writings appear not as eccentric but as central. His early recognition of the dangers of atomic science have attracted to his memory the status of a pioneer of responsible science, and his economic writings have been extremely influential in the area of ecological economics. LINDA MERRICKS

Sources L. Merricks, *The world made new: Frederick Soddy, science, politics, and environment* (1996) • M. Howarth, *Pioneer research on the atom* (1958) • G. B. Kauffman, ed., *Frederick Soddy, 1877–1956* (1985) • J. Martinez-Alier, *Ecological economics* (1987) • *CGPLA Eng. & Wales* (1956)

Archives Bodl. Oxf., corresp. and papers • MHS Oxf., lecture notes and papers • U. Sussex, MSS of the Frederick Soddy Trust | CUL, corresp. with Lord Rutherford • Royal Institution of Great Britain, London, letters to Royal Institution • University of Strathclyde, Beilby MSS

Likenesses W. Stoneman, photograph, 1920, NPG [*see illus.*] • O. Edis, photograph, 1920–29, NPG

Wealth at death £36,725 9s.: probate, 30 Nov 1956, *CGPLA Eng. & Wales*

Sodington Blount, de. For this title name *see* Blount, Elizabeth Anne Mould de Sodington, Lady de Sodington Blount (1850–1935).

Soest [Zoust], **Gilbert** (*c.*1605–1681), portrait painter, was probably born in the Netherlands, or perhaps in England of immigrant parents. His first name was not Gerard as traditionally recorded. He was known to his contemporaries as Zoust and his name is still pronounced in this way. Soest was living in Lincoln's Inn Fields, London, in 1657, and in Tucks Court, off Cursitors Street, from 1658 until his death. He painted only in London. There is circumstantial evidence to suggest that he was a Roman Catholic. There are no known records either of any marriage or of children (nor of any will or administration) although

George Vertue mentioned that he had a wife (Vertue, *Note books*, 4.29). She appears, perhaps, in the unfinished *Mother and Infant* (*c.*1664; priv. coll.). The probability that the infant in this painting is dead confirms its personal nature, to which Sir Oliver Millar drew attention when it was exhibited at the Royal Academy in 1956 (exhibition catalogue, RA, 1956, p. 58). His only self-portrait shows a belligerent, plump-faced man of about fifty-five (*c.*1662; National Gallery of Ireland, Dublin). Soest's style seems to be derived from the portrait work of Gerrit van Honthorst, as practised in The Hague during the 1640s. Painted in oils, his sitters are well-characterized, life-size, conventionally posed, with smoothly finished faces. The backs of the sitters' hands often appear swollen. The adults are always serious, the men usually tense. About 1706 Buckeridge noted that 'The Portraits he drew after Men are admirable, having in them a just, bold Draft, and good Colouring; but he did not always execute with a due regard to Grace, especially in Women's Faces' ([Buckeridge], 480). More recently, Millar described Soest's best portraits as providing the closest parallel in power and sympathy to the best male miniatures of Samuel Cooper (M. Whinney and O. Millar, *English Art, 1625–1714*, 1957, 95). Drapery and hair are depicted by Soest in characteristic, full sweeping curves; his highlighting of drapery at its extreme was aptly described by Waterhouse as 'crumpled zinc' (E. Waterhouse, *The Dictionary of 16th & 17th Century British Painters*, 1988, 64). The painter John Riley was Soest's pupil.

Of Soest's total output, 107 canvases are extant of which seventeen are signed 'Soest'. The only reliable price we have for one of his works is the £30 paid for the grand full-length portrait of Sir Joseph Sheldon, recorded by the Drapers' Company in 1678 (MS, wardens' court book, 4 Aug 1678, Drapers' Hall, City of London). This is on a par with works by the best of his contemporaries, other than Lely who dominated the period and was charging twice as much at this date. Soest's earliest pictures, dating from about 1649—including the double portraits of Viscount and Viscountess Fairfax (NPG, on loan to Tate) and that of John Egerton and his wife and Brilliana Harley with a lamb (both at Welbeck Abbey, Nottinghamshire)—are ambitious works marred by badly drawn hands. They clearly show, however, that he was already a highly accomplished face painter. In the 1650s his output consisted mainly of bust portraits set in a painted oval such as those of six members of the Lyttelton family (1651; priv. coll.). The only other double portrait, of unknown sitters (*c.*1658), is in a private collection. The 1660s were Soest's most productive years: he produced many larger canvases, and his treatment of drapery folds became larger and almost schematic. George Vertue related that

> Zoest the Painter. who haveing been much disgusted with painting Womens pictures. he haveing a dutch taste of designing … it remarkably happen'd, two Gentlewoman came to him to set for their pictures … when they knockt at the door. he accidentally oppen'd it him self. they askt if Mr. Zoest the painter livd there. yes he answer'd. (was he at home.) yes, & he showd them the way up stairs to his painting room. and at the same time turn'd out of doors. left the house & them to wait till they were tyer'd—when his wife told the Ladies. that he had had so ill success in painting the pictures of the fair Sex. that he was resolv'd to paint, or flatter them no more. (Vertue, *Note books*, 4.29)

It appears that his refusal to paint women relates to the period 1660–67. Soest's larger portraits include those of Sir Thomas Tipping (*c.*1661; Tate collection) and of Dr Thomas Bulwer (*c.*1667; Art Institute of Chicago). Several others date from about 1669: *Inspiration of an Artist* (Museum of Fine Arts, Boston), almost certainly a likeness of Edward Pierce the sculptor; *John Hay* (Glasgow Museum and Art Gallery, Kelvingrove); his sons, *Charles and John Hay* (Yale U. CBA); *Henry Howard* (Tate collection); and *Cecil Calvert* (Enoch Pratt Library, Baltimore). Later works include *Portrait of a Woman as a Shepherdess, Formerly called Jane Needham, Mrs Middleton* (*c.*1675; NPG, on loan to Tate)—it is not certain that the sitter was Jane Myddelton—and *Ann Bankes* (*c.*1675; National Gallery of Art, Washington). Soest was buried in St Andrew's, Holborn, on 12 February 1681. Charles Beale recorded in his diary on 11 February that Soest was nearly eighty when he died, at his home in Tucks Court. It is possible that the Anne Soest buried in St Andrew's on 16/17 July 1679 was his wife.

R. H. Merley

Sources R. H. Merley, 'Gilbert Soest: an account of the 17th c. portrait painter', MPhil diss., U. Birm., 1999 • [B. Buckeridge], 'An essay towards an English school of painters', in R. de Piles, *The art of painting, with the lives and characters of above 300 of the most eminent painters*, 2nd edn (1744), 354–430 • Vertue, *Note books* • parish register, Holborn, St Andrew's, GL, 12 Feb 1681 [burial] • parish register, Holborn, St Andrew's, GL, 25 May 1658 [burial: Soest's servant] • parish register, Holborn, St Andrew's, 16/17 July 1679, GL [burial: Anne Soest] • tax records, PRO, E179 143/336; E179/393; E179/267; E179 252/32; E179 253/28; E179 143/370 • C. H. C. Baker, *Lely and the Stuart portrait painters: a study of English portraiture before and after van Dyck*, 2 vols. (1912) • M. K. Talley, *Portrait painting in England: studies in the technical literature before 1700* (1981)

Likenesses G. Soest, oils, *c.*1662, NG Ire. • A. Bannerman, line engraving (after painting by G. Soest), BM, NPG

Soissons, Louis Emmanuel Jean Guy de (1890–1962), architect and town planner, was born in Montreal, Canada, on 31 July 1890, the younger son of Charles de Soissons and his wife, Julie, *née* Rozwadowska. When he and his brother and sister were small, the family moved to London.

De Soissons's early education was at Bewshers and Colet Court, the preparatory school for St Paul's, but he did not continue on to a public school. He knew early that he would be an architect and at the age of sixteen was articled to J. H. Eastwood. From 1906 to 1911 he attended evening classes at the Royal Academy. He became the Royal Institute of British Architects' Tite prizeman (1912) and then their Henry Jarvis student at the British School at Rome (1913). He next went to the École des Beaux-Arts, attending the atelier Duquesne and winning three medals, but returned from Paris when the First World War broke out. Back in Britain, he tried to enlist in a line regiment but short sight precluded this. Instead, he served with the Army Service Corps and later undertook liaison

Louis Emmanuel Jean Guy de Soissons (1890–1962), by Elliott & Fry, 1953

duties with the Italian army. He was mentioned in dispatches, appointed OBE in 1918, was awarded the *croce di guerra*, and was made a *cavaliere* of the order of the Crown of Italy. He also worked with the War Claims Commission where his fluent French and Italian were useful.

After the war de Soissons returned briefly to his studies at the Beaux-Arts. There followed a short-lived partnership with Philip Hepworth, followed by a longer-lasting but informal arrangement with George Grey Wornum. In 1919 destiny placed a finger upon de Soissons. Ebenezer Howard, the doyen of the garden-city movement, had in 1919 impetuously decided to start a second town for 40,000–50,000 near Welwyn to take up the torch from his first experiment at Letchworth. The initial sketch-plan came from a Letchworth architect, but the sapient Sir Theodore Chambers, chairman of Welwyn Garden City Ltd, then asked the Royal Institute of British Architects (RIBA) to recommend an architect-planner. In April 1920 de Soissons was appointed to produce a revised plan, with the duty also of company architect. He presented his plan in June. Its subsequent development and implementation revealed a breadth of interests and skills of design and decision-making which proved to be in excellent balance. Besides laying out the whole plan of Welwyn Garden City, de Soissons designed a high proportion of its civic buildings, its early factories, and its housing. On behalf of the company he had the final decision about the work of other architects in the town, which he always exercised with respect for his fellow professionals. When in 1948 Welwyn Garden City was expanded into one of the government's post-war new towns, de Soissons was confirmed as planner and his firm laid out the large extension scheme.

On 29 April 1922 de Soissons married Elinor Maude Charlotte Penrose-Thackwell, with whom he had three sons. They set up their first home in the embryo new town and he lived in or near it from then on, believing that such a responsibility should not be discharged from a distance. He knew that while a plan could provide a strategy, it was the detail that would touch people's feelings. The results are evident in the pleasure of moving around the town and in the active affection that it generates among its inhabitants.

What is known of de Soissons's architectural philosophy has to be derived mainly from his work and conversation, for he wrote little. He perceived architectural quality without prejudice about style, but had a personal affection for the Italian Renaissance, the eighteenth-century English and American classical vernacular, especially the buildings of Nantucket, and Regency Brighton, Cheltenham, and Leamington. He was too independent to be greatly influenced by any of this or by Welwyn Garden City's immediate predecessors, Letchworth (which he did not much like) and Hampstead Garden Suburb. Like them, his town was conceived as having a formal civic centre surrounded by informal residential areas. The latter were innovatively planned and invested with exceptional natural charm. Yet it was one of his main contributions to the garden-city movement that despite their relaxed and natural character, his streets and housing are distinctively urban in idiom and are not villages writ large. This was a lesson de Soissons had absorbed from the Liverpool school of architect-planners such as Stanley Adhead and Patrick Abercrombie. He developed their neo-Georgian style with suavity and flexibility, but could design flat-roofed houses when asked to. His industrial buildings at Welwyn Garden City were also notable: he attempted, for instance, to confer architectural quality upon the banal 'sectional factories' hitherto built for leasing on trading estates.

De Soissons did much other inter-war housing for people of low and middle incomes, in part through the patronage of Sir Theodore Chambers. He was architect to the duchy of Cornwall estate in Kennington, London, and was one of a small group with whom Edward VIII as prince and king discussed housing problems. He served on the Central Housing Advisory Committee and the Burt committee, appointed after 1945 to promote innovation in construction. He was greatly pleased by an invitation just before the war to design barracks for the brigade of guards and after 1945 to rebuild Carlton House Terrace for the Foreign Office—but sadly both had to be cancelled. He did popular work at Cheltenham. As senior partner in the extended post-war firm of Louis De Soissons, Peacock, Hodges, and Robertson, he participated in rebuilding the bombed centre of Plymouth, as well as further housing in the west country. Among much other work he was responsible for the George VI memorial in Carlton Gardens, the

Hobbs memorial gates at the Oval, the restoration of the Nash terraces in Regent's Park, and buildings at Cheltenham College. He was architect to the Imperial War Graves Commission for Greece and Italy, where his firm meticulously designed and planted war cemeteries rivalling the best built after the First World War; one of the largest and most moving is at Cassino. He believed in personal commitment in design and was the final arbiter in the office. He conveyed his ideas with decisive comments and quick sketches, and expected them to be carried out exactly. He was, however, more open-minded about modern work in the office than his personal tastes might suggest.

In 1923 de Soissons was made a fellow of RIBA and a member of both the Town Planning Institute and the Société des Architectes Diplômés par le Gouvernement. But he was not an 'institute' man and preferred to put effort into the Architectural Association School (1929–33) where he was a vice-principal of the upper school and a tough, incisive critic. He was also active at the Royal Academy, to which he was elected in 1953 (having become an associate in 1942) and where he served as treasurer from 1959, and at the Royal Fine Arts Commission (1949–61). He was also involved with F. R. Yerbury in founding the Building Centre. He was awarded the RIBA distinction in town planning in 1945 and was made CVO in 1956, the honour that he most greatly valued.

De Soissons dressed like a Frenchman, sporting a moustache, round glasses, and a beret, frequently with the addition of a bow-tie. He loved good food and wine, sculpture, and paintings (James Woodford and Charles Cundall were among his close friends), but he did not particularly enjoy theatre or music. He read quickly and enjoyed the best current architectural journals, especially French, Italian, and Scandinavian. He was a devotee of whodunits and of the novels of Dickens, Dumas, and Zane Grey. Though averse to publicity, he was gregarious and friendly with anyone who gained his respect, whatever they were and wherever he found them. He made every day an event for those with him at the time, for he had great vitality and a strong sense of fun. Religious or political compatibility was irrelevant. When he walked into a pub he would look quickly around and give a greeting, and he resented any lack of response. Not a sporting man himself, he enjoyed the idea of field sports, and walking holidays gave him pleasure at one stage. He was a member of the Athenaeum and the Arts Club, but not a club devotee. Among his architectural contemporaries he admired Sir Edwin Lutyens, with whom he once worked briefly, Sir Giles Gilbert Scott, H. S. Goodhart-Rendel, Charles James, and Frank Lloyd Wright. His own closest collaborator in his firm was Kenneth Peacock, with whom he designed the war cemeteries.

De Soissons was first, last, and always a practical architect; and although he wanted the challenge of major set-piece architecture, Welwyn Garden City is likely to be viewed in history as his great achievement, especially its plan and its residential areas. He died at the London Clinic on 23 September 1962.

WILLIAM ALLEN, *rev.* ANDREW SAINT

Sources personal knowledge (1981) · private information (1981) · private information (2004) · C. B. Purdom, *The building of satellite towns* (1949) · M. de Soissons, *Welwyn Garden City: a town designed for healthy living* (1988) · *The Times* (24 Sept 1962) · *The Times* (3 Oct 1962) · m. cert. · d. cert. · *CGPLA Eng. & Wales* (1962)

Archives Louis de Soissons Partnership, London, MSS · priv. coll., MSS | Commonwealth War Graves Commission, Maidenhead, papers relating to work for Imperial War Graves Commission · Welwyn Garden City Library, corresp. with Sir Frederic Osborn

Likenesses Elliott & Fry, photograph, 1953, NPG [*see illus.*]

Wealth at death £47,828 5*s.* 1*d.*: probate, 30 Nov 1962, *CGPLA Eng. & Wales*

Solander, Daniel (1733–1782), botanist, was born in Piteå, northern Sweden, on 19 February 1733, one of four children of Carl Solander (1699–1760), Lutheran clergyman, and his wife, Magdalena Bostadia (1713–1789), the daughter of a high-ranking official in Västerbotten. Only Daniel and a younger sister, Anna Magdalena, reached adulthood. (Daniel is often erroneously called Daniel Carl or Charles Solander, if his unofficially adopted patronymic Carlsson is mistaken for a second forename.) Solander was probably educated at home by his father, an accomplished amateur scientist, and in 1750 he matriculated at Uppsala University where he initially lived with his paternal uncle who was professor of law. He abandoned his humanistic studies and under the tutelage of Linnaeus 'giort större progresser uti Historia naturali … än någon annor af alla some jag kiänner' ('made greater progress in natural history … than anyone else I know'; *Daniel Solander: Collected Correspondence*, 44). Linnaeus later wrote that 'I looked after him like a son, under my own roof' (Fries, 60). Solander worked with Linnaeus on the most important natural history collections in the country, which were in the hands of the monarchy and aristocracy.

In 1753 and 1755 Solander visited the northern shores of the Gulf of Bothnia to study the unusual flora of the Piteå and Torneå districts, returning with collections which were preserved in the Naturhistoriska Riksmuseet (National Museum for Natural History) in Stockholm. In 1756 he published *Caroli Linnaei elementa botanica*, a little piece mainly of interest because it shows the very close relationship between master and pupil. Although often referred to as 'Doctor Solander' he did not complete his degree at Uppsala, since by 1759 he was already making his way to England for what was intended to be a temporary visit. Delayed by illness he finally arrived in London in June 1760 where introductions from Linnaeus ensured his welcome to scientific circles and the particular regard of the naturalist John Ellis. He found it easy to learn foreign languages and could soon communicate well in English. He spent his time visiting botanical gardens and museums, and sent back to the Hortus Upsalienis much useful material including seeds and plants. In constant contact with Linnaeus, he promoted his sexual classification system, the use of which grew rapidly despite initial opposition. He was highly regarded in England, and his English acquaintances, particularly the botanist and entomologist Peter Collinson, helped persuade him in 1762 to decline the offer of a professorship in St Petersburg which Linnaeus had secured for him, and in 1763 to take on the

Daniel Solander (1733–1782), by John Flaxman, 1775

work of cataloguing the natural history specimens in the British Museum, where he devised for his slips the Solander case, which soon became standard in libraries. The same year he declined to accept Linnaeus's professorship at Uppsala University which, exceptionally, was in the holder's gift. After this refusal and the marriage to another man in 1764 of Linnaeus's eldest daughter Elisabeth Christina whom Solander hoped to marry, correspondence between teacher and pupil virtually ceased.

In 1767 Solander met Joseph Banks, who became his patron and friend, and under whose auspices he joined the expedition under James Cook to observe the transit of Venus from Tahiti in the Society Islands. The party sailed in the *Endeavour* on 25 August 1768, visiting Madeira and South America before reaching Tahiti. After completing their work on the island they sailed to New Zealand, where Solander Island was named by Cook, and to Botany Bay, flanked by Point Solander. Solander and Banks found rich new fields for collection and description. The journey home was less productive scientifically and Solander suffered from two bad attacks of malaria before the *Endeavour* reached England in 1771 and Solander became the first Swede to circumnavigate the globe.

Solander shared Banks's enthusiastic reception in London and became his secretary and librarian (in effect the curator of his natural history collection) at Banks's home in Soho Square after plans that they should both join Cook's voyage on the *Resolution* had come to nothing. The two spent a month in Iceland in 1772, where they discovered 'a prodigious deal in all Branches of Natural history, Geography, astronomy, &c &c' (*Daniel Solander: Collected Correspondence*, 289). Solander gained an established position in English scientific circles. Elected fellow of the Royal Society in 1764, in 1771 he was made honorary DCL of the University of Oxford, and in 1773 became keeper of the natural history collections in the British Museum, and also after 1779 curator of the second duchess of Portland's natural history collection.

Solander is remembered primarily as a botanist whose main contribution lay in systematic description and classification, and who worked at an unusually favourable time when the introduction of the Linnaean system coincided with unprecedented discoveries of new lands: however, his reputation was clouded by early accounts of his life which portrayed him as lazy and ungrateful to Linnaeus, and, since he published so little himself, much of his work went unrecognized. Twentieth-century study of his and Banks's manuscripts show him to have been an accomplished zoologist as well as a botanist, and assiduous, meticulous, and skilful in observation and description. He was responsible for much of the scientific content of the first edition of the *Hortus Kewensis*, but characteristically was not identified as author or contributor. His British Museum catalogue has come to be recognized as a major work of scholarship. His great work, the 'Florilegium', was intended to be a description with Banks of their discoveries on the *Endeavour*, but when 700 of the planned 800 copper plates and much of the text had been prepared Solander suddenly died and the work remained unpublished, although the manuscripts survived; it was finally published, complete, in the 1980s.

The famous portrait by Zoffany shows Solander as somewhat portly, well groomed, and urbane. He was hospitable and convivial, and an avid international correspondent with leading figures in fields as far apart as literature and engineering. He was a valued addition to the literary, artistic, and scientific society of which Banks was the centre, although as Fries points out his conviviality stood in the way of his scientific work and hence his later reputation (Fries, 78). It was at a gathering at Banks's home that Solander suffered an attack, probably a stroke, on 8 May 1782; he died there on 13 May. He was buried at the Swedish church in Princess Square, London, and, when this was demolished in 1913, his remains were reburied by the Vetenskapsakademien (the Swedish scientific academy) in the Swedish section of Brookwood cemetery, Woking.

ELIZABETH BAIGENT

Sources R. E. Fries, 'Daniel Solander', *Levnadsteckningar över Kungl. Svenska Vetenskapsakademiens Ledamöter*, 7 (1939–43), no. 114 • *Daniel Solander: collected correspondence, 1753–1782*, ed. and trans. E. Duyker and P. Tingbrand (1995) • R. A. Rauschenberg, *Daniel Carl Solander, naturalist on the Endeavour* (1968) • E. W. Groves, *Notes on the botanical specimens collected by Banks and Solander on Cook's first voyage* (1962) • J. Cook, *The journal of HMS Endeavour, 1768–71* (1977) • J. A. Diment and A. Wheeler, 'Catalogue of the natural history manuscripts and letters by Daniel Solander (1733–82), or attributed to him, in British collections', *Archives of Natural History*, 11 (1982–4), 457–88 • A. Wheeler, 'Daniel Solander—zoologist', *Svenska Linnésällskapets Årsskrift* (1982–3), 7–30 • S. Rydén, *The Banks collection: an episode in eighteenth-century Anglo-Swedish relations* (1963) • J. B. Marshall, 'Daniel Carl Solander: friend, librarian and assistant to Sir Joseph Banks', *Archives of Natural History*, 11 (1982–4), 451–6

Archives Bergianska Herbariet, Stockholm • BL, corresp. and diaries, Add. MSS 29533, 45874–45875 • CUL, notes on *Flora suecica* of Linnaeus • Linn. Soc., corresp. and papers • Naturhistoriska Riksmuseet, Stockholm • NHM, papers • RBG Kew • SOAS, Tahitian vocabulary • University of Uppsala Library, Sweden | Linn. Soc., letters to John Ellis • NRA, letters to Sir Joseph Banks • Statens etnografiska museum, Stockholm, Alström collections

Likenesses line engraving, caricature, pubd 1772 (*The Simpling Macaroni*), NPG • J. Flaxman, jasper medallion, 1775, Wedgwood Museum, Barlaston, Staffordshire [*see illus.*] • jasper medallion, *c*.1779, Wedgwood Museum, Barlaston, Staffordshire • Cl. and J. Alströmer, medal, 1783 • J. Newton, stipple, pubd 1784 (after

J. Sowerby), BM, NPG • J. Zoffany, oils, Linn. Soc. • coloured sketch (Daniel Solander with Joseph Banks), Linn. Soc. • print, Linn. Soc.

Solanke, Oladipo Felix [*known as* Ladipo Solanke] (*c.***1886–1958**), student activist, was born in the Yoruba town of Abeokuta, Nigeria. He was the second child and only son of Adeyola Ejiwunmi and her husband, who had adopted the name of Paley from the Scottish missionary who had raised him. He was educated at St Andrew's Training Institution, Oyo, Nigeria, and at Fourah Bay College in Sierra Leone, where he obtained a bachelor's degree in 1922. Later that year he travelled to England, completed his legal studies at University College, London (1923–8), was temporarily employed as a teacher of Yoruba at London University, and subsequently qualified as a barrister.

Solanke's experiences of poverty and racism inspired him to organize other Nigerian students in Britain, and with the assistance of Amy Ashwood Garvey he formed the Nigerian Progress Union in London in 1924. In 1925 Solanke and Dr Bankole-Bright founded the West African Students' Union (WASU) in London. Under Solanke's leadership WASU became the main social, cultural, and political focus for west Africans in Britain for the next twenty-five years. It served as a training ground for many future political leaders, and played an important role agitating for an end to colonial rule in Britain's west African colonies.

Solanke became one of the main propagandists of WASU, and in 1927 published *United West Africa at the Bar of the Family of Nations*, a demand for the recognition of equal political rights for Africans. Throughout his life he wrote many letters and articles demanding self-government for the west African colonies, especially Nigeria, and essays on traditional Yoruba institutions and culture. He was the first person to make a radio broadcast in Yoruba in June 1924, and, styling himself Omo Lisabi, made some of the first Yoruba records for Zonophone in 1926. In 1945 in Nigeria he was awarded the Yoruba chieftancy title atobatele of Ijeun.

Solanke was at the forefront of WASU's attempts to establish a hostel for west African students in London. Between 1929 and 1932 he embarked on a fund-raising tour of west Africa, and became the warden of the WASU hostel that was opened in Camden in 1933. He returned to Britain with his future wife, whom he married in 1932, Opeolu, *née* Obisanya (*b.* 1910), the first matron of the hostel and mother of his three children. As a result of this tour, WASU branches were formed throughout the region, and Solanke and WASU were able to establish significant political contacts with anti-colonial forces in west Africa, and provide the link between them and the anti-colonial movement in Britain. Solanke also completed a further fund-raising tour of west Africa during 1944–8, prior to the opening of WASU's third London hostel at Chelsea Embankment in 1949.

Solanke's activities on behalf of WASU periodically brought him into conflict with the Colonial Office and sometimes with other black leaders in Britain. However, as WASU secretary-general, he was also able to establish the union as a significant anti-colonial and anti-racist organization in Britain. During the Second World War Solanke established closer relations between WASU and several leading members of the Labour Party's Fabian Colonial Bureau, including Reginald Sorensen, who subsequently became godfather to one of his children. As a result of these links a west African parliamentary committee was established, with Labour MPs as members, that enabled WASU to act as a more effective parliamentary pressure group.

During the 1950s, due to political differences within WASU, Solanke was gradually marginalized from the central role he had once enjoyed. He continued to run a student hostel in London and formed his own breakaway organization, WASU Un-incorporated, which he led until his death from lung cancer at the National Temperance Hospital, St Pancras, London, on 2 September 1958. His funeral and burial took place on 6 September at Great Northern London cemetery, Southgate. HAKIM ADI

Sources private information (2004) • H. Adi, *West Africans in Britain, 1900–1960: nationalism, pan-Africanism and communism* (1998) • G. O. Olusanya, *The West African Students' Union and the politics of decolonization, 1925–1958* (1982) • *Makers of modern Africa*, 2nd edn (1991), 716 [biographical dictionary] • d. cert.

Archives University of Lagos, Gandhi Library, MSS | BL, West African Students' Union journal

Likenesses photographs, University of Lagos, Nigeria, Gandhi Library, MSS • photographs, repro. in *The Journal, West Africa*

Wealth at death £4104 9s. 9d.: administration, 30 Dec 1958, *CGPLA Eng. & Wales*

Solanus, Moses [Moïse du Soul] (*d.* before **1737?**), Greek scholar, was the grandson of Paul du Soul of Tours, professor of theology and rector of the academy at Saumur between 1657 and 1661. As a protestant he was driven from France by persecution, and seems to have settled at Amsterdam, from where he came to England.

Solanus's fine Greek scholarship recommended him to the notice of scholars at both Oxford and Cambridge universities. Encouraged by the classicist Richard Bentley, he projected an edition of Lucian, of which in 1708 he printed a specimen at Cambridge; he also collected materials for a life of that writer, though nothing came of this 'famous and accurate' edition. In the same year he was employed in the family of the earl of Wharton. In 1722 and 1723 he was at The Hague, where 'he may have gone to negotiate with the Wetsteins' (Mayor). In conjunction with Brutel de la Rivière he translated Humphrey Prideaux's *An Historical Connection of the Old and New Testaments* into French, as *Histoire des Juifs et des peuples voisins* (1722). After his return to England, he completed a splendid five-volume edition of Plutarch's *Lives* (1729), which had been started by Augustine Bryan and which Thomas Bentley, Richard's nephew, had, in the first instance, proposed to continue. The precise details of Solanus's death are unknown. A passage in the preface (p. xi) of Karel Koenraad Reitz's edition of Lucian shows that he was living after 1733, though he appears to have died before 1737.

J. B. MULLINGER, *rev.* PHILIP CARTER

Sources E. Haag and E. Haag, *La France protestante*, 10 vols. (Paris, 1846–59) • J. E. B. Mayor, 'Note on Moïse du Soul (Moses Solanus)',

Report and Communications of the Cambridge Antiquarian Society, 5 (1881–4), 167–82

Soldene, Emily [*performing name* Miss FitzHenry] (**1838?–1912**), singer and theatre manager, was allegedly born in Clerkenwell on 30 September 1838, and was brought up as the daughter of Edward Fuller Solden (1805–1873) and his apparently bigamous wife, Priscilla, *née* Swain (1812–1900). She married law clerk John Powell (1834?–1881) on 17 March 1859, and was a mother before she began to study singing (1861) with William Howard Glover. She made her first public appearance in a concert given by Glover in 1862, and her professional début, performing operatic selections and mezzo-soprano ballads at the Oxford Music Hall under the name Miss FitzHenry, in 1863. Miss FitzHenry established herself as one of the outstanding vocalists of the 1860s music halls, and Miss Soldene's classical career was allowed to fade away.

In 1869, with the first vernacular productions of French *opéra bouffe* being mounted in England, attractive actresses who could combine sophisticated comedy and vocal talents of an operatic level were at a premium, and Miss FitzHenry was hired from the halls by Covent Garden's John Russell to take over the star role in his tour of *La grande-duchesse*. For the occasion she returned to being Miss Emily Soldene. She scored a hit, and Miss FitzHenry was duly buried.

Soldene made her West End theatre début in 1870, playing Marguerite in Hervé's *opéra bouffe Le petit Faust*, but superstardom came only in 1871, when Charles Morton produced Offenbach's *Geneviève de Brabant* at the Islington Philharmonic. The show caused a sensation, the theatre became the Mecca of high society and the well-heeled theatregoer, and Emily Soldene, who played the star role of the little pastry-cook Drogan, became the toast of the London musical stage. She confirmed this success as the lusciously plotting Mlle Lange in *La fille de Madame Angot* (1873), before leading a company playing both shows, along with *La grande-duchesse*, Hervé's *Chilpéric*, and Offenbach's new *Madame l'archiduc*, to America (1874–5) to similar triumph.

In the following years Soldene toured her repertory through Britain, America, and, with memorable success, New Zealand and Australia (1877–8), adding, at various times, *Barbe-Bleue*, *La belle Hélène*, *Trial by Jury*, *The Waterman*, *Poulet et Poulette*, *Giroflé-Girofla*, *La Périchole*, and *La jolie parfumeuse* to her list of shows. On returning to Britain in 1879 she starred in three productions at the Alhambra before taking her own company on the road, memorably introducing the English-language version of Bizet's *Carmen* to the British provinces.

The death of Soldene's husband, an underfunded and unsuccessful third tour of America, and an ill-fated attempt to run the Gaiety Theatre, Hastings (1883), put a temporary hitch in her career, but she continued successfully and starrily to tour her hit shows, until age and embonpoint forced her to abandon the sexy sophistications of *opéra bouffe*. She was forty-eight years old and 13 stone when she switched to playing a character role for the first time, in *Frivoli* at Drury Lane (1886). Hired out of *Frivoli* by America's top musical manager, John McCaull, she returned to America and played there in comic opera, vaudeville, variety musical, and briefly on Broadway in a self-adapted French melodrama, before settling in San Francisco, where from 1890 to 1892 she played heavy ladies in comic opera repertoire at the Tivoli and the Orpheum.

In 1892 Emily Soldene was persuaded to return to the scene of her 1877 triumphs, Australia, for a season, but the venture was a disaster and the underfunded singer had to look for alternative employment. An old admirer, a well-connected newspaper man, got her hired as music and drama critic on the Sydney *Evening News*, and Emily Soldene—Madame, as she was fondly known to all—stepped out of the theatre and into journalism. For the next seventeen years she turned out several heavily bylined weekly columns of cheerful, idiosyncratic London social chatter for the *Evening News* and later *The Sun* in a second career almost as successful as her first. She died at her lodgings, 21 Upper Woburn Place, Bloomsbury, on 8 April 1912, while her last column was in the mail to Sydney.

KURT GÄNZL

Sources K. Gänzl, *In search of a singer* [forthcoming] · E. Soldene, *My musical and theatrical recollections* (1897) · K. Gänzl, *The encyclopedia of the musical theatre*, 2 vols. (1994) · *Evening News* [Sydney] · *The Era* · *The Sun* [Sydney] · m. cert.

Likenesses photographs, repro. in Gänzl, *In search of a singer* · photographs, repro. in E. Soldene, *My musical … recollections* · photographs, repro. in Gänzl, *Encyclopaedia* · photographs, British Musical Theatre Collection

Wealth at death £893 3*s*. 4*d*.: probate, 9 May 1912, *CGPLA Eng. & Wales*

Sole, William (**1741–1802**), apothecary and botanist, was born at Thetford, Norfolk, the eldest son of John Sole and his wife, Martha, the daughter of John Rayner, banker, of Ely. The family claimed to have originated at Soules in Normandy, and to have settled in east Kent during the reign of Richard I. Sole was educated at the King's School, Ely, and then apprenticed for five years to Robert Cory, apothecary, of Cambridge. He afterwards practised as an apothecary at Bath, subsequently in partnership with Thomas West.

Sole specialized in the cultivation of mints, trying to reproduce natural conditions, 'in my Botanic Garden, nor has it for upwards of twenty years been manured, if ever' (Savage, 53). Among his botanical correspondents were the Quaker William Curtis and John Pitchford of Norwich, who was a friend of the eminent botanist Sir James Edward Smith. Sole considered his own identifications of the various mints more secure than those of Sir James, or even of Linnaeus, each of whom relied on a different diagnostic feature when identifying the species. Sole drew up a manuscript flora of Bath in 1782; when the Linnean Society was founded in 1788, he was one of the first to be elected as an associate.

In 1798 Sole published his chief work, *Menthae Britannicae*, a folio illustrated with twenty-four copperplates. For a century thereafter several British mints were known by the names which he had given them, though it is now evident that neither Sole nor his contemporaries appreciated the capacity of mint species to vary in their habit. For his account of the British grasses and their agricultural uses, with specimens, which he presented to the Bath and West of England Agricultural Society in 1799, he received a silver tankard. Sole died, unmarried, at his home in Trim Street, Bath, on 7 February 1802, and was buried at Batheaston. Sprengel commemorated him in the species *Solea*, now merged in *Viola*.

G. S. Boulger, *rev.* Anita McConnell

Sources S. Savage, 'William Sole's unpublished notes on his *Menthae Britannicae*, 1798', *Proceedings of the Linnean Society of London*, 150th session (1937–8), 52–8 • *GM*, 1st ser., 72 (1802), 274 • J. G. L. Burnby, *A study of the English apothecary from 1660 to 1760* (1983), 67
Archives Bath and West and Southern Counties Society, Bath • University of Bath Library, drawings and papers

Solicita (*fl. c.*1200). *See under* Women medical practitioners in England (*act. c.*1200–*c.*1475).

Sollas, William Johnson (1849–1936), geologist and anthropologist, was born in Birmingham on 30 May 1849, the eldest son of William Henry Sollas, shipowner, and his wife, Emma (*née* Wheatley). He was educated at the City of London School, the Royal College of Chemistry (under Sir Edward Frankland), and the Royal School of Mines (where, Sollas later averred, he owed most among his teachers to Thomas Henry Huxley). After becoming an Associate of the Royal School of Mines, Sollas proceeded to St John's College, Cambridge, where, under the influence of Thomas Bonney, he specialized in geology, taking a first class in the natural sciences tripos in 1873. From 1873 to 1878 Sollas was engaged in university extension lecturing before appointment as lecturer in geology at University College, Bristol, and as curator of the Bristol Museum, becoming professor of geology and zoology in May 1880.

Already known as a palaeontologist, with unique knowledge of fossil and modern sponges, Sollas was appointed professor of geology and mineralogy at Trinity College, Dublin, in December 1883. There the range of his interests broadened to encompass petrology and mineralogy, interests stimulated by problems posed by the study of some of Ireland's igneous rock complexes.

In 1897 Sollas was elected to the professorship of geology at Oxford, succeeding Alexander Green (1832–1896). In 1874 he had married Helen Coryn (*d.* 1911) of Redruth. Their two daughters, Igerna and Hertha, both collaborated with their father at Oxford, the former in his palaeontological researches and the latter in the translation into English of Eduard Suess's great work *Das Antlitz der Erde*. As well as his teaching and museum duties, Sollas's researches at Oxford continued to expand and diversify: in a single year, 1908, he published papers on topics as disparate as the internal structures of the isomorphs and polymorphs of titanic acid, and on Neanderthal man.

Sollas's best work was done in the period up to about 1920; as he became older, he became increasingly eccentric and erratic, but in his prime he was a fine and strikingly innovative scientist. His 180 published papers span an incredible range and, in the words of one of his obituarists, are not infrequently tinged with genius. He published a book of fine essays under the title *The Age of the Earth* in 1905 and perhaps the best-known of his works, *Ancient Hunters and their Modern Representatives*, in 1911 (3rd edn, 1924). There was also a celebrated petrological memoir on the *Rocks of the Cape Colville Peninsula, New Zealand* (2 vols., 1905). Sollas is remembered for the development of his 'diffusion column' for the separation of mineral grains and micro-fossils of varying specific gravity by flotation in liquids of graded density; for his technique (frowned upon by latter-day museum curators) of investigating the internal structure of fossils by means of serial sectioning; for his (inconclusive) investigation in 1896 of the structure of the Funafuti coral atoll in the Pacific; and for his contributions to hominid evolution. He was posthumously accused, on scant evidence, by J. A. Douglas (his demonstrator and his successor in the Oxford professorship) of having been the moving spirit behind the notorious Piltdown skull fraud.

Sollas was elected a fellow of the Royal Society in 1889, receiving a royal medal in 1914, as well as the Bigsby (1893) and Wollaston (1907) medals from the Geological Society, of which he was president from 1908 to 1910. He held a fellowship of St John's College, Cambridge, from 1882 to 1884, and a fellowship of University College, Oxford, from 1901 until his death. Sollas held honorary doctorates from four universities. He re-married in 1914, his second wife being Amabel Nevill, daughter of John Gwyn Jeffreys, and widow of Professor H. N. Moseley. She died in 1928.

Sollas is described as short and wiry, with a leonine head. He was a man of wide culture and learning, a considerable conversationalist, and a considerate host. His writings are models of lucidity and fine English style; despite inevitably being overtaken by more recent scholarship, many are well worth reading today. After a period of deteriorating physical health and mental state, Sollas died, still in office, at his home, 104 Banbury Road, Oxford, on 20 October 1936.

E. A. Vincent

Sources A. Smith Woodward and W. W. Watts, *Obits. FRS*, 2 (1936–8), 265–81 • W. W. Watts, *Nature*, 138 (1936), 959–60 • J. A. Douglas, transcripts of notes, Oxf. U. Mus. NH • E. A. Vincent, *Geology and mineralogy at Oxford, 1860–1986* (1994) • *WWW* • *CGPLA Eng. & Wales* (1937) • Valter's and Kelly's directories [of Oxford ?]
Archives Bodl. Oxf., corresp. • ICL, archives, lecture notes | BGS, letters to W. W. Watts • BL, corresp. with Macmillans, Add. MS 55222 • Bodl. Oxf., corresp. with Sir Aurel Stein • Oxf. U. Mus. NH, corresp., notebooks and papers • TCD, letters to John Joly • U. Edin. L., letters to Sir Archibald Geikie
Likenesses A. H. Bodle, photograph (in old age), U. Oxf., department of earth sciences • photographs, Oxf. U. Mus. NH, Geological collections
Wealth at death £15,749 18*s.* 9*d.*: resworn administration with will, 9 Feb 1937, *CGPLA Eng. & Wales*

Solly, Edward (1819–1886), chemist, agronomist, and antiquary, was born, probably in London, on 11 October 1819, the son of Edward Solly (*c.*1790–*c.*1847), a wealthy Baltic timber merchant of Berlin and St Mary Axe, London. Sarah Solly, who made a significant bequest to the National Gallery in 1879, was his sister.

From about 1830 Solly studied chemistry in Berlin where his father had many intellectual and artistic contacts. In 1836, at the age of seventeen, at which time he was studying at the Royal Institution in London, he published a paper 'On the conducting power of iodine, &c., for electricity' in the *Philosophical Magazine*. Two years later he was appointed chemist to the Royal Asiatic Society and elected a member of the Society of Arts. In 1841 he became lecturer in chemistry at the Royal Institution where he was associated with Faraday. Solly published numerous papers on the chemistry of plants and on agriculture. He was elected an honorary member of the Royal Agricultural Society (1842) and, as honorary professor of the Horticultural Society, investigated the effects of electricity on vegetable growth. He published a valuable work entitled *Rural Chemistry* (1843; 3rd edn, 1850) which dealt with soil composition and fertilizers. On 19 January 1843 he was elected a fellow of the Royal Society, and in 1845 he became professor of chemistry in the East India Company's military college at Addiscombe. A syllabus of his lectures on chemistry appeared in 1849.

On 13 September 1851 Solly married Alice Sarah Wayland; the couple had five daughters. Solly had become a member of the Gresham Life Assurance Society, in 1849 and eventually became director of the firm, which conducted business overseas with a team of international inspectors. He was one of the promoters of the Great Exhibition of 1851, and acted as a juror; for a year from 9 June 1852 he was secretary to the Society of Arts, beginning its *Journal*, increasing membership, and improving finances.

Associated with free trade politics through his father, Solly advocated and attempted to organize a centralized trade museum of raw materials, machinery, and other information to assist investment and manufacture in all parts of Britain (1855). He also collected a large library, which was particularly rich in eighteenth-century literature; and his wide genealogical and literary knowledge made him a valuable contributor to periodicals including *Notes and Queries*, *The Bibliographer*, and *The Antiquary*. In 1879 he edited *Hereditary Titles of Honour* for the Index Society, of which body he was treasurer. An invalid in his later years, Solly died from heart failure at his home, Camden House, Sutton, Surrey on 2 April 1886. His library was sold at Sothebys, London, in November 1886. He presented to the National Gallery an anonymous picture called *A Venetian Painter*, but most of his father's vast art collection was acquired by the Prussian state about 1830, or sold in London in 1847. G. A. J. COLE, *rev.* V. E. CHANCELLOR

Sources *Walford's Antiquarian*, 9 (1886), 224 • *Journal of the Society of Arts*, 34 (1885–6), 579 • E. Solly, 'On the conducting power of iodine, bromine and chlorine for electricity', *London and Edinburgh Philosophical Magazine*, 3rd ser., 8 (1836), 130–34 • *N&Q*, 7th ser., 1 (1886), 300 • *N&Q*, 7th ser., 2 (1886), 340 • *Men of the time* • H. Solly, *'These eighty years', or, The story of an unfinished life*, 2 vols. (1893) • *The correspondence of Michael Faraday*, ed. F. A. J. L. James, [4 vols.] (1991–) • H. A. L. Cockerell and E. Green, *The British insurance business, 1547–1970* (1976) • F. Herrmann, 'Peel and Solly: two nineteenth-century art collectors and their sources of supply', *Journal of the History of Collections*, 3 (1991), 89–96 • D. Hudson and K. W. Luckhurst, *The Royal Society of Arts, 1754–1954* (1954) • personal knowledge (1886)
Archives BL • Bodl. Oxf. • RSA
Wealth at death £8755 10s.: probate, 3 June 1886, *CGPLA Eng. & Wales*

Solly, Henry (1813–1903), social reformer and founder of working men's clubs, was born on 17 November 1813 in the City of London, the youngest of the ten children of Isaac Solly (1768–1853), a trader and company director, and his wife, Mary, the daughter of John Harrison, a London solicitor. His father was descended from Daniel *Neal, the historian of the puritans. Samuel *Solly was his elder brother. The Sollys were religious dissenters, closely associated with the English Presbyterian meeting-houses at Walthamstow and Hackney. Henry was educated by the nonconformist minister Eliezer Cogan (1762–1855) and then in Brighton under Dr John Morell. Solly was one of the first students to be admitted to the nondenominational University College, London, which he attended from 1829 to 1831.

A career in commerce proved uncongenial, and on the advice of the Unitarian minister Robert Aspland in 1840 Solly briefly attended the General Baptist Academy under Revd Benjamin Mardon. This decision was taken in the light of his father's financial ruin in 1837, an occurrence which had far-reaching effects. Unable afterwards to rely on family money, the search for regular income was a dominant factor in his career. Solly entered the ministry of the Unitarian chapel at Yeovil in 1840, though he always disliked the Unitarian label. He came into contact with workers, especially in the glove factories, which made him sympathetic to Chartism, and he was one of the two dissenting ministers who served as a representative (for Yeovil) at the Birmingham Chartist conference of 1842. His novel, *James Woodford, Carpenter and Chartist* (1881), embodies his experiences at this time.

On 22 April 1841 Solly married his cousin, Rebecca (1812–1893), the daughter of Samuel Shaen, a barrister and landowner of Crix, Essex, at the Presbyterian chapel of High Street, Stourbridge. She loyally supported her husband whatever the financial consequences, and they had one son and four daughters.

Solly became a strong advocate of, and activist in, radical causes: universal suffrage and education, anti-corn law agitation, the co-operative movement, early closing for shops and Sunday opening of museums, anti-slavery, and much else. This commitment to radicalism did not endear him to the leaders of Unitarian congregations. He was forced out of Yeovil in 1842, and had a succession of short-term pastorates at Tavistock (1842–4), Shepton Mallet (1844–7), Cheltenham (1847–51), Carter Lane, London (1852–7), and Lancaster (1858–62). At the end of his London ministry, Solly concluded: 'I could not help feeling that my London pastorate, and work there generally, had been rather a failure, and the back of my life at five and forty seemed broken' (Solly, *These Eighty Years*, 2.140). He never held a pastorate again in any denomination.

Solly returned to London in 1862 with little money and little hope of a pulpit. However the twenty years which followed showed him to be one of the most remarkable social innovators of his time. As William Beveridge, the architect of the welfare state, put it: 'He was a restless, inventive, constructive spirit, part author of at least three large living movements; charity organisation, working men's clubs, and garden cities' (Beveridge, 170). Solly was not a socialist, however, and saw himself as a gentleman. He believed in the class order of British society, but was involved in almost every radical initiative to benefit the working class. He formed numerous associations with this aim, the majority of which failed soon after their creation. The centres of his concern were the condition of the respectable working classes and the fostering of a sense of fellowship between the classes. These he expressed in the Working Men's Club and Institute Union, which was founded in London, chiefly at his initiative, on 14 June 1862; he became its first paid secretary in 1863. An ardent teetotaller, Solly became convinced when at Lancaster that working men needed clubs for recreational purposes. Travelling incessantly, he created clubs all over the country and it was soon a genuinely national organization. An excellent organizer and fund-raiser, the movement he created soon became an established part of British life. His infectious enthusiasm led Henry Fawcett to state: 'Here is Henry Solly, who thinks heaven will be composed of Working Men's Clubs' (*The Inquirer*, 7 March 1903). Despite his success in establishing the club movement, his flamboyant and domineering style, along with his insistence that the clubs should maintain a high moral tone, soon led to trouble. He was first forced out in 1867, but returned a few years later only to sever finally the connection with his creation in 1873 following disputes about his salary and the sale of alcohol in the clubs.

Turning next to the indigent element in society, Solly was chiefly instrumental in creating the Charity Organization Society (COS) in 1869. Thrift was at the heart of the doctrine of self-help that was pressed on the Victorian working man. However 'ultimately self-help and charity might be in conflict … the 1860s were inspired with the belief that the poor could be helped, by intelligent charity, to help themselves' (C. L. Mowat, *The Charity Organisation Society 1869–1913*, 1961, 14). Solly in his usual practical style set out this opportunity in a well-attended public lecture which he gave in 1868 that proved to be a trumpet call for action. The London Association for the Prevention of Pauperism and Crime was in operation by November the same year, and from this the COS was formed.

The society's central doctrine was the high responsibility which it attached particularly to the spending of charitable money, and the need to accompany it with personal care. Serving as its first secretary and guiding force, Solly helped the society become a leading body in the administration of charity in London, and the promotion of social casework throughout Britain. Once again, Solly's insistence on more money for himself and control over the organization resulted in his being ousted from the COS.

In the belief that artisans should be well housed, Solly's last initiative was to set up the Society for the Promotion of Industrial Villages in 1884. This venture soon failed, but the novel idea was later considered to have been an important precursor of the work of Sir Ebenezer Howard in the so-called Garden City movement. 'This Society was the last of my forlorn attempts to promote social reforms by means of an organised association, and I mean it to be the last; for which those friends who have helped me, and those whom I have also worried but who have not helped me, will be devoutly thankful' (Solly, *These Eighty Years*, 2.566).

Solly wrote and lectured extensively on numerous subjects, often in a provocative way in order to engage as many people as possible in support of his causes. He had a tempestuous period as joint editor, with the trade unionist George Potter, of *The Beehive* from 1869 to 1870. He was always an earnest enthusiast, impatient and difficult to deal with except on his own terms. He cheerfully and vigorously forced himself and his causes before the attention of the great and the good. To the distress of his family, later in life he rejected the Unitarian name but not the ministerial title, although others, as he admitted, 'only saw [him] as a Unitarian minister' (Solly, *These Eighty Years*, 2.504). His grandson, J. H. Wicksteed, who followed his father as a Unitarian minister, wrote of Henry: 'to him, wrong and suffering were not symptoms of false ideas, but definite evils to be fought with and removed now and on the spot' (Wicksteed, 5).

Solly's vision and obstinate determination led him to found social organizations well in advance of their time. These same qualities, however, rendered him unfit and unable to stay with them and develop their potential, and by 1900 he was a forgotten figure. Solly died of a brain haemorrhage on 27 February 1903 at Childrey, near Wantage, Berkshire, at the home of his daughter and son-in-law, the Revd Philip Wicksteed, with whom he felt a great affinity; he was buried in Childrey churchyard on 4 March. Solly lived long beyond his time but some belated recognition came with his death. The then secretary of the Working Men's Club and Institute Union (B. T. Hall) aptly wrote in 1904: 'If the work that the Clubs do, if their influence on personal character and their contribution to the sum total of human happiness be correctly appreciated … then shall the investigator reckon Henry Solly amongst the constructive statesmen of our time' (Wicksteed, 214).

ALAN RUSTON

Sources H. Solly, *'These eighty years', or, The story of an unfinished life*, 2 vols. (1893) • A. Ruston, 'H. Solly, the omnibus radical: Rev. Henry Solly (1813–1903)', *Transactions of Unitarian Historical Society*, 19/2 (1987–90), 78–91 • *The Inquirer* (7 March 1903), 150–51 • *Christian Life* (7 March 1903), 119 • J. H. Wicksteed, *Working men's social clubs* (1904), 1–11 • W. Beveridge, *Voluntary action* (1948), 168–70 • H. Bosanquet, *Social work in London, 1869–1912* (1914), 18, 20 • T. Williams, 'Solly, the practical dreamer', *The Inquirer* (14 Feb 1987), 4 • H. L. Malchow, *Agitators and promoters in the age of Gladstone and Disraeli: a biographical dictionary* (1983) • K. Woodroofe, 'The irascible Rev. Henry Solly', *Social Science Review*, 40 (March 1975) • G. Cole, *Short history of the British working class movement*, 2 (1927), 46, 112 • D. Stange, *British Unitarians against American slavery* (1984) • *The Inquirer* (17 Dec 1842) • *The Inquirer* (17 May 1845) • *The Inquirer* (6 Jan 1894) • m. cert. • d. cert.

Archives BLPES, papers relating to working classes • Harris Man. Oxf.

Likenesses photograph, 1866, repro. in Wicksteed, *Working men's social clubs*

Wealth at death £1972 19s. 8d.: probate, 27 April 1903, *CGPLA Eng. & Wales*

Solly, Samuel (1805–1871), surgeon, one of the ten children of Isaac Solly (1768–1853), a merchant involved in trade in the Baltic, and his wife, Mary, the daughter of John Harrison, a London solicitor, was born on 13 May 1805 in Jeffrey Square, in the parish of St Mary Axe, London. Solly came from a family with a dissenting tradition: the social reformer, Henry *Solly was his brother, while his father was descended from Daniel *Neal, the historian of the puritans. The family were also linked with Presbyterian meeting-houses at Walthamstow and Hackney. Samuel was educated by Eliezer Cogan of Higham Hill, Walthamstow, where Benjamin Disraeli and Russell Gurney were among his schoolfellows. In May 1822 he was articled to Benjamin Travers, surgeon to St Thomas's Hospital, London. Travers was probably a relative as his sister, Anne, was the wife of a Thomas Solly, and the mother of the philosopher Thomas Solly (1816–1875). Samuel Solly was among the last surgeons in London who in effect bought the reversion of a hospital post by paying a large apprenticeship fee. Had Solly resided with Travers this would have amounted to £1000; because he lived out, his father was obliged to pay £525 to secure his son's future. While still an apprentice Solly served as a demonstrator in anatomy at St Thomas's, the first of a series of teaching posts he held at the hospital. He was admitted a member of the Royal College of Surgeons on 9 May 1828. He then spent some time in Paris pursuing further professional studies.

Solly began practice at his father's house at St Mary Axe in 1831, before moving to St Helen's Place, Bishopsgate, in 1837; he enjoyed only modest success, however, until he took over the premises of a deceased surgeon at St Helen's in 1849. Towards the end of his life Solly moved once more, this time to Savile Row, London. From 1833 to 1839 he was lecturer on anatomy and physiology at St Thomas's. Solly married Jane Barrett, the daughter of a clergyman, on 22 May 1834; they had seven sons and four daughters.

In 1836 Solly published his major work, *The human brain, its configuration, structure, development, and physiology; illustrated by references to the nervous system in the lower orders of animals.* In this work he decried the practice usual in British medical schools of the period of teaching the anatomy of the brain and nervous system without reference to function, development, and comparative studies. Solly believed that there was a unity of structure that unified the most complex with the simplest examples of nervous organization evident in the animal kingdom. He owed a heavy debt to French and German exponents of transcendental anatomy. He also favoured the techniques for dissecting the brain developed by Franz Josef Gall and Johann Caspar Spurzheim, the founders of phrenology. Solly tried to bring his clinical experience to bear on certain contentious physiological questions, though he was well aware of the perils of seeking to make inferences about normal function from phenomena exhibited in disease. He was elected FRS in the same year as his book was published.

In 1841 Solly was appointed assistant surgeon at St Thomas's, and in 1853 he became full surgeon and began to lecture on clinical surgery. The lectures appeared in 1865 in a volume titled *Surgical Experiences*. In the same year Solly was called upon to resign from the post of surgeon under a new regulation that required medical staff at St Thomas's to retire at the age of sixty. Solly successfully appealed against this ruling, insisting upon his right to serve a full twenty years as surgeon. However, ill health finally obliged him to step down in January 1871.

As well as his private practice and hospital work, Solly worked as a medical referee for an insurance company and held a number of lucrative public offices in the City of London. He was elected a fellow of the Royal College of Surgeons in 1843, became a council member in 1856, and twice served as vice-president. He was elected a member of the court of examiners in 1867, and was Arris and Gale professor of human anatomy and surgery in 1862. Solly was reportedly passed over for the presidency of the college in favour of Sir William Ferguson, surgeon-general to the queen, because it was supposed that the latter would be able to wield greater political influence on the college's behalf. Solly was president of the Royal Medical and Chirurgical Society in 1867–8. He proposed an abortive scheme to unify the various London medical societies in a metropolitan academy of medicine.

Solly also had a lifelong interest in art: two of his watercolours were exhibited at the Royal Academy, while many of his own lecture illustrations were purchased by St Thomas's in 1841. He died suddenly, at 9 New Burlington Street, London, on 24 September 1871 and was buried at Chislehurst, Kent. He was survived by his wife.

L. S. Jacyna

Sources *DNB* · *The Lancet* (30 Sept 1871), 489 · *BMJ* (30 Sept 1871), 395 · E. Clarke and L. S. Jacyna, *Nineteenth-century origins of neuroscientific concepts* (1987) · *CGPLA Eng. & Wales* (1871)

Archives Dorset RO · Lincs. Arch.

Likenesses G. B. Black, lithograph, 1863, Wellcome L. · wood-engraving, 1871, Wellcome L. · Moira and Haigh, photograph, Wellcome L. · C. T. Newcombe, photograph, Wellcome L. · photograph, Wellcome L.

Wealth at death under £9000: probate, 10 Nov 1871, *CGPLA Eng. & Wales*

Solly, Thomas (1816–1875), philosopher, was born on 31 January 1816 in Walthamstow, Essex, the eldest son of Thomas Solly of Blackheath, Kent, and his wife, Anne, sister of Benjamin Travers (1783–1858), an eminent surgeon. He was cousin to Henry Solly, Unitarian social reformer, to the surgeon Samuel Solly, and to the chemist, agronomist, and antiquary Edward Solly. The Sollys were dissenters, associated with the Presbyterian meeting-houses at Walthamstow and Hackney. Thomas was educated at Hove, Sussex, under John Morell, a well-known schoolmaster and Unitarian minister, and then (until 1834) at Tonbridge grammar school. He was admitted pensioner at St John's College, Cambridge, in June 1834, but a few months later he moved to Gonville and Caius College, where he acquired the reputation of an able mathematician, fond of metaphysics. Indeed, Solly was a scholar in 1835 but, being a Unitarian, he was precluded from obtaining a degree.

After leaving Cambridge in 1837, Solly was admitted to Lincoln's Inn in 1838 and three years later to the Middle Temple. He was called to the bar on 19 November 1841. However, two years later he decided to study philosophy at Berlin. He took with him letters of introduction of a highly favourable nature from Sir William Hamilton, the Scottish philosopher and logician, and from his uncle Benjamin Travers. He was soon appointed lecturer, and later professor, for English language and literature at Berlin University. He was also English tutor to the Prussian crown prince and the 'Red Prince', a position that was fairly well paid. In 1845 he married Charlotte Augusta, daughter of Hollis Solly of Tott End Hall, Tipton, Staffordshire, with whom he had two daughters and a son. With his second wife, a German woman who survived him, he had no children.

Solly's writings illustrate ability in all fields of his predilection: mathematics, logic, philosophy, literature, and law. He produced a treatise in German on the *English Law of Real Property* (1853), and edited further *A Coronal of English Verse* (1864) for his German students. But his originality was most clearly manifested in his mathematical treatment of logic and philosophy, the subjects of his books *A syllabus of logic, in which the views of Kant are generally adopted, and the laws of syllogism symbolically expressed* (1839) and *The Will, Divine and Human* (1856).

The *Syllabus* was meant as a brief but complete account of Aristotelian logic, which would help at the same time to popularize the fundamental principles of I. Kant's *Critique of Pure Reason*. Sully opened with a review of R. Whately's *Elements of Logic* (1826), and sought to refute the latter's distinction between the 'art' and the 'science' of logic, introducing instead Kant's distinction between 'formal' and 'transcendental' logic, so as to reinforce logic's scientific character, and clearly to define its realm. Eager to extend the realms of syllogistic logic, Solly introduced the quantification of the predicate, anticipated by the botanist and logician George Bentham in 1827, but made principally known by Hamilton around 1846. His most significant innovation, though, was the reduction of the laws of the traditional syllogism to symbolic equations, as a means of exhibiting the symmetry involved in these laws. In justifying his symbolical procedures, Solly echoed the work of George Peacock and D. F. Gregory on symbolical algebra, and anticipated, moreover, the birth of algebraic logic by Augustus De Morgan and, particularly, George Boole, in 1847.

Solly's mathematization of the syllogism was a consequence of his conviction that mathematical methods could be useful in the study of philosophy; indeed, he devoted part of the *Syllabus* to 'transcendental' logic, raising interesting analogies between abstract, philosophical conceptions and mathematical ones. This discussion was fully developed in *The Will*, after an encouraging contact with F. W. J. Schelling, the German philosopher, in 1845. To apply symbolical representations to concepts such as 'causality', 'will' or 'liberty' was but 'a means of conveying the idea thus symbolized with a greater precision and sharpness of outline than is attainable by other means' (T. Solly, *The Will*, vi). Solly pieced together symbolic algebra, analytic geometry, and William Whewell's intuitionist notion of the limit in calculus to frame a sophisticated elaboration of Kant's notions of time and space.

Although the *Syllabus* was Solly's most significant work, this eccentric combination failed to command a following. One reviewer regarded it as 'a clever attempt to combine the systems of Kant and Aristotle; but the dissertations are so very abstract that they are likely to repel all but the most ardent readers' (*The Athenaeum*, 21 Sept 1839, 722). The book had little impact and was not widely read. Solly's main innovations were saved from total oblivion by the interest that De Morgan expressed in his work in 1847. But the new directions thrown up by Boole meant that Solly's mathematization of traditional logic did not leave an influential legacy for the development of algebraic logic. However, his endeavours were pioneering and his application of symbols of differentiation to both philosophical and logical notions as early as 1839 anticipated later developments.

Solly was an amiable, generous, and modest character. He was fond of art and travel, and spoke eloquently of his journeys in the Saxon Alps and the Hartz Mountains. He had a quiet sense of fun and was given to unsparing but good-humoured satire. His cousin Henry Solly said that 'he had almost the strongest and most resolute will of any man I have ever known, combined with an amount of pluck and courage rarely equalled' (H. Solly, 1.327). In 1848, during the revolutionary action in Berlin, he could not resist going into the streets and assisting in the construction of a barricade. He died in Berlin on 8 June 1875, following a long and painful illness. MARIA PANTEKI

Sources M. Panteki, 'T. Solly: an unknown pioneer of the mathematization of logic in England, 1839', *History and Philosophy of Logic*, 14 (1993), 133–69 • H. Solly, *'These eighty years', or, The story of an unfinished life*, 2 vols. (1893), vol. 1, pp. 274, 294–5, 298–9, 310–12, 325–8; 2.4, 64–70 • J. Venn and others, eds., *Biographical history of Gonville and Caius College*, 2: *1713–1897* (1898), 229 • J. Hutchinson, ed., *A catalogue of notable Middle Templars: with brief biographical notices* (1902), 230 • Boase, *Mod. Eng. biog.* • Venn, *Alum. Cant.* • review of Solly's *Syllabus of logic*, *The Athenaeum* (21 Sept 1839), 722 • T. Solly, *A syllabus of logic* (1839) • T. Solly, *The will, divine and human* (1856) • *DNB*
Archives UCL, letters to A. De Morgan
Wealth at death under £12,000: probate, 28 April 1876, *CGPLA Eng. & Wales*

Solme [Some], **Thomas** (*b.* **1509/10**, *d.* in or after **1553**), protestant divine, was born in 1509 or 1510, as he indicates in his Latin letter of 1535 to Thomas Cromwell, sent in the context of Thomas Legh's monastic visitation. Writing as an Augustinian canon of St Osyth's, Essex, Solme craves release from the monastic habit which, following his pedagogue's insistence in his fourteenth year, he has now endured for twelve years. In November 1538 St Osyth's was included in a closure order sent to Legh. Direct biographical evidence for the course of Solme's subsequent career is slender, but his adoption of distinctly protestant views shines through his *Traetys callyde the Lordis Flayle Handlyde by the Bushops Powre Thressere Thomas Solme*, printed, purportedly, at Basel, *c.*1540.

Contending first that fallen mankind can through works accomplish nothing, Solme counsels utter reliance upon 'remission of sin by grace only'. An exposition of the ten commandments misses no chance either to 'stop the mouth of boasters and crakers rejoicing in works' or to deride the idolatry of the 'popish priesthood'. Alleged distortion of Christ's last supper by those who would replace an institution of remembrance with a rite in which 'they like cruel tyrants do crucify him daily' attracts his special wrath. Allusions to 'the Pope and his sect', the bishops with their 'forked caps', 'Sir Anthony Lack-Latin' the hawking and hunting but non-preaching clergyman, and 'the whore of Babylon' are reminiscent of William Turner's invective, while his yearning for 'Erasmus' eloquence and Zwingli's spirit godly' attests Solme's doctrinal leanings.

However, Cromwell's fall and the 'Catholic reaction' had now produced a changing religious and political background. Despite the *Flail*'s fulsome tribute to Henry VIII's wisdom of Solomon, the name of 'Some, a Priest' appears among those 'imprisoned upon the thirty-nine articles' (Strype, 566), while the books prohibited by royal proclamation on 8 July 1546 include 'the Lord's Flail made by T. Solme' (*Acts and Monuments*, 5.568). Edward VI's accession ensured a more congenial ambience, and Solme reputedly became a popular preacher. In 1549, having 'gathered, writ, and brought to light, the famous Friday Sermons of Master Hugh Latimer', Solme published them as *Seven Sermons*. His dedication of this publication, by 'her humble and faithful orator', to Katherine, duchess of Suffolk, fourth wife of Charles Brandon and, since his death in 1545, dowager duchess, pays fervent tribute to her 'most godly disposition', virtuous conduct, and Christian charity (Solme, *Sermons*, 81–3).

In January 1552 'Thomas Somus Ecclesiastes Lectoris' appended brief Latin verses to William Turner's work, *A preservative … agaynst the poyson of Pelagius, lately renued, & styrred up agayn by the furious secte of the Annabaptistes*. Whether or not Solme shared Turner's exiles, Henrician or Marian, remains conjecture, but the empathy with this very combative divine is significant. So, too, is his support of Turner's purpose in defending the 'sacred rites of baptism' (Turner, N.vi.b), as indicating the dread inspired by the radical sectaries even among the members of the short-lived Edwardian religious establishment. These soon encountered a more immediate and perilous doctrinal adversary. Thus A. F. Pollard's assumption that Solme 'appears to have fled on Mary's accession, and to have died abroad' (*DNB*) remains credible. Certainly, though clearly of the second rank when compared with Latimer or even Turner, Solme had acquired sufficient notoriety in Catholic eyes to invite punishment; yet his name does not appear in any list of Marian martyrs. Neither did Christina Garrett include him in her list of Marian exiles—unlike, ironically, his erstwhile (presumed) patron. Katherine had, in 1552, married Richard Bertie who, two years later, was examined by Gardiner and permitted to go abroad. Joined by his wife, the couple's exile took them as far as Poland. Sadly, no such specific documentation has been found for Thomas Solme, whose end, as yet, remains as shrouded in conjecture as his origins.

WHITNEY R. D. JONES

Sources T. Solme, *A traetys callyde the Lordis flayle* (c.1540) • T. Some [T. Solme], dedication, in *Sermons by Hugh Latimer*, ed. G. E. Corrie, Parker Society, 16 (1844), 81–3 • W. Turner, *A preservative … agaynst the poyson of Pelagius* (1552) [Lat. verses by T. Solme, N.vi.b] • Solme to Cromwell, 1535, BL, Cotton MS Cleopatra E.IV 25 (now 26) • J. Strype, *Ecclesiastic memorials*, 1/1 (1822) • *The acts and monuments of John Foxe*, ed. S. R. Cattley, 8 vols. (1837–41), vols. 5, 8 • Wood, *Ath. Oxon.*, new edn, 1.149 • *Life and letters of Thomas Cromwell*, ed. R. B. Merriman, 2 (1902) • D. Knowles [M. C. Knowles], *The religious orders in England*, 3 (1959) • *STC, 1475–1640* • *DNB* • C. H. Garrett, *The Marian exiles: a study in the origins of Elizabethan puritanism* (1938)
Archives BL, Cotton MS Cleopatra E. IV 25 (now 26)

Solms, Count Hendrik Trajectinus van (1636–1693), army officer, was descended from an ancient German family that had settled at Schloss Braunfels on the River Lahn in Hesse in 946. He was the younger son of Johann Albert, count of Solms-Braunfels (*b.* 1599), governor of Maastricht (1641–8), and his wife, Anna Elisabeth, gravin van Falkensteyn. His aunt Amalie van Solms was married to Prince Frederik Hendrik van Nassau (1584–1647), the younger brother of Prince Maurice and grandfather of William III. Solms entered the Dutch army about 1670 and distinguished himself leading the Dutch foot guards at the battle of Seneffe in 1674. Two years later, on the death of Karl Florentius van Salm at the siege of Maastricht, he was given command of the prestigious Dutch blue guards. The disciplinarian Solms, in company with Georg Friedrich von Waldeck, trained and drilled the blue guards into an élite formation earning William of Orange's admiration as expressed in his promotion to major-general in 1680 and lieutenant-general in 1683. He sailed with William on the *Briel* during the invasion of England in 1688 and was the first senior soldier to step ashore at Brixham on 5 November. On 17 December he led the blue guards and the six regiments of the Anglo-Dutch brigade down King Street to occupy Whitehall. As one of William's principal military advisers, he took the blue guards to Ireland in June 1690. At the battle of the Boyne (1 July 1690) he commanded the corps of Dutch, Huguenot, and English infantry in the attack across the river at Oldbridge which incurred the highest casualties. When William left the camp at Carrick-on-Suir in order to return to England, Solms was appointed commander-in-chief in Ireland with orders to attack Limerick, but his reign was brief: on reaching Dublin William heard better news concerning the overall strategic situation and rode back to the army to take command of the abortive siege of Limerick. William again left him in charge in Ireland when he finally departed on 29 August 1690, but Solms himself returned to England in October, leaving Godard van Reede, heer van Ginkel, as commander-in-chief.

Solms did not endear himself to the English soldiers during his time in Ireland, advising William to disband five British battalions that were in poor condition. He was described, by an admittedly hostile English source, as 'a proud, haughty man and not at all grateful to your men nor treats your officers with any civility' (MS Ballard 39, fol. 87). At the battle of Steenkerke (24 July 1692) he commanded the main body of the infantry but failed to deploy sufficiently rapidly to support the heavily engaged vanguard, composed largely of British battalions, commanded by the duke of Württemberg. Although this was probably the fault of bad planning, the terrain, and poor staff work, he was accused of deliberately standing off and allowing the British soldiers to bear the brunt of the casualties. More temperate observers, such as Lieutenant-Colonel John Blackader of the Cameronians, who was in the heat of the action, simply mentioned that Solms could not advance his men because of the 'narrow ways' (MS Ballard 39, fol. 87). Solms's conduct at Steenkerke provided the necessary personification for the debate in the House of Commons on 23 November 1692 on the whole question of William's favouring foreign general officers at the expense of the English. At the battle of Landen (18 July 1693) he was struck by a cannon ball and lost a leg, a wound from which he died, a prisoner in the French camp, within a few days. JOHN CHILDS

Sources B. L. Müller, 'Solms, Heinrich Maastricht', *Allgemeine deutsche Biographie*, ed. R. von Liliencron and others, 24 (Leipzig, 1892) • *Correspondentie van Willem III en van Hans Willem Bentinck*, ed. N. Japikse, 5 vols. (The Hague, 1927–37) • S. B. Baxter, *William III* (1966) • J. G. Simms, *Jacobite Ireland, 1685–91* (1969) • Bodl. Oxf., MS Ballard 39 • J. C. R. Childs, *The British army of William III, 1689–1702* (1987) • A. Grey, ed., *Debates of the House of Commons, from the year 1667 to the year 1694*, new edn, 10 vols. (1769) • P. J. Müller, ed., *Willem von Oranien und Georg Friedrich von Waldeck* (1880) • F. J. G. ten Raa, F. de Bas, and J. W. Wijn, eds., *Het staatsche leger, 1568–1795*, 8 vols. in 10 (Breda, 1911–64) • *The parliamentary diary of Narcissus Luttrell, 1691–1693*, ed. H. Horwitz (1972) • H. Mackay, *Memoirs of the war carried on in Scotland and Ireland*, ed. J. M. Hog and others, Bannatyne Club, 45 (1833)

Solomon. *See* Cutner, Solomon (1902–1988).

Solomon, Abraham (1823–1862), genre painter, the second son of Michael Solomon (*b.* 1779) and his wife, Catherine, *née* Levy (*d.* 1886), was born at Sandys Street, Bishopsgate, London, on 14 May 1823. The Solomon family was Jewish and originally of Dutch or German origin. Aaron Solomon, Abraham's grandfather, started a hat business in London in 1779, the year of Michael (also known as Meyer) Solomon's birth. Michael Solomon followed his father into the hat business, but his wife was an amateur painter, and three of their eight children—Abraham, Rebecca *Solomon (1832–1886) [*see under* Pre-Raphaelite women artists], and Simeon *Solomon (1840–1905)—became professional artists. Financial security and his father's prominent position within the Jewish community in London enabled Abraham Solomon to enter the art world with relative ease. He enrolled at Henry Sass's School for Drawing and Painting in Bloomsbury in 1836, and that same year was awarded the Isis silver medal from the Society of Arts. On 8 December 1839, recommended by Sass, he entered the Royal Academy Schools, where he gained medals for drawing from the antique, and from life. His first exhibited work, *Rabbi Expounding the Scriptures*, was shown at the Society of British Artists in 1840. In the following year he exhibited two works at the Royal Academy: *My Grandmother* and a scene from Sir Walter Scott's *Fair Maid of Perth*. He continued to exhibit there each year until 1862.

Like other contemporary artists, Solomon derived many of his subjects from popular literary sources, such as *The Vicar of Wakefield*, *Peveril of the Peak*, and Crabbe's *Parish Register*. In 1858, for example, he exhibited *The Lion in Love* (Owen Edgar Gallery, London; engraved by W. H. Simmons), taken from an old fable, which illustrates 'his flair for painting costumes' (Reynolds, 47). Solomon's work was, however, considered superior to similar popular works because he conveyed the psychological drama, in which he incorporated his personal observations about human nature.

Solomon's most successful paintings included familial dramas such as *The Breakfast Table* (exh. RA, 1846), which shows the family servant discreetly delivering a love letter to the daughter of the house while she sits at the breakfast table. In 1850 he showed *Too Truthful*, a sardonic view of the degree of sycophancy needed in order to become a successful portraitist. He later painted a pendant to this painting, which he never exhibited and which was probably commissioned by the buyer of the original work. Solomon employed this formula again in 1854, when he exhibited a pair of paintings: *First Class—the Meeting* (National Gallery of Canada) and *Second Class—the Parting* (National Gallery of Australia). Both works were engraved in mezzotint by Simmons and thus became widely known. These modern moral narratives are noted for their contemporary setting and dress, as well as for their original conception and design. Two versions of the first painting exist. The first shows an encounter between a young woman and man in a railway carriage while the older gentleman who accompanies the young woman is asleep. The moral concern to which this gave rise was eased when Solomon created a revised and more modest (though less piquant) version in 1855 (priv. coll.; replica, together with a replica of *Second Class—the Parting*, National Railway Museum, York). Solomon also made two small oil sketches (*c.*1853–4; priv. coll.) of this pair of paintings that demonstrate his 'technical mastery' of the medium (Daniels and others, 53).

Solomon's best-known painting, *Waiting for the Verdict* (Tate collection), was exhibited at the Royal Academy in 1857 and generated huge public interest. *'Not Guilty': the Acquittal* (exh. RA, 1859; Tate collection) resolved the dramatic tension at the centre of the narrative, but proved an anti-climax. Both pictures were nevertheless so popular that he was commissioned to paint at least two replicas of each, and numerous copies were sold of the engraving of each one by Simmons. The 'before and after' formula which Solomon used so successfully was also used by his contemporaries W. P. Frith and Augustus Egg.

Solomon exhibited in addition several paintings of French subjects: *Ici on rase, Brittany* (exh. RA, 1859); *Art Critics in Brittany* (exh. British Institution, 1861); and *Departure of the Diligence, Biarritz* (Royal Holloway College collection, Royal Holloway, University of London), which was finished shortly before his death. He married Ella (*b.* 1847/8), the daughter of Abraham Septimus Hart and the sister of

Dr Ernest Hart, at 69 Wimpole Street on 10 May 1860. They had no children. Solomon died at Biarritz of tuberculosis on 19 December 1862, the same day he was elected an associate of the Royal Academy.

Described by his younger brother Simeon as 'of a kind and amiable disposition' (*Art Journal*, 25, 1863, 29), Solomon lived in London for most of his life, variously at 3 Sandys Street, Bishopsgate Without, 8 Percy Street, Rathbone Place, 21 Howland Street, and 50 Upper Charlotte Street, before moving to 18 Gower Street, a house which he shared with his sister Rebecca and their brother Simeon from 1856. Solomon was well known for his musical parties, at which many leading professional musicians appeared, including the singer Jenny Lind, of whom Solomon painted a portrait (*c.*1849). Examples of his paintings are held in the Guildhall Art Gallery, London; Oldham Libraries, Galleries and Museums; the Ashmolean Museum, Oxford; Leicester Museums and Art Galleries; and Tunbridge Wells Museum, Kent. CHLOE JOHNSON

Sources *DNB* • J. Daniels and others, *Solomon: a family of painters* (1985) [exhibition catalogue, Geffrye Museum, London, and Birmingham Museum and Art Gallery] • Graves, *RA exhibitors* • Wood, *Vic. painters*, 3rd edn, 489 • *The Tate Gallery, 1982–84: illustrated catalogue of acquisitions* (1986) • *Art Journal*, 24 (1862), 73–5 • *Art Journal*, 25 (1863), 29 • *Art Journal*, 21 (1859), 170 • *Literary Gazette* (16 May 1857), 476 • *The Critic* (2 July 1859), 16 • *The Critic* (15 May 1857), 233 • *The Critic* (1 June 1857), 255 • *The Critic* (7 May 1859), 447 • *The Critic* (28 May 1859), 520 • F. T. Palgrave, *Descriptive handbook to the fine art collections in the International Exhibition of 1862*, 2nd rev. edn (1862), 61 • *Daily News* (5 May 1857), 2 • *Daily News* (11 May 1857), 2 • *Daily News* (30 April 1859), 2 • *Morning Star* (23 May 1859), 2 • *Universal Review*, 1 (1859), 581 • *Blackwood*, 86 (1859), 137 • *The Times* (18 May 1857), 9 • *The Times* (18 May 1859), 12 • *The Spectator* (23 May 1857), 55 • *ILN* (9 May 1857), 444 • *ILN* (20 June 1857), 613–14 • *ILN* (21 May 1859), 498 • m. cert. • *CGPLA Eng. & Wales* (1863) • S. Reynolds, 'Abraham Solomon', *The dictionary of art*, ed. J. Turner (1996)

Likenesses A. Solomon, self-portrait, *c.*1845, repro. in Daniels and others, *Solomon*, 37 • Cundall, Downes & Co., photograph, carte-de-visite, NPG

Wealth at death under £1500: probate, with codicil, 11 Feb 1863, *CGPLA Eng. & Wales*

Solomon [Soloman], **Haym** (1740–1785), financier in America, was born in Lissa (Lezno), Poland, of humble parentage. He left about 1767 as a result of a fire which made many of the poor homeless. Travelling in Europe he acquired facility in a number of languages, and also made commercial contacts. In the early 1770s he arrived in New York city and may have set up in business as a distiller. In June 1776 he was serving as a sutler to the American forces at Lake George under General Philip Schuyler, to whom he had been recommended as warmly attached to the revolutionary cause. Shortly after the British occupation of the city in September Solomon came under suspicion as an American spy; he was imprisoned but was released at the request of Lieutenant-General Philip von Heister, commander of the Hessian mercenaries, to serve as commissary to his troops. Solomon was probably chosen because of his knowledge of German. He also carried on a business of his own as a ship's chandler and distiller. On 6 July 1777 he married fifteen-year-old Rachael Franks (*b.* 1761/2, *d.* in or after 1785).

Solomon once more came under suspicion, for allegedly helping to free American and French prisoners and encouraging Hessian soldiers to desert. He fled New York in 1778 for Philadelphia, leaving his family behind. He petitioned the continental congress for assistance, without success, and then began serving as broker to the French consul and the French army paymaster, again, presumably, because of his knowledge of the language. By March 1780 he had made enough money to bring his family to Philadelphia.

When Robert Morris was appointed American superintendent of finance in 1781 he turned to Solomon to aid him in selling foreign bills of exchange for cash, desperately needed by the American army. This association lasted for three years. Solomon was frequently employed because of his extensive commercial contacts, his known integrity, and his willingness to accept a commission of only 0.5 per cent, less than that charged by other brokers. When Morris arranged to organize the Bank of North America on 31 December 1781, Solomon became one of its subscribers. He also negotiated public securities and bills of exchange for local merchants, and carried on a business of his own, selling and buying a variety of goods, slaves, and real estate. He also loaned money at no interest to several delegates to congress, including James Madison and Edmund Randolph, and to various American army officers, for which they expressed their gratitude.

Solomon was also active in the Jewish community, helping to organize Philadelphia's first synagogue, Mikveh Israel, and becoming one of its most generous benefactors. He was wealthy enough to send money to his parents, but not to other relatives who sought his assistance. He lived modestly in quarters above his shop on Front Street. With other Jews he protested in 1783 against the provision of the Pennsylvania constitution of 1776 that barred Jews from the general assembly, and when in 1784 a local Quaker, Miers Fisher, justified the attempted formation of another bank by claiming that usurious Jews dominated the brokerage business, Solomon denounced him publicly as a British loyalist during the revolution, and defended the patriotism of American Jews.

Solomon died on 6 January 1785, presumably at home, after a 'lingering illness'. He left a considerable estate, largely in government currency and certificates of indebtedness, but depreciation reduced the value so vastly that when a final accounting was made the estate was in debt. He was buried, probably on 7 January, in the cemetery of the Jewish synagogue in Philadelphia, without even a headstone to mark the spot. Efforts by his son years later to secure congressional repayment of what were allegedly large loans to congress proved fruitless. No evidence was ever adduced to prove the claim by his partisans that he was the 'financier of the revolution', even though congress recognized his zealous devotion to the revolutionary cause. The only honours eventually accorded to him were statues erected in Chicago in 1941 and in Los Angeles in 1944, and a commemorative postage stamp issued in 1975. MILTON M. KLEIN

Sources E. Wolf and M. Whiteman, *The history of the Jews in Philadelphia from colonial times to the age of Jackson* (1956) • S. Rezneck, *Unrecognized patriots: the Jews in the American Revolution* (1974) • J. R. Marcus, *United States Jewry, 1776–1985*, 4 vols. (1989–93), 1 • M. J. Kohler, *Haym Salomon: the patriot broker of the revolution: his real achievements and their exaggeration* (1931) • J. R. Marcus, *American Jewry: documents, eighteenth century* (1959) • R. A. East, *Business enterprise in the American revolutionary era* (1938) • N. M. Kaganoff, 'The business career of Haym Solomon as reflected in his newspaper advertisements', *American Jewish Historical Quarterly*, 66 (1976), 35–49 • *The papers of Robert Morris, 1781–1784*, ed. E. J. Ferguson and others, 9 vols. (1973–99) • A. J. Karp, ed., *The Jewish experience in America*, 5 vols. (1969), 1 • M. U. Schappes, ed., *A documentary history of the Jews in the United States, 1654–1875* (1950) • L. R. Schwartz, *Jews and the American revolution: Haym Solomon and others* (1987) • E. Faber, *The Jewish people in America: a time for planting: the first migration, 1654–1820* (1992) • L. M. Friedman, *Pilgrims in a new land* (1948); repr. (Westport, CT, 1979?) • S. Wolf, *The American Jew as patriot, soldier, and citizen*, ed. L. E. Levy (1895); repr. (1972)

Archives American Jewish Archives, Cincinnati, Ohio, papers • Archives of the American Jewish Historical Society, Waltham, Massachusetts, letter-book | Archives of the American Jewish Historical Society, Waltham, Massachusetts, Oppenheim papers

Wealth at death approx. $353,000—with depreciation, $44,732 when accounts settled 1789; $45,292 debts, leaving $560 net deficit: Rezneck, *Unrecognized patriots*; Wolf, *American Jew as patriot*

Solomon, Lewis (1848–1928), architect, was born on 14 March 1848 at 59 Great Queen Street, London, the son of Abraham Solomon, furniture dealer and later silversmith, and his wife, Julia Isaacs. He lost his mother when very young and was sent off to Neumegen's boarding-school in Kew. Like other middle-class Anglo-Jews of his generation, he attended University College School and from 1864 to 1866 University College, London, the first institute of higher education in England that did not operate a religious test. Architecture, however, was then still an unusual career choice for Jews. Solomon showed early promise, and was awarded the Royal Institute of British Architects Donaldson silver medal in 1865–6. He was immediately articled for four years (1866–70) to Sir Matthew Digby Wyatt (1820–1877). He studied at the Royal Academy Schools in 1869. From 1871 to 1872 he acted as Wyatt's clerk of works on the India Office and Ottoman Bank projects and qualified as a district surveyor in 1872. In that year he travelled on the continent, in Italy especially, for three months. He also worked for a short period as assistant to Mr Meakin of Clement's Lane in the City before setting up in independent practice as both architect and surveyor in 1872, working out of a series of offices in Bloomsbury, Gray's Inn Square, Finsbury Pavement, and Moorgate.

Solomon was elected an associate of the Royal Institute of British Architects on 9 January 1871 and a fellow on 11 June 1883, with Wyatt as one of his proposers on both occasions. He was active in the institute, where he served in a number of capacities: on the council (1904–5), as a member and vice-president both of the board of examiners and of the board of architectural education, and as chairman of the science standing committee (1903–8). Solomon's practice was largely domestic and commercial; he designed shops, warehouses, and factories as well as private houses and flats, mainly in London. He also designed synagogues, a fact completely ignored in his obituary in the *RIBA Journal*. He served as honorary architect to the Federation of Synagogues. The Federation of Minor Synagogues had been set up in 1887 by the West End banker Samuel Montagu (afterwards the first Lord Swaythling) as an umbrella organization for the multiplicity of congregations founded by immigrant Jews in the East End of London. The task of the honorary architect was to inspect the premises used by congregations that wished to apply for membership of the federation. Squalid, overcrowded, and ill-ventilated rooms, serving in many cases as tiny synagogues, were not deemed acceptable and the congregations concerned were encouraged to merge into larger groupings in order to improve conditions for worship. Based on Solomon's reports, the federation advanced loans for the renovation or conversion of existing properties. The federation also underwrote construction of small-scale 'model synagogues' in the East End. New Road (1892), Great Garden Street (1896), and Notting Hill (1900; a conversion), all now closed, were typical examples.

The federation model, as devised by Solomon, was a modest building, usually rectangular in shape, with a traditional Ashkenazi floor plan, with centrally placed *bimah* (reading platform) surrounded by pews and with an upstairs gallery running around three sides. Frequently these buildings were lit from above by skylights rather than by many windows, reflecting their often mean placement in a crowded urban environment where light and air were at a premium. Decoration was kept to a minimum, both inside and out, for the sake of economy. Very often these synagogues were set back behind a nondescript brick street elevation.

Solomon succeeded Nathan S. *Joseph as architect-surveyor to the United Synagogue in 1904, having already designed both the New Hambro (1899) and Stoke Newington (1903) synagogues for that organization, which represented the English-born Jewish establishment. Stoke Newington was his largest synagogue commission. He himself was a member of the Central Synagogue, Great Portland Street (actually one of Nathan Joseph's buildings, 1868–70). Solomon acted as architect for improvements at several Jewish schools and was responsible for the purpose-built Industrial School for Jewish Boys at Hayes, Middlesex (1901), and the Soup Kitchen for the Jewish Poor (1902), whose slightly arts and crafts, grade II listed terracotta façade can still be seen in Brune Street, Spitalfields.

Solomon lived at Hamilton Terrace, St John's Wood. He married on 28 March 1883 Caroline (*b*. 1862/3), daughter of Samuel Abrahams, jeweller, and they had two sons and a daughter. One son was killed in action in 1917 and the other, Digby Lewis Solomon (1884–1962)—who was in all probability named after Sir Matthew Digby Wyatt, who had done so much to advance Solomon's career—carried on the architectural practice of Lewis Solomon & Son.

Lewis Solomon died at St Mary's Hospital, Paddington, London, at the age of almost eighty, on 15 February 1928, after being 'knocked down by a motor-car while crossing Maida Vale'. His wife was also hit but survived. He was buried four days later at Willesden Jewish cemetery.

SHARMAN KADISH

Sources biography file, RIBA BAL · *Dir. Brit. archs.* · *Jewish Chronicle* (17 Feb 1928) · H. D. Searles-Wood, *RIBA Journal*, 3rd ser., 35 (1927–8), 312 · *Jewish Year Book* · J. Glasman, 'London synagogues in the late 19th century: design in context', *London Journal*, 13 (1988), 143–55 · J. Glasman, 'Assimilation by design: London synagogues in the 19th century', *The Jewish heritage in British history*, ed. T. Kushner (1992), 171–209 · b. cert. · m. cert.

Wealth at death £20,619 12*s.* 2*d.*: probate, 8 May 1928, *CGPLA Eng. & Wales*

Solomon, Rebecca (1832–1886). *See under* Pre-Raphaelite women artists (*act.* 1848–1870s).

Solomon, Sir Richard Prince (1850–1913), politician in South Africa, was born in Cape Town on 18 October 1850, the third son of Edward Solomon, a Congregational missionary, and his wife, Jessie Matthews, sister of James Matthews, architect and at one time lord provost of Aberdeen. He was educated at the Lovedale Mission and Bedford public school, both in Cape Colony, and at the South African College, Cape Town. He entered Peterhouse, Cambridge, in 1871, passed out as twenty-third wrangler in 1875, and became mathematical lecturer at the Royal Naval College, Greenwich. After being called to the bar at the Inner Temple in 1879, he returned home to practise at Grahamstown, Cape Colony. In 1881 he married Mary Elizabeth, the daughter of John Walton, a Wesleyan minister, of Grahamstown; they had one daughter.

As became a nephew of Saul Solomon (editor of the *Cape Argus* and sympathizer with the African cause in the Cape parliament), he took a keen interest in race relations. He served on the Cape native law and customs commission of 1882, and the Transkei criminal code was largely his work. In 1886 he was legal adviser to the royal commission which inquired into the administration of Mauritius. Three years later he settled at Kimberley, where he worked for De Beers. In 1893, after having been appointed QC, he entered the Cape house of assembly as independent member for Kimberley. At the elections of 1894 he was defeated by a supporter of Cecil Rhodes, but he was returned once more for Kimberley at a by-election at the end of 1896. In 1898 he became attorney-general in the ministry of William Philip Schreiner, as member for Tembuland. In the Second South African War he supported Schreiner in the policy of punishing Cape rebels, which brought about the downfall of the cabinet in June 1900.

Early in 1901 Solomon was appointed legal adviser to the Transvaal government. He took part in the negotiations which led to the peace of Vereeniging, and was created KCMG. As attorney-general of the Transvaal from June 1902 onwards he exercised his powers of persuasion, his moderating influence, and his industry in the work of reconstruction. He revised the Transvaal native labour regulations, presided over the gold laws commission, and reorganized the statute book and the administration of justice. He represented the South African colonies at the Delhi durbar of 1903, and twice served as acting lieutenant-governor of the Transvaal.

In 1906 Solomon helped to draft the letters patent by which responsible government was established in the Transvaal, and was much talked of as the first prime minister of that colony, leader of a moderate English–Africaner coalition. He resigned the attorney-generalship, and stood for Pretoria South with the support of Het Volk (the party of Louis Botha), but was unexpectedly defeated (1907) by the Progressive candidate Sir Percy Fitzpatrick. He refused a post in Botha's ministry and became agent-general for the Transvaal in London, where from 1910 until his death he was high commissioner for the Union of South Africa.

Solomon was elected an honorary fellow of Peterhouse in 1904, and in the next year was appointed KCB. He was created GCMG in 1911. He died at his home, 42 Hyde Park Square, London, after a very short illness, on 10 November 1913, survived by his wife.

E. A. WALKER, *rev.* CHRISTOPHER SAUNDERS

Sources A. M. Davey, 'Solomon, Sir Richard Prince', *DSAB* · R. A. Solomon, *The Solomons* [n.d.], 33–9 · R. Staples, 'Sir Richard Solomon: outline of a biography', Honours diss., University of Cape Town, 1972 · *The Times* (11 Nov 1913) · *Cape Times* (11 Nov 1913) · *The Milner papers*, ed. C. Headlam, 2: *South Africa, 1899–1905* (1933) · L. M. Thompson, *The unification of South Africa, 1902–1910* (1960) · *Selections from the Smuts papers*, ed. W. K. Hancock and J. van der Poel, 7 vols. (1966–73), vol. 2 · P. Lewson, *John X. Merriman* (1982) · E. van Heyningen, 'The relations between Sir Alfred Milner and W. P. Schreiner's ministry, 1898–1900', *Archives Yearbook for South African History, 1976* (1978) · E. Walker, *W. P. Schreiner* (1937) · D. Denoon, *A grand illusion* (1973) · *CGPLA Eng. & Wales* (1914)

Archives Bodl. Oxf., corresp. with Lewis Harcourt · National Library of South Africa, Cape Town, Innes MSS · National Library of South Africa, Cape Town, Schreiner MSS · University of Cape Town, letters to Patrick Duncan

Likenesses F. D. Wood, marble bust, exh. RA 1922, Cape Town Legislative Assembly · likeness, repro. in *Royal Academy Pictures* (1922) · photograph, repro. in Solomon, *The Solomons* · photograph, repro. in L. S. Amery, *The Times History of the war in South Africa*, 6 (1909) · photograph, repro. in *Men of the times: old colonialists of the Cape Colony and Orange Free State* (Johannesburg, 1906) · photograph, repro. in *South Africa* (15 Nov 1913)

Wealth at death £6093 15*s.* 6*d.*: probate, 24 Jan 1914, *CGPLA Eng. & Wales*

Solomon, Samuel (1768/9–1819), manufacturer of patent medicines, was born in 1768 or 1769. Neither the identity of his parents nor the place of his birth is known, but he was of Jewish origin. He is said to have been a street urchin, hawking either black-ball shoe cleaner in Newcastle upon Tyne or hair curlers in Birmingham on Saturday nights after the sabbath was over. He then became a protégé of the quack medicine seller William Brodum (*fl.* 1795–1814), who had bought an MD from Marischal College, Aberdeen. Like Brodum, he early turned his back on Judaism and joined the established church.

By about 1789 Solomon was affluent enough to marry; with his wife Elizabeth he had three sons and seven daughters. In 1796, as a Liverpool resident, he obtained from Marischal College an MD, though the registrar strongly suspected that his certificates from two local doctors had been forged. That same year he launched his Cordial Balm of Gilead, craftily linking it with a biblical quotation (Jeremiah 8: 22). This cure-all, selling at 10*s*. 6*d*. for less than half a pint, apparently consisted of fine old brandy laced with herbs. About 1796 Solomon first published his *Guide to Health*. This work comprised both sensible advice on personal hygiene and some very frank passages on, for example, onanism in both sexes and intimate diseases of women, all readily curable by his nostrum. He later claimed to have published sixty-six editions, running to 120,000 copies in all. However, he brazenly jumped ahead with the editions, from the second to the forty-second and then to the fifty-second.

With an elaborate distribution system and an advertising bill of £5000 a year from 1800 onwards, Solomon did very well out of his remedy, soon adding two other varieties, a liquid tonic named Solomon's Drops to cleanse all impurities from the blood—including scurvy and the pox—and an 'abstergent lotion' to treat skin diseases and beautify the complexion. In 1807 he claimed to be paying £6000 annually in patent medicine tax, equivalent to a home turnover of about £40,000. His sales overseas were alleged to be extensive, through agents in all major European capitals, in India, and in most American states. He boasted of having saved many lives by shipments to the United States during a yellow fever epidemic of 1800–01.

In 1805 Solomon moved to the newly built Gilead House, Liverpool, where he took in resident patients and manufactured his nostrums in a rear wing. He charged a guinea for every personal consultation and half a guinea for written advice. All his ventures made him a rich man, and he ensured that he was widely talked about; he is said to have made a splash in Paris shortly after the peace of Amiens in 1802. At home he entertained the top people of the district lavishly, aped the four-in-hand equipage of the local landowner, the earl of Sefton, and spent £1000 on a failed bid to have Sefton (an Irish peer) elected to the House of Commons.

Solomon's business had apparently begun to decline by about 1814, as the later editions of his *Guide to Health* became coy about its success. In 1815 his wife died. Three months later he married Jane Martin, who died childless at the end of 1818. Within a month he had married his third wife, Sarah, who survived him without issue when he died at lodgings in North Parade, Bath, on 21 May 1819. He had already built a family mausoleum of white sandstone, surmounted by a large central obelisk and four smaller ones, at Mossley Hill, Liverpool. This hideous erection was flattened and Solomon's remains re-interred elsewhere when a railway company purchased the site in 1840.

Solomon's business was run after his death by the manager, Ebenezer Daniell, who received a life interest in the estate. That was valued at £30,000, the firm and its secret formulae being worth a further £30,000. After Daniell died in 1842, the firm clearly collapsed. When in 1857 an enquirer in *Notes and Queries* asked what had become of 'this once famous quack medicine', no one seemed to know. Yet at least his literary gifts descended to his great-grandsons, Henry James Byron, the dramatist, and Sir Henry Newbolt, the poet. T. A. B. CORLEY

Sources S. Solomon, *A guide to health* (c.1792) · W. A. Helfand, 'Samuel Solomon and the cordial balm of Gilead', *Pharmacy in History*, 31 (1989), 151–9 · J. Corry, *Quack doctors dissected* (1810) · J. A. Picton, *Memorials of Liverpool*, rev. edn, 2 vols. (1875) · R. Whittington-Egan, 'Solomon in all his glory', *The Liverpolitan* (Oct 1951), 21–3 · R. Porter, *Health for sale: quackery in England, 1660–1850* (1989) · papers of Catherine Hutton, Wellcome L., MS 5270/61-2 · *Fasti academiae Mariscallanae Aberdonensis: selections from the records of the Marischal College and University, MDXCIII–MDCCCLX*, 2, ed. P. J. Anderson, New Spalding Club, 18 (1898), 137 · *N&Q*, 2nd ser., 3 (1857), 187 · *N&Q*, 4th ser., 2 (1868), 36–7 · will, PRO, PROB 11/1620/441, 295 · valuation of estate, PRO, IR 26/804/1451–74 · *Bath Chronicle* (27 May 1819)

Likenesses Ridley, Holt, and Bloed, engraving (after portrait by I. Steel), repro. in S. Solomon, *A guide to health*, 2nd edn (c.1796)

Wealth at death £30,000 investments bequeathed: will, PRO, PROB 11/1620/441, 295 · £30,000 'recipes of medicines and copyright of *Guide to health*': PRO, death duty registers, IR 26/804/1451–74

Solomon, Saul (1817–1892), newspaper proprietor and politician in Cape Colony, was born on 25 May 1817 at St Helena, the son of Joseph Solomon, merchant of Solomon, Moss, and Gideon and his wife, Hannah, *née* De Mitz. Born into a Jewish merchant family, his parents, in the absence of a synagogue, were married in the island's Anglican church where their children were later baptized, though their liberal dualism meant that the marriage was recorded in the family's Hebrew prayer book and the eldest sons briefly attended a Jewish boarding-school in Ramsgate, Kent. In Cape Town, Solomon's brothers became members of the Congregational church but there is no record of Saul formally joining them even though he was a friend of its leading clergyman and missionary, Dr John Phillip. Nor, though a friend of Cape Town's Jewish minister, did he practise Judaism.

Solomon's liberal political views were respected in Cape Town, even by those opposing them. It was believed in the colony that any legislation he found unacceptable had little prospect of endorsement by the Colonial Office or the Westminster parliament. In practice he was far more radical than either body. Although he read the classical political economists, much history, and the blue books of metropolitan and colonial legislatures, Solomon was as likely to have acquired his beliefs in political representation, personal freedom, and social justice from Cape Town newspapers of the 1830s and 1840s. His influence and standing are best understood in the context of metropolitan and colonial societies of his time.

Solomon's convictions, though they made him a British patriot, did not make him an imperialist. He was often highly critical of the metropolitan government and its representatives in South Africa, and of the majority of settlers. Nevertheless, for thirty years, up to the early 1880s, Solomon was extolled as the colony's pre-eminent parliamentarian. When he rose to speak in the colony's parliament word flew around Cape Town, 'Saul is up', and the public galleries filled (Solomon, 206). Solomon's eminence was the more remarkable given his physical frailty.

He had contracted rheumatic fever and rickets at school in England and his legs had been encased in iron supports which possibly had stunted their growth. This required him to mount a stool in the legislature in order to be seen. Poor health determined that he never held office, and he declined Governor Henry Barkly's 1872 invitation to become the first prime minister of the Cape. Yet, according to W. E. Gladstone Solomon, he 'served on every committee, framed nearly every Bill, and virtually led the House on every great occasion' (Solomon, 71).

The Cape to which Solomon was sent in 1829 was stratified by ethnic, racial, religious, and linguistic distinctions. British settlers were outnumbered by the Dutch and at variance with them. Initially, therefore, crown colony rule, without elected representation, was seen as a way of ensuring that Britain's primary interests, whether economic or strategic, remained paramount. This did not satisfy those under whom Solomon served. His political and commercial apprenticeship began when, aged fourteen, he left school because of his father's straitened circumstances. His seniors wanted greater control over their own affairs; however, although they aspired to representative government, they nevertheless recognized the need to establish a diverse coalition to ensure that when it came, it would not result in British economic and strategic interests being overthrown. Solomon attended the South African College from 1829 to 1831, after which he joined the printer and publisher John Greig; this led to a lifelong association with the colony's liberal and radical journalists, missionaries, and businessmen. In 1834 the *South African Commercial Advertiser*, published by his firm, called for 'English, Irish, and Scotch mechanics, the Malays, and freed Coloured people of every description … the English and Foreign merchants … and the better educated and more liberal portion of the Afrikanders' to unite to 'extinguish the last remnant of the high Dutch Oligarchy' (*South African Commercial Advertiser*, 18 Oct 1834). There was no question of power passing out of British hands.

Nevertheless, by the late 1840s Cape Town's British and Dutch middle classes had begun to form a homogeneous capitalist class with the printing and publishing firm of Solomon & Co. as one of its leading members. The consolidated settler middle class had become increasingly resentful of the colony's still unelected legislative council, which was dominated by officials but contained a minority of nominated members drawn from an older, more entrepôt-orientated British mercantile class who shared government patronage with a small cabal of officials surrounding the Cape's colonial secretary, John Montague. Montague's opponents saw this as undermining the colony's probity and consequently its creditworthiness in the City of London. Opposition became a mechanism for intensifying the colony's social and constitutional crisis, threatening stability and helping to advance the milieu which proved so conducive to Solomon's liberal political philosophy. In addition, the destabilizing effects of the colonial government's frontier policy gave cause for alarm, being seen as provocative of external wars with the independent Xhosa and of disaffection among the increasingly creolized Khoisan. Thereafter, the refusal of colonial militias to serve in the 1847 Cape Frontier War meant the maintenance of an expensive metropolitan army at the Cape. Colonial apprehension about this army, when combined with the anti-convict movement, encouraged a territory-wide coalition crossing ethnicity, class, and race. A leading Cape Afrikaner called for unity between 'Africanders of Dutch, French, German, English, Danish, Portuguese, Mozambiquan, Malay, and Hottentot extraction' (*Cape Town Mail*, 16 April 1852).

The coalition fell short of threatening revolution, but ultimately persuaded the colonial administration that representative institutions would be the cheapest way to restore consent for British rule. In this political climate, Saul Solomon made his address to the Cape Town electors: 'I shall consider it a sacred duty', he told them, 'to give my decided opposition to all legislation tending to introduce distinctions either of class, colour or creed' (Solomon, 22). The coalition broke up, but Solomon's liberal opinions continued to gain respect long after it ceased to dominate Cape politics. His reforming zeal incorporated the advocacy of the abolition of state aid to the two privileged Christian churches and promotion of the economic and political rights of women. He endorsed a proposal for suffrage in 1870 and established a workshop for women printers, bringing a qualified craftswoman to the Cape to instruct white and coloured women apprentices. Confronting considerable opposition, in and out of parliament, he persuaded fellow legislators to repeal a Contagious Diseases Act, writing to Josephine Butler, his great admirer, that the act practised, 'injustice to an outcast class', created a system of 'police espionage', and was 'pernicious and degrading' to the 'unhappy women who came under its operation' (Butler, 67–8). On 21 March 1874 he married Georgina Thomson (1848–1933), a school teacher and afterwards headmistress of advanced feminist views.

Although he did not question the initial colonization of the Cape, Solomon opposed almost any extension of its existing borders, believing that this must lead to an arbitrary and despotic system for the control of the populations brought under the colonial state. When African peoples suffered from the capricious rule of colonists or administrators, he used the legislative assembly to denounce such actions. He opposed the illegal trial of Chief Langalibalele and attacked British policy in Natal and the Transvaal. He was, nevertheless, one of the earliest proponents of a South African federation.

While unable to determine the programme of the Cape parliament, Solomon was perceived as an arbiter of what was acceptable to the Colonial Office and the British parliament. Visiting the Cape in 1878, Anthony Trollope claimed that, 'it would have been nearly impossible to pass any measure of importance through the Cape parliament to which he offered a strenuous opposition' (Trollope, 95). This was borne out in 1881 when Solomon led the successful opposition to Cecil Rhodes's attempt to introduce flogging into a bill aimed at curbing illegal diamond sales. Rhodes acknowledged Solomon's eminence in seeking to make him, along with General Gordon and himself, members of a three-man commission to determine the fate of Basutoland.

Yet times were changing. In the late 1870s, as the diamond fields began to transform the economic potential of South Africa, settlers and the imperial government became increasingly bent on expansionist policies determined to break the independence of the chiefdoms. Solomon and his newspaper the *Cape Argus* were extremely critical of the wars and atrocities which followed. The Cape ministry, largely supported by eastern Cape British settlers, became hostile to Solomon, causing him to lose the government printing contract and to suffer a drastic decline in his commercial well-being. Financial disaster was followed by personal tragedy when a child was drowned. His health deteriorated and he withdrew from parliament, retiring to Kilcreggan, Scotland, where he died on 16 October 1892. His widow, Georgina Thomson, afterwards became an important campaigner for women's rights in South Africa and a suffragette who went to prison in England. STANLEY TRAPIDO

Sources W. E. G. Solomon, *Saul Solomon, 'The member for Cape Town'* (1948) · A. Trollope, *South Africa* (1878) · R. W. Murray, *Pen and ink sketches in parliament*, 2 (1864) · R. W. Murray, *South Africa reminiscences* (1904) · J. Butler, 'Brief recollections of one of my fellow workers, Saul Solomon', *Women's Signal* (2 Feb 1899), 67–8 · *Cape Argus* · *Cape Town Mail* · *South African Commercial Advertiser*

Archives National Library of South Africa, Cape Town | Bodl. RH, Aborigines Protection Society archives

Likenesses H. Schroeder, portrait (*Saul Solomon in his seat in the Cape House of Assembly*), parliament, South Africa

Solomon, Simeon (1840–1905), painter and draughtsman, was born at 3 Sandys Street, Bishopsgate, London, on 9 October 1840, the son of Michael Solomon (*b.* 1779) and his wife, Catherine Levy (*d.* 1886). His father, who had inherited the family hat business and who had started a paper embossing firm, was a prominent member of the Jewish community in the City of London. Both his brother Abraham *Solomon (1823–1862) and his sister Rebecca *Solomon (1832–1886) [*see under* Pre-Raphaelite women artists] were painters specializing in history and genre pictures.

Artistic training and early career Solomon trained as a painter in his brother's studio and at F. S. Cary's academy until his admission to the Royal Academy Schools on 24 April 1856. He was something of a prodigy. His extant juvenilia depict scenes from the scriptures, notably the stories of Abraham and Isaac and of David and Saul, rendered in an ambitious outline style with complex poses and gestures. These subjects were to reappear in paintings and drawings throughout his life. He made his début at the Royal Academy in 1857 at the age of seventeen. His oil painting *The Mother of Moses* (exh. RA, 1860; priv. coll., New York) was noted approvingly by Thackeray in the *Cornhill Magazine* while the art critic of the *Illustrated London News* greeted it with marked enthusiasm: 'Let us not be niggardly in our praise of this work, which we have glanced at again and again with curiosity and admiration … A more touching, a more impressive domestic group it would almost be impossible to imagine' (23 June 1860) Despite his youth and relative inexperience, Solomon's

Simeon Solomon (1840–1905), self-portrait, 1859

talent was recognized by the editors of such magazines as *Once a Week* (in 1862) and the *Leisure Hour* (in 1866), both of whom commissioned illustrations of Jewish rituals and customs from him. Solomon was never to lose interest in Jewish themes. There are three important versions, in either oils or watercolours, of a painting which represents a young rabbi bearing the Torah, *Carrying the Scrolls of the Law* (1867; Whitworth Art Gallery, Manchester; exh. Dudley Gallery 1871; Baroda Art Gallery; exh. RA, 1871; West London Synagogue).

Solomon became identified with the Pre-Raphaelites through his friendship with D. G. Rossetti and Edward Burne-Jones although his closeness to Algernon Charles Swinburne from 1863 to 1872 was to be more significant, strengthening his ties to Pre-Raphaelite poetry and offering new, highly controversial subject matter. Rossetti's influence is clearly apparent both in the subject matter and technique of Solomon's watercolours of the late 1850s and early 1860s, such as *The Painter's Pleasaunce* (1861; Whitworth Art Gallery, Manchester), and in complex pencil drawings like *Dante's First Meeting with Beatrice* (1863; Tate Collection). The young artist's originality can be seen more clearly in the highly detailed pen-and-ink drawing *Babylon hath been a Golden Cup* (1859; Birmingham City Art Gallery) where Solomon delights in the new and daring theme of sexual ambiguity while retaining a pictorial format derived from Rossetti. He was one of several notable artists in the Pre-Raphaelite circle commissioned by the Dalziel brothers to produce drawings for their projected illustrated Bible, for which he was allocated twenty subjects. The project was never completed, although the illustrations appeared in *Dalziel's Bible Gallery* (1880) with narrative captions. During the early period of his professional career Solomon produced designs for stained glass for

Morris, Marshall, Faulkner, & Co., for Middleton Cheney church, Northamptonshire (1864–5).

Mid-career, 1860s–1870s Solomon's career became more distinctly separate from the Pre-Raphaelites in the latter half of the 1860s when, as well as exhibiting at the academy, his works were regularly seen at the newly opened Dudley Gallery. Reception of these works in such newspapers and periodicals as *The Times* and the *Art Journal* was often critical of the painter's 'eccentricities' and 'aberrations'. The changes in his style are apparent in the largest of his oil paintings, *Habet!* (exh. RA, 1865; priv. coll., on loan to Bradford Art Gallery) where Rossettian ideals of feminine beauty are transposed from the medieval world to that of ancient Rome. It depicts the contrasting expressions of a group of women watching a gladiatorial contest. Such subjects as *The Bride, the Bridegroom and the Friend of the Bridegroom* (exh. Dudley Gallery, 1869), *The Sleepers and the one who Watcheth* (exh. Dudley Gallery, 1870; Leamington Spa Museum and Art Gallery), and *A Youth Reciting Tales to Ladies* (exh. RA, 1870; Tate Collection) were seen as typical of a new school of English subject painting. The subjects of these works were derived from a variety of sources: biblical, classical, medieval, and modern; their emphasis was on the mystical and sensual.

Several paintings in oils and watercolours explore the relationship of art to music or literature as in *A Prelude by Bach* (*c.*1865; priv. coll., Norfolk) and *Poetry* (1865; Grosvenor Museum and Art Gallery, Chester). The figures in many of these paintings look sad and dreamy and are often androgynous. Other works depict religious rituals from the ancient to the modern worlds—*Heliogabalus, High Priest of the Sun* (exh. Dudley Gallery, 1866; Forbes Magazine Collection, New York), *Two Acolytes, Censing, Pentecost* (1863; AM Oxf.), *A Saint of the Eastern Church* (exh. Dudley Gallery, 1869; priv. coll., New Zealand). These are among the most beautiful and most completely realized compositions of Solomon's entire career, delicate in colour and innovative in handling. He was influenced by three trips to Italy (1866, 1869, 1870) and by exposure there to Renaissance religious and mythological painting. Traces of the influences of Botticelli and Sodoma can be found in works such as *Love in Autumn* (exh. Dudley Gallery, 1872, as *Autumn Love*; priv. coll., London) and *Bacchus* (exh. RA, 1867; Birmingham City Art Gallery).

During the 1860s Solomon was taken up by various collectors—Lord Battersea, Eleanor Tong Coltart, and James Leathart, wealthy patrons of Pre-Raphaelite and early aesthetic movement artists. His outgoing personality and sense of humour made him popular with young artists including Edward Poynter, Henry Holiday, Walter Crane, and Robert Bateman. He was elected a member of the Savile Club in 1868. He became part of an informal network of gay men which included Walter Pater, Oscar Browning, George Powell, and Lord Houghton, some of whom were friends and confidants, others patrons and collectors of his work. His paintings began to explore a different sensibility in English culture, the visual equivalent of the homoerotic elements of Swinburne's poetry or Pater's ruminations upon images and sculpture. Although the main figures in his paintings are men, their sex is often doubtful, particularly in facial features and expression. This quality, shared with Burne-Jones, became a feature of much late Pre-Raphaelite figure painting towards the end of the century but was taken to extremes by Solomon. Arthur Symons noted of the faces of Solomon's subjects that 'the lips are scarcely roughened to indicate a man, the throats scarcely lengthened to indicate a woman. These faces are without sex; they have brooded among the ghosts of passions till they have become ghosts of themselves' (Symons, 61).

Solomon's prose poem *A Vision of Love Revealed in Sleep* published in 1871 and reviewed by Swinburne for the *Dark Blue Magazine* (July 1871) was an attempt to write about desire and sexuality using concepts from Jewish and Christian mystical writings and classical mythology. The literary images are related to the new themes in his drawings and paintings as, for example, in *Until the Day Break and the Shadows Flee Away* (1869; BM). The combination of mysticism and sexuality helped fuel the adverse criticism launched at Rossetti and his followers in Robert Buchanan's essay 'The fleshly school of English poetry'. Buchanan observed that in 'pretty pictures of morality, such as *Love Dying by the Breath of Lust*, … painters like Mr Solomon lend actual genius to worthless subjects' (Maitland). His exhibited works of 1872 were received badly: *Autumn Love* was noted by *The Times* as 'one of those allegorical designs [of Simeon Solomon's] which usually suggest something unwholesome in sentiment' (11 Nov 1872).

Disgrace and reemergence In 1873 Solomon was arrested in a public lavatory and charged with committing buggery. Although the incident was not reported in the newspapers his public career was effectively at an end; he did not exhibit at either the Dudley or Royal Academy exhibitions that year nor thereafter. Most of his former friends disowned him and he began an obscure and precarious existence which led him to the workhouse and financial dependence upon institutional and family charity. Solomon continued to work sporadically and to sell his drawings and watercolours privately. His drawings were sold in the form of photographic prints by Frederick Hollyer (1838–1933) who became famous for his photographs of works by Rossetti, Burne-Jones, and G. F. Watts. Hollyer stocked some two hundred images from Solomon's works from various dates and these appear to have sold well. Some of them were in the form of sequences of line drawings illustrating biblical themes often reinterpreted by the artist to include homoerotic imagery, for example in *The Song of Solomon* (1878) and *The Book of Ruth* (1879).

During the 1880s and 1890s Solomon's career became emblematic of a certain sensibility and its fate. In part this reputation was formed out of the awareness of an emerging homosexual connoisseurship but in the wilfully anti-establishment London-based 'decadent' circles Solomon's alcoholic, bohemian lifestyle had its own appeal, too. He began to re-emerge gradually from obscurity into a kind of celebrity. Oscar Wilde owned two works by him; J. A. Symonds, Walter Pater, and Eric, Count Stenbock, collected works during the 1880s and 1890s; and Lionel Johnson lined his flat with reproductions after his paintings. Solomon was represented by five paintings at the Royal Jubilee Exhibition of contemporary British painting in Manchester in 1887. In the 1890s he was taken up by Herbert Horne in the relaunched periodical the *Hobby Horse*, to which Solomon contributed two images, notably *Corruptio optimi pessima* (vol. 8, 1893) which was drawn specially for the periodical. In 1897 two of his works were shown at the London Guildhall exhibition 'Victorian painters' and were noted approvingly by the critic of *The Academy*.

Despite these limited successes Solomon continued to live in poverty. He sold works to family members for small amounts of money or agreed to commissions for small advances. Accounts of his final years note his alcoholism and fecklessness, his interest in Catholic mysticism, and his greatly reduced technical and imaginative powers. Certainly none of the extant works of the period has the power or shows the technical inventiveness of his early work. In these years he preferred drawing to painting, the medium being pastel or crayon, with vague religious but supradenominational subject matter, for example *Heads of Christ and Apollo, Facing Each Other* (1888; V&A). Many of our impressions of the last phase of his life depend on Bernard Falk's *Five Years Dead* (1937), in which the author recounts his meetings with the destitute artist on the streets of London. A colourful story about a plot to burgle the home of Burne-Jones is related in Charles Ricketts's *Self-Portrait* (1939) where Solomon's 'case' is described as one of 'blackguardism by preference'. In May 1905 he collapsed in the street in High Holborn and was taken back to St Giles's workhouse, Endell Street, suffering, as the coroner's court was told at the inquest, 'from bronchitis and alcoholism'. He died at the workhouse on 14 August 1905. According to his death certificate, the cause of death was 'syncope, sudden heart failure, disease of the aortic valves' (d. cert.). He was buried in the Jewish cemetery, Willesden, on 16 August.

Posthumous reputation Two memorial exhibitions were held in the winter of 1905–6. The Baillie Gallery, London, showed 122 works in a variety of media as a broad survey of Solomon's output. The Royal Academy winter exhibition had a special display of sixteen works which included some of the notable works of the 1860s and early 1870s. These exhibitions were a triumph, given the extent of the artist's fall from favour thirty-two years before, and are evidence of the fascination with his fate as well as a recognition of his talents.

Although Solomon enjoyed a cult reputation in the early twentieth century his work underwent a new critical appraisal from the 1980s onwards, chiefly due to the emphasis on rediscovering marginalized figures in art history following the growth in women's and gay studies. The serious re-examination of his life and works coincided with a wider interest in the historical significance of symbolist and late Pre-Raphaelite art. Several critics have pointed to the similarity of Solomon's work to that of Gustave Moreau, Odilon Redon, and other contemporary French painters. He shared with them an emphasis on the head and face of a single character, religious and mythological source material, an intimate scale, and experimental handling of materials. While many works of the 1860s and 1870s are striking in the beauty of their colour and originality of their conception, the weakness of the potboiler drawings of his later career cannot be overlooked. Laurence Housman, writing in the *Manchester Guardian* (5 Jan 1906, 14), believed that Solomon would be remembered as a colourist. It is, however, for the particular use of his literary sources, both scriptural and literary, for his depiction of the male figure as the object of sexual desire, and for his allegories that he has continued to enjoy critical re-examination. Solomon took issue with the prevailing moral code and, some twenty years before the trials of Oscar Wilde, dared to express in art his own sexual preferences, however obliquely. COLIN CRUISE

Sources J. Daniels and others, *Solomon: a family of painters* (1985) • S. Reynolds, *The vision of Simeon Solomon* (1985) • B. Falk, *Five years dead* (1937) • S. Colvin, 'English painters of the present day: Simeon Solomon', *The Portfolio*, 1 (1870), 33–5 • A. Symons, 'Painting in the nineteenth century', *Studies in seven arts* (1906), 33–68 • T. Maitland [R. Buchanan], 'The fleshly school of English poetry', *Contemporary Review*, 18 (1871) • T. E. Morgan, 'Perverse male bodies', *Outlooks*, ed. P. Horne and R. Lewis (1997), 61–85 • G. Seymour, 'Simeon Solomon and the biblical construction of marginal identity in Victorian England', *Reclaiming the sacred: the Bible in gay and lesbian culture*, ed. R.-J. Frontain (1997), 97–119 • C. Cruise, '"Lovely devils": Simeon Solomon and Victorian masculinity', *Reframing the Pre-Raphaelites: historical and theoretical essays* (1996), 195–210 • R. Ross, 'Simeon Solomon', *Masques and phases* (1909), 135–47 • J. Ellesworth Ford, *Simeon Solomon: an appreciation* (1908) • *The Times* (18 Aug 1905) • b. cert. • d. cert. • RA • gravestone

Archives JRL, letters to C. A. Howell • King's AC Cam., letters to Oscar Browning • U. Wales, Aberystwyth, George Powell MSS • University of British Columbia, letters to James Leathart • Yale U., Beinecke L., corresp. with Frederick Locke and Charlotte Locke

Likenesses S. Solomon, self-portrait, pencil drawing, 1859, Tate collection [*see illus.*] • D. W. Wynfield, photograph, 1860?–1869, V&A

Solomon, Solomon Joseph (1860–1927), painter, was born in the Borough, London, on 16 September 1860, the fourth son of Joseph Solomon, leather merchant, and his wife, Helena Lichtenstadt, from Vienna. He was educated at Thomas Whitford's South London School, Great Dover Street, and was taught Hebrew and German by Rabbi Simeon Singer, of the Borough synagogue. As a boy he sang in the synagogue choir and showed an early interest in both music and art. Art took precedence, and at sixteen he enrolled at Heatherley's Art School in Newman Street, where his contemporaries included John Lavery and the much older Samuel Butler. In 1877 he entered the Royal Academy Schools, where his tutors included Frederic Leighton (then president of the RA), John Everett Millais, and Lawrence Alma-Tadema. A year later he enrolled at the École des Beaux-Arts in Paris, studying under Alexandre Cabanel, and he also spent three months at the Akademie der Bildenden Künste in Munich. With his fellow student Arthur Hacker he travelled in the Netherlands, Italy, Spain, and Morocco, and returned to London in 1880.

Solomon exhibited for the first time at the Royal Academy in 1881 and began to make a name for himself as a portraitist and as a painter of biblical, mythological, and genre subjects. His first outstanding success was in 1887 with *Samson* (Walker Art Gallery, Liverpool), a dramatic representation of violent action which displayed his technical virtuosity in painting the nude. A series of allegorical nudes followed: *Niobe* (1888) and *Sacred and Profane Love* (1889; both later destroyed by the artist), *The Judgment of Paris* (1891; Lady Lever Art Gallery, Port Sunlight, until 1958), *Echo and Narcissus* (1895; sold to a Russian collector), and *The Birth of Love* (1896). In 1891 Solomon became a founder member of the Society of Portrait Painters and began to specialize in portraiture. Early successes included, in 1894, portraits of Israel Zangwill (State Gallery, Budapest) and *Mrs Patrick Campbell as the Second Mrs Tanqueray* (the Arts Club, Dover Street, London). He later painted notable portraits of Herbert Asquith (1909, National Liberal Club, London) and Ramsay MacDonald (1910, National Portrait Gallery, London). His public commissions included a panel for the royal exchange (1897), a panel for the houses of parliament entitled *The Commons Petitioning Queen Elizabeth to Marry* (1911), and a picture for the Guildhall to celebrate the coronation luncheon given for George V and Queen Mary (1911).

In his painting Solomon remained faithful to the academic traditions in which he was educated. He considered himself above all a skilled craftsman, and he became a capable composer of group portraits and large subject pictures, often experimenting with unusual effects of lighting. Although painting proficiently in many styles, he differentiated between his private and his public art. With the latter he painted to please a conservative public, and, sure of his technical skills, he made a point of exhibiting them. His portraits are well balanced and often perceptive, and the best of his work has considerable dramatic power. He was elected an ARA in 1896 and an RA in 1906. In 1910 he published a book, *The Practice of Oil Painting and Drawing*.

Solomon had married Ella, daughter of Hyman Montagu, solicitor and numismatist, in 1897. They had one son, and two daughters, the younger of whom, Iris Rachel, married the Hon. Ewen Edward Samuel Montagu. Solomon became a prominent figure in Anglo-Jewish society, with a keen interest in Jewish affairs, and was a founder member and president of the Maccabeans Society. At the outbreak of the First World War he communicated his view on the importance of camouflage to the War Office, and in 1916 he was sent, with the rank of lieutenant-colonel in the Royal Engineers, to help the French with their work on camouflage and to set up a British camouflage section in Flanders. Two years later he set up a camouflage school in Kensington Gardens, London, working on concealment from the air of very large areas of terrain. His book *Strategic Camouflage* was published in 1920.

After the war, in 1918, Solomon was elected president of the Royal Society of British Artists. He died at his country home, White Cliffe, Birchington, Kent, on 27 July 1927; his wife survived him. Examples of his work are in the Tate collection, the National Portrait Gallery, the Imperial War Museum, the Royal Academy, the Walker Art Gallery, Liverpool, the Central Museum and Art Gallery, Dundee, the Leighton House Museum, London, and the Wellcome Institute Library. H. B. Grimsditch, *rev.* Jenny Pery

Sources O. S. Phillips, *Solomon J. Solomon* (1933) · S. J. Solomon, *The practice of oil painting* (1910) · S. J. Solomon, *Strategic camouflage* (1920) · J. Collier, *The art of portrait painting* (1905) · C. Spencer, *The immigrant generations: Jewish art in Britain, 1900–1945* (1983) · W. Rothenstein, *Men and memories: recollections of William Rothenstein*, 2 vols. (1931–2) · R. Ormond, *Early Victorian portraits*, 2 vols. (1973) · G. Hartcup, *Camouflage: a history of concealment and deception in war* (1979) · J. Pery, *Solomon J. Solomon* (1990) [exhibition catalogue, Ben Uri Art Gallery, London] · *CGPLA Eng. & Wales* (1927) · E. Morris and F. Milner, *And when did you last see your father?* (1992), 33 [exhibition catalogue, Walker Art Gallery, Liverpool, 13 Nov 1992 – 10 Jan 1993] · *DNB*

Archives IWM · priv. coll. | People's History Museum, Manchester, corresp. with labour party · Richmond Local Studies Library, London, Sladen MSS

Likenesses S. J. Solomon, self-portrait, *c*.1896, priv. coll. · H. von Herkomer, group portrait, oils, 1908 (*The council of the Royal Academy*), Tate collection · J. Russell & Sons, photograph, *c*.1915, NPG · W. Stoneman, photograph, *c*.1917, NPG · Elliott & Fry, photograph, NPG · H. Furniss, pen-and-ink caricature, NPG · S. J. Solomon, self-portrait, pen-and-ink drawing, NPG · group portrait (with family; *Papa painting*), Tate collection

Wealth at death £16,478 11*s*. 10*d*.: probate, 24 Sept 1927, *CGPLA Eng. & Wales*

Solomons [*married name* Starkey], **Estella Frances** (**1882–1968**), landscape and portrait painter, was born on 2 April 1882 at 32 Waterloo Road, Dublin, the elder daughter of Maurice E. Solomons, optician, and his wife, Rosa Jane Jacobs. As a girl she attended the Misses Wades' school in Morehampton Road, Dublin. She then went to a school in Hanover, Germany, and on her return spent some time at Alexandra College, Dublin. She studied under William Orpen at the Dublin Metropolitan School of Art and at the Royal Hibernian Schools under Walter Osborne. She first exhibited with the Young Irish Artists in 1903 and at the Royal Hibernian Academy in 1905. Her visit to Amsterdam in 1906 to see the Rembrandt tercentenary exhibition was deeply influential. It has been claimed that the exhibition turned her from 'the subdued impressionist manner of her early landscapes to *chiaroscuro* in portraits, and a quality of introspection which she retained even after her portrait style lightened to become colourful and expressive' (*Irish Women Artists*, 187). She returned to Holland in 1911, and sketched at Volendam. In Ireland Solomons painted in Dublin, in the Dublin hills, and in Donegal and co. Kerry. In her landscape paintings her manner 'is rapid and expressionist, using wedges of gleaming colour, with brilliant highlights' (ibid., 118).

Solomons joined the nationalist organization Cumann na mBan ('Council of Women') in 1915. It was through this organization that she met Kathleen Goodfellow (1891–1980), whom she painted several times, and who became a lifelong friend. Goodfellow was to provide funding for the *Dublin Magazine*, founded by the poet James Sullivan *Starkey (pseudonym Seumas O'Sullivan) (1879–1958), Solomons's companion and later husband. The couple did not marry until 1926, after the deaths of Solomons's parents, who would not have accepted her marrying outside the Jewish faith. Both Solomons and Starkey were at the centre of Irish cultural and artistic life until the 1950s. After the 1916 rising various men 'on the run' were sheltered in her family home, and she painted some of them. She became widely known as a portraitist. She painted the writers James Stephens, George Russell, and Alice Milligan. Of her portrait painting it has been observed that she was 'never interested in background, only in the personality she painted, and often attempted a peremptory thrust of the figure so as to create a moment of immediacy' (*Irish Women Artists*, 118).

Solomons taught etching at the Dublin municipal technical schools, and in 1922, refusing to take the obligatory oath of allegiance to the British crown, she resigned from her post. Etchings by her illustrated J. S. Starkey's *Mud and People* (2nd edn, 1918); Padraic Colum's *The Road Round Ireland* (1926); and the third edition of D. L. Kelleher's *The Glamour of Dublin* (1928). In 1925 she was appointed an associate of the Royal Hibernian Academy. She exhibited there at the annual members' exhibition for sixty years. Solomons ceased painting in the mid-1950s. She was bedridden for some time before her death at her home, 2 Morehampton Road, Dublin, on 2 November 1968. An exhibition of her work entitled '"Works from an artist's studio": Estella Solomons, 1882–1968' was held at the Crawford Municipal Art Gallery, Cork, in 1986. Her life was the subject of a film, *Estella*, directed by Steve Woods and screened at the Galway Film Fleadh in 2000. Her works can be found in many public collections including the Ulster Museum, Belfast, the Crawford Municipal Art Gallery, Cork, the Sligo County Museum and Library, the Hugh Lane Municipal Gallery of Modern Art, the Irish Jewish Museum, and the National Gallery in Dublin.

MARIA LUDDY

Sources T. Snoddy, *Dictionary of Irish artists: 20th century* (1996) • H. Pyle, *Estella Solomons, HRHA, 1882–1968* (Dublin, 1999) [exhibition catalogue, Frederick Gallery] • H. Pyle, *Portraits of patriots* (Dublin, 1966) • *Irish women artists: from the eighteenth century to the present day* (1987) [exhibition catalogue, NG Ire., the Douglas Hyde Gallery, TCD, and the Hugh Lane Municipal Gallery of Modern Art, Dublin, July–Aug 1987] • B. Fallon, 'Portrait of a lady', *Irish Times* (9 Nov 1999) • L. Miller, ed., *Retrospect: the works of Seumas O'Sullivan, 1879–1958, and Estella F. Solomons, 1882–1968* (1973) [incl. bibliography] • *Works from an artist's studio: Estella Solomons, 1882–1968* (Cork, [1986]) [exhibition catalogue, Crawford Municipal Art Gallery, Cork, 15 May – 7 June 1986]

Archives TCD, corresp. and papers | TCD, corresp. mainly with Seumas O'Sullivan | FILM *Estella* directed by Steve Woods, Ireland, 2000

Likenesses E. F. Solomons, self-portrait, repro. in *Irish women artists*; priv. coll. • E. F. Solomons?, self-portrait?, drawing, repro. in www.d-netsales.com/AllTheFilms, 27 March 2001 • group portrait, photograph (with family), repro. in *Estella Solomons, HRHA*

Wealth at death £18,793: probate, 1969, *CGPLA Éire*

Solomons, Isaac [Ikey] (*c.*1785–1850), receiver of stolen goods, was born in London, probably in Houndsditch, one of three known children of Henry Solomons, an immigrant in his youth from Würzburg, Bavaria. Always known as Ikey Solomons, he became a notorious East End Jewish fence, and was reputedly the model for Fagin in Charles Dickens's novel *Oliver Twist* (1838). Arthur Morrison described him as 'the prince of fences' in *A Child of the Jago* (1896). The family were living at 24 Gravel Lane in 1827; and in that year, at the age of about sixty-nine, Henry Solomons was imprisoned for six months, convicted of receiving stolen goods from his son. Solomons senior seems to have trained as a glass-engraver, but earned his living as a dealer in his younger days, possibly acting as a merchant buying on commission for the Goldsmidt banking brothers.

Ikey Solomons married Ann (Hannah), daughter of Moses Julian, a coachmaster of Aldgate, at the Ashkenazi Great Synagogue in Duke's Place, Houndsditch, on 7 January 1807; four sons and two daughters were born between 1807 and 1826. Ann was described in the prison records as being 5 feet 1 inch tall, 'stoutish', with black hair and hazel eyes. Ikey, at 5 feet 9 inches tall, was 'slender' and 'dark', with brown hair and hazel eyes. A police portrait sketch certainly depicts a man with a prominent aquiline nose, but Ikey appears to have had none of the supposedly stereotypical Jewish features, 'sallow complexion', or 'sharp hooked nose' ascribed to him in some of the more colourful contemporary accounts of his adventures. Indeed, Ikey was able to pass under the gentile names of Jones or Slowman while on the run.

As a child Solomons served an apprenticeship in crime as a pickpocket in a neighbourhood famous for its rogues and gangs of thieves. His first known conviction was for stealing a pocket-book from a gentleman at Westminster Hall on 17 April 1810. However, as an adult he became a receiver of stolen goods, operating out of his house in Bell Lane, Spitalfields. By the mid-1820s he was well known to the police as perhaps the largest dealer in stolen bank notes in London, possibly exploiting a connection with Jewish dealers in the Netherlands for the purpose. He was arrested, gaoled at Newgate, and tried at the Old Bailey in well-publicized cases three times over, in 1810, in 1827, and 1830. On the first occasion Solomons was sentenced to transportation for life, the maximum sentence for pickpocketing. However, owing to the shortage of shipping during the Napoleonic wars, he served his sentence between July 1810 and June 1816 on rusting hulks moored in the Medway near Sheerness. He was then released in error due to a case of mistaken identity, but apparently gave himself up voluntarily and was briefly returned to ship. As a reward he was granted a free pardon on 26 October 1816.

In contrast, on the occasion of his second imprisonment in 1827, Solomons effected a spectacular escape from police custody and went into hiding. He surfaced in Rio de Janeiro in July 1828 and arrived in Hobart Town, Van Diemen's Land, on 6 October of that year. Meanwhile his wife Ann had also been arrested, tried, and convicted of possession of stolen goods and counterfeit money. She was transported in a convict ship to Van Diemen's Land with her four younger children and the whole family were subsequently reunited in the southern hemisphere. However, amid controversy, Ikey Solomons was recaptured and returned to England for his third and final trial. This resulted in his own transportation back to Van Diemen's

Land in 1831, where he was employed as a lowly convict official. He never served as forced labour in a penal settlement, possibly reflecting the fact that he could read and write. In 1838 he was allowed to settle in Hobart Town, where he opened a shop and was finally declared a free man in 1844.

Solomons's wife, Ann, with whom he had made such strenuous efforts to be reunited, became unfaithful, and the quarrelsome family apparently disintegrated. Ikey Solomons was buried on 3 September 1850 in Hobart Town. Rumours that he had made a fortune in Van Diemen's Land proved unfounded: letters of administration revealed an estate of under £70.

SHARMAN KADISH

Sources *AusDB*, 2.457–8 · J. J. Tobias, *Prince of fences: the life and crimes of Ikey Solomons* (1974)
Archives Archives Office of Tasmania · GL · LMA, Middlesex records, legal records
Likenesses sketch, 1827, repro. in Tobias, *Prince of fences*, frontispiece
Wealth at death under £70: administration, Tobias, *Prince of fences*; *AusDB*

Soltau, Henrietta Eliza (1843–1934), evangelist and promoter of missionary work, was born on 8 December 1843 at Plymouth, the second of the eight children of William Soltau (1805–1875), Plymouth Brethren teacher and author, and his wife, Lucy. She had five sisters and two brothers. Baptized as a believer by Robert Chapman on 1 August 1854, she became a Sunday school teacher and, because of her religious zeal, became known as Little Evangelist. When the family moved to Exeter Henrietta, with her elder sister Lucy, assisted a local Brethren evangelist, George Brealey. Henrietta conducted a Sunday school for 100 young children in an attic room. In 1868 the family moved to Newport, near Barnstaple, where evangelistic meetings were held in their house in a large room with a separate entrance which became known as the Meeting Room. The women's Bible class which she ran reached a membership of 170, and she was active in various forms of social and evangelistic work. Despite Victorian—and Brethren—reservations about the role of women in public life, William Soltau allowed her (and her sister Lucy) to give evangelistic addresses to mixed congregations, though only in the Meeting Room or the open air. From 1882, following a spiritual experience then known as a 'second blessing', Henrietta entered into a full life of public activities.

Her work was connected with the China Inland Mission (CIM), whose founder, James Hudson Taylor, she had met in 1866. Prevented on health grounds from going herself to China, she set up a home for the children of missionaries (mainly, but not exclusively, CIM missionaries), first at Tottenham, then at Hastings. She also set up a YWCA institute and holiday home at Hastings, where she conducted evangelistic services for railwaymen (at the Railway Mission Hall), busmen, and children on holiday. At the invitation of Hudson Taylor, she served as secretary to the newly formed ladies' council of the CIM, and in 1889 set up a women's training home in north London. Here up to forty applicants for service in China from Britain and the continent lived under her tutelage while their suitability for missionary service was assessed. Of those who passed through her hands (1889–1916) 547 joined the CIM, besides those who went to other parts of the world. She made one extended visit to China (1897–8), spending thirteen months there informing herself of conditions and addressing groups of missionaries. Though not a member of the mission, she followed its policy of not openly appealing for funds, relying on unsolicited gifts.

As a local YWCA secretary, she continued to hold Bible classes and evangelistic services, and was in great demand as a speaker at meetings and missions for young women. Herself influenced by evangelical feminists like Fanny Grattan Guinness and Catherine Booth, she in turn influenced Jessie Penn-Lewis, secretary of the Richmond branch of YWCA, who was later to become a powerful preacher and writer. After retirement in 1916 she continued to support the CIM, becoming chair of the women's council. Following a stroke she died on 5 February 1934 at 77 Highbury New Park, London, the CIM nursing home, and was buried in Finchley cemetery.

HAROLD H. ROWDON

Sources M. Cable and F. French, *A woman who laughed* (1934) · A. J. Broomhall, *Hudson Taylor and China's open century*, 7 vols. (1981–9) · 'In memoriam—Miss Henrietta E. Soltau', *China's Millions*, 60 (1934), 55

Solti, Sir Georg (1912–1997), conductor, was born György Stern in Vérmezö utca, in the Buda district of Budapest, on 21 October 1912, the younger of the two children of Moricz (later Móric) Stern, a businessman originally from Balatonfökajár in southern Hungary, and his wife, Teréz, *née* Rosenbaum, from Ada in the Bácska region of what later became Croatia. Like many families with German surnames in the post-war Magyar republic, the Sterns felt it advisable to replace theirs with something more patriotically Hungarian. Rather than opting for a simple translation, however, as most did, Moricz Stern was more idiosyncratic: leaving his and his wife's surnames unchanged, he renamed György and his sister Lilly after the small Hungarian town of Solt, a place with which they had no connection and which he apparently chose at random.

Early career in Hungary, Switzerland, and Germany The children both showed considerable musical talent, Lilly as a singer, and György as a pianist. In this capacity he was enrolled at ten at the Ernö Fodor School in Budapest, and two years later moved to the city's more prestigious Franz Liszt Academy, where his teachers included Béla Bartók for piano, Leó Weiner for chamber music, and Ernö Dohnányi for composition (after he had been turned down by the more sought-after Zoltán Kodály). Conducting, however, was taught by a lesser figure, Ernö Unger, who, Solti remembered, 'instructed his pupils to use rigid little wrist motions. I attended the class for only two years, but I needed five years of practical conducting experience before I managed to unlearn what he had taught me' (Solti, 19). (The contrast in his style after he had 'unlearnt' these lessons was considerable: 'His motions are jittery; his whole body is in motion; his shoulders as well as his

Sir Georg Solti (1912–1997), by Anne-Katrin Purkiss, 1987

hands are responding to the rhythm; his beat is a series of jabs, and he looks as though he is shadow-boxing' according to Harold C. Schonberg, *New York Times*, 28 Nov 1976.)

As many conductors found, repetiteuring—coaching opera singers from the piano—proved for Solti a much more valuable learning experience. He took up the first of several positions at the Budapest State Opera House in 1931, and moved on to assist Josef Krips in Karlsruhe a year later. Krips insisted, however, that the Jewish Solti should return home at the end of 1932, when it became clear that Hitler would win the following year's election. Budapest soon became a centre for Jewish and otherwise anti-Nazi musicians, and Solti found himself working with, and learning from, many major figures, including Otto Klemperer, Fritz Busch, and Erich Kleiber. He also worked for Arturo Toscanini, playing the celeste in *Die Zauberflöte* at the 1936 Salzburg Festival.

Whether the result of circumstance or design, this was an unusually long apprenticeship, and it seemed initially that the career for which it was preparing would not materialize: Solti's first—and, for many years, only—complete opera performance, *Le nozze di Figaro* in Budapest in March 1938, was interrupted by reports that German troops had crossed the Austrian border in preparation for the *Anschluss*. He was once more in serious danger, and at his family's behest he soon left the country, initially for London, to conduct for the Ballets Russes de Monte Carlo. He went on to Switzerland, in the hope that Toscanini, who was conducting in Lucerne, would be able to find him a position in America. When the great man was unable to help, Solti was saved by a chance meeting with the Swiss tenor Max Hirzel, who, needing to be coached in the role of Wagner's Tristan, offered him a room in his house in Zürich, and, more importantly, his protection.

Solti remained in Switzerland until the end of the Second World War. This period was not entirely grim—he met Hedwig (Hedi) Oeschli (daughter of a teacher of chemistry at Zürich University), whom he married in 1946, and also won the piano division of the Swiss Music Competition in 1942—but he was deeply frustrated by the lack of opportunities to conduct. Things improved with the return of peace: Edward Kilényi, a fellow Hungarian then working for the US army in Munich, offered Solti a job at the opera house there, providing an open jeep which carried him through a freezing night from the Swiss border into the ruined city. Initially finding himself surplus to requirements, he moved on to Stuttgart to conduct *Fidelio*. The performance was attended by the US music officer for Munich, John Evarts, who recommended his superiors to engage Solti with immediate effect, reporting that 'the improvement in the playing of the orchestra was little short of miraculous' (Solti, 66).

Solti was, by his own admission, 'incredibly lucky' (Solti, 69): at no other time would a conductor with so little practical experience have been considered for a post as prestigious as music director of the Bayerische Staatsoper: the leading German conductors of the time—Wilhelm Furtwängler, Herbert von Karajan, Hans Knappertsbusch, and Clemens Krauss—were forbidden, under the conditions of de-Nazification, from working there, while many of the main non-German candidates, including Solti's compatriots George Szell, Fritz Reiner, and Eugene Ormandy, had emigrated to the USA. The job was fortunate in other ways: in a company forced to rebuild virtually from scratch, Solti was able both to learn a wide repertory at enormous speed—notably many scores by the city's most famous son, Richard Strauss, at whose funeral in 1949 he conducted the trio from *Der Rosenkavalier*—and also to mould a musical and dramatic ensemble precisely as he wished. While at Munich, Solti made his first recordings for Moritz Rosengarten's Decca company, initially as a pianist, accompanying the violinist Georg Kuhlenkampff, and then conducting the Zürich Tonhalle Orchestra in Beethoven overtures.

Despite much critical and popular success, Solti's position in Munich as a non-German (and effectively an American appointee) was never secure and was becoming untenable when in 1951 he was offered the equivalent position at the Frankfurt Opera. The city's new opera house had opened only the year before, and, as he had in Munich, Solti built a new company of young singers to match it, with such a high proportion of Americans that they were soon nicknamed the 'Amerikanische Oper am Main'. Solti spent nine years in Frankfurt, and, although it was a happy and fruitful period for him, he was not universally popular. In particular, he was frequently accused of neglecting the company for engagements with houses and orchestras elsewhere, and he did indeed consolidate his symphonic career with regular appearances in New York, San Francisco, Los Angeles, and Vienna. He also made two very successful visits to the Royal Opera House, Covent Garden (conducting *Der Rosenkavalier* and Britten's *A Midsummer Night's Dream*).

Covent Garden Following Rafael Kubelík's resignation, Solti was offered the directorship of the Covent Garden Opera Company in 1961. His tenure began controversially: coming from the well-organized houses of middle Europe and expecting their most prestigious British counterpart to be run in a similar way, he was surprised to find 'cramped rehearsal space, crowded rehearsal schedules, a phlegmatic chorus master and the absence of what he regarded as basic professional standards'. Moreover, as far as he was concerned, '[m]any of the conductors were inadequate and he was not going to waste his time performing operas in English when there were not enough first-class native singers to cover all the roles' (Lebrecht, 228–9). He demanded change: if he was going to turn this 'beautifully kept semi-amateur' theatre into 'the best opera house in the world' (Robinson, 38), as he announced to his somewhat incredulous first press conference, the fundamental structures of the organization would have to be radically overhauled.

First and foremost, the company's habit of presenting a few popular pieces many times a year, with a new cast change almost every night, would have to stop. It would be replaced with a version of the *stagione* system with which Solti was used to working in Europe: no more than three or four works would be in the repertory at any one time, and each production would be given with a settled and thoroughly rehearsed cast for a maximum of six or seven performances. To the board's slightly shocked insistence that no more than four new productions would be possible in any one year, Solti responded by programming ten in his first season. To effect this new scheme, a proper system of planning was needed: singers were being booked only a few months ahead instead of the years that were necessary to ensure that the best were available. Solti therefore engaged his London agent, Joan Ingpen, who, unlike the Covent Garden management, shared his preference for first-rate European singers, and who introduced five-year casting plans.

Although these systems became standard in British houses, reaction to such radical change was, to put it politely, mixed, and Solti's fierce, if not arrogant, manner did not help matters, particularly when he was seen to berate members of staff, such as the technical director, who thought they did not come under his jurisdiction. Like Kubelík, who had been virtually hounded from the place, he came under attack. He was assailed both by the press—the satirical magazine *Private Eye*, who popularized (though the tenor John Lanigan coined) his nickname 'The Screaming Skull' (Lebrecht, 229), as well as (possibly anti-semitic) music critics—and by his own chorus and orchestra, who, to his great disgust, 'called me a Prussian—me, a Hungarian Jew' (ibid., 231). Matters came to a head after a deeply flawed production in 1962 of Verdi's *La forza del destino*, marred by serious disagreements between conductor and the producer, Sam Wanamaker. Rotten vegetables were thrown at Solti both inside and outside the theatre and, most unsettling of all, his car was vandalized. That he did not straightaway resign and return to the continent was the result of considerable diplomacy and coaxing by his chief supporter at the house, the general administrator, Sir David Webster. Instead, after presenting a lengthy list of demands—for a bigger and better trained orchestra, a new chorus master, the removal of the hard-pressed technical director—Solti not only honoured his initial three-year contract, but remained as music director for a further seven years.

His radical instincts undimmed, Solti introduced to London audiences operas by Gluck, Britten, and Strauss and, in December 1965, Schoenberg's *Moses und Äron*, a difficult work both intellectually and musically, whose fearsome reputation had put paid to Solti's attempts to stage it in his previous houses. The Covent Garden production was not only a major vindication of the work, but also one of the Royal Opera's greatest post-war successes. This was in part a tribute to Solti's passionate advocacy of a score which even he found hard to assimilate. Then again, the *succès de scandale* of Peter Hall's production undoubtedly helped, complete with dozens of naked 'virgins' disporting themselves around the golden calf. Solti, in the pit, complained that from his vantage point he was the one person in the house who could never see them.

In 1964 Solti separated from Hedi, citing differences in their attitudes to his social life, and moved into the Savoy Hotel. Soon afterwards a young television presenter, (Anne) Valerie Sargant (*b.* 1936/7), daughter of William Pitts, chartered secretary, came to the hotel to interview him for the BBC. The meeting sparked a 'passionate love affair' (Solti, 142) with a woman twenty-five years his junior, who was herself married. After a 'ruthless' pursuit across more than one country (ibid.) he persuaded her to divorce, and they married on 11 November 1967. The marriage lasted until his death and produced two daughters, Gabrielle and Claudia. It also persuaded him to settle permanently in Hampstead and, in 1972, to take up British citizenship, allowing him to use the honorary knighthood (KBE) bestowed on him in 1971 (he had already been made an honorary CBE in 1968), although he was not pleased when the Home Office insisted on re-spelling his name 'Georg', as though he really were a 'Prussian'. He got his own back, subtly, by ensuring that it was always pronounced as the English 'George', which in many accents returned it to its Hungarian original.

As well as Schoenberg and Strauss, Solti conducted a new *Ring* cycle for Covent Garden, the first for more than a decade. The production, directed by Hans Hotter, who sang Wotan, and featuring a new generation of British singers, all of them Solti protégés, opened in 1964, and was revived, unusually, in five of the next six seasons. That the company should allow it so many performances in such a short period was due in no small part to Solti's own increasing fame as a Wagner conductor; this in turn reflected the success of his pioneering recording of the four operas made for Decca in collaboration with the visionary producer John Culshaw. A combination of economics, logistics, and received industry wisdom had made previous attempts to record the work impossible, and it would have seemed achievement enough, so soon after the war, simply to have committed all fifteen hours of the work to disc. But Culshaw, whose initiative it had been, saw, as others had not, that the recent innovations of long-playing records and stereo sound provided an unprecedented opportunity to present these colossal, intensely theatrical works in a purely aural form without any loss of vividness. He created what he termed a 'Sonicstage', which allowed his characters to move freely across the stereo image, as if behind a visible proscenium; and he hunted throughout Vienna (where the recordings were made) and beyond for properties and sound effects—Hagen's steerhorns, Mime's anvils, even the collapsing Valhalla itself—which would bring the potentially complicated and esoteric story most directly into the average home.

Culshaw required a conductor who could match his zeal for narrative, and Solti's technique, which promoted the moment over the grand design and urgency over patience, although musically controversial, proved ideally suited. His experience in the leading houses of Germany and England was invaluable in creating a cast which blended the finest exponents of the major roles—Hotter as Wotan, Birgit Nilsson as Brünnhilde, Wolfgang Windgassen as Siegfried—with experienced character actors, such as the *Rheingold* Mime, Paul Kuen, and rising stars imaginatively cast, including Dietrich Fischer-Dieskau as Gunther and Joan Sutherland as the Woodbird. Perhaps most importantly, Solti was also acutely aware of how the recording process should be managed—as one of his producers, Michael Woolcock, recalled:

> One of the revolutionary things about his *Ring* cycle was the amazing planning and attention to detail, meticulous within each session and addressing each section of the work, listing objectives and what needed to be achieved in relation to the whole work. (Quinn, 22–3)

The first part of the *Ring* to be issued, *Das Rheingold*, sold 'like a fireball' (Solti, 113) when it was issued in 1958, and over the next seven years its three successors blazed the same unparalleled trail. While it is perhaps too simplistic to state, with one modern critic, that Solti 'was a much finer conductor when singers were involved than when they weren't' (Hayes), it was his operatic recordings, particularly those of Strauss, which showed him at his most sympathetic, tempering the unforgiving energy and drive often found in his symphonic work with an instinctive accompanist's lyricism and grace.

Chicago In 1969, two years before he finally left Covent Garden, Solti took up the music directorship of the Chicago Symphony Orchestra, succeeding Jean Martinon. On the surface, the Chicago Symphony Orchestra seemed in very good shape: its nucleus remained the brilliant group of musicians assembled by Fritz Reiner in the early 1960s, and its subscription series still attracted large audiences. But morale had fallen under Martinon's leadership, and playing standards with it, while the orchestra's books showed a potentially disastrous debt of $5 million. Solti, a music director much more in the strict, inspirational Reiner mould, swiftly tackled the problems among the players, although he found them magnified by festering personal disputes. To cancel the debt, he saw that the orchestra required a much more international profile. He achieved this partly by engaging them for his Decca recordings, but also, more radically, by leading a series of ambitious foreign tours. The first of these took place in 1971, covering ten European countries, and including the sessions in Vienna's Musikverein for Solti's celebrated recording of Mahler's eighth symphony. At the end of a highly successful tour, the orchestra was welcomed home with a ticker-tape parade: the city recognized that the orchestra's burgeoning international reputation was single-handedly erasing the city's enduring image as a home for gangsters and, as at the democratic convention three years before, riots. As the city benefited, so did the players. Salaries greatly increased and recording fees (from work with others as well as Solti) grew with them, while lost broadcasting rights were restored and prominent sponsors attracted, notably Standard Oil of Indiana, which offered $500,000.

As early as 1973, *Time* magazine declared the Chicago Symphony Orchestra to be the top American orchestra 'sine qua non' and put a portrait of Solti on its cover, over the caption 'The Fastest Baton in the West'; while in 1977, to celebrate his importance to the entire city's economy, his picture was printed on the cover of the Chicago directory of the Illinois Bell Telephone Company. Solti's twenty-two years with the orchestra—his longest period in charge anywhere and 'the happiest time in my professional life' (Solti, 164)—as well as improving its fortunes and vastly increasing its discography, greatly expanded its repertory. He led its first Mahler and Bruckner cycles, encouraged major commissions including Tippett's fourth symphony and Lutosławski's third, and matched his commitment to Bartók, performing virtually his entire orchestral output, with a new-found interest in the American repertory of Charles Ives, Elliott Carter, and George Rochberg.

Although Solti was a hero in Chicago, his interpretative style remained controversial: some commentators celebrated his 'great sense of musical geography' and his rhythmic precision and drive:

> His whole sound world has a rhythmic basis and component to it and the energy that comes from that is the real cornerstone of his sound. He likes the edge, the steeliness and brassiness and general sense of tension and energy in everything that that gives him. (Quinn, 22–3)

Others, notably in London, complained that this sound world produced shallow, if not vulgar, performances, even of works such as Walton's *Belshazzar's Feast*, to which it might have seemed suited:

> Once again going for the dramatic effect and once again ignoring moments of lyricism and bulldozing his way through the score, he seemed concerned only to generate thrills, and instead produced a brash and nasty rush across the surface of the music which was anything but thrilling. (N. Kenyon, quoted in Robinson, 148)

Solti himself, strangely perhaps for such an ambitious man, considered his art in much simpler, more practical terms: 'I think I can make any orchestra, good or bad, perform to the best of its abilities. This is probably my greatest talent' (Solti, 215).

Final years In his later years, and especially after his retirement from Chicago in 1991, Solti seems to have relaxed, both personally and interpretatively. His later recordings, particularly the 1990 *Zauberflöte*, 'exquisite and quite "unSoltian"' in its 'immense humanity' (Jolly, 1), and the celebrated *Traviata* of 1994, possessed a lightness of touch, even a good humour, arguably absent before. His final recording, made in Budapest in June 1997, coupled in an unplanned symmetry works by Bartók and Weiner (who had taught him), with music by Kodály (who perhaps should have done). Three months later, while on holiday in Antibes, Solti suffered two heart attacks, and he died in hospital there on 5 September 1997. His ashes were buried in plot 470 of the Farkaskreti cemetery in Budapest, next to the grave of Bartók. He was survived by his wife, Valerie, and their two daughters. Among numerous honours he received were honorary doctorates from several universities in Britain and America (including Leeds, Oxford, London, Yale, and Harvard), an honorary fellowship of the Royal College of Music, and the gold medal of the Royal Philharmonic Society (1989); for his recordings he received the Grand Prix Mondiale du Disque fourteen times, and thirty-one Grammy awards (including a special trustees' award for his recording of the *Ring* cycle).

STEPHEN FOLLOWS

Sources A. Blyth, ed., *Opera on record* (1979) • M. Hayes, 'Dynamo Budapest', *The Gramophone* (Oct 2002) • J. L. Holmes, *Conductors on record* (1982) • A. Jacobs, 'Sir Georg Solti', rev. J. Bowen, *New Grove*, online edn • J. Jolly, editorial, *The Gramophone* (Nov 1997), 1 • N. Lebrecht, *Covent Garden—the untold story* (2000) • M. Quinn, 'Through other ears', *The Gramophone* (Oct 1997), 22–3 • P. Robinson, *Solti* (1979) • G. Solti, *Solti on Solti: a memoir* (1997) • J. Tooley, 'Sir Georg Solti, 1912–97', *Opera* (Nov 1997) • *The Times* (8 Sept 1997) • *Daily Telegraph* (8 Sept 1997) • *The Guardian* (8 Sept 1997) • *The Independent* (8 Sept 1997) • *WWW* • m. cert. [Anne Valerie Sargant]

Archives FILM BFI NFTVA, *Omnibus*, BBC 1, 28 Sept 1997 • BFI NFTVA, documentary footage • BFI NFTVA, performance footage | SOUND BL NSA, performance recordings • BL NSA, recorded interviews

Likenesses photographs, 1961–86, Hult. Arch. • Y. Karsh, photograph, 1987, NPG • A.-K. Purkiss, photograph, 1987, NPG [*see illus.*] • photograph, repro. in *The Times* • photograph, repro. in *Daily Telegraph* • photograph, repro. in *The Guardian* • photograph, repro. in *The Independent*

Solus. *See* Sualo (*d.* 794).

Sombre, David Ochterlony Dyce (1808–1851), traveller and putative lunatic, was born in Sardhana, a semi-autonomous princely state near Meerut, India, on 18 December 1808, the eldest of the three surviving children of Colonel George Alexander Dyce (*d.* 1838), of mixed Scottish and Indian ancestry, and Julianne Reinhard (*d.* 1820), of mixed French and Indian ancestry. His maternal great-grandfather's second wife, Begum Sombre (*d.* 1836), raised him as a Roman Catholic and had him educated privately with the Revd John Chamberlain and then the Revd Henry Fisher. She eventually entrusted the management of Sardhana to him, appointed him a colonel in her army, and declared him her heir. She also ceded Badshahpur (an *altumgha jagir* or personal estate) to him, and gave him 3,600,000 rupees (£360,000) in East India Company bonds. He added Sombre to his name in 1835, indicating his acceptance of this inheritance, which was derived from her husband, Walter Reinhard or Reinhardt, alias Somru or Sombre (*d.* 1778), a German Catholic mercenary. In addition to composing poetry in Persian and Urdu, Dyce Sombre kept mistresses: Dominga (*d.* 1838), a Catholic who bore him three children, Walter George (1832–1833), Laura Celestine (1834–1835), and Penelope (1836–1838);

David Ochterlony Dyce Sombre (1808–1851), by Charles Brocky

and Hoosna, a Muslim who bore him Josephine Urbana (1834–1835). In 1835, on receipt of a donation of £15,000 from the begum, Pope Gregory XVI named him chevalier of the order of Christ.

At the begum's death (27 January 1836) the East India Company seized Sardhana and its army, confiscating their accoutrements, leaving Dyce Sombre only her extensive personal property (worth about £150,000). He began a series of law suits (which lasted thirty-seven years) against these seizures. In October 1836 he left Sardhana, touring north India, Calcutta, Penang, Singapore, Macao, and Canton (Guangzhou). He returned to Calcutta, settled his affairs in India, including marrying off his mistresses, and left for England. He arrived there on 2 June 1838, and entered high society through the influence of a friend, Stapleton Cotton, Viscount Combermere, and that of Lady Cork. His large fortune made him an eligible bachelor; within months he became engaged to Mary Anne Jervis (1812–1893), third daughter of the second Viscount St Vincent, a Jamaica plantation owner. An accomplished singer, dancer, and composer, she had long associated with the duke of Wellington and Samuel Rogers. Soon after their engagement, he travelled to Italy, where he commissioned for the begum both a vast cenotaph by Adamo Tadolini and a memorial mass by Nicholas Wiseman. On Dyce Sombre's return to London, he quarrelled with his fiancée over her continued social engagements, then over their future children's religious affiliation (Mary Anne was an Anglican). Nevertheless they married on 26 September 1840 in the fashionable St George's Church, Hanover Square, and then in a private Roman Catholic ceremony.

In 1841 Dyce Sombre made £3000 available for the election campaign which he and Frederick Villiers undertook in the radical-Liberal interest in Sudbury, Suffolk. They were elected, but on 14 April 1842 parliament controverted their elections for 'gross, systematic, and extensive bribery' and (in 1844) disenfranchised Sudbury. During tours of England, Scotland, Ireland, and the continent Dyce Sombre's behaviour appeared increasingly antisocial, including his frequent challenges to duels (never accepted) and violent accusations against his wife of promiscuous adultery with her friends, servants, and father. On 30 March 1843 Dr James Clarke supervised his confinement for lunacy, first in the Clarendon Hotel, then, from April 1843, in Hanover Lodge, Regent's Park. After his sisters, Anna May (1812–1867) and Georgiana (1815–1867), and their husbands, John Rose Troup (1802–1862) and Baron Paolo Solaroli (1796–1878), reached London, they agreed with his wife to a commission of lunacy. Despite Dyce Sombre's protests against the validity of the inquiry (held under Francis Barlow in Hanover Lodge in July 1843), public examination of his private papers, and his lack of legal representation, a special jury found him of 'unsound mind', retroactively to 27 October 1842. The lord chancellor seized his property and ordered him confined in Hanover Lodge.

In September 1843 Dyce Sombre was allowed to tour Bath, Bristol, Gloucester, Birmingham, and then Liverpool under the custody of Dr John Grant. Early on 21 September 1843 he fled Liverpool, reaching Paris via London in thirty hours. Living on credit and pawning his jewellery, he appealed to French authorities for protection. A board of leading Paris physicians unanimously declared him of perfectly sound mind. With this evidence, he resisted English efforts to return him to custody and obtained a small portion of his income from the lord chancellor. He began legal appeals—for control over his property and for supersedeas of the lunacy judgment—that lasted until his death. In 1844, 1846, 1847, 1848, and 1851 he returned to England, under protections from the lord chancellor, for a series of extensive mental examinations by various court-appointed doctors. These panels repeatedly confirmed the original judgment of lunacy, but, from 1846, allowed him his income, reserving £4000 per annum for his wife. His defenders excused his actions as not lunatic but rather due to his 'Indian blood' and upbringing; his accusers argued he knew enough of European manners that he must have been lunatic to act as he had done. He consistently maintained he was European, since each parent had some European blood.

In 1849 Dyce Sombre wrote and published his 592-page *Refutation of the Charges of Lunacy in the Court of Chancery*, and also a pamphlet, *The Memoir*, in English, French, and Italian—later found libellous by a French court—excoriating his brother-in-law, Solaroli, and asserting the illegitimacy of his sister Georgiana. Meanwhile, he accomplished his project of visiting every European capital, including St Petersburg and Constantinople, plus Cairo. His obesity, irregular lifestyle, and frequent venereal diseases broke his health. While in London for yet another court-appointed lunacy examination a sore on his foot mortified, and he died on 1 July 1851 at 8a Davies Street, Berkeley Square. His body was buried in Kensal Green cemetery on 8 July, although, as his will (dated 25 June 1849) specified, his heart was apparently later interred with the begum in Sardhana. His wife inherited by successfully challenging (on grounds of his lunacy) his will, which left most of his estate, under the management of the East India Company's directors, for a school for Indians in Sardhana. In 1873 the privy council found the East India Company had been justified by administrative need—but not by treaty—in annexing Badshahpur, but that it owed £63,618 for its illegal seizure of the Sardhana army's accoutrements. Dyce Sombre's widow married on 8 November 1862 George Cecil Weld Forester, later third Baron Forester. MICHAEL H. FISHER

Sources legal advisers' boxes, case of Dyce Sombre, BL OIOC, L/L/63–65, nos. 429–43, 446–8, 450–52 · N. Shreeve, *Dark legacy* (1996) · H. Clarey, 'Lady Forester: a nineteenth century woman of wealth', MA diss., University of Keele, 1986 · D. O. D. Sombre, *Refutation of the charges of lunacy in the court of chancery* (1849) · *Hansard 3* (1841–73), vols. 59–217 · E. C. Archer, *Tours in upper India*, 2 vols. (1833) · A. Barron, *Reports of cases of controverted elections, in the fourteenth parliament of the United Kingdom* (1844) · *Memoirs and correspondence of Field Marshal Viscount Combermere, from his family papers*, ed. M. W. S. Cotton [Viscountess Combermere] and W. Knollys, 2 vols. (1866) · 'Genealogical memoir of the Hon. Miss Jervis', *Court Magazine and Belle Assemblée*, 4 (May 1834), 162–4 · [A. Deane], *Tour through the upper provinces of Hindostan, comprising a period between the years 1804 and 1814* (1823) · *GM*, 2nd ser., 36 (1851), 201–2 · *ILN* (12 July 1851), 42 · 'Some remarks on the principality of Sirdhanah', *Meerut Universal Magazine*, 4 (1837), 274–9 · m. cert. · d. cert. · private information (2004)

Archives BL OIOC, legal advisers' boxes, case of Dyce Sombre · PRO, Dyce Sombre, contested wills

Likenesses M. Azam, group portrait, *c.*1820–1825 (Begum Sombre's court scene, with Dyce-Sombre near centre), Charles Beatty collection, Dublin · Italian artist, portrait, *c.*1838, governor's mansion, Lucknow · C. Brocky, drawing, Stoke-on-Trent City Museum [*see illus.*] · double portrait, governor's mansion, Lucknow

Wealth at death approx. £500,000: BL OIOC, legal advisers' boxes, case of Dyce Sombre

Some, Robert (1542–1609), college head, was born at King's Lynn, Norfolk, the third son of Thomas Some or Soame of Betley, Norfolk, and his first wife, Anne, the daughter and heir of Francis Knighton of Little Bradley in Suffolk. His brother was Sir Stephen Soame, lord mayor of London in 1598. Robert Some attended Cambridge University, where he matriculated as a pensioner of St John's College at Easter 1559 and graduated BA in 1562. He became a fellow of Queens' College, Cambridge, in 1562, proceeded MA there in 1565, and acted as college bursar from 1567 to 1569. He was selected as one of two orators to compose and read Latin verses in honour of Elizabeth I on the occasion of her visit to Cambridge in August 1564, and was appointed a university preacher in 1567. He received the degree of BTh in 1572 and the doctorate in 1580.

During the early part of his university career Some was notably radical in religion. In a sermon at Great St Mary's in 1570, it was reported, he preached against pluralism and non-residence and attacked corrupt church institutions. In particular 'the court of faculties was damnable, devilish and detestable', and 'he hoped to live to see it trodden under foot and overthrown' (Cooper, *Ath. Cantab.*, 510). A preference for eldership over the existing hierarchy was reflected in his dislike of excommunication by one man, and his belief that those with a pastoral charge should not leave it without the consent of their parish. William Chaderton wrote to the chancellor complaining against the sermons of Edmund Chapman of Trinity College and Robert Some of Queens', which he understood to complement the heterodox teaching of Thomas Cartwright. Some was a strong supporter of Cartwright, then locked in conflict with the authorities, and probably attended his lectures. In July and August 1570 three testimonials were sent on Cartwright's behalf to William Cecil, Lord Burghley; of the many subscribers Robert Some was one of only five who set their hands to all three.

Some's early promotion probably moderated his early radicalism. In 1572 he was appointed vice-president of Queens'. On 18 April 1573 he was instituted to the rectory of Girton, Cambridgeshire, on the presentation of Francis Hynde. He became chaplain to Robert Dudley, earl of Leicester, patron of many puritans. The preface dated 20 April 1580 reveals that *A Godly Sermon Preached in Latin at Great S. Maries in Cambridge* (1580) was the translation by Some of his sermon before 'the Earl of Leicester, my singular good lord and master' (sig. Aii). Some also wrote 'Certaine points', issued in response to Archbishop Whitgift's efforts to enforce subscription to the three articles drawn up by him in 1584. It stressed the need to 'further, favour, and encourage the number of true, painful watchful and zealous preachers, in no wise to devise and lay snares or stumbling blocks to put them to silence' (Peel, 1.175).

Some, it should be stressed, thought of himself as a loyal member of the Church of England. His leadership of the literary offensive against the radical separatists, which opened in 1588 with attacks upon John Penry, may have been partly motivated by a need to prove this in the increasingly conservative atmosphere of the church under Whitgift. It is clear, however, from *A Godly Treatise, wherein are Examined and Confuted … H. Barrow and J. Greenewood* (1589), that this was also a labour which Some regarded as a most necessary duty. As he remarked of his opponents in the preface addressed to Christopher Hatton and William Cecil: 'If they will not be won, they may and ought to be repressed, lest men's souls be poisoned, and the Church rent in pieces and the commonwealth disturbed. They which will preserve the sheep may not spare the wolf' (A2*v*). It may be that such polemical labours, and the influence of his patron Leicester, were both factors in Whitgift's decision to overlook Some's early radicalism. It was on his recommendation that on 11 May 1589 Some was admitted to the mastership of Peterhouse, vacated by the death of Anthony Perne.

Some defended the established church as an institution, and especially the Calvinist orthodoxy which had come to dominate its theology. He and other puritan masters such as Roger Goad and William Whitaker were extremely sensitive to the threat of ideas which they saw as covertly popish, and these three men wrote to Burghley in 1593 asking for special powers to deal with the problem. Such fears underlay the efforts, in which Robert Some played a central role, to silence a succession of critics of Calvinism as it was then understood—Peter Baro, William Barrett, and John Overall. Barrett, of Gonville and Caius College, advanced arguments later associated with Jacobus Arminius thirty years before they became fashionable in England. On 29 April 1595 he challenged several tenets of orthodoxy, most notably averring that man's sin was first cause of reprobation. On 5 May, Some chaired consistory court proceedings against Barrett, who on 10 May was forced to suffer the humiliation of a public recantation in Great St Mary's. Called again before the consistory, Barrett wrote to Whitgift naming Some as the orchestrator of a concerted campaign against him. When he had complained against such pulpit attacks, Some 'answered me that he had countenanced and would contenance all those that would appear against me to the uttermost of his power' (Porter, 347).

Robert Some had indeed been active in mobilizing Cambridge puritan opinion against Barrett. Driven by a forceful petitioning campaign, the controversy soon enveloped Peter Baro, whose heterodox views had long been recognized, and which could no longer be tacitly tolerated. In June 1595 eight heads of houses, Some among them, wrote to Whitgift calling for his censure against not only Barrett, but also 'some others whose disciple he is' (Porter, 378). On 7 July Baro was called before the consistory. Asked to give an account of his views, he offered to prepare a critique of the published teaching of Robert Some. But Some, the presiding judge, insisted he set down his opinions in writing in answer to those points specified by the court. Baro prevaricated for several months. Meanwhile, the Barrett case continued. The college heads feared the supervention of Whitgift, whose sympathies could not be relied on, but they needed his support for their own proceedings. Some was sent to London, with a copy of Barrett's sermon for Whitgift, and a letter for Burghley, which represented Barrett's opinions as popish. Some was able to convince Burghley that Whitgift's proposal to call both parties before high commission would be resented as a breach of university privileges.

On 2 July 1595, aware that the authorities were divided, Barrett had revoked his recantation. A few days later Some, filling at short notice a sudden vacancy in the list of university preachers, launched a ferocious attack on him. Barrett's request that his assailant be called before the consistory court could not be denied, but the hearing was dominated by Some's allies, who wrote to the archbishop in his defence. Whitgift was furious, and summoned

Some to Lambeth, where he was 'in friendly sort reasoned with by myself and some one or two other' (Lake, 328), words which may overstate somewhat the bonhomie of the occasion. Some, however, remained convinced of the righteousness of his stand, and on his return to Cambridge he delivered a sermon widely understood to represent as Jewish persecutors the court of high commission—and its head. Whitgift complained to the college heads against 'Dr Some's intemperate and indiscreet sermon' (Strype, 2.254). The cases of Baro and Barrett continued inconclusively for several more months.

Some also took the offensive against a more dangerous opponent, John Overall, the regius professor of divinity at St John's. In 1599 Overall was preaching along similar lines to Baro and Barrett, insisting on the centrality of sin, and on man's individual responsibility for it, as the basis of reprobation. According to Overall it was Some whose complaints persuaded Vice-chancellor Jegon to set up on 20 June 1599 a committee of investigation into his doctrines. In September Overall was examined inconclusively, and sensibly prevaricated when asked to set down his views on paper. On 21 September, in an attempt to force him out into the open, Some preached on the contended issues despite a ban issued by Jegon. No action was taken against Overall, but early in 1600 he expressed himself on transubstantiation in terms which his opponents considered to be popish. In November 1599 Some had entered upon his third term as university vice-chancellor, and on 4 June 1600 Overall was called before the consistory again. Some, presiding, urged him to subscribe to doctrinal points set down by Goad and Chaderton in response to his earlier teaching. No agreement could be reached on a way of dealing with Overall's refusal. On 30 June during a disputation Some sharply attacked popish ideas concerning private confession and purgatory. Overall responded with a violent speech of refutation, which was silenced by Some. Overall, however, survived the assaults upon him.

Robert Some may now seem a narrow-minded bigot, but he pursued his objectives with passionate sincerity. For Some in 1600, 'the university is a precious fountain' whose corruption would be 'a grievous blow to truth and peace' (Lake, 239). His capacity for persuasive advocacy is evident in *Three Questions* (1596), a work which has been described as 'vivid, clear, with an imaginative use of imagery in the best Puritan tradition' (Porter, 315). In it Some restated the nub of high Calvinist doctrine, that Christ died not for all but for the elect few, who could not fall away. The faith of Jonas:

> very far gone in sin … was lulled asleep, and eclipsed for a time, but at length it shined again like the sun from behind a black cloud, and lifted up itself like a palm tree the more it was pressed down. (Some, *Three Questions*, 6)

For those whose agony of uncertainty as to their own salvation led to suicidal despair, he had this counsel: 'They which have most grievously offended the majesty of God, ought not to despair of his mercy' (ibid., 31).

Some's relations with the archbishop were not permanently soured by the Barrett controversy: in 1597 Whitgift unsuccessfully nominated Some for the see of Exeter, characterizing him as 'a very honest man, well learned, an ancient Doctor of Divinity, and one that governeth the college whereof he is master with good commendation' (Collinson, 61). The college historian T. A. Walker comments that Some was 'a man of quick temper and endowed with a shrewd humour' (Walker, 98–9). Walker also reports that Lady Mary Ramsay, founder in 1601 of two new fellowships and four scholarships at Peterhouse, offered a new endowment on condition that 'St Mary' be incorporated into the name of the college. Some is said to have responded tartly that 'Peter has been overlong a bachelor to think of now taking a mate' (Walker, 120). The flow of Lady Ramsay's generosity was abruptly staunched.

Some died unmarried in Cambridge on 14 January 1609 while serving his fourth term as university vice-chancellor. His funeral was held on 20 January with elaborate ceremony:

> all orders of academics attending in their formalities. Great St Mary's was hung with black, as also with verses and escutcheons of his arms and those of the college. The funeral sermon was preached there by Laurence Chaderton, master of Emmanuel, and a funeral oration was there performed by John Cotton of the same college. A procession was then made to Peterhouse where Mr Derham Jr made another oration. The hearse was borne by six ancients of Peterhouse assisted by the four senior doctors of divinity. (Cooper, *Ath. Cantab.*, 512)

Some was buried at Little St Mary's in Cambridge.

STEPHEN WRIGHT

Sources H. C. Porter, *Reformation and reaction in Tudor Cambridge* (1958) · Venn, *Alum. Cant.* · Cooper, *Ath. Cantab.* · J. H. Gray, *Queens'* (1899) · T. A. Walker, *Peterhouse* (1906) · P. Lake, *Moderate puritans and the Elizabethan church* (1982) · T. A. Walker, *A biographical register of Peterhouse men*, 2 (1930) · J. Burke and J. B. Burke, *A genealogical and heraldic history of the extinct and dormant baronetcies of England, Ireland and Scotland*, 2nd edn (1841); repr. (1844) · R. Some, *A godly treatise, wherein are examined and confuted … H. Barrow and J. Greenewood* (1589) · R. Some, *Three questions* (1596) · A. Peel, ed., *The seconde parte of a register*, 2 vols. (1915) · P. Collinson, *The religion of protestants* (1982) · J. Heywood and T. Wright, eds., *Cambridge University transactions during the puritan controversies of the 16th and 17th centuries*, 2 vols. (1854) · J. Heywood, ed., *Early Cambridge University and college statutes* (1855) · J. Ayre, ed., *The works of John Whitgift*, Parker Society (1853)

Some, Thomas. *See* Solme, Thomas (*b.* 1509/10, *d.* in or after 1553).

Somer, Henry (*d.* 1450), administrator, was a kinsman and heir of George Somer of Dartford in Kent. On 11 February 1383, as a king's servant, he was granted 100*s.* yearly from the exchequer, and his appointments as attorney and executor of John Slegh, the king's chief butler (1379–86), suggest that it was in the butler's department that his service to the crown began. In 1398–9 he was a collector of customs in Southampton, and thenceforward a clerk in the receipt of the exchequer, entrusted in December 1399 with the task of taking 8000 marks to Calais for the payment of the garrison. On 13 February 1405 he was appointed keeper of the privy wardrobe in the Tower of London, but soon returned to the exchequer, as a baron, in November 1407, until June 1410, when he became chancellor of the exchequer, an office he was to hold for twenty-nine years.

Despite his clerkships Somer remained a layman, one of the first to hold such offices, and by November 1402 he was married to Katharine, widow of John Newman or Nyeman of Salisbury, and daughter of Mark Faire, a leading Winchester merchant. On 19 July 1408 he added to his other offices that of clerk of the treasurer. It was while Somer was in this office, which he held until 29 September 1410, and again from 17 December 1411 to 2 March 1413, that the poet Hoccleve described him as a sociable member of his 'Court of Good Company'. On 29 November 1411 Somer added the keepership of the exchange and mint in the Tower to the chancellorship, both of which offices he was to retain almost for life. Their profits, added to his business capacity, enabled him to acquire lands, mainly in Cambridgeshire, to the yearly value of perhaps £260, and to serve as a JP and knight of the shire for that county and for Middlesex. He died on 23 March 1450. His heir was James Veer, who was the son of his daughter Agnes, and was then aged ten or eleven. For him he left £3000, his books, and other goods. According to his will he wished to be buried in St Stephen's Chapel in the hospital (soon to be replaced by the college) of St John the Evangelist in Cambridge, where a monument had already been prepared for him. Another monument to a Henry and Katharine Sommer in the London church of St Helen's, Bishopsgate, was recorded by John Stow but has long since disappeared. J. L. KIRBY

Sources *Chancery records* • PRO, Issue Rolls, E 403 • PRO, Chancery, Inquisitions Post Mortem, C 139/138, no. 21 • register of Archbishop Stafford, LPL, fols. 183*v*–184*v* [will] • H. L. Gray, 'Incomes from land in England in 1436', *EngHR*, 49 (1934), 607–39 • J. L. Kirby, 'The rise of the under-treasurer of the exchequer', *EngHR*, 72 (1957), 666–77 • HoP, *Commons, 1386–1421* • J. Stow, *A survey of London*, rev. edn (1603); repr. with introduction by C. L. Kingsford as *A survey of London*, 2 vols. (1908); repr. with addns (1971) • *VCH Cambridgeshire and the Isle of Ely*, vols. 2–3 • *Hoccleve's works*, ed. F. J. Furnivall, 3: *The regement of princes*, EETS, extra ser. 72 (1897)

Wealth at death approx. £60 p.a., total assets of £3000 left to heir together with books and other goods: PRO, C 139/138/21

Somer, John (*d.* in or after **1409**), Franciscan friar and astronomer, belonged to the Franciscan convent at Bridgwater. Although one copy of his *Kalendarium* suggests that at some time before 1384 he was warden of the priory at Bodmin in Cornwall, from at least 1380 to 1395 he was attached to the Oxford convent, on whose behalf he received alms from the king in 1394 and 1395. It was at the request of Thomas Kingsbury, the provincial minister of the Franciscans in England, that in 1380 he composed his *Kalendarium* for Joan of Kent (*d.* 1385), the mother of Richard II. A calendar with astronomical tables attached, covering the four Metonic (nineteen-year) cycles for the period 1387 to 1462, the *Kalendarium* survives in thirty-two complete and eight fragmentary copies. However, the copy preserved in BL, Royal MS 2 B.viii, formerly believed to have been the presentation copy, was not written until *c.*1462. Somer also wrote a chronicle of events in the three 'great cycles' from 64 BC to 1532, in tabular form alongside an Easter table. This survives in BL, Cotton MS Domitian ii, fols. 1–7, where a heading added in the fifteenth century attributes it to Somer. Many hands added historical entries to this copy of the chronicle after Somer's death. Similar chronicles, which are not, however, attributed to Somer, survive in Bodl. Oxf., MS Digby 57, fols. 24–31 and BL, Royal MS 13 C.i, fols. 43–51.

Evidence that Somer was known as an astronomer at Oxford is to be found in the manuscript Cambridge, Peterhouse, MS 75.I, fol. 63*v*, where he is referred to as 'J. Somer Oxonia' in the heading to astronomical calculations for 31 December 1393. The entry in his chronicle for 1395 suggests that he may have incepted in theology at Oxford in that year. He may also have been in attendance on Richard II in 1394 and 1395, since his chronicle entries reveal an intimate knowledge of the king's journeys to Ireland and Calais in those years. In 1399 he received from Richard a grant for life of 8 ells of russet cloth and 8 ells of blanket, to be received every year at Christmas; this grant was confirmed by Henry IV in 1400. Somer was still living on 10 October 1409 when he last collected his royal grant; he probably died soon afterwards, since he left 200 marks for building the new friary church at Bridgwater (where work began in 1412, according to a note in his chronicle by another hand). However, William Worcester assigned his death to 1419, on the evidence of a Franciscan martyrology.

John Somer's *Kalendarium*, along with that of Nicholas Lynn, is cited by Chaucer as a source for the tables in the third part of his *Treatise on the Astrolabe*; however, this third part either was never written or does not survive. Somer's star catalogue may also have been intended as a source; this has been edited by L. Mooney as appendix C of *The 'Kalendarium' of John Somer*, and other astronomical texts and tables ascribed to Somer are edited in appendix D. John Bale attributes to Somer a 'Castigation of former Calendars collected from many sources' (Bale, *Cat.*, 7.viii), but this is now lost. LINNE R. MOONEY

Sources L. Mooney, *The 'Kalendarium' of John Somer* (1998) [incl. full list of MSS] • *CPR*, *1396–9*, 532; *1399–1401*, 344, 434 • PRO, E403/549; E403/554 • Bale, *Cat.*, 7.viii • *Itineraries [of] William Worcestre*, ed. J. H. Harvey, OMT (1969), 78–80, 124–6 • J. H. Wylie, *History of England under Henry the Fourth*, 4 vols. (1884–98); repr. (New York, 1969), vol. 4, p. 218 • G. Chaucer, 'A treatise on the astrolabe', *The Riverside Chaucer*, ed. L. D. Benson, 3rd edn (1987), 661–83 • Emden, *Oxf.* • D. J. Price, ed., *The equatorie of the planetis* (1955), pl. VI

Archives BL, Cotton MS Domitian ii, fols. 1–7 • BL, Royal MS 2 B.viii

Wealth at death bequeathed 200 marks for building of friary church in Bridgwater; 40 marks for books at the friary: *Itineraries*, ed. Harvey, 78–80

Somer, Paul [Pauwels] **van** [Paul Vansommer] (**1577/8–1621/2**), portrait painter, was probably born in Antwerp, perhaps the son of Lambert van Someren. In 1604 the artist and author Karel van Mander wrote about two brothers from Antwerp, Bernaert and Pauwels van Somer, who were at that time working as artists in Amsterdam. Bernaert, a portraitist who had spent some years in Italy, was married to the daughter of the painter Aert Mijtens. Pauwels, or Paul, was still a bachelor and 'excellent in all aspects of art, in invention as well as portraiture' (Mander,

1.458). Paul was recorded in Leiden in September 1612, when his age was given as thirty-four, and again in April 1614. In 1615 he passed through The Hague and in 1616 he was in Brussels where, according to J. de Maere and M. Wabbes, he was commissioned by the Brabant audit office to paint a portrait of the archdukes, Albert and Isabella. By December the same year he had settled in London. Although his working life in England was to last only five years, he seems to have been working for court patrons almost from the outset. His signed portrait of the lord chamberlain, *William Herbert, Third Earl of Pembroke* (Royal Collection), is dated 1617, and this or another similar portrait of Herbert by van Somer was engraved by Simon van de Passe (Hind, 265). Also dated 1617 is van Somer's important full-length portrait of Queen Anne of Denmark (Royal Collection), which presumably postdates July of that year, when the classical gateway at Oatlands Palace, shown in the background, was completed. In this work he reinvented the queen's visual image in terms of the more advanced Netherlandish technique and with a complex iconographical programme.

The date 1618 is inscribed on van Somer's full-length portrait of James I (Royal Collection) with the royal regalia on a table at his side. This, like the image of the queen, offered a fresh presentation of the monarch, and various copies and versions of it survive. On his visit to London in 1618, the English agent in Brussels, William Trumbull, discussed the commission of some portraits with Edward Norgate, who acted as an intermediary for him with van Somer. Van Somer queried the measurements requested for these full-lengths, for which he said he was usually paid £25 or £30, and which appear to have been portraits of the king and the queen (*Downshire MSS*, 447, 601). In July 1619 Lady Anne Clifford wrote that her five-year-old daughter Margaret 'began to sit to Mr Vansommer for her Picture' at their residence in Kent, Knole (*Diaries of Lady Anne Clifford*, 78–9); on 30 August her husband, Richard, third earl of Dorset, 'sat much to have his picture drawn by Van somer, & one picture was drawn for me' (ibid.). None of these pictures is known to survive. In the same year van Somer signed the paired canvases *Second Earl of Devonshire and his Son* and the *Countess of Devonshire and her Daughter* (both North Carolina Museum of Art, Raleigh), and in 1620 the head and shoulders portrait of *Thomas Windsor, Sixth Baron Windsor* (1591–1642) (priv. coll.).

In March 1619 van Somer attended Anne of Denmark's funeral as her 'picture maker', and his documented portrait of her former attendant Elizabeth Talbot, countess of Kent (Tate collection), attired in black, was probably painted about this time. The eighteenth-century engraver and writer George Vertue recorded seeing van Somer's signed and dated portrait of Robert Kerr, earl of Ancram of 1619, now lost. Van Somer was also documented as working for the earl of Rutland, and between 1619 and 1621 there are records of official payments to him for images of James I, Anne of Denmark, Prince Charles, and a posthumous copy of a portrait of Prince Henry. These include a warrant issued on 4 February 1620 for a payment of £170 to him for pictures made for 'the late Queen'.

In London, van Somer lived in St Martin's Lane, as did two other Netherlandish painters employed by the Jacobean court, Daniel Mytens (his kinsman, through his brother's marriage) and Abraham van Blyenberch. James I's Swiss physician, Dr Turquet de Mayerne, who was deeply interested in artists' materials and techniques, questioned all three of them. The opening page of his manuscript 'Pictorja sculptorja & quae subalternarum artium' (BL, Sloane MS 2052) is dated 1620, and names van Somer as one of his initial sources. Van Somer told de Mayerne about the handling of various blue pigments, the properties of lavender and other oils, how to make a drying oil (by bleaching it in the spring sunshine), and how to create an 'incomparable varnish'. A recently rediscovered portrait of Dr Mayerne in classical attire (NPG) has been attributed by Karen Hearn to van Somer.

Van Somer was buried in St Martin-in-the-Fields, London, on 5 January 1622. Payments for his last royal portraits were subsequently made to his widow, Cornelia. A portrait of van Somer was engraved by Simon van de Passe in 1622 (Hind, pl. 160b).

Eighteenth- and nineteenth-century connoisseurs, particularly Vertue, tended to attribute to van Somer almost any early seventeenth-century English portrait that contained Netherlandish elements, especially if full-length. As a result, his name continues to be linked to works by other, now unidentified, hands. In reality, the short duration of his career in England means that his *œuvre* there must necessarily have been fairly small. No work painted by van Somer prior to his arrival in London has yet been identified. KAREN HEARN

Sources K. van Mander, *The lives of the illustrious Netherlandish and German painters*, ed. H. Miedema, 1 (1994), 458 · E. Auerbach, *Tudor artists* (1954), 134, 186 · C. H. C. Baker, *Lely and the Stuart portrait painters: a study of English portraiture before and after van Dyck*, 1 (1912), 26–33 · Vertue, *Note books*, 1.44, 83, 115; 4.48 · E. Waterhouse, *Painting in Britain, 1530–1790*, 5th edn (1994), 51–3 · K. Hearn, ed., *Dynasties: painting in Tudor and Jacobean England, 1530–1630* (1995), 206–7, no. 193 [exhibition catalogue, Tate Gallery, London, 12 Oct 1995 – 7 Jan 1996] · A. M. Hind, *Engraving in England in the sixteenth and seventeenth centuries*, 2 (1955), 27, no. 55, repr. pl. 160b · O. Millar, *The Tudor, Stuart and early Georgian pictures in the collection of her majesty the queen*, 2 vols. (1963), vol. 1, pp. 15, 80–83 · J. Steegman, 'Two signed portraits by Paul van Somer', *Burlington Magazine*, 91 (1949), 52–5 · O. Millar, 'A little known portrait by Paul van Somer', *Burlington Magazine*, 92 (1950), 294 · *The diaries of Lady Anne Clifford*, ed. D. J. H. Clifford (1990), 78–9 · M. K. Talley, *Portrait painting in England: studies in the technical literature before 1700* (1981), 74–84, 325 · M. Faidutti and C. Versini, *Le manuscrit de Turquet de Mayerne* (Lyons, [n.d.]), 13, 19, 112–13, 151 · A. Bredius, ed., *Künstler-Inventare*, 8 vols. (The Hague, 1915–22), vol. 3, pp. 807ff.; vol. 7, pp. 210ff. · C. C. Stopes, 'Daniel Mytens in England', *Notes on pictures in the royal collections*, ed. L. C. Cust (1911), 86 · J. de Maere and M. Wabbes, *Illustrated dictionary of 17th century Flemish painters* (1994), 369–70 · *Report on the manuscripts of the marquis of Downshire*, 6 vols. in 7, HMC, 75 (1924–95), vol. 6, pp. 447, 601 [papers of William Trumbull the elder, Sept 1616 – Dec 1618]

Likenesses S. de Passe, line engraving, 1622, BM; repro. in Hind, *Engraving in England*, pl. 160b

Somer, Paul van (*fl.* 1670–1694), etcher and engraver, was a Frenchman, presumably of Dutch ancestry, who settled in London about 1675. Nothing is known about his origins and training, and he first appears in Paris between 1670

and 1674 making etchings of religious subjects and portraits. A plate of *Hagar in the Wilderness* is signed 'Londini' and dated 1675, but forms part of a set that was published in Paris. For several years van Somer maintained his links with France by sending plates back for publication there, and in 1676 he made two title-pages for books published in Amsterdam. George Vertue says that van Somer was a protestant refugee, and this is confirmed by a series of etched portraits of French ministers of the Huguenot Savoy Chapel, of which the only recorded impressions are in the Pepys Library in Magdalene College, Cambridge. His first mezzotints were made in Paris; a plate made in London in 1676 is one of the earliest dated mezzotints made in England. But his output of thirty-three mezzotints does not begin to approach the total of 209 etchings listed in F. W. H. Hollstein's catalogue of early modern Dutch and Flemish etchings, engravings, and woodcuts.

During the 1680s van Somer was publishing his own and others' plates at his address at the Eagle and Child, near Leicester Fields. He made some prints after the paintings of Paul Mignard (1639–1691), the nephew of Pierre Mignard, who spent a few years in London, and published a few plates of a fellow Huguenot refugee, Simon Gribelin. He was naturalized on 5 March 1691. The last appearance of his name is in the *London Gazette* of 16 July 1694, when 'Paul van Somer's sale of fine plate, pictures and other curiosities' by lottery was advertised. It is not clear whether he was then still alive.

Van Somer's career overlaps with that of Jan van Somer (*fl.* 1660–1687), who is stated by Vertue to have been one of the most prolific, albeit usually anonymous, of the early mezzotint engravers working in London. There are hardly any records of his career, and his relationship, if any, to Paul is unknown, although it has often been asserted that the two were brothers. ANTONY GRIFFITHS

Sources G. Vertue, 'Catalogue of English and foreign engravers', *c.*1730–*c.*1750, Add. MS 23078, fol. 51*v* • W. A. Shaw, ed., *Letters of denization and acts of naturalization for aliens in England and Ireland, 1603–1700*, Huguenot Society of London, 18 (1911), 226 • D. De Hoop Scheffer and G. S. Keyes, *Hollstein's Dutch and Flemish etchings, engravings and woodcuts, c. 1450–1700*, ed. K. G. Boon, 27 (1983), 157–202 • A. Griffiths and R. A. Gerard, *The print in Stuart Britain, 1603–1689* (1998), 231, 272–3 [exhibition catalogue, BM, 8 May – 20 Sept 1998]

Somer [Sommers], **William** (*d.* **1559**), court fool, is of unknown parentage and place of origin. According to James Granger, Somer 'was some time a servant in the family of Richard Farmor, esq. of Eston Neston, in Northamptonshire' (Granger, 149), but there is no independent evidence to verify this claim. He was in Henry VIII's service by 28 June 1535, and went on to serve Edward VI, a warrant of whose reign dated 1551 authorized payment of 40*s.* to one William Seyton, 'whom his Majestie hath appointed to keape William Somer' (Nichols, 1.xliv–xlv n.c.). Mary Tudor also found a place for Somer in her court, providing him with clothing for both ordinary and ceremonial occasions, including a supply of 'handkerchevers of Holland', presumably intended for wiping nose and mouth to deal with a natural condition or illness. Somer was in attendance at the coronation of Elizabeth on 15 January 1559, but is not known to have served her as court fool. He died later that year, on 15 June, and was buried at St Leonard, Shoreditch, London.

We know more of his clothes than of Somer the man. Aside from the possibly indicative supply of lesser linen mentioned above, there are numerous records of gifts of clothing, especially for ceremonial and masquing events. He was provided with a royal livery for wear at court, and with sometimes lavish costume for disguisings. At Henry's court he is most often mentioned in connection with the musical *schola* Henry drew together. Whether his association with these professionals was collaborative or, more likely, in the nature of comic burlesque is not known.

There are excellent visual sources for Somer's appearance. A psalter prepared for Henry's use by the French artist Jean Mallard in 1540 (BL, Royal MS 2.A.XVI) contains a colour illustration (fol. 63*v*) referring to a verse from Psalm 52: 'Dixit insipiens in corde suo non est Deus' ('The fool has said in his heart there is no God'). Henry is depicted as the psalmist David, while Somer is shown as a stocky man, dressed in a green knee-length coat and wearing a purse at his belt, with short-cropped hair, hands clasped in front of him, staring anxious eyes, and raised and perhaps slightly deformed shoulders. A second illustration, a fictionalized portrait of Henry's family painted about 1545 by an unknown artist (Royal Collection), confirms Somer's physical characteristics. He occupies an archway at extreme right of the painting, remote from the main tableau but still in the picture. A pet monkey perched on his shoulder may represent one of the animated props associated with the court fool.

The layout of the family portrait reflects the position of Somer as favoured royal retainer. John Southworth places him in the category of 'innocent', or mental inadequate, rather than professional fool, in accordance with the visual sources and the payment, mentioned above, to his 'keeper'. The familiar account of him as witty adviser and corrector of royal excesses, appearing in plays such as *Misogonus* (first performed 1564–77?), in Thomas Nashe's *Summer's Last will and Testament* (1592), and in Samuel Rowley's *When You See Me, You Know Me* (1605), probably owes more to posthumous myth making than to fact. Nashe's punning use of the proper name with its final 's' may be responsible for fixing in the popular and scholarly mind a usage for which there is no warrant in documents contemporary with Somer. Two jest books offered as biographical histories, Robert Armin's *Foole upon Foole* (1600, expanded as *A Nest of Ninnies*, 1608) and the anonymous *A Pleasant History of the Life and Death of Will Summers* (1676), provide numerous anecdotes, many of them representing standard jests. Armin's account of Somer's tendency to fall into sudden sleep in unexpected places may nevertheless reflect a genuine and progressive illness.

J. R. MULRYNE

Sources J. Southworth, *Fools and jesters at the English court* (1998) • E. Welsford, *The fool: his social and literary history* (1935) • S. Billington, *A social history of the fool* (1984) • A. Feuillerat, ed., *Documents relating to the revels at court in the time of King Edward VI and Queen*

Mary (1914) • J. Granger, *A biographical history of England from Egbert the Great to the revolution*, 5th edn, 1 (1824) • *LP Henry VIII, addenda* • *Literary remains of King Edward the Sixth*, ed. J. G. Nichols, 2 vols., Roxburghe Club, 75 (1857) • A. Rudd, *Misogonus* (1564–1577?) • T. Nashe, *Summer's last will and testament* (1592) • S. Rowley, *When you see me, you know me* (1605) • R. Armin, *Foole upon foole* (1600) • *A pleasant history of the life and death of Will Summers* (1676)

Likenesses J. Mallard, illuminated psalter, 1540, BL • oils, *c*.1545 (with the family of Henry VIII), Royal Collection

Somercote, Lawrence. *See* Somercotes, Laurence of (*fl.* 1245–1258).

Somercote, Robert. *See* Somercotes, Robert of (*d.* 1241).

Somercotes [Somerton], **Laurence of** (*fl.* 1245–1258), ecclesiastic and canonist, may have been related to Cardinal Robert of Somercotes (*d.* 1241) and to his contemporary John of Somercotes, a king's clerk. From 1245 until 24 February 1247 he appears in the *familia* of Walter of Suffield, bishop of Norwich (*d.* 1257). In March 1247 he was appointed canon of Chichester and official to the bishop of Chichester, Richard of Wyche. He had relinquished the officiality by 1251, but as a member of the chapter he played a leading role in the election of a successor to Bishop Richard, who died in April 1253. No doubt it was his experience on this occasion which lay behind his well-known treatise on canonical procedures for the election of bishops. Composed primarily for the guidance of his fellow canons, it was completed in July 1254 and was widely circulated. Somercotes then received a commission from the bishops of Chichester and Norwich, ratified by the king on 4 August 1254, to collect the crusading tenth levied on ecclesiastical benefices in Ireland, which the pope had assigned to the king. As a king's clerk, he was authorized to take £100 from the proceeds of the tax for his salary and expenses; but he wrote from Dublin on 20 May 1256 begging to be relieved of his thorny task, saying he was unwilling to serve any longer in Ireland even at double the salary. In fact, he was discharged, having rendered his accounts, on 17 December 1258. It is not known when he died. C. H. LAWRENCE

Sources A. von Wretschko, *Der traktat des Laurentius de Somercote* (1907) • C. H. Lawrence, 'St Richard of Chichester', *Studies in Sussex church history*, ed. M. J. Kitch (1981), 35–55, esp. 48–50 • LPL, MS 49, fol. 104v [for dating of Laurence's treatise] • B. Dodwell, ed., *The charters of Norwich Cathedral priory*, 1, PRSoc., 40, new ser., 78 (1974), 161 • L. F. Salzman, ed., *The chartulary of Sele Priory* (1923), 32 • Castle Acre Cartulary, BL, Harley MS 2110, fol. 133 • W. D. Peckham, ed., *The chartulary of the high church of Chichester*, Sussex RS, 46 (1946), 221, 224, 286 • T. Arnold, ed., *Memorials of St Edmund's Abbey*, 3, Rolls Series, 96 (1896), 81–2 • *Close rolls of the reign of Henry III*, 14 vols., PRO (1902–38), vol. 8, pp. 92–3, 145–6; vol. 9, pp. 8–9, 393–4; vol. 10, pp. 169–70, 465 • *CPR, 1247–58*, 187, 372, 524, 606 • W. W. Shirley, ed., *Royal and other historical letters illustrative of the reign of Henry III*, 2, Rolls Series, 27 (1866), 117–19

Somercotes, Robert of (*d.* 1241), cardinal, probably took his name from Somercotes in Lincolnshire. He was related to the well-connected Foliot family, of which there was a Lincolnshire branch, and William, Walter, and Laurence of Somercotes were possibly his relatives. In 1214 he was in the service of Archbishop Stephen Langton, from whom he received a rent in the archiepiscopal church of Croydon. He attended the schools of Paris as well as those of Bologna. It was when he was a student at Bologna that the pope provided him with the church of Castor in Northamptonshire, belonging to Peterborough Abbey; efforts were later made to obtain it for his kinsman John of Somercotes.

Somercotes's career illustrates how a man with education and legal training could rise to a powerful position within the papal curia. By 23 May 1236 he was a papal subdeacon. From at least 1 March to 20 May 1238 he was *auditor litterarum contradictarum*, the judge of a court that dealt with the issue of papal mandates and the selection of judges-delegate to hear cases locally. In 1239 he was created cardinal-deacon of St Eustace by Pope Gregory IX. It was also in 1239 that he intervened on behalf of Haymo of Faversham, pleading with Pope Gregory IX to hear Haymo's complaints against Elias, the Franciscan minister-general, with the words 'He is an old man. It is right that you should hear him: he will be brief' (*De adventu*, 66–8). The pope declared against Elias, whom he had previously favoured, and deposed him. From 1239 to 1241 Cardinal Robert acted frequently as a papal auditor, hearing important appeal cases. As a cardinal he stuck loyally by Gregory IX and he was incensed by the remark of Master Simon d'Ételan that Englishmen were not loyal. He himself was not among those cardinals who deserted to the imperial cause on the death of Gregory. Between 1235 and 1237 he had been in the service of the English crown, expediting the royal business at the papal court, and there is little doubt that as a cardinal he was targeted by English petitioners to the curia. There is no reason to reject the statement that he died in the course of the conclave that finally elected Celestine IV on 25 October 1241, though he may not have died of poison, and he may not have stood out among all candidates for election to the papal chair, as Matthew Paris alleges. A contemporary monumental inscription over the interior door into the north-west aisle on the inside of the church of St Chrysogonus in Trastevere, Rome, records that he died on 26 September 1241 and was buried there. JANE E. SAYERS

Sources K. Major, ed., *Acta Stephani Langton*, CYS, 50 (1950), no. 9 • *Les registres de Grégoire IX*, ed. L. Auvray, 4 vols. (Paris, 1896–1955), nos. 946, 3155, 3171, 4123, 4709, 6046, 6091 • P. Bruno Griesser, 'Registrum epistolarum Stephani de Lexinton', *Analecta Sacri Ordinis Cisterciensis*, 8 (1952), 315 n.101 • *Fratris Thomae vulgo dicti de Eccleston tractatus de adventu Fratrum Minorum in Angliam*, ed. A. G. Little (1951), 66–8 • Paris, *Chron.*, 4.5, 16, 64, 164–5, 168; 5.194 • W. W. Shirley, ed., *Royal and other historical letters illustrative of the reign of Henry III*, 1, Rolls Series, 27 (1862), 463 • *Chancery records* • N. da Calvi, 'Vita Innocentii Pape IV', *Rerum Italicarum scriptores*, ed. L. A. Muratori, 1 (1723), 592 • V. Forcella, *Iscrizioni delle chiese e d'altri edificii di Roma dal secolo XI fino ai giorni nostri*, 2 (1873), 170 • J. E. Sayers, 'Canterbury proctors at the court of "*audientia litterarum contradictarum*"', *Traditio*, 22 (1966), 311–45, esp. 325 (n. 87)

Somerled (*d.* 1164), king of the Hebrides and *regulus* of Argyll and Kintyre, was the son of Gille-Brigde, son of Gille-Adomnain. His own name, later Gaelicized as Somhairle, is Scandinavian—appropriately meaning 'summer warrior'—and his father's and grandfather's names are Gaelic, indicative of the hybrid Gaelic–Norse culture of the west highlands and islands at that time. No contemporary pedigree for Somerled survives, but within a century of his death his ancestry was being traced from Colla Uais, one of the legendary founders of the Airgialla in northern Ireland. Later and more detailed accounts derive Somerled from the Airgialla via Godfrey, son of Fergus, said to have been a contemporary of Kenneth mac Alpin (*d.* 858) and to have held power in the Hebrides. The fact that some of the Airgialla appear to have been attached to the division of Loarn in Dalriada as early as the seventh century suggests that there may be some historical basis behind these claims.

It is difficult, in fact, to detach the historical Somerled from the Somerled (Somhairle Mor mac Gille-Brigde) of later Gaelic tradition, in which he is associated with his most famous descendants, the MacDonald lords of the Isles; it was there claimed that his forebears had been lords in Argyll, but had been dispossessed in the time of his grandfather. Tradition also portrayed Somerled as a great champion of the Gael against Scandinavian dominion. This last is certainly misleading. Whatever his paternal ancestry, it is clear that the milieu in which he operated was as much Scandinavian as Gaelic, and that his lordship should be compared with that of rulers of Orkney, Dublin, and the Isle of Man, all of undoubted Scandinavian ancestry, as much as with Gaelic kings and rulers.

The first contemporary mention of Somerled, described as *regulus* of Argyll, occurs in 1153, when he rebelled against the new king of Scots, Malcolm IV (*r.* 1153–65). However, as Somerled rose with his nephews, the sons of Malcolm *Macheth [*see under* Macheth family], the dispossessed claimant to Moray, who had been imprisoned since 1134, it is clear that he must already have been a man of mature years. It has been conjectured that Somerled may have been present at the battle of the Standard in 1138, when the men of Argyll are known to have supported David I, and this is not unlikely. During King David's reign (1124–53) Somerled, like Fergus, prince of Galloway, seems to have acknowledged the king's strong lordship.

Somerled remained opposed to King Malcolm for several years, but reached a settlement with him in 1160, when a royal charter to Kelso Abbey is dated 'in Natali Domino post proximo concordiam Regis et Sumerledi' (*Regesta regum Scottorum*, 1, no. 175). It must have been on the occasion of this reconciliation that Somerled received the sobriquet 'sit-by-the-king'. Three years earlier, in 1157, Malcolm MacHeth had been released from prison and made earl of Ross in compensation for Moray.

In the meantime Somerled had extended his rule into the kingdom of Man and the Hebrides, at that time subject to a rather shadowy Norwegian overlordship. He married Ragnhild, daughter of Olaf (*d.* 1153), son of Godred (or Godfrey) Crovan, and they had three sons, Dugald, Ranald, and Angus, and perhaps a fourth, Olaf. For forty years until his death in 1153 Ragnhild's father ruled the kingdom of the Isles, which encompassed the Isle of Man and the Hebrides, extending from the Calf of Man to the Butt of Lewis. Olaf adopted the Latin style *rex insularum* in his charters, a translation of the Gaelic title *rí Innse Gall* (literally 'king of the foreigners' isles'), which had been in use since the late tenth century. Olaf's son Godred proved an unpopular ruler. A leading chieftain, Thorfinn, son of Ottar, came to Somerled offering to make his son Dugald king in Godred's place. A naval battle ensued between Godred and Somerled in January 1156, as a result of which Godred agreed to part with half of his kingdom. Judging from the territories later under the control of his descendants, Somerled's share included the Mull and Islay groups of islands at least, and perhaps also the Uists and Barra. In 1158 he expelled Godred from the Isles altogether. Godred did not return until after Somerled's death, and then only to a divided kingdom.

Like his father-in-law, Olaf of Man, and Fergus of Galloway, Somerled was a patron of the church. In 1164 he tried to persuade Flaithbertach Ó Brolchain, the successor of St Columba in Ireland, to come to Iona as abbot, but was unsuccessful. He may also have founded the Cistercian monastery of Saddell in Kintyre, although the credit for this more probably belongs to his son Ranald. Somerled's daughter Bethoc became the first prioress of the Benedictine nunnery of Iona.

In 1164 Somerled rose again in opposition to Malcolm IV. He launched a major expedition with men drawn from the Hebrides, Argyll, Kintyre, and Dublin, and sailed up the Clyde with many galleys before landing at Renfrew. The purpose of this expedition is unknown. Could Somerled have been rising in favour of Donald MacWilliam (*d.* 1187), grandson of Duncan II and claimant to the Scots throne? In the *Carmen de morte Sumerledi*, composed by one William, who alleged he was an eyewitness, resistance to Somerled was led by Herbert, bishop of Glasgow. Somerled was killed at the very outset of battle, and his head, severed by a clerk, was brought to the bishop, who wept and gave credit for the victory to St Kentigern. Later Gaelic tradition, however, claimed that he died by treachery. The continuator of the annals of Tigernach styles Somerled 'king of Innse Gall and Kintyre' (Anderson, 2.254) at his death. Somerled was probably buried on Iona, rather than at Saddell Abbey as has sometimes been suggested.

From Somerled's son Dugald descend the thirteenth-century lords of Argyll and the clan MacDougall, and from his son Ranald the later MacDonald lords of the Isles and also the MacRuaris. Gille-Brigte, a son by another union, died with Somerled at Renfrew. W. D. H. SELLAR

Sources A. A. M. Duncan and A. L. Brown, 'Argyll and the Isles in the earlier middle ages', *Proceedings of the Society of Antiquaries of Scotland*, 90 (1956–7), 192–220 • R. A. McDonald and S. A. McLean, 'Somerled of Argyll: a new look at old problems', *SHR*, 71 (1992), 3–22 • W. D. H. Sellar, 'The origins and ancestry of Somerled', *SHR*, 45 (1966), 123–42 • J. W. M. Bannerman, 'The lordship of the isles: historical background', in K. A. Steer, J. W. M. Bannerman, and G. H. Collins, *Late medieval monumental sculpture in the west highlands* (1977) • C. M. MacDonald, *History of Argyll* (1950), 73–80 • G. W. S. Barrow, *Kingship and unity: Scotland, 1000–1306* (1981), 105–21 • 'Carmen de morte Sumerledi', Symeon of Durham, *Opera*, 2.386–8 • G. W. S. Barrow, ed., *Regesta regum Scottorum*, 1 (1960) • A. O. Anderson, ed. and trans., *Early sources of Scottish history, AD 500 to 1286*, 2 vols. (1922) • R. A. MacDonald, *The kingdom of the isles: Scotland's western seaboard, c.1100–c.1336* (1997), 39–67 • S. Duffy, 'Irishmen and

Islesmen in the kingdoms of Dublin and Man, 1052–1171', *Ériu*, 43 (1992), 93–133

Somers. For this title name *see* individual entries under Somers; *see also* Cocks, Arthur Herbert Tennyson Somers-, sixth Baron Somers (1887–1944).

Somers, Edmund Sigismund (1759?–1824), physician, born in Dublin, was the son of William Somers, a mechanic. He entered Trinity College, Dublin, on 7 June 1779, to study for a BA degree. He afterwards studied medicine at Edinburgh University and graduated MD on 12 September 1783. After visiting the medical schools of Paris and Leiden he returned to Dublin and was elected to the membership of the Royal Irish Academy. On 22 December 1791 Somers became a licentiate of the Royal College of Physicians, and he began to practise medicine in London.

On 18 March 1795 Somers was appointed physician to the forces. In this capacity he proceeded to the Cape of Good Hope as director of hospitals. After several years he retired to England, served in the home district, and then went as staff physician to Jamaica. After two years he returned to England because of ill health. On recovery Somers joined the army in the Iberian peninsula, where in 1812 Wellington appointed him physician-in-chief to the allied forces. He served at the principal depots in Portugal and Spain, and was present at the battle of Waterloo. On 18 January 1816 he was nominated deputy inspector of hospitals, and retired on half pay.

While in retirement, Somers published a treatise on dysentery and fevers which he had observed during his military career. *Medical suggestions for the treatment of dysentery, of intermittent and remittent fevers, as generally prevalent at certain seasons among troops in the field*, was published in 1816, appearing in both Latin and English versions. Somers died on 3 February 1824.

E. I. Carlyle, *rev.* Claire E. J. Herrick

Sources Munk, *Roll* • A. Peterkin and W. Johnston, *Commissioned officers in the medical services of the British army, 1660–1960*, 1 (1968), 87 • N. Cantlie, *A history of the army medical department*, 2 (1974), 391 • *Army List* • *The pantheon of the age, or, Memoirs of 3000 contemporary public characters, British and foreign*, 2nd edn, 3 (1825), 418–19

Somers, Sir George (1554–1610), privateer and colonial adventurer, was born in Lyme Regis, Dorset, the son of John Somer (as the name was then spelt) and his wife, Alice (*d.* 1591). He first comes to notice in 1587 when he used prize money to buy 106 acres of land in Dorset. No record exists of his taking part in the Armada battle (1588), but in 1589 he was in command of the *Flibcote* which, with three other vessels, brought Spanish prizes into Dartmouth valued at £8000. Before that, at some time before 1583, he married Joan (*d.* 1618), daughter of Phillip Heywood, a yeoman of Lyme Regis. There were no surviving children. In 1595 he joined Sir Amyas Preston, a hero of the Armada, as second in command of an expedition to what is now Venezuela, where after an arduous march they captured San Jago de Leon, now Caracas. Their efforts to hold the town to ransom failed, and San Jago was burnt before the expedition returned to their boats. Off Cuba, on the way home, they met, by chance, Sir Walter Ralegh, but the two small fleets soon lost each other.

Somers took part in an expedition to the Azores in 1597, and for a time was thought to be lost. His safe return in a small vessel merited a letter to the earl of Essex from Sir Walter Ralegh, Lord Thomas Howard, and Lord Mountjoy. In 1600 the crown gave him command of the *Vanguard*, and the following year of the *Swiftsure*, and then the great ship *Warspite* which Ralegh had commanded five years before. He was knighted on 23 July 1603, a year before the war with Spain ended. He became mayor of Lyme Regis and a member of parliament, but in February 1610 his seat was declared vacant—apparently it was thought that he had left England to be governor of Virginia.

On 10 April 1606 Somers, Sir Thomas Gates, and others received a royal patent for two Virginia companies to settle colonies in America. In 1607 Captain Christopher Newport made the first voyage under the patent and conveyed colonists to Jamestown, Virginia. In 1609 a major fleet was sent out with Sir George as admiral on board the *Sea Venture* (he invested £300 in the voyage), with Newport as captain and Sir Thomas, governor-designate of the colony, as a passenger. On Wednesday 26 July, when the voyage was nearing its end, the fleet was struck by a hurricane and the ships separated. The *Sea Venture* began to leak badly and Gates organized the crew and passengers into three groups to pump and bail for an hour each, with two hours off. Somers stayed on the poop, guiding the ship as best he could in the tumultuous seas. On Thursday night St Elmo's fire sparkled in the rigging. On Friday the ship's company were exhausted, and were giving up, when Sir George looked out from the high poop and saw land. It was Bermuda. The ship was headed toward a beach, but hit a reef, and then lodged between two reefs which held her upright, and everyone reached shore safely. One of the accounts of the wreck, by William Strachey, later secretary of Virginia, reached England and is thought to be an inspiration for William Shakespeare's *The Tempest*—the storm scene, with Ariel flaming in the rigging, has many similarities to Strachey's account, and the butler Stephano recalls a passenger, Stephen Hopkins, who led one of several attempted mutinies, for the stay on Bermuda saw the ship's company divide into estranged factions.

This occurred despite the abundance of hogs (perhaps landed by Spaniards), fish, and birds, eked out with a little meal saved from the *Sea Venture*. Perhaps it started at the landing when Gates, going ashore first, declared as he landed 'Gates, his Bay' and took command. His relations with Somers deteriorated, and Somers apparently tried to distance himself from the main settlement where Gates undertook the building of a vessel, the *Deliverance*, at an exposed beach, still known as Buildings Bay. At first Sir George busied himself in fishing for the company, and then in circumnavigating and mapping the island in a small boat. No doubt he picked out Somerset Island (Somers Seate) for himself during this expedition. Gates took a strong line in dealing with the mutinies, and Somers withdrew himself and some of the sailors to build a smaller second vessel which he called the *Patience*—perhaps a reflection of his state of mind, for much of it he built himself. The mutinous feeling in Gates's camp reached serious proportions when a group planned to raid the storehouse and get away on their own. A ringleader, Henry Paine, was arrested and executed by a firing squad. When news reached Somers's camp all his sailors ran away.

At Gates's request Somers succeeded in recalling his men and completed the *Patience* as Gates's group completed the *Deliverance*, and the two vessels sailed together on 12 May 1610 and reached Jamestown ten days later. They found that during the winter a colony of 500 persons had suffered so severely from starvation, disease, and Indian attacks that only 60 were left alive. The castaways became the rescuers with their ships' supplies, but all decided to abandon Jamestown, and were setting out down the James River when, in the nick of time, another supply fleet commanded by Lord De La Warr arrived, and the colonists returned to Jamestown.

Somers took the *Patience* and another vessel up the coast to fish, and then went back to Bermuda where two men had stayed behind. Somers kept his men busy catching fish and hogs and preparing them for the voyage back to Jamestown, but died on 9 November 1610, 'of a surfeit of eating of a pig' according to his biography in Alexander Brown's *Genesis of the United States* (pp. 1018–19); Captain John Smith's *Historie of Virginia* says that he died of exhaustion. His nephew Matthew Somers decided to go against Somers's wishes that he return to Jamestown with supplies, and, burying his uncle's heart and entrails in Bermuda, carried his body back to England, where it was buried at Whitchurch Canonicorum, Dorset, with pomp and ceremony in 1611.

Somers's contemporaries thought well of him, and Fuller's *Worthies* gives a glib characterization: 'This Sir George Sommers was a lamb on land, so patient that few could anger him: and (as if entering a ship he assumed a new nature) a lion at sea, so passionate few could please him' (Lefroy, 52n.). He seems to have been delighted with Bermuda and may have written to friends suggesting they take part in colonizing the archipelago, as well as picking out an island for himself. He was so highly regarded that the archipelago itself was called by the English the Somers Isles, and the first capital St Georges—linking his name and the patron saint of England. On a personal level he commanded the respect of the sailors on the *Sea Venture* and was able to deal with the malcontents on shore. An inquisition into his estate and will showed that his estate, which included two manors, produced an estimated £19 18*s*. 4*d*. per annum. WILLIAM SEARS ZUILL SEN.

Sources J. H. Lefroy, *Memorials of the discovery and early settlement of the Bermudas or Somers Islands, 1515–1685*, another edn, 2 vols. (1981), 10–53 • R. Hakluyt, *A selection of the principal voyages, traffiques and discoveries of the English nation*, ed. L. Irving (1926), 172–82 • A. Brown, ed., *The genesis of the United States*, 1 (1890), 52; 2 (1890), 1018–9 • F. J. Pope, 'Sir George Somers and his family', *Bermuda Historical Quarterly*, 4 (1947), 57–61 • A. T. Gosling, ed. and trans., *Royal Gazette* [Hamilton, Bermuda] (7–8 July 1959) [inquisition into Somers's estate and will] • J. Smith, *The general historie of Virginia, New England and the Summer Isles*, 2 vols. (1907), vol. 1 • [N. Butler ?], *The historye of the Bermudaes or Summer Islands*, ed. J. H. Lefroy, Hakluyt Society, 1st ser., 65 (1882); facs. edn (New York, 1964) [photographic repr. of orig. Hakluyt Society edn of 1882] • *DNB* • K. R. Andrews, *Elizabethan privateering: English privateering during the Spanish war, 1585–1603* (1964) • H. C. Wilkinson, *The adventurers of Bermuda: a history of the island from its discovery until the dissolution of the Somers Island Company in 1684*, 2nd edn (1958) • O. H. Darrell, 'Admiral Sir George Somers', *Bermuda Historical Quarterly*, 16 (July–Sept 1959), 117–21 • D. F. Raine, *Sir George Somers: a man and his times* (1984)

Likenesses attrib. P. van Somers, oils, Bermuda Historical Society Museum, Hamilton, Bermuda

Wealth at death est. income at £19 18*s*. 4*d*. p.a.: Gosling, ed. and trans., *Royal Gazette*

Somers, John, Baron Somers (1651–1716), lawyer and politician, was born on 4 March 1651, either at White Ladies, Claines, near Worcester, formerly his grandfather's house and at that time owned by his aunt, or at his parents' house in College Churchyard, adjacent to St Michael's Bedwardine, Worcester. His father, also John Somers (1620–1681), a Worcester lawyer, had fought on the parliamentarian side in the civil war, and in 1648 had married Catharine (*c*.1625–1710), daughter of John Severne of Powick, Worcestershire. Somers was the only son of the marriage but he had four sisters, two of whom married political allies: Mary (*b*. 1653), who married Charles Cocks MP; and Elizabeth (*b*. 1655), who married Sir Joseph Jekyll, MP and master of the rolls.

Early life and career Somers was educated at the cathedral school in Worcester, and then possibly at a private school in Sheriffhales, Shropshire, and Walsall grammar school in Staffordshire. He then went to Trinity College, Oxford, matriculating on 23 May 1667. He did not take a degree, his mind being set, it would seem, on the law. He was admitted to the Middle Temple on 24 May 1669 and found an able patron in Sir Francis Winnington, a future solicitor-general. Somers was called to the bar on 5 May 1676 and took chambers in Pump Court the following year.

These were exciting times for a young barrister in London and Somers soon became involved in politics on the whig side, a number of tracts being ascribed to his pen although Somers never explicitly acknowledged authorship. One of these, *A Brief History of the Succession* (1681), was a defence of the Exclusion Bill using historical precedents to reassure conservative thinkers that parliament's altering the succession was not a revolutionary action, but a way of proceeding sanctioned by ancient parliamentary rights going back to Saxon times. In June 1681 Somers took a practical political role for the first time when the king's supporters in the Middle Temple attempted to promote an address of thanks for the royal declaration justifying the dissolution of the two previous parliaments, and he was put up as chair of the meeting by those opposed to such a gesture of support for royal policies. There is also some evidence that he was involved in drafting one of the printed rebuttals of the king's declaration, *A Just and Modest Vindication of the Proceedings of the Last Two Parliaments* (1681), although historians are divided on the extent of his contribution.

John Somers, Baron Somers (1651–1716), by Sir Godfrey Kneller, *c.*1715–16

Somers's growing prominence led to his being appointed standing counsel for the dean and chapter of Worcester Cathedral in 1681. His first major role in a legal trial was as part of the defence team in 1683 which sought to defend several prominent whigs charged with riot at the shrieval elections of June 1682 in the city of London. With the whigs facing political eclipse after 1683 Somers kept a low profile, and at this time may have written several contributions to classical scholarship including the 'Life of Alcibiades', in *Plutarch's Lives by Several Hands* (1683–6). He maintained this interest long afterwards, being the general editor of the 1702 edition of *Several Orations of Demosthenes*.

Somers's next major case was as counsel for the seven bishops who had refused to co-operate with James II's religious policies in June 1688. Henry Pollexfen had insisted on Somers because of his diligence in researching the case: he was the 'man who would take the most pains, and go deepest into all that depended on precedents and records' (Schwoerer, 49). During his short speech at the trial Somers cited a precedent from *Thomas* v. *Sorrel* in 1674, in which the judges had rejected the dispensing power unless sanctioned by parliament. Therefore, the charge of seditious libel against the bishops could not be true as there was no sedition and no libel. Following the acquittal of the bishops Somers was perceived as a potential whig 'collaborator' of James II's policies by some of the king's advisers such as the second earl of Sunderland, and he was seen as a possible MP for several Worcestershire constituencies, but this seems to have been merely wishful thinking on the part of royal agents. Somers did, however, begin to reap the rewards for his part in the cause célèbre of the bishops' trial. Upon the restoration of the City of London's charter in October 1688 he was offered the recordership, but declined. In November 1688 he was elected recorder of Worcester, and then on 11 January 1689 chosen as MP for the city in the elections to the convention. Shortly afterwards, on 10 May, he was made a bencher of the Middle Temple, where he seems to have lived.

Career in the Commons, 1689–1693 For a new member Somers was very active in the Convention Parliament, being appointed to eighty-five committees and making thirteen recorded speeches. When the Commons considered the fate of James II in the committee of the whole house on 28 January 1689 Somers was clearly on the side of those wishing to see William III declared king. To this end he cited the precedent of the expulsion of King Sigismund of Sweden in 1599 in support of those arguing that James II had by his actions incapacitated himself from being king, and that the throne was vacant. There is, however, no evidence that Somers actually proposed the motion that James II had deserted the throne and that it was therefore vacant. On 6 February, when the Commons and Lords met in a conference in an attempt to solve the impasse over whether James II had abdicated the throne and the crown was therefore 'vacant', Somers spoke 'very learnedly' (Schwoerer, 216) on the terms 'abdication' and 'desertion', and on the question of a vacancy, although one of his precedents concerning the assumption of the throne by Henry IV was challenged and he had to be rescued by Sir George Treby, who proved the precedent to be valid after all.

Somers had also been heavily involved in the committee assigned the task of drawing up what was to become the Bill of Rights, a task to which he was well suited given his interest in the history of the constitution, and on 8 February he reported from the committee charged with reconciling into a single text the revised declaration of rights and the votes setting out that James II had abdicated and that the throne was vacant. Although he was not prominent in the passage of the Bill of Rights into law, Somers has been accorded a considerable degree of credit for it because of his earlier work in helping to bring it into being. He also felt the need to go into print with *In Vindication of the Proceedings of the Late Parliament of England … 1689* (1690), which argued that the settling of the crown and the enactment of the Bill of Rights were achievements for which all Englishmen ought to feel indebted to parliament. His reward for supporting the government came on 4 May 1689 when he was named solicitor-general, an office which brought him greater involvement in supply legislation in particular, especially from November 1689 when he began chairing the committee of ways and means. In August 1689 he was elected as recorder of Gloucester, and on 31 October he was rewarded by the king with a knighthood. All of these honours enhanced his status and increased his employability as a lawyer in private practice.

Somers was re-elected to the Commons in the 1690 election and again played a major part in managing the legislation of the parliament and as a spokesman for the government. Nor did he neglect party matters, speaking on 8 April in support of the whigs' proposal that the 1683 *quo warranto* judgment against the City of London be declared void, rather than just reversed as 'I will never give my consent to countenance such illegal and cursed judgements, to bring in popery and arbitrary power' (Grey, 10.43). He also spoke on the Indemnity Bill and the Regency Bill, both measures affecting the security of the new regime. His legal duties as solicitor-general included on 16–19 January 1691 the successful prosecution for treason of the Jacobite Richard Graham, Viscount Preston, although Graham was pardoned later by the king. On 11 December 1691 Somers spoke in the Commons on the House of Lords amendments to the bill regulating treason trials, specifically on the clauses in which the peers claimed special privileges relating to impeachments and the trials of members of the upper house, matters to which he would return in subsequent sessions. On 2 May 1692 he was promoted to the post of attorney-general, although he continued to practise privately acting as counsel for the duke of Norfolk in his suit for damages of £100,000 against Sir John Germaine for adultery with his wife. In the Commons on 14 December 1692 he supported the bill for the 'preservation of their majesties' persons and government', which was ostensibly to further secure William and Mary on the throne but was suspected of being a party political measure against the tories. As attorney-general he was prosecutor at the trial on 31 January–4 February 1693 of Charles, Baron Mohun, who was acquitted of the murder of William Mountford. On 23 March 1693 Somers was advanced to the post of lord keeper of the great seal and made a privy councillor.

Lord keeper and lord chancellor Somers moved into Powys House in Lincoln's Inn Fields as his official residence, and as a figure of major importance in the ministry he was soon put to good use, raising £300,000 from his whig friends in the City to help the king over a crisis of credit. Somers was now speaker of the House of Lords (although he could not speak in debates, as he was not a peer), a judge in the court of chancery, and a politician whose advice William III sought, especially in his role as a manager of the whig party. It was in this role that Somers was useful in conciliating a group of country whig MPs with Worcestershire connections who were dallying with the tories. One old presbyterian, the somewhat rigid Sir Edward Harley, had this to say about a 'great feast' he had been invited to with the lord keeper in January 1694: 'no health drank no profane word uttered, thanks given before and after meat' (Sir Edward to Robert Harley, 16 Jan 1694, BL, Add. MS 70235). In May 1695 Somers refused a peerage on the grounds that he had an insufficient estate to support such a dignity, but his position as a key government minister was reinforced when William appointed him one of the lords justices to administer the kingdom during the king's absence abroad (a position to which Somers was reappointed each year until 1699).

In the debate over the deterioration of the kingdom's silver coinage during the 1690s Somers was an advocate of the position adopted by John Locke, who dedicated two of his pamphlets on the issue to Somers: *A Consideration of Lowering of Interest and Raising the Value of Money*, which was an early contribution to the debate on an emerging problem in 1692, and *Further Consideration Concerning the Raising the Value of Money* (1695). In June 1696 Somers delivered his most elaborate judgment as lord keeper; it concerned the relief of the government's creditors who had suffered by the stop of the exchequer in 1672 and thus had become known as *The Bankers' Case*. Somers found against the bankers, but his decision was overturned in 1700 upon appeal to House of Lords. Along with Locke and other members of 'the College', a group of whig friends, Somers was concerned in setting up the Board of Trade in 1696. Somers was also a key participant once the assassination plot had been uncovered and Sir John Fenwick had attempted to save himself by implicating prominent members of the ministry such as the duke of Shrewsbury; Somers's chief role was to ensure that Fenwick's claims were refuted in public, which was eventually done by means of a bill of attainder, and to prevent Shrewsbury from resigning and thereby weakening the ministry.

As a result of the successful 1696–7 session Somers was made lord chancellor on 22 April 1697 and, on 2 December, just prior to the next session of parliament, he was raised to the peerage as Baron Somers of Evesham. To uphold the dignity of his new position he was granted the manors of Reigate and Howleigh in Surrey, plus £2100 per annum in fee farm rents (which, although they turned out to have already been granted to the earl of Portland, he had managed to acquire by 1699). This increase in wealth from royal grants was one of the grounds on which the tories attacked Somers when they assailed those whigs remaining in the ministry after 1698. The impetus which the peace of Ryswick had given to campaigners against the standing army may have enticed Somers into print as the author of *A letter balancing the necessity of keeping a land force in times of peace: with the dangers that may follow on it*, which appeared before the 1697–8 session. Somers took his seat in the Lords on 14 December and was soon enjoying the freedom of his new dignity to contribute to debate and oppose the land qualification bill for membership of the House of Commons.

In August 1698 Somers had been informed by the king of the negotiations dealing with the fate of the Spanish monarchy in preparation for the imminent death of Carlos II and was requested to affix the great seal to a commission to negotiate the first partition treaty but, unusually, leaving the names of the commissioners blank. Despite some reservations Somers did as he was asked and co-operated in further measures to keep the treaty secret. After the treaty was signed in September he received a warrant for all his actions. These proceedings, especially the sealing of the commission, were subsequently the main justification for his impeachment. Meanwhile, the incapacity and then resignation of Shrewsbury and the retirement of Sunderland had left an increasing burden on Somers to hold the ministry together. This proved to be no easy task as the government was assailed by opponents freed from the need to show unity now that England was at peace.

The king's speech of 9 December 1698 was drafted by Somers and was noticeable for its conciliatory tone. However, the opponents of the standing army carried a motion for a total force of only 7000 men, and this figure remained when the house passed its disbanding bill on 18 January 1699. Somers was now in a quandary because the disbanding bill was a money bill, something with which the Lords were not supposed to interfere, and to amend it would provoke a crisis with the Commons; thus, although he criticized it, the bill was allowed through the Lords on 30 January 1699 without a division. Not the least of Somers's services at this time was to put forcibly to the king the arguments against his carrying out his threat to withdraw from the kingdom because of the Commons refusal to pay for an adequate number of troops or even allow him to retain his cherished Dutch guards.

The upshot of the 1698–9 session was a more mixed ministry, and more tory pressure on the remaining whig ministers, in particular Somers, who became the tories' prime target. In November 1699 his appointments to the commissions of the peace were under scrutiny, but although Somers no doubt had an eye to strengthening the whigs in the counties when he sealed 103 commissions of the peace during 1693–6, there had been no systematic purge of justices. In December, however, Somers had to admit affixing the great seal to Captain Kidd's commission of 1697 which authorized his expedition against piracy. Unfortunately, once at sea, Kidd turned pirate himself. Worse still Somers had been one of the investors (to the tune of £1000) in Kidd's venture. Fortunately for Somers, on 6 December 1699 the Commons voted the commission to Kidd not illegal by 189 votes to 133. Somers was then attacked on 13 February 1700 for passing grants for his own use, but survived the vote by 232 to 182, and he escaped again on 10 April 1700, when a motion for an address to the king to remove him from the royal presence was lost by 167 to 106.

The king seems to have been surprised and somewhat displeased at the survival of Somers while his own legislation was defeated or mangled by the parliamentary opposition. At a privy council meeting on 25 April he asked for Somers's resignation, which the lord chancellor refused on the grounds that such an offer had been made and not accepted earlier in the session. The king then dismissed Somers on 27 April, although there was no-one readily available to replace him. By September 1700 Somers had moved out of Powys House to 21 St James's Square.

Impeachment No sooner had Somers been dismissed than Sunderland was at work trying to include him in a new ministry. In the event a predominantly tory ministry was installed, and a general election held in January 1701. The new parliament was not willing to leave the old ministers in peace. Somers had affixed the great seal to the second partition treaty in March 1700 and he only escaped censure for this on 29 March 1701 by 189 votes to 182. During questioning by the Commons on 8 April, however, the secretary of state, James Vernon, revealed the existence of the first partition treaty. This gave the Commons fresh grounds to attack Somers and, despite a personal appearance before the lower house on 14 April, the Commons voted 198 to 188 to impeach him for his role in the treaty.

The Commons eventually exhibited fourteen articles against Somers which were sent up to the Lords on 19 May 1701. Apart from his role in the partition treaties the main articles concerned his sponsorship of Captain Kidd, his use of the great seal to pass grants of Irish land to royal favourites and for his own benefit, and his manipulation of the commissions of the peace. Somers replied on the 24th: to the articles on the partition treaty he denied promoting it and pleaded that in sealing it he was following the king's order; all his grants had been legal; nor was the grant to Kidd illegal, just unwise. With a whig majority in the upper house, the impeachment procedure became a source of conflict between the two houses, especially when Lord Haversham accused the Commons of ignoring the involvement of tory lords in the treaty. On 17 June 1701 Somers was acquitted by 55 votes to 33 after the Commons failed to appear in Westminster Hall to prosecute their case.

Interests outside politics, character, and religion Freed from office after 1701 Somers had more time to indulge in his many intellectual interests. From 1698 he was a member of the Royal Society, serving as president in 1698–1703, and from about that time he was also a member of the Kit-Cat Club, which brought him into regular contact with a host of whig literary men such as William Congreve, Sir John Vanbrugh, William Walsh, Jacob Tonson, and also Sir Godfrey Kneller, who painted his portrait on several occasions. He was able to help the nonjuring scholar George Hickes by setting aside the legal proceedings against him, and encouraged both Thomas Rymer, author of the *Foedera*, and Thomas Madox, author of works on ancient charters and the exchequer. Dedications to Somers are found in Jonathan Swift's *A Tale of the Tub*, an issue of Richard Steele's *Spectator* in 1712, *The Letter Concerning Enthusiasm* by the third earl of Shaftesbury, and the works of Joseph Addison, John Cary, and John Evelyn. As well as being a patron of literature, Somers was above all a collector and he accumulated more than 9000 books, hundreds of manuscripts, about 4000 drawings, and many more prints. This collection was housed in two properties which Somers acquired in 1701: 28 Leicester Square and Brookmans Manor, Hertfordshire, which became his permanent country residence.

As James Vernon succinctly put it in 1701, Somers was criticized 'for adultery, socinianism, and I know not what besides' (*Letters Illustrative*, 3.156). In 1700 Sir Edward Seymour, fourth baronet, had accused him of being a 'Hobbist' and in 1711 Jonathan Swift echoed this in *The Examiner* with charges of his being a 'deist' or 'socinian' (*Letters Illustrative*, 3.13; Ellis, 215). In fact, although Somers may have been sympathetic to dissent, he was a regular churchgoer. In 1696 he was called out from St Giles's Church by the arrival of a messenger, and Bishop Nicolson wrote in his notes on the occasional conformity debates in December 1702: 'Lord Somers, never at a conventicle'. Furthermore, in December 1704 Nicolson noted that Somers was part of the vestry at St Martin-in-the-Fields, and that he was present there when Nicolson preached in 1705 and 1708.

Of Somers's personal morals there is more evidence. In 1690–91 he had been expected to marry Anne Bawden, the daughter of Sir John Bawden, a wealthy City alderman (and kinsman of John Oldmixon, later an anonymous biographer of Somers), but the match was broken off over a dispute over the portion and Somers remained unmarried. He apparently contracted syphilis in the 1690s and opponents made much of his sexual excesses. Mrs Manley in *The New Atlantis* attacked Somers as 'Cicero', and Swift followed suit in *The Examiner*. The main accusation centred on Somers's household in Queen Anne's reign which was run by his niece, Margaret Cocks, and included one Elizabeth Blount, daughter of the Restoration diplomat Sir Richard Fanshawe. Somers, it was alleged, had caused her husband, Christopher Blount, to be imprisoned in order to secure her services but whether she really was a nurse or a mistress is difficult to determine. He was also linked to a scandal with Lady Harriet Vere, who was reported to have a 'ruined reputation' (Sachse, 81n.) and never married. According to John Macky's character sketch of Somers aged about fifty, he was 'of a grave deportment, easy and free in conversation; something of a libertine, of middle stature, brown complexion' (*Memoirs of the Secret Services*, 50). Addison also referred in *The Freeholder* to Somers's 'masterly and engaging manner of conversation', which he used to good purpose:

> By approving the sentiments of a person … in such particulars as were just, he won him over from those points in which he was mistaken; and had so agreeable a way of conveying knowledge, that whoever conferred with him grew the wiser, without perceiving that he had been instructed. (*The Freeholder*, 210–11)

Political activity out of office, 1701–1707 Somers was out of office but that did not mean he had retired from the political battle. The controversies of this time led to many pamphlets, some of which, such as *Jus regium* (1701), a defence of the king's right to dispose of the Irish forfeitures, and *Jura populi Anglicani, or, The Subject's Right of Petitioning Set Forth* (1701), a defence of the Kentish petitioners, might have been written by Somers. Indeed, by the time the latter was published Somers's political prospects were already rising given the change in foreign affairs which followed James II's death and Louis XIV's recognition of the Pretender (James Stuart) as his heir. In September 1701 Sunderland had urged the king to consider admitting the whigs back into office and advised that he should send for Somers, 'the life, the soul, and the spirit of his party, and can answer for it' (Horwitz, 295). Somers joined with Sunderland in successfully urging a dissolution of parliament, and composed the king's speech delivered to the newly assembled parliament on 30 December 1701, but William III did not recall Somers to office before his death in March 1702. The accession of Queen Anne altered Somers's immediate prospects. She had an aversion to Somers, possibly because of his role in the dispute in 1689 over granting her a separate income independent of William III, and had her own chief ministers ready in Lord Godolphin and the duke of Marlborough. Furthermore, she had greater sympathy with the tories and so Somers was struck off the privy council and was not admitted into the royal presence.

Somers remained in the background for a number of years but he continued to exercise influence with the whigs, and to support the war policy of Godolphin and Marlborough. On more partisan matters he continued to lead the whigs in the Lords. According to Bishop Nicolson, on 2 December 1702 Somers failed in an attempt to move an amendment to the bill against occasional conformity which would have removed corporate office-holders from the scope of the bill. On 9 December, in debate on the third reading, Nicolson recorded that Somers was 'more passionate than usual, for discharging a good conscience and leaving it to posterity to judge of the cause' (*London Diaries*, 137, 141). Somers was then a leading member of the Lords sent on 16 January 1703 to a conference with the Commons on the bill. In the next session he was again to the fore in December 1703 when the whigs decided to launch their own investigation into the Jacobite conspiracy known as the Scotch plot, and the dispute it occasioned with the Commons over the removal of prisoners without a royal warrant. Lord Ossulston's diary indicates that Somers attended at least four conclaves with his fellow whigs concerning this matter in February and March 1704. Similarly, when the *Ashby* v. *White* case over the 1702 Aylesbury election came before the Lords in January 1704 Somers played a major role in arguing the case for an individual elector's right to vote to be cognizable before the law courts rather than the Commons. When the third Occasional Conformity Bill reached the Lords on 15 December 1704, Somers was one of those who spoke in the debate urging its rejection; indeed, there is some evidence that he acted as a sort of 'whip' in soliciting the attendance of peers such as Ossulston for this important vote. When Lord Treasurer Godolphin came under attack in the Lords over his role in advising royal assent to the Scottish Act of Security (which empowered the Scottish parliament to choose its own successor upon the queen's death) Somers managed to divert the debate on 29 November 1704, and on 6 December he proposed the countermeasure which resulted in the Aliens Act. It was this support for Godolphin over Scotland, as well as the defeat of the Occasional Conformity Bill and general support for the war effort, which gradually forced Godolphin to be more accommodating towards whig claims to office.

The problem of Scotland and the succession continued to concern Somers in the 1705–6 session. It was Somers who outflanked the tories on 22 November 1705 by proposing that all the clauses of the Act of Security be repealed bar that allowing for the appointment of commissioners to negotiate a union. Somers was also involved in the promotion of the Regency Bill in the Lords in November 1705, and on 31 January 1706 when the Lords considered the amendments made to the bill by the Commons. In particular, Somers was concerned that the place clauses in the original Act of Settlement of 1701 were not strengthened in the new bill but weakened so that only a specified few were disqualified from sitting in the Commons. The 1705–6 session also saw him pilot through the Lords a measure dealing with law reform in both common law and equity jurisdictions.

In April 1706 Somers was duly appointed a commissioner for negotiating a union with Scotland, and subsequently attended forty out of the forty-five meetings which took place after the end of the session and which eventually led to the Act of Union in 1707. He then took a major role as a manager of the parliamentary debates over ratifying the treaty.

Lord president Somers was at this time increasingly working with the Godolphin ministry—indeed, so in tune was he with ministerial policy that he did not enter a single 'protest' in the Lords between 1704 and 1711. As early as 1706 Godolphin had thought it might be advantageous for the ministry that Somers be employed as an ambassador at any forthcoming peace conference. Marlborough partially concurred: 'he is certainly very capable, but I should think he would object his not being master enough of the French language' (Snyder, 595)—a comment which may suggest that Somers was better at reading than speaking the seven languages with which he was reputed to be familiar. Both Marlborough and Godolphin thought that the presence of Somers in the ministry would make the government easier to manage in the legislature, where the queen's aversion to the whigs was making it more difficult to hold on to whig support. Increasingly the whigs, including Somers, began to flex their muscles in an attempt to demonstrate to the court the necessity of complying with their demands for office. Thus, on 5 February 1708, Somers joined with other whigs and the tories in opposing the court's plans to preserve the Scottish privy council, and on the 17th they supported an attack on the Admiralty, nominally headed by Prince George. By April 1708 Godolphin was impressing upon the queen Somers's suitability as lord president, but she stubbornly held out against their demands until after her husband's death. Eventually Somers was admitted to the cabinet on 25 November 1708 as lord president of the council. Ironically, the queen soon warmed to Somers despite years of having blocked his appointment.

Somers appears to have had reservations concerning the impeachment of Doctor Henry Sacheverell following an inflammatory sermon he had preached before the mayor of London on 5 November 1709. He would have preferred a prosecution in queen's bench, in order to avoid a possible loss of votes in parliament, but he duly voted in favour of the impeachment on 20 March 1710, although he was too ill to attend and vote on the question of Sacheverell's punishment which took place on the following day. Somers, however, had not foreseen the furore caused by the impeachment and the subsequent opportunity it provided for Robert Harley to undermine the ministry. Like most of his junto colleagues Somers was somewhat irresolute when faced with Harley's manoeuvres and he may have been tempted to make a deal to remain in office. In the event Somers was dismissed on 21 September 1710.

Declining years Somers was thus thrust into the ranks of the opposition during 1710–14. He attended the Lords fairly regularly in the 1710–11 session, and signed 'protests' in defence of the conduct of the war in Spain. However, he was suffering increasingly from ill health. Although he signed a protest on 28 May 1712 against the 'restraining' orders issued to the duke of Ormond, the commander of the army in Flanders, he was stricken by a stroke soon afterwards and in July was reported to be beyond recovery. He was able to attend the Lords on 4 May 1713 to oppose the commercial treaty with France, but his powers were in evident decline: according to one of Sir William Trumbull's correspondents on 9 June, 'my Lord Sommers has attempted to speak but once this session and then he faltered and his memory failed him and he was fain to break off with a scrap of a motion' (Jones, 'Party rage', 169). He still attended the whig conclaves on important matters, advising against supporting the motion to dissolve the union with Scotland which was proposed by the earl of Findlater on 1 June. Somers rarely attended the Lords during the opening months of the 1714 session, but he was present more regularly in June and July, notably joining in the protest against the Schism Bill, which was designed to suppress dissenting academies.

Somers attended the privy council meeting on the eve of the queen's death, and on the following day, 1 August 1714, he signed the proclamation of her successor. He was not one of the regents named by George I under the Regency Act, presumably because of the poor state of his health, but he was named to the new privy council, being sworn in again on 1 October, was included in the cabinet, although without a portfolio, and was granted a pension of £2000 per annum. He attended about half of the privy council meetings during the remainder of his lifetime, making a special effort during the crisis of the 1715 Jacobite rising. The last meeting he attended was on 27 January 1716.

Somers died on 26 April 1716 at Brookmans and was buried in the nearby parish church of North Mimms. He left no will and his estate was divided between his sisters: Reigate and Brookmans went to the Jekylls, and the Worcestershire property to the Cocks family. His papers were lost in 1752 when the chambers of Charles Yorke (the son of Somers's niece, Margaret Cocks) were destroyed by fire. The Somers barony was revived in 1784 for Charles Cocks, the grandson of Somers's sister, Mary.

Assessment Somers's contemporaries recognized his significance. Burnet wrote of him: 'he was very learned in his own profession, with a great deal more learning in other professions, in divinity, philosophy, and history. He had a great capacity for business' (*Bishop Burnet's History*, 4.193). Others stressed his pre-eminence as a party politician, one MP even referring to the 'Summerian Whigs' in 1706 (G. S.

Holmes, *British Politics in the Age of Anne*, 14). His legal abilities, constitutional achievements in helping secure the union with Scotland and the Hanoverian succession, and his belief in religious toleration excited extravagant praise from whig historians throughout the eighteenth and nineteenth centuries, from Addison in *The Freeholder*, no. 39 (4 May 1716), and *Memoirs of the Life of John, Lord Somers* (1716), probably by John Oldmixon, to Richard Cooksey, *Essay on the Life and Character of John Lord Somers* (1791), and then T. B. Macauley, L. von Ranke, and G. M. Trevelyan.

Modern historians have concurred in assessments of his abilities. G. S. Holmes called him one of the 'brightest ornaments of the bar in the late seventeenth century' (Holmes, *Augustan England*, 117). L. K. J. Glassey believed him to be 'a cultivated man of wide interests and an outstanding lawyer-statesman' (Glassey, 112); and J. P. Kenyon considered Somers a 'constructive, if self-interested statesman' (Kenyon, 251). All have placed Somers firmly at the centre of the whig party in the twenty-five years following the revolution of 1688. STUART HANDLEY

Sources W. L. Sachse, *Lord Somers: a political portrait* (1975) • E. Rowlands, 'Somers, John', HoP, *Commons, 1660–90* • 'Somers, Sir John', HoP, *Commons, 1690–1715* [draft] • R. M. Adams, 'In search of Baron Somers', *Culture and politics from puritanism to the Enlightenment*, ed. P. Zagorin (1980), 165–93 • H. Horwitz, *Parliament, policy and politics in the reign of William III* (1977) • L. G. Schwoerer, *The declaration of rights, 1689* (1981) • *The London diaries of William Nicolson, bishop of Carlisle, 1702–1718*, ed. C. Jones and G. Holmes (1985) • *Joseph Addison; The Freeholder*, ed. J. Leheny (1979), 207–14 • A. Grey, ed., *Debates of the House of Commons, from the year 1667 to the year 1694*, new edn, 10 vols. (1769), vol. 10 • P. W. J. Riley, *The union of England and Scotland: a study in Anglo-Scottish politics of the eighteenth century* (1978) • *Report on the manuscripts of the late Reginald Rawdon Hastings*, 4 vols., HMC, 78 (1928–47), vol. 2, p. 270 • C. Jones, 'The parliamentary organization of the whig junto in the reign of Queen Anne: the evidence of Lord Ossulston's diary', *Parliamentary History*, 10 (1991), 164–82 • D. W. Hayton and C. Jones, 'Peers, placemen: Lord Keeper Cowper's notes on the debate on the place clause in the Regency Bill, 31 January 1706', *Parliamentary History*, 18 (1999), 65–79 • C. Jones, '"Party rage and faction"—the view from Fulham, Scotland Yard and the Temple: parliament in the letters of Thomas Bateman and John and Ralph Bridges to Sir William Trumbull, 1710–1714', *British Library Journal*, 19 (1993), 148–80 • M. Knights, *Politics and opinion in crisis, 1678–81* (1994), 326n., 376–89 • M. Goldie, 'Restoration political thought', in L. K. J. Glassey, *The reigns of Charles II and James VII and II* (1997), 32 • L. K. J. Glassey, *Politics and the appointment of justices of the peace, 1675–1720* (1979), 112–33 • F. H. Ellis, ed., *Swift vs. Mainwaring: The Examiner and The Medley* (1985), 215 • G. S. Holmes, *The trial of Doctor Sacheverell* (1973), 85–8, 286 • *The Marlborough–Godolphin correspondence*, ed. H. L. Snyder, 3 vols. (1975), 583, 595, 958–9 • Sir Edward Harley to Robert Harley, 16 Jan 1693, BL, Add. MS 70235 • *Letters illustrative of the reign of William III from 1696 to 1708 addressed to the duke of Shrewsbury by James Verno*, ed. C. P. R. James, 3 vols., 3 (1841), 13, 156 • *Memoirs of the secret services of John Macky*, ed. A. R. (1733), 50 • J. P. Kenyon, *Robert Spencer, earl of Sunderland* (1958), 251 • G. Holmes, *Augustan England* (1982), 177, 124

Archives BL, corresp., Add. MS 4223 • BL, legal papers, Add. MS 36116 • BL, library catalogue, Add. MSS 40751–40752 • NYPL, corresp. and papers [transcripts] • PRO NIre., corresp. and papers relating to Ireland [copies] • Surrey HC, corresp., MSS, and papers • Worcs. RO, corresp. and papers [microfilm] | Herts. ALS, letters to Lord Chancellor Cowper • Northants. RO, corresp. with duke of Shrewsbury • NYPL, Hardwicke MSS • U. Nott. L., letters to earl of Portland

Likenesses G. Kneller, oils, *c*.1690, Eastnor Castle, Herefordshire • watercolour miniature, *c*.1690–1700, NPG • G. Kneller, oils, *c*.1700–1710, Knole, Kent • J. Smith, mezzotint, 1713 (after J. Richardson), BM, NPG • G. Kneller, oils, *c*.1715–1716, NPG [*see illus.*] • J. Houbraken, line engraving (after G. Kneller, *c*.1690), BM, NPG; repro. in T. Birch, *The heads and characters of illustrious persons of Great Britain*, 2 vols. (1743–51) • P. Lely?, oils, Eastnor Castle, Herefordshire • attrib. J. Riley, oils (as a young man), Dulwich Picture Gallery

Somers, Robert (1822–1891), journalist, son of Robert Somers and his wife, Jane Gordon Gibson, was born at Newton Stewart, Wigtownshire, on 14 September 1822. He was of English extraction on his father's side and Scottish on his mother's. In early life he was well known as a lecturer on social and political questions. In 1844 he published *Scottish Poor Laws*, a pamphlet that criticized the Poor Law Amendment Act then passing through parliament. He then accepted an offer of the post of editor of the *Scottish Herald*, a new weekly newspaper in Edinburgh. The management of the *Scottish Herald* was merged with that of Hugh Miller's *Witness*, and Somers soon became Miller's assistant.

In 1847 Somers went to Glasgow to join the staff of the *North British Daily Mail*. In the autumn he went to the highlands, as commissioner for that paper, to inquire into the distress in the north-west of Scotland caused by the failure of the potato crop in 1846. He published the results of his inquiry as *Letters from the Highlands* (1848). From 1849 to 1859 Somers was editor at Glasgow of the *North British Daily Mail* and, for the next eleven years, of the *Morning Journal*. He turned his attention to the study of monetary and commercial questions, in which he became a recognized authority, and from time to time he published pamphlets on contemporary social issues.

In 1870–71 Somers travelled for six months in America investigating the effect of the political changes following the civil war on the economy of the southern states. On his return he published *The Southern States of America* (1871). He was the author of works on Scottish education, banking, and the judiciary, and contributed articles on economics for the *Encyclopaedia Britannica* (9th edn). He also wrote a romantic novel. After several years of impaired health, Somers, who was married and had a son, died at his residence, 334 Wandsworth Road, London, on 7 July 1891. E. I. CARLYLE, *rev.* JOSEPH COOHILL

Sources Boase, *Mod. Eng. biog.* • Allibone, *Dict.* • private information (1897)

Wealth at death £378 13*s*.: administration, 16 Sept 1891, *CGPLA Eng. & Wales*

Somerset. For this title name *see* Mohun, William de, earl of Somerset (*d. c*.1145); Beaufort, John, marquess of Dorset and marquess of Somerset (*c*.1371–1410); Beaufort, John, duke of Somerset (1404–1444); Beaufort, Edmund, first duke of Somerset (*c*.1406–1455); Beaufort, Henry, second duke of Somerset (1436–1464); Beaufort, Edmund, styled third duke of Somerset (*c*.1438–1471); Seymour, Edward, duke of Somerset (*c*.1500–1552); Seymour, Anne, duchess of Somerset (*c*.1510–1587); Carr, Robert, earl of Somerset (1585/6?–1645); Seymour, William, first marquess of Hertford and second duke of Somerset (1587–1660); Howard, Frances, countess of Somerset (1590–1632); Seymour, Charles, sixth duke of Somerset (1662–1748); Seymour,

Elizabeth, duchess of Somerset (1667–1722); Seymour, Algernon, seventh duke of Somerset (1684–1750) [*see under* Seymour, Charles, sixth duke of Somerset (1662–1748)]; Seymour, Frances, duchess of Somerset (1699–1754); Seymour, Edward Adolphus, eleventh duke of Somerset (1775–1855); St Maur, Edward Adolphus, twelfth duke of Somerset (1804–1885).

Somerset, Lady Blanche. *See* Arundell, Blanche, Lady Arundell of Wardour (1583/4–1649).

Somerset [*formerly* Beaufort]**, Charles, first earl of Worcester** (*c.***1460–1526**), courtier and magnate, was the illegitimate son of Henry *Beaufort, second duke of Somerset (1436–1464), and his mistress Joan Hill. His mother was still alive in 1493, when Henry VII gave her an annuity. He was thus a cousin both of King Henry and of his mother, Lady Margaret Beaufort, and subsequently acted as one of the latter's executors. His childhood was spent in exile, in Flanders and then in France, until in 1485 he returned to England with Henry Tudor, who knighted him at Milford Haven on 7 August 1485, barely a fortnight before the battle of Bosworth. At this time he bore the name Beaufort, but soon afterwards took that of Somerset, presumably to avoid blurring the royal claim to the Beaufort interest. The new king looked after his kinsman and companion in arms. On 1 March 1486 he made Somerset captain of the yeomen of the guard and shortly after appointed him royal cup-bearer. On St George's day 1496 Somerset was made a knight of the Garter. He was present at a meeting between Henry VII and Archduke Philip which took place outside Calais on 9 June 1500, and his close personal connection with the king secured his appointment in 1501 as vice-chamberlain of the household. In this capacity he took part in the ceremonies connected with the reception of Katherine of Aragon in October and November that year. In September 1503 he was made a knight of the body and by early 1505 he was a councillor.

Although he had no hereditary connections with Wales, Somerset established that country as the principal sphere of his political and economic influence when on 2 June 1492 he married Henry VII's ward Elizabeth (*d.* 1507), sole heir of William Herbert, earl of Huntingdon (*d.* 1490), the son of the king's childhood guardian, and Mary Woodville, the dowager queen's sister. Through his wife Somerset acquired a substantial part of the lordships of Gower, Kilvey, Crickhowell, Tretower, and Raglan. The main authority in Wales was the king's uncle, Jasper Tudor, duke of Bedford, the chief justice of south Wales; and on his death in December 1495 his lands in Wales reverted to the crown. However, Henry, duke of York (the future Henry VIII), was too young to administer Bedford's lands, and the marcher lordship of Glamorgan was leased to Somerset in March 1501. He was responsible for the implementation of justice in this marcher lordship, which operated as a separate judicial system until the Act of Union in 1536. The king, however, had driven a hard bargain, and Somerset claimed in 1502 that the lease was not profitable without the grant of offices. Accordingly in September

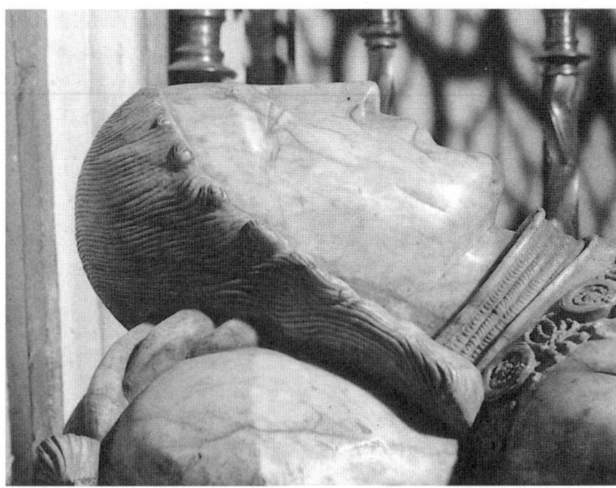
Charles Somerset, first earl of Worcester (*c.*1460–1526), by unknown sculptor

1503 he was granted the lordship of Ewyas Lacy and a month later the stewardship of the lordship of Monmouth. Somerset's influence in the south marches was strengthened following the death of his wife's uncle Sir Walter Herbert in September 1507, when he acquired the lordships of Chepstow and Tudenham and the lease and lordship of the castle of Caldicot. The combination of lands, offices, and title made him the most powerful man in south Wales and the crown's principal agent for its government. This was ratified when he was created Baron Herbert in January 1504.

Henry VII had ensured that no one outside the royal family exerted the sort of authority in Wales exercised by Jasper Tudor. However, within little more than a year of his accession in 1509 Henry VIII had reversed his father's policy of making grants only during pleasure and greatly extended Herbert's influence in the marches. On 19 May 1509 he received the stewardship of the lordship of Ruthin and the constableship of Ruthin Castle, thus extending his authority into north Wales. Two days later he was made steward for life of the lordship of Monmouth and Grosmont and constable of Monmouth Castle, and on 29 May he became sheriff of Glamorgan. In May 1510 he received the reversion for life of the office of chief steward of the lordship of Abergavenny, and in June 1510 all offices previously granted to him (except the stewardship of Monmouth) were included in new grants to be held for life by Herbert and his heir.

Herbert was also closely involved in national politics and international diplomacy. One of Henry VII's closest advisers, he performed a variety of military and diplomatic offices. When the king attempted to mediate between Brittany and France early in his reign, a fleet was fitted out under the command of Somerset, who was made admiral on 20 February 1488 and given captaincy of a ship called *Le Soveraigne*. He was commissioned to go to sea on 9 October when Henry was contemplating supporting the late duke of Brittany's daughter Anne against the French king, Charles VIII. In September 1490 Somerset was sent to invest Emperor Maximilian with the Order of the Garter, and after Charles VIII died on 7 April 1498, he was dispatched to France to renew the treaty of Etaples with the new king, Louis XII. Four years later he undertook an embassy to Maximilian to secure the banishment of Yorkist rebels. Discussions in Antwerp resulted on 19 June 1502 in a general treaty of commerce and a promise by the emperor to keep the Yorkists under supervision in return for a payment of £10,000. Somerset was also entrusted with the delicate negotiations arising from suggestions that Henry VII, widowed in 1503, might make a French marriage; and he was at Blois with Louis XII early in June 1505, when the French king gave him a full briefing on his views, including a proposal that Henry VII might marry his niece, Marguerite of Angoulême.

Baron Herbert remained an influential figure under Henry VIII, who on 30 May 1509 made him lord chamberlain, the nominal head of the entire royal household. He also took part in the expedition to France of 1513. The king's army comprised three divisions, and Herbert had charge of the middle division and was involved in the siege of Thérouanne, captured on 23 August. On 1 February 1514 he was rewarded by being created earl of Worcester. In August following he accompanied the king's sister Mary to France for her marriage to Louis XII and also took part in negotiations aiming at the expulsion of Ferdinand of Aragon from Navarre. In 1515 he was chiefly occupied in seeing to the fortifications of Tournai, captured shortly after Thérouanne. He was involved in unfruitful negotiations with Maximilian in 1516–17. Worcester eventually had to inform Henry that Maximilian was insincere in his desire to maintain an alliance with England and advised his sovereign to send him no more money.

England and France were now drawing closer together and Worcester's finest moments came between 1518 and 1520 when he was put in charge of the negotiations for a truce between the two nations. In 1518 he negotiated the surrender of Tournai to the French in return for 600,000 crowns. In December that year he met King François I at St Denis and he subsequently acted as an intermediary between Wolsey and the French court in negotiations which culminated in the meeting of Henry and François at the Field of the Cloth of Gold. This was largely organized by Worcester, who used the occasion to display his ceremonial and organizational skills. Having landed in Calais on 13 April 1520, he and his French counterpart agreed that the meeting should take place at Val d'Or ('Golden Vale') between the English town of Guînes, where Henry VIII was based, and the French town of Ardres, where François was staying. Guînes Castle was deemed too small to entertain the king and queen of France in, and under Worcester's direction commissioners were appointed to construct a private gallery connected to a temporary palace, 'a honorable lodging' erected by several thousand labourers and craftsmen (Russell, 31). Five thousand people were shipped across the channel. Timber was floated down from the Netherlands and Kent and 4000 feet of glass was brought from St Omer. An Italian observer thought that even Leonardo da Vinci could not have improved upon it, and it was described as the eighth wonder of the world. The temporary palace, one of the lost treasures of the reign, is shown in a painting by an unknown artist at Hampton Court. After some argument the French accepted Worcester's proposed location for the feat of arms, on English soil about a mile from Guînes between two 'eminences', and the details were then left to him, though with the help of a 'platt' by Henry himself. He organized the building of lists and galleries. The tilting yard had been designed by Henry VIII, but was constructed following Worcester's advice to put the lists closer to the viewing gallery. The jousts, which involved 300 contestants, took place on 11 and 22 June and the earl was one of the judges. In the following year he was present at the reception of Emperor Charles V, attesting the Anglo-imperial treaty of Windsor, on 20 June, while in 1525 he helped negotiate the treaty of the More between France and England.

Worcester died on 25 April 1526, probably at his preferred residence at Kew. He was buried in St George's Chapel, Windsor, doubtless in accordance with the arrangements he had dictated in his will. He there showed his love of ceremony by requesting that if he died near London, his body was to be taken down the Thames, covered by a black cloth with a white cross, for interment at Windsor next to his first wife. Elizabeth Herbert, the mother of the earl's son and heir, Henry, died on 27 August 1507, and by November 1511 he had married Eleanor, daughter of Edward Sutton, second Baron Dudley, who survived him. They had a son and a daughter. (Claims that Worcester married three times probably derive from an error by Dugdale.) The earl's wealth cannot be quantified, but an account of 1520 shows that his lands in the Welsh marches yielded about £850 per annum. Raised largely by court service to an earldom, he was the ancestor through his eldest son of an important aristocratic dynasty, successively earls and marquesses of Worcester and dukes of Beaufort. JONATHAN HUGHES

Sources *LP Henry VIII*, vols. 1–4 • GEC, *Peerage*, 12/2.846–50 • P. Williams, *The Tudor regime* (1979) • S. B. Chrimes, *Henry VII* (1972) • J. C. Russell, *The Field of Cloth of Gold* (1969) • W. R. B. Robinson, 'Early Tudor policy towards Wales: the acquisition of lands and offices in Wales by Charles Somerset, earl of Worcester', *BBCS*, 20 (1962–4), 421–38 • *CPR*, *1485–1509* • *CClR*, *1485–1500*, *1500–1509* • W. R. B. Robinson, 'The Welsh estates of Charles, earl of Somerset in 1520', *BBCS*, 24 (1970–72), 384–411 • W. R. B. Robinson, 'Family and fortune: the domestic affairs of Edward Sutton (*d*.1532), Lord Dudley', *Staffordshire Studies*, 10 (1998) • M. K. Jones and M. G. Underwood, *The king's mother: Lady Margaret Beaufort, countess of Richmond and Derby* (1992)

Archives BL, Cotton MSS, letters to Thomas Wolsey

Likenesses marble tomb effigy, St George's Chapel, Windsor [*see illus.*] • oils (posthumous), Badminton House, south Gloucestershire • portrait, priv. coll.

Wealth at death at least £850 p.a.: Robinson, 'Welsh estates'

Somerset, Sir Charles (1587/8–1665), traveller and writer, was the third surviving son of Edward *Somerset, fourth earl of Worcester (*c*.1550–1628), and his wife, Elizabeth Hastings (*d*. 1621), the daughter of Francis *Hastings, second earl of Huntingdon. After attending Eton College from 1598 to 1602 he matriculated, along with his brother Edward (*b*. *c*.1590), from Magdalen College, Oxford, on 16

April 1605, aged seventeen, and was awarded a BA degree on 10 February 1607. When in August 1605 Prince Henry, King James's eldest son, was enrolled among the scholars at Magdalen College, Somerset performed in disputations held before the royal party, and his name was appended to a lavish presentation manuscript containing a Latin address to the king (BL, Royal MS 18 A.lxxiii, fol. 9). In 1606 a collection of Latin verses, containing poems by Charles and Edward Somerset (BL, Royal MS 12 A.lxiv, fol. 50), was presented to the queen's brother, Christian IV of Denmark, to commemorate his visit to Oxford.

About 1609 Somerset married Elizabeth, reputed daughter and heir of Sir William Powell of Llansoy, Monmouthshire. They took up residence at Troy House, near Monmouth, one of the family's most impressive Welsh properties. Charles and Elizabeth had three daughters: Elizabeth, who married Sir Frances Anderton, Mary, and Frances, who married Sir Henry Browne. In 1610 Charles and Edward Somerset were made knights of the Bath at the creation of Henry Frederick as prince of Wales (1–10 June). Their elder brother, Thomas (1579–*c*.1650), had already been made a knight of the Bath in 1605 and was a trusted confidant of the prince.

On 2 April 1611 Somerset left England for an extended tour abroad, from which he returned to London on 4 June 1612. Doubtless undertaken for educational reasons (his brother Thomas was already an experienced European traveller), this tour was probably also prompted by King James's recent restrictive measures against Catholics, following the murder of Henri IV of France, which appeared to open the way for a Catholic dynasty there. Spending a total of £1315 7*s*. 2*d*. Somerset travelled extensively through France, Italy, Austria, Germany, the Spanish Netherlands, and Flanders. His travel diary (University of Leeds, Brotherton Collection, MS Trv.q.3) contains detailed accounts of his visits to such major locations as Paris, Nevers, Marseilles, Genoa, Pisa, Florence, Rome, Venice, Innsbruck, Munich, Heidelberg, Antwerp, and Brussels. The importance of Somerset's travel diary lies primarily in its wealth of detail and lucidly presented eyewitness observations on both major and minor locations. His firsthand descriptions of Paris, Florence, Rome, and Venice, for example, are no less informative than the more famous accounts by Coryate, Moryson, and Evelyn. On a lesser level many of his comments merit further consideration, such as his description of the Huguenot temple at Dieppe as almost indistinguishable in design from 'one of the play-houses in London'—a comment of some significance to English theatre historians since Somerset was undoubtedly a playgoer (probably at the Blackfriars) and his father, the earl of Worcester, was a leading patron of acting companies. Given his high rank (which often granted him privileged access) and his education, coupled with a naturally scholarly nature, Somerset was an informed and often penetrating commentator on local matters of religion (such as the aftermath of the French religious wars and the impact of the Catholic League with Spain, established in 1609 by Maximilian I of Bavaria), civil government (such as the Medici domination of Florence and the notorious Council of Ten at Venice), and culture (the antiquities of Rome, Tintoretto's *Paradise* in the Palazzo Ducale at Venice, and the flourishing arts in the Spanish Netherlands under Archduke Albert and his wife, Isabella, the daughter of Philip II of Spain). He also paid attention to subjects of particular interest to Prince Henry, which included military and naval affairs, civic administration, antiquities, and garden design. The entries vividly bring to life the sheer discomfort and dangers of early seventeenth-century travel with grim descriptions of the scorpions, bloodsucking bed bugs, and filthy mattresses of Orange, immediately followed by a stoically endured but almost fatal bout of smallpox at Orange.

Somerset's Catholicism would have restricted the kinds of public duties entrusted to him on his return to England and he spent much of his time either on his own Welsh estates or at the family's London home, Worcester House. An inventory of his books compiled about 1622 (Badminton House, Muniments Room, OC/2) reveals his wide interests in the classics, contemporary English literature, geography and travel writings, foreign languages, and music. During the civil war Somerset was denounced both as an opponent of the parliamentarian forces in Monmouthshire and as a papist. At about the time of Charles I's execution (30 January 1649) Somerset travelled to Spain and, according to two letters which he wrote to Charles II, he was based at Saragossa, where he may have been investigating the possibilities of Spanish military assistance for the royalist cause. Somerset returned to England about 1651, when Spain formally recognized the Commonwealth, and from then until 1656 he was under constant harassment from the committee for compounding. His Catholicism continued to be a ruinously expensive loyalty throughout the 1650s although after the Restoration he was able to reside quietly on his Troy estate until his death in 1665. MICHAEL G. BRENNAN

Sources *The travel diary (1611–1612) of an English Catholic, Sir Charles Somerset*, ed. M. G. Brennan (1993) • M. G. Brennan, 'Sir Charles Somerset's music books', *Music and Letters*, 74 (1993), 501–18 • W. R. B. Robinson, 'The earls of Worcester and their estates, 1526–1642', BLitt diss., U. Oxf., 1958 • Badminton House, Muniments Room, Sir Charles Somerset personal and estate MSS, OC/1–4 • W. Sterry, ed., *The Eton College register, 1441–1698* (1943) • Foster, *Alum. Oxon.*, 1500–1714 [Sir Charles Somersett] • *Reg. Oxf.*, vol. 2/2 • J. Nichols, *The progresses, processions, and magnificent festivities of King James I, his royal consort, family and court*, 4 vols. (1828) • BL, Royal MSS 12 A.lxiv, fol. 50; 18 A.lxxiii, fol. 9 • *CSP dom.*, 1644–5, 18 • M. A. E. Green, ed., *Calendar of the proceedings of the committee for advance of money, 1642–1656*, 3, PRO (1888), 1218 • M. A. E. Green, ed., *Calendar of the proceedings of the committee for compounding … 1643–1660*, 4, PRO (1892), 2887–8 • *Report on the Pepys manuscripts*, HMC, 70 (1911), 288, 307 • *Collins peerage of England: genealogical, biographical and historical*, ed. E. Brydges, 9 vols. (1812) • Gillow, *Lit. biog. hist.* • GEC, *Peerage*, new edn, vol. 12/2

Archives Badminton House, Gloucestershire, personal MSS, OC/1–4

Somerset, Lord Charles Henry (1767–1831), colonial governor, was born at Badminton, Gloucestershire, on 12 December 1767, the second son in the family of nine sons and four daughters of Henry Somerset, fifth duke of Beaufort (1744–1803), and his wife, Elizabeth (1747–1828), daughter of Admiral Edward *Boscawen. Among his brothers were the army officers Lord FitzRoy *Somerset, first Baron Raglan, Lord (Robert) Edward Henry *Somerset, and Lord John Thomas Henry *Somerset [*see under* Somerset, FitzRoy James Henry].

Educated at Westminster School and at Trinity College, Oxford (MA 1786), Somerset became a colonel in the 1st West India regiment (major-general 1798), and attained the rank of a full general in 1814. In June 1788 he married Elizabeth (*d.* 1815), daughter of William Courtenay, second Viscount Courtenay; they had three sons and four daughters. His second wife, whom he married on 9 August 1821, was Lady Mary Poulett (*d.* 1860), daughter of John Poulett, fourth Earl Poulett; they had two daughters and a son, Poulett George Henry *Somerset [*see under* Somerset, FitzRoy James Henry] He was appointed gentleman of the bedchamber to the prince of Wales in 1791, represented Scarborough (1796–1802) and Monmouth (1802–13) in the House of Commons, was sworn of the privy council in 1797 and was comptroller (until 1804) of the household, then joint paymaster-general of the forces under the premiership of William Pitt and the third duke of Portland in 1804–13, before accepting the governorship of Cape Colony, where he arrived on 6 April 1814.

Lord Charles Somerset's governorship was marked by important developments on the colony's unsettled eastern frontier, in the administration of affairs related to the transfer from Dutch to British rule, and in political conflict with radical elements on the issue of freedom of speech, and was also distinguished by poor relations with both British and Dutch settlers. In 1815 the authorities put down a rebellion by landless Dutch-speaking colonials and mismanaged the execution of convicted ringleaders—in four of the five hangings, the ropes broke and the proceedings had to be repeated. Somerset tried to placate colonists' feelings by persuading Xhosa chiefs to allow them to follow the spoor of stolen cattle across the frontier and exact compensation. But Chief Ngqika, through whom Somerset worked, did not have power to carry this out, and the incident was long remembered by frontiersmen as a grievance against the British. Somerset then cleared a buffer zone east of the Fish River, but a later decision to allow a military settlement there ensured further conflict. Meanwhile Somerset had sought to stabilize the frontier by establishing British immigrants, the 1820 settlers, on the west bank of the Fish.

Somerset's governmental changes included the legalization of the English language as the official medium, the introduction of British currency, the setting up of a council of advice, and attempts to ameliorate the treatment of slaves in accordance with new policies laid down in London. Doctrinaire Anglicization marked some of these changes, but Somerset's enduring reputation was rather that of an autocrat, as appeared from his conflict with leaders of English-speaking opinion in the colonial community, George Greig, John Fairbairn, and Thomas Pringle, who successfully used the governor's quarrels with two reprobate settlers to demand press freedom. The commissioners of eastern inquiry, who included the Cape in their brief, found little justification for personal criticism of Somerset, though they were critical of the form of government in which the colony's governor exercised the sole authority. A council of advice was appointed in 1825. After overreacting to criticism, in March 1826 Somerset returned to Britain, where his critics kept up pressure on him. He did not return to the Cape, and died in Brighton on 20 February 1831.

T. R. H. Davenport, *rev.* K. S. Hunt

Sources A. K. Millar, *Plantagenet in South Africa* (1965) · *DSAB* · G. McC. Theal, *Records of the Cape Colony from 1799 to 1831*, 3–36 (1898–1905)

Archives BL, corresp. with Sir Hudson Lowe, Add. MSS 20116–20128, 20147–20150, 20226, *passim* · Bodl. RH, letters to John Thomas Bigge · Derbys. RO, letters to Sir R. J. Wilmot-Horton

Likenesses Dighton, caricature, 1811, NPG · I. M. Barberton, bust · R. Cosway, oils (after an original formerly in possession of Henry Somerset, Bordon, Hampshire), National Library of South Africa, Cape Town · oils (as a young man); priv. coll.

Somerset, Charles Noel, fourth duke of Beaufort (1709–1756). *See under* Somerset, Henry, second duke of Beaufort (1684–1714).

Somerset, Edward, fourth earl of Worcester (*c*.**1550–1628**), nobleman and courtier, was the only son of William *Somerset, third earl of Worcester (1526/7–1589), and his first wife, Christian North (*b.* 1533), daughter of Edward *North, first Lord North. The Somersets were a grand marcher family who staunchly supported the Tudors and lived in expansive medieval style at Raglan Castle. In December 1571 Lord Herbert, as Edward was styled, married Elizabeth Hastings (*d.* 1621), fourth daughter of Francis *Hastings, second earl of Huntingdon, with whom he had at least five sons and six daughters. Their third surviving son was the traveller and writer Sir Charles *Somerset (1587/8–1665). He succeeded his father as earl of Worcester in February 1589 and in May 1590 was sent to congratulate James VI of Scotland on his return from Denmark with his bride, also informing James that he had been nominated a knight of the Garter along with Henri IV. Worcester and James struck up a friendship that later became significant. In December 1590 he became a member of the council of Wales and the marches. He was admitted to the Middle Temple in 1591, created MA by Oxford University in 1592, and elected knight of the Garter in 1593. In December 1597 Worcester was appointed deputy master of the horse in the absence of the earl of Essex, and in June 1600 he was a member of the court of peers who heard the charges against Essex after his return from Ireland.

On 8 February 1601 Worcester was sent with three senior privy councillors to Essex House to demand why men were assembling there. The four were kept under guard for three hours while Essex attempted to raise London against his enemies at court. Worcester's eyewitness account of events formed part of the indictment of Essex and Southampton; after being sentenced to death Essex asked his pardon for holding him prisoner. In April 1601

Edward Somerset, fourth earl of Worcester (*c.*1550–1628), by Federico Zuccaro

Elizabeth appointed Worcester her master of the horse. He was promoted to the privy council in June and made joint commissioner of Essex's former office of earl marshal in December. He became lord lieutenant of Monmouthshire and Glamorgan in July 1602.

Worcester rose to even greater favour under James VI and I. As earl marshal he oversaw the coronation in July 1603, the baptism of Princess Mary in 1605, and the unique ceremony creating Prince Henry prince of Wales during the parliamentary session of 1610. He became master of the horse for life in January 1604, and was sufficiently competent as a huntsman to accompany the king daily in the field at Royston and Newmarket. However, Worcester tended to weary of the interminable chase and on occasion longed for the summer break when he could retire to Raglan. On these hunting sojourns he frequently acted as one of the royal secretaries, writing to the privy council and particularly to Robert Cecil, earl of Salisbury, with details of James's views, mood, and state of health. The king valued Worcester's advice and regarded him as one of his 'honest society' of leading privy councillors, along with Salisbury, Northampton, and Suffolk (*Letters of King James VI and I*, 271). In 1610 these trusted four peers debated with James at Theobalds on the last stages of the negotiation of the great contract, and later, in November 1610, they made every effort to obtain parliamentary taxation after the king authorized them to accept any reasonable offer from the House of Commons.

After the Reformation, generations of the Somerset clan were divided over religion. Worcester was impeccably conformist, taking the oath of allegiance to the royal supremacy and attending sermons at court. He was placed on a commission for the expulsion of the Jesuits in September 1604. In May–June 1605 he was sent to Raglan, after a period of riotous disturbances in the marches, to summon his county neighbours, including the bishop of Hereford, and urge them to greater efforts in establishing true religion and suppressing recusancy. Later in 1605 he was employed in the interrogation of the gunpowder plotters in the Tower. Yet in 1592 he gave shelter at Raglan to the Jesuit superior Robert Jones, and about 1600 granted the order some Welsh lands and farms. His wife was widely regarded as a Catholic. The earl employed as his children's tutor the noted Welsh protestant Thomas Pritchard, but several if not all of them grew up to be crypto-Catholics who revealed their sympathies on their tours of Europe or visits to Spa near Liège, a resort of Catholic émigrés. Worcester escorted the Catholic-leaning Anne of Denmark to Bath in 1613, and his younger son Thomas served as her master of the horse.

After the death in 1612 of his ally Salisbury, whose private funeral he attended, Worcester became one of the six commissioners for the treasury. Thereafter his career stalled, since his access to the king dwindled with the rise after 1611 of the favourite Sir Robert Carr. By 1614 it was rumoured that he would have to forfeit the mastership of the horse; he surrendered it in January 1616 but received an annuity of £1500 as compensation. He was also given the office of lord privy seal for life, and continued to be named to various commissions, including that which examined Ralegh in 1618 after the Guiana voyage. In 1621 he was appointed judge of requests, and though there were frequent rumours that he would relinquish the post of lord privy seal to make way for a client of Buckingham, he retained it until his death.

Worcester was a cultivated man who supported a theatre company. He completed the suite of grand state rooms at Raglan begun by his father, modernizing the castle's living quarters, and was probably responsible for the recasting of part of the moat into a sunken promenade with shell-lined niches for statues of Roman emperors. His extensive rents benefited from the developing coal industry in Glamorgan, and his tenants were obliged to carry coal to Raglan as part of their leases. Less successful, however, was his patent for the sole making of gunpowder and saltpetre in England, granted in May 1607 and extended to include exports of powder in 1610, but withdrawn in February 1620 after numerous complaints. Worcester's last significant appearance was in February 1626 as lord great chamberlain at the coronation of Charles I. He died at Worcester House in Westminster on 3 March 1628 and was buried on 30 March at Raglan parish church, but his monument there was destroyed in 1646 along with other family tombs. PAULINE CROFT

Sources GEC, *Peerage*, new edn • M. G. Brennan, ed., *The travel diary, 1611–12, of an English Catholic: Sir Charles Somerset* (1993) • *CSP dom.*, 1581–1628 • *Calendar of the manuscripts of the most hon. the marquis of Salisbury*, 24 vols., HMC, 9 (1883–1976), vols. 15–22 • *CSP Scot.*, 1589–93 • J. Newman and others, *Gwent/Monmouthshire* (2000) • L. Stone, *The crisis of the aristocracy, 1558–1641* (1965) • *Letters of King James VI & I*, ed. G. P. V. Akrigg (1984) • P. Croft, 'The parliamentary installation of Henry, prince of Wales', *Historical Research*, 65 (1992), 177–93

Archives Hatfield House, Hertfordshire, letters and papers | Badminton House, Gloucestershire, Badminton MSS

Likenesses S. de Passe, line engraving, 1618 (after oil painting by F. Zuccaro), BM, NPG • F. Zuccaro, oils, Gorhambury, Hertfordshire [*see illus.*] • F. Zuccaro, oils, second version, Badminton House, Gloucestershire

Somerset, Edward, second marquess of Worcester (*d.* **1667**), courtier and scientist, was the first son of Henry Somerset, fifth earl and first marquess of Worcester (1577–1646), and his wife, Anne (*d.* 1639), daughter and heir of John, Lord Russell, and Elizabeth, daughter of Sir Anthony Cook of Gidea Hall, Essex. Styled Lord Herbert from 1628 when his father inherited the earldom, he was educated privately at Raglan Castle, Monmouthshire, and brought up as a Catholic. Granted a pass to travel abroad for three years from 5 August 1619, he visited Germany, France, and Italy. In 1627 the MA degree of Cambridge University was bestowed upon him, although he attended no college.

Scientific interests and military career During the years of the mid-1620s Lord Herbert was admitted to the circle of courtiers around the new king, Charles I, and began to take an active interest in experimental science: these two developments were to form the most important dimensions of his life. About 1628 he married Elizabeth (*d.* 1635), daughter of Sir William Dormer and his wife, Alice, whose father was Sir Richard Molyneux. They had one son, Henry *Somerset, first duke of Beaufort, and two daughters before Elizabeth's death on 31 May 1635. Although he held public office, such as membership of the council in the marches of Wales (12 May 1633) and a deputy lord lieutenancy in Monmouthshire from November 1635, Herbert's principal interests before 1640 were private, and scientific. At Raglan, from the time of his marriage, he employed a Dutch engineer, Caspar Calthoff, to assist him with experiments at the castle. Although no surviving trace of it was ever found during twentieth-century conservation work there, it is possible that a machine employing the propulsive properties of steam was constructed to raise water to the full height of the great tower. Another interest of Lord Herbert was perpetual motion, and he claimed to have devised a machine to demonstrate that principle. In August 1639 he married Margaret (*d.* 1681), second daughter of Henry O'Brien, fourth earl of Thomond; the marriage brought him into contact with members of the Irish peerage. During 1641 he was acting as one of the king's retinue, and on 7 December he was assured by Charles, setting out for the north, that if the king lived, Herbert would 'neither be a loser in, nor repent you for the services you have done me' (Dircks, 33).

As early as January 1642 the citizens of Gloucester feared the consequences for their city if the Catholic Raglan interest were to be mobilized against them. On the outbreak of civil war the Somerset family was an important financial resource for the king, its estates being valued in December 1641 at between £40,000 and £100,000. The controller of this fabulous wealth was Herbert's father, the fifth earl, created first marquess of Worcester on 2 March 1643 in recognition of his major contribution to Charles's war chest. Herbert acted as agent between the king and his father for some of these advances. As early as 3 September 1642 the House of Commons demanded Herbert's presence as a corollary of the Lords' attempts to disarm his father, and in February 1643 parliament called upon the king to rid himself of the services of both father and son. In the opening months of the war Herbert was busy fortifying Raglan, first moving the Monmouthshire powder magazine from Monmouth to Caerleon, and thence to Raglan; and setting up garrisons in Cardiff, Brecon, Hereford, and at Goodrich Castle. These movements heightened the mood of anxiety among the aldermen of Gloucester, who reported to parliament their interrogation of Herbert's servants. News circulated in November 1642 that a force of 7000 Welsh led by the marquess of Hertford and Herbert had engaged the parliamentarian earl of Stamford near Tewkesbury in a fierce battle. Herbert was supposedly personally prominent, but the reports were propaganda, probably manufactured in Gloucester. Recriminations between Herbert and Hertford developed not as a consequence of military defeat but through personal rivalry exacerbated by Herbert's role as Hertford's paymaster. The king sent a representative to try to repair the breach between them.

Edward Somerset, second marquess of Worcester (*d.* 1667), by unknown artist

By January 1643 Herbert was substituting for Hertford as a field commander, and he became general of south Wales. In any assessment of regional military objectives the taking of Gloucester was bound to figure strongly. After an incident at Coleford in the Forest of Dean when some villagers killed three of his officers, a force of 1500 foot and 500 horse under Herbert's command camped at Highnam, outside Gloucester, in preparation for an assault on the city. On 24 March 1643 they allowed themselves to be ignominiously taken prisoner by Sir William Waller. Herbert, who was not present, blamed others for the disaster, which marked the end of royalist plans to take Gloucester. Nothing daunted by this setback, which might have called Herbert's competence as a commander into question, on 6 April Charles appointed him lieutenant-general, and added Monmouthshire to his command. At Abergavenny on 15 April royalists from Herbert's associated counties were summoned to Hereford, but there was local reluctance to flock to the standard. The earl of Clarendon, while admitting that 'many men loved and very few hated' Herbert (Clarendon, *Hist. rebellion*, 2.479), recognized that his Roman Catholicism and his habit of keeping away from his own forces were an obstacle to any success he might have had as a field commander. Clarendon dismissed Herbert's hastily assembled 'mushrump [mushroom] army' (ibid., 2.483) as a wasted opportunity, and Herbert failed subsequently to re-establish himself as a general, despite some evidence of successes in small skirmishes in the Welsh border country. His relations with the two other royalist leaders in his region, Prince Rupert and the marquess of Hertford, were never better than polite. The height of his achievement down to the spring of 1645 was thus in quelling local unrest and helping repair garrisons in Monmouthshire.

A secret mission to Ireland Given his disappointing performance as a military leader it may appear odd that Lord Herbert was selected by Charles I in 1644 for a secret mission to Ireland that called for extraordinary personal and persuasive powers. The story of his mission to Ireland has since the nineteenth century exercised the judgements of historians, and has provoked sharply differing responses among them. Herbert's first association with Irish service dates from 1 April 1644, when he was apparently commissioned to take command of troops to be raised in Ireland and shipped to England in the interest of the king. Herbert was to be 'generalissimo' (Dircks, 70) of three armies from England, Ireland, and the continent of Europe. The authenticity of this commission (and that of many other documents produced by Herbert in connection with his later Irish mission) was brought into question as long ago as 1735 by Thomas Carte, biographer of James Butler, duke of Ormond, but modern commentators tend cautiously to consider it genuine. What qualified Herbert for this service were his long association with the king, who liked at least to be considered loyal to his friends, his work in making available the Raglan fortune for the king's cause—the contribution acknowledged on 12 February 1645 by the king to amount by that time to £250,000—and his Irish contacts through his wife. The king's dealings with the Somersets had always been characterized by a noble, perhaps romantically chivalrous generosity on the part of the family, rewarded by Charles with promises that were difficult to keep and usually accompanied by an enjoinder to secrecy. Privileges promised to Herbert in return for this command included the hand of the king's daughter, Elizabeth, for his son Henry, and the dukedom of Somerset. The whole scheme collapsed, however, when in May agents of the Irish Catholic confederation were dismissed from Charles's court at Oxford, and negotiations with the Irish were placed in the hands of the protestant marquess of Ormond. The king wrote to Ormond, lord lieutenant of Ireland, on 27 December 1644, implying that Lord Herbert was to be subordinate to him when the latter was to visit Ireland, primarily on his own business. At this point Charles did everything to confirm to Ormond his confidence in him and his lack of any formal investment of trust in Herbert. To Ormond, he wrote of Herbert: 'His honesty or affection to my service will not deceive you; but I will not answer for his judgment' (Carte, 5.7–8). Nevertheless, from January 1645 onwards, a series of rather oddly worded commissions were issued to Herbert, who from this point was styled earl of Glamorgan. The title itself, along with that of Baron Beaufort of Caldecot Castle which he claimed from the same time, has always been controversial. No patent passed the great seal until 31 January 1646, and even then doubts remain as to whether it was ever more than a titular earldom: it was probably originally conceived by Charles as an inducement, to be bestowed in the event of Herbert's success in Ireland.

Charles's intention seems to have been that Glamorgan should have full power to negotiate a treaty with the confederates on terms dictated by them, which would have been unacceptable to the protestant Ormond. Most modern assessments of Charles's character have agreed on his principled commitment to the Church of England, so it seems less likely that the king had settled on selling out the Anglican church in Ireland than on allowing the Glamorgan mission to proceed as a dimension in a complex royal game of diplomacy. On 12 February 1645 Charles gave Glamorgan a further warrant for the title of duke of Somerset, and on 12 March the earl received a warrant empowering him to negotiate a secret treaty with the Catholic confederates. On 25 March he sailed for Ireland. After being shipwrecked on the coast of Cumbria after his departure, he was inevitably delayed, and did not reach Dublin until late June. By this time the king's need for an injection of more troops and an opening of a new front in the civil war was acute, in the wake of his defeat at Naseby on 14 June.

Before Glamorgan's arrival in Ireland Ormond had been engaged in peace negotiations with the confederates, in which he had insisted that the Catholic church should not be allowed to retain its property: his refusal to move on this point appeared to be strengthening the hand of the peace party. On 6 August Glamorgan set out for Kilkenny and first appeared to be assisting Ormond in his discussions with the confederates there, but within three weeks he had concluded on 25 August a separate, secret treaty of his own. It went beyond anything previously in the public domain in making concessions to Catholics. All penal laws in Ireland were to be abandoned, Irish Catholics were to be exempt from protestant clerical jurisdiction, and in return the confederates were to provide 10,000 soldiers under Glamorgan's command for use anywhere in the three nations of the British Isles. The principal beneficiaries of the Glamorgan treaty would have been the Irish Catholic clergy, and despite the misgivings of the papal representative, Scarampi, a majority in the Catholic episcopate endorsed it when details leaked out. That Charles himself had not been consulted in detail on the terms of Glamorgan's concessions is suggested by the king's warning of 31 July to Ormond against too readily satisfying Irish Catholic expectations; but the yielding to confederate demands by Glamorgan was not an unreasonable surrender by one who was after all himself a devout Catholic. There is compelling evidence that Glamorgan shared his thinking with others in Ormond's negotiating team, who imposed an oath of their own on Glamorgan to compel him to deploy his promised army only when Charles had expressly given instructions for its use. Between 7 August and 24 December 1645 Glamorgan wrote fourteen letters to Ormond, couched in vague, extravagant terms, but broadly adhering to the line that he had come to help Ormond, not to open rival negotiations: this evidence can be taken to mean that Ormond himself was thus kept in the dark. An alternative reading of the Byzantine correspondence between the two is that Ormond knew of Glamorgan's plans, but had to maintain an official ignorance of them. Glamorgan's 'defeasance', a document he drew up on 26 August, was probably designed as his plan to protect Charles should his scheming fail, rather than as simply an admission by Glamorgan that he had strayed way beyond his commission.

In the event the details of negotiations in Kilkenny proved harder to conclude than the simplistic Glamorgan predicted, and it was mid-September before he could return to Dublin to rejoin the alternative negotiations pursued by Ormond. A further setback arrived in the shape of the new papal nuncio, Rinuccini, who was sceptical that Glamorgan could through his own dubious authority implement the religious concessions to the confederates at the core of the treaty. Even before Rinuccini's arrival Scarampi had distrusted Glamorgan's insistence that the treaty should be secret. Such secrecy that did prevail was already compromised by the diffusion of details of the treaty among the confederate general assembly and the Catholic episcopate, beyond the confederate treaty committee. Rinuccini appears to have suborned Glamorgan to his own proposals for even greater concessions to the Catholic church than those in the secret treaty. A sympathetic view of Glamorgan in his collapse before the nuncio's demands must stress the immediacy of the need for Irish troops to arrive in Chester before it fell, perhaps for ever, to parliament, and Glamorgan virtually alone among the royalist negotiators saw the virtue of persisting in negotiations with the nuncio. His critics, by contrast, will note this episode as further evidence of Glamorgan's hare-brained and quixotic character.

On 28 November 1645 Ormond was evidently still not willing to acknowledge the secret treaty, but its terms found their way to the English parliament after 17 October, when a copy was seized from the baggage train of the ambushed Catholic archbishop of Tuam by a Scots raiding party. On 26 December Glamorgan was brought before Ormond and was charged with treason by Lord Digby. After a theatrical demonstration at this meeting by Ormond that he knew nothing of Glamorgan's activities, it was decided to keep the earl in custody. Letters written by Glamorgan during his captivity strongly suggest that he had every confidence that his detention would be brief, and that he believed himself to be carrying out a scheme that the king must approve of. The pressing military considerations that had quickly wrung concessions from Glamorgan by Rinuccini now worked to secure the earl's release, and on 22 January 1646 he was freed on bail of £40,000. Glamorgan continued to play a part in the negotiations with the confederates, unaware that Charles had repudiated his treaty. Rinuccini now refused to accept the earl's credentials, on the grounds that he had never been formally cleared of treason. During February Glamorgan bent his efforts towards bringing the Ormondists and Rinuccini to the negotiating table, and managed to secure the prolongation of the cessation of arms. On 24 February he set out for Waterford to arrange for the ferrying of troops to England. He planned to send 6000 immediately and another 4000 in May. The date of departure from Ireland was fixed for 18 March: three ports of embarkation were identified. But Chester fell to parliament on 3 February, money and ships did not appear in the necessary quantities, and news broke that Charles had repudiated Glamorgan's commission. This marked the virtual collapse of Glamorgan's plans and of his personal credit in Ireland. On 3 February Charles wrote to the earl to distance himself from what had occurred, asserting that none of these misfortunes would have happened if Glamorgan had listened to Ormond. Three Irish regiments raised by Glamorgan for deployment in England were diverted on 8 April by the confederate council for service in co. Clare. When in June 1646 Glamorgan's father threatened the Monmouthshire parliamentarian committee with the forces his sons were bringing from Ireland, they were dismissed by his local opponents as 'jesuitical inventions' (*Letter from the Marquess of Worcester*).

The interregnum and inventions Until March 1648 Glamorgan remained in Ireland as a member of a new council of the confederates. He was admitted to civic honours in Waterford and Galway, and commanded an army in Munster from September 1646 until June 1647, when he was displaced by Lord Muskerry. He assured the Spanish agent in Ireland that he would send men to serve in Spain under Philip IV, but his offer was politely declined on the grounds that there seemed little substance to the proposals other than as a bargaining ploy with the Spanish. In the aftermath of the collapse of the king's cause Raglan had surrendered on 19 August 1646, and Glamorgan's father and wife were in the castle at the time. The subsequent sequestration of the family estates in south Wales and elsewhere made a return to Monmouthshire impossible for him. He had inherited his patrimonial title of marquess of Worcester in December 1646, on the death of his father, and the new marquess made for France in March 1648, spending most of the remainder of the 1640s in and around Paris.

On 14 March 1649 the Commonwealth government named Worcester among those royalists who were to suffer banishment and the confiscation of estates, but in practice, the republican government conducted itself towards him with more leniency than his history of plotting with the confederates might have deserved. In April 1651 Oliver Cromwell, the principal beneficiary of the confiscation of the Somerset family's estates, warned his wife of a possible visit from Worcester's son, and was particularly anxious lest receiving a member of the family should be construed as a form of political corruption. Despite the order of banishment Worcester was back in England by 28 July 1652, when a parliamentary order confined him to the Tower of London. With the advent of the Cromwellian protectorate, Worcester was treated with greater leniency. On 5 October 1654 he was released from the Tower on bail, and on 26 June 1655 an order under Cromwell's hand was signed for him to receive a weekly pension of £3. This could do little more than blunt the extremity of his circumstances, but he was free to resume his scientific work, in which the government took some interest. Worcester's former collaborator, Calthoff, had left England for the Netherlands, where he resumed experiments involving the motive power of steam to raise water. The English government wanted in February 1652 to interview Calthoff with a view to sponsoring him, and set aside Vauxhall, south of the Thames in London, as a space for scientific and related experimentation.

Apart from personal sympathy towards Worcester shown by Cromwell, the intellectual curiosity which marked interregnum regimes may have accounted for Worcester's rehabilitation. By 1655 Worcester's old partnership with Calthoff had resumed, and the marquess wrote a catalogue of his inventions (eventually published in 1663), in the self-justifying mode that was typical of him, and probably designed to attract sponsorship. *A century of the names and scantlings of … inventions* is an eclectic mixture of detail and the sketchiest of outlines, and even Worcester's most determined apologist, Henry Dircks, writing in 1865, was unable to provide explanatory glosses for all the inventions listed. However, it is the 'water commanding engine' which has excited most interest among historians of science, because its inventor claimed to have found a way to 'drive up water by fire' (Dircks, 475). Although the word 'steam' was not used as a term in science or engineering until after Worcester's death, the water commanding engine appears to have been powered by that means, and thus the marquess has been promoted, most vigorously by Dircks, as an inventor of the steam engine. Victorian commentators, writing in the great age of steam power, were more ready to dismiss Worcester's claims than their successors of a century later. In the continuing absence of any archaeological or other physical evidence, a definitive verdict seems as elusive as ever, but it seems that Calthoff's contribution was probably greater than that of his employer, that steam power was indeed deployed at Vauxhall in a prototype of the water commanding engine, but that it was ultimately unsuccessful.

The Restoration and last years In June 1660 Worcester provided the earl of Clarendon with an account of his activities in Ireland, which emphasized his own motives of self-sacrifice in the interests of the late king, and placed his London residence, Worcester House, in the Strand, at his disposal. The same month he petitioned Charles II for the return of his estates, and the House of Lords accordingly ordered their restitution. There was no heaping of rewards on the Somerset family, however, probably because of Clarendon's continuing suspicions of the marquess. His son was imprisoned briefly in 1660, and in September the title of duke of Somerset was removed from him after an investigation by the Lords of its dubious legality. In July 1661 he successfully pleaded parliamentary privilege to stave off his creditors, and on 3 June 1663, the royal assent was given to an act which provided Worcester with a patent for his water commanding engine.

While his son, Henry, Lord Herbert, was busy reconstructing the Somerset family's political interest, now based at Badminton, across the three counties of Herefordshire, Gloucestershire, and Monmouthshire, the marquess confined himself to scientific experiments at Vauxhall, and to attempts at extricating himself from the debts he estimated at £20,000, which kept him 'not only from a competent maintenance, but even from sleep' (Dircks, 280). He and his wife continued to petition the king for relief from his financial distress. In the final months of his life he wrote for the Lords an autobiographical review of his dealings on behalf of Charles I, inhibited from delivering it verbally through 'prolixity of speech, and a natural defect of utterance' (*Beaufort MSS*, 56). Ever inclined to the grand gesture Worcester declared that he would establish a horse troop, build new highways into London, and provide £10,000 for rebuilding St Paul's Cathedral, all presumably from the profits of the water commanding engine. These meaningless announcements were but an ornament to his real motives: to reveal his calculation that he had spent £918,000 in public service, and to declare himself bewildered that he had been unrewarded since the restoration of the king. The marquess died on 3 April 1667. His remains were conveyed to Raglan where he was buried on 19 April. He was survived by his wife, and his son, Henry, succeeded to the title. Calthoff died soon afterwards, and no more is heard of the water commanding engine after the faith in it of its promoters died with them. Dircks cites a letter from a Catholic priest which discouraged the marquess's widow from pursuing the potential benefits of the 'great machine' (Dircks, 304), but the limitations of available technology are more likely to have proved fatal to its survival than the criticisms of any perceived opponents of rational inquiry.

Reputation At first glance Worcester's careers as a scientific entrepreneur, civil war commander in the Welsh marches, and as a diplomat in Ireland appear sharply differentiated. Running through all these activities in the public sphere, however, was a lofty, quixotic ambition which outran his powers of judgement. He was imaginative, perhaps even visionary in his patronage of hydraulic engineering, but was never able wholly to persuade the scientific community in his own age of his achievement. It was left to Victorian commentators to rescue his reputation as an engineer. As a military commander and as a diplomat his dedication to the cause of Charles I was conceived in high-flown terms and was ill-requited by his king. The special status of his family as the king's prime private source of finance did not help Worcester take a realistic view of what he could achieve, nor did it endear him to his military colleagues in the royal cause. Even after 1660 he was genuinely anguished that his commitment and boldness were never properly rewarded, but under the restored monarchy his chivalrous, studious, but enterprising character seemed less suited than ever to the worldly, cynical spirit of the times.

STEPHEN K. ROBERTS

Sources *The manuscripts of the duke of Beaufort … the earl of Donoughmore*, HMC, 27 (1891) • H. Dircks, *The life, times and scientific labours of the second marquis of Worcester* (1865) • J. Lowe, 'The Glamorgan mission to Ireland, 1645–6', *Studia Hibernica*, 4 (1964), 155–96 • Clarendon, *Hist. rebellion* • R. Hutton, *The royalist war effort, 1642–1646* (1982) • J. R. Phillips, *Memoirs of the civil war in Wales and the marches, 1642–1649*, 2 vols. (1874) • S. R. Gardiner, *History of the great civil war, 1642–1649*, 4 vols. (1893); repr. (1987) • G. Doorman, 'The marquis of Worcester and Caspar Calthoff', *Transactions of the Newcomen Society for the Study of Engineering*, 26 (1953), 269–71 • [T. Carte], *The life of James, duke of Ormond*, new edn, 6 vols. (1851) • *CSP dom.* • GEC, *Peerage* • *DNB* • M. A. McClaire, '"I scorn to change or fear": Henry Somerset, first duke of Beaufort and the survival of the nobility following the English civil war', PhD diss., Yale U., 1994 • *A letter from the marquesse of Worcester* (1646) • J. R. Kenyon, *Raglan Castle*, rev. edn (1994) • M. Ó Siochrú, *Confederate Ireland, 1642–1649* (1999) • G. Aiazzi, *The embassy in Ireland of Monsignor G. B. Rinuccini*, trans. A. Hutton (1873) • *APC*, *1619–21*, 23 • M. Ó Siochrú, ed., *Kingdom in crisis* (2001) • J. H. Ohlmeyer, *Civil war and Restoration in the three Stuart kingdoms: the career of Randal MacDonnell, marquis of Antrim, 1609–1683* (1993) • Venn, *Alum. Cant.*

Archives Badminton House, Gloucestershire, Badminton MSS • NL Wales, Badminton MSS • Wigan Archives Service, Leigh, corresp. and papers

Likenesses Hanneman, group portrait (with his second wife and their daughter), Badminton House, Gloucestershire; repro. in Dircks, *Life, times and scientific labours* • A. Van Dyck, oils, Badminton House, Gloucestershire; repro. in Dircks, *Life, times and scientific labours* • portrait, Badminton House, Gloucestershire [*see illus.*]

Wealth at death died in debt; but had repaid £50,000, 1660–67: petition, quoted by Dircks, *Life, times and scientific labours*, 288

Somerset, Lord (Robert) Edward Henry (1776–1842), army officer, usually known as Lord Edward Somerset, was born on 19 December 1776, the fourth surviving son of the thirteen children (nine boys and four girls) of Henry Somerset, fifth duke of Beaufort (1744–1803), and his wife, Elizabeth (1747–1828), the daughter of Admiral Edward *Boscawen; Lord Charles Henry *Somerset was his elder brother; Lord FitzRoy James Henry *Somerset, first Baron Raglan, and Lord John Thomas Henry *Somerset [*see under* Somerset, FitzRoy James Henry] were his younger brothers. Following his education at Westminster School, on 4 February 1793 he became a cornet in the 10th light dragoons, advancing to lieutenant in December 1793 and captain on 28 August 1794. After having been made aide-de-camp to the duke of York, commander of the expedition to the Helder peninsula, he took part in actions on 19 September and 2 and 6 October 1799. On 21 November 1799 Somerset was promoted major in the 12th light dragoons, and the following year moved to the 28th light dragoons. He was promoted lieutenant-colonel on 25 December 1800, and transferred to the 4th dragoons in that rank on 3 September 1801. He sat as MP for Monmouth (1799–1802) and Gloucestershire (1803–29), and defended his brother Lord Charles Henry in the House of Commons in 1826 and 1827 against charges of professional misconduct as governor of the Cape of Good Hope. Two years later, after initially opposing it, he supported Roman Catholic emancipation.

Meanwhile, the 4th dragoons had gone to Portugal in April 1809, where Somerset commanded it at Talavera (27–8 July 1809) and Busaco (27 September 1810), having been promoted colonel and appointed aide-de-camp to the king on 25 July 1810. At Usagre (25 May 1811) the 4th dragoons, with the 3rd dragoon guards, rode down two French cavalry regiments, causing 170 casualties and taking ninety-five prisoners. Somerset led the regiment in the charge of Le Marchant's heavy brigade at Salamanca (22 July 1812), breaking through three columns of infantry and capturing five guns, for which he earned special mention in Wellington's victory dispatch.

On 4 June 1813, on Wellington's recommendation, Somerset was promoted major-general and presented with a sword of honour by the officers of his regiment. He was given command of the hussar brigade (7th, 10th, and 15th), with which he fought at Vitoria (21 June 1813), the Pyrenees (28–30 July 1813), Orthez (27 February 1814), and Toulouse (10 April 1814). At Orthez his brigade decisively charged the retreating French infantry, securing a large number of prisoners, and once more he was praised in Wellington's post-battle dispatch. He received the thanks of parliament (26 June 1814) and the Peninsular gold cross with one clasp for his services at Talavera, Salamanca, Vitoria, Orthez, and Toulouse. He was also made KCB in January 1815.

At the battle of Waterloo Somerset commanded the household brigade of cavalry, consisting of the 1st and 2nd Life Guards, the Royal Horse Guards (Blue), and the 1st dragoon guards, totalling 1135 rank and file. Shortly after 2 p.m., led by Lord Uxbridge, the brigade charged downhill against d'Erlon's corps of massed infantry, which had attacked Wellington's left, east of the Charleroi–Brussels road. It swept through Dubois's brigade of Milhaud's cuirassiers, which was on d'Erlon's left, but, imprudently, pursued the broken enemy across the valley until attacked by lancers and by a fresh brigade of cuirassiers, losing heavily as it retired. Somerset had a horse killed under him and a flap of his collar struck by a cannon ball, but he was otherwise unscathed. Despite incurring heavy loss in this action, the brigade acquitted itself well later that afternoon as French cavalry and infantry probed in strength west of the Brussels road. During the early evening it was joined by the Union brigade, which had charged d'Erlon on Somerset's left and suffered even more severely, and guarded the part of the British line immediately to the west of La Haye-Sainte. Here the two brigades suffered such further loss from the enemy's fire that their seven regiments ultimately formed only one squadron of about fifty files. The fire was so severe that Uxbridge, the overall cavalry commander, urged Somerset to withdraw his men, who were extended in single rank to show a larger front; but Somerset feared that, if he moved, the Dutch cavalry behind him would not stand firm.

To his brother Beaufort, Somerset referred to 'so dreadful a battle', adding that 'fine alarm and confusion' had reigned in Brussels on 18 June with many families fleeing to Antwerp. Lord FitzRoy, who had lost his right arm, was 'doing as well as possible' (Badminton Muniments, Fm 3/4/1), and he solicitously informed his mother that her youngest son 'mends wonderfully' (Raglan MSS, RPP 1/28). In his dispatch Wellington recommended Somerset's 'highly distinguished' conduct for the prince regent's 'approbation' (*Dispatches*, 12.482–3); Somerset received the thanks of parliament (29 April 1816) as well as the orders of Maria Theresa (Austria), St Vladimir (Russia), and the Tower and Sword (Portugal).

Somerset was appointed to command the 1st brigade of cavalry in the army of occupation in France on 30 November 1815, and he held this command until the army was withdrawn at the end of 1818. He afterwards held the post of inspecting-general of cavalry until his promotion to the rank of lieutenant-general on 27 May 1825. Having been appointed colonel of the 21st light dragoons on 15 January 1818, on its disbandment he became colonel of the 17th lancers (9 September 1822), then of the 1st dragoons (23 November 1829). On 31 March 1836 he was appointed colonel of his old regiment, now the 4th light dragoons. He served as lieutenant-general of the ordnance in 1829–30 and as surveyor-general of the ordnance for a short time in 1835. Somerset was made GCB in 1834 and became general on 23 November 1841. He died in London on 1 September 1842 from a long-standing heart complaint after a recent 'violent' attack in Geneva, and was buried a week later, on 8 September. He had married, on 17 October 1805, Louisa Augusta (*d.* 1823), the twelfth daughter of William, second Viscount Courtenay. They had two sons, Edward Arthur and Augustus Charles Stapleton, both commissioned into the army, and five daughters, three of whom were unmarried at their father's death.

E. M. LLOYD, *rev.* JOHN SWEETMAN

Sources *Army List* • Burke, *Peerage* • Gwent County RO, Newport, Raglan MSS, RPP 1/28 • Badminton muniments, Badminton, Gloucestershire, Fm 3/4/1 • D. S. Daniell, *4th hussar: the story of the 4th queen's own hussars, 1685–1958* (1959) • J. Sweetman, *Raglan: from the Peninsula to the Crimea* (1993) • *The dispatches of … the duke of Wellington … from 1799 to 1818*, ed. J. Gurwood, new edn, 13 vols. (1837–9) • E. Longford [E. H. Pakenham, countess of Longford], *Wellington*, 1: *The years of the sword* (1969)

Archives Badminton House, Gloucestershire • Bodl. Oxf., diary [copy] • Gwent County RO, Newport, Raglan MSS • NRA, priv. coll., letters describing the battle of Waterloo

Likenesses J. W. Pieneman, oils, 1821, Wellington Museum, London • J. W. Pieneman, group portrait, oils, 1824 (*Battle of Waterloo*), Rijksmuseum, Amsterdam • T. Heaphy, watercolour drawing, NPG • W. Salter, group portrait, oils (*The Waterloo banquet at Apsley House*), Wellington Museum, London • W. Salter, oils, NPG

Somerset, FitzRoy James Henry [*known as* Lord FitzRoy Somerset], **first Baron Raglan (1788–1855)**, army officer, was the ninth and youngest son of Henry Somerset, fifth duke of Beaufort (1744–1803), and Elizabeth (1747–1828), daughter of Admiral Edward *Boscawen (1711–1761). Lord Charles Henry *Somerset (1767–1831), Lord (Robert) Edward Henry *Somerset (1776–1842), and Lord John Thomas Henry Somerset [*see below*] were older brothers. Born at Badminton, Gloucestershire, on 30 September 1788, Somerset was educated at Goodenough's School, Ealing (1795–1801), and Westminster School (1802–3).

The Peninsular War Somerset was commissioned cornet, by purchase, in the 4th light dragoons on 9 June 1804, and became lieutenant, by purchase, on 30 May 1805. In 1807 he accompanied the mission of Sir Arthur Paget to the Ottoman empire, which sought unsuccessfully to detach the sultan from his alliance with France. Of Somerset, Paget wrote: 'He is a most excellent Lad—I have the sincerest Regard for him' (Sweetman, 19). Somerset obtained a company as captain in the 6th garrison battalion on 5 May 1808, and on 18 August was transferred to the 43rd foot. Meanwhile, in July 1808, through the duke of Richmond's influence, he went to Portugal with Sir Arthur Wellesley as aide-de-camp, and was at the battles of Rolica (17 August 1808) and Vimeiro (21 August 1808). In action for the first time at Rolica he responded to Wellesley's query 'how do you feel under fire?' with 'better, sir, than I expected' (Sweetman, 23). On 27 August Wellesley wrote: 'Lord FitzRoy has been very useful to me, and I have this day lent him to Sir H. Dalrymple to go to the French headquarters' (Sweetman, 24) to assist peace negotiations.

After the defeated French had left Portugal, Somerset went home with Wellesley, but returned to the Peninsula with him in the spring of 1809, and served on his staff continuously until the close of the war. He was bearer of the dispatches after Talavera (28 July 1809), and was wounded at Busaco (27 September 1810). Appointed military secretary to the duke of Wellington on 1 January 1811, he established direct relations with the battalion commanders, by means of which he acquired, Sir William Napier observed in his *History*, 'an exact knowledge of the moral state of each regiment, rendered his own office important and gracious with the army, and with such discretion and judgment that the military hierarchy was in no manner weakened' (Sweetman, 32). He secured a brevet majority on 9 June, after Fuentes d'Oñoro.

Somerset distinguished himself at Badajoz, where he helped to persuade the French governor to surrender, and at Wellington's special request he was made brevet lieutenant-colonel on 27 April 1812. During the siege of

FitzRoy James Henry Somerset, first Baron Raglan (1788–1855), by Roger Fenton, 1855

Pamplona he succeeded in deciphering a message from its governor to Marshal Soult which came into Wellington's hands, leading to allied success. After the victory at Toulouse on 10 April 1814 Somerset went with Wellington to the victory parade in Paris and on to Spain before reaching England. Somerset received the gold cross with five clasps and silver war medal, also with five clasps, for the Peninsula, and was made KCB on 2 January 1815. On 25 July 1814 he was transferred to the 1st guards as captain and lieutenant-colonel. On 6 August 1814 he married Emily Harriet (1792–1881), second daughter of Wellington's brother, William Wellesley-Pole (later third earl of Mornington).

The battle of Waterloo After Napoleon's first abdication Wellington went to Paris as ambassador, and Somerset accompanied him as secretary to the embassy. He was left in charge of the embassy as minister-plenipotentiary from 18 January 1815, when Wellington went to Vienna, until Napoleon's return. On 14 March—the day Joseph Fouché made his remarkable prediction that the empire would be restored but would last only three months—Somerset wrote to Wellington: 'I see no reason why it should be at all expected that Napoleon should not succeed' (Sweetman, 51–2). On the 20th Napoleon reached Paris, and on the 26th Somerset left it to join Wellington in the Netherlands as his military secretary.

At the battle of Waterloo (18 June 1815), while he was accompanying Wellington, about seven o'clock in the evening, Somerset's right elbow was hit by a bullet from the roof of La Haye-Sainte, and the arm had to be amputated. After the operation Somerset said, 'Hey, bring my arm back. There's a ring my wife gave me on the finger' (Sweetman, 65–6). Wellington wrote to Somerset's brother, the duke of Beaufort, 'You are aware how useful he has always been to me, and how much I shall feel the want of his assistance, and what a regard and affection I feel for him' (Sweetman, 66). He recommended him warmly soon afterwards for the appointment of aide-de-camp to the prince regent. This was given to him with the rank of colonel in the army on 28 August. He was awarded Austrian, Russian, Bavarian, and Portuguese orders.

Secretary to the ordnance, 1819–1827 Heeding advice from Wellington, Somerset returned to the British embassy at Paris. When the allied armies were withdrawn from France, Wellington was made master-general of the ordnance in London, and, early in 1819, Somerset became his secretary. He accompanied Wellington to the congress of Verona in 1822. In January 1823 he was sent on a special mission to Spain to explain the duke's views upon the constitutional crisis to some of the leading politicians, in the hope of averting French intervention, but spent two months at Madrid ineffectually. Promoted major-general on 27 May 1825, in 1826 he went with Wellington on the accession of Nicholas I to St Petersburg, where negotiations were conducted for common action against Turkey on behalf of Greece. During this period Somerset twice sat in parliament as a tory MP for the corporation borough of Truro on the interest of his first cousin, Edward, fourth Viscount Falmouth—in 1818–20 and in 1826–9—but took no active part in any debate. Somerset demonstrated deep paternal interest in the welfare of his children, and Lady Somerset began to suffer the first of many ailments which thenceforth afflicted her.

Military secretary at the Horse Guards, 1827–1852 Having resigned from the Ordnance with Wellington in April, shortly after the duke became commander-in-chief on 28 August 1827, Somerset was made military secretary at the Horse Guards, a post that he held until 30 September 1852. He was noted for his quickness and accuracy, for impartiality, and for his tact and urbanity. In those twenty-five years he served Wellington and Rowland, first Viscount Hill, both of whom devolved more and more responsibility due to their increasing infirmity. He exercised considerable influence over military appointments, co-ordinated opposition to the proposal of Lord Howick in 1837 to enhance the powers of the secretary at war to the detriment of the commander-in-chief, and became officially embroiled in the controversial activities of James Thomas Brudenell, seventh earl of Cardigan, which attracted widespread press condemnation. Lady Somerset's health determined that he decline separately the offer of the captaincy of Cowes Castle and the post of governor-in-chief of British North America. Somerset was made colonel of the 53rd foot on 19 November 1830, and became lieutenant-general on 28 June 1838. He was awarded a DCL degree in June 1834 when Wellington was installed as chancellor at Oxford. On Wellington's death (14 September 1852) Lord Hardinge succeeded him as commander-in-chief and a disappointed Somerset became master-general of the ordnance on 30 September 1852. He was made GCB on 24 September 1852, a privy councillor (on 16 October), and Baron Raglan of Raglan, Monmouthshire, on 18 October. As master-general he continued Hardinge's policy of increasing the artillery and arming the horse and field artillery with heavier guns.

Victory on the Alma In February 1854, when war against Russia seemed imminent, Raglan was selected to command the expeditionary force sent to the east. Though sixty-five he had the strength and vigour of a much younger man. He had never led troops in the field, but Hardinge pointed to his 'great professional experience under the Duke' (Sweetman, 169). His diplomatic skills, as well as his personal character and charm of manner, marked him out for an expedition with the difficulties of both combined operations and alliance warfare. On 27 March, Britain declared war. Raglan left London on 10 April, his primary task to defend Constantinople but warned by Henry Fiennes Pelham-*Clinton, fifth duke of Newcastle, secretary of state for war and the colonies, that 'no blow … would be so effective for this purpose as the taking of Sebastopol' (Sweetman, 179). After spending some days in Paris he reached Constantinople on 29 April. There he resisted attempts by the French commander (Marshal Saint-Arnaud) to assume overall direction of the allied forces, travelled to Schumla to meet the Turkish commander-in-chief (Omar Pasha) and agreed to move troops into Bulgaria, as Russian units were south of the Danube. By the end of June most of the British and French armies were in camp near Varna; but by then the Russian army had recrossed the Danube, and the European provinces of Turkey were no longer threatened.

On 29 June instructions were sent to Raglan that he should prepare to besiege Sevastopol, 'unless with the information in your possession, but at present unknown in this country, you should be decidedly of opinion that it could not be undertaken with a reasonable prospect of success' (Hibbert, 56). In view of Newcastle's comments in April this could not have completely surprised Raglan, but he and Saint-Arnaud had grave misgivings about the enterprise, and they had no such information as the letter mentioned. However, they regarded the instructions as 'little short of an absolute order', and they acquiesced. The ravages of cholera and the need to concentrate men, equipment, and sea transport caused some delay. Not until 14 September did the first troops land without opposition at Calamita Bay, on the west coast of the Crimea, a beach chosen by Raglan himself. Due to bad weather it took four days more to land the horses and guns, and to collect transport. Eventually, on 19 September, the invaders advanced south. That afternoon only Raglan's vigilance prevented the British cavalry from being attacked by superior enemy forces at the Bulganek River.

The following day, on 20 September 1854, the battle of the Alma was fought. The allies' right comprised 28,000 French and 7000 Turkish infantry, with sixty-eight guns; the left 23,000 British infantry, 1000 British cavalry, and sixty guns. The bulk of the Russian army—21,000 infantry, 3000 cavalry, and eighty-four guns—were in front of the British; while they had only 12,000 infantry, 400 cavalry, and thirty-six guns to oppose the French, whose advance could be supported by the fire of the fleet. Crucially, twenty-one guns in two redoubts on Kurgan Hill barred the British path. It was agreed, therefore, that the French should begin the battle, and turn (or threaten to turn) the Russian left. But before this movement was sufficiently developed to make itself felt, Raglan, partly because his waiting troops were incurring mounting casualties, but also at the urgent instance of the French commanders, ordered the British infantry to attack the redoubts. He then rode forward with his staff across the stream, through the French skirmishers, and up to a knoll well within the Russian position. He gained an admirable point of view, which enabled him to observe progress of the action, bring up guns and infantry to enfilade the enemy, and evaluate the situation as the Russians withdrew. Paying tribute to Raglan's bravery Saint-Arnaud wrote that in the midst of cannon and musket fire he displayed a calmness which never left him.

Attack on Sevastopol Victory on the Alma raised high hopes of the prompt capture of Sevastopol, both in the armies and at home. The enemy's works on the south side of the fortress were thought to be weak, whereas the strength of those to the north was obvious. The allied armies, therefore, marched east of Sevastopol to occupy upland to the south. Once established there, the commanders determined that a bombardment by siege guns must precede an assault. Already 172 guns were mounted on the works, and the garrison, after the withdrawal of the field army under Prince Menshikov, numbered 30,000, mostly seamen and marines. Trenches were dug and batteries built. The French, on the left, attacked the works of the town, and the British, on the right, those of the Korabelnaya suburb. On 17 October the allies opened fire with 126 guns, but by this time, through the energy of Lieutenant-Colonel Todleben, the enemy's works had been greatly strengthened, and 341 guns were mounted on them, of which 118 bore on the besiegers' batteries. Lack of co-ordination with the naval bombardment that day and early explosion of a French magazine signalled failure. All thoughts of an assault had to be postponed, and the allies needed to look to their own defence against the growing strength of the Russian field army. Raglan had both to protect the allied right flank and to hold his supply port of Balaklava.

Balaklava and the charge of the light brigade On 25 October came the unsuccessful Russian attack on Balaklava, and the disastrous charge of the light brigade [*see* Nolan, Lewis

Edward]. All agreed that 'some one had blundered'. Raglan, in his dispatch, blamed Lord Lucan: 'From some misconception of the order to advance, the lieutenant-general considered that he was bound to attack at all hazards' (Sweetman, 253). But he himself did not escape blame on the grounds that the wording of the order did not make his intention clear.

Victory at Inkerman On 5 November the Russians concentrated on the allied right, sending 35,000 men onto the upland while another 22,000 manoeuvred on the plain below, and the battle of Inkerman was fought. Aware of British weakness in this area, Raglan had pleaded in vain for French reinforcements. The main attack, upon the 2nd division under Sir John Lysaght Pennefather, began at 6.30 a.m. Raglan was on the field an hour later, but he did not interfere with Pennefather in his conduct of the fight. However, he decisively ordered up two 18-pounder guns, which did much to reduce the Russian preponderance in artillery. He also sent off for French assistance, showing better judgement than two of his divisional generals, who declined Bosquet's offer of aid. He watched the course of the battle from the ridge which formed the main position, where Strangways, the artillery commander, was killed while talking to him, and Canrobert (Saint-Arnaud's successor) was wounded. 'I am not at all aware of having exposed myself either rashly or unnecessarily, either at Alma or Inkerman', he wrote afterwards in reply to Newcastle's remonstrances.

Raglan had been gazetted colonel of the Royal Horse Guards (the Blues) on 8 May 1854, and had been promoted general on 20 June. He was made field marshal from 5 November. The notification was accompanied by a letter from the queen, in which she said:

> The queen cannot sufficiently express her high sense of the great services he has rendered and is rendering to her and to the country by the very able manner in which he has led the bravest troops that ever fought. (Martin, 3.154)

It was a last ray of sunshine.

Winter in the Crimea The allies had narrowly escaped destruction at Inkerman, after which wintering in the Crimea became inevitable, and want of men made it impossible to press actively the siege of Sevastopol. On 14 November a hurricane in the Black Sea wrecked twenty-one vessels laden with urgently needed stores. Next day Raglan informed Newcastle, 'you cannot send us too many supplies of all kinds'. Immediately afterwards the cold weather set in. The sufferings and losses of the troops increased, and criticism at home increased.

Unaware of Raglan's efforts to secure French reinforcements the *Times* correspondent, William Howard *Russell, resentful of Raglan's ignoring him, had already attributed the absence of trenches covering the allies' right to indolence and overweening confidence. He alleged that if central depots had been established while the fine weather lasted, much, if not all, of the misery and suffering of the men and of the loss of horses would have been averted. Anonymous letters from officers and men added more complaints and before Christmas *The Times* charged Raglan and his staff with neglect and incompetence.

The commander of the forces had no direct responsibility for supply and transport. Up to 22 December, when a change was made, the commissariat was a branch, not of the war department, but of the Treasury, and so far as any one cause could be named for the terrible hardships of the troops, it was Treasury failure to comply with the requisitions it received for forage. The horses were starved, and there were inadequate means of transporting stores from Balaklava to the camps. But in face of the rising storm of indignation at home, the government blamed the staff in the Crimea. In an official dispatch of 6 January 1855, as in earlier private letters, the duke of Newcastle censured the administration of the army, and pointed especially to the quartermaster-general, James Bucknall Estcourt, and the adjutant-general, Richard Airey. But Raglan refused to make them scapegoats.

Raglan knew from his war experience under Wellington the importance of military intelligence. He had been sent to the East in 1854 without any intelligence organization, and it was lack of intelligence which had resulted in the fatal decision not to attack Sevastopol immediately from the south, and the British being surprised at the battle of Balaklava. Thereafter intelligence significantly improved, with the secret intelligence department improvised and run by Charles Cattley (alias Calvert)—a civilian member of Raglan's staff and formerly British vice-consul at Kerch, who died of cholera in July 1855—using largely Tartar agents and Polish deserters. Raglan encouraged and utilized competently Cattley's department, and British military intelligence was largely successful. Concerned to prevent the Russians gaining intelligence, Raglan complained to the government of W. H. Russell's reports which published information which 'must be invaluable to the Russians, and in the same degree detrimental to H. M.'s troops' (Hankinson, 99). In January 1855 he complained, 'The Enemy at least need spend nothing under the head of "Secret Service"' (Harris, 76).

On 30 January 1855 the Aberdeen government was defeated upon the motion of J. A. Roebuck for an inquiry into the condition of the army in the Crimea. It fell, and Palmerston formed a ministry, with Lord Panmure as secretary for war. On 12 February Panmure wrote to Raglan: 'It would appear that your visits to the camp were few and far between, and your staff seems to have known as little as yourself of the condition of your gallant men' (Sweetman, 284). He added in a private letter that a radical change of the staff was the least that would satisfy the public. In a long and dignified reply on 3 March, Raglan wrote:

> I have served under the greatest man of the age more than half my life, have enjoyed his confidence, and have, I am proud to say, been ever regarded by him as a man of truth and some judgment as to the qualifications of officers, and yet, having been placed in the most difficult position in which an officer was ever called upon to serve, and having successfully carried out difficult operations, with the entire approbation of the queen, which is now my only solace, I am charged with every species of neglect; and the opinion

> which it was my solemn duty to give of the merits of the officers, and the assertions which I made in support of it, are set at naught, and your lordship is satisfied that your irresponsible informants are more worthy of credit than I am. (Hibbert, 289–90)

The charge brought against Raglan of not visiting the camps was vigorously rejected by homecoming wounded in press interviews. As regards his staff, Lieutenant-General Simpson (who was sent out to report upon it) declared to Panmure that Raglan was 'the worst used man I have ever heard of', the staff 'very much vilified'. According to Raglan's daughter Charlotte, 'Papa is a good deal annoyed' at the unwarranted slurs on his staff (Sweetman, 289). In 1855 he was awarded the order of the Mejidiye (first class).

Siege of Sevastopol Siege operations were actively resumed at the end of February 1855. The French had been greatly reinforced, and were now much stronger than the British. Still responsible for the allied left, they had also taken over the extreme right, where the battle of Inkerman was fought. On 9 April the second bombardment began, and the assault was fixed for the 28th; but Canrobert drew back on the 25th. An expedition against Kerch, at the entrance to the Sea of Azov, was then arranged, to cut the line of communication of the Russians from the east, but it had no sooner started than Canrobert insisted on its recall. It was successfully carried out, though, at the end of May, when Pélissier had replaced Canrobert. Meanwhile, there had been a third bombardment of Sevastopol, the Mamelon (an advanced work in front of the Malakhov) had been taken by the French, and the Quarries before the Redan by the British. The 18 June, the anniversary of Waterloo, was chosen for the general assault.

It was to be preceded by two hours' bombardment, but Pélissier decided at the last moment to attack at 3 a.m., and Raglan reluctantly concurred. The result was disastrous. Due to a misunderstanding the French columns for the assault of the Malakhov, numbering in all 25,000 men, attacked piecemeal. They were met by a storm of fire and were driven back with heavy loss. Seeing their plight Raglan ordered the British forward against the Redan, though the chance of success there was much less. He knew that otherwise 'the French would have attributed their non-success to our refusal to participate in the operation' (to Panmure, 19 June). The two leading British columns, about 500 men each, 'had no sooner shown themselves beyond the trenches than they were assailed by a most murderous fire of grape and musketry. Those in advance were either killed or wounded, and the remainder found it impossible to proceed' (official dispatch).

Death and burial Raglan described 'the failure' as 'a great affliction to me' and 'a great disappointment' (Sweetman, 315). On the 23rd one of the staff wrote: 'He looks far from well, and has grown very much aged lately'. He was further distressed by the death of Estcourt the following day. Although apparently suffering physically only from mild diarrhoea, Raglan's strength was undermined by all he had endured, and he was very depressed. On the 26th he wrote his last dispatch, and on the evening of the 28th he died, at camp before Sevastopol, 'the victim of England's unreadiness for war', Sir Evelyn Wood remarked. Apparently he died, in Victorian terms, of a broken heart. Raglan's unexpected death caused grief and gloom in the army. Pélissier, in his general order next day, paid tribute to Raglan's courage in battle and greatness of character. In the words of the general order issued from the Horse Guards,

> By his calmness in the hottest moments of battle, and by his quick perception in taking advantage of the ground or the movements of the enemy, he won the confidence of his army, and performed great and brilliant services. In the midst of a winter campaign—in a severe climate and surrounded by difficulties—he never despaired.

This last characteristic well deserved emphasis. Saint-Arnaud had often been tiresome, Canrobert despondent, and Omar Pasha frequently at odds with his own government. One of Raglan's divisional commanders—Sir George de Lacy Evans—strongly urged him after Inkerman to give up the siege and embark the army. His capacity as a general was questioned, and he had been the object of much undeserved blame; but belatedly the nobility of his character had made itself felt even by those who had been loudest in complaint (for example, *The Times*, 2 July). His successor as British commander in the Crimea, Sir James Simpson, wrote: 'His loss to us here is inexpressible', and the prince consort observed: 'Spite of all that has been said and written against him, an *irreparable* loss for us!' Florence Nightingale wrote, 'It was impossible not to love him … He was not a very great general, but he was a very good man' (Hibbert, 342).

The body was embarked on the paddle gunboat *Caradoc* with full military honours, the 7 miles of road from his headquarters to Kazatch Bay being lined with troops. It reached Bristol on 24 July, and was buried privately at Badminton on the 26th. A pension of £1000 was voted to his widow (who died on 6 March 1881), and £2000 to his heir; £12,500 was subscribed for a memorial to him, and Kefntilla estate, near Usk, was bought and presented to his heir. He left one son, Richard Henry FitzRoy Somerset, second Lord Raglan (1817–1884), and two daughters, Charlotte Caroline Elizabeth and Katherine Anne Emily Cecilia. His eldest son, Major Arthur William FitzRoy Somerset, had died on 25 December 1845 of wounds received four days before at the battle of Ferozeshahr; Frederick John FitzRoy had died in infancy.

Of 'spotless reputation' (Sweetman, 338), 'the most modest and least vain of men' (Lady Westmorland, his sister-in-law, quoted in Sweetman, 348), with 'too good and kind a heart' (Captain H. Keppel RN, quoted in Sweetman, 348), Raglan was a devout high-church Anglican, socially popular, and an accomplished rider and shot. Of medium height, with, in his younger years distinctive ash blond hair, he was unostentatious and in the Crimea moved with a minimum of military display. With an average annual turnover of £4000 and credit balance of £800, he showed, his bankers noted, 'no sign of his having been embarrassed at any time or in any way'. In the Crimea he was a better general than his critics allowed. Balaklava did not fall on 25 October 1854. Had he lost that battle, either the Alma or Inkerman, the allies would have been faced with ignominious withdrawal from the peninsula. Shortly before his death Raglan referred to having 'served the Crown for above fifty years' (Sweetman, 338). Duty guided his public life, devotion to his family the private part.

W. H. Russell's and *The Times*'s criticisms were long influential, and for many years Raglan was considered a blundering failure in the Crimea, an image repeated in cinematic portrayal. However, after 1960 revisionist studies—Christopher Hibbert's *The Destruction of Lord Raglan* (1961), John Sweetman's *Raglan* (1993), and Stephen Harris's *British Military Intelligence in the Crimean War* (1999)—have provided more balanced and favourable portrayals.

Raglan's nephew and aide-de-camp, Colonel **Poulett George Henry Somerset** (1822–1875), was the fourth son of General Lord Charles Henry *Somerset (1767–1831), colonial governor and second son of the fifth duke of Beaufort, and Mary (*d.* 1860), daughter of the fourth Earl Poulett. He was born on 19 June 1822, was educated at the Royal Military College, Sandhurst, was commissioned as ensign in the 33rd foot on 20 March 1839, exchanged into the Coldstream Guards on 1 May 1840, and became captain and lieutenant-colonel on 3 March 1854. He acted as aide-de-camp to Lord Raglan in the Crimean War, received the order of the Mejidiye (fourth class), and was made CB on 5 July 1855.

His uncle declared himself 'very much pleased with Poulett', sending him, for example, after Russian withdrawal from Silistria 'to desire' Lord Cardigan to take the light brigade 'as far as he could in order to discover what the enemy's left was about'. Poulett rode for a short distance on that lengthy, painful reconnaissance towards the Danube. Once in the Crimea he lived at British headquarters, was present at Raglan's death, travelled home with his body to take part in the funeral procession through Bristol, and joined family mourners for the burial at Badminton. He had a narrow escape at Inkerman, where a shell burst in the body of his horse. Somerset exchanged into the 7th fusiliers on 2 February 1858, became colonel five years later, and went on half pay on 21 June 1864. He was a JP and Conservative MP for Monmouthshire from 1859 to 1871.

Somerset was twice married: first, on 15 April 1847, to Barbara Augusta Nora, daughter of John Mytton of Halston, Shropshire, who died on 4 June 1870; second, on 10 September 1870, to Emily, daughter of J. H. Moore of Cherryhill, Cheshire. There were two sons and one daughter from the first marriage, and one daughter from the second. He died at Homestead, Dundrum, near Dublin, on 7 September 1875.

Raglan's brother, Colonel **Lord John Thomas Henry Somerset** (1787–1846), the eighth son of Henry Somerset, fifth duke of Beaufort (1744–1803), and Elizabeth (1747–1828), daughter of Admiral the Hon. Edward Boscawen, was born on 30 August 1787. He attended Goodenough's School, Ealing, and Westminster School at the same time as his younger brother, FitzRoy. Commissioned as cornet in the 7th light dragoons on 4 August 1804, he advanced to lieutenant on 14 August 1805 and transferred to the 23rd light dragoons as captain on 15 April 1808. He served with the regiment in the Peninsula, taking part in the battle of Talavera (28 July 1809) with his brothers Edward and FitzRoy. He married, on 4 December 1814, Lady Catharine Annesley (*d.* 1865), daughter of the earl of Mountnorris, and they had one son and three daughters. Somerset joined the 60th foot on 15 May 1815, advancing to major on 18 June, the day that he fought at Waterloo, where he reputedly 'saved a brother officer's life' (Durant, 174). On 25 July he went on half pay, progressing to brevet lieutenant-colonel (19 July 1821), lieutenant-colonel (16 July 1830), and colonel (10 January 1837). In 1843 he was restored to full pay on appointment as inspecting field officer to Bristol recruiting district, a post that he held until his death. Suffering from a persistent cough and violent rheumatic pains in his shoulder and neck, he then developed a tumour between his legs, according to his younger brother 'due to the inactive state of his liver'. He moved from Bristol to Weston-super-Mare, Somerset, in the hope that the sea air would improve his health. However, he died there on 3 October 1846, to the grief of FitzRoy: 'I have lost an affectionate brother … the companion of my youth' (Sweetman, 135). FitzRoy believed that, although frugal, Somerset left little money because of his wife's extravagance. He was buried in a vault in the nave of Bristol Cathedral.

E. M. LLOYD, *rev.* JOHN SWEETMAN

Sources J. Sweetman, *Raglan: from the Peninsula to the Crimea* (1993) • C. Hibbert, *The destruction of Lord Raglan* [1961] • *Army List* • A. W. Kinglake, *The invasion of the Crimea*, 8 vols. (1863–87) • S. J. G. Calthorpe, *Letters from headquarters, or, The realities of the war in the Crimea*, 2nd edn, 2 vols. (1857) • *Colburn's United Service Magazine*, 2 (1855) • GEC, *Peerage* • Burke, *Peerage* (1967) • *Supplementary despatches (correspondence) and memoranda of Field Marshal Arthur, duke of Wellington*, ed. A. R. Wellesley, second duke of Wellington, 15 vols. (1858–72), vols. 5–6 • T. Martin, *The life of … the prince consort*, 5 vols. (1875–80), vols. 2–3 • *GM*, 2nd ser., 44 (1855) • H. Durant, *The Somerset sequence* (1951) • A. Hankinson, *Man of wars: William Howard Russell of the Times* (1982) • S. M. Harris, *British military intelligence in the Crimean War, 1854–1856* (1999) • H. Strachan, *From Waterloo to Balaclava: tactics, technology and the British army, 1815–1854* (1985) • A. D. Lambert, *The Crimean War: British grand strategy, 1853–56* (1990) • HoP, *Commons, 1790–1820* • *GM*, 2nd ser., 26 (1846), 645 • Boase, *Mod. Eng. biog.*

Archives Badminton House, Gloucestershire, family corresp. • Gwent RO, Cwmbrân, corresp. and MSS; Raglan private papers • NA Scot., corresp., GD172 • NAM, department of archives, corresp. and MSS, 6807/279–305 • NAM, Raglan military papers • University of Keele, corresp. | All Souls Oxf., corresp. with Sir Charles Vaughan, C • BL, corresp. with J. W. Croker, Add. MS 41124 • BL, corresp. with Sir Robert Peel, Add. MSS 40278–40594, *passim* • BL, corresp. with Lord Strathnairn, Add. MS 4808 • BL, corresp. with earl of Westmorland, M/512/1 [copies] • BL OIOC, letters to marquess of Tweeddale, MS Eur. F 96 • Bodl. Oxf., corresp. with Napier family, MS Eng. lett c248–249, d235 • Bodl. Oxf., Phillipps-Robinson MSS, corresp. with Sir Thomas Phillipps • Cumbria AS, Carlisle, corresp. with Sir James Graham, D/GN3 • Derbys. RO, letters to Sir R. J. Wilmot-Horton • Dorset RO, letters to Sir Rowland Hill • Durham RO, letters to Lord Londonderry, D/Lo • Lpool RO, letters to fourteenth earl of Derby, 920 Der 14, box 137 • NA Scot., letters to G. W. Hope, GD 364 • NA Scot., corresp. with Sir Andrew Leith-Hay, GD 225 • NA Scot., letters to Fox Maule, GD 45 • NL Scot., corresp. with Sir George Brown, MSS 1847–1859, 2837–2854, *passim* • NL Scot., letters to Lord Lynedoch, MSS 3609–3623, *passim* • NL Wales, letters to Louisa Lloyd • NRA, priv. coll., letters to Lord Cathcart • PRO, corresp. with Stratford Canning, FO 352 • PRO, letters to Lord Cowley, FO 519 • PRO, corresp. with Lord John Russell, PRO 30/22 • U. Durham L., corresp. with third Earl Grey, GRE/B120/5 • U. Nott. L., corresp. with duke of Newcastle, NE • U. Southampton L., corresp. with Lord Palmerston, MS 62 • U. Southampton L., corresp. and MSS as secretary to the duke of Wellington, 9/2 • U. Southampton L., letters to the duke of Wellington, MS 61 • U. Southampton L., letters to duke of Wellington, MS 61 • W. Sussex RO, letters to Lady Caroline Maxse • W. Sussex RO, letters to the duke of Richmond, vol. 3 • Woburn Abbey, Bedfordshire, letters to Lord George William Russell

Likenesses T. Heaphy, watercolour drawing, 1813–14, NPG • F. Grant, oils, 1853; formerly at the United Service Club, London • R. Fenton, group portrait, photograph, 1855, NPG • R. Fenton, photograph, 1855, NPG [*see illus.*] • oils, *c*.1858 (after F. Grant), Army and Navy Club, London • T. J. Barker, group portrait, oils (*Duke of Wellington writing for reinforcements at the bridge at Sauroren*), Stratfield Saye, Hampshire • Edwards, bust • J. W. Pieneman, group portrait, oils (*The battle of Waterloo*), Rijksmuseum, Amsterdam • J. W. Pieneman, oils, Wellington Museum, London • W. Salter, group portrait, oils (*The Waterloo banquet at Apsley House*), Wellington Museum, London • W. Salter, oils, NPG • memorial tablet, Badminton estate church, Gloucestershire • memorial tablet, Great Bookham church, Surrey

Somerset, FitzRoy Richard, fourth Baron Raglan (1885–1964), anthropologist, was born at 12 Albert Mansions, Victoria Street, Westminster, on 10 June 1885, the eldest son of George FitzRoy Henry Somerset, third Baron Raglan (1857–1921), and Lady Ethel Jemima (1857–1940), daughter of Walter William Brabazon Ponsonby, seventh earl of Bessborough. He was educated at Eton College and at the Royal Military College, Sandhurst, and joined the Grenadier Guards in 1905, advancing to captain in 1914 and to major in 1919. In 1912–13 he served as aide-de-camp to the governor of Hong Kong. Between 1913 and 1919 he was seconded to the Egyptian army, and was invested with the order of the Nile by the Egyptian (khedival) government. Somerset then served as a political officer in Palestine (1919–21), and resigned from the army in 1922 after succeeding to the barony. He had also served with the Monmouthshire militia from 1902 to 1904, and was later named as lieutenant-colonel and then brevet colonel in that regiment (1930–35). On 9 April 1923 he married the Hon. Julia Hamilton (*d.* 1971), daughter of Robert Archibald Hamilton, eleventh Lord Belhaven and Stenton; they had two sons and two daughters.

Lord Raglan took a keen interest in the county of Monmouth, where the family estate was located at Cefn Tila Court, Llandenni, near Usk, serving as justice of the peace and as lord lieutenant of the county from 1942 until his death. He also served on the county council from 1928 to 1949. His interest in the antiquities of Monmouthshire led him to write, with Sir Cyril Fox, three volumes on the county's medieval and later domestic architecture. He was chairman of the art and archaeology committee of the National Museum of Wales (1949–51) and president of the National Museum of Wales from 1957 to 1962. He was also president of the Royal Anthropological Institute from 1955 to 1957.

Lord Raglan's interests ranged widely: he was seen as a folklorist and antiquarian as well as a student of myth and ritual in all societies. From time to time he became embroiled in controversies that showed his individualistic bent. In 1938 he declared his wish to give up his job at the Ministry of Information on the grounds that he was not doing enough work to justify his salary. In 1958 he agitated Welsh nationalist feelings by declaring Welsh a 'moribund' language. Demands were made for his resignation from the National Museum of Wales, but he stood fast. (The motto of the Raglan barony is *Mutare vel timere sperno*: 'I scorn to change or to fear').

In his published work, Raglan concentrated much of his attention on the nature of history and the relationship between myth and ritual. He located himself in that camp which declared that myth-making—as distinct from mere story-telling—sprang from and was dependent on ritual. *Jocasta's Crime* (1933) bears his hallmarks: a clear, jargon-free and almost chatty style, evidence of wide reading (there is a neat and witty puncturing of Freud's position in *Totem and Taboo*), and at the same time a disorganized and episodic approach, and a bland, unquestioning self-assurance in his analysis. Raglan's position on myth and ritual never changed much and is evident in its clearest form in the chapter he contributed to the collection *Myth: a Symposium* (1955), where he saw, typically, 'a simple scientific principle that similar causes produce similar effects'—and thus a worldwide, transcultural inclination toward ritual-making which *must* produce similar myths. In *The Hero: a Study in Tradition, Myth and Drama* (1936), Raglan's major work, specific thoughts on the hero (in 'Myth') are presented between two sections ('Tradition' and 'Drama') of little enduring merit. In this central section he lays out a pattern of twenty-two 'well-marked features and incidents' that make up the biography of a hero-king, an analysis which continues to have value, and may even be called a classic contribution to the study of the hero-type. The book has remained in print almost continuously since. Raglan's other anthropological works included *How Came Civilisation?* (1939), *Death and Rebirth* (1945), *The Origin of Religion* (1949), and *The Temple and the House* (1964); this series was interrupted by two volumes on public affairs: *The Science of Peace* (1933) and *If I were Dictator* (1934).

The endurance of Raglan's reputation remains a moot point. Critics, especially from the universities, were not impressed by Raglan's amateur status, and possibly resented his broad appeal and wide readership. Certainly he belongs to a mostly discredited school of myth analysis, but he was of his time and his class. He died at his home, Cefn Tila Court, on 14 September 1964, and his *Times* obituarist approvingly quoted a reviewer, for whom Raglan exemplified 'that characteristic disdain for received ideas which is a precious eccentricity of the British aristocracy'. Another reviewer (Edmund Leach, in the *New York Review of Books*) was perhaps more usefully acute: though Raglan never followed up his insights, and though much of what he put forward was simply 'poppycock', in *The Hero* he can be said to have anticipated by twenty years 'the seriously professional analysis of the structure of myth', later made 'academically respectable' by Claude Lévi-Strauss (Leach, 16–17).

DEAN A. MILLER

Sources Lord Raglan, *The hero: a study in tradition, myth, and drama* (1936) • Lord Raglan, *Jocasta's crime* (1933) • *The Times* (15 Sept 1964) • Lord Raglan, 'Myth and ritual', *Myth: a symposium*, ed. T. Sebeok (1955), 122–35 • E. Leach, 'Testament of an English eccentric', *New York Review of Books*, 5 (16 Sept 1965), 16–17 • D. A. Miller, *The epic hero* (2000) • J. Fontenrose, *The ritual theory of myth* (1966) • GEC, *Peerage* • b. cert. • d. cert.

Likenesses D. Levine, caricature, repro. in Leach, 'Testament of an English eccentric'

Wealth at death £151,233: probate, 15 Feb 1965, *CGPLA Eng. & Wales* • 1100 acres in Monmouthshire

Somerset, Lord Granville Charles Henry (1792–1848), politician, was born on 27 December 1792, the second of ten children of Henry Charles Somerset, sixth duke of Beaufort (1766–1835), and his wife, Charlotte Sophia (1771–1854), daughter of Granville Leveson-Gower, first marquess of Stafford (1721–1803), and his third wife, Susannah. His mother was an evangelical Methodist known for her piety. The estates and influence of the dukes of Beaufort, whose seat was at Badminton, ranged from the counties and boroughs of Brecon and Glamorgan to Monmouth, Gloucester, Wiltshire, and Oxfordshire. Assured of a parliamentary seat, Somerset was encouraged to become his father's man of business and to pursue a political career. Disfigurement by a riding accident early in life did not impair his prowess as a sportsman and rider after hounds, but to save him embarrassment he was not sent away to school with his elder brother, Henry, marquess of Worcester [*see below*]. He matriculated at Christ Church, Oxford, on 19 January 1811, and graduated BA on 4 November 1813 with the second prize in classics, MA on 29 March 1817, and DCL on 10 June 1834. Nothing is known of Somerset's attachments prior to his marriage on 27 July 1822 to Emily Smith (*d.* 1869), the youngest daughter of Robert *Smith, first Baron Carrington (1752–1838), of the Smith family of bankers; £30,000 was settled on her to accompany Somerset's portion of £10,000.

On 20 May 1816 Somerset succeeded his uncle Lord Arthur Somerset (1780–1816) as MP for Monmouthshire, and he retained the seat for life. A committed tory and opposed to parliamentary reform, he was appointed a junior Treasury lord by Lord Liverpool in March 1819; he resigned when the pro-Catholic Canning became prime minister in April 1827. He dated his lifelong commitment to the cause of the insane, whom he served from August 1828 as a metropolitan lunacy commissioner, to his service on the select committee of 1827 on pauper lunatics. He returned to the Treasury under the duke of Wellington in January 1828, declared with him for Roman Catholic emancipation in January 1829, and chaired Peel's London committee at the ensuing Oxford University by-election. Ousted with Wellington in November 1830, he proposed Peel as their party leader in the House of Commons.

From 1830 to 1834 Somerset played a leading part in organizing parliamentary and constituency opposition to Lord Grey's reform administration, being involved from the outset in establishing and managing the Charles Street committee and the Carlton Club. His own unopposed election in 1831, after voting against parliamentary reform on 22 March and 19 April, was attributed to his popularity as a hardworking MP attentive to his constituents' interests. He failed on 7 September 1831 to extend Monmouthshire's borough representation under the Reform Act, and was incensed at the forfeiture of the county's intended third seat to provide separate representation for Merthyr Tudful from 1832. However, he secured boundary changes favourable to the Beaufort interest in East and West Gloucestershire and Stroud. Perceiving voter registration, active local committees, and suitable, well-funded candidates as the keys to electoral success, from June 1831 onwards he oversaw the establishment and maintenance of networks of agents, attorneys, barristers, and Conservative landowners in constituencies influenced by his aristocratic relations. Undeterred by defeats in Gloucestershire and in the Monmouth district of Boroughs in 1832, he persevered and gained a reputation as an outstanding party manager at the general elections of 1835, 1837, and 1841, when his system was adopted throughout England and Wales.

From December 1834 to April 1835 Somerset was commissioner of woods and forests in Peel's ministry, with a seat on the privy council. As one of Peel's inner circle he gave advice on election matters, acted with Thomas Francis Fremantle, afterwards Baron Cottesloe (1798–1890), Charles Ross (1800–1860), and Francis Robert Bonham (1785–1863) as a semi-official party whip, and was instrumental in ensuring that the tory veteran William Holmes (1779–1851) resumed that role in 1838. From September 1841 to July 1846 he was chancellor of the duchy of Lancaster in Peel's administration—passed over for the Irish secretaryship he coveted and for the governor-generalship of India lest caricaturists capitalize on his deformity and burlesque manner. On his appointment to the cabinet on 16 May 1844 Gladstone commended him as an excellent administrator, good tempered and good humoured but scarcely a statesman. Loyalty to Peel over corn-law reform in December 1845 cost Somerset the electoral support of his brother Henry, who spent £20,000 promoting the candidature of their protectionist cousin Captain Arthur Somerset against him at the general election of 1847. Winning by 2235 to 2188 votes, Somerset was none the less broken by the ordeal, and died on 23 February 1848 at his home in Clarges Street, London, attended by his brother. He was buried a few days later at Kensal Green cemetery. His will, which provided for his widow and five children, was proved under £2000 on 26 May 1848 and was executed by his widow and by Lord Sandon.

Somerset's brother **Henry Somerset**, seventh duke of Beaufort (1792–1853), sportsman and courtier, was born on 5 February 1792. He was tutored by the Revd Walter Fletcher of Dalston, Cumberland, and Edward Vernon, archbishop of York, entered Westminster School in 1805, and matriculated at Christ Church, Oxford, on 21 October 1809. Styled marquess of Worcester (1803–35), he was renowned for his amorous escapades and as the founder in 1819 of the 'four-in-hand club' and leader of the Badminton and Windsor hunts. He joined the 10th hussars in 1810 and almost immediately began an affair with the courtesan Harriette Wilson, which, as his parents intended and her *Memoirs* (published in 1825) confirm, languished while he was aide-de-camp to the duke of Wellington in the Iberian peninsula from 1812 to 1814. On 25 July 1814 he married Wellington's niece Georgiana Frederica Fitzroy (1792–1821) at the house of her stepfather, Charles Culling Smith (1775–1853). He was devastated by her death on 11 May 1821 from an inflammation of the lungs, but was soon portrayed in caricature as suitor to the widow of the wealthy banker Thomas Coutts, to the pregnant Miss Calcraft, and to Lady Jane Paget, daughter of the marquess of Anglesey, to whom he was briefly engaged. On 29 June 1822 he married his late wife's half-sister Emily Frances (1800–1889), daughter of Anne and Charles Culling Smith, and went to France. The marriage, although not illegal, was voidable under the consanguinity laws, placing the legitimacy of any issue at risk. Attempts to have their union validated under the act of 1823 failed, and a second ceremony at Constance on 21 October 1823 was not recognized as a foreign marriage because it was conducted under Lutheran rites. In 1825 the couple, on whom over £50,000 had been settled, returned to England with Somerset's two daughters and their only son, Henry Charles Fitzroy Somerset (1824–1899), for whom the sixth duke of Beaufort was godfather. Six daughters were subsequently born to the marriage, which was safeguarded retrospectively under the act of 1835.

Excluding a three-month period, April to July 1831, Worcester was tory MP for Monmouth Boroughs from December 1813 until his defeat by Benjamin Hall, afterwards Baron Llanover (1802–1867), in December 1832. He sat for Gloucestershire West from January to 23 November 1835, when he succeeded his father as seventh duke. Undistinguished as an Admiralty lord from May 1815 to March 1819, his main political contribution, for which on Peel's recommendation he was made KG on 11 April 1842, lay in his sponsorship of his brother's electioneering activities. He died of gout on 17 November 1853 at Badminton and was buried in the chapel there on 24 November.

MARGARET ESCOTT

Sources HoP, *Commons, 1790–1820* • HoP, *Commons, 1820–32* [draft] • BL, Peel Papers, Add. MSS 40395–40599 [letters indexed to Henry Somerset, seventh duke of Beaufort, Lord Granville Somerset, and F. Bonham] • priv. coll., Badminton Muniments, Fm M 4/1, O 1/9/2 • *The Times* (1795–1838) [CD-ROM] [Lord Granville Somerset (1816–48), the marquess of Worcester (1803–35), and the duke of Beaufort (1835–53)] • *Hansard 2* (1820–30), vols. 1–25 • *Hansard 3* (1830–48), vols. 1–100 • *GM*, 2nd ser., 29 (1848), 432 • *GM*, 2nd ser., 41 (1854), 80 • *The Times* (24 Feb 1848) • *The Times* (19 Nov 1853) • *The Times* (26 Nov 1853) • *Monmouthshire Merlin* (26 Feb 1848) • *Monmouthshire Merlin* (3 March 1848) • *Harriette Wilson's memoirs of herself and others*, ed. J. Laver (1929) • W. T. Morgan, 'County elections in Monmouthshire, 1705–1847', *National Library of Wales Journal*, 10 (1957–8), 175–84 • N. Gash, *Politics in the age of Peel* (1953); repr. (1962) • N. Gash, 'The organisation of the conservative party, 1832–1846', *Parliamentary History*, 1 (1982), 137–59; 2 (1983), 131–52 [in 2 pts] • U. Southampton, Hartley Library, Wellington MSS, WP1, WP2 • *GM*, 1st ser., 92/2 (1822), 178 • A. Aspinall, ed., *Three early nineteenth-century diaries* (1952) [extracts from Le Marchant, E. J. Littleton, Baron Hatherton, and E. Law, earl of Ellenborough] • *The diary of Philipp von Neumann, 1819–1850*, ed. and trans. E. Beresford Chancellor, 2 vols. (1928) • letters to Ralph Sneyd from Lord Granville Somerset, Keele University, Ralph Sneyd MSS, SC/ • Burke, *Peerage*

Archives Badminton House, Gloucestershire | BL, corresp. with Sir Robert Peel, Add. MSS 40395–40599; 40396–40555 • Bucks. RLSS, Fremantle MSS • Derbys. RO, letters to Sir R. J. Wilmot-Horton • Keele University Library, letters to Ralph Sneyd • Lpool RO, letters to Lord Stanley • NL Wales, Bute, Twiston-Davies, Llangiby Castle, and Tredegar MSS • U. Southampton L., letters to the duke of Wellington

Likenesses R. Cosway, watercolour, *c.*1812 (Henry Somerset), Badminton • G. Cruickshanks, caricature, 1822 (Henry Somerset), BL • I. R. Cruikshank, caricature, 1822 (Henry Somerset), BL • W. Heath, caricature, 1822 (Henry Somerset), BL • IRC, caricature, 1822 (Henry Somerset), BL • Williams, caricature, 1822 (Henry Somerset), BL • caricatures, 1823–5 (Henry Somerset), BL • J. Fairburn/R. Cruikshank, caricature, 1825 (Henry Somerset), BL • W. H., caricature, 1825 (Henry Somerset), BL • W. Gush, portrait, *c.*1837 (Henry Somerset), Badminton House, Gloucestershire • Count D'Orsay, pencil and black chalk drawing on blue paper, 1838 (Henry Somerset), NPG • E. Landseer, 1839 (Henry Somerset), Badminton, Beaufort collection • W. Behnes, bust, 1841 (Henry Somerset), Badminton, Beaufort collection • H. Aitken, oils, 1845 (Henry Somerset), NPG • H. Alken, portrait, 1845? (Henry Somerset), NPG • J. Doyle, drawing, 1848 (Henry Somerset), BM • G. G. Adams, bust, 1854 (Henry Somerset), Badminton, Beaufort collection • J. R. Swinton, drawing, 1854 (Henry Somerset), Badminton • N. Schavoni, 1858 (Henry Somerset), Badminton, Beaufort collection • H. & W. Barraud, portrait (Henry Somerset), repro. in S. Sitwell, *Conversation pieces* (1936) • J. Doyle, two caricatures, pencil drawings, BM • G. Hayter, group portrait (*The trial of Queen Caroline, 1820*), NPG • G. Hayter, group portrait, oils (*The House of Commons, 1833*), NPG • F. C. Lewis, stipple (for Grillion's Club series; after J. Slater), BM, NPG • F. X. Winterhalter, portrait (Henry Somerset), Badminton • G. Zobel, engraving (after drawing by J. R. Swinton, 1854) • caricatures (Henry Somerset), BL • engraving (Henry Somerset), repro. in *ILN* (26 Nov 1853)

Wealth at death under £2000: will, PRO, PROB 11/2075, fol. 434; PRO, death duty registers, IR 26/1818/398 • under £25,000—Henry Somerset: will, PRO, PROB 11/2187, fol. 182; PRO, PROB 8/248

Somerset, Henry, first duke of Beaufort (1629–1700), nobleman, was born at Raglan Castle, Monmouthshire, the only son of Edward *Somerset, sixth earl and second marquess of Worcester (*d.* 1667), and his wife, Elizabeth (*d.* 1635), daughter of Sir William Dormer. His grandfather thought Lord Herbert, as he was styled, 'the only hope' of his Roman Catholic family, and sent him to France and Italy in 1644 with his tutor John Clarke (Badminton muniments, P4/3). He returned in 1650 to find Raglan destroyed, the Somerset estate sequestrated by parliament, and his inheritance wasted largely as a result of wartime loans to the king. He spent the next twenty years trying to restore his family's fortune. In 1651 he negotiated a settlement with Cromwell, confirming the latter's ownership of many south Wales properties in return for the right to compound. Hostile observers later suggested that he became 'a great Favourite' with the lord protector and 'had 2,000*l. per. Ann.* given him, and Lodgings assign'd him at *Whitehall*' (Rogers, 79–80).

In 1655 Herbert acquired by devise from his cousin Elizabeth, daughter and heir of Thomas Somerset, Viscount Somerset of Cashel, an estate at Badminton, Gloucestershire. Here he took up residence when, on 17 August 1657,

Henry Somerset, first duke of Beaufort (1629–1700), by Sir Godfrey Kneller, *c.*1680

he married, before a Clerkenwell JP, Mary [*see* Somerset, Mary (*bap.* 1630, *d.* 1715)], eldest daughter of the royalist martyr Arthur *Capel, Lord Capel of Hadham, and widow of Henry Seymour, Lord Beauchamp. His marriage enhanced his standing among royalists such as Sir Edward Hyde, who later resided at Worcester House in London. It also confirmed his conversion to the protestant faith. Only later did he stand accused of crypto-Catholicism by Monmouthshire natives who could not forget that his grandfather had established a Jesuit mission at Raglan and that his father had tried to raise an Irish Catholic army for Charles I. Herbert's father's wartime activities and his wife Mary's active royalism led to his arrest during the Gloucestershire plot. He spent two months in the Tower before being released on 1 November 1659. He sat in the Convention Parliament and was chosen one of the twelve commissioners from the Commons to attend Charles II at Breda (7 May 1660).

After the Restoration, Herbert was MP for Monmouthshire from 1660 to 3 April 1667, when he succeeded his father as third marquess of Worcester. In 1660 the king appointed him to serve as constable of St Briavels Castle, warden of the Forest of Dean (18 June), and lord lieutenant of Gloucestershire, Herefordshire, and Monmouthshire (30 July). He spent the next several years seeking out potential rebels and undermining plots against the government. In 1662 he saw to the demolition of the walls and fortifications at Gloucester. The following year he persuaded the king of the importance of maintaining a garrison at Chepstow Castle, describing it as 'the key' to south Wales and as 'a bridle to the ill-affected who abound in those parts' (*CSP dom.*, *1663–4*, 359). He even paid many of the costs himself. Not surprisingly, Monmouthshire residents claimed that he used it as a private army. When Sir Trevor Williams was returned for parliament in 1667, 'six files of musketeers were sent to Monmouth to awe the town', according to a report by local MPs fourteen years later. They claimed that soldiers who had guarded the marquess's property rights in Wentwood Forest in 1678 had been 'employed to rob the country of their wood'.

In 1672 Worcester was appointed lord president of the council of the marches of Wales, privy councillor (17 April), and knight of the Garter (29 May). He took his responsibilities seriously, attending nearly half of the privy council meetings during Charles II's reign. His opposition to the Exclusion Bill led the Commons to call for the abolition of the council in the marches and to petition the king for his removal from office in January 1681. Instead, Charles II advanced him to the title of duke of Beaufort (2 December 1682), reminding contemporaries that he was descended, albeit illegitimately, from King Edward III through John de Beaufort, eldest son of John of Gaunt. Beaufort was also given public recognition by Nahum Tate in his second part of *Absalom and Achitophel* (1682) in which he was characterized as Bezaliel, designer of the Tabernacle (Exodus 31:3)

> To Aid the Crown and State his greatest Zeal,
> His Second Care that Service to Conceal.

Beaufort played a leading part in the tory reaction of the 1680s, reforming the county and borough magistracies, remodelling militia commands, and encouraging the surrender of corporate charters in Wales and the border counties. To this end, in 1684 he took a month-long ducal progress through Wales which was chronicled by Thomas Dingley in *Notitia Cambro-Britannica: a Voyage of North and South Wales* (printed eventually in 1864). The progress was marked by considerable pageantry, and onlookers marvelled at the 'splendour of the great man's equippage' (BL, Add. MS 70013, fol. 209). Lord Keeper Guilford, who visited Badminton in the early 1680s, noted the:

> princely way of living, which that noble duke used, above any other, except crowned heads, that I have had notice of in Europe; and, in some respects greater than most of them, to whom he might have been an example. (North, 1.169–73)

During the 1670s Badminton had been rebuilt in the fashionable Palladian style, with formal gardens and landscaped walks that imitated Louis XIV's Versailles. Here, Mary Somerset created a celebrated botanical garden with plants from Africa, Japan, the East Indies, and the Americas.

Beaufort supported the prince of Denmark as chief mourner at the funeral of Charles II (14 February 1685) and he bore the queen's crown at the coronation of James II (23 April). He was appointed gentleman of the bedchamber (16 May) and colonel of the 11th regiment of foot (20 June). In June he defended Bristol against the duke of Monmouth, raising twenty-one companies of foot and four troops of horse. He praised his Welsh troops as 'another complexion than that of theirs in Somersetshire, and being better disciplined, and more soldier-like than militias usually are' (BL, Add. MS 15892, fol. 214). James II spoke of his service with 'the greatest kindness' and honoured him with a visit to Badminton on 24 September 1685, but he could not command his continued loyalty (Badminton muniments, FmE 4/1/19). When the Chepstow Castle garrison was disbanded at the end of 1685 the duke wrote angrily of the 'great rejoicing it will cause among the factions, that have so often bragged they have got me out from my command there' (BL, Add. MS 15892, fol. 241). In 1688 Beaufort surrendered Bristol to troops led by the earl of Shrewsbury and Sir John Guise, claiming that the city was 'incapable of defense' (BL, Add. MS 41805, fols. 156–7). He tried instead to keep Gloucestershire safe from invading forces, particularly as William, prince of Orange, had threatened to 'lay Badminton in ashes' (Bodl. Oxf., MS Carte 130, fol. 307). Meanwhile, Beaufort's eldest surviving son and heir, Charles Somerset (1660–1698), furnished himself with horses at his father's house in London and joined William at Exeter.

Beaufort was 'received very coldly' when he tried to transfer his loyalties to William (Singer, 2.227–8). He took the oaths in March 1689 but refused to declare William and Mary his 'right and lawful' sovereigns. He was removed from his lieutenancies in 1689 and thereafter retired from public life. On 7 September 1690 he entertained the king with a 'noble, but not satisfactory' reception at Badminton (*Memoirs of … Ailesbury*, 1.268). His refusal to sign the Association caused him to be suspected of conspiratorial activities, and government officials searched his house at Chelsea in 1696. In July 1698 his son died as a result of a coach accident in Wales, leaving Beaufort's fourteen-year-old grandson Henry *Somerset (1684–1714) heir to the Somerset estate. Beaufort himself died at Badminton on 21 January 1700 and was buried in the Beaufort chapel in St George's Chapel, Windsor; in 1878 his enormous baroque funeral monument was removed to Badminton. He was survived by his wife, Mary, who died in 1715. Apart from Henry, who had died young, and Charles, they had three younger sons and four daughters, of whom the second, Mary (*d.* 1733), had married, in 1685, James, duke of Ormond; the third, Henrietta (*d.* 1715), had married first, in 1686, Henry, Lord O'Brien, and second, Henry, earl of Suffolk; while the fourth, Anne [*see* Coventry, Anne, countess of Coventry], had married, on 4 May 1691, Thomas, earl of Coventry. MOLLY MCCLAIN

Sources M. McClain, *Beaufort: the duke and his duchess, 1657–1715* (2001) • M. McClain, '"I Scorn to Change or Fear": Henry Somerset, first duke of Beaufort and the survival of the nobility following the English civil war', PhD diss., Yale U., 1994 • M. W. Helms and J. P. Ferris, 'Somerset, Henry', HoP, *Commons, 1660–90* • *The manuscripts of the duke of Beaufort … the earl of Donoughmore*, HMC, 27 (1891) • *CSP dom.* • R. North, *The lives of … Francis North … Dudley North … and … John North*, ed. A. Jessopp, 3 vols. (1890) • Badminton Muniments • N. Rogers, *Memoirs of Monmouth-shire, 1708* (1983) • *The correspondence of Henry Hyde, earl of Clarendon, and of his brother Laurence Hyde, earl of Rochester*, ed. S. W. Singer, 2 vols. (1828) • *Memoirs of Thomas, earl of Ailesbury*, ed. W. E. Buckley, 2 vols., Roxburghe Club, 122 (1890) • GEC, *Peerage* • BL, Add. MSS 70013, 15892, 41805 • Bodl. Oxf., MS Carte 130, fol. 307

Archives Badminton House, Gloucestershire, family corresp. and MSS • BL, pedigree, Add. MS 43378 • Glos. RO | Herefs. RO, letters and commissions • NL Wales, corresp. with Edward Mansell • Yale U., Beinecke L., letters to Sir R. Southwell

Likenesses P. Lely, oils, *c.*1660–1662, Badminton House, Gloucestershire • P. Lely, oils, *c.*1671, Badminton House, Gloucestershire • G. Kneller, oils, *c.*1680, Badminton House, Gloucestershire [*see illus.*] • S. Browne, group portrait, oils, 1685 (with family), Badminton House, Gloucestershire • S. Browne, group portrait, oils, 1685, Badminton House, Gloucestershire • R. White, line engraving, *c.*1700 (after G. Kneller), BM, NPG; repro. in J. Guillim, *A display of heraldry* (1679) • W. Faithorne, line engraving, BM • attrib. G. Gibbons, tomb effigy on monument, St Michael's Church, Badminton • J. Roettier, silver medal, BM • oils, Badminton House, Gloucestershire

Wealth at death over £100,000: Badminton muniments, D2700 FmF 4/2/2 (1710); memorandum in the case of *Granville* v. *Mary, dowager duchess of Beaufort*

Somerset, Henry, second duke of Beaufort (1684–1714), politician, was born on 2 April 1684 at Monmouth Castle, the son of Charles Somerset, marquess of Worcester (1660–1698), and his wife, Rebecca (1665/6–1712), the daughter of Sir Josiah *Child of Wanstead. His father having died in a coach accident in July 1698, Henry became the second duke of Beaufort on the death of his paternal grandfather, Henry *Somerset, first duke, on 21 January 1700. He married his first wife, Mary (1683–1705), the daughter of Charles Sackville, earl of Dorset, on 7 July 1702 at Knole, Kent. In the same year he entertained Queen Anne and Prince George at the family's residence at Badminton. As a 'thorough-going tory' Beaufort removed himself from mainstream court politics during the years of the whig junto, establishing instead a high-tory drinking society, the Honourable Board of Loyal Brotherhood, in 1709.

The collapse of the whig administration in the following year prompted Beaufort to take an active role in the new ministry of Robert Harley. It was only now, as he informed Anne, that he 'could call her Queen in reality'. On 13 December 1710 he was sworn of the privy council, and in the same year he became lord lieutenant of Hampshire (he was made lord lieutenant of Gloucestershire in 1712). Beaufort's wealth, an estimated annual rent roll of £30,000, was directed towards promoting tory fortunes in Monmouthshire, and in the final years of Anne's reign was concentrated on the Bolingbroke/Jacobite interest. His first wife died in childbirth on 18 June 1705, and on 26 February 1706 Beaufort married Rachel Noel (*d.* 1709), the daughter and coheir of Wriothesley, second earl of Gainsborough. She also died in childbirth, on 13 September 1709. His third wife was Mary Osborne (1688–1722), the daughter of Peregrine, second duke of Leeds, whom he married on 14 September 1711. He died at Badminton, Gloucestershire, on 24 May 1714 from an inflammation brought on by having drunk considerable amounts of alcohol after exercise, and was buried there. The title passed first to his son, also Henry Somerset (1707–1745), from his second marriage and then, in February 1745, to the second duke's third but next surviving son, **Charles Noel Somerset**, fourth duke of Beaufort (1709–1756), politician.

Charles Noel Somerset was born on 12 September 1709 and educated at Westminster School and University College, Oxford, where he matriculated in June 1725 and graduated MA (1727) and DCL (1736). A staunch tory like his father, Charles was elected MP for Monmouthshire in 1731 and sat for Monmouth borough between 1734 and 1745, when he assumed the dukedom on his brother's death. A determined critic of the Walpole administration and an advocate of the Jacobite cause, Somerset emerged in 1744 as the head of the parliamentary tory party after Lord Gower's move to join the broad-bottom ministry. Despite his support of the Stuarts, Beaufort's involvement in the planning for French involvement in the 1745 Jacobite rising went unpunished. Towards the close of the decade he was active in securing the support of Frederick, prince of Wales, for the tories, though in these years the duke never matched the dynamic leadership that he achieved in the period immediately after 1744. On 1 May 1740 he had married Elizabeth (1718/19–1799), the daughter of John Symes Berkeley of Stoke Gifford, Gloucestershire, and the sister of the colonial governor Norbone Berkeley, Lord Botetourt. Beaufort died on 28 October 1756 and was buried at Badminton, whereupon the dukedom passed to his son, Henry Somerset (1744–1803).

PHILIP CARTER

Sources *DNB* • GEC, *Peerage* • G. S. Holmes, *British politics in the age of Anne*, rev. edn (1987) • L. Colley, *In defiance of oligarchy: the tory party, 1714–60* (1982) • E. Cruickshanks, 'Somerset, Lord Charles Noel', HoP, *Commons, 1715–54*

Archives PRO, legal papers, C 107/22 30 • W. Yorks. AS, Leeds, Yorkshire Archaeological Society, papers

Likenesses M. Dahl, oils, *c*.1712–1714, Badminton House, Gloucestershire • P. Angelis, group portrait, oils, 1713 (*Queen Anne and the knights of the Garter*), NPG • attrib. M. Dahl, oils, Badminton House, Gloucestershire • G. Vertue, line engraving (after M. Dahl, *c*.1712–1714), BM

Somerset, Henry, seventh duke of Beaufort (1792–1853). *See under* Somerset, Lord Granville Charles Henry (1792–1848).

Somerset, Henry Hugh Arthur Fitzroy, tenth duke of Beaufort (1900–1984), founder of Badminton horse trials and huntsman, was born at 19 Curzon Street, Mayfair, London, on 4 April 1900, the only son and youngest of the three children of Henry Adelbert Wellington Fitzroy Somerset, ninth duke of Beaufort (1847–1924), and his wife, Louise Emily (*d.* 1945), widow of Baron Carlo de Tuyll and daughter of William Henry Harford, of Oldown, Almondsbury, Gloucestershire. As marquess of Worcester he was educated at Eton College and at the Royal Military College, Sandhurst. He was then commissioned into the Royal Horse Guards, with special leave to hunt two days a week. He regretted that he was too young to have seen active service in the First World War.

Worcester was given his own pack of harriers at the age of eleven and was known as 'master' by his friends and family for the rest of his life. As master of a great family pack, fox-hunting became 'a permanent love affair … the basis of my very existence'. Like his father and grandfather before him Beaufort (he became duke in 1924) was 'a sportsman by profession', hunting his own pack for forty-seven years, an unparalleled record. His knowledge of every aspect of the sport from kennel management to the correct position of a tie-pin (he regarded the word stock as an unacceptable neologism) and first aid on the hunting field was displayed in his *Fox Hunting* (1980). His long mastership he regarded as a time consuming and expensive duty rewarded by the 'exhilaration and excitement and, what is more, the sense of achievement that is experienced when a successful hunt is concluded'. He was a great breeder and judge of hounds and his proudest possessions were his old established female lines.

Like most of his forebears Beaufort took little interest in politics: 'local leadership in country sports and agricultural matters', he wrote, 'took precedence'. His own leadership was more than local. As chairman of the Master of Foxhounds Association and president of the British Field Sports Association he was the first figure in the hunting world. As such he was the chosen target of those who opposed his sport. In December 1984 a group of people opposed to hunting attempted to dig up his body in order to present his severed head to the daughter of the queen, Princess Anne, since he was considered guilty of introducing the royal family to fox-hunting.

Beaufort was a natural and bold rider from childhood. As president of the British Olympic Association he was appalled at the performance of the British team as a 'bunch of amateurs' in the Olympic games of 1948. It was to improve standards that in 1949 he established at the family home, Badminton, the three-day trials that were to become the most important event in the British equestrian calendar. His other activities—he was president or chairman of some seventy associations and charities—ranged from the chancellorship of Bristol University (1966–70) to the presidency of the Battersea dogs' home. He was president of the MCC when England regained the Ashes in 1953. On 14 June 1923 he married Lady (Victoria Constance) Mary Cambridge (*d.* 1987), daughter of Adolphus Charles Alexander Albert Edward George Philip Louis Ladislaus (son of the prince of Teck), first marquess of Cambridge and governor and constable of Windsor Castle. She was the favourite niece of George V and Queen Mary; the latter spent the years of the Second World War as a guest at Badminton. The duke and his duchess resisted with tact Queen Mary's eccentricities, which included the tearing down of ivy and the removal of established trees. The duke's close personal connection with the royal family was cemented by his appointment as master of the horse, a post that he held longer than any of his predecessors. As the third great officer of the household he was the sovereign's personal attendant on state occasions. He was proud that the same office had been held by his ancestor in the reign of Elizabeth I and that Elizabeth II valued the counsel of his sound common sense.

Beaufort regarded his father as the inspiration of his life. But whereas the ninth duke was somewhat autocratic his son, apart from the occasional sharp rebuke provoked by bad behaviour in the hunting field, was an amiable man, loved by his family and friends, an admirer of ladies and much admired by them. He took his great possessions and duties as a matter of course. When it was suggested that his heir's son be called John, he remarked that it was a good family name for, as a Plantagenet, he was a direct, though illegitimate, descendant of John of Gaunt. He did not relish change. He had been lord lieutenant of Gloucestershire and when Badminton was absorbed in the newly created county of Avon he protested that he had no desire to live in a four-letter county.

He was appointed GCVO in 1930, sworn of the privy council in 1936, and created KG in 1937. He was high steward of Bristol, Gloucester, and Tewkesbury. He died on 5 February 1984 at Badminton and was buried in the churchyard of St Michael and All Saints, Badminton, three days later. He had no children and was succeeded as duke of Beaufort by his cousin David Robert Somerset (*b.* 1928), an art dealer and formidable horseman, who had served with the tenth duke as joint master of the Beaufort.

RAYMOND CARR, *rev.*

Sources Duke of Beaufort, *Memories* (1981) • Duke of Beaufort, *Fox hunting* (1980) • O. Sitwell, *Queen Mary, and others* (1974) • B. Campbell, *The Badminton tradition* (1978) • R. Carr, *English fox hunting* (1976) • *The Times* (6 Feb 1984) • *The Times* (9 Feb 1984) • private information (1990)

Archives FILM BFI NFTVA, current affairs footage • BFI NFTVA, news footage

Wealth at death £4,074,537: probate, 13 June 1984, *CGPLA Eng. & Wales* • £1,405,200: further grant, 14 Aug 1984, *CGPLA Eng. & Wales*

Somerset [*née* Somers-Cocks], **Lady Isabella Caroline** [Lady Henry Somerset] (**1851–1921**), temperance activist and campaigner for women's rights, was born in London on 3 August 1851, the eldest of the three daughters of Charles Somers Somers-Cocks (1819–1883), Viscount Eastnor and (from 1852) third Earl Somers, and his wife, Virginia (1829–1910), daughter of James Pattle, an official in the Bengal civil service, and his wife, Adelaide de l'Etang. After a private education and two London seasons Lady Isabella married on 6 February 1872 Lord Henry Richard Charles Somerset (1849–1932), son of Henry Charles Fitzroy Somerset, eighth duke of Beaufort (1824–1899), and his wife, Lady Georgiana Charlotte Curzon (*d.* 1906). The match seemed ideal, and produced in 1874 a son, Henry Charles Somers Augustus, but soon Lord Henry's homosexual proclivities broke up the marriage. Lady Henry Somerset rejected divorce as contrary to church teaching, and opted for a separation. A custody battle ensued over their only child, which she won in 1878; she thereafter adopted the style of Lady Isabella Somerset. Because of the adverse publicity over the case she retreated from society life and took up charity work in Ledbury, Herefordshire, near her family home. Christian piety, her personal tragedy, and experience of charity work brought her to the cause of temperance after a close friend committed suicide while intoxicated.

Lady Isabella Somerset entered the national stage in

Lady Isabella Caroline Somerset [Lady Henry Somerset] (**1851–1921**), by Hayman Selig Mendelssohn, pubd 1893

1890, when she was elected president of the British Women's Temperance Association (BWTA). This organization, founded in 1876, affiliated with the newly organized World's Woman's Christian Temperance Union (WCTU) in 1886. Lady Isabella brought to the job eloquence as a speaker and her compelling personality. Yet her major assets were her large reserves of cash and the aristocratic pedigree that gave prestige and financial support to the fledgeling movement. Her father had died in 1883 and she inherited his large estates, including Eastnor (a Norman baronial castle), fashionable properties in London, estates in Surrey and Gloucestershire, and slums in the East End. Equally important to her credentials as a temperance leader, Lady Isabella was baptized an Anglican but worshipped in a Methodist chapel after 1885. This made her views congenial to women temperance advocates who, if not evangelical Anglicans themselves, came mainly from the nonconformist churches.

In 1891 Lady Isabella Somerset visited the United States, where she met—and forged a strong personal friendship with—Frances Willard (1839–1898), president of the World's and the American Woman's Christian Temperance Unions. She spoke at the first World's WCTU convention in Boston in November 1891. There Willard engineered Lady Isabella's election as World's WCTU vice-president. For her part Willard visited Britain for extended periods in the 1890s and lived with her friend.

Back in Britain Lady Isabella Somerset's period in office saw BWTA membership rapidly expand, and its social and political influence grow. She served during this period as the fifth-ranked member of the Women's Liberal Federation, and her politics were always closely linked with the Liberal Party. Lady Isabella forged important alliances with other reformers, including Lord Roberts, former commander of the British army in India and founder of the Army Temperance Association, and with the Salvation Army's William Booth. Her friendship with Church of England Temperance Society leader Canon A. Basil Orme Wilberforce brought her back to the fold of the Anglican church by 1897. Yet her leadership also entailed controversy for the formerly staid BWTA. Opponents felt that American influence was excessive through Somerset's friendship with Willard. More important, they objected to the 'do-everything policy' of the American Union, which involved the introduction into the BWTA of a range of activities including purity (anti-prostitution) work, foreign missions, and campaigns for peace, labour reform, and women's suffrage. Frances Willard and Lady Isabella Somerset became Fabian socialists and preached against the gospel of wealth, which they claimed was destroying Anglo-American society. Though Lady Isabella denied that she intended to turn the organization into a suffrage society, she was, along with Willard, a force within the WCTU's worldwide affiliates for the extension of women's 'emancipation', as they termed it, in all areas of life. As founder and editor of the BWTA journal, the *Woman's Signal*, Lady Isabella pursued a broad reform agenda. Disaffected BWTA members split from the organization and formed in 1894 the British Women's Total Abstinence Union, devoted narrowly to the drink question, but this organization never rivalled the BWTA's membership, which continued to grow strongly to 1914.

Feeling vindicated by the healthy increase in membership, Lady Isabella Somerset became more ambitious. She advocated in 1896 a modification in the policy of prohibition which the BWTA supported, and admitted that she served wine at parties for her son. She publicly expressed the idea that licensed prostitution in selected cantonments in India, for the benefit of the British army, was the most practicable means of dealing with the spread of venereal disease. While this view was common in the aristocracy, it was anathema to her organization. Lady Isabella clashed with Josephine Butler over the issue, and was forced in 1898 to recant her views to prevent the WCTU from disintegrating worldwide. Nevertheless, when Frances Willard died the same year Lady Isabella became World's WCTU president, a post she held until 1906. She visited the United States for the last time in 1903 and, still controversial, argued that the WCTU should adopt a system of public management of hotels similar to that introduced in Scandinavia. Only as a result of this final controversy did she give up her leadership of the British temperance movement.

Lady Isabella Somerset left the national scene in 1903, and devoted her remaining years to the Colony for Women Inebriates, Duxhurst, that she had established in Reigate, Surrey. While she sank her own fortunes into the venture, Duxhurst also received support from the BWTA and the World's WCTU. Formally opened by Princess Mary in July 1896, Duxhurst bore the influence of the Booths' idea that the poor of industrial cities should be sent to 'farm colonies' to relieve social problems. Lady Isabella believed that 'working in the open air and among fruit and vegetables would be the best cure for intemperance' (*Bath Herald*, 2 June 1896). She saw Duxhurst as a personal refuge and an alternative to her controversial public campaigns for temperance reform; she regarded it as her most lasting and effective work, though even here she could not entirely escape controversy. She faced ridicule at the outset when forced to eject one of the first inmates, a recidivist alcoholic woman named Jane Cakebread (*d.* 1899), who disrupted the facility and brought its methods into disrepute.

Lady Isabella Somerset died at 4 Gray's Inn Square, London, on 12 March 1921 after a short illness. She was a charismatic leader who brought the temperance movement from the margin of British life to as close to the centre as was possible without full voting rights. Along with Rosalind Howard, countess of Carlisle, who succeeded her as BWTA president, Somerset was one of the two most important woman temperance reformers in British history. IAN TYRRELL

Sources K. Fitzpatrick, *Lady Henry Somerset* (1923) • I. Tyrrell, *Woman's World/Woman's Empire: the Woman's Christian Temperance Union in international perspective, 1880–1930* (1991) • Woman's Christian Temperance Union Series (1977) [microfilm edn of the Temperance and Prohibition Papers] • R. Bordin, *Frances Willard: a biography* (1980) • Woman's Christian Temperance Union, Evanston, Illinois, USA, Woman's Christian Temperance Union MSS, scrapbook • Castle Howard, Yorkshire, Rosalind Stanley Howard MSS • B. Strachey, *Remarkable relations: the story of the Pearsall Smith family* (1980) • Indiana University, Lilly Library, Hannah Whithall Smith MSS • *DNB* • *Woman's Herald* (1893) • *Woman's Signal* (1894–1903) • *Annual Report of the British Women's Temperance Association* (1890–1904) [United Kingdon Alliance, London] • Women's Library, London, Butler MSS • Burke, *Peerage* • m. cert.

Archives Castle Howard, Yorkshire, Rosalind Stanley Howard MSS • Herefs. RO, corresp. relating to the Eastnor estate • Indiana University, Bloomington, Lilly Library, Hannah Whithall Smith MSS • Women's Library, London, Butler MSS • Evanston, Illinois, Woman's Christian Temperance Union MSS

Likenesses G. F. Watts, double portrait, oils, 1861 (with her sister Adeline), Eastnor Castle, Herefordshire • J. M. Cameron, photograph, 1864 (with her sister Adeline), NPG • G. F. Watts, oils, 1871, Eastnor Castle, Herefordshire • H. S. Mendelssohn, photograph, pubd 1893, NPG [*see illus.*] • Canavari, drawing, Eastnor Castle, Herefordshire • J. Russell & Sons, photograph, NPG • photograph, repro. in A. A. Gorgon, *The beautiful life of Frances Willard* (1898) • portraits, repro. in *Woman's Herald* (1893)

Wealth at death £2593 15*s.* 1*d.*: administration, 3 Dec 1921, *CGPLA Eng. & Wales*

Somerset, James (*b. c.*1741, *d.* in or after 1772), slave, was born in Africa. He was bought by European slave traders and left Africa on 10 March 1749. He must have reached Virginia either on 23 May on the *William* (from Liverpool via Calabar and Antigua) or, more likely, on 26 June on the *Susanna* (probably from Liverpool via an unknown African port). On 1 August he was sold in Virginia to Charles Stewart or Steuart, a successful Scottish merchant who became a senior colonial customs official. During his captivity he was known simply as Somerset.

In summer 1768 Stewart requested leave to return to

England, explaining that his health had been impaired by extensive travelling. He arrived in England on 10 November 1769, accompanied by Somerset, probably in the capacity of a trusted personal servant. On 10 February 1771 Somerset, who was then living (presumably with Stewart) in Baldwin's Gardens, Holborn, was baptized James Summersett at the church of St Andrew, Holborn. The baptismal register describes him as an 'adult black', aged about thirty. Although the baptism may reflect a genuine religious experience, it also had a wider significance, since it was popularly believed to confer manumission. There was no legal precedent either to confirm or dispel such a belief, but it was so pervasive that almost all British colonies that tolerated slavery had passed legislation explicitly repudiating it. It is likely therefore that Somerset's baptism signalled his first step in asserting his freedom: perhaps he was already being advised by abolitionists.

In what was later described as 'a singular instance of ingratitude' (*GM*, 443), Somerset left Stewart's service on 1 October 1771 and refused to return. His freedom lasted a bare two months: on 26 November he was seized and imprisoned. His friends promptly applied for a writ of habeas corpus to free him and his plight attracted the attention and support of Granville Sharp. Somerset's case posed considerable difficulties. Precedents concerning the legality of slavery in England were confused and contradictory, and slavery was deeply embedded into the economic fabric of the British empire. William Murray, Lord Mansfield, the then lord chief justice, did his best to persuade the parties to settle. Only when it became clear that it had become a test case did he agree to a hearing.

The return to the habeas corpus was carefully constructed to make the issues as simple as possible. It did not mention Somerset's baptism and so did not raise the question of manumission. It stated that 'negro slaves' were chattel goods, that Somerset was a slave according to the laws of Virginia and Africa, and that he was detained by order of his master in order to be sent to Jamaica and sold. The legal argument was therefore focused on whether slavery was legal in England and whether an English court could uphold colonial laws if they conflicted with English ones. Mansfield's carefully worded judgment, however, concentrated on the legality of forcible deportation. Since this was governed by a statute of 1679 (31 Charles II c.2 s.12), this enabled Mansfield to sidestep the wider issues. His judgment, delivered in July 1772, conceded an important but limited advancement of slave rights, in that invoking the 1679 statute established that slaves were servants, rather than chattels. It freed Somerset from imprisonment but left his status as a slave unresolved. However, it was widely believed that Mansfield had freed Somerset from slavery and this interpretation of the judgment has passed into Anglo-American legal mythology. Somerset himself believed that Mansfield had declared slavery to be illegal, and wrote to at least one other slave encouraging him to desert his master, on the grounds that 'Lord Mansfield had given them their freedom' (Oldham, 'New light on Mansfield', 66).

As for Somerset himself, there is little to add. When he stepped out of Westminster Hall in July 1772 he also stepped out of the historical record. Nothing is known, as yet, of his life (or death) after that date, and he remains very much a shadow at the centre of events controlled by others. RUTH PALEY

Sources D. Eltis and others, eds., *The transatlantic slave trade* (1999) [CD-ROM] · F. Hargrave, *An argument in the case of James Sommersett a negro lately determined in the court of king's bench* (1772) · J. Oldham, *The Mansfield manuscripts and the growth of English law in the eighteenth century*, 2 vols. (1992) · M. S. Weiner, 'New documentary evidence on James Somerset', unpublished paper · *Somerset v. Stewart* (1772), Lofft 1, 98 ER 499 · PRO, T 1/468 · parish register, Holborn, St Andrew's, GL, 10 May 1771 [baptism] · J. Oldham, 'New light on Mansfield and slavery', *Journal of British Studies*, 27 (1988), 45–68 · *GM*, 1st ser., 68 (1798), 442–4 [obit. of Charles Steuart (Stewart)]

Somerset, John (*d.* 1454), physician and courtier, was a Londoner by birth. His origins are obscure, although he may have been related to Robert Somerset, a London draper active during the late fourteenth century. That his sister, Alice, became prioress of Wintney, Hampshire, while he himself attended Oxford University, suggests a comfortable background. Fear of plague led him to move to Cambridge before 1410, when he appears as a fellow of Pembroke College. By 1418 he had graduated as master of arts and bachelor of medicine, qualifications which brought rapid preferment. Thomas Beaufort, duke of Exeter, made him master of the grammar school at Bury St Edmunds; and just five years later he was named as a governor of a proposed joint college of medicine and surgery in London. So also was the eminent royal surgeon, Thomas Morstede (*d.* 1450), who attended Beaufort with him, in December 1426, during the duke's last illness.

Such connections found Somerset a place in the household of Henry VI, where he served continuously from Easter 1427 until about 1451. Early in 1428, in response to the first of many complaints about poverty, he was promised fees worth £100 a year. By then a doctor of medicine, whose duties included tutoring the young king as well as 'preserving his health' (*CPR, 1429–36*, 241), his influence was incalculable. He spent nearly two years with Henry in France between 1430 and 1432, probably then earning the great reputation as a physician about which he was later to boast. A note, in his hand, in the Bedford book of hours, records its presentation to the king in his presence at Rouen on Christmas eve 1430.

Fur-trimmed robes were regularly assigned to Somerset from the royal wardrobe throughout the 1430s and 1440s, marking his arrival at the pinnacle of his profession. He secured gifts of cash and goods, corrodies, an additional fee of £40 a year, and land in Cambridgeshire and Yorkshire. In 1437 part of his pension was exchanged for the manor of Ruislip in Middlesex, prompting him to acquire an additional estate of over 750 acres and a mansion nearby at Osterley, where he lived as a country gentleman when not at his London residence. Most English physicians took holy orders, but Somerset was twice married, first to Agnes, by the early 1440s, and then, by February 1448, to Alice; and in 1442 he became the first medical practitioner to sit in parliament, as a shire knight for Middlesex. He served on the county bench, discharged many royal commissions, and acted as keeper of various royal properties. The chancellorship of the exchequer and wardenship of the royal mint, awarded in 1439, further increased his authority.

Medical training made Somerset an expert astrologer; and in 1441, when horoscopes had been used by a group of conspirators to forecast the king's early death, he arranged for counter-propaganda to be produced. Henry's secretary, Thomas Beckington (*d.* 1465), a close friend, enlisted Somerset's support during royal marriage negotiations, one year later, while the king sought his advice on educational projects. Somerset helped to draft the statutes of both King's and Queens' colleges, Cambridge, and was also involved in the running of Eton College, near Windsor. He did not, as has been suggested, compose a manual on *The Rule of Princes*, but he was an avid bibliophile, who wrote and collected medical treatises. Some may have been acquired dishonestly: after the death in suspicious circumstances of Humphrey, duke of Gloucester, in 1447, he was made administrator of the duke's estate and incurred considerable opprobrium for failing to hand over part of the ducal library to Oxford University.

Somerset sold his office as warden of the mint at this time, allegedly under pressure from William de la Pole, duke of Suffolk, who, he maintained in a later petition, held him 'not gretely in luf and affeccion' (PRO, C1/19/65). But this was after Suffolk's fall and death in 1450, when Somerset himself had been satirized as the duke's creature and parliament had demanded his removal, as an undesirable influence, from the royal presence. His claim in the same petition never to have taken 'brybes for forderaunce of men' (ibid.), is belied by the fact that in 1445 the rulers of London assigned £66 in cash and a substantial lifetime annuity to him for 'labour with the king' (CLRO, Journal 4, fol. 84*r*) on their behalf. Yet protestations that he spent much of his wealth on charity ring true. In 1446 Henry VI permitted him to found a hospital and religious fraternity at Brentwood; and a fulsome eulogy then addressed to him by an anonymous chronicler dwells upon his concern for the poor.

Although he was not immediately expelled from court, as parliament wished, Somerset's last years were clouded with bitterness. His sense of grievance towards King's College (which had already deprived him of the manor of Ruislip) led him to compose a *Queremonia*, itemizing his woes in Latin hexameters. Nevertheless, he retained substantial holdings in Middlesex and made generous provision for his elderly mother. He died intestate on 4 June 1454, leaving no children. CAROLE RAWCLIFFE

Sources Emden, *Oxf.* • J. H. Wylie and W. T. Waugh, eds., *The reign of Henry the Fifth*, 3 (1929), appx O • *Chancery records* • C. H. Talbot and E. A. Hammond, *The medical practitioners in medieval England: a biographical register* (1965) • exchequer, exchequer of pleas, plea rolls, PRO, E13/146, rot. 51*r* • R. A. Griffiths, *The reign of King Henry VI: the exercise of royal authority, 1422–1461* (1981) • *Thomae de Elmham Vita et gesta Henrici Quinti, Anglorum regis*, ed. T. Hearne (1727) • CLRO, journals 4–5 • H. Anstey, ed., *Epistolae academicae Oxon.*, 1, OHS, 35 (1898) • C. Rawcliffe, *Medicine and society in later medieval England* (1995) • chancery, early petitions, PRO, C1/19/65 • inquisitions *post mortem*, PRO, C145/319/20 • *CPR, 1429–36*, 241

Archives PRO, C1/19/65

Wealth at death see PRO, C 145/319/29

Somerset, Lord John Thomas Henry (1787–1846). *See under* Somerset, FitzRoy James Henry, first Baron Raglan (1788–1855).

Somerset [*née* Capel], **Mary, duchess of Beaufort** (*bap.* **1630**, *d.* **1715**), gardener and botanist, was baptized on 16 December 1630 at Hadham Parva, Hertfordshire, the eldest daughter of Arthur *Capel, first Baron Capel of Hadham (1604–1649), and Elizabeth (*d.* 1661), daughter and heir of Sir Charles Morrison and his wife, Mary Hicks.

On 28 June 1648 Mary married Henry Seymour, Lord Beauchamp (*c.*1626–1654), which short but happy union produced a son and a daughter. Like Mary's father, who died for his royalist sympathies, Lord Beauchamp spent time in the Tower for his support of Charles I.

The young widow married again, on 17 August 1657, opting for a 'republican' marriage in front of a justice of the peace. Her groom, Henry *Somerset (1629–1700), then styled Lord Herbert, proved a second loving husband. They had many children: five sons, three of whom survived to adulthood, and four daughters, three of whom also survived, including the fourth, Anne *Coventry. On 2 December 1682 Somerset was created duke of Beaufort.

About 1660 Henry Somerset inherited the Badminton estate from a female cousin and beginning in 1664 embarked on a major building project there. Mary, meanwhile, focused her attention on the gardens and by 1678 had installed conservatories, the fashion for which is sometimes credited to her brother Sir Henry Capel (*d.* 1696). The duchess also built almshouses and the Badminton School. In 1681 the Somersets bought a home in Chelsea, which they remodelled, and Mary once again took charge of the gardens.

From early 1699, for eighteen months, William Sherard (1659–1728) was at Badminton as tutor to Mary's grandson. While there, through his correspondence with John Ray (1627–1705), James Petiver (1664–1718), Hans Sloane (1660–1753), and others, he added 1500 plants to her collection. He believed that 'no place raises or preserves plants better' (BL, Sloane MS 4063, fol. 44), making Badminton a natural destination for exotic seeds, many of which were unknown elsewhere in Britain. After her husband's death in 1700 Mary redoubled her attentions to gardening and amassed thousands of exotic plants from around the globe. These rare specimens brought the duchess into correspondence with the foremost botanists of her time, linking her to a network of foreign suppliers and ensuring that her plants were identified and published. During this period she also collected insects.

Two illustrated albums of plants in Mary Somerset's gardens were produced by Kychique and Daniel Frankcom, who had visited Badminton between 1703 and 1705. Frankcom also viewed her Chelsea garden. These albums, in addition to the images, contain information about provenances and the treatment of particular plants in the dowager duchess's care.

In 1709 a suit was filed in chancery against Mary Somerset by her children, demanding the distribution of the balance of the late duke's personal estate. The initial ruling against her was overturned on appeal in 1710. The dowager duchess died on 7 January 1715 at Beaufort House in Chelsea, and was buried in St Michael and All Angels' Church, Badminton. She bequeathed her twelve-album herbarium to Sloane and it is now in the Natural History Museum. About twenty-five years after Mary's death, Sloane also bought Beaufort House, which he demolished. The duchess of Beaufort is commemorated in the genus *Beaufortia* of the myrtle family, several species of which are grown as ornamentals. P. E. KELL

Sources H. Durant, *Henry, first duke of Beaufort and his duchess, Mary* (1973) • H. Durant, *The Somerset sequence* (1951) • GEC, *Peerage*, new edn, vol. 2 • Desmond, *Botanists* • 'Somerset, Henry (1629–1700)', *DNB* • 'Sherard, William', *DNB* • J. Petiver, correspondence, BL, MSS Sloane 4063, 4064, 4065 • letter, Sherard to Petiver, 21 Sept 1700, BL, Sloane MS 4063, fol. 44 • W. L. Tjaden, 'William and James Sherard and John James Dillenius: some errors in their biographies', *Journal of the Society of the Bibliography of Natural History*, 8 (1976–8), 143–7

Archives Badminton estate office, Gloucestershire, family corresp. and papers | NHM, plants

Likenesses S. Browne, group portrait, oils, 1685 (first duke and his family), repro. in Durant, *Henry, first duke of Beaufort*, facing p. 61 • Dahl, oils, repro. in Durant, *Henry, first duke of Beaufort*, facing p. 21

Wealth at death £50,000; plus property: Durant, *Somerset sequence*

Somerset, Poulett George Henry (1822–1875). *See under* Somerset, FitzRoy James Henry, first Baron Raglan (1788–1855).

Somerset, Protector. *See* Seymour, Edward (*c*.1500–1552).

Somerset, William, third earl of Worcester (1526/7–1589), nobleman, was the eldest of the four sons of Henry Somerset, second earl of Worcester (1495/6–1549), and his second wife, Elizabeth (*c*.1502–1565), daughter of Sir Anthony Browne. William's grandfather Charles *Somerset, the first earl of Worcester (*c*.1460–1526) of the Somerset creation, acquired extensive lands in south Wales through his marriage with a Herbert heiress, and his influence as Henry VIII's lord chamberlain ensured that his heir, Henry, was granted life tenure of many royal offices in the marches of Wales. Lord Herbert, as he was styled, probably spent his unrecorded early years mainly on his father's lands in Monmouthshire. In 1544 he served with his father in the English army in France, carrying the king's helm and spear at Calais on 25 July, and in December 1545 he attended the king at Westminster. In May 1546 he was among those who 'brake their staves and did very honestly' in a skirmish near Boulogne, but he was too diffident to revenge an insult when visiting Fontainebleau in July 1546 with the English embassy. In 1546 he appears as a member of the privy chamber and was bequeathed £200 in Henry VIII's will. He attended Henry VIII's funeral and was knighted by Edward VI at his coronation.

William Somerset, third earl of Worcester (1526/7–1589), by unknown artist, 1569

Following his father's death on 26 November 1549, the young Earl William, who was then twenty-two, failed to secure appointment to his father's valuable offices in Wales. His landed income was smaller than that of most contemporary earls, and in the 1550s family and other expenses led to land sales and debts. These were relieved by royal pardons in 1552 and 1558 and by assistance from his father-in-law, Sir Edward *North, created Lord North in 1554, who was later credited with disbursing £2000 or £3000 for his relief. His marriage to North's daughter Christian (*b*. 1533) probably took place late in 1549. They had three children, Edward *Somerset, fourth earl of Worcester, Elizabeth, and Lucy. In November 1563 Worcester's disagreement with his wife came to the queen's notice, and in December 1563 they separated on terms which required Worcester to pay the countess £100 a year, rising to £133 6*s*. 8*d*. after his mother's death. Three illegitimate children are also recorded for Worcester.

In May 1551 Worcester accompanied the marquess of Northampton's embassy to the French court. He was one of many signatories of the letters patent of 21 June 1553 settling the crown on Lady Jane Grey, but was present at the proclamation of Queen Mary on 19 July 1553 and served as carver at her coronation. In February 1554 the Spanish ambassador reported that when Wyatt's rebellion threatened London, Worcester had fled the court crying all was lost. Soon afterwards, possibly to counter suspicions that his action at that time reflected opposition to the queen's marriage, he sought leave to visit Spain and was one of those who escorted Prince Philip from Spain to his wedding with the queen. In 1557 he showed his commitment to the reigning monarchs by serving in the army in France commanded by the earl of Pembroke.

In Elizabeth's reign Worcester continued to undertake public duties and regularly attended parliament. He was reputed to be a Catholic and this probably explains his omission until about 1577 from the Elizabethan commissions appointing the council in the marches of Wales, of which he had been a member since 1551. Until his reappointment to that council he was also omitted from all Elizabethan commissions of the peace except those for Monmouthshire, despite his importance as a landowner in Glamorgan, Brecknockshire, and Gloucestershire. His Catholic sympathies were shown in 1566 by his opposition to the bill affirming the validity of the consecration of bishops appointed since Elizabeth's accession. In 1569 the northern insurgents spread unfounded rumours that he was raising men in Wales, but his nomination as a knight of the Garter on 23 April 1570 may be seen as recognition of his loyalty.

On 16 January 1572 Worcester was appointed one of the peers for the trial of the duke of Norfolk. In January 1573 he was sent to France to be proxy for Queen Elizabeth at the christening of Charles IX's daughter, and when in Paris demonstrated his loyalty to the queen by refusing to meet his sister Anne, the widow of the attainted earl of Northumberland. In October 1586 he was one of the commissioners at Fotheringhay for the trial of Mary, queen of Scots, and in July 1588 he undertook to bring into the field six lances and twenty-four light horse for the queen's defence. He died at his house at St John's, in or near the parish of Clerkenwell, Middlesex, on 21 February 1589, and was buried in Raglan parish church, having directed in his will that he was 'there to lye alone'.

After 1551 Worcester was the only peer who mainly resided in Wales. In the 1560s he moved his permanent residence from Chepstow Castle to Raglan Castle, where in the 1580s he undertook extensive rebuilding reflecting the recovery of his finances. The long gallery built at that time incorporates caryatids based on illustrations in a French architectural book in his possession, which he probably acquired in France in 1573. His local influence was shown in the election of his brothers as members of parliament for Monmouthshire: Thomas in 1553 and 1554, Francis in 1558, and Charles in 1571 and 1572. His letters show him on sociable terms with several peerage and gentry families. He was patron of a company of players which performed widely in the provinces from 1556 until 1585, and also of the poets Lewys Morgannwg (Llywelyn ap Rhisiart) and Dafydd Benwyn. W. R. B. Robinson

Sources GEC, *Peerage* • W. R. B. Robinson, 'The earls of Worcester and their estates, 1526–1642', BLitt diss., U. Oxf., 1958, Bodl. Oxf. [and 'Additional notes', filed with thesis] • W. R. B. Robinson, 'Sir William Herbert's acquisition of offices in Wales on the death of Henry, earl of Worcester in 1549', *Historical Research*, 69 (1996), 266–83 • J. R. S. Phillips, ed., *The justices of the peace in Wales and Monmouthshire, 1541 to 1689* (1975) • *JHL*, 1 (1509–77), 388ff.; 2 (1578–1614), 7–148 • *LP Henry VIII*, 21/2, no. 769(12) • [J. Hooker], 'The lyffe of Sir Peter Carewe', *Archaeologia*, 28 (1840), 96–151, esp. 114 • J. G. Nichols, ed., *The chronicle of Queen Jane, and of two years of Queen Mary*, CS, old ser., 48 (1850), 99 • *The manuscripts of the Right Honourable F. J. Savile Foljambe, of Osberton*, HMC, 41 (1897), 5–6 • *CSP Venice, 1556–7*, 1271 • D. Digges, *The compleat ambassador* (1665), 314, 328–9 • *A collection of state papers … left by William Cecill, Lord Burghley*, ed. S. Haynes, 1 (1740), 193 • PRO, PROB 11/48, will-register Morrison, fol. 200; PROB 11/74, fols. 306v–307 • 'Liber Caerulus', Records of the knights of the Garter, St George's Chapel Archives, Windsor Castle • Bodl. Oxf., MS Ashmole 809 • E. J. Saunders, 'Gweithiau Lewys Morgannwg', MA diss., U. Wales, 1922, 251–4, 254–7 • J. A. Bradney, *A history of Monmouthshire*, 2/1 (1911), 14 • E. K. Chambers, *The Elizabethan stage*, 4 vols. (1923), vol. 2, pp. 220–25 • J. M. Traherne, ed., *Stradling correspondence: a series of letters written in the reign of Queen Elizabeth* (1840) • H. Colvin, *Essays in English architectural history* (1999), 116, figs. 90, 91, and frontispiece • W. A. Shaw, *The knights of England*, 1 (1906), 26, 150 • PRO, C 142/90/113

Archives Glos. RO, letters to Lord Berkeley • NL Wales, Badminton MSS; corresp. with Mansell family; Penrice and Margam corresp. • PRO, Scudamore corresp., chancery masters' exhibits, C 115/104; C 115/101

Likenesses oils, 1568, Parham House, Sussex • oils, 1569, Badminton House, Gloucestershire [*see illus.*] • attrib. N. Hilliard, miniature, *c.*1575, Badminton House, Gloucestershire • M. Gheeraerts, senior, etching, 1576, BM • portrait, oils, 1581, Badminton House, Gloucestershire; repro. in H. Durant, *The Somerset sequence* (1951), facing p. 52

Wealth at death probably over £2000 p.a. from landed estate

Somervell, Sir Arthur (1863–1937), composer and educationist, was born on 5 June 1863 at Hazelthwaite in Applethwaite, Cumberland, the youngest of six sons and nine children of Robert Miller Somervell, leather merchant and founder of Somervell Brothers (manufacturers of K Shoes), and his wife, Anne Wilson. After a short period at Uppingham School (1878–9) he entered King's College, Cambridge, where he took an ordinary BA in history (1884). While at the university he studied composition under Sir Charles Stanford and, as an active member of the Cambridge University Musical Society, was introduced to Joseph Joachim and Sir Hubert Parry. At Stanford's recommendation he worked under Friedrich Kiel (Stanford's former teacher) and Woldemar Bargiel at the Berlin Hochschule für Musik (1884–5). On returning to England he studied (again at Stanford's recommendation) for two years with Parry (1885–7) at the Royal College of Music before he began to make a living as a teacher, composer, and examiner, joining the staff of the Royal College of Music in 1894. Somervell married Edith Lance (*b.* 1862) (herself an educationist), daughter of James Collet, civil engineer, on 5 August 1890. They had twin sons (who both joined the shoe-manufacturing company) and two daughters. On his return from Australia in 1900, where he had been examining for the Associated Board, he succeeded John Stainer as inspector of music to the Board of Education, a controversial appointment, in that W. G. McNaught, Stainer's assistant, had considered himself the natural heir. In 1920 he became chief inspector, a position that he held until retirement in 1928. The following year he was knighted for his services to music education.

During the 1890s Somervell produced the majority of his large-scale choral works for provincial festivals—the mass in C minor (Bach Choir, 1891) and the cantatas *The Forsaken Merman* (Leeds, 1895), *The Power of Sound* (Kendal,

1895), and *Ode to the Sea* (Birmingham, 1897)—though arguably his finest work in this genre was *Ode on the Intimations of Immortality* (1907) from Wordsworth's *The Prelude*. He also produced two orchestral works, an orchestral ballad *Helen of Kirkconnel* (1893) and the suite *In Arcady* (1897), but it was not until much later in life that he turned seriously to the composition of instrumental music, even if his stylistic vision was by then rather dated. In 1912 he produced both the symphonic variations *Normandy* and the more nationally inspired maritime symphony *Thalassa*, replete with programme (premièred by Arthur Nikisch); the slow movement of *Thalassa* enjoyed a modicum of popularity through its frequent hearing on occasions of national mourning. Somervell's other orchestral essays, in spite of their temporary approbation from those such as Tovey and their pedigree—the *Concertstück* for violin and orchestra (1913) was written for Jelly d'Arányi, and the later violin concerto (1932) commissioned by her elder sister, Adila Fachiri—failed to make an impression, which Somervell blamed on his broad reputation as a composer of songs. Nevertheless, it is as a songwriter and, more particularly, as the author of several song cycles, that his name has endured. The first cycle, *Maud* (1899), a special favourite of Harry Plunket Greene, its dedicatee, was a highly successful selection of verse from Tennyson's dark monodrama in which the tensions of love and death are skilfully retained in the narrative. In *A Shropshire Lad* (1904) Somervell's lyrical gifts reached their zenith (even though Housman's biting irony lay beyond his grasp), while *James Lee's Wife* (1907) and, arguably his finest achievement, *A Broken Arc* (1923), articulate a sympathy for Browning's unorthodox, and at times complex, world of faith and morality. Indeed, such was Somervell's fascination for the song cycle that he might easily be dubbed the English Schumann, a label that would also be a fair summary of his stylistic parameters. In 1903, on the strength of his compositions, he was awarded the MusDoc at Cambridge.

Somervell's period in office as an inspector of music coincided with a major shift in education away from utilitarianism towards educational and artistic liberalism. His philosophy of musical education, derived from Plato and Aristotle, stressed the link between music and moral values, the essence of music as rhythm (reflecting the Edwardian preoccupation with the secular 'life force'), and a vision of childhood that emphasized emotion and instinct. Somervell hoped that music could instil a sense of emancipation for the many, notably for the manual worker; in practical terms he believed that such educational aims could be realized through the development of sight-singing, familiarization with notation, and the singing of traditional and national songs (proselytized through Hadow's *Songs of the British Islands* of 1903 and Stanford's *National Song Book* of 1906). But most importantly Somervell campaigned tirelessly for music to be considered an indispensable constituent of the school curriculum at a time when the Board of Education remained cautious in its commitment—work for which he is now largely forgotten. After retirement, his experience in musical education was still called upon, notably as the chairman of the School Orchestra Festivals at Queen's Hall, which he undertook from 1932 until his death at his home, 105 Clifton Hill, St John's Wood, London, on 2 May 1937. He was buried in his beloved Lake District.

JEREMY DIBBLE

Sources F. Hudson, 'Somervell', *Die Musik in Geschichte und Gegenwart*, ed. F. Blume (Kassel and Basel, 1949–86) · G. Cox, *A history of music education in England, 1872–1928* (1993) · M. Hurd, 'Somervell, Sir Arthur', *New Grove* · H. C. Colles, 'Somervell', Grove, *Dict. mus.* (1927) · S. Banfield, *Sensibility and English song* (1985) · S. Banfield, 'The immortality odes of Finzi and Somervell', *MT*, 116 (1975), 527–31 · b. cert. · m. cert. · d. cert. · G. Humphreys, sleeve notes, *English song series*, 6 (1998) [audio CD, Collins Classics 1522]
Archives priv. coll., family MSS · Royal College of Music, London, MSS | NL Wales, letters to Madame Lucie Barbier
Likenesses photographs, Royal College of Music, London
Wealth at death £3163 5s. 11d.: probate, 18 Aug 1937, *CGPLA Eng. & Wales*

Somervell, Donald Bradley, Baron Somervell of Harrow (**1889–1960**), politician and judge, was born at Harrow, Middlesex, on 24 August 1889, the second son of Robert Somervell (1851–1933), master and bursar (1888–1919) of Harrow School, and his wife, Octavia Paulina, daughter of the Revd John Churchill. He himself went to Harrow, and then to Oxford in 1907 with a demyship at Magdalen. He obtained first-class honours in chemistry (1911), a choice of subject surprising in light of his subsequent career, but typical of his exceptional mental energy and versatility. In 1912 he was elected a fellow of All Souls College, an event which, like his first election to parliament, he himself regarded as particularly memorable, since he was the first man who, having taken a degree in chemistry, was later elected to an All Souls fellowship. He joined the Inner Temple but his projected career was interrupted by the outbreak of war in which he served in India (1914–17) and Mesopotamia (1917–19), with the 1/9 Middlesex regiment and as staff captain with the 53rd infantry brigade; he was appointed OBE in 1919.

Somervell had been called to the bar *in absentia* in 1916 and began practice in the chambers of W. A. Jowitt, whose pupil he had been. Somervell's mental agility and temperament did not attract him to the ordinary run of the mill common law practice; the art of cross-examination did not appeal to him, seeming indeed to his naturally kind heart apt to be unfair. His arguments were expressed briefly and lucidly, without any emotional or histrionic quality. He applied himself to the mentally exacting problems created by the commercial clauses of the treaty of Versailles, gaining a considerable practice before the mixed arbitral tribunal established under the treaty.

He took silk in 1929 and soon began his political career. Politics had a special fascination for him since boyhood and his choice of profession was largely governed by his belief that the bar would provide a ready introduction to politics. At Oxford his friendship with Cyril Asquith had much inclined him to the Liberals, but the serious decline of that party, his disapproval of the performance of the Labour Party, and above all his admiration for Stanley Baldwin, whom he particularly respected for his freedom from class bitterness, self-esteem, or ambition, converted

Somervell to the Conservative cause. He was defeated at Crewe in 1929 but was successful in 1931 and again, by a narrow majority, in 1935 when he characteristically refused a safer seat, preferring to remain where he had made and valued many local contacts.

To Somervell the House of Commons was both a goal and a home. In his view it was a truly democratic institution in which the ministers were in a real sense subject to the influence of the elected representatives of the nation. He was an assiduous attender, particularly in committees, and he genuinely enjoyed the discussions on public affairs. 'Having got a seat he sat in it.' His maiden speech was on the Statute of Westminster Bill, when he found himself (as often, before 1940) in a measure of disagreement with Winston Churchill.

In 1932 Somervell appeared as one of the leading counsel for the Bank of Portugal in the important case of *Waterlow & Sons* v. *Banco de Portugal* in the House of Lords. In the autumn of 1933 he succeeded Sir Boyd Merriman as solicitor-general and was knighted accordingly. Sir Thomas Inskip was attorney-general. As attorney-general himself from 1936 he had under him first his old friend Sir Terence O'Connor, who had greatly influenced and helped him early in his political career; then Jowitt; and later Sir David Maxwell Fyfe. Somervell was sworn of the privy council in 1938.

The functions of a law officer *vis-à-vis* the heads of the various ministries, a subject on which he addressed the Holdsworth Club in the University of Birmingham in 1946, gave exceptional scope to Somervell's qualities. His emphatic view was that, as a law officer, he should always be available to informal approach by the legal advisers of the various ministries, a view which bore remarkable fruit during the Second World War. Never afraid of quick decision, he was confident in his judgement, which was undoubtedly sound and based on a robust common sense. He wished especially to avoid having to say 'if only you had told me of this before'. Nor was he a man ever to worry over hypothetical situations.

The exceptionally long period of his law officership included problems such as the budget leakage in 1936, the abdication of Edward VIII, and the form of the oath appropriate to the coronation of George VI, a matter involving him in successful negotiations with the representatives of the Commonwealth countries. He also played an important part in debate on such measures as the Incitement to Disaffection Bill and the Government of India Bill. He strongly supported the line taken by Neville Chamberlain at Munich. He was involved in a controversy in 1938 when he threatened Duncan Sandys, Churchill's son-in-law, with prosecution under the Official Secrets Acts for framing a parliamentary question on the state of anti-aircraft defences based on secret information. The majority of a select committee acquitted Somervell of a breach of privilege in making the threat, but a minority was critical.

During the Second World War Somervell's considerable energies were greatly called upon in connection with the very numerous statutory instruments which the exigencies of war demanded, with such legislation as the War Damage Act, and with the vexed problem of war crimes. In respect of all these exacting duties his lucidity, friendliness, and above all his quickness of mind gained him the respect of members of all parties. He applied himself to his duties, in back-bencher opinion, 'without publicity and with great ability and diligence'. However, in Lord Atkins's dissenting judgment in *Liversidge* v. *Anderson* (1942), concerning the powers conferred upon the home secretary under wartime regulations, the arguments used by Somervell, in defence of an encroachment by the executive upon individual liberty, were likened to those of Charles I's attorney-general.

Somervell frequently began his day at the law courts at 8.30 a.m. and remained in the house until late risings, finding none the less time to prepare fully for his appearance in a complicated case next day. His remarkable energy was assisted by his capacity for decision without worry. But his intellectual capacities were not even exhausted by his pressing duties as a member of the bar, as a law officer, or later as a judge. He was an insatiable reader and found time to study diverse and complex subjects, upon which he would summarize his conclusions in papers prepared not for publication but for his own clarification, such as 'Christian art 12th–15th centuries', 'The background to the New Testament', and 'Relativity'.

From 1940 to 1946 Somervell was recorder of Kingston upon Thames. His twelve years as a law officer ended with his appointment as home secretary in the caretaker government of 1945. The defeat of the Conservative Party put an end to his political career, but in 1946 he was appointed by Attlee, on the recommendation of the lord chancellor, Jowitt, as a lord justice of appeal, a position which he held until 1954; for most of this time he presided over one of the divisions of the Court of Appeal. When Churchill's government was formed in 1951 he had strong claims to be lord chancellor, but was passed over, probably because of Sir Albert Napier's preference for Gavin Simonds. Somervell's pre-war clashes with Churchill and identification with the Chamberlainite policy of appeasement also damaged his claims. 'Better be a man of Munich than a man of Yalta', Somervell later reflected (Heuston, *Lives, 1885–1940*, 554).

After the exertions of his ministerial work Somervell felt judicial life to be relatively unexacting since he was able to reach clear conclusions rapidly and to deal speedily with the cases which came before his court. Frequently he would shorten the argument of counsel, not by putting questions critical of their arguments, but rather by summarizing them and then asking: 'That is your case, is it not?' or 'Do you see what I mean?' If Somervell's judgments were not always framed in careful literary style and were, in his own words, inclined to be slapdash, they were notable for lucidity and absence of prolixity. It was his strong view that the law suffered from too much verbal inflation, and of one of his colleagues he observed that 'he would never use one word when ten would do'. As in his political career he earned the affection of his colleagues both in the court and at the bar.

On 29 July 1933 Somervell married Laelia Helen, daughter of Sir Archibald Buchan-Hepburn. They had no children. If 1933—the year of his marriage and his appointment as solicitor-general—had been a triumphant year for Somervell, 1945 was, by contrast, a bleak one. In that year the death of his wife after a long illness ended a perfect partnership, and about the same time the defeat of the Conservative Party ended his career in politics, which had been the principal focus of his mind and energies. Somervell tried to maintain as his home the Old Rectory at Ewelme in Oxfordshire, which he had bought shortly after his marriage (and where he was buried), but in 1955 he felt compelled to abandon it. Thereafter he lived in chambers in the Inner Temple, and paid frequent visits to All Souls. In 1953 he suffered a slight thrombosis. From this he recovered but in 1954 he assumed the less arduous work of a lord of appeal in ordinary, with a life peerage; he later became afflicted with a cancer which caused his judicial retirement in 1960 and his death at the Hospital of St John and St Elizabeth, Marylebone, London, on 18 November of the same year. Meanwhile he had served in 1957 as treasurer of his inn and in 1959 was made an honorary DCL of Oxford; he had been elected an honorary fellow of Magdalen in 1946 and received an honorary LLD degree from St Andrews in 1947. He had also been a governor of Harrow from 1944 to 1953 and for the last six years a most energetic and influential chairman of the governors.

Apart from reading Somervell derived great pleasure from music, especially from gramophone records of chamber music by the classical masters. He was for many years on the governing body of the Royal College of Music. He was also chairman of the Reviewing Committee on the Export of Works of Art and from 1944 to 1949 a trustee of the Tate Gallery. His pleasures throughout his life had never been the playing of games, although at one time he was an enthusiastic if not greatly skilled horseman. For him the greatest enjoyment, whether alone or in company, lay in travel and the open countryside and its wild bird and animal life. He bore his last illness with extraordinary cheerfulness and courage, spending more and more of his time at All Souls, his love of which was demonstrated by his gift of the iron gate in the north-west corner of the Great Quadrangle, which he did not live to see in place. EVERSHED, *rev.* MARC BRODIE

Sources personal knowledge (1971) • private information (1971) • *The Times* (21 Nov 1960) • R. F. V. Heuston, *Lives of the lord chancellors, 1940–1970* (1987) • R. F. V. Heuston, *Lives of the lord chancellors, 1940–1970* (1987) • J. Charmley, *Churchill: the end of glory* (1993) • *CGPLA Eng. & Wales* (1961)

Archives Bodl. Oxf., corresp. and papers | U. Hull, Brynmor Jones L., letters to Irene Forbes Adam

Likenesses W. Stoneman, photographs, 1934–45, NPG • photograph, All Souls Oxf.

Wealth at death £48,174 2*s*. 8*d*.: probate, 1961

Somervell, (Theodore) Howard (1890–1975), medical missionary and mountaineer, was born on 16 April 1890, the eldest of three children and elder son of William Henry Somervell, of Brantfield, Kendal, and his wife, Florence Howard. W. H. Somervell was then directing the affairs of Somervell Brothers of Kendal, later more widely known as K Shoes. A business career did not attract Howard Somervell, though he was fully grateful to his father for giving him an income and the key of the house at seventeen. At Rugby School (1904–9) he was unhappy, leaving school labelled 'unbusinesslike and forgetful'. But his mother's comfort and their common solace in music gave him the kind of courage fit for the great mountains. By twenty he knew the Beethoven symphonies by heart, and would cycle 150 miles to hear a Promenade Concert. When he was eighteen he became a member of the Keswick-based Fell and Rock Climbing Club and thus started a lifetime's devotion to the mountains of the English Lake District.

(Theodore) Howard Somervell (1890–1975), by Howard Coster, 1936

Somervell went on to Caius College, Cambridge, where he obtained first classes in both parts of the natural sciences tripos (1911 and 1913) and where he developed his essentially personal approach to the Christian faith. He then served with the British expeditionary force in France (1915–18) as a captain in the Royal Army Medical Corps, and was mentioned in dispatches. After the war he graduated from London's University College Hospital (MB, BCh, 1921) and became FRCS in 1920.

Somervell's Everest ambitions were stimulated during 1921 by much mountaineering in Britain and Europe. Somervell was a tough physical product of the Cumbrian heights and of the Alps, but he realized that the Himalayan region called for constant movement above 20,000 feet. Everest was to be his physical test in 1922 and 1924, but his colleagues commented too on his mental endurance.

> When one shares [Somervell wrote about George Leigh Mallory, his fellow mountaineer] a tent for days on end throughout the better part of six months with a man one gets an insight into his character such as is vouchsafed to few other men. These many days of companionship with a man whose outlook on life was lofty and choice, human and loving and in a measure divine still remain for me a priceless memory.

Even when in 1924 Somervell was in danger of choking, E. F. Norton wrote: 'Somervell very nearly choked, and was handicapped for three days. Only saved by coughing up the obstructing matter with a lot of blood. That he achieved what he did in this condition was a remarkable performance'.

After the 1922 Everest expedition and with £60 in his pocket Somervell set out to see India from the northern frontier to Cape Comorin; what he saw changed his life. He saw a continent ill-equipped medically and poorly provided for in those skills which he possessed; it was something more powerful than the Himalayas and more compelling than the 'call of the mountains'. He described it as the 'unrelieved suffering of India'. When he visited the main hospital of the south Travancore medical mission and its group of outstations centred on Neyyoor, he found only one qualified surgeon, Stephen Pugh, struggling with a queue of waiting patients which would take ten days to reduce. There and then Somervell offered to perform those overdue operations; then, within a fortnight, he was back in London telling his friends in London hospitals of his decision to devote his life to India after another attempt on Everest. He joined the 1924 expedition on which Mallory died and Somervell and E. F. Norton climbed to within 1000 feet of the summit.

From 1924 to 1949 Somervell was deep in the affairs of the south Travancore medical mission which, with its branch hospitals, could claim to be the largest of its kind in the world. He attracted young surgeons to work with him, especially in the surgery of the stomach. He established a confidence between surgeon and patient by building a gallery in the operating theatre where visitors and relatives could watch what was going on.

> Many thousands have seen us at work [he wrote], and know that a surgical operation is a careful and intelligent procedure. They have been shown the disease inside and been given an explanation of how the operation cures it. Thus not only have we spread a little knowledge among the people around, but they have learned to come to us for treatment far earlier than was their custom in the past.

In 1934, out of 2000 major operations performed at Neyyoor, 590 were for cancer.

Somervell also pioneered the modern treatment of leprosy and practised the modern belief that leprosy can be cured. His home for leprosy patients had four big dormitories for eighty patients, and there was also a leprosy settlement for permanent residents. By 1936 several scores of patients had been sent home 'cured and free from all symptoms of the disease which was once considered incurable'. Describing a day's visit to a branch hospital Somervell wrote:

> The amount of work one has to do here is appalling. Yesterday and the day before over 150 patients who had come five miles and more to the hospital had to go home without seeing me. From 7 a.m. to 8.30 p.m. I saw 153 sick folk continuously.

In 1938 he was awarded the kaisar-i-Hind gold medal, and he was appointed OBE in 1953.

India continued to tug at Somervell's heart and he accepted the post of associate professor of surgery at the Vellore Christian Medical College (1949–61), then at a crucial stage of its development as a teaching hospital. It was a fitting climax to his forty years' service in India. From 1961 to 1964 Somervell was president of the Alpine Club. When the news of his death at Ambleside, on 23 January 1975, reached Neyyoor, the whole community broke into a spontaneous public procession. In London the Royal Geographical Society showed some of Somervell's magnificent Everest paintings, as did his own Lake District friends. In all, he fulfilled the description of him given by Sir Francis Younghusband as 'a man of science, a man of art, a man of warm humanity and of strong religious feeling'.

In 1925 Somervell married Margaret, daughter of Sir James Hope Simpson, director of the Bank of Liverpool, and his wife, Mary, *née* Wilson; they had three sons.

CECIL NORTHCOTT, *rev.*

Sources SOAS, Archives of the Council for World Mission (incorporating the London Missionary Society) · H. Somervell, *After Everest* (1936) · H. Somervell, *Knife and life in India* (1940) · F. Younghusband, *The epic of Mount Everest* (1926) · T. H. Somervell, 'Climbing north of Kangchenjunga', *The Journal of the Fell and Rock Climbing Club of the English Lake District*, 6/2 (1923), 222–6 · G. L. Mallory, 'The first high climb', *GJ*, 60 (1922), 400–12 · *Indian Medical Journal* (1938) · personal knowledge (1986) · *WWW* · *CGPLA Eng. & Wales* (1975)

Likenesses H. Coster, photograph, 1936, NPG [*see illus.*] · H. Coster, photographs, NPG

Wealth at death £45,459: probate, 21 March 1975, *CGPLA Eng. & Wales*

Somervile [Somerville], **William** (1675–1742), poet, was born on 2 September 1675 and was baptized the next day at Colwich, Staffordshire, the eldest son of Robert Somervile (1647–1705) of Edstone, Warwickshire, and Elizabeth (1644–1742), eldest daughter of Anne (*d.* 1704) and Sir Charles *Wolseley (*d.* 1714). He was first educated at Stratford upon Avon and then admitted to Winchester College on 8 August 1690 as founder's kin, his grandmother Anne Fiennes being descended from the sister of William of Wykeham. In 1694 he entered New College, Oxford, matriculating on 24 August, and later became a fellow. On 3 October 1696 he also became a student of the Middle Temple.

On the death of his father in early October 1705 Somervile took up residence at the family home at Edstone and spent the rest of his life there. On 1 February 1708 he married Mary (*d.* 1731), daughter of Hugh Bethell of Rise, Yorkshire. His life was taken up with his responsibilities as a

William Somervile (1675–1742), by unknown artist, *c*.1695–1710

country squire both at Edstone and also at Aston Somerville, Gloucestershire, where his family had long had property. Fair, 6 foot tall, and handsome, he established a reputation as a sociable generous man, popular with his neighbours, and skilful and upright as a local magistrate. He observed his commitments as patron to the parishes of Wootton Wawen, near Edstone, and Aston Somerville, and appreciated the loyalty of those who worked for him, as is evident in the plaque to his servant, Thomas Malbone (*d*. July 1718), at Aston Somerville, and in the epitaph at Wootton Wawen to his butler James Boeter who died in January 1719 after a hunting accident.

Somervile had two major interests, writing poetry and hunting. His first major work written by 1708 was 'The Wicker Chair', a lively recollection by the character of a Vale of Evesham farmer of his exploits at Robert Dover's Cotswold Games. Like the drafts of many of his poems, the text circulated in manuscript before being published, with revisions, as *Hobbinol, or, The Rural Games*, a burlesque dedicated to Hogarth, in 1740. Other early poems reflected his whig sympathies, typical being his 1712 tribute to the duke of Marlborough when the ministers of Queen Anne removed him from all his offices. His first published poem was *The Two Springs, a Fable* (1725). The title of his second published work, *Occasional Poems, Translations, Fables, Tales, &c* (1727) indicated the variety of his output.

Somervile's major poem was *The Chace*, published in 1735 and dedicated to Frederick, prince of Wales. In four books of blank verse he conveyed the excitement and dangers of the chase as well as its place in history. This poem was followed less successfully with *Field Sports* in 1742. Dr Johnson was grudging in his comments on Somervile as a poet, saying that he 'set a good example to men of his own class' (*British Poets*, 36.6), but Somervile was at his best when writing with vitality and enthusiasm about a topic he knew well, especially if it conveyed his love of the countryside. His occasional poems have a genuine but mannered control, whereas in his fables and tales, the moral tends to be laboured.

Somervile's poetry brought him into contact with other writers. He developed a lengthy literary relationship with Allan Ramsay, the Scottish poet who admired his works. He encouraged William Shenstone and Richard Jago. He exchanged ideas about literature and landscape gardening with Lady Luxborough, Bolingbroke's half-sister, who lived nearby at Barrels, Ullenhall, Warwickshire.

Somervile's hunting exploits were well known in the locality. He disapproved of coursing, but he took an active part in hunting, his favourite horse Old Ball being used three days a week during the season. His kennels included twelve couples of beagles, six couples of fox-hounds, and five couples of otter-hounds. Such an establishment cost money, and Somervile was beset with financial problems during his years at Edstone. The income from his estates amounted to £1500 a year but he had to provide an annuity of £600 for his widowed mother who lived to the age of ninety-eight and died a month before him. By 1730 he was so much in debt (and had no children to inherit his property), that he arranged that his friend and cousin, James, thirteenth Lord Somerville of the Scottish peerage, would underwrite him financially with a reversion of his estates after his death.

On 5 September 1731 Somervile's wife died and was buried at Wootton Wawen. 'My House is now a House of Mourning', he wrote to Lord Somerville (BL, Add. MS 44885A). His financial position did not improve, and his kind nature did not help. In September 1734 he was owed more than £1000 by his Aston Somerville tenants. By 1737 he felt he was growing too old for field sports, but he continued to circulate poetic compositions and his translation of Voltaire's *Alzire* was well received. He was still well-respected locally, two hundred attending a dinner in his honour when he was sixty-five.

Somervile died at Edstone on 17 July 1742 and was buried on 20 July alongside his wife in the chantry chapel of the church at Wootton Wawen. An epitaph composed by him marks the stone. Shenstone most aptly summarized the feeling of his friends, much of the expression being later used by Dr Johnson:

> Our old friend Somervile is dead! I did not imagine I could have been so sorry … I can now excuse all his foibles; impute them to age, and to distress of circumstances … For a man of high spirit, conscious of having (at least in one production) generally pleased the world, to be plagued and threatened by wretches that are low in every sense; to be forced to drink himself into pains of the body in order to get rid of the pains of the mind, is a misery … I loved him for nothing so much as his flocci-nauci-nihili-pili-fication of money. (*Letters*, 55–6)

F. D. A. Burns

Sources parish register, Colwich, 3 Sept 1675, Staffs. RO [baptism] · parish register, Colwich, 18 Nov 1674, Staffs. RO [marriage] · parish register, Cherry Burton, Yorkshire, 1 Feb 1708 [marriage] · parish register, Wootton Wawen, Warks. CRO, 20 July 1742 [burial] · parish register, Aston Somerville, Gloucestershire, 18 Nov 1674 [marriage] · T. F. Kirby, *Winchester scholars: a list of the wardens, fellows, and scholars of … Winchester College* (1888), 210 · Foster, *Alum. Oxon.* · H. A. C. Sturgess, ed., *Register of admissions to the Honourable Society of the Middle Temple, from the fifteenth century to the year 1944*, 1 (1949), 240 · W. Somervile, letters to Lord and Lady Somerville, 1728–41, BL, Add. MS 44885A, fols. 3–42 · W. Somervile, poems, Bodl. Oxf., MS Ballard 47, fols. 2–25 · G. W. Campbell, 'The family of Somerville, and the poet of the chase', *The Genealogist*, new ser., 13 (1896–7), 73–81, 152–7 · W. Cooper, *Wootton Wawen: its history and records* (1936), 67–73 · J. Somerville, *Memorie of the Somervilles: being a history of the baronial house of Somerville*, ed. W. Scott, 2 vols. (1815) · R. D. Havens, 'William Somervile's earliest poem', *Modern Language Notes*, 41 (1926), 80–86 · F. G. Waldron, 'The wicker chair', *The Shakespearean miscellany: containing a collection of … tracts … anecdotes of theatrical performers … scarce and original poetry; and curious remains of antiquity* (1802), 3rd section, 25–84 · G. Forester, 'Brief memoir of Somervile', *Sporting Magazine*, 2nd ser., 4 (1832), 22.264–9 · F. L. Colvile, *The worthies of Warwickshire who lived between 1500 and 1800* [1870], 701–6 · *The letters of William Shenstone*, ed. M. Williams (1939) · *The British poets*, 100 vols. (1822), vol. 36

Archives BL, letters to Lord and Lady Somerville, Add. MS 44885A, fols. 3–42

Likenesses oils, *c*.1695–1710, NPG [*see illus.*] · Dahl, portrait, 1702; formerly in possession of Mrs Ralph Smyth, 1897 · R. Rhodes, line engraving, pubd 1815, NPG · Worthington, engraving, pubd 1821 (after a drawing by Thurston; after Kneller) · engraving, 1821, Birm. CL; repro. in W. Somervile, *The chace* (1735) · Kneller, portrait; formerly in possession of Catherine Piggott, 1897 · Worlidge, portrait · engraving (after Dahl, 1702), repro. in Somerville, *Memorie of the Somervilles*, vol. 2 · portrait, priv. coll.

Somerville, Alexander (1811–1885), journalist and soldier, was born on 15 March 1811, at Springfield, Oldhamstocks, East Lothian, the youngest of eleven children of James Somerville, a farm labourer, and Mary Orkney, who before marriage had been a servant in a farmer's house. Somerville grew up in poverty. His father lacked the 1*s.* required to register his birth, and his mother sewed rags together to clothe him. At the age of eight he was put to work herding, cleaning stables, loading corn sheaves, and ploughing; later he harvested hay, broke stones in a quarry, drained land, and worked in a garden nursery. His parents, who were members of the Anti-Burghers, or General Associate Presbyterian Synod, conducted religious worship each day, and Somerville's religious convictions remained unshaken throughout his life.

Somerville learned to read at home, where he was exposed to religious books, the only kind his father possessed. His formal education was limited to at the most six years, and his attendance at school was irregular as it had to be combined with paid employment. He had anything but fond memories of school, where he was thrashed frequently. He was an avid reader and acquired considerable knowledge, but essentially he was self-taught.

Somerville joined the army in December 1831 and within seven months had become a celebrity and a hero to the many supporters of parliamentary reform. With part of his regiment, the Scots Greys, he was at Birmingham, the site of the largest public meetings in support of the Reform Bill, to aid the civil authorities in the event of disturbances. In May 1832 the fate of the bill was uncertain: there were rumours that an anti-reform tory ministry under Wellington would be appointed, in the event of which large numbers of Birmingham citizens might march to Westminster to present a petition for reform. There were also rumours that in the event of a clash between the civil authorities and the people, the Scots Greys would support the populace. In the midst of this turmoil Somerville wrote to a newspaper asserting that the soldiers would protect property but would not prevent citizens from exercising their liberties, nor would they lend their support to a military government.

Somerville had not violated military regulations, but his officers were outraged and were determined to punish him. Circumstances were contrived to provoke him to be disobedient. At the riding school he was ordered to ride an unfamiliar and difficult horse: after he had dismounted and refused to remount, he was court-martialled and punished with 100 lashes. It became a *cause célèbre*: there were protests in newspapers and in parliament, for many assumed that Somerville had suffered punishment for having written the letter. A court of inquiry was convened which exonerated the commanding officer, but through Somerville's interrogation of several officers the suspicion grew that he had been punished for his political action. The publicity surrounding his case contributed to demands for the abolition of flogging in the army.

A subscription was raised to purchase Somerville's discharge from the army, and with his name widely known he had an opportunity to carve out a career that already had attracted him: he acknowledged being 'filled with ambition to be an author' (Somerville, *Autobiography*, 1st edn, 429). Initially this desire led to his becoming a soldier again, as he served in a British mercenary force in Spain for two years in search of adventures that would allow him to write a book. After his return in 1837 he published newspaper accounts of his war experiences and subsequently a 700 page volume, *History of the British Legion, and War in Spain* (1839). This was followed by two somewhat autobiographical novels, *Memoirs of Serjeant Paul Swanston, being a Narrative of a Soldier's Life* (1840) and *Life of Roger Mowbray* (1853). He also wrote pamphlets and numerous articles for various newspapers. He was pleased to describe himself as engaged in 'political authorship' (Somerville, *Cobdenic Policy the Internal Enemy of England*, 17) and to say, 'I am a literary man' (ibid., 14).

A major theme in Somerville's writing harkened back to his experience during the Reform Bill crisis—the relationship of the army to the government and to the people in circumstances of popular uprising. Somerville argued that the populace, lacking training, organization, and adequate arms, would be helpless in any conflict against a disciplined body of soldiers. He insisted, moreover, that it was fantasy to assume that soldiers engaged in such conflicts would support working-class political movements. He applied this analysis to the Chartist agitations in 1839,

1842, and 1848, and he was especially worried that the tactics of 'physical-force' Chartists would lead to the repression of all working-class political activity. Somerville warned working people about leaders who encouraged street violence, and he severely criticized working-class leaders who used revolutionary rhetoric. His abhorrence of civil conflict and fear of revolution led him to develop what he called a 'conservative science of nations', based on a 'logic of revolutions', according to which revolution led to despotism and the end of civil liberty (Somerville, *Conservative Science of Nations*, 9). This historical theory, which had a long provenance, underpinned Somerville's opposition to revolutionary activity, but it did not lead him to oppose gradualist parliamentary reform that would extend the franchise to increasing numbers of the populace.

Interpreting his own conduct in light of this understanding of working-class political agitation, Somerville developed an image of himself as a saviour of his country. Looking back to 1832 he claimed that his letter 'gave the gathered storm that direction which conducted it to peaceful serenity, and saved the unwilling aristocracy from … the irretrievable disaster of revolution' (Somerville, *Conservative Science*, 13), and thereby saved the country from what would have become Wellington's military despotism. In 1834, when he was in touch with those organizing trade unions, he warned the home secretary of a conspiracy to seize government offices, and ever after he claimed that he had forestalled a revolutionary conspiracy by some of the union leaders. In 1839 he published *Dissuasive Warnings to the People on Street Warfare* and claimed that it undermined the efforts of the physical-force Chartists. He also fantasized about preventing the assassination of Queen Victoria at the exhibition of 1851, a theme he included in his novel, *Life of Roger Mowbray*. His exaggerated sense of his own significance rested upon an assumption that revolution originated in conspiracy.

Somerville was employed by the Anti-Corn Law League in August 1842, after Richard Cobden read his articles signed 'One who has whistled at the plough' and was 'struck with the graphic force' of his writing (Cobden to Parkes, 12 Jan 1854, Parkes MSS). He was hired to promote the cause of free trade in agricultural districts where protectionist sentiment was especially strong. To this end Somerville became an itinerant journalist and travelled over the entire country for much of four years, writing a prodigious number of articles for newspapers. In the spirit of a social anthropologist he described farming communities—work habits, the condition of the soil, crops, prices, rents, wages, the state of the roads, diets, dwellings, crime, discontents, religious beliefs—all laced with arguments for free trade. He also included accounts of actual conversations on these topics: one, revealing strong resentments against the clergy among farm labourers, was quoted by Engels in *The Condition of the Working Class in England* (1845). Somerville's reports have been compared to William Cobbett's *Rural Rides* (1830), and there are patterns of resemblance in the courses of their lives. Many of these writings were published in Somerville's *Whistler at the Plough and Free Trade* (1852–3), a three-volume work that included biographies of notable figures in the free-trade movement and those, such as Adam Smith, who had anticipated their efforts. Somerville served the Anti-Corn Law League well and was kept on in spite of periods when he was incapacitated by heavy drinking. He was also sent to Ireland in 1847 to report on the effects of the famine. Later he quarrelled with Cobden and published *Cobdenic Policy the Internal Enemy of England* (1854), in which he accused Cobden of unscrupulous tactics and of supporting policies such as pacifism that weakened the country.

From the late 1840s Somerville's journalism became desultory, and he faced financial ruin. In 1857 he suffered a psychiatric episode in which he had delusions of persecution, and the following year he emigrated to Canada. With him travelled his wife, Emma, *née* Binks (1825–1859), daughter of a London cabinet-maker, whom he had married on 10 January 1841, and their six children, but he was left a widower only a year later. His journalism revived and was based largely in Hamilton; he wrote about Canada for several English papers and edited the *Canadian Illustrated News* from 1862 to 1864. In 1866 he reported on the Fenian disturbances and published his *Narrative of the Fenian Invasion of Canada*, having lost much of his sympathy for the cause of reform in Ireland in the process.

Somerville had hoped to return to England in 1868, but the assassination of Thomas D'Arcy McGee prevented this; Somerville had been counting on payment from McGee for an 'emigrant's handbook'. He went on to edit the *Church Herald*, from 1873 to 1875, and continued to report on the Fenian disturbances. The Canadian government commissioned articles from him to encourage immigration, and awarded him a pension in 1876. During the last decade of Somerville's life, however, he was isolated, impoverished, and became increasingly eccentric.

Somerville's politics cannot be encompassed with a single label. He had a good deal of class feeling—he had shown 'the martinets of the Scots Greys that, although my parents were poor … and their parents rich … yet I was a man, and that they were, if quite as much, nothing more' (*Political Soldier*, 7 Dec 1833, 1). Throughout his life he sympathized with the working classes and was eager for a democratic suffrage. At the same time he upheld established authority and feared civil conflict, defended the monarchy, and regarded atheists with abhorrence. He also criticized unbridled commerce, and, in spite of his support for free trade, he wished to rescue political economy from the 'soulless materialism which had made it … odious to the People' (Somerville, *Conservative Science of Nations*, 22). He felt great national pride that Britain had achieved reform without sacrificing either order or liberty. His political sentiments reflected his love of 'dear old rural England' (Somerville, *Cobdenic Policy*, 18), and he acknowledged that his 'mental constitution sympathises with a reasoning conservatism' (ibid., 38–9).

Somerville was distinguished by his broad Scottish accent and his mountainous size, and Cobden described how 'the doorway was literally darkened with the huge awkward hulking figure that came lumbering head-foremost into the room' (Cobden to Parkes, 12 Jan 1854, Parkes MSS). In old age he weighed more than 20 stone. He was capable of immense physical stamina. There were times when he went on drinking sprees, but they were followed by 'fits of penitential remorse' (ibid.). He was fiercely independent, and throughout his adult life he was obsessively concerned with issues of loyalty and betrayal as they related to social order and revolution. For all his flaws Somerville is memorable for being a self-educated working man who, in spite of great poverty and an unpromising start in life, conducted himself in difficult circumstances with moral seriousness and a sense of honour, and who wrote prodigiously and thoughtfully with a clear and forceful prose style on important economic and political subjects.

Somerville died on 17 June 1885 at his home in York Street, Toronto, Canada, and was buried in the cemetery of the St Andrew's Society at Toronto.

JOSEPH HAMBURGER

Sources [A. Somerville], *The autobiography of a working man* (1848), chap. 24 · A. Somerville, *Conservative science of nations, being the first complete narrative of Somerville's diligent life in the service of public safety in Britain* (1860) · A. Somerville, *The whistler at the plough*, 3 vols. (1852–3) · A. Somerville, *Cobdenic policy the internal enemy of England* (1854) · A. Somerville, *Public and personal affairs* (1839) · A. Somerville, *Dissuasive warnings to the people on street warfare*, 7 numbers (1839) · J. Carswell, introduction, in A. Somerville, *The autobiography of a working man*, new edn (1951) · E. Waterston, 'Somerville, Alexander', *DCB*, vol. 11 · W. M. Sandison, 'Alexander Somerville', *Border Magazine*, 18, no. 207 (March 1913), 49–55 · A. Somerville, *The whistler at the plough*, 3 vols. (1852–3); facs. edn with introduction by K. D. Snell (1989), iii–xxxi · J. Hamburger, *James Mill and the art of revolution* (1963) · M. C. Satre, 'Somerville, Alexander', *BDMBR*, vol. 2 · Parkes MSS, Cobden to Parkes, 12 Jan 1854

Archives UCL, Parkes MSS · W. Sussex RO, Cobden MSS

Likenesses photograph, 1871 (Montreal), repro. in Sandison, 'Alexander Somerville', 51 · W. Wood, stipple and line engraving (after P. Wilkinson), NPG; repro. in Somerville, *The whistler*, frontispiece · lithograph (after photograph), NPG · photograph, repro. in Somerville, *Autobiography*, frontispiece

Wealth at death probably nil: *Waterston*, 'Somerville, Alexander'

Somerville, Alexander Neil (1813–1889), Free Church of Scotland minister and evangelist, was born in Edinburgh on 29 January 1813, the eldest of eight children of Alexander Somerville, a wine merchant and his wife, Eliza Munro. He was educated at Edinburgh high school and Edinburgh University, where Robert Murray McCheyne became an inseparable friend. Licensed by the presbytery of Jedburgh in December 1835, he worked as a missionary at Stockbridge, Edinburgh, before succeeding McCheyne as assistant to Dr John Bonar of Larbert and Dunipace. In November 1837 he was ordained as minister of Anderston, a *quoad sacra* charge in Glasgow. His connection with this congregation was to last in various forms for the next fifty-two years. On 6 June 1841 he married Isabella Mirrlees Ewing (*d.* 1900); they had two daughters and three sons.

In 1843, at the Disruption of the Church of Scotland, Somerville joined the Free Church and his congregation built a new church in Cadogan Street. Like McCheyne he had felt a missionary impulse early in life, but he channelled it instead into revivals and home-mission work. There was much to do in Anderston, where drunkenness and prostitution were rife. He became home secretary of the Glasgow African Missionary Society and a director of the Glasgow Bible Society. His interest in the latter led him to become one of the founders of the National Bible Society of Scotland. His urge to travel and his skills as a propagandist were exploited by the Free Church, which sent him to Canada on its behalf in 1845. In 1848–9 he went on a visit to the Holy Land. He took a great interest in the cause of protestantism in Spain, where he spent each summer for six years. He drew up a constitution and confession of faith for Spanish protestants in 1870. In the same year the ancient Scottish barony of Somerville fell vacant and Somerville was a claimant. No claim was upheld, however, and the peerage became dormant.

Somerville's tireless work led to a physical breakdown, but he recovered to be galvanized by the visit of the American revivalists Moody and Sankey to Scotland in 1873. He resolved to become a full-time evangelist, and went on a missionary tour in India in 1874–5. He visited Canada in 1876; in the following year he formally became a missionary there and the Glasgow United Evangelistic Association released him from ministerial duties. In May 1877 he received the honorary degree of DD from Glasgow University. Thereafter he travelled to Australia, New Zealand, France, Italy, Germany, Russia, South Africa, Greece, western Asia, Bohemia, Hungary, Serbia, and Romania. His practice was to preach, when necessary through an interpreter, at meetings where hymns were sung. Although understandably most effective in the English-speaking world, his gatherings in other countries invariably attracted an audience and, less often, some local opposition. Somerville's unorthodox methods and nondenominational approach did not prevent him from being honoured by his own church when, in 1886, he became moderator of the Free Church of Scotland general assembly. He was invited to address the general assembly of the established church on the question of converting the Jews, the last of his enthusiasms, in 1889. He died on 18 September 1889 at 11 South Park Terrace, Hillhead, Glasgow, and was buried nearby at the western necropolis, Maryhill.

Although hardly orthodox in his missionary methods, which were not confined to one continent, let alone one country, Somerville was an effective missionary who used modern evangelistic techniques. His efforts were helped by his commanding appearance: he had a tall and athletic build, a lofty brow, and a piercing eye, and his hair, bushy and black in youth, turned to a venerable, flowing white.

E. I. CARLYLE, *rev.* LIONEL ALEXANDER RITCHIE

Sources G. Smith, *A modern apostle* (1890) · A. N. Somerville, *Precious seed* (1890) · J. Smith, *Our Scottish clergy*, 2nd ser. (1849) · *Fasti Scot.* · *Free Church of Scotland Monthly* (1 Jan 1890), 8–10 · W. Ewing, ed., *Annals of the Free Church of Scotland, 1843–1900*, 1 (1914), 323 · GEC, *Peerage*

Likenesses photograph (in old age), repro. in Smith, *A modern apostle*, frontispiece · photograph, repro. in Somerville, *Precious seed*, frontispiece

Wealth at death £4997 9*s*. 10*d*.: confirmation, 22 Oct 1889, *CCI*

Somerville, Andrew (1808–1834), painter, was born in Edinburgh, the son of a wireworker. He was educated at the Edinburgh high school, and then trained at the Trustees' Academy. He studied under the historical and landscape painter William Simson, whom he subsequently assisted in teaching drawing. He exhibited publicly for the first time at the Institution for Encouragement of Fine Arts in 1826 with a chalk drawing of a young man. In the course of his career with the Royal Scottish Academy he exhibited a total of twenty-seven works, was elected an associate on 9 November 1831, and, on 10 February 1833, a full member. His early death at the age of twenty-six in Edinburgh on 7 January 1834 cut short the promising career: as was stated in the minutes of the academy's general meeting on 10 February 1834, Somerville was 'a most esteemed member of the academy the excellence and quality of whose pictures, exhibited at an early age gave high promise of future eminence in the walk of art'. As he died intestate an inventory of his effects was drawn up and signed on 5 June 1834 by his brother James Somerville, an engraver in Edinburgh. Few examples of Andrew Somerville's work are known; he painted chiefly subjects drawn from border ballads and literary sources such as James Hogg. His *Cottage Children* and *Bride of Yarrow* (1833) are in the National Gallery of Scotland, Edinburgh, and portraits by him are in the collection at Balnagown Castle, Scotland. TINA FISKE

Sources *Annual Report of the Council of the Royal Scottish Academy of Painting, Sculpture, and Architecture*, 7 (1834) · minutes books of general meetings, 1831–2, 1834, Royal Scot. Acad. · A. Somerville, letter of acknowledgement on election as academician, 14 Feb 1832, Royal Scot. Acad., ALS collection · *Scottish Nation* (1834) · R. Brydall, *Art in Scotland, its origin and progress* (1889) · J. L. Caw, *Scottish painting past and present, 1620–1908* (1908) · E. Gordon, *The Royal Scottish Academy of painting, sculpture and architecture, 1826–1976* (1976) · P. J. M. McEwan, *Dictionary of Scottish art and architecture* (1994) · W. D. McKay and F. Rinder, *The Royal Scottish Academy, 1826–1916* (1917) · B. Stewart and M. Cutten, *The dictionary of portrait painters in Britain up to 1920* (1997) · Redgrave, *Artists* · [J. Lloyd Williams], *National Gallery of Scotland: concise catalogue of paintings* (1997) · Intestate, SC 70/1/50, 724–5
Archives Royal Scot. Acad., Royal Scottish Academy records

Somerville, Edith Anna Œnone (1858–1949), writer and artist, born on 2 May 1858 in Corfu where her father was stationed with his regiment, was the eldest of the eight children of Lieutenant-Colonel Thomas Henry Somerville (1824–1898) and his wife, Adelaide Eliza Coghill (1831–1895).

An independent girl The Somerville family experienced extreme pecuniary difficulties in the years after the famine; the colonel's children had to make their own way in life, using family connections in the army and navy freely. To maintain their home, Drishane House, Skibbereen, co. Cork, all hands were needed and sisters joined their brothers in the effort to keep the old place up. In 1859 Colonel Somerville retired home to Drishane. He—and his father—liked independence in women and encouraged it. Edith completely dominated her siblings who, despite

Edith Anna Œnone Somerville (1858–1949), by unknown photographer, 1922

this, developed into two admirals, two colonels, one master of foxhounds, and the celebrated cattle breeder and farmer Lady Coghill. The forcing house of such a family background naturally produced women who would be self-confident rather than submissive. In this Edith and her sister were no different from any other sporting soldier's daughters; Edith's skill as a rider was developed in hunting with men, where she felt it was important to show that women could do as well as men in the hunting field. Her only sister, Hildegarde, born in 1867, came too late on the scene to be an ally in childhood. Her close companion in childhood was her first cousin and 'twin' Ethel Coghill.

Schooling was not at that time thought to be absolutely necessary for girls, but the female cousinhood at Castletownshend was gathered in a 'schoolroom' where a series of governesses taught them the rudiments. Edith snatched one term at school at Alexandra College in Dublin before developing into a serious art student. Her strength of character won her unusual independence for she was determined enough to fund herself for professional training in Paris at the studios of Colarossi and Délécluse. Her status as an artist was important to her all through her life, in creating her own space within the Somerville family of which she was intensely proud and which she had no desire to leave. In the group of families descended from Chief Justice Charles Kendal Bushe, who was great-grandfather of both Edith Somerville and her cousin and colleague Violet *Martin (1862–1915), there was a high incidence of the type of woman known as *maîtresse femme*, and as mothers the type could be over characterful but certainly encouraged in their daughters great powers of speech. Edith's language, both in conversation and in writing, was vigorous, pithy, and well structured, and she venerated good talkers, habitually recording them in writing.

Edith put aside thoughts of marriage following an emotional crisis in 1878, when an unsuitably impecunious suitor, a cousin Hewitt Poole, was seen off by Edith's parents. She had a second relationship, with Captain Barry Yelverton (*d.* 1885), son of the notorious William Yelverton, fourth Viscount Avonmore. After this she vowed to be self-supporting, to work, and remain unmarried. Following training at the West Kensington School of Art and at Colarossi's studio in Paris she supported herself as an illustrator, though her first love was always to remain painting. Finding it difficult to bring in an income solely from art, when she had ventured to write a 'shilling shocker' with Violet Martin, she wrote to her brother Cameron in 1888 on the advisability of having more than one iron in the fire. With the success of their experimental *An Irish Cousin* published in 1889, she resigned herself to the more remunerative principal occupation of writing.

An Irish Cousin Although they met on 17 January 1886 it was some time, quite contrary to her later account in the idealized *Irish Memories*, before Edith Somerville contemplated a working partnership with her cousin. At first the Somerville family had taken Mrs Martin and her reserved daughter for spongers, and it took some time for their charm to take hold all round. Edith was highly popular in the throng of cousins that flowed through Castletownshend, and revelled in riotous assemblies. She did not, at first, particularly mark out Violet Martin, who was superficially restrained and subtle, as a congenial soulmate. It was Martin who positively fostered a special relationship and who set in motion their first playful work of collaboration: a spoof dictionary of family slang that sent up the scholarly work of Edith's faithful suitor and cousin Herbert Greene, Oxford classics don and contributor to Liddell and Scott's *Greek Lexicon*. This light-hearted effort gave such pleasure and amusement that they dared to think of larger things: payment and publication.

Edith made more of her modest talents as an artist than might have been expected—her talent as a writer far exceeded them—because she was generally used, as a matter of course, as the natural choice of artist to illustrate the writing of Somerville and Ross. Her income, including as it did fees from the illustration as well as from the writing, was proportionately greater than that of Violet Martin. Both as a writer and as an illustrator she had a tendency to Dickensian zaniness that marked her work with a bluntness entirely in contrast to her superfine colleague. Though feminists, they were not separatists, they gave support to men, and received it from them throughout their lives. Their novels persistently describe pairing between a liberated female and a sympathetic male. It was the less refined and fastidious Somerville who wrote the romantic passages of their work.

An Irish Cousin gave them a reputation, and in the 1890s, trading on their excellent connections in the world of journalism, they were commissioned to write travel books, touring Connemara in 1890 for the *Lady's Pictorial*, and Wales and Denmark in 1893. All through that period of light-hearted journalistic work they were piecing together a novel that was, after some years in the wilderness, to place them in the first rank: *The Real Charlotte*, published in 1894. To begin with it was not the great pecuniary or critical success that they had hoped for, however, and after *The Silver Fox* of 1897, and a severe talking-to by their agent J. B. Pinker, they undertook a major overhaul of their style and aims and came up with *The Irish RM*, a set of comic tales that was to bring them the fame, and much more importantly the fortune, that was so badly needed to keep up their homes. Hunting and the maintenance of a pack of hounds was also a major drain on Edith's income. With the West Carbery foxhounds Edith had the distinction of being the first woman master of foxhounds in Ireland, from 1903 to 1908 and again from 1912 to 1919. She undertook this onerous position not only from love of the sport but as she felt it gave her writing on the chase an added authority.

Writing *The Irish RM* They began on the RM series when Martin was recovering from a bad injury sustained in a hunting accident and much of the responsibility for the management of their literary career fell on Edith. As Martin was sofa-bound they hit upon the dodge of reworking their old letters and weaving RM stories around tracts of prose describing Martin's infiltration into the society of west Cork twelve years before. One of the peculiarities of their working relationship was that it was carried on at a distance, Edith being based at Drishane and Martin at Ross House, co. Galway, for a large part of the year. For twenty years they wrote together in instalments by post or when travelling. In February 1906, however, Martin's mother died and she left Ross for Drishane. That year, much troubled by the future of Drishane, Edith had the shock of discovering that Cameron, the heir, had an overdraft of £1000, and in consequence her letters are understandably fixated on staving off pecuniary disaster. As professional women authors Somerville and Ross belonged to a community of working women; pairing between women in this society was common and for economic and social reasons as well as sexual ones. Edith had a harmonious business partnership for more than thirty years in running a farm with her sister. Edith was president, and Martin vice-president, of the Munster Women's Franchise League, until the split in the league brought about by the First World War.

Farm affairs permitting, Martin worked in Castletownshend with Edith for nine years during which time they produced some excellent light essays, but more importantly *Further Experiences of an Irish RM* in 1908, *Dan Russell the*

Fox in 1911, and in 1915 the final RM series, *In Mr Knox's Country*. At the end of that year with very little warning Martin fell gravely ill, immobilized by a brain tumour, and in a few weeks she wasted away. Edith was unable to bear the thought of animals or humans in great suffering and with her animals aided the release of death when she could. She knew that Martin would not recover, and sat writing in her sick-room three days before Martin eventually died on 21 December 1915, organizing her burial. Edith was not distraught as she had been at her mother's death, but was stunned and inert with shock. Unable even to make diary entries Edith could not write or paint and moved after the funeral on 23 December to Lismore to be with her cousin and childhood 'twin' Ethel Coghill, and later went to her brother Jack in London. She was staying with him when the Easter rising broke out in Dublin. With all of her brothers serving in the armed forces in the war, and not wishing to offend them, she wrote anonymously to *The Times* to plead for clemency to be shown to the leaders of the uprising, the first such appeal in those pages.

In Edith's absence Cameron supplied to E. V. Lucas some material regarding the nature of the cousins' collaboration that exaggerated its mystery. Edith wrote to correct Cameron, explaining that it was perfectly easy to differentiate between their two hands, but, perhaps because it was more convenient to publicists to have a mystery, this was never corrected in the press, and the passage, manufactured by Cameron and printed by E. V. Lucas in his memorial to Martin in *The Spectator*, has continued to be quoted. Edith did not at first contemplate continuing a career in writing—she had disparagingly referred to herself as the 'hack and amanuensis' to the genius of Martin. Some unknowing obituarists regretted that, as Edith was the illustrator and Martin the writer, Somerville and Ross could be no more. But as Edith recovered her composure, a novel solution to the survival of the writing partnership presented itself. Coming from a family that had been prominent in the early years of the Society for Psychical Research, of which her uncle Joscelyn Coghill had been one of the first vice-presidents, and that took with utmost seriousness the existence of a parallel world of spirit beings, Edith became convinced that Martin was still with her in spirit and her self-appointed role as amanuensis was continued through the medium of automatic writing.

Writings without Martin The quick-fire verbal exchange that had accompanied their writing process now became an interior dialogue. Edith eased herself back into the writing profession with a memoir of Martin, *Irish Memories*, in 1917, and, as it contained material written by both, she justified the continuance of the dual authorship. The adulatory portrait of Martin is a surprisingly soft-hearted and sentimental tribute given the sharp and sometimes savage humour of their paired wit. Taking a step further, in maintaining to be the representative of two authors in one person, Edith incorporated notes of projected works and discussions of plots from their letters, as she did for *The Big House of Inver* (1925), as further justification for continuing to publish under the name of two authors, one living, one dead.

In 1919 Edith met the composer Ethel Smyth, who had privately assumed Edith to be a fellow lesbian from the tone of *Irish Memories*, and began a stimulating and consoling friendship, although it did not survive Edith's refusal to entertain the enthusiastically passionate Ethel as anything other than a friend. The necessity of earning an income remained pressing. Edith published fifteen titles, and one privately circulated family history, in the thirty-four years following Martin's death. If she did not become wealthy, she did have public recognition for her literary work: in 1932 Trinity College, Dublin, awarded an honorary LittD and in 1941 the Irish Academy of Letters awarded her the Gregory gold medal. She had always kept more than one iron in the fire and raised some money from horse-coping, and from selling her paintings at exhibitions organized for her by Ethel Smyth in London and New York. In 1940, to shield her brother Cameron from shame, Edith cashed in her untouched stocks and shares to prevent Drishane lands from falling into the hands of the Bank of Ireland. Her movement increasingly restricted by sciatica, she moved from Drishane in 1946, where she had been mistress since her mother's death in 1895, and went with her sister Hildegarde to Tally Ho, on the main street of Castletownshend, a more convenient house for her invalid existence. On her ninetieth birthday in 1948 she took immense pleasure in the BBC broadcast of a birthday tribute made by her nephew, Hildegarde's son Professor Nevill Coghill. In the same year Oxford University Press included *The Real Charlotte* in its World's Classics series. In her last months she was much entertained by conversation with Father Lamb, a parish priest and old friend. She died at Tally Ho, a protestant, on 8 October 1949, having been cared for by her sister and the young Mrs Ambrose Coghill, who had feared conversion to Catholicism up to the last moment. She was given a wake in Tally Ho by her close attendants, and was buried on 11 October at St Barrahane's Church, Castletownshend.

Writing of a hybrid Anglo-Irish world that was long gone, and crammed into a 'rollicking tales' pigeon-hole with Lever and Lover, Somerville and Ross declined in reputation after the establishment of Irish independence. New Ireland looked on them with appalled disgust: there was a time in the 1950s and 1960s when to admit to enjoying the RM series or *The Real Charlotte* caused real offence. But slowly an appreciation of their style and genuineness has grown, and of their record of Irish speech, which was exact, voluminous, and incorporated verbatim into their work.

Born out of impecunious necessity, Edith's confidence in the sphere of arts and crafts knew no bounds: at various times she designed a house, whose building she supervised, tombstones, books, and book jackets. An active parishioner, she was the organist in the parish church for seventy-five years. The mosaic that she designed for the floor of the apse in Castletownshend church, adapted from a motif in the Book of Kells of two serpents with intertwined tongues, celebrates the writing life of Somerville and Ross, and is strikingly successful in contrast to their two headstones in the graveyard. Martin has a restrained and formal cross, chosen by her brother Jim who suggested that it would be better for Martin to lie in the village where she had been so happy, rather than in the decayed graveyard at Ross, of which she had a horror. In contrast beside it Edith has a monolith of local stone similar to the memorial she designed for her brother Aylmer, her fellow master of foxhounds. The two stones are inharmonious together and show that Edith, true to her beliefs, had given no thought to the combined appearance of those final full stops. GIFFORD LEWIS

Sources diaries of E. A. Œ. Somerville, Queen's University, Belfast • E. A. Œ. Somerville, correspondence with M. Ross, NYPL, Humanities and Social Sciences Library, Berg collection • review scrapbooks, Coghill family papers • Buddh dictionary, Coghill family papers • E. Œ. Somerville, automatic writing, Queen's University, Belfast • letters from Ethel Smyth to E. Œ. Somerville, Queen's University, Belfast • E. Œ. Somerville and V. Martin, *Irish memories* (1917) • O. Rauchbauer, *The Edith Œnone Somerville archive in Drishane: a catalogue and an evaluative essay*, IMC (1995) • G. Lewis, *Somerville and Ross: the world of the Irish RM* (1985) • *The selected letters of Somerville and Ross*, ed. G. Lewis (1989) • G. Lewis, *Edith Somerville: a biography* (2003)

Archives Drishane, Castletownshend, co. Cork, archives • Harvard U., Houghton L., corresp. and literary MSS • NRA, priv. coll., corresp. and papers • Queen's University, Belfast, corresp. and papers • TCD, corresp. • TCD, notebook | BL, corresp. with Society of Authors, Add. MSS 56814, 63329 • NL Ire., letters to J. B. Pinker • NYPL, Berg collection • Queen's University, Belfast, letters to Geraldine Cummins • TCD, corresp. with Thomas McGreevy • U. Reading, letters to Longmans, Green & Co. • Sourden, Rothes, Fife, Coghill family MSS

Likenesses J. Coghill, photograph, 1875, repro. in *Selected letters*, ed. Lewis • H. Coghill, double portrait, photograph, *c*.1891 (with Martin Ross), repro. in *Selected letters*, ed. Lewis • photograph, 1922, NPG [*see illus.*] • double portraits, photographs (with Martin Ross), repro. in Lewis, *Somerville and Ross*, pp. 64, 78

Wealth at death £967 4*s*. 6*d*.: probate, 1950, *CGPLA Éire* • £706 15*s*. 7*d*.—in England: probate, 9 Jan 1950, *CGPLA Eng. & Wales*

Somerville [*née* Gibb], **Euphemia Gilchrist** (1860–1935), social worker and local politician, was born on 19 September 1860 in New Town, Dollar, Clackmannanshire, the daughter of William Gibb, a draper, and his wife, Margaret Scott McMinn. She was educated at Dollar Academy, where she won a number of prizes. On 28 June 1893 she married Alexander Somerville (1841/2–1907), a retired East India merchant, the son of Alexander Neil *Somerville, a Free Church minister. They had two sons and a daughter. Her husband, a widower with three daughters, had taken up the study of botany after his retirement from business. After his death in 1907 Euphemia Somerville and her children moved to Edinburgh and from 1911 lived in Colinton. The introduction to *A Child Lover* (1937), an appreciation published after her death, stated that her experience of child poverty in Glasgow was the motivation for all her work. Her first public role was in Glasgow where, in response to high rates of infant mortality, she organized voluntary health visitors on behalf of the city council. She was asked to develop a similar scheme in Edinburgh in 1908, and with Mrs Hamilton Maxwell started the Edinburgh Voluntary Health Workers' Association, under the auspices of the council child welfare scheme.

Euphemia Somerville was elected to the town council for the Merchiston ward in 1919 as an independent, actively supported by the Edinburgh Women Citizens' Association (EWCA). The EWCA was set up in 1918, after women were partially enfranchised, to educate and organize the new women voters. It was ambitious, with interests encompassing women's political representation at local and national level, equal pay, and social welfare, especially for women as mothers and for children, but also mental handicap, social housing, and public health. When she was first elected she went to live for a month in the Craiglockhart poorhouse 'in order that she might obtain first-hand information on this side of Social Service' (*A Child Lover*, 11), and then took a diploma at the new school of social study and training at the University of Edinburgh, a course that was aimed at both professional and voluntary social workers and taken by many women active in social reform. On the council, she was a member at various times of the education, public health, housing, and town planning and public parks committees. A colleague said that she was seen as 'a party of one—viz. herself' (ibid., 41), and that this limited her influence and preferment. Mrs Hamilton Maxwell saw her, however, as 'unconfused by political interest or side issues' (ibid., 14). As well as being the second woman councillor in the city, holding her seat until her death, she also became in 1932 the city's second woman bailie, or magistrate, after several attempts. When she took this position, the 'woman of the streets was the subject of Mrs Somerville's special personal attention' (ibid., 44).

Somerville chaired the executive committee of the EWCA from 1922 to 1930. Her multiple roles illustrate a mutually reinforcing relationship between women in local politics and women's organizations. By 1926 she was pushing for more council housing within the corporation and had set up the EWCA subcommittee on housing, through which she launched the Edinburgh Welfare Housing Trust in 1928 to build 'good houses for the very poor' (*A Child Lover*, 55) as a model of what councils could do. By 1934 the trust had built on four city sites. Accounts of that work hint that her determination over housing, particularly slum clearance, bordered on the obsessive. After her death it was said that 'the vast new housing schemes that now detract from the landscape around Edinburgh' were her reward (*The Scotsman*, 1 Dec 1937)—an ambiguous legacy but one that indicated a response to housing conditions of the time. In the introduction to a survey of the St Andrews ward in Edinburgh (just behind the smart shops in Princes Street), commissioned by the EWCA in 1931 and undertaken by two women chartered surveyors, Somerville wrote that they wanted 'to bring out in strong relief the environment of the child in overcrowded insanitary areas' (E. E. Perry and I. T. Barclay, *Behind Princes Street*, 1931, 5). Such concerns were also acted on by the Edinburgh corporation public health committee. After May 1930 the committee's responsibilities included administration of the municipal hospitals and all services for mental health and handicap. As the first convener of the new mental diseases subcommittee (1930–32), which administered two major institutions, Bangour Mental Hospital and Gogarburn, and their auxiliary services, Somerville championed progressive approaches to the care and treatment of the mentally ill and handicapped.

Somerville was best known in Edinburgh for the toddlers' playgrounds of which, at her death, there were nineteen. They grew out of her work in health visiting, as toddlers were often neglected when a new baby came and also had high rates of mortality. The playgrounds offered supervision, 'exercise, fresh air, and happy occupation' (*A Child Lover*, 18). Edinburgh was a pioneer in pre-school provision, having established in 1903 the first free kindergarten in Scotland, at Reid's Court, Canongate, and by 1913 it had five voluntarily funded child gardens, as they were called, there being only fourteen in the rest of Britain. However, with an estimated 4000 children under five living in crowded rooms in densely populated districts, cheaper provision was needed through the playgrounds and after-school play centres. From 1930 Somerville convened a special committee on the care and education of children up to five. She commissioned a survey of children's health in the poorer areas, information that was used to argue for council nursery schools, the first of which was built in 1930 and is still open.

Somerville was similarly assiduous in the cause of equal pay and promotion for women employees of the council, on which the EWCA lobbied. In 1928 she was described as steadily and persistently pursuing equal increments for corporation clerical employees. She also argued for women and men to be represented on all boards and charitable bodies, and for council advisory committees in key areas with equal numbers of men and women members.

The boundary between voluntary work, voluntary associations, and the local state was permeable at this time and one which many 'organized women' (as the EWCA called itself) crossed. In Edinburgh Somerville was the pre-eminent example of this activity, as she brought into local government her own early experience of voluntary health visiting. The influence of women and women's organizations on welfare policy was arguably at a height during the inter-war period, when poor relief, voluntary hospitals, public health, and children's health and welfare (through educational provision) were all locally administered. Somerville espoused campaigns for aged persons, rent rebates according to the number of children in a family, social centres in the new housing areas, and the appointment of women police officers. She was also a director of the Royal Maternity and Simpson Memorial Hospital, where she was seen as possessing expertise in maternal mortality, birthrate fluctuations, and venereal disease; she was a link between the hospital and the council's public health department. Although babies and small children were undoubtedly a priority in her work, to emphasize her role as a 'child lover' is to underplay her organizational and leadership skills and the expertise she developed in several areas of health and welfare. She was a 'practical visionary' (*A Child Lover*, 15), with immense vitality, a notable thoroughness, and, according to Mrs Hamilton Maxwell, 'a genius for accuracy'. What she called practical Christianity was a central motivation, and in *Citizenship* (n.d.), a pamphlet she wrote for the EWCA, she emphasized the importance of collectivity and citizenship as 'the gospel and practice of inter-relationships'.

Euphemia Somerville died at her home, 27 Colinton Road, Edinburgh, on 27 September 1935. The herbarium of British plants she and her husband had collected was presented to the University of Edinburgh.

SUE INNES

Sources *A child lover* (1937) • S. Innes, 'Love and work: feminism, equality and citizenship, Britain, 1900–1939', PhD diss., U. Edin., 1998 • *The Scotsman* (28 Sept 1935) • *The Scotsman* (1 Dec 1937) • *Edinburgh Evening News* (3 Dec 1937) • b. cert. • m. cert. • d. cert. • Edinburgh city libraries, Edinburgh Room • EWCA annual reports, 1919–35, NA Scot., GD 333/2 • EWCA minutes of executive committee and general meetings, 1918–25, NA Scot., GD 333/7, 333/8, 333/9 • J. Stewart, *Organisation of education in Edinburgh* (1925), esp. 76–7 • minutes of the Edinburgh education authority, 1919–30, Edinburgh City Archives • minutes of the Edinburgh corporation education committee, 1930–34, Edinburgh City Archives • M. Rackstraw, ed., *A social survey of the city of Edinburgh* (1926) • J. Lewis, 'Women's agency, maternalism and welfare', *Gender and History*, 6/1 (1994) • J. Lewis, 'Gender, the family and women's agency in the building of "welfare states": the British case', *Social History*, 19 (1994)

Archives NA Scot., Edinburgh Women Citizens' Association

Likenesses photograph, Edinburgh City Archives; repro. in *The Scotsman* (28 Sept 1935)

Wealth at death £9961 12*s*. 3*d*.: confirmation, 26 Nov 1935, *CCI*

Somerville, Hugh, fourth Lord Somerville (*c.*1484–1549), nobleman, was the second son of William, master of Somerville, and his second wife, Janet Douglas of Drumlanrig. His father died in 1491, a few months before his grandfather John, second Lord Somerville, who died in November. His elder brother, also John, thus succeeded, but died childless in 1522, and so Hugh took his seat in parliament as the fourth lord on 16 November 1524. He married twice. His first wife, Anna, an illegitimate daughter of James Hamilton, first earl of Arran, whom he married on 20 December 1510, died of smallpox with their two young sons in 1516. In July 1517 he married Janet, daughter of William Maitland of Lethington, with whom he had six sons and three daughters.

A major landowner in Lanarkshire, Somerville was often entangled in territorial disputes. In August 1525 his cousin John Somerville of Cambusnethan sought to usurp the lands of Carnwath, at the centre of Hugh's inheritance. Cambusnethan had the support of the sixth earl of Angus, the effective head of the government, and eventually Lord Somerville had to give way. Instead he took up residence in Cowthally, an ancient family strength, which he largely rebuilt. On 4 September 1526 he was involved in the fight at Linlithgow in which the twelfth earl of Lennox was killed, following an unsuccessful attempt to remove the young James V from Augus's custody. That in 1531

Somerville was declared innocent of any complicity in Lennox's death, faring better than others who had to pay substantial fines, was probably owing to royal favour. In 1528 he had supported James V at Stirling when the king finally broke free of Angus's control, and he subsequently became something of an intimate with James, who in 1532 resolved his dispute with Cambusnethan.

Somerville frequently entertained James V at Cowthally, where in July 1532 the king attended the marriage of Hugh's daughter Agnes. Royal friendship brought few visible rewards, but some sort of warmth clearly existed: Somerville was on Leith docks when the king returned from France with his first wife, Madeleine, on 19 May 1537, having spent lavishly to bedeck himself and his retainers in new liveries for the occasion: according to family tradition it was to pay for this that he sold rents worth £60 from Carnwath to St Mary Magdalene hospital, Edinburgh, and indeed two charters from 1540 record just such a sale. In 1540 he served the king by sitting on the assize which condemned Hamilton of Finnart for treason; he may also have served his own interests, since Finnart's accumulation of estates was making him a potential rival in Lanarkshire. On 30 December 1540 James granted Somerville the bailiary of the lands and barony of Carstairs, forfeited by Finnart. Somerville was not just a courtier, however, for he fought in James V's army at Solway Moss on 24 November 1542 and was among the many Scottish nobles captured by the English. Taken to London considerably more slowly than his fellows (he did not arrive until about 19 December), there he became one of the Assured Scots, pledged to press for the marriage of the infant Mary, queen of Scots, to Henry VIII's son, Prince Edward, and to promote the English cause in Scotland. His ransom, assessed on lands valued at £800 and goods worth £1000 Scots, was accordingly reduced and he was promised a pension. But like his fellows he had to hand over his eldest son as a hostage.

Back in Scotland early in 1543, Somerville participated in that year's confused manoeuvring, as an opponent of Cardinal David Beaton and his policy of alliance with France. Instead he collaborated with the earl of Angus, at this time pro-English, and even went to Douglas on 8 September to subscribe a band contracting to support the English marriage. Assigned with the fifth Lord Maxwell to represent the views of his associates to Henry VIII, he ill-advisedly went via Edinburgh, where he was arrested on 1 November, to be briefly imprisoned there before being taken to Blackness Castle on the 6th. Although his dispatches were used by Beaton as evidence for the treason of his enemies, the services implicit in Somerville's captivity secured the release from England of his eldest son. He was himself freed from Blackness by 2 April 1544.

Somerville's political position remained ambivalent for the rest of his life. He was present in the Scottish army at Coldingham in December 1544 and at Ancrum Moor on 27 February 1545, while on 10 June 1546 he attended the convention at Stirling which made provision for the government of Scotland after the murder of Beaton. But on 21 March 1549 he was once more presenting himself as a supporter of England and an enemy of the governor, the second earl of Arran. His stance at this point may have been influenced by his protestantism in religion, or may have resulted from one of his son's being an English prisoner. Somerville died later that year, sometime before 11 November, and was buried at Carnwath. His wife, who died sometime after 19 August 1559, was interred beside him.

The fourth lord's eldest son from his second marriage, **James Somerville** (*c.*1519–1569), succeeded as fifth Lord Somerville, having sasine of Carnwath by 19 February 1550. Like his father he married twice. His first wife, Jean Hamilton, whom he had married by 26 March 1529, was another illegitimate daughter of the first earl of Arran. They had no children, and the marriage may have been ended by divorce. Then, some time after 8 April 1536, James married Agnes, daughter of Sir James Hamilton of Finnart, with whom he had two sons and two daughters; he probably also had an illegitimate son. In the late 1550s the fifth lord, like his father in the previous decade, seems to have favoured a Scottish alliance with England, but unlike his father he remained a Catholic. In 1560 he signed the treaty of Berwick of 22 February and the Leith bond of 27 April, and he supported proposals that Queen Elizabeth should marry the earl of Arran, but according to Knox he was one of three peers who voted against the reformed confession of faith in August, declaring 'We will believe as our fathers believed' (*History of the Reformation*, 1.339). Later he was a firm supporter of Mary, queen of Scots, whom he entertained at Cowthally from 24 to 26 August 1563. He took part in the suppression of the chaseabout raid in 1565, and fought for Mary at Langside on 13 May 1568, when he was wounded. He died at Cowthally in December 1569 and was buried at Carnwath, as was his wife, who was still alive in August 1597. His heir was his elder son, Hugh. MARCUS MERRIMAN

Sources *Scots peerage* · GEC, *Peerage* · J. Somerville, *Memorie of the Somervilles*, 2 vols. (1815) · J. Cameron, *James V: the personal rule, 1528–1542*, ed. N. Macdougall (1998) · M. Merriman, *The rough wooings: Mary queen of Scots, 1542–1551* (2000) · J. M. Thomson and others, eds., *Registrum magni sigilli regum Scotorum / The register of the great seal of Scotland*, 11 vols. (1882–1914), vol. 3 · G. Donaldson, *All the queen's men* (1983) · *John Knox's History of the Reformation in Scotland*, ed. W. C. Dickinson, 2 vols. (1949) · *State papers published under … Henry VIII*, 11 vols. (1830–52), vol. 5

Wealth at death in 1542 lands assessed at £800 Scots p.a; goods at £1000 Scots: *State papers of Henry VIII*, 5.242

Somerville, James, fifth Lord Somerville (*c.*1519–1569). *See under* Somerville, Hugh, fourth Lord Somerville (*c.*1484–1549).

Somerville, James (*bap.* 1632, *d.* 1693), family historian, was baptized on 24 January 1632 at Newhall, Lanarkshire, the eldest son of James Somerville (1596–1677) of Drum and his wife, Lilias Bannatyne (1607/8–1675). The elder Somerville, who was by right the ninth Lord Somerville but never assumed the title as he felt that he lacked the wealth to support it, travelled widely and gained martial experience with the French and Venetian forces. Returning to Scotland, he sided with the presbyterian covenanters against Charles I, serving under General Leslie. He was made a major and held a command at the siege of Edinburgh Castle in 1640. James Somerville was with his father at that siege, although he was only nine. In 1645 he was in the cavalry muster held by David Leslie on Gladsmuir to deal with the royalist threat from Montrose.

In 1647 smallpox and consumption killed Somerville's two brothers, leaving him the only surviving male heir of the house of Somerville. His father became more reluctant to risk his son's life and resolved that he should never leave Scotland. In 1648 Somerville senior was persuaded by his relations to purchase the decayed family barony of Cambusnethan in Lanarkshire; he moved there with his family at Easter in that year.

The elder Somerville's political views changed with the execution of Charles I and the Cromwellian threat to Scotland. Despite his concern for his son's safety he took him to Edinburgh, where royalist forces were gathering, and placed him at the service of Charles II, who had recently (June 1650) arrived in Scotland. Somerville was attached to the retinue of the earl of Eglinton, who commanded the King's horse guards, and saw much of the action that followed Cromwell's march into Scotland, including the Scottish defeat at Dunbar on 3 September 1650. While he was in this service, Somerville met John Bannatyne of Corhouse and his daughter Martha (1633–1679), his future wife. After Dunbar, Somerville returned to Cambusnethan, which was threatened by the forces of the Association, the hard-line presbyterians who, while opposed to Cromwell, were also hostile to the royalists. He clashed with them briefly.

The next period of Somerville's life was taken up with military concerns. After visiting the court of Charles II at Perth, in November 1650 he joined the cavalry of his cousin Major-General Robert Montgomery, which was charged either to defeat or come to terms with the Association forces of colonels Ker and Strachan. Montgomery entrusted Somerville with the task of negotiating with these forces but by the time Somerville reached Renfrew events had gone too far for negotiations, and he joined the royalist forces on Ruglen, which were mustered to stop Cromwell taking Hamilton. The Cromwellian troops briefly took the town in a night attack but were driven out shortly afterwards. Soon after this Somerville returned to Cambusnethan.

Cromwell was not long in reoccupying Hamilton, and his forces made life increasingly unsafe for royalists in the area. Somerville and his father moved north to safety, and attended the coronation of Charles II at Scone on 1 January 1651. They then visited, at Struthers in Fife, the duke of Hamilton who offered the elder Somerville a command in the royalist forces. This he declined, but again placed his son in royal service, as a volunteer. He regretted this when Charles II decided to invade England, and wrote to his son, telling him to leave the army, but the young Somerville was resolved to go. A stratagem was employed to prevent him: he was lured into the home of his betrothed, Martha Bannatyne, after which the gate was locked and kept so until the army had gone. Somerville thus escaped involvement in the Scottish defeat at Worcester, which ended the royalist cause.

This was the end of Somerville's military career. He spent the years of Cromwellian occupation quietly, and married Martha Bannatyne at Leshamahago church in Lanark on 13 November 1651. His father was involved in the abortive royalist rising of 1653, but Somerville himself took no part in this. His father's death on 3 January 1677 left him the *de jure* tenth Lord Somerville, but, for the same reasons as his parent, he refused to assume the title.

Somerville studied family records, and completed his 'Memorie of the Somervilles' by 1679, the year of his wife's death; the work, edited by Walter Scott, was published in 1816. A large portion of the work deals with his father's life, and describes the turbulent mid-century events in Scotland, with a markedly royalist and episcopalian bias; he regarded his father's adherence to the presbyterian covenanter cause as an unfortunate aberration. This royalism did not prevent Somerville from speaking against abuses of power by royal government. In March 1684 he served on a jury in the trial of Campbell of Cessnock for treason and, with two other jurors, protested against royal proceedings in the case. He and his associates were indicted for riot in interrupting the court, but the charge was later dropped.

Somerville married again on 15 March 1685. His new wife was Margaret Jamieson. On 15 June the next year he was appointed a commissioner of supply for Edinburgh. Despite his loyalty to the Stuarts, he does not seem actively to have opposed the revolution of 1688. He died on 7 February 1693 and was buried in Liberton church, Edinburgh, on 9 February. His eldest son by his first marriage had been accidentally killed in 1682 when trying to separate two friends who were fighting, and he was succeeded as head of the house of Somerville by his grandson, also called James. Margaret Somerville died some time before 19 October 1717. ALEXANDER DU TOIT

Sources J. Somerville, *Memorie of the Somervilles: being a history of the baronial house of Somerville*, ed. W. Scott, 2 vols. (1815), vol. 2, pp. 127–478 · GEC, *Peerage*, new edn · R. Douglas, *The peerage of Scotland*, 2nd edn, ed. J. P. Wood, 2 (1813), 509

Archives NL Scot., Neilsen collection

Wealth at death estates of Drum and barony of Cambusnethan, in an impoverished state: Somerville, *Memorie of the Somervilles*

Somerville, Sir James Fownes (1882–1949), naval officer, was born at Weybridge, Surrey, on 17 July 1882, the second son of Arthur Fownes Somerville, of Dinder House, Wells, Somerset, and his wife, Ellen, daughter of William Stanley Sharland, of New Norfolk, Tasmania. A descendant of a great naval family, the Hoods, Somerville himself chose a naval career, entering the Royal Naval College, Dartmouth, in January 1897, together with Andrew Cunningham, who became a lifelong friend. Promoted lieutenant in 1904, he qualified in the new field of wireless telegraphy in 1907. In the next twenty years he occupied a series of important posts in signalling, including fleet wireless officer during the Gallipoli operations (in which he was appointed DSO for his exceptional service in ship-to-shore communications), experimental work, and director of the signal division. His superiors noted his all-round ability, organizing skill, zeal, tact, good judgement, and determination. In January 1913 he married Mary Kerr, daughter of Colonel Thomas Main, of Curdridge Croft, Botley, Hampshire. They had one son, John, also a naval officer and later at GCHQ, and a daughter, Rachel, a Women's Royal Naval Service officer in the Second World War. Lady Somerville died in August 1945. Promoted captain in 1921, Somerville commanded the battleships *Benbow*, *Barham*, and *Warspite*. In 1931, in the wake of the Invergordon mutiny, together with Captain John Tovey, another officer of great promise, he undertook an inquiry in the Atlantic Fleet which heard the men's grievances and established the causes of the mutiny. He then took command of the cruiser *Norfolk*.

Somerville, initially a shy man, developed a personality of great richness, founded upon a boisterous and infectious sense of humour, a deep sense of obligation and fairness to those who served under him, unflagging energy, and the capacity for inspiring and imaginative leadership. He possessed a wide range of technical interests and skills and was an expert handler of ships with an acute sense of appropriate tactics. Following his successful role in restoring the Royal Navy's confidence after Invergordon, his talent for dealing justly and sympathetically with ratings was recognized by successive postings as commodore of the royal naval barracks, Portsmouth, and director of personal services. Promoted rear-admiral in 1933, he initiated major improvements in the domestic economy of naval families. In 1935 he was appointed CB and in 1936 succeeded the formidable destroyer leader Andrew Cunningham as rear-admiral (D), Mediterranean Fleet. Following the outbreak of the Spanish Civil War, Somerville spent most of the next two years as the senior British naval officer off the Spanish Mediterranean coast, where his astute diplomacy, firm defence of British interests, and ability to get on with others were of inestimable benefit to his country; he never put a foot wrong in a difficult situation. Promoted vice-admiral in 1937, he became commander-in-chief, East Indies, in October 1938 but was compelled to retire from the active list in July 1939 with suspected pulmonary tuberculosis (a verdict which he vigorously opposed, with Harley Street testimony); it was a blow scarcely softened by his promotion to KCB.

Fortunately for Somerville, the Second World War broke out shortly after his retirement and, after a highly successful stint as a radio commentator on the war, he took on the task of developing naval radar and securing its installation on ships; that it was developed successfully and installed rapidly was due chiefly to Somerville's technical mastery, drive, and determination. During the evacuation of Dunkirk, he volunteered to assist Admiral Ramsay at Dover; his ability to assess a situation accurately and speedily and his capacity for initiating action were of immense value.

The defeat of France presented the Churchill government with many problems: specifically that of fighting the Italians single-handed and, more immediately, of neutralizing the French fleet, then located chiefly in north and west African ports. Somerville, the only senior flag officer immediately available who had recent experience of a seagoing command and intimate knowledge of the western Mediterranean, was appointed to the command of force H, a detached squadron under the operational control of the Admiralty and based on Gibraltar. His first task, on 3 July 1940, was to secure the demobilization of the major portion of the French fleet at Mers al-Kebir, by negotiation if possible, by force if necessary. Somerville had little room for manoeuvre, the French Admiral Gensoul was unbending and, at the end of the day, pressures of time, fuel, possible French reinforcements, and Churchillian insistence forced Somerville to open fire and cripple three capital ships at a cost of 1600 French casualties. No one was more distressed by this assault on erstwhile allies than Somerville himself. On this and several subsequent occasions, the outspoken Somerville was at odds with the Admiralty and the prime minister. Force H acted as gatekeeper to the Mediterranean and defended convoys in the central Atlantic. Its most important Atlantic foray was the pursuit of the *Bismarck* in May 1941, in which Somerville's masterly handling of his squadron led to *Ark Royal*'s Swordfish crippling the giant battleship, handing her on a plate to Admiral Tovey's Home Fleet. However, force H, constantly at sea and with flying taking place almost every day, spent most of its time on twenty 'club runs' to Malta with troops, stores and, above all, fighters. These operations, conducted between the summer of 1940 and the autumn of 1941, played a major part in sustaining Malta's resistance to axis attacks and helped to provide it with naval and air striking forces against Rommel's convoys. In the course of these sorties, Somerville's balanced, up-to-date but small force (*Renown*, *Ark Royal*, *Sheffield*, and a flotilla of destroyers) successfully fought off Italian air attacks, drove off superior Italian surface forces and mounted air attacks on shore targets, together with a bombardment of Genoa. Somerville proved himself a first-rate 'fighting admiral' in his handling of force H. Not only was he an admired leader, a tireless trainer, and a subtle tactician, he demonstrated also a capacity to think critically about sea warfare in the modern age. In particular, he grasped quickly the essential principles of carrier air power, often flying in Swordfish to gain understanding of the problems and possibilities, and displaying a sophisticated deployment of *Ark Royal*'s air component. He developed fighter direction, night operations, and anti-submarine patrols.

When disaster overtook the Far Eastern empire in December 1941, Somerville was sent out in February 1942 with a new Eastern Fleet, powerful on paper but with many obsolete units and untrained as a force. A defensive role was forced upon him and he could only shepherd his ragbag fleet to safety when the Japanese Pearl Harbor striking force swept into the Indian Ocean in April 1942. Thereafter, Somerville, now a full admiral, saw his fleet drained away to support vital operations elsewhere and for most of 1942 and 1943 he was reduced to making bricks without straw, endeavouring to build up base facilities and protect convoys. Following the defeat of Italy and the loss of German capital ships, the Eastern Fleet was strengthened by carriers and battleships and Somerville was at last able to strike at Japanese bases with his planes and ships. He also experienced a somewhat troubled relationship with the new supreme allied commander in south-east Asia, Admiral Lord Mountbatten; in wrangles over operations, command, and staff duties, Somerville was generally in the right.

In August 1944 Somerville was asked by his old friend Cunningham, now first sea lord, to head the British Admiralty delegation in Washington. The Americans, increasingly preoccupied with their triumphant drive across the Pacific and now clearly the dominant partner in the western alliance, seemed reluctant to make available resources to Britain, now reduced to the role of a suppliant. Somerville, renowned for his charm, humour, energy, forthrightness, and reputation as a 'fighting admiral', seemed to Cunningham just the man to tackle the redoubtable but unpredictable Admiral Ernest J. King, the American chief of naval operations. Somerville, characteristically, enhanced the Royal Navy's prestige, obtained the required resources and co-operation, and made a host of American friends—King included—in his sojourn in Washington (October 1944 to December 1945). The crowning point in his distinguished career came on VE-day when he was promoted admiral of the fleet. He had earlier been restored to the active list and had also been created GCB and GBE. On ceasing active service in 1946, he retired to the family estate in Somerset and became an energetic county alderman and lord lieutenant, dying at Dinder on 19 March 1949 from a coronary thrombosis. He was buried in Dinder churchyard later that month. Somerville was a sailor of immense gifts—he had a wide range of technical and nautical skills and accomplishments of the highest order, the capacity for leadership with an ability to take hard decisions swiftly and firmly, the warm personality to engender high morale and affection in those who served with him, strategic insight and tactical acumen, abundant energy, and dedication to high standards of efficiency and selfless service. Given his distinguished tenure of three of the Royal Navy's most taxing commands in the Second World War, it was entirely fitting that his career should climax with promotion to admiral of the fleet. MICHAEL SIMPSON

Sources CAC Cam., Somerville MSS • private information (2004) [in possession of son, John Somerville] • BL, Cunningham MSS • CAC Cam., North MSS • CAC Cam., Edwards MSS • NMM, Tennant MSS • D. Macintyre, *Fighting admiral: the life of admiral of the fleet Sir James Somerville* (1961) • M. Simpson, *The Somerville papers* (1995) • *DNB* • Royal Navy service record of Sir J. F. Somerville, PRO, ADM 196/47

Archives CAC Cam., corresp. and papers | BL, corresp. with Viscount Cunningham, diary, Add. MSS 52563–52564 [copy] • PRO, Admiralty records | FILM BFI NFTVA, news footage • IWM FVA, actuality footage • IWM FVA, news footage | SOUND BL NSA, recorded talk ['Coventry: six hundred years young']

Likenesses W. Stoneman, photograph, 1942, NPG • O. Birley, oils, *c.*1945–1948, NMM

Wealth at death £20,663 13*s.* 11*d.*: probate, 5 Aug 1949, *CGPLA Eng. & Wales*

Somerville, John, second Lord Somerville (*c.*1430–1491). *See under* Somerville, William, first Lord Somerville (*c.*1400–1456).

Somerville, John (1560–1583), convicted conspirator, was the son of John Somerville (*d.* in or after 1579), of Edstone, Warwickshire, and Elizabeth Corbett of Lee, Shropshire. After studying at Hart Hall, Oxford, between 1576 and 1579, he married Margaret Arden, the daughter of Edward *Arden of Park Hall, Warwickshire. They had two daughters, Elizabeth and Alice. His father died some time after late 1579, leaving his properties in Warwickshire, Gloucestershire, and Worcestershire to his wife, until John should take possession at the age of twenty-four.

Somerville and his family were members of the Roman Catholic church, and he presumed its restoration if Mary, queen of Scots, should supplant Elizabeth I. In early October 1583 Somerville had been examined regarding an acquaintance imprisoned in the Tower for associating with Mary. On 24 October 1583 he was ill in bed at his father-in-law's home. Yet early the next morning he began to journey alone to London, where he was said to have 'meant to shoot her [Elizabeth] with his dagg [pistol], and hoped to see her head on a pole, for that she was a serpent and a viper' (*CSP dom., 1581–90*, 126). Somerville publicized his intention to fellow guests at an inn, and he was arrested and questioned for the next few days. On 31 October he spoke to Sir John Conway, a relation of the Ardens, regarding 'the trouble of his mind' (ibid., 126). On 7 November Thomas Wilkes, secretary to the privy council, reported to Sir Francis Walsingham that 'nothing could be learned except from the confessions' of Somerville and his family (ibid., 129). Some scholars have presumed that this last statement implied the use of torture. In any event Somerville, as well as his wife's parents, and Hugh Hall, a priest resident at Park Hall, whom he was said to have implicated as the instigators of this 'conspiracy', were imprisoned in the Tower of London and convicted of high treason on 16 December 1583. On 19 December Somerville and Arden were moved from the Tower to Newgate prison. Within two hours of this move Somerville was found strangled in his cell. It was stated that he had committed suicide. His head was cut off and placed on Tower Bridge, and his body buried in Moorfields outside the city of London.

Many contemporaries of Somerville believed that he had been the means for Robert Dudley's vengeance for the public contempt with which he was held by Edward Arden. That Somerville was mentally ill seems beyond doubt. Cecil admitted as much in his *Execution of Justice in England*, and William Allen drew attention to this fact in his *True Defense of English Catholics*. Like other Roman Catholics, he questioned whether John Somerville had died in his cell 'for prevention of the discovery of certain shameful practices about the condemnation' of his father-in-law (Allen, 108–9). WILLIAM WIZEMAN

Sources *CSP dom.*, *1581–90*, 124–6 • *Report of the Deputy Keeper of the Public Records*, 4 (1843), appx 2, pp. 272–3 • J. Stow, *The annales of England … untill this present yeere 1592* (1592), 1189 • W. Cecil, *The execution of justice in England* (1584); repr., ed. R. M. Kingdon (1965) • W. Allen, *A true, sincere and modest defence of English Catholiques that suffer for their faith at home and abrode* (1584); repr., ed. R. M. Kingdon (1965) • C. C. Stopes, *Shakespeare's Warwickshire contemporaries* (1897), 39–47 • W. Dugdale, *The antiquities of Warwickshire illustrated*, rev. W. Thomas, 2nd edn, 2 (1730); facs. edn [1973], 830 • W. Camden, *Annales: the true and royall history of the famous Empresse Elizabeth*, trans. A. Darcie (1625), bk 3, p. 47 • Foster, *Alum. Oxon.*, *1500–1714* [John Somervile] • will of John Somerville the elder, PRO, PROB 11/67, sig. 11 • *N&Q*, 3rd ser., 5 (1864), 352, 463, 492

Somerville, John Southey, fifteenth Lord Somerville (1765–1819), agriculturist, was born on 21 September 1765 at Fitzhead Court, near Taunton, Somerset, the only child of Hugh Southey Somerville (1729–1795), younger son of James, thirteenth Lord Somerville, head of the Scottish branch of the family, and his first wife, Elizabeth Cannon (*d.* 1765), daughter of Christopher Lethbridge, of Westway, Devon. From his father's second marriage there were four sons and three daughters. In 1730 William Somerville, head of the older (English) branch of the family, granted the reversion of his remaining English estates to the thirteenth Lord Somerville, who therefore united the estates of the two families, the Scottish estate in Roxburgh, and the English estate at Aston-Somerville in Warwickshire. William Somerville died childless in 1742. The family hoped to buy the château of Somerville, in Normandy, but this plan was abandoned because of the French Revolution.

Somerville was educated at Harrow School, and then studied with a private tutor for three years in Peterborough, before entering St John's College, Cambridge, as a fellow-commoner on 28 June 1782. He graduated MA in 1785, and then went on the grand tour, meeting Francis Russell, fifth duke of Bedford, in Nice, and travelling with him to Leghorn and through Italy, Switzerland, and France. His inheritance of some of his mother's property in Somerset was disputed, but during the six years in which the case was in chancery, he improved the one farm of which he had possession. During the Napoleonic wars he became colonel of the West Somerset yeomanry, and continued to serve until a carriage accident forced him to resign.

Somerville succeeded to the title in 1796, on the death of his uncle, the fourteenth lord, and he was elected a representative peer of Scotland in the House of Lords. He was re-elected to the parliaments of 1802 and 1806. In 1793 he was appointed one of the first members of the board of agriculture, and on 23 March 1798 he was elected president of the board through Pitt's influence, ousting Sir John Sinclair; he remained president until 1800.

In 1799 Somerville became a lord of the king's bedchamber, and this brought him into close contact with George III, who took a keen interest in agriculture. Apart from the king, who was responsible for introducing merino sheep into England in 1788, Somerville became the largest breeder and owner of merinos in England. In 1802 he visited Spain, and managed to buy a flock of pure merinos. He was one of the leaders of the English merino movement; its members were mainly wealthy landowners, who formed the Merino Society of Great Britain in 1811 with Sir Joseph Banks as president. They wanted to cross the Spanish merino, which produced the best wool in Europe, with British Ryeland and Southdown sheep, to produce a superior animal. But English merino fleeces were inferior to the Spanish; moreover, the new crossbreeds could not compete in carcass quality with the improved English breeds such as the Shorthorns, and with the arrival of wool from Australia there was no future for the English merino. By 1850 there were no merino flocks left in Great Britain.

Somerville also invented several improved agricultural implements, including a plough. He was a patron of the Smithfield Club, founded in 1799, which was concerned with the fattening of cattle. In 1802 he started an annual show of cattle, sheep, and pigs in London, which he carried on at his own expense for many years, providing the prizes. He also promoted the replacement of horses as work animals with draught oxen. Among his publications were *The System Followed during the Last Two Years by the Board of Agriculture* (1800) and *Facts and Observations Relative to Sheep, Wool, Ploughs, Oxen* (1803).

Somerville spent the winter of 1818 in Italy, and the following summer in France, for the benefit of his health, but while travelling through Switzerland he died of dysentery at Vevey, on 5 October 1819. He was buried at Aston-Somerville, Warwickshire. He was unmarried, and was succeeded by his half-brother.

ERNEST CLARKE, *rev.* ANNE PIMLOTT BAKER

Sources E. Clarke, 'John, fifteenth Lord Somerville', *Journal of the Royal Agricultural Society of England*, 3rd ser., 8 (1897), 1–20 • R. Trow-Smith, *A history of British livestock husbandry, 1700–1900*, 2 vols. (1957–9) • J. Thirsk, ed., *The agrarian history of England and Wales*, 6, ed. G. E. Mingay (1989) • H. C. Cameron, *Sir Joseph Banks* (1952), 200–08 • Burke, *Peerage*

Archives NL Scot., letters to Sir Walter Scott

Likenesses R. Rhodes, line engraving (after S. Woodforde), BM, NPG; repro. in J. Somerville, *The memorie of the Somervilles*, ed. W. Scott (1815) • S. Woodforde, portrait, repro. in Clarke, 'John, fifteenth Lord Somerville'; formerly at Matfen Hall, Northumberland, 1897

Somerville [*née* Fairfax; *other married name* Greig]**, Mary (1780–1872)**, science writer and mathematics expositor, was born on 26 December 1780 at the manse, Jedburgh, Roxburghshire, the fifth of seven children (three of whom died young) of Lieutenant (later Vice Admiral Sir) William George *Fairfax (1739–1813) and his second wife, Margaret (1741–1832), daughter of Samuel Charters, solicitor of customs for Scotland. She grew up in the small port town of Burntisland, Fife. Apart from one year at Miss Primrose's boarding-school, Musselburgh (1791–2), she mainly taught herself, using the small family library; her uncle, Thomas Somerville, helped her learn Latin. In her early teens she acquired Euclid's *Elements of Geometry* and Bonnycastle's

Mary Somerville (1780–1872), by Thomas Phillips, 1834

Algebra which she studied in secret, her father having forbidden her to read mathematics. Small and shy, but very good-looking, attractive, and sociable, in 1804 Mary married a cousin, Samuel Greig (1778–1807). A captain in the Russian navy, he became commissioner for the Russian navy and Russian vice-consul for Britain in London. In the capital she continued to study mathematics (without encouragement from Greig) and took French lessons. She had two sons, born in 1805 and 1806. Following Greig's death in 1807 she and her children returned to Burntisland.

With the independence brought by her status as a widow with a small inheritance, and family connections which gave her access to Edinburgh social and intellectual circles, Mary was able to talk with people who could help her with her studies. John Playfair of Edinburgh University put her in touch with his protégé William Wallace, who provided mathematics instruction by correspondence. She was also tutored by Wallace's brother, John. In 1812 she remarried, her second husband being another cousin, William *Somerville (1771–1860), an army doctor of liberal outlook who was interested in science and encouraged her studies. With continued guidance from the Wallaces she became familiar with much of the work in advanced mathematics, especially analysis, being pioneered in France. She also assembled a small but good mathematics library.

In 1816, following a change in William Somerville's army appointment, the Somerville family (which now included two small daughters) moved to London. With introductions from Scottish friends they quickly made their way into scientific society where they came to know several leading figures, including William Wollaston, Henry Kater, Thomas Young, Henry Warburton, and William Blake. Mary's serious enthusiasm for science and obvious talent led to her being accepted as a protégée by these men; the frequent close interaction she had with them, typically at private social gatherings, became her equivalent of formal instruction. She also established connections with several visiting French scientists at this time, connections expanded during a visit to the continent in 1817–18. Somerville's first scientific publication appeared in 1826, a report of her observations on the magnetizing power of sunlight, a topic then of much interest. Although her deductions were incorrect, the paper established her as someone active in scientific work.

The following year Somerville was asked by Henry Brougham, an influential figure in London educational circles, to prepare for publication in an educational books series a condensed English version of Laplace's *Mécanique céleste* (1798–1827). This 5 volume treatise in applied mathematical analysis presenting Laplace's nebular hypothesis of the solar system was one of the great guidebooks for nineteenth-century theoretical astronomers—the completion of the gravitational part of Newton's *Principia*. The version Brougham envisaged required substantial introduction and explication; his request to Somerville was hardly minor. She worked on the project for three years, consulting often with astronomer Sir John Herschel and mathematicians Augustus De Morgan and Charles Babbage. Her completed work covered the first four of Laplace's volumes. Brougham decided it was too long for his low cost series, but on Herschel's recommendation the publisher John Murray accepted it. *The Mechanism of the Heavens* appeared in 1831 and was generally well received. The following year the largely non-mathematical introduction, which Somerville considered her most important contribution, was published separately as *Preliminary Dissertation to the Mechanism of the Heavens*. Sales of the *Mechanism* were slow, but its adoption in 1837 as an advanced mechanics textbook at Cambridge guaranteed a small but steady demand. Recognition came quickly, the Royal Society commissioning a marble bust of her for its apartments, and Cambridge University entertaining her and her husband as official guests for a week. In 1834 the Royal Irish Academy made her a member and a year later the Royal Astronomical Society elected her and Caroline Herschel its first women honorary members.

Impressed by the overlap between the branches of science covered in her first project, and anxious to make clear her ideas about the interconnections she saw between the subjects discussed, Somerville started a second book. *On the Connection of the Physical Sciences* was published by Murray in 1834. Thanks to close consultations with leading scientists in both England and France (including Brougham, Faraday, Lyell, Whewell, Ampère, and Becquerel), the work was an up-to-date account of what would later be classed as astronomy and traditional physics, with, in addition, sections on meteorology and physical geography (then linked with heat). Supplemented with concise introductions to the technical material, it presented all in straightforward prose backed by mathematical notes. It was immensely successful. A pirated American edition and French, German, and Italian translations quickly appeared. Subsequent editions, incorporating the most recent research findings, came out in 1835, 1836, and 1837. Soon an established scientific classic and best-seller, it functioned for a time as an annual progress report for physical science.

In 1835 Mary was awarded a civil list annual pension of £200, increased to £300 two years later because of her family's financial difficulties. In 1838, William Somerville's health being poor, they went to Rome for the winter, and except for two brief visits Mary never returned to Britain. They had no settled home, but lived for periods in various Italian cities. She continued her writing, nine editions of the *Connection* appearing during her lifetime and a tenth in 1877; 15,000 copies were sold. In 1848 her third work appeared, her 2 volume *Physical Geography*, the first English language textbook in the field. Although preceded by the first volume of von Humboldt's acclaimed *Kosmos* (1845), it was an immediate success. Running to seven editions and for long on university textbook lists, it was her most popular work. In geographical writing it was pioneering since it discarded old constraints of political boundaries and anticipated the regional approach. A fourth work, *On Molecular and Microscopic Science* (1869), though its science was largely out of date, was kindly received out of deference to its author, then in her eighty-ninth year. Her autobiography, *Personal Recollections, from Early Life to Old Age*, finished just before her death, was edited and published by her daughter Martha in 1873.

In addition to her early honours, Mary Somerville received in 1869 the patron's gold medal of the Royal Geographical Society and the Victor Emmanuel gold medal of the Geographical Society of Florence. She was honoured by one Swiss, two American, and at least twelve Italian scientific societies. At Oxford, Somerville College (founded in 1879 as a non-denominational women's college) and a Somerville scholarship for women commemorate her name.

Although she was not among those nineteenth-century women who contributed to original work in science, Mary's long sustained and immensely successful scientific writing was unquestionably outstanding. Perhaps no woman of science until Marie Curie was as widely recognized in her own time. Her books were remarkably influential; not only did they bring scientific knowledge in a broad range of fields to a wide audience, but thanks to her exceptional talents for analysis, organization, and presentation, they provided definition and shape for an impressive spread of scientific work. She died at 66 Riviera-di-Chiaja, Naples, on 29 November 1872 and was buried in the English cemetery there. MARY R. S. CREESE

Sources E. C. Patterson, *Mary Somerville and the cultivation of science, 1815–1840* (1983) • M. Somerville, *Personal recollections, from early life to old age, of Mary Somerville* (1873) • M. Sanderson, 'Mary Somerville: her work in physical geography', *Geographical Review*, 64 (1974), 410–20 • M. Oughton, 'Mary Somerville, 1780–1872', *Geographers: biobibliographical studies*, 2, ed. T. W. Freeman, M. Oughton, and P. Pinchemel (1978), 109–11 • E. C. Patterson, 'Mary Fairfax Greig Somerville (1780–1872)', *Women of mathematics*, ed. L. S. Grinstein and P. J. Campbell (1987) • G. Sutton and Sung Kyu Kim, 'Mary Fairfax Greig Somerville (1780–1872)', *Women in chemistry and physics*, ed. L. S. Grinstein, R. K. Rose, and M. H. Rafailovich (1993) • M. T. Brück, 'Mary Somerville, mathematician and astronomer of underused talents', *Journal of the British Astronomical Association*, 106 (1996), 201–6 • *DNB* • *CGPLA Eng. & Wales* (1873)

Archives Bodl. Oxf., corresp. and papers | BL, letters to Charles Babbage, Add. MSS 37185–37201 • Bodl. Oxf., corresp. with Lovelace and Byron families • CUL, Noel MSS • CUL, Whewell MSS • GS Lond., letters to Sir R. I. Murchison and his wife • priv. coll., Murray archives • RS, corresp. with Sir John Herschel; letters to Sir John Lubbock • Somerville College, Oxford, letters mainly to Agnes Greig • Somerville College, Oxford, Edmonds MSS • Trinity Cam., corresp. with William Whewell

Likenesses J. Jackson, portrait, 1831, Somerville College, Oxford • F. Chantrey, marble bust, 1832, RS • T. Phillips, oils, 1834, Scot. NPG [*see illus.*] • S. Laurence, drawing, 1836, Girton Cam. • L. MacDonald, bronze medallion, 1844, Somerville College, Oxford • J. R. Swinton, chalk drawing, 1848, NPG • F. Chantrey, two pencil sketches, NPG • D. D'Angers, bronze medallion, Musée des Beaux Arts, Angers • P. S. D. D'Angers, bronze medallion, NPG • C. Vogel, drawing, Staatliche Kunstsammlungen, Dresden • portrait, Somerville College, Oxford

Wealth at death under £4000: probate, 14 Jan 1873, *CGPLA Eng. & Wales*

Somerville, Mary (1897–1963), educationist and broadcasting executive, was born in New Zealand on 1 November 1897, the eldest daughter of the Revd James Alexander Somerville, of Gullane, East Lothian, Scotland, who at one time had been chairman of a Scottish school board, and his wife, Agnes Fleming. Though born in New Zealand she was brought up in Scotland, very much a daughter of the manse and greatly influenced by the atmosphere of her home, where she was always conscious of lack of money but where she was able to establish contact with people of eminence whose interests were literary, educational, and philosophical.

Mary Somerville became a passionate believer in the importance of education, and, having an adventurous mind as well as a great deal of self-confidence, wanted equally passionately to modify the practices of most schools so that these would include the development of children's imagination in addition to the giving of normal scholastic training. She hoped to make a career for herself which would allow her to play a part in achieving this change and, incidentally, earn enough money to ensure her own financial security and that of her family.

This required courage as well as determination, for throughout Mary Somerville's energetic life she had to struggle with ill health. Ill health was the main reason why most of her early education took place at home. She also attended the Abbey School, Melrose, and Selkirk high school. She did not go to Oxford, where she attended Somerville College, until she was twenty-four. While she was still an undergraduate she met a fellow Scot, John (later Lord) Reith, then managing director of the British Broadcasting Company but soon (1927) to be the first director-general of the newly created British Broadcasting Corporation.

By the time Mary Somerville met Reith she was already convinced that the new medium of radio broadcasting should be used in schools in order to supplement what she

Mary Somerville (1897–1963), by unknown photographer

regarded as the over-rigid scholasticism of current teaching methods. On 24 February 1925 she wrote to Reith suggesting that she should work in radio for nothing or for a nominal sum during her forthcoming long vacation and then be considered for a permanent post at a salary that would meet her needs. Reith was sufficiently impressed by her intelligence and enthusiasm to put her suggestion to J. C. Stobart, his director of education. As a result, and in spite of the fact that she was too ill to sit for her finals in June 1925 and received an *aegrotat*, not, as expected, first-class honours in English, she was appointed in July 1925 to the post of schools assistant to Stobart and embarked upon the work to which she was to dedicate her life.

The timing of Mary Somerville's entry into broadcasting was fortunate. In those early days the BBC, under Reith, regarded the function of broadcasting in general terms as educational and was already endeavouring to form an alliance between broadcasters and established educationists so that the BBC could fulfil its educational purposes not only in its routine programmes but in the more specialized areas of school and adult education. Reith's appointment in 1924 of Stobart, previously a Board of Education inspector, as the company's director of education was an early example of this intention, and Stobart, a classical scholar, proved to be as ready as Mary Somerville to embark upon a new career in broadcasting with an enthusiasm equal to, if different from, hers.

It was significant that Stobart had accepted Mary Somerville's unusual suggestion of a trial period of work in broadcasting before agreeing to her appointment because he was uncertain of her willingness to settle down to office routine. This was perceptive, for during the whole of her professional life she was, in a sense, a rebel. She fought unceasingly for the money and the tools she considered necessary to do her job properly, for her own rights, and for those of any of her staff she believed to be unfairly treated as a result of the workings of the BBC's administrative machinery.

But what made Mary Somerville so considerable a figure in what Asa Briggs has labelled 'the golden age of wireless' (Briggs, vol. 2) was not her battling with the corporation but her identification with what, under Reith, were its fundamental aims. Her great contribution to broadcasting was, in practice, her insistence upon the duality of the high standards for which the corporation stood: on the one hand the upholding of what she regarded as Oxford standards of thought, but equally (and after continuous monitoring of the effect of any broadcast at the receiving end) upon the observance of the professional broadcasting standards necessary for any broadcast communication. It is said that she was once rebuked by her seniors for having had the impertinence to ask a distinguished Oxford professor of literature to rewrite a broadcast script. But it was precisely in this duality of approach that her strength lay. She wanted for broadcasting the standard of thinking that, for her, Oxford represented. Yet, in her judgement, even Oxford professors had to observe the professional standards of the medium of expression they chose to employ.

It is a tribute to both Mary Somerville and the corporation that she could be promoted so consistently in spite of their differences about administrative detail. In 1929 she became responsible for all programmes of broadcasting to schools and secretary to the Central Council of School Broadcasting. In 1947 she was made assistant controller to the entire talks division of the BBC and in 1950 controller, talks (home sound), and so became the first woman to rise to the exalted rank of controller within the BBC.

When Mary Somerville retired in December 1955 the corporation formally stated that 'the BBC's service of broadcasting to schools is Miss Somerville's great monument' and also that 'during her last five years in office' she had brought her mature wisdom to bear upon the difficult and exacting problems that face controller, talks. Outside the corporation the value of her work was given increasing public recognition. In 1935 she was appointed OBE; in 1943 the University of Manchester awarded her an honorary MA degree. During 1947 she accepted invitations to visit Australia and the USA to speak and advise upon educational broadcasting; in April 1955 she was presented with a twenty-fifth anniversary award from the Institute of Education by Radio-Television in America for her 'outstanding contribution to the development of educational broadcasting during the past quarter of a century'.

Mary Somerville was a very feminine figure, lavishing upon a devoted circle of admirers and friends her continuing intellectual energy and her warmly generous hospitality. She was twice married: on 3 July 1928 to Ralph Penton Brown (*b.* 1900/01), a journalist, with whom she had a son, her only child. She divorced her husband in 1945. Her second marriage, to a BBC producer and old friend, Eric Rowan Davies (*b.* 1896/7), took place on 30 July 1962, seven years after she had retired from the BBC and only a year before her death at her home, 5 Macaulay Buildings, Bath, on 1 September 1963. GRACE WYNDHAM GOLDIE, *rev.*

Sources A. Briggs, *The history of broadcasting in the United Kingdom*, 1–2 (1961–5) · personal knowledge (1981) · private information (1981) · *CGPLA Eng. & Wales* (1964) · I. McIntyre, *The expense of glory: a*

life of John Reith (1993) · m. cert. [Ralph Penton Brown] · m. cert. [Eric Rowan Davies]
Likenesses photograph, BBC Picture Archives, London [*see illus.*]
Wealth at death £21,813: probate, 3 Jan 1964, *CGPLA Eng. & Wales*

Somerville, Thomas (1741–1830), Church of Scotland minister and historian, was born at Hawick, Roxburghshire, on 15 February 1741, the fifth child and only son of the parish minister, William Somerville (1691–1757), and Janet Grierson (*d.* 1749), daughter of John Grierson, the minister of Queensferry. He left behind a valuable autobiographical memoir, written in 1813–14 and published posthumously in 1861 as *My Own Life and Times, 1741–1814*, which documents the first seventy-three years of his life and contains perceptive observations on the cultural, social, and ecclesiastical history of the Scottish lowlands, especially the borders, during the late eighteenth century. According to that account, Somerville attended local schools in Hawick and then the school in Duns, Berwickshire, where his education was supervised by the local minister, his relative Adam Dickson, the agricultural historian. From November 1756 he studied arts and subsequently divinity at the University of Edinburgh, benefiting particularly from participation in two student clubs, the Theological Society and the Belles Lettres Society. The unexpected death of his father during his first year at university caused him to move to Edinburgh with his sisters, relying largely on the support of his father's friends and relations, including his father's patron, Lord Somerville. George Burges, the latter's son-in-law, brought young Thomas to Somerville House from 1759 to 1767 as the tutor of his son, James Bland Burges. During this difficult period Thomas and his three surviving siblings petitioned the courts to recover 6000 merks allegedly owed to their father's second wife, Isabel Scott, who had died in 1759.

Having been licensed by the presbytery of Edinburgh on 28 November 1764, Somerville gained clerical experience substituting for George Wishart at the Tron Church, Edinburgh, for a period of nine months, as we know from a joint recommendation letter of 28 April 1766 sent to Sir Gilbert Elliot of Minto, in Roxburghshire, by Wishart and his colleague at the Tron, John Jardine (Minto MS 11016, fols. 72–3). In December 1766 Elliot presented Somerville to the little parish of Minto, where he was ordained on 24 April 1767. During his six years there he tutored Elliot's two sons (one of whom would become the first earl of Minto), met David Hume and many of Sir Gilbert's other friends, made the first of his five visits to London in 1769, and married on 5 June 1770 Martha Charters (*d.* 1809), daughter of the solicitor of customs Samuel Charters and cousin of Somerville's closest friend, the Revd Samuel Charters of Wilton. The couple had five surviving children, including William *Somerville (1771–1860), an eminent physician and traveller, whose wife, the mathematician Mary *Somerville, was Thomas Somerville's niece by marriage and received her earliest intellectual encouragement from him. On 13 August 1771 Samuel Charters senior wrote to Elliot to promote the placement of his son-in-law in Jedburgh, 'one of the best Livings being above £100 besides the Gleeb and Manse', which was formally in the gift of the crown but actually at the disposal of the marquess of Lothian (Minto MS 11019, fol. 1). Elliot accordingly wrote to Lothian, who gave him a promise of support on 14 September 1771 (ibid., fol. 3), and on 27 July 1772 Somerville was presented to Jedburgh, where he would remain for the rest of his life, though the parishioners' opposition to ecclesiastical patronage delayed his admission until 1 July 1773.

Somerville was affiliated with the politically conservative 'moderate' party, which supported ecclesiastical patronage and the British policy in the American War of Independence. In 1781 he published a pamphlet, *Candid Thoughts, or, An Enquiry into the Causes of National Discontents*, which supported the policies of Lord North against the colonists and was answered the following year by Thomas Tod's *Consolatory Thoughts on American Independence*. But he disappointed moderate leaders, and cost himself a chance to be moderator of the general assembly, by increasingly refusing to toe the party line. For example, he backed the 'popular' party candidate for moderator in 1783 and campaigned aggressively for repeal of the Test Act in 1790–91. He initially supported the French Revolution, though he eventually changed course and in 1793 published two pamphlets against the revolution and its feared consequences in Britain: *The Effects of the French Revolution* and *Observations on the Constitution and Present State of Britain*. In regard to the slave trade, which the moderates also opposed, he stirred up controversy simply by being so zealous, as his memoir relates, concerning his published sermon *A discourse on our obligation to thanksgiving, for the prospect of the abolition of the African slave-trade* (1792).

Somerville was a diligent pastor and a well-respected preacher. Two of his sermons were selected for inclusion in the *Scotch Preacher* (vol. 2, 1776, and vol. 3, 1779), and a volume of his sermons was published at Edinburgh in 1813. He wrote the accounts of two parishes, Jedburgh and Ancrum, in Sir John Sinclair's *Statistical Account of Scotland* (1791–9). His greatest accomplishment as an author, however, was the publication of two large quarto histories: *The history of political transactions, and of parties, from the Restoration of King Charles the Second, to the death of King William*, published in London in early spring 1792 by Andrew Strahan and Thomas Cadell, and its sequel, *The History of Great Britain during the Reign of Queen Anne*, published in 1798 by Strahan along with the firm of Cadell and Davies. Based on extensive research in London and Edinburgh, these volumes contained much new information and analysis, including a discussion of the Union of 1707 that dealt frankly with its initial unpopularity in Scotland. There were good reviews, and William Robertson praised the first work and encouraged the second. Yet neither book sold well, and both have been largely neglected by scholars of British and Scottish historiography. Somerville was indignant at being branded a tory historian by Charles James Fox, and he defended his whig credentials in an updated pamphlet, *Observations on a passage in the preface to Mr Fox's historical work, relative to the character of Dr Somerville as an historian*. Having been motivated to become a historian by 'pecuniary embarrassments', as he wrote in his memoir (T. Somerville, 205), Somerville was disappointed to receive only £300 for his first history and attributed its failure to reach a second edition (which would have brought him an additional £200) to the 'horrors of the French Revolution' (ibid., 256). His second experience was still more frustrating, for he turned down an initial offer of £300 for *Queen Anne* in hopes of getting more, but ended up earning far less when the 200 copies of the book that he finally received as compensation proved more difficult to sell by subscription than he had anticipated.

Somerville received an honorary DD degree from the University of St Andrews on 17 July 1789. The publication of his first history, along with his political pamphlets, gained him a £50-a-year sinecure in 1793 as one of his majesty's chaplains-in-ordinary, which was upgraded to a more prestigious chaplaincy in 1798 and finally, in 1800, to a pension worth £100 per annum. One week after preaching an animated sermon and dispensing the Lord's supper to his congregation, he died 'Father of the Church' aged eighty-nine on 16 May 1830, and was buried in Jedburgh Abbey. RICHARD B. SHER

Sources T. R. Adams, *The American controversy: a study of the British pamphlets about the American disputes, 1764–1783*, 2 vols. (1980) • G. M. Ditchfield, 'The Scottish campaign against the Test Act, 1790–1791', *HJ*, 23 (1980), 37–61 • *Fasti Scot.*, new edn, 2.127–8, 115, 133 • T. Somerville, *My own life and times, 1741–1814*, ed. W. Lee (1861); repr. with new introduction by R. B. Sher (1996) • R. B. Sher, *Church and university in the Scottish Enlightenment: the moderate literati of Edinburgh* (1985) • *Unto the right honourable, the lords of council and session, the petition of Thomas, Agnes, Helen and Janet Somervilles, children of the deceased Mr. William Somerville, minister at Hawick* (1761) • *DNB* • NL Scot., Minto MS 11016, fols. 72–3; Minto MS 11019, fols. 1, 3 • M. Somerville, *Personal recollections, from early life to old age, of Mary Somerville* (Boston, MA, 1876)

Archives Bodl. Oxf., family corresp. | NA Scot., Melville MSS • NL Scot., corresp. with Lord Minto

Somerville, William, first Lord Somerville (*c*.1400–1456), courtier, was the eldest son of Sir Thomas Somerville of Carnwath (*c*.1370–*c*.1440), a valued servant of James I, and probably his first wife, Janet Stewart (*fl.* 1391–*c*.1405). William was apparently knighted at the baptism of the future James II in October 1430. His estates lay in Lanarkshire, Roxburghshire, Stirlingshire, and Haddingtonshire. They were extensive enough for him to rank as one of the more important Scottish barons of the early fifteenth century and to justify his assumption of a peerage title, as first Lord Somerville, in mid-1445 (at the same time as a number of other prominent Scottish nobles). He was seldom at court during its domination by the Livingston faction, but after its fall in late 1449 he is normally found as a witness to crown charters. Following in his father's footsteps, Somerville served the crown briefly as justiciar in the early 1450s and also as one of the king's council or auditors of causes in parliament to whom legal disputes were referred. On 14 March 1452 he witnessed a charter issued by James II at Stirling, shortly after the killing of the eighth earl of Douglas. James II created Carnwath a free burgh of barony for him in 1451. No later than 1456 the conditions on which the Somervilles held Carnwath included that of presenting a pair of red stockings to the winner of a race from the east end of the town to the Cawlo Cross. The eccentric, but detailed, late seventeenth-century family account *Memorie of the Somervilles* asserts that Somerville married Janet, daughter of Sir John Mowat of Stenhouse, *c*.1428, though a contemporary source shows that in 1438 he was married to Elizabeth (surname unknown). The *Memorie* also states that he died at Cowthally, his principal castle, of a surfeit of fruit on 20 August 1456; the service of his heir, however, has the date of death as 3 July 1456. He was apparently buried in the college aisle of Carnwath church, as was Janet on her death about two years later. They had three sons and two daughters.

Their eldest son, **John Somerville**, second Lord Somerville (*c*.1430–1491), fought among the successful Scottish forces against the English at the battle of Sark on 23 October 1449. He was seldom at court after he succeeded his father, but he took part in the abduction of the young James III from Linlithgow to Edinburgh on 9 July 1466, for which he, Robert, Lord Boyd (*d.* 1482), and others were pardoned later that year. He regularly attended parliament, served occasionally on the king's council or as an auditor of causes, like his father, and was himself a frequent litigant there. He married first Helen, daughter of Sir Adam Hepburn of Hailes, on 10 July 1446. They had probably two daughters and a son, William, who married Marjory Montgomery, sister of Hugh Montgomery, earl of Eglinton; William predeceased his father in 1491, and his sons John and Hugh succeeded as third and fourth lords Somerville. The second Lord Somerville married again in March 1456, and he and his second wife, Marion (*fl.* 1456–1506), daughter of Sir William Baillie of Lamington, had at least one son and two daughters. Somerville had one further daughter, but it is not known whether Helen or Marion was her mother. He died in November 1491 and was also buried at Carnwath. Marion outlived him and about 1496 married John Ross, first Lord Ross of Hawkhead, from whom she obtained a divorce; she was still alive in January 1506. ALAN R. BORTHWICK

Sources J. M. Thomson and others, eds., *Registrum magni sigilli regum Scotorum / The register of the great seal of Scotland*, 11 vols. (1882–1914), vol. 2 • *APS*, 1424–1567 • G. Burnett and others, eds., *The exchequer rolls of Scotland*, 23 vols. (1878–1908) • [T. Thomson], ed., *The acts of the lords auditors of causes and complaints, AD 1466–AD 1494*, RC, 40 (1839) • [T. Thomson] and others, eds., *The acts of the lords of council in civil causes, 1478–1503*, 3 vols. (1839–1993) • *RotS*, vol. 2 • J. Somerville, *Memorie of the Somervilles: being a history of the baronial house of Somerville*, ed. W. Scott, 2 vols. (1815) • M. McNeill, *The silver bough*, 4 (1968) • NA Scot., GD 17/1; GD 40/4/63, 64

Archives NA Scot., Lothian muniments • NL Scot., Lockhart of Lee and Carnwath MSS

Somerville, William. *See* Somervile, William (1675–1742).

Somerville, William (1771–1860), military surgeon, eldest son of the Presbyterian minister and historian Thomas *Somerville (1741–1830) and his wife, Martha, daughter of Samuel Charters, was born in Edinburgh on 22 April 1771. He trained as a surgeon, entered the army as a hospital assistant on 25 March 1795, accompanied the expedition of Sir James Henry Craig to the Cape of Good Hope in 1795, and was appointed garrison surgeon of Cape Town on its capture by the British. He was employed on confidential missions by the government in the negotiation of treaties with the Xhosa peoples, who continued to make inroads on the farms of the Dutch colonists. In the course of his wanderings, he and his native guide were at one time sentenced to death by a chief, and owed their lives to the intercession of the chief's wife. During an interval in his African travels Somerville graduated as doctor of medicine in the University of Aberdeen, on 27 June 1800. His longest and most important journey was undertaken in 1801–2, as co-commissioner with John Trüter, member of the court of justice, for the Cape government, to negotiate the purchase of cattle from the tribes of the interior, to replace those lost by the colonists in the Cape Frontier War. The expedition reached Lithako, the kraal of the Batlapin people, 700 miles from their starting point, and 300 from the frontier of the colony, in a region then rarely visited by Europeans. The journey is described in an appendix to Sir John Barrow's *Voyage to Cochin China* (1806).

Somerville accompanied Sir James Craig on his expedition to the Mediterranean, part of the operations against Napoleon in 1805. When failing health compelled Craig to resign his command at the end of a year, during which Naples and Sicily had been successively occupied, Somerville returned to England with him, and was again on Craig's staff when his partial recovery enabled the latter to go out to Canada as governor-in-chief in 1807. The post of inspector-general of hospitals in Canada was held by Somerville, together with the comptrollership of the customs in Quebec, until 1811, when he returned to England with his chief, and remained in attendance on him until Craig's death in February 1812. His prospects abroad were renounced for a home appointment on his marriage, in 1812, to his cousin, Mrs Greig, *née* Fairfax, who became better known as the scientist and mathematician Mary *Somerville (1780–1872); they had two daughters, Martha and Mary.

After holding for a short time the post of deputy inspector of hospitals at Portsmouth, Somerville became in 1813 head of the army medical department in Scotland, and resided in Edinburgh until his appointment in 1816 as one of the principal inspectors of the army medical board in England, when he moved to London. Admitted LRCP on 27 June 1817, he was elected FRS on 11 December, and, on 13 November 1819, gazetted physician to the Royal Hospital, Chelsea. His serious illness in 1838 compelled his family to winter abroad, and from then to live mainly on the continent. He died suddenly at Casa Capponi, Florence, on 25 June 1860, aged eighty-nine. A man of considerable endowments, Somerville shared the scientific interests as well as the social success of his wife, and after his marriage seemed to merge all personal ambition in the interest of her career.

E. M. Clerke, *rev.* Roger T. Stearn

Sources T. Somerville, *My own life and times, 1741–1814*, ed. W. Lee (1861) • Munk, *Roll* • J. Barrow, *A voyage to Cochin China* (1806) • Boase, *Mod. Eng. biog.* • *CGPLA Eng. & Wales* (1860)

Archives Bodl. Oxf., corresp. and papers, incl. log of voyage to Brazil and South African notes | BL, letters to C. Babbage, Add. MSS 37188–37201 • RS, corresp. with Sir John Herschel

Likenesses F. Chantrey, pencil sketches, NPG

Wealth at death under £300: probate, 11 Sept 1860, *CGPLA Eng. & Wales*

Somerville, Sir William (1860–1932), agriculturist, was born at Cormiston, Lanarkshire, on 30 May 1860, the only child to survive infancy of Robert Somerville (*d.* 1879), farmer, and his wife, Margaret Alexander. The Somerville family seems to have settled in Lanarkshire in the twelfth century, and at one time held very extensive landed estates, but the 400 acre farm of Cormiston, bought in 1820, was Robert Somerville's only land.

Somerville was educated at the Royal High School, Edinburgh, and soon after leaving attended a short course of lectures in agriculture at Edinburgh University. Following his father's death he spent six years farming Cormiston. This practical experience of running a poor farm in a period of agricultural depression was an important part of his education, and later helped him win the confidence of farmers and agricultural workers.

In 1885 Robert Wallace was appointed to the chair of agriculture at Edinburgh. When the university instituted a degree in the subject, Somerville returned to college, graduating in 1887. He then went to Munich in order to study forestry under Heinrich Mayr and Robert Hartig, and graduated DŒc in 1889. During his studies, he married, in 1888, Margaret Elizabeth, fourth daughter of George Gaukroger, of Southfield, East Lothian; they had two daughters, the younger of whom predeceased her father.

In 1889 Somerville returned to Edinburgh as the first lecturer in forestry. During his brief stay in that post he did much to awaken interest in the new German scientific approach to forest problems both by his contacts with foresters and by his translation of Hartig's book *Timbers, and How to Know Them* (1890) and afterwards of his *Text-Book of the Diseases of Trees* (1894). However, in 1891 he went to the Durham College of Science (later Newcastle University) as professor of agriculture and forestry. There he at once began a programme of field experimental work that was to prove fruitful to British farming. In 1899 he moved to Cambridge as the first Drapers' professor of agriculture, and was elected a fellow of King's College. Next, in 1902, he joined the Board of Agriculture and Fisheries as assistant secretary, but found the work of a government department far from satisfying. Thus, in 1906 he accepted the Sibthorpian chair of rural economy at Oxford, and became a fellow of St John's College. He remained at Oxford until his retirement in 1925.

As a teacher of agriculture Somerville made a strong and lasting impression on his pupils. In middle life he was probably the most effective, among all academic agriculturists, as a speaker at farmers' gatherings. Indeed, no one contributed more than Somerville to removing the suspicion of research in agriculture which was entertained by farmers at the outset of his career. Moreover, he was a notable 'improver', for he bought two derelict farms (Poverty

Bottom, near Hastings, and Compton Cassey, near Northleach, in Gloucestershire) and brought both back into full and profitable production.

Among Somerville's many contributions to agricultural progress, three deserve special mention. The first is the evidence which he produced that phosphate deficiency was the commonest cause of low productivity in pasture land, and that in basic slag (until then regarded as a worthless by-product) lay the means of improvement. The second is the development of the field experiment as a means of discovering the grass and crop response to fertilizers, of testing the adaptability of different species and varieties, and of comparing the long-term results from various systems of cropping. The third is the use of the animal as a direct measure of the feeding value of pasturage. In all his experiments Somerville so contrived the layout that the plots provided striking visual demonstrations, and he invariably stated his results in terms of profit and loss.

Although agriculture became Somerville's main concern, his interest in trees was maintained to the end. He was twice president of the Arboricultural Society (1900–01 and 1922–4), and was editor of its *Journal* for thirteen years (1910–23). His last book was *How a Tree Grows* (1927). He received an honorary LLD from Edinburgh University in 1922. He was appointed KBE and elected an honorary fellow of St John's College, Oxford, in 1926.

Somerville was a very complete countryman: among other things a competent field botanist, a student and a lover of birds, and a notable fisherman. Even after his health gave way, he maintained his lifelong interest in alpine gardening. He died at his home, Rye House, Boars Hill, Berkshire (near Oxford), on 17 February 1932.

J. A. S. Watson, *rev.* Peter Osborne

Sources *The Times* (18 Feb 1932) · *Nature*, 129 (1932), 389–90 · private information (1949) · personal knowledge (1949) · *CGPLA Eng. & Wales* (1932)

Likenesses G. Hall-Neale, portrait; formerly in school of rural economy, Oxford · portrait (after G. Hall-Neale), St John's College, Oxford

Wealth at death £29,371 5s. 2d.: probate, 14 May 1932, *CGPLA Eng. & Wales*

Somerville, William Meredyth, first Baron Athlumney and first Baron Meredyth (1802–1873), politician, was the son of Sir Marcus Somerville, third baronet (*d.* 1831), and his first wife, Mary Anne, daughter and heir of Sir Richard Meredyth, bt. He was educated at Harrow School and matriculated at Christ Church, Oxford, in February 1822, but did not take a degree. He succeeded to the baronetcy on the death of his father in 1831. After a short period in the diplomatic service, on 22 December 1832 Somerville married the Hon. Maria Harriet Conyngham, with whom he had one son and one daughter surviving. His wife died on 3 December 1843.

In January 1835 Somerville stood unsuccessfully as a Liberal candidate for Wenlock. In August 1837 he was returned for Drogheda, which he represented for fifteen years. From his second session onwards he spoke frequently on Irish questions from the viewpoint of a Liberal landlord. In 1841 (3 June) he made a strong speech in support of Lord Melbourne, whose ministry was overthrown by a vote of one in Peel's motion for a vote of censure. Somerville was of the view that the repeal of the corn laws was the best way to modernize the Irish farming system. Later, in 1846 (30 March), he opposed the postponement of Peel's Corn Bill in favour of the Protection of Life in Ireland Bill. The motion was rejected by 147 to 108 votes. However, when, on 17 April, the repressive measure was introduced, he denounced it as unnecessary and likely to be ineffective. On 8 June he moved its rejection on the second reading, and after six nights' debate succeeded, with the aid of the protectionists, in defeating the bill and overthrowing the tory government.

In Lord John Russell's new whig government Somerville became under-secretary for the Home department. In July 1847 he was appointed chief secretary for Ireland and sworn of the privy council. During his term of office he had to deal with the Irish famine and the Young Ireland movement. He was appointed to the new, separate, Irish poor-law commission in 1847. In September of that year he was alarmed at the prospect that poor-law guardians would have to finance the fever hospitals set up in the wake of the famine 'knowing as I do that the cessation of the accustomed [government] funds even for one day may cause effects the most deplorable and disastrous' (Woodham-Smith, 314). The Treasury eventually agreed to a subsidy. In 1848 he introduced a land bill that would have given a measure of security to tenants in Ireland, but it foundered amid opposition from landlords. Two years later he was more successful in piloting the Irish Franchise Act (13 & 14 Vict. c. 69), 'the single most important legislative influence upon the make up of the electorate and the course of electoral politics in nineteenth century Ireland', according to one authority (Hoppen, 17). The act made voter registration a process of automatic renewal, and established a new franchise on the basis of the occupation, rather than the ownership, of property.

When Lord John Russell's ministry fell in February 1852, Somerville ceased to be chief secretary, and at the general election in the following July lost his seat for Drogheda. After a two years' absence from parliament, he was returned at a by-election for Canterbury on 18 August 1854. During the next few years he spoke on many topics in the house: favouring the abolition of church rates (1855); considering the bill dealing with dwellings of Irish labourers; supporting Roebuck's motion for the abolition of the Irish viceroyalty 'for imperial as well as Irish reasons'; and bringing in a bill whose aim was to remove legal impediments to Roman Catholics who might wish to become Irish chancellor (1859). The bill received the support of leaders of both parties, but, after reference to a select committee, was withdrawn. On 16 October 1860 in Paris Somerville married Maria Georgiana Elizabeth Jones (1831–1899), with whom he had several daughters and two sons. On 14 December 1863 he was created a peer of Ireland, with the title of Baron Athlumney of Somerville and Dollardstown; on 3 May 1866 he was raised to the peerage of the United Kingdom as Baron Meredyth of Dollardstown, co. Meath, in which county lay his family estates of some 10,000 acres. In his last speech in the House of Commons (21 June 1864) he expressed his opinion against any further interference between landlord and tenant in Ireland. In the House of Lords he supported Lord Clanricarde's bill of 1867 to simplify tenure of Irish land, declaring his preference for emigration over legislative interference. Nevertheless, he supported Gladstone's Land Bill of 1870, taking considerable part in the discussions in committee. He also gave a warm support to the Irish Church Bill, having been an early supporter of concurrent endowment. He died at Waterloo Crescent, Dover, on 7 December 1873, and was buried at Kentstones, co. Meath, on 13 December. He was survived by his second wife and was succeeded in the peerage by his son James Herbert Gustavus Meredyth Somerville.

G. Le G. Norgate, *rev.* Sinéad Agnew

Sources L. G. Pine, *The new extinct peerage, 1884–1971: containing extinct, abeyant, dormant, and suspended peerages with genealogies and arms* (1972), 17 • *The Times* (10 Dec 1873), 7 • *ILN* (20 Dec 1873), 614 • GEC, *Peerage*, vol. 7 • Boase, *Mod. Eng. biog.*, 1.102 • L. C. Sanders, *Celebrities of the century: being a dictionary of men and women of the nineteenth century* (1887), 68 • E. Lodge, ed., *The genealogy of the existing British peerage and baronetage*, new edn (1859), 826 • R. B. O'Brien, *Fifty years of concessions to Ireland, 1831–1881*, 2 vols. (1883), vol. 2, chs. 5 and 6, 149, 154, 159 • *Hansard 3* (1840), 54.179–88 • C. B. F. Woodham-Smith, *The great hunger: Ireland, 1845–1849* (1962) • C. Kinealy, *This great calamity: the Irish famine, 1845–52* (1994) • K. T. Hoppen, *Elections, politics, and society in Ireland, 1832–1885* (1984)
Archives PRO NIre. | Bodl. Oxf., letters to earl of Clarendon • Borth. Inst., letters to Sir Charles Wood
Wealth at death under £10,900: probate, 20 Jan 1874, *CGPLA Ire.* • under £300 in England: probate, 20 Jan 1874, *CGPLA Ire.*

Somes, Joseph (1787–1845), shipowner, was born in Stepney, London, on 9 December 1787, the younger son (there were also four daughters) of Samuel Somes (1758–1816), victualler, waterman, coal merchant, and shipowner, of east London, and his wife, Sarah Green (1762–1835), the daughter of a coal-meter. Apprenticed to his father as a lighterman, and sent to sea at the age of fifteen, Somes's early experience was in the coal and coastal trades.

At the age of twenty-one he became a captain of his father's ships and remained at sea until 1818, acquiring a worldwide knowledge of shipping and navigation. The death of Somes's father in 1816 left him as partner with his elder brother, Samuel, in what was by then a prosperous family shipping firm. This firm continued to prosper during the more difficult post-war years, and by the time of Samuel's death in 1829 Joseph was operating extensively as owner, charterer (especially for the East India Company), sailmaker, and chandler.

It was under Somes's sole ownership in the 1830s that the firm rose to become the largest in England. Somes seized the opportunity offered by the breakup of the fleet of the East India Company to purchase a number of its best ships, for example, the *Lowther Castle* and *Earl of Balcarres*. His ships sailed primarily to the East Indies but entered vigorously into the newly opening trade of Australasia, including whaling, sailing more rarely to Africa and the Americas, and occasionally to the Baltic. By 1842 the Somes shipping empire, that of the largest private shipowner in the world, embraced about forty ships registered at Lloyd's. Somes specialized in chartering ships to the government for the transport of convicts, stores, and troops.

Somes's prominence and wealth led him to develop an interest in the colonies, and he invested in the Western Australian Company, the North American Colonization Society of Ireland, and, above all, the New Zealand Company. Somes joined the latter company when it was refounded in 1838, sold to it its first ship, the *Tory* (sent to New Zealand in 1839 with a shipload of settlers without government permission), and became governor of the company in 1840. As governor, Somes was the figurehead for an aggressive and ruthless campaign aimed at securing government recognition for the New Zealand Company. This onslaught won financial concessions but not the decisive part in the colonization of New Zealand which the company sought.

Somes entered the House of Commons as Conservative MP for Dartmouth in December 1844. He was obliged to transfer the ownership of his ships to his nephews in order, narrowly, to avoid disqualification as a government contractor. His political aims were unclear, and his closest allies believed that in 1845 he was about to betray the company, which was in a state of virtual collapse at the time of Somes's death.

Somes was well known on the stock exchange and at Lloyd's, and was one of the originators of the new *Lloyd's Register of Shipping* in 1834. He was also active within the General Shipowners' Society. Often called to give evidence before government inquiries, he was a stout defender of the part played by the Navigation Acts and mercantile marine in the prosperity and defence of the nation.

In 1811 Somes married Mary Ann (1788–1835), daughter of Thomas Daplyn of Stepney. They had one surviving daughter. Second, in 1837, Somes married Maria (1816–1911), daughter of Charles Saxton. She was the sister of both the Revd Charles Waring Saxton, an early migrant to New Zealand, and of Somes's solicitor, Edward Saxton. Somes died on 25 June 1845 at his home, New Grove, Mile End Road, London. He was buried in the family vault in St Dunstan's parish church, Stepney, on 2 July.

A. C. Howe, *rev.*

Sources CKS, Colyer-Fergusson papers • *Horace Fildes notebooks*, Victoria University of Wellington • 'Select committee on the Dartmouth election petition', *Parl. papers* (1845), 12.32, no. 164 • *The Times* (26 June 1845) • *The Times* (3 July 1845) • P. Burns, *Fatal success: a history of the New Zealand Company* (1989)
Likenesses portrait, NL NZ, Turnbull L.; repro. in Burns, *Fatal success*, 74
Wealth at death £434,000: *DNB*

Somes, Michael George (1917–1994), ballet dancer and teacher, was born on 28 September 1917 at Horsley, Gloucestershire, the younger son of Edwin Joseph Somes (1882–1973), church organist and schoolteacher, and his wife, Ethel Mary Marie, *née* Pridham (1889–1972), also a

Michael George Somes (1917–1994), by Baron, *c.*1950

schoolteacher. As a small boy he accompanied his mother and her pupils to dancing classes in Taunton, 'probably', as he said, 'to keep me out of mischief' (priv. coll.), and revealed unexpected talent. He was educated at Huish's Grammar School, Taunton. Unusually for a time when there was no established British ballet company, and extreme prejudice against English male dancers, his parents encouraged him to take up ballet professionally and he left school at the age of fourteen to study full time with Katherine Blott in Weston-super-Mare. In 1934 he was the first boy to be given a scholarship to the Vic-Wells School, founded by Ninette de Valois to train dancers for the Vic-Wells (later Royal) Ballet. Somes claimed, with characteristic modesty and cynicism, that male dancers were so rare that they would take anything and anyone they could.

Somes joined the Vic-Wells Ballet in 1935. An exceptional jump, unusual musicality, a forceful virility then rare in male dancers, and matinée idol good looks attracted the attention of the company's choreographer, Frederick Ashton, who in 1937 created several eye-catching roles to display Somes's talents, notably in *Les patineurs* and *A Wedding Bouquet*. In 1938 Ashton created *Horoscope* for Somes and the young Margot *Fonteyn, exploiting Somes's intensity, elevation, and raw, youthful energy, clearly demonstrating that here was a potentially great English male dancer. In 1940 Ashton made two other major roles for him, with Fonteyn as the Children of Light, tormented by the evil in the world, in *Dante Sonata*, and the sensitively erotic 'Lovers' *pas de deux* in *The Wanderer* with Pamela May.

The Second World War was a serious setback to the development of male dancing in Britain. Despite appeals for exemption, Somes joined the Royal Artillery in 1941 and became a physical training instructor, but in 1944 a fall ruptured his spleen and threatened to put an end to his career. He was discharged from the army on medical grounds and returned to the Sadler's Wells Ballet (as the Vic-Wells Ballet was now called) in 1945. In 1946 the Sadler's Wells Ballet became resident at the Royal Opera House, where, in April, Somes was one of the original six dancers in Ashton's masterpiece *Symphonic Variations*. It seemed that he might never regain his previous form, but over the next five years he made steady progress. His innate nobility perfectly fitted him for the princes in *Swan Lake*, *The Sleeping Beauty*, and Ashton's *Cinderella* (1947), and in Balanchine's *Ballet Imperial* (1950). Rather than detailed characterizations, he projected an emotion or mood and the 'essence' of an attribute—nobility, youthful love, stern authority. By the early 1950s he was dancing at his peak, acclaimed in London and on the highly successful Sadler's Wells Ballet tours of America. He developed into a great *danseur noble* and one of the finest partners in the world, his one aim to display his ballerina to utmost advantage. In the 1940s he partnered several of the company's ballerinas, including Margot Fonteyn, and when her regular partner, Robert Helpmann, left in 1950 Somes was his obvious successor.

Throughout the 1950s Fonteyn and Somes were *the* ballet partnership, perfectly matched both stylistically and physically. Ashton created ballets for them enshrining their lyricism, elegance, exceptional musicality, and instinctive rapport, notably *Daphnis and Chloë*, *Sylvia*, the great *pas de deux* in *Birthday Offering*, and *Ondine*, ballets which defined not only Ashton's style but that of the Royal Ballet (as Sadler's Wells Ballet became in 1957). Somes's superb partnering was a major factor in Fonteyn's success. They danced all over the world, acclaimed not only for their dancing, but also for their dedication and professionalism. They were important cultural ambassadors for Britain, and such visits involved myriad official functions, which Somes, a very private person, loathed, but which he survived by exercising his considerable natural charm. On and off stage, his uncompromising masculinity did much to dispel the myth that male dancing equalled effeminacy.

On 7 July 1956 Somes married Deirdre Annette Dixon (*d.* 28 May 1959), a young dancer with the company. In 1959 he was the first male dancer to be made a CBE, official recognition of a new attitude towards the male dancer and of the leadership and example he had given to the men of the Royal Ballet. His pride in the award was, however, overshadowed by the death of his wife later the same year. He retired from major roles in 1961 and from 1963 to 1970 was an assistant director of the Royal Ballet, responsible for the development of young dancers. Under his eagle eye, Royal Ballet standards reached new heights and the *corps de ballet* became one of the finest in the world. In particular, he was architect of the Antoinette Sibley-Anthony Dowell partnership, which, in popularity and excitement, came almost to rival that of Fonteyn and Nureyev. Somes and Antoinette Sibley (*b.* 1939) married on 22 June 1964. Somes continued performing character roles; as Armand's Father in Ashton's *Marguerite and Armand* in 1963 (Armand being Fonteyn's new partner Rudolf Nureyev) he created a supreme authoritarian figure, and he was a stern, uncompromising Capulet in Kenneth MacMillan's *Romeo and Juliet* (1965). He created one last leading role, a poignant Oscar Wilde in the short lived Joe Layton ballet *O.W.* in 1971.

In 1970 Somes became principal *répétiteur* of the Royal Ballet, a job which he described as a cross between 'nurse, office boy, Mother Superior' and 'butcher' (priv. coll.). He had particular responsibility for Ashton's ballets and his total commitment to Ashton's genius ensured the maintenance of the true Ashton style. His reverence for tradition and his phenomenal memory also made him the proud custodian of the Diaghilev Ballet repertory, notably Bronislava Nijinska's masterpieces *Les biches* and *Les noces*, and Fokine's *The Firebird*, in which he had been an outstanding Ivan Tsarevich. His loyalty to the Royal Ballet was absolute, seeing his role as one of 'stewardship' in striving to uphold its ideals and traditions.

Somes made huge demands upon himself and his dancers, and his unpredictable temper, iron discipline, and ferocious pursuit of excellence became legendary. He advocated that 'All Ye That Enter Here, Be Prepared for Ninety-Nine-Per-Cent Failure Every Day' should be inscribed in every rehearsal room, and his famous rages were probably born of frustration in the unattainable search for perfection. His especial anger was reserved for talented but lazy dancers. Despite his irascibility, sarcasm, heavy humour, and, some said, sadism, dancers respected and revered him, realizing that there was nothing personal in his outbursts and that he could make them achieve more than they could have believed possible. Less publicized were his many acts of kindness and generosity.

Somes and Sibley divorced in 1973 and in the 1970s Somes established a relationship with his young protégée Wendy Rose Ellis (*b.* 1951/2). In 1985 a disagreement with choreographer Kenneth MacMillan led to his dismissal from the company. He married Ellis, the daughter of Clive Richard Ellis, shop manager, on 15 May 1987. He returned to oversee Ashton ballets, both for the Royal Ballet and for companies abroad, and it was after mounting a superb revival of *Enigma Variations* for Birmingham Royal Ballet in 1994 that he collapsed and died of a brain tumour, in London, on 19 November 1994. He was survived by his third wife.

His work is preserved in the films *The Royal Ballet* (1959) and *Romeo and Juliet* (1966), in the archives of BBC television, and in photographs by Gordon Anthony and Houston Rogers preserved in the Theatre Museum, London.

SARAH C. WOODCOCK

Sources M. Clarke, *The Sadler's Wells Ballet: a history and appreciation* (1955) • P. W. Manchester, *Vic-Wells: a ballet progress* (1942) • H. Fisher [C. Swinson], *Michael Somes* (1955) • J. Gruen, 'Michael Somes', *The private world of ballet* (1975), 162–7 • J. Percival, 'Michael Somes', *Dance and Dancers* (March 1959), 16–17 • J. Percival, 'Michael Somes', *Dance and Dancers* (April 1959), 18–19 • *The Independent* (21 Nov 1994) • *The Guardian* (21 Nov 1994) • *The Times* (21 Nov 1994) • *Dancing Times* (Jan 1995) • private information (2004) • priv. coll. • d. cert. [E. J. Somes] • d. cert. [E. M. M. Somes] • m. cert. [Wendy Rose Ellis] • m. cert. [E. J. Somes and E. M. M. Pridham] • *CGPLA Eng. & Wales* (1995)

Archives priv. coll. | Royal Opera House, Covent Garden, London • Theatre Museum, London | FILM BBC WAC • BFI NFTVA, performance footage | SOUND BL NSA, oral history interview

Likenesses Baron, group portrait, photograph, 1946, Hult. Arch. • Baron, photograph, *c.*1950, Hult. Arch. [*see illus.*] • Baron, photograph, 1951 (with Margot Fonteyn), Hult. Arch. • Baron, photograph, 1953 (with Margot Fonteyn), Hult. Arch. • Baron, photograph, 1954 (with Svetlana Beriosova), Hult. Arch.; *see illus. in* Beriosova, Svetlana (1932–1998) • Baron, photograph, *c.*1955, Hult. Arch. • Baron, photograph, 1955 (with Svetlana Beriosova), Hult. Arch. • H. Rogers, photograph, 1956, repro. in *The Independent* • J. Bratby, oils, priv. coll. • photograph, repro. in *The Times* • photographs, Theatre Museum, London • photographs, Royal Opera House, Covent Garden, London • photographs, Hult. Arch.

Wealth at death £1,003,689: probate, 2 Feb 1995, *CGPLA Eng. & Wales*

Sommers, William. *See* Somer, William (*d.* 1559).

Somner, William (*bap.* **1598**, *d.* **1669**), antiquary and Anglo-Saxon scholar, was baptized on 5 November 1598 at St Margaret's, Canterbury, one of three sons of William Somner, registrar of the court of Canterbury, and his wife, Anne Winston. His widow and son believed his birth date to be 30 March 1606 (Kennett, 3.119). He was educated by Mr Ludd at the free school of Canterbury. He became a clerk to his father, and was subsequently appointed registrar of the ecclesiastical courts of Canterbury by Archbishop Laud.

Somner was twice married, first on 12 June 1634 to Elizabeth (*b.* 1599), daughter of William Thurgar of Teversham, Cambridgeshire, and second on 1 December 1659 to Barbara (*d.* 1706), daughter of John Dawson, the chief searcher of Kent. After Somner's death she married Henry Hanningham, vicar of Elham, Kent. His first marriage produced one son and three daughters, the second one daughter and three sons.

Canterbury was Somner's home throughout his life, and the focus of his antiquarian endeavours. These were encouraged by his colleague Meric Casaubon, whom Somner described as his 'precious friend and ever-honoured Mecoenas' (*Treatise of Gavelkind*, 1660, preface). His first publication was *The antiquities of Canterbury, or, A survey of that ancient citie, with the suburbs and cathedrall, etc.* (1640, reissued 1662; 2nd edn by Nicholas Batteley, 1703). The book was dedicated to his patron Laud, praised for his preservation of antiquities. The text is thoroughly Laudian, describing Becket's shrine as the 'glory' of Canterbury 'cut down' at the Reformation (pp. 245–51), and calling for the restoration 'to each Parochial Church and Chapell the forgotten name and memory of such Saint or Saints, as at their dedication … were given (and are therefore proper) to them' (p. 510). It is said to be the first book

William Somner (*bap.* **1598**, *d.* **1669**), by Michael Burghers, pubd 1693

published with an appendix containing original records (S. Pegge, *Anonymiana*, 1809, 7). Somner made further collections for a history of Kent. In 1647 he wrote 'A treatise of gavelkind, both name and thing' (1660), noting in the preface his failure to produce a county history since the civil war had necessitated 'other thoughts, chiefly how I might secure my self against the fury … of the present storm'.

Somner, a keen royalist, attempted to hide the muniments of Canterbury from iconoclastic parliamentary soldiers, and was responsible for preserving the pieces of the cathedral's font, smashed in 1642, for reconstruction in 1660. The loss of patronage after Laud's fall did not deter Somner from promoting the royal cause. Early in 1649 he published a passionate elegy entitled 'The in-securitie of princes, considered in an occasionall meditation upon the kings late sufferings and death', describing Charles as 'a myrror fit for all posterity' and 'three Kingdoms choicest treasure'. This was followed by 'The frontispiece of the kings book opened' (1650?), an exposition of the portrait of Charles I in *Eikon basilike* and a call to recognize Charles II as king.

The turbulence of the period hampered Somner's access to libraries, as he complained to Sir Simonds D'Ewes in 1649 (BL, Add. MS 22916, fol. 57). Nevertheless, at Casaubon's suggestion Somner devoted himself to learning Anglo-Saxon. Together with legal skills gained from his employment, this enabled him to complete a Latin commentary and glossary on the laws of Henry I (BL, Harleian MS 684). The work was dedicated to Sir Roger Twysden, who in 1644 had published the Henrician statutes. In 1650 Casaubon published Somner's 'Ad verba vetera Germanica' as an appendix to his *De quatuor linguis commentationis*. Somner's varied talents were employed by William Dugdale and Roger Dodsworth in the first volume of *Monasticon Anglicanum* (1655), for which he translated Anglo-Saxon documents into English and provided information on Kent's religious houses. In 1656 he published *Iulii Caesaris portus Iccius*, a reply to J. J. Chifflet on the Roman expeditions to Britain, which survives in E. Gibson's 1694 edition of both works.

In 1657 Archbishop Ussher persuaded Roger Spelman to present Somner with the Anglo-Saxon lectureship at Cambridge founded by his grandfather Henry Spelman. This provided financial support for his most important work, the magisterial *Dictionarium Saxonico-Latino-Anglicum, voces, phrasesque praecipuas Anglo-Saxonicas … cum Latina et Anglica vocum interpretatione complectens* (1659). Although, as the author admitted, it was not without errors, the dictionary enabled Anglo-Saxon studies to flourish. Demand for it caused the issue of a second edition in 1701 by Thomas Benson entitled *Vocabularium Anglo-Saxonicum*.

In 1659 Somner was imprisoned in Deal Castle after soliciting petitions for a free parliament, but was rewarded at the Restoration with the mastership of St John's Hospital, Canterbury, and the office of auditor of Canterbury Cathedral, a position he occupied until his death. The breadth of Somner's interests, his linguistic abilities, and the disciplined scholarship of his publications, led to a well-deserved reputation. He corresponded with many renowned antiquaries and he was the first port of call for anyone interested in Anglo-Saxon. Some of his Kent collections were published posthumously as *Chartham news, or, A brief relation of some strange bones there lately digged up, in some grounds of Mr. J. Somner's, of Canterbury* (1669), and *A Treatise of the Roman Ports and Forts in Kent* (1693) which included a 'Life of Somner' by Bishop Kennett. Somner died in Canterbury on 30 March 1669 and was buried on 2 April at St Margaret's, Canterbury, where a tablet was erected several years later in praise of his scholarship, piety, and royalism. PETER SHERLOCK

Sources W. Kennett, 'Life of Somner', in W. Somner, *Treatise of gavelkind*, 2nd edn (1726) • D. C. Douglas, *English scholars, 1660–1730*, 2nd edn (1951), 55–7 • G. J. Armytage, ed., *A visitation of the county of Kent, begun … 1663, finished … 1668*, Harleian Society, 54 (1906), 152 • parish register, St Margaret's, Canterbury, 2 April 1669 [burial] • G. Parry, *The trophies of time: English antiquarians of the seventeenth century* (1995)

Archives BL, collections, Harley MS 684 • BL, corresp., Add. MSS 22916, 28004, 32093, 33924; Harley MS 374 (175) • Bodl. Oxf., copies of extracts from chartulary of Monks Horton priory and list of errors in Spelman's *Concilia* • Bodl. Oxf., corresp. • Bodl. Oxf., notes on Roman ports and forts in Kent • Bodl. Oxf., transcript of his *Dictionarium* with MS additions by George Ballard and Edward Thwaites • Canterbury Cathedral, archives, collections

Likenesses M. Burghers, line engraving, pubd 1693, BM, NPG, V&A [*see illus.*]

Son, Adrian van (*d.* **1604x10**), painter, is of obscure origins. He was married to Susanna de Cologne and had five children, one of whom, very probably, was the painter Adam de *Colone. He may be the Adriaen Jacops van Sonne who purchased a house in Breda on 12 December 1579 but the first secure reference to him is in a payment from the treasurer of James VI of Scotland in June 1581 for two portraits which were sent to Geneva to be engraved for Theodore Beza's *Icones*. These were of John Knox and of either James VI or the king's tutor, George Buchanan. In May 1582 van Son received £20 for 'certane paintrie' and, as he received a regular fee between May 1584 and Martinmas 1586, he had probably succeeded Arnold Bronckhorst as court painter. On 30 December 1585 he was made a burgess of Edinburgh on the condition that he instructed apprentices. In 1588 the will of his cousin, the painter Pieter Matheeusen (or Mattheus), left him three portraits as well as a copy of Hilliard's *The Arte Concerning Limning*. In 1594 van Son was listed twice in the register of the privy council of Scotland and described as painter to the king in documents of 24 and 27 May of that year which record him standing part surety for the enormous sum of £3000 for three Dutch sailors. Two portraits of James VI by van Son respectively dated 1586 and 1595 survive (Scot. NPG). James VI's accession to the English throne in 1603 prompted van Son to move to London and he is last recorded as being paid by the Dutch colony in London for work on decorations for the triumphal entry of James VI on 15 March 1604. The painter must have died between this date and 6 July 1610 when his widow lodged a claim at court for outstanding wages and debts.

P. G. MATTHEWS and ELIZABETH DREY-BROWN

Sources D. Thomson, ed., *Painting in Scotland, 1570–1650* (1975), 25–32 [exhibition catalogue, Scot. NPG] • K. Hearn, ed., *Dynasties: painting in Tudor and Jacobean England, 1530–1630* (1995), 172–3, no.117 [exhibition catalogue, Tate Gallery, London, 12 Oct 1995 – 7 Jan 1996] • D. MacMillan, *Scottish art, 1460–1990*, 42–6 • D. Thomson, *The life and art of George Jamesone* (1974), 45–8

Son, Jan Frans van (*b.* **1658**, *d.* in or after **1705**), painter, born at Antwerp on 16 August 1658, was son of the still-life painter Joris van Son (1623–1667) and Cornelia van Heulem. Van Son was too young to have learned much from his father before the latter's death, but he may have studied with his father's friend, the still-life specialist Jan Pauwel Gillemans the elder. His name does not appear in the Antwerp guild registers, and so it seems likely that—as Vertue claimed—he came young to England, perhaps not long after Gillemans's death in 1675. He painted flowers, fruit, and game for a wealthy London clientele which included the earls of Dover and Ranelagh, and he decorated the earl of Radnor's house in St James's Square. He married the niece of Robert Streater, the king's sergeant-painter, and, according to Walpole, inherited much business after Streater's death in 1680. He signed his paintings J. van Son, which has led to confusion with his father's work, albeit that Jan's style is less polished. Vertue maintained that van Son died in St Alban's Street in 1700, at the age of about fifty. Weyerman went to London in late 1702 or early 1703, and wrote that the flower and fruit painter 'N. van Zon' had died shortly before. This, apparently, was the result of a heart broken with grief by the death of a daughter. Both sources are probably wrong, since a painting in Lille is signed and dated 1705; and van Son may not have died in St Alban's Street since his name has not been found in the burial register of St James's Piccadilly.

PAUL TAYLOR

Sources A. van der Willigen, *Netherlandish still-life painters, 1500–1725*, ed. F. Meijer [forthcoming] • Vertue, *Note books*, vols. 1–2 • J. C. Weyerman, *De levens-beschryvingen der Nederlandsche konst-schilders en konst-schilderessen*, 4 vols. (The Hague, 1729–69), vol. 3 • T. J. Broos, *Tussen zwart en ultramarijn: de levens van schilders beschreven door Jacob Campo Weyerman (1677–1747)* (1990) • *DNB* • H. Walpole, *Anecdotes of painting in England: with some account of the principal artists*, ed. R. N. Wornum, new edn, 2 (1849)

Likenesses A. Bannerman, line engraving, BM, NPG; repro. in H. Walpole, *Anecdotes of painting in England* (1762)

Sondes, George, first earl of Feversham (**1599–1677**), politician, was born in November 1599 at Lees Court, in the parish of Sheldwich, near Feversham in Kent, the son and heir of Sir Richard Sondes (1571–1645) of Throwley in the same county and afterwards of Lees Court, and his wife, Susan, daughter of Sir Edward Montagu (1532–1602) of Boughton in Weekley, Northamptonshire. He was of an old Kentish family, and his grandfather Sir Michael Sondes lived in Sheldwich from 1576 to 1587. George was educated at Emmanuel College, Cambridge, where he entered in 1615 and where his tutor was Dr Preston, but he does not appear to have proceeded to a degree. On 10 September 1620 he married Jane (1603–1637), daughter and heir of Ralph Freeman of Aspeden, Hertfordshire, lord mayor of London in 1633–4. They had three children—Freeman, who died in infancy, George, and a younger son, also called Freeman. Sondes was created KB on 1 February 1626 upon Charles I's coronation, and he represented Higham Ferrers in Northamptonshire in the parliament of 1628–9, while as a staunch royalist he was made sheriff of Kent in 1637–8. He sought election as knight of the shire in 1640, but failed. On the outbreak of the civil war he was named a deputy lieutenant for Kent, and was on the royalist committee for the county in 1643, despite having resolved, as he later claimed, 'to sit still, and not do' (Ferris, 457).

When the parliamentary cause proved triumphant Sondes suffered greatly in his estate, and was imprisoned from 1645, first in Upnor Castle and then in the Tower; he was released in May 1650, but not finally discharged until 25 June following, after compounding for his estate by a payment of £3350. Altogether he computed that he lost not less than £30,000 by the civil war. On his release, however, he began rebuilding Lees Court from the plans of Inigo Jones, but his pursuits were interrupted by a terrible calamity which befell him in 1655. On 7 August in that year his younger son, Freeman, a sullen youth of eighteen or nineteen, apparently actuated by jealousy, killed his elder brother, George, who was asleep in an upper room in Lees Court, by a deadly blow on the back of the head with a cleaver. The murderer, who at once apprised his father of his crime, was taken to Maidstone next day and arraigned at Maidstone assize on 9 August. He pleaded guilty, was sentenced to death, and was hanged at Maidstone on 21 August, meeting his end with resignation. The fratricide proved a fruitful theme for the pulpit, and is still memorable on account of the curious pamphlet literature that it evoked. Robert Boreman at once issued *A mirrour of mercy and judgment, or, An exact true narrative of the life and death of Freeman Sonds, esq.* (1655). Other ministers and godly men of the vicinity, less compassionate than Boreman, traced the 'visitation' to Sondes's own moral remissness. He had failed (it was said) to continue the endowment of Throwley Free School as purposed by his father, had improperly executed the will of his father-in-law, Sir Ralph Freeman, and had generally mismanaged his sons' education. Sir George answered the charges with humility in a *Plaine Narrative to the World of All Passages upon the Death of his Two Sonnes* (1655); this is scarcely less steeped in religious sentiment than Robert Boreman's avowedly edifying tract. There followed from other pens *The devils reign upon earth: being a relation of several sad and bloudy murthers lately committed, especially that of Sir George Sonds his son upon his own brother* (1655) and *A funeral elegie upon the death of George Sonds, esq. … by William Annand Junior of Throwllgh, whereunto is annexed a prayer compiled by his sorrowful father* (1655).

On 25 February 1656 Sondes married Mary (*d.* 1688), daughter of Sir William Villiers, bt, of Brooksby. They had two daughters, Mary (*bap.* 1657), who on 19 March 1676 married Louis Duras, Baron Duras of Holdenby, and Katherine (*bap.* 1658), who married Lewis Watson in 1677. On the Restoration, Sondes was again appointed deputy lieutenant for Kent. In a bid to avoid forfeiture of property in consequence of his youngest son's felony, he returned to parliament for the first time in thirty-two years, representing Ashburton, Devon, from 1661 to 1676. An almost entirely inactive parliamentarian, it was due solely to the services of his son-in-law, Lord Duras, favourite and close confidant of the duke of York, that in 1676 he was created baron of Throwley, Viscount Sondes of Lees Court, and earl of Feversham, with remainder to Duras, who succeeded him when he died at Lees Court on 16 April 1677; Sondes was buried at Throwley on 30 April. Thomas Southouse had dedicated his *Monasticon Favershamiense* to him in 1671. Sondes's second son-in-law, Lewis Watson, in 1689 became Baron Rockingham, and upon the death of the second earl of Feversham was created Baron Throwley, Viscount Sondes of Lees Court, and earl of Rockingham (19 October 1714).

THOMAS SECCOMBE, *rev.* SEAN KELSEY

Sources GEC, *Peerage*, 5.364–5 • J. P. Ferris, 'Sondes, Sir George', HoP, *Commons, 1660–90*, 3.456–7 • W. A. Shaw, *The knights of England*, 2 vols. (1906) • Venn, *Alum. Cant.* • *IGI*

Archives CKS, letter seeking patronage in election of knights of the shire

Likenesses G. P. Harding, pencil drawing, NPG

Wealth at death est. £2000 p.a. before civil war: Ferris, 'Sondes, Sir George', 3.457

Sonmans [Sunman], **William** [Willem] (*d.* **1708**), portrait painter, was born in Dordrecht. He was one of the Dutch artists who followed Sir Peter Lely to England during the reign of Charles II, and gained a tolerable reputation. After Lely's death he obtained permission to paint the king's portrait, but

> having not the success he expected, nor his picture so well likt as Mr. Rileys picture of the King by many of the conoiseurs at that time he was so disgusted that he went to Oxford, where he came into good repute & was much imploy'd. (Vertue, *Note books*, 1.62)

Thereafter it was his custom to spend term time in Oxford and the rest of the year in London.

Sonmans's portrait of Robert Morison, the botanist (Oxford Botanic Garden), was engraved by Robert White as a frontispiece to Morison's *Plantarum historiae universalis Oxoniensis* (1680); Sonmans also made the drawings for many of the plates to that work. The frontispiece to the third volume of John Wallis's *Opera mathematica* is a portrait of Wallis by Sonmans (1698), engraved by Michael Burghers (1699).

A number of Sonmans's portraits are in the Bodleian Library, Oxford, including *Thomas Creech* (engraved by Michiel Van der Gucht and Robert White), *John Hudson* (engraved by Simon Gribelin), and *Thomas Bouchier?* (1698). John Taylor, not Sonmans, is now believed to have painted many of the Bodleian's copies of the founders portraits. Other portraits ascribed to Sonmans are at the Examination Schools, Christ Church, Wadham, and Trinity colleges, Oxford. Wadham has a portrait of a college servant named Mrs Alice (Mother) George (1691), which he painted and presented to the college.

Sonmans was living in Gerrard Street, London, when he was named as an executor of the will of Simon Du Bois, painter, in May 1708. He died in Greek Street, Soho, London, in July 1708, and was buried in St Anne's churchyard on 15 July.

F. M. O'DONOGHUE, *rev.* ARIANNE BURNETTE

Sources Vertue, *Note books*, vol. 1 • Mrs R. Lane Poole, ed., *Catalogue of portraits in the possession of the university, colleges, city and county of Oxford*, 3 vols. (1912–25) • *Engraved Brit. ports.* • C. H. C. Baker, *Lely and the Stuart portrait painters: a study of English portraiture before and after van Dyck*, 2 (1912) • H. Walpole, *Anecdotes of painting in England: with some account of the principal artists*, ed. R. N. Wornum, new edn, 2 (1849); repr. (1862) • Thieme & Becker, *Allgemeines Lexikon* • E. K. Waterhouse, *The dictionary of British 16th and 17th century painters* (1988) • *DNB* • will of Simon Du Bois, PRO, PROB 11/501, sig. 113 • parish register, Westminster, St Anne, 15 July 1708 [burial]

Sonnenschein, Edward Adolf (**1851–1929**), classical scholar, was born on 20 November 1851 in Holloway, London, the eldest son of Adolphus (Adolf) Sonnenschein and his first wife, Sarah Robinson, daughter of the Congregationalist missionary the Revd Edward *Stallybrass. One of Sonnenschein's younger brothers was William Swan Sonnenschein, founder of the publishing house of that name. Born Abraham Sonnenschein in Eisgrub, Moravia, in 1825, Edward's father emigrated in 1848 to England

Edward Adolf Sonnenschein (1851–1929), by Vandyk, *c.*1921

after the revolutions of that year. He taught mathematics both in schools and at Bedford College, London, and wrote textbooks of mathematics, German, and English. He also campaigned for educational reform, using his knowledge of continental educational provision to good effect.

Edward Sonnenschein was educated at University College School and at University College, London, proceeding from there as a scholar to University College, Oxford, in 1871. In 1873 he gained a first class in classical moderations (1873), and then won a Taylorian scholarship in modern languages. In the following year, however, he was deprived of this and rusticated for four terms after voluntarily confessing that he had been shown the scholarship papers in advance by his coach, a compositor at the University Press. He went on to gain first-class honours in *literae humaniores* in 1875. From 1877 to 1881 he acted as assistant to G. G. Ramsay, professor of humanity at Glasgow; in November 1881 he was appointed headmaster of the recently founded Kelvinside Academy there, but resigned before the end of the school year. In 1883 he became professor of Greek and Latin at the newly founded Mason College, Birmingham (which became Birmingham University in 1900), where he remained until retirement. On 23 December 1884 he married Edith Annesley (1855–1942), daughter of Ogden Bolton, barrister, of Liverpool, and younger sister of Adolphine, who had become Adolf Sonnenschein's second wife in 1872; they had three sons.

Perhaps influenced by T. H. Key, his old headmaster and professor at University College, London, Sonnenschein had a long-standing interest in Plautus. Already in 1879 he had published an edition of the *Captivi*, notable for an account of Richard Bentley's emendations, which he had found in the British Museum. This account he afterwards elaborated into a volume of the *Anecdota Oxoniensia* (1883). More independent was his edition of the *Mostellaria* of Plautus (1884), which included contributions from his former London teacher Robinson Ellis, who became a lifelong friend. This book led to his long friendship with the German classical scholar Oskar Seyffert, who spoke of Sonnenschein as his 'literary heir'; Seyffert's influence is seen in the edition of the *Rudens* (1891). After this, work on Plautus was thrust into the background by other calls on Sonnenschein's time, but he continued to publish journal articles on the subject, and contributed the articles on Plautus to the eleventh and later editions of the *Encyclopaedia Britannica*.

His experiences as a headmaster in Glasgow made Sonnenschein aware that the various ancient and modern languages were taught without any common terminology. As he put it in an article entitled 'The parallel study of grammar' published in the *Educational Review* in 1892, 'Every classroom had a different set of grammatical terms'. Sonnenschein determined on a campaign to remedy this, and once in Birmingham enlisted the support of colleagues at Mason College and teachers at the King Edward VI School in founding the Grammatical Society, which drew up rules for the standardized teaching of grammar (1886). He then set up the Parallel Grammar series, published by his brother's firm Swan Sonnenschein, which he edited and to which he contributed Latin and Greek grammars. The series, which began to appear in 1888, covered several modern languages, including Welsh, 'Dano-Norwegian', and Dutch, and was notable for the attention paid to the presentation of text. Different stages of learning were indicated by the use of three distinct typefaces, while elementary material was distinguished by marginal lines. Sonnenschein's concern with teaching methods also led to the publication of two Latin narrative readers, *Ora maritima* (1902) and *Pro patria* (1903).

Sonnenschein responded enthusiastically to the call to arms in defence of the classics issued in the *Fortnightly Review* in November 1902 by John Percival Postgate. Together they founded the Classical Association (1903), and served as its joint secretaries. Sonnenschein chaired the association's curricula committee (1904–9), and in pursuance of his grammatical campaign, founded and chaired the joint committee on grammatical terminology. Using the Classical Association as a campaigning base, he enlisted the help of other subject associations, and was largely successful in promoting standardized usage in textbooks. The stiffest resistance came from within the English Association, where some objected to what they saw as the imposition of Latinate terminology on English. The resistance came in particular from W. W. Skeat, and from his ally the leading textbook writer John Collinson

Nesfield. Nesfield conducted a campaign against Sonnenschein's proposals, and had a pamphlet criticizing them bound into several of his English textbooks, but was eventually forced to revise the books in accordance with Sonnenschein's terminology. The joint committee, later the standing committee on grammatical terminology, maintained a watching brief under Sonnenschein's chairmanship, but was wound up on his death in 1929. His plan to bring non-European languages into the same terminological framework, developed in the early 1920s, remained unrealized.

For some years Sonnenschein wrote the article 'Grammar, lexicography and metric' for *The Year's Work in Classical Studies* (founded in 1906). His projected work on Plautine metre never saw light, but the results of his wider metrical studies appeared in *What is Rhythm?* (1925). Much of his grammatical research was summed up in *The Unity of the Latin Subjunctive* (1910) and *The Soul of Grammar* (1927). The latter argued for the unity of internal structure in Aryan languages, and was intended, in Sonnenschein's words, to 'demolish the arch-enemy, Jespersen'—the celebrated Danish linguist Otto Jespersen, who by contrast stressed the autonomous development of vernacular languages. Jespersen's fame initially outlived Sonnenschein's among linguists, but later revaluations rescued the latter from undeserved obscurity.

Sonnenschein's talents as a reformist campaigner were not deployed only in his work for classics and for uniform grammatical terminology. Beginning in 1897 he fought a long, and ultimately successful, campaign to secure a charter for the University of Birmingham, which was granted in March 1900 and gave considerable rights to the academic faculties, as opposed to the lay governors from the local business community. The crucial moment in this campaign came when he enlisted the help of Joseph Chamberlain. The resultant document, which recognized academic autonomy, guaranteed security of tenure, and acknowledged the importance of research, became a model for other modern universities.

During the First World War, besides being, with his wife, prominent among those who organized relief for Belgian refugees, Sonnenschein was the first to call attention to the manifesto of the German academics on war guilt, which led to the publication of a rejoinder by English scholars, circulated in both English and German. He also wrote two of the Oxford war pamphlets, *Through German Eyes* (1914) and *Idols of Peace and War* (1915), and numerous letters in the press on the question of war guilt. Others with Germanic surnames changed them, but Sonnenschein declared that he had made his name as Sonnenschein, and Sonnenschein he would remain, unlike his brother William who chose to become William Stallybrass. One of Sonnenschein's sons, Christopher Edward, had died in a mountaineering accident in Switzerland in 1914. Of the other two, one became Edward Jamie Somerset in 1916, and the other, Edward Oliver, a naval officer, changed his surname to Stallybrass with his uncle in 1917.

Sonnenschein's interest in and publications on grammar and metre led some to see him as a version of Browning's grammarian, concerned only to 'settle hoti's business'. He was in fact a good talker with a fund of humour, though this was not revealed on public occasions. In Birmingham, and later in Bath, where he retired in 1918, he founded and led 'Socratic' societies for the discussion of philosophy. At Birmingham in 1914, he and his wife had appeared at the lord mayor's fancy-dress ball as Socrates and Xanthippe (or as the local newspaper reported, 'Socrates and Christian Thippe'). A particular interest was the later influence of Stoicism, on which he published in the *Hibbert Journal* (1907) and the *Contemporary Review* (1923). Sonnenschein died at his home, 4 Sion Hill Place, Bath, on 2 September 1929. He was survived by his wife and his two remaining sons. His character was summed up in the *Dictionary of National Biography*:

> In scholarship, as in other things, Sonnenschein prided himself on being 'a conservative of the right sort'. He was minutely accurate, and averse to loose quotations and incorrect innovations in language; for instance, he objected to the expression 'post-graduate'. He was a loyal friend, but uncompromising in condemning anything which fell short of his own exacting standards. As a correspondent, he was conscientious in answering questions or discussing difficulties, and never spared himself in promoting the cause of good scholarship or helping fellow students. A certain absent-mindedness in society and indifference to correctness in dress only served to endear him the more to several generations of pupils.

CHRISTOPHER STRAY

Sources *DNB* • E. J. Somerset, *The birth of a university* (1934) • *The Times* (3 Sept 1929) • *The Times* (7 Sept 1929) • *Classical Review*, 43 (1929), 161 • J. B. Walmsley, 'E. A. Sonnenschein and grammatical terminology', *English traditional grammars*, ed. G. Leitner (1991) • J. B. Walmsley, 'The Sonnenschein v. Jespersen controversy', *Meaning and beyond*, ed. U. Fries and M. Heusser (1989) • b. cert. • *CGPLA Eng. & Wales* (1929) • b. cert. [Edith Annesley Bolton]

Archives Bodl. Oxf., letters to Gilbert Murray • Bodl. Oxf., Round Table corresp. • Society for Psychical Research, London, corresp. with Sir Oliver Lodge • U. Birm. L., letters to H. G. Fiedler

Likenesses Vandyk, photograph, *c.*1921, repro. in Somerset, *The birth of a university*, frontispiece [*see illus.*] • C. Gere, portrait; formerly in family possession, 1937 • photograph, repro. in Somerset, *The birth of a university*

Wealth at death £9128 3*s.* 4*d.*: resworn probate, 9 Nov 1929, *CGPLA Eng. & Wales*

Sonnenschein, William Teulon Swan. *See* Stallybrass, William Teulon Swan (1883–1948).

Sonntag, Jacob (1905–1984), journal editor and translator, was born on 15 April 1905 at Vijnita (Wiznitz), northern Bukovina, then a part of the Austro-Hungarian empire (and now in Ukraine), the eldest child (there were three younger brothers and one younger sister) of Ben-Zion Singer-Sonntag, a bookbinder, and his wife, Edel David. (As a young writer, Jacob Sonntag sometimes called himself Jacob Singer, after his grandfather.) Born to poverty, his family moved to Kosov, in eastern Galicia, where he attended the local elementary schools, and then, during

Jacob Sonntag (1905–1984), by unknown photographer, early 1970s

the early stages of the First World War, moved to Innsbruck and then to Vienna, where he attended a local *Gymnasium* to the age of about sixteen. He had also received a traditional Jewish religious education in Orthodox *cheders*, but abandoned this outlook for secular pursuits in literature and philosophy. He also became a convinced Zionist, attending a *hachshara* (training in agriculture for intending migrants to Palestine). Here he met Berta (Batyah), daughter of Israel and Chaja Weinraub of Czernowitz, then in Romania, whom he married in Vienna in January 1927. During the 1920s he contributed prose and verse to German-language Jewish newspapers in Vienna and, in 1930, moved briefly to Palestine but returned to Vienna after six months. For the next five years he worked as a freelance journalist in Vienna, contributing mainly to Jewish newspapers and periodicals and also working as a foreign correspondent for Jewish newspapers in France and the United States. After the fascist coup in Austria in 1934, he moved to Czechoslovakia, where he worked as a freelance journalist for three years, first in Brno and then in Prague.

With the invasion of Czechoslovakia by the Nazi regime, Sonntag was fortunate to escape to Britain (Berta's parents perished in the Holocaust). He arrived in England in November 1938 among the first group of refugees who emigrated with the help of the Czech Trust Fund and the National Union of Journalists. After internment on the Isle of Man and spells of unemployment and menial work, he resumed work as a freelance writer and translator, chiefly for Jewish publications in Britain. He also edited *Zeitspiegel*, a small publication of the Austrian Centre, consisting of translations from the English press. As a survivor of the decimated Jewish communities of eastern Europe, Sonntag was acutely aware that Jewish literary culture and commentary could only be carried on if the seeds of the vanished Jewish civilization of Europe were somehow replanted, and flourished, in Britain. Berta Sonntag was active in the field of children's education and in 1941–2 was honorary secretary of the refugee teachers association of the National Union of Teachers. After the Second World War, Britain contained one of the largest remaining Jewish communities in Europe, in a democratic society with a literate culture. Yet the Anglo-Jewish community was lamentably lacking in a continuing tradition of Jewish literature and commentary, containing few organs in which Jewish writers could feel at home or speak freely. Nor had Anglo-Jewry many close ties with any of the vigorous intellectual and political traditions of Jewry on the continent. It was this situation that Sonntag spent the rest of his life attempting to ameliorate. In 1947 he launched an illustrated monthly, *New Life*, intended to provide a platform for Jewish writers and artists who had survived the Holocaust. This lasted for less than two years before it was unfortunately discontinued because of paper restrictions. He also edited two other short-lived publications, the *Jewish Literary Supplement* and the *Jewish Literary Quarterly*.

In spring 1953 Sonntag founded the *Jewish Quarterly*, the periodical with which his name is associated. It provided a distinguished forum for Anglo-Jewish writers and intellectuals who wished to emphasize the Jewish component of their outlook, or to comment on Jewish affairs. Many of the most notable Anglo-Jewish writers of the post-war decades published in the *Jewish Quarterly*, particularly younger authors who were increasingly concerned with their Jewish roots, among them such notables as Danny Abse, Brian Glanville, Wolf Mankowitz, Alexander Baron, Frederic Raphael, Jon Silkin, and Arnold Wesker (whose first published works appeared there). The *Jewish Quarterly* also featured vigorous commentary on key Jewish issues such as secular Jewish identity in Britain, the central role of Israel in contemporary Jewish affairs, and the persecution of Jews in the Soviet Union. Although ever aware of Jewish history and tradition, Sonntag was a liberal intellectual who was uncomfortable with the growth of Jewish religious fundamentalism and right-wing Israeli nationalism since the 1960s. Two anthologies of notable works from the *Quarterly* were published in his lifetime; these were *Caravan: A Jewish Quarterly Omnibus* and *Jewish Perspectives: 25 Years of Modern Jewish Writing* (1980). Sonntag edited the *Quarterly* almost single-handedly, always on a shoestring budget, and operating from his own home in north London. It was widely noted that for its range and quality the *Quarterly* was without equal in the English-speaking world. The Jewish Literary Trust Ltd was established in 1976 to fund the periodical, allowing it to be published without desperate financial worries. The *Quarterly* continued to be published after Sonntag's death.

Sonntag also published a number of translations from the Yiddish, in particular a narrative poem by Abraham Sutzkever, *Siberia* (1953), which appeared with original illustrations by Marc Chagall. He edited two anthologies of Jewish writing, much of which had not appeared in the *Quarterly*, namely *Jewish Writing Today* (1974) and *New Writing from Israel* (1980). He contributed several surveys of Yiddish literature to encyclopaedias of world literature, and organized many symposia on topics of Jewish interest. He was renowned for his absolute integrity and editorial independence, and was sometimes compared to the *maskilim* of nineteenth-century Europe who sparked the so-called Jewish enlightenment. Britain has not known another figure like Sonntag either before him or since his death. Jacob Sonntag died at 68 Worcester Crescent in north London on 27 June 1984. W. D. RUBINSTEIN

Sources private information (2004) [Ruth Sonntag] · 'Jacob Sonntag', *The Blackwell companion to Jewish culture*, ed. G. Abramson (1989) · *Jewish Chronicle* (6 July 1984) · *Jewish Quarterly*, 31/2 (1984), 3–8 · R. Sonntag, 'Jacob Sonntag: a personal memoir', ed. S. W. Massil, *The Jewish Year Book 2003*, xiii–xviii
Archives priv. coll., family papers
Likenesses photograph, 1970–74, priv. coll. [*see illus.*] · photograph, repro. in Sonntag, 'Jacob Sonntag' · photographs, priv. coll. · portrait, priv. coll.
Wealth at death £12,347: principal probate registry index

Soone, William (*fl.* 1545–*c.*1575), civil lawyer and map maker, was of unknown parentage. He graduated BA at Cambridge in 1545 and proceeded MA in 1549. He became a doctor of canon and civil law, probably at a university on the continent. The bursar's accounts at Gonville and Caius College, Cambridge, show that he was resident at Gonville Hall, probably as a fellow, from 1548 to 1555. In 1561 he became regius professor of civil law and in June he was admitted as a fellow of Trinity Hall. He had probably left Trinity Hall by 1563, when he was succeeded in his professorship by William Clerke. His reason for leaving was that he would not conform to the new protestant service.

Soone is said to have lived in Paris, Dôle, Freiburg, and Padua and was professor of law for some time at Louvain. From there he moved to Antwerp where he probably acted as Abraham Ortelius's assistant, perhaps because of his expertise as a map maker. In 1572 he was at Cologne, where he published *Gulielmi Sooni Vantesdeni auditor, sive, Pomponius Mela disputator de situ orbis*, a copy of which is in the British Library. Ortelius complained to Soone that part of the book, the 'Novi incolae orbis terrarum', was copied from that of Arnold Mylius published by Ortelius in his 1570 version of the *Theatrum*. Soone wrote to Ortelius from Cologne on 31 August 1572, and offered some rather weak explanations for this. Soone also copied the map of Cambridge drawn by Richard Lyne for Thomas Caius's *History of the University* (1574) and published it in Braun's and Remigius Hogenberg's *Civitates orbis terrarum* (*c.*1575) along with a description of the university. He was working as an auditor in Cologne by 1573 but decided that his legal and administrative skills could be put to better use in Rome, where Gregory XIII appointed him *podestà* of a town within the Papal States. JOHN F. JACKSON

Sources Cooper, *Ath. Cantab.* · R. Willis, *The architectural history of the University of Cambridge, and of the colleges of Cambridge and Eton*, ed. J. W. Clark, 4 vols. (1886) · W. Soone, *Gulielmi Sooni Vantesdeni auditor, sive, Pomponius Mela disputator de situ orbis*, Cologne, 1572, BL, 569.c.32 · C. Koeman, *The history of Abraham Ortelius and his 'Theatrum orbus terrarum'* (1964)

Soper, Donald Oliver, Baron Soper (1903–1998), Methodist minister, was born on 31 January 1903 at 36 Knoll Road, Wandsworth, London, the first son and first child of the three children of Ernest Frankham Soper (1871–1962), an average adjuster in marine insurance, the son of a tailor, and his wife, Caroline Amelia, *née* Pilcher (*b.* 1877), a headmistress and daughter of a builder.

Donald Oliver Soper, Baron Soper (1903–1998), by Hans Schwarz, 1987

Early life Donald Soper's home inculcated the nonconformist gospel of duty, hard work, sabbatarianism, and teetotalism. His father was Sunday school superintendent at the local Wesleyan Methodist church, where the family worshipped. His parents enjoyed controversy. His father was an accomplished open-air speaker, skilled with hecklers. His forthright mother took Donald to a suffragette meeting as a child. He inherited humour from his mother and concern for the needy from both parents. At the age of thirteen he declared his intention of becoming a minister of the church.

When the First World War broke out, Soper uncritically accepted the patriotism instilled by his Sunday school and through the cadet corps at Aske's School, Hatcham, to which he went in 1915. But a number of experiences forced him to think more deeply about war and violence. He was horrified when he caused the death of a batsman by fast bowling. On the first armistice day, Soper, as head of the school, strongly defended the right of the son of a local communist to refuse to observe it. When he went up to St Catharine's College, Cambridge, as an exhibitioner in 1921, war veterans were confident that such a war would never happen again. His historical studies convinced him that they were wrong. During his first term he was unwell and lonely. For the first time he found the arguments against Christianity compelling and for a while became an atheist. But he continued to play the hymns for a Sunday school. Gradually he realized what he would lose as an atheist. But the faith to which he returned was more questioning. Meanwhile, his skills in music, sport, and entertainment made him a popular member of his college. He received a lower second for part one and an upper second for the second part of the history tripos.

Early ministry At the conference on politics, economics, and citizenship in 1924 Soper realized that goodwill was not a private attitude but involved a new relationship to neighbours and neighbourhoods. He joined an evangelistic mission in Derby which gave him confidence to speak in the open air and an experience of factory life which converted him to socialism. By the time of the general strike in 1926 he was studying for the Methodist ministry at Wesley House, Cambridge. He opened a centre for strikers. Through his study of the philosophy of religion he was learning to think lucidly and quickly and was awarded a first. He enjoyed public speaking, which both drew people to him and yet kept them at a distance, thus protecting himself from intimacy.

In 1926 Soper was appointed as probationer minister to the mainly working-class congregation at Oakley Place Wesleyan Church, off the Old Kent Road. The poverty of the area shocked and challenged him. Many people appreciated his pastoral zeal, social concern, and fun, but his liberal theology on issues such as the Virgin Birth impelled local officials to try to remove him. Meanwhile he was writing a thesis on Gallicanism under Harold Laski at the London School of Economics, for which he was awarded a PhD in 1929.

In 1927 Soper accepted a church member's suggestion that he should offer his reasoned Christianity to outsiders on Tower Hill. This ministry was to last over seventy years. On the first occasion a question about Marxism floored him. He went home and read Marx, Lenin, Trotsky, and economics. Each week he looked forward to what he called the fellowship of controversy which set his adrenalin flowing. His repartee with hecklers became legendary. The majority of questions were about the Bible, science, and the hypocrisy of the churches. Acutely aware of the challenges of secularism and science, he wrestled with the issues that mattered to ordinary people and answered them with pithy sayings and parables from everyday life.

On 30 July 1929 Soper was ordained at Plymouth. On 3 August that year he married Marie Dean (1908–1994) at Streatham. She had an Anglican background, Roman Catholic education, and was strikingly beautiful. She found it difficult sometimes to be married to a public figure, but he valued his home and family where he could find privacy. For most of his ministry his home was at some distance from his place of ministry. Their four daughters went to Methodist public schools. In 1929 Soper moved to Islington Central Hall, Highbury, where he cleared the debt, developed children's cinema, organized breakfasts for 500 each Christmas morning, and sponsored concerts and variety evenings. He founded a centre where unemployed men could barter their skills. In 1936 he took charge of the west London mission centred on Kingsway Hall. Unlike most Methodist ministers, who are itinerant, Soper stayed there for forty-two years. The mission's work was extensive: a holiday home, a crèche, a hostel for discharged prisoners, a maternity hospital, and girls' hostels. Congregations grew. He taught the centrality of the eucharist, developed the Good Friday three hours' devotion, and began to wear a cassock regularly. In 1942 he started a weekly Sunday open-air session at Hyde Park.

Pacifist campaigner In the early 1930s Dick Sheppard, the Anglican pacifist whom Soper greatly admired, drew him into the peace movement. Soper became a familiar speaker at peace rallies and demonstrations. Gandhi convinced him that goodness could be a powerful force if mobilized by demonstrations and pressure groups. Soper supported the Fellowship of Reconciliation, the Methodist Peace Fellowship, created by a fellow minister Henry Carter in 1933, and the Peace Pledge Union, founded by Sheppard in 1936.

Soper wrestled neither with Reinhold Niebuhr's challenge to pacifism nor with the Augustinian *realpolitik* of the Methodist historian Herbert Butterfield. Some of Soper's judgements seem startlingly naïve. In 1933 he claimed that 'pacifism contains a spiritual force strong enough to repel any invader' (Ceadel, 98). In 1936 he asserted that there was 'a real yearning for peace' in Germany and Italy (ibid., 249). He wrote in 1936 that there was only a small possibility that a nation which renounced violence would suffer crucifixion. As late as November 1937 he predicted that Europe was on the verge of a pacifist landslide.

Soper greeted the outbreak of the Second World War with a mixture of despair and action. He often quoted, 'He that doeth the will shall know of the Gospel'. For most of the war he and others ran a canteen for those sleeping in the shelters. He befriended conscientious objectors and vouched for their characters at tribunals, the judgments of which Soper thought almost always correct. Since 1934, when Sheppard had invited Soper to broadcast from St Martin-in-the-Fields, he had been popular on the radio. But in 1941, together with other pacifists, he was banned from the airwaves. However, he continued to preach pacifism. Sometimes a man from special branch came and took notes. Soper realized that a pacifist could not opt out of society, so he was ready to compromise by fire-watching and by choosing his words carefully when he conducted services for the forces. Some pacifists abandoned their pacifism. But Soper stated: 'I am alone sustained by the Christian faith which assures me that what is morally right carries with it the ultimate resources of the universe' (Ceadel, 212). He wanted the allies to win but continued to regard war as a greater evil than Nazism. 'Auschwitz was produced by the war … the actual enormity of mass genocide was the result of going to save the Jews' (Purcell, 136).

Soper had joined the Labour Party at Cambridge. Only a socialist society could bring peace, because capitalism depended 'on violence for its ultimate authority and sanction' (Purcell, 133). His socialism was derived from the teaching of Jesus and the writings of the Anglican socialists Temple and Tawney. From the 1950s Soper became a familiar and controversial figure through his high-profile support for the Labour Party and nuclear disarmament, and through his regular appearances on radio and television.

In 1945 Soper became chairman of the Methodist Peace Fellowship. In 1957 the Campaign for Nuclear Disarmament was founded and Soper became a member of the executive. He led the first Aldermaston march of 1958 for part of the way, in drenching rain. It was the first of many such marches, yet they left him exhausted because of his growing physical disabilities. He explained in 1950, 'You don't know what would happen if one country were to repudiate its capacity to fight, and then make its claim to moral leadership' (Purcell, 139). After a visit to Russia in 1954 he praised its care for children and old people. He did not discover one Christian dissatisfied with the regime. The labour camps, he thought, were little different from any other prisons.

Labour activist During the war Soper had supported Temple's crusade for a more just post-war society. He regarded the Attlee government as more truly socialist than the Wilson or Callaghan administrations. For Soper, Labour was a movement of protest, and therefore his natural allies were those such as Aneurin Bevan, Tony Benn, and Michael Foot—all with nonconformist roots. For him there was no permanent place for a mixed economy in a socialist society. Clause 4 of the party constitution about common ownership expressed 'what I believe to be the ultimate principle that emerges from our Lord's teaching, that this world ought to be conceived as a home, the goods of this world ought to be set on a family table' (Purcell, 111). He was horrified when Hugh Gaitskell attempted to drop Clause 4 in 1959. In the following year Soper rejoiced when the Labour conference voted for unilateralism. Soper thought 'the kingdom had come' (Purcell, 144). He was bitter when Gaitskell got the decision reversed. Soper championed Bevan as his replacement. When Bevan died in 1960 Soper conducted an act of remembrance on a Welsh mountainside.

Soper became Labour's unofficial chaplain. In 1953 he preached the conference sermon. In 1954 he began a regular column for the left-wing *Tribune*. In 1958 he became Labour alderman of the London county council. He participated in a party broadcast in the 1959 general election. In 1960 he was chosen as chairman of the new Christian Socialist Movement. Most of its members identified socialism with nationalization.

Soper and Harold Wilson were neighbours in Hampstead Garden Suburb, where the Wilsons attended the Free Church. In 1964 Wilson, on becoming prime minister, asked Soper to lead prayers at a service for his ministers; Bishop Mervyn Stockwood preached. In 1965 Soper accepted a life peerage. Wearing his cassock by special permission, he spoke in the Lords on more than 230 occasions. In 1966 he said prayers for Wilson's second government; Wilson subsequently quoted one of these in a speech defining Labour's ethical vision. Nevertheless, Soper concluded that Wilson's governments were not truly socialist, and sometimes he wondered whether Labour would ever be an instrument for socialism. Yet he was at ease with the establishment. He criticized the queen for attending races and the duke of Edinburgh for playing Sunday polo, but happily agreed to preach at Sandringham in 1971.

Soper supported many pressure groups, campaigned against apartheid, alcohol, and gambling, and for the homeless, prisoners, and immigrants, chaired the League against Cruel Sports and Shelter, and supported the Voluntary Euthanasia Society. Though in 1957 he welcomed the Wolfenden committee's recommendation for the decriminalization of adult homosexual conduct, he commented strangely: 'I believe that a disarmed world would be a world in which homosexuality would die out' (Purcell, 99). Later he became more sympathetic.

Methodism Soper's relationship with the Methodist church was ambiguous and sometimes strained. Methodists were proud that the best-known English Christian was a Methodist, someone who could fill any building and bring laughter and controversy to any event. Evangelical Methodists objected to his liberal theology, the priestly implications of his cassock, his sacramentalism, and his criticism of the Billy Graham campaigns. Traditionalists disliked his identification of Christianity with left-wing socialism and were horrified by his statement in 1950 that a Russian invasion would be preferable to war. Many were gratified when Lord Hailsham in 1956 criticized Soper for declaring that Conservatives had 'no philosophy of life as is demanded by Christianity' (Frost, *Goodwill on Fire*, 74).

Soper's attraction to Anglicanism alarmed some Methodists, especially when he said he was ready to be reordained by a bishop to break the deadlock in Anglican–Methodist negotiations. To some he was an unwelcome reminder of Methodism's radical past; others had been wounded by his dismissive remarks. As a result, Soper suffered 'almost ostracism' from official Methodist circles (Purcell, 25). This delayed his election as president of the conference until 1953. On the other hand, the Order of Christian Witness which Soper created in 1946, and which offered a style of theologically open, socially concerned, and eucharistically focused evangelism, drew into its ranks some remarkable missioners who became gifted Methodist ministers. But after twenty years it was in decline. It was too dependent on Soper, lacked devotional discipline and the communal life which enabled the Iona community to flourish.

Later years In 1978 over 1000 people gathered to pay tribute to Soper, now seventy-five, for his forty-two years of ministry at Kingsway Hall. The building was deteriorating, so the mission moved to Hinde Street Methodist Church, where Soper continued to exercise a ministry. Because of severe arthritis he had to be lifted up onto his open-air podium twice a week. When he could no longer stand, he spoke with small groups from a wheelchair. Predictably he was a fierce critic of Thatcherism, and disliked the policies of Denis Healey, Neil Kinnock, and 'new' Labour. Lord Soper had acquired something of a new lease of life in these later years by his frequent appearances on radio discussion programmes, where his distinctive speaking voice, quick wits, and ready tongue were manna to serious broadcasters; as a radio personality he reached a new audience. His literary selections on the Radio 4 programme *With Great Pleasure* on 27 October 1997 included the comic history *1066 and All That*, by Sellar and Yeatman, which he had read in the 1930s and, he maintained, 'cured me … of the evangelism of privilege and confirmed the iniquity of violence'. On 31 January 1993 he celebrated his ninetieth birthday with a eucharist at Hinde Street recorded by television and packed with admirers, including Benn and Foot. After an afternoon session in Hyde Park he was the focus of a live broadcast of *Songs of Praise*, during which tributes were paid by Archbishop Runcie, Cardinal Hume, and others. In the following year his wife died. He was devastated, but he believed, 'things that are eternally true and good will be in abundance beyond the grave' (Frost, *Vintage Soper*, 128). He died at his home in Hampstead Garden Suburb on 22 December 1998. After the funeral at Hinde Street Church on 30 December 1998 he was cremated at Golders Green, where his ashes were buried.

Character and influence Soper described himself as merely a 'would-be Christian', but many experienced him as 'goodwill on fire' (Frost, *Goodwill on Fire*, viii, 3). A restless matador always on the look-out for a likely bull, he was liable to be swept away by his enthusiasms. He became the type of rebel which the British are skilled at domesticating and neutralizing. 'The man talks in quotes', exclaimed a delighted journalist (ibid., 152). But his ability to coin a memorable phrase learned in the open air, limited his capacity for sustained exposition.

Theologically, Soper was a liberal modernist who developed a catholic understanding of church, ministry, and sacraments. The Christian calling was to action not speculation. The Sermon on the Mount was a better introduction to God than the Nicene creed. Yet he greatly valued the scaffolding of liturgical worship. Central to his message was the kingdom of God. Though he wanted a rational theology, like Pascal he also knew that the heart had reasons. Wesley's phrase 'that dear disfigured face' in his hymn about Jesus moved him to tears. His Good Friday and ordination addresses inspired many. Everyone was a brother or sister for whom Christ died. Latterly he spent an hour in silence in All Hallows Church before his dialogues on Tower Hill. He was very selective about the Bible, but believed that the church was vital to the Christian life. He joined the Methodist Sacramental Fellowship and became its president in 1950. He wrote, 'eucharistic worship is objective, universal and apostolic' (Soper, *All his Grace*, 92). When he was president of the Methodist Conference the eucharist was the central act of worship wherever he went. He was in the tradition of the nineteenth-century nonconformist conscience, embodied in the founder of the west London mission, Hugh Price Hughes, which believed there was no boundary between politics and religion and that social evils should be denounced in vivid language at mass rallies.

Soper was one of the last links with the pioneers of Christian pacifism—Dick Sheppard, Vera Brittain, Charles Raven, and George Lansbury—and he continued the tradition of those Victorian nonconformists who were Labour stalwarts. Foot praised Soper for recalling Labour to first principles. But he supported factionalism, was naïve about Soviet society, and uncritically adopted statism, despite the nonconformist voluntarist tradition. He described the political process as 'a long, desperate, continuously disappointing road' (Frost, *Vintage Soper*, x).

A journalist remarked that there

> is in Soper's life so much of an England which is lost or half-forgotten. Joseph Rank's Methodist Central Halls, outdoor meetings, pacifism, ethical socialism, passionate discussion of issues, working men's missions, and a belief in the perfectibility of men in society. (Frost, *Goodwill on Fire*, 229)

Brian Frost suggests he was perhaps one of those who bear for society 'hopes and aspirations which in its better moments it yearns to accept, while remaining ambivalent about the consequences of their implementation' (ibid., 254). His faith, courage, humour, and persistence transcended the battles he fought. 'The end is not death. The end is not injustice. The end is love', he said in a sermon in 1980 (Frost, *Vintage Soper*, 132).

Among Soper's publications were *Christ and Tower Hill* (1934), *All his Grace* (1957), *The Advocacy of the Gospel* (1961), and his autobiography, *Calling for Action* (1984). He was made an honorary fellow of St Catharine's College, Cambridge, in 1966; in 1981 he received the world Methodist peace award; and in 1988 he received an honorary DD at Cambridge and became a freeman of the City of London and of the Haberdashers' Company.

ALAN WILKINSON

Sources B. Frost, *Goodwill on fire: Donald Soper's life and mission* (1996) · W. Purcell, *Odd man out: a biography of Lord Soper of Kingsway* (1983) · B. Frost, ed., *Vintage Soper, God, faith and society* (1997) · D. Soper, *Calling for action: an autobiographical enquiry* (1984) · D. Soper, *All his grace* (1957) · M. Caedel, *Pacifism in Britain, 1914–1945: the defining of a faith* (1980) · A. Wilkinson, *Dissent or conform? War, peace and the English churches, 1900–1945* (1986) · A. Wilkinson, *Christian socialism: Scott Holland to Tony Blair* (1998) · private information (2004) · personal knowledge (2004) · *The Times* (23 Dec 1998) · *The Guardian* (23 Dec 1998) · *The Independent* (23 Dec 1998) · *The Scotsman* (23 Dec 1998)

Archives BBC WAC · JRL, Methodist Archives and Research Centre, papers as President of Methodist Conference · NRA, priv. coll., papers · University of Bristol Library, corresp. and statements relating to trial of *Lady Chatterley's lover* | SOUND BL NSA, tapes

Likenesses stained-glass window, 1937, Muswell Hill Methodist Church · H. Schwarz, drawing, 1987, NPG [*see illus.*]

Soper, William (*d.* 1459), administrator and merchant, was the son of Robert and Clemency Soper. The family may have been connected with Salisbury: a John Soper traded with that city, and William himself had a house there *c.*1445; another possible place of origin is the area round Totnes in Devon. Soper was probably apprenticed in Southampton, where he is recorded as town steward in 1410, and for which he sat regularly in parliament, being returned thirteen times between May 1413 and February 1449. In 1413 he was appointed collector of subsidy and other royal dues at Southampton, continuing as customer there for thirty years. Also in 1413, his *annus mirabilis*, he stepped onto the ladder of royal service after a vessel of his captured a Castilian vessel, which became the royal ship *Holy Ghost*. He made this prize over to the crown, and his future career as a royal official at Southampton, and especially in connection with Henry V's navy, may have started from that transaction. Soper was certainly a key figure in the revival of the English navy under Henry V. In 1416 he administered the building of the *Gracedieu*, *Falcon*, and *Valentine*, all at Southampton. The *Gracedieu* weighed 1400 tons, and was the largest and most impressive of

King Henry's ships. Facilities for its building at Southampton under Soper, who was appointed surveyor of the king's ships at 1*s.* a day in 1418, contributed to the creation of a dockyard workshop, which included a forge and storehouse costing £200 and made of ragstone and 'holyngston'. Southampton effectively replaced Greenwich as England's principal naval base after 1420. Following active service in 1420 the *Gracedieu* came to Soper who managed it. The great ship was laid up at Hamble in 1432 and burnt out in 1439. Marine archaeology has shown it was 125 ft long and clinker-built. It was excluded from the sale of ships under Henry V's will.

On 3 February 1420 Soper became keeper of the king's ships. His surviving accounts, now at Greenwich, have been published, and record the details of naval administration, maintenance, and equipment of the years around 1420 in the context of the development of the Lancastrian navy and of Soper's life. However, he also undertook a number of other tasks on behalf of the government. These included holding inquisitions and musters, and being a verderer of the New Forest, where he went to live. Trade in his own right—recorded from 1412, when the commodity was La Rochelle wine—probably became relatively less significant after he obtained royal preferment in 1413. But in 1417 he sent wool to Pisa, and in 1419 to Spain 'and foreign parts'. He owned the 140 ton *Julian of Hampton* in 1418, and was sending wine to the dean of Salisbury and to the king's house at Guildford as late as 1440. There is evidence that the Southampton town government was aware of developments in financial practice as early as 1441, and was in the forefront of bookkeeping practice in England by the end of the century. Soper may have been influential in this area, since he was handling financial instruments and letters of payment in the 1420s and 1430s.

With an annual income of £50, Soper was one of the wealthiest men in Hampshire in 1436. He certainly had cordial relations with Luca di Maso degli Albizzi, who was captain of the Florentine galleys in 1429. Albizzi visited Soper's rich New Forest home at Newton Bury (now Bury Farm), Hampshire, and declared of the *Gracedieu* that 'in truth I have never seen so large and beautiful a construction' (Mallett, 259). His account of his visit provides a vivid view of the pleasures—feasting, hunting, receipt of gifts—which accompanied business with Soper. In 1436 Soper may himself have gone to north Italy on pilgrimage. He developed financial interests which may have included moneylending and banking, perhaps operating from properties he had in Southampton. This could help to explain his slackening interest in trade after 1413. He continued in royal service under Henry VI until 1442. Having become one of the new administrative squirearchy of late medieval England, he died in 1459 at his country house as William Soper esquire. His association with Southampton continued in death, as his will tells of his marble tomb at the town's Franciscan church. Recent excavations may have uncovered his remains, but not his tomb. He apparently left no children, though he married twice: first the pious, and perhaps older, Isabel, whose surname is unknown, and second, *c.*1438, his former mistress, Joan Chamberlain. TOM BEAUMONT JAMES

Sources S. Rose, *The navy of the Lancastrian kings: accounts and inventions of William Soper keeper of the king's ships, 1422–1427*, Navy Records Society, 123 (1982) • C. Platt, *Medieval Southampton: the port and trading community, AD 1000–1600* (1973) • A. B. Wallis Chapman, ed., *The Black Book of Southampton*, 2, Southampton RS, 14 (1912) • M. E. Mallett, *The Florentine galleys in the fifteenth century with the diary of Luca di Maso degli Abizzi captain of the galleys, 1429–30* (1967) • B. C. Turner, 'Southampton as a naval centre, 1414–58', *Collected essays on Southampton*, ed. J. B. Morgan and P. S. Peberdy (1958) • W. J. C. Turner, 'The building of the *Gracedieu*, *Valentine* and *Falconer* at Southampton, 1416–20', *Mariner's Mirror*, 40 (1954), 55–72 • M. Oppenheim, *A history of the administration of the Royal Navy* (1896) • T. B. James, 'The geographical origins and mobility of the inhabitants of Southampton, 1400–1600', PhD diss., U. St Andr., 1977 • private information (2004) • HoP, *Commons, 1386–1421*, 4.405–8

Archives PRO, accounts various, E101 *temp.* Henry V, Henry VI

Sophia, princess palatine of the Rhine (1630–1714), electress of Hanover, consort of Ernst August, was born on 4 October 1630 in The Hague, the youngest of five daughters and the youngest but one of the thirteen children of Frederick V (1596–1632), elector palatine (1610–32) and the 'winter king' of Bohemia (1619–21), and his wife, *Elizabeth (1596–1662), the daughter of James I. Born in exile because of Frederick's expulsion from Bohemia and the Palatinate, Sophia's importance in history was derived from her parentage and from the unpredictable fate of the Stuarts.

Brought up at Leiden until 1641, Sophia was taught French, German, English, Dutch, Latin, Greek, theology, history, mathematics, and law before moving in 1641 to her mother's court at The Hague, an environment where learning was encouraged. Her mother suggested that Sophia marry the exiled Charles II, but he was not interested, and, her pride hurt, in 1650 she moved to the court of her eldest brother, *Charles Lewis (Karl Ludwig), now restored to Heidelberg.

Sophia married Ernst August of Brunswick-Lüneburg (1629–1698) in 1658, on 17 October NS according to some biographers, after his elder brother had withdrawn an offer. Ernst August and Sophia had six sons and one daughter; their eldest son, Georg Ludwig [*see* George I], was born in 1660; among their other children was *Ernest Augustus, duke of York and Albany. Ernst August benefited from the failure of his three elder brothers to father any legitimate sons, and, from prince bishop of Osnabrück in 1661, he progressed to duke of Calenberg (1679) and elector of Hanover (1692). As the territories of the different branches of the house of Brunswick-Lüneburg were consolidated, Ernst August became a more powerful individual. Sophia was proud of her husband and delighted by his rise. She had made a lengthy visit with him to Italy in 1664–5 and enjoyed the company of learned men, including G. W. Leibniz. Sophia was not intolerant in religious matters.

The death of William, duke of Gloucester (1689–1700), the last surviving child of Queen Anne, led to fresh concern over the succession in Britain. In 1701 by the Act of

Settlement, Catholics were debarred from the English succession, and Sophia and her heirs were named heirs to William III and Anne. The Act of Union of 1707 ensured that this succession would extend to Scotland. The granddaughter of James I, Sophia was the nearest protestant claimant by blood; fifty-seven Roman Catholics nearer in blood were passed over.

After William III's death in 1702 and Anne's succession Sophia became the immediate heir to the throne. The relationship between Sophia and the monarch was never free from tension, and the succession also created difficulties between Sophia and her eldest son, Georg, a particularly serious crisis occurring in 1706 over Sophia's attempt to intervene in English politics. Expectation about becoming queen helped to give Sophia a powerful interest in her last years, but she was denied her chance, dying on 28 May 1714 after hurrying to shelter from sudden rain during a walk in the palace gardens at Herrenhausen. Anne died two months later, on 1 August 1714. Thus the British were denied the chance of a monarch who would have been more cultivated than any of the other Hanoverians, while Sophia, born in exile, died without ever visiting the country to whose throne she was heir. Her eldest son, Georg Ludwig (George Lewis), became George I, king of Great Britain and Ireland in 1714. JEREMY BLACK

Sources A. Ward, *The electress Sophia and the Hanoverian succession*, 2nd edn (1909) • R. Hatton, *George I, elector and king* (1978) • *Memoiren der Sophie Kurfürstin von Hannover*, ed. A. Köcher (1879) • *Memoirs of Sophia, electress of Hanover*, ed. and trans. H. Forester (1888) • *Correspondenz von Leibniz mit der Prinzessen Sophie*, ed. O. Klopp, 3 vols. (1873) • *Aus den briefen der Herzogin Elisabeth, Charlotte von Orleans an die Kurfürstin Sophie von Hannover*, ed. E. Bodemann, 2 vols. (1891) • *Briefe der Kurfürstin Sophie von Hannover an die Raugrafinnen und Raugrafen zu Pfalz*, ed. E. Bodemann (Leipzig, 1888) • *Briefwechsel der herzogin Sophie von Hanover*, ed. E. Bodeman (Leipzig, 1885) • *Briefe der Königin Sophie Charlotte von Preussen und der Kurfürstin Sophie von Hannover*, ed. R. Doebner (1905)

Archives BL, corresp., Stowe MSS 222–227, 241–242, *passim* | BL, letters to Lord Craven, Add. MS 63743 • NRA Scotland, priv. coll., letters to Thomas Burnett • U. Nott. L., corresp. with earl of Portland

Likenesses G. Honthorst, oils, *c*.1643, Wilton House, Wiltshire • G. Honthorst, oils, *c*.1645, Staatliche Schlösser und Gärten, Schloss Charlottenburg, Berlin • G. Honthorst, oils, 1650, Ashdown House, Oxfordshire • W. Faithorne junior, mezzotint, BM, NPG • J. Smith, mezzotint (after F. Weideman), BM, NPG • W. Vaillant, etching, BM • line engraving, BM • marble bust, NPG • medals, BM • miniature (in old age), Royal Collection • oils, Royal Collection

Sophia, Princess (**1777–1848**). *See under* George III, daughters of (*act*. 1766–1857).

Sophia Dorothea [Princess Sophia Dorothea of Celle] (**1666–1726**), electoral princess of Hanover, was born in the castle of Celle, Germany, on 15 September 1666 OS, the eldest child of Georg Wilhelm, duke of Brunswick-Lüneburg (1624–1705), ruler of the Celle portion of the duchy from 1665, and Eléonore Desmier d'Olbreuse (1639–1722), an exiled French protestant aristocrat. At the time of Sophia Dorothea's birth her mother and father were of unequal status; their legal union in 1665 was less than a marriage, consisting of a promise by Georg Wilhelm never to leave Eléonore and not to marry anyone

Sophia Dorothea [Princess Sophia Dorothea of Celle] (**1666–1726**), by Jacques Vaillant, *c*.1690 [with her children, the future George II and Sophia Dorothea, queen of Prussia]

else. None the less, Georg Wilhelm and Eléonore continually worked to regularize their union. Sophia, the only surviving child, gradually transformed from an illegitimate daughter into an eligible heiress. In 1674 her mother became a reigning princess as countess of Wilhelmsburg. On 2 April 1676 Georg Wilhelm and Eléonore were formally married; as part of the marriage settlement Sophia Dorothea was fully legitimized as a Brunswick-Lüneburg princess.

Georg Wilhelm fielded several proposals for his daughter's hand. Sophia Dorothea was at first engaged to Friedrich August, son of Anton Ulrich, duke of Brunswick-Wolfenbüttel, but the young prince was killed in battle in 1676. In the succeeding years Georg Wilhelm negotiated with his brother Duke Ernst August, reigning at Hanover from 1679, on behalf of his eldest son Georg Ludwig (1660–1727), later *George I of Great Britain. The marriage of Sophia Dorothea to Georg Ludwig was designed to secure the succession of Ernst August and his heirs to Celle. The union of Celle and Hanover was a vital part of Ernst August's scheme to become an imperial elector. The marriage took place in Celle on 22 November 1682.

The couple formally resided together in Hanover but Georg Ludwig was frequently away on military campaigns. Many of Sophia Dorothea's biographers have seen the contrast between her arranged marriage to Georg Ludwig and the love match of her parents as the root of her later disaffection. Despite the long absences of her husband, the couple had two children, Georg August (later

*George II of Great Britain) and Sophia Dorothea, subsequently queen of Prussia to Frederick William I and mother of Frederick the Great.

Sophia Dorothea was introduced to Philipp Christoph, Count von Königsmark (1665–1694), during 1689 soon after he had been granted a commission by Ernst August. The count was from a distinguished Swedish military family and has been contrasted as 'ardent' and 'poetic' alongside the 'matter-of-fact' Georg Ludwig (Hatton, 54–5). The two began corresponding in July 1690 and were lovers by early 1692.

The relationship alarmed the Hanoverian court because of the couple's lack of discretion. They ignored warnings and began to prepare for an independent life away from Hanover. Sophia Dorothea agitated for control over some of her inheritance, signed away by her father in her marriage contract, while in June 1694 Königsmark accepted a commission from his friend Friedrich August I of Saxony. He returned to Hanover to wind up his affairs, but disappeared on 1 July 1694 after leaving for the Leine Palace to visit Sophia Dorothea.

The disappearance of Königsmark was never satisfactorily explained. Georg Schnath, based on a study of circumstantial evidence, suggested that Königsmark was mortally wounded soon after entering the palace, probably on the orders of Ernst August's mistress Clara von Platen. Königsmark's house was searched and his papers seized. Sophia Dorothea was placed under guard but proved eager to accept the divorce arranged by Ernst August and Georg Wilhelm and consented to be named the guilty party without admitting to her adultery. The consistorial court of Hanover pronounced the divorce on 28 December 1694 and Sophia Dorothea was forbidden to remarry.

Sophia Dorothea remained a political liability. As she could not be allowed to seek help from the emperor or from Saxony should she wish to revise the divorce settlement, Georg Wilhelm and Ernst August agreed to confine her at the manor house of Ahlden in the territory of Celle, built in 1613 as a magistrate's residence. The 'castle' was fortified, supposedly for Sophia Dorothea's own protection, and she was guarded by a marshal and forty infantry and cavalry. On 28 February 1695 Sophia Dorothea arrived at Ahlden, where she was to be imprisoned, with a brief interlude, for the rest of her life. She was allocated the title duchess—or princess—of Ahlden. Her mother was the only visitor from her old life permitted to see her, and correspondence with her children was forbidden.

The duchess of Celle sought to improve Sophia Dorothea's condition but her efforts—which included negotiations with both Louis XIV and William III—came to nothing. From April to September 1700 Georg Ludwig (who had succeeded his father in 1698) allowed Sophia Dorothea to live at Celle in the face of a French invasion of the Brunswick duchies. Once the threat subsided Georg Wilhelm, who had refused to see his daughter, sent her back to Ahlden.

Sophia Dorothea had been marginalized to reduce any damage she might do to the dynastic fortunes of the house of Brunswick. At the time of her divorce it was feared that any action she took against the family would jeopardize both recognition of the Hanoverian electorate and acceptance of the Electress Sophia as heiress presumptive to Great Britain. The danger did not abate once the Act of Settlement had been passed as it was conceivable that Sophia Dorothea would use any freedom she was granted to attack her husband's character and so help the Jacobite cause. Conscious that his divorce was a political and religious embarrassment in Great Britain, Georg Ludwig never explained the absence of his wife to British visitors. However, the story of Sophia Dorothea's relationship with Königsmark and her imprisonment at Ahlden circulated widely, most sensationally through the sixth volume of Duke Anton Ulrich's epic *roman-à-clef* the *Roman Octavia* (1708), which emphasized the brutality of Georg Ludwig and the virtue of Sophia Dorothea. Opponents of the Hanoverian succession in Great Britain used the Königsmark story to allege that the future George II was not the son of Georg Ludwig.

Georg Ludwig succeeded to the British throne in 1714 as George I, but this brought no change in Sophia Dorothea's position. She began a clandestine correspondence with her daughter soon after her wedding, but the queen of Prussia failed to arrange her mother's freedom as Sophia Dorothea had hoped. The discovery that her financial adviser the count de Bar had embezzled the money she had entrusted to him to invest on the Amsterdam stock exchange further reduced her confidence. Depressed, she died at Ahlden, possibly following a stroke or heart attack, on 13 November 1726 NS; George I intended that she should be buried in the castle grounds at Ahlden but the soil was too waterlogged and her remains were placed in a lead coffin until further instructions were received from London. George eventually conceded that she be interred in the ducal vaults in the Old Church, Celle, where her body was placed in May 1727.

Sophia Dorothea's legend continued to grow after her death. It was said that the death of George I in 1727 was brought on by reading a final letter from Sophia Dorothea written shortly before her death. Variations on her life story continued to appear and she became a measure for the Hanoverian dynasty's immorality. When George IV began divorce proceedings against his wife, Caroline, in 1820, an attack on his conduct was published as *Sophia, Princess of Zell, to George the First, on his Accession to the Throne of England*. The discovery by historians of Sophia Dorothea's correspondence with Königsmark ended the myth that Sophia Dorothea had been falsely accused of adultery but did nothing to dispel the romantic allure of her story. This continued to be the basis for several historical novels in the twentieth century, most famously *Saraband for Dead Lovers* (1935) by Helen Simpson, filmed in 1948. MATTHEW KILBURN

Sources *DNB* · R. Jordan, *Sophia Dorothea* (1970) · W. H. Wilkins, *The love of an uncrowned queen* (1900); rev. edn (1910) · C. Schnath, 'Die Sophie-Dorotheen-Trilogie', *Angewählte Beträge zur Landgeschichte Niedersachsens* (1968), 52–257 · R. Hatton, *George I: elector and king* (1978) · 'Verses on the death of Sophia Dorothea',

1726, BL, Add. MS 4455, fol. 87 • *Some queries proposed to civil, canon and common lawyers publish'd in London, July 1712. In order to prove the legitimacy of the pretender* (1712) • *Sophia, princess of Zell, to George the first, on his accession to the throne of England* (1820) • M. Kroll, *Sophie, electress of Hanover* (1973) • A. W. Ward, *The Electress Sophia and the English succession* (1909) • D. Schwennicke, ed., *Europäische Stammtafeln*, new ser., 1/1 (Frankfurt am Main, 1998), table 25

Archives Lund University, corresp. with Philip Christopher Königsmark • Royal Secret State Archives, Berlin, corresp. with Philip Christopher Königsmark

Likenesses J. Vaillant, group portrait, oils, *c*.1690, Bomann-Museum, Celle [*see illus.*] • J. Smith, mezzotint, pubd 1706 (after F. W. Weidemann), NG Ire. • A. Birell, stipple, pubd 1802 (after F. Kerseboon), BM, NPG • stipple, pubd 1845, BM • W. Faithorne junior, mezzotint (after F. Kerseboon), BM • oils, Gripsholm Castle, Stockholm

Sopwith, Thomas (1803–1879), surveyor and civil engineer, was born on 3 January 1803 in Pilgrim Street, Newcastle upon Tyne, possibly the only son of Jacob Sopwith (1770–1829), builder and cabinet-maker, and his wife, Isabella, daughter of Matthew Lowes. Sopwith developed early aptitudes for writing, drawing, and the cataloguing of minerals. He was educated privately, but briefly, on Tyneside, before being apprenticed to his father as a cabinet-maker.

In 1822 Sopwith commenced a diary (which he continued until his death), designed a new gaol for Newcastle, for which he was awarded 10 guineas, and was admitted a free burgess of the corporation of Newcastle. Despite his training as a cabinet-maker, Sopwith was determined to become a land surveyor; accordingly, as soon as his apprenticeship was completed, he joined Joseph Dickinson of Alston in his survey of the Greenwich Hospital's Alston Moor mines, and soon went into partnership with him. By 1824 or 1825, while he was still based at Alston, Sopwith had already undertaken surveys for the Newcastle and Carlisle Railway and the corporation of Newcastle; he also learned to play the organ. In 1826 his *Account of All Saints Church* [*Newcastle*] was published. On 2 September 1828 he married Mary Dickenson of Alston, daughter of a principal agent to the Greenwich Hospital; their only child, Jacob, was born on 24 July 1829. Mary died seven days later, and Sopwith's father died in October of the same year. Although concentrating on surveying, Sopwith and his cousin, John Sopwith, continued the cabinet-making business. This was not just out of filial piety, as Sopwith was particularly proud of his 'monocleid writing cabinet' design with its central locking system.

Sopwith returned to Newcastle in 1830 and surveyed a new line for the Ponteland turnpike. On 1 February in the following year he married Jane Scott (*c*.1807–1855) of Ross, Northumberland; they had three sons and four daughters. In 1832 Sopwith was elected to the Institution of Civil Engineers and took an office in the newly opened Royal Arcade, Newcastle, embarking on a busy life as a consulting surveyor. He published his *Account of Alston Moor* in 1833, and his *Treatise on Isometric Drawing* in 1834, the latter following systematic study over two years. He was also to publish about eighteen articles. He undertook many commissions in the years 1832–45, including street improvements in the city of Newcastle, surveys of the minerals in the Forest of Dean (leading to his appointment as crown commissioner for the forest), and work on several railways in England and on the Sambre and Meuse Railway in Belgium. Through all these activities he came to know, and sometimes to work with, engineers such as George and Robert Stephenson, Isambard Kingdom Brunel, William Cubitt, and W. G. Armstrong; and among his friends he included Decimus Burton, Charles Landseer, Charles Barry, Rowland Hill, and professors Sedgwick and Faraday.

At the 1838 British Association meeting in Newcastle, Sopwith argued for the necessity of preserving mining records. In 1845 he was elected fellow of the Royal Society and became chief agent to the W. B. [Lead] Company centred at Allenheads, whereupon he agreed to give up all other professional interests except that of commissioner for woods and forests. He accepted this radical change because the post at Allenheads offered him an important job for the rest of his life, with the provision of comfort in old age. It would also take him back to an area he had come to love, and it would enable him to make Allenheads his main family home. However, he continued to keep a house in Newcastle, and one in London from about 1845. As agent at Allenheads, Sopwith developed the mines; built schools, libraries, and chapels; improved cottages; and encouraged mutual improvement and benefit societies for the workers and their families. He introduced a system of mine surveying and plan production of considerable intricacy, producing some of the earliest detailed mine plans. The limitations of two-dimensional plans, even when drawn isometrically, led him to develop highly regarded three-dimensional geological models in wood, which were constructed in the cabinet-making works. His only setback, in an otherwise successful professional life, came with the Allenheads strike in 1849, when he insisted on enforcing time clauses in miners' bargains. Some miners, led by local Primitive Methodists, refused to accept these bargains and a strike ensued. It was a time of labour surplus, and while the miners hoped for concessions he made none. Described by a friend as the very soul of order and of exactitude, he was in fact obsessive about punctuality. The strike collapsed after four months, and thereafter work was denied to many: some sixty men, women, and children left the dale on one day in May to seek work in America.

Sopwith was not vindictive after the strike and helped various Methodist societies, for example; but he remained uneasy about the strike even in his last years. Although not active in politics, he supported universal suffrage and annual elections, and welcomed the entry of working-class MPs into the Commons, believing that they would lead to an extension of liberal views or a new political party. He was able, no doubt, to express such views both among his influential friends and within some of the twenty-six learned societies to which he belonged.

A dispute with the owner of the Allenheads company, W. B. Beaumont, caused Sopwith to offer his resignation in 1857 (the year in which the University of Durham awarded him an honorary MA), though this was not accepted. He was subsequently allowed to undertake the management from London and returned to Allenheads in 1860. His third marriage, to Anne, daughter of Addison Longhorne Potter of Heaton Hall, took place on 29 September 1858. Sopwith finally retired from his position, and all professional life, in 1871. He died from heart disease at his house, 103 Victoria Street, London, on 16 January 1879, and was buried at Norwood cemetery. His third wife survived him. One of his grandsons was the pioneering aviation engineer Sir Thomas *Sopwith (1888–1989).

STAFFORD M. LINSLEY

Sources T. Sopwith, diary, U. Newcastle, Robinson L. • B. W. Richardson, *Thomas Sopwith* (1891) • *DNB* • R. Welford, *Men of mark 'twixt Tyne and Tweed*, 3 vols. (1895) • 'Thomas Sopwith', *Monthly Chronicle* (April 1889) • S. Turner and W. R. Dearman, 'Thomas Sopwith's large geological models', *Proceedings of the Yorkshire Geological Society*, new ser., 44 (1982–4), 1–28 • *IGI*

Archives Hunt. L., journal • U. Newcastle, Robinson L., diaries [microfilm copies] | Bodl. Oxf., letters to Mary and Martha Somerville • U. Newcastle, Robinson L., letters to Sir Walter Trevelyan • Wellcome L., letters to Henry Lee

Likenesses autotype, repro. in Richardson, *Thomas Sopwith* • sketch, repro. in 'T. Sopwith', *Monthly Chronicle*

Wealth at death under £12,000: probate, 12 March 1879, *CGPLA Eng. & Wales*

Sopwith, Sir Thomas Octave Murdoch (1888–1989), engineer and airman, was born on 18 January 1888 at 92 Cromwell Road, Kensington, west London, the eighth child and only son of Thomas Sopwith (1838–1898), managing director of the Spanish Lead Mines Company of Linares in southern Spain, and his wife, Lydia Gertrude, daughter of William Messiter of Wincanton, Somerset. Sopwith was educated at the Cottesmore School, Hove, Sussex, and, from 1902, the Seafield Park Engineering College at Lee-on-Solent, where he pursued his already deep interest in early motor cars, motor cycles, and all things mechanical. His childhood was deeply affected by an incident on a boating expedition during the family's annual summer holiday on the Isle of Lismore, off Oban in Scotland, when a gun, lying across the ten-year-old Sopwith's knee, went off and killed his father. This haunted Sopwith for the rest of his life. A substantial inheritance of £52,000 was divided chiefly between Sopwith and his mother, because five of the seven daughters had already married well.

Thus provided, on leaving Seafield Park in 1905 without academic attainments but with a good practical grasp of basic engineering, Sopwith plunged into the enjoyable pursuits of ballooning, motor racing at Brooklands, and sailing in channel waters. He bought a single-seat Avis monoplane and taught himself to fly (he gained the aviator's certificate no. 31). Before the end of 1910 he set up a British distance and duration record of 107 miles and 3 hours 10 minutes and, in December, with a flight of 169 miles in 3¾ hours, won the £4000 Baron de Forest prize for the longest flight of the year from Britain into Europe. He won further prize money in America, which enabled him,

Sir Thomas Octave Murdoch Sopwith (1888–1989), by unknown photographer, 1910

in February 1912, to found the Sopwith School of Flying and, in June, the Sopwith Aviation Company Ltd.

By the outbreak of the First World War in August 1914 the Sopwith Aviation Company had become one of the leading early British aircraft manufacturers, supplying aircraft to both the Admiralty and the War Office. Moreover, a Sopwith Tabloid on floats—a precursor of all subsequent single-seat fighters—had won for Britain the second Schneider Trophy air race at Monaco. Between August 1914 and November 1918 more than 18,000 Sopwith aircraft, of thirty-two different types, were designed and built for the allied air forces. They included 5747 Sopwith Camel single-seat fighters. The Camel was one of the most successful military aircraft of the First World War, with 1294 confirmed victories in air combat.

Sopwith's contribution to the war was recognized by his appointment as CBE in 1918, but from the end of the war until September 1920 the Sopwith company built only fifteen aircraft, while vainly endeavouring to maintain the employment of as many of its workers as possible by building motor car bodies, motor cycles, and even aluminium saucepans. In September 1920 Sopwith put the company into liquidation while he was still able to pay creditors in full. Two months later he launched the H. G. Hawker Engineering Company Ltd, with himself as chairman, Fred Sigrist as chief engineer, and Harry Hawker as designer/test pilot. In June 1928 the Hawker company's fortunes were truly founded, following the first flight at Brooklands of the outstanding Hawker Hart, a two-seat day bomber, designed by Sydney Camm, who had joined the Hawker company in 1923. During the next ten years 3036 Harts, including seven variants of the design, were built to form a substantial portion of the Royal Air Force.

Until 1963, under Sopwith's leadership and with Camm's design team, 26,800 aircraft of fifty-two different types flowed from the production lines of Hawkers and its associated companies. Chief among them was the Hawker Hurricane, a single-seat fighter, first flown on 6 November 1935, and put into production by Sopwith three months before an Air Ministry order had been received. Thanks to that hazardous but calculated risk, an additional 300 Hurricanes were able to be in service when the battle of Britain began in 1940—a factor which contributed to Britain winning the world's first decisive air battle.

In July 1935, with acumen and skill, Sopwith had begun to weld a major portion of the British aircraft industry into the Hawker Siddeley group—a combination of the Armstrong-Whitworth, Avro, Gloster, and Hawker aircraft companies, with the Armstrong Siddeley aero-engine and motor car company and Air Service Training. During the Second World War the group delivered more than 40,000 aeroplanes of fifteen different types. They ranged from the Avro Lancaster bomber to the Gloster Meteor jet fighter. In 1959 the De Havilland Aircraft Company was added to the group and, in 1963, Blackburn and General Aircraft Ltd. Sopwith remained steadfastly in charge as chairman of the board, skilfully delegating his responsibilities until in 1963, at the age of seventy-five, he retired as chairman, but remained on the board until, on his ninetieth birthday, he was elected founder and life president. He was knighted in 1953.

Throughout his long life Sopwith maintained his cherished pursuits of fishing, shooting, and boating. In 1913 he set up a world speed record for power boats of 48 knots, and between 1928 and 1930, with seventy-five first prizes, he became the leading British 12 metre yachtsman. In 1930 he was elected a member of the Royal Yacht Squadron. With his J-class sloop, *Endeavour*, he came close to winning the America's Cup for Britain in 1934. In 1937 he tried again, with *Endeavour II*, but lost to a better boat. In later years he confided: 'My one great regret is that I didn't bring home that Cup'. Between 1937 and 1939 Sopwith revelled in the ownership of the 1600 ton, ocean-going diesel yacht *Philante*, built to his own requirements.

Sopwith was 6 feet tall, somewhat chubby-faced, with full cheeks, and a high, broad, and clear forehead, topped by a mass of thick dark hair, always parted to the right. He had somewhat heavy eyebrows, hazel eyes, a broad, straight nose, a wide mouth, and a rather thin upper lip. In 1914 he married the 43-year-old Beatrix Mary, divorced wife of Charles Edward Malcolm and daughter of Walter James Hore-Ruthven, eighth Lord Ruthven. To his great distress she died of cancer in 1930. In 1932 he married Phyllis Brodie Leslie, daughter of Frederick Philip Augustus Gordon, inspector of gaols in the Indian Civil Service. She died in 1978. They had one son. In his ninetieth year Sopwith became completely blind, but he lost none of his memory, nor his interest in aviation, sport, and meeting old friends. In 1988 a great assembly of Sopwith's legion of friends attended a 100th birthday party held for him at Brooklands, at which they contacted him in Hampshire by land line. He died at his home, Compton Manor, King's Somborne, Hampshire, on 27 January 1989. A memorial service was held at St Clement Danes Church, London, on 12 April 1989. PETER G. MASEFIELD, *rev.*

Sources B. Robertson, *Sopwith: the man and his aircraft* (1970) • H. F. King, *Sopwith aircraft, 1912–1920* (1981) • A. Bramson, *Pure luck: the authorized biography of Sir Thomas Sopwith* (1990) • private information (1996) • personal knowledge (1996) • *The Times* (28 Jan 1989) • *The Independent* (19 Jan 1989) • *The Independent* (13 April 1989)
Likenesses photograph, 1910, Hult. Arch. [*see illus.*] • I. Opffer, chalk drawing, 1934, NPG • photographs, repro. in *The Independent* (19 Jan 1989)
Wealth at death £690,749: probate, 9 March 1989, *CGPLA Eng. & Wales*

Sorabji, Cornelia (1866–1954), barrister and social reformer, was born at Nasik in the Bombay Presidency, India, on 15 November 1866, the fifth daughter of the Revd Sorabji Karsedji, a Parsi Christian convert, and his wife, Franscina Ford, who had been brought up by an English couple. The Sorabji children were taught to respect all that was best in Indian and British cultural tradition. They also imbibed from their mother a spirit of social service. Early in childhood Cornelia Sorabji became acquainted with the injustice and servitude experienced by Indian women, especially the *purdahnashins* who led a secluded life behind the veil. Most of these women in purdah owned considerable property, but were unable to protect it since they were forbidden to communicate with the outside male world and were denied the necessary legal expertise and knowledge. Sorabji's concern for such women largely determined the course of her career: she resolved to fight the legal battles of wives, widows, and orphans, who were unable to do so in their customary seclusion.

The first woman student of Deccan College, Poona, Sorabji became the first female graduate in western India. She received a first-class degree in literature in 1888 from Bombay University which, but for her sex, would have entitled her to a scholarship to study at a British university. Instead, she had to content herself with a teaching job in Gujarat College, Ahmadabad. However, determined not to be bound by discrimination, Sorabji joined Somerville College, Oxford, in 1889 with the help of English friends. She was given special permission to sit for the examination in bachelor of civil law in 1892, the first woman ever to do so, and was placed in the third class. But Sorabji was not admitted to the degree because women in Oxford gained this right only in 1919. It was not until 1922 that she was able to return to Oxford and receive her law degree. She was called to the bar from Lincoln's Inn the following year.

Cornelia Sorabji's student days in Oxford moulded her views on politics, social issues, and Indo-British relations. At Oxford she enjoyed the friendship of Benjamin Jowett, through whom she was introduced to leading contemporary figures in politics, law, social service, and literature. Sorabji met the aged Florence Kent and was presented at court. She acquired a deep appreciation for British civilization and culture, and believed in Britain's civilizing role in India. Exposure to late nineteenth-century Conservative philosophy also made her detest democracy and popular politics.

On her return to India in 1894 Sorabji was initially involved with educational work in the principality of Baroda since her gender denied her the right to plead before

Cornelia Sorabji (1866–1954), by Lafayette, 1930

the Indian courts of law. She could appear only with special permission in cases concerning proprietary rights of Hindu women before the British agents of Kathiawar and Indore principalities. But determined to secure professional standing in the Indian legal world, Sorabji presented herself for the LLB examination of Bombay University in 1897 and pleader's examination of Allahabad high court in 1899. Despite her success she was denied registration as a practising lawyer.

In these circumstances Sorabji turned to the colonial bureaucracy in order to put her legal knowledge to practical use. With great difficulty she persuaded the India Office to appoint her in 1904 lady legal adviser to the court of wards in Bengal, Bihar, Orissa, and Assam, as a kind of liaison officer between women in purdah and the outside world to deal with the problems connected with women and minors whose estates were being administered by the courts. Sorabji was nevertheless herself much influenced by the customs and rituals of the upper-caste Hindu women with whom she dealt, and she subsequently involved herself with women's organizational and social service work. She contributed to infant welfare and district nursing programmes and became associated with the Bengal branch of the National Council for Women in India, the Federation of University Women, and the Bengal League of Social Service for Women. She was awarded the kaisar-i-Hind gold medal in 1909. However, while carrying out this work Sorabji continued to face discrimination against her as a woman and an Indian—at which she protested.

In 1924 the legal profession was opened to women in India and Sorabji began practising in the Calcutta high court. Unfortunately, constant battling against male bias and stereotypes made it an uphill struggle. Faced with such obstacles Sorabji had no option but to confine herself to preparing opinions on cases, rather than pleading before the courts of law.

Sorabji's allegiance to late-nineteenth-century imperial culture made her disapprove both of post-1905 Indian nationalism and of Mahatma Gandhi's strategy of mass mobilization against the British raj. She opposed the nationalist demand for self-rule, believing that it should only follow a period of training in democracy and citizenship. Sorabji dubbed the twentieth-century nationalists 'progressives' and accused them of violating the beliefs, customs, and tradition of the country's Hindu 'orthodox'. She feared a clash between these two groups of Indians and urged the British to provide constitutional safeguards for the Hindu orthodox. Sorabji condemned, too, those Indian women who joined the nationalist struggle as subordinate partners of Indian men and disregarded the difficulties of the 'orthodox Indian women'. From 1927 Sorabji was engaged in propaganda work for the empire and the Hindu orthodox. She further made herself appear a 'natural imperialist' in nationalist eyes when she favourably reviewed Katherine Mayo's *Mother India* (1927), a controversial book on India's social and political life. Proclaiming herself as an 'Empire Citizen', Sorabji toured India extensively and visited the USA in 1929 to propagate her political ideas. While she was in the United States, her eyesight began seriously to fail. She was awarded the Coronation Medal and a certificate in 1937 by the king-emperor.

From the mid-1930s Sorabji spent most of her time in London, which she loved, going to India only in the winters. She concentrated on writing, and produced many vivid, moving sketches. Her works included a biography of her parents, *Therefore* (1924), as well as the story of her educationist sister, Susie Sorabji (1932), and two autobiographical works, *India Calling: the Memories of Cornelia Sorabji* (1934) and *India Recalled* (1936). Her last literary project was to edit *Queen Mary's Book for India* (1943), a small anthology of articles connected with India and published in support of the Indian Comforts Fund. In addition, she maintained regular correspondence with her parents, with Lady Elena Richmond, and also with the Allahabad high court judge Harrison Falkner Blair. These letters vividly capture Sorabji's dilemmas, frustration, and aspirations.

At the end of her life Sorabji suffered from acute rheumatism and was almost blind. She died at her London home, Northumberland House, Green Lanes, Finsbury Park, on 6 July 1954. Despite her relatively marginal impact as a female lawyer in India, she became a well-known figure in Britain. An obituary in the *Manchester Guardian* described her as:

> an arresting figure with a superb profile, always perfectly dressed in the richly coloured silk sari to which the modern Parsee woman has remained faithful. Her English speech was distinguished. She talked and spoke in public with equal

brilliance, and her gifts of phrase remained with her to the end. (9 July 1954)

SUPARNA GOOPTU

Sources S. Gooptu, 'Cornelia Sorabji, 1866–1954: a woman's biography', DPhil diss., U. Oxf., 1997 • C. Sorabji, *Therefore: an impression of Sorabji Kharsedji Langrana and his wife* (1924) • C. Sorabji, *India calling: the memories of Cornelia Sorabji* (1934) • C. Sorabji, *India recalled* (1936) • A. Burton, *Burdens of history: British feminists, Indian women, and imperial culture, 1865–1915* (1994) • A. Burton, *At the heart of the empire: Indians and the colonial encounter in late Victorian Britain* (1998) • N. Chaudhuri and M. Strobel, *Western women and imperialism: complicity and resistance* (1992) • J. H. Mair, *Behind the curtain: India's first woman lawyer* (1961) • R. Symonds, *Oxford and empire: the last lost cause?* (1986) • S. Tharu and K. Lalita, eds., *Women writing in India: 600 B.C. to the present century*, 1 (1991) • *The Times* (8 July 1954) • *Manchester Guardian* (13 April 1903) • *CGPLA Eng. & Wales* (1954) • *Manchester Guardian* (9 July 1954) • BL OIOC, Sorabji MSS

Archives BL OIOC, corresp., diaries, and papers, MS Eur. F 165/1–235 • priv. coll. | FILM BBC WAC, television programme, July 1966 • BFI NFTVA

Likenesses Lafayette, photograph, 1930, NPG [*see illus.*]

Wealth at death £3163 4s. 7d.: probate, 7 Oct 1954, *CGPLA Eng. & Wales*

Sorabji, Kaikhosru Shapurji (1892–1988), composer and music critic, was born on 14 August 1892 in Buxton Road, Chingford, Essex, as Leon Dudley Sorabji, the only child of a Parsi father, Shapurji Sorabji, mining engineer and iron merchant, and his wife, Madeline Matilda Korthy, a Spanish-Sicilian opera singer. He adopted the baptismal Parsi name by which he was universally known early in life, though near the beginning of his career he signed himself with various forms combined with Leon and Dudley. Latterly he rejected enquiries into his nomenclature, as into the date of his birth, with the jealousy of his privacy that characterized his life. This refusal to countenance journalistic curiosity, coupled with the challenging letters with which he would bombard those who displeased him, was in contrast to the good humour, humanity, and generosity which he would show to those who came into personal contact with him.

Sorabji had a number of teachers, both as pianist and as composer, but no formal education. His keyboard technique was admired as 'fabulous' in the early part of his career, when he played in London, Paris, Vienna, Glasgow, and Bombay; but he came to dislike the circumstances of public music-making, and withdrew from the concert platform in December 1936. In part this was a product of his distaste for playing to listeners of whom he knew nothing, and of a preference for addressing himself to a circle of like-minded friends. Modest private means enabled him to pursue a life free from the commercial considerations he despised, though he continued to compose (up to 1982) and won himself a reputation as a trenchant and forceful critic. He wrote especially for the *New English Weekly* and for A. R. Orage's *New Age*. Some of these articles were later reprinted in two collections, *Around Music* (1932) and *Mi contra fa* (1947).

The allusion in the latter title is to the medieval theorists' description of two harmonically opposed notes: 'mi contra fa, diabolus in musica'. However, Sorabji's criticism was generally on the side of the angels. Composers he championed included those who later won international recognition, such as Karol Szymanowski, Nicolai Medtner, Ferruccio Busoni, and Charles-Henri Alkan (all influences on him), and some who have remained neglected even in their homeland, such as Francis George Scott and Bernard van Dieren. Though he had strong opinions his attacks were mostly reserved for individuals and organizations whose attitudes he saw as betraying the loftiest standards. He expressed himself forcefully, even vituperatively, but always with an expressive bravura in his widely ranging sentences that made his prose an entertainment to read. A characteristic sally is contained in the dedication of what is probably his masterpiece, the *Opus clavicembalisticum*, to his friend Hugh MacDiarmid: 'likewise to the everlasting glory of those few men blessed and sanctified in the curses and execration of those many whose praise is eternal damnation'.

The elaborate richness of Sorabji's own music reflects not so much the oriental luxuriance often attributed to it (nothing enraged him more than being described as Indian) as the profusion of his mind. His earliest music, such as *In the Hothouse* (1918), is sensuously chromatic in a manner that might have appealed to Frederick Delius (who admired his *Le jardin parfumé* of 1923). His first piano sonata (1919) makes some use of thematic cells, but the second (1920) lacks any clear controlling form; his fourth (1929) was accompanied by a rare analytical account (probably written as a concert introduction) and gave the music more traditional forms, such as passacaglia. He claimed to have found his direction with the first organ symphony (1924), a work lasting two hours (the later organ symphonies are longer). In this, an opening passacaglia provides an admirable tether for his far-ranging fantasy, a fugue develops some ideas strictly, and in the complex finale all the ideas are woven into a complex tapestry. Other works drew, with great technical virtuosity, on established forms as providing the basis for elaborate fantasizing. The *Opus clavicembalisticum* (1930) for solo piano combines into its time-span of four and a half hours a wide range of disciplines, of which the principal is fugue.

Sorabji gave the first performance himself in Glasgow in December 1930. It caused a sensation, but then an inadequate London performance of the first part by an inferior pianist contributed to Sorabji withdrawing his music from being performed without his express permission. This ban was relaxed when, in the 1970s, there began to emerge virtuosi with the technique to master the music's difficulties and the intellectual curiosity to explore its substance. Sorabji was happy with performances by John Ogdon, Yonty Solomon, Michael Habermann, Geoffrey Douglas Madge, and the organist Kevin Bowyer.

He had by now long since withdrawn to what he called his 'granite tower', a small house on the outskirts of Corfe Castle in Dorset, from which he repelled casual visitors with fierce notices, but welcomed friends with warmth and wit. Short of stature and bespectacled, with a shock of wild black hair that in later life became a heavy white mane, he was a delightful conversationalist whose independence of mind remained intact. Though he denied any formal doctrinal persuasion, he had a religious temperament that inclined towards Roman Catholicism while not excluding an interest in Parsi mysticism. He never married, and died in Marley House Nursing Home, Winfrith Newburgh, Dorchester, on 15 October 1988.

JOHN WARRACK, *rev.*

Sources Sorabji archive [organized by Alistair Hinton, Easton Dene, Bailbrook Lane, Bath, BA1 7AA] · *The Times* (17 Oct 1988) · *The Independent* (17 Oct 1988) · personal knowledge (1996) · b. cert. · P. Rapoport, *Sorabji: a critical celebration* (1992) · *CGPLA Eng. & Wales* (1988)

Archives Easton Dene, Bailbrook Lane, Bath, Sorabji archive, corresp. and music MSS | BL, letters to Bernard Stevens, Add. MS 69025

Likenesses J. Grayson, photograph, repro. in *The Independent*

Wealth at death £89,893: probate, 28 Nov 1988, *CGPLA Eng. & Wales*

Sorby, Henry Clifton (1826–1908), geologist, was born on 10 May 1826 at Woodbourne, on the Orgreave estate on the eastern outskirts of Sheffield, Yorkshire. He was the only child of Henry Sorby (*d.* 1846) and Amelia Lambert (*d.* 1872) of London, a woman said to have had much force of character. Henry Sorby was a partner in the firm of John and Henry Sorby, edge-tool makers, a trade with which the family had been connected since the sixteenth century. One ancestor, who died in 1620, was the first master cutler and Henry Clifton Sorby's grandfather filled the same office. Henry Sorby owned an extensive tract of land around Woodbourne and mined the productive coal seams beneath the Orgreave estate.

Sorby received his early education at a private school in Harrogate and at the collegiate school in Sheffield. Later he was tutored by the Revd Walter Mitchell who fostered Sorby's love of natural science. Like many of his contemporaries he was not sent to university, but unlike them he neither entered the family business nor indulged in their pastimes. With his father's encouragement he associated with local men of learning, and he also converted an outhouse into a well-equipped chemical laboratory. Sorby's father died in 1846 and in 1853 he and his mother moved to 6 Beech Hill Road, Broomfield, a house about a mile west of the centre of Sheffield. This house, like Woodbourne, was well equipped with a laboratory and a workshop.

Microscopy and optical techniques Sorby's early training in chemistry and mathematics considerably influenced his approach to all his researches. To analyse and to measure, especially by the use of the microscope, was to him an essential part of research. This application of the microscope to his researches appears to have resulted from a chance meeting on a train, some time before 1842, with William Crawford Williamson (1816–1895), then a Manchester surgeon, who taught him to make sections of fossil wood, scales, teeth, and bones. It occurred to Sorby that a great deal might be learned by applying a similar method to the study of rocks. He made numerous thin sections, over 1000 of which are preserved in the University of Sheffield, the earliest being dated 1849. It is interesting to note that his slides of non-calcareous rocks were made to a thickness of 30 microns (still the standard thickness

Henry Clifton Sorby (1826–1908), by unknown photographer, pubd 1908

over one hundred and fifty years later) using the technique of judging the thickness by the pale yellow or white colour of quartz grains viewed between crossed Nicol prisms (polarizers). The calcareous rocks were usually rather thicker in order to examine shell fragments contained within them.

In 1851 Sorby described the microscopical structure of the Calcareous Grit of the Yorkshire coast in the *Quarterly Journal of the Geological Society of London*. Not only did he measure the linear dimensions of the many small reniform bodies forming the bulk of the rock, but he calculated their volume and the numbers of them present in the rock. By the use of polarized light, he showed that some of the particles were calcite, some were quartz, and yet others were agate. This method of examining rocks did not find favour among most of the geologists of the day and it was ridiculed by many. It was not until Sorby described his methods of making thin sections to Zirkel in Germany in 1861 that microscopical petrography began to be established as an invaluable tool for the examination of rocks.

Composition of rocks and crystals In 1853, seeking to determine the proportions of minerals in a rock, Sorby used a camera lucida to trace the outline of the grains in a thin section onto a sheet of tinfoil. He realized that the total weight of the fragments representing each mineral species was proportional to the area of that species in the rock and, apparently intuitively, he realized that the total area of each species was proportional to the volume of that mineral in the rock. Knowing the density of each mineral, he could thus calculate its percentage weight in the rock. This he called 'physical analysis'. Whether he was aware that Delesse had used a similar method on coarse grained syenites (using the naked eye rather than the microscope), he does not reveal. Sorby, however, made the crucial step of applying the microscope to the method on which the whole science of stereology was later founded.

Some time in the 1850s Sorby turned his attention to the microscopical study of crystals and showed that the liquid contained in tourmaline crystals, which had been observed by Sir David Brewster in 1824, was liquefied carbon dioxide. Again his work met a chilly reception, but he persisted with this line of investigation and was able to estimate the temperature at which certain minerals had been formed, and hence the temperature and depth at which igneous rocks had been emplaced.

Sorby devised improved methods for the identification of the component grains of rocks and developed methods for the precise measurement of the refractive index of grains in thin sections and invented the quartz wedge used for distinguishing the positive and negative directions (the slow and fast rays) in doubly refracting minerals. He also studied the microscopical characteristics of crystals formed by fusion in beads of microcosmic salt, hoping to develop a qualitative method of chemical analysis of minerals.

Spectroscopy In the 1860s the science of spectroscopy was advancing rapidly, but this was always by means of the emission spectra of substances heated in a flame. Fortunately Hoppe (1862) and Stokes (1864) observed that substances in solution could yield an 'absorption' spectrum when illuminated with white light. This caught Sorby's attention (and imagination) and in 1866 he devised a direct vision spectroscope to replace the microscope eyepiece. Very few mineral grains yielded a characteristic absorption spectrum, but far from abandoning his new instrument, Sorby modified his apparatus to enable him to examine small amounts of liquids, in particular, blood and plant pigments in solution. This occupied him for many years, but must ultimately be regarded as one of his less productive lines of investigation.

Other geological investigations It is almost impossible to treat Sorby's studies in a simple chronological manner: ideas seemed to have flooded into his mind at every turn. For example, his study of igneous rocks led him to the study of meteorites, and to explain the structure of meteoric irons he began the study of 'artificial irons', that is, iron and steel from the local iron works in Sheffield. Using the methods of grinding and polishing, which he had developed for the preparation of thin sections of rocks, Sorby produced polished surfaces on metals and meteorites which could be examined microscopically using reflected light. He was able to show that iron, steel, and meteorites were mixtures of well-defined substances and that their structure was in many ways analogous to that of igneous rocks. His work on iron and steel subsequently had great industrial value.

In 1847 Sorby made an observation of profound significance to the development of geology. While sheltering from a shower of rain in a local sandstone quarry, he recognized the association between the current structures in the quarry face, the movement of the sand grains in the rainwash, and the deposition of the alluvium in rivers. In one afternoon, at the age of twenty-one, he had laid the foundations of modern sedimentology, though late in life he lamented that no one had taken up and developed his ideas.

Following an extensive tour of Wales in 1851 and south-west England in 1852 studying the structure of sedimentary rocks, Sorby commenced an investigation of slaty cleavage in rocks, and his evidence that this was due to the effect of pressure brought him into serious conflict with some of the eminent geologists of the day, notably Sir Henry De la Beche. Nevertheless, Sorby's views gained ground and in 1857 he was elected to the Royal Society in acknowledgement of this work.

Sorby's studies of limestones caused him to reject the widely held belief that these were always the product of chemical precipitation, a view still held by some many years later. He showed that they were, in fact, sandstones and mudstones composed of carbonate particles produced by abrasion of shell fragments. He also showed that the Cretaceous chalk was made up essentially of *Coccolith* remains, long before this was confirmed by studies with the electron microscope.

Later researches In 1872 Sorby's mother died and, though he was seriously affected by the loss of her companionship (he was unmarried), he was at last free to associate more with his fellow scientists in London. Indeed, Sorby contemplated moving to London, but ultimately he did not. Instead he bought a yacht, the *Glimpse*, on which he spent the summer months of almost every year until about 1900. His intention had been to live on board in some quiet place and devote himself to the task of writing up for publication the investigations of the preceding years. Instead, he kept finding new subjects and new lines of investigation. He spent much time in dredging and in making biological and physical investigations in the estuaries of Suffolk and Essex and in studying the architecture of the churches of the region. In 1882 he was asked to investigate the mud deposits of the Thames estuary with a view to giving evidence before a royal commission on the discharge of sewage into the river. This marked the beginning of the efforts to improve the quality of Thames water which had become very heavily polluted.

The winter months were spent in Sheffield where Sorby did much to stimulate the intellectual life of the place. As early as 1876 (when he was fifty) he was beginning to ponder how best to endow original scientific research. He had no dependants and obviously was concerned that his assets should be used in the best possible way after his death. From his own experience he firmly believed that research was best carried out by an investigator freed entirely from all obligation to carry out other duties. From this sprang the Sorby fellowship of the Royal Society. He continued to take an active part in the learned societies of

London and in the north of England, and in particular he helped to found Firth College, which ultimately became the University of Sheffield.

Recognition and the final years The importance of Sorby's diverse researches was recognized with the award of three gold medals. The first was the Wollaston medal from the Geological Society of London in 1869, the second was the Boerhaave medal from the Royal Dutch Society of Science in 1872, and the third, in 1874, was the royal medal of the Royal Society. He was president of the Royal Microscopical Society (1875–7), of the Mineralogical Society (1876–9), and of the Geological Society of London (1878–80). In 1879 he was made an honorary LLD by the University of Cambridge.

In 1903 Sorby broke his hip and was confined to bed or a wheelchair for the rest of his life. Nevertheless, he continued to be involved in his scientific work, as well as with the preparation for the new university. In 1907, when Sorby was too ill to visit London for the centenary celebrations of the Geological Society, the society sent an address to 'the father of microscopical petrology' signed by the world's leading petrologists. His willingness to help fellow workers, his modesty and his freedom from self-seeking, had won him many friends. Sorby died on 9 March 1908, still working on his great stock of accumulated observations. He was buried on 13 March at Ecclesall churchyard, Sheffield. Only a few days after his death, his last great contribution on the application of quantitative methods to the study of the structure and history of rocks was published by the Geological Society of London. He 'ranks as one of the real Titans of science' (Folk, 43).

D. W. HUMPHRIES

Sources N. Higham, *A very scientific gentleman* (1963) · D. W. Humphries, 'The father of microscopical petrography', *The Sorby centennial symposium on the history of metallurgy*, ed. C. S. Smith (1965), 17–41 · D. W. Humphries, 'A bibliography of publications by H. C. Sorby', *The Sorby centennial symposium on the history of metallurgy*, ed. C. S. Smith (1965), 43–58 [repr. in Summerson, *Sorby on geology*] · C. S. Smith, *A history of metallography* (1960) · *Sorby on sedimentology: a collection of papers from 1851–1908*, ed. C. H. Summerson (1976) · *Sorby on geology: a collection of papers from 1853-1906*, ed. C. H. Summerson (1978) · M. J. Bishop, 'New biographical data on Henry Clifton Sorby (1826–1908)', *Earth Sciences History, Journal of the History of the Earth Sciences Society*, 3 (1984), 69–81 · R. L. Folk, *Journal of Geological Education*, 13/2 (1965), 43–7 · *CGPLA Eng. & Wales* (1908) · *Floreamus: a chronicle of the University of Sheffield* (1908) · *The Engineer* (13 March 1908), 267 · *Engineering* (13 March 1908), 339 · *Journal of the Iron and Steel Institution*, 76 (1908), 217–19

Archives Sheff. Arch., corresp. and papers · Sheffield Central Library, corresp. and sketches · University of Sheffield, diaries, papers, and photographs | CUL, letters to Sir George Stokes

Likenesses M. L. Walker, oils, 1898, Cutlers' Hall, Sheffield; copy, M. L. Walker, 1906, University of Sheffield · marble bust, 1898, University of Sheffield · photograph, repro. in *Geological Magazine*, 5 (1908), pl. 8 [*see illus.*]

Wealth at death £46,328 1s.: resworn probate, 24 April 1908, *CGPLA Eng. & Wales*

Sorell, William (*bap.* **1773**, *d.* **1848**), army officer and administrator in Australia, the son of Jane and Lieutenant-General William Alexander Sorell, was baptized at St Mary's Church, Marylebone, Middlesex, on 2 September 1773, by the rite of the Church of England, his lifelong formal allegiance. After attending Westminster School, he joined the army in 1790. In the ensuing decade he fought in the West Indies and Europe. He became a major in 1804 (later lieutenant-colonel) and trained under Sir John Moore. In 1807 he went to the Cape of Good Hope, where he excelled as deputy adjutant-general. Yet in 1811 he returned to Britain and the following year resigned from the army.

These moves resulted from strange personal circumstances. Between 1800 and 1807 Sorell had seven children with Harriet Coleman, an illiterate. The couple were married in 1807, but Harriet did not accompany her husband to the Cape. There Sorell entered into a liaison with the wife of a fellow officer, Louisa Matilda Kent, *née* Cox. From 1811 or 1812 the couple lived as man and wife, and by 1824 they had eight children.

Backed by superiors and patrons, Sorell in 1816 was appointed lieutenant-governor of Van Diemen's Land. The move coincided with official rethinking as to the Australian colonies finding a larger imperial role. Sorell's new post was a challenging one, since the mixed population of Van Diemen's Land consisted of about 600 convicts still under bond, 3000 free white people (largely former convicts), and probably as many Aborigines. Runaway convicts ('bushrangers') formed an alternative society, ignoring and challenging authority, while sloth and corruption permeated officialdom.

Sorell, accompanied by Louisa Kent and her children of mixed paternity, assumed government in April 1817. He attended first to the bushrangers, and then to the fundamentals of colonial expansion: arbitrating disputes, harrying bureaucrats into efficiency, and fostering economic growth. Convicts now started arriving direct from Britain in considerable numbers (1397 in 1820). Sorell distributed most of these as 'assigned' labourers to the likewise increasing free immigrants, generally boasting some social standing and/or ambition. All this was done with great efficiency: Sorell was an exemplar of how the wars provided training for a generation of outstanding imperial managers.

At times Sorell could appear ruthless. He had no qualms in punishing miscreants: the station he established at Macquarie Harbour for further disciplining convicts became a byword of cruel severity. Towards Aborigines, suffering as a result of European expansion, he evinced some philanthropy, but he gave them little place in either policies or dispatches. He rightly perceived that his major problems lay elsewhere. Regional particularism proved salient in Tasmanian affairs: Sorell found it difficult to bring a sub-colony in the island's north under his sway, and became fierce in denouncing the local commandant, Captain Gilbert Cimitiere. Likewise he had to confront potentially over-mighty subjects. Chief among these was Anthony Fenn Kemp, formerly captain of the New South Wales Corps and now a leading merchant and grazier in Van Diemen's Land, who was evidently ready to repeat his role in deposing Governor William Bligh in Sydney in 1808.

Generally, however, Sorell succeeded in overcoming problems and critics. His gracious manner and accessibility, coupled with a sense of humanity, even of natural justice, proved valuable assets, but the irregularity of his union with Louisa Kent proved his downfall. In 1817 Lieutenant Kent won £3000 in damages against Sorell. Kemp and other opponents cited the matter when fighting the lieutenant-governor, notably in writing to British authorities. Harriet Sorell proved to the secretary of state, Lord Bathurst, that her husband had broken promises to sustain their family, and Bathurst put Sorell's private life before J. T. Bigge, whom he sent out in 1819 on a general commission of Australian inquiry. Bigge found much to admire in Sorell, as both man and governor, but added his own moral rebuke. Essentially because of these matters, Bathurst recalled Sorell.

Uniquely in Australian history, such news aroused more dismay than pleasure among colonists affected. Leading citizens petitioned for Sorell's continuance; ironically A. F. Kemp inspired this move. It was to no avail, however, and Sorell resigned office on 13 May 1824. He retained some influence in Australian affairs, provoking Ralph Darling—the tory governor of New South Wales from 1825 to 1831—to disparage 'the Convenient pliancy of his disposition [which] made him a favourite at Van Diemen's Land' (*Historical Records of Australia*, 1st ser., 13.190). However, Sorell's hopes for renewed appointment bore fruit only in his service as consul at Oporto in 1832–3. After periods living in Europe and Ireland he died in London on 4 June 1848. His estate of £200 went to Louisa Kent, described as his widow (they had probably married about 1840).

In 1823 Harriet's eldest child with Sorell, William, joined his father in Hobart. He settled, and in 1825 married a daughter of A. F. Kemp. Their daughter Julia married Thomas Arnold junior in Hobart in 1850. Descendants of that marriage included Mary Augusta Ward, Janet Penrose Trevelyan, and Julian and Aldous Huxley.

MICHAEL ROE

Sources [F. Watson], ed., *Historical records of Australia*, 1st ser., 13 (1920); 3rd ser., 2–4 (1921) • J. Sorell, *Governor William and Julia Sorell* (1988) • R. W. Giblin, *The early history of Tasmania* (1928–39) • A. Alexander, *Governors' ladies: the wives and mistresses of Van Diemen's Land governors* (1987) • *AusDB* • J. Ritchie, *Punishment and profit: the reports of Commissioner John Bigge* (1970)

Likenesses portrait, repro. in J. W. Beattie, *Glimpses of the life and times of the early Tasmanian governors* (1905), 22

Wealth at death £200: *AusDB*

Sorensen, Reginald William, Baron Sorensen (1891–1971), politician and Unitarian minister, was born at 25 Ronalds Road, Islington, north London, on 19 June 1891, the eldest son in the family of two sons and two daughters of William James Sorensen (1868–1925), a silversmith of Danish paternity, and his wife, Alice Jemima (*d.* 1934), daughter of John Tester, a fisherman of Worthing, Sussex.

Early evidence of Sorensen's rebellious spirit came when Reg (as he was universally known) was sent home from Sunday school for 'disturbing' the class with his questioning. He left a local elementary school at the age of fourteen and worked as an errand-boy, as a manual worker in a factory, and then in a shop. He fell under the spell of the Revd Reginald John Campbell of the City Temple, London, an influential dissenting preacher who combined radical politics with liberal theology. Sorensen joined Campbell's Liberal Christian League; he later acknowledged the impact made on him by Campbell's *The New Theology* (1907). He spent four years living in a religious community run by Campbell: the Order of Pioneer Preachers. In 1914 he became the Unitarian minister of the Free Christian Church, Walthamstow, an area with which he was associated until his death. On 22 January 1916 he married Muriel (*b.* 1891), daughter of the Revd William Harvey-Smith, a Unitarian minister, of Long Sutton, Lincolnshire. They had a daughter and two sons, one of whom died during the Chinese revolution, when working as a missionary.

In 1908 Sorensen joined the Finsbury branch of the Independent Labour Party, of which Campbell was president. He never forgot when, as a boy, he had been sent by his mother to collect money owed by a neighbour. He had entered an unhealthy tenement to find the wretched, emaciated woman, with a baby sucking at her shrivelled breast, in a room bare of furniture—the bailiffs had called. During the First World War he was exempted from military service as a minister of religion, but declared himself a pacifist. He experimented with a guild shop and was involved with a co-operative colony.

After the war Sorensen combined his duties as a Unitarian minister with tuition for the Workers' Educational Association. From 1921 to 1924 he was a member of the Walthamstow urban district council, where he was chair of the education committee. In 1924 he was elected an Essex county councillor, and he served until 1945. After twice unsuccessfully contesting Southampton as a Labour parliamentary candidate at the general elections of 1923 and 1924 he was elected for Leyton West in 1929. During the two years of the second Labour government his neighbouring MP, in Leyton East, was his brother-in-law Fenner Brockway. Both lost their seats in the electoral débâcle of 1931. Sorensen had by then left the Independent Labour Party, probably because he had no sympathy with Jimmy Maxton's leadership. After failing to win Lowestoft at a by-election in 1934, he recovered his Leyton West seat by a small majority in the general election of 1935 and represented the area until 1964 (when, in 1950, the constituency was redrawn he became MP for Leyton).

As an MP Sorensen combined pacifist anti-militarist sentiments with loyalty towards the Labour Party leadership. He joined the Peace Pledge Union in 1936 and remained rather uneasily a member despite declaring his support for rearmament on the ground that a majority of the people supported it: 'a virile people must defend itself', he told the House of Commons, 'there are certainly worse things than war' (*Hansard 5C*, 309, 12 March 1936, 2389). In 1939 he accepted the political case for the war. Although in the 1950s he continued to support anti-militarist positions, he latterly moderated his views, and 'pacifist' was not a term he would have applied to himself, even if some others continued often to do so.

Sorensen was much involved in the movements for colonial liberation, being particularly identified with India, the Caribbean, and, later, Africa; he chaired the Fabian Colonial Bureau and the India League, which supported Indian nationalism. As a member of the parliamentary deputation to India in 1946, he was impressed by the urgent need for Britain to transfer power. He welcomed Indian independence in 1947, though he regretted partition and hoped that the princely states would develop democratic institutions. However, his attachment to the right of the Labour Party caused Aneurin Bevan once to say (unfairly) to him: 'Your trouble, Reg, is that you believe in liberation in every country but your own' (personal knowledge).

Sorensen held his seat at the general election of 1964 but reluctantly agreed soon afterwards to stand down in favour of Patrick Gordon Walker, then foreign secretary, who had been defeated in Smethwick. While Sorensen went to the Lords in December 1964 with a life peerage, as Baron Sorensen, the controversies about his reluctance to stand down and local dissatisfaction with his emotionally and geographically distant successor as candidate (Gordon Walker lived away from the constituency) helped the Conservatives to win the seat at the resultant by-election. The Lords amused, exasperated, and interested Sorensen, and in 1966 he proposed its abolition in favour of a senate of experts in administration. He attained ministerial office as a government whip and resigned in April 1968.

Sorensen's varied interests can be seen in the bodies with which he was associated: he chaired the National Peace Council and was president of the World Congress of Faiths, treasurer of Help the Aged, and chairman of the trustees of the West African Students' Union Board. He espoused many causes and did so more modestly than many. He was also a dedicated constituency MP, and his wife, Muriel, was a full and willing partner in that work; their home at Woodside Park Avenue, Walthamstow, London, served as hostel, office, and advice bureau. He once said that his membership of the Herbert committee, which led to the Matrimonial Causes Act of 1937, an early loosening of the divorce laws, was the task that gave him most satisfaction.

Sorensen's philosophical roots were eclectic, ranging from Buddha and the founders of other Eastern religions to Thomas Paine. The idea of 'sacred reality' conceived by the humanist Julian Huxley was one he made his own. He was open-minded and sceptical, and sought to apply his theological understanding to daily action. Several of his eleven books were devoted to religion. While he had no time for dogma, in his last book, *I Believe in Man* (1970), he said that we 'should not be seduced into thinking that the only reality is the tangible and the sensuous, but that reality is vaster and more permeative of our material environment than we can neatly tie up with intellectual string'. He was an early supporter of women's suffrage—he was a friend of Sylvia Pankhurst—and birth control. He had known Nehru and Gandhi and the young London pastry cook from Indo-China later known to the world as Ho Chi Minh.

Sorensen had a puckish sense of humour, a lively intelligence, and a fund of recollections. He became a freeman of the borough of Leyton in 1958 and in 1963 was awarded the grand cross of the order of merit of the Federal Republic of Germany. He died on 8 October 1971 at Whipps Cross Hospital, Leytonstone, and was cremated at the City of London cemetery on 15 October. His wife survived him. A memorial meeting was later held at Waltham Forest town hall.

TERRY PHILPOT

Sources W. D. Rubinstein, *The biographical dictionary of life peers* (New York, 1991) · T. Philpot, *The Humanist* (Dec 1971), 379 · Baron Sorensen, *I believe in man* (1970) · *WWW* · b. cert. · m. cert. · d. cert. · *The Labour who's who* (1927) · Burke, *Peerage* (1967) · M. Caedel, *Pacifism in Britain, 1914–1945: the defining of a faith* (1980) · S. Howe, *Anticolonialism in British politics: the left and the end of empire, 1918–1964* (1993)

Archives Bodl. RH, papers relating to colonialism · HLRO, MS autobiography · HLRO, personal and political papers | Labour History Archive and Study Centre, Manchester, minutes of Christian socialists · Scott Bader Company Ltd, Wollaston, Wellingborough, corresp. with Ernest Bader

Likenesses photograph, repro. in *The Humanist*

Wealth at death £9618: probate, 15 Aug 1972, *CGPLA Eng. & Wales*

Sorley, Charles Hamilton (1895–1915), poet, was born in Aberdeen on 19 May 1895, the elder twin son and third surviving child in the family of two sons and two daughters of William Ritchie *Sorley (1855–1935), professor of moral philosophy at Aberdeen University, and his wife, Janetta Colquhoun Smith. When Sorley was five his father was appointed Knightbridge professor of moral philosophy at Cambridge University and elected a fellow of King's College, and from then on Sorley was brought up in Cambridge, where until he was nine he was taught at home by his mother. From 1906 to 1908, with his twin brother Kenneth, Sorley attended King's College choir school as a day boy, and it was there, at the age of ten, that he wrote a publishable poem, 'The Tempest', in form and content a clear portent of his adult work. Compulsory regular attendance at services in King's College chapel may account for numerous biblical references in later poems; Sorley was deeply religious in the philosophical sense but always remained out of tune with conventional belief. When he was thirteen, despite an erratic academic performance at King's, Sorley gained an open scholarship to Marlborough College, where he developed two abiding sensual passions, for food and cross-country running. His poetry began to appear in *The Marlburian* in 1912, influenced by John Masefield and by the Wiltshire downs, with their irresistible evocation of the past. Impending death was an early subject, and one of his most accomplished schoolboy poems is 'The River', based on an actual suicide.

In his last year at Marlborough, Sorley won the senior Farrar prize for English literature and language, the Buchanan prize for public reading, and a scholarship to University College, Oxford. It was decided that before going up to Oxford, which in fact he never did, he should spend time with a German family in Mecklenburg and three months studying at the university in Jena, where he attended lectures on philosophy and political economy and made many close friends among German Jews. Hence his stay on the continent strongly influenced the ambivalent feelings he was to entertain towards the war, reflected so strikingly in his poetry. He had rashly embarked on a walking tour in the Moselle region when war was declared, and he spent the night of 2 August 1914 in prison at Trier. Although Sorley was to make light of the experience, he had been in considerable danger. On his release he made his way back to England through Belgium, sailing from Antwerp in the hastily requisitioned *Montrose*.

Sorley was deeply divided in his loyalties, but, believing the war to be an evil necessity, he immediately enlisted and received a commission in the 7th battalion of the Suffolk regiment. He was promoted first lieutenant in November 1914 and captain nine months later. He arrived in France with his battalion on 30 May 1915, having told his mother, 'I do wish people would not deceive themselves by talk of a just war. There is no such thing as a just war. What we are doing is casting out Satan by Satan.' He served for several months in the trenches around Ploegsteert, and displayed considerable courage in saving the lives of two men. When his battalion moved south to take part in the battle of Loos, Sorley commanded an attack on two trenches known as the Hairpin, south of the Hohenzollern redoubt, and was killed by a sniper on 13 October 1915. He was buried near the spot where he fell. He was twenty.

A posthumous collection, *Marlborough and other Poems*, was published in 1916 and went into six editions in the first year. Robert Graves pronounced Charles Sorley 'one of the three poets of importance killed during the war', rating him alongside Wilfred Owen. Sorley is certainly remarkable for rejecting the prevailing enthusiasm for war so early on, and for forecasting, through a mixture of irony and pity, the horrors of Flanders before ever he reached the front. Typical of his best work, much of which he had no opportunity to revise, are 'Barbury Camp', written at Marlborough, 'The Song of the Ungirt Runners', and his last poem, 'When you see millions of the mouthless dead', scribbled in pencil and discovered in his kitbag after he had been killed. His parents published a collection of his letters in 1919, *The Letters of Charles Sorley*, which the *Manchester Guardian* thought 'contained the first mature impressions of a nature which was all vigour and radiance, a boy who may be said to have had a genius for truth'. His collected poems appeared in 1985.

MICHAEL DE-LA-NOY, *rev.*

Sources *TLS* (28 Oct 1915) • T. B. Swann, *The ungirt runner* (1965) • J. M. Wilson, *Charles Hamilton Sorley: a biography* (1985) • *The letters of Charles Sorley*, ed. W. R. Sorley (1919) • *Friends' Quarterly Examiner* (1937) • *CGPLA Eng. & Wales* (1916)
Likenesses C. Jameson, chalk drawing, 1916, NPG
Wealth at death £201 8*s*. 6*d*.: administration, 1 April 1916, *CGPLA Eng. & Wales*

Sorley, Sir Ralph Squire (1898–1974), air force officer, was born in Hornsey, London, on 9 January 1898, the son of James Graham Sorley, a soft goods manufacturer, of Stroud Green, and his wife, Ellen Merson. He was educated at the University School, Hastings, and by a private tutor. He joined the Royal Naval Air Service on 4 December 1914, and rose to the rank of flight commander before transferring to the Royal Air Force as captain (air) on its formation in 1918. He was awarded the DSC in 1918 and the DFC while commanding 6 squadron in Mesopotamia in 1920.

Sorley's extended and invaluable connections with future aircraft and weapons began with his posting as a test pilot to Felixstowe in 1924 and then to 22 squadron at Martlesham Heath in 1925. These stations were the centres of development of seaplanes and land planes. In 1927 he went to the Air Ministry in the directorate of technical development, and in 1929 he went to the Staff College. He was then posted to Aden to command 8 squadron for two years before returning to the Air Ministry in 1933.

Sorley's crusading dedication and drive ensured that the eight-gun fighter was a reality when the Second World War began. His calculations had showed that a mere two seconds would be available to destroy a high-speed monoplane fighter and that eight guns would be necessary to achieve a lethal burst in that time. Sorley, only thirty-five years old and a wing commander, against immense opposition persuaded the Air Ministry and the designers, Sydney Camm and R. J. Mitchell, of the importance of the 'two-second squirt', which was possibly the biggest single factor of the many which contributed to Britain's victory in the battle of Britain.

At the outbreak of war Sorley was posted to command RAF Upwood, but very soon he went to command the Aeroplane and Armament Experimental Establishment, for which all his experience had trained him. From 1943 to 1945 he worked in the Ministry of Aircraft Production, and he became controller of research and development and a member of the Air Council. After the war he was promoted air marshal and given command of technical training in the RAF until he retired at his own request in 1948.

In 1948 Sorley became managing director of De Havilland Propellers Ltd, Hatfield. The advent of the jet engine made the future look bleak and the possibility of entering the helicopter field was studied and rejected. Instead it was decided to concentrate on guided weapons. Sorley formed the nucleus of a design team to study the new technology and seek research and development contracts from the Air Ministry, the first of which was obtained in 1951—for an infra-red homing head which became the guidance system for the Firestreak air-to-air weapon, the RAF's first airborne missile. Sorley played a large part in the initial discussions with the RAF which formulated its operational requirements and specifications.

The respect in which he was held caused Sorley to be appointed head of the industrial team for a new project in 1955—a British independent deterrent consisting of a ballistic missile, code-named Blue Streak, with a range of 2000 miles and carrying a thermo-nuclear warhead. Sorley formed a separate design team with design offices in London, assembly facilities at Stevenage, and test sites at Hatfield, Spadeadam (in present-day Cumbria), and

Woomera (Australia). In 1960, however, a government decision was made to cancel Blue Streak and in the same year Sorley retired.

Sorley was a fellow of the Royal Aeronautical Society and of the Royal Society of Arts and was appointed OBE (1936), CB (1942), and KCB (1944). On 6 June 1925 he married Mary Eileen (*d.* 1977), the daughter of Ernest Robert Gayford, of Hadleigh, Suffolk, and the sister of Wing Commander Oswald Robert Gayford (1893–1945), DFC, AFC, who held the world long-distance flying record (1930) and then commanded the long-range development which regained the record for Great Britain. There were two daughters of the marriage. Sorley died on 17 November 1974 at the RAF Hospital, Wroughton, Wiltshire.

GEOFFREY TUTTLE, *rev.*

Sources private information (1986) • personal knowledge (1986) • *The Times* (20 Nov 1974)
Archives Royal Air Force Museum, Hendon, corresp., papers, diaries, and logbooks
Likenesses W. Stoneman, photograph, 1942, NPG
Wealth at death £17,809: probate, 27 June 1975, *CGPLA Eng. & Wales*

Sorley, William Ritchie (1855–1935), philosopher, was born at Selkirk on 4 November 1855, the younger son of William Sorley, a minister of the Free Church of Scotland, and his wife, Anna Ritchie. He was educated at a school kept by an uncle at Birkenhead, and entered Edinburgh University when about fifteen years old. After taking his degree, he studied theology for several years at New College, Edinburgh, Tübingen, and Berlin, with a view to entering the ministry, but was not ordained. At the age of twenty-four he began a further course of study, in moral science, at Trinity College, Cambridge, where he obtained a first class in the moral sciences tripos of 1882.

Sorley was elected into a fellowship at Trinity in 1883, and from 1882 until 1887 he lectured in the university and elsewhere on ethics. In 1888 he became professor of logic and philosophy at University College, Cardiff, where he remained until 1894. In 1889 he married Janetta Colquhoun Smith, a lively and witty woman, daughter of George Smith, journalist and author, and sister of George Adam Smith, Old Testament scholar. They had two daughters and two sons. In 1894 Sorley was appointed regius professor of moral philosophy at Aberdeen University. In 1900 he succeeded Henry Sidgwick in the Knightbridge chair of moral philosophy at Cambridge: this post he held until his resignation in 1933. He was elected a fellow of King's College, Cambridge, in 1901.

Sorley inherited from his father both administrative and literary ability. At Cardiff he took an active part in the formation of the University of Wales, and at Cambridge he served on the council of the borough as well as on that of the senate of the university: he welcomed the experience that various kinds of business brought him, despite the distraction from intellectual work. Besides editing works by the philosophers Robert Adamson and James Ward, he wrote several books, and more than fifty articles. Sorley's primary interest was in ethics. He was initially influenced by the philosophical idealism of T. H. Green and F. H. Bradley; he contributed an essay on historical method to a collection, published in 1883 to commemorate Green, which was widely regarded as a statement of the idealist position. But Sorley became increasingly critical of philosophical idealism, which he regarded as unable to account for the existence of evil. For example, he criticized idealists for describing an individual's moral activity as the reproduction of an eternal reality even though selfish interests so often prevailed over the common good. He found deeply unsatisfactory attempts by all non-theistic theories to explain the struggle between good and evil. His chief work, containing the Gifford lectures delivered at Aberdeen in 1914–15 and published in 1918 as *Moral Values and the Idea of God*, has played an important part in the education of students of philosophical theology. Sorley's philosophical and theological position was that of theism. His main theistic argument was based on considerations concerning moral values. These, he maintained, are objective in that they are not constituted by feeling or desire and in that they form one of the factors which a comprehensive philosophy should co-ordinate: the relations between moral values and reality he believed to be inexplicable by any non-theistic theory. Sorley's explanation of why individuals realize moral values so imperfectly and why the natural order of the world displays such indifference to the standard of good and evil appealed to the Kantian argument that good cannot be achieved except in circumstances that make evil possible as well as good. These philosophical problems became all the more urgent for Sorley in the context of the First World War: his eldest son, Charles Hamilton *Sorley, a promising poet, was killed in the battle of Loos in 1915. William Sorley edited two volumes of Charles Sorley's verse and a collection of his literary and prescient letters from the front.

Sorley also had a long-standing interest in the ethical significance of evolutionary theory, a subject he first addressed in the Shaw fellowship lectures given at the University of Edinburgh in 1884, published the following year as *The Ethics of Naturalism*. This was at the time a fashionable subject, but Sorley reached a rather less fashionable conclusion when he judged evolution 'unable either to set up a comprehensive ideal for life, or to yield any principle for distinguishing between good and evil in conduct' (*The Ethics of Naturalism*, 309). Sorley's argument anticipated T. H. Huxley's famous Romanes lecture of 1893. Sorley also rejected attempts by contemporaries to rehabilitate utilitarianism in the light of evolutionary theory. While he held himself aloof from the prevailing schools of thought in his time—both philosophical idealism and the new realism—and accordingly stood for much of his life at the periphery of philosophical debate, his writings had an impact on philosophers of religion and churchmen, such as W. R. Inge.

Sorley was a conservative with a strong belief in the nation-state and in the empire. He was awarded the degree of LittD by Cambridge University (1905), the honorary LLD degree by Edinburgh University (1900), and the fellowship of the British Academy (1905). Following a bout of pneumonia, he died at his home, St Giles House, Chesterton Lane, Cambridge, on 28 July 1935. His ashes were buried at the west end of King's College chapel, Cambridge. His wife survived him.

F. R. TENNANT, *rev.* S. M. DEN OTTER

Sources F. R. Tennant, 'William Ritchie Sorley, 1855–1935', *PBA*, 21 (1935), 393–405 · G. F. Stout, *Mind*, new ser., 45 (1936), 123–5 · *The letters of Charles Sorley: with a chapter of biography*, ed. W. R. Sorley (1919) · *The Times* (30 July 1935) · private information (1949) · personal knowledge (1949)
Archives King's Cam., letters to Oscar Browning · NL Scot., letters to Lord Haldane
Likenesses J. P. Clarke, photograph, 1902–12, King's Cam., coll. photo. 467
Wealth at death £19,353 15*s.* 7*d.*: probate, 18 Nov 1935, *CGPLA Eng. & Wales*

Sorocold, George (*c.*1668–1738?), engineer, was the son of James Sorocold (1627–1675), a Lancashire gentleman who moved to Derby. Little else is known of Sorocold's life until on 7 December 1684 he married Mary, the daughter of Henry Franceys, a prosperous Derby apothecary. By 1702 they had thirteen children, of whom eight then survived.

The earliest known engineering work undertaken by Sorocold was connected with the supply of water to Macclesfield between 1685 and 1687, and the recasting and rehanging of the bells at All Saints' Church in Derby in 1687. Although he had a varied engineering career, he is best-known for his pioneering work in water supply; and one of his innovations in this area was the introduction of pumps worked by water-wheels which rose and fell in accordance with the level of the stream. In 1693 a patent along these lines was granted to his working colleague, John Hadley, so there is a possibility that it was a joint venture.

Sorocold was particularly associated with waterworks in provincial towns such as Derby, Bridgnorth, Bristol, Deal, King's Lynn, Leeds, Newcastle upon Tyne, Norwich, Portsmouth, Sheffield, and Great Yarmouth; but he also worked in London, improving London Bridge waterworks and the New River, and constructing Marchant's waterworks. At many sites his pumping machinery was adapted to other uses as well, and on occasion put to draining mines, such as at Alloa in 1710. His sole patent, a horse- or water-powered machine for sawing planks, was probably another variation.

Sorocold was more involved in river improvement work than is often realized. His work on the early unimplemented schemes on the River Derwent is well known, but a letter he wrote in 1711, when advising on problems along the lower tidal River Lea, cites his involvement on the River Aire, probably after the death of Hadley in 1701, and on the River Cam a few years later. He expounded a philosophy of river improvement, whereby a series of locks with a fall of only 3 or 4 feet was preferred to fewer locks with larger falls, as the latter were more harmful to mills and meadows. For the non-tidal Lea, which he had surveyed at his own expense in 1702, he made the novel suggestion that it be improved by the construction of several temporary seasonal flash locks, but such recommendations were not implemented.

There is also evidence of Sorocold's involvement in erecting iron forges, and in setting up atmospheric engines, and he had some interest in dock engineering. Statements about his involvement in the construction of Howlands Dock in Surrey cannot be substantiated by contemporary evidence, but he did give advice to the corporation of Liverpool on their first wet dock scheme, a dock built by Thomas Steers. He also erected the mill work at Cotchetts' silk mill at Derby in 1702, an enterprise taken over in 1719 by John Lombe, and then Sir Thomas Lombe. This mill was one of the most important early modern factories. In 1699 Thomas Surbey noted that when Sorocold was showing some gentlemen round the corn mill at Derby waterworks he fell into the mill race and although swept under the water-wheel, was not hurt. However, Daniel Defoe, in his *Tour thro' the Whole Island of Great Britain* (1727), reported this accident as having occurred at Lombe's silk mill.

Sorocold made several trips to Scotland between 1710 and 1715, and he assisted John Adair in surveying the route of a proposed canal between the Forth and the Clyde. In 1717 he was described as the 'ingenious, unfortunate, mathematician' (Williamson, 45), but it is not known why. His engineering skills were undoubtedly valued by his contemporaries: he was characterized as 'one of the two engineers of this age who never failed in what they undertook because they considered perfection and success of their work first and their profit afterwards' (private information).

The date of Sorocold's death is not known, but the lease to Derby waterworks was still in his name as late as 1738.

K. R. FAIRCLOUGH

Sources F. Williamson, 'George Sorocold of Derby: a pioneer of water supply', *Journal of the Derbyshire Archaeological and Natural History Society*, 57 (1936), 43–93 · R. Jenkins, 'George Sorocold: a chapter in the history of public water supply', *Links in the history of engineering and technology from Tudor times: the collected papers of Rhys Jenkins* (1936), 149–53 · F. Williamson and W. B. Crump, 'Sorocold's waterworks at Leeds', *Thoresby Miscellanea*, 11/2 (1941), 166–82 · C. Hadfield, *The canals of Yorkshire and north-east England*, 1 (1972), 96–100 · [D. Defoe], *A tour thro' the whole island of Great Britain*, 3 (1727) · M. Craven, *John Whitehurst of Derby: clockmaker and scientist, 1713–88* (1996) · M. A. Clarke, 'Thomas Steers', *Dock engineers and dock engineering* [Papers presented at a Research Day School at Merseyside Maritime Museum, 13 Feb 1993] · parish register, Derbys. RO, M151 [marriage] · private information (2004) [M. Craven] · P. Hughes, 'Some civil engineering notes from 1699', *Local Historian*, 26/2 (May 1996), 102–14 · P. G. Vasey, 'The Forth-Clyde canal: John Adair, progenitor of early schemes', *Journal of the Railway and Canal Historical Society*, 30/7 (March 1992), 373–7 · A. Calladine, 'Lombe's mill: an exercise in reconstruction', *Industrial Archaeology Review*, 16 (1993–4), 82–99
Archives GL, Bridge House committee, reports and papers

Sorocold, Thomas (1561/2–1617), Church of England clergyman, was born in Lancashire. Of his parents it is known only that his father survived him and must therefore have lived to a very great age indeed. Sorocold may have been related to Ralph Sorocold, a wealthy merchant of Manchester, and have come under the tutorship of Oliver Carter, fellow and subdean of Manchester collegiate church. On 10 December 1579 the executors of the will of Philip Nowell, the educational benefactor, provided 10*s*. for 'Thomas Sorrocold, scholare of Manchester, commended by certen gentlemen and Mr Carter' (Grosart, 2.170). Sorocold matriculated on 18 July 1580, aged eighteen, from Brasenose College, Oxford, graduating BA on 6 February 1583 and MA on 8 July 1585. After his ordination he returned to Lancashire and became a preacher there; among his more illustrious hearers was the earl of Derby, at his chapel at Lathom House in July 1587. On 22 October 1590 Sorocold was instituted to the rectory of St Mildred Poultry in London. On 4 August 1592 he was granted a licence to marry Susan, daughter of Richard Smith, a grocer of St Benet Sherehog, with whom he had a daughter, also named Susan, baptized on 12 March 1597. Susan Sorocold was buried in the chancel of St Mildred's on 16 March 1605.

The work for which Sorocold is chiefly remembered is his *Supplications of Saints*, a devotional aid containing a meditation on Christ's life, death, and passion, aimed at a wide audience. Registered with the Stationers' Company in 1608, it went through nearly fifty editions by 1723; in the third edition of 1617, dedicated to Prince Charles, Sorocold recalled that Princess Elizabeth, before going with her husband to the Palatinate in 1613, had consented to sponsor the work. In his will, dated 7 December 1617, Sorocold requested that he be buried as near as possible to 'my deceased wife' Susan. To Elizabeth, his wife at the time of his death, he bequeathed a little house and garden 'neer the Moorefeildes in the suburbs of London' (LMA, DL/C/360/Thomas Sorocold, X19/5, fol. 313), while her son Thomas Methwold received a gold piece. Sorocold's interest in property in Salford, near Manchester, where his father was still living, went to his daughter Susan. Sorocold was buried at St Mildred Poultry on 12 December 1617. STEPHEN WRIGHT

Sources [C. B. Heberden], ed., *Brasenose College register, 1509–1909*, 2 vols., OHS, 55 (1909) • A. Grosart, ed., *The spending of the money of Philip Nowell* (1877) • W. Ffarrington, *The Stanley papers, pt 2*, ed. F. R. Raines, Chetham Society, 31 (1853) • T. Milbourne, *History of St Mildred's Church* (1872) • Foster, *Alum. Oxon.* • will, LMA, DL/C/360/Thomas Sorocold, X19/5, fol. 313 • I. Green, *Print and protestantism in early modern England* (2000)

Wealth at death exact sum unknown: will, LMA, DL/C/360/Thomas Sorocold, X19/5, fol. 313

Sorrell, Alan Ernest (1904–1974), artist and writer, was born on 11 February 1904 at Tooting Graveney, south London, the second child of Ernest Thomas Sorrell (1861–1910), watchmaker and jeweller, and his wife, Edith Jane Doody (1867–1951). The family moved to Southend-on-Sea in Essex when he was two years old. He was a sickly and nervous boy; his childhood was spent confined to a bath chair with a suspected heart condition. These years were further shadowed by the early deaths of his father, an amateur artist, and of his only sister, Doris.

As a young man Sorrell steadily pursued his determination to become an artist. He trained at the Southend Municipal School of Art and, after a brief spell as a commercial artist in London—an experience which gave him a perhaps exaggerated fear of 'facility' in his work—at the Royal College of Art (1924–8). Here he came under the influence of the principal, William Rothenstein, who greatly encouraged him and became a good friend. In 1928 Sorrell won the prix de Rome in mural painting and spent until 1931 at the British School at Rome. This was a crucially formative time: he mingled with classical scholars, engravers, painters, and architects, and the twin themes of his work—the depth of history and the fragility of the present—began to assert themselves.

Sorrell returned to England in 1931 and was invited by Rothenstein to join the teaching staff at the college as a drawing-master (1931–48). He became known affectionately to students in the life class as Old Angles because of his insistence on the importance of structure and form. His contemporaries on the teaching staff—Gilbert Spencer, Charles Mahoney, and others—were lifelong friends. About 1932 he married (Irene Agnes) Mary Oldershaw; however, the marriage ended in divorce in 1946.

At this stage Sorrell thought of himself as a mural painter. His first large commission was a decorative scheme (1932–6) for the central library in Southend-on-Sea—four tall panels with historical subjects, one of which was *The Refitting of Admiral Blake's Fleet at Leigh, 1652*. He evolved a characteristic working method, a period of intense questioning and study which preceded the development of the painting. The landscape transformed itself in front of his eyes:

> The problem was to pierce the skin of building which had spread over the hillsides, plant them again with trees, mentally demolish that ugly gasometer and the railway that has cut through the fishing village, and then rebuild the wharves, people them with those oddly dressed Cromwellian figures, fill the estuary with white-sailed ships-of-the-line—and there would be the picture. (Sorrell, 10)

This unusual (for an artist) historical perspective is what informs his best-known work. Other decorative schemes, in a variety of settings, occupied him at intervals throughout his life, for example the chancel arch at St Peter's Church in Bexhill, Sussex; panels for the Festival of Britain (1951); and a wall-length mural for the entrance hall of Warwick Oken County secondary school.

However, when Sorrell 'found himself', it was not as an oil or tempera painter but, *par excellence*, as a draughtsman. He was never happier or more assured than when working directly with pen and ink, pencil, charcoal, and brush on a subject which challenged him. Journeys abroad to Iceland (1935), to Greece and Istanbul (1954), and, finest of all, to Egypt and Nubia to record the riverside temples and villages before their inundation by Lake Nasser (1962), produced a crop of drawings. He showed similar verve working at his 'reconstruction' drawings, whistling snatches of the 'Kreutzer' sonata as he leant over his board in his studio, with papers, books, paints, chalks, and brushes piled around him.

His first reconstruction drawing, in 1936, arose from a chance visit to the excavation by Kathleen Kenyon of the

Roman 'basilica' at Leicester. It was published in the *Illustrated London News* (*c.*May 1936) and, among archaeologists, stimulated an immediate response. He soon found himself working with Mortimer Wheeler (the result of which was a dramatic drawing of the Roman assault on the eastern entrance of Maiden Castle, Dorset) and with Cyril Fox and V. E. Nash-Williams on a series of drawings of Roman and prehistoric sites for the National Museum of Wales (1937–40). So began a partnership with two generations of archaeologists, which only ended with his death in 1974. For nearly forty years he 'reconstructed' with his lively pen numerous sites in Britain and continental Europe, including Stonehenge and Avebury; Roman forts on Hadrian's Wall; Roman towns, villas, and temples; Dark Age brochs and viking settlements; medieval castles in England, Scotland, and Wales; and great monastic foundations like Tintern, Rievaulx, and Fountains. He was an artist working productively with scientists. In an age much vexed by the 'two cultures', he seemed effortlessly to be able to bridge the gap without compromising his own acute sensibilities. In these works (many of which were commissioned by the ancient monuments branch of the Ministry of Works—which then became English Heritage—as well as by the Scottish Office and the Welsh Office) he played a not inconsiderable part in the popularizing of historical sites and buildings in Britain which was such a feature of the twentieth century. But he was more than a popularizer. He expressed his own aspiration for the form in these words: 'the reconstruction which is conceived as a work of art has that super-realism, the realism of the dream, which fixes for ever the image of the scene or incident or personage depicted' (Sorrell, 25). His drawings were frequently reproduced *in situ*, giving the visitor to the site a striking image of how it might have looked.

Sorrell served in the RAF during the Second World War as a camouflage officer, and by-products of these years were drawings and paintings of aerodromes and barrack-room life. Many of these were purchased by the war artists' commission and eventually became part of the collections of the Tate and the Imperial War Museum in London. In 1947 he married (Mabel) Elizabeth Tanner (1916–1991) who, working under her married name, Elizabeth Sorrell, was a distinguished watercolourist. They bought and converted a redundant chapel on Daws Heath, Thundersley, Essex, formerly belonging to The Peculiar People, and made it their workplace and home. Of the three children of this marriage—Richard, Mark, and Julia—Richard and Julia followed their parents in becoming professional artists.

Sorrell was a neo-Romantic. Recruits marching down to the station, in a wartime painting, proceed under a haloed moon. His reconstruction drawings are invested with dramatic cloud formations, swirling rainstorms, and smoke. In his more imaginative compositions, not tied down to immediate reality, a brooding oppressive atmosphere often prevails. They are images of a violently broken civilization—earthquake-shattered cities, jungle-invaded monuments, propped façades. In spite of this pessimistic attitude, he was a man with a gusto for life, naturally sociable and gregarious, with a witty manner which was hindered but never stifled by a stammer.

He wrote with pleasure and apparent ease. His more personal writing—records of his life as a student in Rome and of his journeys to Greece and Nubia—are a revelation of his character as an artist and man. He compiled several books, illustrated with reconstruction drawings and published by Batsford, with titles such as *Living History* (1965), *Roman London* (1969), and *British Castles* (1973); and a very successful series of school books based on his drawings was published by Lutterworth: *Roman Britain* (1961), *Saxon England* (1964), *Norman Britain* (1966), *Prehistoric Britain* (1968), and *Imperial Rome* (1970). His Nubian drawings are reproduced in *Nubia—a Drowning Land* (1967) by Margaret Drower.

Sorrell was a member of the Royal Society of Painters in Watercolour and regularly exhibited at the Royal Academy. His work is represented in many public and private collections. Alan Sorrell died in Southend-on-Sea on 21 December 1974. MARK SORRELL

Sources M. Sorrell, *Reconstructing the past* (1980) • D. W. Sykes, ed., *Alan Sorrell: early Wales re-created* (1980) • *CGPLA Eng. & Wales* (1975) • personal knowledge (2004) • private information (2004)
Archives priv. coll.
Likenesses A. Sorrell, self-portrait, oils, 1972, priv. coll.
Wealth at death £23,281: probate, 19 June 1975, *CGPLA Eng. & Wales*

Soskice [*formerly* Soskis], **David Vladimirovich** (**1866–1941**), journalist and campaigner for freedom in Russia, was born on 27 March 1866 in Berdichev, near Kiev in Ukraine, the son of Wolf Soskis, merchant, and his wife, Bassia Liuba Soskis (1844–1923). His parents were Jewish but he did not follow their religious faith. He first encountered tsarist oppression at school in Kiev in 1880: 'in the gymnasium I heard of three young students being hanged for distributing socialist literature … [then] considered myself a socialist—or a revolutionist, which is the same thing'. In 1881 he witnessed an anti-Jewish pogrom and hid 'revolutionists who were trying to escape … took part in meetings of secret circles … was constantly watched by spies and [his] rooms repeatedly searched'. Police harassment continued and Soskice led a forced peripatetic university life at Kiev, St Petersburg, and Odessa, where he graduated in law. He practised in Kazan but his continuing revolutionary activities led to his arrest in 1890 and imprisonment for three years without trial (Perris, 266–73). After his release he was warned of re-arrest and escaped to France.

Soskice settled in England in 1898 and on 1 November 1899 married Anna Sophia Johansen, daughter of a Russian judge of Norwegian descent, with whom he had been living; they had a son, Victor (1895–1986). They were divorced in August 1902. Soskice's friendships with Russian refugees and their English sympathizers brought him into contact with Edward and Constance Garnett and their circle, where he met Juliet Catherine Emma Hueffer (1881–1944), a musician and later a writer, whom he married on 20 September 1902. He was fifteen years older and according to David Garnett was 'squarely built ... with a curly black beard and a square forehead but with a literal mind and no imagination' while she was 'a ravishingly beautiful blonde ... with golden hair', highly intelligent and gifted in languages and music (D. Garnett, 37–9). She was fresh and lively, he earnest and serious and said to be without humour, although Perris says that he had 'wide culture and fine spirit and [was] as unlike the conventional conspirator as possible' (Perris, 267–77). Their backgrounds, too, could not have been more different. Her father, Francis *Hueffer, was a noted music critic; her mother, Catherine, was the daughter of Ford Madox Brown; her aunt, Lucy Madox, to whom she was close, was married to Michael Rossetti; Ford Madox Ford was her brother. Their union was happy and they had three sons of whom the first, Frank *Soskice, was born on 23 July 1902 before their marriage in September. Their home became a meeting place for writers, artists, refugees, and politicians. Later in life Juliet translated Nekrasov and wrote five novels; her autobiographical *Chapters from Childhood* (1921) is a minor classic.

In London, Soskice contributed, under pseudonyms, to Russian newspapers and journals on British affairs and wrote on Russian affairs in English publications. He joined the Agrarian Socialist League and the Socialist Revolutionary Party and was particularly active in the Society for Friends of Russian Freedom, whose aims were to publicize the evils of the tsar's regime and to encourage peaceful democratic change in Russia. (Although publicly for peaceful change, some figures engaged in such activities as gun-running, in which Soskice may have taken some part.) The society published a monthly journal, *Free Russia*, to which Soskice contributed; he became editor in 1904 and through his contacts was able to provide full accounts of the events of 1905 in Russia. In January 1905 Father Gapon, the leader of the 'bloody Sunday' march in St Petersburg, escaped to England and lived secretly, mainly with the Soskices, in Hammersmith. While in London, Soskice and G. H. Perris combined to write, from Gapon's dictation, his *The Story of my Life* (1905).

Late in 1905 Soskice was appointed St Petersburg correspondent for the short-lived Liberal daily newspaper *The Tribune*. Perris was foreign editor and they arranged such a comprehensive and accurate coverage of Russian affairs that Benckendorff, the Russian ambassador in London, described the newspaper as his 'bête noire' and its St Petersburg correspondent as 'execrable' (Hollingsworth, 'Benckendorff', 107). He was particularly irritated over the episode of the memorial to the Russian Duma of 1906 which *Tribune* journalists initiated. It was drawn up immediately after the Duma's dissolution as a statement of support from many public figures in British life, with Soskice making arrangements for its reception in St Petersburg.

In 1908 Soskice returned to England and resumed a busy life in journalism and lecturing, developed business interests in Russia, and established a Russian Law Bureau. In 1908–9 he worked in support of the Parliamentary Russian Committee. In 1909 he took part in an attempt to save the *English Review* (to which he himself was a contributor), which was in financial difficulties after an auspicious start under Ford's editorship.

After the collapse of the tsar's government in March 1917 Soskice promoted support for the new regime and in May was appointed a second St Petersburg correspondent for the *Manchester Guardian*. He participated vigorously in political debate and action and in August joined Kerensky's secretariat. He was thus able to report and analyse events as they unfolded. He was present during the Kornilov affair, when he feared for his life, and was in the winter palace in November when it was besieged by Bolshevik red guards but managed to escape. He remained loyal to Kerensky and, on his return to London, wrote about the events surrounding Kerensky's fall.

After the triumph of the communist regime Soskice lost hope of any immediate change in the government of Russia, and his final years were spent in Britain on his business affairs and in writing, although he and Juliet remained lively hosts. He was naturalized in 1924 and died at his home, 5 Woodlands Road, Barnes, Surrey, on 28 June 1941 of a duodenal ulcer. He was cremated at Golders Green. ROBERT GOMME

Sources B. Hollingsworth, 'David Soskice in Russia in 1917', *European Studies Review*, 6 (1976), 73–97 • G. H. Perris, *Russia in revolution*, 2nd edn (1905), 267–77 • B. Hollingsworth, 'The Society of Friends of Russian Freedom: English liberals and Russian socialists, 1890–1917', *Oxford Slavonic Papers*, new ser., 3 (1970), 45–64 • B. Hollingsworth, 'British memorial to the Russian Duma, 1906', *Slavonic and East European Review*, 53 (1975), 539–57 • B. Hollingsworth, 'Benckendorff's *bête noire*: *The Tribune* and Russian internal affairs, 1906–8', *Poetry, prose, and public opinion ... essays presented in memory of Dr N. E. Andreyev*, ed. W. Harrison and A. Pyman (1984), 106–32 • D. Garnett, *The golden echo* (1954), 37–9 • D. Goldring, *A record of the life and writings of F. M. Ford* (1948), 139–51 • *DNB* • *Manchester Guardian* (May–Dec 1917) • *Free Russia* (1890–1917) • *The Tribune* (1906–8) • J. Soskice, 'Father Gapon', *New Leader* (1 Dec 1922), 10 • J. Soskice, 'Father Gapon', *New Leader* (8 Dec 1922), 12–13 • R. Garnett, *Constance Garnett: a heroic life* (1991) • m. certs. • d. cert. • private information (2004) [family]

Archives HLRO, corresp. and papers | UCL, school of Slavonic and east European studies, historical notes

Likenesses double portrait, photograph (with Juliet Soskice), repro. in W. Harrison and A. Pyman, eds., *Poetry, prose, and public opinion: aspects of Russia, 1850–1970* (1984) • photograph, repro. in Perris, *Russia in revolution* • photographs, HLRO, Stow Hill MSS

Wealth at death £5375 17s. 11d.: probate, 18 Oct 1941, *CGPLA Eng. & Wales*

Soskice, Frank, Baron Stow Hill (1902–1979), politician and lawyer, was born on 23 July 1902 in Geneva, the eldest of the three sons of David Vladimirovich *Soskice (1866–1941) and his second wife, Juliet Catherine Emma (1881–1944), daughter of Francis *Hueffer, music critic of *The Times*. He was educated at St Paul's School, London, as a foundation scholar and then won a classics scholarship to Balliol College, Oxford, where he obtained a first class in classical moderations in 1922 and then a third in philosophy, politics, and economics in 1924. In the same year he was naturalized. He was called to the bar by the Inner Temple in 1926. As an advocate, he is said to have pressed his cases with vigour and persistence and to have inspired

Frank Soskice, Baron Stow Hill (1902–1979), by Walter Bird, 1963

complete trust in his clients. His success was such that several foreign governments—India, Greece, and Cambodia—instructed him to act for them at the International Court of Justice at The Hague (*DNB*). On the outbreak of the Second World War he joined the Oxfordshire and Buckinghamshire light infantry. The following year he married Susan Isabella Cloudesley, daughter of William Auchterlony Hunter, of Spean Bridge in Inverness-shire. They had two sons. He served first in east Africa and then, as political welfare executive, in Cairo. Later he worked with the Special Operations Executive in London.

In 1945 Soskice resumed his legal career, taking silk. He also entered parliament as Labour MP for East Birkenhead, and Attlee made him solicitor-general and conferred on him a knighthood. In 1948 he was sworn of the privy council. He lost his seat in February 1950, when the East Birkenhead constituency was abolished in boundary changes. Yet he was kept on as solicitor-general, despite becoming UK delegate to the United Nations general assembly for a short time, and by April 1950 was found a safe seat, the incumbent MP for Sheffield Neepsend (Harry Morris) being persuaded to take a peerage. Soskice held Neepsend until 1955, when it too was abolished. He failed to win the nomination for Gorton in Manchester, but in 1956 he won a by-election at Newport, Monmouthshire, which he continued to represent until 1966.

As solicitor-general Soskice showed himself an able figure. He advised on a wide range of domestic and international disputes, and appeared for the crown in many cases, especially concerning revenue matters. He was also becoming a valued parliamentarian. In June 1948 he took a leading role in carrying the Gas Bill through the Commons, winning high praise from Hugh Gaitskell for his 'extraordinary capacity': he took tory amendments for two nights running and yet 'remained patient, lucid and polite to the end and looked as fresh as a baby' (*Diary of Hugh Gaitskell*, 66). Another colleague, Douglas Jay, judged that with his return to the Commons in April 1950 the debating strength of the Treasury team increased by 50 per cent: 'Probably Soskice was at that moment more indispensable than any other member of the Government' (Jay, 197). During a debate on the Finance Bill, he was 'ever present, inexhaustible and almost omniscient' (Jay, 198). In April 1951 Attlee promoted him to become attorney-general. In this position he replaced the emergency wartime Order 1305, prohibiting strikes and lockouts, which had been introduced in 1940 and maintained by Attlee's government, with a milder decree that was less objectionable to the trade unions. In July 1951 he argued that Morrison's projected use of force to regain the Abadan oil refinery from the Iraqis might well break international law.

In opposition from October 1951, Soskice was elected to the shadow cabinet in 1952. Gaitskell noted that he was as popular as ever and that he managed to combine a heavy work load at the bar with onerous political duties. A 'good linguist, a good mixer, hard-working and conscientious', he was a possible future foreign secretary (*Diary of Hugh Gaitskell*, 334). As a prominent member of the 'Hampstead set', whose own house in Church Row was only 200 yards from that of Gaitskell, Soskice's political career received a boost with Gaitskell's election as Labour leader in December 1955. Here was some compensation for the party's general election defeat earlier in the year. Yet Labour lost again in 1959, and Soskice must have felt justified in not having sacrificed his legal career. General election victory when it did come, under Harold Wilson in October 1964, was in many ways too late for Soskice.

Wilson had spoken of his intention of giving Soskice a peerage and making him leader of the House of Lords (Benn, 82). Instead he decided to make him home secretary; but Wilson remarked privately that his 'real' cabinet would be formed in 1966 (Benn, 131). Soskice's performance at the Home Office did nothing to change the prime minister's mind. He reacted indecisively to the results of an electoral boundary commission for Northamptonshire. At first he accepted its results, which would have benefited the Conservatives, but then changed his mind and appointed a public inquiry—a volte-face that led to a motion of censure in the Commons, which he survived by 299 votes to 291 (*Diaries of a Cabinet Minister*, 1.160, 170). After he slipped out of a meeting with Wilson and Crossman on boundary decisions, Wilson 'raised his hands … in horror' (ibid., 1.189). Soon Wilson was referring to him as an incubus (*Castle Diaries, 1964–70*, 79).

Soskice also failed to impress in his handling of the politically sensitive issue of Commonwealth immigration.

The Race Relations Act of 1965 banned racial discrimination in public places, but the left wing of the Labour Party was dismayed when Soskice accepted a Conservative amendment to substitute conciliation for criminal sanctions. He gained the reputation for being a hard-liner on immigration, and Labour issued fewer 'C' vouchers (for unskilled workers) under the Commonwealth Immigrants Act of 1962 than had their predecessors, although in fact he had argued in favour of a liberal approach. Bert Bowden (the lord president) marshalled the cabinet committee against the views of its chairman.

Soskice minuted: 'Poor old Home Office. We are not always wrong, but we always get the blame' (Jenkins, 181). Certainly the consensus was that he failed as home secretary. His successor, Roy Jenkins, judged that he had 'practically no political sense and an obsessive respect for legal precedent' (Jenkins, 175). Yet a major cause of his failure was wretched health. He suffered badly from arthritis and a twisted shoulder. The newspaper magnate Cecil King judged in July 1965 that he was 'slowly seizing up' (King, 19). One of his few successes was that he was the first home secretary during whose term of office no one was hanged. He reprieved all those found guilty of murder before the Murder Act abolished the death penalty in 1965.

It was rumoured that, rather than agreeing to become a backbencher, Soskice would resign his seat and force a by-election (*Diaries of a Cabinet Minister*, 411). But in Wilson's first cabinet reshuffle, in December 1965, he was made lord privy seal and in 1966 he took a seat in the upper house as Baron Stow Hill of Newport (a life peerage). In 1967 he led a parliamentary delegation to Australia and the following year became treasurer of the Inner Temple. He died in Hampstead on 1 January 1979.

ROBERT PEARCE

Sources *DNB* · *The Guardian* (4 Jan 1979) · *Daily Telegraph* (3 Jan 1979) · *The Times* (16 Nov 1979) · *The diary of Hugh Gaitskell, 1945–1956*, ed. P. M. Williams (1983) · D. Jay, *Change and fortune: a political record* (1980) · R. H. S. Crossman, *The diaries of a cabinet minister*, 1 (1975) · R. Jenkins, *A life at the centre* (1991) · T. Benn, *Out of the wilderness: diaries, 1963–67* (1987) · *The Castle diaries, 1964–1970* (1984) · K. O. Morgan, *Labour in power, 1945–1951* (1984) · D. Dean, 'The Wilson government and the Smethwick factor', *Twentieth-Century British History*, 11/2 (2000) · *CGPLA Eng. & Wales* (1979) · C. King, *The Cecil King diary, 1965–1970* (1972), 19

Archives HLRO, political and family papers | FILM BFI NFTVA, documentary footage

Likenesses W. Bird, photograph, 1963, NPG [*see illus.*]

Wealth at death £134,820: probate, 2 March 1979, *CGPLA Eng. & Wales*

Sosnow, Eric Charles (1910–1987), journalist and businessman, was born on 18 August 1910 in Kolno, eastern Poland, the second son in the family of three boys and two girls of David Sosnow, a Jewish produce merchant, and his wife, Libby Markewitz. He spent his early years in Poland and was educated at Łomża secondary school, Vilna University, and law chambers in Warsaw. In 1934 he left Poland for England and was employed as a foreign correspondent for Polish newspapers.

Sosnow worked briefly for Nahum Sokolov as his private secretary. In 1936 he became a graduate research student at the London School of Economics. As a foreign journalist he joined the Foreign Press Association and with his knowledge of politics and command of languages (he spoke eight) he specialized in articles on eastern Europe. In 1938 he started writing for *The Economist* under Donald Tyerman and in 1940 became an overseas correspondent for the *Sunday Times* and *Sunday Chronicle*. He was to continue writing for these papers for a further twenty years. His reputation grew and in 1944 he was asked to interview the Polish prime minister and, later, the president of Czechoslovakia before the latter's ill-fated journey to Moscow. He mixed easily with foreign journalists of every nationality and political persuasion. He loved journalism for the contact it gave him with people and the outlet it provided for his writing. He was naturalized in October 1947.

While travelling and reporting Sosnow built a network of contacts around the world. Although his first love was journalism, the most obvious outlet for his talents and energy was international trade. On his arrival in England he worked with his uncle in the importation of fruit juices. In 1945 he took over a redundant orange juice factory and started, together with his wife, the manufacture of inexpensive fashion clothing under the name Estrava.

In 1955 Sosnow was asked by Joe Bradley, with whom he had developed a very close association, to take over the management of Carters Merchants, an import–export company. In 1961 Estrava and Carters Merchants were combined into Whiteley Stevens, a textile company quoted on the London stock exchange. In the same year the group bought Gordon Woodrofe, with its trading interests in India, China, Japan, and Africa. In 1962 Sosnow changed the name of the group to United City Merchants. He now had an international trading group, which was to continue to grow and keep him travelling.

Gaining a reputation for barter, Sosnow became a central figure in international trade, and particularly trade behind the iron curtain. When he retired as chairman in 1981, United City Merchants was an international trading company, with offices worldwide, involved in banking, shipping, leather, raw materials, industrial machinery, cars, and turnkey projects. He had hoped that his very talented son, Norman, would take over from him, but he was killed in an air crash in 1967, at the age of twenty-three, while working for the company.

From 1981 onwards Sosnow devoted more of his time to predominantly educational charities. He became a governor and honorary fellow of the London School of Economics and was elected a fellow-commoner of Christ's College, Cambridge. He endowed chairs and travelling scholarships in both universities in his son's name; he had a great affection for and understanding of young people. He was very much involved in the Hebrew University of Jerusalem and the Weizmann Institute in Israel, and was closely associated with the Oxford Centre for Postgraduate Hebrew Studies and with the Institute of Jewish Affairs in London. Among his decorations were the Polish order of merit (1985) and the rank of comendador of the republic of Portugal (1973). He became a freeman of the City of London in 1960.

Sosnow was a short, affable, and energetic man, always immaculately dressed, and with a great sense of humour. He was never prepared to take 'no' for an answer. As a journalist he searched for the scoop. As a businessman he expanded his company, which grew, not only in spite of the controls in the 1960s and 1970s, but because of them. He was never prepared to contest take-over bids but was willing to fight the system. When dividend controls were instituted he used them as an opportunity to conserve cash with which he bought businesses. He developed a technique for issuing tax-free bonus shares to his shareholders which was widely copied. He enjoyed the pomp and ceremony of the City and was happy when he was made a freeman of the City of London. He believed the basic tools necessary for success in international trade were a knowledge of and aptitude for languages, training in economics and international law, a love of travel, and an interest in modern history and people.

Sosnow was a voracious reader and an excellent academic lawyer, from whom solicitors and counsel learned many lessons. As a lawyer he derived immense satisfaction from his successful appeal to the House of Lords in 1982, *United City Merchants Investments Ltd* v. *Royal Bank of Canada*, which decided that where a letter of credit was in order on its face, refusal by a banker to pay on presentation did not extend to fraud to which the seller was not party.

In 1943 Sosnow married Sylvia, daughter of Mark Tafler, an authority on late nineteenth-century English engraved glass. As well as their son they had a daughter. They were a remarkable couple, Sylvia being an active partner in the business and contributing greatly to its success. Sosnow died at the Hospital of St John and St Elizabeth, London, on 20 February 1987, and his wife died in 1988. A memorial service for Sosnow was held in July 1987 at the New West End Synagogue, London. E. S. Birk, *rev.*

Sources *The Times* (26 Feb 1987) • *The Times* (9 July 1987) • personal knowledge (1996) • private information (1996) • *CGPLA Eng. & Wales* (1988)

Wealth at death £122,494: probate, 22 June 1988, *CGPLA Eng. & Wales*

Sotheby family (*per.* **1778–1861**), auctioneers and book collectors, came to prominence in the book trade in the mid-eighteenth century with **John Sotheby** (1740–1807). The Sothebys stemmed from Pocklington in Yorkshire, where a nineteenth-century wall plaque in the local church of All Saints details the family members. A bookish interest can be traced back to James Sotheby (1682–1742), a keen collector of manuscripts and incunabula, and to William Sotheby (1757–1833), a poet and author. Three generations of the Sotheby family were to be associated with the celebrated auction house which was subsequently established; two centuries later the firm still bore their name.

The family's involvement in auctioneering came about through the marriage of John Sotheby (1703–1775) to Anne, sister of Samuel Baker (1711–1778), a young bookseller. Baker began in business on his own in 1733 and started holding book auctions in 1744. Even sixty years after they had been introduced into England from the Netherlands, auctions were still a relatively unusual method of selling books. Although Baker eventually faced strong competition in London, his firm flourished. In 1767 he took George Leigh (1742–1816) into partnership. Baker died in 1778; Leigh continued as a partner in the firm until his own death in 1816.

Baker, whose own marriage was childless, left a share of the business to his nephew, John Sotheby (1740–1807), the only child of his sister and John Sotheby. Born in 1740, the younger John Sotheby married Elizabeth Cotton (daughter of Thomas Cotton and Mary Barnett) on 6 September 1770 at St George's, Bloomsbury. He joined his uncle's auction house at the age of thirty-eight on the latter's death. A serious but competent administrator, he worked very harmoniously with George Leigh: in fact they issued a fixed-price catalogue under the names Leigh and Sotheby as early as 23 July 1778.

In the last two decades of the eighteenth century under the joint management of Leigh and John Sotheby, the firm's sale catalogues became noticeably more elegant and the detail of the cataloguing improved greatly. The frequency of sales went up too and prices, particularly for manuscript material and prints, rose. By the end of the century the firm needed assistance to deal with the increased workload. In the summer of 1800 it arrived in the form of John Sotheby's son, **Samuel Sotheby** (1771–1842). He was the eldest of nine children and was born at Woodford in Essex on 14 July 1771. Baker had been his godfather. The firm now changed its style to Leigh, Sotheby & Son. After his uncle's death in 1778 John, who had lived in Charlotte Street, Bloomsbury, inherited Baker's house in Chigwell and moved there.

For some reason, never fully explained, a serious altercation occurred between the two senior partners in 1804, as a consequence of which George Leigh and young Sam took themselves off to new premises at 145 Strand. John Sotheby remained in the firm's original premises in York Street, Covent Garden; he held two more sales there, then closed the business and retired. He sold his library through another auctioneer and died four years later on 11 November 1807. He was buried in St Paul's churchyard, Covent Garden.

Samuel Sotheby married Harriet Barton on 13 October 1803, and they lived in Hampstead. Harriet gave birth to two sons and two daughters before she died on 7 July 1808. Nine years later, on 12 May 1818 at Cheltenham, Sotheby married again. His second wife was Laura Smith, daughter of Christmas Smith of Bideford, Devon, and Oporto, Portugal. Although she had two children, both died in infancy and she herself died on 30 April 1827.

Continuing growth forced the firm to move again to 3 Waterloo Bridge Street (later renamed 13 Wellington Street). It was now selling not only libraries, but also increasing numbers of prints, coins, drawings, watercolours, even paintings, as well as other forms of the decorative arts. Soon after George Leigh's death, Samuel Sotheby took into the business his second son, **Samuel Leigh Sotheby** (1805–1861), who was born on 31 August 1805 in Hampstead; George Leigh had been his godfather. S. L. Sotheby married in 1842 or 1843 his first cousin, Julia Emma Pitcher (1818–1898), youngest of the six children of Henry Jones Pitcher (1779–1849) of Northfleet, Kent, a book dealer, and Anne Sotheby.

Samuel Leigh had a keen analytical mind and soon proved to be an adept partner in the business. It was a happy partnership, for father and son shared many interests, and indeed they became virtually fused into a single personality in the public mind. One of their strongest interests was the study of early printing and typography. They were in a wonderful position to appreciate it, for a constant stream of relevant raw material passed through their rooms and had to be scrutinized very carefully before being catalogued.

In the troubled economic circumstances after the Napoleonic wars the firm ran into difficulties. According to a notice that appeared in *The Times* on 25 November 1825, Samuel Sotheby of Wellington Street, Strand, auctioneer, was declared insolvent, and this was followed on 5 December with the dates of the proceedings in the bankruptcy court. It was presumably for this reason that Samuel Leigh began to take a more prominent role; Samuel Sotheby retired from the business, and in 1828 the firm sold its own entire run of bound and annotated copies of its sale catalogues down to that year. Over 700 of these sales—which included many of the most important libraries in the land—had taken place since Samuel Sotheby had begun to work in the auction house. Perhaps the most notable catalogue produced by him was that of the library of the first marquess of Lansdowne (*d.* 1805), who had been a passionate collector of state papers and owned 120 folio volumes of the Burleigh papers. The catalogue was in two volumes, the second running to 444 closely set pages. It aroused so much interest that the British Museum stepped in and bought the collection in its entirety for £4925, granted for this purpose by parliament, and thus no auction ever took place.

Despite his effective retirement, Samuel Sotheby was declared bankrupt a second time, and the 1836 insolvency may have been the cause of the anonymous sale of his huge library on 9 February 1837. Samuel Sotheby died at Cleves Lodge, Chelsea, on 6 January 1842. He was buried alongside Samuel Baker in St Paul's churchyard. The *Gentleman's Magazine* was clearly aware of these events when its obituarist wrote:

> the character of the late Mr Sotheby was strictly exemplary in all the relations of private life; and though not so happy as he deserved in realising his fortune in a very arduous profession he retired from it with the good wishes and regret of very many who had long known and highly respected him. (*GM*, 17, 1842, 444)

In 1837 Samuel Leigh had changed the firm's title to S. L. Sotheby. Although he now faced the world alone, after nearly a hundred years in existence the firm had achieved an enviable reputation. During the following sixty years it consolidated its standing as the premier auctioneer of antiquarian books. For much of that time Sotheby had the able assistance of John Wilkinson (1803–1895), who had originally joined the firm in 1821 as an accountant but became a brilliant auctioneer, and later its sole manager. He retired in 1885.

Because he was so familiar with their contents, Samuel Leigh completed and published a number of books on which his father had already spent years of research, including *The Typography of the Fifteenth Century* (1845). The principal bibliographical work begun by Samuel and completed by Samuel Leigh (after sixteen years' further labour) was *Principia typographica* (3 vols., 1858). This concerned the early forms of book printing, such as block books, but both father and son had also been fascinated by the watermarks used on paper in the early days of printing and devoted much time to their collection and study. This topic was another important part of the book. There was also collaboration with William Young Ottley, a family friend, and Ottley's son over the eventual publication of each family's own book on this subject.

In 1835 Samuel Leigh's own curiosity was much excited when the firm received from Frankfurt the 5000 volumes of the library of Dr Georg F. B. Kloss (1787–1854), mostly printed before 1536. Many of these volumes contained marginal annotations which Sotheby thought to be in the hand of Philip Melanchthon, the friend of Martin Luther. His deductions (now not regarded as correct) were published in volume form in 1840 under the title *Unpublished Documents*, but they continued to occupy him for many years.

In a different vein, Sotheby produced *Ramblings in the Elucidation of the Autograph of Milton* (1861), and for more than thirty years he was at work on an unpublished 'Bibliographical account of the English poets to the period of Restoration'. His widow, Julia Emma, endeavoured to complete the work, but never did so, and the manuscript was eventually sold to Chetham's Library in Manchester, where it remains.

Samuel Leigh was also something of a collector. In 1859 he staged an exhibition on the firm's premises of his 'cabinet pictures'. They were mostly the work of a wide range of English artists, including Richard Parkes Bonington, George Cattermole, William Collins, John Sell Cotman, John Constable (*A View of Windsor Castle*), Richard Dadd, William Etty, and A. V. Copley Fielding, many of them given by relatives of the artists. On other occasions he bought them at auction, 'paying more than others'. An informative catalogue survives. He also took a great interest in the management of the Crystal Palace, which had been re-erected near his home, Woodlands, in Norwood.

Samuel Leigh died suddenly and quite unexpectedly on 19 June 1861. He was subject to fainting fits, and during a ramble near Buckfastleigh Abbey he appears to have fallen into the River Dart and drowned. His library, including all his Melanchthon papers, was sold at Wellington Street on 8 February 1862. He was a man of enormous and diverse enthusiasms who had changed the character of the firm's establishment in Wellington Street into an altogether more interesting and wide-ranging business, where scholarship and, above all, accuracy were regarded as of primary importance. In John Wilkinson he was fortunate to have a partner whose solid but intelligent objectivity tempered his own idiosyncrasies and who was also able to consolidate, profitably, the many innovations that the last of the Sothebys had brought about.

The very different characters of the three generations of the Sotheby family set the seal on the business that survives to this day. They established the essential methodology of successful auctioneering, creating and consolidating sound administration, scholarship, and precision in cataloguing. This was particularly true of Samuel Leigh, whose questing mind gave the firm a new impetus on which his successors were able to build.

FRANK HERRMANN

Sources F. Herrmann, *Sotheby's: portrait of an auction house* (1980) • private information (2004) [C. S. Pitcher, Sotheby family archive] • A. Weeden, 'The Sotheby family', DLitB [forthcoming] • *DNB* • *GM*, 2nd ser., 17 (1842), 442–4 • *GM*, 3rd ser., 11 (1861), 446–7
Archives BL, Add. MSS 34572–34581 • CUL, material on Sothebys • priv. coll., family archive
Likenesses portrait (John Sotheby), repro. in F. Herrmann, *Sotheby's: portrait of an auction house* (1980) • portrait (Samuel Leigh Sotheby), repro. in F. Herrmann, *Sotheby's: portrait of an auction house* (1980)
Wealth at death under £14,000—Samuel Leigh Sotheby: probate, 30 July 1861, *CGPLA Eng. & Wales*

Sotheby, Charles (1782/3–1854). *See under* Sotheby, William (1757–1833).

Sotheby, Sir Edward Southwell (1813–1902), naval officer, born at Clifton, Bristol, on 14 May 1813, was the second son of Admiral Thomas Sotheby (1759–1831) and his second wife, Lady Mary Anne (*d.* 1830), fourth daughter of Joseph Deane Bourke, third earl of Mayo and archbishop of Tuam. William Sotheby (1757–1833) was his uncle. After attending the Royal Naval College, Portsmouth, Edward went to sea in 1828. He passed his examination in 1832, was promoted lieutenant on 3 October 1835, and in December was appointed to the *Caledonia* (120 guns), flagship in the Mediterranean. In April 1837 he joined the corvette *Dido* as first lieutenant, and in her served during the war on the coast of Syria in 1840, for which he was, on 30 October 1841, promoted commander. In June 1846 he was appointed to command the sloop *Racehorse*, in which he took part in the later operations of the New Zealand War of 1846–7, and served in China until 1848. He commissioned the *Sealark* for the west coast of Africa in June 1850, and cruised to suppress the slave trade. On 6 September 1852 he was promoted captain, and in December 1855 was appointed to the corvette *Pearl*, which he commanded on the East Indies and China station until 1858.

In July 1857 the *Pearl*, with the frigate *Shannon* (Captain William Peel), was sent from Hong Kong to Calcutta on the receipt of news of the outbreak of the Indian mutiny. While on passage, the *Pearl* rescued the crew of the wrecked transport *Transit*. Sotheby himself took command of the *Pearl*'s brigade; they were thirteen times mentioned in dispatches relating to the operations in Oudh, and received the thanks of both houses of parliament and of the governor-general of India. Sotheby was made a CB and served as an extra aide-de-camp to the queen (1858–67).

In 1860 Sotheby commissioned the battleship *Conqueror*, serving in the channel until late 1861, when he was dispatched with reinforcements to the West Indies. The ship was wrecked on Rum Cay, in the Bahamas, on 29 December 1861, without loss of life, the master having failed to allow for the local currents. At the court martial Sotheby argued that he was not responsible for the navigation of the ship. The court accepted this, admonishing the master. Admiral Milne, the commander-in-chief, disagreed, and wrote to the Admiralty, attributing the loss to carelessness, and blamed Sotheby for failing to supervise the master. The Admiralty concurred, and on 20 March 1862 altered the regulations to place the final responsibility for a ship's safety on the captain. Thereafter Sotheby had no further seagoing commands. In 1863 he commanded the Portland coastguard division, after which he was not again actively employed. He married, on 24 June 1864, Jane Lucy Elizabeth, daughter of Henry John Adeane, of Babraham, Cambridgeshire, and granddaughter of John Thomas, first Baron Stanley of Alderley. They had three sons, and she survived her husband.

Sotheby reached flag rank on 1 September 1867, and retired on 1 April 1870. He was promoted vice-admiral on the retired list on 25 August 1873, was made a KCB in 1875, and became admiral on 15 June 1879. After leaving the sea Sotheby devoted himself to philanthropic work; in 1886 he was a commissioner for investigating and reporting on the condition of the blind, and was for many years chairman of the Blind Institute in Tottenham Court Road, London. Sotheby died at his residence, 26 Green Street, London, on 6 January 1902, and was buried at Ecton, Northamptonshire. He was a brave officer, but better suited to irregular warfare than to the discipline of peacetime service.

L. G. C. LAUGHTON, *rev.* ANDREW LAMBERT

Sources W. B. Rowbotham, ed., *The naval brigades in the Indian mutiny, 1857–58*, Navy RS, 87 (1947) • R. A. Courtemanche, *No need of glory: the British navy in American waters, 1860–1864* (1977) • M. Lewis, *The navy in transition, 1814–1864: a social history* (1965) • C. I. Hamilton, *Anglo-French naval rivalry, 1840–1870* (1993) • Burke, *Peerage* (1879) • O'Byrne, *Naval biog. dict.* • *CGPLA Eng. & Wales* (1902) • *The Times* (8 Jan 1902)
Archives Royal Naval Museum, Portsmouth | NL Scot., corresp. with Charles Graham
Wealth at death £15,655 0s. 4d.: probate, 14 Feb 1902, *CGPLA Eng. & Wales*

Sotheby, John (1740–1807). *See under* Sotheby family (*per.* 1778–1861).

Sotheby, Lionel Frederick Southwell (1895–1915), army officer, was born at Burnham, Buckinghamshire, on 16 August 1895, the elder son of William Edward Southwell Sotheby (*b.* 1865), electrical engineer, and his first wife, Margaret (*d.* 1922), eldest daughter of William Williams of Parciau, Anglesey. The family were landed gentry with a tradition of military and naval service. Sotheby's paternal grandfather, Admiral Sir Edward Southwell *Sotheby

(1813–1902), commanded the *Pearl*'s naval brigade in the Indian mutiny. Sotheby's paternal uncle, Lieutenant-Colonel Herbert George Sotheby (*b.* 1871) of Ecton, Northampton, was a regular army officer in the Argyll and Sutherland Highlanders and served in the Second South African War and the First World War. At the time of Sotheby's birth his parents lived at Cippenham House, Burnham, Buckinghamshire. In 1896 they moved to Sussex Lodge, Slough, and later to Menaifron, Dwyran, Llanfair Pwllgwyngyll, Anglesey, where they were in 1914.

Sotheby was educated at Langley and, like his father, at Eton College (1909 to December 1913). He was devoted to Eton—he later concluded his will with 'Floreat Etona'—but, though he played football for his house and won his house colours, he was undistinguished there. According to the *Eton College Chronicle* obituary he played and rowed hard and worked conscientiously, but had not 'more than average brains' (*Eton College Chronicle*, 1915, 900). He served in the Officers' Training Corps. Intending a business career from 10 January to 19 July 1914 he was in Germany, learning German at the Institute Tilly, Berlin. He admired German organization and zeal. Back in London he attended Brooks's, Boodle's, and the Carlton.

Following the outbreak of war, in August 1914 Sotheby was commissioned second lieutenant in the 4th battalion of his uncle's regiment, the Argyll and Sutherland Highlanders. After training with them in England, on 2 January 1915 he sailed to France. There he was attached to the 1st battalion, the Black Watch, in 1st division, 1st corps. A Seaforth officer he met said of the Black Watch that 'it was as good as signing your death warrant to join them, as they were practically in all the worst fighting' (Richter, 5). On 28 February he went to the front-line trenches at Festubert and Artois, and he fought in the battles of Neuve Chapelle (March) and Aubers Ridge (May). Brave, resilient, and cheerful, he endured rain, lice, discomfort, illness, and narrow escapes from death. He admired the 'Kitchener's army' men he saw, but believed conscription essential to defeat Germany. He knew he might well be killed. He wrote in March 1915 that a platoon commander 'has to encourage his men and expose himself more than anyone. For an attack he has to be in the front and first in everything' (Richter, 83). On 4 June, following an old Etonian dinner at Béthune, he wrote a farewell letter to be opened after his death, stating:

> To die for one's school is an honour … To die for one's country is an honour. But to die for right and fidelity is a greater honour than these … be thankful that such an opportunity was given to me … Floreat Etona. (Richter, 142)

Still a second lieutenant—in a 'Kitchener' battalion he probably would have been promoted—Sotheby in late July was attached to the 2nd battalion, the Black Watch, in the Bareilly brigade, Meerut division. On 25 September 1915 his brigade attacked at Aubers Ridge, Artois, an action subsidiary to the battle of Loos. They advanced through British chlorine gas, released from cylinders but not blown away by the wind as intended—the first British use of chemical warfare—with Sotheby's platoon in the first line, and captured the German first and second lines, then the Germans counter-attacked. The battalion suffered heavy casualties, among them Lionel Sotheby, aged twenty: according to his battalion commander he was wounded, then killed by a grenade. His body was never recovered. The public schools and ancient universities, from which so many young officers came, suffered disproportionate losses: Sotheby was among 1131 Etonians killed in the war. His family preserved his diaries and letters, and in 1997 an edition of them was published as *Lionel Sotheby's Great War*. ROGER T. STEARN

Sources *Lionel Sotheby's Great War: diaries and letters from the western front*, ed. D. C. Richter (1997) • *Eton College Chronicle* (21 Oct 1915) • *Eton College Chronicle* (2 Oct 1912) • *The Eton register*, 7 (privately printed, Eton, 1922) • Burke, *Gen. GB* (1937) • J. M. Winter, *The Great War and the British people* (1985) • H. Cecil and P. H. Liddle, *Facing Armageddon: the First World War experienced* (1996) • I. F. W. Beckett and K. Simpson, eds., *A nation in arms: a social study of the British army in the First World War* (1985) • T. Wilson, *The myriad faces of war: Britain and the Great War, 1914–1918* (1986) • B. Bond, ed., *The First World War and British military history* (1991) • B. Bond, *A victory worse than defeat? British interpretations of the First World War* (1997) • E. M. Spiers, *Chemical warfare* (1986) • P. Parker, *The old lie: the Great War and the public-school ethos* (1987) • W. J. Reader, *At duty's call: a study in obsolete patriotism* (1988) • b. cert.

Archives U. Leeds, Brotherton L., Liddle collection, letters and diaries

Likenesses photograph, *c.*1915, U. Leeds; repro. in *Lionel Sotheby's Great War*, ed. Richter, frontispiece

Sotheby, Samuel (1771–1842). *See under* Sotheby family (*per.* 1778–1861).

Sotheby, Samuel Leigh (1805–1861). *See under* Sotheby family (*per.* 1778–1861).

Sotheby, William (1757–1833), poet and translator, was born in London on 9 November 1757, the eldest son of William Sotheby (*d.* 1766), colonel of the Coldstream Guards, and his wife, Elizabeth (*d.* 1790), daughter of Sir William Sloane, of Stoneham, Hampshire. Sotheby's younger brother Thomas (1759–1831) entered the navy, rose to be an admiral of the white, and was captain of the *Marlborough* when she was wrecked off the Île de Gioua t, France (*GM*, 1831). His father died when Sotheby was eight, and his guardians then became Charles *Yorke (1722–1770), lord chancellor, and his maternal uncle, Hans Sloane (1739–1827). Sotheby succeeded to the estate of Sewardstone, on the borders of Epping Forest, Essex, which had been the property of the family since 1673. He was educated at Harrow School, but at the age of seventeen purchased a commission as ensign in the 10th dragoons and went to study at the military academy of Angers. He was subsequently stationed with his regiment at Edinburgh, where he made the acquaintance of the young Walter Scott. On 17 July 1780 he increased his financial resources by marrying Mary (1759–1834), youngest daughter of Ambrose Isted of Ecton, Northamptonshire, and his wife, Anne, sister and coheir of Sir Charles Buck, of Hamby Grange, Lincolnshire. They had five sons, William, Charles, George, Hans, and Frederick, and two daughters, Maria and Harriet Louisa. Sotheby then retired from the army; purchasing Bevis Mount, near Southampton, he

William Sotheby (1757–1833), by Sir Thomas Lawrence, *c.*1807

began to devote himself to literature, and in particular to a close study of the Latin and Greek classics.

Sotheby's first publication was a volume of *Poems* (1790), which comprised an account of a walking tour which he and his brother Thomas had made through north and south Wales in 1788, and a number of sonnets and odes with a heroic epistle to a friend, on physiognomy. The volume was reprinted in 1794, with thirteen engravings by J. Smith.

Meanwhile, in 1791 Sotheby moved to London, and began to divide his time between the City and his property at Sewardstone, where he occupied Fair Mead Lodge. Like previous owners of Sewardstone, he acted as a master keeper of the adjoining Epping forest.

Sotheby soon became a prominent figure in London literary circles. He joined the Dilettante Society in 1792, and in 1794 was elected fellow of the Royal Society and of the Society of Antiquaries. He entertained the best-known literary figures of the day, and had a benevolent interest in the struggles of young authors. Scott, Wordsworth, Coleridge, Samuel Rogers, Sir George Beaumont, Mrs Siddons, Joanna Baillie, Maria Edgeworth, Byron, Thomas Moore and Southey were numbered among his guests and intimate associates. Scott, who 'ever retained for him a sincere regard', owed to him on his visits to London 'the personal acquaintance of not a few of their most eminent contemporaries in various departments of literature and art' (Lockhart, 1.452).

Sotheby made extensive corrections to the proofs of *Richard I*, a poem by his friend Sir James Bland Burges, published in 1800, and in 1809 joined another friend, Sir George Beaumont, in encouraging Coleridge to bring out a literary periodical, entitled *The Friend*. In 1812 Sotheby, with Beaumont and Sir Thomas Barnard, received subscriptions for Coleridge's 'Lectures on the drama' at Willis's Rooms.

Sotheby's skill in translation secured for him a wide literary reputation. In 1798, after rapidly acquiring a knowledge of German, he published *Oberon: a Poem*, a translation of Christoph Martin Wieland's *Oberon*, which had already achieved popularity in Europe. Wieland, to whom Sotheby sent a copy of his translation, expressed great satisfaction. A second edition, with illustrations by Fuseli, appeared in 1805. In 1802 Sotheby adapted it as a masque in five acts of blank verse called *Oberon, or, Huon of Bourdeaux*, which he dedicated to George Ellis.

An equally good reception awaited Sotheby's verse translation of Virgil's *Georgics*, which appeared in 1800 with further editions in 1815 and 1830. Jeffrey, in the *Edinburgh Review*, declared it possibly 'the most perfect translation of a classic poet now extant in our language' (*EdinR* 4, 1804, 303). John Wilson (Christopher North) thought it 'stamped' Sotheby 'the best translator in Christendom' (R. S. Mackenzie, ed., *Noctes Ambrosianae*, 5 vols. (1863–6), 3.456–7). It was reprinted in the sumptuous *Georgica Publii Virgilii Maronis hexaglotta* in London, at the translator's expense, in 1827. Besides Sotheby's English version of the *Georgics*, it included a Spanish version by John de Guzman; a German version by J. H. Voss; an Italian version by Francesco Soave; and a French version by James Delille. Despite Sotheby's appeals, however, Scott refused to review it.

Although Byron described Sotheby in his *English Bards and Scotch Reviewers* (1809) as one who wrote poetry with sincerity, Sotheby's large poetic output was not well received. His verse includes *The Battle of the Nile* (1799), an ode dedicated to Lord Spencer, first lord of the Admiralty, whose second son was involved in the battle; *A poetical epistle to Sir George Beaumont, bart., on the encouragement of the British school of painting* (1801); *Saul* (1807), a blank-verse epic written in two parts; and *Constance de Castille* (1810), a poem in ten cantos in imitation of Scott's *Lady of the Lake*.

Sotheby's attempts at writing tragedy also met with little success. His tragedy *Bertram and Matilda* was acted privately at Winchester by himself and his friends some time before 1790. He subsequently published at least six other historical tragedies, all in five acts and in blank verse. Only one of these plays appeared on the stage. *Julian and Agnes, or, The Monks of the Great St Bernard*, was acted on 25 April 1800 at Drury Lane, with Sarah Siddons and John Philip Kemble in the leading roles. At a memorable point in the play Sarah Siddons accidentally struck the head of a dummy infant she was carrying against a doorpost, and both the audience and the actress herself were convulsed with laughter. There was no second performance.

Sotheby's other tragedies were offered to Drury Lane, but were rejected by the actors. In 1816 Byron persuaded the management to accept *Ivan*, but after three or four rehearsals it was withdrawn, as Kean felt unable to make anything of the title-role (Genest, *Eng. stage*, 10.233). Sotheby at once republished the piece as *Ivan, a Tragedy …, Altered and Adapted for Representation* (1816). Byron insisted at the time, in a letter to Samuel Rogers, that Sotheby had been 'capriciously and evilly entreated' (Clayden, 1.239), but afterwards regretted having befriended Sotheby's 'trash' (Clayden, 1.255). With the exception of Byron, Sotheby retained his many literary friendships throughout his life. In 1818 Byron wrote scathingly of Sotheby's 'airs of patronage which [he] affects with young writers, and affected both to me and of me many a good year' (Clayden, 1.255). Others were more tolerant, however. Coleridge spoke on Homer at one of Sotheby's dinner parties in 1828, and Sotheby visited Scott at Abbotsford as late as autumn 1829.

Sotheby, who had been greatly distressed by the death of his eldest son, William, colonel in the guards, on 1 August 1815, went on a long tour of Italy in May 1816 with his family and two friends, Professor Elmsley and Dr Playfair. They returned via Germany at the end of the following year. Sotheby published his impressions of his journey in *Farewell to Italy, and Occasional Poems* (1818), most of which he republished with additions in *Poems* (1825), and in *Italy and other Poems* (1828). On returning to London, Sotheby mainly devoted himself to a verse translation of Homer. *The First Book of the 'Iliad', a Specimen of a New Version of Homer* appeared in 1830, and the whole of the *Iliad* (in heroics) followed in 1831. Christopher North praised the work in five articles in *Blackwood's Magazine*. The *Odyssey* followed in 1834, with a new edition of the *Iliad*, and seventy-five illustrations engraved by Henry Moses from Flaxman's designs. As a translator of Homer, Sotheby, who was much influenced by Pope, was considered by Matthew Arnold to have failed to reproduce Homer's directness of style and diction (Arnold, 10–11).

Sotheby, wrote Byron, 'has imitated everybody, and occasionally surpassed his models.' Although his poems and plays were held in high esteem by his friends, he is chiefly remembered for his translations of Virgil and Wieland, and for his friendships with the distinguished literary figures of his age. Sotheby died at his home in Lower Grosvenor Street, London, on 30 December 1833, and was buried on 6 January 1834 in the family vault in Hackney churchyard, Middlesex. His wife survived him; she died on 14 October 1834. Wordsworth wrote to Rogers of his grief at the death of 'the veteran Sotheby' (Clayden, 2.87).

Of Sotheby's other sons, George (1787–1817) entered the East India Company's service, and was killed at Nagpur during the Third Anglo-Maratha War, on 27 November 1817. Hans, also in the service of the East India Company, died on 27 April 1827; Frederick was a colonel in the Bengal artillery and CB, and died in 1870.

Charles Sotheby (1782/3–1854), William Sotheby's second and eldest surviving son, who succeeded to Sewardstone Manor, entered the Royal Naval Academy in 1795. He was a midshipman at the battle of the Nile in 1798, took part in the operations in Egypt in 1801, and fought against the Turks in 1807. He was appointed to the acting command of the *Pilot* in March 1809, and confirmed in the rank of commander on 8 January 1810, going on to serve on several vessels. On 15 February 1819 he married the Hon. Jane Hamilton (*d.* 1820), third daughter of William, seventh Lord Belhaven and Stenton. Charles Sotheby was appointed to the *Seringapatam* in 1824, and was active in suppressing piracy in the Mediterranean. After the death of his first wife, he later married his cousin Mary Anne, daughter of Admiral Thomas Sotheby, and Lady Mary Anne Sotheby, on 18 November 1830. He attained flag rank on 20 March 1848, and died rear-admiral of the red at his home at 38 Lowndes Square on 26 January 1854. Charles's and his first wife's eldest son, Charles William Hamilton Sotheby (1820–1887), high sheriff of Northamptonshire in 1881, succeeded to the Ecton estates in that year on the death of his cousin, Ambrose Isted, and sold Sewardstone in 1884; his half-brother, Major-General Frederick Edward Sotheby, succeeded to Ecton on his death in 1887.

William Sotheby's grandson, Hans William Sotheby (1827–1874), the son of Hans, was a man of erudition, referred to in Jeaffreson's *Recollections* as 'scholarly, fastidious, chivalric Hans Sotheby' (1.189). He was a fellow of Exeter College, Oxford, from 1851 to 1864, and was a contributor to *Fraser's Magazine* (December 1860 and January 1861), and to the *Quarterly Review* (July 1875).

SIDNEY LEE, *rev.* MELANIE ORD

Sources *N&Q*, 8th ser., 8 (1895), 411 · *GM*, 1st ser., 101/2 (1831) · *GM*, 2nd ser., 42 (1854), 191–2 · *BL cat.* · *EdinR*, 4 (1804), 296–303 · Nichols, *Illustrations*, 8.324–5 · P. W. Clayden, *Rogers and his contemporaries*, 2 vols. (1889), vol. 1, p. 22, 239, 255; vol. 2, p. 87 · J. G. Lockhart, *Memoirs of Sir Walter Scott*, 1 (1914), 452; 5 (1914), 193 · M. Arnold, *On translating Homer* (1896) · J. C. Jeaffreson, *A book of recollections*, 2 vols. (1894), vol. 1, pp. 152, 189 · *Memoirs, journal and correspondence of Thomas Moore*, ed. J. Russell, 2 (1853), 306 · *The letters of Charles Lamb*, ed. A. Ainger, 1 (1888), 255 · O'Byrne, *Naval biog. dict.* · d. cert. [Charles Sotheby]

Archives BM · Ecton, Northamptonshire | BL, letters to Royal Literary Fund, Loan 96 · Bodl. Oxf., letters to Richard Heber

Likenesses T. Lawrence, chalk drawing, *c.*1807, NPG [*see illus.*] · T. Lawrence, crayon drawing, 1814, Ecton, Northamptonshire · T. Lawrence, oils, Ecton, Northamptonshire · F. C. Lewis, engraving (after T. Lawrence)

Sothel, Seth (*d.* **1693/4**), colonial governor, was born in England; his parents' identity is unknown. By 1675, however, he had sufficient status for the Carolina proprietors to identify him as 'a person of considerable estate here in England' (Cheves, 468–9) who intended to acquire 12,000 acres in Carolina, on which he would establish settlers from England. That plan never came to fruition, but Sothel bought the earl of Clarendon's share of the proprietorship in 1677, and because of the political chaos in the Albemarle settlement (North Carolina), which culminated in 'Culpepper's rebellion', he agreed to serve as governor of the area. On the voyage out north African pirates captured and held him for ransom at Algiers, where he spent time at hard labour before being freed two years later. Characteristically, he failed to recompense those who had posted bond for him until forced to do so by legal action.

In 1682 Sothel arrived at Albemarle, where he governed relatively well at first. He also received land grants for two seignories totalling 24,000 acres, participated in the American Indian trade, and in the second half of 1686 married a wealthy widow, Anna Blount, *née* Willix. The marriage remained childless but, behaving as if he had a large family to support, Sothel soon became extraordinarily avaricious. At least, according to the testimony of his enemies, he preyed upon his political opponents and the powerless, imprisoning them and seizing their property. In 1689 Thomas Pollack, whom he had jailed, led an armed force that overthrew and arrested Sothel. The local assembly then tried and sentenced him to a year's banishment and permanent disbarment from political office in the colony. A Virginian, Philip Ludwell, became governor.

Sothel went to Charles Town in South Carolina, arriving in 1690 while this settlement was also in the middle of a political crisis. Aligning himself with factional opponents of Governor James Colleton, he maintained that the fundamental constitutions of Carolina gave him the right as a proprietor to claim the governorship. Although the legal status of this document was debatable, Sothel's support was strong enough that the threat of an armed confrontation enabled him to prevail in a bloodless coup. He then called a local parliament which passed several constructive acts. It also, however, banished Colleton and barred him, as well as some of his supporters, from future public office. Simultaneously Sothel resumed his avid and questionable pursuit of wealth. Ordering the survey of 24,000 acres for himself was probably legitimate; apparent preparations for acquiring a monopoly of the West Indian trade were more doubtful; and trafficking with pirates was clearly prohibited. News of these actions prompted the proprietors to disallow all acts passed by Sothel's parliament and in November 1691 remove him from office. Once again, they turned to Philip Ludwell, who on 13 May 1692 officially informed Sothel that he was out. Sothel remained in the area for about a year, futilely claiming the office, but by November 1693 he was back in Albemarle. At some time before 3 February 1694, when his will was proved, he died, apparently in Virginia, where he was presumably buried. Most of his property went to his wife, Anna, but a bequest to his father-in-law, Edward Foster of Albemarle county, indicates that he had been previously married. Final settlement of his extensive and complex estate required prolonged litigation. After his death his widow married John Lear but she died at some time before May 1695.

Sothel's political career produced significant constitutional changes in Carolina. Partly because his claims to the governorship at Charles Town rested on the fundamental constitutions, the proprietors in 1691 suspended it and restructured the government by reducing membership in the council and permitting the lower house to meet separately. These steps influenced the configuration of local government for the rest of the colonial period and laid the foundation for the rise to power of the assembly.

ROBERT M. WEIR

Sources M. E. E. Parker, 'Sothel, Seth', *Dictionary of North Carolina biography*, ed. W. S. Powell (1979–96) • C. H. Lesser, *South Carolina begins: the records of a proprietary colony, 1663–1721* (1995) • L. S. Butler, 'Sothel, Seth', *ANB* • W. L. Saunders and W. Clark, eds., *The colonial records of North Carolina*, 30 vols. (1886–1907), vols. 1–2 • M. E. E. Parker and others, eds., *North Carolina higher-court records*, 1: *1670–1696* (1968) • M. E. E. Parker, ed., *North Carolina higher-court records, 1697–1701* (1971) • will, PRO, PROB 11/436, sig. 39 • L. S. Butler, 'The governors of Albemarle county, 1663–1689', *North Carolina Historical Review*, 46 (1969), 281–99 • *CSP col.*, vols. 10, 12 • A. S. Salley jun., ed., *Commissions and instructions from the lords proprietors of Carolina to public officials of South Carolina, 1685–1715* (1916) • L. Cheves, ed., *The Shaftesbury papers and other records relating to Carolina* (1897) • M. E. Sirmans, *Colonial South Carolina: a political history, 1663–1763* (Chapel Hill, NC, 1966)

Wealth at death wealthy: will, PRO, PROB 11/436, sig. 39

Sothern, Edward Askew (1826–1881), actor, born in Liverpool on 1 April 1826, made his mark playing eccentric comic roles on the British and American stage. The son of a collier, he initially studied for a career in medicine, but claimed to have been disgusted by the dissection work at St Bartholomew's Hospital in London, where he attended operations. In the late 1840s he worked as a clerk in a Liverpool shipping office. However, his personality seemed better suited to the stage, and he soon tried his hand as an amateur at the Theatre Royal, Jersey, in 1848, before moving on to Guernsey, under the stage name of Douglas Stewart. About this time he married Fannie (Frances Emily) Stewart (*d.* 1882), the daughter of an Irish merchant. The couple had four children—Lytton Edward [*see below*], Edward Hugh [*see below*], George Evelyn Augustus T., and Eva Mary—all of whom appeared on the stage.

Sothern worked in theatres at Portsmouth, Wolverhampton, and Birmingham before heading to Boston, Massachusetts, where he was employed by John Lacy at the National Theatre. He first appeared there as Dr Pangloss in *The Heir-at-Law*—to miserable reviews. Struggling to establish himself in the United States, he worked at the Howard Athenaeum in Boston and Barnum's Museum in New York. It was in Boston that he met a lifelong friend, the actress Mrs R. H. Vincent. His break finally came when he took on the unlikely role of Armand in *Camille* opposite Mathilde Heron at Wallack's in New York. Sothern was tall and slender, with blue eyes and wavy brown hair, but despite his good appearance he was not a natural for romantic roles. According to Clement Scott he was 'as handsome a man as ever stood on the stage'; however, Scott continued, 'he had not the voice, the touch, the tone or the persuasiveness requisite for a Romeo, a Ruy Blas, or a Lagardière' (Scott, 1.392). Despite this early success as Armand, Sothern did not make a stage career as a romantic hero, but as a result he was given a part in Tom Taylor's *Our American Cousin*, staged at Laura Keene's Theatre in New York in October 1858.

Taylor's farce, now best known as the play President Lincoln was watching when he was assassinated in Ford's Theatre in Washington, DC, provided Sothern with the role that would define him as an actor. The play follows the adventures of an American, Asa Trenchard (first played by the American actor Joseph Jefferson), when he goes to England to claim the family estate. Lord Dundreary was not intended to be a major part in the play—Sothern claimed that it was originally a scant forty-seven lines—but Sothern created a notable image of an eccentric, weak-minded fop, featuring an eye-glass, droopy side-whiskers that became known as 'Dundrearys', a lisp, elaborate mannerisms, and verbal

Edward Askew Sothern (1826–1881), by Bassano [as Lord Dundreary in *Our American Cousin* by Tom Taylor]

nonsense. Lord Dundreary's nonsensical references to the life and wisdom of his 'bwother' Sam delighted audiences. The character launched a craze on both sides of the Atlantic (although it completely puzzled the French, who disdained the 1867 Paris production), and the style of walking, dressing, and speaking displayed by Sothern's Dundreary was much imitated and lampooned. In the USA, in particular, Dundreary became the type of the 'silly ass Englishman' of title or rank.

Our American Cousin was given its première at Laura Keene's Theatre on 15 October 1858 and ran for 150 performances; when the play opened in London, at the Haymarket, in 1861, Sothern played the role of Dundreary 196 times. His appearance in this play was also his London début. The London critics adored his Dundreary: 'his embodiment was a veritable creation, well-proportioned, consistent, finished to the nails' (Towse, 29); 'it is certainly the *funniest* thing in the world … a vile caricature of a vain nobleman, intensely ignorant, and extremely indolent' (*The Athenaeum*, 16 Nov 1861).

In the minds of audiences in the United States and England, Sothern would eternally be associated with Dundreary: 'Dundreary was Sothern, and Sothern Dundreary afterward, and the identity could never be destroyed' (Reignolds-Winslow, 85). The Dundreary craze did not die quickly, and was to have various dramatic resuscitations in such works as John Oxenford's *Brother Sam* and H. J. Byron's *Dundreary Married and Done For*. But Sothern was ready to move on to new roles. His next major part was the title role in T. W. Robertson's *David Garrick* (Haymarket, 1864); this was a more sentimental, pathetic character, a break from the rather grotesque caricature of Dundreary. 'The critics cut me up root and branch', said Sothern. But the show was a success anyway. The review in *The Times* noted that the role 'is the first that has really tested Mr Sothern's powers beyond the Dundreary sphere' (6 May 1864); Sothern's performance in the 'drunk scene' of the second act was in fact admired by the critic of *The Times*, who praised 'the most extravagant form of drunkenness … perpetually brought into contact with the real agony of mind which is now on the point of casting aside the mask of debauchery'. Sothern would later claim in *The Era* to have written some of the best scenes in *David Garrick*—and in Robertson's *Home*—much to Robertson's disgust. Lester Wallack backed up Sothern in the dispute, but Sothern's contribution to the plays remains unclear.

Sothern's manic energy had social as well as professional outlets; he was well known as a club man, sportsman, and bon vivant, as often in the press for his hunting activities, jokes, magic tricks, and conversation as for his work on stage. F. G. De Fontaine termed him 'a Prince of Fellows'. He was also a notorious prankster, as befits someone born on 1 April. In London he was known as part of a lively theatrical circle including J. L. Toole, J. B. Buckstone, T. W. Robertson, and H. J. Byron. The group apparently had an endless taste for low jokes and stunts, such as staging mock disputes on public omnibuses, putting fake advertisements in newspapers, paying street urchins to harass passers-by in the streets, and the like. On one occasion Sothern entered an ironmonger's establishment, accompanied by fellow prankster Mrs Vincent, and persistently demanded a copy of the second edition of Macaulay's *History of England*, reducing a clerk to fits. On another occasion Sothern and Toole panicked a waiter by tossing the silver out of a window and hiding under the table; when the waiter, finding the room empty and the silver gone, ran to report the theft, Toole and Sothern restored the settings and resumed their places at table, languidly discussing their meal.

In the 1860s and 1870s Sothern appeared in London and the provinces in such plays as Westland Marston's *A Hero of Romance* and T. W. Robertson's *Home*; he toured the USA in the mid-1870s. His next great role was as the comically 'tragic' actor Fitzaltamont in Byron's *The Crushed Tragedian* (1878). Of Fitzaltamont, Sothern said, 'I have simply boiled down all the old-school tragedians as I boiled down all the fops I met before I played Dundreary' (Pemberton, 89). If Sothern was not ultimately suited for tragic roles, he could none the less mock them expertly: *The Era* of 19 May 1878 referred admiringly to 'the sepulchral tones, the glaring eyeballs, the long hair, the wonderful "stage walk", the melodramatic attitudes'. Despite this favourable report, the production was not a success in London, and the Haymarket soon replaced it with another of Byron's plays, *The Hornet's Nest*, in which Sothern also appeared. In New York, however, *The Crushed Tragedian* was very warmly received. The Philadelphia *Inquirer* praised the production:

> With what elaboration of detail does the actor embody his conception! There is not a gesture, not an intonation, not a movement, but seems to illustrate the character portrayed. He strides across the stage and it is as though he were wading through a sea of gore; he mutters to himself 'Ha! ha!' and you know that he is cursing fate with a bitterness loud and deep. … always and in all things poor Altamont is exquisitely, indescribably ludicrous. (Pemberton, 91–2)

Despite these successes in other roles, Sothern continued regularly to play Dundreary in *Our American Cousin* and its offshoots until his death, at his home, 1 Vere Street, Cavendish Square, London, of a lung inflammation on 20 January 1881. He was buried in Southampton cemetery on 25 January. According to his biographer T. Edgar Pemberton, one role he regretted not having played was that of Cheviot in W. S. Gilbert's *Engaged* (1877).

Of Sothern's children, Eva had a brief career, as did George (*b.* 1870)—who was known professionally as Sam Sothern. He was closely associated with his father's roles (as his choice of stage name indicates), although he later had some success in secondary parts in Henry Arthur Jones's *The Case of Rebellious Susan* (1894) and *The Liars* (1897). **Lytton Edward Sothern** (1851–1887), born on 27 June 1851, enjoyed his first prominent appearance on the stage in the role of Captain Vernon in a production of *Our American Cousin* at Drury Lane in 1872; later that year he made a mark in the USA playing the role of Bertie in H. J. Byron's *Home* at the Walnut Street Theatre in Philadelphia. With his dark good looks (Lytton was thought the handsomest of the Sothern men), he was considered a promising comedian. But he worked in his father's shadow and often played roles made famous by the elder Sothern; he took on the parts of Dundreary, Brother Sam, and Garrick during tours of Australia (beginning in 1878) and the United States (in 1883). Of his Dundreary, one critic wrote that 'the imitation was exact enough, yet an indescribable "something" was wanting to make the part what it was in the elder Sothern's hands' (*The Dramatic Calendar*, 27 June 1881). He did, however, show some promise in other comic roles, such as Cecil Leighton in G. R. Sims's *Crutch and Toothpick* (Royalty, 1879) and as Arthur Spoonbill in Byron's *Fourteen Days* (Criterion, 1882). He died at his home, St James's Chambers, Duke Street, London, on 11 March 1887 of peritonitis, and was buried on 19 March in Brompton cemetery.

It was **Edward Hugh Sothern** (1859–1933), born in New Orleans on 12 June 1859—his father called him a 'handsome little creole'—who made his mark independently of his father. He was educated in England and made his stage début in an American production of *Brother Sam* in a minor role; his father, in a letter to Lucy Derby Fuller in October 1879, wrote: 'Eddy, my second son, is at the Boston Museum, playing very small parts by my advice. … I wish him to commence at the bottom of the ladder' (E. H. Sothern, 32). He was somewhat shorter than his father and rather thin lipped, but dark haired and good-looking. After touring in the USA and England, he was engaged by Daniel Frohman at his Lyceum Theatre in New York, and for the remainder of his career he was associated with the New York theatre, though he toured occasionally in Britain. He began to make his mark in heroic, romantic roles such as that of Prince Rudolph in *The Prisoner of Zenda* (1895), but he also showed a flair for romantic comedy, most notably as the lovesick auctioneer in *The Highest Bidder* (1887). William Winter remained convinced that 'the realm in which he has most naturally, and therefore most freely, moved, is that in which light comedy is commingled with romance' (W. Winter, *Vagrant Memories*, 1915, 432). It was during this period, in 1896, that Sothern met and married his first wife, the actress Virginia Harned (1872–1946).

In the early twentieth century Sothern became a highly popular actor in Shakespearian tragedies, foremost among them *Hamlet* (1900). It was as a Shakespearian actor that he was associated with the actress Julia Marlowe (1866–1950), and beginning in 1904 the two regularly performed in Shakespeare's plays, including the comedies—critics considered Benedick and Malvolio to be among Sothern's best roles. But some reviewers were unimpressed by his appearances in Shakespeare. Winter lamented 'his complete lack of weirdness' in playing Hamlet (W. Winter, *Shakespeare on the Stage*, 1911, 392); J. Ranken Towse asserted that 'anxiety over "points" betrayed him occasionally into violence of speech and gesture and painfully abrupt transitions of mood' (Towse, 393). Sothern and Marlowe were married in 1911 after his first marriage ended in divorce. The two performed in revivals of their favourite plays at the Shubert and Century theatres in 1919 and 1921, but Marlowe's health was failing. During this time Sothern also appeared in early films, including *The Chattel* (1916) and *The Man of Mystery* (1917). After repeatedly threatening to retire and move to England, he finally did so in 1927. He died of pneumonia in New York on 28 October 1933. HEIDI J. HOLDER

Sources T. E. Pemberton, *A memoir of Edward Askew Sothern*, new edn (1890) · E. A. Sothern, *Birds of a feather flock together, or, Talk with Sothern*, ed. F. G. De Fontaine (1878) · C. Reignolds-Winslow, *Yesterdays with actors* (1887) · J. W. Marston, *Our recent actors*, 2 vols. (1888) · E. H. Sothern, *A melancholy tale of 'me'* (1916) · C. E. Pascoe, ed., *The dramatic list*, 2nd edn (1880) · J. R. Towse, *Sixty years of theatre* (1916) · H. G. Fisk, *The New York Mirror annual and directory of the theatrical profession for 1888* (1888) · C. Scott, *The drama of yesterday and today*, 2 vols. (1899) · T. A. Brown, *History of the American stage* (1870) · L. Hutton, *Plays and players* (1891) · *The Times* (22 Jan 1881) · *New York Tribune* (22 Jan 1881) · *CGPLA Eng. & Wales* (1887) [Lytton Edward Sothern] · *The Times* (25 Jan 1881)

Archives Col. U., Edward H. Sothern and Julia Marlowe collection · Harvard TC · NYPL, Billy Rose theatre collection · Players' Club, New York, Hampden-Booth Library

Likenesses G. E. Tuson, oils, 1862, Garr. Club · D. H. Friston, woodcut, 1879 (as David Garrick), Harvard TC · Bassano, photograph, NPG [*see illus.*] · C. R., oils over a photograph (as Lord Dundreary), Garr. Club · Elliott & Fry, cartes-de-visite, NPG · J. Fleming, woodcut (as Lord Dundreary), Harvard TC · M. Morgan, lithograph (as Delancey Fitzaltamont), Harvard TC · M. Morgan, lithograph (as Sidney Spoonbill), Harvard TC · caricatures, Harvard TC · cartes-de-visite, NPG · engraving (after photograph by Sarony), NYPL, New York, Billy Rose theatre collection · engraving (as David Garrick; after photograph by Sarony), NYPL, New York, Billy Rose theatre collection

Wealth at death under £16,000: probate, 31 May 1881, *CGPLA Eng. & Wales* · £76—Lytton Edward Sothern: administration, 31 May 1887, *CGPLA Eng. & Wales*

Sothern, Edward Hugh (1859–1933). *See under* Sothern, Edward Askew (1826–1881).

Sothern, Lytton Edward (1851–1887). *See under* Sothern, Edward Askew (1826–1881).

Sotherton, John (1562–1631), judge, born in London, was the son of John Sotherton (*c.*1525–1605), from 16 June 1579 until his death baron of the court of exchequer, and his second wife, Mary or Maria, daughter of Edward Wooton MD. The Sotherton family originally came from the village of Sotherton in Suffolk, and many of its members were mercers in London or Norwich, active in the Merchant Taylors' Company and in political life.

Sotherton matriculated from Christ Church, Oxford, on 20 November 1580, graduated BA on 22 January 1583, was in the same year incorporated at Cambridge, and proceeded MA in April 1586. He was admitted in November 1587 a member of the Inner Temple, where he was called to the bar in 1597, and elected a bencher in 1610. Appointed receiver-general for the counties of Bedford and Buckingham in July 1604, he was advanced to the post of cursitor baron of the exchequer on 29 October 1610. He sat regularly as one of the commissioners of gaol delivery for the City of London, was joined with Sir Julius Caesar, Sir Francis Bacon, and others in a commission of ways and means in August 1612, and at a later date was one of the assessors of compositions for defective titles and an inspector of nuisances for Middlesex. His first wife was Ann Bray, his second Elizabeth, *née* Cook, widow of Sir John Morgan of Chilworth, Surrey. Their son John (*b.* 1599/1600) inherited the manor of Wadenhall, Kent, which Sotherton had purchased from the crown in 1600. Sotherton died in 1631, administration of his estate being granted on 8 October; his successor on the bench, James Pagitt, was appointed on 24 October that year. Sotherton was buried at St Alban, Wood Street.

J. M. Rigg, *rev.* Anita McConnell

Sources 'Boyd's citizens of London', Society of Genealogists, London · Foss, *Judges*, 6.364–5 · Foster, *Alum. Oxon.* · F. A. Inderwick and R. A. Roberts, eds., *A calendar of the Inner Temple records*, 5 vols. (1896–1936) · F. Blomefield and C. Parkin, *An essay towards a topographical history of the county of Norfolk*, [2nd edn], 11 vols. (1805–10), vol. 3, p. 359; vol. 4, pp. 59, 198; vol. 10, p. 428 · *CSP dom., 1598–1601*, 383; *1603–10*, 135, 613, 639; *1611–18*, 248; *addenda, 1580–1625*, 461 · J. J. Howard and G. J. Armytage, eds., *The visitation of London in the year 1568*, Harleian Society, 1 (1869) · St Alban, Wood Street, churchwarden's accounts, 1584–1639, GL, MS 7673/1 · admon, PRO, PROB 6/14A, fol. 56r

Soubise, Julius [*formerly* Othello] (*c.*1754–1798), man of fashion, was born on the Caribbean island of St Kitts. His mother was a black slave, and his father probably a free white man. The first record of his existence was his entry on 2 April 1764 under the name Othello aboard the royal naval vessel *Richmond*, commanded by his owner, Captain Stair Douglas. The young slave first reached England on 25 June 1764, when he was discharged from the ship with his master at Plymouth. The boy quickly gained the favour of Catherine Hyde, the 64-year-old wife of his owner's cousin, Charles Douglas, third duke of Queensberry. Captain Douglas soon gave the child to the duchess as a gift.

Though his fellow servants continued to refer to him as 'the young Othello', the duchess renamed him, perhaps after Charles de Rohan, prince de Soubise (1715–1787), a general with a mixed record during the Seven Years' War, and since 1763 a Parisian man of fashion and courtier in the court of Louis XV and Madame de Pompadour. The duchess had Domenico Angelo teach Soubise fencing and riding, and Soubise attended Angelo as his usher at Eton and other colleges. Observers felt the duchess was spoiling the youth. For example, Lady Mary Coke noted in her journal entry for 31 March 1767:

> Made a visit to the Duchess of Queensberry, & found her at home half dress'd & half undress'd; She was talking to her Black Boy, who indeed seems to have a very extraordinary capacity, something very uncommon; She told me She had him taught everything he had a mind to learn, She thought it better than keeping him to serve in the House; in that I think her Grace judged right, but When She told me he learnt to ride & fence, I could not help thinking those exercises too much above his condition to be useful, & wou'd only serve to give him expectations that cou'd not be answer'd. (*Letters and Journals*, 1.194–5)

The duchess's generosity allowed Soubise to live a life of womanizing and fashion and soon led to widespread talk of a scandalous relationship between the young Soubise and his elderly mistress. Through the duchess he became a friend and correspondent of Ignatius Sancho, the most famous African Briton of his day. The avuncular Sancho affectionately wrote of and to Soubise in unsuccessful attempts to dissuade the younger man from continuing to indulge in the mistakes of Sancho's own youth. Soubise was also the favourite of David Garrick and Thomas Sheridan. An amateur violinist, composer, singer, sonneteer, and actor, and calling himself the Black Prince, Soubise soon became the subject of satiric engravings as a macaroni or fop. He ran up large debts, ignored Sancho's advice to reform, and finally caused his patron to send him to Calcutta to repair his fortunes as a fencing and riding instructor.

Soubise departed on 15 July 1777, aboard the East India Company ship the *Bessborough*, and arrived at Madras, India, on 9 February 1778. The duchess died two days after he left. An additional motive for his leaving England may have been the desire to shield him from prosecution for rape. The *Morning Post, and Daily Advertiser* reported on 22 July 1777 that about two months earlier Soubise had

> enticed one of the house-maids under the pretence of her meeting with a country acquaintance, to call at a house in the Strand, where he had previously secreted himself, and having fixed upon a notorious bawdy-house for the accomplishment of his designs, threatened the girl to murder her, if she refused to yield up her person.

Because of the duchess's 'unaccountable attachment' to

Soubise, she tried to bribe the maid into dropping charges. When she failed, she gave him money to enable him to flee the country. Soubise never returned to England. He remained part of the landscape of London celebrity for a little longer: 'A Love Letter' to 'the Honourable Miss G— a celebrated toast, with a fortune of 30,000l.' appeared in the second volume of the scandal-mongering *Nocturnal Revels, or, The History of King's Place*, published anonymously in London in 1779. The 'letter', which may well be a forgery, depicts Soubise as aspiring to lighten his complexion in order to win the love of 'Miss G—'.

By the end of 1779 Soubise was living in Calcutta. On 24 June 1784 he advertised the opening of his fencing school in the *Calcutta Gazette*. On 15 November 1784 he announced in the *India Gazette* that he was moving his fencing school and combining it with a riding school. On 7 January 1788 he advertised in the same newspaper for women students as well as men, and again on 21 April 1788 that his new riding school for men and women, 'built by subscription', was about to open. On 16 June 1788 he advertised that he was also selling Charles Thompson's popular *Rules for Bad Horsemen* (1762; 5th edn, 1787), making him the first known African-British bookseller of works by others. Soubise advertised his skill at breaking unruly horses in another Calcutta newspaper, *The World*, on 10 March 1792. He expanded his business further with the opening of his 'Calcutta Repository' for horses announced in the *Calcutta Gazette* on 12 February 1795. His success in India was abruptly ended by his death on 25 August 1798 from injuries sustained in a fall from a horse he was trying to subdue. He was buried the following day in Calcutta.

On 6 September 1798 the *Calcutta Gazette* advertised the sale of a horse 'for the benefit of Mrs. Soubise', presumably the widow of Julius. No record of her given name or their marriage has been found, and the sale suggests that Soubise left little wealth. Soubise fathered at least two children: Mary Soubise, baptized on 20 June 1785, aged two years and four months; and Frederick William Soubise, baptized on 7 August 1785, aged nine months. The only parent listed in the Mission Church register for both children is Julius Soubise. A Henry Soubise, aged fifteen years, was baptized on 14 January 1800, though neither the church nor any parent is identified.

VINCENT CARRETTA

Sources H. Angelo, *Reminiscences*, 1 (1828) • H. Angelo, *Angelo's pic nic* (1834) • *Nocturnal revels, or, The history of King's Place and other modern nunneries. Containing their mysteries, devotions, and sacrifices. Comprising also, the ancient and present state of promiscuous gallantry: with their portraits of the most celebrated demireps and courtezans of this period: as well as sketches of their professional and occasional admirers. By a monk of the order of St. Francis* (1779), 2.210–32 • *Calcutta Gazette* (1784) • *Calcutta Gazette* (1795) • *Calcutta Gazette* (1798) • *The letters and journals of Lady Mary Coke*, ed. J. A. Home, 4 vols. (1889–96) • *India Gazette* (1784) • *Morning Post* (1777) • *Letters of the late Ignatius Sancho, an African*, pbk edn, ed. V. Carretta (1998) • *The World* (1792) • PRO, ADM 36/6496, 6497; ADM 52/1421 • BL OIOC, L/MAR/B/259 A&B; N/1/3/ff60–61; N/1/5/f153; N/1/5/f272; N/1/9f343

Likenesses engraving, 1772 • W. Austin, double portrait, engraving, 1773 (with the duchess of Queensberry)

Soulbury. For this title name *see* Ramsbotham, Herwald, first Viscount Soulbury (1887–1971).

Soulemont, Thomas (*b.* in or before **1500**, *d.* **1541**), administrator, was born in Jersey, the eldest son of the jurat Pierre de Soulemont of St Helier and his wife, Marguerite Messervy. As early as the fourteenth century his family lived in the island parishes of St Helier and Grouville. As a young man Soulemont left the Channel Islands for England; little is known of his education, although Anthony Wood (who confuses him with the cleric and controversialist Thomas Solme) claims that Soulemont studied for a time at Oxford. Despite settling in England, Soulemont retained close ties with his native island. Rector of Grouville from 1533, he was named dean of Jersey by the bishop of Coutances the following year and, although non-resident, he vigorously defended his decanal jurisdiction against encroachment by the states of Jersey.

By late 1532 Soulemont had entered royal service as one of the king's French secretaries, when he was needed at Calais to prepare for meetings with François I. He was one of the senior clerks employed by Thomas Cromwell, whom he served as chief secretary from 1537. Soulemont's fluency in French naturally involved him in a variety of extra duties, in addition to drafting and translating routine diplomatic correspondence. Such special assignments included examining witnesses to assaults upon members of the French ambassador's household, and investigating complaints from French merchants trading in England. In April 1539 he met with the French ambassador to discuss foreign policy developments, in place of his master Cromwell, who was ill. That same year he served as deputy clerk of parliaments, in which position he sought to rationalize and simplify the records. On 21 September 1540 he was appointed clerk of parliaments, and his journal describes the closing of the 1540 parliament in exceptional detail.

Both Cromwell and the king rewarded their secretary's energetic labours. In April 1537 Soulemont was collated to the prebend of Knaresborough at York, while in July of the same year Cromwell persuaded the bishop of Hereford to collate his clerk to the vacant prebend of Moreton Magna. Having already acquired the Cornish manors of Forwood and Fowey from his friend and colleague Thomas Wriothesley in early 1538, Soulemont subsequently secured from the crown leases of the site of Canonsleigh convent, Devon, as well as property at the London Greyfriars.

In addition to his administrative work Soulemont was a keen antiquary, collecting and transcribing records (from the royal library and elsewhere) relating to the history of Jersey and the Channel Islands, on which he was an authority. He supplied manuscripts to John Leland, who praised Soulemont's scholarship in his *Encomia*, while John Bale mentioned two unpublished works by Soulemont (now lost): the 'Select antiquities of Great Britain', and a life of Thomas Becket. Thomas Soulemont died, probably in London, on 12 July 1541 and was buried at the Carmelite convent in the city.

P. R. N. CARTER

Sources G. R. Balleine, *A biographical dictionary of Jersey*, [1] [1948] • *LP Henry VIII*, vols. 5–16 • M. McKisack, *Medieval history in the Tudor age* (1971) • G. R. Elton, *The Tudor revolution in government* (1952) • *Fasti Angl., 1300–1541*, [Hereford] • *Fasti Angl., 1300–1541*, [York] • Emden,

Oxf. • Bale, *Index* • J. Leland, *Principum, ac illustrium aliquot et eruditorum in Anglia virorum* (1589) • S. E. Lehmberg, *The later parliaments of Henry VIII, 1536–1547* (1977) • J. A. Messervy, 'Liste des doyens de l'Île de Jersey', *Annual Bulletin* [Société Jersiaise], 9 (1919–22) • Wood, *Ath. Oxon.*, new edn

Soulis, Sir John (*d.* before **1310**), administrator and guardian of Scotland, was the second son of Nicholas de Soulis, lord of Liddesdale and butler of Scotland, and younger brother of William, justiciar of Lothian, who died *c.*1292–3. John appears from about 1280 in the shadow of his elder brother, but from 1284, by then a knight, as a royal servant on the embassy which arranged the marriage of Yolande de Dreux to Alexander III; by 1289, and perhaps before 1286, he was sheriff of Berwick, and he was among the magnates present in negotiations at Birgham in 1290. In the Great Cause he and William were auditors nominated by Robert (V) de Brus (though William's son, Nicholas, was a claimant). John is found in the two records of King John's parliaments of 1293, including acting as surety for the young Robert Bruce, earl of Carrick, and in 1295 was one of two magnates sent by the government which had taken power from King John to make an alliance with France. He is not named in the Ragman rolls among those submitting to Edward I in 1296, and the charter which he is said to witness at this time is an undated but earlier private charter contained in a royal *inspeximus* of 1296. There is no trace of him in Scotland or England from 1295, and he seems to have been in France for some five years. He received payments from Philippe IV in February and May 1299 and was reported to be at Damme in July 1299, awaiting passage to Scotland, just at the time when King John had been released from English into papal custody.

It has been assumed that Soulis returned to Scotland in 1299, but there is no evidence to that effect, and it is more probable that he was left behind by the other ambassadors because the Scottish king could now be contacted, and that he eventually spent time with the king. Fordun states that during the time of John Comyn's guardianship, that is, from 1298, Soulis was associated in office with him by King John, who was then freed from prison and living at Bailleul; King John was released by the pope into French custody some time after September 1300, and was sent to Bailleul at a date which seems to have been late in the summer of 1301. Despite Fordun, the timetable is such that the king must have appointed Soulis guardian before his release to the French and before going to Bailleul, for Soulis is found acting as sole guardian in Scotland in May 1301. He took the remarkable step of issuing charters and other acts in the name of King John, and responded decisively to the evasive arguments deployed at the papal court by Edward I by holding a council and sending two proctors to join Baldred Bisset at the curia with a dossier of cogent counter-arguments.

The war of deeds was less effective than the war of words, though in the summer of 1301 Soulis and Ingram Umfraville successfully harassed the prince of Wales in the south-west, attacking the stronghold of Lochmaben on 7–8 September 1301 and then mustering at Loudoun in the vain hope of relieving Bothwell Castle, besieged by Edward I. Nevertheless Edward achieved so little that in January 1302 he agreed to a nine-month truce. All now depended upon the involvement of Edward I in France, or on an Anglo-French peace which incorporated Scotland, and in the autumn of 1302 Soulis went again to France with a powerful embassy to try to hold Philippe IV to the Scots' cause. In 1303 they wrote home with a mixture of despair and hope, but the despair alone was justified: Philippe deserted the Scots, and in February 1304 their leaders decided to sue for peace. Soulis, punished with just two years of exile, could have been included, but would have none of it. He remained in France until his death at an unknown date before 1310. He married Margaret, daughter of Merleswain, lord of Ardross in Fife, and widow of Hugh de Perisby, probably before 1295; they had a daughter, Muriella. Fordun had no high opinion of Soulis, but he should be judged as a politician, or statesman, not a commander. For a man of small resources and minor standing he clearly impressed his social betters with his diplomatic skills.

His nephew, Nicholas de Soulis, lord of Liddesdale, died at the end of 1296, leaving two sons from his marriage to Margaret, daughter of Alexander Comyn, earl of Buchan. The elder, **Sir William Soulis** (*d.* 1320/21), was probably sympathetic to the patriotic cause, but still young when received to Edward I's peace in 1304. He was knighted by 1312. From 1306 he served in the English interest, and was rewarded in 1312 with the lands of Sir Robert Keith, but after Bannockburn and the threat of forfeiture he adhered to Robert I. It was probably he, not John as the Lanercost chronicle says, who accompanied Edward Bruce and James Douglas in a great raid into northern England in August 1314, for William had a grant of Wark in Tynedale from King Robert before 1315. Yet not until the very end of 1319 does he appear in a royal act, being sent as negotiator of the truce made in December of that year. Early in 1320, as a witness to a royal charter, he is described as butler of Scotland, and he also has that designation in the declaration of Arbroath on 6 May 1320.

Within weeks Soulis was discovered to be involved in a plot against the king, along with others formerly associated with the Balliol camp. According to Barbour, Soulis had 360 esquires in his livery, as well as knights, at Berwick, suggesting that he had recruited a gang of men-at-arms there. When arrested and brought before parliament in August 1320, he confessed and was sent to Dumbarton Castle for life imprisonment. Barbour's claim that the conspirators meant to make Soulis king is to be discounted as an attempt to explain an episode for which his source gave no explanation. The aim may have been to replace Robert I by Edward Balliol, but not to restore English lordship. It is also likely that Barbour has exaggerated Soulis's part and diminished the importance in the conspiracy of Sir David Brechin, who was executed. Each was the son of a daughter of Alexander Comyn, earl of Buchan. Soulis had died by 20 April 1321. He and his wife, whose name is unknown, had two daughters and possibly a son, the man of the same name killed at Boroughbridge on 16 March 1322, according to the Lanercost chronicle.

Sir William's younger brother, **Sir John Soulis** (*d.* 1318), emerged from obscurity in November 1314 when, already a knight, he came from France to ransom kinsmen taken prisoner at Bannockburn. He gave allegiance to King Robert and in the following year joined Edward Bruce on the Irish adventure, a typical landless younger son seeking endowment in this risky business. He was back in Scotland when Sir Andrew Harclay invaded Eskdale from Carlisle in 1316 and was routed and taken prisoner by a small force under Sir John, an exploit famous in ballad in the fourteenth century. By 1318 Soulis had returned to Ireland, where he took part in the last campaign of Edward Bruce and was killed with him in a foolish battle at Faughart, near Dundalk, on 14 October 1318. He had no known children. A. A. M. DUNCAN

Sources T. McMichael, 'The feudal family of de Soulis', *Transactions of the Dumfriesshire and Galloway Natural History and Antiquarian Society*, 3rd ser., 26 (1949), 163–93 · G. W. S. Barrow, *Robert Bruce and the community of the realm of Scotland*, 3rd edn (1988) · R. J. Goldstein, 'The Scottish mission to Boniface VIII in 1301: a reconsideration of the context of the *Instructiones* and *Processus*', *SHR*, 70 (1991), 1–15 · N. Reid, 'The kingless kingdom: the Scottish guardianships of 1286–1306', *SHR*, 61 (1982), 105–29 · *CDS*, vols. 2–3, 5 · J. Barbour, *The Bruce*, ed. A. A. M. Duncan (1997) · J. Stevenson, ed., *Chronicon de Lanercost, 1201–1346*, Bannatyne Club, 65 (1839) · G. W. S. Barrow and others, eds., *Regesta regum Scottorum*, 5, ed. A. A. M. Duncan (1988) · T. W. Moody and others, eds., *A new history of Ireland*, 2: *Medieval Ireland, 1169–1534* (1987)

Soulis, Sir John (*d.* **1318**). *See under* Soulis, Sir John (*d.* before 1310).

Soulis, Sir William (*d.* **1320/21**). *See under* Soulis, Sir John (*d.* before 1310).

Soulsby, Lucy Helen Muriel (**1856–1927**), headmistress, was born in London on 18 July 1856, the only daughter of Christopher Percy Soulsby and Susan Sybilla Thompson, who had married the year before. In November 1860 they emigrated to New Zealand, where Christopher Soulsby was appointed to the land office. He died in January 1867. Lucy Soulsby's younger brother Basil was born in 1864 (*d.* 1933). Her mother, by this time running a small school, provided all Lucy's education as a child, and indeed formed the major influence in her life. The two discussed such issues as religious education, literature, and women's questions until Susan Soulsby's death on 9 February 1904 (Soulsby edited and published a selection of her mother's papers, *Home is Best*, 1904). They returned to London late in 1867 and, after periods in Ramsgate, Leominster, and, briefly, Cheltenham, lived at Salcombe, Devon, from 1879 to 1884, where Soulsby started to write short articles for, among other publications, *Work and Leisure*. During her late adolescence and early womanhood Soulsby studied independently for a number of public examinations.

In 1885 Dorothea Beale offered Soulsby a place on the staff of Cheltenham Ladies' College, where she remained for two years before being appointed headmistress of Oxford High School for Girls (1887–97). She later acknowledged her considerable debt to Beale, and contributed 'The moral side of education' to Beale's *Work and Play in Girls' Schools* (1898). In 1897 she became headmistress of a small private school for girls aged between fifteen and eighteen at Manor House, Brondesbury, which she ran according to ideals which owed a great deal to her close relationship with her mother and to her reverence of the power of the home. She prioritized 'character-building' over academic matters, preparing 'a race of leisured girls' for their probable married futures and claiming 'I try to make fine women who will be fine wives and fine mothers' (Barclay, 159); 'my interest is not primarily in education, but in making you as grateful to your mother as I am to mine' (*Impressions*, 82). She maintained that 'Brondesbury stood for a belief in the old-fashioned idea that a child's sympathies, memories, aspirations should be coloured and dominated by her mother' (ibid., 80). Many testimonies from former pupils recall her personal magnetism and her intensely personal care for each girl (there were never more than forty in the school) as well as her somewhat whimsical methods.

While in Oxford, Soulsby sat on the council of Lady Margaret Hall (1889–1905): she was a friend of Elizabeth Wordsworth, principal of the college. Her experience in this city, however, firmed up her opposition to academic education for women. In 1895 she opposed the opening of the Oxford degree to them, the only Girls' Public Day School Company headmistress to do so, and the period strengthened her feelings that women and men should have different types of education.

Soulsby drew her principles from the works of John Keble, Charlotte M. Yonge, and Elizabeth Sewell (publishing an edited and revised edition of her *Principles of Education*, 1914). She emphasized the importance of cultivating spirituality and encouraging the drawing up of individual plans of prayer, Bible reading, and self-discipline. Publishing *Two Aspects of Education* in 1899, she chose to highlight 'I. Self-Control II. Fortitude, Humility and Large-Heartedness'. Although sympathetic to evangelical teaching until her mid-twenties, she drew increasingly towards the post-Pusey high church during her time in Oxford. Her spiritual heroes were John Bunyan and Samuel Rutherford, and she greatly revered St Teresa of Avila, not just for her devotion but for her practicality. While she placed great stress on the power of women's influence, she did not support women's suffrage, signing Mrs Humphry Ward's petition against it in 1889, and considered women's and men's spheres to be essentially different. She favoured educated girls taking up elementary school teaching if a career was necessary. She preferred to take advice from men, although Mrs Henry Grenville was a close friend for some twenty years before her death in 1923. Soulsby retired from Brondesbury in 1915, by which time her ideas were seeming increasingly dated.

In addition to teaching, Soulsby served on the council of the Mothers' Union and the National Union of Women Workers; she served on educational committees, spoke at church congresses in Britain and America, and wrote about sixty pamphlets and books dealing with the education of girls and with devotional issues. These include *Stray Thoughts for Girls* (1893), *Stray Thoughts for Invalids*

(1896), *Stray Thoughts for Mothers and Teachers* (1897), *Suggestions on Prayer* (1902), *Suggestions on Bible Reading* (1904), and *Talks to Mothers* (1916). She travelled extensively in Europe (spending more than thirty summers in Venice, and drawing on her foreign experiences when it came to introducing examples of European art and architecture into her teaching), Norway, South Africa, and Egypt. An extended visit to the United States was written up as *The America I Saw in 1916–18* (1920). After some years of ill health (she had had serious operations in 1905 and 1908, and was never as robust as she appeared), Lucy Soulsby died unmarried at her home, Mentmore, 7 Bath Road, Reading, on 19 May 1927. KATE FLINT

Sources [S. S. Soulsby and L. H. M. Soulsby], *The letters of S. S. S. and L. H. M. S. (Mrs and Miss Soulsby)*, ed. E. A., B. H. S., and P. H. (1929) • E. A. and B. H. S., eds., *Impressions of L. H. M. S.* (1927) • E. A. and B. H. S., eds., *Further impressions of L. H. M. S. by E. A. and B. H. S.* (1928) • *The Times* (24 May 1927) • *The Guardian* (3 June 1927) • Mrs H. Barclay [E. N. D. Barclay], 'Lucy Soulsby', *Mothers in Council*, 39 (July 1927), 157–60 • R. Waterhouse, 'L. H. M. S.', *Mothers in Council*, 39 (July 1927), 160–62 • M. D. Chitty, *Workers' paper* [published by the Mothers' Union] (July 1927) • E. L. Soulsby, ed., *The autobiography of Elizabeth M. Sewell* (1907) • G. Battiscombe, *Reluctant pioneer: a life of Elizabeth Wordsworth* (1978) • St Anne's College, Oxford, Annie Rogers MSS

Likenesses photographs, 1867–1913, repro. in [Soulsby and Soulsby], *The letters of S. S. S. and L. H. M. S.* • group portrait, photograph, *c.*1896 (with her staff), repro. in V. E. Stack, ed., *Oxford High School, Girls Public Day School Trust, 1875–1960* (1963)

Wealth at death £19,672 4*s.* 1*d.*: probate, 8 Aug 1927, *CGPLA Eng. & Wales*

Soutar, William (1898–1943), poet and diarist, was born on 28 April 1898 at 2 South Inch Terrace, Perth, the only child of John Soutar (1871–1958), master joiner, and his wife, Margaret Smith (1870–1954), who were both Scottish. Soutar's mother wrote poetry, and her athletic, handsome son followed suit, regularly composing verses while still a schoolboy. He attended the Southern District School, Perth, from 1903 to 1912 and Perth Academy from 1912 to 1916.

Soutar joined the Royal Navy in 1916, and spent the next two years with the North Atlantic Fleet. The life was taxing, but it was a stimulating challenge. He enjoyed the rough comradeship of fellow sailors but became increasingly aware of the politics of war and the human suffering that it caused. The experience developed his democratic instincts and his doubts about the values of empire, conquest, and class-ridden society. He was demobilized in November 1918, but at that time of rejoicing was ill and unable to walk, due to an unidentifiable ailment. In 1919 he had recovered sufficiently to begin a course in medicine, which he did not enjoy, before switching to honours English at Edinburgh University, but he never regained full mobility.

Soutar's university career was undistinguished. Anglo-Saxon bored him, and he challenged the university establishment and distinguished Donne scholar Herbert Grierson, his professor, asserting its irrelevance to his future career. He dressed in a dandified fashion, alienating his peers, many of whom were prejudiced against former forces students. He graduated in 1923 with a third-class

William Soutar (1898–1943), by James A. Finlayson

degree, which he was lucky to get, having been perversely arrogant throughout, refusing for example to study the novel. 'I'm not a "Varsity bird"—one is apt to get cobwebs on one's wings', he commented on the years when he:

> walked with stiffening bones
> among the academic stones.

Continuing, however, to write English poetry, he contributed to the magazine *The Student*. His first book, *Gleanings by an Undergraduate* (1923), was produced, like most of his subsequent slim volumes, at his father's expense. On 18 April 1919 he also began his lifelong practice of keeping a daily dairy: 'Carpe Diem!' heralded that commitment, followed the next day with 'Remember to seize every opportunity. Reverence Truth: Chastity and Love'. A belief that his thoughts might have wider relevance and significance is already implicit in those words.

During this period Soutar made contact with Hugh MacDiarmid (C. M. Grieve), at that time a journalist in Montrose, and Ezra Pound, among others. His letters indicate determined ambitions as a poet and contempt for the fashionable poetry of the day. MacDiarmid was abandoning writing poetry in English in favour of 'synthetic Scots', eclectically gleaned from old Scots, especially the medieval 'makars' Henrysoun and Dunbar, and all current dialects. This evolved into the Scottish literary renaissance, its aim to revitalize Scottish culture by replacing dominant stereotypes, mostly distorted caricatures, with genuine images and concepts rooted in, but not bound by, genuine Scottish traditions and connecting with the European modernist mainstream. Soutar initially disagreed with the linguistic spearhead of MacDiarmid's agenda but became increasingly excited by the possibilities of Scots. He had an effortless grasp of the language, having grown up in a Scots-speaking environment. By 1930 he was fervently writing Scots poetry for adults as well as his superb 'bairnrhymes' for children, believing that 'if the Doric is to come back alive, it will come on a cock-horse' (letter to C. M. Grieve, 1931).

Unfortunately for Soutar his mysterious illness advanced during his university career; his hopes of becoming a journalist with *The Scotsman* were dashed. He began teacher training in October 1924 but had to return to Perth to undergo medical treatment for his now diagnosed ankylosing spondylitis. His parents were happy to keep him, but from 1924 he became increasingly stiff and paralysed, and in 1930 finally bedridden. One bright spot in this darkening picture was his parents' adoption of an orphaned Australian cousin, Evelyn, aged six. Soutar doted on her, and she inspired his bairnrhymes.

From 26 November 1930, and the onset of permanent invalidity, to his death, thirteen years later, Soutar's life entailed predictable routine. Lovingly looked after, with his bedroom and bed always immaculate, he was a dandy to the last, dressing with care and bravado in velvet jacket and bow tie, his black hair fanned out on the supporting pillows. Nature had always been his great passion, and the window of his long room was enlarged so that he could observe the outside world: the garden, the sycamore tree at its foot, and Craigie Hill beyond, wrenchingly nostalgic for memories of his previous active life, the hill being a natural haven for courting couples. Eventually Soutar couldn't move even his head; his father furnished the room with bookshelves and an elaborate system of mirrors so that he could identify to a mobile helper the books that he required.

October 1924 had witnessed a poignant moment when Soutar, walking one lovely evening in Edinburgh and contemplating the prospect of his future, restricted life, stopped under the pillars of St George's West Church and said to himself: 'Now, I can be a poet'. Throughout his bedridden years he set himself a strict daily routine of writing poetry, adding to his diary, and making many other jottings: commonplace books for noting (often humorously) trivial events; journals for more extensive, philosophical explorations; dream books; and letters. He read voraciously, believing that 'the poet should know everything', at one point setting himself to read the *Encyclopaedia Britannica*—a task that he accomplished.

The invalid's room became a magnet for visitors: family, friends, local worthies, well-intending sick-visitors. Soutar was always cheery and welcoming to his uninvited guests but secretly was irritated and frustrated when hours each week were inevitably passed in 'mindless conversation'. He was also sexually frustrated and often fantasized about women who might somehow provide relief. His parents' strict religious views rendered any such satisfaction out of the question. One of his finest poems, 'The Tryst', takes the form of a haunting fantasy about receiving a nubile, willing night visitor. Many literary figures also called: Hugh MacDiarmid, George Bruce, Tom Scott, William Montgomery, Helen B. Cruickshank, the artist and school friend Jim Finlayson, and others. With them he could relish real conversation.

Though brought up in the Free Church of Scotland (Auld Lichters) Soutar departed from the strict beliefs of his parents and became virtually an atheist. He became more nationalistic and socialist, and his own predicament combined with his outgoing nature and love of life to generate in him a passionate pacifism. The Spanish Civil War horrified him, especially the bombing of Guernica, inspiration for his outstanding poem 'The Children'. As the Second World War proceeded he was increasingly weakened by tuberculosis, first contracted in 1929. His decline in energy and well-being from 1942 onwards is noticeable in all his writings, and he knew by July 1943 that his condition was terminal. It was then that he began a special diary, *The Diary of a Dying Man*, to document that last journey. It is a masterpiece.

William Soutar died on 15 October 1943 at his home—27 Wilson Street, Perth—and was buried at Deanfield cemetery, Perth. There is a tendency still for the Scottish literary orthodoxy to dismiss him as a poetic miniaturist whose best achievement was a few Scots poems and the bairnrhymes, and as an old-fashioned figure in the male-dominated literary renaissance. His poetic achievement, however, extends to many fine poems in English, and even a large proportion of his Scots writing still goes ignored. After Soutar's death Hugh MacDiarmid edited his *Collected Poems* (1948) but, perhaps because he felt Soutar essentially a rival and threat, he left out many fine pieces. W. R. Aitken edited *Poems in Scots and English* in 1961, but not until 1988 was there a substantial edition, *Poems of William Soutar: a New Selection*, also edited by Aitken, who decided, misguidedly, that Soutar would not be best served by a proper edition of the complete poems. Soutar's diaries must also be considered in any assessment. In 1954 Alexander Scott published a small selection from the diaries of 1930 to 1943, unfortunately entitling it *Diaries of a Dying Man*, virtually appropriating the title of that unique, last diary. It was thanks to American diarist scholar Thomas Mallon, moved by the tragic story of the diaries and amazed at their literary quality and Soutar's obscurity, that a process began that brought *Diaries of a Dying Man* back into print in 1988.

A biographical television film, *The Garden Beyond*, was broadcast in 1977 but a real awakening of interest in Soutar did not occur until the late 1980s, with an article in the *Scots Magazine*. A selection from *Diaries of a Dying Man* was broadcast on BBC Radio Scotland in 1987, and in 1989 Soutar House, bequeathed by Soutar's father to the town as a memorial to his son, was refurbished, designated a listed building, and a writer in residence installed. In 1990 Perth Theatre produced a play about Soutar's life, *Gang doun wi' a Sang*. But the fact that in his centenary year, 1998, none of his poems was in print shows that the unique achievement of his contribution is not yet properly appreciated, in Scotland or internationally.

Soutar as a literary figure must be examined in his entirety: the poetry in Scots and English, the diaries, the letters, and other writings, mostly still unpublished. His literary output must be seen against the background of his life story and the suffering that he endured, his courage, and the sheer sensitive intelligence that he brought to everything. At its best the poetry exhibits a perfection and lyrical resonance that few poets achieve, while the intellectual power and insight represented by the diaries is of international significance. Seen in this context Soutar is a major figure in Scottish literature. JOY HENDRY

Sources A. Scott, *Still life: William Soutar (1898–1943)* (1958) · W. Soutar, *Diaries of a dying man*, ed. A. Scott (1988) · *Poems of William Soutar: a new selection*, ed. W. R. Aitken (1988) · W. Soutar, *The diary of a dying man* (1991) · *Collected poems of William Soutar*, ed. H. MacDiarmid (1948) · J. Hendry, *Gang doun wi' a sang* (1995) [a play about William Soutar] · *Chapman*, 53 (1988), 1–56 · J. Hendry, 'The Soutar we knew', *Scots Magazine* (Feb 1988), 493–503 [contains photographs] · T. Mallon, *A book of one's own* (1985)

Archives NL Scot., corresp. papers | NL Scot., corresp. with George Bruce · NL Scot., letters to Mairi Campbell Ireland · NL Scot., letters to William Montgomerie [copies] · NL Scot., letters to Margaret Hay Scott · NL Scot., letters to David Stephens | FILM Scottish Film Archive, Glasgow, *The garden beyond*, Book Film Productions Ltd, 1977 | SOUND BBC Radio Scotland, 'Journey in a single room', Oct 1987

Likenesses J. A. Finlayson, oils, 1926, Soutar House, Perth · J. A. Finlayson, two pencil drawings, 1931–3, Soutar House, Perth · B. Schotz, bronze bust, 1959, Perth Museum and Art Gallery · H. B. Cruickshank, photograph, repro. in Soutar, *Diary of a dying man* · J. A. Finlayson, portrait, Perth Museum and Art Gallery [*see illus.*]

Wealth at death nothing but literary artefacts

Souter, Alexander (1873–1949), patristic scholar and lexicographer, was born at Croft Park, Perth, on 14 August 1873, the eldest of four sons and two daughters of Alexander Souter (*d*. in or after 1899) and his wife, Elsie Cruickshank (*d*. in or after 1899). His father, a commercial traveller and clothier by trade, was a studious Congregationalist, a confessional commitment which his son maintained throughout his own life. Until the age of twelve he attended Sharp's Educational Institute, Perth; when the family moved back to Aberdeen he attended Robert Gordon's College in the town, until he went up to Aberdeen University in 1889 to read classics under William Mitchell Ramsay. A classmate was Alexander William Mair, later professor of Greek at Edinburgh. After gaining a first in classics and winning three university prizes Souter proceeded in 1893 to Cambridge, where he obtained a first in part 1 and a second in part 2 of the classical tripos, in 1896 and 1897 respectively. Two scholars furthered his career there: James Smith Reid, at his own college, Gonville and Caius, and J. E. B. Mayor, at St John's, who awoke in him an enthusiasm for lexicographical study of the Latin fathers. (Mayor's lectures on Tertullian were attended by a minority audience of two: Terrot Reaveley Glover and Souter.)

Following graduation at Cambridge, Souter was recalled to Aberdeen as assistant to Ramsay. On 7 July 1899 he married Elizabeth Barr Anderson (*b*. 1878/9), elder daughter of William Blair Anderson of Aberdeen, a photographer, and sister of the eminent Latinist William Blair Anderson; they were to have three daughters. His publications during these six years at Aberdeen related to his Latin teaching and were minor. But he had already turned his attention to the study of Latin manuscripts, and this was signalled in 1903 by his appointment as lecturer in medieval palaeography; he published a paper entitled 'Palaeography and its uses' in the *Journal of Theological Studies* in that year.

At the early age of thirty Souter was appointed Yates professor of New Testament Greek and exegesis at Mansfield College, Oxford, where he also held the post of librarian. His eight years in Oxford (1903–11) brought him into close contact with other students of patristics; this and superior library facilities enabled him to proceed rapidly to publication in his chosen field. In 1905 he published *A Study of Ambrosiaster*. This commentator on the Pauline epistles, earlier erroneously identified as Ambrose, had been little studied by English-speaking scholars; Souter's edition has remained influential and was reprinted in 1967. An edition of Pseudo-Augustine, *Quaestiones veteris et novi testamenti CXXVII*, followed (1908; repr. 1963). These editions, supplemented by about twenty articles in the *Journal of Theological Studies*, established Souter in the forefront of patristic scholarship, and he won wider recognition with his edition of the Greek New Testament (1910). Remarkably his father, though no academic, had collected thirty earlier editions of the Greek New Testament, later lodged in Aberdeen University Library, and these underpinned Souter's text ('textui a retractatoribus anglis adhibito adnotationem criticam subiecit Alexander Souter'). The volume was regularly reprinted, and a revised edition was issued in 1947.

In 1911 Souter returned to Aberdeen to fill the regius chair of humanity vacated by Ramsay—at this distance a curious move career-wise, but the chair was then internationally famous, though it was later abolished, and Souter was keen to return to Scotland. As a teacher he was not distinguished; he was not concerned to impart to students a vision of the literary, historical, or philosophical merits of the main-line Latin authors. Instead he offered textual and lexicographical observations on lesser-known figures, pointing out to his bewildered classes the inadequacies of the Latin dictionary of Lewis and Short. During these twenty-six years at Aberdeen he became a dominant figure in the university as dean of arts (1917), curator of the university library (1919–24), and briefly vice-chancellor (1925–6). Meanwhile his fame had spread to North America; he was invited to Princeton Theological Seminary as Stone lecturer (1924–5, 1927–8), to Southern Baptist Seminary as Norton lecturer (1924–5), and to Auburn Theological Seminary as Russell lecturer (1932–3).

But research and publication remained Souter's primary activity. Initially he extended his studies on the Greek texts of the scriptures in his *The Text and Canon of the New Testament* (1912; often republished), and his *Pocket Lexicon to the New Testament* (1916 and frequently republished thereafter) was a boon to divinity students. He edited

Tertullian's *Apology* (1917) and published translations of other treatises of Tertullian (1919–22). Next followed *Pelagius's Expositions of Thirteen Epistles of Saint Paul* (1922, 1926, and 1931). This three-volume publication of the commentaries composed by the celebrated British theologian at Rome shortly before 410 was Souter's supreme scholarly achievement. He extended his studies of patristic commentaries on the Pauline letters in *The Earliest Latin Commentaries on the Epistles of Saint Paul* (1927). Perhaps mindful of his obligations to classical Latin in the tenure of his chair he wrote a dozen brief pieces on Cicero, Lucan, and other authors for the *Classical Review*, as well as *Hints on Translation* and *Hints on the Study of Latin*, pamphlets which both appeared in 1920.

Souter retired to Oxford in 1937. He had received honorary degrees from Aberdeen, Dublin, and St Andrews; he had also been elected a fellow of the British Academy in 1926 and awarded its medal for biblical studies in 1932; he served on its council from 1938 to 1947. His energies at Oxford were now concentrated on the proposed *Oxford Latin Dictionary*, of which he had been appointed editor in 1933, with his former student J. M. Wyllie as assistant editor. Wyllie's war service delayed the project. Disharmony later ensued, and after Wyllie's appointment was terminated in 1954 he circulated scurrilous pamphlets alleging incompetence against Souter and other figures involved; copies are preserved in Aberdeen University Library. Earlier it had been decided that Christian Latin should not be covered by the dictionary, and Souter then decided to produce as a supplement *A Glossary of Later Latin to 600 AD*. He compiled this from 27,470 slips composed in his own hand. The work was published by Oxford University Press in 1949 and was well received by such savants as Marouzeau ('Une mine invraisemblablement riche'; *Revue des Études Latines*, 29, 1949, 279) and Ernout ('son glossaire est précieux'; *Revue de Philologie*, 29, 1951, 115). Sadly Souter did not survive to see the publication. He died at 3 Canterbury Road, Oxford, on 17 January 1949.

In his heyday at Aberdeen, as his students recalled, Souter was a handsome and distinguished figure with fresh complexion and silver-grey hair, a familiar sight as he strode out each Sunday with his family to the Congregationalist church. He was very much 'the lad o' pairts': a talented musician; a seasoned traveller, fluent in French, German, and Spanish; and an addict of the cinema. One former pupil speaks of his prodigious industry and Teutonic thoroughness, aptly comparing him to the elder Pliny, who 'believed that all time was wasted that was not given over to study'. P. G. WALSH

Sources R. J. Getty, 'Alexander Souter, 1873–1949', *PBA*, 38 (1952), 255–68 · J. M. R. Cormack, 'Alexander Souter, professor of humanity, 1911–1937', *Aberdeen University Review*, 38 (1959–60), 334–6 · 'Pelagianism', *The Oxford dictionary of the Christian church*, ed. F. L. Cross, 3rd edn, ed. E. A. Livingstone (1997), 1248–9 · *Oxford Latin dictionary* (1982), publisher's note · private information (2004) [W. S. Watt, emeritus professor of humanity, U. Aberdeen] · b. cert. · m. cert. · Venn, *Alum. Cant.*

Archives Bodl. Oxf., corresp. · King's Lond., working MSS and notebooks

South, Sir James (1785–1867), astronomer, born at Southwark, London, in October 1785, was the eldest son in the large family of James South (*d.* 1823), a prosperous dispensing chemist of High Street, Southwark, and his first wife, Sarah. His half-brother, from his father's second marriage, was the surgeon John Flint *South. James studied surgery, became a member of the Royal College of Surgeons, and embarked on a profitable career; but his friendship with Joseph Huddart aroused his interest in astronomy, and he began observing with a 6 inch Gregorian reflector. His marriage, in 1816, to Charlotte (*d.* 1851), the niece and sole heir of Joseph Ellis of South Lambeth, relieved him of the need to earn a living and allowed him to abandon his large surgical practice. He established an observatory attached to his house in Blackman Street, Borough, London, which he equipped with two equatorials of 5and 7 feet focal length respectively, besides a first-rate transit instrument by Troughton. Here, between 1821 and 1823, he observed, in collaboration with John Frederick William Herschel, 380 double stars. In presenting him with the gold medal of the Astronomical Society in 1826, Francis Baily spoke of his 'princely collection of instruments, such as have never yet fallen to the lot of a private individual' (*Memoirs of the Royal Astronomical Society*, 2, 1826, 547).

In 1825 South took his 5 foot telescope to Passy, near Paris, where he came to know Humboldt and Arago, and convinced Laplace of the reality of orbiting double stars by visual demonstration. In only a few months there he carried out what Herschel called 'a noble series of measures' on 458 compound stars, of which 160 were new; for this work, together with his paper 'On the discordances between the sun's observed and computed right ascensions', presented to the Royal Society on 8 June 1826, South was awarded the society's Copley medal in 1826. He had been elected a fellow of the society in 1821.

South was one of the founders of the Astronomical Society; he was elected president in 1829, and the royal charter granted to it in 1831 was made out in his name. By this time he was no longer president, however, and the confusion of formalities that resulted gave his enemy Richard Sheepshanks the opportunity to provoke the irascible South into behaviour that made his position in the society untenable. South withdrew, and became alienated from most of his early scientific friends.

South was by no means alone in regarding science in England as decadent, and he actively considered emigrating to France. Both governments saw him as a notable prize and competed for his favour, but the knighthood conferred on him on 21 July 1830 by William IV, and the civil-list pension of £300 in aid of his astronomical researches that soon followed, persuaded him to remain in England.

In 1826 South equipped a splendid observatory on Campden Hill, Kensington, adding to his array of instruments an 8 foot achromatic, the transit circle used by Stephen Groombridge, and a clock presented by the king of Denmark. But he was handicapped in his friendly rivalry with Wilhelm Struve of Dorpat, Estonia, in the

Sir James South (1785–1867), by Maull & Polyblank, 1855

study of double stars by his lack of a large object-glass of high quality. Then, in 1829, he heard that a 12 inch object-glass by the great Paris optician Cauchoix was for sale. He hastened to Paris, paid the asking price of about £1000, and returned in triumph with the lens.

The mounting he entrusted to Troughton, but the work, finished in 1831, proved a failure. South, bitterly disappointed, refused to pay; and Troughton, vigorously encouraged by Sheepshanks, brought an action. The matter was referred to arbitration, and there ensued a trial that involved almost every British astronomer of note. From 1834 to 1838 Sir William Henry Maule presided over the court; John Elliot Drinkwater Bethune acted as counsel for South, while Sheepshanks advised Troughton. In 1838 Maule gave judgment in favour of Troughton, whereupon South smashed the mounting in dispute, and sold the wood and iron by public auction in 1839 and the brass in 1842, on each occasion advertising the sale with scurrilous posters. The first sale resulted in a small loss, and the second in a profit of £11 for South to set against the many thousands of pounds he had spent on the instrument and the ensuing legal costs. His mind had been well-nigh unhinged by the protracted episode. The 12 inch lens that had been the ruin of his astronomical career was eventually presented by him in 1862 to the observatory of Trinity College, Dublin.

After 1838 South attempted only casual pieces of work, experimenting with clocks and pendulums, and executing at Watford in 1846 a series of observations on the disturbance, by passing railway trains, of star images reflected from mercury. They were reported to the government and presented in 1863 to the Royal Society. South observed Encke's comet in 1828 and 1838, Mauvais's comet in 1844, and Vico's in 1845. He was a friend and confidant of William Parsons, third earl of Rosse, and in February 1845 had the privilege, with Thomas Romney Robinson of Armagh, of trying the performance of Rosse's 6 foot reflector, by far the largest telescope ever built. The impetuous Robinson made exaggerated public claims for the scientific implications of what the instrument revealed, which he regarded as a triumph for Irish astronomy, and South found himself in the unaccustomed role of restraining influence. He was a member of a number of scientific academies, including those of St Petersburg and Brussels, and in 1863 he received an honorary LLD from the University of Cambridge.

In two papers, presented to the Royal Society on 16 June 1831 and 13 December 1832, South detailed observations of Mars that showed a complete absence of planetary atmospheric effects. He published a number of astronomical papers in later life, but these were of a minor nature. He was a frequent contributor, at times acrimoniously, to the daily and weekly press, and was the author of a number of critical pamphlets. In one, published in 1822, he pointed out defects in the *Nautical Almanac*, and he presided over a committee of the Astronomical Society appointed in 1829 to find ways of bringing the publication up to standard. He took a prominent role in attempts to make the membership of the Royal Society more professional, but his *Thirty-Six Charges Against the President and Council of the Royal Society*, printed as a tract in 1830, were officially ignored, notwithstanding his protest at a stormy meeting of the society. His feud with Sheepshanks led him to join with Charles Babbage, another of Sheepshanks's victims, in 1852 in a successful attempt to embarrass Sheepshanks over a youthful customs deception of his that had come to light. Sheepshanks was defended by his ally the astronomer royal, George Biddell Airy, and when Airy renewed his defence in an obituary, published after Sheepshanks's death in 1855, South defied convention by pursuing his adversary beyond the grave in a printed rejoinder.

During his later years South became partially blind and deaf. He died at his home at Observatory, Campden Hill, on 19 October 1867. His instruments were sold on 4 August 1870. A. M. Clerke, *rev.* Michael Hoskin

Sources T. R. R. [T. R. Robinson], *PRS*, 16 (1867–8), xliv–xlvii · *Monthly Notices of the Royal Astronomical Society*, 28 (1867–8), 69–72 · M. Hoskin, 'Astronomers at war: South *v.* Sheepshanks', *Journal for the History of Astronomy*, 20 (1989), 175–212 · d. cert.

Archives Kensington Central Library, London, corresp. and accounts · RAS, observations and papers | BL, corresp. with Charles Babbage, Add. MSS 37182–37201, *passim* · BL, corresp. with Sir Robert Peel, Add. MSS 40401–40562, *passim* · CUL, letters to Sir George Stokes · Devon RO, letters to duke of Somerset and Lord Edward Seymour · RS, corresp. with Sir John Herschel

Likenesses Maull & Polyblank, photograph, 1855, NPG [*see illus.*] · photograph, RAS

Wealth at death under £4000: probate, 17 Sept 1868, *CGPLA Eng. & Wales*

South, John Flint (1797–1882), surgeon, was born on 5 July 1797 in London, probably at Lant Street, Southwark, the son of James South (*d.* 1823), druggist, and his second wife, Mary (*d.* 1865). His half-brother was the astronomer Sir

James *South. From October 1805 until June 1813 South attended Dr Samuel Hemming's school at Hampton, Middlesex. He then received tuition in the classics from the Revd William Fancourt, and he also attended the lectures of Astley Cooper and practice sessions at St Thomas's Hospital, London. Here in 1813 he met Joseph Henry Green, who became a lifelong friend. On 18 February 1814 South was apprenticed to the surgeon Henry Cline the younger, and in 1815 he started work as a dresser. From 1819 he served as prosector for the anatomy lecturers at St Thomas's, and in 1820 he was appointed conservator of the museum and assistant demonstrator of anatomy for three years on a salary of £100. The next year he established his own practice above a cork shop in St Thomas Street, but he later moved to Adelaide Place, near London Bridge.

After some ill health, South was appointed in 1823 as joint demonstrator of anatomy with Bransby Cooper (which led to a dispute between Sir Astley Cooper and Green), and he retained this position until he became lecturer on anatomy in 1825. In 1834 he was elected assistant surgeon at St Thomas's, but severe illness caused him to resign his lectureship in January 1841. However, in July of the same year he was made full surgeon at the hospital, and with his health restored was able to lecture again. In 1843 he was appointed surgeon to the Female Orphan Asylum in Westminster Road, and in 1855 he served as a royal commissioner enquiring into the condition and operation of Dublin hospitals. He also acted as surgeon to the South Eastern Railway Company for many years.

South held many positions at the Royal College of Surgeons, which he joined in 1819. In 1841 he was appointed a member of the council, and in 1843 he became a fellow. The following year he was Hunterian orator, and in 1845 he acted as Arris and Gale professor of human anatomy and surgery. In 1849 he was elected to the court of examiners, and in 1851 and 1860 he served as president of the college. He was also a member of many other learned societies and regularly corresponded with scientists in Germany, France, and Stockholm.

South married twice. His first wife, whom he married in 1832, was Mrs Annie Wrench (*d.* 1864), second daughter of Thomas Lett of Dulwich House, Surrey. After her death he married, in 1865, Emma Lemmé, daughter of John Louis Lemmé of Antwerp and London, and niece of his friend Green. There were five children from the first marriage, and two daughters from the second. From 1841 the family lived at Blackheath Park in Kent.

South wrote several medical works and also revised two editions of *A Description of the Bones* (1828 and 1837). His *Household Surgery, or, Hints on Emergencies* (1847) ran to several editions, was hugely popular, and served as an early form of first-aid manual. Fluent in both French and German and realizing the importance of overseas medicine, South published *A Compendium of Human and Comparative Pathological Anatomy* (1831), translated from the German of A. W. Otto; and *A System of Surgery* (2 vols., 1847), translated from M. J. Chelius's *Handbuch der Chirurgie*, to which he added many valuable notes and observations of his own surgical experiences. He also wrote a religious tract, as well as articles on zoology and anatomy for the multi-volume *Encyclopaedia metropolitana* (completed 1845); and, with Joseph Henry Green, he revised *The Dissector's Manual* (1825).

In appearance South was thin, with a 'handsome face, bright eyes and smile of unabated intellect' (Feltoe). He was a lifelong diarist, and deeply religious. He carried out church work and was a keen supporter of Sunday schools. Restless and never idle, his many interests included horticulture. In 1831 South helped to establish the Surrey Zoological and Botanical Society's 'Surrey gardens' at Kennington in London, and after a visit to Sweden in 1852 he was awarded the fellowship of the Linnean Society and a medal of the Swedish Horticultural Society for introducing the vegetable marrow to that country. In 1859, largely through South's efforts, the body of the eminent surgeon John Hunter was removed from the church of St Martin-in-the-Fields and reinterred in Westminster Abbey.

In 1860 South retired from his lectureship at St Thomas's, and in 1863 he also resigned the post of surgeon. He then became a governor of the hospital. The last twenty years of his life were spent collecting material for a history of English surgery. However, *Memorials of the Craft of Surgery in England*, edited by Power, did not appear until 1886, after his death. South died on 8 January 1882 at his home, 7 Morden Road, Blackheath Park, London. He was buried in Charlton cemetery.

CHRISTOPHER F. LINDSEY

Sources *Memorials of John Flint South*, ed. C. L. Feltoe (1884) • *BMJ* (14 Jan 1882), 71 • *The Lancet* (14 Jan 1882) • *The Times* (12 Jan 1882) • *DNB* • V. G. Plarr, *Plarr's Lives of the fellows of the Royal College of Surgeons of England*, rev. D'A. Power, 2 vols. (1930) • parish register, 22 April 1798, City of London, Scots Church, London Wall [baptism] • *Medical Directory* (1880)

Archives RCS Eng., lecture notes; letters • Wellcome L., memoranda on the history of surgery

Likenesses T. H. Maguire, portrait, 1840, RCSL • T. H. Maguire, lithograph, 1848, Wellcome L. • H. Weekes, bust, 1872, St Thomas's Hospital, London • W. E. Abbott, photograph, Wellcome L. • Beynon and Co., coloured lithograph (*Buildings and famous alumni of St. Thomas's Hospital*), Wellcome L. • M. and N. Hanhart, lithograph (after T. Maguire) • C. T. Newcombe, photograph, Wellcome L. • steel engraving, repro. in *Memorials*, ed. Feltoe

South, Mary Anne. *See* Atwood, Mary Anne (1817–1910).

South, Robert (1634–1716), Church of England clergyman and theologian, was born on 4 September 1634 at Hackney, Middlesex, the son of Robert South, a London merchant with roots in Lincolnshire, and his wife, Elizabeth, *née* Berry, daughter of Captain John Berry of Lydd, Kent. He attended Westminster School and was elected a king's scholar in 1647. Like his schoolmates John Dryden and John Locke he became a favourite of Dr Richard Busby, its staunchly royalist headmaster. On the morning of King Charles's execution, 30 January 1649, Busby kept his students indoors; according to the memoir prefaced to the 1717 edition of his sermons South read the day's Latin prayers to the school, which would have been an extraordinary favour for a fourteen-year-old pupil. With Busby's blessing, in 1651 South took the closed route laid out for king's scholars between Westminster and Christ Church, Oxford. He was elected head of the list of scholars bound for Christ Church, and matriculated from there on 11 December 1651. A relative, Dr John South of New College, regius professor of Greek, contributed to his studentship of £30. Unlike Locke, who followed him to Christ Church a year later, South bridled under John Owen, its Cromwellian dean. South graduated BA on 24 February 1655 and took his MA in June 1657.

While an undergraduate South attended illegal services according to the rites of the Church of England which were conducted by three ejected members of Christ Church, Richard Allestree, John Dolben, and John Fell, in rooms above Merton Street in Oxford. Here South secretly entered holy orders, probably in 1658. The royalist episcopal clergy of Oxford were rewarded at the Restoration. While Fell replaced Owen as dean of Christ Church, South's sermons of 1659–60, tastefully furnished with Laudian railings against the presbyterians, had earned him the attention of the newly restored king's commissioners for ecclesiastical appointments: in August 1660 Edward Hyde, earl of Clarendon, lord chancellor of England and chancellor of Oxford University, made South the university's public orator and his own domestic chaplain. Clarendon disappointed South by not simultaneously granting him a canonship of Christ Church, which had been annexed to the oratorship under the Laudian and Caroline code for the reformation of Oxford in the 1630s. Clarendon, helped by Nathaniel Crew, fellow of Lincoln College and later bishop of Durham, and John Wallis, Savilian professor of mathematics at Oxford, did however see that South gained formal credentials in divinity: despite some grumblings, South was admitted both BD and DD on 1 October 1663.

The ejections which followed the 1662 Act of Uniformity supplied more provisions of pluralism for Laudian avengers such as South. In 1663 he was installed prebendary of Westminster. In 1667 he became vicar of a parish in the diocese of St Asaph, north Wales, perhaps that of Llanrhaeadr, Denbighshire; there is little recorded of his involvement with the parish, but he probably maintained a curate there. On 29 December 1670 South finally received a canonship of Christ Church, and held it along with the university oratorship until 1677, when he resigned the latter. In the same year he travelled to Poland as chaplain to Clarendon's son, Laurence Hyde, the ambassador-extraordinary to John Sobieski, king of Poland; the purpose of the visit was to present gifts to Sobieski's daughter, who was Charles II's goddaughter. South described his travels in Poland in a long letter to Edward Pococke, regius professor of Hebrew at Oxford and a fellow canon of Christ Church. South respected the piety of Polish Catholics, echoing the respect with which high Anglicans were treating the devotional writing of Cardinal Robert Bellarmine by the late seventeenth century. South noted the generous livings of the Polish church and its widespread pluralism, but also pointed out the lack of pastoral care which resulted from absenteeism, avoided in the Church of England by the appointment of curates to deputize for absentee clergy. While South lived comfortably upon the inheritance of his father's estate in Caversham, Oxfordshire, his own will suggests that he provided for his curates well. In 1678 he became rector of Islip in Oxfordshire, a parish in the gift of Westminster School worth £200 p.a. South directed £100 to his curate and the rest towards educating the children of the parish. He rebuilt the chancel of Islip parish church in 1680, founded a school that still survived as a Church of England aided state funded school at the start of the twenty-first century, and in 1689 built a grand rectory which featured an expansive garden walled off from the street. With genuine Laudian sadness South often lamented the dispersal of church property which had followed the Reformation, and he believed that God avenged those who had built houses upon church ruins, houses 'gilded with the name of reformation' (South, *Twelve Sermons*, 339); his sermons mentioned stories of how providence routinely punished the enemies of the church, ranging from Cardinal Thomas Wolsey to the parliamentary defacers of Lichfield Cathedral during the civil wars. The mortar of South's Islip rectory was barely dry by 1695, but White Kennett included an illustration of it in his *Parochial Antiquities* of that year, perhaps to show the Anglican commitment to rebuilding church infrastructure following the wars.

South had been appointed a chaplain to James, duke of York, brother of Charles II, in 1667, and remained one through the Popish Plot. The Popish Plot and the exclusion crisis only strengthened South's opinions. In a sermon delivered in July 1678 and printed in 1679 he praised the rigours of a Jesuit education, while attacking Socinians as Epicureans who believed only what pleased them. Throughout his career South feared protestant nonconformity more than Catholicism. His royalist ridicule of the social inversions wrought by the 'sectarian barbarisme' (South, *Interest Deposed*, sig. A4v) of the interregnum, together with his belief in the divine right of kings, endeared him to both Charles II and James II. Following the accession of James II in 1685 both the younger Hydes became senior ministers. Laurence Hyde, earl of Rochester, was lord high treasurer, and Henry Hyde, second earl of Clarendon, lord lieutenant of Ireland, and with their patronage combining with the king's knowledge of him, South appeared poised to gain what he most wanted, a bishopric. Yet despite his views and his connections South never received one. Between 1681 and 1685 he had apparently been offered several offices which he had declined by citing the burden of his other duties, but there is a strong possibility that South simply was not offered an office that he wanted. He may have been offered an Irish bishopric early in James's reign, for the see of Cashel became vacant in 1685, but if so he declined it. In July 1686 he wrote to William Sancroft, archbishop of Canterbury, imploring him for high office, perhaps the bishopric of Oxford, which South would have preferred above any other. Nothing came of South's request.

Neither South's professional ambitions nor his scruples were troubled by James's Catholicism, but circumstances eventually forced him to reconsider his sacramental view of kingship. His 1721 biographer claimed that South had promised to 'change his black Gown for a Buff-Coat' (*Memoirs of the Life of the Late Reverend Dr. South*, 112) in order to suppress the rising of James Scott, duke of Monmouth, in 1685, and in 1688 he showed no enthusiasm for the proposed invasion of William of Orange. Once William had landed he delayed declaring for either James or William for as long as possible. Flummoxed like many Anglicans by the conflict between legitimacy and orthodoxy he delivered sermons which offered ecumenical jeremiads but conclusively evinced a more passionate hatred of protestant rebels than of Catholics. James might have failed England, but South feared more the consequences of William, who combined military aggression with a Calvinist protestantism alien to South's vision of the established church, ascending the throne. South strained to change his colours, and he took the new oaths of allegiance on 31 July 1689, the last day possible to do so without incurring suspension as a nonjuror. His confidence in divine right grudgingly fell beneath the accommodationist fiction that James had abdicated the throne by failing to protect his subjects, and so was consequently owed no obedience. By 1691–2 South had fully finessed his transition into compliance with William and Mary: England, the chosen nation of God, had replaced the king as God's chosen vicegerent on earth, and the sovereignty of the conscience had displaced that of James II. These were dramatic changes for South, given his fervent espousal of divine right during the Restoration. Yet he retained the Augustinian dismissal of dissenters' consciences, holding that these were merely inferior consciences that needed coercion to improve them into orthodoxy. These changes may account for his redoubled hatred of the dissenters, the 'sly, sanctified sycophants' (South, *Twelve Sermons*, 2.547) of 1689, whom he genuinely believed sought nothing less than the destruction of the church itself.

South accommodated, but the politics of religion following the revolution of 1688 effectively excluded him from a bishopric for the next two decades, which he spent writing and preaching against the various, but in his mind related, enemies of the high-church position. First and most visible were the heirs of both civil war puritanism and Restoration presbyterianism: these South routinely depicted as unredeemably ignorant, of too low a social station to qualify for the ministry, and made literally insensible in the light of their extemporaneous preaching and their delusional claims to divine inspiration. The royalist memory of the civil wars consistently informed his polemic: such dissenters South frequently compared to the unread shop-hands who in his memory had seized the pulpits at knifepoint during the interregnum. South's attacks upon extemporaneous preaching and divine inspiration made him a royalist, but they did not make him a rationalist. For second among his foes came the dissenters who had embraced rationalism instead: these threatened South's mystical Christianity as the revolution had destroyed his sacramental view of kingship. Just as he blamed a French Dominican for introducing extemporary prayer into England, South blamed the philosophy of René Descartes, the 'rational world' (South, *Tritheism*, sig. A2v) and its dependence on 'impartial reason' (ibid.) for the church's sufferings. For South the introduction of rationalism into theology, such as the Socinians' argument against the Trinity, had caused the church as much trouble as had the puritans and their radical brethren.

South hated inspired dissenters and rational Socinians with equal intensity, but he is most renowned for his attack upon William Sherlock, a fellow Anglican who sought to defeat the same enemies. Since 1690 Sherlock had been embarked upon a quixotic effort to demonstrate the reality of the Trinity with rationalist methods. This, he hoped, would unhand the Socinians with their own weapons. Yet for South mystery and incomprehensibility were the essence of the Trinity and of Christianity itself: Christianity was manifestly not reasonable. In 1693 and again in 1695 South gleefully dismembered Sherlock's argument in *Animadversions upon Dr. Sherlock's Book* (1693), and *Tritheism Charged upon Dr. Sherlock's New Notion of the Trinity* (1695). John Wallis, his old ally from Oxford and a fellow nemesis of Thomas Hobbes, attacked Sherlock as well. Yet the witty invective and genteel irony of South's performances should not conceal his resolute conviction that the end of Anglican orthodoxy could never justify the means of rationalism. His defence of the Trinity against Sherlock may be seen as a Laudian riposte to John Locke's similarly robust attack upon Robert Filmer in the first treatise: Lockean epistemology could dismantle divine right, but rationalism could never comprehend Christian mystery, however much it claimed to support orthodox doctrine. Yet South never took on Locke, whom he admired despite their many differences; Sherlock was dean of St Paul's and thus a dangerous insider, but Locke's Socinianism put him beyond the boundary of toleration itself.

South's health began to decline after 1698, and during Anne's reign he remained for the most part inactive, living in his house near Westminster Abbey, attending its services, and preparing volumes of his sermons for the press. South urged leniency for Henry Sacheverell during the latter's trial in March 1710, and with the downfall of the ministry of Sidney Godolphin, earl of Godolphin, and John Churchill, duke of Marlborough, later that year, his hopes for a bishopric revived for the first time since the 1688 revolution. When in 1713 he was offered the bishopric of Rochester, made vacant by the death of Thomas Sprat, South declined on the basis of his infirmity. Francis Atterbury, dean of Christ Church, prolocutor of convocation, and high-church champion, took that mitre instead in June 1713, and South fully approved. South died on 8 July 1716. After lying in state at the Jerusalem Chamber and then at the college hall of Westminster, South's corpse was attended by Atterbury to Westminster Abbey, where he was buried on 12 July near the steps of the altar, adjacent to the tomb of his beloved Busby. South's Laudian loyalties survived his accommodation with the revolution, and they ruled beyond the grave: he left £200 in his will for twenty ejected nonjurors, while requiring other beneficiaries to conform to the prayer book worship as decreed by the 1662 Act of Uniformity. Such stubbornness earned him the praise of the nonjuror Thomas Hearne, who described South as 'pretty honest, though he was a Complyer' (*Remarks and Collections* of Thomas Hearne, ed. C. E. Doble and others, 5, 1901, 264).

BURKE GRIGGS

Sources R. South, *Sermons preached upon several occasions*, 7 vols. (1823) • R. South, *Animadversions upon Dr. Sherlock's book*, 2nd edn (1693) • R. South, *Tritheism charged upon Dr. Sherlock's new notion of the Trinity* (1695) • J. Spur, *The Restoration Church of England* (1991) • G. Reedy, *Robert South (1634–1716): an introduction to his life and sermons* (1992) • G. V. Bennett, *The tory crisis in church and state, 1688–1730* (1975) • *Memoirs of the life of the late Reverend Dr. South* (1721) • R. South, *Interest deposed*, 2nd edn (1668) • R. South, *A sermon preached at Lambeth Chapel* (1666) • R. South, *A sermon preached before the court* (1665) • R. South, *Sermons preached upon several occasions* (1679) • R. South, *Twelve sermons preached upon several occasions*, 3 vols. (1692–8) • *Old Westminsters* • Foster, *Alum. Oxon.*

Archives BL, commonplace book, Lansdowne MS 695

Likenesses oils, *c.*1660–1669, Bodl. Oxf.; version, Christ Church Oxf. • G. Vertue, line engraving, 1711–16, Westminster Abbey, dean and chapter • attrib. F. Bird, tomb effigy on monument, Westminster Abbey • G. Vertue, line engraving (after R. White), BM, NPG • R. White, line engraving, NPG • portrait, Oriel College, Oxford

Southall. For this title name *see* Pearson, Alexander, Lord Southall (*d.* 1657).

Southall, Joseph Edward (1861–1944), painter and pacifist, was born on 23 August 1861 in Albert Street, Nottingham, the son of Joseph Sturge Southall (1835–1862), grocer, and Elizabeth Maria Baker (1833–1922). His parents, both Quakers, had married the previous year. When his father died in September 1862, his mother took him to Edgbaston, Birmingham, to live with his maternal grandmother. From 1872 he attended Friends' schools in Ackworth, Bootham in York, and Scarborough, and received lessons in watercolour painting from Edwin Moore in York. In 1878 he became articled to Martin and Chamberlain, one of Birmingham's leading architectural practices, where he stayed until 1882, keeping himself through an inheritance from his father and an uncle. He found the training too narrow: a true architect, he thought, should be able to carve and paint. About 1882 he returned to Edgbaston to live at 13 Charlotte Road, a house which had belonged to his uncle, George Baker, and where he was to spend the rest of his life. While an architectural apprentice Southall studied in the evenings at the Birmingham School of Art, then one of the country's leading art schools, where he absorbed the principles of the arts and crafts movement, particularly in drawing from nature, and won various prizes in national competitions. In 1883 he spent eight weeks in Italy, having taken with him John Ruskin's *St Mark's Rest* (3 pts, 1877–84). He became an ardent admirer of the Italian primitives and developed a great interest in egg tempera painting.

On Southall's return to England, George Baker, master of Ruskin's Guild of St George, showed some of his nephew's drawings to Ruskin, who, according to the artist, 'praised them highly and said he had never seen architecture better drawn' (MS autobiography, private information). Baker had given to the guild land adjoining his property at Bewdley, near Kidderminster, and in 1885 Ruskin commissioned Southall to design a museum there for the guild, since he had quarrelled with Sheffield council over the original site. Before the museum could be constructed, however, Ruskin made up his quarrel with Sheffield council and the original plans went ahead. Southall wrote in his manuscript autobiography: 'my chance as an architect vanished and years of obscurity with not a little bitterness of soul followed' (ibid.).

The year 1893 was a key one in Southall's development: he had the first of several highly influential interviews with the Birmingham-born artist Edward Burne-Jones and, with his fellow art student and lifelong best friend, Arthur Gaskin, he visited William Morris at Kelmscott Manor, his home in the Cotswolds. Southall returned to tempera painting with renewed vigour, though his first exhibit at the Royal Academy was a watercolour, *Cinderella* (1895, Tate collection). He began to exhibit regularly at the annual exhibitions held by municipal art galleries and the Arts and Crafts Exhibition Society and, from 1904, abroad. Having become firmly established as a tempera painter, he was a co-founder, in 1901, of the Society of Painters in Tempera, and he gave lessons at home in the technique. He preferred natural paints, and usually painted on linen, but occasionally on wood, paper, and silk. The hatched brushstrokes typical of his tempera paintings were mainly a consequence of the properties of the egg tempera medium. From this time he began to be elected to art bodies in Britain and France, and he held the presidency of the Royal Birmingham Society of Artists from 1939 to 1944.

Like other members of the arts and crafts movement Southall frequently designed his own frames for his paintings. These were usually gilded by his wife, Anna Elizabeth (Bessie) Baker (1859–1947), his first cousin whom he married on 23 June 1903. They had known each other since their youth, though because of their existing family relationship they decided to have no children of their own. His wife frequently accompanied him on his regular visits to Southwold, Suffolk, or Fowey, Cornwall, and to Italy or France, where Southall produced many boat studies and landscapes. In Italy he saw many examples of mural painting and was keen to promote the use of *buon fresco*, or true fresco, in Britain to enhance public buildings as they did in Italy. His most famous fresco, still *in situ*, is *Corporation Street, Birmingham, in March 1914* (1916, City of Birmingham Museum and Art Gallery).

The main body of Southall's work was his easel paintings in tempera of mythological and romantic subjects, which often took up to two years to complete owing to their large size. He exhibited these works, including his largest, *Beauty Receiving the White Rose from her Father* (1898–9, City of Birmingham Museum and Art Gallery), again and again, but painted few after 1910, doubtless partly because of the time they took and consequent high price, and partly because his reputation was secure. The majority were exhibited together at the influential Galeries Georges Petit in Paris in 1910, certainly his single most important exhibition, which received critical acclaim as well as good sales. Southall's tempera work showed clear and precise outlines and bright and clear colour, and had a permanence he believed to be greater than that which could be achieved by oil-based paint.

Since the latter part of the nineteenth century large numbers of Quaker families, in Birmingham particularly, had been commissioning portraits of themselves from Southall. His Quaker background and connections led him to become a pacifist of deep conviction, and following the outbreak of war in 1914 he became chairman of the Birmingham city branch of the Independent Labour Party, a position he held until 1931. The majority of his public correspondence was concerned with politics and especially pacifism. His commitment to pacifism meant that his painting output suffered considerably during the First World War, though his political cartoons, mostly published in pamphlets, are among his most poignant, powerful, and acerbic work.

Joseph Southall died of heart failure at his home, 13 Charlotte Road, Edgbaston, Birmingham, on 6 November 1944 and was interred in the Society of Friends' part of Witton cemetery, Birmingham, four days later. He was survived by his wife. In his life Southall brought together the gathered stillness of a Quaker meeting, the jewelled calm of tempera painting, and the peace sought by pacifism. A memorial exhibition was held in 1945 at the City of Birmingham Museum and Art Gallery, which has examples of his work. GEORGE BREEZE

Sources private information (2004) [family MSS] · G. Breeze, *Joseph Southall, 1861–1944: artist-craftsman* (1980) [incl. technical notes by J. Dunkerton; exhibition catalogue, Birmingham City Museum and Art Gallery, and the Fine Art Society, London] · letters from Joseph Southall to Arthur Gaskin, priv. colls. · A. Crawford, ed., *By hammer and hand: the arts and crafts movement in Birmingham* (1984) · H. Stokes, 'A modern Gozzoli', *Lady's Realm*, 17 (1904), 17–24 · J. E. Southall, 'Grounds suitable for tempera', *Papers of the Society of Painters in Tempera*, 2nd edn, 1 (1928), 1–7 · M. M. Harvey, 'A Quaker artist and rebel', *Friends' Quarterly*, 14 (1963), 353–61 [reprinted] · M. Armfield, introductory notes, *Memorial exhibition of works by the late Joseph Edward Southall* (1945), 1–8 [exhibition catalogue, City of Birmingham Museum and Art Gallery, 27 March – 24 April, 1945] · V. Massey, *A testimony to the life of Joseph Edward Southall* (Warwickshire Society of Friends, 1945); repr. (1946) · J. E. Southall, 'The graphic arts in education', *Friends' Quarterly Examiner*, 59 (1925), 130–45 · C. Napier-Clavering, 'Birmingham painters and craftsmen at the Fine Art Society's galleries', *The Studio*, 42 (1907–8), 215–22 · C. Gere, *The earthly paradise* (1969) [exhibition catalogue, The Fine Art Society, London] · *CGPLA Eng. & Wales* (1945) · Mallalieu, *Watercolour artists*

Archives Birm. CA, notebooks and papers · Birmingham Museums and Art Gallery, collection of material relating to his works; collection of material relating to 1980 exhibition organized by G. Breeze for Birmingham and The Fine Art Society, London · priv. coll., family MSS · Religious Society of Friends, Birmingham, corresp. and papers | priv. coll., letters to Arthur Gaskin

Likenesses J. E. Southall, self-portrait, tempera on wood panel, 1896, priv. coll. · J. E. Southall, self-portrait, tempera on linen, 1911 (the artist with his wife), priv. coll. · J. E. Southall, self-portrait, buon fresco in a wooden case, 1925, University of Central England, faculty of art and design archive · J. E. Southall, self-portrait, tempera on wood panel, 1933, Society of Friends, Birmingham

Wealth at death £13,707 7s. 11d.: probate, 23 Jan 1945, *CGPLA Eng. & Wales*

Southampton. For this title name *see* Fitzwilliam, William, earl of Southampton (*c*.1490–1542); Wriothesley, Thomas, first earl of Southampton (1505–1550); Wriothesley, Henry, second earl of Southampton (*bap*. 1545, *d*. 1581); Wriothesley, Henry, third earl of Southampton (1573–1624); Wriothesley, Thomas, fourth earl of Southampton (1608–1667); FitzRoy, Charles, second duke of Cleveland and first duke of Southampton (1662–1730); FitzRoy, Charles, first Baron Southampton (1737–1797).

Southborough. For this title name *see* Hopwood, Francis John Stephens, first Baron Southborough (1860–1947).

Southcote, John (1510/11–1585), judge, was the son of William Southcote and Alice Tregonwell, a niece of the civilian John *Tregonwell. The Southcotes were a Devon family. William's father, Nicholas, lived at Chudleigh, and William's brother John (*d*. 1556), clerk of the peace for Devon, lived at Bovey Tracey. There is some evidence that the younger John Southcote lived for a time at Bodmin in Cornwall. He was admitted to the Middle Temple between 1535 and 1537, probably after studying at Lyon's Inn, which sued a John Southcote (possibly his uncle) for dues in 1543. In 1553 he was twice returned to parliament, by Lewes and Steyning respectively. By that time he had settled in London and been appointed one of the under-sheriffs, which made him a judge of the sheriffs' court; and in 1554 he became a justice of the peace for Middlesex. It was about this time that he married Elizabeth, daughter of the London alderman William Robins. In 1556 he was elected autumn reader of the Middle Temple, and only two years later was offered the coif by Queen Mary. The writs for the serjeants' call abated on the queen's death, but Southcote's writ was renewed by Elizabeth and he was created serjeant in April 1559, having read for a second time in Lent as serjeant-elect.

On 10 February 1563 Southcote was appointed a justice of the queen's bench, and from about that time began to acquire an estate at Witham, Essex, where he lived until his death. In 1575 he purchased Petworth's in Witham, and it is believed that he was responsible for building Witham Place there soon afterwards. He also had a well-furnished house in Carter Lane in the parish of St Gregory by Paul, London. He served as a puisne judge under Sir Robert Catlin and Sir Christopher Wray, and his opinions were noted by Plowden, Dyer, and other Elizabethan reporters. Coke related a story that when Chief Justice Catlin suggested altering a record, Southcote refused to assent, 'and said openly, that he meant not to build a clock-house' (Coke, *Third Institute*, 72), referring to the legend that a fine imposed on Chief Justice Hengham in the time of Edward I was reputedly used to build the clock house of Westminster Palace. He served as an assize judge on the home circuit for twenty years, even though the circuit included Essex. He retired from circuit work in 1582, and was formally discharged from his judicial office on 1

June 1584. Although there was a family tradition that he had resigned to avoid condemning a priest, there is no contemporary evidence of recusancy and he may simply have been allowed to retire on grounds of illness or age. He died on 18 April 1585 and was buried at Witham, where there is a grand monument with his effigy in judicial robes. The inscription gives his age at death as seventy-four and records that he had thirteen children, but only one son, John, and two daughters survived him. He was remembered as 'a good natured man … governed by his wife' (HoP, *Commons, 1509–58*, 3.351). J. H. Baker

Sources HoP, *Commons, 1509–58*, 3.350–51 • Baker, *Serjeants*, 171, 538 • Sainty, *Judges*, 30 • P. R. P. Knell, 'The Southcott family in Essex, 1575–1642', *Essex Recusant*, 14 (1972), 1–38 • PRO, CP 40/1116, m. 621 [Lyon's Inn] • C. H. Hopwood, ed., *Middle Temple records*, 1: *1501–1603* (1904) • W. C. Metcalfe, ed., *The visitations of Essex*, 1, Harleian Society, 13 (1878), 491–2 • PRO, KB 29/212–213 [house in Carter Lane] • J. S. Cockburn, *A history of English assizes, 1558–1714* (1972) • pedigree roll (MS), 1572, priv. coll. [in the possession of Professor J. H. Baker] • will, PRO, PROB 11/69, sig. 24 • monument, Witham church, Essex • inquisition post mortem, PRO, C142/206/25
Likenesses oils, *c*.1563–1582, Ingatestone Hall, Essex

Southcote, Philip (1697/8–1758), landscape gardener, was the son of Edward Southcote, head of an influential Roman Catholic family, originally from Chudleigh, Devon, but then living at Albery, Surrey. His early life is chronicled in the memoirs of his mistress, (Teresa) Constantia Phillips, published in 1748 as *Apology for the Conduct of Mrs Teresa Constantia Phillips*. As a young man he went to the University of Lorraine (which was probably located at Pont-à-Mousson), returning to England in 1723. Edward Southcote, financially impoverished and with five male children who had survived to manhood, was hard pressed to fund their lifestyles. The manor of Albery, which had been in the family for 150 years, was sold in 1727 with the exception of an interest in a number of farms retained by Philip's brother Edward.

In 1727 Southcote met (Teresia) Constantia *Phillips and two years later went to Italy with his patron, thought to have been the eighth duke of Norfolk. He renewed his relationship with his mistress in 1730, by which time Philip was well known in the upper ranks of society since he had acquired a veneer of culture from his residence in France and travels in Italy. He was acquainted through his uncle with Alexander Pope and closely associated with the Petres, another prominent Roman Catholic family.

In 1732, Southcote's income was augmented following his marriage on 3 February to Anne Fitzroy (*d.* 1745), a much older wealthy widow, daughter of Sir William Pulteney of Misterton, Leicestershire, whose first husband had been Charles Fitzroy, duke of Cleveland (son of Charles II and Lady Castlemaine). After their marriage, Southcote had use of the duchess's house in St James's Square, London. Social convention dictated that it was necessary for them to acquire a country residence. As he had no estate of his own, they purchased the 116 acre Wooburn Farm (later known as Woburn), located to the west of Weybridge, Surrey. As a precaution against fine or sequestration or the imposition of a capital levy on Roman Catholics, the conveyance, dated 15 April 1735, was in the name of Lord Lichfield.

Southcote began to develop the estate with an assurance and flair that was unexpected, extending the ornamentation from the garden to the more utilitarian aspects of the surrounding fields. 35 acres were planted with trees, shrubs, and flower borders. The rest remained as farmland interspersed with ornamental walks and coverts. His novel approach was widely praised in many contemporary accounts. Joseph Spence, who knew Southcote and his farm intimately, claimed that Philip pioneered the garden farm or 'ferme ornée'. George Mason, in *An Essay on Designing Gardening* (1768), also credited Southcote with coining the term 'ferme ornée', which was not used in France at that time. He noted that 'the elegance of Woburn Farm was so conspicuous that even its faults were imposing'. Wooburn soon became a fashionable place visited by the leisured classes. Its popularity was enhanced by the writings and lyrics of William Shenstone, a minor poet of the pastoral school. Not all visitors, though, were well behaved. Horace Walpole observed that at one time 'Mr. Southcote was forced to shut up his garden for the savages who came as connoisseurs, scribbled a thousand brutalities in the buildings upon his religion' (King).

Following the death of his first wife on 2 February 1745, Southcote married Bridget (*d.* 1783), daughter of Sir Francis Andrew. He himself was buried on 2 October 1758 at Witham, Essex. The estate was maintained more or less in the way he had left it until the death of his second wife in 1783. Although the Petre family, who acquired the estate from his wife, attempted to maintain it, by the 1820s it appeared significantly different from Southcote's initial aspirations.

After William Kent, Southcote was the second most important contributor to this new style of landscape gardening. Unlike Kent, who strove to create an elysium or classical paradise, his efforts focused on creating an arcady or ideal countryside. Twentieth-century texts have been more sceptical of his long-term contribution since, after the estate had decayed after his second wife's death, there were few surviving written records of his achievements. The high upkeep of ornamental farms based on his principles became commercially unacceptable for even the wealthy classes by the early nineteenth century. An objective evaluation of Southcote's input to new natural gardening by R. W. King has suggested that he developed at least two original ideas of his own: the lavish use of flowers, particularly away from the main house; and the ornamental peripheral walk. Changes in gardening fashion banished flower, fruit, and vegetable gardens to hidden walled enclosures. His concept of a peripheral walk, although shorn of its ornament to become more utilitarian, still remained popular in the twentieth century.

John Martin

Sources R. W. King, 'The *ferme ornée*: Philip Southcote and Woburn Farm', *Garden History*, 2/3 (1974), 27–60, 28a • J. Sambrook,

'Wooburn Farm in the 1760s', *Garden History*, 7/2 (1979), 82–101 • D. Jacques, 'Southcote's Wooburn', *Garden History*, 3/2 (1975), 3–6 [letter to the ed.] • D. Jacques, 'Two notes on James Sambrook's article on Wooburn Farm', *Garden History*, 7/3 (1979), 9–12 • M. Hadfield, R. Harling, and L. Highton, *British gardeners: a biographical dictionary* (1980) • M. Hadfield, *A history of British gardening*, 3rd edn (1979) • T. C. Phillips, *Apology for the conduct of Mrs Teresa Constantia Phillips* (1748) • T. Whately, *Observations on modern gardening* (1770) • E. Malins and the Knight of Glin, 'Landscape gardening by Jonathan Swift and his friends in Ireland', *Garden History*, 2/1 (1973), 69–93, esp. 74–5 • J. Spence, *Observations, anecdotes, and characters, of books and men*, ed. J. M. Osborn, new edn, 2 vols. (1966) • *The Shell gardens book* (1964) • O. Manning and W. Bray, *The history and antiquities of the county of Surrey*, 3 vols. (1804–14) • G. Dawson, 'The Jacobite Southcotes of Witham', *Essex Review*, 63 (1954), 143–65 • M. Lefevre, *St George's College, Weybridge, 1869–1969* (1969) • G. Mason, *An essay on design in gardening* (1768)

Archives St George's College, Weybridge, archives | Essex RO, Petre MSS

Likenesses double portrait, photograph (Philip and Bridget Southcote), repro. in King, 'The *ferme ornée*', 28a

Wealth at death see King, 'The *ferme ornée*' • will, Essex RO

Southcott, Joanna (1750–1814), prophet and writer, was born on 25 April 1750 in Taleford, near Ottery St Mary, Devon, the fourth of six children, and was raised in the village of Gittisham, 16 miles from Exeter. Her father, William Southcott (*d.* 1802), was a tenant farmer, and her mother, Hannah, *née* Godfrey (*d. c.*1770), was the daughter of a respectable farmer from Ottery St Mary. William, who continued to be aggrieved over his grandfather's loss of the Southcott family estate in Herefordshire, instilled in his daughter a strong sense of pride in her ancestry and in the quality of her work, however humble. As a girl, Joanna developed a lifelong habit of reading scripture and interpreting everyday events within a spiritual frame. Although inclined when about twenty to high spirits and a taste for pretty clothes and romance, she promised her dying mother that she would commit herself to a life of piety. During her twenties and thirties, Southcott held various positions in different households in and around Exeter, mostly as a farm labourer, maidservant, and upholsterer. Although Southcott did not start publishing her writings until 1801, when she was fifty-one, most of her texts are enlivened by fascinating fragments of village lore and autobiographical detail from her early life in Devon. In *What manner of communications are these?* (1804) she recalls various encounters with desirable suitors (and at least one impudent footman) in order to elaborate on the intricate progress of her spiritual life; this is evident in the story of her first boyfriend, Noah Bishop, the farmer's son from Sidmouth, whom she teased and rejected for some time, about 1768, before regaining her holy bearings (pp. 27–40; Seymour, 1.143–52). The more dramatic experiences of others could also be turned to similar effect. For example, when questioned on the propriety of including such materials in her books, especially the racy ballad of Lord Burnet's discovery and murder of his wife's lover in their marriage bed (now known as the 'Ballad of Mattie Groves'), Southcott was convinced that even this narrative could be transformed into a spiritual sign that the Lord

Joanna Southcott (1750–1814), by William Sharp, in or before 1812

would return in just fury against the nation that had betrayed him with Satan.

Origins of a visionary Southcott's millenarian visions first began in 1792 when she was forty-two years old. Day and night, she was spoken to by a 'voice' predicting what would happen on earth, from the coming war in France to food shortages in the west country. These communications first happened while she was working in the household of the Taylors, who found it to their profit, both materially and spiritually, to heed her providential advice to lay in stores. Along with other Exeter witnesses, Lucy Taylor later corroborated Southcott's claim that a number of her predictions had come true during the 1790s (*The Trial of Joanna Southcott*, 1804, 59–60). To prove the authenticity of her mission, Southcott developed the bold stratagem of sealing her prophecies and sending them to clergymen or other dignitaries, so that her predictions could be tested against future events. In her first book, *The Strange Effects of Faith* (1801), she recounts her persistent efforts (between 1792 and 1800) to have her prophetic role and the truth of her visions examined and accredited by the clergy. She accuses the religious leaders she approached—including a Methodist (John Eastlake), a Calvinist-Methodist (Henry Tanner), a dissenter (Mr Leach), and an Anglican (Joseph Pomeroy)—of returning or burning her letters, of belittling her humble station and bad handwriting, and of forbidding her to publish her writings, even though she had been ordered to do so by her 'voice'. Southcott saw herself as appointed to speak for the poor and working classes during a time of war and crisis, when their acute distress was being ignored by the clergy and the privileged classes. Typically, in a letter dated 23 March 1800, she attacks the Revd Pomeroy, vicar of St Kew, Cornwall, who had at first heard her petitions with respect, for his proud indifference: 'I hear the cries of the poor, complaining they are starving to death, for want of food' (*Copies of Letters Sent to the Clergy of Exeter*, 1813, 27). Her confidence grew, as did her local fame, when her predictions—regarding the date of the death of Bishop Buller of Exeter in December 1796, and the crop failures and ensuing famines of 1799 and 1800—were fulfilled.

Finally, in 1801, weary of admonishing the local clergy to no avail, Southcott used up her life savings, supplemented by loans, to print 1000 copies of the first part of her book, *The Strange Effects of Faith; with Remarkable Prophecies (Made in 1792)*, five more parts of which were published by the end of 1802. This first work attracted the attention of some followers of the prophet Richard Brothers, who had been at the height of his influence about 1795, when his extravagant warnings—for example, that George III must surrender his crown to Brothers as God's chosen one—led to an eleven-year incarceration for insanity (1795–1806). In December 1801 six followers of Brothers and a seventh man (Peter Morrison, a cotton printer from Liverpool) travelled to Exeter to examine the new prophet's credibility. The seven stars, as Southcott called her judges, included three Anglican clergymen: Stanhope Bruce, vicar of Inglesham; Thomas Webster, a London cleric; and Thomas Philip Foley, rector of Old Swinford near Stourbridge, Worcestershire, who became one of Southcott's most loyal friends. The other four were Morrison; John Wilson, a coach-maker of Kentish town; George Turner, a merchant of Leeds, who became a prominent regional recruiter; and William Sharp (1749–1824), the master engraver, who later created the best-known portrait of Southcott. By the next year, these men had arranged for Southcott to move to London, where they provided her with lodgings and began to promote her work. The Exeter trial of Southcott's claims was followed by two more public trials; one in a house in Paddington rented by Foley, and the third at Neckinger House, Bermondsey, at the home of Elias Carpenter, a wealthy papermill owner, who was, for a time, a tireless promoter of her mission. By 1803 the nucleus of Brothers's followers had declared their convincement. Southcott had been careful not to attack Brothers and seemed to advocate his release, but once she had secured his main followers, she declared the superiority of her mission. After consolidating her following in London during 1803 and 1804, Southcott went on a missionary tour and was particularly successful in Yorkshire and the west country in attracting people to her stunning promise of a redeemed England in which the true heirs would soon come to possess the land.

The Southcottian movement One of the most significant of her London converts was Jane Townley, who not only invited Southcott, in April 1804, to become part of her household, but also did all she could to promote Southcott's writings and cause, including providing her maidservant, Ann Underwood, to act as Southcott's accomplished and devoted amanuensis. With the steadfast assistance of Foley, Sharp, and others, the three women became the nerve centre for the Southcottian movement, which generated an astonishing degree of interest, correspondence, and debate regarding Southcott's prophetic claims. Between 1801 and 1814, Southcott published some sixty-five pamphlets, totalling almost 5000 pages; moreover, her unpublished manuscripts amount to twice the number of pages in print. By one conservative estimate, a total of 108,000 copies of her various works were published and circulated from 1801 to 1816, making her one of the most popular writers of her time (Hopkins, 84). One reason for the immediate appeal of her texts is their unique mix of apocalyptic optimism with down-to-earth narratives about everyday life, which she converts to spiritual account. Particularly vivid are her narratives of what it was like to be an unmarried maidservant negotiating the sexual politics of a household. During the early 1780s, she stayed for five years with the Wills family from whom she learned the upholstering trade. Complaining of his adulterous wife, her master Wills had tried to seduce Southcott by declaring his desire to be her Christian lover. She rejected him in no uncertain terms: 'no tongue can paint the horror I felt, to hear of love from a married man' (*Copies and Parts of Copies of Letters and Communications, Written … to Mr W. Sharp*, 1804, 18–19). She agreed to stay in his household, however, after Wills arranged to bring a Methodist minister into the house as a lodger to restore moral order. Unfortunately, the lodger turned out to be the charismatic preacher Hugh Saunderson, who violated Wills's trust by seducing the obliging Mrs Wills and by trying to turn the couple's children against their father. Southcott intervened by trying to have the Methodists remove Saunderson from the house without scandal. This ploy proving ineffectual, she was forced to inform Wills directly. Flying into a violent fit, Wills unaccountably accused Southcott of lying and drove her from his household. His malice was so great that he vindictively spread lies to prevent her from obtaining a new position. Her good name being her chief capital, she sued Wills and won the case because, although many false witnesses were paid to defame her, Wills's own son refused to come to bear false witness. Her triumph in going to court and being found trustworthy became a model of success by which her credibility as a prophet could be put to public trial.

Early on, Southcott developed the practice of sealing as a way to bind her scattered followers into one community of believers. The practice entailed drawing a circle on a piece of paper, within which was written a simple message of acceptance; the believer signed at the top, Southcott signed below; then the paper was folded and sealed with Southcott's special seal, which contained two stars and the initials IC (Iesu Christi). Southcott initially cast her sealing net wide, but soon it became a prerequisite that all those wishing to be sealed read two of her booklets, *Sound an Alarm in my Holy Mountain* (1804), and *A Caution and Instruction to the Sealed* (1807), to familiarize themselves with what was required of the heirs to the new Jerusalem. A safe estimate of the total number of sealed followers achieved by 1815 is around 20,000 (Harrison, 109). The practice also left Southcott open to abuse, as can be seen in the notorious case of the fortune-teller and con-artist Mary Bateman (1768–1809), who obtained one of Southcott's seals in order to capitalize on the spirit of the age. In 1806 Bateman charged admission to see her display of three millennial eggs, hatched from a miraculous hen, inscribed with the message 'Christ is Coming'. Bateman defrauded, bullied, and bribed a number of victims from York to Leeds, before being convicted and hanged in 1809 for poisoning one of her clients with arsenic. Southcott eventually denounced not only Bateman, but also the newspapers that malevolently deceived the public by insinuating that Southcott herself was somehow connected to fraud and murder (*A True Picture of the World and a Looking Glass for All Men*, 1809?, 7–8; Seymour, 1.243–4).

Mother of Shiloh One key element of Southcott's sect was its insistence that a female figure would bring about millennial change. Similar to Jane Lead and the Philadelphians of the 1690s, Southcott underlined the significance of such biblical passages as Genesis 3, in which God promises that the woman's seed shall bruise the serpent's head, and Revelation 12, in which the Woman clothed in Sun brings about a new order. This point was reinforced also by several strategic visions. In June 1804, full of self-doubt and wounded by the vicious public attacks on her character, Southcott retreated from London to a house in Bristol. She was pacing up and down when the whole house began to shake with her fury and despair, frightening those living with her; Southcott fell into a frenzy—'words flew too fast to utter'—but then she recomposed herself. Her prophetic 'voice' asserted that, just as the house trembled, the whole earth would tremble, and powerful men and doubting clergy would fall; then the 'voice' re-established Southcott's authority, saying: 'I will conquer in woman's form' (*Copies and Parts of Copies of Letters and Communications, Written … to Mr W. Sharp*, 79; Seymour, 1.52). In 1814 Southcott carried the claim to a new level when she announced that she was about to become the mother of Shiloh, the name given to the expected divine incarnation. The revelation was made explicit in *The Third Book of Wonders, Announcing the Coming of Shiloh* (1814), and *Prophecies Announcing the Birth of the Prince of Peace* (1814), which collected extractions from earlier writings that seemed to anticipate this new revelation. Public incredulity reached new heights in April of that year when it was rumoured that a number of physicians were being called in to examine Southcott's body, which was said to be showing signs of pregnancy, although, as she freely admitted to her doctors, she was a virgin and sixty-four years old. In fact, for believers, the very absurdity of the situation seemed to confirm its miraculous potential. The popular press exploded with laughter and scorn as can be seen in Thomas Rowlandson's cartoon 'A Medical Inspection, or, Miracles will Never Cease', which shows an obese Joanna lifting her skirts to be examined by leering medical men. By November Southcott was overdue, and she was said to be enduring terrible labour pains. In hope that all that was wanting to effect delivery was a legal father, on 12 November 1814 Southcott married John Smith (1758–1829) of Blockley, a respectable friend of her own age and a former steward to the earl of Darnley, who offered himself in the role of Joseph, the adopted father of the expected Shiloh.

The marriage was to be annulled if Shiloh did not appear; however, Southcott died on 27 December 1814 at 38 Manchester Street, London. Given the possibility that she was only in a trance, her body was wrapped in flannel and kept warm for four days. At the time, according to Dr Richard Reece, the engraver William Sharp believed that her body could be resuscitated and Shiloh produced. When Reece protested at such a delusion, Sharp retorted, 'Ah, Sir, you take only a *professional* view of it, but I take a *spiritual* one' (Seymour, 2.389). Finally on 31 December an autopsy took place at 38 Manchester Street at which were a number of her followers and several medical men, including James Sims, Joseph Adams, and Richard Reece. Southcott was buried at St John's Wood, Middlesex on 1 January 1815. However, her body continued to be the site of conflicting and confusing interpretations. Dr Mathias, who was also present at the autopsy, sought to give physical explanations for the symptoms of pregnancy in his *The Case of Johanna Southcott* (1815): the body, he argued, was already livid and putrid; he found four inches of fat on the abdomen, and glandular enlargement of the breasts; and he blamed the supposed quickness felt in her abdomen on extreme flatus in the intestines. On dissecting the uterus, no foetus was found. Or, as the believers put it, Shiloh had mysteriously disappeared.

After Southcott's death the movement splintered and prophets of Shiloh proliferated, among which John Ward's Shilohites and John Wroe's Christian Israelites were the most prominent. A core of her inner circle kept the faith quietly, remaining loyal to Southcott's work, as signified by their protection of the 'great box', which contained the sealed prophecies that were to be opened some time in the unspecified future by the bishops. The box had been made by William Sharp in 1801 to contain Southcott's prophecies and letters, which were opened at her second and third trials. In 1816 the box was passed to Jane Townley, and upon her death in 1825 to Thomas Philip Foley, and finally in 1835 to Foley's son, the Revd Richard Foley (*d.* 1861). In 1839, in order to gain control of Southcott's legacy, Lavinia Taylor Jones (niece of Lucy Taylor, Southcott's Exeter employer) dressed as a man to enter Richard Foley's rectory, where she tried to steal the 'great box'. Sometime after that, rival boxes began to appear. As recently as 1977, the Panacea Society, a twentieth-century millenarian group dedicated to rehabilitating Southcott's reputation, claimed to know the secret whereabouts of the true box (Exell, 55–62). In 1966 interest of a different and scholarly sort was enkindled, when E. P. Thompson, in full appreciation of

Southcott's working-class origins and enduring appeal, called her England's 'greatest prophetess of all' (Thompson, 382). SYLVIA BOWERBANK

Sources A. Seymour, *The Express … containing the life and divine writings of the late Joanna Southcott*, 2 vols. (1909) • J. Hopkins, *A woman to deliver her people: Joanna Southcott and English millenarianism in an era of revolution* (Austin, 1982) • J. F. C. Harrison, *The second coming: popular millenarianism, 1780–1850* (1979) • A. W. Exell, *Joanna Southcott at Blockley and the Rock Cottage relics* (1977) • G. R. Balleine, *Past finding out: the tragic story of Joanna Southcott and her successors* (1956) • P. Mathias, *The case of Johanna Southcott, as far as it came under his professional observation, impartially stated* (1815) • E. P. Thompson, *The making of the English working class* (New York, 1966) • E. P. Wright, *A catalogue of the Joanna Southcott collection at the University of Texas* (Austin, 1968) • D. Jones, *Catalogue of books published by Joanna Southcott* [n.d., after 1852] • C. Garrett, *Respectable folly: millenarians and the French Revolution in France and England* (Baltimore, 1975), 215–23, *passim* • C. Lane, *Life of Joanna Southcott and bibliography of Joanna Southcott*; repr. from *Transactions of the Devonshire Association for the Advancement of Science, Literature and Art*, 44 (1912), 732–809 • W. H. Oliver, *Prophets and millennialists: the uses of biblical prophecy in England from the 1790s to the 1840s* (Auckland, NZ, 1978) • R. Matthews, *English Messiahs: studies of six English religious pretenders, 1656–1927* (1936)

Archives BL, corresp. and papers, Add. MSS 26038–26039, 27919, 32633–32637, 47794–47803, 57860; Egerton MS 2399 • Blockley Antiquarian Society, Gloucestershire, Joanna Southcott collection and Rock Cottage relics • City Westm. AC, letters and writings • Glos. RO, corresp. and papers • JRL • LMA, papers • LUL, Harry Price Library • NRA, priv. coll., corresp. and papers • Ransom HRC, collection • Worcs. RO, papers and pamphlets | BL, index to writings relating to Joanna Southcott, Add. MS 65137 • Exeter Central Library, Westcountry Studies Library, Burnet Morris collection • Princeton University Library, New Jersey, Miriam Y. Holden Collection on the History of Women

Likenesses W. Sharp, engraving, 1812, repro. in Seymour, *The Express*, vol. 1, frontispiece • W. Sharp, pencil drawing, in or before 1812, NPG [*see illus.*] • A. Flat, etching, pubd 1814 (*The cunning woman*; after G. L.), BM • T. Rowlandson, caricature, 1814 (*A medical inspection, or, Miracles will never cease*) • stipple, pubd 1814 (*A correct view of the superb crib, presented to Joanna Southcott*), NPG • line engraving, repro. in Wright, *A catalogue*, facing p. 66

Southerey, Simon (*b*. *c*.1342, *d*. in or after 1420), Benedictine monk, was born possibly on the Norfolk estates of St Albans Abbey. He probably entered Hertford Priory, a dependency of St Albans, shortly after 1360, because he was ordained priest as a monk of the priory on 28 February 1366. He studied at Gloucester College, Oxford, during the 1370s, and was a doctor of theology by 1388 when, together with other graduates, he was cited to appear in chancery following serious disturbances between northerners and southerners at the university. Bale suggests he was present at the second session of the Blackfriars Council, convened in 1382 to condemn the work of John Wyclif, but may have confused him with his St Albans contemporary Nicholas Radcliffe. In 1389, as *prior studentium* of Gloucester College, Southerey defended the community against the attempts of William Courtenay, archbishop of Canterbury (*d*. 1396), to subject it to visitation. The St Albans chronicler, Thomas Walsingham, suggests that it was the force of Southerey's arguments that deterred the archbishop. In 1390 he was appointed prior of Belvoir, another dependency of St Albans, and remained there until the death of the abbot, Thomas de la Mare, in 1396. In addition to these responsibilities he was in constant demand as a representative of his order. In 1392 he was the only Benedictine to be present at the trial at Stamford of the suspected Wycliffite Henry Crump, and throughout the 1390s he was involved in the work of the Benedictine general chapters, serving as elector of the presidents in 1393 and as preacher at a chapter meeting *c*.1396. Soon after the election of Abbot John Moot in 1396, Southerey became prior of St Albans, and remained in office at least until 1401, when he supervised the election of William Heyworth as abbot. From 1396 to 1399 he was in receipt of a royal pension and in 1419 he became a papal chaplain; these were both unusual distinctions for a monk who was not an abbot, and are therefore an indication of Southerey's prestige.

Southerey was distinguished as a theologian, an opponent of the works of John Wyclif, an astronomer, and a poet whose work perhaps prefigured the humanists of the later fifteenth century. Walsingham wrote that not only were 'many turned away from the errors of John Wyclif as a result of his preaching', but also that Southerey was 'very able in the art of versification, and in astronomy and astrology, and in the study of poetry is considered the most learned in the whole kingdom' (*Annales … Amundesham*, 2.305). Southerey may have been the author of several theological works; Bale attributes three texts to him without incipits, *Super ecclesie auctoritate*, *De sacramento altaris*, and *Contra Wyclevistas*, but none of these survives. A fragment of an astrological almanac attributed to Southerey survives in a single manuscript (Bodl. Oxf., MS Digby 98, fol. 32), and it was perhaps for his astrological writing that he attracted the attention of Richard II and received a royal pension. Although none of his literary works is known to survive, he was praised by other writers for his knowledge of grammar, poetry, and classical literature. Walsingham dedicated his *Archana deorum*, a commentary on Ovid's *Metamorphoses*, to Southerey, and praised him for his great knowledge of classical fables. In the same way, the London grammar-master John Seward (*d*. 1435), who wrote a lengthy treatise, the *Somnium*, in Southerey's honour, presents him as a distinguished teacher of the rules of grammar and the art of metre. Through his association with Seward, Southerey may have been linked to other scholars who were also friends of the grammar-master, including Richard Courtenay, bishop of Norwich (*d*. 1415), and John Leyland, another celebrated grammarian.

Southerey was still alive in September 1420 at the election of Abbot John Whethamstede, although he was then among the sick confined to the infirmary. He probably died soon after; the year is unknown, but the day, 3 November, is recorded in the martyrology of Belvoir Priory. JAMES G. CLARK

Sources *Gesta abbatum monasterii Sancti Albani, a Thoma Walsingham*, ed. H. T. Riley, 3 vols., pt 4 of *Chronica monasterii S. Albani*, Rolls Series, 28 (1867–9), vol. 3, pp. 425–36, 479–90 • *Thomae Walsingham, quondam monachi S. Albani, historia Anglicana*, ed. H. T. Riley, 2 vols., pt 1 of *Chronica monasterii S. Albani*, Rolls Series, 28 (1863–4), vol. 2, pp. 190–92 • [T. Netter], *Fasciculi zizaniorum magistri Johannis Wyclif cum tritico*, ed. W. W. Shirley, Rolls Series, 5 (1858) • H. T. Riley, ed.,

Registra quorundam abbatum monasterii S. Albani, 2, Rolls Series, 28/6 (1873), 305 • V. H. Galbraith, 'John Seward and his circle', *Medieval and Renaissance Studies*, 1 (1941), 85–104 • Bale, *Cat.*, 1.496 • W. A. Pantin, ed., *Documents illustrating the activities of … the English black monks, 1215–1540*, 3 vols., CS, 3rd ser., 45, 47, 54 (1931–7), vol. 2 • *Registrum Simonis de Sudbiria, diocesis Londoniensis*, AD 1362–1375, ed. R. C. Fowler, 2, CYS, 38 (1938), 40 • T. Walsingham, *Archana deorum*, ed. R. A. Van Kluyve (1968) • *CEPR letters*, 7.1, 21 • PRO, E 403/556 m.4, E 403/559 m.9, E 403/562 m.3 • Unclassified MS fragments, Clare College, Cambridge, fol. 1v • Bodl. Oxf., MS Digby 98, fol. 32r–v • U. Edin. L., MS 136 • Trinity Cam. • *Annales monasterii S. Albani a Johanne Amundesham*, ed. H. T. Riley, 2 vols., pt 5 of *Chronica monasterii S. Albani*, Rolls Series, 28 (1870–71)

Archives Bodl. Oxf., MS Digby 98, fol. 32 | U. Edin., MS 136

Southern, Henry (1799–1853), journalist and diplomatist, was born at York, the son of Richard Southern, a barber. After attending school in York he entered Trinity College, Cambridge, as a sizar on 31 December 1814, graduated BA in 1819 as twenty-second senior optime, and proceeded MA in 1822. On 23 January 1822 he became a member of the Middle Temple, but he was not called to the bar. Meanwhile, he had founded the *Retrospective Review*, whose first number appeared in January 1820. Dedicated to the promotion of early English literature, most particularly of the sixteenth and seventeenth centuries, the *Review* provided 'valuable criticisms upon, analyses of, and extracts from curious, valuable, and scarce old books' (Introduction, *Retrospective Review* 1, 1820). Southern wrote a good deal of the material himself but also managed to recruit a number of talented, and often young, contributors, including Charles Wentworth Dilke, Thomas Noon Talfourd, the Unitarian William Johnson Fox, John Hamilton Reynolds, and Charles Barker, a friend from Trinity College (and possibly a schoolfellow), who acted as his assistant. Southern was sole editor of the *Review* until 1826, when the antiquary Sir Nicholas Harris Nicolas became his partner. The magazine folded in 1828.

By this time, however, Southern had been associated with other journals. When Jeremy Bentham founded the *Westminster Review* in 1824, he invited him to take charge of its literary pages alongside John Bowring, who was the political editor. Charles Barker again agreed to share Southern's duties. By now a confirmed Benthamite and a Unitarian, Southern took a distinctly utilitarian view of contemporary literature, tending to dismiss much of it as irrational, sentimental, and anti-progressive. He especially denigrated fashionable novels and light verse. Nevertheless, he impressed many, including Henry Crabb Robinson who was struck early on by his 'talent and learning'. The two became friends, though it was not an entirely happy relationship, Crabb Robinson often complaining in his diary of Southern's insobriety (which Francis Place also noticed) and his habit of not paying his debts. His friend's unwillingness to pay him for contributions to the *Westminster*, added to Southern's attack in its pages on Crabb Robinson's friend Ayrton, led to a final break. Crabb Robinson declared in exasperation that Southern had become a 'fanatic of reform' and an 'iconoclast'. Southern relinquished his role as co-editor of the *Westminster* in 1827, though he continued to write for it.

For nearly three years Southern had been associated with the *London Magazine*, first as associate editor, then from January 1825 as the editor of a new series. He took over the ownership of the magazine in the following September. Under its new proprietor the once celebrated *London*, which had been steadily losing readers, went into an even steeper decline principally because Southern used it as a medium for the social and political concerns of utilitarianism, rather than for promoting the best of contemporary literature. To Charles Lamb, Southern's February number of 1825 was 'all trash'. By the following August, when Lamb's final article appeared, the *London* had 'fallen'. A drastic loss of readers necessitated Southern's sale of the magazine to Charles Knight in April 1828, by which time he was busily employed as a freelance. He contributed to early issues of *The Atlas* newspaper and wrote on literature for *The Spectator* at a reported £5 a week under the sobriquet of O'Higgins, after the former dictator of Chile.

From September 1828 Southern was a regular contributor to the *Foreign Quarterly Review*, where he evinced a special interest in French politics and literature, and also in the reform of education and prison discipline. He embraced Jean-Joseph Jacotot's system of education which was critical of 'mechanical' learning. He also promoted the American system of prison discipline that relied on solitary, rather than communal, detention, and he approved of the American privatization of prisons. Southern was an opponent of transportation to Australia and forced labour, and he frequently held up Bentham's Panopticon scheme as an ideal. His tastes at this time were 'most miscellaneous', according to a letter he wrote to Macvey Napier, editor of the *Edinburgh Review*, to whom he offered an article on Aboriginal life in Australia and an account of the Belgian communes. His interest in foreign politics had already been reflected in his freelance contributions to the *Westminster* and when, in August 1830, revolution broke out in Belgium he lost no time in visiting Brussels, talking to politicians and reporting on the trial of De Potter. He later published graphic accounts of his experiences in the *Foreign Quarterly Review*, *Fraser's Magazine*, and the *Westminster*. At this time Southern was also writing for the *New Monthly Magazine*, the *United Service Journal*, and, like many of his fellow utilitarians, for the radical *Examiner*.

In 1833 Southern's former colleague on the *Westminster*, John Bowring, recommended him to Sir George Villiers, ambassador to Spain, as his private secretary. Southern duly accompanied Villiers to Madrid and by the following year had been promoted at the minister's request to an unpaid post as attaché to the legation. He was made paid attaché in August 1835 when his predecessor, Newton Savile Scott, moved to The Hague. Villiers regarded Southern as his 'right-hand man' and thanked Palmerston for giving him an attaché with 'worth and abilities … of no ordinary kind' (Bullen and Strong, 281). He proved invaluable in helping Villiers draw up a trade treaty, and his close contacts with the Spanish, particularly the liberals, enabled him to handle the Cadiz junta effectively in 1836.

An attack on Southern in the *Journal des Débats* of 1 September 1837 alleged that he had taken part in the military insurrection which had made the queen a prisoner, but this was publicly scotched by Villiers and Southern. In April 1838 Southern's intervention on behalf of the gaoled George Borrow contributed to his early release. By 1839 Southern was looking for a post outside diplomacy and Villiers arranged for him to be proposed for the governorship of Mauritius, which had to be taken up immediately. Unfortunately, the resignation of Villiers soon afterwards demanded that Southern, as his deputy, remain behind in Madrid, and the governorship went to another.

With the arrival of a replacement for Villiers, Southern was appointed secretary of the legation at Lisbon in the autumn of 1839. Here too he felt unfulfilled, and by February 1842 was seeking more active employment from Aberdeen. In the following May he wrote again to Aberdeen requesting to be reconsidered for the vacant governorship of Mauritius, as the 'great object' of his ambition was to have 'the political management and administration of a Colony' (Southern to Aberdeen, BL, Add. MS 43229, fol. 141), but was again unsuccessful. He was an assiduous secretary and ensured that his former master Villiers was kept informed of events in Portugal and elsewhere. One report of forty-four pages on the September 1843 conclave at Château d'Eu was based on a confidential communication from Aberdeen himself. During the civil war of 1846–7 in Portugal, Southern's strong sympathy for the Septembrists (in opposition to Howard de Walden's equally fervent support for Queen Isabella) prompted Palmerston to reassure the governments of Spain and France that the Septembrists were not Miguelites. On 31 May 1848 Southern was appointed minister to the Argentine confederation and on 29 August 1851 was promoted to the court of Brazil, having been made a companion of the Bath in the previous March. He died a bachelor on 28 January 1853 at Rio de Janeiro. R. M. HEALEY

Sources G. L. Nesbitt, *Benthamite reviewing* (1934) • *Palmerston*, ed. R. Bullen and F. Strong, 1: *Private correspondence with Sir George Villiers … as minister to Spain, 1833–1837* (1985) • J. Bauer, *The London Magazine, 1820–29* (1953) • W. Thomas, *The philosophic radicals: nine studies in theory and practice, 1817–1841* (1979) • *Henry Crabb Robinson on books and their writers*, ed. E. J. Morley, 3 vols. (1938) • H. E. Maxwell, *Life and letters of George William Frederick, fourth earl of Clarendon*, 2 vols. (1913) • *Autobiographical recollections of Sir John Bowring*, ed. L. B. Bowring (1877), 66 • J. Ridley, *Lord Palmerston* (1970), 318, 393 • W. I. Knapp, *Life, writings and correspondence of George Borrow*, 2 vols. (1899) • *GM*, 2nd ser., 39 (1853), 547 • *The Athenaeum* (19 March 1853), 353 • Administrations, 1854, PRO

Archives BL, Add. MSS | Bodl. Oxf., letters to Lord Clarendon • NMM, letters to Sir William Parker • Norfolk RO, letters to Sir Henry Bulmer • U. Southampton L., corresp. with Palmerston • UCL, letters to Society for the Diffusion of Useful Knowledge

Wealth at death likely that Brazilian government took a large part of his wealth: administration, PRO

Southern [Soowthern], **John** (*fl.* 1584), poet, is known primarily for his translations and imitations of the poetry of the Pléiade. It has been speculated that he was either born or educated in France; however, contemporary courtly references and his own identification as an exemplary English poet, 'a well learned voice' in 'our England', suggest an English nationality, perhaps connected to the Shropshire family of Southern.

In 1584 Southern published his only volume of verse, *Pandora, the Musyque of the Beautie, of his Mistresse Diana*, dedicated to Edward de Vere, seventeenth earl of Oxford. This collection of lyrics largely consists of acknowledged and unacknowledged translations of the poetry of Pierre de Ronsard and Philippe Desportes, and is characterized by distinct technical anomalies for the period—the use of arrhythmic metres, idiosyncratic principles of rhyming, and abbreviated forms of proper nouns. This unconventional style also characterizes four sonnets and two sestets attributed in the text to the countess of Oxford, Anne Cecil de Vere, epitaphs written 'after the death of her young sonne the Lord Bulbecke', as well as a single sonnet attributed in the text to Elizabeth I, an epitaph for the martial protestant princess of the Netherlands, Philippine-Christine de Lalaing. The sonnets attributed to both women contain substantial sections of translation from Desportes's *Cartels et masquarades, épitaphes*, but the stylistic eccentricities of these sonnets, coupled with their presence in a volume of similar translations, suggest that the women's texts are both examples of prosopopoeia written by Southern.

Southern's methods of translation attracted Puttenham's criticism in *The Arte of English Poesie* (1589). Although the entry for Southern opens with his description as one 'of reasonable good facilitie in translation', Puttenham's criticism centres upon Southern's use of French terms in the place of English words, seen as a corruption of the vernacular with 'no maner of conformitie with our language either by custome or derivation which may make them tollerable'. Puttenham takes exception to Southern's claim to be the first to imitate Pindar—not because of the claim itself but because of its phrasing as an exact translation of Ronsard's identical claim, and uses him as an example of the vice of unattributed translation: 'for in deede as I would wish every inventour which is the very Poet to receave the prayses of his invention, so would I not have a translatour be ashamed to be acknowen of his translation' (Puttenham, 252–3). Informed by a particularized opposition to the admonitory protestant politics of Southern's text and its unauthorized appropriation of Elizabeth's poetic voice, Puttenham's criticisms are countered by Drayton's qualified praise in 'Southerne an English Lyrick' in *Poemes Lyrick and Pastorall* (1603):

Southern, I long thee spare,
Yet wish thee well to fare,
Who me pleased'st greatly,
As first, therefore more rare,
Handling thy harpe neatly.

Two copies of *Pandora* survive: one in the Huntington Library, which belonged to Richard Heber, and a second in the British Museum, which belonged to George Steevens and which contains copious annotations in his hand.

ROSALIND SMITH

Sources S. W. May, 'The countess of Oxford's sonnets: a caveat', *English Language Notes*, 29/3 (1992), 9–19 • R. Smith, 'The sonnets of the countess of Oxford and Elizabeth I: translations from Desportes', *N&Q*, 239 (1994), 446–50 · E. Moody, 'Six elegiac poems, possibly by Anne Cecil de Vere', *English Literary Renaissance*, 19 (1989), 152–70 · L. Schleiner, *Tudor and Stuart women writers* (1994) · J. Soowthern, *Pandora, the musyque of the beautie of his mistresse Diana* (1584) [BL copy; G. Steeven's annotated copy, BL, C.39.e.35] · [G. Steevens], letter to the editor, *European Magazine and London Review*, 13 (1788), 389–91 · J. Ritson, *Bibliographia poetica* (1802), 1.337, 363–8, 380 · L. C. John, *The Elizabethan sonnet sequences: studies in conventional conceits* (1938) · J. G. Scott, *Les sonnets élisabéthains* (1929) · G. Puttenham, *The arte of English poesie*, ed. G. D. Willcock and A. Walker (1936) · M. Drayton, *Poemes lyrick and pastorall* (1603) · P. Desportes, *Cartels et masquarades, épitaphes*, ed. V. E. Graham (Geneva, 1958)

Southerne, Thomas (1660–1746), playwright, was born at Oxmantown, near Dublin, the third son of Francis Southerne (*d.* 1678), a brewer. His mother's name is not known. He attended the grammar school of Edward Wetenhall in Dublin, then Trinity College, Dublin, though there is no record of his having been awarded a BA degree. He was, however, awarded an MA degree in 1696.

Southerne left Dublin for London in 1680 and on 15 July of that year was admitted to the Middle Temple. Right from the start his chief interest was not the law but the theatre, and in 1682 he prevailed on the management of Drury Lane to stage his first play, *The Loyal Brother*, with tory-leaning prologue and epilogue supplied by Dryden. The play, like many others of that time, pillories Shaftesbury and exalts the reputation of James, duke of York, as 'the loyal brother'—all this in the most transparent and facile political allegory, written partly in prose and partly in blank verse. It was well received in its day and was followed two years later by *The Disappointment, or, The Mother in Fashion* (1684), also acted at Drury Lane, with a special command performance for Charles II and his queen given only two weeks before the king's death. This play, a typical enough imitation of the Restoration intrigue play, shows also some signs of the new tendency towards sentimentalism which was to reach its full flowering in the work of Cibber, Steele, and the eighteenth-century writers generally.

Southerne's next play suffered a violent and lengthy interruption, as he himself explains in its preface: 'This tragedy was begun a year before the Revolution [that is, in 1687] and near four acts written … Many things interfering with those times, I laid by what I had written for seventeen years.' The play was called *The Spartan Dame* and it did not reach the stage until 1719. Southerne had joined the army in June 1685 and, making profitable use of his good standing with the duke of York, later James II (accruing from the flattery lavished on the duke in *The Loyal Brother*), had climbed from ensign to lieutenant between 1685 and 1688. After 1688 Thomas Southerne was not moved, either by his enthusiasm for his former patron or by his general sympathy with the tory faction, to continue actively in the Jacobite cause and by December 1690 he was back in the theatre with his first comedy, *Sir Anthony Love, or, The Rambling Lady*. Gerard Langbaine, in *An Account of the English Dramatic Poets*, said of it: 'This play was acted with extraordinary applause, the part of Sir Anthony being most masterly play'd by Mrs. Montfort: and certainly, whoever reads it, will find it fraught with true wit and humour' (Langbaine, 184). The 'extraordinary applause' apparently encouraged Southerne. During the next five years he produced four plays, all presented at Drury Lane: *The Wives' Excuse, or, Cuckolds Make Themselves* (1692), *The Maid's Last Prayer, or, Any Rather than Fail* (1692), *The Fatal Marriage, or, The Innocent Adultery* (1694), and *Oroonoko, or, The Royal Slave* (1696). The first was not a success at the time and failed to secure its place in repertory, despite having a potent advocate in Dryden, who wrote a ludicrously complimentary verse epistle to accompany its publication in 1692. Its reputation revived somewhat in the twentieth century, however, and it was staged by the Royal Shakespeare Company in 1973. The last two, both tragedies and both adapted (rather freely) from novels by Aphra Behn, were particularly successful with audiences and both remained in the standard repertory well into the nineteenth century.

Thomas Southerne (1660–1746), by John Simon (after James Worsdale, 1734)

After the sudden spate of plays from 1690 to 1695 there was a gap of five years in Southerne's writing before *The Fate of Capua* appeared in 1700: a run-of-the-mill 'heroic tragedy' of a mediocre kind, there has never been, either in its own time or since, any critical debate about its undoubted mediocrity. Nineteen years elapsed before another new Southerne play appeared, and even then it was not really a new play but the resuscitated *The Spartan Dame*, long suppressed for political reasons but finally revised, sanitized, completed, and produced in 1719. And for the whole of that long interval there is very little solid information about Southerne's life and activities. There are occasional passing mentions of him—always kindly, always admiring: he seems to have been, uniquely among the public figures of the age, quite free from either malice or envy. Especially was he known for being ready to help other playwrights, particularly the young and as yet untried, with their plans and ambitions. It was he, for example, who recommended Colley Cibber's first play—*Love's Last Shift*—in 1696 to Christopher Rich, the manager of Drury Lane.

From an anonymous satire written in 1703 it appears that about that time Southerne married:

> For since the Marriage-Yoke he has put on,
> He drinks *Champaign* and quits the Helycon.
> (*Religio poetae, or, A Satyr on the Poets*, 1703, 9)

Whether married or not, Southerne certainly had a daughter because his will, dated 6 November 1731, makes 'my dear daughter Agnes' sole executrix, responsible for paying 'all my Just and lawfull debts' (Dodds, 'Appendix', 218).

Increasingly Southerne became a welcome guest and a trusted friend of the rich and famous. Dryden had long been his close acquaintance: as early as 1691 the elder poet, who fell ill while struggling to complete his play *Cleomenes*, had asked his young colleague to complete the last act for him, and this Southerne has successfully achieved. Through his middle years Southerne is frequently mentioned—and never other than kindly—in the *vers de société* with which poets and poetasters alike littered literary London in the early eighteenth century. And in his old age he remained, still, quite literally the toast of the town. For the greater part of that time he lived with Mr Whyte, an oilman, in Tothill Street, against Dartmouth Street, until he moved to his final home in Smith Street, also in Westminster. On his eighty-first birthday he was invited to dine with Lord Orrery where he received a graceful verse panegyric from Pope.

Southerne, almost alone among Restoration dramatists, made playwriting pay. *Oroonoko* and *The Fatal Marriage*, in particular, made him quite wealthy. But whatever the magic touch was, it deserted him finally: his last play, *Money the Mistress*, a comedy written when he was sixty-six, was hissed off the stage, but by then (1725) he was secure enough financially to absorb the loss without its threatening his lifestyle. In 1733 Swift wrote from Dublin to Pope in London:

> Our old friend Southern [*sic*], who has just left us, was invited to dinner once or twice by a judge, a bishop, or a commissioner of revenue, but most frequented a few particular friends, and chiefly the Doctor, who is so easy in his fortune, and very hospitable. (*Correspondence of Jonathan Swift*, ed. H. Williams, 1965, 4.170; the 'Doctor' referred to is Dr Delaney)

John Boyle, earl of Orrery was one of Southerne's especial friends. In the summer of 1733, for example, he wrote to Southerne from Ireland with genuine warmth and affection. Addressing him as 'dear Brother poet' he begged Southerne not to risk another journey to Ireland but instead to 'go and regale thyself amongst my Ancestours at Marston. Pillard shall open my Cellars, and Marston shall be your own house as long as you will think it worth making it so' (Dodds, 17).

Another of Southerne's distinguished friends in later life was the poet Thomas Gray, who in 1737 wrote to Horace Walpole:

> We have old Mr. Southern [*sic*] at a gentleman's house a little way off, who often comes to see us; he is now seventy-seven years old and has almost wholly lost his memory; but is as agreeable as an old man can be, at least I persuade myself so when I look at him and think of Isabella [in *The Fatal Marriage*] and Oronooko.

Gray was by no means the only one to remember Southerne's career chiefly for these two plays, both of which remained in the English theatre repertory throughout the eighteenth century and one of which continued to hold the stage much longer than that: Garrick played Oronooko in 1759, Kean played it in 1817 (Hazlitt thought it 'one of his best parts' (see *Works*, ed. A. R. Waller and A. Glover, 12 vols., 1902–4, 11.301)), Junius Brutus Booth played the first American performance of it in New York in 1832—and Ralph Richardson played it at the Malvern festival in 1932.

Thomas Southerne died in London, aged eighty-six, on 26 May 1746. He was buried on 29 May at St Margaret's, Westminster. ERIC SALMON

Sources J. W. Dodds, *Thomas Southerne, dramatist* (1933) • Burtchaell & Sadleir, *Alum. Dubl.* • G. Langbaine, *An account of the English dramatick poets* (1691) • M. Cordner and R. Clayton, eds., *Four Restoration marriage plays* (1995) • *Gentleman's Journal* (Jan 1691) • M. Banham, *Cambridge guide to theatre* (1992) • J. H. Smith, *The gay couple in Restoration comedy* (Cambridge, MA, 1948) • *Review of English Studies*, new ser., 41 (1990) • O. G. Brockett, *History of the theatre* (Boston, 1982) • P. Hartnoll, *The theatre: a concise history* (1985) • P. Hartnoll, ed., *The Oxford companion to the theatre* (1951); 2nd edn (1957); 3rd edn (1967) • M. Elwin, *Playgoer's handbook to Restoration theatre* (1928) • T. Southerne, *Collected plays*, 2 vols. (1721)

Likenesses J. Simon, mezzotint (after J. Worsdale, 1734), BM, NPG [*see illus.*] • J. Worsdale, oils, priv. coll.

Southesk. For this title name *see* Carnegie, David, first earl of Southesk (1574/5–1658); Carnegie, James, sixth earl of Southesk (1827–1905).

Southey, Caroline Anne Bowles (1786–1854), poet and writer, was born on 6 December 1786 at Buckland Manor near Lymington, Hampshire, the daughter of Captain Charles Bowles (1737–1801), who had retired from the East India Company, and Anne Burrard (1753–1817), the sister of Lieutenant-General Sir Harry *Burrard (*bap.* 1755, *d.* 1813). Some sources give Caroline Bowles's birth date as 1787, and she herself in later life claimed not to know which was correct; the confusion arose because she was not christened until January 1787 as the weather was too severe earlier to take an infant to church. The Burrard family were powerful local dignitaries, and had provided shire councillors and mayors for Lymington as early as the sixteenth century. Charles Bowles was initially backed by the Burrard family (he served as mayor three times), but proved ineffectual as a country squire and later subsided into melancholia, moving his family from the extensive manor farm to the much more modest Buckland Cottage while his daughter was very young. She grew up as an only child in a largely female household (her mother's mother and Jersey grandmother lived with them) in idyllic rural surroundings on the edge of the New Forest, with summers spent by the sea at her uncle Harry's home at Calshot Castle. She learned to read and write very early, and relished parental encouragement for her efforts at verse and also at drawing and painting, for which she also had a gift. This was developed through lessons she received from the local vicar at Boldre church, who happened to be the celebrated 'picturesque' author and artist William Gilpin (1724–1804). Some of her later paintings survive: they are held by the Wordsworth Trust and owned by Keswick School.

Devoted to her family, Caroline Bowles was devastated by her parents' deaths. Most of her Burrard boy cousins, too, were killed very young on active service. By 1817 she was left to live alone with only her faithful old nurse for company. Threatened with loss of her home in 1818, owing to mismanagement by a guardian, she sought advice about publication of her 'metrical verse tale' first from the poet laureate Robert Southey, whose publisher John Murray admired it but feared it would not sell; next from the poet and editor James Montgomery. At this point one Colonel Bruce, a mysterious adopted son of her father's, made his appearance from India, coming to the rescue by settling on his 'sister' an annuity of £150. She went ahead with (anonymous) publication of her verse tale, and *Ellen Fitzarthur: a Poem in Five Cantos* went through two editions (1820, 1822) when eventually brought out by Longmans.

Robert *Southey (1774–1843) became Caroline Bowles's mentor and friend first by correspondence, later in person: they met in London in 1820, and she visited him at home with his family in the Lake District in 1823. Their correspondence and friendship continued, and finally, after his first wife died, he became her husband: they married on 4 June 1839 when she was fifty-two and he was sixty-five, thinking to spend their declining years working side by side. Before her marriage she had published five volumes of poetry, two of prose sketches, *Chapters on Churchyards* (2 vols., 1829), and one of mixed prose and verse, *Solitary Hours* (1826). Most of her work was published initially in *Blackwood's Edinburgh Magazine*—where she built a wide reputation as the author of the *Chapters* in particular—followed by volume publication with the same firm. She felt a strong kinship with William Blackwood senior whose brand of old-fashioned toryism matched her own (her lively letters to Blackwood are preserved in the National Library of Scotland). Gradually she learned to assert herself as a professional writer, although, disliking publicity, she clung to anonymity until 1836 when she brought out over her own name her major work, an (unfinished) autobiography, *The Birth-Day*. Written in blank verse of suppleness, authority, and conversational ease (though with moments of diffidence), it brought her mixed censure and praise; John Wilson (Christopher North) being one of her major champions. It recounts the story of her solitary childhood among a loving family and a menagerie of animal friends, as well as (more mutedly) her frustration with an anti-intellectual environment and limited educational opportunities. The sombreness of the poet's viewpoint as a lonely and bereaved adult provides throughout a constant counterpoint to the often humorous narrative of the child's experiences.

Unlike many of her female contemporaries, Caroline Southey rarely made romantic love the subject of her writings: the beauties of the natural world seemed to hold more charm for her, although she disliked sentimentality. Her work varied in genre from prose fiction (more popular than her verse during her lifetime), through verse satire (*The Cat's Tail*, 1830), dramatic monologue (*Tales of the Factories*, 1833), and verse narrative (*Ellen Fitzarthur*, *The Birth-Day*) to lyric poetry. Although physically tiny and often plagued by ill health, she possessed great personal courage, ready to repel intruders with her father's pistols while living alone at Buckland during the threshing-machine riots of the early 1830s, and never hesitating to speak out against injustice. Her *Tales of the Factories* were among the earliest of that kind of protest poetry, preceding both Caroline Norton's and Elizabeth Barrett's works in the genre. Her surviving correspondence gives the salty flavour of her character, with her gift for expressing herself with down-to-earth immediacy and pungent turns of phrase: 'It is no use to stand shivering and *shilly shallying* under the shower Bath—Best pull the string, and get the shock over …' (this to her aunt, about her own forthcoming marriage; see Blain, 200). Her correspondence with Southey was published in 1881.

Possessing a fine ear equally for metre and for natural speech rhythms, Caroline Southey mastered the traditional difficulties of blank verse in *The Birth-Day* (more than 3000 lines long), as well as a variety of lyric forms in her shorter poems. Robert Southey recognized her genius long before he came to love her. However, she was never able to fulfil his dearest wish that they should jointly write an epic on Robin Hood: mainly because she could not abide the ungainly metre he insisted upon (the same as for his *Thalaba*, which Coleridge once described as a kind of dumb-bell exercise). 'Robin Hood' remained unfinished at Southey's death, and in 1847 Caroline Southey published the fragment in a jointly authored volume of that name, the bulk of which however, consisted of her own work, including her fine, sad sonnets on the marriage. Invariably, however, the volume is catalogued as his.

'The last three years have done on me the work of twenty', Caroline Southey wrote to Lydia Sigourney (Sigourney, 39) shortly before her husband's death, and indeed she never fully recovered from the emotional trauma of finding soon after their marriage that Robert Southey's endearing absent-mindedness was but the first stage of a rapidly advancing senile dementia. She threw herself loyally into full-time caring for him, but her situation as second wife in the household at Greta Hall in Keswick was virtually untenable. Robert Southey's daughter Kate, who was his housekeeper, hugely resented her intrusion, and she fought so bitterly with his son Cuthbert, whom she felt to be neglectful of his father, that he all but obliterated her from his published account of his father's life. The tensions at Greta Hall became the subject of widespread gossip, harming Caroline Southey's literary as well as her personal reputation. Wordsworth, for example, initially an admirer, sided with the children against her. Many assumed incorrectly that Caroline Bowles had married for money—in fact, she had forfeited Colonel Bruce's annuity on her marriage, and was forced to dip into her own savings to pay the household bills when her husband became very quickly incapacitated. She spent her days by his side in his study, although he could no longer write or even read much: his dependence was total. Her tactless possessiveness did not help the situation with his children, though she made firm friends with his eldest daughter Edith and her husband John Wood Warter, later editor of Southey's letters and of her own *Poetical Works* (1867).

After Robert Southey's death from typhus in March 1843, Caroline Southey was obliged to leave Greta Hall immediately and return to Buckland, where she spent her remaining years in increasing ill health, writing no more. In 1852 she was awarded a civil-list pension of £200. She died at Buckland Cottage, Lymington, on 20 July 1854, and was buried among Burrard family members in St Thomas's churchyard, Lymington.

VIRGINIA H. BLAIN

Sources V. Blain, *Caroline Bowles Southey (1786–1854): the making of a woman writer* (1998) • *The correspondence of Robert Southey with Caroline Bowles*, ed. E. Dowden (1881) • E. Orlebar, 'Robert Southey's second wife', *Cornhill Magazine*, 30 (1874), 217–29 • V. L. Schonert, ed., 'The correspondence of Caroline Anne Bowles Southey to Mary Anne Watts Hughes', PhD diss., Harvard U., 1957 • [H. N. Coleridge], 'Modern English poetesses', *QR*, 66 (1840), 374–418 [review] • J. E. Courtney, 'Caroline Southey', *The adventurous thirties: a chapter in the women's movement* (1933) • L. H. Sigourney, *Pleasant memories of pleasant lands* (1844) • *The Athenaeum* (5 Aug 1854), 969–70 • *GM*, 2nd ser., 42 (1854) • parish register, Lymington, 10 Jan 1787, Hants. RO [baptism] • letters, NL Scot., Blackwood MSS • correspondence with Anna Bray, University of Rochester

Archives BL, poetical notebooks, Add. MS 47892 • NL Scot., corresp. | BL, letters to Emma Burrard, Add. MS 45185 • Bristol RO, corresp. with John King and his daughter, Zoe • Hants. RO, letters to John May • Harvard U., Houghton L., letters to Mary Hughes • NA Scot., corresp. with Dr Bell • NL Scot., corresp. with Blackwoods and literary MSS • University of Rochester, New York, Rush Rhees Library, letters, mainly to Anna Stothard Bray • University of Rochester, New York, Robert Southey collection

Likenesses C. A. B. Southey, self-portrait, crayon, Wordsworth Trust, Grasmere

Southey, Henry Herbert (1784–1865), physician, son of Robert Southey (1745–1792), linen draper, and Margaret Hill (1752–1802), and younger brother of the poet Robert *Southey, was born at Bristol on 17 January 1784. He was educated at private schools in and around Great Yarmouth, and in particular with George Burnett, a Unitarian minister in Great Yarmouth, and with Mr Maurice of Normanstown, near Lowestoft. His older brother Robert wanted to bring him up to his house in London so that he could study anatomy under Sir Anthony Carlisle at Westminster Hospital and go on to university at Edinburgh or in Germany. This plan fell through and Henry studied at Norwich under Philip Meadows Martineau, uncle of Harriet Martineau and a distinguished surgeon. While there he became friendly with William Taylor, a Unitarian, who supervised his extra-professional studies. In November 1803 he entered Edinburgh University to study medicine. There he made lifelong friends with a group of fellow medical students, William Knighton, Lockyer of Plymouth, Fearon of Sunderland, and Robert Gooch; the five of them acquired an unusual facility in colloquial Latin and used to speak it together. Southey also wrote Latin elegantly, a skill highly prized at the time, and rarely travelled without a copy of Horace or Virgil in his pocket. He graduated MD on 24 June 1806, producing an interesting dissertation on the origins and course of syphilis which suggested an American origin for the disease.

Southey then studied for a year at one of the London hospitals, as was common on graduating from Edinburgh, and in 1807 settled in Durham as a general physician, although the opportunities were limited. In 1812 he moved back to London on the advice of Knighton and became a licentiate of the Royal College of Physicians on 22 December 1812. In 1814 he published 'Observations on pulmonary consumption', which may have helped in his attempt to obtain a position in one of the London hospitals. Southey was finally elected physician to the Middlesex Hospital on 17 August 1815, and four days later married his first wife, Louisa Gonne (*d.* 1830), at St Leonard's Church, Streatham. Southey remained at the Middlesex until April 1827. In the meantime, owing to considerable support from Knighton, he was appointed physician-in-ordinary to George IV in 1823, and in 1830 physician-extraordinary to Queen Adelaide. He became FRCP on 25 June 1823 and he took on a variety of roles in the college throughout his life. He was elected FRS on 25 April 1825. In 1828, on the recommendation of Sir Henry Halford, he was appointed a metropolitan lunacy commissioner under the 1828 Madhouse Act, one of the reasons being that although he had a reputation as a good physician with a knowledge of mental illness he was not 'overwhelmed with private practice'.

In 1830 Southey's wife, Louisa, died in childbirth, little Louisa being their tenth child. This left him in a desperate position, both financially and in terms of pursuing a career. His role as a metropolitan lunacy commissioner paid only expenses. However, by mid-1833 he had met and married his second wife, Clara (1798–1858), and although they went on to have a further five children his appointment the same year as a lord chancellor's medical visitor in lunacy, with a salary of £1500, gave him the financial security he needed. Writing in July to thank his friend Lord Brougham for appointing him, he commented, this 'will relieve me from pecuniary anxiety for the rest of my life'. Together with John Bright he simultaneously held office in the Lord Chancellor's Department and the metropolitan lunacy commission until 1845. In that year Southey was named as one of the full-time lunacy commissioners under Lord Shaftesbury's Lunacy Act, but it was clear that he could not perform the duties of both salaried posts. He promptly resigned from the new commission, preferring to remain a lord chancellor's visitor in lunacy, a post he held until his death. From 1834 to 1865 he was also Gresham professor of medicine, and on 16 June 1847 was created honorary DCL at Oxford.

As a young man Southey was noted for his good looks, athletic prowess, and fondness for field sports. He was an accomplished society physician, discreet, polite, and with a kind heart. Despite only a short period of practice in the north of England he attracted the support of a number of great aristocratic families there. He was also the grateful recipient of three significant legacies from non-relatives, a testament to his popularity. He was one of a number of London physicians who built up private practices which they extended to the private care of the mentally ill, but most importantly he helped carve out a strong role for the lord chancellor's medical visitors. This body ensured a high degree of privacy for wealthy families with mentally ill relatives, although it came into conflict with Lord Shaftesbury's lunacy commission. Southey was one of those who opposed amalgamation of the two authorities.

In June 1858 Southey's second wife, Clara, died at their home in Queen Anne Street, Cavendish Square, London. He himself died at 1 Harley Street on 13 June 1865 and was buried in Highgate cemetery. NICK HERVEY

Sources Munk, *Roll*, 3.272 • *GM*, 3rd ser., 19 (1865), 125 • *The Lancet* (17 June 1865), 665 • *Robberd's memoir of William Taylor of Norwich with his correspondence with Robert Southey* (1843) • *IGI* • H. Southey, letters to Lord Brougham, UCL, Brougham collection • *CGPLA Eng. & Wales* (1865) • Boase, *Mod. Eng. biog.*

Archives UCL, Brougham collection, letters to Lord Brougham

Likenesses photograph, RCP Lond.

Wealth at death under £50,000: probate, 13 July 1865, *CGPLA Eng. & Wales*

Southey, Sir Richard (1808–1901), colonial governor, the second son of George Southey (*b.* *c.*1781), a farmer, and Jane Baker (*c.*1782–1835), was born at Culmstock, Devon, on 25 April 1808. He was educated at Uffculme grammar school until 1820, then went in a settler party led by his father to South Africa. The family settled as farmers near Clumber, east of Grahamstown, Cape Colony. In 1824 Richard joined Heugh and Fleming, Grahamstown merchants, as a clerk, but not enjoying the life, he went in 1829 on a cross-border trading and hunting expedition. It failed, and he returned home and bought a nearby farm, to breed cattle. In 1830 he married Isabella (*d.* 1869), daughter of John Shaw of Albany; they had five sons and two daughters.

Southey volunteered for military service after rumours of invasion in 1828, and took part in the Cape Frontier War of 1834–5. He formed and led a corps of guides on orders from Colonel Harry Smith (1787–1860). It provided the escort for Smith during the escape of the Gcaleka (Xhosa) chief Hintsa (who was shot by Southey's brother George). At the close of the war he was appointed resident agent with the Ndhlambe chiefdom in annexed territory to the east, until Sir Benjamin D'Urban's annexation policy was reversed in September 1835. Southey and his brothers then moved to Graaff-Reinet, where they farmed and traded until 1846.

On his return to South Africa in 1847 as governor and high commissioner, Sir Harry Smith made Southey, whom he rated highly, secretary to the high commission. Southey was present when Smith broke the resistance of émigré Voortrekkers at Boomplaats in 1848. After Smith's extension of British rule to Transorangia, Southey was left at Bloemfontein to collect fines levied on the Boers, to handle continuing Boer opposition, and to assist Major H. D. Warden, the British resident, in the difficult task of fixing boundaries between the Boer and Sotho settlements which also took into account the interests of other chiefdoms in the Caledon river valley.

In 1849 Southey entered Cape Colony administration as resident magistrate of Swellendam, though he was temporarily diverted during the Cape Frontier War of 1850–53 to the raising of African levies and the procurement of military supplies. After Smith's retirement he was drawn back to Cape Town as acting government secretary by Sir George Cathcart in 1852–4. In Cathcart's absence on the eastern frontier Southey was impetuously suspended by Lieutenant-Governor Darling for the indiscreet release of official documents likely to undermine proposed constitutional reforms, but honourably restored on appeal to the secretary of state. A second spell as magistrate at Swellendam ensued (1854–5), followed by a return to Grahamstown as secretary to Lieutenant-Governor Jackson (1855–8). But he was soon brought back to the centre of power, backed by an accolade from Governor Sir George Grey, with successive appointments as auditor-general (January–April 1859), treasurer-general with a seat in the executive council (1862–4), and colonial secretary (1864–72) during the governorships of Sir Philip Wodehouse and Sir Henry Barkly.

Southey was now playing a major role in public life. Having once failed to undermine constitutional reform in 1853 by adopting a posture of which Wodehouse approved but Barkly did not, he fought the introduction of responsible government with well articulated arguments, until the acceptance of autonomy by parliament in 1872 led to the termination of his non-elective office. In October 1872 he declined a proposal by Barkly that he should seek a seat in parliament in order to form a responsible ministry. Developments at the Orange–Vaal confluence offered him an alternative, for Southey had acquired a passion for the expansion of British rule, as he later put it in 1876, 'from coast to coast, from Walwich Bay to Delagoa Bay, and as far inland as it could be carried, but certainly north to the Zambesi' (Campbell, 152), for—unlike Cecil Rhodes—Southey mistrusted colonies as well as republics as managers of imperial estates. Isabella, his first wife, had died in 1869; in 1872 he married Susanna Maria Hendrika Krynauw (*d.* 1890) of Grabouw, near Cape Town; they had a daughter and a son.

Barkly supported Southey when he began to work for the British annexation of the diamond fields. In close association with the land speculator David Arnot, who contrived to detach large parts of Nicholas Waterboer's lands for white settlement, Southey persuaded Waterboer, after his sovereignty had been safeguarded under the Keate award of 1871, to transfer his territory to British control. The crown colony of Griqualand West was duly set up in

1873, with Southey as lieutenant-governor and J. B. Currey as colonial secretary.

The record of Southey's brief rule (January 1873 to August 1875) has been debated. It is clear that he worked to prevent the infiltration of settlers from the republics and other land-grabbers onto tribal land, thus conserving some tribal land for the indigenous people, and that he did not indulge in significant land speculation himself, as was alleged. But his plans for commercial farming did intrude on Africans' territory, and openings were not created for enterprising black farmers. It is clear also that Southey and Currey worked to protect black claimholders' rights at the diggings—at the cost of inadequate control over smuggling. They did little to control the traffic in firearms, despite its destabilizing effect, because the chiefs demanded guns as a price for supplying labour. Southey's concern to ensure the flow of labour from outside can also be seen in his idea for the purchase by Englishmen of farms in the Transvaal to ensure safe passage for people travelling through that country to seek work in the mines. All this brought him onto a collision course with white diggers, led by ruffians such as Alfred Aylward, whose 'black flag' revolt of 1875 nearly toppled the government. The Colonial Office, working in association with Barkly, who had withheld effective military support from Southey, decided to terminate Southey's appointment. This time his appeal failed.

On 4 December 1876 Southey filled a vacancy in the house of assembly as a member for Grahamstown and an opponent of the Molteno ministry. But he did not seek re-election in 1878, and took no further part in public affairs.

Southey had been a keen freemason, and was elected provincial grand master for South Africa in 1862. He was created CMG on 30 November 1872, and KCMG on 30 May 1891. He died at his residence, Southfields, Plumstead, on 22 July 1901, and was buried in St John's cemetery, Wynberg. T. R. H. Davenport

Sources *The Times* (23 July 1901) · *Cape Argus* (23 July 1901) · *Cape Times* (24 July 1901) · J. A. I. Agar-Hamilton, *The road to the north: South Africa, 1852–1886* (1937) · J. A. Benyon, *Proconsul and paramountcy in South Africa: the high commission, British supremacy and the sub-continent, 1806–1910* (1980) · *John Blades Currey, 1850–1900: fifty years in the Cape Colony*, ed. P. Brooke Simons (1986) · W. B. Campbell, 'The South African frontier, 1865–1885: a study in expansion', *Archives Year Book for South African History*, 1 (1959) · H. E. Hockly, *The story of the British settlers of 1820 in South Africa* (1957) · B. A. Le Cordeur, *The politics of eastern Cape separatism, 1820–1854* (1981) · M. Macmillan, *Sir Henry Barkly* (1970) · L. L. Minott, 'Sir Richard Southey, lieutenant-governor of Griqualand West, 1872–1875', MA diss., University of Capetown, 1973 · E. Morse-Jones, *Roll of the 1820 settlers*, 2nd edn (1971) · K. Shillington, *The colonisation of the Southern Tswana, 1870–1900* (1985) · *The autobiography of Lieutenant-General Sir Harry Smith*, ed. G. C. Moore Smith, 2 vols. (1901) · K. Smith, *Alfred Aylward, the tireless agitator* (1983) · A. Wilmot, *The life and times of Sir Richard Southey* (1904) · *DSAB*

Archives National Archives of South Africa, Cape Town, corresp. and papers · Rhodes University, Grahamstown, South Africa, Cory Library for Historical Research, family MSS

Likenesses F. Wolf, oils, Civil Service Club, Cape Town · photographs (in middle age and old age), repro. in Wilmot, *Life and times* · portrait, National Library of South Africa, Cape Town · portrait, Macgregor Museum, Kimberley

Southey, Robert (1774–1843), poet and reviewer, was born in Wine Street, Bristol, on 12 August 1774. He was the second son of Robert Southey (1745–1792), a linen draper descended from a family of Somerset woollen manufacturers and farmers. Robert the elder was not successful in business, and in 1792 became bankrupt. The poet's mother, Margaret (1752–1802), daughter of Edward and Margaret Hill, belonged to a higher social class: minor gentry from Herefordshire and Somerset. Her brother, Herbert Hill, was chaplain to the British factory in Oporto, Portugal, and was an important influence on Robert during his adolescence and young manhood. But it was Margaret's half-sister Elizabeth Tyler who took responsibility for Robert in his childhood: he lived with her almost exclusively until the age of seven, and even after that she exerted a dominating authority. She lived in Bath, thus distancing herself from her socially inferior relatives in Bristol, and took pains to keep the boy away from playmates and the usual activities of childhood. In compensation she had a passion for the theatre which she allowed Robert to share: he saw his first play at the age of four, and was early seized with the ambition to write plays himself.

Education and early writings The informal autobiography that Southey wrote in letters to a friend between 1820 and 1825 vividly conjures up his varied experiences of repression and bullying. The picture he gives of the schools he attended (a dame-school, two grammar schools in Bristol, and a boarding-school at Corston) is one of incompetence and brutality, though he felt that the years at his second grammar school, while unprofitable, were not unhappy. He early took to the writing of poetry, his first effort, at the age of nine or ten, being a sequel to the *Orlando Furioso*. Subsequent projects included historical epics, heroic epistles, a satire, some translations, and a play about the Trojan war. At the outset he thus displayed the versatility which was to mark the whole of his literary career. His reading, too, was immense. He particularly admired the great romantic epics of Ariosto, Tasso, and Spenser.

In 1788 Southey's uncle Herbert Hill had him entered at Westminster School, with a view to gaining admission to Oxford University and so to a career in the church. Here again he had to suffer the bullying and brutality of the kind experienced at his earlier schools, but he also made lasting friendships, recorded in a mass of carefully preserved correspondence. One of these friends was Charles William Watkins Wynn, who came from a prominent whig family in Wales. In due course he was sufficiently affluent to help Southey with a modest annuity, and in 1808 sufficiently influential to replace this with a government pension. Southey's other close friend, Grosvenor Charles Bedford, lived near London, and his family's collection of modern books was available to Southey when he visited. Voltaire, Rousseau, Gibbon, and Goethe's *Sorrows of Young Werther* combined to unsettle his religious beliefs, and to produce the subversive state of mind that led to his expulsion from the school. He and his friends produced a periodical after the manner of *The Spectator*

Robert Southey (1774–1843), by Henry Edridge, 1804

and *The Rambler*, entitled *The Flagellant*, and at the end of March 1792 Southey contributed an attack on corporal punishment as an invention of the devil. This was too much for Dr Vincent, the headmaster, who not only expelled Southey forthwith but also warned Christ Church, the Oxford college where he expected to be enrolled, that he was an undesirable character.

Although Dr Vincent had done his best to protect Oxford from Southey's malign influence, Balliol College took a more relaxed view, and he matriculated there in November 1792, coming into residence in the following January. In the months after his expulsion from Westminster his state of mind fluctuated between near despair and exhilaration. He was encouraged by the way in which the ideas of Paine and the power of the French Revolution seemed to be triumphing over the corrupt old order, but the political atmosphere changed abruptly at the end of the year with the prospect of war between France and Britain. Southey remained faithful to his radicalism, but it was an anxious fidelity. His insecurity was heightened by his father's bankruptcy and death in the autumn of 1792.

At Balliol College, Southey found little to stimulate him, apart from some congenial new friends, notably another prospective ordinand, Edmund Seward, whose austere Christian stoicism was to be a lifelong influence. But Southey's own rejection of orthodoxy made him increasingly resistant to the idea of becoming a clergyman, and he evidently put a good deal more energy into his literary projects than into his studies. It was in 1793 that he wrote the first version of *Joan of Arc*, a democratic epic that celebrated a woman who was also an enemy of England. Still, he could not make a living by such outrageous challenges to convention, and by the end of 1793 he decided that he would have to make a career for himself in medicine. (His younger brother Henry Herbert *Southey became a physician.) But sessions in the dissecting-room disgusted and disenchanted him, and he then wondered if he might follow Grosvenor Bedford into government service in the exchequer. He soon discovered that his reputation as a republican put this out of the question.

Pantisocracy In despair Southey's thoughts turned to emigration, an idea which was the more attractive since he found himself in love with a Bristol seamstress, Edith Fricker (1774–1837), and wanted to marry her. And then in June 1794 Samuel Taylor *Coleridge (1772–1834) visited Oxford and was introduced to Southey. They took to each other at once, gave each other confidence in their speculations, and by the following month had devised the scheme of pantisocracy—the establishment of an egalitarian settlement in North America. Southey was mainly responsible for persuading people to join the enterprise. He recruited members of his family and a number of his friends, including Edith Fricker and her sisters. Coleridge provided most of the theory underpinning the project, and confirmed his commitment by marrying Edith's younger sister Sara.

Southey had been reading William Godwin's recently published treatise *Political Justice*. Its faith in the inevitable triumph of a society based on reason attracted him, as did the role which Godwin saw literature playing in this desirable process. Pantisocracy would provide a foretaste of this triumph, and it gave him 'new life, new hope, new energy'. All the faculties of his mind, he said, were dilated (letter of 12 Oct 1794, *New Letters*, 1.81–2). He left Oxford and spent the next year and a quarter in the west of England, much of it in the animating company of Coleridge. While planning emigration the two men gave ingeniously subversive public lectures. Their conversation, too, seems to have been downright audacious. They collaborated in writing a verse play on the death of Robespierre, and Southey composed a similar piece on Wat Tyler, who he supposed (thinking of his aunt) might be one of his forebears. It was at this time that he wrote his 'Botany Bay Eclogues', exposing the injustices of the English legal system, and the experiments in classical metres ('The Soldier's Wife', 'The Widow') so mercilessly parodied by George Canning in *The Anti-Jacobin*.

But the exhilaration of this period could not be sustained. Pantisocracy failed because Southey and Coleridge lacked the money even to travel to Pennsylvania, let alone establish their settlement. Southey himself was in increased financial difficulties because Miss Tyler had cast him off when she learned of the emigration plan and the engagement to a seamstress. As time went on, too, Coleridge's flamboyant radicalism, coupled with his less stable temperament, created tensions which led to an estrangement. Southey's uncle in Portugal helpfully invited his nephew to spend some months in that country, and he left Bristol for Lisbon on 19 November 1795, having secretly married Edith Fricker on the 14th. She took up residence in the family of Joseph Cottle, the bookseller who had agreed to publish *Joan of Arc* and who later proved to be exceedingly generous in his assistance to both Southey and Coleridge.

Portugal and beginnings of literary career Southey's stay in Spain and Portugal lasted from mid-December to early May in the year following. He visited Madrid, but spent most of his time in and around Lisbon. He obtained a good grounding in both Spanish and Portuguese, but was repelled by his encounter with the Roman Catholic church, a repulsion that proved permanent. In spite of this, and his disgust at the lack of cleanliness that he encountered, Southey enjoyed himself on this visit, an enjoyment manifest in *Letters Written during a Short Residence in Spain and Portugal* (1797), a miscellany of verse and prose which proved quite popular and soon went into a second edition.

On his return to England, Southey and Edith began their married life in lodgings, and he embarked on his career as a professional writer. He worked on his Spanish and Portuguese *Letters*, wrote poetry for the *Monthly Magazine*, enjoyed the favourable reception that *Joan of Arc* received in the reviews, and, thus encouraged, went on with his next epic projects, *Madoc* and (somewhat later, though published first, in 1801) the Arabian tale *Thalaba the Destroyer*. *Joan of Arc*, though it had been innovative in subject, was traditional in its blank verse form. But *Thalaba* was written in an irregular metre that Southey had learned from Frank Sayers's *Dramatic Sketches of Northern Mythology*. It illustrated some aspects of Islam as Southey understood it, commending the virtues of endurance and faithfulness. The poem at its best suggests an irrepressible buoyancy, as in the hero's journey in the little boat downstream, where:

The flowing current furrow'd round
The water-lily's floating leaf
(11.34, *Poems*, 107)

Southey at this time needed all the resilience he could command, as his circumstances remained disquietingly unsettled. The annuity from Wynn had been offered on the understanding that Southey would study law, so when the first instalment was paid early in 1797 he moved to London and was admitted a member of Gray's Inn. But London suited neither Southey nor Edith, and after some intermediate moves they settled for a few months in Burton in Hampshire, where he made another new friend who became important to him in later years. This was John Rickman, soon to become secretary to the speaker of the House of Commons, and organizer of Britain's first census in 1801. In the next two and a half years Southey was often on the move, staying sometimes in London but more often in various parts of the south and west of England, finding indeed some sense of permanence in Martin Hall, the house he rented in Westbury-on-Trym, near Bristol, from mid-1798 to mid-1799. Throughout this time he was studying law, but devoting more and more time to literature. He had a contract to send poetry to the *Morning Post*, which led to his writing some of his most characteristic short lyrics. Here he showed, like Wordsworth, how far the language of the middle and lower classes was adapted to poetry. His work has less vitality, and is more conventional, than that of his rivals, which may account for his notoriously depreciatory assessment of *Lyrical Ballads* in the *Critical Review*.

Although this was a productive period, its unsettled restlessness weakened Southey's health, and made a visit to a warmer climate desirable. Once again help came from his uncle in Portugal, and he and Edith spent over a year there. By now he had conceived an ambitious project to write a history of Portugal, and he took every opportunity to collect materials, forming the nucleus of his remarkable collection of books in Spanish and Portuguese. This became a lifelong preoccupation, though the only part published was his *History of Brazil* (1810–19). His health much improved, he returned to England in July 1801.

Southey's friend Rickman now put him in the way of a post in the government of Ireland, recently reorganized under the Act of Union. He accepted the position of secretary to Isaac Corry, the chancellor of the exchequer there, and spent a fortnight in Dublin in October 1801. But there was no work to be done, and no prospect of any apart from serving as a tutor to Corry's son. So he resigned, the more confidently because he could already feel that his literary reputation, even notoriety, was well established. Thus, when the newly founded and instantly influential *Edinburgh Review* wanted to attack poetic innovation, it was by way of reviewing *Thalaba* (1801). Then, too, he had some unusual qualifications: in particular, his knowledge of Spanish and Portuguese, which enabled him to undertake moderately well-paid translation work, notably of *Amadis of Gaul* (1803), after the original by Vasco Lobeira. He was recruited by Arthur Aikin to deal with a wide range of topics for his *Annual Review*, and for several years this periodical was an important source of income for him.

The move to Keswick Southey passed the winter of 1801–2 in London. It was an unhappy time, as his mother died at the beginning of January, and Edith's health was poor. In May he and Edith returned to Bristol, where in August their first child, Margaret, was born. It now became more pressing for them to find a settled residence, and Coleridge, already occupying Greta Hall in Keswick in the Lake District, urged the couple to join him and Sara there. Southey was at first unwilling because he mistrusted the climate, but when Margaret died in her first year he thought it best for Edith to be with her sister, and they moved to Keswick. It was to be the Southey home for forty years.

Coleridge's marriage had long been under severe strain, and a few months after the Southeys' arrival he left for Malta in quest of a place in the government there. Southey thus had the responsibility of looking after Coleridge's wife and three children as well as his own. In 1803 Southey, with Joseph Cottle, brought out an edition of Chatterton's poems for the benefit of the poet's family. He later performed the same service for Henry Kirke White in 1807. A second daughter, Edith May, was born to the Southeys in 1804, a son, Herbert, in 1806, then four more daughters, Emma, Bertha, Katharine, and Isabel, and, last of all, a second son, Charles Cuthbert. Southey took great pleasure in his family. As he put it in one of his last books, the rambling miscellany published as *The Doctor*, 'a house is never perfectly furnished for enjoyment, unless there is a child in it rising three years old, and a kitten rising six weeks' (chap. 130, 4.328). Few things distressed him more than the mistreatment of children, and in the same work he deplores the wanton, wicked suffering too often inflicted on them out of obduracy, caprice, stupidity, malignity, cupidity, and cruelty. He made sure that Greta Hall was a good place for young people, and the boisterous good humour that is one of the most attractive features of his work was evidently fostered by his home life. It enabled him to compose the one work of his which has proved unquestionably enduring (admittedly now in a range of corrupted texts), his magnificent version of the story of the Three Bears. Perhaps one might also add the flamboyant evocation of the cataract of Lodore:

curling and whirling and purling and twirling,
And thumping and plumping and bumping and jumping,
And dashing and flashing and splashing and clashing.
(*Poems*, 349)

Settled in Keswick, Southey came to know the Wordsworths well, at first because of their association with Coleridge, but soon, living as they did not far away in Grasmere, out of neighbourly sympathy. Through the Wordsworths he was introduced to the young Thomas De Quincey, whose vivid memories of the lake poets were later to cause great resentment. In 1805 he met Walter Scott and liked him very much, finding his conservative political outlook increasingly congenial. From the time of Southey's withdrawal from the pantisocracy scheme, his radical enthusiasm had weakened, but there were considerable fluctuations in his political sentiments. Until perhaps 1808 or 1809 he liked to think of himself as a Jacobin. Certainly many of the poems he wrote for the *Morning Post* in 1798 are emphatically subversive. He always insisted on free and fearless thinking in religious matters. He never modified his disparagement of William Pitt, whose war policy he abominated. In 1807 he and Wordsworth shocked De Quincey with their cheerfully irreverent republican views (De Quincey, 204–5). With the breakdown in 1803 of the brief peace of Amiens, however, he adopted the traditional British hostility to the French with enthusiasm. The hostility reached a climax in 1808 when the French invaded his beloved Spain and Portugal. From then onwards he saw the war as a crusade, and those who opposed it as little better than traitors. His most ambitious publication during this period was *Madoc* (1805), a long narrative celebrating the civilizing mission of virtuous Europeans in overcoming an inhumane culture in Mexico. He attached particular importance to this poem, regarding his previous work as exercises to prepare him for its composition. 'I looked to this', he wrote in a draft preface (prudently discarded) 'as the monument to perpetuate my memory' (Keswick Museum and Art Gallery, MS 221.1). The indifference of the reading public on this occasion disappointed him.

Southey's state of mind in his first years at Greta Hall emerges clearly from *Letters from England* (1807), the supposed work of an imaginary Spanish traveller, Don Manuel Alvarez Espriella. The temper is generally relaxed, but he finds some aspects of English life alarming, particularly in its industrial and commercial expansion. He compares commerce to a witch who has cast a baleful spell on the entire population, tainting every aspect of society. There is too much wealth and too much poverty. Only a taxation policy aimed at breaking down great properties might serve to break the enchantment. The theme of sinister magic is one to which Southey recurs in his poetry, and in this respect he may have spoken to a rather pervasive anxiety at the time. Meanwhile his work as a translator of Portuguese and Spanish came to fruition in *Palmerin of England* (1807) and *Chronicle of the Cid* (1808), a skilful fusion of several sources.

Southey would have given up writing his own poetry altogether had it not been for Walter Savage Landor, whom he met in 1808. Landor offered to subsidize the publication of any future epics, an encouragement which prompted Southey to continue writing his next major poem, *The Curse of Kehama* (1810). This was a romance, like *Thalaba* in irregular verse, taking Hinduism as a background to a story of resilient endurance. The invulnerability of the hero, Ladurlad, profoundly gratifies Southey's imagination, as does the eternal punishment inflicted on the aspiring Kehama:

And while within the burning anguish flows,
His outward body glows
Like molten ore, beneath the avenging Eye,
Doom'd thus to live and burn eternally.
(24.18, *Poems*, 206)

The *Quarterly Review* and Conservative politics *Kehama* was published some two years after the outbreak of the Peninsular War, and by that time the euphoria attending its first phase was beginning to give way to an anxiety deepening to panic when he contemplated the political scene in Britain. His earlier Jacobinism ceased to appeal once he was forced to recognize that it was allied with opposition to the war. He was eager to take part in producing a new periodical, the *Quarterly Review*, dedicated to countering the influence of the widely read *Edinburgh Review*, which was proving lukewarm in its support of the Spanish patriots. While he had grave suspicions of the new journal's links with government ministers, the war issue took precedence over everything else. Besides, he was glad to strengthen the opposition to the *Edinburgh* politically since it had been hostile to his poetry. The pay, too, was excellent.

At the outset the tory management of the *Quarterly* did not trust Southey with political subjects. His first contribution was a defence of the Baptist Missionary Society, in effect a reply to a scornful article in the *Edinburgh*. Even here the editor excised any indication of indifference to theological orthodoxy, and Southey was furious when he saw how cruelly his article had been mutilated. He hoped for better things when, in 1811, he reviewed Charles W. Pasley's *Essay on the Military Policy and Institutions of the*

British Empire. Pasley argued for a more aggressive war policy, with fewer scruples about conquest. Southey called in Rickman to help him with economic arguments to support Pasley's views, and although the resulting article contradicts Southey's enduring hostility to the industrial revolution, he was still gratified at the idea that he was establishing a new and less inhibited habit of thinking about the war. But once again the editor intervened: he called in J. W. Croker to tone down the more offensive passages. Southey refused to acknowledge the review as his when he saw the published version.

Southey had more freedom of expression in another publishing enterprise. This was the 'history of the year' that he contributed to the *Edinburgh Annual Register*, beginning with 1808. What he wrote in the first volume, which occupied him through the winter of 1809–10, illustrates the final phase of his radical commitment. He strongly supported the Spanish patriots, showed goodwill to the British radical reformers, censured government patronage, and admired (with some reservations) Cobbett's vigorous and fearless journalism. While he was, of course, scornful of Samuel Whitbread and the peace campaigners, and disturbed when radicals like Sir Francis Burdett supported them, the continuity with his former views is still unmistakable. But when he came to write the history of the following year, during the winter of 1810–11, he adopted an altogether different tone. He had to record the exposure of the duke of York's corrupt disposal of army commissions through his mistress, and the resulting 'political Saturnalia' which gave the mob an unwelcome taste of power (*Edinburgh Annual Register for 1809*, 1.230). As he was writing, the renewed mental illness of George III opened up the prospect of a regency and hence of a change of government, a change which might mean some weakening in the conduct of the war. By the time he had finished he was convinced that what the country needed was above all a strong leader. A regular opposition was absurd, and reform an invitation to anarchy.

This was Southey's political creed for the next two decades. It gave him little comfort, as increasingly he felt that events were moving inexorably towards a destructive revolution. His fears were reinforced in May 1812 when a failed businessman assassinated the prime minister, Spencer Perceval, and crowds rejoiced in the streets. In a succession of articles in the *Quarterly* he called for stern measures against agitators coupled with an attempt to reverse the fatal dependence on manufacturing industry. There were now extremes of inequality which undermined social cohesion and were intolerable. It was this revulsion against the commercial spirit that led him to endorse the egalitarian plans of Robert Owen, and to listen sympathetically to the young and fiercely radical poet Shelley when he visited Keswick in 1812.

Poet laureate In 1813, partly through the efforts of Walter Scott, Southey was offered and accepted the post of poet laureate. His immediate predecessor, Henry James Pye, was extremely undistinguished, but Southey saw the appointment as an opportunity to offer much needed leadership to a nation threatened by catastrophic disruption. Though some of his odes dealt with traditional laureate subjects like a royal marriage, he lost no opportunity of making a (lofty) political point. He denounced the idea of negotiating with Bonaparte, celebrated the victory over France in 1814, commended programmes of emigration, and warned the nation of the dangers of faction and sedition. His last major narrative poem, *Roderick, the Last of the Goths* (1814), reinforced this martial message, evoking warlike passions strangely at variance with the pacifism implicit in poems like 'The Battle of Blenheim' of some fifteen years earlier. Admittedly the mood is very different in his *Poet's Pilgrimage to Waterloo* (1816), where a sad visit to the battlefield is followed by an inspiring vision of the future, of a world transformed by beneficent British rule. The *Life of Nelson* (1813) belongs to this period, a book which continued to find readers long after most of Southey's work was forgotten. This is understandable, for Nelson was congenial to both sides of Southey's character, the kindly and the aggressive, being a war hero who was both indomitable and affectionate.

Southey was a poet laureate who took his duties as a bulwark of good order very seriously—duties which inevitably exposed him to ridicule by those who were in opposition to the tory government. Critics accused him of absurd self-importance, and were quick to point out the contrast between his former radicalism and his present role as a courtier. The contrast was underlined in 1817 when a mischievous publisher obtained a copy of Southey's youthful play *Wat Tyler* and printed it. The publication was enormously successful, and was acutely embarrassing to a poet laureate, although he defended himself forcefully. In his *Letter to William Smith* (1817) he argued that his basic convictions had never changed. His concern had always been to remove obstacles to human progress.

The sympathy that Southey felt for Nelson does not inform the more ambitious *Life of Wesley* (1820), impressive though this is as a conscientious account of the rise and progress of an important religious movement. Southey is stern about Methodism's enthusiasm and extravagance, and hopes that it will see its way to becoming an auxiliary of the established church.

On one occasion, at least, Southey's standing as a champion of established institutions gained him recognition that gave him unmixed pleasure. In June 1820 his old university awarded him the degree of LLD, and at the ceremony he told his daughters, 'there was a great clapping of hands and huzzaing at my name' (Southey, *Life and Correspondence*, 5.41). But there were few cheers a year later when his laureate career reached an unhappy climax with *A Vision of Judgement*. This was an elaborate poem in hexameters describing the king's triumphant entry into heaven. His manifest innocence put to shame those who had so troubled him during his lifetime. Rather rashly, Southey identified political opposition with discipleship of Satan, and in the preface further attacked what he called the satanic school of poetry. Lord Byron took this personally, and in his own hugely entertaining *Vision of Judgment* interpreted the events imagined by Southey in a way far less flattering to the dead king. Southey's reputation has never recovered from Byron's ridicule.

Southey was unfortunate in coming to the laureate's office at a time of acute social disruption, when political conflicts were savage and apocalyptic hopes and fears all too plausible. The harsh tone of his political writing after 1812, though ugly, was a natural enough reaction to a pervasive sense of insecurity. The insecurity was intensified by distresses nearer home. His much loved son Herbert died in 1816 when only nine years old, and with his death Southey lost something of his hopes for the future.

In Southey's view the threats to order and good government continued to multiply through the 1820s. The main focus of his concern was the so-called Catholic question. Until 1829 Roman Catholics in Britain and Ireland were excluded from many public offices and were forbidden to sit in parliament. Southey strongly defended these exclusions, mainly on the ground that Ireland, where most of the Catholics lived, was a barbarous country, and Catholicism a characteristic element in the barbarity: inherently, incurably, and restlessly intolerant. Unchecked, it would threaten the whole fabric of the British constitution, and attempts at conciliation served only to whet destructive appetites. Southey's contribution to the defence was to publish *The Book of the Church* (1824), a history of Christianity in England. It celebrated the emergence of an established church which had shown itself the guardian of religious and political liberty. The book became the focus of fierce controversy, to which Southey responded in *Vindiciae ecclesiae Anglicanae* (1826), making its political significance explicit. The Catholic claims were, he said, supported by every faction, 'every demagogue, every irreligious and every seditious journalist, every open and every insidious enemy to Monarchy and to Christianity' (p. xvi). One of the most active opponents of concessions, the earl of Radnor, thought so well of Southey's exertions that in 1826 he had him returned as MP for Downton in Wiltshire, a borough he controlled. This happened without Southey's knowledge, and as he had no wish to embark on a career in parliament he declined the honour. Certainly he would have found it painful to witness at close quarters the spectacle, some three years later, of a tory ministry under the duke of Wellington conceding Catholic emancipation.

Man of letters and last years, 1829–1843 None the less, as the pressure towards a major reform of parliament became irresistible, Southey's alarm seems to have decreased. His *Colloquies of Society* (1829) is a calm exposition of his mature social and political convictions: rejection of the Catholic claims and of constitutional reform, support for high taxation to redistribute wealth, and so on. The conversations are conducted with the ghost of Sir Thomas More, whose *Utopia* was a remote ancestor of pantisocracy. They are set in the neighbourhood of Keswick, and the beauty of the countryside tempers the generally gloomy tone of the conversation, as does the quiet of his splendid library. 'When I go to the window there is the lake, and the circle of the mountains, and the illimitable sky' (*Colloquies*, 2.343).

This quieter mood is typical of the last phase of Southey's life. It can already be detected in his last published narrative poem, *A Tale of Paraguay* (1825), which shows him exploring, in greater depth than elsewhere in his work, the insecurity of the human condition, the prolonged suffering to which so many are condemned. But he could still take pleasure in the vigorous ballad mode which he had always found congenial, in such poems as 'All for Love' and 'The Young Dragon' (1829). His edition of Bunyan's *Pilgrim's Progress* appeared in 1830, and in 1831 he published the poems of an 'old servant', John Jones, with an essay on 'uneducated poets'. His substantial edition of Cowper's works (1835–7) includes a sympathetic biography.

Byron said that Southey

> had written much blank verse and blanker prose,
> And more of both than anybody knows.
> (*The Vision of Judgment*, stanza 98)

The conscientious industry needed to write works like the *History of Brazil* (1810–19) and the *History of the Peninsular War* (1823–32) is impressive, and the curious reader can still find in them much engaging anecdote and odd information. But they show a poor narrative grasp, and little sense of a broad historical perspective. Southey was more at home with his last assignment, *Lives of the British Admirals* (1833–7). His last poem to be published was *Oliver Newman: a New-England Tale* (1845). He had been working on it for many years, but it was never finished. It was a story with an unconventional hero, a near Quaker caught up in a war with Native Americans. It appeared posthumously, as did his *Commonplace Books* and his various travel journals.

Vehement feelings were never far from the quiet surface, even in Southey's last years, sometimes bursting out in a startling way. When Thomas Carlyle met him in 1835 something provoked his anger, and his face became '*slaty* almost, like a rattle-snake, or fiery serpent' (Carlyle, 2.284). He came to know Thomas Sadler and Lord Ashley (later Lord Shaftesbury), and was horrified by their accounts of child labour. He was much alarmed by 'the devouring principle of trade' (*Colloquies*, 2.253), and one of his last articles for the *Quarterly* warned his readers of the danger of an appalling social cataclysm if that devouring principle went unchecked (*Quarterly Review*, 51/279, March 1834). But checked it could be, by the corn laws and factory legislation.

The man of letters Throughout his adult life until his mind failed at the end, Southey followed his vocation as a man of letters with a quiet diligence. He never overworked, never carried on any task until it wore him out, but passed from one assignment to another, from poetry to history to reviewing, with an equable temper. He was a strikingly handsome man, tall with aquiline features. He took regular exercise, was hospitable to visitors, and valued the time he spent with his children. He was conscientious in responding to requests for advice from aspiring writers, most famously in his letters to Charlotte Brontë in 1837. While his concern that she might be neglecting her womanly duties reflected views widely held at the time, it is also evidence of a depressed state of mind, which indeed informs much of his work. 'My days among the Dead are past', he said in a once famous lyric (*Poems*, 347), and the fact is often too apparent.

This was in part a sign of ageing. Southey had much to dispirit him. His youngest daughter, Isabel, died at the age of fourteen in 1826, and his wife was even more severely affected by this loss than he. In 1834 her mental illness became acute, and although treatment at the Quaker hospital in York did some good, she never recovered her sanity, and died in 1837. Two years later, on 4 June 1839, Southey married again. His new wife was Caroline Anne Bowles (1786–1854) [*see* Southey, Caroline Anne Bowles], whom he had known for some twenty years. He had helped her in finding publishers for her poetry, and had even collaborated with her in writing a poem on Robin Hood. But he was already suffering a loss of his faculties, and the last few years of his life were passed in senility. Robert Southey died on 21 March 1843 at Greta Hall and was buried on 23 March at Crosthwaite church in Keswick.

Southey's status as a writer has always been uncertain. He never gained from his long narrative poems the reputation he hoped for. The *Life of Nelson* and a few of his shorter poems were familiar to many readers for up to a century after his death, but by the late twentieth century were familiar no longer. Yet he remains an important figure for students of Romanticism, and his private letters have an enduring value. They provide an unsurpassed insight into the stresses of life in the England of his time.

GEOFFREY CARNALL

Sources *The life and correspondence of Robert Southey*, ed. C. C. Southey, 6 vols. (1849–50) [incl. autobiography] · *Selections from the letters of Robert Southey*, ed. J. W. Warter, 4 vols. (1856) · *New letters of Robert Southey*, ed. K. Curry, 2 vols. (1965) · *Poems of Robert Southey*, ed. M. H. Fitzgerald (1909) · *The correspondence of Robert Southey with Caroline Bowles*, ed. E. Dowden (1881) · J. Simmons, *Southey* (1945) · G. Carnall, *Robert Southey and his age* (1960) · M. Storey, *Robert Southey: a life* (1997) · O. Williams, *Lamb's friend the census-taker: life and letters of John Rickman* (1911) · T. De Quincey, *Recollections of the lake poets*, ed. E. Sackville-West (1948) · T. Carlyle, *Reminiscences*, ed. C. E. Norton, 2 (1887) · W. Haller, *The early life of Robert Southey* (1917) · K. Curry, *Southey* (1975) [systematic discussion of works, with bibliography] · E. Bernhardt-Kabisch, *Robert Southey* (1977) · J. W. Robberds, *Memoirs of the life and writings of the late William Taylor*, 2 vols. (1843) · R. Southey, *The doctor*, 7 vols. (1834–47) · *The contributions of Robert Southey to the Morning Post*, ed. K. Curry (1984) · R. Southey, *Letters written during a short residence in Spain and Portugal* (1797) · R. Southey, *Journal of a tour in the Netherlands in the autumn of 1815*, ed. W. R. Nicoll (1903) · R. Southey, *Journal of a tour in Scotland in 1819*, ed. C. H. Herford (1929) · R. Southey, *Journals of a residence in Portugal, 1800–1801, and a visit to France, 1838*, ed. A. Cabral (1960) · M. Lefebure, *The bondage of love* (1986) [on the Fricker sisters]

Archives BL, corresp., literary MSS, and papers, Add. MSS 28096, 30927, 47883–47892, 49529; M/621; RP 202, 254, 487, 1222, 2544, 4533(ii) · Bodl. Oxf., corresp. and literary MSS · Boston PL, corresp. and literary MSS · Bristol Reference Library, diaries in Portugal and France, corresp. and papers · Col. U., Rare Book and Manuscript Library, papers · Cornell University, Ithaca, New York, papers · Cowper Memorial Library, Market Place, Olney, letters and literary MSS · Duke U., Perkins L., corresp. and papers · FM Cam., letters to his publisher relating to his *Life of Cowper* · Harvard U., Houghton L., corresp. and papers, incl. commonplace books, literary MSS · Hunt. L., corresp. and papers, incl. notebooks and literary MSS · Inst. CE, journal · JRL, letters · Keswick Museum and Art Gallery, corresp., literary MSS, and papers · McGill University, Montreal, McLennon Library, corresp. and papers · Morgan L., papers · Newnham College, Cambridge, letters · NL Scot., corresp. · NL Wales, corresp. · Ransom HRC, papers · Saffron Walden Museum, Essex, literary MSS and papers · U. Leeds, Brotherton L., letters and notes; literary MSS · U. Leeds, Brotherton L., letters in his *Life of Nelson* · University of Rochester, New York, Rush Rhees Library, corresp., literary MSS, and papers · University of Waterloo, Ontario, letters, notes, and literary MS; corresp. and papers relating to Samuel Taylor Coleridge · Wordsworth Trust, Dove Cottage, Grasmere, corresp. and notebooks | BL, letters, mostly to Anna Eliza Bray [copies], MS Facs. 615 · BL, letters to Sir John Taylor Coleridge, Add. MS 47553 · BL, letters to Charles Danvers, Add. MS 30928 · BL, letters to John May, microfilm M/596 · BL, letters to William Peachey, Add. MS 28603 · BL, letters to his brother, Thomas Southey, Add. MS 30927 · BL, letters and poems to Daniel Stuart, Add. MS 34046 · Bodl. Oxf., corresp., mainly with Grosvenor Bedford; other MSS · Bodl. Oxf., letters to Charles Danvers and Caroline Bowles [copies] · Bodl. Oxf., corresp. with Isaac D'Israeli · Bodl. Oxf., letters to Francis Douce · Bodl. Oxf., letters to Robert Gooch · Bodl. Oxf., letters to Richard Heber · Bodl. Oxf., letters to Nicholas Lightfoot · Bodl. Oxf., letters to H. H. Southey · CKS, letters to Lord Stanhope · Cumbria RO, Carlisle, letters to Lord Lonsdale · DWL, letters to Henry Crabb Robinson and others · FM Cam., letters to Baldwin & Cradock · Hunt. L., letters to Edward Locker · Hunt. L., letters to John Rickman · Keswick Museum and Art Gallery · Man. CL, Manchester Archives and Local Studies, letters to James Crossley · Man. CL, Manchester Archives and Local Studies, letters to Charles Swain · Mirehouse, Keswick, corresp. with John Spedding · NL Scot., letters to J. G. Lockhart · NL Scot., corresp. with Sir Walter Scott · NL Wales, corresp. with C. W. W. Wynn · NRA Scotland, priv. coll., letters to John Swinton · U. Edin. L., letters to David Laing · U. Leeds, letters to John May · U. Lpool L., corresp. with Joseph Blanco White · University of Rochester, New York, Rush Rhees Library, letters to Humphrey Senhouse [copies] · University of Toronto, Victoria University, letters to Samuel Taylor Coleridge · V&A NAL, letters and literary MSS sent to W. S. Landor · Yale U., Beinecke L., corresp. with John Taylor

Likenesses P. Vandyke, oils, 1795, NPG · R. Hancock, pencil and wash drawing, 1796, NPG · H. Edridge, pencil, chalk, and wash drawing, 1804, NPG [*see illus.*] · M. Betham, watercolour miniature, 1812, Bristol City Museum and Art Gallery · E. Nash, oils, 1820, NPG · S. Lane, oils, exh. RA 1824, Balliol Oxf. · T. Lawrence, oils, 1828, National Gallery of South Africa, Cape Town; repro. in K. Garlick, *Sir Thomas Lawrence* (1954) · F. Chantrey, marble bust, 1828–32, NPG · E. W. Wyon, wax medallion, 1835, NPG · J. G. Lough, marble effigy, 1845, Crosthwaite church, Cumberland · D. Aguirre, drawing, NPG · E. H. Baily, bust, Bristol Cathedral · W. H. Egleton, stipple (after J. Opie), BM, NPG; repro. in Southey, *Life and correspondence* (1849) · J. G. Lough, marble bust, NPG · S. W. Reynolds, mezzotint (after T. Phillips, 1815), John Murray collection, London · H. Weekes, bust, Westminster Abbey · miniature, NPG

Southgate, Henry (1818–1888), anthologist and auctioneer, was born in London, the son of James Webb Southgate, floor cloth manufacturer and auctioneer. Little is known of his early life or education, but on 4 June 1840 he married Elizabeth Lawson Robertson (*b.* 1819/20). Southgate entered his father's business, and from 1840 to 1866 carried on his practice as an auctioneer of prints and engravings at 22 Fleet Street. The firm was known as Southgate and Barrett from 1845 until 1860, when the partnership was dissolved, and Southgate began gradually to take over the business. He had by this time made a considerable reputation as a compiler of selections in prose and verse from English classics.

Southgate's works include *Many thoughts on many things:*

being a treasury of reference, consisting of selections from the known great and the great unknown, published in London in 1857; the third edition was extensively revised, and published under the title, *Many Thoughts of Many Minds* in November 1861. It had a large circulation and was frequently reprinted. The first edition was denounced by *The Athenaeum* in 1857 as 'an enormous book, an enormous blunder'. It did, however, receive commendations from the *London Examiner* and the *Gentleman's Magazine* (5, 1858, 196), and in the nineteenth century was considered equal to Bartlett's *Familiar Quotations*. A second series was published in London in 1871. In 1864 appeared *What Men have said about Woman: a Collection of Choice Thoughts and Sentences*, which was reprinted in 1865 and 1866, while 1866 also saw the publication of *Musings about Men, Compiled and Analytically Arranged from the Writings of the Good and Great*, illustrated by Birket Foster and Sir John Gilbert; this was reprinted in 1868. *Noble thoughts in noble language: a collection of wise and virtuous utterances in prose and verse* appeared in 1871 and was reprinted in 1880. The book was arranged alphabetically from 'Ability' to 'Zeal', and, after *Many Thoughts of Many Minds*, was the most popular of Southgate's compilations.

More thematic compilations included *Christus redemptor, being the life, character and teachings of Jesus Christ; illustrated in many passages from the writings of ancient and modern authors* (1874, 1880). Southgate also produced a book dedicated to his daughter Julia, entitled *Things a Lady would Like to Know Concerning Domestic Management and Expenditure* (1874, 1875); and in 1876 he dedicated *The Way to Woo and Win a Wife, Illustrated by a Series of Choice Extracts* to his wife, editor of her own anthology, *The Christian Life: being Thoughts in Prose and Verse from the Best Writers of All Ages* (1883).

During the last fifteen years of Southgate's life a collection of 'plates, cuttings, and extracts, printed and manuscript', was compiled by him for publication as *The Wealth and Wisdom of Literature, or, A Dictionary of Suggestive Thought*. A title-page was printed, but Southgate sought in vain to find a publisher for this huge anthology, which eventually extended to forty weighty volumes (with an alphabet from 'Abandoned' to 'Zymotic').

From 1870 Southgate lived first at Salcombe and then at Sidmouth in south Devon. He afterwards moved to Ramsgate, Kent, where he died on 5 December 1888 at 32 Hardres Street. THOMAS SECCOMBE, *rev.* MELANIE ORD

Sources Allibone, *Dict.* • *BL cat.* • S. Low, *The English catalogue of books*, 1–4 (1864–93) • *Nineteenth century short-title catalogue: series II, 1816–1870*, 37 (1994), 393 • d. cert. • m. cert.
Archives BM

Southgate, Richard (1729–1795), numismatist, was born at Alwalton, Huntingdonshire, on 16 March 1729, the eldest of ten children of William Southgate (*d.* 1771), farmer, and his wife, Hannah Wright (*d.* 1772), daughter of Robert Wright, canal engineer. He went to schools in Uppingham and Fotheringhay, where he began to display a retentive memory and taste for study, and to Peterborough grammar school. Thence in 1745 he went as an exhibitioner to St John's College, Cambridge, under Thomas Rutherforth, and graduated BA in 1749. Through great economy he was able to begin collecting books and coins, of the latter only specimens in the finest condition.

After taking holy orders in 1752, Southgate became curate of Weston, Lincolnshire. He was elected a member of the nearby Spalding Gentlemen's Society on 24 May 1753. From 1754 he held the rectory of Woolley, Huntingdonshire, during the minority of the patron, who was himself intended for the church. Southgate resigned in 1759, although under no obligation to do so. He then served the curacies successively of Upton and Leighton Bromswold, Wootton and Wykeham, Coveney and Maney, Godmanchester, Louth, Raithby, Tathwell and Calkwell, and Doddington and Newnham in Kent; but the want of books and persons of literature in country villages were insurmountable objects to improving his knowledge. In 1763, having been recommended to the rector of St James's, Westminster, he was appointed one of his subcurates, and, on Christmas day 1765, curate of St Giles-in-the-Fields, a post he held until his death.

As a parish priest Southgate was indefatigable in his attendance on the poor, in the cellars or the garrets of St Giles's, at any hour of the day or night. Occasionally he was imposed upon; but a contemporary observed that the poorest of his Irish parishioners, although Roman Catholics, treated him with good manners which they paid no one else (Reid, 51–2). He inherited an estate in Whitechapel worth £100 p.a., and in addition to St Giles's he was presented by the duke of Ancaster in 1783 to the rectory of Little Steeping, which he exchanged in 1790 for the living of Warsop, worth £1400 p.a. He was thus able to enlarge both his collecting and his charity, and to give away almost double what he received from St Giles's, including on one occasion his last shirt but one.

Southgate's main areas of collecting were Anglo-Saxon coins, English town pieces and tradesmen's tokens, of which he formed a collection superior to any in the kingdom, and dollars of the world, from which he acquired his knowledge of the history of Europe. On 3 November 1784 he was appointed assistant librarian at the British Museum, succeeding Andrew Gifford in responsibility for the coins and medals. He was elected fellow of the Society of Antiquaries on 6 June 1793, and was a member also of the Linnean Society.

Southgate advised William Hunter on Anglo-Saxon coins. He collected material for a treatise on the history of the Saxons and Danes in England, illustrated by their coins, but his progress in it was retarded by his diffidence (Nichols, *Lit. anecdotes*, 6.112). Among the contributions he did make was a plate of coins struck at Leicester, printed in J. Nichols's *The History and Antiquities of the County of Leicester*. The Revd Rogers Ruding stated that from Southgate's collection he first derived a practical knowledge of the English coinage, that his 'entertaining and instructive conversations' led Ruding to study English coins historically, and that by Southgate's encouragement he was induced to prepare for publication his great *Annals of the Coinage* (Ruding, 1.xix). Ruding illustrated about 200

Anglo-Saxon coins in Southgate's collection, the importance of which has been discussed by J. S. Martin and H. E. Pagan.

Southgate was 5 feet 10 inches tall, very upright, latterly corpulent, of a cheerful disposition, active in mind yet slow and inactive in body. He died apparently unmarried, of 'an asthmatical and dropsical complaint' (*GM*, 171–2) at his residence in the British Museum on 21 January 1795. He was buried on 3 February in St Giles-in-the-Fields, where a memorial tablet by John Hinchliffe the younger was placed on the south-east pillar. Southgate's *Sermons Preached to Parochial Congregations*, with a biographical preface by George Gaskin, was published in 1798. He left no will, and his property went to five surviving brothers. His 'elegant and valuable library' was sold by Leigh and Sotheby from 27 April to 9 May 1795, for £1,332 12*s.*, and his small collection of shells and other natural curiosities on 12–13 May. The sale of his coins was planned for May, but the whole collection was purchased by Samuel Tyssen for 1800 guineas before the sale, with the resulting duplicates being auctioned in July. Southgate became thereby a source for the British Museum collection of coins, and the Anglo-Saxon coins from his collection have subsequently been identified by Martin. R. H. THOMPSON

Sources *GM*, 1st ser., 65 (1795), 171–2, 252–3 · *Museum Southgatianum: being a catalogue of the valuable collection of books, coins, medals and natural history, of the late Rev Richard Southgate: to which is prefixed, memoirs of his life* (1795) [printed for Leigh and Sotheby] · R. Ruding, *Annals of the coinage of Great Britain and its dependencies*, 2nd edn, 6 vols. (1819) · J. S. Martin, 'Some remarks on eighteenth-century numismatic manuscripts and numismatists', *Anglo-Saxon coins: studies presented to F. M. Stenton*, ed. R. H. M. Dolley (1961), 227–40 · H. E. Pagan, 'Presidential address', *British Numismatic Journal*, 55 (1985), 208–19 · J. Nichols, *The history and antiquities of the county of Leicester*, 4 vols. (1795–1815) · W. H. Reid, *The rise and dissolution of the infidel societies in this metropolis* (1800) · Nichols, *Lit. anecdotes*, 6.112–13, 359–79 · G. Macdonald, *Catalogue of the Greek coins in the Hunterian collection, University of Glasgow*, 3 vols. (1899–1905) · W. E. Riley, *The parish of St Giles-in-the-Fields*, ed. L. Gomme, 2, Survey of London, 5 (1914) · R. Gunnis, *Dictionary of British sculptors, 1660–1851*, new edn (1968) · H. E. Manville and T. J. Robertson, *British numismatic auction catalogues, 1710–1984* (1986) · *DNB*

Archives BL, Ruding MSS, Add. MS 18093

Likenesses T. Trotter, line engraving, 1785, BM; repro. in Leigh and Sotheby, *Museum southgatianum*

Wealth at death £3222 12*s.*: sales of library and coins; also shells and natural curiosities

Southrey, Simon. *See* Southerey, Simon (*b. c.*1342, *d.* in or after 1420).

South Saxons, kings of the (*act.* 477–772), rulers in the area of modern Sussex, with portions of Kent and Hampshire, are for the most part obscure, their names supplied by the occasional charter and their dates a matter for abstruse calculation. The traditional founder of the kingdom was *Ælle, said to have arrived on the South Saxon coast in 477 with his three sons, Cymen, Wlencing, and Cissa. The last that is heard of Ælle is his storming of the Roman fort of Anderida, near Pevensey, supposedly in 491; his partner in the assault was his son Cissa. From the omission of any reference to the other two sons, it might be deduced that Cissa succeeded his father; but there is no firm evidence of this, and indeed nothing to show that Ælle founded a dynasty.

The next South Saxon ruler of whom anything is known is King **Æthelwealh** (*d. c.*685), who was the first to accept Christianity. He was baptized in Mercia, at the suggestion of his overlord, King Wulfhere (*r.* 658–75), who acted as his sponsor and subsequently presented him with the Isle of Wight and the land around the Meon valley as a token of their new relationship in God. Æthelwealh may have been more ready to accept Christianity because he had a Christian wife, Eafe, who was originally from the kingdom of the Hwicce (roughly the present counties of Gloucestershire and Worcestershire); this marriage was probably also engineered by Wulfhere, to strengthen his overlordship over the South Saxon kingdom. In the early 680s Æthelwealh received Bishop Wilfrid of Northumbria, then in exile from his native land, and encouraged him to organize the mass conversion of the South Saxons and to set up a permanent church in the kingdom; he granted Wilfrid a large estate in the Selsey area, where the bishop founded a monastery which he used as his base for the short period he remained in the kingdom. Æthelwealh's reign ended about 685, when Sussex was invaded by a young West Saxon prince named Cædwalla, himself an exile. Æthelwealh was killed in the course of this incursion, but Cædwalla was driven out by two of the king's noblemen, Berhthun and Andhun. Shortly afterwards, in 686, Cædwalla managed to establish himself as ruler of the West Saxons, and with his additional resources he once more invaded Sussex, killing Berhthun. Sussex now became for some years subject to a period of harsh West Saxon domination.

By 692 the people were under the rule of a certain Nothhelm, usually known as **Nunna** (*fl.* 692–714?), who acknowledged the overlordship of the new West Saxon king, Ine. According to one version of the Anglo-Saxon Chronicle, Nunna was a kinsman of King Ine, and collaborated with him in an assault on Cornwall in 710. Two of Nunna's earlier charters are also attested by a King **Watt** (*fl.* 692), while a later one has the subscription of a King **Æthelstan** (*fl.* 714?) (*AS chart.*, S 45, 1173, 42). It would appear that Sussex was now being ruled by West Saxon nominees; they may have been joint kings (with Nunna as the probable senior ruler), or there may have been some kind of territorial division. If the latter, then Nunna, who could dispose of land around Selsey and Chichester, is likely to have ruled the western part of the kingdom; Watt, followed by Æthelstan, may have been in charge of the eastern part (from which no charters survive). There is evidence from later in the century that the area around Hastings, occupied by the people known as the Hæstingas, existed as a territory distinct from the rest of the South Saxon kingdom; it may have been settled by colonists from Kent. The suggestion that Watt was the ruler of the Hæstingas is attractive, but unsupported by any evidence. Nunna's last appearance is in a charter dated 714 (possibly for 717 or 721), but he may have gone on ruling for some time after this.

The next South Saxon king to emerge in the sources is

Æthelberht (*fl.* 733–747?), donor of two charters (*AS chart.*, S 46 and 47, the latter being a fabrication); all that can be said for certain about him is that he was a contemporary of Sigefrith, bishop of Selsey, who was consecrated in 733 and who died at some point between 747 and 765. By the latter date Sussex had a new bishop, and at least three or even four new kings had come to power. Determining the sequence and relationship of these rulers proves very difficult. One was **Osmund** (*fl.* 765–770x72), who made grants of land at Ferring in 765, at Henfield in 770, and at Peppering near Amberley probably between 770 and 772 (S 48, 49, 44); all these places are within 20 miles of each other, and provide some indication of the areas which Osmund controlled. None of Osmund's charters is attested by another king. By contrast, a charter (S 50) in the name of a King **Ealdwulf** (*fl. c.*760), which seems to belong to the 760s, is attested by a King **Ælfwald** [Ælhuald] (*fl. c.*760) and a King **Oslac** [Osiai] (*fl. c.*760).

The independent existence of the South Saxon kingdom came to an end in the early 770s. In 771 Offa, king of the Mercians, conquered the territory of the Hæstingas; he may have entered Sussex from Kent, where he was already dominant. By 772 he apparently controlled the whole kingdom. In that year he issued a diploma granting land at Bexhill to the bishop of the South Saxons (*AS chart.*, S 108), which was witnessed by four men described as *dux*: Oswald, Osmund, Ælfwald, and Oslac. There is reason to suspect that at least three of these men were former kings of Sussex. Osmund was probably the ruler who issued diplomas in the 760s and early 770s, while Ælfwald and Oslac seem likely to have been the Ælhuald and Osiai who attested King Ealdwulf's charter in the 760s. Nothing is known of Oswald, although judging from the position of his subscription in the witness list to Offa's diploma he would appear to have been the most senior of the four. It would seem that after his conquest of Sussex Offa had come to an agreement with its former rulers, who continued to rule as Offa's representatives, with the reduced status of *dux*. In subsequent years Oslac and Ælfwald both made grants of land as *dux* of the South Saxons, but in each case the grants were made with Offa's permission or were later confirmed by him (S 1178, 1183, 1184). Sussex remained a Mercian possession until *c.*825, when it was absorbed into the West Saxon kingdom. S. E. KELLY

Sources *ASC*, s.a. 477, 491, 710 • Bede, *Hist. eccl.*, 4.13, 15 • E. Stephanus, *The life of Bishop Wilfrid*, ed. and trans. B. Colgrave (1927), caps. xli–xlii (pp. 80–85) • S. E. Kelly, ed., *Charters of Selsey*, Anglo-Saxon Charters, 6 (1998) • Symeon of Durham, *Opera*, 2.44 • M. Welch, *Early Anglo-Saxon Sussex*, 2 vols. (1983) • M. Welch, 'The kingdom of the South Saxons: the origins', *The origins of Anglo-Saxon kingdoms*, ed. S. Bassett (1989), 75–96 • P. Brandon, ed., *The South Saxons* (1978)

Southward, John (1840–1902), printer and writer, was born on 28 April 1840, the son of Jackson Southward, printer, of Liverpool, a native of Corney, Cumberland, and his wife, Margaret Proud of Enniscorthy, co. Wexford. After education at the Liverpool Collegiate Institution (later to become Liverpool College), he gained a thorough practical knowledge of printing in his father's office in Pitt Street, Liverpool. At seventeen he became co-editor with the Revd A. S. Hume of the *Liverpool Philosophical Magazine*, and from November 1857 until its closure in 1865 he edited the *Liverpool Observer*, the first penny weekly issued in the town, which was printed in Jackson Southward's office. On the failure of the paper John Southward moved to London to increase his experience, and was reader successively for Cox and Wyman and for Eyre and Spottiswoode.

In 1868 Southward travelled in Spain for a firm of English watchmakers, throughout all parts of the country, visiting every newspaper office and securing copies of all serial publications. While there he was a close observer of the Spanish revolution which took place in September of that year and he described his experiences in four articles in the *Printers' Register* in 1869. Many further contributions to this and other trade organs followed.

Southward soon became recognized as the leading authority on the history and processes of printing. His *Dictionary of Typography and its Accessory Arts*, after being issued as monthly supplements to the *Printers' Register*, was published as a book in 1872. It was printed simultaneously in the Philadelphia *Printers' Circular*, and formed the basis of Ringwalt's American *Encyclopædia of Printing*. A revised edition appeared in 1875. *Practical Printing: a Handbook of the Art of Typography*, a much larger work, which also first appeared monthly in the *Printers' Register*, was first published independently in 1882, and became a standard textbook. The series was reprinted in American and Australian printing journals. Southward prepared revised editions in 1884 and 1887; it reached its sixth edition by 1911. From 1886 to 1890 Southward was also the editor of the *Printers' Register* and then editor of *Paper and Printing Trades Journal* from 1891 to 1893, having taken over from Andrew Tuer. Southward's illustrated *Progress in Printing and the Graphic Arts during the Victorian Era* appeared in 1897. *Modern Printing*, which he edited in four profusely illustrated sections between 1898 and 1900, was designed to be at once a reference book for the printing office and a manual of instruction for class and home reading. The work, in which leading experts co-operated, was adopted as a textbook in the chief technological institutions, and reached its eighth edition by 1954.

Southward also published *Authorship and Publication*, a technical guide for authors, in 1881, and *Artistic Printing: a Supplement to Practical Printing*, in 1892. His first wife, Rachel Clayton of Huddersfield, with whom he had three sons and four daughters, died in 1892. He remarried in 1894; his second wife was Alice King, widow of J. King. He contributed the article 'Modern typography' to the ninth edition of the *Encyclopaedia Britannica* and wrote technical articles for *Chambers's Encyclopaedia*. The *Bibliography of Printing*, issued under the names of Edward Clements Bigmore and C. W. H. Wyman (3 vols., 1880–86, one volume reprinted 1969), was to a large extent his work. Southward compiled the *Catalogue of the Passmore Edwards Library* (1897) and the *Catalogue of the William Blades Library* (1899).

Southward was active in philanthropic work and in 1888 founded, and for a short time edited, a monthly paper called *Charity*. During his later years he lived at Streatham, and died at St Thomas's Hospital, London, after an operation, on 9 July 1902. He was buried in Norwood cemetery. G. LE G. NORGATE, *rev.* A. P. WOOLRICH

Sources E. C. Bigmore and C. W. H. Wyman, *Bibliography of printing*, vol. 3 • private information (2004) • *Printers' Register* (6 Aug 1902) • *The Times* (11–12 July 1902) • *The Times* (17 July 1902) • *Streatham News* (19 July 1902) • *CGPLA Eng. & Wales* (1903)
Archives St Bride Printing Library, London
Likenesses photograph, repro. in J. Southward, *Modern Printing*, 1 (1899)
Wealth at death £275 9*s*. 6*d*.: administration, 8 April 1903, *CGPLA Eng. & Wales*

Southwark. For this title name *see* Causton, Richard Knight, Baron Southwark (1843–1929); Causton, Selina Mary, Lady Southwark (1852–1932) [*see under* Causton, Richard Knight, Baron Southwark (1843–1929)].

Southwell [*née* Harris], **Anne, Lady Southwell** (*bap.* **1574**, *d.* **1636**), poet, was born at Cornworthy Priory, Cornworthy, Devon, the eldest child of Elizabeth Pomeroy (*d.* 1634) and Thomas Harris MP (1547–1610, knighted by 1604). She was baptized at St Peter's, Cornworthy, on 22 August 1574. Her siblings included Sir Edward, who became chief justice of the king's bench in Munster, Ireland; Sir Christopher, who was killed at Ostend, and Honor, who married Sir Hugh Harris of Scotland. Because Thomas Harris was serjeant-at-law at the Middle Temple Inn and MP for four towns, the family may have lived in London occasionally. No record of Anne's education remains, although her compositions illustrate an understanding of theology, literature, rhetoric, and music.

Anne married Thomas Southwell (1575?–1626), of Spixworth, Norfolk, at the church of St Clement Danes in London on 24 June 1594. He was knighted on 23 July 1603 and at a later date sent to Munster for the plantation of Ireland. Through Thomas's mother, Alice Southwell (*née* Cornwallis), Anne may have met the essayist William Cornwallis and his friends John Donne and Thomas Overbury. The Southwell family also enjoyed other literary and courtly connections, the most famous being Robert Southwell, poet and martyr for the Roman cause. Anne Southwell, however, was herself a staunch protestant who mocked Roman 'Popelings'. Her early writing included 'Answere[s]' to two 'Newes' reports, one by Donne and the other by Overbury, that were published, with her initials, in Overbury's notorious book *A Wife now the Widow of Sir Thomas Overburye* (1614).

After Sir Thomas's death in 1626 Anne married Captain Henry Sibthorpe, who probably gave her the folios of Folger, MS V.b.198 that with his help she turned into an uncommon commonplace book. The two collected her compositions as well as works they liked by others, some of which could prove useful as models. Occasionally Sibthorpe served as a scribe and, as is clear from marginalia (fol. 49*r*), he also mentored his wife's writing. After Anne's death he may have added some explanatory titles and inserted a few of the works, especially those to or about prestigious people, to make the volume a 'monument of an Endlesse affection', as he described it on the folios he added (fols. 73 and 74).

In 1628 Anne and Henry Sibthorpe settled in Clerkenwell, Middlesex, and, in 1631, they moved to Acton. They lived near St Mary's Church, in 'tenaments' rented from Robert Johnson, court lutenist and composer. Entries in the commonplace book show Anne's interaction with her neighbours, and especially with the curate Roger Cocks.

Lady Southwell's compositions suggest that she was an intelligent and spirited woman. She claimed lethal ladies of the Bible, Jael and Judith, as her role models. With a voice of authority, she wrote to and about people such as Henry Cary, Viscount Falkland; Bishop Adams of Limerick; the duchess of Lennox; and the kings of Bohemia and Sweden. She could also banter with politicians, as she did in petitioning Richard Boyle, earl of Cork, for the land rights of Sir Richard Edgcumbe (Chatsworth, Lismore MSS, box 14, fol. 160; see also fol. 174). Her greatest contribution may be the way that she often urged mutuality in marriage, based on Christ's example with his spouse, the church. She warned against dangers such as the 'heresy' that females have so little wit, 'as but to serve men they are only fitt' (Folger MS V.b.198, fol. 26*v*). BL, MS Lansdowne 740, fols. 142–167*v*, includes Anne's two long meditations on the third and fourth commandments, expansions from poems in the Folger volume. Although at first the meditations probably were meant to honour James I, the final dedication evidently addressed Charles I. Lady Southwell died at the home owned by Robert Johnson's widow in Acton on 2 October 1636 and was buried on 5 October in the chancel of St Mary's Church, where a plaque on the back wall still commemorates her. Her husband survived her. JEAN KLENE

Sources F. Steer, *Woodrising Church and other families connected with the parish* (1959) [with a foreword by the earl of Verulam] • F. Blomefield, *A history of the county of Norfolk*, 11 vols. (1809), vol. 10 • Burke, *Gen. GB* (1838) • J. Lodge, *The peerage of Ireland*, 4 (1754) • HoP, *Commons, 1558–1603* • R. P. Mahaffy, ed., *Calendar of state papers, 1615–1632* (1900), vol. 1 • J. L. Vivian, ed., *The visitations of the county of Devon, comprising the herald's visitations of 1531, 1564, and 1620* (privately printed, Exeter, [1895]) • A. Southwell and H. Sibthorpe, *The Southwell–Sibthorpe commonplace book: Folger MS.V.b.198*, ed. J. Klene (1997)
Archives Devonshire collection, Chatsworth House, Derbyshire, Lismore MSS
Wealth at death Sibthorpe paid little for keeping of his men in Cork: *CSP Ire.* • rented 'tenements' in Acton; therefore probably little money left; costly clothing in inventory of 'Aparel' suggests former wealth

Southwell, Charles (**1814–1860**), freethinker and journalist, was born in London, the thirty-third (and last) child of a piano maker, William Southwell (*c.*1758–1825/6), and the only child of Fanny, his former servant and third wife, who was at least thirty years his junior. William Southwell had taken out early patents in the search for a small upright piano suitable for domestic use. At school Charles was rebellious and intractable but read widely. After his father's death, the eleven year old became a piano finisher at Broadwood & Sons, having rejected the more genteel occupation of a tuner which his brothers had arranged for him. A copy of Timothy Dwight's *Sermons* (1828), lent by a pious fellow workman, led Southwell to follow his father in repudiating Christianity.

Southwell abandoned factory work during the reform crisis of the early 1830s. He opened an ultra-radical bookshop in Westminster, where he participated in opening a 'rational school' and defended the seditious press from clerical attacks. His youthful marriage to Mary Seaford around 1832 was marked by separation and mutual infidelity (on Southwell's side with his wife's aunt, in a relationship which raised accusations of bigamy). Unhappily reunited, the couple ran the shop, which failed after two years when Mary became terminally ill. Following her wishes, when she died (*c*.1835) Southwell watched a surgeon open her body to ensure that she was dead and remove her heart as an anatomical specimen. Only the intervention of the police prevented a riot.

Hoping to make a new start, Southwell joined the British Legion in 1835 to fight as a royalist mercenary in Spain against the Carlists. He returned two years later, half-starved and nearly penniless, to work once more at Broadwoods. Attracted to radical debate rather than making pianos, Southwell created a sensation with his open-air addresses on Kennington Common. In 1840 the central board of the Association of All Classes of All Nations (AACAN) confirmed him as a socialist missionary, first in London, then in Birmingham. However, Southwell chafed at Robert Owen's attempts to curb uninhibited attacks on theology, and he resigned in 1841, soon after bringing the campaign to Bristol. Together with William Chilton and John Field, Southwell began the *Oracle of Reason*, a penny weekly advocating atheism. Aggressively confrontational, the *Oracle* featured a pro-evolutionary series (begun by Southwell, continued by Chilton) using science to prove the bestial origins of the human race. Southwell's antisemitic diatribe against the Bible, 'The Jew book', led to his arrest in 1842. In one of the most celebrated blasphemy trials of the century he was fined £100 and sentenced to a year in prison.

After his release Southwell refused to resume the *Oracle* editorship, much to the annoyance of his associates, launching instead the more temperate (but short-lived) *Investigator*. He campaigned for free thought in Edinburgh and especially in London, where in 1844 he opened the Paragon Hall and Coffee House in Lambeth. The dampness of the rooms, combined with Southwell's ambitions as an actor, led him to sell up in 1848 and take a lease on the Canterbury Theatre. This failed almost immediately, and Southwell returned to London where he managed a lecture hall at Blackfriars.

Throughout this period, Southwell lived with a Mrs Gordon (formerly Mrs Rowen), a married woman who managed his finances. Deeply affected by her death from uterine cancer in 1849, and harassed by the Inland Revenue which fined him £150 for serving alcohol without a licence, Southwell prepared to sail for the United States. However, freethinkers in Manchester convinced him to take over their Hall of Science, which he did with great (though temporary) success, baiting evangelicals, organizing displays of religious idolatry and issuing the weekly *Lancashire Beacon*. After this 'vain attempt to revolutionize Lancashire' (Southwell, 98), he returned in 1850 to London, where he lectured on theological and literary subjects. He became convinced of the futility of debating abstract questions such as the existence of a deity, although he continued to denounce Christianity and the church.

Southwell was a brilliant platform speaker, free thought's most electrifying and entertaining advocate in the 1830s and 1840s. Reckless and impulsive, he drew huge working- and lower-middle-class crowds with his verbal pyrotechnics and outrageous vulgarity. He published dozens of pamphlets, including an attack on marriage (1840), and revealing *Confessions* (1850), written to counter scurrilous diatribes by former associate and fellow blasphemer Thomas Paterson. Southwell also worked with William Chilton, Robert Cooper, Walter Cooper, George Jacob Holyoake, and Lloyd Jones, but quarrelled with all of them and hated ties with any organized movement. As radicals sought respectability and institutional security after 1848, Southwell's racy individualism looked increasingly out of place.

In 1855 Southwell emigrated to Melbourne, where he lectured, engaged in radical politics, and acted in his favourite role, Shylock. In the following year he went on a theatrical tour, first to Sydney and then to Auckland, where he began lecturing after the company folded. Southwell ridiculed missionary attempts to protect the lands and rights of Aboriginal peoples, whom he dismissed as racially inferior barbarians. In 1856 he started a weekly newspaper, the *Auckland Examiner*, which ran for four years before closing through financial difficulties. Once again penniless, Southwell died of consumption on 7 August 1860 at Wynyardton Villa, Symonds Street, Auckland, leaving a widow, and was buried in the Symonds Street cemetery in Auckland. J. A. SECORD

Sources C. Southwell, *The confessions of a free-thinker* [n.d., 1850?] • E. Royle, 'Southwell, Charles', *BDMBR*, vol. 2 • H. H. Pearce, 'Charles Southwell in Australia and New Zealand', *New Zealand Rationalist*, 18–19 (1957–8) • T. Paterson, *Letters to infidels* (1846) • E. M. Good, *Giraffes, black dragons, and other pianos* (1982) • A. Desmond, 'Artisan resistance and evolution in Britain, 1819–1848', *Osiris*, 2nd ser., 3 (1987), 77–110 • *The Reasoner* (2 Dec 1860), 385–6

Archives Bishopsgate Institute, London, Holyoake MSS • Co-operative Union, Holyoake House, Manchester, letters to G. J. Holyoake

Wealth at death see *The Reasoner*

Southwell, Edward (1671–1730), politician and government official, was born on 4 September 1671, the only surviving son of Sir Robert *Southwell (1635–1702), diplomat and government official, of King's Weston, in Gloucestershire, and of Kinsale, co. Cork, and his wife, Elizabeth (1649–1682), daughter of Sir Edward *Dering of Surrenden Dering in Kent. His father was a career bureaucrat, resident in Westminster, and Edward was sent to schools in Kensington and Bloomsbury before going up to Merton College, Oxford, in 1687. In the previous year he had been admitted to Lincoln's Inn, his father's inn of court, but did not pursue a legal education. Nor did he stay long at Oxford, his father ordering him home in 1688 in alarm at

King James's interventions in the government of the university. In any case Sir Robert envisaged a public rather than an academic career for his clever son. At his prompting Edward attended the prince of Orange during the revolution of 1688, observed the military campaign in Ireland in 1690, and accompanied his maternal cousin Lord Nottingham in 1691 to the allied conference at The Hague. Southwell's intellectual precocity received recognition in his election to the Royal Society in 1692. In that same year he took his first step into public service when he was made joint prothonotary of common pleas in Ireland and was elected to the Irish parliament. Then in 1693 he followed in his father's footsteps as a clerk of the privy council. There followed a succession of other posts, but it was in the council offices that Southwell made his mark, as a diligent and skilful administrator.

His father's death in 1702 seems to have coincided with a sudden flowering of Southwell's career. First he succeeded to the prestigious but largely honorific post that Sir Robert had held, of secretary of state for Ireland. Within a year he had been elected to the Westminster parliament for the cinque port of Rye, on the Ashburnham interest; had concluded a highly advantageous marriage, on 29 October 1703, to Lady Elizabeth Cromwell (*b.* after 1672, *d.* 1709), daughter and heir of Vere Essex, fourth earl of Ardglass (1625–1687); and had been appointed chief secretary to the new lord lieutenant of Ireland, the second duke of Ormond. His Irish background and connections (the family fortune had been made in plantation in Munster) and his father's long association with the Ormond family made him a natural choice, and he served in both Ormond's viceroyalties, in 1703–7 and in 1710–13. Although a highly efficient secretary, and in that respect just the type of servant the indolent Ormond needed, he was not particularly effective in the political aspects of the chief secretary's role and tended to leave parliamentary management in Ireland to local politicians. Inevitably he was associated with the tory policies followed by Ormond, and in British politics too he seems to have been identified as a tory, although a very moderate one, and naturally inclined towards administration, so much so that he was unable to find a constituency willing to return him in the tory landslide of 1710. When he recovered his Westminster seat in the general election of 1713 he sat as a 'Hanoverian tory', and he was continued in all his offices under the incoming dynasty in 1714, though he did not sit in either parliament thereafter.

Some time after the death of 'Lady Betty' in 1709 Southwell took as his second wife, in 1716, Anne, daughter of another 'civil servant', William *Blathwayt (*bap.* 1650, *d.* 1717); she died in the following year. Cultivated and pious, Southwell was a keen supporter of the Society for the Propagation of the Gospel, and founded charity schools on his Irish estates. His later years were blighted by ill health, following injuries sustained in a road accident, and he eventually died, of a stroke, on 4 December 1730. He was buried at King's Weston. His cousin Lord Perceval, later first earl of Egmont, commented: 'No man led a more pleasant life. He was beloved by all his acquaintance for his cheering, obliging temper, and esteemed for his experience in business' (*Egmont Diary*, 1.119). His namesake, Edward, his eldest son from his first marriage, who shared various Irish patentee offices with him and eventually succeeded him as secretary of state in Ireland, sat as MP for Bristol from 1739 to 1754. D. W. HAYTON

Sources HoP, *Commons, 1690–1715* • E. Cruickshanks and B. D. Henning, 'Southwell, Sir Robert', HoP, *Commons, 1660–90* • S. R. Matthews, 'Southwell, Edward', HoP, *Commons, 1715–54* • D. W. Hayton, 'Ireland and the English ministers, 1707–16', DPhil diss., U. Oxf., 1975 • T. G. Doyle, 'The politics of protestant ascendancy: politics, religion and society in protestant Ireland, 1700–1710', PhD diss., University College Dublin, 1996 • BL, Southwell MSS • W. King, correspondence, TCD, Lyons collection • W. King, letter-books, TCD • *The manuscripts of the marquis of Ormonde, the earl of Fingall, the corporations of Waterford, Galway*, HMC, 14 (1885), viii • *CSP dom., 1703–4* • *Report on the manuscripts of the earl of Egmont*, 2 vols. in 3, HMC, 63 (1905–9) • *Manuscripts of the earl of Egmont: diary of Viscount Percival, afterwards first earl of Egmont*, 3 vols., HMC, 63 (1920–23), vol. 1 • T. C. Barnard and J. Fenlon, eds., *The dukes of Ormonde, 1610–1745* (2000) • GEC, *Peerage*

Archives BL, corresp. and papers, Add. MSS 9710–9715, 11759, 20720, 21131, 21135–21138, 21494, 21553, 22130, 34358, 34773–34778, 36771, 37673–37674, 38015, 38147–38157, 38173, 38861, Egerton MSS 1628–1629, 1631 • NA Ire., corresp., MS M3036 • NAM, naval corresp. and papers • NL Ire., corresp., MSS 698, 991–993, 2260 • TCD, corresp. and papers relating to Ireland, MSS 1179–1181 • University College, Cork • Yale U., Beinecke L., journals and papers | BL, Blathwayt MSS • BL, corresp. with M. Coghill, Add. MSS 21122–21123 • BL, corresp. with William Cole, Add. MSS 18598–18599 • BL, Egmont MSS • BL, letters to J. Ellis, Add. MSS 28880–28898 • BL, letters to Lord Halifax, c9 • BL, corresp. with Lord Nottingham, Add. MSS 28569–28595 • BL, corresp. with Sir William Petty • BL, letters to Sir Hans Sloane • Blackburn Central Library, corresp. with R. Southwell • NL Ire., corresp. with duke of Ormond • TCD, Lyons collection, corresp. with William King

Likenesses J. Smith, mezzotint (after G. Kneller, 1708), NG Ire., NPG

Wealth at death £35,000 in property from first marriage; plus estates in Gloucestershire, co. Cork, and co. Down: HoP, *Commons, 1690–1715*

Southwell, Nathanael. *See* Bacon, Nathaniel (1598–1676).

Southwell, Sir (Charles Archibald) Philip (1894–1981), petroleum geologist and industrialist, was born at Oak Royce, Calverley Lane, Rodley, Calverley, Yorkshire, on 6 June 1894, the only son of Charles Edward Southwell, medical practitioner, and his wife, Clare, *née* Beaumont. Educated at Newcastle under Lyme high school between 1904 and 1912, his academic achievements were overshadowed by his prowess at cricket, rugby, and hockey. Encouraged by his father's friend, the geologist Dr Wheelton Hind (1859–1920), he enrolled at Birmingham University as one of the first students on the new petroleum technology course set up there by John Cadman (1877–1941). His training was interrupted by the First World War, throughout which he served mostly in the Royal Artillery; he was awarded the MC in 1918. He then returned to Birmingham and graduated in 1920.

Southwell's long and fruitful career in the oil industry, often in Cadman's footsteps, began when he joined S. Pearson & Son, engineering contractors. Between 1922 and 1929 he worked for the Trinidad government petroleum office. He returned briefly to marry on 17 August 1926 Mary Burnett (*d.* 1981), daughter of Thomas Scarratt of Belmont Hall, Ipstones, Staffordshire. In 1930 he accepted Cadman's offer of the post of local manager of oil fields and geology with the Anglo-Persian Oil Company (later British Petroleum). His subsequent experience in the Persian Gulf led Southwell to predict the existence of the great oil reserves of Kuwait. Few other geologists were optimistic, and in only one well had oil been discovered in Kuwait prior to the Second World War. Southwell was then recalled and put in charge of exploring for oil reserves in England, using imported American technologies and organizing British experiments on horizontal drilling.

In 1946 Southwell became managing director of the new Kuwait Oil Company, jointly owned by BP and the American company Gulf Oil. His task was to open up Kuwaiti fields with American partners who had no previous experience of conditions in the Middle East. He built up the company workforce to 15,000 men, who initially lived under canvas, and he went on to develop the oilfields with great success, in line with his earlier forecasts. Kuwaiti oil replaced much of that lost to Western nations when the Iranian government nationalized its oilfields in 1951. Southwell was an early advocate of the need for local control of production from Middle East fields, and he anticipated the eventual formation of the Organization of Petroleum Exporting Countries (OPEC). He deplored the invasion of Suez in 1956 and campaigned behind the scenes for its early end.

Southwell was president of the Institute of Petroleum from 1950 to 1952, and an honorary fellow from 1959. As one of Cadman's first students, the award of the institute's Cadman memorial medal in 1954 gave him particular pleasure. He was awarded the Royal Society of Arts silver medal in 1953 for his paper on Kuwait, and he sat on the RSA council from 1958, in which year he was also knighted. He was a liveryman in the Shipwrights' Company. Southwell left BP and Kuwait Oil in 1959 having reached the age of sixty-five. Retirement was, however, far from his mind and he threw himself energetically into developing the oilfields newly discovered under the North Sea, where conditions were very different and vastly more difficult than those of the Middle East. In 1960 he became chairman of Brown and Root (UK) which laid the first pipeline from BP's West Sole field in 1966. Southwell played a pioneering role in constructing North Sea oil and gas platforms, as first chairman of Brown and Root's joint venture with George Wimpey Ltd—Highland Fabricators from 1973, based at Nigg Bay—and as director of the Halliburton Company in Dallas from 1973. He became president of Brown and Root (UK) in 1978 and only relinquished this and the post with Highland Fabricators on 1 January 1981.

Southwell attributed his good health, energy, and longevity to his early passion for water polo, another sport at which he excelled. He was active in work for charities in Britain and in the Middle East, where the Southwell Hospital at Ahmadi in Kuwait was opened in 1960. He was director-general of the St John Ambulance Brigade from 1960 to 1968, a commander of the order of the Cedar of Lebanon and bailiff grand cross of the order of St John of Jerusalem, for whose eye hospital he also raised funds. Mary Southwell, who had shared enthusiastically in his interests, died in September 1981; Southwell died at the Queen Elizabeth Military Hospital, Woolwich, London, after a minor operation on 30 November 1981 and was buried at Tendring parish church in Essex on 4 December. Two sons survived him. H. S. TORRENS

Sources [D. C. Payne], *Petroleum Review* (Jan 1982), 44–5 · Autobiography covering 1894–1938, *c.*1980 [owned by his son] · G. H. Woodward and G. S. Woodward, *The secret of Sherwood Forest* (1973) · *WW* (1982) · *The Times* (21 Aug 1926) · *The Times* (10 Dec 1981), 14 · *Brown and Root News (Europe/Africa)*, 3/1 (March–April 1981), 1, 6 · *Brown and Root News (Europe/Africa)* (Jan–Feb 1982), 6 · *Journal of the Royal Society of Arts*, 130 (1981–2), 102–3 · N. L. Falcon, *List of fellows of the Geological Society of London* (1983), 260 · *Register of Newcastle under Lyme high school, 1910–1932*, Register of Newcastle under Lyme High School, 2 (1933) · b. cert. · d. cert. · *Financial Times, who's who in world oil and gas, 1981–1982*, ed. J. Comber (1981), 488 · *Staffordshire Advertiser* (21 Aug 1926) · *East Essex Gazette* (4 Dec 1981) · *Essex County Standard* (4 Dec 1981)
Archives priv. coll.

Southwell, Sir Richard (1502/3–1564), administrator, came of a family which originated in Suffolk and had recently prospered in government service. He was the eldest son of Francis Southwell (*d.* 1512), an auditor of the exchequer, and his wife, Dorothy, daughter of William Tendring of Little Birch, Essex. The lawyer Sir Robert *Southwell was one of his younger brothers. Richard became heir not only to his father, but also to his uncle Sir Robert Southwell, chief butler to Henry VII, who died in 1514 leaving an estate based on the manor of Woodrising, Norfolk. In 1515 Richard became the ward of Sir Robert's widow and William Wootton. Four years later the wardship was acquired by Sir Thomas Wyndham, who married Richard to his stepdaughter Thomasin, the sister of Sir Thomas Darcy.

The Southwells and the Wyndhams were both clients of the Howards, in whose household Richard may have been brought up, perhaps latterly alongside Henry Howard, from 1524 styled earl of Surrey. There is no record that Southwell attended university, but in 1526 he entered Lincoln's Inn, and he must have been well educated since he became tutor to Thomas Cromwell's son Gregory, who for a time lived with him in Norfolk. Southwell is said to have instructed him in pronunciation and etymology. In 1525, presumably now of age, he had livery of his lands. In 1531 he became a JP for Norfolk and Suffolk, a position he retained until 1554.

On 20 April 1532, with accomplices who included his brothers Robert and Anthony, Richard killed Sir William Pennington in sanctuary at Westminster. Pennington had married a cousin of Charles Brandon, duke of Suffolk, and was the latter's tenant of the manor of Costessey, and the crime may have arisen from a competition for pre-eminence in East Anglia between Brandon and the Howards. The Howards and Cromwell were able to obtain

Sir Richard Southwell (1502/3–1564), by Hans Holbein the younger, 1537

a pardon for Southwell and his followers on 15 June 1532, though his crime cost Richard a fine of £1000, subsequently confirmed by act of parliament. Instead of money he gave the king his Essex manors of Coggeshall and Filolls Hall. The affair did not prevent Southwell from being made sheriff of Norfolk and Suffolk in 1534, while in 1536, thanks to Cromwell's patronage, he and his brother Robert were named receivers in the court of augmentations. In this office Southwell dealt with the lands of dissolved monasteries in East Anglia. He himself obtained lands formerly held by several religious houses in Norfolk, but nevertheless displayed his conservative religious sympathies by writing an appeal on behalf of Pentney Priory. He also acquired lands which had belonged to the priory of St John of Jerusalem. During the Pilgrimage of Grace he assisted the duke of Norfolk in raising forces from that county. Knighted in 1540, from 1542 until the death of Henry VIII he was one of the three general surveyors of the king's lands.

Southwell's parliamentary career may have begun in 1536: the returns for this election are lost, but it is possible that he succeeded Sir James Boleyn as one of the knights of the shire for Norfolk following Anne Boleyn's fall. He was certainly elected in 1539, but only after a fracas with Sir Edmund Knyvet, who also coveted the seat and chose to disregard the king's nomination of Southwell and Edmund Wyndham. He probably sat again in 1542.

Southwell played a part in the fall of both Sir Thomas More and Thomas Cromwell. Roper's life of More records that Southwell was sent to More's room in the Tower to take away his books. While there he heard the famous exchange between More and Sir Richard Rich in which the former chancellor denied that parliament could make the king head of the church. When asked to give evidence against More, however, he said that he was appointed only to deal with the books and 'gave no ear' to the conversation (Roper, 244–8). In March 1540 Southwell (who was presumably still loyal to Cromwell) was one of six men who took a deposition from one Thomas Molton, who was charged with having said that the world would never be quiet so long as one so base in birth as Cromwell served on the king's council.

Southwell was several times sent on administrative and diplomatic missions. In 1542 Henry VIII dispatched him, together with Lord Lisle, the deputy of Calais, to view the fortifications at Berwick; they reported that the new works did not conform to the designs approved by the king although 20,000 marks had been spent and much more would be required to complete the project. In January 1543 he was again involved in Scottish affairs, being sent with Bothwell to Darlington, for discussions with Scottish nobles who had recently pledged loyalty to Henry VIII. In the king's war with France he was treasurer of the 'battle' ward and in 1544 received more than £65,000 for wages and other expenses. Shortly before Henry VIII's death Southwell was granted an annuity of £100, and the king's will included a bequest of £200 in token of his 'special love and favour' (*LP Henry VIII*, vol. 20, pt 2, no. 634).

Named one of the assistant executors of Henry's will, Southwell was probably hoping to ingratiate himself with the Seymours when he helped bring about the fall of the earl of Surrey, notwithstanding his own previously close relationship with the Howards. It was Southwell who on 2 December 1546 notified the privy council 'that he knew certain things of the Earl that touched his fidelity to the King' (Starkey, 157), leading to Surrey's arrest for treason, and he later gave evidence against the earl. But perhaps because of his religious conservatism he was not made a member of the privy council (as has been claimed) following the king's death, being only one of 'certen of the counsell at large' (Hoak, 49). In October 1549 he was among the conservatives who supported John Dudley, earl of Warwick, and his allies against the protector, and he now briefly became a privy councillor, but once Warwick had gained firm control of government Southwell lost his place on the council and in January 1550 he was sent to the Tower, charged with writing seditious bills. Bishop John Ponet claimed that Southwell had done enough to be hanged for, a charge possibly arising from allegations that in the previous summer he had given royal money to the Norfolk rebels, but he was soon released. He did not, however, sit in either of Edward VI's parliaments.

In 1553 Southwell at first accepted Lady Jane Grey as Edward VI's heir, but he soon resolved to stand by Princess Mary, and by 12 July brought her 'reinforcements of men, a store of provisions and moreover money … not to mention his own skill in counsel and long experience'; in acting thus he claimed to be mindful of 'the many favours heaped on him by Henry VIII' (MacCulloch, 254). For his services he was rewarded on 4 December with an annuity of £100. He remained loyal to Mary at the time of Wyatt's rising early in 1554, guarding the rear of Whitehall with 500 men. The new queen restored him to the privy council and made him master of the ordnance. Within her administration Southwell served on a number of commissions. A follower of the chancellor, Bishop Stephen Gardiner, he supported the latter in favouring her marriage to Edward Courtenay rather than to Philip of Spain. But though returned to parliament as a knight of the shire for Norfolk in the first three parliaments of Mary's reign (he is said to have announced the queen's supposed pregnancy to the Lords in 1554), he became less active in public affairs after Gardiner's death at the end of 1555. His religious position remained staunchly conservative: according to John Foxe he exclaimed against protestants 'to the rack with them, one of these knaves is able to undo a whole city' (Loach, 177).

Southwell was not reappointed to the privy council following Elizabeth's accession and in 1559 surrendered his offices in exchange for an annuity of £165. He was too weak to sign his long will, dated 24 July 1561 (PRO, PROB 11/47, fols. 144*r*–152*r*), but did not die until 11 January 1564, probably at Woodrising. His landholdings were substantial and included more than thirty manors in Norfolk alone, together with over 10,000 sheep. Succession to his estates was complicated by the fact that his two sons were illegitimate. He and his first wife, Thomasin Darcy of Danbury, Essex, had a daughter, Elizabeth, who married George Heneage. His second wife was Mary, the daughter of Thomas Darcy of Danbury and a relative of Thomasin. They had two sons, Richard and Thomas, who were born of their adulterous relationship while Mary was still married to the Norwich alderman Robert Leeche, and a daughter, Katherine, born following her marriage to Southwell. Sir Richard had settled land on his elder son (who was the father of Robert Southwell the Jesuit) before his death, and in his will he made no distinction between his legitimate and illegitimate offspring. Should Elizabeth attempt to break the will she was to be disinherited. Southwell left his personal armour to his cousin and friend Sir Henry Bedingfield and other armour to the young fourth duke of Norfolk, whom he named as an executor, together with Sir Thomas Cornwallis and Francis Gawdy. The will records a well-furnished household, containing such items as 'hangings of imagry worke' bought for Woodrising, where they were 'accustomed to hange my hawle at highe and solempe feastes', and 'a tester of cloth of silver tynsell and crimsen vellet enbrodered wheruppon myne armes ar sett'. Sir Richard also disposed of large quantities of plate, including 'one rounde balle wherwith to warme colde handes'. A lengthy codicil provided for payments to a number of servants and friends. Southwell asked to be buried in the chancel of Woodrising church, where the Easter sepulchre once stood, but that was the limit of his religious traditionalism. Though he left £100 to be distributed to the poor and indigent of the village and of 10 miles around, he did not request the beneficiaries of this gift to pray for his soul, and in the preamble to his will he referred to Queen Elizabeth as defender of the faith and entrusted his soul to the Trinity alone.

A loyal councillor and efficient administrator under Henry VIII, Southwell was never in the top echelon of advisers who made or directed policy. The reasons for his failure to achieve true eminence may be implicit in his portrait by Holbein, which suggests a man both haughty and indecisive. Painted in 1536 when Southwell was thirty-three, the picture formerly belonged to the fourteenth earl of Arundel, who gave it to Cosimo (II) de' Medici, grand duke of Tuscany. It is now in the Uffizi Gallery, Florence. Holbein's drawing of Southwell remains in the Royal Collection at Windsor. STANFORD LEHMBERG

Sources *LP Henry VIII*, vols. 1–21 · HoP, *Commons, 1509–58*, 3.352–4 · W. Roper, 'The life of Sir Thomas More', *Two early Tudor lives*, ed. R. S. Sylvester and D. P. Harding (1962) · PRO, PROB 11/47, fols. 144*r*–152*r* · P. Ganz, ed., *Holbein: the paintings* (1956) · W. C. Richardson, *Tudor chamber administration* (1952) · W. C. Richardson, *History of the court of augmentations* (1961) · W. K. Jordan, *Edward VI*, 1: *The young king* (1968) · W. K. Jordan, *Edward VI*, 2: *The threshold of power* (1970) · D. E. Hoak, *The king's council in the reign of Edward VI* (1976) · *DNB* · S. J. Gunn, *Charles Brandon, duke of Suffolk, c.1484–1545* (1988) · D. Starkey, *The reign of Henry VIII: personalities and politics* (1991) · J. Loach, *Edward VI* (1999) · D. MacCulloch, 'The *Vita Mariae Angliae Reginae* of Robert Wingfield of Brantham', *Camden miscellany, XXVIII*, CS, 4th ser., 29 (1984), 181–301 · D. Loades, *The reign of Mary Tudor: politics, government and religion in England, 1553–58*, 2nd edn (1991) · D. MacCulloch, *Thomas Cranmer: a life* (1996)

Archives Holkham Hall, Norfolk, surveys of his estates

Likenesses H. Holbein the younger, chalk drawing, 1536, Royal Collection; copy, Louvre, Paris · H. Holbein the younger, oils, 1536, Uffizi, Florence; copy, Louvre, Paris · H. Holbein the younger, portrait, 1537, Galleria degli Uffizi, Florence [*see illus.*]

Wealth at death very rich; thirty manors in Norfolk alone; also 10,000 sheep: will, PRO, PROB 11/47, fols. 144*r*–152*r*; *CIPM, Elizabeth*, 6, no. 142, cited *DNB*

Southwell, Sir Richard Vynne (1888–1970), mechanical and aeronautical engineer, was born on 2 July 1888 at Norwich, the only son and the second of the three children of Edwin Batterbee Southwell, a director of J. and J. Colman Ltd, Norwich, and his wife, Annie, daughter of Richard Vynne, a farmer and corn merchant of Swaffham. His family was in Norfolk even in Tudor times, when Sir Richard *Southwell, an ancestor, was a court official and Robert *Southwell, a Jesuit poet, was executed in 1595 (he was beatified in 1929 and canonized in 1970). Southwell was educated at King Edward VI School, Norwich, where he received an excellent classical grounding, but turned to mathematics in the last two years. He won an exhibition to Trinity Hall, Cambridge, but instead entered Trinity College as a commoner in 1907. After winning scholarships and prizes there he graduated with first-class honours in both parts of the mechanical sciences tripos (1909 and 1910). He was fortunate to be coached by H. A. Webb, an excellent tutor with a lively interest in the theory of structures. It was thus natural that Southwell's first paper, published in 1912, was on the strength of struts.

Southwell left Trinity College, where he had become a fellow in 1912, in August 1914 to join the army, and was in

France by the end of the year. But in May 1915 he was withdrawn to work on the development of non-rigid airships and later moved to the Royal Aircraft Establishment at Farnborough. There, as Major Southwell, he was placed in charge of the aerodynamics and structural departments until he was demobilized in March 1919. This experience, which brought him in touch with the leading aeronautical engineers of the time, including Leonard Bairstow and A. J. S. Pippard, started his lively and enduring interest in the problems of aircraft structures.

Southwell returned to Trinity College but in 1920 became superintendent of the aeronautics department of the National Physical Laboratory, where he stayed for five years. During the war his researches had ranged over problems of dynamic and static stability, but now he began his classic work on space frames. The biplanes and rigid airships of the time had structures which were essentially intricate space frames, and for the next ten years the problems of the great spider-web-like structures of rigid airships stirred Southwell's mind. This period saw the production of six papers on stress determination in space frames, and some related ones on tension coefficients, strain energy, and St Venant's principle, for which he is particularly remembered. Under him, a department which was primarily aerodynamic produced also a whole series of papers on the critical stability of space frameworks.

When Southwell returned to Trinity College in 1925 his personal research work widened again and papers on vibration and hydrodynamic problems appeared. But from 1924, when the last British airship building programme started, until its cessation in 1931, his heart was in airship structures. He had become a friend of Colonel V. C. Richmond, the designer of the R100, and acted as his structural consultant at Cardington, Bedfordshire, while A. J. S. Pippard acted in a similar capacity to Barnes Wallis, the R101 designer. All frequently met together with Bairstow on the airship stressing panel of the Aeronautical Research Committee, where the stressing problems of airships were thoroughly discussed and appropriate airworthiness requirements developed.

In 1929 Southwell was invited to succeed C. F. Jenkin as professor of engineering science at Oxford. Engineering at Oxford was then scarcely viable and Southwell accepted only after considerable hesitation, but he soon found a way to appoint a reader, E. B. Moullin, to strengthen his small department. He showed himself an outstanding teacher with a flair for clarity and precision, and attracted junior staff of notable ability. He was rightly concerned, however, that engineering had too small an Oxford base and that staff would leave. At Brasenose College, as at Trinity, he engaged the interest of non-engineering colleagues by his lively mind and felicitous humour. He was greatly helped in this by his wife, Isabella Wilhelmina, daughter of William Warburton Wingate, a medical practitioner. They were married in Cambridge in 1918 and had four daughters.

It was at Oxford that Southwell's deep understanding and appreciation of the earlier work of Lord Rayleigh and A. E. H. Love became generally apparent. Rayleigh's Principle in applied mechanics became a feature in his teaching and he never tired of delving into Love's monumental book on elasticity. Although his first book, *Introduction to the Theory of Elasticity for Engineers and Physicists*, did not appear until 1936, he had already written a number of papers in the field.

But the major work of Southwell's Oxford period was the development of his relaxation method of analysis. It was known that the simultaneous equations of equilibrium and of compatibility of strains necessary to determine the loads in the members of a highly redundant framework were numerous and often ill-conditioned, and these characteristics became acute in the analysis of the complex space frames of airships. As a result, the solution of the simultaneous equations involved became impossible without the adoption of some simplifying physical assumptions. Mathematically this problem invited the use of iterative methods, but the process could be lengthy and the results uncertain. It was Southwell's great contribution in his relaxation method to devise a successive approximation process that at any stage could be physically understood and guided by engineering experience. He started the work in relation to frameworks, but quickly realized the general applicability of the process and, aided by a succession of able research assistants at Oxford and London, developed the method for many fields of engineering science and physics. A whole generation of engineering scientists thus benefited and became adept in using the method. It was only the coming of computers that rendered the method largely unnecessary, though still physically enlightening.

Southwell left Oxford in 1942 to become rector of Imperial College, London, in succession to Sir Henry Tizard. He still carried on the development of the relaxation process in spite of the administrative work of his office, and published his second book on the subject (his first appeared in 1940) in 1946. He retired in 1948 and returned to an earlier home at Trumpington, Cambridge. He continued to be fruitful with papers on engineering science for the next ten years. He died after a long illness in St Andrew's Hospital, Northampton, on 9 December 1970.

Southwell was honoured by many universities and learned societies. He was elected FRS in 1925 and was knighted in 1948. He was made an honorary fellow of Brasenose College, Oxford (1943), and of Imperial College, London, and Trinity College, Cambridge (both 1950). He won many awards, among them the James Alfred Ewing medal in 1946. For many years he was one of the moving spirits of the International Congress of Applied Mechanics, of which he was president in 1948–52 and treasurer in 1952–6. He was general secretary of the British Association from 1948 to 1956. Throughout his life his colleagues, in whatever capacity, found him a man of great charm and wit; as a Trinity College colleague wrote, 'no one has ever had for me so exquisite a choice of mirth-provoking phrase'.

A. G. Pugsley, *rev.* H. C. G. Matthew

Sources D. G. Christopherson, *Memoirs FRS*, 18 (1972), 549–65 · *The Times* (12 Dec 1970) · *WWW* · *Hist. U. Oxf.* 8: *20th cent.* · *CGPLA Eng. & Wales* (1971)

Likenesses W. Stoneman, photographs, 1930–53, NPG · H. Lamb, oils, 1954, ICL · R. Guthrie, drawing, 1962, Trinity Cam.

Wealth at death £12,833: probate, 3 June 1971, *CGPLA Eng. & Wales*

Southwell, Sir Robert (*c.*1506–1559), lawyer and member of parliament, was the second son of Francis Southwell (*d.* 1512) of Norfolk, and Dorothy, daughter and coheir of William Tendring of Little Birch, Essex. He was a younger brother of Sir Richard *Southwell (1502/3–1564), the privy councillor. His uncle Sir Robert Southwell (*d.* 1514), of Woodrising, Norfolk, was an auditor of the exchequer and, like Francis, a member of Lincoln's Inn. By coincidence another Robert Southwell died in 1514; he was a bencher of Gray's Inn who lived in Suffolk. Francis Southwell's son was still a boy when these namesakes died. He entered the Middle Temple in the mid-1520s, and as early as 1529, about the time of his call to the bar, he was returned to parliament for Bishop's Lynn, in Norfolk. He was to serve in parliament, representing six different constituencies, for the remainder of his life. In 1535 he became doubly established in the world, both by securing the hand of Margaret, daughter and heir apparent of Sir Thomas *Neville (*d.* 1542), bencher of Gray's Inn and privy councillor, and by obtaining an appointment as common serjeant of London. In 1536 he moved to the less lucrative but more promising position of solicitor-general to the new court of augmentations, set up to handle the revenue arising from the dissolution of the monasteries, and in 1537 he became its attorney-general.

His marriage, and the death of his father-in-law, provided Southwell with a seat at Mereworth in Kent, and he was added to the commission of the peace for that county (and for Norfolk) in 1538. His office in the augmentations enabled him to acquire numerous parcels of monastic land, much of which he sold at a profit. In 1540 he surrendered that office and was sworn of the privy council, with a stipend of £100, in order to serve as a master or receiver of requests in place of Sir Nicholas Hare. In the same year he delivered the autumn reading at the Middle Temple. The height of his legal career was reached on 1 July 1541, when he was appointed master of the rolls, with a knighthood following in 1542. After sitting in chancery for ten years he resigned in December 1550, though the reason is not apparent. He does not seem to have fallen out with the Edwardian regime, since he continued to serve actively on commissions and in parliament throughout the reign, and indeed through Mary's, proving his religious flexibility by managing to participate in heresy investigations under both monarchs. He died on 26 October 1559 and was buried on 8 November in Kent, presumably at Mereworth. Among other provisions in his will he left to his eldest son, Thomas, the manors of Chickering and Hoxne, in Suffolk, which he had purchased in the 1540s from his profits on land sales, a capital messuage in Bermondsey, Surrey, pieces of plate including 'a greate pott all gilt which Kinge Henrye the eight myne olde master gave me for my last new yeres gift', and hangings embroidered with the family arms and badges. His 'olde frende' Sir Nicholas Bacon was made supervisor of the will jointly with Dame Margaret. J. H. Baker

Sources HoP, *Commons, 1509–58*, 3.354–6 · will, PRO, PROB 11/43, sig. 53 · Sainty, *Judges*, 149 · *The diary of Henry Machyn, citizen and merchant-taylor of London, from AD 1550 to AD 1563*, ed. J. G. Nichols, CS, 42 (1848), 217 · inquisition post mortem, PRO, C142/128/55

Southwell, Robert [St Robert Southwell] (**1561–1595**), writer, Jesuit, and martyr, was born towards the end of 1561, the third son of Richard Southwell (*d.* 1600), gentleman and courtier, of Horsham St Faith, Norfolk, and Bridget (*d.* 1583x7), daughter of Sir Roger Copley of Roughway, Sussex, and his second wife, Elizabeth, daughter of Sir William Shelley, judge of the common pleas. Richard Southwell was the illegitimate elder son of Sir Richard *Southwell (1502/3–1564) of Woodrising, Norfolk. Sir Richard was married to Thomasine, daughter of Sir Robert Darcy of Danbury, Essex, but his two sons and three of his daughters were born as a result of his liaison with Mary Darcy, Thomasine's cousin, daughter of Thomas Darcy of Danbury.

As one of the visitors for the suppression of the monasteries in Norfolk, Sir Richard obtained some monastic properties for himself, among them the priory of St Faith, with its surrounding farms, assigned to him outright in 1545. The conveyance bears the note 'To remayne with mistres Leche', a gift to Mary Darcy, who had been married off to a man called Leech from Norwich. From his immense wealth Sir Richard provided for all his children, his one legitimate daughter, Elizabeth, married to Sir George Heneage, and his children with Mary Darcy, whom he may have married before the birth of her third daughter, Katherine. In his will, dated 24 July 1561, she is described as 'Dame Marye Southwell my late wief', and his sons Richard—'late of Lincolnes Inne'—and Thomas are identified as 'Darcy alias Southwell'.

Childhood and education Richard Southwell inherited the property at Horsham and for the rest of his life was identified with it. Robert probably spent his childhood mainly in the house created from the refectory of the priory. When he returned to England as a mission priest, he spoke of his regret at being unable to visit his father, so that 'banishing myself from the sent of my cradle, in myne owne country, I have lived like a foreyner, findinge emong straungers that which in my neerest bloude I presumed not to seeke' (Stonyhurst College, MS A. v. 27, fol. 4). He also reminded his father that 'even from my infancy yowe were wonte in merimente to call me father R. which is the customary stile nowe allotted to my present estate' (ibid., fol. 7). Robert may also have stayed with his parents at the Copley house at Gatton, Surrey, while Sir Thomas *Copley, Bridget's eldest brother, was in exile. In a letter to Burghley in 1583 begging that Bridget Southwell might be allowed to return to the house, Sir Thomas described her as 'her Majestie's ould servant of neer fortie yeeres continuance'.

In 1576 Robert Southwell set out on the long journey that was to fulfil his father's teasing title for him. On 10

June he arrived at the English College, Douai, accompanied by John Cotton, one of his mother's Catholic cousins. He was admitted to Anchin College, the Jesuit school in the town, while continuing to board at the English College. In a later letter Southwell gives an account of the beginning of his friendship with John Deckers, a Flemish student at the school, whom he saw walking with Leonard Lessius, then on the staff, and later a theologian at the Jesuit college in Rome. The boys' education was interrupted after the summer months by the movement of French and Spanish forces, and Southwell was sent to Paris for greater safety, probably as a student at the Collège de Clermont under the tutelage of the Jesuit Thomas Darbyshire. He returned to Douai on 15 June 1577, but left again with Deckers early in 1578, travelling to Rome with the intention of joining the Society of Jesus.

Deckers was sent on to Naples for training in the noviciate, but to Southwell's bitter disappointment he was at first refused entry. His reaction was to write an emotional appeal that his case might be heard again. He wrote in English, but the text survived only in a Latin redaction by Henry More, entitled 'Querimonia', until a section of the original was discovered in a catalogue of the early Jesuits compiled in 1640. In his hurt Southwell pours out his distress: 'How can I but wast in anguish and agony that find myself disjoyned from that company severed from that Society, disunited from that body wherein lyeth all my life my love my whole hart and affection' (Archivum Romanum Societatis Iesu, Anglia 14, fol. 80, under date 1578). His plea was heard, and he was admitted to the probation house of Sant' Andrea on 17 October 1578, when he was almost seventeen.

Rome, 1578–1586 During the two years of his noviciate Southwell wrote a series of personal meditations, 'Exercitia et devotiones', which has survived in three early manuscript copies. The brief passages are not collected in their original order. The only dated section, written after he had taken his vows on 18 October 1580, is numbered 21, out of more than 70 passages relating to the course of training: to times of sickness, to self-accusation and doubt, to the reaffirmation of Jesuit teaching regarding obedience, to resolutions taken in the last week of the Ignatian *Spiritual Exercises*.

On the completion of the noviciate Southwell started courses in philosophy and theology at the Jesuit college in Rome. He lived at the English College, where he appears to have acted as secretary to the rector, Alphonsus Agazzari. His handwriting is to be found from 1580 in both parts of the *Liber ruber*, the college history. In the first part, he copied the entries of the arrival of students. In the second part, the annual letters are mainly in his hand and perhaps compiled by him until 1585. It is likely also that on behalf of Agazzari he wrote the life of Edward Throckmorton, a childhood friend in England who died at the college on 18 November 1582 and who was received into the society on his deathbed. The account contains details unlikely to have been known to the rector, to whom the work is sometimes ascribed, particularly details concerned with boyhood incidents and later events as a member of the sodality of the Blessed Virgin of which Southwell was prefect. Other letters from this period include a draft of a long narrative written to Deckers in 1580, and a letter to Robert Persons, written in Italian as if to a merchant. A newsletter in Italian dated 3 February 1584, recounting sufferings of priests and lay Catholics in England, addressed to the provincial of Naples, also survives, an early example of the regular reports Southwell later sent from England.

Southwell completed his course in philosophy, was admitted BA in 1584, appointed 'repetitor' or tutor at the English College for two years, and finally made prefect of studies. His ordination took place in spring 1584, when his title changed from Frater to Pater. Throughout these years in Rome he maintained his habit of keeping small notebooks, some containing student notes, others used for drafts of poems and translations. Some of these are now preserved, bound in a single volume, at Stonyhurst College (MS A. v. 4). The collection, comprising 64 leaves, is all that has survived from a longer sequence, indicated by Southwell's numbering of pages to 256. Included in the group of theological notes and Latin poems and prayers is the beginning of a translation into English of Luigi Tansillo's *Le lagrime di San Pietro*, entitled 'Peeter Playnt'. It is the earliest version of a subject to which he would return at least twice during his work in England, and which would be developed as his longest poem, 'Saint Peters Complaint'.

The last section of the compilation consists of two attempts to translate into English the medieval homily, then attributed to Origen, known as 'Audivimus Mariam' from its first words. Southwell translated about two-thirds of the sermon, using it as an exercise to regain fluency in English. After this effort he abandoned the translation and started again, this time completing only a few lines. When he was in England he secured another copy of the sermon and incorporated the whole of it into his prose study *Marie Magdalens Funeral Teares*.

The holograph manuscript also contains a single page of English prose, beginning 'Alas, why doe I lament his losse that must needes be lost?' Like the 'Querimonia' it is an extremely personal outpouring of emotion. It records the sense of failure that overwhelmed him after a young man rejected his attempts to lead him into greater spiritual awareness, and at the same time Southwell asked himself whether his disappointment was based on the loss of a soul or a 'sensuall lykynge'. The young man who so disturbed him may have been William Cecil, son of Sir Thomas Cecil and grandson of Lord Burghley, who visited Rome without family permission in 1585. Inevitably rumour circulated that he had become a Catholic, but there is no evidence that he had, and Southwell felt it helpful to draw upon their friendly relationship and their shared adventure with a runaway carriage when he wrote to Sir Robert Cecil from the Tower in 1593. It would certainly not have been tactful to have reminded Cecil of this occasion if William Cecil had indeed embraced Catholicism while he was in Rome.

Another group of small notebooks kept by Southwell during his studies as a scholastic has recently come to light (Bodl. Oxf., MS Arch. F. g. 4). Three are bound together, and one remains unbound, with two leaves uncut. The three bound notebooks are all concerned with his theological training; the unbound notebook, of sixteen leaves, outlines the daily life of a scholastic in Rome. A note, written upside down, is particularly revealing for the way it suggests the strain of the regime. Under the title 'Assequi' he wrote: 'hoc assequi posse diffido hoc efficere non possum eo progredi nequeo' ('here I find it difficult to make progress; I am not able to carry this out; in that I do not know how to go on'). But Southwell, though greatly tested, did not break.

Southwell's last year in Rome was accompanied by difficulties at the English College. As prefect of studies he wrote to Claudio Acquaviva, general of the society, about the situation, ending the letter with a request that he should be allowed to serve on the English mission: 'in the same way as Your Paternity approves of my present work among the English, so by the inspiration of God may you also approve of my service in England itself, with the highest hope of martyrdom' (Archivum Romanum Societatis Iesu, Fondo Gesuitico 651/648).

Return to England, 1586 On 8 May 1586 the two Jesuit priests Henry Garnet and Robert Southwell rode out of Rome. Their journey was not without travellers' difficulties, as Southwell recorded in letters to Agazzari and to Acquaviva, but they reached Douai safely and passed on to St Omer. Their route may have taken them through Switzerland, the way Edmund Campion and Persons had travelled, and the way John Gerard and Edmund Oldcorne followed in 1588. One of Southwell's most poignant poems, 'A Vale of Teares', may recall its wild and forbidding landscape, suitable for the torments of a soul conscious of sin and longing for the way of penitence:

A vale there is enwrapt with dreadfull shades,
Which thicke of mourning pines shrouds from the sunne,
Where hanging clifts yeld short and dumpish glades,
And snowie floud with broken streams doth runne.
(*Poems*, 41)

One of Southwell's last letters from the continent was to Deckers. He wrote 'e portu', from Calais or Boulogne, on 15 July, just before the crossing to England. It is a letter full of apprehension, ending once more with the hope of martyrdom.

The two priests landed on the south coast near Folkestone, and made their way separately to London. Both wrote accounts of their first adventures. Southwell's letters of 25 July to Acquaviva and to Agazzari were intercepted. The letter to Acquaviva gives news of his arrival in London, where he met his first Catholics 'inter gladios'—under armed guard—and in prison. He reports their meeting with William Weston, the only Jesuit priest active in England, and their journey with him into the country. The letter is the first of Southwell's reports, written out in his neat Italian hand. Of those that reached Rome four were sent in 1587, seven in 1588, and one in January 1590. A few other letters are preserved in transcripts. Henry More, gathering materials for his *Historia provinciae Anglicanae Societatis Jesu* (1660), spoke of a collection of 150 letters, but no similar treasure remains. No letters survive after 1590.

In the aftermath of the Babington plot that burst upon the government a few weeks after Southwell's arrival, Weston was arrested, and Garnet succeeded him as superior. In his organization of the mission Southwell was assigned to the London area, and as he became established there priests arriving from the continent came to him before departing to their posts in various parts of England. In December 1586 he reported that he had made some journeys into the country, and spoke of being in grave danger twice. On one occasion he escaped a search while he was behind panelling for four hours, possibly in the town house of Lord Vaux in Hackney. The house was raided on 5 November 1586, on information given by the spy Anthony Tyrrell, who reported to Justice Young, the Middlesex priest-hunter, that a priest called Sale (possibly a mishearing of the elided form of Southwell) was sheltered there. Two letters signed 'Robertus' were found in the possession of Henry Vaux, starting a rumour that Persons had returned to England, but Tyrrell identified them as Southwell's. A connection with the Vaux family may account for the coincidence that poems of Henry Vaux are bound in with a volume of the first edition of Southwell's poems (Washington, DC, Folger Shakespeare Library, Harmsworth MS).

The prose works During these first months in England it is likely that Southwell wrote the *Epistle to his Father*, pleading with him to return to the Catholic faith. The forceful arguments expressed in the letter made it a most suitable tool to supplement the work of the priests, and it became one of the most widely disseminated of Southwell's writings. It has survived in eight manuscripts and in several others in part; other early copies were made from the printed edition, issued from Garnet's second press. Some copies are dated 22 October 1589, almost certainly an early scribal error for 1586. The central section was printed by Benjamin Fisher as *The Dutiful Advice of a Loving Sonne to his Aged Father*, the second part of *Sir Walter Raleighs Instructions to his Sonne* (1632). It later appeared in Raleigh's *Remains* (1657).

When Robert Southwell approached his father, this man of property had made his peace with the Church of England. The letter has a formality indicating the distance now dividing father and son, separated for ten years, and cut off still further by the danger to which Robert would be exposed if he visited Horsham. His language is more Latinate than in any other prose writing, the phrases more classically turned. Southwell mentions the support he has from his brothers, but there is no mention of his mother, and her death at some time after 1583 is confirmed by the second marriage of his father in 1587, to Margaret, the young daughter of John Style, a well-to-do farmer from Ellingham, Norfolk. If Richard Southwell was moved by his son's persuasiveness he apparently delayed committing himself. Two manuscripts of the *Epistle* include a short letter making the same passionate plea. In March 1588, however, Richard Southwell, with his son Richard, is listed among recusants in Norfolk. In 1600 Garnet reported to Acquaviva that Richard Southwell had died a Catholic.

After his narrow escapes Southwell's position in London stabilized. He had been fortunate in obtaining the protection of Anne Howard, countess of Arundel and Surrey. She permitted him the use of a house, probably the house she owned in the enclave of Spitalfields, and there he set up a printing press. He was able to keep up a correspondence with her husband, Philip Howard, who was imprisoned in the Tower, and according to the preface these letters formed the basis of his longest prose work, *An epistle of comfort, to the reverend priestes, and to the honorable, worshipful, and other of the laye sort, restrayned in durance for the Catholicke fayth*. Although the first edition (1587–8) announces that it was 'Imprinted at Paris', it was printed from the secret press. Its structure of letters is obscured in the final text, which comprises a series of nine 'Comfortes in tribulation', followed by chapters which attempt to strengthen the courage of prisoners facing martyrdom. It is lengthily illustrated with excerpts from the Bible and from the fathers of the church, and enlivened with images from the natural world, sometimes in its most extraordinary manifestations. In the last pages Southwell turns again to the glories obtained through martyrdom:

> And we have God be thanked such martyrquellers now in authoritye, as meane if they may have theyre will, to make Saynctes enough to furnishe all our Churches with treasure when it shall please God to restore them to theyre true honoures. (Southwell, *Epistle of Comfort*, sig. Cc5v)

It was to the earl of Arundel also that Southwell addressed his letter of consolation on the death of the earl's half-sister, Lady Margaret Sackville, in August 1591. He advises against unrestrained grieving, seeing it as the indulgence of 'the seliest women … who make it their happiness to seeme most unhappie, as though they had onely bene left alive, to be perpetuall mapps of dead folkes misfortunes' (Stonyhurst College, MS A. v. 27, fol. 21*v*). He soon turns, however, to a consideration of the fine traits that he acknowledges in the Lady Margaret: 'She was by birth second to none, but to the first in the realme, yet she measured onely greatnes by goodnes, making nobilitye but the mirrhour of vertue' (ibid., fol. 22). It is difficult to determine whether Southwell had known her personally. The splendid qualities he praises are those of which he may have heard from her friends and from those who cared for her. With regard to her husband, Robert Sackville, later Lord Buckhurst and earl of Dorset, he says only 'how dutifully she discharged all the behoofes of a most loving wife' (ibid., fol. 23*v*). Nothing is said of her as a mother except that she would have wished her children to live after her, although her eldest children had already died 'as pledges of her owne comming' (ibid., fol. 28*v*). Four survived her, and in the first printed edition in 1595, when it was given the title *The Triumphs over Death*, the editor, John Trussell, dedicated the work to them.

In persuading the earl to be reconciled to his sister's death, Southwell was also preparing him for his own death, for Arundel had been impeached in 1589, condemned to death, and his goods confiscated. Southwell believed that the earl was better able to bear his sister's death than she would have been able to bear his. With a delicate play upon her name he reaches his conclusion:

> The base shell of a mortall body, was an unfit roome for so pretious a margarite. And the Jeweller that came into this world to seeke good perles, and gave not onely all he had, but himself also to buy them, thought it nowe tyme to take her into his bargaine, finding her growen to a Margarites full perfection. (Stonyhurst College, MS A. v. 27, fol. 35)

Sheltered in the household of the countess of Arundel as chaplain and confessor, Southwell prepared for her *A Shorte Rule of Good Life*, an outline of conduct suitable for a pious lay woman under continual threat of persecution at the queen's whim. The countess used the work as a spiritual guide for the rest of her life, and copies were made for other aristocratic Catholic families. Of the seven manuscripts now known, some have been revised, some casually copied, and only one contains all the items in the original text. A printed version was issued by Garnet's second press about 1596–7. In the 'Preface to the reader' Garnet speaks of it as 'even amongst the last of his fruitefull labours', referring not to the original text but to a revision that Southwell was working on before his arrest. The changes in the printed version, however, are unlikely to be authoritative.

In providing the *Shorte Rule* Southwell acknowledged that the return of Catholicism to England was now a distant hope. It was a faith to be followed in secret, without the support of the traditional structure of the church. In *Marie Magdalens Funeral Teares* he led the Catholic who felt abandoned and desolate through the agony endured by Mary Magdalen in the hours following the crucifixion. Once more Southwell translated the medieval homily, and greatly expanded the incidents of St John's gospel into a meditation of penetrating exegesis. It becomes a dialogue in which Mary's grief takes her to the very edge of hysteria, and the steady voice of the observer questions and comforts her in an exposition of Christian hope.

The *Funeral Teares* was the first of Southwell's writings to be printed commercially. The work was carried out by John Wolfe for Gabriel Cawood in 1591. It is well printed, and Southwell may have read proof on it. The dedication, signed 'S. W.', was addressed to 'Mistres D. A.', who may possibly be identified with Dorothy Arundell, daughter of Sir John Arundell of Lanherne, Cornwall. She was a young woman then living in London, later becoming one of the founding members of the English Benedictine community in Brussels in 1599. The popularity of the *Funeral Teares* among both Catholics and members of the established church is shown by its reprinting six times before 1609, and by its inclusion in the 'collected' editions of Southwell's work, both Catholic (1616 and 1620) and protestant (1620, 1630, and 1636). It is the culmination of his imaginative writing, and together with 'Saint Peters Complaint' and some of the lyrics it introduced the phenomenon of the 'literature of tears' to England.

The last complete work that Southwell undertook in the course of his ministry was his only political statement. *An Humble Supplication to her Majestie* was written in response to the proclamation 'A declaration of great troubles pretended against the realme by a number of seminarie priests and Jesuists', dated 18 October 1591 and published in November. The proclamation was Burghley's work, and he prefaced the penal orders with an attack on the personal qualities of the young men who went overseas to submit themselves to training for the priesthood. The Jesuits had been expressly instructed to avoid all political action, but the abusive diatribe from 'this heavy adversary of our good names' (Inner Temple Library, Petyt MS 538.36, fol. 60) fired Southwell to make a rebuttal. Point by point he responds to the charges. He reiterates the religious nature of their purpose: 'The whole and only intent of our comming into this Realme, is noe other, but to labour for the salvation of soules, and in peaceable and quiet sort to confirme them in the auntient Catholique Faith' (ibid., fol. 61). He answers the specific issue of the Babington plot that may be brought against them, and in a long central section he sets out the details of the way in which the government manipulated the players and destroyed Mary, queen of Scots, claiming that it was 'both plotted, furthered and finished by Sir *Francis Walsingham* and his other Complices' (ibid., fol. 64).

Throughout his appeal Southwell addresses the queen with the most formal respect, acknowledging her as an anointed sovereign, and presenting his arguments as if she knew nothing of the barbarous treatment ordered by her ministers. But the plea was in vain, and there is no evidence that the queen ever read the *Supplication*. Many of the points made in the work are to be found in a report originating with Southwell and sent on by Richard Verstegan in Antwerp (Stonyhurst College, MS Anglia I, 70). 'Caput 2' is made up largely of material that was used in the *Supplication*, including a brief history of the Babington plot.

The *Supplication* was a work that was too dangerous to publish. Burghley's fury was to be expected; a year later, on 20 September 1592, he wrote to Archbishop Whitgift of the 'multitude of sclaunders dispersed in Bookes against the State and government' (LPL, Fairhurst MS 2004, fol. 45). Garnet was aware of the danger, and acknowledged in a letter to Persons on 5 May 1602, 'Fa. S. wrote a very good answer to the Proclamation but it could never be set forth' (Stonyhurst College, MS A. iv. 2). Nevertheless it circulated in manuscript, of which four substantive copies remain. Its later history is one of political exploitation. A printed edition, falsely dated 1595, was produced in 1600 by the Appellants, a group of secular priests opposed to the appointment of George Blackwell as arch-priest. Short extracts were translated into Latin and presented to Pope Clement VIII to demonstrate that the over-zealous expressions of loyalty to the queen indicated a willingness on the part of the Jesuits to collude with the government. The passages quoted, however, were ineffective in securing for the complainants the ruling they hoped for. The edition was fiercely suppressed in England, and the three distributors in London were seized and hanged.

Arrest, 1592 The publication of the proclamation increased the severity of the persecution that had been most rigorous throughout 1591. Garnet and Southwell barely escaped capture at a house in Warwickshire where the Jesuits had met to renew their vows in October. Southwell's physical appearance, with his distinctive auburn hair, was made known to the authorities through the depositions of John Cecil, alias Snowden, a priest from the seminary at Valladolid, captured shortly after his arrival. In a letter of 11 February 1592 Garnet reported that he had taken Southwell's place in London and that Southwell had been sent into the country. By the summer Garnet had returned to Warwickshire, and sent for Southwell to join him. Accompanied by Thomas Bellamy, he set out from London on 25 June 1592 to say mass and to spend the first night of the journey at the Bellamy house at Uxenden, near Harrow. That night, on information given by Anne Bellamy, Thomas's eldest sister, who had become the tool of Richard Topcliffe, the most vicious of priest-hunters, the house was raided and Southwell captured. Topcliffe used Southwell's alias, Cotton, but he knew whom he had found.

Southwell refused to give his name or to acknowledge that he was a priest, hoping to give the Bellamys time to escape. He was taken first to Topcliffe's house, where he was tortured, and on 28 June he was sent to the Gatehouse nearby. On 28 July he was committed to the Tower.

The poems After his arrest Southwell's papers were gathered together, probably by Garnet. Fifty-two lyrics were put into order, enclosing groups linked by subject or moral purpose, and prefaced by a prose dedication 'to his loving Cosen' and a verse address 'To the Reader' that had been written for a smaller collection. The same order is followed in the five manuscripts that have survived, and it underlies the printed editions. The long poem, 'Saint Peters Complaint', although still needing revision, was set at the head of the selection of poems made by the first publisher, John Wolfe, in 1595. More poems were added in his second edition, and the same group was included with others in the third edition printed by John Roberts for Gabriel Cawood. Seven further printings appeared before 1615. A second collection, entitled *Mœoniæ*, was printed by Valentine Simmes for John Busby in 1595, and twice more (all dated 1595) within five years. Busby chose to head his volume with the sequence on the Virgin and Christ that stood first in the manuscripts. All publishers avoided poems that revealed their Catholic origins.

As in his prose work, Southwell's poems are an extension of his ministry. He has an unerring sense of word-music and rhythm, and an apparent simplicity that belies the subtlety of meaning. A great deal of his imagery is based on the natural world, frequently with reference to the iconography of the Bible. This polished work is a remarkable development from the stumbling translation of the years in Rome. The versatility with which he uses a commonplace stanza form may be demonstrated in the recounting of Peter's despair after his denial of Christ:

At sorrowes door I knockt, they crav'de my name;
I aunswered one, unworthy to be knowne:
What one? say they, one worthiest of blame.
But who? a wretch, not Gods, nor yet his owne.
A man? O no, a beast? much worse, what creature?
A rocke: how cald? the rocke of scandale, Peter.
(*Poems*, 97)

The five lyrics on the nativity are those which are found most frequently in anthologies, and of these 'The Burning Babe' is by far the best known. Its succinct lines present a glowing vision of the suffering Christchild on Christmas morning when, in a series of paradoxes and allegorical figures recalling the play of Petrarchan conceits, the direct speech of the Child creates a luminescence in which the reader sees 'mens defiled soules' within a purifying furnace, looking to the salvation to be achieved at the crucifixion:

For which, as now on fire I am
To worke them to their good,
So will I melt into a bath
To wash them in my blood.
(*Poems*, 16)

Ben Jonson is said to have commented: 'That Southwell was hanged yett so he had written that piece of his the burning babe he would have been content to destroy many of his' (McDonald, 134). The setting of two of the poems in Benjamin Britten's *Ceremony of Carols* is most sensitive to the imagery of the verse, as in the marching rhythms of 'This little Babe so few dayes olde', whom Southwell represents as a military leader, the final lines echoing Jesuit spirituality, 'My soule with Christ joyne thou in fight' (*Poems*, 15).

Trial and execution Southwell's solitary confinement lasted two and a half years. After eight months in the Tower, when he reckoned that the Bellamys had had time to disappear, he asked for pen and paper to write to Sir Robert Cecil. The letter, dated 6 April 1593, provided Cecil with the necessary information to bring him to trial. He presents his case, arguing that he had returned to England in order to minister to his family:

I was the childe of a Christian woman, and not the whelpe of a tygar; I could not feare, and foresee, and not forewarne; I had not a crueller harte then a damned caytiffe, to despise their bodies and soules, by whome I received myne. But this was an inveigled zeale, a blinde, and a now abolished faithe; A zeale notwithstanding, and a faithe yt was; and god almightie is my wittnes I came with no other intention into the realme. (Washington, DC, Folger Shakespeare Library, MS V. a. 421, fol. 57*v*)

He asks not for condemnation but for leniency: 'I have heere sent you a sharpe sworde, yet, as I suppose, well sheathed' (ibid., fol. 60). The existence of the letter was known to Garnet; he sent an inaccurate report of its contents to Acquaviva in the letter of 7 March 1595. No action was taken by Cecil.

The long months of imprisonment, called by Garnet 'this blessed solitude', stretched out. In February 1595 Southwell was taken to Newgate, and on the 20th he was brought before the queen's bench for trial for treason under the act of 1585. Details of his last days are contained in the four letters sent by Garnet to Rome, and two eyewitness reports, one by Thomas Leake, a seminary priest (Stonyhurst College, MS Anglia VI, 125–8), and one entitled *A Brefe Discourse of the Condemnation and Execution of Mr. Robert Southwell* (Stonyhurst College, MS Anglia A. III, 1–11). Sir Edward Coke, attorney-general, conducted the prosecution, and much was made of the Jesuits' advocacy of equivocation. Southwell had written an explanation of this way of avoiding incrimination. It was never published and apparently never widely distributed. Garnet was unable to find a copy when he was asked to give an account of equivocation for the instruction of Catholics in 1598, and he was forced to write his own treatise.

Southwell was very weak, and he excused any memory lapses as caused by the torture he had had to endure on ten occasions. All his answers were scorned by Topcliffe, who had to be restrained several times. Anne Bellamy alone gave evidence, saying that she had been instructed not to reveal the presence of a priest in the house, an example of equivocation he roundly defended. He was found guilty, and returned to Newgate. The next day, 21 February 1595, he was taken to Tyburn to face the horror of being hanged, drawn, and quartered. All his adult life he had prepared himself for such a death, and those who wrote of his last sufferings spoke of the resignation he showed. For the last time he acknowledged that he was a priest of the Society of Jesus. He prayed for the queen, for the country, and for his soul, asking that he might find perseverance 'unto the end of this my laste conflicte' (Janelle, 89).

From the moment of his death, Robert Southwell was regarded as a martyr of the Roman Catholic church. He was remembered by his Jesuit fellow-priests with the greatest affection. John Gerard, who occasionally travelled with him, spoke of his success in saving souls: 'He was so wise and good, gentle and loveable' (Gerard, 17). Garnet's letters reveal the distress he felt at the suffering of his friend. In a letter to Rome of 16 July 1592 he spoke of his sense of being bound with him in a mystical union in which all tortures might be endured. Before Garnet's letter arrived Acquaviva wrote to express understanding of his particular sorrow, his 'loneliness and grief of mind and heart' (Caraman, 158). The loneliness never left him.

What Janelle called 'The Apostolate of Letters' continued, and its influence permeated the religious writing of the last years of the sixteenth century and the work of the metaphysical poets in the first part of the seventeenth. After 1636, however, all publication ceased with the growth of puritan distrust of Catholic and Laudian attitudes. Southwell's reputation was stifled, and with the changing fashion he became no more than a distant outrider in the procession of literary figures. In more recent years a powerfully original body of work has been reassessed with the recovery of texts, the publication of volumes of his work, and perceptive critical comment.

Robert Southwell was canonized as one of the forty English martyrs in 1970.

Although it is unlikely that a likeness was made during

Southwell's lifetime a portrait painted soon after his death was preserved at the Jesuit house in Fribourg, Switzerland. It survives in a copy, a crayon drawing by Charles Weld, now at Stonyhurst College. It was reproduced in *The Triumphs over Death*, edited by J. W. Trotman (1914), and since that time it has been generally assumed to be an authentic likeness. NANCY POLLARD BROWN

Sources Stonyhurst College, MS A. v. 4 • letters of Robert Southwell, Archivum Romanum Societatis Iesu, Fondo Gesuitico 651/648 • *Liber ruber*, English College, Rome • Bodl. Oxf., MS Arch. F. g. 4 • letters of Henry Garnet, Archivum Romanum Societatis Iesu, Fondo Gesuitico 651 • J. H. Pollen, ed., *Unpublished documents relating to the English martyrs*, 1, Catholic RS, 5 (1908), 293–337 • J. H. McDonald, *The poems and prose writings of Robert Southwell, S. J.: a bibliographical study* (1937) • P. Beal, *Index of English literary manuscripts*, ed. P. J. Croft and others, 1/2 (1980), 498–522 • A. F. Allison and D. M. Rogers, eds., *The contemporary printed literature of the English Counter-Reformation between 1558 and 1640*, 2 vols. (1989–94) • *STC, 1475–1640* • *The poems of Robert Southwell, S. J.*, ed. J. H. McDonald and N. P. Brown (1967) • *Two letters and 'Short rules of a good life'*, ed. N. P. Brown (1973) • R. Southwell, *An humble supplication to her majestie*, ed. R. C. Bald (1953) • R. Southwell, *Spiritual exercises and devotions*, ed. J.-M. de Buck, trans. P. E. Hallett (1931) • H. More, *Historia missionis Anglicanae Societatis Iesu* (St Omer, 1660), 172–201 • P. Janelle, *Robert Southwell the writer* (1935) • J. Gerard, *The autobiography of an Elizabethan*, trans. P. Caraman (1951) • P. Caraman, *Henry Garnet, 1555–1606, and the Gunpowder Plot* (1964) • C. Devlin, *The life of Robert Southwell, poet and martyr* (1956) • 28 April 1545, Norfolk RO, MS 16385 32c3 h8 • will, PRO, PROB 11/47, sig. 19 • H. Spelman, *The history and fate of sacrilege* (1698) • *Letters of Sir Thomas Copley … to Queen Elizabeth and her ministers*, ed. R. C. Christie, Roxburghe Club, [130] (1897) • J. Morris, ed., *The troubles of our Catholic forefathers related by themselves*, 2 (1875) • *The letters and despatches of Richard Verstegan, c. 1550–1640*, ed. A. G. Petti, Catholic RS, 52 (1959) • T. G. Law, ed., *The archpriest controversy: documents relating to the dissensions of the Roman Catholic clergy, 1597–1602*, 2 vols., CS, new ser., 56, 58 (1896–8) • 'The letters of Robert Southwell, S.J.', *Archivum Historicum Societatis Iesu*, 63 (1994), 101–24

Archives Archivum Romanum Societatis Iesu, Fondo Gesuitico 651/648 • Bodl. Oxf., MS Arch. F. g. 4 • English College, Rome, *Liber ruber* • NRA, letters and literary MSS • Stonyhurst College, Lancashire, MS A. v. 4, Anglia I, Anglia VI, Anglia A. III | Archivum Romanum Societatis Iesu, Rome, Fondo Gesuitico 651, Anglia 14, Fland. Belg. i, Anglia 8, Anglia Necrol. II 1573–1651 • Bodl. Oxf., MS Laud misc. 655 • English College, Rome, Christopher Grene, *Collectanea F*, Liber 1422 • Folger, MS V. a. 421, Harmsworth MS

Likenesses W. J. Alais, stipple and line engraving, BM; repro. in R. Southwell, *The complete poems of Robert Southwell*, ed. A. B. Grosart (privately printed, London, 1872) • C. Weld, crayon drawing (after portrait), Stonyhurst College, Lancashire; repro. in R. Southwell, *The triumphs over death*, ed. J. W. Trotman (1914) • line engraving, BM, NPG

Southwell, Robert (*bap.* **1608**, *d.* **1677**), administrator and local politician, was baptized on 29 March 1608 in St James, Bury St Edmunds, Suffolk, the son of Anthony Southwell (*bap.* 1579, *d.* 1623), undertaker in the plantation of Munster, and Margaret, daughter of Sir Ralph Shelton of Norfolk. Nothing is known of his early years or education, and at an unknown date he married Helena (1613–1679), daughter of Major Robert Gore of Shereton, Wiltshire. On 22 July 1631 he was appointed collector of customs for the port of Kinsale, where he remained throughout the Irish rising of 1641, during which time it is said that he 'took his share in the defence of the town against the Irish' (*DNB*). On the conclusion of Ormond's treaty with the Kilkenny confederates Southwell helped to provision the fleet of revolted English ships with which Prince Rupert arrived in the port in January 1649. Although it is said that he suffered for his loyalty to the Stuart cause, the commissioners subsequently appointed for the government of Ireland by the Rump Parliament were evidently reliant upon Southwell for cash loans by June 1652. On 26 November 1653 he was appointed one of the commissioners for surveying lands in the baronies of Kinalea and Kerrykuhirry in co. Cork. On 10 March 1656 he was added to a commission set up for transplanting to Connaught those liable who had not yet vacated co. Cork. At Mallow later that year, during the trial of 'ancient inhabitants of Cork, Kinsale and Youghal', Irish Catholics who laid claim to exemption from the transplantation orders on grounds of constant loyalty to the English interest throughout the rebellion, Southwell gave evidence as to the fidelity and good affection of those many Catholics who had remained in English quarters, and whose loyalty only came in question after their technical disqualification by right of Inchiquin's general defection in 1648. Evidently he was motivated, at least in part, by his ownership of estates purchased from such individuals in the period 1641–52, properties which were themselves liable to confiscation. In 1655 Southwell's daughter Catherine (*d.* 1679) married John Percivall (Perceval), who was knighted by Henry Cromwell in 1658 and elevated to an Irish baronetcy in 1661. Another daughter, Anne, married Ralph Barney of Wyckingham, Norfolk. By 1657 Southwell shared responsibility for provisioning ships of the Commonwealth navy. On 5 October of that year he was elected chief officer, or sovereign, of the corporation of Kinsale.

After the restoration of Charles II, Southwell received pardon by order of the king on 25 April 1661. He resumed his services to the state in the administration of maritime and naval affairs. In October he petitioned for an award of certain forfeited lands belonging to James Mellefont and Philip Barryoge in satisfaction for a debt incurred supplying the king's fleet at a time apparently unspecified. A grant of Barryoge's property in the liberty of Kinsale, including Ringcurran, was confirmed to Southwell by letters patent on 16 June 1666, and he became governor of the fort erected there in defence against the Dutch; during the Second Anglo-Dutch War he incurred considerable personal expense in dealing with enemy seamen taken prisoner. As of 1 April 1662 he was customer for the port of Kinsale within the establishment for civil affairs in Ireland. By August 1665 he was deputy vice-admiral of Munster, and on 20 September 1670 he was appointed vice-admiral of the province, and admitted as a member of the provincial council. In 1671 he was sovereign of Kinsale once more. In 1675 order was given that the town's new charter incorporate a saving in respect of land from the fee farm rent recently granted to Southwell, on which he had built housing and other accommodation to the advantage of the port and harbour there. He died on 3 April 1677 after a long illness (probably dropsy), during which his second but only surviving son, Sir Robert

*Southwell, diplomat and future secretary of state for Ireland, took comfort from his stoic discourse, remarking that 'Socrates and Seneca did by the help of Words and Witt, leave greater Monuments of their Firmity when they came to this great experiment; but I believe hee will expire as little concerned as either of them' (Marquis of Lansdowne, 11–12). Southwell was buried alongside his infant son Thomas in the family tomb in the eastern aisle of Kinsale church. His wife and their daughter Catherine, who both died in 1679, were buried next to him.

SEAN KELSEY

Sources *DNB* · *CSP Ire., 1660–69* · *CSP dom., 1660–76* · GEC, *Baronetage*, 3.314–15 · R. Dunlop, *Ireland under the Commonwealth*, 2 vols. (1913) · *The Petty-Southwell correspondence, 1676–1687*, ed. marquis of Lansdowne [H. E. W. Petty-Fitzmaurice] (1928) · *IGI* · will, PRO, PROB 11/355, fols. 56*v*–58*v*

Archives BL, corresp. with Perceval family, Add. MSS 46934–46955, *passim*

Wealth at death real and personal estate; sum of £5385 plus interest held by East India Co. towards purchase of real estate in England: will, PRO, PROB 11/355, fols. 56*v*–58*v*

Southwell, Sir Robert (1635–1702), diplomat and government official, was born near Kinsale in co. Cork on 31 December 1635, the second but only surviving son and heir of Robert *Southwell (*bap.* 1608, *d.* 1677) and Helena (1613–1679), daughter of Major Robert Gore, of Shereton, Wiltshire. His father, from the second generation of a family settled in the recently planted province of Munster, had acquired the post of collector of customs in the port of Kinsale in 1631. Even before this Robert Southwell the elder, and his father of the same name, had been accumulating property in and around the town. They continued to add to their holdings in the locality. Southwell the elder, in common with other Munster planters, was endangered by the uprising of 1641 and spent the next decade trying to suppress it. Unlike some protestant leaders in the region, notably Broghill, he looked to the king and his Irish lord lieutenant, Ormond, to end the rebellion. Faithful to the royal cause even after Charles I had been defeated in England, in 1648 Southwell assisted Prince Rupert, who was harrying the victorious parliamentarians at sea. Kinsale was notable as a safe harbour and was also developing as a victualling centre for shipping. Southwell put it at Rupert's disposal, and thereby incurred the hostility of the English authorities.

Education and foreign travel Once the formidable army of the new English Commonwealth had disembarked in Ireland in August 1649, royalists among the Irish protestant community were liable to harassment and punishment. It may have been to escape this uncongenial atmosphere that Southwell dispatched his young heir to Christchurch in Hampshire in 1650. Already Robert the younger had received some schooling in the city of Cork. In 1653 the youth matriculated at Queen's College in Oxford, where he graduated BA in 1655. In 1654 Southwell was entered at Lincoln's Inn. Some signs of his versatility were precociously apparent in verses which he wrote between 1654 and 1656. Some celebrated his contemporaries among the undergraduates at Oxford, but one was occasioned by the death of John Selden, 'the grave and famous antiquary' (Bodl. Oxf., MS Eng. poet. f.6, fol. 44).

Sir Robert Southwell (1635–1702), by Sir Godfrey Kneller, in or before 1695

The past affiliations of the elder Robert Southwell in 1654 threatened him with the forfeiture of one-fifth of his Irish holdings. However, he ingratiated himself with the new regime. From 1655, with Henry Cromwell as effective governor, prospects for older established settlers in Ireland brightened. Under this friendlier administration Southwell added to his property in Kinsale, attracted government contracts for provisioning ships, and so improved his finances. As a result, his heir was able to undertake an extended foreign tour. One motive for travelling at this juncture may still have been a wish to avoid too close contact with the usurpers; another, to improve links with the exiled royalists. But the principal purpose seems to have been to educate the promising young man who, as yet, had not chosen a career. Between 1659 and 1661 his travels took in France, the Netherlands, parts of central Europe, and Italy. An obvious result was a facility in languages which would soon be applied in foreign embassies. Welcomed by grandees, Southwell developed and exhibited a courtliness which was much admired. In 1660 he had spent three months in Florence, where he was warmly received by the grand duke and his brother, reviving a contact between the Medicis and Southwells which stretched back to the early sixteenth century and which would be extended in the improbable setting of Kinsale in 1669. In Florence and Bologna he frequented the circles of virtuosi, encountered a pupil of Galileo, and met mathematicians, astronomers, and antiquaries. Southwell followed a similar routine in Rome during 1661. There he counted the scientist Father Athanasius Kircher a particular friend and, on behalf of an acquaintance from Munster, Robert Boyle, questioned the Jesuit closely. He conversed with cardinals and English expatriates, exiled on account of religion and political principles. Among the last was the republican Algernon Sidney. The table talk in Rome ranged widely. It even embraced the attributes—including dissimulation—needed to thrive in state and diplomatic service, which Southwell seems to have heeded. These peregrinations also allowed the traveller to send back to his friends in Ireland and England rarities, from books and artefacts to a Parmesan cheese. It left him with an enthusiasm for the continent which he not only indulged during his own life but which he passed to his descendants. In successive generations the enlightening effects of the grand tour were appreciated.

Public office Equipped by this protracted preparation, Southwell returned home, there to consider his future. The Restoration had improved the standing of the family. The gains of recent years were likely to be confirmed, and the possible penalties had been averted. The elder Southwell wanted his heir to find a profitable occupation which would keep him in Ireland. The advent of Ormond to the lord lieutenancy made this a realistic ambition, since Ormond was accounted a friend and patron of the Southwells. However, the younger Southwell, uninterested in a military post, doubted that Ormond had anything in his gift which fitted his qualifications. Moreover, he argued that his knowledge of the wider world was more relevant to possible employments in England than in Ireland. The first office which he acquired, in 1664, was a secretaryship to the commission of prizes. This may have come his way thanks to his family's connections, as owners of the docks at Kinsale, with the naval administrators in London. But it also owed something to support from Ormond and his circle.

On 26 January 1665 Southwell married Elizabeth (1649–1682), the eldest daughter of Sir Edward *Dering, a baronet from Kent. Dering had recently served in Ireland as one of the English commissioners charged with adjudicating on the claims of those who wished to be restored to their confiscated estates. No doubt the opportunity for this alliance arose during Dering's stay in Dublin. With the bride came a portion of £1500. The expectation of the dowry may have enabled Southwell late in 1664 to buy one of the four clerkships of the privy council for £1600 or £2000. The seller was another Irish protestant, Sir George Lane, secretary to Ormond. It was reckoned that a clerk could earn £450 per annum. The office also introduced Southwell into the innermost workings of government. From his vantage point he maintained a watching brief for friends back in Ireland and Dublin University as the new land settlement was drafted. He soon attracted plaudits, being described by Arlington as 'an ingenious young gentleman and very well qualified for the employment' (BL, Add. MS 34336, fols. 1–2). In particular, his linguistic proficiency rapidly brought him more work. In November 1665 he was appointed as emissary to Portugal, with the mission of concluding peace between the Portuguese and Spain. The next month he was knighted. He travelled to Lisbon early in 1666, and helped to bring about the peace of Lisbon, which was signed on 13 February 1668. Soon he was ordered to return to that country, again as envoy. His task was now to negotiate a commercial treaty between England and Portugal. Negotiations detained him for more than a year and left him financially embarrassed. More foreign missions soon followed. In October 1671 he was dispatched to Brussels as ambassador.

Back in England by 1672, Southwell was elected the next year to parliament for the Cornish borough of Penryn, which he represented until 1679. In 1672 he was reappointed secretary to the commission of prizes, having relinquished the post in 1667. Profitable involvement in maritime affairs increased with his being named as deputy to his father as vice-admiral of the province of Munster: no sinecure, but, with its chances to share in the sale of prizes and wrecks, lucrative to the family. In 1677 Southwell succeeded to the vice-admiralty itself following his father's death on 3 April. Another valuable post, a commissioner for the excise, was gained in 1671: it carried a salary of £500 per annum. Throughout the 1670s Southwell distinguished himself as a diligent and adroit administrator. Loyal to the court, he hardly ventured into partisan politics. For much of the decade his original patron, Ormond, was in eclipse, but this did not slow the protégé's steady progress. As a result of his greater prosperity and rank, by 1672 he had acquired a property in Spring Gardens in Westminster. By the 1670s he was enquiring what country estates were on offer. Like other purchasers from southern Ireland, he opted for one in south-western England, at King's Weston outside Bristol, handy for rapid movement between Ireland and England. In 1671 he had revisited his ancestral home; his father's death in 1677 obliged him to return to settle affairs in Kinsale. He drew approximately £1000 annually from Irish property, almost all of which was concentrated in the town, and so watched vigilantly over his own and the port's interests. In particular, he used his official connections to urge on the Treasury and Admiralty the claims of Kinsale as the centre where ships could most expeditiously be provisioned. In 1682 he was prepared to lease his little-used house there as a navy office. In addition, he frequently bestirred himself to place the sons of tenants and kinsfolk from the district in the navy or government service. As such he remained a useful patron even after he had permanently absented himself from Ireland.

The furore over the Popish Plot embarrassed Southwell. Although a compliant servant of the administration throughout the 1670s, his Irish upbringing and property in Ireland gave him strong reasons for resisting the demands of the Catholics for better treatment. Yet in 1679 he was criticized in the House of Lords. In connection with his duties as clerk to the council he was reputed to have suppressed pertinent information about the conspiracy.

He felt it best to leave the sensitive public post. Seemingly with the help of Ormond (since 1677 back in favour), Southwell was allowed to sell his clerkship in December 1679 for £2500. His choice in the spring of 1680 for an embassy to the elector of Brandenburg showed that he was still highly regarded. The mission was connected with a scheme to construct an alliance against France, and it took Southwell to the prince of Orange and the court of Brunswick–Lüneburg. But such diplomacy was not to the taste of Charles II, moving in the orbit of France. Southwell was soon recalled. In 1681 his place in the excise commission was terminated. He was returned to the 1685 parliament, this time for another Cornish seat, Lostwithiel.

Estates and scholarly interests Otherwise, without public employments, Southwell busied himself about private and family matters. King's Weston (bought in 1679) was improved; Kinsale, albeit from a distance, was overseen. Almshouses were endowed and the parish church ornamented with a monument to his parents from the workshop of Grinling Gibbons. The education of his heir, Edward *Southwell, born on 4 September 1671, preoccupied him, the more so as his wife had died in 1682. He attended also to the upbringing of other young kinsmen, the Percevals, Kings, and Sir Thomas Southwell. All were entrusted to the expert Southwell. Also, the ageing Ormond, who was restored to the Irish viceroyalty and held the post from 1677 to 1685, confided much in him. Probably the honorary doctorate of civil law which Southwell received from Oxford University in 1677 had been prompted by Ormond, the chancellor of the university. The management of his errant grandsons, especially the eldest—James Butler, future duke of Ormond—after his father, Lord Ossory, died in 1680, was delegated to Southwell. In 1682, when the duke became embroiled in an acrimonious and potentially damaging controversy with Anglesey, he turned to Southwell to construct a detailed defence of his conduct during the 1640s. The project expanded into an authorized biography. Although Southwell worked on it intermittently between 1682 and 1688, being accorded access to the archives of aristocrats other than Ormond, nothing was published in the lifetime of either the duke or Southwell. The life, eventually published in 1792, showed how the discretion which brought Southwell such respect could be carried to extremes.

Southwell's preferences, always sedentary, increasingly inclined to the cerebral. In 1662, sponsored by his friend Robert Boyle, he had been elected a fellow of the Royal Society. Absences overseas interfered with his attendance at meetings, but when in London he participated with enthusiasm. Furthermore, a close friendship with the polymath Sir William Petty stimulated an interest in utilitarian improvements and speculations on the natural world. Together they reflected on the demography, topography, and politics of Ireland. It indicated Southwell's tact and self-effacement that he could keep the affection of two such divergent figures as the haughty Ormond and the touchy Petty.

Southwell and the revolution of 1688–1689 These same qualities stood Southwell in good stead during the developing crisis of 1688. Edward Southwell acted more impetuously than his cautious father by joining the forces of William of Orange shortly after they had landed in November 1688. Soon, although an uneasy calm descended on England once William and Mary had been accepted, the danger to protestant proprietors in Ireland, such as Southwell, worsened. James II, indeed, landed at Kinsale on 12 March 1689 at the start of his bid to use Ireland to regain his other two kingdoms. The absent, and those from Ireland who had embraced William, stood to forfeit their properties. Southwell had met William during his mission in 1680 and may covertly have kept in touch thereafter. He readily accepted from William appointment as principal secretary for Ireland. In this office, it seemed, Southwell's intimacy with the country was married to his administrative expertise. He accompanied the king to Ireland, and landed with him at Carrickfergus on 14 June 1690. In the field with William he was primarily concerned with the commissariat, not tactics. However, he may have proposed that William repeat the ploy tried by Cromwell in 1650: to seek to detach the humbler Irish Catholics from their leaders with offers of clemency. It did not succeed. Southwell's secretaryship, important while the kingdom had still to be subdued, occupied its holder less once more conventional rule through lords deputy or lords justices was resumed. He was not long detained in Ireland, being back in London by October 1690. High standing with the new order had also been shown in his appointment, on 19 April 1689, as a commissioner for managing the English customs, a post he held until he relinquished it on 12 June 1697. Further acknowledgement of his standing, and perhaps of his skills as organizer and diplomat, was shown in his election in December 1690 as president of the Royal Society. He was re-elected annually until 1695.

Much in demand for his good sense, Southwell shrewdly advised a nephew, Sir John Percival, about to take possession of his co. Cork estate, how to comport himself. An understanding of men and affairs generally made him treat with equanimity the foibles of his fellows. Yet, having advanced himself largely through his own exertions, he could be sensitive on questions of honour. A Brandenburger, Schwerin, whom—as a favour—Southwell had helped in the supervision of his Monmouthshire estate, provoked Southwell's wrath. Schwerin had accused him of malpractices. Southwell insisted that he had acted honourably, and warned Schwerin that he had 'other use of my time and ill health than to serve you and to displease you at once' (R. Southwell to Baron De Schwerin, 9 Feb 1698[9], Cardiff Central Library, MS 4.11/103). For once, the passionless mask had slipped. Southwell, deferential towards superiors and elders in his early years, once he had climbed to some eminence was himself accorded (and expected) respect and trust. He died at King's Weston on 11 September 1702 and was buried near by in Henbury church in Gloucestershire, where his wife had earlier been interred. He had not severed his links with Ireland, not least because it remained a vital source of remittances. Yet he had transformed himself from Irish protestant to English country gentleman in receipt of about £1000 per annum from Irish property.

TOBY BARNARD

Sources BL, Egerton MS 917; MS 1632 • Carte MSS, Bodl. Oxf., MS Eng. lett. C. 53 • NL Ire., MS 664, MS 14910 • *The Petty–Southwell correspondence, 1676–1687*, ed. marquis of Lansdowne [H. E. W. Petty-Fitzmaurice] (1928) • CKS, Dering–Southwell papers, U1713/C 1–4 • *Report on the manuscripts of the earl of Egmont*, 2 vols. in 3, HMC, 63 (1905–9) • *The manuscripts of the marquis of Ormonde*, [old ser.], 3 vols., HMC, 36 (1895–1909) • V&A NAL, Forster Library, Ormonde papers • TCD, MUN P/1/470/20 and 36; MS 1181 • *The works of the Honourable Robert Boyle*, ed. T. Birch, 5 (1744) • Bodl. Oxf., MS Eng. poet. f.6 • Southwell–Schwerin letters, Cardiff Central Library, MS 4.11 • Kinsale manorial MSS, National University of Ireland, Cork, Boole Library, MS U 20 • NMM, Southwell MSS, SOU/1; SOU/8; SOU/10 • M. Hunter, *The Royal Society and its fellows, 1660–1700: the morphology of an early scientific institution* (1982) • D. M. Gardener, 'The work of the English privy council, 1660–1679, with respect to domestic affairs', DPhil diss., U. Oxf., 1992 • E. Cruickshanks and B. D. Henning, 'Southwell, Sir Robert', HoP, *Commons, 1660–90* • A. M. Crino, ed., *Un principe di Toscana in Inghilterra e in Irlanda nel 1669* (1968) • T. C. Barnard, 'The political, material and mental culture of the Cork settlers', *Cork: history and society—interdisciplinary essays on the history of an Irish county*, ed. P. O'Flanagan and C. G. Buttimer (1993), 309–52 • *The history of the revolution of Portugal … with letters of Sir Robert Southwell* (1740)

Archives BL, corresp. and papers, Harley MSS; Egerton MSS 1627–1633; Add. MSS 9708–9709, 9748–9749, 11759, 19670 • BL, corresp. and papers, Add. MSS 21494, 34329–34346, 35099–35101, 38105, 38146–38157, 38536, 47038–47039 • BL, corresp. and papers, Add. MSS 58219, 60581–60583 • Blackburn Central Library, corresp. and papers • Bodl. Oxf., papers • Bodl. Oxf., verses and papers • CKS, letter-book (list of correspondents only) • Georgetown University, Washington, DC, papers relating to Roman Catholicism • NMM, naval corresp. and papers • priv. coll., list of correspondents • RS, corresp. and papers • TCD, corresp. and papers relating to Ireland • Yale U., Beinecke L., corresp. and papers | BL, corresp. with William Cole, Add. MSS 18598–18599 • BL, letters to J. Ellis, Add. MSS 28875–28876 • BL, letters to Lord Essex • BL, letters to Sir J. Kempthorne, Egerton MS 928 • BL, corresp. with Perceval family, Add. MSS 46936–47042, *passim* • BL, corresp. with Sir William and Lady Petty • BL, letters to Hans Sloane • Bristol RO, letters to Sir Hugh Smyth • CKS, letters to Sir Edward Dering • Cumbria AS, Carlisle, letters to Sir John Lowther • Glos. RO, corresp. with William Blathwayt • Leics. RO, corresp. with the earl of Nottingham • NL Ire., corresp. with duke of Ormond • priv. coll., corresp. • TCD, corresp. with William King • U. Nott. L., corresp. with Lord Portland • University College, Cork, Boole Library, official and Cork estate papers • V&A NAL, Forster Library, papers relating to dukes of Ormond

Likenesses G. Kneller, oils, in or before 1695, RS [*see illus.*] • J. Smith, mezzotint (after G. Kneller), BM, NPG

Southwell, Thomas. *See* Bacon, Thomas (*c.*1592–1637).

Southwell, Thomas, first Baron Southwell (*c.*1665–1720), politician, was born at 'Glanamorohe Rhaiaile', co. Limerick, Ireland (Foster, *Alum. Oxon., 1500–1714*, 4.1393), the eldest son of Richard Southwell (*d.* before February 1680), politician, and his wife, Lady Elizabeth O'Brien (*d.* 1688). Richard Southwell's father, Thomas Southwell of Castle Mattress (now Castle Matrix), co. Limerick, had been created a baronet in 1662. On his grandfather's death in May 1681, the younger Thomas succeeded him in his title and estates. Responsibility for Sir Thomas's estates and education was placed in the hands of guardians, who requested the advice of his kinsman Sir Robert Southwell, later Irish secretary of state. Sir Thomas landed in England in October 1681, and matriculated at Christ Church, Oxford, two months later. He left in 1684 without a degree. After finding that he was unable to afford a journey to the continent, and was forbidden to enter the inns of court by his guardians, Southwell probably returned to Ireland.

In late 1688, anticipating an invasion by James II, Southwell and his brother William [*see below*] raised a troop of one hundred horse in co. Limerick, in an attempt to secure Munster for William III. Facing opposition, Southwell and his party retreated north towards Ulster but were captured by the Jacobite sheriff of Galway, James Power, tried for and found guilty of treason, and imprisoned for fifteen months. The psychological torture and other privations they endured provided material for William King's anti-Catholic *The State of the Protestants of Ireland under the Late King James's Government* (1691). Although attainted by the Irish parliament in May 1689, Southwell was released from Galway in April 1690 into the custody of the earl of Seaforth, who took him to Scotland and allowed him to return to the government forces. Southwell's colleagues remained imprisoned until after the battle of the Boyne. In 1692 Southwell successfully petitioned William and Mary for £500 to cover the costs he had incurred in maintaining the poorest prisoners and buying reprieves from the death sentences passed upon them.

Southwell then devoted himself to the Williamite reconstruction of Ireland. In April 1693 he was made a commissioner to inspect and collect arrears on crown lands. More importantly, by August of that year he was already involved in settling continental protestant families in Ireland, initially from France. A Treasury letter of 19 August authorized the provision of victuals for the families for a month, and another of 14 July 1695 a grant to Southwell of £180 7*s.* 6*d.* for the cost of transporting the families from London. Most of the protestants were linen manufacturers, the most prominent being Samuel-Louis Crommelin. The majority did not settle in co. Limerick but in Ulster where there was already a substantial protestant population. Southwell remained an active campaigner for the cause of linen manufacturing in Ireland. In correspondence with Charles Montagu from about 1698 (BL, Add. MS 4761, fols. 183–93) he discussed the influence of English legislation encouraging the export of wool from Ireland to England, and suggested further measures to encourage Irish linen and discourage the sale of Irish wool outside the British Isles. One of the consequences was the establishment of the royal corporation, by which the government gave financial support to Crommelin's investment. The correspondence reveals Southwell to have been anxious to promote voluntary co-operation between Ireland and England on economic matters, as the basis for a secure protestant settlement in both countries.

On 4 April 1696 Southwell married Meliora Coningsby (*d.* 1735), daughter of the first Earl Coningsby; the couple had six sons and five daughters, seven of whom survived infancy. In the previous year he had been elected member of the Irish parliament for co. Limerick which he represented until 1699 and again in the years 1703–13 and 1715–17. As an active whig, Southwell continued to enjoy several administrative positions. From 1697 to 1713 and from 1714 to his death he was a commissioner of the revenue. On 12 February 1701 he was appointed a trustee for the erection of barracks in Ireland, and on 4 December 1702 he became a trustee for the establishment of the linen manufacture, as provided for in the legislation he had supported setting up the royal corporation. He was sworn of the Irish privy council in 1710. The arrival in England of the protestant exiles from the Palatinate, Germany, inspired Southwell to further action; by 1712 he had settled 130 German protestant families in co. Limerick, but encountered difficulty in acquiring compensation for his expenses from the government. It was not until 1718 that George I agreed to discharge Southwell's debts and support the Palatine families on his estates for seven years. Despite Southwell's efforts the settlement was not a success.

Although Southwell seems to have been out of favour and office at the end of Anne's reign, the accession of George I helped to restore his political fortunes, and he was created an Irish baron, as Baron Southwell of Castle Mattress, co. Limerick, on 4 September 1717. He died suddenly in Dublin on 4 August 1720, and was buried at Rathkeale, co. Limerick. His widow died in London on 22 October 1735.

William Southwell (1669–1720), army officer and politician, was the younger brother of the first Baron Southwell. After his release from imprisonment in Galway following the defeat of James II, he continued his military career. He was commissioned in Colonel Hamilton's regiment of foot on 1 September 1693, and was promoted to captain-lieutenant the following August. He was severely wounded at Terra Nova, Namur, but survived and was promoted to captain in September 1695. On half pay after the Nine Years' War, he returned to service for the War of the Spanish Succession. He was made a major in Colonel James Rivers's regiment of foot in February 1702, and a lieutenant-colonel in January 1704. His distinguished leadership during the siege of Barcelona in September 1705 ensured the capture of the fortress of Monjuich; Southwell was the first officer through the breach and he obtained the surrender. He was rewarded with the temporary governorship of the fortress and the colonelcy of his old regiment, Hamilton being reassigned. Ill health prevented him from commanding the regiment at Almanza in April 1707, when he was in England; on 14 June 1708 he sold his regiment to Colonel Harrison for 5000 guineas. The duke of Marlborough obtained his horse as a gift for the duchess (Snyder, 965). He returned to Ireland where he had been elected MP for Kinsale, co. Cork, in 1703, and supported the whigs. He was returned for Castlemartyr, co. Cork, in 1713. In 1714 he was captain of the lord lieutenant of Ireland's honour guard, and from the next year until his death he was MP for Baltimore, co. Cork.

Southwell was married to Lucy (*d.* 1733), youngest daughter and coheir of William Bowen of Ballyadams, Queen's county; they had five sons and eight daughters. William Southwell died on 23 January 1720.

MATTHEW KILBURN

Sources J. Lodge, *The peerage of Ireland*, rev. M. Archdall, rev. edn, 6 (1789) · Thomas Southwell, letters to Charles Montagu, *c.*1698, BL, Add. MS 4761, fols. 183–93 · Sir Robert Southwell, letter, 18 Oct 1684, BL, Add. MS 46961, fol. 121 · W. King, *The state of the protestants of Ireland under the late King James's government* (1691) · C. Gill, *The rise of the Irish linen industry* (1925) · *CSP dom.*, 1691–2 [S. P. Dom Petition Entry Book 1, 226] · Southwell, memorials to earl of Galway and King George I, BL, BL Add. MS 35933, fols. 24, 29, 246 · C. Dalton, ed., *English army lists and commission registers, 1661–1714*, 3 (1896) · Lord Peterborough [C. Mordaunt], *Letters from the earl of Peterborough to General Stanhope in Spain*, ed. Lord Mahon (1834) · *The Marlborough–Godolphin correspondence*, ed. H. L. Snyder, 3 vols. (1975) · A. Parnell, *The war of the succession in Spain during the reign of Queen Anne, 1702–1711* (1888); repr. (1905) · GEC, *Peerage* · 'Southwell, Thomas', E. M. Johnston-Liik, *History of the Irish parliament, 1692–1800*, 6 vols. (2002) · 'Southwell, William', E. M. Johnston-Liik, *History of the Irish parliament, 1692–1800*, 6 vols. (2002)

Archives BL, Add. MSS 4761, 35933, 46961 | PRO NIre., letters to Lord Coningsby · TCD, corresp. with William King

Wealth at death manuscripts and state papers: GEC

Southwell, Thomas (1831–1909), naturalist, was born on 15 June 1831 at King's Lynn, the son of Thomas Elmer Southwell, chief cashier at the King's Lynn branch of Gurney's Bank, and his wife, Jane Castell. After private education at King's Lynn, Southwell entered the service of Gurney & Co. in that town on 14 September 1846. In 1852 he was transferred to Fakenham, and in November 1867 to the headquarters of the bank at Norwich, from which he retired in 1896 after fifty years' service. He married on 15 June 1868, Martha (1832/3–1903), daughter of Joseph Fyson, a draper, of Great Yarmouth; they had two daughters.

Almost all Southwell's life was spent in Norfolk and all his leisure was devoted to the natural history of the county. He was also an authority on the topography and archaeology of the fen district adjacent to his birthplace. When the Norfolk and Norwich Naturalists' Society was founded in 1869 Southwell became an active member; he was president in both 1879 and 1893, and his contributions to the society's *Transactions*, numbering more than 100, covered a wide range.

From Southwell's earliest years he showed a keen interest in birds. He wrote:

> I have myself talked with men who have taken the eggs of the avocet and blacktailed godwit, and who have seen the bustard at large in its last stronghold. The bittern was so common in Feltwell Fen that a keeper there has shot five in one day, and his father used to have one roasted for dinner every Sunday. I have found the eggs of Montagu's harrier, and know those who remember the time when the hen harrier and short-eared owl bred regularly in Roydon Fen, and who have taken the eggs of the water-rail in what was once Whittlesea Mere.

Southwell devoted much attention to the preservation of birds. For the educational series of the Society for the Protection of Birds he wrote papers on the swallow (no. 4), and the terns (no. 12). His most useful achievement was considered to be the completion of *The Birds of Norfolk* by

Henry Stevenson FLS, of which the two earlier volumes had been published between 1866 and 1870. Stevenson died on 18 August 1888, and in 1890 Southwell brought out the third volume, thus completing 'a model county ornithology', from letters and manuscripts left by the author, but largely supplemented by information supplied by himself.

Southwell was elected a fellow of the Zoological Society on 22 February 1872, the proposer for his election being the zoologist Alfred Newton (1829–1907). In 1881 Southwell published *The Seals and Whales of the British Seas*, comprising papers reprinted from *Science Gossip*. From 1884 onwards he contributed annually to *The Zoologist* a lucid report with authentic statistics on the seal and whale fisheries. He closely identified with the work of the Norwich museum, serving on the committee from 1893, when the old museum was transferred to Norwich Castle. He compiled the admirable *Official Guide to the Norwich Castle Museum* in 1896, and contributed an article entitled 'An eighteenth-century museum' to the *Museum Journal* in 1908.

Southwell, in addition to many other contributions to periodicals, published a revised edition of Richard Lubbock's *Observations on the Fauna of Norfolk* (1879), and *Notes and Letters on the Natural History of Norfolk, More Especially on the Birds and Fishes* (1902), from the manuscripts of Sir Thomas Browne (1605–1682) in the British Museum (part of the Sloane collection), and the Bodleian Library. Southwell died at his home, 10 The Crescent, Chapel Field Road, Norwich, after a cerebral haemorrhage, on 5 September 1909. He was survived by his two daughters.

James Hooper, *rev.* Yolanda Foote

Sources *Eastern Daily Press* (6 Sept 1909) • *The Field* (11 Sept 1909) • S. H. Long, 'Mr Thomas Southwell', *Transactions of the Norfolk and Norwich Naturalists' Society*, 9 (1909–14), 134–7 • *Annals of an East Anglian bank* (1900), 347 • *The Ibis*, 9th ser., 4 (1910), 191 • private information (1912)
Archives Norwich Castle Museum, diary, notebooks, and papers • Scott Polar RI, corresp., notes, and papers
Likenesses portrait, repro. in Long, 'Mr Thomas Southwell', 134
Wealth at death £7886 15*s*. 4*d*.: probate, 23 Sept 1909, *CGPLA Eng. & Wales*

Southwell, William (1669–1720). *See under* Southwell, Thomas, first Baron Southwell (*c*.1665–1720).

Southwood. For this title name *see* Elias, Julius Salter, Viscount Southwood (1873–1946).

Southworth, John [St John Southworth] (1592–1654), Roman Catholic priest and martyr, was born into an unflinchingly recusant family at Samlesbury, Lancashire. A government spy reported about the time of his birth that there was a popish schoolmaster in Samlesbury, and it is quite possible that this man educated Southworth. He was the third member of the family in a generation to offer himself for the priesthood at Rheims or Douai. He entered the latter in 1613 and was ordained as a secular priest on Holy Saturday 1618, offering his first mass on Easter morning. He was sent to England in December 1619 and spent most of the next thirty-five years in London, except for a twelve-month recall in 1624–5, when he was asked to act as chaplain to the Benedictine nuns in Brussels, and for a brief period in 1627–8 in Lancashire. This culminated in his arrest, trial, and conviction under the Elizabethan statute making it treasonable to be a Catholic priest in England. His execution was stayed, however, and he was transferred to the Clink prison in London. In 1630 he was one of twelve priests who, at the behest of the queen and to mark the peace treaty between England and France, had their sentences commuted to perpetual banishment—with the king's 'express will and pleasure' that if they remained in or returned to England and Wales, then 'the Law should pass on every several person without further favour' (Reynolds, 38).

Southworth simply ignored this threat and remained in London, serving in some of the poorest areas of Clerkenwell and Westminster. He is lost to historical view for most of the next twenty-five years, but can be regularly glimpsed signing petitions for the return of Bishop Smith or the appointment of a coadjutor to bring discipline and to instil a common practice among the clergy. He was especially prominent during the plague years in the mid-1630s, when he raised money for the victims and their families, and complained that his co-worker, Henry Morse SJ, administered the sacraments of penance and holy communion but not of extreme unction (since touching the victims of plague would incur unnecessary personal risk). He was arrested four times on the sworn evidence of spies between his release from the Clink in 1630 and the outbreak of civil war, but he was three times released after intervention by secretary of state Windebank. On the fourth occasion, in 1640, he escaped. He is completely lost to view throughout the following decade, but can be traced again, operating from the house of the Spanish ambassador in the early 1650s. He was arrested at a private house on 19 June 1654, brought twice before the common serjeant of London on 24 and 26 June, and ordered to be hanged, drawn, and quartered, a sentence carried out at Tyburn on the 28th. In his final speech he begged that 'Catholics, being free-born subjects should enjoy that liberty [of conscience] as others do as long as they live obedient subjects to the Lord Protector and the laws of the nation' (*Last Speech*, 2).

Southworth was the only Catholic priest executed during the protectorate, and the last ever to be executed simply for being a priest in England. His arrest is probably connected with the discovery in the previous month of an assassination plot against the protector, and the establishment of links between the leading plotters and the French ambassador. This in turn provoked a spasm of heightened anti-popery. The speed of his arraignment and execution, the fact that he was brought before the common serjeant and not the high court of justice (which had been granted sole jurisdictions over treasons), and the fact that he was hanged, drawn, and quartered (a recent ordinance had restricted the manner of execution to hanging only, or to beheading) all point to the fact that he died under his 1627 conviction and under the terms of his 1630 commuted sentence. This bound the hands of the judge, who had only to establish that he was the John Southworth, priest, previously condemned. Certainly Serjeant Steele tried very hard to persuade Southworth to deny, or at least to equivocate over, his priesthood, 'assuring him that if he would so plead his life would be safe, as they had no evidence which could prove him to be a priest' (Challoner, 507). Instead, Southworth 'confessed himself a priest and a condemned man many years since' (Purdie, 116). Foreign ambassadors pleaded for his life, and Cromwell (who had no power of pardon under the 'Instrument of government') made it clear that he was unhappy about this execution. As a grim acknowledgement of this the protector ordered surgeons to be present so that once the law had taken its course, the eviscerated and quartered body could be sewn together and returned to Douai College for burial, on 14 July 1654—the only corpse of an English Catholic martyr to survive into modern times. He was beatified by the Vatican in 1929, and in 1970 he was proclaimed one of forty English martyr-saints of the Reformation era. When Douai College was pulled down in the 1920s John Southworth was exhumed and taken to a place of honour in Westminster Cathedral, close to the very spot where he had fearlessly anointed plague victims three hundred years before. JOHN MORRILL

Sources R. Challoner, *Memoirs of missionary priests*, ed. J. H. Pollen, rev. edn (1924), 505–10 • A. B. Purdie, *The life of Blessed John Southworth* (1930) • E. E. Reynolds, *John Southworth, priest and martyr* (1962) • E. H. Burton and T. L. Williams, eds., *The Douay College diaries, third, fourth and fifth, 1598–1654*, 1–2, Catholic RS, 10–11 (1911) • G. F. Nuttall, 'The English martyrs, 1535–1680', *Journal of Ecclesiastical History*, 22 (1971), 191–7 • S. R. Gardiner, *History of the Commonwealth and protectorate, 1649–1656*, new edn, 4 vols. (1903), vol. 3, pp. 149–52 • *The writings and speeches of Oliver Cromwell*, ed. W. C. Abbott and C. D. Crane, 3 (1945), 320–21 • *CSP Venice, 1653–4*, 233–4 • Thurloe, *State papers*, 2.376 • W. Prynne, *The popish royal favourite* (1643) • *The last speech and confession of John Southworth a popish priest at his execution at Tyburn … printed from a true copy found among other papers at the search of a papist's house* (1679)

Souttar, Sir Henry Sessions (1875–1964), surgeon, was born at Birkenhead on 14 December 1875, the only son of Robinson Souttar, member of parliament for Dumfriesshire (1895–1900), and his wife, Mary Ann, daughter of Philip Dixon Hardy. He was educated at Oxford high school and the Queen's College, Oxford (1895–8), where he acquired a double first in mathematics and was also interested in engineering. In 1904 he married Catharine Edith (*d.* 1959), daughter of Robert Bellamy *Clifton, professor of experimental philosophy at Oxford. They had a son and a daughter.

Souttar qualified in medicine at the London Hospital, where he became MRCS, LRCP in 1906; in the same year he graduated BM at Oxford. He then held a number of resident hospital appointments, became FRCS in 1909, and continued his career as a surgical registrar. He was appointed to the staff of the West London Hospital and in 1915 he became assistant surgeon to the London Hospital.

At the outbreak of war in 1914 Souttar was appointed surgeon to the Belgian field hospital at Antwerp and he later described the siege and withdrawal from that city to the coast. He was awarded the order of the Crown of Belgium, and later, when deputy consultant to the southern command, he was appointed CBE.

Souttar's mathematical background and his engineering skills gave him a broad interest in the world of surgery. He had his own workshop where he designed and made many surgical instruments, with the aim of simplifying or enlarging the scope of existing operative procedures. One invention of his, which remained in use and became known by his name, was a flanged tube made of a soft wire spiral which was introduced down the gullet to overcome obstructions. He also devised a steam cautery to sterilize and clean breaking-down tumours and ulcers on the surface of the body, and he devised and used a most ingenious craniotome (an instrument used to open the skull in brain operations). With the introduction of radium in the treatment of malignant tumours, Souttar was again well in advance of many of his contemporaries. His mathematical skill in assessing both dose and range was very valuable and he chaired many committees in connection with the use of radiation in the treatment of cancer. For implantation he designed a 'gun' by which radon seeds could be implanted in or around a tumour with comparative simplicity.

Souttar's most dramatic venture in surgery and the one by which he became best known was in connection with the heart. In 1925 surgery of the chest was in its infancy and operations on the valves of the heart were unknown. Souttar operated successfully on a young woman with mitral valve disease, devising an approach to the heart which enabled him to make the exploration. He did this by making an opening in the appendage of the left atrium and inserting a finger into this chamber in order to palpate and explore the damaged mitral valve. This was a pioneer operation on the heart which was not repeated for nearly a quarter of a century. The patient in this case survived for a number of years and the operation was regarded as one of the great landmarks in cardiac surgery. In a lesser way Souttar made medical history by being one of the first people to fly abroad to perform an operation. In 1933 he and his anaesthetists went to India by air, a journey which took them nearly a week in each direction.

Souttar was a good linguist and a competent musician. It is said that he constructed a violin and played it himself. His artistic talents were shown in his illustrations for his well-known textbook, *The Art of Surgery* (1929).

Souttar was a member of the council of the Royal College of Surgeons from 1933 to 1949 and was vice-president in 1943–4. He was the college's Bradshaw lecturer in 1943 and the Hunterian orator in 1949. He was instrumental in the foundation of the faculty of dental surgery and the faculty of anaesthetists in the college, and was elected an honorary fellow of both these bodies. He was president of the British Medical Association in 1945–6 and was an honorary fellow of the Australasian and the American colleges of surgeons. Trinity College, Dublin, awarded him an honorary MD in 1933. He was knighted in 1949.

After his retirement in 1947 from the London Hospital

Souttar retained his active interest in surgery, and at surgical meetings his advice was often sought and always graciously given. He was a very tall and powerfully built man, dark in his younger days, and impressive looking. He was noted for his extreme courtesy and kindness, and for his ingenuity and ideas. He was undoubtedly a great surgeon, but his interests both within surgery and outside it were possibly a little too diffuse to allow him to concentrate on any one area. Following the death of his first wife in 1959, Souttar married again in 1963; his second wife was Amy Bessie, widow of Harry Douglas Wigdahl. Souttar died at his London home, 9 Cambridge Gate, on 12 November 1964; the funeral service was held at St Marylebone Church, of which he had been a warden for many years.

T. Holmes Sellors, *rev.* Tom Treasure

Sources *BMJ* (21 Nov 1964) · *The Lancet* (21 Nov 1964) · personal knowledge (1981) · private information (1981)
Archives RCS Eng., corresp.
Wealth at death £11,483: probate, 1965, *CGPLA Eng. & Wales*

Soutter, Francis William (1844–1932), political agent and activist, was born at 38 Canterbury Street, Lambeth, London, on 23 April 1844, the second child of Francis Soutter (*d.* 1855), manager of a tobacco manufactory, and his wife, Harriet, *née* Hancock (*d.* 1854), daughter of a London publican. After the early death of his parents, Soutter was cared for by a foster mother, and briefly attended the British and Foreign School, Borough Road, before earning his living in a sawmill. He attended the Surrey Chapel Sunday school, and, swayed by Sir George Livesey, took the temperance pledge aged twelve. Most formatively, he came under the influence of the theist and radical Dr P. W. Perfitt, 'a world wide humanitarian of the broadest type' (Soutter, *Recollections*, 23), and regularly attended the South Place Chapel, the leading metropolitan ethical society. After a short apprenticeship to a carpenter, he joined his foster brother in a sawmill business, his pound a week enabling him to marry, on 29 April 1867, Arabella Amelia (1842/3–1918), daughter of Alexander Campbell, farmer. She was a vital helpmeet especially in his later life as well as mother of four children.

Shortly after his marriage, Soutter joined William Stafford in business and in politics, for they were soon at the heart of Southwark radicalism. In February 1870, with the aid of William Allan, they managed the by-election campaign of George Odger, in a pioneering, if unsuccessful, campaign to return the first 'Labour' MP independent of the local Liberal notables. Soutter was also a close associate of the feminist Helen Taylor in her campaign for the Southwark school board in 1876 and in 1885 encouraged her candidacy for parliament at North Camberwell. He took a prominent part in campaigning against the church rates (under private acts) which had survived the general abolition in 1868 and remained a focal issue for London radicals and secularists. An early supporter of the Workman's Peace Association, Soutter won the prize offered by the National Association for the Promotion of Social Science congress in 1873 for his essay on international arbitration. He was also a keen member of the National Sunday League, acting as secretary of its south London branch, and as honorary editor of the *Free Sunday Advocate* in the mid-1870s.

A leading participant in London's radical club life, Soutter was committed to removing the restrictions on working-men's right to vote and purportedly he became the first 'latchkey' voter in 1878. He also remained keen to encourage labour representation in parliament and in February 1880 ran the campaign of George Shipton in Southwark. This failed badly and in April at the general election, Soutter supported the 'official' Liberal candidates, Thorold Rogers and Arthur Cohen. On this occasion his incautious libelling of the Conservative candidate Sir Edward Clarke contributed to his suffering a severe nervous breakdown. On his recovery, he launched into a strident campaign against coercion in Ireland, helping to form the Anti-Coercion Association and setting up a weekly paper, *The Radical*, run on 'radical democratic republican' principles. Soutter visited Ireland and won the esteem of the home-ruler T. P. O'Connor. To Soutter personally *The Radical* proved a costly and short-lived failure, but those with whom he had been closely associated in it went on to found the Social Democratic Federation (SDF) in 1884.

Soutter himself returned once more to saw-milling and Southwark radicalism, although having become an early exponent of Henry George's ideas in *The Radical* he served on the executive of the English Land Restoration League. But vestry politics became his mainstay and he led the 'progressive' opposition to what he saw as a clerical and reactionary regime in Bermondsey. His forceful stance and populist tactics incurred much local enmity and entwined him in several lengthy legal cases. In particular, in 1889 he was charged, with the SDF activist Harry Quelch, with riotous assembly and was briefly imprisoned for contempt of court. But he returned triumphantly to be elected to the vestry and to chair its general purposes committee in the early 1890s. Much of Soutter's time was now taken up with political campaigning, on issues ranging from the Employers' Liability Act and parish councils to housing and the adulteration of food, while in September 1899 he organized a notable anti-war rally with the SDF. But ill health having led him to give up saw-milling, he now depended on his wife's corner-shop earnings and his own registration work for the local Liberal association. As secretary of the Bermondsey Labour League, he helped to secure a large lodger vote for the Liberals in Bermondsey, although he was unable to break the tory stranglehold on the seat between 1895 and 1906, when his close associate Dr G. J. Cooper won the seat.

But Soutter's career moved on to a new plane in October 1903 when he was employed by the Free Trade Union and became its most successful speaker and agent. Short, swarthy, and vigorous, his stentorian voice and knowledge of registration work proved major assets in the campaign against tariff reform during a series of by-elections that preceded the general election of 1906. Thereafter he was briefly employed as Liberal agent in North Cumberland, before returning to stump the country for the Free Trade Union until 1914. The defence of free trade proved congenial to Soutter as a popular democrat preferring to advocate general rather than party or class interests while he took great pride in the role it opened to women lecturers. But the First World War much reduced the scope for professional agitators of his type and Soutter secured only temporary work for the War Savings Association and in recruiting labour for munitions factories. Having lost both his wife and his son in 1918, he subsequently produced two volumes of memoirs, *Recollections of a Labour Pioneer* (1923) and *Fights for Freedom* (1925). These well depicted the milieu of London's radical working men, promoting the interests of the poor but resistant to the appeal of socialism. Soutter died in relative poverty at his home at 13 Stonecroft Way, Mitcham Road, Croydon, Surrey, on 9 May 1932, but as late as the 1950s he was upheld as a vigorous pioneer of democracy by the *Daily Worker* (22 September 1953). A. C. Howe

Sources F. W. Soutter, *Recollections of a labour pioneer* (1923) · F. W. Soutter, *Fights for freedom* (1925) · *The Radical* (1880–82) · *South London Press* (1891–5) · *The Star* (1889–1932) · *Southwark Recorder* (1889–93) · *Free Sunday Advocate* (1873–9) · minutes of evidence in the case of Soutter *et al.*, July 1889, BLPES, Coll. misc. 230 · correspondence, BLPES, Mill-Taylor MSS, vol. 18 · *Daily Worker* (22 Sept 1953) · b. cert. · m. cert. · d. cert.

Archives BL, John Burns corresp., papers · BLPES, Mill-Taylor corresp., papers · priv. coll., Sir Edward Clarke corresp., papers

Likenesses photograph, 1917, repro. in Soutter, *Recollections of a labour pioneer*, frontispiece

Wealth at death £116 15*s.* 0*d.*: administration, 31 May 1933, *CGPLA Eng. & Wales*

Souvestre, Marie Claire (1835–1905), headmistress, was born in Brest on 28 April 1835, the second of three children (all daughters) of (Charles-) Emile Souvestre (1806–1854) and his second wife, Angélique-Anne (Nanine) Papot (1806–1886). The father was the prolific, Morlaix-born, republican-inclined author who, making his name with *Les derniers bretons* (1836) and subsequently settling in Paris, achieved European fame through a plethora of writings of various genres, notably the best-selling *Un philosophe sous les toits* (1850). Marie's vivacious mother edited a *Journal des femmes* and wrote stories for children under the name Nanine Souvestre.

The sole surviving glimpse of Marie Souvestre's childhood and early life is a visit paid by father and fourteen-year-old daughter to his friend the historian Jules Michelet early in February 1850. At some stage she learned German and English, translating into French *Deux jeunes femmes* (1858) by Mme Carlen from the former and *Paul Ferroll* (1859), Caroline Clive's best-seller, from the latter.

In 1864, with Caroline Adelaïde Dussaut (1832–1887), a qualified teacher, Souvestre opened a pioneering girls' boarding-school, Les Ruches, at Avon, Fontainebleau, at which forty or so girls from well-to-do non-French families received, in French, a liberal, secular, intellectual, and social education of high quality. The venture was supported by Victor Duruy, the education minister of the day, who foresaw its contribution to the global diffusion of French culture. Caroline Dussaut brought to the enterprise her professional expertise, Marie Souvestre her money, social flair, and acute intellect and the cultural contacts inherited from her father. The two women, who seem previously to have spent some time together in Germany, had been lovers at least since 1862, the fragile Caroline constantly cosseted by her more forceful younger partner. Of the two, Marie was also to reveal herself as by far the more demanding and charismatic teacher.

To learn at Les Ruches came Anna (Bamie) Roosevelt, the favourite sister and later adviser of Theodore Roosevelt; Natalie Clifford Barney; Helen Vacaresco, the Romanian poet; Dorothy Strachey, future author of *Olivia*; Beatrice Chamberlain, daughter of Joseph and half-sister of Neville; and the daughters of Stuart Rendel, Charles Kegan Paul, T. H. S. Escott, and Richard Potter—though Beatrice Potter (later Webb), then antipathetic to the Frenchwoman's energetic atheism, declined to follow her sister Rosy. John Morley's sister briefly taught at the school. All fell under the intellectual spell of Marie Souvestre, an excitingly incisive and intuitive teacher of history, politics, and literature and a riveting reader of French poetry.

The English intake to the school stemmed largely from the recruiting talents of, on the one hand, Lady Jane Strachey, and, on the other, Frederic Harrison. Jane Strachey, wintering in Florence in 1870–71, made the acquaintance there of Marie Souvestre, who had closed her school owing to the Prussian advance and, with Caroline, accompanied her friends, the elderly Michelet and his wife, into temporary Italian exile. Ardent friendship and the eventual attendance of Jane's daughters, Elinor and Dorothy, at Les Ruches, ensued. *Olivia* (1949) by Dorothy Bussy (*née* Strachey) is a scarcely fictionalized account of schoolgirl life in Fontainebleau and a posthumous homage from pupil to teacher. With Marie, Dorothy lost her heart and found her mind.

The positivist Harrison had known Souvestre, perhaps through the Paris positivists or the Michelet connection, also since the early 1870s. They met at intervals—she kept him abreast of French politics—and corresponded. He rented holiday quarters at Les Ruches for the summer of 1877, when she introduced him to Fontainebleau society and took him to see the painter Millet at work in Barbizon.

Professional and emotional jealousies between the two teacher-partners, exacerbated by Dussaut's increasing neurotic invalidism, eventually led Marie to abandon Les Ruches to her and, with the support of Lady Jane Strachey and her other English friends, to open, in 1884, Allenswood, a similarly 'French' international girls' boarding-school, in a grand house in Albert Road, Wimbledon Park, Surrey—'a very highly esteemed school for girls at high, breezy Wimbledon', Henry James wrote to his brother in 1900 (L. Edel, *Henry James: the Master*, 1972, 83–4). Finance (the fees by 1904 were £54 7*s.* 0*d.* a term) and administration were run by the devoted Paolina Samaïa, who had followed Marie from Les Ruches—and who perhaps supplanted Caroline.

Isabel Fry, Helen Gifford, and Dorothy Bussy taught at Allenswood, as did Lloyd George's lover, later his secretary and eventual wife, Frances Stevenson. Among the pupils were Pernel and Marjorie Strachey, Marjorie North (Mack) (whose *The Educated Pin* of 1944 contains a long account of Souvestre at Allenswood), Helen Gifford, Hester Ritchie, Olive Harrison, Megan Lloyd George, and Marie's most famous favourite, Eleanor Roosevelt. Roosevelt's autobiography *This is my Story* lengthily describes her debt to and affection for the inspirational teacher, who took her travelling in Europe, and with whom she corresponded to the last—and from whom, in addition, she may have indirectly learned her lesbian proclivities. She described Marie in her sixties: 'beautiful, with clear-cut, strong features, a very strong face and broad forehead … her eyes looked through you and she always knew more than she was told' (Roosevelt, 58). The young Lytton Strachey, too, who met her in the role of family friend, was in part her intellectual creature: a number of his views—on religion, education, and French literature—were coloured by her ideas. This is particularly true of his receptivity to the dramatic poetry of Racine—Marie's readings were renowned—of whom he was the first authentically insightful English critic in the modern sense. Marie thus stands at the source of modern English Racine criticism.

In London, Souvestre became intimate, as well as with the Harrisons and Stracheys, with Leslie Stephen, the Morleys, the Chamberlains, Mrs J. R. Green, and a wider circle of radicals and freethinkers, including the young Beatrice Webb. A convinced humanist, candidly pro-Boer, anti-imperialist, and anti-clerical—though she also frequented and liked the Mandell Creightons—she impressed with her intellect and charmed with her personality.

Souvestre died, unmarried, aged sixty-nine, of liver cancer, at Allenswood School on 30 March 1905, having named Paolina Samaïa her executor, and was buried, alongside her parents, in the Père Lachaise cemetery, Paris, on 5 April, beside Balzac and close, as she had been in life, to Michelet. Funeral orations were given by her friends Pastor Charles Wagner and Alexandre Ribot, a former *président du conseil*. 'A brilliant woman', wrote Webb in her diary for 31 March, 'handsome, warm-hearted—the very soul of veracity—and keen-witted; she must have counted for much in the lives of many women coming from the best of the governing class in England, America, France and Germany' (Webb, *Diary*, 2.340–41). Allenswood School continued, under Mlle Samaïa, then different proprietor-heads, at least until 1948. D. A. STEEL

Sources B. W. Cook, *Eleanor Roosevelt*, 1 (1993) • J. Michelet, *Journal* (Paris, 1962) • E. Roosevelt, *This is my story* (1937) • J. P. Lash, *Love, Eleanor: Eleanor Roosevelt and her friends* (1982) • M. Mack, *The educated pin* (1944) • Olivia [D. Bussy], *Olivia* (1949) • M. Holroyd, *Lytton Strachey: a new biography* (1994) • *The diary of Beatrice Webb*, ed. N. MacKenzie and J. MacKenzie, 4 vols. (1982–5), vol. 2 • B. Webb, *My apprenticeship* (1926) • M. S. Vogeler, *Frederic Harrison: the vocations of a positivist* (1984) • F. Harrison, *Autobiographical memoirs*, 2 (1911) • E. B. Harrison, 'In memoriam Marie Souvestre', *Positivist Review*, 13 (1905), 115–16 • F. L. Lloyd George, *The years that are past* (1967) • N. Clifford Barney, *Souvenirs indiscrets* (1960) • B. Webb, *Our partnership* (1948) • d. cert. • *CGPLA Eng. & Wales* (1905) • Marquis de Granges de Surgères, *Deux incidents de la vie littéraire d'Émile Souvestre* (Nantes, 1911) • d. cert. [C. A. Dussaut] • Archives départementales de Seine-et-Marne, France • Merton Local Studies Centre, London • interment register, Père Lachaise cemetery administrative archives, 16 rue du Repos, 75020 Paris • b. cert.

Archives Franklin D. Roosevelt Library, New York, Eleanor Roosevelt MSS • Harvard U., Houghton L., Joe Lash MSS

Likenesses photograph, repro. in Cook, *Eleanor Roosevelt*, 140

Wealth at death £6536 19*s*. 2*d*.: administration, 30 June 1905, *CGPLA Eng. & Wales*

Sowerbutts, William Edmund [Bill] (**1911–1990**), nurseryman and broadcaster, was born on 4 January 1911 at Moss Side Nurseries, Ashton under Lyne, Lancashire, the son of John Sowerbutts, nurseryman and seedsman, and his wife, Catherine, *née* Shuttleworth. Always known as Bill, he was born into a market gardening family and at an early age followed his father in growing vegetables on the rich peaty soil of the family nursery at Ashton under Lyne. He was also responsible for the family's numerous chickens. As a young man he fostered an ambition to be a journalist. This was curtailed, however, by the early death of his father, and so, from the age of sixteen he had to work both on the nursery and on the family stalls where the produce was sold at Oldham, Ashton, and Rochdale markets. On 24 April 1934 he married a local girl, Dorothy (Doris) Postle (*b*. 1911/12), a designer, and daughter of Ernest Postle, a cashier. They had one son. Sowerbutts soon became a successful businessman. He later delighted in telling of how his fortunes took an upward turn once it was pointed out to him that by selling his vegetables in heavier paper bags his profit margins would increase.

Sowerbutts would have remained unknown outside his local circle were it not for a BBC radio producer named Robert Stead. He had the idea of capitalizing on the popularity of vegetable growing after the end of the Second World War and the government's wartime dig for victory campaign, which had encouraged the home growing of produce. Stead began a programme in which gardeners put questions to a panel of experts, recordings taking place with gardening societies, women's institutes, and similar groups. The programme was called *How does your Garden Grow*, and the first recording took place at the Broad Oak Hotel, Ashton under Lyne, near Sowerbutts's home. He was one of a panel of four including a fellow Lancastrian, Fred Loads, and with Stead himself as chairman. It was broadcast on the north and Northern Ireland Home Service of the BBC on the evening of Wednesday 9 April 1947. The programme ran until 1951 when the four became three with the Scot, Dr Alan Gemmell, joining Sowerbutts and Loads. At the same time it moved to Sunday at 2 p.m. and was retitled *Gardeners' Question Time*. It was first broadcast nationally on 29 September 1957. Sowerbutts and his colleagues soon became a national institution and, especially in the years before widespread television, the programme became obligatory listening for the nation's gardeners. Despite the deep practical knowledge of Sowerbutts and Loads especially, much of the appeal lay in the interplay between three strong and sometimes abrasive characters with fine regional voices.

William Edmund Sowerbutts (1911–1990), by unknown photographer

Disagreements between Sowerbutts and Gemmell became legendary.

Sowerbutts was a tall man with a long lugubrious face, rarely smiling and instantly recognizable, even from behind, by his enormous ears. He was seldom without his pipe. He had a very dry Lancastrian sense of humour which was displayed to good effect in the stories that *Gardeners' Question Time* panel members were called on to tell before each programme recording in order to warm up the audience. But he was always aware of his monetary worth and once, when a new panel member was reminded by the producer at the last minute that he would need a story, Bill instantly offered (only slightly tongue in cheek) to sell him one.

Sowerbutts appeared occasionally on the BBC regional television programme *Gardeners' Direct Line*, but radio was his real medium. He was the last of the three to retire from *Gardeners' Question Time*, making his last broadcast as a panel member at Horsforth, Leeds, on 4 September 1983. At a press reception to mark his retirement he was asked which, of all the flowers he had ever grown, was his favourite. Without hesitation he replied 'The cauliflower; it's the only one that makes you any money'. His final appearance came over five years later when he attended a programme recording at Hayfield in Derbyshire as a member of the audience and a questioner asked about growing loofahs, the vegetable sponge. This was a plant that had always fascinated Sowerbutts and he was called on by the chairman to answer the question from the floor.

Latterly, Sowerbutt's 2½ acre garden was made available as a local nature reserve and he spent much time in his final years gardening in his heated greenhouses. His business had by then expanded to include florists' shops which he ran in conjunction with his son Peter. Retirement allowed him more time for two of his other passions, golf and music. He was a talented pianist and would sometimes entertain his fellow panel members if there was a piano in the village hall where a programme recording was to take place. He died at Ashton under Lyne on 28 May 1990. He was survived by his wife and son.

STEFAN BUCZACKI

Sources *The Times* (30 May 1990) • 'Bill Sowerbutts, British gardening expert and broadcaster', *Annual Obituary* (1990), 326–8 • b. cert. • m. cert. • personal knowledge (2004) • *CGPLA Eng. & Wales* (1990)

Archives SOUND BBC Sound Archives, selected recordings of *Gardeners' question time*

Likenesses photograph, News International Syndication, London [*see illus.*]

Wealth at death £405,937: probate, 20 Oct 1990, *CGPLA Eng. & Wales*

Sowerby, George Brettingham, the first (1788–1854), conchologist and natural history dealer, was born at Lambeth, London, on 12 May 1788, the second son among the nine children of James *Sowerby (1757–1822), botanical artist and natural history periodical publisher, and his wife, Anne de Carle (1764–1815). His elder brother was James De Carle *Sowerby (1787–1871). The first G. B. Sowerby is thought to have been educated at home by private tutors, but, as with all the children, he was soon caught up in the production and publication of the Sowerby natural history works, contributing descriptions to the *Mineral Conchology* (1812–22).

On 16 May 1811 G. B. Sowerby the first married Elizabeth Meredith. The couple had nine children, including George Brettingham Sowerby the second and Henry Sowerby [*see below*]. It seems likely that an estrangement from his father at about this time, thought by some to be due to business matters (Sowerby, *Saga*, 43; Macdonald, 395) was, instead, due to his marriage. Whatever the cause, the estrangement led to G. B. Sowerby establishing himself as a dealer in natural history objects at King Street, Covent Garden. He was elected a fellow of the Linnean Society in 1811. An early interest in entomology provided his first paper (1812) but, on being persuaded that the study was cruel, he turned to other subjects. On his father's death in 1822 he became responsible for completing *The Genera of Recent and Fossil Shells* (1820–22).

The *Catalogue of the Shells in the … Tankerville Collection* (1825) influenced the illustration and nomenclature of conchology and helped to establish the first G. B. Sowerby's reputation in that field. His acquisition of the Tankerville collection in the 1820s, followed by the purchase of that of George Humphreys, caused him considerable financial embarrassment when the removal of import duty reduced the resale value of that stock. In a letter to Royer, in Paris, he wrote:

> I am at this moment in the midst of two enormous collections of Shells, Minerals and Fossils that I have purchased and actually know not which way to turn myself. I believe I shall go distracted unless I can find some person to assist me, or dispose of the whole concern together. (12 Oct 1824, G. B. Sowerby MS 208)

These transactions marked the first G. B. Sowerby's entrance into the commercial market, which caused considerable anxiety to other dealers and later led to rivalry over the quality of shells that were used for illustrations.

Correspondence from 1822–46 indicates the complexity of his dealings in shells, minerals, and fossils, as well as his role as a publisher and/or agent for other European dealers and publishers. His wide knowledge and good reputation meant that his opinion was frequently sought in making valuations. Between 1825 and 1830 he became involved with the *Zoological Journal*, a periodical dealing with new and exotic discoveries produced by a group of zoologists anxious to establish their own society, for which he wrote a succession of short papers on Mollusca. Further contributions were made to its successor, once the Zoological Society had been formed, and to other natural history periodicals.

In the 1830s, collaborating with his brothers, Sowerby tried numerous subscription schemes to raise finance (including an attempt to dispose of the Yorkshire meteorite in 1835) for a 'Sowerby Museum'. He also founded the *Malacological and Conchological Magazine* and financed it for twelve months until it failed through lack of support. His own collection of natural history objects and stock of shells had to be sold by Thomas and Stevens on 27 May 1833.

Through his conchological reputation, Sowerby was involved in the description and illustration of recent and fossil molluscs collected on expeditions made during the late 1830s and 1840s (Beechey, 1839; Darwin, 1844; Strzelecki, 1845; and Adams, 1850). In particular he collaborated with Hugh Cuming in describing and marketing extensive collections from South America, but it was later realized that many 'new species' were created solely as commercial opportunities.

In a sales leaflet (*c*.1841) 'GBS' observed that his exertions for many years had been devoted to advance natural history, but that owing to ill health and with a numerous family, he now sought assistance from the 'Friends of science' in order to continue. His health had been weakened by an inflammation of the lungs before 1811 and this condition was aggravated by the stress of a dealer's life. He died on 26 July 1854 at Hanley Road, Hornsey, London. Shortly before his own death, Gideon Mantell wrote, in his last journal entry (27 October 1852): 'Called on poor Mr. G. Sowerby, a decrepit and paralytic old man! and I remember my first interview with him at his father's when he was a laughing healthy youth—life is a sad enigma' (G. Mantell, diary, Lewes, Sussex Archaeological Society).

The first G. B. Sowerby's oldest son, **George Brettingham Sowerby the second** (1812–1884), conchologist and artist, was born in Lambeth on 25 March 1812. He was probably educated at Harrow School and then assisted his father with publications and the natural history business. On 25 December 1835 he married Margaret Hitchen, the daughter of the Revd Thomas Hitchen.

He collaborated with his father in the production of *The Conchological Illustrations* (1841), a work that was initially intended to be a companion volume of coloured figures to a 'descriptive catalogue' of hitherto unfigured shells described by J. E. Gray. He also published other significant conchological works with various members of the Sowerby family: *The Conchological Manual* (1839), *Thesaurus conchyliorum* (1848–87), *Popular British Conchology* (1854), and *Illustrated Index of British Shells* (1859). He was persuaded to produce *The Popular History of the Aquarium* (1857) by Lovell Reeve, but not having the necessary knowledge he was criticized for incorporating material published by other authors and labelled as 'one of the greatest proficients in the art of "scissors and paste"' (*Annals and Magazine of Natural History*, 20, 1857, 139).

The second G. B. Sowerby is renowned for the illustrations he produced for the works of other specialists. A volume of drawings, *Palaeontology of the Vicinity of Cheltenham* (*c*.1844), showing fossils in the collection of Charles Fowler, suggests that he ought to be regarded as the most artistically talented of the Sowerbys. Crosse in a review (Crosse, 260) commented that he was a mediocre naturalist, a shocking Latinist, but an excellent draughtsman and concluded 'Faites des planches, faites des planches … mais pour l'amour de Dieu ne décriver point de coquille!' ('Make plates, make plates, … but for the love of God don't describe any shells!'). Sowerby died at Wood Green on 26 July 1884.

Henry Sowerby (1825–1891), librarian and draughtsman, the second son of G. B. Sowerby the first, was born in Kensington on 28 March 1825. He was educated at Bickerdike's School, Kentish Town, and then at University College, London. Between 1843 and 1853 he served part-time as assistant librarian to the Linnean Society. Later his carelessness as sub-curator was thought to have been partly responsible for 'serious injury' to the collection of shells (Gage, 128). During that period he published his only work *Popular Mineralogy* (1850) as one of Reeve's popular handbooks. In his preface, Henry Sowerby claimed that the plates were the first illustrations of minerals to be produced by lithography. He married Annie Faulkner in April 1847 and they had two children. In 1854 he went to Australia where he became a draughtsman at Melbourne University. After teaching drawing in various state schools he became occupied in gold mining for the last twenty years of his life. He died on 15 September 1891 in Doylesford, Victoria.

R. J. CLEEVELY

Sources R. J. Cleevely, 'A provisional bibliography of natural history works by the Sowerby family', *Journal of the Society of the Bibliography of Natural History*, 6 (1971–4), 482–559 • R. J. Cleevely, 'Some "malacological pioneers" and their links with the transition of shell-collecting to conchology during the first half of the nineteenth century', *Archives of Natural History*, 22 (1995), 385–418 • A. De C. Sowerby and others, *The Sowerby saga: being a brief account of the origin and genealogy of the Sowerby family* (1952) • H. Crosse, 'Variéties: ne sutur ultra crepidam!', *Journal de Conchyliologie*, 18 (1870), 251–60 • J. B. Macdonald, 'The Sowerby collection in the British Museum (Natural History): a brief description of its holdings and a history of its acquisition, 1821–1971', *Journal of the Society of the Bibliography of Natural History*, 6 (1971–4), 380–401 • S. P. Dance, *Shell collecting: an illustrated history* (1966) • S. P. Dance, *A history of shell collecting*, rev. edn (1986), pl. 27 • A. T. Gage, *A history of the Linnean Society of London* (1938) • C. Matheson, 'George Brettingham Sowerby the First and his correspondents [pts I–II]', *Journal of the Society of the Bibliography of Natural History*, 4 (1962–8), 214–25, 253–66 • C. D. Sherborn, 'On "the conchological illustrations" by George Brettingham Sowerby, jun., London, 1832–41', *Proceedings of the Malacological Society*, 8 (1909), 331–2 • J. F. Sowerby, *List of exhibits: Sowerby exhibition at the Royal Botanic Gardens, Regent's Park, London, December 5th and 6th 1908* (1908) • *GM*, 2nd ser., 42 (1854), 406 • *Proceedings of the Linnean Society of London*, 2 (1848–55), 415–16 • H. Crosse and P. Fischer, *Journal de Conchyliologie*, 3rd ser., 25 (1885),

80 • NMG Wales, G. B. Sowerby MSS, nos. 207–8 • *CGPLA Eng. & Wales* (1884) [George Brettingham Sowerby the second] • *IGI* [George Brettingham Sowerby the second]

Archives NMG Wales | Institute of Geological Sciences, Keyworth • Linn. Soc. • NHM

Likenesses photograph, *c*.1870 (George Brettingham Sowerby the second), University of Amsterdam, Westerman album; repro. in Dance, *History of shell collecting*, pl. 27 • photograph, NHM

Wealth at death £266—George Brettingham Sowerby the second: probate, 6 Sept 1884, *CGPLA Eng. & Wales*

Sowerby, George Brettingham, the second (1812–1884). *See under* Sowerby, George Brettingham, the first (1788–1854).

Sowerby, Henry (1825–1891). *See under* Sowerby, George Brettingham, the first (1788–1854).

Sowerby, James (1757–1822), natural history artist, publisher, and collector, was born on 21 March 1757, at 2 Bolt-in-Tun Passage, Fleet Street, London, the son of John Sowerby (1719–1766), a lapidary, and his wife, Arabella Goodreed (1725–1782). He was educated at a day school, where he often made models during his lessons that he could sell. When he was fourteen friends provided £100 to indenture him to Richard Wright, the marine painter, who following a paralytic stroke referred him to a Mr (William?) Hodges. Eventually, despite his diffidence in submitting a work to gain admittance, he became a student at the Royal Academy on 1 December 1777.

Initially Sowerby supported himself by teaching drawing or by painting portraits and miniatures, but he disliked the inaccuracy involved in pleasing his subjects and decided to try landscape painting. The resulting sketches persuaded William Curtis to employ him as a botanical illustrator for his publications including the *Flora Londinensis* (1783–8) and, in return, to instruct him in botany. Sowerby illustrated many of the plants featured in the *Botanical Magazine*. After observing the processes of etching and engraving, he acquired sufficient knowledge to undertake his own publications and began with the abortive *Flora luxurians* (1789), which was followed by *An Easy Introduction to Drawing Flowers According to Nature* (1788), and its second edition, *A Botanical Drawing Book* (1791). When working for William Curtis, he had completed illustrations for several other authors including L'Heritier (1784, 1787, 1788) and Withering (1785).

While a student Sowerby visited the Norwich home of his friend Robert de Carle, and met Anne de Carle (1764–1815), the subject of a portrait he had once drawn solely from her brother's description. At Norwich, he was introduced to several influential botanists and zoologists, including James Edward Smith and Dawson Turner. Through these connections and by soliciting drawing commissions from members of the nobility attracted to natural history pursuits, he was able to increase his income. Ultimately he co-operated with Smith to produce *English Botany* (1790–1814)—the first extensive description of the British flora, which owing to Smith's caution over admitting authorship of this work, became known as 'Sowerby's Botany'. This enterprise ended his association with Curtis. Its success encouraged him to publish a companion work, *Coloured Figures of English Fungi* (1797–1815), for which he was solely responsible, and to produce a series of models of British fungi for display. After becoming a member of the Linnean Society in 1789 (made fellow in 1793), he became involved with the work of Sir Joseph Banks.

James Sowerby (1757–1822), by J. C. Edwards (after Thomas Heaphy, 1816)

In order to obtain material for description in *English Botany*, Sowerby requested botanists throughout the country to submit suitable specimens. By appealing to their vanity, or willingness to serve science, he established the network of naturalists that enabled his family to produce a succession of natural history publications. Dawson Turner (1755–1858), an early contributor, joined him on a botanical tour of Cornwall in 1799—one of the few occasions that Sowerby carried out fieldwork and did not use pressure of work as an excuse to hide a dislike of travelling.

Following his marriage to Anne de Carle on 9 February 1786, which produced nine children, among them James De Carle *Sowerby and George Brettingham *Sowerby the first, and the gift of a house in Lambeth by his father-in-law, Robert Brettingham de Carle, Sowerby started to form his own museum and planned to achieve a complete collection of British natural history. Seeking further publishing outlets, he produced the *British Miscellany* (1804–6), a work that featured new and rare animal, bird, and insect subjects, many from his own specimens. He then produced a work on crystallography (1805) and, when rheumatism prevented him engraving for a while, published *A New Elucidation of Colours …* (1809). The acquisition and exploitation of the Yorkshire meteorite in 1804 demonstrates his business acumen, persistence, and resourcefulness, while the complete disregard for his fungi drawings when adapting them to unsuitable copper plates indicates his very thrifty nature. The fashion for geology led to the part publications of *British Mineralogy* (1802–17), *Exotic Mineralogy* (1811–20) and to his commencing *The Mineral Conchology of Great Britain* (1812–46). In 1808, he became a fellow of the Geological Society, formed the previous year.

In both his publications and correspondence, Sowerby assisted and encouraged naturalists, or advised uninformed collectors of minerals, fossils, plants, birds, and insects; many maintained that they were completely dependent upon him for such information. Specimens were sent for identification, description, and illustration, or as additions to his museum, and in return he sent duplicate specimens or parts of his various publications. He was often used as a clearing house by distant correspondents or asked to conduct other errands. Fully occupied, he wrote 'as one letter &c. … so frequently comes upon another … my avocation will not allow me to answer all' and claimed 'I have been such a recluse that I scarcely know what is doing out of doors!' (Wellington, NZ, Mantell Archive, ATL MS 83, folder 90). The publications became irregular or incomplete, or had errors, which caused widespread criticism and dissatisfaction among subscribers. Apart from the *Genera of Recent and Fossil Shells* (1820–34), no attempt was made to arrange the contents of his works systematically, but in providing the first scientific description, name, and illustration for many British taxa, they established a framework for several branches of natural history as well as encouraging methodical collection. Sowerby, always fully involved in some aspect of illustration, publication, or communication, regarded pursuits such as the playing of musical instruments, or entertainment, as 'a loss of time' (Simpkins, 'Biographical sketch', 409).

After the death of his wife in September 1815 Sowerby concentrated on increasing his collections but still directed the various members of the family in the continuation of the serial publications. The following year, he published the first part of Smith's *Strata Identified by Organized Fossils* (1816–17), a project which had been in hand since 1808. In December 1820 he married the widow of Admiral Reynolds, Maria Catherine, who then upset the rest of the family by trying to interfere with their established publishing procedures.

In his portrait, James Sowerby appears to be small and slight; for most of his life he enjoyed good health, but in the last few years he suffered from the urinary problems commonly experienced in old age and after an illness of some four months, died at his home, 2 Mead Place, Lambeth, on 25 October 1882. Sowerby had a considerable influence on the development of natural history. Although he did not achieve the goal of acquiring a complete collection of the British flora and fauna, he made a substantial contribution to its scientific description. *Sowerbaea*, an Australian genus known as the 'vanilla lily', was named by J. E. Smith in Sowerby's honour, and the cetacean *Mesoplodon bidens*, first described in the *British Miscellany*, is still commonly known as 'Sowerby's whale'.

R. J. CLEEVELY

Sources D. M. Simpkins, 'Biographical sketch of James Sowerby, written by his son James De Carle Sowerby, 1825', *Journal of the Society of the Bibliography of Natural History*, 6 (1971–4), 402–15 • R. J. Cleevely, 'A provisional bibliography of natural history works by the Sowerby family', *Journal of the Society of the Bibliography of Natural History*, 6 (1971–4), 482–559 • R. J. Cleevely, 'The Sowerbys, the *Mineral conchology*, and their fossil collection', *Journal of the Society of the Bibliography of Natural History*, 6 (1971–4), 418–81 • R. J. Cleevely, 'The Sowerbys and their publications in the light of the manuscript material in the British Museum (Natural History)', *Journal of the Society of the Bibliography of Natural History*, 7 (1974–6), 343–68 • A. De C. Sowerby and others, *The Sowerby saga: being a brief account of the origin and genealogy of the Sowerby family* (1952) • J. Collins, ed., *Supplementa Sowerbiana, or, A catalogue of books and manuscripts written or illustrated by members of the Sowerby family* (1969) [suppl. to Quaritch's catalogue no. 894] • J. M. Eyles, 'Sowerby, James', *DSB* • D. M. Simpkins, 'Childhood reminiscences of James Sowerby', *Journal of the Society of the Bibliography of Natural History*, 6 (1971–4), 416–17 • J. F. Sowerby, *List of exhibits: Sowerby exhibition at the Royal Botanic Gardens, Regent's Park, London, December 5th and 6th 1908* (1908) • K. van W. Palmer, 'Who were the Sowerbys?', *Hawaiian Shell News*, 14/1 (1965), 4–5; 14/2 (1965), 5; 14/3 (1966), 7; repr. in *Sterkiana*, 23 (1966), 1–6 • Desmond, *Botanists* • *GM*, 1st ser., 92/2 (1822), 568 • *Cottage Gardener*, 5 (1850–51), 29 • B. Henrey, *British botanical and horticultural literature before 1800*, 2 (1975), 145–8

Archives Carnegie Mellon University, Pittsburgh, Hunt Institute for Botantical Documentation • Institute of Geological Sciences, Keyworth, Nottinghamshire • Linn. Soc. • NHM • NL Scot. • NMG Wales • RGS • RS • Trinity Cam. • University of Bristol Library | Linn. Soc., letters to Sir James Smith; corresp. with Sir James Smith • NL NZ, Turnbull L., corresp. with G. A. Mantell • NL Wales, letters to Hugh Davies • U. Leeds, Brotherton L., letters to James Dalton • U. Oxf., department of plant sciences, Sherard MSS • Ulster Museum, Belfast, corresp. with John Templeton • Wiltshire Archaeological and Natural History Society, Devizes, letters to William Cunnington

Likenesses portrait, *c*.1822 (after watercolour by T. Heaphy, 1816), repro. in J. De C. Sowerby, 'Preface to general indexes', *Mineral Conchology*, 6/105 (1 Aug 1835), frontispiece • J. C. Edwards, engraving (after T. Heaphy, 1816), NPG [*see illus.*] • J. Sowerby, self-portrait (with brother Charles and sister Arabella), priv. coll.; repro. in *British paintings 1500–1850* (1985) [sale catalogue, Sotheby's, 20 Nov 1985, lot 48] • D. Turner, etching (after T. Heaphy), BM, NPG

Sowerby, James De Carle (1787–1871), naturalist and artist, was born in London on 5 June 1787, the eldest of the nine children of James *Sowerby (1757–1822), botanical artist, and his wife, Anne de Carle (1764–1815). George Brettingham *Sowerby was his younger brother. He was educated at home by private tutors, but in science was largely self-taught with the help of his father's scientist contacts. He was attracted to chemistry and mineralogy and conducted his own analytical experiments encouraged by Faraday, Humphry Davy (under whom he studied with Faraday), and Wollaston, in whose house he was a welcome visitor. He is said independently to have proposed the classification of minerals according to their chemical composition and also to have supplied the analyses of many minerals described in his father's mineralogical works. Accompanying his father on field excursions around London, he also acquired a knowledge of natural history.

James De Carle Sowerby soon became involved in his family's publications. In his teens he was sent to organize and utilize the collections of other naturalists and to teach drawing and etching to their families. His earliest published illustrations appeared in Dawson Turner's *Muscologiae Hibernicae spicilegium* (1804), and he described many of the fossils illustrated in the *Mineral Conchology* (1812–46). On 25 September 1813 he married Mary Edwards (1786–1852); all their eight children were born while the family lived in Lambeth.

Writing to Dawson Turner, James De Carle Sowerby explained the progression of the family's publications:

> we go on in the old plodding way, the vegetables of our country being exhausted, we must live upon the rocks, with a few shells for a treat now and then, or any thing else that comes in our way. (J. de C. Sowerby to D. Turner, 23 Feb 1816, Dawson Turner MSS)

James De Carle Sowerby inherited the family business with his brother Charles Edward on their father's death in 1822, and the two went into partnership. Although solely responsible for *Mineral Conchology*, Sowerby assisted Charles with the other periodicals until the partnership was dissolved in 1831. Even later he was to supply many plates and some text for the supplement to *English Botany* (1831–49). However, the majority of Sowerby's time was soon devoted to describing and illustrating material for leading geologists, including Sedgwick, Murchison, Buckland, and Fitton, who employed him to deal with their fossils. Between the 1820s and the 1860s he also produced illustrations for monographs, books, and papers on many other subjects, ranging from anatomical plates in veterinary journals to the engravings of turtles in Bell's *Monograph of the Testudinata* (1836–41). A few descriptive papers in the *Zoological Journal* and others, or notes in periodicals, were all that he published under his own name.

In 1838, with his cousin Phillip Barnes, James De Carle Sowerby founded the Royal Botanic Gardens at Regent's Park, becoming its first secretary, a post he held until retirement in 1869. However, the garden, intended to be a public establishment for the general study of the vegetable kingdom, became merely a stage for London's fashionable society and earned the name 'Royal Botanical Humbug' from the *Gardeners' Gazette*. In 1846 Sowerby was appointed librarian and curator of the Geological Society, on 'partial duty' to enable him to retain his post at Regent's Park. He resigned in 1848 when the salary was limited to £50. He became a fellow of the Linnean Society in 1823 and was a founder member of the Zoological Society in 1826. The Geological Society awarded him the Wollaston fund in 1840.

A generous nature and financial needs led to James De Carle Sowerby's undertaking too many commitments. His work at the Botanical Society led to considerable delay to every publication with which he was involved. Lindley, Bell, and Darwin were among those who suffered, with the last complaining 'I did not know how dreadfully dilatory he was when I picked him out as most capable of doing the work' (Burkhardt and Smith, 367). Darwin eventually turned to his nephew G. B. Sowerby the second to complete the task. The irregularity of the Sowerbys' *Mineral Conchology* was a factor that led to the formation of the Palaeontographical Society in 1847, but such was Sowerby's expertise that the society often found itself employing him to illustrate and produce engravings for its monographs, in spite of his reputation.

In 1861 James De Carle Sowerby sold the Sowerby collection to the British Museum. He stopped working at the Royal Botanic Gardens in 1867 through ill health, declaring 'I feel the effects of age and am growing very feeble' (J. De C. Sowerby, letter, 27 Dec 1867, Sowerby archive, London, Natural History Museum). He retired officially in 1869 and died on 26 August 1871 at his home, 18 St George's Road, Kilburn.

James De Carle Sowerby was arguably the most prolific and accomplished member of the Sowerby family, and although responsible for the description of many taxa, his main contribution to natural history had been 'the portraits of natural objects he has left behind him … delineated faithfully from … acquaintance with their form and structure' (W. Sowerby, cited in Simpkins, 393), 'which no pencil or burin, but those of a scientific artist could possibly accomplish' (Buckland). An obituarist described him as: 'Gentle, earnest, conscientious, ever ready to help others out of his wealth of knowledge, Mr Sowerby's name will be remembered with affection and reverence by all who knew him. His was a truly blameless and useful life' (*Gardeners' Chronicle*). R. J. CLEEVELY

Sources A. De C. Sowerby and others, *The Sowerby saga: being a brief account of the origin and genealogy of the Sowerby family* (1952) · D. M. Simpkins, 'Biographical sketch of James Sowerby, written by his son James De Carle Sowerby, 1825', *Journal of the Society of the Bibliography of Natural History*, 6 (1971–4), 402–15 · R. J. Cleevely, 'A provisional bibliography of natural history works by the Sowerby family', *Journal of the Society of the Bibliography of Natural History*, 6 (1971–4), 482–559 · R. J. Cleevely, 'The Sowerbys, the *Mineral conchology*, and their fossil collection', *Journal of the Society of the Bibliography of Natural History*, 6 (1971–4), 418–81 · W. Buckland, presidential award of the Wollaston fund to Mr James de Carle Sowerby, *Proceedings of the Geological Society of London*, 3 (1838–42), 208–9 · *The correspondence of Charles Darwin*, ed. F. Burkhardt and S. Smith, 4 (1988) · J. De C. Sowerby, letter, *Magazine of Natural History*, new ser., 3 (1839), 418–20 · *Gardeners' Chronicle* (30 Sept 1872), 1260 · *The Lancet* (23 Sept 1871), 451–2 · J. Prestwich, presidential address, *Quarterly Journal of the Geological Society*, 28 (1872), xlv · G. Meynell, 'The Royal Botanic Society's garden, Regent's Park', *London Journal*, 6 (1980), 135–46 · G. Meynell, 'Kew and the royal gardens committee of 1838', *Archives of Natural History*, 10 (1981–2), 469–77 · R. J. Cleevely, 'The Sowerbys and their publications in the light of the manuscript material in the British Museum (Natural History)', *Journal of the Society of the Bibliography of Natural History*, 7 (1974–6), 343–68 · 'Royal Botanic Society's gardens, Regent's Park', *Gardeners' Magazine* (11 Aug 1888), 494–5 · H. B. Woodward, *The history of the Geological Society of London* (1907), 83–4 · Trinity Cam., Dawson Turner MSS · NMG Wales, G. B. Sowerby MSS

Archives American Philosophical Society Library, Philadelphia · Bodl. Oxf. · Bristol City Museum · Bristol University · Institute of Geological Sciences, Nottingham · Linn. Soc. · NHM · priv. coll. ·

RBG Kew · RS | Bodl. Oxf., letters to Sir James Smith · GS Lond., letters to Roderick Impey Murchison · NMG Wales, G. B. Sowerby MSS · Trinity Cam., Dawson Turner MSS · W. Sussex RO, Gordon-Lennox MSS
Likenesses photograph, c.1870, Linn. Soc.; repro. in *Gardeners' Magazine*, 494 · photograph (in old age), repro. in H. B. Woodward, *History of geology* (1911), 53 · photograph, NHM
Wealth at death under £1500: probate, 2 Dec 1871, *CGPLA Eng. & Wales*

Sowerby, John Edward (1825–1870), artist and publisher, was born in Lambeth on 17 January 1825, the eldest son of the botanist and publisher Charles Edward Sowerby (1795–1842) and his wife, Judith Ainsley. A grandson of James *Sowerby (1757–1822), the natural history artist and publisher of *English Botany*, J. E. Sowerby inherited the family talent for botanical drawing.

Few details of J. E. Sowerby's early life and education are available, but it would appear that, like the children of each generation of that family, he was soon involved in the preparation of illustrations for its publications. The plates he produced at the age of sixteen for his father's *Illustrated Catalogue of British Plants* (1841) were his first signed work. On 10 February 1853 he married Elizabeth Dewhurst, the daughter of Roger Dewhurst of Preston, Lancashire.

J. E. Sowerby collaborated with the botanist Charles Johnson (1791–1880) in 1855–7, and his son Charles Pierpoint Johnson (*d.* 1893) from 1857 to 1862, to provide the illustrations for numerous British works for which they had written the text. These dealt with ferns (1855), fern allies (1856), poisonous plants (1856), grasses (1857–61), wild flowers (1858–60, 1863), and 'useful plants' (1861–2). He provided a supplement on 'Ferns, horsetails and club mosses' for Johnson's *British Wild Flowers* (1863, 1894). Other illustrations were provided for the second (1850) and third (1863–72) editions of *English Botany* published by J. T. I. Boswell Syme (1822–1888). *An Illustrated Key to the Natural Orders of British Wild Flowers*, published by Van Voorst (1865), was his only independent work. He used miniature versions of drawings in *English Botany* as typical plants of the principal orders and borrowed descriptions from Babington's *Manual of British Botany*.

All J. E. Sowerby's drawings were on botanical subjects and through publishing economies had a similar multiple arrangement of figures. Among the works he was associated with were those on flowers by Mrs Lankester (1861, 1879) and J. E. Taylor (1878); on ferns—T. W. Gissing (1862); rusts, smut, mildew, and mould—M. C. Cooke (1865, 1878); and a flora of Essex by G. S. Stacey (1862). The extent of his botanical knowledge is not clear, but, surprisingly, not one of the authors acknowledged his contribution other than on the title-page.

Following a short illness, J. E. Sowerby died at his home, Stanley Villa, Poultney Road, Lavender Hill, Clapham, on 28 January 1870, aged forty-five. Shortly after his death an appeal was made through the *Gardeners' Chronicle* to provide funds for his family and to secure the admission of one of his six children to an infants' orphan asylum. His widow was later granted a civil-list pension in recognition of the scientific value of his work. R. J. Cleevely

Sources A. De C. Sowerby and others, *The Sowerby saga: being a brief account of the origin and genealogy of the Sowerby family* (1952) · *Gardeners' Chronicle* (23 April 1870), 559 · R. J. Cleevely, 'A provisional bibliography of natural history works by the Sowerby family', *Journal of the Society of the Bibliography of Natural History*, 6 (1971–4), 482–559 · Desmond, *Botanists*, rev. edn · F. A. Stafleu and R. S. Cowan, *Taxonomic literature: a selective guide*, 2nd edn, 5, Regnum Vegetabile, 112 (1985), 763–4 · J. Collins, ed., *Supplementa Sowerbiana, or, A catalogue of books and manuscripts written or illustrated by members of the Sowerby family* (1969), 18 [suppl. to Quaritch's catalogue no. 894] · J. F. Sowerby, *List of exhibits: Sowerby exhibition at the Royal Botanic Gardens, Regent's Park, London, December 5th and 6th 1908* (1908) · *Journal of Botany, British and Foreign*, 8 (1870), 63 · *CGPLA Eng. & Wales* (1870)
Archives NHM
Wealth at death under £600: administration, 2 March 1870, *CGPLA Eng. & Wales*

Sowernam, Ester (*fl.* 1617), author, published a pamphlet entitled *Ester hath hang'd Haman, or, An answere to a lewd pamphlet entituled 'The arraignment of women': with the arraignment of lewd, idle, froward, and unconstant men, and husbands* in London in 1617. The pamphlet was a response to Joseph Swetnam's 1615 pamphlet *The Arraignment of Lewde, Idle, Froward, and Unconstant Women*, and was one of several published in the same year, including Rachel Speght's *A Mouzell for Melastomus* and Constantia Munda's *The Worming of a Mad Dogge*. Ester Sowernam is clearly a pseudonym: 'Sowernam' presents a witty opposition to Swetnam, while 'Ester' refers to the biblical figure Esther who saved her people, the Jews living in Persia, by revealing the plots against them of the Persian chief minister Haman who was consequently hanged. The actual identity of Ester Sowernam remains unknown. Since the early 1980s, when this text and others relating to early modern controversies about the nature of women attracted much feminist interest, there has been debate as to whether the author was a woman engaged in an early feminist argument, or a man taking a woman's point of view as part of a formal exercise in rhetoric or disputation, or in order to profit from exploitation of a fashionable controversy.

Sowernam's text itself is notable for its logical organization. Its opening contains a concise, lucid statement of purpose and method: first to 'deliver the worthinesse and worth of women; both in respect of their Creation as in the work of Redemption' and to give biblical examples of women as 'gratious instruments' of God; then, in the second part, to show how women have been valued in history; and finally to respond to 'all materiall objections' against women and to 'arraigne' all men such as Joseph Swetnam who are 'lewd, idle, furious and beastly disposed persons' (sigs. A2*v*–A3*r*). Throughout, Sowernam uses logic and wordplay to refute Swetnam's (and traditional) railings against women, and to turn anti-women arguments back on themselves. She argues, for instance, that in the biblical account of the fall Adam was more culpable than Eve and that evil is more associated with masculinity than femininity since the serpent was 'of the masculine gender' (sig. B4*r*).

Sowernam's pamphlet has literary and historical importance as an example of measured, witty polemic. It both employs and self-consciously criticizes seventeenth-century habits of arguing by means of analogy, dispute over biblical interpretation, classical logic, and play with language. It is a significant text, too, in that it has been a focus in the late twentieth century for debates over the importance of signature and the gendering of authorship. Read as a cultural artefact it offers an insight into the concerns and fashionable interests of urban, educated, middle-class women and men in the early seventeenth century. ELSPETH GRAHAM

Sources S. Shepherd, ed., *The women's sharp revenge: five women's pamphlets from the Renaissance* (1985) · K. U. Henderson and B. F. McManus, *Half humankind: contexts and texts of the controversy about women in England, 1540–1640* (1985) · D. Purkiss, 'Material girls: the seventeenth-century woman debate', *Women, texts and histories, 1575–1760*, ed. C. Brant and D. Purkiss (1992), 69–101 · M. Bell, G. Parfitt, and S. Shepherd, *A biographical dictionary of English women writers, 1580–1720* (1990) · *STC, 1475–1640*, no. 22974

Sowle, Andrew (1628–1695), printer, was the son of Francis Sowle, yeoman of the parish of St Sepulchre, London. From 1646 to 1653 he was apprenticed to Ruth Raworth, a widow who was known for printing radical and reforming works. Some time before 1655 he married a woman named Jane [*see below*], whose maiden name is not known. The couple had at least ten children, but only three daughters are known to have lived to adulthood; all three of these daughters became Quaker printers in their own right. Jane, the eldest daughter (*bap.* 6 August 1655), married Jonas Hinde of Shoreditch in 1679. After Hinde died she married John Bradford, a family apprentice, and set up as a printer, managing the business after Bradford's death. Elizabeth Sowle married another family apprentice, William Bradford, in 1685, and emigrated with him to Pennsylvania, where they became the first Quaker printers in the American colonies. Tace *Sowle, born on 29 March 1666, succeeded her father as head of the Sowle press in 1691.

While Andrew Sowle began printing for the Quakers some time before the Restoration, the details of his early activities are not known. Early Quaker publications were perceived as posing a serious threat to the social order, and printers rarely showed their name in imprints. Sowle's name does not appear in imprints before 1680. From that year until 1690 imprints show that he retailed works at his home in Shoreditch 'at the sign of the Crooked Billet' and also at 'Devonshire New Buildings' near Bishopsgate Street, the site of the first public Quaker meetings in London. In 1687 he added a third outlet in Gracechurch Street, near the main Quaker meeting-house. The papers of Quaker leader William Penn, however, reveal that Sowle was printing for the Society of Friends on a regular basis by 1672, and in 1674 minutes of the Quaker morning meeting name him as one of their official printers. Sowle managed to hide his press from government authorities until 1678. His name is conspicuously absent from a government list ('List of the severall printing houses taken the 24 of July 1668', PRO, SP 29/243/126) and, seven years later, 'Andrew Sole a Quaker' is recorded in 'A list of the several printing-houses taken the 29th of March 1675' (PRO, SP 29/369/97) but the location of his press is not recorded. In 1678 the warden of the Stationers' Company, Thomas Vere, searched Sowle's residence in Shoreditch and discovered there 'a Private Printing Press … in two upper Rooms to which there was no passage but through Trapp-doores to it' (PRO, SP 29/403/59, 19 April 1678). Sowle was charged with illegal printing at the Middlesex sessions, but on 9 December a jury declared him not guilty.

As a printer of nonconformist literature Sowle suffered severe treatment and losses at the hands of government agents. In a testimony of 1701 concerning Sowle in *Piety Promoted, in a Collection of the Dying Sayings of many of the People called Quakers*, William Penn records how his friend 'freely gave himself up to the service' of the Quaker movement:

> even in times of the hottest persecution, believing it his duty so to do, though therein he should hazard not only his life but also that outward substance God had blessed him with: being for several years together in continual danger upon that account. (Tomkins, 121)

Early in his career, in 1664, Sowle was arrested under the Conventicle Act. Upon learning that Sowle was a printer Alderman Sir Richard Browne is reputed to have threatened to send him to the same fate as 'his brother Twyn', the printer John Twyn executed that year for treason (Hetet, 143).

In 1691 Tace Sowle succeeded her father, and from this date on her name replaces his in imprints. On 26 December 1695 Andrew Sowle died at his home in Holloway Lane, Shoreditch, from consumption, attended by William Penn. He was buried at Checker Alley, London. His will leaves small sums to his daughters Jane Bradford and Elizabeth Bradford and their children, and designates his unmarried daughter, Tace, and wife, Jane, joint executors and residuary legatees of his modest estate.

The Sowle press was the primary channel through which early Quaker works were published, and Andrew Sowle printed works by nearly all of the founders of Quakerism, including authors such as George Fox, Robert Barclay, George Whitehead, Isaac Penington, and William Penn. (Sowle is estimated, for instance, to have printed more than 90 per cent of Penn's works.) During the eleven years that his name appears in imprints Sowle published well over eighty works for the Friends. The Quakers also relied on the Sowles to organize the distribution of their publications; in this regard, the Sowle press is an important exception to the rule in this period that printing houses generally did not retail their own products. From its beginnings some time near the Restoration until 1829 when it can no longer be traced under any variation of name, this unique publishing operation flourished not only in London but also, through the Bradford connection, in America.

Jane Sowle (*c.*1631–1711) played a key role in the Sowle press both during her marriage to Andrew and for sixteen years after his death. While Tace Sowle officially succeeded her father, Jane remained an important force in the family business. When Tace eventually married in 1706 she ensured that her mother would retain command of her house. At the age of seventy-four Jane Sowle became the nominal head of the business, and imprints after this date read 'J. Sowle'. Even after Jane died at Clapton, Hackney, on 18 June 1711, aged about eighty, Tace (now Tace Raylton) continued to use her mother's name in imprints. From 1711 to 1735 imprints show 'assigns of J. Sowle' (that is, Tace). Jane Sowle is also remembered for having contributed a testimony to the collectively authored *Piety Promoted by Faithfulness … Concerning Ann Whitehead* (1686). She was buried at Bunhill Fields, London, two days after her death. PAULA MCDOWELL

Sources meeting for sufferings minutes, vols. 1–43 (1675–1831); morning meeting minutes, vols. 1–8 (1673–1861); yearly meeting minutes, vols. 1–14 (1672–1723), RS Friends, Lond. • digest registers of births, marriages, and burials, to 1837, RS Friends, Lond. [microfilm, reels 3–5] • P. McDowell, 'Tace Sowle' and 'Andrew Sowle', *The British literary book trade, 1475–1700*, ed. J. K. Bracken and J. Silver, DLitB, 170 (1996), 249–57 • P. McDowell, *The women of Grub Street: press, politics and gender in the London literary marketplace, 1678–1730* (1998) • J. S. T. Hetet, 'A literary underground in Restoration England: printers and dissenters in the context of constraints, 1660–1689', PhD diss., U. Cam., 1987 • A. Littleboy, 'Devonshire House reference library: with notes on early printers and printing in the Society of Friends', *Journal of the Friends' Historical Society*, 18 (1921), 1–16, 66–80 • R. S. Mortimer, 'Biographical notices of printers and publishers of Friends' books up to 1750', *Journal of Documentation*, 3 (Sept 1947), 107–25 • R. S. Mortimer, 'The first century of Quaker printers', *Journal of the Friends' Historical Society*, 40 (1948), 37–49 • J. Tomkins, *Piety promoted … part one* (1701) • *The papers of William Penn*, ed. M. M. Dunn, R. S. Dunn, and others, 1 (1981) • J. C. Jeaffreson, ed., *Middlesex county records*, 4 vols. (1886–92), vol. 4 • will, PRO, PROB 11/467, sig. 185, fols. 135*v*–136*r* • D. F. McKenzie, ed., *Stationers' Company apprentices*, [2]: *1641–1700* (1974)

Wealth at death modest; small sums (4–50s.) to daughters, grandchildren, one friend and one servant; residue to widow and Tace Sowle: will, PRO, PROB 11/467, sig. 185, fols. 135*v*–136*r*

Sowle, Jane (*c.*1631–1711). *See under* Sowle, Andrew (1628–1695).

Sowle [*married name* Sowle Raylton], **Tace** (1666–1749), printer and bookseller, was born on 29 March 1666 at Pye Corner, Smithfield, London, the daughter of the printers Andrew *Sowle (1628–1695) and Jane *Sowle (*c.*1631–1711) of Shoreditch [*see under* Sowle, Andrew]. She had numerous siblings, but only two sisters are known to have lived to adulthood. Like these sisters she was trained in the family trade. By 1690 she had assumed management of the family printing house, and in 1691 she succeeded her father as printer to the Society of Friends. On 7 October 1695 she was formally freed of the Stationers' Company by patrimony. After Andrew Sowle died on 26 December 1695 Tace and Jane Sowle gave up their Shoreditch premises and moved to a new residence and shop in Leadenhall Street at the sign of the Bible. (They also continued to retail works in Gracechurch Street near the Quaker meeting-house.) Tace immediately expanded the production of the press, with her name appearing in nearly 300 imprints during the first fifteen years of her career (1691–1705). The period of her initial take-over was in fact the busiest in the history of the Sowle press. In 1704 William Penn referred to her as the Quakers' 'only Stationer, now, as well as printer' (*Papers of William Penn*, 4.270). In 1715 she abandoned the Leadenhall Street location for new premises in George Yard, Lombard Street, also at the sign of the Bible.

In 1705 the bookseller John Dunton described Tace as

> both a Printer as well as a Bookseller, and the Daughter of one; and understands her Trade very well, being a good Compositor herself. Her love and piety to her aged Mother is eminently remarkable; even to that degree, that she keeps herself unmarried for this only reason … that it may not be out of her power to let her Mother have always the chief command in her house. (Dunton, 1.222–3)

Tace did in fact marry the following year on 10 October 1706, but she ensured that her mother would retain significant power in her house. At the age of seventy-four Jane Sowle became the nominal head of the Sowle press the year her daughter was married, and imprints after this date read 'J. Sowle' and then 'assigns of J. Sowle' (that is, Tace). Tace never gave up her name for that of her husband, Thomas Raylton (1666/7–1723), but instead used the compound Tace Sowle Raylton. Thomas Raylton was not a member of the Stationers' Company and he had no training or experience as a printer. While he assisted with warehousing and accounting, Tace continued to oversee the printing business as she had done for sixteen years before she was married, and as she would do for another twenty-six years after she was widowed. In 1723 Thomas Raylton died of asthma aged fifty-six, and Tace continued to manage her press without employing a foreman until she was seventy years old. In 1736 she employed a relative, Luke Hinde, and imprints changed from 'assigns of J. Sowle' to 'T. Sowle Raylton and Luke Hinde': after thirty years of invisibility, her name once more appeared in imprints. In 1739 she made Hinde her partner.

As the leading Quaker printer and bookseller for more than half a century (1691–1749), Tace Sowle Raylton printed and distributed the major works of the founders of Quakerism, including George Fox, Margaret Askew Fell Fox, William Penn, and Robert Barclay (to name a few). She printed two of the three volumes of the first folio edition of George Fox's *Works* (1694–1706), and in 1726 she produced a collected edition of William Penn's works. Other landmark works in the history of Quakerism which she printed include John Whiting's *Catalogue of Friends Books* (1708), the first Quaker bibliography, and William Sewel's *History of the … Christian People called Quakers* (1722). She served as the primary printer of Quaker women's writings—the single largest category of English women's writings in this period—printing more than one hundred works by thirteen different women (including one non-Quaker, the leader of the Philadelphian Society, the visionary Jane Lead). Last, but not least, she handled virtually all routine business printing for the Quakers, such as the *Yearly Meeting Epistle*, printed in 1000 copies annually.

The Quakers relied on Sowle Raylton to oversee the national and international distribution of their books and tracts, and she shipped several thousands of items every year, not only throughout Great Britain and Ireland but also to continental Europe and other 'foreign partes beyond the seas' (the American colonies and the Caribbean). Her expert knowledge of market demands meant that she sometimes made publication recommendations to the Friends. Upon taking over her family press in 1691, for instance, she immediately recommended that Elizabeth Bathurst's works (including her 'Sayings of Women') be reprinted in the form of a collection. At this time of strict internal control of Quaker publications, when Quaker elders served as an official review board for all authorized Quaker works, the Friends' occasional willingness to trust Sowle Raylton with publishing matters is remarkable.

On 1 November 1749, Tace Sowle Raylton died in the parish of St Edmund the King, London, a wealthy, independent businesswoman with houses in London and Clapton and additional real estate in Blackfriars. (By this time she had already conveyed to her nephews William and Andrew Bradford a deed for 1000 acres of land she owned in Pennsylvania.) Her will left sums of up to £400 to friends and relatives; for instance, £30 to the London Quaker women's meeting and £50 to 'my nephew William Bradford of New York … printer' (PRO, PROB11/774, fol. 345*v*). Her printing house went to Luke Hinde, who succeeded her. She was buried at Bunhill Fields on 6 November 1749.

The half century spanned by Tace Sowle Raylton's career was a formative period in the history of Quakerism and in the history of the British press. As the chief printer for one of England's largest nonconformist sects she published nearly 600 items over a period of fifty-eight years. By the end of its 150-year history the Sowle press (under several variations of name) was one of the longest running printing houses in Britain. It was under Tace Sowle Raylton's management that the house saw its greatest development. PAULA MCDOWELL

Sources RS Friends, Lond. [meeting for suffering minutes, vols. 1–43 (1675–1831); morning meeting minutes, vols. 1–8 (1673–1861); yearly meeting minutes, vols. 1–14 (1672–1723)] • digest registers of births, marriages, and burials, to 1837, RS Friends, Lond. [microfilm, reels 3–5] • P. McDowell, 'Tace Sowle', *The British literary book trade, 1475–1700*, ed. J. K. Bracken and J. Silver, DLitB, 170 (1996), 249–57 • P. McDowell, 'Andrew Sowle', *The British literary book trade, 1475–1700*, ed. J. K. Bracken and J. Silver, DLitB, 170 (1996), 249–57 • P. McDowell, *The women of Grub Street: press, politics and gender in the London literary marketplace, 1678–1730* (1998) • A. Littleboy, 'Devonshire House reference library: with notes on early printers and printing in the Society of Friends', *Journal of the Friends' Historical Society*, 18 (1921), 1–16, 66–80 • R. S. Mortimer, 'Biographical notices of printers and publishers of Friends' books up to 1750', *Journal of Documentation*, 3 (Sept 1947), 107–25 • R. S. Mortimer, 'The first century of Quaker printers', *Journal of the Friends' Historical Society*, 40 (1948), 37–49 • J. Dunton, *The life and errors of John Dunton … written by himself* (1705), 222–3 • J. Field, ed., *Piety promoted, in a collection of the dying sayings of many of the people called Quakers*, 6 (1728) • M. Treadwell, 'London printers and printing houses in 1705', *Publishing History*, 7 (1980), 5–44 • *The papers of William Penn*, ed. M. M. Dunn, R. S. Dunn, and others, 4 (1987) • D. F. McKenzie, ed., *Stationers' Company apprentices*, [2]: *1641–1700* (1974) • will, PRO, PROB 11/774, sig. 354, fols. 345*v*–346*r* [Tace Sowle Raylton] • will, PRO, PROB 11/595, fols. 128*v*–129*r* [Thomas Raylton]

Wealth at death property in London, Clapton, and possibly Blackfriars; bequests of several hundred pounds: will, PRO, PROB 11/774, sig. 354, fols. 345*v*–346*r*

Sowthernes, Elizabeth (*c.*1532–1612). *See under* Pendle witches (*act.* 1612).

Soyer, Alexis Benoît (1810–1858), chef, was born on 4 February 1810 at Meaux-en-Brie, near Paris, the youngest of three sons of Emery Roch Alexis Soyer, a shopkeeper, and his wife, Marie Madeleine Françoise, *née* Chamberlan; his parents were both thirty-one when he was born. He was sent to the local cathedral with the intention of becoming a priest, but he did not take to this vocation and, after ringing the cathedral bells at night, which brought out the town garrison and the fire brigade, he was expelled. In 1821 he joined his brother Philippe, a chef in Versailles, and was apprenticed as a cook. At the age of seventeen he joined a M. Douix, a restaurateur in the boulevard des Italiens, where he stayed for three years. He then went as second chef to the prince de Polignac, but left Paris in 1831 and moved to England where his brother was then chef to the duke of Cambridge. Soyer worked in several noble households, including those of the duke of Sutherland and the marquess of Waterford, and then for four years with William Lloyd of Aston Hall, near Oswestry. In 1837 he was appointed chef to the newly created Reform Club in Pall Mall. On 12 April in the same year he married, at St George's Hanover Square, Emma Jones [*see* Soyer, (Elizabeth) Emma (1813–1842)], an artist with a modest reputation for her portraits.

At the Reform Club Soyer installed modern kitchens: he was one of the first to use gas for cooking, and his culinary domain became a showplace, and the venue for a number of magnificent displays of his art. On the day of Queen Victoria's coronation, 28 June 1838, he prepared a breakfast for two thousand guests. He also prepared a massive dinner for Ibrahim Pasha at the Reform Club on 3 July 1846. In 1842 he was asked to Belgium to meet the king, and left his wife at home although she was expecting a child. Unfortunately during the few days he was away she had a miscarriage and died. Soyer was deeply distressed and never fully recovered from his grief and guilt at having left his wife alone. He became even busier in his work, producing new dishes, such as his *côtelettes à la Reform*, and providing for private banquets. He also wrote a small book entitled *Délassements culinaires* (1845), followed in 1846 by *The Gastronomic Regenerator*, written primarily for the grander households with a kitchen staff. Soyer was approached by the government in 1847 and asked to go to Ireland to install soup kitchens, in order to help alleviate the famine. This kind of work suited him well, and he set up a kitchen at the Royal Barracks in Dublin capable of feeding a thousand people an hour; the soup was cheap and tasty even if it did not constitute a balanced diet. On his return to London he published *Soyer's Charitable Cookery, or, The Poor Man's Regenerator* (1848), sold for 6*d.*, 1*d.* being returned to the poor fund. He also continued his soup kitchens by providing for the Huguenot silk weavers of Spitalfields, who were then being affected by a treaty with France that allowed cheap imported silk into this country.

Soyer was never out of the public eye for long and, apart from his banquets, produced a series of kitchen gadgets that were the forerunners of many modern utensils, as well as selling a range of bottled sauces and relishes. His most ingenious production was the Magic Stove, on which

Alexis Benoît Soyer (1810–1858), by Henry Bryan Hall, pubd 1858 (after Emma Soyer, 1843)

food could be cooked at the table, essentially the same device used in restaurants today. This was not entirely his own invention, but he improved and marketed one that he had been shown.

Soyer continued to write, and his next book, *The Modern Housewife* (1849), was aimed at the middle classes. It took the form of letters between two housewives, and gave an interesting insight into domestic life of the time. In 1850 he left the Reform Club and was asked to tender for the catering at the Great Exhibition planned for the following year. He found this to be too restrictive and instead rented Gore House, now the site of the Albert Hall, where he created the Gastronomic Symposium of All Nations. This was not only a restaurant but a place of magical entertainment, the gardens being filled with fountains, statues, and replicas of the seven wonders of the world, and offering much else, including fireworks, music for dancing, and other noisy frolics. Visitors averaged a thousand a day and the food was good and affordable, but Soyer was never very skilful with accounts, and the Symposium closed with a loss of £7000. Also in 1850 a young Frenchman, Alexis Lemain, wrote to Soyer claiming to be his son. Soyer had had an early liaison when a young man in Paris, and in due course he accepted Lemain as his son.

Shortly after the closure of the Symposium, the Admiralty, well aware of the scandals surrounding the navy rations, asked Soyer to investigate the preservation of food for long voyages. He did this with success and his recommendations were accepted. Soyer also produced at that time a scholarly work entitled *The Pantropheon* (1853), covering every aspect of food production, preparation, and history. This was in a completely different style from his previous work, and it is now known that it was not written by him, but by a Frenchman, Adolphe Duhart-Fauvet, who sold it to Soyer to translate and complete. This he did, but published it under his own name without acknowledgement to the original author. Soyer was a generous man, but craved publicity and, at that time, money, so it seems likely that, as with the Magic Stove, he considered the additions he made justified him in claiming the work as his own. *A Shilling Cookery for the People* (1855) followed, designed for the working classes. This contained basic recipes for plain dishes, boiled meats, puddings sweet and savoury, offal, and leftovers though not, oddly, many ideas for soups, the usual standby for cheap eating.

In 1855 reports of appalling conditions in the war in the Crimea were reaching London, and Soyer offered his service, without payment, to the government. This was accepted and he went out to Scutari to reorganize the catering in the hospitals there. His practical skills were put to good use, and he later went with Florence Nightingale to Balaklava and Sevastopol to continue the work. The field stoves he had devised before leaving London were sent out and installed in the camp kitchens. They proved so efficient and economical that the army used them, in modified form, for at least a century.

Soyer returned home in 1857 and published *A Culinary Campaign*, mainly about his own adventures in the Crimea and the way he simplified and improved the army catering. It contained a selection of recipes for hospital and invalid diets, as well as hearty dishes, such as salt meat, for large numbers, under the heading of 'Field and barrack cookery'. He also wrote a pamphlet in that year, *Instructions to Military Cooks*. He was then asked to redesign the kitchens at Wellington barracks, which were opened in July 1858.

Alexis Soyer was a flamboyant, warm-hearted man with a strong sense of humour and a love of practical jokes. Ingenious and inventive, with a talent for organization, he was sometimes carried away by his insatiable desire for publicity. He took his work seriously and was very much aware of those less fortunate, and tried to help when he could. He was unbusinesslike in money matters and never patented any of his inventions, so made little from them financially. He was well known and easily recognized, largely because of his unconventional appearance. Portraits show him to be of middle height, bearded, and always wearing a floppy cap, usually made of velvet, which he made his trade mark. His clothes were cut on the bias, or '*à la zoug-zoug*' as he called it (Ray, 12), and designed by himself. Thackeray, an admirer and friend, used him as the model for Mirabolant in *Pendennis*. Soyer died on 5 August 1858, of a stroke, at his home, 15 Marlborough Road, St John's Wood, and was buried on 11 August at Kensal Green cemetery in the same grave as his beloved Emma. ELIZABETH RAY

Sources F. Volant and J. R. Warren, *Memoirs of Soyer* (1859); repr. (1985) · *The Times* (3 July 1844) · *The Times* (11 March 1847) · *The Times*

(14 May 1847) • *The Times* (21 Feb 1848) • *The Times* (30 July 1850) • *The Times* (28 April 1851) • *The Times* (16 May 1851) • *The Times* (22 Jan 1855) • *The Times* (3 Feb 1855) • *The Times* (16 May 1855) • *The Times* (10 Jan 1856) • *The Times* (20 March 1858) • *The Times* (6 Aug 1858) • *ILN* (22 Sept 1855) • *ILN* (7 Aug 1858) • *ILN* (14 Aug 1858) • *Punch*, 18 (1850), 17, 244 • *Punch*, 21 (1851), 180, 189 • G. A. Sala, *Things I have seen* (1894) • E. Ray, *Alexis Soyer: cook extraordinary* (1991) • H. Morris, *Portrait of a chef: the life of Alexis Soyer* (1938) • M. Aylett and O. Orlish, *First catch your hare: a history of the recipe-makers* (1965) • *DNB* • b. cert. [French] • d. cert.

Archives BM, letters

Likenesses J. Barrett, group portrait, oils, *c*.1856 (*Florence Nightingale at Scutari*), NPG; study, NPG • J. Barrett, oils, 1857, NPG • Bingham, photograph, repro. in A. Soyer, *A culinary campaign* (1857) • H. B. Hall, stipple (after E. Soyer, 1843), BM, NPG; repro. in Volant and Warren, *Memoirs* (1858) [*see illus.*] • H. G. Hines, illustrations, repro. in A. Soyer, *A culinary campaign* (1857) • Hogg, photograph, repro. in A. Soyer, *A shilling cookery for the people* (1855) • E. Soyer, portrait • portrait, priv. coll.

Wealth at death under £1500: administration with will, *CGPLA Eng. & Wales*

Soyer [*née* Jones], **(Elizabeth) Emma** (1813–1842), portrait and figure painter, was born in London. Little is known of her parents, other than the fact that her father died in 1818 and her mother remarried in 1820 and died in 1839. A precocious child who learned French and Italian and excelled in music, she devoted herself to art after early exclusive instruction from the Flemish painter François Simoneau, who married her mother. She first exhibited at the Royal Academy at the age of ten, and two years later she had produced more than one hundred portraits drawn from life. Her crayon portrait sketches were popular with the aristocracy. On 12 April 1837 she married Alexis Benoît *Soyer (1810–1858), cook at the Reform Club in London.

Emma Jones's works comprise portraits and genre paintings depicting the young and very old, sometimes in a French or Italian context, chiefly in oil, and reputedly in the style of the seventeenth-century Spanish painter Murillo. Between 1823 and 1843 fourteen of her pictures were exhibited at the Royal Academy, thirty-eight at the British Institution, fourteen at the Society of British Artists, twenty-five at the Liverpool Academy, and five at the Paris Salon. Her most celebrated works were *The Young Israelites* ('The Jew Lemon Boys'; exh. British Institution 1837 and at Paris Salon 1841 as *Jeunes Israélites*), *The Young Bavarians* (exh. Society of British Artists 1838), *Une glaneuse anglaise* ('The English Ceres') and *La centenaire d'Edimbourg* ('The Centenarian'; both exh. Paris Salon 1840 and engraved by Gérard), and *Savoyards Resting* (exh. British Institution 1842). One of her largest works, *Italian Boys* ('The Alpine Wanderers'; exh. British Institution 1839), measuring 5 feet 10 inches by 5 feet, was sold in 1839 for 100 guineas. Her work was appreciated in France for its vigour of execution, correct drawing, and lifelike expression, and in Belgium by the king and queen and the duke of Saxe-Coburg and Gotha.

Although exhibiting occasionally from Canterbury and Ramsgate, Emma Jones lived chiefly in London, at addresses in Fitzroy Square between 1833 and 1837 and at 26 Charing Cross from 1840 to 1842. She died on 29–30 August 1842 after a premature confinement induced by a thunderstorm and was buried on 8 September at Kensal Green cemetery in London, where her husband erected a monument to her memory. Her total output amounted to 403 pictures. In June 1848 Alexis Soyer organized a memorial exhibition—with an accompanying catalogue—of 140 of her works, called Soyer's Philanthropic Gallery, at the prince of Wales's bazaar.

CHARLOTTE YELDHAM

Sources F. Volant and J. R. Warren, *Memoirs of Alexis Soyer* (1859) • C. R. Dodd, *The annual biography: being lives of eminent or remarkable persons, who have died within the year MDCCCXLII* (1843), 477 • *GM*, 2nd ser., 18 (1842), 441 • *Morning Post* (2 Sept 1842), 4 • *Art Union*, 4 (1842), 257 • *Engraved Brit. ports.* • Graves, *Artists* • J. Johnson, ed., *Works exhibited at the Royal Society of British Artists, 1824–1893, and the New English Art Club, 1888–1917*, 2 vols. (1975) • Graves, *Brit. Inst.* • Graves, *RA exhibitors* • E. C. Clayton, *English female artists*, 1 (1876), 382–3 • D. Foskett, *A dictionary of British miniature painters*, 2 vols. (1972) • T. P. Grinsted, *Last homes of departed genius* (1867), 291–2 • H. Morris, *Portrait of a chef: the life of Alexis Soyer* (1938) • E. Ray, *Alexis Soyer: cook extraordinary* (1991), 15–19 • E. Morris and E. Roberts, *The Liverpool Academy and other exhibitions of contemporary art in Liverpool, 1774–1867* (1998)

Archives Courtauld Inst., Witt Library • NPG

Likenesses H. B. Hall, stipple engraving (after self-portrait, crayon drawing), BM, NPG

Spagnoletti, Charles Ernest Paolo della Diana (1832–1915), electrical inventor, was born at Brompton, London, on 12 July 1832, the eldest son of Ernesto Spagnoletti, a musician, and his wife, Charlotte, *née* Stohwasser (1809–1901). The family was descended from the ancient Italian noble house of della Diana. The surname Spagnoletti originated as a variant of Spagnoletto, a nickname bestowed on one of his ancestors. Charles attended Blemmell House School, Brompton, until the age of fourteen, when he left to take up a post in the National Debt Office. After a few months he became a pupil of the electrical and telegraph engineer Alexander Bain. In 1847 Spagnoletti joined the Electric Telegraph Company, and in 1855 became telegraph superintendent of the Great Western Railway (GWR) at a salary of £100 per annum. His main achievement there was to introduce the block system whereby train movements were controlled by electric telegraph. Following a serious illness, he retired from the GWR in 1892, but remained consulting electrical engineer to the company. Spagnoletti made many electrical inventions. Besides signalling and telegraph equipment, he designed bells, bridges, clocks, and a fire alarm, all worked by electricity. He installed the first electric light at several London termini, and advised on the use of electricity at the Crystal Palace. For Ascot racecourse he designed a board to show the starters, winners, and prices. In 1890 the City and South London Railway, acting on Spagnoletti's advice, became Britain's first electric underground railway. He was also consultant to the London Electrical Omnibus Company, and invented a new system of road building, using pre-cast concrete blocks, which was widely used by the London county council.

After leaving the GWR, Spagnoletti became managing director of the Phonophore Company, and worked on telephone development. Following the act of 1868 to nationalize the telegraph system, Spagnoletti had advised the government on the compensation to be paid. In 1872 he became a founder member of the Society of Telegraph Engineers, served on its council from 1874 to 1880, and as its vice-president from 1880 to 1884. Meanwhile the title had been changed to the Society of Telegraph Engineers and Electricians, and it was of that body that Spagnoletti became president in 1885. In 1912 he was made an honorary member of the society's successor, the Institution of Electrical Engineers. He had become a member of the Institution of Civil Engineers in 1875, and belonged to several other scientific bodies. In 1884 he was elected president of the Conference of Railway Companies' Telegraph Superintendents. From 1878, when he served as a member of the international jury on electrical exhibits at the Paris Universal Exhibition, he was much involved in work of this type.

Spagnoletti continued the musical interests of his father and grandfather. He wrote and composed many songs, and had a good tenor voice. When Sir William Preece showed the first Edison phonograph at a meeting of the Society of Telegraph Engineers in 1878, Spagnoletti sang the national anthem into it. He was one of the first supporters of the Electro-Harmonic Society. As 'Mr Sprigalilly' he appears in Simmons's *Memoirs of a Station Master*. The portrait is vivid and malicious, but not necessarily accurate. In 1853 Spagnoletti married a widow, Caroline Charlotte Duffield (1829–1903), daughter of Robert Vincent Dawson, a veterinary surgeon. They had two sons and three daughters. Spagnoletti died of pneumonia on 28 June 1915 at 16 Frognal Lane, Hampstead, where he had lived for more than ten years. He was buried on 2 July at Hampstead cemetery. At least four other members of the family made careers in electricity. They were Charles's son, James, his brother, Hylton, his great-nephew, Philip, and Philip's son, Robert. When in 1907, James transformed his business into a private company, he gave £2000 worth of shares from his own allocation to his father, who thus became the second largest shareholder.

HENRY PARRIS

Sources H. Parris, 'Spagnoletti, Charles Ernest Paolo della Diana', *DBB* • T. S. Lascelles, 'C. E. Spagnoletti', *Proceedings of the Institution of Railway Signalling Engineers* (1941) • A. Vaughan, 'C. E. Spagnoletti—the father of telegraphs', *Newsletter of the Signalling Record Society*, 55 (1979) • *Electrical Review*, 77 (1915), 18, 52 • *The Electrician* (2 July 1915), 459 • *Great Western Railway Magazine* (1915), 223 • *Journal of the Institution of Electrical Engineers*, 54 (1916) • *PICE*, 201 (1915–16), 394–5 • *Railway Gazette* (9 July 1915) • *Railway Gazette* (13 Aug 1915) • A. Vaughan, *A pictorial record of Great Western signalling* (1984) • T. S. Lascelles, *The City and South London Railway* (1955) • E. T. Macdermot and O. S. Nock, *History of the Great Western Railway*, rev. C. R. Clinker, 3 vols. (1964) • H. A. Simmons, *Memoirs of a station master*, ed. J. Simmons (1974) • PRO, Rail/1005/454/5 • *Electrical Trades Directory and Handbook* (1899) • private information (2004) • 'Spagnoletti's electrical fire alarm', *The Electrician* (12 Aug 1882), 296–7 • 'Application de l'electricité à la manoeuvre des signaux de chemins de fer', *Journal Universel d'Electricité* (1885), 451–61 • 'Spagnoletti's electrical fire alarm', *Telegraphic Journal*, 8 (1880), 381–2 • m. cert. • d. cert. • *CGPLA Eng. & Wales* (1915)

Archives PRO, Great Western and Metropolitan railways, records

Likenesses photograph, priv. coll.

Wealth at death £35,070 4*s*. 7*d*.: probate, 7 Aug 1915, *CGPLA Eng. & Wales*

Spaight, James Molony (1877–1968), lawyer and theorist of air power, was born at Affock, co. Clare, Ireland, on 7 October 1877, the younger of the two sons (there were also two daughters) of Robert Spaight JP (1845–1888), a gentleman farmer, and his wife, Alice Maud, *née* Molony (*d*. 1906). He attended Trinity College, Dublin, and in 1905 graduated with an LLD. Meanwhile, he had joined the civil service in 1901, and soon after served with the Civil Service volunteer rifles in South Africa. He married on 5 November 1907 Constance Elizabeth (Dolly; *d*. 1962), the daughter of Colonel William FitzHenry Spaight RE, of Ardnatagle, co. Clare. They had one daughter.

Spaight specialized in the international law of war, and in 1911 he published *War Rights on Land*. In 1918 he was appointed OBE and transferred to the recently formed Air Ministry, where he remained until his retirement in 1937. During that time he served as the British delegate to the Commission of Jurists at The Hague (1923), was appointed CBE (1927), became the Air Ministry's director of accounts (1930) and principal assistant secretary (1934), and was made a CB (1936). He specialized in the law of air war—a field that had attracted much speculation but little informed examination. Specifically, he focused on the aerial bombing of urban areas.

Although cities were often shelled in war, many hoped that a precedent could be set to bar aeroplanes from also conducting such operations. To Spaight, this hope was delusory: given what was permitted to armies and fleets, there was nothing in the law that prohibited the aerial bombing of cities. In his *Aircraft in War* (1914) he noted that in virtually every siege in modern times the attackers' guns had been turned on civilian portions of a town, non-military property was destroyed, and non-combatants were killed. The right to do so under certain circumstances was well established in the law, and was thus incorporated into British manuals for land and sea warfare. Given this precedent, Spaight sought to identify those situations that made aerial bombing of civilian areas similarly legal or illegal.

In *Air Power and War Rights* (1924; 3rd edn 1947), *Air Power and the Cities* (1930), and *Air Power in the Next War* (1938) Spaight argued that it was permissible to destroy 'private' property, that bombing was legal even though civilian deaths would occur as a result, and that it was permissible to attack certain targets for the express purpose of causing civilian hardship so as to induce war weariness in the population and a desire to surrender. Land and naval war had engaged in such actions for centuries through blockades, sieges, raids, and the shelling of coastal cities.

Spaight therefore focused primarily on the issues of military objectives and targets. Some targets, such as banks, railway stations, and public utilities—although they had military implications—were not traditional military objectives. Consequently he concluded that it was not permissible to attack them, especially if they were located in urban areas where a significant loss of life would occur as the result of attack. He especially condemned bombing whose primary purpose was to terrorize the civilian population. Instead, he argued that air power offered new opportunities to win wars with far less death and destruction than through traditional methods. Air warfare, in his view, was a form of economic war that, like sea power, was fundamental to the British tradition. Thus aircraft should be used for 'direct attacks' on the war-making potential of the enemy—munitions factories, dockyards, arsenals, steelworks, and so on. These were legitimate targets, but the strictures against bombing other targets, or even bombing military targets located within cities, must be maintained. Spaight was soon to change his mind.

The Second World War was more vicious and total than Spaight or most others had anticipated. In *Bombing Vindicated* (1944), a revised edition of *Air Power and War Rights* (1947), and *Air Power can Disarm* (1948) he now argued that war had become so total and so dependent on mass industrialization that the line between military and civilian objectives had blurred. The major cities of all the belligerents had become 'battle-making towns', so he now made a distinction between civilians who were true noncombatants, and therefore immune from attack, and civilians such as factory workers who contributed directly to a nation's war-making potential and were thus 'warriors'. They had forfeited their civilian immunity status. Moreover, the law had always made a distinction between cities that were defended and those that were undefended. Defended cities, especially those containing military facilities, were liable to artillery or naval bombardment. Spaight argued that German and Japanese cities had become so militarized and so heavily defended that they had become fair game for aerial bombardment as well—even the area bombing of the allies was permissible. Nevertheless, he still drew a line at terror bombing, while also stating that cities of no military significance were protected from indiscriminate attacks. In truth there was a fine line between area bombing and indiscriminate terror bombing. Given Spaight's position as a British civil servant, his defence of allied bombing strategy could be seen as motivated more by loyalty to his government than by a rigorous interpretation of the law that he himself had helped to establish.

Spaight was perhaps the most important and influential expert of his era on the law of air war. Colleagues remembered him as 'delightful and distinguished' with 'an acute and original mind'. After retiring in 1937 Spaight continued to write on air power matters, although now he focused more on its theoretical than its legal aspects. He died at his home, 35 Forester Road, Bath, on 8 January 1968. PHILLIP S. MEILINGER

Sources *WWW, 1971–80* · R. Higham, *The military intellectuals in Britain, 1918–1939* (1966), 230–33 · *The Times* (10 Jan 1968) · *The Times* (19 March 1968) · [J. Macdonnell], 'The laws of war', *TLS* (27 April 1911) · *The Times* (31 July 1914) [review] · [J. Macdonnell], 'Aircraft in peace', *TLS* (12 Feb 1920) · *TLS* (22 May 1930) [review] · *The Times* (18 Oct 1938) [review] · b. cert. · Burke, *Gen. Ire.* (1912)

Archives BL, corresp. with Society of Authors, Add. MS 63330 · CUL, corresp. with Sir Samuel Hoare · King's Lond., Liddell Hart C., corresp. with Sir B. H. Liddell Hart

Wealth at death £50,587: probate, 11 March 1968, *CGPLA Eng. & Wales*

Spain, Nancy Brooker (1917–1964), journalist and broadcaster, was born on 13 September 1917 at 1 Archbold Terrace, Jesmond, Newcastle upon Tyne, the second and youngest daughter of Lieutenant-Colonel George Redesdale Brooker Spain (1877–1961), land agent and volunteer soldier, and his wife, Norah Elizabeth (1886–1964), daughter of William Holmes Smiles of Belfast and his wife, Lucy. Her grandfather was the eminent Victorian writer and philosopher Samuel *Smiles (1812–1904), author of *Self-Help* (1859). She was the great-niece of Isabella Mary Beeton (1836–1865), author of the classic *Mrs Beeton's Book of Household Management* (1861); in 1948 she wrote a biography of her great-aunt's short but eventful life. From 1931 to 1935, she was educated at the world-famous girls' school Roedean in Sussex, a place she loathed.

After leaving school, Spain turned her hand to amateur sports on her native Tyneside, excelling in ladies' tennis, lacrosse, and cricket. This led her into journalism; she became a cub sports reporter for the *Newcastle Journal* and other north-country papers, and she combined this with regular performances in local radio drama productions. Her sporting activities introduced her to Winifrid (Bin) Sargeant (1912–1939), a well-known Tyneside sportswoman with whom she had her first serious love affair. Shortly after the outbreak of the Second World War she joined the Women's Royal Naval Service, serving as a driver, before becoming an officer and working for its press office in London. She was invalided out of the service in early 1945. Her early service days inspired her first book, the autobiographical *Thank you Nelson* (1945), which became a best-seller and paved the way for her subsequent light literary career as a self-styled 'trouser-wearing character called N. Spain' (Spain, *A Funny Thing Happened on the Way*, 45). She wrote a series of camp detective novels, including *Poison for Teacher* (1949), inspired by her Roedean days and set in an all-girls school called Radcliffe Hall.

In 1950, while editing the literary magazine *Books of Today*, Spain met Joan Ann Werner *Laurie (1920–1964), a book and magazine editor, who became her life partner and with whom she established an unorthodox household, consisting of Joan's son Nicholas; Thomas, passed off as Joan's youngest son, but in fact Nancy's son from a brief liaison with Philip Youngman Carter, the husband of the crime novelist Margery Allingham; and Sheila Van Damm, the racing driver.

After a spell at *Good Housekeeping* magazine, Spain joined the *Daily Express* in 1952, becoming one of the brightest stars in Lord Beaverbrook's firmament of 'personality' journalists, first as books editor and then as celebrity interviewer, peppering her articles with references to 'my friend Noel Coward' and 'my friend Marlene Dietrich' (with whom she had a brief romance). She cut a striking figure on Fleet Street, with her cropped hair, monogrammed men's shirts, baggy jumpers, and trousers. However, when more formal occasions required, she would borrow couturier dresses from her designer sister

Nancy Brooker Spain (1917–1964), by Francis Goodman, 1962

Liz Hulse or from her close friend and lover Ginette Spanier (1904–1988), directrice of Balmain.

In 1956 Spain and her employers were successfully sued for libel by Evelyn Waugh, as she had claimed that his brother Alec outsold him. She survived this hiccup and continued with the paper until 1961, when she left to join the *News of the World* as a 'stunt/personality' journalist. Throughout the fifties and early sixties she became one of the most popular and recognizable radio personalities; she was a regular and much-requested contributor to *Woman's Hour* and a panellist on the internationally famous literary quiz *My Word*, from 1954 to 1964, alongside Frank Muir and Denis Norden. Her unconventional appearance and mischievous personality also made her a hit on television panel games, most notably *What's my Line?* and *Juke Box Jury*. Her appearances with the irascible Gilbert Harding (1907–1960) helped fuel the long-running and implausible rumour that the pair were to be married.

Spain was due to cover the Grand National on 21 March 1964 when the Piper Apache plane carrying her, Joan Werner Laurie, and two other passengers crashed outside Aintree racecourse, killing everyone on board. As she and Joan had interchangeable wills, this resulted in both estates passing to Joan's son Nicholas; Nancy's son Thomas inherited nothing. Noël Coward wrote in his diaries: 'It is cruel that all that gaiety, intelligence and vitality should be snuffed out when so many bores and horrors are left living' (*Coward Diaries*, 560). Spain was cremated at Golders Green on 26 March, and her ashes were placed in the family grave in Horsley, Northumberland.

ROSE COLLIS

Sources R. Collis, *A trouser-wearing character: the life and times of Nancy Spain* (1997) • personal knowledge (2004) • private information (2004) • N. Spain, *A funny thing happened on the way* (1964) • *The Noël Coward diaries*, ed. G. Payn and S. Morley (1982) • b. cert. • m. cert. • Northumbd RO

Archives BBC WAC • BL, Colindale, London, Newspaper Library • BL | HLRO, Beaverbrook MSS | FILM BBC WAC • BFI NFTVA | SOUND BBC WAC • BL NSA

Likenesses photographs, 1944, IWM • photograph, 1954, Hult. Arch. • F. Goodman, photographs, 1962, NPG [*see illus.*] • L. Morley, photographs, 1962, NPG • photographs, repro. in N. Spain, *Why I'm not a millionaire* (1956) • photographs, repro. in Spain, *A funny thing happened*

Wealth at death £28,260: probate, 14 Aug 1964, *CGPLA Eng. & Wales*

Spalding, Adalbert of (*fl. c.*1160), supposed theological writer, was a creation of the confusion of the bibliographer John Bale (*d.* 1563), who placed him around the middle of the twelfth century. Bale's contemporary John Leland (*d.* 1552) had recorded the presence at the abbey of Spalding, Lincolnshire, of a copy of a letter to the priest Herman prefacing a work generally known as *Speculum Gregorii*. Bale did not recognize this as the compilation of extracts from Gregory the Great's *Moralia in Job* which survives in numerous manuscripts, mostly of continental provenance, the earliest of which dates from the late tenth century. It is now firmly attributable to the continental writer Adalbert of Metz (*d. c.*980). Bale simply, and erroneously, took the presence of a manuscript of the work at Spalding to indicate the origin of the author at that abbey. The 'Homilies' that Bale also ascribed to this Adalbert cannot now be identified, if indeed they ever existed. The speculation in the *Dictionary of National Biography* that Bale's attribution of this latter work to an Adalbert of Spalding may indicate the existence of such a writer places too much faith in the testimony of this uncertainly reliable Tudor bibliographer.

MARIOS COSTAMBEYS

Sources R. Sharpe, *A handlist of the Latin writers of Great Britain and Ireland before 1540* (1997) • P. Wasselynck, 'Les compilations des *Moralia in Job* du VIIe au XIIe siècle', *Recherches de Théologie Ancienne et Médiévale*, 29 (1962), 27–8 • Bale, *Cat.*, 205–6

Spalding, Douglas Alexander (1841–1877), comparative psychologist, was born on 14 July 1841 at 2 St James Street, Islington, London, the only son of Alexander Mitchell Spalding, office clerk, and his wife, Jessey Fraser. Shortly after his birth, Douglas Spalding's parents relocated the family to Aberdeenshire, where they had previously lived. As G. C. Robertson noted, Spalding 'began life under great material disadvantages, and raised himself through his own exertions' (Robertson, 154). While working as a slater in Aberdeen, Spalding obtained Alexander Bain's permission to attend lectures in literature and philosophy, free of charge, at the University of Aberdeen in 1862. Spalding subsequently returned to London, where he supported himself by teaching, and embarked on a career in law. He entered the Middle Temple on 12 November 1866 and was called to the bar on 7 June 1869. Perhaps in the hope of alleviating the symptoms of pulmonary tuberculosis, which he had contracted in London, Spalding travelled to France, where he made the acquaintance of John Stuart Mill. This proved to be a propitious encounter. Through Mill, Spalding met the freethinkers John Russell, Viscount Amberley, and his wife, Kate, who wished to employ him as a tutor for their children. They first proposed this scheme at a dinner party at Mill's London home in April 1871, but they could not convince Spalding to give up law.

Spalding's commitment to law, however, may not have been vocational. An obituary noted that although he kept up his terms as a barrister, he never actually practised (*Nature*, 36). His principal interest lay in experimental physiological psychology. He gained notoriety in the field after delivering a paper entitled 'Instinct with original observations on young animals' to the British Association for the Advancement of Science at Brighton in August 1872. Convinced that the introspective methodology and the associationist theory of natural theologians and analytical psychologists were scientifically inaccurate, he used rigorous experimentation to challenge George Berkeley's theory of human vision. Specifically, he sought to demonstrate that spatial perception was not acquired or learned, but was inherited as instinct. He achieved his goal by subjecting approximately fifty developing chicks to sensory isolation. In addition to this experimental work on perceptual motor maturation, Spalding made significant observations on early social behaviour. His delineation of the 'instinct to follow', for example, was identified by later ethologists as 'imprinting'. Similarly, he recognized that instincts could be lost if not used within a given period. Upon the publication of the complete paper in *Macmillan's Magazine* in February 1873, Spalding received the public approbation of Charles Darwin and George Henry Lewes. As an acknowledged expert in psychology, Spalding began a minor career as a regular reviewer for *Nature* and the *Examiner*, which ended only upon his death. He consistently evaluated texts in relation to his own materialist, Spencerian evolutionary perspective.

The Amberleys continued their pursuit of Spalding. After dining with him at Mill's house on 1 April 1873, they invited him to join Mill, Helen Taylor, R. W. Emerson, John Tyndall, and Alexander Bain at their London home for a dinner party two weeks later. Spalding undoubtedly realized the potential social, intellectual, and economic benefits of an association with the Amberleys. As he explained in *Nature* (8, 1873, 289), he enlisted Lady Amberley as a research assistant three months later for his experiments on flight maturation in swallows at the Amberleys' Monmouthshire home, Ravenscroft (later Cleddan Hall). At the completion of these experiments, he promised to become a resident tutor to their eldest son, John Francis (Frank).

Like most of the Amberleys' friends and relations, Frank took an immediate dislike to Spalding. Years later he asserted that his tutor, 'with hollow sunken cheeks, a sallow complexion and rather long black hair' 'exercised a sinister influence' over the household. When not fleeing Spalding to evade beatings, Frank 'was much intrigued by a little wooden tube which he always kept in his mouth to breathe through' (Russell, *Life and Adventures*, 24). Apparently only a nominal tutor, Spalding used the opportunity to continue his experiments on physiological psychology; chickens wandered freely through the drawing-room and library.

Within months of moving into Ravenscroft, Spalding accompanied the Amberleys on a holiday to Italy, where he proclaimed his love for Lady Amberley. Intent on demonstrating his commitment to complete openness in marriage Lord Amberley gave his approval to a sexual relationship between his wife and Spalding. On rational grounds the Amberleys contended that this arrangement would satisfy Spalding's needs and circumvent the dangers engendered in a consumptive man reproducing. These unusual relations came to an abrupt end with the death of Lady Amberley from diphtheria in June 1874. Spalding continued to reside and work at Ravenscroft, presenting papers on 'Instinct and acquisition' and on 'Free trade and labour' to the meeting of the British Association for the Advancement of Science at Bristol in August 1875. This was his last report of original experimental research. Five months later Lord Amberley died. Under the terms of his will, he appointed two agnostics, Spalding and T. J. Sanderson, as guardians of his surviving children, Frank and Bertrand Russell. Amberley's father, Lord John Russell, successfully contested the will and gained guardianship of his grandchildren. Although he guaranteed Spalding a lifetime wage, this proved to be a short-term commitment. In pursuit of a healthier climate, Spalding fled to Cabrolles, near Menton, in France, and died in Dunkirk on 30 October 1877.

Although his life was tragically cut short, Spalding helped to transform psychology from a sub-discipline of philosophy into a natural science. In this respect his demonstration of the importance of experimentation for the study of animal behaviour proved especially significant. His work on instinct and 'imperfect instincts' inspired early comparative psychologists, such as George John Romanes, Conwy Lloyd Morgan, Wesley Mills, and William Preyer. More generally, he contributed to the shift from an environmentalist to a hereditarian emphasis within animal psychology. And a little over half a century later, in 1954, J. B. S. Haldane introduced emergent ethologists to Spalding's contributions after reading about them in William James's enduring *Principles of Psychology* (1890).

J. F. M. Clark

Sources *Nature*, 17 (1877–8), 35–6 · [G. C. Robertson], 'News', *Mind*, 3 (1878), 153–4 · H. A. C. Sturgess, ed., *Register of admissions to the Honourable Society of the Middle Temple, from the fifteenth century to the year 1944*, 2 (1949), 555 · J. B. S. Haldane, 'Introducing Douglas Spalding', *British Journal of Animal Behaviour*, 2 (1954), 1 · *The Amberley papers: the letters and diaries of Lord and Lady Amberley*, ed. B. Russell and P. Russell, 2 vols. (1937) · Earl Russell [J. F. S. Russell], *My life and adventures* (1923) · P. H. Gray, 'Douglas Spalding: the first experimental behaviorist', *Journal of General Psychology*, 67 (1962), 299–307 · P. H. Gray, 'Verification of Spalding's method for controlling visual experience by hooding chicks in the shell', *Proceedings of the Montana Academy of Sciences*, 21 (1962), 120–23 · P. H. Gray, 'Spalding and his influence on research in developmental behavior', *Journal of the History of the Behavioral Sciences*, 3 (1967), 168–79 · P. H. Gray, 'Prerequisite to an analysis of behaviorism: the conscious automaton theory from Spalding to William James', *Journal of the History of the Behavioral Sciences*, 4 (1968), 365–76 · R. J. Richards, *Darwin and the emergence of evolutionary theories of mind and behavior* (1987) · R. Boakes, *From Darwin to behaviourism: psychology and the minds of animals* (1984) · B. Russell, *The autobiography of Bertrand Russell*, 1 (1967) · *The later letters of John Stuart Mill, 1849–1873*, ed. F. E. Mineka and D. N. Lindley, 4 vols. (1972), vols. 14–17 of *The collected works of*

John Stuart Mill, ed. J. M. Robson and others (1963–91), vol. 4 • b. cert. • *CGPLA Eng. & Wales* (1878)
Archives BLPES, J. S. Mill MSS
Wealth at death under £1500 in England: probate, 15 Jan 1878, *CGPLA Eng. & Wales*

Spalding, John (*b.* 1624?, *d.* in or after 1669), historian, was the son of Alexander Spalding, an Aberdeen lawyer, and possibly of his first wife, Christian Hervie, but in January 1624 Alexander Spalding was disciplined for being the father of a child being carried by Euphame (Effie) Lillie, and for having tried to procure the unborn child's abortion. If John Spalding was this child and was thus born illegitimate, he was subsequently legitimized by his parents' marriage, for Alexander and Euphame were married by 1649.

Spalding was from the outbreak of the revolt against Charles I in Scotland in 1637 a committed royalist and episcopalian, and signed the king's covenant in October 1638. He entered King's College, Aberdeen, in 1640, just after it had been purged of its royalist staff by the covenanters, and graduated MA there in 1644. He then made his living as a clerk. On the defeat of the engagers' army in England in 1648 Spalding acted as clerk for the remnants of their forces in Scotland in September when they were negotiating terms under which they would disband.

Spalding is best-known through his *Memorialls of the Trubles*, but the title, inflicted by later editors, misrepresents the nature of the work and its author's intentions. He appears to have begun writing after the outbreak of the 'troubles' in Scotland in 1637, but begins for no obvious reason with entries for 1624. A likely explanation was that this was the year of his birth, and that he thus intended his manuscript to cover events in his own lifetime. The early sections of his work are derivative accounts of occurrences during his childhood, mainly relating to rivalries and feuds in the north-east of Scotland, but after the beginning of rebellion against the king Spalding concentrates on detailing its progress, with a strong emphasis on Aberdeen and the north in general. He was an eyewitness to much of what happened in Aberdeen, but he rarely mentioned this, preferring to remain silent about himself. Thus while he furiously denounces the conduct of William Guild, the covenanting principal imposed on King's College (who even interfered with students' 'naturall eisment' by roofing over the toilets, provoking a dirty protest of indiscriminate easement), he never mentions that he was a student at the university at the time (Spalding, 2.188). This personal reticence may have been based both on his father's notoriety as a repeated adulterer and on the fact that his sisters (or half-sisters) showed an unfortunate taste for enemy soldiers. One was disciplined for fornication with a covenanter, and after the English conquest of Scotland two of them married members of the Cromwellian garrison. The distinctive name of Spalding was perhaps not one to boast of in Aberdeen.

Spalding provides a detailed account of the impact of civil war in the north-east, unrivalled by surviving sources for any other part of Scotland, and his rough, unpolished chronicle of events compensates for lack of sophistication by giving a sense of immediacy. In general the closer events were to Aberdeen, the more reliable Spalding's accounts of them are, though occasionally he widens his focus by inserting the texts of documents relating to national affairs. The manuscripts that survive end in 1644, but the text originally continued until at least 1647.

After the Restoration in 1660 Spalding was made a burgess of Edinburgh at the request of the new bishop of Aberdeen, whose servant he was (August 1661), and the following month he became a burgess of Aberdeen. Soon afterwards he was appointed clerk of the commissary court, but he resigned in 1663, having sold the right to the office to his successor. He settled in Edinburgh, and is last heard of there in 1669. His name was subsequently commemorated by three Aberdeen clubs devoted to publishing historical sources, the Spalding, New Spalding, and Third Spalding clubs (active 1839–1960).

David Stevenson

Sources J. Spalding, *Memorialls of the trubles in Scotland and in England, AD 1624 – AD 1645*, ed. J. Stuart, 2 vols., Spalding Club, [21, 23] (1850–51) • D. Stevenson, 'Who was John Spalding?', *Aberdeen University Review*, 51 (1985–6), 102–15 • D. Stevenson, 'The secretive chronicler: Mr John Spalding', *King or covenant?* (1996), 95–103

Spalding, Samuel (1807–1843), philosopher, born in London on 30 May 1807, was the son of Thomas and Ann Spalding. His father was the founder of the firm of Spalding and Hodge, wholesale stationers, in Drury Lane, in which Samuel became a partner. Subsequently he studied for the Congregational ministry at Coward College, and graduated BA from London University in 1839; he proceeded MA in May 1840, with special distinction in mental and moral science. In an attempt to recover from excessive studying he travelled first in Italy, and then to the Cape of Good Hope, where he died on 14 January 1843.

Spalding's only work, *The Philosophy of Christian Morals*, was published posthumously in London in 1843. Influenced by Sir James Mackintosh's *Dissertation on the Progress of Ethical Philosophy*, Spalding seeks to derive all moral virtue from the supreme 'principle of benevolence', which he identifies with Christian charity and with God's love. What distinguishes his appeal to benevolence from that which is to be found in much eighteenth-century British moral philosophy is his claim that benevolence has to include an element of conscious volition in order to be distinctively moral, so that it is a fusion of intellect and emotion. Spalding uses this account of virtue to sketch a new theology of the atonement, arguing that the atonement cannot be adequately explained as a mere propitiation of God's vengeance for sin, since the demand for justice is a moral principle which is not independent of benevolence but subordinate to it. For Spalding, this new atonement theology implies the forgetting of denominational differences in the common fight against poverty.

J. M. Rigg, *rev.* Gavin Budge

Sources *DNB* • S. Spalding, *The philosophy of Christian morals* (1843) • *GM*, 2nd ser., 19 (1843), 557

Spalding, William (1809–1859), author, was born in Aberdeen on 22 May 1809, son of James Spalding, advocate, of

Aberdeen, and his wife, Frances Read. He graduated MA at Marischal College, Aberdeen, in 1827 and was afterwards writer to the signet for some years in Edinburgh, where he passed advocate in 1833. In the same year he published a notable *Letter on Shakespere's Authorship of the Two Noble Kinsmen*, which was reissued in 1876 and 1994. He made an extensive study of Shakespearian and Elizabethan drama, and in the 1840s contributed several articles on the subject to the *Edinburgh Review*. On 22 March 1838 he married Agnes Frier; they had a daughter, Mary, who was his constant literary companion and amanuensis.

After having failed to get the chair of logic at the University of Edinburgh in 1836, Spalding was elected to the chair of rhetoric and *belles-lettres* there on 2 November 1840. In 1841 he published *Italy and the Italian Islands* (3 vols.), the fruits of his earlier travels in Italy. On 22 October 1845 he became professor of logic, rhetoric, and metaphysics at St Andrews, a post he held until his death on 16 November 1859, at South Street, St Andrews, after a long period of delicate health.

Spalding was short and plain in appearance and he suffered from chest complaints. He was a popular, if exacting, teacher and wrote on numerous literary, biographical, and historical subjects. His most important work, other than those mentioned above, was his *History of English literature, with an outline of the origin and growth of the English language* (1853) which went to numerous English editions and was translated into German. His work in many subjects was much praised in his lifetime and in the years immediately following his death.

J. M. RIGG, *rev.* ELIZABETH BAIGENT

Sources J. H. Burton, 'Life of Spalding', in W. Spalding, *Letter on Shakespeare's authorship of the Two noble kinsmen*, New Shakespeare Society's Publications, 8th ser., 1 (1876), preface • private information (1897) • *GM*, 3rd ser., 8 (1860), 191 • *The Scotsman* (19 Nov 1859) • Allibone, *Dict.* • M. F. Conolly, *Biographical dictionary of eminent men of Fife* (1866) • Boase, *Mod. Eng. biog.* • W. A. Knight, *Some nineteenth century Scotsmen* (1903)

Archives Mitchell L., Glas., letters | NL Scot., corresp. with John Lee • NL Scot., letters to John Burton • UCL, letters to Society for the Diffusion of Useful Knowledge

Spang, William (1607–1664), Presbyterian minister in the Netherlands, was born in Glasgow, the son of Andrew Spang (*d.* 1638), merchant burgess of the city, and his wife (*d.* in or after 1638). He graduated MA from the University of Glasgow in 1625 and studied divinity in Edinburgh. Spang then taught at Edinburgh high school until 27 January 1630, when the convention of royal burghs appointed him minister of the Scottish church in the staple town of Veere, in the south-west corner of the Netherlands.

Spang is best-known as a correspondent of his cousin, the well-known Glasgow University principal Robert *Baillie (1602–1662), and their exchange contributes much to what is known of the latter. Baillie wrote regularly, keeping his cousin informed of affairs in his homeland, while in return Spang wrote about European news and sent over books. Both men were committed presbyterians and Baillie was keen for Spang to obtain the assistance of the Dutch in the name of the cause. In 1641 Veere was the first foreign congregation to be recognized by the general assembly as a component part of the Church of Scotland and the following year Spang was persuaded to attend the assembly. During the 1640s fasts and days of prayer were held in support of Scottish success and on 29 May 1644 the solemn league and covenant was subscribed by members of the congregation in the church.

In turn Spang did much to promote Scottish presbyterianism in the Netherlands. He was involved in the publication of Scottish works, including Baillie's *Operis historici et chronologici libri duo* (1668) and an edition of Arthur Johnstoun's poems. He himself publicized the history of the Scottish church with *Brevis et fidelis narratio in regno et ecclesia Scotica* (1640, reprinted as *Rerum nuper in regno Scotiae gestarum historia* in 1641), and published *Motuum Britannicorum verax Cushi ex ipsis Joabi et oculati testis prototypis totus translatus* in 1647. Spang's relationship with Dutch theologians was of most interest to his cousin. He distributed copies of Baillie's works, constantly reminded his peers of Scottish affairs, and undertook propaganda work which persuaded the local *classis* to commission a book in aid of presbyterianism against English Independency during the deliberations of the Westminster assembly in 1644.

Spang's attachment to the covenanting movement probably contributed to the major dispute of his Veere incumbency. In July 1643 Elizabeth Cant, mother-in-law of the Scots conservator Sir Patrick Drummond, died, and her relatives announced the intention (in accordance with Dutch practice) of placing a memorial stone with her coat of arms in the church. The memorial was erected, notwithstanding the dissent of the kirk session, led by Spang, which argued that the house of God should not have its walls covered with such badges of pride. In an escalation of the dispute, Cant's two sons then accused the minister of persecuting their mother to death. The issue was referred to the general assembly, which in October backed the view of the kirk session. The memorial was removed and in 1644 the pro-covenanting merchant Thomas Cuningham replaced Drummond as conservator. Spang's first wife, whose name is unknown, died in 1647. He then married Anna Meese; they were to have two sons and three daughters.

In 1649 Spang was involved in the ultimately successful negotiations to persuade Charles II to sign up to the covenants and return to Scotland. After serving the Veere congregation for twenty-three years, Spang was appointed minister at Middelburg, on 10 November 1652 (though he did not move to his new charge until May 1653). Here he seems to have upset some of the English members of his church by referring to it as a British or Scottish church. He also had to contend with English Quakers who interrupted his sermons in 1655 and 1657, the latter resulting in a Quaker's being sentenced to two years' hard labour by the magistrates. Spang was appointed *classis* scribe in 1657, and remained at Middelburg until his death there on 17 June 1664. His son William (*c.*1658–1683) followed in his father's footsteps, as minister of Middelburg between 1682 and 1683.

GINNY GARDNER

Sources *Fasti Scot.*, new edn, 7.540–41, 547–8 • *DSCHT*, 51, 788 • *The letters and journals of Robert Baillie*, ed. D. Laing, 3 vols., Bannatyne Club, 73 (1841–2) • J. Davidson and A. Gray, *The Scottish staple at Veere* (1909) • W. Steven, *The history of the Scottish church, Rotterdam* (1832, 1833) • K. L. Sprunger, *Dutch puritanism: a history of English and Scottish churches of the Netherlands in the sixteenth and seventeeth centuries* (1982)
Archives NL Scot., Wodrow MSS

Spankie, Robert (1774–1842), lawyer, was born on 17 April 1774 at Falkland, Fife, the second (but eldest surviving) son of Thomas Spankie (1743–1783), Church of Scotland minister at Falkland, and his wife, Margaret, daughter of Robert Boyce of Perthshire. He matriculated to St Andrews University in 1789 but though 'considered by far the cleverest man of his year' (Hardcastle, 1.45) he left without graduating and migrated to England about 1792. He became a reporter on Joseph Perry's *Morning Chronicle*, and was noted for the unmatched speed of his handwriting (and long remembered for a daring leap into the lobby of the House of Commons when a crowded staircase impeded the delivery of his report on a crucial division).

Spankie became editor, and possibly part proprietor, but having assisted the future Lord Campbell (a student acquaintance) to enter the law, Spankie followed suit, being admitted to the Inner Temple on 27 January 1803 and called on 1 July 1808. He did not prosper initially, but his marriage to Euphemia (1785?–1872), the daughter of John Inglis, an East India Company director, on 29 December 1813 opened up opportunities in India, and on 2 July 1817 he was made advocate-general in Bengal. The post was worth about £3000 a year, and conditions were highly propitious for the few British barristers practising in the superior court at Calcutta, so he was amassing a sizeable fortune when a disease of the liver made him return home in July 1823.

Once his health recovered Spankie resumed his practice in England, the first man to do so, and soon had a home at 36 Russell Square, London. Tallish and athletic in his youth, pale-complexioned and with a nose that 'partakes of the cock-up form' (Grant, 2.183), he was convivial and popular. He was not in the top flight as an advocate and was handicapped by a 'most discordant voice and a revoltingly coarse Scottish accent' (Hardcastle, 1.142), but he was fluent and animated, and against moderate competition became one of the leaders in the common pleas and went the home circuit. He also proved effective at the parliamentary bar in support of the Liverpool and Manchester Railway bills of 1825–6. He had been made a serjeant in July 1824 and on 8 December 1830 the lord chancellor, Lyndhurst, to the indignation of the other serjeants, gave patents of precedence to Spankie and C. C. Jones. In 1832 he became a king's serjeant.

At the general election of December 1832 Spankie stood successfully as a Liberal in the new and tumultuous constituency of Finsbury Boroughs. He proved decidedly conservative on legal questions, opposing both the abolition of imprisonment for debt on mesne process and the Prisoners' Counsel Bill in 1834, and staunchly defending the Irish judge Baron Smith from the government's censure for making political speeches. His constituents were disenchanted by his equivocal stance on the motion to repeal the window tax (1833), and especially by his stern disapproval of their 'excitement' and out-of-doors agitation. He also gave a qualified support to Peel's minority government, and the result of this drift towards Conservatism was the loss of his seat at the election of 1835. In 1837 he stood as a Conservative for Bury but was soundly beaten, and so ended his political career. Lyndhurst considered making him a judge for his party services but it was thought that, partly because of the time he had spent in India, his legal knowledge was insufficient.

Spankie's position at the bar went into decline in the 1830s with the arrival in the common pleas of more talented men such as Wilde and Talfourd, and with the loss of the serjeants' monopoly in 1834. He joined the other leading serjeants in petitioning the crown to declare Brougham's warrant unlawful but took no prominent part in the legal proceedings which they instituted. His declining practice was cushioned by his role as standing counsel for the East India Company from 1832. He had a large family to provide for, and this connection enabled him to send three sons to India, where Robert became a judge of the high court of Allahabad. The other son, John, was called to the bar from Lincoln's Inn. Spankie died at his house in Russell Square on 2 November 1842. His widow survived him by thirty years and died on 30 May 1872. The tradition, encouraged by Ballantine, that Spankie, perhaps bigamously, married a Miss Smith—

> Then came Serjeant Spankie
> And Miss Smith said 'Thankie'.
> (Veitch, 54)

—has no substance and reflects Spankie's name rather than his morals. Patrick Polden

Sources G. S. Veitch, 'Mr Serjeant Spankie', *Transactions of the Historic Society of Lancashire and Cheshire*, 82 (1930), 42–67 • [J. Grant], *The bench and the bar*, 2nd edn, 2 (1838) • *Life of John, Lord Campbell, lord high chancellor of Great Britain*, ed. Mrs Hardcastle, 2 vols. (1881) • *GM*, 2nd ser., 18 (1842), 654 • W. Ballantine, *Some experiences of a barrister's life*, 4th edn, 2 vols. (1882) • Baker, *Serjeants* • Sainty, *King's counsel* • J. Whishaw, *A synopsis of the English bar* (1835) • F. W. S. Craig, *British parliamentary election results, 1832–85*, 2nd edn (1989) • M. F. Conolly, *Biographical dictionary of eminent men of Fife* (1866) • Venn, *Alum. Cant.*, 2/5 • Foster, *Alum. Oxon.* • J. M. Anderson, ed., *The matriculation roll of the University of St Andrews, 1747–1897* (1905) • J. B. Atlay, *The Victorian chancellors*, 1 (1906) • *London Directory*
Likenesses I. Spankie, group portrait, sketch, *c.*1816 (with family), priv. coll.; repro. in Veitch, 'Mr Serjeant Spankie' • silhouette, priv. coll.; repro. in Veitch, 'Mr Serjeant Spankie', facing p. 46
Wealth at death under £35,000: PRO, death duty registers, IR 26/1656, fols. 55*v*–58*v*

Spare, Austin Osman (1886–1956), artist and occultist, was born on 30 December 1886 at 10 Bloomfield Place, King Street, Snowhill, near Smithfield, London, the fourth of the five children of Philip Newton Spare (1857–1928), a City of London policeman, and his wife, Eliza Ann Adelaide, *née* Osman (1860–1939). He was educated at St Sepulchre's School, Smithfield. The family moved in 1894 to Kennington, where Spare attended St Agnes School and took evening classes at Lambeth Art School.

On leaving school at fifteen Spare worked for a poster

manufacturer before going to a stained-glass firm, where he was recommended for a scholarship to the Royal College of Art. In 1904 he attracted attention as the youngest exhibitor at the Royal Academy summer exhibition and was profiled in several newspapers. A serious and autodidactic youth, he told a *Daily Chronicle* journalist that he was inventing his own religion ('Boy artist at the R.A.', *Daily Chronicle*, 3 May 1904).

Spare attracted patrons as an illustrator and bookplate designer, but was an *enfant terrible* at the Royal College of Art, where he was a friend of Sylvia Pankhurst. He left in 1905 without completing the course. The same year, aged eighteen, he published his first book, *Earth: Inferno*. His first West End showing at the Bruton Galleries in 1907 was widely condemned as unhealthy, and George Bernard Shaw is alleged to have said that 'Spare's medicine is too strong for the average man' (Grant, 16). His early work is often compared to that of Aubrey Beardsley—a comparison of limited usefulness—and to that of the book illustrator E. J. Sullivan. He took something from both, but he struck an off-key note of the cracked, decayed, and corrupt which was all his own.

In some respects an heir to the 1890s, Spare was taken up by Canon John Gray. He attended André Raffalovitch's salon, and drew Beardsley's sister Mabel. In 1915 John Lane agreed to publish a new quarterly edited by Spare and Francis Marsden, perhaps hoping for another *Yellow Book*; the first issue of *Form* appeared in 1916, with an article, 'Automatic drawing', by Spare and Frederick Carter. A second issue appeared in 1917, the year in which Spare was conscripted into the Royal Army Medical Corps. In 1911 Spare had married the theatre actress Eily Gertrude Shaw (1888–1938), but they separated during the First World War.

Spare became a war artist, going to France in 1919 to illustrate the medical history of the First World War. In 1921 he revived the title *Form*, co-editing it with the poet W. H. Davies, and in 1922 he became co-editor with Clifford Bax of the luxurious new quarterly the *Golden Hind*, which folded in 1924. Spare underwent a crisis and wrote his *Anathema of Zos*, attacking conventional society. By now he had retreated south of the Thames, living as 'a swine with swine', as he told Grace Rogers (Spare, 9). He remained there for the rest of his life.

Spare claimed to have come under the influence of a Kennington witch named Mrs Paterson when he was a child, and he was briefly an associate of Edward Alexander (Aleister) Crowley, joining Crowley's Argenteum Astrum in 1909. However, Spare's originality lies in dispensing with the conceptual paraphernalia of ritual magic in favour of more free-form, psychically orientated practices. He felt that conscious belief and desire were weak compared with their unconscious counterparts, so he sought to manipulate and programme the unconscious. This often involved graphic techniques: he condensed verbal ideas into monogram-like forms called sigils, and developed an idiosyncratic and eroticized 'alphabet of desire'. His sorcery also relied on a complex redefinition of elemental spirits and familiars. His major magical work was *The Book of Pleasure (Self-Love)*, which he published himself in 1913: this is graphically radical in its drawings of sensations, which accompany more conventional allegorical pictures.

Spare increasingly parted company with fame and fortune during the 1920s, and between the wars he held selling exhibitions in his council flat. He drew intense pastels of Southwark locals from life, art deco pictures of film stars from magazines, and he experimented with anamorphic distortion, which he termed siderealism. Hitler tried to commission a portrait from him in 1936, but Spare refused. Spare was devastated when his studio was blitzed in 1941, but achieved a post-war renewal with exhibitions in south London public houses and at the Archer Gallery in Westbourne Grove. He died on 15 May 1956 in the South Western Hospital, Landor Road, Stockwell, London, following appendicitis, and was buried at St Mary's, Ilford, Essex.

Spare's work often featured pagan and occult imagery such as satyrs and witches, but his portraits and nudes have a less circumscribed appeal. He was a draughtsman of exceptional power, and some of his work has an almost Pre-Raphaelite degree of finish. His skills enabled him to produce remarkably separate styles, and he was popularly compared at different times with Beardsley, Albrecht Dürer, William Blake, Michelangelo, and Rembrandt. He also produced automatic drawings and grotesques.

Spare's life has been mythologized, beginning with his own extensive confabulations; as befits a man who sought to dissolve the borders between fantasy and reality, he was very flexible with the truth. It is unlikely that he spent time in Egypt, as he claimed, and even the existence of Mrs Paterson, a cornerstone of the Spare myth, is not universally agreed.

Described by Mario Praz as a 'Satanic occultist' (*The Romantic Agony*, 2nd edn, 1951, 396 n. 59) and condemned by Crowley as a black magician, Spare was none the less a keen member of the RSPCA. Urban but unworldly, he stayed eccentrically close to working-class life, and in the mid-1930s produced a set of Surrealist Racing Forecast Cards for picking winners. Misleadingly promoted as a proto-surrealist, or pigeon-holed as an Edwardian decadent, Spare was a maverick artist whose best work carries an exceptional charge. He was above all a prodigious draughtsman, and a prime candidate for inclusion in what Peter Ackroyd has often termed 'the Cockney visionary tradition' (*Blake*, 1995, 92). Examples of Spare's work are in the Victoria and Albert Museum and the Imperial War Museum, London, and the Ashmolean Museum, Oxford. PHIL BAKER

Sources F. Letchford, *Michelangelo in a teacup: Austin Osman Spare* (1995) · K. Grant, *Images and oracles of Austin Osman Spare* (1975) · R. Ansell, *The bookplate designs of Austin Osman Spare* (1988) · G. Semple, *Zos-Kia: an introductory essay on the art and sorcery of Austin Osman Spare* (1995) · A. O. Spare, *Two tracts on cartomancy* (1997) · G. Semple, 'Austin Osman Spare', *A collection of watercolours and drawings by Austin Osman Spare* (1994) [sale catalogue, 12 May 1994, Christies, South Kensington, London] · *The Times* (16 May 1956) · K. Grant, *The magickal revival* (1972) · K. Grant and S. Grant, *Zos speaks* (1998)

Likenesses A. O. Spare, self-portrait, pastel drawing, 1937, NPG · A. O. Spare, self-portrait, pastel drawing, Man. City Gall. · photographs, repro. in Letchford, *Michelangelo in a teacup*
Wealth at death £618 9s. 3d.: administration with will, 1 Jan 1957, *CGPLA Eng. & Wales*

Spark, Thomas (*bap.* 1655, *d.* 1692), Church of England clergyman and classical scholar, was baptized on 21 June 1655 at Northop, Flintshire, the youngest child of Archibald Spark (*c.*1610–1670), vicar of Northop, and his wife, Katharine Jones. From Westminster School, where he was a king's scholar between 1668 and 1672, Spark hopefully addressed Joseph Williamson with Latin poems on 'Rome and other subjects' (*CSP dom.*, *1670*, 643). He was elected to Christ Church, Oxford, in May 1672 (matriculating on 17 July), held a Bostock exhibition, and was tutored by Richard Roderick. He graduated BA in 1676 and proceeded MA in 1679. He enjoyed Dean John Fell's generosity but disparaged it in a begging letter sent to his old schoolmaster Richard Busby. Fell nominated him to deliver the first annual Bodleian oration, endowed by John Morris, on 8 November 1682. He was Greek praelector (1682–3) and senior censor (1684).

Spark's published scholarship is unimpressive. His editions of Herodian (1678) and Zosimus (1679)—possibly two of the 'New year books' whose publication Fell sponsored—deserve the same criticism Thomas Hearne makes of his edition of Lactantius (1684): 'a poor Performance, the Text being very uncorrect and the Notes from MSS. very mean, he having taken no pains to collate them accurately' (*Remarks*, 2.71). A Latin poem by Spark appears in *Pietas universitatis Oxoniensis … Caroli II* (1685). Two rather longer ones were printed posthumously in *Musarum Anglicanarum analecta* (vol. 2, 1699): the first on the restoration of St George's Hall, Windsor Castle, with a concluding attack on Shaftesbury and rebellion; the second on Christ Church's newly recast bell Great Tom.

Wood describes Spark as 'confident and forward without measure' (Wood, *Ath. Oxon.*, 2.893), and, as chaplain to Lord Chancellor George Jeffreys, his advancement in the church may have seemed assured. He became prebendary of Lichfield (9 April 1686), rector of Ewhurst, Surrey (1 March 1687), and of Norton, Leicestershire, and prebendary of Rochester (2 June 1688). However, on 12 September 1687 Oxford's convocation denied Jeffreys's request, by 118 votes to 53, that Spark and his other chaplain, Luke de Beaulieu, receive DD degrees. Spark did become BD on 18 February 1688 and eventually obtained his DD degree in 1691. That year he published in Oxford *A Sermon Preached at Guildford*. He married Dorothy Blaker at Chidnam, Sussex, on 16 April 1691. Having gone to Bath for his health, he died there on 7 September 1692 and was buried in Bath Abbey four days later. Wood attributes his early death to 'his Excesses and too much Agitation in obtaining Spiritualities' (Wood, *Ath. Oxon.*, 2.893). His widow was granted letters of administration on 31 October 1692.

HUGH DE QUEHEN

Sources Wood, *Ath. Oxon.*, 2nd edn, 2.751 · *Old Westminsters*, vol. 2 · F. Madan, *Oxford literature, 1651–1680* (1931), vol. 3 of *Oxford books: a bibliography of printed works* (1895–1931); repr. (1964) · J. R. Bloxam, ed., *Magdalen College and James II, 1686–1688: a series of documents*, OHS, 6 (1886) · *Remarks and collections of Thomas Hearne*, ed. C. E. Doble and others, 2, OHS, 7 (1886) · *Fasti Angl., 1541–1857*, [Canterbury] · archives, Christ Church Oxf. · E. G. W. Bill, *Education at Christ Church, Oxford, 1660–1800* (1988) · BL, Burney MS 520, fol. 31 · *Flint parish registers*, 1/1 (1994) · *IGI*

Sparke, Edward (*d.* 1693), Church of England clergyman, was a native of Kent; the names of his parents are as yet unknown. He matriculated as a sizar at Clare College, Cambridge, in Easter term 1626, graduated BA in 1630, and proceeded MA in 1633. He was created BD in 1640 and was incorporated at Oxford on 12 July 1653. He was created DD in 1660. On 15 September 1641 his first wife, Sarah (1615/16–1641), aged twenty-five, 'dy'dst to give another life!' according to one of Sparke's verses, 'Tears and Flowers Strew'd upon the Hearse of Mrs S.S.' (Sparke, *Appendix sacra*, sig. C4).

Sparke was preacher at St Mary's, Islington, in January 1638 when he delivered the funeral sermon of the herald Henry Chitting. He was instituted to the rectory of St Martin Pomeroy, Ironmonger Lane, London, on 28 September 1639, but was ejected during the civil war and according to a royalist newsletter was 'plundred by the Rebels' (Newcourt, 1.412). On 1 December 1646 a fifth of the income of the living was granted to his second wife, Martha. On 30 November 1650 the living was declared vacant by his resignation. In 1650 he was vicar of the Isle of Grain, Kent, to which he had been presented by Sir Edward Hales. By 1654 he was minister at St James's, Clerkenwell, where in July he buried a daughter, Elizabeth, and three years later his third wife, Judith. He retained this living until 1665; at the Restoration he also regained St Martin Pomeroy, Ironmonger Lane, and became a chaplain to Charles II. He resigned from St Martin's on 5 June 1661 and was instituted to the vicarage of Walthamstow in December 1662, which he held until he resigned and exchanged it for the vicarage of Tottenham, Middlesex, where he remained for the rest of his life.

Sparke's most important work was *Scintillula altaris, or, A pious reflection on primitive devotion, as to the feasts and fasts of the Christian church, orthodoxally revived*, first published in 1652 and reprinted seven times between 1660 and 1700. A long work, much of it written in poetic form, it detailed the lives of saints and various feast and fast days. The verses, many of which found the pun on Sparke's name irresistible (and whose authors included Thomas Fuller and Isaak Walton) underlined the work as an assertion of Anglican values in a time of adversity. Henry Delaune lauded the 'Bright shining Sparke of consecrated fire', while Thomas Shirley, mourning the distressed state of the church, proclaimed:

> In her eclipse no Herbert, not a Donne,
> SPARKE only sings her Resurrection.
> (Sparke, *Scintillula altaris*, no pagination)

Sparke's book was a positive celebration of the rites and religious calendar of the Church of England: 'All being done decently and in Order, and tending only to Gods Honour, his Saints Memory, and our Edification', but without these, he warned, '('tis too visible) Religion will soon languish, and even die away be degrees, into Profanenesse,

Heresie and Atheisme' (ibid., 5). Later editions of the work contain an engraved portrait of the author.

Sparke died in 1693, between the making of his will on 2 May 1693 and its proving by his executors on 25 September. He requested to be buried on the site of his old church (which after the great fire had become the churchyard of St Olave Jewry), in a black-marble-topped tomb where the chancel had been. A son, Edward Sparke, a graduate of St John's College, Oxford, had died in 1675, and his will mentions only one child living, a daughter, Sarah Lister, wife of Matthew Lister. Sparke was survived by his (presumably fourth) wife, Ruth. CAROLINE L. LEACHMAN

Sources J. Walker, *An attempt towards recovering an account of the numbers and sufferings of the clergy of the Church of England*, pt 2 (1714), 175 • Wood, *Ath. Oxon.: Fasti* (1820), 178–9 • Foster, *Alum. Oxon.* • E. Hasted, *The history and topographical survey of the county of Kent*, 2 (1782), 93 • Venn, *Alum. Cant.* • *Walker rev.* • R. Newcourt, *Repertorium ecclesiasticum parochiale Londinense*, 2 vols. (1708–10) • R. Hovenden, ed., *A true register of all the christenings, mariages, and burialles in the parishe of St James, Clarkenwell, from … 1551 (to 1754)*, 6 vols., Harleian Society, register section, 9–10, 13, 17, 19–20 (1884–94) • G. Hennessy, *Novum repertorium ecclesiasticum parochiale Londinense, or, London diocesan clergy succession from the earliest time to the year 1898* (1898) • will, PRO, PROB 11/416, sig. 147 • E. Sparke, *Appendix sacra* (1652) • E. Sparke, *Scintillula altaris, or, A pious reflection on primitive devotion* (1652) • E. Sparke, *The Christians map of the world* (1637)

Likenesses A. Hertochs, line engraving, 1662, BM, NPG; repro. in Sparke, *Scintillula altaris* • engraving, repro. in Sparke, *Scintillula altaris* (1700) • engraving, repro. in Wood, *Ath. Oxon.: Fasti*, vol. 2, p. 179 • line engraving, BM, NPG; repro. in Sparke, *Scintillula altaris*

Wealth at death wife to receive *c.*£35 p.a. rents from properties in Wapping, Middlesex; £150 to each of three grandchildren, from mortgage in their father's hands; 'Assignments' with £144 p.a. annuities/rents: will, PRO, PROB 11/416, sig. 147

Sparke, Joseph (1682–1740), Church of England clergyman and antiquary, was born at Peterborough on 16 December 1682, the son of John Sparke, a feoffee of the town. He was educated at the town grammar school and in 1699 entered St John's College, Cambridge, graduating BA in 1704. He was appointed under-master at his old school in 1704, ordained deacon in 1705, and made a minor canon of the cathedral on 2 September 1706. He was ordained priest on 23 September 1710 and served the curacy of Eye. On 29 June 1710 he married Rebecca Wigmore (1692–1747), a widow, at Peterborough.

On 22 June 1714 Sparke was appointed registrar, chapter clerk, and master of the works at Peterborough Cathedral, succeeding John Brown, who had got into financial difficulties and to whom Sparke remitted some of the fees attached to the office. His responsibilities included the care of the books belonging to the dean and chapter and the making of a full index of their contexts. He had already entered into correspondence with White Kennett, the antiquarian bishop of Peterborough, and soon began to co-operate with him on the history of the cathedral, correcting the work of Simon Gunton. He remained a close collaborator of Kennett, though they quarrelled over fees due to Sparke in 1720, by which date he had been appointed cathedral librarian, charged with the care of the extensive library presented by the bishop. Sparke had already recatalogued the library of the earl of Cardigan at Deene. In 1723 Sparke published *Historiae Anglicanae scriptores varii*, comprising the chronicles of John of Peterborough, Hugh Candidus, and Robert of Swaffham, and Fitzstephen's life of Becket, though the text owed more to White Kennett's work than was suggested in the volume. The volume was published from a transcript provided by the Northamptonshire historian John Bridges (in whose house he wrote the preface to part two of the volume); despite containing a number of errors, it was a significant contribution to local history.

Sparke was appointed rector of Paston in 1719, where his wife's former husband had also served, but moved to the valuable capitular living of Northborough on 18 June 1723, continuing as rector until his death. He was a founder member of the Gentlemen's Society of Peterborough, founded by a fellow minor canon and St John's man, Timothy Neve, and also belonged to the more famous society at Spalding in Lincolnshire. In 1726 he was given extended leave of absence from his cathedral duties on account of ill health, and from 1731 these were performed by a more or less permanent deputy. Sparke had proposed a second volume of Peterborough chronicles but it remained unpublished, though almost ready for the press at his death. He died at Peterborough on 20 July 1740 and was buried in the cathedral on 25 July. There is a monument to him in the choir of the cathedral, but perhaps the best epitaph comes from the pen of the Oxford antiquary Thomas Hearne, who described Sparke thus in 1725:

> Mr Sparke is an excellent scholar, of a great memory, admirably well versed in the Editions of Books, that he is mad a quarter of a year together every year … that he is very sober … & that he is always among his Books, wholly delighting in Study. (*Remarks*, 8.382)

G. LE G. NORGATE, *rev.* WILLIAM JOSEPH SHEILS

Sources J. D. Martin, ed., *The cartularies and registers of Peterborough Abbey*, Northamptonshire RS, 28 (1978) • H. I. Longden, *Northamptonshire and Rutland clergy from 1500*, ed. P. I. King and others, 16 vols. in 6, Northamptonshire RS (1938–52), vols. 12, 16 • *Remarks and collections of Thomas Hearne*, ed. C. E. Doble and others, 8, OHS, 50 (1907) • *The Peterborough chronicle of Hugh Candidus*, trans. W. T. Mellows and C. Mellows (1941)

Archives BL, notes relating to English religious houses and cathedrals, Add. MS 5828 | BL, letters to White Kennett, Lansdowne MS 990 • Bodl. Oxf., letters to John Bridges

Sparke, Michael (*b.* in or before **1586**, *d.* **1653**), bookseller, was the son of Richard Sparke, husbandman, of Eynsham, Oxfordshire. It seems likely that he had at least a grammar-school education since he could read and write Latin, and made a bequest to an Oxfordshire grammar school in his will. He was apprenticed on 7 June 1603 to the London bookseller Simon Pauley, but was transferred successively to two other stationers, the latter of whom, Bartholomew Downes, freed him on 10 June 1610.

Sparke later described himself as a 'wholesaleman' and in 1652 claimed that he had 'dealt in *Books* above 40 yeares for my self' (Sparke, *Second Beacon*, 5). He may have spent some years as a journeyman since his first entry in the Stationers' Company register was in 1617; by his own account he had sold books through the countryside with Pauley and was well acquainted with provincial networks of chapmen, pedlars, and mercuries. From 1617 onwards he was dwelling and working at the sign of the Blue Bible in Green Arbour Court, London, near the Old Bailey. He sold books printed by the university printers at Oxford and Cambridge with whom he had a sustained working relationship. Sparke's brother Thomas and nephew Nathaniel were colonists in Virginia and Bermuda respectively, which may have inspired his interest in publishing works about colonization, including those of Captain John Smith and the first English edition of Mercator's *Atlas*. His will indicates that he also exported books to the American colonies.

In later life Sparke denounced Pauley as a papist who sold '*Popish Books, Pictures, Beads*, and such *Trash*' in the countryside (Sparke, *Second Beacon*, 6). He also denounced a notorious papist bookbinder and other papists in the trade who had defrauded him. Indeed, Sparke's life and work were characterized by his maniacal devotion to the protestant religion. He later reminisced about visiting Leiden, probably about 1630, to line up books, especially bibles, for importation. In the 1620s he published *Crumms of Comfort*, a collection of prayers intended to serve as a daily prayer book, perhaps as an alternative to the official prayer book of the state church. Sparke's little volume proved immensely popular and went into forty-four editions through the early eighteenth century.

From 1626 Sparke was the dedicated publisher of the religious radical William Prynne and, according to Prynne, it was about this time that Sparke's troubles with church and crown regulatory authorities began. He was first in trouble in the aftermath of the parliament of 1626 for publishing Bishop Carleton's book refuting Richard Mountague. Following his arrest in April 1631 for publishing unlicensed books, Sparke was described as having been 'within 10 years past several times committed in prison and admonished, and although he promised to submit to his governors as other moderate men do, has as yet been more refractory and offensive than ever' (Rostenberg, 261). On a number of occasions Prynne and Sparke were in trouble together, notably at the appearance of *Histriomastix* in 1633 for which both author and publisher were publicly pilloried, Sparke 'with a Paper in his Hat' (Jackson, 256). In addition, Sparke was fined £500 by the Star Chamber and suspended from the livery of the Stationers' Company to which he had been admitted in December 1626. He also published the works of the Revd Henry Burton, another religious radical and associate of Prynne. Sparke was frequently in trouble for selling imported bibles to the detriment of the king's printer, and was still ranting about the monopoly over bibles in *Scintilla*, which he wrote and published in 1641. At other times he ran foul of the church, state, and Stationers' Company for printing unlicensed books. He was prosecuted also for having printed at Oxford books registered to other stationers in London.

From 1636 Sparke was in business with one of his sons, Michael, who was freed of the Stationers' Company on 1 March 1641, although their names continued also to appear separately in imprints and the son owned no copyrights. Not much is known of the son except that he died on 17 November 1645, 'Wounded by his unnaturall Brother [Philip] causelesly' according to an acrostic ballad memorial (Vere).

The convening of the Long Parliament in 1641 was something of a turning point for Sparke. His clients and friends, Prynne and Burton, were reprieved and hailed as heroes. Sparke's £500 fine from the *Histriomastix* case was remitted and he was granted a licence by the committee for printing to publish and republish Prynne's works. Sparke was also called on as an expert witness for the parliamentary government as, for example, in the trial of Archbishop William Laud: the publisher cuts a prominent figure in Hollar's engraving of the trial.

But as with many religious radicals of the period, Sparke became disillusioned with the Long Parliament and its godly revolution. He was also frustrated with his chosen trade. Between 1641 and 1645 he was a leader of a group of 'rebel Stationers' who unsuccessfully sought reform in the governance of the company and in particular in the allocation of monopolies and the power the monopolists exercised within the trade. He continued to protest as an individual. In 1652 he upbraided stationers who would print and sell anything for profit, and who had no dedication to the protestant religion. He lamented that 'our Reformation is now a Desolation' and that '*Poor honest Stationers*' could not pay their rents or feed their families (Sparke, *Second Beacon*, 9).

Sparke died in December 1653 in Hampstead, Middlesex, and was buried on the 29th. He left a will indicative of his religious fervour and his moderate success in the book business. Sparke was married twice, and while he left a generous settlement to his second wife, Isabel, he requested to be buried in St Sepulchre's, Holborn, London next to his first wife, Elizabeth, who may have been connected to the Warwickshire gentry. To his 'good frend' William Prynne, Sparke bequeathed his 'seale ring of gold'. He specified that the livery of the Stationers' Company, along with all women save his daughters and grandchildren, should be excluded from his funeral, and further, that there should be no funeral sermon; his favoured devotional books rather than refreshments were to be distributed to those who attended. S. A. BARON

Sources *CSP dom.* • PRO, state papers domestic, Charles I, SP 16 • H. R. Plomer, 'Michael Sparke, puritan bookseller', *The Bibliographer*, 1 (1902), 408–19 • will, PRO, PROB 11/199, sig. 52 [Michael Sparke, son] • will, PRO, PROB 11/236, sig. 153 • [M. Sparke], *Scintilla, or, A light broken into darke warehouse* (1641) • [M. Sparke], *A second beacon fired by Scintilla* (1652) • W. A. Jackson, ed., *Records of the court of the Stationers' Company, 1602 to 1640* (1957) • C. Blagden, 'The Stationers' Company in the civil war period', *The Library*, 5th ser., 13 (1958), 1–17 • D. F. McKenzie, ed., *Stationers' Company apprentices*, 3 vols. (1961–78), vols. 1–2 • W. Prynne, *Canterburies doome, or, The first part of a compleat history of the commitment, charge, tryall, condemnation, execution of William Laud, late arch-bishop of Canterbury* (1646) • T. Vere, *To the never dying memory of his ever honor'd friend Mr Michael Sparke jun.* [1645] • *The obituary of Richard Smyth … being a catalogue of all such persons as he knew in their life*, ed. H. Ellis, CS, 44 (1849) • L. Rostenberg, 'Michael Sparke', *The British literary book trade, 1475–1700*, ed. J. K. Bracken and J. Silver, DLitB, 170 (1996), 258–65

Likenesses Hollar, engraving (Laud's trial), repro. in W. Prynne, *A breviate of the life of William Laud* (1644)

Sparke, Thomas (1548–1616), Church of England clergyman, is said by Wood to have originated at South Somercotes, Lincolnshire. Elected to a demyship at Magdalen College, Oxford, in 1567, he was a fellow there from 1569 to 1572. He graduated BA in October, proceeding MA in January 1574, BTh on 8 July 1575, and DTh on 1 July 1581. Rector of South Somercotes as early as 1571, on 26 January 1576 he was collated archdeacon of Stow by Thomas Cooper, bishop of Lincoln, whose chaplain he had become. In 1578 he was presented to the rectory of Bletchley, Buckinghamshire, by Arthur, fourteenth Baron Grey of Wilton, where he is said to have been 'held in great esteem for his piety' (Wood, *Ath. Oxon.*, 2.189). But on 6 March 1582, conscience-stricken that this living was far removed from the duties of his archdeaconry (apparently the pangs were not about pluralism as such), he resigned the latter office, having already found compensation in presentment to the Lincoln prebend of Sutton in Marisco.

Although he was a beneficed clergyman, Sparke's sympathies lay with the puritan wing of the Church of England. In December 1584, along with Walter Travers, he represented the interests of the godly in a meeting with Archbishop Whitgift and Bishop Cooper at Lambeth Palace, primarily about subscription to the Book of Common Prayer. The conference was held at the insistence of the earl of Leicester, who was joined by Walsingham, Burghley, and Sparke's patron Grey for two days of deliberations. Though keenly anticipated by the puritans, not least because it tacitly set their ministry on a par with that of the bishops, the meeting was disappointing in its effects. Sparke and Travers confined themselves to matters concerning lectionary readings from the Apocrypha, and to certain perceived abuses in the baptismal rite, and refused to engage in debate with Whitgift over matters of polity and the Christian ministry, let alone the large puritan objections to the prayer book *in toto*. Ultimately the meeting achieved only a further easing of subscription to the prayer book, already limited since the summer, and that seems to have been effected by Walsingham and to have owed little or nothing to the debate.

Sparke's second appearance as a puritan champion proved even more disappointing for the precisians than that of 1584. On 1 November 1603 he was one of the representatives of the godly cause to appear before James I at the Hampton Court conference. Though still noted as 'a great nonconformist and a pillar of puritanism', who refused to attend in clerical garb but wore 'such that Turkey merchants wear' (Wood, *Ath. Oxon.*, 2.190), he none the less remained silent during the whole of the first day's proceedings. Next day, following a private audience with James (for whose right of succession he had earlier been an advocate), Sparke completely abandoned his nonconformity. His conversion led to the publication in 1607 of *A Brotherly Perswasion to Unity and Uniformity in Judgement and Practice*. Sparke dedicated it to James I, giving the king credit for his being persuaded 'by your majesties owne most readie and apt answers' and addressing him as 'over all persons, and in all causes Ecclesiasticall as civil in these his dominions' (Sparke, *Perswasion*, sig. A3r). Not only is the royal supremacy proclaimed, but Sparke also recants even those marginal scruples he had maintained in 1584, and goes on to allow *jure divino* status for bishops, for 'in respect of their ministry and spiritual iurisdiction in the Church, they wel may be said to be of God's own ordinance' (ibid., 78). Sparke's treatise was answered by Samuel Hieron in the following year.

Sparke also published funeral sermons preached for the second earl of Bedford in 1585 and for his patron Lord Grey in 1593, and a rebuttal of Jean d'Albin de Valsergue's *Discourse Against Heresies*, entitled *An Answere to Master John De Albines, Notable Discourse* (1591). As was customary, Sparke reproduces the entire text of d'Albin's work in his own, replying to it section by section. Dedicated to Lord Grey, the book is more a defence of protestantism in general than of the Church of England in particular.

Sparke is recorded by Wood as having been so respected at Oxford for his learning and exemplary manner of living 'that the sages of the university thought it fit, after his death, to have his picture painted on the wall in the school-gallery among the English divines of note' (Wood, *Ath. Oxon.*, 2.190). He died at Bletchley on 8 October 1616 and was buried in the chancel of the parish church, where he is commemorated by a monument. With his wife, Rose Inkforbye (*d.* 1615), the youngest daughter of an Ipswich merchant, he had ten children, of whom five survived their parents. Three of Sparke's sons followed him into the ministry of the church, including **William Sparke** (1587–1641), who was born at Bletchley and followed his father to Magdalen in 1603, becoming first a demy and then a fellow, both in 1606. Graduating in 1607, he proceeded MA in 1609 and BTh in 1629. He resigned his fellowship in 1616 to succeed his father as rector of Bletchley. He also became a chaplain to the duke of Buckingham. He published two treatises, *Vis naturae et virtus vitae explicatae* (1612) and *The Mystery of Godlinesse* (1628). He is recorded as living at Bletchley in 1630, but indebtedness forced him to resign the living; on 20 May 1641, however, he became rector of Chenies, also in Buckinghamshire. He died in October that year. He is not known to have married.

GARY W. JENKINS

Sources Wood, *Ath. Oxon.*, new edn, 2.189–91, 495 · Tanner, *Bibl. Brit.-Hib.* · P. Collinson, *The Elizabethan puritan movement* (1967) · A. Peel, ed., *The seconde parte of a register*, 2 vols. (1915) · *STC, 1475–1640* · *Fasti Angl., 1541–1857*, [Lincoln] · *DNB* · Foster, *Alum. Oxon.*

Likenesses attrib. R. Haydock, brass effigy, St Mary's Church, Bletchley, Buckinghamshire · engraved plaque, Bletchley church, Buckinghamshire · line engraving, BM, NPG

Sparke, William (1587–1641). *See under* Sparke, Thomas (1548–1616).

Sparkes, John Charles Lewis (1832/3–1907), educationist and college head, was among the most prominent art educationists of the Victorian period. He was the son of John Sparkes, but little is known of his early life except that he was first taught by Paul Naftel in Guernsey and, on arriving in London, pursued his studies at Leigh's academy and the Royal Academy Schools. Advised by Leigh to take up teaching, he entered the art masters' training class at

Marlborough House, run by the fledgeling Department of Science and Art, about 1853. A year later, he took charge of the art classes formed by the Revd Robert Gregory at the schools of St Mary-the-Less in Lambeth. From these classes developed the successful Lambeth School of Art, which soon established itself as a leader in the provision of instruction in applied art and design to working artisans, many of whom were employed by local manufacturing firms. Through his friendship with Henry Doulton, Sparkes cultivated a special relationship between the Lambeth School and Doulton's pottery manufactory: from about 1869, the school developed coursework geared to the pottery trade, and the firm provided rooms for students to carry out the work, a link that was maintained until the 1880s when these advanced classes were taken over by the City and Guilds Institute. The result of this collaboration was a new line of 'art-pottery', known popularly as Doulton ware, many items of which were designed by Sparkes.

As an educator, Sparkes proved to be both innovative and resourceful, being among the first art instructors to teach mechanical drawing by setting students to draw actual pieces of machinery as opposed to merely copying flat examples. Despite the technical flavour of such an experiment, he was actually a firm traditionalist in matters of art and design education, espousing throughout his life the approved academic belief that life drawing was the best training for any kind of artistic work. Although his students were generally quite successful in examinations and competitions, his methods were not fully endorsed by his superiors in the Department of Science and Art. When its head, Henry Cole, introduced full payment on results into the national system of art education in 1863, an association of art masters was formed to contest the new minutes, led by Sparkes. A nationwide revolt of art masters managed to attract a great deal of political momentum, projecting Sparkes to the fore of the debate. The masters were eventually defeated, as Cole's system survived a parliamentary inquiry in 1864, but Sparkes had begun to make his mark administratively.

In 1875 (after Cole's retirement) Sparkes was invited by Edward J. Poynter to become headmaster of the National Art Training School at South Kensington and was promoted to principal when Poynter relinquished the position in 1881. He remained in this post until retiring in 1898, having reached the age limit. Many famous names can be counted among his pupils, including W. W. Ouless, George Frampton, and Stanhope Forbes. During these years he published works on a wide range of artistic subjects, including *A Handbook to the Practice of Painting* (1877), *The Classical Composition of John Flaxman, Sculptor* (1879), *Hints on Pottery Painting* (1885), *A Manual of Artistic Anatomy* (1888), *Wild Flowers in Art and Nature* (1894), and *Potters: their Arts and Crafts* (1897). He also contributed to the descriptive catalogue of the Dulwich Picture Gallery (1876–1905) and edited the Fine-Arts Library series from 1884.

On 1 August 1868 Sparkes married the painter and illustrator Catherine Adeline Edwards (*d.* 1891), who had been his student at Lambeth and who exhibited many pictures at the Royal Academy between 1866 and 1890, first under her maiden name and then as Mrs C. A. Sparkes after 1870. After her death in 1891, and a few years before his own, Sparkes made arrangements with the Royal Academy to bequeath the proceeds of his Surrey estates towards founding scholarships for female students, in memory of his wife. Afflicted with blindness in his later years, he died on 12 December 1907 at Heathside, Ewhurst, Surrey.

R. C. DENIS

Sources *The Times* (19 Dec 1907) · *Art Journal*, new ser., 28 (1908), 60, 128, 370 · 'Select committee on … schools of art', *Parl. papers* (1864), 12.47–54, 72–87, no. 466 [minutes of evidence] · J. C. L. Sparkes, 'Schools of arts: their origin, history, work and influence', *The Health Exhibition literature* [London 1884], 7 (1884), 721–880 · Wood, *Vic. painters*, 2nd edn · m. cert. · *CGPLA Eng. & Wales* (1908) · d. cert.

Archives V&A NAL, corresp.

Wealth at death £14,513 16*s*. 7*d*.: resworn probate, 1 Feb 1908, *CGPLA Eng. & Wales*

Sparks, Hedley Frederick Davis (1908–1996), biblical scholar, was born on 14 November 1908 at 2 Sydner Road, South Newington, London, the only child of the Revd Frederick Sparks (1847–1908), curate of West Hackney, and his second wife, Blanche Barnes (1871–1951), daughter of William Jackson. His father died about six weeks before Sparks was born, and his mother was left in straitened circumstances. He was educated at St Edmund's School, Canterbury (where tuition, lodging, food, and clothing during term time was provided by the Clergy Orphan Corporation) and at Brasenose College, Oxford. He took a first in theology in 1930 and various university prizes, a BD in 1937, and a DD in 1949. Ordained deacon in 1933, he combined a curacy at the City Church with work on the Vulgate and a (non-stipendiary) chaplaincy at Ripon Hall, where he had done his ordination training. The increasingly strident tone of the Modern Churchmen's Union and its links with Ripon Hall led to his resignation in 1936. He was, however, later chairman of the governors. From 1936 to 1946 he was lecturer in the theology department at Durham University; he took an active part in the maintenance of discipline in the absence of lay colleagues during the Second World War, and enjoyed doing so. He then went to Birmingham as the first Cadbury professor of theology (1946–52); there he developed the syllabus and gave the faculty an ecumenical basis, breaking new ground in the appointment of a Roman Catholic (H. Francis Davis) as lecturer. In 1952 he became Oriel professor of the interpretation of holy scripture in Oxford. Although he regretted the severance of the chair from a canonry at Rochester, the appointment fulfilled a long ambition. He was elected a fellow of the British Academy in 1959. Until her death in 1951 he had provided a home for his mother. On 25 August 1953 he married Margaret Joan (*b.* 1930), daughter of C. H. Davy. They had two sons and a daughter. In 1976 he retired to Canterbury.

In 1933 Sparks was recruited by H. J. White, dean of Christ Church, to assist him on the critical edition of the Vulgate New Testament begun by J. Wordsworth. The first fascicule of the work had been published in 1889; by 1926 it had reached 2 Corinthians. Sparks helped White with the proofs of Ephesians (published with Galatians in 1934) and after White's death became editor, originally under the supervision first of F. C. Burkitt and then of B. H. Streeter, but from 1937 on his own. He completed volume 2 in 1941 and the final volume in 1954. Towards the end there was an increasing amount of work to be done, since some of the collations he inherited were incomplete and there were more patristic commentaries to be incorporated. Sparks in turn recruited the assistance of A. W. Adams, who helped with the proofs from 2 Timothy onwards and to whom Sparks handed over the editorship of the Johannine epistles. In 1942 Sparks was asked to help with what became known as the Critical Greek Testament. This project dated back to 1926 and the volumes on Matthew and Mark had already been published. Luke was eventually to appear in two parts in 1984–7. Sparks was responsible for the citations of the Vulgate and for part of the Old Latin material (in connection with which he went to Beuron in 1976 and 1977). From 1959 he was also involved with the preparation of the Stuttgart edition of the Vulgate (published in 1969).

Apart from his work on the Latin text of the Bible, Sparks was engaged on two other long-term projects. His *Synopsis of the Gospels* (in English) showed not only the parallels between different sections in the synoptic gospels but also parallels between identical and alternative words or phrases within the sections, and included the Johannine parallels. Part 1 appeared in 1964, part 2 in 1974, with John printed as the main text and the synoptic parallels noted on the right-hand side of the page. *The Apocryphal Old Testament* (1984 [actually 1985]) was designed as a handy replacement for the work of R. H. Charles, published in 1913. Omitting the Apocrypha, it contained revisions of the translations by Charles or new translations, with some new items; while the translations were the work of different scholars, the introductions and bibliographies were all done by Sparks, providing the book with uniformity and a high standard of accuracy. He also wrote *The Old Testament in the Christian Church* (1944), *The Formation of the New Testament* (1952), and a number of learned articles in journals, contributed to various co-operative enterprises, including *Chambers' Encyclopedia* and *The Cambridge History of the Bible*, and was responsible for the biblical material (in a wide sense) in the second edition of *The Oxford Dictionary of the Christian Church*.

Beyond the field of textual criticism, Sparks exercised wide influence through his teaching, his wise counsel in the bodies with which he was associated, and his editorship of the *Journal of Theological Studies* from 1954 to 1977. He recruited Henry Chadwick, then young and little known, as co-editor, insisting that they should appear as equals. For twenty-four years he devoted infinite care to the journal, teaching generations of beginners how to handle and present scholarly material, and reading with a sharp and critical eye the whole of every issue. In Oxford he was but one of eight professors of theology, but his sane views carried weight in the affairs of both faculty and college. From 1961 to 1968 he was also rector of Wytham; until 1975 he usually took a locum during the long vacation and almost everywhere he lived he regularly helped with services in church. His strong sense of duty found expression in meticulous scholarship and an expectation of high standards in others (coupled with a certain intolerance when these were not met), and in a pastoral care even for the most unattractive. He was short in stature, but could dominate an audience. He was devoted to railways and music, and was a good practical gardener. He died on 22 November 1996 in the Nunnery Fields Hospital, Canterbury, and was buried on 28 November in New Romney churchyard, after a funeral service in Canterbury Cathedral. He was survived by his wife and three children.

ELIZABETH A. LIVINGSTONE

Sources H. F. D. Sparks, autobiography, priv. coll. • S. P. Brock, *PBA*, 101 (1999), 513–36 • personal knowledge (2004) • private information (2004) [S. P. Brock; M. J. Sparks] • *The Times* (29 Nov 1996) • *Daily Telegraph* (3 Dec 1996) • *WWW* [forthcoming]

Likenesses photograph, British Academy, London • photograph, repro. in *The Times*

Wealth at death £229,423: probate, 27 March 1997, *CGPLA Eng. & Wales*

Sparrow, Anthony (1612–1685), bishop of Norwich, was born in 1612 at Depden, near Bury St Edmunds, Suffolk, the son of Samuel Sparrow, and baptized on 7 May at nearby Wickhambrook. He matriculated from Queens' College, Cambridge, in 1625, graduated BA in 1629 and proceeded MA in 1632. He was a junior fellow by 13 February 1633, and was ordained priest at Ely on 22 February 1635. On 24 June 1637 Sparrow preached *A Sermon Concerning Confession of Sins and the Power of Absolution* (1637), in which he made the typically Laudian claim that priests might hear confession and pronounce absolution, with the proviso that God would actually absolve only the truly penitent. Insisting that the individual must accept responsibility for sin, without blaming God, nature, or the devil, Sparrow's sermon effectively advanced the idea of free will, and was too far distant from Calvinist predestinarian doctrine to be regarded as simply Arminian. It has been persuasively argued that it should be regarded instead as one in a rapidly growing number of frankly papist theological and sacramental pronouncements made from various quarters within the university at this time. Within two weeks of preaching the sermon was in print. Contemporaries were outraged, but Sparrow remained untouched, evidently enjoying at least the tacit protection of Archbishop William Laud's press censors, and perhaps the bishop of London himself, William Juxon.

Sparrow was Hebrew praelector from 1638 to 1639, with a stipend of £5 per annum, and proceeded BD in 1639. In 1640–41, however, Sparrow and a number of his contemporaries at Cambridge came under the scrutiny of a parliamentary committee set up to investigate religious innovations at the universities. Despite his close association with the scandalous disclosures of popish doctrine and adornments corrupting a number of colleges and their chapels Sparrow remained at Queens'. He was Greek praelector, 1640–41; Hebrew praelector again in 1642–3; bursar, 1640–42; censor theologicus and examinator,

Anthony Sparrow (1612–1685), by unknown artist, *c.*1670

1641–2; and censor philosophicus, 1642–3. But on 8 April 1644 he fell victim to the parliamentarian purge of the university. He was ejected from his fellowship by the orders of Edward Montagu, second earl of Manchester, for non-residence and failure to comply with a summons to return to his college.

On 1 August 1645 Sparrow married Susanna Orrell (*d.* in or after 1693) at Withersfield, Suffolk. On 30 September 1647 he was instituted to the rectory of Hawkedon, near Depden, but he was ejected within five weeks for using the proscribed Book of Common Prayer. In 1655, shortly after a protectoral proclamation was issued upholding the prohibition of the prayer book, Sparrow published, anonymously, his *Rationale upon the Book of Common Prayer* which described and justified the liturgy in every detail. Undoubtedly a courageous publication Sparrow's book formed a direct answer to the denigration that had been heaped upon the prayer book and renewed the confidence of the adherents of orthodox usage. Sparrow also formulated a cogent theology of morning prayer in terms of access to the presence of God which gave the daily service a clear purpose and articulated its basic theological structure. The *Rationale* subsequently went through perhaps as many as eight editions before Sparrow's death, and enjoyed a minor revival in the nineteenth century.

In 1660 Sparrow was reinstated as rector of Hawkedon, and was also elected to a preachership at Bury St Edmunds. On 7 August he was appointed to the archdeaconry of Sudbury. On 31 August Sparrow, with Thomas Fuller and other eminent loyalists, graduated DD from Cambridge at the express command of the king. On 15 April 1661 he was appointed to the second prebendal stall at Ely. That year he also published *A Collection of Articles, Injunctions, Canons of the Church of England*, constructed broadly to evince that the reform of the church had been, and rightly ought to be 'orderly and synodical' and because Sparrow felt that 'without a definitive and authoritative sentence, controversies will be endless, and the churches peace unavoidably disturbed' (1671 edition, preface). But for Sparrow it seems that there would be little escaping the disturbance of the peace, whether that of the church or of the college to which he had now returned.

In 1662 Charles II and Clarendon bore down heavily on the majority of fellows at Queens', who had elected Simon Patrick to be their president, preferring Sparrow for the position instead. Patrick took the matter before the court of king's bench. He eventually withdrew from the contest to take up the benefice of St Paul's, Covent Garden, offered him by William Russell, earl of Bedford, but not before the king and his ministers had shown 'the lengths to which [they] were prepared to go to defend the interests of the high churchmen within the university' (Gascoigne, 35). As vice-chancellor of the university in 1664–5 Sparrow himself sought to intervene on behalf of the king's chosen candidate for a fellowship at Trinity Hall. He was also ever vigilant for the spread of religious heterodoxy within the university, showing no interest whatever in the case for latitude or moderation.

Sparrow's reward for his services at Cambridge came in 1667 with his promotion to the see of Exeter, where he was consecrated on 3 November. From 1668 to 1676 he also held the archdeaconry of Exeter and the sinecure deanery of St Buryan. Sparrow's episcopacy was characterized by deep concern at the growth of dissent. His primary visitation charge, preached in a sermon at Truro, was published in 1669 as *The Bishop of Exons Caution to his Diocese Against False Doctrines*. The indulgence of 1672 seems to have come as something of a betrayal, Sparrow complaining to Archbishop Gilbert Sheldon: 'I see daily to my heart's grief the poor sheep committed to my trust snatched out of the fold by cunning wolves and I know not how to bring them back' (Spurr, 63).

In 1676 Sparrow was transferred to the no less difficult, but considerably more valuable, see of Norwich. The city was descending at that time into a period of factional conflict which one contemporary compared with pardonable exaggeration to that between Guelphs and Ghibellines in medieval Italy. Sparrow's appointment probably contributed to the polarization of opinion between the church and crown loyalists who had welcomed the appointment of Lord Yarmouth as lord lieutenant in 1675, and the sizeable nonconformist minority fearful of the rising tide of aggressive Anglicanism. However, before long Sparrow appears to have found himself caught in the crossfire between the extremists of the tory and whig parties. He found 'some clamouring loud against me for prosecuting schismatics, and some who profess great loyalty and zeal for the church, as loud complaining because we do not proceed violently beyond the rule of law' (Spurr, 82). Sparrow died at the episcopal palace at Norwich on 19 May 1685; a monument and inscription mark the spot where he lies buried in the nearby chapel. In his will he left £100 to the rebuilding of St Paul's Cathedral, £100 to Queens' College, and smaller sums to Norwich Cathedral and the widows and orphans of diocesan clergy. His widow and sole executor was still alive in 1693. They had numerous children, three daughters marrying dignitaries of Exeter Cathedral. RICHARD J. GINN and SEAN KELSEY

Sources *DNB* • Venn, *Alum. Cant.* • *Walker rev.* • D. Hoyle, 'A Commons investigation of Arminianism and popery in Cambridge on the eve of the civil war', *HJ*, 29 (1986), 419–25 • J. Gascoigne, *Cambridge in the age of the Enlightenment* (1989) • J. Spurr, *The Restoration Church of England, 1646–1689* (1991) • J. Miller, *After the civil wars: English politics and government in the reign of Charles II* (2001) • will, PRO, PROB 11/380, sig. 75 • *IGI*

Archives Bodl. Oxf., corresp. | Bodl. Oxf., letters to Gilbert Sheldon

Likenesses portrait, *c.*1670, Norwich Castle Museum and Art Gallery [*see illus.*] • W. Richardson, line engraving, 1798 (after portrait formerly at the bishop's palace, Exeter, 1897), BM, NPG • oils, Queens' College, Cambridge; version, bishop's palace, Exeter • print, repro. in A. Sparrow, *Rationale upon the Book of Common Prayer* (1657)

Wealth at death see will, PRO, PROB 11/380, sig. 75

Sparrow, John (1615–1670), translator and lawyer, was born on 12 May 1615 at Stambourne, Essex, the first son of John Sparrow, a military man. He matriculated from Trinity College, Cambridge, in 1631 but did not graduate. He was admitted of the Inner Temple in November 1633 and became a barrister. His law career was an active one: he took an interest in legal reform and was a member of the parliamentary civil service. He married Hester (*bap.* 1621), daughter of Joseph Norgate of Norwich, on 8 June 1641. They had six children, the eldest of whom, John, followed his father to Trinity College in 1659.

Between 1647 and 1662 Sparrow and his cousin John Ellistone translated and published the complete works of the Silesian mystic Jacob Boehme (1575–1624) from German into English; Sparrow took over the project at Ellistone's death in 1652. Boehme's theosophist philosophy blended mystical religious experience based on an understanding of the soul, alchemy, and Paracelsian medicine which found a ready audience of those disaffected by religious factionalism. Boehme's ideas of a personal spiritual relationship with God predated and were similar to those of George Fox; the Behemists eventually amalgamated with the Quakers, who downplayed Boehme's enthusiasm for astrology. The Silesian's hermetic philosophy was also popular among natural philosophers who responded to his vision that science was the way to understand the workings of the universe. Boehme was not an easy author to understand, as Sparrow himself admitted in his preface to his translation, *XL Questions Concerning the Soule* (1647): 'some will think it so hard to attaine … when they read the answer to the first Question … that they will forbeare to take so much paines as they suppose it requisite' (sig. A3*v*). Sparrow went on to encourage his readers to overcome their hesitation, and provided alternate translations or interpretations in the margins to help with difficult concepts. Boehme himself had provided

John Sparrow (1615–1670), by David Loggan, 1659

glossaries to his works which Sparrow included in his translations.

Sparrow was buried at Gestingthorpe, Essex, on 8 December 1670. K. GRUDZIEN BASTON

Sources J. S. [J. Sparrow], 'To the reader', in J. Behmen, *XL questions concerning the soule*, trans. J. Sparrow (1647) • R. R. A. Walker, 'John Ellistone and John Sparrow, the English translators of Jacob Behmen', *N&Q*, 167 (1934), 312 • K. Thomas, *Religion and the decline of magic* (1971); repr. (1991) • C. Webster, *The great instauration: science, medicine and reform, 1626–1660* (1975) • E. Vipont, *The story of Quakerism through three centuries*, 2nd edn (1960) • F. L. Cross and E. A. Livingstone, eds., *The Oxford dictionary of the Christian church*, 2nd edn (1974) • E. Bysshe, *A visitation of the county of Essex*, ed. J. J. Howard (1888) • W. H. Cooke, ed., *Students admitted to the Inner Temple, 1547–1660* [1878] • W. W. Rouse Ball and J. A. Venn, eds., *Admissions to Trinity College, Cambridge*, 2 (1913) • Venn, *Alum. Cant.* • *IGI* • *DNB*

Likenesses D. Loggan, line engraving, 1659, BM, NPG [*see illus.*]

Sparrow, John Hanbury Angus (1906–1992), college head, was born in New Oxley, near Wolverhampton, on 13 November 1906, the eldest son of Isaac Saredon Sparrow (1871–1964), barrister, and his wife, Margaret, *née* Macgregor (1871–1963). His father, who practised somewhat ineffectually on the midland circuit, was descended from a wealthy family of Black Country ironmasters; his mother's family, originally from the highlands, was in trade in Birmingham. Sparrow was a scholar at Winchester and New College, Oxford, where he took firsts in both classical moderations and *literae humaniores*. He had already displayed a precocious literary talent, which

John Hanbury Angus Sparrow (1906–1992), by Janet Stone

seems to have alarmed his schoolmasters and was associated with a lifetime passion for book collecting. A copy of Donne's *Devotions upon Emergent Occasions*, bought when he was thirteen, led to an edition published by Cambridge University Press in 1923. Two years later he edited *The Poems of Bishop Henry King* for the Nonesuch Press, followed in 1926 by a collection of poems by Abraham Cowley. In 1929 he was elected a prize fellow of All Souls College, Oxford, and won the Eldon law scholarship. He spent the next decade at the chancery bar, in chambers headed by Wilfrid Greene and then Cyril Radcliffe. During these years he wrote one short work of classical scholarship, *Half-Lines and Repetitions in Virgil* (1931), and a rather acerbic study of contemporary poetry, *Sense and Poetry* (1934). He also wrote numerous reviews and short articles for the *Times Literary Supplement*, *The Spectator*, and other periodicals.

At the outbreak of the Second World War Sparrow enlisted as a private soldier, but was soon commissioned in the Coldstream Guards. He moved to the War Office in 1941, ultimately becoming assistant adjutant-general with special responsibility for morale. He left the army in 1946 with the rank of lieutenant-colonel and an OBE. He then returned to the bar until he was elected as warden of All Souls in February 1952, a position he held until his retirement in September 1977. Between 1943 and 1975 he published eight volumes of *Lapidaria*, collections of inscriptions with designs by Stanley Morison and Reynolds Stone, as well as a study on the subject, *Visible Words* (1969). The Clark lectures given at Cambridge in 1965 were published in 1967 as *Mark Pattison and the Idea of a University*, and the 1976 Sara Schaffner lectures at Chicago were published in 1977 as *Too much of a Good Thing*. Sparrow's combination of book collecting and literary scholarship was exemplified in the anthology *Renaissance Latin Verse*, edited with Alessandro Perosa (1979). Two collections of shorter pieces appeared as *Independent Essays* (1963) and *Controversial Essays* (1966). His own poems were collected in 1981 under the characteristic title *Grave Epigrams and other Verses*.

The formal outlines of Sparrow's life and writings, and even those writings themselves, give a very inadequate impression of a most remarkable man. He was essentially a bundle of contradictions: a passionate and independent person who outwardly took highly conventional positions, a scholar and college head who had little sympathy for most academics, a lover of literature and the arts with a curiously narrow range of taste, a master of English prose who wrote no major book, and a believer in high moral standards who occasionally behaved very badly. His hatred of mediocrity and his intermittent snobbery were combined with an ability to relate to 'ordinary' people which made him a great success in his wartime career and was often evident in his dealings with college servants. He had a special talent for friendship which marked his whole life, was often both generous and perceptive, yet at times allowed a streak of deep selfishness to damage both himself and others. Some of these paradoxical qualities probably went back to his childhood, for his devotion to his mother and siblings contrasted with his dislike of his difficult father. The only common ground between father and son was a love of football: Sparrow was a talented player himself, and a keen supporter of Wolverhampton Wanderers who watched football enthusiastically to the end of his life.

Sparrow had a marvellously quick and precise intelligence, allied to a fine ear for words, so that those who debated with him risked being caught out on matters of both substance and style. Many of Sparrow's friends, like Maurice Bowra, felt that the powerful influence of his philosophy tutor, H. W. B. Joseph, had been harmful, cramping the more imaginative and creative side of his character, but his adult personality was unimaginable without his love of a good argument. It may well be that some part of him never fully accepted his own rational judgement, early in adult life, that he lacked the stuff of a major creative artist and must abandon his childhood ambitions in that direction. His letters reveal a growing sense of unease about his apparently successful legal career, probably sharpened by his notable wartime service. Once the idea that he might become warden of All Souls had been mooted, it is plain that he coveted the position above anything else, although it was only a series of unexpected illnesses and deaths which culminated in what might a couple of years earlier have been thought a most unlikely election.

In time it became evident that all parties, not least Sparrow himself, had failed to envisage the enormous changes which would overtake both society and the university over the next quarter century, still less how he might react to them. He had seen the wardenship as an ideal post for a scholarly man of letters, outside the academic mainstream, who could easily cope with routine college business. His colleagues, who had chosen him largely to avoid the alarming prospect of A. L. *Rowse, hoped that his intellectual powers and social gifts would flourish once he took up office. Sparrow did have real virtues as warden: he was an urbane and charming host, he was usually fair-minded in dealing with individual cases, and he stood up firmly to any college grandees who tried to pull rank. Unfortunately, by the 1960s the situation called for positive leadership, coupled with an understanding of both university politics and academic aspirations. Sparrow, who had revealingly declined to take up the vice-chancellorship in 1959, retreated into an instinctive (and at times provocative) conservatism. All Souls became mired in a long and confused debate about its future policy, which led to a public rebuke from the Franks commission and some unseemly controversy, before surplus college income was used to create a visiting fellowships scheme.

This public relations fiasco, together with Sparrow's attacks on the bearded and unkempt student generation he detested, exposed many of his weaknesses and prejudices. Another failing was his inability to conceal his personal likes and dislikes for individual fellows, sometimes accompanied by an unexpected touch of cruelty. He was capable of alarming outbursts of temper, which revealed something of the unhappiness and pessimism beneath the outward charm. Yet he was devoted to All Souls, and his effect on its affairs was often far from malign. He was instrumental in the appointment of outstanding professionals as bursar and librarian, while in his time the academic activity of the college grew enormously. Despite his own conservatism he was not the Machiavellian enemy of all change that some thought him; he had sufficient sense of duty to avoid that, and he was surprisingly ready to accept practical suggestions from others, particularly if they were not accompanied by what he saw as progressive cant.

Nothing aroused Sparrow's pugnacious instincts more than sloppy or sentimental arguments. His frequent forays into print to rebut instances of such failings made him a well-known public figure. At his best, when exploring the moral complexities of the trial of Adolf Eichmann, destroying conspiracy theories about the assassination of President Kennedy, or revealing the true sexual message of *Lady Chatterly's Lover*, he was a brilliant polemicist. These performances, and much of his literary criticism, also emphasized that he was generally more comfortable in destructive than in constructive mode. It was telling that in his superbly economical lectures on Mark Pattison he faltered at the same point as his subject, when it came to giving a convincing and coherent explanation of his own idea of a university. This was typical of a man who preferred debate to action, would invent an argument against himself if no one else obliged, and had little sympathy for general or abstract ideas. He was infinitely happier with the particular, as when solving a textual problem, or sharing his delight in association copies and rare editions with the Oxford Society of Bibliophiles, whose patron he became.

Sparrow's outward conventionality was in many respects a mask: he hated humbug, lacked any kind of religious faith, and was a lifelong homosexual. The notoriety he achieved in the 1960s and 1970s as an icon of conservatism depended on a certain degree of play-acting on his part, for he undoubtedly enjoyed striking public attitudes at variance with his private beliefs and conduct. This went with an infectious taste for practical jokes and a polished wit, qualities treasured by his many friends and most of his colleagues; one ambition he did fulfil was to be the author of memorable jokes. He inspired great affection even from many who saw his faults clearly, and the long list of his close friends included such figures as Maurice Bowra, Kenneth Clark, John Betjeman, L. P. Hartley, and Isaiah Berlin. It is sad to record that after so long a period as warden he found great difficulty in relinquishing the role and declined into alcoholism, from which he was rescued only after a long unhappy period. He died at his home, Beechwood House, Iffley Turn, Iffley, Oxford, on 24 January 1992. ROBIN BRIGGS

Sources *The warden's meeting: a tribute to John Sparrow*, ed. [Oxford University Society of Bibliophiles] (privately printed, 1977) · J. Lowe, *The warden: a portrait of John Sparrow* (1998) · *The Times* (25 Jan 1992) · *The Times* (29 Jan 1992) · *The Times* (5 Feb 1992) · *The Independent* (25 Jan 1992) · *The Independent* (29 Jan 1992) · *The Independent* (4 Feb 1992) · *The Independent* (14 Feb 1992) · *Daily Telegraph* (27 Jan 1992) · *WWW, 1991–5* · personal knowledge (2004) · private information (2004) · *CGPLA Eng. & Wales* (1992)

Archives Bodl. Oxf., corresp. with R. W. Chapman · Bodl. Oxf., corresp. with L. G. Curtis · King's Cam., letters to G. H. W. Rylands · Tate collection, corresp. with Lord Clark | SOUND BL NSA, documentary recording

Likenesses J. Stone, photograph, NPG [*see illus.*] · photograph, repro. in *The Times* (25 Jan 1992) · photograph, repro. in *The Independent* (25 Jan 1992) · photograph, repro. in *Daily Telegraph* · photographs, repro. in Lowe, *The warden*

Wealth at death £1,716,649: probate, 24 June 1992, *CGPLA Eng. & Wales*

Spartali, Marie. *See* Stillman, Marie (1844–1927).

Spartas, Reuben Ssedimbu Sebanjja Mukasa (1899–1988), politician in Uganda and Orthodox priest, was born at Masooli village, Kyadondo county, Buganda, on 16 December 1899, the son of Yakobo Damulira Mugimbalume (*d.* 1915), a village headman, and his wife, Maliza Mukomutibwa (*d.* 1935). The sixth of eight children, he was baptized at Gayaza into the Anglican church in December 1906, and in 1907 an older brother helped him to begin school. His intelligence was noticed, and in 1912 he was taken into the household of a missionary, Archdeacon Daniel, of Bishop Tucker College, Mukono, so that he could attend Bishop's School, Mukono. A teacher nicknamed him Sparta because of his sporting prowess, and he added an 's' when told that Greek masculine forms ended thus. He left school on the outbreak of the First World War, intending to enlist, but was too young to do so until 1917. After two years in the army he returned to Bishop's School, and then, having won a post office scholarship, attended King's School (later College), Budo, from 1920 to 1922. He served only briefly with the post office before rejoining the King's African rifles. He spent three years in the army at Bombo, and before long was appointed to instruct the troops and start a school for their children.

At Bombo, Spartas met Obadiah Basajjakitalo, who shared his growing resentment that the Anglican church treated them like 'boys'. Through his reading in Archdeacon Daniel's library Spartas had realized that the Orthodox church had a longer history than the Anglican church, which he learnt had originated in Henry VIII's divorce proceedings. Orthodoxy might offer a Christianity that was independent of the mission-founded Anglican or Catholic churches. Moreover the Orthodox church had a pedigree that local independent churches had not. In 1929 the two men announced that they were setting up the African Orthodox church, and they sought Orthodox ordination. In 1932 Bishop Alexander of the African Orthodox Church of South Africa agreed to ordain them. His orders were, however, irregular, and a Greek who took his child to be baptized by Spartas noticed that he knew little of Orthodox liturgy or practice. This led to a South African Orthodox priest coming to instruct Uganda's nascent Orthodox church, and in 1946 a link was also made with the patriarchate of Alexandria. The patriarch sent Spartas a copy of the liturgy of St John Chrysostom in English, which Spartas rendered into excellent Luganda. When he appointed Spartas his vicar in Uganda, the patriarch clearly did not realize that his ordination was irregular.

On 7 July 1926 Spartas married Eseri Namuyiga; she died childless on 5 December 1933. Following Orthodox custom, Spartas did not remarry, but he had a liaison with Ekiria Kezia Namyonga, and acknowledged her daughter, born in 1947, as his child.

Spartas continued active both in education and in Buganda politics. In 1926 he and Basajjakitalo founded Anonya private school, and other schools followed, in particular that now known as Chwa II Memorial College, Uganda's leading Orthodox school. In the early days the church struggled to bring these up to an acceptable standard. In 1938 Spartas and Ignatius Kangaye Musazi founded the Bana ba Kintu (sons of Kintu), a Ganda populist protest movement. From 1946 he was active in the Bataka party, a protest movement of peasants and small traders in Buganda and Busoga. After the 1949 Bataka riots in Buganda, Spartas and other leaders were sent into internal exile in northern Uganda. He spent four years there, followed by a year's restriction on his return home. He considered that he was treated very well by the British during his imprisonment, and being a 'prison graduate' enhanced his reputation among his compatriots. In 1955 he was a founder member of the Progressive Party and in 1956 the kabaka nominated him a member of the lukiiko (assembly of chiefs).

In 1959 a Greek metropolitan for east Africa was appointed, and Spartas was invited to visit Greece, where he was received as an honoured guest. Although the Greeks came to realize that the Orthodox church in Uganda was far from Orthodox, they decided to assist and educate it, providing theological education. Spartas, to his great disappointment, was passed over as bishop, Ireneo Magimbi Nyankyama being preferred, and for a while Spartas remained outside the main body of the church, which was increasingly accepted by the other churches in Uganda. Towards the end of his life he became reconciled with his position and gained a reputation as an elder statesman. He died in 1988. M. Louise Pirouet

Sources F. B. Welbourn, *East African rebels: a study of some independent churches* (1961) · Dam-Tabajjwa, 'The biography of Archpriest Spartas Reuben Sebbanja Ssedimbu Mukasa, politician, educationalist and founder of the African Greek Orthodox church', research paper, Makerere University College, 1969 · A. Hastings, *A history of African Christianity, 1950–1975* (1978) · B. Sundkler and C. Steed, *A history of the church in Africa* (2000) · *Who's who in Uganda, 1988–89* (1989) · personal knowledge (2004) · private information (2004) [K. Ward]

Spavens, William (1735/6–1799), seaman and autobiographer, was born in Stewton, near Louth, Lincolnshire. In May 1754, at the age of eighteen, his curiosity about distant lands prompted him to apprentice himself to the master of the snow *Elizabeth and Mary*, trading between Hull and the Baltic. He contracted smallpox on his first voyage, but quickly recovered. At the beginning of the Seven Years' War he was pressed into the *Buckingham* (70 guns), in which he first went aloft; and he then spent two years cruising in the West Indies in the *Blandford* (24 guns), taking many prizes. From January 1759 he was in the *Vengeance* (28 guns), pressing at Dublin and Liverpool, and witnessed the battle of Quiberon Bay on 20 November 1759.

When he was moved to the *Flora* (32 guns) at Plymouth, Spavens deserted and travelled overland to Deptford, where he entered the East Indiaman *Elizabeth* about December 1761. At Sumatra in August 1762 Spavens, with three others, took a boat and deserted the *Elizabeth*, planning to join a 'country ship' at Calcutta and make his fortune. But he ended up a prisoner of the Dutch, until he escaped and joined the *Panther* (60 guns). In January 1764 he seriously injured his leg while loading casks at Batavia. After reaching home in July 1765 he spent four months in Haslar Hospital, and received a small pension from the Chatham chest for his injury.

Finding that his wages had been claimed by his former master and that he had been cheated out of his prize money, and being unfit for the sea, Spavens returned to Louth, married, and learned to make gloves and breeches. His injured leg had to be amputated in May 1793. In 1796 he wrote his autobiography, *The Narrative of William Spavens*, which offers some rare insights into the life of a common seaman. He died in 1799. Randolph Cock

Sources W. Spavens, *The narrative of William Spavens* (1796) · W. Spavens, *The narrative of William Spavens*, new edn (2000)

Speaight, Robert William (1904–1976), actor and literary scholar, was born on 14 January 1904 at the Corner Cottage, St Margaret's Bay, Kent, the eldest of three sons of Frederick William Speaight and his wife, Emily Isabella, daughter of Frederick Elliott. His father ran a Bond Street photographer's but had varied artistic interests, designing the decorations for Edward VII's funeral, the Marble

Arch improvement scheme of 1905, and restoring old houses, including a Georgian mansion at Hatfield to which he moved his family in 1910.

Speaight's first contact with the stage was at the age of nine when he saw Sir H. Beerbohm Tree play Henry VIII. He went to school at The Wick, Hove, and then to Haileybury College, where he played Mark Antony, audaciously writing to Sybil Thorndike for advice. She replied: 'Acting is one of the greatest studies in the world: whether it is your living or not, the study of it helps you in every walk in life' (Speaight, 39), a truth which proved exceedingly apt for Speaight's career.

It was the great age of the country-house theatre and when Bobby, as he was known, played Macbeth at Hatfield, aged seventeen, his father persuaded Charles Morgan of *The Times* and W. A. Darlington of the *Daily Telegraph* to review the performance. At Oxford, where he won a scholarship to Lincoln College, Speaight's Falstaff (1926) reduced James Agate to tears: the great critic told him, 'You are the best Falstaff I have seen since Louis Calvert' (Speaight, 77), and gave him a glowing notice in the *Sunday Times*.

After that there was no doubt about a theatrical career. Having taken a third-class degree in English in 1926, Speaight spent a year with the Liverpool Repertory, followed by a tour of Egypt (1927) with Ernest Milton, whom he regarded as one of the finest actors of his day. In 1928 the scholar–director William Poel (whose biography Speaight published in 1954) invited him to play Arruntius in the *Sejanus* of Ben Jonson, and that autumn he created Smerdyakov in the dramatization of *The Brothers Karamazov* by Theodore Komisarjevsky.

Speaight's first West End success was in the all-male trench drama, *Journey's End*, by R. C. Sherriff, in which he played the coward Hibbert, first with Laurence Olivier in the lead, later with Colin Clive in an eighteen-month run (1929–30). He recalled: 'We gave one performance to an audience exclusively of VCs. We almost came to believe that we had been through the war ourselves' (Speaight, 105). Then followed a clutch of Shakespearian roles: First Player in the *Hamlet* of Henry Ainley, Edmund in John Gielgud's *King Lear* (1931), and in the 1931–2 Old Vic season he shared leads (and a dressing-room) with Ralph Richardson, playing Hamlet, King John, Cassius ('I won the best notice I have ever received from an English critic in a Shakespearian part') and Fluellen, which remained his favourite minor part (ibid., 142–3).

By this time Speaight's interests had broadened with the publication of a novel, *Mutinous Wind* (1932), the first of four, and deepened with his religious conversion. Speaight's parents had been fervent protestants and both his godfathers were Anglican clergymen, but after a visit to Bavaria and the Oberammergau passion play, 'I suddenly felt with quite overwhelming force that I wanted to become a Catholic' (Speaight, 115). In October 1930 he was received into the church at Farm Street, following instruction by Father Martin d'Arcy and Father C. C. Martindale. His new faith, and his growing interest in writing, brought him into contact with a wide circle of Catholic intellectuals: Hilaire Belloc and G. K. Chesterton, Douglas Woodruff and Tom Burns (in turn editors of *The Tablet*, to which Speaight contributed for nearly forty years), Compton Mackenzie, and Christopher Hollis. In 1935 Michael de la Bedoyere sent him to Rome to report the canonization of Sir Thomas More and John Fisher for the *Catholic Herald*, and on his return he seemed a natural choice to create the part of Thomas à Becket in *Murder in the Cathedral*, which T. S. Eliot had written for the Canterbury Festival.

Thus Speaight entered what he later wryly called 'the crypt of St. Eliot's'. His acting career had already reached a plateau. Short and stocky, he lacked the ideal physique for what he called the *optique du théâtre* and he had, as *The Times* put it, 'an interesting and mobile but not handsome face'. On the other hand, his voice had operatic power, stamina, and control, so that he adjusted easily to the acoustics of a cathedral or concert hall. He spoke verse with great intuitive skill, perfected by much study. He liked to quote Jean Cocteau's dictum: 'There are actors who think what they are saying, and actors who think about what they are saying', and Speaight was certainly among the latter. He was the first to discover how to recite Gerard Manley Hopkins's poems in such a way as to bring out both their full meaning and their sprung rhythm, though as Eliot said, 'he would have made a laundry-list sound like great poetry' (private information). In short he was the ideal festival actor.

Thanks to Speaight, *Murder in the Cathedral* was a surprising popular success, and he played it over 1000 times throughout the British Isles and North America. His performance evoked a characteristic 'compliment' from W. B. Yeats: 'Long before I saw you act I divined that you were important—because your acting was derided by all the people I most dislike' (Speaight, 177). In 1941 it won Speaight the coveted role of Christ in the twelve-part adaptation of the gospels for the BBC by Dorothy L. Sayers. In those days representation of Christ in a place of public entertainment was forbidden, but broadcasting was not covered by the law. Though each episode was vetted by C. F. Garbett, the bishop of Winchester, *The Man Born to be King* (1942) was a sensational success. Unfortunately it typecast Speaight for good: thereafter he found it hard to get parts which were not saints or clerics. He played Christian in *The Pilgrim's Progress* at Covent Garden (1948), Gerontius in Newman's *The Dream of Gerontius* (1951), St Peter at Westminster Abbey (1953) and, the same year, Cardinal Pole at Canterbury. Oddly enough the most enviable post-war role, for which he was ideally suited, Thomas More in Robert Bolt's *A Man for All Seasons*, eluded him in the West End, though he played it with distinction in Australia (1962–3).

Speaight did not regret the etiolation of his acting career. He directed plays, adjudicated drama festivals, and published many books about the theatre, especially on Shakespeare. As J. C. Trewin said, 'No one wrote as he did about the plays in performance.' His *Nature in Shakespearian Tragedy* (1955) struck many as the best study of its kind since that of A. C. Bradley; he put all his practical knowledge of Elizabethan stagecraft into *Shakespeare on the Stage* (1973); and his delightful *Shakespeare: the Man and his Achievement* (1977), published posthumously, has been well described as 'the actor-scholar's legacy to his friends'. But though he called his autobiography *The Property Basket* (1970), he noted in it: 'Stage doors no longer have the slightest magic for me. … My roots and my freedom are elsewhere.'

They were indeed. Speaight was a Catholic intellectual in the great European tradition. Among his mentors the man he most admired was Maurice Baring because he was 'the most spontaneously international person I have ever known' (Speaight, 160). He could not emulate Baring's astonishing command of languages, but no other actor of his day was capable, as he was, of performing in German or of directing a French version of *Antony and Cleopatra*. It was typical of Speaight that his novel *The Unbroken Heart* (1939) was 'inspired by a gnomic saying of Leon Bloy … and by a sculpture … on the outside of Chartres Cathedral' (ibid., 205), and who else would have described Jaques at the end of *As You Like It* 'wandering off like Proust returning to a monastery'?

In 1935 Speaight married Esther Evelyn Bowen; they had one son. In 1951 he married Bridget Laura Bramwell, a painter and musician. She was the daughter of Nevil Digby Bosworth-Smith, under-secretary in the Ministry of Education. They had one adopted son. They shared a passion for Joseph Conrad, Henry James, and Proust, and a delight in Campion House, the engaging Tudor house they found and adorned near Benenden in the Kentish weald.

Like Belloc, whose official life he wrote in 1957, Speaight enjoyed tramping through the French countryside exploring the vineyards, and his *The Companion Guide to Burgundy* (1975) is a model of its kind. But his chief interest was in French literature, especially the neo-Thomism of Jacques Maritain, of whom he wrote 'his philosophy … is as hard and clear as a diamond … But his heart is a mine of charity' (Speaight, 212). Thomism led him to join with Christopher Dawson in the 'Sword of the Spirit', a thirties ecumenical movement which adumbrated Pope John XXIII's *aggiornamento*. After the war he became a familiar figure in the Maritain circle at Meudon and the Paris salons, where he got to know Valéry, Claudel, Malraux, Mauriac, and Bernanos. In 1967 he published a study of *Teilhard de Chardin*, whom he admired, though not as a philosophical guide, and in 1973 and 1976 the rather more weighty *Georges Bernanos* and *François Mauriac*. Bernanos he revered as the finest novelist of his generation, but Mauriac he loved as a friend. Speaight was thus a close observer of the last great phase of European Christian culture, which gave joy to his life and meaning to his religion, and whose strength and pathos he captured in his best critical writing. Speaight died at Campion House, near Benenden, Kent, on 4 November 1976. PAUL JOHNSON, *rev.*

Sources *The Times* (6 Nov 1976) · R. Speaight, *The property basket* (1970) · personal knowledge (1986) · private information (1986) · *CGPLA Eng. & Wales* (1976)

Archives FILM BFI NFTVA, performance footage | SOUND BL NSA, documentary recordings · BL NSA, performance recordings
Likenesses A. Buckley, photograph · Karsh of Ottawa, photograph · M. Laurencin, oils; now lost
Wealth at death £8696: probate, 16 Dec 1976, *CGPLA Eng. & Wales*

Spear, (Thomas George) Percival (1901–1982), historian, was born on 2 November 1901 at Bath, the younger son and fourth and last child of Edward Albert Spear, provision merchant, of Bath, and his wife, Lucy, *née* Pearce. He was educated at Monkton Combe School, Somerset, and St Catharine's College, Cambridge, where he was an exhibitioner. He read history, and was placed in the upper division of the second class in part one of the tripos in 1921 and also in part two in 1922. He then took part two of the theological tripos in 1923, when he was placed in the undivided second class. He went to India in 1924 to teach at St Stephen's College, Delhi, under the auspices of the Cambridge Mission to Delhi. (His elder brother, the Revd Edward Norman Spear, later a canon of Gloucester Cathedral, was also a missionary in India.)

Spear began at St Stephen's College by teaching British and European history, but he was quickly drawn to the history of India, and of the British connection with it. He later became head of the history department and reader in history at Delhi University. He soon found a highly congenial subject for his own research—English social life in eighteenth-century India. He read widely, both in libraries and in the government archives, which were then in Calcutta, and he continued this research while on leave in England. He successfully completed a Cambridge PhD thesis on this subject in 1931, and it was published in a revised form under the title *The Nabobs: a Study of the Social Life of the English in Eighteenth Century India* (1932). It was an informative survey—witty, anecdotal, but descriptive rather than analytical. It lasted well, and was republished as a paperback in 1963, with an introduction in which Spear outlined the Indian context of the growth of British power in the eighteenth century.

In 1933 Spear married (Dorothy) Margaret Gladys, daughter of the Revd Frederick Harry Roberts Perkins, an Anglican clergyman. They had no children. They set up house in Delhi, and quickly established good relations with their Indian neighbours. In their reminiscences, *India Remembered* (1981), Percival and Margaret Spear portrayed their married life in Delhi as a time when they widened and deepened their understanding of Indians of different communities. In these years also Percy was extending his knowledge of Indian, and especially Indo-Muslim, history and culture. Delhi itself always fascinated him. He published a concise but vivid historical survey, *Delhi: an Historical Sketch* (1937), and a guide to its buildings, *Delhi: its Monuments and History* (1943). The latter book was originally designed for schoolchildren, but a visitor to Delhi today could still learn from it.

During the Second World War Spear and his wife joined the staff of the director-general of information in India, he as a writer, she as librarian. This unit was absorbed into the department of information and broadcasting in 1941, and he was then appointed deputy director of counter-propaganda. In 1943 he became deputy secretary to the government of India in the department of information and broadcasting. He also served for a time in 1944 as government whip in the legislative assembly. He was appointed OBE in 1946. Although he had been mildly critical of the aloofness of members of the Indian Civil Service, after his experience in the secretariat he paid tribute to what he had seen of their alertness, energy, and resourcefulness in times of difficulty.

Spear returned to England after the war, and turned to academic administration when he was appointed bursar and fellow of Selwyn College, Cambridge, in 1945. He also continued his research into the history of Delhi and its surroundings, which culminated in his *Twilight of the Mughuls: Studies in Late Mughul Delhi* (1951), which has become an acknowledged classic of historical writing on India. In the course of it he accepted the argument first put forward in Western scholarly writing by F. W. Buckler ('The political theory of the Indian mutiny', *Transactions of the Royal Historical Society*, 4th ser., 5, 1922), that the British had no right, after they had suppressed the mutiny and revolt of 1857, to try the Mughal emperor, or king of Delhi, as a rebel, since he was not a British subject. Spear reinforced this view with an eloquent analysis of Indian attitudes to the fallen Mughal ruler. The book is also remarkable for its portrayal of the life of the people of Delhi and of the villages in the neighbourhood. It is outstanding above all for its literary style and for the sensitive restraint with which Spear expressed a sense of nostalgia for past Mughal splendours.

Spear rewrote the third part of the *Oxford History of India* in 1958. This was republished as *The Oxford History of Modern India, 1740–1947* (1965). In contrast to Vincent A. Smith, the author of the previous *Oxford History of India*, Spear paid considerable attention to socio-economic history and provided a sympathetic account of the nationalist movement. Then he wrote *India: a Modern History* (1961), one of fifteen volumes of the *University of Michigan History of the Modern World*. He also wrote the second volume of *A History of India* published as a paperback by Penguin Books in 1965. He had little more to say of significance in these latter two books, but they occupied much of his time, and distracted him from other projects, such as a study of India in the time of the governor-generalship (1828–35) of Lord William Henry Cavendish-Bentinck, and a large-scale history of Delhi, neither of which he completed.

Spear also taught when he could and did what he could to spread a knowledge of Indian history in Cambridge. He resigned office as bursar in 1963, when he was appointed university lecturer in history, a post which he filled with distinction until 1969. Thereafter he continued to take a lively interest in the affairs of the Centre for South Asian Studies at Cambridge, and his services as an external examiner were often sought by other universities. Quiet in manner, and reticent about himself, Spear was always ready to advise and encourage younger scholars. He was alert and witty to the end, especially when the conversation turned to Delhi, as it usually did. He died in Cambridge on 16 December 1982.

KENNETH BALLHATCHET, *rev.*

Sources personal knowledge (1990) · private information (1990) · *CGPLA Eng. & Wales* (1983)

Wealth at death £136,700: probate, 26 April 1983, *CGPLA Eng. & Wales*

Spear, (Augustus John) Ruskin (1911–1990), artist and teacher of art, was born on 30 June 1911 in Hammersmith, London, the only son and youngest of five children of Augustus Spear, coach builder and coach painter, and his wife, (Matilda) Jane Lemon, cook. He acquired his unusual and appropriate forenames by being named Augustus after his father, John after his maternal grandfather, and Ruskin after a member of the artistically inclined family with whom his mother was in service at the time of his birth. Disabled by polio at an early age, Spear attended the Brook Green School, Hammersmith, for afflicted children, where his artistic talent was recognized. He went on to study at the Hammersmith School of Art on a scholarship, aged about fifteen, and then at the Royal College of Art in London (1930–34), on another scholarship, under Sir William Rothenstein.

Spear subsidized his own work by teaching, stating that he 'tried to believe money unimportant', and he noted wryly: 'first teaching appointment Croydon School of Art. Fee for 2½ hours, 16 shillings plus train fare. The Principal, interested in palmistry, read my hand, deciding it was promising, offered me four days per week'. He taught at Croydon, Sidcup, Bromley, St Martin's, Central, and Hammersmith schools of art, and—notably—as a visiting teacher in the painting school at the Royal College of Art (1952–77). He was also a gifted musician, and added to his income by playing jazz piano.

Throughout his life Spear regarded himself as 'a working-class cockney', while pursuing an extensive career as one of the liveliest members of the art world, loved by the public, fellow artists, and students, but only occasionally by the critics, by whom he was not taken seriously. He was a robust character, direct, colourful, pipe-smoking, and bearded. Known as a man with a prodigious thirst, he frequented his local pubs in Hammersmith and Chiswick, where his fellow drinkers formed a substantial proportion of his subject matter. He summed up his life view thus: 'Painting, breathing, drinking, ars longa, vita brevis'. His polio caused a permanent limp and prevented active service in the Second World War. He did, however, contribute noteworthy paintings of working life on the home front, commissioned and purchased by the War Artists' Advisory Committee.

Spear became an associate of the Royal Academy in 1944 and Royal Academician in 1954. This enabled him as of right to contribute to the academy's summer exhibitions, where he had first exhibited in 1932. His facility with paint, and his fascination with low life and high life, and the foibles of both, often made his contributions newsworthy. Pub characters, members of the royal family, and

(**Augustus John) Ruskin Spear** (1911–1990), self-portrait, 1982

politicians were his favourite subjects for academy presentation, with the portraits of public figures often based on newspaper photographs. He was a gentle satirist, exaggerating what was there rather than turning to stereotypes. He also portrayed ordinary life with vivid sympathy; a painting of a mother potting a baby caused the president of the Royal Academy, Sir Alfred Munnings, such displeasure in 1944 that it was not shown. In 1942 Spear was elected to the London Group, and was its president in 1949–50.

Spear had a thriving portrait practice among prominent figures. His subjects, which he proudly listed in his *Who's Who* entry, included lords Butler, Adrian, Olivier as Macbeth (painted from life), and Ramsey of Canterbury, Sir John Betjeman in a rowing boat, and lords Goodman and Howe of Aberavon. He was a portrayer of the human comedy with a light touch, in spite of often using a dark palette. He never had regular showings or a contract with a commercial gallery. He did occasionally exhibit abroad, but the only substantial exhibition of his work ever held in Britain (or anywhere) was the retrospective in the Diploma Galleries in the Royal Academy in 1980. The National Portrait Gallery has several of his portraits.

In spite of the relatively conventional, if exuberant, nature of his own work Spear promoted what he called the 'modern chaps', and was instrumental in turning the academy away from its unhealthy nostalgia; he was assisted by his outstanding success as a teacher during a golden age at the Royal College (Ron Kitaj, Frank Auerbach, David Hockney, and Peter Blake were his students). 'We did a lot of teaching. The atmosphere tingled with the excitement of being *free*.' Spear himself produced portraits endowed with sympathy; he was also a fascinating reporter, but his portrayals often appeared skin-deep rather than profound, and his talent was 'made in England' and not for travel. He was appointed CBE in 1979.

In 1935 Spear married (Hilda) Mary, artist and only child of William Henry Freer Hill, civil engineer, and Hilda Anne Grose; they had a son. The existence of his long-lasting liaison with Claire Stafford, an artist's model whom he met in 1956 when she was sixteen, was posthumously publicly revealed in 1993. They had a daughter, Rachel Spear-Stafford (*b.* 1957). Spear died in Hammersmith on 17 January 1990. A memorial service was held at St James's, Piccadilly, London, on 14 March 1990.

MARINA VAIZEY, *rev.*

Sources *Ruskin Spear RA: a retrospective exhibition* (RA, 1980) · M. Levy, *Ruskin Spear* (1985) · private information (1996) · personal knowledge (1996) · *The Times* (18 Jan 1990) · *The Independent* (19 Jan 1990) · *The Independent* (20 Jan 1990) · *CGPLA Eng. & Wales* (1991)
Likenesses K. Hutton, photograph, 1943, Hult. Arch. · M. Levy, pencil drawing, 1982, NPG · R. Spear, self-portrait, oils, 1982, NPG [*see illus.*] · photograph, repro. in *The Times* · photograph, repro. in *The Independent* (19 Jan 1990)
Wealth at death £514,428: probate, 9 Sept 1991, *CGPLA Eng. & Wales*

Spearhafoc (*fl.* **1047–1051**), abbot of Abingdon and craftsman, is first recorded as a monk of Bury St Edmunds. His name, meaning 'sparrowhawk', also occurs in Domesday Book in Suffolk and Nottinghamshire and may represent Anglo-Scandinavian usage. It was almost certainly a byname, even though no other name is recorded for him; perhaps it refers to the craftsman's sharp eyes.

About 1047 Edward the Confessor made Spearhafoc abbot of Abingdon. The Abingdon chronicle implies that he bribed the worldly Bishop Stigand to further his cause with the king; at all events Edward appointed him to the bishopric of London in 1051. He was, however, disapproved of by Robert of Jumièges, Edward's new archbishop of Canterbury, who had just returned from Rome with his pallium. The Anglo-Saxon Chronicle E text recounts that Spearhafoc met Robert

> with the king's writ and seal to the effect that he was to be consecrated bishop of London by the archbishop. But the archbishop refused and said that the pope had forbidden it him. Then the abbot went to the archbishop again about it and asked for ordination as bishop, and the archbishop refused him resolutely and said that the pope had forbidden it him. Then the abbot went back to London and occupied the bishopric that the king had given him; he did this with the king's full permission all that summer and autumn. (*ASC*, s.a. 1048, *recte* 1051, text E)

In the autumn of 1051, immediately after he had banished the rebellious Godwine family, Edward expelled Spearhafoc from the bishopric; Spearhafoc left the country, never to be seen again.

As abbot and bishop Spearhafoc epitomizes the faults of the late Anglo-Saxon church, but as craftsman he is of much interest. Goscelin of St Bertin calls him 'an exceptional artist outstanding in painting, gold-engraving and goldsmithing', and describes events when Spearhafoc was working at Canterbury at Abbot Ælfstan's request (that is, before 1046): as a thank-offering for the miraculous recovery of a precious ring belonging to Queen Eadgyth, he made images 'of enormous size and beauty' of Bishop Liudhard and Queen Bertha (Goscelin, col. 46). It was remembered at Abingdon that he was 'a marvellous worker in the fashioning of gold and silver', and that in 1051 he absconded with a great store of gold and gems which the king had given him to make an 'imperial crown' (*Chronicon monasterii de Abingdon*, 1.462–3). It may be that Spearhafoc, like Mannig, abbot of Evesham, supervised a goldsmithing workshop based in his abbey: Abingdon tenants in Edward the Confessor's time included Leofwine *aurifaber* or 'goldsmith' (*Domesday Book*, 1.58v). The careers of Spearhafoc and Mannig show that manual skills were esteemed in even the highest-ranking late Anglo-Saxon churchmen, and indeed were a means to advancement: in Spearhafoc's case there is no record of any other qualities that might have commended him to the king. JOHN BLAIR

Sources J. Stevenson, ed., *Chronicon monasterii de Abingdon*, 2 vols., Rolls Series, 2 (1858), 1.462–3 • Goscelinus Cantuariensis, 'Historia translationis Sancti Augustini', *Patrologia Latina*, 155 (1854), 46 • *ASC*, s.a. 1048, 1051 [text E]; s.a. 1050–51 [text D] • John of Worcester, *Chron.*, 2.552–4, 614 • C. R. Dodwell, *Anglo-Saxon art: a new perspective* (1982), 46–7, 213 • F. Barlow, *The English church, 1000–1066: a history of the later Anglo-Saxon church*, 2nd edn (1979), 47–50 • O. von Feilitzen, *The pre-conquest personal names of Domesday Book* (1937), 369

Wealth at death only assets known to have been in his possession when he absconded in 1051 are a quantity of gold and jewels stolen from the king: Stevenson, ed., *Chronicon monasterii de Abingdon*

Spearman, Sir Alexander Young, **first baronet** (1793–1874), civil servant, was born on 13 September 1793 at Pentridge, Dorset, the eldest son in the family of seven boys and two girls of Alexander Young Spearman (1762–1808), of Thornley, Durham, major in the Royal Artillery, and his wife, Agnes, daughter of James Morton, of Bonar Hill, Lanarkshire. Nothing is known of his education. He entered the public service at the early age of fifteen in 1808, serving as deputy assistant commissary-general in the last years of the Napoleonic wars. His chief in this capacity was John Charles Herries, with whom he formed a lasting friendship. When Herries was appointed auditor of the civil list in October 1816 Spearman became his chief clerk. He first came to prominence in 1822 when he was appointed to investigate and report upon irregularities in the Stationery Office. His recommendations were accepted and in the following year he was made controller of that department. In February 1824 he was transferred to the Treasury as assistant clerk in the revenue department and clerk of parliamentary accounts with responsibility, under Herries, now the financial secretary, for the classification of the miscellaneous estimates. This office, which he held for more than ten years, gave him an intimate knowledge of the procedures for securing parliamentary authority for public expenditure. In addition Spearman served as private secretary to Herries as chancellor of the exchequer between September 1827 and February 1828. He married on 29 December 1826 Jane Campbell (*d*. 1877), daughter of Duncan Campbell of Inverawe, Argyll, with whom he had four sons.

In February 1831 the decision was made to incorporate the civil-list audit department into the Treasury, and Spearman, who had continued to serve as chief clerk in that department, was appointed auditor. This represented a considerable promotion since, in addition to his specialized responsibility for the work of audit, he became one of the principal officers of the Treasury, ranking from 1834 immediately after the assistant secretary, its most senior permanent official. In January 1836 Spearman himself became assistant secretary. After only four years, overwork led to a breakdown in his health which obliged him to resign at the age of forty-six. His labour earned him a high reputation not only for industry but also for wise judgement and mastery of Treasury business. In recognition of his services he was created a baronet on 28 April 1840.

Spearman spent the next ten years in virtual retirement, emerging only in 1848 to give evidence to the select committee on miscellaneous expenditure, where his emphasis on the merits of familiarity with the routines of business when considering fitness for recruitment to and promotion in the public service contrasted with the views of his successor at the Treasury, Charles Edward Trevelyan. By July 1850 his health had recovered sufficiently to enable him to be appointed secretary and comptroller of the National Debt Office. In this capacity he was much concerned with the problems of savings banks and he was instrumental in promoting the legislation which led to the establishment of the Post Office Savings Bank in 1861 and the passage of the Trustee Savings Bank Act of 1863. He also served as deputy chairman of the Public Works Loans Board and as one of the commissioners for the exhibition of 1851. His stature as a public servant of exceptional ability was widely recognized and led to his appointment as a privy councillor in November 1869. He finally retired in March 1873. At the end of his life he was described by Rivers Wilson as 'one of the old school and always wore a jabot or frilled shirt front' (Winnifrith, 320). Spearman died at his home, The Spring, Hanwell, Middlesex, on 20 November 1874. J. C. SAINTY

Sources J. Winnifrith, 'The Rt Hon. Sir Alexander Spearman, bart. (1793–1874)', *Public Administration*, 38 (1960), 311–20 • J. C. Sainty, ed., *Treasury officials, 1660–1870* (1972) • Boase, *Mod. Eng. biog.* • d. cert.

Archives BL, corresp. with W. E. Gladstone, Add. MS 44305 • BL, corresp. with John Charles Herries, Add. MS 57374 • Bodl. Oxf., letters to Benjamin Disraeli • LMA, letters to clerk of Hanwell Asylum

Wealth at death under £18,000: probate, 14 Dec 1874, *CGPLA Eng. & Wales*

Spearman, Charles Edward (1863–1945), psychologist, was born on 10 September 1863 at 39 Upper Seymour Street, London, the younger of the two sons of Alexander Young Spearman (1832–1865), a man of independent means, and his second wife, Louisa Anne Caroline Amelia (1842/3–1933), daughter of Edward Pellew Mainwaring of Whitmore, Staffordshire. Sir Alexander Young *Spearman was his grandfather. In 1870 the widowed Louisa

Spearman married Henry Harrington Molyneux-Seel, an official of the College of Arms. The family lived in Leamington Spa, Warwickshire, and Charles was educated from the age of twelve to eighteen as a day boy at Leamington College. Recalling his schooldays in 1930 Spearman tells of his 'excessive but secret devotion to philosophy', despite outwardly affecting a 'seemingly exclusive devotion to games and sports of all kinds' ('C. Spearman', 299). Thus, it was probably by choice and necessity (as his mother was widowed once more) that Spearman turned to 'a short spell of military service' ('C. Spearman', 300), on leaving school in 1882. This 'short spell' in the Royal Munster Fusiliers, which actually lasted until 1897, was spent mainly in India where, despite the diversions of polo, poker, and some active campaigning in Burma, he still found time to pursue his boyhood passion for philosophy. Later on his reading extended into psychology, where he apparently found greater affinity with the more scientific approach that was flourishing in Germany than with the empiricist and associationist stance of contemporary British psychology. Shortly after completing a two-year course at the Army Staff College, Camberley, in December 1896 Captain Spearman resigned his commission to study experimental psychology in Wilhelm Wundt's laboratory at Leipzig University.

Spearman's studies were interrupted by the Second South African War when the army recalled him to serve as deputy assistant adjutant-general to Guernsey. There he met Frances Henrietta Priaulx (1880?–1955), daughter of John Aikman MD, whom he married on 4 September 1901; their four daughters and a son were born between 1902 and 1918. During the few months between his release from military duties and returning to Germany in late 1902 Spearman embarked on the pioneering work which led to his two-factor theory of human intelligence with its notion of a single quantifiable element, a common intellective function *g*, underlying every intellectual activity, and its idea that different activities both relied on *g* to differing degrees and also called on a specific function, *s*, unique to the particular activity. How well people performed on any task would be determined by their individual levels of *g* and *s*. The correlational method that he devised at this time to demonstrate the existence of *g* (and incidentally to measure it) was the earliest version of the statistical method now known as factor analysis. Not surprisingly, this work, with its promise of an index of general intelligence, attracted considerable critical attention when it was published in 1904.

Nevertheless, Spearman pursued a broad curriculum over his remaining five years in Germany, interesting himself, for instance, in spatial perception (for which he obtained a PhD from Leipzig in 1906). Although making some progress with the correlational work, it was only on his return to England in 1907 that the two-factor theory, and its theoretical implications for psychology, became the focus of his research. This work, which reached its zenith in 1927 with the publication of *The Abilities of Man*, was gradually eclipsed by more complex representations of the structure of human intelligence. None the less, defending the two-factor theory against its many detractors kept Spearman and his myriad recruits busy for the best part of three decades.

Spearman had returned home in 1907 to a part-time appointment as reader and head of the small psychological laboratory at University College, London, a post relinquished by his acquaintance William McDougall. Apart from service during the First World War, Spearman remained at University College until his retirement in 1931, having become Grote professor of mind and logic and head of psychology in 1911, then professor of psychology in 1928, and finally emeritus professor.

Over some forty years Spearman published six books and more than a hundred journal articles, the last appearing after his death. He also received many honours including fellowship of the Royal Society (1924), an Hon. LLD from Wittenberg, USA, as well as honorary membership of the British Psychological Society (1934) and of several foreign academies of science. He served also as president of the British Psychological Society (1923–6) and of section J (psychology) of the British Association for the Advancement of Science (1925).

Although his name was later almost exclusively identified with factor analysis, test reliability, and the famous rank correlation measure, to Spearman himself this statistical and psychometric work was of secondary importance. Indeed, even the two-factor theory was but a part of his search for fundamental laws of psychology. For instance, in *The Nature of 'Intelligence' and the Principles of Cognition* (1923), Spearman proposed an epistemology founded on what he called noëgenetic principles. In essence, these laws, derived from eighteenth- and nineteenth-century philosophical notions, characterized people as actively educing relationships between events and then generalizing these relationships to deal with new situations. Despite Spearman's own claims, however, these notions offered little more than the embryo of a fundamental system.

Spearman's intellectual and organizational powers were formidable. He founded the so-called London school of psychology, distinguished by its scientifically and statistically rigorous approach to studying human ability, though naturally having the doctrine of the two-factor theory, especially *g*, at its heart. In fact, so attractive was this new line that students came from all over the world to work within Spearman's carefully co-ordinated research programme, thereby creating the first centre of psychological research of any note in Britain. It should be added that, despite Spearman's association with the eugenics movement, he held no strong hereditarian views. Indeed, according to members of his family, he believed that everyone was a genius at something.

Though ferocious with academic opponents, Spearman engendered a high degree of loyalty from his many followers and was remarkably adroit at persuading colleagues and acquaintances to work for the cause—establishing *g*. Colleagues generally found him personally affable and courteous, though his children thought him rather stern and remote. Notorious absentmindedness about briefcases, umbrellas, and the like contrasts sharply with his meticulously ordered academic life. He loved to travel and made many visits to the USA (his favourite) and Europe, as well as touring in India and Egypt. Beyond academic work, Spearman's passion was tennis.

Spearman's health and spirits deteriorated in the early 1940s: besides the loss of his son, killed in action in Crete, sudden and frequent fainting fits made working, and therefore life, almost impossible. He developed pneumonia after a bad fall during one of these blackouts and he was admitted to University College Hospital, London. Spearman died on 17 September 1945 after throwing himself from a fourth floor window of the hospital; he had long believed that individuals had the right to determine when their own lives should end. He was survived by his wife. P. Lovie and A. D. Lovie

Sources 'C. Spearman', *A history of psychology in autobiography*, ed. C. Murchison, 1 (1930), 299–331 • P. Lovie and A. D. Lovie, 'Charles Edward Spearman, FRS (1863–1945)', *Notes and Records of the Royal Society*, 50 (1996), 75–88 • private information (2004) [Spearman family] • British Psychological Society, London, British Psychological Society archives, Spearman MSS • G. Thomson, *Obits. FRS*, 5 (1945–8), 373–85 [incl. bibliography] • b. cert. • d. cert. • Burke, *Peerage* • *DNB* • *The Times* (18 Aug 1865)

Archives British Psychological Society, London, British Psychological Society archives | BL, corresp. with Macmillans, Add. MS 55251 • Wellcome L., C. S. Myers MSS

Likenesses photograph, 1920?–1929, UCL, department of psychology • W. Stoneman, photograph, 1931, NPG • photographs, repro. in Lovie and Lovie, 'Charles Edward Spearman', following p. 75

Wealth at death £33,710 5s. 5d.: probate, 15 Dec 1945, *CGPLA Eng. & Wales*

Spearman, Robert (*bap.* **1703**, *d.* **1761**), theologian, was baptized at St Mary-le-Bow, Durham, on 4 March 1703, the eldest son of Robert Spearman (1657–1728), attorney, of the city of Durham, and his wife, Hannah (*d.* 1737), daughter of William Webster, merchant, of Stockton-on-Tees. He was educated at Durham School and matriculated from Corpus Christi College, Oxford, as a gentleman commoner, on 2 June 1720 but seems to have left in spring 1723 without having taken a degree.

Spearman lived a retired life on his estate, Old Acres, in the large parish of Sedgefield, co. Durham, where, as his epitaph records, he 'employed the leisure and abilities which God had given him in the study of His Word and His Works'. He was one of the first followers of the physico-theologian John Hutchinson, whose brief life he wrote and whose complete works he co-edited in twelve volumes (published 1748) with his friend the Revd Julius Bate. Spearman's own two books explained his belief that Hutchinson had a unique key to knowledge. His *Enquiry after Philosophy and Theology*, published anonymously in 1755, contained an attack on the perceived contemporary primacy of natural religion that had resulted in Christianity's being in a 'cool and lukewarm state' (p. 402); a repetition of the Hutchinsonian belief that Trinitarian unity is demonstrated in the combination of fire, light, and spirit; and a sustained engagement with some of Sir Isaac Newton's published writings. Spearman concluded with a plea to his readers to look to Hutchinson, where 'they will, to their inexpressible satisfaction, both as Christians and men of sense, find the scriptures made one, uniform, compleat system of theology and philosophy, consistent with themselves and nature' (p. 424). His last major work, *Letters to a Friend Concerning the Septuagint Translation and the Hebrew Mythology* (1759), was a defence of the Hutchinsonian approach to scripture and a plea for the accuracy and stability of the existing printed Hebrew text of the Old Testament against revisers like Kennicott, for here was 'the original record, the *Magna Charta*, as I may call it, of our eternal inheritance' (R. Spearman, *Letters to a Friend*, 1759, 371). He also made further attacks on natural religion and argued that 'Paganism was nothing else but the *great truths* of Christianity split and debased into a legend of fables, such as we meet with in their mythology' (ibid., 151).

Spearman was genuinely learned and had some gift for popularizing and shaping Hutchinsonian thinking. He introduced it to many clergy and laity in the north east of England and was respected both for his adherence to the master's views and his willingness to listen to the reservations held by those who could not enter 'into all the depths of the Hutchinsonian philosophy' (Surtees, 3.398). These included his friend Dr Thomas Sharp, archdeacon of Northumberland, who dedicated his *Two dissertations concerning etymology & scripture-meaning of the Hebrew words Elohim and Berith* (1751) to Spearman and saluted his 'moderation and candour' (Sharp, iv).

Spearman married, first, Mary Lewen, who died on 18 March 1748, aged forty-two, and, second, Ann (*b.* 1725/6, *d.* 1821), the daughter of Robert Sharp (or Sharpe), gentleman, of Hawthorn, co. Durham. He died on 20 October 1761 and was buried on 30 October at Sedgefield parish church, leaving five daughters as coheirs. His widow survived him for almost sixty years; she died in Durham, and was buried at Sedgefield on 24 August 1821, aged ninety-five. Nigel Aston

Sources C. S. Earle and L. A. Body, eds., *Durham School register: to June, 1912*, 2nd edn (1912) • Foster, *Alum. Oxon.* • CCC Oxf. • T. Sharp, *Two dissertations concerning etymology and scripture-meaning of the Hebrew words Elohim and Berith* (1751) • W. Hutchinson, *The history and antiquities of the county palatine of Durham*, 3 (1794), 55, 72–3 • R. Surtees, *The history and antiquities of the county palatine of Durham*, 1 (1816), 96; 3 (1823), 29, 48, 398 • W. Fordyce, *The history and antiquities of the county palatine of Durham*, 2 (1857), 345, 378, 384 • *VCH Berkshire*, 3.336 • Nichols, *Lit. anecdotes*, 4.171 • *DNB* • parish register, Durham, St Mary-le-Bow, 4 Mar 1703 [baptism] • parish register, Sedgefield, 30 Oct 1761 [burial] • parish register, Sedgefield, 24 Aug 1821 [burial: Ann Spearman]

Wealth at death see will dated 10 Nov 1756, probate 19 Nov 1763 (bishop of Durham's consistory court); all his MSS to Rev. John Price; Durham RO, D/X487 2/5

Spears. For this title name *see* Borden, Mary [Mary Spears, Lady Spears] (1886–1968).

Spears [*formerly* Spiers], **Sir Edward Louis**, **baronet** (**1886–1974**), army officer and diplomatist, was born in the Passy district of Paris, at 7 Chaussée de la Muette, on 7 August 1886, the only son and elder child of Charles McCarthy Spiers (1858–1912), commission agent, and his

Sir Edward Louis Spears, baronet (1886–1974), by Lafayette, 1928

wife, Marguerite Melicent Hack (1864–1927), daughter of Edward Louis Hack, a railway engineer. C. M. Spiers was one of the five sons of Alexander *Spiers, lexicographer and teacher of English in Paris, and the grandson of Isaac Spiers and his wife Hannah Moses of Gosport and a descendant of Jewish immigrants from Germany. E. L. Spiers grew up in France where his parents' unhappy marriage and his unstable mother meant that he lived mostly with his grandmother, Lucy Harriet Hack (1841–1922), a member of the Anglo-Irish family of Aylmer, and his cousins by marriage, the Rafinesques, at Voutenay, their property in Burgundy. He was educated privately, and at a boarding-school in Neuwied, Germany (1901–2), and he stayed often with the Aylmers at Donadea Castle in co. Kildare; he joined the Kildare militia in 1903 before being gazetted into the 8th hussars in 1906. A polo accident stopped him from accompanying the 8th hussars to India and he transferred to the 11th hussars in 1910.

Peacetime soldiering did not suit the restless Spiers (known to his friends as Louis), although he translated two French books on cavalry tactics and, as a bilingual British officer, worked on an Anglo-French code book. On the eve of the First World War he was in Paris, working at the French war office and with British agents in Belgium; then in August 1914 he was made liaison officer between General Lanrezac of the French Fifth Army and Sir John French, the British commander-in-chief. On 23 August he alerted Sir John to Lanrezac's retreat towards Rethel on the British expeditionary force's right flank, thus saving the isolated British from almost certain annihilation. Spiers continued as a liaison officer with the French army, admiring its heroism and endurance. He won the MC in 1915 and was wounded four times before becoming head of the British military mission to the French war office in Paris in May 1917. At the front in 1916 he met Mary *Borden (1886–1968), daughter and heir of William Borden of Chicago, running her own field hospital; she divorced her husband, George Douglas Gordon Turner (with whom she had three daughters), and married Spiers on 31 March 1918 at the British embassy in Paris, before living with him in a house in the rue Monsieur. He changed his name to Spears, claiming that Spiers was frequently mispronounced. This Anglicization was significant; his ambitions were growing through contact with the French and British high commands and, most important, Winston Churchill.

In 1915 Spiers had met Winston Churchill, then out of office, on the western front. Churchill admired Spiers's courage and ability and supported him against French and British jealousy and suspicion: Sir Henry Wilson saw Spears as an intriguer and Clemenceau thought he knew too many French secrets. Spears emerged from the war as an acting brigadier-general with a CBE (1919), a CB (1921) and a considerable but controversial reputation. Hard work and anxiety led to a nervous breakdown, showing an underlying fragility, and Spears left the army for business in 1920. Mary Borden and he moved to London, to a house in Little College Street, but found it less friendly than Paris. Then, with Churchill's encouragement, he stood for parliament as a National Liberal, becoming member for Loughborough in 1922, a seat he held until 1924, and following Churchill into the Conservative Party to sit for Carlisle from 1931 to 1945. From the 1930s he lived at St Michael's Grange at Warfield in Berkshire, and also at 12 Strathearn Place, London.

In support of Churchill, Spears opposed the foreign policy of the Chamberlain government. He remained a firm Francophile and published two books of great descriptive power about the First World War: *Liaison, 1914* (1930), on his experiences during the retreat; and *Prelude to Victory* (1939), on the Nivelle offensive of 1917. Then on 22 May 1940 Churchill, as prime minister, made Spears his personal representative to the doomed French government of Paul Reynaud. Horrified at the humiliation and defeatism of his beloved France, Spears left Bordeaux for London in an aeroplane on 17 June with de Gaulle, recently one of Reynaud's junior ministers. A myth grew, nurtured by Spears, that he had gathered the general up and led him to Churchill, thus creating the leader of the Free French; in fact the plane had been lent to de Gaulle by the British prime minister. But once in London Spears, as Churchill's representative with de Gaulle, used his domineering personality to further de Gaulle's cause, accompanying him on the Dakar expedition of September 1940 and to Africa and the Middle East.

Tall, thick-set, and dark haired, with a prominent nose, narrow eyes, and a clipped moustache, Spears had charm, wit, an imposing manner, courage, and piercing intelligence but his aggression hid an acute sense of himself as an outsider in British life. He was not suited to the diplomacy that followed the victory over the Vichy forces in Syria by the allies in June 1941 when, as head of the British Mission to the Free French, he had to implement the agreement between Free France and Britain that the Levant states of Syria and Lebanon, hitherto French mandated territories, should get their independence: a promise to the local populations who detested the colonial regime. De Gaulle, however, was desperate to keep French influence and power.

Spears was appointed the first British minister to Syria and Lebanon in January 1942, and promoted KBE. Encouraged by Churchill, he worked to bring about their independence, conceiving an idea of himself, fed by local flattery and the antagonism towards the allies of former Vichyite French officials, as the liberator of an oppressed Arab people. The French, led subtly on the spot by General Catroux and more brutally from afar by de Gaulle, opposed him; in London and Algiers Anthony Eden, Duff Cooper, and Harold Macmillan thought Spears was offending the French unnecessarily. The end was unsatisfactory for Spears and for his critics: in December 1944 Churchill made him resign and in 1945 the Levant states became independent amid scenes that brought Britain and France close to war. Henceforth the name of Spears was abominated by many in France.

In 1945 Spears lost his seat in parliament and resumed his business activities and his writing. He became chairman of Ashanti Goldfields in 1945 and resuscitated the Institute of Directors as its chairman from 1948 to 1966, making it a formidable advocate of free enterprise. His vivid and personal account of the fall of France, *Assignment to Catastrophe*, was published in two volumes in 1954; while scathing about the embryonic spirit of Vichy, it is admiring of de Gaulle. His other books were *Two Men who Saved France* (1966), a study of Pétain and de Gaulle; *The Picnic Basket* (1967), a volume of mostly childhood memories; and *Fulfilment of a Mission* (1977), the posthumously published account of his time in the Levant. In 1953 he was created a baronet.

Spears's marriage to Mary Borden was turbulent. The Borden fortune, founded on mining and dairy products, suffered in the Wall Street crash of 1929 and Mary lost her money. She ran field hospitals and ambulances with the French in both world wars and Spears greatly admired her courage; each gave outward support to the other and their son Michael was born in 1921. However, in the decade following the First World War he began an affair with Nancy Maurice (1901–1975), daughter of Major-General Sir Frederick Barton Maurice, who worked as Spears's secretary from 1920, and this hurt his wife deeply. Another sadness was that Michael Spears contracted osteomyelitis in 1934 and never wholly recovered. He died in 1969.

After Mary Borden's death in 1968 Spears married Nancy Maurice on 19 December 1969. Mary Borden had a life of her own as a writer whereas Spears was Nancy Maurice's whole existence and she worked ruthlessly to further his career, encouraging him in the pursuit of vendettas and strong dislikes. The second Lady Spears accompanied her husband regularly to the Asante goldmines in Ghana where he became increasingly out of touch with post-colonial Africa.

Those who knew Spears in old age remember his inimitable anecdotes, his charm as a host, and the tenacity with which he held to his opinions. There was, however, a note of disappointment, particularly over his break with France where the return to power in 1958 of de Gaulle, who could scarcely bear to speak of Spears, dashed hopes of an official reconciliation. Spears died on 27 January 1974 of a haemorrhage and thrombosis at the Heatherwood Hospital at Ascot, and the baronetcy became extinct. He was cremated at Bracknell crematorium on 1 February. MAX EGREMONT

Sources M. Egremont, *Under two flags: the life of Major-General Sir Edward Spears* (1997) · E. L. Spears, *The picnic basket* (1967) · M. Borden, *Journey down a blind alley* (1946) · E. L. Spears, *Liaison, 1914: a narrative of the great retreat* (1930) · E. L. Spears, *Prelude to victory* (1939) · King's Lond., Spears MSS · CAC Cam., Spears MSS · St Ant. Oxf., Middle East Centre, Spears MSS · Boston University, Mary Borden MSS · E. L. Spears, *Fulfilment of a mission* (1977) · E. L. Spears, *Assignment to catastrophe*, 2 vols. (1954) · E. L. Spears, *Two men who saved France* (1966) · *CGPLA Eng. & Wales* (1974) · b. cert.

Archives CAC Cam., corresp., diaries, and papers · King's Lond., Liddell Hart C., papers relating to First World War, literary papers, photographs · St Ant. Oxf., Middle East Centre, corresp., diaries, and papers relating to Middle East | Boston University, Mary Borden MSS · HLRO, corresp. with Lord Beaverbrook · IWM, corresp. with Sir Henry Wilson · King's Lond., Liddell Hart C., corresp. with Sir B. H. Liddell Hart · Lpool RO, corresp. with seventeenth earl of Derby | FILM BBC WAC · IWM FVA, actuality footage | SOUND BBC WAC · BL NSA, oral history interview · IWM SA, *The Great War*, BBC interviews, BBC, 1963

Likenesses W. Stoneman, three photographs, 1922–53, NPG · Lafayette, photograph, 1928, NPG [*see illus.*] · double portrait, photograph, 1940 (with de Gaulle), Hult. Arch. · photographs, 1940, IWM · M. Codner, oils, *c*.1966, Institute of Directors, Pall Mall, London · W. Bird, photograph, NPG · M. Borden (Lady Spears), oils, NPG · photograph (in later years), Camera Press · photographs, Spears MSS

Wealth at death £60,211: probate, 25 March 1974, *CGPLA Eng. & Wales*

Spears, Robert (1825–1899), Unitarian minister, was born on 25 September 1825 at Lemington, in Newburn, some 5 miles west of Newcastle, the fifth of six sons and two daughters born to John Spears (1765–1849), who was an ironworker, and his second wife, Mary Glenn (1782/3–1874). He was baptized on 30 September in the Ebenezer Chapel in Swalwell, co. Durham, on the opposite bank of the Tyne. The Presbyterian baptism reflects John Spears's background as a Scottish Calvinist, but Mary Spears was a Methodist and while for a time Robert Spears worshipped in the Newburn parish church, he eventually joined the New Connexion Methodists. He was apprenticed as an engineering smith, and on 1 January 1846, then living in Sugley, Newburn, he married Margaret Kirton (1818–1867), also of Sugley, the daughter of John Kirton, a watchman. Five children were born in the marriage; the youngest daughter, the only one to live past childhood, survived him.

Disliking his work and having been encouraged in self-

Robert Spears (1825–1899), by unknown photographer

education by his mother, Spears discovered a gift for teaching and later in 1846 began teaching at a New Connexion school in Scotswood-on-Tyne, also serving as a local preacher. He was, however, denied formal ministerial enrolment because of heterodox tendencies which he traced to attending a debate in Newcastle the previous year between the Revd William Cooke DD (1806–1884) of the New Connexion and the Revd Joseph Barker (1806–1875), who had been expelled from that denomination and was at the time closely associated with Unitarians.

By 1849 a friendship with the Revd George Harris (1794–1859) of Newcastle led Spears to avow Unitarianism, but he continued to teach for the New Connexion while supplying Unitarian pulpits. In 1852 he entered the Unitarian ministry at Sunderland, where a successful school compensated for the lack of a stipend. In 1856 he established a monthly magazine, the *Christian Freeman*, which he edited until his death. In 1858 he moved to Stockton-on-Tees at a salary of £65, successfully reviving a declining congregation. The next year he founded a weekly newspaper, the *Stockton Gazette*, which under other names and ownership eventually became a daily paper.

Spears was invited to become sub-editor and day-to-day manager of the weekly *Unitarian Herald*, established in Manchester in 1861 as a counter, both geographical and theological, to the more advanced views of the London-based *Inquirer*. The negotiations failed, but he eventually served for a time as the paper's London agent. His move to London that year was encouraged by Robert Brook Aspland (1805–1869), since 1857 secretary of the British and Foreign Unitarian Association (BFUA). The London District Unitarian Association, through the generosity of Sir James Clark Lawrence (1820–1898), assured Spears a salary of £100 as minister at Stamford Street Chapel, Blackfriars. In 1867 he became co-secretary of the BFUA and in 1870, following Aspland's death, general secretary; he revived the publishing programme and nearly quadrupled the association's income. In October 1867 his wife, Margaret, had died, and on 5 January 1869 he married Emily Glover (1835–1917), the daughter of Joseph Glover, a Dorking butcher; the couple had two sons and four daughters.

Spears's loyalty to an undiluted, biblically based Unitarianism made him an invaluable recruit for Aspland and his allies in their opposition to the transcendentalist reconstruction of Unitarianism identified with James Martineau, who called Spears the orchestrator of sectarian 'bluster' (letter to John Gordon, 28 Dec 1872, Unitarian College MSS, JRL). The 'new school' was making generational progress, however. Spears had successfully republished early Unitarian classics and the works of the eloquent American minister William Ellery Channing (1780–1842), but in 1876 the committee of the BFUA decided to republish the works of the radical American Unitarian Theodore Parker (1810–1860) and Spears resigned; a testimonial subscription of £1800 provided him an income for life. He immediately founded *Christian Life*, a weekly newspaper which, drawing on talented contributors like Samuel Sharpe (1799–1881) and Alexander Gordon (1841–1931), offered a lively alternative to *The Inquirer* until it was finally merged with its rival in 1929.

Spears was an irrepressible missionary. At Stamford Street in 1866 he founded the first lay preachers' union. In 1874 he left Stamford Street for his new foundation at College chapel, Stepney, and he encouraged new or revived congregations in the metropolis and elsewhere in the country. He assisted in the founding in 1886, by Florence Hill (1843–1935) and others, of the Central Postal Mission, to cater to Unitarians without ready access to a chapel. A strong supporter of Indian missions, in 1870 he organized the English tour of Keshab Chandra Sen, the leader of Brahmo Samaj, a Westernizing reformist movement within Hinduism. Ecumenical enthusiasm led him in 1881 to organize the Sion College conferences, which brought together eminent representatives of a wide range of faiths. He was an untiring advocate of Sunday schools, and in 1886, with the help of Matilda Sharpe (1830–1916), he founded Channing House School for Girls in Highgate, having moved there the year before from Stepney to establish a new—and again successful—congregation.

Spears was a man of imposing presence and unfailing energy. Despite his lack of formal education, an unpolished style, and the Northumbrian accent which he thought a disadvantage, he charmed and influenced men and women from all walks of life, notably the wealthy Unitarians who subsidized his many initiatives. He had wide contacts among liberal Christians on the continent, and an extended visit to the United States in 1887 brought him a new circle of friends and admirers. He died at home at Arundel House, The Bank, Highgate Hill, from bladder cancer, on 25 February 1899 and was buried on 1 March in Nunhead cemetery in London. R. K. WEBB

Sources *Memorials of Robert Spears* (1900) · *Christian Life* (4 March 1899) · *The Inquirer* (4 March 1899) · *The Inquirer* (11 March 1899) · *The Inquirer* (18 March 1899) · *The Inquirer* (22 April 1899) · *Unitarian Herald* minute book, 1861, DWL · private information (2004) · A. R. Ruston, *A history of lay preaching in the Unitarian movement* (1973) · m. certs. · d. cert. · *CGPLA Eng. & Wales* (1899) · register, Ebenezer Chapel, Swalwell, co. Durham

Likenesses oils, *c.*1846, priv. coll. • S. Cooper, pencil or charcoal drawing, 1899 (after photograph in DWL) • oils • photograph, repro. in *Christian Life* • photograph, repro. in *Memorials*, frontispiece [*see illus.*] • portrait, DWL, trustees' album

Wealth at death £3319 8*s.* 11*d.*: probate, 11 June 1899, *CGPLA Eng. & Wales*

Speckman [*alias* Brown], **Charles** (1734?–1763), confidence trickster, was probably born in London in 1734, although one account reports a slightly earlier birth about 1728 in either Antigua or Barbados (*The Ordinary of Newgate*). In keeping with his chosen profession he adopted various aliases, and it is therefore difficult to be entirely confident that his name really was Speckman. He was tried in 1763 as Charles Brown, and was also known as Spackman, Woodward, Evans, Saunders, Tafrail, and Dougan. He was reported to have been one of eighteen children, but the names of them and of his parents are unknown; nor is it known if he married or had children. The only descriptions of him are tainted by the different perspectives of their authors, but nevertheless seem to corroborate one another in essentials: the Revd Stephen Roe, the ordinary of Newgate, with whom he quarrelled, wrote that Speckman was 'thin, tall, and of a sallow complexion … close and crafty' (*The Ordinary of Newgate*, 10), while the editor of his autobiography more sympathetically described him as

> of genteel appearance, a likely person, thin narrow face, somewhat cloudy brow'd, about five feet nine inches high, of a spare slender make, his demeanour courteous and affable, and his countenance, though pale, carried the vestigia not only of serenity but innocence. (*Life*, 48–9)

In an autobiography which Speckman appears to have written just before his death he claimed that he was sent by his father to be educated by a clergyman with whom he boarded, probably in London. Around 1748 he ran away and made his living by committing petty thefts. He was eventually arrested, but avoided prosecution by appearing as a witness for the crown at the trial in February 1750 of Abraham Crown, John Beaumont, Campbell Hamilton, and Catherine Hall. However, his admission that he had been a party to the offences charged led to the acquittal of the defendants because at that time the evidence of an accomplice had to be corroborated. According to his autobiography, this experience led him to work on his own rather than lay himself open to the sort of betrayal in which he had engaged. He also turned to confidence tricks, typically adopting the guise of a gentleman or a gentleman's servant so as to obtain goods on credit or approval which he then sold or pawned. In November 1750 he was arrested trying to pawn a watch he had stolen from a shop in Fleet Street, London, and was committed to New prison. He was sentenced to death at the Old Bailey in December 1750, but this was reduced to transportation for fourteen years and he sailed to Virginia in the summer of 1751.

According to his autobiography, Speckman soon escaped from the master to whom he had been sold and travelled extensively throughout the American colonies over the next ten years: he joined the British army and then deserted on at least three separate occasions, was whipped for stealing lace in New York, and was an overseer of slaves in Charlestown, South Carolina. He claimed to have had relationships with several women, which ended as abruptly as they began, and, indeed, to have married three times while in America, although the identities of these wives are not known: two he abandoned and one died. It is a matter of speculation how accurate much of this material is, or whether it was included in his autobiography simply to boost sales, although Roe recorded that when challenged Speckman claimed that, aside from some stories concerning horses, it was 'pretty right' (*The Ordinary of Newgate*, 16).

Speckman seems to have returned to England in 1761, landing at Falmouth and then travelling around England, Scotland, and Ireland defrauding tradespeople and occasionally committing highway robberies. In September 1763 he stole 12 yards of lace from a milliner's shop near Golden Square in London. He passed the lace to Maria Rogers and Ann Davis, and they took it to two pawnbrokers, one of whom, Frank Rotchford, recognized it as having been advertised as stolen. Speckman was arrested by Richard Fuller, a thieftaker connected with John Fielding, the Bow Street magistrate, committed to New prison, and in October 1763 condemned to death at the Old Bailey. It was while in Newgate that he met and quarrelled with Roe. According to Roe, Speckman demanded a payment for his life story sufficient to cover his funeral expenses, but Roe felt the amount requested was excessive—sufficient for Speckman to have been 'buried like a Lord' (*The Ordinary of Newgate*, 10)—and, indeed, seems to have felt that he should have confessed without expecting any payment as an act of contrition necessary for his salvation. Speckman claimed that Roe applied pressure on him by refusing the sacrament. Rather than buckle, Speckman appears to have written his own account, which he delivered to an editor on the day before his execution and which was published as *The Life, Travels, Exploits, Frauds and Robberies of Charles Speckman, alias Brown* (1763). Neglected by Roe, he was, along with the other condemned prisoners, visited by the theologian Alexander Cruden. On the day he was hanged, Speckman was said to have emerged from Newgate prison, lifted his arms, and declared, 'This is the finest Morn, that ever I have seen'. His editor claimed he behaved 'with patience and resignation' (*Life*, 51), praying and telling the spectators at the gallows at Tyburn that he deserved to die. He was hanged on 23 November 1763 and was probably buried on 27 November in Tindall's burial-ground, Bunhill Fields, London.

PHILIP RAWLINGS

Sources *The life, travels, exploits, frauds and robberies of Charles Speckman, alias Brown* (1763) • *The ordinary of Newgate's account of the behaviour confession, and dying words, of five malefactors … who were executed at Tyburn on Wednesday Nov 23, 1763* (1763) • P. Rawlings, *Drunks, whores and idle apprentices: criminal biographies of the eighteenth century* (1992), 181–216 • *The whole proceedings on the king's commission of the peace* (1762–3) [Old Bailey sessions papers, 19–21 Oct 1763]

Spedding, James (1808–1881), literary editor and biographer, was born on 26 June 1808 in Mirehouse, Cumberland, the son of John Spedding and Sarah Gibson, eldest

James Spedding (1808–1881), by George Frederic Watts, *c.*1853

daughter of Henry Gibson of Newcastle upon Tyne. After attending grammar school at Bury St Edmunds, he entered Trinity College, Cambridge, in 1827, where he won a prize for a declamation delivered on commemoration day 1830. Although he was a good classical scholar, and in the second class of the classical tripos of 1831, his greater merits were recognized by his contemporaries. As one of the Apostles at Cambridge, he became a lifelong friend of Lord Houghton, Edward Fitzgerald, Arthur Hallam, Archbishop Trench, W. M. Thackeray, and Alfred Lord Tennyson, who said of Spedding, 'He was the Pope among us young men—the wisest man I know' (Hallam, Lord Tennyson, *Alfred Lord Tennyson: a Memoir by his Son*, 1867, 1.38). In 1835, in an appointment made by James Stephen, Spedding entered the Colonial Office where he established a reputation with 'quite a genius for business'. The appointment was never made permanent and Spedding left in 1841 and spent the next year in the United States as secretary to the Ashburton commission negotiating a settlement of the boundary dispute between that country and Canada. After that period, Spedding began what was to be his main employment for over thirty years, his edition of the works of Francis Bacon, refusing in 1847 the office of permanent under-secretary of state for the colonies and serving on the civil service commission only when it was first instituted in 1855 and resigning when the office was in working order. The first result of his Bacon studies, *Evenings with a reviewer, or, A free and particular examination of Mr Macaulay's article on Lord Bacon*, written in 1845 but not published until 1848, demonstrates a precise method contrasting the generalized attacks and misrepresentations of Macaulay with quiet humour and a shrewd critical faculty which, to a careful reader, make the book more interesting than its rival. By 1847 Spedding had negotiated with Robert Lesie Ellis and D. D. Heath to bring out a complete edition of Bacon. Ellis, the editor of the philosophical works, was soon disabled by illness, leaving completion of his task to Spedding in 1853. Although Heath edited the legal texts, Spedding took on almost all the other editing of *The Letters and the Life of Francis Bacon* from 1857 to 1859 and was solely responsible for volumes 8–14 which appeared from 1861 to 1874. As Victorians themselves recognized immediately and all generations have since, Spedding's labour of a lifetime became a model of complete and precise scholarship and editing. If he did not prove Bacon a model hero of the kind Victorians and the nineteenth century tended to worship, he revealed an intelligible Bacon out of careful documentation and critical realism. A new cultural model thus appeared not from the grandeur and dramatic wills the century sought in its heroic models but from unflagging industry (slowed down only about 1863 when Spedding had to take a long rest), familiarity with every possible source of information, and slow but sure-footed judgement based on the most careful balancing of evidence. A new kind of hero thus emerged, the ambiguous and mixed hero of the twentieth century, to which Spedding's scholarship and editing was a clear prelude. Writing to Spedding's close friend the poet and translator Edward Fitzgerald in 1874, Thomas Carlyle, whose heroes tended towards the Victorian ideal, praised the volumes of *The Letters and the Life* as 'the hugest and faithfullest bit of literary navvy work I have ever met with in this generation' for in these texts, 'Bacon is washed clean down to the natural skin' so that, for Carlyle, 'There is a grim strength in Spedding, quietly, very quietly, invincible, which I did not quite know of before this book' (*Letters*, 2.175–7). The result of such labour revealed the human figure behind the cultural and scientific origination the Victorians ascribed to Bacon. In one of his brilliant prefaces, to the philosophical and autobiographical work by Bacon in middle age, *De interpretatione naturae proemium*, Spedding could be exact about one of Bacon's failures and reveal its ironic genesis in his own greatest talents:

> Bacon failed to devise a practicable method for the discovery of the Forms of Nature, because he misconceived the conditions of the case; he expected to find the phenomena of nature more easily separable and distinguishable than they really are; a misconception into which a discursive intellect, an enterprising spirit, and a hopeful nature, would most naturally fall.

This open understanding of human character was found in Spedding's entire life, whether in his personal relationships or his final essays in his 1879 *Reviews and Discussions, Literary, Political, and Historical not Relating to Bacon*, where he discusses the authorship of Fletcher and Shakespeare in the play *Henry VIII* and reveals not only his ardour for the novels of Jane Austen, for example, but also his liberal politics (although rarely roused to enthusiasm after the Hungarian struggle of 1848–9). In the last year of his life Spedding published *Studies in English History* (1881), a volume co-authored by the historian James Gairdner. A lifelong bachelor, he occupied chambers from 1835 until 1864 at 60 Lincoln's Inn Fields, just around the corner from the Public Record Office and only a short walk from the British Museum and library, his main centres of research. For his friends from the whole spectrum of Victorian intellectual society, Spedding's quiet sense of humour and incisive perceptions of their world always made him a delightful companion. Physically noteworthy (as revealed in the Victorian photograph by Julia Margaret Cameron) for his high-domed bald head, he was a good swimmer, walker, and player of archery and billiards, though not a brilliant performer of either. On the resignation of Charles Kingsley in 1869, Spedding was offered the professorship of modern history at Cambridge; in 1874 the university offered him an honorary degree. He refused both, accepting only an honorary fellowship at his beloved Trinity College. From 1864 on, he lived with a niece at Westbourne Grove. On 1 March 1881 Spedding was knocked down by a hansom cab and taken to St George's Hospital, where he died on 9 March. Tennyson, whose poems Spedding read in manuscript and reviewed in 1842 in the *Edinburgh Review* and whose early drawing by Spedding appeared in Tennyson's son's biography of the poet, rushed to the hospital but was refused admission. The end of Spedding's life revealed his essential nature. While still conscious, he was characteristically anxious to make it clear that he considered the accident that was killing him due not to the driver, but to his own deafness and carelessness. LESLIE STEPHEN, *rev.* W. A. SESSIONS

Sources D. Alexander, 'Benevolent sage or blundering booby?', *Dickens Quarterly*, 8 (Sept 1991), 120–27 • C. Drinker Bowen, *Francis Bacon: the temper of a man* (Boston, 1966) • R. Dellamora, *Masculine desire: the sexual politics of Victorian aestheticism* (1990) • D. Du Maurier, *The winding stair: Francis Bacon, his rise and fall* (New York, 1977) • J. J. Epstein, *Francis Bacon: a political biography* (Athens, USA, 1977) • K. J. Fielding, 'Carlyle and the Speddings: new letters', *Carlyle Newsletter*, 7 (spring 1986), 12–20 • K. J. Fielding, 'Carlyle and the Speddings: new letters II', *Carlyle Newsletter*, 8 (spring 1987), 51–66 • C. Ricks, 'Spedding's annotations of the Trinity MS of *In memoriam*', *Tennyson Research Bulletin*, 4 (Nov 1984), 110–13 • L. Stephen, 'James Spedding', *Living Age*, 233 (28 June 1902), 797–809 • G. S. Venables, preface, in J. Spedding, *Evenings with a reviewer, or, Macaulay and Bacon*, 1 (1881) • *IGI*

Archives BL, letters to Maevey Napier, Add. MSS 34617–34626, *passim* • Bodl. Oxf., corresp. with Sir Henry Taylor • Trinity Cam., letters to J. W. Blakesley • V&A, corresp. with John Forster and reviews, etc., for *The Examiner*

Likenesses attrib. A. C. Sterling, salt print, *c.*1846–1849, NPG • G. F. Watts, chalk drawing, *c.*1853, NPG [*see illus.*] • J. M. Cameron, photograph, 1864, NPG • S. Laurence, oils, 1881–2, Trinity Cam. • T. Woolner, marble medallion, 1882, Trinity Cam.

Speechly, William (1723–1819), agriculturist, was born near Peterborough, Northamptonshire, the son of a farmer. He began work as a gardener at Milton Abbey, Dorset, and after working at Castle Howard in Yorkshire he became head gardener to Sir William St Quintin of Harpham, Yorkshire. In 1767 he became gardener to William Henry Cavendish Cavendish-Bentinck, third duke of Portland, at Welbeck Abbey in Nottinghamshire. In 1771 he visited the Netherlands. He married, and had at least two sons.

In 1776 the duke asked him to write a description of the method of planting trees on the Nottinghamshire estates for Alexander Hunter's edition of John Evelyn's *Silva*. This later appeared as an article in Hunter's *Georgical Essays* (1803). Speechly also contributed a note on the possibility of raising the pineapple without the use of tanner's bark.

Speechly was mainly known for his skill in growing pineapples and grapes. He revolutionized the cultivation of the pineapple, and was particularly concerned that it should not be kept at too hot a temperature in the winter. He introduced new methods for cultivating grapes. In 1779 he issued a *Treatise on the Culture of the Pine Apple*; this was followed in 1790 by a *Treatise on the Culture of the Vine*. Both works were republished, in one volume, in 1820. In 1797 Sir John Sinclair (1754–1835), president of the board of agriculture, thought about bringing out a comprehensive work on agriculture, and, at his request, Speechly prepared the sections on gardening and domestic rural economy. But in 1798 the project was laid aside, and in 1800 Speechly's manuscript was returned to him at his own request.

In 1801 his younger son died, and Speechly retired from Welbeck Abbey to manage his son's farm. During this time he neglected his manuscript on rural economy, but on his retirement to Great Milton in Oxfordshire he completed and enlarged it, and it was published in 1820, with several other essays appended, under the title *Practical Hints in Domestic Rural Economy*. This work was devoted to the management of cottage gardens. Speechly died at Great Milton in Oxfordshire on 1 October 1819.

E. I. CARLYLE, *rev.* ANNE PIMLOTT BAKER

Sources R. P. Brotherston, 'Speechly and his books', *Gardeners' Chronicle*, 3rd ser., 47 (1910), 193, 211–12 • Desmond, *Botanists*, rev. edn • *GM*, 1st ser., 84/2 (1814), 140

Speed, Adolphus (*fl.* 1647–1659), agriculturist, has been often referred to as 'Adam' Speed from the title-page of his only acknowledged work, *Adam out of Eden* (1659) where he signs himself 'Ad. Speed'. That this stands for Adolphus, and not Adam, however, is proved by his autograph on an earlier publication. On the same title-page he claims gentle birth. There is nothing to prove it, or the assertion, made later, that he was a descendant of the historiographer John Speed. It is, however, just possible that he was a kinsman of the Chichester minister, William Speed. If so, this helps to explain his contact with, and support from, the intelligencer Samuel Hartlib, for the latter had known William Speed during his brief and unsuccessful attempt to establish an academy in Chichester in 1630.

The discredit and collapse of the system of patents and monopolies in England during the 1640s left the way open to enterprising 'projectors' to advertise their passports to prosperity. For Speed, 'how excellent and how innocent the art of Husbandry is' needed no demonstration (*Adam out of Eden*, 3). That 'calling' offered the prospect of endless prosperity, a Virginia 'within'. He would be the agent for its realization. Already, in 1647, he was retained (through Hartlib) by Sir Cheney Culpeper, the inheritor of the Leeds Castle estate in the Kentish weald, to advise him on rabbit-farming on the Isle of Elmley. Speed appreciated the advantages of Hartlib's scheme for an 'Office of Address' to advertise his skills and, in 1650, 'made hard shift to print some few Pages' (*Hartlib Papers*, 46/5/1A) under the title *Generall Accommodations by Addresse*. The latter extolled the virtues of the proposed agency. At the same time, Speed tempted the public with enticing, risk-free opportunities of dazzling returns on landed investment through implementing his innovations. The pamphlet ended with a somewhat domestic design for a gentlemen's (and gentlewomen's) academy and a retirement home for elderly widows and spinsters.

It was probably about 1650 that Speed had to ask Hartlib to pay off his debts in order to release him from prison. 'Hartily ashamed' (*Hartlib Papers*, 46/5/8A), he retired in poverty from London to the provinces, where he claimed to 'gaine excellent discoveries constantly' to 'make myself famous' (ibid., 46/5/2A). In 1652 the pamphlet *Cornu copia* appeared. Often ascribed, either in sum or in part, to Hartlib, it was in reality the product of Speed's enterprising imagination. Subtitled 'A miscellanium of lucriferous and most fructiferous experiments, observations, and discoveries, immethodically distributed', it itemized fifty-four diverse schemes. These proposals can only be fully understood in the light of *Adam out of Eden*, which Hartlib helped Speed publish in 1659, but which must have existed in manuscript by at least 1652. Some of them involved new root crops (turnips and potatoes); others offered the potential benefits of new grasses (lucerne, clover-grass, and so on). He was particularly open to the possibilities for cash crops on farms within reach of the London market and commended the development of the industrially orientated products (hops, liquorice, saffron, mustard, teasels, and French furze). He was a strong advocate of liquid manure ('muck-water') and claimed to have devised an engine 'in part like they use in London, when houses are on fire', to spray it on to fields (*Adam out of Eden*, 45). He added legitimacy by referring to 'Sir Richard Weston', 'A Gentleman of Richmond', 'An Honourable Knight in Kent' and so on, whose experiments confirmed the veracity of his claims.

Walter Blith, a sober agronome, distrusted Speed, 'that superlative Improver' (Blith, 174). The second and enlarged edition of his *The English Improver Improved* (1652) was published in response to Speed's prospectus. Blith ridiculed the latter

> I being once so weake as to come to an agreement with Mr. Speed, who writes such high things, as reason cannot fathom, to discover his particulars to me, which he gave me in writing … all of which (except the Pompion) were as well known before to myselfe as to hym, but not, that from them to raise so great advantages, I never knew nor shall.
> (ibid., 276)

Speed's exaggerated and naïve claims for agricultural innovation risked its protagonists being 'accompted or at least … Scandalized as a projector' (ibid., preface). Despite Blith's scepticism, however, Speed's reliance on empirical observation (including his respect for women's recipes and medicinal cures) was genuine; and his exalted aspirations for innovative husbandry accurately reflect the enthusiasm of a network of agricultural improvers in Commonwealth England.

Ernest Clarke, *rev.* M. Greengrass

Sources A. Speed, *Adam out of Eden, or, An abstract of divers excellent experiments touching the advancement of husbandry* (1659) • A. Speed, *Generall accommodations by addresse* [1650] • [A. Speed], *Cornu copia: a miscellanium of lucriferous and most fructiferous experiments, observations, and discoveries, immethodically distributed* (1652) • *The Hartlib papers*, ed. J. Crawford and others (1995) [CD-ROM] • W. Blith, *The English improver improved, or, The survey of husbandry surveyed*, another edn (1653) • T. Speed, *Records and memorials of the Speed family* (1890), 17 • 'The letters of Sir Cheney Culpeper, 1641–1657', ed. M. J. Braddick, *Camden miscellany, XXXIII*, CS, 5th ser., 7 (1996), 105–402

Archives University of Sheffield, Hartlib MSS

Speed, John (1551/2–1629), historian and cartographer, was born at Farndon, Cheshire. He was the son (born before their marriage) of John Speed (1526–1584x1603), merchant tailor, and Elizabeth Cheynye (*b.* 1530). Speed was made free of the Merchant Taylors' Company on 10 September 1580 through patrimony, with no occupation given; meanwhile, he had married Susanna (1557/8–1628), daughter of Thomas Draper, freeman of the city of London, in 1570 or 1571 and become a father: the couple had twelve sons and six daughters. Both father and son had property in St Paul's Churchyard: by 1567 the father was leasing from the dean and chapter of St Paul's a sizeable house on the north side in St Gregory's parish; by 1602 the son was leasing two houses on the south-east side in St Faith's parish, adjoining the south-east end of the cathedral (possibly the two ruinous tenements Speed leased from the dean and chapter of St Paul's in 1592). In one of these houses seven books tending towards papistry were found in 1584.

By the late 1580s the younger Speed had theological interests, was associated with Hugh Broughton, and in 1588–9 saw the printing of Broughton's *Concent of Scripture* through the press. This work contained maps, including one engraved by William Rogers (who was later to engrave Speed's map of Cheshire of 1602–3) and one attributed to Jodocus Hondius (engraver for Speed's *Theatre*). Shortly afterwards, Broughton fled to the continent, leaving his genealogies of the scriptures with Speed, who had helped to compile them. These *Genealogies Recorded in the Sacred Scriptures* were published in 1592 and probably formed the basis of those for which Speed was granted the privilege in 1610 to insert in every copy of the Authorized Version of the Bible for ten years. This patent was renewed twice; after much correspondence, the Stationers' Company bought out Speed's son John [*see below*] in 1638 for £700. Speed's theological interests continued: about 1595 he published *A direction to finde all those names expressed in that large table of genealogies of scripture, lately gathered*. His other main theological publication was *A Clowd of Witnesses: and they the Holy Genealogies of the Sacred Scriptures* (1616), republished in 1620 and 1628.

Speed was also developing his historical and cartographic interests. In the 1590s, possibly at the behest of the bookseller Bonham Norton, he went to Ewelme and Wickham to gather genealogical information about Chaucer's descendants and arms, which were assembled round the portrait published in Thomas Speight's edition of Chaucer's works in 1598. In 1595 he published a wall map of biblical Canaan. By 1598 Speed had presented maps to Queen Elizabeth; in that year she appointed him a customs waiter, a position whose duties it is unlikely he carried out himself. Sir Fulke Greville probably recommended Speed for the post; Speed acknowledged his help and that of many others in his publications.

In 1600 Speed presented three of his maps to the Merchant Taylors' Company, which praised his skill as a map

John Speed (1551/2–1629), by Salomon Savery, pubd 1632

maker and genealogist. He collected material for *A Description of the Civill Warres of England*, published soon after as a broadside with a map dedicated to Sir Oliver St John. A reduction of a manuscript map, a four-sheet version was published in 1603, probably to celebrate the accession of James I. About this time Speed was responsible for three genealogical engravings, in 1605 and 1608 he was paid for making maps for the king, and about 1606 he was granted a coat of arms. He joined the circle which included members of the original Society of Antiquaries, and met scholars such as William Camden, Robert Cotton, and William Smith. These all helped Speed with his researches, being engaged in methodically studying the history of the British people and institutions. Speed participated; through Cotton, he developed an interest in coins, and was responsible for those in Camden's *Britannia* (1600). Speed was also compiling material for his *History of Great Britain* with its accompanying atlas volume, *The Theatre of the Empire of Great Britaine*. As Speed acknowledged, both text and maps were the result of industrious research and reading: from manuscript and printed sources of contemporary topographers such as Christopher Saxton, William Smith, John Norden, Sir Henry Spelman, and others; from Sir Robert Cotton's collection of manuscripts and maps; from records of crown officials in the shires; from field observation; and from illustrations of coins, antiquities, and armorial designs.

The Theatre of the Empire of Great Britaine followed the model of Ortelius's *Theatrum orbis terrarum*—first published in English in 1606—in its title and its format, with map sheets backed by historical and geographical texts and gazetteers of place names. This was the earliest English attempt at producing an atlas on a grand scale, with the first detailed maps of the provinces of Ireland, the first set of county maps consistently attempting to show the boundaries of territorial divisions, and the first truly comprehensive set of English town plans—a notable contribution to British topography. Perhaps as many as fifty of the seventy-three towns had not previously been mapped, and about fifty-one of the plans were probably Speed's own work. In 1606 Speed might have been helped by his son John in surveying towns. A balance is struck between the modern and historical, with information placed on the edges of the maps about antiquarian remains, and sites and vignettes of famous battles, together with arms of princes and nobles. This additional information is one of the *Theatre*'s most significant contributions. Scotland is covered in less detail, as Timothy Pont was surveying there. Individual maps for the *Theatre* were prepared from about 1602, plates were engraved by Jodocus Hondius—noted for his skills in decoration—from 1607, George Humble was granted a privilege to print the *Theatre* for twenty-one years from 1608, and the *Theatre* and *History* were published together in 1611–12. They were an immediate success: three new editions and issues of each appeared during Speed's lifetime, and a miniature version was first published about 1619–20. The maps in the *Theatre* became the basis for subsequent folio atlases until the mid-eighteenth century.

In 1614 Speed negotiated on behalf of the Merchant Taylors' Company to renew its lease of the Mora prebendal estate from the chapter of St Paul's. In the following year he was granted the renewal of a lease of land at Moorfields, upon which he had built a new house valued at £400, and which had been let in 1594 to George Sotherton. Three years later, in 1618, he secured a lease on adjoining land.

By 1625 Speed had lost his sight. Nevertheless, in 1627 he published *A Prospect of the most Famous Parts of the World*, which shared a title-page with the 1627 edition of the *Theatre*. The *Prospect*, the earliest world atlas by an Englishman (though not the first to be published in England), seems to have been primarily a commercial venture, in which Speed was probably not closely involved. It lacks the organization and methodical preparation of his earlier works, with thin and haphazard map coverage. The twenty-one maps are mostly Anglicized versions of examples engraved in Antwerp or Amsterdam; the text on the reverse draws heavily on Peter Heylyn's *Microcosmus* (1625, 1627).

Speed's wife died on 28 March 1628 and he followed her on 28 July 1629, aged seventy-seven. His funeral was held in St Giles Cripplegate: the sermon was preached by Josias Shute and a monument was put up in his memory. He left his leaseholds in St Giles Cripplegate and St Faith the Virgin to his sons Samuel, John, and Nathan, the profits from printing his *Genealogies* to his children in turn, and bequests to his descendants and the poor of the parishes where he held property.

John Speed (1595–1640), anatomist, son of John and Susanna Speed, was born in London in January 1595 and entered Merchant Taylors' School in January 1604. He matriculated at St John's College, Oxford, on 30 October 1612, proceeding BA in 1616, MA in 1620, and BM and DM in 1628. In 1624 he resigned his fellowship and married Margaret Warner (*d.* 1685); they had five children, including Samuel *Speed (1630/31–1682). In 1632 he renewed the lease of his house in Moorfields, London, from the Merchant Taylors' Company and he became a member of Gray's Inn in 1633. Speed was the first anatomy lecturer in Oxford, and wrote a treatise which relates to two skeletons which he made and gave to his college library. He was also the author of 'Stonehenge: a Pastoral', acted in the college hall in 1635. He died in May 1640 and was buried in the college chapel, leaving a house in London and land in Oxford and its surroundings.

John Speed (1628–1711), physician and poet, was the second child and eldest son of John and Margaret Speed, and was born in Oxford on 4 November 1628 and baptized four days later. He attended Merchant Taylors' School, London, in 1640 and was elected a scholar at St John's College, Oxford, in June 1644. He became a fellow there in 1647, proceeded BA on 1 February 1648, but was ejected that May. He was invited to Southampton by Thomas Knollys of Grove Place near Nursling and stayed there until the Restoration, taking his MA in 1660 and BM and DM in 1666. Meanwhile, he had renewed from the Merchant Taylors' Company the lease he had inherited of land in Moorfields, London, in 1652. In 1667 Speed married Elizabeth Barker-Bernard (1628–1678), widow of William Bernard, and moved to Southampton where he established a medical practice. They had four children. In 1680 he married Philadelphia Knollys (*d.* 1725), with whom he had seven children. His satirical poem, *Batt upon Batt: a poem upon the parts, patience and pains of B.K., clerk, poet, cutler of Holyrood-parish in Southampton … to which is annexed the vision*, was published in 1680; another six editions were issued, the last about 1740. He was mayor of Southampton in 1681 and again in 1694 and was granted a coat of arms. Speed died on 21 September 1711 and was buried in Holy Rood Church, Southampton, on the 27th. He left to his widow the tithes of Eling, which he had bought from Lord Henry Sandys, and his house in St Lawrence parish, Southampton, and bequests to her and his six children of £3800, to the poor of the parishes of St Lawrence and Holy Rood, and to his servants. His grandson, John Speed (1703–1781) MD, made extensive manuscript collections relating to Southampton.

Sarah Bendall

Sources R. A. Skelton, introduction, in J. Speed, *A prospect of the most famous parts of the world*, facs. edn (1966) • R. A. Skelton, *County atlases of the British Isles, 1579–1830: a bibliography* (1970) • A. M. Hind, *Engraving in England in the sixteenth and seventeenth centuries*, 2 (1955) • C. M. Clode, *The early history of the Guild of Merchant Taylors of the fraternity of St John the Baptist, London*, 2 (1888) • Foster, *Alum. Oxon.* • G. Ormerod, *The history of the county palatine and city of Chester*, 2nd edn, ed. T. Helsby, 2 (1882) • R. A. Skelton, 'Tudor town plans in John Speed's *Theatre*', *Archaeological Journal*, 108 (1951), 109–20 • R. W. Shirley, *Early printed maps of the British Isles*, rev. edn (1980) • A. Baynton-Williams, 'John Speed', www.mapforum.com, nos. 2–4, 1999 • will, GL, MS 25626/4, fols. 363*v*–369*r* • will, PRO, PROB 11/183 [John Speed, 1595–1640] • will, PRO, PROB 11/524 [John Speed, 1628–1711] • G. Schilder and H. Wallis, 'Speed military maps discovered', *Map Collector*, 48 (1989), 22–6 • H. Wallis, 'England re-discovered', *British Museum Society Bulletin*, 9 (1972), 20 • N. Nicholson, introduction, in J. Speed, *The counties of Britain: a Tudor atlas* (1988) • W. C. Costin, *The history of St John's College, Oxford, 1598–1860*, OHS, new ser., 12 (1958) • *CSP dom.*, *1581–90*, 198; *1598–1601*, 62; *1603–10*, 425, 639; *1625–6*, 308 • C. J. Robinson, ed., *A register of the scholars admitted into Merchant Taylors' School, from AD 1562 to 1874*, 1 (1882) • J. L. Chester and J. Foster, eds., *London marriage licences, 1521–1869* (1887) • E. Kell, 'On the castle and other ancient remains at Southampton', *Journal of the British Archaeological Association*, 21 (1865), 285–93 • *N&Q*, 5th ser., 10 (1878), 327, 453 • *N&Q*, 5th ser., 11 (1879), 139 • J. T. Smith, *Antiquities of London and environs* (1791) • A. Chalmers, ed., *The general biographical dictionary*, new edn, 28 (1816), 263–6 • A. Maunsell, *The … catalogue of English printed bookes* (1595) [in 2 pts] • J. S. Davies, *A history of Southampton* (1883) • Fuller, *Worthies* (1662) • Wood, *Ath. Oxon.*, new edn, 4.699 • *Biographia Britannica, or, The lives of the most eminent persons who have flourished in Great Britain and Ireland*, 6 (1763) • M. J. Simmonds, *Merchant Taylor fellows of St John's College, Oxford* (1930) • monument, St Giles Cripplegate, London • parish register, Oxford, All Saints [John Speed, 1595–1640] • parish register, Oxford, St Michael's [John Speed, 1595–1640] • parish register, Oxford, St Michael's [baptism: John Speed, 1628–1711] • monument, Southampton, Holy Rood [John Speed, 1628–1711] • parish register, Southampton, Holy Rood [burial: wives of John Speed, 1628–1711] • *IGI*

Archives BL, notebook relating to *History of Great Britain*, Add. MS 57336 • Merton Oxf. • St John's College, Oxford [John Speed, 1595–1640 and John Speed, 1628–1711] • St John's College, Oxford, archives, MS | BL, Lawrence MSS

Likenesses S. Savery, line engraving, BM, NPG; repro. in J. Speed, *A prospect of the most famous parts of the world* (1632), frontispiece [*see illus.*] • W. Ward, mezzotint (after J. Jackson), NPG • marble effigy on monument, St Giles Cripplegate, London; repro. in Smith, *Antiquities of London and environs* • oils (after S. Savery), Bodl. Oxf.

Wealth at death property in Moorfields and St Faith the Virgin, London; annuities of £100; bequests of *c.*£55: will, GL, MS 25626/4, fols. 363*v*–369*r* • John Speed (1595–1640): land in London and Oxfordshire: will, PRO, PROB 11/183 • John Speed (1628–1711): tithes Eling, house in Southampton, bequests of £3800: will, PRO, PROB 11/524

Speed, John (1595–1640). *See under* Speed, John (1551/2–1629).

Speed, John (1628–1711). *See under* Speed, John (1551/2–1629).

Speed, John (1703–1781), physician and antiquary, was born on 7 September 1703 at Southampton, where he was baptized at Holy Rood Church, six days later. He was the son of Dr John Speed (*bap.* 1671, *d.* 1747), physician, and Anne Crosse (*bap.* 1680, *d.* 1769), and great-great-grandson of the cartographer John Speed (1551/2–1629). He was the third generation of John Speeds to practise medicine in Southampton. He was educated at Merchant Taylors' School, London, and from 1722 at St John's College, Oxford, where he graduated doctor of medicine in 1740 and was a fellow until 1741. He married his cousin the heiress Anna-Maria Crosse (*c.*1700–1787) at Jesus Chapel, Pear Tree Green, Southampton, on 13 September 1741; of their four children only Elizabeth (1754–1836) and John Milles Speed (1747–1792) reached maturity. Having returned to Southampton, where his father had almost drunk away his practice, he resided first at the former Holy Rood vicarage, then at 1 High Street, and finally in the family house in St Lawrence's parish. He became a burgess in 1752. He inherited the rectory and advowson of Eling, Hampshire, which was served as vicar in turn by his uncle Richard (1714–57), his brother Samuel (1757–75), and his son (1775–92), and estates in Headley, Hampshire, and Marsh Gibbon, Buckinghamshire.

Speed's practice benefited from Southampton's role as a watering-place patronized by royalty. His *A Commentary on the Use of Sea-Water* (1750) was a supplement to the translation of a Latin treatise by Dr Russell of Leiden, to which he added accounts of his own cases; it ran through four editions. Under the pseudonym Statutophilus, he also published *An impartial by-stander's review of the controversy concerning the wardenship of Winchester College* (1759). Speed was a cultured man who read and wrote fluently both Latin and Greek. He left about thirty unpublished and voluminous poems, plays, and treatises on subjects as varied as Pyrrhus, king of Sicily, Anglo-Saxon grammar, mushrooms, Methodism, the revolution of 1688, and Chaucer's *Miller's Tale*. His historical interests antedated 1759, when he gave Southampton corporation a transcript and translation of Charles I's borough charter, copiously annotated from the town records. He had trawled through all the corporation's archives by 1770, when he wrote his 'History and antiquities of Southampton', which organized a mass of miscellaneous material into sixteen coherent chapters and twenty appendices. It was a remarkable pioneering achievement. Speed was acquainted with the best antiquarian scholarship, if not with the national archives. He was not afraid to differ from authorities like Camden, sometimes mistakenly, and with others. The published edition of 1909 omits the preface, which proclaimed 'the great usefulness of instituting Corporate Bodies, tho' they are now very muchy dislik'd and decry'd' and hoped that reminders of 'Ancient glory' would prompt Southampton's corporation to exercise their powers 'or at least pay some regard to the solemn obligation they be under to preserve those few shadows of their ancient rights that are still left them' (Southampton RO, MS SP 2). Although anxious to avoid extra rates it was civic pride that prompted him to deplore the Waterworks Act (1747) and to oppose the Paving Act (1770) that overrode the corporation when, as he argued, the existing facilities were satisfactory. He blamed the water issue on 'captious people' in 'mutinous uproar' (J. Speed, *The History and Antiquities of Southampton*, ed. E. R. Audrey, 1909, 38) and the paving issue on his genteel patients, who despised residents and corporation alike. Against the Paving Act he wrote two unprinted satirical treatises, 'An account of the ancient town of Gotham' and 'A curious account of a nondescript species of negroes', in which the aristocratic visitors to Southampton spa were black-hearted rather than black-skinned.

Although limited by previous settlements Speed's will of 10 August 1780 bought out the rights of his daughter, Elizabeth, with £5000 worth of stock but on 5 January 1781, because of 'her undutiful resolution … in spight of my Teeth and in defiance of the laws of God and Man to marry a person of whom I very much disapprove', he disinherited her (will). He died in Southampton on 15 March 1781 and was buried two days later at Holy Rood Church. In the settlement of 25 June relating to Elizabeth's marriage to George Goring (*d.* 1828), surgeon and apothecary of Southampton, her brother guaranteed her £5000 on her mother's death in return for her renunciation of all other rights. Speed's widow was buried at Eling on 22 September 1787.

MICHAEL HICKS

Sources J. S. Davies, *A history of Southampton* (1883) · *VCH Hampshire and the Isle of Wight* · A. Temple Patterson, *A history of Southampton, 1700–1914*, 1, Southampton RS, 11 (1966) · Foster, *Alum. Oxon.* · B. W. Greenfield, 'Pedigree of the Speed family', *Miscellanea Genealogica et Heraldica*, 3rd ser., 2 (1896–7), 18–21 · will, PRO, PROB 11/1077, sig. 212 · Southampton RO, Speed papers, Acc 180/4; 180/5a; 180/6 · Hants. RO, M79/128 · U. Southampton L., MS 3/1

Archives Southampton RO, historical papers relating to Southampton · Southampton RO, MS history and notes on Southampton · Southampton RO, papers, Acc 177, 180, 181, 182 · Southampton RO, papers, BRA 171, 842 · Southampton RO, papers, SC 1/S | Hants. RO, documents relating to Speed

Wealth at death £5000 in stock; estates: will, PRO, PROB 11/1077, sig. 212

Speed, Samuel (1630/31–1682), Church of England clergyman, was the eldest son of the anatomist John *Speed (1595–1640) [*see under* Speed, John] and his wife, Margaret Warner (*d.* 1685). He was a grandson of the famous cartographer, historian, and genealogist John *Speed. Elected to Christ Church, Oxford, from Westminster School in 1645, Samuel Speed matriculated on 1 February 1647, aged sixteen, graduating BA on 8 July 1649 and proceeding MA on 30 October 1660. On 14 July 1648 he formally refused to submit to the parliamentary visitors, but must have done so later, for in March 1651 it was recorded that he was absent on leave from the university.

Anthony Wood notes, obscurely, that Speed suffered for his loyalty to the Stuarts. Family tradition had it that he was forced to flee the country for complicity in a plot against Cromwell, and that he sailed to the West Indies and engaged there in piracy against the forces of the protectorate. Perhaps, therefore, he was the same Samuel Speed who was released from the custody of the serjeant-at-arms by an order of the council of state, dated 8 December 1653, on giving his bond not to act for the future to the prejudice of the Commonwealth. At an unknown date, he married Maria, a daughter of Howard Layfield, rector of Chiddingfold, Surrey. There appear to have been no children; after Speed's death his widow was in financial distress and lived at Bishop George Morley's foundation for the widows of clergy at Winchester.

In 1664, probably through the influence of his elder brother, John *Speed of Southampton (1628–1711) [*see under* Speed, John], Samuel was presented by Richard Baylie, dean of Salisbury, to the vicarage of Godalming, Surrey, after the crown had withdrawn its nominee. He was appointed a naval chaplain in 1666 and served in the Second Dutch War (and possibly also the third if there is any truth in the garbled account that he was shipboard chaplain to the earl of Ossory). He earned himself a reputation as 'the famous and valiant sea-chaplain and seaman' (Wood, *Ath. Oxon.: Fasti*, 2.347) and on 25 April 1670 the bishop of Lincoln urged Secretary Williamson to use 'your influence in behalf of Mr Speed, whom I might call Captain Speed, as he fought as well as those that are so called' (*CSP dom.*, *1670*, 181). On 27 June he was duly presented by the king to the prebend of Caistor in the diocese of Lincoln and installed by proxy on 20 September 1670. On 6 May 1674 he was installed as a prebendary of Christ Church, Oxford, on the presentation of the crown. In the same month the king wrote to Oxford University, ordering that the degree of DD be conferred upon Speed, since he 'has not had the opportunity of taking it in the usual course, chiefly by reason of his constant adherence to the King's service' (*CSP dom.*, *1673–4*, 269). On 30 May 1675 a letter from the chancellor of the university to that effect was read in convocation at Oxford, but the degree seems not to have been awarded. Besides his benefice of Godalming, Speed also held the rectory of Whitburn, co. Durham, from 1673 to 1675, and that of Alverstoke, Hampshire, from 1675.

Speed died on 22 January 1682 in the parish of St Michael Queenhithe, in the City, and was buried on the 25th in the chancel of the parish church. Two published works have commonly been attributed to him, one a translation of the *Romae antiquae descriptio* of Valerius Maximus (1678), and the other *Prison-Pietie* (1677). But there is reason to believe that both books, and therefore the biographical facts revealed in the second, were actually the work of his cousin and namesake, the printer and publisher Samuel *Speed. STEPHEN WRIGHT

Sources O. Manning and W. Bray, *The history and antiquities of the county of Surrey*, 1 (1804) • *Old Westminsters* • *The visitation of London, anno Domini 1633, 1634, and 1635, made by Sir Henry St George*, 2, ed. J. J. Howard, Harleian Society, 17 (1883), 256 • administration, PRO, PROB 6/57, fol. 25 • *Fasti Angl.*, *1541–1857*, [Lincoln] • Foster, *Alum. Oxon.* • Wood, *Ath. Oxon.*, new edn, 2.660–61 • Wood, *Ath. Oxon.: Fasti* (1820), 347 • M. Burrows, ed., *The register of the visitors of the University of Oxford, from AD 1647 to AD 1658*, CS, new ser., 29 (1881) • *Fasti Angl.*, *1541–1857*, [Bristol] • *CSP dom.*, *1670* • private information (2004) [N. Rodger]

Speed, Samuel (*bap.* **1633**, *d.* **1679?**), printer and bookseller, was baptized on 23 October 1633 at St Giles Cripplegate, London, the son of Samuel Speed (*d.* before 1661), a citizen and member of the Merchant Taylors' Company—himself the second surviving son of John *Speed, the historian and cartographer—and his wife, Jane, daughter of Richard Joyner alias Lloyd of Abingdon, Berkshire. He was the cousin of Samuel *Speed, the clergyman. Speed was neither (as has been suggested) the son of Daniel Speed, a publisher between 1603 and 1620, nor the father of Thomas Speed, a London bookseller from 1689. On 29 September 1649 young Samuel Speed was bound apprentice to a London stationer, Edward Blackmore, who was probably his uncle, the husband of his father's sister Sarah. He was made free on 5 October 1657 and became a printer and publisher in London. His business was located at St Paul's Churchyard from 1658 to 1662, but moved the following year to the Rainbow, Fleet Street, and after 1669 to Threadneedle Street near the Royal Exchange. The printer was almost certainly the Samuel Speed of St Gregory's, London, a bachelor aged twenty-seven who on 20 February 1661 was granted a licence to marry Rose (*b.* 1642/3), spinster, aged eighteen, daughter of John Underwood, gentleman, of the Middle Temple.

On 8 May 1666 Speed was arrested on charges of publishing and distributing seditious books; specific mention was made of *The Power and Practice of Court Leets* by 'Ag Ph' in which was reproduced material originally issued in Cromwell's time. This was thought by a nervous government to encourage the spread of dangerous ideas. He was discharged on 26 May on provision of a bond for £300 against repeating the offence. It seems possible that this brush with the law affected Speed's trade; perhaps he had enemies in the Stationers' Company, but however that may be he was soon in trouble again. On 15 April 1669, company officials testified that he had 'surreptitiously' obtained licences for two books, *The King's Primer* and its replacement, *The King's Psalter*, from Samuel Parker, chaplain to Archbishop Sheldon (*CSP dom.*, *1668–9*, 280). On 8 October 1672 Speed wrote to the archbishop himself, outlining his project of revising and updating his grandfather's history; he also complained of his own imprisonment in Newgate, which had arisen partly from losses sustained in the great fire of London and partly through legal actions against him, apparently in respect of *The King's Psalter* and *The King's Primer*.

The appeal to Sheldon was unsuccessful. In 1673 Speed issued *The prisoners compaint to the king's most excellent majestie, or, The cries of the king's bench. With Advice to the disconsolate gentlemen prisoners in the several prisons of England especially the king's bench* 'By SS a fellow of King's Colledge in Southwark'. There followed the following year *Fragmenta carceris, or, The King's Bench Scuffle, with the Humours of the Common Side*, an account in verse of a prison brawl witnessed by the author, 'Samuel Speed, a member of the Royal Society'. Despite these ironic shafts, his books reveal Speed not as a radical but as an ultra-loyalist cavalier, seeking to inspire in his readers a sense of outrage that gentlemen such as himself should suffer the indignities of 'the common side'. In the frontispiece of *The King's Psalter* there appears a portrait of Charles II, with the verse,

> First Worship God, and his commands obey,
> And next the King, who doth his sceptre sway:
> Observe his Laws, no innovators trust,
> And to thy neighbour as thyself be just.

It appears from his *Prison-Pietie* (1677) that Speed's financial and legal difficulties had continued unabated: 'London's too late and fatal Judgements, the Plague and Fire, having made me uncapable to manage my Affairs with the like success as formerly, some Creditors forced me to a Confinement in *Ludgate*'; and he observed sadly that 'Many when they grow rich in Temporals, wax poor in Spirituals: As their outward man increaseth, so their inward man decayeth; and as the flesh flourishes, the spirit withers: yet prosperous wickedness is accounted vertue' (sig. A3r, A6r). But his verse, though not of the highest quality, had improved somewhat, and his political loyalty was immovable. In an appended panegyric to Henry Compton, bishop of London, Speed advised:

But if the many headed beast should rise
To pluck King's plumes, and peck out prelates eyes,
Teach them to crumble, like a tottering wall,
Or Dagon crippled with a second fall;
Or heads on London bridge, exposed to sight,
That grin, and shew their teeth, but cannot bite.
(p. 191)

In 1678 there appeared Speed's translation of *Romae antiquae descriptio* by Valerius Quintus Maximus, dedicated to Heneage Finch, lord chancellor, and lately attorney-general, from whom Speed had 'lately experienc'd the Influences of your Honours Favours' (sig. A1r). This may suggest a recent intervention in his legal difficulties which had led to his release. Nothing further is certainly known of Samuel Speed; but there is some reason to suspect that his death may have occurred the following year.

STEPHEN WRIGHT

Sources *The visitation of London, anno Domini 1633, 1634, and 1635, made by Sir Henry St George*, 2, ed. J. J. Howard, Harleian Society, 17 (1883) • D. F. McKenzie, ed., *Stationers' Company apprentices*, [2]: 1641–1700 (1974) • J. L. Chester and G. J. Armytage, eds., *Allegations for marriage licences issued from the faculty office of the archbishop of Canterbury at London, 1543 to 1869*, Harleian Society, 24 (1886) • T. Speed, *Records and memorials of the Speed family* (1892) • S. Speed, *Prison-pietie, or, Meditations divine and moral* (1677) • *CSP dom., 1665–6, 1668–9* • H. R. Plomer and others, *A dictionary of the booksellers and printers who were at work in England, Scotland, and Ireland from 1641 to 1667* (1907) • H. R. Plomer and others, *A dictionary of the printers and booksellers who were at work in England, Scotland, and Ireland from 1668 to 1725* (1922) • *IGI*

Speedy, Tristram Charles Sawyer (1836–1910), army officer and colonial official, was born on 26 November 1836 in Meerut, India, the elder son of Dublin-born Major James Speedy (*b.* 1811) of the Buffs and his wife, Sarah, *née* Squire. Speedy was exceptionally tall (6 feet 5 inches) and strong, and despite his mild manner with courage befitting his size. He was also energetic, with the ability to improvise in difficult situations. He was, however, restless, with little liking for routine, extravagant with both his own and public money, and there was an affectation in his personality and appearance. He had a particular talent for languages.

Speedy entered the army as an ensign in India in 1854, and was adjutant of the 10th Punjab regiment in August 1858; his army reports noted his patience and good temper with his troops. He resigned his commission at the end of 1860, and went to Abyssinia to assist King Tewodros in training his army. Tewodros was engaged in wars against rival rulers and treated the Europeans in his entourage with casual brutality. With Speedy he established a rapport, admiring Speedy's size and courage, and his ability to speak Amharic. From Tewodros Speedy acquired a taste for wearing Abyssinian dress.

In early 1863 Speedy became British vice-consul at Massawa in the Sudan, and then, when the consul was captured by Tewodros, acting consul. In January 1864 he resigned and went to New Zealand. Land disputes between settlers and Maori had resulted in war, and from June 1864 to December 1866 Speedy served as a captain in the Waikato militia, using that title for the rest of his life. He moved to Australia, returning to Abyssinia at the beginning of 1868 as civilian interpreter to General Sir Robert Napier, who commanded the British–Indian military expedition to release British subjects held prisoner by Tewodros. Speedy was a valued member as an interpreter in diplomatic negotiations, riding in advance of the troops and talking to chieftains. In April the British took Magdala, the prisoners were released, and Tewodros committed suicide. Napier, in dispatches, praised Speedy's services, and entrusted him with Tewodros's young son Alamayu (1861–1879). The British government as official guardian left the prince in Speedy's care. Early in 1869, when Speedy took up an appointment as district superintendent of police in Oudh, India, Alamayu accompanied him. Also with him was his wife, Cornelia Mary (*d.* 1917), the daughter of Benjamin Cotton, a well-to-do land owner in Freshwater, Isle of Wight, whom he had married on 15 December 1868. The Speedys treated Alamayu as a son, establishing an affectionate, trusting relationship; but in 1871, when Speedy moved to Penang in the Straits Settlements, Malaya, the British government insisted that Alamayu return to England. Alamayu was educated at Cheltenham College, at Rugby School, and at the Royal Military College, Sandhurst, but died of pleurisy at Headingley, Leeds, on 14 November 1879.

Tristram Charles Sawyer Speedy (1836–1910), by Julia Margaret Cameron, 1868 [with Alamayu, prince of Ethiopia]

In Penang, Speedy, as superintendent of police, was caught up in the deteriorating situation arising from civil war in neighbouring independent Perak, where disputes between Malay chiefs and among Chinese factions had devastated the tin-mining region of Larut. An arms embargo was enforced, and Speedy was involved in confrontations with the Chinese, the boarding of junks and chases along the coast and up rivers, yet he maintained the confidence of the Chinese in Penang. By the end of 1872 mining production had stopped, and the Malay chief of Larut, in an effort to regain control, approached Speedy with offers of financial rewards if he would recruit troops to settle the conflicts among the Chinese. Speedy accepted, with tacit approval from the British authorities, resigned his post, and left for India in July 1873. By September he was back with a force of Sepoys, and was successful against the Chinese. An armistice followed, because of Speedy's blockade and because the political situation had changed. The British government had determined to restore order and began negotiations with Malay chiefs and Chinese headmen. On 20 January 1874 the Pangkor treaty was signed, whereby Perak remained independent but overall responsibility for administration was assigned to British residents who would advise the Malay chiefs and collect and control state revenues. Priority was to establish an assistant resident in Larut to restore mining production. Speedy, who had the confidence of the Straits Settlement authorities, the Malay chiefs, and the Chinese headmen, was appointed. By the end of 1874 Speedy had succeeded in re-establishing law and order, had settled the mining disputes, and had built a new town and administrative accommodation, including a residency for himself. The Colonial Office considered his administration successful, without acknowledging that he had not only advised but had also administered directly.

In 1875 James W. Birch became resident of Perak, an appointment senior to Speedy. Birch, with enthusiastic support from Sir William Jervois, governor of the Straits Settlements, imposed measures for revenue collection. His actions were seen as further British intervention, unrest returned, and Birch was murdered in November. British military action (the Perak War) followed, in which Speedy built roads for the troops. He recruited a Chinese workforce, but construction was slow. When the column was delayed the British commander complained that Speedy's workforce had been insufficient and unproductive, blaming Speedy for his soft treatment of the Chinese. These complaints were reiterated by Governor Jervois when justifying his support for Birch's actions and war expenses. When the war ended in February 1876 the Colonial Office suggested Speedy as permanent resident of Perak. Jervois responded by damning Speedy, whom he considered inferior and extravagant with public money; Jervois hinted at his disloyalty, noting his dealings with the Malay chief in 1873. Speedy was reappointed as assistant resident, but his responsibilities were restricted.

Towards the end of 1877 Speedy resigned, disgusted with the constant belittlement of his post and his abilities. In 1876–7 the Colonial Office published parliamentary papers on Malaya which included Jervois's documents about Speedy; as such they were public but privileged, and Speedy had no redress. However, his wife, on the death of her father in 1875, had become an heiress, and Speedy was now independent with access to a considerable private income. In 1878 Speedy and his wife went on an extensive shooting tour of eastern Sudan, travelling with a camel caravan. For Mrs Speedy it was a stimulating if wearying experience. Her long descriptive letters were published as *My Wanderings in the Soudan* in 1884, when her husband was back in Abyssinia.

Speedy went to Abyssinia as political adviser to Vice-Admiral William Hewett on a diplomatic mission following Mahdist successes in the Sudan: Hewett's task was to offer trade concessions to King Yohannes in return for permission for Egyptian troops to retreat through his country. Yohannes accepted the British proposals, and Massawa became a free port. Hewett and his party left in June, but Speedy stayed on until 1885 to ensure that the agreement was kept. In his report Hewett acknowledged Speedy's invaluable assistance. Speedy returned to Abyssinia in 1897, again as interpreter and adviser, with another diplomatic mission which related to the British campaign to re-conquer the Sudan; the objective was to settle the Sudan–Abyssinia frontiers. The mission was partly successful, but Speedy's contribution was less effective: his expertise was no longer so relevant, and at sixty he was physically less capable.

The Speedys moved to Chatsworth, Church Stretton, Shropshire. There were financial misfortunes in 1883, but under the terms of her father's will a trust fund in Mrs Speedy's name provided sufficient income for them to live in modest comfort. Speedy died at Chatsworth, Church Stretton, on 9 August 1910 and was buried at Church Stretton. Mrs Speedy, a worthy and generous companion of a complex and restless personality, died in 1917. Speedy's career with the Colonial Office might well have been longer and more productive but for the disrepute brought about by Jervois. He had much ability and his language skills were considerable: he was able to communicate in Amharic, Arabic, Malay, Urdu, Hindustani, French, German, Greek, and some Chinese. He was also patient, considerate, and persuasive, and won the confidence of many of those with whom he dealt. DOROTHY ANDERSON

Sources J. M. Gullick, 'Captain Speedy of Larut', *Journal of the Malayan Branch of the Royal Asiatic Society*, 26/3 (1953), 1–103 • C. M. Speedy, *My wanderings in the Soudan*, 2 vols. (1884) • F. Swettenham, *British Malaya: an account of the origin and progress of British influence in Malaya*, rev. edn (1955) • F. Myatt, *The march to Magdala: the Abyssinian war of 1868* (1970) • J. M. Gullick, *Malaysia* (1969) • *The Times* (11 Aug 1910) • D. Anderson, 'Captain Speedy of Abyssinia, Malaya — and Church Stretton', *Bulletin for the Association for the Study of Travel in Egypt and the Near East: Notes and Queries*, no. 8 (Oct 1999), 18–20 • D. Anderson, 'Henry Morton Stanley meets Captain Speedy in Abyssinia, 1868', *Bulletin for the Association for the Study of Travel in Egypt and the Near East: Notes and Queries*, no. 13 (spring 2002), 21–3

Archives BL, English–Amharic dictionary, Add. MSS 7945–7947 | BL, letters to G. F. Wise, Add. MS 45726

Likenesses J. M. Cameron, photograph, 1868, priv. coll. [*see illus.*] • photograph, 1868 (after woodcut), repro. in Speedy, *My wanderings*, pl. 1 • photograph, 1897, repro. in Speedy, *My wanderings*, pl. 6 • J. Hughes, double portrait, photograph, NPG • photograph, Army Museums Ogilby Trust; repro. in Myatt, *March to Magdala*, pl. 11

Wealth at death £227 3*s*. 4*d*.: probate, 10 Sept 1910, *CGPLA Eng. & Wales*

Speght [*married name* Procter], **Rachel** (*b.* 1597?), polemicist and poet, was the daughter of James Speght (*d.* 1637), a Calvinist minister in London who was rector of St Mary Magdalen, Milk Street (1592–1637), and of St Clement Eastcheap (1611–37); nothing is known of her mother or of any siblings. Her father was the author of religious tracts and had some associations with the Goldsmiths' guild and the City establishment; Thomas Speght, editor of Chaucer (1598 and 1602), may have been a kinsman. One of Rachel's works was dedicated to her godmother Mary Moundford 'as a testimonie of my true thankefulnesse for your fruitfull love'; Mary was the wife of Thomas Moundford, a renowned London physician who was six times president of the College of Physicians.

Speght was the first Englishwoman to identify herself, by name, as a polemicist and critic of contemporary gender ideology. Her tract defending women, *A Mouzell for Melastomus* (1617), is the first, and maybe the only, female contribution to the vigorous Jacobean pamphlet war over women's place and role. She also published, in 1621, a long poetic meditation on death, *Mortalities Memorandum*, together with an allegorical dream-vision poem, *The Dreame*, that is remarkable for its account of her rapturous encounter with learning and for its impassioned defence of women's humanistic education. Her writings indicate that she had acquired a classical education very rare for seventeenth-century women of any class; she knew Latin and had some training in logic and rhetoric, and had at least encountered a wide range of learned authorities. Her minister father may have conducted or supervised that education, or she may have attended one of the few schools for young gentlewomen at that period. In the preface to *Mortalities Memorandum* and *The Dreame* she offers her new book in part to reassert her authorial rights against those who (refusing to credit female achievement) attributed her tract to her father. As a member of the London bourgeoisie she seems not to have been much troubled by the anxieties about authorship and publication common among the upper classes in early modern England, and especially among women. She may indeed have hoped to earn money from writing as a quasi-professional author.

The immediate stimulus to Speght's writing was the publication in 1615 of an anonymous attack on women: the rambling, boisterous, tonally confused but lively *Araignment of Lewde, Idle, Froward, and Unconstant Women* by Joseph Swetnam. This tract inaugurated the rancorous Jacobean skirmish in the centuries-old *querelle des femmes*, or debate over the nature and worth of womankind. Two years later, in 1617, Speght's answer, *A Mouzell* [muzzle] *for Melastomus* [black mouth], was published; of the eight major contributors to the Swetnam and cross-dressing controversies of 1615–20 only Speght (then nineteen) published under her own name and insisted on her authorial identity. Most of the tracts in these controversies recycled hoary arguments pro and con, and the male writers saw themselves as participants in an ongoing game of wit. Speght's tract breaks the mould of such rhetorical gamesmanship and, inserting herself into the male preserve of protestant biblical exegesis, reinterprets biblical texts—especially the creation–fall story from Genesis—so as to make them yield a more expansive and equitable concept of gender.

Speght attacks Swetnam on particular points, as the genre and readership of such polemics required, but her sometimes trenchant invective against his logic and style is restricted to the prefatory matter and a few poems, and to an appended small tract, *Certaine Quaeres to the Bayter of Women*, with separate title-page, epistle, and preface. In the *Mouzell* proper she looks past Swetnam to engage ministers and other commentators who find in scripture some basis to devalue and wholly subjugate women. Her most radical claims are extrapolations from Galatians 3:28, that under the New Testament 'male and female are all one in Christ Jesus'. On that authority she applies the parable of the talents to women, inferring that 'no power externall or internall ought woman to keep idle, but to imploy it in some service of God', while her own act of writing this tract makes the case that some talents ask employment beyond the domestic sphere. She concludes with a stern warning to men who invite God's certain revenge for reviling his best gift and excellent handywork—'women I meane, whom God hath made equall with themselves in dignity, both temporally and eternally'. A copy of the *Mouzell for Melastomus* at the Beinecke Library, Yale University (1h Sp 617m), contains in the margins some eighty-seven harsh and derogatory manuscript annotations in a contemporary hand. These are probably Swetnam's notes, prepared with a view to answering Speght's tract, although no such answer was published.

Most of what is known about Speght's life must be deduced from *The Dreame*, which prefaces her long meditative poem, *Mortalities Memorandum* (1621). The latter offers itself as an example of a proper Christian meditation on death and indicates that her mother's death prompted it. *The Dreame* allegorizes in a romance mode the obstacles that Speght encountered and overcame in her pursuit of learning—her own fears, the dissuasions of others, the distractions of domestic duties—as well as the encouragement she apparently found from (perhaps) her father and mother, or the Moundfords. It is enlivened by the dialogue of the speaker with allegorical characters: Thought, Age, Experience, Truth, Dissuasion, Industry. Rachel the speaker has to overcome difficulties mounted by Dissuasion:

> As dulnesse, and my memories defect;
> The difficultie of attaining lore,
> My time, and sex, with many others more
> (ll. 106–8)

but once entered into Erudition's garden she delights in the 'taste of science' and desires to 'reape this pleasure more and more'. Truth delivers a paean to knowledge, forcefully countering the conventional arguments in contemporary tracts for limiting woman's education to what is of practical use in her life—the Bible, religious treatises, grammar, handwriting, domestic skills (and, for aristocrats, music, dancing, and modern languages)—with the progressive argument that the very nature of humankind makes all knowledge useful for all humans. At length some unspecified 'occasion' forced her, regretfully, to end her studies, to return

to that place …
From whence I came

and to use her time 'other-ways' (ll. 238–40), presumably in domestic offices. Soon afterwards she encountered a 'full fed Beast' [Swetnam] attacking women and was prompted to muzzle him; and some time after that [1621] another devouring beast [Death] that depopulated countries and took her mother.

In the *Mouzell* Speght does not attack patriarchy as a social arrangement but she does deny any essential basis for it in nature or in the spiritual order. She also represents the family in terms very different from conventional views of it as an analogue of monarchy in the state. *The Dreame* offers an uncompromising defence of woman's education on the same basis as man's education. Speght's serious effort to rethink the implications of the dominant biblical discourse in regard to women was provoked by Swetnam but *The Dreame* suggests that it was also provoked by her own situation as a learned young woman hedged about by restrictions. Both tract and poem strongly, cogently, and subversively argue her own and all good women's worth and substantial equality with men.

On 6 August 1621, at the age of twenty-four, Speght married William Procter (1593–1653) of Somerset, also a Calvinist cleric (and the author of published sermons) at St Mary Woolchurch, London. In 1624 the Procters were living at Upminster in Essex, just outside London, and soon after that in the parish of St Giles Cripplegate, where two children were baptized: Rachel (26 February 1627) and William (15 December 1630). William Procter died in 1653 and was buried at All Hallows, Lombard Street; there is no record of Rachel Speght's death.

BARBARA K. LEWALSKI

Sources T. Teltroth [J. Swetnam], *Araignment of lewde, idle, froward, and unconstant women: or the vanitie of them, choose you whether* (1615) • W. Procter, *The watchman warning: a sermon preached at Pauls Crosse the 26. of Septembere, 1624* (1625) • E. Sowernam [pseud], *Ester hath hang'd Haman, or, An answere to a lewd pamphlet, entituled The arraignment of women* (1617) • C. Munda [pseud], *The worming of a mad dogge, or, A soppe for Cerberus the jaylor of hell* (1617) • B. K. Lewalski, ed., *The polemics and poems of Rachel Speght* (1996) • K. U. Henderson and B. F. McManus, *Half humankind: contexts and texts of the controversy about women in England, 1540–1640* (1985) • parish register, St Mary Woolchurch, 6 Aug 1621 [marriage] • parish register, St Giles Cripplegate, GL, 26 Feb 1627; 15 Dec 1630 [baptism: Rachel Procter; baptism: William Procter] • parish register, St Mary Magdalen, Milk Street, 7 April 1637 [burial: James Speght]

Speght, Thomas (*fl.* **1566–1602**), literary editor, was probably of a Yorkshire family and may himself have been born in Yorkshire. He matriculated sizar at Peterhouse, Cambridge, at Easter in 1566 and received a scholarship from Lady Mildred Cecil, to whose son, Elizabeth I's secretary of state Robert Cecil, he dedicated his two Chaucer editions. Speght graduated with his BA in 1569–70 and took his MA in 1573.

It seems certain that Speght was a schoolmaster and he was perhaps the Speyght who is recorded as having been a minor canon of Ely in 1572 and headmaster of the attached grammar school. He contributed commendatory verses in Latin to two books of instruction, Abraham Flemming's *A Panoplie of Epistles, or, A Looking Glasse for the Unlearned* (1576) and John Baret's *An Alvearie, or, Quadruple Dictionarie* (1580). A survey of London made about 1612 shows the house and chapel of St James in the Wall, near Cripplegate, and records that much of the house was rented by a Thomas Speght who used the highest part of the building as a schoolhouse.

Laurence Speght, of the surveyor-general's office in the time of Charles I, was probably Thomas's son; his epitaph in the church of St Peter in Clopton, Northamptonshire, refers to his father as 'Thomas Speght Schoole-master Paragon' (P. Whalley, ed., *History and Antiquities of Northamptonshire*, 1791, 2.372). The Calvinist minister and author, James Speght, and his daughter, the writer Rachel Speght, may have been relatives but Rachel was certainly not Thomas's daughter, as was earlier thought (Lewalski, xi–xii).

Speght became interested in Chaucer at Cambridge and shared his enthusiasm with at least one friend, Francis Beaumont (not the dramatist but the future master of Charterhouse), who later contributed a prefatory letter to Speght's Chaucer edition. It is possible that they formed part of a circle of Chaucerians at Peterhouse and it is perhaps significant that they overlapped with the Cambridge years of another noted Chaucerian, Edmund Spenser (1569–76). After Cambridge, Speght appears to have maintained a private interest in Chaucer. In October 1592 a reprint of Chaucer's works was entered in the Stationers' register and by the time this work appeared under the title *The Workes of our Antient and Lerned English Poet, Geffrey Chaucer, Newly Printed* early in 1598, Speght was the editor.

In preparing the edition Speght certainly had the help of the antiquary John Stow and the 1598 edition of Chaucer is in some ways not much more than a revision of Stow's own edition of 1561. Although Speght lists works of Chaucer's which he claims were 'never before imprinted' (Speght, *Workes*, sig. Aiiiv) most of them in fact appeared in Stow's edition, suggesting the extent to which he saw his task as simply presenting anew what Stow had done. Nevertheless, Speght's notes and introductory material are far more elaborate than in any previous edition and he was the first to provide a substantial glossary. While this suggests that Chaucer's language was becoming difficult to read, it is also part of the process whereby the Chaucerian text was dignified by the kind of extensive apparatus a classical author might receive.

Speght also contributed new annotations to the text of Chaucer, of which the most famous is his comment on a reference to the legendary hero Wade. Speght wrote, 'because the matter is long and fabulous, I passe it over' (Speght, *Workes*, sig. Bbbb.iiiiv), an unfortunate omission as all knowledge of stories of Wade has subsequently been lost.

Also among the introductory material was an extensive biography, which informed all subsequent accounts of the poet's life until the 1840s. Several common beliefs about Chaucer were established here, some of them on the basis of texts attributed to the poet, but spurious. Hence, Chaucer was thought (as supposed author of Thomas Usk's *The Testament of Love*) to have spent time in exile in the 1380s and was claimed as a fellow Cantabrian on the basis of *The Court of Love*. Speght played up Chaucer's links with John of Gaunt and enhanced the image of the poet as a man who 'alwaies held in with the Princes, in whose daies he lived' (Speght, *Workes*, sig. Bviv). He was also the source of the biographical detail that Chaucer was once fined 2*s.* for beating a Franciscan friar in Fleet Street. The document supposedly recording this was found in the Inner Temple, leading Speght to suggest that the poet studied law there.

While the beating of the friar has never been disproved, it is suspiciously convenient evidence of an early and vigorous tendency to anti-clericalism on the poet's part, which, making him appear at odds with the Church of Rome, helped to refashion a Chaucer acceptable to Reformation England.

Criticisms of the 1598 edition were forthcoming from Francis Thynne, son of the earlier Chaucer editor William Thynne, in his *Animadversions uppon the Annotacions and Corrections … of Chaucers Workes*. Speght took heed of the criticisms, though they were not always accurate, and in a new edition of Chaucer appearing in 1602 he departed more decisively from Stow. In this work the Chaucerian *œuvre* was augmented by the *ABC*, in print for the first time, and the anti-clerical (but non-Chaucerian) *Jack Upland*, which further bolstered the poet's reputation as a Wycliffite.

In 1687 a reprint of this work with a few alterations appeared, and remained in use even after the publication of John Urry's much reviled Chaucer edition of 1721. Thomas Tyrwhitt, editing the *Canterbury Tales* in the 1770s, used the 1602 and 1687 editions of Speght, taking the latter as his base text. With a period of influence stretching from the late sixteenth century to the late eighteenth, then, Speght's Chaucer has been the most durable of any Chaucer edition. DAVID MATTHEWS

Sources Cooper, *Ath. Cantab.*, vol. 2 • *The visitation of London, anno Domini 1633, 1634, and 1635, made by Sir Henry St George*, ed. J. J. Howard and J. L. Chester, 2 vols., Harleian Society, 15, 17 (1880–83) • D. E. Wickham, 'An early editor of Chaucer reidentified?', *N&Q*, 240 (1995), 428 • J. Schofield, ed., *The London surveys of Ralph Treswell* (1987) • B. Willis, *A survey of the cathedrals of Lincoln, Ely, Oxford and Peterborough* (1730) • J. Stow, *A survay of London*, rev. edn (1603) • Venn, *Alum. Cant.* • Wood, *Ath. Oxon.*, new edn, vol. 1 • Rymer, *Foedera*, 2nd edn, vol. 20 • Arber, *Regs. Stationers*, vol. 2 • F. Thynne, *Animadversions uppon the annotacions and corrections of some imperfections of impressiones of Chaucers workes*, ed. F. J. Furnivall and G. H. Kingsley, EETS, 9 (1865); repr. (1875) • B. K. Lewalski, ed., *The polemics and poems of Rachel Speght* (1996) • B. A. Windeatt, 'Thomas Tyrwhitt', *Editing Chaucer: the great tradition*, ed. P. Ruggiers (1984), 117–43 • D. Pearsall, 'Thomas Speght', *Editing Chaucer: the great tradition*, ed. P. Ruggiers (1984), 71–92 • D. Brewer, ed., *Chaucer: the critical heritage*, 2 vols. (1978) • T. W. Machan, *Textual criticism and Middle English texts* (1994)

Speight, John [Johnny] **(1920–1998)**, comedy writer, was born on 2 June 1920 at 111 Dale Road, Canning Town, east London, the eldest of the three children (two sons and one daughter) of John Speight, a boiler scaler, and his wife, Johanna, *née* Sullivan. Educated locally at St Helen's Roman Catholic School, he left, aged fourteen, without any formal qualifications.

A succession of menial jobs followed at several East End factories along the Silvertown Way, but what enthusiasm Speight exhibited during this period was reserved for his fledgeling career as a jazz musician, playing drums in two minor London-based bands before forming his own outfit, Johnny Speight and His Hot Shots. When the Second World War intervened he joined the Royal Corps of Signals, serving as a cook, and then, following demobilization, he tried and failed to forge a full-time career as a drummer, and had to settle instead for spells as a milkman and an insurance salesman.

The idea of writing as a vocation came to Speight through his regular visits to Canning Town Public Library. John Steinbeck was an early influence, because Speight felt he wrote of real, believable worlds, but it was a novel by George Bernard Shaw, *Immaturity*, which had an impact that the stocky, stammering, but sharp-witted Speight likened to a 'divine revelation', acting as if 'a light had been turned on and every dark recess lit by sweet reason' (Speight). He proceeded to devour all things Shavian, as well as works by Strindberg, Chekhov, and Ibsen, and he joined the Unity Theatre, where he wrote several overtly left-wing plays which he later dismissed as 'a load of crap' (ibid.).

Speight's move into comedy came in the mid-1950s, when in a jazz club one of his sardonic remarks was overheard by Spike Milligan and Eric Sykes. With their encouragement he started developing more humorous material. After meeting Frankie Howerd, a great patron of comic writers, Speight committed himself to his new craft. His work was first heard on a 1955 BBC radio show entitled *Mr Ross—and Mr Ray*, starring bandleaders Edmundo Ross and Ray Ellington, and at the end of that year he began contributing scripts to *The Frankie Howerd Show*.

Speight married a secretary from Dagenham, Constance Beatrice Barrett (*b.* 1929/30), the daughter of Edward Barrett, a bus conductor, on 3 April 1956. They had two sons and one daughter.

Speight's writing career started to advance in 1957 when he began a nine-year engagement as principal scriptwriter of ITV's *The Arthur Haynes Show*. Haynes came to television without an established comic persona, so Speight created one for him: an aggressive, argumentative, know-all tramp by the name of Hobo Haynes. It was also during this period that Speight wrote several class-conscious plays for television, including *The Compartment* (1961), for which he won the first of his four Screen Writers' Guild awards, and *Playmates* (1962). On 22 July 1965 Speight's half-hour satire, *Till Death Us Do Part*, about a white, working-class, ill-educated, tory-voting East End bigot named Alf Ramsay (played by Warren Mitchell) and his stoical wife, saucy daughter, and left-wing Liverpudlian son-in-law, was broadcast on BBC1 as part of its *Comedy Playhouse* season. It struck a chord, and a series (the first of seven) was commissioned.

Till Death Us Do Part, which ran from 1966 to 1975,

brought social commentary to the genre of situation comedy. Each week Alf Garnett (the surname was changed in deference to England's football manager) would swear (although the BBC limited him to twenty 'bloodys' per episode), and shout as he said the unsayable about liberal modern Britain's sacred cows. Some viewers failed to see Speight's satirical intention, but the writer remained unrepentant: 'I didn't create Alf Garnett', he protested. 'Society did. I just grassed on him' (Speight).

The show, which Speight described as 'the longest play I have written' (Speight), spawned two movies—*Till Death Us Do Part* (1969) and *The Alf Garnett Saga* (1972)—and served as the basis for milder versions in Holland, Germany, and, most notably, America, where *All in the Family* ran from 1971 to 1992. It made Speight a wealthy man, but he never came close to equalling its success. *Curry and Chips* (1969), a racial-conflict comedy co-written with Sykes and Milligan, was dropped by London Weekend Television after six episodes, while two other sitcoms, *Spooner's Patch* (1979–82), set in a police station, and *The Nineteenth Hole* (1989), set in a golf club, failed to catch on. In 1985 Speight brought back the characters from *Till Death Us Do Part* for *In Sickness and in Health*, which ran for seven years without recapturing its old bite.

Johnny Speight died on 5 July 1998 of pancreatic cancer, at his home, Four Acres, Nottingham Road, South Heronsgate, Chorleywood, Hertfordshire. His achievement was in encouraging television comedy to develop sharper eyes, as well as a sharper tongue. GRAHAM McCANN

Sources D. Nathan, *The laughter makers* (1971) • J. Speight, *It stands to reason* (1973) • D. Bradbury and J. McGrath, *Now that's funny!* (1998) • b. cert. • m. cert. • d. cert.

Likenesses photograph, 1981, Mirrorpix, 13113838 • photograph, 1982, NPG, P512 [20] • photograph, repro. in *The Guardian* (6 July 1998), 15 • photograph, repro. in Speight, *It stands to reason*

Wealth at death £215,848 gross; £212,737 net: probate, 1998, *CGPLA Eng. & Wales* • £75,000—further grant: 1999

Speight, Sadie [*married name* Sadie Martin, Lady Martin] (**1906–1992**), architect and designer, was born on 26 May 1906 at 65 Church Street, Standish, Lancashire, one of two daughters of Alfred Speight, a doctor, and his wife, Mary Annie, *née* Urmston. Both she and her sister, Kathleen, studied at Manchester University. Speight graduated from the school of architecture with first-class honours in 1929. She was a prix de Rome finalist and spent time studying abroad, as holder of the Zimmern travelling scholarship in 1929. In 1930 Speight received the Royal Institute of British Architects' (RIBA) silver medal for drawing and was elected an associate; in 1932 she held the Faulkner fellowship at Manchester University and gained her master's degree in 1933. Between 1930 and 1934 she was also working as an architectural assistant to Halliday and Associates in Manchester. As recipient of the RIBA Neale bursary in 1934 she conducted research into Isabelline architecture in Spain.

On 3 January 1935 Speight married John Leslie *Martin (1908–2000), who had been a fellow student at Manchester University, and they collaborated on the design of a number of private houses, including one for the textile designer and painter Alastair Morton, and a kindergarten at Northwich, Cheshire (1937–8). Speight, who continued to work under her maiden name, and Martin were part of the group of modernist architects and artists, including Ben Nicholson and Naum Gabo, who produced *Circle: an International Survey of Constructive Art* in 1937. The couple's interest in contemporary design was further developed through the Good Form range of modular furniture which they produced for W. Rowntree & Sons of Scarborough *c.*1938 and the publication, in 1939, of *The Flat Book* (commissioned by Herbert Read) which offered advice on all aspects of the creation of the modern home. Many of the designers whose work they recommended, including Barbara Hepworth, Serge Chermayeff, and Milner Gray, were leading exponents of modernism in Britain; some of the products they illustrated, such as chairs by Finnish designer Alvar Aalto, they had purchased for their own home. Speight was an invaluable chronicler of the modern movement in architecture and design in Britain, as well as one of its practitioners. Her achievements in product design and shop layout reveal a particular flair for the use of colour and the grouping of objects, which surely owed much to her early contact with the champions of abstract art in Britain.

After the Second World War Speight was a founder member of the Design Research Unit, set up to enable the skills of designers to be utilized to the full in the post-war recovery. Her designs for household appliances included an electric kettle and iron for Beethoven Electric Equipment. For the Festival of Britain in 1951, in collaboration with Leonard Manasseh, she designed the Rosie Lee cafeteria at the 'Live Architecture' exhibition in Lansbury, London. From the 1950s onwards she continued to work on architectural, interior, and exhibition design commissions while bringing up two children, Christopher and Susan, both of whom were to train as architects themselves. These projects included interiors for Swansea University in the 1950s and various Cambridge colleges in the 1960s. In this latter part of her career she also documented her husband's work as a leading architect and emeritus professor at Cambridge; he was knighted in 1957. She designed the layout of his book *Buildings and Ideas* (1983) in which he acknowledged her contribution to his career, and was involved in the planning of 'Leslie Martin and Associates', an exhibition organized by the Gulbenkian Foundation in 1990. Almost until the end of her life, Speight continued to work on house conversion projects in Norfolk for family use. In her final months she suffered from motor neurone disease; she died on 23 October 1992 at her home, The Barns, Church Street, Great Shelford, Cambridgeshire. JILL SEDDON

Sources private information (2004) • L. Walker, 'British women in architecture', *Women architects: their work* (1984), 19–20 • L. Walker, 'Concrete proof: women, architecture and modernism', *Feminist Arts News*, 3/4 (1986), 6–8 • M. Parkin, *The Independent* (27 Oct 1992) • d. cert. • b. cert. • m. cert.

Archives RIBA BAL, 'Isabelline architecture in Spain, 1474–1504', MS, 1934

Likenesses photograph, repro. in Parkin, *The Independent*

Wealth at death £70,325: probate, 30 Nov 1992, *CGPLA Eng. & Wales*

Speke, Charles (*d.* 1685). *See under* Speke, George (1623–1689).

Speke, George (1623–1689), politician and political activist, was born on 1 May 1623, the eldest son of George Speke (*d.* 1637), landowner, and his wife, Joan, daughter of Sir John Portman, first baronet, of Orchard Portman. Speke's ancestors were Devon knights who came into possession of the manor house at White Lackington parish in Ilminster, Somerset, in the mid-fifteenth century. Through royal service to the Tudors the family had prospered and although they lost their influence at court in the seventeenth century they remained powerful within Somerset. When he was thirteen Speke's father died and his wardship was sold to Sir Robert *Pye of Faringdon, Berkshire, for £1800. Speke travelled abroad in 1639, and on 21 May 1641, at St Mary Abbots, Kensington, he married Mary *Speke, Sir Robert Pye's eldest daughter. George and Mary Speke had six sons and three daughters. Of their nine children three died young: their eldest son, George; the second youngest son, Thomas; and their youngest daughter, Elizabeth. Their youngest son, William, of Shipton Beauchamp, did not engage in political affairs. Their other children, Philip, John, Hugh, Mary, and Charles all followed their parents' politics.

During the civil wars Speke supported the king, sending Prince Rupert a thousand broad pieces during the siege of Bridgwater and raising regiments of horse and foot for the royal cause. After the fall of Bridgwater in July 1645, Speke was taken prisoner by Sir Thomas Fairfax and his goods were sequestrated. Through the intervention of his brother-in-law, Colonel Robert Pye, a New Model Army officer, Speke was able to win his freedom although he paid a large fine of £2390. Speke remained under suspicion during the interregnum. He was imprisoned again in 1655 for possible complicity in a royalist conspiracy and two years later was required to rebuild with his own resources a hospital that had been demolished in the 'late troubles' (*Exeter MSS*, 279).

Shortly after the Restoration, Speke became an outspoken critic of Charles II. His conversion to the politics of opposition was undoubtedly influenced by his strong-willed wife, Mary. She, like her parliamentarian brother Colonel Pye, was a presbyterian. In 1663 Mary was arrested at a conventicle. To his dismay Speke soon found that neither his royalist credentials nor his authority as a deputy lieutenant and a JP could protect her. Indeed, having publicly declared that he would not disturb any presbyterian meetings he was dismissed as JP. Speke and his wife supported various dissenting preachers and a conventicle at White Lackington House, which became known as a 'receptacle for all the malcontents' in the heated atmosphere of the 1670s and 1680s (*CSP dom., July–Sept 1683*, 8).

Along with three of his sons, John, Hugh *Speke, and Charles, Speke joined the notorious whig Green Ribbon Club. He was elected a knight of shire for Somerset in the second election of 1679 and sat in the short-lived third Exclusion Parliament of 1681. Although he left no traces in the records of his parliamentary activity his obnoxious behaviour in the west, where he and his family were known as 'grand fanatics', left little doubt as to where he stood (*CSP dom., July–Sept 1683*, 16). Following his election in 1679 he supposedly declared that he 'would not fight for the Duke of York, who was a Papist, but for the Duke of Monmouth, who was a Protestant' and that he could furnish Monmouth with men and arms. Speke was called before Charles II to answer for his comments. In his defence he reminded the king that he had been a 'great sufferer' in Charles I's cause and that he wished only to defend the protestant religion (*CSP dom., 1680–81*, 690–91). Apparently Speke was forgiven but the encounter served only to further embolden him. In May 1680 his son John described his father's behaviour in a letter to his brother Hugh: 'Since his return, notwithstanding the numberless entreaties and advices to be silent and not concern himself with public affairs, he gives himself more liberty, and talks more at random and dangerous than formerly' (*CSP dom., 1679–80*, 471).

Speke was notorious for his violent talk and the government had no trouble compiling a list of 'abusive and scandalous expressions' uttered by Speke to anyone who would listen. Following the death of the earl of Essex in the Tower in 1683 he told his neighbours the earl had been murdered. When one neighbour argued with Speke he called him a 'Cursed Tory and struck him in the face with a stick'. He also supposedly declared 'that the nation was governed by a company of whores', and that the king 'was no more fit to govern than an ass' (*CSP dom., July–Sept 1683*, 430–31). On another occasion Speke asserted that all 'the bishops were popishly affected and the betrayers of their country' (*CSP dom., 1683–4*, 1). Upon the discovery of the Rye House plot in June 1683, 'old Mr. Speke' came under suspicion and was ordered to come to London. A few months later, in October, Speke absconded, possibly to the Netherlands, 'for horrible words' (*CSP dom., Jan–June 1683*, 363; *1683–4*, 20). His house was searched time and again for arms and papers throughout 1683 and even the house of his mother, 'a rigid sectarian', was searched although little was uncovered (*CSP dom., July–Sept 1683*, 212–13).

By a marriage licence dated 10 November 1682 George Speke married his second daughter, who had the unusual name of Philip [**Philip Trenchard** (1663/4–1743)], to John *Trenchard (1649–1695), politician, fourth son of Thomas Trenchard of Wolverton, Dorset. She was eighteen; he was thirty-three. While the Spekes and the Trenchards had intermarried throughout the sixteenth and seventeenth centuries, George and Mary were particularly fond of John Trenchard, who lived at Lytchett Matravers, Dorset, but was often at White Lackington and an intimate with their sons. Trenchard was one of the pall bearers at the funeral of the Spekes' youngest daughter, Elizabeth, who died in 1681. John Trenchard's politics certainly matched those of the Spekes. He had acted as the chairman of the Green Ribbon Club and was deeply implicated in the Rye House plot. When Speke was questioned by a neighbour for marrying his daughter to Trenchard he exclaimed 'my son Trenchard is so brave and forward a man that I do not question but to see him Lord Chancellor in a little time' (*CSP dom., July–Sept 1683*, 430). Like her mother and sister Philip frequented conventicles. She also stayed as a close prisoner with her husband in the Tower when he was arrested in 1683 and later followed him to Amsterdam during his exile.

In early 1685 George Speke was arrested and heavily fined for creating a riot in order to rescue Trenchard from the custody of a messenger. A few months later the Spekes were involved in Monmouth's rebellion. Trenchard was at White Lackington when he received notice of Monmouth's landing at Lyme Regis. Recognizing the dangers ahead he prepared to flee to the continent, urging the Spekes to join him. Instead, George and Mary spread the good news of Monmouth's coming and sent him encouragement and support. But shortly afterwards Speke fled to Utrecht. He, his wife, son John and daughter Mary were all exempted from James II's general pardon of March 1686. Speke eventually obtained a pardon for himself and his family for a fine of £8000 in February 1687. Not surprisingly he joined William of Orange's march to London in November 1688. Speke unsuccessfully petitioned the House of Commons twice in 1689 for financial compensation for the losses his family had incurred under James II. He died in debt on 2 December 1689. Philip and John Trenchard had four sons and three daughters. The only son to survive into adulthood, George, sat for Poole in the House of Commons as a whig from 1713 to 1754. John Trenchard died of consumption in 1695. Philip, who lived until 1743, married Daniel Sadler, esquire, of London, in 1701 although she continued to use Trenchard as her surname.

Speke's eldest surviving son, **John Speke** (1651/2–1728), politician and Monmouth rebel, matriculated from Wadham College, Oxford, on 6 April 1666 aged fourteen, entered Lincoln's Inn in 1669, and travelled abroad in 1671. He married Katherine, daughter of Edmund Prideaux of Forde Abbey, Devon, a family with which the Spekes had close ties. They had no children. In 1679 John Speke was one of the deputy lieutenants for Somerset. He was returned for Ilchester in the first election of 1679, was listed as 'honest' by the earl of Shaftesbury, and voted for the bill to exclude the duke of York from the throne. John was friendly with the notorious informer Titus Oates and, along with his brother Hugh, he was probably involved in fomenting the Popish Plot. He was elected again for Ilchester in August 1679 but failed to be re-elected in 1681. In June 1685 John Speke joined Monmouth's rebellion, riding to Chard with a group of 'ordinary fellows' to link up with the duke's army (BL, Lansdowne MS 11, 52A, fol. 240). Monmouth made him a colonel with his own regiment. Other rebels later ridiculed John as a 'silly and insignificant man', who 'gave orders to his regiment from the top of a tree with his handkerchief' during battle (BL, Add. MS 41819, fol. 58). At Frome John learned that James II had issued a general pardon for all those who laid down their arms and so he stole away from Monmouth's camp at night and escaped to Amsterdam. In 1687, with the help of Trenchard, John secured a pardon and willingly co-operated with James's administration. On 25 June 1687 John, now a widower, married Elizabeth, daughter and coheir of Robert Pelham of Compton Valence, Dorset. They had one son. In 1688 he was deemed a suitable court candidate for Ilchester but following the prince of Orange's invasion he failed to win election to the Convention. He did sit as a whig in 1690 and 1695 and signed the Association in 1696. He died in 1728. His son George carried on the family's whig tradition in parliament in 1722 and 1747.

The Spekes' eldest daughter, **Mary Jennings** (*bap.* 1649?), Monmouth supporter, married a Quaker, Thomas Jennings, of Burton Pynsent in Curry Rivel, Somerset, son of Marmaduke Jennings and Elizabeth (formerly Trevilian). They had three children, Thomas, Mary, and Elizabeth. After her husband died in 1680 Mary as, 'the widow Jennings', remained in close contact with her family and was known as an outspoken critic of the government. When Monmouth's band marched through Taunton in 1685 she sent him four horses, and the Quaker John Whiting who visited her at the time, later wrote that she 'was all afloat about the Duke [of Monmouth], thinking the day was their own' (Whiting, 141). Mary was exempted from James II's general pardon of 1686 for supporting Monmouth. It is not known when she died.

The Spekes' third son, **Charles Speke** (*d.* 1685), political activist, was not as deeply involved in whig politics as his elder brothers, John and Hugh, but he did join the Green Ribbon Club and was a dissenter. He also read and spread whig propaganda. On 6 August 1677 Charles was admitted to Lincoln's Inn and although never called to the bar, in the early 1680s he had an office and chambers in Lincoln's Inn and purchased the office of filazer (filing writs) for several western counties for the hefty sum of £3000. In June 1685 Charles apparently shook hands with Monmouth as he passed through Ilminster although he did not join the rebellion. His obeisance to Monmouth was enough later to have him imprisoned and Judge Jeffreys sentenced him to death for treason at Wells in late September 1685. When Jeffreys was informed that there were two Spekes and that he had convicted the wrong Speke brother Jeffreys supposedly replied, 'His family owes a life and he shall die for his namesake' (Roberts, 2.222). Charles was hanged in September or October in the market place, Ilminster, from a large tree. His attainder was reversed after the revolution of 1688. He was remembered in the whig martyrologies of the post-revolution era as a young man who 'came from that good pious family which always have been opposers to popery and suffered deeply for their courage that way' (Tutchin, 34). MELINDA ZOOK

Sources J. Collinson, *The history and antiquities of the county of Somerset*, 3 (1791), 67–8 • T. G. Barnes, *Somerset, 1625–1640: a county's government during the personal rule* (1961), 18–20, 24–5 • G. Roberts, *The life, progresses and rebellion of James duke of Monmouth*, 2 vols. (1844), vol. 1, p. 293; vol. 2, pp. 315–40 • *Report on records of the city of Exeter*, HMC, 73 (1916), 279 • H. Speke, *Some memoirs of the most remarkable passages and transactions of … 1688* (1709), 33–5 • Burke, *Gen. GB* • *CSP dom., 1663–4*, 116; *1679–80*, 175–6, 185, 322, 471; *1680–81*, 690–91; *Jan-*

June 1683, 363; *July–Sept 1683*, 8, 16, 212–13, 389–99, 402, 416, 430–31; *1683–4*, 1, 2, 25, 178 • F. N. MacNamara and A. Story-Maskelyne, eds., *The parish register of Kensington, co. Middlesex, from AD 1539 to AD 1675*, Harleian Society, register section, 16 (1890), 71 • J. Tutchin, *New martyrology, or, The Bloody Assizes* (1693) • E. Green, *The march of William of Orange through Somerset* (1892) • J. Whiting, *Persecution exposed in some memoirs relating to the suffering of J. W.* (1715), 141–2 • G. Agar-Ellis, ed., *The Ellis correspondence: letters written during the years 1686, 1687, 1688, and addressed to John Ellis*, 2 vols. (1829), 1.194 • BL, Lansdowne MS 11, 52A • N. Luttrell, *A brief historical relation of state affairs from September 1678 to April 1714*, 1 (1857), 346, 355, 365, 399, 531 • M. S. Zook, *Radical whigs and conspiratorial politics in late Stuart England* (1999) • I. Cassidy, 'Speke, George', 'Speke, John', J. P. Ferris, 'Trenchard, John', HoP, *Commons, 1660–90* • *IGI* • M. J. Hawkins, ed., *Sales of Wards in Somerset, 1603–1641*, Somerset RS, 67 (1965) • W. P. Baildon, ed., *The records of the Honorable Society of Lincoln's Inn: admissions*, 1 (1896) • marriage agreement, Dorset RO, D/BLXD60/F54 [Philip Trenchard and Daniel Sadler] • P. Trenchard, lettter to George Speke, 1741, Dorset RO, D/BLXD60/F55

Speke, Hugh (1656–*c.*1724), whig agitator, was the second son of George *Speke (1623–1689), a civil-war royalist turned whig MP, of White Lackington, near Ilminster, Somerset, and his wife, Mary *Speke, daughter of Sir Robert Pye. Speke matriculated at St John's College, Oxford, on 1 July 1672; he did not take a degree and in 1680 entered at Lincoln's Inn. During the era of the Exclusion Crisis (1679–83) Speke, along with his father and brothers, John *Speke (1651/2–1728) [*see under* Speke, George] and Charles *Speke (*d.* 1685) [*see under* Speke, George], who was later hanged for his part in the Monmouth rebellion, joined the Green Ribbon Club. He was active in London whig politics and associated with such men as William, Lord Russell, Sir Robert Atkyns, and John Trenchard, who later married Speke's sister, Philip. In 1679 Speke was warned by a friend that to go 'so open amongst them' (meaning whigs) was dangerous (*CSP dom.*, 21.281). But Speke was impervious to any advice and he led a colourful life in London, making himself not only obnoxious to the court for his outspoken whig politics, but also to his dissenting family in Somerset for his gaming, gambling, and passion for 'half-mad, extravagant, expensive, and drunken' women. 'Keep out of debauched company', Speke's elder brother, John, warned him in 1682, 'though Whigs and great men' (ibid., 23.121–2). In June 1683 an indictment was brought against Speke for proclaiming in the presence of others that Thomas Pilkington's remark of 1679—that the duke of York had set fire to London in 1666 and wanted to cut protestant throats—was true (ibid., 24.338–9). Speke was the author of *Enquiry into and Detection of the Barbarous Murder of the Late Earl of Essex* (1683), in which he hinted that Essex had been assassinated by partisans of the duke of York. Pilkington had been sued by James for his comments and was still languishing in prison.

In the summer of 1683 Speke was active in the defence of those accused of conspiring against the royal brothers in the so-called Rye House plot. In July he served as a go-between in the defence of William, Lord Russell, bringing Lady Russell the legal advice of Sir Robert Atkyns. On 18 August he also visited Francis Charlton at the Tower, offering 'the best advice and directions I can' (*CSP dom.*, 25.304). Two weeks later a warrant was issued for Speke's arrest. He had finally landed himself in real trouble by agreeing to assist Laurence Braddon in his quest to uncover the truth about the earl of Essex's death. Braddon, a whig lawyer, was interviewing witnesses and collecting evidence, aiming to prove that Essex had been murdered in the Tower. At the time of Braddon's arrest letters of introduction by Speke to persons of quality, including Atkyns, were discovered on him. Speke later claimed he was drinking at the time he wrote the letters and 'knew not well what I writ'. But the letters were plainly incriminating, informing Atkyns that, 'we hope we can bring on the earl of Essex's murder on the stage, before they can any of those [Rye House plotters] in the Tower to a trial' (*State trials*, 9.1196, 1162). Speke was arrested in an action of *scandalum magnatum* at the suit of the duke of York. The charge was later changed to sedition and he was prosecuted along with Braddon before Judge Jeffreys in February 1684. Speke was fined £1000. Unwilling, as he claimed, or simply unable to pay the fine, Speke spent the next four years in the king's bench prison at great expense. There he met the Revd Samuel Johnson, the late Lord Russell's chaplain, who was condemned for seditious libel in 1684 for his notorious attack on the duke of York, *Julian the Apostate*. Speke had various prison liberties, including access to a printing press which enabled Johnson to continue publishing anti-papist diatribes. In March 1686 Johnson and Speke decided to arouse the consciences of the protestant soldiers serving in James II's army who were encamped outside London on Hounslow Heath. Speke had Johnson's *A Humble and Hearty Address to All English Protestants in this Present Army* printed and, he later boasted, 20,000 copies were distributed among the soldiers in one night. The tract exhorted the men to abandon their Catholic officers and defend the protestant religion. Although 500 copies of the address were found in Speke's chambers, it was Johnson who paid dearly for their boldness. He was defrocked and whipped from Newgate to Tyburn. He refused to name Speke during his ordeal, and Speke was merely placed under stricter confinement.

In 1687, when James II began a new policy of courting dissenters, Speke achieved his liberty. He paid £5000 to the exchequer as a pledge of his own and his family's good behaviour and, for a time, he retired to Exeter, where he became a member of the city council. In 1688, as rumours of the prince of Orange's intended invasion began to circulate, Speke headed for London where he appeared daily at 'Whitehall to show myself zealous in James II's cause' (Speke, *Memoirs*, 40). As someone with connections to both the disaffected gentlemen in western England and those gathered about the prince of Orange, Speke was seen as particularly useful to James's court at that critical moment. Soon after Prince William had landed at Torbay, the king himself met with Speke at Chiffinch's lodgings, requesting him to spy on the prince's camp and report back its strength. Speke was given several blank passes, so that he might travel freely, and offered £10,000, which he declined, having no intention of serving the king's interest. He set out on 8 November and proceeded to Exeter, where he came upon an advance guard of the prince of Orange's army. Speke was soon able to arrange a meeting with William and convince him of his loyalty. He gave the prince an account of the king's strength and designs and wrote letters to James, perused by William, magnifying the strength of the prince's army and warning the king that many of his own officers would eventually desert him. The subsequent desertions of the prince of Denmark and the duke of Ormond served to assure James of the reliability of Speke's intelligence.

Speke may have also had a hand in instigating the anti-papist hysteria that gripped London in early December. Fearing an invasion of French and Irish troops bent on massacring protestants, Londoners set about arming themselves, disarming Catholics, and, in the process, looting some Catholic homes and chapels. Their panic had been fed by rumours and letters sent throughout England warning protestants of their impending demise at the hands of roving papist soldiers. Speke later claimed that he had not only sent those letters on his way to Exeter but that he was also the true author of the spurious *Third Declaration of the Prince of Orange* (dated 'Sherburn Castle, 28 Nov. 1688'). The *Third Declaration* fuelled hysteria by stating that armed papists in and around London were going to 'make some desperate attempt' upon the inhabitants 'by fire or sudden massacre' (*Third Declaration*, Cobbett, *Parl. Hist.*, 4, 1809, 14). Speke also asserted later that it was he who advised James, with Prince William's consent, to retire to France. How much of Speke's memoirs of the revolution of 1688 (first published in 1707 as *Some Memoirs of the most Remarkable Passages and Transactions on the Late Happy Revolution*, and again in 1715 with some modifications as *The Secret History of the Happy Revolution in 1688*) can be trusted is unclear. It seems likely that he was the author of the *Third Declaration*. None of the other possible candidates for the job, including Samuel Johnson, who also liked to exaggerate his influence on the revolution, and Robert Ferguson, the notorious plotter and pamphleteer who was certainly capable of the task, ever claimed it.

Speke's relationship with William and Mary's government is not entirely clear. Unlike so many whigs active on the part of the prince, Speke was not given a public office as a reward for his services. Speke himself claimed that this was because he kept a correspondence with James, with William's knowledge, and wanted to keep up the façade of his loyalty to the exiled monarch. But he was also in dire straits financially and received very little support from the new administration. From 1692 to 1694, during his brother-in-law John Trenchard's term as secretary of state, Speke occupied himself with zealously chasing down suspected Jacobites. But by 1698 he was begging for money, and in 1703 he petitioned parliament for some monetary compensation, considering all that he and his family had suffered and paid in fines before the revolution. He was rewarded with £100. He later solicited George I for £500, but it is unclear if he had any success. In his later years Speke was living at High Wycombe, Buckinghamshire. He died about 1724. MELINDA ZOOK

Sources H. Speke, *The secret history of the happy revolution in 1688* (1715) • H. Speke, *Some memoirs of the most remarkable passages and transactions on the late happy revolution in 1688* (1707) • *CSP dom.*, 1679–80, 281; 1682, 121–2; *Jan–June 1683*, 338–9; *July–Sept 1683*, 304 • N. Luttrell, *A brief historical relation of state affairs from September 1678 to April 1714*, 1 (1857), 286–7, 299–300, 306; 3 (1857), 313 • J. R. Jones, *The revolution of 1688 in England* (1972), 301–2 • T. B. Macaulay, *The history of England from the accession of James II*, new edn, ed. C. H. Firth, 6 vols. (1913–15), vol. 2, pp. 760–61; vol. 3, pp. 1212–15 • *The humble petition of Hugh Speke* (1703) • M. S. Zook, *Radical whigs and conspiratorial politics in late Stuart England* (1999) • *A supplement to Burnet's History of my own time*, ed. H. C. Foxcroft (1902), 122–3, 299–300 • Burke, *Gen. Ire.* • G. Agar-Ellis, ed., *The Ellis correspondence: letters written during the years 1686, 1687, 1688, and addressed to John Ellis*, 2 vols. (1829), vol. 1, p. 194; vol. 2, p. 356 • *N&Q*, 12 (1855), 403 • G. Roberts, *The life, progresses and rebellion of James duke of Monmouth*, 2 vols. (1844), 315–37 • Evelyn, *Diary*, 4.367, n. 1 • Foster, *Alum. Oxon.* • *Report on the manuscripts of the marquis of Downshire*, 6 vols. in 7, HMC, 75 (1924–95), vol. 1, p. 617 • *State trials*, 9.1196, 1162 • M. Zook, 'Hugh Speke' • Greaves & Zaller, *BDBR*

Archives BL, letters to Robert Harley, Add. MS 70316

Speke, John (1651/2–1728). *See under* Speke, George (1623–1689).

Speke, John Hanning (1827–1864), explorer in Africa, was born on 4 May 1827 at Orleigh Court in the parish of Buckland Brewer, near Bideford, Devon, the second son of William Speke (1798–1887), an army captain in the 14th dragoons and landowner, and his wife, Georgina Elizabeth, *née* Hanning. The family later moved to Jordans in Somerset.

Education and entry into the army Speke attended Barnstaple grammar school and then Blackheath proprietary school. He detested his schooling, possibly partly because of a latent tubercular condition which caused eye troubles, which were to affect him again in 1858. It seems that he had little aptitude for languages; nor, later, was his written English beyond reproach. On the other hand, he had the ability to calculate longitudes from observed lunar distances and was to take the trouble to enhance his understanding of other sciences when preparing for his Nile expedition in 1859. At the age of seventeen, in 1844, he was accepted for a commission in the Indian army and joined the 46th native Bengal infantry. He took part in the First and Second Anglo-Sikh wars of 1845–6 and 1848–9. There is little information on his military career, but he remarked that peacetime soldiering bored him. Consequently, from 1848 onwards, the young lieutenant spent all the time he could on hunting trips in Tibet, combining his avid collecting of trophies to send home with a little geographical enquiry. James Augustus Grant was with him on at least one of these trips and provides some information.

At the end of his first ten-year commission in 1854 Speke wished to extend his trophy hunting to Africa, and was fortunate in finding that a Bombay presidency expedition under Richard Burton was just leaving Aden for the Somali coast opposite. The plan was to penetrate southwards into east Africa, but the only success was Burton's solo venture westwards to Harar. Given the task of reconnoitring the area south of Bunder Gori, Speke found his inexperience told against him: he became involved in clan

John Hanning Speke (1827–1864), by Southwell Brothers, *c.*1863

disputes he did not understand, although he eventually realized that his guide and 'protector' was using the trip for his own purposes. At least there were some useful lessons about the realities of African travel, but little ground was explored. Speke rejoined the rest of the expedition at Berbera, where they were attacked in April 1855 by the Har Owel tribe. Speke was captured and escaped but had been so badly wounded that he almost died. In the longer run it was even more significant that, at one point in the mêlée, Burton seemed to accuse him of cowardice. This rankled as the first of the breaches between them which were so greatly to affect the careers of both men.

The expedition to the great lakes of east Africa, 1856–1859 Although he was invalided to England in June 1855, Speke almost immediately volunteered for the Crimea, where he was attached to a Turkish regiment just before the war's end. In the midst of his plans for a hunting trip to the Caucasus came news of the chance to rejoin Burton on another east African venture. This was being organized by the Royal Geographical Society (RGS) with limited financial and logistical support from the British and Indian governments. A new era was beginning in Britain's relations with east Africa, this coinciding with important internal developments. The RGS was now powerful and influential enough to contemplate solving the problems of east Africa's geography, about which 'armchair geographers' such as Cooley and McQueen had speculated and upon which the missionary Krapf and his companions based near Mombasa had thrown some limited but confusing light. A large lake or lakes, snow-capped mountains, and, above all, the possible source of the Nile seemed to exist in the interior. Although the Foreign Office said it was simply 'supporting geographical science', with the Suez route in use and the Suez Canal soon to open, the western Indian Ocean region was becoming of much greater concern to both the Indian and British governments, who needed more information on political and economic realities in the region—not forgetting the slave trade to which David Livingstone was currently drawing attention. Whatever the motives of those involved, the days of solo travels such as those Burton had hitherto undertaken were over; comparatively large and well-equipped expeditions imitating Zanzibar Arab trade caravans seemed appropriate. This was all the more necessary as east Africa itself was becoming more disturbed and prone to violence as Indian-financed Arabs undercut African traders, new forms of political authority based on force developed, and Ngoni groups from the south taught how to live by war and plunder.

The expedition, with both men now holding captaincies, set off from the coast opposite Zanzibar in June 1857 and reached Lake Tanganyika in February 1858. Both Europeans were ill with the effects of malaria or relapsing fever, and Speke's ophthalmic problems recurred so that he could not properly see the lake. During his attempt to cross it by canoe, Speke also suffered when a beetle entered his ear, causing intense discomfort and longer-term problems of deafness. No boat large enough to examine the lake properly could be secured and so the possibility of an outlet to the north could not be tested, thus leaving scope for Burton later to be able to claim that 'his' Lake Tanganyika was the source of the Nile. By the time the explorers were back in Tabora, the Arab traders' headquarters, Burton remained ill but Speke was sufficiently recovered to want to make a trip northwards to another reported lake. Directly in charge now of his own sub-expedition, Speke reached the southern end of what he christened Lake Victoria on 3 August 1858. He immediately decided that this lake must be the source of the Nile. Local political rivalries prevented him from exploring very extensively in the area and he regained Tabora, whence the whole expedition returned to the coast. Burton's previously tolerant and friendly attitude to Speke began to change; he could not accept the Nile claims, and there were differences of opinion about how much the porters deserved to be paid and about how the deficit in the funding of the whole venture should be made up from their own pockets. Underneath these arguments there lay the problem of incompatibility between the socially unconventional and highly intellectual Burton and the rather unimaginative and certainly unintellectual Speke. The difficulties were compounded when Speke returned to England before Burton in May 1859 and, probably as a result of mischief-making counsel from Laurence Oliphant and the anxiety of Roderick Murchison to have a hero for the RGS, made his Nile claims public. This, in effect, belittled Burton's achievement. Speke published his account of the expedition in *Blackwood's Edinburgh*

Magazine and the breach with Burton became almost complete.

The Nile expedition, 1860–1863 Although the RGS offered Burton the chance to return to east Africa, their first priority for an expedition was clearly to send Speke back to prove his Nile claims. They obtained £2500 from the government and raised a public subscription of £1200 to enable the Nile ivory trader John Petherick to meet Speke with supplies at Gondokoro on the upper Nile. J. A. Grant was invited to join Speke. In addition, mules and an escort of Cape mounted riflemen were provided by Sir George Grey, the governor of Cape Colony, although they proved unsuitable and had to be sent back.

The expedition left the coast in September 1860 with 176 men, including Bombay and Baraka, two former slaves who had learned Hindi and so could act as interpreters and negotiators for Speke. Unfortunately, these two talented men were frequently at loggerheads and their disputes complicated management problems in the caravan and the all-important business of negotiating with local political leaders through whose jurisdictions the expedition had to pass. Most difficult was the situation at Tabora, where the relationship between the Arab traders and the Nyamwezi chiefdom of Unyanyembe had broken down, with the result that Speke found it difficult to recruit porters and get supplies. He was not powerful enough to impose a solution but he did try to arbitrate. However, Manua Sera, the chief whom the Arabs had deposed, wanted unequivocal support, which the explorer could not afford to give knowing that he still needed Arab help. As in many similar situations, Speke had to learn to be patient and act in the light of the advice of Bombay and Baraka. Negotiating a way northwards towards the western shores of Lake Victoria continued difficult, with Speke and Grant forced to separate for long periods, and it took until November 1861 to reach Karagwe and its friendly king, Rumanika.

The nature of the problems then began to change. The powerful kings of the 'interlacustrine' region could disregard Arabs or petty chiefs and provide an easy passage for the travellers—if it suited them to do so. In fact, Speke's presence and his petitions for permission to go on northwards presented them with dilemmas. Here was someone representing a power apparently even greater than Zanzibar or Egypt. Would that power be deployed? Speke's constant questions about his friend Petherick and his Nile boats suggested it might be. More immediately, should Rumanika help him to open a Nile route if that diminished his own importance as 'gatekeeper' on the route from the south? Yet he could not risk displeasing Mutesa, the *kabaka* of the most powerful kingdom, Buganda, by keeping Speke back. Mutesa himself was also worried about the Nile route, since this would enhance the importance of the rival kingdom of Bunyoro. And the rulers of Buganda and Bunyoro were already both worried by the encroachments of the Khartoum-based slave and ivory traders from the north. In short, Speke's presence presented something of a foreign-policy dilemma for all these potentates, and this largely explains the long delays between the arrival of the travellers in Karagwe in November 1861 and their emergence from the lake region in February 1863 to reach Gondokoro, where they expected Petherick to be waiting. For his part, Speke was fascinated by the peoples and especially their rulers. These, surely, were different in race and history from their subjects and from other Africans in east Africa. He encouraged their claims that they were an aristocracy who had come from the north. So was born the 'Hamitic myth' which helped to direct particular European attention to this region as having potential collaborators who would be receptive to European economic, political, or religious initiatives—initiatives which Speke himself was later to try to develop.

From November 1861 Speke remained in Karagwe, learning much of the kingdom and hearing Rumanika's testimonies on the geography of the region. Then in February 1862 came Mutesa's peremptory order for him to proceed to Buganda, although Grant had to remain with an ulcerated leg until May. Mutesa presided over a court system which involved constant intrigue and competition between the country's great men. Both consciously and unconsciously, Speke became part of the system, seeking various favours from Mutesa, including permission to go on to the Nile, and sometimes playing off the queen mother's court against her son's. For his part, Mutesa was fascinated by Speke's guns and also by the knowledge Speke imparted to him. He used Speke in his own political ploys, for example, against the priests of certain cults. What Speke learned in Buganda was perhaps as significant a 'discovery' as the source of the Nile. Eventually Speke was allowed to go on to that source—the point where the Nile issues from Lake Victoria—which he reached on 28 July 1862 and which he named Ripon Falls. This was the crowning moment of the expedition and of Speke's career. Unfortunately, Grant, who was still suffering with his leg, had been sent off directly north and so did not confirm the discovery, no doubt to his own disappointment and certainly to the detriment of Speke's subsequent reputation. Nor did the party follow the Nile stream closely as they went north to Bunyoro and beyond. Although this left scope for Samuel Baker to discover Lake Albert a few months later, it also allowed critics to question whether Speke's river really was the Nile. In Bunyoro the ruler Kamurasi's distrust of anyone who had come from Buganda and his fears about a rival allied with Nile traders meant further delays, but the expedition reached Gondokoro in February 1863. This was long after the November 1861 target date set with Petherick, who had left supplies but was trading elsewhere. Before he returned, it was Baker who now welcomed Speke and provided material help. Speke reacted to Petherick's absence in a very intemperate and unfair way, subsequently destroying the man's career by his vilification. By May 1863 the explorers, with eighteen remaining 'faithfuls' from the porters, had reached Cairo and let the world know that the Nile was 'settled'.

The return home and the dispute with Burton Having returned to London, Speke certainly became the 'lion';

windows were broken as crowds tried to get into the special meeting of the RGS, and there was an enthusiastic welcome at his father's home in Somerset. The situation was to change. The *Journal of the Discovery of the Source of the Nile* was published in December 1863. Speke's draft had been very heavily 'improved' for grammar and bowdlerized of its too sexually explicit passages by John Hill Burton, who also made Speke appear more in charge of situations than had actually been the case. The book was not a literary landmark and ultimately did not sell as well as Blackwood hoped. Its first edition included a large historical error. McQueen, a friend of Petherick's father-in-law, wrote a very hostile review, and Burton began to question the Nile discovery, especially after Speke republished in 1864, as a book entitled *What Led to the Discovery of the Source of the Nile*, his own accounts of the earlier Somali and Lake Tanganyika expeditions. Murchison became lukewarm, partly because of the Petherick affair but mainly because Speke had chosen to publish his account through Blackwood and not the RGS. Murchison's wavering support almost certainly explains why Speke received no honour from the crown and perhaps why Speke's own plans for the 'regeneration' of Africa received no significant institutional support. Even so, it was probably mischievous or worse for Murchison and the RGS to arrange that the geographical section of the British Association's September 1864 meeting include a debate on the Nile question between Burton and Speke. The two men were now completely estranged. On 15 September, the day before the planned debate, Speke left a lunch where Burton was present and went off to shoot partridges at Neston Park, his uncle's nearby estate at Corsham, Wiltshire. In getting over a wall with his gun cocked he shot himself, with fatal result. Ever since 1864 it has continued to be asserted that Speke, knowing that Burton was almost certain to worst him in debate, must have committed suicide. The evidence, although not incontrovertible, is very much against this possibility. The tragic death and the attendant controversy further undermined Speke's credibility. Although Murchison immediately relented, attending the funeral at Dowlish Wake church, near Jordans, on 26 September and later arranging for the erection of a memorial in Kensington Gardens, the doubts about both Speke's geography and his character remained. Even the wording on the memorial is equivocal: Speke is not described as the discoverer of the source of the Nile.

Speke's later reputation It was not until about twelve years later that the work of H. M. Stanley and others made it clear that Speke was right about Lake Victoria and the Nile.

Speke, who was 'the boldest explorer of the age' and than whom no man was 'safer for immortality', according to one of his obituaries (*Blackwood*, 514–16), has, nevertheless, not become a household name. By 133 years after his death there had been only one book-length biography. It is true that he burnt many of his personal and exploration papers. It is also arguable that his books have little literary merit and that their cause has not been helped by reprints which are either ill-edited or based on the corrupt Everyman edition of his *Journal*. Yet there are adequate manuscript records of his correspondence and exploratory activities, and his work was important in the history of discovery and, to some extent, in the history of Africa. The reasons for Speke's comparative eclipse have something to do with the peculiar circumstances of his discoveries and of his death, but perhaps also something to do with his character. It has been said that he was a repressed homosexual with a mother fixation and a death drive, that he was fastidious and priggish and full of egotism and intolerance. Modern observers find his slaughter of animals—in which there seems to have been something of a ritual element—especially unattractive. On the other hand, the only substantial evidence on his sexuality is that he fathered a child in Buganda, and there is much contemporary testimony that he was liked by children, respected by adults, whether African or European, and had a genuine scientific interest in the fauna of Africa.

In retrospect it can be seen that, even if Speke was not altogether a great man, he was a great discoverer whose achievement was a landmark in the systemization of knowledge about the world. The source of the Nile itself became a great focus for European strategic interests twenty-five years after his visit, while his making known the existence of Buganda and its people had even greater implications for both European imperialists and the Ganda themselves. More generally, Speke's accounts of his expeditions remain absolutely vital sources of evidence on the history of east Africa in the nineteenth century. ROY BRIDGES

Sources A. Maitland, *Speke* (1971) · R. C. Bridges, 'John Hanning Speke: negotiating a way to the Nile', *Africa and its explorers*, ed. R. I. Rotberg (1970), 95–137 · R. C. Bridges, 'Speke and the Royal Geographical Society', *Uganda Journal*, 26 (1962), 23–43 · J. H. Speke, *Journal of the discovery of the source of the Nile* (1863) · J. H. Speke, *What led to the discovery of the source of the Nile* (1864) · Journal of discovery, NL Scot., MSS 4872–4874 [MS and proofs] · correspondence files, 1851–60, 1861–70, RGS · list of observations, no. 10, RGS · J. H. Speke, correspondence with Grant and Rigby, NL Scot., MSS 17910, 17931 · J. H. Speke, letters to Blackwood, 1859–64, NL Scot., MS 4143 · A. Mifsud, 'Medical history of J. H. Speke', *The Practitioner*, 214 (1975), 125–30 · *DNB* · R. C. Bridges, 'Nineteenth century east African travel records', *Paideuma*, 33 (1988), 179–96 · *Blackwood*, 96 (1864), 514–16 · *Proceedings* [Royal Geographical Society], 9 (1864–5), 196–9 · K. Ingham, 'John Hanning Speke…', *Tanganyika Notes and Records*, 49 (1957), 301–11 · J. A. Casada, 'J. H. Speke's youth', *Devon and Cornwall Notes and Queries*, 32 (1971–3), 121–2 · J. A. Casada, 'The birthplace of Speke', *Devon and Cornwall Notes and Queries*, 32 (1971–3), 55–8 · J. A. Casada, 'Sir George Grey and the Speke–Grant Nile expedition', *Quarterly Bulletin of the South African Library*, 25 (1971), 137–46 · J. A. Casada, 'A further look at Grey's contributions', *Quarterly Bulletin of the South African Library*, 26 (1971), 41–50 · J. A. Casada, 'Sir George Grey and the "Hottentot" contingent', *Quarterly Bulletin of the South African Library*, 40 (1985), 71–84 · 'Captain Speke's welcome', *Blackwood*, 94 (1863), 264–6 · R. F. Burton, *The Nile basin* (1864) · F. Welbourn, 'Speke and Stanley at the court of Mutesa', *Uganda Journal*, 25 (1961), 220–23 · H. Mukasa, 'Speke at the court of Mutesa', *Uganda Journal*, 26 (1962), 97–9 · H. B. Thomas, 'The death of Speke', *Uganda Journal*, 13 (1949–50), 105–7 · *ILN* (4 July 1863)

Archives NL Scot., map of Tibet, MS 17923 · NL Scot., MS and proofs of *Journal of discovery*, MSS 4872–4874 · RGS, scientific observations on the Nile region | NL Scot., corresp. with Blackwoods, papers, and proofs · NL Scot., letters to J. A. Grant · NL Scot.,

corresp. with J. A. Grant and Rigby, MSS 17910, 17931 • RGS, list of observations, no. 10 • RGS, MS file • RGS, correspondence files, 1851–60, 1861–70, Speke • RGS, letters to Royal Geographical Society • RGS, The family of Speke…, College of Arms, MS c.1923
Likenesses Southwell Bros., sepia photograph, *c.*1863, NPG [*see illus.*] • J. W. Wilson, oils, *c.*1863, RGS • L. Gardie, plaster bust, 1864, NPG • H. W. Phillips, group portrait, oils, *c.*1864, priv. coll. • photograph, 1864, priv. coll. • L. Gardie, bust, 1865, RGS • E. G. Papworth, senior, bust, exh. RA 1865, Taunton shire hall, Somerset • Disderi, carte-de-visite, NPG • M. Gardis, bust, RGS • S. Hollyer, stipple and line engraving (after photograph by Southwell Bros), NPG • A. Paul, carte-de-visite, NPG • S. G. Pieroni, bust, Royal Albert Memorial Museum, Exeter, Devon • memorial, Kensington Gardens, London • portrait (after photograph), repro. in *ILN* • prints, NPG • tomb, Dowlish Wake church
Wealth at death £2000 said to have been passed by family to Dr Livingstone: letters, NL Scot.

Speke [*née* Pye], **Mary** (*fl.* **1641–1697**), nonconformist patron and political activist, was the eldest daughter of Sir Robert *Pye (*bap.* 1585, *d.* 1662) of Faringdon, Berkshire, and his wife, Mary Croker. She may be the Mary Pye who was baptized at Richmond, Surrey, on 10 November 1625. Her father, an auditor of the exchequer, was a client of the duke of Buckingham in the 1620s. In the 1640s he was a lukewarm parliamentarian suspected of royalist sympathies, presbyterian in his religion, and a victim of Pride's Purge. Her brother, Sir Robert *Pye, married Anne Hampden, daughter of John Hampden. An active soldier during the civil war, he shared his father's political and religious presbyterianism, though not his lukewarmness. After the Restoration he retired to his father's Berkshire estate, where he was reportedly in league with other 'fanatics' families' (*CSP dom., July–Sept 1683*, 338).

Mary Pye married George *Speke (1623–1689) of White Lackington, Ilminster, Somerset, on 21 May 1641 at St Mary Abbots, Kensington: George had been the ward of her father (who had purchased the wardship for £1800). She was probably responsible for his conversion from civil war royalist to Restoration radical. Of their six children, Hugh *Speke, John *Speke, Charles *Speke [*see under* Speke, George], and their eldest daughter, Mary Speke [*see* Jennings, Mary, *under* Speke, George], were active whig supporters. Their youngest daughter, Philip Speke [*see* Trenchard, Philip, *under* Speke, George], married John *Trenchard of Bloxworth, Dorset, chairman of the notorious Green Ribbon Club, pro-exclusion MP, and Rye House conspirator.

Mary Speke was an ardent supporter of protestant dissenters and of whig politics in Somerset. She led conventicles at the Speke houses at White Lackington and Dillington, supported numerous presbyterian teachers, and frequented dissenting meetings throughout Somerset. She was indicted in 1663 for keeping conventicles, but fearlessly, and without protection from her husband, who was dismissed as a JP for refusing to disturb presbyterian meetings, pursued nonconformist devotion. She was widely known for her religious enthusiasm, and in 1675 the presbyterian preacher James Strong dedicated an edition of his sermons to her. She was obviously a strong-willed and influential woman, the force at the centre of her turbulent and notorious family. She strove to control her grown sons, scolding Hugh Speke so violently in 1682 that he declared he was unwell for weeks. Her movements were closely watched by Peter Mews, bishop of Bath and Wells. When Mary visited her sons in London in July 1683, the bishop warned Secretary Jenkins of her arrival, asserting that 'there is not a more dangerous woman in the west than she, and what her sons are I need not tell you' (*CSP dom., July–Sept 1683*, 8). Later the bishop wrote:

> I need give you no character of their family. I suppose it is sufficiently known how actively of late years they have all appeared against his Majesty's interest, especially the mother and the son, Hugh. … It is a wonder that Whitelackington House is not searched by particular order, not only for arms but papers for the lady keeps great correspondence, and her son-in-law, Trenchard, is her darling. (ibid., 178)

In August 1683 Mary was called before the privy council investigating her son Hugh's involvement in an effort to uncover the supposed murder of the earl of Essex in the Tower. The council was interested in Hugh's connection to the prominent whig lawyer Sir Robert Atkyns. Mary testified that her son had 'lost great sums' gambling and had borrowed money from Sir Robert Atkyns (ibid., 342).

The Speke family were great supporters of the duke of Monmouth and entertained him lavishly during his 1680 progress through the west. Not surprisingly, Mary Speke and George, and their sons John and Charles, were all implicated in Monmouth's rebellion in 1685, and Charles was executed. Mary was excepted from James II's general pardon of March 1686, although her husband obtained a pardon for the entire family in 1687. Her family supported the prince of Orange's invasion in 1688. George Speke appointed Mary his executor in his will of 1689. She made her own will on 22 September 1697, in which (apart from some small bequests to her servants) she left all her estate to her youngest son, William. He proved the will on 9 November 1706. MELINDA ZOOK

Sources Burke, *Gen. GB* (1972) • state papers, Charles II, PRO, SP 29 • G. L. Turner, ed., *Original records of early nonconformity under persecution and indulgence*, 2 (1912), 111–12 • J. Strong, *Lydia's heart opened* (1675), dedication • *CSP dom.*, 1663–4, 116; 1682, 121–2; *Jan–June 1683*, 338; *July–Sept 1683*, 8, 173–4, 178, 342 • W. H. Rylands, ed., *The four visitations of Berkshire*, 1, Harleian Society, 56 (1907), 270 • J. Collinson, *The history and antiquities of the county of Somerset*, 1 (1791), 66–8 • 'Pye, Sir Robert (1585–1662)', *DNB* • HoP, *Commons, 1660–90* • PRO, PROB 11/491, fol. 133*r* [will of Mary Speke] • PRO, PROB 11/410, fols. 171*v*–172*r* [will of George Speke] • *IGI*
Archives Dorset RO, undated petition to parliament, D60/L18

Spelman, Clement (*bap.* **1598**, *d.* **1679**), judge, was baptized on 4 October 1598 at Sedgeford, Norfolk, the fourth and youngest son of Sir Henry *Spelman (1563/4–1641), and his wife, Eleanor (*d.* 1620), daughter and coheir of John L'Estrange of Sedgeford. Sir John *Spelman (1594–1643) was his eldest brother. Spelman was admitted to Gray's Inn on 20 March 1614, and to Queens' College, Cambridge, on 16 September 1616. He was called to the bar in 1624. On 16 July 1628 he married Mary, daughter and coheir of Francis Mason of St Leonard's, Shoreditch. They had two sons and two daughters.

Spelman performed in a masque on 24 February 1635 at the Middle Temple. On 22 August 1638 he was named a member of the commission charged with inquiring into the breach of the statute of 31 Eliz. that required every new cottage to have 4 acres of land attached, and also into usury. He became an ancient of Gray's Inn on 4 May 1638.

Spelman wrote a preface to the 1646 Oxford edition of his father's *De non temerandis ecclesiis*, and in 1647 he published anonymously *Reasons why we should admit the king to a personall treaty in parliament, and not treat by commissioners*. In 1648 he wrote *A letter, to the assembly of divines at Westminster: shewing the conversion of church-lands to lay-uses, to be condemned by Luther, Calvin, Knox, and the whole assemblies of Scotch divines*. Either Spelman or a namesake was named on a list of sequestrated delinquents on 24 April 1648.

Spelman was elected a bencher of Gray's Inn on 6 July 1660. He may have been the author of *A Character of the Oliverians* (1660). He was appointed cursitor baron of the exchequer on 9 March 1663. Anthony Wood reported that Spelman had died in Fleet Street after Whitsuntide 1679. He had certainly died by 30 May 1679, when his successor was appointed. Spelman was buried in St Dunstan's Church, Fleet Street. He should not be confused with his second cousin and namesake, Clement, the recorder of Nottingham, whose will was proved in 1680.

William Carr, *rev.* Stuart Handley

Sources Sainty, *Judges* • Venn, *Alum. Cant.* • Foss, *Judges* • J. Foster, *The register of admissions to Gray's Inn, 1521–1889, together with the register of marriages in Gray's Inn chapel, 1695–1754* (privately printed, London, 1889), 134 • W. Harvey, *The visitation of Norfolk in the year 1563*, ed. G. H. Dashwood and others, 1 (1878), 252–7 • *The life and times of Anthony Wood*, ed. A. Clark, 2, OHS, 21 (1892), 453 • *CSP dom.*, 1637–8, 602 • R. J. Fletcher, ed., *The pension book of Gray's Inn*, 1 (1901), 330, 431 • *Brief lives, chiefly of contemporaries, set down by John Aubrey, between the years 1669 and 1696*, ed. A. Clark, 2 (1898), 231

Spelman [*formerly* Yallop], **Edward** (*d.* **1767**), writer and translator, was the son of Charles Yallop (*d.* *c.*1736), gentleman, of Bowthorpe Hall, Norfolk, and his wife, Ellen Barkham. Some indication of his reasons for rejecting his father's surname and adopting that of his great-grandfather Clement *Spelman (*bap.* 1598, *d.* 1679) can be gleaned from a manuscript diary, 'Annales miserarium' (1724). The diary details his incarceration for non-payment of a £5000 mortgage. His exiled father, who had contracted the debt, was forced to send the conveyance for the Yallop estates from Rotterdam. Having cleared the mortgage, Spelman settled £100 a year on Jenny, the mother of his natural daughter, and £150 on his disgraced father, Charles. The diary also records, in salacious Latin, Edward's Boswell-like adventures among the prostitutes and drinking-dens of London, and, in French, his plans to flee to France if the mortgager Naish proceeded with the suit.

There is no record of Spelman having spent time at university—his literary executor remembered him once shouting: 'Good God! doth any fellow of a college know anything of Greek?' (*DNB*)—but the classical scholarship for which he is remembered was formidable. In 1742 Spelman published *The Expedition of Cyrus*, his translation of Xenophon's *Anabasis*. Pope was then making the final revisions of his *Iliad*, and Spelman attacked those 'paraphrasers' who 'find less Difficulty in clothing modern Thoughts in a modern Dress, than in making Those of an Ancient appear graceful'. Edward Gibbon, who had a copy of the *Expedition* with him in Lausanne, testified to Spelman's own success in this respect, as does the fact of the *Expedition*'s remaining in print until 1849.

During the following year Spelman published *A Fragment out of the Sixth Book of Polybius*. He intended to parallel the balanced, tripartite constitution of Rome described by Polybius with that of modern Britain. The *Fragment* includes an introduction demanding the repeal of the Septennial Act, 'the severest Stab the liberties of the People of England ever received', and an appended 'Dissertation' on the constitution (as opposed to the powers) of the Roman senate. An indication of the volume's high reputation is that Nathaniel Hooke condescended to attack its historiography in his *Observations* (1758). It was thus measured against the writings of Hooke's other authoritative targets: Vertot, Lord Hervey, Thomas Chapman, and Conyers Middleton, whose hugely successful *Life of Cicero* had originally inspired Spelman's adaptation of Polybius.

Spelman proved a reluctant controversialist in *A Short Review of Mr. Hooke's 'Observations'* (1758), which replied to Hooke's main charge: that not one of the above five writers had produced reliable evidence for their shared assumption that the early Roman senates were elected by a democratic vote. Spelman was then completing a translation of *The Roman Antiquities of Dionysus Halicarnassensis*, due to be published in four sumptuous volumes later in 1758. Since Dionysus was the authority that Hooke deemed unreliable and sophistic, both past and future publications required defence. Spelman emphasized the obvious point that Hooke had rejected Dionysus's account 'because his political principles (no more to be concealed than the itch, though very luckily they are not so catching) lead him to look upon the appointment of a senate to be the dismembering of his darling prerogative'. Spelman was in turn answered by William Bowyer the younger, whose *Apology* for Hooke was published posthumously in 1783.

Even before his controversy with Hooke, Spelman had settled on the remnants of his family estates near East Acre, Norfolk. He had started building High House, at West Acre, before 1756, and great attention to the details of its construction is evident in his correspondence with Sir William Browne. This project must have exhausted his already diminished income, since Spelman sold the entire estate to Richard Hammond in 1761, on condition of his being allowed to remain at High House. He died there, unmarried, on 12 March 1767, and was buried at the Barkham vault in East Acre church. During his last years Spelman began *The History of the Civil War between York and Lancaster* (1792), which was completed by G. W. Lemon. The editor's press-copy of this book, interleaved with voluminous manuscript notes and corrections, is in the Bodleian Library. Lemon also published the last fruits of Spelman's scholarship, a tract on Greek accents, in 1773.

Patrick Bullard

Sources E. Spelman, 'Annales miserarium', 1724, Norwich City Archives, HMN 7/277, 772–5 • F. Blomefield and C. Parkin, *An essay towards a topographical history of the county of Norfolk*, [2nd edn], 11 vols. (1805–10), vol. 2, p. 384; vol. 6, p. 201; vol. 9, pp. 145, 163 • Nichols, *Lit. anecdotes*, 2.305–411, 616; 3.661; 8.135 • *GM*, 1st ser., 37 (1767), 144 • J. Aikin and others, *General biography, or, Lives, critical and historical of the most eminent persons*, 10 vols. (1799–1815) • W. Rye, *Norfolk families*, 2 (1913), 1074 • 'Particulars of Spelman's estate', Norwich City Archives, HMN 2/1/1–52, 736–8 • letters to Sir William Browne, Norwich City Archives, HMN 2/6/1–56, 736–7 • E. Gibbon, *Memoirs of my life and writing*, ed. A. O. J. Cockshut and S. Constantine, bicentenary edn (1994), 75 • *Norfolk: south and west*, Pevsner (1999) • *DNB*

Archives Norfolk RO, diary mainly relating to his imprisonment for debt

Spelman, Sir Henry (1563/4–1641), historian and antiquary, was born at Congham, near King's Lynn, Norfolk, the eldest son of Henry Spelman (*d.* 1581) of Congham and his second wife, Frances (*d.* 1622), daughter of William Saunders of Ewell, Surrey. He was educated at Walsingham grammar school, where later tradition had it that he was a poor student. Spelman was admitted to Trinity College, Cambridge, on 15 September 1580; he matriculated in his seventeenth year on 17 March 1581 at Trinity College, Cambridge, and graduated BA in 1583, despite the interruption to his studies caused by the death of his father in October 1581. He then went to Furnival's Inn, and entered Lincoln's Inn on 14 May 1586 'with a design of studying the law, but disliking the drudgery necessary for attaining to the lucrative part of the profession he applied himself to the history and antiquities of his native land' (Mirrlees, 147). Thus it was about this time that he helped to found the Society of Antiquaries, to which he delivered several extant papers on such topics as the state of the kingdom's coinage. It was through the society that Spelman made the acquaintance of other devoted antiquaries, including Sir Robert Bruce Cotton, first baronet.

Norfolk, 1590–1612 After three years at Lincoln's Inn Spelman returned to Norfolk and on 18 April 1590 he married Eleanor (*d.* 1620), daughter and coheir of John L'Estrange of Sedgeford, Norfolk. They had four sons, two of whom predeceased him, and four daughters: Sir John *Spelman (1594–1643), the eldest son, was a royalist author, and Clement *Spelman (*bap.* 1598, *d.* 1679) was cursitor baron of the exchequer. Most of his wife's inheritance remained with her mother, who married Richard Stubbe, but Spelman secured the wardship of Hamon L'Estrange, son of Sir Nicholas L'Estrange (*d.* 1591), his wife's cousin. This allowed him to live at the L'Estrange property of Hunstanton, Norfolk; its proximity to Castle Rising probably explains his return to parliament for that borough in 1593 and 1597. It was during Spelman's sojourn in Norfolk as a country gentleman that he wrote what may have been his first work, 'Aspilogia', a Latin treatise on coats of armour, which, although probably written before 1595, remained unpublished until 1654. His 1604 tract, 'Of the union', declared support for the general principle of union, but was opposed to proposals which sought a more perfect union through free trade, mutual naturalization, and a common legal system. Spelman was knighted in 1604 and served as

Sir Henry Spelman (1563/4–1641), after Cornelius Johnson, 1628?

sheriff of Norfolk from November 1604 until February 1606 and as justice of the peace until 1616. He transcribed many of the deeds and charters relating to Norfolk and Suffolk monasteries and, according to Thomas Hearne, he wrote the description of Norfolk printed in John Speed's *Theatre of the Empire of Great Britain* (1611).

In 1594 Spelman's purchases of the leases of Blackborough and Wormegay abbeys from the crown lessees caused him to be involved in extensive litigation in chancery, which was not settled until 1625 by the lord keeper, Sir Thomas Coventry. When Sir Francis Bacon heard the case, he found against Spelman, which perhaps explains his involvement in petitioning parliament against the lord chancellor. It was in his unhappy tribulations over these former church properties that Spelman 'first discerned the infelicity of meddling with consecrated places' (H. Spelman, *The History and Fate of Sacrilege*, 1853, 247). He was still collecting material on the punishment meted out to those committing sacrilege in 1633, but his work, *The History and Fate of Sacrilege*, although sent to the printers in 1663, was delayed in the press and temporarily lost during the fire of London. It was subsequently recovered by Edmund Gibson, but remained unpublished until 1698.

London, 1612–1630 The end of Hamon L'Estrange's minority presumably coincided with Spelman's decision in 1612 to move his permanent residence to Tothill Street in London. Within a year of his arrival in the capital he had completed and published *De non temerandis ecclesiis: a Tract of the*

Rights and Respect due unto the Churches (1613), which, according to the title, was written to 'a gentleman [his maternal uncle, Francis Saunders], who, having an appropriate parsonage, employed the church to profane uses, and left the parishioners uncertainly provided of Divine service in a parish near there adjoining'. Spelman had collected numerous cases showing that ill fates awaited those who enjoyed church property; his examples included three of William I's children, and the disappearance of King John's plunder from Peterborough and Croydon abbeys, which were lost in quicksand. The book's advocacy was sufficiently powerful, according to Bishop Gibson, to ensure a steady stream of converts willing to return their impropriations to the church. It also helped to stimulate John Selden's response, *The Historie of Tithes* (1618), which refuted the contention that tithes were justified by both history and constant usage.

On 2 March 1617 Spelman was named a commissioner to determine unsettled titles to lands and manors in Ireland, business which necessitated three visits to Ireland. In July 1620 he had to recover from the death of his wife, a son, and a grandson all within the space of nine days. That year he became a member of the New England Company, an association which was to last until 1635 and which saw him heavily involved in the legal battles with the rival Virginia Company. In July 1621 the archbishop of Canterbury, George Abbot, accidentally shot and killed a park-keeper with a cross-bow while hunting. Perhaps in response to a request from the resultant commission charged with investigating whether the archbishop was now capable of carrying on his archiepiscopal duties, Spelman undertook an analysis of the case. His views appeared in 'An answer to the foregoing apology', which as the title suggests was a reply to 'A short apology for Archbishop Abbot'. Spelman was critical of Abbot, noting that as he had intended to kill a deer, the death of the keeper was not truly accidental, and dismissing the argument that Abbot was merely hunting for his health. In finding Abbot's conduct irregular he lined up with bishops Williams and Laud, who refused to accept consecration from Abbot.

Following the agitation in the parliament of 1621 over the reform of the courts of justice, in October 1622 James I appointed a commission to investigate the fees taken in both civil and ecclesiastical courts since 1588. Spelman was an assistant to the privy councillors named in the commission, but he shouldered most of the immediate administrative burden. When the commission was renewed in March 1623 Spelman was named a commissioner, and he became a mainstay of that and the other commissions appointed in 1627, 1630, 1634, and 1637. He wrote most of the reports to the king and council, including 'Considerations touching the suppression of unjust fees' in 1630, and attended as many as ninety meetings a year. In 1625 he was elected to parliament for Worcester, but he relinquished his seat to his son John at the election held in the following year. Indeed by 1628 Spelman was writing to Archbishop James Ussher of Armagh, 'I am no parliament man' (BL, Add. MS 25384, fol. 15).

Spelman's antiquarian labour increased during his residence in London, where he was part of a community of scholars such as John Selden and Sir Robert Cotton, and where he had the use of Cotton's magnificent library located in Westminster. His study of both the common law and the church forced him to confront the problem of the meaning and definition of the terms used in the past, especially Anglo-Saxon and Latin terms. With the encouragement of foreign scholars, such as Peiresc, to whom he submitted samples of his work, in 1626 he published *Archaeologus* (which covered the letters A–L). This was the first part of his glossary of 'obsolete and barbaric words in the ecclesiastical and legal vocabularies' (Pocock, 93). It encompassed the study of the usages, offices, ranks, ceremonies, and rules in the medieval church and law in the context of the words used in Europe. However, he had to bear the full cost of its publication.

In June 1627 Spelman was appointed by letters patent to the Guiana Company and elected as its treasurer. That same year he completed his *Codex legum veterum*. This work studied the origins of feudalism, in that it discussed the Norman introduction of feudal tenures, while also supporting the traditional view that the Normans had confirmed the laws already in being in Anglo-Saxon England. Spelman designed to publish this material in 1640, possibly as an antidote to the more extreme claims of those who saw parliament's rights as existing from time immemorial. Such a theme ran through his unpublished 'Of parliaments', which was written after 'having seen more parliaments miscarry, yea suffer, shipwreck, within these sixteen years past, than in many hundred heretofore' (probably therefore written about 1630), and 'The original, growth, propagation and condition of feuds and tenures by knight-service in England', which found its way into print in *Reliquiae Spelmannianae*.

Final years, 1630–1641 Simonds D'Ewes described Spelman in 1630 as 'a learned and studious gentleman, now very aged and almost blind' (Cooper, 106), but John Aubrey was less sure of his physical decline, recording a contemporary opinion that he 'wore always his sword till he was about 70 or more' (*Brief Lives*, 2.231). In any case Spelman spent most of the 1630s working on another large project, a plan to document all the church councils held in Britain or attended by British representatives. This would show the development of the church in all its facets since Roman times. Assisted by Jeremy Stephens and his own son John Spelman, he published part 1 of the work in 1639 as *Concilia*. It covered the period before 1066 and was used in evidence before the House of Commons in 1641 to argue against the sole jurisdiction of the bishops.

In January 1632 Spelman was described by the Norfolk justices in a letter to the privy council as 'a grave person, well knowing the state of their country and well known to their lordships' (*CSP dom., 1631–3*, 258). In November 1636 he was granted £300 by the king in recognition of his extraordinary 'labour and pains taken by him on sundry occasions in his majesty's service' (*CSP dom., 1636–7*, 210).

About February 1638 he declined the offer of the mastership of Sutton's Hospital, Charterhouse, preferring to solicit the place for his son John.

Spelman maintained his contact with Cambridge University and began discussions at some point around 1635 concerning the endowment of a chair in Anglo-Saxon. This was established by 1640 when Abraham Wheelock was professor, although the chair lapsed with his death in 1657. Spelman's scholarly reputation may explain his candidature, at such an advanced age, for the university in the elections to the Long Parliament, when he was defeated. His supporters included some youthful Laudians, attracted no doubt by his works on the church, although it is doubtful if Spelman himself could be characterized as such. The last work published by him before his death appeared in 1641: *De sepultura* was a result of his appointment to the commission of 1627 into the taking of exorbitant fees.

Death and reputation On 8 October 1641 Spelman's assistant, John Walden, reported that his master had died on 1 October 1641 at the house in the Barbican of his daughter and her husband, Sir Ralph Whitfield. Walden recorded that Spelman was to be buried on the 14th in Westminster Abbey, although the printed registers indicate that interment took place on the 24th.

Much of Spelman's work remained unpublished at his death. As well as assisting with *Concilia*, Jeremy Stephens helped other of Spelman's later endeavours. Stephens saw to the publication of *Tithes too Hot to be Touched* in 1646, republished the following year as *The Larger Treatise on Tithes*. Another antiquary, William Dugdale, whom he met in 1638, was responsible for the publication after the Restoration of the remainder of the glossary. In 1694 Edmund Gibson gained possession of five bundles of Spelman's papers, which, together with those preserved in the library of Sir Charles Spelman, formed the basis of Gibson's *Reliquiae Spelmannianae*, published in 1698.

Spelman was known by contemporaries as a scholar and antiquary. His subsequent reputation has been enhanced by the knowledge that his determination to comprehend fully English institutions laid the groundwork for future methodology and understanding. In particular, he managed to link separate pieces of evidence together in order to explain the development of feudalism, rather than merely accumulate and present a series of unrelated facts. For many historians his comparative work on the language and terms of northern Europe led to the 'discovery' that feudalism developed as a consequence of the Norman conquest, and that English institutions had not existed from time immemorial. STUART HANDLEY

Sources R. Virgoe, 'Spelman, Henry', HoP, *Commons, 1558–1603* • F. M. Powicke, *Sir Henry Spelman and the Concilia* (1930) • Venn, *Alum. Cant.* • J. S. Wilson, 'Sir Henry Spelman and the royal commission on fees, 1622–40', *Studies presented to Sir Hilary Jenkinson*, ed. J. Conway Davies (1957), 456–70 • J. G. A. Pocock, *The ancient constitution and the feudal law* (1987), 57–123 • *Reliquiae Spelmannianae* (1698) • G. Parry, *The trophies of time: English antiquarians of the seventeenth century* (1995), 157–81 • W. Harvey, *The visitation of Norfolk in the year 1563*, ed. G. H. Dashwood and others, 1 (1878), 253, 256 • J. L. Chester, ed., *The marriage, baptismal, and burial registers of the collegiate church or abbey of St Peter, Westminster*, Harleian Society, 10 (1876), 116, 135 • P. A. Welsby, *George Abbot: the unwanted archbishop, 1562–1633* (1962), 91–104 • C. H. Cooper, 'On an early autograph of Sir Henry Spelman', *Cambridge Antiquarian Society*, 2 (1864), 101–12 • H. A. Cronne, 'The study and use of charters by English scholars in the 17th century: Sir Henry Spelman and Sir William Dugdale', *English historical scholarship in the 16th and 17th centuries*, ed. L. Fox (1956), 73–91 • H. Ellis, ed., *Original letters of eminent literary men of the sixteenth, seventeenth, and eighteenth centuries*, CS, 23 (1843), 163–4, 170 • W. P. Baildon, ed., *The records of the Honorable Society of Lincoln's Inn: admissions*, 1 (1896), 104 • *Brief lives, chiefly of contemporaries, set down by John Aubrey, between the years 1669 and 1696*, ed. A. Clark, 2 vols. (1898), 231 • D. R. Woolf, *The idea of history in early Stuart England* (1990) • H. Mirrlees, *A fly in amber: being an extravagant biography of the romantic antiquary Sir Robert Bruce Cotton* (1962), 147 • G. A. Carthew, *The hundred of Launditch and deanery of Brisley, in the county of Norfolk*, 1 (1877), vol. 1, pp. 144–5 • N. Sykes, *Edmund Gibson bishop of London, 1669–1748* (1926), 20–22 • C. J. Somerville, *The secularization of early modern England* (1992) • F. S. Fussner, *The historical revolution: English historical writing and thought, 1580–1640* (1962) • B. R. Galloway and B. P. Levack, eds., *The Jacobean union: six tracts of 1604*, ser. 4, Scottish History Society, 21 (1985) • J. Morrill, 'A British patriarchy? Ecclesiastical imperialism under the early Stuarts', *Religion, culture and society in early modern Britain*, ed. A. Fletcher and P. Roberts (1994), 209–37

Archives BL, biographical papers, Add. MS 33751 • BL, corresp., Add. MSS 25384, 34599–345601 • Bodl. Oxf., drafts of *De sepultura* • Bodl. Oxf., papers • Norfolk RO, papers incl. heraldic and genealogical notes and papers relating to political matters • Suffolk RO, Ipswich, papers incl. 'life of Cardinal Wolsey' by G. Cavendish | BL, Harley MSS, collections • Bodl. Oxf., Tanner MSS, corresp. • CUL, letters to Wheelock and corresp. • U. Edin. L., *Archaismus graphicus* and corresp.

Likenesses oils, 1628? (after C. Johnson), NPG [*see illus.*] • oils, second version, 1628?, Plymouth City Museum and Art Gallery [on loan] • W. Faithorne, line engraving, BM, NPG

Spelman, Sir John (*c*.1480–1546), judge and law reporter, was the fourth son of Henry Spelman (*d.* 1496) and his second wife, Ela, daughter of William Narborough of Narborough, Norfolk, and widow of Thomas Shouldham (*d.* 1472) of Marham. His father was a reader of Gray's Inn, and is portrayed in his robes as recorder of Norwich on a brass at Narborough; his reading was printed in 1951. John Spelman followed his father to Gray's Inn about 1500. On becoming a bencher in Lent 1514 he read on the first five chapters of the Statute of Westminster I. Several cases argued on this occasion survive in manuscript. In Lent 1519 he delivered his celebrated second reading, on the Statute of *Quo warranto*. This was not printed until 1997, but it circulated widely in manuscript, and the disputed cases are also preserved. In Lent 1521 he delivered a third reading, as serjeant-elect; this was on *Prerogativa regis*, and a manuscript text survives in Gray's Inn.

Spelman was created serjeant on 1 July 1521, elected to his father's old office of recorder of Norwich the following year, and on 28 November 1526 became one of the king's serjeants. On 3 July 1531 he was appointed to the judgeship of the king's bench which had been vacant since the death of Sir John More, the chancellor's father, and on 8 July was sworn in by Sir Thomas More. He was knighted the following year. As a judge of assize he went on the arduous northern circuit until 1537, when he changed to the home. In 1540 he stopped going on circuit, and the cessation of his reports at the same time suggests that he was becoming decrepit. There was indeed a garbled later recollection that he had retired to the country on grounds of age; but he seems in fact to have continued sitting in Westminster Hall until 1545, and died in office on 26 January 1546. Sir Robert Brooke described him as 'valde peritus in lege' ('mightily learned in the law'; Brooke, 1, fol. 182*v*). He was buried at Narborough, where there is a brass depicting him in judicial robes, coloured red, with his wife and children, and a picture of the resurrection. The inscription describes him as 'Secundary Justice of the Kinges Bench' but gives his date of death incorrectly as 26 February.

Spelman is renowned for his reports of cases, which run from about 1502 until 1540 and were known to Stanford and Coke. The reports begin with the Christmas festivities in Gray's Inn which Spelman attended as a young student, and include readings and moots in the inn as well as cases observed in Westminster Hall. After he became a serjeant in 1521, the reporting emphasis shifted to the common pleas, and when he became a judge in 1531 to the king's bench. He was the first reporter to note legal discussions 'at table' in Serjeants' Inn, Chancery Lane, these being the first indications of a nascent procedure for discussing reserved crown cases. He also reported some private judicial sessions in the exchequer chamber, the most important of which is his account of *Lord Dacre's case* (1535), the case which enabled Henry VIII to force the Statute of Uses on an unwilling Commons. Among several notes on matters of state are accounts of the fatal proceedings against Wolsey ('home de graund pompe et riches'), the coronation, trial, and execution of Anne Boleyn, and the trials of Fisher and More. The autograph of the reports is lost, but the corpus which remains, rearranged in its original alphabetical format, was published for the first time in 1977.

On the death of his half-brother Thomas Shouldham in 1514, Spelman obtained the estate at Narborough where he became established. After some litigation with the Shouldhams, his title was perfected by final concord in 1526 and he thereupon built Narborough Hall, where his descendants lived until 1773. The house still displays a stone tablet with the judge's arms, impaling Frowyk, and the date 1528. The impalement commemorated his only marriage, to Elizabeth (*d.* 1556), daughter of Chief Justice Frowyk's brother Henry, with whom he had a remarkable number of offspring. The judge left his law books to his seventh son, Erasmus, with an exhibition to study in Gray's Inn, but none of his children made any mark in the law. His grandson Sir Henry *Spelman (1563/4–1641) was the celebrated antiquary, and Sir Henry's son Clement *Spelman (*bap.* 1598, *d.* 1679), bencher of Gray's Inn and cursitor baron of the exchequer, was the last-known owner of Spelman's autograph reports. Another Clement Spelman (*d.* 1680), the great-grandson of Sir John's second son, John, was a king's counsel and recorder of Nottingham; his standing effigy in robes is in Narborough church, and his library is preserved as a parochial library in Swaffham church.

J. H. BAKER

Sources *The reports of Sir John Spelman*, ed. J. H. Baker, 2 vols., SeldS, 93–4 (1977–8) · J. H. Baker, ed., *John Spelman's reading on Quo warranto*, SeldS, 113 (1997) · will, PRO, PROB 11/31, sig. 5 [Lady Elizabeth Spelman] · inquisition post mortem, PRO, C 142/95/14 · PRO, E 101/209/4 [patent as king's serjeant] · R. Brooke, *La graunde abridgement* (1573) · *The English works of Sir Henry Spelman*, ed. E. Gibson (1727)

Likenesses brass effigy on monument, Narborough church, Norfolk

Spelman, Sir John (1594–1643), royalist author, was born in Hunstanton, Norfolk, the eldest son of the historian and antiquary Sir Henry *Spelman (1563/4–1641) and Eleanor L'Estrange (*d.* 1620). Clement *Spelman was his younger brother. He was admitted at Gray's Inn on 16 February 1608 and entered Trinity College, Cambridge, the following year. About 1620 he married Anne Townshend. He represented the City of Worcester in the 1626 parliament. He had inherited his father's literary and antiquarian interests, and he made several trips abroad, including to Paris (1619) and Italy (1628–9), during which he met a number of continental scholars. He also published, from manuscripts in his father's library, *Psalterium Davidis Latino-Saxonicum vetus* (1640).

Spelman, who was knighted on 18 December 1641, sat in neither the Short nor Long parliament and in January 1642 Charles I ordered him to remain in Norfolk. However, Spelman was later summoned to Oxford, where he occupied rooms in Brasenose College while he studied there. During 1642–3 he published four tracts which eloquently express moderate royalist political and religious attitudes, and which constitute his principal claim to fame.

In the earliest of these, *A Protestants Account of his Orthodox Holding in Matters of Religion* (1642), Spelman presented a sustained defence of existing forms of church government. He attacked the exponents of root-and-branch reform as 'fighters against the Spirit of God' and insisted that 'the liturgy of our Church' had been established 'by the laws of this kingdom' (*A Protestants Account*, 23–4). A similar concern for the rule of law loomed equally large in Spelman's other treatises. In *Certain considerations upon the duties both of prince and people, written by a gentleman of quality, a wel-wisher both to the king and parliament* (1642), he argued, in terms reminiscent of the king's *Answer to the Nineteen Propositions*, that 'the composite forme' was 'the only firme and durable forme', and that 'of the three powers, regall, aristocraticall or popular, any of them prevailing so far as to be wholly free from being qualified or tempered by some operation of the other two, corrupted the legitimate forme into a tyrannicall' (*Certain Considerations*, 18). The monarch's authority was therefore not 'without law' but subject to limitations: the laws were 'most sacred and binding even to Kings themselves'. However, this was 'to be understood in safety, in honour, in conscience betweene God and them', and there was no way that 'in their default, the people can become authorised' (ibid., 18–20).

This last point in turn led Spelman to compose a refutation of Henry Parker's *Observations*, entitled *A View of a Printed Book Intituled 'Observations upon His Majesties Late Answers and Expresses'* (1642). Spelman began by insisting that although the king and the houses of parliament formed one body, 'yet is the King the head of that body' (*A View of a Printed Book*, 8). This was not to claim 'a power to make lawes and lay taxes without the consent of Parliament', but only 'a negative voice, that they without him may not make any lawes, or charge his subjects, but that all be done by the joynt consent of him and his people' (ibid., 23). Although certain powers, such as control over the militia, were 'by the fundamentall law immovably setled in the Crowne' (ibid., sig. F3*r*), Spelman wrote that:

> monarchy … tempered and mixt … is the constitution of government in England, so well poysed and molded by the wisdome of our ancestors as that it gives to this kingdome the conveniences of all [forms] without the inconveniences of any one. (ibid., sig. E2*v*)

Spelman developed these points at greater length in his last political work, *The case of our affaires, in law, religion, and other circumstances briefly examined, and presented to the conscience* (1643). He reiterated that 'even by the declaration of our lawes', the king was 'a supreme head, a soveraigne', whose crown was 'an imperiall crown, the kingdom *his* kingdom, *his* realme, *his* dominion, the people *his* people, the subject *his* subject' (*The Case of our Affaires*, 1). Hence 'the soveraignity of this State' was 'clearly vested in the King, by law established in him, and inseparably annexed to his person' (ibid., 2). By the same token, the houses of parliament were 'meerly instruments of regulation and qualification of the King's legislative absolutenesse' and 'no sharers with him in the soveraignity'. Royal powers were thus 'not as properly said to be restrained as regulated' (ibid., 5). Here, as in his other writings, Spelman argued that mixed monarchy did not imply shared sovereignty, and that the concept of legally limited monarchy involved a regulation rather than a restriction of the monarch's powers.

While resident in Oxford, Spelman also compiled *Alfredi magni Anglorum regis invictissimi vita*, published posthumously in 1678. Spelman's abilities won the king's favour and he was about to be appointed secretary of state when he died of camp fever on 25 July 1643, at Brasenose. He was buried in Great St Mary's Church the next day, and James Ussher preached his funeral sermon.

David L. Smith

Sources Foster, *Alum. Oxon.* • J. Foster, *The register of admissions to Gray's Inn, 1521–1889, together with the register of marriages in Gray's Inn chapel, 1695–1754* (privately printed, London, 1889), 119 • Venn, *Alum. Cant.* • I. D. Brice, 'Political ideas in royalist pamphlets of the period 1642–1649', BLitt diss., U. Oxf., 1970 • D. L. Smith, *Constitutional royalism and the search for settlement, c. 1640–1649* (1994) • BL, Sir Henry Spelman correspondence, Add. MS 34599 • state papers domestic, Charles I, PRO, SP 16 • J. Spelman, letter to Sir John Potts, 2 Feb 1643, Bodl. Oxf., MS Tanner 64, fol. 145*r* • *DNB*

Spence, Sir Basil Urwin (1907–1976), architect, was born on 13 August 1907 in Bombay, the elder son of Urwin Archibald Spence (*d*. 1927), chemist in the Indian Civil Service, and his wife, Daisy Crisp (*b*. 1881). The Spences, originally from Orkney, maintained ties with Scotland by sending their son in 1919 to George Watson's College, Edinburgh, at the age of twelve. From here, having

Sir Basil Urwin Spence (1907–1976), by Howard Coster, 1954

obtained his school certificate and a report which mentioned his facility for drawing, Spence went in 1925 to Edinburgh College of Art, initially to study sculpture but eventually to take up architecture.

Architectural education and early practice At the college Spence came under key influences: he was taught architectural history by John Summerson and town planning by Frank Mears, and came in contact with the architect Robert Lorimer, who, as a college governor, was a frequent visitor and examiner of student work. During Spence's period of study at the college of art, two distinguished international architects lectured: Walter Gropius in 1929 and Eric Mendelsohn a year later. Spence thrived in the stimulating atmosphere of Scotland's premier art college (by the 1920s Glasgow's supremacy had been eclipsed) and was elected secretary of the students' association in 1928. By his second year college records show he was winning drawing prizes and had sufficient potential to be awarded a bursary. This and the small income Spence earned by preparing perspective drawings for some of the larger Edinburgh practices were essential following the death of his father in 1927.

In 1929 Spence was awarded the college certificate in architecture and left Edinburgh to work in the London office of Sir Edwin Lutyens for his 'year out'. There he came under further important influences. From Lutyens, Spence experienced the geometric vigour of that blend of free classicism and modernism which Lutyens had by then made his own. While in London, Spence read Le Corbusier's *Towards a New Architecture*, to which he was introduced when attending evening classes at the Bartlett school of architecture under Albert Richardson between October 1929 and April 1930. Spence spent the year in Lutyens's office preparing furniture and garden designs for Viceroy House in New Delhi, no doubt using to advantage his knowledge of both the Indian Civil Service and local customs. Spence later acknowledged his admiration for Lutyens's handling of space, volume, and light, describing the elder architect as his 'patron and master' (personal knowledge). Lutyens in turn appreciated Spence's talents, calling him my 'Scots boy' (ibid.).

In 1930 Spence returned to Edinburgh to complete his architectural training. He quickly gained prizes confirming his promise as a student: the Rowand Anderson medal (1930); the RIBA silver medal (1931); the Pugin prize (1933); and with Robert Matthew the Arthur Cates prize for town planning (1933). These prizes give a glimpse of the early talent for drawing, building, and civic design that Spence displayed. In September 1931 he obtained his diploma in architecture and joined the well-established Edinburgh practice of Rowand Anderson, Balfour Paul, & Partners. His student friend and collaborator William Kininmonth had joined the practice a year earlier and both continued to dabble in private commissions. At this time Spence led something of a double life: in his work with the practice he was busy with country house designs and department stores in Edinburgh, but his evenings were spent entering competitions and building modernist extensions to Edinburgh houses for Kininmonth's doctor brother and circle of friends. The conservative nature of the commissions undertaken by the office of Rowand Anderson, Balfour Paul, & Partners, such as Broughton Place near Biggar, which Spence designed in 1935 for Professor Thomas Elliot, in a free baronial style influenced by Lorimer, stand in contrast to the international style houses which the practice of Kininmonth and Spence designed on their own account. For example, 11 Easter Belmont Road, Edinburgh, for Dr John King, is a play of smooth white cubes, semicircular drums, sun terraces, and horizontal bands of windows.

The pre-war years were happy and productive for Spence. Edinburgh provided a mix of professional and social contacts which proved invaluable later in life. The work was varied and demanding and, typically of the period, there was no single style to adopt. He was appointed a junior partner in the practice of Rowand Anderson, Balfour Paul in 1935. Balfour Paul, the senior partner under whom Spence worked, entrusted Spence with designs for some of the practice's most important clients, such as Gribloch (1938) near Loch Lomond for the steel magnate John Colville, and Quothquhan (1936) near Lanark for Alexander Erskine-Hill MP. These were large country houses for clients whose own architectural tastes had to be accommodated. In them Spence combined with dexterity the two principal themes of British architecture of the 1930s—tradition and modernity. From Lorimer he drew upon the legacy of the arts and crafts movement, blending a fondness for textured materials such as rough stone, flint, slate, and pantiles, and from Lutyens an underlying geometric monumentality.

The plans of these houses and those of the commercial designs in Edinburgh prepared by Spence (such as a car showroom in Causewayside, 1933) develop a theme which recurred throughout the architect's career. That is the abandonment of the simple rectangle or square in favour of angled and circular projections. The plan or figure on the ground is invariably disrupted by the activities within, resulting in rooms, wings, or drums which break free of simple perimeter containment. The deliberate disruption of plan and cross-section gives these early buildings a distinctive sculptural quality. Spence captured this three-dimensional quality in his presentation perspectives and strove to express it on site using the indigenous materials of the Scottish landscape.

The year 1938 was a high point for Spence: working at first with Kininmonth and later on his own account, he was commissioned independently of the Anderson and Paul practice to design the Scottish pavilion at the Empire Exhibition in Glasgow, under the direction of Thomas Tait. Here in the rarefied atmosphere of a world fair Spence could express himself with the suave sophistication of his student projects. The Scottish pavilion, noted by critics at the time as a landmark of the exhibition, consisted of a white cube with a pair of detached penetrating circular drums and a dramatic tower. It is the closest Spence came between the wars to the abstract spatial ideas promulgated by Le Corbusier. He was also commissioned to design the ICI pavilion and a country cottage intended as a model for agricultural workers. In these commissions Spence ensured that artists were also employed, including Thomas Whalen, who provided plaster murals for the ICI pavilion, and Archibald Dawson whose sculptured figures of industrial workers stood prominently in the glazed rotunda of the Scottish pavilion. Exhibition work in Glasgow, Edinburgh, Johannesburg, and later London provided the 'forcing house for experiment' which Spence hoped would take on 'more solid form at some later date' (Black, 114).

On 6 September 1934 Spence married Mary Joan Ferris (1912–1989), daughter of John Ferris, a butcher of Tiverton, Devon, with whom he had corresponded for five years. They had met as members of the London badminton club and achieved championship status in mixed doubles. Honeymooning in Germany, Spence had a glimpse of the direction in which that country was heading and enrolled with the Territorial Army on his return. With an increasing volume of work on his own account, the outbreak of the Second World War came at an inopportune time for Spence. He joined the Royal Artillery and rose to the position of major in the camouflage unit, where his talent for design and landscape composition were put to advantage. He later became a staff captain in intelligence. While on duty in Normandy he witnessed the destruction of ancient religious structures, and declared in his diary the ambition to build a church of his own time if he was lucky enough to survive (L. Campbell, *To Build*, xiv).

Post-war years in Edinburgh With few commissions available and an embargo on construction except for wartime repairs, Spence found his former practice unable to re-employ him. The following lean years were spent undertaking house extensions, exhibition and furniture design (mainly for Morris & Co. in Glasgow), and in teaching part-time at Edinburgh College of Art. In 1946 the practice of Basil Spence & Partners was formed mainly out of assistants from Balfour Paul's office and bright students from the college. The new practice was engaged initially on designing exhibition pavilions such as the Enterprise Scotland Exhibition in Edinburgh (1946), the Scottish Industries Exhibition in Glasgow (1947), the Britain Can Make It Exhibition in London (1949), and various British industry fairs overseas. However, by the late 1940s the practice received several more substantial commissions in the area of local authority housing. The projects Spence undertook at Bannerfield, Selkirk (1948), Dunbar (1949), Sunbury-on-Thames and Feltham (1950), and Shepperton (1951), are marked by a subtle interlocking of courtyards and quasi-modern detailing of vernacular forms. Large concrete-framed metal windows, delicate steel balconies, and smooth wall surfaces counterbalanced by areas of rough textured stonework are a feature of the work. Spence's design for working-class housing was sufficiently regarded for him to receive the Festival of Britain award for housing in 1951.

The exhibition work drew Spence to the attention of the organizers of the Festival of Britain (1951), who commissioned him to design the Sea and Ships Pavilion, Skylark Restaurant, Nelson Pier, and the heavy industries stand. Spence was the only architect from outside the close circle of London designers to be given work on any scale at the festival. The designs he developed from his office at 40 Moray Place, Edinburgh, using angled steel columns and curved roofs, signalled the emergence of an architect who had more than a Scottish outlook.

Success at Coventry Cathedral Soon after the Festival of Britain had opened Spence learned, in August 1951, that he had won the competition to rebuild the cathedral at Coventry which had been reduced to a shell by incendiary bombs in 1940. The competition attracted over 100 entries, and followed the abandonment in 1947 of the rather conservative proposals for a new cathedral to designs by Giles Gilbert Scott. The brief called for retention of the existing tower and chapels beneath the nave, but Spence went further and retained the ruins of the whole. Several other architects had adopted a similar approach, but none produced a composition which was so balanced or so attentive to historic detail. Few others addressed the wider environs in a fashion which created an attractive sequence of pedestrian routes and semi-enclosed urban spaces which stitched the cathedral into the city fabric. Spence was also alone in exaggerating the perspective of the new nave by bringing the columns subtly together so that they enhanced the drama of the progression to the altar.

The design at Coventry was typical of Spence: the new cathedral was placed at right angles to the ruins of the old, whose column spacing rhythms and buttressed perimeter influenced the spirit of new arrangement. The burnt-out structure symbolized 'Faith, Courage, and Sacrifice', while the new building represented the 'Resurrection' (Spence and Snoek, 3). Old and new buildings, mirroring the Old and New testaments, were linked by a grand conception which Lewis Mumford applauded for its fusion of continuity and creativity. Spence had a rare ability to absorb the essence of place and make it a vital element of a new design. The right-angled realignment at Coventry allowed Spence to exploit the former nave as an open-air narthex to the new, setting a double-height porch in the space between the two structures. The new cathedral was long and majestic, with sawtooth-shaped walls and two nearly free-standing circular structures: the Chapel of Unity to the west and Chapel of Industry to the east, providing vertical articulation. The tall slot-like windows set in massive stone mullions, the circular drums projecting onto surrounding lawns, and the gaunt fire-damaged shell of the former cathedral made for a powerful composition which Spence exploited with understandable enthusiasm in several presentation perspectives. The best views were those which allowed the old tower and spire to act as a counterpoint to the chapels, giving the whole composition a repose which few other designs could match.

Success at Coventry and his presidency of the RIBA from 1958 to 1960 threw Spence into public prominence. He was much engaged in public speaking in support of his cathedral design, both defending its principles and helping to raise money for the construction. He contributed to articles in newspapers and magazines, appeared on radio and television, and travelled to Canada and the USA to gain support for the project from wealthy benefactors. The flair Spence displayed in drawing was matched by an equal facility for public speaking. He talked in terms the general public would understand, making modern architecture seem attractive and understandable. In this he helped pave the way for a wider acceptance of the principles of modern architecture. His 'fantastic fluency with words, draftsmanship and architecture' (*The Guardian*, 20 Nov 1976) prepared post-war Britain for the wider adoption among clients and individuals of the discipline of modernity. The resolution of traditional values and progressive spirit at Coventry marks a high point for twentieth-century architecture in Britain. Lewis Mumford, who accompanied Spence around the building in 1961, observed that it 'vibrates longer and with deeper resonance than many other works of modern architecture' (*New Yorker*, 10 March 1962).

By the time Coventry Cathedral was consecrated by the queen in 1962, Basil Spence had become a household name. His cathedral, though orthodox in plan and structurally more theatrical than essential for the needs of gravity, had a modern spirit and one which was distinctly British in character. This owed much to the works of art which were incorporated into the building: a fine tapestry by Graham Sutherland, stained glass by John Piper, and sculpture by Jacob Epstein and Elisabeth Frink both celebrated and brought to public attention modern British art. Spence's training at Edinburgh College of Art provided a basis for commissioning artists of like mind and at Coventry the partnership between architect, craftsman, and artist allowed each to flourish in the manner of the medieval cathedral.

The combination of success in the Coventry Cathedral competition and the praise surrounding the Festival of Britain buildings led Spence to open an office in Buckingham Street, London, in 1951, followed by a larger undertaking at 48–52 Queen Anne Street a year later. Although the firm of Basil Spence & Partners existed throughout, an Edinburgh practice known as Spence, Glover, and Ferguson was formed in 1958 and a London practice known subsequently as Spence, Bonnington, and Collins two years later. In addition, from 1964 Spence maintained a small select office known as Sir Basil Spence OM RA, which worked from rooms above his London home in Canonbury Place. The various Spence offices employed a degree of design independence and were seen at the time as important stopping-off points for young architects passing through the architecture schools of London or Edinburgh. Many of the partners developed designs on their own account, notably Andrew Renton with Thorn House in London (1959), Hardie Glover with Glasgow airport (1962), and John Bonnington with the Sunderland civic centre (1970). A great deal of design output was generated in the offices under the direction of partners but Spence maintained control over quality by requiring key projects to be sent to Canonbury Place before submission to clients. In total, the various Spence offices in London and Edinburgh produced 160 major buildings and master plans over a forty-year period.

Public commissions in the 1960s After Coventry Cathedral Spence was much in demand. He was appointed to design at least a dozen churches in England (of which at least three were in Coventry) and a further group in Scotland. These develop the earlier theme: an orthodox if irregular plan punctuated by shafts of light designed to focus upon the pulpit, free-standing bell-towers, integration of church architecture and liturgical art, and a rugged materiality of construction. Mortonhall crematorium outside Edinburgh, with its irregularly coursed sandstone, severe angularity, and twists in plan, is among the best. Some were favourably reviewed in architectural journals, others ignored for their aping of traditional configuration when modern churches were increasingly in the round.

Spence benefited considerably from the expansion of higher education in the UK following the Robbins report of 1963. He was appointed to master-plan the new University of Sussex and provide the framework for the expansion of many others: Southampton, Nottingham, Liverpool, Edinburgh, Newcastle, Durham, and Exeter. The Spence offices in London and Edinburgh also provided designs for a variety of faculty buildings, including the libraries at Sussex University (1962), Edinburgh University (1964), and Heriot-Watt University (1970). The projects in which Spence took a personal interest—for example, Falmer House, Sussex University (1962), and St Aidan's College, Durham (1963)—display characteristic visual power and bold construction. Structure was something Spence approached with the eye not of an engineer but of a sculptor. Huge oversailing segmental arched roofs, walls of rough brick or stone, and massive double-height columns gave these buildings a primitive quality which owed an increasing debt to Le Corbusier. His expansion of Queens' College, Cambridge, in mellow red brick built upon a pilotis was, in 1959, the first building in the modernist style along the Backs.

In parallel with the expansion of university provision, Spence received many commissions from public bodies. These included central-area redevelopment schemes in Newcastle, Sunderland, Hampstead, and Chelsea and work on the development of Basildon New Town. From these master plans grew much subsequent work: the Swiss Cottage Library and public baths (1960–62); the new public library in Newcastle (1969); the civic centre, Sunderland (1970); Kensington town hall (1974), and many lesser works. He also designed the Knightsbridge barracks overlooking Hyde Park (1967–70), as a muscular thirty-storey tower block. It was much criticized at the time, but Spence said 'I did not want this to be a mimsy-pimsy building. It is for soldiers. On horses. In armour' (private information).

Spence was also much involved in housing projects, and won a Saltire award for harbourside housing in Dunbar, Scotland, and in more heroic spirit for the now demolished Gorbals tower blocks in Glasgow. In the 1960s he was the most sought-after architect for public buildings in the UK, and where he could not provide detailed design services he acted as 'consultant', especially on overseas commissions. In this capacity he advised the New Zealand government on the design of the new parliament building in Wellington, the United Nations on its new offices in Geneva, and the trustees of the Kennedy memorial. He was involved in the design of the Riverstaete Building in Amsterdam, and new banks and airports from Greece to Iraq. The reports Spence furnished in his capacity as consultant were invariably supported by perspective sketches full of mood and drama, and pregnant with architectural possibility.

Among the avalanche of work two projects in particular required close attention. The first was the Rome embassy for the British government, commissioned in 1960 and opened a decade later. The site stood alongside Michelangelo's Porta Pia, the structural proportions of which Spence adopted for his design. Spence had always been fascinated by the play of light on walls and in the Rome embassy manipulated sunlight and shadows to give the building the presence needed to stand alongside its distinguished neighbour. As with Coventry Cathedral a close examination of context provided the basis for a design which, though modern in materials and construction, added subtly to the wider composition. As with the cathedral, the Rome embassy was seen in some architectural circles as too traditional and picturesque and hence out of step with the growing brutalism of modern architecture. The other project of note from this period was the British pavilion designed by Spence for Expo '67 in Montreal. Here a composition of pyramids, platforms, and towers (largely devoid of structural logic) provided exhibition space in which British goods (including the Mini) and works of art (including sculpture by Henry Moore) could be displayed. The basic form, a huge fractured crystal surrounded by an extensive moat, allowed light to penetrate in triangular shafts, providing that touch of panache necessary in exhibition pavilions.

Awards at home and abroad tainted by growing criticism By the early 1970s Spence was highly regarded by the general public and professional peers, though architectural critics led by the *Architectural Review* were becoming more vocal. His rise to eminence had been swift and he received an unprecedented number of public and professional awards. Knighted in 1960, he was awarded the Order of Merit in 1962 and received honorary awards from the French Academy, the American Institute of Architects, and the Rome Academy, as well as the Royal Academy in London, and doctorates from many universities. Spence rose to the highest professional office in the UK, by becoming president of the Royal Institute of British Architects (1958–60), and was given the title Royal Designer for Industry in 1960. Inevitably over a career of forty years Spence could not always adapt to changing fashions or client demand. His image also became tarnished by a reputation for a scale of architectural ambition that often exceeded his clients' budgets (the nickname Sir Basil-Expense was coined following cost overruns at Sussex University). Some critics dismissed his buildings as over-theatrical and lacking in technological substance. Of his British pavilion at Expo '67 the *Architectural Review* said it 'looked like a shape designed for its own sake, with the means of construction decided afterwards' (*Architectural Review*, August 1967, 157).

The criticism cut deep: Spence sought refuge in his wife, Joan, and their two children, Milton and Gillian. Joan, who had earlier given Spence resolution in the face of criticism over the design for Coventry Cathedral, again supported her husband in the later years. But increasingly they withdrew to the holiday homes he had designed overlooking the river at Beaulieu in Hampshire and in Majorca and Malta. Here he painted, designed buildings for admiring clients, sailed, and entertained surrounded by works of art.

An appraisal Basil Spence brought flair to the colourless world of post-war British architecture. His bow-ties, dapper suits, ready smile, and talent for publicity helped revitalize the profession in the 1950s. Largely uninterested in the technology of building construction, suspicious of system building and even at times of functionalism itself, he was supremely an architect of the senses. The visual world was Spence's main concern: how things looked was no less important than how well they performed their task. If the aesthetics of architecture ran deep in the Spence consciousness, they found particular expression in the handling of light, in geometrical composition, and in the relationship between buildings and landscape. In this he shared affinity with other artists of his age—the sculptor Henry Moore and the painters Graham Sutherland, Victor Pasmore, and John Piper. Spence was the most painterly in outlook of mid-twentieth-century British architects. The eye was the dominant sense and when doubt arose he trusted his visual judgement. The large formal perspective drawing was prepared by Spence not just to win over clients and committees but also to confirm to himself the validity of his initial vision. He died at Yaxley Hall, near Eye, Suffolk, on 19 November 1976, and was buried at St Michael's Church, Thornham Parva, Eye, Suffolk.

After a period of disfavour Spence's reputation began to revive in the 1990s and many of his buildings, savaged at the time, are now listed. The protected structures include some of his more controversial projects: Swiss Cottage Library, Knightsbridge barracks, Coventry Cathedral, Mortonhall crematorium, and most of Sussex University.

Brian W. Edwards

Sources A. Birks, *Building the new universities* (1972) • M. Black, *Exhibition design* (1950) • D. Daiches, *The idea of a new university* (1964) • M. Emanuel, ed., *Contemporary architects* (1980) • P. Fawcett, 'Basil Spence', *International dictionary of architecture and architects* (Detroit) • *DNB* • B. Spence, *Phoenix at Coventry* (1962) • B. Edwards, *Basil Spence 1907–1976* (1995) • L. Campbell, *Coventry Cathedral: art and architecture in post-war Britain* (1996) • L. Campbell, *To build a new cathedral* (1987) • J. Thomas, *Basil Spence* (1992) • R. Sheppard, *RIBA Journal*, 84 (1977) • F. Gibberd, *ArchR*, 161 (1977), 254–5 • C. Campbell, *Scottish Review* [Edinburgh] (spring 1977) • *The Times* (20 Nov 1976) • *The Guardian* (20 Nov 1976) • *Daily Telegraph* (20 Nov 1976) • B. Spence and H. Snoek, *Out of the ashes* (1963) • private information (2004) • d. cert. • m. cert.

Archives Anthony Blee Associates, London, drawings and family MSS • Coventry City Art Gallery, MSS • priv. coll., family MSS • RIBA, index to architects • RIBA, presidential file • Royal Commission on the Ancient and Historical Monuments of Scotland, Edinburgh, National Monuments Record of Scotland, designs and MSS | RIBA BAL, designs for British pavilion at Expo '67, Montreal

Likenesses H. Coster, photograph, 1954, NPG [*see illus.*] • G. Epstein, bronze sculpture, 1960, RIBA • photographs, NPG

Wealth at death £110,325: probate, 10 Jan 1977, *CGPLA Eng. & Wales*

Spence, Benjamin Evans (*bap.* 1823, *d.* 1866), sculptor, was born probably in Liverpool and was baptized on 3 January 1823 at St Peter's, Church Street, Liverpool, the eldest son of William Spence (1792–1849), sculptor, and his wife, Elizabeth. His father was a partner in Spence and Franceys (monumental masons) and was in the circle of the Liverpool art patron William Roscoe. In 1838 Benjamin attended the Liverpool Academy Schools, exhibiting busts there from 1838 to 1841 and in 1843. In 1844 he showed, at the Westminster Hall exhibition in London as well, *The Death of the Duke of York at the Battle of Agincourt*, which was awarded the Heywood silver medal by the Royal Manchester Institution in 1846. In that year he went to Rome and entered the studio of his father's friend John

Gibson, who observed that 'he is sadly behind in art' (23 June 1846, Crouchley papers). Sensing that Gibson's strict neo-classical style was not his métier, Spence joined the studio of Richard James Wyatt, the sculptor of serene nymphs, after whose death in 1850 he completed the works sold at Christies in London on 22 June 1861.

Spence's initial exhibit at the Royal Academy in 1848, *Lavinia* (on the London art market 1990), from James Thomson's *Seasons* (commissioned by the Liverpool builder Samuel Holme), displays the tranquillity characteristic of Wyatt's work. Subjects taken from favourite authors of the day, such as Robert Burns, Shakespeare, or Sir Walter Scott, became a hallmark of Spence's sculpture. *Highland Mary*, a sculpture of Burns's early love, first carved around 1852 for Charles Meigh of Grove House, Shelton, was his most popular work in this vein. Often repeated, a version was given as a birthday present by Prince Albert to Queen Victoria in 1853 (Royal Collection). Similar works include *The Angel's Whisper* (version *c.*1857, Musée d'Orsay, Paris), illustrating a lyric by Samuel Laver, and *The Lady of the Lake* (1861, Royal Collection), from Scott's poem, commissioned by Victoria and Albert as a companion to *Highland Mary* and *Oberon and Titania* (1866, Victoria and Albert Museum, London). These figures, while recognizably within Wyatt's classical style, are given precise identity by the addition of realistic details such as a plaid or thistle—in 'a new and popular character', according to William Bell Scott (Scott, 132). Although Spence showed at the RA six times, most sales came through contacts made in Rome: he did 'a good trade', commented Alfred Gatley, a fellow sculptor, as a result of his 'evening parties' (Gatley MSS). The Liverpool banker Richard Naylor, his most loyal patron, owned a version of *Highland Mary*, *Dora and Margaret Naylor*, *Mrs Naylor with Rowland and Christopher*, and *The Finding of Moses* (all Walker Art Gallery, Liverpool), the last of which was shown at the 1862 International Exhibition in London, and *The Seasons*. His only public commission, for St George's Hall in Liverpool, was *Reverend Jonathan Brooks (1775–1855), Rector of Liverpool* (*in situ*, St George's Hall); it was delivered in 1858 for £1200. For the Crystal Palace at Sydenham, Kent, he appropriately carved a monumental figure *Liverpool*.

After Spence's death from consumption and pulmonary disease at his father-in-law's house in Leghorn, Italy, on 28 October 1866, his widow, Rosina, daughter of G. H. Gower, the British consul there, gave twelve plasters from his studio to Liverpool (three survive in Picton Library, Liverpool). The remaining marbles were sold at Christies on 4 June 1870. Spence was among the last of the British artists who made a living in Rome by selling primarily to their visiting countrymen. His career represents the final phase of Rome's dominance on the visual arts in Britain.

TIMOTHY STEVENS

Sources T. J. Stevens, 'Roman heyday of an English sculptor', *Apollo*, 94 (1971), 226–31 · *Art Journal*, 28 (1866), 364 · W. B. Scott, *The British school of sculpture* (1871), 132 · S. C. Hall, T. K. Hervey, and others, *The gallery of modern sculpture*, unpaginated · exhibition catalogues [Liverpool Academy] · Graves, *RA exhibitors* · sale catalogue [Spence studio sale; Christies, 4 June 1870] · Richard James Wyatt studio sale catalogue [Christies, 22 June 1861] · Harris Museum and Art Gallery, Preston, John Crouchley papers · letters concerning royal commissions, Royal Arch. · priv. coll., Alfred Gatley MSS · *IGI* · Liverpool Academy, minute books, 1830–48, Walker Art Gallery, Liverpool · J. A. Picton, *Memorials of Liverpool*, rev. edn, 2 (1875), 218

Archives Royal Arch., letters · Walker Art Gallery, Liverpool, MSS and collection of his sculpture | Harris Museum and Art Gallery, Preston, John Crouchley MSS · Liverpool Central Library, Law Courts and St George's Hall Committee minutes, 1/2 452 · Liverpool Central Library, museum and education committee minutes, 1/8: 17, 20, 74, 75 · NRA, priv. coll., Alfred Gatley MSS

Likenesses oils · photograph, Walker Art Gallery, Liverpool

Spence, Catherine Helen (1825–1910), writer and reformer in Australia, was born on 31 October 1825 near Melrose, Scotland, the fifth of the eight children of David Spence (1789–1846), a writer, solicitor, and banker, and Helen Brodie (1791–1887). Her parents were both Scots and members of the established Church of Scotland. She attended Miss Sarah Phinn's protestant day school, St Mary's Convent, in Melrose, but plans for her to attend an advanced school for girls in Edinburgh failed when financial collapse compelled the family to emigrate to South Australia in 1839.

Determined not to add to the numbers she believed predestined to eternal damnation, and pleased at her first earnings from working as a governess, Spence decided against marriage and motherhood, though she brought up three families of other people's children in the course of her life. After a brief attempt to set up a school, she embarked upon the multifaceted career which led, by her eightieth birthday, to the announcement that she was 'the most distinguished woman they had had in Australia' (Sir Samuel James Way, quoted in *Catherine Helen Spence*).

Spence's career as a novelist stretched from the publication of *Clara Morison: a Tale of South Australia during the Gold Fever*, in 1854, until 1888–9, when her future-vision novella 'A Week in the Future' appeared in the *Centennial Magazine* in Sydney. During the intervening years she produced five novels and a religious allegory. Neglected from the late nineteenth century, these works underwent critical reassessment during the 1970s and 1980s, and all but three were either published for the first time or reprinted. Spence was hailed as the founder of a genre of realist fiction in Europe as well as Australia, and *Clara Morison* was described as 'the first colonial work that may fairly be compared with that of George Eliot or Elizabeth Gaskell' (Perkins, 146). Some, noting the critiques of gender-segmented labour markets in *Mr Hogarth's will* (1865), and of conventions governing marriage, most particularly in *Handfasted* (first published 1984)—the judges of a competition to which Spence submitted this novel in 1880 rejected it on the grounds that 'it was calculated to loosen the marriage tie—it was too socialistic, and consequently dangerous' (Spence, 63)—have claimed for her a pioneering place in feminist writing.

Her religious doubts banished by her conversion to Unitarianism in the 1850s, Spence embarked on work with the Boarding-Out Society, established in 1872, which led to her appointment to the new state children's council in 1887, and to the government destitute board in 1897. At

Catherine Helen Spence (1825–1910), by Bond & Co., 1890s

the invitation of the new state education department, she composed *The Laws we Live under* (1880), the first social studies textbook used in Australian schools. In 1878, after thirty years of publishing occasional press and journal articles under the pseudonym 'a Colonist of 1839', she was jubilant at being appointed 'a regular outside contributor' to the daily *South Australian Register*: 'I felt as if the round woman had got at last into the round hole which fitted her' (Spence, 55). This provided her not only with 'a very decent income' of around £300 a year, but also with a broad and influential canvas for the causes she wished to promote (Spence, 61). Principal among them was electoral reform, through the introduction of proportional representation, or, as she called it, 'effective voting' (ibid., 68). For this she took the skills in public speaking that she had developed as a preacher in the Unitarian church to public platforms throughout South Australia, in Melbourne, Sydney, and (in 1893–4) across the United States and in London. In promoting this cause she stood for election to the Federal Convention of 1897, thus becoming Australia's first female political candidate.

A latecomer to the campaign for female suffrage in South Australia, in 1894 the first Australian colony to grant to women the right to vote and also to stand for election, Spence nevertheless provided active support to suffragists throughout Australia, in the United States, and in England, and to other feminist organizations around the turn of the century. In 1905, this short, stout, eighty-year-old announced: 'I am a new woman, and I know it' (*Catherine Helen Spence*, 33). When she died, of heart failure, at her home in Queen Street, Norwood, Adelaide, on 3 April 1910 she was mourned as 'the Grand Old Woman of Australia' (Henry, 117). 'No more noteworthy woman ever lived in the Southern hemisphere', wrote the *Adelaide Register* (4 April 1910). She was buried on the following day at the Anglican cemetery, Glenelg. Spence is commemorated by a statue in Light Square, Adelaide, a scholarship, a section of a school, and an occasional-care centre.

SUSAN MAGAREY

Sources C. H. Spence, *An autobiography* (Adelaide, 1910) • E. J. Gunton, *Bibliography of Catherine Helen Spence* (1967) • S. Magarey, *Unbridling the tongues of women: a biography of Catherine Helen Spence* (1985) • J. F. Young, *Catherine Helen Spence: a study and an appreciation* (Melbourne, Australia, 1937) • D. Modjeska, *Exiles at home: Australian women writers, 1925–1945* (1981); repr. (North Ryde, New South Wales, 1991) • F. Giles, 'Romance: an embarassing subject', *The Penguin new literary history of Australia*, ed. L. Herganhan (1988), 223–37 • E. Perkins, 'Colonial transformations: writing and the dilemma of colonisation', *The Penguin new literary history of Australia*, ed. L. Herganhan (1988), 139–53 • S. Magarey, 'Feminist visions across the Pacific: Catherine Helen Spence's *Handfasted*', *Antipodes: A North American Journal of Australian Literature*, 3/1 (1989), 31–2 • H. Thompson, 'Love and labour: marriage and work in the novels of Catherine Helen Spence', *A bright and fiery troop: Australian women writers of the nineteenth century*, ed. D. Adelaide (1988), 101–11 • S. Magarey, 'Catherine Helen Spence — novelist', *Southwords: essays on South Australian writing*, ed. P. Butterss (1995), 27–45 • L. S. Morice, 'Auntie Kate', State Library of South Australia, Adelaide, Mortlock Library of South Australiana • A. Henry, 'Catherine Helen Spence: the grand old woman of Australia', *Survey* [New York] (1910), 117–18 • *The Register* [Adelaide] (4 April 1910) • *The Advertiser* [Adelaide] (4 April 1910)

Archives State Library of South Australia, Adelaide, Mortlock Library of South Australia | Mitchell L., NSW, Scott family MSS, Rose Scott MSS • Mitchell L., NSW, Miles Franklin MSS

Likenesses Bond & Co., photograph, 1890–99, NL Aus. [*see illus.*] • M. Preston, oils, 1911, Art Gallery of South Australia, Adelaide • I. Poscius, bronze statue, 1986, Light Square, Adelaide • M. Gordon, watercolours, State Library of South Australia, Adelaide, Mortlock Library of South Australiana • photograph, Mitchell L., NSW • photograph, repro. in Young, *Catherine Helen Spence* • photograph, repro. in *Adelaide Observer* (8 April 1893) • photograph, priv. coll. • two photographs, State Library of South Australia, Adelaide, Mortlock Library of South Australiana

Wealth at death £215: *AusDB*

Spence, Elizabeth Isabella (1768–1832), writer, was born on 12 January 1768 at Dunkeld, Perthshire, the only child of Dr James Spence (*d.* 1786), physician at Dunkeld, and his wife, Elizabeth (*d.* 1777), youngest daughter of George Fordyce, provost of Aberdeen (*d.* 1733), and sister of James Fordyce (1720–1796). Losing her parents early, Elizabeth Spence went to live in London with an uncle and aunt, and was by their death left destitute of relatives. She had already begun writing as a pastime, and now carried it on as a livelihood, producing works of fiction and travel narratives. Her first novel, published in 1799, was *Helen Sinclair*. Her books of travel include *Summer Excursions through Part of England and Wales*, published in 1809, and *Sketches of the Present Manners, Custom, and Scenery of Scotland*, of which the second edition bears the date 1811. The latter work was ridiculed in *Blackwood's Magazine* (3, 1818, 428–38) in an article entitled 'Miss Spence and the Bagman'.

Among Elizabeth Spence's friends were Lady Anne Barnard, Elizabeth Ogilvy Benger, the Porters, Laetitia Elizabeth Landon, and Sir Humphry Davy. Her other works include *Nobility of the Heart* (1804), *The Wedding Day* (1807), *The Curate and his Daughter: a Cornish Tale* (1813), *The Spanish Guitar* (1815), *Letters from the North Highlands* (1816), *A Traveller's Tale of Last Century* (1819), and *How to be Rid of a Wife* (1823). Elizabeth Isabella Spence died, unmarried, at Chelsea on 27 July 1832 of a paralytic stroke.

ELIZABETH LEE, *rev.* REBECCA MILLS

Sources Blain, Clements & Grundy, *Feminist comp.* • A. Dingwall Fordyce, *Family record of the name of Dingwall Fordyce in Aberdeenshire* (1885), 228 • *Annual Biography and Obituary*, 17 (1833), 367–71 • *GM*, 1st ser., 102/2 (1832), 650 • Watt, *Bibl. Brit.*, vol. 2 • Allibone, *Dict.*
Likenesses engraving, repro. in *La belle assemblée*, no. 185

Spence, George (1787–1850), jurist, was the second son of Thomas Richard Spence, surgeon, of Hanover Square, London. Educated at a private school at Richmond, Surrey, he matriculated at the University of Glasgow in 1802 and graduated MA in 1805. He was for a period in the office of a London solicitor before joining the Inner Temple in 1806. He was called to the bar on 28 June 1811. After a pupillage with John Bell (1764–1836), he was in good practice at the chancery bar. In 1819 he married Anne Kelsall, the daughter of a solicitor in Chester. He entered parliament, being elected in the tory interest for Reading (20 June 1826), but was unseated on petition (26 March 1827). He was later returned for Ripon (2 March 1829) and held that seat until the dissolution of December 1832, when he did not seek re-election, having voted for the Reform Act of 1832 against his party.

Spence took silk in December 1834 but he was not successful as a leading counsel and ceased to retain an active practice. Elected bencher of the Inner Temple in 1835, he became reader in 1845 and treasurer in 1846. He devoted the rest of his life to the cause of law reform and to the study of legal history, particularly the history of the chancery jurisdiction. He had raised the issue of chancery reform on several occasions in parliament and in pamphlets published in 1830 and 1839, and he was an original member of the Society for Promoting the Amendment of the Law, founded in 1844. His interest in legal history was evident as early as 1812 in an essay read to the Society of Clifford's Inn on the origin of English laws and institutions. In 1826 he published *An Inquiry into the Origin of the Laws and Political Institutions of Modern Europe*. The culmination of his researches was *The Equitable Jurisdiction of the Court of Chancery, comprising its Rise, Progress and Final Establishment*, the first volume of which appeared in the year of his Inner Temple treasurership (1846) and was dedicated to his fellow benchers. In two parts, it included a general historical survey and a historical and analytical account of the equitable jurisdiction. With the aid of Cecil Monro, registrar of the court of chancery, Spence was able to include some original material drawn from the court's records. The second volume (1849) was in the nature of a textbook on the substantive law of the court as it had developed by the middle of the nineteenth century. Spence was a jurist of wide interests, and though time has rendered some of his writing on general history and Roman law parallels somewhat obsolete, this work as a whole continued to serve as an important source of information on the development of equitable jurisdiction in England, surpassing everything previously published in that field. It was also a pioneering work in the field of comparative legal history.

Spence's health had been affected by his literary labours and in a fit of insanity he took his own life on 12 December 1850 at his home, 42 Hyde Park Square, London. His wife and two sons survived him.

D. E. C. YALE

Sources *The Times* (17 Dec 1850) • *Law Review*, 13 (1850–51), 431–3 • *Law Magazine*, 45 (1851), 130–31 • *GM*, 2nd ser., 35 (1851), 435 • Sainty, *King's counsel*, 105 • Holdsworth, *Eng. law*, 13.316–17, 496–8, 15.342–4
Likenesses T. Bragg, line engraving (after A. J. Oliver), NPG, BM

Spence, James (1812–1882), surgeon, son of James Spence, a merchant of Edinburgh, and his third wife (*née* Edwards), was born on 31 March 1812 in South Bridge Street, Edinburgh. He was educated in Galashiels, at a large boarding-school, and then at the high school, Edinburgh. He entered the University of Edinburgh in 1825, and began to study medicine with the intention of becoming an army surgeon. His medical studies were interrupted, and he was apprenticed to Messrs Scott and Orr, an eminent firm of chemists, of Princes Street, Edinburgh. He completed his medical education at the university and in the extramural school, and in 1832 he received the diploma of the College of Surgeons, Edinburgh, having previously spent some time in Paris studying anatomy and surgery.

As soon as he was qualified Spence made two voyages to Calcutta in 1833 as surgeon to *Protector*, a ship of the East India Company. He then returned to Edinburgh, where he had a severe attack of typhus fever. There he set up practice at 14 Rankeillor Street and began to teach anatomy as the university demonstrator under Professor Alexander Monro tertius; he held the position for seven years. He resigned his post in 1842 and joined P. D. Handyside and Henry Lonsdale in the extramural school of anatomy at 1 Surgeons' Square, to act as demonstrator in place of Allen Thomson, who had been appointed to the chair of physiology in the university. There Spence (who was nicknamed 'dismal Jemmy') took part in the lecture-room course of demonstrations on regional anatomy, as well as in the dissecting-room teaching. His teaching proved invaluable to the school, at that time the chief school of anatomy in Edinburgh. He was a remarkably dexterous dissector, and some of his beautiful preparations of the vascular system were preserved in the university.

Spence, who was in surgical practice while teaching anatomy, left the dissecting room in 1846 and began lecturing on surgery. On 13 October 1847 he married Margaret Sarah, the daughter of Thomas Fair of Buenos Aires. They had six sons and three daughters.

In 1849, on becoming a fellow of the College of Surgeons, Edinburgh he lectured first at High Schools Yards, adjoining the Royal Infirmary, where Robert Liston and

James Miller had lectured, and, on the death of Richard Mackenzie in 1854, at the school at Surgeons' Hall. In 1864, on the death of Professor James Miller, he was appointed professor of surgery in the university. He had been appointed assistant surgeon to the Royal Infirmary in 1850, full surgeon in 1854, clinical lecturer in 1856, and he continued, as professor of surgery, to act as surgeon at the infirmary until his death. He also served as surgeon to the Royal Public Dispensary and the Lock Hospital, and as consultant surgeon to the Royal Sick Children's Hospital and the Leith Hospital. He was appointed surgeon-in-ordinary to the queen in Scotland in 1865, fellow of the Royal Society of Edinburgh in 1866, president of the Royal College of Surgeons of Edinburgh in 1867 and 1868, and member of the General Medical Council in 1881, as a representative for the Royal College of Surgeons of Edinburgh.

Spence has been described as one of the great operating surgeons who made Edinburgh famous throughout the world. Like Liston, Fergusson, and Syme, he had an intimate knowledge of anatomy. He specialized in tracheotomy, herniotomy, urinary diseases, and amputations, yet he was essentially a conservative surgeon, and, like his great contemporary Sir William Scovell Savory, he maintained that, in skilled hands, the simple methods of the older school were preferable to, and gave as good results as, the more complicated system adopted by the disciples of the antiseptic school of Lister. After the death of James Syme in 1870 Spence became the leading consulting and operating surgeon at Edinburgh, and he occupied that position until his death. He died at his home, 21 Ainslie Place, Edinburgh, on 6 June 1882, and he was buried in the Grange cemetery, Edinburgh, on 9 June.

The work upon which Spence's reputation as a writer chiefly rests is his *Lectures on Surgery* (2 vols., 1868–9, 1871). He also contributed many papers on anatomical and surgical subjects to various Scottish, English, and Irish scientific journals. D'A. POWER, *rev.* KAYE BAGSHAW

Sources *Edinburgh Medical Journal*, 28 (1882–3), 89–96 • *The Lancet* (17 June 1882), 1011–13 • *BMJ* (17 June 1882), 928–9 • A. Boyle and F. Bennet, eds., *The Royal Society of Edinburgh: 100 medical fellows elected 1841–1882* (1983), vol. 4 of *Scotland's cultural heritage* (1981–4) • parish register (marriage), St Cuthbert's, Edinburgh, 1847

Archives U. Edin. • U. St Andr.

Likenesses Durand, etching (after Irvine); replica, formerly at Royal College of Surgeons, Edinburgh, 1897 • J. Irvine, oils (after portrait by unknown artist, exh. 1881), RCS Eng. • photograph, U. Edin.

Wealth at death £3978 4*s*. 2*d*.: confirmation, 18 Oct 1882, *CCI* • £122 13*s*. 0*d*.: additional estate, 2 March 1883, *CCI* • £1070 16*s*. 7*d*.: additional estate, 7 Feb 1907, *CCI*

Spence, Sir James Calvert (1892–1954), paediatrician, was born in Queen Street, Amble, Northumberland, on 19 March 1892, the fourth son and seventh child of David Magnus Spence, an architect, and his wife, Isabella Turnbull, both of old Northumbrian stock. He was educated at Elmfield College, York, and then studied medicine in Newcastle upon Tyne at the Durham University College of Medicine, starting in 1909. He was an undistinguished student academically but made up for it by his prowess as a soccer player, captaining both the college and the university as a centre half. It was a matter of some surprise when he graduated in 1914 with second-class honours.

Spence had always been active in the Officers' Training Corps as a student and on the outbreak of war in August 1914 he immediately joined up. He was posted to a field ambulance and stayed with it until after the end of the war in 1919. He served at Gallipoli and later in Belgium. In August 1917 Revere Osler, son of the famous physician Sir William Osler (and the great-great-grandson of Paul Revere), was brought into his casualty clearing station; in spite of all efforts Revere died. Spence's bravery in the field was rewarded with the Military Cross and later with a bar.

Spence returned to civilian life as a house physician at the Royal Victoria Infirmary in Newcastle and then casualty officer at the Hospital for Sick Children, Great Ormond Street, London. He became interested in the emerging subject of clinical biochemistry and went to work on sugar metabolism at St Thomas's Hospital, London. While in London he met and, on 28 September 1920, married Kathleen Margaret (*b*. 1892/3), daughter of Robert Downie-Leslie, an advocate; the couple had a son and four daughters. They returned to Newcastle in 1922, and Spence took up the post there of medical registrar and chemical pathologist to the Royal Victoria Infirmary. He was able to resume his interest in children when he joined the medical staff of a day nursery which had been set up by a wealthy local woman to look after the children of munitions workers. This day nursery eventually developed into the Babies Hospital and was the foundation of Spence's work with children. He quickly realized the important role that mothers can play in the care of their sick children. At a time when mothers were generally allowed to visit their sick children only once each week, and then only to view them through a window, he encouraged mothers to 'room in'. This was the foundation of social paediatrics, with which Spence will always be associated.

In 1926–7 Spence spent a year as a Rockefeller fellow at Johns Hopkins Hospital in Baltimore. Here he laid the foundations of many American friendships. He spent the year in Baltimore with a colleague from Newcastle, D. A. F. Bernard Shaw, a lecturer in pathology and nephew of George Bernard Shaw. They both admired the scientific approach to medicine they saw in Baltimore, and brought many new ideas back to Newcastle. In 1928 Spence was appointed assistant physician to the infirmary, but his practice was largely with adults. Until 1931 his scientific papers had related mainly to laboratory work, but in that year he published a report on seventeen children with nutritional xerophthalmia and night-blindness. In 1933 Spence was invited by the Medical Research Council to undertake a study of calciferol in rickets. The study proved the effectiveness of calciferol and laid further foundations for his lifelong interest in the nutrition and welfare of children in his native north-east.

In 1933 Spence made his first scientific study in community and social paediatrics. Newcastle, like much of the north, was suffering from the effects of the economic depression. There was concern in the city about increasing poverty and the great increase in sickness and malnutrition. The city council asked Spence to undertake a comparative study of 'the health and nutrition of the children in Newcastle upon Tyne between the ages of one and five years'. He showed that thirty-six per cent of children from the poorer districts of the city were unhealthy or physically unfit and apparently malnourished, and suggested that because he was unable to find similar ill health in the well-off areas of the city there might be preventable factors. A subsequent study of infant mortality, again commissioned by the city council, found very high levels of mortality in the poorer areas of the city. The main cause seemed to be infection. These two studies led to one of the first longitudinal cohort studies. The outbreak of the Second World War meant that it was 1947 before the 'thousand families' were recruited. The study was intended to look at the social correlates of morbidity and mortality in the first year of life. Spence, with his junior colleague Fred Miller, harnessed the considerable resources of the city's health visitors, who visited every one of the thousand families on at least a monthly basis and kept meticulous records. The study clearly showed links between poverty and ill health. It was so successful that it was extended to the end of the school years, long after Spence's death. The four books of the study are a tribute to his vision and to the inspiration of Fred Miller. The results of the thousand families study shaped the practice of community paediatrics for the next fifty years. In 1997 the detailed records initiated by Spence half a century earlier allowed a further follow-up on the cohort at the age of fifty. This study showed once again that adult ill health is greatly influenced by lifestyle factors.

In the first half of the twentieth century paediatrics was just emerging as a separate discipline, and Spence was at the forefront of its evolution. One of his great strengths was his recognition that there could be no progress without scientific study, and this was the subject of his lecture to the British Postgraduate Medical Federation in 1953 entitled 'The methodology of clinical science'. In 1942 the Nuffield Foundation had decided to establish in Newcastle the first department of child health in England, and Spence was appointed professor. Wartime conditions prevented the department from functioning properly, but immediately after hostilities ceased Newcastle became the mecca for aspiring paediatricians from all over the world. Spence made several visits to Australia and was the inspiration behind the establishment of the Australian College of Paediatrics. He greatly influenced Eric Saint, the foundation professor of medicine in Perth and later dean in Queensland. Saint thought that Spence 'had the enviable capacity to communicate the excitement of science and medicine, and … prompted us to consider its social relevance'. He described him as 'slim built with fine features, a penetrating gaze of the eye, remarkably articulate using a conversational style which embraced wit and irony'.

Spence had also been at the forefront of the British Paediatric Association when it was set up in 1928, but it was not until 1950 that he was elected its president. During the Second World War Spence's administrative talents came to the fore, and he was called upon to undertake many important national roles. He was appointed chairman of the social medicine committee of the Royal College of Physicians, and joined the advisory committee of the Nuffield Provincial Hospitals Trust. This was followed by membership of the University Grants Committee and (twice) of the Medical Research Council. He took part in many of the discussions which led to the formation of the National Health Service in 1948 and was on the original Ministry of Health Central Health Services Council.

Spence's department in Newcastle grew rapidly and his teaching was greatly sought after by medical students as well as paediatricians in training. He had a particular skill in bringing a social context to illness. His Babies Hospital had been evacuated to the country during the war, but it was re-established in Newcastle and became a focus for his work on caring for children and their mothers, as well as for teaching. Spence's reputation as a paediatrician, educationist, and philosopher led to many invitations from abroad. He visited Belgium, Czechoslovakia, Australia, New Zealand, Canada, and the United States. In 1949 he delivered the Cutter lecture at Harvard entitled 'Family studies in preventive paediatrics'. This was based on the early results of the thousand families study. He made many important contributions to the literature, and his two lectures to the Royal College of Physicians, the Bradshaw and the Charles West lectures, have continued to be influential. They were entitled 'The nature of disease in infancy' and 'The care of children in hospital'.

Spence was universally accepted by his contemporaries as a wise counsellor, moderate in presenting his views but enthusiastic and a practical-minded visionary. As a clinician he was of the highest calibre, and his sensitivity to the needs and fears of patients and parents made him a supremely understanding and sought-after physician. He had a whimsical charm which made him a most attractive personality. His scientific ability was probably overshadowed by his clinical interests, but as a teacher, a leader, and an inspiration to younger men he was exceptional. He wrote: 'the first aim of my department is comradeship not achievement' (*DNB*). His achievements were great and his constructive and far-sighted aims for British medicine were recognized by a knighthood in 1950.

Spence was a lover of the countryside and especially the mountains and fells. He was an experienced alpinist and conquered the Matterhorn. He died at his home, 25 Brandling Park, Newcastle upon Tyne, from haemorrhage, exhaustion, and bronchogenic carcinoma on 26 May 1954. He was survived by his wife. ALAN W. CRAFT

Sources *The purpose and practice of medicine: selected writings of Sir James Spence* (1960) · *BMJ* (5 June 1954) · *The Lancet* (5 June 1954) · F. J. W. Miller, 'Sir James Spence', *Journal of Medical Biography*, 5 (1997), 1–7 · E. G. Saint, *On good doctoring* (privately printed, 1998) · *DNB* · m. cert. · d. cert.

Wealth at death £13,992 12s. 0d.: probate, 15 Dec 1954, *CGPLA Eng. & Wales*

Spence, Joseph [*pseud.* Sir Harry Beaumont] (**1699–1768**), literary scholar and anecdotist, was born at Kingsclere, north Hampshire, on 28 April 1699. His father, Joseph (*bap.* 1661, *d.* 1715), was rector of Winnal in Winchester and precentor of the cathedral. His mother, Mirabella, *née* Collier (1670–1755), was granddaughter of Sir Thomas Lunsford (1610–1653). Joseph was their eldest son; two other boys and a girl survived to adulthood.

In 1709 Joseph was sent to school in Mortimer, close to his birthplace, after which he was briefly at Eton College before moving to Winchester College in 1715; his early education was paid for by Mrs Fawkener, a relative. He matriculated at Magdalen Hall, Oxford, on 11 April 1717, but did not go up until he was admitted as scholar or probationary fellow at New College on 22 April 1720. He was advanced to full fellowship on 30 April 1722, took his BA on 9 March 1724 and MA on 2 November 1727, and was ordained in the Oxford diocese on 5 June 1726. His early literary friends included fellow Wykehamists Robert Lowth, Christopher Pitt, Glocester Ridley, and Edward Young.

Spence's *Essay on Pope's 'Odyssey'* (1726) brought its author the friendship of Pope, who commented upon the manuscript of part two of the *Essay* (published 1727). Thanks partly to the *Essay* and partly to Pope's influential friends, Spence was elected to the Oxford chair of poetry (stipend £180 p.a., later increased to £200) on 11 July 1728; he held the post for ten years, the maximum allowed. Also in July 1728 he was presented to the New College living of Birchanger, Essex; but he continued to hold his fellowship and live mostly in Oxford when not travelling abroad. He became a regular visitor to Pope's house and began taking notes of conversations with Pope and other literary and public figures.

Recommended by Pope, Spence was travelling companion of Charles Sackville, Lord Middlesex (later second duke of Dorset), on a grand tour which lasted from December 1730 to July 1733 and included stays of several months each in Dijon, Lyons, Venice, and Florence. During Spence's absence abroad, his *Account* of Stephen Duck was published (1731): the first of his studies of 'natural genius'. Back in Oxford he lectured and made unremarkable contributions to poetry collections marking royal weddings, births, and deaths. He wrote 'The Charliad', a feeble imitation of Pope's *Dunciad*, and, in prose, a Scriblerian-satirical 'Life of Charles Magot' (both unpublished). In honour of his first pupil and at Pope's suggestion he published *An Account of Lord Buckhurst* (1736) and an edition of *Gorboduc*, censured as spurious by the antiquary Thomas Coxeter.

Between May 1737 and February 1738 Spence was in the Netherlands, Flanders, and France as travelling companion of John Morley Trevor (1717–1743), a distant relative of the duke of Newcastle, and between September 1739 and November 1741 he travelled in Italy with Henry Fiennes Clinton, earl of Lincoln, later second duke of Newcastle under Lyme. During each tour Spence wrote frequent lively, graphic, and amusing letters to his mother, which he later edited for publication but never published.

Joseph Spence (**1699–1768**), by Rosalba Carriera, 1741

Lord Lincoln's powerful relatives brought patronage Spence's way. On 4 June 1742 he became regius professor of modern history at Oxford (worth £400 p.a.), an appointment confirmed under the new reign in 1761. Also in 1742 Spence exchanged Birchanger for the richer New College living of Great Horwood, Buckinghamshire (about £500 p.a.). He did not reside at Horwood, but made annual visits, when he distributed generous charity. He relinquished his New College fellowship and settled with his mother in London about 1742, whence he often visited Pope.

Spence wrote occasionally for his friend Robert Dodsley's periodical, *The Museum* (1746); he contributed advice (and one poem) to Dodsley's *Collection of Poems* (1748–58). His long gestated *Polymetis* was published as a lavishly illustrated folio in February 1747 and earned him at least £1450 by subscription and sale of copyright. Conceived during Spence's first visit to Italy and with much of its material collected there, *Polymetis* was intended to show how the works of ancient artists and of Roman poets illustrate and explain one another. It was attacked in Gotthold Ephraim Lessing's *Laokoon* (1766) and, though new editions appeared in 1755 and 1774, and abridged versions for the use of schools were current until the 1820s, it sank fairly quickly from serious notice. However, it proved an invaluable guide to mythological images for Keats.

In 1748 Lord Lincoln gave Spence the lifetime use of a house he owned at Byfleet, Surrey. Spence moved there with his mother (aged nearly eighty) and, using profits from *Polymetis*, developed his long-standing interest in landscape gardening. Already he had laid out at Birchanger a small, simple version of Pope's Twickenham garden, he had planted extensively at Great Horwood, and, in London, had provided garden plans and notes for friends. Now at Byfleet he developed his 30 acre estate as a *ferme ornée* (like nearby Wooburn, home of Philip Southcote), and improved his own views when neighbours asked his advice about landscaping their estates. Though he never completed his gardening treatise, 'Tempe', for which he made many notes, he translated Jean-Denis Attiret's influential account of the emperor of China's gardens, which praises 'beautiful disorder'. This translation was published (1752) as the work of Sir Harry Beaumont, a pen name Spence adopted also for *Crito* (1752), a slight, genteel, classically inspired work on aesthetics, and *Moralities* (1753), a miscellany of prose essays, Aesopian fables, and translations, mostly reprinted from Dodsley's *Museum*. *Crito*, like the *Essay on Pope's 'Odyssey'* and *Polymetis*, was in dialogue form because the first person singular seemed arrogant to Spence.

In 1752 Spence procured the living of Byfleet for his friend Stephen Duck. In the next two years he published accounts of two other 'natural geniuses' of humble origin: Robert Hill, the learned tailor, and Thomas Blacklock, the blind poet. Spence promoted a subscription edition of Blacklock's poems and in 1758 travelled with Dodsley to see Blacklock in Scotland, visiting William Shenstone at The Leasowes for a week *en route*. In the same year he arranged for the printing at Horace Walpole's Strawberry Hill Press of his *Parallel in the Manner of Plutarch* (1758) between a famously learned Florentine librarian and Robert Hill, in order to raise funds for Hill. Spence also contributed notes to the edition of Virgil (1753) by Joseph Warton and edited the *Remarks on Virgil* (1768) of another Wykehamist friend, Edward Holdsworth.

On 24 May 1754 Spence was installed as a prebendary of Durham, a preferment in the gift of the bishop, Richard Trevor. Byfleet continued to be Spence's main home but he spent more than the minimum of three weeks' residence annually at Durham, where he improved the garden of his prebendal estate and those of neighbours, including the bishop and the earl of Darlington at Raby. His travels took him, weeks at a time, to landscape gardens where his advice was solicited. Sometimes Dodsley travelled with him; it was on one of their northern excursions in 1764 that Dodsley died at Spence's Durham house.

In June 1766 Spence suffered a mild stroke during his annual journey north. He made his will at Sedgefield, Durham, on 4 August 1766, and on 24 March 1767 sold his copyrights (including rights over unpublished works) to James Dodsley for £100. On 20 August 1768 he was found lying on his face in the shallow ornamental waters of his garden at Byfleet, probably drowned in a fit. He was buried at St Mary's, Byfleet, four days later. His wealth at death was more than £1800, not counting the voluminous unpublished writings bequeathed to his executors and residuary legatees (Lowth, Ridley, and the Revd Edward Rolle) with the request that nothing further of his should be printed, unless by their joint judgement and approbation.

Spence's unpublished writings included edited 'travelling letters', notes for a gardening treatise, notes for a biographical history of English poetry, and valuable 'Anecdotes' noted from conversations with Pope and others. The executors decided that nothing should be printed, and cancelled the agreement with James Dodsley. A handsomely bound transcript of the 'Anecdotes' was presented to Spence's patron the duke of Newcastle (formerly Lord Lincoln); other papers, including a fuller text of the 'Anecdotes' than the Newcastle transcript, were lost to view until they were acquired by a bookseller named Carpenter, who commissioned Samuel Weller Singer to prepare an edition. By the end of the century material from the Newcastle transcript had appeared in Warburton's edition of Pope, Joseph Warton's *Essay* on Pope, Ruffhead's biography of Pope, Johnson's *Lives of the Poets*, Malone's biography of Dryden, and elsewhere. The copy of much of the Newcastle transcript made by Malone came into the hands of John Murray (1778–1843): he and Carpenter raced to print, and rival editions of the *Anecdotes* were published in January 1820 on, it was said, the same day. As Singer had very much more material, his version was incomparably better than Murray's. The authoritative edition is by James M. Osborn (1966).

Spence's *Anecdotes* is his chief claim to fame. Primarily valuable as a rich biographical source for others, it reflects its scribe: self-effacing, conscientious, discriminating, knowledgeable, and kindly. His friends commended his sweet temper and amiability; he is portrayed as the benevolent Phesoi Ecneps in *Tales of the Genii* (1764) by James Ridley, son of his friend Glocester. Spence was about 5 feet tall and spindly; he was a valetudinarian; he never married. JAMES SAMBROOK

Sources A. Wright, *Joseph Spence: a critical biography* (1950) · J. Spence, *Observations, anecdotes, and characters, of books and men*, ed. J. M. Osborn, new edn, 2 vols. (1966) · J. Spence, *Letters from the grand tour*, ed. S. Klima (1975) · J. Spence, *Anecdotes, observations, and characters, of books and men*, ed. S. W. Singer, 2nd edn (1858) · *The correspondence of Alexander Pope*, ed. G. Sherburn, 5 vols. (1956) · registers of admissions and of business transacted, New College, Oxford · P. D. Mundy, 'Extracts from letters from Joseph Spence, 1739–1762', *N&Q*, 189 (1945), 252–5, 271–3 · Nichols, *Lit. anecdotes*, 1.643–5, 2.373–7, 8.98 · M. Laird, *The flowering of the landscape garden: English pleasure grounds, 1720–1800* (1999) · R. W. King, 'Joseph Spence of Byfleet', *Garden History*, 6/3 (1978), 38–64; 7/3 (1979), 29–48; 8/3 (1980), 44–65, 77–114 · Walpole, *Corr.*, vols. 17, 20, 30, 40 · Foster, *Alum. Oxon.* · Venn, *Alum. Cant.* · T. F. Kirby, *Winchester scholars: a list of the wardens, fellows, and scholars of … Winchester College* (1888), 225 · *Fasti Angl.* (Hardy), 3.315, 530

Archives BL, corresp. and accounts of tours, Egerton MSS 2234–2235 · BL, lectures, Add. MS 17281 · Hunt. L., corresp. and literary MSS · U. Nott., corresp. and papers · Yale U., Beinecke L., bound literary MSS and papers · Yale U., Beinecke L., letters and papers | Bodl. Oxf., corresp. with Christopher Pitt

Likenesses R. Carriera, pastel drawing, 1741, priv. coll. [*see illus.*] · T. Cook, engraving (after engraving by G. Vertue), repro. in Spence, *Observations*, vol. 2, frontispiece · G. Vertue, line engraving (after I. Whood), BM, NPG; repro. in J. Spence, *Polymetis* (1747)

Wealth at death £1813 15*s*. 10*d*.: Wright, *Joseph Spence*, 175–6, 247

Spence, (James) Lewis Thomas Chalmers (1874–1955), poet and Scottish nationalist, was born at Darlington Cottage, Seafield, Broughty Ferry, Forfarshire, on 25 November 1874, the eldest of four children of James Edward Kendall Spence, insurance agent and house proprietor, and his wife, Barbara Charlotte Chalmers. His grandfather was James *Spence, professor of surgery at the University of Edinburgh. Other relatives included Thomas Chalmers, leader of the Free Church of Scotland, and James Spence, inventor of the adhesive postal stamp. Spence was educated at the collegiate school, Broughty Ferry, and privately at Ongar School, Essex, before studying dentistry at the University of Edinburgh, where he took his MA. He chose journalism as a career, and from 1899 to 1904 was a sub-editor on *The Scotsman*. On 25 November 1899 he married Helen (1876/7–1942), daughter of George Bruce, cabinet-maker, of Edinburgh. They had a son and three daughters. He edited a short-lived *Edinburgh Magazine* before moving in 1906 to London to work for the *British Weekly* which, under William Robertson Nicoll, was a vehicle for the kailyard school of Scottish writing.

In 1909 Spence returned to Edinburgh to work as a freelance, as he would do for the rest of his life. He prospered best from feeding public taste for the occult and supernatural, with a special sideline on the lost continent of Atlantis. But he was also a genuine, scholarly expert on mythology and folklore, especially of Central and South America, and became a fellow of the Anthropological Institute of Great Britain and Ireland. He wrote many books on these matters, notably *Myths and Legends of Mexico and Peru* (1913), *An Encyclopaedia of Occultism* (1920), *An Introduction to Mythology* (1923), and *The Magic Arts in Celtic Britain* (1945).

Poetry was less lucrative but more satisfying. After publishing two early, somewhat precious, volumes of verse Spence started composing in Scots. He was thus among the first to set about raising the modern language to the literary stature it had lost, by enriching it with archaic words and phrases. In doing so, he reacted against what he called the 'gutter Scots' of some vernacular verse, such as Charles Murray's, which sought to echo the voice of the people in sub-Burnsian fashion. His borrowings from the past also extended to poetic forms such as sonnets or roundels, though his range of themes was conventional and generally limited to nature or mythology. He aimed at a magical quality, such as he thought to find in the English romantics and in Scottish ballads. The praises he sang to various suburbs of Edinburgh, 'Ae dawin, frae Corstorphine lea', 'The Fute Fa's Kind at Craigentinnie', 'Now June has hid Craigmillar's wa', did not always hit the elevated note he sought. Near the end of his life he brought out his *Collected Verse* (1953) and there—though it by no means contained his whole output—he let the English outnumber the Scots poems by two to one. His efforts had once been praised by Christopher Murray Grieve (Hugh MacDiarmid) for their exquisite sensory and intellectual quality. But bitter argument on art and politics afterwards destroyed the early friendship of the pair.

As a youth Spence had already become a member of the

(James) Lewis Thomas Chalmers Spence (1874–1955), by David Foggie, 1933

Scottish Home Rule Association and he wrote numerous articles or essays about its cause. Feeling, like other contemporary writers, the need for a deeper political commitment, he joined the Scots National League in the 1920s. It came together with three other bodies to form in 1926 the Scottish National Movement, of which he was elected president. In 1928 this in turn combined with remaining splinter groups into the National Party of Scotland, parent of the Scottish National Party. Spence became a vice-chairman. He was the first to try its strength at the hustings. As candidate in a four-cornered by-election in North Midlothian in January 1929, he polled 842 votes and lost his deposit. The party remained fissile. In 1932 Spence made a public avowal of his personal convictions, including unreserved loyalty to the crown. The consequence was a motion of censure on him in the party's national council, which he forestalled by resigning his post. He took the chance to denounce tendencies distasteful to him, the utopianism of the pan-Celticists round Compton Mackenzie and the socialist leanings, as he saw them, of adherents of the social credit propounded by Major C. H. Douglas. Before long he left the party altogether. He played no further role in politics, but devoted himself exclusively to writing. In later years he turned to short stories and plays, and also edited the *Atlantean Journal*.

Spence attached high importance to the revival of Scots poetry, but his own work seldom rose above an undemanding, often historical romanticism. He died on 3 March 1955 at his home, 34 Howard Place, Edinburgh.

MICHAEL FRY

Sources *Glasgow Herald* (4 March 1955) · *The Scotsman* (4 March 1955) · *The Times* (4 March 1955) · *Scottish biographies* (1938) · *WWW* · b. cert. · m. cert. · d. cert. · T. Royle, *The Macmillan companion to Scottish literature* (1983)
Archives NL Scot., corresp. and papers | NL Scot., letters to J. P. McGillivray · NL Scot., letters to Robert Muirhead
Likenesses D. Foggie, chalk drawing, 1933, Scot. NPG [*see illus.*] · photographs, *Glasgow Herald* Library · photographs, *The Scotsman* Library
Wealth at death £807 11*s*. 3*d*.: confirmation, 7 Oct 1955, *CCI*

Spence, Peter (1806–1883), industrial chemist and alum manufacturer, was born on 19 February 1806 in Brechin, Forfarshire, Scotland, the younger son of a hand-loom weaver of Brechin, and his wife, whose family had been farmers for generations. Spence was educated at the parish school in Brechin, but began his working life very early, apprenticed to a grocer, an uncle, in Perth. After finishing his apprenticeship he set up a business with this uncle, but it failed.

In 1832 Spence married Agnes (*d*. 1883), second daughter of Francis Mudie, linen manufacturer, of Dundee. They had four sons and four daughters. In the same year he joined a gasworks in Dundee, where he acquired a good knowledge of practical chemistry and patented minor innovations in manufacture (for example, of Prussian blue). In 1834 he set up on his own in London as a general chemical manufacturer. He did not prosper, and moved to Burgh by Sands, near Carlisle. There his fortune changed after his discovery in 1845, after much experimentation, of a new and rapid method of making alum from coal shale (colliery refuse) and the ammoniacal liquor by-product of gasworks. Alum, an outstanding mordant, was an essential chemical for the printing and dyeing of textiles and was also used in the treatment of sewage and in paper manufacture. In 1846 he moved his main manufacture to Pendleton, near Manchester, and became the principal supplier of this important substance. He opened a second factory in Gode in 1854. His ammonium alum gradually displaced the potash alum which had been made principally at Whitby. Spence was awarded a medal for his process at the exhibition of 1862. In the 1860s he had become interested in copper smelting, and in 1866 he set up a company in Gode to develop his ideas. He was forced to sell this in the 1870s, after the failure in Redonda, in the West Indies, of his company formed to mine phosphate deposits and convert them to fertilizers.

As a staunch Congregationalist Spence was active in social reform, notably in promoting total abstinence. He also campaigned against pollution but suffered the irony of being prosecuted himself for pollution in 1857, which caused him to move his works to Miles Platting. He never forgave the chemist Edward Frankland, who had been a colleague, for appearing for the prosecution. He was an active member of the Manchester Literary and Philosophical Society, his papers to it showing a wide range of interests. Spence died at his home, Erlington House, Whalley Range, Manchester, on 7 July 1883.

FRANK GREENAWAY, *rev.*

Sources J. Fenwick Allen, *Some founders of the chemical industry: men to be remembered* (1906) · D. W. F. Hardie, 'Chemical pioneers 9: Peter Spence', *Chemical Age*, 78 (1957), 219 · P. J. T. Morris and C. A. Russell, *Archives of the British chemical industry, 1750–1914: a handlist* (1988) · *CGPLA Eng. & Wales* (1884)
Likenesses portrait, repro. in C. Singer, *The earliest chemical industry* (1948), 285
Wealth at death £15,661 6*s*. 5*d*.: probate, 25 June 1884, *CGPLA Eng. & Wales*

Spence, Robert (1905–1976), chemist, was born on 7 October 1905 in South Shields, co. Durham, the only child of Robert Spence, a marine engineer, and his wife, Rebecca Robertson. He was educated at the Stanhope Road elementary school (1911–17) and the Westoe secondary grammar school (1917–22) at South Shields, before going in 1922 to Armstrong College (then part of the University of Durham) in Newcastle upon Tyne. He obtained a first-class BSc in chemistry in 1926, and was awarded a Department of Scientific and Industrial Research grant (1926–8) to work with G. R. Clemo in research on the production and constitution of some polynuclear compounds derived from naphthalene.

In 1928 Spence became a Commonwealth Fund fellow at Princeton University, USA, for three years. He studied the vapour phase oxidation of ethylene (ethene) and acetylene (ethyne) in collaboration with Hugh Stott Taylor and G. B. Kistiakowsky, taking his PhD in 1930. He received an excellent physico-chemical training there, and found that the American ideals of self-help and respect for hard work influenced his personal outlook on life.

In 1931 Spence was appointed as a lecturer in physical chemistry at the University of Leeds. There he investigated a number of thermal and photo-oxidations and the photodecomposition of gaseous acetone (propanone), showing that the production of an acetyl radical is an essential step in the decomposition process. On 25 July 1936 he married Kate Lockwood, one of his students, with whom he shared a close and happy partnership. They had three children: Alan, Catherine, and James.

During the Second World War Spence, who had joined the Territorial Army in 1936, was seconded to the RAF and sent to Egypt, in July 1942, as a scientific adviser (chemical warfare). He developed a new method of dispersing dense clouds of smoke from aircraft, and showed that, contrary to contemporary opinion, mustard gas attacks in hot climates presented a serious vapour hazard. The following year, in Italy, he pioneered anti-malaria spray techniques, and after returning to Britain in November 1944 he worked on fuels for jet engines.

After the war Spence worked for two years in the Anglo-Canadian Atomic Energy Laboratories, at Montreal and Chalk River, on the development of a continuous process for the large-scale recovery of plutonium from irradiated uranium; before a plant could be designed, every detail of the chemistry had to be known. This complicated engineering task (laboratory methods had to be scaled up by a factor of many millions to produce the kilogram quantities needed) proved so successful that separation began on the planned date (February 1952) and proceeded quickly: the plutonium required for the first British atomic bomb was delivered six months later. In recognition of his contribution to Britain's early atomic development Spence was appointed CB in 1953.

While in Canada Spence was responsible for recruiting staff for the research that would later be carried out in England in the radiochemical laboratory constructed to his design at Harwell, Berkshire. In 1946 he became head of the chemistry division of the Atomic Energy Research Establishment at Harwell. He was later chief chemist (1950–60), deputy director (1960–64), and director (1964–8). There he was responsible for the chemical aspects of nuclear power, including the production of fuel elements and special reactor materials, waste disposal, processing of irradiated materials, and coolants. His successes lay in conceiving and organizing major industrial processes, but he maintained a personal interest in problems of an experimental nature, particularly the extraction of uranium from sea water.

Spence served on a number of technical committees at Harwell, together with terms on the councils of the Chemical Society, the Faraday Society, and the Royal Institute of Chemistry. He was elected FRS in 1959 and participated in the Royal Society's government grant board and its scientific research in schools committee. Most of his published work (over fifty papers, 1928–72) appeared in British science journals.

Spence was quiet and unassuming, devoted to his family and his profession. He was unfailingly courteous, but determined and always well prepared. His friendliness, foresight, example, and enthusiasm were an inspiring influence on junior colleagues. A tall man, he enjoyed outdoor pursuits such as rowing, walking, and canoeing. In 1968 Spence left Harwell, where economic and political pressures had made his job increasingly uncongenial, and became master of Keynes College and professor of applied chemistry in the University of Kent at Canterbury. His main interest focused on the college and its students: he implanted an attitude of tolerance and mutual forbearance into a young institution composed of disparate elements. He played a vital role in the creation of an honours degree in chemistry with control engineering, and supervised experimental projects. At his retirement in 1973 Spence returned to Ranger Cottage, 5 Jennings Lane, his home in Harwell village, where he died of lung cancer on 10 March 1976. He was survived by his wife.

K. D. WATSON

Sources E. Glueckauf, *Memoirs FRS*, 23 (1977), 501–28 · W. A. Campbell and N. N. Greenwood, *Contemporary British chemists* (1971), 211–12 · *WWW* · *The Times* (12 March 1976), 16g · *The Times* (23 March 1976), 16g · M. Gowing and L. Arnold, *Independence and deterrence: Britain and atomic energy, 1945–1952*, 2 vols. (1974) · A. G. Debus and others, eds., *World who's who in science* (1968)

Archives U. Leeds, Brotherton L.

Likenesses W. Bird, photograph, repro. in Campbell and Greenwood, *Contemporary British chemists*, 211–12

Wealth at death £51,316: probate, 22 April 1976, *CGPLA Eng. & Wales*

Spence, Thomas (1750–1814), radical and bookseller, was born on the Quayside of Newcastle upon Tyne on 21 June 1750. His father, Jeremiah Spence, had arrived in Newcastle from Aberdeen about 1739, while his mother, Margaret Flet, his father's second wife, came from the Orkneys. Jeremiah, who fathered nineteen children, was at first a net-maker and later sold hardware goods from a booth on the Sandhill. Always a poor but hard-working man, he was deeply religious and encouraged his children to read the Bible daily. Denied a formal education and forced to work even as a child, Thomas began to read widely, and gradually educated himself enough to advance from being a clerk to becoming a schoolmaster in Haydon Bridge and Newcastle. While at Haydon Bridge he married a Miss Elliott from Hexham in the early 1780s. Although the marriage was apparently not a happy one, a son, William, was born soon afterwards. This son later went to London with his father and there helped him to distribute his radical tracts; he died as a teenager about 1797. Within two years of the death of his first wife in 1792 Spence married a servant girl in London, but this marriage soon broke down irretrievably, though Spence appears to have paid this second wife, about whom further details are unknown, a small weekly allowance after they separated.

Early career, 1775–c.1788 Although in many ways a committed educator, Spence was more interested throughout his life in educating poor adults than children, and he was not a great success as a schoolteacher. Barely 5 feet tall, slightly built, very poorly dressed, and physically unimpressive (a situation made worse by a stroke or attack of palsy which left him with a limp and a speech impediment), he did not immediately command respect. Very enthusiastic in putting over his own point of view, he was not very good at listening to others, and he could be aggressive when faced with disagreement or opposition. Once convinced of the rightness of his opinions, he could be obstinate in their defence and unwilling to countenance any objections. He insisted on speaking his mind freely and fearlessly, a practice which was admired by some and deplored by others. Warm in his attachment to his friends, he could be abrasive and hostile to those not convinced of what he regarded as the obvious rationality, truth, and benefit of his ideas and schemes for reform. Quite early in his career as a teacher he developed ideas on the teaching of English by means of a phonetic alphabet. He published several works explaining the virtue of his new alphabet for both the uneducated poor and foreigners learning the English language. The most important of these was *The Grand Repository of the English Language*, published in 1775. Despite the cool reception which this work received, Spence continued to propagate his phonetic alphabet for the rest of his life. Several of his later radical works were printed in this alphabet as well as in standard

English, and modern philologists now treat his efforts seriously.

Spence's parents' and his own lifelong experience of poverty taught him to sympathize with the plight of the industrious poor and to condemn the idle rich. Influenced also by his wide reading, especially of James Harrington, he developed notions about the natural rights and the natural equality of all men, and he had a strong belief in the power of reason and the idea of progress. There was undoubtedly a secular and enlightened aspect to his thinking as well as a millenarian and religious streak that he gained not only from his father but from the sermons and published works of the Revd James Murray, an extreme Presbyterian who made congregational autonomy an article of faith. Murray was a Scot, educated at the University of Edinburgh, who was invited to establish a meeting-house in Newcastle, where he was an active preacher and writer from 1765 until his death in 1782. Spence became one of Murray's greatest admirers, and was influenced by his use of scriptures and his appeal to reason in order to justify the claim that all men were naturally equal in the sight of God and had an equal claim to the same natural and inalienable rights. In his sermons and his published works Murray taught the benefits of civil and religious liberty, sympathized with John Wilkes's campaigns, and criticized the government's handling of the American crisis. He and Spence combined in the early 1770s in a prolonged and eventually successful campaign to preserve the customary rights of the Newcastle freemen threatened by the town corporation's efforts to make money by enclosing and engrossing parts of the large Town Moor.

The protracted Newcastle Town Moor affair had a profound effect on Spence and led him to develop his land plan, which was to be the focus of all his later radical political writings. In 1775 he became a member of Newcastle's newly established philosophical society. The society showed an interest in liberal ideas and occasionally debated political questions. On 8 November 1775 Spence created some dissension when he gave a lecture to the society on 'the real rights of man'. This was the first public occasion on which Spence vehemently denounced the evils of private property and proposed that each parish should control the land within its boundaries for the benefit of every inhabitant of the parish. Although his lecture was not well received when it was delivered, Spence proceeded to publish it without the permission of the society and, worse still, to hawk it about the streets of Newcastle. Despite the protests of some members, especially James Murray, Spence was expelled from the society. This did not prevent him from repeating his views in *The Poor Man's Advocate* (1779) and in *A Supplement to the History of Robinson Crusoe* (1782), nor from engaging in violent disputes in the several informal clubs and debating societies springing up in Newcastle.

London radical Increasingly isolated in Newcastle following the death of Murray and, in 1788, of his publisher, Thomas Saint, in an unhappy marriage, and discharged for reasons unknown from his teaching post at St Ann's School in Sandgate, Newcastle, on 17 December 1787, Spence and his son moved permanently to London. Although he is often reputed to have arrived in London in 1792, there is some evidence that he was settled there by early 1788, but that he was unknown as he eked out a living in a series of casual labouring jobs. By 1792 he had emerged as a radical bookseller and author just as popular radicalism was reviving in London because of the excitement generated by the French Revolution. The ideas behind and example of events in France increased Spence's attachment to reason, natural rights, and progress, but also reinforced the millennial streak in his writings. It seems likely that he mixed with the various millenarian, deistical, infidel, and apocalyptic groups then flourishing in parts of the capital. Moreover, although more of a political theorist and propagandist than an activist, Spence also associated with the more extreme political radicals. He allowed the 12th division of the *London Corresponding Society (LCS) to meet on his premises, while he was the first member of the 30th division, was elected to the general committee of the society, received subscriptions and collected signatures for petitions, and published the society's *Report of the Committee of the Constitution* in June 1794. He also signed the first *Address* of the Society of the Friends of the Liberty of the Press, allowed the militant and shadowy Lambeth Loyal Association to perform military drill in a large room above his bookshop, and in 1796 he acted in concert with Thomas Evans, the secretary of the LCS and also one of the leaders of the more revolutionary Society of United Englishmen.

From 1792 Spence endeavoured to maintain himself by printing and selling handbills, tracts, periodicals, and pamphlets (many of his own composition), by producing copper coins, tokens, and medallions, and by keeping a bookstall or bookshop. His first stall was at the eastern corner of Chancery Lane and Holborn, from where he also sold saloop (a hot drink of milk, sugar, and powdered sassafras). He later moved to a bookshop, the Hive of Liberty, at 8 Little Turnstile, Holborn, and by early 1797 he was based at 9 Oxford Street and also kept a stall near the Pantheon in Oxford Street. Many of Spence's publications were developments and variations on his land plan. His Newcastle lecture was republished as *The Real Rights of Man* in 1793 and as *The Meridian Sun of Liberty* in 1796. Variations on the same theme appeared in many other pamphlets, including *The End of Oppression* (1795), *Thomas Spence's Recantation of the End of Oppression* (1795), *A Letter from Ralph Hodge to his Cousin Thomas Bull* (1795), *Description of Spensonia* (1795), *Rights of Infants* (1797), *The Constitution of a Perfect Commonwealth* (1798) (republished in 1803 as *The Constitution of Spensonia*), and *The Restorer of Society to its Natural State* (1801). He also produced between 1793 and 1795 a periodical, *One Penny Worth of Pig's Meat: Lessons for the Swinish Multitude*, later reprinted in three volumes, which reproduced selections from such writers as Harrington, Philip Sydney, John Locke, Richard Price, Joseph Priestley, and William Godwin, as well as a further version of his own *The Real Rights of Man*. Although somewhat repetitious, all of Spence's works were written in a fresh, vigorous, and direct manner. While he was undoubtedly fixated with his land plan, his writings could be ironic and humorous, and they invariably had attractive titles. His style was deliberately tailored to reach, inspire, and convert poor men, who were his target readers.

The land plan and other political ideas Despite his emphasis on rational argument, his clear and vigorous prose, and his tireless efforts to publicize his land plan, Spence failed to make the details of it clear to his contemporaries or many later historians. Many believed that he advocated the nationalization of land so that it could be placed under the control of the central government, although administered by parish councils. In fact, Spence was always hostile to giving so much power to central government and wished to devolve as much power as possible to the local level. Convinced that political rights alone, however extensive, could never prevent the rich landowners from dominating the poor masses, he wanted to place what he regarded as the source of all power—land—into the hands of all citizens, men, women, and children alike. Spence insisted that all private property had been secured by force, fraud, or theft. Its return to the people as a whole was a simple act of justice. All the land should be owned by parish corporations composed of every person who lived within the parish boundaries. At first he suggested that this land would be rented out annually to applicants chosen by lot, but after 1782 he decided that the land should be rented out annually to the highest bidder, who would not be able to pass this leased land on to their heirs or to sell it. Rivers, lakes, mines, forests, and other natural resources would be rented out in a similar fashion. From the rents which it received, each parish corporation would make a contribution to the limited costs of the national government and its courts of justice, would use a proportion of its income for a wide variety of parochial needs, including houses, roads, harbours, and bridges, for such public amenities as a parish hall, school, library, and hospital, and for the care of the sick, aged, and unemployed. On occasion Spence suggested that the national government might maintain a small professional army, but more often he favoured a citizen militia supported by each parish. After all its expenses were met, the rest of the rent collected by the parishes would be divided, every three months, between every man, woman, and child in the parish. Dire poverty would be virtually eliminated, since no one paid taxes and everyone received a proportion of the parish rent. Although Spence planned to eliminate utter destitution, he did not advocate complete economic equality. While he was prepared to see the people confiscate the land and all natural resources from the rich, he was ready to see the latter retain all their movable property, and he accepted that some citizens would be more active, resourceful, and fortunate than others and so their income and personal possessions might well differ. Industry and talent would be rewarded, but land, the true source of political power, would always be communally owned, and the tyranny of the few over the many would be ended for ever. While Spence possessed an inadequate understanding of the social, economic, and demographic complexities of the day and he was far too optimistic about the practicality of his land plan, he did reveal a greater awareness than all his radical contemporaries of the true sources of political power and the desperate plight of the industrious poor. His vision of a welfare state was more extensive even than that outlined by Thomas Paine.

Aside from his land plan, Spence did not neglect other more overtly political questions. His writings were full of comments on constitutional and political arrangements. He clearly rejected monarchy, aristocracy, and an established state church, and he favoured a democratic republic. He favoured a limited and cheap national government, the complete separation of the executive, legislative, and administrative branches of government, and a system of election for all those in positions of authority. He favoured annual elections, the secret ballot, the abolition of any property qualification for, and the payment of, representatives, and universal suffrage. He was quite prepared to grant the vote to all women as well as all men, though he believed women should be excluded from positions of political responsibility because of what he termed the delicacy of their sex. Although he hoped to achieve his aims by reasoned argument and peaceful means if possible, and he did not personally engage directly in any revolutionary conspiracy, he did realize that the landed élite would probably not tamely surrender their property. In *The End of Oppression* he suggested that a few thousand men, guided by a leadership of honest, firm, and intelligent officers, who would themselves be inspired by a noble cause (Spence's land plan), would relatively easily overcome the resistance of the landed élite, when the mass of the people clearly supported this cause.

Spence's radical publications and his involvement in radical politics got him into a great deal of trouble with the authorities. He was arrested three times between December 1792 and December 1793, but was released each time without going to trial. He was again arrested on 20 May 1794, on suspicion of treasonable practices, and was kept in Newgate prison for seven months without trial, an injustice the authorities could perpetrate because habeas corpus had been suspended. He was arrested again in 1798 and released soon afterwards, but was arrested again and this time convicted for publishing *The Restorer of Society to its Natural State*. Accused of seditious practices and disaffection, he defended himself with great courage and impudence. None the less, he was sentenced to a year in Shrewsbury gaol, where he suffered severely. This punishment did not silence him, because on his release he published *The Important Trial of Thomas Spence* (1803), complete with a reprint of the offending pamphlet and a reworking of his land plan.

Final years Spence was not easily intimidated, and he kept his ideas alive and in limited circulation in the inhospitable political climate of the early nineteenth century. In 1805 he published *The World Turned Upside Down*, and this was followed by several political broadsides and volumes of political songs. He reissued some of his earlier pamphlets in 1807 and as late as 1814 he began a new periodical,

The Giant Killer, or, Anti-Landlord. Only two issues of this appeared in August before he died of a bowel complaint in Castle Street, off Oxford Street, London, on 1 September 1814. During his last years Spence attracted to him a group of disciples, who met as a Free and Easy Club in local taverns to discuss his ideas and sing his songs. This group included Thomas Evans, Arthur Thistlewood, and Allen Davenport. About forty of his followers attended Spence's funeral procession to the burial-ground of St James's, Hampstead Road, London, on 8 September 1814.

Although his last years were spent in obscurity compared to the years between 1792 and 1803, Spence's death was noted in many leading newspapers and magazines. After his death his small group of disciples, known as the Spencean Philanthropists, kept alive his ideas and were involved in such revolutionary activity as the Spa Fields riots of 2 December 1816 and the Cato Street conspiracy of 23 February 1820. Supporters of Spence's land plan were active in the 1830s in both the National Union of the Working Classes and the Chartist movement. Later still, he was wrongly acclaimed as an early socialist and as an advocate of the nationalization of land by the state.

H. T. DICKINSON

Sources T. Evans, *A brief sketch of the life of Mr Thomas Spence* (1821) · A. Davenport, *The life, writings, and principles of Thomas Spence: author of the Spencean system, or agrarian equality* [1836] · O. D. Rudkin, *Thomas Spence and his connections*, reprint of 1927 edn (1966) · P. M. Ashraf, *The life and times of Thomas Spence* (1983) · *Pigs' meat: the selected writings of Thomas Spence, radical and pioneer land reformer*, ed. G. I. Gallop (1982) · *The political works of Thomas Spence*, ed. H. T. Dickinson (1982) · A. W. Waters, *The trial of Thomas Spence in 1801* (1917) · T. R. Knox, 'Thomas Spence: the trumpet of jubilee', *Past and Present*, 76 (1977), 75–98 · T. M. Parsinnen, 'Thomas Spence and the origins of English land nationalization', *Journal of the History of Ideas*, 34 (1973), 135–43 · T. M. Parsinnen, 'Spence, Thomas', *BDMBR*, vol. 1 · M. Chase, *The people's farm: English radical agrarianism, 1775–1840* (1988) · Olivia Smith, *The politics of language, 1791–1819* (1984)

Archives BL, pamphlets [copies]

Likenesses T. Bewick, engraving, 1810, Newcastle upon Tyne Central Public Library

Spence [*alias* Butler], **William** (1650/51–1699), conspirator and private secretary, was 'born of mean parents' (*CSP dom.*, *1683*, 370) at Sandreford in Fife, the son of Margaret Millar, though Spence is an Orcadian name and local tradition has it that his family hailed from the Orkney Isles. On 19 August 1684 he was said to be aged about thirty-three. He had a brother, Thomas, and four sisters. About 1676–7 he entered the service of Sir Daniel Carmichael, in whose employ he remained for about a year, before becoming secretary to the earl of Argyll. He served as courier for Argyll at the time of the Rye House plot and Monmouth rebellion, operating under the name of Butler. He travelled to London in October 1682, possibly to meet with the English dissidents who were planning an insurrection, and left for the Netherlands on 8 November, where Argyll, by now a condemned traitor who had fled justice, had taken refuge. Spence was back in London by June 1683, and was apprehended at his lodgings at the Pewter Pot, in Leadenhall Street, on the early morning of the 27th, following the arrest the day before of Major Abraham Holmes, who was taken in possession of a number of ciphered letters from Argyll which he said he had received from Butler (Spence). Spence insisted he knew nothing of any political plots, claiming that he was a student of divinity at the College of Utrecht and had come to London to buy books, though he did admit that he recognized one of the letters to be in Argyll's hand.

Spence was imprisoned in the Marshalsea in heavy irons, but he continued to protest his innocence and so was deported to Scotland in November 1683, where the government had the option of using torture. Although Charles II wrote to his Scottish council ordaining Spence to be put to the boots 'to extort a discoverie of the late designes' (*Historical Notices*, ed. Laing, 463), and despite the fact that Holmes, in his examination of December 1683, had revealed that Spence knew how to decipher Argyll's letters, the Scottish chancellor, the earl of Aberdeen, refused to put Spence to the question. English experts managed to decipher enough of the correspondence to confirm that it contained highly incriminating material, and, following the replacement of Aberdeen as chancellor by the earl of Perth and the receipt of a further letter from Charles II in the summer of 1684 authorizing torture, the Scottish council finally decided to proceed against Spence. Torture could be used in Scotland in capital cases when there was a solid presumption of guilt but only one witness to the crime, instead of the required two (the so-called *semiplena probatio*, or half-proof). However, enduring the torture was supposed to purge one of all suspicion; the suspect was not to be put to the torture again. There was no half-proof against Spence for a capital offence, but he was subjected to three different types of torture on different occasions: first, on 26 July 1684, he was put to the boot; then he was deprived of sleep for several days and nights; and finally, on 7 August, he was subjected to the thumbscrews. At last he agreed to co-operate. He helped decipher a letter written by Argyll from the Netherlands dated 21 June 1683 which talked about plans for a co-ordinated uprising in Scotland and England, and although he was probably telling the truth when he said that he did not know what was in it, he nevertheless confessed that he did 'truly believe there was an Insurrection intended', the grounds being 'the defence of the Protestant Religion' and 'the Liberties of the Kingdom' (Mackenzie, 26).

After a brief spell in Dumbarton Castle, Spence was set at liberty in January 1685, whereupon he rejoined Argyll and the exiled dissident community in the Netherlands, becoming secretary to Argyll's council of war. In early February he was arrested at Harwich, posing as an art buyer, carrying letters from English malcontents in Utrecht, though the letters appear to have been devoid of political information (the more important messages were to be transmitted orally) and he was soon released. Later that month, back in the Low Countries, he sent a letter to the duke of Monmouth in Brussels informing him that Argyll was preparing to launch an invasion and inviting him to lend his support. Spence sailed with Argyll's invasion force in May, which stopped first at the Orkney Isles, where Spence, who had an uncle living at Kirkwall, was sent ashore to enlist recruits. Spence was captured along with his co-conspirator, Dr William Blackader, and the pair were subsequently sent as prisoners to Edinburgh in early June. Spence was tried for treason on 16 July 1685, found guilty, and condemned to be hanged on 22 July, but was reprieved at the intercession of Lord Dumbarton in the hope that he might be made use of to make a fuller discovery of the plot or to secure convictions against other leading Scottish malcontents. According to Robert Wodrow, he remained in prison until the revolution; he was certainly still in custody in April 1686, though he may have been free by August 1687, when 'two parcels containing scandalous libels against the King and his Government' (*CSP dom.*, *1687–9*, 61) and intended for William Spence or his assigns were found on board a ship recently arrived in England from the Netherlands.

After the revolution, the Williamite regime made some attempt to compensate Spence for his sufferings. In January 1690 he was appointed principal warden of the mint in Scotland, and in December of the following year receiver-general of the bullion: positions which together probably carried a salary of £1250 Scots. Marriage followed position and income, and on 17 October 1692 Spence married Jean Alexander, the widow of an Edinburgh brewer named Alexander Inglis. Spence died in 1699: he was explicitly described as deceased when the successors to his offices were appointed on 26 October. Twelve years later his widow and son William sought (eventually successfully) to be released from a debt of £310 still owing to the crown on Spence's account as receiver-general, pleading against it £160 that he had spent in 1691 in getting the instruments and materials necessary for setting up the mint in Scotland, and also that he had died leaving his widow with several small children unprovided for. The clause in the Scottish Claim of Right (1689) regulating the use of torture was in part a response to the treatment meted out to Spence in 1684. TIM HARRIS

Sources T. Sprat, *A true account and declaration of the horrid conspiracy against the late king* (1685) • *Bishop Burnet's History of his own time*, new edn (1850) • *Calendar of the manuscripts of the marquess of Ormonde*, new ser., 8 vols., HMC, 36 (1902–20), vol. 7 • [G. Mackenzie], *A true and plain account of the discoveries made in Scotland, of the late conspiracies against his majesty and the government* (1685) • *Historical notices of Scotish affairs, selected from the manuscripts of Sir John Lauder of Fountainhall*, ed. D. Laing, 2 vols., Bannatyne Club, 87 (1848) • *CSP dom.*, *July–Sept 1683*; *1683–4*; *1686–92*; *1699–1700* • R. Morrice, 'Ent'ring book', DWL, Morrice MS P • R. L. Greaves, *Secrets of the kingdom: British radicals from the Popish Plot to the revolution of 1688–89* (1992) • R. Ashcraft, *Revolutionary politics and Locke's two treatises of government* (1986) • J. Willcock, *A Scots earl in covenanting times: being life and times of Archibald, 9th earl of Argyll (1629–1685)* (1907) • R. Wodrow, *The history of the sufferings of the Church of Scotland, from the Restauration to the revolution*, 1 (1721), vol. 2 • W. A. Shaw, ed., *Calendar of treasury books*, 25/2, PRO (1954), 413; 27/2 (1954), 227–8 • H. Paton, ed., *The register of marriages for the parish of Edinburgh, 1595–1700*, Scottish RS, old ser., 27 (1905)

Wealth at death left widow unprovided for

Spence, William (*bap.* **1782**, *d.* **1860**), political economist and entomologist, was baptized on 1 October 1782 at All Saints, Bishop Burton, Yorkshire, the son of Robert Spence, husbandman, and his wife, Anna. He received his early education in natural history from the Revd Robert Rigby, vicar of St Mary's, Beverley, who instructed him in the Linnaean classification of plants. After attending Beverley grammar school, Spence served as an apprentice to merchants and shipowners, Carlill, Greenwood & Co. at Hull. This combination of a rural upbringing and a commercial apprenticeship influenced his development both as a political economist and as an entomologist.

A year after taking up residence in the Drypool district of Hull in 1806, Spence produced his *Radical Cause of the Present Distresses of the West-India Planters Pointed out* (1807) and his *Britain Independent of Commerce* (1807). An avowed follower of the physiocrats or 'French economists', he proclaimed that agriculture was the most important source of a nation's wealth. Extremely contentious, *Britain Independent of Commerce* passed through six editions and netted Spence a profit of £230 by late 1808. As one of about three dozen books and pamphlets spawned in reaction to Spence's opinions, James Mill's *Commerce Defended* (1808) laid the intellectual underpinnings of classical political economy. Moreover, Mill identified Spence's purportedly wartime, nationalistic cant as a critique of capitalism and an *apologia* for the landed interests. Spence responded with his *Agriculture the Source of the Wealth of Britain* (1808).

Inspired by Thomas Marsham's *Entomologia Britannica* (1802), Spence took up the study of entomology in 1805 and in the same year became acquainted with the Revd William Kirby. In 1808 Spence and Kirby began work on a popular introduction to entomology. About this time, Spence married Elizabeth Blundell (1779/80–1855). In 1811 he entered a commercial partnership with Elizabeth's brother Henry, founding Messrs Blundell, Spence & Co., paint and colour makers and general merchants. Despite these commitments Spence's interest in agriculture continued—he was elected to the Holderness Agricultural Society in December 1811. The paper that he presented at his first meeting appeared as *Observations on the Disease in Turnips, Termed in Holderness 'Fingers and Toes'* the following year. He subsequently served as both a vice-president (1814) and president (1815) of the society; and he dedicated his *Objections Against the Corn Bill Refuted* (1815) to his fellow members.

Pursuing entomological research, Spence spent the summer of 1812 in London at the library of Sir Joseph Banks. Having been elected a member of the Linnean Society in 1806, Spence published his first entomological paper in the society's *Transactions* in 1815. The first volume of his and Kirby's *Introduction to Entomology* appeared in the same year; and, following the battle of Waterloo, he took a four-month tour on the continent. After the publication of volume two of the *Introduction* in 1817, work on projected further volumes was seriously curtailed by Spence's affliction with severe headaches. With special permission from the commandant, he sought solace through solitary strolls along the ramparts of the citadel at Hull. Continued ill health, however, forced him to submit his unfinished manuscripts to Kirby, and to remove himself and his family to Exmouth, Devon, about 1820.

With the publication of the final two volumes of the *Introduction* in 1826, Spence and his family left Devon for the continent, where they enjoyed a semi-peripatetic existence for the next eight years. Summers were generally spent in Geneva, Lausanne, and Bern, and winters were spent in Florence, Pisa, and Rome. Often drawing on his continental experiences, Spence continued to publish articles on natural history. In the early 1830s, for instance, the *Magazine of Natural History* published his meteorological observations for Switzerland and Italy. In 1834 he read his paper, 'Observations on a mode practised in Italy of excluding the common house-fly from apartments', before the Entomological Society of London.

Spence and family returned from the continent in 1833, in time for the official launch of the Entomological Society of London. With his two sons, William and Robert Henry, Spence attended the first sitting of the society in November 1833. At Kirby's behest, he was elected honorary English member, in recognition of his contribution to the *Introduction*. His election marked the beginning of a long association with the society. In addition to serving on the council (1844, 1850, 1852–3), the publication committee (1844–52), and the library committee (1847–9), he was a vice-president (1844–6, 1853), and president (1847–8). On his death, his son, William, presented his library to the society.

After his return to England, Spence resided briefly at Bristol, and sought improved health through excursions to Leamington. Eventually he settled at 18 Lower Seymour Street, Marylebone, and took a fairly active role in London's scientific life. He was elected a fellow of the Royal Society in 1834, and subsequently served on both its council and that of the Linnean Society. He published approximately twenty articles on natural history, his principal interests lying in physiology, economic entomology, and instinct/intelligence disputes. Although admired by Charles Darwin, his liberal, secular interpretation of animal instinct and intelligence had led to his one open disagreement with Hutchinsonian Kirby.

In late 1842, a sixth edition of volumes one and two of the *Introduction* appeared. Because of Kirby's age and declining health, Spence had been solely responsible for the necessary revisions. *The Gardeners' Chronicle* acknowledged it 'as the most entertaining accounts of the habits of insects that has ever been put into popular form' (2, 3 Dec 1842, 808). Perhaps again exhausted, Spence and his wife returned to Italy for 1843. By this time, Spence's many sojourns to Italy had made their mark on his family. In 1833 one of his two daughters, Eliza, married Louis Schmid, the *chargé d'affaires* to the court of Tuscany; two years later, his son, William, married a Florentine woman.

Although the *Introduction to Entomology* continued to be popular, Spence's declining health precluded active participation in scientific circles. The death of his wife in April 1855 and the onset of deafness resulted in his increasing reclusiveness. Consequently, by the time of his death, at his home in Lower Seymour Street on 6 January 1860, contemporaries had confused the details of his intellectual career. Perhaps misled by his early work on political economy, a number of obituaries erroneously eulogized him as a former member of parliament for Hull. Spence was buried at Bishop Burton. J. F. M. Clark

Sources T. Sheppard, 'Bygone Hull naturalists, III: William Spence', *Transactions of the Hull Scientific and Field Naturalists' Club*, 3 (1906), 285–90 · W. Spence, 'Mr Kirby's acquaintance with Mr. Spence: origin and progress of the "Introduction to entomology"', in J. Freeman, *Life of the Rev. William Kirby* (1852), 265–327 · A. Rollinson, 'William Spence', *The Paint Pot* [Hull] (Aug 1979), 12–13 · J. F. M. Clark, 'Science, secularization, and social change: the metamorphosis of entomology in nineteenth-century England', DPhil diss., U. Oxf., 1994 · R. L. Meek, *The economics of physiocracy: essays and translations* (1962) · *ILN* (4 Feb 1860) · *Proceedings of the Linnean Society of London* (1859–60), xxxi–xxxii · *PRS*, 11 (1860–62), xxi–xxxi · S. A. Neave, *The centenary history of the Entomological Society of London, 1833–1933* (1933) · B. Semmel, *The rise of free trade imperialism: classical political economy, the empire of free trade and imperialism, 1750–1850* (1970) · W. G. B. Page, *Historic Hull houses* (1907), 5–6 · W. Bethel, ed., *Extracts from the minutes of the Holderness Agricultural Society* (1883) · K. Tribe, *Land, labour and economic discourse* (1978) · parish records, Bishop Burton, East Riding of Yorkshire Archives Service, Beverley, PE 140/4, p.10 · d. cert.

Archives BL, Add. MSS 32439, fol. 323; 37951, fols. 15–16; 32166, fol. 96 · Royal Entomological Society of London | Bodl. Oxf., Phillipps-Robinson MSS · Linn. Soc., Alexander and William S. McLeay MSS · Oxf. U. Mus. NH, Hope Library, corresp., mainly letters to F. W. Hope

Likenesses W. Raddon, line engraving, pubd 1839 (after J. J. Masquerier), BM, NPG · T. H. Maguire, lithograph, 1849, BM, NPG; repro. in *Portraits of honorary members of the Ipswich Museum* · W. T. Fry, engraving (after J. J. Masquerier), repro. in W. Kirby and W. Spence, *An introduction to entomology or elements of the natural history of insects*, 4 (1826), frontispiece · Marochetti, marble bust, repro. in Sheppard, 'Bygone Hull naturalists', 287 · engraving, repro. in *ILN*, 109 · portrait (destroyed in Second World War), Hull Museum · portrait, Messrs. Blundell, Spence &. Co., Hull

Wealth at death under £100,000: probate, 1860, *CGPLA Eng. & Wales*

Spencer. *See also* Spenser.

Spencer family (*per. c.*1647–1765), ironmasters, of Cannon Hall, in the parish of Cawthorne, near Barnsley, sat at the heart of the interlocking partnerships which controlled the greater part of iron production in Yorkshire between the mid-seventeenth and mid-eighteenth centuries. The Spencers ran a string of furnaces, forges, and slitting mills in the West Riding and their interests extended into neighbouring parts of Derbyshire and Lancashire. They also ventured into secondary manufacturing, being heavily involved in the nail trade in the first half of the eighteenth century. The forges in the area south and west of Leeds were first drawn together when Sir Francis Fane, the future earl of Westmorland and son of the Kentish ironmaster Sir Thomas Fane of Badsell, acquired the leases of the new forge at Kirkstall in 1618 and of the ancient bloomery forge at Wortley in 1621. However, it was not until these forges and the associated furnaces were in the hands of the Spencer family that they became of regional significance.

The Spencer family came from Criggion in Montgomeryshire. A connection between this family and south Yorkshire was established in 1605, when Walter Spencer, son of John Spencer (*d.* 1632), gentleman, married Frances, daughter of Thomas Barnby of Barnby (PRO, C2 Jas I B6/68). A younger brother of Walter was the London merchant **John** [i] **Spencer** (*c.*1600–1658), who was involved in the Shrewsbury drapery trade. John mentioned his Yorkshire forges and furnaces in his will and his contact with the iron industry may have arisen from the marriage of his sister Elizabeth to the ironmaster William Fownes in 1625. In turn, it seems possible that the interests of William Fownes in the Yorkshire ironworks arose through his brother-in-law Walter Spencer, especially as one of the partnership's blast furnaces was established at Barnby, on land belonging to Walter's brother-in-law, Sir Charles Barnby.

William Fownes and his brother Gilbert were involved in the Yorkshire ironworks by the 1640s; these comprised Wortley forges, Colne Bridge forge, and Barnby and Bank furnaces, with the lease of Kirkstall forge being agreed in the late 1650s. John [i] Spencer possessed a three-fifths share in these works for about ten or twelve years before his death, so his involvement dated perhaps from the death of William Fownes, whose will was proved in 1647.

John [i] Spencer died in August 1658 and was buried at Wortley. He and his wife, Elizabeth, had one son and two daughters. Himself a younger son, Spencer wished to assure genteel standing for his own children and in his will he charged the Yorkshire works with raising £1500 to fulfil the marriage settlement of his son, Edward, and £1000 as a marriage portion for his daughter Mary. He also directed his brother, another Edward Spencer, and his son-in-law, Russell Alsopp, to administer the works on behalf of his son and heir, who retired to an estate purchased by his father at Huntington in Cheshire and never played an active role in the iron industry. John [i] Spencer was survived by his wife, who by his will was to receive £150 out of the drapery trade and possession of some land. Elizabeth Fownes died before her brother; in her own will (1655) she described herself as of Wortley forge, and it was at Wortley that she too was buried in February 1658. Monuments in the church commemorated both her and her brother.

The third member of this family to establish Yorkshire connections was **John** [ii] **Spencer** (1629–1681), the son of John [i] Spencer's elder brother Randolph, who in 1650 was sent by his father to join Walter in Yorkshire, where he acted as a clerk in the ironworks. John [ii] Spencer's first wife, Sarah, had died in 1657 and through his second wife, Margaret (*née* Clayton), widow of Robert Hartley of Cannon Hall, who died without male heir in 1656, John [ii] Spencer acquired a wooded and iron-bearing estate near Cawthorne and firmly established his family in Yorkshire. Randolph Spencer, having moved to join his son, was buried at Cawthorne in July 1658.

Elizabeth Fownes's share in the ironworks devolved via her son-in-law William Cotton (*d.* 1675), who was general manager of the works, on John Bancks. The share of Gilbert Fownes had gone to his son, William Fownes, while by buying one of Edward Spencer's shares Russell Alsopp himself became a partner. Until 1667, during the managership of Cotton, the partnership prospered, acquiring a slitting mill near Wigan to supply the Lancashire market. Thereafter, perhaps because Edward Spencer resided in Cheshire and Alsopp, Bancks, and the younger Fownes were London merchants, all remote from the works, mutual suspicion disrupted the partnership. Suit was followed by counter-suit, in both chancery and the Chester exchequer court, and during the 1670s the first Spencer partnership was wound up. The link with the Fownes family had been important for the development of the Spencer interest in the iron industry and rivalry with the *Cotton family was a constant theme of its continuation, but the lessons of the 1670s appear to have been learned and the risk of ruin through litigation was henceforth avoided.

Meanwhile, William Cotton and his cousin, Thomas Dickin, had acquired Colne Bridge forge from the former partnership in 1665 and a slitting mill was built there. In 1675 Cotton's son and heir, William Cotton (*c.*1648–1703), of Haigh Hall, and Thomas Dickin also bought the unexpired leases of Kirkstall forge and Barnby furnace. John [ii] Spencer took the first step in retrieving his family's fortunes the following year, when he joined Cotton and Dickin in a one-third share of Kirkstall and Barnby for £836, and they also began to operate a slitting mill at Kirkstall forge. John [ii] Spencer died on 19 April 1681, probably at Cannon Hall.

It was mainly due to the energy of Spencer's son, **John** [iii] **Spencer** (*c.*1655–1729), that the family was able to re-establish its dominance in south Yorkshire. Thomas Dickin died in 1692 and in 1695 it was to his son of the same name that the new lease of Wortley forges was granted. However, Spencer now acquired a half share at Wortley for £2000. He also extended his influence to the south of Sheffield by acquiring a share in the former Sitwell works (Foxbrooke and Staveley furnaces, Staveley and Carburton forges, and Renishaw slitting mill) which Denis *Hayford and partners took over about 1700.

Spencer was provided with a great opportunity by fatalities among his partners. The second Thomas Dickin died childless in 1701, only nine years after his father's death and in 1703 Spencer's main rival, William Cotton of Haigh Hall, died, leaving as heir a minor, William Westby Cotton. Dickin's heirs were his five sisters, so Spencer's half share left him the dominant partner at Wortley. Matthew Woodhead, who was not only the adopted son of Thomas Dickin and manager of Wortley forges and Barnby furnace, but also the husband of one of the Dickin sisters, was persuaded to let Spencer buy half the Dickin share in Colne Bridge. Spencer also induced Robert Wilmott, the husband of another sister, Mary Dickin, to sell him half their share in the Kirkstall partnership, thus gaining a quarter share at Colne Bridge and Bank furnace and increasing his influence at Kirkstall forge and Barnby furnace.

In 1680 John [iii] Spencer married Anne (1659–1699), daughter of John Wilson of Wortley; they had two sons. When Matthew Woodhead died in 1704, Spencer had his brother-in-law Matthew Wilson installed as managing partner at Wortley. In 1713, through the Wilmott connection, Spencer obtained a share in Holme Chapel furnace, near Burnley in Lancashire, which Wilmott had established in 1693. He also extended the Spencer iron-bearing estates by purchasing from the Allott family of Bentley half the former estates of Sir Charles Barnby. Spencer's position as the most influential figure in the iron trade of south Yorkshire was consolidated in 1727 by the acquisition of five shares out of thirty-two in the duke of Norfolk's works (Chapel furnace, Attercliffe and Wadsley forges, and Masborough slitting mill), the only remaining major iron interest in the area. John [iii] Spencer died on 13 April 1729.

The markets of the south Yorkshire ironworks had included York itself, Hull, and the east coast as far south as Norfolk, with large sales in London. Rod iron from Colne Bridge slitting mill went chiefly to the Lancashire nail trade, through warehouses in Burnley and Rochdale. The slitting mills at Kirkstall and Wortley supplied the local nail trade, for which some of the ironmasters, including John [iii] Spencer's elder son, **William Spencer** (*c.*1690–1756), acted as factors. London was the main market for the bulk nail trade, but these distant markets became steadily more difficult to retain. Even in Lancashire, rod iron had to be delivered at Chowbent, in the centre of the nail-making area, in the effort to maintain that market.

Meanwhile, William Westby Cotton (*bap.* 1689, *d.* 1749) had laid claim to the Cotton interest in Colne Bridge in 1717. During the 1720s he organized a rival partnership, based on a new furnace at Bretton, Kilnhurst forge on the Don, and a lease of Rockley furnace obtained in 1726. This was unwelcome to the Spencers, because the scarcity of cordwood in south Yorkshire made it difficult to apportion charcoal between the works. Though William Spencer acquired the remainder of the Barnby inheritance, his own estates were insignificant in comparison with those of the duke of Norfolk, the marquess of Rockingham, and the Wortley Montagu family, all of which needed to be laid under contribution to satisfy the charcoal needs of the ironworks. Wood agreements with Cotton, whom William Spencer characterized as an 'unreasonable wasp' and contemptuously called 'the little gentleman', rarely lasted more than a few months (Butler, 14). Writing to John Watts, the managing partner at Kirkstall forge, Spencer described Cotton as his 'greatest enemy but yourself' (ibid., 18), and it was with Watts that he was involved in an exasperating feud concerning the price to be paid by Kirkstall forge for pig iron, a dispute which continued until just before Watts died in 1751.

William Spencer was a scholar of Christ's College, Cambridge (1706–7), and about 1715 he married Christiana (*d.* 1737), daughter and heir of Benjamin Ashton of Hathersage, Derbyshire. They had one son and one daughter. His father, perhaps knowing the uncertain temper of his eldest son, left the Spencer share in the partnership (which included Wortley slitting mill) divided between William and his younger brother, Edward. Edward died in 1729 and he left his share in this partnership not to his brother William, with whom he had been on bad terms, but to their uncle Matthew Wilson. William Spencer challenged the validity of the will, and seized the forges on Wilson's death in 1739. In 1743 the matter went before arbitrators, one of them the hated Westby Cotton. However, by March 1746 Spencer was persuaded to accept the unfavourable arbitration and to relinquish control at Wortley slitting mill to John Cockshutt, Wilson's nephew and heir.

William Spencer was not the only ironmaster in south Yorkshire interested in the nail trade, but he was perhaps the largest, with two-thirds of his Wortley iron going into rod iron for nails. Between 1742 and 1747 he employed 120 nailers and sent some 4465 bags of nails worth £10,000 via Hull to London. However, there were constant difficulties in maintaining quality control, some nails being without points, others without heads, and some having neither, as his clerk complained. Towards the end of the period slitting had to be done for him by John Fell at Masborough and John Cockshutt at Wortley, both of them competitors in the nail trade, so he finally withdrew from it in 1748.

William Spencer's frustrations were small inducement to his son, **John** [iv] **Spencer** (1719–1775), to retain an interest in the iron trade. Life as a country gentleman held more attractions for this product of Winchester School and University College, Oxford. He was unmarried, the last of his line, and announced his withdrawal from the business in 1765, his father, William, having died on 30 January 1756. His principal heir was his nephew Walter Stanhope of Horsforth and Leeds, who, in honour of his uncle, prefixed the name Spencer to his own. It is through this family that the accounts and documents relating to the various ironworks in which the Spencer family had an interest survived.

Apart from the interlude of Cotton dominance between 1675 and 1703 the Spencer family played the leading role in establishing the charcoal iron industry in the area between Leeds and Sheffield and continuing it for 120 years. John [iii] Spencer was clearly the ablest of his line and it is sad that the survival of diaries and letter-book give a better insight into the life and character of William Spencer than into that of his father. However, William Spencer saw the concern through until within two years of the establishment of the Walker ironworks at Masborough; and the decision to withdraw made by John [iv] Spencer was probably a judicious one, because a quite special talent for innovation and change would have been needed to survive in the era of coke-smelted iron.

BRIAN G. AWTY

Sources [R. Butler], *The history of Kirkstall forge*, 2nd edn (1954) • J. Hunter, *South Yorkshire: the history and topography of the deanery of Doncaster*, 2 vols. (1828–31) • G. G. Hopkinson, 'The charcoal iron industry in the Sheffield region, 1500–1775', *Transactions of the Hunter Archaeological Society*, 8 (1960–63), 122–51 • B. G. Awty, 'Charcoal ironmasters of Cheshire and Lancashire, 1600–1785', *Transactions of the Historic Society of Lancashire and Cheshire*, 109 (1957), 71–124 • R. A. Mott, 'The early history of Wortley forges', *Historical Metallurgy*, 5 (1971), 63–70 • A. Raistrick and E. Allen, 'The south Yorkshire ironmasters, 1690–1750', *Economic History Review*, 9 (1938–9), 168–85 • A. Raistrick, 'The south Yorkshire iron industry,

1698–1756', *Transactions* [Newcomen Society], 19 (1938–9), 51–86 · A. Raistrick, *Quakers in science and industry* (1950) [more reliable on technological matters than on intricacies of family history] · Sheff. Arch., Spencer-Stanhope papers

Archives Sheff. Arch., Spencer-Stanhope papers | PRO, state papers, domestic, Charles I SP 16

Spencer, Miss. *See* Woodham, Mrs (*d.* 1803).

Spencer, Mrs. *See* Pope, Maria Ann (1775–1803).

Spencer [*married names* Stanley, Egerton], **Alice, countess of Derby (1559–1637)**, noblewoman, the youngest of eight daughters of Sir John Spencer (*d.* 1586) of Althorp, Northamptonshire, and Katherine Kytson, eldest daughter and heiress of Sir Thomas Kytson of London, was born at Althorp on 4 May 1559. The family acquired great wealth through skilful land management and sheep farming, and all the daughters were amply provided for in their marriages. Alice lived in Spencer homes in Althorp, Wormleighton, and London, where she was probably schooled in music, literature, and religion. Musicians and minstrels made regular visits to the family. In her late teens she moved into court life with her elder sisters, who married nobles and landed gentlemen.

Alice married Ferdinando *Stanley, Lord Strange, heir to the earldom of Derby, secretly in 1579/80. Since he and his mother, Margaret, countess of Derby, were potential successors to Elizabeth I, the marriage caused considerable suspicion, especially as it had been promoted by the earl of Leicester (Fogle, 9–10). It brought Alice a significant dowry. They had three daughters, Anne (1580–1647), Frances (1583–1636) [*see* Egerton, Frances], and Elizabeth *Stanley (*bap.* 1587, *d.* 1633). Anne went on to marry Grey *Brydges, fifth Baron Chandos, and Mervin *Touchet, the notorious second earl of Castlehaven.

A beautiful, well-educated, and cultured woman, Alice entered the queen's household and became prominent at court. Ferdinando, one of the richest noblemen in the country, sponsored actors and playwrights and wrote poetry. She became particularly fond of Ferdinando's London residence in Holborn, and of the family seat in Lancashire at Knowsley, known as the northern court, which had a staff of 143 by 1590. She encouraged the visitation of acting companies in the 1580s, when the Queen's Men, Earl of Leicester's Men, and Earl of Essex's Men appeared there many times.

After Ferdinando's death in 1594, his own company, Lord Strange's Men, became the Countess of Derby's Men. This was the company that merged with the Lord Chamberlain's Men in 1594, with Shakespeare as chief playwright. In the years 1584–94 Alice and Ferdinando were celebrated by Robert Greene, Thomas Nash, and Edmund Spenser as great sponsors of music, poetry, and literature. Spenser dedicated works to Alice and her sisters for their patronage, and to her daughters, thanking Alice for her 'private bands of affinitie'. She performed frequently in masques before the court, and was a masquer in Ben Jonson's *Blackness*, performed in the winter of 1605. A number of writers patronized by Alice and Ferdinando reciprocated by dedicating works to the noble couple. These included John Davies of Hereford, John Harrington,

Alice Spencer, countess of Derby (1559–1637), by unknown artist

Henry Lok, John Marston, Greene, Nash, and Spenser. Alice received special dedications to herself from Davies, Harrington, Lok, and Spenser.

Ferdinando died without male heirs, making Alice a highly eligible young dowager countess sporting three attractive unmarried daughters. While Ferdinando left his unentailed lands to Alice and his daughters, his younger brother William succeeded to an earldom that was deep in debt. He decided not to give over title to any Stanley lands to Alice and her daughters, and a series of bitter legal contests ensued that were not resolved until an act of parliament in 1609. After a complicated series of transactions in October 1600 Alice secretly married Sir Thomas *Egerton, her daughter Frances being betrothed to his son and heir, John. Sir Thomas had a chancery decree confirm the descent of the Derby lands in the midlands to Alice for her life, passing to Frances and John and their heirs. Once the couple obtained the queen's dispensation, Egerton purchased for Alice in 1601 Harefield House in Middlesex, which she refurbished. They entertained Elizabeth at York House, London, in 1601, and in 1602 they hosted her royal progress at Harefield with one of the most lavish entertainments of the era that cost over £2000.

Alice brought a number of books to Egerton's library, and shared in building the famous collection. She also used York House as her central London abode, entertaining ladies Bedford, Carey, Clifford, Montgomery, and others. The couple's relationship, however, was not always pleasant as Egerton, a careful counter of coin, did not appreciate her lavish spending and entertaining. He did, however, purchase the Stanley manor of Ellesmere in 1600 for the family title, and forced William, Ferdinando's successor, to settle £20,000 upon Alice and her daughters in 1600. William's inability to meet these stiff conditions led to Egerton's forcing his buy-out of the heirs for nearly £30,000 in 1609. This included Alice's alleged title to the descent of the Isle of Man (Coward, 45–9).

After the death of Egerton in 1617 Alice lived at Harefield House as a 'rural queen'. She travelled between there and the estates of her daughters and sons-in-law (the countess and earl of Bridgewater and the countess and earl of Huntingdon) at Ashridge, Hertfordshire, and Ashby-de-la-Zouch, Leicestershire. Harefield House became a cultural community. Preparing her grandchildren for social and public life, she employed schoolteachers and musicians, and provided for lavish masques in which the grandchildren acted. Henry Lawes, a neighbouring musician, was hired as their music master. It has been suggested that Alice patronized the young John Milton for a non-clerical career (Brown, 12–14), and that the success of *Arcades* for her seventy-fifth birthday on 4 May 1634 led to the family's approval of his collaboration on *Comus* for Bridgewater's installation as lord president of the council of Wales at Ludlow Castle. Milton had written *Arcades* in her honour near Harefield in 1632. When it was staged and directed by William Lawes at Harefield, Alice played a part in pastoral habit and was joined by her grandchildren. Milton wrote:

> Mark what radiant state she spreads,
> In circle round her shining throne,
> …
> Sitting like a Goddess bright, In the centre of her light.
> …
> Such a rural Queen All Arcadia hath not seen.
> (*Milton: Complete Poems*, 77)

Alice died in January 1637 at Harefield House and was buried at the church of St Mary the Virgin in Harefield, Middlesex. She wrote the directions for her burial in her will. A devout woman, she gave clothes and money to the poor of Cobham, Harefield, Hillingdon, and Weybridge, and created a charitable trust for a hospital for the poor with religious education to be built in Hillingdon with her arms as its seal. She also set out in the will whom her grandson George, Baron Chandos, would marry, and the monetary penalties if the marriage did not take place. Providing carefully for each of her servants, children, and many grandchildren, she charged them to live in peace without altercation. An independent woman who dedicated her life to bringing up her children and grandchildren, often in tragic circumstances, the countess pursued the cultural life with zest, striving to attain the highest standards of an Elizabethan woman in an age of declining moral values. LOUIS A. KNAFLA

Sources F. R. Fogle, '"Such a rural queen": the countess dowager of Derby as patron', *Patronage in late renaissance England*, ed. F. R. Fogle and L. A. Knafla (1983), 3–29 · T. Heywood, *The Stanley papers, pt 1: the earls of Derby and the verse writers and poets of the sixteenth and seventeenth century*, Chetham Society, 29 (1853) · W. Ffarrington, *The Stanley papers, pt 2*, ed. F. R. Raines, Chetham Society, 31 (1853), 35–49 · *Milton's 'Comus', being the Bridgewater manuscript with notes and a short family memoir*, ed. A. Egerton (1910) · C. C. Brown, *John Milton's aristocratic entertainments* (1985), 12–26, 41–56, 154 · J. S. Diekhoff, ed., *A maske at Ludlow: essays on Milton's 'Comus'* (1968) · D. Masson, *The life of John Milton*, rev. edn, 1 (1894) · *J. Milton: complete poems and major prose*, ed. M. Y. Hughes (1857), 77 · J. Nichols, *The progresses and public processions of Queen Elizabeth*, new edn, 3 (1823), 581–6 · BL, Sloane MS 848, fol. 9 [entertainment at Ashridge, 1607] · BL, Add. MS 11406 · BL, Add. MSS 25079–25080 · will, PRO, PROB 11/174, fols. 90v–97r · B. Coward, *The Stanleys, lords Stanley and earls of Derby, 1385–1672: the origins, wealth and power of a landowning family*, Chetham Society, 3rd ser., 30 (1983), 34–5, 44–50 · C. Herrup, *A house in gross disorder: sex, law, and the second earl of Castlehaven* (1999) · L. A. Knafla, *Law and politics in Jacobean England* (1977), 32–4, 59 · *The diaries of Lady Anne Clifford*, ed. D. J. H. Clifford (1990), 23, 44–5, 51, 97 · B. Falk, *The Bridgewater millions: a candid family history* (1942), 15, 30–31, 34–5, 56–8, 60–62, 65 · J. P. Collier, *A catalogue, bibliographical and critical, of early English literature … at Bridgewater House* (1837) · L. Marcus, 'The milieu of Milton's *Comus*: judicial reform at Ludlow and the problem of sexual assault', *Criticism*, 25 (1983), 293–327 · R. K. Mundhenk, 'Dark scandal and the sun-clad power of chastity: the historical milieu of Milton's *Comus*', *Studies in English Literature*, 15 (1975), 141–52 · B. Breasted, '*Comus* and the Castlehaven scandal', *Milton Studies*, 3 (1971), 201–24 · A. Lister, 'The Althorp library of second Earl Spencer, now in the John Rylands University Library of Manchester: its formation and growth', *Bulletin of the John Rylands Library of Manchester*, 7/2 (1989), 67–86 · J. Orrell, 'Antimo Galli's description of "The mask of beauty"', *Huntington Library Quarterly*, 43/1 (winter 1979), 13–23 · A. Harbage, *Annals of English drama*, ed. S. Schoenbaum (1964), 297, 301–2 · P. McLane, 'Spenser's Choloris: the countess of Derby', *Huntington Library Quarterly*, 24/2 (1961), 145–50 · E. Williams, *Early Holborn and the legal quarter of London*, 1 (1927), para. 690 · L. H. Cust, *The Bridgewater Gallery: one hundred and twenty of the most noted paintings at Bridgewater House* (1903) · J. O. Halliwell, *Observations on the Shakespearian forgeries at Bridgewater House* (1853) · *The letters and epigrams of Sir John Harington*, ed. N. E. McClure (1930), 251

Likenesses drawings, repro. in Brown, *John Milton's aristocratic entertainments*, pls. 2–3, 11, 14 · oils, unknown collection; copyprint, NPG [*see illus.*]

Spencer, Aubrey George (1795–1872), bishop of Newfoundland, born on 8 February 1795, was the son of William Robert *Spencer (1770–1834) author, and his wife, Susan, the widow of Count Spreti and the daughter of Francis *Jenison, Count Jenison Walworth. His brother was George Trevor *Spencer, bishop of Madras. He was educated at St Albans Abbey School and in Greenwich, and matriculated from Magdalen Hall, Oxford, on 28 March 1817, but did not graduate. After being ordained in 1819 Spencer worked for the Society for the Propagation of the Gospel in Newfoundland and the Bermudas, of which in 1825 he was appointed archdeacon. At about that time he married Eliza Musson, daughter of a rich Bermuda merchant; they had one son and three daughters.

In 1829 Spencer's devotion to Bermudan welfare and education led him to reject the offer of the archdeaconry of Newfoundland. However, in 1839, when Newfoundland was constituted a separate diocese, with the Bermudas under its care, Spencer was appointed its bishop. He was consecrated in London at Lambeth Palace on 4 August 1839; during his visit to Britain he was created DD of Oxford University. Spencer undertook the organization of his diocese, founded the theological college, and laid the first stone of the cathedral of St John's, besides helping to found twenty other churches. But his health was affected by the severe winters of Newfoundland, and on 28 November 1843 he was relieved to be appointed bishop of Jamaica, which included British Honduras and the Bahamas. Here his health improved a little, though a good deal of travelling was necessary. In October 1848 he visited the Bahamas and some years later he went to Havana. But in 1855 further poor health required him to resign.

Spencer returned to Britain and retired to Torquay, where he published *A Brief Account of the Church of England* (1867). He died at Torquay on 24 February 1872, his wife surviving him. C. A. HARRIS, *rev.* H. C. G. MATTHEW

Sources *The Times* (27 Feb 1872) · *DCB*, vol. 10 · C. F. Pascoe, *Two hundred years of the SPG*, rev. edn, 2 vols. (1901) · O. R. Rowley, *The Anglican episcopate of Canada and Newfoundland* (1928)
Archives LPL, corresp.; letter-book | NL Wales, letters to Johnes family · U. Birm. L., letters to Church Missionary Society · U. Durham L., corresp. with third Earl Grey; letters to Miss E. Copley
Likenesses M. Gauci, lithograph (after F. Rochard), BM · oils, Hertford College, Oxford
Wealth at death under £4000: probate, 12 April 1872, *CGPLA Eng. & Wales*

Spencer, Sir Augustus Almeric (1807–1893), army officer, was the third son of Francis Almeric *Spencer, first Baron Churchill [*see under* Spencer, George (1739–1817)], and Lady Frances Fitzroy, fifth daughter of Augustus, third duke of Grafton. George *Spencer, fourth duke of Marlborough, was his grandfather. He was born on 25 March 1807 at Blenheim Palace, Oxfordshire, and was one of the pages when Alexander I visited Blenheim after the peace of 1815. He lived from 1817 at Cornbury, Oxfordshire, the seat of his father in Wychwood Forest, and was privately educated by the Revd Walter Brown, rector of Stonesfield, Oxfordshire, formerly chaplain and librarian at Blenheim. In 1825 he entered the army as ensign of the 43rd light infantry, and was with the regiment at Gibraltar. In 1827 he was under Sir George de Lacy Evans in Portugal. A few years later he accompanied the regiment to Canada, and on 6 February 1836 married, at Fredericton, Helen Maria (*d.* 1899), second daughter of Sir Archibald Campbell, governor of New Brunswick.

In 1845 Spencer was appointed to the command of the 44th, and served throughout the Crimean War. He was present at the battles of Alma and Inkerman, the occupation of the cemetery and suburbs of Sevastopol (18 June 1855), where he was wounded, and as brigadier-general of the 4th division in the night attack at the fall of Sevastopol (8 September 1855). In October 1855 he commanded the land forces in the expedition to Kinburn, in conjunction with General Bazaine. He was thus with the army from the first landing at Varna until its return to England, was ten times mentioned in dispatches, received the Mejidiye (third class) and was made CB and officer of the Légion d'honneur.

After his return to England in 1856 Spencer was placed in command of a brigade at Aldershot. In 1860 he was made major-general, and appointed to a division of the Madras army at Bangalore. On 28 March 1865 he was made KCB. In 1866 he was appointed to the command of the western district (Devonport), and in 1869 he was again in India as commander-in-chief of the Bombay army. In this year also he became colonel of his old regiment, the 43rd. Returning from India in 1874, he commanded the 2nd army corps in the manoeuvres on Salisbury Plain in the following year, and was promoted to the rank of general. This was the close of his active service. He was made GCB on 29 May 1875. He died on 28 August 1893 at his home, 51 Ennismore Gardens, London. His wife survived him.

H. L. BENNETT, *rev.* M. G. M. JONES

Sources *The Times* (13 Aug 1893) · *Hart's Army List* · *Army List* · Boase, *Mod. Eng. biog.*
Wealth at death £74,466 16*s.* 3*d.*: probate, 12 Oct 1893, *CGPLA Eng. & Wales*

Spencer, Sir (Walter) Baldwin (1860–1929), biologist and anthropologist, was born on 23 June 1860 at Stretford, Lancashire, the second of eleven children of Reuben Spencer (1830–1901) and his wife, Martha (1832–1906), *née* Circuit. Reuben, a pillar of Manchester congregationalism, rose from clerk to managing director of John Rylands & Sons, textile manufacturers, bequeathing over £200,000 to his family in 1901. Baldwin was educated at Old Trafford School. A year at the Manchester School of Art developed his artistic talents, later enhancing his notebooks and publications.

Spencer entered Owens College, Manchester, in 1879, to study medicine, but was diverted to science by the inspiring evolutionary biologist Milnes Marshall. Following the award of a scholarship at Exeter College, Spencer moved to Oxford University in 1881, already well grounded in biology and geology; he rejected his father's conventional religion for unobtrusive agnosticism. He received stimulating evolutionary instruction also at the University Museum where, following his *Challenger* voyage experiences, Professor H. N. Moseley combined biology with enthusiastic ethnology.

Oxford life nourished this slight, energetic scholar, who attended Ruskin's art and E. B. Tylor's anthropology lectures, and co-founded the Junior Scientific Club, attracting distinguished scientific speakers. Spencer shared rooms for some months with Halford Mackinder; this possibly influenced his biogeographical approach to Australian fauna and his dedicated involvement in Victorian public education.

Spencer graduated in 1884, and was appointed a demonstrator in Moseley's laboratory. His research successfully applied recent microscopy and histological techniques to the parietal (pineal) eye in reptiles. He assisted Moseley and Tylor in transferring the Pitt Rivers ethnographic collection from Bethnal Green in London to its new Oxford building. This provided invaluable experience in artefact typology, classification based upon evolutionary assumptions of simple to complex forms. When honorary director of the National Museum of Victoria from 1899 to 1928, Spencer gave these now outmoded concepts classic expression in his *Guide to the Australian Ethnographical Collection* (1901).

Elected a fellow of Lincoln College in 1886, Spencer formed a friendship with the Roman historian and naturalist W. Warde Fowler. They tramped the Cotswolds

Sir (Walter) Baldwin Spencer (1860–1929), by unknown photographer

together, while Fowler expounded upon the countryside, ornithology, and the values of humane education. Such precepts were later exemplified when, in 1890, Spencer, with a Melbourne classicist, T. G. Tucker, co-edited the innovative journal *Australasian Critic*.

Shortly after Spencer's election at Lincoln the University of Melbourne advertised the foundation chair of biology. Moseley and Tylor wrote strong references supporting the youthful Spencer, who was selected from a strong field which included A. C. Haddon; T. H. Huxley was a selector. Prior to sailing, Spencer married Mary Elizabeth (Lillie) Bowman (1862–1935), the daughter of Richard Bowman, a family friend, at Hatherlow Chapel, Stockport, on 18 January 1887. They had two daughters, but their third child, a boy, died at birth in 1896, which affected Lillie's health.

Spencer disembarked at Melbourne on 30 March 1887. His arrival followed shortly after David Orme Masson occupied the chemistry chair at Melbourne. Both proved dynamic forces in university affairs and public science. Within a year Spencer designed and occupied the biology building, notable for its well-lit laboratories, where he attracted young researchers on Australian biota. Despite his formidable moustache and busy teaching schedule, he proved approachable, inaugurating field excursions. He was a memorable lecturer, filling Melbourne's town hall in 1902 for a lecture on Aborigines.

Spencer's espousal of feminist causes was exceptional, commencing with sponsorship of a women's university club. His was the first Australian university department to appoint female lecturers and associate professors; by 1919 all colleagues were female. Spencer encouraged undergraduate social and sporting activities, serving as popular president of the Sports Union, precursor to his presidency of the Victorian football league (1919–26). His administrative talents ensured his election as president of the professorial board, the university's senior executive post, which he held from 1903 to 1911. His office followed serious misappropriations necessitating a royal commission; his activities assisted recovery of the institution's reputation and finances.

As a public figure, Spencer pioneered nature conservation during the 1890s, and through university extension lectures popularized science in country centres. He played crucial roles in reviving the Field Naturalists' Society and the Royal Society of Victoria. On broader fields Masson and Spencer promoted the Australasian Association for the Advancement of Science, for which Spencer twice edited handbooks, and he was elected president of its 1921 congress. Masson and Spencer were the Melbourne architects of the 1914 British Association Australian Congress. When Masson initiated moves to establish the future Commonwealth Scientific and Industrial Research Organisation, Spencer supported the early negotiations.

Membership of the 1894 Horn scientific exploring expedition to central Australia, as zoologist, transformed Spencer's career. In Alice Springs he met F. J. Gillen, the overland telegraph stationmaster, whose Aboriginal knowledge stimulated him. After editing the four-volume expedition report, Spencer returned to Alice Springs in 1896, where he and Gillen completed the most sustained participant observation of Aboriginal rituals yet attempted. Spencer's ability to cross class bounds and establish rapport with unorthodox frontiersmen enriched the lives of many, as reflected in their letters, their search for data for 'the prof', and the flow of ethnographic items to his museum. None was more important than Gillen, whose voluminous correspondence testifies to the innovative strength and mutual independence of their intellectual partnership.

Although Gillen's and Spencer's Darwinian preconceptions were highlighted by later anthropologists who, as a result, neglected their work, their powers of critical observation, data cross-checking, and commonsense approach are appreciated today. Their *Native Tribes of Central Australia* (1899) set a standard which influenced overseas social theorists, notably James Frazer and Émile Durkheim. Frazer raised a petition which obtained them a year's leave. Spencer virtually funded their expedition which, in 1901–2, crossed Australia from Oodnadatta to Borroloola. It is memorable for the use of wax cylinder sound recording and cinematography under incredible hardships, but, more significantly, for the hundreds of sharp, artistic photographs of people and rituals, together with their documentation providing resources for Aboriginal people and anthropologists alike. Their *Northern Tribes of Central Australia* and a popular 1912 version drawn from Spencer's newspaper articles, when read in the light of Gillen's correspondence, testify to their broad thematic coverage, appreciation of linguistic requirements, and use of photographs to document and supplement field notes.

The commonwealth government invited Spencer to lead a scientific party to report on developmental aspects once it controlled the Northern Territory from 1911. Following its report he was appointed as special commissioner and chief protector of aborigines through 1912. A leg injury restricted his fieldwork, yet he published an indispensable ethnographic account (1914), a year after his blueprint for Aboriginal welfare was tabled in parliament, but thereafter forgotten. His recommendations were paternalistic, authoritarian, social Darwinist, but innovative, including the establishment of extensive Aboriginal reserves. The government sought and ignored Spencer's advice again in 1923, relating to welfare concerns at Alice Springs and Hermannsburg Lutheran mission.

Spencer's indirect role in anthropology merits record. Without his assistance it is unlikely that Alfred William Howitt would have published his compendious volume on the tribes of south-east Australia (1904). When Bronislaw Malinowski was marooned in Australia by the First World War, Spencer's advice to government, personal hospitality, and intercession for funding were critical factors behind Malinowski's celebrated Papuan research. In 1917 Spencer donated his ethnographic collection to the National Museum of Victoria, including films, wax cylinders, and some 1700 photographic negatives. His 220 Arnhem Land bark paintings constitute a unique early collection.

Hindsight suggests that these paintings were Spencer's greatest contribution to Australian art, though his contemporaries judged otherwise, for Spencer championed white Australian artists. He established enduring friendships with many prominent artists, including Arthur Streeton, Tom Roberts, Hans Heysen, George Lambert, and the three Lindsay brothers. He entertained them and purchased from both the celebrated and the needy; their letters to him comprise a national archive of aesthetic tastes and aspirations. His was among the largest private collections; when he sold it in 1919, he immediately amassed another. On behalf of the Victorian Art Gallery's Felton bequest committee, he visited England in 1916 to select advisers, resulting in significant acquisitions. His patronage was recognized in 1926 by the award of the Society of Artists' medal, Sydney.

Spencer was elected a fellow of the Royal Society in 1900 and an honorary fellow of his Oxford colleges, Exeter (1906) and Lincoln (1916) and he was awarded honorary doctorates from Manchester (DSc, 1914) and Melbourne (DLitt, 1916). He became CMG (1904), and was appointed KCMG (1916). He retired from his Melbourne chair in 1919, his workload finally impairing his health, although other factors caused his stressed condition. His marriage had failed although his wife still shared their home. They followed separate ways, probably since their son's death. Lillie was prominent in Melbourne society, but she played no part in Spencer's university life; she disapproved of his bohemian friends, and frequently visited England. Both his daughters spent the war years overseas, one never returning, so he lacked a balanced family life. He had imbibed freely with his early bush mates; now he sought solace in alcohol. In 1921 he was hospitalized with alcoholism, though ostensibly for an injured leg.

Spencer's rehabilitation was rapid: he revisited Alice Springs for fieldwork in 1923 and 1926, and wrote two two-volume books by 1928. Possibly his rejuvenation was related to his discreet association with (Alice) Jean Hamilton (*c.*1890–1961), a librarian thirty years his junior, officially his secretary. They lived in London from 1927 until voyaging to Tierra del Fuego to undertake fieldwork. Spencer died there on Navarin Island, on 14 July 1929, from angina pectoris. Jean Hamilton took his body for burial to Punta Arenas, Chile, then returned his possessions to Melbourne. A stained glass window in Exeter College hall commemorates him. D. J. MULVANEY

Sources D. J. Mulvaney and J. H. Calaby, *So much that is new: Baldwin Spencer, 1860–1929* (1985) • J. Mulvany, H. Morphy, and A. Petch, eds., *'My dear Spencer': the letters of F. J. Gillen to Baldwin Spencer* (1997) • private information (2004) • R. R. Marett and T. K. Penniman, eds., *Spencer's last journey* (1931) • R. Vanderwal, ed., *The Aboriginal photographs of Baldwin Spencer* (1982) • *CGPLA Eng. & Wales* (1930) • M. P. Byrne, *From the frontier: outback letters to Baldwin Spencer*, ed. A. Petch, J. Mulvaney, and H. Morphy (2000)

Archives Mitchell L., NSW, MSS • Museum of Victoria, Melbourne, MSS, journals, ethnographic collection • U. Oxf., Pitt Rivers Museum, anthropology MSS, corresp. and notebooks | BL, corresp. with Macmillans, Add. MS 55158 | FILM Australian Institute of Aboriginal and Torres Strait Islander Studies, Canberra • BFI NFTVA, *Strangers abroad*, ITV, 11 Oct 1986 • ScreenSound Australia | SOUND Australian Institute of Aboriginal and Torres Strait Islander Studies, Canberra, tape recording • BL NSA, wax cylinder recording, 1901 [transferred sound] • Museum of Victoria, Melbourne, wax cylinder recording, 1901 [transferred sound] • ScreenSound Australia, Canberra, tape recording

Likenesses G. Lambert, oils, 1917–21, Museum of Victoria, Melbourne • W. B. McInnes, oils, 1923, University of Melbourne • W. B. McInnes, oils, 1924, Exeter College, Oxford • photographs, South Australian Museum, Gillen collection • photographs, Museum of Victoria, Melbourne, Spencer collection [*see illus.*]

Wealth at death £6734 5*s.* 5*d.*: effects in England: administration with will, 29 Nov 1930, *CGPLA Eng. & Wales*

Spencer [*married name* Dowling or Dawlin], **Barbara** (*c.***1697–1721**), coiner, was born of 'mean parents' in the parish of St Giles Cripplegate, in London (*Lives*, 1.46). One of the more obscure figures in the criminal annals of the eighteenth century, very little is known of her early life. Spencer's father died when she was very young; her mother was reported, variously, to have kept a brandy shop, an alehouse, and a 'Boiling Cook-shop' (*Ordinary*, 19 Sept 1716; 5 July 1721). However, such business ventures were, it seems, not the family's only, or perhaps even primary, source of support: in 1721 Barbara Spencer informed the ordinary of Newgate that her mother had been 'lately executed' (5 July 1721) at Tyburn. While she did not volunteer any more information, it seems likely that Barbara's mother was one Mary Williams, alias Spencer, who in 1716 was hanged for theft; and was, moreover, an old offender, having been condemned and later pardoned for a similar offence nine years previously (ibid., 19 Sept 1716).

None the less, the only two detailed contemporary accounts of Barbara Spencer's life conform closely to the formula of the typical early eighteenth-century criminal biography, casting her as a disobedient child whose vicious inclinations frustrated all efforts on the part of well-meaning (if too tender) 'Friends' to keep her within bounds. She is described as being 'headstrong' and of a 'naturally … violent Temper', in short, too wild and unruly to be 'manag'd' by an overly 'fond' mother, who was 'too indulgent to curb her as she ought to have done' (*Ordinary*, 5 July 1721). Barbara was so 'incapable of bearing restraint' and so apt to '[fly] out into the wildest excesses of Passion and Fury' that, after a 'very slight difference at home', she left her mother to serve as an apprentice to a 'Mantua Maker' (*Lives*, 1.47). After serving only two years, Spencer 'ran Home again to her Mother', complaining of the 'cruel Usage she had met with' (*Ordinary*, 5 July 1721). Nor, it seems, was Barbara's 'Temper' much improved by her stint in service: refusing to do any work about the house, she insisted that her mother hire a maid. Quarrelling shortly thereafter with the latter, and piqued at her mother's attempts to 'interpose' between them, Barbara once again absconded from her long-suffering, but all too obliging parent. Mother and daughter soon reconciled, but reached a final (and, as it turned out, fatal) parting of the ways when—with an irony unlikely to have been lost on contemporary readers—Barbara defied her parent by going to see some malefactors hanged at Tyburn.

After leaving home Spencer married one William Dowling or Dawlin, a butcher, and although Barbara would later express to the ordinary of Newgate her 'satisfaction' that her husband—who had 'liv'd in Credit'—was dead (and hence spared any grief or shame on her account), the evidence suggests that he was still living in late 1717, when Barbara fell in with a group of coiners who instructed her in the 'Secrets' of their 'Trade' (*Ordinary*, 5 July 1721). In December 1717 she was convicted at the Old Bailey for issuing counterfeit money and sentenced to pay a fine of 5 marks. In May 1721 she was again tried at the sessions house: this time not for a misdemeanour but on charges of coining, a species of high treason. She was found guilty and sentenced to be burnt at the stake at Tyburn—the punishment meted out to women convicted of either petty or high treason (although customarily mitigated by strangling the offender with a cord before the flames had reached her body).

Spencer's claim on the interests of later chroniclers of crime rests largely on the fact that she seems to have been the first woman to have been burnt for coining in the eighteenth century. While this offence had been rigorously prosecuted in the 1680s and 1690s, burning women for high treason had become rare by Spencer's time (although the practice was not abolished until 1790). Yet Barbara Spencer proved to be, if nothing else, at least a woman of remarkable fortitude. She persisted to the last in refusing to divulge the names of other coiners of her acquaintance, vowing 'that tho' there lay the Faggots and Brushes to burn her, she would not take away the Life of any one, tho' a Magistrate was to come in Person, and offer her a Pardon to do it' (*Ordinary*, 5 July 1721).

But despite all her 'Resolution', Spencer was at the place of execution treated most unkindly by the assembled crowd, who threw 'clods of Dirt and Stones' until she was quite 'beat down and wounded' (*Lives*, 1.51; *Ordinary*, 5 July 1721). While we may suppose—as did the editors of the 1773 *Newgate Calendar*—that the crowd's 'resentment against her arose from the many losses they had sustained from counterfeit money' (1.285), it seems that such hostility could be better explained in terms of a reaction to Spencer's general demeanour, or what was known of her character. She was, after all, described as being 'very outragious and turbulent in her Behaviour' while awaiting sentence in Newgate (*Ordinary*, 5 July 1721) and as a known counterfeiter and pickpocket at her first trial (where we learn that she had attempted to dispose of incriminating evidence by swallowing a false shilling in the presence of a witness for the prosecution). Barbara Spencer may well have seemed too bold and hardened in her carriage to elicit much sympathy from spectators. Yet by all accounts, she made a good end—dying at Tyburn on 5 July 1721 'in perfect charity' with 'all the world', and 'chearfully' forgiving even those 'Vagabonds' who had pelted her with mud and stones (ibid.; *Lives*, 1.51).

ANDREA MCKENZIE

Sources P. Lorrain, *The ordinary of Newgate: his account of the … malefactors that were executed … 19th of September, 1716* (1716) • P. Lorrain, *The ordinary of Newgate: his account of the … malefactors that were executed … 5th of July 1721* (1721) • *The lives of the most remarkable criminals who have been condemn'd and executed*, 3 vols. (1735) • *The proceedings … of the peace, and oyer and terminer and gaol delivery of Newgate … at justice-hall in the Old Bailey*, 25–7 May 1721, 4–7 Dec 1718, 6–10 Sept 1716 • *Select trials … at the sessions house in the Old Bailey*, 2 vols. (1734–5) • *Select trials at the sessions house in the Old Bailey*, 4 vols. (1742) • *The Newgate calendar, or, Malefactor's bloody register*, 5 vols. (1773) • A. Knapp and W. Baldwin, *The Newgate calendar, comprising interesting memoirs of the most notorious characters*, 4 vols. (1824–6) • *Daily Journal* (6 July 1721)

Spencer, (Charles) Bernard (1909–1963), poet and broadcaster, was born on 9 November 1909 in Madras, India, the third of three children of Charles Gordon Spencer (1869–1934), a high court judge in the Indian Civil Service who was later knighted, and Edith Mary (*d.* 1936), daughter of Colonel Hugh Pearce Pearson, of the Indian army.

In 1911 Bernard, as he was habitually known, joined his brother, John (*b.* 1907), and sister, Cynthia (*b.* 1904), in England, where he was brought up by relatives and guardians in Hampshire and Oxfordshire. Spencer's education followed an expected course for a young man of his background. He attended Heddon Court preparatory school in Stevenage and Marlborough College (1923–7), where his contemporaries included Louis MacNeice, John Betjeman, and Anthony Blunt. Aesthete rather than athlete, he filled his spare hours at Marlborough with poetry and painting, and pursued these interests at Corpus Christi College, Oxford (1928–32), where he read classics. He contributed poems, reviews, and art criticism to *Oxford Outlook*, and in

1930 co-edited the influential annual *Oxford Poetry* with Stephen Spender. Spencer left university with a third class in classical moderations and a second in Greats and no clear ambitions. From 1932 to 1940 he held temporary posts teaching at preparatory schools in London and the home counties, all the while continuing to publish poems in periodicals and anthologies. His pre-war reputation as a junior member of the Auden generation was secured with contributions to *New Verse*, the most important poetry magazine of the 1930s, where he also served as assistant editor under Geoffrey Grigson from 1935 to 1938. He confirmed a quiet but resolute rebellion against class expectations by marrying a repertory actress, Nora Kathleen Gibbs (1909/10–1947), on 1 August 1936.

Spencer's first British Council appointment, in January 1940, as a lecturer at the Institute of English Studies in Salonika, changed his life and art. He discovered the major inspiration for his poetry, the Mediterranean south, the cultures and landscapes of this 'explosive, crushed-blue, nostril-opening sea' (Spencer, 19). Poems like 'Delos', 'Aegean Islands, 1940–41', and 'Greek Excavations' explore the region's ancient past, often identifying the melancholy continuities of history, as they celebrate the tactile immediacy of a living world. Greece also offered him a more cosmopolitan literary circle, with his fellow British exile Lawrence Durrell, and, in the vanguard of contemporary Greek poetry, George Seferis and Odysseus Elytis. The German invasion cut short Spencer's idyll, and he was evacuated in January 1941 to Egypt, where he spent the war years teaching at Fuad I University in Cairo. He, Durrell, and Robin Fedden edited *Personal Landscape* from 1942 to 1945, 'one of the rare "little" magazines that have made literary history in our time' (Lehmann, 339). The editors enshrined a distinctive poetry of exile, at once modernist and European, with the best of their own work, many of the important war poems of Keith Douglas, as well as translations of Rilke and Cavafy, and contributions from Seferis.

In London after the Second World War, Spencer did occasional broadcasting as a presenter, reader, and scriptwriter for the BBC Third Programme and the Home Service, but the expatriate life had taken a hold, and the particular allure of the Mediterranean beckoned once again. Spencer secured an appointment with the permanent overseas service of the British Council and was posted to Palermo in September 1946, the year that his first volume of poems, *Aegean Islands*, appeared. His duties in Sicily came to an abrupt end when his wife succumbed to tuberculosis and died in Rome on 13 June 1947. After three months working at the British Institute in Turin, Spencer, now suffering from the disease himself, underwent treatment at a clinic in Leysin, Switzerland. A long convalescence delayed a new assignment until September 1949, when he was posted to the British Institute in Madrid. Spencer served there until 1955, returning in 1958 for another four years after two interludes teaching in Athens (1955–6) and Ankara (1958). He adapted well to the western end of the Mediterranean as he had before to the Aegean. With his trim figure, casual elegance, and patrician good looks, he was a popular teacher, wry, self-deprecatory, and an elegant raconteur. His reputation as good company had followed him from pre-war London to Greece to Egypt, and now to Spain.

Spencer was never prolific, and he could be reticent about publication, but in the last five years of his life there was a new creative energy at work. His second and third volumes, *The Twist in the Plotting* and *With Luck Lasting*, appeared in 1960 and 1963 respectively. These later poems, vivid with sensuous particulars, record both the anomie and the unexpected miracles of urban life. During his second posting to Spain he met Anne Margaret Helen Marjoribanks (*b*. 1938), an English teacher and secretary at the time of marriage, whom he married in Madrid on 29 September 1961. His final posting, in January 1962, was to Vienna. Despite the unaccustomed distance from 'the promise of the South' (Spencer, 34), it was a hopeful time. His only child, Piers Bernard, was born there in July 1963, and a collected edition was planned. What seemed like a new beginning was once again undone. In the summer of 1963 he began to suffer from blackouts and memory loss, and on 10 September, now seriously ill, he was admitted to a clinic for tests. He apparently wandered away, undetected, and was found dead the following morning on a railway line in Vienna, having been struck by a train. The nature of his illness and the exact circumstances of his death have never been established. He was cremated on 17 September in Vienna, and his ashes were returned to England, where they lie beside his parents' grave in the estate church of Wheatfield House, Wheatfield, Oxfordshire. He was survived by his wife, Anne.

Bernard Spencer's *Collected Poems* was published in 1965, and a substantially expanded volume appeared in 1981. Approximately 100 poems appear in the later edition, and show the continuity of his vision over thirty years and the landscapes of seven countries. Spencer's very rootlessness—he was always the alert stranger—offered a bracing alternative to the dictates of settled metropolitan taste. He is a poet of exact momentary observation and of the long historical view, and that apparent paradox is his great strength. ROGER BOWEN

Sources B. Spencer, *Collected poems*, ed. R. Bowen (1981) · R. Bowen, *'Many histories deep': the personal landscape poets in Egypt, 1940–45* (1995) · P. Orr, ed., 'Bernard Spencer', *The poet speaks* (1966), 233–7 · L. Durrell, 'Bernard Spencer', *London Magazine* (Jan 1964), 42–7 · R. Bowen, 'The edge of a journey: notes on Bernard Spencer', *London Magazine* (Dec 1979–Jan 1980), 88–102 · R. Bowen, 'Native and exile: the poetry of Bernard Spencer', *Malahat Review*, 49 (1979), 5–27 · R. Fedden, *Personal landscape* (1966) · J. Betjeman, 'Louis MacNeice and Bernard Spencer', *London Magazine* (Dec 1963), 62–4 · O. Manning, 'Poets in exile', *Horizon* (Oct 1944), 270–79 · M. Dodsworth, 'Bernard Spencer', *The modern poet* (1968), 90–100 · J. Lehmann, *In my own time: memoirs of a literary life* (1969) · *The Times* (13 Sept 1963) · m. cert. [Nora Kathleen Gibbs] · *WW* (1933) · private information (2004) [Cynthia Peppercorn, sister; British Council]

Archives American School of Classical Studies, Athens, Gennadius Library, George Seferis archive, MSS and poem · BBC WAC, contributions to the Third and the Home Service · Ransom HRC, *London Magazine* collection and John Lehmann papers, corresp., galleys, and carbons · State University of New York, Buffalo, poetry and rare books collection, typescript and galley · U. Reading L., MSS, transcripts, notes, unpublished lectures, and corresp. | Southern Illinois University, Carbondale, Morris Library, corresp. with L. Durrell | SOUND BL NSA

Likenesses A. Nimr (Lady Smart), charcoal, 1941, repro. in Spencer, *Collected poems*, jacket · photographs, 1961?, repro. in Bowen, 'The edge of a journey', 88, 97 · photograph, repro. in *Britain Today* (Oct 1950), 12

Spencer, Sir Brent (1760–1828), army officer, was the son of Conway Spencer of Trumery, co. Antrim. On 18 January 1778 he was commissioned an ensign in the 15th foot, which was sent that year to the West Indies, and took part in the capture of St Lucia. He was promoted lieutenant on 12 November 1779, and was taken prisoner in February 1782, his regiment being part of the small garrison of Brimstone Hill, St Kitts, which had to surrender after nearly a month's siege.

After returning to England Spencer was given a company in the 99th (or Jamaica) regiment on 29 July 1783, from which he exchanged back to the 15th on 4 September. In 1790 the 15th was again sent out to the West Indies, and on 6 March 1791 Spencer obtained a majority in the 13th, then stationed in Jamaica. He served in the expedition to St Domingo, and distinguished himself at the capture of Port-au-Prince in 1794, but went home soon afterwards to join the 115th, a newly raised unit, in which he had been made lieutenant-colonel on 2 May.

On 22 July 1795 Spencer exchanged to the 40th (or 2nd Somersetshire) regiment, and went for a third time to the West Indies, landing at St Vincent at the end of September. He commanded the 40th there in the operations against the Caribs, and afterwards at Jamaica and St Domingo. At the latter he was made brigadier on 9 July 1797, and commanded the troops at Grande Anse. In the early part of 1798 he had 8000 British and colonial troops under him, and was actively engaged against Toussaint L'Ouverture until the evacuation of the island.

Spencer had been made colonel in the army and aide-de-camp to the king on 1 January 1798. At the end of that year he returned with the 40th to England, and in August 1799, when it had been raised to two battalions, he commanded it in the expedition to The Helder under the duke of York. On 10 September he defended the village of St Martin 'with great spirit and judgment', as Abercromby reported, against the Dutch troops which formed the right column of Brune's army. The republicans were attacked in their turn on 19 September, and Spencer with the 40th, forming part of Pulteney's column, drove the Dutch troops through Oudt Carspel, and along the causeway to Alkmaar. The advance had to be made along a dyke swept by artillery fire, and cost the regiment eleven officers and 150 men. Eventually the British troops had to fall back, owing to the defeat of the Russians at Bergen. The duke of York praised Spencer's conduct. The attack on the French positions was renewed on 2 October, but Pulteney's division was not actively engaged.

The British forces returned to England in November. At the end of March 1800 the 40th embarked for the Mediterranean, Spencer commanding the 2nd battalion. After some months in Minorca, and after the abandonment of the attempt upon Cadiz, it went to Malta; the four flank companies, under Spencer, accompanied Abercromby's expedition to Egypt. They formed part of the reserve under Moore, and in the landing at Abu Qir Bay, on 8 March 1801, they were among the first troops ashore. In front of them was a sandhill from which the fire was very severe.

> With Moore and Spencer at their head, the 23rd and 28th regiments, and the four flank companies of the 40th, breasted the steep sandhill. Without firing a shot they rushed at one burst to the summit of the ridge, driving headlong before them two battalions of the enemy, and capturing four pieces of field artillery. (Bunbury, 95)

Spencer's conduct was praised by Moore and Abercromby.

Spencer and his men were in the hottest part of the battle of Alexandria (21 March), and helped to disperse the cavalry who were pressing on the 42nd. On 2 April he was sent to Rosetta with 1000 British infantry, accompanied by 4000 Turks. The French evacuated it on his approach, and on 19 April he took Fort St Julien, which commanded the western branch of the Nile. Hutchinson, in his dispatch, praised Spencer's zeal, activity, and military talents. On 17 August, shortly before the fall of Alexandria, he was in command of a detachment of the 30th, under 200 men, which held an advanced post, known as 'the green hill,' on the east side of the city. Six hundred French sortied to cut off this detachment; but by Spencer's order it charged them with the bayonet, and drove them back.

After his return to England Spencer served on the staff in Sussex, first as brigadier-general, and from 1 January 1805 as major-general. George III, with whom he was a favourite, made him an equerry, and he spent much time at court. He was rumoured to have secretly married the king's daughter, Princess *Augusta, known as Puss [*see under* George III, daughters of (*act.* 1766–1857)]. In July 1807 he was appointed to the command of a brigade in the expedition to Copenhagen. The expedition returned in October, and shortly afterwards he was sent to the Mediterranean with about 5000 men. Their secret instructions were to co-operate with Moore against the Russian fleet in the Tagus, to take the French fleet at Cadiz, to assault Ceuta, and to attack the Spanish fleet at Port Mahon. Delayed by bad weather, which dispersed his force, he did not reach Gibraltar until March 1808. He went on to Port Mahon, but, on the outbreak of the Spanish insurrection, returned to Cadiz. Spain and England were nominally at war, and the Spaniards refused to let British troops enter Cadiz. Spencer would not risk his small force by advancing inland; but his appearance off the mouth of the Guadiana encouraged the insurgents in the south of Portugal, and prevented the detachment of troops from Junot's army from aiding Dupont in his attempt on Seville.

The surrender of Dupont at Baylen on 19 July made it unnecessary for Spencer to remain longer near Cadiz, and on 5 August he joined Wellesley's force at the mouth of the Mondego, anticipating an order which Wellesley had sent him. He was present as second in command at the actions of Roliça and Vimeiro. Wellesley acknowledged his assistance in his dispatches, and recommended him for some mark of the king's favour. 'There never was a braver officer, or one who deserved it better' (*Dispatches*, 6.124). It was deferred because of the inquiry into the convention of Cintra, but on 26 April 1809 he was made KB. He also received the gold medal.

Spencer returned to England in October 1808, as his health would not let him share in Moore's campaign in Spain. He was one of the witnesses at the inquiry into the convention. His evidence was in its favour; but he supported Wellesley's contention that more might have been made of the victory of Vimeiro. He had been made colonel of the 9th garrison battalion on 25 November 1806, and transferred to the 2nd West India regiment on 25 June 1808; and on 31 August 1809 he was made colonel-commandant of the 2nd battalion of the 95th (later the Rifle brigade).

In May 1810 Spencer went back to the Peninsula to succeed Sir John Coape Sherbrooke as second in command under Wellington, but on the understanding that Graham, who was then at Cadiz, would fill that post if summoned to the army, and would be Wellington's successor in case of need. Spencer was given the command of the first division and the local rank of lieutenant-general (5 May 1810). He commanded his division at Busaco, in the lines of Torres Vedras, in the pursuit of Masséna, and at Fuentes d' Oñoro. Wellington repeatedly mentioned in his dispatches the able and cordial assistance which Spencer afforded him. He was left in command of the British troops in the north of Portugal, when Wellington was with Beresford near Badajoz, in the latter half of April 1811, and again from the middle of May to the middle of June. He had to watch Marmont; and when the latter moved southward to join Soult and relieve Badajoz, Spencer made a corresponding movement and joined Wellington.

Napier speaks of Spencer as vacillating when left in separate command, and as 'more noted for intrepidity than for military quickness'. He was one of the officers who wrote despairing letters home at the time of the retreat to Torres Vedras, and helped to shake the faith of the government in Wellington's scheme of defence. In July Graham joined the army from Cadiz, superseding Spencer as second in command. The latter obtained leave to go home, and Wellington reported it without expressing regret. Spencer received the Portuguese order of the Tower and Sword.

Spencer saw no further service, and passed the rest of his life in retirement. He had become lieutenant-general in the army on 4 June 1811, and was made general on 27 May 1825. He was given the colonelcy of the 40th on 2 July 1818. He was appointed a member of the consolidated board of general officers, and was also made governor of Cork. He died at The Lee, near Great Missenden, Buckinghamshire, on 29 December 1828.

E. M. LLOYD, *rev.* ROGER T. STEARN

Sources *United Service Journal*, 2 (1829) • *GM*, 1st ser., 99/1 (1829) • J. Philippart, ed., *The royal military calendar*, 3rd edn, 5 vols. (1820), vol. 2 • R. H. R. Smythies, *Historical records of the 40th regiment* (1894) • H. Bunbury, *Narratives of some passages in the great war with France, from 1799 to 1810* (1854) • *The dispatches of … the duke of Wellington … from 1799 to 1818*, ed. J. Gurwood, 13 vols. in 12 (1834–9) • W. F. P. Napier, *History of the war in the Peninsula and in the south of France*, new edn, 6 vols. (1886) • J. J. Stockdale, *Enquiry into the convention of Cintra* (1809) • E. Longford [E. H. Pakenham, countess of Longford], *Wellington*, 1: *The years of the sword* (1969) • A. J. Guy, ed., *The road to Waterloo: the British army and the struggle against revolutionary and Napoleonic France, 1793–1815* (1990) • R. Muir, *Britain and the defeat of Napoleon, 1807–1815* (1996)

Archives Sheff. Arch., estate papers, leases, deeds, etc. relating to family property at Bramley Grange | BL, corresp. with Sir James Willoughby Gordon, Add. MS 49489 • U. Nott. L., Hallward Library, letters to Lord William Bentinck

Spencer, Charles, third earl of Sunderland (1674/5–1722), politician, the second son of Robert *Spencer, second earl of Sunderland (1641–1702), and his wife, Lady Anne Digby (1645/6–1715), the youngest daughter of George *Digby, second earl of Bristol, was born into politics and never left that arena from his earliest youth. He was educated at home; his tutor, Charles Trimnell, later bishop of Norwich and bishop of Winchester, remained a close friend and ally throughout his life. The death of his elder brother, Robert, in September 1688, made Spencer the heir to the peerage, and from then until his father's death he was known as Lord Spencer. The elder Sunderland, despised and reviled as the tool of James II, fled to the Netherlands in December 1688, and was followed by his family in April 1689, where Spencer studied at the University of Leiden. This was a formative period of his upbringing, and the political principles he imbibed in the Netherlands had much to do with his early political radicalism. Spencer was a precocious and highly intelligent young man. He mastered a number of foreign languages and developed a passion for learning and books that was to be a notable attribute throughout his life.

Entry into active politics In April 1690, on the family's return to England, Spencer's father re-entered politics as political manager to William III, though his infamy was such that he could not be given office. His father's connections and eminence brought Spencer into contact with virtually all the leading politicians of the age. It also led to two successive marriages which brought him both wealth and important political liaisons. The first, on 12 January 1695, to Lady Arabella Cavendish (1673–1698), the daughter of Henry *Cavendish, second duke of Newcastle upon Tyne, brought him a rich dowry of £25,000 and a brother-in-law who was the greatest boroughmongerer of the age—John *Holles, later duke of Newcastle upon Tyne of the second creation. When Arabella died in 1698, his father contracted an even more important marriage for him with Lady Anne Churchill (1683–1716), the second and favourite daughter of his long-time political associate John *Churchill, first duke of Marlborough. The marriage took place on 2 January 1700.

As soon as he came of age in 1695, Spencer entered the House of Commons as member for Tiverton. His strong party loyalty has been commented on so widely by contemporaries that it cannot be questioned. He was characterized as a violent whig of 'a disagreeable impetuosity and ungrateful manner of speaking' (*Buckinghamshire MSS*,

Charles Spencer, third earl of Sunderland (1674/5–1722), by Sir Godfrey Kneller, 1720

508). At the same time he showed a natural talent for politics and quickly mastered the intricacies of parliamentary practice. His father had joined the tories following the death of Mary II in December 1694, but Spencer remained firmly attached to the whig leaders, especially the lord chancellor and their head, John Somers, Baron Somers.

By 1701 the tide of public opinion was turning against the tories, accelerated by Louis XIV's recognition of the Pretender on the death of James II in September 1701, and the whigs were returned to power. The change of the ministry was short-lived. The death of William in March 1702 and the accession of Anne resulted in her putting herself into the hands of her friends Marlborough and Sidney Godolphin, first Baron Godolphin. The two ministers endeavoured to steer a middle course between the two parties, though the queen's own predilections determined the return of the senior tory leaders to office as well. At this juncture the elder Sunderland died, on 28 September 1702, and Spencer succeeded to his estate and honours and took his seat in the Lords in the new parliament.

A junto whig in opposition Sunderland, by his intelligence, the strictness of his principles, his record in the Commons, his keenness in debate, and his grasp of foreign and domestic affairs, sharpened by his stay in the Netherlands and his omnivorous reading, was marked out for a position of prominence. Above all he had a claim to membership in the chief counsels of the party because of his relationship with Marlborough. The whig leaders undoubtedly saw him as a means to return to power. Thus the junto, the ruling council of the whig party, gained a fifth member, replacing the defecting Charles Talbot, duke of Shrewsbury. For the next thirteen years this structure of leadership remained unchanged, a powerful testimony to the durability of party even in its embryonic stage. Sunderland was also much in the confidence of Sarah Churchill, duchess of Marlborough, an outspoken whig and the confidante of the queen. Lady Sunderland, too, was the most actively political of the four Churchill daughters, and was widely celebrated and touted as the Little Whig.

Though the whigs were broken after their brief return to power in the autumn of 1701, they continued to hold the balance of power in the Lords. It was in this body, in which all their leaders were members, that they began to rebuild their party. Sunderland immediately took an active role in the Lords, though, with the conduct of the main business out of the hands of his party, he had little influence. He was active as a manager in the Lords to defeat the Occasional Conformity Bill in February 1703, to the embarrassment of his father-in-law, for the queen had the measure dear to her heart. He incensed the queen even more when he opposed the bill to allow her consort an allowance in the event she predeceased him. In the next session the whigs were presented with a golden opportunity to compromise Daniel Finch, second earl of Nottingham, the most active tory minister in the cabinet. In the summer of 1703 a French design to raise an army in Scotland to support an uprising was revealed. Dispatches from and to Nottingham were turned over to Sunderland by his former brother-in-law Newcastle, into whose hands they fell. Sunderland arranged a meeting of the junto lords in December to determine how to exploit Nottingham's apparent effort to conceal elements of the plot. A committee of whig lords was formed to investigate and Sunderland was actively involved. Although they were unable to pass a motion of censure, Nottingham was roughly handled and much incensed.

When the Occasional Conformity Bill was again passed by the Commons, Sunderland was one of the managers who defeated it in the Lords in December 1703. His detailed estimates on the vote testify to his assiduity and care for detail. Finally, when the tory commissioners of accounts put another junto lord, Edward Russell, earl of Orford, under fire, Sunderland unearthed a precedent from the reign of Charles II that encouraged the Lords to alter the panel when it came up for renewal, thus ensuring the bill's rejection and the lapse of the commission. When the session was over in spring 1704, Nottingham and his tory allies demanded the removal of Archbishop Thomas Tenison and Charles Seymour, sixth duke of Somerset, from the cabinet and another whig peer from office for opposing the Occasional Conformity Bill. In response Nottingham's offer of resignation was accepted, his allies dismissed, and the ministry altered. Sunderland was the leading whig candidate for office and was proposed as secretary to succeed Nottingham. But the queen was not ready to accept the whigs and the post went to Robert Harley, laying the grounds for the bitter enmity which later arose between him and Sunderland. In the autumn the whigs tried to install him as comptroller but were no more successful than before. When parliament reassembled in October, Godolphin and his colleagues were in a dilemma. The tory leaders were now bent on their destruction for being evicted from office. The whigs, likewise disappointed in being promoted, joined them in denouncing the queen's servants. At a critical debate in the Lords on 29 November on the state of the nation, principally on the implications of Scotland's Security Act, which seemed to ensure the end of the personal union, Godolphin capitulated, the whigs switched sides, and the government was saved. Sunderland was in the chair and helped to steer and temper the debate, which began the process leading to the Act of Union of 1707 and settled the whig-leaning character of the ministry.

Office under Anne One proof of the rapprochement was the appointment of Sunderland as envoy-extraordinary to the Holy Roman emperor. The embassy was originally intended to mediate, in conjunction with the Dutch, between the insurgents in Hungary and the emperor. It was considered a thankless and unrewarding assignment, and Godolphin had been unable to recruit anyone for it. But with the death of Leopold I and the accession of Joseph I it was combined with a mission of condolences and congratulations. The junto lord Charles Montagu, Baron Halifax, proposed Sunderland as a means of edging him into office, and the queen agreed. The appointment, made on 17 June, gave him valuable insight into foreign affairs and first-hand knowledge of England's principal allies.

On his return at the beginning of 1706 Sunderland immediately attended parliament, where he was caught up in the debates on the Regency Act and spoke strongly on behalf of the court whig measure, allowing office-holders to retain their seats in the Commons during the six-month period for which parliament was to survive a dead monarch. When the session was over the whigs once more pressed their demands for a seat for Sunderland in the cabinet as secretary, the opening wedge in their return to office. Throughout the summer and autumn the pressure mounted. Godolphin, seeing no other option, advised the queen to capitulate, but secretly advised by Harley she adamantly refused. Harley also worked successfully to detach some of the moderate whigs from the junto, which weakened their efforts. Even when Marlborough returned from the continent he was unable to budge her. It was only resolved when Sir Charles Hedges resigned voluntarily as southern secretary to make way for him. On 3 December 1706 he finally received the seals of office.

As soon as Sunderland entered office he attacked his new duties with all the energy and enthusiasm that always characterized his activities. The job was demanding, requiring long hours in the office, preparing and often writing fair copies of letters to the English envoys abroad assigned to his department, acting as the queen's and cabinet's conduit to foreign powers and commanders in the field—especially onerous in wartime—co-ordinating preparations for expeditions, handling a large flow of domestic correspondence, and attending cabinet meetings. He also had to be in regular attendance on the queen, even when she was out of town at Windsor or elsewhere, and assiduously appear in parliament, where he was a principal government spokesman. On taking office, he was immediately engaged in preparing reinforcements to send to Spain, and it gave him an early exposure to the frustrations of dealing with bureaucrats. Initially he seemed to have moderated his behaviour, to the pleasant surprise of the queen. In the Lords he was a principal manager in the passage of the treaty of union with Scotland in 1707. He also was heavily involved in negotiations for the management of Scotland after the union, though when he was sidetracked for several weeks by illness he and the other whig leaders were outmanoeuvred by Godolphin, who kept control in his own hands. During 1707 Harley, violently opposed to Sunderland's appointment and the admission of more junto members to the cabinet, fought a rearguard action against them. Senior appointments in the church were the most visible battleground. As Harley had the ear of the queen, Godolphin and the junto were on the defensive. Sunderland entered into cabal with his whig colleagues several times during the summer, where they considered ways of forcing the queen's hand. It was not until early 1708 that the crisis was resolved. The espionage of one of Harley's clerks compromised him badly and the whigs took up the attack in parliament. Harley, garnering support from moderate whigs and tories, almost pulled off a coup, removing Godolphin, Sunderland, and their adherents, but it was finally aborted by the intervention of Marlborough.

The seeds for the destruction of the ministry were sown, however, and the alienation of the queen from the duchess of Marlborough, who was replaced in the queen's confidence by her dresser, Abigail Masham, exacerbated the situation. When parliamentary elections were held in May 1708, the tories and Harley, in disarray following their removal from office and embarrassed by the aborted Jacobite invasion of Scotland in February, were routed. Sunderland, who managed the transfer to London of Scots implicated in the invasion, used their presence to intrigue against Marlborough and Godolphin and elect a whig slate of representative peers for the new parliament. Marlborough and Godolphin triumphed over the whig challenge, returning twelve of the sixteen. The queen was so incensed that she demanded Sunderland's resignation, and only with the greatest difficulty was Godolphin able to persuade her to accept an apology instead. Sunderland was more successful in supporting a whig bill to abolish the Scottish privy council, considered a creature of the treasurer's. Aside from the elections and the Jacobite invasion, Sunderland's main concerns were foreign and military affairs. He had responsibility for France and southern Europe and was heavily engaged in planning and supervising the campaigns in Spain and Italy and an abortive attempt to land an expeditionary force on the Atlantic coast of France.

Flushed with their victory at the polls, the whigs were now determined to gain admittance for more of their leaders into the cabinet. When James Butler, second duke of Ormond, had resigned as lord lieutenant of Ireland, Godolphin was able to refuse their demands to replace him with Thomas Wharton, earl of Wharton, adding the post to the existing responsibility as lord president of Thomas Herbert, eighth earl of Pembroke. Sunderland now acted as intermediary between the whigs, Marlborough and Godolphin, and the queen. In return for the resignation of the queen's husband, Prince George, as lord high admiral, to be replaced by Pembroke, and the appointment of Somers as lord president and Wharton as lord lieutenant of Ireland, the whigs agreed to support the government's financial legislation. When the queen's obduracy put the whole scheme in jeopardy, it was saved by the death of Prince George on 28 October and the breakdown of her resolve. The appointments were made, Peter King, the whig nominee, was selected for speaker, and the legislative session at least started smoothly. But the contest for power between the treasurer and the court party and the whigs continued unabated. The whigs were able to dominate the hearings on controverted elections in the Commons, nullifying the elections of a number of tories, though Harley escaped their net. They also displaced several nominees of the treasurer in key committee posts. Sunderland continued to try to wrest control of Scotland from the treasurer, but appeals to seat the remaining whig candidates as representative peers failed. He did work actively to relocate the protestant refugees, known as the Palatines after their homeland, driven out of the Rhineland by France, and guided their Naturalization Bill through the house. The majority were sent on to Ireland and ultimately to North America. As his responsibilities extended to those territories, Sunderland also worked closely with Wharton in Dublin and spent long hours planning an expeditionary force to seize French Canada, only to see it held up and abandoned because of the pending peace negotiations. After the success of the allied campaign in 1708 and the bankruptcy of the French treasury, Louis XIV had made overtures for peace. This resulted in another apple of discord between Marlborough and Godolphin and the junto. The whigs wanted to secure Dutch support for the protestant succession and were willing to guarantee a series of Dutch-occupied fortresses in the Spanish Netherlands as a bar against a surprise invasion. The admission of Somers to the cabinet as lord president was especially important to the whigs, as it would give the former chancellor a role in any peace negotiations. Marlborough, who controlled British diplomacy in northern Europe, was wary of a barrier treaty which could be grounds for reprisal by the tories if they regained control of the government. The general found it expedient to accept a co-envoy to avoid sole responsibility. After several candidates were considered for the post, including Sunderland, the choice went to Charles Townshend, second Viscount Townshend. Townshend returned with a barrier treaty, but Louis XIV rejected the peace terms he was offered and the war continued. Meanwhile Sunderland and his junto colleagues were involved in a continuing series of disputes with Godolphin and the queen. They came to a head over the queen's reluctance to replace Pembroke with an Admiralty commission headed by Orford. Orford himself insisted upon certain guarantees that almost sank the scheme until he finally gave way, and the new commission passed the great seal in November.

When parliament met in autumn 1709, Sunderland and his colleagues had good reason to be pleased. Sunderland finally found the queen easy with him, though Marlborough attributed her co-operativeness to resignation rather than contentment. Sunderland had the pleasure of seeing the queen ratify the barrier treaty, which was essentially a whig project. Though the negotiations had technically lain in the department of Harley's successor, Henry Boyle, as northern secretary, Sunderland and Somers, in conjunction with Godolphin, had been responsible for its direction. Over Marlborough's strenuous objections they did not include a clause binding the Dutch to 'no peace without Spain', and the general, though a co-plenipotentiary, refused to sign. In parliament the spirit of the tories appeared to be broken. Legislation passed so quickly that all the money bills were in by Christmas and the funds voted were the greatest yet given. What finally undid Sunderland and his colleagues was an inflammatory high-church parson.

Sacheverell and the return to opposition Dr Henry Sacheverell delivered a flaming sermon before the lord mayor of London on 9 November 1709. A high-church diatribe, it provoked the ministry into impeaching him to try to put quietus to the tory opposition. Opinion is divided as to whether Godolphin, who was singled out for attack by Sacheverell, or Sunderland was the strongest proponent, although the latter is usually given the responsibility for the débâcle that followed. Unquestionably Sunderland was on the attack. He made strenuous efforts to curb the tory press, closing down two short-lived newspapers and arresting Delariviere Manley for her slander against the government in the *New Atlantis*. Concurrently Harley was building a new coalition to challenge Godolphin and working secretly with the queen to undermine him. The first challenges came early in January, when the queen ignored Marlborough's recommendations in two senior military appointments. In retaliation the incensed Marlborough threatened to resign his commissions if the queen did not dismiss Mrs Masham. The general even proposed an address by the Commons to the queen for Masham's removal and, more audaciously, demanded his appointment as captain-general be made for life. The queen bestirred herself, however, and Sunderland alone among the chief ministers supported the ultimatums, so the duke gave way, and the queen and Harley won the first test. The next contest came over two church appointments, for two bishoprics which fell vacant in February. Sunderland immediately proposed candidates on behalf of the junto, but they were rejected.

It was the Sacheverell trial which now occupied everyone's attention. The government mobilized a strong team of prosecutors and won the battle but lost the war. For though Sacheverell was found guilty the punishment was so mild as to be without effect. The tories used the occasion of the trial to whip up demonstrations and riots. Sunderland as secretary was responsible for maintaining public order. He marshalled troops to quell the rioters and conducted several months of investigations to try to determine responsibility for the disturbances, but to no avail. Emboldened by her recent successes, the queen now peremptorily informed Godolphin that she was appointing Shrewsbury as lord chamberlain. Soon afterwards she insisted on adding Masham's brother to the list of colonels to be promoted general over Marlborough's objections. Most ominously of all, rumours began to circulate that Sunderland was to be dismissed. As the special object of both Harley's and the queen's hatred, the most vehement of the junto and the son-in-law of Marlborough, he was an ideal wedge to dislodge the government. Anne, acting on the advice of Harley, who in turn had won over Shrewsbury and the difficult Somerset, ordered Sunderland to turn in his seals of office on 13 June 1710. She offered him a pension of £3000 a year, as there was no proper reason for discharging him, which he refused. Godolphin was the next to go, replaced by a commission including Harley, who was also appointed as chancellor of the exchequer. The dissolution of parliament and a call for new elections brought the resignation of the rest of the whig ministers. Marlborough alone, isolated and abroad, remained.

For the next four years Sunderland now took on the leadership of the whigs in opposition. Godolphin was old and ailing, and died in 1712. Somers, though younger than Godolphin, was also increasingly infirm. The vain Halifax was wooed by Harley (who became earl of Oxford) and his colleague Henry St John, Viscount Bolingbroke, and Orford went into retirement. Only Wharton displayed his usual energy and partisanship. Marlborough, urged by his friends to retain his command, could do so only by remaining detached from politics at home, and he eventually went into exile on the continent in November 1712. Sunderland worked vigorously for the party in the elections that took place in the autumn of 1710. When Marlborough, too, was disgraced, Sunderland was the natural person to reconstitute the alliance between his family and his friends. He seemed to have learned to exercise more self-control. Once out of office he became a frequent and respected speaker in the Lords. He was a consistent and effective debater during the dark days of the whigs from 1710 to 1714.

The last four years of Anne's reign, dominated by an Oxford-led ministry, were frustrating and even dangerous times for Sunderland and his colleagues. The tories were bent on destroying their opponents, no less vindictive than the whigs had been when in power. In investigations into the Spanish campaign, particularly the defeat at Almanza in 1707, Sunderland, as secretary responsible for Spain, was singled out for criticism. The whig concern for the Palatines and their naturalization also incited tory ire. The repeal of the naturalization was passed in the Commons in autumn 1710 but failed in the Lords, where the whigs possessed a frail majority. The Commons, frustrated by the rejection of the bill, passed condemnatory resolutions on Sunderland as the principal protector of the Palatines and even considered his impeachment. The idea was dropped when it was not supported by the court, as was consideration of an address to the queen asking that Sunderland be excluded from her councils forever. Another reversal of a whig landmark in which Sunderland had been heavily involved came with the repeal of the barrier treaty in 1711. In autumn 1711 Sunderland was one of the leaders in the Lords of the successful effort to pass a 'No peace without Spain' resolution to be sent to the queen as a threat to the tory ministry if they compromised the long-standing British war aims. As a quid pro quo for the support of Nottingham and his relations, Sunderland and the whigs agreed to betray their dissenter allies, and the infamous Occasional Conformity Bill was now passed. Other minor victories were won in parliament in the remaining years of the reign, notably the rejection of the commercial treaty with France proposed as part of the peace settlement, but it was divisions within the tories themselves, notably the competition between Oxford and Bolingbroke, that eventually denied them the support of the queen and prepared the way for the restoration of Marlborough and the whigs to power—thwarted only by the death of the queen herself before it could be consummated.

Office under George I When George I succeeded to the throne in August 1714, Sunderland and Marlborough must have thought that their restoration to favour was at hand, but they soon discovered this was not to be the case. The king was wary of Sunderland's impetuous behaviour and Marlborough's ambition. Both found themselves excluded from the list of lords justices appointed to manage the country until the new king arrived. While the other junto leaders were assigned seats in the cabinet, Sunderland, though sworn of the privy council on 1 October 1714, was sidetracked with an appointment as lord lieutenant of Ireland and the prospect of political exile by having to take up his post in Dublin. The new whig ministry was headed by Townshend as northern secretary, the post to which Sunderland had made his claim, with James Stanhope as southern secretary. Though Townshend and Halifax, first lord of the Treasury, were the senior ministers in terms of influence with the new king, they were joined by the two Hanoverian ministers, Bothmer and Bernstorff, along with Marlborough, to make up the inner circle of advisers. Marlborough's diplomatic skills and personal charm allowed him to extend his influence with George I, which was to Sunderland's benefit.

When Wharton died in 1715 (in the same year as Somers and Halifax) Sunderland was encouraged by messages sent via the duchess of Marlborough through his wife that a more congenial post would be found him in London. Sunderland never made the voyage to Ireland, on the grounds of poor health, and on 28 August 1715 he succeeded Wharton as lord privy seal. Still frustrated by his exclusion from real power, he began to build a connection of other discontented whigs and some tories. At the same time he shared the distrust of Townshend and others of the prince and princess of Wales and the prince's favourite, John Campbell, second duke of Argyll, long a rival to Marlborough in the army. Sunderland and his father-in-law now worked behind the scenes to oust Townshend and assume control of the ministry. Their machinations were disrupted for a time in the first part of 1716, first by the death of Lady Sunderland, the duke's favourite daughter, on 29 April 1716. The duke in turn was felled by a paralytic stroke on 28 May, and though he made a partial recovery he never regained his health and influence. Nevertheless, the plans had been concerted, the king had been seduced, and after frequent consultation with his former in-laws and General William Cadogan, Marlborough's long-time deputy, Sunderland and Cadogan embarked for the continent. Sunderland travelled ostensibly to Aix-la-Chapelle, to take the waters, but from there went on to Hanover, where the king was in residence. During the king's absence the prince of Wales, as regent, along with his more popular and astute wife, ingratiated themselves with the public and the politicians. Able to converse comfortably in English, and much more social and hospitable than the reclusive king, they were represented by Sunderland as trying to curry favour with the public at the expense of the king. Townshend, who had remained in London in charge of the government, was further represented as being in conspiracy with the prince and princess. Townshend was also accused of working with his brother-in-law Robert Walpole, now first lord of the Treasury, to hold up the signing of a commercial treaty with France, to which the king was committed and for which Stanhope was responsible. Sunderland, following Marlborough's advice, won over the suspicious king and James Stanhope, the secretary in residence, as well. As a result, soon after the king returned Townshend was dismissed and Walpole and their followers resigned. The way was now clear for a wholesale reconstitution of the ministry. Stanhope moved to the Treasury, Sunderland succeeded Townshend as northern secretary on 15 April 1717, and, with Cadogan now the *de facto* head of the army, Argyll was also deprived of access to power. Stanhope, the son of a diplomatist, had spent a good part of his life abroad and was far more interested and comfortable with responsibility for foreign affairs than finance and patronage. Even though Sunderland had served in this capacity in the previous reign, Stanhope remained the dominant voice in foreign affairs. When the ministers presented to the imperial representative the draft of what became the Quadruple Alliance, in which the emperor, Charles VI, renounced all claims to the crown of Spain, Stanhope joined Sunderland in presenting the draft. As a consequence of Stanhope's clear preference to deal with foreign affairs, within a year he and Sunderland traded posts, on 20 March 1718, four days after Sunderland also assumed the post of lord president of the council. He was now in his element, in charge of patronage, domestic policy, and the management of parliament.

Joint head of the ministry For the next three years Sunderland and Stanhope, with the king's full confidence, controlled the ministry, both at home and abroad. It is difficult to determine the respective roles and authority of the two senior ministers. Stanhope was fully occupied with foreign affairs, a charge he found congenial. It also permitted him to resume his trips abroad to negotiate directly on behalf of the king. Sunderland, who was also experienced in diplomacy, found domestic politics more to his liking and took the lead mending fences at home, managing patronage, entertaining members of parliament, and acting as the ministry's chief liaison to the parties. As secretary Stanhope had shared that office with Joseph Addison, a weak and ineffectual minister. When Stanhope was elevated to the peerage, on 12 July 1717, this left the leadership of the house in weak hands and unable to withstand the attacks of Walpole and his party. When Sunderland took the Treasury he was replaced by James Craggs the younger, a much more supple and able politician, who shared the management of the Commons with John Aislabie as chancellor of the exchequer. But then the split in the whig ranks was soon followed by a split in the royal family.

In December 1717 the prince of Wales, in arranging for the christening of his son, decided that the child would have only royal sponsors. But Thomas Pelham-Holles, duke of Newcastle, as lord chamberlain, and with the king's support, asserted his prerogative and also stood sponsor at the ceremony, to the prince's dismay. Words were exchanged, the duke misinterpreting the prince's remarks, and the prince was ordered to apologize by the king. Failing to do so, the prince was banished from court, care of his children was assumed by the king, and the prince and princess were isolated from the court and the ministers for more than two years. Walpole, Townshend, and their adherents now rallied around the prince, who thus legitimized their opposition and began a tradition that was to create a precedent repeated in the next two reigns. For Sunderland and Stanhope it left their ministry in a precarious position, as the opposition was joined by the lord chancellor, William, first Earl Cowper, and other politicians loyal to the heir apparent and his supporters. Though Stanhope tried to dissuade Cowper from resigning, it was Sunderland who delivered him the king's ultimatum, that he either absent himself from the prince's court or give up his post. The ministers now planned a series of measures to bolster their position. The Septennial Act, passed in 1716, gave the whigs an extra four years to consolidate their power before submitting to elections for the Commons. Early in 1717 the ministers began to sound their supporters among the bishops about plans to repeal the Occasional Conformity Act. They also discussed a plan to reform the two English universities, both tory strongholds, by placing the appointment of all officers, heads of houses, members of colleges, and so on, in the hands of the king. Stanhope even wanted to repeal the Test and Corporation Acts in so far as they affected protestant dissenters, but Cowper was equivocal and Sunderland was opposed. No action was taken at the time. In December 1718 Stanhope, now more confident, introduced a bill repealing both the Occasional Conformity and Schism Acts as well as modifying the Test Act. Sunderland seconded it, but, in its course through the Lords, Cowper, now in opposition, moved to strike the clause affecting the Test Act, and Stanhope, under pressure from Sunderland, gave way. In this altered state it passed both houses, though not without vociferous opposition from Walpole. The Relief Act of 1719 clarified provisions of the Corporation Act and, in conjunction with regular Indemnity Acts, allowed many protestant dissenters to remain members of corporations without having to conform to the established church. A bill to reform the universities was drawn up but not submitted after other reform schemes were rejected in parliament. But the great *cause célèbre* of the session was the Peerage Bill, a measure to limit the number of members in the Lords and convert the sixteen representative peers of Scotland into a hereditary group of twenty-five. The ostensible justification was to forestall a repeat of Oxford's simultaneous creation of twelve peers in 1711 to gain a majority in the Lords. But the real justification had as much to do with the desire of Sunderland and Stanhope to bar the prince of Wales from adopting a similar scheme on his accession with the potential of overturning their base of power in the Lords. It was also a means to prevent the king's German favourites from acquiring peerages. The opposition was so strong that Stanhope withdrew the bill in April. But the ministers were determined to persevere. The Peerage Bill, the Universities Bill, and even the repeal of the Septennial Act were considered over the summer. In the last-named case this probably meant permitting parliament to sit at the pleasure of the king with a mandatory dissolution only upon the death of the sovereign, which was the practice in Ireland. When the Peerage Bill was reintroduced the following session it passed the Lords but was voted down in the Commons, the victorious opposition once again led by Walpole. With this defeat Sunderland and Stanhope abandoned the rest of their reform measures. Sunderland's attention now turned to consolidating the national debt and reducing the burden of interest, a process begun by Walpole before his departure from the Treasury. At the beginning of 1720 the chancellor of the exchequer, John Aislabie, introduced into the Commons a scheme proposed by the South Sea Company to take over the unfunded national debt, which passed in April, over the strong opposition of the Bank of England, and sent South Sea stock soaring.

After their setbacks in parliament, Sunderland and his colleagues now realized the danger of their position and the need to bring back the dissident whigs in order to maintain their control of the government. A further issue was the interference of the king's Hanoverian ministers, especially Bernstorff, who it was believed was working to unseat them. For their part Walpole and Townshend recognized that, however effective they were in debate and in thwarting the ministry's measures, it was unlikely they would return to power so long as Sunderland and Stanhope retained the king's confidence. An accommodation was reached. In April Walpole was readmitted as paymaster-general and Townshend as lord president. Though still in lesser roles, they were at least back in office; Stanhope and Sunderland had consolidated the ministry's control of parliament, the Germans were forced to decamp, and the king and his son were reconciled, though barely so.

The contest for the king's favour and control of the government now was focused in the court rather than in parliament. But a new crisis caused a dramatic change in the political scene. After South Sea stock skyrocketed in price in June 1720, following its assumption of the unfunded national debt, the price began a rapid decline in July. By September its bankers ceased payments, a panic ensued, and parliament, which convened in December, was out for blood. Sunderland, as first lord of the Treasury, was especially vulnerable. A series of accidents combined with parliamentary hostility to weaken the ministry. Stanhope died on 5 February 1721, following a stroke while vigorously defending the government in the Lords the previous day, and was succeeded as northern secretary by Townshend. The younger James Craggs died of smallpox on 16 February and was succeeded as southern secretary by a Sunderland ally, John Carteret, second Baron Carteret. Aislabie was expelled from the Commons on 8 March, and the elder James Craggs died (a possible suicide) on 16 March. Though Sunderland was cleared of corruption after a long debate in the Commons on 15 March, thanks to a brilliant defence by Walpole, the price of his deliverance was his resignation. He was succeeded by Walpole.

Death and assessment Sunderland was now on the defensive, but by taking the post of groom of the stole he retained his access to and also the confidence of the king. For the next year there was a running battle between Sunderland and Walpole for control. Each had supporters in key cabinet posts. The final test came with the dissolution of parliament in March 1722 and the ensuing elections. Sunderland sought support wherever he could find it. Most significant was his concerted effort to win the backing of the tories, even the Jacobites. To do so he resumed negotiations with Bolingbroke, exiled since 1715 in France. Bolingbroke had negotiated with successive ministers for a pardon and in turn offered to bring the Jacobites into the fold and declare allegiance to George I and his successors. The pardon was drafted, and in the election contests Sunderland entered into cabal with the Jacobites and every possible ally to return members of parliament who would follow his lead rather than Walpole's. But the success of his efforts was never to be determined, for Sunderland fell ill and died of pleurisy on 19 April 1722 at his London residence, Sunderland House, Piccadilly, just as the returns began to trickle in. By default Walpole now succeeded as premier minister. Sunderland was buried on

1 May at Brington, Northamptonshire, near his country seat of Althorp.

Sunderland is a study in contrasts. In his youth a fierce and vehement partisan, in his maturity he became a supple, if not devious, skilled politician, in contrast to Stanhope, who was never at ease in the Commons and never learned to curb his temper. Sunderland's dealings with the Jacobites raises questions about his principles, but he was regarded as personally honest in office, a rare quality in an Augustan politician. Though he was married three times, questions have been raised about both his and Stanhope's sexual preferences. He and his first wife, Lady Arabella Cavendish, had one daughter, Frances (*d.* 1742), who married Henry *Howard, afterwards fourth earl of Carlisle (1694–1758) [*see under* Howard, Charles, third earl of Carlisle]. With his second wife, Lady Anne Churchill, he had three sons and two daughters. His eldest son, Robert (*b.* 1701), succeeded him as fourth earl of Sunderland, but died on 15 September 1729. His second son, Charles *Spencer (1706–1758), succeeded his brother as fifth earl of Sunderland, and in 1733 became, in succession to his aunt (Marlborough's eldest daughter, Henrietta), third duke of Marlborough. The third son, John (1708–1746), succeeded to the Althorp estate when Charles became duke of Marlborough, and was father of John Spencer, first Earl Spencer. Sunderland's daughter Anne (*d.* 1769) married William Bateman, first Viscount Bateman, and Diana (*d.* 1735) became the first wife of John *Russell, fourth duke of Bedford. His three children with his third wife, Judith Tichborne, whom he had married on 5 December 1717, all predeceased him. After his death Judith married Sir Robert *Sutton (1671/2–1746). She died on 17 May 1749.

Condemned by Jonathan Swift and others for his intemperate and precipitate behaviour, Sunderland became the most subtle and successful of politicians. Although devious and pragmatic, he was a zealous defender of liberty in his youth and eschewed corruption in terms of personal enrichment from government coffers. He was a man of learning and taste, vying with his arch-rival Oxford for the mantle of the greatest book collector and connoisseur in Britain of his time. Because of the confiscation and destruction of his personal papers on the orders of Walpole, and the similar fate of the papers of many of his colleagues, including Somers, Halifax, Cowper, and Walpole himself, the full extent of his management and manoeuvres in the troubled and dangerous political tempests of the early Hanoverian period will never be precisely known. It is safe to say that few equalled him for sheer brilliance, audacity, astuteness, and shrewdness in the politics of his age. HENRY L. SNYDER

Sources H. L. Snyder, 'Charles Spencer, third earl of Sunderland, as secretary of state, 1706–1710: a study in cabinet government and party politics in the reign of Queen Anne', PhD diss., U. Cal., Berkeley, 1963 • A. F. B. Williams, *Stanhope: a study in eighteenth-century war and diplomacy* (1932) • J. P. Kenyon, *Robert Spencer, earl of Sunderland, 1641–1702* (1958) • W. Michael, *England under George I*, 2 vols. (1936–9) • *The manuscripts of the earl of Buckinghamshire, the earl of Lindsey … and James Round*, HMC, 38 (1895) • A. Cunningham, *The history of Great Britain*, 2 vols. (1787) • H. L. Snyder, 'Godolphin and Harley: a study of their partnership in politics', *Huntington Library Quarterly*, 30 (1967), 241–71 • H. L. Snyder, 'The duke of Marlborough's request of his captain-generalcy for life: a reexamination', *Journal of the Society for Army Historical Research*, 45 (1967), 67–83 • H. L. Snyder, 'The defeat of the Occasional Conformity Bill and the tack: a study in the techniques of parliamentary management in the reign of Queen Anne', *BIHR*, 41 (1968), 172–92 • H. L. Snyder, 'The pardon of Lord Bolingbroke', *HJ*, 14 (1971), 227–40 • H. L. Snyder, 'Queen Anne versus the junto: the effort to place Orford at the head of the admiralty in 1709', *Huntington Library Quarterly*, 35 (1972), 323–41 • W. Coxe, *Memoirs of the life and administration of Sir Robert Walpole, earl of Orford*, 3 vols. (1798) • *The Marlborough–Godolphin correspondence*, ed. H. L. Snyder, 3 vols. (1975) • *Diary of Mary countess Couper, lady of the bedchamber to the princess of Wales, 1714–1760*, ed. S. Couper, 3rd edn (1865) • J. H. Plumb, *Sir Robert Walpole* (1956–61), vol. 1 • W. A. Speck, *The birth of Britain* (1994) • P. Langford, *Public life and the propertied Englishman, 1689–1798* (1991) • W. Coxe, *Memoirs of John, duke of Marlborough*, 2nd edn, 3 vols. (1818–19) • *The Wentworth papers, 1705–1739*, ed. J. J. Cartwright (1883) • J. Carswell, *The South Sea Bubble* (1961) • G. M. Trevelyan, *England under Queen Anne*, 3 vols. (1930–34); repr. (1948) • H. R. Snyder, 'Party configurations in the early eighteenth century House of Commons', *BIHR*, 45 (1972), 38–72 • Evelyn, *Diary* • F. Harris, *A passion for government: the life of Sarah, duchess of Marlborough* (1991)

Archives BL, letters, Add. MS 28056 • BL, household and personal accounts, A18 • Bodl. Oxf., journal • Hunt. L., papers relating to New York and New Jersey | BL, Blenheim MSS • BL, letters to James Dayrolle, Add. MS 15866 • BL, corresp. with Francis Manning, Add. MSS • BL, corresp. with Sir John Norris, Add. MSS 28141, 28153, 28155, *passim* • BL, Portland MSS • BL, corresp. with George Stepney, Add. MSS 61502, 61534, 61651 • CAC Cam., corresp. with Thomas Erle • CKS, corresp. with Lord Stanhope • Herts. ALS, letters to Lord Cowper • Herts. ALS, Panshanger MSS • NA Scot., letters to duke of Montrose • NA Scot., corresp. with Lord Polwarth • Spencer Research Library, Lawrence, Kansas, Simpson–Methuen corresp. • TCD, corresp. with William King

Likenesses G. Kneller, oils, *c.*1700, NPG • G. Kneller, portrait, 1720, Blenheim Palace, Oxfordshire [*see illus.*]

Spencer, Charles, third duke of Marlborough (1706–1758), politician and army officer, was born on 22 November 1706, the third of the five children of Charles *Spencer, third earl of Sunderland (1674/5–1722), a politician, and his second wife, Lady Anne Churchill (1683–1716). As the grandson of the first duke, John *Churchill, 'stat magni nominis umbra' ('he stands the shadow of a mighty name') would have been an appropriate motto. His path to the Sunderland peerage was blocked by an elder brother, Robert, and to the Marlborough peerage by a cousin, but the first died of fever in 1729 and the second, William Godolphin, marquess of Blandford, died in 1731 after a drinking spree at Oxford. In 1733 Spencer inherited the dukedom on the death of his aunt Henrietta (duchess in her own right), but since the redoubtable dowager duchess Sarah Churchill retained possession of Blenheim Palace during her lifetime, he was dependent upon her precarious favour.

After schooling at Hampstead and at Eton College Spencer made the conventional grand tour, and on his return adopted a lavish lifestyle, largely on expectations. His grandmother, the dowager duchess, intended to bring him into parliament for Woodstock in 1727 but was warned of a possible petition against him since he was still just under age: she substituted his cousin Lord Blandford, and Charles Spencer never served an apprenticeship in the Commons. He took his seat in the upper house as

Lord Sunderland in January 1730. His close associates were the Fox brothers and their friend Lord Hervey, but his grandmother's hatred of Walpole took him into opposition. Although he was neither a ready debater nor a good speaker (his grandmother complained that he spoke through his teeth), his rank made him a valuable recruit and the glory of his grandfather's name lent him a vicarious authority in military matters. In his first session he voted for a place bill, a favourite nostrum of the opposition, and signed a protest, but his interest soon waned: he attended only five days in his first session and eight in 1731. His elevation to the dukedom raised his profile, and after taking his seat again in January 1734 his attendance increased considerably.

In February 1734, in the aftermath of the excise crisis, during which Walpole had secured the dismissal of several army officers who were opposition MPs, Marlborough was put up to move that the king should be deprived of the power to dismiss officers without recourse to parliament. Lord Hervey, an ally of Walpole, reported to Henry Fox that Marlborough had been 'extremely frightened, said but little, and what he did say was neither remarkably well or ill' (*Lord Hervey and his Friends*, 193). Condemned as an unwarrantable encroachment on the royal prerogative, his motion was defeated by 100 votes to 62. Marlborough continued in opposition and was a frequent visitor at the court of Frederick, prince of Wales. In 1737, when the prince had a spectacular quarrel with the king and was turned out of St James's Palace, Marlborough was reported at Carlton House with Chesterfield and Carteret distributing printed copies of the king's forthright message. But his financial position, as a result of gambling, fox-hunting and building, was becoming desperate, and he had quarrelled violently with his grandmother, who complained that he was stolid and far from entertaining, and whose preference for his younger brother John was marked. A further cause of bad feeling had been his marriage, on 23 May 1732, to Elizabeth (*d.* 1761), the daughter and heir of Thomas Trevor, second Baron Trevor, and his wife, Elizabeth Burrell. She was a granddaughter of an erstwhile enemy of the great duke and one of the tory peers created in 1712 to carry the peace of Utrecht. In March 1738 Marlborough abandoned opposition, signalling his adherence to Walpole by accepting the colonelcy of the 38th foot, and embarked, belatedly, on a military career. 'The Fox has stolen my goose' (Walpole, *Reminiscences*, 90), was his grandmother's tart comment. She retaliated by changing her will yet again to his disadvantage, and a series of legal actions followed, culminating in her appearance before Lord Hardwicke to declare that she would never trust Marlborough with his grandfather's diamond-studded sword, since he would only pick out the diamonds and pawn them.

Marlborough's political conversion brought quick rewards. Within six months he was made a lord of the bedchamber; he was appointed lord lieutenant of Oxfordshire and Buckinghamshire in 1739 and given the Garter in 1741. He repaid Walpole by defending him against Carteret's motion of dismissal in February 1741, moving that to attempt 'to inflict any kind of Punishment, on any person without allowing him an opportunity of his Defence, or, without proof of crime, is contrary to natural justice, the fundamental laws of this realm, and the ancient, established usage of parliament' (Cobbett, *Parl. hist.*, 11, 1739–41, 1218). His motion put the opposition into some disarray, and at length they decided to treat it as a truism, allowing it to pass *nem. con.* His attendance in parliament improved again, and in the critical session 1741–2, which saw the fall of Walpole, he was present on thirty-four days. His connection with Henry Fox, who described him as 'the most intimate and dear friend from childhood' (Fox-Strangways, 2.106), and whose secret wedding he attended in 1744, brought him into the duke of Cumberland's orbit and improved his career chances. He was promoted brigadier-general in 1743 and fought with some distinction at Dettingen, but in the recriminations after the battle followed his commander-in-chief Lord Stair by resigning his bedchamber place and colonelcy in protest against the conduct of the Hanoverian troops. His motives, however, were mixed. A private reason was to avoid further separation from his wife, to whom he was devoted, explaining to her that he had forced 'a pretext to quit' by demanding a promotion which the king emphatically refused (Rowse, 49–50). He signed a Lords protest against the Hanoverians in December 1743 and in January 1744 seconded Sandwich's motion, arguing that to employ Hanoverians in future would risk the allies turning their arms on each other in 'a scene of slaughter' (Cobbett, *Parl. hist.*, 13, 1743–7, 566). Behaviour so pointedly offensive to the king is not easily explained. Horace Walpole thought he was still paying court to the dowager duchess. That scarcely explains Lord Stair's conduct. If true, Marlborough's grandmother was unimpressed, remarking that, like most recruits, her grandson had joined the army when drunk and left it when sober. The step would have ruined Marlborough's prospects, but in February 1744 reports of an imminent Jacobite invasion gave him the opportunity to move a loyal address and to join Stair in an audience with George II, when he pledged his life and fortune (of which there was little left) to the king. Stair was reappointed commander-in-chief, and Marlborough was reinstated and promoted major-general in 1745 and lieutenant-general in 1747. The reconciliation was complete when in 1746 Marlborough moved the Lords' congratulations on Cumberland's victory at Culloden.

The peace of Aix-la-Chapelle in 1748 brought a change in Marlborough's career, following Henry Fox's political progress. In 1749 he was brought in by the Pelhams as lord steward of the household, a post he held until 1755, when he became a privy councillor. In 1750, 1752, and 1755 he was one of the lords justices who acted as regents during the king's absences in Hanover. This suggests that George II was at last getting over the detestation he had felt in the 1730s, when he seldom referred to Marlborough without some opprobrious epithet—'scoundrel, rascal or blackguard' (Hervey, *Some Materials*, 246). His electoral interests were not negligible. In 1754 he was a leader in seizing

Oxfordshire for the whigs, and, though the coup could not be repeated, he retained one seat on a compromise. To his two seats at Woodstock, which gave little trouble after 1734, he added an interest in Oxford city and property at Heytesbury, and he also looked after the Spencer interest at St Albans during the minority of his nephew John from 1746 to 1755. In the political reshuffle after Pelham's death in 1754 he became lord privy seal, which post he retained from January to December 1755. When that office was needed for Lord Gower, Marlborough became master of the ordnance, which brought him into prominence at the outbreak of the Seven Years' War in 1756. The following year there was an unpleasant political skirmish, when he was sharply criticized for taking £10 a day in pay and allowances and was obliged to repay the excess on £4. The same year he was appointed with Lord George Sackville and General Waldegrave to investigate the fiasco of the attack upon Rochefort. Their report was highly critical of Sir John Mordaunt, who was subsequently court-martialled but acquitted. It was therefore understandable that Marlborough should be offered the command of a similar expedition against St Malo in 1758, with Sackville as his second in command but widely regarded as director of the enterprise. Despite a major effort involving eighteen ships of the line and 14,000 men, little was achieved, though a number of French ships and stores were burnt. The British withdrawal was so hasty that Marlborough left his silver spoons behind, which the French commander politely returned. As soon as the troops reached home Marlborough was appointed to command the army in Germany, again with Sackville as his immediate subordinate, to collaborate with Prince Ferdinand. Once more his strong dislike for the Hanoverians showed itself, and soon after arriving at Emden he threatened resignation rather than be outranked by the Hanoverian General Spoerchen: he was not prepared, he told Pitt, to be no more than 'cleavers of wood and drawers of water to the Hanoverians' (*Correspondence of William Pitt*, 1.337–8). Pitt hastily sorted out the problem, and Marlborough was gazetted 'general over all' on 29 August (*GM*, 1st ser., 28, 1758, 379). He died in camp at Munster on 20 October 1758 and was buried at Blenheim in the chapel on 21 November.

Marlborough's death attracted attention for a bizarre reason. In November 1757 he had received an anonymous letter demanding money and threatening to destroy him without fear of discovery. Clearly poison was hinted at. More letters were received and meetings arranged, and in May 1758 William Barnard, the son of a respectable London merchant, was arrested and put on trial. After producing character witnesses and evidence that his financial affairs were by no means desperate, he was acquitted. Five months later the duke was dead. But the cause of death was almost certainly dysentery, and Calcraft reported to Henry Fox that Marlborough's lungs were so decayed that he could not have survived another year.

Contemporary references to Marlborough were often disparaging. We do not have to accept the dowager duchess's view of her 'ungrateful and very foolish grandson' (Yorke, 1.219), since admiration did not come easily to her. Lord Shelburne, just beginning his army career when Marlborough commanded in Germany, described him later as:

> an easy-going, good-natured, gallant man, who took a strange fancy for serving, to get rid of the ennui attending a private life, without any military experience or the common habits of a man of business, or indeed capacity for either, and no force of character whatever. (*Life*, ed. Fitzmaurice, 1.349)

Horace Walpole thought him personally brave, but inexperienced—'capable of giving the most judicious advice and of following the worst … bashfulness and indistinctness in his articulation … confirmed a very mean opinion of his understanding' (Walpole, *Memoirs*, 2.114; 3.24). Smollett was kinder: the duke was 'brave beyond all question, generous to profusion, and good-natured to excess' (Smollett, 3.8). The late start to his army career and his comparatively early death meant that Marlborough achieved supreme command only at the end of his life: though the St Malo campaign was hardly a success, no blame fell upon the duke, who was at once appointed to the German command.

Marlborough was succeeded by his eldest son, George *Spencer (1739–1817), as fourth duke. His daughter Diana (1734–1808) became known as an artist [*see* Beauclerk, Lady Diana]. His younger sons, **Lord Charles Spencer** (1740–1820) and Lord Robert (1747–1831), both had long political careers. The former, who was born on 31 March 1740 and educated at Eton (1747–54) and Christ Church, Oxford (1756–9), sat for Oxfordshire from 1761 to 1790 and again from 1796 to 1801. He held office as a lord of the Admiralty under Lord North, adhered to the Fox–North coalition, and went over with Portland in 1794 to support Pitt. From 1801 until 1806 he was joint postmaster-general and from 1808 until his death a lord of the bedchamber. He married on 2 October 1762 Mary Beauclerk (*d.* 1812), the daughter and heir of Vere, first Baron Vere, and had two sons. His later life was a desperate effort to find and retain some office that would keep him financially afloat, and he was obliged to flee to the continent in 1818, at the age of seventy-eight, to escape his creditors. He died in Petersham, Surrey, on 16 June 1820. JOHN CANNON

Sources GEC, *Peerage* • *JHL*, 24–9 (1731–60) • Cobbett, *Parl. hist.*, 11.1218; 13.566 • *GM*, 1st ser., 14 (1744), 105 • *GM*, 1st ser., 28 (1758), 240, 379 • *GM*, 1st ser., 10 (1740), 203 • *GM*, 1st ser., 90/1 (1820), 573 • *Annual Register* (1758) • A. L. Rowse, *The later Churchills* (1958) • HoP, *Commons, 1715–54* • I. R. Christie, 'Spencer, Lord Charles', HoP, *Commons, 1754–90* • H. Walpole, *Memoirs of King George II*, ed. J. Brooke, 3 vols. (1985) • John, Lord Hervey, *Some materials towards memoirs of the reign of King George II*, ed. R. Sedgwick, 3 vols. (1931) • Earl of Ilchester [G. S. Holland Fox-Strangways], *Henry Fox, first Lord Holland, his family and relations*, 2 vols. (1920) • F. Harris, *A passion for government: the life of Sarah, duchess of Marlborough* (1991) • Walpole, *Corr.* • *Correspondence of John, fourth duke of Bedford*, ed. J. Russell, 3 vols. (1842–6) • *The political journal of George Bubb Dodington*, ed. J. Carswell and L. A. Dralle (1965) • *Lord Hervey and his friends, 1726–38*, ed. earl of Ilchester [G. S. Holland Fox-Strangways] (1950) • *Report on the manuscripts of Mrs Frankland-Russell-Astley of Chequers Court, Bucks.*, HMC, 52 (1900) • *Report on manuscripts in various collections*, 8 vols., HMC, 55 (1901–14), vol. 8 • *Correspondence of William Pitt, earl of Chatham*, ed. W. S. Taylor and J. H. Pringle, 4 vols. (1838–40) • L. B. Namier, *The structure of politics at the accession of George III*,

2nd edn (1957) · *Life of William, earl of Shelburne … with extracts from his papers and correspondence*, ed. E. G. P. Fitzmaurice, 3 vols. (1875–6) · P. C. Yorke, *The life and correspondence of Philip Yorke, earl of Hardwicke*, 3 vols. (1913); repr. (1977) · *Reminiscences written by Mr Horace Walpole in 1788*, ed. P. Toynbee (1924) · T. Smollett, *History of England* (1828)

Archives priv. coll., Blenheim MSS · priv. coll., Althorp MSS | BL, corresp. with Lord Holland, Add. MS 51386 · BL, corresp. with duke of Newcastle, etc., Add. MSS 32698–32992, *passim* · U. Hull, Brynmor Jones L., corresp. with Charles Hotham · U. Nott., corresp. with third duke of Portland

Likenesses W. Hogarth, oils, *c*.1737 (*The Holland House group*), Ickworth House and Garden, Suffolk · S. Slaughter, oils, 1737, Althorp, Northamptonshire · J. M. Rysbrack, marble bust, 1750, Blenheim Palace, Oxfordshire · T. Hudson, oils, *c*.1754 (with family), Blenheim Palace, Oxfordshire · J. Reynolds, oils, 1757, Wilton House, Wiltshire · R. Houston, mezzotint, 1758 (after J. Reynolds), BM · Turner, engraving (Lord Charles Spencer; after Ashby) · J. B. van Loo, oils, Blenheim Palace, Oxfordshire · oils, Gov. Art Coll.

Wealth at death had inherited dowager duchess' estates; Althorp estate made over to younger brother; heavily in debt; mortgaged many properties: Harris, *A passion*, appx. ii

Spencer, Lord Charles (**1740–1820**). *See under* Spencer, Charles, third duke of Marlborough (1706–1758).

Spencer, Lady Diana. *See* Beauclerk, Lady Diana (1734–1808).

Spencer [*née* Sidney], **Dorothy**, **countess of Sunderland** [*known as* Sacharissa] (**1617–1684**), subject of poetry, was born early in October 1617 at Syon House, the London seat of her grandfather Henry *Percy, earl of Northumberland (1564–1632), and baptized in the nearby village of Isleworth on 5 October 1617. She was the eldest of thirteen children of Robert *Sidney, second earl of Leicester (1595–1677), and Dorothy Percy (1598–1659). Her brothers included Philip *Sidney, third earl of Leicester (1619–1698), the republican Algernon *Sidney (1623–1683), and, her favourite brother, Henry *Sidney, earl of Romney (1641–1704).

Dorothy Sidney spent her youth in the beautiful and peaceful surroundings of Penshurst, the family estate in Kent, eloquently praised in Jonson's 'To Penshurst' as representing a harmonious ideal of natural abundance and social order. During her early years, until her paternal grandfather's death in 1626, Dorothy and her mother resided at Penshurst while her father spent much of his time on military service in the Netherlands. When her father succeeded to the earldom he inherited the estate, and his wife, now countess of Leicester, continued to reside there, occasionally complaining about the 'solitariness' of 'this lonely life' in the country (Cartwright, 42).

Several letters from the countess to her husband, absent on ambassadorial duties in France between 1636 and 1639, discuss the relative merits of possible suitors for Dorothy's hand. Although in October 1636 she anxiously writes, 'it greeves me ofne to see that our poore Doll is sought by none, and that shee will shortly be called a staile maide', she was soon actively engaged in negotiations with the families of two young noblemen, Lord Lovelace and Lord Devonshire, after conceding that a third, Lord Russell, about whom she had had 'some hopes', was 'disposed on' elsewhere (*De L'Isle and Dudley MSS*, 60–61, 68,

Dorothy Spencer, countess of Sunderland (1617–1684), by Sir Anthony Van Dyck, *c*.1640

92). Lord Lovelace, who had the advantage of an estate of £6000 a year and a mother 'who is rich, and loves him very much' but the disadvantages of a 'breeding' which 'hath not been precisely of the best', with a tendency to keep 'extreame ill company' and to 'drink to distemper himself', was put forward by Lady Leicester's brother Henry Percy. The proposed match foundered on Dorothy's dislike—'she abhorred the man'—and his own 'wildness' and 'idle' nature, which made the countess 'studie how to break off with him' without giving offence (Cartwright, 58, 60–61). Lord Devonshire, the brother of Dorothy's close friend, Lady Anne Cavendish, the 'Amoret' of Waller's poems, was a more plausible candidate. But here Lord Devonshire's mother had other plans for her son: she and her emissaries, the countess complained, were 'so full of desaite as it is inpossible to know what thaie meane by that they saie', while her son, though 'a verie honest man … has no will of his owne' and 'dairs not eat or drinke but as she apoints' (*De L'Isle and Dudley MSS*, 101, 106). The earl of Holland, who professed to be acting in their interest, was secretly intriguing 'in makeing a Mariage for an other', a wealthy French heiress, and the countess concluded that 'he is so weak, and so unfaithfull, as his Friendship is not worth the least Rushe' (Collins, 2.472).

The name of Edmund Waller does not appear in the countess of Leicester's list of eligible suitors. Aubrey claims that 'he was passionately in love with Dorothea, the eldest daughter of the Earle of Leicester, who he haz eternized in his Poems' and also that 'the Earle loved him, and would have been contented that he should have had one of the youngest daughters' (*Brief Lives*, 308), but there is no supporting evidence that he was considered seriously by the family as a possible husband for Dorothy or her sister Lucy. Waller's poems to and about 'Sacharissa' are characterized by courtly praise, in poems to be circulated among a coterie audience, rather than by burning, unrequited passion. Waller's poetic courtship of Sacharissa began in 1635, before the earl of Leicester's departure for France, when he wrote:

That beam of beauty, which began
To warm us so, when thou wert here.
(*Poems of Edmund Waller*, 1.xxiv, 48, 57)

These praises continued until 1638, during which time Waller was a regular visitor at Penshurst. As Johnson remarks, the sugary name Dorothy was given is somewhat inappropriate for one described consistently as haughty and remote, the 'cruel fair' of the Petrarchan tradition, 'inviting fruit on too sublime a tree', unmoved by her servants' protestations of love (Johnson, 1.253; *Poems of Edmund Waller*, 1.43, 52). On 20 July 1639 Dorothy Sidney was married to Henry, Lord *Spencer (*bap.* 1620, *d.* 1643) at Penshurst. Waller wrote a graceful letter of congratulation to Lucy Sidney:

May she that always affected silence and retiredness, have the house filled with the noise and number of her children, and hereafter of her grandchildren, and then may she arrive at that great curse so much declined by fair ladies, old age; may she live to be very old, and yet seem young. (*Poems of Edmund Waller*, 1.xxix)

In autumn 1639 Lord and Lady Spencer, with the countess of Leicester, joined the earl of Leicester in Paris, where two children were born in the next two years. Their daughter, Dorothy, born in 1640, married Sir George Savile, later the marquess of Halifax, in 1656. Their son Robert *Spencer, later second earl of Sunderland (1641–1702), like his brother-in-law became an important statesman during the Restoration period. After the return of Lord and Lady Spencer to England in 1641, at which time they took up residence in Althorp, Northamptonshire, two more children were born: Penelope in 1642 and Harry in 1643. In June 1643 Lord Spencer was created earl of Sunderland, possibly as a consequence of a loan of £5000 to Charles I.

At the outbreak of the civil war the Sidney family was bitterly divided. Dorothy's brothers Philip (Lord Lisle) and Algernon took up arms for the parliament, and the earl of Leicester, 'suspected and distrusted of either side', wrote gloomily from the king's camp, 'we know not what we do, nor what we would have, unless it be our own destruction' (Cartwright, 83–4). Sunderland served in the king's army as a volunteer, and, in spite of 'having no command in the army, attended upon the King's person under the obligation of honour' (Clarendon, 3.177). In a series of letters written to his wife in 1642 and 1643 he expresses a longing for peace and a deep suspicion of the queen's party and the king's advisers, but a loyalty to the royalist cause despite these reservations: 'If there could be an expedient found, to save the punctilio of honour, I would not continue here an hour. The discontent that I, and many other honest men, receive daily, is beyond expression' (Cartwright, 88–9). In September 1643 he was killed, at twenty-three, at the battle of Newbury, 'having often charged the enemy before that fatall shott befell him', and the news of his death caused the pregnant Lady Sunderland to fall 'into a great passion of griefe'; 'Doll thinkes of nothing but her great los[s]e', her mother writes (*De L'Isle and Dudley MSS*, 434–5). Sunderland left legacies of £10,000 and £7000 to two of his children, and Lady Sunderland and her father were awarded joint wardship over her son Robert.

For the next seven years the widowed Lady Sunderland and her children lived with her parents at Penshurst, where in March 1649 her youngest child, Harry Spencer, died at the age of five. After the execution of Charles I, two of the royal children, the duke of Gloucester and Princess Elizabeth, were placed under the care of the earl and countess of Leicester, and after Elizabeth's death in 1650 a diamond necklace and other keepsakes were bequeathed to Lady Sunderland and her mother as a token of the care the princess had received at Penshurst. In 1650 Lady Sunderland and her children left Penshurst, to live at Althorp, where she remained for most of the next twelve years managing her son's estate until he came of age in 1662. One contemporary account says that in the 1650s she provided sanctuary as well as maintenance at Althorp for ejected Anglican clergymen (Cartwright, 126). In 1652 she surprised a number of observers by marrying for a second time; her second husband was Robert Smythe (1613–1664x7) of Boundes, near Penshurst; he was later knighted. The earl of Leicester declined to attend the wedding, though other members of the family were present. Dorothy Osborne, teasing Sir William Temple about his long-standing admiration for Lady Sunderland, whose portrait he owned, remarked caustically:

My Lady Sunderland is not to bee followed in her marrying fashion … Whoe would ere have dreamt hee should have had my Lady Sunderland, though hee bee a very fine Gentleman … I shall never forgive her one thing she sayed of him, which was that she marryed him out of Pitty … To speak truth 'twas convenient for neither of them … She has lost by it much of the repute she has gained, by keeping herself a widdow. It was then believed that Witt and discretion were to be Reconciled in her personne that have soe seldome bin perswaded to meet in any Body else: but wee are all Mortall. (Osborne, 52–4)

The second marriage appears to have been happy, producing one child, Robert Smythe (1653–1695), who eventually inherited his father's estates at Boundes and Sutton-at-Hone.

During her second marriage Lady Sunderland lived partly at Althorp and partly at Boundes, and after 1663 spent much of her time at Rufford, the seat of her son-in-law, the marquess of Halifax. She was widowed a second time in the mid-1660s. After the death of her daughter, Lady Halifax, in 1670, she assumed responsibility for the care of her daughter's four children until Halifax's second marriage two years later. She was always on close terms with Halifax, and twelve of her letters to him, all written in 1680, survive. She also remained friendly with 'old Waller'. When she asked him in 1680 when he would write some more 'beautiful verses' to her, he replied, with unsentimental realism, 'When, Madam, your Ladyship is as young and as handsome again' (*Poems of Edmund Waller*, 1.lxvii). There are several reports of serious illnesses and injuries: an injured hand in 1666 and a dangerous attack of ague in 1679, about which Halifax reports she 'hath been very ill, and is not yet out of danger' (*Savile Correspondence*, 77).

Lady Sunderland's letters of 1679–81 to Halifax and her brother Henry Sidney provide a detailed commentary on the politics of the Exclusion Bill crisis. Her own views were much closer to Halifax's than to those of her son the earl of Sunderland. In November 1680 she expressed disquiet that her son was in league with Shaftesbury and the whigs against Halifax ('that is the thorn in my side'). She despised Shaftesbury ('this great value he puts on himself is more than anybody else does'), had a low opinion of the duke of Monmouth, and disapproved of her brother Algernon's republican politics, though she remained on friendly terms with him. In writing to Halifax in July 1680 she expressed her hope that 'the moderate, honest people' would prevail, as against those 'who have designs that can never be compassed, but by the whole nation being in a flame' (Cartwright, 255, 281–2, 296).

Lady Sunderland died in February 1684, three months after the execution of her brother Algernon, and was buried on 25 February 1684 in the chapel of the Spencers at Brington church, Northamptonshire. She left no will, but letters of administration were granted in March 1684 to a creditor, John Benn, rather than to her two surviving children, the earl of Sunderland and Robert Smythe. There are many portraits of Lady Sunderland, including four from 1639–40 by Van Dyck (at Petworth, Althorp, Chatsworth, and Penshurst), two later paintings by Lely and Riley, a miniature by Cooper, and engravings, after Van Dyck, by Lombart, Vertue, and others.

WARREN CHERNAIK

Sources J. Cartwright, *Sacharissa* (1893) • *The poems of Edmund Waller*, ed. G. Thorn-Drury, 2 vols. (1905) • *Report on the manuscripts of Lord De L'Isle and Dudley*, 6, HMC, 77 (1966) • D. Osborne, *Letters to William Temple*, ed. K. Parker (1987) • H. Sydney and others, *Letters and memorials of state*, ed. A. Collins, 2 vols. (1746) • *Diary of the times of Charles the Second by the Honourable Henry Sidney (afterwards earl of Romney)*, ed. R. W. Blencowe, 2 vols. (1843) • B. Berry, ed., *Some account of the life of … Lady Russell … to which are added, eleven letters from Dorothy Sidney, countess of Sunderland, to George Savile, marquis of Halifax* (1819) • *Savile correspondence*, ed. W. Cooper (1858) • *Aubrey's Brief lives*, ed. O. L. Dick (1962) • S. Johnson, *Lives of the English poets*, ed. G. B. Hill, [new edn], 3 vols. (1905) • W. Chernaik, *The poetry of limitation: a study of Edmund Waller* (1968) • Clarendon, *Hist. rebellion* • *Eighth report*, 3 vols. in 5, HMC, 7 (1881–1910) • *Ninth report*, 3 vols., HMC, 8 (1883–4) • W. A. Shaw, ed., *Calendar of treasury books*, 1, PRO (1904) • *DNB* • *IGI*

Archives BL, letter, Add. MS 15914, fol. 90 | BL, letters to H. Sidney, Add. MSS 32680, 32681 • BL, Althorp papers, letters to Sir Justinian Isham and to Halifax, A8 and C17 • Penshurst Place, Kent, Sidney papers, De L'Isle and Dudley MSS

Likenesses A. Van Dyck, oils, *c*.1639, Penshurst, Kent; version, Althorp, Northamptonshire • A. Van Dyck, oils, *c*.1639, Chatsworth House, Derbyshire • A. Van Dyck, oils, *c*.1640, Petworth House, West Sussex [*see illus.*] • studio of A. Van Dyck, oils, *c*.1643, Althorp, Northamptonshire • P. Lely, oils, *c*.1650; Christies, 1935 • S. Cooper, watercolour miniature, 1653, Starr collection, Kansas City • J. Riley, oils, *c*.1680 • P. Lombart, engraving (after Van Dyck at Petworth), NPG • G. Vertue, engraving (after Van Dyck), NPG

Wealth at death see administration, PRO, PROB 6/59, fol. 40v

Spencer, Francis Almeric, first Baron Churchill of Wychwood (1779–1845). *See under* Spencer, George, fourth duke of Marlborough (1739–1817).

Spencer, Frederick, fourth Earl Spencer (1798–1857). *See under* Spencer, Sir Robert Cavendish (1791–1830).

Spencer, George, fourth duke of Marlborough (1739–1817), politician, born on 26 January 1739, was the eldest son of Charles *Spencer, third duke of Marlborough and fifth earl of Sunderland (1706–1758), and his wife, Elizabeth Trevor (*d.* 1761), the daughter of Thomas Trevor, second Baron Trevor. The artist Lady Diana *Beauclerk was his sister. Following education at Eton College he obtained an ensigncy on 14 June 1755 in the Coldstream Guards, and on 12 June 1756 was gazetted captain of the 20th foot. On succeeding to the peerage two years later he left the army.

In politics, Marlborough shook off the influence of his father's leader, Henry Fox, and 'flung himself totally on Lord Harcourt to direct his conduct in the County of Oxford' (*Grenville Papers*, 1.297–8), of which he was named lord lieutenant on 21 March 1760. At the coronation of George III, on 22 September 1761, he was bearer of the sceptre and cross. On 22 November the following year he was appointed lord chamberlain and sworn of the privy council. On 23 August 1762 he married Lady Caroline Russell (1743–1811), the only daughter of John *Russell, fourth duke of Bedford, and his second wife, Gertrude Leveson-Gower. They had three sons and five daughters. Marlborough's marriage ensured that he was an important member of the Bedford faction, and in the Grenville ministry, though still under thirty, he held office as lord privy seal from April 1763 to July 1765. On 27 July, after some delay occasioned by George III's attempts to induce them to stay in—a delay which was thought 'rather extraordinary'—he and his brother Lord Charles *Spencer [*see under* Spencer, Charles, third duke of Marlborough] resigned their offices. In November 1766 he assured his uncle and father-in-law, the duke of Bedford, that he should 'not join Lord Temple to oppose your grace' (*Correspondence of John, Fourth Duke of Bedford*, 3.357), and for the present did not desire office. He was, however, ambitious of obtaining the Garter, and Bedford obtained from Chatham the promise of it on the next vacancy. But Cumberland was given the next Garter—in order to spite the Bedfords, according to Horace Walpole—and Marlborough did not obtain the coveted honour until 12 December 1768 and was not installed until 25 July 1771.

On 29 January 1779 Walpole wrote to Horace Mann that Marlborough and Lord Pembroke had declared against 'the First Lord of the Admiralty' (the earl of Sandwich) in the celebrated politico-naval dispute that followed Admiral Keppel's action off Ushant. Marlborough even forbade his brother Lord Charles Spencer to attend parliament during Keppel's trial (Walpole, *Journal*, 2.325–6). Marlborough took relatively little part in political affairs after his early years, and for the most part lived quietly at

Blenheim, although he remained a figure of some importance in electoral terms on account of his influence in the boroughs of Woodstock, Oxford, and Heytesbury and in the county of Oxfordshire. In 1762 he had purchased most of Zanetti's gems at Venice. From 1764 to 1774 he employed Capability Brown to remodel the grounds at Blenheim. He was created DCL of Oxford University on 6 July 1763 and high steward of Oxford on 23 November 1779. He presented to the university a large reflecting telescope made by James Short in 1742 and fine copies of Raphael's cartoons. In 1766 he was made high steward of Woodstock. He became an elder brother of Trinity House in 1768 and master on 22 May 1769. He was also ranger of Wychwood forest, a governor of the Charterhouse, and FRS (1786), his chief scientific interest being astronomy. He continued the income given by his father to the classical scholar Jacob Bryant. Marlborough was found dead in bed at Blenheim on 29 January 1817, and was buried there on 7 February. On his death Marlborough House, St James's, reverted to the crown, according to the terms of the original grant.

Of Marlborough's five daughters, Lady Caroline (1763–1813) married Henry, second Lord Mendip; Anne (1773–1865), the Hon. Cropley Ashley, the brother of Lord Shaftesbury; Amelia (1785–1829), Henry Pytches Boyce; Elizabeth (1764–1812), her cousin the Hon. John Spencer; and Charlotte (1769–1802), Edward Nares, regius professor of modern history at Oxford.

His eldest son, **George Spencer-Churchill**, fifth duke of Marlborough (1766–1840), politician and book collector, born George Spencer on 6 March 1766, took the additional name of Churchill by royal licence in May 1817. He was educated at Eton and Christ Church, Oxford, graduating MA on 9 December 1786 and DCL on 20 June 1792. He was MP for Oxfordshire from 1790 to 1796 and for Tregony from 1802 to 1804, and during the second ministry of William Pitt the younger he was a lord of the Treasury (from 7 August 1804 until 11 February 1806). On 12 March 1806 he was called to the upper house as Baron Spencer of Wormleighton. He married, on 15 September 1791, Lady Susan Stewart (1767–1841), the second daughter of John Stewart, seventh earl of Falloway, and his wife, Anne Dashwood. They had four sons and two daughters; in addition he had a further six children with Matilda Glover (*c.*1802–1876) and one with Mary Anne Sturt (1768–1854). He spent great sums on his gardens and his library at White Knights, near Reading. In 1812 he gave £2260 for Valdarfer's edition of the *Decameron* at the duke of Roxburghe's sale, and in 1815 he bought from the library of James Edwards the celebrated Bedford missal. Most of his collections were dispersed during his lifetime, and his extravagance compelled his retirement during his later years. He died at Blenheim on 5 March 1840 and was buried there on 13 March. He was succeeded as sixth duke of Marlborough by his eldest son, George Spencer-*Churchill (1793–1857).

Lord Henry John Spencer (1770–1795), diplomatist, the second son of the fourth duke, was born on 20 December 1770 and educated at Eton and Christ Church, Oxford, where he gave great promise. He entered public life in April 1790, before he came of age, as secretary to Lord Auckland, ambassador at The Hague. He was left from September 1791 to May 1792 in sole charge of the embassy at a critical period, and established so high a reputation for discretion and vigour that he was again appointed minister-plenipotentiary to the Netherlands in May 1793. In July 1793 he went to Sweden as envoy-extraordinary. In 1795 he was appointed envoy-extraordinary and plenipotentiary to Prussia, but he died of fever at Berlin on 3 July, in his twenty-fifth year.

Marlborough's youngest son, **Francis Almeric Spencer**, first Baron Churchill of Wychwood (1779–1845), politician, born on 26 December 1779, was MP for Oxfordshire from 1801 to 1815, and, during the ministry of Spencer Perceval, a member of the Board of Control (from 13 November 1809 to July 1810), although he was never sworn in. In August 1815 he was created a peer as Baron Churchill of Wychwood. He married, on 25 November 1801, Lady Frances Fitzroy (*d.* 1866), the fifth daughter of Augustus Henry Fitzroy, third duke of Grafton. Sir Augustus Almeric *Spencer was their third son. He died in Brighton on 10 March 1845. G. Le G. Norgate, *rev.* Stephen M. Lee

Sources A. L. Rowse, *The later Churchills* (1958) • GEC, *Peerage* • J. E. Doyle, *The official baronage of England*, 3 vols. (1886) • *Annual Register* (1817) • *Annual Register* (1840) • *Annual Register* (1845) • *GM*, 1st ser., 65 (1795) • *GM*, 1st ser., 87/1 (1817) • *GM*, 2nd ser., 23–4 (1845) • R. G. Thorne, 'Spencer, George', HoP, *Commons, 1790–1820* • R. G. Thorne, 'Spencer, Lord Henry John', HoP, *Commons, 1790–1820* • R. G. Thorne, 'Spencer, Lord Francis Almeric', HoP, *Commons, 1790–1820* • M. Soames, *The profligate duke: George Spencer-Churchill, fifth duke of Marlborough, and his duchess* (1987) • *Reports on the manuscripts of the earl of Eglinton*, HMC, 10 (1885), 391–3 • *The Grenville papers: being the correspondence of Richard Grenville … and … George Grenville*, ed. W. J. Smith, 1 (1852), 297–8; 3 (1853), 210, 297–8 • *Correspondence of John, fourth duke of Bedford*, ed. J. Russell, 3 (1846), 355–7 • H. Walpole, *Journal of the reign of King George the Third*, ed. Dr Doran, 2 (1859), 325–6 • *The letters of Horace Walpole, fourth earl of Orford*, ed. P. Toynbee, 5 (1904), 163; 7 (1904), 154; 10 (1904), 366

Archives MHS Oxf., scientific MSS | BL, corresp. with Lord Auckland, Add. MSS 34412–34461 • BL, letters to Lord Grenville, Add. MS 58990 • BL, corresp. with duke of Newcastle, Add. MSS 32885–32963 • PRO, letters to William Pitt, PRO 30/8

Likenesses T. Hudson, group portrait, oils, *c.*1754, Blenheim Palace, Oxfordshire • J. Reynolds, oils, 1762, Blenheim Palace, Oxfordshire • J. Reynolds, oils, 1764, Wilton House, Wiltshire • G. Romney, portrait, 1771?, Blenheim Palace, Oxfordshire • J. Reynolds, group portrait, oils, 1777, Blenheim Palace, Oxfordshire • J. Downman, portrait, 1781 (George, marquess of Blandford), Courtauld Inst. • J. Ogborne, stipple, pubd 1795 (after F. Bartolozzi), BM, NPG • R. Cosway, oils, Blenheim Palace, Oxfordshire • W. Owen, portrait (Lord Francis Spencer), Blenheim Palace, Oxfordshire • J. Reynolds, double portrait (Lord Henry Spencer and Lady Charlotte Spencer, known as *The little fortune teller*), Hunt. L. • J. Smith, oils (after J. Reynolds), Blenheim Palace, Oxfordshire

Wealth at death under £12,000—Francis Almeric Spencer: *GM*, 2nd ser., 668

Spencer, (William) George (*bap.* **1790**, *d.* **1866**), schoolmaster, was baptized on 8 February 1790 in the parish of St Werburgh, Derby, the son of Wesleyan Methodists, Matthew Spencer (1762–1831), a schoolmaster, and his wife, Catherine Taylor (1758–1843). Spencer was the eldest of five surviving brothers and a sister; he was known as

George after the birth of his youngest brother, also William. His brother Thomas *Spencer (1796–1853), a Cambridge mathematics wrangler, became notable as a social reformer. Spencer was educated at his father's school, where he also started to follow his father's career, including work from 1807 as a private tutor in the Derby area.

In his twenties Spencer ran his own private school alongside his private tutoring. He taught a wide range of subjects, including English language, arithmetic, accounts, drawing, algebra, geometry, mechanics, astronomy, and the sciences. Such subjects were not part of the normal classics-based, public-school curriculum and Spencer's teaching business thrived. Further income came from some inherited and purchased property. He advanced his own informal education through political, social, religious, and ethical discussions with his brothers and other acquaintances. In mathematics, the sciences, and medicine he also benefited from the meetings and literature of the Derby Philosophical Society, for which he acted as honorary secretary from his mid-twenties.

Spencer married Harriet Holmes (1794–1867), the daughter of a plumber and glazier, on 6 January 1819 and they first lived at 12 Exeter Row, Derby. It was not a happy relationship. He commanded attention through his physical presence, being a well-built man about 6 feet tall, his abundant energy and strength of character, displaying independence and originality, and his notable lack of reticence. By contrast, she was gentle, conforming, and conservative. Of nine children only Herbert *Spencer (1820–1903), the eldest, survived beyond infancy to become a well-known philosopher and sociologist.

Pressure of work gradually affected the balance of Spencer's mind and, in 1824, forced him temporarily to give up teaching. The family moved to New Radford, near Nottingham, and Spencer became involved with the then new lace-manufacturing business. This commercial venture failed and, in 1827, the Spencers moved to 8 (later 17) Wilmot Street, Derby, where they remained and Spencer resumed private tutoring.

Spencer's historical significance rests on two related aspects of his teaching: his seminal contribution to pedagogy; and his influence on his son Herbert's intellectual development. Herbert's autobiography (2 vols., 1904) is permeated with references to his father's contributions to his developing thought and tributes to his father's individuality, inventiveness, and idealism. Spencer's pedagogy was based on respect for pupils, motivation, and active rather than passive learning to promote understanding, as opposed to rote memorizing. This self-help method of teaching through guided discovery was eventually exemplified as *Inventional geometry: a series of questions, problems, and explanations, intended to familiarize the pupil with geometrical conceptions, to exercise his inventive faculty, and prepare him for Euclid and the higher mathematics* (1860). This small work of thirty-two pages on practical geometry was over thirty years ahead of its time in England; it was first reprinted through his son's efforts in 1892. As early as the 1870s, an American edition made some impact in the USA. The pedagogy gained prominence in England during the 1900s, when the use of editions of Euclid for school geometry was eventually abandoned.

Spencer also had some artistic talent and his inventiveness extended to the elaboration, over much of his life, of a new system of shorthand. Again through his son's efforts, this work was posthumously published as *A System of Lucid Shorthand* (1893). Spencer died of a lung infection and an overdose of morphia, on 27 April 1866 at 17 Wilmot Street, Derby. MICHAEL H. PRICE

Sources H. Spencer, *An autobiography*, 2 vols. (1904) · D. Duncan, *The life and letters of Herbert Spencer* [1908] · T. Mozley, *Reminiscences: chiefly of towns, villages and schools*, 2 vols. (1885), vol. 2, pp. 144–74 · T. Mozley, *Reminiscences, chiefly of Oriel College and the Oxford Movement*, 1 (1882), 145–9 · parish register, Derby St Werburgh, Derby Local Studies Library, microfilm 168, 8 Feb 1790 [baptism] · parish register, Derby St Werburgh, Derby Local Studies Library, microfilm 169, 6 Jan 1819 [marriage] · d. cert. · W. G. Spencer, *Inventional geometry: a series of questions, problems, and explanations, intended to familiarize the pupil with geometrical conceptions, to exercise his inventive faculty, and prepare him for Euclid and the higher mathematics*, 2nd edn (1892) · W. G. Spencer, account book, 1866, Derby Local Studies Library, MS 9487 · *DNB* · 'Spencer, Herbert', *DNB* · 'Spencer, Thomas (1796–1853)', *DNB* · [P. S. Jones], ed., *A history of mathematics education in the United States and Canada* (Washington, DC, 1970), 31–2

Archives Derby Local Studies Library

Likenesses W. G. Spencer, self-portrait, 1818, repro. in Spencer, *Autobiography*, 1, facing p. 52 · drawing, *c.*1860 (after photograph), repro. in Spencer, *Autobiography*, 1, facing p. 56

Wealth at death under £600: administration, 20 Dec 1866, *CGPLA Eng. & Wales*

Spencer, George [*name in religion* Ignatius of St Paul] (**1799–1864**), Roman Catholic priest, was born at Admiralty House, London, on 21 December 1799, the youngest of the eight children of George John *Spencer, second Earl Spencer (1758–1834), first lord of the Admiralty, and his wife, Lavinia (1762–1831), daughter of Charles Bingham, first earl of Lucan. He had four brothers, including John Charles *Spencer, Robert Cavendish *Spencer, and Frederick *Spencer [*see under* Spencer, Robert Cavendish], and three sisters, including Sarah *Lyttelton; one brother and a sister, however, died in infancy. After education at home, Spencer went to Eton College, before proceeding in 1817 to Trinity College, Cambridge, to read classics, mathematics, and divinity. Placed in the first class in both the 1818 and the 1819 examinations, he received his MA in 1819. He was ordained a deacon of the Church of England on 22 December 1822 and priest on 13 June 1824; in January 1825 he became rector of St Mary's, Brington, on the family's Althorp estate. After a chance encounter with Father William Foley of Northampton and subsequent discussions with him and with Ambrose Phillipps De Lisle, Spencer was received into the Roman Catholic church in Leicester by a Belgian Dominican priest, Father Charles Caestryck, on 30 January 1830. He then went to the English College, Rome, to study for the Catholic priesthood and was ordained on the feast of St Augustine of Canterbury, 26 May 1832, in the church of St Gregory the Great on the Coelian Hill. While he was in Rome he met Father Dominic Barberi, professor of theology at the Passionist retreat

George Spencer [Ignatius of St Paul] (1799–1864), by unknown artist

of SS Giovanni e Paolo. Spencer returned to England and was appointed to Walsall in August 1832, and in November 1832 to West Bromwich, with responsibility also for Dudley.

Although massively built, Spencer was physically delicate, and it was a serious illness in 1838 which brought about the beginning of his life's work: his Crusade of Prayer for Unity in the Truth. Sent to the continent to recuperate, he was invited to address the French clergy at St Sulpice in Paris. When his request for prayers for the conversion of England was favourably received, he extended it wherever he travelled and, on his return to England, throughout the British Isles. In January 1840 he went to Oxford to ask John Henry Newman and his followers to pray for unity in the truth. Newman later wrote in his *Apologia pro vita sua* that he could have 'laughed for joy' to see him. He refused to dine with him, however, because he regarded him as '*in loco apostatae* [an apostate] from the Anglican Church'. Nevertheless he did draw up prayers for reunion. The modern movement for Christian unity may be said to date from their meeting. The decree on ecumenism, *Unitatis redintegratio*, issued by the Second Vatican Council in 1964, owed much to Spencer's inspiration and writings.

In 1839 Spencer was appointed to St Mary's College, Oscott, as spiritual director. In 1839–41 he was largely responsible for facilitating Father Dominic Barberi's foundation of the Passionist congregation in England, and in 1846–7 he entered the Passionist noviciate at Aston Hall near Stone, Staffordshire, taking the religious name Ignatius of St Paul. From his profession of vows in January 1848 he travelled throughout the British Isles and Europe, preaching the passion and seeking prayers for the conversion of England and the sanctification of Ireland. He also advocated temperance. Between 1849 and 1864, in co-operation with Father Gaudentius Rossi, CP, and Elizabeth Prout, he was instrumental in founding the Sisters of the Cross and Passion, a new religious congregation with no dowry requirements for admission and no class distinctions. He also assisted this congregation to provide homes for factory girls.

Spencer died suddenly from a heart attack at Monteith House, Carstairs, Lanarkshire, on 1 October 1864. His remains were conveyed to St Anne's Passionist Retreat, Sutton, St Helens, where he had been rector, and his funeral took place on 5 October 1864. He was interred in the crypt, but in 1973 his remains were removed to a side chapel in the new church of St Anne and Blessed Dominic in Sutton, where they lie beside those of Blessed Dominic Barberi and Elizabeth Prout. The cause for his canonization was introduced in June 1992. E. HAMER

Sources *Life of Father Ignatius of St Paul, Passionist (the Hon. and Rev. George Spencer)*, ed. Pius Devine (1866) · J. V. Bussche, *Ignatius (George) Spencer, Passionist (1799–1864), Crusader of Prayer for England and pioneer of ecumenical prayer* (1991) · U. Young, *Life of Father Ignatius Spencer C.P.* (1933)

Archives Birmingham Oratory · BL, corresp. and papers · Colwich Abbey · Congregation of the Passion, Rome, general archives · Congregation of the Passion, Minsteracres, co. Durham, provincial archives · English Province of Passionist Fathers, London · NRA, corresp. and papers · Sisters of the Cross and Passion, Salford, Lancashire, general archives

Likenesses portrait, *c*.1825–1829 (as an Anglican clergyman), chapel, Althorp House, Northamptonshire · photograph, *c*.1862, Congregation of the Passion, Sutton, St Helens, Provincial Archives · portrait (after photograph, *c*.1862), SS Giovanni e Paolo, Rome, Passionist Retreat · portrait (after portrait), English College, Rome · watercolour?, NPG [*see illus.*]

Spencer, George Alfred (1873?–1957), trade unionist and politician, was born at Sutton in Ashfield, Nottinghamshire, probably in 1873, the second son in a mining family which eventually numbered eighteen children. His parents, John Spencer and his wife, Eliza, moved around a lot when Spencer was a boy and this may explain why no record of his birth has been found. The family moved to Worksop and at the age of eight Spencer was working on local farms. His parents later kept a public house at South Normanton in Derbyshire and the eleven-year-old boy worked as a half-timer at a coal mine in Pleasley. The following year he began work underground at Blackwell colliery. Spencer was later to compensate for an intermittent early education by attending evening classes organized by the Workers' Educational Association. He also became a Wesleyan Methodist preacher.

In 1896 Spencer married Emma, daughter of Richard Carlin of Sutton in Ashfield. They had two children, one daughter and a son who later became a doctor. By this time Spencer was working at New Hucknall colliery where the miners elected him checkweighman. He soon became president of the local branch of the Nottinghamshire Miners' Association (NMA), a delegate, and then permanent official, and was of sufficient standing in the coalfield by 1910 to be nominated as an arbitrator when cutting machines were introduced at Eastwood collieries. He narrowly failed to be elected to the post of NMA assistant secretary in the same year but in 1912 became the union's president.

Spencer had also become active in labour politics and was voted onto the urban district council in Sutton in Ashfield, eventually becoming its chairman. His support for the war was reflected by his membership of the local military tribunal. In general he was not on the left of the Labour Party, although he opposed intervention in Russia after the revolution and called for the withdrawal of British troops from Ireland. In the general election of 1918 he won Broxtowe in Nottinghamshire for Labour and held the seat at the elections of 1922, 1923, and 1924. He resigned the Labour whip in 1927 and did not stand in 1929.

Like many miners' leaders Spencer believed strongly in the idea of the independence of the county associations. In 1915 he supported the attempt of J. G. Hancock MP to disaffiliate the NMA from the Miners' Federation of Great Britain (MFGB) and in 1918 he spoke strongly against a proposal for national wage negotiations. He was very conscious that Nottinghamshire was one of the most prosperous coalfields in contrast to the economic difficulties of most of the others. He was not always consistent, however, and at the annual conference of the MFGB in 1920 he seconded the resolution in favour of the nationalization of the mines. The turning-point in his career came with the general strike in 1926 and the long drawn out stoppage in the coal industry which followed.

The miners' unions had barely recovered from the strike of 1921. In Nottinghamshire, 6000 miners were in arrears with their subscriptions and 23,000 were not in the union. Spencer hoped that the report of the royal commission on the coal industry, chaired by Sir Herbert Samuel, would form the basis for an agreement on its future. A strike began in May 1926, however, and by August there was growing contact between groups of miners and local colliery companies, and a steady drift back to work began in Nottinghamshire. Spencer did not instigate this movement but intervened in its later stages in order to get the best possible terms for the men. As this was not the policy of the MFGB he was summoned before their national conference where he was called a coward and a blackleg and expelled. He was suspended by the NMA. His decision to lead a breakaway union quickly followed and on 20 November the Nottinghamshire Miners' Industrial Union (NMIU) reached an agreement with the local coal employers.

The Spencer union was anti-socialist. It was an industrial organization whose funds were not to be used for politics. Spencer characterized the miners' strike of 1926 as an 'experiment in elementary communism' (Waller, 111). The rules of the NMIU barred from membership communists or members of the Minority Movement. Nor was it a particularly democratic organization. The holding of branch meetings was at the discretion of the branch committee and difficult matters were often referred to the union's central office or to Spencer himself. The aim was to co-operate with the employers in a relatively prosperous coalfield. Spencer was especially concerned with the plight of the old miners and he persuaded the owners to subsidize a pension fund. He was well known for his handling of compensation cases and in 1930 alone won over £10,000 for NMIU members. He was often called in by branches to talk personally to colliery managements. It was not a bosses' union. As Spencer said, 'in my view there can be no improvement in the lot of the worker unless and until there is co-operation between the two, but while I am co-operating with the owners, I shall see to it that the workers get their share of the wealth that their joint efforts create' (Griffin and Griffin, 152).

Outside Nottinghamshire, the non-political trade union movement had little success. Spencer became president of the Federation of Non-Political Unions but he was not a national leader, being much more concerned to do the best he could for Nottinghamshire miners. The national strength of the MFGB recovered with the economy in the second half of the 1930s, so much so that an attempt was made to re-form an NMA branch at Harworth colliery in 1936. The strike which followed provided the opportunity for the negotiations which led to the fusion of the Spencer union and the NMA as the Nottinghamshire Miners' Federated Union in 1937. The terms were largely dictated by Spencer. He became president of the new amalgamated organization as well as its representative on the MFGB. He was also able to insist that the existing district wages agreement should continue for five years and that there should be no strikes in that time. He retired in 1945.

Spencer rose to be a member of the Nottinghamshire élite from the humblest of beginnings. He was deputy lieutenant of the county from 1941 and a member of the freemasons. He was interested in art and sport, and was president of Nottinghamshire County Cricket Club in 1949–50. He once scored eighty runs playing for the House of Commons at the Oval. He liked to dress in formal suits and had little time for the traditional cloth cap of the working man. He died in Nottingham City Hospital on 21 November 1957. He was survived by his wife.

TONY MASON

Sources *Guardian Journal* [Nottingham] (22 Nov 1957) • *The Times* (23 Oct 1957) • *Colliery Guardian* (28 Nov 1957) • *DLB* • A. R. Griffin and C. P. Griffin, 'The non-political trade union movement', *Essays in labour history, 1918–1939*, ed. A. Briggs and J. Saville (1977), 133–62 • R. J. Waller, *The Dukeries transformed: the social and political development of a twentieth century coalfield* (1983) • d. cert. • census returns, 1881

Likenesses portrait, repro. in *Nottingham Guardian Journal*

Wealth at death £20,471 15s. 3d.: probate, 27 Jan 1958, *CGPLA Eng. & Wales*

Spencer, George John, **second Earl Spencer** (**1758–1834**), politician and book collector, was born at Wimbledon Park in Surrey on 1 September 1758, the only son of John *Spencer, first Earl Spencer (1734–1783), politician and landowner, and his wife, (Margaret) Georgiana *Spencer

George John Spencer, second Earl Spencer (1758–1834), by John Singleton Copley, 1799–1806

(1737–1814), the daughter of Stephen Poyntz of Midgham in Berkshire. When his father was elevated to an earldom in 1765 Spencer took the courtesy title Viscount Althorp.

From 1765 to 1770 Althorp was privately tutored by the orientalist Sir William Jones, who instilled in him a love of the Greek and Roman classics and an appreciation of fine books that he retained until the end of his life. In 1770 he entered Harrow School, where he remained until 1775. Having been admitted in 1776 to Trinity College, Cambridge, he proceeded to a nobleman's MA degree in 1778. He then went on the grand tour of Europe for nearly two years. Tall and athletic but gentle and reserved in demeanour, he had neither the bearing nor the scintillating personality of his elder sister Georgiana *Cavendish, duchess of Devonshire (1757–1806), nor the vivacity of his younger sister Henrietta *Ponsonby, countess of Bessborough (1761–1821). He was, however, agreeable, polished in manners, and temperate in conduct. His intellectual acuity was recognized when, on Sir William Jones's recommendation, he was welcomed in 1778 as an active member of Johnson's Literary Club, and in 1780 he became a fellow of the Royal Society. The University of Oxford awarded him the honorary degree of DCL in 1793.

Althorp married on 6 March 1782 Lady Lavinia Bingham (1762–1831), the eldest daughter of Charles Bingham, first earl of Lucan, and his wife, Margaret *Bingham, *née* Smith (*c.*1740–1814), a miniature painter. Lavinia Spencer was a strong-minded and strong-willed woman of great erudition and charm and was perhaps the pre-eminent hostess in London society. Both at Althorp and Spencer House in London the Spencers delighted in entertaining the foremost intellectual and political leaders of their time. Of their eight children, four sons and two daughters reached maturity: John Charles *Spencer, Viscount Althorp and third Earl Spencer, politician; Sir Robert Cavendish *Spencer and Frederick *Spencer, fourth Earl Spencer [*see under* Spencer, Sir Robert Cavendish], who were both naval officers; the Revd George *Spencer; Sarah *Lyttelton, Lady Lyttelton, governess to Queen Victoria's children; and Lady Georgiana Charlotte Quin.

Althorp's family connection was staunchly whig, and in that tradition he began his political career. He was returned to parliament on the family interest for Northampton borough in 1780. After vacating that seat in 1782, he was then returned for Surrey. Never an impressive speaker, he seldom spoke in the Commons but diligently attended to his parliamentary duties. He supported Rockingham's attack on North's government in 1782 and served as a junior lord of the Treasury in the Rockingham administration. Having declined to serve under Shelburne, he supported the Fox–North coalition in 1783 but refused the offer to become lord lieutenant of Ireland. On his father's death, on 31 October 1783, he succeeded to the earldom. He also became high steward of St Albans, where he managed his family's borough interest, as well as at Northampton and Okehampton in Devon. The management of his vast estates, especially the renovation by Henry Holland of his ancestral seat at Althorp in Northamptonshire and the rebuilding of the Spencer villa at Wimbledon Park, diverted his attention from politics. His involvement in political management was also diminished by its demands on his time and the resources of his heavily encumbered estate. The repercussions of the French Revolution on British politics, however, stirred his sense of public duty, and with the duke of Portland and other whig leaders Spencer broke with Fox and Grey and joined the government of William Pitt in 1794. He was sworn of the privy council and became lord keeper of the privy seal on 11 July 1794. Shortly thereafter he was sent as ambassador-extraordinary to Vienna in a futile effort to persuade the Austrians to increase their efforts in the war against France. On his return from Vienna, Pitt shifted his ineffective and lethargic brother, the earl of Chatham, from the Admiralty to the office of privy seal and on 17 December 1794 made Spencer first lord.

Without any administrative experience or knowledge of the navy, Spencer considered his appointment a patriotic duty for the public benefit. Despite his youth and inexperience, he required his subordinates, especially the professional navy men serving as lords commissioners, to recognize the prerogatives and civilian authority of his office. Finding the office routine of the Admiralty in disarray, he immediately restored order and set an example by being punctual and methodical in the conduct of business. He maintained that in the shaping of overall strategy the views of the first lord be considered by the foreign secretary and the secretary of state for war and the colonies. Strongly opposed to misdirected colonial expeditions, he urged that naval strength be concentrated in European waters. His influence was decisive in appointing capable commanders in major theatres, such as Jervis to the Mediterranean command in 1795 and to the channel in 1800, Duncan to the North Sea in 1795, and Nelson to an independent command that won the battle of the Nile in 1798. For all naval officers, Spencer sought an improved system of promotion and recognition by merit. He was quick to recognize outstanding service, and he recommended Jervis for a peerage in 1797 because of the efficiency and good order of his command. He also demonstrated magnanimity and deference to senior officers, who had rendered many years of distinguished service, by postponing in 1797 for two years his acceptance of the Garter for himself in favour of Lord Howe. While he and Lady Spencer always sought to maintain cordial social relations with naval officers and their wives, he did not hesitate to reprimand Nelson in 1800 for dallying too long with Lady Hamilton at Naples.

Aware of the corruption and waste in the navy, Spencer was unable in time of war to effect significant reform, though some progress was made in improving dockyard efficiency. He was interested in Samuel Bentham's innovations in the dockyards, and his support of Bentham's work as inspector-general of navy works laid the foundations for reform in later years. Always attracted to any scientific endeavour, especially if it could be made applicable to the dockyards, Spencer was an early patron of the engineer Marc Isambard Brunel. In the naval mutinies of 1797 he acted promptly, decisively, and fairly. By going himself to Spithead, and by enlisting the aid of Lord Howe, he succeeded in persuading the seamen to return to their duty by promising increase in pay and improvement in the conditions of service. At the Nore he was compelled to act with greater severity in quelling the mutiny because he recognized that there was evidence of political incendiarism that had not been present at Spithead. Spencer's six-year tenure at the Admiralty was unprecedented not only in length, but in having been entirely during wartime; during his period there the three great naval victories at St Vincent, Camperdown, and the Nile were won. After leaving the Admiralty, when Pitt went out of office in February 1801, he remained interested in the Royal Navy and its personnel, especially the welfare of destitute seamen. Two of his sons became naval officers with his blessing, and a grandson, the fifth Earl Spencer, served as first lord of the Admiralty at the end of the nineteenth century.

Although out of office, Spencer continued to voice his opinion on public affairs in the House of Lords, and in 1802 he was one of sixteen peers speaking and voting against the treaty of Amiens. He renewed his ties with Fox and Grey and in 1806 was home secretary in the coalition ministry of Grenville and Fox. While in that office he served as a member of the special commission investigating the conduct of Caroline, princess of Wales. When the ministry resigned in 1807, Spencer retired from national politics, though he regularly attended the House of Lords; when his health did not permit attendance he gave Lord Grey his proxy. By 1807 the Spencer family interest at Northampton, Okehampton, and St Albans had ended, and Spencer relinquished his political role to his heir, Viscount Althorp.

From 1807 until the end of his life Spencer devoted his time mainly to local affairs in Northamptonshire, and to his literary, philanthropic, and scientific interests. For more than thirty years he served as chairman of quarter sessions and as colonel of the Northamptonshire regiment of yeomanry. He supported the establishment of a savings bank in Northampton, helped to found an institution for deaf mute people, and promoted the building of the Northampton Infirmary and an asylum for the insane. From 1820 he was a patron of the peasant poet of Northamptonshire, John Clare, to whom he provided an annuity; the latter was continued after Spencer's death by his son. As a governor of the Charterhouse and as president of the Royal Institution he promoted education and the advancement of scientific knowledge. He was interested in the improvement and safety of navigation and served as an elder brother of Trinity House and as master from 1806 to 1807. A fellow of the Society of Antiquaries, his concern to preserve the national heritage led to his appointment in 1831 as a commissioner of the public records. Spencer was a staunch Anglican and a patron and officer in several evangelical societies, such as the British and Foreign Bible Society. He favoured Catholic emancipation, and when, much to his displeasure, his youngest son became a Roman Catholic priest, he nevertheless provided financial support for him.

Spencer's chief interest after retiring from public life, and perhaps his pre-eminent achievement, was collecting the greatest private library in Europe. By 1834 the collection consisted of upwards of 40,000 volumes valued at more than £60,000. It was sold in 1892 for £250,000 to become the principal collection of the John Rylands Library at Manchester. The nucleus of the collection was the small ancestral library at Althorp, but the purchase of the Hungarian Count Reviczky's library in 1790 was the first of many valuable acquisitions that Spencer continued to make until about 1830. The library was especially important for books that illustrated the evolution of the art of printing during the fifteenth and sixteenth centuries. The incunabula in the collection, especially books printed by Aldus Manutius, William Caxton, and Christopher Valdarfer, equalled the collections of the greatest public libraries at that time. As the foremost bibliophile of his era, it was fitting that Spencer was one of the founders and the first president of the Roxburghe Club, the first of the great bibliophilic societies.

Spencer died on 10 November 1834 at Althorp Park and was buried on 19 November in the Spencer chapel in the church of St Mary the Virgin at Great Brington. Ever faithful to his responsibilities as a privileged aristocrat, he willingly performed the duties of public office, both locally and nationally, as a public trust. First lord of the Admiralty at a critical time, he rendered distinguished service to his country as an organizer of naval victory. A philanthropist, patron of arts and letters, and bibliophile, he left his mark on English culture. MALCOLM LESTER

Sources BL, Althorp MSS • BL, Add. MS 35155 • *Private papers of George, second Earl Spencer*, ed. J. S. Corbett and H. W. Richmond, 4 vols., Navy RS, 46, 48, 58–9 (1913–24) • PRO, Admiralty MSS • GEC, *Peerage*, new edn • *GM*, 2nd ser., 3 (1835), 89–93 • I. R. Christie, 'Spencer, George John, Viscount Althorp', HoP, *Commons, 1754–90* • HoP, *Commons, 1790–1820* • W. L. Clowes, *The Royal Navy: a history from the earliest times to the present*, 7 vols. (1897–1903) • G. J. Marcus, *A naval history of England*, 2: *The age of Nelson* (1971) • S. De Ricci, *English collectors of books and manuscripts* (1930) • C. Spencer, *The Spencer family* (1999) • C. B. Arthur, *The remaking of the English navy by Admiral St Vincent — key to the victory over Napoleon* (1986)

Archives BL, Add. MS 35155 • BL, Althorp MSS • BL, corresp. and papers | BL, corresp. with Jeremy Bentham, Add. MSS 33541–33542 • BL, letters to Philip Bliss, Add. MSS 34567–34571 • BL, corresp. with Lord Bridport, Add. MSS 35195–35220 • BL, letters to John Clare, Egerton MSS 2246–2249 • BL, letters to Henry Dundas • BL, corresp. with Lord Grenville, Add. MSS 58932–58933 • BL, letters to Thomas Grenville, Add. MSS 41854, 42058 • BL, letters to Lord Hardwicke, Add. MSS 35642–35666, *passim* • BL, corresp. with Lord Holland, Add. MS 51724 • BL, corresp. with Lord Nelson, Add. MSS 34902–34917, *passim* • CKS, letters to Lord Camden • CKS, letters to William Pitt • CKS, corresp. with Lord Stanhope • Cumbria AS, Carlisle, letters to first earl of Lonsdale • HLRO, letters to J. G. Shaw-Le Fevre • Hunt. L., letters to Grenville family • JRL, letters to T. F. Dibdin • NA Scot., corresp. with Henry Dundas • NL Scot., corresp. with Sir Alexander Cochrane • NL Scot., letters to Henry Dundas • NL Scot., corresp. with William Elliott • NMM, letters to Lord Nelson • PRO, Admiralty MSS • Royal Arch., letters to George III • U. Durham L., letters to second Earl Grey • U. Nott., corresp. with duke of Portland • Warks. CRO, corresp. with Lord Hugh Seymour

Likenesses A. Kauffmann, group portrait, oils, 1771–4, Althorp, Northamptonshire • J. Reynolds, oils, exh. RA 1776, Althorp, Northamptonshire • J. S. Copley, group portrait, oils, 1779–80 (*The collapse of the earl of Chatham in the House of Lords, 7 July 1778*), Tate collection; on loan to NPG • J. S. Copley, oils, 1799–1806, Althorp, Northamptonshire [*see illus.*] • J. S. Copley, oils, 1800, NPG • M. A. Shee, oils, exh. RA 1802, Althorp, Northamptonshire • J. Hoppner, oils, *c*.1807–1808, Althorp, Northamptonshire • T. Phillips, oils, 1810, Althorp, Northamptonshire • F. Chantrey, pencil drawing, NPG • G. Clint, portrait, Althorp, Northamptonshire • J. Downman, chalk drawing, FM Cam. • H. Edridge, pencil and watercolour drawing, BM • H. Raeburn, ivory miniature, Althorp, Northamptonshire • C. Read, three pastel drawings, Althorp, Northamptonshire

Wealth at death £95,791 10*s*. 6*d*. personal property; excl. landed estate; debts of £147,806 11*s*.: inventory, 1838, BL, Althorp MSS, G.171

Spencer, George Trevor (1799–1866), bishop of Madras, India, was born on 11 December 1799 at Curzon Street, Mayfair, Westminster, the third son of the Hon. William Robert *Spencer (1770–1834) and his wife, Susan, widow of Count Spreti and daughter of Francis *Jenison (known as Jenison Walworth). Aubrey George *Spencer (1795–1872), bishop of Newfoundland, was his brother. Having gained prizes for Latin alcaics and an English essay at Charterhouse School, he went to University College, Oxford, where he graduated BA in 1822.

In the following year he was ordained deacon, and also married Harriet Theodora, daughter of Sir Benjamin *Hobhouse; they had two sons and three daughters. In 1824 he was ordained priest and held the perpetual curacy of Buxton until 1829. From 1829 until 1837 he was rector of Leaden Roding in Essex.

On 19 November 1837, through the influence of his brother-in-law Sir John Cam Hobhouse, president of the Board of Control, Spencer was consecrated second bishop of Madras, and enthroned in St George's Cathedral, Madras, on 4 November 1838. In 1842 he published a *Journal of a visitation to the provinces of Travancore and Tinnevelly in the diocese of Madras, 1840–41*. In 1845 he also published *Journal of a visitation tour, in 1843–4, through part of the western portion of his diocese*. Besides places in his own diocese, he visited during this tour Poona, Ahmednagar, and Bombay. In the autumn of 1845 Spencer visited the missions of the Society for the Propagation of the Gospel and the Church Missionary Society, and published his *Journal* in the following year, together with charges delivered at St George's Cathedral, Madras, and at Palamcottai, and appendices containing statistical tables. In 1846 he also published *A brief account of the C.M.S.'s mission in the district of Kishnagur, in the diocese of Calcutta*. In the diocese of Madras he established three training colleges for Indian converts.

The whole of Spencer's episcopate was fraught with tensions between himself and the Madras diocesan committee of the Society for the Propagation of the Gospel in Foreign Parts. Relations were equally strained with the Church Missionary Society and its forceful chief secretary, Henry Venn. Spencer's stress upon the authority of the bishop rather than the missionary societies, especially in theological matters, was bound to cause problems in a diocese where many of the missionaries were either German or Danish Lutherans or were influenced by Tractarian beliefs. Dogged by ill health, by 1847 Spencer could no longer cope and returned to England on leave. On 16 June 1847 he was made doctor of divinity, and at some time during the course of his stay in England he decided to resign the episcopate, though this was not carried into effect until 1849.

On 4 October 1852 Spencer was appointed commissary or assistant to Richard Bagot, bishop of Bath and Wells. Once again he entered an area of theological controversy, this time with the Ven. George Denison, archdeacon of Taunton, examining chaplain to Bagot. They differed strongly over their understanding of the 'real presence' in the eucharist, Denison taking an extreme Tractarian position, and over the extent of Spencer's powers to test whether the beliefs of those presented to him for ordination were in accordance with those sanctioned by the Church of England. The controversy was brief but acrimonious and led to an angry correspondence which ended in Denison's declining 'any further communication by word or writing', and both men's publishing their correspondence in an attempt to vindicate themselves. The result was the resignation of both men, Spencer on 10 May and Denison on 4 June 1853.

In 1860 Spencer was appointed chancellor of St Paul's

Cathedral in London, and in the next year became rector of Walton on the Wolds, Leicestershire. He died of dropsy on 16 July 1866 at his home, Edge Moor, Hartington Upper Quarter, near Buxton, Derbyshire, his wife surviving him. G. LE G. NORGATE, *rev.* CLARE BROWN

Sources T. E. Yates, *Venn and Victorian bishops abroad: the missionary policies of Henry Venn and their repercussions upon the Anglican episcopate of the colonial period, 1841–1872* (1978) • H. Cnattingius, *Bishops and societies: a study of Anglican colonial and missionary expansion, 1698–1850* (1952) • M. E. Gibbs, *The Anglican church in India, 1600–1970* (1972) • G. T. Spencer, *Journal of a visitation to the provinces of Travancore and Tinnevelly in the diocese of Madras, 1840–1841* (1842) • G. T. Spencer, *Journal of a visitation-tour, in 1843–4, through part of the western portion of his diocese* (1845) • G. T. Spencer, *Journal of a visitation-tour, through the provinces of Madura and Tinnevelly, in the diocese of Madras, in August and September, 1845* (1846) • G. T. Spencer, *Letter to the Hon. and Right Rev. the Lord Bishop of Bath and Wells* (1853) • G. A. Denison, *Notes of my life, 1805–1878* (1878) • *GM*, 4th ser., 1 (1866), 281 • Foster, *Alum. Oxon.* • d. cert. • *CGPLA Eng. & Wales* (1866)

Archives BL, letters to J. C. Hobhouse, Add. MSS 36460–36472, *passim* • BL OIOC, letters to Lord Tweeddale, MS Eur. F 96 • Bodl. RH, Madras Diocesan Committee Series, Society for the Propagation of the Gospel archives • LPL, corresp. with A. C. Tait • U. Birm. L., corresp. with Church Missionary Society

Wealth at death under £16,000: probate, 5 Oct 1866, *CGPLA Eng. & Wales*

Spencer [*née* Poyntz], **(Margaret) Georgiana, Countess Spencer (1737–1814)**, philanthropist, was born on 8 May 1737 at St James's Palace, London, the fourth surviving child of Stephen *Poyntz (*bap.* 1685, *d.* 1750), steward to the household of the duke of Cumberland, and Anna Maria Mordaunt (*d.* 1771), daughter of Brigadier-General the Hon. Lewis Mordaunt and granddaughter of the earl of Peterborough. Her paternal grandfather was a successful linen draper who sent his clever son to Eton College, and thereby launched him into a career and a life in society. Her mother was a maid of honour to Queen Caroline and 'a great royal favorite' (Friedman, 52), and her godfather was George II. Charles *Poyntz (1734/5–1809) was her brother. On 20 December 1755 she married John *Spencer (1734–1783), later first Earl Spencer, who through the inheritance from his great-grandmother, Sarah Churchill, was one of the richest young men in England.

The countess lived a varied and active life, corresponding with an enormously divergent series of people. Her correspondence with her friend the Hon. Mrs Howe is reputed to be the largest single private collection of letters in the British Library. Exceptionally intelligent and well educated, she could write and speak faultless French and Italian, make puns in Greek, and was accomplished in botany and skilled at the viola de gamba, hunting, and billiards. Above all, however, she was known by her contemporaries as a woman of a philanthropic bent, actively involved in projects both among her neighbours, in the world of associated or charitable institutions, and as a founding member of the Ladies Society, one of the first philanthropic organizations systematically to investigate the characters and circumstances of those who appealed to them for assistance. This technique was later to be embodied in the work of the Mendicity Society (in which

(Margaret) Georgiana Spencer, Countess Spencer (1737–1814), by Sir Joshua Reynolds, 1759–61 [with her daughter Lady Georgiana Spencer, later duchess of Devonshire]

her son, George John *Spencer, the second earl, was an important and early member) and ultimately in the Charity Organization Society.

Lady Spencer was a meticulous keeper of files; she remarked of herself that 'method was [her] passion'. In her correspondences, as well as in the published subscription lists, we can see how much time and effort she devoted to charitable activities. One of the most remarkable parts of her papers is a file that she described as her 'charity letters', which she kept as 'a Cordial—to remind me of my Lord's [her husband's] never failing Generosity and Humanity and of the earnestness with which I executed and sometimes endeavored to imitate his benevolence' (Althorp MS F130). These words were probably written shortly after her husband's untimely death in 1783 and were a modest, though not entirely accurate, reflection of the couple's charitable practices. For even if the initial impulse were her husband's, Lady Spencer served as his agent many years before his demise. Among her friends and acquaintances, she was renowned for her philanthropy. Elizabeth Montague noted: 'The history of La Fee Bienfaisante is not half so delightful as seeing the manner in which Lady Spencer spends her day. Every moment of it is employed in some act of benevolence and charity' (Doran, 332–3). Lady Spencer also corresponded with and advised a number of philanthropists and charitable institutions. Jonas Hanway, perhaps the eighteenth century's most active founder of charities, was one such correspondent. She also took great interest in, and gave minute advice to, those charitable organizations to which she donated. She sent, for example, the secretary of the Asylum for Orphaned Girls a detailed letter of instruction about how mealtimes should be conducted at the asylum.

A committed, and perhaps somewhat overbearing, philanthropic involvement permeated many of her activities. She felt she knew what was best for people, and was prepared to put her money and her efforts behind her plans for them. Her condescension was to mankind in general; only her husband and son were never criticized. Despite this attitude of knowing best, she was without obvious class prejudice, and her Christian piety, which flirted with but never succumbed to Methodism, best expressed itself in her hard work and interest in the needy and deserving. She died at St Albans on 18 March 1814, and was buried on 30 March at Brington, Northamptonshire. After her death the *Gentleman's Magazine* said of her:

> No one was ever better formed by nature, not only to become, but to shed a grace and ornament upon the high station in which she was placed … and to exert the noblest prerogative which rank, and wealth confer, by giving a high example of virtue and piety, united with a proper display of splendour … which naturally belonged to her situation … Her words and her actions bore, in their general and unfailing benevolence, the stamp of the characteristic virtue of her religion, and shewed how intimately Christian charity was blended with her manners, her feelings and her opinions …. Amidst the pleasures and occupations of the world, she never had forgotten the offices of benevolence and piety. (*GM*, 309)

In addition to her three surviving children, Lady Spencer had two who died in childhood. Her eldest daughter, Georgiana *Cavendish, duchess of Devonshire, was perhaps the most famous aristocratic woman of her day, a noted trendsetter, gambler, and leader of the female wing of the whig party. Her sister, Harriet, Lady Bessborough [*see* Ponsonby, Henrietta Frances], was less flamboyant but also involved in both the beau monde and in aristocratic politics. Their brother, the second Earl Spencer, was as prominent as his sisters, serving as first lord of the Admiralty during the Napoleonic wars; he, however, was a sober-living, religious Pittite. Lady Spencer wrote voluminously to her children (as to everyone else) and much of this correspondence has been published. She wrote just as frequently, if not as warmly, to her daughter-in-law Lavinia, whom she disliked despite the latter's piety and charity. Throughout her long life she engaged in various activities of disciplined usefulness, and helped usher in an era of 'personal nobility' in which she was the 'exemplar of aristocratic female virtue' (Langford, 571).

DONNA T. ANDREW

Sources *Letters of David Garrick and Georgiana, Countess Spencer, 1759–1779*, ed. Earl Spencer and C. Dobson, Roxburghe Club, 226 (1960) • P. Langford, *Public life and the propertied Englishman* (1991) • B. Masters, *Georgiana* (1997) • J. Friedman, *Spencer House: chronicle of a great London mansion* (1993) • Walpole, *Corr.* • B. Rizzo, *Companions without vows: relationships among eighteenth-century British women* (1994) • *GM*, 1st ser., 84/1 (1814), 309 • J. Doran, *A lady of the last century, Mrs Elizabeth Montagu* (1873) • GEC, *Peerage* • BL, Althorp MSS

Archives BL, letters from her son, second Earl Spencer; personal and estate corresp. and papers • Chatsworth House, corresp. and journals • Northants. RO, Althorp MSS

Likenesses J. Reynolds, double portrait, oils, 1759–61, Althorp, Northamptonshire [*see illus.*] • Batoni, portrait, repro. in Friedman, *Spencer House* • Liotard, portrait miniature, repro. in Friedman, *Spencer House* • Reynolds, portrait, repro. in *Letters of David Garrick and Georgiana*

Spencer, Gervase (*c.*1715–1763), miniature painter, is of unknown parentage. According to Edwards he 'was originally a gentleman's servant, but, having a natural turn to the pursuits of art, amused himself with drawing' (Edwards, 18–19). Spencer apparently suggested that he copy a recently completed miniature of one of his master's family, 'a hint [that] was received with much surprise, but he was indulged with permission to make the attempt' (ibid.). His success meant that he 'acquired the encouragement and patronage of those he served, and by their interest, became a fashionable painter of the day' (ibid.). Spencer's contemporary George Vertue also commented on his training; in July 1749 he noted:

> Lately I was shewn some watercoloured limnings—womens heads—done by a young man, Mr Spencer, who a few years ago was in the capacity of a footman to Dr W.—and now professes limning with some success, which demonstrates a genius pracizing [*sic*] by degrees of himself,—and really is in a curious neat manner and masterly. (Vertue, *Note books*, 3.51)

In the first half of the eighteenth century it was the norm for British miniaturists to be self-taught rather than to undergo formal apprenticeships. Enamel painting, however, demanded a significant outlay in terms of equipment for firing and involved unpredictable procedures. It is not known if Spencer received formal training in enamel. Samuel Finney noted in his memoirs that, when in 1760 he wanted to try enamel painting, there was 'only one Artist in that Branch, Mr Spencer … and he was excellent, though the knowledge he had gained in that Art was almost purely his own'. Finney believed he was emulating Spencer when he chose to 'attempt this difficult Art too without a Master' (Finney, 'Autobiographical account', 287–313).

Spencer established his practice in London, presumably through newspaper advertisements and word of mouth; his earliest miniatures date from about 1745. Only late in his career did the first public exhibiting society open, the Society of Artists; he exhibited in 1761 number 111, *Two Ladies in Enamel*, and in 1762 number 106, *Two Miniatures, in Enamel*. Graves gives Spencer's dates of exhibition as 1761–74 (Graves, *Artists*, 262) and Foskett gives an address for Spencer of 28 Suffolk Street (Foskett, 527). But the Mr Spencer of 28 Suffolk Street who exhibited in 1774, at the same society, number 242, *An Old Man's Head, Kit-Kat*, is clearly another artist. Gervase Spencer's name also appears in *Mortimer's Universal Director* (1763), an early trade directory advertising the services of artists and others.

By the 1760s aspiring miniaturists were, in contrast to Spencer's generation, taking lessons with established miniaturists. According to Samuel Redgrave, Henry Spicer (1743–1801) was Spencer's pupil (Redgrave, *Artists*, 408). However, Edwards noted of Spicer, 'Although the author was acquainted with this artist, yet he knows not who was his master' (Edwards, 287–8). Joseph Farington, however, in a note in his diary in 1796 about the Carwardine family, remembered that one of the '3 or 4 daughters … who afterwards married Mr Butler was some time with Spencer the Miniature Painter who taught her

Gervase Spencer (*c.*1715–1763), self-portrait

that art and she instructed her brother' (Farington, *Diary*, 2.651–2); this was presumably Penelope Carwardine.

Spencer's standing among his contemporaries is attested to by his fellow miniaturist Samuel Finney. Finney wrote that when he moved to London in 1748/9 to learn more about miniature painting 'There were at that time only two Miniature Painters of Eminence in London, Spencer who was excellent', and another whom Finney despised and identified only as 'T' (Finney, 'Autobiographical account', 267–87). Finney 'admired' Spencer and 'wished to arrive to his excellence, and be his Rival' (ibid.). Spencer also knew Sir Joshua Reynolds, whose oil portrait of Spencer painting a miniature was in the sale of Spencer's effects in 1797; its whereabouts are now unknown though Edwards noted that it was 'late in the possession of [the] artist, Mr Edridge' (Edwards, 18–19). Spencer made a brush drawing in grey wash of this portrait (British Museum) and etched it himself, showing the sitter in reverse to the drawing; a number of impressions are in the British Museum, one lettered, presumably by Spencer, 'Sr I Reynolds pinx … se ipse sculp' and subsequently (and clearly not by the etcher) 'George [*sic*] Spencer Miniature Painter'.

It is not known when or whom Spencer married but Edwards noted that when Spencer died he left

> a daughter, who married a person of the name of Lloyd … and at his death, Mr. Spencer's remaining collection of neglected miniatures, unfinished performances, together with his painting materials, were sold by auction by Hutchins, Wells, and Fischer [Fisher] in King-street, Covent-garden, in December 1797. (Edwards, 18–19)

(A copy of the catalogue is recorded in the cabinet des estampes of the Bibliothèque Nationale, Paris.) The sale catalogue also included a now lost portrait, *Mrs. Spencer, by Barwell* (presumably Thomas Bardwell). In addition Spencer executed a number of small etchings, including a half-length of a woman in a hood, inscribed 'No. 1 Jan 27 1757 London' and identified in later inscriptions as Mrs Spencer (British Museum). According to Edwards, Spencer died on 30 October 1763 'at his house in Great Marlborough-street, where he had resided some years' (ibid.).

Spencer was prolific and is represented in many public and private collections. The quality of the work attributed to him is variable and as he often signed his work it is possible that some of the unsigned works attributed to Spencer are by other artists. Some of Spencer's works indicate that he borrowed poses and costumes from the portraits of the French artist Jean-Étienne Liotard (1689–1762), for example, the portrait of Elizabeth Bradshaw at the Yale Center for British Art, New Haven, Connecticut.

KATHERINE COOMBS

Sources E. Edwards, *Anecdotes of painters* (1808); facs. edn (1970) · Vertue, *Note books*, 3.151 · S. Finney, correspondence, Ches. & Chester ALSS, Finney of Fulshaw MSS, DFF 28–39 · S. Finney, 'Autobiographical account', in 'An historical survey of the parish of Wilmslow', 1785, Ches. & Chester ALSS · Graves, *Artists*, 3rd edn · D. Foskett, *A dictionary of British miniature painters*, 2 vols. (1972) · Farington, *Diary*, 2.651–2 [28 Aug 1796] · Redgrave, *Artists* · E. Croft-Murray, MS catalogue entry on Spencer drawings, BM · P. J. Noon, *English portrait drawings and miniatures* (New Haven, CT, 1979) [exhibition catalogue, Yale U. CBA, 5 Dec 1979 – 17 Feb 1980]

Archives Ches. & Chester ALSS, Finney of Fulshaw MSS, DFF 28–39

Likenesses G. Spencer, miniature, 1749 · G. Spencer, drawing, BM [*see illus.*] · G. Spencer, grey wash painting (after lost oils by J. Reynolds), BM

Spencer, Gilbert (1892–1979), painter, was born at Cookham, Berkshire, on 4 August 1892, the eighth son and youngest of the eleven children of William Spencer, organist and music teacher, and his wife, Anna Caroline Slack. His brother Stanley *Spencer was thirteen months older. There was little money and their formal education was sketchy, but what they lacked in schooling was made up for by the talk they heard between their elders at meal times. Gilbert followed Stanley to the Slade School of Fine Art, London, in 1913, having previously attended the Camberwell School of Arts and Crafts and the Royal College of Art.

At the Slade Gilbert Spencer came under the powerful influence of Henry Tonks, which stayed with him to the end of his life. He won the coveted life drawing prize in 1914 and was runner-up for the summer competition prize with a huge mural, *The Seven Ages of Man* (Hamilton Art Gallery, Canada).

The outbreak of war in August 1914 interrupted Spencer's career. He left unfinished the picture he was working on, *Sashes Meadow* (later acquired by the Tate), enlisted in the Royal Army Medical Corps, and was drafted out to Macedonia. After the war, in 1919 Spencer returned to the Slade with a scholarship for another year.

By the early 1920s Gilbert Spencer was producing some of his best pictures, at first much under the influence of Stanley, such as *Crucifixion* (Tate collection) and *Shepherds Amazed* (Leeds Art Gallery). Family links between the brothers remained strong for the rest of their lives, yet in

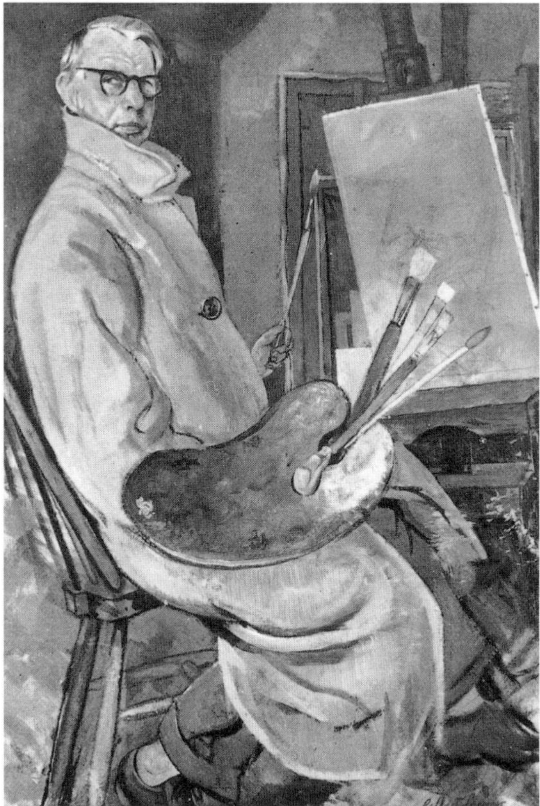

Gilbert Spencer (1892–1979), self-portrait, 1967 [*Activity at Tree Cottage no. 2*]

the course of time the fact that they followed the same vocation inevitably caused a certain tension in their relationship. In time Gilbert was to mark out a special place for himself, chiefly as a very English landscape painter.

While at the Slade in 1919 Spencer met Hilda *Carline, later to become the wife of Stanley, and her brother Sydney *Carline [*see under* Carline family], Ruskin master of drawing at Oxford, who invited Gilbert to join his staff there in 1922. This provided him with a happy *modus vivendi* until he could put on his first one-man show at the Goupil Gallery, London, in 1923. There he met Lady Ottoline Morrell who solved his domestic problem by arranging a room for him in the village of Garsington and giving him what he called 'tap and enter' rights at the manor. Thus he came into contact with many notable artists and members of the 'Bloomsbury set'. His paintings of this time, such as *Trees at Garsington* (Ashmolean Museum, Oxford), *Garsington Roofs*, and *The Sheep Fold at Upper Farm*, have a characteristic directness of line and clarity of colour.

When the Morrells gave up Garsington, Spencer moved with Sydney Carline from lodgings in Oxfordshire and Berkshire to Hampstead where he painted a remarkable portrait of Mrs Carline and started an 8 foot canvas which was to prove his best-known painting, *A Cotswold Farm* (Tate collection), first exhibited at his highly successful one-man show at the Goupil Gallery in 1932. In 1930 he was appointed to the staff of the Royal College of Art by Sir William Rothenstein, and on the strength of it married in the same year (Margaret) Ursula (*d.* 1959), daughter of John Gerald Bradshaw, headmaster of Packwood Haugh Preparatory School for Boys, Warwickshire. They had one daughter.

In 1934 Spencer was commissioned by Balliol College to paint murals for its new building at Holywell Manor, Oxford. On completion of the work in 1936 the Spencers left Oxford with their only daughter and made their home at Tree Cottage, Upper Basildon, near Reading, Berkshire, spending the long holidays from the Royal College of Art in a much-loved Dorset farmhouse. The college was evacuated to Ambleside in 1941, which gave Spencer yet another landscape to paint. Also, to escape from the restrictions of the time, he made a series of watercolour paintings of semi-imaginary comic episodes in the Home Guard.

In 1948, with the advent of Robin Darwin, Spencer was peremptorily dismissed from his post at the Royal College of Art, but happily he was immediately appointed head of the department of painting and drawing at the Glasgow School of Art, where he spent two rewarding years. In 1950 he was elected an associate of the Royal Academy on the strength of a small picture, *Culcrenth*. That year, for his wife's sake, he went south and became head of the department of painting at the Camberwell School of Arts and Crafts for the next six years. This proved to be a less happy appointment, but while still at Camberwell his frustrations were relieved by a commission from the Abbey Trust for a mural in the students' union of University College, London, for which he chose the subject of *The Scholar Gypsy*. He greatly enjoyed the work, but his fee was so small that, to make up, the president of the Royal Academy commissioned him to paint a mural, which he called *An Artist's Progress* (RA restaurant). He was elected Royal Academician in 1959; like his brother he was a somewhat stormy member of that body, resigning from time to time, but always glad to return.

In 1959 both his wife and brother died, a double blow which resulted in his writing and illustrating a book, *Stanley Spencer* (1961). In 1964 he held a retrospective exhibition at Reading of his life's work, and ten years later a further retrospective was arranged by the Fine Art Society in London. He left his beloved Berkshire in 1970 for a farm cottage in Walsham-le-Willows, Suffolk, and, though he could no longer paint, he wrote his *Memoirs of a Painter* (1974) and entered ardently into family and village life to the end. He died at Lynderswood Court, Black Notley, Braintree, Essex, on 14 January 1979. His work is also represented in the Victoria and Albert Museum and the Imperial War Museum, London; Manchester City Galleries; the Graves Art Gallery, Sheffield; and Belfast City Art Gallery. CATHERINE MARTINEAU, *rev.*

Sources G. Spencer, *Stanley Spencer: by his brother Gilbert* (1961) • G. Spencer, *Memoirs of a painter* (1974) • personal knowledge (2004) • *The Times* (19 Nov 1979) • F. Spalding, *20th century painters and sculptors* (1990), vol. 6 of *Dictionary of British art* • *CGPLA Eng. & Wales* (1979)

Likenesses G. Spencer, self-portrait, oils, 1919, NPG • G. Spencer, self-portrait, oils, 1928, Tate collection • H. Coster, two photographs, 1932–54, NPG • G. Spencer, self-portrait, 1967, RA [*see illus.*]

Wealth at death £11,298: probate, 7 March 1979, *CGPLA Eng. & Wales*

Spencer, Henry, first earl of Sunderland (*bap.* 1620, *d.* 1643), politician and royalist army officer, was born at Althorp and baptized on 23 November 1620 at Brington, Northamptonshire, the eldest son and heir of William Spencer, second Baron Spencer of Wormleighton (*bap.* 1592, *d.* 1636), and his wife, Lady Penelope Wriothesley (1598–1667), daughter of Henry *Wriothesley, third earl of Southampton, and his wife, Elizabeth, daughter of John Vernon of Hodnet, Shropshire. The family's wealth derived from sheep farming during the Tudor period. Spencer was educated at home at Althorp by private tutors before matriculating from Magdalen College, Oxford, on 8 May 1635. He was created MA on 31 August 1636 on the king's visit to the college and succeeded his father as third Baron Spencer of Wormleighton on 19 December of that year. In what was probably a love match he married the admired Lady Dorothy Sidney [*see* Spencer, Dorothy (1617–1684)], daughter of Robert *Sidney, second earl of Leicester (1595–1677), and Dorothy, daughter of Henry Percy, ninth earl of Northumberland, at Penshurst, Sussex, on 20 July 1639; his wife was the Sacharissa of Edmund Waller's poem. Until late 1641 the couple passed the years with Spencer's father-in-law, then ambassador to France, in Paris, where their eldest children, Dorothy and Robert *Spencer (1641–1702), who succeeded him as second earl, were born in July 1640 and September 1641 respectively. The family settled at Althorp in late 1641.

On his return to England Spencer took his seat in the House of Lords and initially supported parliament's struggle with the king. He was nominated to the lord lieutenancy of Northamptonshire on 5 March 1642 and, with parliament's prompting, reviewed the muster of the county's trained bands in the following month. By the summer of 1642, however, he had clearly aligned himself with the beleaguered peace party in the Lords. Clarendon claims Spencer was 'recovered to a right understanding, of which he was very capable, by his uncle [the earl] of Southampton' (Clarendon, *Hist. rebellion*, 2.181), and he had left Westminster by August 1642.

Spencer may have left parliament to support the king, but he hated the war and ranged himself with those constitutional royalists who were searching for a settlement. Along with Lord Falkland he presented unsuccessful proposals to parliament on 5 September 1642. Weeks later he wrote to his pregnant wife at Penshurst 'How much I am unsatisfied with the Proceedings here' and of his distaste for the 'Insolency of the Papists' who urged hardline policies on Charles. Honour drew him to the king's side and impelled him to stay there:

> Neither is there wanting, Daily, handsome occassion to retire, were it not for Grinning Honour. For let occassion be never so handsome, unless a Man were resolved to fight on the Parliament Side, which, for my part, I had rather be hanged, it will be said without doubt, that a man is afraid to fight. If there be an expedient found, to salve the Punctillio of Honour, I would not continue here an Hour. (Collins, 2.667)

His explanation for his allegiance has attracted historians' interest.

Despite his longing for peace, Spencer was a volunteer in the king's guard at the battle of Edgehill (23 October 1642). The following winter he visited Penshurst, where another daughter, Penelope, was later born to him posthumously. On 6 June 1643 he was created earl of Sunderland, partly, it has been suggested, in acknowledgement of a loan to Charles I. He participated in the attack on Bristol in July, and in August he was in the trenches at the siege of Gloucester. From there he wrote to his wife describing how the activity temporarily dispelled thoughts of 'how infinitely more happy I should esteem myself, quietly to enjoy your company at Althorp, than to be troubled with the noises, and engaged in the factions, of the Court, which I shall endeavour to avoid' (Collins, 2.669–70). His solitude was briefly alleviated by dining with friends from the Great Tew circle, Falkland and Chillingworth.

Sunderland was in the king's horse guard at the first battle of Newbury, on 20 September 1643, when he was fatally wounded by a cannon bullet, shortly before Falkland's fatal charge; he was twenty-three. He was buried at the battlefield, though his heart is supposedly kept in an unmarked lead casket in the Spencer vault at Brington. His will provided a jointure on Wormleighton, Warwickshire, for his wife, and £10,000 and £7000 respectively for his daughters. His two-year-old son was his main heir.

S. L. Sadler

Sources H. Sydney and others, *Letters and memorials of state*, ed. A. Collins, 2 (1746), 625, 667–72 • D. Lloyd, *Memoires of the lives … of those … personages that suffered … for the protestant religion* (1668), 432–3 • *JHL*, 4 (1628–42), 625 • *JHL*, 5 (1642–3), 338 • *Fifth report*, HMC, 4 (1876), 162 • *The manuscripts of his grace the duke of Portland*, 10 vols., HMC, 29 (1891–1931), vol. 1, p. 89 • Clarendon, *Hist. rebellion*, 2.181; 3.177 • GEC, *Peerage* • J. Cartwright, *Sacharissa* (1901), 71–104, 160–61 • S. D'Ewes, 'The diary of Sir Simonds D'Ewes', BL, Harley MS 163 • A. Steele Young and V. F. Snow, eds., *The private journals of the Long Parliament*, 3: *2 June to 17 September 1642* (1992), 86, 167, 172n., 240 • M. A. E. Green, ed., *Calendar of the proceedings of the committee for advance of money, 1642–1656*, 3 vols., PRO (1888), 98, 355, 1291 • *CSP dom.*, *1641–3*, 352 • J. P. Kenyon, *Robert Spenser, earl of Sunderland* (1958), 1–3 • Foster, *Alum. Oxon.*, *1500–1714*, 4.1397 • A. Fletcher, *The outbreak of the English civil war*, rev. edn (1985), 276, 406 • D. L. Smith, *Constitutional royalism and the search for settlement, c. 1640–1649* (1994), 111, 210 • A. Fraser, *The weaker vessel: women's lot in seventeenth-century England* (1984); repr. (1993), 91–2 • S. R. Gardiner, *History of the great civil war, 1642–1649*, new edn, 1 (1893); facs. repr. (1987) • C. V. Wedgwood, *The king's war, 1641–1647* (1958), 121, 230, 237

Archives CKS, De L'Isle and Dudley MS, U 147

Likenesses R. Walker, oils, repro. in Cartwright, *Sacharissa* • R. Walker?, oils, probably Althorp, Northamptonshire • engraving (after R. Walker), repro. in E. Lodge, *Portraits of illustrious personages of Great Britain*, 4 vols. (1821–34), vol. 2 • portrait, Penshurst, Kent • portrait, Althorp, Northamptonshire

Spencer, Sir Henry Francis (1892–1964), iron and steel industrialist, was born at 6 Earl Street, Wallbrook, Coseley, Staffordshire, on 8 April 1892, the middle child of three but only son of Henry Francis Spencer, boat loader, and his wife, Alice Wassell. His mother was illiterate, and

Spencer came from a very poor background. Despite having only a rudimentary education behind him, he left school at thirteen with a burning resolve to better himself. His first employment, however, was as a sandboy in the Cannon iron foundry at Bilston, Staffordshire, and he then spent some time as a clerk. His ambition to go into business on his own account was achieved in 1914, when, having volunteered for the armed forces, but been rejected on health grounds, he joined together with his future wife, Ethel May Southall, and her father, William, to start a small iron and steel merchants' business at Fullwoods End, Coseley. Spencer and Ethel May were subsequently married in 1916; they had one daughter.

Finally called up in 1916 to serve with the Royal Engineers, Spencer was seconded to the Admiralty. On his discharge in 1918 he set about improving himself by attending night school in order to acquire knowledge of accountancy, law, engineering, and metallurgy. This, together with his tremendous drive, strong personality, a formidable native common sense, and instinctive business acumen, helped him to develop the business, which initially had been an extremely simple and primitive operation, into a flourishing concern after the war. Some twenty years later it was said that the business, which by then had moved to Wolverhampton, was the largest distributor of flat-rolled steel products in Europe. Most significantly, however, his business interests brought him into contact with several important concerns within the steel industry, most notably the Ebbw Vale Steel, Iron, and Coal Company Ltd, and John Lysaght & Co. Ltd, the two principal manufacturers of flat-rolled steel products. His interests also widened to include the tin-plate sector, located in south Wales, and it was here that he was eventually to make such a significant impact.

The expansion of the Wolverhampton business led to Spencer's acquiring a higher profile in the Black Country. He started to take an interest in public affairs, and was elected to Coseley council, subsequently to become chairman of its education committee—education and training were to remain a lifelong and absorbing interest. More significantly, however, together with other leading industrialists in the region he became involved in an imaginative scheme to create a wide strip mill near Wolverhampton, in order to serve the rapidly expanding motor industry, in which flat-rolled steel products were to play a major part. The plans, however, were overtaken by a government decision, in order to alleviate severe unemployment problems in south Wales, to have a strip mill built in the severely distressed Ebbw Vale area.

This new strip mill was to be built by Richard Thomas & Co. Ltd, which, in 1935, had acquired the iron and steel assets of the Ebbw Vale Company, which had gone into liquidation. Because of his links with the former Ebbw Vale Company and his expertise in marketing flat-rolled products, Spencer was appointed as sheet sales controller of Richard Thomas, later becoming commercial manager, assistant managing director (1949), and, finally, managing director (1952) of what had, by then, become Richard Thomas and Baldwins. In these roles Spencer played a major part in the formation, in 1947, of the Steel Company of Wales Ltd, being one of its founder directors, which was to be an important development in the restructuring of the post-war steel industry in south Wales.

In the mid-1950s the Iron and Steel Board decided that the three British strip mills would be insufficient to meet future requirements. Harold Macmillan, then prime minister, decided that two new strip mills should be built, one in Scotland and one on a greenfield site at Llan-wern, near Newport, in south Wales. Spencer became the prime mover in the creation of the giant steelworks at Llanwern, which later became known also as the Spencer works. From the start he planned to build the works in two-thirds of the time thought sensible for such a project and, with maximum efficiency and determination, he succeeded; the works were opened by the queen in October 1962. The works materially increased productive capacity in the industry just at a time when there was a world surplus of steel, which initially threatened the project. Resolved that success would be achieved, Spencer set in motion a trading operation to ensure the works would be viable.

Through his commercial and business life Spencer displayed a ruthless dynamism, yet this was tempered with broad humanity and complete approachability, by no means common among men who have clawed their way to the top from humble origins. His relations with the trade union movement, while firm, were always notable for the degree of co-operation he was able to sustain by reason of the respect accorded to his integrity. He had a keen sense of humour and a wide interest in subjects outside his immediate business life, notably the British Institute of Management, of which he became vice-president, although his business was always the dominating influence. In addition to the business connections already noted, he was also a member of the council and executive committee of the British Iron and Steel Federation, of a number of policy-making committees within the larger orbit of the steel industry, and a director of the Development Corporation for Wales.

Spencer enjoyed family life and the company of his friends, and numbered among his recreations golf, gardening, and stamp collecting. Although a ruthless and formidable (although always fair) opponent, he would spare no pains to help his friends, colleagues, and subordinates, and sometimes indeed his opponents and enemies. He was knighted in 1963 for services to the steel industry, and died of a heart attack in London at University College Hospital on 31 May 1964, having been in poor health for several months. He was survived by his wife.

R. A. CROMARTY, *rev.* TREVOR BOYNS

Sources *The Times* (2 June 1964) · *Western Mail* (1 June 1964) · *WWW*, *1961–70* · G. Williams, ed., *Glamorgan county history*, 5: *Industrial Glamorgan from 1700 to 1970*, ed. A. H. John and G. Williams (1980) · private information (1981) · b. cert. · d. cert. · *CGPLA Eng. & Wales* (1964)

Wealth at death £70,990: administration, 1964, *CGPLA Eng. & Wales*

Spencer, Lord Henry John (1770–1795). *See under* Spencer, George, fourth duke of Marlborough (1739–1817).

Spencer, Herbert (1820–1903), philosopher, social theorist, and sociologist, was born at 12 Exeter Road, Derby, on 27 April 1820. He was the eldest son of (William) George *Spencer (*bap.* 1790, *d.* 1866), the proprietor and headmaster of a small private school, and his wife, Harriet, *née* Holmes (1794–1867): he was the only one of their nine children to survive beyond infancy.

Family background and formative influences Spencer's maternal ancestors were reputed to include Hussite and Huguenot refugees, who had fled religious persecution in France and Bohemia some centuries before. Both the Spencer and Holmes families had been settled in Derbyshire for several generations, and all four grandparents had been early recruits to Wesleyan Methodism (Herbert himself was baptized as an infant into the Methodist connexion, despite the misgivings of his father, who inclined to a strictly unceremonial form of 'inner light' religion). On his mother's side his immediate forebears had been artisans and tradesmen, while his paternal grandfather had been a schoolmaster turned pin manufacturer whose business failed, leaving the Spencer family in reduced circumstances and the grandfather in a state of permanent nervous melancholia. When Herbert was three his father also ventured into business, engaging in lace manufacture in Nottinghamshire; but this too ended in failure, and in 1827 the Spencers moved back to Derby, where the father spent the rest of his life coaching private pupils. The family income was secured, however, by the rents of thirteen tenements which Spencer's parents had inherited from various relations.

Despite the detailed accounts of his life in his *Autobiography* and his *Life and Letters*, there is much in Herbert Spencer's background, personality, career, and public reputation that remains elusive and not easy to interpret. Many commentators have stressed the seminal importance of his upbringing in the town of Derby, which in the 1820s was the hub of a very vibrant radical, scientific, and nonconformist culture, centring upon the Derby Philosophical Society, of which William George Spencer acted as honorary secretary. The multiple strands in this culture—the pursuit of free trade, political reform, rational religion, technical innovation, and experimental science—all flowed powerfully into the mainstream of English national life during the second quarter of the nineteenth century. The lasting effects of this environment on Herbert Spencer's personal development cannot be denied; yet there were to be other aspects of his future beliefs (such as his preference for theory rather than practice, and his dislike of exertion and hard work) that implicitly challenged many elements in this bracing provincial background.

The same was true of the often stressed influence of Herbert Spencer's father. Despite his business failure, which was accompanied by mental breakdown and prolonged depression, William George Spencer was a man of 'exacting' intellect, constantly devising new alphabets,

Herbert Spencer (1820–1903), by unknown photographer, *c.*1898

inventing new mechanical devices, promoting an alternative system of non-Euclidean geometry, striving to be 'a useful member of society', and pressing these interests upon his only son (Spencer, 1.94–101, 2.240). Some of these concerns were undoubtedly reflected in the son's later career, but again there were other elements in Herbert Spencer's outlook—his resistance to all forms of personal constraint, his lack of interest in practical experiment, and his scepticism of 'self-sacrifice' in the cause of public service—all of which stemmed from reaction against his father's influence rather than emulation of him. Moreover, though both father and son spent their lives in search of rational and 'purified' religious truth, William George always pursued his quest within the bounds of dissenting Christianity whereas his son from an early age rejected all possibility of belief in an immanent or personal God. There were other ways too in which the family inheritance appears to have been negative rather than constructive. The atmosphere of 'chronic alienation' between the Spencer parents, his father's unpredictable 'irritability', and his mother's excessive fussiness and caution all helped to foster Herbert Spencer's lifelong proneness to anxiety, insecurity, and hypochondria; while the mental stresses and traumas of his middle life seem to have been precipitated, not by any painful readjustment of basic beliefs, but by some form of chronic psychological malaise or personality disorder akin to that suffered by his father and grandfather. The very fact that Spencer, much of whose scientific career was devoted to theorizing about psychological causation, frequently 'could not remember' many of his own thoughts and feelings suggests an element of repression or inner reserve that was in some degree unusual.

Nevertheless, the reader of Spencer's labyrinthine works has constantly to keep in mind that this was a man who came to be treated as an equal by philosophers and scientists of the calibre of Mill, Darwin, Huxley, Sidgwick, and Romanes, and who for several decades enjoyed an outstanding scholarly and popular reputation, not just in Britain but in Europe and North America. The central narrative of Spencer's career—his unexpected ascent from obscure, autodidactic, provincial roots into the inner circles of a metropolitan and international scientific élite—poses some major questions about the man and his context, as does the equally unexpected decline of his reputation and influence in the later years of his life.

Education and civil engineering Spencer's education was unusual but academically undistinguished. Unlike his father and grandfather he was not sent to Derby grammar school, probably because his father disliked the rote learning and unscientific character of the classical curriculum. He was late in learning to read, and spent much of his spare time day-dreaming, fishing, drawing, and listening to 'instructive' conversations between his father and uncles, 'now on politics, now on religion, now on scientific matters, now on questions of right and wrong' (Spencer, 1.96–7). For a time he attended a small private school run by one of the uncles, which specialized in teaching by 'reason' rather than by 'rote'. Undoubtedly, however, the major educational influence on Spencer's early life was his father, whom he later recalled as teaching him to look for patterns of causation in the structures of the physical world. 'Always the tendency … was to regard everything as naturally caused', Spencer recalled. 'I do not remember my father ever referring to anything as explicable by supernatural agency … his remarks about the surrounding world gave no sign of any other thought than that of uniform natural law' (ibid., 101). His mother's role in his education, by contrast, appears to have been virtually nil; and Herbert from an early age picked up his father's habit of treating her merely as an amiable and pious nonentity.

This largely informal education came to an end when Spencer was thirteen. In 1833 he was sent away (ostensibly for a holiday) to the household of his father's elder brother the Revd Thomas *Spencer, who was a Cambridge wrangler, ultra-radical reformer, and evangelical rector of Hinton Charterhouse, a rural parish near Bath. When it transpired that he was to remain there permanently as one of his uncle's private pupils, Herbert responded by running home to Derby: he reached his parents' house in great distress after a journey on foot of over 100 miles in three days. Sent back to Hinton Charterhouse by his father, he was to continue under his uncle's tutelage for the next three years, during which he worked on Euclid, Latin, algebra, chemistry, and physics, with a smattering of political economy, French, and Greek. Relations with his uncle soon improved into mutual affection and respect, to such an extent that Herbert's first publication was a letter to a local newspaper defending his uncle's strict application of the controversial new poor law of 1834. Moreover, his uncle's tuition, though more systematic than his father's, largely endorsed and strengthened the intellectual traits and biases of his early childhood. By the age of sixteen Herbert Spencer was a young man with a deep-rooted dislike of systematic reading (other than of occasional novels): instead he preferred to dip into books selectively, in order to find confirmation for ideas and conjectures already taking shape in his own head. His education left him with a powerfully developed faculty for speculation and for questioning received wisdom (such as the theory of *vis inertia*, which he scornfully rejected at the age of fourteen); but it left him also with very little disciplined capacity or inclination for putting his ideas and conjectures to any serious practical test.

It is probable that the purpose of sending Spencer to study with his uncle had been to prepare him for entry to the University of Cambridge. However, his resistance to all mental activity that did not immediately interest him, particularly Latin and Greek (he found the *Iliad* 'torture'), soon ruled this out of the question. His uncle remarked upon the absence of a 'main spring' in his nephew's self-motivation, which undermined his prospects of serious academic success (Spencer, 1.124). On leaving Hinton Charterhouse at the end of 1836 he toyed with the notion of training as an architect, then taught for a time as an assistant in a Derby private school before becoming apprenticed as a civil engineer to one of his father's former pupils, the railway builder Charles Fox. Railway construction at the end of 1837 was on the brink of a massive entrepreneurial and technological expansion that was to last for the next quarter-century, and Spencer's letters to his parents at the start of his new employment showed him 'fully alive to the responsibilities of my post, and resolute to succeed' (ibid., 145–57). Over the next four years he was employed by the London–Birmingham and Birmingham–Gloucester rail companies in a variety of roles, including station design, track building, and general surveying. These experiences are often portrayed as a major influence in the shaping of his social thought; and it is certainly true that Spencer acquired far more direct grass-roots knowledge of the industrial revolution than the vast majority of Victorian social theorists (such as Mill and Carlyle) and that his later theoretical writings were often peppered with examples drawn from that firsthand experience.

Nevertheless, the claim that Spencer's railway career was an important catalyst of his later social beliefs—a conjunction of 'civil engineering and social buccaneering' (S. E. Finer, quoted in Peel, 214)—is difficult to sustain. His experience of railway management can scarcely have been responsible for his defence of private enterprise and freedom of contract, since he was to become a lifelong critic of the inefficiency and semi-fraudulent practices of many railway directors. As a trainee engineer his constant criticism of the technical skills and moral code of the engineering profession did not win popularity with his fellow employees; they indulged, he complained, in 'stories not of an improving kind' and 'glances down on the passengers, especially the females', to the 'continuous accompaniment of whistling and singing, chiefly of sentimental ballads' (Spencer, 1.159–62). Likewise, what had initially been good relations with his immediate superior, a Captain Moorsom, gradually deteriorated; though it is unclear whether this happened because of Spencer's critical and abrasive manner or because he had the misfortune to fall in love with Moorsom's coquettish niece. This young woman vigorously pursued the young Spencer throughout the summer of 1840, but then turned out to have been engaged all along to somebody else. Her heartless treatment seems to have left a permanent mark on Spencer, for he recalled it with quite uncharacteristic clarity half a century later, and there is no record of his ever again becoming emotionally attached to any other woman (ibid., 191–5). In the intellectual sphere the main legacy of his engineering training seems to have been to confirm his earlier preference for working out solutions to problems from 'first principles' rather than from practical experiment. In 1841 he refused a permanent post with the Birmingham–Gloucester company on the ground that he needed to complete his engineering training by studying higher mathematics; but this in turn was soon abandoned as a result of his 'inability to persevere in labour which has not an object at once large and distinct' (ibid., 215).

Then followed nearly a decade of restless and apparently aimless dilettantism, in which Spencer toyed with various schemes for mechanical inventions, dabbled in drawing, modelling, and phrenology, returned to occasional temporary posts in railway building and promotion, and spent much time with his uncle at Hinton Charterhouse discussing philosophy, political economy, and radical politics. Out of these discussions came a series of letters from Spencer to *The Nonconformist* newspaper on such topics as free trade, the poor laws, the established church, public health, and national education, all arguing that 'society' if left to its own devices was naturally 'self-adjusting', and that the sole proper aim of government was the defence of individual rights. These writings (reissued as a pamphlet on *The Proper Limit of Government*) brought Spencer into close contact with many of the burgeoning dissident movements of the day, including the constitutionalist wing of Chartism and the Complete Suffrage Union, and with leading provincial radicals such as Lawrence Heyworth and Edward Miall. They also awakened a feeling that his own true vocation might lie in philosophy and literature rather than civil engineering; and they fostered in him a secret conviction that 'the moral Euclid'—a philosophical work that would articulate the basic unifying principles of social, political, and moral science—did not yet exist and was waiting to be written.

Nevertheless, dreaming of the moral Euclid was one thing, actually writing it quite another. Literary openings were slow to materialize, and when they came were usually transient or unpaid. Several projects for starting new radical journals came to nothing, while a newly founded suffragist newspaper, *The Pilot*, on which Spencer obtained a post as sub-editor in 1844, folded after a month. Occasional short articles in provincial journals about his various 'inventions' (such as a 'velocimeter' for measuring the speed of trains) did nothing to earn him a living; indeed the fact that Spencer was able to survive for so long without settled employment suggests that financial support from his father and uncle must have been more substantial than he ever openly acknowledged. At one stage he contemplated emigration to New Zealand, but was deterred by the fact that his parents felt unable to go with him. Not until November 1848 did an opportunity arise of the kind he had long been hoping for: the offer of a sub-editorship on *The Economist* at a salary of £150 a year, including free accommodation at the journal's London office and the chance to write leading articles at an extra guinea a week. The fact that the journal's proprietor, James Wilson, a bastion of the Anti-Corn Law League and the Complete Suffrage Union, was a friend of his uncle indicates how far Herbert Spencer had still to go in establishing himself as an independent literary figure.

London literary life Nevertheless, Spencer's entry into London journalistic circles at the end of 1848 came at an opportune moment for one of his social and intellectual outlook, occurring as it did just two years after the adoption of free trade, and only a few months after the final collapse of organized Chartism. Spencer's emerging conception of 'society' as a co-operative, cross-class, self-regulating organism, tended at a distance by a minimal state, was to have far more plausibility in the booming 1850s than at any moment during the previous half-century. At the same time many familiar theological, philosophical, and scientific ideas were in a state of critical debate and flux—trends exemplified by the rise of Comtean positivism, by rumours of new 'development theories' spreading from the continent, and by J. S. Mill's triumphal onslaught on the 'intuitionist' theories of Dr William Whewell. Within this rising ferment Herbert Spencer soon discovered a receptive and expanding audience, eager to give a hearing to anyone who could articulate and make sense of this powerful but tangled confluence of new ideas.

Despite his long-drawn-out engineering apprenticeship, Spencer was still only twenty-eight when he joined *The Economist*, but he already showed signs of many of the fixed habits and attitudes that were to characterize him in later life. He was 5 feet 10 inches tall, thin and wiry with a compulsive need for regular exercise, and a nervous and somewhat irritable disposition. His thick brown hair was already receding, accentuating the enormous cranial dome that became his most striking feature in later portraits. As in earlier years he was very averse to sustained work of a routine kind and, although he wrote some distinguished leaders, he valued his post on *The Economist* primarily for the leisure it gave him to pursue his own private interests. In all such matters he was overwhelmingly preoccupied with his own thoughts and found it difficult to give concentrated attention to the ideas of other people, except when they fed directly into his own prior concerns. He prided himself on 'speaking his mind', was constantly surprised when others took offence at this, and yet was thrown into a state of nervous agitation and dejection whenever his own opinions came under attack. In his reactions to new experiences he practised a studied refusal to be impressed by anything that was generally admired by his contemporaries, be it the landscape of Switzerland ('colourless'), Florentine painting ('grotesque'), Paris ('dull'), the operas of Mozart ('pretty airs and duets'), or John Ruskin's *The Stones of Venice* ('sheer barbarism').

Despite his self-preoccupation, however, Spencer was very fond of social life and domestic sociability. Since the mid-1840s he had been the frequent house guest of the railway promoter Richard Potter, staying up far into the night to discuss theology and philosophy with Potter's studious wife, Lawrencina: he was to remain for more than forty years the Potter family's perennial 'philosopher on the hearth' (Webb, *Apprenticeship*, 1.47). His five-year period on *The Economist* saw a great expansion in this social circle, bringing him into close contact with many leading literary and scientific figures. He attended the salon run by John Chapman, editor of the *Westminster Review*, where he met many prominent men and women of the day, among them James Froude, Francis Newman, H. T. Buckle, Anna Swanwick, Eliza Linton, and Barbara Leigh Smith. Early in 1850 he made the acquaintance of G. H. Lewes, with whom he pursued engrossing conversations on the fallacies of 'creationism', on Milne-Edwards's theory of the 'physiological division of labour', and on the model of universal transition from 'homogeneity to heterogeneity' advanced by the German physiologist K. F. von Baer (Spencer, 1.436–7, 445–6). He paid several visits to Carlyle's house in Chelsea, though that relationship did not flourish: 'I found that I must either listen to his absurd dogmas in silence, which it was not in my nature to do, or get into fierce argument with him, which ended in our glaring at one another' (ibid., 440). Other new acquaintances of this period included Charles Kingsley, Leigh Hunt, and the physicist Dr John Tyndall; and in 1852 he met T. H. Huxley, newly returned from his voyage on *The Rattlesnake*, who introduced him into advanced scientific circles and was to become a close friend. For a time he became the constant companion of Marian Evans, the recent translator of Strauss's *Leben Jesu* and better known by her later literary pseudonym, George Eliot. Marian Evans fell in love with him and hinted at marriage, but Spencer, who greatly admired her mind and moral character, reputedly rejected her because she was too ugly. She was long believed to have avenged herself by parodying him as Dr Casaubon in her novel *Middlemarch*, though recent literary criticism has reinterpreted this work as an extended and largely favourable exposition of many of Spencer's philosophical ideas.

Spencer's post on *The Economist* meant that he could now launch himself upon his literary career. His first book, *Social Statics*, appeared in 1850; as its title indicated, it was concerned with the 'equilibrium of a perfect society' in the future, rather than the forces (or 'dynamics') by which society was struggling towards perfection in the immediate present (p. 229). Although the book attracted little attention at the time, it contained some important pointers to the ways in which Spencer's thought was developing. The most important of these were his treatment of human society as governed by immutable natural laws, his vision of the role of the state as confined to the enforcement of those natural laws, his emphasis on continuous functional adaptation in both institutions and organisms, and his formulation of a law of 'equal freedom' for each individual, limited only by 'the similar freedoms of all' (p. 35). The book also reflected the strain of utopian radicalism in Spencer's thought inherited from his early background: it denied the legitimacy of private property in land, held out equality of the sexes as a moral ideal, and advocated the training of children by persuasion and rational argument rather than discipline and coercion. This was followed two years later by two short but seminal articles. In 'The development hypothesis', published in *The Leader*, Spencer attacked 'special-creationism', and argued for an evolutionary model of the natural world, based on a process of continuous minuscule structural modification: 'Surely if a single cell … may become a man in the space of twenty years … there is nothing absurd in the hypothesis that … a cell may, in the course of millions of years, give origin to the human race' (H. Spencer, *Essays: Scientific, Political and Speculative*, 1891, 1.6). This article was later praised by Charles Darwin as having made a seminal contribution to the crystallization of evolutionary thought. The second article, 'A theory of population deduced from the general law of animal fertility', appeared in the *Westminster Review* early in 1853. It propounded the law that 'the degree of fertility is inversely proportionate to the grade of development', from which Spencer concluded that, as human societies progressed in civilization, birth-rates would inevitably decline. Development itself he portrayed as determined in all spheres by success or failure in adapting to environment, a process that he succinctly summarized in a much quoted phrase as the 'survival of the fittest' (Spencer, 1.449–52; Peel, 137–8).

Spencer's articles attracted much more attention than his book, and he was soon under pressure from editors to produce more of them. Early in 1853 the death of his uncle Thomas Spencer, who left him a legacy of £500, enabled him to resign his post on *The Economist* in order to pursue an independent literary career. First, however, he went on an extended holiday to Switzerland, where he engaged in strenuous bouts of walking and climbing. This left him with the conviction that he had permanently strained his heart, though no medical corroboration for this fear was ever to be forthcoming. For the next three years he led a 'wandering, unsettled life' in Derby, London, Paris, Eastbourne, and Dieppe, searching for good doctors and congenial climates. It was also, however, a period of intense intellectual activity, when Spencer made serious efforts to master Mill's *Logic*, which he criticized on the ground that Mill glossed over the need for an ultimate 'criterion of belief'. He also studied the positivist philosophy of Auguste Comte, which he dismissed as a 'pseudo-scientific cosmogony', useful only for the two new concepts of 'altruism' and 'sociology', that he henceforth adopted for his own purposes (Duncan, 544; Spencer, 1.537–8).

Such works served to nurture the slowly gestating secret ambition to produce his own grand synthesis of scientific and philosophical theory, based on the premise of a 'Universal Postulate' which he increasingly conceived as the indispensable prerequisite of all forms of knowledge. His second full-length book, *The Principles of Psychology*, which portrayed 'mind' in all its forms as the product of environmentally generated organic evolution, appeared in 1855 and evoked much hostile criticism of its supposed atheism and materialism. Over the same period Spencer was writing a stream of articles for the major London journals on such themes as progress, anthropology, positivism, metaphysics, and scientific method—all of which contributed to the furore of impassioned intellectual debate that preceded publication of Darwin's *The Origin of Species* (1859). Well before this event, however, Spencer had become seriously ill with a paralysing nervous breakdown from which he never fully recovered. One morning in July 1855, 'soon after beginning work, there commenced a sensation in my head—not pain, nor heat, nor fulness, nor tension, but simply a sensation, bearable enough but abnormal'. This 'sensation', for which doctors initially prescribed 'sea-air', rendered him unfit for work for the next eighteen months, and unable ever again to work for more than three hours a day. 'The pursuit of health, now commenced, was fated to be unsuccessful; for health, in the full sense of the word, was never again to be overtaken' (Spencer, 1.545).

Spencer's breakdown left him in a position of some financial embarrassment, for during eighteen months of continuous medical treatment and total rest in quiet seaside towns his uncle's legacy was rapidly exhausted. As his health improved, he began to look around for some administrative sinecure that might enable him to continue his writing career, but, unsurprisingly in the circumstances, no such post was forthcoming. In 1858–9 he wrote a series of articles on education, which denounced cramming, the dominance of Latin and Greek, and the history of kings and queens, and proposed their replacement by a regime of 'self-development', based on problem-solving, 'empirical geometry', healthy exercise, drawing from observation, and natural science. In all spheres children should be taught and disciplined, not by artificial rewards and punishments but by having to accept the consequences of their actions, with the 'impersonal agency of Nature' replacing 'the personal agency of parents' (H. Spencer, *Education: Intellectual, Moral and Physical*, 1861, 118–26). These articles later formed the core of a best-selling book, but in the meantime they left him with no money and no energy for pressing on with more systematic work; and it was perhaps characteristic of Spencer that his breakdown in health had in no way diminished his belief that the world needed his Synthetic Philosophy. When his fortunes seemed at their lowest ebb, however, he was rescued by a patron from North America. Professor Edward L. Youmans, a long-standing admirer of Spencer's work, and himself a popular lecturer on scientific subjects, proposed to market his books in the United States by mass subscription, a procedure that for the rest of his life secured to Spencer a substantial regular income from North American sales. At the same time a boom in demand for 'evolutionary' writings after 1859 led to a series of English reprints of his works, and the beginning of extensive translation of his writings into French, German, and Russian. The year 1860, when Spencer reached forty, saw him relieved of immediate financial anxiety but committed to a twenty-year programme of philosophical writings that would link together theology, epistemology, thermodynamics, astronomy, biology, psychology, ethics, and political thought. 'When I look back on all the circumstances', Spencer later commented,

> when I recall the fact that at my best I could work only three hours daily—when I remember that … I from time to time had a serious relapse; I am obliged to admit that to any unconcerned bystander my project must have seemed almost insane. (Spencer, chap. 32)

Writing the Synthetic Philosophy Spencer now settled into a pattern of life that lasted for several decades. He briefly considered living near his parents in Derby, but he was by now too accustomed to independence for this to be a success (though he continued to visit the parental home regularly until his mother's death in 1867). The advice of Huxley and George Eliot—that he should look for a suitable wife—was also rejected, perhaps because he cherished his privacy and solitude, but more probably because he still recalled his painful experience of rejection in the summer of 1840. For a time he maintained his own bachelor establishment, but had difficulty finding servants who could put up with his eccentric manners and valetudinarian habits. He then moved to a series of genteel lodging-houses before eventually settling in a boarding-house near Lancaster Gate and taking a room in neighbouring Leinster Square for use as his study. He lived there for many years, writing for three hours every morning, then walking across Hyde Park to his club (he was elected in 1867 to the Athenaeum, which became his 'second home'). There he lunched, read the newspapers, played billiards, and 'killed time' for the rest of the day. In the evening he returned to his lodging or dined quietly with friends. This pattern was punctuated by occasional visits to the continent, walking tours with friends such as Tyndall and G. H. Lewes, and frequent holidays in Scotland, at various seaside resorts, or at the country home of the Potters in the Wye valley. The main preoccupation of Spencer's daily life became to avoid all stress and nervous excitement, which he feared would precipitate a recurrence of the breakdown of 1855–6. Above all he went to great lengths to avoid contact with anyone who might disagree with him, the strain of even polite argument being more than his nervous constitution could withstand. Even so, he felt himself to be living in a state of permanent illness, characterized by headaches, depression, heart strain, and chronic insomnia (all regarded as largely imaginary by many of his friends). Recollections of this period suggest that he was truly happy only in the company of small children, particularly the nine daughters of the Potter family, who relished his tirades against discipline, book learning, grammar, and governesses, and who became his 'firm friends' (Webb, *Apprenticeship*, 1.39–44).

Given his poor health and reclusive habits, what is surprising about this period of Spencer's life is his flowering as a productive and increasingly popular writer, and the respect and personal friendship that he gained from so many eminent contemporaries. Although he refused to join the Metaphysical Society (where he feared to meet people such as Cardinal Manning, R. H. Hutton, and others who would certainly have 'disagreed' with him), he was a member and active attendant at meetings of the X-club, the exclusive forum of mid-Victorian Britain's most eminent natural scientists (all of whom, apart from Spencer himself, were fellows of the Royal Society). He corresponded regularly with J. S. Mill, whose tact and gentleness in dealing with their deep philosophical differences were quite exemplary. In the late 1860s he was invited to apply for two major professorial chairs, in mental philosophy at University College, London, and in moral philosophy at the University of Edinburgh; and although he did not accept these invitations, the fact that they were made was a measure of his standing at this time among academic philosophers. Moreover, despite his almost complete withdrawal from radical politics, he was sufficiently moved by the Governor Eyre controversy to join the famous Jamaica committee that called for Eyre's prosecution for his suppression of the Morant Bay rebellion; this act of piety was prompted by Spencer's father, who, as a lifelong crusader for the rights of subject peoples, had denounced Governor Eyre from his deathbed in May 1866.

What was most remarkable about Spencer's life in this period, however, was the tenacity with which he pursued the writing of his Synthetic Philosophy, a project that was eventually to occupy him for more than forty years. The physical act of writing had become almost as stressful for him as concentrated reading, and from the early 1860s he began to dictate all his compositions to an amanuensis (he was as thrilled as his father would have been by the invention of Pitman's shorthand). Some years later the shorthand writer was supplemented by a series of research assistants, whose job was to trawl through empirical and descriptive scientific and sociological materials, selecting and organizing them so as to provide supporting evidence for Spencer's deductions and theories. The longest-lasting of these assistants was David Duncan, Spencer's eventual biographer, who became a professor at the University of Madras, and was to spend a lifetime accumulating data designed to illustrate Spencer's hypotheses about the links between ethnicity, human physiognomy, and levels of civilization.

The first volume of Spencer's Synthetic Philosophy, dealing with the metaphysical and epistemological underpinnings of his general theory, appeared in 1862, under the title *First Principles*. Although written while he was still seriously depressed, it was the best-selling and most often reprinted of Spencer's works; and more clearly than any of his other writings it revealed the full range and depth of his philosophical concerns. Its popularity may have lain partly in the fact that it dealt more directly than his other writings with the philosophical underpinnings of religious belief, for which there was a ready market among the mid-Victorian reading public. But it stemmed also from the nature of the subject matter, which particularly lent itself to Spencer's deductive and speculative methodology, and did not require the kind of detailed empirical support and demonstration for which he had very little knack. Spencer's point of departure was that, despite the epic battles waged for centuries between science and religion, there was really no contest between them: the apparent antagonism stemmed simply from failure to define the logical boundaries between the 'Knowable' and the 'Unknowable'. Everything in the former sphere was the proper province of science, while everything in the latter sphere was the proper province of religion, including those a priori assumptions about the objective character of existence (the 'Universal Postulate'), which science could not dispense with and yet was incapable of proving. The task of philosophy was the largely secondary one of identifying and sorting out the difficulties of language and perception that led to confusion between the two spheres; in the last resort 'ultimate religious ideas and ultimate scientific ideas, alike turn out to be merely symbols of the actual, not cognitions of it' (p. 50). In applying these arguments to the 'actual world' Spencer drew heavily upon the notion of an 'unconditioned Absolute' underpinning all reality, which had been developed in the 1850s by Christian metaphysicians such as Sir William Hamilton and Dr Mansel; but unlike them he vigorously denied that the absolute was to be in any way identified with a personalized creator-God who could be moved by prayer and supplication. ('Let those who can, believe that there is eternal war set between our intellectual faculties and our moral obligations. I, for one, admit no such radical vice in the constitution of things.') Instead he claimed that the concept of an impersonal 'Ultimate Cause' restored 'the truly religious element of Religion', by purifying it of all 'those dogmas by which mystery was made unmysterious' (pp. 74–5, 80). And it also enabled theorists and scientists to acknowledge and demarcate all those non-empirical aspects of the more concrete sciences that were, in Spencer's view, fundamental and essential to the understanding of how nature worked, but nevertheless ultimately imponderable.

Part 2 of *First Principles* attempted to demonstrate how these ideas might be applied to the study of 'the Knowable'. Here he drew upon themes in the physical and biological sciences that had been engaging him since the

1840s. Of these the most important were: first, the various competing models of development and evolution; second, ideas about the nature of matter and motion derived from theoretical mechanics; and third, von Baer's model of the progression from homogeneity to heterogeneity in the structure of cells—all of which Spencer envisaged as having application far outside the specialist disciplines in which they had first arisen. As shown above, he had been a firm adherent of the 'development hypothesis' or 'theory of evolution' from the early 1850s; and like many other theorists of the period he had learned about 'competition' within and between species from Malthus's *Essay on Population*. He was also closely acquainted with Lamarck's account of a process of organic change generated by use, practice, and adaptation to environment: 'adaptation' in particular was a central theme in Spencer's seminal articles of the mid-1850s. After 1859 he rapidly incorporated Darwin's theory of 'natural selection' into his own model of evolution; but in *First Principles* and all subsequent works he insisted that it was by no means the only element, and that selection operated alongside other evolutionary mechanisms, such as adaptation to environment, acquired characteristics, and the multiplication of cells. In addition he claimed that all progressive development was governed by the mechanical principle of the 'persistence of force' (what other theorists usually referred to as the 'indestructability of matter', though Spencer denied that they were identical). This implied that nothing in the natural world, either organic or inorganic, could be added or newly created: progress and development entailed simply the structural 'reorganization' of existing material in a more complicated manner. Thus, in the organic world single cells in lower organisms multiplied into clusters of cells in higher organisms; in the inorganic world single molecules fused into compounds; while in the social world the (supposedly simple) structures of primitive peoples evolved into the complex institutional arrangements of modern life: in all cases the evolution consisted of new structures, not of new material. Moreover, in all spheres structural development was accompanied by ever-increasing specialization of functions; hence, while evolution in the organic sphere constantly generated new species, in the 'super-organic' sphere it was constantly replacing social systems whose members were all much the same by social systems where everyone was individual and different. Thus, not just biology but physics, psychology, anthropology, ethics, and government all demonstrated the tendency towards a 'physiological division of labour' that Spencer had noted in the work of Milne-Edwards; a process that also coincided with the transition from 'homogeneity to heterogeneity' which he had discovered in the writings of von Baer.

These key principles were elaborated by Spencer in a long series of books, the last of which was not published until he was nearly eighty. Two volumes applying them to biology were published in 1864 and 1867; and two volumes applying them to psychology (incorporating and updating the materially based theory of mind set out in his earlier *Principles of Psychology*) appeared in 1870 and 1872. Three volumes of *The Principles of Sociology* (incorporating political, ecclesiastical, and economic institutions, as well as social structure) appeared between 1876 and 1897. These sociological volumes traced the evolution of religious belief and institutions from what Spencer believed to have been their origins in the cult of ancestors through to his own conception of an 'unknowable' First Cause. They also identified a universal law of socio-political development, from regimes based on military organization through to regimes based on industrial production (analogous to, and tacitly borrowed from, Sir Henry Maine's account of the transition from status to contract). Two further volumes portrayed social evolution as tending inexorably towards greater individualism, greater altruism, greater co-operation, and a complete realization of the 'law of equal freedom'—the latter underpinned by a minimalist but powerful state, strictly confined to its generic functions of defence, police, and enforcement of civil contracts (*The Principles of Ethics*, 1879–93).

All these volumes were issued simultaneously in Britain and North America, and several of them were reprinted in popular or abridged editions. They were translated into many European languages, and were to find new audiences in Japan, China, India, and Latin America after Spencer's death. A popular abridgement of his ideas, *The Study of Sociology*, which Spencer wrote for the Paris-based International Scientific Series in 1873, had gone into no fewer than twenty-one editions by 1894. Towards the end of his life Spencer was receiving £1300 a year in royalties (perhaps equivalent to between £80,000 and £100,000 at the beginning of the twenty-first century). In the 1870s and 1880s he was showered with offers of academic and ceremonial honours, most of which he rejected on the ground that he disapproved of such honours on principle. In 1873 he would certainly have been elected a fellow of the Royal Society if he had not refused to permit his name to go forward. In 1875 he was elected to the academy of Rome, but only because this was done without his foreknowledge; and in 1883 he turned down his election as a member of the French Académie des Sciences Morales et Politiques. In 1882 he was persuaded by Youmans to go on a literary tour of American universities, which could have been repeated many times over, had he not loathed the travel and public-speaking engagements, which left him convinced that he had 'made another step downwards towards invalid life' (Spencer, 2.481). He refused many offers of honorary degrees and invitations to the rectorships of the universities of Aberdeen and Edinburgh; and many more such honours would doubtless have been forthcoming if his stalwart refusal to accept them had not become common knowledge. On his deathbed in 1903 Spencer was to be nominated as a candidate for the newly founded Nobel prize for literature. Moreover, despite his reclusiveness, there was a time in the 1870s and early 1880s when he was viewed as something of a cult figure, not just in intellectual circles but in fashionable London society: 'you could not mention his name in many companies high or low without exciting a thrill of interest, and even in the most unlikely quarters his name would be known as that of a distinguished man' (Duncan, 497–8). In 1883 a leader of the English co-operative movement, Arthur Hughes, described Spencer's *The Study of Sociology* as the 'introduction to this great master, as Walküre, Act 1, was to Wagner' (inscribed in Hughes's copy, in possession of the author).

Retreat and eclipse The mass sales and public esteem of the 1870s were, however, a deceptive index of Herbert Spencer's real influence and standing. His major impact on the vital core of intellectual life almost certainly came earlier, in the 1850s and early 1860s, when he was still struggling to find an audience but was a creative and often original contributor to some of the cutting-edge controversies of the day. Despite the flood of recognition that came to him in later years, in the early 1880s the tide of intellectual fashion in Britain turned against Herbert Spencer; and the storehouse of ideas that he had forged out of the seething cross-currents of his youth suddenly began to look repetitive and *passé*. The causes of this downturn lay partly in Spencer himself, and partly in the emergence of new ideas and circumstances that he was unwilling or unable to accommodate. The underlying principles of the Synthetic Philosophy which, if not wholly plausible, had seemed immensely audacious and ambitious in 1862 began to seem tendentious and over-familiar when reiterated through volume after volume of what was supposed to be supporting evidence, but often seemed like little more than rows of random examples. As the natural sciences made more and more use of laboratories, Spencer's lack of interest in controlled experiment meant that his deductive method became increasingly remote from advanced scientific research. And as the momentum in intellectual life moved away from the quarterlies and salons into the universities, Spencer's lack of an academic platform severely limited his opportunities for transmitting ideas to the leaders of a younger generation. His inability to engage in friendly interchange with other theorists—always a major weakness—now became a serious liability, as not just biology, physics, and philosophy but also political thought, economics, and theology all began to move away from the familiar landmarks of his early career. In later middle age Spencer increasingly appeared not so much unaware of as simply unable to take account of new data and new theories that could not be slotted into the structure of the Synthetic Philosophy. These included such diverse developments as the growth of anthropological evidence about the immense complexity of 'primitive' tribal structures; the rise or revival of idealist, socialist, and communitarian political thought; and the tendency to equilibrium and entropy in the physical universe posited by refinements in the second law of thermodynamics. Most crucially of all, developments in cell biology conclusively undermined the theories of adaptation, 'purpose', and 'inheritance of acquired characteristics', which Spencer had portrayed as equally if not more important than 'natural selection' throughout *A System of Synthetic Philosophy*.

Similarly, many developments in the social world failed to live up to Spencer's earlier confident prediction that as 'an essential principle of life … evil perpetually tends to disappear' (H. Spencer, *Social Statics*, 1850, 27). The 'equilibrium' promised by political economy failed to materialize; while successive extensions of the franchise seemed to have led not to the dissolution of interest-group politics but to their re-emergence in other more deeply entrenched forms (such as the demand of trade unionists for certain immunities from the common law). National and local government, instead of leaving social evolution to take its course, increasingly succumbed to the demands of a mass electorate for regulation, intervention, subsidies, and measures that treated citizens like infants. Opposition to these trends became the central theme of Spencer's journalistic writings of the late 1870s and early 1880s, and culminated in his famous polemic against 'the new Toryism' (that is, the social reformist wing of Gladstonian Liberalism), published in 1884 as *The Man versus the State*. In this he denounced the Liberals for having lost their *raison d'être* of defending personal liberty, and engaging instead in a long sequence of paternalist social legislation: a sequence that included Irish land reform, compulsory education, safety at work, temperance and licensing laws, free libraries, mitigation of the rigours of the poor law, and a host of other issues. In all these spheres Spencer argued that the substantive content of the measures in question was not at issue; if achieved through altruism and voluntary co-operation, as part of spontaneous adaptation of the social organism, then all of them would have claims to be 'progressive'. What was objectionable was the use of the coercive powers of the state, the discouragement given to voluntary self-improvement, and the disregard of the 'laws of life' relating to individuation and natural selection; all of this was tantamount to 'socialism', which in Spencer's view meant the same as 'slavery'. And above all he was horrified by the all-party enthusiasm for annexation of colonies and imperial expansion—the trend for 'white savages' to make war on indigenous peoples—which seemed to subvert all he had predicted about evolutionary progress from 'militant' to 'industrial' societies and states.

The result was that, despite his continuing wide readership and his mass popularity in North America, Spencer found himself gradually cut off from the advanced intellectual circles with whom he had mingled for three decades. A series of attacks on his work by leading intellectuals of the 1880s and 1890s—T. H. Green, Henry Sidgwick, F. R. Maitland, Frederic Harrison—left many aspects of the Synthetic Philosophy in tatters. Many of his more radical disciples were shocked and disappointed by his abandonment of the view set out in *Social Statics* that there could be no 'absolute right of property' in a natural resource such as land. To a new generation of advanced Liberals, faced with the poverty, homelessness, unemployment, and mass disorder of the late 1880s, Spencer's blanket condemnation of state aid began to look not just irrelevant but positively immoral. The deaths of several of Spencer's dearest friends—G. H. Lewes, George Eliot, Lawrencina and Richard Potter—left him bereft of the surrogate domestic life which he had always particularly enjoyed; while several of his younger followers, such as Grant Allen and Beatrice Potter (later Beatrice Webb), became converts to Fabian socialism. The X-club virtually ceased to meet, and Spencer became estranged from his old friend Thomas Huxley, who had concluded in his Romanes lecture that there was no necessary connection between natural phenomena and ethics—a conclusion which, if true, threatened the very foundations of Spencer's conception of an objective and universal 'agnostic metaphysics'. Another old acquaintance, Alfred Russel Wallace, attacked what he saw as Spencer's obstinate attachment to Lamarckianism as 'a glaring example of taking the unessential in place of the essential and drawing conclusions from a partial and altogether insufficient survey of the phenomena' (Taylor, *Contemporary Assessments*, 497). Spencer himself, however, in his *Autobiography* fully acknowledged the intellectual pre-eminence of Darwin, and blamed himself for the combination of *idées fixes* and failure to look at the evidence that had debarred him from cottoning on to the hypothesis of 'natural selection' forty years before.

The last decade and a half of Herbert Spencer's life was spent in a great deal of 'mental misery' and social isolation. For some years he shared a house with two maiden ladies in St John's Wood; but this initially amicable arrangement ended in failure, and he again moved into a series of temporary lodgings before finally settling in Brighton, at 5 Percival Terrace. To Beatrice Potter, who visited him regularly during this period out of family piety and personal affection, it seemed that he was 'living a living death'. She recorded that he was 'poisoned by morphia and self-absorption', cared for only by calculating sycophants, and reduced to a 'strangely crude vision of all human life as a series of hard bargains', in which 'even illness and death seem a nasty fraud perpetrated by nature'. He was obsessed, she believed, with the fear that his whole life's work was a delusion, yet still clung to the belief that the Synthetic Philosophy was the clue to definitive truth (Webb, *Apprenticeship*, 48–52; *Diary of Beatrice Webb*, 2.172, 285–6, 306). These were harsh judgements on a man whose domestic staff later wrote warmly of the fun and good humour they had enjoyed in his household and who himself wrote to a friend only weeks before his death, 'The Why? and the Why? and the Why? are questions which press ever more as the years go by' (Duncan, 472; *Home Life*, *passim*). But Herbert Spencer remained to the end an enigmatic figure. He died at his house at 5 Percival Terrace, Brighton, on 8 December 1903, and was cremated on 14 December at Golders Green. Shortly after his death a petition signed by many leading natural and social scientists called for a memorial to be raised in Westminster Abbey. But this was politely declined by the abbey authorities, and Spencer's remains were more fittingly interred in accordance with his own wishes in a sarcophagus in Highgate cemetery, not far from the grave of his fellow system-builder and ideological antithesis Karl Marx.

Spencer's serious reputation was waning long before his death, but his most damning obituary was to be pronounced thirty years later by Professor Talcott Parsons: 'Dead by suicide or at the hand of person or persons unknown' (Parsons, 3). Spencer's 'death', Parsons suggested, signified not just the end of a life but the closing of an epoch; it was the terminal point of the 'individualist' and 'positivistic-utilitarian' tradition which had played such an important part in 'the intellectual history of the English-speaking peoples', and of which Herbert Spencer had been a 'typical representative' (T. Parsons, *Theory of Social Action*, 1937, 3–5). This highly tendentious judgement dominated approaches to the study of Spencer for more than half a century; and only in recent decades has it become possible to examine his life and work in a less stereotyped and more genuinely historical fashion. Recent reassessments have been much less concerned with Spencer's reputation as one of the 'founding fathers' of sociology, and much more interested in locating his role in nineteenth-century intellectual history, as a mirror of certain aspects of the Victorian age and as a contributor to specific debates on physiology, psychology, epistemology, political and social theory, ethics, and religious belief (for example, the work of Mark Francis, T. S. Gray, J. D. Y. Peel, Michael W. Taylor, Paul Weindling, and David Wiltshire).

Looked at from these more precise perspectives, Spencer has been slowly resurfacing not as the triumphal author of a holistic 'total structure', but as an innovative and significant figure on a number of different fronts. Current writing on the history of science has re-emphasized his contribution to the intellectual debates that precipitated *The Origin of Species*, his role in importing continental 'cell theory' and embryology into English debate, and his seminal influence in promoting study of the biological basis of mind (Weindling, *passim*; Rylance, 203–50). His theory of the 'Universal Postulate' has been reinterpreted as providing a post-Christian metaphysic for those mid-Victorian scientists who could no longer accept the 'natural theology' framework of the earlier generation of Adam Sedgwick and William Whewell (Francis, *passim*). Much of his more ephemeral writing on such themes as language, speech, manners, beauty, and fashion anticipated the recent awakening of interest in reconstructing the history of human culture. Attempts to trace a conscious historical pedigree between Spencer's political thought and that of late twentieth-century neo-liberals and libertarians such as Hayek and Nozick have been largely inconclusive. But there can be no doubt that he anticipated many of the analytical standpoints of these later theorists, most notably in his 'law of equal liberty', his insistence on the limits to predictive knowledge, his conception of a spontaneous social order, and his emphasis on the 'unintended consequences' of collectivist social action. There can be no doubt also that Spencer's 'law of equal liberty' was derived from an enlightenment assumption of the universality of 'human rights', a principle which he viewed as perfectly compatible with such 'natural' phenomena as an evolutionary stepladder of civilized and primitive peoples, and with biologically determined distinctions of language, race, and gender. Spencer's seemingly paradoxical ideas about race (favouring the principle of absolute equality between races, yet disapproving of racial intermarriage and miscegenation as culturally and biologically regressive) deserve more attention in reconstructions of the history of racial theories than they have so far received.

In all these different spheres, however, Spencer was much less lastingly influential than he might have been if he had not been so contemptuous or indifferent towards other theorists whose interests bore some relation to his own. This applied particularly to the philosophy of Kant, whose a priori categories Spencer loftily dismissed as (unlike his own!) mere subjective rubbish. His critique of J. S. Mill's inadequate treatment of supra-empirical truths would have been very much more telling if he had shown any awareness that philosophers of other schools (such as idealists and neo-Kantians) had raised similar or parallel objections (H. Spencer, *Essays: Scientific, Political and Speculative*, 1891, 2.188–217). Spencer's writings constantly cited the authority of 'natural law'; yet he appears to have been almost wholly ignorant of the vast body of natural law theory, both ancient and modern, that had long anticipated many of his own ideas. He was also largely indifferent to the study of history. He believed that historical events were meaningless without deductive theory, and that where such theory was available historical detail was largely redundant; yet again and again his assumptions about individuals, institutions, peoples, and nations were undermined or made meaningless by their lack of reference to inconvenient historical facts. He appeared to envisage, for example, that the growth of international free trade could come about as a purely economic phenomenon, perhaps accelerating the 'organic evolution' of different groups, but in no way modifying or dissolving the existing boundaries between different ethnic, national, and cultural identities. And his social theories were rooted in the assumption that industrialization and militarism were mutually exclusive (although the most cursory glance at the history of nineteenth-century Europe and America might have suggested otherwise).

Herbert Spencer has often been portrayed as both the prophet and the paradigm of classic 'Victorian values', as someone who preached the virtues of hard work, self-help, abstinence, and thrift, and at the same time transplanted the industrial and entrepreneurial ethic into scientific and social theory. The reality, however, was very different from the reputation. Spencer in his own day was widely viewed as an unusual and eccentric character, even by contemporaries who admired him greatly; and he was very far from being a 'typical' or 'representative' Victorian figure, in either his way of thought or way of life. Despite his background in radical nonconformity, he was in many ways a critic of and rebel against that tradition; and, despite the fame he achieved in the 1860s and 1870s, his attitudes and ultimate beliefs were profoundly different from those of many of the mid-Victorian intellectual aristocracy. He lacked a classical training and was largely indifferent to the great landmarks of British history, and many of his theoretical concerns were more in tune with those of continental philosophers than with the British tradition (though Spencer himself showed little awareness of this fact). Even his 'agnosticism' was different in kind from the religious outlook of other Victorians who embraced that term (that is, Spencer believed that an ultimate power definitely existed but was inscrutable, whereas most Victorian agnostics were simply uncertain whether God existed or not). And, perhaps most important of all, he singularly failed to attain for himself what G. M. Young and others identified as the most fundamental of all 'Victorian values', the social and psychological resource of settled family life.

Moreover, despite his theoretical emphasis on work, struggle, enterprise, and self-help, and on the laws of competition, adaptation, co-operation, and natural selection, there was little evidence of these principles being prominent in Spencer's own life. On the contrary, Herbert Spencer came from a family whose recurrent business ventures appear always to have ended in failure. He himself disliked and even despised hard work; he was dependent for financial support, first from his father and uncle, and later from the patronage of Professor Youmans. He was notoriously unco-operative in all private affairs, and—as his *Autobiography* attests again and again—he was driven to nervous frenzy and mental and physical illness by the slightest signs of personal criticism or intellectual competition. Perhaps Spencer's most characteristically 'Victorian' attribute was precisely this: that he succumbed throughout his adult life to long periods of undiagnosed physical ailments, neurasthenia, and melancholia (leading eventually to chronic dependence on sedatives, morphine, and other painkilling drugs). This culture of invalidism was shared by many other major nineteenth-century figures, such as Coleridge, Darwin, Ruskin, J. S. Mill, and Harriet Taylor. But there was a peculiar element of paradox and pathos in the fate of the philosopher of the 'survival of the fittest', who believed that for more than fifty years he had been 'pursued by demons', and whose personal struggle for existence was waged against prolonged inertia, nervous breakdown, and mental depression (Spencer, *passim*; Webb, *Apprenticeship*, 1.47–50).

Spencer left an estate of £18,635, together with the proceeds of his royalties, to a charitable trust set up for the pursuit of 'Descriptive Sociology', which until the 1930s published anthropological data compiled by David Duncan and others, designed to illustrate and corroborate Spencer's social theories. Many of his writings on ethics, science, government, sociology, education, and even on the principles of aesthetic taste, continued to be reprinted regularly in Britain, America, and many other parts of the world throughout the twentieth century. A series of annual lectures in the University of Oxford, endowed in his honour by an Indian admirer, Shyarmaji Krishnavarma, in 1907, continues to be delivered by eminent natural and social scientists down to the present day.

Spencer was a man of handsome and striking appearance, who was painted, sculpted, and photographed on several occasions. The most distinguished portrayal, painted by Hubert von Herkomer to celebrate the completion of the Synthetic Philosophy, was executed in 1897 and hangs in the Scottish National Portrait Gallery in Edinburgh. JOSE HARRIS

Sources H. Spencer, *An autobiography*, 2 vols. (1904) • D. Duncan, *The life and letters of Herbert Spencer* (1908) • B. Webb, *My apprenticeship*, 2 vols. (1938) • *The diary of Beatrice Webb*, ed. N. MacKenzie and J. MacKenzie, 4 vols. (1982–5), vols. 1–2 • *Home life with Herbert Spencer* (1906) • J. D. Y. Peel, *Herbert Spencer: the evolution of a sociologist* (1971) • D. Wiltshire, *The social and political thought of Herbert Spencer* (1978) • M. W. Taylor, *Men versus the state: Herbert Spencer and late Victorian individualism* (1992) • M. W. Taylor, ed., *Herbert Spencer: contemporary assessments* (1996) • T. Parsons, *The structure of social action* (1936) • T. S. Gray, 'Herbert Spencer: individualist or organicist', *Political Studies*, 33 (1986), 236–53 • M. Francis, 'Herbert Spencer and the mid-Victorian scientists', *Metascience*, 4 (1986), 1–21 • P. Weindling, 'Conceptualising biology: the contribution of Herbert Spencer', *La Lettre de la Maison Française*, 7 (1997), 84–90 • R. Rylance, *Victorian psychology and British culture, 1850–1880* (2000)

Archives Knox College, Galesburg, Illinois, corresp. • LUL, corresp. and papers • Royal Institution of Great Britain, London, letters | BL, corresp. with W. E. Gladstone, Add. MSS 44441–44785, *passim* • BLPES, letters to Frederic Harrison • BLPES, letters to Sidney Webb and Beatrice Webb • Co-operative Union, Holyoake House, Manchester, letters to George Jacob Holyoake • Harvard U., Houghton L., letters to Roland G. Hazard • Hunt. L., letters, mainly to John Fiske • ICL, letters to Thomas Huxley • L. Cong., letters to Andrew Carnegie • NL Scot., letters to Alexander Campbell Fraser • NL Scot., corresp., mainly with Sir Patrick Geddes • Northwestern University, Illinois, corresp. with John Stuart Mill • RS, corresp. with Sir John Herschel • TCD, corresp. with Elizabeth Lecky • UCL, letters to Sir Francis Galton • UCL, corresp. with George Croom Robertson • UCL, letters to James Sully • University of Chicago, Illinois, letters to Sir Percy Bunting • University of Exeter, letters to Sir J. Norman Lockyer

Likenesses J. B. Burgess, oils, 1872, NPG • J. E. Boehm, marble bust, *c.*1884, NPG • J. M. Hamilton, oils, *c.*1895, NPG • J. McLure Hamilton, oils, *c.*1895, NPG • H. von Herkomer, oils, 1897, Scot. NPG • A. Grant, oils, 1898 • photograph, *c.*1898, NPG [*see illus.*] • E. Gulland, Herkomer type, pubd 1899 (after H. von Herkomer), BM • A. Grant, oils, 1904, Athenaeum, London • Barraud, cabinet photograph, NPG • Barraud, photograph, NPG; repro. in *Men and Women of the Day*, 1 (1888) • CG [F. C. Gould], caricature study, watercolour, NPG; repro. in *VF* (26 April 1879) • Elliott & Fry, cabinet photograph, NPG • H. Furniss, pen-and-ink caricature sketch, NPG • J. Hanson Walker, copy (after J. B. Burgess), Derby public library • London Stereoscopic Co., cabinet photograph, NPG • Mayall, photograph, NPG • J. Watkins, carte-de-visite, NPG

Wealth at death £18,635 7*s.* with proceeds of royalties: probate, 28 Jan 1904, *CGPLA Eng. & Wales*

Spencer, Sir John (*d.* 1610), merchant and lord mayor of London, was the son of Richard Spencer of Waldingfield in Suffolk, but details of his family background and early years are not known. There is no record of his London apprenticeship or freedom, but he entered the livery of the Clothworkers' Company in 1570. By that date he was already a successful merchant trading to Spain, importing raisins, oil, iron, and wine. He was among the founder members of the Spanish Company in 1577, and a pioneer, with fellow clothworkers Sir Edward Osborne and Richard Staper, of the Levant trade (chartered from 1582). Dizzying fortunes could be made in the exchange of cloth, rabbit skins, and tin for the spices, dyestuffs, cotton wool, and silks of the Levant, but Spencer was in the forefront of those anxious to limit membership of the company in the

Sir John Spencer (*d.* 1610), by unknown sculptor, *c.*1610 [with his wife, Alice]

1590s. In 1599 he was one of the leading investors in the East India Company. In later years he seems to have turned to moneylending, counting the crown and the earls of Essex and Northumberland among his creditors. His subsidy assessments (£300 in the 1570s, £410 in 1589) placed him at the pinnacle of the city's pyramid of wealth, and at his death his estate was variously (and implausibly) estimated at between £300,000 and £800,000. His wealth was legendary. An unsubstantiated mid-seventeenth-century account records a plot by Dunkirk pirates to kidnap and ransom him, only foiled by his being detained in the city on business. Although he was regarded as parsimonious (a libel circulating after his death alleged that he 'spent by the dramme and laid up by the pound' (Bodl. Oxf., MS Ashmole 781, p. 152), he lived in some style. From the sons of William Bond (*d.* 1576) he purchased Crosby Place in Bishopsgate, a late fifteenth-century mansion described by Stow as very large and beautiful. Although Spencer kept his mayoralty at Crosby Place, and spent large amounts on it, he does not seem to have resided there in his later years, and it was regularly used to house visiting foreign dignitaries. His preferred residence was at Canonbury in Islington, purchased from Lord Wentworth for £2000. The surviving long gallery (still *in situ*, with a plaster ceiling dated 1599 decorated with medallions of classical heroes) and three of the chimney-pieces (removed in 1865 to Compton Wynyates and Castle Ashby) show him to have been a man of some taste.

Spencer was a difficult man who, although attaining the highest offices, clearly lacked enthusiasm for his civic obligations, and he proved a truculent colleague. As a junior liveryman of his company he repeatedly refused to serve as steward for the lord mayor's feast and, unusually for a man of his standing, he never served as master of his livery company, refusing the office when elected in 1580. He was a common councillor for Bishopsgate ward between 1576 and 1583, and was elected to the court of aldermen on 27 June 1583, serving successively in the wards of Bridge Without (1583–7), Langbourn (1587–94), and Bassishaw (1594–1610). He was sheriff of London in 1583–4 (but only after having been nominated three times) and lord mayor in 1594–5. His mayoralty took place in the difficult circumstances of the social distress caused by escalating prices, heavy wartime taxation, and trade disruptions. But the situation seems to have been aggravated by his noxious personality. He was at loggerheads with his fellow aldermen over patronage matters, and rumours of his corruption circulated widely. Unusually for the sixteenth century when the lord mayor usually took a mediatorial role in popular disturbances, his character was an issue in the apprentice riots of June 1595. Libels circulated comparing him unfavourably with another alderman, Sir Richard Martin, and it was rumoured that apprentices had set up a gallows outside his house. So great was his loss of control that martial law was humiliatingly imposed by the privy council on the city in July. Although reports of Spencer's partiality had reached the crown's ministers, they did not endanger the customary knighthood, bestowed on the lord mayor at some point between 27 May and 13 June 1595.

Spencer married Alice (*d.* 1610), daughter of Thomas Bromfield of London and widow successively of Henry Leake (*d.* 1563), a wealthy Southwark brewer, and of William Cockes, citizen and haberdasher of London (*d.* 1569). Their only surviving offspring was a daughter, Elizabeth (*d.* 1632), who became a target for fortune-hunters such as Spencer's colleague on the aldermanic bench Anthony Ratcliffe. Spencer saw him off with little difficulty but the heavily indebted Henry, first Lord Compton and later earl of Northampton (*c.*1570–1630), proved a more serious challenge. By January 1599 it was widely reported that they were to marry but that Spencer was doing all in his power to hinder the match, hiding Elizabeth and alleging a precontract with Sir Arthur Heveningham. Spencer was committed briefly to the Fleet prison and on his release his daughter was taken out of his care, allegedly because of his cruelty. The marriage took place shortly after 15 March 1599. The bitterness between Spencer and his feckless son-in-law intensified when Compton delivered a spectacular snub to the merchant at a tournament in the queen's presence soon after the wedding. In spite of the efforts of Sir Robert Cecil (and possibly even the queen) to mediate, Spencer 'the hardhead' (*Letters of John Chamberlain*, 1.124) remained obdurate, even when his daughter gave birth to a son in 1601.

Spencer died in the parish of St Helen, Bishopsgate, on 3 March 1610, followed a few weeks later by his wife. He was buried in St Helen's Church on 22 March. Given that there are no indications that he was reconciled with his son-in-law, who continued his improvident lifestyle after the marriage, it is difficult to understand why he died intestate, his estate thereby passing to Compton. This was a stroke of good fortune so extraordinary as to turn Compton's wits. After a brief orgy of conspicuous consumption, he was 'oppressed with the greatnes of his sudaine fortune [and] fell madde' (*Abergavenny MSS*, 83–4), apparently necessitating a brief spell in the Tower. It was in fact alleged by Spencer's nephews in a Star Chamber lawsuit that Compton had suppressed the will, and they had the testimony of Sir Henry Montague, the recorder of London, in their favour. The sad episode perhaps contributed to Spencer's reputation for avarice, for there were no charitable bequests. And yet contemporaries were impressed by the extraordinary largesse to the poor at his funeral on 22 March 1610 (conscience money from Compton or a sign of Spencer's more conventionally charitable instincts?), and it was rumoured that the suppressed will contained bequests to his poor kindred amounting to £20,000 and as much again to charities. Spencer's was unquestionably one of the most controversial sixteenth-century mercantile careers, but his reputation as the 'old usurer' (PRO, SP 14/53/107) may have been exploited by his unscrupulous son-in-law to further his own ends. IAN W. ARCHER

Sources King's remembrances, PRO, SP 14/53/107; STAC 8/112/9 • court minutes and wardens' accounts, Clothworkers' Company, London • journals, CLRO, court of common council • repertories of the court of aldermen, CLRO • A. B. Beaven, ed., *The aldermen of the City of London, temp. Henry III–[1912]*, 2 vols. (1908–13) • *The letters of John Chamberlain*, ed. N. E. McClure, 2 vols. (1939) • *Memorials of affairs of state in the reigns of Q. Elizabeth and K. James I, collected (chiefly) from the original papers of … Sir Ralph Winwood*, ed. E. Sawyer, 3 vols. (1725) • *Calendar of the manuscripts of the most hon. the marquis of Salisbury*, 24 vols., HMC, 9 (1883–1976) • D. Papillon, *The vanity of the lives and passions of men* (1651) • J. E. Cox, ed., *The annals of St Helen's, Bishopsgate, London* (1876) • M. Reddan and A. W. Clapham, *The parish of St Helen, Bishopsgate*, 1, Survey of London, 9 (1924) • H. W. Fincham, *An historical account of Canonbury House* (1926) • P. Norman and W. D. Caröe, *Crosby Place* (1908) • Bodl. Oxf., MSS Ashmole • BL, Lansdowne MSS • GEC, *Peerage*, new edn • M. Benbow, 'Index of London citizens involved in city government, 1558–1603', U. Lond., Institute of Historical Research, Centre for Metropolitan History • L. Stone, 'The peer and the alderman's daughter', *History Today*, 11 (1961), 48–55 • 'Abstract of sundry deeds relating to houses in the parishes of St Saviour and St Olave Southwark', *Collectanea Topographica et Genealogica*, 5 (1838), 45–61 • *The manuscripts of the marquess of Abergavenny, Lord Braye, G. F. Luttrell*, HMC, 15 (1887)

Likenesses effigy on monument, *c.*1610, St Helen's Bishopsgate, London [*see illus.*]

Wealth at death est. between £300,000 and £800,000: *Memorials of the affairs of state … collected chiefly from the originals of Sir Ralph Winwood*, 3.136

Spencer [Spenser; *alias* Tyrwhitt], **John** (**1600–1671**), Jesuit and religious controversialist, was born in Lincolnshire on 10 August 1600. On the basis of Spencer's alias, Foley and Gillow suggest that his mother may have been from the Tyrwhitt family of Ketilby. He matriculated at Christ's College, Cambridge, in 1618 and during his time in Cambridge converted to the Roman Catholic church. He joined the Society of Jesus in Watten on 14 March 1626. From the noviciate he moved to Liège to study theology in either 1628 or 1629. He was ordained priest on 18 March 1632. He completed his final year of Jesuit formation, tertianship, in Ghent in 1634. From 1635 until either 1636 or 1637 he worked in Watten as prefect of the church, catechist, and missionary. In 1637 or 1638 he was sent to England to work in the residence of St Dominic (Lincolnshire). By 1641 he was back in Flanders as professor of moral theology or convener of discussions on controversial theology at Liège. He was professed of the four vows at Liège on 5 August 1641. Sent to Antwerp in 1644 he served there as procurator of the English province until late 1646 when he was transferred to Ghent. From that base he served as a military chaplain until 1655, when he returned to Antwerp as procurator. Between 1655 and 1658 when he reappeared at Antwerp, he is not listed in the official provincial catalogues, but from his involvement in a disputation with the Anglican divines Peter Gunning and John Pearson it is known that he spent some of that time in England.

Although Spencer had presided over controversial theological discussions at Liège in 1643 he published nothing in the field until *Scripture Mistaken* (Antwerp, 1655). It is possible that he returned to controversial theology because of proselytizing Anglicans during his years as Roman Catholic chaplain to the English forces in Flanders. Protestants, according to Spencer, conceded that they could not withstand Catholic arguments based on historical succession, tradition, patristics, and so on. But scripture, the word of God, was a more powerful weapon and it was firmly held in protestant hands. However, Spencer argued that protestants tortured scripture to support their arguments which, upon detailed examination, rested on nothing but errors, mistakes, and faulty translations. His work was intended to demonstrate the veracity of traditional Catholic teaching on justification by faith, good works, purgatory, and real presence. Henry Ferne replied with *An Answer to Mr. Spencer's Book Intituled Scripture Mistaken* (London, 1660).

For reasons unknown Spencer revived an old debate in his second book, *Questions propounded for resolution of unlearned pretenders in matters of religion, to the doctors of the prelatical pretended reform'd church of England* (Paris, 1657). It was a reply to William Laud's *A Relation of the Conference* (2nd edn, London, 1639).

According to Charles Dodd (that is Hugh Tootell), Spencer 'was an able controvertist: and recommended himself to the world by a controversy, he and doctor [John] Lenthal[l] (formerly a Protestant divine of Cambridge) had with doctor Peter Gunning, and doctor John Pearson, anno 1657' (Dodd 3.312, col. 2). In May 1657 the four disputants argued 'Whether those of the Roman Church, or those of the English Protestant Church be Schismatiques'. Through personal encounters or letters the debate continued until June 1658. At the start all promised that the discussions would be published only with the consent of all, but 'if either Party were guilty of a culpable neglect, or delay, in the prosecution of the business, the other Party should be at liberty to print' (J. Spencer, *Scisme Unmask't*, Paris, 1658). The account, thus named, accused Gunning of procrastination and negligence. Gunning's rejoinder, *A Contention for Truth* (London, 1658), appeared shortly thereafter. During the reign of James II extracts from *Scripture Mistaken* on the schismatic state of the Church of England were published separately.

From 1659 until 1667 Spencer was at the residence of St George (Worcestershire) and from 1659 until 2 August 1666 he was superior. In either 1668 or 1669 he moved to London. During his final illness he was taken into Grafton Manor, a house of the earl of Shrewsbury in the residence of St George, where he died on 17 January 1671.

THOMAS M. MCCOOG

Sources T. M. McCoog, *English and Welsh Jesuits, 1555–1650*, 2 vols., Catholic RS, 74–5 (1994–5) • T. M. McCoog, ed., *Monumenta Angliae*, 1–2 (1992) • H. Foley, ed., *Records of the English province of the Society of Jesus*, 7 vols. in 8 (1875–83) • Venn, *Alum. Cant.* • C. Dodd [H. Tootell], *The church history of England, from the year 1500, to the year 1688*, 3 vols. (1737–42) • T. H. Clancy, *A literary history of the English Jesuits: a century of books, 1615–1714* (1996) • Gillow, *Lit. biog. hist.*

Archives Archives of the British Province of the Society of Jesus, London • Archivum Romanum Societatis Iesu, Rome

Spencer, John (*c.*1600–1658). *See under* Spencer family (*per.* *c.*1647–1765).

Spencer, John (1629–1681). *See under* Spencer family (*per.* *c.*1647–1765).

Spencer, John (*bap.* 1630, *d.* 1693), college head and Hebraist, was baptized in Boughton under Bleane, Kent, on 31 October 1630, possibly the son of Adam Spencer, fellmonger. He became a king's scholar at King's School, Canterbury. From the age of fourteen he lived mainly in or near Cambridge. Spencer was admitted as a Parker scholar of Corpus on 25 March 1645 and graduated BA in 1648/9, MA in 1652, BD in 1659, and DD in 1665. He was chosen fellow of the college (1655) and master (3 August 1667), and was vice-chancellor of the university in 1673–4. As a young fellow he served the Cambridge parishes of St Giles and St Bene't where he was vicar from 1657 to 1662. Like other masters before him, he was also rector of the college living of Landbeach, near Cambridge (1667–83), and dean of Ely (from 1677); he was also archdeacon of Sudbury, in the Norwich diocese, from 1677.

Spencer married Hannah (*d.* 1674), daughter of Isaac Puller of Hertford and sister of Timothy Puller, the author of *The Moderation of the Church of England*. Their children, Elizabeth and John, were baptized on 25 March 1672 and 19 December 1673 respectively. Hannah Spencer was buried in St Bene't's chancel on 21 April 1674. Elizabeth was buried next to her mother on 9 December 1688. Spencer's nephew William Spencer, his curate and successor at Landbeach, also died in 1688.

Wainscoting attributed to the beginning of Spencer's mastership can be seen in the old master's lodge. The years when he lived there as a widower with his daughter, before her untimely death, form the theme of a college ghost story current by the early nineteenth century.

Benefaction and writing characterized the last decade of Spencer's life. In 1683–5 he issued at Cambridge the first edition of his great work *De legibus Hebraeorum ritualibus et earum rationibus*, comprising three books 'on the ritual laws of the Hebrews, and the reasons for them'. In 1687 he settled the valuable Elmington estate on Corpus, and gave books to the college library. In 1691–2 he made an entirely new fourth book of *De legibus* ready for printing, together with revisions of the earlier books. His will of 20 April 1693 details further benefactions to the college, the cathedral (including the singing men and vergers), the three parishes which he had served, the poor of Ely, relations, and servants. The marble font which this will directed to be made for the cathedral is now in Prickwillow parish church. Spencer died on 27 May 1693, and was buried in Corpus Christi College chapel, where a black marble floor stone bears his epitaph.

Spencer fully accepted the Restoration settlement, but

was a friend and benefactor of dissenters. In outlook he resembled his close friend and executor Thomas Tenison, archbishop of Canterbury. Moreover, the Socinian writer Samuel Crell claimed, probably rightly, that Spencer received him when he visited Cambridge. Suspicion of Spencer's latitudinarianism as doctrinally lax will then have sharpened criticism of his writings.

W. Robertson Smith called Spencer 'one of the greatest English theologians … whose Latin work on the ritual laws of the Hebrews may justly be said to have laid the foundations of the science of Comparative Religion'. Spencer urged that on investigation these laws and customs could be seen in every case to derive from the surrounding paganism, especially that of Egypt. This bold historical conclusion was invaluable theologically, Spencer argued, for even the greatest writers who had contended for the rationality of Old Testament law—Spencer instanced Maimonides among the Jews and Aquinas among the Christians—had judged the reasons for many particular laws to be irrecoverable. Now, however, Spencer claimed, the ritual laws could be fully understood as a divine concession to human frailty, and a kind of inoculation against paganism. Spencer noted that such divine concession to ward off idolatry was envisaged by church fathers, including Eusebius, and in the Jewish tradition by Maimonides. He thus integrated his philological and historical work with an argument for the concord of scripture and reason.

Spencer's argument was not unparalleled in his time on either the historical side, by John Marsham, or the theological, by Edward Stillingfleet; but he united the two with unrivalled learning and insight, and with the cumulative force of a series of detailed inquiries into ancient religion. He had prepared the way by *Dissertatio de Urim et Thummim* (1669), which elicited the first of many continental and British criticisms of his argument. *De legibus* was twice reprinted (The Hague, 1686; Leipzig, 1705). The unpublished fourth book was eagerly awaited after Spencer's death (letter of Newton to Otto Mencke, 22 Nov 1693, *Correspondence*, no. 416). Tenison's efforts to issue it were in vain, but he himself left money to provide for editorial work. The second edition, now including the fourth book (ed. L. Chappelow, Cambridge, 1727, with portrait), was also twice reprinted (Tübingen, 1732; Venice, in parts, 1757–67). WILLIAM HORBURY

Sources will, PRO, PROB 11/418, fols. 116*v*–118*r* • R. Masters, *The history of the College of Corpus Christi and the B. Virgin Mary … in the University of Cambridge* (1753), 163–70 and *passim*, and appx, 8, 23, 75 • *Masters' History of the college of Corpus Christi and the Blessed Virgin Mary in the University of Cambridge*, ed. J. Lamb (1831), 193–201 and *passim* • Venn, *Alum. Cant.*, 1/4.133 • *Cambridgeshire*, Pevsner (1954), 52, 365, and pl. 38b • C. H. E. Smyth, 'The Very Reverend Dr John Spencer (1630–93)', *Letter of the Corpus Association*, 54 (1975), 12–21 • W. Robertson Smith, *Lectures on the religion of the Semites* (1889), 6 • *The correspondence of Isaac Newton*, ed. H. W. Turnbull and others, 7 vols. (1959–77), vol. 3, no. 416 • J. Assmann, *Moses the Egyptian: the memory of Egypt in Western monotheism* (1997), 55–79 and *passim* • M. Mulsow, 'Orientalistik im Kontext der sozinianistischen und deistischen Debatten um 1700: Spencer, Crell, Locke und Newton', *Scientia poetica*, 2, ed. L. Danneberg and others (Tübingen, 1998), 27–57 • W. Horbury, 'John Spencer (1630–93) and Hebrew study', *Letter of the Corpus Association*, 78 (1999), 12–23 • G. G. Stroumsa, 'John Spencer and the roots of idolatry', *History of Religions*, 41 (2001) • epitaph, Corpus Christi College chapel, Cambridge

Archives LPL, Tenison MSS, corresp., Lambeth MSS 674, 870 • LPL, Gibson MSS, papers, Lambeth MS 942

Likenesses G. Vertue, line engraving, 1727 (after unknown artist), repro. in J. Spencer, *De legibus Hebraeorum ritualibus et earum rationibus libri quatuor*, ed. L. Chappelow, 2 vols. (1727), i • van der Myn, oils, CCC Cam. • oils, CCC Cam.

Wealth at death see will, PRO, PROB 11/418, fols. 116*v*–118*r*

Spencer, John (*c*.1655–1729). *See under* Spencer family (*per. c*.1647–1765).

Spencer, John (1719–1775). *See under* Spencer family (*per. c*.1647–1765).

Spencer, John, first Earl Spencer (1734–1783), politician, was born on 19 December 1734, the only son of John Spencer (1708–1746), a landowner, and his first wife, Georgiana Caroline (1716–1780), the third daughter of John *Carteret, second Earl Granville (1690–1763). Since he had not been expected to survive infancy he was educated at home by tutors. His younger sister Diana died aged only eight.

Spencer was just eleven and a half when in the summer of 1746 his father died and he succeeded to the considerable family estates. He also inherited the bulk of the property, including the new house and park at Wimbledon, left by the will of Sarah *Churchill, duchess of Marlborough, but with the strict proviso that if he accepted any office or pension from the crown this inheritance was to pass to the next heir. Until he came of age, however, he could not take control of this fortune. His estates and finances were managed by trustees, while he went on a grand tour of France and Italy and gained a lifelong interest in art and architecture.

On 20 December 1755, the day after his twenty-first birthday, Spencer married Margaret Georgiana Poyntz (1737–1814) [*see* Spencer, (Margaret) Georgiana], the eighteen-year-old daughter of a leading diplomatist, Stephen *Poyntz, of Midgham House, Berkshire, and his wife, Anna Maria, *née* Mordaunt. The marriage ceremony, unusually, took place in private. While five hundred guests were being entertained at a ball at Althorp, those privy to the secret withdrew to a large upstairs room for the marriage. Not until Christmas was the news made public. In the new year husband and wife drove to London and were presented at court, where they became close friends of the royal family. They soon had a growing family of their own: Georgiana (1757–1806), later duchess of Devonshire [*see* Cavendish, Georgiana], George John *Spencer (1758–1834), who succeeded his father as the second earl, and Henrietta, known as Harriet (1761–1821) [*see* Ponsonby, Henrietta Frances], who married Viscount Duncannon, heir to the earl of Bessborough.

Although his political prospects were rendered nugatory by the terms of Sarah Churchill's will, Spencer, after an expensive by-election defeat at Bristol in 1756, entered the House of Commons later that year as MP for Warwick. He was a member of the old whig corps, and the duke of Newcastle secured him a viscountcy in 1761. He followed Newcastle into opposition in 1762, and when the former

Newcastle party returned to office in 1765 was rewarded with an earldom. He rarely attended the House of Lords on account of his poor state of health.

By this time Spencer was the owner of a magnificent London house. Designed by John Vardy, this Palladian mansion overlooked Green Park, and took ten years, from 1756 to 1765, to build. Its beautiful rooms, some the work of Vardy's rival James 'Athenian' Stuart, became the centre for great entertainments and the home of a fine collection of Italian paintings and family portraits by Sir Joshua Reynolds and Thomas Gainsborough. Spencer and his wife, however, preferred life at the family home, Althorp. There, looked after by eighty servants, he built up a fine library, especially strong in history, literature, and classical mythology. But his chief passion was hunting. As master of the Pytchley hunt, he spent more on the sport and his stables than on the day-to-day running of his houses. Despite all this considerable expenditure on top of an excessive love of gambling, Spencer still found the resources to improve his main inheritance from Sarah Churchill, the house and park at Wimbledon. In 1760 he commissioned Capability Brown to transform the park into a place described in one newspaper of 1785 as 'perhaps as beautiful as anything near London'. He held garden parties on the lawns, and enjoyed himself shooting, as well as fishing in the new lake. He also employed Stuart to redecorate the house in the latest neo-classical style. Wimbledon thus became the perfect country retreat from the noise, dirt, and disease of London, especially in the spring and at midsummer. Lady Spencer, writing to her son in the spring of 1781, expressed her delight in 'the beauty of the scene, the birds, the flowers, the verdure and every other charms the country abounds with' (BL, Althorp MSS, G275).

Throughout the 1760s and the 1770s Spencer suffered from a series of illnesses—crippling chest and stomach pains, gout, and various fevers and nervous palpitations. To restore his health he paid frequent visits to Bath to drink the waters and to Scarborough to bathe and take the sea air. He often crossed the channel to stay at Spa or to go on grand tours with his family. In all these troubles he was supported by his strong Anglican faith and the devotion of his wife. During the summer of 1783, however, even Georgiana confessed in a letter to her son that she became 'quite discouraged' as 'all his old complaints returned' (BL, Althorp MSS, G276). She took him to Margate and finally in late September back to Bath. Spencer seemed no better for taking the waters, but managed to ride every day. Then on 25 October Georgiana, 'sadly alarmed', wrote to her son that his father 'now wanders when he wakes and is not sure where he is' (BL, Althorp MSS, G276). Six days later, on 31 October 1783, he died in Bath. He was only forty-eight years old. He was buried on 9 November in the family vault at St Mary's Church, Great Brington, just outside the gates of Althorp Park. 'Handsome with dark romantic looks' (Friedman, 38), Spencer was said to be 'generous and amiable' (Le Marchant), although very extravagant and at times bad-tempered because of almost continuous ill health. He left his son massive debts, yet greatly increased his family estates and also its prestige by being the employer of leading architects, the collector of Italian paintings, and the friend and patron of Sir Joshua Reynolds, Laurence Sterne, David Garrick, and Thomas Linley. His widow died in St Albans on 18 March 1814 and was buried in St Mary's Church, Great Brington, on 30 March. RICHARD MILWARD

Sources BL, Althorp MSS • R. Milward, *The Spencers in Wimbledon, 1774–1994* (privately printed, 1996) • J. Friedman, *Spencer House: chronicle of a great London mansion* (1993) • K. Garlick, ed., *A catalogue of pictures at Althorp*, Walpole Society, 45 (1974–6) • G. Battiscombe, *The Spencers of Althorp* (1984) • D. Le Marchant, *Memoir of John Charles, Viscount Althorp, third Earl Spencer*, ed. H. D. Le Marchant (1876) • D. Stroud, *Capability Brown*, rev. edn (1957) • Seventh Earl Spencer, *A short history of Althorp and the Spencer family* (1949) • HoP, *Commons* • GEC, *Peerage*

Archives BL, Althorp MSS | BL, corresp. with duke of Newcastle, Add. MSS 32868–32989, *passim*

Likenesses G. Knapton, portrait, *c.*1742–1743 (as child with sister), Althorp House, Northamptonshire • G. Knapton, portrait, 1745 (as boy with father), Althorp House, Northamptonshire • J. Liotard, twin miniature portraits, *c.*1754 (of earl and wife), probably Althorp House, Northamptonshire • T. Gainsborough, oils, *c.*1763, Althorp House, Northamptonshire • J. Nollekens, funerary monument, *c.*1786, Great Brington, Northamptonshire • engraved miniature (copy), Wimbledon Society Museum • line engraving, NPG

Wealth at death approx. £20,000 from rents and profits of estates; approximately £10,000 in plate, furniture, jewels, horses, carriages, etc.: BL, Althorp MSS • £40,000–£60,000: Friedman, *Spencer House*

Spencer, (Edward) John, eighth Earl Spencer (1924–1992), landowner and courtier, was born on 24 January 1924 at 24 Sussex Square, London, the only son of Albert Edward John Spencer, seventh Earl Spencer (1892–1975), and his wife, Lady Cynthia Elinor Beatrix Hamilton (1897–1972), second daughter of the third duke of Abercorn. Queen Mary and the prince of Wales were his godparents. As Viscount Althorp he was educated at Eton College and the Royal Agricultural College, Cirencester. He served briefly as a captain in the Royal Scots Greys during the Second World War and was mentioned in dispatches. He then served as aide-de-camp to Lieutenant-General Sir Willoughby Norrie, governor of South Australia, from 1947 to 1950.

The Spencer family was steeped in royal service. Althorp's mother and several aunts were ladies-in-waiting to the queen, and so he moved easily into the job of temporary equerry to King George VI, from 1950 to 1952, and, on the king's death, to the queen until 1954. He served as acting master of the household and equerry on her coronation tour of the Commonwealth from 1953 to 1954. He was appointed MVO (later LVO) in 1954. A keen cameraman, he made cine-films of the tour, which he showed in Norfolk on his return, raising £2500 for charity.

On 1 June 1954 Althorp married Frances Ruth Burke Roche (*b.* 1936), daughter of the fourth Baron Fermoy and his wife, Ruth Gill, later a lady-in-waiting to the queen mother. They farmed quietly at Park House, on the Sandringham estate in Norfolk, and had two sons, one of

(Edward) John Spencer, eighth Earl Spencer (1924–1992), by Rodrigo Moynihan, *c.*1945

whom died in infancy, and three daughters. He divorced his wife for desertion in 1969 and was given custody of his young family.

Althorp was a county councillor in Northamptonshire, high sheriff in 1959, and a deputy lieutenant from 1961. He was deputy honorary colonel of the Royal Anglian regiment (TA) from 1972, and chairman of the Nene Foundation. He was chairman of the National Association of Boys' Clubs from 1962 to 1980, and later deputy president. He was a member of the UK council of European architectural heritage year in 1975. He succeeded his father in 1975 and moved his family into Althorp, the Spencers' ancestral home in Northamptonshire.

In the following year, on 14 July 1976, Spencer married Raine Legge, *née* McCorquodale, countess of Dartmouth (*b.* 1929), who was divorced from the ninth earl of Dartmouth earlier that year. She was daughter of the romantic novelist Dame Barbara Cartland. Theirs was a controversial union, leading to divisions within the family—Spencer's children were never reconciled to his marriage—and her attempts to restore the fortunes of Althorp were subject to contradictory interpretation. There is no doubt that Althorp required a lot of attention, but conservationists became increasingly alarmed when the sales of family heirlooms became frequent. Van Dycks and Gainsboroughs were sold, as was furniture, china, porcelain, silver and gold, the Spencer family archives, and various properties. In due course the Spencers opened a shop in the stables at Althorp, where they both acted as salesmen, Lord Spencer selling his 'own-label' champagne, and even postcards of the house, signed by him.

When Spencer suffered a serious stroke in 1978, his wife nursed him daily. By her efforts, including the employment of an untested drug, he was restored to remarkably active health for his remaining fourteen years. He celebrated his recovery with a service of thanksgiving.

As a couple Earl and Countess Spencer were propelled into the full spotlight of media attention when his youngest daughter, Diana [*see* Diana, princess of Wales], became engaged to the prince of Wales in February 1981. Both Spencer and Diana's maternal grandmother, Ruth, Lady Fermoy, had promoted the marriage. Spencer was by no means a fit man, but he rose valiantly to the challenge of taking his daughter to St Paul's Cathedral to give her away. The ceremony was relayed by television to far corners of the globe, and he won much respect for the courage with which he went through the day: his chauffeur assisted him up the steps of the cathedral, and his daughter supported him as they walked the length of the aisle. He took considerable pride in his grandsons, Prince William and Prince Harry, who bore strong Spencer traits in looks and character.

In the years that followed, the work at Althorp continued apace and Spencer supported his wife in all her fund-raising endeavours. With her he produced two books, *Spencers on Spas* (1984) and *Japan and the East* (1986), which contained his photographs. They entertained lavishly and travelled extensively.

Johnnie Spencer was a tall man, a mixture of the bluff and the shy, inherently gentle, and one of the world's innocents. The press sometimes mocked his statements about his daughter—'a fine specimen', he said of her as a baby—but every word was uttered with the same paternal pride which remained with him to the end. His rather sudden death in the Humana Hospital, Wellington, St John's Wood, London, on 29 March 1992 spared him knowledge of the revelations concerning Diana by Andrew Morton, and of the sharp decline in fortune and favour of his daughter, let alone her separation, divorce, and tragic death a mere five years later. Lord Spencer was buried at the church of St Mary the Virgin, Great Brington, on 1 April. The estate he had worked so hard and so controversially to protect was valued at some £89 million. He was survived by his second wife, three daughters, and one son, Charles Edward Maurice Spencer (*b.* 1964), who succeeded as ninth earl.

HUGO VICKERS

Sources *The Independent* (30 March 1992) · *The Times* (30 March 1992) · *The Times* (20 Oct 1992) · Burke, *Peerage* (1999) · A. Levin, *Raine and Johnnie* (1993) · T. Clayton and P. Craig, *Diana: story of a princess* (2001)

Archives Bodl. Oxf., corresp. with William Clark

Likenesses R. Moynihan, portrait, *c.*1945, priv. coll. [*see illus.*]

Wealth at death approx. £89,000,000

Spencer, John Charles, **Viscount Althorp and third Earl Spencer** (**1782–1845**), politician, agriculturalist, and

John Charles Spencer, Viscount Althorp and third Earl Spencer (1782–1845), by Charles Turner, 1832

sportsman, was born on 30 May 1782 at Spencer House, St James's Place, London, the eldest child of George John *Spencer, second Earl Spencer (1758–1834), and Lavinia Bingham, daughter of the first earl of Lucan. Of his four brothers and three sisters, five survived to adulthood, four being noticed in the *Oxford Dictionary of National Biography*: Sir Robert Cavendish *Spencer, captain RN, surveyor-general of the ordnance, who died at sea in 1830; Frederick *Spencer, fourth Earl Spencer [*see under* Spencer, Sir Robert Cavendish], who retired from the navy as a vice-admiral; George *Spencer, an Anglican cleric who converted to Rome in 1830; and Sarah *Lyttelton, Lady Lyttelton, who served as governess of Queen Victoria's children.

A brutal upbringing Spurred to excel by their formidable but controlling mother the Spencer siblings sought to escape her repressive regime quickly. Robert and Frederick fled to sea. Althorp, as he was known, was sent away to school at eight, but not before experiencing a kind of Gothic childhood which included drunken servants, extended periods of parental desertion, and ferocious verbal abuse. Lord Spencer, though an affectionate father, did nothing to protect his son from the singularly unmaternal brutality of his wife. Althorp was permanently maimed: a profound sense of personal inadequacy undermined an otherwise physically robust and intellectually gifted personality. He did not marry until the age of thirty-four, and he did not begin to unleash his exceptional powers as a politician until he was nearly fifty.

Althorp's years at Harrow School (1790–98) offered him some respite from the terrors of home, but were otherwise undistinguished. His contemporaries there included the future prime ministers Goderich, Peel, Aberdeen, and Palmerston. He was close to his cousin, Viscount Duncannon, a friend and political ally in adulthood. Lord Spencer became dissatisfied with the school's instruction and withdrew Althorp for two years of private tutoring to prepare him for Cambridge.

Althorp spent several years at Trinity College, Cambridge, under the supervision of Joseph Allen, later bishop of Ely. The torpid intellectual atmosphere of the university left little mark on the young nobleman. His encounter with Allen was of the first importance. The don was sensitive to the fragile nature of Althorp's emotional development. He could do nothing about Althorp's rejection of his mother's cosmopolitan values, but Allen's influence prevented a retreat into country bumpkinism. He succeeded in nurturing Althorp's intellectual curiosity and deepening religious faith, tempering both with a gentle worldliness.

The peace of Amiens in 1802 allowed Lord Spencer to send his son on a grand tour. The journey became a parody of traditional practice. Althorp hurried from one Italian city to another searching for a bolt-hole to England. But the shock of encountering raw despotism on its home ground was vital to the gestation of his political ideology. 'They have no more idea of a limited monarchy on the Continent', he told his father, 'than a horse has of the Scriptures' (Wasson, 14).

This fillip to his whiggism helped Althorp emerge from a Pittite chrysalis. Lord Spencer had deserted Fox in 1794 in reaction to the excesses of the French Revolution and only gradually returned to his native party. Althorp had no clear political beliefs until his tour sparked a revulsion towards conservative ideology. However, his entry into parliament for the pocket borough of Okehampton in April 1804 did not presage a dynamic Commons career. Most of Althorp's life for the next fourteen years was devoted to hunting and shooting. By this means he sought to escape his mother and adult responsibility, and to everyone's surprise he found a wife and the will to lead.

Fox-hunting and marriage After a few years of preparation Althorp ascended to the mastership of the Pytchley hunt, already something of a national institution. He took office because of his rank. He achieved fame by intelligent, courageous, and innovative leadership. Through unremitting and arduous effort he built the organization into the premier hunt in England just at the moment when the political and social élite were embracing fox-hunting as a core element of English culture. For ten years Althorp provided superb sport not only to local yeomen and gentry, but also to a membership that increasingly encompassed a significant portion of the high aristocracy. Senior statesmen obeyed the commands of this ungainly youth. Nearly a century later an authority judged that although twenty masters had reigned since 'not one more completely realized the idea of what a master of hounds should be' (H. O. Nethercote, *The Pytchley Hunt: Past and Present*, 1888, 40). He brought the Pytchley, another sporting writer declared, to 'the zenith of its glory' (H. H. Dixon, *Silk and Scarlet*, 1895, 73–4). The mastership gave Althorp confidence and experience that neither his nominal service as junior lord of the Treasury in the 'ministry of all the talents' (1806–7) nor his aimless years in the political wilderness of opposition could confer.

Lord Spencer obliged Althorp to stand as Pitt's successor for the parliamentary seat of Cambridge University in 1806. This absurd project ended in defeat. The Spencers met with more appropriate success later in the year by gaining one of the Northamptonshire seats, where Althorp Park and the Pytchley were located. The brief but vigorous election campaign antagonized many tory squires, but strong support from the whig grandees and potent nonconformist plumpers left Althorp secure until the famous battle of 1831 in the midst of the Reform Bill crisis, which became the last great electoral contest of the *ancien régime*. He held a county seat (southern division after 1832) until his elevation to the Lords in 1834.

Althorp's maiden speech came in 1809 during a debate over the extent to which the duke of York's mistress influenced military appointments made by the prince in his capacity as commander-in-chief of the army. The 'York affair' was decisive in binding Althorp to a group of young whig magnates (including lords Milton, Folkestone, Tavistock, Ebrington, Duncannon, and Lyttelton) increasingly attached to the radical 'Mountain', whom the conservative Grenvillites called 'enragés'. The failure of the senior whigs, notably lords Grey and Grenville, to condemn royal malfeasance and, perhaps even more importantly, immorality, radicalized Althorp's political thought. He broke decisively with the established leadership and isolated himself under the tutelage of the radical Samuel Whitbread to the consternation and incomprehension of the older generation.

In 1814 Althorp fell passionately in love with Esther Acklom, a plump and unsophisticated heiress, daughter of a minor country gentleman, Richard Acklom of Wiseton Hall, Nottinghamshire, and his wife, Elizabeth; he married her on 13 April that year. She returned unstinting devotion. Her death at the age of twenty-nine, after giving birth to a stillborn child in June 1818 was a catastrophe Althorp almost did not survive. His devout religious faith wavered. Possibly suicidal, he withdrew into a period of black depression and social isolation. He wore mourning clothes for the rest of his life. As a penance he gave up fox-hunting, by which means he fashioned a psychological hair shirt producing potent and prolonged misery. He found the sound of a hunting horn almost unbearable even in old age.

Althorp reconciled himself to Esther's death through a belief in their eventual reunion in heaven, which he could earn only by personal atonement. 'I have abstracted myself from all worldly considerations perhaps more than you will think right', he confessed to Lord Milton, 'but my prospects are so completely annihilated in this world that I only wish to make use of it as a stepping stone to the next' (Wasson, 98). His passion for service became the controlling force of his life. Coupled with his courage and skill as a leader, it overcame his diffidence and stimulated his submerged ambition. This explains the paradox of his bumbling, unprepossessing demeanour and his steely drive to excel.

Agriculture and education Oxen replaced foxes as Althorp's chief objects of pursuit in 1818. Agriculture allowed him to devote his wealth and energy to public service and to enjoy animals. By shrewd purchase and careful breeding he quickly built up one of the most important herds of cattle in Britain. He assisted the development of a lighter boned, quicker fattening strain, which launched shorthorns on the road to bovine supremacy in Britain and America. His skill as a breeder was honed with canines, and bloodlines from both his foxhounds and cattle were still being sought a century after his death. Much of his energy, however, was devoted to promoting research and the dissemination of applied science to farming. He founded his first agricultural association the year after Esther's death. In 1825 he took over the moribund Smithfield Club and transformed it into a national association for animal breeders. By the 1840s its shows were attracting 60,000 visitors a year. He became the founder or president of several county societies and spoke regularly at agricultural meetings throughout the country. In 1838 he chaired the organizational meeting and became the first president of the Royal Agricultural Society, and with his close friend, the duke of Richmond, managed its affairs for most of the next decade. He helped to found and edit the society's journal, planned the giant annual shows, established the library, and authored five articles on breeding and feeding. An indication of his stature in the agricultural world came with the request of Thomas Coke of Holkham that he supervise the great Norfolk estate during the minority of the second earl of Leicester.

Althorp's philanthropic activities in other realms were equally vigorous though less well known. He attended the preliminary discussions in 1825 to establish London University and later took an active part in the meetings of its council. The next year he participated in the foundation of the Society for the Diffusion of Useful Knowledge. Coupled with the mechanics' institutes, the society was strongly Benthamite in cast. It issued publications Althorp called 'works of great Utility', most notably the *Penny Magazine*, under the motto 'Knowledge is Power'. For twenty years he edited publications, sought contributions, suggested series, and censored antisemitism, and in 1840 became managing director. In that year he tried unsuccessfully to replicate his achievement at Smithfield by restoring a declining institution to health, but he failed and it collapsed on his demise.

After Esther's death Althorp designed a programme for self-improvement the better to prepare himself for life after fox-hunting. He read theology and economic theory in alternate doses. Later he extended his investigations to new works on biology and geology and made himself an expert on current developments in these fields. His focus on God, science, and Mammon served as yet another reason for the Augustans of the whig leadership to find his interests suspicious. Althorp moved on from reading to meeting the classical economists. In 1823 he joined the Political Economy Club, presided over by Malthus, Ricardo, McCulloch, and the Mills, and participated in its debates.

Althorp's activities in agriculture and education also led to encounters and friendships with an extraordinary array of scientists, engineers, abolitionists, utilitarians, and radicals, with whom few aristocrats consorted. Leigh Hunt, Francis Place, Elizabeth Fry, Joseph Hume, Lyon Playfair, Josiah Parkes, I. K. Brunel, George Grote, Henry Warburton, Daniel O'Connell, Harriet Martineau, Nassau Senior, and both Macaulays numbered among his associates in various projects. They came to understand and trust him, perhaps alone among the great whigs of his day. He in turn honestly and openly listened and learned.

Opposition years, 1818–1830 Althorp devoted much of his political activity in the decade after Esther's death to legal and economic reform. He chaired a number of committees and succeeded in modestly emulating the work that Romilly, Huskisson, and Peel were also accomplishing. 'Committee is my forte', he once bragged, and his dazzling performance during the second readings of the Great Reform Bill confirmed this assessment. However, it was the harsh measures taken by Liverpool's administration to restrain dissent in the difficult years after Waterloo that made Althorp a politician. He believed the ministers were driving a wedge between the people and the ruling class that would provoke further unrest.

Althorp responded to the crisis in two ways. First, in the Commons he mounted a sustained and vociferous opposition to government measures of repression. Sometimes virtually alone—for many whigs, even liberal ones, lacked his confidence in the ability of the aristocracy to ride out the storm unaided by suspension of habeas corpus and stronger laws against sedition—Althorp fought the measures clause by clause trying to limit the application and duration of the legislation. Second, he took the extraordinary step of appearing alongside Burdett and Major Cartwright at an anti-government rally in Covent Garden in December 1819, standing under a banner proclaiming: 'Let us die like men and not be sold like slaves' (Wasson, 89). He spoke against withdrawing from parliament as a means of protest, but he also associated the grand whiggery directly with the radical movement against the six acts. He won respect, even from opponents, for consistency and courage. Walter Bagehot, who was not a sympathetic judge of Althorp's career, noted later that in these years he 'said things that the best of that majority [in favour of repression] understood in a rugged English way, which changed feelings, even if it did not alter votes'. 'He was always there, always saying what was clear, strong, and manly' (N. St J. Staves, ed., *Bagehot's Historical Essays*, 1965, 159).

Sidmouth's suppression of dissent made Althorp a parliamentary reformer, as it did many of his closest associates. Unlike some colleagues, however, he did not abandon calls for electoral changes after the emergency was over. Among the great whigs only Russell and Althorp sustained this policy throughout the 1820s. The latter came to see a constitutional revolution as the means by which all his other goals could be achieved. For Althorp parliamentary reform became 'the great aim and object of his political life' (Le Marchant, 290). He also came to see that only a strong whig party could achieve office. This realization brought a gradual end to his isolation and the mentality of permanent opposition. Even though he still refused to countenance his own assumption of the leadership of the party in the Commons, a step which others increasingly pressed upon him, his conduct during the next decade, especially from 1827 onwards, led inevitably in that direction.

In part Althorp's elevation was due to the elimination of all other suitable candidates. Character flaws, ill health, and suicide removed Brougham, Tavistock, Lambton, Milton, Ponsonby, Tierney, Horner, Russell, Romilly, and Whitbread from contention. Althorp's refusal in 1827 to take office in the Canning administration, though initially seen as divisive, ultimately confirmed his claim to the leadership. It also led to his reconciliation with Lord Grey and to the disgrace of Lord Lansdowne, which unified the whig party, as much as its aristocratic nature allowed, and placed its leadership in the hands of the two strongest patrician reformers of their respective generations. This decisively shifted the centre of whiggery leftwards and forged a party capable of seizing power.

Office, 1830–1834 On 3 March 1830 a meeting held in Althorp's rooms in the Albany formally proposed that he should lead the whig party in the Commons. George IV's death and the ensuing election, followed by Wellington's implacable declaration against reform, altered the political landscape. In November William IV summoned Lord Grey to form a government, which Grey could not promise to do until he had secured Althorp as leader of the House of Commons, chancellor of the exchequer, and chief lieutenant. Although in some respects a coalition ministry, on every important occasion Lord Grey's will was decisive during the next four years but only in close consultation and rarely in conflict with the man he called his 'right hand', Lord Althorp. Indeed, Grey tried on several occasions to make Althorp his co-leader through the eccentric device of appointing him first lord of the Treasury while the premier took the Foreign Office. Althorp consistently refused to accept this proposal. The older man groomed the younger one as his successor, not because he agreed with Althorp's radical views, but in the hope of holding a whig–liberal–radical coalition together in the aftermath of reform.

Althorp's power in the cabinet was demonstrated by his refusal to serve unless the reckless and undisciplined Henry Brougham was removed from the Commons, which was done. And, although both the king and Grey had the final say on what went into the Reform Bill, it was Althorp's draft proposal which formed the basis for the legislation. He did not insist on triennial parliaments and universal suffrage, which he advocated but knew the Commons would never swallow, but in other respects the boldness of the plan, with its sweeping disfranchisement of smaller boroughs and uniform £10 householder qualification, were for him a *sine qua non* and only reluctantly accepted by some members of the cabinet.

In early 1831 Althorp was well into middle age. A journalist described his expression as 'soft and stupid-like'. He was stout, broad-whiskered, and round-faced. His farmer-like figure dressed in homely, black, rumpled clothes created an impression of placidity and pedestrian dullness. Creevey nicknamed him Clunch. His speaking style was awkward, full of hesitations, and oddly off-key. Moreover, his orations were sometimes bewildering. 'I forget my topics', he confessed (Aspinall, 123). Yet it was this seeming ordinariness and lack of elegance which won the trust of the country gentlemen, and along with his mastership of the Pytchley convinced many of them that the whig government would not commit any irretrievable enormities.

There was nothing feigned about Althorp's unprepossessing manner. But many contemporaries and subsequent observers failed to look beyond the superficial appearance of squirearchical bonhomie. Althorp observed the world from the pinnacle of wealth and power and as the hereditary custodian of a potent ideology. His sense of personal unworthiness drove him to prodigies of exertion uncharacteristic of most grandees. His able mind gave him mastery in parliamentary debate. Peel understood this, noting: 'he never failed on every question to say a few words entirely to the point, and no argument open to reply escaped him' (*Greville Memoirs*, 86). His style of management was loose and unassertive, but this proved useful both in forcing the unreformed Commons to accept its own demise and in bringing as much unity as was likely to be achieved in the house after 1832. His mastery of the job won universal praise during the reform debates, when his knowledge, persuasive candour, and coolness in emergencies secured the passage of the bill virtually intact. Some kind of reform bill would have been passed whoever was in the lead. That a sweeping measure came through almost unscathed was Althorp's personal achievement. He earned the sobriquet 'Honest Jack' because of his disarming truthfulness and the essential Englishness of his character.

Althorp carried into effect economic reforms to the extent that the whig legislative agenda and Lord Grey would allow. The latter was adamantly opposed to abolition of the corn laws, which meant that free-trade principles could only be introduced in moderate amounts. His first budget in 1831 was a disaster owing to constraints of time and Althorp's inexperience. Subsequent years saw more effective legislation that gradually reduced tariffs. His bills dealing with the East India Company and the Bank of England charter reflected *laissez faire* tempered by political realism. He was successful in slashing sinecures and streamlined the operation of the Treasury. In the 1840s Peel continued his work and complemented his achievements.

Under Althorp's leadership in 1833 the reformed House of Commons enacted abolition of slavery in the British empire. His factory reform, called Althorp's Act, was too limited for Lord Ashley's taste, but it included two crucial precedents that the chancellor of the exchequer insisted upon and defended vigorously: mandatory provisions for the education of children and the founding of a factory inspectorate. The latter opened the door for even more dramatic state intervention with the new poor law of 1834. Althorp worked with Senior and Chadwick to draft this legislation and carried it through the Commons. Workhouses came to be known as 'Althorp's bastilles'. He was blamed for accepting the harsh principle of 'less eligibility'. On the other hand, he blocked the doctrinaire Edwin Chadwick's appointment as a commissioner of the centralized London bureaucracy set up to manage the system. Althorp advocated an overhaul of the poor law based on Benthamite and classical economic principles, but he also insisted on a balance between efficiency and humanity. He kept Chadwick out of power in order to check dogmatic enforcement.

The reform ministry came unstuck over the issue of Ireland. In 1833 Althorp enthusiastically introduced legislation to reform the Church of Ireland, and won Daniel O'Connell's praise. He execrated 'ascendancy' arrogance and English misrule, which he once called 'a disgrace to a civilized country' (*Hansard* 3, 81, 4 June 1845). Grey's insistence on strong coercive measures to accompany concessions led to internal convulsions from which the ministry did not recover. Stanley and other conservatives resigned, and Grey soon followed them. Althorp was obliged to resign after his father's death on 10 November 1834 translated him to the House of Lords. William IV used the excuse of Russell's inability to compensate for the loss of Althorp from the Commons as an excuse to exercise for the last time the royal prerogative of dismissing a ministry.

Retirement Spencer escaped the premiership after Grey's resignation in 1834 and Peel's failure to gain the confidence of the Commons in 1835 because of the king's repugnance and his own refusal to become the head of a radical–liberal 'movement' party organized by O'Connell, Hume, Warburton, and others. Though ambitious, he knew himself well enough to understand that he lacked the temperament and strategic vision to hold the first place. Many remained ardent for his leadership, but Spencer lay low in order to give no encouragement to his followers. He made 'rare appearances for serious purposes' (J. Morley, *The Life of William Ewart Gladstone*, 1903, 1.292) in the Lords, and a few times he organized a cabal of grandees to moderate Palmerston's aggressive foreign policy. His support for abolition of the corn laws sometimes made it awkward for him to speak before large assemblages of farmers.

Spencer devoted his retirement to agricultural propaganda, educational philanthropy, and salvaging the Spencer estate, which he was shaken to learn was half a million pounds in debt. Interest payments alone consumed three-quarters of his income. He lived frugally at his deceased wife's modest dwelling at Wiseton Hall, Nottinghamshire, shut up Althorp and Spencer houses, and sold off property not connected with the core of the estate. He sacrificed his comfort and dignity to ensure that his successors would enjoy splendour for at least another couple of centuries. The philistine of the grand tour preserved the glories of the Spencer collections, sacrificing the ease of his old age rather than sending Caxtons and Holbeins to the salerooms. Indeed, in later years Spencer carried on the family tradition of patronage. He sponsored a trip to Rome made by the sculptor William Butlin, funded the poet John Clare, and continued to make additions to his father's great library, which was made available to scholars.

In the autumn of 1845 Spencer fell ill and died of kidney failure on 1 October at Wiseton. His body was taken by rail to Northamptonshire where he was interred among the glory of the Tudor and Jacobean Spencer tombs at Great Brington near Althorp Park. Queen Victoria noted: 'He will be a great loss, not only to his family, but to the country' (Wasson, 349) His friend Lord Fitzwilliam proposed a subscription for a public monument, but Frederick Spencer demurred at his older brother's instruction. 'On long consideration,' the new earl told his correspondent, 'it was [Althorp's] opinion that for a public man the history of his country would be the best memorial of his character and acts' (ibid.).

The Victorians grasped the importance of the Reform Act they called 'great'. Later whig historians continued to tout its importance but saw Durham, Brougham, Holland, or Russell as the progenitors of change. Then for a time the reformers' reputations were in eclipse as revisionists struggled to combine sociology with historical analysis. Lively debate continues to surround the origins and implications of parliamentary reform and the great wave of accompanying legislation of the early 1830s. Historians now better understand the complex mixture of Anglicanism, *laissez faire* economics, confident paternalism, incipient collectivism, radical utilitarianism, Irish nationalism, and developing party consciousness in the making of reform. The Reform Act itself has been successfully rehabilitated as the great political watershed of the first half of the nineteenth century. Among the whig magnates Althorp was the most committed and potent reformer. Bagehot and some later commentators portrayed Althorp as a simpleton or a blundering rustic. On the other hand, most of his contemporaries accorded him respect and affection. His unique mastery of the Commons was greatly admired by both Gladstone and Salisbury. He conveyed to the Victorians a notion of public virtue and moral government that melded whiggery and Liberalism. His life work laid the foundations of the Liberal Party and the modern state. ELLIS ARCHER WASSON

Sources E. A. Wasson, *Whig renaissance: Lord Althorp and the whig party, 1782–1845* (1987) • D. Le Marchant, *Memoir of John Charles, Viscount Althorp, third Earl Spencer*, ed. H. D. Le Marchant (1876) • E. Myers, *Lord Althorp* (1890) • G. Battiscombe, *The Spencers of Althorp* (1984) • D. O. Madden, 'The age of Pitt and Fox', *EdinR*, 83 (1846), 240–73 • W. Bagehot, 'Lord Althorp and the Reform Act of 1832', *The collected works of Walter Bagehot*, ed. N. St John-Stevas, 3 (1968), 200–31 • M. Brock, *The Great Reform Act* (1973) • Lord Holland [H. R. V. Fox] and J. Allen, *The Holland House diaries, 1831–1840*, ed. A. D. Kriegel (1977) • *Correspondence of Sarah Spencer, Lady Lyttelton, 1787–1870*, ed. Mrs H. Wyndham (1912) • A. Aspinall, ed., *Three early nineteenth-century diaries* (1952) [extracts from Le Marchant, E. J. Littleton, Baron Hatherton, and E. Law, earl of Ellenborough] • *The Greville memoirs, 1814–1860*, ed. L. Strachey and R. Fulford, 8 vols. (1938) • Baron Broughton [J. C. Hobhouse], *Recollections of a long life*, ed. Lady Dorchester [C. Carleton], 6 vols. (1909–11) • J. Parry, *The rise and fall of liberal government in Victorian Britain* (1993)

Archives BL, corresp. and papers | BL, corresp. with George Appleyard • BL, corresp. with Lord Broughton, Add. MSS 47226–47227 • BL, letters to John Clare, Egerton MSS 2249–2250 • BL, corresp. with Lord Holland, Add. MS 51724 • Devon RO, Fortescue MSS • Harrowby Manuscript Trust, Sandon Hall, Staffordshire, corresp. with earl of Harrowby and Viscount Sandon • HLRO, letters to J. G. Shaw-Lefevre • Lpool RO, letters to Lord Stanley • Northants. RO, Fitzwilliam MSS • Northants. RO, corresp. with J. C. Gotch • PRO, corresp. with Lord John Russell, PRO 30/22 • Royal Arch., Melbourne MSS • Staffs. RO, letters to Lord Hatherton • U. Durham L., corresp. with second Earl Grey • U. Southampton L., corresp. with Lord Palmerston • UCL, corresp. with Sir Edwin Chadwick • UCL, letters to Society for the Diffusion of Useful Knowledge • W. Sussex RO, Goodwood MSS, letters to duke of Richmond

Likenesses J. Reynolds, double portrait, oils, 1783–4 (with his mother), Hunt. L. • J. Reynolds, oils, 1786, Althorp, Northamptonshire • M. A. Shee, oils, 1800, Althorp, Northamptonshire • G. Hayter, oils, 1816, Althorp, Northamptonshire • W. Butlin, bust, 1832, Althorp, Northamptonshire • C. Turner, chalk drawing, 1832, NPG [*see illus.*] • F. Chantrey, portrait, *c.*1833, Holkham Hall, Norfolk • R. Andsell, group portrait, oils, 1843, Althorp, Northamptonshire • photograph, 1845, Althorp, Northamptonshire • G. Hayter, group portrait, oils (*The House of Commons, 1833*), NPG • T. Phillips, oils, Althorp, Northamptonshire

Wealth at death under £160,000; estate of over 30,000 acres in Northamptonshire, Warwickshire, and Norfolk: GEC, *Peerage*

Spencer, John Poyntz, fifth Earl Spencer (1835–1910), politician and viceroy of Ireland, was the son of Frederick *Spencer (1798–1857) [*see under* Spencer, Sir Robert Cavendish], a distinguished naval captain, who became fourth Earl Spencer on his brother's death in 1845. As member of parliament for Worcestershire and Midhurst, Sussex, between 1831 and 1841, Frederick invariably voted with the whigs. In this he followed the tradition of his elder brother, John Charles Spencer, third earl, who was chancellor of the exchequer in Grey's ministry from 1830 and played a leading part in the passing of the Reform Bill two years later. Frederick had married Elizabeth Georgiana Poyntz of Midgham House, Berkshire, and Cowdray Park, Sussex, in 1830, and there were three children, Georgina, Sarah, and a boy, John Poyntz, born on 27 October 1835 at the family's London mansion, Spencer House. Their mother died in 1851 and the fourth earl married secondly Adelaide Horatia Seymour in 1854. A daughter, Victoria Alexandrina, was born in 1855 and a boy, Charles Robert (Bobby), in October 1857.

Spencer, styled Viscount Althorp until 1857, entered Harrow School in Easter 1848 and, though not prominent in his academic studies, developed his lifelong interest in cricket and took an active part in the debating society. Althorp made a number of friends, including H. Montagu Butler, later headmaster of Harrow, and Lord Frederick Cavendish. After a spell with a tutor at Brighton, Althorp went up to Trinity College, Cambridge, in 1854 to read for

John Poyntz Spencer, fifth Earl Spencer (1835–1910), by Frank Holl, 1888

a nobleman's degree. He made no mark academically—a major distraction was his growing passion for riding—and graduated MA in January 1857.

Early political career Althorp was elected for one of the two seats in the southern division of Northamptonshire in the general election of March 1857, pledging his support for Palmerston. This was followed by a three-month tour of North America, where he observed the growing tensions between the northern and southern states. He arrived back in England in mid-December: on 27th of that month his father died suddenly, and Althorp became the new Earl Spencer at the age of twenty-two.

Because of Spencer's desire to remain active in the political field on his appointment to the royal household, first as groom of the stable to Prince Albert, 1859–61, and then to the prince of Wales (later Edward VII), 1862–6, he required assurances that his participation in politics would still be possible. Spencer made a number of contributions to the debates in the Lords in the early 1860s. He was made a knight of the Garter in 1864, an appropriate acknowledgement of his gift to the nation at this time of Wimbledon Common. In the following year he chaired a royal commission to suggest means of dealing with the cattle plague. Other members of the commission included Lord Cranborne (later the marquess of Salisbury), Robert Lowe, and Lyon Playfair. He gained further experience in public life when he served on a special committee, set up in November 1867 by the War Office, to report on a suitable breech-loading rifle.

The introduction of a reform bill by Lord Russell in 1866 had led to a split among his own supporters. A group opposed to reform was led by Earl Grosvenor, Robert Lowe, and Lord Elcho in the Commons, and the marquess of Lansdowne, Earl Grey, and Lord Lichfield in the Lords. Elcho and Grosvenor tried to persuade Spencer to lead the moderate Liberal faction but he refused, expressing his confidence in mainstream Liberalism, and especially Gladstone.

Viceroy of Ireland, 1868–1874 Spencer's loyalty was not forgotten when Gladstone formed his ministry in December 1868. The offer of lord lieutenant of Ireland came as a surprise both to Spencer and to many others. He had previously held no official political post and had had no experience of Irish affairs. The appointment was largely due to the influence of Chichester Fortescue, later first Baron Carlingford, who had been chief secretary in 1865–6 and again in 1868, with a seat in the cabinet. Spencer's correspondence with his ministerial colleagues on the Land Bill of 1870 first displayed his grasp of the Irish problem. Himself a model landlord, Spencer favoured the restoration of goodwill between landlords and tenants. He suggested the setting up of tribunals with jurisdiction on questions of rent and proposed that tenants-at-will should enjoy a period of five to seven years at a fixed rent. Spencer regarded the Land Act as a prerequisite for settling agrarian crime and for regaining the confidence of the Irish people. This approach went further than those put forward by government colleagues, many of whom represented the landlord interest, although Fortescue, who held property in Ireland, to a large extent shared his views. However, Spencer's proposals clashed with Gladstone's principle that the state should be given as few responsibilities as possible under the Land Act.

Between the time when the bill was first discussed in cabinet in late 1869 and its introduction in the Commons in February 1870, agrarian crime rose considerably. Spencer and Fortescue pressed for greater powers to deal with crime and contemplated resignation when it seemed unlikely that the cabinet would sanction coercive legislation in Ireland. Although a Peace Preservation Bill granting such powers was rapidly enacted, matters did not go smoothly with the Land Bill. It was much weakened in the course of its passage through parliament and the act failed to pacify Ireland. A second Land Act was required eleven years later.

When Fortescue moved to the Board of Trade early in 1871, his place as chief secretary was taken by Spencer Compton, marquess of Hartington, Spencer's second cousin. At the end of 1870 Spencer believed that it was safe to release the remaining Fenian prisoners. However, there was a further outbreak of agrarian violence, especially in co. Westmeath, where secret societies flourished, and Spencer was obliged to ask for the suspension of habeas corpus. Spencer and Hartington were heavily involved in drawing up the Westmeath Bill, granting them the necessary powers. It received the royal assent in June 1871.

When Gladstone turned his attention to remodelling the Irish university education system in 1872–3, Spencer had the task of pacifying the Roman Catholic hierarchy.

Hartington expressed grave dissatisfaction with the inherent contradictions in the Irish University Bill, though Spencer supported Gladstone. The bill and the government were defeated in the Commons on 11–12 March 1873. Spencer favoured resignation rather than a dissolution, a course which was agreed upon by the cabinet. However, Disraeli, not wishing to be head of a minority government, refused to take office and the Liberal administration continued, though much weakened. When the general election led to a Conservative victory in February 1874, Spencer was relieved to be out of office after five years in Ireland and returned to his country seat, Althorp, in Northamptonshire. Looking back over his time as lord lieutenant, he considered his achievements. Only two men were in prison under his warrant when he left Ireland, life and property in co. Meath and co. Westmeath were secure, and Fenianism appeared to be diminishing.

Out of office and marriage On leaving office Spencer was offered a marquessate by Gladstone, but after consulting Granville and Hartington refused it. He was now free to pursue his hobbies, rifle shooting and fox-hunting. In 1860 he was the chairman of a committee which met at Spencer House to form the National Rifle Association, and he was closely connected with that body until his death—as chairman 1867–8 and member of the council for almost fifty years. He frequently shot in the Lords' team in the Lords and Commons match, and presented the Spencer cup, to be competed for at the annual meeting by boys at public schools. Like his ancestors before him, he had been master of the Pytchley hounds (1861–4), and once more resumed in 1874. Spencer expended much time and effort in enhancing the hunt's reputation. One notable visitor to Northamptonshire was Elizabeth, empress of Austria, reputedly one of the most beautiful women in Europe. She was an excellent rider and enjoyed flouting convention, preferring beer to other drinks, and shocking guests at Althorp one night after dinner by smoking a cigar. She hunted with the Pytchley in March 1876 and again in 1878 and Spencer was subsequently invited to Gödöllö, the empress's favourite hunting seat in Hungary. The cost of being master was extremely heavy: in 1879, a year after he resigned the position, he had to seek a loan of £15,000 on account of the excess expenditure for the hounds.

Spencer also embarked on large-scale alterations to the house in the years 1876–8, including a new dining-room to house the collection of Reynolds paintings. In 1872 he had become lord lieutenant of Northamptonshire, and Spencer fully participated in the duties which holding this office entailed.

It was in the 1860s that Spencer first grew the large red beard which gave rise to his nickname, the Red Earl, a characteristic which cartoonists of the Irish press during his second viceroyalty were quick to exploit. In manhood he was a tall, commanding figure, some 6 feet 3 inches in height. His fortitude and stamina in the hunting field belied a basically weak constitution. Spencer was subject to sporadic illnesses, arising out of a weakness in one of his lungs, and he frequently visited German spas in search of better health.

To the outside world Spencer often appeared aloof and withdrawn. In 1904 Edmund Gosse, then librarian of the House of Lords, wrote down his impressions after meeting Spencer.

> I found him very intimidating; one looks up in despair for his face at the top of a white cliff of his great beard. He was possibly shy, he certainly made me feel so, but he gives the impression of great dignity, and the temper of a very fine gentleman. I admire him intensely, but he is certainly the most alarming figure I have yet encountered here.
> (E. Gosse, diary, 14 March 1904, HL, MS L32)

Spencer's reserved manner in public stemmed mainly from a nervous disposition, but privately, when relaxed, his natural sense of fun was given full rein. He laid little claim to intellectual pursuits but was an industrious and conscientious administrator. His handwriting was exceptionally difficult to decipher, and in his speech-making his delivery lacked forcefulness. He accepted invitations to speak in public with reluctance and depended heavily upon notes. In religious matters he disliked extreme views; he was a patron of thirteen livings.

Spencer married Charlotte Frances Frederica Seymour (*d.* 1903), youngest of three daughters of Lady Augusta and Frederick Seymour, on 8 July 1858. All three sisters were noted beauties in London society. There was already a family link, as Adelaide, Spencer's stepmother, and Charlotte were cousins. Although from a Conservative background, she supported Spencer in his career and expressed herself trenchantly on political matters. Her private diaries contain memoranda on, for example, aspects of Fenianism and the Eastern question. There were no children of the marriage.

When Beaconsfield appointed the royal commission on agricultural depression in July 1879, chaired by the duke of Richmond, Spencer was the only Liberal peer out of the twenty members appointed, together with one Liberal commoner, G. J. Goschen. As a landowner of 27,185 acres, 16,800 of which were in Northamptonshire, with lesser holdings in Warwickshire, Hertfordshire, Buckinghamshire, Leicestershire, and Surrey, Spencer took a keen interest in the commission's deliberations. In November he was advised to recuperate from an illness, and, with rumours of a dissolution in the air, left for Algiers in December.

Lord president and Ireland, 1880–1882 When Gladstone formed his second administration in 1880, Spencer joined the cabinet as lord president of the council with a seat in the cabinet. It was envisaged by Gladstone that Spencer would be able to advise on Irish matters as well as carry out the duties of lord president. The post carried formal responsibility for supervision of the education department, but in practice the vice-president was in charge of its day-to-day running.

One of the first tasks of the new government was to complete the existing legislation relating to compulsory education. The 1870 Education Act had allowed school boards to have ambiguous permissive powers on compulsion: the 1876 act created school attendance committees, which were able to make by-laws for the enforcement of attendance. Spencer calculated that in 1880 about a quarter of the population were still outside the influence of the by-laws. Spencer, A. J. Mundella, the vice-president, and W. E. Forster, vice-president in Gladstone's first government, discussed and approved a new bill. By August 1880 an act establishing attendance was on the statute book and was an immediate success.

Another major educational reform with which Spencer is associated is the new code of 1882. This was the first major reconstruction of the grant award system to schools since Robert Lowe, then vice-president, had introduced the notorious 'payment by results' system some twenty years previously. Besides altering the basis for payment, the code encouraged a wider curriculum and more intelligent teaching in elementary schools; it also gave an impetus to the development of higher grade schools which enabled older and more advanced elementary pupils to continue their education. An important series of royal commissions was instigated, which investigated medical and technical education, and the provision of secondary and higher education in Wales.

While carrying out these duties, Spencer was at the same time heavily involved in advising on Irish affairs. W. E. Forster, the chief secretary, advocated strong measures to repress the Land League, especially the suspension of habeas corpus, and was supported in this view by the viceroy, Lord Cowper. Early in 1881 a Coercion Bill and a Peace Preservation Bill were steered through the Commons by Forster, though Gladstone's Land Bill, aimed at pacifying the Irish nationalists, became law in August. Parnell's defiance led to his arrest on 12 October. Secret negotiations with Chamberlain as intermediary led to Parnell's release on 1 May. The following day, Forster resigned. On 3 May Spencer replaced Cowper as lord lieutenant while retaining his post as lord president of the council.

Viceroy of Ireland, 1882–1885 Spencer was not unprepared for his return to Ireland. At Gladstone's request he had made two visits, in October and December 1881, to discuss matters with Cowper and Forster and to report back on the situation. After crossing to Ireland on 5 May with the new chief secretary, Frederick Cavendish, Hartington's younger brother, Spencer made his official entry into Dublin the following day. He attended a meeting at the castle in the afternoon with Cavendish and T. H. Burke, the under-secretary. Walking back across Phoenix Park later, Cavendish and Burke were brutally murdered by members of the Invincibles, a secret organization whose purpose was to assassinate British officials in Ireland. Spencer, who had left the castle on horseback and was in the viceregal lodge when the murders took place, told Gladstone, 'I must have crossed the road riding either behind or in front of them within a minute of them' (BL, Add. MS 44308, fol. 217).

The news of the assassinations was received in England with a mixture of shock and fury. A Prevention of Crime Bill, already sanctioned in principle by the cabinet, received the royal assent on 12 July and was rigorously enforced. For the next three years, near siege conditions prevailed at the castle. Spencer was everywhere accompanied by a detective, and on subsequent tours of Ireland the cavalcade included eight hussars and eight mounted police at the front, while behind were two armed constables in a car followed by two more detectives.

The Irish crisis dramatically and unexpectedly thrust Spencer into the limelight. His wishes were met whenever possible and his handling of the new situation was widely admired. Gladstone told the queen on 27 May, 'He possesses all the fine and genuine qualities of his excellent Uncle Althorp, and exercises them with heightened powers'. Within a few days of the assassinations, there was a complete turnabout in the real power of Irish administration. G. O. Trevelyan was appointed as Irish chief secretary. The previous holder, Forster, had been the main spokesman for Irish affairs in the cabinet and in the Commons. His lord lieutenant, Cowper, was outside the cabinet and played a subordinate role in Irish affairs. Now the positions were reversed.

Two immediate tasks faced Spencer: the reorganization of the police forces and the destruction of secret societies responsible for political murders. The Royal Irish Constabulary and the Dublin Metropolitan Police were inadequate for the range of duties required of them and new leadership was found. Spencer also secured permission from Gladstone to appoint an under-secretary for police and crime, responsible for creating a secret intelligence section to monitor potential terrorists and to infiltrate their ranks. The reform of the magistracy was also undertaken. By the end of the year, the situation in Ireland was relatively quiet largely because of Spencer's prompt action.

One law case which was to cause great controversy followed the murder of the Joyce family at Maamtrasna, Galway, earlier in the year. Ten men were accused of the crime: two of these turned informers, five were given a late reprieve, but one of them, Myles Joyce, declared his innocence throughout the trial. He was hanged in December and came to be regarded as a political martyr. Spencer admitted to Harcourt after the executions had been carried out that 'the Maamtrasna decision worried me dreadfully up to the last' (MS Harcourt 40).

From early in 1883 Spencer once more began to attend cabinet meetings in London, where matters concerning Ireland were on the agenda, and in March he readily agreed to relinquish the lord presidency to Carlingford. Spencer was able to make tours of Ireland, partly for recreation and partly to gather information on the state of the country at first hand. His views on methods of dealing with the distress of Irish tenants were not sentimental. He strongly favoured the workhouse system and supported the view that the government should help unions in cases where people wished to emigrate.

In July 1884 Spencer let it be known that he was willing

to be considered for the post of viceroy of India, as the incumbent, Ripon, was contemplating giving it up. However, Trevelyan, after two years as chief secretary, urgently requested to be relieved of his position and Spencer was involved in finding a suitable successor. Campbell-Bannerman replaced Trevelyan in October, and Spencer continued as lord lieutenant.

In outlining a plan of desired legislation to Gladstone in January 1885, Spencer stated that the most urgent matter was the renewal of the Crimes Act, due to expire at the end of the session. One of Spencer's cherished hopes was for the prince and princess of Wales to visit Ireland, and he was closely involved in the delicate negotiations with the queen. The visit, which took place between 8 and 27 April, with the Spencers accompanying their visitors, was a success in the loyal north, though the party ran into trouble in the south. Spencer was now emboldened to raise with the queen the issue of a royal residence in Ireland, but this was instantly rejected. 'I feel inclined', Spencer gloomily told Ponsonby in May, 'to throw up the sponge and retire to my plough in Northamptonshire.'

The crises in the cabinet engendered by the Egyptian question and the fall of Khartoum, with differences on policy within the cabinet, raised doubts on the survival of the government. Spencer's programme of legislation for Ireland, the renewal of the Crimes Act and a Land Purchase Bill, was not discussed in cabinet until the end of April. The search for a solution to the Irish problem brought Spencer into sharp conflict with Chamberlain and Dilke, who demanded in place of the Land Bill a large measure of local government. While these matters were awaiting settlement, Gladstone was defeated on the budget in the early hours of 9 June and the government resigned.

However, Spencer's troubles were not quite over. On 17 July Parnell's motion censuring Spencer for the administration of law and order in Ireland, especially the handling of the Maamtrasna murders case, was strongly supported by Randolph Churchill and others. While in opposition, the Conservatives had supported Spencer's firm line on the case. Members from both parties were highly critical of this attack, and within a week a banquet in honour of Spencer, attended by more than 200 Liberals from both houses, under the chairmanship of Hartington, was held at Westminster Palace Hotel.

Home Rule, 1885–1886 Commenting on Gladstone's address to his Midlothian constituents, issued on 17 September 1885, Spencer told a friend:

> Suppose we could 1. Get security for the landlords 2. Prevent a civil war with Ulster 3. Make the Irish nation our friends, not enemies, it would be worth while giving them Home Rule, but I don't see my way to the three conditions or any of them being secured. (Spencer to C. Boyle, 20 Sept 1885, Althorp MSS)

Spencer was closely involved with the autumn consultations on Ireland. After meeting Hartington at Chatsworth on 5 December, he joined Rosebery at Hawarden on 8 December, where they talked at length with Gladstone. This was followed by meetings with Goschen and Northbrook. Spencer also sounded out a number of Irish landlords on Gladstone's behalf. On the last day of the year, he wrote to Mundella:'I must confess to you that I look on the old methods of dealing with Ireland … as gone and hopeless. … There seems nothing but a big measure, Home Rule with proper safeguards, or at no distant day, coercion stronger than we have ever had before. The latter cannot be thought of now' (Mundella MSS, MP 6P/18).

Following Gladstone's adoption of the policy of home rule, he sketched out with his two most trusted colleagues, Spencer and Granville, the strategies to be pursued if they were returned to office. After the Salisbury government's defeat in the Commons on 27 January 1886, Spencer was much occupied in advising Gladstone on candidates for office in the new ministry, a difficult task in view of the secession of so many moderate Liberals in both houses of parliament. He had hoped to have been offered the Admiralty but, because of difficulties over Granville, reluctantly resumed his former post of lord president of the council. His main task, however, was to help in the preparation of Irish legislation.

Two bills were submitted to the cabinet: one proposing a new Irish legislature, the other dealing with land purchase on a large scale. Chamberlain and Trevelyan thereupon resigned. The Government of Ireland Bill was presented to the Commons on 8 April by Gladstone, and the Land Purchase Bill eight days later. The vital debate on the second reading of the Government of Ireland Bill in May extended over fourteen nights, and encountered opposition from Irish Unionists and a strong minority of Liberals; the scheme for land purchase, unpopular with Irish landowners, also weighed against the success of the Home Rule Bill. On 7 June the government was defeated by 341 to 311, with 93 Liberals voting with the Conservatives. Defeated at the subsequent general election, Gladstone resigned on 20 July.

Personal finances and opposition politics Politics were not the only worry for Spencer at this time. His two spells as lord lieutenant of Ireland had been a heavy financial drain. The depressed state of agriculture throughout the country affected the Althorp estate, with agricultural prices unprecedentedly low. By late 1885 Spencer calculated that his net income was 40 per cent less than it had been ten years previously.

Perhaps the most painful consequence of Spencer's acceptance of home rule was the social ostracism and hurtful public criticism which long dogged him. Edward Hamilton, Gladstone's former secretary, noted that 'his [Spencer's] friends actually cut him and won't meet him'; these sentiments were shared by the queen, who pointedly no longer invited Spencer, as a leading member of the opposition, to Windsor.

Spencer closely followed events in Ireland and the attempts of the Salisbury government to control them. Greater demands were being made on politicians for public speeches, and at great cost to himself Spencer accepted many invitations to address rallies. He caused unintentional consternation in the Liberal camp by stating during a speech at Stockton in October 1889 that Irish members should be retained in an imperial parliament. Earlier in the year, Spencer had been in the public eye when he had shaken hands with Parnell at a dinner given by Liberals. In December 1891 Althorp was the setting for a meeting between the Liberal leaders, Gladstone, Harcourt, Morley, Rosebery, and Spencer, to discuss aspects of the Newcastle programme, announced in October, which dealt with future Liberal policy.

Spencer continued to participate in Northamptonshire affairs. With the establishment of county councils following the 1888 Local Government Act, Spencer became first chairman of the Northamptonshire county council, efficiently and conscientiously carrying out his duties. When the Liberals were returned to power in August 1892 it was obvious that he could not carry a double burden, and he relinquished this post at the end of the year. However, he continued to take a close interest in county council affairs and retained his councillorship until 1907.

With little prospect of improvement in rent and land values, Spencer was obliged to seek a dramatic solution to his financial problems. The Althorp Library, long acknowledged as one of the great European collections, had been mainly amassed by his grandfather, George John, second Earl Spencer. It included many fifteenth- and sixteenth-century volumes, among them the Gutenberg Bible, the first Mainz psalter, and fifty-three Caxtons. The purchase, for £210,000, was made by Mrs Enriqueta Rylands, widow of John Rylands, the Manchester millionaire, who wished to found a theological library in that city in memory of her husband. In August and September 1892, 600 cases of books were packed and dispatched to Manchester. In October 1899, when the John Rylands Library was opened, Spencer, as chancellor of the Victoria University (1892–1907), was awarded an honorary degree by the library's benefactress.

At the Admiralty, 1892–1895 After the general election of 1892, in which the Liberals were returned with a small majority, Spencer was delighted to be appointed to the post of first lord of the Admiralty. He assumed office at a time when there was widespread concern over the expansion by other European powers of their navies: Britain's long undisputed supremacy was now being challenged, particularly by France and Russia. The large shipbuilding programme embodied in the Naval Defence Act of 1889 had already begun, and continuity of administration was of prime importance. Spencer was the first to set the precedent of retaining in office the professional members of the board who had been appointed by his predecessor.

Spencer handled the administrative and political aspects of his post with great skill. An early set-back while the Spencer programme was being discussed occurred in 1893 when the *Victoria*, the flagship of Vice-Admiral Sir George Tryon, was rammed by another battleship, the *Camperdown*, with the loss of more than 350 officers and men. Spencer came into conflict with Harcourt, the chancellor of the exchequer, over his demands, backed by the sea lords, for seven more first-class battleships, six cruisers, and thirty-six destroyers. In December 1893 Lord George Hamilton, Spencer's predecessor, moved in the Commons for immediate action to increase the size of the navy. Harcourt informed the house that the sea lords were satisfied with the present expenditure. This led the following day to the admirals entirely repudiating this interpretation. On 6 January 1894 Gladstone sent for Spencer and told him that he could not accept the estimates and would resign rather than do so. Spencer, for his part, refused to yield further. Gladstone resigned from office on 1 March and a week later the cabinet, under Rosebery, formally approved the estimates.

It may seem surprising, in the light of fundamental disagreements on naval policy, that Gladstone was prepared to nominate Spencer as his successor. On 2 March, as he was setting out for Windsor, he confided in John Morley that if invited by the queen to advise on his successor, he would nominate Spencer. However, at the subsequent interview Gladstone's advice was not sought, and the queen chose Rosebery. Spencer was happy to serve under the new prime minister until the government fell in June 1895. In preparing the naval estimates for his last year in office, Spencer was able to state that the shipbuilding programme far outstripped those of France and Russia.

Final years and death Freed from the responsibilities of office, Spencer resumed hunting with the Pytchley, having taken over the mastership for the third time in 1890. Always a keen and progressive farmer, he was president of the Royal Agricultural Society in 1898.

The outbreak of the Second South African War in 1899 deepened the divisions within the Liberal Party, a group of leading members, known as Liberal Imperialists, having been formed under Rosebery's leadership. Spencer supported Campbell-Bannerman, the opposition leader in the Commons, who adopted a central position over the war. During Kimberley's illness in 1901 Spencer acted as leader of the opposition in the Lords, and was elected leader in April 1902. He spearheaded the attack on the Education Bill in the Lords but without success. The death of Lady Spencer on 31 October 1903 was a severe blow. In the following year, on 23 September, Spencer suffered a heart attack and was advised to rest for the remainder of the year.

This did not dispel rumours of the probability of Spencer's appointment to the highest office. Salisbury had resigned in July 1902 and his nephew, Balfour, presided over a party divided by the free-trade controversy. A return of the Liberals to power seemed likely. Much speculation was aroused by the appearance in the press on 10 February 1905 of a letter, the day after Spencer had presided at a conference of Liberal leaders, stating his views on the policy of a future Liberal government. Spencer protested in vain at the interpretation placed on the letter by both the politicians and public. The *Times's* reaction was that, in the event of a Liberal victory, Spencer would be offered the premiership (11 Feb 1905).

Spencer returned to London from Marienbad on 18 September in great spirits, and at the end of the month he was at the family's property at North Creake, Norfolk, for shooting. On 11 October he suffered a severe stroke which removed him from the political scene. 'Poor Lord Spencer', wrote the young Winston Churchill to Rosebery, 'it was rather like a ship sinking in sight of land' (19 Oct 1903, Rosebery MSS, 10009, fol. 171). He retained a keen interest in naval and political developments, and was delighted at the appointment of Campbell-Bannerman as prime minister in December 1905 and at the impressive general election victory of the Liberals in January 1906, when they gained 226 seats.

Spencer resigned from the chancellorship of Manchester University and the lord lieutenancy of Northamptonshire in 1908. Now in failing health, he attended the Garter ceremony at Windsor in November 1909. On 5 July 1910 Spencer suffered a further stroke and died on 13 August at Althorp. He was buried beside his wife at Great Brington, Northamptonshire, on 18 August. His half-brother, Robert, succeeded him as sixth earl.

Assessment Spencer's prominent role in Liberal politics over a period of almost four decades has not received the recognition it deserves. First coming to prominence in 1867 over franchise reform, he was a member of successive Liberal governments for the rest of the century, and a member of the cabinet in all except the first. As lord lieutenant of Ireland during the crucial periods 1868–74 and 1882–5, Spencer was given the difficult task of carrying out the provisions of the Land Acts and a Coercion Act. Spencer's stubborn opposition to Chamberlain's central board scheme was crucial in the cabinet's rejection of it in May 1885.

His subsequent conversion to the cause of Irish home rule was regarded with astonishment by members of both parties. In fact, Spencer's decision was entirely consistent with his character: once convinced of the necessity of a course of action, he was willing to pursue it, however uncomfortable the consequences. Another example was the support given to the admirals in 1893 for the navy estimates, in spite of Gladstone's protests. Spencer rarely courted popularity for its own sake, but he treated political opponents with courtesy. Loyalty was another quality which he prized highly. It seems unlikely that Gladstone could have successfully formed a government in 1886 without Spencer's assistance, and his support for home rule remained critical, as Gladstone made it a test of loyalty to Liberalism.

Two other areas of Spencer's activities are worthy of note. His shipbuilding programme and steps taken to improve naval defences were of immense value when the First World War broke out; and, as lord president, he promoted compulsory attendance through the 1880 Education Bill and the drawing up of more enlightened codes, which affected the status and work of inspectors, teachers, and children, and encouraged the development of a national system of schools and higher education for Wales.

The likelihood of a Spencer ministry in 1903 and 1904 if Balfour had resigned was widely accepted at the time. Although he inspired few with his oratory, he possessed many of the qualities needed for a prime minister. Reflecting on the merits of rival contenders, Harcourt, Rosebery, and Spencer, for the post in July 1894, Gladstone chose Spencer:

> Less brilliant than either, he has far more experience … he has also decidedly more of that very important quality termed weight, and his cast of character I think affords more guarantees of the moderation he would combine with zeal, and more possibility of forecasting the course he would pursue. (W. E. Gladstone, memorandum, 25 July 1894, BL, Add. MS 44790, fols. 145–6)

Spencer's reserved manner was sometimes mistaken for aloofness. He told his wife in 1892, 'Granville once said that no one who had been Viceroy altogether lost its effect on his manners. I always kept that before me, and tried to be natural, but there may be something in it' (6 June 1892, Althorp MSS). Though he never gained the highest office, Spencer was content to have served his party with a loyalty which both friends and foes alike acknowledged. His achievements were many, and, like a true whig, without being a leader of popular movements he worked for changes through constitutional means which would ultimately benefit the country. PETER GORDON

Sources *The Red Earl: the papers of the fifth Earl Spencer, 1835–1910*, ed. P. Gordon, 2 vols., Northamptonshire RS, 31, 34 (1981–6) · J. Morley, *The life of William Ewart Gladstone*, 3 vols. (1903) · A. G. Gardiner, *The life of Sir William Harcourt*, 2 vols. (1923) · J. A. Spender, *The life of the Right Hon. Sir Henry Campbell-Bannerman*, 2 vols. (1923) · R. O. A. Crewe-Milnes, *Lord Rosebery*, 2 vols. (1931) · Gladstone, *Diaries* · A. B. Cooke and J. Vincent, *The governing passion: cabinet government and party politics in Britain, 1885–86* (1974) · *The political correspondence of Mr Gladstone and Lord Granville, 1876–1886*, ed. A. Ramm, 2 vols. (1962) · R. R. James, *Rosebery: a biography of Archibald Philip, fifth earl of Rosebery* (1963) · Bodl. Oxf., Harcourt MSS · BL, Althorp MSS · NL Scot., Rosebery MSS · Sheffield University Library, Mundella MSS

Archives BL, Althorp MSS, corresp. and papers · BL, travel journals, Add. MSS 62917–62918 | BL, corresp. with Sir Henry Campbell-Bannerman, Add. MS 41229 · BL, corresp. with Sir Charles Dilke, Add. MS 43891 · BL, letters to Lord Gladstone, Add. MS 46017 · BL, corresp. with W. E. Gladstone, Add. MSS 44306–44314 · BL, corresp. with Sir Edward Walter Hamilton, Add. MS 48613 · BL, corresp. with Lord Ripon, Add. MS 43538 · Bodl. Oxf., corresp. with Herbert Asquith · Bodl. Oxf., corresp. with Sir William Harcourt · Bodl. Oxf., letters to Lord Kimberley · Chatsworth House, Derbyshire, letters to Lord Hartington, etc. · Hove Central Library, Sussex, letters to Lord Wolseley · ICL, college archives, letters to Lyon Playfair · ING Barings, London, corresp. with earl of Northbrook · NL Scot., letters to Lord Kimberley · NL Scot., corresp. with Lord Rosebery · NL Scot., corresp. mainly with Lord Rosebery · NRA, priv. coll., letters to Lord Aberdeen · NRA, priv. coll., corresp. with Lord Monck · PRO, corresp. with Lord Granville, PRO 30/29 · PRO NIre., corresp. with Lord O'Hagan · Som. ARS, letters to Lord Carlingford · U. Birm. L., corresp. with Joseph Chamberlain · University of Sheffield, letters to A. J. Mundella

Likenesses H. T. Wells, 1867, Althorp, Northamptonshire · F. Holl, portrait, 1888, Althorp, Northamptonshire [*see illus.*] · J. Brown, print (after H. T. Wells), NPG

Wealth at death £642,454 10s. 2d.: probate, 22 Dec 1910, *CGPLA Eng. & Wales*

Spencer, Leonard James (1870–1959), mineralogist and geologist, was born in Worcester on 7 July 1870, the eldest of eight children of James Spencer, schoolmaster, and Elizabeth Bonser. He was educated at Keighley trade and grammar school and from the age of thirteen at Bradford Technical College where his father was headmaster of the day school department. Aged sixteen he gained a royal exhibition to the Royal College of Science in Dublin, taking a first-class degree in chemistry in 1889. With a scholarship to Sidney Sussex College, Cambridge, he subsequently obtained a first class in both parts of the natural science tripos in 1892–3 and won the Harkness scholarship for geology in 1893. At Cambridge he also studied mineralogy and geology and, successful at examination for a vacancy in the department of mineralogy of the British Museum (Natural History), he took up an appointment there on 1 January 1894, priming himself in advance with three months' study of mineralogy and petrology in Munich under Groth, Weinschenk, and Muthmann.

On 5 April 1899, at the church of Stratfield Mortimer, Spencer married Edith Mary Close (1872–1954) daughter of Islip J. Close, farmer, of Mortimer in Berkshire. They had one son and two daughters, one of whom was the dancer Penelope *Spencer.

In 1889, possibly out of financial necessity, Spencer spent a brief period abstracting papers for the Patent Office, working on abridgements of specifications of philosophical instruments for the years from 1855. His work henceforth was to be similarly detailed and descriptive. As a child he had avidly collected minerals and fossils; by 1892 his collection numbered 3000 specimens, all labelled and catalogued. This collection was donated to Bradford Technical College. His work at the British Museum lay chiefly in establishing a system for registering, labelling, and cataloguing the mineral collection, but he was also extremely active as an original investigator and as an editor and bibliographer. He was to publish over 150 papers in the field of descriptive mineralogy and many early papers (he published twenty-seven in his first decade at the museum) came out of the curatorial work he did on the crystallographic catalogue. In 1902 the Geological Society of London awarded him the Wollaston Fund. He named eight new minerals—miersite, tarbuttite, parahopeite, chloroxiphite, diaboleite, schulterite, aramayoite, and bismutotantalite (all nonsilicates)—and supplied much new information on hitherto incompletely described minerals such as plagionite, heteromorphite, and semseyite.

In 1921 Spencer became ScD of Cambridge and in 1925 was elected fellow of the Royal Society. The following year he became a correspondent, later an honorary fellow, and in 1940 Roebling medallist of the Mineralogical Society of America. He also became in 1927 an honorary member of the German Mineralogical Society. He was awarded the Murchison medal of the Geological Society in 1937 and was that society's vice-president in 1945–6 and a senior fellow for many years. He was president of the Mineralogical Society of Great Britain from 1936 to 1939 and its foreign secretary from 1949 to 1959. He was also an honorary member of the Royal Geological Society of Cornwall and a recipient of its Bolitho gold medal. Spencer travelled to Canada in 1924 for the British Association's Toronto meeting, which afforded him the opportunity to collect minerals in the eastern United States and Canada. Similarly in 1929 he travelled to South Africa for its meeting in Johannesburg and Pretoria and for the International Geological Congress.

Spencer's later interests centred on meteorites, particularly the origin of tektites. In succeeding G. T. Prior as keeper of minerals in 1927 he continued his predecessor's work on the museum's collection of meteorites. The discovery of silica-glass fragments in meteorite craters at Henbury in central Australia in 1931 and at Wabar in Arabia in 1932 enabled him to study material new to science. Finding meteoritic iron at both locations provided increased support for the still controversial meteoritic origin of Meteor Crater in Arizona. Rare silica glass was found at Wabar, apparently due to the fusion of quartz sand, and at Meteor Crater, due to the fusion of underlying sandstone, providing an argument against a volcanic origin for the craters, as the melting of quartz requires a temperature higher than any known to occur in volcanic processes.

Spencer suspected that vaporization of some terrestrial and meteoritic material had occurred but his calculations of heat generated by the impact of a large, high-velocity meteorite suggested such high temperatures that he thought them absurd, that he had made an error. His mineralogical investigation of silica glass from Wabar revealed that slaggy bombs and small 'black pearls' consisted of snow-white silica glass coated with a thin skin of jet-black silica glass, which he felt were formed by ejection from a pool of molten silica into an atmosphere of silica, iron, and nickel vapours. Proof was later provided by the microscope, which showed that the black silica glass contained minute spheres of nickel iron, as many as 1⅓ million per cubic centimetre, caused, Spencer said, by a 'fine drizzle' of vaporized metal. He found support for his 'absurd' figures in an earlier paper by A. C. Gifford which contained a table of energy in calories per gram for meteorites moving at various velocities, indicating the immense amount of energy released on impact by large, high-velocity meteorites. This confirmed his opinion that meteorite craters are explosion craters and that whatever the angle of impact they must be round due to the symmetrical explosive forces. However, he overlooked the fact that relatively small, slow-moving meteorites may strike the earth without generating enough energy to cause explosions. He published nineteen papers dealing with meteorites or meteorite craters and gave evidence of the very high temperatures produced by the impact of large meteorites, drawing comparisons between the known craters on earth and those on the moon.

In 1934, the year he was appointed CBE, and but a year before he retired from the museum, Spencer was asked to join the survey of Egypt expedition to the Libyan desert to investigate the site where P. A. Clayton had discovered masses of yellow silica glass of unknown origin but thought to be connected with meteorites. He was unable to find evidence of meteorite craters and he was forced to return with the problem of the origin of the glass unsolved. Spencer made a major contribution to the field of mineralogical literature and bibliography. He succeeded Henry Miers, a former colleague at the British Museum, as editor of the *Mineralogical Magazine* in 1900, continuing in the role for fifty-five years. He had abstracted papers on mineral chemistry for the Chemical Society since 1894 and reviewed that field for the society's annual *Report on the Progress of Chemistry*. He had already catalogued mineralogical literature for the Royal Society's *Catalogue of Scientific Papers*, fourth series (1884–1900) and for the mineralogy volumes of the *International Catalogue of Scientific Literature* (1900–14) when, in 1920, he volunteered to prepare and edit *Mineralogical Abstracts*, a new publication of the Mineralogical Society. It aimed, in covering the period 1915 onwards, to preserve continuity with the *International Catalogue*. For many years Spencer contributed the bulk of the abstracts himself and compiled all the indexes for twenty volumes; they appeared in two issues in 1895 and 1926. He supplied triennial lists of new mineral names, twenty-one lists in all, and three supplementary lists of British minerals, as well as obituary notices of mineralogists (eight series). He devoted most of his spare time to this work which he continued long after his retirement from the museum. In November 1950 his colleagues at home and abroad contributed articles to an editorial jubilee number of the *Mineralogical Magazine* and a dinner was given in his honour to celebrate fifty years of his editorship. He ceased to edit the magazine and the abstracts in 1955 but lived to see the latter appear in a new format as a joint publication of the British and American mineralogical societies. He continued to write occasional papers and prepare abstracts, particularly on meteorites, almost until the day of his death. His last paper, on meteorites, appeared in *Nature* only a month before he died. As an editor Spencer:

> had a remarkable capacity for attention to every detail of a paper and had a sufficiently good knowledge of many languages [he possessed dictionaries in forty-one] and a good enough memory to enable him to detect every flaw in the spelling or printing of titles. (Tilley, 245)

Although meticulous and exacting in his work, Spencer nevertheless possessed a wicked sense of humour. On receiving a complaint from a neighbour about the visibility of the Spencer bathroom, he replied by dispatching a toy telescope to improve the view further.

Spencer died of a cerebral thrombosis and arteriosclerosis at St James's Hospital, Balham, London, on 14 April 1959. Among his other activities he had been a special constable in the Metropolitan Police from 1915 to 1918. In the academic years 1899–1900 and 1931–2 he was an examiner for the natural science tripos at Cambridge, and in 1907–8 and from 1912 to 1914 an examiner at Durham University. In connection with recording the weights of large diamonds he was partly instrumental in the introduction, in 1914, of the metric carat as the legal unit of weight for precious stones. A token of the high esteem in which he was held was that a zinc phosphate and an iron carbide were named spencerite after him. He always worked extremely long hours and rarely took a holiday; when he did it usually became a collecting trip to some English mines. One outside interest was gardening, in which he would indulge at his cottage at Chobham near Woking in Surrey, where the family would spend weekends. He also owned a motor launch which was kept moored on the Thames near his four-storey house at Albert Bridge.

Spencer wrote two textbooks, *The World's Minerals* (1911) and *A Key to Precious Stones* (1936). He also translated, with his wife's assistance, M. Bauer's *Edelsteinkunde* (1904) and R. Braun's *Das Mineralreich* (1908–12). He contributed the articles on minerals to the *Encyclopaedia Britannica* (eleventh to fourteenth editions) and to Thorpe's *Dictionary of Applied Chemistry*. Spencer's elder daughter established a fund, in memory of her father, to provide travel and research grants to students in the department of mineralogy and petrology at Cambridge.

Robert Sharp and Kathleen Mark

Sources C. E. Tilley, *Memoirs FRS*, 7 (1961), 243–8 • *DNB* • *DSB*, 12.572–3 • *The Times* (16 April 1959), 17 • *WWW* • W. Campbell Smith, *Nature*, 183 (1959), 1564–5 • W. Campbell Smith, 'L. J. Spencer's work at the British Museum', *Mineralogical Magazine and Journal of the Mineralogical Society*, 29 (Dec 1950), 256–70 • J. Phemister, 'Leonard James Spencer, editor 1900–55: an appreciation', *Mineralogical Magazine and Journal of the Mineralogical Society*, 31 (March 1956), 1–4 • W. Campbell Smith, 'Leonard James Spencer', *Mineralogical Magazine and Journal of the Mineralogical Society*, 32 (Sept 1959), 181–4 • private information (2004) • m. cert. • d. cert. • *Kelly's London Directories*

Archives NHM, corresp., diaries, and papers • NRA, priv. coll., scientific and personal corresp. and diaries

Likenesses W. Stoneman, photograph, 1930, NPG • photograph, repro. in Tilley, *Memoirs FRS* • photograph, repro. in W. Campbell Smith, *Mineralogical Magazine and Journal of the Mineralogical Society*, 29 (Dec 1950) • photograph, repro. in W. Campbell Smith, *Mineralogical Magazine and Journal of the Mineralogical Society*, 32 (Sept 1959)

Wealth at death £8592 13*s*. 8*d*.: probate, 22 July 1959, *CGPLA Eng. & Wales*

Spencer [*married name* Barman], **Penelope** (1901–1993), dancer and choreographer, was born on 30 December 1901 at 39 Albert Mansions, Albert Bridge Road, Battersea, London, the daughter of Dr Leonard James *Spencer (1870–1959), mineralogist, then working as an assistant at the British Museum, and his wife, Edith Mary, *née* Close, schoolteacher. Her mother's infant school was attended by the children of Augustus John, George Lambert, and Bertrand Russell, and Penelope Spencer was exposed early to interesting contacts. More of these occurred during her training at the Italia Conti School and, importantly, with the great modern dance pioneer Margaret Morris. Later, her special friends included Constant Lambert, Lord Berners, Rex Whistler, and Oliver Messel.

In 1921 Rutland Boughton engaged Spencer to stage dances for the Glastonbury festival, including some which he incorporated into a new staging of his opera *The Immortal Hour*, brought to London in 1922. From 1922 to 1924 she was principal dancer of the British National Opera Company at Covent Garden, London, and in June 1926 performed there in *The Jewels of the Madonna*. When *Tannhäuser* (act II) was staged at the London Coliseum in June 1923 she created a ballet for a cast of fifty. From 1924 to 1928 she composed dances for plays starring Sybil Thorndike and

Penelope Spencer (1901–1993), by Frank Davis, 1926

worked for Nigel Playfair's Lyric Theatre Hammersmith productions. As a teacher of dance and movement at the Royal College of Music she arranged dances for the first performance of Vaughan Williams's *Hugh the Drover* (July 1924).

Spencer's first success as a recitalist, in 1924, was the solo that was considered her most striking: *Funeral March for the Death of a Rich Aunt*, with theme and music by Berners. This richly ironic piece used movement and mime impressively, and the costume she designed for herself was a lugubrious *mélange* of loose patterned jacket, white trousers, top hat, and outsize black-edged handkerchief. Arnold L. Haskell remarked on her comic range: 'she can show us wit, humour, caricature and the grotesque' (Haskell, *Penelope Spencer*, 14). She could also express lyricism—*Laideronette*, to music from Ravel's *Mother Goose* suite, was an enchanting impression of a young oriental woman bathing in a pool near a pagoda. Both dances were shown on BBC television on 4 February 1932. A third important creation was *Elegiac Blues* to music by Constant Lambert, a tribute to the memory of the exceptional black dancer Florence Mills.

With Hedley Briggs, Spencer appeared in her satirical *Baedeker* (about American tourists in Europe) and the sinister *Parisian Dolls* (about puppets that imitated their owners). They were also associated, in January 1930, in a rare presentation of James Shirley's masque *Cupid and Death*. In the same year, on 19 October, they took part in the first performance of the Camargo Society. For this Spencer developed a work staged for the Royal College of Music in 1927, and now called *A Toothsome Morsel: Scenes from a Dentist's Waiting Room* (with music by Gavin Gordon). The dowager's solo from this, danced by her, was televised by the BBC on 20 February 1933. On 4 December 1932 the Camargo Society presented another of her ballets, *The Infanta's Birthday*, based on Oscar Wilde's story. This had music by Elisabeth Lutyens, and designs by Rex Whistler (his first for the stage), and was also initially choreographed for the Royal College of Music.

On 8 March 1930 Spencer married Harry Lowis Barman (1901/2–1972), engineer, later a director of Rolls Royce, the son of Harry Drummond Dawson Barman, gentleman. The demands of a husband and later of three sons led her to retire from the theatre, although she later taught mime for the Royal Academy of Dancing. In an obituary in the academy's *Dance Gazette*, Clement Crisp wrote: 'An old dance injury was to make her increasingly immobile but her humour, her gentleness, her modesty—she never felt that she had "done very much"—remained unaltered and inspiring'. She died of bronchopneumonia at Knowle Park Nursing Home, Knowle Lane, Cranleigh, Surrey, on 3 October 1993. She was survived by her three sons, her husband having predeceased her in 1972.

Evaluating a stage artist of the 1920s means relying on the facts of a career and the comments of contemporary writers. Penelope Spencer's important contribution to British dance cannot be studied on video, and relatively few people can recall her choreography or her performances. The evidence, however, makes it abundantly plain that hers was a valuable talent employed outside the mainstream of classical ballet or central European modern dance. Haskell classified her as 'the most interesting of all our English non-ballet dancers … the greatest of her type I have yet seen in any country' (Haskell, *Penelope Spencer*, 11–12). Spencer holds a unique place in British dance history. Most dancers of the time worked in opera, drama, and revues, and some of them had the classical ballet skills that she largely lacked; but she was outstanding for possessing histrionic magnetism, and for being able to dance and choreograph with imagination and variety in her own freestyle terms. She also had a lucid and ably considered approach to dance composition. In *Dancing Times* (November 1929) she analysed the structure of a dance—original idea, opening section, development of themes, and a conclusion 'drawing all the threads together and ending on a definite and interesting note'. One comment is even more relevant now than it was then:

> So many dancers are occupied exclusively by their technique, they seem to think that technical perfection and the ability to follow a producer is their goal in dancing, forgetting that their dance language is not an end in itself but the medium for the expression of ideas, the opening to a new world. (Spencer, 146)

KATHRINE SORLEY WALKER

Sources A. L. Haskell, *Penelope Spencer, creative artist, and other studies* (1930) · P. Spencer, 'Dance composition', *Dancing Times* (Nov 1929), 146–7, 159 · A. L. Haskell, 'Further studies in ballet (Penelope Spencer)', *Dancing Times* (Feb 1930), 574–6 · *The Times* (7 Oct 1993) · *Daily Telegraph* (14 Oct 1993) · *The Independent* (12 Oct 1993) · *Dance Gazette*, 1 (1994), 8 · *Dancing Times* (Nov 1993), 141 · b. cert. · m. cert. ·

d. cert. • M. Hurd, *The immortal hour: the life and times of Rutland Boughton* (1962) • R. Boughton, *The self-advertisement of Rutland Boughton* (privately printed, 1909)

Likenesses F. Davis, photograph, 1926, Theatre Museum, London [*see illus.*] • H. Lambert, woodcut, repro. in *The Independent* • photograph, repro. in *Dancing Times* (June 1922), title page, 757 • photograph, repro. in *Dancing Times* (June 1923), 895 • photograph, repro. in *Dancing Times* (March 1924), 578 • photograph, repro. in *Dancing Times* (June 1926), 236 • photograph, repro. in *Dancing Times* (July 1926), 393 • photograph, repro. in *Dancing Times* (April 1927), 246 • photograph, repro. in *Dancing Times* (Sept 1927), 602 • photograph, repro. in *Dancing Times* (Jan 1929), 535 • photograph, repro. in *Dancing Times* (Aug 1929), 435 • photograph, repro. in *Dancing Times* (Nov 1929), 147 • photograph, repro. in *Dancing Times* (Feb 1930), 575 • photograph, repro. in *Dancing Times* (May 1930), 140 • photographs, repro. in Haskell, *Penelope Spencer*, facing pp. 8, 12, 14, 20 • woodcut, repro. in *The Times*

Wealth at death £160,692: probate, 1994, *CGPLA Eng. & Wales*

Spencer, Robert, first Baron Spencer (1570–1627), politician and sheep farmer, was the son of Sir John Spencer (*c.*1545–1600) of Althorp, Northamptonshire, and his wife, Mary Catlin (*d.* 1621), daughter of Sir Robert *Catlin. He was educated at Oxford University and on 15 February 1588 married Margaret (*c.*1570–1597), daughter of Sir Francis *Willoughby of Wollaton, Nottinghamshire. He was knighted in 1601 and created Baron Spencer of Wormleighton on 21 July 1603. He sat as MP for Brackley in 1597 and was a justice of the peace and musters commissioner for Northamptonshire from about 1601.

The Spencer family's fortunes were founded in the early sixteenth century by Robert's great-great-grandfather Sir John Spencer, who made large profits out of sheep farming in south-west Warwickshire. He was able to purchase two blocks of manors centred on Wormleighton in Warwickshire and Althorp in Northamptonshire which were to remain the family's principal residences. By the time Robert inherited the estate from his father in 1600 it had expanded considerably as a result of advantageous marriages and growing income from the carefully managed sheep flocks. He continued the family tradition and remained first and foremost a sheep farmer. At the time when he received his baronage, he was 'reputed to have by him the most money of any person in the kingdom' (Finch, 38), which presumably referred to reserves of ready money at his disposal. His income was between £6500 and £8000 a year, but there were several contemporary landowners wealthier than him.

Like other landed families whose wealth had been acquired recently, the Spencers were anxious to present themselves as long established. In 1595 Robert's father acquired a pedigree from the College of Arms which traced their descent back to the Despensers, earls of Gloucester and Winchester. This did not impress some members of the ancient peerage, however, and during the 1621 parliament Spencer's origins were denigrated by the earl of Arundel, who recalled that his own ancestors had suffered 'for doing the king and country good service, and in such time as when perhaps the lord's ancestors that spake last kept sheep' (Gardiner, 4.114). The insult was prompted by Spencer's challenging Arundel over Sir Henry Yelverton's right to a hearing in the Lords, after Yelverton had implicitly compared the duke of Buckingham to Edward II's favourite, Hugh Despenser. Arundel argued that he had said enough to warrant condemnation, but Spencer—who must have been acquainted with Yelverton, a fellow Northamptonshire landowner and recorder of Northampton—urged that he be allowed to explain himself. Arundel refused to apologize for the insult and was confined to the Tower.

This speech was Spencer's most significant intervention in parliament and did much to confirm his image among contemporaries as a 'patriot' peer. Arthur Wilson, writing in the 1650s, described him as someone who:

> made the countrie a vertuous court where his fields and flocks brought him more calm and happy contentment than the various and mutable dispensations of a court can contribute; and when he was called to the Senate was more vigilant to keep the people's liberties from being prey to the incroaching power of monarchy than his harmless and tender lambs from foxes and ravenous creatures. (Wilson, 162–3)

Spencer's record in national politics generally bears out Wilson's verdict. In 1603, soon after he was made a peer, a career at court beckoned when he was sent to Germany as ambassador to invest the duke of Württemberg with the Order of the Garter, but nothing came of this. In the Lords he was not a prominent speaker, but he attended assiduously and in his speeches generally supported 'country' causes. In 1621 he urged that the recusancy statutes be vigorously enforced and that the notorious monopolist Sir Giles Mompesson be openly indicted; in 1624 he proposed that Lord Treasurer Cranfield's estates be made liable for the damages he had incurred; and in 1626 he drew attention to criticisms of Buckingham's performance as lord admiral. Where Spencer made his greatest mark, however, was in the local politics of Northamptonshire.

Spencer's wealth, prestige, and extensive landholdings made him the most influential figure in the western half of the county, if not in the shire as a whole. He used this to good effect in parliamentary elections. In 1603 he campaigned for county seats for himself and Sir Edward Montagu (later first Baron Montagu of Boughton), against opposition from Sir Anthony Mildmay, and seems to have been more or less assured of election at the point when he was granted his peerage. In the election of 1624 he succeeded in overturning the convention that one knight be chosen from each half of the shire by securing election for his puritan friend Richard Knightley, and his son Sir William Spencer. The reason he gave for this to Montagu—that 'the papists will work hard in this parliament' and it was therefore necessary to support candidates who would staunchly oppose them (*Montagu of Beaulieu MSS*, 106)—revealed much about his political priorities. In the election of 1626 he again clashed with Montagu and the magnates in the east of the shire and again came out on top, using his influence to help secure the election of another puritan, Sir John Pickering. Later in the year he made perhaps his most significant intervention in local politics by resisting the forced loan. During November it was widely reported that he was refusing to co-operate with the levy, along with fifteen other peers, including two of his closest friends, the Leicestershire magnates Henry, Lord Grey of Groby, and Henry Hastings, fifth earl of Huntingdon. He probably shared the views of his son Sir William, who early in 1626 was alleged to have declared at a meeting of the deputy lieutenants that 'the king wanted no money, and if he did he might call a parliament' (BL, Spencer MS A2). His defiance went unpunished and set an example for widespread refusal of the loan in Northamptonshire early in 1627.

Such evidence of his religious views as survives suggests that Spencer was a staunch Calvinist, although rather less zealous than someone like his friend Knightley. He was described in his funeral sermon, by the Calvinist Richard Parre, as one of 'God's Saints' and was praised for 'the great encouragement and countenance he gave to the ministers of God' (Parre, 21–2). When account is taken of the extent of his patronage, his support of godly ministers was not in fact as conspicuous as it might have been. Nevertheless, as his interventions in county elections demonstrated, there was little doubt that he broadly aligned himself with the godly.

In other respects, too, Spencer sought to present himself as the archetypal country peer. According to Parre he was renowned for his 'careful frugality'. He did not get caught up in the Jacobean fashion for showy building projects, and in 1618 turned down an earldom when it was offered to him for £10,000. His hospitality was said to be bountiful but not ostentatious, something borne out by his household accounts. He also had a reputation for generously helping the poor, and as a wise master to his tenants and servants and a trusted arbiter of local disputes. When Grey and Huntingdon became locked in a quarrel in the early part of James's reign he intervened to mediate between them. Finally he shared the contemporary passion for genealogy, corresponding with William Camden about tracing his family tree and earning a tribute for his 'singular … skill in antiquities, arms, alliances' (Parre, 24). His funeral elegy described him as 'the pattern of a perfect man' (*The Muses Thankfulness*).

Spencer did not marry again after his wife, Margaret, died in August 1597 leaving him with four sons and three daughters. He died at Wormleighton on 25 October 1627 and his body was taken back to the family chapel at Great Brington, Northamptonshire, where he was buried on 6 November next to the monument he had erected to his wife. He was succeeded by his second, and eldest surviving, son, Sir William. RICHARD CUST

Sources HoP, *Commons, 1558–1603*, 3.426–7 • M. E. Finch, *The wealth of five Northamptonshire families, 1540–1640*, Northamptonshire RS, 19 (1956), 38–65 • R. Parre, *The end of the perfect man: a sermon preached at the buriall of the Right Honorable Sir Robert Spencer* (1628) • *The muses thankfulness, or, A funerall elegie consecrated to the memory of Robert Baron Spencer* (1627) • A. Wilson, *The history of Great Britain: being the life and reign of King James the First* (1653) • BL, Spencer MSS, Add. MS 25079 • *Report on the manuscripts of his grace the duke of Buccleuch and Queensberry … preserved at Montagu House*, 3 vols. in 4, HMC, 45 (1899–1926), vols. 1 and 3 • *Report on the manuscripts of Lord Montagu of Beaulieu*, HMC, 53 (1900) • F. H. Relf, ed., *Notes of the debates in the House of Lords … AD 1621, 1625, 1628*, CS, 3rd ser., 42 (1929) • W. B. Bidwell and M. Jansson, eds., *Proceedings in parliament, 1626*, 1: *House of Lords* (1991) • S. R. Gardiner, *History of England from the accession of James I to the outbreak of the civil war*, new edn, 10 vols. (1904–9) • A. E. J. Spencer, seventh Earl Spencer, 'Lord Spencer's Garter embassy to the duke of Württemberg in 1603', *Northamptonshire Past and Present*, 1/2 (1949), 1–11 • P. Norman and W. D. Caröe, *Crosby Place* (1908)

Archives BL, corresp., papers, and household accounts, Add. MSS 25079–25082 | BL, corresp. with Sir T. Tresham, Add. MS 39829 • BL, papers relating to his mission to duke of Württemberg • Northants. RO, Montagu MSS

Likenesses M. Gheeraerts, oils, Althorp, Northamptonshire; repro. in Finch, *Wealth*, 19 • funeral monument, Great Brington church, Northamptonshire • miniature, Althorp, Northamptonshire

Wealth at death £6500–£8000—income p.a.: Finch, *Wealth of five Northamptonshire families*

Spencer, Robert, second earl of Sunderland (1641–1702), politician, son of Henry *Spencer, third Baron Spencer (*bap.* 1620, *d.* 1643), and his wife, Lady Dorothy Sydney (1617–1684), daughter of the earl of Leicester, was born in Paris on 5 September 1641 'and was christened Robert after his grandfather Leicester' (Kenyon, *Sunderland*, 2). Two years after his birth his father was made earl of Sunderland by Charles I, only to die fighting for the king at Newbury in September. Robert therefore succeeded to the earldom as an infant, which was to mean that, unlike many politicians of the period, he never served as a member of the House of Commons.

Marriage and early career Sunderland's widowed mother brought him up as a staunch Anglican, employing an ejected fellow of Magdalen College, Oxford, Thomas Pierce, as his tutor. After going together to the continent in 1658 they returned in 1660 when Pierce was restored to his fellowship at Magdalen. Robert possibly accompanied him there as a student, for he was associated with the protest William Penn made at Christ Church against the wearing of the surplice. Certainly he accompanied Penn on a visit to France in 1661. Apart from a brief visit home in 1663 he remained on the continent until April 1665, spending time in Spain, Switzerland, and Italy as well as in France. His interlude in England was spent courting Lady Anne Digby (1645/6–1715), younger daughter of George *Digby, earl of Bristol, with whom a marriage was arranged that summer. At the last moment, however, the groom panicked and fled abroad. By the time he got back to England his mind was made up, and he married Lady Anne on 9 June 1665. When they settled at Althorp, their seat in Northamptonshire, they virtually rebuilt it and used it for glittering social gatherings. Among those they entertained were prominent courtiers and politicians, including the dukes of York and Monmouth. This lavish lifestyle, and Robert's penchant for the gaming table, where he gambled for sums as big as £5000 a night, ran them into debt.

It also brought them into the world of high politics, with which their families were naturally connected. Sunderland and his countess were related to several leading figures, including Algernon *Sidney and Henry *Sidney, who were his uncles, George *Savile, earl of Halifax, who became his brother-in-law, and the Russells, earls of Bedford, of whom the fourth was the countess's maternal

Robert Spencer, second earl of Sunderland (1641–1702), by Sir Peter Lely, 1666?

grandfather. The most political animal in late Stuart England, Robert Spencer was attracted into this world soon after his marriage, when he attached himself to the earl of Arlington, a friend of his wife's family. As long as the first earl of Clarendon was in power Arlington's influence was not an asset which could further his career, since the secretary of state led those who sought to remove the leading minister. After he succeeded in that task in 1667, however, his protégé could be advanced. In 1668 Arlington began to seek for Sunderland a diplomatic post, the usual appointment for an apprentice courtier. In June 1670, following the conclusion of the secret treaty of Dover, Sunderland went to France to convey Charles II's compliments to Louis XIV. Next year he went as envoy-extraordinary to Madrid, briefed with the task of preventing an alliance between the Dutch and the Spanish against the French. Although this was a useful experience of diplomacy it got nowhere, and Sunderland was relieved to be transferred to Paris from Madrid in May 1672. There he replaced Ralph Montagu as English ambassador. After spending time, and money, in Paris to little purpose Sunderland complained that the embassy was costing him too much. Although his complaints brought some financial relief from the Treasury, he was again relieved when, in March 1673, he received instructions to go as envoy to the Congress of Cologne. He never got there, however, being prevented by illness, which led him to ask to be discharged from his official duties, and to return to England in September.

Shortly after his return Sunderland was made gentleman of the bedchamber with a salary of £1000, though this was never paid in full. For an ambitious and spendthrift politician neither the post nor the salary could be satisfactory. Now that his patron, Arlington, had fallen from favour Sunderland looked round for another, and found one in the king's new mistress, Louise de Kerouaille, duchess of Portsmouth. 'As I have always found your Lordship knew her better than any,' observed Danby in 1679, 'so I found that nobody knew so well how to manage her' (Kenyon, *Sunderland*, 18n.). His ability to manage her got him noticed not only by Danby but also by the king. Charles II used Sunderland as a go-between with the duchess in 1675 when he recognized her son as his and ennobled the child as duke of Richmond. In April 1677 and again in July 1678 Sunderland was employed as an envoy to Louis XIV. Though he failed to persuade the French king to renew his alliance with England, his diplomatic activities apparently impressed Charles II, for in February 1679 Sunderland became secretary of state.

Court politician Sunderland's appointment placed him at the forefront of affairs. John Dryden recognized this when he dedicated his play *Troilus and Cressida* to the new 'principall Secretary of State'. The playwright claimed that he could:

> say without flattery [that] he had all the depth of understanding that was requisite in any able statesman, and all that honesty which commonly is wanting; that he was brave without vanity, and knowing without positiveness; that he was loyall to his Prince and a lover of his Country; and his principles were full of moderation, and all his Councils such as tended to heal and not to widen the breaches of the Nation. (*Works of John Dryden*, 13.220–21)

This was of course, despite Dryden's disclaimer, the grossest court flattery. Sunderland was more renowned for his hypocrisy than for his honesty, while so far were his principles 'full of moderation' that, as his biographer puts it, he 'was nothing if not a man of extremes' (Kenyon, *Sunderland*, 332). He was an arrogant, cynical, hard-nosed politician, whose irascibility frequently wounded those who felt the lash of his tongue. 'He wanted not this farther quality to make him universally odious', commented Arthur Onslow (*Bishop Burnet's History*, 4.412n.). Bishop Burnet agreed that 'he raised many enemies to himself by the contempt with which he treated those who differed from him' (ibid., 2.18) yet acknowledged that 'he had indeed the superior genius to all the men of business that I have yet known' (ibid.). By this he meant a genius for appreciating the big picture rather than for taking pains. For Sunderland was a poor administrator, impatient of detailed application, which he left to subordinates. A hostile observer, of whom there were many, claimed to have been told by one of his underlings that 'he never came to the secretary's office, but they carried the papers to him at his house, where he was usually at cards, and he would sign them without reading, and seldom asked what they were about' (ibid.). Yet even his opponents admired the intellect of the 'Proteus Sunderland':

> The deep Reserves of whose Apostate Mind,
> No Skill can reach, no Principles can bind;

Whose working Brain does more Disguises bear
Than ever yet in Vision did appear.
('Advice to a painter', Lord and others, 18)

Sunderland was 'at the helm', as Dryden put it, for the greatest crisis following the Restoration. The Danby ministry had collapsed under pressure from a country party which accused the minister of systematic bribery and corruption in order to create a court party to pursue policies inimical to England's interests. In particular it charged him with encouraging popery and arbitrary power by aligning England with France. The prospects of the accession of James after the death of his brother, Charles, however, had transcended concerns about Danby's policies following the outbreak of the Popish Plot in 1678. This raised the whole question of the succession of the Catholic duke, and brought on a campaign to exclude him from the throne. The first Exclusion Bill was to be introduced into parliament following the general election, which was under way when Sunderland was appointed secretary. Charles was so concerned at the threat it posed that he sent his brother out of the country to Brussels.

Sunderland played a major role in other moves made by the king to stave off the crisis. Thus he negotiated with leading opponents of the court a deal which led to the formation of a new privy council including them. Although the scheme was the idea of Sir William Temple, to whom it is usually attributed, Sunderland was responsible for its detailed implementation. His first involvement in high politics was to bring dissident elements, including Shaftesbury, leader of the first whigs, into government in an attempt to buy them off. Although this scheme failed to resolve the exclusion crisis, it gave Sunderland valuable experience in wheeling and dealing with politicians ostensibly opposed to the court. It was of these negotiations that Roger North recorded a curious anecdote about Sunderland's affecting a 'court tune': 'Whaat, my laard, if his Majesty taarn out faarty of us, may not he have faarty athors to saarve him as well? And what maatters who saarves his Majesty, so lang as his Majesty is saarved?' (*DNB*). North used the story to illustrate an affectation of Sunderland's which he claimed was adopted by others at court. It also records a very revealing maxim of Sunderland's, who clearly did not think it mattered who served the king as long as the king was served. It was one he was to apply not only to the circumstances of the exclusion crisis but to other political crises in the next two reigns.

Over the summer of 1679 Sunderland was associated with the earls of Essex and Halifax in a so-called triumvirate. They tried to sell to the whigs an idea of the king's to obviate exclusion. This was a scheme of limitations, whereby a Catholic successor would have to uphold the Church of England and work with parliament. James himself, who thought the whole whig campaign aimed ultimately at a republic, disliked limitations even more than the Exclusion Bill, arguing that they would transform the monarchy into a quasi-republic under the titular kingship of the duke of Monmouth, Charles II's illegitimate son. When the idea failed to stop the Exclusion Bill in its tracks Charles prorogued parliament. Sunderland then persuaded him to dissolve it and hold fresh elections. When the privy council met to discuss this decision on 10 July, Shaftesbury and his cohorts angrily criticized those responsible for it. The dissolution put a strain on the coalition scheme, but it was the return of James from exile in Brussels that September which brought about its collapse.

Sunderland invited the duke back because the king had become dangerously ill. Although on his recovery Charles ordered his brother to remove himself again, this time to Scotland, he also sent Monmouth out of the country and dismissed Shaftesbury. James was furious at being exiled in Edinburgh, and accused Sunderland of failing to fulfil a promise that he should stay in England. He was prepared to attribute this to inexperience rather than treachery, telling the French ambassador 'that Lord Sunderland, being new to politics, found himself in difficulties, and he lacked the boldness so necessary in these difficult times' (Kenyon, *Sunderland*, 32). He nevertheless ensured that Sunderland's influence in the ministry would be counterbalanced by that of his own protégé Laurence Hyde, who became first lord of the Treasury in November. Hyde was no more experienced in office than Sunderland. Indeed so green were they and their colleague Sidney Godolphin, with whom they formed the ministry, that they were known as 'the Chits'. Throughout 1680 the ministry laboured to try to offset the results of the parliamentary elections, which had gone again in favour of the exclusionists. They persuaded the king to keep proroguing parliament to avoid an early meeting which would play into the hands of the whigs. This was not mere procrastination as they also made efforts to bring moderate members of both houses to accept the court line.

Sunderland's role in this strategy was to espouse an anti-French foreign policy, reversing his previous reliance on France and making a treaty with Spain. He even hoped that William of Orange could be persuaded to come to England before parliament met in order to demonstrate the court's commitment to an eventual protestant succession. In June 1680 the Chits held a conference at Sunderland's country house, at which they negotiated a deal with Halifax to lay before the houses when they met. Not only was William to be invited over but a scheme of limitations on a popish successor was to be proposed. When William refused to accept an invitation unless it was issued by the king, Charles obliged and sent one over to the Netherlands. Sunderland sent three letters about this on the same day, 21 July, to his uncle Henry Sidney at The Hague. These document the degree to which he was acting deviously in that tense summer. The first, known only to himself and his close colleague Godolphin, stressed that they alone knew 'the best reasons for this journey', whose aim was to ensure that 'the King and his People must agree at their next meeting, and the King is convinced of it'. As the architect of the new alignment of England with Spain and the Dutch republic against France, Sunderland stressed that the most important point of the imminent session of parliament was to get it 'to support the alliances the King has made for which it will be necessary to let them see that the thing is in earnest that those most concerned think so'. The most concerned, of course, was the prince of Orange. His presence was to show the houses the visible embodiment of the new anti-French foreign policy. 'Another great point', Sunderland continued, 'is to settle Religion without meddling with the Succession'. This apparently referred to the limitations which Charles proposed to place on his brother's prerogative when he became king. The prince's presence was presumably to give his blessing to this scheme. He was also intended to mediate between:

> the king and his people, by whose means all Jealousies may be removed either that the King has any intentions but what are for the good of the people or they any but to support the Government and religion now established. (Kenyon, 'Charles II', 99, 101)

The meaning of many passages in these letters is cryptic, partly because the context in which they were written, and which Sunderland assumed Sidney was aware of, cannot now be reconstructed, and partly because they were meant to be. But it seems that Sunderland wanted William to reconcile Charles with the whigs by showing that the king was not a supporter of popery and arbitrary power, while they were not crypto-republicans intent on making Monmouth a puppet king.

It was Sunderland's determination to demonstrate his commitment to William and to dish whig support for Monmouth which apparently lay behind his otherwise inexplicable decision to support the second Exclusion Bill. For on the face of things it was to commit political suicide. The king had made it clear on more than one occasion that he would not stand for any alteration in the succession. Though he was persuaded by the privy council, led by Sunderland, to send his brother to Scotland on the eve of the parliamentary session, he did so with an ill grace, and again reiterated that he would not assent to exclusion. The whigs nevertheless eschewed limitations and introduced an exclusion bill in the new parliament. When the bill was first debated in the Commons on 6 November it did not name a successor. But in committee a clause was added to it to provide that the crown should descend as though James had died, which ensured the succession of William's wife, Mary, and scotched Monmouth's chances. Although it cannot be documented it can be deduced that Sunderland had worked hard behind the scenes to carry this clause. He apparently agreed with his uncle Henry Sidney that James 'would never inherit the Crown … and if the succession is not settled somewhere, it will certainly turn to a Commonwealth' (*Diary of … Sidney*, 2.129). When the bill went up to the House of Lords, therefore, Sunderland was committed to its passage despite the king's disapproval. As he put it to Temple, who tried to dissuade him, ''twas too late, his honour was engaged, and he could not break it' (Kenyon, *Sunderland*, 64). Sunderland duly voted with the minority when the bill was thrown out. The king, who was present in the house, observed that his speech in support of the bill was 'the kiss of Judas' (ibid., 66). Charles marked the secretary down for destruction, but waited until he dissolved parliament on 18 January 1681 before dismissing him on the 24th. Sunderland was mortified, though he went to the third Exclusion Parliament at Oxford 'with as good resolutions as if my usage had been contrary to what it was' (*Diary of … Sidney*, 2.180).

Within two years Sunderland was restored to favour. On 27 July 1682 he was allowed an audience by the king, when he kissed hands. In September he was readmitted to the privy council and on 31 January 1683 he again became secretary of state. This was the first of two returns to power which gave him the reputation of being the indispensable courtier, twice bounding back to the centre of politics after a disgrace. His redemption after being an exclusionist, however, was less spectacular a feat than his becoming the principal adviser to William III, after serving James II in the same capacity. Supporting exclusion could be forgiven even by Charles II, who allowed Godolphin to remain at the Treasury despite his also voting for the second bill. Admittedly the king excused him on the grounds that he had been misled by Sunderland. But if Sunderland's sin was unforgivable by Charles at the time, it was a lesser offence to James than support of limitations. Halifax, the architect of the defeat of the bill in the upper house, was paradoxically less appealing to James because he advocated limitations, even to the point of suggesting the duke's permanent exile in Scotland unless he converted to Anglicanism. When Sunderland cynically justified his vote on the grounds that the bill was bound to fail anyway, and that the alternative was to limit the prerogative, James was prepared to overlook his disloyalty and support his return to office. It was also supported by the duchess of Portsmouth, whose influence with the king had never been greater.

His acceptance at court meant that Sunderland was identified with the reaction which set in against the whigs. Although he took little part in the proceedings against them, he nevertheless acquiesced in the trials and executions of the Rye House plotters. These included his wife's cousin, Lord William Russell, and his uncle Algernon Sidney, whose death apparently hastened that of his own mother in 1684. This break with former political allies extended to the prince of Orange. When William saw Sunderland after his disgrace in 1681 he expressed appreciation of the earl's efforts on his behalf. On becoming secretary of state, however, Sunderland fell in with the court's rapprochement with France, reversing his previous pro-Dutch foreign policy. Thus along with the French he backed the Danes in their quarrel with the Dutch, a policy which led to the marriage of Princess Anne, James's younger daughter, to Prince George of Denmark in July 1683.

Sunderland's willingness to fall in with measures of the court he had not supported when in office inevitably makes his motives appear cynical. It could even seem that he missed the emoluments of office at a time when his extravagant social life was running him ever deeper into debt. At the time of his dismissal he had mortgaged estates in two counties to raise the collateral for debts of £16,000. His wife complained 'we are on the point of ruin' (*Diary of … Sidney*, 2.185). Yet Sunderland was not in politics for the money. Had he embarked on a political career in order to enjoy its financial rewards he would have made survival a top priority. In fact he was in it for power, and he was prepared to gamble as recklessly in politics as he was at the gaming table. He had staked a lot on the last throw of the dice and had lost. Now he was back at the court casino he was determined to recoup his losses.

In order to do so Sunderland had to beat a formidable rival, Laurence Hyde, now the earl of Rochester. As first lord of the Treasury, Rochester was high in the king's favour for presiding over a significant improvement in the royal finances, which helped Charles manage without parliament. He was also the confidant of the duke of York, and when James returned from Scotland worked closely with him on the commission for ecclesiastical promotions. At first Sunderland ingratiated himself with his rival, claiming the 'realest friendship imaginable' (*Correspondence of … Clarendon*, 1.87). But when the first lord fell foul of the king, following accusations of peculation in the management of the hearth tax, Sunderland distanced himself from him and helped to manoeuvre Rochester out of the Treasury into the post of lord president in August 1684. Godolphin, Sunderland's closest colleague, succeeded as first lord. The following month Judge Jeffreys, whose appointment as lord chief justice Sunderland had procured, was admitted to the cabinet council. In the closing weeks of Charles II's reign, therefore, Sunderland came close to being the chief minister.

Then, in February 1685, Charles II suddenly died. Once again Sunderland had gambled and lost. Like many politicians of the day he assumed that the king would outlive his brother. He had gone along with Charles when he cooled towards James, even being implicated in the rumours that Monmouth was to be rehabilitated at court. He thus found himself wrong-footed at the outset of the new reign, and had to do some nimble footwork to earn the approval of James II. It seems that his preparations for the elections to parliament found favour with the king, especially when they contributed to the return of the most loyal House of Commons ever to sit under the Stuarts. Whatever the reason, Sunderland was retained in the office of secretary of state.

Agent of absolutism Perhaps the main reason why Sunderland survived the crisis of James II's accession and remained at the very centre of his affairs until just before the revolution was that he was more sympathetic to the king's religious aims than other close advisers such as Rochester. Anglican tories were devoted to the hereditary succession and the Church of England, a devotion which would put intolerable pressure on them when they had to choose one or the other. Most chose the church. Sunderland, who had no strong religious beliefs, and was certainly not a staunch Anglican, felt no such dilemma. His loyalty was to the crown. As Bonrepos, a French envoy, observed:

> the King is well aware of Lord Sunderland's character, that he is ambitious and capable of any sacrifice for ambition's sake; but though he has no great confidence in him he makes use of him, because he is more devoted to him than others and because he unhesitatingly falls in with all his plans for the establishment of the Catholic religion—though for himself he professes no faith at all and speaks very loosely about it. (Kenyon, *Sunderland*, 155)

Realizing that the king's attempt to obtain relief for his co-religionists from Anglicans was doomed to failure, he cultivated the Catholics at court. These were divided. Moderate Catholics, like Lord Belasyse, worried that James's zeal would cause a backlash when he died, and his protestant daughter, Mary, and her husband, William of Orange, would succeed. Extreme Catholics, like Father Petre and Tyrconnell, were prepared to push the drive to Rome as fast as they could. Sunderland, perhaps realizing that the latter were more appealing to the king, threw in his lot with them. Thus early in the reign he made approaches to the earl of Tyrconnell and Father Petre. Above all he insinuated himself into the favour of the queen, Mary of Modena. 'The Queen was artificially possessed by this lord' maintained Sir John Reresby:

> that the relations and friends of the King's first wife were in greatest favour, and had the best places, as Rochester, Clarendon, Dartmoth etc., whilst her friends, that was Queen Regent, had none soe considerable, of which nomber were reckned Lord Sunderland, Lord Chancellor, Lord Churchill etc. (*Memoirs of Sir John Reresby*, 401)

Ultimately Sunderland's cabal was to triumph over James's Anglican tory ministers, led by the king's Hyde brothers-in-law, the earls of Rochester and Clarendon. Rochester used the king's mistress, Catherine Sedley, as a counterpoise to the queen. Although it was to take him nearly two years to remove his rivals, Sunderland showed that in the end he had backed the right horse.

Over the summer of 1685 Sunderland entrenched himself in power. He presided over the suppression of Monmouth's rebellion and rewarded Jeffreys, the judge responsible for the brutal aftermath, by persuading the king to appoint him as lord chancellor. In October a dangerous rival, Halifax, was removed when James dismissed him for refusing to support the repeal of the Test and Habeas Corpus Acts. Sunderland was appointed to the post of lord president made vacant by Halifax's dismissal, a position he held together with the secretaryship. The only serious rival to Sunderland's ascendancy at the end of 1685 was the lord treasurer, Rochester. Although it was to take Sunderland another year to see him off, Rochester dated his decline and fall from the prorogation of parliament that November for not endorsing the commissions given to Catholics by the king, using his prerogative to dispense them from the Test Act. Rochester apparently disapproved of the dispensing power being used for that purpose. While Sunderland later insisted that he too objected to the practice, he does not appear to have registered his objections at the time. Nor does he seem to have done so with regard to the commission for ecclesiastical causes set up in 1686, on which he and Rochester sat, himself apparently accepting its legality, while his rival made clear his unease. It would have been a curious gnat to strain at when that summer Sunderland swallowed the camel of conversion to Catholicism. He finally undermined Rochester's credibility with the king by inducing James to attempt the treasurer's conversion too. Rochester responded by agreeing to hear a disputation between Anglican and Catholic divines, but when he declared that he had not been persuaded by the latter his days at the Treasury were numbered, and he was dismissed in January 1687. Meanwhile Sunderland had engineered the removal of Rochester's brother Clarendon from the lord lieutenancy of Ireland, and his replacement as lord deputy by the Catholic earl of Tyrconnell.

The breach with the Hydes shifted the balance of power in James's counsels from the Anglicans to the Catholics. Thus the Treasury was put into commission headed by the Roman Catholic peer Lord Belasyse, though the effective business was done by Sunderland's ally Godolphin. Although Sunderland's conversion had not yet been made public, the announcement by his eldest son, Robert, in April 1687 that he had converted to Rome helped to keep him well in with Catholic ministers. At the same time Sunderland was aware that a government which rested solely on Catholic support was too narrowly based to be viable. Having broken with the Anglicans he advised the king to make a conciliatory gesture to protestant dissenters. This was a difficult policy to advocate since James was convinced that most nonconformists were republicans who would disturb the peace of his kingdom. Sunderland had to persuade him that some at least would co-operate with the regime. James had already made an exception of the Quakers, doubtless because he accepted that as pacifists they were scarcely likely to rebel. Thus in 1686 he had released many from gaol, and had sent the Quaker leader, William Penn, to The Hague, but the mission was abortive. The prince and princess would agree to toleration, even for Catholics, but not to doing away with the Test Act. Sunderland capitalized on this concession by persuading the king to make his old acquaintance Penn deputy lieutenant in Buckinghamshire in November. Thus even before the dismissal of the Hydes there were signs of a rapprochement with dissenters. Sunderland was aware that they suffered along with the Catholics from the penal laws and Test Act. He therefore sought to consolidate the alliance with them by pursuing the goal of relieving them from the oppressive statutes.

Given the intransigence of the Anglicans in parliament to this measure Sunderland declined to advise the reconvening of that body, although he did string James along with the hope that they could be persuaded to change their minds. He did not, however, approve of the king's policy of closeting members. As he himself put it, 'who was to get by closeting I need not say, but it was certainly not I, nor any of my friends' (*Diary of … Sidney*, 2.374–5). Nor did he support James's interference in the election of a president of Magdalen College, Oxford. His intervention in that business, which dragged on from April 1687 to the end of the year, was an exercise in damage limitation. Despite these disagreements with James the king still held him in high esteem, installing him as a knight of the Garter in May. This was perhaps because he did approve the king's declaration of indulgence or edict of toleration in April 1687. This concession suspended the penal laws against protestant nonconformists and Catholics alike. Aware that a principal objection to an edict as distinct from a statute was that it depended on the will of the king who issued it, and could be revoked by his successor, Sunderland sought to assuage dissenting scruples on that score by trying to get the heirs apparent, William and his wife, Mary, to agree to support the king in his repudiation of the acts when they came to the throne. To this end he pleaded with the Dutch envoy Dykvelt, but got no further than Penn had done the year before.

The failure to persuade William and Mary to acquiesce in the king's proposals for religious toleration temporarily lost Sunderland credit at court. He found himself outmanoeuvred by Catholic advisers, who urged James that the only way forward was to dissolve the parliament and to take steps to pack another with members who would support the repeal of the penal laws and Test Act. Sunderland was appalled by this strategy. He was more aware than his Catholic colleagues how damaging a dissolution would be to England's foreign relations. He also was less sanguine, and more realistic, about the prospects of packing a parliament to the extent that would be required. Consequently he held up the decision to dissolve for several weeks, and absented himself from the meeting of the privy council in July which took it. By the end of the month, however, he was back at court. He seems to have decided that, since parliament had been dissolved, then, despite the auspices being unfavourable, everything should be done to try to ensure that a general election would result in a House of Commons more inclined to do the king's bidding.

Sunderland's hand can be detected behind the preliminary changes in the lord lieutenancies, and the restoration of whigs to London livery companies from which they had been ousted by Charles II. In August he accompanied the king on an electoral tour of the west country. The result as far as Sunderland was concerned was to confirm him in his view that the prospects for a compliant parliament were bleak. Although some dissenters indicated their support, the bulk of the gentry were lukewarm or even hostile. But the king was convinced that his cause was popular. He even devised a crude public opinion poll, in which three questions were put to the magnates in the localities to test their approval of his policies. These began to be circulated by Sunderland in October, though it was to take months to sound out opinion throughout the country. Meanwhile in November a commission for regulation was established to preside over the purging of corporations, with a view to influencing parliamentary elections. Its work was supervised by Sunderland and his ally Jeffreys, together with Catholic regulators including Father Petre. Sunderland went along with this to the point of approving Father Petre's admission to the privy council in November, to the alarm even of moderate Catholics. Then in December Sunderland assured James that he would make his own conversion public whenever it seemed to be advantageous for the king.

Sunderland's apparent rashness at this point was another calculated gamble. Since the summer he had been concerned that James would not achieve his objectives before he died, and that the king's whole enterprise would collapse, taking him down with it. By December, however, it became known that the queen was pregnant. If she produced a girl, then the effect on the succession would be minimal. But if she gave birth to a boy, he would have precedence over James's daughters with his first wife. In the words of Sunderland's biographer 'he had a fifty-fifty chance: double or quits on the turn of a card' (Kenyon, *Sunderland*, 168).

The campaign to pack parliament led to tensions in the cabinet council early in 1688. James, egged on by the Catholic cabal, was eager to put it to the test of an election as soon as possible. Sunderland, realizing that the outcome would be disastrous, advised postponing the polls as long as possible. In March he persuaded the king to put them off until after the summer. This victory for common sense was soon offset, however, by James's fateful decision, on reissuing the declaration of indulgence in April, to require the clergy to read it from their pulpits: 'of which I most solemnly protest', Sunderland claimed later, 'I never heard one word till the King directed it in Council' (*Diary of … Sidney*, 2.375).

As in the Magdalen College case Sunderland tried to limit the damage that the refusal of the clergy to read the edict produced. Thus, when the issue of the seven bishops who petitioned the king to be excused from the duty was discussed in the cabinet, he argued that they had broken no law and should therefore not be prosecuted. But he was overruled by the Catholic cabal 'and so unanimously that I was just sinking', he observed, adding significantly, 'and I wish I had then sunk' (*Diary of … Sidney*, 2.375). He surfaced at the birth of a son to James and his queen, at which he and his wife were present. A few days later he publicly announced his conversion to the Catholic faith. For his pains he was denounced as a 'Popish dog' by the mob as he made his way to give evidence at the trial of the bishops. The acquittal of the seven bishops created a crisis of confidence at court, discrediting those who had insisted on their prosecution. This played into Sunderland's hands. In July a Scottish observer wrote from London that he 'is certainly the premier minister and tho in truth the King is not governed by any body I believe he hath more power with his Majesty than anybody' (NL Scot., Yester MS 7011, James Hays to Tweeddale, 14 July 1688). His renewed influence was felt when the commission for ecclesiastical causes postponed its next meeting from August until December. Because of the revolution it never met again.

On 27 August, Sunderland wrote to Bevil Skelton in Paris 'I believe there never was in England less thought of a rebellion, and when the parliament meets this will, I doubt not, be evident to all the world' (Kenyon, *Sunderland*, 208). The parliament, like the commission for ecclesiastical causes, never met. Sunderland wrote streams of letters in September endorsing some 105 candidates right up to the 16th, when writs were issued for an election. On 21 September, however, the rumours that the prince of Orange planned to invade, which had been circulating all summer, were finally confirmed. On 25 September the writs were recalled. The election was off. Both James and Sunderland panicked, and sought hastily to mend fences with the Anglican tories. 'I laid hold of the opportunity to press the King to do several things which I would have done sooner' Sunderland claimed later:

> the chief of which were to restore Magdalen College and all other ecclesiastical preferments which had been diverted from what they were intended for; to take off my Lord Bishop of London's suspension; to put the counties into the same hands they were in some time before; to annul the Ecclesiastical Court; and to restore entirely all the Corporations of England. (*Diary of … Sidney*, 2.376)

When the prince of Orange's task force was turned back by storms in mid-October James resented having made these concessions. 'I see God Almighty continues his Protection to me by bringing the wind westerly again', he told the earl of Dartmouth on 20 October (*Dartmouth MSS*, 1.169). His resentment was taken out on Sunderland, whom the Catholic cabal accused of ruining him 'by persuading him to make such shameful condescensions' (*Diary of … Sidney*, 2.377). On 27 October, James dismissed him. The dismissal took people by surprise. 'This remove is somewhat misticall' noted Sir John Bramston:

> there are those that say he was not true to the King as he ought, and that the King, when he dismissed him, sayd 'You have your pardon; much good doe it you. I hope you wilbe more faithfull to your next master than you have been to me'. (*Autobiography*, 327)

The comeback courtier Between his dismissal and his flight to the Netherlands in December, Sunderland was swept along in a welter of events over which nobody had any control. At first he seems to have accepted that William's invasion left him with no alternative but to share the same fate as the king. Sensing that James would seek refuge in France for his wife and their infant son, he tried to ingratiate himself with the royal couple and also with Louis XIV. Thus he assured Mary of Modena that he would remain a staunch Catholic, which led the queen to regret his dismissal. He then sought asylum in France, but Louis declined to offer it. That led him to seek refuge in the Dutch republic instead. This sudden shift, while it can be ascribed simply to panic, also admits of a more profound explanation. Whether Sunderland read Hobbes's *Leviathan* or not, he certainly acted as though he had imbibed Hobbesian maxims. His allegiance was owed to the sovereign only so long as he could protect him. When protection was no longer forthcoming then allegiance was forfeited and could be transferred to another sovereign who could offer it. It was perhaps this philosophical outlook which led Sunderland to be described as 'a second Machiavel' ('Faction display'd', Lord and others, 662). His decision to escape to a protestant country delighted his wife, who put pressure on him to renounce his conversion to Catholicism. They spent much of November in London raising funds for a protracted exile. Quite when they decided to cut and run is uncertain, but early in December they made their way to Rotterdam.

Sunderland seems to have regretted his flight almost immediately, for his wife went back to England on 19 December. She took with her copies of a manuscript he had written justifying his collaboration with the regime of James II. One of these was left with a printer for publication in England, while Sunderland himself arranged for it to be printed in the Dutch republic. His *Letter to a friend in London, plainly discovering the designs of the Romish party and others for the subverting of the protestant religion and the laws of the kingdom* was an attempt to gain a sympathetic audience for his version of events. 'I know I cannot justify myself by saying, though it is true', he wrote, 'that I thought to have prevented much mischief' (*Diary of … Sidney*, 2.370). He nevertheless sought to demonstrate that he had tried to restrain the more extravagant schemes of the king. Some of his claims were justified, for he did attempt to limit the damage of James's attacks upon the Church of England. He also sought to mend fences with William, praising 'the miracles he has done by his wonderful prudence, conduct and courage, for the greatest thing which has been undertaken these thousand years, or perhaps ever, could not be effected without virtues hardly to be imagined till seen nearer hand' (ibid., 376).

Soon after his wife returned to Rotterdam in January 1689 Sunderland was arrested, after a tip-off to the authorities from Admiral Herbert, and thrown into prison. The indomitable Lady Sunderland appealed to Princess Mary to help release him, and when Mary got word to William his release was ordered. Sunderland was sycophantic in his gratitude, assuring the prince, who had just been offered the crown by the Convention in England, that he wished he could have been there to vote for it. It was too early, however, even for a chameleon like Sunderland to change his colours to the court of William and Mary. The best he could hope for was to be allowed to return to England undisturbed, which could not be effected until April 1690. Even then he was *persona non grata* at court, being exempted from the Act of Indemnity given the royal assent on 23 May. The Sunderlands had to retire to Althorp. In April 1691, however, they were summoned from their country house to the king's presence. There were rumours that William was going to appoint Sunderland to office, and these seemed to be confirmed when on 28 April he went to the House of Lords and took the oaths. Nothing came of them immediately, however, and the earl and countess returned to Althorp. There they found themselves in desperate financial circumstances. Their income was largely confined to the rents from their estates.

Shortly after the Sunderlands' return to England the Treasury sued Sunderland in the court of exchequer for the return of plate he had borrowed from the Jewel House. He wrote to the king to protest that he would have to sell land to pay the sum due, and William obliged by ordering the process to be suspended. In December, however, the commissioners for public accounts brought the matter up in the House of Commons, and also questioned the validity of a pension of £1000 a year which was paid to Sunderland. He went up to take his seat in the Lords in January 1692, presumably to look after his own interests. The king again intervened on his behalf, securing the payment of the pension in February, and waiving the requirement to return the plate in March.

Sunderland's increasing dependence on William perhaps partly explains why he was exempted from James's proclamation of pardon, which was proclaimed at St Germain in April. This removed the option of reconciliation with the former monarch, and made the earl totally dependent upon the new king. William realized this, and that not all English politicians, even those in office, were as free from Jacobitism. Sunderland's political instincts could be invaluable for the survival of the post-revolution regime, and his advice was increasingly sought from the spring of 1692. He urged William to drop his policy of offsetting tory and whig ministers in order to achieve a balanced ministry, and instead to swing the balance decisively in favour of the whigs. Arthur Onslow recalled many years later having:

> heard from a great personage that when the earl of Sunderland came afterwards to be in king William's confidence, and pressing him very much to trust and rely more upon the whigs than he had done, the king said, he believed the whigs loved him best, but they did not love monarchy; and although the tories did not like him so well as the others, yet as they were zealous for monarchy, he thought they would serve his government best: to which the earl replied, that it was very true that the tories were better friends to monarchy than the whigs were, but then his majesty was to consider that he was not their monarch. (*Bishop Burnet's History*, 4.5n.)

William resisted Sunderland's advice until 1693. At the beginning of that year he made a partial move towards the whigs by appointing John Somers as lord keeper and Sir John Trenchard as secretary of state. Although Sunderland kept on insisting throughout the spring and summer that this was not enough, and that the other secretary, the earl of Nottingham, should be replaced by a whig too, William kept the tory peer in office, still retaining his penchant for employing ministers of both parties. That summer, however, the policy exploded in his face when a merchant fleet *en route* for Turkey was captured by the French. The loss of the Smyrna fleet provoked recriminations between Nottingham and the whigs, who blamed the secretary for having forced out of office the whig Admiral Russell, replacing him with incompetent tory cronies. William returned from the continent that autumn determined to get a grip on these divided counsels by following Sunderland's advice. Much to the dismay of Queen Mary, Nottingham was dismissed and the vacant secretaryship given to the whig earl of Shrewsbury. Russell was reinstated as lord admiral. 'But the person that had the king's confidence to the highest degree' observed Bishop Burnet:

> was the earl of Sunderland, who, by his long experience, and his knowledge of men and things, had gained an ascendancy over him, and had more credit with him than any Englishman ever had: he had brought the king to this

> change of councils, by the prospect he gave him of the ill condition his affairs were in, if he did not entirely both trust and satisfy those, who, in the present conjuncture, were the only party that both could and would support him. (*Bishop Burnet's History*, 4.222)

Sunderland's scheme paid dividends in the parliamentary session of 1693–4. For, though the king had to accept the Triennial Act, after vetoing a bill the previous year, as the price of Shrewsbury's appointment as secretary, he also gave his assent to the bill creating the Bank of England. This whig measure showed William that the party meant business when it claimed to support his war effort more wholeheartedly than did the tories. But they began to demand more ministerial posts as the price of their continued support, and this challenged Sunderland's control. The first indirect attack upon him came in the next session, 1694–5, when his long-time ally Henry Guy, the secretary to the Treasury, was found guilty of accepting a bribe. The whigs began a campaign against corruption which resulted in Guy's being sent to the Tower and dismissed from his post. They then turned their attention to the venal speaker of the Commons, Sir John Trevor, another of Sunderland's allies, who was also found guilty of bribery and expelled the house. Sunderland attempted to retrieve his grip on the government by having the king dissolve parliament in the summer of 1695, hoping to influence the elections to his advantage. The campaign began with a visit from the king to Althorp, a visible sign of Sunderland's support in high places.

The elections resulted in a whig majority in the Commons, but one which saw a division between court and country whigs. The court whigs supported the whig ministers whom Sunderland had helped to promote, but who now wished to elbow him aside to make room for more of their type. The country whigs were suspicious of the whig ministers, dubbing them the junto, and accusing them of betraying their principles for power. Sunderland apparently saw in the country whigs allies in his own struggle with the junto. Thus in the new session of parliament he went along with their schemes to create a commission of trade nominated by the Commons, rather than a Board of Trade appointed by the crown, and to set up a land bank to offset the Bank of England. Neither scheme succeeded in anything other than irritating the king and the junto. In 1696 these divisions in whig ranks temporarily closed in response to the issues raised by the Jacobite Sir John Fenwick. Fenwick accused members of the government of plotting to restore James II. Sunderland, one whose loyalty to William was undoubted, conducted the government's answer to Fenwick's charges. But where he wanted Fenwick to be repudiated the junto wanted him to be eliminated. They introduced the bill of attainder against him which eventually resulted in his execution, a procedure which Sunderland opposed.

Once Fenwick was out of the way the rift between Sunderland and the junto re-opened. The earl outmanoeuvred the whig leaders by allying with the duke of Shrewsbury against them. Shrewsbury had been reluctant to be appointed secretary of state in 1693, and, though he had been elevated in the peerage to a dukedom the following year, still was semi-detached from the court. He had been the most alarmed at Fenwick's allegations, even threatening resignation over them until warned that this would make him appear guilty of them. When the affair resulted in exonerating him he felt grateful to Sunderland rather than to the junto. Early in 1697 he went to London, where he and Sunderland were quickly regarded as the two most powerful men in the government. At that time Sunderland held no ministerial post, being regarded as a minister behind the curtain. On 19 April, however, he was appointed to the office of lord chamberlain, which the king had purchased from the earl of Dorset for £10,000 to offer him as a gift. On 22 April, two days before the king's departure from England, he was named as one of the lords justices to govern the country in William's absence. He spent the summer handling the English end of the negotiations which were to result in the peace of Ryswick in September.

Sunderland expected trouble when parliament met in December. There had already been murmurings about his appointments as lord chamberlain and lord justice in the fag end of the previous session. The peace strengthened the hands of the country whigs, who came to town determined to attack the government's intention of retaining a large peacetime army, and singled out Sunderland as their chief target. On 11 December a member linked the retention of the army with that of Sunderland as chief minister, 'a man who was the standard bearer of despotism in the last two reigns' (Kenyon, *Sunderland*, 297). Similar remarks were made in subsequent debates. They seem to have rattled Sunderland, who tried to hand in his resignation to the king three times in December, but was refused. In desperation he handed his gold key of office to James Vernon, one of the secretaries of state, on 26 December, saying he had the king's permission to resign. This was a subterfuge, for William had made no such commitment. Indeed he still refused to accept Sunderland's resignation, and Vernon kept the key until 1699. But Sunderland never officiated again as lord chamberlain.

Elder statesman If Sunderland felt that by stepping down he would be removed from the political firing range he was soon to be undeceived. For early in 1698 he found himself caught up in a scandal involving his Jacobite son-in-law, the earl of Clancarty. Clancarty had gone through a marriage ceremony with Elizabeth Spencer, the daughter of the Sunderlands, in 1684. But he had quickly repented of it, and returned to his native Ireland, where he declared himself a Roman Catholic and married again according to the rites of that church. In 1690 he had been captured by the English at the siege of Cork and imprisoned in the Tower. He had escaped in 1694, however, and joined James II as his gentleman of the bedchamber at St Germain. In December 1697 he was in London, where he sought out his first, protestant, wife and was reconciled with her to the point of consummating their marriage. Her brother Charles *Spencer, following the death of Robert in 1688 now the eldest son of the Sunderlands, was informed of Clancarty's presence with Elizabeth at Norfolk House.

Lord Spencer obtained a warrant for his brother-in-law's arrest, which was promptly executed, confining Clancarty to Newgate prison. 'This heady mixture of sex and treason', writes Sunderland's biographer, 'intoxicated the public, who did not know which to denounce as the greater monster, Clancarty or Spencer' (Kenyon, *Sunderland*, 302). Sunderland took his son's side against his son-in-law, though he did ask the king to pardon Clancarty. His daughter then enlisted Godolphin and Lord and Lady Marlborough on her side. The affair thus split the family and threatened to alienate some of Sunderland's political allies. Fortunately for him it ended in March when William pardoned Clancarty and granted the unfortunate couple a pension of £1000 a year, on condition that they lived abroad. In May, therefore, they left England to live in Germany.

The problems raised by the Clancarty affair occupied Sunderland for the first six months of 1698 to the exclusion of other political concerns. It was not until 8 July that he appeared at court. While in London he announced that he still thought that only the junto could do the king's business, and that 'if he was disagreeable to them, or any way obnoxious, he would return to Althorp and not come to town for seven years' (Kenyon, *Sunderland*, 306). In fact they wanted little to do with him, especially as they were planning their campaign in the general election which was held that summer. Sunderland therefore did retire to Althorp, not for seven years but for eighteen months. However, he did not retire completely from politics in Northamptonshire, his advice being frequently given and occasionally sought, so that he was still thought of as a grey eminence behind the turbulent ministerial changes between 1698 and 1700. His next appearance in London in December 1699 was to attend to the final arrangements for the marriage of his son Charles to Lady Anne Churchill, daughter of the earl and countess of Marlborough. Lord Spencer's first wife, Lady Arabella Cavendish, daughter of the duke of Newcastle, had died in June 1698. Where he was said to be inconsolable his mother lost no time in seeking out another desirable match, putting the proposition to Lady Marlborough that July. The negotiations were held up by Lord Marlborough's objections to Spencer's radical whig politics, but eventually the wedding took place in January 1700.

Sunderland stayed in town for the rest of the parliamentary session. The king apparently asked him to stay to use his skills as a manager to try to persuade Robert Harley, the leader of the country whigs, to enter the government. At this stage Harley was not tempted, though the following year he was to be brought into the administration. Sunderland strengthened his ties with Harley to the extent of voting in the Lords in support of the country bill to resume William's grants in Ireland to courtiers. This so annoyed the king that Sunderland felt it best to stay out of his way after the bill received his reluctant assent. William's difficulties that spring, however, were such that he sought out Sunderland to help bolster his collapsing ministry. On 14 May they had an audience at Hampton Court in which the earl agreed to do his best to bring the duke of Shrewsbury back into business. But when his overtures to Shrewsbury were rebuffed he retired to Althorp at the end of the month. In response to the king's entreaty to return he replied that he would keep 'his resolution of not stirring from Althorp and … by the grace of God that he will meddle no more' (Kenyon, *Sunderland*, 317).

In fact Sunderland was meddling once more by the beginning of August. The death of the duke of Gloucester, Princess Anne's only son and heir, on 30 July reopened the question of the succession. William was determined to settle it in the house of Hanover. Sunderland advised him that the only way to secure that objective was to reconstruct the ministry around Harley, and to dissolve parliament so as to give the reconstructed ministry a majority in the House of Commons. William followed the advice, Sunderland handled the approach to Harley through his old colleague Henry Guy, a largely tory ministry was duly appointed, and early in 1701 a new parliament was convened. When it met it passed the Act of Settlement which provided for the accession of the house of Hanover. The tories, however, used the opportunity to pay off scores with William, for example by inserting clauses forbidding the Hanoverian monarchs from going abroad without the consent of parliament, and prohibiting foreigners from holding office under them or receiving property from them. They also unleashed an attack upon the junto, impeaching them for their part in the negotiation of the partition treaty in 1700, whereby William had attempted to prevent the whole of the Spanish empire from descending to one claimant on the death of Carlos II. Their partisanship was made blatantly obvious when they included the earl of Portland in the impeachment proceedings, but not the tory earl of Jersey who had been as involved in the treaties. Sunderland, though he was on good terms with Portland, had no high opinion of him. Nevertheless he felt that by including the earl in their censures of the junto the tories had overreached themselves. 'O silly, silly—had they left alone Lord Portland', he protested, 'they might have hanged the other three in a garret' (Kenyon, *Sunderland*, 315).

William was mortally offended at these flagrant attacks upon himself and his favourite, and wrote from the Netherlands to ask Sunderland's advice. He advised him to reinstate the junto. The king did not immediately accept this advice, but when Louis XIV played into whig hands by recognizing James II's son as king of England he determined to make ministerial changes and to dissolve parliament. Somers wrote to Sunderland inviting him to London to help in the reconstruction of the ministry, but he declined, sending a detailed memorandum instead.

William's death in March 1702 must have reminded Sunderland of his own mortality. For he was clearly suffering from a heart condition which left him short of breath on exertion of any kind. The accession of Queen Anne also brought to power his allies Godolphin and the Marlboroughs. On 11 March he wrote to the earl of Marlborough 'all I wish is to die quietly, with the hopes that my country may not be miserable, which I shall do, if the Queen governs as she says' (Kenyon, *Sunderland*, 326).

Sarah, Marlborough's countess, used her influence with the queen to obtain for him a pension of £4000 a year. His wife wrote to Sarah on 1 June to ask if the arrears owing to him from William's reign could also be paid. To the end Sunderland was in financial difficulties. His last letter, written on 26 August, was to thank Sarah for her kindness. Soon afterwards his heart condition confined him to bed at Althorp, where he died on 28 September. He was buried at Brington on 7 October. W. A. Speck

Sources J. P. Kenyon, *Robert Spencer, earl of Sunderland, 1641–1702* (1958) · J. P. Kenyon, 'Charles II and William of Orange in 1680', *BIHR*, 30 (1957), 95–101 · *Diary of the times of Charles the Second by the Honourable Henry Sidney (afterwards earl of Romney)*, ed. R. W. Blencowe, 2 vols. (1843) · *Bishop Burnet's History* · G. de F. Lord and others, eds., *Poems on affairs of state: Augustan satirical verse, 1660–1714*, 7 vols. (1963–75), vol. 6 · *The works of John Dryden*, 13: *Plays: All for love, Oedipus, Troilus and Cressida*, ed. M. E. Novak and others (1985) · *The autobiography of Sir John Bramston*, ed. [Lord Braybrooke], CS, 32 (1845) · *The correspondence of Henry Hyde, earl of Clarendon, and of his brother Laurence Hyde, earl of Rochester*, ed. S. W. Singer, 2 vols. (1828) · *Memoirs of Sir John Reresby*, ed. A. Browning, 2nd edn, ed. M. K. Geiter and W. A. Speck (1991) · *The manuscripts of the earl of Dartmouth*, 3 vols., HMC, 20 (1887–96) · NL Scot., Yester MS 7011 · *DNB*

Archives BL, Althorp papers, Add. MSS 61126, 61486–61490, 61501 | BL, corresp. with T. Chudleigh, B. Skelton, and others, Add. MSS 32680–32681, 41803, 41809–41811, 41823–41824, 41831–41835, *passim* · BL, corresp. with Lord Danby, Egerton MS 3326 · BL, corresp. with H. Sydney, Add. MSS 32680–32681 · PRO, Baschet transcripts, 31/3/144–178 · U. Nott., letters to earl of Portland and William III, MSS PWA 1208–1280 · Yale U., Beinecke L., letters to Edmund Poley, OSB MS 1

Likenesses P. Lely, portrait, 1660, Althorp, Northamptonshire · P. Lely, portrait, 1666?, Althorp, Northamptonshire [*see illus.*] · school of Kneller, *c.*1680, Blenheim Palace, Oxfordshire · N. Dixon, miniature, *c.*1690, Boughton House, Northamptonshire · P. Lely, portrait (as a young man), Knole, Kent · C. Maratti, portrait, Althorp, Northamptonshire · portrait, Penshurst Place, Kent

Spencer, Sir Robert Cavendish (1791–1830), naval officer, born on 24 October 1791, was the third son of George John *Spencer, second Earl Spencer (1758–1834), and his wife, Lady Lavinia, eldest daughter of Charles Bingham, first Earl Lucan, and the brother of John Charles *Spencer, Viscount Althorp and third Earl Spencer, Frederick Spencer, fourth Earl Spencer [*see below*], George *Spencer, and Sarah *Lyttelton. He was educated at Harrow School. In August 1804 he entered the navy on the *Tigre* (Captain Benjamin Hallowell, afterwards Carew), and served continuously with him, in the *Tigre* and afterwards in the *Malta* (being promoted lieutenant on 13 December 1810) until appointed to command the brig *Pelorus* in October 1812. On 22 January 1813 he was promoted commander of the *Kite*, from which he was moved into the *Espoir*, one of the squadron off Marseilles, under the command of Captain Thomas Ussher. He was afterwards appointed to the *Carron*, employed on the coast of North America, served in the operations against New Orleans, and was promoted to post rank by the commander-in-chief, Sir Alexander Forrester Inglis Cochrane, on 4 June 1814. In 1815 he commanded the *Cydnus* on the home station, and from 1817 to 1819 the frigate *Ganymede* (26 guns) in the Mediterranean, where he successfully negotiated with the bey of Tunis. From 1819 to 1822 he commanded the *Owen Glendower* on the South American station, and from 1823 to 1826 the frigate *Naiad* (46 guns) in the Mediterranean, where he took an active part in the operations against Algiers in the summer of 1824, and himself concluded the agreement with the bey. He was later employed on the coast of Greece during the Greek War of Independence. During these years of peace service, and especially in the *Naiad*, Spencer acquired a reputation in the service as a first-rate gunnery officer and disciplinarian. When the *Naiad* was paid off, she was spoken of as the perfection of a man-of-war. Spencer's reputation in the service ensured that his ships were always crowded with young aristocrats and the sons of senior naval officers. Had he lived, his career, which had been remarkably good under his political opponents, would have prospered.

From August 1827 to September 1828 Spencer was private secretary and groom of the bedchamber to the duke of Clarence, then lord high admiral. Spencer worked closely with Clarence on important reforms concerning gunnery, steam power, and manning. However, his liberal politics and advanced views ensured that he was widely blamed for the breakdown of relations between Clarence and Sir George Cockburn, the leader of his council. In October 1828 he was nominated a KCH, and he was knighted on 24 November. In September 1828 he was appointed to command the *Madagascar*, again in the Mediterranean. He had just been recalled to England on his appointment as surveyor-general of the ordnance, when he died, off Alexandria, on 4 November 1830, from 'an inflammation of the bowels' (*GM*, 82). He was buried at Malta. He never married.

His younger brother, **Frederick Spencer**, fourth Earl Spencer (1798–1857), naval officer, born on 14 April 1798, entered the navy on 18 September 1811. After serving as lieutenant under his brother in the *Owen Glendower*, Spencer commanded the brig *Alacrity* on the South American station. After promotion to captain on 26 August 1826, he was appointed to the frigate *Talbot*; he commanded her with distinction at the battle of Navarino on 20 October 1827, and in subsequent operations on the coast of the Morea. For these services he was made a CB (13 November 1827) and was decorated by the kings of France and Greece, and by the tsar. On 23 February 1830 he married his second cousin, Elizabeth Georgina (*d.* 10 April 1851), daughter of William Stephen Poyntz MP, of Cowdray Park, Midhurst. They had three children; the only son, John Poyntz *Spencer, later became the fifth Earl Spencer.

In 1831 Spencer was MP for Worcestershire, and afterwards for Midhurst (between 1832 and 1834, and 1837 and 1841). On the death of his eldest brother, he succeeded as fourth Earl Spencer, on 1 October 1845. From 1846 to 1848 he was lord chamberlain of the queen's household; he was made a KG on 23 March 1849, and in 1854 was appointed lord steward. On 9 August 1854 he married Adelaide Horatia Elizabeth (*d.* 29 Oct 1877), daughter of Sir Horace

Beauchamp Seymour. They had two children: Charles Robert became in 1910 the sixth Earl Spencer. A lifelong whig, Spencer was regarded by his children as a serious and reserved man. He died a vice-admiral on the retired list on 27 December 1857.

J. K. LAUGHTON, *rev.* ANDREW LAMBERT

Sources *The Red Earl: the papers of the fifth Earl Spencer, 1835–1910*, ed. P. Gordon, 2 vols., Northamptonshire RS, 31, 34 (1981–6) · J. B. Hedderwick, *The captain's clerk* (1957) · *The letters of King George IV, 1812–1830*, ed. A. Aspinall, 3 vols. (1938) · S. M. Eardley-Wilmot, *Life of Vice-Admiral Edmund, Lord Lyons* (1898) · L. M. S. Pasley, *Admiral Sir T. S. Pasley* (1900) · *GM*, 1st ser., 101/1 (1831), 82 · O'Byrne, *Naval biog. dict.* · Burke, *Peerage* (1959)

Archives Beds. & Luton ARS, letters to Thomas, second Baron Grantham · BL, corresp. with Lord Spencer · U. Durham L., corresp. with Charles, second Earl Grey

Likenesses C. Allingham, oils, Althorp, Northamptonshire · F. Chantrey, marble bust, Althorp, Northamptonshire · H. Edridge, drawing, Althorp, Northamptonshire · M. Gauci, lithograph (after T. Phillips), BM, NPG · T. Phillips, oils, Althorp, Northamptonshire · portrait, repro. in Hedderwick, *The captain's clerk* · statue, between Valletta and Citta Vecchia, Malta

Spencer, Sir Stanley (1891–1959), artist, was born on 30 June 1891 at Fernlea, High Street, Cookham-on-Thames, Berkshire, the seventh son in a family of eleven children, of whom two died in infancy, of William Spencer (*d.* 1928), music teacher and organist, and his wife, Anna Caroline, *née* Slack (*d.* 1922). Fernlea, a semi-detached villa in Cookham High Street, had been built by Stanley's grandfather, a local master builder. The family history was intertwined with that of the immediate community. Stanley Spencer himself became closely identified with Cookham through his lifelong sequences of visionary paintings which drew on village life and topography, transforming the local into the epic with an oddness and intensity unparalleled in twentieth-century British art.

Early years and the Slade Spencer, known in the family as Stan, was brought up in a close, cosy, moralistic household in which William Spencer, described by an acquaintance as 'a patriarchal figure who cycled around Cookham reciting Ruskin aloud' (Collis, 18), set the tone of self-improvement. 'Pa', bearded and frock-coated, is recognizable in many of Spencer's later paintings. William Spencer was organist at nearby Hedsor church. His Church of England affiliations were balanced by the more literal, emotional Methodism of his wife, who took the child Stanley to religious meetings at the Wesleyan chapel in Cookham (now the Stanley Spencer Gallery). The 'Bible life', as he described it, was his everyday existence: 'It came into my vision quite naturally, like the sky and rain' (Bell, 1992, 12).

Music was the other dominant influence of Stanley Spencer's childhood. Stanley's elder brother William was a child prodigy pianist who went on to become a professor at the Bern Music Institute. Listening to Bach being played at home gave Stanley 'such a desire to paint great pictures' (MS letter to Florence Image, 1917, Tate collection, archives). He and his brother Gilbert *Spencer, who became a respected British painter on his own account, were the

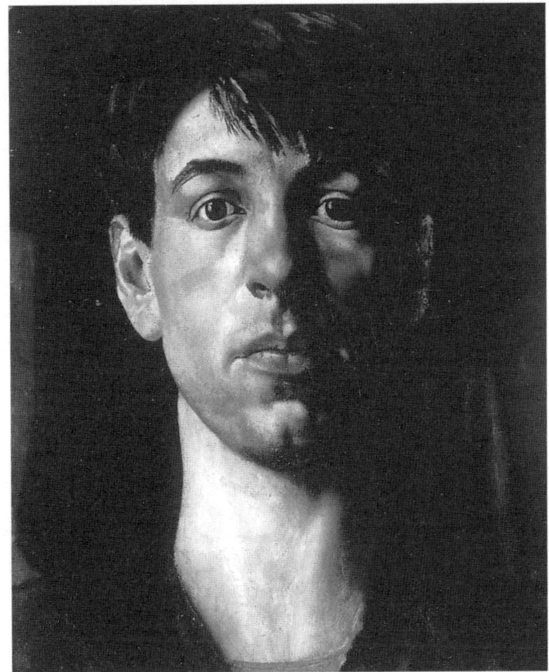

Sir Stanley Spencer (1891–1959), self-portrait, 1914

most visually orientated children of this inordinately talented family. In addition to the general education provided by their sister Annie, who gave classes to her siblings in the corrugated iron hut at the bottom of the garden at Fernlea, Stanley and Gilbert took lessons from Dorothy Bailey, daughter of the local artist William Bailey. In 1907 Stanley Spencer became a full-time art student at the technical school in Maidenhead.

In 1908 Spencer progressed to the Slade School of Fine Art, the leading London art school of the period, where his contemporaries included Edward Wadsworth, Paul Nash, Christopher Nevinson, David Bomberg, William Roberts, Mark Gertler, and Dora Carrington. His four years at the Slade were not altogether happy. He was marked out as a misfit by his physical appearance: his diminutiveness (he was only 5 feet 2 inches), his heavy fringe, and pudding-basin haircut. His aura of other-worldliness was enhanced by the fact that he commuted daily by train from Berkshire. He was known jeeringly as Cookham, and terrified by being put upside-down in a sack.

But artistically Spencer flourished. Professor Henry Tonks's regime at the Slade emphasized the importance of drawing from life. Spencer's skill as a draughtsman is evident in such exquisite early works as *The Fairy on the Waterlily Leaf* (1910; Stanley Spencer Gallery, Cookham), and drawing was always to remain essential to his artistic practice. A drawing was his starting point in formulating ideas for a painting already in his mind.

In the Slade years Stanley Spencer immersed himself in study of the old masters, discovering Masaccio, Giotto, Donatello, and Fra Angelico from the monochrome plates of Gowans and Gray Art Books. At the same time he was responding to the modern European painters then beginning to be exhibited in London under the aegis of Roger Fry. Spencer's oil painting *John Donne Arriving in Heaven* (priv. coll.; on loan to FM Cam.) and two of his drawings were shown in 1912 in the second post-impressionist exhibition at the Grafton Galleries, alongside work by Matisse, Picasso, and Cézanne. Already Spencer's ambitiousness was impressive. Tonks judged him as having the most original mind of any student he could remember at the Slade.

In 1912 Spencer returned to live and work in Cookham, which he saw more than ever as 'a kind of earthly paradise' (Tate collection, archives, 733.2.4). *Zacharias and Elizabeth* (Sheffield City Art Gallery and Tate collection) was started on the dining-room table at Fernlea in December 1913. His close personal involvement with the subjects of his paintings, the quality he would describe as their 'me-myselfness', is precociously obvious in two works of 1914: the strange biblical scene *The Centurion's Servant* (Tate collection), centred around the curly cast-iron bed in the room occupied by the Spencers' maidservant, and the searching *Self-Portrait*, precursor of Spencer's uncompromisingly honest nude portraits of the 1930s. The *Self-Portrait* was immediately bought by Sir Edward Marsh, the well-known London connoisseur.

The First World War and Sandham Memorial Chapel Spencer's natural progression as an artist was interrupted by Britain's declaration of war against Germany in 1914. He enlisted in the Royal Army Medical Corps and from July 1915 worked as a hospital orderly in Beaufort War Hospital in Bristol, looking after the war wounded. He became intensely interested in the human body under duress, observing operations with careful fascination, and made an important friendship with the young Roman Catholic intellectual Desmond Chute.

The following summer Spencer was sent to Macedonia to join the British forces fighting the Bulgarians and Greeks. He had never been abroad before. At first he served with the field ambulance divisions, but in August 1917 volunteered for the infantry, joining the 7th battalion, the Royal Berkshires, and spending several months in the front line. Private Spencer's delicate physique and unpredictable temperament made his military service problematic (unlike that of his brother Sydney, who was awarded the MC before being killed in France). After a recurrence of malaria Stanley Spencer was finally invalided out of the army, returning to Cookham in December 1918. His painting *Swan Upping at Cookham* (1915–19; Tate collection), left unfinished when he had enlisted, was lying on the bed at home.

Spencer revivified his deeply absorbed wartime experiences in a sequence of paintings over the next decade which must rate as among the most original and moving of European artistic responses to the First World War. Although the army had refused to release him in time to take up his appointment as official war artist, Spencer carried out a number of post-war commissions for the Ministry of Information. Studies made in Macedonia were mislaid in the Berkshire regiment's last big offensive of the war, but Spencer recreated these from memory in a small series of preparatory wash drawings. In January 1919 he started work on the magnificent large-scale painting *Travoys Arriving with Wounded at a Dressing Station, Smol, Macedonia, 1916* (IWM).

The jagged Macedonian landscape erupts into Spencer's visionary biblical paintings of the period, notably *The Crucifixion* (Aberdeen Art Gallery) of 1921. In 1922 Spencer returned to Yugoslavia on a painting holiday, spending a productive month in Sarajevo. What he found in this wild country had 'something equal in degree of intensity' to Cookham, stark intimations of purgatory (MS letter to Florence Image, 24 Feb 1918, Tate collection, archives).

Spencer's most substantial post-war commission was the cycle of nineteen paintings for the Sandham Memorial Chapel in Hampshire. These were commissioned in 1923 by Louis and Mary Behrend in memory of Mrs Behrend's brother Lieutenant Henry Willoughby Sandham who had died in 1919 after an illness contracted in wartime. He too had served in Macedonia. The Behrends bought a specific site at Burghclere, instructing the architect, Lionel Pearson, to construct the building as Spencer envisaged it. The idea of a sequence of paintings 'at home' in a purpose-built setting delighted him, familiar as he was (albeit through reproduction) with Giotto's Arena Chapel in Padua. While working on this cycle almost continuously between 1926 and 1932, Spencer lived in a cottage alongside the chapel. For Spencer, as for his admired pre-Renaissance painters, the painting of the cycle became his way of life.

The paintings at Burghclere brought Spencer into public cognizance for the first time. He carried out much of the work visibly *in situ*, on wide bolts of canvas stretched along the chapel nave. The narrative of Stanley Spencer's war—the wounded arriving at Beaufort, the training camp at Tweseldown, the day-to-day routines of service in Macedonia—climaxes in the crowded, joyful central composition *The Resurrection of the Soldiers* covering the whole east wall. It is a highly personal sequence that transcends the anecdotal, treating the grand themes of glory and redemption in an extraordinary fusion of grandiloquence and homeliness.

Marriage, *Resurrection, Cookham*, divorce Spencer's obsessive need for a domestic framework for his work found a new outlet when he met and, on 23 February 1925, married at Wangford parish church, Suffolk, Hilda *Carline (1889–1950) [*see under* Carline family], herself a Slade-trained painter and a member of a gregarious, well-connected Hampstead family of artists and intellectuals. Spencer's innocence of upbringing was such that, at the age of thirty-three, he was sexually inexperienced. His early years of marriage, spent mainly at Burghclere, were almost deliriously happy. He and Hilda had two daughters: Shirin (*b*. 1925) and Unity (*b*. 1930).

Stanley Spencer's great painting *The Resurrection, Cookham*, most convincing of several contemporaneous attempts at the resurrection theme, was painted between 1924 and 1926 in a studio in Hampstead borrowed from Henry Lamb. The painting, set in Cookham churchyard, is an anthem to his altered state, in which his childhood sense of 'the richness that underlies the Bible in Cookham' (Bell, 1992, 15) merges with his new-found delight in the adult mysteries of love, sex, and cohabitation. *The Resurrection, Cookham* was the work that established Stanley Spencer's reputation. The *Times* critic described it as 'the most important picture painted by any English artist in the present century … It is as if a Pre-Raphaelite had shaken hands with a Cubist' (28 Feb 1927). The painting is now in the Tate collection.

Early in 1932 Spencer brought his young family to live in Cookham, buying Lindworth, a relatively substantial semi-detached house in the centre of the village. It was a year of increased optimism, in which Spencer was elected an associate of the Royal Academy and an agent, Dudley Tooth, was appointed to take charge of his hitherto chaotic professional affairs. But Spencer's marriage was showing signs of strain: his suffocating dependence upon Hilda gave her no scope to continue her own painting or to express her views. There were warnings of the mental instability from which she later suffered so tragically. Fervent Christian Science principles impelled her to desist from sex for protracted periods.

Perhaps partly in retaliation, Spencer focused his creative energy on a vastly ambitious project known as the Church House, a successor to the Sandham Memorial Chapel but designed to contain celebratory cycles of love, sacred and profane. His inherent interest in ideas of the primitive sacredness of erotic art had been stimulated by his reading of Sir Edwin Arnold's *The Light of Asia* and by his friendship with the artist James Wood, a devotee of Islam. From now on Spencer's graphically imagined explorations of sexual permissiveness, both delicate and *outré*, would dominate his paintings, although the Church House as such was never built.

Spencer's growing preoccupation with the erotic was encouraged by a friendship, which quickly flared up into an infatuation, with Patricia Preece, glamorous but impecunious daughter of an army officer who lived in Cookham with her friend and sexual partner Dorothy Hepworth. Preece and Hepworth, who had both trained at the Slade, evolved a curious *modus vivendi* by which Hepworth—the better artist—sold her paintings under the signature 'Patricia Preece'. Spencer's persistent advances seem to have been encouraged by Preece in the hope of financial gain. Hilda's refusal to accede to demands for a *ménage à trois* demanded by the increasingly unrealistic Stanley forced her eventually to file for a divorce which was granted on 25 May 1937.

Four days later Stanley Spencer married at Maidenhead register office Patricia (formerly Ruby Vivian) Preece (1894–1966). They never lived together, and the marriage was almost certainly unconsummated. The legacy of his disastrous relationship with Preece is a series of nude portraits painted between 1935 and 1937, including the now famous *Double Nude Portrait: the Artist and his Second Wife* (Tate collection) of 1937, known familiarly as 'The "leg of mutton" nude'. These portraits were painted directly from the model, with inquisitive candour compared by Spencer to that of an ant exploring the contours of the human body. They confront a relationship already proving emotionally arid and sexually non-negotiable.

This was a decade of humiliation and disappointment. Two paintings, *St Francis and the Birds* (1934; Tate collection) and *The Dustman* (also called *The Lovers*; 1934; Laing Art Gallery, Newcastle upon Tyne), were rejected in 1935 by the hanging committee of the Royal Academy's summer exhibition on the implied grounds of their obscenity. Spencer resigned in anger. Financial problems dogged him, and Spencer was sued by Hilda several times for arrears of maintenance. The accumulated tensions of producing saleable landscapes, flower paintings, and portraits at speed, on Dudley Tooth's instructions, in preference to his more esoteric paintings no doubt contributed to his serious breakdown in 1938.

Spencer still yearned for the love and companionship of Hilda, writing screeds of letters to her and unravelling their past in a series of nine paintings intended for the Church House, the poignantly detailed so-called *Domestic Scenes* (1935–6; various priv. colls.; one, *At the Chest of Drawers*, on long loan to the Stanley Spencer Gallery, Cookham). He explored more sombre themes of love, anguish, incompatibility, and the ageing of desire in a further Church House cycle, *The Beatitudes of Love* (1937–8; various priv. colls.; one, *Romantic Meeting*, in the National Art Gallery and Museum, Wellington, New Zealand), which Spencer called his 'couple' paintings. Here Spencer's lifelong contention that the ugly is redeemable is emphasized by his conscious distortion of technique.

In 1938 Patricia Preece rented out Lindworth, which Spencer had unwisely made over to her while continuing to live there. Homeless, he moved back to London on his own. A final Church House sequence, *Christ in the Wilderness* (1939–53; full series, Art Gallery of Western Australia, Perth), was planned to contain forty paintings, one for each of Christ's days of torment in the desert, of which Spencer completed the first eight. He began working on the series in his rented room in Adelaide Road, Hampstead. As he was the first to notice, he had entered a Christ-like wilderness himself.

In spite of these vicissitudes, the doggedly productive Spencer exhibited twenty-two canvases in the British pavilion at the Venice Biennale in 1938.

Port Glasgow in the Second World War Soon after the declaration of war on Germany, the War Artists' Advisory Committee commissioned Spencer to record shipbuilding on the Clyde. He and his Slade contemporary Paul Nash were rare in being official war artists whose works span two world wars. Spencer's second great public project occupied him from May 1940 to March 1946. His work was based at Lithgow's shipyard in Port Glasgow on the Firth of Clyde, concentrated on merchant ships under construction, and Spencer spent extended periods in Scotland during and immediately after the war. Spencer's war work came as a reprieve from his anxious isolation. He was able to immerse himself in the day-to-day activities of ordinary working people, intimately involved in the highly skilled processes of making with which he had always felt an innate sympathy. The Clyde shipbuilding paintings were conceived on an epic scale. Spencer's proposal was for a three-tier frieze 70 feet long. Eight of the projected thirteen canvases had been completed by the time the war artists were disbanded in 1946. All except two are in the Imperial War Museum. Spencer's Port Glasgow paintings lack the concentration of energy of his earlier cycle for the Sandham Memorial Chapel. But they have enormous human warmth and interest, not least in the evidence they give us of the artist creatively identified with the waging of a war. Spencer became a familiar figure of the shipyards, photographed making his preparatory sketches on a gradually unfurled toilet roll, and appearing as a Chaplinesque hero in Jill Craigie's documentary *Out of Chaos*, filmed on Clydeside in 1944.

His uplifting years in Scotland inspired Spencer to embark on a *Port Glasgow Resurrection* series (1945–50; various locations; preparatory drawings, Tate collection). These eight paintings mark a post-war return to his loved themes of reunion and rediscovery, in which mystic events are translated into an affectionate, idiosyncratic visual language that renders them 'as real as going shopping' (Bell, 1992, 497). Spencer had intended the paintings to be hung together, but he was, once again, frustrated in this wish and the *Resurrection* sequence was broken up.

Final Cookham years In September 1945 Spencer returned to Cookham, settling in Cliveden View, a small house in Cookham Rise belonging to his brother Percy, in which his now ailing elder sister Annie had previously lived. Much of his time was now expended on a vast new cycle, *Christ Preaching at Cookham Regatta* (1955–9; various locations including Tate collection and Stanley Spencer Gallery, Cookham). These paintings emanate from the colourful and curious English summer ritual of the annual regatta that had intrigued small Stan Spencer as a child. They have the weird ebullience many people would regard as quintessential Spencer, although they lack the grand originality of the best of his earlier work.

In 1950 Stanley's former wife Hilda, whose mental illness had led to her confinement in Banstead Mental Hospital in Epsom, died of cancer of the breast. He was present at her death, after which he continued to write her his long, hectic, erotic, often incoherent letters. He returned with new energy to his Church House scheme, designating a Hilda Chapel—the 'you-me' room—and painting a series of pictures in which Hilda appears in the guise of the cosily responsive wife and mother that she still represented in his imagination.

Through the 1950s Spencer's artistic powers were waning, though he could still occasionally rise to his old creative force, as in his Cookham rooftop *Crucifixion* (1958; priv. coll.) and his wonderful late-in-life *Self-Portrait* (Tate collection) of 1959. In general his thin, flat quality of paint looked more than ever meagre in contrast with contemporary American abstract painters' techniques, which deployed paint expressively on the surface of their canvases. Much of Spencer's subject matter was appearing merely quaint.

But Spencer's public personality was flourishing as never before. The biblically inspired and at times unstoppably loquacious Stanley Spencer had matured into the village prophet and English eccentric on a cosmic scale, his pyjama trousers peeping out from underneath his trousers, his Woolworth's glasses tipping off his nose, as he trundled his painting equipment around Cookham in a dilapidated ancient black pram, living proof of his claim that he was 'on the side of the angels and of dirt' (C. Neve, *Unquiet Landscape*, 1990, 37). In 1954 he spent a month in China as an enthusiastic if obstreperous member of an official British party of intellectuals and artists promoting cultural exchange. After the formal programme had ended he stayed on in China by himself to paint.

Death and reputation In the last year of his life Spencer moved back into his old childhood home, Fernlea (now renamed Fernley). In July 1959 he was knighted by Elizabeth II, an honour of which Patricia Preece took full advantage, becoming Lady Spencer. Five months later, on 14 December 1959, Stanley Spencer died of cancer in the Canadian Red Cross Memorial Hospital at Taplow. He was cremated on 17 December and his ashes buried in the churchyard at Cookham on 18 December. The address at his memorial service in St James's Church, Piccadilly, was given by Sir Charles Wheeler, president of the Royal Academy which had rejected his work in 1935. The Stanley Spencer Gallery in Cookham was opened by the Friends of Stanley Spencer Trust in 1962.

Biographers, of whom the first was Maurice Collis, attempted not wholly successfully to grapple with the conflict in Spencer's personality between the abnormally sensitive and the cruelly obtuse. Pam Gems's biographical play *Stanley* opened at the National Theatre in London in 1996 and was revived later in New York.

The serious reassessment of Spencer's work began with the major retrospective exhibition at the Royal Academy in 1980. The excellence of many of the landscapes the artist himself had deprecated came to be appreciated, along with a new recognition of the beauty and originality of Spencer's drawings. By the year 2000, Stanley Spencer was generally regarded as the most important British painter in the first half of the twentieth century—treating the great contemporary themes of war and love, destruction and redemption, with his extraordinary freshness of vision and his monumental creative energy. In the breadth of his engagement he provides a link backwards to such earlier visionary artists as Henry Fuseli and William Blake as well as prefiguring in unexpected ways the portraiture of Lucian Freud and Francis Bacon, giving Spencer an essential involvement in the often anguished history of twentieth-century confrontation with self.

FIONA MACCARTHY

Sources K. Bell, *Stanley Spencer: a complete catalogue of the paintings* (1992) · K. Pople, *Stanley Spencer: a biography* (1991) · G. Spencer, *Stanley Spencer: by his brother Gilbert* (1961) · F. MacCarthy, *Stanley Spencer: an English vision* (1997) · M. Collis, *Stanley Spencer: a biography* (1962) · D. Robinson, *Stanley Spencer* (1990) · D. Robinson, *Stanley Spencer at Burghclere* (1991) · R. Carline, *Stanley Spencer at war* (1978) · *Stanley Spencer, the man: correspondence and reminiscences*, ed. J. Rothenstein (1979) · K. Bell, ed., *Stanley Spencer RA* (1980) [exhibition catalogue, RA, 20 Sept – 14 Dec 1980] · *Stanley Spencer: the apotheosis of love* (1991) [exhibition catalogue, Barbican Art Gallery, London, 1991] • *The art of Hilda Carline, Mrs Stanley Spencer* (1999) [exhibition catalogue, Usher Gallery, Lincoln, 1999] • D. Sylvester, introduction, *Drawings by Stanley Spencer*, ed. D. Sylvester (1954) [exhibition catalogue, Arts Council of Great Britain] • A. Glew, *Stanley Spencer: letters and writings* (2001) • T. Hyman and P. Wright, eds., *Stanley Spencer* (2001) [exhibition catalogue, Tate Gallery, London] • b. cert. • m. certs. • d. cert.

Archives Art Gallery of Western Australia, Perth • Berks. RO, corresp. and diaries of Spencer family (Stanley, William, Percy, Sydney, and Florence) • IWM • Leeds City Art Gallery • Sandham memorial chapel, Burghclere, Hampshire • Stanley Spencer Gallery, Cookham, Berkshire • Tate collection, fragments, drawings, photographs • Tate collection, papers • Tate collection, sketchbook papers, manuscripts, and drawings | RA, letters to the Royal Academy • Stanley Spencer Gallery, Cookham, Berkshire, letters to Desmond Chute; memorabilia • Tate collection, letters to Mary Behrend and Louis Behrend • Tate collection, letters to Henry Lamb • Tate collection, corresp. with Charlotte Murray • Tate collection, letters to Gwen Raverat • Tate collection, letters to Sir John Rothenstein and notes about his art • Tate collection, letters to Sir Michael Sadler • Tate collection, corresp. with Dudley Tooth of Arthur Tooth & Sons | FILM BBC Television Archives, 'In the National Trust', Sandham Memorial Chapel, BBC 2, 3 Feb 1995 • BFI, *Out of chaos*, by Jill Craigie at Port Glasgow, 1944 | SOUND Tate collection, Gilbert Spencer interviews, 1970 and 1975

Likenesses S. Spencer, self-portrait, sanguine drawing, *c*.1912–1913, Williamson Art Gallery and Museum, Birkenhead • S. Spencer, self-portrait, oils, 1913, Tate collection • S. Spencer, self-portrait, 1914, Tate collection [*see illus.*] • S. Spencer, self-portrait, pencil drawing, 1919, NPG • S. Spencer, group portrait, oils, *c*.1923–1927 (*The resurrection, Cookham*), Tate collection • S. Spencer, self-portrait, pencil drawing, *c*.1926, Arts Council of Great Britain, London • H. Lamb, oils, 1928, NPG • H. Spencer, pencil drawing, 1931, Scottish Gallery of Modern Art, Edinburgh • W. Rothenstein, sanguine drawing, 1932, NPG • S. Spencer, double portrait, oils, 1936 (with his second wife, Patricia Preece), FM Cam. • S. Spencer, self-portrait, 1936, Tate collection • S. Spencer, self-portrait, oils, 1936, Stedelijk Museum, Amsterdam • S. Spencer, self-portrait, *c*.1936–1937, FM Cam. • S. Spencer, double portrait, 1937 (with his second wife, Patricia Preece), Tate collection • S. Spencer, self-portrait, oils, 1939, FM Cam. • photographs, 1943–59, Hult. Arch. • S. Spencer, self-portrait, oils, 1944, National Gallery of Canada, Ottawa • I. Penn, photograph, 1950, NPG • S. Spencer, self-portrait, oils, 1959, Tate collection • J. Hedgecoe, photograph, NPG • H. Lamb, oils, Art Gallery of Western Australia, Perth • McCoombe, photographs, repro. in *Picture Post* (2 Oct 1943) • photographs, Stanley Spencer Gallery, Cookham, Berkshire

Wealth at death £8448 15*s*. 9*d*.: probate, 29 Feb 1960, *CGPLA Eng. & Wales*

Spencer [*née* Armitage], **Sybil Beatrice** (1908–1994), gardener, was born at 114 Tong Road, Armley, Leeds, on 29 March 1908, the daughter of Nathaniel Newburn Armitage, pharmacist, and his wife, Mary Jane, *née* Ellis. She trained at the Royal Academy of Dramatic Art (RADA) and hoped to become an actress, but left in order to marry Frederick Henry Spencer (*d*. 1963), a chartered surveyor, in 1928. In 1951 they bought a grey-stone farmhouse called York Gate, in Back Church Lane, Adel, Leeds. There, she and her son Robin, who was in his last year at school at the time of the purchase, created the garden which made them both well known.

Like many women gardeners of her generation, Spencer was a dutiful wife and mother, and deferred to both her husband and her son's tastes. Her gardening career began only in middle age, when the family acquired York Gate, which at that time was an unassuming house surrounded by an acre of scrubby, sandy ground, sheltered, but in a frost pocket. Spencer took to gardening with enthusiasm and energy: 'I'd bring some sandwiches and garden all day' (Spencer, 79). Most of the planning for the garden was undertaken with Robin, who from an early age showed an interest in garden design and garden artefacts and antiques. Spencer, like so many women gardeners, was self-taught. In 1957 she began to keep a loose-leaf horticultural scrapbook, where she stored and commented on articles on planting and design, and Robin did likewise with antiques, and these served as a reference and resource for their work.

Local craftsmen, stonemasons, builders, and joiners were hired to execute the designs of mother and son. As Spencer wrote, 'we have a lot of circles at York Gate—the millstones, the grindstones, the font and even a circular window in the potting shed' (Spencer, 86). The centrepiece of these circular designs was a cobblestone and gravel maze near the entrance to the garden, from which many pathways radiated. Spencer had wanted a conservatory attached to the house, where she could propagate seedlings and cuttings, but her husband objected, saying that conservatories 'were like warts on houses' (Spencer, 84). So a greenhouse was built at the end of the garden, and she traversed the winding paths to reach it. Robin gradually filled the garden with strange and eye-catching *objets trouvés*, which served as foci for his mother's planting. But one of her most prized objects, a bronze Chinese vase, came not from Robin, but from the director of parks in Leeds. Spencer planted it with purple cordyline, and had the stonemason make a seat around it. Her favourite part of the garden was an area with a sharp slope with a 4 feet drop, which she had levelled in the middle and planted with her favourite shrubs—golden Irish yews, *Acer palmatum* 'Senkaki', *Acer palmatum* 'Ozakazuki', and *Eucryphia nymansensis*.

Frederick Spencer died in 1963, and Robin died suddenly in 1982. Sybil Spencer, though bereft, continued to garden. She had already quietly worked around Robin, for example pruning trees—which he objected to—when he went on trips; but writing in the journal *Hortus* she commented sadly after his death, 'I have to make my own decisions now' (Spencer, 85). She had already employed a local man, Brian Noble, as a gardener for the heavy work, and with his help she set about extending the garden.

Even before Robin died the garden was becoming extremely well known in gardening circles. York Gate was first opened to the public under the National Gardens scheme in 1968. In the *National Gardens Handbook* the garden was described as 'an orchard with pool, an arbour, miniature pinetum, dell with stream, folly, nutwalk, peony bed, iris borders, fern border, herb garden, summerhouse, alley, white and silver garden, pavement maze and vegetable garden' (*National Gardens Handbook*, 1992). This extraordinary variety of plantings and gardens within a garden were fitted into the 1 acre site in a succession of vistas so cleverly designed that the area seemed infinitely larger than it was. The use of evergreens and the continual dramatic pleasure of the carefully placed objects, together with the stonework, ironwork, and other building materials which were so carefully used to complement and enhance the planting, meant that the garden was as elegant and exciting in winter as in summer.

Spencer continued to work in the garden despite advancing age and increasing ill health. 'It is a poor sort of day when I don't do some sort of gardening', she commented in a television programme filmed a year before her death (Penn, 206). Her garden attracted visitors from all over England and even further afield. Amateur and professional gardeners, planners, and landscape artists came to visit it. Just before her death one group came from Russia, to measure and draw the garden and to dissect its extraordinary spatial qualities. Gardening brought Spencer many friends and admirers. She had a slightly theatrical manner, perhaps left over from her RADA days, but she remained essentially modest and unassuming. She died at Leeds General Infirmary on 14 December 1994. She left her home and garden to the Gardeners' Royal Benevolent Society, together with an income to maintain it, with the stipulation that it must continue to remain open to the public. HELEN PENN

Sources S. Spencer, 'York Gate: the making of an English garden', *Hortus*, 38 (summer 1996), 78–91 • H. Penn, *An Englishwoman's garden* (1993) • *The Times* (31 Dec 1994) • b. cert. • d. cert. • *National Gardens Handbook* (1992)

Archives FILM An Englishwoman's garden, BBC (PM Productions) (September 1993)

Likenesses photograph, repro. in Penn, *Englishwoman's garden* • photograph, repro. in *The Times*

Wealth at death £740,495: probate, 28 Feb 1995, *CGPLA Eng. & Wales*

Spencer, Thomas (1791–1811), Independent minister, second son of a worsted weaver, was born at Hertford on 21 January 1791. His mother died when he was five. He had to leave school, where he had acquired some Latin, at the age of thirteen 'to twist worsted every day with a heavy heart'. For some months he was apprenticed to a firm of glovers in Poultry, London. Here he was introduced to Thomas Wilson, treasurer of the Hoxton Academy. To prepare him for entry to this ministerial training college he was sent for a year to study with William Hordle at Harwich: here he learnt Hebrew and abridged Parkhurst's *Hebrew Lexicon*. He entered Hoxton in January 1807 at the age of sixteen, and in June took his first service at Colliers End, near Hertford. He at once became a popular preacher and was in great demand throughout the home counties. On 10 January 1810 he addressed 'an immense congregation' from Rowland Hill's pulpit in Surrey Chapel. He visited Liverpool in the summer of 1810, and on 26 September accepted an offer of the pastorate of Newington Congregational Church, much against his will, as he really wanted a southern church. His Liverpool ministry began in February 1811.

The 'boy preacher' had a youthful appearance, with a sensitive face and deep-set eyes. His voice was melodious, his memory extraordinary, and his delivery fluent and powerful—he reminded many of George Whitefield. There was, however, always some concern about his state of health. He at once attracted a vast congregation, far too large for the building. A new chapel was designed for him, to be erected in George Street; the foundation stone was laid on 15 April 1811, with no fewer than 8000 people in attendance. Spencer's promising career was brought to an abrupt end on 5 August 1811 when he was drowned while bathing in the Mersey off the Herculaneum Pottery. He was buried in Liverpool two days later. Thomas Raffles succeeded him in the pastorate of Great George Street. A collection of his sermons was published in 1829 and a volume of his tracts in 1853.

G. LE G. NORGATE, *rev.* IAN SELLERS

Sources T. Raffles, *Memoirs of the life and ministry of Rev. T. Spencer* (1811) • E. Robinson, *Poems on the death of Thomas Spencer* (1811) • *Funeral discourses on Thomas Spencer* (1811) • B. Nightingale, *Lancashire nonconformity*, 6 vols. [1890–93], vol. 6

Likenesses E. Scriven, stipple (after N. Branwhite), BM; repro. in *Life* (1812) • portrait, repro. in Raffles, *Memoirs of the life and ministry of Rev. T. Spencer*

Spencer, Thomas (1796–1853), writer, son of Matthew Spencer (1762–1831) and his wife, Catherine Taylor (1758–1843), was born on 14 October 1796, at Derby, where his father kept a large school. William George *Spencer was his elder brother, and Herbert *Spencer was his nephew. For some time Thomas taught at Quorn School, near Derby, and in October 1816 entered St John's College, Cambridge. He graduated as ninth wrangler in 1820, and, after taking pupils for a term, was ordained deacon. While at Cambridge he fell under the influence of Charles Simeon, the evangelical. For eighteen months in 1821–2 he was curate of Anmer in Norfolk, living in the house of the village squire, to whose son he was tutor. For a while he held the college living of Stapleford, near Cambridge. He was also a curate in Penzance, and had sole charge of a church at Clifton for a year or two. He was elected to a fellowship of St John's College in March 1823, which he retained until his marriage in September 1829 to Anna Maria, daughter of Major James Henry Brooke of the Bengal artillery.

In March 1826 Spencer was presented by George Henry Law, bishop of Bath and Wells and the father of Spencer's college friend Henry Law, later dean of Gloucester, to the perpetual curacy of Hinton Charterhouse, between Bath and Frome. He took pupils, among whom was the Revd Thomas Mozley, whose *Reminiscences* (1885, 2.174–85) contains anecdotes of Spencer. The population of the parish of Hinton was about 737, and there had been no clergyman and no parsonage since the Reformation. The income was about £80. Spencer built a house, erected cottages, and established a school, a clothing club, a village library, and field gardens. He fought against intemperance and pauperism; through his efforts the rates were reduced from £700 to £200 a year. Wages increased and outdoor relief gradually diminished. He described this achievement in *The Successful Application of the New Poor Law to the Parish of Hinton Charterhouse* (1836). When Hinton was incorporated in the Bath union, Spencer was elected a guardian, and was the first chairman.

Spencer's energies were not confined to local claims. He

travelled about the country preaching and lecturing, chiefly as a temperance advocate. For Spencer, every teetotaller 'was a policeman engaged in repressing crime'. He was a member of the Anti-Slavery Conference, he said grace at the first as well as at the last banquet of the Anti-Corn Law League, and he was chairman of the Conference of Ministers of Religion. His many pamphlets—on church reform, the poor law, education, and the corn laws—had an immense circulation; of some, as many as 27,000 copies were printed. He resigned his curacy in September 1847, moved to London, and devoted himself to the pulpit and platform. In March 1851 he was appointed secretary of the National Temperance Society and editor of the *National Temperance Chronicle*.

Spencer died at Notting Hill, Middlesex, on 26 January 1853 and was buried at Hinton. He was, Tom Mozley recalled, a 'decidedly fine-looking man, with a commanding figure, a good voice and a ready utterance' (Mozley, 2.176). H. R. TEDDER, *rev.* H. C. G. MATTHEW

Sources *GM*, 2nd ser., 39 (1853), 317 • Venn, *Alum. Cant.* • Boase, *Mod. Eng. biog.* • T. Mozley, *Reminiscences, chiefly of Oriel College and the Oxford Movement*, 2 vols. (1882) • private information (1897)
Archives Som. ARS, Robertson Glasgow MSS • UCL, letters to Edwin Chadwick
Likenesses H. Spencer, head, 1842 • W. G. Spencer, crayon (as a youth)

Spencer, William (*c.*1690–1756). *See under* Spencer family (*per. c.*1647–1765).

Spencer, William Robert (1770–1834), poet and humorist, was born in Kensington Palace, London, on 9 January 1770, the younger son of Lord Charles *Spencer (1740–1820), second son of the third duke of Marlborough [*see under* Spencer, Charles, third duke of Marlborough] and the Hon. Mary Beauclerk (*d.* 1812), daughter of Lord Vere. He was educated at Harrow School before matriculating on 13 October 1786 from Christ Church, Oxford. He did not take a degree, but had an exceptional memory which he proved while at Oxford by betting that 'he would learn a whole newspaper by heart, and recite it from beginning to end without displacing one word. He won his bet, but said he was never so bored as while preparing himself for this' (*Poems*, 11).

Spencer's wit and accomplishments made him very popular in London society, and he was a frequent guest of the prince of Wales. At his house in Curzon Street Pitt and Fox met, and among his other friends were R. B. Sheridan, Sydney Smith, and Francis Horner. He sought no prominence in public life, but was content with the reputation of a wit and a writer of *vers de société*. In 1796 he published a translation of Bürger's *Leonore*, which was highly thought of by Scott and others. Byron said of him that 'His was really what your countrymen call an elegant mind, polished, graceful and sentimental' (Staunton, 344). Wilson, in *Noctes Ambrosianae*, has Hogg say, 'That chiel's a poet. Thae verses hae muckle o' the auld ballant pathos and simplicity' (Wilson, 487).

On 13 December 1791 Spencer married Susan, widow of Count Spreti, and daughter of Count Francis Jenison Walworth, chamberlain to the elector palatine. It was rumoured that 'the countess was first married to an old man, who, perceiving an attachment gradually increasing between her and young Spencer, destroyed himself that he might not be a bar to their union' (*Portion of the Journal*, 294). This story was said to have suggested Madame de Souza's tale of *Adèle de Sénange*, although the husband there dies of apoplexy.

Spencer had five sons and two daughters; his sons included Aubrey George *Spencer (1795–1872) and George Trevor *Spencer (1799–1866). His large family caused him to give up his briefly held seat in parliament to become a commissioner of stamps from 1797 until 1826. In 1825, owing to financial difficulties, Spencer withdrew to Paris, where Scott on a visit the following year invited him to breakfast. In a state of poverty and ill health he remained in Paris until his death on 22 or 23 October 1834. He was survived by his wife and six children (one son, Charles, having died in 1793), and was buried in Harrow church.

Spencer's work also includes *Urania*, a satire on German ghost literature which was performed at Drury Lane in 1802; *The Year of Sorrow* (1804); a volume of poems (1811); and a prologue to Miss Berry's play *Fashionable Friends* (1802). J. G. ALGER, *rev.* S. C. BUSHELL

Sources *Poems by the late Hon. W. R. Spencer* (1835) • *GM*, 2nd ser., 3 (1835), 98–9 • H. Staunton, *The great schools of England* (1865), 343–4 • *A portion of the journal kept by Thomas Raikes from 1831–1847: comprising reminiscences of social and political life in London and Paris during that period*, 1 (1856), 293–4 • J. G. Lockhart, *Memoirs of the life of Sir Walter Scott*, [2nd edn], 9 (1839), 30 • J. Wilson, 'Noctes ambrosianae', *Blackwood*, 21 (1827), 487 • Foster, *Alum. Oxon.* • D. Bank and A. Esposito, eds., *British biographical index*, 4 vols. (1990) • Allibone, *Dict.* • *Annual Biography and Obituary*, 19 (1835), 457
Archives Powerhouse Museum, Sydney, corresp. with Chinnery family and Giovanni Battista Viotti • RA, corresp. with Thomas Lawrence • Yale U., Beinecke L., corresp. with Chinnery family

Spencer-Churchill. For this title name *see* Churchill, Clementine Ogilvy Spencer-, Baroness Spencer-Churchill (1885–1977).

Spender, John Alfred (1862–1942), journal editor and writer, was born at 37 Gay Street, Bath, on 23 December 1862. He was the eldest of four sons and third of the eight children of John Kent Spender, physician, and his wife, Lily (1835–1895), *née* Headland, novelist [*see* Spender, Lillian]. Both Spender's parents valued education and literary achievement highly, and two of his younger brothers, Edward Harold Spender (1864–1926) and Hugh Frederick Spender (1873–1930), followed him to Oxford and into journalism. He was educated as a day boy at Bath College. His headmaster, T. W. Dunn, noted the boy's unusual sobriety of judgement. His equable temperament belied his youth and the impression suggested by impish features and a shock of red hair. In 1881 Spender won a classical exhibition to Balliol College, Oxford. He excelled in his studies, as well as playing a full part in every aspect of university life.

Journalism in Hull and London In 1885 illness narrowly robbed Spender of his expected first in Greats. Jowett, Balliol's formidable master, proposed the bar as a suitable future career for Spender. Journalism he dismissed as 'an impossible profession ... foolishly partisan ... fatal to good manners and honest thought' (Spender, *Life, Journalism and Politics*, 1.22). Spender's father shared these sentiments. Yet it was journalism that Spender chose, and not inappropriately considering that his uncle William Saunders owned both the *Western* and the *Eastern Morning News*, and the central press agency in London.

Saunders gave Spender his first job, as his general factotum. This lasted a few months before peremptory dismissal. But Spender's tyro journalistic efforts had impressed Passmore Edwards, who offered Spender the post of leader writer for his *Echo*, a London, evening, halfpenny newspaper with radical sympathies and cultural pretensions. Five months later Spender resigned, ostensibly because he refused to obey Edwards's instruction to write a leader censuring Gladstone's Irish policy. Their relationship had all along been difficult and experienced journalists, from whom Spender sought advice, had counselled him that he would do better beginning in the provinces rather than London. Then, unexpectedly, Spender's uncle proposed that his nephew become editor of his Hull property the *Eastern Morning News*. This last was too good an offer to refuse. From October 1886 to February 1891 Spender served what effectively was a gruelling apprenticeship in every aspect of the newspaper business. He was obliged to be not only editor but also sales manager, financial director, reporter, leader writer, and literary critic. J. E. Taylor, owner of the *Manchester Guardian*, impressed by Spender's versatility, offered him the post of manager. Wisely he refused, recognizing that 'his true inclination was not towards management but literary work' (Ayerst, 289). Spender's reward for restoring the *Eastern Morning News* to profitability was unemployment. His uncle sold the newspaper over his head.

Not unwillingly, Spender returned to London. He lived at Toynbee Hall, Whitechapel, oldest, most celebrated of the university settlements. Samuel Barnett, the warden, a benign mentor, encouraged Spender to persevere with his freelance journalism. Soon established as a regular contributor to several journals, Spender also published in 1892 his first book, a brief monograph on the state provision of old-age pensions. This elicited the enthusiastic approval of John Morley and thereafter the two men remained firm friends for life.

While still at Oxford Spender had published the occasional article in the *Pall Mall Gazette*. It was, however, entirely fortuitous that in June 1892 the *Pall Mall*'s editor, E. T. Cook, should propose Spender as his assistant. Spender gladly accepted. Assured of a regular salary, the next month he married Mary (May; *d.* 1946), eldest daughter of William George Rawlinson, the art collector. There were no children born to this close, harmonious, mutually supportive marriage that lasted a month short of fifty years. May contributed enormously to Spender's domestic happiness and successful professional life. She was 'his gifted, constant help-meet and inspirer' (Lord Crewe, speaking at the Reform Club, July 1937, Harris, 63).

The *Westminster Gazette* and Liberal politics Within a month, editor and staff of the *Pall Mall* were obliged to resign because a new proprietor brought a change of political allegiance. But as swiftly fortune smiled. George Newnes, who had made his name and fortune with *Tit-Bits*, agreed to finance a new Liberal journal. Editor and staff were re-engaged. The first issue of the *Westminster Gazette* appeared on 31 January 1893.

Spender served three years as Cook's assistant before he was appointed editor. His influence was soon apparent, and knowledgeable critics confidently asserted that the *Westminster* was now 'the best edited paper in London' (Frederick Greenwood, Koss, *Rise and Fall*, 1.376). Under Spender the sober traditions of an earlier journalism continued, while he encouraged some aspects of the so-called 'new' journalism that made it possible to stimulate debate about previously ignored social problems. Spender's partnership with his assistant editor, the distinguished cartoonist F. C. Gould, was described as 'the most notably successful instance of all that was most enterprising in the new journalism combined with all that was best and worth preserving in the old' (Escott, 257). Indubitably the leading evening newspaper, the *Westminster* was never, as the Liberal chief whip claimed, 'the most powerful organ in England', as it never challenged the primacy of *The Times* (draft memorandum by Ellibank, 25 June 1906, Ellibank MSS, NL Scot.). It never made a profit, for its circulation rarely exceeded 20,000 copies. But this did not worry the proprietors so long as their property enjoyed widespread prestige and political influence.

Friend and foe alike acknowledged that it was Spender who gave the *Westminster* its distinction. His leaders were required reading for serious politicians, whatever their party. Spender's writing was invariably scrupulously fair and moderate in expression. He always treated the arguments of his opponents courteously and seriously. In debate, wherever possible, he sought to be constructive. It was not that he eschewed controversy, but he possessed to an unusual degree a sense of the common good which tempered any inclination to political partisanship. His declared ambition had been from the first 'to make the *Westminster* a serious political paper expounding Liberalism' (Spender, *Life, Journalism and Politics*, 1.63). Not every Liberal shared Spender's particular notion of just what constituted Liberalism. H. W. Massingham chided the *Westminster*'s editor for, 'invariably adopting a ministerialist pose'; for failing to distinguish between the political philosophy and the political party when in power. Spender's sweet reasonableness merely served to exasperate the irascible Massingham. He did not doubt the admirableness of Spender's mind, but that never stopped him from 'disagreeing with his argument that all is for the best' (Havighurst, 175–6).

Spender's constant priority was Liberal unity. The Second South African War he had considered 'unnecessary but not unjust' (Gooch, 79). His balanced editorials contrasted sharply with the impassioned polemic in which other Liberal editors indulged. He later admitted that to choose 'the unheroic course ... pouring oil on troubled waters, was not simple' (Spender, *Life, Journalism and Politics*, 103). It earned him the reproaches of both Liberal factions. Similarly, after the 1906 Liberal electoral triumph, he confessed that 'invariably playing the Government's loyal supporter was a wearying business' (ibid., 134). He generally chose to keep private reservations concerning Liberal politicians or policies. Thus he publicly lauded Rosebery's estimable qualities but never published his conviction that the earl constituted the single greatest impediment to Liberal unity. He was not, however, reticent in expressing doubts about Lloyd George's plan to reform land ownership, the exception that proved the rule.

When Asquith succeeded Campbell-Bannerman as prime minister in 1908 he forcibly expressed concern at how ill served the Liberal Party was by its carping press. He never had cause to complain about Spender, an ever dependable ministerial loyalist. Senior cabinet ministers freely shared their confidences with the editor, a practice the radical lord chancellor, Loreburn, condemned as 'a monstrous, hole and corner system'. Loreburn's paranoia was fuelled by the conviction that a 'small group of Liberal jingoes', which included the prime minister, foreign secretary, and the editor of the *Westminster Gazette*, was pursuing and advertising an aggressive, anti-German foreign policy (Morris, 293–8). So far as Spender was concerned, the censure was undeserved, but his attempted rebuttal of Loreburn's charge did not acknowledge that his private political allegiance was always closer to Liberal Imperialist than radical cabinet ministers, a fact notorious to disgruntled back-benchers who routinely added Spender's name to those of Asquith, Grey, and Haldane, condemning them collectively as 'the usual crew of quidnuncs who fear strong courses' (Mallet to Ponsonby, 29 Jan 1910, *Liberal Chronicle*, 156 n.1). Spender certainly did grow more cautious after the 1910 elections had eroded the Liberal parliamentary majority. He urged restraint upon impatient colleagues, 'lest we go smash' (Spender to Bryce, 3 Feb 1910, Bryce MSS, Bodl. Oxf.). A. G. Gardiner was not alone among Liberal editors in censuring what he judged to be 'timid alarmism … excessive caution' (Koss, *Fleet Street Radical*, 126).

The outbreak of war in 1914 brought Spender particular problems as key staff left to serve in the armed forces, and damaged machinery could be neither adequately repaired nor replaced. But Spender's references to the war as a time of extraordinary difficulty concerned his growing disillusionment with Asquith as a wartime leader. Characteristically he did not publish his concern, but confided in a friend. It could no longer be doubted that 'the source of much public discontent is the Prime Minister's laziness and lack of ideas' (E. T. Cook's diary, 1 and 3 April 1915, Koss, *Rise and Fall*, 276). When Asquith's government fell, Spender—speaking and writing to friends in obvious dejection—suggested that he would remain in harness, at the most, a few more years.

Change of proprietor and resignation Always sensitive about editorial authority, Spender would never allow his independence to be compromised. While Newnes remained owner of the *Westminster* there was never any question of a clash of opinion. But in 1908 Newnes sold out to a syndicate of Liberal politicians and businessmen. The new board was not always compliant, and Spender's relationship with the chairman, Alfred Mond, was guarded and uneasy. There had been several earlier alarms when Spender learned that Mond and Sir Charles Henry, at Lloyd George's instigation, were plotting his removal. Lloyd George saw capturing the *Westminster Gazette* as the most effective cure for Spender's wounding, critical barbs. The plot failed because the board was divided in its loyalties between Lloyd George's allies and Asquith's friends. But the uncertainty engendered damaged staff morale; sales and revenue declined. It was decided that for the *Westminster* to survive it must become a morning newspaper. The change was effected in November 1921. Although urged by friends to remain as editor, Spender resigned in February 1922. He recognized the tolling of the death knell for his kind of reflective journalism.

The *Westminster* lasted six more inglorious years before it was absorbed in 1928 by the *Daily News*, which, in its turn, was swallowed by the *Chronicle* in 1930. Just like the party, the Liberal press was thoroughly enfeebled by the Lloyd George/Asquith schism. Further weakness and uncertainty were induced by doubts about whether it was better to woo or to oppose the Labour Party. For Spender it was intellectually and emotionally impossible to countenance intimacy with Labour. His opposition made it increasingly difficult for him to contribute to the *Westminster*'s several successors. Eventually, in February 1935, by mutual agreement, the contract with the *News Chronicle* was severed. Spender was clearly unhappy; he deplored the changes overtaking journalism and admitted to friends that he looked forward to the time when 'no longer' would he have to 'argue, preach, try to convert anybody to anything' (Spender to A. G. Gardiner, Koss, *Fleet Street Radical*, 305). Deservedly his career ended upon a much happier note, as a regular contributor to the *Sunday Times* and the Westminster group of provincial newspapers. He also broadcast for the BBC.

Biographer and public life between the wars In his last two decades Spender wrote many books on a variety of subjects: travel, current affairs, history, biography. All were admired for their impeccable scholarship, judicious analysis, and lucid narrative. He wrote two official biographies of prime ministers. Radical readers found his life of Sir Henry Campbell-Bannerman (1923) not entirely satisfactory, claiming that Spender did not sufficiently emphasize the distinctiveness of Sir Henry's perception of foreign policy. The biography of Asquith (1932), the writing of which was seamlessly shared with the subject's youngest son, Cyril, was a generous and detailed appreciation of a friend's effortless superiority as the supreme parliamentarian of his generation. In 1930 he published two shorter but no less competent biographies of his friends Cowdray and Hudson. Spender thoroughly deserved John Morgan's sobriquet as 'the Nestor of Liberal journalism' (Morgan, 70). The biographies still afford valuable historical insights, for Spender had an unrivalled and intimate knowledge of contemporary politics and politicians, but they have been largely overtaken by modern studies plundering the revelations afforded by the release of private papers. Spender's *Life, Journalism and Politics* (1927) remains particularly valuable. Invariably reticent concerning his private life, these volumes are as near as he ever came to writing an autobiography. *The Public Life* (1925) affords sprightly and informed reflections upon various subjects, most valuably, the press.

Spender served on numerous public committees, royal commissions and inquiries, including two royal commissions, on divorce and matrimonial causes (1909–12) and on the private manufacture of armaments, and Milner's mission to Egypt in 1919–20. He self-deprecatingly observed, despite all the effort, 'I never succeeded in ever inducing any Government to take my advice' (Spender, *Life, Journalism and Politics*, 2.124). He three times refused public honours—in 1906, 1916, and 1934. In 1937 he accepted appointment as a Companion of Honour. In 1940 fellow journalists acknowledged his unique status in their profession by electing him charter president of their institute. His 'immense value' (Oxford and Asquith, telegram to Spender, June 1926, Harris, 213) to the political party to which he gave a lifetime's unwavering allegiance was acknowledged in June 1926, when he was made president of the National Liberal Federation. That body did not survive the year, destroyed by the quarrels over the Lloyd George fund. He was elected chairman of the Liberal council by a small rump of Liberals with neither suffix nor affix, but that body became moribund with the outbreak of war in 1939. Spender was, at the time, much out of favour with the Sinclairite Liberals. They counted him an appeaser because, aware of the shortages and the inadequacy of British armaments, he pleaded 'for some coherence and distinction between what we *wish* and what with our resources and liabilities we *can* perform' (Spender to Meston, 12 Oct 1938, Harris, 216–17). The war supposedly submerged the differences of opinion within the Liberal ranks. That the bitterness remained unassuaged is apparent from Violet Bonham Carter's letter of 10 September 1940 to Churchill, describing her father's great friend and loyal advocate as 'a cocoa-blooded, old Munichite' (*Champion Redoubtable*, 228).

Liberal editor For forty years Spender was a prominent member of the coterie of distinguished literary and political figures that regularly convened at 'the table' or in 'the corner' of his much loved club, the Reform. In his last years a painful and increasingly disabling illness ended Spender's visits to his club. Bravely he continued writing up to within a few days of his death, at Bromley, Kent, on 21 June 1942. In the history of modern journalism C. P. Scott, J. L. Garvin, and Spender alone share the distinction of their names being inseparably coupled with the newspapers they edited, in Spender's case his 'pea-green, incorruptible' *Westminster Gazette*. The qualities of Spender's personality were those of his journalism: moral sensitivity, discretion, intelligent idealism, sagacity, responsibility. But above all else, integrity. A. J. A. Morris

Sources J. A. Spender, *Life, journalism and politics*, 2 vols. (1927) • J. A. Spender, *The public life*, 2 vols. (1925) • W. Harris, *J. A. Spender* (1946) • *DNB* • S. E. Koss, *The rise and fall of the political press in Britain*, 2 vols. (1981–4) • A. J. A. Morris, *Radicalism against war, 1906–14* (1972) • J. H. Morgan, *John, Viscount Morley* (1924) • D. Ayerst, *Guardian: biography of a newspaper* (1971) • T. H. S. Escott, *Masters of English journalism* (1911) • G. P. Gooch, *Under six reigns* (1958) • *A liberal chronicle: journals and papers of J. A. Pease*, ed. C. Hazlehurst and C. Woodland (1994) • *Champion redoubtable: the diaries and letters of Violet Bonham Carter, 1914–1945*, ed. M. Pottle (1998) • A. F. Havighurst, *Radical journalist: H. W. Massingham* (1974) • S. E. Koss, *Fleet Street radical: A. G. Gardiner and the 'Daily News'* (1973) • M. Bentley, *The liberal mind, 1914–1929* (1977) • H. C. G. Matthew, *The liberal imperialists: the ideas and politics of a post-Gladstonian élite* (1973) • *CGPLA Eng. & Wales* (1942)

Archives BL, corresp. and papers, Add. MSS 46386–46394 • BM, papers • priv. coll., letters | BL, corresp. with Lord Herbert Gladstone, Add. MS 46042 • BL OIOC, corresp. with Sir Harcourt Butler, MS Eur. F 116 • BL OIOC, letters to Lord Reading, MSS Eur. E 238, F 118 • BLPES, letters to Violet Markham • BLPES, corresp. with E. D. Morel • Bodl. Oxf., corresp. with Herbert Asquith • Bodl. Oxf., corresp. with Gilbert Murray • CAC Cam., Esher papers, letters • CAC Cam., letters to Lord Fisher • HLRO, letters to Herbert Samuel • HLRO, corresp. with John St Loe Strachey • NA Scot., corresp. with Lord Lothian • NL Scot., corresp. with Lord Haldane • NL Scot., corresp. mainly with Lord Rosebery • priv. coll., corresp. with Lord Fitzmaurice • Ransom HRC, corresp. with John Lane • U. Birm. L., corresp. with Austen Chamberlain • U. Newcastle, corresp. with Walter Runciman

Likenesses M. Bone, pencil drawing, IWM • C. Gardiner, oils, Reform Club, London • photographs (as old man), repro. in Harris, *J. A. Spender* • portrait (as undergraduate)

Wealth at death £4795 4*s.* 4*d.*: probate, 29 Aug 1942, *CGPLA Eng. & Wales*

Spender [*née* Headland], **Lillian** [Lily; *known as* Mrs John Kent Spender] (**1835–1895**), novelist, born on 22 February 1835, was the second daughter of Edward Headland (1803–1869), a well-known physician of Portland Place, London, and his wife, a daughter of Ferdinand de Medina, a Spaniard. Lily Headland was educated privately for her first fourteen years and then attended classes at Queen's College, Harley Street, London. As a child she wrote rhymes and started a manuscript magazine with her friends. Until her marriage she studied French, German, and Italian at home and, with her brothers' help, Latin, Greek, and natural science.

On 28 October 1858 Lily Headland married John Kent Spender (*d.* 1882), a physician and medical researcher who was attached to the Mineral Water Hospital in Bath, and she moved to Bath. It was then that she started writing—as Rev. L. Spender—and she sent essays to magazines, on German poets as well as on social issues such as women's employment and the evils of the imprisonment of children. She was a contributor to the *London Quarterly Review*, the *Englishwoman's Journal*, the *Dublin University Review*, and *Meliora*, a magazine concerned with social work. She worked on several committees for educational and social work in Bath and, for ten years, was the secretary of the Oxford examination for girls.

Lily Spender's first novel, *Brothers-in-Law* (1869), was

written with a desire to provide an alternative to sensation fiction as well as to supplement the family income for her sons' education (she also sent one daughter to Somerville Hall at Oxford), family holidays, and her husband's early retirement. An early novel, *Parted Lives* (1873), was reviewed in *The Spectator* as the best novel of the year after George Eliot's *Middlemarch*, and most of her other novels received very favourable criticism. She wrote some twenty-one novels—about one every year until her death—in between housekeeping, raising her eight children, and various social service interests. *The Recollections of a Country Doctor* (1885) was based on her early experiences with her father. Later works such as *A Strange Temptation* (1893) and *A Modern Quixote* (1894) have leading characters of committed ideals, socialistic or otherwise, whose loyalty to friends leads them into serious difficulties in forming love relationships. Although intelligently written, her novels often have endings which fall into banal romance. They were, however, very popular and most went into several editions.

Lily Spender died at her home at 17 The Circus, Bath, on 4 May 1895. Two of her seven surviving children, John Alfred *Spender (1862–1942) and Harold Spender, were well-known London journalists. The poet Stephen Spender (1909–1995) was her grandson.

E. I. CARLYLE, *rev.* SAYONI BASU

Sources J. A. Spender, *Life, journalism and politics*, 2 vols. (1927) · Blain, Clements & Grundy, *Feminist comp.* · F. Hays, *Women of the day: a biographical dictionary of notable contemporaries* (1885) · *DNB* · Boase, *Mod. Eng. biog.* · J. Sutherland, *The Longman companion to Victorian fiction* (1988) · *CGPLA Eng. & Wales* (1895)

Likenesses portrait, repro. in *The Sketch* (22 May 1895), 180

Wealth at death £3472 18*s.* 5*d.*: probate, 28 June 1895, *CGPLA Eng. & Wales*

Sir Stephen Harold Spender (1909–1995), by Humphrey Spender, 1932

Spender, Sir Stephen Harold (1909–1995), poet, was born on 28 February 1909 at 47 Campden House Court, London, the son of (Edward) Harold Spender (1864–1926), a journalist and author, and his wife, Violet Hilda, *née* Schuster (1878–1921), daughter of Ernest Joseph Schuster (1850–1924), barrister, and his wife, Hilda Weber, daughter of Sir Herman Weber, physician.

Origins, childhood, and university Stephen Spender sprang from a mixed English Liberal and richly cosmopolitan stock. His father was, with his brother J. A. Spender (1862–1942), a well-known political journalist. The Spenders were a long-established professional family in Bath and Stephen's paternal grandmother, Lily Kent Spender (1835–1895), was a fluent Victorian novelist. Of the Spender brothers, 'J. A.' enjoyed the better career, becoming editor of the influential *Westminster Gazette*. Harold's Liberalism was more radical and his career less steady. In January 1904 he married Violet Schuster. She was university educated, a published poet, and rich. The Schusters emigrated to Britain in 1866 and set up a bank that became the National Provincial in 1919. 'That we were of Jewish as well as German origin', Spender recalls in *World within World*, 'was passed over in silence or with slight embarrassment by my father's family' (Spender, *World within World*, 13).

The Spenders' first child, Michael (1907–1945), was followed by Christine (1908–2001), Stephen, and Humphrey (*b.* 1910). After a distinguished university performance, Michael made his name as an explorer and scientist and was a leader in the field of photo-interpretation during the Second World War. Humphrey went on to become a distinguished photojournalist.

In 1913 the Spenders moved to The Bluff, Sheringham, on the Norfolk coast, where they sat out the First World War. Here it was that Stephen's parents 'kept me from children that were rough' (S. Spender, *Poems*, 1933). The family's financial circumstances were (thanks to the Schusters) comfortable, but Stephen's childhood was unhappy. He felt overshadowed by Michael. His father (overshadowed by *his* brother) felt himself a failure and Violet Spender was a chronic invalid. The family regime was one of 'Puritan decadence'—evangelical, but culturally oppressive. Oppression was relieved by a pair of servants, Bertha and Ella Mills (nicknamed Berthella), and enlivened by the occasional sight of Zeppelins over Sheringham. It was on a family holiday in 1917, in the Lake District, that eight-year-old Stephen had his 'first sustained experience of poetry' and decided to become a poet (Spender, *World within World*, 87).

Spender was sent to Gresham's preparatory school in

1918. There he was bullied by schoolfellows and comforted by the music teacher, Walter Greatorex, who predicted (accurately) that Stephen would be unhappy until 'you are about to go to University' (Spender, *World within World*, 334). In 1920 the Spenders moved to 10 Frognal, Hampstead, and in October of that year Stephen was returned from Gresham's as unteachably 'backward'. His misery at this trying period of his life is recorded in his novel *The Backward Son* (1940). Greater misery followed. He and Humphrey were dispatched to Charlcote boarding-school in Worthing where they were bullied by their classmates as 'Huns' (as Schusters). Their suffering here ended in December 1921 with domestic tragedy, the death of their mother, during a routine surgical operation. The boys were brought back to Frognal. Being a day boy suited Stephen. He joined University College School in October 1922 where he thrived in the 'liberal' atmosphere (as the opening paragraph of *World within World* indicates, Spender's definition of 'liberalism' was idiosyncratic). At this period (when he was most at odds with his 'Victorian' father) he came under the beneficent influence of his maternal grandmother, Hilda Schuster, who introduced him to modern art and literature. Spender published his first poems (influenced by Humbert Wolfe) for the University College School magazine, *The Gower*. He was introduced to socialism and D. H. Lawrence (both would be lifelong allegiances) by one of the masters, Geoffrey Thorp.

Harold Spender died on 13 April 1926. Stephen summed up his complex filial emotions in a later poem, 'The Ambitious Son' (1939), with its Oedipal opening, 'Old man, with hair made of newspaper cutting'. On Harold Spender's death, the Schusters decided to keep the three younger children (Michael was now at Oxford) at Frognal, under the care of a housekeeper, Winifred Paine (called Caroline in *World within World*). This arrangement lasted until 1933. Spender left school in 1926. Before going to university, he spent some unhappy months in Nantes, followed by an interlude at Lausanne, where—as his first published short story, 'By the Lake', records—he had a significant sexual experience with another English boy resident there. He went up to University College, Oxford, in October 1927 enrolling for the politics, philosophy, and economics degree.

Spender disliked Oxford's public-school ethos and took refuge in an intense friendship with Gabriel Carritt (Tristan in *World within World*). In his first year Spender was also embroiled in a love affair with another undergraduate, John Freeman (Marston in *World within World*), for whom he wrote good poems, unavailingly. In summer 1928 he had his momentous first meeting with W. H. Auden, then a finalist at Christ Church, and through him Spender met Christopher Isherwood. These older comrades later enthused him with the idea of living in Germany.

Over the 1928 summer vacation Spender printed his first collection (*Nine Experiments*) and a booklet of Auden's poems on a small hand press of a kind used for printing chemist's labels. In his second year, with Auden gone, Spender formed what became a lifelong friendship with Isaiah Berlin.

Spender spent the long vacation of 1929 in Hamburg, an experience memorialized in his novel *The Temple* (1989). Particularly formative was his friendship with the photographer Herbert List and his connection with the eminent German critic Ernst Robert Curtius through whom he cultivated a passion for Rilke, Hoelderlin, Schiller, and Goethe.

Lyric poet of the 1930s In May of his final year at Oxford Spender published *Twenty Poems*, which was well received. T. S. Eliot invited him to contribute to *The Criterion*. Having spectacularly failed his final exams he left for other education in Hamburg in June 1930. Over the next few years he wrote and rewrote his *Bildungsroman*, *The Temple*. Its frank depiction of homosexual love rendered it unpublishable in the UK. Eliot, meanwhile, urged him to write poetry. On a visit to England at Christmas 1930 Spender met John Lehmann, and embarked on a long and often vexed friendship. Early in 1931 he moved from Hamburg to Berlin, to be with Isherwood; this was a relationship which, if not always harmonious, was important to both men until after the Second World War.

Spender's reputation was lifted by the appearance of his poems (notably 'I think continually of those who were truly great') in Michael Roberts's *New Signatures* in February 1931. Late in 1932 Spender returned to England to see his Faber collection (*Poems*, 1933) through the press. A temporary rift with Isherwood led to a withdrawn dedication. On publication in January 1933 the book was a huge success confirming Eliot's verdict that 'If Auden is the satirist of this poetical renascence, Spender is its lyric poet' (dustjacket).

Late in 1933 Spender embarked on a permanent love relationship with a Welsh former guardsman, Tony Hyndman (1911–1980) (Jimmy Younger in *World within World*). Settled in Maida Vale, Spender cultivated relations at this period with the Bloomsbury set. Among his younger friends were J. R. Ackerley, William Plomer, Cecil Day Lewis, and the Lehmanns (Rosamond and John).

Early in spring 1934, holidaying with Hyndman near Dubrovnik (and working on his study of Henry James, *The Destructive Element*, published in 1935), Spender met Muriel Gardiner (1901–1985). She was American, rich, a divorcée, and studying to be a psychoanalyst. When Hyndman, a few weeks later in May, fell ill with appendicitis she arranged for treatment in Vienna. The Austrian capital was seething with street battles between the communists and the fascists. Gardiner was involved with the leftist underground smuggling of refugees to safety. She and Spender became lovers. 'I find boys much more attractive, in fact I am rather more than usually susceptible, but actually I find the actual sexual act with women more satisfactory, more terrible, more disgusting, and, in fact, more everything', Spender informed a disapproving Isherwood (MS letter, 14 September 1934, Huntington Library). Spender's relationship with Gardiner was complicated by the presence of Hyndman and ended when, in spring 1935, she fell in love with the Austrian socialist Joseph Buttinger, whom she later married.

Spender finished *The Destructive Element* in July 1934 and

went on to publish his long political poem *Vienna* for Faber in November. This eminently unlyrical work pleased neither T. S. Eliot nor the reviewers, but his critical writing was well received and led to a lifelong friendship with Cyril Connolly.

Between November 1935 and March 1936 Spender embarked on an experiment in communitarian living in Cintra, Portugal, with Christopher Isherwood, and their partners Hyndman and Heinz Neddermeyer. The experiment failed. In April 1936 Faber published Spender's book of short stories *The Burning Cactus*, to mixed reviews (Rosamond Lehmann found them brilliant, but 'terribly cranky').

Germany had collapsed into fascism and Spain was embroiled in civil war. Spender seized the moment with a 'political book' for Victor Gollancz's Left Book Club, *Forward from Liberalism* (1937). In September 1936 Spender broke with Hyndman and the two men ceased living together. A few weeks later, early in October, he fell in love with Inez Maria Pearn (1914–1977), a modern languages postgraduate at Oxford. They married on 15 December. In the same month Hyndman joined the International Brigade in Spain.

Forward from Liberalism brought Spender to the notice of the Communist Party. They needed, as Harry Pollitt put it, 'their Byron'. Spender was disinclined to lay down his life, but he agreed to undertake an investigatory trip to southern Spain. On his return, in February, he announced in the *Daily Worker* that he had joined the party, but he almost immediately let his membership lapse. In April 1937 he went to Spain again, ostensibly to work for a republican radio station in Valencia. He was increasingly concerned about the fate of Hyndman who, after the battle of the Jarama, had deserted and was in custody. Spender's experiences in Spain were profoundly disillusioning. They produced the finest of his (anti-)war poems: 'The Coward' and 'Ultima ratio regum'. He finally succeeded in extricating Hyndman in July 1937. His marriage during these months came under strain. Spender made one last trip to Spain in July 1937 as a delegate to the second international congress of writers in Madrid. It led to his total severance from the Communist Party.

On his return to Britain, Spender studied painting with the Euston Road group and undertook a course of psychoanalysis with Karen Stephen. He worked with J. B. Leishmann on a translation of Rilke, published as *Duino Elegies* in 1939, and joined Rupert Doone's Group Theatre as literary director. In March 1938 the company produced his verse play, *Trial of a Judge*. His long-awaited second collection of verse, *The Still Centre* (1939), established him as the leading poet of his generation still in Britain, Auden having left for America.

War, peace, and America The strains in Spender's marriage climaxed in August 1939 when Inez eloped with the poet Charles Madge, whom she later married. The Second World War broke out a fortnight later. Out of this period of breakdown Spender produced his confessional *September Journal*. At the same time he completed his novel *The Backward Son* (published in April 1940) and joined with Connolly, and the rich patron Peter Watson, to set up the literary magazine *Horizon*.

In summer 1940 Spender met the 21-year-old concert pianist Natasha Litvin (*b.* 1919), whom he subsequently married on 9 April 1941. Slightly over-age and wholly unfit for military service, he failed his medical exam twice and spent the winter of 1940 teaching at Blundell's School in Devon. By 'pulling strings' he finally contrived to get himself in the Auxiliary Fire Service and began his basic training in September 1941. In slack periods over the next three years' service he wrote poetry, reviewed extensively, and organized educational programmes for his fellow firemen. His publications include *Ruins and Visions* (1942, chronicling his recent breakdown and recovery), the sonnet sequence *Spiritual Explorations* (1943), and the manifesto *Life and the Poet* (1942).

In July 1944 Spender transferred to the Foreign Office's political intelligence department. In March 1945 he and his wife had their first child, Matthew, and moved to the house in St John's Wood which was their home for the next fifty years. On 11 May 1945 Squadron Leader Michael Spender was killed in a flying accident. A deeply affected Stephen wrote the elegy 'Seascape' for a brother with whom his relationship had always been difficult.

With peace, Spender took up service with the control commission—charged with restoring civil order to Germany. Out of his work in 1945 for this body he wrote his reportage volume *European Witness* (1946). His personal life was meanwhile darkened by the lingering death of his brother Humphrey's wife, Margaret, from Hodgkin's disease, at Christmas 1945. His 'Elegy to Margaret'—an ambitious sequence—headed *Poems of Dedication*, was published in 1947.

On leaving the control commission late in 1945 Spender was appointed literary counsellor to the newly established UNESCO in Paris. He held this post until early in 1947 when he accepted an invitation to teach (from September 1947 to July 1948) at Sarah Lawrence College in New York State. After teaching ended Spender undertook an extensive travel and lecturing itinerary across the US. Through Auden he met Frieda Lawrence in Taos, New Mexico, and she invited him to use the remote 'Lawrence Ranch' for writing. This he did, from September to October 1948, producing the first drafts of *World within World* and his political memoir for Arthur Koestler's and Richard Crossman's collection *The God that Failed* (published in January 1950). *World within World* (published in April 1951) is candid about his relations with his father, his brother Michael, his friends Auden and Isherwood, his wives, and—most controversially—Tony Hyndman. The book was a best-seller, clearing 50,000 copies in its first year.

In December 1949 Spender brought out *The Edge of Being* and the critical tide turned against him. He resolved 'not to run the gauntlet of another volume of poetry ever again' (unpublished journal). Over the next years Spender would undertake numerous international trips for the British Society for Cultural Freedom, the Congress for Cultural Freedom, and PEN.

In 1952, following a trip to Israel, Spender published a

book on the new state, *Learning Laughter*, and from February to June 1953 he occupied the Elliston chair at the University of Cincinnati giving the lectures on modernism published as *The Creative Element* (1953). Later in 1953 he accepted (from the CCF) the invitation to serve as 'English editor' for the new monthly magazine *Encounter*. His co-editor was the American Irving Kristol. The first issue of the magazine came out in October 1953 and for the fourteen years of his co-editorship, Spender was hoodwinked as to the financing of the journal.

International man of letters; last years Spender's *Collected Poems* (stringently winnowed down to seventy-five lyrics) came out in 1955. In that year he wrote in his journal, 'things I do other than writing seem to take up a larger and larger place in my life'. In 1958 Spender enjoyed considerable success with his translation from Schiller *Mary Stuart*, which was performed at the Edinburgh festival and the Old Vic. In 1959 he took a sabbatical from *Encounter* to take up the Beckman chair at the University of California at Berkeley. There he wrote *The Struggle of the Modern* (1963). His relationship with his colleagues at the magazine became increasingly difficult. In 1963, following allegations about the funding, Spender successfully had the management of *Encounter* transferred to a visibly British proprietor, Cecil King. In the same year he distanced himself from direct control of the magazine by accepting a three-year, one-semester teaching appointment at Northwestern University, in Chicago. He was, thereafter, a 'corresponding editor'.

Spender's absence from the UK was extended by his accepting the post of poetry consultant to the Library of Congress (effectively the US laureateship) from April 1965 to June 1966. In February 1966 he gave the Clark lectures in Cambridge on British and American literature, later published as *Love-Hate Relations* (1974). In April 1966 the crisis at *Encounter* exploded with the allegation in the *New York Times* that the magazine had been the 'indirect beneficiary' of CIA funds. When these allegations substantiated by *Ramparts Magazine* in April 1967 Spender resigned. In January 1968, following an open letter from Pavel Litvinov in *The Times* about the legal persecution of writers in the USSR, Spender launched a campaign which in October 1971 resulted in the setting up of *Index on Censorship*, to monitor oppression of writers. In March 1968 he gave a series of Mellon lectures on painting and literature in Washington, but was, at this period, as interested in what was happening in the streets as in the lecture halls. Following a trip to Paris, New York, Berlin, and Prague he published in May 1969 *The Year of the Young Rebels*.

During the late 1960s Spender was a frequent academic visitor to the University of Connecticut at Storrs, which he later claimed had the 'most congenial teaching faculty' he had encountered in America (Spender, *Journals*, 259). In October 1970 Spender accepted a chair of English at University College, London (UCL). In 1971 his volume of poems *The Generous Days* was published to mixed reviews. Spender confided to a colleague that 'reviewers don't know they are killing you bit by bit'. In summer 1972, through Auden, he formed a close friendship with the exiled Russian poet Joseph Brodsky. With the death of Auden in September 1973, a chapter in Spender's life closed. Connolly died in 1974 and Spender wrote elegies for both men. His memorial collection of essays, *W. H. Auden: a Tribute*, appeared in 1975. The UCL years also produced a monograph on T. S. Eliot (1975) and a symposium entitled *D. H. Lawrence: Novelist, Poet, Prophet* (1973). The autobiographical *The Thirties and After* (1978) blazed a trail for the collected *Journals, 1939–83* (1985). Spender's translation of Sophocles' *Oedipus* trilogy was published (and performed) in 1983 and a second *Collected Poems* was also published. His belated and much revised 1930s novel *The Temple* appeared in 1989. Spender's last collection of new verse, *Dolphins*, came out in 1994.

Spender's last years were troubled by the publication of an unauthorized biography by Hugh David (*Stephen Spender: a Portrait with Background*, 1992) which he tried and failed to suppress. He was successful in having David Leavitt's novel *While England Sleeps* (1993) withdrawn after its publication in the UK, on the ground that it borrowed illegitimately from the Jimmy Younger (that is, Tony Hyndman) episode in *World within World*.

Spender received numerous honours. He was awarded a CBE in 1962, made a companion of literature by the Royal Society of Literature in 1977, and knighted in 1983. Four honorary doctorates were also conferred on him. He retired from UCL in 1975, but continued to teach in America. Spender was much photographed, and had his portrait done by, among others, Lucian Freud, Wyndham Lewis, Robert Bückler, William Coldstream, Henry Moore, and David Hockney. He was tall, handsome in youth, and looked distinguished in later life. His hair silvered early, adding to the distinction. His personality is often described as 'enigmatic': famously Cyril Connolly (reviewing *World within World*) discerned 'two Spenders', one naïve, one calculating. Spender's mobility was curtailed by a serious accident in 1980, and a collapse of health in 1994, after which he did not travel again.

Stephen Spender died at his home, 15 Loudoun Road, St John's Wood, London, of heart failure, on 16 July 1995; he was cremated and his ashes were subsequently buried at St Mary's, Paddington Green, on 21 July. Although he was subjected to more satire and sarcasm than most famous modern poets (particularly by the followers of F. R. Leavis), few who knew him well seem not to have loved him.

JOHN SUTHERLAND

Sources S. Spender, *World within world* (1951) · S. Spender, *Journals, 1939–1983* (1985) · S. Hynes, *The Auden generation* (1976) · S. Spender, *The thirties and after* (1978) · C. Isherwood, *Christopher and his kind* (1976) · D. Leeming, *Stephen Spender: a life in modernism* (1999) · N. Page, *Auden and Isherwood: the Berlin years* (1998) · [S. Spender], *Letters to Christopher*, ed. L. Bartlett (1980)

Archives BL, Stephen Spender xerox archive of occasional writings, journalism, and essays · BL PES, address on European unity · Harvard U., Houghton L., corresp., literary MSS, and papers · Ransom HRC, notebooks · Stephen Spender Memorial Trust Archive, London · Virginia Polytechnic Institute, Blacksburg, corresp. and literary MSS | Bodl. Oxf., letters to Jack W. Lambert · Georgetown University, Washington, DC, Lauinger Library, letters to Elizabeth Jennings · Hunt. L., corresp. with Christopher Isherwood · King's AC Cam., letters to G. H. W. Rylands, incl. some draft poems · NL

Scot., corresp. with J. B. Singer • Rice University, Houston, Texas, Woodson Research Center, corresp. with Sir Julian Huxley • Tate collection, Tate Gallery archive, corresp. with Lord Clark • U. Leeds, Brotherton L., letters to the *London Magazine* • U. Sussex, corresp. with Leonard Woolf • U. Sussex, corresp. with Virginia Woolf and Leonard Woolf • U. Warwick Mod. RC, corresp. with Victor Gollancz • University of Bristol Library, corresp. and statements relating to trial of *Lady Chatterley's Lover* | FILM BFI NFTVA, *South Bank Show*, ITV | SOUND BBC WAC • BL NSA, documetary recordings • BL NSA, performance recordings

Likenesses H. Spender, photograph, 1932, NPG [*see illus.*] • photographs, *c.*1940–1975, Hult. Arch. • B. Brandt, photograph, 1941, NPG • I. Penn, photograph, 1947, NPG • D. Low, chalk drawing, *c.*1952, NPG • D. Moore, photograph, 1992, NPG • F. Topolski, portrait, NPG

Spender, Sir Wilfrid Bliss (1876–1960), army officer and civil servant, was born in London on 6 October 1876, the last of the five children of Edward Spender (1834–1878) and his wife, Ellen Rendle. His father was co-founder of the *Western Morning News* in Plymouth, and at the time of his death was chief proprietor and managing director of the newspaper. Wilfrid was one year old when his father, and two of his older brothers, Reginald (thirteen) and Sidney (eleven), were drowned while bathing at Whitsands Bay outside Plymouth. He was educated at Winchester College (1889–92) and thereafter at the Staff College, Camberley. He obtained a commission first in the Devon artillery and then in 1897 in the Royal Artillery. He saw service in Bermuda, Canada, Malta, England, Ireland, and India, mostly on the north-west frontier. After Camberley he was nominated to attend a naval war course, one of the first two army staff officers to be so chosen. In 1908 he was posted to the general staff at the War Office in London, and in 1909 became a member of the home defence section of the imperial defence committee, then involved with the general defence of the United Kingdom. It was in this context that his interest in Irish affairs was thoroughly awakened. His father had been a strong Liberal Unionist, and the family was seriously divided over home rule in the 1870s.

But it was in the context of imperial defence in the years immediately leading up to the First World War that Spender's own lively and, in the end, all-consuming interest in Irish affairs developed. His War Office post involved him in the preparation of a defence scheme for the United Kingdom in the light of a probable European war. It was his discovery that, in the event of war, two regular divisions would still be needed to maintain order in Ireland which, by his own account, drew his attention to the importance of Ireland in the defence of the British empire (account of Sir Wilfrid Spender's career, MS, *c.*1950, Spender MSS, D/1295/14b/5). His concern led him into public and political opposition to home rule. He approached Conservative central office and embarked on a speaking tour drawing public attention to the threat home rule would pose to the security of the empire. He organized and partly financed a national petition against home rule, and helped found the Junior Imperial League. He accepted an invitation to stand for parliament, but withdrew when the rules were changed to place officers on half pay if they

Sir Wilfrid Bliss Spender (1876–1960), by Lafayette, 1929

entered parliament. He signed the Ulster covenant when it was opened for signature in England.

Involvement in Ulster In 1912 Spender returned to India to a staff appointment on the north-west frontier. On arrival he felt it his duty to inform his commanding officer that he had signed the covenant, with its undertaking that his services would be placed at the disposal of the Ulster people, if they were coerced under an Irish government. The War Office promptly directed him to relinquish his staff appointment and return to duty with his regiment at a mountain battery elsewhere in India. After much manoeuvring, including special leave home to argue his case, the offer of a staff post in Australia, and an appeal to the king, Spender was allowed to retire—he had refused to resign—in 1913, with the rank of captain and a pension of £120 a year. He was thirty-six. A confidential inspection report of 1913 commented that Captain Spender had been led away by a 'too active conscience' and had been very injudicious, risking his prospects in life. In all other respects, the report said, he was an excellent and accomplished officer (Spender MSS, D.1295/1a/23). Also in 1913, while on leave from India, he had renewed acquaintance with a childhood friend, Lilian Dean (1880–1968), herself on leave from a post in Canada, and they had married within a few weeks. She was a devoted wife and constant support for the rest of his varied life.

During his dispute with the army Spender had sought legal advice from Sir Edward Carson, a distinguished barrister as well as leader of the Irish Unionists. This would appear to have been Spender's first personal contact with the men who were to lead Ulster initially into open and armed defiance of the government of the United Kingdom, and then as a devolved province of that kingdom. Barely six months later, in mid-1913, Carson was inviting Spender to come to Belfast to assist the Unionist cause, and help organize the Ulster Volunteer Force (UVF). The Ulster Unionist Council had already persuaded Lieutenant-General Sir George Richardson to accept the command of this recently formed, and technically not illegal, citizens' army, and it was Richardson who formally invited Spender to join his staff, which he did in September 1913, after travelling to Belfast with his new wife straight from a ten-day honeymoon. He did so on a voluntary basis, intending his involvement to be temporary, and stipulating that he would be able to continue his growing business interests in England. (He was a director of the *Western Morning News*, and remained so until the paper was sold in 1920.) In Belfast he acted as quartermaster-general to the new force, and was closely concerned with preparations then being made to enable the Unionists to take over the administration of Ulster in an emergency. By 1914 he was working with Colonel Fred Crawford on a plan to import arms from continental Europe. He was present at Larne on the night of Friday 24 April 1914, when 80 tons of rifles were landed, and more transferred for shipment to other ports. The guns were distributed throughout Ulster by motor vehicles in a remarkable logistical operation planned and directed by Spender. This dramatic arming of the UVF added a new factor to the situation, but as elsewhere events in Ulster were overtaken by the growing threat and then the reality of European war.

Service in France In July 1914 Spender, as a retired officer, was told to hold himself ready to take up an appointment with the eastern command in Chatham. He returned immediately to England, and a short time later, after the outbreak of war, was transferred as general staff officer to the new 36th (Ulster) division, formed after Carson had pledged the loyalty of the UVF to the war effort. He served with the Ulster division until 1916, and was present at the battle of the Somme, when he won the Military Cross for his part in the assault on Thiepval; in his correspondence he left a remarkable eyewitness account of the conduct of the Ulstermen on that July day. He also won the DSO and was mentioned in dispatches four times. In 1916 he was promoted lieutenant-colonel, and served with Lord Cavan's corps, and then at advanced general headquarters working under Lord Haig. He was still following events in Ireland, and remained in contact with the Unionist leadership. His correspondence shows he was strongly opposed to accepting a six-county option for partition in Ireland, and on these grounds he declined an invitation from Carson to consider contesting an Ulster constituency at Westminster. About the same time he gave some support to moves to launch a national party in England—'to promote Reform, the Union and Defence'—and considered seeking nomination for parliament in a constituency in Devon or Cornwall.

The end of the war brought a diversion from Irish affairs, by way of an invitation from Lord Haig to join the Ministry of Pensions in London, as officers' friend, or, adviser on the interests of demobilized officers and of officers' widows and families. His nomination may well have been suggested by Sir James Craig MP, soon to take over the leadership of unionism from Carson, who was then parliamentary secretary to the Ministry of Pensions. It was on Spender's advice that Haig set up a committee, of which Spender was a member, to co-ordinate the various organizations working for ex-servicemen—a move which led to the foundation of the British Legion. In 1920 he was approached by Carson and Craig and asked to return to Belfast to help reorganize the UVF, an action deemed necessary by the Unionist leadership to preserve law and order in the north of Ireland in the run-up to the creation of Northern Ireland, now inevitable under the terms of the Better Government of Ireland Bill published in February 1920. He agreed immediately, and took extended leave from the ministry. Again he saw the move as temporary, and his own long-term future in business in England.

After the First World War the UVF remained formally in existence, though it had lost many of its members in action during the war and had ceased to operate in any organized sense. Sir George Richardson had resigned from its command in 1919. Early in 1920, as Sinn Féin opposition to the proposed partition of Ireland intensified and the operations of the Irish Republican Army increasingly affected Ulster, Unionists—particularly in Fermanagh and Tyrone—began to organize armed vigilante groups to protect property and to defend Unionist interests. In June 1920 the Unionist Party decided to revive the UVF. By July 1920 Spender was back in Belfast, and commandant of the UVF. It was familiar ground, but the circumstances differed fundamentally from 1913. Then the UVF existed primarily to defy the government of the United Kingdom and oppose its policy in Ireland; by 1920 the Ulster Unionists had become the only significant group in Ireland ready to accept the partition settlement embodied in the Government of Ireland Bill, and part of the role of the UVF was to defend that policy. It was still, however, a somewhat irregular body, unlikely to be accepted and armed by government. In October 1920 the situation was regularized by the official announcement of the creation of a new special constabulary. This was based on a plan drawn up by Spender, using the UVF as the foundation of the new force.

Cabinet secretary By early 1921, his task completed and having once again declined an invitation to run for parliament, Spender was ready to return to his post in the Ministry of Pensions. His plans were altered when Craig succeeded Carson as Ulster Unionist leader in February 1921, thereby also becoming the prime minister designate of the new entity of Northern Ireland, due to come into existence in May 1921. Craig asked Spender to stay on as secretary to the new Northern Ireland cabinet. Spender, by his own account, agreed with reluctance, intending to remain for no more than twelve months, until the new administration was established. In fact, he was to remain for the next twenty-three years, an important if somewhat incongruous figure at the heart of the Unionist administration of Northern Ireland. In the early years, as cabinet secretary, his role was highly political, both as a close personal adviser to Craig and as a senior figure in the Unionist ranks—minister without portfolio, his wife confided to her diary. He accompanied Craig to negotiations with the Sinn Féin leaders in London in 1921, and with Michael Collins, head of the provisional government, in Dublin in 1922. While his advice was not always taken, he played a significant political role in the early years of Northern Ireland's existence.

Spender's move in 1925 from cabinet secretary to permanent secretary at the ministry of finance and head of the Northern Ireland civil service was surprising and not entirely welcome to him. He had no personal expertise in public finance, and he was aware of the inevitable loss of political influence the move would involve. However, he was once again persuaded by Craig, and he set about the double challenge of consolidating a professional civil service for Northern Ireland, and managing the persistently difficult financial relations between the provincial administration and the Treasury in London. In neither task was he entirely successful, but in 1929, in recognition of his contribution, he was knighted. It is widely acknowledged that he was mainly responsible for setting up the nucleus of a first-class civil service in Northern Ireland, but that service was much criticized for the absence of Catholics from its upper ranks, and for an unacceptable degree of political interference in appointments and promotions. In fact, Spender ensured that entry to the top administrative grade was, from 1929 on, by way of the London civil service commission examination, which in practice resulted in many top posts going to Oxford and Cambridge graduates with no Northern Ireland connections. He himself opposed any discrimination on religious grounds, but was unable to prevent Unionist members of the Northern Ireland parliament dominating the selection boards for other ranks. He was never a friend, let alone a member, of the Orange order.

In dealing with London, Spender found himself increasingly at odds with Craig, who, he thought, was too concerned with the immediate interests of Northern Ireland rather than with the union itself and the overall British interest. As he put it himself, looking back on his career: 'Lord Craigavon was guided in his policy by his desire to ensure the prosperity of his province and its people, whereas I followed Lord Carson's line of thought in thinking far more of the general effect upon the Empire of any change in the Irish situation' (Fisk, 483–4). In this he was consistent. It was concern with the effect upon the empire that had led him in 1913, despite his 'too active conscience', to throw in his lot with Unionists plotting open defiance of the government. In various notes and interviews he repeatedly justified his actions then by the benefits they brought to the empire. He insisted that the arming of the UVF had strengthened the hand of government in dealing with the nationalists, had deprived the Germans of arms for three divisions (the UVF guns were purchased in Germany), and had allowed Britain to send to France in August 1914 one of the two divisions earmarked for the defence of Ireland, and finally had provided the British army with a new division already trained.

Death and significance In 1939, aged sixty-three, Spender contemplated early retirement, but again a European war intervened, and he remained in post until 1944. He finally left Northern Ireland and returned to England in 1955. He died of heart failure on 21 December 1960 at the East Hill Hotel, his home at Liss in Hampshire. He was survived by Lady Spender and their only child, Daffodil, born in Belfast in 1923.

Descriptions of Spender portray him towards the end of his civil service career. In 1937 one young recruit saw him as 'remote, kindly, lisping, out of touch, hospitable, croquet-playing, correct … a survivor from a bygone era of English colonial life' (Oliver, 17). Another has portrayed him as 'a very tall, gangling man, with eager, uncomprehending blue eyes … his appearance and demeanour suggested guileless innocence' (Shea, 138). That he was a survivor from a bygone era is true, and he may at times have played the innocent abroad—as when, in 1935, he suggested to the Northern Ireland cabinet that it might consider changing the name of the province to 'north-west Britain' to help remind the average Englishman that it was still part of the United Kingdom (letter of 20 Dec 1935, Spender MSS, D715/7). But he was also a shrewd observer of events and, at times, an uninhibited and sardonic commentator on them. His view of Northern Ireland, and of things Irish in general, confided to his 'Financial diary' at the end of 1939, remains quotable:

> In Northern Ireland we claim that we have the biggest shipyard, the biggest ropeworks, the biggest linen manufacturers and the biggest tobacco factory in the world: I am afraid there is one other factory in which we could probably claim that we, or the Free State, are the largest manufacturers—namely the factory of grievances. I am not at all sure that this particular factory isn't the most paying one in the Province. ('Financial diary', 84, Spender MSS, D 715)

An inveterate writer of notes and memoranda, Spender kept a personal account of his administrative and political involvement from 1931 to 1944 ('Financial diary'), and he was the author, sometimes anonymously, of articles in newspapers and magazines. In 1933, for instance, he contributed to the *Western Morning News*, under a pseudonym, a series of articles critical of the relations between the Unionist administration in Belfast and government in London, while he himself was head of the Northern Ireland civil service. Before leaving Northern Ireland he presented a large collection of his papers to the Public Record Office of Northern Ireland. These, together with the diaries of Lady Spender, give unique glimpses of forty years of Irish history, and of the part played in them by a remarkable if somewhat eccentric Englishman with a too active conscience.

DENNIS KENNEDY

Sources I. L. Maxwell, 'The life of Sir Wilfrid Spender, 1876–1960', PhD diss., Queen's University, Belfast, 1991 · A. T. Q. Stewart, *The*

Ulster crisis (1967) • P. Buckland, *The factory of grievances* (1979) • J. A. Oliver, *Working at Stormont* (1978), 17 • P. Shea, *Voices and the sound of drums* (1981), 138 • R. Fisk, *In time of war: Ireland, Ulster and the price of neutrality, 1939–1945* (1983) • PRO NIre., Spender MSS
Archives PRO NIre., corresp., diaries, and papers | PRO NIre., Lady Spender diaries | SOUND PRO NIre., interview recording
Likenesses Lafayette, photograph, 1929, NPG [*see illus.*]

Spens, Henry [Harry] (**1714–1787**), university professor and translator, was born Henry Spence on 10 September 1714 in Edinburgh, the son of James Spens of Kirkton of Alves, an Edinburgh writer to the signet who is credited with a broadside against the Jacobite rising of 1715. His mother was Anne Robertson. Educated at King's College, Aberdeen, where he graduated MA on 1 April 1730, Spens trained for the ministry and was licensed by the presbytery of Dalkeith on 3 October 1738. In November 1744 he was ordained to the parish of Wemyss, on the coast of Fife, where he served for thirty-five years. While there he is believed to have co-authored, with John Chalmers, minister of the nearby parish of Elie, a brief pamphlet titled *An Inquiry Concerning a Plan of a Literary Correspondence* (1751). In 1763 Spens produced the first English translation from the Greek of Plato's *Republic*, which was frequently reprinted from 1906 onward in the popular Everyman's Library edition. The original edition was published in Glasgow by Robert and Andrew Foulis, with a preface that was identified on the title page as 'a Preliminary Discourse concerning the Philosophy of the Ancients, by the Translator'. There Spens praises the ancients, and especially Plato, for joining philosophy with 'politeness', virtue, and religion. Writing of Socrates and Plato, he asserts that 'Divine Providence seems to have raised up these illustrious philosophers, to be advocates for virtue, and to give some check to the progress of prevailing corruption, and impiety' (*The Republic of Plato*, trans. H. Spens, 1763, xviii).

On 29 October 1765 Spens married Anne Duncan, the widow of a Captain Home RN. Their only child, James, was born on 1 October 1771 but died later that month. Spens was admitted to the chair of divinity at St Andrews on 29 December 1779 and remained there until his death in 1787. His connection with the moderate party in ecclesiastical affairs was an important factor in his selection for the chair. When promoting Spens's candidacy in a letter to London of 15 November 1779, William Robertson, the historian and leader of the moderates, wrote:

> He is learned, decent, and worthy, and eminent for an uniform adherence to … moderate and rational principles both concerning Ecclesiastical and civil policy. … It is indeed of great importance to have a person of his character in such a station, at a time when a spirit of fanaticism and disorder, is spreading among our Order. (W. Robertson to Lord —, PRO, SP 54/47, fols. 364–5)

Spens was then put up for moderator of the general assembly by the moderates, and on 25 May 1780 he secured that office in a significant test of party strength by narrowly defeating Sir Henry Moncreiff Wellwood, the popular party leader, 112 to 106. According to Scott he received an honorary DD degree from King's College, Aberdeen, on 1 October 1781, but he was already styled 'H. Spens, D.D.' on the title page of his translation of Plato's *Republic* in 1763. Spens was a non-resident member of the Royal Society of Edinburgh. He died on 27 November 1787.

RICHARD B. SHER

Sources P. Gaskell, *A bibliography of the Foulis Press*, 2nd edn (1986) • M. Price, *Philosophical dialogue in the British Enlightenment* (1996) • *Fasti Scot.*, new edn • R. B. Sher, *Church and university in the Scottish Enlightenment: the moderate literati of Edinburgh* (1985)
Archives PRO, Robertson to Lord —, SP 54/47, fols. 364–5

Spens, James, of Wormiston, Baron Spens in the Swedish nobility (*d.* **1632**), diplomat and army officer in the Swedish service, was the eldest son of three known children of David Spens, laird of Wormiston (*d.* 1571), and his wife, Margaret Lermonth (*d.* in or after 1574), daughter of the laird of Dairsie, Fife. He was probably born during the 1560s, but little is known of his early years and education. His father, a leading supporter of Queen Mary's party, was killed at Stirling Castle on 4 September 1571 during a botched attempt to abduct the regent, Matthew, fourth earl of Lennox. As punishment the Spens estates centring on Wormiston House near St Andrews were confiscated and awarded to the queen's gaoler, Patrick Lindsay, sixth Lord Byres. In 1574 or soon afterwards James's mother married Sir John Anstruther of that ilk and it was largely thanks to his standing at court that the family returned to grace. The young Spens slowly reacquired the family lands and perhaps the office of constable of Crail, which had been in his family for generations, but he never regained Wormiston.

In 1589 Spens's sister Lucretia married Patrick *Forbes of Corse, an influential theologian and future bishop of Aberdeen (1618–35). About this time Spens himself married Agnes Durie, with whom he had at least four daughters and two sons who survived into adulthood. Spens's status was improving: in February 1593 he attended privy council sessions at St Andrews, and in 1594 and again in 1607 was provost (mayor) of the burgh of Crail, Fife.

On 29 June 1598 Spens was one of eleven 'gentilmen adventuraris' from Fife contracted by James VI to 'plant policy and civilisation in the hitherto most barberous Isle of Lewis' (*Reg. PCS*, 1592–9, 462–3). The project—similar to the plantation of Ulster—was expected to bring the king rental income by 1600, though the financial risk fell on the adventurers. In November 1598 they landed with 500–600 troops, built a fortified camp near Stornoway, and began to 'civilize' the islanders, not always by peaceful methods. By December 1601 a bitter dispute had erupted with the local Macleods, and when Spens attempted to capture Neil Macleod he was ambushed and nearly sixty colonists were killed; the settlement in Stornoway was burnt and Spens was kept hostage until the colonists had abandoned the island. A second colonization attempt was made in summer 1605, supported by royal troops; houses were built and crops planted, but raiding by the islanders and financial problems again forced the settlers to leave. A third attempt in 1609 came to the same end. Dispirited, Spens and the two other surviving shareholders sold their rights to the island in 1610 to Lord Kintail for 10,000 merks Scots.

By this time, Spens's attentions had switched to Sweden. In October 1605, following a costly defeat by the Poles at Kirchholm in Latvia, Karl IX of Sweden commissioned Spens and his younger brother David to raise 1600 mercenary foot and 600 horse in Scotland. Due to finance and shipping problems the levy was only partly completed by 1608, but Spens accepted a further commission in 1609 for 1000 foot and 500 horse. This time recruitment fared better, largely because the British authorities welcomed the opportunity of ridding Ireland of troublemakers after the Nine Years' War. In February 1610 Spens's Scots, Irish, and English recruits marched from Finland across the frozen ice of the Bothnian Gulf to join a Russian-led army, only to be defeated by the Poles at Klushino, near Moscow, on 4 July 1610 NS; weeks later the Poles marched unopposed into Moscow. The Russians were quick to blame their defeat on the treachery of Spens's recruits, although one English officer complained that the Swedes had traded the British soldiers to the Russians 'as horses are in Smythfield' (*EngHR*, 29, 1914, 246–56). Spens was technically colonel of the British, but had not joined them in the field and escaped blame.

Spens's shuttling between Sweden and Britain acquired a diplomatic character. He was also an indispensable courier for correspondence between Gustavus Adolphus of Sweden and Henry, prince of Wales, and their younger brothers Charles Phillip and Charles, duke of York. No later than 1609 Spens was knighted, and from May 1609 he became Britain's special ambassador to Sweden. As he was returning to Sweden in March 1611 from a mission to recruit 3000 Scottish and Dutch mercenaries the Danes arrested him half a mile into Swedish soil and killed one of his party. The incident outraged the Swedes and contributed to the outbreak of the Kalmar War in April 1611. Spens was also instrumental in bringing the conflict to a close: in peace talks at Knäred, brokered by James I, Spens represented Sweden, while his stepfather's grandson Sir Robert *Anstruther (1578/9–1644/5?) acted for Denmark. On 18 January 1613 the two Scots reported to James I that peace had been agreed 'chiefly thanks to their own abilities' (*CSP Venice*, 1610–13, xxix).

Appointed Sweden's ambassador to Britain in December 1613, Spens spent several years in London channelling British policy towards Denmark and Poland in favour of Sweden. He intended to return to Sweden in 1618, and even received diplomatic instructions in 1619, but his departure was repeatedly delayed. He finally reached Sweden in spring 1621 as Britain's special ambassador to Sweden. Gustavus Adolphus, who had embarked on a string of attacks on Polish possessions across the Baltic, chose Spens as his chief recruiting master for soldiers from Scotland. Despite Gustavus Adolphus's complaints about nepotism among the Scots, Spens was allowed a free hand and did not hesitate to install kith and kin in plum jobs. In 1624 Spens obtained permission to raise a regiment of 1200 Britons for Sweden, and passed the colonelcy to his eldest son, also James. Of the two regiments which he was to levy in 1627 he gave one to Sir James *Ramsay, husband of his daughter Isobel (married in Scotland in 1619). Another daughter, Cecily, married another famous 'Swedish' Scot, General-Major Sir David Drummond. There were also blood ties (difficult to disentangle) to officers of the Monypenny family. More than once Spens's standing with Gustavus Adolphus saved his protégés. On one occasion Colonel Ramsay had been shackled in irons after 'hard words' with the Swedish king, and 'if not for his father-in-law, … his life had been forfeit' (I. Hoppe, *Geschichte des ersten schwedischen-polnischen Krieges in Preussen*, 1887, 419). Nevertheless the Swedish king and the chancellor, Axel Oxenstierna, developed a deep affection for their Scottish soldiers and for Spens in particular.

As Sweden's wars began to merge with the Thirty Years' War in Germany, Spens's diplomatic remit shifted to the European mainland. His trips from London to Stockholm usually followed a route via The Hague, Hamburg, and Copenhagen, during which he called on notables including the family of the count palatine of the Rhine, exiled in the Netherlands, and Sir Robert Anstruther, now Britain's main representative in Denmark, with whom he often swapped royal letters and information before it was made public.

In 1624 Spens became involved in protestant attempts to organize a grand alliance against the Habsburgs, a project that depended on British financial commitment. Spens's main remit was to obtain for Sweden the leadership of the alliance's army, but although constantly reporting back from the Netherlands he played a secondary role in the diplomacy. His knowledge of languages was limited, and he preferred to write in turgidly phrased Scots (sometimes deliberately in lieu of a code) which often required translation. He was soon outwitted by Robert Anstruther, who obtained English promises of a subsidy for a Danish-led intervention in Germany. Hopes for a grand alliance faded further in 1625 when a conference in The Hague was postponed after the deaths of Maurice of Nassau and James I. When Charles I came to power he came under the influence of the duke of Buckingham who favoured war with Spain rather than involvement in Germany. Spens reported Buckingham's 'papist' machinations with displeasure to the Swedish monarch, amid perceptive observations on the rift between king and parliament.

Though Spens was a strict Calvinist, he was not opposed to a religious settlement to the Thirty Years' War. Among his protégés were two champions of ecumenism: his onetime secretary, John Durie (possibly a relative of his wife), and his chaplain, Eleazar Borthwick (sent in 1628 by Spens's brother-in-law, the bishop of Aberdeen). Both got hearings with the Swedish monarch thanks to Spens, and went on to have considerable influence in Europe.

On 28 April 1627, as reward for his services to Sweden, Spens was made Baron Spens, of Orreholm near Skaraborg in Västergötland. The jealousy of a Swedish rival, Riksråd Johan Skytte, meant the grant was not officially countersigned until early 1629. On 23 September 1627, as ambassador-extraordinary from Charles I, Spens personally presented Gustavus Adolphus with the Order of the Garter and St George Cross in an elaborate ceremony in the presence of English heralds at Dirschau in Polish Prussia.

In March 1629 Spens arrived in London to raise troops for Gustavus Adolphus's invasion of Germany. He shipped to Polish Prussia 3000 recruits in three new regiments and from about July 1629 was appointed honorary general over all the English and Scots in Swedish service.

Early in 1631 the death of his son James nearly killed Spens, who complained of a 'deadlie illnesse' in his will drafted in Stockholm on 31 May (Spens, 51). His health improved after his second wife, Margretta Forath, gave birth to a son, Jakob (their first son, Axel, had been named for the Swedish chancellor). By 3 September 1631 Spens was well enough to join Gustavus Adolphus in Germany as his legate to James Hamilton, marquess of Hamilton's 6000-strong 'English army'. Having landed near Stettin in August, Hamilton's grandiose goal was to recover the palatinate, but he lacked the financial support of Charles I and the trust of Gustavus Adolphus, and his force quickly melted away. Spens could do little to help: often complaining of gout the last of his increasingly scrawly official letters, dated 1 September 1632, was to request Hamilton's presence before the Swedish king on the winding up of his command.

Spens continued to follow the Swedish court in Germany, and reassumed the colonelcy of his son's old Scots regiment (though there is no record of him serving in the field with it, nor with any other of the units he nominally commanded). He was in Frankfurt-am-Main when Gustavus Adolphus was killed at Lützen on 16 November and he himself died at Frankfurt on the morning of 27 November, apparently at the shock of the news. His body was transported to Stettin, where it remained for half a year before being shipped to Stockholm; he is said to have been buried in Riddarholm church, Stockholm, the resting-place of Swedish royalty. He was survived by his wife, who married, in 1637, Hugh Hamilton, a colonel in Swedish service, later Baron Hamilton of Glenlawley. Spens was succeeded in his barony by his son William. The senior branch of the family was introduced into the Riddarhus (house of nobles) in 1635 but died out in 1665. A junior branch, elevated to greve (count) from 1712, survived in Sweden until the end of the twentieth century.

Spens made a far bolder impression overseas than in Britain. He was the leading figure in the diaspora of Scots who abandoned their impoverished homeland for Sweden's rising star and in shipping in excess of 10,000 Britons to serve in the Swedish army made a significant contribution to the building of Sweden as a great power. Despite his status as double ambassador, there can be little doubt that Spens eventually became more Swedish than British in his affiliations.

RICHARD ZYGMUNT BRZEZINSKI

Sources A. Duncan, *The diplomatic correspondence of Sir James Spens of Wormiston*, c.1970, U. Glas., department of history • E. Spens, 'A Scots lady in Älghut', *Scottish Genealogist*, 31/2 (June 1984), 44–53 • T. A. Fischer, *The Scots in Sweden* (1907) • H. Cook, 'The Fife adventurers', *Scots Magazine*, 134/6 (March 1991), 640–45 • H. D. Watson, 'Sir James Spens of Wormiston, 1571–1632: a Scoto-Swedish genealogy', *Scottish Genealogist*, 28/4 (Dec 1981) • V. Donaldson, 'Mr Harry Watson's article on Sir Jas. Spens of Wormiston', *Scottish Genealogist*, 29/2 (June 1982), 56–9; 29/4 (June 1982), 127 • *Rikskansleren Axel Oxenstiernas skrifter och brefvexling*, 15 vols. (Stockholm, 1888–1977) • A. Grosjean, 'Scots and the Swedish state: diplomacy, military service and ennoblement, 1611–1660', PhD diss., U. Aberdeen, 1998 • G. M. Bell, *A handlist of British diplomatic representatives, 1509–1688*, Royal Historical Society Guides and Handbooks, 16 (1990) • A. A. v. Stiernman, *Matrikel öfver Svea rikes adel-och ridderskap*, 2 vols. (Stockholm, 1754–5) • W. Wood, *The East Neuk of Fife*, 2nd edn (1887) • *The manuscripts of the duke of Hamilton*, HMC, 21 (1887) • J. H. McMaster and M. Wood, eds., *Supplementary report on the manuscripts of his grace the duke of Hamilton*, HMC, 21 (1932) • PRO, SP 81/39, fols. 197, 228v • *CSP dom.* • *CSP Venice*, 1610–13 • *Reg. PCS*, 1st ser., vol. 5 • *Register of the privy seal of Scotland*, 1546–80, 1582, 1593–1608 • *APC* • PRO, SP 95 (Sweden), bundles 1–3 • Riksarkivet, Stockholm, biographica collection, Spens • Riksarkivet, Stockholm, Anglica collection, Spens • riksregistraturet, Latin registraturet, and Tysk registraturet, Riksarkivet, Stockholm

Archives PRO, SP 95 (Sweden), bundles 1–3 • Riksarkivet, Stockholm, Anglica collection, Spens • Riksarkivet, Stockholm, biographica collection, Spens • Riksarkivet, Stockholm, riksregistraturet, Latin registraturet, and Tysk registraturet

Wealth at death little in Britain; land and money in Sweden: Spens, 51–3

Spens, Janet (1876–1963), literary scholar, was born on 23 January 1876 at Bellevue, Hamilton, Lanarkshire, the second daughter of Walter Cook Spens (1842–1900), a Glasgow advocate and sheriff-substitute of Lanarkshire, and his wife, Helen (*d.* 1927), daughter of Sir John Gillespie of Edinburgh. Janet was one of eleven children, only seven of whom survived to adulthood. She and a sister were sent to live with an aunt, Mrs Lizzie Robertson, in Edinburgh. Until she was fourteen she was educated by governesses and thereafter she attended private classes in Edinburgh. She then returned to Glasgow and enrolled at Glasgow University, graduating MA in 1899.

In 1901 Miss Spens went to Versailles as a *répétitrice*. The following year she returned to Glasgow, where she held a class for adults and gave a series of lectures on nineteenth-century poets. In 1903 she and Margaret Hannan Watson founded Laurel Bank School for Girls in Glasgow. During her five years teaching at Laurel Bank, she continued her adult literature classes. She was happiest teaching adults: to her, the quintessence of things was revealed only in art, especially literature, and above all in poetry. Great literature was written by adults, for adults, and chiefly about adult experiences. In 1908 she was appointed assistant lecturer in the English department at Glasgow University and in 1909 she was appointed tutor to the women students in arts. Her first work, *Two Periods of Disillusion*, was published the same year and the following year she gained the degree of DLitt.

In 1911 Miss Spens was appointed tutor in English literature at Lady Margaret Hall, where she remained for twenty-five years, latterly as a fellow. She was unusual in holding such a post without having been a student at one of the Oxford or Cambridge women's colleges; her appointment was a reflection of the high opinion of her work held by her teachers and colleagues, including Gilbert Murray and A. C. Bradley. She enjoyed Greek and French literature and was interested by metaphysics and theology. Her subtle mind expressed itself either in ingenious suppositions or imaginative penetration. She published three more books, *An Essay on Shakespeare's Relation to Tradition* (1916), *Elizabethan Drama* (1922), and *Spenser's Faerie Queene: an Interpretation* (1934), the last of which was the most original and provocative. She also wrote a number of articles, reviews, and essays. She did not publish as much as she may have wished, partly because she never found writing easy. Her lecturing, too, was rather strained. She was best in small groups, or tutoring, though her sharp mind and forthright criticism could make it rather an ordeal for her students. She regarded the contemporary emphasis on self-expression and self-development in educational theories as mistaken. She was keenly interested in all aspects of education and with Eleanor *Lodge, the history tutor at Lady Margaret Hall, she started the Oxford National Education Association to provide contacts between teachers in elementary and secondary schools and university academics.

Janet Spens and Eleanor Lodge formed a lifelong friendship. They shared holiday cottages and bought a house in Oxford to which they intended to retire. Miss Spens was devotedly nursed by Eleanor Lodge through a protracted period of severe illness, which began shortly after her arrival at Lady Margaret Hall and lasted through the First World War. Eleanor Lodge died in 1936, but Janet Spens remained for the rest of her life at their house at 5 Fyfield Road, Oxford. During the Second World War she was an indefatigable air-raid warden and had a houseful of evacuee children.

Miss Spens was described by friends as unshockable, for her scrupulous sincerity led her to question moral and literary values. Her sincerity also resulted in a 'ruthlessness in criticism which made her formidable as a tutor and extremely candid in friendship' (K. M. L., *The Brown Book*, 33). But she was enormously kind and would go far out of her way to help others, while her originality was heightened by her idiosyncrasies. Her unintentional remarks provided sheer comedy, and she was notoriously absent-minded. But she was always the first to laugh at herself.

The Oxford National Education Association ended in the 1930s and Janet Spens retired as tutor at Lady Margaret Hall in 1936, but she continued teaching part-time and discussing education into her seventies. Each term she invited the university English women tutors for a literary evening with papers and discussions. She was created an Oxford MA by decree when women were admitted to full membership of the university. In 1944 Glasgow University awarded her an honorary LLD and in 1954 she was elected an emeritus fellow of Lady Margaret Hall. She died at the Radcliffe Infirmary, Oxford, on 14 January 1963, having suffered near-blindness in her last few years.

Lindy Moore

Sources K. M. L. [K. M. Lea], 'Janet Spens, 1876–1963', *Brown Book* (1963), 33–5 • E. Mitchell, ed., *Laurel Bank School, 1903–1953* (1953) • E. C. Lodge, *Terms and vacations*, ed. J. Spens (1938) • *The Times* (16 Jan 1963) • K. M. L., 'Janet Spens', *Oxford Magazine* (30 May 1963), 328–9 • V. M. Brittain, *The women at Oxford: a fragment of history* (1960) • matriculation album, women, 1896–7, U. Glas., Archives and Business Records Centre • *General register of the University of Glasgow* (1945) • register of D.Litt., U. Glas., Archives and Business Records Centre • enrollment book, 2, U. Glas., Archives and Business Records Centre, Queen Margaret College archives, DC 233/2/7/1/2 • Burke, *Peerage* (1967) • b. cert. • d. cert.

Archives Bodl. Oxf., corresp. with Gilbert Murray

Likenesses group portrait, photograph (at Laurel Bank School, 1904), repro. in Mitchell, ed., *Laurel Bank School*, frontispiece • photograph, repro. in *Brown Book* (1963), 35 • photographs, Lady Margaret Hall, Oxford

Wealth at death £8560 12*s*. 0*d*.: probate, 29 April 1963, *CGPLA Eng. & Wales*

Spens, John, of Condie (*d*. 1573), lawyer, was the son of James Spens of Condie, Perthshire. He had a brother, Lawrence, but nothing is known of their mother. A determinant at St Salvator's College, University of St Andrews, in 1535, by 1539 Spens was appearing as an advocate before the lords of session, and a decade later had become one of the nine leading advocates licensed to act in all matters before the college of justice.

From 1554 Spens acted as one of the assessors (or legal advisers) of Edinburgh town council, and between 1558 and 1564 he was regularly either one of the bailies of the burgh or on the council. In October 1555 he was promoted to act as queen's advocate jointly with Henry Lauder, and received a pension in consequence. In 1560 he acted as a spokesman for Mary of Guise in her last negotiations with the lords of the congregation. On 12 November 1561, following Lauder's death, Spens took his place on the bench, *ex officio* as queen's advocate, and thereafter also attended the privy council. He still held the office of queen's advocate jointly, being now associated in that office with Robert Crichton of Eliok, but after Lauder's death he was the senior figure. In 1566 he was appointed to a commission for the revision of the laws.

Spens married Jane Arnot and they had three daughters, Euphemia, Margaret, and Jean. He also had two natural children, John and Grizel. Spens was described by John Knox as 'a man of gentle nature, and one that professed the doctrine of the Evangel' (Knox, 2.401). In May 1555 he acquired the lands of Condie pursuant to an entail in which it had been stipulated that if his uncle, John Spens of Condie, died without male heirs, then the lands would be disponed to him as the son and heir of James Spens. He therefore inherited the lands at the expense of two female cousins. He also owned lands in Gilmerton, near Edinburgh, where he appears to have lived while working in Edinburgh. On his way home in 1564 he and his servants were attacked by nine men who were later forced to apologize before the lords of council. He referred in his testament to Sir John Wemyss, laird of Wemyss, as his 'special gud friend and chief' (NA Scot., register of testaments). Wemyss was a supporter of Queen Mary in the 1560s. Spens retained his position during all the changes of government from 1560 onwards. His estate, including arrears of pensions, exceeded £4000 at his death. His last will and testament is dated 16 June 1573, and he was dead by the end of the month. His wife, Jane, was his executor, and he also made provision for his natural children.

John Finlay

Sources MS acts of the lords of council and session, NA Scot., CS6 • MS register of testaments for Edinburgh commissary court,

NA Scot., CC8/8/3 • MS register of deeds, NA Scot., RD1 • MS books of *sederunt*, NA Scot., CS1 • R. K. Hannay, ed., *Acts of the lords of council in public affairs, 1501–1554* (1932) • *APS, 1424–1592* • *Reg. PCS*, 1st ser., vols. 1–2 • J. M. Thomson and others, eds., *Registrum magni sigilli regum Scotorum / The register of the great seal of Scotland*, 11 vols. (1882–1914), vols. 3–4 • M. Livingstone, D. Hay Fleming, and others, eds., *Registrum secreti sigilli regum Scotorum / The register of the privy seal of Scotland*, 2–6 (1921–63) • J. Knox, *History of the Reformation in Scotland*, vols. 1–2 of *The works of John Knox*, ed. D. Laing, Wodrow Society, 12 (1846–8) • J. M. Anderson, ed., *Early records of the University of St Andrews*, Scottish History Society, 3rd ser., 8 (1926) • J. Finlay, *Men of law in pre-Reformation Scotland* (2000) • A. I. Dunlop, ed., *Acta facultatis artium universitatis Sanctiandree, 1413–1588*, 2 vols., Scottish History Society, 3rd ser., 54–5 (1964) • R. K. Marshall, *Mary of Guise* (1977)

Wealth at death approx. £4000: NA Scot., register of testaments for Edinburgh commissary court, CC 8/8/3

Spens, (William) Patrick, first Baron Spens (1885–1973), lawyer and politician, was born on 9 August 1885 at Frimley Park, Surrey, the eldest in the family of three sons and three daughters of Nathaniel Spens, chartered accountant, and his wife, Emily Jessie Connal, both of whom were of Scottish descent. Spens was educated at Rugby School and New College, Oxford, which he entered as a commoner in 1904. He obtained second classes in both classical honour moderations (1905) and *literae humaniores* (1907).

Spens was called to the bar by the Inner Temple in January 1910 and was commissioned in a Surrey territorial unit, the 5th battalion of the Queen's Royal regiment, in 1911; he served with them as adjutant throughout the First World War, first in India, then in Mesopotamia, then in India again. He was thrice mentioned in dispatches and appointed OBE (1918). On 15 September 1913 he married Hilda Mary (*d.* 1962), daughter of Lieutenant-Colonel Wentworth Grenville Bowyer; they had two sons (the younger of whom was killed in 1942 during the Second World War) and two daughters.

On his return from India in 1919 Spens appeared before the Chancery bar, specializing in company work. He took silk in 1925. In May 1929 he stood as Conservative candidate in a by-election for St Pancras South-West but was unsuccessful. He was chosen as National candidate in a by-election for the Ashford division of Kent in March 1933. He held the seat with 48 per cent of the vote against a strong Liberal challenge. At the general election of 1935 he increased his majority (against the national trend), obtaining 59 per cent of the vote. As an MP he was popular though not prominent in the house. Leo Amery observed: 'Spens is not in any sense an active party politician … He hasn't spoken often and though universally liked and respected has never been a conspicuous figure in the cut-and-thrust of parliamentary debate.'

Unexpectedly, at the age of fifty-eight, Spens attained high office. The chief justice of India, Sir Maurice Gwyer, was due to retire in 1943. Three eminent counsel were invited to succeed—Sir Walter Monckton, Sir Cyril Radcliffe, and Sir William Jowitt—but none felt able to leave his current position. An offer was then made to Spens. When the outgoing chief justice was informed he bitterly opposed the selection, insisting that under the agreed procedure he ought to have been invited to suggest names

(William) Patrick Spens, first Baron Spens (1885–1973), by Elliott & Fry, 1950

first. He objected to Spens on three main grounds: an Indian should have been considered initially; a party-political appointee would not be deemed impartial; and, finally, Spens's professional qualifications were inadequate. Gwyer observed testily that no lord chancellor had thought to consider him for a High Court judgeship. The viceroy, the second marquess of Linlithgow, acknowledged that there had been 'a serious error in procedure', but he was not disposed to make this an issue. Spens took up the appointment in June 1943.

Spens's personal relations with successive viceroys were good: Linlithgow described Spens as 'quick, sensible' and Viscount Wavell called him 'sensible and helpful … practical'. However, his judicial experiences proved frustrating. The federal provisions of the Government of India Act (1935) had not been implemented and the court had no explicit role. Between 1937 and 1943 only forty-six cases were decided, and on his arrival Spens reported a 'lack of confidence' in the court throughout India. He proposed to amend this by enlarging its sphere so as to include appeals from the Indian high courts which had gone up to the privy council. Legislation was drafted, but opposition was soon expressed. The newspaper *Dawn* described the federal court as 'a queer bottleneck in the political system' and advised Spens to 'curb his missionary zeal'. Wavell concluded that the proposals had aroused an 'adverse verdict by organized opinion in India', and the initiative lapsed. Spens also produced elaborate proposals for the reform of the system of high courts but these too failed to find favour: Wavell observed that 'his knowledge of India is inadequate' and nothing further was done.

After the return of peace the political tempo in India became urgent with increasing rivalry between Congress and the Muslim League. Communal tensions exploded in 'the great Calcutta killing' of August 1946. Wavell asked Spens to head a judicial inquiry into its causes. Spens informed the viceroy privately that 'there was Hindu incitement and a sudden and concerted attack without provocation on the Muslims', but in the deteriorating political situation any agreed report became impossible. The commission of inquiry was adjourned *sine die* and then dissolved. When partition between India and Pakistan was agreed in June 1947 it appeared probable that disputes would arise between the two new states over the division of assets. It was decided to appoint an arbitral tribunal. Once again Radcliffe was approached and this time agreed to serve, but he was reserved for the more vexing task of determining the boundary between the two new states. Jawaharlal Nehru proposed that the federal court should constitute the tribunal but M. A. Jinnah was adamant in opposing this, saying of the federal court judges 'the present lot were particularly poor'. As a compromise, Spens was asked to chair the tribunal, with India and Pakistan each nominating their own assessors. The tribunal considered fifty-eight references; its last award was made on 25 April 1948. Thereafter, Spens returned to London and by March 1949 was again in practice in King's Bench Walk.

For the general election of February 1950 Spens was adopted as candidate for the safe Conservative seat of South Kensington. In a three-cornered contest he obtained 75 per cent of the vote. At subsequent elections in 1951 and 1955, in straight fights with Labour, he increased his share of the poll to 79.5 per cent and then to an astonishing 82.5 per cent. He decided not to contest the next general election and in August 1959 moved to the House of Lords, receiving one of the last hereditary peerages.

Spens was knighted in 1943, appointed KBE in 1948, admitted to the privy council in 1953, and made treasurer of the Inner Temple in 1958. His first wife died in 1962 and on 25 May 1963 he married Kathleen Annie Fedden, daughter of Roger Dodds, of Northumberland and Bath. In retirement he lived in Kent. Spens died at his home, Beacon Cottage, Benenden, Kent, on 15 November 1973, and was succeeded in the title by his elder son, William George Michael (*b*. 1914). HUGH TINKER, *rev.*

Sources Burke, *Peerage* (1970) · Burke, *Peerage* (1999) · *The Times* (16 Nov 1973) · private information (1986)
Archives SOUND BL NSA, documentary recording
Likenesses Elliott & Fry, photograph, 1950, NPG [*see illus.*]
Wealth at death £73,295: probate, 18 Feb 1974, *CGPLA Eng. & Wales*

Spens, Thomas (*c*.1415–1480), diplomat and bishop of Aberdeen, was the third son of John Spens of Glen Douglas and Lathallan and his wife, Isabel, daughter of Sir John Wemyss. Having allegedly been educated in Edinburgh in the 1430s, he took his first steps in a long diplomatic career when on 16 December 1439 he was granted a safe conduct by Henry VI to go to England. He also came to hold a number of church offices; by 10 June 1444 he was archdeacon of Moray, and he was appointed to the positions of apostolic protonotary and succentor of Moray by the following year. In the late 1440s, in an ambassadorial role, Spens was instrumental in opening the negotiations which secured the eventual marriage of James II to Mary of Gueldres, niece of the duke of Burgundy. His provision to the bishopric of Galloway, which took place on 8 January 1450, had the effect of placing a loyal king's man in an area of Black Douglas influence.

Spens was sent by James II on an embassy to Charles VII of France in 1450 and was in turn commissioned by the French king to urge James II's support for Henry VI of England against Richard of York. In the crucial period of tension between James II and the Black Douglases, Spens gave consistent support to the king. He attended the parliament held in July 1451, at which William, eighth earl of Douglas, resigned and received formal regrants of his possessions. Spens was in Newcastle by 24 August, when a three-year truce between Scotland and England was ratified, but he was back in Scotland by 1 September; he appeared then with the king at Falkland, and he witnessed a number of royal charters throughout the winter. He was with James as late as January 1452, shortly before the king killed the earl of Douglas on 22 February. As bishop of Galloway, Spens was the senior churchman in the heartland of Black Douglas influence, but his loyalty to the king appears to have been unwavering. James II sent him to France to explain in person the king's position regarding the Black Douglases, just before the forfeiture of the family in 1455.

Spens was received at Bourges on 19 May 1455, and was largely engaged in diplomatic activity on the continent until 1458. He was present when the betrothal between James II's sister Annabella and Count Louis of Geneva, arranged in 1444, was formally broken off in 1456. Between 30 January 1458 and 18 April 1459 Spens held the office of keeper of the privy seal. When Ingram Lindsay, bishop of Aberdeen, died on 24 August 1458, Spens was translated from Galloway to Aberdeen before 15 December, and it was as bishop of Aberdeen that on 16 April 1459 he witnessed a charter by Mary of Gueldres, in which she founded the collegiate church of the Holy Trinity, Edinburgh. On 2 June 1460 Spens received a safe conduct for himself and Andrew Durisdeer, bishop of Glasgow, to go to England on matters concerning the existing truce, but the overthrow of the Lancastrian dynasty on 10 July resulted in turmoil and the renewal of Anglo-Scottish hostilities, in the course of which James II was killed.

Spens was mainly occupied with the business of his diocese during the following year, although he was part of a Scottish embassy once more by 24 September 1461. A safe conduct for one year was issued to him by Edward IV on 25 June 1463, but in spite of this Spens, in company with Alexander, duke of Albany, James III's younger brother, was captured on a return voyage from Bruges in an act of piracy by an English barge and subsequently held captive in England. This had occurred before 8 July 1464, and Spens was not released until the next year; he appeared back at court on 2 July 1465. His detention was designed by Edward IV to exert pressure on the Scots to abandon support for the Lancastrian cause, and the bishop was set free once proposals for a truce, including the projected marriage of James III to an English bride, were put forward. He was sufficiently in favour with Edward IV to receive from that king a large annuity and several gifts.

Spens was involved in the Stirling agreement of April 1468, whereby the Boyds attempted to secure acceptance for their recent elevation; however, the forfeiture of the family in November 1469 rendered the document ineffective. Upon the death of James Lindsay in 1468 Spens resumed the office of keeper of the privy seal, and appears to have been unaffected by the fall of the Boyds. By 12 June 1469 he had returned from another diplomatic mission to England, in time for the marriage of James III to Margaret of Denmark on 13 July. On 17 August 1472 St Andrews was erected into a metropolitan see, with Patrick Graham as the first archbishop. Spens then petitioned Pope Sixtus IV for exemption from metropolitan jurisdiction for the diocese of Aberdeen during his own lifetime, and received a papal bull granting this on 14 February 1474.

Spens became embroiled in a protracted dispute over compensation claimed from the English for the seizure of Bishop Kennedy's barge, the *Salvator*, which was wrecked near Bamburgh in March 1473. The issue was settled on 25 October 1474 and on 3 February 1475 Spens took payment of 500 marks on behalf of the Scots merchants whose goods had been plundered. Negotiations for a marriage between Prince James of Scotland and Edward IV's daughter Cecilia saw Spens playing a central role in the preliminary discussions on 25 June 1474, but he was not present when the negotiations were concluded in October 1475.

Spens was assiduous as a witness to royal charters and was a constant member of the committee of the articles throughout the 1470s. But the fact that he does not appear to have engaged in diplomacy after the mid-1470s may indicate that his health was now declining. He made a number of gifts and improvements to St Machar's Cathedral in Aberdeen, and fortified the bishop's palace as well. He also founded St Mary's Hospital in Leith shortly before his death, which took place in Edinburgh on 15 April 1480. Spens was buried on the following day in the collegiate church of the Holy Trinity, whose foundation he had witnessed twenty-one years earlier.

C. A. McGladdery

Sources J. Dowden, *The bishops of Scotland … prior to the Reformation*, ed. J. M. Thomson (1912) · Rymer, *Foedera*, new edn, vols. 10–11 · *RotS*, vol. 2 · *APS*, 1424–1567 · J. M. Thomson and others, eds., *Registrum magni sigilli regum Scotorum / The register of the great seal of Scotland*, 11 vols. (1882–1914), vol. 2 · *Hectoris Boetii murthlacensium et aberdonensium episcoporum vitae*, ed. and trans. J. Moir, New Spalding Club, 12 (1894) · *CDS*, vol. 4 · G. Burnett and others, eds., *The exchequer rolls of Scotland*, 5–6 (1882–3) · [C. Innes], ed., *Liber cartarum Sancte Crucis*, Bannatyne Club, 70 (1840) · C. Innes, ed., *Registrum episcopatus Aberdonensis*, 2 vols., Spalding Club, 13–14 (1845) · A. I. Dunlop, ed., *Calendar of Scottish supplications to Rome*, 4: 1433–1447, ed. D. MacLauchlan (1983) · C. Innes, ed., *Registrum episcopatus Moraviensis*, Bannatyne Club, 58 (1837)

Spens, Sir William (1882–1962), educationist, was born on 31 May 1882 at 7 Woodside Place, Glasgow, the eldest of the four sons of John Alexander Spens (1847–1928), writer to the signet and a leading layman in the Scottish Episcopal church, and his wife, Sophia Nicol (*d.* 1940), daughter of Hugh Baird. He was educated at Rugby School (*c.*1895–1901) and King's College, Cambridge, where he was elected a scholar in 1901. He obtained a first class in part one of the natural sciences tripos, and went on to read theology. After a serious illness, he was appointed in 1906 director of studies in natural sciences at Corpus Christi College and early in 1907 was elected to a fellowship—the first natural scientist to join the governing body of the college. His administrative and organizational qualities soon came to be recognized and in 1911 he was appointed a tutor. On 9 July 1912 he married Dorothy Theresa (*d.* 1973), daughter of John Richardson *Selwyn, formerly bishop of Melanesia; they had a son and three daughters, one of whom died in infancy. Spens contemplated taking holy orders, and although he did not do so, his course of lectures, published in 1915 as *Belief and Practice*, indicated his strong interest in theology and helped to establish his reputation as a liberal Anglo-Catholic thinker. He later contributed an essay on the eucharist to *Essays Catholic and Critical*, edited by Edward Gordon Selwyn (1926), and one on birth control to *Theology* (1930).

Being medically unfit for military service, Spens took up a temporary wartime post at the Foreign Office in 1915 and two years later became secretary of the foreign trade department which was responsible for the 'black list' of blockaded items. After the armistice his services were recognized by his appointment as CBE. The French government appointed him chevalier of the Légion d'honneur and he was also appointed an officer of the order of the Crown of Italy.

After the war Spens returned to Cambridge, where he held a succession of administrative offices; 'for him university management and intrigue were of the essence' (*DNB*). He was elected to the council of the senate (1920) and to the financial board of the university. He became a member of the statutory commission (1923) and played a major part in drafting new statutes for the university and the colleges. In 1927 he was appointed master of his college and remained in that post until retirement in 1952. Inter-war Corpus, one of the smallest colleges in the university, has been described as 'a Conservative–Anglican plot' (Cowling, 73), Spens's own politics being high tory. In the years before the Second World War he did much to strengthen the position of the college with major improvements to its buildings and amenities and by making use of additional benefactions to attract able students with awards and scholarships. Admission was restricted to men intending to read for honours. The annual Corpus Christi feast was seen as an occasion to form or strengthen links with public figures, and the guests included the archbishop of Canterbury, Stanley Baldwin, and Neville

Sir William Spens (1882–1962), by Henry Lamb, 1939

Chamberlain. The resources of the college were strengthened considerably in the longer term by a timely transfer of capital out of gilt-edged securities into land, house, and commercial property. From 1931 to 1933 he was vice-chancellor and from 1930 to 1939 he was chairman of the university appointments board.

Apart from serving on various university bodies in Cambridge, Spens was a member of the commission on Christian doctrine appointed by the archbishops of Canterbury and York (1922–38), of the royal commission on Durham University (1934), and of a War Office departmental committee. From 1934 to 1938 he was chairman of the Universities Bureau of the British Empire.

In February 1934 Spens was appointed to succeed W. H. Hadow as chairman of the consultative committee of the Board of Education. In October 1933 the committee had been requested to consider and report upon the organization and interrelation of schools, other than elementary, providing for pupils over the age of eleven. It took five years to conclude its deliberations—the board had apparently expected it to take two—but the resulting report on secondary education, published on 30 December 1938, and generally known as the Spens report, has been reckoned 'one of the most remarkable state papers of the inter-war period' (*The Times*). That all the committee's members were brought around to supporting the final recommendations owed much to Spens's powers of persuasion and management.

Following the earlier Hadow report on the education of the adolescent (1926), the Spens report recommended a differentiated, tripartite system of grammar schools, technical high schools, and modern schools, each providing a complete curriculum of secondary education for pupils above the age of eleven. It recommended that the school-leaving age be raised to sixteen. Particular emphasis was placed on improvements to technical schools, to make them effective alternatives to grammar schools. The report aspired to achieve parity of esteem and staffing between the three different types of school. It accepted contemporary expert opinion that innate intellectual ability could be objectively measured, and recommended that pupils be allocated to these separate institutions on the basis of written intelligence tests. The possibility of providing secondary education in 'multilateral' (comprehensive) schools was considered at some length, though the idea was rejected other than as an expedient in sparsely populated rural areas.

Despite its rejection of multilateralism, the Spens report was in many respects a radical document, and its proposals went a good deal too far for the Board of Education (which had not yet implemented the provision in the 1936 Education Act to raise the leaving age to fifteen). Well before the outbreak of the war, Spens's proposals had been pigeon-holed. But the social and political impact of war soon made many of the report's ideas a part of reconstruction thinking, and they underlay the 1944 Education Act, which provided secondary education for all. Indeed the Ministry of Education subsequently arranged for the report to be reprinted and reissued in 1947 on the grounds that it was likely to be valuable when the new policy (in secondary education) was being developed in practice. Spens himself was given a knighthood in 1939.

With the outbreak of war Spens was appointed regional commissioner in charge of civil defence in the eastern region, which was thought to be one where an enemy invasion was probable. The arrangement was that if any part of the country was cut off from the central government by invading forces, then the regional commissioner was to exercise very wide powers, delegated from the king, without responsibility to parliament. In practice the post involved keeping a balance between the competing claims of the civil and military authorities in the region. His legendary powers of administration and efficiency were brought to bear in the king's name, and after the war the borough of Great Yarmouth in gratitude installed him as high steward.

Against a background of political strife and accompanied by a considerable degree of professional fear and manoeuvring, Spens chaired three interdepartmental government committees on the remuneration of general practitioners, of dentists, and of medical consultants from 1946 to 1948 in preparation for the full implementation of the National Health Service. From 1947 to 1956 he was chairman of the National Insurance Advisory Committee, whose main task was to consider draft regulations under the National Insurance Act. On his retirement from the mastership of Corpus in 1952 he was appointed steward of the cathedral chapter at Ely.

Spens had always retained an active interest in his old school and was nominated by Cambridge University in

1944 as its representative on the governing body, immediately becoming chairman on the death of Archbishop William Temple in 1944. He remained a governor until 1958, and helped bring about the controversial appointment of Sir Arthur Fforde as headmaster in 1948. He was deputy chairman of the Governing Bodies' Association from 1954 to 1959 and chairman of the joint committee of governors, headmasters, headmistresses, and bursars from 1948 to 1959. Philip Snow, who knew him in this capacity, described him thus:

> Six feet tall, wearing rimless pince-nez, with a highly domed head, a slow tread, a tight-lipped expression, and little small-talk, Spens was a formidable personality. Napoleonic and Machiavellian were adjectives applied to him by those with whom he worked. His mastery of detail was supreme. He was punctilious to the last comma in the recording of proceedings. Insistent on having the consideration of all possible relevant data, he would brief himself with the most minute fact. One of the most experienced chairmen in the country, with a rather autocratic manner, he would encourage the same select number in a committee to speak, tending to ignore the presence of persons in whose appointment he had not a hand and disregarding their eminence or distinction in any field other than that which he considered relevant to the committee. Scrutinizing draft minutes, he would sometimes deny that people had been present at a meeting over which he had presided, when in fact they had been there but had been discouraged by him from making any contribution. He would lay his gold watch on the table at the beginning of a meeting and, without appearing to rush the tempo, conclude it, having completed all the agenda, on the exact minute upon which he had decided at the outset. His intellect was so sharp that nothing escaped his notice in any memorandum, although he was short-sighted and not so observant of things off paper, albeit interested in on-the-spot assessments. (*DNB*)

The same writer added that although Spens was 'invariably serious and very much to the point', he 'was surprisingly susceptible to feminine presence. His wife in this atmosphere helped to humanize him: he enjoyed it when the large bubble of an over-ponderous statement of his was pricked by female comment' (ibid.). Spens died at his home, the Old Sacristy, The College, Ely, on 1 November 1962, following a stroke. PETER GOSDEN

Sources *DNB* · *The Times* (2 Nov 1962) · J. Simon, 'The shaping of the Spens report on secondary education, 1933–38; an inside view', *British Journal of Educational Studies*, 25 (1977), 63–80, 170–85 · P. Bury, *The college of Corpus Christi and of the Blessed Virgin Mary: a history from 1822 to 1952* (1952) · R. McKibbin, *Classes and cultures: England 1918–1951* (1998) · G. Sutherland and S. Sharp, *Ability, merit and measurement: mental testing and English education, 1880–1940* (1984) · R. Barker, *Education and politics, 1900–1951: a study of the labour party* (1972) · M. Cowling, *Religion and public doctrine in modern England*, 1 (1980) · C. Webster, *The health services since the war*, 1 (1988) · b. cert. · m. cert. · d. cert.

Archives BL, letters to Albert Mansbridge, Add. MS 65257B · King's Lond., Liddell Hart C., corresp. with Sir B. H. Liddell Hart | FILM BFI NFTVA, current affairs footage · BFI NFTVA, news footage

Likenesses H. Lamb, oils, 1939, CCC Cam. [*see illus.*] · W. O. Hutchinson, oils, *c.*1955, Rugby School, Warwickshire

Wealth at death £35,103 3*s*.: probate, 21 Feb 1963, *CGPLA Eng. & Wales*

Spenser, Edmund (1552?–1599), poet and administrator in Ireland, was born in London but his family possibly came from Burnley in north-east Lancashire. His origins are unclear and his immediate family not established beyond doubt, although a number of possible ancestors and relatives are recorded. The Spensers are noted at the end of the thirteenth century, holding a freehold at Hurstwood, in Worsthorne, 3 miles south-east of Burnley. An Edmund Spenser, head of this branch of the family, is recorded deceased in 1587. He married twice and by each marriage had a son named John, both of whom had sons named Edmund. Spenser publicly claimed kinship with a more exalted line of the family name, the Spensers of Althorp. In *Prothalamion* he claims that:

> from another place I take my name,
> An house of auncient fame
> (ll. 130–31)

and in *Colin Clouts Come Home Againe* he notes his relation to the three daughters of Sir John and Lady Katherine Spenser of Wormleighton and Althorp:

> Ne lesse praiseworthy are the sisters three,
> The honor of the noble familie:
> Of which I meanest boast my selfe to be,
> And most that unto them I am so nie.
> (ll. 536–9)

He dedicated three of the poems contained in his *Complaints* to the three ladies: *Mother Hubberds Tale* (published separately in 1612) was dedicated to Anne, Lady Compton and Monteagle; 'The Teares of the Muses' to Alice, Lady Strange; and 'Muiopotmos' to Elizabeth, Lady Carey. Spenser also addressed to Lady Carey one of the dedicatory sonnets to *The Faerie Queene*, which contains a reference to the poet's 'remembraunce of your gracious name'—probably a sly hint at their kinship and her maiden name.

Edmund's father may have been the John Spenser who moved from Hurstwood to London, where he became a member of the Merchant Taylors' Company. John is recorded working as a free journeyman clothmaker in the service of Nicholas Peele, 'sheerman', of Bow Lane, London, in October 1566. He may have been the John Spenser who became an alderman in 1583, owned a house formerly in the possession of the duke of Gloucester, near the Merchant Taylors' Hall, constructed a warehouse nearby, was made lord mayor in 1594, and subsequently received a knighthood. It is also possible that Edmund was the son of an ordinary journeyman, as his claims to gentleman status came through his own achievements—a university degree—and acquisition of land in Ireland. Nothing is known of his mother other than her name, Elizabeth, to which he refers in *Amoretti*, sonnet 74. Spenser probably had a number of siblings. Gabriel Harvey refers to him as 'your good mother's eldist ungracious son' in his *Letter Book*. There were perhaps two sisters, named Elizabeth and Sarah, the latter of whom later lived in Ireland. A John Spenser who matriculated as a sizar at Pembroke College, Cambridge, at Easter 1575 and graduated in 1577–8 may well have been a younger brother. A John Spenser, perhaps the same person, is recorded as attending Merchant Taylors' School in 1571, and a John Spenser is recorded as serving as constable of Limerick in 1579, the coincidences suggesting, assuming both are the same person, that he was probably related to Spenser in some way.

Early years and education It is not certain where in London Spenser was born. Early eighteenth-century antiquarians claimed that he came from East Smithfield but, given the low population of this area, it is more plausible that he was born in West Smithfield. He was probably born in 1552, since he matriculated at Cambridge University in 1569, at a time when the usual age at matriculation was sixteen or seventeen. First he attended the recently founded Merchant Taylors' School, probably from 1561, the year in which it opened, although the sole record of his attendance is for his last year there, 1569. The headmaster was the humanist educational theorist Richard Mulcaster, whose rigorous pedagogical methods and intellectually demanding approach to the curriculum strongly influenced Spenser. Mulcaster was also interested in the development of the English language, advocating its widespread use but recognizing its need to borrow words and phrases from other languages. It is perhaps significant that this problem was one which Spenser examined throughout his literary career. The school was housed in an old mansion, the Manor of the Rose, in the parish of St Laurence Pountney. Other pupils included Thomas Kyd, Lancelot Andrewes, and Thomas Lodge.

On 26 February 1569 Spenser was one of thirty-one 'certyn poor schollers of the scholls aboute London'—six from his school—who were left 1*s*. and a gown to wear at the funeral of Robert Nowell, a rich lawyer from Lancashire and brother of Alexander Nowell, dean of St Paul's, in the will of the deceased. This may indicate that the Spensers were poor, and so suggests that Spenser's father was the less rather than the more successful John Spenser mentioned above. Spenser subsequently received three payments from Nowell's bequest: 10*s*. on 7 November 1569, 6*s*. on 7 November 1570, and 2*s*. 6*d*. on 24 April 1571. He also received five other payments while at university, between 1571 and 1574, which may have been on account of ill health or further indications that he was a scholar in need of funds.

Shortly before he went to university Spenser translated a series of twenty-one poems: six 'epigrams', which were stanzas from Petrarch's canzone 'Standomi un giorno solo a la finestra', and fifteen sonnets from Du Bellay's 'Visions'. These were published with accompanying woodcuts as an introduction to *A theatre wherein be represented as wel the miseries and calamities that follow the voluptuous worldlings*, a translation of a work by the major Dutch protestant poet Jan Van Der Noot by Henry Bynnemann, a prominent publisher, who had entered the work in the Stationers' register on 22 July 1569. Van Der Noot's preface suggests that the translations are his but Spenser later reworked both sequences as 'The Visions of Petrarch, Formerly Translated' and 'The Visions of Bellay' in *Complaints* (1591). These works indicate that his was regarded as a precocious talent, as it is unusual for a schoolboy to contribute to such an important volume. They also suggest that Mulcaster, who was friendly with Van Der Noot's cousin Emanuel Van Meteren and had other Dutch contacts, may have been instrumental in launching Spenser's writing career.

Spenser matriculated at Pembroke College, Cambridge, on 20 May 1569 as a sizar—a poor scholar who earned his bed and board by performing a series of servant's duties. Spenser wrote little about his life at college but he did refer to 'My mother Cambridge' in *The Faerie Queene* (book 4, canto 11, stanza 34). He appears to have read widely in a variety of languages, and could read Latin, Greek, French, and Italian, and probably other tongues. His contemporaries included Lancelot Andrewes, who followed him to Pembroke from school two years later; Gabriel Harvey, who became a fellow in 1570 and was to be Spenser's most significant mentor for the next ten years or so; and Edward Kirke, admitted as a sizar in 1571, who may have made some contribution to the notes published with *The Shepheardes Calender*, or at least have been party to their complex humour and eccentric nature. On 18 October 1569 a bill was signed to an Edmund Spenser for bearing letters from Tours for Sir Henry Norris, ambassador to France, to Queen Elizabeth, indicating that Spenser was already involved in secretarial work for powerful patrons. Norris was father of John and Thomas Norris, whom Spenser later served in Ireland.

Spenser graduated with a BA in 1573, his name placed eleventh in a list of 120, and an MA in 1576, when he was placed fourth from last out of seventy (the lists may not be in order of merit). It is not clear how he spent the next three or four years. He may have travelled back to Lancashire, where he fell in love with 'Rosalind'; E. K., in *The Shepheardes Calender*, encourages readers to identify the love-sick Colin in the January and June eclogues with Spenser—'[Rosalynde] is … a feigned name, which beyng wel ordered, wil bewray the very name of hys love and mistresse, whom by that name he coloureth' (January); 'this is no poetical fiction, but unfeynedly spoken of the Poete selfe' (June)—but taking such material at face value is a hazardous enterprise. It is possible that Spenser was in Ireland in the mid-1570s. In *A View of the Present State of Ireland* (written *c*.1596) Irenius claims to have witnessed the execution of Murrough O'Brien (July 1577). Such evidence is also problematic, as it depends upon an exact identification of Spenser with Irenius, a fictional character in a dialogue. However, there is corroborating evidence: Spenser is recorded delivering letters and a 'cast of falcons' to Robert Dudley, earl of Leicester, from Sir William Drury, president of Munster (8 July 1577). It is possible that Spenser was working for the lord deputy, Henry Sidney, Leicester's brother-in-law, as he had for Sir Henry Norris.

Some time after 1 April 1578 Spenser was employed in the household of Dr John Young, bishop of Rochester, and former master of Pembroke College when Spenser was a student (Young was installed on the above date). Gabriel Harvey possessed a copy of Jerome Turler's *The Traveller* (1575), which has the inscription 'Ex dono Edmundi Spenserii, Episcopi Roffensis Secretarii' ('a gift of Edmund Spenser, secretary of the bishop of Rochester'). It is likely that Spenser lived at the bishop's residence in Bromley, which would account for E. K.'s statement in the June eclogue that 'Colin' had 'for his more preferment removing out of the Northparts came into the South'.

Gabriel Harvey records that he and Spenser met in London on 20 December 1578. Spenser presented Harvey with four 'foolish bookes' that he had to read before 1 January 1579 or give Spenser his four volumes of Lucian. The four volumes were Till Eulenspiegel's *A Merye Jest of a Man that was called Howleglas* (*c.*1528), Andrew Borde's *Jests of Scoggin* (*c.*1566), *Merie Tales … by Master Skelton* (1567), and *The Pleasaunt Historie of Lazarillo de Tormes* (trans. D. Rowland, *c.*1569). The outcome of the contest is not recorded. Harvey also noted in his *Letter Book* that Spenser looked like a 'young Italianate signor and French monsieur', a description that gives a sense of the humorous banter established between the two friends.

Early works Spenser was clearly writing poetry throughout the 1570s. The prefatory epistle to *The Shepheardes Calender*, signed E. K., claims to have been written 'From my lodging at London thys 10. of April'. E. K. may have been Edward Kirke, Spenser's contemporary at Pembroke, but it is more likely that the epistle was written by Harvey or by Spenser himself, and possibly both. E. K. refers to a series of other works that are now lost: 'Dreames, Legendes, Courte of Cupide', a translation of Moschus; 'Idyllion of Wandering Love, Pageaunts, Sonnets'; and 'The Englishe poete', a critical treatise. It is likely that some of these works were revised and reappeared as parts of longer poems published later (commentators speculate that the 'Courte of Cupide' was revised as *The Faerie Queene*, book 3, cantos 11–12). Certainly this would accord with other information about Spenser's habits of composition. Lodowick Bryskett records, in his *Discourse of Civill Life* (1606), an exchange—which may be in part fictional—between a number of intellectuals at his house near Dublin in 1582. Spenser begs to be excused from a discussion of moral philosophy because he has already completed such a task in *The Faerie Queene*, which suggests that his works were often written a long time before they were published and that they were carefully revised.

Spenser wrote to Harvey on 5 October 1579 from 'Leycester House' to say that he had entered the earl's service and was ready to travel abroad for his master. It is likely that he had entered the Leicester circle some time between September 1578 and April 1579. On 15 October he wrote to Harvey again, from the house of 'Mystresse Kerkes' in Westminster, to say that he was in 'some use of familiarity' with Sir Philip Sidney and Edward Dyer, and that they debated how to reform English metre and bring it in line with the standards of the ancients. In another letter Harvey writes that both he and Spenser are friendly with Daniel Rogers, another acquaintance of Sidney's. Commentators have suggested that Spenser and Sidney enjoyed a close relationship and discussed poetic matters, before Sidney's untimely death in 1586. Others argue that the evidence is slim and that it is unlikely that someone of Sidney's social status would have been keen to spend a great deal of time with a commoner such as Spenser (Heninger).

On 27 October 1579 Spenser married Maccabaeus Childe at St Margaret's, Westminster. They had two children, Sylvanus and Katherine—Richard Mulcaster, Spenser's former headmaster, had a child named Sylvanus. Spenser married again, in 1594, but his poetic persona, Colin Clout, refers to being 'Vassall to one, whom all my dayes I serve' (*Colin Clouts Come Home Againe*, 1591), which suggests that Maccabaeus Spenser died between *c.*1590 and *c.*1593.

The Shepheardes Calender was entered into the Stationers' register on 5 December 1579 and was published by the protestant publisher Hugh Singleton soon after that date, as the poem bears the imprint 1579 (indicating that it must have appeared before the end of February). The *Calender* was a popular work and was reprinted in 1581, 1586, 1591, and 1597, demonstrating that Spenser did make an impact as 'our new poet'. It contains twelve poems, complete with prefatory comments and notes by E. K., which may or may not have been written by Spenser himself and Gabriel Harvey, and a series of emblematic woodcuts of allegorical significance. The poems describe events in the lives of a series of fictional shepherds and vary from apparently personal laments on the nature of loss and unrequited love to stringent ecclesiastical satire and attacks on corruption and court patronage. They comment on the nature of love and devotion, the pains of exile, praise for the queen, forms of worship, the duties of church ministers, forms of poetry, the merits of protestantism and Catholicism, and impending death. Equally important is the showy technical proficiency of the works and the ways in which the poems and commentary serve to announce the arrival of a major new English poet.

The *Calender* was soon followed by another work, presumably as part of the same plan to launch Spenser as a significant English poet. On 30 June 1580 his and Harvey's *Three Proper, and Wittie, Familiar Letters* were entered into the Stationers' register; the epistle 'To the Curteous Buyer, by a Welwiller of the Two Authors' is dated 19 June 1580. To these letters were attached 'Two other very commendable letters, of the same mens writing … more lately delivered unto the printer'. Spenser's letters are purportedly written from Leicester House and are dated 5 October 1579 (containing further material dated 15–16 October) and 2 April 1580. They discuss a variety of intellectual and literary matters, concentrating especially on the need to reform English poetry and, especially, the desirability of quantitative metre. The tone, in H. R. Woudhuysen's words, is 'familiar and intimate, knowing and rather jokey, secret and yet clearly assembled with publication in mind' (Hamilton, 435), in line with the textual apparatus of *The Shepheardes Calender*. The letters contain more references to lost works: 'My Slomber', 'The Dying Pellican', 'Nine Comoedies', 'Stemmata Dudleiana', 'Dreames' (also referred to in *The Shepheardes Calender*), and 'Epithalamion Thamesis' (probably reworked as part of *The Faerie Queene*, book 4, canto 11). Spenser refers to 'Dreames' and 'Dying Pellican' as 'fully finished'. There is also the first reference to *The Faerie Queene* when Harvey writes that, for Spenser, '"The Faerye Queene" be fairer in your eie than the *Nine Muses*, and *Hobgoblin* runne away with the Garland from *Apollo*' (p. 628).

Secretary to Lord Grey in Ireland In 1580 Spenser became private secretary to Arthur, Lord Grey of Wilton, who was appointed lord deputy of Ireland in July. Spenser probably arrived with Lord Grey on 12 August. His salary, as recorded on 31 December, was £20 p.a. He was also paid £43 19*s.* 3*d.* for carrying messages, and paid out £18 16*s.* 10*d.* to messengers (12 December). He now lived in Ireland until his death, returning to England at regular intervals for official and literary business. He may not have wished to leave for Ireland, as some have conjectured. It is likely that he incurred the wrath of William Cecil, Lord Burghley, for his hostile portrait in *Mother Hubberds Tale*, which appears to have circulated in manuscript in the late 1570s or 1580. No copies of this manuscript survive and there is no contemporary corroborating evidence, apart from internal references, added later, lamenting the fate of an unsuccessful courtier—presumably Spenser himself—who has 'thy Princes grace, yet want her Peeres' (l. 901). The last lines of *The Faerie Queene* have also been taken to refer back to this incident; Spenser hopes that his work will be read fairly, unlike his 'former writs', and so be:

> free from all that wite [blame],
> With which some wicked tongues did it backbite,
> And bring into a mighty Peres displeasure.
> (book 6, canto 12, stanza 41)

The peer in question was Burghley and the work *Mother Hubberds Tale*.

It seems likely that the work was controversial because of its direct satire of the queen's projected marriage to François, duke of Alençon. John Stubbs, author of *The Discoverie of a Gaping Gulf* (1579), an aggressive treatise urging Elizabeth not to make her subjects obey a foreign, probably Catholic, monarch, had just had his right hand severed for publishing his work. Stubbs's book was translated into French and Italian, and a manuscript was sent to the pope, precipitating an international incident. Spenser could hardly have chosen a less apposite time to circulate a topical satire of the incident, in which he seems to show that the queen is in danger of being duped by the French ambassador, Simier, represented as an ape (Elizabeth's name for him) in league with her chief minister, represented as a fox. The disastrous effect of *Mother Hubberds Tale* probably explains why Spenser, who had promoted himself as the most important new English poet earlier in the year, did not publish another significant work for ten years and concentrated instead on his career in the Irish civil service.

It is possible that Spenser accompanied Grey on some military expeditions and he may have been present at the notorious massacre at the Fort d'Oro, Smerwick, on the Dingle peninsula, on 9 November 1580, when Lord Grey ordered the slaughter of some 600 Spanish and Italian troops who had surrendered to the lord deputy. The state papers contain letters in Spenser's hand from Grey to Elizabeth and Lord Burghley, vigorously defending his actions. Spenser later defended Lord Grey himself in *A View of the Present State of Ireland* (*c.*1596).

Spenser may also have accompanied Grey on expeditions against the O'Mores of Connaught in February 1581 and the O'Tooles, O'Byrnes, and Kavanaghs in co. Wicklow and co. Wexford in May–June; on his northern tour of duty in August, when Grey negotiated peace with Turlogh Lynagh O'Neill and fought in Leinster; and in his campaign against the Munster rebels in September. On 14 March Spenser was appointed clerk of the chancery for faculties, as successor to Lodowick Bryskett. The seven-year appointment required the drafting of the licences and dispensations issued by the archbishop of Dublin. Spenser undoubtedly employed a deputy and kept part of the salary for himself. At the end of the month he was paid £52 4*s.* 10*d.* for carrying messages and paid out £39 3*s.* 8*d.* to messengers. The total that Spenser was paid for organizing messengers during Grey's deputyship was £430 10*s.* 2*d.* He is referred to as 'gent … secretary of the deputy', affirming that his position in Ireland had changed his status, probably through his ability to purchase and rent land.

Spenser was undoubtedly living in Dublin or close outside throughout this period. It is likely that his intellectual circle in Dublin was wide and varied, as indicated in Lodowick Bryskett's *Discourse of Civill Life*. As well as Bryskett and Grey, Spenser undoubtedly knew Geoffrey Fenton, translator of prose romances and of Guicciardini's history of Italy, who married into the Boyle family, as Spenser was to do later; Barnaby Rich, soldier and author of numerous romances and political treatises; and Barnaby Googe, author of *Eglogs, Epytaphs, and Sonettes* (1563)—pastoral poems that may have had some influence on *The Shepheardes Calender*—and numerous translations.

On 6 December 1581 Spenser was granted the official lease for the abbey and manor of Enniscorthy, co. Wexford, a former Franciscan monastery, 'and a ruinous castle and weir there'. The lands were leased out to Richard Synnot, a previous owner who may have been living there all the time, for £11 13*s.* 4*d.* In 1581–2 Spenser also leased a house in Dublin; a former monastery at New Ross, co. Wexford, which he later sold to Sir Anthony Colclough (*d.* 1584); and another ruined Franciscan monastery, New Abbey, near Kilcullen, co. Kildare, 25 miles from Dublin (15 July 1582). He signed a twenty-one-year lease on the last property for £3 a year but forfeited this in 1590. There is only one record of Spenser paying rent (August 1583), which suggests that he probably moved to Munster soon after that date. Spenser's transactions indicate how easy it was for 'new' English civil servants, soldiers, and adventurers to acquire land and wealth well beyond what they could have expected to gain had they remained in England. It is unlikely that Spenser would have been able to become a gentleman in England, and this change in status may also explain why he chose to pursue a career in Ireland. Many of the properties in question were confiscated from Irish 'rebels'. New Abbey was forfeited by James Eustace after his rebellion.

Ireland, 1582–1589 Lord Grey was recalled and left Ireland on 31 August 1582, so ending Spenser's secretaryship. Grey's appointment was ended partly due to criticism at court of his harsh treatment of Irish rebels, most notably at Smerwick, but he was to remain a heroic figure for many of the 'new' English, who approved of his stern and decisive actions and looked back to his example during the Nine Years' War in the 1590s. Eudoxus, in *A View of the Present State of Ireland*, tries to refute claims that the 'good Lo. Grey … was a blodye man, and regarded not the life of her [majesty's] subjectes no more then dogges' (*Works*, 10.159). Such partisan support indicates that Spenser thought highly of Lord Grey and respected him as a master. He may have accompanied Grey on his final expedition to King's county in May–June 1582.

In May 1583 Spenser was appointed a commissioner for musters in co. Kildare for two years, with twenty-six others. The commissioners were expected 'to summon all the subjects of each barony, and then so mustered in warlike apparel' (Maley, 38), when necessary. Spenser's address is given as New Abbey, implying that this was his principal residence. Spenser was summoned to perform his duties on 4 July 1584, with twenty-five others.

On 6 November 1583 Lodowick Bryskett, whose career in the Irish civil service appears to have been more advanced than Spenser's and who seems to have acted as patron to the younger man, was officially installed as clerk of the council of Munster and secretary to Sir John Norris, president of the council. Spenser served as his deputy, probably from this time or soon afterwards, on a salary of £7 10*s*., but undoubtedly employed a deputy himself. Assuming that the new lord deputy, Sir John Perrot, required secretaries to follow him on expeditions and tours of duty, Spenser may have accompanied Perrot and Sir John Norris on a tour through Munster and Connaught in July 1584 to install Norris and Sir Richard Bingham in their respective presidencies. He may also have travelled north to Ulster with Norris in August and September to confront Sorley Boy MacDonnell, who had landed on the Antrim coast with a large force of Scots in July, and returned to Dublin in October.

In 1585 Spenser became prependary of Effin, a benefice attached to Limerick Cathedral, which probably made few, if any, demands on his time. A prepend was a pension or plot of land granted to a cathedral to fund a secular priest or a regular canon; Effin, west of Balingaddy, consisted of 1052 acres. In the May and July eclogues of *The Shepheardes Calender* Spenser had attacked such practices as corrupt. In *Mother Hubberds Tale* he makes a direct reference to the problematic nature of prepends:

> How manie honest men see ye arize
> Daylie thereby, and grow to goodly prize;
> To Deanes, to Archdeacons; to Commissaries,
> To Lords, to Principalls, to Prependaries?
> (ll. 414–17)

How Spenser performed his duties is not recorded.

Spenser would have attended the sessions at the presidency court of Munster in Limerick and Cork throughout 1585 and 1586. A few years earlier plans had been made to establish a plantation of English settlers in Munster using the lands confiscated from the native Irish after the Desmond rebellion (1579–83). The forfeited lands were surveyed in September–November 1584 with the purpose of selling them off to settlers; the plan for the plantation was drafted in December 1585 and, having passed through the Irish parliament of 1586, which Spenser would have attended, the articles for the Munster undertakers received royal assent in June.

At some point in 1586 Spenser acquired an estate of 3028 acres connected to the ruined Norman castle of Kilcolman, in co. Cork, one of the smaller portions of land granted to English settlers on the plantation from over half a million acres confiscated from the earl of Desmond's lands. It is likely that he used one Andrew Reade to claim the property on his behalf. Kilcolman was described as 'a large castle, old, and dilapidated, which at the present time has no use except to shelter cattle at night' (Maley, 43). Spenser would have lived in an adjoining house, not in the castle itself. Like Dublin, Munster would have supplied Spenser with numerous intellectual contacts, allies, and companions. Sir Walter Ralegh was his immediate neighbour, occupying an enormous estate of 42,000 acres in co. Cork and co. Waterford, although he may not have spent much time in Ireland. Richard Beacon, the queen's attorney for Munster and author of *Solon his Follie* (1594), occupied land also in the counties of Cork and Waterford. Meredith Hanmer, protestant polemicist and historian, whose history of Ireland was included in Sir James Ware's edition of Irish chronicles, together with Spenser's *View*, was archdeacon of Ross from 1591 until his death in 1604. Sir William Herbert, author of 'Croftus, sive de Hibernia liber', occupied land in co. Kerry and acted as vice-president of Munster in the absence of Sir Thomas Norris while living in Ireland from 1586 to 1589. Spenser's life was to be closely connected to the fate of the plantation until his death.

Spenser was probably in Dublin for much of 1586, attending the Irish parliamentary session, which opened on 26 April and closed on 14 May. A sonnet written to Gabriel Harvey, and later included in Harvey's *Foure Letters* (1592), is dated 18 July from Dublin, suggesting that Spenser spent most of the year in Dublin, probably returning to attend sessions of the presidency court of Munster held in September in Dungarvon and in October in Lismore and Youghal. The third edition of *The Shepheardes Calender* was published in London, indicating that Spenser's work was still in demand in England.

Spenser undoubtedly attended a session of the Munster council in Cork in March and two others in Limerick in June and November 1587. He probably spent most of the year in various parts of Munster. By October he was serving as deputy to Bryskett, clerk of the council of Munster. Records indicate that he must have taken up residence at Kilcolman some time in 1588, probably around September, when Lord Roche, a local Irish landowner, complained to the queen's commissioners that some of his land had been occupied by English planters. It is likely that Spenser spent some of the year with Ralegh, who was resident in his house at Youghal, and was serving as mayor of the town. Spenser sold on his post as clerk of the court of chancery to Arland Uscher (22 June).

There was general panic in Ireland in 1588, when the Spanish Armada tried to sail home round the Irish coast and out into the Atlantic. Fearing Atlantic storms, many sailed close to the coast and, because their maps were not accurate enough to navigate through the treacherous waters, most were wrecked—twenty-five in February alone. The English authorities in Ireland, fearing an invasion triggered by an alliance between Irish and Spanish, swiftly mobilized to deal with any survivors. Spenser probably accompanied Sir Thomas Norris's military expedition to Ulster and Connaught in October and November. He would have been in Dublin in December to see Norris knighted by the lord deputy, Sir William Fitzwilliam.

Spenser would have returned with Norris to Munster in January 1589, as a letter in his hand indicates (Maley, 48–9). He obtained official possession of the Kilcolman estate on 22 May, for which he paid an annual rent of £20 and on which he established a colony of six householders and their families. Meanwhile Lord Roche was making further complaints about the confiscation of his lands, naming Spenser, with George Browne, Hugh Cuffe, Justice Smythes, and Arthur Hyde. On 12 October he wrote directly to Elizabeth, alleging that:

> Edmund Spenser falsely pretending title to certain castles and 16 ploughlands, hath taken possession thereof. Also by threatening and menacing the said Lord Roche's tenants, and by seizing their cattle, and beating Lord Roche's servants and bailiffs, he has wasted 6 ploughlands of his lordship's lands. (ibid., 52)

The undertakers countered with a bill against Roche, alleging that he had:

> relieved one Kedagh O'Kelly, his foster brother, a proclaimed traitor, has imprisoned men of Mr. Verdon's, Mr. Edmund Spenser and others. He speaks ill of Her Majesty's government and hath uttered words of contempt of Her Majesty's laws, calling them unjust. He killed a fat beef of Teig Olyve's, because Mr. Spenser lay in his house one night as he came home from the sessions at Limerick. He also killed a beef of his smith's for mending Mr. Peer's plough iron. He has forbidden his people to have any trade or conference with Mr. Spenser or Mr. Piers or their Tenants. He has concealed from Her Majesty the manor of Crogh, being the freehold of one who was a rebel. (Maley, 52)

The case was to haunt Spenser throughout the next decade, and was arguably a significant influence on the 'Two cantos of Mutabilitie', published after his death (P. Coughlan, 'The local context of Mutabilitie's plea', *Irish University Review: A Journal of Irish Studies*, 26, 1996, 320–41).

The Faerie Queene Spenser had clearly been working hard on his poetry, even though he had published next to nothing since his initial success with *The Shepheardes Calender*. It is likely that his busy job as a civil servant precluded extensive publication—although we cannot be sure how onerous his duties really were. Perhaps now that he was a landowner of some substance he could find more time to write, or to prepare what he had written for publication, as he produced a large body of work in the last decade of his life. The first edition of *The Faerie Queene* must have been ready for publication in 1589, for in October he left for England with Ralegh, leaving Richard Chichester as a substitute deputy. Spenser's visit is recorded in *Colin Clouts Come Home Againe* (first published 1596)—although as usual we should be wary of taking anything Spenser wrote in his work at face value. The preface to that poem, dated 27 December 1591, 'From my house of Kilcolman', thanks Ralegh 'for your singular favours and sundrie good turnes shewed to me at my late being in England'.

Spenser may have brought a copy of *The Faerie Queene* with him in order to see the proofs through the press, as he appears to have been careful to do this for other works. The poem was entered into the Stationers' register on 1 December 1589 and published in early 1590. The appended 'Letter to Raleigh' is dated 23 January 1589 (that is, 1590), suggesting that it may have been inserted at the proof stage. *Colin Clouts Come Home Againe* claims that Spenser (Colin Clout) was granted an audience with Elizabeth and was able to read out sections of *The Faerie Queene*. It is quite likely that this did occur, as Elizabeth is the main dedicatee of the poem. Spenser writes that the encounter was a great success:

> Unto that Goddesse grace me first enhanced,
> And to mine oaten pipe enclin'd her eare,
> That she thenceforth therein gan take delight,
> And it desir'd at timely houres to heare …
> And wondrous worth she mott my simple song,
> But joyd that country shephearde ought could fynd
> Worth harkening to, emongst the learned throng.
> (ll. 359–67)

Although it is unsafe to assume that Spenser's audience with Elizabeth went as well as Colin Clout claims, on 25 February 1591 she did grant him a life pension of £50 a year.

The Faerie Queene was a new departure in the history of English poetry, being a combination of Italian romance, classical epic, and native English styles, principally derived from Chaucer. Spenser signalled this by inventing a new stanza (which has come to be known as the Spenserian stanza), a hybrid form adopted from the Scots poetry of James I, 'rhyme royal', and Italian 'ottava rima'. It contained nine lines, the first eight being pentameters and the last line an alexandrine, and employed the rhyme scheme *ababbcbcc*. It was accompanied by seventeen dedicatory sonnets to a variety of figures. Unusually for an Elizabethan poem these were appended, rather than prefaced, to it. They were addressed to a range of important courtiers: Sir Christopher Hatton; Robert Devereux, second earl of Essex; Sir William Cecil, Lord Burghley; Edward de Vere, seventeenth earl of Oxford; Henry Percy, ninth earl of Northumberland; George Clifford, third earl of Cumberland; Thomas Butler, tenth earl of Ormond; Charles, Lord Howard of Effingham; Sir Henry Carey, first Lord Hunsdon; Arthur, Lord Grey of Wilton; Thomas Sackville, Lord Buckhurst; Sir Francis Walsingham; Sir John Norris; Sir Walter Ralegh; Mary Sidney, countess of Pembroke; Lady Carew; and 'all the gratious and beautifull Ladies of the Court'. It is clear from this list that Spenser had chosen to dedicate the poem to friends and employers—Ralegh, Norris, and Grey—and figures who were especially concerned with matters in Ireland—Ormond, Burghley, and Essex—as well as to a variety of powerful politicians and potential patrons, such as Mary Sidney and

Walsingham. It would be stretching a point to read personal relationships into this miscellaneous group of people, especially if one bears in mind that works could be dedicated to patrons without their knowledge (as was the case with Stephen Gosson's dedication of *School of Abuse* (1579) to Sir Philip Sidney, and Sir John Hayward's dedication of *The First Part of the Life and Reign of King Henry IV* (1599) to the earl of Essex).

The poem has survived as a long fragment of six completed books, each of twelve cantos, of lengths varying from forty to eighty stanzas. A further fragment of a seventh book, published after Spenser's death, consisted of two complete cantos and two stanzas from a third. There was also a letter appended from the author to Ralegh, dated 23 January 1589, explaining the allegorical method of the 'Poet historical'. Scholars are divided on the question of the extant nature of the poem, some concluding that Spenser never really intended to complete it, others that had he lived longer all twelve books would have emerged. Equally the relationship between the 'Two cantos of Mutabilitie' and the rest of the poem has not been satisfactorily resolved, some regarding these as a key to the whole work, others reading them as a minor episode not fully worked through.

The Faerie Queene tells a series of discrete but interrelated stories based around the quests of six knights who each represent a particular virtue. Its allegory is flexible and moves easily from the historically specific to deal with theological, philosophical, and ethical questions, many based on readings of Aristotle's *Nicomachean Ethics*, a stated source of the poem. Book 1 tells the story of the redcross knight, eventually revealed to be the patron saint of England, St George, who has to destroy the dragon who holds captive the parents of his lady, Una. As with all romances the narrative moves sideways as much as forwards (a process known as dilation), and a whole series of episodes represent events and problems precipitated by the Reformation. The lovers are united but, significantly, the knight is recalled to his service to Gloriana, the faerie queen, before they can get married. Book 2 charts the progress of the knight of temperance, Sir Guyon, culminating in the famous description of his destruction of the Bower of Bliss, an episode which has inspired commentators, artists, and writers ever since. Guyon's undoubted virtue is shown to be limited when he is defeated by the knight of chastity, Britomart, the heroine of book 3. While Guyon can only refuse and oppose bodily temptation Britomart is able to experience corporeal ecstasies and agonies, and so point to a way beyond the limits of temperance for those who have to live in the ordinary world. Britomart, in pointed contrast to the real queen of England, the virginal Elizabeth, sees her husband-to-be, Artegall, in Merlin's magic mirror, and the dynasty that she will found stretching into the future. The first edition of *The Faerie Queene* concluded with the striking image of the hermaphrodite created through the passionate embrace of the rescued lovers, Amoret and Scudamore, a sign that human experience could be equal and satisfying through the institution of marriage.

The second edition of the poem (1596) is generally agreed to be a darker and more diffuse work. Book 4, the legend of Friendship, has two central figures, Cambel and Telamond, who occupy only a small section of the narrative. Many commentators argue that the original version of the poem that circulated in manuscript in the early 1580s consisted of portions of books 3 and 4, later worked into the printed version with varying success. The book contains the famous description of the marriage of the Thames and the Medway—again probably adapted from an earlier work or version of the poem. Book 5, the legend of Justice, follows the adventures of Artegall, Britomart's future spouse. This has generally been the least popular section of the poem because of its disturbing defence of English policy in Ireland and, more overtly, its historical allegory, but it has recently received far more attention for the very reason that it was previously ignored. Artegall, abandoned by his tutor, Astrea, has to resolve a number of difficult disputes, foolishly falls prey to the Amazon Radigund, and has to be rescued by Britomart before his violent suppression of rebellion in Ireland is prematurely truncated by Gloriana. Book 6, the legend of Courtesy, depicts the adventures of Sir Calidore, a confused and misdirected knight who tries to give up his elusive quest for the Blatant Beast when he stumbles across a pastoral world at odds with the courtly world he is less than keen to defend. The book, like its predecessor, is replete with disturbing images of violent disruption, principally of disguised rebels ambushing small peasant communities (undoubtedly an echo of Spenser's experience in Ireland). It ends when Calidore finally manages to capture the Blatant Beast, but it escapes to terrorize the world with its awful slanders, which include attacks on the poet himself.

Spenser may have spent much of 1590 in London, or he may have returned to Ireland, owing to his protracted lawsuit with Lord Roche. A letter from Richard Whyte to Lord Burghley, dated 8 May, suggests that Richard Chichester was still serving as Spenser's deputy as clerk of Munster. A 'bill of imprest' made out by Sir Henry Wallop, treasurer at wars in Ireland, on 30 May may have been made out to Spenser in person, in which case he was clearly back in Ireland. On 6 May Elizabeth granted Spenser and his heirs the manor, lands, castle, and town of Kilcolman in fee-farm forever, confirmed on 26 October. The royal grant notes that part of the estate went by the name Hap Hazard (Maley, 55).

Other publications of the early 1590s The volume *Complaints* was entered into the Stationers' register on 29 December 1590. The publisher, William Ponsonby, included a preface to the reader, which states that his last publication for Spenser, *The Faerie Queene*, 'hath found favourable passage with you [the readers]' and that therefore he has attempted to:

> get into my handes such smale Poemes of the same Authors; as I heard were disperst abroad in sundrie hands, and not easie to bee come by, by himselfe: some of them having bene diverslie imbeziled and purloyned from him, since his departure ouer Sea.

Ponsonby claims that he has gathered the volume together 'for that they al seeme to containe like matter of argument in them'. He also refers to other works that he understands are circulating:

> namelie *Ecclesiastes*, and *Canticum canticorum*, translated *A Senights Slumber, The Hell of Lovers, his Purgatorie*, being all dedicated to ladies. Besides some other Pamphlets looslie scattered abroad: as *The Dying Pellican, The Howers of the Lord, The Sacrifice of a Sinner, The Seven Psalmes, &c.* which when I can either by himselfe, or otherwise attaine too, I meane likewise for you your favour sake to set forth.

From this preface it has been argued that Ponsonby simply went ahead on his own without the poet's consent and that arguments for Spenser's involvement in the physical process of publishing his work should be discounted (see Brink, 'Who fashioned Edmund Spenser?'). It might equally be a means of disguising the fact that he and Spenser worked in close co-operation (Johnson, 27). As well as providing another confirmation of the existence of 'The Dying Pellican' and naming other lost works Ponsonby's comments read like an advertisement for future publications of Spenser's works, suggesting a relationship in print that we should place alongside Spenser's published correspondence with Gabriel Harvey, Sir Walter Ralegh, and the enigmatic E. K. It is implausible that Spenser was not aware of Ponsonby's comments.

Complaints, like *The Shepheardes Calender*, is a complex and puzzling volume. Critics who want to claim that Spenser was attempting to follow a poetic career based on the model of Virgil, progressing from the pastoral *Eclogues* to the epic *Aeneid*, have to ignore *Complaints*, treating it as a detour between the serious business of *The Shepheardes Calender* and *The Faerie Queene*, often taking Ponsonby's prefatory comments that he, not Spenser, compiled the poems, at face value. *Complaints* gathers together a series of poems 'being all complaints and meditations of the worlds vanitie, verie grave and profitable': 'The Ruines of Time', 'The Teares of the Muses', 'Virgil's Gnat' (an adaptation of the pseudo-Virgilian *Culex*), *Prosopopia, or, Mother Hubberds Tale*, 'The ruines of Rome: by Bellay' (a translation of Du Bellay's *Antiquitez de Rome*), 'Muiopotmos, or, The fate of the butterfly' (dated 1590 and dedicated to Lady Carey), 'Visions of the Worlds Vanitie', and 'The Visions of Bellay' and 'The Visions of Petrarch, Formerly Translated', the last two being revised versions of the material published in Van Der Noot's *Theatre* over twenty years earlier.

The volume, evidently published early in 1591, appears to have landed Spenser in more trouble, owing to its satire of Lord Burghley. It was quickly called in. Given that Burghley was one of the dedicatees of *The Faerie Queene* Spenser may have assumed that the offence taken at the manuscript of *Mother Hubberds Tale* about 1580 was now forgotten. His mistake, which reflects his lack of knowledge of court life, might have fostered his adoption of an Anglo-Irish identity. This was publicly expressed in *Colin Clouts Come Home Againe*, dated 27 December 1591—that is, soon after the publication of *Complaints*—where the 'home' that Colin refers to rather bitterly in the poem is Ireland, not England. Gabriel Harvey noted: 'Mother Hubberd in heat of choller, forgetting the pure sanguine of her sweete Faery Queen, willfully over-shott her malcontented selfe' (E. Spenser, *The Faerie Queene*, ed. A. C. Hamilton, 1977, x). The Catholic recusant Sir Thomas Tresham, in a letter of 19 March 1591, also refers to the furore surrounding the publication of the volume, while noting the effect that the scandal had on its price:

> The whole discourse of that ould weoman [Mother Hubberd] ys (as I have heard reported) to showe by what channce the apes did loose their tayles. Thowghe this be a jest, yett is itt taken in suche earnest, that the booke is by Superior awthoritie called in; and nott to be had for anie money. Where ytt was att the first sould for vi. D. it is nowe of redie money a Crowne. The bookebynders have allreadie gotten by the vent of this booke, more then all the Apes in Parys garding is worthe. I did never see ytt myselfe; neither would I read ytt nowe, yf I might have ytt, becawse yt is forbidden. (Peterson, 22–3)

Tresham also attests to the popularity of Spenser, noting that *The Faerie Queene* 'was so well liked, that her ma:tie gave him ane hundred marks pencion forthe of the Exchequer: and so clerklie was yt penned, that he beareth the name of Poet Laurell'. Now, however, Spenser was 'in hazard to loose his forsayd annuall reward: and fynallie hereby proove himselfe a Poett Lorrell' (ibid., 23). The title poet laureate was evidently an unofficial one but indicates that Spenser did indeed make a significant impact at court in 1589–90, one which he appears to have spoilt rather with the publication of *Complaints*. This may explain the extent of his bitterness towards the court—and the queen—in some of his subsequent writings.

Spenser continued to produce poetry at an impressive rate. *Daphnaida: an elegie upon the death of the noble and vertuous Douglas Howard, daughter of Lord Howard and wife of Arthur Gorges*, an imitation of Chaucer's *Book of the Duchess*, was published by Ponsonby on 1 January 1592. There is no evidence to suggest how close Spenser was either to Arthur Gorges, later translator of Lucan's *Pharsalia*, or to Douglas Howard herself, daughter of John Howard, fifth duke of Norfolk. The poem is dedicated to Lady Helena, marchioness of Northampton, another figure whose relations with Spenser are unknown. The pseudo-Platonic *Axiochus: a most excellent dialogue, written in Greeke by Plato the phylosopher, trans. by Edw. Spenser* was entered into the Stationers' register on 1 May and published later in the year. The work is a translation from a Greek dialogue between Socrates and Axiochus, an old man, about the fear of death. It is not certain that the translation was by Spenser, as the attribution is based on verbal echoes in Spenser's other works, most of which could be coincidence (although there is a substantial echo of an entire clause in the dialogue in *The Faerie Queene*, book 2, canto 12, stanza 51). The attribution to 'Edw.' may simply be a mistaken expansion by the publisher but remains a troubling detail for those who want to include it in the Spenser canon. Some scholars attribute the work to Anthony Munday.

There is little record of Spenser in the next two years. He appears to have travelled to England in August–September 1592 and is referred to in a list of colonists who have paid their rent in December of that year. The lawsuit with Lord Roche was still proceeding, with claims and counter-claims. In 1593 Roche petitioned Adam Loftus, lord chancellor of Ireland, that Spenser had falsely claimed his land at Shanballymore (east of Doneraile). He also petitioned against Joan Ny Callaghan on the grounds of his 'supportation and mayntenance of Edmond Spenser, gentleman, a heavy adversary unto your suppliant' (Maley, 60). Spenser sold his office as deputy clerk of Munster to Nicholas Curtis. There were a large number of references to Spenser and his work, borrowings, quotations, and citations in the early 1590s, indicating his popularity and influence as a poet. These include works by Barnaby Barnes, Nicholas Breton, Samuel Daniel, John Florio, Abraham Fraunce, Sir John Harington, Christopher Marlowe, Thomas Nashe, Henry Peacham, George Peele, and Thomas Watson.

Spenser served as queen's justice for Cork in 1594. The legal battle with Lord Roche continued with Roche complaining in February that Spenser had occupied and damaged his land at Ballingerath, destroying woods and corn to the value of £200. Spenser appeared in court on 12 February and Roche was granted possession of the disputed lands.

Marriage and later works On 11 June 1594, St Barnabas day, Spenser married, as his second wife, Elizabeth Boyle, a relative of Richard Boyle, later earl of Cork. They had one child, Peregrine ('Lat. Strange or outlandish', according to William Camden), born possibly in 1595. The courtship and marriage are represented in the sonnet sequence *Amoretti* and the marriage hymn *Epithalamion*, entered into the Stationers' register on 19 November 1594 and published as a single volume in early 1595, when they were advertised as poems 'Written not long since'. The dedicatory note by Spenser's usual publisher, William Ponsonby, to Sir Robert Needham claims that he has taken responsibility for publishing the poems in the absence of the poet. Needham, according to Ponsonby's dedication, had brought them from Ireland to London, and it is possible that he also brought over the completed second edition of *The Faerie Queene*. Sonnet 80 of *Amoretti* states that Spenser had already finished the six completed books of *The Faerie Queene*, which were to be published in 1596, giving the newly married Spenser time to turn his attentions from Elizabeth, the queen, to his wife of the same name.

Colin Clouts Come Home Againe, another poem that draws on Spenser's life, was published in the same year, though it states that it was written 'From my house of *Kilcolman* the 27. of December. 1591' (*The Poetical Works of Edmund Spenser*, ed. J. C. Smith and E. de Selincourt, 1912, 536). The poem fits neatly into a tradition of advice literature that exempts the monarch from the general failings of his or her courtiers, and includes strong criticisms of the court, as well as attacks on the vanity, ignorance, and greed of courtiers in general. It is possible that *Colin Clout* was intended as a criticism of Elizabeth's regime in the 1590s, especially if we bear in mind Spenser's own lack of preferment in England and his posthumous criticisms of the queen in 'Two cantos of Mutabilitie' (A. Hadfield, *Edmund Spenser's Irish Experience*, 1997, chap. 6). 'Astrophel: a pastorall elegie upon the death of the most noble and valorous knight, Sir Philip Sidney' was published in the same volume and dedicated to the countess of Essex, Sidney's widow, Frances Walsingham, with six other elegies, by Lodowick Bryskett and others; again Spenser's poem was undoubtedly written earlier. He also published a commendatory sonnet prefixed to William Jones's translation of *Nennio, or, A Treatise of Nobility* (1595).

The second edition of *The Faerie Queene* was entered into the Stationers' register on 20 January 1596, and it is possible—although no evidence survives—that Spenser was in London to supervise its publication. The work consisted of three new books, 4–6, and a revision of the first three books, with the ending altered to allow the plot to continue; like the first edition it was dedicated to Elizabeth. As in the case of *Mother Hubberds Tale* it plunged Spenser into considerable trouble and triggered a diplomatic row. Robert Bowes, the English ambassador in Scotland, wrote to Lord Burghley on 1 November 1596 that James VI was extremely angry at the portrayal of his mother, Mary, queen of Scots, and her execution in book 5, canto 9. The poem was withdrawn from sale in Scotland and James signalled his intention to complain to Elizabeth. Bowes wrote to Burghley again, on 12 November, claiming that he had persuaded the king that *The Faerie Queene* had not been published with royal approval but warned that 'he still desires that Edward [*sic*] Spenser for his fault may be tried and duly punished' (*CSP Scot.*, *1589–1603*, 723). Nothing appears to have come of James's complaints but in March 1598 he commissioned the poet George Nicolson to write a response to Spenser's book, which was either never completed or has not survived. James's furious reaction indicates that Spenser's work was read seriously and carefully by those with political power and influence.

Later in the year Spenser published *Fowre Hymnes*, the first two ('Of Love' and 'Of Beautie'), dated 1 September 1596, written 'in the greener times of my youth' and dedicated from the court at Greenwich to Lady Margaret, countess of Cumberland, and Lady Mary, countess of Warwick; the volume also contained the second edition of *Daphnaida*, and *Prothalamion*, a marriage hymn celebrating the betrothals of the two daughters of the earl of Worcester, Lady Elizabeth and Lady Katherine Somerset. The earl was a close associate of Robert Devereux, second earl of Essex, in whose capacious circle Spenser appears to have been moving in the last years of his life. The marriage took place at Essex House, London, on 8 November 1596 and Spenser may have attended, given his presence in London recorded in the *Fowre Hymnes*. He also published a commendatory sonnet prefacing Zachary Jones's translation *History of George Castriot, Surnamed Scanderbeg* (1596), from the French of de La Vardin.

A View of the Present State of Ireland It is likely that Spenser completed *A View of the Present State of Ireland* in June and July 1596, possibly before he travelled to London to attend the weddings celebrated in the *Prothalamion*. The work recommends that a lord lieutenant be appointed to oversee Irish affairs and refers to 'such an one I Coulde name uppon whom the ey of all Englande is fixed and our last hopes now rest' (p. 228). Many commentators have suggested that Spenser—through his character, Irenius—was referring to the earl of Essex, a supposition made plausible by other indications that he had started to move in the large Essex circle.

A View is a work which poses a number of questions. It was not published until 1633, when it formed part of Sir James Ware's *Ancient Irish Histories*, alongside works by Edmund Campion and Meredith Hanmer. It was entered into the Stationers' register on 14 April 1598 with the note 'Mr Collinges / pray enter this Copie for mathew Lownes to be printed when he do bringe other authoritie' (Arber, *Regs. Stationers*, 3). Commentators have sometimes assumed that this means that the work was censored but this was not necessarily the case. Other works entered in the register were queried in the same way, often owing to disputes between printers and stationers. Given that Matthew Lownes, a printer with a record of literary piracy (most notably over Sir Philip Sidney's *Astrophil and Stella*), entered the work and not Spenser's usual publisher, William Ponsonby, it is more probable that *A View* was the subject of a dispute between printers than that it was carefully read and censored. Some twenty manuscript copies survive, including one that belonged to the earl of Essex, which indicates that this work also was read by powerful and influential figures. It is unlikely that Spenser would have been keen to have a political treatise dealing with such a dangerous issue bearing his name circulating to a wide audience in print, considering the dearth of works published that discussed Ireland in the later 1590s when the Nine Years' War was being fought; he had, after all, had his fair share of brushes with the authorities before 1598. The chances are that Lownes wanted to make a profit out of Spenser's name, given the impact of the recently published *Faerie Queene*.

Later claims have been made that Spenser did not write *A View* (Brink, 'Constructing the *View of the Present State of Ireland*', *Spenser Studies*, 11, 1994, 203–28; 'Appropriating the author'); the work was definitely attributed to Spenser only after his death, by Sir James Ware, although one of the manuscripts bears the initials E. S. Such claims, if substantiated, would cause numerous scholars to revise their interpretation of Spenser's relationship to Ireland. But they have not found much favour with other critics and historians who have defended the attribution of the work to Spenser on a variety of grounds: verbal and stylistic echoes between *A View* and Spenser's poetry; lack of suitable alternative authors; dating; widespread circulation of manuscripts; and the attribution by Ware. In short it cannot be proved that Spenser wrote *A View* but the wealth of corroborating evidence suggests that only a bizarre series of coincidences would force scholars to attribute the work to somebody else.

Final years Spenser was still active in acquiring land, despite the mounting threat to the Munster plantation from Hugh O'Neill's forces in the Nine Years' War. In 1597 he purchased the castle of Renny, in the south of co. Cork, and its surrounding lands for his young son, Peregrine, for £200. Buttevant Abbey also came into his possession. On 7 February 1598 he was noted as being in arrears for the rent of this property. On 30 September, with the Munster plantation on the brink of being overrun by O'Neill's forces, he was made sheriff of Cork by the privy council (which included the earl of Essex) 'for his good and commendable parts (being a man endowed with good knowledge in learning and not unskilful or without experience in the service of the wars)' (Judson, 200).

Spenser's lands were under serious threat from the rebels when he was appointed, indicating that his elevation was a desperate measure and might not have happened in quieter times. On 4 October Sir Thomas Norris, James Goold, and George Thornton wrote to the privy council from Kilmallock that a force of 2000 Irish rebels were marching towards the area of Kilcolman. By 7 October the plantation was effectively overrun. On 15 October Kilcolman was sacked and burnt. A letter by Sir Thomas Norris of 23 October noted that the son of the Lord Roche with whom Spenser had been in dispute, David Roche, was one of the prominent rebels in the area. Spenser and his family escaped through an underground tunnel, known as the fox hole, leading to caves north of the estate (the tunnel is still recorded as extant in 1840). The family fled to Cork for refuge.

Spenser, in his new official role as sheriff, is recorded as being in Cork on 7 December. He left the city on 9 December to deliver a letter from the president of Munster, Sir Thomas Norris, to the privy council, detailing the desperate situation in the province. He was probably in Whitehall about 24 December, when he delivered letters from Norris and a host of other documents from the English inhabitants of Munster, some of which were later collected as *A Briefe Note of Ireland* and attributed to Spenser. This work consisted of three documents: 'A briefe note of Irelande'; an address to the queen beginning 'Out of the ashes of disolacon and wastnes of this your wretched Realme of Ireland'; and 'Certaine pointes to be considered of in the recovery of the realm of Ireland'. Though these have been reproduced in the standard works of Spenser it is now generally agreed that the first two are probably not by Spenser, and the attribution of the third has been disputed. Given that all three short pieces do little more than echo the sentiments and pleas of a desperate people who want more military aid to repel the Irish rebels they could have been written by any number of literate Munster planters, and probably are all that survive of a larger batch of similar documents brought over by Spenser in December 1598. Including or excluding any or all of *A Briefe Note of Ireland* in the Spenser canon does little to affect his reputation either way.

On 8 December Spenser was paid £8 for delivering the letters from Norris to the privy council (the official document, as elsewhere, calls him Edward). He died on 13 January 1599 in Westminster. Ben Jonson told William Drummond of Hawthornden 'that the Irish having robbed Spenser's goods and burnt his house and a little child new born, he and his wife escaped, and after he died for lack of bread in King Street' (C. H. Herford and others, eds., *Ben Jonson*, 1925–52, 1.137). There is no other evidence of the dead child and, given that it is unlikely that Spenser starved to death in Westminster, having been paid a pension of £25 and £8 for delivering letters in the previous month, Jonson's comments have usually been discounted. Spenser was buried in Westminster Abbey, near Chaucer, on 16 January, at the expense of the earl of Essex, further evidence of the relationship between the two men. William Camden noted 'his hearse being attended by poets, and mournful elegies and poems, with the pens that wrote them, thrown into the tomb' (Maley, 80). The queen ordered that a monument be erected to his memory but this was not carried out until 1620, at the expense of Ann Clifford, countess of Dorset (*Fowre Hymnes* had been dedicated to her mother and her aunt), who commissioned Nicholas Stone to produce the work. The inscription reads:

> Heare lyes (expecting the Second comminge of our Saviour Christ Jesus) the body of Edmond Spencer, the Prince of Poets in his tyme; whose Divine Spirrit needs noe othir witnesse then the works which he left behinde him. He was borne in London in the yeare 1510. And Died in the yeare 1596. (Judson, 207)

A folio edition of *The Faerie Queene* was published in 1609 by Matthew Lownes, who acquired the papers of William Ponsonby after his death, in 1604. This was the first work to contain 'Two cantos of Mutabilitie', supposedly the basis for a seventh book of the uncompleted work that the 'Letter to Ralegh' stated would run to twelve books. The discovery may have inspired James Ware's comment in 1633 that 'the latter part' of *The Faerie Queene* had been lost by a careless servant. The date of these cantos is unknown but they were probably written in the late 1590s, as they contain allegorical material relating to Ireland in line with Spenser's other later writings. Lownes published a folio edition of the collected works in 1611 entitled *The faerie queene: The shepheardes calender: together with the other works of England's arch-poet, Edm. Spenser.* This was reprinted in 1617.

Spenser was survived by his widow, Elizabeth, who married Richard (or Roger) Seckerstone in 1603. They had a son called Richard. After Seckerstone's death she married Captain Robert Tynt. Spenser had three children: Sylvanus and Katherine from his first marriage, and Peregrine from his second. Sylvanus, who died in 1638, married Ellen Nagle (or Nangle) and they produced two children, Edmund and William. Sylvanus sued his stepmother successfully for possession of Kilcolman. William inherited the property but, having been converted to Catholicism, was labelled an 'English papist' and transplanted to Connaught in 1654; his lands were assigned to Captain Peter Courthope. William sued for the restoration of the estate, a suit favourably received by Cromwell, but the disputed property only returned to his possession after the Restoration. He became a loyal supporter of William of Orange and received further grants of land (including those forfeited by his cousin Hugoline) before his death *c.*1720. His son Nathaniel died in 1734 and his grandson Edmund was recorded 'of Kilcolman', indicating that the property remained in the Spenser family for several generations. Peregrine married Dorothy Maurice and was granted the lands surrounding the castle at Renny by his elder brother. He died at some point before 1656. His son Hugoline sided with James II against William of Orange, and his estates were transferred to his cousin William after he was attainted and outlawed on 11 June 1691. Katherine Spenser married William Wiseman of Bandon but there is no record of their having any children.

Reputation Spenser's work has had an enormous influence over the course of English poetry in the four centuries since his death. His most widely read poem has been *The Faerie Queene*, which any aspiring English poet has felt obliged to read carefully and imitate. But *The Shepheardes Calender* and much of *Complaints* have also had a major impact (it is one of the great clichés of literary criticism that Spenser's shorter poems would be far better known had he not written *The Faerie Queene*). Spenser's principal strands of influence have been to create an oppositional, protestant-inspired, anti-courtly poetry in the seventeenth century; to define the style and subject matter of mainstream canonical writers within a central tradition of English writing; to establish the Gothic in art and literature in the eighteenth century; and to help fashion a protestant Anglo-Irish identity in Ireland.

Many writers of the early Stuart period looked back to the age of Elizabeth with envy and nostalgia. One particular group were the self-styled 'shepheards nation', who modelled their verse on Spenser's pastorals, so forming a community of dissident writers opposed, as their mentor had been, to what they saw as the corrupt, false values of the court. The principal writers were George Wither, William Browne, Christopher Brooke, and, most significant of all, Michael Drayton, whose *Pastorals* and long chorographical poem *Poly-Olbion* reuses and adapts numerous episodes from *The Faerie Queene*. Other imitators of Spenser's style include Phineas and Giles Fletcher.

At the same time that Spenser was being used as the focus for opposition to the Stuart regime he was also being canonized as the most important Elizabethan poet, having already been lavishly praised by contemporaries such as Sir Philip Sidney, William Webbe, George Puttenham, and Samuel Daniel. Sir Kenelm Digby, for example, extravagantly praised him as 'our English *Virgil*' in a Neoplatonic reading of *The Faerie Queene*, book 2; Alexander Gill suggested that he was 'more correct in beautifying his language' than Homer; and for Henry Peacham he was 'our excellent *Spenser*' (Cummings, 126, 144, 147–59). Spenser was to influence virtually all major poets writing in English before the twentieth century. He had a decisive impact on the career of John Milton, who referred to 'our sage and serious Poet *Spenser*, whom I dare to be known to think a better teacher then *Scotus* or *Aquinas*' in *Areopagitica* (1664; ibid., 164). Milton planned to write his epic on the Arthurian legends but changed his mind and switched to the story of the fall for fear of allowing himself to become simply an imitator of Spenser.

In Ireland *A View of the Present State of Ireland* was undoubtedly influential in helping to establish a protestant Anglo-Irish identity when it was published, with some of its fiercest comments removed, in 1633 by the Dublin antiquarian Sir James Ware. Spenser drew a clear line between the embattled 'new' English settlers in Ireland, who were opposed and undermined by the native, 'wild' Irish and, worse still, the 'degenerate' 'old' English, the descendants of the twelfth-century Anglo-Norman settlers who had become Irish and Catholic. Spenser is adamant that Ireland must be purged and then properly governed before peace can return to the island, a political message that was influential throughout the seventeenth century, as the numerous references to his work indicate.

In the eighteenth century Spenser began to be seen as an antique and eccentric poet whose marvellous fictions inspired visions of a vanished, Gothic England of knights, fairies, and castles. Such a case was argued in John Hughes's six-volume edition of Spenser's works (1715), where the perceived irregularities of the poet were made a cause for celebration rather than criticism. This interpretation of Spenser was expanded by subsequent critics such as John Jortin, Thomas Warton the younger, John Upton, and Richard Hurd. Also influential were William Kent's illustrations for Thomas Birch's edition of *The Faerie Queene* (1751), which used Kent's knowledge of garden design, architecture, painting, and interior design to construct for the poem a Gothic world of mystery, intrigue, and the supernatural. The poem most clearly inspired by this vision of Spenser was James Thompson's *The Castle of Indolence* (1748). In essence the Romantic version of Spenser was similar, as is demonstrated in the work of the most Spenserian of the English Romantics, John Keats, whose 'Eve of Saint Agnes' clearly owes much to the reading of *The Faerie Queene* established in the previous century. Spenser was also an important influence on William Blake's art and poetry.

Spenser's work became more obviously moralized in the nineteenth century and it is significant that numerous editions of *The Faerie Queene* were produced for children, the complex verse rewritten as prose to draw out the perceived moral of selected episodes. Spenser was an important author for the Pre-Raphaelites, and numerous representations of his work were produced. A fascinating example of Spenser's wide readership is represented by the stained-glass windows commissioned for the entrance to Cheltenham Ladies' College in 1880; these were the brainchild of the headmistress, Dorothea Beale, who wished to provide the young ladies in her charge with suitable ideals of womanhood to inspire them. She selected Britomart as an 'ideal of woman' because she seemed to combine a devotion to duty, motherhood, and marriage with an assertive independence and male virtues. Charles Kingsley's novel *Westward Ho!* (1855) contains a portrait of Spenser as a vigorous and daring adventurer in both life and writing—alongside Sir Walter Ralegh—thus transforming him into a Victorian imperialist and muscular Christian. He was also starting to have an impact in America, and was the subject of a famous essay by the Harvard scholar James Russell Lowell (1819–1891), who emphasized the puritan and Platonic strains in his work.

Spenser was still read by poets and authors in the twentieth century, a notable devotee being the war poet Wilfred Owen, who writes in his journals of reading Spenser as a means of transporting himself away from the horrors of the front line. W. B. Yeats, who edited an important selection of Spenser's poetry in 1906, wrote an influential preface to that work arguing that Spenser has to be divided up into the sensitive poet who appreciated the beauties of Ireland and the brutal colonizer who sought to impose his narrow-minded English will on the natives. Yeats's version of Spenser is essentially repeated in the critical works of C. S. Lewis, undoubtedly the most widely read Spenser critic of the twentieth century. Spenser featured more in the work of Irish and Scottish writers than of English at the end of the twentieth century, notably in that of Seamus Heaney, George MacBeth, and Brendan Kennelly, who regarded Spenser in the same ambiguous way as Yeats did.

But perhaps it is true to suggest that Spenser became more of a scholar's poet in the twentieth century and had little impact on a wider reading public. As David Hill Radcliffe has pointed out, 'In the first three decades of the twentieth century, more was written about Spenser than in the previous three hundred years' (Radcliffe, 157). Spenser became one of the key major authors central to university English courses and a writer with whom the aspiring university teacher was expected to struggle.

ANDREW HADFIELD

Sources W. Maley, *A Spenser chronology* (1994) · G. Harvey, *Letter book, 1573–1580*, ed. G. L. J. Scott (1884) · A. C. Hamilton, ed., *The Spenser encyclopedia* (1990) · A. C. Judson, *The life of Edmund Spenser* (Baltimore, 1945) · F. R. Johnson, *A critical bibliography of the works of Edmund Spenser printed before 1700* (Baltimore, 1933) · *The works of Edmund Spenser*, ed. E. Greenlaw and others, 11 vols. (1932–57) · *The complete works in verse and prose of Edmund Spenser*, ed. A. B. Grosart, 9 vols. (1882–4) · L. Bryskett, *A discourse of civill life* (1606); ed. T. E. Wright (Northridge, California, 1970) · S. K. Heninger, 'Spenser and Sidney at Leicester House', *Spenser Studies*, 8 (1990), 239–49 · J. R. Brink, 'Appropriating the author of *The faerie queene*', *Soundings of things done*, ed. P. E. Mepine and J. Wittreich (Newark, Delaware, 1997), 93–136 · R. Peterson, 'Laurel crown and ape's tail: new light on Spenser's career from Sir Thomas Tresham', *Spenser Studies*, 12 (1991), 1–35 · J. Brink, 'Who fashioned Edmund Spenser? The textual history of *Complaints*', *Studies in Philology*, 88 (1991), 153–68 · N. P. Canny, 'Edmund Spenser and the development of an Anglo-Irish identity', *Yearbook of English Studies*, 13 (1983), 1–19 · R. M. Cummings, ed., *Edmund Spenser: the critical heritage* (1971) · A. Hadfield, 'Spenser, Drayton, and the question of Britain', *Review of English Studies*, new ser., 51 (2000), 599–616 · A. Hadfield, 'William Kent's illustrations of *The faerie queene*', *Spenser Studies*, 14 (2000), 1–81 · M. O'Callaghan, *The 'shepheardes nation': Jacobean and early Stuart political culture, 1612–1625* (2000) · D. H. Radcliffe, *Edmund Spenser: a reception history* (1996) · M. MacCarthy-Morrogh, *The Munster plantation* (1986) · Venn, *Alum. Cant.*

Archives PRO, state papers

Likenesses attrib. A. Allori, portrait; formerly in possession of Rev. Sabine Baring-Gould, 1897 · B. Wilson, oils (after portrait by unknown artist; now lost), Pembroke Cam. · oils; at Dupplin Castle in 1897 · oils; at Bretby Park in 1897

Spenser, John (1558/9–1614), college head, was born in Suffolk, the son of John Spenser, gentleman. He attended Merchant Taylors' School in London from 3 August 1571, and then Corpus Christi College, Oxford, where he graduated BA on 29 October 1577. Soon afterwards, on 9 June 1578, despite lacking a master's degree (he was hurriedly admitted as a fellow the following day), Spenser was elected by the president and seniors to the post of Greek reader.

At this time Spenser was reported variously to have been acting as clerk or a *famulus collegii*. Both descriptions are consistent with his most likely role—as a private secretary, probably to the college's president, William Cole, whose wife was Spenser's sister. The president claimed not to have pressed but merely to have acquiesced in his brother-in-law's nomination, but the unprecedented promotion aroused sharp resentment among older and better qualified fellows. Letters were dispatched to the visitor, Bishop Horne of Winchester, pointing to Spenser's lack of qualifications and his youth; his appointment was not only ill-judged but was also in breach of college statutes. But Horne confirmed the legality of the appointment. Spenser graduated MA on 16 March 1581.

In 1588 Spenser resigned the Greek lectureship, having served the minimum ten years required to retain his fellowship free from the duty of lecturing. He may have been the John Spenser who on 5 June 1589 was instituted to the vicarage of Alvely, Essex, which he held until 1592, when he was presented to Broxbourne, Hertfordshire; it was certainly he who on 12 June 1599 was instituted to the vicarage of St Sepulchre, Newgate. On 21 March 1590 Spenser graduated BTh, and he was awarded his doctorate on 20 April 1602. A chaplain-in-ordinary to King James, he was among the translators of the King James Bible, serving on the Westminster group which worked on the epistles of St Paul. It has been remarked that in his sermons he did not adopt the colloquial style common among Elizabethan puritans but spoke with 'a more formal sober and gracious elegance, sometimes falling into excess of wit' (MacLure, 164). Spenser was married to George Cranmer's sister, a favourite pupil of Richard Hooker. He was the first editor of Hooker's *Of the Lawes of Ecclesiasticall Politie*, published in 1604, and there is no doubt about his sympathy with Hooker's approach. Spenser's preface to the 1604 edition lamented 'this unhappy controversy about the received ceremonies and discipline of the church of England' which had 'rent the body of the church into divers parts, and divided her people into divers sects', and had 'taught the sheep to despise their pastors, and alienated the pastors from the love of their flocks' (Hooker, preface).

On 9 June 1607 Spenser took the oaths as president of Corpus Christi College, Oxford, in succession to John Rainolds. His presidency seems to have been peaceful and uneventful. In 1610 he became one of the founding fellows of Chelsea College, Middlesex, and on 13 November 1612 he was collated to the prebend of Ealdstreet in St Paul's Cathedral. He died aged fifty-five on 3 April 1614, and was buried in the chapel of Corpus Christi College. A monument to his memory stands next to one of his predecessor, 'each being attired in his doctor's habits, and each holding a book, Reynolds a closed one, Spenser an open one' (Fowler, 175). His death seems greatly to have distressed his widow and children. STEPHEN WRIGHT

Sources T. Fowler, *The history of Corpus Christi College*, OHS, 25 (1893) · J. Spenser, *A learned and gracious sermon* (1615) · M. MacLure, *The Paul's Cross sermons, 1534–1642* (1958) · R. Hooker, *Of the lawes of ecclesiasticall politie* (1604), preface · *Hist. U. Oxf.* 3: *Colleg. univ.*, pl. XXII b · will, PRO, PROB 11/123, sig. 65
Likenesses bust on monument, CCC Oxf.

Sperling, John (1793–1877), army officer, was born at Tottenham, Middlesex, on 4 November 1793, the son of Henry Piper Sperling of Park Place, Henley-on-Thames, and afterwards of Norbury Park, Surrey, and his wife, Sarah Ann (*d.* 28 May 1850), daughter of Henry Grace of Tottenham. Sperling attended the Royal Military Academy, Woolwich, and spent some time in the Ordnance Survey before being commissioned second lieutenant in the Royal Engineers on 14 December 1811. He joined at Chatham in March 1812 and was promoted lieutenant on 1 July 1812.

At the end of 1813, when the Dutch rebelled against French occupation, a British expeditionary force under Sir Thomas Graham was sent to their aid. Sperling was one of the engineer officers under Lieutenant-Colonel Carmichael Smyth who accompanied the expedition, which landed at Williamstadt on 18 December 1813. Sperling distinguished himself in the ensuing operations, and most particularly, in the unsuccessful attempt to storm Bergen-op-Zoom with four columns on 8 March 1814. Headed by Sperling the first column effected an entrance by surprise at the Watergate and seized the guard, the French officer surrendering his sword to Sperling, who kept it as a trophy. The party then swept the ramparts for some way, but not being supported by the main body of their own, and encountering a large force of the enemy, it was obliged to fall back after the death of its two commanders, Carleton and Gore. In the course of this operation it came across the second column, and together they made a stand for the night. At dawn next day it should have been possible to take Bergen-op-Zoom, but instead of support came the order to retire. Sperling was specially commended by the master-general of the Board of Ordnance for his 'gallantry and ability' shown while attached to the advanced party of stormers.

On 23 March 1814 Sperling was appointed adjutant and quartermaster of the Royal Sappers and Miners and joined the headquarters staff. On 11 April 1814 the news arrived of the entry of the allies into Paris and of the change of government, which ended hostilities. During May Sperling was employed in taking possession of the fortresses assigned for British occupation, and in June he was sent to London to report on the border fortifications to the Board of Ordnance. In August he made a survey and plan of Liège citadel for Lord Lynedoch, who was about to hand over command to the prince of Orange.

Sperling's duties were greatly increased after news was received of Napoleon's escape from Elba. He inspected many defence works and Wellington, who inspected the border fortresses, was well satisfied with Sperling's preparations. After accompanying Colonel Carmichael

Smyth on an inspection of the fortifications Sperling made a sketch of a defensive position at Hal against a French advance; it was laid before Wellington on 17 May and received his approval.

Napoleon crossed the frontier into the Southern Netherlands on 15 June 1815. Sperling joined Carmichael Smyth on 17 June as the British fell back from Quatre Bras. They remained close to Wellington during the early part of the battle of Waterloo, but later became separated from him, although they remained on the battlefield throughout. From time to time they were forced to take refuge in one of the infantry squares. They returned to Brussels after the battle, moving with the headquarters to Le Cateau on 24 June, and later towards Paris. Sperling reconnoitred the Seine on 2 July to find a suitable bridging site and recommended one at Argenteuil, which was later selected. He entered Paris with the headquarters staff on 7 July and remained there until 27 January 1816, when Wellington moved his headquarters to Cambrai.

Sperling returned home in November 1818. He retired on permanent half pay on 24 January 1824, and resided at Great Doods, near Reigate, Surrey. Later he lived in a house which he built for himself at 16 Kensington Palace Gardens, London, where he died on 14 February 1877. On 12 March 1819 he married Harriet Hanson; they had one son, John (1825–1894). R. H. Vetch, *rev.* James Lunt

Sources J. Sperling, *Letters of an officer of the Corps of Royal Engineers, from the British army in Holland, Belgium and France, to his father, from the latter end of 1813 to 1816* (1872) • War Office records • records, Royal Engineers, Brompton barracks, Chatham, Kent • *Jackson's Woolwich Journal* (April 1877) • *Royal Engineers Journal* (1877) • *Record* (1877) • C. Smyth, *Chronological epitome of the wars in the Low Countries* (1825) • Burke, *Gen. GB* • W. Porter, *History of the corps of royal engineers*, 1 (1889); repr. (1951) • Fortescue, *Brit. army*, vol. 10

Archives Royal Engineers, Brompton barracks, Chatham, Kent

Wealth at death under £60,000: resworn probate, Sept 1877, *CGPLA Eng. & Wales*

Spert, Sir Thomas (*d.* **1541**), naval administrator, of unknown parentage, must have distinguished himself in naval service well before 1512. His marine skills are attested by payment to him from January 1512 of 8*d*. a day from the petty customs of London for looking after the king's new ship, *Mary Rose*. Sir Edward Howard's appointment as lord admiral on 7 April 1512 brought Spert to prominence as Howard immediately sought competent captains for his fleet of eighteen ships. On 16 April Thomas Spert of Stepney was paid 'conduyte money' at the rate of 6*d*. per man recruited for each 12 miles of distance travelled in 'garderying together' mariners. By 12 June Spert had recruited men at distances of between 130 and 150 miles from London. The significance of that wartime allowance (later raised to 30*s*. a month under Sir William Fitzwilliam) emerged six months later when Spert together with three other expert masters were paid 100*s*. for horse hire during the week that they journeyed from Southampton to Eltham and back to share with the king 'their mynde in bestowyng the Kyng's shippes this winter'—that is from 28 October 1512 until 11 February 1513. As 'Master of the *Mary Rose*', Spert had a budget of £200 for her winter care, approving payment of £132 4*s*. 3½*d*. to John Hopton, then clerk controller, for organizing her hard standing near Woolwich between 28 October 1512 and 11 February 1513, and to pay John Brown, painter, for fourteen flags and pennants with St George's cross. On 15 March 1513 Spert was paid 100*s*. for his 'lodesmanshippe' or pilotage to Danzig; £4 for the lodging of himself and another pilot in Zeeland (Thomas Frende, purser of the *Dragon*, for whom he had signed a petition to the lord chancellor seeking diplomatic protection as he had retained his services for the war effort); plus 60*s*. for piloting the *Mary Rose* into the Thames. On 21 April 1513 Spert assumed a similar role for the bigger *Henri Grace a Dieu* procuring her new rigging and decking, and also flags and pennants. On 10 November 1514 Spert was granted an annuity of £20 in succession to Master Woodless for keeping the secret of the newly discovered Black Deep Channel into the Thames.

From 1511 to 1514 Spert petitioned to transform the body administering Trinity House's almshouses in Deptford into an important marine corporation, and to initiate a census of all English shipping over the next decade he acted with Robert Brygandyne, clerk of the ships, and others when charging the treasury of the chamber for naval repairs. A letter from the lord high admiral, William Fitzwilliam, to Wolsey of 16 August 1522 reveals Spert had found at Portsmouth 'a place nearly a mile within the haven where the *Henry* and the *Great Galley* can lie without spending half as much tackle as now, and they will be safer from rafts'. In April 1523 Spert was consulted by Fitzwilliam on how to destroy Scottish vessels at Boulogne.

Spert was promoted clerk comptroller of the king's ships in 1524 to work with 'the rule of all the foresaid ships maisters, and maryners with the advise of Brygandine'. From 1524 he worked closely with William Gonson authorizing many repairs—for example approving payment of £79 13*s*. 4*d*. in August 1529 for rigging and trimming for the *Minion* and the *Mary Guildford*, and making payments for the victuals and wages of the keepers of the king's ships while the ships were wintering. Spert was knighted for his part in such matters at Whitehall Palace in 1529 and received a grant of arms. Until 1533 he acted as master of the *Henri Grace a Dieu*. From 1527 Thomas Jermyn, Trinity House pilot, who had found the Black Deep Channel, succeeded Brygandyne as his deputy and paymaster. In 1535 Spert was described as master of the king's ships while undertaking a seagoing command to curb 'certain rovers active in the Channel'.

During 1536 Spert sat as an assessor in the high court of admiralty when Trinity House's right to levy pilotage charges for the Thames was upheld. In 1536 he saw the Trinity House of Newcastle upon Tyne chartered and in 1537 had its charter of 1514 slightly amended. During 1538 and 1539 as the captain of Portsmouth he supervised the fortification of Gosport later known as 'Spert's bulwark'. In March 1539 he led a formal naval inspection of the *Great Nicholas* of Bristol because Gonson was incapacitated by gout.

Spert's version of the charter of 1514 (London, Guildhall, MS 3001A, later misdated 20 May 1513) follows a woodcut of two carracks flying St George's crosses and a waterside chapel. Another element drafted on 21 February 1541 shows him as the master of Trinity House devising an educational regime for children of the brotherhood free of charge to their parents or friends, to which duty he appointed the chaplain (first envisaged in 1514) to teach for £8 a year plus lodging and clothing. His piety is apparent as these pages are bound with *Horae beatissme virginis* and woodcuts by Wynkin de Worde printed between 1509 and 1534.

In August 1541 Spert acted for the last time as an assessor in the high court of admiralty. He had married three times, first Margery, then Anne Salkell, and last Mary, with whom he had two children, Anne, who married Thomas Brook and later John Skott, and Richard, who later married Grissell Salkell of King's Wood, Wiltshire. Mary was the executor named when on 28 November 1541, 'sick in bodie', Spert made his will . He died at Stepney in the following December (not, as erroneously stated on his monument in St Dunstan and All Saints, Stepney, on 8 September). Under the terms of the will, Mary received his profitable Blackwall pasturage until Richard should come of age. Lesser bequests went to his married daughter and to his cousin, Margaret Spert, married to the famous Guinea seaman, John Lok. R. C. D. Baldwin

Sources R. Eden, 'preface', *A treatyse of the New India … translated out of the Latin by Richard Eden* (1533) • R. Hakluyt, *The principall navigations, voiages and discoveries of the English nation* (1589), 515 • R. Hakluyt, *The principal navigations, voyages, traffiques and discoveries of the English nation*, 2nd edn, 3 vols. (1598–1600), vol. 3, pp. 498–9 • *LP Henry VIII*, 1, nos. 1044(14), 1372(30), 1602, 1805(1), 2305, 2478, 2865, 2964(59), 3137, 3499, and pp. 1502–3; 4, nos. 309, 3656, 6138; 14, no. 540; 16, no. 220(41) • A. W. Clarke, 'Trinity House and its relation to the Royal Navy', *Journal of the Royal United Service Institution*, 72 (1927), 512–20 • C. R. Barratt, *The Trinity House at Deptford Strond* (1893), 1–14 • A. A. Ruddock, 'The Trinity House at Deptford in the sixteenth century', *EngHR*, 65 (1950), 458–76 • G. G. Harris, *The Trinity House of Deptford, 1514–1660* (1969), 24–7, 50, 59, 129, 174, 185, 273 • A. Spont, ed., *Letters and papers relating to the war with France, 1512–1513*, Navy RS, 10 (1897), 3, 68, 70 • D. M. Loades, *The Tudor navy* (1992), 75–9, 83, 101, 115 • M. Oppenheim, 'Maritime history', *VCH Kent*, 2.243–336, esp. p. 286 • W. A. Shaw, *The knights of England*, 2 (1906), 47 • J. Maclean and W. C. Heane, eds., *The visitation of the county of Gloucester taken in the year 1623*, Harleian Society, 21 (1885), 150–51 • H. M. Colvin and others, eds., *The history of the king's works*, 4 (1982), 409 • PRO, HCA 13/1, no. 162, fols. 5–6 • letters patent to Trinity House and draft, PRO, C 66/622, membrane 10; C 82/366, no. 38A [draft] • surveys of English shipping, PRO, SP 1/129, fols. 197–202; E 122/195/10 • PRO, E 101/55/22 [chapter house accounts, 16 April 1512]; E 101/56/5 [Robert Sand's naval accounts, 1513–14] • Magd. Cam., Pepys Library, Pepys MS 2869, fol. 6 • Hawksworth to Plantagenet, March 1539, BL, Arundel MS 97 • BL, Cotton MS Appendix xviii.i.10 • BL, Harley MS 1041, fol. 946*v*.; 1543, fol. 118 • will, PRO, PROB 11/20, fol. 2

Speyer, Sir Edgar, baronet (1862–1932), railway financier and patron of music, was born in New York on 7 September 1862, the second son of Gustavus Speyer, a Jewish banker, of Frankfurt, and his wife, Sophia, daughter of Rudolph Rubino, of Fritzlar, Prussia, and Frankfurt.

Educated at the Realgymnasium, Frankfurt, at the age of twenty-two Speyer became a partner in his father's three associated companies in Frankfurt, New York (established 1837), and London (1861). In 1887 he went to London as director of Speyer Brothers, who were interested in exchange arbitrage with the continent and the United States of America and in railway finance. He was naturalized in 1892.

Sir Edgar Speyer, baronet (1862–1932), by Sir William Orpen, exh. RA 1914

With electric traction becoming financially attractive in the 1890s, Speyer Brothers turned their attention to the electrification of the Metropolitan District Railway, part of London's existing steam underground. C. T. Yerkes, a world authority on all aspects of urban transport, arrived from the United States in 1900. He and Speyer headed an international consortium which eventually managed to raise £15 million to electrify the Metropolitan District Railway, build three tube railways, and acquire an electric tramway. Yerkes, who had become chairman of Underground Electric Railways of London Ltd in 1902 to oversee the whole venture, died at the end of 1905. Speyer succeeded him, only to inherit a dreadful economic situation, for revenue did not cover costs.

In 1902 Speyer married a widow, Leonora, daughter of Ferdinand, Count von Stosch, of Mantze, Silesia. She had been a professional violinist, and Speyer shared her musical interests, becoming chairman of the Queen's Hall concert board, and paying out £2000 a year for many years to make up the deficit on the Promenade Concerts. At his home in Grosvenor Street there were many concerts, at several of which Richard Strauss and Debussy conducted their own works. Speyer also took a lively interest in philanthropic and cultural causes. He was on the board of King Edward's Hospital Fund, president of Poplar Hospital, and a trustee of the Whitechapel Art Gallery. In the years before the First World War he led the life of a wealthy banker, socially well considered and lavish in entertainment, whether at Grosvenor Street or at Overstrand, near Cromer.

Very soon after the Underground Electric Railways of London Ltd (UERL) started to make money in 1912–13, Albert Henry Stanley having acquired London's recently motorized omnibuses, Speyer (who was created a baronet in July 1906) was in trouble again. Although a friend of Asquith and a privy councillor from 1909, when war broke out in 1914 his German origins were remembered, his patriotism was called into question, and he was even accused of signalling to German submarines from his Norfolk home. His brother James in New York was known to be pro-German, and Lady Speyer, incensed by the ostracism of those who had claimed to be her friends, spoke scathingly of their ingratitude. He was obliged to resign from the UERL board and to give up his hospital work. Crowds assembled outside his house and jeered at visitors. On 17 May 1915 he wrote to the prime minister offering to resign his baronetcy and membership of the privy council, but Asquith replied that the king was unwilling to accept the offer, and added: 'I have known you long and well enough to estimate at their true value these baseless and malignant imputations upon your loyalty to the British Crown.' This view was upheld later in the year, when a court case was unsuccessfully brought by Sir George Makgill to require Speyer and Sir Ernest Cassell to justify their membership of the privy council. But Speyer and his family had left for America on 26 May. There he was in regular touch with the Frankfurt part of the business and at that stage in the war was in no doubt that he wanted to live in Berlin when it was over. After Germany's defeat, however, he preferred the USA.

In December 1921, as a result of proceedings of the nationalization (revocation) committee, his name was struck off the list of privy councillors, and his naturalization, and those of his wife and three daughters, were revoked. A white paper, published in January 1922, accused Speyer Brothers of engaging in 1915 in exchange arbitrage with the firm of Teixeira, of Amsterdam, knowing that this would involve traffic with Germany. There were other charges, but in a long statement to Reuter's agency Speyer characterized them as 'trivial beyond words'.

Speyer lived on in New York, but died at Pauls Borner Strasse 4, Berlin, on 16 February 1932, having arrived there a fortnight before for a minor operation. He was a director of Speyer-Ellissen, the Berlin part of the family bank. His services to London's transport, music, and hospitals need not be obscured by the events of 1915; but, though it may be that he was guilty of no more than minor technical offences against the laws of his adopted country, there can be no doubt of his pro-German sympathies.

THEO BARKER

Sources A. C. Salter and others, 'Speyer report revelations', *The Times* (7 Jan 1922), 5 • *The Times* (18 Feb 1932) • *The Times* (29 March 1932) • T. C. Barker and M. Robbins, *A history of London Transport*, 2 (1974) • D. Kynaston, *The City of London*, 1 (1994) • *CGPLA Eng. & Wales* (1932) • E. F. Benson, *As we are* (1932) • private information (1949) • *Daily Telegraph* (17 Oct 1921) • *Daily Telegraph* (9 Jan 1922) • *Daily Herald* (14 Dec 1921) • *Daily Herald* (7 Jan 1922) • *Morning Post* (18 Feb 1932)

Archives Elgar Birthplace Museum, Worcester, letters to Edward Elgar • Broadheath, Elgar MSS

Likenesses W. Orpen, oils, exh. RA 1914, unknown collection; copyprint, NPG [*see illus.*] • M. Beerbohm, caricature, repro. in M. Beerbohm, *Fifty caricatures* (1913)

Wealth at death £3362 19*s.* 1*d.*: administration with will, 8 Oct 1932, *CGPLA Eng. & Wales*

Spicer, Sir Albert, first baronet (1847–1934), paper merchant and wholesale stationer, was born on 16 March 1847 at Clapham, Surrey, the second of four sons and sixth of ten children of James Spicer (1807–1888), a wholesale stationer of Woodford Green, Essex, and his wife, Louisa (*née* Edwards). He was educated at Mill Hill School and was then sent to Heidelberg where he learned to speak German fluently.

Shortly after Spicer returned to England in 1864 his grandfather, John Edward Spicer, died leaving his stationer's business at 182 New Bridge Street, London, to his three sons. They fell out, however, and James started another paper merchant firm, James Spicer & Sons, at 50 Upper Thames Street, London. His two brothers, meanwhile, continued the existing business in New Bridge Street under the name Spicer Bros. Both branches of the Spicer family were influential Congregationalists. On James Spicer's side they were linked to the Unwins, the publishing family, through the marriage of two of his daughters, one of whom, Elizabeth, became mother of Sir Stanley Unwin.

Albert Spicer became the dynamic figure in James Spicer & Sons. With just eight employees in 1865, the firm tapped new markets for printing and writing paper by acting as an intermediary between the paper manufacturers on one side and retailers and consuming organizations on the other. The company developed a regional branch house system, moved swiftly when new markets (such as school boards or county councils) appeared, and vigorously sought foreign markets, mostly in the British empire, Albert himself making overseas tours. In 1879 he married Jessie Stewart Dykes (1857–1934); they had three sons and eight daughters.

Albert and his brother Evan (1849–1937) strengthened their competitive position by increasing the capital investment in their London facilities, rebuilding the Upper Thames Street premises, and in 1886 acquiring an envelope factory in Southwark. In 1910 the partnership was converted into a private company, James Spicer & Sons Ltd, with an authorized capital of £450,000. It continued to build up its British and empire distribution network so that in 1913 it had warehouses in London, Birmingham, Manchester, Leeds, Glasgow, Bristol, Melbourne, and Durban, and offices in Belfast, Liverpool, Edinburgh, Sydney, Brisbane, Adelaide, Perth, Wellington (New Zealand), Cape Town, and Paris.

The slump after the First World War increased the pressures on specialist wholesalers and dealers. James Spicer & Sons protected their position by reuniting with their cousins. The two Spicer firms merged in 1922 with the formation of Spicers Ltd with an authorized and issued capital of £1.15 million. It owned Eynsford Mills in Kent and the Sawston Mills, Cambridgeshire; two factories in Southwark; and a new factory at Brimsdown, Middlesex. Albert Spicer received 4966 of the 50,000 £10 ordinary shares and 5162 of the 65,000 5 per cent £10 preference shares in Spicers and, in addition, an annuity of £3000 for five years. He remained chairman of the new company for one year before retiring from business in 1923.

In London's business community Albert Spicer was a considerable figure. He was president of the London chamber of commerce from 1907 to 1910 and in 1909 visited Sydney as president of the Chambers of Commerce of the Empire. For ten years, from 1907, he sat on the commercial intelligence advisory committee of the Board of Trade. During the First World War he was a member of the royal commission on paper supplies.

Outside business Spicer's interests centred on Congregationalism and Liberal politics. He was elected to the Essex Congregational Union and then, in 1873, to the London Missionary Society's board, serving as chairman from 1882 and as treasurer from 1885 to 1910. Spicer was also instrumental in the building of Mansfield College, Oxford, a Congregational theological college, of which he was treasurer from 1888 to 1921. In 1892 Spicer was elected the second lay chairman of the Congregational Union of England and Wales and in 1899 moderator of the International Congregational Council held at Boston. He attempted to inject greater social concern into his denomination but made little headway. In 1919–20, as chairman of the laymen's commission on ministerial stipends, he visited local Congregational churches, encouraging lay support for the local ministry. It was calculated that his gifts, chiefly but not only to the Congregational cause, averaged 26 per cent of his income during his active life. He became vice-president of the British and Foreign Bible Society in 1896, president of the Sunday School Union in 1900, and for seven years served on the army council's advisory committee on the spiritual and moral welfare of the army.

Spicer entered politics by sitting on the Woodford school board from 1877 to 1892. By 1888 he had held every official position connected with Liberal organizations in Essex. He founded and was vice-president of the London and Counties Liberal Union and by 1888 was a trustee of the National Liberal Club. He unsuccessfully contested the Walthamstow division of Essex in 1886 but sat as Liberal MP for Monmouth Boroughs from 1892 to 1900, and for Central Hackney from 1906 to 1918. For public services Spicer was created a baronet in 1906 and sworn of the privy council in 1912.

In 1912 Spicer chaired the Marconi inquiry committee which investigated the dealings between Godfrey Isaacs and leading Liberal politicians. Partly because of his deafness he failed to dominate the committee, and the Liberal members glossed over what all agreed was at least ministerial impropriety, and what tories saw as corruption. To his credit, Spicer issued his own report departing from both sides. He died on 20 December 1934, at his home, 24 Palace Court, Bayswater, London, his wife having died before him, in May 1934. He was cremated at Golders Green crematorium. DAVID J. JEREMY

Sources D. Jeremy, 'Spicer, Sir Albert', *DBB* • DWL, Albert Spicer MSS • *Albert Spicer, 1847–1934: a man of his time … by one of his family* (1938) • D. W. Bebbington, *The nonconformist conscience: chapel and politics, 1870–1914* (1982) • b. cert. • m. cert. • d. cert.

Archives DWL | DWL, letters and papers relating to commission on ministerial stipends

Likenesses photograph, repro. in *Paper Record* (Aug 1888)

Wealth at death £76,964 4s. 0d.: resworn probate, 11 Feb 1935, *CGPLA Eng. & Wales*

Spicer [*married name* Pearce], **Dorothy Norman** (**1908–1946**), aviator and aeronautical engineer, was born on 31 July 1908 at Hadley Wood, Middlesex, the only daughter of Norman Spicer (*d.* 1936), a stockbroker, and his wife, Hilda Mary Sisterson. She was educated at the Godolphin School in Brussels and at University College, London, before learning to fly in 1929 at the London Aeroplane Club, Stag Lane. During her flying training she met Pauline Gower who was there to study for her 'B' (commercial) pilot's licence. They became great friends and decided that as soon as they had finished training they would form a business partnership.

In July 1931 Dorothy Spicer and Pauline Gower went to work; Pauline was licensed to carry passengers for 'hire or reward', and Dorothy qualified as a ground engineer (only the second woman in the world to do so) and the holder of an 'A' (private) pilot's licence. They started with a hired Gipsy Moth but soon had a plane of their own. However, times were not easy and often they had barely enough money to buy food. Dorothy and her partner were determined to prove that it was possible for an aeronautical business run entirely by women to succeed, despite the severe economic depression.

With the idea of increasing their income Dorothy and Pauline decided to join the Crimson Fleet air circus and later the British hospitals' air pageant. The work was hectic, as in common with traditional circuses they were constantly on the move. While the pilots flew the planes the engineers were extremely busy maintaining them, doing running repairs, helping passengers into the aircraft, collecting the money, and organizing the queues. During this period Dorothy gained valuable experience especially as she had to strip down, repair, and rebuild the Spartan's engine on several occasions. Her skills became so well known that she was much sought after as a speaker and contributor to various aeronautical publications. She decided to add to her qualifications and to study for the 'B' engineer's licence. As a woman it was very difficult to acquire this type of training because institutions offering advanced courses were restricted to men. However, she persuaded the manufacturers of their Spartan plane to allow her to obtain the necessary practical and theoretical training at their workshops and thus earned her 'B' licence, becoming the first woman in the world to do so. Rather than return to touring Dorothy and Pauline decided to provide joyrides and aerial taxi trips from the

Dorothy Norman Spicer (1908–1946), by Bassano, 1938

holiday town of Hunstanton, Norfolk, where the constantly changing population would provide regular customers. Their business was going well so they decided to list it as a commercial company, thus giving birth to the first registered aeronautical company staffed and owned by women.

By early 1935 Dorothy Spicer was again keen to add to her impressive list of qualifications. Already she was the only woman in the world to hold 'A' and 'B' licences and a recently acquired 'C' engineering licence. The goal this time was a 'D' licence. At the time it was not possible for a woman to study at such an advanced level and it became so only when Air Vice-Marshal A. E. Borton persuaded Sir Harold Snagge, the chairman of the Napier Engineering Company Ltd, to make special arrangements. Six months later she won an award not possessed by any other woman and became authorized to inspect, pass out, and repair both engines and airframes. She was in fact qualified to build all aspects of an aircraft, airframe, and engine from scratch, and to approve the materials required for the work. It was an extraordinary achievement for anyone, let alone someone who had literally so many 'man-made' barriers to overcome.

After two very successful years at Hunstanton, Dorothy and Pauline opted to accept an invitation from Tom Campbell Black to tour with his British empire air display with Dorothy as senior engineer and Pauline the chief pilot. While on tour Dorothy learned that her father had died from injuries sustained from a bad fall, and later in the year Pauline's mother also died. As both wanted to be more available to support their surviving parents they established an aerial garage on Hayling Island where pilots could bring their aircraft for service and repair. However, the work was not satisfying and the business was wound up. The final task was to write an account of their flying days together, *Women with Wings* (1938).

Dorothy Spicer was well known and admired in the aviation world, so when it became known that she was available she was offered several jobs. She finally accepted a position with the Air Registration Board in London, thereby becoming the first woman in the British empire to receive a technical appointment in civil aviation. On 2 March 1938 she became engaged to Flight Lieutenant Richard Pearce (*d.* 1946). They were married on 26 April 1938 at Holy Trinity, Brompton, with Pauline Gower as chief bridesmaid. The Pearces' only child, Patricia Mary, was born at Farnham Common, Surrey, on 15 May 1939.

War broke out just months after the baby's birth. Richard first served in Coastal Command but was soon appointed as a test pilot to the Royal Aircraft Establishment, Farnborough. In late 1940 Dorothy joined him, took on flying work as an air observer and research assistant, and became involved in the development of a variety of new aircraft types and items of equipment. After the war Richard accepted the job of South American representative of British Aviation Services Ltd in Rio de Janeiro. In December 1946 they left their daughter with family and flew out as passengers in a British-built Avro York of the Argentinian airline Flota Aerea Mercante Argentina. The trip was uneventful until bad weather forced the plane to be diverted from a scheduled landing at Rio de Janeiro. Ten miles from the airport, in thick fog, the plane flew into a mountainside, killing all on board. MICHAEL FAHIE

Sources M. Fahie, *A harvest of memories* (1995) · C. B. Smith, *Amy Johnson* (1967) · D. B. Walker, *Spreading my wings* (1994) · E. C. Cheesman, *Brief glory* (1946) · L. Curtis, *The forgotten pilots: a story of the Air Transport Auxiliary, 1939–45* (1971) · P. Gower, *Women with wings* (1938) · A. King, *Golden wings: the story of some of the women ferry pilots of the Air Transport Auxiliary* (1956) · A. H. Narracott, *Unsung heroes of the air* (1943) · private information (2004) · b. cert.

Archives priv. coll., MSS · Royal Air Force Museum, Hendon, MSS · Royal Society for the Prevention of Cruelty to Animals, London, MSS · Tunbridge Wells Library, MSS

Likenesses photograph, 1931, Hult. Arch. · Bassano, photograph, 1938, NPG [*see illus.*]

Spicer, Eulalie Evan (1906–1997), lawyer and legal aid administrator, was born on 20 April 1906 at 19 Elm Road, Beckenham, Kent, the daughter of Charles Evan Spicer, a wholesale stationer, and his wife, Elsie Mary, *née* Williams. Her family were well-to-do paper manufacturers. One of her uncles was dean of Manchester. She was educated at St Helen's School, Northwood (of which she subsequently became a governor), King's College, London, where she graduated BA in philosophy, and University College, London, where she gained the degree of PhD, her thesis being on Aristotle's conception of the soul. After taking a law degree she qualified as a solicitor in June 1938, at a time when an annual average of only fifteen women were qualifying, and practised from premises at 5–6 Clement's Inn, London, close to the law courts.

In December 1942 Spicer joined the Law Society's staff in Chancery Lane, London, as supervising solicitor in the newly created services divorce department, which had been established to deal with the large number of marriage breakdowns during the Second World War and in the absence of many solicitors on war service. By the end of hostilities in 1945, she had become the most notable of the seven solicitors and hundred staff involved. She was involved in the preparations for thousands of divorces, and travelled all over the country to local assizes where divorce petitions were heard. The work involved taking statements, organizing the necessary papers, compliance with procedural rules, and briefing counsel for the undefended hearings.

With the increase in the divorce rate it was obvious that there could be no return to dealing with these cases under the charitably based poor persons' procedure. Following the report of the Rushcliffe committee in 1945 the Labour government decided to establish a state-funded legal aid scheme, administered by the Law Society. Spicer was heavily involved in the large-scale preparations for introducing the new arrangements, which came into force in a limited form in October 1950. She was soon appointed secretary of no. 1 (London) area, the largest of the twelve legal aid divisions into which the country was divided.

As area secretary Spicer was responsible not only for the effective administration of her area, but also for arranging the appeals by applicants for legal aid from decisions of local committees. Her frequent contacts with the legal profession ensured that many practitioners became involved in legal aid work through inclusion on the voluntary panels and serving on area committees. When she emerged from her room laden with files, the committee—whose servant she nominally was—would stand when she entered. She kept a strict hold over the subsequent proceedings. Considerable extensions to the jurisdiction of the legal aid scheme were made in 1960 when county court and summary jurisdiction cases came within its scope. When Spicer retired in 1966, no. 1 area was handling 25,000 applications for legal aid a year, and was subsequently divided into two.

On retirement Spicer went back into private practice for a further seven years. She jointly edited the fifteenth edition of *Latey on Divorce* (1973), having edited the fourth edition of *Phillips Practice of the Divorce Division* (1951). She was involved in church affairs, becoming secretary of the legal aid committee of the general synod of the Church of England as well as a lay reader. At seventy she took the degree of BD at King's College, London, as well as playing a role with local churches near her Dolphin Square flat. She died of heart disease at St Thomas's Hospital, Lambeth, London, on 29 March 1997. She was unmarried.

Miss Spicer, as she was always called (except by her staff, who knew her as EES), was probably the highest-ranking woman lawyer in the immediate post-war period. Masculine in appearance, she wore her hair in an Eton crop, never used make-up, and sometimes wore a suit and tie. She smoked cigarettes through an amber holder, and rode a motor scooter to her Red Lion Street legal aid office. In spite of her unconventional appearance she established a reputation for efficiency and management which became legendary. She played a crucial role in establishing the success of the legal aid scheme in its initial phase.

CYRIL GLASSER

Sources *The Times* (30 April 1997) • *The Guardian* (7 May 1997) • *Daily Telegraph* (31 May 1997) • *Law List* (1939) • S. Pollock, *Legal aid: the first 25 years* (1975) • *Seventeenth legal aid annual reports* (1966–7) • b. cert. • d. cert.

Likenesses photograph, repro. in *The Guardian* • photograph, repro. in *Daily Telegraph*

Wealth at death £1,274,196: probate, 22 Aug 1997, *CGPLA Eng. & Wales*

Spicer, Henry (1742/3–1804), miniature and enamel painter, was born at Reepham, Norfolk; of his parents, nothing is known. He became a pupil of the miniature painter Gervase Spencer. A member of the Incorporated Society of Artists of Great Britain, he exhibited with the society from 1765 to 1783. In 1773 he was appointed secretary to the society; in 1770 he had been elected a fellow of the Society of Antiquaries. He exhibited for the first time at the Royal Academy in 1774. Approximately three years later he travelled to Dublin, where he lived for some years and earned several commissions from prominent patrons. He had returned to London by 1782. From 1792 to 1804 Spicer was an annual contributor to the Royal Academy. He suffered ill health for some years before his death, at the age of sixty-one, at 7 Great Newport Street, London, on 8 June 1804. He was survived by his wife, details of whom are unknown.

Spicer's distinguished sitters included the duke of Northumberland, the earl of Moira, Sir Joshua Reynolds, Edmund Burke, and Lord Nelson. Among his friends were the artists George Stubbs, J. H. Mortimer, William Hamilton, and Ozias Humphry, whose portrait Spicer painted and who lodged with Spicer's widow at 39 Lower Thornhaugh Street until his own death in 1810. Despite his appointment as painter in enamel to the prince of Wales (the royal warrant is in the possession of his descendants), Spicer died a poor man. His works are of admirable quality, full of character, and finely coloured. His miniature of George IV (exh. RA, 1796) and his enamel of the first marquess of Hastings (exh. RA, 1802) are in the National Portrait Gallery, London. The interesting history of his fine enamel of Marie Antoinette (1789, priv. coll.), signed on the front '5/89', is given in D. Foskett's *Miniatures: Dictionary and Guide* (1987). His portraits of the actors John Moody and William Smith, the dramatist George Downing, Charlotte Augusta, princess of Wales, and of Mrs Chambers were engraved. Examples of his theatrical portraits are in the Garrick Club Collection, London. Both his daughters, F. and M. A. Spicer, went on to become artists.

EMMA RUTHERFORD

Sources D. Foskett, *A dictionary of British miniature painters*, 2 vols. (1972) • B. S. Long, *British miniaturists* (1929) • B. S. L., 'Two miniatures by Henry Spicer', *The Connoisseur*, 78 (1927), 229–30 • H. Blättel, *International dictionary miniature painters / Internationales Lexikon Miniatur-Maler* (1992) • artist's notes, NPG, Heinz Archive and Library • D. Foskett, *Collecting miniatures* (1979) • Redgrave, *Artists* • Graves, *Artists* • R. Bayne-Powell, ed., *Catalogue of portrait miniatures in the Fitzwilliam Museum, Cambridge* (1985) • W. G. Strickland,

A dictionary of Irish artists, 2 vols. (1913) • G. Ashton, *Pictures in the Garrick Club*, ed. K. A. Burnim and A. Wilton (1997) • *DNB*

Likenesses attrib. J. Reynolds, oils, priv. coll.

Spicer [*née* Gibbon], **Joanna Ravenscroft** (1906–1992), television executive, was born on 29 April 1906 at Ranmoor, St Albans, Hertfordshire, the second of the three daughters of Andrew Owen Gibbon, a Post Office engineer, and his wife, Alice Mary, *née* Smith. She was educated at St Paul's Girls' School, from which in 1924 she won an exhibition to Somerville College, Oxford, where she gained a second-class degree in history in 1927. She spent a fourth year working for a diploma in education, and then became secretary of the Oxford University women's appointments board. In 1935 she joined the staff administration of Selfridges Ltd. She married Robert Henry Scanes Spicer (1897–1956), a publisher, in 1937, and after her son John was born she returned to Selfridges as personal assistant to Gordon Selfridge jun.

When her husband was called up for active service in 1939 Spicer joined the broadcasting division of the Ministry of Information, dealing particularly with the BBC's overseas finances and its wartime expansion. Subsequently she was asked by the BBC to transfer to its overseas service, where she worked for the next nine years. In 1949 the recently appointed director of BBC television, Sir George Barnes, invited her to join him at Alexandra Palace with the task of 'stopping fires', as he put it, in the new service. Two years later she became head of programme planning, television, which meant coping effectively with all the problems of programme development and administrative control in a service which had to comply with complicated governmental restrictions on the amount and nature of its programmes. Moreover, television resources always fell short of demand. She was the housekeeper who made certain that the heads of the programme departments cut their requirements to match what was then a chronic shortage of studios, crews, and film effort. She was the power behind the throne for many controllers of programmes, including Cecil McGivern, Kenneth Adam, Stuart Hood, Huw Wheldon, and David Attenborough. She was in charge of programme planning for fourteen years, finally becoming assistant controller, television development. As such she advised various managing directors of television on the production resources they needed, and on their best use.

Spicer also represented the television service on the programme committee of the European Broadcasting Union, the focal point for Eurovision and satellite programme operations. She was a forceful voice there, in fluent French. She was also effective in Italian. On one occasion she reprimanded a Venetian waiter so imperiously that he scurried away profusely apologizing, 'Si Contessa, si Contessa'. Independent Television, a relative newcomer to the Eurovision club, was keen to employ her as its Eurovision representative and made her many attractive offers. But Sir Charles Curran, the director-general of the BBC and also the president of the European Broadcasting Union, kept extending her contract well beyond the normal BBC retirement age.

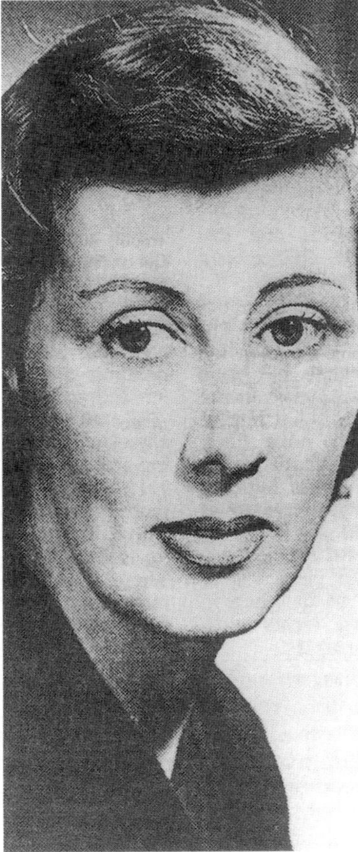

Joanna Ravenscroft Spicer (1906–1992), by unknown photographer

Spicer was the first woman to be made a fellow of the Royal Television Society. In 1957 she was made an OBE and in 1974 a CBE. She was always a compulsive worker. The sudden death of her husband in 1956 had left her responsible for financing the education of their son at Oxford. In 1967 she suggested to David Attenborough that colour television, the new technical development he was about to introduce for the coverage of Wimbledon, should also be used to enrich the television fare offered to serious viewers. That conversation led to the BBC's first great success in colour—Kenneth Clark's series *Civilisation*. Spicer finally retired from the BBC in 1973, but continued to work full time in the field of international communications, with a wide range of assignments in the UK and abroad, notably in Greece and Brazil. For ten years she was closely associated with Asa Briggs on the research programme of the International Institute of Communications, and they collaborated in writing *The Franchise Affair* (1986), a study of the fortunes and failures of independent television programme companies.

Spicer managed to retain her slim good looks, her charm, and her skill as a cook even into her eighties, when she continued to write a newsletter for the British Friends of UNESCO. Although virtually unknown to the general public, she had a profound influence on the growth of British and European television. She died on 17 March 1992 in the Charing Cross Hospital, Fulham Palace Road,

London, after a stroke. She was cremated and her funeral was held on 27 March 1992 at the church of St Peter and St Paul, Eye, Herefordshire, where her ashes were buried beside those of her husband. LEONARD MIALL

Sources personal knowledge (2004) · private information (2004) [John Spicer] · *The Times* (19 March 1992) · L. Miall, *The Independent* (18 March 1992), 33 · A. Briggs, 'In memory: Joanna Spicer, 1906–1992', *Intermedia*, 20/2 (1992), 8 · D. Attenborough, 'Joanna Spicer: a life in television', *Television: the Journal of the Royal Television Society* (April 1992), 15–16
Likenesses photograph, repro. in *The Independent* · photograph, News International Syndication, London [*see illus.*] · photograph, repro. in Briggs, 'In memory: Joanna Spicer'
Wealth at death £373,893: probate, 4 March 1993, *CGPLA Eng. & Wales*

Spiers, Alexander (1807–1869), lexicographer, was born at Gosport in Hampshire. He studied in England, at Leipzig, and in Paris, and graduated doctor of philosophy at Leipzig. On the advice of the poet Andrieux (*d.* 1833), he settled in Paris as a professor of English, and found employment at the École de Commerce, at the École des Ponts et Chaussées, at the École des Mines, and at the Lycée Bonaparte. He spent fourteen years on his *General English and French dictionary, newly composed from the English dictionaries of Johnson, Webster, Richardson, &c., and from the French dictionaries of the French Academy, of Laveaux, Boiste, &c.* (1846). It proved superior to its predecessors and was at once 'autorisé par le conseil de l'instruction publique', on 3 July 1846. The twenty-ninth edition, in two volumes, appeared in 1884 (remodelled by H. Witcomb, Spiers's successor at the École des Ponts et Chaussées). An abridgement, under the title of *Dictionnaire abrégé anglais–français et français–anglais, abrégé du dictionnaire général de M. Spiers*, was published in 1851 and supplied to almost every school and *lycée* in France. In 1853 he married Victoire Dawes Newman. They had five sons.

In November 1857 Spiers brought an action against Léon Contanseau and his publishers, Longmans & Co., for pirating his dictionaries in a work entitled *A Practical Dictionary of the French and English Languages*. However, Vice-Chancellor Sir William Page Wood (afterwards Lord Hatherley), in his decision on 25 February 1858, maintained that, though great use of Spiers's books had been made without due acknowledgement, as such publications could not be entirely original a charge of piracy could not be sustained (*Weekly Reporter*, 1857–8, 352–4; *The Times*). Spiers's other publications included a *Manual of Commercial Terms in English and French* (1846), a *Study of the English Prose Writers, Sacred and Profane* (1852), and a *Study of English poetry, a choice collection of the finest pieces of the poets of Great Britain* (1855). They were all issued in both English and French editions in London, Paris, and America. Spiers also printed and edited for French students Sheridan's *School for Scandal* and *The Essays of F. Bacon, Viscount St. Albans* (1851).

Spiers was nominated an *agrégé de l'université, officier de l'instruction publique, examinateur à la Sorbonne*, and *inspecteur général de l'université*. He received the cross of the Légion d'honneur from Napoleon III. He died at the rue de la Faisanderie, avenue de l'Imperatrice, Paris, on 27 August 1869. G. C. BOASE, *rev.* JOHN D. HAIGH

Sources P. Larousse, ed., *Grand dictionnaire universel du XIXe siècle*, 17 vols. (Paris, 1866–90), vol. 14, p. 1009 · *The Times* (26 Feb 1858), 10 · private information (1897) · Boase, *Mod. Eng. biog.* · Allibone, *Dict.* · T. Cooper, *A new biographical dictionary: containing concise notices of eminent persons of all ages and countries*, [pt 2] (1873), 106 · *CGPLA Eng. & Wales* (1869)
Wealth at death under £600: resworn probate, Oct 1872, *CGPLA Eng. & Wales* (1869)

Spiers [*née* Davis], **Dorothy Beatrice** (1897–1977), actuary, was born on 25 May 1897 at 34 Downs Park Road, Hackney, London, the second of three daughters of Samuel Davis, schoolmaster and later head of the Jewish Free School, and his wife, Sarah, *née* Samuel. She was educated at the London county council Wilton Road School and the City of London Girls' School; in 1915 she entered Newnham College, Cambridge, where she graduated BA in mathematics in 1918 and MA in 1923. While employed by the Guardian Assurance Company from 1918 to 1931 Davis was allowed, in 1918, to attend the lectures for the examinations held by the Institute of Actuaries. In 1919 a resolution was passed by the institute's governing body, admitting women to the fellowship on the same conditions as men; Davis was the first woman to be admitted a fellow of the institute, in 1923. She married on 25 October 1931 Henry Michael Spiers, an industrial chemist, with whom she had two sons. Between 1931 and 1954 she returned to the Guardian Assurance for short periods; between 1932 and 1938 she worked on the continuous mortality investigation for the Institute of Actuaries, and from 1943 to 1946 with the Eagle Star Insurance Company. Spiers had wide-ranging interests and in retirement she devoted much time and energy to the League of Jewish Women, serving on the council and as national treasurer, where her common sense and mathematical ability were much appreciated. She made small bequests to the Jewish Welfare Board and to the Jewish Blind Society. Having been predeceased by her husband Dorothy Spiers died at the Central Middlesex Hospital, Park Royal, on 2 September 1977. ANITA MCCONNELL

Sources A. Crawford and others, eds., *The Europa biographical dictionary of British women* (1983), 375–6 · R. C. Simmonds, *The Institute of Actuaries, 1848–1948* (1948), 177 · [A. B. White], ed., *Newnham College register*, 2: *1924–1950* (1964), 301 · *Jewish Chronicle* (2 Dec 1977), 26 · b. cert. · m. cert. · d. cert. · *CGPLA Eng. & Wales* (1977)
Wealth at death £32,029: probate, 27 Oct 1977, *CGPLA Eng. & Wales*

Spiers, Richard Phené (1838–1916), architect, was born in Oxford on 19 May 1838, the eldest son of Alderman Richard James Spiers, a bookseller and stationer who was a leading citizen of Oxford and its mayor in 1854, and his wife, Elizabeth Phené, daughter of Thomas Joy, of Oxford. Walter Lewis *Spiers (1848–1917), a younger brother, was curator of Sir John Soane's Museum, Lincoln's Inn Fields, from 1904 to 1917. Richard Phené Spiers was educated at King's College School and in the engineering department of King's College, London. From 1858 to 1861 he was a student at the École des Beaux-Arts, Paris, a most unusual

Richard Phené Spiers (1838–1916), by unknown photographer

course for an English architect but one recommended to his father probably by Thomas Henry Wyatt. The American architect H. H. Richardson was a fellow pupil. On returning to Britain he became assistant to Sir Matthew Digby Wyatt, who was then engaged on works, particularly the grand staircase and internal courtyard, at the India Office, Whitehall. Spiers's relations with Wyatt were close and sympathetic.

In 1861 Spiers was elected an associate of the Royal Institute of British Architects; in 1863 he gained the silver and gold medals of the Royal Academy, and in 1864 the travelling studentship. In 1865 he won the Soane medallion and £50 for his designs for an 'Institute for the Study, Practice, and Performance of Music'. In the same year, in company with some artist friends, he set out on a tour of eighteen months through France, Germany, Greece, Constantinople, Palestine, Syria, and Egypt. His companions worked in watercolours, and Spiers followed their example. He became, in fact, very expert, and was well known for his drawings of architecture in colour, which for many years were sold at good prices. He always felt, however, that his professional pursuits prevented him from keeping up with the artistic and technical advance of watercolour painting.

On his return to Britain in 1866 Spiers assisted William Burges in his Gothic design (which was not successful) for the new law courts in the Strand; in conjunction with Charles John Phipps in 1874 he submitted a modern French design for the war memorial church of the Sacré Cœur at Montmartre; and with Professor Robert Kerr he competed in a design for the Criterion restaurant and theatre in Piccadilly; he also assisted in designing and building the synagogue in Seymour Street, Edgware Road.

Spiers's executed works are not numerous. They include additions to Umberslade Park, Warwickshire; restorations of the churches of Hampton Poyle and Weston on the Green, Oxfordshire; studios in Campden Hill Square and elsewhere; two board schools in London; and alterations and additions to Beckett Hospital, Barnsley. In conjunction with Auguste Tronquois, of Paris, he designed Château Impney, near Droitwich, Worcestershire (1869–75). His house in the 'Queen Anne' style on the Chelsea embankment (1878) for Robert Collier (later Lord Monkswell) suffered from being adjacent to the Clock House by Norman Shaw, whom he greatly respected but who, he complained, worked to a radically different system of proportion from that which Spiers had learned in Paris.

With his appointment in 1870 as master of the Royal Academy architectural school a fresh phase of Spiers's career opened; but, although he held the post for thirty-six years (until 1906), the outcome disappointed his friends. His reputation as an architectural designer and as a watercolourist, his skill as a draughtsman, his close touch with continental tradition, and, above all, his gifts as a teacher, raised hopes that a fresh lead in the development of English architecture would be inspired by the new master of the academy school. These hopes were not fulfilled. Partly because he allowed his personality and ideas to be overshadowed by those of his brilliant contemporaries George Edmund Street and Richard Norman Shaw, but mainly because he felt that his influence with and authority over the students were subject to interference by the academy visitors, Spiers did not give the lead expected of him and he found that the students did not have time for the Beaux-Arts curriculum which he attempted to teach. It is probable, indeed, that his best teaching was done outside the academy school; and it was perhaps a matter of regret to his friends that he did not found a private school of his own, where his inspiration and undoubted gifts would have had free play. One pupil, W. R. Lethaby, recalled that 'Spiers was in much a follower of Cockerell, and he was not able to accept the narrowly concentrated point of view of the Gothic revivalists' (*RIBA Journal*, 23, 21 Oct 1916, 334).

In addition to his teaching Spiers pursued his study of the architecture of all periods and countries. He collected and abstracted a mass of material of all kinds bearing on the subject. His point of view was scientific and highly cautious, and he was tireless in ascertaining exact data. His papers thus embodied the results of years of research, and were very carefully compiled, but are apt to be found rather dry. He was in his element in the work of preparing new editions of texts written by others, such as James Fergusson's *History of Architecture* (1893); though characteristically his respect for the author prevented the necessary firm editing of the text. His own book *Architectural Drawing* (1887) gives a clear explanation of technical methods, but some of the illustrations were not happily chosen (the frontispiece was his own design for the Sacré-Cœur church in Paris). His collected papers in *Architecture, East and West* (1905) contain some of his most valuable work. The book was published on his retirement, by past students of the Royal Academy School when he was given a bronze plaque with his portrait, modelled by Edouard

Lantéri. He was also presented with a commemorative medal by the Société Centrale des Architectes Français, of which body Spiers was an honorary and corresponding member. He was president of the Architectural Association in 1867–8, served on the council of the Royal Institute of British Architects from 1888 to 1903, and was chairman and member of the literature committee for twenty-two years. He died in London on 3 October 1916. He was unmarried.

Spiers is remembered for his modest and disinterested devotion to the study and teaching of architecture. He was a discriminating critic who tolerated no lowering of a high artistic standard. He regarded architecture as a rational art, and believed in the prevalence, in all periods and styles, of definite principles not to be transgressed. When he died, Beresford Pite observed that the school which Spiers represented and which had seemed so old-fashioned 'is practically, again the dominant school of architectural thought' (*RIBA Journal*, 24, 11 Nov 1916, 13). For Lethaby 'he was a true cosmopolitan' (*RIBA Journal*, 23, 21 Oct 1916, 334). A. T. BOLTON, *rev.* GAVIN STAMP

Sources *The Builder*, 46 (17 May 1884), 725; 51 (13 Jan 1887), 715; 52 (7 May 1887), 701 · *ArchR*, 40 (1916), 98 · R. Chafee, 'The *École des Beaux-Arts* and British architecture, 1817–1940', PhD diss., U. Lond., 1983 · *RIBA Journal*, 23 (1915–16), 334; 24 (1916–17), 13 · *CGPLA Eng. & Wales* (1916)
Archives V&A NAL, notes on Syrian architecture
Likenesses photograph, RIBA BAL, photographic collection [*see illus.*]
Wealth at death £10,761 3*s*. 8*d*.: probate, 22 Nov 1916, *CGPLA Eng. & Wales*

Spiers, Walter Lewis (1848–1917), museum curator and architect, was born on 27 July 1848 in Headington, Oxford, and baptized on 1 October at St Giles', Oxford, the youngest in the family of five sons and two daughters of Richard James Spiers, stationer, and his wife, Elizabeth Phené Joy. In 1858 he won a choristership at Magdalen College, Oxford, and entered the college's school. In 1864 he entered the engineering department of King's College, London. He was articled to his brother, Richard Phené *Spiers, in 1866, when he also joined the Architectural Association, later gaining first prize in the class of design. He became a student at the Royal Academy in 1868.

From 1870 to 1880 Spiers was at the office of the architect Thomas Henry Wyatt and later went into partnership with the latter's son Matthew. In 1875 he was elected an associate of the Royal Institute of British Architects. In 1887 he was appointed district surveyor for Charlton, Lee, and Kidbrooke under the Metropolitan Board of Works and continued in this post under the London county council. In 1888–9 he was involved with the building of the headquarters of the Artists' volunteer corps (the Artists' Rifles), of which he was an enthusiastic member for many years, retiring with the honorary rank of major.

Spiers's appointment as curator of Sir John Soane's Museum at a salary of £300 per annum was announced on 16 July 1904; he had been acting curator while his predecessor George H. Birch had been on sick leave. His successor as curator, Arthur T. Bolton, claimed that 'it is no disrespect to his distinguished predecessors in that office to assert that he was the best curator that ever held that position of trust', an opinion that was shared by John Summerson, who succeeded Bolton. Spiers did much to make the museum's collections more accessible to students and placed his wide-ranging knowledge ungrudgingly at the service of enquirers. The inventory of the museum's contents that he drew up with such meticulous care, accompanying his sections for each room with an admirable sketch showing the location of each item, remained in use and he also took an invaluable series of photographs recording the interiors of the museum and some of the objects. Spiers also catalogued the museum's large collection of drawings by Robert Adam and did preliminary work on the arrangement and classification of Soane's archive, laying the foundations on which Arthur Bolton was to build.

Spiers enjoyed the ardours of research. While at the Soane he edited and wrote a commentary on two small books in the museum, *The Notebook and Account Book of Nicholas Stone, Master Mason to James I and Charles I* (*Walpole Society*, 7, 1919), which he illustrated with photographs of that sculptor's monuments taken during numerous journeys devoted to studying Stone's work. He also contributed several important articles to the *Journal of the London Topographical Society*, of which he was one of the earliest members and to the council of which he was elected in 1902. As a result of this special interest he made a topographical index to the drawings in the Soane museum. His own large personal collection of prints and maps, some of them annotated by him and much consulted in his lifetime, was sold at auction by his family after his death. He was elected fellow of the Society of Antiquaries in 1916. Spiers was trained in the Gothic school, but Bolton, who knew him well, insists that he never referred to any buildings of his own and little is apparently known about his work as an architect. The announcement of his appointment as curator in the *Builders' Journal and Architectural Record* for 13 June 1904 included the information that he would relinquish his private practice. He did, however, carry out some repairs to the fabric of the Soane museum. Bolton stated that Spiers 'disliked his name being quoted in any way' and that it was 'difficult for his services to be adequately acknowledged'. Spiers was an unassuming and kindly man, whose painstaking scholarship was greatly admired by those who knew him.

Spiers refused to take a holiday of even a single day during the German air attack on London in 1916–17, wishing to be present should any emergency arise. This confinement apparently affected his health and, after a short illness, he died suddenly at the museum on 28 May 1917. He was unmarried. He was buried at Brookwood cemetery, Surrey, on 31 May.

PETER THORNTON, *rev.* SUSAN PALMER

Sources A. J. Finberg, preface, in W. L. Spiers, *The notebook and account book of Nicholas Stone*, Walpole Society, 7 (1919) · *The 18th Report of the Council of the London Topographical Society for 1917* (April 1918) · *Architects' and Builders' Journal* (4 July 1917) · *IGI*
Archives Sir John Soane's Museum, London, curatorial papers relating to his period as curator

Likenesses photograph, Sir John Soane's Museum, London · photograph, RIBA; repro. in *Architects' and Builders' Journal*
Wealth at death £7634 4s. 3d.: probate, 13 July 1917, *CGPLA Eng. & Wales*

Spigurnel, Sir Henry (*b*. in or before **1261**, *d*. **1328**), justice, was the eldest son of Philip Spigurnel, who held the manor of Dagnall near Edlesborough in Buckinghamshire. The family surname came from a hereditary office in the royal chapel and chancery, and Philip was a younger son either of the Godfrey Spigurnel who died in 1240, or of the Nicholas Spigurnel who succeeded Godfrey in office and in the family lands in Nottinghamshire and Essex, and who died in 1266. Henry had at least one younger brother, Thomas, and possibly a second brother, Simon. Since Henry Spigurnel was old enough to be appointed as an attorney by 1282, he cannot have been born later than 1261. He was active as an attorney in the common bench only between 1282 and 1285, and probably undertook this activity only while attending the court to listen to litigation as part of his legal education. By the autumn of 1285 he is to be found speaking as a serjeant in the Northamptonshire eyre, and surviving reports show him acting as a serjeant in a number of other counties on the northern eyre circuit during 1286 and 1287. His first appearance as a serjeant in the common bench was late in 1287, and he soon became one of the court's most prominent and active serjeants. Between 1292 and 1294 he left the common bench to appear as a serjeant on the southern eyre circuit, but he returned to the court when the eyre circuits were suspended in the summer of 1294.

In October 1295 Spigurnel was appointed a regular assize and gaol delivery justice on a circuit with Robert Retford, covering the south-east midlands and East Anglia. He managed to combine this with a continuing common bench practice as a serjeant, and only ceased acting as a serjeant when he was appointed a justice for the Cambridgeshire and Ely eyre of 1299. The following year he went with the former royal justice William of Brompton to Holland, in connection with the assignment of dower to the king's daughter Elizabeth, countess of Holland and Zealand. Brompton was also among his colleagues on the Cornwall eyre of 1302 where Spigurnel heard crown pleas and took some part in hearing civil pleas. By March 1303 he had become a knight. In 1305 and 1306 he was prominent among the justices appointed to the trailbaston commissions, being one of the 'cruel' justices threatened with violence in the 'Song of Trailbaston'. Spigurnel had sat on a temporary basis in the court of king's bench in the Hilary and Easter terms of 1301 but became one of its permanent justices only at the very end of Edward I's reign (in Trinity term 1307). He then served in the court almost continuously until 1323, apart from apparently brief overseas embassies for Edward II in 1307, 1311 (to the papal curia), and perhaps 1314, and when serving as one of the justices of the Kent eyre in 1313–14. During the same period he also continued active service as a justice of assize, gaol delivery, and oyer and terminer. After he had retired from the king's bench he was commissioned to head an eyre in the Channel Islands, which took place in the autumn of 1323, and he continued to receive judicial commissions until September 1327.

In or before 1294 Spigurnel married Sara, the daughter and heir of John le Brun, who brought him the Oxfordshire manor of Brize Norton, the Bedfordshire manor of Clapham, and lands at Passenham in Northamptonshire. His home was at Dagnall. In 1297 he received a licence from Bishop Sutton to have a private chapel there, and in 1322 he received permission to assign property to support a chaplain celebrating daily in the chapel. In May 1328 Spigurnel was allowed to delay performing homage to the young Edward III on the grounds that he was too decrepit to travel without danger to his life, and by 26 July 1328 he was dead. His death probably occurred at Dagnall; his heir was his elder son, Thomas. He also had a second son, Master Robert Spigurnel, who was going abroad to study in 1322, 1327, and 1330, and who in 1325 exchanged his living of Keyston in Huntingdonshire for that of Tring in Hertfordshire with Master Robert Inge, a relative of the William Inge who was a contemporary of Robert's father as a serjeant and as a royal justice, and whose connections with Henry Spigurnel went back to the time when they were jointly appointed as attorneys by a number of clients in the 1280s. PAUL BRAND

Sources P. A. Brand, ed., *The earliest English law reports*, 2, SeldS, 112 (1996) · unpubd law reports, BL; CUL · *Chancery records* · *CIPM*, 7, no. 128

Spillan, Daniel (**1796/7–1854**), classical and medical writer, was the son of Daniel Spillan, a butcher. A Roman Catholic by religion, he entered Trinity College, Dublin, as a sizar on 3 June 1817, graduated BA in 1822, and proceeded MA and MB in 1826. On 13 April 1826 he was admitted licentiate of the King and Queen's College of Physicians in Ireland, and was elected a fellow on 7 June 1830.

Shortly thereafter Spillan moved to London, but he was unable to earn a living as a physician, and, having already published some medical texts in Ireland, now sought to maintain himself as a writer. He produced several short books each year, some on medical subjects and written by himself or translated from continental authors, and others translated from classical texts. He was equally unsuccessful in these literary enterprises and was eventually reduced to destitution. He died in St Pancras workhouse of 'disease of the brain' on 26 June 1854, leaving a wife and family. One of his sons also died in the workhouse, probably of tuberculosis, immediately afterwards.
E. I. CARLYLE, *rev.* ANITA MCCONNELL

Sources *The Lancet* (5 Aug 1854), 116 · *GM*, 2nd ser., 42 (1854), 203 · Allibone, *Dict.* · Boase, *Mod. Eng. biog.* · d. cert.

Spiller, James (**1692–1730**), actor and dancer, was born in Gloucester, the son of a carrier. According to George Akerby, a painter and purported friend who wrote an early biography of him, his father had aspirations to educate him as a gentleman; but Spiller had other intentions. He was apprenticed to a landscape painter, but soon tired of a sedentary life and joined a company of strolling players, in spite of his father's disapproval. He began with them as a low comedian, which suited his earthy and irreverent temperament; later he came to specialize also in old men's parts. There are anecdotes about his patience in making up for these and his success in deceiving even near acquaintances whom he met while in character.

Spiller's life with the strollers gave him a lifelong taste for drink, which led him into debt, and into imprisonment from time to time. By December 1709 it had also given him a wife, one Elizabeth Thompson (*c.*1690–*c.*1740), an actress, described as 'a good pretty woman, with a little too much affectation' (Akerby, 10). His provincial experience can hardly have lasted long, for he appeared for the first time on the London stage on 6 December 1709, playing the Porter in a Drury Lane revival of John Crowne's *The Country Wit* under the management of Aaron Hill. His wife made her début there three days later.

Spiller's career at Drury Lane was intermittent. A personal rivalry shaped its early stages, since his parts duplicated those of William Pinkethman, an older and more established comedian. After a reorganization of the theatre companies in 1710 he was forced to leave Drury Lane to accommodate performers displaced from the now exclusively musical Queen's Theatre, and according to Akerby he went strolling again. But he was back at Drury Lane once or twice in each of the next two years, and was apparently a full member of the company again in the 1712–13 season, when he played among others the part of Ananias, an addition to Shakespeare's *Macbeth*.

Spiller was now an actor in demand. When John Rich opened the Lincoln's Inn Theatre in 1714 he reminded Spiller of a promise made to his father, the former Drury Lane patent holder Christopher Rich, that he would join his company. Spiller and Pinkethman were again rivals at Drury Lane, and this was another reason for him to move over. He remained with Rich for the rest of his short life. In his first season his parts included Setter in *The Old Bachelor* and Jeremy in *Love for Love*, both plays being by William Congreve, and Harlequin in *The Emperor of the Moon* by Aphra Behn. (He had played this part at Drury Lane in 1709; in February 1715 Pinkethman undertook it at Drury Lane, and Spiller sought to reclaim it at the other house in April.) In subsequent seasons he played a further wide range of parts, including Sir Politick in Ben Jonson's *Volpone* and minor roles in Shakespeare; but his forte was the comic. A ferocious squint, which he developed after the loss of the sight of one eye through smallpox, was an undoubted asset. He was paid well, at £1 6*s.* 8*d.* a day, but not enough to keep pace with his extravagancies. In these years Rich, an outstanding Harlequin, was developing the English pantomime, again in rivalry with Drury Lane. Spiller was a popular Harlequin too. He also gained a niche as a speaker of epilogues, quite frequently mounted on an ass and once (unprovably) on an elephant.

For most of his career Spiller regularly played in the booth theatres set up in the London fairs, Smithfield, Greenwich, and Southwark particularly, when the major theatres closed for the summers. Here his gifts for low comedy found full expression. Pinkethman also ran a theatre booth. Sometimes Spiller joined him, and sometimes he ran against him. On a personal level, the two comedians seem to have been drinking companions, and the story in Akerby that Spiller stole a draft of Charles Johnson's *The Cobbler of Preston* from Pinkethman's pocket, after he had drunk him into oblivion, rings true, for Christopher Bullock anticipated the Drury Lane production by a week or two with a spoiling version at Lincoln's Inn Fields.

Spiller separated from his wife at some point, and lived with his mistress, a Dinah Stratford, of Wild Street, who when the 14*d.* a week he allowed her was insufficient was occasionally reduced to the undignified trade of selling asparagus, or sometimes hot baked faggots. Another of his mistresses was a Mrs D., whom he shared with a duke until the duke found Spiller wearing one of his own shirts.

Spiller's extravagant life kept him in debt, and in 1722 he had to shelter in The Mint, a refuge in Southwark; later, after The Mint was suppressed, he found himself in the Marshalsea. But The Mint gave him the name of his part in John Gay's *The Beggars' Opera* (1728)—Matt of the Mint, in which character Gay gave him the appropriate song 'Fill every glass, for wine inspires us'. In this role he was also depicted on the special benefit ticket engraved for him by William Hogarth. One of his gaolers in the Marshalsea retired and took an inn in Clare Market, renaming it the Spiller's Head.

Spiller's death was sudden. Frederick, prince of Wales, commanded a performance at Lincoln's Inn Theatre of Lewis Theobald's *The Rape of Proserpine* on 7 February 1730, and Spiller, cast as Clodpole, rose from his sickbed to appear. He died on stage of apoplexy. He was buried on 10 February at St Clement Danes, London, at Rich's expense. Akerby's *Life of Mr James Spiller, the Late Famous Comedian* was hastily written, being dated '1729' and hence clearly in print before 24 March, when the new year would have officially begun. Many of the anecdotes in it appear also in *Spiller's Jests* (*c.*1730), which is one of the less amusing joke books of the period. JOHN LEVITT

Sources G. Akerby, *The life of Mr James Spiller, the late famous comedian* (1729) • S. Rosenfeld, *The theatre of the London fairs in the eighteenth century* (1960) • J. Loftis, *The politics of drama in Augustan England* (1963) • Highfill, Burnim & Langhans, *BDA* • E. L. Avery, ed., *The London stage, 1660–1800*, pt 2: *1700–1729* (1960) • A. Nicoll, *Early eighteenth centry drama, 1700–1750*, 3rd edn (1952), vol. 2 of *A history of English drama, 1660–1900* (1952–9); repr. (1969) • *Spiller's jests* (*c.*1730) • C. Leech, T. W. Craik, L. Potter, and others, eds., *The Revels history of drama in English*, 8 vols. (1975–83), vol. 5 • Genest, *Eng. stage* • *DNB*

Likenesses I. Bell, engraving, repro. in Akerby, *Life* • W. Hogarth, engraving, repro. in R. Paulson, *Hogarth's graphic works* (1965)

Spiller, Joel (1804–1853), corn factor and miller, was born in Bridgwater, Somerset, the son of an ironmonger there. The family was, allegedly, of Flemish origin. In April 1829 Spiller married Sarah Taylor Durston, and in the same year he set up in business as a corn factor and dealer from a shop in St Mary Street, Bridgwater.

Spiller was a free-trade activist in Bridgwater, supporting the Liberal cause as did his friend, the shipowner James Sully, whose main business was transporting bricks to south Wales and returning with coal. The potential for carrying corn and flour to the expanding coal and iron communities of south Wales was obvious and was exploited by Joel Spiller during the 1830s; his mercantile business prospered and in 1840 he went into partnership with Samuel Woolcott Browne, son of Captain Charles Browne RN, a Bridgwater banker. A substantial four-storey warehouse was built on West Quay and the office was in Castle Street. The opening of a new dock in Bridgwater in 1841 enabled vessels of 500 tons to reach the town, but the town bridge and the vagaries of the tides were to be a limiting factor to the local ambitions of Spiller and Browne and to the industrial development of the city.

In the early 1840s Spiller and Browne diversified into milling, building a steam mill in Chilton Street. On the repeal of the corn laws in 1846 they expanded the business, renting three local water mills. However, as Britain increased her imports of North American wheat, ports on the west coast and in south Wales became prime locations for steam-driven flour mills. Cardiff was clearly a more promising location for business expansion and in 1852 Spiller and Browne leased a site on which to build a 1200-sack steam mill, at the head of the new west dock, from the marquess of Bute.

Joel Spiller died, aged forty-nine, during the construction of the Cardiff mill. On one of his visits to the site, in June 1853, he grazed his shin. The injury did not seem to demand attention but within a day or so the wound had turned septic. Spiller returned home to Bridgwater where he died on 7 June leaving a widow and three children. Highly esteemed locally, he was widely acknowledged to have been the architect of his own fortune. He was buried in Wembdon Road cemetery, Bridgwater.

After Spiller's death, Browne took two of their brothers-in-law into partnership: Charles Thompson, husband of Browne's sister Marian, and William Allen, who had married Spiller's sister. Both men were to make important contributions to the management of the concern, which became a limited liability company in 1887 with a paid-up capital of £440,000. JENNIFER TANN

Sources 'Spillers Petfoods', MS history of Spillers, Spillers Petfoods, New Malden, Surrey • W. Rees, *Cardiff: a history of the city* [1962] • '150 years of Spillers, 1829–1979', *Milling Feed and Fertiliser* (Dec 1979) • 'Spillers Limited: a story of progress', *The Miller* (6 Nov 1933) • C. J. Holmes, 'Spillers' history from 1880 to 1929', *Milling* (1978) [centenary issue]

Archives Spillers archives, Spillers House, 1 Blagden Road, New Malden, Surrey

Spiller, John (1833–1921), chemist and inventor of photographic techniques, was born on 20 June 1833, one of at least two sons of John Horatio Spiller, an architect. Educated at a private school at Crouch End, London, and the City of London School, he then entered the Royal College of Chemistry and stayed on after his coursework as a junior assistant to Professor A. W. Hoffman. At the age of twenty he assisted Dr John Percy at the Royal School of Mines in analysing British iron ores, and the results of their important work were published in the *Memoirs of the Geological Survey*. Within three years, in 1856, his growing reputation led to an appointment as an assistant chemist at the Woolwich arsenal. In 1861 he founded a department there to teach the new art/science of photography; he also lectured on the art at the Royal Military Institute and the Royal Military Repository. He left Woolwich in 1868 to join his brother's colour firm, Messrs Brooke, Simpson, and Spiller, as their chief chemist: it was the first British firm to manufacture synthetic (coal-tar) dyes. His retirement after twenty years there led to no diminishment of activity. Spiller was one of the first to embrace the volunteer movement, achieving his commission in 1859 and finally retiring in 1877 as a captain of the 26th (Kent) rifles.

In spite of achievements in many areas of chemistry and geology, it is for his work in photography that Spiller is best-known. It was in his youth at the Royal College of Chemistry that he met and formed a close friendship with William Crookes. Photography was their common interest and their first experiments together started about 1850 with the calotype process. Within two years Henry Talbot's pioneering invention was beginning to give way to the new negative process of wet collodion. Although this was much more sensitive and finely detailed than the calotype process, it involved a chemically volatile glass plate which had to be exposed and processed while wet, a great limitation for field or spontaneous use. In an 1854 issue of the *Philosophical Magazine* Crookes and Spiller published their first paper on photography, on a 'Method of preserving the sensitiveness of collodion plates'. This described how, if a deliquescent salt was incorporated to keep them sufficiently moist, the plates could be made up ahead of time, packaged in light and tight containers, used in the field, and processed at a more convenient time. This presaged the later factory-made dry plates and the *Art Journal* in 1854 rightly celebrated the improvement as one of the greatest importance.

Spiller also published papers on methods of making photographs more permanent (a matter of enormous concern at the time), artificial lighting for photography, and the photography of solar eclipses. His scientific essays, of which nearly thirty were published, were dominated by photographic topics. He continued a close working relationship with Crookes until the latter embraced spiritualism in the 1870s, a development which proved a strain on the scientific beliefs which had been the basis of their association: their personal friendship, however, lasted late into their long lives.

Spiller married (Caroline) Ada, the daughter of the well-known microscopist Andrew *Pritchard FRSE; they had a daughter and two sons. Her brother, H. Baden Pritchard, succeeded Spiller in the photographic department at Woolwich and was later an influential editor in photography and a preserver of some of the earliest history of photography. Almost four years after Ada's untimely death (in October 1873) Spiller married, on 5 June 1877, Emma Davenport, daughter of Samuel Thomas Davenport, assistant secretary of the Society of Arts; they had one son.

Born at a time when the stagecoach was the most common means of travel, Spiller came of age just as the art/

science of photography was coming of age as well. His activity in this field spanned seven decades of enormous change. His formal admission into the Photographic Society of London (later the Royal Photographic Society) was delayed until 1867, but he rapidly gained the distinction of being the only person ever to fill all their major offices, rising from treasurer-secretary to vice-president to president in 1874–5. He was also the editor of the *Photographic Journal*, sometimes in conjunction with Pritchard and sometimes with Dr Hugh Welch Diamond, and was designated 'Lord Uriel of the Solar Club'. Most of his photographic output primarily recorded his technical experiments in the medium, but some competent amateur pictorial work which he did about 1857 with Dr John Percy survives.

Spiller, who bore an uncanny physical resemblance to Field Marshal Lord Roberts, also took an active interest in church and civic matters. He died on 8 November 1921 at his home, 2 St Mary's Road, Canonbury, London. He was survived by his second wife. Chapman Jones, his obituarist, in a 1922 issue of the *Photographic Journal*, remembered him as being 'of a most kindly disposition, ever ready to lend a helping hand or step into a gap that needed filling … there are … many in the chemical and photographic world who are indebted to him' (Jones, 23–4). His photographs are in the Royal Photographic Society collection at the National Museum of Photography, Film and Television, Bradford, and the Gernsheim collection in the University of Texas at Austin. LARRY J. SCHAAF

Sources Wellcome L., Spiller MSS • *JCS*, 121 (1922), 748–9 • C. Jones, *Photographic Journal*, new ser., 46 (1922), 23–4 • m. cert. [J. Spiller and E. Davenport] • d. cert. • *CGPLA Eng. & Wales* (1922)
Archives Wellcome L., corresp.
Likenesses F. Lewis, photograph, National Museum of Photography, Film and Television, Bradford, Royal Photographic Society collection
Wealth at death £8815 16*s*. 8*d*.: probate, 14 Jan 1922, *CGPLA Eng. & Wales*

Spilman, James (*bap.* **1680**, *d.* **1763**), merchant, was baptized at Yarmouth on 6 December 1680, second son of the merchant Benjamin Spilman (*c*.1644–1719) and his third wife, Susan Robins. An uncle, Samuel Spilman, shipped presents from the Russia Company to Peter the Great at Yarmouth in 1693. Spilman probably went to Russia in the wake of the tsar's European recruitment drive of 1697–8, trading on his own account in 1701 or earlier. The tsar, having granted a lucrative monopoly of the Russian tobacco trade in 1698 to the London-based Tobacco Company, transferred it in 1704 to Moscow burgomasters. They signed a contract in February 1705 with Spilman and Samuel Martin, his co-factor, agents for a group of London businessmen, to supply tobacco and equipment, but the project was abandoned following an export ban. After the murder of Martin in 1709, Spilman, co-executor of his will, spent some time in England and was admitted to the freedom of the Russia Company on 8 June 1711.

When St Petersburg became the Russian capital in 1712, Spilman replaced Henry Stiles as senior English merchant, responsible to the tsar for recruiting English naval and industrial personnel, and for training Russians in England. Simultaneously he partnered Henry Hodgkin, a factor merchant, trading with several north European countries as well as with Britain. Their intervention helped to secure the election on 29 July 1714 to the Royal Society of Prince Menshikov, Russia's second most powerful figure and its leading industrial entrepreneur.

Although appointed to the Russia Company's court of assistants in March 1718, Spilman continued with his business concerns in Russia until 1721. On 13 April 1723 he married Hester, daughter of William Willys, a Hamburg and Russia merchant, the sister and coheir of Sir Thomas Willys (*d*. April 1732), sixth baronet, of Fen Ditton, Cambridgeshire. Their only child, Julia, was baptized in September 1724, when they were living at Park Place, near St James's Palace. By the 1730s they had moved to Conduit Street, close to Hanover Square.

Spilman was on the Russia Company's court of assistants for many years, becoming its auditor (1729–40) and consul (1733–5). His considerable knowledge and expertise was utilized on various committees: Baltic lightships (1725), management of the company's trade and legal affairs (1728), and briefing the Board of Trade on Russian court contracts (1736); however, his major contributions were in drawing up an Anglo-Russian treaty of commerce (1732–4) and drafting a memorial to the Treasury for importing Persian silk through Russia (1735). In 1742 he published *A Journey through Russia into Persia*, containing an account by John Elton and Mungo Graeme (or Graham) of their exploring in 1739 the prospects for British trans-Caspian trade from Astrakhan to Persia. The treatise was dedicated to Spilman's colleague, Sir John Thompson, a prominent cloth merchant, shipowner, and Russia Company governor (1740–49). Spilman received the freedom of Yarmouth in 1750.

A long-serving director of the Bank of England (1730–62), Spilman was concurrently an active commissioner of the Royal Hospital at Greenwich (1732–62), attending its committee meetings on eighty occasions and, with Sir John Thompson, acting as trustee to the Derwentwater estates. Spilman was elected fellow of the Royal Society on 31 October 1734 and council member in 1743. When admitted on 14 November 1734, he presented the society with three items given to him by Peter the Great: a snuff-box of granadilla wood made by the tsar, a fragrant stick of golden birchwood from Samarkand, and a piece purported to be of Noah's ark, but 'undoubtedly brought from Mount Ararat'. The society's journal books and certificates (1734–49) provide evidence of Spilman's interest in Russian and general natural history, and of his significant Anglo-Russian connections. Six book subscriptions (1735–57) partly reflect the promotion of experimental philosophy, stressed as a qualification in his election certificate (4 April 1734).

Spilman's wife, Hester, died on 23 August 1761, aged seventy-two, and his own death followed in London on 21 November 1763. He was buried at Waltham Abbey Holy Cross, Essex, commemorated by a marble monumental inscription in the north aisle wall. Their daughter, Julia, who married George Richard Carter of Chilton, Buckinghamshire, in 1753, was granted an administration in December 1763. JOHN H. APPLEBY

Sources J. H. Appleby, 'James Spilman, FRS (1680–1763), and Anglo-Russian commerce', *Notes and Records of the Royal Society*, 48 (1994), 17–29 • GL, Russia Co. MSS, 11/741/2–6 • journal books, RS, vols. 15–18 • council minutes, RS, vol. 2, pp. 285–6 • J. M. Price, *The tobacco adventure to Russia: enterprise, politics, and diplomacy in the quest for a northern market for English colonial tobacco, 1676–1722* (1961), 62–7, 105–10 • BL, Add. MSS 33357, fols. 361, 381–2, 37360, fol. 389 • RS, Box file 48, nos. 52, fols. 1–2, 166, fols. 1–2 • Greenwich Hospital minutes, PRO, MS ADM 67/10 [1735–62] • *The correspondence of Isaac Newton*, ed. H. W. Turnbull and others, 6 (1976), 171–2, 184 • *Sbornik imperatorskago Russkago Istoricheskago Obshchestva* [Compendium of the Imperial Russian Historical Society], 61 (1888), 163–4 • F. J. G. Robinson and P. J. Wallis, *Book subscriptions lists* (1975) • A. Compling, *East Anglian pedigrees*, Harleian Society, 91 (1939) • private information (1994) • *IGI* • administration, PRO, PROB 6/139, fol. 356r

Spilsbury, Sir Bernard Henry (1877–1947), forensic pathologist, was born on 16 May 1877 at 35 Bath Street, Leamington Spa, Warwickshire, the eldest of the three children of James Spilsbury, a manufacturing chemist, and his wife, Marion Elizabeth, formerly Joy, of Stafford.

Education and early career Spilsbury studied at Leamington College, University College School, Manchester grammar school, and Owens College, Manchester, prior to his undergraduate career at Magdalen College, Oxford, where he took a BA in natural science in 1899, and proceeded MA in 1908. His academic performance was unexceptional; he was remembered by school contemporaries for his pleasant disposition, care with dress, and penchant for hard work. His goal was general medical practice, though he had some interest in bacteriology when he began his medical studies in London in 1899. At St Mary's Hospital at the turn of the twentieth century, however, he came under the influence of three brilliant forensic practitioners: the toxicologists Arthur Pearson Luff and William Willcox, and Augustus Joseph Pepper (1849–1935), pathologist.

Eventually Spilsbury worked under Pepper as joint assistant demonstrator of pathology (1904–5) and as pathologist and morbid anatomist in 1907. He succeeded Pepper upon the latter's retirement in 1908. He had received his medical qualifications in 1905 after a relatively long period of study and, with Pepper's guidance, pursued his interest in microscopy.

Forensic medicine When Spilsbury completed his medical training in 1905 and began working with Pepper, Willcox, and Luff at St Mary's, those three more senior men had a special working relationship with the Home Office, which administered the Metropolitan Police. Luff was Home Office analyst 1892–1908, and Willcox 1904–19. The Treasury solicitor often asked for advice from these forensic medical experts, and by 1909 all three were being regularly called in by the coroner, the Home Office, or the director of public prosecutions, who, among other duties, was vested with the authority to request the Home Office to order exhumations.

Sir Bernard Henry Spilsbury (1877–1947), by Edward Cahen

Through his connections with Pepper at St Mary's, Spilsbury early on was trusted by the Home Office as an adviser. This in its early days coincided with the tenure of Edward Henry, commissioner of the Metropolitan Police from 1903 to 1918, and a key figure in the history of Scotland Yard. Henry was dedicated to making criminal investigations more efficient and modern. Spilsbury, who argued that England's pathologists ought to have access to the finest laboratories and mortuary equipment, found in Henry a powerful ally.

The mid-Victorian practice of forensic medicine had fallen into disrepute as a result of controversial trials at which forensic evidence had been handled sloppily by toxicologists. Pepper, Luff, and Willcox, and their predecessor Sir Thomas Stevenson, had managed to restore some of the prestige of forensic medicine. Within the medical profession, however, when Spilsbury was a young physician, forensic medicine still was called 'that beastly science' (Browne and Tullett, 22).

Though Spilsbury became famous in connection with the resolution of cases of violent crimes, the fees paid for autopsies in connection with the twenty or thirty murder cases that occurred annually in London would not have supported him as a young pathologist. More routine autopsies, on persons who had died in hospital unexpectedly, or accidentally, remained at the centre of his practice.

On 3 September 1908 Spilsbury married Edith Caroline Mary (*b*. 1878/9), daughter of William Henry Horton, a surgeon-dentist. They had four children. Spilsbury had close working relationships with his sons Peter, who became a surgeon, and Alan, who despite ill health assisted him in his laboratory. Work and devotion to his family kept Spilsbury living in London for all of his career, with rare holidays but constant travel as a consultant.

Spilsbury was a lecturer in pathology at St Mary's (between 1907 and 1919) and morbid anatomy (1919–47) at St Bartholomew's Hospital. At University College Hospital medical school and the London School of Medicine for Women he lectured on forensic medicine and toxicology, and lectured on forensic medicine at St Thomas's. He was an examiner in pathology at the University of London, and forensic medicine at several other universities. He was elected a fellow of the Royal College of Physicians in 1931. A detailed but uninspiring lecturer, he was best with students when he meticulously demonstrated technique in the mortuary.

Fame and controversy Early in his career as a forensic pathologist Spilsbury became widely known outside his profession as a riveting expert witness in a series of notorious murder cases. Assiduous in conducting fieldwork and performing post-mortem examinations, Spilsbury testified only about facts on which he was certain. His demeanour in court won the respect of counsel, judges, juries, and the public. The Crippen case of 1910 made him famous; other criminal investigations in rapid succession enhanced his prestige. Hawley Harvey Crippen was an American doctor accused of poisoning his wife, Belle Elmore. Crippen had tried to dispose of his victim's body with lime. A key aspect in proving Crippen's guilt lay in the identification of the body. Very little of the remains were left upon which to base a physical appraisal about identity. Through examination of a scarred section of the victim's skin Spilsbury established to the jury's satisfaction that the victim was in fact Belle Elmore. Spilsbury's testimony went a long way toward ensuring Crippen's conviction and execution.

In the Seddon case of 1911–12 Spilsbury demonstrated his expertise with regard to arsenic poisoning. Frederick Henry Seddon stood accused of administering arsenic to an acquaintance named Eliza Barrow, from whose demise he expected to profit financially. Under extremely able cross-examination from Seddon's attorneys Spilsbury maintained that Barrow had died from acute rather than chronic (and thus perhaps self-administered) arsenic poisoning. Furthermore his examination of Barrow's body indicated that Barrow could not have died of any other complaint, such as heart disease. Those arguments proved decisive: Seddon was hanged for his crime.

In 1915 Spilsbury helped to convict the multiple murderer George Joseph Smith. Smith stood accused of drowning three women over a period of several months. Smith had been romantically involved with each woman in turn. Each had died, the defence contended, as a result of accident or illness while in her bath; the newspapers referred to the trial as the 'brides in the bath' case. Spilsbury coolly repudiated each argument by the defence. He was able to convince the jury, for example, that one victim (whom Smith maintained had suffered an epileptic seizure and drowned), could not have been immersed in water during a faint or seizure, due to her height and the size of the bath.

Herbert Rowse Armstrong, a solicitor in Hay-on-Wye, on the Welsh border, was tried in 1911 at the summer assizes at Hereford after an extensive police investigation. Armstrong was suspected of poisoning his wife and planning the murder of a business associate. Spilsbury's contentions on the stand about the effects of acute arsenic poisoning again were influential in securing a conviction. A striking feature of the trial was a glowing tribute given to Spilsbury by the experienced trial judge, Mr Justice Darling, in his charge to the jury.

Spilsbury's honorary Home Office appointment was formalized as such in 1922—though he received only case fees and £100 per annum towards his laboratory at Bart's over and above his teaching and examining fees. Knighted in 1923 he was renowned not only as a valuable witness but as a pathologist who helped to establish his profession as worthy of being called a science. When Spilsbury was at the peak of his professional influence during the 1910s to the 1930s, his opinion was virtually unquestioned among many jurors. Newspapers frequently reported his testimony, solidifying the impression that the appearance of 'Sir Bernard in the Box' was a turning point in inquests and criminal trials. His reputation for invincibility evoked comment and some professional jealousy. The misstatement by one defence counsel—who called him 'Saint Bernard'—reinforced the perception among the public that Spilsbury could not be gainsaid, even by an array of other expert witnesses.

It is remarkable that Spilsbury testified successfully in so many well-publicized cases. Equally noteworthy is the fact that in nearly forty years as an expert witness his opinion on a medical point of any consequence was never contradicted, though many talented advocates attempted to do so. Some modern scholars have disparaged Spilsbury's professionalism. Those who think that Spilsbury was overrated as an expert witness point to his reluctance to rely on statistics, his lack of interest in research and publication of his own work for peer review, and several of his opinions on the stand which seemed outdated at the time.

The most controversial moment in Spilsbury's career was during and just after the Thorne case of 1926. Norman Thorne was accused of fatally beating Elsie Cameron, arranging her death to make it seem a suicide by hanging; the defence, while admitting that Thorne had attempted to conceal the body, argued that Cameron had hanged herself. Arrayed against Spilsbury, who argued that death had been caused by trauma to the skull, were at least eight medical witnesses who testified to the contrary. Not the least of those experts was Dr Robert Patrick Bronte, who prior to 1922 had been crown analyst in Ireland. Bronte often testified for the defence in cases where Spilsbury served as the chief witness for the crown.

The jury sided with Spilsbury and Thorne was executed. In the wake of the trial Spilsbury's influence was questioned by authorities such as Arthur Conan Doyle, the legal writer Edgar Lustgarten, Helena Normanton (who edited the Thorne trial for the Notable British Trials series), and the *Law Journal*.

Reputation Spilsbury's success was due not only to his careful work habits and power as a witness. He was unfailingly courteous in his dealings with persons with whom he worked—from mortuary attendants, whom he compensated graciously, to police officers, whom he treated with great respect as fellow professionals. He got along well with coroners, and convinced many of them to employ more and better trained pathologists. He made provincial physicians feel at ease, in spite of the fact that sometimes his findings about causes of death were in disagreement with their original death certificates. Although he could appear aloof among strangers, his friends and close associates described him as shy and humble.

At his most productive, in the 1930s, Spilsbury was performing between 750 and 1000 post-mortem examinations per year. His little black books, filled with notes from field observations, autopsies, and trials, included more than 6000 separate medico-legal cases on which he worked. He performed more than 25,000 post-mortems in his career.

His vast experience yielded knowledge about unusual causes of death. Spilsbury, for example, eventually saw dozens of cases of poisoning; the regular practitioner—or even coroner—might see none during a career. Besides poisoning, other unnatural causes of death with which Spilsbury had great familiarity were deaths due to firearms (still rare in England in his day), illegal abortions, suicide, and asphyxia. He also became well versed in the identification of human remains, even in cases of dismemberment. This talent was to serve him well at the time of the sensational Mahon case of 1924, in which he literally pieced the victim's body together.

At the time of his death Spilsbury's professional colleagues lamented that he never had written the textbook for which he had been compiling notes throughout his career. In contrast to contemporaries such as Willcox, Spilsbury's output of original scholarship was meagre. Among his professional accomplishments were research which he did with Willcox on toxic jaundice, his presidential lecture on illegal abortion before the Medico-Legal Society (1933), and the Lettsom lectures of 1923, 'Wounds and other injuries', to the Medical Society of London.

Spilsbury belonged to the Junior Carlton and United Universities clubs. A longtime freemason, he was a member of the Rahere, Abernethy Mark M., and Sancta Maria lodges. He joined the Medico-Legal Society in 1908, and served as its secretary, treasurer, and president (1933–4). He was a member of two select professional groups, the Organon Club and the Sydenham Medical Club. One of his most cherished associations was with a group of criminologists and amateur crime buffs called Our Society or the Crimes Club. Those club meetings focused on medical and legal discussions of historical cases, such as the murder of Sir Edmund Godfrey (1621–1678) by Roman Catholics.

Several of Spilsbury's attributes as a pathologist were peculiar to him. In the early 1920s, for example, he had begun to lose his sense of smell. As a younger man he had been known to distinguish odours (such as the smell of arsenic in a newly exhumed body) which others could not perceive. The loss of that ability, ironically, made him more capable as a pathologist in one sense: later in his life he could tolerate offensive working conditions which others could not bear. He experienced arthritis from his forties onward, and was affected by the cold. He suffered a stroke in 1940, which led to a loss of finger dexterity in one hand, so that he learned to be ambidextrous. The deaths of his sister and two sons during the 1940s (Alan from disease and Peter in a bombing raid during the blitz) were devastating personal blows.

Spilsbury was discovered unconscious on 17 December 1947 in his gas-filled laboratory at University College, London; he could not be revived. The coroner at the subsequent inquest, his former colleague Bentley Purchase, noted that Spilsbury's sadness concerning his declining health must have been a key factor in his decision to commit suicide. Lady Spilsbury, his son Richard, and daughter Evelyn survived him. ELISABETH A. CAWTHON

Sources D. G. Browne and E. V. Tullett, *Bernard Spilsbury: his life and cases* (1951) • *The Times* (18–19 Dec 1947) • *The Times* (22 Dec 1947) • G. Roche Lynch, 'Obituary, Sir Bernard Spilsbury', *Medico-Legal Journal*, 16 (1948), 13–14 • 'Sir Bernard Spilsbury', *BMJ* (3 Jan 1948), 29 • *Trial of H. H. Crippen*, ed. H. Hodge and J. H. Hodge, Notable British Trials (1920) • *Trial of G. J. Smith*, ed. H. Hodge and J. H. Hodge, Notable British Trials (1922) • *Trial of H. R. Armstrong*, ed. H. Hodge and J. H. Hodge, Notable British Trials (1927) • M. A. Green, 'Is Sir Bernard Spilsbury dead?', *Crime investigation: art or science?*, ed. A. R. Brownlie (1984), 23–6 • K. Simpson, *Forty years of murder* (1978) • b. cert. • m. cert. • d. cert. • *CGPLA Eng. & Wales* (1948) • Z. Cope, *The history of St Mary's Hospital medical school* (1954) • P. H. A. Willcox, *The detective-physician* (1970) • *The Times* (1 Jan 1923)

Likenesses G. Belcher, cartoon, charcoal drawing, repro. in Browne and Tullett, *Bernard Spilsbury*, following p. 252 • E. Cahen, photograph, NPG [*see illus.*] • Elliott and Fry, photograph, repro. in Browne and Tullett, *Bernard Spilsbury*, following p. 252

Wealth at death £9932 4s. 10d.: probate, 25 March 1948, *CGPLA Eng. & Wales*

Spilsbury, John (1739–1769). *See under* Spilsbury, Jonathan (*bap.* 1737, *d.* 1812).

Spilsbury, Jonathan (*bap.* 1737, *d.* 1812), printmaker and portrait painter, was born at Worcester, where he was baptized on 6 February 1737, the eldest of three sons of Thomas Spilsbury (*d.* 1741) and his second wife, Mary Wright (*d.* 1773), a young widow. He was followed by John [*see below*] and a third son, Thomas, who became a printer. All three brothers and their mother eventually settled in London. The careers of Jonathan and John were closely connected and ever since 1785, when the publisher John Boydell mistakenly printed the name John Spilsbury on the title-page of Jonathan Spilsbury's *Collection of Fifty Prints … from Antique Gems*, the brothers' work has been confused.

From 1750 to 1757 Jonathan was apprenticed to his cousin George Spilsbury of Birmingham, a japanner and box painter. He then moved to London, where his aunt Sarah had married the court painter Jonathan Richardson who probably facilitated his invitation to work in Thomas Hudson's studio before practising as a painter of portraits in oils, watercolours, and chalk, and as a printmaker. Jonathan worked chiefly in mezzotint but also on occasion using etching, dry-point, and stipple techniques. He exhibited three works at the Society of Artists between 1763 and 1771, and thirteen paintings at the Royal Academy between 1776 and 1784. His large mezzotint of George, prince of Wales (later George III), first published in 1759 is, according to its title inscription, after Spilsbury's own portrait of the prince. This royal sitting, which would have considerably furthered Spilsbury's career, must have been arranged through Thomas Jefferys, geographer to the prince of Wales, to whom John Spilsbury was apprenticed.

In 1761 Jonathan was awarded a premium by the Society of Arts for a mezzotint after Joshua Reynolds of Esther Jacobs. These early mezzotint portraits and another of Reynolds's pupil Giuseppe Marchi, after Reynolds and published in 1761, are among his most accomplished known works. Between 1763 and John's death in 1769 he appears to have worked from John's shop in Covent Garden, and his brother frequently acted as his publisher. A copy of his strongly modelled mezzotint of the Revd Richard Baxter is priced at 1*s.* 6*d.* and was published by John Spilsbury in 1763.

Jonathan frequently visited Bristol, where he met in 1765 Rebecca (1748–1812), daughter of Walter Chapman, prebendary of Bristol Cathedral. After ten years' courtship they married at St Marylebone on 13 February 1775, setting up home at 28 Great Ormond Street. Their daughter (Rebecca) Maria Ann *Spilsbury (1777–1820), a surviving twin, was taught by her father and became a notable painter and musician; there was also a younger son. About 1785–9 Jonathan taught drawing at Harrow School where his pupils included the sons of Mrs Sarah Tighe of co. Wicklow, who invited him to Ireland to instruct her daughters. Jonathan's family accompanied him on this mission; they returned to London in 1791 and settled in St George's Row, off Oxford Street. In later life Jonathan produced many rather lifeless mezzotints, some after his own portrait paintings and drawings. A preponderance of clerics, many of Wesleyan persuasion, may reflect his own religious inclinations. While Rebecca stayed within the Church of England, Jonathan had long been drawn to nonconformity and in 1781 he joined the Moravian church, but his ambition to become a Moravian minister was not fulfilled.

Between March 1781 and December 1784 Boydell published Spilsbury's prints of *Antique Gems*, with a complete octavo set with title-page issued in 1785. For this project Jonathan closely followed the formula employed nearly twenty years earlier by Thomas Worlidge for his *Select Collection of Drawings from Curious Antique Gems* (published in parts from 1765), using a dry-point Rembrandtesque technique. Jonathan's small dry-point heads in the manner of Rembrandt, dated 1776, are also strongly reminiscent of Worlidge's work, although no record has been found of any formal connection between the two artists. Jonathan was living in St George's Row, Oxford Street, at the time of his death; his last print, of Mary Fletcher, after a portrait by himself, being published in October that year. Rebecca died in February 1812, Jonathan in October that same year; they were interred in the same grave (not following Moravian practice, in separate graves) in the nonconformist Bunhill Fields, on the northern margin of the City of London.

John Spilsbury (1739–1769), printmaker, was apprenticed, probably from 1753 to 1760, to Thomas Jefferys (1719–1771), engraver, cartographer, and map and print publisher of St Martin's Lane, Westminster. In 1761 he married Sarah May of Newmarket, Suffolk, and found a source of income in the increasing children's educational book trade. The commercial success of Jefferys's 'geographical race game' suggested to John the possibility of mounting a map on thin mahogany board, cutting it along the county borders, and selling it, boxed, for children to reassemble. The advertisements for his business, which was established at Russell Court, off Drury Lane, mentioned prints, maps, and charts, and other books and stationery, plus 'all sorts of dissected maps, for teaching geography'. He also took advantage of the brief fashion for printed silk kerchiefs, offering one with a 'New and most accurate map of the roads of England and Wales; with distances by the milestones'. John also became interested in the Moravian church, where he and his mother attended services, but neither became a member. He died on 3 April 1769 and was interred on 9 April in the burial-ground of St Mary-le-Strand, which lay alongside Russell Court.

John's widow ran the business for a short time, then married Harry Ashby, who had been apprenticed with John Spilsbury and later worked with him at Russell Court. Ashby was still advertising 'Dissected Maps for teaching geography … on the original Plan of the late Mr Spilsbury' in 1785 (*Morning Chronicle*, 16 Jan 1785).

SUSAN SLOMAN

Sources L. Hannas, *The English jigsaw puzzle, 1760–1890* (1972) · J. C. Smith, *British mezzotinto portraits*, 3 (1880), 1323–35 · C. W. King, *Antique gems and rings*, 2 vols. (1872), vol. 1, p. 468 · Graves, *RA exhibitors* · private information (2004) [Colin Davies, Rita M. Gibbs] · J. Strutt, *A biographical dictionary, containing an historical account of all the engravers, from the earliest period of the art of engraving to the present time*, 2 (1786), 333–4 · T. Dodd, 'Memorials of engravers in Great Britain, 1550–1800', BL, Add. MS 33405, fols. 113–18 · apprenticeship records, PRO, IR 17 · BM, department of prints and drawings, Banks collection of trade cards · R. Young, *Father and daughter: Jonathan and Maria Spilsbury* (1952) · G. Hill, *Cartographical curiosities* (1978)

Likenesses J. Spilsbury, self-portrait, repro. in Young, *Father and daughter*, frontispiece

Spilsbury [*married name* Taylor], **(Rebecca) Maria Ann** [Mary] **(1777–1820)**, painter, was born at 68 Great Ormond Street, London, the daughter (her twin brother died) of Jonathan *Spilsbury (*bap.* 1737, *d.* 1812), engraver, and his wife, Rebecca (1748–1812), daughter of Dr Walter Chapman, senior prebendary of Bristol Cathedral. She had a younger brother, Jonathan Robert Henry Spilsbury, who was baptized on 7 December 1779 at St Marylebone, London. Maria Spilsbury received art instruction from her father who, about 1785–9, was drawing-master at Harrow School. His pupils included the sons of Mrs Sarah Tighe of Rossana, co. Wicklow. In 1789, having been employed to teach drawing to Mrs Tighe's daughters, he took his family to Ireland. About May 1791 they moved back to London and settled at 10 St George's Row, Hyde Park. Sir William Beecher gave Maria Spilsbury lessons in colour and she was taught music by Charles Wesley the younger (1757–1834), who considered her the best amateur performer on the organ in London.

Maria Spilsbury exhibited forty-seven works at the

Royal Academy as an honorary exhibitor (1792–1808), and thirty-two at the British Institution (1806–13). Her contributions, primarily oil paintings, included portraits, often of children, such as *Miss Elizabeth Angerstein Attended by Guardian Angels* (exh. RA, 1805; ex Phillips, 13 June 1997); genre scenes comprising picturesque subjects such as *The Schoolmistress* (1803; Tate collection) and *Confusion, or The Nursery in the Kitchen* (exh. British Institution, 1811; Williamson Art Gallery and Museum, Birkenhead) and others revealing an interest in charitable initiatives, an example of which is *The House of Protection for Destitute Females of Character; Two Girls Applying for Admission* (exh. RA, 1806 and British Institution, 1807); she also exhibited biblical subjects and literary themes from Dr Johnson, William Cowper, Richard Bloomfield, James Thomson, and Mrs Row. Her most ambitious and celebrated works depicted crowd scenes on fête days, holidays, and at open-air meetings: *Christ Feeding the Multitude, the Second Miracle of the Loaves and Fishes—St. Matthew, xv* (exh. RA, 1804), *The Fourth of June* (exh. RA, 1807 and British Institution, 1808), and *The Royal Jubilee, as Celebrated at Great Malvern, 1809* (exh. British Institution, 1811) were all large-scale works, the last measuring 4 ft 6 in. by 5 ft 6 in.

Although Maria Spilsbury and her mother were both members of the Church of England, the family had early associations with nonconformity. Jonathan Spilsbury was received into the Moravian church in 1781; Mrs Tighe, a close friend of the family, was a supporter of John Wesley. Through the Wesleys, the Spilsburys became acquainted, about 1798, with the family of Walter Taylor, a nonconformist who ran a successful engineering business in Southampton. By 1807 Maria was engaged to his son, John Taylor (1785–1821)—dissenter, Calvinist, philanthropist, and unrecognized inventor of the box wheel or Collinges patent axle—who was her junior by eight years, and whom she married at St George's, Hanover Square, London, on 3 November 1808. They lived in rooms at 8 Collyer's Buildings, Blackheath Road, London.

During the year of her engagement Maria Spilsbury worked extremely hard (possibly to finance her forthcoming marriage), exhibiting a total of thirteen paintings in 1807 and twelve in 1808. Her work became fashionable and on private view days at her studio in 10 St George's Row over twenty carriages would sometimes wait outside. The prince regent (George IV) and the marquess of Stafford were regular purchasers of her pictures. For these she charged up to 40 guineas, and such was her success that the family was able to depend upon her income. After the death of her parents in 1812 (both were buried at Bunhill Fields, a nonconformist burial-ground near Wesley's Chapel in London), the Taylors moved into 10 St George's Row with the first of their five children.

In 1814 the Taylors settled in Ireland, where they lived initially with Mrs Tighe in Rossana and from 1817 at her town house in Upper Dorset Street, Dublin. Maria Taylor is said to have exhibited in Dublin at the Hibernian Society (1814, 1816) and at Hawkins Street (1816, 1817, 1819). She continued to paint multiple-figure subjects, such as *John Wesley Preaching in the Open Air at Willybank, Rossana* (1814/15; Museum of Methodism at Wesley's Chapel, London), which included representations of her family. This painting is probably *The Irish Fair in the Vale of Glendalough or the Seven Churches*, commissioned by the prince regent). *Patron's Day at the Seven Churches, Glendalough* (exh. Hawkins Street, 1816; National Gallery of Ireland, Dublin), in which the artist painted herself sketching the scene, is another example of her multi-figured subjects. She also executed numerous portraits including *Mrs. Henry Grattan* (National Gallery of Ireland, Dublin), *Alexander Hamilton and his Wife and Daughters*, and *Francis Synge*, who founded the Pestalozzi School in Dublin. Many of these remain in private collections in Ireland. A number of her subject pictures and her *Portrait of the Reverend Benjamin Williams Mathias (1772–1841) Chaplain of Bethesda, Dublin* were engraved by Charles Turner (1774–1857). Henry Edward Dawe (1790–1848) engraved her *Portrait of the Rev. William Kingsbury*. Maria Spilsbury also executed a few original etchings. Other examples of her work are in private collections in New Zealand. She died on 1 June 1820 at her home in Upper Dorset Street, Dublin, and was buried in Drumcondra churchyard. Her husband, John Taylor, died in London the following year. CHARLOTTE YELDHAM

Sources R. Young, *Father and daughter: Jonathan and Maria Spilsbury* (1952) • R. Young, 'Maria Spilsbury, 1777–1820: a woman artist of the Regency', *Country Life*, 83 (1938), xliv–xlvi • W. G. Strickland, *A dictionary of Irish artists*, 2 vols. (1913) • Graves, *RA exhibitors* • Graves, *Brit. Inst.* • *The Connoisseur*, 84 (1929), 159, 194, 227 [illustrations] • artist's file, archive material, Courtauld Inst., Witt Library • J. W. A. Taylor, 'A family history', priv. coll. • *IGI*

Likenesses R. M. A. Spilsbury, self-portrait, 1793, repro. in Young, 'Maria Spilsbury', xliv

Spinckes, Nathaniel (1654–1727), bishop of the nonjuring Church of England, was born on 9 May 1654 at Castor, Northamptonshire, where his father, Edmund Spinckes (1606/7–1671), was the rector. His mother, Martha (*bap.* 1623, *d.* 1693), was the second daughter of Thomas Elmes, esquire, of Lilford and Warmington, Northamptonshire, whom Edmund Spinckes served as a chaplain. Edmund evidently had links with New England, where he had a share in an ironworks at the time of his death as well as property in Ireland. He took the solemn league and covenant and was faced with the threat of nearby royalist troops; he needed a troop of horse to guard him when he preached at Castor and was forced to flee from Warmington on the day before his eldest son was born because enemy parties had twice raided the house that day. Edmund Spinckes was ejected for his nonconformity at the Restoration. Indeed much was made later of Spinckes senior's support for parliament: 'nobody being more zealous for the rebels', and consequently Spinckes junior's achievement in overcoming 'the errors of his father' and conquering the 'prejudice of his first education' (*Remarks*, 9.5). In fact, Spinckes senior conformed to the Church of England, and Nathaniel's early schooling was undertaken by Samuel Morton, the rector of Haddon, Huntingdonshire.

Nathaniel Spinckes (1654–1727), by George Vertue, pubd 1731 (after John Wollaston)

On 9 July 1670 Nathaniel Spinckes matriculated at Trinity College, Cambridge. As the eldest surviving son, on his father's death in 1671 Spinckes inherited his father's estate. This 'disqualified him from preferment in his college, according to the statutes' (BL, Sloane MS 4225, fols. 107–11), so Spinckes transferred to Jesus College on 12 October 1672, aged eighteen, where he was elected a Rustat scholar. He graduated BA in 1674. He was ordained deacon on 21 May 1676 by Bishop Henry Compton of London, proceeded MA at Cambridge in 1677, and was ordained priest on 22 December 1678 by Bishop Thomas Barlow of Lincoln.

Spinckes became chaplain to Sir Richard Edgcumbe at Mount Edgcumbe, Devon, in June 1677, leaving to become curate at Stibbington, Huntingdonshire, in August the following year. In early 1679 he moved to Petersham in Surrey, where he served as curate and as chaplain to John Maitland, earl of Lauderdale, staying there for the next two and a half years. His fellow chaplain was George Hickes, another future nonjuror. He was appointed to the vicarage of Eckington in Worcestershire through the offices of the influential Anglican polemicist Simon Patrick, but was never instituted and, returning the living to its patrons, moved to London. He was curate of St Stephen Walbrook, London, from about March 1683 to September 1685; he also served as lecturer there for some months in 1684 and assisted William Clagett as afternoon preacher at Gray's Inn in 1685. On 17 September 1685 he was instituted as rector of Peakirk-cum-Glinton, Northamptonshire, by the dean (Simon Patrick again) and chapter of Peterborough. On 1 December 1686 he married Dorothy Rutland (*bap.* 1660, *d.* 1727), daughter of William Rutland, citizen of London, who brought with her a portion of £1000. On 21 July 1687 he was made a prebendary of Salisbury, and on 24 September he became rector of St Martin's, Salisbury.

The revolution of 1688 changed Spinckes's comfortable existence. He lost his livings on 1 February 1690 for refusing to take the oaths of allegiance to the new regime. Much respected by fellow nonjurors such as John Kettlewell, Robert Nelson, and George Hickes for his piety, learning, and sweet disposition he was actively involved in Kettlewell's scheme to raise money to relieve indigent deprived clergy, for which he was one of those hauled before the privy council in 1695, and came to be the chief manager of the fund. However, Spinckes was, it seems, slow to take up his pen as a controversialist. In August 1705 Thomas Hearne recorded that Spinckes had written 'one book already about patience', presumably *Of trust in God, or, A discourse concerning the duty of casting our care upon God in all our difficulties* (1696). Now Hearne was informed that 'Mr Spinckes is a very prudent man and … well qualified to answer Mr Basset's *Essay for Catholic Communion*', a polemical work by Joshua Basset who had been the Catholic master of Sidney Sussex College, Cambridge, appointed by James II (*Remarks*, 1.30). This Spinckes duly did with his *Essay towards a Proposal for Catholic Communion* (1705) which he followed up with *The Case Truly Stated* (1714), *The Case Further Stated* (1718), and *The Article of Romanish Transubstantiation Inquired into and Disproved* (1719). According to Hearne, in 1705 he was also employed in the distribution of money 'given by the chief Jacobites for charitable purposes' (*Remarks*, 1.30). Spinckes also entered the controversy against the French prophets with *The New Pretenders to Prophecy Re-Examined* (1709). In 1712 he published a more popular work, *The sick man visited and furnished with instructions, meditations and prayers suitable to his condition*, the fourth edition of which in 1731 contained a short life of the author by John Blackbourne.

On 3 June 1713 Spinckes, Jeremy Collier, and Samuel Hawes were consecrated bishops 'at large' by the nonjuring Bishop Hickes, assisted by bishops Campbell and Gadderar. In 1713 he wrote the preface to the published sermons of Hickes. In October 1716 he was taken into custody in Norwich on suspicion of Jacobite activity. From 1716 Spinckes was an important participant in the 'usages' dispute over the proposals of some nonjurors like Collier to return to the first liturgy used by Edward VI. At least four pamphlets were published by Spinckes on this issue, including *No Reason for Restoring the Prayers and Directions of Edward VI's First Liturgy* (1717) and *No Just Grounds for Introducing the New Communion Office* (1719). Indeed, Spinckes was to be an intractable opponent of a compromise with the usagers which would have ended the schism between the nonjurors.

Not all of the work of Spinckes was explicitly acknowledged. His Greek scholarship was put to good use in translating the proposals for unity with the Greek church. In 1721 Spinckes published *The True Church of England Man's Companion to the Closet* (1721), which became known as Spinckes's Devotions during its long usage in the eighteenth century. In 1726 he published more discourses by Hickes with a preface.

Spinckes died on 18 July 1727, aged seventy-four; his wife followed seven days later. He was buried in the cemetery of the parish of St Faith under St Paul's, London. Although Spinckes had a large family, seven children died in infancy while an eighth, Robert, drowned in a shipwreck sailing from Bengal to Bombay in 1712. Only William, a merchant, and Anne, who married Anthony Cope, survived their parents. *The Historical Register* rather sympathetically recorded that Spinckes 'had no wealth, few enemies, many friends … His patience was great, his self-denial greater, and his charity still greater; though his temper seems to be his cardinal virtue' (*Historical Register*, 12.29–30).

STUART HANDLEY

Sources Venn, *Alum. Cant.* • J. H. Overton, *The nonjurors: their lives, principles, and writings* (1902), 119, 129–33, 394, 493 • J. Blackbourne, 'A short account of the life', in N. Spinckes, *The sick man visited*, 4th edn (1731), i–xl • *Fasti Angl., 1541–1857*, [Salisbury], 56 • BL, Sloane MS 4225, fols. 107–11 • *IGI* • H. Broxap, *The later non-jurors* (1924), 14–15, 31, 78, 111, 114 • *The historical register*, 12 (1727), appx, 29–30 • T. Lathbury, *A history of the nonjurors* (1845), 365 • N. Rogers, 'Popular Jacobitism in a provincial context: eighteenth century Bristol and Norwich', *The Jacobite challenge*, ed. E. Cruickshanks and J. Black (1988), 140n. • *Calamy rev.* • *Corrections and additions to the Dictionary of National Biography*, Institute of Historical Research (1966) • H. I. Longden, *Northamptonshire and Rutland clergy from 1500*, ed. P. I. King and others, 16 vols. in 6, Northamptonshire RS (1938–52), vol. 13, pp. 19–21 • *Remarks and collections of Thomas Hearne*, ed. C. E. Doble and others, 11 vols., OHS, 2, 7, 13, 34, 42–3, 48, 50, 65, 67, 72 (1885–1921), vol. 1, p. 30; vol. 11, p. 5

Likenesses G. Vertue, line engraving (after J. Wollaston), NPG; repro. in Blackbourne, 'A short account' [*see illus.*]

Spinks, Alfred (1917–1982), chemist and biologist, was born in the fens village of Littleport, Cambridgeshire, on 25 February 1917, the only child of Alfred Robert Spinks, manager of a Littleport brewery, and his wife, Ruth Harley. He was educated at Soham grammar school, was awarded an Isle of Ely major scholarship, and entered University College, Nottingham, in 1935 to read chemistry. In the 1938 University of London BSc external degree examination he gained the highest chemistry marks of any candidate and was awarded the Neil Arnott studentship for postgraduate studies. He chose to go to Imperial College under Ian Heilbron, where he worked with A. W. Johnson on vitamin A synthesis. He gained his PhD in 1940.

For the next two years Spinks was employed by ICI, but continued to work under Heilbron at Imperial College. In 1942 he moved to ICI's dyestuffs division at Blackley, and worked under F. L. Rose in the new medicinal chemistry section, determining concentrations of sulphonamides in animal tissues. Over the next eight years he made an intensive study of the behaviour of organic compounds in animals as relationships between chemical structure and drug absorption became an important concept in new drug design at ICI. In 1946 Spinks married Patricia, daughter of Frederick Charles Kilner, an engineer with Manchester corporation waterworks; they had two daughters.

By 1950 Spinks was self-educated in biochemistry, pharmacology, and physiology, and a far-sighted divisional research director, Clifford Paine, sent him to Worcester College, Oxford, to study physiology. Taking a degree was not a requisite but he did so, obtaining a first after two years' study. When he returned to Blackley plans for the independent pharmaceuticals division were well advanced and Spinks became head of the new pharmacology section.

Spinks's promotion to research manager of the first ICI biochemistry department in 1961 marked the beginning of his career as an administrator. Based at Alderley Park he became divisional research director in 1966 and then, after a brief period as deputy chairman, he joined the ICI main board, becoming responsible for research and development throughout the whole of the company. Spinks believed that scientists in the laboratory were the driving force in research, and often found time to visit and encourage them even though they worked in fields remote from his personal experience. He was particularly sensitive to the problems of chemicals in the environment, and established procedures to ascertain the possible mutagenic or carcinogenic risk of compounds made by the company. His more general responsibilities extended to pharmaceuticals, Nobel and agricultural divisions, and to certain countries overseas, particularly South Africa, where during the years of apartheid he took an active part in introducing a unified pay scale for all employees irrespective of colour or race.

Spinks retired from the board of ICI in 1979 but his multidisciplinary mastery and wide experience ensured that his advice remained widely sought. He was a founder member in 1976 of the Advisory Council for Applied Research and Development (ACARD), of which he was chairman from 1980 until his death. His impact on science policy was most notably evident in the report of a joint working party of ACARD, the Advisory Board for Research Councils, and the Royal Society on the emerging field of biotechnology—the Spinks report. On his retirement he was appointed to the royal commission on environmental pollution, to the boards of Dunlop and Johnson Matthey, and as chairman of Charter Consolidated. He was involved in the affairs of many learned societies and especially of the Chemical Society of which he became president in 1979–80. He was elected FRS in 1977 and appointed CBE the following year. His great natural ability was augmented with vast knowledge and wide experience, and he developed keen interests in music, the arts, photography, and gardening. He was regarded as a large, kindly, sociable man, whose intellect, nevertheless, bordered on the intimidating. Spinks died at his home, Woodcote, Torkington Road, Wilmslow, Cheshire, on 11 February 1982.

E. R. H. JONES, *rev.*

Sources *The Times* (13 Feb 1982) · A. W. Johnson, F. L. Rose, and C. W. Suckling, *Memoirs FRS*, 30 (1984), 567–94 · personal knowledge (1990) · private information (1990) · *CGPLA Eng. & Wales* (1982)

Likenesses H. Coster, photographs, NPG · B. Wilkinson, photograph, RS, record

Wealth at death £219,406: probate, 14 May 1982, *CGPLA Eng. & Wales*

Spinola, Benedict (1519/20–1580), merchant, was one of the six children, the second son, of Battista Spinola of Genoa and his wife, Elisabetta, daughter of Giacomo Spinola. The Spinolas had long been prominent in Genoa (in 1556 Battista would decline the dogeship), and Benedict was born there. His early history is unknown but he appears in London in 1541, employed by Bastian Bony, postmaster, as a clerk at £2 a year: working for the postal service of London's foreign merchants gave Spinola ready access to the world of commerce and finance. He resided in St Gabriel Fenchurch parish (where he remained until he died) with his nephews Hannibal and Ascaneo Spinola. His property in Shoreditch, Middlesex, was popularly known as 'Spinola's pleasure'. During 1544–52, at least, he was associated with Acelin Salvago, a Genoese merchant.

Unusually, Spinola was granted full denization in 1552, a privilege allowing him to pay taxes and customs dues at the Englishman's rates. By 1559 he was exporting woollen cloth at customs dues up to £200, and importing sweet wines to £40, a year. Illegally, he exported another's goods on his own licence (1561), and his signed confession survives; but his 1566 grant permitted this, and raised his limits to £2000 and £400 over a longer period. He had shipped his full quota of 4800 cloths by the end of 1569 but imported only 3845—out of 5342—butts of wine by Michaelmas 1570. Moreover, important communities of Italian merchants had been established in Antwerp and London, largely because of the luxury textiles and other wares carried from Italy overland to 'Flanders' (mostly Brabant), often for trans-shipment: hence, while his brothers Francisco, Pasquale, and Giacomo resided in Antwerp, Spinola himself lived in London, where he was in the very top rank of merchants. Requiring hangings for the dining chamber at Kenilworth Castle, the earl of Leicester told his man to 'deal with Mr Spinola', who was 'able to get such stuff better cheap than any man' (Jackson, 92). In 1572 Leicester asked Francis Walsingham, then in France, to favour Spinola in his (unspecified) 'great cause', as 'he is my dear friend and the best Italian I know in England' (BL, Harley MS 260, fol. 363).

Spinola objected when, about 1550, Michael Angelo Florio, the minister of the (Calvinist) Italian church, preached against 'Popish' doctrines; but in 1566 the Spanish ambassador reported to Philip II that Spinola was now confirmed in his Anglicanism. Inclusion of his name in a list of suspected 'papists' (1578) was doubtless an error. By 1568 he and his household, inclusive of the French cook, were attending their parish church. Spinola's growing affluence is evident from his assessments for subsidy: in 1544, on £5; 1549, £20; in 1559, Spinola 'and his company' were assessed on £500; in 1564, £200; and in 1576, £100. The later reductions hint at his improved, favoured, status as an adviser to the government, gathering intelligence through his foreign correspondents and as an important negotiator in political and financial matters, as in the settlement of the Antwerp embargo, 1564–5. By virtue of his state and business interests, he often handled immense sums, so that, on 24 June 1574, he was owed amounts totalling £27, 879 9*s*. 8*d*.

In 1568 the ships carrying the money for paying the duke of Alva's troops were forced into English ports by Huguenot raiders. For safety, the silver was conveyed ashore, whereupon Alva denounced this as an English plot for stealing the money, at Spinola's suggestion. When the government repaid the Genoese lenders, Spinola acted for it. In 1578 Spinola, with Horatio Palavicino, was an agent for arranging the loan to the Union of Brussels. On his eventual return from the Netherlands he made his Italian will on 6 July 1580. He was then somewhat infirm, *alquanto indisposto del corpo*: in fact he died of plague, and was buried in the choir—a mark of his high standing locally—of St Gabriel's Church on 15 August 1580. He had never married, and probate was granted to his nephew, Giacomo Spinola, on 29 October. JOHN BENNELL

Sources R. Cooke, *Visitation of London, 1568*, ed. H. Stanford London and S. W. Rawlins, [new edn], 2 vols. in one, Harleian Society, 109–10 (1963), 102–3 · R. E. G. Kirk and E. F. Kirk, eds., *Returns of aliens dwelling in the city and suburbs of London, from the reign of Henry VIII to that of James I*, 4 vols., Huguenot Society of London, 10 (1900–08) · G. D. Ramsay, *The queen's merchants and the revolt of the Netherlands* (1986), 91–2, 157–8, 187 · G. D. Ramsay, 'The undoing of the Italian mercantile colony in sixteenth century London', *Textile history and economic history: essays in honour of Miss Julia de Lacy Mann* (1973), 33, 41–3 · *CPR, 1550–53*, 281; *1558–60*, 110; *1563–6*, no. 2621 · J. W. Burgon, *The life and times of Sir Thomas Gresham*, 1 (1839), 411–13 · BL, Lansdowne MS 13, fol. 50 · *CSP for.*, *1572–4*, no. 1458 · J. E. Jackson, 'Amye Robsart', *Wiltshire Archaeological and Natural History Magazine*, 17 (1878), 47–93, esp. 92 · BL, Harley MS 260, fol. 363 · *CSP dom., addenda, 1566–79*, 550 · will, PRO, PROB 11/62, 294–5 · parish register, London, St Gabriel Fenchurch, GL, MS 5293 [burial] · J. Stow, *A survay of London*, rev. edn (1603); repr. with introduction by C. L. Kingsford as *A survey of London*, 2 vols. (1908), 288 · M. A. S. Hume, ed., *Calendar of letters and state papers relating to English affairs, preserved principally in the archives of Simancas*, 1, PRO (1892), 1558–67 · Baron Kervyn de Lettenhove [J. M. B. C. Kervyn de Lettenhove] and L. Gilliodts-van Severen, eds., *Relations politiques des Pays-Bas et de l'Angleterre sous le règne de Philippe II*, 11 vols. (Brussels, 1882–1900), vol. 11, nos. 4257, 4259, 4298, 4299, 4324

Spittall, Henry (*d.* 1536). *See under* College of justice, procurators of the (*act.* 1532).

Spittlehouse, John (*bap.* 1612, *d.* in or after 1657), Fifth Monarchist, was the son of John Spittlehouse (*d.* 1638), of Gainsborough, saddler, and his wife, Mary, *née* Waterhouse (*d.* before 1636), and was baptized at Gainsborough on 10 June 1612. He was perhaps educated at the grammar school, possibly by the future Baptist Hanserd Knollys, who taught there in the late 1620s. Spittlehouse fought in the action at Gainsborough in 1643, at his own charges, at Newark in 1644, and thereafter in the parliamentary army until after the battle of Worcester (1651). In 1650 he was assistant to the marshall-general, responsible for military security. In July 1649 he joined other radical officers in Whitehall in a day of solemn humiliation over religious divisions within the army. Spittlehouse and his wife,

Mary, were both active members of the London gathered General Baptist congregation led by Peter Chamberlen in the 1650s.

A prolific pamphleteer, Spittlehouse published polemical tracts against Samuel Oates, John Brayne, and John Simpson, but most of his output was inspired by zeal for the approaching millennium. In *Rome Ruined* (1650) he justified the regicide, but condemned the failure of parliament and council to promote Christ's reign. He welcomed the overthrow of the Rump Parliament in April 1653 in *The Army Vindicated*, calling for Cromwell to rule as a new Moses with an assembly elected exclusively by godly army officers. The work was republished in a Dutch translation. A few weeks later Spittlehouse suggested that Cromwell himself should nominate every member of the new government. He had some hopes of Barebone's Parliament, and published a tract in September anticipating the speedy abolition of tithes. He clashed with the authorities, however, apparently over fen drainage in the Isle of Axholme, and on 5 December the council ordered his arrest over petitions he had presented, including one to parliament attacking John Thurloe. In March 1654 he begged Cromwell for release, and he was freed on 6 April. Despite this appeal Spittlehouse regarded the new protectorate as a gross betrayal, and he predicted that Cromwell would meet the same fate as the king. He responded to Cromwell's denunciation of the Fifth Monarchists to parliament in September 1654 by publishing a staunch defence and condemning Cromwell as a turncoat. This prompted his rearrest in October, though he was never charged. In *The Royall Advocate* (1655) Spittlehouse accused the army too of apostasy, called for a radical programme of reforms including the abolition of excise, customs, and tithes and the establishment of the Mosaic law code, and demanded that the army should pay its own way by conquests in Roman Catholic Europe instead of being supported by the taxpayer. He was in custody again in the winter of 1655–6 with John Jones, a Fifth Monarchist conspirator, but was released on 1 February 1656 on entering a bond in £200 to live peaceably.

An inveterate polemicist, Spittlehouse at various times attacked Presbyterians, Independents, seekers, ranters, and Quakers, but he denied that magistrates had any right to meddle in religious affairs and wanted even the Koran to circulate unhindered. Well read in puritan literature, old and new, he dismissed as worthless both classical languages and universities. His last publication, with William Saller, in spring 1657, championed the seventh-day sabbath. The date of John Spittlehouse's death is unknown; a widow Spittlehouse living in Whitehall, London, in 1659 was almost certainly the relict of a William Spittlehouse, formerly a minor council official and Whitehall doorkeeper. BERNARD CAPP

Sources will, Lincs. Arch., Stow wills 1638–40/34 [J. Spittlehouse, father] · *CSP dom.*, *1653–9* · churchbook of the Baptist church at Lothbury Square, London, Bodl. Oxf., MS Rawl. D. 828 · J. Spittlehouse, *Rome ruined* (1650) · J. Spittlehouse, *The army vindicated* (1653) · J. Spittlehouse, *An answer to one part of the Lord Protector's speech* (1654) · J. Spittlehouse, *The royall advocate* (1655) · Worcester College, Oxford, Clarke MS 18 · H. Knollys, *The life and death of that old disciple of Jesus Christ and eminent minister of the gospel, Mr Hanserd Knollys*, ed. W. Kiffin (1692) · B. S. Capp, *The Fifth Monarchy Men: a study in seventeenth-century English millenarianism* (1972) · private information (2004) [Ian Wilson] · Greaves & Zaller, *BDBR* · parish register, Gainsborough, 10 June 1612, Lincs. Arch. [baptism]

Spode, Josiah (1755–1827), potter and merchant, was born on 8 May 1755 at Stoke-on-Trent, the son of Josiah Spode (1733–1797), founder of the Spode pottery factory there, and Ellen, *née* Finley (1726–1802). He was trained in the art of ceramic manufacture by his father and entered the family firm. On 9 July 1775 he married Elizabeth Barker (*d.* 1782) of Lane Delph, daughter of the potter Thomas Barker. They had five children: William (1776–1834), Josiah (1777–1829), Elizabeth (*b.* 1778, *d.* after 1835), Saba (1780–1811), and Mary (*b.* 1781, *d.* after 1834). Both William and Josiah were to become involved in their father's trade.

In 1778 a London outlet was decided on as the most profitable manner of retailing to the fashionable and lucrative metropolitan market. In that year Spode became a freeman of the City and a member of the Worshipful Company of Spectacle Makers, there being no company of potters or pot sellers. A retail outlet was established in 1778 at 29 Fore Street. Business flourished and the firm moved to successively larger establishments at 46 then 45 Fore Street before settling, in 1794, at 5 Portugal Street, a better address adjacent to Lincoln's Inn Fields. Domestic residences accompanied the premises. These premises were rented, but in 1802 Spode bought the Portugal Street warehouse and the adjoining domestic residence. Such expansion was in response to the firm's growing success and in readiness to market the new bone china his father was producing. The Portugal Street establishment provided the wares for both the London retail market and international trade. The success of the bone china, called Stoke China, can be accredited to Spode's marketing prowess. A shrewd businessman, he was able to capitalize on the demands of fashionable London society. It has been suggested that without his retail ability bone china may not have reached such levels of popularity. The recent reductions in the tax payable upon imported tea also served to widen the demand for tea wares.

While living in London, Spode maintained his links with Stoke. In 1790 he took a lead role in the formation of the Fenton Park colliery which was the first joint potters' coal company. On the death of his father he returned to Stoke and lived in Fenton Hall. By 1803 he had acquired a 17 acre site in Penkhull on which to build his own mansion, The Mount, half a mile from the Stoke potworks. It was a suitably grand home for a man of his standing and wealth, with extensive grounds that had been enlarged by the time of his death. He also built many houses for his workforce in the vicinity of the large factory works. The London business, while remaining in the name of Spode, was in 1805 put into the charge of a partnership between Spode's son William and William Copeland (1765–1826), who had joined the London firm in 1784. The partnership was dissolved on 31 December 1811 when William Spode retired. Copeland and Spode went into partnership, with

Josiah Spode (1755–1827), by unknown artist, *c.*1785–90

Copeland possessing three of the four shares. In 1824 Copeland's son William Taylor Copeland (1797–1868) was admitted to the partnership with his father giving him one of his shares. Following the death of his father, William Taylor Copeland entered into an equal partnership with Spode, each possessing two shares, to run for seven years, and he succeeded Spode as the owner of the firm in 1833.

Spode's own achievements were as a merchant and in the consolidation of the success of his father to whom is given the credit for the perfection of underglaze transfer-printing on earthenware in blue in 1784 and the development of bone china. Blue printed earthenware, designed to meet the demand for painted blue and white Chinese porcelain, was a highly popular product, perhaps the most famous pattern being the willow design of about 1790, itself a derivative of Chinese scenes. Spode introduced bone china about 1798. It proved popular and successful for the production of dinner ware. It was an elegant white body, translucent yet strong. From 1800 until 1822 Henry Daniel was in charge of Spode's enamelling studio, producing finely designed and painted scenes, often with exquisite gilding. Spode achieved a great accolade in 1806 following a visit by the prince of Wales when he was allowed to title himself 'Potter and English Porcelain Manufacturer to H.R.H. Prince of Wales'. In 1813 Spode adopted the body called by him 'Stone China', which he matched with elaborate Chinese porcelain designs. This was a superior formula to earthenware, proving a stronger body, and its decorations required several firings. Spode was also committed to the technical side of the business, promoting the continued use of steam engines and a partnership with other potters for the lease, in 1799, of the Carloggas china clay and stone pit in Cornwall, thereby securing the supply of essential raw materials. The Spode family is perhaps second only to the elder Josiah Wedgwood in English ceramic history. The introduction of bone china and the popular success of transfer-printed earthenware helped to expand and develop the pottery industry in the Staffordshire Potteries into one of world renown. Josiah Spode died on 16 July 1827 in Stoke-on-Trent and was buried in the churchyard of St Peter ad Vincula there. He was perhaps the most successful bone china manufacturer of the early nineteenth century.

HELEN L. PHILLIPS

Sources L. Whiter, *Spode* (1970) · R. Copeland, *Spode and Copeland marks* (1993) · P. A. Halfpenny, ed., *Spode-Copeland, 1733–1983: potters to the royal family since 1806* (1983) [exhibition catalogue, City Museum and Art Gallery, Stoke-on-Trent, 1983] · private information (2004)

Archives Keele University

Likenesses miniature, *c.*1785–1790, NPG [*see illus.*] · W. McCall, oils, *c.*1818, City Museum and Art Gallery, Stoke-on-Trent, Staffordshire · bone china plaque, Spode Museum, Stoke-on-Trent, Staffordshire · oils, City Museum and Art Gallery, Stoke-on-Trent, Staffordshire

Spofforth, Frederick Robert (1853–1926), cricketer, was born on 9 September 1853, probably in Balmain, a suburb of Sydney, Australia, the fourth child and second son of Edward Spofforth (1805–1875), a Yorkshire-born banker who had travelled to the infant colony of Perth, Western Australia, in 1836, and Anna McDonnell, who came from a pioneering New Zealand family. Spofforth's parents were married in New Zealand, where his father lived for a time in the mid-1840s. Fred Spofforth, as he was known, grew up in Glebe, another Sydney harbour-side suburb. He attended Eglinton College and then, briefly, Sydney grammar school, where he helped the second eleven defeat the first eleven, before following his father into banking. He was a fine all-round athlete, and in 1881 ran the 100 yards in 10.2 seconds, a New South Wales resident record.

Spofforth initially bowled underarm, then round-arm and finally overarm. After watching the English fast bowler George Tarrant bowl at the Sydney Domain in 1864, he was inspired to bowl fast. A tearaway fast bowler, he took nine for 10 against the Sydney University side in 1873–4, with seven batsmen clean bowled: the batsman he failed to dismiss was Edmund Barton, who became Australia's first prime minister in 1901. He was selected to play for New South Wales in 1874–5 as a right-arm fast bowler and contributed to an emphatic New South Wales win by 195 runs against Victoria the following season, when he took four for 22 and five for 50. An independent spirit, he withdrew from what is now defined as the first test against England, in 1876–7, because Jack Blackham of Victoria was preferred to his colony's keeper, Billy Murdoch. Spofforth made his test début in the second test of 1876–7, when Murdoch was selected, though Blackham was retained as keeper.

Spofforth developed his craft and established his reputation on the 1878 tour of England and the four subsequent tours (1880, 1882, 1884, 1886). On the first tour he

Frederick Robert Spofforth (1853–1926), by unknown photographer

bowled day in and day out for about fifteen months, developing his technique as a fast bowler and assuming the role of both strike and stock bowler. He bowled almost twice as many overs as any other bowler, and took more than double the number of wickets. During this period he added subtle and well-disguised variations of pace to his bowling repertory. He was a fine athletic fieldsman but only a tail-end batsman who occasionally played an entertaining innings, such as in 1885, when he hit lustily to score his only test fifty.

Partnered by Harry Boyle, Spofforth took match figures of ten for 20 at Lord's on 27 May 1878—in only the second match of the tour—to demolish a powerful Marylebone Cricket Club side and assure the tour's success. He bowled the English champion W. G. Grace for a duck in the second innings. His reputation was built on his ability to challenge Grace and to rival him as one of the first stars of international cricket. Like Grace, he was a great presence on the field: tall and gaunt and with a prominent nose, Spofforth was thought to be the personification of the demon (which became his nickname). He proved a fine foil to the ebullient Grace.

Spofforth took the first test hat-trick in 1878–9 at Melbourne and, on two other occasions, took three wickets in four balls. He was a fine performer in a crisis and is best remembered for his courageous fourteen for 90 at the Oval in 1882, which enabled Australia to win its first test in England by just seven runs, the original 'Ashes' game. He bowled consistently well through all five tours of England from 1878 to 1886, though an injury to his hand restricted his achievements on the last tour.

Spofforth enjoyed the media spotlight and kept them guessing to the last minute as to whether he would tour England in 1884 and 1886. A forthright individual, he was never afraid to express his views and defended himself against the charge of cutting up the pitch unfairly with the spikes of his boots in 1883. He married Phillis Marsh Cadman (*d.* 1951), the daughter of Joseph Cadman, a Derbyshire tea merchant, at Breadsall, Derbyshire, on 23 September 1886. They had two sons and two daughters. He settled in England in 1887, and took over his father-in-law's business, the Star Tea Company, the following year. A believer in Anglo-Australian ideals, he was prepared to play for England against Australia, but did not actually do so. Although he played nine games for Derbyshire and club cricket for Hampstead until 1903, the demands of running a business occupied most of his time. He was a successful tea merchant and died a wealthy man at his home, Ditton Hill Lodge, Long Ditton, Surrey, on 4 June 1926. He was buried on 8 June in Brookwood cemetery, Surrey.

Spofforth wrote a number of brief but informative magazine articles, including 'In the days of my youth: chapters of autobiography' (*MAP: Mainly about People*, 28 November 1903, 672–4) and 'Australian cricket and cricketers: a retrospect' (*New Review*, 10, 1894, 507–16), which contain some colourful anecdotes about the early history of Australian cricket. Jas Scott, an acute observer of the sport in Australia, noted however that Spofforth 'often deviated from the truth for entertainment' and was a 'confirmed leg puller' (Scott, 65).

By modern standards Spofforth was not a fast bowler, but he operated at a time when wickets were less well prepared and the ball was different. However, he bowled fast enough to intimidate the batsmen, though his first test wicket was a stumping achieved in his fourth over. Spofforth's stock ball was an off-cutter and he took a number of wickets caught at short leg. He bowled with pinpoint control and more than half his test wickets were bowled. His action was not a classical one, but his high athletic leap as he delivered the ball has been admired. It was captured in a remarkable 1904 photograph by George Beldam, a pioneer of action photography, when Spofforth was fifty-one.

Fred Spofforth was one of the first great overarm bowlers, who more than any other player helped to establish the popularity of international cricket and to put Australian cricket on the map. He was the first great thinking fast bowler and took this craft to a new level. C. B. Fry stated that 'he appears to have been the first naturally fast bowler to discover that the subtle variations of pace and deceptive tricks practised by a slow-medium bowler … might with advantage be imitated and developed in conjunction with sheer speed' (Cashman, 238).

RICHARD CASHMAN

Sources R. Cashman, *The 'demon' Spofforth* (Kensington, NSW, 1990) • R. L. Arrowsmith, 'Brief lives: F. R. Spofforth', *Journal of the*

Cricket Society (1983) · R. Barter, *Ten great bowlers* (1907) · J. Scott, 'A cricketing miscellany', MS, New South Wales Cricket Association · *DNB* · d. cert. · bap. reg., Balmain, Sydney, 1853

Likenesses G. Beldam, photograph, 1904 · Spy [L. Ward], caricature, chromolithograph, NPG; repro. in *VF* (13 July 1878) · photograph; Christies, 18 June 1997, lot 132 [*see illus.*] · portrait, Australian cricket board · portraits, repro. in Cashman, *The 'demon' Spofforth*

Wealth at death £169,268 9*s*. 7*d*.: probate, 6 July 1926, *CGPLA Eng. & Wales*

Spofforth, Markham (1825–1907), lawyer and political agent, was the second son of Samuel Spofforth of Newfields, near Howden in Yorkshire, and his wife, Anne, only daughter of Thomas Richardson of Market Weighton, Yorkshire. He was educated at Barnsdale. On 26 December 1858 he married Agnes, only daughter of John Claudius *Loudon, the landscape gardener. She died in 1863. Elizabeth (*d*. 1896), his second wife, whom he married in 1889, the youngest daughter of Thomas Peters, was the widow of Colonel Walter Meller (1819–1886), Conservative MP for Stafford from 1865 until he was unseated in 1869.

Admitted a solicitor in 1850, Spofforth joined the firm of London solicitors, Baxter, Rose and Norton, in 1853 to assist one of the partners, Philip Rose, Disraeli's personal lawyer, in acting as central agent for the Conservative Party. He helped to rebuild the system of Conservative agents in the constituencies, shattered by the split of 1846. He encouraged local parties to fight seats, found them candidates, and was involved in disbursing money from the central party fund. This exposed him to the corrupt side of electioneering. Following election petitions, on which he was a specialist, he sometimes had to appear before committees of inquiry into corrupt practices. He acted as principal agent from 1859, when accusations of corruption had forced Rose to withdraw.

Spofforth saw the need to broaden the party's appeal, helped to form the National Union of Conservative Associations in 1867, and wrote for *The Day*, a short-lived Conservative paper. He had considerable influence with Disraeli, to whom he was deeply loyal. In the 1868 election he forecast victory and advised Disraeli to play the protestant card by making low-church ecclesiastical appointments. He was furious when Disraeli tried to redress the balance by professing his respect for the high-church party and always remained suspicious of Romanizing tendencies in the Church of England. Continuing accusations of electoral corruption were among the reasons for his resignation as party agent in March 1870, when he was succeeded by J. E. Gorst. In 1876 Disraeli secured him an appointment as senior taxing master in chancery. Spofforth had a commanding presence, was on familiar terms with many leading political and social figures, and was a frequent guest at country house parties, but his lack of discretion attracted criticism. He died on 26 January 1907 at his home, 27 Knightsbridge, London. E. J. Feuchtwanger

Sources *WWW* · *The Times* (28 Jan 1907) · *The Times* (13 Feb 1907) [appreciation] · Kelly, *Handbk* (1893) · R. Stewart, *The foundation of the conservative party, 1830–1867* (1978) · E. J. Feuchtwanger, *Disraeli, democracy and the tory party: conservative leadership and organization after the second Reform Bill* (1968) · 'Royal commission to inquire into … corrupt practices at elections', *Parl. papers* (1867), 29.979, 1003, no. 3776 [Totnes]; (1870), 29.9, C. 15 [Beverley] · m. cert. · d. cert. · H. J. Hanham, *Elections and party management: politics in the time of Disraeli and Gladstone* (1959)

Archives Bodl. Oxf., Hughenden MSS

Likenesses Ape [C. Pellegrini], cartoon, repro. in *VF* (20 March 1880), 220

Wealth at death £7955 3*s*. 7*d*.: probate, 25 March 1907, *CGPLA Eng. & Wales*

Spofforth, Reginald (1768x70–1827), composer, was born in Southwell, Nottinghamshire, the son of a currier. His uncle, Thomas Spofforth, was organist of Southwell Minster and gave him his first musical tuition. Encouraged by Sir Richard Kaye, a prebendary of Southwell who was also dean of Lincoln, he went to Lincoln and became deputy organist at the cathedral. He then moved to London and studied composition with Benjamin Cooke and the piano with Daniel Steibelt. His first success as a composer came in 1793, when he won two prizes offered by the Noblemen's and Gentlemen's Catch Club for the glees 'See! smiling from the rosy east' and 'Where are those hours?'.

Although his earliest publications were of solo songs, Spofforth's importance as a composer is based on the numerous glees (about seventy-five in number) that he published from 1796, many of which also appeared in anthologies. One of them, 'Hail! smiling morn' (no. 6 of *Six Glees*, 1818), was the most popular item in the entire repertory of glees. Spofforth composed many songs and duets and left three books of nursery-rhyme settings, but no instrumental or sacred music.

Spofforth was chorus master at Covent Garden for a time, and wrote various songs and glees for productions there, but turned down an invitation to succeed William Shield as musical director in 1797. He also served as organist at Fitzroy Chapel and later at Eltham parish church, and was active as a teacher. Some of his unpublished works were issued after his death as *A Collection of Glees* (1830), with a memoir by his former pupil William Hawes. Spofforth died in Kensington on 8 September 1827, and was buried in the parish church there. A tablet to his memory was erected in Brompton cemetery.

A younger brother, Samuel Spofforth (1780–1864), composed some sacred music and was organist of Peterborough Cathedral and, from 1807, of Lichfield Cathedral.

J. C. Hadden, *rev*. David J. Golby

Sources *The Harmonicon*, 11 (1833), 186–7 [biographical sketch] · N. Temperley, 'Spofforth, Reginald', *New Grove* · W. Hawes, memoir, *A collection of glees*, ed. W. Hawes (1830) · [J. Bayley], *A sketch of the life of Reginald Spofforth* (1880) · W. A. Barrett, *English glee and madrigal writers* (1877), 36 · D. Baptie, *Sketches of the English glee composers: historical, biographical and critical (from about 1735–1866)* [1896], 74–6

Spohr, Louis (1784–1859), composer, violinist, and conductor, was born on 5 April 1784 at what is now Spohrplatz 7, Brunswick, the first of the seven children of Carl Heinrich Spohr (1756–1843), a medical doctor, and his cousin Juliane Ernestine Luise Henke (1763–1840). His baptismal name was Ludewig, but his parents, following the fashion of the day, called him Louis; it was by that name he signed himself in later life and under which his compositions were generally published. Spohr's mature height was about 6 feet 6 inches, and he was powerfully

Louis Spohr (1784–1859), by Friedrich Jentzen (after C. Arnold)

built. His upright character enhanced his reputation in England; the anonymous translator of his *Autobiography* observed: 'he has left us an example of high morality, great amiability, and bright domestic virtues, too rare, alas! among artists and men of genius' (ii). He was twice married: first, on 2 February 1806, to Dorothea Scheidler (1787–1834), and second, on 3 January 1836, to Marianne Pfeiffer (1807–1892).

Little of Spohr's music seems to have been known in England before he first visited London in 1820, to participate as both violinist and composer at the Philharmonic Society. The immediate impact of this five-month stay was limited. As a violinist he was considered to 'equal, if not to exceed, any player that has lately been heard in England' (*London Magazine*, 1, 1820, 444). At a Philharmonic rehearsal he caused a sensation by conducting with a baton and in public by conducting with his violin bow. Among his many compositions performed during the visit was his second symphony, written early in his stay in London. The general reaction to his music is reflected in the *Quarterly Musical Magazine*'s comment that the new symphony was 'well received but did not excite extraordinary sensation' (2, 1820, 383); yet his distinctive musical style made a far greater impression on musicians, laying the foundations for his future popularity and influence in the country. Spohr's music became steadily more familiar in England during the nineteen years that elapsed before his second visit, but it was more popular with musicians than with the public: the inclusion of three of his works in a Philharmonic concert in 1831 prompted the suggestion that the subscribers were 'not yet sufficiently advanced in taste to comprehend it' (*The Atlas*, 6, 1831, 140). However, his oratorio *Die letzen Dinge* (*The Last Judgement*), hailed as 'one of the greatest musical productions of the age' (*The Harmonicon*, 8, 1830, 466), stimulated more widespread enthusiasm after its introduction at the Norwich festival of 1830. Edward Taylor recalled, 'Perhaps there is no instance of a similar work, under like circumstances, having attained such speedy celebrity and such high estimation' (preface to Spohr's *Calvary*, 1836).

The vicissitudes of Spohr's reputation in the 1830s were neatly summarized by H. F. Chorley's comment:

> By some he has been extolled to the seventh heaven, as surpassing Mozart, Weber, and Beethoven, in right of sweet melodies, rich harmonies, and magnificent conceptions—by others, degraded to the level of those respectable, but most wearisome persons, who produce a multitude of carefully-executed works, upon the liberal allowance of half an idea. (*The Athenaeum*, 13, 1840, 421)

Spohr's visit to Norwich to conduct his oratorio *Des Heilands letzte Stunden* (*The Crucifixion*, later *Calvary*) in 1839, however, was a triumph that did much to reinforce his standing in England as 'the greatest living musician' (*Morning Chronicle*, 20 Sept 1839). *The Times* observed:

> there is no cold musical criticism here; no questioning or calculating, 'ought we to admire this, and is Spohr the great composer we have heard him described to be?' We saw in the countenances of the immense multitude the most unequivocal evidences of the composer's genius. Hundreds were melted to tears, and the deep and breathless silence, which from first to last reigned throughout the vast assembly, betokened the heartfelt sympathy which thus enchained them. (21 Oct 1839)

Spohr's presence dominated the London season of 1843. He played and conducted his own works at two Philharmonic Society concerts (one a special command performance for the queen and prince consort), and directed two performances of *The Fall of Babylon* (commissioned for the 1842 Norwich festival), the second attended by more than three thousand people. At Spohr's farewell dinner, William Horsley observed that 'His reputation ranks with the greatest genius of the present day and would take its position with that of past ages, with Bach, with Handel, Haydn, Mozart and Beethoven' (*Musical World*, 18, 1843, 231).

Spohr was similarly lionized during his last three sojourns in England, in 1847, 1852 (for which he revised his opera *Faust* for Covent Garden), and 1853. After Mendelssohn's death he was almost universally acknowledged as the greatest living composer. But much of his later work, including the eighth symphony, written for the Philharmonic Society in 1848, was more coolly received, and increasing criticism was levelled against the 'mannerism' of his works.

Obituaries, following his death on 22 October 1859 in Kassel (where he was buried on 25 October in the Neue Friedhof), stressed his position as 'the last of the Teutonic family of musical giants' (*Musical World*, 24, 1859, 713), yet by the centenary of his death his music occupied a significantly smaller place on concert programmes. Nevertheless, his influence on the generation of English composers coming to maturity between 1820 and 1840 was profound. William Spark observed that in the 1830s Spohr's

> rich, original, luscious harmonies quite fascinated our English musicians, who, in many instances, failed not to avail themselves of Spohr's style, so that the term 'Spohrish' soon became associated with a large number of the compositions which were produced at that and subsequent periods by our native composers. (*Musical Memories*, 1888, 55–6)

One of these composers, Sir George Macfarren, recalled, 'Few if any composers have exercised such influence on their contemporaries as Spohr did, and many living writers may be counted among his imitators' (*Imperial Dictionary of Universal Biography*). Among those whose music was seen to exhibit Spohr's influence were George Rodwell, Henry Bishop, John Barnett, Henry Smart, William Sterndale Bennett, Macfarren, Samuel Sebastian Wesley, Edward J. Loder, John Lodge Ellerton, Edwin J. Nielson, and many other minor composers. CLIVE BROWN

Sources *Louis Spohr's autobiography: translated from the German* (1865) • *Lebenserinnerungen: erstmals ungekürzt nach den autographen Aufzeichnungen*, ed. F. Göthel (Tutzing, 1968) • C. Brown, *Louis Spohr: a critical biography* (1984) • J. C. A. Brown, 'The popularity and influence of Spohr in England', DPhil diss., U. Oxf., 1980 • F. Göthel, *Thematisch-bibliographisches Verzeichnis der Werke von Louis Spohr* (1981) • H. Homburg, *Louis Spohr: Bilder und Dokumente seiner Zeit* (1968) • H. Becker and R. Krempien, eds., *Louis Spohr: Festschrift und Ausstellungskatalog zum 200. Geburtstag* (1984)

Archives Louis Spohr- Gedenk- und Forschungsstätte, Kassel, Germany • Murhardsche Bibliothek der Stadt Kassel und Landesbibliothek, Kassel, Germany | Archiv des Musikverlags VEB Edition Peters, Leipzig, Germany • Bibliothèque Nationale, Paris • BL • Kunigliga Musikaliska Akademiens Biblioteket, Stockholm, Sweden • Mitteldeutscher Sängerbund, Kassel • Staatsarchiv, Marburg, Germany, Akten des Kurfürstlichen Hoftheaters Kassel • Staatsbibliothek, Berlin • Stadt- und Universitätsbibliothek, Frankfurt-am-Main

Likenesses F. Jentzen, lithograph (after C. Arnold), NPG [*see illus.*]

Sponlee, John (*d.* 1382?). *See under* Wynford, William (*d.* 1405).

Spooner, Charles (*d.* 1767), engraver, a native of co. Wexford, Ireland, learned mezzotint engraving as a pupil of John Brooks in Dublin. After Brooks went to London, Spooner worked for the Dublin printsellers. Five mezzotints and three engravings and etchings published in the years 1749–52 are known. Spooner went to London before 1756, where he scraped a wide variety of portraits and genre subjects. A few of his engravings were after his own drawings, but the bulk of his output consisted in copying popular prints of his contemporaries for the printsellers Robert Sayer and Thomas, John, and Carington Bowles. Like several of his countrymen, Spooner took to drink; he died in London on 5 December 1767 and at his own request was buried in Hampstead churchyard near his friend James Macardell.

TIMOTHY CLAYTON and ANITA MCCONNELL

Sources W. G. Strickland, *A dictionary of Irish artists*, 2 vols. (1913); repr. with introduction by T. J. Snoddy (1989), vol. 2, pp. 398–400 • Redgrave, *Artists* • J. C. Smith, *British mezzotinto portraits*, 4 vols. in 5 (1878–84) • Dodd, history of engravers in Britain, BL, Add. MS 33405

Spooner, Charles (1806–1871), veterinary surgeon, born on 19 October 1806, was the youngest of the three sons of John Spooner of Fordham, Essex. His father at the time of his birth occupied the dairy farm at Mistley Park, near Manningtree, Essex. On leaving school Charles Spooner was apprenticed to a chemist, George Jervis of Westbar, Sheffield, and at the end of his apprenticeship he entered the Royal Veterinary College, London, as a student, in November 1828. He obtained his diploma on 21 July 1829, and shortly afterwards was appointed veterinary surgeon to the Zoological Society, chiefly through the influence of Professor William Sewell (1780–1853).

Spooner's appointment extended his knowledge of anatomy and physiology and increased his perception of the inadequacies of the course taught, at that time, at the Royal Veterinary College. While working in his capacity as veterinary surgeon to the Zoological Society, he established a school of veterinary anatomy in a house opposite the college, where he gave private lectures and demonstrations to college students. *The Veterinarian* reports that Spooner was already 'well known as one of the best veterinary anatomists, perhaps the best, of which the profession could boast' (*Veterinarian*, 8.646), and thus a gap which had long existed in the official college training was efficiently filled. Spooner was associated with Sewell in the formation, in 1836, of the Veterinary Medical Association, of which he became treasurer and in 1839 president, an office to which he was subsequently re-elected annually. Spooner's post at the Zoological Society was eventually taken over by William Youatt.

Early in 1839 Spooner reluctantly accepted the post of demonstrator of anatomy at the Royal Veterinary College, and terminated his private classes. His advancement at the college was rapid. In the same year he became assistant professor in the place of Sewell, who was now made professor of the college on the death of the former chief, Professor Edward Coleman (1764–1839). Spooner delivered his first lecture on 19 November 1839. On 9 January 1840 he was elected by the medical committee of the college to become an examiner of the college students. On 22 July the same year he married Mary Anne, daughter of William Boulton. They subsequently had eight children—five sons and three daughters. In 1842 he became deputy professor of the college, and during the 1843–4 session the students presented him with a marble bust of himself in recognition of his teaching abilities. In 1853, on the death of Sewell, Spooner became chief professor and secretary, with residence in the college. He now stood at the head of his profession, and in 1858 he became president of the incorporated Royal College of Veterinary Surgeons, of which he had been an original petitioner in 1844.

In 1865 Spooner was a member of the cattle plague commission. His judgement as a witness had by then been frequently appealed to in the law courts in cases of veterinary jurisprudence. He was held in extremely high regard both by his students and by many of his contemporaries within the emerging veterinary profession, and *The Lancet*, reporting on his abilities as a legal witness, claimed 'his testimony and opinion were highly valued by judge, jury and client' (*The Lancet*, 869). In 1864, as a tribute to his administrative abilities, a special meeting of the governors of the Royal Veterinary College recorded in the minute book 'that at no time since the foundation of the college has the average number of students in the theatre, or patients in the infirmary, been so large … nor the resources of the college so prosperous as at the present time … since it came under his [Spooner's] superintendence' (minute books, RVC). However, though for some time joint editor of the *Veterinary Review*, Spooner wrote little. It was rather as a surgeon, where he was aided by his accurate knowledge of anatomy, as a lecturer, and as a demonstrator on anatomy, that his talent was shown. Numerous reports of his speeches and lectures may be found in *The Veterinarian*, and in the *Proceedings of the Veterinary Medical Association*. Spooner was considered the chief authority on horse matters in Britain and a lecture by him entitled 'Horses', delivered before the members of the Farringdon Agricultural Library, was published as the pamphlet *Horses and Sheep* (1861).

Spooner died in the Royal Veterinary College on 24 November 1871 and was buried in Highgate cemetery five days later. He was survived by his wife.

ERNEST CLARKE, *rev.* LINDA WARDEN

Sources J. B. Simonds, *The foundation of the Royal Veterinary College, 1790–1, with biographical sketches of St. Bel, Edward Coleman, William Sewell and Charles Spooner* (1897) • *CGPLA Eng. & Wales* (1872) • F. Smith, *The early history of veterinary literature and its British development*, 4 vols. (1919–33); repr. (1976), vol. 4 • *The Veterinary Record and Transactions of the Veterinary Medical Association*, 1 (1849), 84 • E. Cotchin, *The Royal Veterinary College, London: a bicentenary history* (1990) • d. cert. • I. Pattison, *The British veterinary profession, 1741–1948*, [another edn] (1984) • minute book, 1844–69, Royal College of Veterinary Surgeons, London • minute books, 1853–67, Royal Veterinary College, London • *The Lancet* (16 Dec 1871), 869 • *The Veterinarian*, 45 (1872), 89–90 • *The Veterinarian*, 7 (1834), 665 • *The Veterinarian*, 8 (1835), 646 • *The Veterinarian*, 12 (1839), 817 • *The Veterinarian*, 31 (1858), 349 • burial register, Highgate cemetery, London • m. cert.
Likenesses marble bust, Royal Veterinary College, London
Wealth at death under £4000: probate, 19 Dec 1872, *CGPLA Eng. & Wales*

Spooner, Charles Easton (*bap.* **1818**, *d.* **1889**), railway engineer, was born at Maentwrog, Merionydd, and baptized on 25 May 1818 at Maentwrog church, the fourth of ten children of James Spooner (1790–1856), surveyor and civil engineer, and his first wife, Elizabeth, *née* Easton (1787–1850). His father was English, his mother English or perhaps Scottish. At the age of twelve or thirteen, he helped his father to survey the Ffestiniog Railway (FR); James Spooner then supervised construction, and in 1836 the line was opened from slate quarries near Blaenau Ffestiniog to Porthmadog harbour. Its gauge was very narrow, less than 2 ft, which enabled the track to follow a serpentine route along steep mountainsides; this in turn facilitated a continuous gradient down which laden trains ran by gravity. Horses hauled the empty wagons uphill.

From about 1834 until 1840 Charles Spooner trained as a civil engineer and surveyor, successively under his father, under Joseph Locke, and under I. K. Brunel. In 1856 he succeeded his father as manager and engineer of FR. On 14 September 1848 he married Mary (1823–1860), daughter of George Barker; sadly, she died just twelve years later, leaving him with four young children.

If, as seemed probable, a standard-gauge steam railway was to be built to Blaenau Ffestiniog, FR would have been unable to compete. Its route inhibited conversion to standard gauge, but no public railway of so narrow a gauge was then worked by steam. None the less, in 1860 Spooner was instructed by his board to enquire into the practicability of using locomotives. George England eventually built two small locomotives—the first of several for FR—in 1863. With these, Spooner was able to replace horses, and to introduce steam-hauled passenger trains in 1865.

Traffic increased rapidly and was catered for by the introduction in 1869 of the double engine *Little Wonder*, the first wholly successful locomotive built to the patents of Robert *Fairlie. The spectacle of *Little Wonder* as it hauled a train 400 yards long, up grade through curves as sharp as the sweep of Oxford Circus (as a contemporary put it), was rendered the more dramatic owing to the Railway Regulation (Gauge) Act (1846). This act had made 4 ft 8½ in. the standard gauge and had had the effect of prohibiting the construction of new passenger railways to narrow gauges.

Nevertheless, railways in Britain had cost too much, it seemed, and cheaper railways were needed, particularly for overseas territories then being opened up. Engineers, often trained in Britain, were already starting to build railways overseas to narrow gauges such as 3 ft 6 in., which was still far wider than that of FR. The Ffestiniog Railway, cheap and very profitable, demonstrated what could be done, and its example led to the construction of narrow-gauge railways all over the world. As Spooner's obituary in *Engineering* eventually put it, 'hundreds of engineers have been received with kindness by Mr Spooner and courteously conducted over the Ffestiniog Railway … his experience was freely put at the service of all'. Much of that experience was incorporated into Spooner's book, *Narrow Gauge Railways*, published in 1872.

In Britain, where the railway system was already extensive, comparatively few narrow-gauge railways were built. Although Spooner was closely concerned with promotion of the North Wales Narrow Gauge Railways Company in 1872, this company completed only one line of an intended network. His greater contribution to home railways was probably his introduction, on the Ffestiniog Railway in 1872–3, of the first bogie passenger coaches to go into regular service in Britain. The use of bogie coaches was already standard practice in North America, and before long it became so in Britain also. The original two coaches still ran on the Ffestiniog Railway more than a century later, as did Fairlie's double engines.

Spooner was also consulting engineer to many slate quarry companies. He remained manager of FR until shortly before his death, on 18 November 1889, at Bron-y-garth, his Porthmadog residence. He was buried on 23 November at Beddgelert, Caernarvonshire.

P. J. G. RANSOM

Sources M. J. T. Lewis, 'Archery and spoonerisms: the creation of the Ffestiniog railway', *Journal of the Merioneth Historical and Record Society*, 12 (1994–7), 263–76 • J. I. C. Boyd, 'In the beginning', *Festiniog Railway Magazine*, 73 (1976), 14–17 • D. H. Wilson, 'The Spooners up to date', *Festiniog Railway Magazine*, 77 (1977), 19–25 • A. Spooner, 'In the beginning', *Festiniog Railway Magazine*, 77 (1977), 28 • D. H. Wilson, 'The Spooner connection', *Festiniog Railway Magazine*, 127 (1989), 300–01 • C. E. Spooner, *Narrow gauge railways*, 2nd edn (1879) • *Engineering* (29 Nov 1889) • J. I. C. Boyd, *The Festiniog railway*, 2 vols. (1975) • P. J. G. Ransom, *Narrow gauge steam: its origins and world-wide development* (1996), chaps. 2, 3, 5, 6 • H. Ellis, *Railway carriages in the British Isles* (1965), 182–3 • *CGPLA Eng. & Wales* (1890) • m. cert. • Festiniog Railway Company archives, Gwynedd Archives, Caernarfon

Archives Gwynedd Archives, Caernarfon, Festiniog Railway Company archives

Likenesses T. Fall, photograph, *c*.1880–1889, Festiniog Railway Company photographic collection, no. P/01A

Wealth at death £4696 19*s*. 9*d*.: resworn probate, Nov 1890, *CGPLA Eng. & Wales*

Spooner, William Archibald (1844–1930), college head, was born at 17 Chapel Street, Grosvenor Place, London, on 22 July 1844, the eldest son of William Spooner, barrister and county court judge for north Staffordshire, of Walton Lodge, Stafford, and Jane Lydia Spooner, daughter of John Wilson, of Seacroft Hall, Leeds. Archibald Campbell Tait, subsequently archbishop of Canterbury, was an uncle by marriage to his aunt Catherine Spooner, and his godfather. Spooner was an albino, with characteristic pink complexion and white hair. The poor eyesight that albinism brought with it is suggested by the charming portrait that hangs in New College hall. He was educated at Oswestry School, Shropshire, and in 1862 won an open scholarship to New College, Oxford. He was the first scholar in the college's history to be elected other than from Winchester College, college statutes having restricted admission to boys educated at Winchester until 1857, when commissioners appointed by parliament to give new statutes to Oxford and Cambridge colleges had removed the restriction.

From 1862 Spooner's life was bound up with that of New College, as scholar, fellow, tutor, and warden, and after his retirement in 1924 as an honorary fellow. In his memoirs, he describes himself as 'a moderately useful man', but it is clear that he played an important part in transforming New College from the Wykehamist backwater that it had been in the first half of the century into one of the three or four largest and most important colleges in Oxford. The prime mover in this change was Edward Charles Wickham, Gladstone's son-in-law, Spooner's undergraduate tutor, and a man whom Oxford traditionalists thought of as possessed by 'a spirit of abominable restlessness', to quote his admiring colleague Hereford George. From 1865 Wickham was joined by Alfred Robinson; he had been an undergraduate at University College, and was described by Spooner himself as an overwhelmingly powerful moral force in the affairs of the college. Spooner's role in the changes they wrought was essentially to second their efforts while smoothing the feathers they had ruffled.

Wickham invented the modern Oxford lecture system in 1868 by forming an alliance with Balliol whereby New College and Balliol undergraduates could share classes. Spooner benefited even before the event by reading logic with Henry Wall and philosophy with Benjamin Jowett. He thought less well of Henry Mansel, perhaps the most distinguished Oxford philosopher of the day, whose 'philosophy of the conditioned' he deplored as a philosophy of 'pure nescience'. Spooner's appearance made for some amusing moments; when a visiting preacher took the text 'Ye who have grown grey in sin' as the basis for his sermon, Spooner's friends found the thought that he was its target quite irresistible. He took first classes in moderations in 1864 and in *literae humaniores* in 1866. He became a fellow in 1867, lecturer in 1868, and tutor in 1869; from 1876 to 1889 he held the office of dean. He was extremely well liked by the undergraduates; his cherubic face and white hair unsurprisingly attracted the nickname of The Child; when he married the imposing Frances Wycliffe Goodwin, third daughter of Harvey *Goodwin, bishop of Carlisle, on 12 September 1878, she was equally unsurprisingly nicknamed The Madonna. The Madonna and Child had a happy and successful marriage, which produced two sons and five daughters. Of these, William Wycliffe Spooner (*d*. 1967) was an inventor of industrial machinery, Frances Catharine *Dodgson a portrait painter, and Rosemary Spooner a Labour councillor on Oxford city council. A granddaughter, Dame Alice Rosemary Murray (*b*. 1913),

William Archibald Spooner (1844–1930), by unknown photographer

was the first woman vice-chancellor of Cambridge University (1975–7).

As a tutor and lecturer, Spooner taught both the historical and the philosophical sides of the *literae humaniores* syllabus. Many generations of undergraduates were grateful for his tuition, which was always patient and kindly; the moral authority which Spooner praised in Alfred Robinson did not endear Robinson in quite the same way to undergraduates, though Spooner, too, could be severe on the idle. He was one of the first generation of married dons. Although the college had ceased to require the ordination of fellows after 1858, Spooner was ordained deacon in 1872 and priest in 1875. He was examining chaplain to Edward Carr Glyn, bishop of Peterborough, from 1902 to 1916, and was made an honorary canon of Christ Church in 1899 by William Stubbs, bishop of Oxford. He was a better speaker extempore than he was a preacher: his poor eyesight led him to stumble over the written text of his sermons, but his affection for his audiences and his great good nature made him a much loved speaker at college and other occasions.

The fellows of New College had expected to elect Alfred Robinson as warden well before the end of the century. James Edwards Sewell had been warden since 1860, and was fifty years old at his election. But Robinson died in 1895, and Sewell not until 1903. At that point the fellows unanimously elected Spooner to succeed Sewell. At least one of their juniors disapproved: the historian Charles Oman thought Spooner did not look the part and that the college should have had a head who looked like a head. Events proved that the college had chosen wisely. The bachelor Sewell had occupied two small rooms in the warden's lodgings, but to accommodate a bishop's daughter, seven children, and a flock of servants, the lodgings were reconstructed wholesale. They became, what they had not been for a century, the social heart of the college. The college and the outside world rather than the university received the benefit of Spooner's energy; he was pro-vice-chancellor but refused the vice-chancellorship, and did little on hebdomadal council. He supported the promotion of natural science studies and welcomed the foundation in 1901 of the Wykeham chair of physics at New College. He served on several boards, among them the council of Lady Margaret Hall (1901–7) and that of Oxford House in Bethnal Green (1908–20). He was an active member of the Oxford branch of the Charity Organization Society, a poor-law guardian, and chairman of the council of the Warneford Hospital. He was a keen member of the Political Economy Club and its secretary for many years. He retired from the wardenship in 1924 at the age of eighty, and died at his home, 1 Canterbury Road, Oxford, on 29 August 1930. His wife survived him.

Spooner was not a scholar of great distinction, and published little beyond an edition of Tacitus and two small volumes on Bishop Butler and William of Wykeham. His name has endured because of the verbal slip now known as a Spoonerism. The connection of the slip with Spooner is suspect. In particular, the most famous example, 'Kinquering kongs their titles take', appears to have no foundation in fact. His daughter Rosemary has pointed out that New College chapel used printed service sheets; her father would never have had cause to tell a congregation what they were about to sing. Others are evidently student inventions ('You have hissed my mystery lectures; you have tasted a whole worm; you must leave at once by the town drain'), as must be such gems as 'Who has not nourished in his bosom a half-warmed fish?' and 'Our Lord is a shoving leopard'.

There is better evidence for the perpetration of physical Spoonerisms: on one occasion he spilt salt on the tablecloth and poured claret on top of it, and on another he remarked on the darkness of a staircase before turning off all the lights and attempting to lead a party down the stairs in the dark. In writing, too, he perpetrated odd slips of the pen, as though his mind ran ahead of his hand. It seems that he had some mild developmental disorder, but that it rarely resulted in such felicitous slips as those with which he is credited. Other stories hint at an agreeable touch of malice in Spooner's make-up—'I see your book has filled a much needed gap'—and yet others only at confusion in the face of distress—'Was it you or your brother who was killed in the war?' Spooner knew all the stories about him. At his final college dinner the undergraduates called for a speech; Spooner stood up and said, 'You want me to say one of those things; but I shan't', and sat down.

Spooner's politics, like his religion, were quietly middle of the road. He suffered no crises of faith, and no agonies of doubt. His wardenship was, however, marked by an act of considerable moral courage. In the First World War, New College had more old members killed in action than any other Oxford college. Against opposition Spooner insisted that the German dead were to be remembered on the war memorial erected in the college chapel, alongside the allied dead. His view prevailed. Spooner is buried at Grasmere, where his family had always taken their summer holidays at his wife's house of How Foot. The portrait by Hugh Riviere that hangs in New College hall was said by contemporaries to be an excellent likeness. A. RYAN

Sources W. Hayter, *Spooner: a biography* (1977) • H. B. George, *New College, 1856–1906* (1906) • *The Times* (1 Sept 1930) • W. A. Spooner, 'Fifty years in an Oxford College', MS, New College, Oxford • J. M. Potter, 'Dr Spooner and his dysgraphia', *Proceedings of the Royal Society of Medicine*, 69 (1976), 639–48 • J. Potter, 'What was the matter with Dr Spooner?', *Errors in linguistic performance*, ed. V. A. Fromkin (1980) • b. cert. • m. cert. • d. cert. • *CGPLA Eng. & Wales* (1930)

Archives New College, Oxford, corresp. and papers | Bodl. Oxf., letters to Gilbert Murray • Cumbria AS, Carlisle, letters to Lord Howard of Penrith • LPL, letters to *Church Quarterly Review* • New College, Oxford, letters to H. L. Henderson

Likenesses H. G. Riviere, oils, 1913, New College, Oxford • W. Stoneman, photograph, 1924, NPG • S. P. Hall, pencil sketch, NPG • Spy [L. Ward], caricature, NPG; repro. in *VF* (21 April 1898) • photograph, NPG [*see illus.*]

Wealth at death £17,526 19*s*. 2*d*.: resworn probate, 29 Oct 1930, *CGPLA Eng. & Wales*

Spooner, William Charles (1809?–1885), veterinary surgeon, was born at Blandford, Dorset, where his father is said to have been an innkeeper. He was in no way related to his namesake, Charles Spooner (1806–1871), with whom he has frequently been confused. He entered the Royal

Veterinary College, London, in November 1827, and obtained his diploma on 7 March 1829. While at the college he presented two papers to the London Veterinary Medical Society, one on glanders and farcy and the other on staggers. He went into practice at Southampton, where he established a veterinary infirmary, forge, and register office for the sale of horses, at Vincent's Walk, Hanover Buildings.

In 1845, however, Spooner largely gave up his veterinary practice and entered into partnership with a Mr Bennett, manufacturer of chemical manures at Eling Hill Farm, near Eling, in Hampshire. Spooner subsequently purchased the Old Bone Mill at Eling, and the Spooner and Bailey Chemical Manure Works became perhaps the most complete of their kind in the south of England. Spooner lectured regularly at various clubs and societies in Hampshire and the adjoining counties. He also played a leading part in the Botley and South Hampshire Farmers' Club.

Spooner was a frequent contributor to the earlier numbers of *The Veterinarian* and the *Journal of the Royal Agricultural Society*, and he gained a prize from the society for two essays in the *Journal*—'On the use of superphosphate of lime produced with acid and bones for manure' (1846, 7.143), and 'On the management of farm horses' (1848, 9.249). In 1852 he was awarded a prize by the Bath and West of England Agricultural Society for his essay 'On the most economical and profitable method of growing and consuming root crops'. This essay was printed among the society's proceedings for 1854. In the same year a water drill that he had invented was exhibited at Pusey, and was much praised.

> Mr Spooner has been a writer, lecturer, public-spirited promoter in every way of agricultural improvement … His strong commonsense, well tempered enthusiasm, sound judgement and wide intelligence, had for years exerted a most useful influence on both local and general agricultural progress.

Spooner wrote many books and articles on veterinary and agricultural subjects, of which *The History, Structure, Economy and Diseases of Sheep* (1844) is perhaps the most well known. However, several other titles should also be mentioned, for example, *A Treatise on the Influenza of Horses* (1837), *A Treatise on the Structure, Functions, and Diseases of the Foot and Leg of the Horse* (1840), and *A Treatise on Manures* (1847). For the *Encyclopaedia metropolitana* Spooner wrote the article 'Veterinary art', which was subsequently published separately. He contributed to John Morton's *Encyclopaedia of Agriculture*, which was published between 1848 and 1853. He edited, and in part rewrote, in 1842, James White's two treatises, *A Compendium of the Veterinary Art*, and *A Compendium of Cattle Medicine*, which contained 'the first short account in the English language of the foot and mouth disease which prevailed in England and Ireland from about 1838 to 1840'. Spooner also wrote on a wide range of other agricultural topics.

Towards the end of his life Spooner concentrated his attention almost solely on the manufacture of superphosphate and other artificial manures. He suffered greatly throughout life from deafness, which eventually led to his retirement from active life. He died of apoplexy on 3 May 1885 at Eling House, his residence at Eling. He left a widow, Caroline, and a son, Albert.

Ernest Clarke, *rev.* Linda Warden

Sources F. Smith, *The early history of veterinary literature and its British development*, 4 vols. (1919–33); repr. (1976), vol. 4 · d. cert. · *CGPLA Eng. & Wales* (1885) · *The Veterinarian*, 58 (1885), 448 · *Veterinary Journal*, 20 (1885), 461 · E. Cotchin, *The Royal Veterinary College, London: a bicentenary history* (1990) · *Mark Lane Express* (11 May 1885), 584 · *Bell's Weekly Messenger* (11 May 1885), 5 · *Bell's Weekly Messenger* (18 May 1885), 5 [list of his works] · *Agricultural Gazette* (11 May 1885), 597–8 · *Livestock Journal* (8 May 1885) · I. Pattison, *The British veterinary profession, 1741–1948*, [another edn] (1984) · P. Dingley, *Historic books on veterinary science and animal husbandry* (1992) · communications, Royal Veterinary College, London · papers discussed at the London Veterinary Medical Society, 1827–8 and 1828–9, Royal Veterinary College, London · register of pupils, 1794–1907, Royal Veterinary College, London

Archives Royal Veterinary College, London, essays discussed session 1840–41; papers discussed 1827–8; papers discussed 1828–9; communications

Likenesses portrait, repro. in *Agricultural Gazette*

Wealth at death £118,233: probate, 8 July 1885, *CGPLA Eng. & Wales*

Sporborg, Henry Nathan (1905–1985), banker and intelligence officer, was born on 17 September 1905 in Rugby, the elder son of Henry Nathan Sporborg, an electrical engineer, and his wife, Miriam A. Smaith, who were Americans by origin. His younger brother died accidentally in 1928. He went, like his brother, from Rugby School to Emmanuel College, Cambridge; there he took a second class (division II) in history part one (1926) and a third in law (part two, 1927), and rowed. He was admitted as a solicitor in 1930. He joined Slaughter and May, the City solicitors, and became a partner in 1935. He married in that year Mary, the daughter of Christopher Henry Rowlands, engineer. They had a son and three daughters.

Early in the Second World War, Sporborg joined the Ministry of Economic Warfare, and from it soon moved into its secret branch, the Special Operations Executive (SOE), when it first needed legal advice. Most of his partners joined him; hence the unkind quip about SOE's starting troubles, 'Seems to be all may and no slaughter'. Sporborg first worked, under Charles Hambro, in the Scandinavian section, where they encountered a mixture of failures and successes. He also took over supervision of several sections working into north-west Europe: one each for Belgium and the Netherlands, two for France, and an escape section to help all four. Some of the foundations for future clandestine work he helped to lay were sound, although troubles shortly developed in the Netherlands. When Hambro became SOE's executive head, Sporborg too was promoted.

Under the cover appointment of principal private secretary to the minister in charge, the third earl of Selborne, Sporborg acted for eighteen months in 1942–3 as SOE's principal liaison officer, both with him and with several large departments in Whitehall, none of which wished SOE well: the Foreign Office, the Ministry of Supply, and those for the three other fighting services. He also looked after SOE's relations, which were sometimes turbulent, with the other secret services. He continued the latter task while, from September 1943 until SOE was disbanded in January 1946, he was deputy to Major-General Colin Gubbins, its last executive head. Gubbins handled most military business, while he left political affairs to Sporborg. One or other of them was always in London, where Sporborg was prepared to face the chiefs of staff, the foreign secretary, or the prime minister if SOE's needs required it. He saw the permanent under-secretary at the Foreign Office, Sir Alexander Cadogan, almost daily. He became a strong advocate of the role of subversion—SOE's main task—as a tool for unseating the governments of axis-occupied countries, although he felt the subject was too delicate and too secret for him ever to be able to give a publishable account of it. Under Gubbins's and his direction, SOE secured several significant triumphs, particularly in France, Greece, Italy, Norway, Denmark, and Burma, and ended up with a tidy monetary profit as well.

Sporborg then returned to the City, as a businessman. He joined Hambro's Bank, of which he was a director for nearly thirty years, and for a time general manager. His main expertise lay in financing takeovers and mergers. His judgement was so widely respected that several large firms took him on as chairman or vice-chairman—Thorn Electrical Industries and the Sun Group of assurance companies among them; and he served on the Port of London Authority for eight years (1967–75). He was also active in the Fishmongers' Company and in various charities; he spent a decade as chairman of St Mary's Hospital, Paddington.

Sporborg had held the wartime rank of lieutenant-colonel on the general list, and was appointed CMG in 1945. He was also a chevalier of the Légion d'honneur, and held a French Croix de Guerre, the order of St Olaf of Norway, the King Christian X liberty medal, and the United States medal of freedom. A solidly built, burly man with an affable manner, set off by a drooping eyelid, he also had an active life as a country squire, riding to hounds from Upwick Hall, Albury, near Ware in Hertfordshire, the house where he died of heart failure on 6 March 1985.

M. R. D. Foot, *rev.*

Sources *The Times* (9 March 1985) • *The Times* (8 Aug 1985), 12 [will details] • A. H. Maude and A. Archer, eds., *Rugby School register, 1911–1946*, rev. edn (1957), 1171, 1448 • private information (1990) • B. Bramsen and K. Wain, *The Hambros, 1779–1979* (1979) • *WWW* • *CGPLA Eng. & Wales* (1985)

Archives Bodl. Oxf., Palmer MSS • Bodl. Oxf., corresp. with third earl of Selborne

Wealth at death £618,728: probate, 22 July 1985, *CGPLA Eng. & Wales*

Sporley, Richard (*b.* before **1410**, *d.* **1491**), Benedictine monk and historian, entered the abbey of St Peter at Westminster in 1428–9, and was ordained priest on 15 March 1432. If canonically qualified for ordination, he was then at least twenty-four years old, and must have been born before 1410. He held the minor office of granger three times (1445–6, 1453–63, and 1470–71), but never held a major office with financial responsibilities. The precentorship, which he held from 1464 to 1466, and perhaps longer, and which entailed responsibility for the abbey's books, was probably more suited to his capacities. The receipt of a pension of 20s. per annum from 1474/5 until his death early in 1491 indicates that he now lived privately, in a chamber. His annals of the kings of England from 1043 to 1483 (BL, Harley MS 692, fols. 198–204*v*) were completed, and may have been begun, in this late period. Now valueless, they retained an interest into the sixteenth century, when the text down to 1135 was included by John Joscelyn in his larger collection of annals (BL, Cotton MS Vitellius E.xiv, fol. 254). Sporley may have compiled his history of Westminster Abbey at a much earlier date, and, if later entries in the surviving manuscript can be accepted, did so as early as 1450 (BL, Cotton MS Claudius A.viii, fol. 22*r*). His own contribution to this work was an account, of no intrinsic value, of early abbots and priors (ibid., fols. 40–41*v*). The rest (ibid., fols. 22–39*v*, 42–70*r*) derives from the history of the abbey by John Flete.

Barbara F. Harvey

Sources BL, Harley MS 692, fols. 198–204*v* • BL, Cotton MS Vitellius E.xiv, fol. 254 • BL, Cotton MS Claudius A.viii, fol. 22*r* • register of Robert Fitzhugh, bishop of London, 1431–6, GL, MS 9531/4, fol. 219*r* • E. H. Pearce, *The monks of Westminster* (1916), 143 • J. Flete, *The history of Westminster Abbey*, ed. J. A. Robinson (1909)

Spotswood [Spottiswood], **Alexander** (**1676–1740**), army officer and colonial governor, was born on 12 December 1676 in Tangier, the son of Robert Spotswood (*d.* 1688), a physician serving with the English regiment, and his wife, Catherine, formerly Elliott, *née* Mercer (*d.* 1710). He came to England at the age of seven, one year before the garrison was abandoned, and was educated at Westminster School. His family—Scottish, royalist, and members of the Church of England—had seen better times than those of the 1680s, when anti-Scottish, anti-royal sentiments were sweeping the nation.

Patronage and opportunism marked Spotswood's distinctive military and political careers. He spent seventeen years in the army, receiving his first commission as an ensign in an infantry regiment in 1693 serving under the earl of Bath, and was promoted lieutenant in 1696. When wounded at Blenheim in 1704 he was already a captain. At Oudenarde in 1708 he was captured and exchanged.

In 1710 Spotswood was appointed lieutenant-governor of Virginia, sharing the salary with his army patron, titular governor George Hamilton, first earl of Orkney. At that time the colony faced problems on all sides. For five years Spotswood enjoyed the support of the colony's council but thereafter relations deteriorated. His attempt to reform the collection of land quitrents alienated Philip Ludwell and cut across the gubernatorial ambitions of the locally powerful William Byrd. Furthermore he unsettled the wily James Blair, commissary of the bishop of London, by attempting to use his full powers over the church. Conflicts over precedence, appointments, and the creation of a new court of oyer and terminer also undermined relations with the council. Relations with the lower house of the legislature were never good either. Spotswood's agenda was costly and his attitude towards the burgesses (members of the lower house) openly contemptuous. In 1718 a petition to the king signed by the speaker, Daniel

McCarty, accused Spotswood of subverting the constitution and sought his removal.

Spotswood's efforts did have benefits, however. When the notorious pirate Edward Teach (Blackbeard) threatened to bottle up the colony's trade in 1718, Spotswood dispatched an expedition to Ocracoke Inlet, though outside his jurisdiction, which led to Teach's death. Thirteen of Teach's men were tried for piracy in Virginia and hanged. Spotswood sought not only to improve colonial defences but to reform abuses in trade with the Native Americans which he believed were a factor in the late war with the Tuscaroras. His policy towards the Native Americans was farsighted though ultimately unsuccessful. In 1714 he persuaded a number of smaller tribes to settle at Fort Christanna with support from the newly created Virginia Indian Company, which received a twenty-year monopoly on trade south of the James River. He also promoted a system of tobacco inspection and the construction of public warehouses in an attempt to boost Virginia's languishing economy. But the system undermined the interests of small planters, and it was further damaged by Spotswood's attempt to use it as a source of patronage by appointing sitting burgesses to agencies at salaries of £250 a year. Most of his appointees were turned out at the next election in 1715, and in 1717 the privy council disallowed both the Tobacco Inspection Act and the Indian Trade Act. Lasting elements of Spotswood's time in office included the policy of settling foreign protestants on the Virginian frontier. He also carried forward the development of Williamsburg, originally laid out by Francis Nicholson, and his famous excursion across the Blue Ridge Mountains in 1716 captured the imagination of nineteenth-century writers.

Spotswood's career in Virginia illustrated the limitations on the exercise of royal power in the colonies even when in the hands of an able and dynamic official. His attempt to build a power base independent of the traditional sources of authority in the colony alienated Virginians, while his failure to consolidate his relationship with leading families made him vulnerable to complaints from both houses and lost him support among the merchant community in Britain. Caught between a hostile colonial assembly, their friends and representatives in London, and the ambivalence of British merchants, Spotswood was unable to realize many of his most cherished projects. Although relations with the assembly improved in the last years of his governorship, he was removed from office in 1722, by which time he had amassed vast landholdings in the colony. Spotswood spent the period 1724–30 in England securing his land titles on favourable terms, not all of which had been patented in his name. In 1724 he married Anne Butler (*d.* 1750), daughter of Richard and Anne Brayne of St Margaret's, Westminster, with whom he had four children. In 1729 he was appointed postmaster-general at a salary of £300 a year. Returning to Virginia in 1730, Spotswood lived the life of a Virginia planter, land speculator, and ironmaster. From his ironworks at Tubal he exported pig iron to England. When war broke out with Spain in 1739 Spotswood was appointed quartermaster-general and second in command to Charles, eighth Baron Cathcart. As colonel of the American regiment in 1740, he was travelling north to confer with colonial governors, when he fell ill at Annapolis, Maryland, where he died on 7 June 1740. GWENDA MORGAN

Sources L. Dodson, *Alexander Spotswood, governor of colonial Virginia, 1710–1722* (1932) · W. M. Billings, J. E. Selby, and T. W. Tate, *Colonial Virginia: a history* (1986) · W. R. Hofstra, '"The Extension of His Majesty's Dominions": the Virginia backcountry and the reconfiguration of imperial frontiers', *Journal of American History*, 84 (1998), 1281–312 · C. Dowdy, *The Virginia dynasties: the emergence of 'King' Carter and the golden age* (Boston, Massachusetts, 1969) · R. L. Morton, *Colonial Virginia*, 2 (1960) · B. P. Lenman, 'Alexander Spotswood and the business of empire', *Colonial Williamsburg*, 13 (autumn 1990), 44–55 · *The official letters of Governor Alexander Spotswood … 1710–1722*, ed. R. A. Brock, 2 vols. (1882–5) · R. B. Davis, 'Arthur Blackmore: the Virginia colony and the early English novel', *Virginia Magazine of History and Biography*, 75 (1967), 22–34 · W. Havighurst, *Alexander Spotswood: portrait of a governor* [1967] · *The writings of 'Colonel William Byrd of Westover in Virginia'*, ed. J. S. Bassett (1901), 356–470 · *The journal of John Fontaine: an Irish Huguenot son in Spain and Virginia, 1710–1719*, ed. E. A. Porter (Williamsburg, Virginia, 1972) · L. J. Cappon, *Iron works at Tubal* (Charlottesville, Virginia, 1945) · J. P. Greene, *The quest for power: the lower houses of assembly in the southern royal colonies, 1689–1776* (1963) · G. Hood, *The governor's palace in Williamsburg: a cultural study* (1991) · G. Hood, *Charles Bridges and William Dering: two Virginia painters, 1735–1750* (1978) · *Pennsylvania Gazette* (12 June 1740) · *Daily Post* [London] (22 July 1740) · Colonial Williamsburg Foundation, Rockefeller Library, Alexander Spotswood papers · 'Correspondence of Alexander Spotswood with John Spotswood of Edinburgh', *Virginia Magazine of History and Biography*, 60 (1952), 211–40

Archives Colonial Williamsburg Foundation, Rockefeller Library, papers · NYPL, letter-book [transcript] · Virginia Historical Society, Richmond, corresp. | PRO, governor's corresp., CO5

Likenesses attrib. C. Bridges, oils, *c.*1735–1740, Colonial Williamsburg Foundation, De Witt Wallace Building · C. Bridges, oils, Commonwealth of Virginia, Richmond · miniature (as young man), Virginia Historical Society, Richmond

Wealth at death entailed estate upon eldest son; left £3000 to his other son and £2000 each to his two daughters: will, Orange County will book, 1, pp. 181–6

Spottiswood, James (1567–1645), Church of Ireland bishop of Clogher, was born at Calder in Scotland on 7 September 1567, the second son of John *Spottiswoode (1509/10–1585), superintendent of Lothian, and his wife, Beatrix Crichton, and the younger brother of John *Spottiswoode (1565–1639), archbishop of St Andrews. He was educated at home with a tutor called William Strange, later minister of Kirkliston. He subsequently attended Edinburgh grammar school and a school at Linlithgow. In 1579, then aged twelve, he entered the University of Glasgow, graduating in 1583. After his father's death he entered the service of James VI in 1588, and one of his first tasks was to accompany the king to meet his future wife, Anne of Denmark. He also raised the alarm which prevented the earl of Bothwell from seizing the king in 1591. He was secretary to the ambassadors to the king of Denmark and the German princes in 1598. After the succession of James to the crown of England he was sent to John Whitgift, archbishop of Canterbury, who persuaded him to take orders in the Church of England. He was ordained and presented by the king to the rectory of Wells, in Norfolk. He remained there until 1616, when he formed part of a visitation to the University of St Andrews with Patrick Young, dean of Winchester. There he was made DD for a thesis later published as *Concio J Spottiswodii ... quam habuit as celrum Andreanopoli ... pro gradu doctoratus* (1616). In the same year he also published at Edinburgh *The execution of Neshech and the confyning of his brother Tarbith, or, A short discourse shewing the difference betwixt damned usurie and that which is lawful: wherunto there is subjoyned an epistle of ... J Calvin touching that same argument ... translated out of the Latine*.

In 1620 Spottiswood became involved in a dispute in Norfolk involving admiralty rights which took him to the court in London. While there George Montgomery, bishop of Meath and Clogher, who acted as agent for the Irish church at court, died, and Spottiswood's friends persuaded him to petition the king for the bishopric. Through the influence of the duke of Buckingham this was granted. He was nominated on 20 January 1621, arrived in Dublin in April, and the mandate for his consecration was dated 22 October 1621. The delay in issuing the mandate gave rise to a dispute with James Ussher, archbishop of Armagh, about his exercise of the jurisdiction of the see of Clogher.

By 1625 Spottiswood had become entangled in a dispute with a prominent co. Fermanagh landowner, Lord Balfour, over the right to appoint a schoolmaster to the Royal School at Enniskillen. Under the terms of the Ulster plantation scheme such rights, and the lands of the schools, had been vested in local bishops as trustees of the schools. Geoffrey Middleton, Balfour's chaplain and schoolmaster at Enniskillen, petitioned the king to grant him the school lands in fee. Spottiswood, suspecting that Balfour was attempting to seize the lands for himself, objected, and Balfour began to create a complicated network of rumour and intrigue at court against Spottiswood. The result was a fist fight between the two men and arbitrators were called in. However, a dispute over the meaning of the arbitration led to a chancery suit which was settled in 1627. More serious was the fatal wounding in 1626 of Sir John Weymss, sheriff of co. Fermanagh, by Humphry Galbraith, rector of Derrybrusk, during a raid to seize cattle distrained for non-payment of rent due on land belonging to Spottiswood. The result was a set of actions and counter-actions taken in the Dublin courts between Balfour and Spottiswood—each trying to bankrupt the other by having higher and higher sureties demanded for appearance at court. In November 1627 Spottiswood was tried for his servants' actions, since the servants did not appear. The jury brought in a verdict of 'ignoramus', but not before Spottiswood had made accusations of witchcraft against Sir John Weymss's daughter. Balfour again tried to blacken Spottiswood's name at court in London but the king intervened, setting up a commission to determine the case. Tensions between the two men persisted in the 1630s, each taking a different side in the factional politics of co. Fermanagh. Spottiswood's own account of the disputes was published in 1811 as *A Breefe Memorial of the Lyfe and Death of Doctor James Spottiswood*, which a later hand continued into the 1630s.

Spottiswood spent a considerable amount of time and effort in the 1630s recovering alienated church land in the diocese of Clogher and he improved church income considerably. After the outbreak of the rising of 1641 in Ulster he fled to London, where he lived until his death at Westminster in March 1645, being buried in St Benedict's Chapel, Westminster, on 31 March 1645. He left a son, Sir Henry Spottiswood, and a daughter, Mary.

RAYMOND GILLESPIE

Sources [J. Spottiswood], *A breefe memorial of the lyfe and death of Doctor James Spottiswood, bishop of Clogher in Ireland*, ed. A. B. [A. Boswell] (1811) · R. Gillespie, 'The trials of Bishop Spottiswood, 1620–40', *Clogher Record*, 12 (1987), 320–33 · J. B. Leslie, *Clogher clergy and parishes* (1929) · J. L. Chester, ed., *The marriage, baptismal, and burial registers of the collegiate church or abbey of St Peter, Westminster*, Harleian Society, 10 (1876) · T. W. Moody and others, eds., *A new history of Ireland*, 9: *Maps, genealogies, lists* (1984)

Likenesses oils, Clogher Cathedral, Clogher, co. Tyrone; repro. in Gillespie, 'The trials of Bishop Spottiswood', 325

Spottiswood, John. *See* Spottiswoode, John (1509/10–1585); Spottiswoode, John (1565–1639); Spottiswoode, John, of that ilk (1667–1728).

Spottiswood [Spottiswoode], **Sir Robert**, **Lord Dunipace** (**1596–1646**), judge and politician, was the second son of John *Spottiswoode (1565–1639), archbishop of St Andrews, and Rachel, daughter of David Lindsay, bishop of Ross. He was educated at grammar school in Glasgow and at the University of Glasgow (1609–13), where he graduated as master of arts. He then moved to Exeter College, Oxford, becoming a fellow, before embarking on nine years of travel and study in France, Italy, and Germany. During this period he greatly helped his father's work on the history of the church in Scotland by recovering many documents carried abroad by Roman Catholic refugees after the Scottish Reformation. It was presumably on his return to Scotland that he married Bethia (*d*. 1639), daughter of Sir Alexander Morison of Prestongrange.

Spottiswood's abilities, and his father's position, brought him quick advancement. He was admitted to the privy council of Scotland on 11 July 1622, and was appointed the next day to be an extraordinary lord of the court of session, in place of his father. He took the judicial title Lord New Abbey from lands bought for him by his father, and was knighted in 1624. On 14 February 1626 he was made an ordinary lord of session, and in 1634 changed his title to Lord Dunipace when the New Abbey lands were restored to the crown as a patrimony for the new bishopric of Edinburgh. In October 1633 he was elected president of the court of session, having been nominated by Charles I. After 1625 he never took his seat on the privy council, preferring to concentrate on his judicial duties, and he was omitted from the new council appointed in 1631.

When open resistance to the king began in Scotland in 1637 Spottiswood became a hated figure, as much because he was the son of an archbishop as because of his political views. Late in that year he travelled to court in England, and it was rumoured that he had gone to inform the king of the incompetence of his officials, being regarded as 'almost a professed enemie' to the noble councillors and 'an agent for the bishops' (*Letters and Journals of Robert Baillie*, 1.47). He was back in Scotland by 28 February 1638, when he took his seat on the session, and he continued to sit in court until 22 March 1639, by which time the country was on the verge of civil war between the king's supporters and the covenanters. He withdrew eventually to England, but returned to Scotland with Charles I in 1641. Denounced by the Scottish parliament as an 'incendiary' responsible for sowing discord between king and people, he was imprisoned in Edinburgh Castle by parliament on 17 August, but was released on 16 November. The threat to bring him to trial at a later date was abandoned, and, omitted from the new commission to the court of session in October, he returned to England with the king.

In January 1644 Spottiswood was appointed secretary of state for Scotland by Charles at Oxford, his civil war headquarters, but the Scottish parliament, which had just allied itself with its English counterpart against the king, refused to recognize the appointment, denouncing him as a usurper on 22 July. Spottiswood had formed a close friendship with the marquess of Montrose and in May 1645, having sealed the king's commission to the marquess to be the king's lieutenant-governor and captain-general of Scotland, he set out to deliver the document to Montrose himself. His role was no doubt intended to be much more than that of a messenger. Montrose had raised hopes that his army would soon win control of Scotland from the covenanters, and if that happened moves would need to be made to establish a royalist regime under the powers granted in the new commission. Spottiswood's presence as secretary of state would lend credibility to this transition from conquest to administration. Travelling by way of Wales and the Isle of Man, Spottiswood landed in Lochaber, finally joining Montrose's army at the beginning of September. The timing seemed perfect, for Montrose's victory at Kilsyth a few weeks earlier had left no army in Scotland to oppose him, and he was indeed preparing to establish a regime. But the failure of lowland royalists to rally to Montrose, desertions from his army, and the news of the approach of the cavalry of the Scottish army in England made the situation perilous. As Spottiswood wrote on 10 September, 'All these were great Disheartenings to any other but to him [Montrose], whom nothing of this kind can amate [deject]' (Spottiswoode, xxxvi). When Montrose's forces were crushed at Philiphaugh on 13 September, Spottiswood fled, but was captured, and the fact that he had drawn his sword was used as evidence that he had been 'in arms'.

Spottiswood was at first imprisoned in Glasgow, where a list of charges against him was delivered to him on 5 November. The main accusations were having accepted office as secretary without parliamentary consent and having served in arms against the state. His defences that he owed natural allegiance to his king, that he had not been in arms, and that he had been promised quarter were rejected in a debate in parliament at St Andrews, and he was found guilty of high treason. He was sentenced to death on 16 January 1646, orders being issued for bringing 'the maiden'—the Scottish beheading machine—to St Andrews. On 19 January, the day before his death, Spottiswood wrote to Montrose reaffirming his loyalty, and on the day itself he wrote to his children: all he had to bequeath to them was 'the example of my loyalty, which as yow looke for a blessing from heaven or will have mine to light on you I command you to imitate' (NL Scot., MS 2933, 24*r*).

On 20 January 1646, on the scaffold, Spottiswood's attempt to make a speech was interrupted by covenanting ministers, who 'tormented him in the last moments of his life with their officious exhortations and rhapsodies' (Maidment, 1.223). Another account speaks of one of the ministers, Robert Blair, being white with fury and breaking 'out into scurrilous abuse' of Spottiswood and his archbishop father, which he bore in 'serene silence' (Wishart, 171). Blair on the other hand records Spottiswood's 'railing discourse', and his own comment that it was no surprise to find the son of a 'false prophet' slandering faithful servants of Christ. Spottiswood, says Blair, 'died railing and raging' (*Life of Mr Robert Blair*, 180). Finally, there is the story that he 'died as he lived, full of malice against the cause and the Covenant', affirming his support for Montrose, 'that matchless mirrour of all true worth and nobility' (Maidment, 1.203–4, 208). On balance, it seems he died with spirit rather than serenity.

Laying aside unsubstantiated charges of corruption as a judge hurled at him by his enemies, Spottiswood seems to have been a scholarly, diligent, and well-liked man. That his father was an archbishop advanced both his career and his death, for in the covenanters' determination to obtain revenge on their enemies Spottiswood was almost a symbolic victim. In hailing him as a 'great man' George Wishart treated him as a symbol of loyalty and martyrdom, but whether he was also 'remarkable for his knowledge of things both human and divine', outstanding as a linguist, and 'deeply versed in history, law and politics' (Wishart, 171) it is impossible to decide through lack of evidence.

David Stevenson

Sources *DNB* · J. Maidment, ed., *The Spottiswoode miscellany*, 1 (1844) · R. Spottiswoode, 'Memoirs of Sir Robert Spottiswood's life', *Practicks of the laws of Scotland* (1706) · G. Wishart, *The memoirs of James, marquis of Montrose, 1639–1650*, ed. and trans. A. D. Murdoch and H. F. M. Simpson (1893) · G. Brunton and D. Haig, *An historical account of the senators of the college of justice, from its institution in MDXXXII* (1832) · *Reg. PCS*, 1st ser. · *Reg. PCS*, 2nd ser. · *APS*, 1124–1707 · acts of sederunt, NA Scot., CS1/5 · *The letters and journals of Robert Baillie*, ed. D. Laing, 3 vols. (1841–2) · *The life of Mr Robert Blair … containing his autobiography*, ed. T. M'Crie, Wodrow Society, 11 (1848) · NL Scot., MS 2933, fol. 24*r*

Archives NL Scot., corresp. and papers

Likenesses oils, 1636, Scot. NPG

Spottiswoode, Arthur Cole (1808–1874), army officer in the East India Company, born on 9 January 1808 at Ganjam, Madras, was the eldest son of Hugh Spottiswoode of the Madras civil service, who died on his passage to the Cape on 4 April 1820, and Harriet, daughter of Burton Smith. He entered the East India Company's service as ensign on 25 February 1824, became lieutenant in the 37th native infantry (Bengal) on 13 May 1825, captain on 14 November 1833, and major on 17 March 1851. He served with distinction at the siege and capture of Bharatpur in 1826, heading the assault, and receiving the personal thanks of Lord Combermere. On 29 July 1834 he married Jessy Eliza (1817/18–1898), daughter of Lieutenant-General Lambert Loveday. They had three sons and three daughters.

In 1835 Spottiswoode began many years' employment in the stud department at Hapur, but left this staff appointment for a time to rejoin his regiment during the Afghan campaign of 1838–9. He was made brevet major on 6 November 1846, and brevet lieutenant-colonel on 20 June 1854.

Spottiswoode succeeded to the command of the 37th as lieutenant-colonel on 22 May 1856. His regiment was at Benares, and on 4 June 1857, as it was believed to be on the point of mutiny, orders were given to disarm it. It was a case for skilful handling, for there were other native troops there, and the British force consisted of only 250 men and three guns. Spottiswoode still had faith in his men, to whom, as the native officers said, he had always been a father; but he had to parade them and tell them to lodge their arms. While they were doing so the British troops were seen to be approaching, and a cry rose that they were going to be shot down. The regiment broke, and some of the men opened fire, but they were soon dispersed by the guns, as were also the Sikh cavalry who sided with them. For a time there was great risk that the city would join them, and much fault was afterwards found with the arrangements made by the general in command, Brigadier George Ponsonby. Spottiswoode carried out the burning of the sepoy lines during the night, and helped to provide for the security of the European women and the treasure. He became colonel in the army on 23 July 1858, and retired with the rank of major-general on 31 December 1861. He died at 5 Verulam Place, Hastings, on 23 March 1874. E. M. LLOYD, *rev.* M. G. M. JONES

Sources V. C. P. Hodson, *List of officers of the Bengal army, 1758–1834*, 4 (1947) • Burke, *Gen. GB* • *Annual Register* (1874) • *East-India Register* • J. W. Kaye, *A history of the Sepoy War in India, 1857–1858*, 2 (1876) • *CGPLA Eng. & Wales* (1874)

Wealth at death under £100: probate, 2 April 1874, *CGPLA Eng. & Wales*

Spottiswoode [Spottiswood], **John** (**1509/10–1585**), Scottish reformer and superintendent of Lothian, has been identified as the second son of William Spottiswoode of that ilk in Berwickshire, who was killed at Flodden in 1513, and Elizabeth Pringle (*d.* 1514/15), daughter of Henry Pringle of Hoppringle or Torsonce in Lothian. Spottiswoode was orphaned when four years old; 'his friends put him to school in Glasgow' (*History of the Church*, 2.336), where he entered the university in 1534, as 'schir' John Spottiswoode (denoting clerical status), and graduated MA. Acting as the rector's servant in 1534, he was licensed in 1536 as a student of Alexander Logan and later reappeared as the rector's deputy in 1543. His intention was to proceed to study divinity, but he was discouraged by the persecution of heretics at home and so left Scotland in favour of England where he was befriended by Archbishop Cranmer, who brought him to 'knowledge of the truth' (ibid.). He returned to Scotland after James V's death in 1542, with released Scottish nobles captured at Solway Moss, and 'stayed a long time' with the fourth earl of Glencairn, an early protestant sympathizer and friend of England. Glencairn introduced him to the fourth earl of Lennox, employed by Henry VIII to foster support for England among the Scots. When Lennox took to arms in the west at Henry's bidding, in an unsuccessful attempt to overthrow the government, Spottiswoode was present at Dumbarton Castle as servitor to the earl's brother, Robert Stewart, bishop elect of Caithness, who became another exile in England and temporarily lost his bishopric.

Spottiswoode remained with Lennox for some months in England (where Lennox was exiled for his unpatriotic activities) and served as a bearer of Lennox's communications with Henry VIII. On obtaining a pardon enabling him to return home, he was already known to James Sandilands of Calder, himself a supporter of the reformer George Wishart and 'assured' to the English cause. Accepting Sandilands's offer of the parsonage of Calder in 1548, a living with an annual income at the Reformation valued at £185, he lived sometimes with Sandilands, who was preceptor of Torphicen (a hospital of St John of Jerusalem), and sometimes with Lord James Stewart, Queen Mary's half-brother and commendator of St Andrews Priory. In September 1550 Spottiswoode and Sandilands received a licence from the crown to visit France. Spottiswoode went in the entourage of Mary of Guise, the queen mother, whose party also included Lord James, and was in France again in April 1558 when the young Queen Mary was married to the dauphin. At Paris, along with Robert Colville of Cleish, he signed a contract on 14 May 1558 with the Parisian master printer Jean Cavalier, who promised, on gaining approval from the Paris faculty of theology, to deliver to them 200 copies of Patrick Cockburn's *De vulgari sacrae scripturae phrasi* (1552).

With the outbreak of the Reformation, Spottiswoode took up residence at Calder, where he served as minister in the reformed church. By then he had been moving in reforming and Anglophile circles for a generation, and a Roman Catholic controversialist depicted him as 'profundlie learnit in the misteriis of the New Testament' (*Works of John Knox*, 6.167). He was certainly well equipped to offer his ideas on reform by contributing to the Book of Discipline and the confession of faith, as he was invited to do in 1560. On 9 March 1561 he was admitted by John Knox, who himself declined the office, as superintendent of Lothian, though he retained his parish ministry at Calder. This led his parishioners to complain to the general assembly in 1562 and again in 1563 that they were deprived of his services for much of the year on account of his duties as superintendent which they wished him to demit; the assembly refused their plea.

In a circular letter written from Edinburgh on 22 March 1561, Spottiswoode showed that he regarded his commission as superintendent to be valid and effective: first, because he possessed the approval and support of the churches in his province; second, because he was so charged by the nobility; and third, because as a consequence of this authorization so to act he had received from the privy council endorsement and added authority for effecting a visitation of his province. Even so he may have felt himself somewhat disadvantaged by Knox, who occupied the pulpit of St Giles in the capital. Knox had authority to call general assemblies, served as a visitor, and had the ear of the English ambassador, who in all his dispatches during Mary's personal rule seems only once to have alluded to Spottiswoode (and even then only in the context of Knox's activities, without mentioning his name). Knox's name also took precedence over Spottiswoode's in a decree granting the earl of Eglinton's divorce in 1562. Nor was Spottiswoode elected moderator of the general assembly, though a regular attender at its meetings.

In May 1565 Spottiswoode, who was by now married to Beatrix Crichton, mother of his two sons John *Spottiswoode and James *Spottiswood, delivered to the queen a petition from the brethren of Edinburgh seeking punishment of adulterers and papists and was assured by the queen in 'fair words' of her desire to satisfy men's consciences (*Knox's History*, 2.147). He also several times presented to Mary petitions for payment of ministers' stipends. In December 1565 he was appointed by the general assembly to seek from the queen redress of grievances, and in 1566 to ask her that Prince James 'be baptized according to the form used in the Reformed Church' (*History of the Church*, 2.40). Although Mary received him graciously, she avoided answering. Yet she allowed him to take the prince in his arms and to offer 'a short and pithy prayer, which was very attentively heard by her'; thereafter 'he spake to the babe, and willed him to say Amen for himself; which she took in so good part, as continually afterwards she called the superintendent her Amen' (ibid.). In the event James was baptized according to Roman Catholic rites, but on 29 July 1567, following Mary's enforced abdication, Spottiswoode officiated at James's protestant coronation at Stirling. With Mary's escape from captivity in Lochleven Castle and the ensuing civil war, he attempted to rally support for the king's cause in a letter in 1569 in which he admonished those nobles who supported Mary and urged them to defect to the king's party, for Mary was an adulterer and murderer who 'deserved more than ten deaths' (Calderwood, 2.482).

A participant in the convention of Leith in 1572, which sought to settle the vexed question of ecclesiastical endowment and assimilate protestant bishops, Spottiswoode continued to discharge his duties as superintendent of Lothian and to convene meetings of the synod of Lothian, despite the appointment of an archbishop of St Andrews. He repeatedly urged the general assembly to let him demit his superintendent's office, but the assembly showed reluctance. Even in 1575, when Spottiswoode was said to have 'become sickly and not altogether able in his own person presently to visit the whole bounds allotted to him in commission' (Thomson, 1.327), the assembly encouraged him to persevere and granted him the support of assistant visitors. In April 1576 he was censured by the assembly for inaugurating Alexander Hepburn to the bishopric of Ross after 'being admonished of the brethren not to doe it' (ibid., 1.349). Yet he remained prominent in the assembly's deliberations until old age and infirmity intervened. Although he seems to have played no part in the preparation of the second Book of Discipline, when the assembly pressed ahead with plans for presbyteries in 1581 it was recommended that a presbytery seat be located at Calder, where Spottiswoode 'might be had to be moderator' (ibid., 2.523). As his son John Spottiswoode, the historian and archbishop of St Andrews, remarked of his father in his declining years:

> When he saw the ministers take such liberty as they did, and heard of the disorders raised in the Church through that confused parity which men laboured to introduce, as likewise the irritations the king received by a sort of foolish preachers, he lamented extremely the case of the Church to those that came to visit him, who were not a few, and of the better sort. (*History of the Church*, 2.336–7)

Spottiswoode died in his seventy-sixth year, on 5 December 1585, 'well esteemed for his piety and wisdom, loving, and beloved of all persons, charitable to the poor, and careful above all things to give no man offence' (ibid.).

James Kirk

Sources J. Spottiswood, *The history of the Church of Scotland*, ed. M. Napier and M. Russell, 3 vols., Bannatyne Club, 93 (1850) • D. Calderwood, *The history of the Kirk of Scotland*, ed. T. Thomson and D. Laing, 8 vols., Wodrow Society, 7 (1842–9) • *John Knox's History of the Reformation in Scotland*, ed. W. C. Dickinson, 2 vols. (1949) • *CSP Scot., 1547–1603* • J. Kirk, ed., *The books of assumption of the thirds of benefices: Scottish ecclesiastical rentals at the Reformation* (1995) • *Reg. PCS*, 1st ser., vols. 1–4 • T. Thomson, ed., *Acts and proceedings of the general assemblies of the Kirk of Scotland*, 3 pts, Bannatyne Club, 81 (1839–45) • R. Wodrow, *Collections upon the lives of the reformers and most eminent ministers of the Church of Scotland*, ed. W. J. Duncan, 1, Maitland Club, 32 (1834) • C. Innes, ed., *Munimenta alme Universitatis Glasguensis / Records of the University of Glasgow from its foundation till 1727*, 4 vols., Maitland Club, 72 (1854) • J. Durkan and J. Kirk, *The University of Glasgow, 1451–1577* (1977) • J. Kirk, *Patterns of reform: continuity and change in the Reformation kirk* (1989) • G. Donaldson, *The Scottish Reformation* (1960) • *The works of John Knox*, ed. D. Laing, 6 vols., Wodrow Society, 12 (1846–64) • M. Livingstone, D. Hay Fleming, and others, eds., *Registrum secreti sigilli regum Scotorum / The register of the privy seal of Scotland*, 4 (1952)

Spottiswoode, John (1565–1639), archbishop of St Andrews and historian, was born in Greenbank, in the barony of Calder, Edinburghshire, the eldest son of John *Spottiswoode (1509/10–1585), the widely respected protestant reformer and superintendent of Lothian and Tweeddale, and Beatrix Crichton, the daughter of Patrick Crichton of Lugton and Gilmerton by Dalkeith. Although there is no extant record appertaining to Spottiswoode's childhood, like his younger brother James *Spottiswood it is likely that he received his initial educational instruction in his father's house under the tutorage of the cleric William Strange. Afterwards he presumably proceeded to grammar school at Edinburgh or Linlithgow, where an introduction to the arts prepared him for entry to university. Spottiswoode matriculated at the University of Glasgow at the early, although not uncommon, age of twelve or thirteen. He graduated MA in August 1581 at the age of sixteen. After graduating he returned to Calder to help his aged father, probably with a view to succeeding to his

John Spottiswoode (1565–1639), by Wenceslaus Hollar, pubd 1655

charge after gaining the requisite experience and having met with the church's thorough exegetical and doctrinal standards.

Early career In 1583, at the age of eighteen, Spottiswoode was officially deemed qualified to assist his father in his pastorate. He duly succeeded to the incumbency after his father's death in December 1585, and in addition was advanced to the nearby charge of Calder-Cleres on 19 July 1594. He demitted this second charge two years later to make way for John Brown, who was presented to the vicarage by James VI on 31 January 1596. The frequency of his name in extant synod and general assembly registers is indicative of his high standing among fellow ministers. Although the synod of Lothian and Tweeddale records reveal that Spottiswoode encountered difficulties with regard to enforcing church discipline within the jurisdictional bounds of the Linlithgow presbytery, in comparative terms his problems were relatively minor and were not peculiar to his pastorate. Moreover, he continued to play a conspicuous role within the higher echelons of the church, which would indicate that his administrative and managerial talents were recognized at a relatively early date. He was among the commissioners nominated by the general assembly to undertake a visitation of the University of Aberdeen in 1593. He was elected moderator of the synod of Lothian and Tweeddale in October 1594, was assigned a prominent part in negotiations between church and state, and played a high profile role in the battle to extirpate Roman Catholic recusancy from Scotland. In May 1601 Spottiswoode, along with his future archiepiscopal colleague James Law, was instructed to effect the proselytization of William Douglas, tenth earl of Angus. However, he was unable to comply 'because he was directit be his Majestie to awaite upon the Duke of Lennox in his ambassadrie to France' (*Booke of the Universall Kirk*, 3.981). He was also appointed by the general assembly on visitations to Galloway in 1596 and Clydesdale in 1601 and 1602.

The available evidence, although inconclusive, implies that Spottiswoode was a firm adherent of the decidedly presbyterian party within the church up until the late 1590s. However, by 1600 there can be no doubt that Spottiswoode favoured the reinstitution of Erastian episcopacy. Indeed, he was chosen secretary of the Erastian party in the church–state debates, which monopolized the Montrose assembly in March of that year. If he needed to be persuaded of the merits of Erastian episcopacy, the answer to his conversion lies in his belief that the power and coercive authority of the crown and state were essential to both the material and spiritual well-being of the reformed faith in Scotland. It is also worth conjecturing that Spottiswoode's father-in-law, the moderate-minded royal chaplain, David Lindsay, who was appointed bishop of Ross in November 1600, might well have had a bearing on Spottiswoode's future Erastian orientation. In 1589 Spottiswoode had married Rachel, the daughter of that vastly experienced and much respected cleric. During the 1590s their marriage produced three children who survived into adulthood. Their eldest son, John, subsequently became Sir John Spottiswoode of Dairsie after his father's accession to the metropolitan see of St Andrews; their younger surviving son was the lawyer and supporter of Montrose, Sir Robert *Spottiswood (1596–1646), and their daughter, Anna, eventually married Sir William Sinclair of Roslin.

In May 1601 Spottiswoode was nominated chaplain to Prince Henry's house and was called upon to join the duke of Lennox's diplomatic mission to France in July of that same year. From extant correspondence between Spottiswoode and Isaac Casaubon, the French classical scholar who was sub-librarian of the royal library in Paris, it is evident that he almost met with a premature death on his return voyage from France. Spottiswoode set sail for England from Dieppe on the afternoon of 3 November 1601 on board an English merchant vessel. However, the ship never reached its destination for it was caught in a storm and badly damaged, forcing her skipper to return to the port of Boulogne. From there Spottiswoode made a safe and uneventful journey back to Scotland via the English court, which he visited with the prime objective of securing official recognition of James's right to succeed the aged Elizabeth I. Spottiswoode had evidently made a favourable impression on James since he was included in the royal party, which, after James's peaceful accession, headed south in April 1603. News reached the king, while at Burleigh House, that the exiled Roman Catholic archbishop of Glasgow, James Beaton, whom he had restored in 1598, had died in Paris. Spottiswoode was immediately appointed to the see, and was instructed to return to Scotland to escort Queen Anne to London as her official almoner. He was officially installed in the archbishopric of Glasgow in July.

Archbishop of Glasgow After the regal union Spottiswoode quickly emerged as the most authoritative and commanding episcopal figure of his generation. As archbishop of Glasgow (1603–15), his ascent was meteoric. Owing to the titular nature of his office and his involvement in more pressing matters on behalf of church and crown, the archbishop did not take up residence in Glasgow until January 1605. However, his acquisition of ecclesiastical, and magisterial authority within Glasgow and its archiepiscopal environs was swift and decisive. The Linlithgow assembly made him constant moderator of the Glasgow presbytery in December 1606, although in practice Spottiswoode rarely attended its meetings until the Glasgow assembly of 1610 restored episcopal ecclesiastical jurisdiction. In his protracted absences from his locality the archbishop relied on the highly competent Patrick Sharp, principal of the University of Glasgow and deputy moderator, to keep him informed of developments and oversee the smooth operation of presbyterial affairs. The same assembly similarly allegedly appointed Spottiswoode moderator of the synod of Clydesdale. Nevertheless, it was not until the following August that the injunction was put into effect after the synod was browbeaten into acceptance of the new constitutional arrangement by the earl of Abercorn at the behest of the king. In a similar manner the archbishop quickly established his grip on the archiepiscopal city as he filled the power vacuum left by the duke of Lennox, who had relocated in England with King James. As early as November 1606 Spottiswoode had gained control of the city administration through his ability to determine the complexion and composition of the burgh council. It was no coincidence that in April 1611 Glasgow was finally accorded royal burgh status through the endeavour of the archbishop.

Spottiswoode's elevation rested on solid financial and legal foundations. Although they were significantly dilapidated, a grant made under the privy seal on 4 June 1604 reallocated the temporalities of the bishopric back into the archbishop's patrimony. The following year he was granted the parsonage and vicarage of the parish church of Glasgow. More important, in August 1608 he was awarded regality jurisdiction throughout his archbishopric. Such an award not only boosted the archiepiscopal coffers with the profits of justice but also placed a vast reservoir of patronage at his disposal. That same year he was additionally granted the parsonages and vicarages of Ancrum, Eskirk, Stobo, Edilstoun, Kilbryde, and Torrence. In August/September 1614 Spottiswoode successfully negotiated the transfer of Kilwinning Abbey into his patrimony. Moreover the archbishop was instrumental in the acquisition of New Abbey for his younger son, Robert, in September 1612 and had the title deeds of Holyroodhouse conferred upon his elder son, John, in March 1613.

From the parliament of July 1604 Spottiswoode was a regular lord of the articles, preparing, scrutinizing, and selecting all legislation presented to parliament for its formal approval. From 30 May 1605 he also sat as a privy councillor. He played a key role in the successful campaign of 1608 and 1609 to have commissariat jurisdiction restored to the episcopate. His timely intervention and involvement in the affairs and procedures of the Scottish exchequer in 1608 led to alterations in its constitution and personnel. During his years in Glasgow, Spottiswoode was also heavily involved in government initiatives to advance the cause of church and crown in the Scottish borders and in the highlands and islands. In May 1610 he was made an extraordinary lord of session. Moreover, following the untimely and premature death of his powerful ally, the earl of Dunbar, in late 1611, Spottiswoode was one of the neo-Octavians appointed by the king in April 1612 to oversee the affairs of the combined offices of the treasurer, collector, and comptroller. He was the crown's principal agent in the re-establishment and defence of an Erastian episcopal settlement. He was moderator of the landmark Glasgow assembly of 1610 which fully restored episcopal ecclesiastical jurisdiction and all but made presbytery a bare name, and his ecclesiastical powers were further enhanced in February of that year by the creation of the Scottish court of high commission. Later that same year Spottiswoode, along with Bishop Andrew Lamb of Brechin and Bishop Gavin Hamilton of Galloway, received episcopal consecration in England at the hands of the bishops of London, Ely, Rochester, and Worcester, although at Spottiswoode's insistence, both English archbishops were excluded from the service, since their inclusion might have left the Church of Scotland open to a renewal of the highly contentious and dubious English archiepiscopal claim to jurisdictional supremacy over Scotland.

In spite of his later assertion incorporated into his will that 'the government episcopall is the only right and Apostolique form', Spottiswoode was, however, no *jure divino* episcopalian. Nor for that matter was he an enthusiastic supporter of the creation of a British church conforming to the Anglican *via media*. The archbishop was first and foremost a Scottish churchman. A highly astute and skilful politician, his talent lay especially in administration and in motivating and managing the affairs of men. In addition to Spottiswoode's continual endeavour to right the Church of Scotland's pecuniary difficulties, the perennial problem of Roman Catholic recusancy occupied much of his time and energy. Most notably he was the crown's chief protagonist and prosecutor in the capture, trial, and subsequent execution of John Ogilvie in 1614 and 1615. He penned *A trve relation of the proceedings against John Ogilvie, a Jesuit, executed at Glasgow, the last of Februarie, anno 1615*, in an attempt to demonstrate that Ogilvie was tried and convicted for treason not heresy. Spottiswoode was also a prominent player in the infamous political fall in 1608 of the crypto-Roman Catholic secretary of state and president of the court of session, James Elphinstone, first Lord Balmerino.

Archbishop of St Andrews Spottiswoode was elevated to the metropolitan see after the death of George Gladstanes in March 1615. As primate he continued to be the main channel through which James VI and later Charles I sought to Anglicize the Church of Scotland through the introduction of doctrinal, liturgical, and ceremonial modifications. Spottiswoode was the author of the *Refutatio libelli de regimine ecclesiae Scoticanae*, 1620, which was an episcopal riposte to the presbyterian polemics of David Calderwood. His forceful and erudite sermon on 1 Corinthians 11: 16, given in defence of the king's five articles at the Perth assembly on 25 August 1618, was similarly published in defence of the untimely and unwarranted alterations. Nevertheless Spottiswoode was no slavish sycophant. Although an advocate of the theory of divine right of kings, the archbishop was often working to a quite independent agenda to that of his royal master. The archbishop's extant sermons as primate clearly reveal that he was an orthodox Calvinist in theology if not ecclesiology. It is telling that he informed Isaac Casaubon that he greatly admired the works of the widely renowned Scottish covenant theologian, Robert Rollock, whom he described as 'worthy of immortality' (Burney MSS 366, fol. 197*r*).

At St Andrews, Spottiswoode continued his quest to secure adequate financial provision for the church. In 1616 he had published a Scottish edition of Sir Henry Spelman's *De temerandis ecclesiis, or, The rights and respects due to churches, written to a gentleman, who having an appropriate parsonage, employed the church to profane uses, and left the parishioners uncertainly provided of divine service in a parish there adjoining*. He added a preface in which he argued that to 'rest upon the benevolence of the people … is a beggarlie thing … not beseeming the dignitie of the Ministrie'. During his early years as metropolitan Spottiswoode purchased the pre-Reformation archiepiscopal estate of Dairsie, which was held in the name of his son John. The archbishop contributed towards the restoration and refurbishment of the castle at Dairsie and had a new parish church erected there in 1621. Shortly after the death of James VI in March 1625 Spottiswoode wrote that 'posteritie wil admire bothe the workes and the persone [of James VI], and looking back into ages past for the lyk pattern, sal not be able to find any thing to be compared with it' (NL Scot., MS 2934, fol. 28). It was testimony to Spottiswoode's loyalty and to his in-depth knowledge and experiences of the Scottish administration that Charles I made him president of the exchequer shortly after becoming king, despite the fact that the archbishop's conscientious opposition to officiating at the funeral of James VI in May 1625 dressed in Anglican ecclesiastical vestments compelled him to relinquish his place in the ceremony.

Eight years later, on 18 June 1633, Spottiswoode did officiate at Charles's Scottish coronation in the Canongate kirk. Between December 1634 and March of the following year the archbishop, with the aid of his youngest son, Robert, was the principal crown prosecutor of John, second Lord Balmerino, on account of the nobleman's opposition to the king's religious policy. In January 1635 the archbishop, by now in his seventieth year, combined the two most powerful offices in the Scottish church and state in his person after he was appointed chancellor of the kingdom. Nevertheless Spottiswoode's influence over the affairs of the crown was evidently on the wane. Not unexpectedly he was involved in the preparation of the new book of canons in 1635 and 1636 and in the innovative Scottish prayer book, which was in circulation by the winter of 1636–7. Nevertheless, the impetus behind their introduction lay with the king and the archbishop of Canterbury, William Laud. Although loyalty and duty to the crown compelled Spottiswoode to implement the highly controversial canonical and liturgical alterations, these were done against his better judgement. Indeed, he had intimated to both Charles and Laud that the Scottish church and nation were ill-prepared, and unlikely to accept these new measures without a fight. In February 1638 he reputedly intimated to the privy council that the aberrant imposition of the prayer book was ill-conceived and should be shelved forthwith. In spite of his overtures to dampen the flames which threatened to raze the episcopal edifice to the ground, his career ended in failure and ignominy. His attempts to mediate between the crown and the covenanting government after the revolution of 1637–8 having fared no better, he was forced to seek exile in England, where he lived out the remaining months of his eventful life.

Having made his will at Newcastle in January 1639, Spottiswoode died in London on 26 November. In spite of his expressed desire to be buried alongside his late wife at Dairsie he was interred at St Benedict's Chapel in Westminster Abbey. The day after his death his *History of the church and state of Scotland from the year of Our Lord 203 to the end of the reign of King James VI, 1625*, was presented to Charles I by John Maxwell, the bishop of Ross. Ironically, the archbishop's *magnum opus* was not published until 1655, during the Cromwellian interregnum. The *History* was unquestionably an apologia for the royalist and episcopal cause in Scotland. Its title is somewhat misleading since its spotlight is largely focused on the reign of the 'British Solomon', James VI and I, who commissioned the work. In contrast to the compositions of his presbyterian detractors, Spottiswoode's *History* is a great deal more guarded and temperate in its use of language. His partisanship, however, is palpably manifest, and his apparent moderation should not obscure the obvious point that the archbishop, unlike his persecuted opponents, could afford to be magnanimous during the years of its compilation. A. S. Wayne Pearce

Sources A. S. W. Pearce, 'John Spottiswoode, Jacobean archbishop and statesman', PhD diss., University of Stirling, 1998 · A. S. W. Pearce, *John Spottiswoode: Jacobean archbishop and statesman* [forthcoming] · J. Spottiswood, *The history of the Church of Scotland*, ed. M. Napier and M. Russell, 3 vols., Bannatyne Club, 93 (1850) ·

Original letters relating to the ecclesiastical affairs of Scotland: chiefly written by … King James the Sixth, ed. D. Laing, 2 vols., Bannatyne Club, 92 (1851) · R. Pitcairn, ed., *Ancient criminal trials in Scotland*, 3, Bannatyne Club, 42 (1833), 332–54 · J. Spottiswoode, *Miscellany*, 1 (1844), 31–62, 65–87 · J. Cooper, 'Archbishop Spottiswoode, 1565–1639', *Transactions of the Glasgow Archaeological Society*, new ser., 7 (1924), 79–104 · A. I. Dunlop, 'John Spottiswoode, 1565–1639', *Fathers of the kirk*, ed. R. S. Wright (1960), 48–61 · A. L. Birchler, 'Archbishop John Spottiswoode: chancellor of Scotland, 1635–1638', *Church History*, 39 (1970), 317–26 · M. Ash, 'Dairsie and Archbishop Spottiswoode', *Records of the Scottish Church History Society*, 19 (1975–7), 125–32 · J. Kirk, ed., *The records of the synod of Lothian and Tweeddale, 1589–1596, 1640–1649*, Stair Society, 30 (1977) · D. Calderwood, *The history of the Kirk of Scotland*, ed. T. Thomson and D. Laing, 8 vols., Wodrow Society, 7 (1842–9) · T. Thomson, ed., *Acts and proceedings of the general assemblies of the Kirk of Scotland*, 3 pts, Bannatyne Club, 81 (1839–45) · *The letters and journals of Robert Baillie*, ed. D. Laing, 1 (1841) · M. Lee, 'Archbishop Spottiswoode as historian', *Journal of British Studies*, 13/1 (1973–4), 138–50 · A. R. Macdonald, *The Jacobean kirk, 1567–1625: sovereignty, polity and liturgy* (1998)

Archives BL, letters | BL, Burney MS 366 · NL Scot., Advocates MSS, MS 2934: 5960–5996

Likenesses W. Hollar, etching, BM, NPG; repro. in J. Spottiswoode, *The history of the church and state of Scotland* (1655) [*see illus.*] · oils, Parliament Hall, Edinburgh · portrait, Faculty of Advocates, Edinburgh; repro. in T. G. Snoddy, *Sir John Scot, Lord Scotstarvit: his life and times* (1968)

Wealth at death was owed much money (never collected): will, Spottiswood, *History of the Church of Scotland*, vol. 1, pp. cxxx–cxxxiii

Spottiswoode, John, of that ilk (1667–1728), lawyer and jurist, was born on 28 November 1667, the son of Alexander Spottiswoode (1636–1675), advocate, designated of Crumstaine in right of his first wife, Isobel, daughter of Sir John Home of Crumstaine in Berwickshire, and his second wife, Helen, seventh daughter of John Trotter of Mortonhall. Alexander Spottiswoode had a son, Alexander, by his first marriage, who died unmarried. The family had distinguished antecedents: Alexander Spottiswoode was the son of Sir Robert Spottiswood, Lord New Abbey, senator and then president of the college of justice, executed for treason in 1646, and the grandson of John Spottiswoode, archbishop of St Andrews, lord chancellor of Scotland, and extraordinary lord of session, of the old Berwickshire family of Spottiswoode of that ilk. Alexander's brother Robert was a doctor of medicine, who served in the army with the British garrison at Tangier; Robert's son, another Alexander, ultimately became governor of Virginia.

Initially schooled in Crumstaine, Spottiswoode attended the Latin school at Duns and then, from 1677, Kelso School, learning Latin and some Greek. From 1683 to 1686 he attended the University of Edinburgh under the regent Herbert Kennedy, though taking classes in mathematics from the famous Newtonian David Gregory. After graduation Spottiswoode was apprenticed on 15 December 1686 to James Hay of Carriber, writer to the signet, in his apprentice's view 'the ablest Conveyancer of the last Age' (J. Spottiswoode, *Introduction to the Knowledge of the Style of Writs*, 1708, sig. a2*r*). Though indented for three years Spottiswoode stayed with Hay until 1692, when, having determined to become an advocate, he left for Leiden in the Netherlands, where he studied law with Gerard Noodt and Ph. R. Vitriarius and chemistry with Jacob Le Mort. He returned to Scotland in January 1694 and was finally admitted advocate on 24 December 1696.

Lying behind much of Spottiswoode's conduct was a determination to restore the fortunes of his family and ensure once more its landed rank, which the vicissitudes of the seventeenth century had affected so badly. With much effort he reacquired the barony of Spottiswoode; he sought unsuccessfully to involve his cousin Alexander, the future governor, in reacquiring the barony of Dairsie (which had belonged to the archbishop); and he sought from the crown the re-grant of New Abbey (which his grandfather had been compelled to resign to the crown to endow the newly erected bishopric of Edinburgh in return for a promise of £3000, which had never been paid but which the crown had kept after the re-establishment of presbyterianism in 1690). Although parliament recognized Spottiswoode's rights to New Abbey in 1695, it was not re-granted by the crown in his lifetime. He finally purchased the superiority of Spottiswoode in February 1700, and, after his infeftment in the lands and barony in March, thereafter proudly styled himself John Spottiswoode of that ilk, although in 1724 he was still involved in litigation relating to the acquisition.

Spottiswoode's account books suggest that he was soon making enough to live in a relatively simple but gentlemanly fashion from his practice at the bar. Yet for someone with such ambitions to restore the family fortune, money must have been a scarce commodity. In 1698 he had thought of offering private classes to the apprentices of writers; he was certainly fascinated by the styles of legal documents, perhaps stimulating his antiquarian interests. In 1701 he decided to offer classes in Scots law and civil (Roman) law, which he started to teach in 1702. His classes on Scots law covered the form of process, the styles of documents, and the substance of the law. The first two of these led to his publishing *Introduction to the Knowledge of the Style of Writs* (1708) and *The Form of Process, before the Lords of Council and Session* (1711), both of which went through several editions. He relied on Sir George Mackenzie's *Institutions of the Law of Scotland* to teach the substance of the law, publishing an edition with notes deriving from his classes in 1723. In Roman law he taught a course on Justinian's *Institutes*, using as his textbook Böckelmann's *Compendium Institutionum Justiniani*. Spottiswoode's classes were initially very successful (his pupils included Duncan Forbes of Culloden), but he seems to have stopped teaching between 1706 and 1710, because of the success of a rival private teacher. After 1710 he taught only his classes on Scots law, probably teaching most years until 1722. Again his classes were successful.

Active in the Faculty of Advocates, Spottiswoode served as clerk of faculty (1697–1702, 1703–6) and keeper of the library (1702–28), Thomas Ruddiman being his underkeeper. He was also appointed in 1724 to a committee of the faculty to consider the examination of all intrants on Scots law. He also maintained a regular practice, the most noted case in which he was involved being the trial of Captain Green and the crew of the *Worcester* before the court of Admiralty. The trial was a popular event in the politically charged years before the Union, and Spottiswoode's defence raised strong feelings against him—particularly troubling to one much given to introspective self-examination.

Growing success led Spottiswoode in 1710 to marry Helen Arbuthnott (1675–1741), widow of John MacFarlane of Arrochar (younger of that ilk), and daughter of Robert, second Viscount Arbuthnott, and his second wife, Katherine Gordon. The couple had four children: John, the heir (1711–1793); Robert (*b. c.*1711/12); Helen, who married John Gartshore of Alderston; and Anne, who married James Dundas. Spottiswoode was at one time close to the famous historian and antiquary James Anderson, sharing the historical and patriotic concerns of those grouped around Sir Robert Sibbald; indeed he compiled *An Account of All the Religious Houses that were in Scotland at the Time of the Reformation* (published posthumously with his edition of Sir Thomas Hope's *Minor Practicks* (1734)). He also briefly ran a printing house. As well as a number of more ephemeral works linked to his teaching and other endeavours, including pamphlets on an election, the Union debate, and the scandal over the Jacobite medal that Henrietta, duchess of Gordon, tried to present to the faculty, he also edited and published in one volume Gilmore's and Falconer's collections of decisions of the session (1701) and his own grandfather's *Practicks* (1706). These last publications obviously reflected his ambitions in the faculty and his pride in his ancestry. His short work *Law of Elections* in 1710 was an evident *pièce d'occasion*, though reflecting his teaching to some extent. He collected a substantial library, and 2982 items were auctioned after his death.

The appointment of his pupil Alexander Bayne as professor of Scots law in the University of Edinburgh in 1722 probably led Spottiswoode to end teaching. He also seems now to have played little part in the running of the Advocates' Library, though still keeper, but he did maintain a practice before the session. He died in Edinburgh on 13 February 1728, having played by his example a major part in the successful re-establishment of legal education in the Scottish universities, though he never gained the chair to which he had once aspired. JOHN W. CAIRNS

Sources NL Scot., MSS 658–60, 2933–53, 10283–6 · NL Scot., Ch. 1492–1568 · J. W. Cairns, 'John Spotswood, professor of law: a preliminary sketch', *Miscellany three*, ed. W. M. Gardy, Stair Society (1992), 131–9 · 'Correspondence of Alexander Spotswood with John Spotswood of Edinburgh', *Virginia Magazine of History and Biography*, 60 (1952), 211–40 · bap. reg. Scot., OPR, ext. 565307 · *Scots Courant* (1700–28)

Archives NL Scot., business journals and family papers and corresp. | Colonial Williamsburg Foundation, Williamsburg, Virginia, corresp. with Alexander Spotswood · GL, letters to Thomas Bourey

Wealth at death see will, 1730, NA Scot., CC 8/8/93, fol. 86*v*

Spottiswoode, William (1825–1883), mathematician and physicist, was born in London on 11 January 1825, the eldest son of Andrew Spottiswoode (1787–1866), member of parliament for Saltash (1826–30) and Colchester (1830–31), and partner in the firm of Eyre and Spottiswoode of New Street Square, queen's printers, and his wife, Mary, eldest daughter of Thomas Norton *Longman [*see under* Longman, Thomas], the publisher. Spottiswoode passed from a school at Laleham to Eton College, from where he was expelled for letting off fireworks in the town, thus offending against a decree by the headmaster, Dr Hawtrey. Transfer to Harrow School proved a gain for Spottiswoode, since Eton had an inferior academic record, and mathematics, a subject which attracted him, was not even compulsory there. He went to Balliol College, Oxford, in 1842, graduated BA in 1846 with a first class in mathematics, and gained his MA in 1848.

In 1845 and 1846 Spottiswoode rowed for Oxford against Cambridge. While he was at Oxford, his father lost his capital through financial speculation and Spottiswoode took over as queen's printer; he showed financial acumen and steadily rebuilt the fortunes of the printing firm, which became a model company of the patriarchal Victorian type. Spottiswoode gave scientific lectures in the school set up for its employees, and throughout his life remained in close contact with the day-to-day working of the company and exercised an interest in the welfare of its employees. He always reserved time for his scientific and literary pursuits. During his annual holidays he travelled widely in other countries, and in 1856 travelled in eastern Russia, publishing in the following year *A Tarantasse Journey through Eastern Russia in the Autumn of 1856*. In 1860 he visited Croatia and Hungary.

Meanwhile Spottiswoode was pursuing the mathematical studies which had first attracted him at university, and in 1847 he issued *Meditationes analyticae*, his earliest scientific publication. This was a miscellany of thirteen chapters including such topics as the curvature of surfaces, the calculus of variations, and physical astronomy. From the first he showed 'extraordinary liking for, and great skill in, what might be called the morphology of mathematics' (*Nature*), according to his tutor at Oxford, Bartholomew Price. By his own account it was W. F. Donkin, the Savilian professor, who 'first inspired [him] with a sense of the magnificence of mathematics' (*Proceedings*, 491). After Sir William Rowan Hamilton discovered quaternions in October 1843, Spottiswoode began contributing papers on the new algebras. He was one of the first English mathematicians to publish work in continental journals and thus break the introspection which had hindered English mathematics for more than a century.

Spottiswoode's *Elementary Theorems Relating to Determinants* (1851) was the first attempt to bring together the main ideas on this topic and to present them in textbook form. At the request of the editor of 'Crelle's journal' (*Journal für die Reine und Angewandte Mathematik*, published from Berlin) he remodelled and expanded this work, taking account of the rapid progress then being made in the theory of determinants. The result was published in the journal in 1856. Spottiswoode's style was neat and precise, reflecting work efficiently executed. His attraction to determinants owed much to his aesthetic sense of symmetry. Like many mathematicians of this period his interests were wide, and he also published on invariant theory, geometry, and the calculus of operations. His high rank as a mathematician was mainly the result of his series of memoirs on the contact of curves and surfaces, contributed to the *Philosophical Transactions* of 1862 and subsequent years. On 27 April 1861 Spottiswoode married Eliza Taylor Arbuthnot, of Bexley, Kent, the eldest daughter of William Urquhart Arbuthnot, member of the Council for India. Their at-homes in Grosvenor Place, held at the height of the London season, attracted the cream of Victorian science and cabinet ministers alike. During these events the latest news in science would invariably be demonstrated in the laboratory which occupied part of the house.

In 1871 Spottiswoode turned his attention to experimental physical science. At first he devoted his researches to the polarization of light; subsequently he studied the electrical discharge in rarefied gases. On these subjects he gave popular lectures to crowded audiences at the Royal Institution, at the South Kensington College of Science, and at the British Association. He was constantly active in the cause of science and was a member of the ginger group known as the X-club which was founded in 1864 and met regularly in the St George's Hotel in Albemarle Street near Piccadilly, the only London club to which he belonged. An inveterate member of scientific societies, he served as an officer on many of their committees. He was elected to the Royal Society on 2 June 1853, and joined the Ethnological Society, the Royal Asiatic Society, the Society of Antiquaries, and the Royal Astronomical Society. During a difficult period in the history of the Royal Geographical Society he acted as its secretary (with Francis Galton). His financial abilities were put to good use in the cause of science—he was treasurer of the British Association for the Advancement of Science (1861–74), of the Royal Institution (1865–73), and of the Royal Society (1871–8). He served as president of the mathematical section of the British Association in 1865 and of the recently formed London Mathematical Society in 1870–72. He reached the top of the administrative side of the scientific establishment by being president of the British Association in 1878, and on 30 November that year was elected president of the Royal Society.

Spottiswoode remained president of the Royal Society until his death. He was awarded the honorary degrees of LLD at Cambridge, Dublin, and Edinburgh, and DCL at Oxford; he became a correspondent of the Institut de France (Académie des Sciences) for the geometrical section after a sharp contest with M. Borchardt in 1876. He was not only a mathematician and physicist but also an accomplished linguist, possessing a remarkable knowledge of both European and oriental languages. He translated *Jewish Literature from the Eighth to the Eighteenth Century* (1857) from Moritz Steinschneider's original, and delved into the history of mathematics and astronomy in India by reading original sources. The results were published by the Royal Asiatic Society. His scientific publications included *The Polarisation of Light* (1874), *Polarised Light* (vol. 2 of *Science Lectures*, published by the Department of Science and Art, 1879), *A Lecture on the Electrical Discharge, its Form and Functions* (1881), and about a hundred scientific memoirs in various journals.

Spottiswoode was described by a contemporary as a 'dark, grave, student like but aristocratic-looking person'. He was a member of the board of visitors of the Royal Observatory, Greenwich, and his chairmanship of a visitation was one of the last official duties he performed. He went to Italy on a short holiday to recuperate from overwork and the after-effects of a tricycle accident but after returning home contracted typhoid, and three weeks later died, on 27 June 1883, at his home, 41 Grosvenor Place. He was fifty-eight years old and his death was regarded as a national loss. In recognition of his position as president of the Royal Society and his contribution to science he was buried on 5 July in Westminster Abbey in the presence of civic dignitaries and the whole scientific establishment. A. J. CRILLY

Sources A. B. K. [A. B. Kempe], *PRS*, 38 (1884–5), xxxiv–xxxix • *Nature*, 27 (1882–3), 596–601 • *The Observatory*, 6 (1883), 231–2 • F. Galton, *Proceedings* [Royal Geographical Society], new ser., 5 (1883), 489–91 • *Encyclopaedia Britannica*, 9th edn, 22 (1887), 431–2 • *The Times* (28 June 1883) • *The Times* (29 June 1883) • *The Times* (30 June 1883) • *The Times* (5 July 1883) • *The Times* (6 July 1883) • R. A. Austen-Leigh, *The story of a printing house*, 2nd edn (1912) • J. E. Ritchie, *Famous city men* (1884), 236–49 • election certificate, RS • Foster, *Alum. Oxon.* • *DNB* • m. cert. • d. cert.

Archives Royal Institution of Great Britain, London, list of apparatus and notes • RS | CUL, letters to Sir George Stokes • ICL, college archives, letters to Thomas Huxley • RAS, letters to Royal Astronomical Society

Likenesses R. C. Belt, marble bust, exh. RA 1880, Royal Institution of Great Britain, London • J. Collier, oils, 1884, RS • G. J. Stodart, engraving, repro. in *Nature*, facing p. 597 • G. J. Stodart, stipple (after photograph by Van der Weyde), NPG • G. F. Watts, portrait, RS • T. Woolner, marble bust, RS • lithograph, NPG • wood-engraving, NPG; repro. in *ILN* (7 July 1883)

Wealth at death £187,077 19*s*. 3*d*.: probate, 15 Aug 1883, *CGPLA Eng. & Wales*

Spragge, Sir Edward (*c*.1629–1673), naval officer, was a son of Lichfield Spragge (*d*. *c*.1645) of Roscommon and Mary Legge, an aunt of George Legge, Lord Dartmouth. Spragge's grandfather had served in Elizabeth's Irish army and his father was killed as governor of Roscommon during the civil war. Little is known of Spragge's early career. He is said to have spent some time as a slave in Algiers, and it is possible that he served in Prince Rupert's royalist squadron between 1648 and 1653. He subsequently married Clara Colaert, daughter of the governor of Dunkirk. In company with Clara's brother, Spragge put to sea about 1655 in command of a French privateer, which was badly damaged by an English frigate off La Rochelle; unable to fund a second voyage, Spragge then took a volunteer's place under the royalist captain Richard Beach. He subsequently commanded the royalist privateer *Charles*, but the Dutch captured this in July 1660, losing him £10,000—or so he claimed. Spragge was always to possess a reputation for avarice, and when he entered the navy shortly afterwards, Charles II's favourite Charles Berkeley remarked 'whether it could be thought safe to put one of the king's ships into his hands, lest he should run away with her, his condition being so necessitous, and his former dealings of

Sir Edward Spragge (*c*.1629–1673), by Sir Peter Lely

no better reputation' (*Samuel Pepys and the Second Dutch War*, ed. R. Latham, 1995, 243).

Despite such concerns Spragge became captain of the *Portland* on 16 March 1661. He served aboard her until the end of 1662, becoming captain of a foot company at Portsmouth in the same year. He commanded the *Dover* from May to October 1664 before moving into the *Lion*, which he commanded at the battle of Lowestoft on 3 June 1665; on 24 June he was knighted for his gallantry in this engagement. Spragge commanded the *Royal James* from August to October 1665. By this time he had abandoned his wife and taken a mistress, probably Dorothy Dennis, with whom he had children. He made the acquaintance of Samuel Pepys at much the same time: the diarist's first impression, not yet clouded by Spragge's later involvement in faction fighting and opposition to Pepys's own patron, Sandwich, was of 'a merry man that sang a pleasant song pleasantly' (Pepys, *Diary*, 11 Jan 1666). During the 1666 campaign Spragge commanded the *Triumph* before moving into the *Dreadnought* on 27 May and fighting in her during the Four Days' Battle (1–4 June 1666). After this engagement he was appointed vice-admiral of the blue on 8 June 1666, flying his flag in the *Victory* and taking a prominent part in the St James's day fight (25 July 1666). At this time Spragge was regarded as the leading naval client of Prince Rupert and was accused, falsely, of instigating the 'division of the fleet' which precipitated the Four Days' Battle (allegedly so that Rupert would not have to share any glory with his joint admiral, Albemarle). In 1667 Spragge served as commander of a squadron attempting to secure the Medway and Sheerness against the Dutch attack on 9–10 June; in the two disastrous days which followed, he moved ashore to take command of some of the gun batteries, and subsequently led a force of frigates and fireships into battle against another Dutch incursion on 23 July. Spragge's background made him a natural scapegoat for the Medway disaster, and he was accused of being an Irish papist. However, he successfully survived a parliamentary inquiry in October 1667, throwing the blame instead onto Peter Pett.

Spragge commanded the *Revenge* in 1668, later serving as ambassador to the Spanish Netherlands from 27 November 1668 to 29 January 1669. In April 1669 he rejoined the *Revenge*, bound for the Mediterranean, where he served as vice-admiral to Sir Thomas Allin in the fleet fighting the Algerine corsairs. When Allin went home Spragge became admiral in his place (24 September 1670). His greatest success in this command was his spectacular victory over the Algerine fleet at Bugia Bay on 8 May 1671. Although the enemy vessels were in a well protected harbour, ships' boats broke the boom, enabling a fireship to enter and wreak havoc. Seven Algerine warships and three prizes were destroyed, and the battle prompted a coup in Algiers which led to the signing of a peace treaty. For his success, Spragge was rewarded with 3000 ounces of plate and a pension of £1000 p.a.

Returning to England in the *Rupert*, Spragge met a squadron under Sir Robert Holmes in the English Channel on 10 March 1672. Holmes had secret orders to attack the Dutch Smyrna convoy, and it was assumed for many years that because he was determined to claim the victory for himself, he failed to pass these on to Spragge, despite allegedly obtaining intelligence of the Dutch fleet's movements from him, and therefore did not maximize his chances of success by uniting the two squadrons. In fact, the two squadrons never communicated with each other at all, as Spragge's journal proves. Nevertheless the relationship between Holmes and Spragge was a bitter one. Holmes by then was Prince Rupert's chief naval client, but Spragge had turned against the prince and thrown in his lot with the duke of York. Spragge was reported to have said that it was for 'the king which he would choose, Holmes or him, and that it would spoil his whole service to make use of them both' (Pepys, *Tangier Papers*, 245). Spragge commanded the *London* during the 1672 campaign against the Dutch, serving successively as vice-admiral of the blue, vice-admiral of the red, and finally admiral of the blue following the battle of Sole Bay on 28 May 1672, in which he again distinguished himself. In February 1673 Spragge undertook a diplomatic mission to France to adjust the terms of the Anglo-French alliance, attending *en route* a by-election at Dover at which he was elected an MP; although the result was initially declared void, he won a second ballot, but never took his seat due to his departure for sea as admiral of the blue, flying his flag in the *Royal Prince*. He fought in the battles of Schooneveld (28 May and 4 June 1673), and was fiercely critical of the tactics of his admiral, Rupert, throughout the campaign. At the battle of the Texel (11 August 1673) Spragge ordered his Blue squadron, in the rear, to back its sails in order to resume a private battle with Tromp, apparently dating from the 1666 campaign. Indeed, among the last words in Spragge's journal, written the night before, were 'Tromp is now in the rear … he will, I hope, fall to my share in the Blue squadron tomorrow' (Anderson, *Journals and Narratives*, 330). The *Prince* was badly damaged in a three-hour battering from Tromp's flagship and shortly after midday Spragge shifted his flag to the *Saint George*. When she lost her main topmast shortly afterwards he attempted another transfer, this time to the *Royal Charles*, but his boat was sunk *en route* and Spragge was drowned.

Spragge was buried at Westminster Abbey on 23 September 1673. By his will dated 22 May 1673 he made bequests totalling £4800, chiefly to his two sons with Dorothy Dennis, William and Edward Spragge, and his daughter Dorothy. Payment of the bequests had to await a grant by the crown in January 1675 of arrears of pay and pensions totalling over £3000. J. D. Davies

Sources Pepys, *Diary* • R. C. Anderson, ed., *Journals and narratives of the Third Dutch War*, Navy RS, 86 (1946) • J. R. Powell and E. K. Timings, eds., *The Rupert and Monck letter book, 1666*, Navy RS, 112 (1969) • HoP, *Commons, 1660–90*, 3.468–9 • BL, Dugdale MSS, grant of arms, Add. MS 14294, fol. 29 • will, PRO, PROB 11/343, fols. 262–3 • J. D. Davies, *Gentlemen and tarpaulins: the officers and men of the Restoration navy* (1991) • *The manuscripts of the earl of Dartmouth*, 3 vols., HMC, 20 (1887–96), vols. 1, 3 • S. R. Gardiner and C. T. Atkinson, eds., *Letters and papers relating to the First Dutch War, 1652–1654*, 6, Navy RS, 66 (1930), 20–21 • *The Tangier papers of Samuel Pepys*, ed. E. Chappell, Navy RS, 73 (1935) • *The journals of Sir Thomas Allin, 1660–1678*, ed. R. C. Anderson, 2 vols., Navy RS, 79–80 (1939–40) • *The journal of James Yonge (1640–1721), Plymouth surgeon*, ed. F. N. L. Poynter (1963), 41 • F. L. Fox, *A distant storm: the Four Days battle of 1666* (1996) • J. S. Corbett, *England in the Mediterranean: a study of the rise and influence of British power within the straits, 1603–1713*, 2 vols. (1904) • G. M. Bell, *A handlist of British diplomatic representatives, 1509–1688*, Royal Historical Society Guides and Handbooks, 16 (1990) • Bodl. Oxf., MS Rawl. A. 174, fols. 372–84 • burial in Westminster Abbey, 182

Archives NMM, commonplace book, MS DAR/2 | PRO, Admiralty MSS

Likenesses P. Lely, oils, Inveraray Castle, Strathclyde [*see illus.*] • engraving, NMM; repro. in Fox, *A distant storm*, 166 • mezzotint, BM, NPG • oils, NMM

Wealth at death £4800 in bequests: will, PRO, PROB 11/343, fols. 262–3 • £3000 owed to him by the crown; bequests could not be made until debt received: J. R. Tanner, ed., *Calendar of Pepysian manuscripts*, 4, Navy Records Society (1922), 129–30

Sprat, Thomas (*bap.* **1635**, *d.* **1713**), bishop of Rochester, was born at Beaminster, Dorset, and baptized there on 20 September 1635, the son of Thomas Sprat and his wife, whose forename is unknown but was of the Strode family of Parham, Devon. His father was probably the man who proceeded BA of Magdalen Hall, Oxford, in 1629 and MA in 1632, was curate of Beaminster from 1631 to about 1641, and then intruded minister of Tallaton, Devon, from 1646. The elder Sprat may also have been vicar of East Greenwich, Kent, from about 1645 to September 1646, and possibly minister of Winterborne Dancy in 1649; he was buried at Tallaton on 12 May 1655.

Thomas Sprat (*bap.* 1635, *d.* 1713), by John Riley, *c.*1690

Background, education, and early career The younger Sprat was educated in Tallaton and matriculated at Wadham College, Oxford, on 12 November 1651. He was elected scholar on 25 September 1652 and took his BA on 25 June 1654 and his MA on 11 June 1657. His BD and DD followed on 3 July 1669; in 1671 he was incorporated at Cambridge. Sprat was a fellow of Wadham from June 1657 to 24 March 1670 and was elected catechist in December 1659.

Sprat's early career was literary. Among his early poems, which soon established him as a wit, were 'Ode on the English Ovid' (1657), about his new friend Abraham Cowley, and his contributions to 'Naps upon Parnassus' (1658). In 1659 Sprat published 'To the happie memorie of the most renowned prince, Oliver, lord protector' in a panegyrical volume which included work by John Dryden and Edmund Waller. Dedicated, with lavish thanks, to John Wilkins, warden of Wadham, it was reprinted in 1682 under the curious title, 'To the happy memory of the late usurper', and appeared in a fifth edition in 1703. The poem was later held against him, yet it may reflect Sprat's wish to impress a useful patron more than his true political beliefs, since in 1659 he also published 'The Plague of Athens'. An allegory on the English revolution the poem turns the plague of the Peloponnesian War into England's sin of disobedience and denounces the 'irreligion' and 'tyrannous … pain'. The style, imitative of Cowley, brought Sprat much praise and earned him the nickname Pindaric. It was reprinted some seven times by 1709. Sprat also vilified the army in a contemporary letter to his friend Christopher Wren. On 20 October 1660 Sprat was installed in the Carlton-cum-Thurlby prebend at Lincoln and, probably on 10 March 1661, he was ordained priest. Through Cowley, Sprat met George Villiers, second duke of Buckingham, whom Sprat served as chaplain from the early 1660s and was one of three trustees for part of his estate from 1675. Sprat may have helped Buckingham write *The Rehearsal*. On 27 September 1663 Sprat delivered a sermon at St Mary's, Oxford, attended by the chancellor and various lords, and on the next day gave a speech before the king and queen at Wadham College.

The History of the Royal Society In 1663, on Wilkins's nomination, Sprat became a fellow of the Royal Society. At about the same time he was commissioned to write a 'history' of the society—a public statement of its aims, methods, and achievements, that might meet criticisms of the Royal Society's limited productivity in the three years since its foundation, and quell fears that experimental science would challenge the belief structures of Restoration society. Neither before nor after writing the *History* did Sprat demonstrate any interest in natural philosophy, even though he remained a member of the society until his death. His post as Buckingham's chaplain afforded him the leisure to write the *History*. Sprat's own motivation was probably that the commission allowed him to display his literary talents and associate himself with a company that afforded a chance to redeem himself politically and perhaps advance his career. The *History* was doubtless heavily influenced by Wilkins, the overseer of the project, but Sprat also built on earlier comments by Abraham Cowley, John Evelyn, and Joseph Glanvill. Sprat's praise of Wilkins in the *History*, often interpreted as evidence of Sprat's limited role as Wilkins's amanuensis, may have been in part the formulaic self-debasement of a client before mentor and patron and thus a trolling device for other patrons, too. As Dr Johnson said, Sprat was 'a very willing and liberal encomiast, both of the living and the dead' (*Johnson's Lives of the Poets*, 2.41).

By November 1664 the *History* was reportedly almost finished and parts of it were probably printed shortly thereafter, but Henry Oldenburg was concerned that it provided insufficient evidence of the society's scientific productivity. In December 1664, therefore, the council of the society established a committee to select pertinent materials for inclusion. These appear as edited versions of fourteen papers read to the society between 1661 and 1664. The technological bent of all the papers expressed the society's wish to establish itself as of immediate, practical assistance to the nation. A further committee was established in May 1665 to review Sprat's text; Wilkins served on both committees. In 1667 Wilkins also produced an abridgement of the society's statutes for inclusion in the *History*.

The council's interventions were a response to Samuel Sorbière's *Relation d'un voyage en Angleterre* (May 1664). While generally complimentary to the Royal Society (of which he was a fellow), Sorbière criticized certain English institutions and implicitly challenged England's leadership in natural philosophy. Charles II forbade the Royal Society to answer the *Relation*. None the less, conscious that a failure to reply might jeopardize the society's prestige and support, Sprat set aside the *History* to write the very critical and unfair *Observations on Monsieur de Sorbier's 'Voyage into England'* (1665), addressed as a letter to Christopher Wren. Sprat twisted Sorbière's comments to permit a more vehement defence. He challenged Sorbière's sketch of Hobbes and Bacon, emphasizing the differences between dogmatism and experimentalism, while privileging the society's Baconian methods. Sprat may have intended to distance the society from Hobbes, whose views were close to those of a number of fellows and had the potential to damage the society's reputation. He also denied that the society relied on books or on any modern authority, such as Pierre Gassendi or René Descartes. Sprat also challenged Sorbière's criticisms of England's mercantile policies. In both the *Observations* and the *History* Sprat was conspicuously silent concerning the scientific Montfort Academy in Paris, officially established in 1657, and thus a challenge to the Royal Society's chronological primacy and England's leadership. Sorbière's *Relation* may also have pushed Sprat to write the contentious third part of the *History*, apparently wholly drafted after this episode, and possibly not overseen by Wilkins or the council. The *Observations*, extensive comments on English religion and politics, thus help to place the *History* in context.

Delayed by the plague and the great fire the book finally appeared in the summer of 1667 and was presented to the society on 10 October. Sprat received the society's thanks but the *History* did not receive their imprimatur. Given the great variety of scientific methods, as well as of political–religious opinions among the fellows, any attempt to portray a corporate ideology of the society, beyond the general language of its charter concerning experiment and utility, was bound to be inaccurate. Sprat portrayed the society as an ideology-free collection of Baconian empiricists, interested only in the discovery and beneficial application of nature's secrets, and uninterested, at least for the present, in theorizing or in establishing laws. In combining a rationalist theology, Anglican and monarchist history, and a normative structure of scientific truth the *History* represented a proclamation (if not an actualization) of a broad consensus in early Restoration cultural politics.

The *History* is divided into three parts. The first part offers an extended critique of various approaches to natural philosophy from ancient times to the current day. Sprat presents three main categories: first, scholastics, but also those moderns who having abandoned Aristotle established another ancient such as Epicurus as the new authority; second, those, principally the Cartesians, who sought to establish a modern authority; third, the modern experimenters. The second part of the *History* provides an explanation of the origins of the Royal Society, its experimental method, and its purposes. Here Sprat argues that co-operative scientific effort, as conducted and encouraged by the society, would lessen the antagonisms that led to civil unrest, and, as it included the manual arts, provide for the economic and social betterment of humanity. The society intended a '*Philosophy*, for the use of *Cities*, and not for the retirements of *Schools*' (*History*, 76). Part three responds to particular social, cultural, and religious objections to experimental philosophy, and predicts future political and economic leadership for England based on the society's contributions. Sprat portrayed the society (and experimental philosophy) as friends of the universities and their form of learning, as well as of rational Christianity and the church, and of the state.

The *History* cannot be relied on as an accurate account of the founding, the breadth of views, or the immediate utility of the society. Sprat drew heavily on the iconic status of Francis Bacon (reinforced by Cowley's ode at the beginning of the *History*), to the point of deprecating other modern influences within the society. He also underplayed the breadth of hypothesizing and of mathematical activity in English natural philosophy in the 1660s. Sprat's construction of the society's Baconianism as almost random fact gathering (though he did criticize Bacon on this score) was contradicted by a number of the scientific 'reports' included in the *History* itself. He was also disingenuous about interest within the society in alchemy and witchcraft. Sprat exaggerated the institutional and English nature of the Wadham group as founders of the society, perhaps as a political legitimation device directed against the foreign, parliamentarian, millenarian, and non-Anglican associations of the contemporary (and overlapping) London group of experimentalists.

Sprat attempted to privilege experimentalism by pushing to an extreme the convention among scientists of emphasizing things rather than words. Reports to the society, even exchanges among the fellows, themselves constituted 'things', since they reflected the scientist's own involvement as the witness of an event and therefore offered accurate representations of nature. In order to help incorporate the society's practices (as represented) into a pre-existing cultural consciousness, Sprat in effect recalibrated the terms 'experimental' and 'witnessing' from an individualistic Christian experience to a formal methodological tool for assessing and assimilating single experiences, involving rules and order. 'Truth' was established through demonstrations at the society's meetings to members of the higher social orders, who were better equipped to reliably construct and approve 'truth'. Since this co-operative experimental process would overcome the inherent problems of error or bias in the individual experimenter, Sprat downplayed any reservations, including even Robert Boyle's, concerning the reliability of experiments. Similarly, the moderate but regulated criticism allowed at meetings was represented as a ritualized harmonization within this public science. The experimental, non-dogmatic study of nature 'never separates us into mortal Factions' and, unlike the enthusiasm and dogmatism of the immediate past, permitted fellows 'to raise contrary imaginations … without danger of a Civil War' (*History*, 56).

Sprat also associated the society with the 'universal Disposition of this Age' (*History*, 374) for a rational religion. He acknowledged the objection that concentration on secondary causes and the growing emphasis on purely mechanistic explanations reduced emphasis on a providential God. Some scientists did seem 'inclinable to irreligion' and had 'brought a discredit on *Knowledge* itself' (ibid., 375), but he argued that those wayward in religion would have held the same views whatever their profession. Experimental knowledge protected church and state against 'the wild amuzing mens minds, with *Prodigies*, and conceits of *Providences* [which] has been one of the most considerable causes of those spiritual distractions, of which our Country has long bin the *Theater*' (ibid., 362). Religion constituted 'the perfection and the crown of the Law of *Nature*' (ibid., 368). According to Sprat the church's increasing emphasis on fundamentals matched the underlying natural truths available to experimental philosophy, while the stress on morality and practical divinity paralleled the society's devotion to utility. The church and the society were thus natural allies.

To overcome remaining doubts Sprat contended that experimentalism constituted a parallel religious exercise. Experimentalism and England's protestant church both dated from, and were defined by, a reformation, that is, an attempt to return to the basic 'things' of nature or 'the plain and unquestion'd parts of the *Word of God*' (*History*, 370). So while the fellows avoided meddling with '*Divine things*', by 'long studying of … the accidents which belong to *humane bodies*', there might, 'without question, be very neer ghesses made' concerning the operations of the soul, 'and that too, without destroying its *Spiritual* and *Immortal* Being' (ibid., 82–3). Christ himself had been an experimentalist, emphasizing the works he performed. Experimentalism even inculcated Christian virtues such as diligence and modesty. As well, the society's utilitarianism would fulfil Christ's insistence upon improving the lot of the poor. The society's admission of Romanists, far from being a mistake, opened the door to a new, non-political eirenicism based on shared knowledge.

In support of the argument for the society's utility, Sprat transformed certain long-standing, authoritative political–religious conventions, including that of England as Israel. Sprat argued that the aggrandizement of England's financial power through experiment and trade was both necessary and moral. God had designed the English to be best able to comprehend and exploit nature, a task Sprat portrayed as part of the race among nations and churches. Evidence of God's continued favour towards England was now to be located in the material realm of wealth rather than in the immaterial sphere of private revelation and sacrifice. Much of this—for example, the anti-Dutch remarks—was set in the developing language of interest, linking the Royal Society and the increasingly fiscally active state in a new political economy. There was, however, a contradiction in Sprat's dual advocacy of international co-operation and England's primacy that also mimicked Bacon.

Wilkins's general influence, in particular the *History*'s

construction of a symbiotic relationship between rational religion and natural philosophy, has led some historians to label the *History* as latitudinarian. While many positions in the *History* are similar to those expressed by people commonly called latitudinarians, they were also fairly conventional, while the term 'latitudinarian' is at least very fluid for the early Restoration. Sprat is not named in contemporary discussions of latitudinarians, nor is there evidence that he participated in comprehension schemes in the 1660s. An overtly latitudinarian stance would also not have suited some members of the society's council. Thus, no such classification can safely be made concerning the *History*, though Sprat's later views were decidedly anti-latitudinarian.

Oldenburg praised the *History* in the *Philosophical Transactions* but still, dissatisfied with Sprat's summary of the society's achievements, encouraged Glanvill to write the *Plus ultra* (1668). There was also much praise of the *History*'s plain style from Oldenburg, Glanvill, and Cowley, the last suggesting that it offered a 'judicious' style incorporating 'all the comely Dress without the paint of Art' (*History*, sig. B3*v*).

Sprat admitted that he had adopted a contentious style to respond to the society's 'Detractors' and their 'Objections and Cavils' (*History*, sig. B4*v*). Opponents reacted sharply. In seven books and pamphlets in 1670–71 Henry Stubbe vilified the society, Sprat, and Glanvill, accusing them of attacking the universities, encouraging vice, even promoting a Catholic plot inspired by the writings of Tommaso Campanella (1568–1639). Sprat's comment that a 'mechanical' education might henceforth be more suitable than the traditional 'methodical' approach brought forth a vehement defence of a humanist, word-based culture and learned values. If the society were to abandon the ancient connection between knowledge and virtue England would lack people trained to offer a rhetorical defence of true religion. Sprat was conciliatory to the work of the universities, even condemning iconoclasts who came 'as furiously to the purging of *philosophy*, as our *Modern Zealots* did to the *Reformation* of *Religion*' (ibid., 328–9), but there was much disapproval in the universities concerning the society's perceived threat to their status.

Stubbe and others also argued that a materialist philosophy fostered 'atheism', an amorphous term commonly associated with personal immorality, scepticism, secularism, republicanism, and 'scoffing'. Sprat had taken pains to dissociate the society from scepticism, but Robert South, preaching at Westminster Abbey in 1667, termed the Royal Society a 'diabolical society' for 'finding out new experiments of vice' which he tied to 'that profane, atheistical, epicurean rabble' (R. South, *Sermons Preached upon Several Occasions*, 1823, 1.375). South delivered a similar diatribe at the dedication of the Sheldonian Theatre in July 1669, at which Sprat may have been present. Meric Casaubon, another forceful critic, alleged that Sprat's mechanist philosophy too easily led to atheism. Several fellows rigorously contravened contemporary moral standards, which made the charge more credible.

Glanvill published two replies to the attacks and there were also anonymous defences of the society and of experimental philosophy, but Sprat himself did not respond. The society refused to amend or disavow the *History*. An unofficial French translation appeared in 1669 and 1670; the absence of a Latin edition (though planned) brought some contemporary complaint. Perhaps because of the society's unease the *History* was not reprinted until 1702, with subsequent reprints in 1722 and 1734.

Sprat also shared the interest of the Royal Society's council in reforming the English language. He argued against Sorbière that much of the corruption of English style in the revolutionary era had already been overcome. That the council desired to direct further reform towards 'Philosophical purposes' is evident in its instructions to a committee established in December 1664 (RS, minutes of council, vol. 1, 1663, 'The Journal Book', p. 83). Sprat did not mention this committee in the *History*, but did note that John Wilkins, appointed to guide the committee, was himself working on a 'universal character', a language based on sense experience which would encapsulate the things-in-themselves. Sprat stressed the society's method of making 'faithful *Records*' and a plain style reporting of observed 'facts', 'barely stated, without any prefaces, apologies or rhetorical flourishes' in order to avoid the 'many mists and uncertainties' that 'specious Tropes and Figures have brought on our knowledg' (*History*, 61). The ideal was to recapture 'primitive purity and shortness, when men deliver'd so many *things* almost in an equal number of *words*' (ibid., 112–13). Against the mythology-based wit of ancient poets the society would provide 'Ornaments which are *Tru* and *Real* in themselves' (ibid., 414). Thus, studying nature, which contained an 'inexhaustible Treasure of *Fancy* and *Invention*' (ibid., 413), could improve wit. The plain style required that '*eloquence* ought to be banish'd out of all *civil Societies*, as a thing fatal to Peace and good Manners' (ibid., 111).

Sprat's interest in language reform was broader than the council's. He praised Pelisson's *History of the French Academy* (1657), on which he perhaps even loosely modelled the structure of the *History*, and supported the founding of an English language academy to act as an 'Impartial Court of Eloquence' (*History*, 43). In a letter to Christopher Wren in 1663 he suggested that wit was not commonly found 'among Men of large and full and high Thoughts' whose strength lay in devising 'general Axioms'. But while axioms were more useful, 'yet they do not affect our thoughts with such an immediate and familiar Delight' (Wren, 2.259). Wit 'must apply itself to the Condition and Inclination of the Company' (ibid., 258) and, as he soon afterwards argued, in its 'true perfection' be 'plyable to all occasions, to walke or flye, according to the Nature of every subject' (T. Sprat, 'An account of the life and writing', *The Works of Mr Abraham Cowley*, 1668, sig. D*v*). That Sprat adopted a more Ciceronian style in his own sermons may indicate that the *History*'s comments on dispassionate rhetoric and mathematically plain language were heavily influenced by the council's instructions and were probably intended by Sprat to be limited to natural philosophy. Sprat's disappointment that Cowley died before undertaking his own work on style also indicates Sprat's belief that his own comments in the *History* were insufficient. Samuel Butler, a contemporary, commented on the contradiction between Sprat's rhetorical recommendations and his own literary style.

Church career, family, and politics In 1668 Sprat wrote a Latin panegyric for Cowley, who had died in 1667. An expanded English version, 'An account of the life and writing', was included in Cowley's *English Works* (1668), published by Sprat in accordance with Cowley's will, though Sprat and Martin Clifford decided against publication of Cowley's letters. Sprat's defence of Cowley's 'Mistress' was denounced by Edmund Elys. In addition to clarifying Sprat's views on language the 'Life' attempted to rehabilitate Cowley by suggesting that anyone who had 'dissembled their Counsels' under Cromwell had been 'one of the greatest helps to the King's Affairs' (Sprat, 'Life', sigs. Av–A2). Given Sprat's own difficulties this perhaps constituted a public *mea culpa*. Sprat also composed Cowley's epitaph in Westminster Abbey.

In February 1669 Charles II nominated Sprat to a prebend of Westminster Abbey. On 22 February 1670 he was instituted to the rectory of Uffington in Lincolnshire (presented by the duke of Buckingham) and, because of a legal technicality, was later instituted (April 1670) on presentation by the king. Sprat was also licensed to preach in the diocese of Lincoln. There is no evidence that he lived at Uffington, though in 1680 he brought a complex tithe case against a parishioner. In July 1670 Sprat received a licence to accompany Buckingham to France and in August 1676 he became a royal chaplain.

Sprat married Hellen Wolseley (1647–1726) in October 1676. She was of the Wolseley family of Ravenstone, Staffordshire; her will mentions her grandfather Sir John Zouch and her grandmother Lady Wolseley. The Sprats had two sons. Thomas, born on 5 April 1679, proceeded BA of Christ Church in 1701 and MA in 1704, and among his clerical posts was a chaplaincy to his father (1704). The younger Thomas Sprat died in May 1720, as archdeacon of Rochester and prebend of Westminster. The Sprats' second son, George, was baptized on 12 October 1682 and died on 1 October 1683.

In September 1679 Sprat became curate and lecturer of St Margaret's, Westminster. He developed a reputation as a preacher, emphasizing the primitive quality of the Church of England and frequently attacking enthusiasm. He was clearly regarded as a close supporter of the king. On 22 December 1680 both Sprat and Gilbert Burnet preached before the House of Commons. Burnet was thanked but Sprat was not, Burnet says, because he had questioned the Commons' sense of duty to the king. Perhaps as a result, on 14 January 1681 Sprat was installed as canon of the Chapel Royal at Windsor. In March 1681 Sprat reputedly supported James, duke of York, in a sermon to the Commons at Oxford; again he received no thanks. A sermon of 1682 argued a duty of 'Christian submission' and the impossibility of a morally just struggle against one's monarch (*A Sermon Preached before the Artillery Company of London*, 1682, 5). In the preface to the printed version Sprat contended that 'Enemies of our Church and State' disliked the sermon. He was installed as dean of Westminster on 21 September 1683, resigning his Westminster canonry and his post at St Margaret's, despite his plea to Archbishop William Sancroft noting the deanery's limited revenues and his fear that he would be unable 'to maintain any tolerable reputation, or even to avoid contempt, if I should be straightened in the support of such a dignity' (Bodl. Oxf., Tanner MS 34*, fol. 119). This may have been one of the roots of Sancroft's jibe that income was all important to Sprat. On 2 November 1684 he was consecrated bishop of Rochester, receiving a royal dispensation to retain his deanery, but he had to resign Uffington and the canonry at Windsor. In 1685 Sprat was bequeathed land worth around £25 per year on condition that he pay £200 towards the discharge of his mother's debts.

Shortly after Sprat's appointment to Westminster the king had asked him to write an account of the Rye House plot. *A True Account and Declaration of the Horrid Conspiracy* (1685) was based on the documentary evidence of the case. It condemned zeal and proved particularly hostile to William, Lord Russell, while also criticizing Burnet. That both Charles and then James II 'made divers alterations' to the text may help to explain the extreme vilification of the conspirators (Bodl. Oxf., Tanner MS 31, fol. 22*r–v*). Despite refusing James's request to write a parallel account of Monmouth's rebellion Sprat became clerk of the closet in December 1685. However, rumours that he might be translated to York, or even to London, proved inaccurate. None the less he proved one of James's loyal servants. In July 1686 he was appointed to the new commission for ecclesiastical affairs, which also had authority to investigate the universities. He was involved in the notorious case against Henry Compton, bishop of London; in October 1686 Sprat and two other bishops were named commissioners to execute Compton's offices. Sprat also assisted at the degradation of Samuel Johnson, a minister who had argued that kings were subject to English law. In 1687 he signed the address from the church to James II, thanking him for his 'royal favours' (*Seventh Report*, HMC, 504). Sprat also wrote prayers celebrating the queen's pregnancy, and, at royal command, later prepared a prayer and service for the new heir.

While many clergy refused to proclaim James II's declaration of indulgence in their churches, Sprat complied at Westminster Abbey. A schoolboy witness later recalled that Sprat had trembled while it was read. Sprat also ordered the abbey bells silenced amid celebrations of the acquittal of the seven bishops. However, on 15 August 1688 he quit the ecclesiastical commission. In his letter of resignation Sprat stressed his unwillingness to participate in punishing others who had acted 'on a principle of Conscience' (BL, Add. MS 28876, fol. 146). Following Sprat's departure the commission immediately adjourned. James soon dissolved the commission; it was possibly Sprat's withdrawal that ended the commission's viability. As the invasion by William of Orange approached, Sprat and other bishops attended several audiences with James II, advancing the cause of a free parliament. As part of a concerted effort to ensure that the bishops' advice to the king was favourably represented Sprat wrote to Sancroft on 12 November offering his own version of the meeting on 6 November ('The bishop of Rochester's relation'). On 11 December, at the Guildhall, Sprat signed the 'Declaration of Lords Spiritual and Temporal about the Cities of London and Westminster', assenting to the provisional government of peers following James's flight. He also helped to write the prayer which gave thanks that 'our holy Reformed Religion was not overwhelmed with Popish Superstition and Idolatry' (*LondG*, 2409, 13 Dec 1688).

In January 1689 Sprat, who preferred a regency, opposed the argument in the Lords that James had abdicated. Yet in the same month he wrote prayers for William stressing gratitude for delivery from popery and the maintenance of England's liberty, as well as decrying further sedition in the state or schism in the church. Sprat's political malleability and public refashioning are again visible in the claims he made in two explanatory letters of his conduct, addressed to Charles Sackville, earl of Dorset and Middlesex, and published in February and March 1689. In the first letter Sprat claimed to have defended the English clergy against the ecclesiastical commission and to have protected Compton and the universities. In quitting the commission, and so in opposing the 'Counsels of Popery then prevailing', he had put himself under the king's 'severe displeasure' (*A Letter from the Bishop of Rochester*, 18). He also recorded his pleasure at being on the 'popular' side for the first time since the Restoration. In the second letter he apologized for his attack on Russell and offered a general defence of his recent actions. He again claimed to have defended the clergy 'from the violent Persecutions of the Popish party', opposed the dispensing power, and called for a free parliament (*Second Letter*, 15). He insisted that the established church had both saved England and suffered most. It was finally the trial of the seven bishops which had taught him 'what unalterable Bounds the Law has fix'd between the Just Prerogatives of the Crown, and the Legal Rights of the Subject' (ibid., 18). He proposed moderation towards those—such as himself—who 'happen'd to be employed in the late Times' (ibid., 59). Two anonymous replies of April and May 1689 attacked Sprat's credibility and called for punishment. Gilbert Burnet said that George, Baron Jeffreys, a co-commissioner, charged that Sprat himself had incited extremism.

On 4 March Sprat took the oath of allegiance to William III and Mary II and on 11 April brought the crowns to the new monarchs and bore the chalice in the coronation ceremony. He was also appointed to a new ecclesiastical commission, established in September 1689, primarily to make the liturgy and prayer book more broadly acceptable. Sprat hosted the new commission at the Jerusalem Chamber in October and November 1689, even though he questioned its legality and soon ceased attending. In concert with Simon Patrick and Compton he suggested some revisions to the office of 5 November. His sermon preached before William and Mary on Good Friday 1690 was published 'by Their Majesties Command'.

In 1692 Sprat, John Churchill, earl of Marlborough, James Cecil, earl of Salisbury, Sancroft, and others, were the intended victims of a plot devised by Robert Young and Stephen Blackhead. Sprat was arrested and examined by the privy council on suspicion of conspiring to restore James II. After ten days' confinement he was released to his residence but was placed under armed guard. At an inquiry on 10 June Sprat confronted Blackhead, who confessed. Each year thereafter Sprat celebrated 13 June, the date of his discharge, as a day of deliverance. Sancroft encouraged William Lloyd to urge Sprat to 'draw up the Narrative' (LPL, MS 3894, fol. 61). The result was *A Relation of the Late Wicked Contrivance of Stephen Blackhead and Robert Young* (1692) and *A Second Part of the Relation* (1692). The *Relation* also provides some personal detail, mentioning Sprat's weak eyes and asserting his methodical record keeping. Sancroft believed that Sprat's 'quick & ready Witt & Memory' kept him from being 'clapt into prison' (ibid., fol. 63).

While Sprat's attendance at the Lords declined in the 1690s he remained active. In November 1692 Sprat disallowed the epitaph for the late poet laureate, Thomas Shadwell, on the grounds that it was too laudatory of plays to be permitted in a church. In 1694 he arranged the repair of the abbey organ at a cost of £200. He performed the office of burial for Mary II on 5 March 1695. Thereafter he was involved in a complex dispute with the College of Heralds, not settled until December 1696, concerning legal rights to the funerary decorations. In February 1696 Sprat signed a manifesto disowning any sympathy for the Jacobite plotters recently executed. While he refused to sign either the association promising revenge if William met a violent death or a proposed loyalty oath, Sprat wrote in November 1697 an address congratulating William on his safe return from Europe, and stressing again the nation's delivery from 'Romish Superstition' (*LondG*, 3344, 29 Nov 1697). Sprat was involved in 1699 in the simony trial of Bishop Thomas Watson but absented himself from court rather than assent to the punishment. In the same year he directed the rebuilding and improvement of the chapel at Bromley Palace, his episcopal residence. Sprat officiated at the funeral of William, duke of Gloucester, on 9 August 1700. He also oversaw the commencement of Wren's extensive repairs to Westminster Abbey and later persuaded Queen Anne to donate a marble altarpiece. In 1700 he arranged for John Dryden to be buried in the abbey. His treatment of the poet John Philips (1676–1709) was less generous. Certain lines on Philips's monument praised the unequalled greatness of Milton in composing blank verse; Philips had been a great admirer and imitator of Milton, but Sprat ordered the lines removed.

In a long-running dispute in convocation Sprat sided with the lower house and opposed the archbishop's right to prorogue convocation. In June 1701 he became a commissioner of the Society for Propagating the Gospel in America. While he did not attend meetings he helped support ministers, partly by sending books. He also helped prepare Clarendon's *History of the Rebellion* for publication, which began in 1702, but denied altering the content. Sprat participated in William III's funeral on 12 April 1702 and read the service at the coronation of Anne on 23 April. Rumours that Anne would make him lord almoner or primate of Ireland proved false. Sprat wrote various addresses to the new queen, including one, in April 1708, which emphasized Anne's 'undoubted Right to your Imperial crown and Dignity' (*LondG*, 4431, 29 April 1708). On 13 November 1708 Sprat officiated at the burial of Anne's husband, Prince George of Denmark. In 1709 he became one of the charitable commissioners for palatine refugees dwelling in London. In the same year Sprat was a member of a number of committees investigating the Sacheverell affair. He supported Henry Sacheverell in the Lords and voted on the minority tory side against both impeachment and sentence. He was also active in seeking funds for the repairs to Westminster Abbey and in September 1711 he became one of the commissioners for building fifty new churches in London. Burnet says Sprat was the lone bishop who in 1712 opposed the resolutions in convocation that only ministers could legally baptize but that no baptism should be repeated.

Assessment and death Collections of Sprat's sermons were published in 1697 and 1710. His writings were not systematic but his various works—including eleven sermons published between 1676 and 1694 and the lengthy *Discourse Made by the Lord Bishop of Rochester to the Clergy of his Diocese* (1695), as well as John Evelyn's notes on many of his unpublished sermons—reveal a consistent support for both political authority and for the Church of England, though he held that the church's duty was always 'to keep itself in a due Submission to the Civil Magistrate' (*History*, 370). His later works built on his comments in the *History* that he favoured a religion composed of 'sound, sober, intelligible Doctrines, in plain, practicable, rational Precepts' (*A Sermon Preached before the King at Whitehall*, 1676, 7). At the same time his sermons and political writings indicate a firmer approach on many questions as his career developed. In his *Discourse* (1695) he blamed the neglect of catechizing for the 'profane enormity of manners' (*Discourse*, 266) which had led to the civil wars.

Sprat's ecclesiastical views and his interpretation of the Reformation seem heavily influenced by Richard Hooker, perhaps as refashioned by Isaak Walton, whose work was known to Sprat. The Reformation emerges as an attempt to liberate both reason and the English throne from illegitimate subjection to the pope, rather than as primarily a doctrinal breach. While Sprat was critical of Romanist theology some way of recognizing the legitimacy of the Roman church was not untoward. Yet he moved from a denunciation of anti-Roman rhetoric as late as 1685 to a position, more political than theological, that the Church of England was 'irreconcilable with the Interests of Popery' (*Discourse*, 67–8). Sprat worried more about dissent. In his view Calvinist doctrine had been added later to an already existing *via media* Church of England. While 'comeliness of worship' (*A Sermon Preach'd before the Lord Mayor*, 1682, 4) was important the basis of faith was the word preached, though not extempore. Sprat rejected double predestination, stressing instead free human co-operation in grace and a moralist theology which downplayed theological differences. Works, while not 'meritorious' (ibid., 7), were of 'absolute necessity to salvation' (ibid., 37). While acknowledging the moral rectitude of individual dissenters he forcefully opposed changes in the church's liturgy to accommodate nonconformists. Ralph Thoresby thought a sermon of Sprat's in 1683 'too full of severity' (*Diary*, 1.157) against dissenters. Sprat also defended the Test Acts and insisted that claims of a 'tender conscience' against the church were specious (*A Sermon Preached at the Anniversary Meeting of the Sons of Clergy-Men*, 1678, 30). Typically, he hoped that one effect of the union of 1707 would be that Scottish presbyterians would 'lay aside all Bitterness and Animosity' (*LondG*, 4350, 21 July 1707).

Sprat followed a reasonably consistent neo-Stoic approach to political obligation and right. His attacks on zeal are consistent with a Lipsian desire to detach oneself from the passion that could jeopardize the existence of either the self or the state. Private interests should be subordinated to those of the commonwealth: hence his denunciation of the German radicals for having set 'inward sanctity, and Inspirations' above the public 'Obligations of Virtue, and Obedience' (*A Sermon Preach'd before the Lord Mayor*, 1682, 12). In England this behaviour had culminated in the civil war and Commonwealth. Sprat linked right-of-resistance theory with presbyterianism, denounced the idea of popular sovereignty, and denied that England had a mixed constitution. Even under an idolatrous ruler passive obedience was required: for the subject to fight 'against the lawful prince for the Cause of God' was to set one religious principle against another (*A Sermon Preached before the Artillery Company of London*, 1682, 22–3). In a dramatic reversal of the resolution of the Commons in 1629 Sprat insisted that 'whoever would subvert the State, they are mortal enemies to Religion' (*A Sermon Preach'd before the Lord Mayor*, 1682, 41). For Sprat, therefore, it was the 'glory of the *Church* of *England*, that it never resist'd Authority, nor engag'd in Rebellion' (*Observations on Monsieur de Sorbier's 'Voyage into England'*, 1665, 114). Yet his common emphasis on 'prudence' drew the line at what Lipsian neo-Stoicism termed 'great deceit' (ibid., 79–80). His explanation for quitting James's ecclesiastical commission was at least consistent with his earlier opinion that 'Law, and … the strict rules of Justice' (ibid., 169–70) bound the exercise of authority. He later allowed, without ever elaborating, that those who held 'Lawful, Public Authority in Church, and State' (*A Sermon Preached at the Anniversary Meeting*, 37–8) might go beyond reproof and complaints.

In June 1712 Sprat attended the Lords for the last recorded time. On 24 February 1713 Atterbury noted that Sprat and another bishop were 'much decayed in their understandings, and have lost all spirit and firmness of mind' (*Epistolary Correspondence*, 3.317–18). On 20 May 1713 Sprat died, reportedly of apoplexy, at his palace at Bromley. He was buried on 25 May in Westminster Abbey, on the south side of St Nicholas's Chapel. A monument with a long inscription by Dr John Freind stands in the south aisle, near the west door, moved there from the chapel. Sprat's will left his small estate to his son, with a life interest for his wife; it also stressed his previous generosity to his family. His wife, Hellen, died on 26 February 1726, and was buried near her husband in St Nicholas's Chapel on 3 March. Atterbury's and the earl of Ailesbury's view that Sprat was very liberal in his hospitality but restrained in his personal appetites contrasts with other contemporary opinion about his love of good living. Sprat also faced much criticism as a time-server. Burnet offered the harsh summary that Sprat's 'lazy, libertine course of life, to which his temper and good nature carried him, without considering the duties, or even the decencies of his profession' (*Bishop Burnet's History*, 6.176) had 'brought no sort of honour' to the party he served (ibid., 4.527).

Sprat's literary style has also excited a range of opinion, his prose generally faring better than his poetry. John Evelyn praised Sprat's pulpit technique, particularly his 'never making use of notes' and his 'most pure and plain style ..., full of matter, readily expressed' (Walcott, 121). John Hughes thought Sprat's language 'united the most Charming Elegance to the strictest Propriety, and is witty without the least shadow of Affectation' (Hughes, 84). Pope listed Sprat among English prose authors from whom an authoritative dictionary for writers might be drawn. Bentley called Sprat 'our English Cicero' (Bentley, xcvi), but the nonconformist Philip Doddridge, while praising Sprat's beautiful language, criticized his Ciceronianism, commenting that 'Tully is translated for many sentences together in some of his Sermons, though not mentioned' (Doddridge, 28). Dr Johnson thought Sprat's epitaph on Cowley 'too ludicrous for reverence or grief, for christianity and a temple' (Johnson, 'Essay', x–xi). Macaulay, too, regarded Sprat's poetry as that of a 'servile imitator' but insisted that his prose writings established him as 'a very great master of our language' (Macaulay, 2.748). At the start of the twenty-first century, Sprat is known almost solely for the *History*.

JOHN MORGAN

Sources H. W. Jones, 'Thomas Sprat (1635–1713)', *N&Q*, 197 (1952), 10–14, 118–23 • R. B. Gardiner, ed., *The registers of Wadham College, Oxford*, 1 (1889) • J. L. Chester, ed., *The marriage, baptismal, and burial registers of the collegiate church or abbey of St Peter, Westminster*, Harleian Society, 10 (1876) • C. L. Sonnichsen, 'The life and works of Thomas Sprat', PhD diss., Harvard U., 1931 • *DNB* • H. Aarsleff, 'Sprat, Thomas', *DSB* • Evelyn MSS and Evelyn papers, BL • Bodl. Oxf., MSS Tanner 27, fol. 13; 28, fols. 186, 233–238*v*, 239, 247, 295*r–v*, 352*r–v*, 353*r–v*, 360; 31, fols. 22*r–v*, 233; 34, fol. 119; 42, fol. 29; 147, fol. 15 • 'The journal book', 1663–81, RS [minutes of council, vol. 1] • *LondG* (13 Dec 1688) • *LondG* (16 March 1702) • *LondG* (21 July 1707) • *LondG* (29 April 1708) • Westminster Abbey, muniments • bishops' registers, Lincs. Arch., Lincoln diocesan archives, registers 33–34 • presentation deeds, Lincs. Arch., PD/1670/1 and PD/1670/15 • C. Wren, *Parentalia, or, Memoirs of the family of the Wrens* (1750), 1.254 • LPL, MS 3894, fols. 61, 63; SPG papers, vol. 6, fol. 12*r–v* • P. B. Wood, 'Methodology and apologetics: Thomas Sprat's *History of the Royal Society*', *British Journal for the History of Science*, 13 (1980), 1–26 • M. Hunter, 'Latitudinarianism and the "ideology" of the early Royal Society: Thomas Sprat's *History of the Royal Society* (1667) reconsidered', *Philosophy, science and religion in England, 1640–1700*, ed. R. Kroll, R. Aschcraft, and P. Zagorin (1992), 199–229 • P. Dear, '*Totius in verba*: rhetoric and authority in the early Royal Society', *Isis*, 76 (1985), 145–61 • B. Shapiro, *John Wilkins, 1614–1672: an intellectual biography* (Berkeley and Los Angeles, 1969) • E. Freeman, 'A proposal for an English academy in 1660', *Modern Language Review*, 19 (1924), 293 • E. Curll, *Some account of the life and writings of the right reverend father in God, Thomas Sprat, D.D., late lord bishop of Rochester, with a true copy of his last will and testament* (1715) • R. Hine, *The history of Beaminster* (1914) • BL, Add. MSS 28876, fol. 146; 61873, fol. 79 • *CSP dom.*, *1670, 1678, 1680–81, 1683–9, 1700–02* • *Fasti Angl.* (Hardy), 3.405 • *Biographia Britannica, or, The lives of the most eminent persons who have flourished in Great Britain and Ireland*, 6 (1763), pt 1 • J. Wells, *Wadham College* (1898) • *The diary of Ralph Thoresby, 1677–1724*, ed. J. Hunter, 2 vols. (1830), vol. 1, p. 157 • A. R. Waller, ed., *Characters and passages from note-books* (1908) • *Johnson's Lives of the poets*, ed. Mrs A. Napier (1890), 41 • J. Hughes, 'Of style', *Critical essays of the eighteenth century, 1700–1725*, ed. W. H. Durham (1915), 79–85 • *The epistolary correspondence, visitation charges, speeches, and miscellanies of Francis Atterbury*, ed. J. Nichols, 5 vols. (1783–90), vol. 3, pp. 317–18 • M. Walcott, *Westminster: memorials of the city, St Peter's College, the parish churches, palaces, streets, and worthies* (1849), 121 • P. Doddridge, *Lectures on preaching, and the several branches of the ministerial office* (1821), 28 • S. Johnson, 'An essay on epitaphs', *A collection of epitaphs and monumental inscriptions*, 1 (1806) • *A new and general biographical dictionary*, 8 (1795) • *The correspondence of Henry Hyde, earl of Clarendon, and of his brother, Laurence Hyde, earl of Rochester*, ed. S. W. Singer, 1 (1828), 91 • R. Bentley, *Dissertation on the letters of Phalaris* (1699) • Foster, *Alum. Oxon.* • *State trials*, 12.501–6, 1051ff. • T. B. Macaulay, *The history of England from the accession of James II*, new edn, ed. C. H. Firth, 6 vols. (1913–15), vol. 2, p. 748 • W. Scott, ed., 'Some reflections upon the humble petition ... of the Lords Spiritual and Temporal', *A collection of scarce and valuable tracts ... Lord Somers*, 2nd edn, 9 (1813), 281 • J. M. Attenborough, 'Bishop Sprat', *Westminster Review*, 159 (1903), 394–409 • *JHL*, 14 (1685–91), 113–38 • *An answer to the bishop of Rochester's first letter to the earl of Dorset, &c. concerning the late ecclesiastical commission* (1689) • *An answer to the bishop of Rochester's second letter to the earl of Dorset* (1689) • *The state letters of Henry, earl of Clarendon lord lieutenant of Ireland during the reign of King James the Second*, 2 vols. (1763), vol. 2, pp. 335–7 • *Bishop Burnet's History* • register of congregation, 1659–69, Oxf. UA, NEP/Supra/Reg. Q b, fol. 176 • *Seventh report*, HMC, 6 (1879), 504 • *The life and times of Anthony Wood*, ed. A. Clark, 1–3, OHS, 19, 21, 26 (1891–4)

Archives Westminster Abbey, muniments, papers [as dean of Westminster] | Bodl. Oxf., corresp. with Sanford, etc.

Likenesses J. Riley, oils, *c.*1690, Walker Art Gallery, Liverpool [*see illus.*] • M. van der Gucht, line engraving, 1710 (after P. Lely), BM, NPG; repro. in Cowley, *Works* (1710), vol. 1, facing p. xliv • M. Dahl, double portrait, oils, 1712 (with his son Thomas), Bodl. Oxf. • J. Smith, mezzotint, 1712 (after M. Dahl), BM, NPG; repro. in *Heads of illustrious and celebrated persons* (1811) • J. Smith, oils, 1825 (after M. Dahl), Wadham College, Oxford • G. Kneller, oils, Christ Church Oxf. • engraving (after D. Loggan) • oils (after M. Dahl), Westminster Abbey, deanery • oils (after M. Dahl), chapter house, Rochester, Kent

Wealth at death see will, PRO, PROB 11/534, sig. 147

Spratt, James (1771–1853), naval officer, a descendant of the Revd Devereux Spratt (*d.* 1688) of Mitchelstown, co. Cork, where the family settled, was born at Harrel's Cross, co. Dublin, on 3 May 1771. After several years in the merchant navy he entered the Royal Navy as a volunteer in 1796, served on the coast of Guinea and in the West Indies, was rated a midshipman on the *Bellona*, and was present at the battle of Copenhagen on 2 April 1801. In 1803 he was rated master's mate on the *Defiance* with Captain Philip Durham, taking part in the action off Cape Finisterre on 22 July 1805 and in the battle of Trafalgar on 21 October. The *Defiance* had been for some time engaged with the

French *Aigle* (74 guns), whose fire had almost ceased, and Durham wished to board her. However, the wind failed, and Spratt, who had volunteered to lead the boarders but was unable to do so from the ship, and finding that all the boats were disabled, called to his men to follow him, dashed overboard, and, with his cutlass between his teeth, swam to the *Aigle*. His men had not heard or not understood, and when Spratt arrived alongside the *Aigle* he found himself alone. He would not, however, turn back; climbing up the rudder chains, he got in through a gunroom stern-port and succeeded in getting onto the poop. Here he was attacked by three men with fixed bayonets. He disabled two of them and threw the third from the poop onto the quarter-deck, where he broke his neck. Spratt, however, fell with him and found himself in the thick of the fight, the *Defiance* having succeeded in throwing her men on board. By the time the *Aigle*'s colours were struck, Spratt's right leg was shattered by a musket bullet, and, swinging himself back on board the *Defiance*, he was carried down to the cockpit. He would not allow his leg to be amputated, and was afterwards sent to hospital at Gibraltar, where, after he had suffered excruciating pain, his wound was cured to the point that he was able to be sent home.

Spratt was promoted lieutenant on 24 December 1805, but as his right leg was now 3 inches shorter than the left, and his general health enfeebled, he was appointed to the charge of the signal station at Teignmouth, Devon, where he remained until 1813. On 4 April 1809 he married Jane, daughter of Thomas Brimage, yeoman, of East Teignmouth. They had three sons and six daughters, of whom Thomas Abel Brimage *Spratt was the eldest son. In May 1809 James Spratt was awarded the silver medal of the Society of Arts for his invention of the 'homograph' system of signalling with a handkerchief, which formed the basis of the semaphore afterwards adopted in England. After his duties at Teignmouth he served for a year on the *Albion* on the North American station; but his wound still caused him acute pain, and he was compelled to invalid. During the early part of 1815 he commanded the prison ship *Ganges* at Plymouth, and in January 1817 he retired on his half pay and a pension of £91 5s. a year. On 17 July 1838 his scanty means were increased by his promotion to commander, and he settled in the neighbourhood of Teignmouth. Even in his last years he was a remarkable swimmer; during his service afloat he had saved, at different times, nine men from drowning and when nearly sixty he is said to have swum more than 14 miles for a small wager. His bravery at Trafalgar would have been of more service to his career had he not been so severely wounded. He died at Teignmouth on 15 June 1853.

J. K. LAUGHTON, *rev.* ANDREW LAMBERT

Sources M. Deacon, *Vice-Admiral T. A. B. Spratt and the development of oceanography in the Mediterranean, 1841–1873* (1978) · O'Byrne, *Naval biog. dict.* · *Army and Navy Gazette* (11 March 1893) · *GM*, 2nd ser., 40 (1853), 311

Likenesses watercolour, NMM

Spratt, Thomas Abel Brimage (1811–1888), naval officer and hydrographer, eldest son of Commander James *Spratt (1771–1853) and his wife, Jane, daughter of Thomas Brimage, was born at East Teignmouth in Devon on 11 May 1811. He entered the navy in June 1827, and from 1832 served in surveying vessels in the Mediterranean, first the *Mastiff* and then the *Beacon*, under Lieutenant Thomas Graves, who had trained as a surveyor under Captain Philip Parker King. Spratt passed his examination in January 1835, but though specially recommended in October 1837 for gallantry in saving a marine who had fallen overboard, as well as for valuable work in the survey, he was not promoted lieutenant until 15 October 1841. Graves had just been promoted commander but remained in the *Beacon*, as also did Spratt until 1847, when he was appointed to command the *Volage* on the same service. On 5 March 1849 Spratt was promoted commander and succeeded Graves in command of the *Spitfire*, in which he continued surveying in the Mediterranean. On 27 February 1844 Spratt married Sophia Dear, only daughter of Edward Price: they had children and she survived him.

During the Crimean War the *Spitfire* was with the Black Sea Fleet, and Spratt's ability as a surveyor was frequently utilized in laying down positions for the ships, especially in the attack on Kerch and Kinburn, and his service was specially acknowledged by the commander-in-chief. On 3 January 1855 he was promoted captain, and on 5 July was nominated CB. He made a major contribution to the strategy of the Black Sea campaigns, especially in 1855, when he was given the wholehearted support of Admiral Lyons. His surveys opened up the Sea of Azov, which, once occupied, cut Russian logistics in the Crimea. After serving on the allied council of war at Paris in January 1856 he surveyed the approaches to the Suez Canal, a project then opposed by the British government.

After the peace Spratt commanded the *Medina*, still on the Mediterranean survey, where he remained until 1863. He had no further service afloat and retired in 1870; he became rear-admiral and admiral on the retired list. From 1866 to 1873 he was a commissioner of fisheries, and from 1879 until his death was chairman of the Mersey conservancy board. Spratt died at his residence, Clare Lodge, Tunbridge Wells, Kent, on 10 March 1888.

Spratt, elected FRS in 1856, was known not only as an accomplished surveyor and hydrographer but one who contributed to knowledge of the classical and geological history of the eastern Mediterranean coasts and islands. He published *Travels and Researches in Crete* (2 vols., 1865) and several other books, and numerous papers in scientific journals. He was also important as an oceanographer, conducting pioneering if ultimately unsuccessful work on currents which brought him into contact with the scientific community. His career demonstrated the low status of surveying work and the limits placed on naval careers, however brilliant, by lack of influence.

J. K. LAUGHTON, *rev.* ANDREW LAMBERT

Sources M. Deacon, *Vice-Admiral T. A. B. Spratt and the development of oceanography in the Mediterranean, 1841–1873* (1978) · A. D. Lambert, *The Crimean War: British grand strategy, 1853–56* (1990) · J. W. D. Dundas and C. Napier, *Russian war, 1854, Baltic and Black Sea: official correspondence*, ed. D. Bonner-Smith and A. C. Dewar, Navy RS, 83

(1943) • A. C. Dewar, ed., *Russian war, 1855, Black Sea: official correspondence*, Navy RS, 85 (1945) • G. S. Ritchie, *The Admiralty chart: British naval hydrography in the nineteenth century* (1967) • O'Byrne, *Naval biog. dict.* • *The Times* (15 March 1888) • *CGPLA Eng. & Wales* (1888)

Archives NMM | Hydrographic Office, Taunton • U. Edin. L., corresp. with Sir Charles Lyell • W. Sussex RO, Lyons MSS

Wealth at death £7041 1s. 8d.: administration with will, 24 May 1888, *CGPLA Eng. & Wales*

Sprengel, Hermann Johann Philipp (1834–1906), chemist, was born at Schillerslage, near Hanover, on 29 August 1834, the second son of a landowner, Georg Sprengel. He was educated at home by a private tutor and then at school in Hanover. He studied natural sciences at Göttingen University, then took his doctorate at Heidelberg, where he concentrated on chemistry and physics, graduating *summa cum laude* on 2 August 1858; about six months later he became assistant to the Oxford chemistry professor Benjamin Brodie. In the summer of 1862 he moved to London to conduct two years' laboratory research at the Royal College of Chemistry and at Guy's and St Bartholomew's hospitals. The following year he described some innovative nitric acid detection methods at the Chemical Society, of which he was elected a fellow in 1864.

In 1865 Sprengel joined Thomas Farmer's sulphuric and nitric acid works at Kennington as a chemist. In the same year he published his first paper, on making unprecedentedly high vacua by reducing residual air in the pump chamber to no more than one millionth of its original volume by using the fall of mercury or other liquids in narrow glass tubes. Sprengel pumps, indispensable tools for a range of physico-chemical researchers, gained early publicity from the eminent chemist Thomas Graham at the Royal Society in 1866. Sprengel's expertise as glass-blower was decisive in his pump designs, subsequently used by Robert Bunsen for fast filtration, by William Crookes in developing radiometers and, from the end of the 1870s, by Thomas Edison and Joseph Swan for incandescent lamps. In 1870 Sprengel left Farmer's firm and set up as an independent London chemist. In 1871 he joined the council of the Chemical Society, on which he served for four years. Despite persistent financial problems and what he considered was widespread prejudice, he continued to pursue accurate and profitable chemical techniques. In 1873 he described a revised water-driven air-pump and also designed a U-tube for precision determination of liquid densities capable of detecting less than 8 milligrams of dissolved mineral per litre of water. The same year Sprengel developed an atomizer to spray water, rather than more costly steam, into sulphuric acid chambers, a process he developed in papers of 1887 which argued that vitriol manufacturers' worries about the feasibility of substituting water for steam at low heats were groundless.

From the early 1870s most of Sprengel's attention focused on explosives research. He investigated liquid explosives, solutions of nitrated hydrocarbons in nitric acid, which were exploded by a detonating cap. At John Hall's powder works at Faversham in March 1871 he demonstrated picric acid, a nitrated hydrocarbon rich in oxygen and thus in no need of an external oxidizing agent. When exploded with nitric acid this explosive, later named lyddite, yielded almost no smoke. His originality challenged by American competitors, Sprengel publicized picric acid in 1873; it became the standard detonating charge for artillery shells by the British army. Safety explosives then became Sprengel's speciality. He designed means of driving reactions to theoretically complete oxidation and rejected the use of water to make explosives non-combustible. In 1871 he patented mixtures of two non-explosive agents, an oxidizer such as commercially available aqueous nitric acid, and a combustible substance, normally a nitrobenzenoid which would absorb heat when mixed with the acid, though he soon let these patents lapse. The two agents could safely be transported separately, then combined and subjected to the percussion of a fulminate cap wrapped in dry gun cotton, a process he named cumulative detonation. Criticized because of the dangers involved at the moment of mixing, Sprengel proposed wrapping the materials in sheet lead or storing them under glass. His recipes for dealing with semi-sensitive explosives such as wet gun cotton, a mixture of 15 per cent water with a nitro-compound, first announced in 1873, soon became popular in military circles. Sprengel often found it necessary persistently to contest others' property claims over explosives, which he did in major publications of 1890 on the origins of lyddite and again in 1902 on cumulative detonation. His projects for solid explosives, using a moistened cake of potassium chlorate rather than nitric acid as the oxidizer, proved hard to promote in Europe. When a mixture of 79 per cent potassium chlorate with 21 per cent nitrobenzol, baptized 'Rackarock', was used by the US army in 1885 to clear a huge rock from New York harbour, Sprengel angrily claimed the prior invention of Rackarock and a range of other novel explosives such as Panclastite and Hellhoffite. These pamphlet wars helped publicize the utility of safety explosives both in military and in mining operations throughout the last decades of the century.

Often disappointed in his commercial ambitions, Sprengel was elected a fellow of the Royal Society on 6 June 1878, and in 1893 he was made a royal Prussian professor by German imperial decree. Though increasingly competing with James Dewar's method to make vacua by absorbing gases on charcoal cooled with liquid air, Sprengel pumps remained decisive resources for work such as the production of Roentgen rays and gas discharge throughout the 1890s. Sprengel continued active chemical work, including a patent for a high-temperature process for making diamonds in later 1905. He died, unmarried, at his home, 54 Denbigh Street, Westminster, London, on 14 January 1906 and was buried in Brompton cemetery.

SIMON SCHAFFER

Sources H. J. P. Sprengel, *The discovery of picric acid* (1902) • H. J. P. Sprengel, 'Researches on the vacuum', *JCS*, 18 (1865) • R. Messel, *JCS*, 91 (1907), 661–3 • *Men and women of the time* (1899) • J. C. Poggendorff and others, eds., *Biographisch-literarisches Handwörterbuch zur Geschichte der exacten Wissenschaften*, 3 (Leipzig, 1898) • O. Guttmann, *The manufacture of explosives*, 2 (1985), 225–6 • S. P. Thompson, *Development of the mercurial air pump* (1888)

Likenesses portrait, repro. in *Seventh International Congress of Applied Chemistry* (1910)
Wealth at death £952 16*s.* 6*d.*: administration, 1 March 1906, *CGPLA Eng. & Wales*

Sprenger, Aloys Ignatz Christoph (1813–1893), orientalist, was born on 3 September 1813 at 3/4 Nassereith, Tyrol, Austria, the ninth of ten children of Christoph Sprenger (1760–1835), collector of customs and storekeeper, and his wife, Theresia (1772–1850), daughter of Johann Dietrich, butcher, and his wife, Johanna. He attended grammar school in Innsbruck (1827–32) and university in Vienna (1832–6). Notwithstanding the support of the famous Austrian orientalist Hammer-Purgstall, he could not find an adequate post. Disappointed, he left Vienna in 1836 and went to London where he approached G. A. Fitzclarence, the earl of Munster. Sprenger became his secretary and contributor to his projected work, 'Military science among the Mussulmans'. In 1838 he obtained British citizenship, which was very useful for his future career. In June 1840 he graduated as doctor of medicine at Leiden with the dissertation 'De originibus medicinae arabicae sub khalifatu'.

After the death of the earl of Munster, Sprenger gained a post in the medical service of the East India Company. On 16 April 1842 he married Catharina Müller (1810–1893), daughter of John Peter Müller of Frankfurt, and in 1843 they went to India. They had three sons, of whom the eldest, Aloys, joined the public works department in India. Sprenger soon started a successful career in the educational system, focusing on the modernization of language training and the development of the native languages. From 1845 to 1847 he was principal of Delhi College. He published the first weekly magazine in Hindustani as well as an *English–Hindustany Grammar* (1845). Besides this he began to edit works of oriental authors, including al-Kasani's *Dictionary of the Technical Terms of the Sufies* (1845) and ʿUtbi's *History of Sultan Mahmud of Ghaznah* (1847). From March 1848 to January 1850 he was in Lucknow, where he examined approximately 10,000 oriental manuscripts. Since nearly all these works were destroyed in 1857, Sprenger's *Catalogue of the Arabic, Persian and Hindústány manuscripts of the libraries of the king of Oudh* (1854) is a unique document of early Hindustani poetry. It is considered to be one of the essential works of the literary history of the Hindustani language and was later also translated into Urdu.

From 1850 to 1854 Sprenger was the head of the Madrasas in Calcutta and Hooghly and translator to the government of India. As a secretary of the Asiatic Society of Bengal (1851–4) he had influence on the Bibliotheca Indica, a series in which he edited the principal works of Persian and Arabic authors, including Nizami's *Iskandarnama* (vol. 12, 1852), at-Tusi's *List of Shy'ah Books* (vol. 19, 1853–5), and others. Besides this he published twenty-three articles in the *Journal of the Asiatic Society of Bengal*, concentrating especially on early Islamic history. In 1854 his wife and sons went to Europe while he travelled for almost two years through the Middle East. In 1856 he returned to India, but when he repudiated a financial agreement with F. Boutras, a former principal of Delhi College, he was removed from all his civil posts and went back to Europe. However, the thirteen years Sprenger spent in oriental countries were not only the happiest in his life, but also of greatest influence on his further scientific works.

From 1856 to 1858 Sprenger lived near Heidelberg, where he completed his *Catalogue of the Bibliotheca Orientalis Sprengeriana* (1857), a collection of nearly 2000 manuscripts and rare lithographs, which he sold to the king of Prussia in 1858. By the late twentieth century the largest part of the collection was in the Preussischer Kulturbesitz, the state library, in Berlin. In 1858 Sprenger was asked to be professor of oriental languages at the University of Bern. During his time in Switzerland (1858–81) he published some of his most valuable works, mainly on ancient geography and early Islamic history. Besides several articles in the *Zeitschrift der Deutschen Morgenländischen Gesellschaft*, he issued *Die alte Geographie Arabiens* (1875), a work which set new standards for research on pre-Islamic Arabia.

The focus of Sprenger's interest was the biography of Muhammad. His exhaustive study *Das Leben und die Lehre des Mohammad* (3 vols., 1861–5) is mainly based on the analysis of Arabic sources which were unknown until then. Sprenger's aim was to show that the emergence of Islam was more a product of the *zeitgeist* than the act of the prophet Muhammad. The importance of this and other works lies primarily in the fact that Sprenger looked at his subject from a global perspective. This, and his insight into oriental society and its way of thinking, distinguished him from many of his contemporaries. Sprenger's theories on the emergence of Islam became, though extremely controversial, of great importance for the further development of Islamic studies. In 1881 Sprenger was divorced and returned to Heidelberg where he married Antonia (1818–1911), daughter of Dr Johann Diehl, physician, and Sofia Diehl, *née* Fleischmann. Sprenger died of influenza on 19 December 1893 at his home, Leopoldstrasse 43, Heidelberg. His ashes were buried on 22 December at the urn cemetery there.

STEPHAN PROCHÁZKA

Sources N. Mantl, *Aloys Sprenger: der Orientalist und Islamhistoriker aus Nassereith in Tirol* (1993) · D. Schönherr, 'Dr. Alois Sprenger in Indien', *Tiroler Schützenzeitung*, 5 (1850), 235–7 · *DNB* · J. Fück, *Die arabischen Studien in Europa bis in den Anfang des 20. Jahrhunderts* (Leipzig, 1955) · S. Procházka, 'Die Bedeutung der Werke Aloys Sprengers für die Arabistik und Islamkunde', *Tiroler Heimatblätter*, 69 (1994), 38–42 · 'Ein österreichischer Arabist: Aloys Sprenger zu seinem 100. Geburtstage', *Österreichische Monatsschrift für den Orient*, 39 (1913), 198–202 · M. H. Zaidi, 'Aloys Sprengers Beitrag zum Urdu-Studium', *Zeitschrift der Deutschen Morgenländischen Gesellschaft*, suppl. 2 (1974), 259–65 · C. von Wurzbach, *Biographisches Lexikon des Kaiserthums Österreich*, 60 vols. (Vienna, 1856–91), vol. 36, pp. 258–63 · A. Haffner, *Aloys Sprenger: ein Tiroler Orientalist: Zur Enthüllung des Sprenger-Denkmales in Nassereith am 19. Oktober 1913* (1913) · M. I. Chaghatai, 'Dr. Aloys Sprenger (1813–1893): his life and contribution to Urdu language and literature', *Iqbal Review*, 36/1 (1995), 77–99 · parish register, Nassereith, Austria, book of baptism III/57 [baptism] · statutory register, Köniz, Switzerland, 17/1893 [death of first wife] · statutory register, Heidelberg, Germany, 1094/1911 [death of second wife] · statutory register, Heidelberg, Germany,

8651/1893 [death] · private information (2004) [Stadtmagistrat, Heidelberg]

Archives Staatsbibliothek, Berlin, Bibliotheca Orientalis Sprengeriana | BL, letters to Sir H. M. Elliott, Add. MS 30789, *passim* · UCL, letters to Society for the Diffusion of Useful Knowledge

Likenesses photograph, 1868, Museum Ferdinandeum, Innsbruck, W 4875 · F. J. Kranewitter, bronze bust, 1913, in front of primary school, Nassereith, Tyrol; repro. in Mantl, *Aloys Sprenger*, 6

Sprigg, Christopher St John [*pseud.* Christopher Caudwell] (**1907–1937**), writer, was born on 20 October 1907 at 53 Montserrat Road, Putney, south-west London, the third child of Stanhope William Sprigg (*d.* 1932), then literary editor of the *Daily Express*, and Jessie Mary Caudwell (1872/1873–1916), a professional artist.

Stanhope Sprigg, an Irish protestant, had converted to his wife's Catholicism upon their marriage, and their three children were brought up as devout members of the Roman communion. Paula, the eldest (*b.* 1899), became a nun. Christopher's childhood was mainly spent at East Hendred in Berkshire. His mother died when he was eight, and he was sent away to the Benedictines' Ealing Priory School. His close schoolfriend Paul Beard, who with his wife, Elizabeth, became Sprigg's closest literary confidant and who edited the posthumous *Poems*, described Sprigg as greatly interested in both poetry and science even as a schoolboy.

Before he had reached fifteen Christopher Sprigg abruptly left school (family financial difficulties were rumoured, Stanhope Sprigg having lost his job at the *Express*), and moved with his father to Bradford, where Sprigg senior became literary editor of the *Yorkshire Observer*, and his son worked on that paper as a cub reporter. In 1925 Sprigg returned south to live with his elder brother, Theodore, and his wife, Vida, at Claygate, Surrey. He went through intensely religious phases—though he lost his faith 'some time before 1932'. His religious turmoils are a main subject of his poems, which he went on writing in spurts all his life. He never married.

Theodore Sprigg was the editor of *Airways*, the first British aeronautical monthly. Christopher threw himself into the burgeoning world of air-minded journalism, reviewing books and films for *Airways*, editing *Airways and Airports*, and writing short air stories for *Popular Flying*. He also found time to edit *British Malaya*. He wrote under a large roster of names—including St John Lewis and Arthur Cave. Arthur Cave's stories in *Popular Flying* were, said Captain W. E. Johns, author of the famous Biggles air-novels, 'some of the best short air stories that have ever been written'.

The Sprigg brothers were busy entrepreneurs, founding Airways Publications Ltd, running an air press agency, starting up *Aeromarine Advertising*, editing the short-lived *Work and Opportunities: the National Advertiser of British Training and Service*. Very keen, too, on motor cars, Sprigg patented in 1930 a variable-speed gear that attracted praise from the motor industry. But his main source of income in the early 1930s—the many Sprigg commercial enterprises having collapsed by then—was writing. He became, essentially, a full-time freelance. He had learned

Christopher St John Sprigg (1907–1937), by unknown photographer

to fly at Brooklands Aero Club, and he produced popular flying handbooks—*Fly with Me* (1932), *Let's Learn to Fly* (1937)—and pot-boiling celebrations of air achievements: *The Airship* (1931), *British Airways* (1934), *Great Flights* (1935). He wrote non-stop, not least a sequence of trashy and patently money-spinning thrillers (some of them, he claimed, knocked off in a fortnight or so each): *Crime in Kensington* (1933), *Fatality in Fleet Street* (1933), *The Perfect Alibi* (1934), *Death of an Airman* (1934), *Death of a Queen* (1935). *The Six Queer Things: Uncanny Stories*, edited by Sprigg, came out posthumously in 1937. But by 1935 this autodidactic hack writer, a relentless wide-reader (he was a keen member of the London Library), endlessly curious about the new sciences, especially psychology, psychiatry, anthropology, modern biology, and quantum physics, was turning to political science and educating himself in socialist texts. All on his own he became a Marxist.

In mid-1935, in Porthleven, Cornwall, this embryonic Marxist started a book to be called *Verse and Mathematics* ('a study in the Foundation of Poetry'). In November of that year Sprigg left his brother's house in Surrey to live in Poplar, in the East End of London, telling Theodore this was to seek local colour for his fiction, but actually intending to share in the proletarian life his new politics were driving him to value. He joined the Poplar branch of the Communist Party. He started learning Russian with an eye to visiting the Soviet Union. He stopped writing every day at 5 p.m. to go out on party work, flyposting, speaking on street corners, selling the *Daily Worker*. His (mainly dock worker) comrades soon lost their suspicions of this loquacious, bourgeois, horse-riding writer ally. He became their delegate on the Poplar Peace Pledge Union council. He was completely unknown to party headquarters in King Street, Covent Garden. He attended some lectures by party intellectuals—Douglas Garman and Alick West—but steered clear of their 'verbosity and dogmatism'.

But in addition to his journalism and the rest, by which he 'scratched a living', Sprigg was engaged on the serious work which distinguished him as perhaps British communism's sharpest intellectual of his time. He wrote plays and sub-Kafkaesque short stories, polishing and splitting up *Verse and Mathematics* into what became *Illusion and Reality* and *The Crisis in Physics*. *Illusion and Reality* was the first extended British attempt at a Marxist analysis of art, self, and literary history. It was conceptually rough-edged, but impressively ambitious and always suggestive, for all its adherence to Moscow's line on socialist realism and the abhorrence of modernism and popular culture. *The Crisis in Physics* boldly linked epistemological problems in science with the perceived threat to bourgeois economics. He also composed the wonderfully alert essays on aesthetics, bourgeois biology, modern thinkers, and cultic heroes (including the especially fine pieces on George Bernard Shaw, D. H. Lawrence, and T. E. Lawrence, comparable in many ways with the essays of the great German Marxist Walter Benjamin) which became *Studies in a Dying Culture* and *Further Studies in a Dying Culture*. In February 1936 the novel *This my Hand* appeared, as by Christopher Caudwell, becoming the only book so to appear in Sprigg's lifetime. It attempted, somewhat weakly, to add social engagement to his crime mode (the usual extreme violences are afforced by some religious and political background analyses, earnest psychologizings, and sentiments against capital punishment). It shows little promise for any future career that Caudwell might have had as a writer of Marxized genre fiction.

Meanwhile practical politics were commanding the attention of Spriggy, as his comrades knew him. In March 1936 he was made branch secretary. He visited Paris to see the new popular front government at first hand. In London he was arrested and beaten up by police while scuffling with Mosley's fascists in Victoria Park, Hackney. When the Spanish Civil War broke out in July 1936 he was, in common with all 1930s leftists, quite magnetized by its significance. In December that year he answered the party's call for all able-bodied men to go and fight for the Spanish republican cause. He drove to Spain the vehicle Poplar people had purchased as an ambulance (usefully this bourgeois communist possessed a passport). Once in Spain he joined up with the International Brigades, trained as a machine-gunner at Albacete, became a machine-gun instructor and group political delegate, and edited a wall-newspaper. Early in February 1937 he and his battalion moved up to the Jarama River in the defence of Madrid. On the afternoon of the chaotic first day of the Jarama battle, 12 February 1937, Sprigg died covering a retreat by his company in the face of overwhelming fascist force. His body was never recovered. The faithful Theodore had tried to have the party in London recall his brother from dangerous action as a valuable intellectual, and did eventually succeed in that by showing General-Secretary Harry Pollitt the proofs of *Illusion and Reality*. The telegram summoning Sprigg home arrived just too late.

Paul Beard's selection from the many poems Sprigg wrote appeared in 1939. By then the name Christopher Caudwell had begun to be known—through *Illusion and Reality* (1937), *Studies in a Dying Culture* (1938), and *The Crisis in Physics* (1939). Caudwell's *Further Studies in a Dying Culture* was published in 1948. He was Britain's foremost pioneer of Marxist literary theory, and gradually his renown as an inspiring, if never not chaotic cultural analyst, spread across the world. A *Collected Poems* came out in 1986, edited by Alan Young, as did a collection of previously unpublished manuscripts, *Scenes and Actions*, edited by Jean Duport and David Margolies.

VALENTINE CUNNINGHAM

Sources V. Cunningham, *British writers of the thirties* (1988) · H. Sheehan, *Marxism and the philosophy of science: a critical history* (1985); repr. (1993) · b. cert.

Archives Ransom HRC, corresp. and papers

Likenesses photograph, priv. coll. [*see illus.*] · photographs, U. Texas, Sprigg MSS

Sprigg, Sir (John) Gordon (1830–1913), politician in Cape Colony, was born at Ipswich, Suffolk, on 27 April 1830, the second son of the Revd James Sprigg, Baptist minister, and his wife, Maria Gardiner. After some schooling then employment in local insurance and shipbuilders' offices, he became in 1846 a parliamentary shorthand writer. In 1858 he travelled to the Cape and in 1861 obtained a free farm on military tenure near East London in British Kaffraria. In 1862 he married Ellen (*d*. 25 Nov 1900), the daughter of a neighbouring farmer, James Fleischer. They had a son and three daughters.

A member of the East London divisional council, Sprigg advocated the annexation of British Kaffraria to the Cape Colony, together with self-government for the enlarged colony (1865–6). In 1869 he was elected member for East London, which he represented until 1904. He supported John Molteno in the successful agitation for self-government (1872), but when Molteno became the first premier of the Cape, Sprigg attacked him for opposing Lord Carnarvon's scheme for South African confederation (1875) and for refusing to accept the findings of Sprigg's committee on the defence of the eastern frontier.

Sprigg, nominated by the governor, Sir Bartle Frere, succeeded Molteno as prime minister upon the latter's dismissal during the Cape Frontier War of 1877–8, and duly carried his defence measures, including a bill for the disarmament of the Africans by proclamation. He supported the confederation policy, harassed though he was by native wars, predominantly caused by the disarmament proclamations. Sprigg's ministry fell in 1881, nominally on the defeat of his measures for local railway construction instead of the Kimberley line desired by Cecil Rhodes, but really because of his lingering and unsuccessful war against the southern Sotho.

In 1884 Sprigg became treasurer in the ministry of

Thomas Upington, and in 1886 prime minister for the second time. In July 1890 he was defeated once more on a railway bill and made way for Rhodes. He joined the second Rhodes ministry in May 1893, and, after the fiasco of the Jameson raid, formed a cabinet in 1896. In 1897, the year of Queen Victoria's diamond jubilee, he attended the premiers' conference in London. Relying on a resolution of the house of assembly to assist the navy he offered the Admiralty a cruiser; he was enrolled as a privy councillor and received an honorary DCL from Oxford and an honorary LLD from Edinburgh, but on his return to South Africa he had to withdraw his unauthorized promise.

In 1898 Sprigg attempted to carry a redistribution bill reducing the advantage enjoyed by the Afrikaner Bond rural constituencies as against the Progressive towns, but was defeated on a motion of no confidence and appealed to the country virtually on the issue of British or Transvaal supremacy. He was defeated and had to resign. On the fall of William Philip Schreiner's ministry in June 1900, Sprigg became premier for the fourth time and governed for two years without parliamentary sanction. He was inclined to approve of a suspension of the Cape constitution as the best means of furthering the federation of South Africa. However, after Rhodes's death, in 1902, he became resolute and at the premiers' conference which took place in London that year he followed Sir Wilfrid Laurier in crushing the scheme.

Sprigg appealed to the country in 1904, but was himself rejected. In 1908 he was returned once more for East London as an independent federalist, and tried to stop the passage of the draft Union Bill. On the clause setting up the parliamentary colour bar he voted with Schreiner in a minority of two (June 1909) and was one of the signatories to an appeal to the British government to preserve the rights of non-Europeans in the Cape.

Sprigg exercised great influence during his thirty-six years in parliament. As head of a department for eighteen years he was industrious and businesslike, and as premier for thirteen years he displayed great powers of party management. He was created KCMG in 1886, GCMG in 1902, and commander of the Légion d'honneur in 1889. He died at his home at Vredenburg, Wynberg, Cape Province, on 4 February 1913, and was buried in St Peter's cemetery, Mowbray. E. A. Walker, *rev.* Lynn Milne

Sources *The Times* (5 Feb 1913) • *Cape Times* (5 Feb 1913) • *DSAB* • T. R. H. Davenport, *South Africa: a modern history*, 4th edn (1991) • L. M. Thompson, *The unification of South Africa, 1902–1910* (1960) • M. Wilson and L. Thompson, eds., *The Oxford history of South Africa*, 2 vols. (1971), vol. 2 • private information (1927)

Archives Rhodes University, Grahamstown, South Africa, Cory Library for Historical Research, corresp. and papers | U. Birm. L., corresp. with Joseph Chamberlain • University of Cape Town Library, corresp. with Henry De Smidt

Likenesses E. Rowarth, oils, probably Parliament Building, Cape Town • Spy [L. Ward], caricature, chromolithograph, NPG; repro. in *VF* (16 Sept 1897) • oils, East London City Hall • photograph, Cape Archives, Cape Town • Sunday family portraits, Rhodes University, Grahamstown, South Africa, Cory Library

Wealth at death £588 2*s*. 3*d*.: administration with will, 14 Sept 1914, *CGPLA Eng. & Wales*

Sprigg [Sprigge], **Joshua** (*bap.* 1618, *d.* 1684), Independent minister, was baptized at Banbury, Oxfordshire, on 19 April 1618, the third son of William Sprigg or Sprigge (*fl.* 1618–1652). His father had been servant to William Fiennes, Lord Saye and Sele, and was later steward of New College, Oxford. Sprigg matriculated at New Inn Hall, Oxford, in 1634 but did not proceed to any degree and went to Edinburgh University, where he graduated MA in 1639. He then returned to England to become a preacher at St Mary Aldermary, London, and after taking the solemn league and covenant was made rector of St Pancras, Soper Lane.

During the early 1640s Sprigg was an active preacher and religious controversialist. Besides his close connection, through his father, with Saye he seems to have enjoyed the patronage of Lady Willoughby of Parham, to whom he dedicated his sermon on the Song of Songs. In most of his preaching he stuck to purely religious themes, disclosing himself as an advanced Calvinist of millenarian tendencies, stressing human sinfulness and the centrality of Christ, whose second coming he interpreted alternatively as an inward experience of each individual and as a literal event in 'these last dayes' when Christ and man would be 'returned into a unity of Concord and agreement' (Sprigge, *Christus redivivus*, 59, 27). A strong advocate of religious toleration, he was almost certainly the author of *The ancient bounds, or, Liberty of conscience, tenderly stated, modestly asserted, and mildly vindicated* (1645). In his early sermons Sprigg revealed his animosity to the bishops, rejoicing that they had been 'made Cyphers, instead of making the Parliament so' (Sprigge, *Solace for Saints*, 28). He also deplored the quarrels over church government that had rocked the Westminster assembly of divines: 'And now is all that truth we expected come to a new forme of government, whether Presbyteriall or Congregational? … Is this the shaking of heaven and earth, to shake men out of an Episcopal prelacy into a Presbyteriall?' (Sprigge, *A Testimony to an Approaching Glory*, sig. B5*r*). In 1648 and 1649, because 'The world hath been witnesse of many hard speeches against me', including the accusation that he denied the divinity of Christ, he decided to publish collections of his sermons so that the world could judge for itself.

One cause of Sprigg's unpopularity in London was undoubtedly his outspoken advocacy of Sir Thomas Fairfax's New Model Army at a time when the City fathers, inspired by Thomas Edwards and other presbyterian clergy, were denouncing it as a breeding-ground of sectarian heresy. He had been hired by Fairfax to be a chaplain and member of the secretariat of the new army. In this capacity he accompanied it on its travels, and wrote a number of dispatches. At the beginning of 1647 he published *Anglia rediviva*, a day-by-day account of the army's successes during the first fifteen months of its existence. In it he provided an unabashedly providential interpretation of the New Model's unbroken string of victories. Whether it was the miraculous draught of fishes near Dartmouth, or the cannon ball that snapped the chain of the drawbridge at Tiverton, or the escape of General Fairfax from a shower of timber, stones, and sheets of lead after the terrible explosion at Torrington, 'you will easily discern a thread of divinity running through the whole proceeding of this army', he wrote in the epistle dedicatory; 'their actions have been nothing else but a copy of the wisdom, power, providence and love of God put forth in men' (Sprigge, *Anglia rediviva*, sig. A3*v*). Mindful of his obligations to his patron Saye, Sprigg also was careful to weave into his account a lengthy justification of Saye's son, Nathaniel Fiennes, who had been court-martialled for his surrender of Bristol in 1643. The apology for Fiennes was so comprehensive that it prompted Clement Walker to refer sardonically to the author as 'Sprigg alias Nathaniel Fines in his legend or romance of this army' (Walker, 1.32). Although the book relies heavily on the pamphlets and newsbooks of the period it is occasionally enlivened by Sprigg's eyewitness accounts, and the whole is shot through with his overarching vision of the New Model Army's providential role in the war against the king. The book was not a commercial success. Four months after its publication the army secretariat paid the publisher John Partridge £150 'for the losses hee sustayn'd by Anglia Rediviva' (Thoresby Society, MS SD ix, unfoliated). In 1648 Sprigg was constituted a fellow of All Souls, Oxford, and the following year he was incorporated MA. At All Souls he exercised his zeal by having a stone carving of Christ's ascension over the college gate defaced. He remained a fellow of the college until 1669.

In December 1648 Sprigg intervened in the debate in the council of officers at Whitehall over the adoption of the Leveller-inspired *Agreement of the People*. While he approved the effort to 'promote the spirituall liberties of the saints' by restraining the power of the magistrate over religion, he thought that devising a constitution for England at that moment was a waste of time; they ought rather to wait upon God who was about to 'bringe forth a New Heaven and a New Earth' (Firth, 2.85, 87).

A few weeks later Sprigg incurred the displeasure of the army high command by his forthright opposition to the execution of the king. On Sunday 21 January 1649 he preached to the members of the court of high commission on the text 'He that sheds blood, by man shall his blood be shed'. Speaking after him in support of the king's execution, Hugh Peters 'made amends' for the disturbing questions raised by Sprigg (*The Moderate*, 16–23 Jan 1649, 271). Sprigg did not give up. Barely three days before Charles went to the scaffold he wrote that 'the end of the Lord's judging is purifying not destroying'; 'To execute the King for what he did in prosecution of the War … is to shed the blood of War in Peace' (*Certaine Weighty Considerations*, 1649, sigs. B1*r*, B2*v*).

After his failure to avert the regicide Sprigg's only other known intervention in public life came on 23 December 1656 when he spoke on behalf of thirty petitioners, asking parliament to reduce the punishment of the Quaker James Nayler, who had been convicted for blasphemously imitating Christ's entry into Jerusalem. He exhorted the MPs to 'leave him to Gospel remedies, as the proper way to reclaim' (*Diary of Thomas Burton*, 1.217).

After the Restoration, Sprigg retired to an estate that he had bought at Crayford in Kent. With the death of James Fiennes, Lord Saye and Sele, in 1673 he married in 1675 that nobleman's widow, Frances (*d.* 1684), daughter of Edward *Cecil, Viscount Wimbledon. They had no children, and kept conventicles in their house. Perhaps owing to local hostility they moved to Highgate near London, where Sprigg died in June 1684, with his wife following him that same month. He was buried in Crayford church. His will showed him to be a man of substance, owning a coach and horses and land in both Crayford and Middle Norton, the latter bought with his wife's dowry of £2000. He distributed £100 to 'poore Christians' and £500 to endow a workhouse in his native Banbury (PRO, PROB 11/376, fol. 262*v*). He directed that upon his wife's death his remaining estate should descend to his brother William *Sprigg, a barrister. IAN J. GENTLES

Sources J. Sprigge, *Anglia rediviva; England's recovery* (1647) · J. Sprigge, *A testimony to an approaching glory* (1648) · J. Sprigge, *Christus redivivus* (1649) · I. Gentles, *The New Model Army in England, Ireland, and Scotland, 1645–1653* (1992) · *The Clarke Papers*, ed. C. H. Firth, 2, CS, new ser., 54 (1894) · B. Kiefer, 'The authorship of *Ancient bounds*', *Church History*, 22 (1953), 192–6 · J. Sprigge, *Solace for saints in the saddest times* (1648) · 'An accompt of contingencies disbursed since December 1646 by warrants from his excellency the Lord General Fairfax', Thoresby Society, Leeds, MS SD ix · diary of Nehemiah Wallington, 1644–8, Tatton Park, Cheshire, MS 104 · C. Walker, *The compleat history of Independency* (1661) · *The Moderate* (16–23 Jan 1649) · *Diary of Thomas Burton*, ed. J. T. Rutt, 4 vols. (1828), vol. 1 · will, PRO, PROB 11/376, fols. 262*v*–263*v* · A. Beesley, *The history of Banbury* (1841) · Foster, *Alum. Oxon.* · Wood, *Ath. Oxon.*, 1st edn, vol. 2 · All Souls Oxf., archives · GEC, *Peerage*

Wealth at death approx. £4000: will, PRO, PROB 11/376, fols. 262*v*–263*v*

Sprigg, William (*bap.* **1633**, *d.* in or after **1701**), political writer, was baptized on 9 July 1633 at Banbury, Oxfordshire, the second son of William Sprigg or Sprigge (*fl.* 1618–1652), steward of New College, Oxford, and subsequently assessment commissioner for Oxfordshire. Sprigg's elder brother Joshua *Sprigg was an Independent minister, and their father procured the rectory of Somerton, Oxfordshire, for their brother-in-law John Fenwick. After matriculating at Lincoln College, Oxford, on 2 October 1652, Sprigg graduated BA ten days later. On the recommendation of Oliver Cromwell (chancellor of the university), Sprigg became a fellow of Lincoln on 11 December 1652. At Oxford he was part of the experimental philosophy circle that included John Locke, Robert Boyle, William Petty, and Christopher Wren. He proceeded MA on 15 June 1655. His first publication, *Philosophicall Essayes with Brief Adviso's*, appeared anonymously in 1657, with discourses criticizing logicians and Galenist physicians, praising natural science, and exploring themes as diverse as melancholy, atheism, the ministry, and antiquity. The same year he was appointed a fellow of the new college at Durham, a position he held until its dissolution in 1659. On 27 November 1657 he was also admitted to Gray's Inn, and in 1659 he was incorporated MA at Cambridge University.

Sprigg's major work, *A Modest Plea for an Equal Common-Wealth Against Monarchy*, was published anonymously in September 1659 and reveals his indebtedness to Francis Bacon and especially James Harrington. In the commonwealth he espoused, offices would be filled by rotation among qualified men, with the highest officers being godly gentry. Castigating hereditary nobles, professional clergy, and lawyers as enemies of a free state, he favoured freedom of conscience as long as people kept within legal bounds, moderation, and morality. He called for the abolition of professional clergy and tithes, and for the expropriation of glebe lands for annexation to workhouses. Sprigg urged legal reform, with simpler laws, land registers, and courts in all counties, and a single, free tenure for all land, with compensation to landlords for relinquishing copyhold. Primogeniture should be replaced by gavelkind or multiple inheritance, but he would permit an eldest son to receive a double portion or the entire personal estate. Sprigg supported the decentralization of higher education, with staff rather than superfluous heads governing schools. Instead of classical and scholastic studies, the curriculum in at least some schools should stress such utilitarian subjects as riding, fencing, dancing, music, modern languages, history, politics, civil and common law, chemistry, anatomy, medicine, agriculture, and animal husbandry. In their spare time, students were to study vocational topics. According to Sprigg's friend Anthony Wood, copies of *A Modest Plea* were 'greedily bought up, and taken into the hands of all curious men' (Wood, *Ath. Oxon.*, 4.560). It prompted an anonymous response, *A Modest Reply, in Answer to the Modest Plea* (1659). Sprigg's last work, *The Royal and Happy Poverty* (1660), a meditation on Matthew 5:3, was a sermon preached at Durham; the copy Sprigg presented to Wood is now in the Bodleian Library.

At the Restoration, Oxford's visitation commissioners ordered Sprigg's removal from his fellowship at Lincoln on 16 August 1660 on the grounds that he had been improperly appointed and had not lived statutably. When he refused to vacate his chamber, they ordered his ejection on 2 October. His petition of 27 December to the House of Commons for restoration of his fellowship was unsuccessful. Returning to Gray's Inn, he was called to the bar in early 1664, and, according to Wood, rendered legal assistance to James, duke of York. Some time thereafter, Sprigg moved to Ireland and married. From 1670 to 1686 he served as recorder of the borough of Galway, where his position was unsuccessfully challenged by the former recorder John Shadwell, attorney-general for Connaught, in 1673. At Lord Kingston's recommendation, Charles ordered Ormond to appoint Sprigg first justice of Connaught in 1672. In 1682 and again in 1683 the government considered appointing Sprigg king's serjeant, but he demonstrated little interest in the position. Following Kingston's death in 1676, Sprigg served as a trustee to settle his debts. Commencing in March 1683, Sprigg received £100 p.a. from the civil list. Following the deaths of his brother and his widow the following year, he inherited their estate at Crayford, Kent, but he opted to remain in Ireland. He also leased land from the Quaker Anthony Sharp in the barony of Coolestown, King's county (co. Offaly). Sprigg sat in Galway's common council in 1686–7 and again in 1701 and in the Irish parliament as MP for Banagher from 1692 to 1699. There is no further record of him after 1701. Although his Irish career was marked by diligent service, his claim to historical significance rests on his authorship of *The Modest Plea* and his linkage of the Baconian and Harringtonian traditions.

RICHARD L. GREAVES

Sources Wood, *Ath. Oxon.*, new edn, 4.137–8, 560–61 • R. L. Greaves, 'William Sprigg and the Cromwellian revolution', *Huntington Library Quarterly*, 34 (1970–71), 99–113 • J. C. Davis, *Utopia and the ideal society: a study of English utopian writing, 1516–1700* (1981) • F. J. Varley, ed., 'The Restoration visitation of the University of Oxford and its colleges', *Camden miscellany, XVIII*, CS, 3rd ser., 79 (1948) • *The manuscripts of the marquis of Ormonde, the earl of Fingall, the corporations of Waterford, Galway*, HMC, 14 (1885), 503–13 • Commons' Journals, 8.227 • *CSP dom.*, 1671–2, 168, 173, 437; 1672–3, 420; 1673, 504, 553; 1676–7, 309–10 • *Calendar of the manuscripts of the marquess of Ormonde*, new ser., 8 vols., HMC, 36 (1902–20), vol. 6, pp. 291, 494, 516; vol. 7, p. 72 • W. A. Shaw, ed., *Calendar of treasury books*, 7, PRO (1916), 1005 • J. Foster, *The register of admissions to Gray's Inn, 1521–1889, together with the register of marriages in Gray's Inn chapel, 1695–1754* (privately printed, London, 1889), 284 • NA Ire., MS T6899 • R. L. Greaves, *The puritan revolution and educational thought: background for reform* (1969) • *DNB*

Sprigge, Sir (Samuel) Squire (1860–1937), medical editor and author, was born at Watton, Norfolk, on 22 June 1860, the eldest son of Squire Sprigge (*d.* 1877), a doctor and small landowner, and his wife, Elizabeth, daughter of John Jackson, solicitor, also from a long-established East Anglian family. He was educated at East Dereham, Uppingham School (1873–8), Gonville and Caius College, Cambridge, and St George's Hospital, London. After graduating BA in 1882 he was awarded the MRCS diploma in 1886 and graduated MB BCh in the following year.

Sprigge then worked briefly as a clinical assistant at Great Ormond Street Children's Hospital, as a house surgeon at the West London Hospital, and as a house physician at the Brompton Hospital. In addition he entered practice in Mayfair. However, Sprigge had little interest in clinical work. Instead, he cultivated his taste for letters and for the company of writers and artists, by becoming secretary to J. Russell Reynolds and, under persuasion from Walter Besant, secretary of the newly formed Society of Authors (1889–92), of which he was later chairman (1911–13). In those years Sprigge wrote articles and reviews for the medical press and short stories for popular magazines. He also made many valuable friendships at the United University and Savile clubs. In 1894 he inherited a family property in Buckinghamshire. Sprigge proceeded MA and MD in 1904.

The turning point in his career came in 1893, when Sprigge, while attending a literary congress in Chicago, received and accepted an invitation to join *The Lancet*. After a short probationary period he was made assistant editor. He had not been with it long when the editors, T. H. Wakley and Thomas Wakley, respectively son and grandson of the founder, Thomas Wakley, gave him the congenial task of tracing the origin and early fortunes of the paper; the result was a book, *The Life and Times of Thomas*

Wakley (1897). Sprigge was married twice: first, in Toronto in 1895, to Mary Ada Beatrice (*d.* 1903), daughter of Sir Charles Moss, chief justice of Ontario. There were two children: Cecil, who became financial editor of the *Manchester Guardian*, and Elizabeth (Mrs Mark Napier), the novelist. Sprigge's second marriage, in 1905, was to Ethel Coursolles, daughter of Major Charles Jones RA. Their daughter Annabel became an artist and sculptor.

Sprigge published in 1905 his Cambridge MD thesis in book form under the title *Medicine and the Public*. The senior editor of *The Lancet* died in 1907, and the junior editor survived him by only two years, during which time the conduct of the journal fell increasingly into Sprigge's hands. In 1909 Sprigge took over the editorship in name as well as in fact. He was the first *Lancet* editor not of the Wakley family. His twenty-eight-year editorship proved him a diplomat and man of the world, upholding the traditions of medicine and keeping on close terms with its leading figures. Unlike the founder of the paper he preferred urbanity to combativeness, and his advice on public medical affairs was frequently sought. As editor Sprigge placed much emphasis on the reform of medical education. His other interests included medical protection and smoke abatement. During the First World War the Belgian Doctors' and Pharmacists' Relief Fund was run from *The Lancet*'s offices. With Dawson Williams he acted to end the 'war' between *The Lancet* and the *BMJ* which had characterized the editorships of the Wakleys and Ernest Hart.

Sprigge wrote an enormous number of unsigned articles for *The Lancet*. His wit and pungency of phrase, so well known in private life, were firmly checked in these careful and balanced writings and in public speech; but flashes of them shone through his early books, *Odd Issues* (1899) and *An Industrious Chevalier* (1902), and in *Physic and Fiction* (1921). Quick judgement of people and an all-round view of situations were notable in his work as an editor; this in turn was reinforced by many social and intellectual contacts beyond the world of medicine. Never populist in his approach to medical journalism, under Sprigge's guidance *The Lancet* enhanced its reputation.

The position which Sprigge came to hold in professional life was recognized by a knighthood in 1921, and by election as FRCS in the same year and as FRCP in 1927. In 1928 he delivered the Hunterian lecture to the American College of Surgeons and was elected a college fellow. His leisure interests included wine, food, and lepidoptery. In youth and early manhood he was an accomplished sportsman, playing rugby for St George's, and football to county standard. Subsequently he became a competent fencer. Sprigge also showed considerable talent as a watercolourist and was an excellent judge of this genre.

Sprigge was a small man with an immaculate dress sense. He retained his youthful looks even in his seventies. In personality he was undemonstrative and shy, never mastering the use of the telephone. Some found him distant and impatient but he could be kind, generous, genial, witty, and humorous. He was a particularly good after-dinner speaker. Sprigge died suddenly and unexpectedly at the Middlesex Hospital in London on 17 June 1937 of a pulmonary embolism, following an operation; he was buried in Norfolk. At the time of his death he was still nominally working and still able to employ his alert and penetrating mind and to keep up his friendships. His second wife survived him. Aside from the works already mentioned Sprigge wrote *The Society of French Authors* (1889), *The Methods of Publishing* (1890), and *Some Considerations of Medical Education* (1910). He edited the *Autobiography of Sir Walter Besant* (1902). N. G. Horner, *rev.* P. W. J. Bartrip

Sources *The Lancet* (26 June 1937), 1550 · *BMJ* (26 June 1937), 1346 · *The Times* (18 June 1937) · *WW* · *WWW* · Venn, *Alum. Cant.* · *Uppingham School roll, 1853–1947* (1948) · V. G. Plarr, *Plarr's Lives of the fellows of the Royal College of Surgeons of England*, rev. D'A. Power, 2 vols. (1930) · *Annual Register* (1937) · Society of Authors, London, archives · personal knowledge (1949) · *Manchester Guardian* (18 June 1937) · *CGPLA Eng. & Wales* (1937)

Archives BL OIOC, papers as chairman of Indian statutory commission | BL, corresp. with Society of Authors, Add. MSS 56816–56817

Likenesses photograph, repro. in *The Times* · photograph, repro. in *The Lancet* · photograph, repro. in *BMJ*

Wealth at death £50,836 3*s.* 6*d.*: probate, 3 Sept 1937, *CGPLA Eng. & Wales*

Sprimont, Nicholas (*bap.* 1715, *d.* 1771), goldsmith and porcelain manufacturer, was baptized in Liège on 23 January 1715, the son of Pierre Sprimont and Gertrude Goffin, and may have been apprenticed there to his uncle Nicholas Joseph Sprimont (*c.*1678–1744). Given his knowledge of French silver and porcelain it is likely that he also trained in Paris. His presence in London is recorded in 1742, when he took on his first apprentice, James Lamistre, and in November married Ann Protin at Knightsbridge Chapel. Sprimont entered his mark at Goldsmiths' Hall on 25 January 1743, when he was working in Compton Street, Soho. In September 1744 he stood godfather to Sophie, daughter of the French sculptor Louis François Roubiliac, at the Huguenot church in Spring Gardens; this suggests that he himself was a Huguenot. It is known that one model used by him while he was proprietor of the Chelsea Porcelain Manufactory was based on a Roubiliac original—that of the painter William Hogarth's pug dog Trump, which dates from 1747–50 (V&A). In 1745 it was stipulated that a large panel of Chelsea porcelain should be incorporated into the base relief of Roubiliac's monument to Bishop Hough in Worcester Cathedral.

The goldsmith Sprimont's documented silver is rare and bears date marks for 1743 to 1747. Of the four salts in the Royal Collection at Windsor Castle (1742–3) one, supported on a crayfish, is similar to salts made in the early years of the Chelsea Porcelain Manufactory. The crayfish are so lifelike that they may well have been cast from nature. The sauceboats and stands in the Royal Collection at Buckingham Palace (1743–5), in the form of shells on dolphins, support figures of Venus and Adonis. These salts and sauceboats form part of a larger service made for Frederick, prince of Wales, on which Sprimont worked in collaboration with the goldsmith Paul *Crespin (1693/4–1770). The centrepiece of 1741–2 bears Crespin's mark but the shell support under the bowl has Turin marks and may

Nicholas Sprimont (*bap.* **1715**, *d.* **1771**), by unknown artist, *c.*1759 [centre, with his wife, Ann (right), and his sister-in-law Susanna Protin (left)]

be the work of Lorenzo Lavi, who later worked in Paris. Dominated by a central figure of Poseidon the bowl is supported by four dolphins and the raised arms of two mermaids. Four dishes that complete the service are unmarked but have been attributed to Sprimont. This royal service was evidently a complex combined effort incorporating the work of several foreign craftsmen. A payment of £149 to Sprimont, recorded in the receipt book of Charles, fifth Lord Baltimore, in January 1745, was probably for this royal service (particularly as Baltimore made an earlier payment to Paul Crespin in April 1743 for £89 3*s*.). Lord Baltimore served as gentleman of the bedchamber to the prince of Wales and may have served as his agent for this commission. Other important commissions include a tea kettle (1745), formerly in the Russian royal collection (Hermitage Museum, St Petersburg); a set of six shell-shaped sauceboats (1746–7) made for Thomas Watson, earl of Winchilsea and Nottingham (Boston Museum of Fine Arts); and the 1747 centrepiece made for the second earl of Ashburnham (V&A). The latter is in the form of a tureen supported by young goats and may have been intended for use as a fruit basket. The Ashburnham centrepiece is close in design to a soup tureen made for the duke of Somerset, dated 1740 and marked by Paul Crespin (Toledo Museum of Art, Ohio). An epergne made by the royal goldsmiths John Parker and Edward Wakelin for the duke of Bolton in 1760 has a similarly complex design. The similarities of these elaborate centrepieces suggest that Sprimont may have designed all three but close examination reveals no connection in their casting, finishing, and facture.

The Chelsea Porcelain Manufactory Sprimont's involvement with the foundation of the Chelsea Porcelain Manufactory probably dates from September 1744, when his presence in Chelsea is first recorded; he leased a house in Church Lane East, for which he took out an insurance policy. He was encouraged to venture into porcelain making by a 'casual acquaintance with a chemist' who has been named as d'Ostermann, a German (Mallet, *Dictionary*, 432). The Huguenot Charles Gouyn (*d.* 1785), a jeweller from Dieppe, was senior partner in the enterprise until about 1748, when he left to set up the 'girl in a swing' factory in the West End. In 1751 Gouyn described himself in a newspaper advertisement as 'late Proprietor and Chief Manager of the Chelsea-House'.

The earliest products of the Chelsea Porcelain Manufactory are marked by an incised triangle and include salt cellars in the form of crayfish based on a silver prototype. By 1747 Sprimont was also occupying Monmouth House, Lawrence Street, Chelsea—at that time the factory showroom—which backed onto the Church Lane property. Although production was in Chelsea sales were later conducted from a warehouse in Pall Mall, and the Lawrence Street site became a manufactory from 1749. The business was closed for a year in 1749–50 for reorganization and expansion.

Contemporary newspapers advertised the range of new stock, which was marked with a raised anchor. The earliest advertisement, of 1749, lists luxury products including tea, coffee, and chocolate services, plates, dishes, and all table utensils. Many of these pieces were based on Meissen prototypes. In 1754 porcelain toys, snuffboxes, smelling bottles, etwees, trinkets, enamel-painted watches, and porcelain hafts for table and dessert knives and forks were also listed. These pieces were marked with an anchor in underglaze red. A scent bottle and candle nozzle found on the site of the property in Church Lane East suggests that the 'red anchor' toys were made there. Such toys had been made in silver for export by Sprimont's former business associate Paul Crespin. Traditionally supplied by jewellers, such stock may have been inspired also by Sprimont's brother Jean Piers, who was a working jeweller in Liège. The Chelsea toys were intended for wholesale to jewellers, goldsmiths, toyshops, and cutlers.

The Chelsea porcelain was designed to appeal to rich, fashionable, and aristocratic clients and to replace expensive foreign imports. Clients included Queen Charlotte, who in 1763 ordered a service for her brother Duke Adolphus Frederick IV of Mecklenburg-Strelitz. About 1752–3 Sprimont addressed an anonymous plea to the government to curb the import of porcelain from the Meissen factory entitled 'The case of the undertaker of the Chelsea manufacture of porcelain ware'. Meissen was brought into the country by patrons for their own use but inevitably sold on at auction and by the London chinamen. Sprimont wrote:

> considerable parcels are now allowed to pass at the Custom House, as for private use, by which means the shops abound with new stock, and public sales are advertised at the very

beginning of the winter, and in large quantities. (Jewitt, 171–2)

About the same time Sprimont deliberately arranged to copy examples of Meissen porcelain. Sir Everard Fawkener wrote to Dresden on behalf of the Chelsea Porcelain Manufactory, asking the British envoy, Sir Charles Hanbury-Williams, to send 'over fifty or threescore pounds' worth of models for copying' (Clarke, 111). Sprimont also arranged to borrow pieces in private ownership, from Henry Fox at Holland House, Kensington. From 1756, during the Seven Years' War, supplies of Meissen porcelain ceased and even French competition was virtually eliminated. Sprimont responded by developing a line in vases in the French manner. He continued to attract financial support for his venture; Sir Everard Fawkener, a rich Turkey merchant and secretary to the duke of Cumberland, paid Sprimont sums totalling £1495 between 1746 and 1748. Fawkener held a large stock in the manufactory until 1757, when it closed for a year due to Sprimont's illness. When it reopened a gold anchor was used as the mark.

Designer and proprietor Sprimont was an accomplished draughtsman. A signed design for a tureen that bears the arms of Thomas Coke, earl of Leicester (Sprimont's landlord in Chelsea; V&A), must date from 1744–59 and could have been intended for silver or for porcelain. Another signed drawing shows two glasses on a silver dish decorated with vine leaves and grapes (Society of Antiquaries, London). Sprimont was also a skilled modeller but, except in the earliest years, it is unlikely that he had time to design and model for the Chelsea manufactory himself as well as manage the enterprise. He directed the design and modelling by recruiting the best foreign craftsmen, including the Brussels-born figure modeller Joseph Willems, who eventually left for Tournai in 1766 after working for Chelsea for over fifteen years. The decorating studio was managed by a member of the Flemish Duvivier family. In the 1760s the modeller responsible for the French-style vases may have been Flanchet, described by a contemporary as a pupil of the French court goldsmith Jean Claude Duplessis. There was a workforce of about a hundred at Chelsea during the early 1750s.

Sprimont used his own skills to promote those of the next generation. He provided training in designing and painting—'arts very much wanted here'—for thirty boys from parish and charity schools (Tait, 26–7). One of these, William Browne, described his experiences in a letter of 1772 to the earl of Charlemont:

> I served an apprenticeship to Mr Sprimont of Chelsea who … was the first person who brought English china to the perfection it now has arrived at. Under him, I was made master of the various branches of this art, and though painting was my particular department in his manufactory, yet with attention I have obtained a thorough practical knowledge of the whole process. (ibid.)

Later years A painting of a man seated with two ladies, flanked by Chelsea porcelain vases, has recently been identified as showing Nicholas Sprimont with his wife and his sister-in-law Susanna Protin. It dates from about 1759 and features elaborate porcelain vases associated with the Chelsea gold anchor period (1758–69), when the addition of bone ash made the paste better able to retain its shape during the firing process. One of these vases is closely based on a French model produced at the Vincennes factory by Duplessis. The lady carrying the pot-pourri vase—identified as Sprimont's sister-in-law Susanna—played an active part in the management of the Chelsea Porcelain Manufactory. In 1751 her signature is found on the apprenticeship indenture of Richard Dyer; in August 1769 she was signatory of the transferral of the lease on the Chelsea factory to the new owner, the jeweller James Cox. Susanna lived with the Sprimonts for the last few years of Nicholas's life, and he recognized her support by leaving her £1500 in his will. The identification of the sitter as Sprimont is reinforced by his evident ill health. Sprimont is thought to have suffered from chronic gout; his lameness is mentioned in a press notice in January 1763, as it impeded development of the manufactory.

Besides his own portrait Sprimont had a considerable collection of Italian, French, Flemish, and Dutch paintings, including works by Poussin and Watteau. These furnished his house in Chelsea and, from 1762, his property in Richmond, Surrey, on the terrace overlooking the bridge. In December 1758 he announced his intention to sell 'all his Pictures … in order to enable him to carry on his great Undertaking in the Chelsea Porcelain Manufactory till March next' (Tait, 27). This sale was cancelled and the paintings were eventually sold at Christies in March 1771, when they raised £1239. The spate of newspaper advertisements for the Chelsea manufactory that mention Sprimont's name demonstrate his ability to promote his venture.

In April 1769 a notice of sale of the Chelsea porcelain factory, including the models, mills, kilns, and presses, appeared in the London press. The finished porcelain was sold to a Piccadilly dealer, Thomas Morgan, who made a considerable profit, and James Cox, jeweller, bought all the workshops and equipment later that year. The death of Sprimont's manager, Francis Thomas, in January 1770 led Cox to sell the factory to William Duesbury and John Heath, of Derby, in the following month. The manufactory continued in their ownership until 1784, when the Lawrence Street buildings were demolished.

After Sprimont's death, on 22 June 1771, Susanna Protin married his friend the upholsterer Francis Deschamps; Sprimont was buried in the Deschamps family vault at Petersham church, near Richmond. Sprimont's wife, Ann, remarried in 1773. She described her first husband as 'a man of the most unsuspecting and benevolent disposition' (Gardner, 140). The couple had had no children. Collections of Sprimont's silver are held in the Victoria and Albert Museum, London, the Boston Museum of Fine Arts, and the Hermitage Museum, St Petersburg.

TESSA MURDOCH

Sources H. Young, *English porcelain: its makers, design, marketing and consumption* (1999) • T. Murdoch, 'The Huguenots and English rococo', *The rococo in England*, ed. C. Hind (1986), 60–81 • P. Glanville,

Silver in England (1987) · J. Fleming and H. Honour, *The Penguin dictionary of decorative art* (1977) · A. Grimwade, 'Crespin or Sprimont? An unsolved problem of rococo silver', *Apollo*, 90 (1969), 126–8 · J. V. G. Mallet, *Hogarth's pug in porcelain* (1971) · N. Valpy, 'Charles Gouyn and the girl-in-a-swing factory', *Transactions of the English Ceramic Circle*, 15/2 (1994), 318–26 · A. Grimwade, *London goldsmiths, 1699–1837: their marks and lives* (1976); 3rd rev. edn (1990) · T. Murdoch, 'Huguenot artists, designers and craftsmen in Great Britain and Ireland, 1680–1760', PhD diss., U. Lond., 1982 · F. S. Mackenna, *The gold anchor wares* (1952) · B. Watney, 'A china painter writes to an earl', *Transactions of the English Ceramic Circle*, 11/1 (1981), 48–9 · 'A painting of Nicholas Sprimont, his family and his Chelsea vases', *Les Cahiers de Mariemont*, 24–5 (1994–5), 76–95 · J. V. G. Mallet, 'Sprimont, Nicholas', *The dictionary of art*, ed. J. Turner (1996) · E. Adams, *Chelsea porcelain* (1987) · M. Snodin and E. Moncrieff, eds., *Rococo: art and design in Hogarth's England* (1984) [exhibition catalogue, V&A, 16 May – 30 Sept 1984] · H. Tait, 'Nicholas Sprimont at Chelsea, his apprentice William Brown, and the "anchor and dagger" mark', *Ars Ceramica*, 15 (1998–9), 24–33 · L. Jewitt, *The ceramic art of Great Britain*, 2 vols. (1878), 1.171–2 · T. H. Clarke, 'Sir Charles Hanbury Williams and the Chelsea factory', *Transactions of the English Ceramic Circle*, 13/2 (1988), 110–20 · B. Gardner, 'Further history of the Chelsea Porcelain Manufactory', *Transactions of the English Ceramic Circle*, 2/8 (1942), 136–41

Archives Maryland Historical Society, Baltimore, receipt book of Charles, fifth Lord Baltimore

Likenesses group portrait, oils, *c.*1759, priv. coll. [*see illus.*]

Spring family (*per. c.*1400–*c.*1550), clothiers, of Lavenham, Suffolk, has as its first representative **Thomas** [i] **Spring** (*d.* 1440). He was the first of three Thomas Springs to be associated with the late fifteenth- and early sixteenth-century East Anglian cloth trade. By the second quarter of the fifteenth century, the Springs were already a prominent clothier family: Thomas [i], with forty-nine out of 555 cloths recorded in the aulnage account for Lavenham from 1424/5, was the most important of the thirty-three clothiers listed there. Two other members of the Spring family, an Agnes and a William, also appear in the same aulnage account, each producing ten cloths for sale. In his will Thomas [i] was able to leave, in addition to 100*s.* for the fabric of Lavenham church and 40*s.* 'for tithes and oblations forgotten', his capital tenement to his widow for the term of her life, as well as £100 'to be raised from my goods and debts', and four separate tenements in Lavenham and Preston to his four children (Dymond and Betterton, appx 2, 67). Two of his children, possibly the youngest, also received £20 each; a priest was to be paid a stipend for four years to pray for Thomas's soul, twelve paupers were to receive 12*d.* each Wednesday for four years after his death, and 9 marks (120*s.*) were left for the repair of the king's highway between Lavenham and Bury St Edmunds. His widow and executor, **Agnes Spring** (*d.* in or after 1457), may also have been actively involved in the cloth trade; it seems likely that she was the Agnes Spring named in the 1424/5 aulnage account. She was summoned, in her capacity as executor, seventeen years after her husband's death, to answer at common bench for 100*s.* owed to a Great Yarmouth merchant, suggesting that the final injunction of Thomas [i]'s will, namely that the executors (who were each paid 40*s.*) should 'pay the debts which I owe', was not performed to the letter.

According to Thomas [i]'s will, he was survived by four children, **Thomas** [ii] **Spring** (*d.* 1486), Katherine, William, and Dionisia. Thomas [ii] was to take the capital tenement upon the death of his mother and was, it appears, his father's eldest son and heir. He is the only Spring listed in the 1468/9 aulnage account for Lavenham and was one of three villagers who each produced eighty cloths for sealing; only Roger Creketot, with the considerable total of 200 broadcloths, surpassed them. That Thomas [ii] continued in the successful vein of his father is evident from his own will: he left bequests of £100 each to three of his children, William, James, and Marion, and 100 marks (£66 13*s.* 4*d.*) to be distributed among 'my spinners, weavers and fullers' (Dymond and Betterton, appx 2, 68). He also bequeathed 300 marks (£200) towards the building of the church tower at Lavenham and 200 marks (£133 6*s.* 8*d.*) towards the repair of the roads; a further 50 marks (£33 6*s.* 8*d.*) were left to three orders of friars and 10*s.* for the rector of the parish to pray for his soul. The remainder of his property he left to his widow, **Margaret Spring** [*née* Appleton] (*d.* in or after 1504), of Waldringfield, and his eldest son, Thomas [iii] [*see below*]. Thomas [ii] instructed that his body be buried in the vestry, the construction of which he had himself financed and in which he now lies with his wife; their son James, who lost his life in a brawl, is also buried there. A memorial brass, known as the 'resurrection brass', survives in the vestry and represents Thomas [ii], his wife, and ten children (four boys and six girls) kneeling, in shrouds. It offers a fine representation of a fifteenth-century merchant family and no doubt, also, it illustrates the growing aspirations of the Spring dynasty as it progressed towards membership of the peerage. The memorial brass was certainly a product of successful dealing in the cloth trade, as were the donations of the Springs and others to the general fabric of the church at Lavenham. The Latin inscription requests the reader to 'pray for the souls of Thomas Sprynge, who caused this vestry to be made during his lifetime, and Margaret his wife' (McClenaghan, 65). Although the date of death of Thomas, 7 September 1486, is given on the brass, Margaret's dates remain blank but for the decade, 148—; in fact, she survived, presumably against all expectations, at least until the first decade of the sixteenth century. Like her mother-in-law, Agnes, Margaret was no stranger to business: in her widowhood she attempted to recover a debt of £16 in 1492 and, in 1504, acted as executor of her brother's will.

It is with **Thomas** [iii] **Spring** (*c.*1456–1523), known as the 'rich clothier', that the fortunes of the Spring family, at least in terms of their involvement in the cloth trade, reached their apex. The last decades of the fifteenth century and the first years of the sixteenth were a highpoint in the history of English cloth, with exports increasing at a steady rate from the early 1480s; it is also at this point that Lavenham appears to have enjoyed a measure of ascendancy over certain other centres of cloth production in eastern England. By the late 1460s over one-fifth of all cloth sealed in Suffolk was registered in Lavenham. Thomas [iii]'s involvement in the cloth trade is evidenced in the details of a general pardon granted by Henry VII in

1508 which includes specific reference to 'offences in the making of woollen cloth' (McClenaghan, 68–9); a good deal of his profits from the trade seem to have been invested in the land market. On occasion, he appears to have shaken long-established tenurial regimes. On Westminster Abbey's manor of Birdbrook, for example, Thomas [iii] was admitted to six copyhold tenements 'free of any punishment, penalty or forfeiture for waste done or to be done in any home, homes or buildings upon these premises' (Schofield, 16). Profit also gave way to piety. Evincing the success of the cloth trade, the decades either side of 1500 saw considerable building activity in Lavenham; in particular, the church, work on which was under way when Thomas [ii] died, was substantially rebuilt in this period. The late Perpendicular nave, tower, porch, and side chapels all date from the forty years after 1485. The vestry, situated to the east of the chancel and separate from this later work, was, as already noted, an early (*c.*1444) addition by Thomas [ii]. It was the clothiers of Lavenham, together with the de Vere lords of the manor, who financed this work and the Springs were in the vanguard of donors and bequeathers. Singularly important in the completion of the work was Thomas [iii]: in his will he left £200 'to the finishing of the steeple' and requested that he should be buried 'before the awter of Saint Kateryn where I will be made a tombe with a parclose therabout' (Dymond and Betterton, appx 2, 68–70). Lavish donations were made both at Lavenham and elsewhere to provide for prayers for Thomas's soul. In carrying out his wishes, his executors spent a further £847 on the church; as well as the elaborately carved parclose, this included a chapel, the 'Lady' or 'Spring' chapel. Throughout the church, bosses and carvings, depicting the merchant marks and the coat of arms (granted just before Thomas [iii]'s death) of the family, testify to the munificence of the Springs. The wealth of Thomas [iii] far surpassed that of any other villager at Lavenham: the 1522 muster roll records that, in addition to £20 worth of land, he possessed £1800 in money and was owed £2200 in debts 'sperat' and 'desperat'. Thomas's widow, **Alice Spring** (*d.* 1538), of Bocking, Essex, paid, as an individual and executor, a combined total of £66 13*s.* 4*d.* in the 1524 lay subsidy, the second largest contribution in Suffolk apart from that of the duke of Norfolk and one that helped hoist Lavenham to the position of fourteenth wealthiest town in England. When Thomas [iii] died on 29 June 1523 he held twenty-five manors scattered throughout East Anglia. Wolsey's taxation of this huge personal wealth drew comments from the poet laureate, John Skelton, in his poem 'Why Come ye Nat to Court'. He writes:

Good Springe of Lanam
Must count what became
Of his clothe makyng
Though his purse wax dull
He must tax for his wul
By nature of a new writ
My Lordes grace nameth it
A quis non satisfacit
In spight of his tethe
He must pay agayne
A thousand or twayn
Of his gold in store
And yet he payd before
An hundred or more
Which pincheth hym sore
My Lordes grace will bryng
Down thys hye sprynge
And brynge it so lowe
It shal not ever flow.
(Skelton, 'Why come ye nat to court', ll. 933–52, ed. Scattergood)

The weight of taxation, which did not bear just upon the Springs and their peers, provoked riots and, in the 1520s, Lavenham became a centre of unrest. The Springs, however, were not to be numbered among the rioters; instead, Thomas [iii], with his son-in-law, Thomas Jermyn, had acted as a commissioner for the collection of lay subsidies in 1512, 1513, and 1517, and his eldest son, **Sir John Spring** (1498–1548), was (again together with Jermyn) instrumental in restraining the populace in 1525 and 1536. Described as a 'gentleman' in the 1524 lay subsidy, John was knighted on the accession of Edward VI in 1547, a year before his death on 7 February 1548. John was executor of Thomas [iii]'s will together with Alice Spring, Thomas's widow. Alice, now widowed for the second time, had brought 600 marks (£400) to her marriage with Thomas and now also received a legacy of 1000 marks (£666 13*s.* 4*d.*). Hers is generally considered to be the last major involvement of the family in the Lavenham cloth trade; in the mid-sixteenth century, when Thomas [iii]'s younger son, Robert, retired from the cloth trade, the family seat moved from Lavenham to Pakenham. If, by the 1550s, the Springs had lost their prominence in the cloth trade, successful marriages ensured that their star did not fall. These included that of Bridget Spring, the only child of the marriage of Thomas [iii] and Alice (Thomas's other children were from a previous marriage, to Anne King), to William Ernely, son of the lord chief justice of the common pleas Sir John Ernely (*d.* 1520), and, most famously, the marriage of Margaret Spring, a niece of Thomas [iii] Spring, to Aubrey de Vere, second son of the fifteenth earl of Oxford. The rise of the family as clothiers, their accumulation of a vast family fortune, and their entry, through marriage, into the ranks of the nobility, encourage the perception of the Springs as an archetypal late medieval success story. That they chose to invest much of this wealth in church rebuilding and the care of their souls also shows them to have been of their time. The family arms were argent on a chevron between 3 mascles gules, 3 cinquefoyles or. PHILLIPP R. SCHOFIELD

Sources B. McClenaghan, *The Springs of Lavenham and the Suffolk cloth trade in the fifteenth and sixteenth centuries* (1924) • D. P. Dymond and A. Betterton, *Lavenham: 700 years of textile making* (1982) • S. H. A. Hervey, ed., *Suffolk in 1524*, Suffolk Green Books, 10 (1910) • transcript of 1522 muster roll for Suffolk, Suffolk RO, (B) J527 • *Chancery records* • *John Skelton: the complete English poems*, ed. J. Scattergood (1983) • R. H. Britnell, *Growth and decline in Colchester, 1300–1525* (1986) • E. M. Dewing, 'Notes on Lavenham and its church', *Proceedings of the Suffolk Institute of Archaeology and Natural History*, 6 (1885–8), 105–30 • E. M. Carus-Wilson and O. Coleman, *England's export* *trade, 1275–1547* (1963) · E. Power, *Medieval people* (1924) · P. R. Schofield, '*Extranei* and the market for customary land on a Westminster Abbey manor in the fifteenth century', *Agricultural History Review*, 49 (2001), 1–16

Likenesses group portrait, memorial brass (Thomas [ii] Spring and Margaret Spring with ten children), St Peter and St Paul, Lavenham

Wealth at death bequests over £155 plus five properties; Thomas [i] Spring: will, Dymond and Betterton, *Lavenham*, appx 2, 67 · bequests over £733 and property; Thomas [ii] Spring: will, Dymond and Betterton, *Lavenham*, appx 2, 68 · executor's account for £8092 11*s*. 9*d*.; Thomas [iii] Spring: PRO, PROB 2/14

Spring, Agnes (*d.* in or after **1457**). *See under* Spring family (*per. c.*1400–*c.*1550).

Spring, Alice (*d.* **1538**). *See under* Spring family (*per. c.*1400–*c.*1550).

Spring, (Robert) Howard (**1889–1965**), novelist and journalist, was born in Tiger Bay, Cardiff, on 10 February 1889, the third of the nine children of William Henry Spring (*d.* 1901) and his wife, Mary Stacey. His father as a boy had run away from his home in co. Cork; he was a jobbing gardener who was often out of work. His mother took in washing to eke out the scant family income.

When his father died Spring left Cardiff board school reluctantly at the age of twelve, worked for a short time for a butcher as an errand-boy, then became an office boy to an accountant in the Cardiff docks. Unhappy with his pay, after a year he found another job as messenger-boy in the office of the *South Wales News*, which was to be the beginning of a distinguished career in journalism. His lack of early formal education was in part countered by memories of his book-loving father, and in 1904 he began the laborious process of self-education which was to dominate his youth. Motivated by his ambition to become a reporter, he became an extremely fast and accurate shorthand writer. This energy and commitment impressed his editor, who paid the tuition fees for him to study English, French, Latin, mathematics, and history at evening classes held by Cardiff University. Meanwhile he had also been promoted from messenger-boy to reporter, and his days were long and busy. He worked full days for the paper collating telephone news reports and then worked as a reporter through the evening. Hours would be snatched from this hectic schedule to attend evening classes; then he would return to the office to write his report; then home to have supper and do homework.

In 1912, after nine years' service on the *South Wales News*, Spring moved to Bradford and joined the staff of the *Yorkshire Observer*. Here he had a less arduous job, which paid almost twice the 30*s*. a week he had earned for working his 'double shift' on the morning and evening papers in Cardiff. This pay rise was vital, as earlier that year his elder brother had died from overwork and malnutrition, and Spring was left to support his mother and younger siblings. He began to specialize in reviewing books on the *Yorkshire Observer*. Freed at last from the regular evening classes, he found the time to read widely and form intellectually fulfilling friendships with his colleagues. In his autobiography he called his time at Bradford his 'university years'.

(Robert) Howard Spring (1889–1965), by Howard Coster, 1932

In the spring of 1915 Spring moved to the *Manchester Guardian*, where C. P. Scott was editor, but he remained only a few months before joining the Army Service Corps as a shorthand-typist, working eventually at general headquarters in France. (He had been turned down for active service because of his frail physique.) After the war he returned to the *Manchester Guardian*, where he met Marion Ursula Pye (1890–1976), daughter of George William Pye, a London cotton merchant. She was also self-educated and was working as a secretary to James Bone, the editor. After a brief courtship the couple married in March 1920; they had two sons.

Spring had an almost superstitious belief in the rare moments which signified a crossroads in his career. In the general election of 1931 he reported on Lord Beaverbrook's speech in Darwen. The approach to the hall lay through the Saturday market swarming with hucksters and pedlars, which suggested the title for his *Guardian* article, 'The pedlar of dreams'; this headline so delighted Beaverbrook that he at once arranged to bring Spring to London to work on the *Evening Standard* where he became book reviewer, following Arnold Bennett and J. B. Priestley. The care and judgement which he brought to this task and the institution of a 'book of the month' selection made him an influential figure in the book world.

Spring did not begin to write novels himself until he was over forty. His first publication was a children's book, *Darkie & Co.*, published in 1932. His first novel, *Shabby Tiger*

(1934), was followed by a sequel, *Rachel Rosing*, in 1935. The modest sales of both did not lead him to predict the great success of his next novel, *O Absalom!* (1938), retitled *My Son, my Son!* for publication in the United States and in subsequent editions in Britain. The *Times Literary Supplement* praised it as 'a long, vigorous novel of frustrated lives … a story that is remorseless in its insistence on futility; pitiless as life itself' (26 March 1938). It was a great success in America, was translated into many languages, and was made into a film. Spring found himself, in middle age, transported from wage-earner to independence. He bought a bungalow on the shores of Mylor Creek in Cornwall and moved there in the early years of the Second World War, giving up his work for the *Evening Standard* in 1939. His next novel, *Fame is the Spur!*, the story of a Labour leader's rise to power and subsequent corruption—a barely disguised commentary on Ramsay MacDonald—was finished in the early months of 1940. In the following year he began reviewing for *Country Life*. He had written *Heaven Lies about Us: a Fragment of Infancy* in 1939 and now followed it with two further autobiographical works, *In the Meantime* (1942) and *And Another Thing …* (1946). In 1972 the three works were published in one volume as *The Autobiography of Howard Spring*. During the Second World War he wrote two more novels, *Hard Facts* (1944) and *Dunkerley's* (1946). Both enjoyed success and were frequently reprinted on both sides of the Atlantic.

In 1947 Spring moved to a large Georgian house in Falmouth, and became president of the Royal Cornwall Polytechnic Society. He also settled down to a regular routine of work. He wrote for five mornings a week, producing a thousand words each morning, and this industriousness provided a steady flow of novels. Within a few years he had achieved a secure position as a well-known popular author. He published *There is No Armour* (1948), *The Houses In Between* (1951), *A Sunset Touch* (1953), *These Lovers Fled Away* (1955), *Time and the Hour* (1957), *All the Day Long* (1959), and *I Met a Lady* (1961). He was a gifted story-teller: his characters were convincing and absorbing, his dialogue easy and natural, and his plots ably crafted. In some books 'perhaps co-incidence played too large a part' (*The Times*, 4 May 1965), but although none of his later novels repeated the success of *O Absalom!*, they all enjoyed respectable sales.

After a slight stroke Spring had to give up reviewing for *Country Life*, but he was determined to go on writing and even before he was allowed to walk he was practising with a notebook and pencil. Soon he could write legible words and before long he was at his desk writing his last book, *Winds of the Day*, published in 1964. He had another stroke and died at his home, the White Cottage, Fenwick Road, Falmouth, on 3 May 1965.

M. H. SPRING, *rev.* KATHERINE MULLIN

Sources M. H. Spring, *Howard* (1967) • *The autobiography of Howard Spring* (1972) • *The Times* (4 May 1965) • *TLS* (26 March 1938) • *CGPLA Eng. & Wales* (1966)
Archives JRL, corresp. and literary papers | BL, corresp. with Society of Authors, Add. MS 56818 • JRL, letters to *Manchester Guardian*
Likenesses H. Coster, photograph, 1932, NPG [*see illus.*] • photographs, repro. in Spring, *Howard*
Wealth at death £23,111 0s. 0d.: probate, 1966, *CGPLA Eng. & Wales*

Spring, Sir John (1498–1548). *See under* Spring family (*per. c.*1400–*c.*1550).

Spring, Margaret (*d.* in or after 1504). *See under* Spring family (*per. c.*1400–*c.*1550).

Spring, Thomas (*d.* 1440). *See under* Spring family (*per. c.*1400–*c.*1550).

Spring, Thomas (*d.* 1486). *See under* Spring family (*per. c.*1400–*c.*1550).

Spring, Thomas (*c.*1456–1523). *See under* Spring family (*per. c.*1400–*c.*1550).

Spring, Tom. *See* Winter, Thomas (1795–1851).

Springett, Mary, Lady Springett. *See* Penington, Mary (*bap.* 1623, *d.* 1682).

Springfield, Dusty [*real name* Mary Isabel Catherine Bernadette O'Brien] (1939–1999), popular singer, was born on 16 April 1939 in Hampstead, north London, the only daughter of Catherine Ann (Kay) Ryle, a housewife, and Gerard O'Brien (also known as OB), a tax consultant. She did not have the happiest or most stable of childhoods: her mother, Kay, was quietly but indomitably dissatisfied with the stereotypical role of mother and wife her upbringing had carved out for her, and had embarked on a lifelong career of generating excitement, travelling, and socializing. OB, on the other hand, was a reserved man who doggedly pinned his own musical aspirations on Mary. From an early age she felt eclipsed by her academically gifted brother Dion and that she was denied the attention her parents lavished on him. Commentators have suggested that Dusty's perfectionism, and her constant need for praise and affirmation, were linked to this early sense of isolation and neglect.

Just before the outbreak of the Second World War, under the threat of air raids, the O'Briens moved from London to High Wycombe. Mary spent her first eleven years in Buckinghamshire before moving back to the London area in 1950; the family settled in Ealing. Mary was schooled at St Anne's Convent and here developed a passion for singing and dreamed of becoming a blues singer like Bessie Smith.

By 1956 Mary had left school and was working in a department store and singing alongside her brother at nightclubs in London's West End. Two years later, however, her life as a part-time entertainer and shop girl was over. She responded to an advert in *Stage* and was auditioned and accepted as the third 'sister' of an all-girl trio, the Lana Sisters, with Riss Chantelle and Lynne Abrams. The Lana Sisters enjoyed some success performing in variety shows and television pop programmes, and released a number of singles, including 'Chimes of Arcady' and 'My mother's eyes' (Fontana, 1959 and 1960 respectively).

Mary left the Lana Sisters in 1960 and joined her brother Dion (now known as Tom) and Tim Field (who was later

Dusty Springfield (1939–1999), by Vivienne, 1962–3

replaced by Mike Longhurst-Pickworth) as lead singer of the Springfields. As a Lana Sister she had taken her first superficial step towards becoming the glamorous Dusty Springfield, dyeing her hair blonde so that she looked more like Riss and Lynne. However, it was as a member of the Springfields that she finally changed her name. This decision, combined with a new image—her trademark beehive and glittering 'panda eyes'—proved essential to her transformation from bookish schoolgirl to striking pop star.

Dusty had been a Lana Sister for only a year, but had gained much experience and made a valuable contribution to the Springfields, dominating the stage with seemingly unselfconscious performances. In April 1961 the Springfields were invited to audition for Johnny Franz at Philips. They played a version of the American Civil War song 'Dear John' and Franz signed them immediately, releasing 'Dear John' as their first single. It was not a major hit, but the Springfields quickly made a name for themselves with their innovative sound, a combination of folk and other musical styles. The band split up in 1963 and Dusty launched her solo career soon afterwards with the classic 'I only want to be with you' (which reached number 4 in the British charts). She released her first album, *A Girl Called Dusty*—recorded in New York and produced by Johnny Franz—in April 1964. The album was a mixture of soul, rhythm and blues, and contemporary pop, marking a radical departure from the folk styles of the Springfields.

In 1964 Dusty provoked much controversy by refusing to play to segregated audiences in South Africa. Contrary to government regulations she performed in front of a mixed audience and was consequently deported. Though she disliked being regarded as a political figurehead, even declaring herself apolitical, her actions—deprecated by members of Equity, who claimed that she had acted foolishly in order to gain publicity—reverberated throughout the British government and the music industry.

Between 1964 and 1968 Dusty worked with some of the most talented songwriters of the sixties, including Carole King and Burt Bacharach, and released six albums: *A Girl Called Dusty* (1964), *Everything's Coming up Dusty* (1965), *Golden Hits* (1966), *Where am I Going* (1967), *Dusty Springfield* (1968), and *Dusty … Definitely* (1968). The year 1969, however, was pivotal in her career. Still with Philips in the UK, she signed a second recording contract with Atlantic Records in the USA. In the 1960s Memphis was recognized by many as the world centre of popular music, boasting racial, musical, and artistic integration. Dusty had always admired the 'Memphis sound'. So when her chance came she flew out to the United States and, produced by Jerry Wexler, Tom Dowd, and Arif Mardin, recorded *Dusty in Memphis*, an album which has since been proclaimed a modern masterpiece.

Wexler had guided Aretha Franklin to the fore of American soul music, having recognized the rawness of her voice and its powerful effect on audiences. With Wexler, Franklin made the sensational transition from girl singer to sexy, mature, soul diva. He saw similar potential in Dusty, and encouraged her to embrace and experiment with the soul music she loved so much. 'Son-of-a-preacher-man' was released as a single in 1971 and entered the top 10 in both the British and the American charts. Ultimately a song about secret love and sexual awakening, 'Son-of-a-preacher-man' was brought to life by Dusty's husky and languorous voice. As 'the seduced' she sounds positively blasé, almost breathless and more comfortable than a young God-fearing child of the church ought to be with such 'teachings'.

In the early 1970s the British press was saturated with rumours about Dusty's sexuality after she declared in an interview that she was 'as capable of being swayed by a woman as by a man' (cited in *Daily Telegraph*, 4 March 1999). She decided to move to Los Angeles, where attitudes to homosexuality were more tolerant and the lifestyle more relaxed. Having escaped the pressures and constraints of fame and the unwanted attentions of the British press, she lived in Los Angeles for more than fifteen years with innumerable adopted cats. However, despite the air of control and confidence she exuded, she was deeply insecure and unfulfilled. Her depressive nature has been well documented: in interviews Dusty spoke of feeling lonely and homesick, but with no real sense of where home was, and of an intangible emotional pain she could not escape. There was something else haunting her. She never forgot the timid and lonely schoolgirl Mary O'Brien, and in later years she found it difficult to reconcile her two identities. In Los Angeles, influenced by a hedonistic social circle, she developed a dependence on alcohol and drugs which helped numb her depression. In 1978 she released *It Begins*

Again, but despite huge efforts to promote the album it was not a commercial success.

After almost fifteen years in semi-retirement in Los Angeles, Dusty's career took an unexpected turn. Neil Tennant and Chris Lowe of the Pet Shop Boys, one of the biggest pop duos of the late 1980s, asked her to perform on their single 'What have I done to deserve this?', which they had written with Los Angeles songwriter Allee Willis. She eventually agreed to the collaboration and flew back to England to meet Tennant and Lowe. The song was recorded and entered the British charts at number 2 in the autumn of 1987. In the same year 'Nothing has been proved' was included on the soundtrack for the film *Scandal*. Dusty recorded a further album, *Reputation* (1990), and a single from it, 'In private', reached the top 20, but her career was interrupted in 1994 when she was diagnosed as having breast cancer shortly after returning from Nashville, where she was recording her final album, *A Very Fine Love* (1995). She remained positive, but despite a period of remission it became clear that the cancer was untreatable.

Towards the end of her life acknowledgements of Dusty's talent and contribution to popular music were finally given an official stamp. In January 1999 she was appointed OBE in the new year honours list. Vicki Wickham, Dusty's long-time friend and manager, collected the award from St James's Palace and presented it to her in a private ceremony at the Royal Marsden Hospital, where she lay critically ill. She eventually lost her five-year battle with cancer and died at home in Henley-on-Thames on 2 March 1999. She was buried at St Mary's Church, Henley-on-Thames, on 12 March.

A revolutionary, Dusty Springfield was a key figure in the 'British invasion' of popular musicians into America. She paved the way for women in pop by her insistence on control over her own work and by maintaining a professional attitude in the recording studio, which earned her a reputation for being difficult. Dusty once claimed that she would only sing a love song if it made her cry. This was indicative of a deeply personal commitment to her music that made her unique and one of the most evocative singers of the twentieth century, whose legacy will live on for many years. ALICE R. CARR

Sources L. O'Brien, *Dusty*, updated and rev. edn (London, 2000) • D. Clarke, ed., *The Penguin encyclopedia of popular music* (London, 1998) • P. Valentine and V. Wickham, *The authorised biography of Dusty Springfield: dancing with demons* (2000) • S. Whiteley, *Women and popular music: sexuality, identity, and subjectivity* (2000) • K. Schoemer, 'Pop chicks: fluff to tough', *Trouble girls: the Rolling Stone book of women in rock*, ed. B. O'Dair (New York, 1997), 71–83 • *Daily Telegraph* (4 March 1999) • *The Independent* (4 March 1999) • *The Times* (4 March 1999) • *The Guardian* (4 March 1999)

Archives FILM BFI NFTVA, 'Definitely Dusty', BBC2, 25 Dec 1999 • BFI NFTVA, documentary footage • BFI NFTVA, performance footage

Likenesses Vivienne, photograph, 1962–3, NPG [*see illus.*] • thirty-four photographs, Hult. Arch.

Spring-Heeled Jack (*fl.* 1837–1838), mystery assailant, was first reported, though not named, in early January 1838, when the lord mayor of London made public a letter he had received, signed 'A resident of Peckham':

> It appears that some individuals (of, as the writer believes, the higher ranks of life) have laid a wager with a mischievous and foolhardy companion (name as yet unknown) that he durst not take upon himself the task of visiting many of the villages near London in three disguises—a ghost, a bear and a devil; and, moreover, that he will not dare to enter gentlemen's gardens for the purpose of alarming the inmates of the house. The wager has been accepted, and the unmanly villain has succeeded in depriving seven ladies of their senses. (*The Times*, 9 Jan 1838)

The publication of this letter elicited a host of reports of incidents, dating from the autumn of the previous year, from all around the periphery of London. Though the correspondents who answered the lord mayor's call for more information shared the belief that a malicious prankster was responsible, plainly many of their informants (frequently their servants) did not, but believed the incidents supernatural. They involved a mysterious figure who appeared, always after dark, chiefly in the forms of a bear, a man in armour, or the devil himself, and either frightened or attacked people by lacerating them or, more commonly, tearing at their clothing with his talons. His most usual target was young women.

By mid-February 1838 the assailant was known as Spring-Heeled Jack. The first first-hand report of an attack was published: an eighteen-year-old named Jane Alsop had answered the door at her father's house in Old Ford, near Bow, and been attacked by a figure who 'vomited forth a quantity of blue and white flames from his mouth' and 'tore at her neck and arms with his claws' before scampering away across the fields (*The Times*, 22 Feb 1838). An inconclusive investigation followed: one witness cast doubt on the severity of the attack and on the possibility of the fire-breathing; another told of seeing an unidentified 'young man in a large cloak' nearby; and the principal suspect, a carpenter called Millbank, was so drunk on the night of the attack that he could remember nothing of what had taken place.

The scare was now at its height. There had been reports from upwards of thirty locations around London. Rewards were posted; the police baffled; and, in parts of London, 'females … afraid to move a yard from their dwellings unless … very well protected'. More incidents followed—some obviously the work of lacklustre imitators (two were arrested); others more serious. In one, Jack breathed blue fire at one Lucy Scales in an alley in Limehouse, leaving her, according to the doctor who was called to examine her, 'suffering from hysterics and great agitation, in all probability the result of fright' (*Morning Post*, 7 March 1838).

Though there were no further attacks in this, the original, panic of 1837–8, Spring-Heeled Jack lodged in the popular consciousness and stuck there. He was celebrated on stage and in penny dreadfuls, and took on a new folkloric persona as a waylayer of solitary travellers. An assault on a woman in Teignmouth in 1847 gave rise to a

'Spring-Heeled Jack investigation'; his name was also associated with the Peckham ghost of 1872 and the Sheffield Park ghost of 1873, and when Aldershot Camp was plagued by series of ghostly visitations in 1877 the perpetrator was labelled Spring-Heeled Jack. He last appeared in Liverpool in 1904 (Dash, 66–97).

In the reports of all the incidents from the second part of his career, after 1838, Jack's principal characteristic is his agility: he moves with incomparable swiftness and leaps over obstacles 6, 8, and even 15 or 20 feet high. Those who believed he was of flesh and blood ascribed this preternatural ability to his wearing boots with springs in their heels. But, curiously, his christening as Spring-Heeled Jack predates any reference to his jumping ability or spring-heeled shoes, and why he was so named is unknown. It may simply have referred to the light elastic shoes which—naturally enough for one so elusive—he was originally described as wearing; it certainly connoted that elusiveness. Later generations, to whom the name's original force had been lost, reinterpreted it, and it informed their reports of his exploits.

Who, then, was the original Spring-Heeled Jack? The notion that he was a nobleman fulfilling the terms of a bet was a popular, and entirely reasonable, contemporary explanation of the scare of 1837–8. It excludes the supernatural; it explains how the perpetrator could manage the logistics of the enterprise and (through intimations of a cover-up) how he had escaped justice; and it makes some sense out of what would otherwise have been entirely random and meaningless events. The chief suspect was (and, for some, remains) Henry de la Poer *Beresford, marquess of Waterford, the hottest blood of the day (*N&Q*; Haining, chap. 4).

Yet there is no direct evidence for this explanation. The notion of a wager was only ever a hypothesis, necessary because the alternative—that a monster, or the devil himself, was walking abroad in Peckham—was 'too absurd for belief'. And the hypothesis fails to explain why, as contemporary reporters complained, no first-hand witness to Spring-Heeled Jack could be found in early February 1838, although the story was on everyone's lips. To the sceptical folklorist, this absence suggests that the story was a rapidly disseminating urban legend—or rather, two legends: among the servant and working classes, from whom Jack selected his victims, a straightforwardly supernatural story of a polymorphous monster (very like traditional accounts of diabolical spirits visiting the earth); and, among the letter-writing middle classes and metropolitan newspaper men, a rationalized version, involving a young blood, a well-stocked costume cupboard, and a wild wager. Viewed in this light, both tales, as befit the products of the mythopoeic imagination, reveal a number of societal concerns—most interestingly, perhaps, given the historical context, a tension between the irrational countryside and the rational town.

The extreme of this sceptical position would be to deny that there was any truth in the story; to label it a narrative of hysteria, sprung from some small trigger that, once sprung, gathered its own momentum. As part of this momentum (to which the lord mayor contributed the decisive shove) imitators abounded, and assaults which appeared to fit the pattern were assimilated to it. The fact that, just before she was attacked, Lucy Scales had been reading about the Alsop case consorts neatly. Corroboration, too, might be found by comparison with the cases of other mystery assailants, such as the Halifax Slasher, who provoked hysteria and vigilantism in equal measure in Halifax in November 1938, or the Monkey Man, who terrorized areas of New Delhi in May 2001. In both cases, in the end, the police stopped looking for the attackers and announced that they did not exist.

Yet this explanation of Spring-Heeled Jack as a hysterical chimera leaves some questions unanswered (why the name? why—and what was—the blue flame?) and simply postpones others. Most importantly, the question of who (the devil) was Spring-Heeled Jack simply metamorphoses into the equally puzzling question of why (on earth) did his story catch on? It may be the most reasonable explanation for the phenomenon available, but it fails to go to the heart of the matter. RUPERT MANN

Sources M. Dash, 'Spring-Heeled Jack: to Victorian bugaboo from suburban ghost', *Fortean Studies*, 3 (1996), 7–125 • *The Times* (9 Jan 1838) • H. Hems, 'Marquess of Waterford as Springheel Jack', *N&Q*, 10th ser., 8 (1907), 455 • P. Haining, *The legend and bizarre crimes of Spring Heeled Jack* (1977) • M. Goss, *The Halifax Slasher: an urban terror in the north of England* (1987) • E. Showalter, *Hystories: hysterical epidemics and modern culture* (1997)

Sprint, John (*d.* 1590). *See under* Sprint, John (*d.* 1623).

Sprint, John (*d.* 1623), Church of England clergyman and religious controversialist, was born in or near Bristol, the son of **John Sprint** (*d.* 1590), also a Church of England clergyman. Sprint the elder, the son of an apothecary of the same name from Gloucester, was admitted to Corpus Christi College, Oxford, in 1560. He became a fellow and vicar of Berkeley, Gloucestershire, in 1563, graduated BA in 1564, and proceeded MA in 1566. He then gained a succession of preferments, becoming rector of Charlton Mackrell, Somerset, in 1567, vicar of Hambledon and dean of Bristol in 1571, canon of Winchester in 1573, and rector of Martyr Worthy, Hampshire, and canon of Old Sarum in 1574. That year on 23 July he proceeded BD and DD from Christ Church, Oxford. Having become archdeacon of Wiltshire in 1578, he gained a number of livings in that county and in Somerset. In 1584 he became treasurer of Salisbury Cathedral, and remained so until his death in 1590.

John Sprint the younger was elected a student of Christ Church in 1592. He graduated BA on 6 March 1596 and proceeded MA on 21 May 1599. He was ordained and soon made it plain that he was a puritan. On 21 November 1602, at a particularly sensitive time in the religious politics of Oxford, he preached in the university church. The sermon does not survive but Anthony Wood claims that he made 'sundry points of Doctrine against the Ceremonies and Discipline now established in the Church of England … also taxing by cavelling speeches the Vice-chancellor, and other Governors of the University' (Wood, 2.272). John

Howson, the vice-chancellor, demanded a copy of the sermon and when Sprint refused the request he was imprisoned. This was part of, and exacerbated, a campaign of partisan sermons, and eventually the disputants were called before a commission of the privy council. In March 1603 Sprint was required to deliver a public submission before the authorities in Oxford.

In 1602 Sprint was appointed vicar of Thornbury, Gloucestershire, and proved himself to be as yet unreconciled to established ritual. About 1604 he wrote a short piece mainly against rituals lacking scriptural authority. Such ceremonies were seen to be invented by Anti-Christ and maintained in the interests of 'Lordly prelacie' with the implication that the government as well as the liturgy of the Church of England was in need of purification. He was finally induced to conform by Samuel Burton, archdeacon of Gloucestershire. Sprint's first published work, *Propositions, Tending to Proove the Necessarie Use of the Christian Sabbaoth* (1607), was both reformed and orthodox, with voguish puritan sabbatarianism but a conciliatory tone toward the establishment. A catechism, *The Summe of Christian Religion* (1613), was followed by *Cassander Anglicanus: shewing the necessity of conformitie to the prescribed ceremonies of our church in case of deprivation* (1618), which became influential among puritan-inclined ministers. Sprint had come to the conclusion, not that the ceremonies were a positive part of worship, but that it was a greater evil to lose the chance to preach than to commit the lesser evil of conducting the ceremonies, providing that these were not imposed in a dictatorial manner. As these arguments came from a writer of proven godliness, they were taken more seriously by puritan clergy than admonitions from the bishops, being cited by moderate puritans in the 1630s.

Sprint married twice. With his first wife he had a son, John, born late in 1605 or in 1606, and with his second a son, Samuel, baptized at Tetbury, Gloucestershire, on 15 January 1622. In 1623 Sprint published a consolatory work, *The Christian Sword and Buckler*, but died the same year, at Thornbury, and was buried at St Anne Blackfriars, London. His son John (*d.* 1658) matriculated from Pembroke College, Oxford, on 26 November 1624 aged eighteen, and after graduation eventually became curate of Hampstead, Middlesex. His son Samuel (*d.* 1690x98), admitted to Trinity College, Cambridge, in 1646, was master of Newbury School and rector of South Tidworth, Hampshire, before his ejection in 1662. Licensed as a congregational minister in 1672, by 1690 he was preaching in Andover and Winton. TOM WEBSTER

Sources Foster, *Alum. Oxon.* • A. Wood, *The history and antiquities of the University of Oxford*, ed. J. Gutch, 2 (1796) • C. M. Dent, *Protestant reformers in Elizabethan Oxford* (1983) • T. Webster, *Godly clergy in early Stuart England: the Caroline puritan movement, c.1620–1643* (1997) • Venn, *Alum. Cant.* • *IGI* [register of Tetbury, Gloucestershire] • *Calamy rev.*, 456–7

Sproson [*née* Lloyd], **Emma** (1867–1936), suffragist and local politician, was born on 13 April 1867 at Pikehelve Street, West Bromwich, one of the seven children of John Lloyd, canal boat builder, and his wife, Ann, *née* Johnson. Her father drank heavily and she had a childhood of extreme poverty. In the mid-1870s the family settled in Wolverhampton. Emma had little formal schooling and joined the casual labour market at the age of eight: picking coal from the pit mounds and running errands. A year later she left home to enter the household of a local milkwoman where she helped with the cooking, cleaning, and evening delivery, though she did attend school four days a week. In 1880 she obtained a full-time position that combined shop work with domestic service. Later she was dismissed without a reference when she reported that her mistress's brother had made sexual advances towards her. Now unemployed, Emma moved to Lancashire to find work. About that time she began teaching in a Sunday school and was introduced to the church debating society.

Emma Lloyd's first experience of public speaking came at a church debate; her second was during a parliamentary campaign by Lord Curzon. This incident was the defining moment in her conversion to women's suffrage. Curzon refused to answer her question because 'she was a woman and did not have the vote' (MS autobiographical notes). By 1895 she had returned to Wolverhampton with enough money to buy a business for herself and her mother. It seems likely that this was a shop in the front room of their house. In this period Emma enrolled in the Independent Labour Party (ILP). On 1 August 1896 she married Frank Sproson, postman and secretary of the Wolverhampton branch of the ILP. The couple had four children, of whom three survived: two sons, Frank (*b.* 1899) and George (*b.* 1906), and a daughter, Chloris (*b.* 1897), who became profoundly deaf.

In 1906 Frank Sproson was instrumental in securing the services of Emmeline Pankhurst, founder of the Women's Social and Political Union (WSPU), to address a meeting of the Wolverhampton ILP on 28 October. On that occasion Mrs Pankhurst stayed at the Sprosons' home and Emma Sproson chaired the meeting. In the first half of 1907 she took part in a series of meetings in London halls and parks. For instance, on 13 February she attended the meeting at Caxton Hall and was among those arrested on the green at Westminster Abbey. Her host in London, Frederick Pethick Lawrence, stood as surety for her and she was bailed to appear before the magistrates on 14 February. From the options of a 20s. fine or fourteen days' imprisonment, she elected to go to prison. The following month she travelled to London to join another suffrage march from Caxton Hall to parliament. In the confusion she was arrested and sentenced to a fine or a one-month prison sentence. While in Holloway, she was visited by Christabel Pankhurst, and on 20 April she participated in a public luncheon organized by the WSPU to celebrate the release of the militants. Press reports of Emma Sproson's activities in the spring and summer of 1907 show that she was in demand as a speaker. For example, shortly after her release from prison she featured alongside Jennie Baines, a working-class organizer for the WSPU, at a meeting in Wolverhampton market place. Later that same year she went on to tour the Black Country on behalf of the WSPU.

Disillusioned with the increasingly autocratic leadership style of the Pankhursts, Emma Sproson subsequently defected from the WSPU to join the Women's Franchise League (WFL). By February 1908 she was a hard-working member of the national executive committee of the league, following an exhausting itinerary of public speaking up and down the country. In 1911 she served two terms of imprisonment in Stafford gaol for the offence of keeping a dog without a licence, carrying out the WFL policy of 'no taxation without representation'. This time she staged a hunger strike and won the right to be reclassified as a political prisoner. In 1912 she resigned from the WFL, in protest at Charlotte Despard's autocratic style of leadership. Thereafter she devoted herself to local politics. Emma Sproson contested two unsuccessful local elections on behalf of the Labour Party in 1919 and 1920, but in 1921 she was elected councillor for Dunstall ward. The first woman councillor in Wolverhampton, she served on the public health committee and the subcommittees that dealt with mental health and homes for unmarried mothers. In the autumn of 1922 she provoked uproar among her colleagues when she exposed financial irregularities in the administration of the local fever hospital. Yet the official report exonerated the officials involved and Emma was removed from the hospital committee and the health committee. She was also censured by the Labour Party. In retaliation she published her own version of events in a pamphlet entitled *Fever Hospital Inquiry—Facts v. Fairy Tales*. In November 1924 she fought a successful by-election but she failed to retain her seat when she stood as an independent in 1927. She attended the annual conference of the ILP in 1924 and again in 1926. Latterly her hearing became severely impaired and public work was increasingly difficult. Emma Sproson died at home, 56 Castlecroft Road, Tettenhall, Staffordshire, on 22 December 1936; she was survived by her husband. Emma Sproson's working-class, midlands-based career provides a vivid counterbalance to the view of the women's suffrage movement which portrays it as predominantly bourgeois and London-centred. JANE MARTIN

Sources S. P. Walters, 'Emma Sproson (1867–1936): a Black Country suffragist', MA diss., University of Leicester, 1993 • b. cert. • m. cert. • d. cert. • MS autobiographical notes, Wolverhampton Archives and Local Studies Library

Archives Wolverhampton Archives and Local Studies Library, autobiographical notes | Women's Library, London, Women's Freedom League

Likenesses photocopy (as a young woman; after photograph), Wolverhampton Archives and Local Studies Library • photograph, Women's Library, London, Women's Freedom League • photograph, Wolverhampton Archives and Local Studies Library • postcard, Museum of London, Women's Freedom League archive • two photographs, Museum of London

Sprot [Sprott], **George** (*d.* **1608**), conspirator and forger, was a notary of Eyemouth, Berwickshire, who by no later than 1600 had become intimate in the affairs of Robert Logan, seventh laird of Restalrig, and a regular guest at his house at Gunsgreen. Logan died in 1606, but two years later Sprot let slip, while drunk, that he had knowledge of the Gowrie conspiracy. When arrested and interrogated by the privy council in April 1608 Sprot confessed to possession of letters written by Logan to the third earl of Gowrie and others suggesting a plot to abduct James VI to Fast Castle. Tortured in iron boots, he recanted and admitted he had forged the letters. The case was nevertheless brought to the attention of George Home, earl of Dunbar, who intervened to halt the torture and persuade Sprot to revert to his original confession implicating Logan, though Sprot continued to maintain that the letters were themselves forgeries. The likely motive for forging the letters appears to have been to blackmail Logan's heir.

Sprot was tried and convicted for his role in the conspiracy in August. At his trial it emerged that he had made a regular business of forging letters and receipts for other clients. He was hanged, broken, and quartered at Edinburgh High Cross on 12 August 1608. The following June Logan's corpse was exhumed for the treason trial conducted to forfeit his son Robert, and Sprot's letters were introduced as evidence. The five letters, dated between 18 and 31 July and variously addressed to Gowrie, Logan's agent James Bower, and an unknown person, disclose intrigue between Logan and the Ruthvens, but do not clearly reveal its purpose. Before he was executed Sprot had clarified earlier contradictory statements to confess that he had copied the letter addressed to Gowrie directly from an original letter penned by Logan which he had seen, but that the others were pure inventions based upon this letter. Sprot's compliance may have been secured by Dunbar's promise to safeguard the welfare of his wife and children after his death. The Logan estates were forfeited, to the ruin of the family but also to the considerable benefit of the earl of Dunbar, who still owed a substantial sum for the purchase of the traitor's Berwickshire lands.

JOHN SIMMONS

Sources *APS, 1593–1625* • R. Pitcairn, ed., *Ancient criminal trials in Scotland*, 7 pts in 3, Bannatyne Club, 42 (1833) • *Reg. PCS*, 1st ser. • M. Kennaway, *Fast Castle: the early years* (1992) • A. Lang, *James VI and the Gowrie mystery* (1902) • W. Fraser, *Memorials of the earls of Haddington*, 2 vols. (1889) • parliamentary records, NA Scot.

Sprott, George Washington (**1829–1909**), Church of Scotland minister and liturgical scholar, was born on 6 March 1829 at Musquodoboit, Nova Scotia, the second of five children of John Sprott (*b.* 1780), a presbyterian minister, and his third wife, Jane Neilson. Both his parents came from Wigtownshire, Scotland. After early education in Nova Scotia, Sprott attended Glasgow University, where he graduated BA in 1849. Having decided to enter the ministry of the kirk, he was licensed and ordained for work overseas by the presbytery of Dunoon in 1852 and returned to Nova Scotia, where he was an assistant minister at Halifax. In 1856 he married Mary (*d.* 29 Dec 1874), daughter of Charles Hill of Halifax. They had nine children.

After a short period in Scotland serving in churches at Greenock and Dumfries, Sprott was appointed in 1857 as chaplain to the Scottish troops based at Kandy in Ceylon. He returned to Britain in 1865, becoming minister of

Chapel of Garioch, Aberdeenshire, in 1866 and then of North Berwick in East Lothian in 1873, where he remained until his retirement in 1904. In 1873 Sprott had applied unsuccessfully for the chair of church history at Edinburgh, but he was appointed in 1879 to a lectureship in pastoral theology in the Scottish faculties of divinity. These lectures led to the award of the degree of DD by the University of Glasgow in 1880, and were published as *The Worship and Offices of the Church of Scotland* (1882).

It was while Sprott was serving in the colonies alongside churches of different traditions that he felt impelled to re-examine the basis of reformed worship. People who lived abroad, in his view, were often attracted to the worship of the Anglican church when the services of their own church were not available. The Church of England loomed large, but he thought that in matters of worship presbyterians should look first to their own traditions and to those of other reformed churches. Sprott was thus led to study the history of the worship of the kirk, especially in the period following the Reformation. Before returning to Scotland he had published a pamphlet, *The Worship, Rites, and Ceremonies of the Church of Scotland* (1863), in which he suggested the formation of a society which would prepare a book of prayers for public worship and the administration of the sacraments. The Church Service Society was formed in 1865 and Sprott became a leading member of its editorial committee. He was one of those principally involved in producing the society's service book, *Euchologion*, and he was responsible for an annotated edition of the book in 1905. He served as vice-president from 1899 to 1907, and as president in 1907. Sprott had brought out a critical edition of the Book of Common Order or 'Knox's liturgy' in 1868, which was published with the *Westminster Directory*, edited by his friend Thomas Leishman. In 1871 he produced an edition of *Scottish Liturgies of the Reign of James VI*, and in 1905 he edited the *Liturgy of Compromise*, the service book used by Knox when he was in exile on the continent. Sprott's Lee lecture in 1897, published as *The Worship of the Church of Scotland during the Covenanting Period, 1638–61*, remained the most authoritative account of the subject a century later. From these studies he was able to show that the Church of Scotland had not been against the use of a service book, and that set forms, such as the creed, the Lord's prayer, and the doxology, had been features of early reformed worship. In addition he maintained that it had been the influence of English puritanism which had led to the abandonment of many liturgical forms during the seventeenth century. Even more important for Sprott, however, was the place of the Lord's Supper: although the sacrament had not been celebrated frequently in Scotland, the order of worship was based on the Lord's Supper as the norm, with the prayers of intercession and the Lord's prayer following the sermon. The ordinary service was thus kept in harmony with that of a communion Sunday and was a testimony to the Lord's Supper as part of the complete service of the house of God.

The importance of the doctrinal basis of worship is seen in Sprott's *Church Principles of the Reformation* of 1877. He showed that the popular view of the sacraments as 'bare' signs had been rejected by the Scots reformers, who had held instead that they were means of Christ's presence with his people. Sprott held a 'high' view of the church as a divine institution and he considered that presbyterian orders were valid. In his view the threefold ministry of ministers, elders, and deacons more faithfully reflected the practice of the early church than its Anglican counterpart. His sermon before the synod of Aberdeen in 1873 was published as *The Necessity of a Valid Ordination to the Holy Ministry*, and at the general assembly in 1882 he objected to the admission of Congregational ministers without presbyterian ordination. Sprott was also a firm advocate of Christian unity, and his Macleod memorial lecture of 1903, published as *The Doctrine of Schism in the Church of Scotland*, was a valuable study of the way in which division in the kirk had been regarded as 'one of the worst of evils'. The society which most closely reflected his views was the Scottish Church Society, formed in 1892 to 'defend and advance Catholic Doctrine'. He served as president on four occasions and gave several papers at its conferences. Sprott's scholarship and his faithful parish ministry ensured that his catholic liturgical outlook came to be accepted as belonging within the reformed tradition of the kirk.

Sprott died at Edinburgh of heart disease on 27 October 1909 and was buried at North Berwick three days later. Memorials were erected to him in the church at North Berwick and in St Oswald's Church in Edinburgh, where he worshipped in his later years. He was survived by a son and five daughters. D. M. MURRAY

Sources H. Sprott, 'The Rev. George Washington Sprott, DD, of North Berwick (1829–1909)', *The Gallovidian*, 50 (1911), 57–61 · G. W. Sprott, ed., *Memorials of the Rev. John Sprott* (1906) · *DNB* · *Fasti Scot.* · J. C. Saunders, 'George Sprott and the revival of worship in Scotland', *Liturgical Review*, 7/2 (1977), 49–54; 8/1 (1978), 11–22 · D. M. Murray, 'Disruption to union', *Studies in the history of worship in Scotland*, ed. D. B. Forrester and D. M. Murray, 2nd edn (1996), 87–106 · D. M. Murray, 'Doctrine and worship', *Liturgical Review*, 7/2 (1977), 25–34 · A. K. Robertson, 'George Washington Sprott: 1829–1909', *Church Service Society Annual*, 36 (1966), 8–12 · J. C. Saunders, 'A Sprott bibliography', *Liturgical Review*, 7/2 (1977), 44–8 · *The Scotsman* (28 Oct 1909) · *The Scotsman* (29 Oct 1909)

Archives U. Glas. L., Church Service Society MSS

Likenesses photograph, repro. in Sprott, 'The Rev. George Washington Sprott', facing p. 57

Wealth at death £1601 19s. 9d.: confirmation, 11 May 1910, *CCI*

Sprott, Thomas (*fl.* 1272), Benedictine monk and chronicler, wrote a history of St Augustine's Abbey, Canterbury—his own house—and its abbots. This is generally taken to be the text that survives in two thirteenth-century manuscripts: LPL, MS 419, folios 111–60, which comes down to 1221 and perhaps represents the earlier state of its composition; and BL, Cotton MS Tiberius A.ix, folios 107–80, which, with a change of hand at 1221, comes down to *c.*1265, and has further additions to about the mid-fourteenth century (ending confusedly and imperfectly, as a result of damage in the Cotton Library fire of 1731). There are also later transcripts: BL, Cotton MS Vitellius D.xi, folios 39–69*v* (abridged from Tiberius A.ix; damaged in the fire of 1731); Cotton MS Vitellius E.xiv, folios 237–252*v* (an epitome made by the Elizabethan scholar John

Joscelyn, perhaps from the Lambeth Palace manuscript); BL, Add. MS 46918 (copied from Vitellius D.xi or its exemplar); and BL, Harley MS 692, folios 75–193*v* (a fair copy of Vitellius E.xiv, made by or for Joscelyn's contemporary the antiquary Arthur Agarde). It has not been printed.

Sprott's chronicle is mentioned twice by the late fourteenth-century St Augustine's chronicler, William Thorne, who in the preface to his own chronicle refers to Sprott's work as ending in 1272; confusingly, just after the end of the portion of his chronicle that relates an event of 1228, Thorne states that he has ceased thereafter to use Sprott's work, and in modern times this has often been thought to mean that Sprott's work came down to no later than 1228.

The chronicle is initially cast in the form of abbatial biographies, with a few entire texts inserted into the narrative; the number of texts (such as royal grants and papal letters) gradually increases, and the history of the house as a whole becomes the author's main focus. For the twelfth and early thirteenth centuries Sprott is both more detailed and, almost certainly, more accurate than William Thorne, who appears to have derived so much from Sprott's work. For instance, where Sprott recounts the dedication of the abbey's chapel on its manor of Kennington, Kent, on 16 April 1258—the first of the abbey's chapels to have two side-altars—Thorne simply states that the chapel was dedicated in 1258; and while Sprott refers to the abbey's old refectory as being pulled down in 1262, Thorne places this event in 1260 along with the arrival in England of the papal legate Otto (which actually took place in 1237).

The fifteenth-century catalogue of the library of St Augustine's Abbey includes both of the thirteenth-century manuscripts of the chronicle, and also eight more of Sprott's books: works of canon law, natural science, philosophy, and theology, some of which he may have compiled as well as owned. Overall, their titles are suggestive of his having lived into the second half of the thirteenth century. John Bale credits Sprott with the authorship of *Cantuariorum historiarum*.

Confusingly and mistakenly, the authorship of two much later chronicles has been attributed to Sprott: a late fourteenth-century summarized history of the world with some material relating to St Augustine's Abbey (now CUL, Add. MS 3578), edited by Thomas Hearne as *Thomae Sprotti Chronica* (Oxford, 1719); and a fifteenth-century abridgement of the *Flores historiarum*, in the Joseph Mayer Collection, Liverpool Museum (no. 12012), printed in translation by William Bell as *Thomas Sprott's Chronicle of Profane and Sacred History* (Liverpool, 1851). NIGEL RAMSAY

Sources J. C. Russell, 'Dictionary of writers of thirteenth century England', *BIHR*, special suppl., 3 (1936) [whole issue], esp. 170 • S. E. Kelly, ed., *Charters of St Augustine's Abbey, Canterbury, and Minster-in-Thanet*, Anglo-Saxon Charters, 4 (1995), lv, xcvii–xcviii • *William Thorne's chronicle of St Augustine's Abbey, Canterbury*, trans. A. H. Davis (1934), xx–xxii, xxvi • T. D. Hardy, *Descriptive catalogue of materials relating to the history of Great Britain and Ireland*, 3, Rolls Series, 26 (1871), 125–6, 208–9 • Thomas of Elmham, *Historia monasterii S. Augustini Cantuariensis*, ed. C. Hardwick, Rolls Series, 8 (1858), xv–xvi • Bale, *Cat.*, 1.326

Sprott, Walter John Herbert [Sebastian] (1897–1971), sociologist, was born at Sillwood Place, Crowborough, Sussex, on 19 April 1897, the son of Herbert Sprott, a country solicitor, and his wife, Mary Elizabeth Williams. He was dominated in infancy by his mother, was sent to Felsted, a boarding-school with a rigorous regime, and then in 1919 entered Clare College, Cambridge, to read the moral sciences, in which he took a double first.

Perhaps this is the central characterization of Edwardian childhood among the English professional classes. But Sprott was eccentric. Charm and wit and oratorical skill led him effortlessly into the magic circle of John Maynard Keynes's close friends; he became an intimate of E. M. Forster, who eventually made him his literary executor, and of Lytton Strachey. He became 'Sebastian' in the overlapping circles of Cambridge and Bloomsbury. He was elected to the exclusive society of the Apostles in 1920. He regularly went riding with Keynes, accompanied him on a holiday to Algeria and Tunisia in 1921, and was probably his last male lover. This intimacy, though not the friendship, ended with Keynes's marriage to Lydia Lopokova in 1925.

In that year Sprott, who had been a demonstrator in the psychological laboratory at Cambridge since 1922, moved to a lectureship in psychology at Nottingham University, though the habit of frequent, almost daily, letters customary between Bloomsberries continued to include the name Sebastian. Much of this correspondence was later destroyed. Thus many of the letters from Sprott were burnt either by Maynard himself or by his brother Geoffrey. However, a few survived. One, written in April 1921 after reading Hirschfield's *History of Sex*, reads 'I suspect I am tainted with Transvestitismus, Autonomosexualität, and Hermaphroditismus … to say nothing of Homosexualität and Onanie … My love, Yours ever Sebastian' (Skidelsky, 35). That was to Keynes.

The combination of intellect with aestheticism was much admired after the First World War—so much so that 'sprott' was generalized in Cambridge argot as a label for fashionable cleverness. Yet Sprott made no secret of his sexual tastes. He pioneered the path to the night-clubs of Berlin, being subsequently followed by Christopher Isherwood and W. H. Auden. Between the wars, with his friend Joe Ackerley, he sought 'low-life adventure' in the pubs of Dover and Portsmouth. In Nottingham he lived in a squalid Victorian terrace, where academic colleagues and their wives were served by discharged prisoners. Here the Bloomsbury appellation Sebastian was dropped in favour of the more matey and proletarian forename Jack.

All this threw a shadow of loneliness and sadness over Sprott's personal life, but it did not darken the charming courtesy or cloud the manners of the old-fashioned don which he unfailingly presented to the respectable world. Nor did it blight his academic performance. He was applauded on every side as a lecturer of outstanding wit and eloquent exposition. Invitations to give public lectures came in a steady flow throughout his career. Caustic and ruthless demolition of theories, especially those promoting salvation through simplistic politics or the 'quick fix', came readily to his lips, and colleagues and students relished his private conversation.

Moreover Sprott ranged freely over a wider intellectual territory than is now academically fashionable. He held chairs in philosophy and in psychology at Nottingham. Above all he held fast to his belief in sociology as an academic discipline throughout the time in which it was resisted by the British establishment—that is, from his translation to a lectureship in psychology at Nottingham in 1925, through his incumbency first in the readership of philosophy there from 1928 to 1948, then in the chair of philosophy from 1948 to 1960. He served Nottingham University with steadfast loyalty and was its public orator from 1948 to 1964.

Sprott published *Physique and Character* (1925) and *New Introductory Lectures on Psycho-Analysis* (1933), translations of works by Kretschmer and Freud respectively. But his sociological writings, though little read today, remain important in sociology's history. All were written with lucid elegance. He was the first English sociologist to offer an informed, critical, and sympathetic view both of European writing in 'the grand manner' and of the sophisticated functionalism of the American R. K. Merton. There were only three named chairs of sociology in the UK when he gave the Josiah Mason lectures at the University of Birmingham in 1953. His *Sociology* (1949), *Science and Social Action* (1954), and *Sociology at the Seven Dials* (1962) form a bridge from Hobhousian evolutionism to the functionalism which dominated the subject after the Second World War; they also link Parsonian general theory to more modest theories of the middle ground. So Sprott challenged functionalism by quoting Talcott Parsons: 'the combination of an occupationally differentiated industrial system and a significantly solidary kinship system *must* be a system of stratification in which the children of the more highly placed come to have differential advantages' (*Social System*, 161). He thereby showed that the evolution of industrial societies has functional limitations (*Science and Social Action*, 139). He was a genial and articulate link between the older founders of sociology in Britain, such as Hobhouse and Ginsberg, and the new professionals emerging in the aftermath of the Second World War. He was hailed by Sir Leon Radzinowicz (*The Times*, 14 Sept 1971) as an influential figure in the development of criminology as an academic subject. Sprott died on 2 September 1971 of acute heart failure at his home in Langham Road, Blakeney, Norfolk. He was childless and unmarried but was mourned by many friends. A. H. Halsey

Sources *The Times* (6 Sept 1971) • *The Times* (9 Sept 1971) • *The Times* (11 Sept 1971) • *The Times* (14 Sept 1971) • personal knowledge (2004) • *WWW* • b. cert. • d. cert. • D. E. Moggridge, *Maynard Keynes: an economist's biography* (1992) • R. J. A. Skidelsky, *The economist as saviour, 1920–1937* (1992), vol. 2 of *John Maynard Keynes* (1983–2000) • D. Felix, *Keynes: a critical life* (1999) • *CGPLA Eng. & Wales* (1971)

Archives King's Cam., corresp. | King's Cam., letters to G. H. W. Rylands

Wealth at death £21,322: probate, 14 Oct 1971, *CGPLA Eng. & Wales*

PICTURE CREDITS

Smillie, Robert (1857–1940)—by permission of the People's History Museum
Smirke, Sir Robert (1780–1867)—© National Portrait Gallery, London
Smith, Adam (*bap.* 1723, *d.* 1790)—© National Portrait Gallery, London
Smith, Albert Richard (1816–1860)—© National Portrait Gallery, London
Smith, (Robert) Angus (1817–1884)—reproduced courtesy of the Library and Information Centre, Royal Society of Chemistry
Smith, Annie Lorrain (1854–1937)—© The Natural History Museum, London
Smith, Arthur Lionel (1850–1924)—© Estate of Francis Dodd; collection National Portrait Gallery, London
Smith, Audrey Ursula (1915–1981)—National Institute for Medical Research
Smith, Benjamin Leigh (1828–1913)—© National Portrait Gallery, London
Smith, Bernard (*c.*1628/9–1708)—Faculty of Music, University of Oxford
Smith, Brian Abel- (1926–1996)—© News International Newspapers Ltd
Smith, Cecil Lewis Troughton [Cecil Scott Forester] (1899–1966)—© National Portrait Gallery, London
Smith, Sir Charles Edward Kingsford (1897–1935)—Getty Images - Hulton Archive
Smith, Charlotte (1749–1806)—© National Portrait Gallery, London
Smith, Cyril Stanley (1903–1992)—© National Portrait Gallery, London
Smith, Donald Alexander, first Baron Strathcona and Mount Royal (1820–1914)—Getty Images - A. J. Ross
Smith, Dorothy Gladys [Dodie] (1896–1990)—© Kenneth Hughes / National Portrait Gallery, London
Smith, Edwin George Herbert (1912–1971)—© National Portrait Gallery, London
Smith, Eric Edward Dorman Dorman- (1895–1969)—private collection
Smith, Florence Margaret [Stevie] (1902–1971)—© Jorge Lewinski; collection National Portrait Gallery, London
Smith, Sir Francis Petit (1808–1874)—© National Maritime Museum, London
Smith, Frederick Edwin, first earl of Birkenhead (1872–1930)—© National Portrait Gallery, London
Smith, George (1713/14–1776)—© National Portrait Gallery, London
Smith, George (1815–1871)—© National Portrait Gallery, London
Smith, George (1831–1895)—© National Portrait Gallery, London
Smith, Sir George Adam (1856–1942)—photograph reproduced by courtesy of The British Academy
Smith, George Albert (1864–1959)—© reserved; British Film Institute
Smith, George Barnett (1841–1909)—© National Portrait Gallery, London
Smith, George Charles Moore (1858–1940)—photograph reproduced by courtesy of The British Academy
Smith, George Joseph (1872–1915)—© National Portrait Gallery, London
Smith, George Murray (1824–1901)—unknown collection / © National Portrait Gallery, London
Smith, Sir George Reeves- (1863–1941)—© reserved; photograph National Portrait Gallery, London
Smith, Goldwin (1823–1910)—© National Portrait Gallery, London
Smith, Sir Henry George Wakelyn, baronet, of Aliwal (1787–1860)—© National Portrait Gallery, London
Smith, Herbert (1862–1938)—by permission of the People's History Museum
Smith, Horatio (1779–1849)—© National Portrait Gallery, London
Smith, Sir Hubert Llewellyn (1864–1945)—© National Portrait Gallery, London
Smith, James, of Jordanhill (1782–1867)—© National Portrait Gallery, London
Smith, Sir James Edward (1759–1828)—by permission of the Linnean Society of London; photograph National Portrait Gallery, London
Smith, John (*bap.* 1580, *d.* 1631)—© National Portrait Gallery, London
Smith, John (1652–1743)—© Tate, London, 2004
Smith, John (1938–1994)—© Scottish National Photography Collection, Scottish National Portrait Gallery
Smith, John Pye (1774–1851)—by permission of Dr Williams's Library
Smith, John Stafford (*bap.* 1750, *d.* 1836)—© National Portrait Gallery, London
Smith, John Thomas (1766–1833)—© National Portrait Gallery, London
Smith, (Lloyd) Logan Pearsall (1865–1946)—© Estate of Roger Fry; collection Haverford College, Pennsylvania; © reserved in the photograph
Smith, Sir Matthew Arnold Bracy (1879–1959)—© National Portrait Gallery, London
Smith, Muriel (1923–1985)—Getty Images - Tracey
Smith, Richard Baird (1818–1861)—The British Library
Smith, Richard John [O Smith] (1786–1855)—Garrick Club / the art archive
Smith, Robert (*bap.* 1689, *d.* 1768)—The Master and Fellows, Trinity College, Cambridge
Smith, Rodney (1860–1947)—© National Portrait Gallery, London
Smith, (Edwin) Rodney, Baron Smith (1914–1998)—reproduced by kind permission of the President and Council of the Royal College of Surgeons of London
Smith, Sir Ross Macpherson (1892–1922)—© reserved; Australian War Memorial negative number ART03179
Smith, Samuel (1836–1906)—Board of Trustees of the National Museums and Galleries on Merseyside (Walker Art Gallery, Liverpool)
Smith, Sarah (1832–1911)—© National Portrait Gallery, London
Smith, (Emily) Sheila Kaye- (1887–1956)—© National Portrait Gallery, London
Smith, Sir (William) Sidney (1764–1840)—© National Portrait Gallery, London
Smith, (Thomas) Southwood (1788–1861)—© National Portrait Gallery, London
Smith, Stanley Alexander de (1922–1974)—photograph reproduced by courtesy of The British Academy
Smith, Sydney (1771–1845)—© National Portrait Gallery, London
Smith, Sydney Goodsir (1915–1975)—Scottish National Portrait Gallery
Smith, Sir Thomas (1513–1577)—© National Portrait Gallery, London
Smith, Thomas (1614–1702)—© National Portrait Gallery, London
Smith, Thomas Daniel (1915–1993)—© News International Newspapers Ltd
Smith, (Lillias Irma) Valerie Arkell- (1895–1960)—by permission of the E. O. Hoppé Trust, Curatorial Assistance, Inc., Los Angeles
Smith, William (1727–1793)—© Collection of The New-York Historical Society. Negative no. 1281
Smith, William (1756–1835)—Norwich Castle Museum & Art Gallery
Smith, William (1769–1839)—© National Portrait Gallery, London
Smith, William Henry (1808–1872)—© National Portrait Gallery, London
Smith, William Henry (1825–1891)—© National Portrait Gallery, London
Smithells, Arthur (1860–1939)—© National Portrait Gallery, London
Smithson, Alison Margaret (1928–1993)—© National Portrait Gallery, London
Smithson, Harriet Constance (1800–1854)—Yale Center for British Art, Paul Mellon Collection
Smithson, James Lewis (1764–1829)—National Portrait Gallery, Smithsonian Institution
Smollett, Tobias George (1721–1771)—© National Portrait Gallery, London
Smuts, Jan Christiaan (1870–1950)—© National Portrait Gallery, London
Smyth family (*per. c.*1500–1680) [Smyth, Sir Hugh, first baronet (1632–1680)]—© reserved
Smyth, Dame Ethel Mary (1858–1944)—© National Portrait Gallery, London
Smyth, Richard (1826–1878)—© National Portrait Gallery, London
Smyth, Robert Brough (1830–1889)—by permission of the National Library of Australia R8321
Smyth, William Henry (1788–1865)—© National Portrait Gallery, London
Smythe, Francis Sydney (1900–1949)—The Royal Geographical Society, London
Smythe, George Augustus Frederick Percy Sydney, seventh Viscount Strangford (1818–1857)—Hughenden Manor (The National Trust) / NTPL / Ben Johnson
Smythe, Patricia Rosemary (1928–1996)—Getty Images - Haywood Magee
Smythe, Sir Thomas (*c.*1558–1625)—© National Portrait Gallery, London
Snagge, John Derrick Mordaunt (1904–1996)—© Roger George Clark; collection National Portrait Gallery, London
Snell, Hannah (1723–1792)—© National Portrait Gallery, London
Snow, Charles Percy, Baron Snow (1905–1980)—© Mark Gerson; collection National Portrait Gallery, London
Snow, John (1813–1858)—© National Portrait Gallery, London
Snowball, Elizabeth Alexandra [Betty] (1908–1988)—Getty Images
Snowden, Ethel (1881–1951)—© National Portrait Gallery, London
Snowden, Philip, Viscount Snowden (1864–1937)—© National Portrait Gallery, London
Soane, Sir John (1753–1837)—by courtesy of the Trustees of Sir John Soane's Museum
Soddy, Frederick (1877–1956)—© National Portrait Gallery, London
Soissons, Louis Emmanuel Jean Guy de (1890–1962)—© National Portrait Gallery, London
Solander, Daniel (1733–1782)—Wedgwood Museum, Barlaston
Solomon, Simeon (1840–1905)—© Tate, London, 2004
Solti, Sir Georg (1912–1997)—© Anne-Katrin Purkiss; collection National Portrait Gallery, London
Sombre, David Ochterlony Dyce (1808–1851)—The Potteries Museum & Art Gallery, Stoke-on-Trent
Somers, John, Baron Somers (1651–1716)—© National Portrait Gallery, London
Somerset, Charles, first earl of Worcester (*c.*1460–1526)—reproduced by kind permission of the Dean and Canons of Windsor
Somerset, Edward, fourth earl of Worcester (*c.*1550–1628)—reproduced by permission of the Earl of Verulam. Photograph: Photographic Survey, Courtauld Institute of Art, London
Somerset, Edward, second marquess of Worcester (*d.* 1667)—reproduced by kind permission of His Grace the Duke of Beaufort. Photograph: Photographic Survey, Courtauld Institute of Art, London
Somerset, FitzRoy James Henry, first Baron Raglan (1788–1855)—© National Portrait Gallery, London
Somerset, Henry, first duke of Beaufort (1629–1700)—reproduced by kind

permission of His Grace the Duke of Beaufort. Photograph: Photographic Survey, Courtauld Institute of Art, London

Somerset, Lady Isabella Caroline [Lady Henry Somerset] (1851–1921)—© National Portrait Gallery, London

Somerset, William, third earl of Worcester (1526/7–1589)—reproduced by kind permission of His Grace the Duke of Beaufort. Photograph: Photographic Survey, Courtauld Institute of Art, London

Somervell, (Theodore) Howard (1890–1975)—© National Portrait Gallery, London

Somervile, William (1675–1742)—© National Portrait Gallery, London

Somerville, Edith Anna Œnone (1858–1949)—private collection / National Portrait Gallery, London

Somerville, Mary (1780–1872)—Scottish National Portrait Gallery

Somerville, Mary (1897–1963)—BBC Picture Archives

Somes, Michael George (1917–1994)—Getty Images - Baron

Somner, William (*bap.* 1598, *d.* 1669)—© National Portrait Gallery, London

Sonnenschein, Edward Adolf (1851–1929)—© reserved

Sonntag, Jacob (1905–1984)—© reserved; private collection

Soper, Donald Oliver, Baron Soper (1903–1998)—© National Portrait Gallery, London

Sophia Dorothea [Princess Sophia Dorothea of Celle] (1666–1726)—© Bomann-Museum Celle

Sopwith, Sir Thomas Octave Murdoch (1888–1989)—Getty Images - Hulton Archive

Sorabji, Cornelia (1866–1954)—© National Portrait Gallery, London

Sorby, Henry Clifton (1826–1908)—© National Portrait Gallery, London

Soskice, Frank, Baron Stow Hill (1902–1979)—© National Portrait Gallery, London

Sotheby, William (1757–1833)—© National Portrait Gallery, London

Sothern, Edward Askew (1826–1881)—© National Portrait Gallery, London

Soutar, William (1898–1943)—reproduced by generous permission of Perth Museum and Art Gallery, Perth & Kinross Council, Scotland; photograph by John Watt

South, Sir James (1785–1867)—© National Portrait Gallery, London

Southcott, Joanna (1750–1814)—© National Portrait Gallery, London

Southerne, Thomas (1660–1746)—© National Portrait Gallery, London

Southey, Robert (1774–1843)—© National Portrait Gallery, London

Southwell, Sir Richard (1502/3–1564)—Galleria degli Uffizi, Florence, Italy / Bridgeman Art Library

Southwell, Sir Robert (1635–1702)—© The Royal Society

Sowerbutts, William Edmund (1911–1990)—© reserved; News International Syndication; photograph National Portrait Gallery, London

Sowerby, James (1757–1822)—© National Portrait Gallery, London

Soyer, Alexis Benoît (1810–1858)—© National Portrait Gallery, London

Spain, Nancy Brooker (1917–1964)—© National Portrait Gallery, London

Sparrow, Anthony (1612–1685)—Norwich Castle Museum & Art Gallery

Sparrow, John (1615–1670)—© National Portrait Gallery, London

Sparrow, John Hanbury Angus (1906–1992)—© Estate of Janet Stone; collection National Portrait Gallery, London

Spear, (Augustus John) Ruskin (1911–1990)—© National Portrait Gallery, London

Spears, Sir Edward Louis, baronet (1886–1974)—© National Portrait Gallery, London

Spears, Robert (1825–1899)—© National Portrait Gallery, London

Spedding, James (1808–1881)—© National Portrait Gallery, London

Speed, John (1551/2–1629)—© National Portrait Gallery, London

Speedy, Tristram Charles Sawyer (1836–1910)—© reserved

Speke, John Hanning (1827–1864)—© National Portrait Gallery, London

Spelman, Sir Henry (1563/4–1641)—© National Portrait Gallery, London

Spence, Sir Basil Urwin (1907–1976)—© National Portrait Gallery, London

Spence, Catherine Helen (1825–1910)—by permission of the National Library of Australia

Spence, Joseph (1699–1768)—private collection / by courtesy of Allemandi & Co., Italy (Bernardina Sani, *Rosalba Carriera*, 1988)

Spence, (James) Lewis Thomas Chalmers (1874–1955)—Scottish National Portrait Gallery

Spencer, Alice, countess of Derby (1559–1637)—© reserved

Spencer, Sir (Walter) Baldwin (1860–1929)—reproduced courtesy of Museum of Victoria, Melbourne

Spencer, Charles, third earl of Sunderland (1674/5–1722)—by kind permission of His Grace the Duke of Marlborough

Spencer, Dorothy, countess of Sunderland (1617–1684)—Collection Lord Egremont; photograph National Portrait Gallery, London

Spencer, George [Ignatius of St Paul] (1799–1864)—© National Portrait Gallery, London

Spencer, George John, second Earl Spencer (1758–1834)—Collection of the Earl Spencer, Althorp / Bridgeman Art Library

Spencer, (Margaret) Georgiana, Countess Spencer (1737–1814)—Collection of the Earl Spencer, Althorp / Bridgeman Art Library

Spencer, Gervase (*c.*1715–1763)—© Copyright The British Museum

Spencer, Gilbert (1892–1979)—© reserved; collection Royal Academy; photograph National Portrait Gallery, London

Spencer, Herbert (1820–1903)—© National Portrait Gallery, London

Spencer, Sir John (*d.* 1610)—© English Heritage. NMR; photograph National Portrait Gallery, London

Spencer, (Edward) John, eighth Earl Spencer (1924–1992)—© reserved; Althorp

Spencer, John Charles, Viscount Althorp and third Earl Spencer (1782–1845)—© National Portrait Gallery, London

Spencer, John Poyntz, fifth Earl Spencer (1835–1910)—private collection; © reserved in the photograph

Spencer, Penelope (1901–1993)—V&A Images, The Victoria and Albert Museum

Spencer, Robert, second earl of Sunderland (1641–1702)—Collection of the Earl Spencer, Althorp / Bridgeman Art Library

Spencer, Sir Stanley (1891–1959)—© Estate of Stanley Spencer 2004. All rights reserved, DACS; photograph Tate Gallery, London

Spender, Sir Stephen Harold (1909–1995)—© Humphrey Spender 1932 / National Portrait Gallery, London

Spender, Sir Wilfrid Bliss (1876–1960)—© National Portrait Gallery, London

Spens, (William) Patrick, first Baron Spens (1885–1973)—© National Portrait Gallery, London

Spens, Sir William (1882–1962)—Estate of Henry Lamb; Corpus Christi College, Cambridge

Speyer, Sir Edgar, baronet (1862–1932)—Witt Library, Courtauld Institute of Art, London

Spicer, Dorothy Norman (1908–1946)—© National Portrait Gallery, London

Spicer, Joanna Ravenscroft (1906–1992)—© reserved; News International Syndication; photograph National Portrait Gallery, London

Spiers, Richard Phené (1838–1916)—RIBA Library Photographs Collection

Spilsbury, Sir Bernard Henry (1877–1947)—Edward Cahen Collection, MS4, University of Exeter Library; photograph National Portrait Gallery, London

Spinckes, Nathaniel (1654–1727)—© National Portrait Gallery, London

Spode, Josiah (1755–1827)—© National Portrait Gallery, London

Spofforth, Frederick Robert (1853–1926)—Christie's Images Ltd. (2004)

Spohr, Louis (1784–1859)—© National Portrait Gallery, London

Spooner, William Archibald (1844–1930)—© National Portrait Gallery, London

Spottiswoode, John (1565–1639)—© National Portrait Gallery, London

Spragge, Sir Edward (*c.*1629–1673)—from the collection belonging to the 13th Duke of Argyll

Sprat, Thomas (*bap.* 1635, *d.* 1713)—Board of Trustees of the National Museums and Galleries on Merseyside (Walker Art Gallery, Liverpool)

Sprigg, Christopher St John (1907–1937)—© reserved

Sprimont, Nicholas (*bap.* 1715, *d.* 1771)—E&H Manners

Spring, (Robert) Howard (1889–1965)—© National Portrait Gallery, London

Springfield, Dusty (1939–1999)—© Vivienne; collection National Portrait Gallery, London